Webster's New World

Word Game Word Finder

Bruce Wetterau

PRENTICE
HALL
PRESS

New York London Toronto Tokyo Singapore

New World Dictionaries/Prentice Hall Press
15 Columbus Circle
New York, NY 10023

PRENTICE HALL PRESS, TREE OF KNOWLEDGE, and
WEBSTER'S NEW WORLD and colophons are trademarks
of Simon & Schuster, Inc.

Manufactured in the United States of America

1   2   3   4   5   6   7   8   9   10

Acknowledgments

I would like to thank the free-lancers who helped in selecting and checking words for inclusion in this book. Editorial assistants, Ann Marr, Sharon Thompson, Cindy Poots Remington, Katherine Somervell, Leila Finn, Mary St. John, and Virginia Kennan all worked long hours on this phase of the project. Donna Packard single-handedly keyboarded the basic word list, while Laurel Adams and Susan Carter keyboarded additions and deletions required to put the database in final editorial order. Finally, my editors Ken Wright and Kate Kelly, and publisher Charles Levine deserve special thanks for making this book possible in the first place.

CONTENTS

Preface

Here is a brand new companion reference and solver for a host of popular word games, including commercially produced word games like Scrabble® Brand Crosswords, Boggle®, and Upwords®; newspaper word game puzzles such as the Jumble® puzzle; organized word game contests for prizes; and impromptu word games that generally require nothing more than a pencil, paper, and some spare time. These games, in one way or another, challenge us to make a word from a set of randomly selected or intentionally scrambled game letters. And, at one time or another, all of us have found ourselves at a loss for that word, despite much shifting of letters back and forth. But there is no need for that to happen any more.

The unique solving system used in *Webster's New World Word Finder* helps you find the word hidden in random letters quickly and easily. All you do is alphabetize your game letters and look them up in the Word Finder section. In seconds, you will find what word can be spelled using your letters. The Word Finder doesn't stop there, however; it also identifies other shorter words that can be made using just some of those letters. And another brand new feature, The Word Builder section, helps you make new words by adding letters on to words that have already been played (as in Scrabble® and Upwords®).

The solving systems, powerful though they are, would not be of much use without the necessary answer words. You'll find no shortage of them here. The three sections of this book list over a half million answer words–more than you are likely to need in a lifetime. Included among the words, which range from 2 to 8 letters long throughout this book, are singular and plural forms of nouns, the various regular and irregular forms of verbs, plus adjectival and adverbial forms, and comparative and superlative forms. You can play any answer word you find here, because words in the original database have been checked for eligibility for word games against *Webster's New World Dictionary, Third Collegiate Edition*. So, there are no proper nouns, foreign words, hyphenated or two word forms, abbreviations, or contractions. In addition, any word you find will be also listed in Webster's, in case you need a definition for it.

If you haven't already guessed it, that word "database" in the last paragraph surely reveals that computers played a part in producing this book. To be sure, the long and tedious job of gathering and checking words for the 45,000-word database was done by hand, and it was a project in itself. So too was the job of programming the computers. But once all that was done, work on actually compiling entries took place electronically, somewhere in the bowels of those powerful microcomputers that are readily available these days.

It is safe to say that this book probably would not have been compiled without them. They performed hundreds of millions, if not billions of electronic checking operations during the compiling of the Word Finder section alone. And it took not one, but three computers operating day and night for about two and a half months to complete the work.

In the end, they produced far too many answer words to be included in a single volume. There are literally hundreds of thousands of answer words for alphabetized letter sequences ranging from 2 to 6 letters long, but every possible answer word for every sequence is covered in this range. To include every single answer word for 7 and 8 letter words, however, would have added another million and half words.

The 7- and 8-letter entries do list all possible 7- and 8-letter words; they just don't show shorter words there at the entry. If you want shorter words, you have only to look up one of the 5- or 6-letter cross-reference sequences listed at the end of these entries. All words that you find at the shorter entries can be made from the original set of 7 or 8 letters. Note that coverage of 7- and 8-letter words includes many, but not all, possible answer words between 2 and 6 letters long.

In closing, I would like to point out again that introductions to each of the sections provide more detailed instructions on using the sections.

Bruce Wetterau
Charlottesville, Virginia

Three Easy Ways to Find Winning Words

The Word Finder

Want to find the word or words a group of scrambled letters will make? Just put the letters into alphabetical order and look up that letter sequence in the Word Finder section. Answer words, all of them eligible for play in word games, are listed at the matching letter sequence in this section.

It's that easy. And you will have plenty of words to choose from, because the Word Finder entry includes words spelled with all the letters you looked up (up to 8 letters), plus the many shorter words that use just some of them (on down to 2 letters).

The Word Finder works wonders for any word game or puzzle requiring you to unscramble game letters. But remember, some random letter sequences don't make words, and it is always harder to get the letters you need for a longer word than a shorter one. If your exact letter sequence isn't listed in the Word Finder, try looking up just the first 4 to 6 letters. Also, eliminate one of any pair of doubled letters, as in AEILNRR. The introduction to the Word Finder section provides more useful tips on using this powerful new word game reference.

The Word Builder

Adding letters to a word already on the board is a great way to increase your score, and this new word game reference makes it unbelievably easy. Just look up the word you want to add on to (from 2 to 5 letters long). Then read through the list of valid answer words until you find one you can make by adding letters you have on hand. See the introduction to this section for more on how it works.

The Word Lists

Be prepared! Avid word game players often memorize special types of words with unusual or high-scoring letters. But the Word List section in this book contains valuable lists that you can use for reference whenever the need arises. For example, suppose you want to make a word using two *Zs* or one ending with *-wise*. It takes only a few seconds to check the appropriate list in this section. And if you use the *Official Scrabble Player's Dictionary* to settle challenges, there is even a list of the 600-plus playable words included in the Word Finder that cannot be found in the OSPD.

I. THE WORD FINDER

For anyone who—like this author—has struggled to make a word from a set of scrambled letters, this new Word Finder is heaven sent. All you have to do is put the scrambled letters into alphabetical order and look that sequence up in this section. Presto! Listed after the sequence are answer words ranging from the length of the sequence you looked up on down to 2 letters. And any of those words can be made with your letters.

Experienced word game players will recognize immediately just how powerful this new reference is, but you don't have to be an expert to make it work for you. When playing the ever-popular Scrabble® Brand Crossword Game, for example, it certainly can help you make a word quickly from your letter tiles. But that is not all. Because this section gives you more than one answer word, you can also decide which word is best to play. Maybe you want a word spelled with higher-scoring letters, one that is long enough to land on a special scoring square, or one that suits some other strategic purpose.

For other word games that require you to make as many new words as possible out of the letters of a game word—well, the arrangement of entries here does exactly that. You can use the Word Finder to see how well you did on your own, to provide additional answers you may have missed, or to provide all the solutions.

Putting the Word Finder to Work

Before looking up your first letter sequence, take a minute to read the rest of these introductory notes. There are some useful pointers here to help you get the most from the Word Finder.

First, this section and all others in this book contain only those words eligible for most word games. So any of the answer words you find with it can be played. You can look up alphabetized letter sequences ranging from 2 letters long on up to a maximum of 8. Listed answer words also fall within this range.

Now, so long as you have letters that make a word (and they are in alphabetical order), the Word Finder will always lead you to the word. But it should come as no surprise to anyone who plays word games that many groups of random letters just don't make words. Generally speaking, it is harder to get the letters you need to make a longer word than a shorter one. Therein lies the source of much shuffling of tiles, scribbling on paper, and the like. Frustration!

Here is where the Word Finder really shines, though. Used correctly, it can actually help you home in on the exact letters you need to make a word from the random letters on hand.

Suppose, for example, you have 7 letters to play and there is one on the game board to include in the proposed word. First, put the letters in alphabetical order (leave a partial space for the one on the game board). Look up all 8 letters in the Word Finder, and if you find a matching sequence, all well and good. If not, look at the other shorter sequences above it on the page. Often, you'll find an entry sequence that has only the first 5 or 6 of your letters. Unless you really need a 7 letter word, you've just found plenty of answer words from which to choose.

Sometimes your letters will prove much more stubborn, so that even the first 3 or 4 of the 8 just won't make a word. Don't give up on them yet. Occasionally, the problem is a single intervening letter in the alphabetized sequence that is holding up a match in the Word Finder. For example, a pair of the same letters is often the problem. Except for a few very common doublings (such as AEE...), it is probably best to always eliminate one of the two identical letters at the very start.

You can also try selectively eliminating other letters. Apart from doubled letters, it is usually better to eliminate from the end or middle of the alphabetized sequence, rather than from the beginning. The simple fact is that the great majority of words in the English language have at least one or two letters from the beginning of the alphabet.

Cross-references

Every letter sequence listed in this book makes at least one word using all the letters in the sequence, and many other shorter words besides. In fact, for sequences ranging from 2 to 6 letters, the lists contain all words in this book that can

INTRODUCTION

be made using letters of the sequences. Longer sequences (of 7 and 8 letters) are a different story, though. All possible answer words for these two lengths alone would amount to far too many to include in one volume. Besides, the answer words are repeated elsewhere under sequences of 6 letters or less.

For these reasons, 7 and 8 letter sequences provide only answer words that are longer than 6 letters. If you want to find shorter words, just look up the cross-reference sequences listed at the end of the entry, as in the example below.

> **ademnoor** marooned doorman doormen
> madrone. *See* **ademno ademnr ademor**
> **admnor**

The first entry for a cross-reference sequence is often right there on the same page, and every answer word it lists can be made using letters of your 8-letter sequence. If you want still more shorter words, just check the other cross-reference sequences (a maximum of five will be listed). Cross-reference sequences are included for all but a handful of 7-letter sequences, which happen to form 7-letter words, but no 5- or 6-letter words. In the unlikely event you match up with one of these and really want shorter words, just eliminate three of your letters and try for a 4-letter sequence (or less) in the Word Finder.

aa

aaaahjmr   maharaja. *See* **aahjr**

aaaaimpr   arapaima. *See* **aaimr**

aaaairtx   ataraxia. *See* **aaaitx**

aaabbelt   abatable. *See* **aaablt**

aaabbkl   kabbala. *See* **aaabkl aabbk**

aaabbkls   kabbalas kabbala kabalas. *See* **aaabkl aabbks**

aaabccr   baccara. *No 6s or 5s*

aaabccrs   baccaras baccara cascara. *See* **aaabcs aabcrs**

aaabccrt   baccarat baccara. *See* **abcrt aacrt aabrt**

aaabchls   calabash cabalas. *See* **aaabcl aaabcs aabchs aabcls**

aaabcl   cabala cabal alba aba ala alb baa cab lab lac ba la

aaabcls   cabalas. *See* **aaabcl aabcls aaabcs**

aaabcn   cabana aba ana baa ban cab can nab an ba na

aaabcnrr   barranca. *See* **aaabcn**

aaabcns   cabanas. *See* **aaabcn aaabcs**

aaabcs   casaba baas cabs scab aba baa cab sac as ba

aaabcss   casabas. *See* **aaabcs abcss**

aaabdnn   bandana. *See* **aaabbn**

aaabdnnn   bandanna bandana. *See* **aaabnn**

aaabdnns   bandanas bandana bananas. *See* **aaabnn**

aaabdnrs   saraband. *See* **abdnrs**

aaabehnr   habanera. *See* **aaenr abehr**

aaabgrtu   rutabaga. *See* **aabrt**

aaabkl   kabala alba balk aba ala alb baa kab kal lab ba ka la

aaabkls   kabalas. *See* **aaabkl aabls abkls**

aaabklsv   baklavas kabalas baklava. *See* **aaabkl**

aaabklv   baklava. *See* **aaabkl**

aaablopr   parabola. *See* **aaablr**

aaablr   labara labra alba alar aba ala alb baa bar bra lab lar ba la

aaablst   balatas. *See* **aaablt aablst**

aaablt   balata alba blat aba ala alb alt baa bat lab tab at ba la ta

aaabnn   banana aba ana baa ban nab an ba na

aaabnns   bananas. *See* **aaabnn abnns**

aaabrsz   bazaars. *See* **aaabrz aabrs**

aaabrz   bazaar aba baa bar bra ba

aaaccepr   carapace. *See* **aacep aacer acepr**

aaacci   acacia ai

aaaccilr   calcaria. *See* **aaacci aacclr aacilr**

aaaccis   acacias. *See* **aaacci**

aaaccrs   cascara. *No 6s or 5s*

aaaccrss   cascaras cascara carcass. *See* **acrss**

aaaccrtt   cataract. *See* **aartt aacrt acrtt**

aaacdeim   academia. *See* **adeim aceim acdem**

aaacdlu   acaudal. *See* **aacdlu**

aaacdmm   macadam. *See* **aadmm**

aaacdnno   anaconda. *See* **acnno**

aaacelnt   analecta. *See* **aacent aaelnt acelnt**

aaacenp   panacea. *See* **aacenp**

aaacenps   panaceas panacea canapes. *See* **aacenp aaenps acenps**

aaacglsw   scalawag. *See* **aagls aclsw**

aaachips   aphasiac aphasia aphasic. *See* **aacips achips**

aaachlsz   chalazas chalaza. *See* **aachls**

aaachlz   chalaza. *No 6s or 5s*

aaacilmn   maniacal almanac. *See* **aacilm aacimn aailmn**

aaacilmr   calamari malaria. *See* **aaacmr aacilm aacilr**

aaacintv   cavatina. *See* **aacitv aacntv**

aaacirrs   sacraria. *See* **aairs aarrs airrs**

aaacjmr   jacamar. *See* **aaacmr**

aaacjmrs   jacamars jacamar maracas marasca mascara. *See* **aaacmr aaamrs**

aaacjn   jacana ana can an na

aaacjns   jacanas. *See* **aaacjn**

aaaclmn   almanac. *See* **aacln**

aaaclmns   almanacs almanac. *See* **aaalms aaclns**

aaaclp   alpaca paca clap ala alp cap lac lap pal la pa

aaaclps   alpacas. *See* **aaaclp aclps aacps**

aaaclpst   catalpas alpacas catalpa. *See* **aaaclp**

aaaclpt   catalpa. *See* **aaaclp aclpt**

aaaclrsz   alcazars alcazar. *See* **aaclrs aalrsz**

aaaclrz   alcazar. *See* **aalrz**

aaacmr   maraca cram marc arc arm cam car mac mar ram am ma

aaacmrs   maracas marasca mascara. *See* **aaacmr aaamrs**

aaacmrss   mascaras maracas marasca mascara samaras samsara sarcasm. *See* **aaacmr aaamrs acmrss**

aaacnrsv   caravans caravan. *See* **aacnsv aanrsv**

aaacnrv   caravan. *See* **aanrv**

aaacnsst   canastas canasta. *See* **acnsst**

aaacnst   canasta. *See* **aanst acnst**

aaacnstt   cantatas canasta cantata. *See* **aanst acnst**

aaacntt   cantata. *No 6s or 5s*

aaacrswy   caraways caraway. *See* **acrsw acrsy**

aaacrwy   caraway. *No 6s or 5s*

aaacssv   cassava. *No 6s or 5s*

aaadefwy   fadeaway. *See* **adewy**

aaadelms   salaamed. *See* **aaalms adelms**

aaadkrrv   aardvark. *See* **aadrr**

aaadmnt   adamant. *See* **aaamnt aadmn**

aaadmr   armada drama dram arm dam mad mar rad ram ad am ma

aaadmrs   armadas. *See* **aaadmr aadmrs aaamrs**

aaaeglst   galateas galatea lastage. *See* **aaegst aeglst**

aaaeglt   galatea. *See* **aaegt aeglt aaelt**

aaaegnpp   appanage. *See* **aaegp aaenp aagnp**

aaaehmnt   anathema. *See* **aaamnt aehmnt**

aaaelnpt   panatela. *See* **aaelnt aaelpt aelnpt**

aaaelsz   azaleas. *See* **aaaelz aelsz**

aaaelz   azalea laze zeal ala ale lea ae el la

aaaffll   alfalfa. *No 6s or 5s*

aaafflls   alfalfas alfalfa. *See* **aflls**

aaafinst   fantasia. *See* **afinst**

aaafirst   ratafias ratafia. *See* **aafirs aairst**

aaafirt   ratafia. *See* **afirt aairt**

aaafrwy   faraway. *No 6s or 5s*

aaaghnty   yataghan. *See* **agnty**

aaaghpr   agrapha. *See* **aaghr aghpr**

aaaginrr   agrarian arraign. *See* **aagin aginr**

aaaglmm   amalgam. *See* **aaagm aagmm**

aaaglmms   amalgams amalgam. *See* **aaagms aaalms aagmms**

aaaglns   lasagna. *See* **aaglns**

aaaglrst   astragal. *See* **aalrst**

aaagm   agama aga gam mag am ma

aaagmnr   anagram. *See* **aagmnr aaagm**

aaagmnrs   anagrams anagram. *See* **aaagms aaamrs aagmnr**

aaagms   agamas agama agas gams mags saga aga gam gas mag sag am as ma

aaagnn   nagana aga ana gan nag an na

aaagnns   naganas. *See* **aaagnn**

aaahimrt   hamartia. *See* **aaimrt**

aaahips   aphasia. *See* **ahips aahps**

aaahipss   aphasias aphasia. *See* **aahpss ahipss**

aaahmmst   mahatmas mahatma. *See* **aahmst**

aaahmmt   mahatma. *No 6s or 5s*

aaahmnrt   amaranth. *See* **aaamnt aamnrt**

aaahnopr   anaphora. *See* **ahnopr**

aaaiinpr apiarian. *See* **aainp**

aaaillmr malarial malaria. *See* **aalmr aailm aallm**

aaaillpt palatial palatal. *See* **ailpt**

aaailmr malaria. *See* **aalmr aailm aaimr**

aaailrt talaria. *See* **aailrt**

aaaimnrr marinara. *See* **aaimnr**

aaainopr paranoia. *See* **aainp anopr ainor**

aaaiprsx apraxias apraxia. *See* **aiprsx**

aaaiprx apraxia. *No 6s or 5s*

aaaiqru aquaria. *No 6s or 5s*

aaaistx ataxias. *See* **aaaitx aistx**

aaaitx ataxia taxi ita tax ai ax it ta ti xi

aaajmp pajama amp jam map am ma pa

aaajmps pajamas. *See* **aaajmp**

aaakkmr markkaa. *See* **aakkmr**

aaaklm kamala lama ala kal lam am ka la ma

aaaklms kamalas. *See* **aaaklm aaalms**

aaaklmsy yamalkas kamalas yamalka. *See* **aaaklm aaalms**

aaaklmy yamalka. *See* **aaaklm**

aaallpst palatals palatal. *See* **aalst allps aapst**

aaallpt palatal. *No 6s or 5s*

aaalms salaam lamas alas alms lama lams slam ala lam sal am as la ma

aaalmss salaams. *See* **aaalms aamss aalss**

aaalwyy layaway. *See* **aalwyy**

aaamnopr panorama. *See* **aamopr**

aaamnst atamans. *See* **aaamnt aamnst**

aaamnt ataman atman manta mana anta ana ant man mat tam tan am an at ma na ta

aaamrs samara arms rams arm mar ram am as ma

aaamrss samaras samsara. *See* **aaamrs aamss**

aaamrsss samsaras samaras samsara. *See* **aaamrs**

aaamrstu tamaraus tamarau traumas. *See* **aaamrs aamrtu amrstu**

aaamrtu tamarau. *See* **aamrtu**

aaannsv savanna. *No 6s or 5s*

aaanqtuu aquanaut. *See* **aanqtu**

aaanrstt tantaras rattans tantara tartans. *See* **aanrtt aarstt**

aaanrtt tantara. *See* **aanrtt**

aaappsy papayas. *See* **aaappy aapps appsy**

aaappy papaya papa pap pay pya yap pa ay

aaapqrtu paraquat. *See* **aaprt aqrtu**

aaarstv avatars. *See* **aaartv aarsv aastv**

aaartv avatar vara art rat tar tav vat at ta

aaartxy ataraxy. *No 6s or 5s*

aab aba baa ba

aabb abba baba aba baa ba

aabbbo baobab abba baba aba baa boa bob ba

aabbbos baobabs. *See* **aabbbo aabbs**

aabbcdeg cabbaged cabbage. *See* **abbcde abbdeg**

aabbcdrs scabbard. *See* **aabcrs**

aabbceg cabbage. *No 6s or 5s*

aabbcegs cabbages cabbage. *See* **aabes abbes aabbs**

aabbceis abbacies cabbies. *See* **abbcei abbeis abceis**

aabbcekr bareback. *See* **abcekr**

aabbcekt backbeat. *See* **aabbck aabet aabbk**

aabbcinr barbican. *See* **aacinr**

aabbcirr barbaric. *See* **aabci abcir abirr**

aabbcy abbacy cabby abba baba baby aba aby baa bay cab cay ay ba by

aabbeelr bearable. *See* **aabelr abbelr**

aabbegn beanbag. *See* **abegn**

aabbegns beanbags beanbag. *See* **aabes abbes aabbs**

aabbellm blamable. *See* **aabem abelm abell**

aabbells baseball salable. *See* **abells**

aabbelry bearably. *See* **aabelr abbelr abbery abelry**

aabbk kabab abba baba aba baa kab ba ka

aabbks kababs kabab babas abba baas baba bask kabs aba ask baa kab kas as ba ka

aabbllmy blamably. *See* **aally ablly ablmy**

aabbs babas abba baas baba aba baa as ba

aabccehk backache. *See* **aabck abceh acceh**

aabccet baccate. *See* **aabet**

aabcckkp backpack. *See* **aabck**

aabccklp blackcap. *See* **aacclp**

aabccmot catacomb. *See* **abcmot**

aabcdein abidance cabined. *See* **aabci abdei acden**

aabcdeit abdicate. *See* **aabdet abdeit**

aabcdell caballed. *See* **aabdll abcdel abdell acdell**

aabcdeln balanced balance. *See* **abcdel acdeln**

aabcdhkn backhand. *See* **aabck**

aabcdhkr hardback. *See* **aachkr**

aabcdkrw backward drawback. *See* **aabck aadrw ackrw**

aabceert acerbate cabaret. *See* **aabert aaeert abeert aceert**

aabcegot cabotage. *See* **aabet aaegt abegt**

aabceilm amicable amiable amical alembic. *See* **aabcim aacilm abcelm aceilm**

aabceirt bacteria cabaret. *See* **aabert abceir abeirt**

aabceklm clambake makable. *See* **abcelm aceklm**

aabcellp placable capable. *See* **aacelp aaellp**

aabcells scalable salable. *See* **aabcls aaclls abcels abells**

aabceln balance. *See* **aabln aabcl abcel**

aabcelnr balancer barnacle balance. *See* **aabelr aacenr aaclnr acelnr**

aabcelns balances balance. *See* **aabcls aaclns abcels**

aabcelor albacore. *See* **aabelr aaelor abelor acelor**

aabcelp capable. *See* **aacelp aabcl abcel**

aabcelt actable. *See* **aabet aaelt abelt**

aabcemr macaber macabre. *See* **aacemr abcemr**

aabcerst cabarets abaters abreast cabaret. *See* **aabcrs aabert aabest aabrst**

aabcert cabaret. *See* **aabert abcer aacer**

aabcessu abacuses. *See* **aabcsu aabess abessu acessu**

aabcfhkl halfback. *See* **aabck aackl abckl**

aabcfkst fastback fatbacks fatback. *See* **aabck aabft abcks**

aabcfkt fatback. *See* **aabck aabft**

aabchilr brachial. *See* **aacilr achilr**

aabchinr branchia. *See* **aacinr abchnr achinr**

aabchkls backlash. *See* **aabchs aabcls aabhks aachls**

aabchksw backwash hacksaw. *See* **aabchs aabhks aabhsw aachkw**

aabchmry chambray. *See* **abmry abchr achmr**

aabchor abroach. *See* **abchor**

aabchs casbah abash baas bach bash cabs cash scab aah aba aha ash baa bah cab has sac ah as ba ha sh

aabchss casbahs. *See* **aabchs abcss**

aabci abaci aba baa cab ba ai

aabciils basilica basilic. *See* **aabcls abiils aciils**

aabciklt tailback. *See* **aabci aabck aackl**

aabcilms cabalism. *See* **aabcim aabcls aablms aacilm**

aabcilmy amicably amiably. *See* **aabcim aacilm abclmy**

aabcilnn cannibal. *See* **aabinn**

aabcilst basaltic cabalist. *See* **aabcls aabist aablst**

aabcim cambia abaci mica aba aim baa bam cab cam mac ai am ba ma mi

aabcinnr cinnabar. *See* **aabinn aacinr**

aabcinns cannabis banians. *See* **aabinn abcins**

aabcistx taxicabs taxicab. *See* **aabist**

aabcitx taxicab. *See* **aabci**

aabck aback back aba baa cab kab ba ka

aabcklpy playback capably. *See* **aabck aackl abkly**

aabckrr barrack. *See* **aackrr aabck**

aabckrrs barracks barrack arracks. *See* **aabcrs aackrr**

aabcksty backstay. *See* **aabck abcks aksty**

aabcl cabal alba aba ala alb baa cab lab lac ba la

aabclpy capably. *See* **aabcl aalpy**

aabcls cabals albas balas balsa basal cabal alas alba albs baas cabs labs scab slab aba ala alb baa cab lab lac sac sal as ba la

aabcmn cabman mana aba ana baa bam ban cab cam can mac man nab am an ba ma na

aabcorst acrobats abators acrobat rabatos. *See* **aabcrs aabort aabrst aacrst**

aabcort acrobat. *See* **aabort**

aabcostt catboats catboat. *See* **acostt**

aabcott catboat. *See* **acott**

aabcrs scarab sabra crabs arcs baas bars bras cabs cars crab scab scar aba arc baa bar bra cab car sac ba as

aabcrss scarabs. *See* **aabcrs aabrss**

aabcrstt abstract tracts.. *See* **aarstt abcrst aacrst aabrst**

aabcsu abacus scuba baas cabs cubs scab aba baa bus cab cub sac sub as ba us

aabddeet deadbeat debated. *See* **aabdet abddee abdeet**

aabddegn bandaged bandage. *See* **aadegn abdden abdegn**

aabddehn headband. *See* **abdden addehn**

aabddel addable. *See* **abddel**

aabdder abraded. *See* **aabder adder**

aabddlns badlands. *See* **aadlns**

aabdeelr readable. *See* **aabder aabelr abdeel abdeer**

aabdeelv evadable. *See* **abdeel adeelv**

aabdegin badinage bandage beading. *See* **aadegn abdegn adegin**

aabdegn bandage. *See* **aadegn abdegn**

aabdegns bandages agendas bandage sandbag. *See* **aabdes aadegn aadegs abdegn**

aabdehs abashed. *See* **aabdes abdehs**

aabdeis diabase. *See* **aabdes abdeis**

aabdeiss diabases diabase. *See* **aabdes aabess abdeis abeiss**

aabdekry daybreak. *See* **aabder abdekr abdery abekry**

aabdellu laudable. *See* **aabdll aaellu abdell abellu**

aabdelor adorable labored. *See* **aabder aabdor aabelr aaelor**

aabdelpt baldpate . *See* **aabdet aadelt aaelpt abdelt**

aabdelry readably already. *See* **aabder aabelr abdelr abdery**

aabdems sambaed. *See* **aabdes aabems**

aabdenu bandeau. *No 6s or 5s*

aabdeors seaboard abrades. *See* **aabder aabdes aabdor abdeos**

aabder abrade ardeb bared beard bread debar abed area bade bard bare bead bear brad brae bred dare dear drab read aba are baa bad bar bed bra dab ear era rad red ad ae ba be er re

aabders abrades. *See* **aabdes aabder abders**

aabdes abased abase based beads abed baas bade base bead beds dabs aba ads baa bad bed dab sad sea ad ae as ba be

aabdet abated abate bated abed abet bade bate bead beat beta data date debt aba aet ate baa bad bat bed bet dab eat eta tab tad tea ted ad ae at ba be ta

aabdghn handbag. *See* **abghn**

aabdghns handbags handbag sandbag. *See* **abghns**

aabdginr abrading bargain brigand. *See* **aadinr abdinr abginr adginr**

aabdgnov vagabond. *See* **abdgno**

aabdgns sandbag. *See* **abdns abgns**

aabdgnss sandbags sandbag. *See* **abdns abgns aagss**

aabdgotu gadabout. *See* **abotu bdotu**

aabdhlln handball. *See* **aabdll**

aabdhllr hardball. *See* **aabdll**

aabdhnst hatbands hatband. *See* **aabhs aanst abhst**

aabdhnt hatband. *No 6s or 5s*

aabdimr barmaid. *See* **abdir aadmr aaimr**

aabdimrs barmaids barmaid. *See* **aabmrs aadmrs abdirs adimrs**

aabdinnr rainband. *See* **aabinn aadinr abdinr**

aabdknns sandbank. *See* **abdns abkns abnns**

aabdll ballad alba bald ball aba ala alb all baa bad dab lab lad ad ba la

aabdllry balladry. *See* **aabdll abdlly**

aabdlls ballads. *See* **aabdll aabls ablls**

aabdlluy laudably. *See* **aabdll abdlly**

aabdlm lambda alba bald balm lama lamb aba ala alb baa bad bam dab dam lab lad lam mad ad am ba la ma

aabdlmny damnably. *See* **aabdlm aabdmn aadlmy aalmny**

aabdlmru adumbral labarum. *See* **aabdlm aadmru ablmru**

aabdlms lambdas. *See* **aabdlm aablms**

aabdloot boatload. *See* **ablot bdloo adlot**

aabdlopr lapboard. *See* **aabdor aadlop**

aabdlorr larboard. *See* **aabdor aaborr**

aabdlory adorably broadly. *See* **aabdor abdory**

aabdlrsw bradawls bradawl. *See* **aadrsw ablrsw adlrsw**

aabdlrw bradawl. *See* **aadrw ablrw adlrw**

aabdmn badman adman band damn mana aba ana and baa bad bam ban dab dam mad man nab ad am an ba ma na

aabdmnns bandsman sandman. *See* **aabdmn aamnns**

aabdmnr armband. *See* **aabdmn abdnr aadmr**

aabdmnrs armbands armband mansard. *See* **aabdmn aabmrs aadmrs abdnrs**

aabdnno abandon. *No 6s or 5s*

aabdnnos abandons abandon. *See* **abdns abnns bdnos**

aabdnntu abundant. *See* **adntu bdntu**

aabdnrry barnyard. *See* **abdnry**

aabdor aboard abroad board broad dobra bard boar bora brad drab orad road aba ado baa bad bar boa bra dab dor oar orb rad rob rod ad ba do od or

aabdorty boatyard. *See* **aabdor aabdrt aabort aabrty**

aabdorv bravado. *See* **aabdor**

aabdorx broadax. *See* **aabdor**

aabdrsst bastards bastard tabards. *See* **aabdrt aabrss aabrst**

aabdrst bastard tabards. *See* **aabdrt aabrst**

aabdrt tabard rabat bard brad brat dart data drab drat aba art baa bad bar bat bra dab rad rat tab tad tar ad at ba ta

aabeegkr breakage. *See* **abeegr abeekr**

aabeegnt abnegate. *See* **aaegnt abeent aeegnt**

aabeehlt hateable eatable. *See* **beehlt**

aabeells saleable salable. *See* **abeels abells beells**

aabeelmn amenable nameable namable. *See* **aabeem abeeln aeelmn**

aabeelrs erasable arables. *See* **aabelr abeels abelrs aeelrs**

aabeelrw wearable. *See* **aabelr abeerw abelrw**

aabeelst eatables eatable. *See* **aabest aablst abeels abelst**

aabeelsv saveable. *See* **abeels aeelsv beelsv**

aabeelt eatable. *See* **aabet abeel aaelt**

aabeem amebae abeam ameba beam bema aba baa bam bee mae ae am ba be em ma me

aabeenor anaerobe. *See* **abeeor**

aabeffl affable. *See* **abeffl**

aabefgl fleabag. *See* **aaegl abegl abefl**

aabefgls fleabags fleabag. *See* **abefls abegls**

aabeflll flabella. *See* **aaflll abefll**

aabeflmu flambeau. *See* **aaeflm beflmu**

aabeggg baggage. *No 6s or 5s*

aabeggr garbage. *See* **abeggr aaeggr aabggr**

aabeghln hangable. *See* **aaegln abegln**

aabegllm ballgame. *See* **aabegm aaeglm abeglm**

aabeglr algebra. *See* **aabelr abeglr aaeglr**

aabeglrs algebras algebra arables garbles laagers. *See* **aabelr aaeglr abeglr abegls**

aabeglru arguable algebra. *See* **aabelr aaeglr abeglr abeglu**

aabegm ambage abeam ameba beam bema gamb game mage aba aga age baa bag bam beg gab gae gam gem mae mag ae am ba be em ma me

aabegmnr bargeman manager. *See* **aabegm aabgmn aaegmn aagmnr**

aabegms ambages. *See* **aabegm aabems**

aabegnor baronage. *See* **aaegor aagnor abegnr abegor**

aabegort abrogate. *See* **aabert aabort aaegor aaeort**

aabegost sabotage. *See* **aabest aaegst**

aabegrr barrage. *See* **abegr**

aabegrrs barrages barrage abegr. *See* **abegrs aberrs**

aabehlpt alphabet. *See* **aaelpt**

aabehlsw washable. *See* **aabhsw aehlsw**

aabehss abashes. *See* **aabess abehss**

aabeilm amiable. *See* **aabem abelm aabil**

aabeilrv variable. *See* **aabelr aaeilr aaelrv abeilv**

aabeilst labiates satiable bestial blastie labiate stabile. *See* **aabest aabist aablst abeilt**

aabeilt labiate. *See* **abeilt aabet aaelt**

aabeiltv ablative labiate. *See* **abeilt abeilv**

aabeirsv abrasive. *See* **abeirs abersv aeirsv**

aabejll jellaba. *See* **abell**

aabejmu jambeau. *See* **aabem**

aabejmux jambeaux jambeau. *See* **aabem**

aabeklm makable. *See* **aabem abelm abekl**

aabekmnr brakeman. *See* **abekmn abekmr abeknr**

aabellmt meatball. *See* **aabemt aaelmt abellt aellmt**

aabelln balneal. *See* **aabln abell**

aabellpp palpable. *See* **aaellp aaelpp**

aabellpy playable payable. *See* **aaellp aellpy**

aabells salable. *See* **abells aabes aabls**

aabellsv salvable salable. *See* **abells**

aabelluv valuable. *See* **aaellu abellu**

aabelmn namable. *See* **aabem abelm aabln**

aabelmny amenably namable. *See* **aalmny aelmny**

aabelmst blastema lambaste lambast malates maltase tamales. *See* **aabems aabemt aabest aablms**

aabelmsu amusable. *See* **aabems aablms abelms abelsu**

aabelmtu ambulate tableau mutable. *See* **aabemt aabetu aabltu aaelmt**

aabelno abalone. *See* **aelno aabln belno**

aabelorr arboreal areolar laborer. *See* **aabelr aaborr aaelor abelor**

aabelosv lavaboes absolve. *See* **aablov aelosv**

aabelovw avowable. *See* **aablov aalovw**

aabelpr parable. *See* **aabelr aaelp aelpr**

aabelprs parables sparable parable arables. *See* **aabelr aaelps aaeprs abelrs**

aabelpss passable. *See* **aabess aaelps aalpss abelss**

aabelpsy payables payable. *See* **aaelps aalpsy abelsy**

aabelpy payable. *See* **abely aalpy**

aabelr arable abler blare blear labra able alar alba area bale bare bear brae earl rale real aba ala alb ale are baa bar bel bra ear era lab lar lea ae ba be el er la re

aabelrs arables. *See* **aabelr abelrs**

aabelrt ratable. *See* **aabert aabelr abelrt**

aabelrty betrayal ratable. *See* **aabelr aabert aabrty abelrt**

aabelstu tableaus ablauts sublate tableau. *See* **aabest aabetu aablst aabltu**

aabelttu tabulate tableau. *See* **aabetu aabltu abeltt abettu**

aabeltu tableau. *See* **aabetu aabltu**

aabeltux tableaux bateaux tableau taxable. *See* **aabetu aabltu aeltux**

aabeltx taxable. *See* **aabet aaelt abelt**

aabelz ablaze blaze able alba bale laze zeal aba ala alb ale baa bel lab lea ae ba be el la

aabem abeam ameba beam bema aba baa bam mae ae am ba be em ma me

aabemns baseman. *See* **aabems aaemns**

aabemo amoeba abeam ameba ambo beam bema aba baa bam boa mae moa mob ae am ba be em ma me mo om

aabemos amoebas. *See* **aabemo aabems**

aabems amebas abase abeam ameba beams bemas samba baas bams base beam bema mesa same seam aba baa bam mae sea ae am as ba be em ma me

aabemt bemata abate abeam ameba abet bate beam beat bema beta mate meat tame team aba aet ate baa bam bat bet eat eta mae mat met tab tam tea ae am at ba be em ma me ta

aabenrrt aberrant narrate. *See* **aabert aaerrt aanrrt abenrr**

aabenrst ratsbane abaters abreast banters. *See* **aabert aabest aabrst aaenrs**

aaberst abaters abreast. *See* **aabert aabest aberst aabrst aaerst**

aabersz zarebas. *See* **abersz aaberz**

aabert abater abate rabat reata abet area bare bate bear beat beta brae brat rate tare tear aba aet are art ate baa bar bat bet bra ear eat era eta rat ret tab tar tea ae at ba be er re ta

aaberz zareba braze zebra area bare bear brae raze aba are baa bar bra ear era ae ba be er re

aabes abase baas base aba baa sea ae as ba be

aabess abases abase bases baas base bass seas aba ass baa ess sea ae as ba be

aabest abates abase abate abets baste bates beast beats betas tabes abet baas base bast bate bats beat best beta bets east eats etas seat seta stab tabs teas aba aet ate baa bat bet eat eta sat sea set tab tea ae as at ba be ta

aabet abate abet bate beat beta aba aet ate baa bat bet eat eta tab tea ae at ba be ta

aabetu bateau abate beaut abet abut bate beat beau beta tabu tuba tube aba aet ate baa bat bet but eat eta tab tau tea tub ae at ba be ta ut

aabetux bateaux. *See* **aabetu**

aabffly affably. *No 6s or 5s*

aabfilu fabliau. *See* **aabilu abfilu**

aabfilux fabliaux fabliau. *See* **aabilu abfilu**

aabfllst fastball ballast. *See* **aablst**

aabflott flatboat. *See* **aaflot**

aabft abaft aba aft baa bat fat tab at ba fa ta

aabggr ragbag agar brag gaga garb grab raga aba aga baa bag bar bra gab gag gar rag ba

aabggrrt braggart. *See* **aabggr aaggrt**

aabggrs ragbags. *See* **aabggs aabggr aaggrs**

aabggs gasbag agas baas bags gabs gaga gags saga aba aga baa bag gab gag gas sag ba as

aabggss gasbags. *See* **aabggs aagss**

aabghkrs shagbark. *See* **aabhks**

aabgilm mailbag. *See* **aabil aailm**

aabgilms mailbags mailbag gimbals. *See* **aablms aagims aailms**

aabgimns sambaing abasing siamang. *See* **aabgmn aagims aaimns abgins**

aabginr bargain. *See* **abginr aagin**

aabginrs bargains abasing bargain sabring sangria. *See* **abginr abgins abinrs aginrs**

aabgins abasing. *See* **abgins aagin aagis**

aabgint abating. *See* **abgint aagin aagit**

aabglruy arguably. *See* **aalry aalru bgluy**

aabgmn bagman bang gamb mana aba aga ana baa bag bam ban gab gam gan mag man nab nag am an ba ma na

aabgnorz garbanzo organza. *See* **aagnor abgnor**

aabhhoru brouhaha. *See* **abhor**

aabhillr hairball. *See* **aabill**

aabhiltu habitual halibut. *See* **aabilu aabltu**

aabhinst habitans habitan abstain. *See* **aabist abhins abhist**

aabhint habitan. *See* **abhit**

aabhintt habitant habitan habitat. *See* **aaintt**

aabhistt habitats habitat. *See* **aabist abhist**

aabhitt habitat. *See* **abhit**

aabhks kasbah abash kasha baas bash bask kabs aah aba aha ash ask baa bah has kab kas ah as ba ha ka sh

aabhkss kasbahs. *See* **aabhks abkss**

aabhlty bathyal. *See* **ahlty**

aabhnotu autobahn. *See* **abotu abnot ahntu**

aabhs abash abahs baas bash aahs aah aba aha ash baa bah has ah as ba ha sh

aabhssw bashaws. *See* **aabhsw ahssw abssw**

aabhsw bashaw abash awash baas bash haws shaw swab wash aah aba aha ash baa bah has haw saw was ah as aw ba ha sh

aabiijlt jailbait. *See* **abiilt**

aabiilx biaxial. *See* **abiil aailx aabil**

aabil labia alba bail aba ail ala alb baa lab ai ba la li

aabill labial labia alba bail ball bill aba ail ala alb all baa ill lab ai ba la li

aabillly labially. *See* **aabill**

aabillst ballista ballast. *See* **aabill aabist aablst**

aabilmy amiably. *See* **ablmy abily aailm**

aabilnnu biannual. *See* **aabilu aabinn aalnnu ailnnu**

aabilnor baronial. *See* **aailnr abilno**

aabilnot ablation. *See* **abilno abinot ailnot**

aabilnty banality. *See* **ailnty**

aabilost sailboat. *See* **aabist aablst ablost**

aabilrrt arbitral. *See* **aailrt abilrt**

aabilrs basilar. *See* **abilrs aabls aails**

aabilrvy variably. *See* **aairvy**

aabilsu abulias. *See* **aabilu aabls aails**

aabilu abulia labia alba bail aba ail ala alb baa lab ai ba la li

aabimmr marimba. *See* **aabmm aaimr**

aabimmrs marimbas marimba. *See* **aabmms aabmrs aaimms**

aabimors ambrosia. *See* **aabmrs aamors abiors**

aabinn banian bani aba ana ani baa ban bin inn nab nib ai an ba in na

aabinnpr brainpan. *See* **aabinn**

aabinns banians. *See* **aabinn abnns abins**

aabinors abrasion. *See* **abinos abinrs abiors abnors**

aabinrtz bartizan tzarina. *See* **aabinz aainrt**

aabinsst abstains abstain. *See* **aabist abinss ainsst**

aabinst abstain. *See* **aabist aanst ainst**

aabinz banzai azan bani aba ana ani baa ban bin nab nib ai an ba in na

aabiortt abattoir. *See* **aabort**

aabist abatis baits baas bait bast bats bias bits stab tabs aba baa bat bit ita its sat sib sit tab ai as at ba is it si ta ti

aabistuz zaibatsu. *See* **aabist**

aabkllpr ballpark. *See* **aaklr aablr aakpr**

aabknrst tanbarks tanbark. *See* **aabrst aaknst aakrst abknrs**

aabknrt tanbark. *See* **aanrt aakrt aabrt**

aabkoosz bazookas bazooka. *See* **aboosz akoosz**

aabkooz bazooka. *See* **abooz akooz**

aabl alba aba ala alb baa lab ba la

aabllppy palpably. *See* **aallpp**

aabllst ballast. *See* **aablst ablls allst**

aabllstu blastula ballast ablauts. *See* **aablst aabltu**

aabllwy wallaby. *See* **aally ablly ablwy**

aablmnor abnormal. *See* **aalmor almnor**

aablmru labarum. *See* **ablmru**

aablms balsam albas balas balms balsa basal lamas lambs samba alas alba albs alms baas balm bams labs lama lamb lams slab slam aba ala alb baa bam lab lam sal am as ba la ma

aablmss balsams. *See* **aablms aabmss**

aablmsst lambasts balsams basalts lambast. *See* **aablms aablst aabmss ablsst**

aablmst lambast. *See* **aablms aablst**

aablmsy abysmal. *See* **aablms abmsy almsy**

aabln banal alba anal aba ala alb ana baa ban lab nab an ba la na

aablntt blatant. *See* **aabln aalnt**

aablov lavabo alba lava oval aba ala alb baa boa lab lob ova ba la lo

aablpssy passably abyssal. *See* **aalpss aalpsy abpssy alpssy**

aablr labra alba alar aba ala alb baa bar bra lab lar ba la

aablrtu tabular. *See* **aabltu ablrtu**

aabls albas balas balsa basal alas alba albs baas labs slab aba ala alb baa lab sal as ba la

aablsst basalts. *See* **aablst ablsst**

aablssy abyssal. *See* **abssy aabls aassy**

aablst basalt albas atlas balas balsa basal blast blats alas alba albs alts baas bast bats blat labs last salt slab slat stab tabs aba ala alb alt baa bat lab sal sat tab as at ba la ta

aablstu ablauts. *See* **aablst aabltu**

aabltu ablaut tubal abut alba blat tabu tuba aba ala alb alt baa bat but lab tab tau tub at ba la ta ut

aabmm mamba mama aba baa bam am ba ma

aabmms mambas mamas mamba samba baas bams mama aba baa bam am as ba ma

aabmnot boatman. *See* **aabmnt**

aabmnst bantams batsman. *See* **aamnst aabmnt**

aabmnt bantam batman atman manta mana anta aba ana ant baa bam ban bat man mat nab tab tam tan am an at ba ma na ta

aabmorsu marabous marabou. *See* **aabmrs aamors abmrsu amorsu**

aabmortu tamboura marabou tambour. *See* **aabort aamrtu abortu**

aabmoru marabou. *See* **amoru aamor abmru**

aabmrs sambar samba sabra arms baas bams barm bars bras rams aba arm baa bam bar bra mar ram am as ba ma

aabmrss sambars. *See* **aabrss aabmrs aabmss**

aabms samba baas bams aba baa bam am as ba ma

aabmss sambas samba amass baas bams bass mass aba ass baa bam am as ba ma

aabnnosz bonanzas bonanza. *See* **aansz abnns**

aabnnoz bonanza. *No 6s or 5s*

aabnny banyans. *See* **aabnny abnns**

aabnny banyan aba aby ana any baa ban bay nab nay an ay ba by na

aabnsw bwanas nawabs bwana nawab awns baas bans nabs sawn swab swan aba ana awn baa ban nab saw wan was an as aw ba na

aabnw bwana nawab aba ana awn baa ban nab wan an aw ba na

aaborr arroba arbor boar bora roar aba baa bar boa bra oar orb rob ba or

aaborrrt barrator. *See* **aaborr aabort**

aaborrs arrobas. *See* **aaborr aborrs**

aaborst abators rabatos. *See* **aabort aborst aaorst**

aabort abator rabato abort aorta rabat tabor boar boat bora bort brat rota taro tora aba art baa bar bat boa bot bra oar oat orb ort rat rob rot tab tar tor at ba or ta to aabrrrty barratry. *See* **aabrty**

aabrrsst brassart. *See* **aabrss aabrst**

aabrrsuv bravuras bravura. *See* **abrrsu**

aabrruv bravura. *No 6s or 5s*

aabrs sabra baas bars bras aba baa bar bra as ba

aabrss sabras sabra brass baas bars bass bras aba ass baa bar bra as ba

aabrst rabats brats rabat sabra arts baas bars bast bats bras brat rats stab star tabs tars tsar aba art baa bar bat bra rat sat tab tar as at ba ta

aabrsty barytas. *See* **aarsty aabrty aabrst**

aabrt rabat brat aba art baa bar bat bra rat tab tar at ba ta

aabrty baryta rabat arty brat bray tray aba aby art baa bar bat bay bra rat ray tab tar try yar at ay ba by ta

aabs baas aba baa as ba

aabsstux saxtubas saxtuba. *See* **abstu absst bsstu**

aabstux saxtuba. *See* **abstu**

aacccruy accuracy. *See* **accruy**

aaccddes cascaded cascade saccade. *See* **acdes**

aaccdei cicadae. *See* **aaccdi**

aaccdeim academic cicadae. *See* **aaccdi**

aaccdelo accolade cloacae. *See* **aacclo acdelo**

aaccdenu caducean. *See* **acden cdenu**

aaccdes cascade saccade. *See* **acdes**

aaccdess cascades saccades cascade saccade. *See* **access**

aaccdi cicada acid cadi cad aid ad ai id

aaccdir cardiac. *See* **aaccdi aacdir**

aaccdirs cardiacs acarids cardiac cicadas. *See* **aaccdi aacdir acdirs**

aaccdis cicadas. *See* **aaccdi acdis**

aaccdovy advocacy. *See* **aacco accdy**

aacceent cetacean catenae. *See* **aacent accent aceent**

aaccelo cloacae. *See* **aacclo**

aaccelor caracole cloacae coracle. *See* **aacclo aacclr aaelor acelor**

aaccenrt carcanet. *See* **aacenr aacent accenr acenrt**

aaccertu accurate arcuate. *See* **aacetu acceru acertu**

aaccest saccate. *See* **acest**

aaccfilr farcical. *See* **aacclr aacfil aacilr**

aaccgilt galactic. *See* **accilt**

aacchir archaic. *See* **accir achir**

aacchllt catchall catcall. *See* **aacll accht achlt**

aacchlor charcoal. *See* **aacclo aacclr achlor**

aacchlot cachalot. *See* **aacclo**

aacchmno coachman. *See* **acchno**

aacciist sciatica sciatic. *See* **accit**

aaccilm acclaim. *See* **aacilm**

aaccilms acclaims acclaim. *See* **aacilm aailms acilms**

aaccilru acicular accrual caracul crucial. *See* **aacclr aacilr acilru**

aacciltt tactical cattail. *See* **accilt accitt**

aaccipty capacity. *See* **acipty**

aaccjoru carcajou. *See* **aacjou**

aacckkps packsack. *See* **aakks aacps ackps**

aaccllst catcalls catcall. *See* **aaclls**

aaccllt catcall. *See* **aacll**

aacclo cloaca cacao coal coca cola ala col lac la lo

aacclp calpac paca clap ala alp cap lac lap pal la pa

aacclps calpacs. *See* **aacclp aclps aacps**

aacclr calcar alar carl ala arc car lac lar la

aacclrsu accruals caraculs accrual accusal caracul. *See* **aacclr aaclrs aaclsu**

aacclru accrual caracul. *See* **aacclr aalru**

aacclsu accusal. *See* **aaclsu**

aaccnn cancan ana can an na

aaccnns cancans. *See* **aaccnn**

aaccnvy vacancy. *No 6s or 5s*

aacco cacao coca

aaccos cacaos cacao cocas coca sac as os so

aaccostt staccato. *See* **aaccos accost acostt**

aaccrss carcass. *See* **acrss**

aacddenv advanced advance. *See* **acdden**

aacddetu caudated caudate. *See* **aacddu aacetu acddeu acddtu**

aacddir radicand rancid.. *See* **acdir aacdnr acddin aacinr**

aacddrsw crawdads crawdad. *See* **aadrsw**

aacddrw crawdad. *See* **aadrw**

aacddu caudad duad add cad cud dad dud ad

aacdeehh headache. *See* **aadeh acdeh**

aacdeehr headrace charade earache reached. *See* **aacder acdehr adeehr**

aacdeels escalade. *See* **acdees acdels adeels**

aacdeem academe. *See* **acdem adeem**

aacdeems academes academe. *See* **acdees adeems**

aacdeeps escapade escaped. *See* **acdeep acdees acdeps aceeps**

aacdeest caseated caseate. *See* **acdees acdest adeest**

aacdef facade faced aced cade cafe dace deaf face fade ace cad fad fed ad ae fa

aacdefs facades. *See* **aacdef acdes acefs**

aacdegkp packaged package. *See* **acdekp**

aacdegmr decagram. *See* **aacder aacemr aadegm acdegr**

aacdehhy headachy. *See* **aadeh acdeh acdey**

aacdehin hacienda chained. *See* **cdehin**

aacdehlp cephalad. *See* **aacehp aacelp acdelp acehlp**

aacdehm chamade. *See* **aadeh acdeh acdem**

aacdehms chamades ashamed chamade chasmed. *See* **acdehs acehms adehms**

aacdehr charade. *See* **aacder acdehr**

aacdehrs charades arcades charade crashed. *See* **aacder aacers acdehr acdehs**

aacdehrt cathedra cathead charade charted trachea. *See* **aacder aaceht acdehr acdeht**

aacdehst cathends cathead scathed. *See* **aaceht acdehs acdeht acdest**

aacdeht cathead. *See* **aaceht acdeht**

aacdehtt attached attache cathead chatted. *See* **aaceht aachtt acdeht acdett**

aacdeinr radiance cairned carinae. *See* **aacder aacdir aacdnr aacenr**

aacdejnt adjacent. *See* **acdent aacent**

aacdeknp pancaked pancake. *See* **aacenp acdekp**

aacdektt attacked. *See* **aacktt acdekt acdett**

aacdelln canalled. *See* **acdell acdeln**

aacdelmn manacled manacle. *See* **aademn acdelm acdeln**

aacdelnr calendar caldera adrenal. *See* **aacder aacdnr aacenr aaclnr**

aacdelos caseload. *See* **acdelo acdels acelos cdelos**

aacdelpt placated placate. *See* **aacelp aadelt aaelpt acdelp**

aacdelr caldera. *See* **aacder acdelr**

aacdelrs calderas arcades caldera cradles. *See* **aacder aacers aaclrs acdelr**

aacdeltt lactated lactate. *See* **aadelt acdett aceltt**

aacdemy academy. *See* **acdem acdey**

aacdensv advances advance. *See* **aacnsv aadnsv acdens**

aacdensz cadenzas cadenza. *See* **acdens**

aacdenv advance. *See* **acden acdev aadnv**

aacdenz cadenza. *See* **acden**

aacdeotv advocate vacated. *See* **aacetv acdeot aceotv**

aacdequy adequacy. *See* **aaequ acdey**

aacder arcade acred arced areca cadre cared cedar raced aced acre area cade card care dace dare dear race read ace arc are cad car ear era rad rec red ad ae er re

aacders arcades. *See* **aacder aacers acders**

aacderst cadaster arcades redacts. *See* **aacder aacers aacrst aaerst**

aacdersv cadavers arcades cadaver. *See* **aacder aacers acders acderv**

aacderv cadaver. *See* **aacder acderv**

aacdettu actuated caudate actuate. *See* **aacetu acdett**

aacdetv caudate. *See* **aacetu acdet acdtu**

aacdetv vacated. *See* **aacetv**

aacdginr cardigan carding. *See* **aacdir aacdnr aacgir aacinr**

aacdhinp handicap. *See* **adhip aainp achin**

aacdhinr arachnid handcar. *See* **aacdir aacdnr aacinr aadhnr**

aacdhkrt hardtack hatrack. *See* **aachkr**

aacdhmr drachma. *See* **aadhmr acdhmr**

aacdhmrs drachmas dharmas drachma drachms. *See* **aadhmr aadmrs aahmrs acdhmr**

aacdhnr handcar. *See* **aacdnr aadhnr**

aacdhnrs handcars canards dharnas handcar. *See* **aacdnr aachns aadhnr acdhrs**

aacdhnrt handcart handcar. *See* **aacdnr aadhnr**

aacdilmt dalmatic. *See* **aacilm**

aacdilno diaconal calando nodical. *See* **acilno**

aacdilnr cardinal cranial laniard radical. *See* **aacdir aacdnr aacilr aacinr**

aacdiloz zodiacal. *See* **acdioz**

aacdilr radical. *See* **aacdir aacilr aadilr**

aacdilrs radicals acarids radials radical. *See* **aacdir aacilr aaclrs aadilr**

aacdimrt dramatic. *See* **aacdir aaimrt**

aacdinst antacids antacid discant satanic. *See* **aadins aadist acdist acinst**

aacdint antacid. *See* **acint acdit aadin**

aacdir acarid acrid caird acid aria arid cadi card raid aid air arc cad car rad ria rid ad ai id

aacdirs acarids. *See* **aacdir acdirs**

aacdirty caryatid. *See* **aacdir aadrty**

aacdituy audacity. *See* **aaituy acituy**

aacdjksw jackdaws jackdaw. *See* **acjks**

aacdjkw jackdaw. *No 6s or 5s*

aacdlno calando. *See* **aacln adlno**

aacdlns scandal. *See* **aaclns aadlns**

aacdlnss scandals scandal sandals. *See* **aaclns aadlns aadlss acdlss**

aacdlor carload. *See* **aclor**

aacdlors carloads carload. *See* **aaclrs aclors adlors**

aacdlort cartload carload. *See* **acort aalrt aaort**

aacdlpr placard. *See* **aaclpr**

aacdlprs placards placard carpals. *See* **aaclpr aaclrs**

aacdlu caudal ducal auld caul clad dual laud ala cad cud lac lad ad la

aacdmmor cardamom. *See* **aamor acmor acmmo**

aacdmp madcap camp damp paca amp cad cam cap dam dap mac mad map pad ad am ma pa

aacdmps madcaps. *See* **aacdmp acmps aacps**

aacdnr canard card darn narc nard rand ana and arc cad can car rad ran ad an na

aacdnrs canards. *See* **aacdnr acdrs adnrs**

aacdoosv avocados avocado. *See* **acdos**

aacdoov avocado. *No 6s or 5s*

aacdrsz czardas. *See* **acdrs acrsz**

aaceeflp paleface. *See* **aacefl aacelp aaeelp**

aaceeglr clearage acreage. *See* **aaeegl aaeglr aceelr aeeglr**

aaceeglv cleavage. *See* **aaeegl aaeglv aceelv**

aaceegr acreage. *See* **aeeegr aacer acegr**

aaceehr earache. *See* **aacer acehr ceehr**

aaceehrs earaches earache reaches. *See* **aacers aceers acehrs aeehrs**

aaceehrt tracheae cheater earache hectare hetaera teacher trachea. *See* **aaceht aaeert aceert aeehrt**

aaceeimt emaciate. *See* **ceeimt**

aaceeinn encaenia. *See* **aceinn**

aaceelrt lacerate treacle. *See* **aaeert aceelr aceert acelrt**

aaceelst escalate caseate celesta lactase. *See* **acelst aeelst ceelst**

aaceemst casemate caseate. *See* **acems aacms acest**

aaceent catenae. *See* **aacent aceent**

aaceentt catenate catenae acetate. *See* **aacent aceent**

aaceeprv precavae. *See* **aeeprv**

aaceepss seascape escapes. *See* **aceeps aceess acepss aeepss**

aaceesst caseates caseate. *See* **aceess acesst aeesst**

aaceest caseate. *See* **acest acees aeest**

aaceestt acetates caseate acetate. *See* **acestt aeestt**

aaceett acetate. *See* **acett**

aaceetuv evacuate. *See* **aacetu aacetv**

aaceetvx excavate. *See* **aacetv aacetx**

aaceffin affiance caffein. *See* **acefin**

aacefis fasciae. *See* **aacfis acefis**

aacefist fasciate fasciae. *See* **aacfis acefis acefst aefist**

aacefl faecal fecal cafe calf clef face flea lace leaf ace ala ale elf lac lea ae el fa la

aaceflt falcate. *See* **aacefl aaelt acelt**

aaceflu faculae. *See* **aacflu aacefl**

aacefr carafe areca facer farce acre afar area cafe care face fare fear race ace arc are arf car ear era far rec ref ae er fa re

aacefrr carfare. *See* **aacefr acerr**

aacefrrs carfares carfare carafes. *See* **aacefr aacers aacfrs acefrs**

aacefrs carafes. *See* **aacers aacefr acefrs aacfrs**

aacefrss fracases carafes. *See* **aacefr aacers aacfrs acefrs**

aacegilt glaciate. *See* **aegilt**

aacegirr carriage. *See* **aacgir acegir aceirr**

aacegirv vicarage avarice. *See* **aacgir aacirv aaegrv acegir**

aacegkp package. *See* **aaegp aacep aaekp**

aacegkpr packager package. *See* **acekpr**

aacegkps packages package. *See* **aaegp aacep aaekp**

aacegnr carnage. *See* **aacenr aegnr acegr**

aacegrst cartages cartage. *See* **aacers aacrst aaegst aaerst**

aacegrt cartage. *See* **aaegt aacer aacrt**

aacehill heliacal challie helical. *See* **aacill**

aacehirz archaize. *See* **acehir aehirz**

aacehlss calashes clashes. *See* **aachls acehls acehss acelss**

aacehmrs marchesa cameras marches mesarch. *See* **aacemr aacers aahmrs acehms**

aacehmst schemata matches. *See* **aaceht aahmst acehms acehst**

aacehnp panache. *See* **aacehp aacenp**

aacehnps panaches apaches canapes panache. *See* **aacehp aacenp aachns aaenps**

aacehp apache apace chape cheap peach ache cape chap each heap paca pace aah ace aha ape cap cep hae hap hep pah pea ae ah eh ha he pa pe

aacehps apaches. *See* **aacehp acehps**

aacehpu chapeau. *See* **aacehp**

aacehrst tracheas trachea. *See* **aaceht aacers aacrst aaerst**

aacehrt trachea. *See* **aaceht aacer aacrt**

aacehrtt reattach attache chatter ratchet trachea. *See* **aaceht aachtt aehrtt**

aacehstt attaches attache hastate. *See* **aaceht aachtt acehst acestt**

aaceht chaeta cheat tache teach theca ache cate chat each etch hate heat tach tech aah ace act aet aha ate cat eat eta eth hae hat het tea the ae ah at eh ha he ta

aacehtt attache. *See* **aaceht aachtt**

aaceilln alliance canaille. *See* **aacill aeilln**

aaceilmn calamine manacle laminae. *See* **aacilm aacimn aaeimn aailmn**

aaceilnz canalize. *See* **aeiln aeinz aacln**

aaceilop alopecia. *See* **aacelp aacilp aceilp ceilop**

aaceilrv cavalier avarice caravel caviler claviar. *See* **aacilr aacirv aaeilr aaelrv**

aaceimns amnesiac amnesia amnesic caimans cinemas maniacs. *See* **aacimn aaeimn aaemns aaimns**

aaceinr carinae. *See* **aacenr aacinr aceinr**

aaceinrs canaries arsenic carinae carnies. *See* **aacenr aacers aacinr aaenrs**

aaceinrt carinate carinae certain. *See* **aacenr aacent aacinr aainrt**

aaceinrv variance carinae avarice. *See* **aacenr aacinr aacirv aceinr**

aaceipps papacies. *See* **aacips aceips**

aaceiqsu acequias acequia caiques. *See* **aceiqu aceqsu**

aaceiqu acequia. *See* **aceiqu aaequ**

aaceirsv avarices avarice caviars viscera. *See* **aacers aacirv aceirs aceisv**

aaceirv avarice. *See* **aacirv aacer acerv**

aaceittv activate. *See* **aacetv aacitv aceitv aeittv**

aacekklw cakewalk. *See* **aackl aaekw**

aaceknp pancake. *See* **aacenp aaekp**

aaceknps pancakes askance canapes pancake. *See* **aacenp aaenps acenps**

aacekns askance. *See* **aceks acens aakns**

aacekost oatcakes oatcake. *See* **acekst aceost cekost**

aacekot oatcake. *No 6s or 5s*

aacekrtt attacker. *See* **aacktt aaekrt acekrt**

aacellot allocate lacteal collate. *See* **acello acelot**

aacellst lacteals lacteal lactase. *See* **aaclls acelst aellst**

aacellt lacteal. *See* **aaelt aacll acell**

aacelmn manacle. *See* **acelm aacln aceln**

aacelmns manacles manacle. *See* **aaclns aaemns acelms acelns**

aacelmr cameral caramel. *See* **acelmr aacemr**

aacelmrs caramels cameral cameras caramel marcels. *See* **aacemr aacers aaclrs aalmrs**

aacelnpr parlance. *See* **aacelp aacenp aacenr aaclnr**

aacelnpt placenta placate. *See* **aacelp aacenp aacent aacnpt**

aacelnpy anyplace. *See* **aacelp aacenp**

aacelnst analects cantles centals lactase lancets sealant. *See* **aacent aaclns aaelnt aaenst**

aacelnsv valances valance. *See* **aaclns aacnsv acelns acelsv**

aacelnu lacunae. *See* **acelnu aaclnu**

aacelnv valance. *See* **acelv aacln aalnv**

aacelp palace apace palea place cape clap lace leap paca pace pale peal plea ace ala ale alp ape cap cep lac lap lea pal pea ae el la pa pe

aacelps palaces. *See* **aacelp acelps aaelps**

aacelpst placates lactase palaces palates placate placets. *See* **aacelp aaelps aaelpt acelps**

aacelpsu scapulae capsule palaces scapula specula. *See* **aacelp aaclsu aaelps acelps**

aacelpt placate. *See* **aacelp aaelpt acelpt**

aacelrsv caravels caravel carvels. *See* **aacers aaclrs aaelrv aalrsv**

aacelrv caravel. *See* **aaelrv acelrv**

aacelst lactase. *See* **acelst**

aacelstt lactates lactase lactate. *See* **acelst aceltt acestt**

aaceltt lactate. *See* **aceltt aaelt**

aacemnps spaceman canapes encamps. *See* **aacenp aaemns aaenps aamnps**

aacemr camera areca cream acme acre area came care cram mace marc mare race ream ace arc are arm cam car ear era mac mae mar ram rec rem ae am em er ma me re

aacemrs cameras. *See* **aacers aacemr acemrs**

aacemrss massacre cameras sarcasm screams. *See* **aacemr aacers acemrs acerss**

aacenotu oceanaut. *See* **aacent aacetu acenot acnotu**

aacenp canape apace apnea paean pecan acne cane cape nape neap paca pace pane pean ace ana ane ape can cap cep nae nap pan pea pen ae an en na ne pa pe

aacenprs pancreas canapes prances. *See* **aacenp aacenr aacers aaenps**

aacenps canapes. *See* **aaenps aacenp acenps**

aacenpsu saucepan canapes. *See* **aacenp aaenps aaensu acenps**

aacenr arcane anear areca arena caner crane nacre acne acre area cane care earn narc near race ace ana ane arc are can car ear era nae ran rec ae an en er na ne re

aacenrvz czarevna. *See* **aacenr acenrv**

aacenssv canvases canvass. *See* **aacnsv**

aacenstt castanet. *See* **aacent aaenst acenst acestt**

aacent catena antae enact acne anta ante cane cant cate cent neat ace act aet ana ane ant ate can cat eat eta nae net tan tea ten ae an at en na ne ta

aaceopst peacoats peacoat capotes. *See* **aceopt aceost acepst**

aaceopt peacoat. *See* **aceopt aacep**

aaceosst seacoast. *See* **acosst acesst ceosst aceost**

aacep apace cape paca pace ace ape cap cep pea ae pa pe

aacer areca acre area care race ace arc are car ear era rec ae er re

aacers arecas acres areas areca cares races scare aces acre arcs area arse care cars case ears eras race rase scar sear sera ace arc are car ear era rec res sac sea ae as er re

aacerstt castrate. *See* **aacers aacrst aaerst aarstt**

aacerswy raceways raceway. *See* **aacers aaeswy acersy aerswy**

aacerttt tractate attract. *See* **aerttt**

aacertu arcuate. *See* **aacetu acertu**

aacerwy raceway. *See* **aacer aaerw aerwy**

aacesttu actuates actuate. *See* **aacetu acestt aesttu cesttu**

aacestv caveats vacates. *See* **aacetv aaestv**

aacesuwy causeway. *See* **aaeswy**

aacettu actuate. *See* **aacetu acett**

aacetu acuate acute cate cute ace act aet ate cat cue cut eat eta tau tea ae at ta ut

aacetv caveat vacate cate cave ace act aet ate ave cat eat eta tav tea vac vat vet ae at ta

aacetx exacta exact cate ace act aet ate cat eat eta tax tea ae at ax ex ta

aacfhmst camshaft. *See* **aahmst**

aacfil facial alif calf fail fila laic ail ala lac ai fa if la li

aacfilly facially fallacy. *See* **aacfil aacill**

aacfils facials. *See* **aacfil aacfis acfils**

aacfinst fanatics caftans fanatic satanic. *See* **aacfis aacfnt acinst afinst**

aacfint fanatic. *See* **aacfnt acint afint**

aacfirrt aircraft. *See* **afirt aairt aacrt**

aacfirtt artifact. *See* **afirt aairt aartt**

aacfis fascia asci fisc fas ifs sac sic ai as fa if is si

aacfiss fascias. *See* **aacfis aaciss**

aacfjklp flapjack. *See* **aacjkl**

aacflly fallacy. *See* **aacll aally**

aacflrst flatcars flatcar. *See* **aacfrs aaclrs aacrst aalrst**

aacflrt flatcar. *See* **aalrt aacrt acfrt**

aacfltu factual. *See* **aacltu aacflu**

aacflu facula faucal calf caul ala flu lac fa la

aacfnst caftans. *See* **aacfnt aanst acnst**

aacfnt caftan anta cant fact act aft ana ant can cat fan fat tan an at fa na ta

aacfrs fracas scarf afar arcs arfs cars scar arc arf car far fas sac fa as

aacggino anagogic. *See* **acggin acgino**

aacghopz gazpacho. *See* **achop**

aacgiimn magician. *See* **aacimn acgimn**

aacgill glacial. *See* **aacill acgill**

aacgilm magical. *See* **aacilm acgim**

aacgilnv galvanic calving. *See* **aagilv acgiln acginv agilnv**

aacgilox coxalgia coaxial. *See* **aaclox**

aacgimmt magmatic. *See* **acgim aagmm**

aacgimnp campaign camping. *See* **aacimn acgimn acginp**

aacginot contagia coating. *See* **acgino acgint acinot**

aacgintv vacating. *See* **aacitv aacntv acgint acginv**

aacgir agaric cigar agar aria crag raga aga air arc car gar rag ria rig ai

aacgirs agarics. *See* **aacgir acgirs**

aacgisty sagacity. *See* **aagist**

aacglmou glaucoma. *See* **aalmo aglmu glmou**

aacglost catalogs catalog coastal. *See* **aclost aglost**

aacglot catalog. *See* **aglot**

aacgnosu guanacos guanaco. *See* **acgnos agnosu**

aacgnou guanaco. *See* **acgno agnou**

aacgnrvy vagrancy. *See* **aacnry aagnry aagrvy**

aachhtwy hatchway. *See* **achht achtw achty**

aachiimr mariachi. *See* **achir achmr ahimr**

aachikn kachina. *See* **achin chikn**

aachikns kachinas kachina. *See* **aachns achins chikns**

aachilnp chaplain. *See* **aacilp achilp**

aachilps calipash aphasic apicals caliphs paschal spacial. *See* **aachls aacilp aacips aahlps**

aachilrv archival. *See* **aacilr aacirv achilr**

aachilt calathi. *See* **achit achlt chilt**

aachimnn chainman. *See* **aacimn**

aachimnr chairman. *See* **aacimn aacinr aacmnr aaimnr**

aachimrr armchair. *See* **achir achmr chirr**

aachimrs archaism charisma charism chrisma. *See* **aahmrs achirs achmrs acimrs**

aachips aphasic. *See* **aacips achips**

aachipss aphasics aphasic. *See* **aacips aaciss aahpss achips**

aachirst citharas cithara. *See* **aacrst aairst achirs achrst**

aachirt cithara. *See* **achit aairt aacrt**

aachkmn hackman. *No 6s or 5s*

aachkr charka arak arch cark char hack hark rack aah aha arc ark car rah ah ha ka

aachkrs charkas. *See* **aachkr aakrs ackrs**

aachkrst hatracks charkas hatrack. *See* **aachkr aacrst aakrst achrst**

aachkrsy hayracks charkas hayrack. *See* **aachkr**

aachkrt hatrack. *See* **aachkr aacrt achrt**

aachkry hayrack. *See* **aachkr achry**

aachkssw hacksaws hacksaw. *See* **aachsw aachkw achssw achkss**

aachksty haystack. *See* **achsty**

aachksw hacksaw. *See* **aachsw aachkw achksw**

aachkw kwacha whack chaw hack hawk aah aha caw haw ah aw ha ka

aachlmno monachal. *See* **aalmo aahlo aacln**

aachlps paschal. *See* **aachls aahlps**

aachlpss paschals paschal. *See* **aachls aahlps aahpss aalpss**

aachls calash clash alas cash lash aah aha ala ash has lac sac sal ah as ha la sh

aachlstu calathus. *See* **aachls aaclsu aacltu aclstu**

aachmnnr ranchman. *See* **aacmnr**

aachmntw watchman. *See* **aamnt achnt aacmw**

aachmnuy naumachy. *See* **aacmny**

aachmpry pharmacy. *See* **aahmpy**

aachmsy yashmac. *See* **aahms aahsy aacms**

aachnry anarchy. *See* **aacnry achry achnr**

aachns ashcan cans cash scan aah aha ana ash can has nah sac ah an as ha na sh

aachnss ashcans. *See* **aachns acnss**

aachoppr approach. *See* **aahppr achopr**

aachrrt catarrh. *See* **aacrt achrt**

aachrsw carwash. *See* **aachsw achrs acrsw**

aachrswy archways carwash archway. *See* **aachsw**

aachrtuy autarchy actuary. *See* **aacrt achrt achry**

aachrwy archway. *See* **achry**

aachsw cashaw awash chaws schwa cash caws chaw haws shaw wash aah aha ash caw has haw sac saw was ah as aw ha sh

aachtt attach chat tach tact that aah act aha cat hat tat ah at ha ta

aaciitv viatica. *See* **aacitv**

aacijm jicama mica aim cam jam mac ai am ma mi

aacijnop japonica. *See* **aainp acnop aajnp**

aacill laical calla lilac laic call ail ala all ill lac ai la li

aacillry racially lyrical. *See* **aacill aacilr acilry**

aacilm calami lamia claim calm clam laic lama mail mica ail aim ala cam lac lam mac mil ai am la li ma mi

aacilmnt claimant actinal clamant matinal. *See* **aacilm aacimn aailmn acilnt**

aacilmty calamity. *See* **aacilm**

aacilnr cranial. *See* **aacinr acilnr aaclnr aailnr aacilr**

aacilnrv carnival cranial. *See* **aacilr aacinr aacirv aaclnr**

aacilnt actinal. *See* **acilnt aacln aailn**

aacilntu nautical actinal lunatic. *See* **aaclnu aacltu acilnt cilntu**

aacilnty analytic actinal. *See* **acilnt ailnty**

aacilos asocial. *See* **acilos aails**

aacilott coattail cattail. *See* **ailtt acitt aciot**

aacilox coaxial. *See* **aaclox aailx acilx**

aacilp apical plica clap clip laic paca pail pica ail ala alp cap lac lap lip pal ai la li pa pi

aacilpru piacular. *See* **aacilp aacilr aaclpr acilru**

aacilps apicals spacial. *See* **aacilp aacips**

aacilpst capitals apicals capital plastic spacial spatial. *See* **aacilp aacips ailpst**

aacilpt capital. *See* **aacilp aclpt ailpt**

aacilpty atypical capital playact typical. *See* **aacilp acipty**

aacilr racial alar aria aril carl laic lair liar lira rail rial ail air ala arc car lac lar ria ai la li

aacilrty alacrity clarity. *See* **aacilr aailrt acilrt acilry**

aacilstt cattails cattail astatic. *See* **acistt**

aaciltt cattail. *See* **ailtt acitt**

aacimn caiman maniac amain anima mania manic main mana mica mina aim ana ani cam can mac man nim ai am an in ma mi na

aacimnor macaroni ocarina. *See* **aacimn aacinr aacmnr aaimnr**

aacimnot anatomic. *See* **aacimn acimno acimnt acimot**

aacimns caimans maniacs. *See* **aaimns aacimn**

aacimort aromatic. *See* **aaimrt acimot aciort**

aacinnst cantinas cantina satanic. *See* **acinnt acinst**

aacinnt cantina. *See* **acinnt**

aacinor ocarina. *See* **aacinr**

aacinors ocarinas ocarina. *See* **aacinr acinos acinrs aciors**

aacinort raincoat ocarina carotin. *See* **aacinr aainrt acinot aciort**

aacinotv vacation. *See* **aacitv aacntv acinot**

aacinpst captains capstan captain catnaps satanic. *See* **aacips aacnpt aainpt acinps**

aacinpt captain. *See* **aacnpt acinpt aainpt**

aacinqtu acquaint aquatic quantic. *See* **aanqtu aciqtu ainqtu**

aacinr carina crania cairn aria narc rain rani air ana ani arc can car ran ria ai an in na

aacinrsz czarinas czarina. *See* aacinr acinrs

aacinrz czarina. *See* aacinr

aacinst satanic. *See* acinst

aaciopst tapiocas tapioca. *See* aacips aciost aiopst ciopst

aaciopt tapioca. *See* aciot ciopt aiopt

aaciprty rapacity. *See* aaipry acipry acipty aiprty

aacips capias aspic pacas spica asci caps paca pica asp cap pas sac sap sic sip spa ai as is pa pi si

aaciqstu aquatics aquatic acquits. *See* aciqtu

aaciqtu aquatic. *See* aciqtu

aacirrtt tartaric. *See* aarrtt

aacirsv caviars. *See* aacirv acirsv

aacirtzz czaritza. *See* aairt aacrt aatzz

aacirv caviar vicar aria vair vara air arc car ria vac via ai

aaciss cassia assai asci sacs ass sac sic sis ai as is si

aacisss cassias. *See* aaisss aaciss acisss

aacistt astatic. *See* acistt

aacitv atavic vatic act cat ita tav tic vac vat via ai at it ta ti

aacjkl jackal jacal alack calk jack lack ala kal lac ka la

aacjklps slapjack jackals. *See* aacjkl aacjls aajlps

aacjkls jackals. *See* aacjkl aacjls

aacjkss jackass. *See* ackss acjks

aacjksty jackstay. *See* acjks aksty ackst

aacjl jacal ala lac la

aacjls jacals jacal alas ala lac sac sal as la

aacjosu acajous. *See* aacjou

aacjou acajou jo

aackknps knapsack. *See* ackkns

aackl alack calk lack ala kal lac ka la

aacklstw catwalks catwalk. *See* aackl

aackltw catwalk. *See* aackl

aackmnp packman. *No 6s or 5s*

aacknrs ransack. *See* acknrs aakrs aakns

aacknrss ransacks ransack. *See* acknrs acknss aknrss

aackorwy rockaway. *See* ackory

aackrr arrack arak cark rack arc ark car ka

aackrrs arracks. *See* aackrr aakrs aarrs

aackstt attacks. *See* aacktt ackst

aacktt attack tack tact act cat kat tat at ka ta

aacll calla call ala all lac la

aacllnry carnally. *See* aaclnr aacnry aallny

aacllrry carryall. *See* aalry aally aarry

aaclls callas calla calls scall alas call ala all lac sac sal as la

aacllsuy casually. *See* aaclls aaclsu aallsy acllsu

aaclltuy actually. *See* aacltu

aaclmnns clansman. *See* aaclns aamnns

aaclmnt clamant. *See* aamnt aacln aalnt

aaclmsu calamus. *See* aaclsu

aacln canal anal clan ala ana can lac an la na

aaclnnsu cannulas cannula annuals. *See* aaclns aaclnu aaclsu aalnnu

aaclnnu cannula. *See* aaclnu aalnnu

aaclnr carnal canal alar anal carl clan narc ala ana arc can car lac lar ran an la na

aaclnrsu lacunars lacunar. *See* aaclnr aaclns aaclnu aaclrs

aaclnru lacunar. *See* aaclnr aaclnu

aaclns canals canal clans nasal alas anal cans clan scan ala ana can lac sac sal an as la na

aaclnu lacuna canal anal caul clan ulna ala ana can lac an la na nu

aaclorru oracular auroral. *See* aaorru aclorr acloru aclrru

aaclorsu carousal arousal oculars oscular. *See* aaclrs aaclsu aclors acloru

aaclost coastal. *See* aclost aalst

aaclotv octaval. *See* aclov

aaclox coaxal coxal calx coal coax cola coxa ala col cox lac lax lox ax la lo ox

aaclpprt claptrap. *See* aaclpr

aaclpr carpal alar carl carp clap crap paca para ala alp arc cap car lac lap lar pal par rap la pa

aaclprs carpals. *See* aaclpr aaclrs

aaclprsu capsular scapular carpals scapula. *See* aaclpr aaclrs aaclsu acprsu

aaclprty calyptra playact. *See* aaclpr aalpry alprty

aaclpssu scapulas casuals causals scapula. *See* aaclsu aalpss aclpss acpssu

aaclpsty playacts playact. *See* aalpsy

aaclpsu scapula. *See* aaclsu

aaclpttu catapult tactual. *See* aacltu

aaclpty playact. *See* alpty aclpt aalpy

aaclrs lascar rascal sacral scalar carls alar alas arcs carl cars scar ala arc car lac lar sac sal la as

aaclrss lascars rascals scalars. *See* aaclrs

aaclrsuv vascular. *See* aaclrs aaclsu aalrsv

aaclrvy cavalry. *See* aalry aclry aalrv

aaclssu casuals causals. *See* aaclsu

aaclstty catalyst. *See* aclsy aalst actty

aaclstuy casualty. *See* aaclsu aacltu aclstu

aaclsu casual causal cauls alas caul ala lac sac sal as la us

aaclttu tactual. *See* aacltu

aacltu actual caul cult talc act ala alt cat cut lac tau at la ta ut

aacmnoor macaroon. *See* aacmnr acmnor acnoor amnoor

aacmnr carman cram mana marc narc ana arc arm cam can car mac man mar ram ran am an ma na

aacmnrsu arcanums arcanum. *See* aacmnr acmrsu amnrsu

aacmnru arcanum. *See* aacmnr amnru

aacmnsy caymans. *See* aacmny aacms aamsy

aacmny cayman cyma mana many maya myna ana any cam can cay mac man may nay yam am an ay ma my na

aacmors sarcoma. *See* aamors acmors

aacmorss sarcomas sarcoma sarcasm. *See* aamors aamoss acmors acmrss

aacmrss sarcasm. *See* acmrss aamss aacms

aacmrsss sarcasms sarcasm. *See* acmrss

aacms camas cams macs scam cam mac sac am as ma

aacmw macaw cam caw mac maw am aw ma

aacnpsst capstans capstan catnaps passant. *See* aacnpt aapsst acnsst

aacnpst capstan catnaps. *See* aacnpt aanst acnst

aacnpt catnap anta cant paca pact pant tapa act ana ant apt can cap cat nap pan pat tan tap an at na pa ta

aacnrstt transact rattans tartans. *See* aacrst aanrtt aarstt acrstt

aacnry canary carny narc nary racy yarn ana any arc can car cay cry nay ran ray yar an ay na

aacnssv canvass. *See* aacnsv acnss

aacnsv canvas cans scan vacs vans ana can sac vac van an as na

aacntv vacant anta cant act ana ant can cat tan tav vac van vat an at na ta

aacoprsu acarpous. *See* acprsu coprsu

aacorttu autocrat. *See* acort aaort aartt

aacp paca cap pa

aacppy papacy paca papa cap cay pap pay pya yap pa ay

aacps pacas caps paca asp cap pas sac sap spa as pa

aacrst carats carat carts acts arcs arts cars cart cast cats rats scar scat star tars tsar act arc art car cat rat sac sat tar as at ta

aacrsttt attracts attract. *See* aacrst aarstt acrstt

aacrstv cravats. *See* aacrst aacrtv

aacrt carat cart act arc art car cat rat tar at ta

aacrttt attract. *See* aartt aacrt acrtt

aacrtuy actuary. *See* aacrt

aacrtv cravat carat cart vara act arc art car cat rat tar tav vac vat at ta

aacstuwy cutaways cutaway. *See* **acstu acsuy**

aactuwy cutaway. *No 6s or 5s*

aacuv vacua vac

aadddeeh deadhead. *See* **addeeh**

aaddden addenda. *See* **addden**

aadddgnr granddad. *See* **adgnr**

aaddefll deadfall. *See* **addell**

aaddegm damaged. *See* **aadegm**

aaddegrt gradated gradate. *See* **addegr addert adegrt**

aaddehhr hardhead. *See* **aadeh adder addeh**

aaddehln headland handled. *See* **addehn addeln adehln**

aaddehmn handmade headman. *See* **aademn addehn**

aaddehrz hazarded. *See* **aadhrz**

aaddeil alidade. *See* **addeil**

aaddeils alidades alidade laddies. *See* **aadils addeil addels adeils**

aaddeirt radiated radiate. *See* **addeir addert adeirt**

aaddelns sandaled. *See* **aadlns addeln addels addens**

aaddeltu adulated adulate. *See* **aadelt addelu**

aaddemnt mandated mandate. *See* **aademn addemn ademnt**

aaddemru maraudened. *See* **aadmru addemr ddemru**

aaddemry daydream. *See* **addery ademry addemr**

aaddenp deadpan. *See* **aaenp aadnp**

aaddenps deadpans deadpan. *See* **aadnps aaenps addens addeps**

aaddepr paraded. *See* **aadepr addepr**

aaddept adapted. *See* **aadpt adept addet**

aadderw awarded. *See* **adderw aadrw aaerw**

aaddhimn handmaid. *See* **aadmn aaimn aadin**

aaddhkr khaddar. *No 6s or 5s*

aaddhkrs khaddars khaddar. *See* **aakrs adhrs ahkrs**

aaddllny landlady. *See* **aallny**

aaddlnrw landward. *See* **aalnrw**

aaddnrst standard dastard. *See* **adnrst**

aaddosu aoudads. *See* **aaddou addsu**

aaddou aoudad dado duad add ado dad dud duo odd oud udo ad do od

aaddrsst dastards dastard. *See* **adrst arsst**

aaddrst dastard. *See* **adrst**

aaddx addax add dad ad ax

aadeeghr headgear. *See* **adeegr adeehr deeghr**

aadeeglt galeated. *See* **aadegl aadelt aaeegl adeelt**

aadeegrv averaged ravaged average. *See* **aaegrv adeegr adeerv aeegrv**

aadeehmt meathead edemata. *See* **adeeht adeemt**

aadeeirt eradiate aerated radiate. *See* **aaeert adeeit adeirt deeirt**

aadeeknw awakened wakened. *See* **aadekw aaeknw adeenw aeeknw**

aadeelnn annealed. *See* **aaelnn adeeln**

aadeelpp appealed. *See* **aaelpp adelpp adeelp aaeelp**

aadeemnt emanated edemata emanate manatee mandate. *See* **aademn adeemn adeemt adeent**

aadeemt edemata. *See* **adeemt**

aadeentt antedate dentate. *See* **adeent adentt deentt**

aadeeppr appeared papered. *See* **aaeppr adeppr aadepr adeepr**

aadeepps appeased appease. *See* **adeeps adepps**

aadeeqtu adequate equated. *See* **aeeqtu**

aadeert aerated. *See* **aaeert deert adeer**

aadefhlt flathead fathead. *See* **aadelt adefht adehlt**

aadefhst fatheads fathead shafted. *See* **adefhs adefht adefst adehst**

aadefht fathead. *See* **adefht aadeh**

aadefirz faradize. *See* **aadefr aadfir adefir**

aadefllr falderal. *See* **aadefr adeflr aeflllr**

aadeflry defrayal already. *See* **aadefr adeflr adefly adefry**

aadefr afeard farad fared afar area dare deaf dear fade fare fear read are arf ear era fad far fed rad red ref ad ae er fa re

aadeg adage aged egad gaed aga age dag gad gae ad ae

aadeginr drainage gardenia grained reading. *See* **aadegn aadinr adegin adegnr**

aadegitt agitated agitate. *See* **aadeg aaegt adegt**

aadegl gelada adage algae galea glade aged alga dale deal egad gaed gala gale geld glad lade lead aga age ala ale dag eld gad gae gal gel lad lag lea led leg ad ae el la

aadegls geladas. *See* **aadegs aadegl adegls**

aadeglsv salvaged geladas salvage savaged. *See* **aadegl aadegs aaeglv aaegsv**

aadegm damage adage gamed aged dame egad gaed game made mage mead aga age dag dam gad gae gam gem mad mae mag ad ae am em ma me

aadegmn managed. *See* **aadegn aademn aadegm aaegmn**

aadegmpr rampaged rampage. *See* **aadegm aadepr adempr**

aadegms damages. *See* **aadegm aadegs**

aadegmss massaged amassed damages massage. *See* **aadegm aadegs adegss ademss**

aadegn agenda adage aged dean egad gaed aga age ana and ane dag den end gad gae gan nae nag ad ae an en na ne

aadegnrr arranged arrange gnarred grander. *See* **aadegn adegnr adegrr adenrr**

aadegns agendas. *See* **aadegn**

aadegpry paygrade drayage yardage. *See* **aadepr adegry adepry**

aadegpss passaged passade passage. *See* **aadegs adegps adegss adepss**

aadegrst gradates gradate. *See* **aadegs aaegst aaerst adegrs**

aadegrsy yardages drayage yardage. *See* **aadegs adegrs adegry aegrsy**

aadegrt gradate. *See* **adegrt aadeg aaegt**

aadegrtu graduate gradate. *See* **aadrtu aaegtu adegrt adegru**

aadegrv ravaged. *See* **aaegrv adegrv**

aadegry drayage yardage. *See* **adegry aadeg**

aadegs adages adage degas agas aged ages dags egad gads gaed saga sage ads aga age dag gad gae gas sad sag sea ad ae as

aadegssu assuaged assuage sausage. *See* **aadegs adegss aegssu**

aadegsv savaged. *See* **aadegs aaegsv**

aadeh aahed ahead hade head aah aha edh had hae ad ae ah eh ha he

aadehiln nailhead inhaled. *See* **aadhil adehil adehln adeiln**

aadehilr railhead airhead. *See* **aadhil aadilr aaeilr adehil**

aadehils headsail dahlias halides. *See* **aadhil aadils adehil adehls**

aadehir airhead. *See* **aadeh adeir adehr**

aadehirr diarrhea airhead hardier harried. *See* **adehrr adeirr**

aadehirs airheads airhead dashier shadier. *See* **adehrs adeirs adhirs aehirs**

aadehiwy hideaway headway. *See* **aadeh adehw adehy**

aadehlmp headlamp. *See* **adelmp**

aadehmn headman. *See* **aademn aadeh**

aadehmns headsman anadems ashamed headman. *See* **aademn aaemns aahmns adehms**

aadehms ashamed. *See* **adehms**

aadehmst masthead ashamed. *See* **aahmst adehms adehst ademst**

aadehps saphead. *See* **adehps**

aadehpss sapheads saphead passade. *See* **aahpss adehps adehss adepss**

aadehrrw hardware warhead. *See* **adehrr aderrw**

aadehrss   harassed dashers. *See* **aahrss adehrs adehss aehrss**

aadehrsw   warheads warhead. *See* **aadrsw adehrs adehsw adersw**

aadehrw   warhead. *See* **aadeh aadrw aaerw**

aadehssy   sashayed assayed. *See* **aahssy adehss**

aadehwy   headway. *See* **aadeh adehw adehy**

aadeilms   maladies malaise misdeal mislead. *See* **aadils aailms adeilm adeils**

aadeilps   palisade alipeds apsidal palsied. *See* **aadils aaelps adeilp adeils**

aadeilrs   salaried aerials derails radials. *See* **aadilr aadils aaeilr adeilr**

aadeilss   assailed aliases. *See* **aadils aadlss aailss adeils**

aadeiltv   validate availed. *See* **aadelt adeilt adeilv adeitv**

aadeilv   availed. *See* **adeilv aailv**

aadeimnn   amandine. *See* **aademn aaeimn adeimn**

aadeimnr   marinade. *See* **aademn aadinr aaeimn aaimnr**

aadeimnt   animated animate mandate mediant. *See* **aademn aaeimn adeimn adeint**

aadeimrv   maravedi. *See* **adeimr adeirv**

aadeimst   diastema. *See* **aadist adeims ademst adimst**

aadeins   naiades. *See* **aadins adeis aeins**

aadeintt   attained tainted. *See* **aaintt adeint adentt**

aadeinz   zenaida. *See* **adeiz aeinz deinz**

aadeiprs   paradise aspired despair diapers parades praised. *See* **aadepr aaeprs adeipr adeirs**

aadeiptv   adaptive. *See* **adeitv**

aadeirst   dataries radiates aristae astride atresia diaster radiate tirades. *See* **aadist aaerst aairst adeirs**

aadeirt   radiate. *See* **adeirt aairt aaert**

aadeisst   diastase. *See* **aadist adeiss adisst aeisst**

aadeistt   satiated satiate. *See* **aadist adestt**

aadeitw   awaited. *See* **adeitw aaitw**

aadejnnp   japanned. *See* **adennp**

aadeklry   kaleyard already. *See* **adeklr adelry adklry**

aadekmnr   mandrake. *See* **aademn adekmr adeknr**

aadekw   awaked awake waked awed wade wake weak weka awe dew wad wed ad ae aw ka we

aadellpp   appalled. *See* **aaellp aaelpp adellp**

aadelly   allayed. *See* **aally aelly adlly**

aadelmnr   alderman adrenal alarmed mandrel. *See* **aademn adelmr adelnr**

aadelmns   leadsman anadems. *See* **aademn aadlns aaemns adelms**

aadelmo   alamode. *See* **adelmo aalmo**

aadelmos   alamodes alamode. *See* **aalmos adelmo adelms adlmo**

aadelmpt   palmated palmate. *See* **aadelt aaelmt aaelpt adelmp**

aadelmr   alarmed. *See* **adelmr**

aadelmyz   amazedly. *See* **aademz aadlmy**

aadelnr   adrenal. *See* **adelnr**

aadelnrs   adrenals adrenal arsenal darnels landers slander snarled. *See* **aadlns aaenrs adelnr adelns**

aadelnyz   analyzed analyze. *See* **adely adeln adelz**

aadelppt   palpated palpate. *See* **aadelt aaelpp aaelpt adelpp**

aadelpry   parlayed already. *See* **aadepr aalpry adelpy adelry**

aadelry   already. *See* **adelry aalry**

aadelstu   adulates adulate saluted. *See* **aadelt adelst adlstu aelstu**

aadelt   alated alate dealt delta lated dale data date deal lade late lead tael tale teal aet ala ale alt ate eat eld eta lad lea led let tad tea ted ad ae at el la ta

aadeltu   adulate. *See* **aadelt adltu deltu**

aadeltuv   valuated adulate valuate vaulted. *See* **aadelt adeluv**

aademm   madame madam dame made mama mead dam mad mae mem ad ae am em ma me

aademn   anadem adman admen amend maned menad named amen dame damn dean made mana mane mead mean mend name ana and ane dam den end mad mae man men nae ad ae am an em en ma me na ne

aademns   anadems. *See* **ademns aademn aaemns**

aademnst   mandates anadems mandate. *See* **aademn aaemns aaenst aamnst**

aademnt   mandate. *See* **aademn ademnt**

aademrru   marauder eardrum. *See* **aadmru ademrr aemrru demrru**

aademss   amassed. *See* **ademss aamss**

aademz   amazed amaze mazed adze dame daze made maze mead adz dam mad mae zed ad ae am em ma me

aadennst   andantes andante. *See* **aaenst adennt**

aadennt   andante. *See* **adennt aaent**

aadenrrt   narrated narrate. *See* **aaerrt aanrrt adenrr adenrt**

aadenrsv   verandas veranda. *See* **aadnsv aaenrs aanrsv adenrs**

aadenrv   veranda. *See* **aaenr aderv aenrv**

aadepr   parade drape padre pared raped aped area dare dear para pard pare pear rape read reap ape are dap ear era pad par pea per rad rap red rep ad ae er pa pe re

aadeprrs   paraders drapers parades sparred. *See* **aadepr aadrrs aaeprs adeprr**

aadeprs   parades. *See* **aadepr aaeprs**

aadeprst   adapters adapter departs parades petards. *See* **aadepr aadpst aaeprs aaerst**

aadeprt   adapter. *See* **adeprt aadepr**

aadepss   passade. *See* **adepss**

aadepsss   passades passade. *See* **adepss adesss**

aadeqrtu   quadrate quadrat. *See* **aadrtu aeqrtu**

aaderrrw   rearward. *See* **aderrw**

aaderry   arrayed. *See* **aderry aarry aadrr**

aaderstw   eastward steward. *See* **aadrsw aaerst aderst adersw**

aadessy   assayed. *See* **aassy aessy**

aadfgnno   fandango. *See* **adgno afnno**

aadfhmnr   farmhand. *See* **aadhmr aadhnr**

aadfinru   unafraid. *See* **aadfir aadinr aafinr aainru**

aadfir   afraid farad afar aria arid fair raid aid air arf fad far fid fir rad ria rid rif ad ai fa id if

aadflllln   landfall. *See* **aaflll**

aadflmnr   farmland. *See* **aadmn aalmr aadmr**

aadflorw   aardwolf. *See* **aadrw adlrw adfrw**

aadfmrry   farmyard yardarm. *See* **aarry aadmr aadfr**

aadfr   farad afar arf fad far rad ad fa

aadfrs   farads farad afar arfs fads rads sard ads arf fad far fas rad sad ad as fa

aadgghr   haggard. *See* **aaghr**

aadgggimn   damaging. *See* **aaggmn aggimn**

aadggglnn   gangland. *See* **aagln adgln**

aadgglr   laggard. *No 6s or 5s*

aadgglrs   laggards laggard. *See* **aaggrs**

aadgiins   gainsaid. *See* **aadins adgiin dgiins**

aadgillo   gladiola. *See* **aadgio**

aadgillr   galliard. *See* **aadilr aagilr**

aadgilmr   madrigal diagram admiral. *See* **aadilr aagilr**

aadgilno   diagonal loading. *See* **aadgio aaglno adgiln adgino**

aadgimpr   paradigm diagram. *See* **aagim aadmr aaimr**

aadgimr   diagram. *See* **aadmr aaimr**

aadgimrs   diagrams diagram. *See* **aadmrs aagims adimrs**

aadginpr   parading grandpa draping. *See* **aadinr aagnpr adginr aginpr**

aadginpt   adapting. *See* **aainpt adgint adinpt aginpt**

aadginru guardian. *See* **aadinr aaginu aainru adginr**

aadginrw awarding drawing. *See* **aadinr adginr adginw adinrw**

aadgio adagio goad agio ado aga ago aid dag dig dog gad gid goa god ad ai do go id od

aadgiqru quadriga. *See* **adgru**

aadgllsw gadwalls gadwall. *See* **aagll aagls aglls**

aadgllw gadwall. *See* **aagll**

aadglnr garland. *See* **aaglnr adgln adgnr**

aadglnrs garlands garland raglans. *See* **aadlns aaglnr aaglns adglns**

aadglru gradual. *See* **aalru adlru adgru**

aadgmnor dragoman gormand grandam grandma. *See* **aagmnr aagnor adgnor admnor**

aadgmnr grandam grandma. *See* **aagmnr aadmn aadmr**

aadgmnrs grandams grandmas grandam grandma mansard. *See* **aadmrs aagmnr adgnrs**

aadgmot dogmata. *See* **adgmo**

aadgnpr grandpa. *See* **aagnpr adgnr aadnp**

aadgnprs grandpas grandpa parangs. *See* **aadnps aagnpr aagnps adgnrs**

aadgnrt gardant. *See* **aanrt agnrt**

aadgnruv vanguard. *See* **adgnr adgru aaguv**

aadgop pagoda goad ado aga ago dag dap dog gad gap goa god pad pod ad do go od pa

aadgops pagodas. *See* **aadgop adgos**

aadhhips padishah. *See* **adhips**

aadhil dahlia dial hail laid aah aha aid ail ala had hid lad lid ad ah ai ha hi id la li

aadhillr halliard. *See* **aadhil aadilr**

aadhilnr handrail laniard. *See* **aadhil aadhnr aadilr aadinr**

aadhils dahlias. *See* **aadhil aadils**

aadhinrr harridan. *See* **aadhnr aadinr**

aadhlpss slapdash. *See* **aadlss aahlps aahpss aalpss**

aadhlrsy halyards halyard. *See* **aahlrs aalrsy adhlry adhrsy**

aadhlry halyard. *See* **adhlry aalry**

aadhmnny handyman. *See* **aadmn adhny aamnn**

aadhmr dharma drama amah dram hard harm aah aha arm dam had ham mad mar rad rah ram ad ah am ha ma

aadhmrs dharmas. *See* **aahmrs aadhmr aadmrs**

aadhnpr hardpan. *See* **aadhnr aadnp**

aadhnprs hardpans hardpan dharnas. *See* **aadhnr aadnps**

aadhnr dharna darn hand hard nard rand aah aha ana and had nah rad rah ran ad ah an ha na

aadhnrs dharnas. *See* **aadhnr adnrs adhns**

aadhnssw handsaws handsaw. *See* **aahsw adnsw adhns**

aadhnsw handsaw. *See* **aahsw adnsw**

aadhrsz hazards. *See* **aadhrz adhrs**

aadhrwy hayward. *See* **aadrw adhry**

aadhrz hazard hard aah adz aha had rad rah ad ah ha

aadhsswy washdays washday. *See* **aahssy**

aadhswy washday. *See* **aahsw aahsy adhsy**

aadikllo alkaloid. *See* **aaikll**

aadilmnn mainland. *See* **aailmn adilnn**

aadilmr admiral. *See* **aadilr aalmr aadmr**

aadilmrs admirals admiral radials. *See* **aadilr aadils aadmrs aailms**

aadilnp paladin. *See* **aainp aailn ailnp**

aadilnpr prandial paladin laniard. *See* **aadilr aadinr aailnr aalnpr**

aadilnps paladins paladin apsidal. *See* **aadils aadins aadnps**

aadilnr laniard. *See* **aailnr aadilr aadinr**

aadilnrs laniards laniard radials radians. *See* **aadilr aadils aadinr aadins**

aadilorr railroad. *See* **aadilr**

aadilpry lapidary airplay rapidly. *See* **aadilr aaipry aalpry adilry**

aadilps apsidal. *See* **aadils adilps**

aadilr radial laird alar aria arid aril dial dirl laid lair lard liar lira raid rail rial aid ail air ala lad lar lid rad ria rid ad ai id la li

aadilrs radials. *See* **aadils adilrs aadilr**

aadils dalasi alias dials salad aids ails alas dais dial lads laid lids said sail slid ads aid ail ala ids lad lid sad sal ad ai as id is la li si

aadilwy waylaid. *See* **adily**

aadimnnr mandarin. *See* **aadinr aaimnr**

aadimnrt tamarind radiant tamarin. *See* **aadinr aaimnr aaimrt aainrt**

aadimnry dairyman drayman yardman. *See* **aadinr aaimnr adimry**

aadimnrz zamindar. *See* **aadinr aadmrz aaimnr**

aadimnuv vanadium. *See* **aadmn aaimn aainv**

aadimor diorama. *See* **aamor aadmr aaimr**

aadimors dioramas diorama. *See* **aadmrs aamors adimrs adiors**

aadin naiad aid ana and ani din ad ai an id in na

aadinops diapason paisano. *See* **aadins aadnps adinos ainops**

aadinopt adaption. *See* **aainpt adinpt**

aadinr radian dinar drain nadir naiad aria arid darn nard raid rain rand rani rind aid air ana and ani din rad ran ria rid ad ai an id in na

aadinrs radians. *See* **adinrs aadins aadinr**

aadinrt radiant. *See* **aadinr aainrt**

aadins naiads naiad aids dais dins said sain sand ads aid ana and ani din ids sad sin ad ai an as id in is na si

aadiorrt radiator. *See* **adiort diorrt**

aadirrsy disarray. *See* **aadrrs aarrsy adirrs**

aadist stadia adits staid tsadi adit aids dais data dits said tads ads aid dit ids ita its sad sat sit tad ad ai as at id is it si ta ti

aadjnttu adjutant. *See* **adntu ajntu anttu**

aadklmnr landmark. *See* **aadmn aalmr aadmr**

aadklnpr parkland. *See* **aalnpr**

aadkms damask dams mask ads ask dam kas mad sad ad am as ka ma

aadkmss damasks. *See* **aadkms aamss akmss**

aadknrst tankards tankard. *See* **aaknst aakrst adnrst**

aadknrt tankard. *See* **aanrt adknr aakrt**

aadkorwy workaday roadway workday. *See* **aadrw dkory dorwy**

aadkrww awkward. *See* **aadrw**

aadllmr mallard. *See* **aalmr aadmr aallm**

aadllmrs mallards mallard. *See* **aadmrs aallms aalmrs**

aadllpu paludal. *See* **aallu**

aadlmnns landsman sandman. *See* **aadlns aamnns**

aadlmnss landmass sandals. *See* **aadlns aadlss**

aadlmnu ladanum. *See* **aalmnu aadlnu**

aadlmnuu laudanum ladanum. *See* **aadlnu aalmnu**

aadlmy malady madly amyl lady lama maya ala dam day lad lam lay mad may yam ad am ay la ma my

aadlnrsy lanyards lanyard. *See* **aadlns aalnsy aalrsy**

aadlnry lanyard. *See* **aalry adlry aalny**

aadlns sandal lands nasal salad alas anal lads land sand ads ala ana and lad sad sal ad an as la na

aadlnss sandals. *See* **aadlns aadlss**

aadlnsu landaus. *See* **aadlns aadlnu**

aadlnu landau anal auld dual land laud ulna ala ana and dun lad ad an la na nu

aadlop apodal load opal plod ado ala alp dap lad lap lop old pad pal pod ad do la lo od pa

aadlopsy payloads payload payolas. *See* **aadlop aalopy aalpsy**

aadlopy payload. *See* **aadlop aalopy**

aadlortu   adulator. *See* aadrtu
aadlppsu   applauds applaud. *See* alppsu
aadlppu   applaud. *See* aalpp alppu
aadls   salad alas lads ads ala lad sad sal ad as la
aadlss   salads salad salsa alas lads lass sals ads ala ass lad sad sal ad as la
aadmm   madam mama dam mad ad am ma
aadmmn   madman madam adman damn mama mana ana and dam mad man ad am an ma na
aadmmnow   madwoman. *See* aadmmn
aadmms   madams madam mamas mama dams ads dam mad sad ad am as ma
aadmn   adman mana damn ana and dam mad man ad am an ma na
aadmnno   madonna. *See* aadmn aamnn admno
aadmnnos   madonnas madonna sandman. *See* aamnns admnos
aadmnns   sandman. *See* aamnns aadmn admns
aadmnort   mandator dormant matador mordant. *See* aamnrt admnor amnort
aadmnrs   mansard. *See* aadmrs
aadmnrss   mansards mansard. *See* aadmrs
aadmnry   drayman yardman. *See* aadmn aadmr adnry
aadmnsy   daysman. *See* aadmn admns aamsy
aadmorst   matadors matador stardom. *See* aadmrs aamors aamost aaorst
aadmort   matador. *See* aaort aamor aadmr
aadmr   drama dram arm dam mad mar rad ram ad am ma
aadmrrsy   yardarms yardarm. *See* aadmrs aadrrs aarrsy
aadmrry   yardarm. *See* aarry aadmr amrry
aadmrs   dramas madras drama drams arms dams dram rads rams sard ads arm dam mad mar rad ram sad ad am as ma
aadmrsu   marauds. *See* aadmrs aadmru
aadmrsz   mazards. *See* aadmrs aadmrz
aadmrszz   mazzards mazards mazzard. *See* aadmrs aadmrz
aadmru   maraud drama aura dram drum dura maud arm dam mad mar mud rad ram rum urd ad am ma mu um
aadmrz   mazard drama dram adz arm dam mad mar rad ram ad am ma
aadmrzz   mazzard. *See* aadmrz
aadnopr   pandora. *See* adnopr aadnp
aadnoprs   pandoras pandora parados pardons. *See* aadnps adnopr adnors anoprs

aadnoswy   nowadays. *See* adnsw dnosw dnowy
aadnp   panda ana and dap nap pad pan ad an na pa
aadnps   pandas panda daps naps pads pans sand snap span ads ana and asp dap nap pad pan pas sad sap spa ad an as na pa
aadnqrtu   quadrant quadrat quartan. *See* aadrtu aanqtu adnrtu
aadnqruy   quandary. *See* adnry
aadnsv   vandas vanda sand vans ads ana and sad van ad an as na
aadnv   vanda ana and van ad an na
aadoprs   parados. *See* adors doprs aaprs
aadoprx   paradox. *No 6s or 5s*
aadopss   passado. *See* adoss aopss
aadopsuy   paduasoy. *See* aopsy opsuy apsuy
aadorswy   roadways roadway. *See* aadrsw dorswy
aadorwy   roadway. *See* aadrw dorwy
aadostt   tostada. *See* aostt adost
aadpst   adapts adapt pasta tapas daps data pads past pats spat tads tapa taps ads apt asp dap pad pas pat sad sap sat spa tad tap ad as at pa ta
aadpsyy   paydays. *See* aadpyy
aadpt   adapt data tapa apt dap pad pat tad tap ad at pa ta
aadpyy   payday dap day pad pay pya yap yay ad ay pa
aadqrstu   quadrats quadrat. *See* aadrtu aaqrsu aqrstu
aadqrtu   quadrat. *See* aadrtu aqrtu
aadrr   radar rad ad
aadrrs   radars radar arras rads sard ads rad sad ad as
aadrssty   daystars daystar. *See* aadrty aarsty arssty
aadrsty   daystar. *See* aadrty aarsty
aadrsw   awards award draws sward wards draw rads sard wads ward wars ads rad raw sad saw wad war was ad as aw
aadrtu   datura aura dart data drat dura turd art rad rat rut tad tar tau urd ad at ta ut
aadrty   datary adyta tardy arty dart data drat dray tray yard art day dry rad rat ray tad tar tray yar ad at ay ta
aadrw   award draw ward rad raw wad war ad aw
aadrwwy   wayward. *See* aadrw
aadt   data tad ad at ta
aadty   adyta data tad day ad at ay ta
aaeeehrt   hetaerae hetaera. *See* aaeert aeehrt
aaeefgl   leafage. *See* aaeegl
aaeefrrs   seafarer. *See* aeerrs eefrrs

aaeegkl   leakage. *See* aaeegl
aaeegkls   leakages leakage. *See* aaeegl aeegls
aaeegl   galeae algae eagle galea agee alee alga gala gale glee aga age ala ale eel gae gal gee gel lag lea lee leg ae el la
aaeegmpr   amperage rampage. *See* aeegmpr aeempr
aaeegrsv   averages average greaves ravages. *See* aaegrv aaegsv aeegrs aeegrv
aaeegrv   average. *See* aaegrv aeegrv
aaeehrt   hetaera. *See* aaeert aeehrt
aaeeilnt   alienate lineate. *See* aeilnt aaelnt aeelnt .aailn
aaeekmns   namesake kamseen. *See* aaemns aeemns
aaeeknrw   reawaken. *See* aaeknw aeeknw aeekrw
aaeekprt   parakeet partake. *See* aaeert aaekrt aeekrt aeeprt
aaeekqsu   seaquake. *See* aekqsu
aaeelllm   lamellae lamella. *See* aeelll aeellm
aaeellpt   patellae patella. *See* aaellp aaelpt aaeelp aellpt
aaeelnps   seaplane. *See* aaeelp aaelps aaenps aeelps
aaeelor   areolae. *See* aaelor aeelor
aaeelort   areolate areolae. *See* aaeert aaelor aaeort aeelor
aaeelp   paleae palea alee leap pale peal peel plea ala ale alp ape eel lap lea lee pal pea pee ae el la pa pe
aaeelrtu   laureate. *See* aaeert aeelrt
aaeeltuv   evaluate valuate. *See* aeeltv
aaeemmtt   teammate. *See* aemtt eemmt
aaeemnst   manatees emanate manatee meanest. *See* aaemns aaenst aamnst aeemns
aaeemnt   emanate manatee. *See* aaent aamnt aeent
aaeennt   antennae antenna. *See* aeennt
aaeenrst   serenata aerates earnest eastern nearest. *See* aaeert aaenrs aaenst aaerst
aaeenrtt   anteater entreat ternate. *See* aaeert aanrtt aeenrt aenrtt
aaeenstu   nauseate. *See* aaenst aaensu aeenst aenstu
aaeepprr   rapparee reappear prepare. *See* aaeppr aeeprr
aaeepps   appease. *See* aapps aeeps eepps
aaeeppss   appeases appease. *See* aeepss
aaeeprst   separate aerates repeats. *See* aaeert aaeprs aaerst aaprst
aaeerst   aerates. *See* aaeert aeerst aaerst
aaeert   aerate eater reata area rate rete tare tear tree aet are art ate ear eat era ere eta rat ret tar tea tee ae at er re ta
aaeffgr   agraffe. *See* aeffgr

aaeffgrs agraffes agraffe gaffers. *See* **aeffgr aeffgs**

aaefflll falafel. *See* **aeflll**

aaeffnr fanfare. *See* **aaenr**

aaeffnrs fanfares fanfare. *See* **aaenrs**

aaeffstt taffetas taffeta. *See* **aefst affst aestt**

aaefftt taffeta. *No 6s or 5s*

aaefglll flagella. *See* **aaflll**

aaefimrr airframe firearm. *See* **aefirr aefmrr efimrr**

aaefkmst makefast. *See* **aefks aefms aefst**

aaeflm aflame flame fleam fame flam flea lama lame leaf male meal ala ale elf elm lam lea mae mel ae am el em fa la ma me

aaeflmot meatloaf oatmeal. *See* **aaeflm aaelmt aaflot**

aaeflrtw flatware. *See* **aeflrt**

aaefnu faunae fauna fane faun ana ane fan fen feu fun nae ae an en fa na ne nu

aaefrrw warfare. *See* **aaerw aerrw aefrw**

aaefrrwy wayfarer warfare. *See* **aefrry aefrwy**

aaefrswy wayfares. *See* **aaeswy aefrsw aefrwy aerswy**

aaegglnu language. *See* **aaegln aeggln aeggnu**

aaeggno anagoge. *See* **aegno**

aaeggnos anagoges anagoge. *See* **aegnos**

aaeggr garage agar ager area gaga gage gear raga rage aga age are ear egg era erg gae gag gar rag reg ae er re

aaeggrs garages. *See* **aaeggr aaggrs**

aaeghlu haulage. *See* **aaegl aghlu aehlu**

aaeghmrx hexagram. *See* **aaghmr**

aaeghnru harangue. *See* **aaghnr aeghnr eghnru**

aaegillr galleria regalia. *See* **aaeglr aaeilr aagilr egillr**

aaegilr regalia. *See* **aaeilr aagilr aaeglr**

aaegilsx galaxies. *See* **aaeilx aegils**

aaegiltt tailgate agitate. *See* **aegilt**

aaegimno egomania angioma. *See* **aaegmn aaeimn aegimn aeimno**

aaegimns magnesia amnesia enigmas manages seaming siamang. *See* **aaegmn aaeimn aaemns aagims**

aaegimnz magazine amazing. *See* **aaegmn aaeimn aegimn agimnz**

aaegimrr marriage armiger. *See* **aegimr**

aaeginpt paginate pageant. *See* **aaegnt aainpt aegint aginpt**

aaeginrt aerating granite ingrate tanager tangier tearing. *See* **aaegnt aainrt aeginr aegint**

aaegintv navigate vantage vintage. *See* **aaegnt aegint aeintv**

aaegirsv vagaries gravies ravages rivages. *See* **aaegrv aaegsv aegirv aegisv**

aaegiss assegai. *See* **aagiss aegis aegss**

aaegisss assegais assegai. *See* **aagiss aaisss**

aaegistt agitates agitate satiate. *See* **aaegst aagist**

aaegitt agitate. *See* **aaegt aagit**

aaegivwy giveaway. *See* **aaegv aeivw**

aaegkos soakage. *No 6s or 5s*

aaegkoss soakages soakage. *See* **aegss egoss aeoss**

aaegl algae galea alga gala gale aga age ala ale gae gal gel lag lea leg ae el la

aaegllpr pellagra. *See* **aaeglr aaellp aagllp**

aaegllst tallages gallets lastage tallage. *See* **aaegst aegllt aegIst aellst**

aaegllt tallage. *See* **aegllt aaegt aaelt**

aaeglm agleam algae galea gleam alga gala gale game lama lame mage male meal aga age ala ale elm gae gal gam gel gem lag lam lea leg mae mag mel ae am el em la ma me

aaegln galena algae angel angle galea glean lagan alga anal gala gale glen lane lean aga age ala ale ana ane gae gal gan gel lag lea leg nae nag ae an el en la na ne

aaeglnou analogue. *See* **aaegln aaglno eglnou**

aaeglns galenas lasagne. *See* **aaegln aaglns**

aaeglnss lasagnes galenas lasagne. *See* **aaegln aaglns aeglns**

aaeglntu angulate. *See* **aaegln aaegnt aaegtu aaelnt**

aaeglop apogeal. *See* **aaegp aaegl aglop**

aaeglr laager algae galea glare lager large regal agar ager alar alga area earl gala gale gear raga rage rale real aga age ala ale are ear era erg gae gal gar gel lag lar lea leg rag reg ae el er la re

aaeglrs laagers. *See* **aaeglr aeglrs**

aaeglssv salvages salvage savages. *See* **aaeglv aaegsv aalssv aeglsv**

aaeglst lastage. *See* **aaegst aeglst**

aaeglsv salvage. *See* **aaegsv aeglsv aaeglv**

aaeglsvy savagely salvage. *See* **aaeglv aaegsv aeglsv aeglsy**

aaeglv lavage agave algae galea gavel vagal alga gala gale gave lava lave leva vale veal aga age ala ale ave gae gal gel lag lea leg lev ae el la

aaegmn manage mange amen game mage mana mane mean name aga age ana ane gae gam gan gem mae mag man men nae nag ae am an em en ma me na ne

aaegmnr manager. *See* **aegmnr aaegmn aagmnr**

aaegmnrs managers manager manages mangers. *See* **aaegmn aaemns aaenrs aagmnr**

aaegmnrv gravamen manager. *See* **aaegmn aaegrv aagmnr aegmnr**

aaegmns manages. *See* **aegmns aaemns**

aaegmnst magentas magnates agnates gateman magenta magnate magnets manages. *See* **aaegmn aaegnt aaegst aaemns**

aaegmnt gateman magenta magnate. *See* **aaegnt aegmnt aaegmn**

aaegmors sagamore. *See* **aaegor aamors aegmos aegmrs**

aaegmpr rampage. *See* **aaegp aegpr aegmr**

aaegmprs rampages rampage. *See* **aaeprs aegmrs aegprs agmprs**

aaegmrrv margrave. *See* **aaegrv aegrrv**

aaegmss massage. *See* **aamss aegms aegss**

aaegmsss massages massage amasses. *See* **aemsss**

aaegmttw megawatt wattage. *See* **aaegt aemtt**

aaegnop apogean. *See* **aaegp aaenp aegno**

aaegnpst pageants agnates anapest pageant peasant. *See* **aaegnt aaegst aaenps aaenst**

aaegnpt pageant. *See* **aaegnt aaegp aaenp**

aaegnrr arrange. *See* **aegnrr**

aaegnrrs arranges arrange garners rangers. *See* **aaenrs aegnrr aegnrs**

aaegnrst tanagers agnates argents garnets strange tanager. *See* **aaegnt aaegst aaenrs aaenst**

aaegnrt tanager. *See* **aaegnt aegnrt**

aaegnrtu runagate tanager. *See* **aaegnt aaegtu aegnrt aenrtu**

aaegnst agnates. *See* **aaegst aegnst aaegnt aaenst aagnst**

aaegnstt stagnate agnates. *See* **aaegnt aaegst aaenst aagnst**

aaegnstv vantages agnates vantage. *See* **aaegnt aaegst aaegsv aaenst**

aaegnt agnate agate agent antae anta ante gate gent gnat neat tang aet aga age ana ane ant ate eat eta gae gan gat get nae nag net tag tan tea ten ae an at en na ne ta

aaegntv vantage. *See* **aaegnt aaegv**

aaegor agorae agora aero agar ager area gear goer gore ogre raga rage aga age ago are ear ego era erg gae gar goa oar ore rag reg roe ae er go or re

aaegorrt arrogate aerator garrote. *See* **aaegor aaeort aaerrt aegort**

aaegp agape gape page peag aga age ape gae gap pea peg ae pa pe

aaegpss passage. *See* **aaegp aepss aegps**

aaegpsss passages passage. *See* **aepsss**

aaegqsuy quayages quayage. *See* **aeqsuy**

aaegquy quayage. *See* **aaequ**

aaegrstt regattas regatta targets. *See* **aaegst aaerst aarstt aegrst**

aaegrstz stargaze. *See* **aaegst aaerst aegrst aegrsz**

aaegrsv ravages. *See* **aaegsv aegrsv aaegrv**

aaegrsvy savagery ravages. *See* **aaegrv aaegsv aagrvy aegrsv**

aaegrtt regatta. *See* **aegrtt aaegt aartt**

aaegrv ravage agave grave agar ager area aver gave gear raga rage rave vara aga age are ave ear era erg gae gar rag reg rev ae er re

aaegsssu assuages sausages assuage sausage. *See* **aegssu**

aaegsstw wastages wastage. *See* **aaegst aegsst aesstw**

aaegssu assuage sausage. *See* **aegssu aagss**

aaegssv savages. *See* **aaegsv**

aaegst agates agate gates stage agas ages east eats etas gate gats gest gets saga sage seat seta stag tags teas aet aga age ate eat eta gae gas gat get sag sat sea set tag tea ae as at ta

aaegsttw wattages wastage wattage. *See* **aaegst**

aaegstw wastage. *See* **aaegst aestw aegsw**

aaegstwy gateways getaways gateway getaway wastage. *See* **aaegst aaeswy aegsty aestwy**

aaegsv agaves savage agave agas ages aves gave saga sage save vase aga age ave gae gas sag sea ae as

aaegt agate gate aet aga age ate eat eta gae gat get tag tea ae at ta

aaegttw wattage. *See* **aaegt**

aaegtu gateau agate gate ague aet aga age ate eat eta gae gat get gut tag tau tea tug ae at ta ut

aaegtux gateaux. *See* **aaegtu**

aaegtwy gateway getaway. *See* **aaegt**

aaegv agave gave aga age ave gae ae

aaegz agaze gaze aga age gae zag ae

aaehhpt aphthae. *See* **aahhpt aehhp aehht**

aaehilp aphelia. *See* **aehlp aahlp aaelp**

aaehimnt anthemia animate. *See* **aaeimn aehmnt aeimnt**

aaehinst asthenia. *See* **aaenst aehnst**

aaehirt hetaira. *See* **aairt aehrt aeirt**

aaehkmry haymaker. *See* **aehmr aakmr aekmr**

aaehknst khanates khanate. *See* **aaenst aaknst aehkns aehnst**

aaehknt khanate. *See* **aaent aehnt aeknt**

aaehlmnw whaleman. *See* **aalmnw aelmnw**

aaehlmt hematal. *See* **aehlmt aaelmt aahlmt**

aaehlpuv upheaval. *See* **aehlp aahlp aahlv**

aaehlpx hexapla. *See* **aehlp aahlp aaelp**

aaehmnrt earthman. *See* **aamnrt aehmnt aehnrt aemnrt**

aaehmopr amphorae amphora. *See* **aamopr aehmpr**

aaehmort atheroma. *See* **aaeort ehmort**

aaehnpr hanaper. *See* **aaenr aaenp**

aaehnprs hanapers hanaper sharpen. *See* **aaenps aaenrs aaeprs aehprs**

aaehnpst pheasant anapest peasant. *See* **aaenps aaenst aehnst aenpst**

aaehnsy hyaenas. *See* **aaehny aehnsy**

aaehny hyaena hyena ayah yeah yean aah aha ana ane any aye hae hay hen hey nae nah nay yah yea yen ae ah an ay eh en ha he na ne ye

aaehrrss harasser sharers. *See* **aahrss aehrrs aehrss**

aaehrsss harasses. *See* **aahrss aehrss aehsss**

aaehrsy hearsay. *See* **aaers aahsy aehrs**

aaehstt hastate. *See* **aehstt**

aaeiiprs apiaries. *See* **aaeprs aeiprs**

aaeiirsv aviaries. *See* **aeirsv**

aaeijlnv javelina javelin. *See* **aeilnv**

aaeikkmz kamikaze. *See* **aaemz aeimz aaimz**

aaeiklln alkaline. *See* **aaikll aeilln**

aaeiklls alkalies. *See* **aaikll aeills**

aaeikllz alkalize. *See* **aaikll**

aaeilllu alleluia. *See* **aaellu**

aaeillpp papillae papilla. *See* **aaellp aaelpp**

aaeillpt palliate patella. *See* **aaellp aaelpt aeillt**

aaeillry aerially. *See* **aaeilr aellry**

aaeillx axillae. *See* **aaeilx aaillx**

aaeilmn laminae. *See* **aaeimn aailmn aeilmn**

aaeilmnt laminate ailment aliment animate laminae matinal. *See* **aaeimn aaelmt aaelnt aailmn**

aaeilmrt material maltier marital martial. *See* **aaeilr aaelmt aailrt aaimrt**

aaeilms malaise. *See* **aailms aeilms**

aaeilmss malaises aimless aliases malaise salamis. *See* **aailms aailss aeilms aeilss**

aaeilnpr airplane plainer praline. *See* **aaeilr aailnr aalnpr aeilnp**

aaeilnpt palatine pantile. *See* **aaelnt aaelpt aainpt aeilnp**

aaeilnsz nasalize. *See* **aailns aeilns aeinsz**

aaeilprt parietal apteral apteria partial. *See* **aaeilr aaelpt aailrt aeilrt**

aaeilprx preaxial. *See* **aaeilr aaeilx**

aaeilr aerial alar area aria aril earl lair liar lira lire rail rale real rial riel rile ail air ala ale are ear era ire lar lea lei lie ria ae ai el er la li re

aaeilrrt arterial retrial trailer. *See* **aaeilr aaerrt aailrt aeilrr**

aaeilrs aerials. *See* **aaeilr aeilrs**

aaeilrss assailer salaries aerials airless aliases sailers serials. *See* **aaeilr aailss aeilrs aeilss**

aaeilrtv varietal travail. *See* **aaeilr aaelrv aailrt aeilrt**

aaeilss aliases. *See* **aeilss aailss**

aaeilstv salivate estival. *See* **aaestv aailsv aeilsv aelstv**

aaeilstx saxatile. *See* **aaeilx aelstx**

aaeiltvx laxative. *See* **aaeilx**

aaeilx alexia axial axile axil axle ilex ail ala ale axe lax lea lei lie ae ai ax el ex la li xi

aaeimmst imamates imamate. *See* **aeimst aaimms aemmst**

aaeimmt imamate. *No 6s or 5s*

aaeimn anemia amain amine anima anime mania minae amen main mana mane mean mien mina mine name aim ana ane ani mae man men nae nim ae ai am an em en in ma me mi na ne

aaeimnrt marinate animate minaret raiment tamarin. *See* **aaeimn aaimnr aaimrt aainrt**

aaeimns amnesia. *See* **aeimns aaeimn aaimns aaemns**

aaeimnss amnesias amnesia inseams samisen. *See* **aaeimn aaemns aaimns aeimns**

aaeimnst animates amnesia animate inmates stamina. *See* **aaeimn aaemns aaenst aaimns**

aaeimnt animate. *See* **aaeimn aeimnt**

aaeimtv amative. *No 6s or 5s*

aaeinort aeration. *See* **aaeort aainrt aeinrt aenort**

aaeinorx anorexia. *See* **aaenr aiorx ainor**

aaeinrrw rainwear. *See* **aeirrw aenrrw**

aaeinrst seatrain antiars aristae artisan atresia nastier retains retinas stainer tsarina. *See* **aaenrs aaenst aaerst aainrt**

aaeinstt astatine attains satiate satinet. *See* **aaenst aaintt ainstt einstt**

aaeinstv sanative natives. *See* **aaenst aaestv aainsv aeinsv**

aaeipprs appraise appears apprise sappier. *See* **aaeppr aaeprs aeiprs aepprs**

aaeiprr pareira. *See* **aeiprr**

aaeiprrs pareiras pareira parries praiser rapiers repairs. *See* **aaeprs aeiprr aeiprs aeirrs**

aaeiprst aspirate parasite apteria aristae atresia parties pastier piaster pirates traipse. *See* **aaeprs aaerst aairst aaprst**

aaeiprt apteria. *See* **aeiprt aaprt aairt**

aaeirsst atresias aristae atresia satires. *See* **aaerst aairst aeirss aeirst**

aaeirst aristae atresia. *See* **aairst aaerst aeirst**

aaeirstt ariettas aristate arietta aristae artiste atresia attires ratites satiate striate tastier. *See* **aaerst aairst aarstt aeirst**

aaeirsvw airwaves waivers. *See* **aeirsv aeirvw aeisvw aersvw**

aaeirtt arietta. *See* **aeirtt**

aaeirttz zaratite arietta. *See* **aeirtt**

aaeisstt satiates satiate. *See* **aeisst aesstt**

aaeistt satiate. *See* **aestt**

aaejopr aparejo. *See* **aejpr aeopr**

aaejoprs aparejos aparejo. *See* **aaeprs aejprs aeoprs**

aaekkrsy kayakers kayaker. *See* **aakksy**

aaekkry kayaker. *See* **aakky**

aaeklmrw lawmaker. *See* **aeklrw**

aaeklmry malarkey malarky. *See* **aalmr aalry aelry**

aaekmrr earmark. *See* **aekmrr**

aaekmrrs earmarks earmark markers remarks. *See* **aakmrs aekmrr aekmrs aemrrs**

aaeknprt partaken partake. *See* **aaekrt aeknrt aenprt**

aaeknsw awakens. *See* **aaeknw aaeksw aeknsw**

aaeknw awaken awake waken anew kana knew wake wane weak wean weka ana ane awe awn ken nae new wan wen ae an aw en ka na ne we

aaekp apeak peak ape pea ae ka pa pe

aaekprrt partaker partake. *See* **aaekrt aaerrt aekprr**

aaekprst partakes partake. *See* **aaekrt aaeprs aaerst aakprs**

aaekprt partake. *See* **aaekrt aaprt aaekp**

aaekrt karate karat reata taker arak area kart rake rate take tare teak tear trek aet are ark art ate ear eat era eta kat rat ret tar tea ae at er ka re ta

aaeksw awakes askew awake wakes wekas awes sake skew wake weak weka ask awe kas saw sea sew was ae as aw ka we

aaekw awake wake weak weka awe ae aw ka we

aaelllm lamella. *See* **aallm**

aaelllpr parallel. *See* **aaellp**

aaellmpu ampullae ampulla. *See* **aaellp aaellu aelmpu**

aaellp paella palea lapel leal leap pale pall peal plea ala ale all alp ape ell lap lea pal pea ae el la pa pe

aaellps paellas. *See* **aellps aaellp aaelps**

aaellpt patella. *See* **aaellp aaelpt aellpt**

aaellrst laterals lateral stellar. *See* **aaerst aalrst aellrt aellst**

aaellrt lateral. *See* **aellrt aaelt aalrt**

aaellu alulae alula alula leal ala ale all ell lea leu ae el la**

aaellwyy alleyway. *See* **aalwyy**

aaelmmno melanoma. *See* **aalmo aelno aelmo**

aaelmmt lemmata. *See* **aaelmt**

aaelmmtu malamute lemmata. *See* **aaelmt aelmtu**

aaelmnrt maternal. *See* **aaelmt aaelnt aamnrt aelmnt**

aaelmnss salesman manless. *See* **aaemns aelmns aemnss**

aaelmnst talesman laments malates maltase mantels mantles sealant tamales. *See* **aaelmt aaelnt aaemns aaenst**

aaelmnu alumnae. *See* **aalmnu**

aaelmost oatmeals malates maltase maltose oatmeal tamales. *See* **aaelmt aalmos aamost aelmos**

aaelmot oatmeal. *See* **aaelmt**

aaelmprt malapert apteral palmate trample. *See* **aaelmt aaelpt aalmpr aelmpr**

aaelmpt palmate. *See* **aaelmt aaelpt**

aaelmpty playmate palmate. *See* **aaelmt aaelpt aelmty**

aaelmrsy lamasery. *See* **aalmrs aalrsy aelmrs aelmsy**

aaelmrtt maltreat martlet. *See* **aaelmt aelmrt aelrtt aemrtt**

aaelmsst maltases atlases malates maltase samlets tamales. *See* **aaelmt aelmst aelsst aemsst**

aaelmst malates maltase tamales. *See* **aelmst aaelmt**

aaelmt malate tamale alate metal lama lame late male malt mate meal meat melt tael tale tame teal team aet ala ale alt ate eat elm eta lam lea let mae mat mel met tam tea ae am at el em la ma me ta

aaelnn anneal anal lane lean ala ale ana ane lea nae ae an el en la na ne

aaelnns anneals. *See* **aaelnn aalnns**

aaelnntu annulate annulet. *See* **aaelnn aalnnu aaelnt aelntu**

aaelnoss seasonal. *See* **aelnos aenoss alnoss elnoss**

aaelnprt parental paternal prenatal apteral plantar planter replant. *See* **aaelnt aaelpt aalnpr aelnpr**

aaelnprw warplane. *See* **aalnpr aalnrw aelnpr**

aaelnpst pleasant anapest palates peasant planets platens sealant. *See* **aaelnt aaelps aaelpt aaenps**

aaelnrs arsenal. *See* **aaenrs aelnrs**

aaelnrss arsenals arsenal. *See* **aaenrs aelnrs aelrss**

aaelnrst asternal antlers arsenal rentals saltern sealant sternal. *See* **aaelnt aaenrs aaenst aaerst**

aaelnrtx relaxant. *See* **aaelnt aelnrt**

aaelnryz analyzer analyze. *See* **aelnry**

aaelnsst sealants sealant atlases. *See* **aaelnt aaenst aalnst aelsst**

aaelnssy analyses. *See* **aalnsy aelnsy**

aaelnst sealant. *See* **aaenst aalnst aaelnt**

aaelnstt atlantes lattens saltant sealant talents. *See* **aaelnt aaenst aalnst aelntt**

aaelnsyz analyzes analyze. *See* **aalnsy aelnsy aelsyz**

aaelnt lanate alate antae leant natal anal anta ante lane late lean lent neat tael tale teal aet ala ale alt ana ane ant ate eat eta lea let nae net tan tea ten ae an at el en la na ne ta

aaelnyz analyze. *See* **aalny**

aaelor areola aero alar aloe area earl lore oral orle rale real role ala ale are ear era lar lea oar ore roe ae el er la lo or re

aaelorr areolar. *See* **aaelor**

aaelors areolas. *See* **aaelor aelos aaers**

aaelorsu aureolas areolas arousal aureola. *See* **aaelor aelrsu aeorsu**

aaelorty aleatory. *See* **aaelor aaeort aelrty**

aaeloru aureola. *See* **aaelor aaeru aalru**

aaelostx oxalates oxalate. *See* **aelost aelstx elostx**

aaelotx oxalate. *See* **aaelt aeltx elotx**

aaelp palea leap pale peal plea ala ale alp ape lap lea pal pea ae el la pa pe

aaelpp appeal apple palea papal pepla leap pale palp papa peal plea ala ale alp ape lap lea pal pap pea pep ae el la pa pe

aaelppr apparel. *See* **aaelpp aaeppr aelppr**

aaelpps appeals. *See* **aaelpp aelpps aaelps**

aaelppst palpates appeals lappets palates palpate. *See* **aaelpp aaelps aaelpt aelpps**

aaelppsu applause appeals papules. *See* **aaelpp aaelps aelpps aelppu**

aaelppt palpate. *See* **aaelpp aelppt aaelpt**

aaelprst palestra apteral palates palters plaster platers psalter stapler. *See* **aaelps aaelpt aaeprs aaerst**

aaelprsv palavers palaver. *See* **aaelps aaelrv aaeprs aalrsv**

aaelprt apteral. *See* **aaelpt aelprt**

aaelprv palaver. *See* **aaelrv aaelp aelpr**

aaelpryz paralyze. *See* **aalpry aelpry**

aaelps salpae lapse leaps palea pales peals pleas salep salpa sepal alas ales alps apes apse laps leap leas pale pals peal peas plea sale seal slap ala ale alp ape asp els lap lea pal pas pea sal sap sea spa ae as el la pa pe

aaelpst palates. *See* **aaelpt aelpst aaelps**

aaelpstu plateaus palates plateau pulsate spatula. *See* **aaelps aaelpt aelpst aelstu**

aaelpt palate alate palea petal plate pleat late leap lept pale pate peal peat pelt plat plea tael tale tapa tape teal aet ala ale alp alt ape apt ate eat eta lap lea let pal pat pea pet tap tea ae at el la pa pe ta

aaelptu plateau. *See* **aaelpt elptu aeptu**

aaelptux plateaux plateau. *See* **aaelpt aeltux**

aaelrv larvae larva laver ravel velar alar area aver earl lava lave leva rale rave real vale vara veal ala ale are ave ear era lar lea lev rev ae el er la re

aaelrwyy waylayer. *See* **aelrwy aalwyy aelryy**

aaelsst atlases. *See* **aelsst**

aaelstuv valuates valuate. *See* **aaestv aelstu aelstv aelsuv**

aaelsux asexual. *See* **aelsux**

aaelt alate late tael tale teal aet ala ale alt ate eat eta lea let tea ae at el la ta

aaeltuv valuate. *See* **aaelt aeltv aeluv**

aaemmm mammae mamma mama mae mem ae am em ma me

aaemmmr maremma. *See* **aaemmm**

aaemmnrt armament. *See* **aamnrt aemmnr aemnrt**

aaemns seaman manes manse means names amen mana mane mean mesa name same sane seam ana ane ens mae man men nae sea sen ae am an as em en ma me na ne

aaemnstu manteaus manteau mantuas. *See* **aaemns aaenst aaensu aamnst**

aaemntu manteau. *See* **aamntu aaent aemnt**

aaemortt amaretto. *See* **aaeort aemrtt aeortt**

aaemottu automate automat. *See* **aemttu**

aaempttu amputate. *See* **aemttu**

aaemrrtu armature amateur erratum. *See* **aaerrt aamrtu aemrru aemrtu**

aaemrstu amateurs amateur matures strumae traumas. *See* **aaerst aamrtu aemrst aemrtu**

aaemrttu maturate amateur. *See* **aamrtu aemrtt aemrtu aemttu**

aaemrtu amateur. *See* **aamrtu aemrtu**

aaemsss amasses. *See* **aemsss aamss**

aaemsz amazes amaze mazes smaze maze mesa same seam mae sea ae am as em ma me

aaemz amaze maze mae ae am em ma me

aaennnst antennas antenna. *See* **aaenst**

aaennnt antenna. *See* **aaent aennt**

aaennott annotate. *See* **aanntt aenntt aenott**

aaennstu nauseant. *See* **aaenst aaensu aenstu annstu**

aaennsz zenanas. *See* **aaennz aansz aenns**

aaennz zenana azan ana ane nae ae an en na ne

aaenops paesano. *See* **aaenps aenops**

aaenopss paesanos paesano. *See* **aaenps aenops aenoss aenpss**

aaenortu aeronaut. *See* **aaeort aenort aenrtu anortu**

aaenp apnea paean nape neap pane pean ana ane ape nae nap pan pea pen ae an en na ne pa pe

aaenpprt apparent parapet. *See* **aaeppr aenppr aenprt**

aaenps apneas paeans paesan apnea aspen napes neaps paean panes peans apes apse nape naps neap pane pans pean peas pens sane snap span ana ane ape asp ens nae nap pan pas pea pen sap sea sen spa ae an as en na ne pa pe

aaenpsst anapests peasants anapest aptness passant patness peasant. *See* **aaenps aaenst aapsst aenpss**

aaenpst anapest peasant. *See* **aaenst aaenps aenpst**

aaenpsv pavanes. *See* **aaenps aaenpv aanpsv**

aaenpv pavane apnea paean pavan nape nave neap pane pave pean vane ana ane ape ave nae nap pan pea pen van ae an en na ne pa pe

aaenr anear arena area earn near ana ane are ear era nae ran ae an er na ne re

aaenrrst narrates narrate. *See* **aaenrs aaenst aaerrt aaerst**

aaenrrt narrate. *See* **aanrrt aenrrt aaerrt**

aaenrs arenas anear areas arena earns nares nears saner snare area arse earn ears eras near rase sane sear sera ana ane are ear ens era nae ran res sea sen ae an as en er na ne re

aaenrsuw unawares unaware. *See* **aaenrs aaensu aenrsw**

aaenrsyy naysayer. *See* **aaenrs aenrsy**

aaenrtvz tzarevna. *See* **aenrtv**

aaenruw unaware. *See* **aaenr aaeru aaerw**

aaenst ansate antae antas antes nates anta ante ants east eats etas neat nest nets sane seat sent seta tans teas tens aet ana ane ant ate ens eta nae net sat sea sen set tan tea ten ae an as at en na ne ta

aaensu nausea sauna sane anus ana ane ens nae sea sen sue sun use ae an as en na ne nu us

aaent antae anta ante neat aet ana ane ant ate eat eta nae net tan tea ten ae an at en na ne ta

aaeopstt apostate teapots. *See* **aeoptt**

aaeorrst aerators aerator roaster. *See* **aaeort aaerrt aaerst aaorst**

aaeorrt aerator. *See* **aaeort aaerrt**

aaeort aortae aorta orate reata aero area rate rota rote tare taro tear tora tore aet are art ate ear eat era eta oar oat ore ort rat ret roe rot tar tea toe tor ae at er or re ta to

aaeppr appear paper area papa para pare pear prep rape reap repp ape are ear era pap par pea pep per rap rep ae er pa pe re

aaepprs appears. *See* **aaeppr aepprs aaeprs**

aaepprst parapets appears parapet. *See* **aaeppr aaeprs aaerst aaprst**

aaepprt parapet. *See* **aaeppr aaprt aeprt**

aaeprs sarape areas paras pares parse pears rapes reaps spare spear apes apse area arse ears eras para pare pars pear peas rape raps rase rasp reap reps sear sera spar ape are asp ear era par pas pea per rap rep res sap sea spa ae as er pa pe re

aaeprtxy taxpayer apteryx. *See* **aeprtx**

aaequ aquae aqua qua ae

aaer area are ear era ae er re

aaerrrs arrears. *See* **aaers aarrs aerrr**

aaerrt errata reata area rare rate rear tare tear aet are art ate ear eat era err eta rat ret tar tea ae at er re ta

aaers areas area arse eras rase sear sera are ear era res sea ae as er re

aaersssy assayers assayer. *See* **aasssy aerssy aesssy**

aaerssy assayer. *See* **aerssy aaers aassy**

aaerst reatas areas aster rates reata stare tares tears area arse arts ears east eats eras erst eras rase rate rats rest rets sear seat sera seta star tare tars tear teas tsar aet are art ate ear eat era eta rat res ret sat sea set tar tea ae as at er re ta

aaersttu saturate stature. *See* **aaerst aarstt aerstt aesttu**

aaert reata area rate tare tear aet are art ate ear eat era eta rat ret tar tea ae at er re ta

aaertwwy waterway. *See* **aertwy**

aaeru aurae area aura urea are ear era rue ae er re

aaerw aware area ware wear are awe ear era raw war ae aw er re we

aaerwx earwax aware waxer area ware wear are awe axe ear era raw rex war wax ae aw ax er ex re we

aaesstv savates. *See* aaestv aesstv

aaesswy seaways. *See* aaeswy aassy aessy

aaestv savate avast stave aves east eats etas save seat seta tavs teas vase vast vats vest vets aet ate ave eat eta sat sea set tav tea vat vet ae as at ta

aaeswy seaway away awes ayes easy eyas sway ways wyes yaws yeas yews awe aye saw say sea sew was way wye yaw yea yes yew ae as aw ay we ye

aaffiln affinal. *See* aailn afiln

aaffilrt taffrail. *See* aaffir aailrt affirt

aaffilx affixal. *See* aailx affix

aaffinpr paraffin. *See* aaffir aafinr

aaffinst affiants affiant. *See* afinst

aaffint affiant. *See* afint

aaffir affair raffia afar aria fair raff riff air arf far fir ria rif ai fa if

aaffirs affairs raffias. *See* aaffir aafirs

aaffrsy affrays. *See* aaffry affrs afrsy

aaffry affray afar fray raff arf far fay fry ray yar fa ay

aafghin afghani. *See* aagin

aafghins afghanis afghani fashing. *See* aagin afgns agins

aafglmn flagman. *See* aagln

aafglnrt flagrant. *See* aaglnr

aafgnrrt fragrant. *See* aanrrt

aafgorr farrago. *See* aagor

aafhlwy halfway. *No 6s or 5s*

aafhrsuu hausfrau. *See* aarsu ahrsu

aafiillm familial. *See* afiill

aafiilmr familiar airmail. *See* aalmr afilr aailm

aafillnr rainfall. *See* aafinr aailnr

aafilmst fatalism. *See* aailms

aafilnst fantails fantail. *See* aailns aalnst afilns afinst

aafilnt fantail. *See* afint aaflt afiln

aafilstt fatalist. *See* aails afils ailtt

aafiltty fatality. *See* ailtt aaflt aflty

aafinnst infantas infanta infants. *See* afinnt afinst

aafinnt infanta. *See* afinnt

aafinr farina afar aria fain fair firn naif rain rani air ana ani arf fan far fin fir ran ria rif ai an fa if in na

aafinrs farinas. *See* aafinr aafirs

aafiprst parfaits parfait. *See* aafirs aairst aaprst aiprst

aafiprt parfait. *See* afirt aaprt aairt

aafirs safari arias fairs afar airs arfs aria fair firs rias rifs sari air arf far fas fir ifs ria rif sir ai as fa if is si

aafirss safaris. *See* aafirs airss aaiss

aafirswy fairways fairway airways. *See* aafirs aairwy

aafirwy fairway. *See* aairwy afiry

aafjlor alforja. *See* aflor

aafjlors alforjas alforja. *See* aflors

aafknst kaftans. *See* aafknt aaknst

aafknt kaftan tanka anta kana tank aft ana ant fan fat kaf kat tan an at fa ka na ta

aaflll fallal fall ala all fa la

aafllls fallals. *See* aaflll aflls

aafllprt pratfall. *See* aalrt aaprt aaflt

aafllty fatally. *See* afllty aally aaflt

aaflnu faunal fauna anal faun flan ulna ala ana fan flu fun an fa la na nu

aaflot afloat aloft fatal float alto flat foal loaf loft lota tola aft ala alt fat lot oaf oat oft at fa la lo of ta to

aaflt fatal flat aft ala alt fat at fa la ta

aafmnsst fantasms fantasm. *See* aamnst

aafmnst fantasm. *See* aamnst

aafnsstt fantasts fantast. *See* aanst afsst

aafnstt fantast. *See* aanst

aafnsty fantasy. *See* aanst ansty

aafnsu faunas fauna fauns sauna snafu anus fans faun ana fan fas fun sun an as fa na nu us

aafnu fauna faun ana fan fun an fa na nu

aafr afar arf far fa

aag aga

aagg gaga aga gag

aaggiln ganglia. *See* aagin aggin agiln

aaggimnn managing. *See* aaggmn aaginn aggimn

aagginrv ravaging graving. *See* agginr aginrv

aagginsv savaging. *See* aainsv aginsv

aagglly lallygag. *See* aagll aally

aaggmn gagman gaga gang mana aga ana gag gam gan mag man nag am an ma na

aaggnswy gangways gangway. *See* aggnsy

aaggnwy gangway. *No 6s or 5s*

aaggqsu quaggas. *See* aaggqu aaqsu agqsu

aaggqu quagga aqua gaga quag aga gag qua

aaggrs saggar agars ragas agar agas gaga gags gars raga rags saga aga gag gar gas rag sag as

aaggrss saggars. *See* aaggrs agrss aagss

aaggrt ragtag agar gaga raga aga art gag gar gat rag rat tag tar at ta

aaghhins shanghai hashing. *See* aagin agins aghns

aaghilnn hangnail anginal. *See* aaginn aghiln

aaghjn ganjah hang aah aga aha ana gan hag jag nag nah ah an ha na

aaghjns ganjahs. *See* aaghjn aghns

aaghkmny gymkhana. *See* aagmy agmny ahmny

aaghlnpy anaglyph. *See* aahlp ghlpy ahlpy

aaghmnn hangman. *See* aamnn

aaghmnoy mahogany. *See* aagmy agnoy agmno

aaghmr graham aargh agar amah gram harm raga aah aga aha arm gam gar hag ham mag mar rag rah ram ah am ha ma

aaghnr hangar aargh agar gnar hang raga rang aah aga aha ana gan gar hag nag nah rag rah ran ah an ha na

aaghnrs hangars. *See* aaghnr aagrs agnrs

aaghr aargh agar raga aah aga aha gar hag rag rah ah ha

aaghrssw washrags washrag. *See* aahrss

aaghrsw washrag. *See* aaghr aahsw aagrs

aaghst aghast ghats aahs agas gash gats ghat hags hast hats saga shag stag tags aah aga aha ash gas gat hag has hat sag sat tag ah as at ha sh ta

aagiilnv availing vailing. *See* aagilv agiiln agilnv giilnv

aagiintw awaiting waiting. *See* giintw

aagiknw awaking. *See* agiknw aagin

aagillny allaying allying. *See* aallny agilny

aagilmno magnolia angioma loaming. *See* aaglno aailmn agilmn aglmno

aagilmnr alarming marginal laminar. *See* aagilr aaglnr aagmnr aailmn

aagilnn anginal. *See* aaginn agiln aagln

aagilpry plagiary airplay. *See* aagilr aaipry aalpry agilry

aagilr argali glair agar alar alga aria aril gala girl lair liar lira raga rail rial aga ail air ala gal gar lag lar rag ria rig ai la li

aagilrs argalis. *See* aagilr agilrs

aagilsv gavials. *See* aailsv aagilv

aagilv gavial vagal avail alga gala lava vail vial aga ail ala gal lag via ai la li

aagimno angioma. *See* aagin aaimn agimo

aagimnos angiomas angioma anosmia siamang. *See* aagims aaimns agimos

aagimnps paganism siamang. *See* aagims aagnps aaimns aamnps

aagimns siamang. *See* aagims aaimns agimns

aagimnss amassing siamangs siamang massing. *See* aagims aagiss aaimns agimns

aagimnz amazing. *See* agimnz aagin aaimn

aagimstt stigmata. *See* **aagims aagist agimst**

aagin again gain aga ana ani gan gin nag ai an in na

aaginn angina again gain aga ana ani gan gin inn nag ai an in na

aaginns anginas. *See* **aaginn agins aagis**

aaginrr arraign. *See* **aagin aginr**

aaginrrs arraigns arraign sangria. *See* **aginrs**

aaginrry arraying arraign granary. *See* **aagnry aginry**

aaginrs sangria. *See* **aginrs**

aaginrss sangrias sangria. *See* **aagiss aginrs aginss**

aaginsst assignat against. *See* **aagiss aagist aagnst aginss**

aaginssy assaying gainsays gainsay sayings. *See* **aagiss aginss aginsy**

aaginst against. *See* **aginst aagnst aagist**

aaginsu iguanas. *See* **aaginu agins agnsu**

aaginsy gainsay. *See* **aginsy aagin aagis**

aaginu iguana again gain guan aga ana ani gan gin gnu gun nag ai an in na nu

aagiortt agitator. *See* **aagor aaort agort**

aagis saiga agas saga aga gas sag ai as is si

aagiss saigas assai sagas saiga agas saga sags aga ass gas sag sis ai as is si

aagist taigas gaits saiga taiga agas gait gats gist saga stag tags aga gas gat ita its sag sat sit tag ai as at is it si ta ti

aagit taiga gait aga gat ita tag ai at it ta ti

aagjrsu jaguars. *See* **aagjru aagjsu**

aagjru jaguar ajuga agar ajar aura gaur juga jura raja ruga aga gar jag jar jug rag raj rug

aagjsu ajugas ajuga agas jags juga jugs saga aga gas jag jug jus sag as us

aagju ajuga juga aga jag jug

aagkkno angakok. *No 6s or 5s*

aagkknos angakoks angakok. *See* **aakks aakns aknos**

aagkly galyak alga gala laky aga ala gal gay kal lag lay yak ay ka la

aagknoor kangaroo. *See* **aagnor aaknor**

aagl alga gala aga ala gal lag la

aagll algal alga gala gall aga ala all gal lag la

aagllnst gallants gallant. *See* **aaglns aagnst aalnst**

aagllnt gallant. *See* **aagll aagln aalnt**

aagllp plagal algal alga gala gall pall aga ala all alp gal gap lag lap pal la pa

aagln lagan alga anal gala aga ala ana gal gan lag nag an la na

aaglno analog lagan along agon alga anal gala gaol goal loan long aga ago ala ana gal gan goa lag log nag nog an go la lo na no on

aaglnor granola. *See* **aaglno aagnor aaglnr**

aaglnors granolas analogs angoras granola raglans. *See* **aaglno aaglnr aaglns aagnor**

aaglnos analogs. *See* **aaglno aaglns aglnos**

aaglnoy analogy. *See* **aaglno agnoy aalny**

aaglnr raglan lagan gnarl agar alar alga anal gala gnar raga rang aga ala ana gal gan gar lag lar nag rag ran an la na

aaglnrru granular angular. *See* **aaglnr aglnru**

aaglnrs raglans. *See* **aglnrs aaglns aaglnr**

aaglnru angular. *See* **aaglnr aglnru**

aaglns lagans galas glans lagan nasal slang agas alas alga anal gala gals lags nags saga sang slag snag aga ala ana gal gan gas lag nag sag sal an as la na

aagls galas agas alas alga gala gals lags saga slag aga ala gal gas lag sag sal la as

aaglv vagal alga gala lava aga ala gal lag la

aaglx galax alga gala aga ala gal lag lax la ax

aaglxy galaxy galax alga gala aga ala gal gay lag lax lay ax ay la

aagmm gamma magma mama aga gam mag am ma

aagmmrr grammar. *See* **aagmm**

aagmmrrs grammars grammar. *See* **aagmms**

aagmms gammas gamma magma mamas agas gams mags mama saga aga gam gas mag sag am as ma

aagmnr ragman agar gnar gram mana raga rang aga ana arm gam gan gar mag man mar nag rag ram ran am an ma na

aagmnpy apogamy. *See* **aagmy**

aagmosu agamous. *No 6s or 5s*

aagmotuy autogamy. *See* **aagmy amoty agmtu**

aagmotyz zygomata. *See* **agmoyz**

aagmrsy margays. *See* **aagmry aagrs agmrs**

aagmry margay gamay agar army gamy gram gray maya raga aga arm gam gar gay gym mag mar may rag ram ray yam yar am ay ma my

aagmy gamay maya gamy aga gam gay gym mag may yam am ay ma my

aagnnstt stagnant. *See* **aagnst aanntt**

aagnopr paragon. *See* **aagnor aagnpr**

aagnoprs paragons angoras paragon parangs. *See* **aagnor aagnpr aagnps agnors**

aagnor angora agora argon groan organ agar agon gnar raga rang roan aga ago ana gan gar goa nag nog nor oar rag ran an go na no on or

aagnorrt arrogant tarragon grantor. *See* **aagnor aanrrt**

aagnors angoras. *See* **aagnor agnors**

aagnorsz organzas angoras organza. *See* **aagnor agnors**

aagnorz organza. *See* **aagnor**

aagnp pagan panga pang aga ana gan gap nag nap pan an na pa

aagnpr parang pagan panga agar gnar pang para raga rang aga ana gan gap gar nag nap pan par rag ran rap an na pa

aagnprs parangs. *See* **aagnps aagnpr agnprs**

aagnps pagans pangas pagan panga pangs spang agas gaps gasp nags naps pang pans saga sang snag snap span aga ana asp gan gap gas nag nap pan pas sag sap spa an as na pa

aagnrry granary. *See* **aagnry aarry**

aagnrstv vagrants vagrant. *See* **aagnst aanrsv aanstv agnrst**

aagnrtuy guaranty. *See* **aagnry agnrty**

aagnrtv vagrant. *See* **aanrt agnrt aanrv**

aagnry angary angry rangy agar gnar gray nary raga rang yang yarn aga ana any gan gar gay nag nay rag ran ray yar an ay na

aagnst satang antas gnats stang tangs agas anta ants gats gnat nags saga sang snag stag tags tang tans aga ana ant gan gas gat nag sag sat tag tan an as at na ta

aagopss sapsago. *See* **agpss aagss agoss**

aagopsss sapsagos sapsago. *See* **agpss aagss agoss**

aagor agora agar raga aga ago gar goa oar rag go or

aagorsss sargasso. *See* **aagrs aagor agrss**

aagorssu saguaros saguaro. *See* **agrssu**

aagorsu saguaro. *See* **aagrs aagor aarsu**

aagppr grappa agar papa para raga aga gap gar pap par rag rap pa

aagpprs grappas. *See* **aagppr aagrs agprs**

aagr agar raga aga gar rag

aagrs agars ragas agar agas gars raga rags saga aga gar gas rag sag as

aagrvy vagary gravy agar gray raga vara vary aga gar gay rag ray yar ay

aags agas saga aga gas sag as

aagss sagas agas saga sags aga ass gas sag as

aagsuv guavas guava vagus agas saga vugs aga gas sag vug as us

aaguv guava aga vug

aah aah aha ah ha

aahhll hallah hall aah aha ala all hah ah ha la

aaiiprst apiarist. *See* **aairst aaprst aiprst iiprst**

aaiirtvx aviatrix. *See* **aiirtv**

aaijlnp jalapin. *See* **aainp aajlp aajnp**

aaikkstz kazatski. *See* **aakks aikks**

aaikll alkali kail kill ail ala all ilk ill kal ai ka la li

aaiklm kalmia lamia kail kami lama mail milk ail aim ala ilk kal lam mil ai am ka la li ma mi

aaiklms kalmias. *See* **aaiklm aailms**

aaikmnn manakin. *See* **aaimn aamnn**

aaikmnns manakins manakin kinsman. *See* **aaimns aamnns aikmns**

aaikmnst antimask stamina. *See* **aaimns aaknst aamnst aikmns**

aaikmrst tamarisk amritas. *See* **aaimrt aairst aakmrs aakrst**

aaikppr paprika. *See* **aakpp aakpr**

aaiksstw swastika. *See* **aaistw aisstw**

aaiktvv akvavit. *No 6s or 5s*

aaillluv alluvial. *See* **aallu aailv aillv**

aaillmmm mammilla. *See* **aalmmm**

aaillmnt mantilla matinal. *See* **aailmn**

aaillmsx maxillas maxilla. *See* **aaillx aailms aallms ailmsx**

aaillmx maxilla. *See* **aaillx aailm aallm**

aaillnsv vanillas vanilla. *See* **aailns aailsv aainsv aillsv**

aaillnv vanilla. *See* **ailnv aailv aainv**

aaillpp papilla. *See* **aallpp ailpp**

aaillrx axillar. *See* **aaillx**

aaillrxy axillary axillar axially. *See* **aaillx**

aaillx axilla axial axil ail ala all ill lax ai ax la li xi

aaillxy axially. *See* **aaillx aally allxy**

aailm lamia lama mail ail aim ala lam mil ai am la li ma mi

aailmmn mailman. *See* **aailmn**

aailmmrs alarmism. *See* **ailms aaimms aalmrs**

aailmmx maximal. *See* **aailx aailm aimmx**

aailmn animal lamina amain anima lamia lanai mania anal anil lain lama limn mail main mana mina nail ail aim ala ana ani lam man mil nil nim ai am an in la li ma mi na

aailmnor manorial laminar. *See* **aailmn aailnr aaimnr aalmor**

aailmnr laminar. *See* **aaimnr aailmn ailmnr aailnr**

aailmns animals. *See* **aailmn aaimns aailns aailms**

aailmnst talisman animals matinal stamina. *See* **aailmn aailms aailns aaimns**

aailmnt matinal. *See* **aailmn**

aailmopt lipomata optimal. *See* **aailmp ailmop**

aailmorr armorial. *See* **aalmor**

aailmp impala lamia lama lamp limp mail pail palm ail aim ala alp amp imp lam lap lip map mil pal ai am la li ma mi pa pi

aailmps impalas. *See* **aailmp aalmps**

aailmrst alarmist amritas lariats marital martial mistral mitrals. *See* **aailms aailrt aaimrt aairst**

aailmrt marital martial. *See* **aaimrt aailrt ailmrt**

aailms salami alias lamas lamia mails salmi ails aims alas alms lama lams mail mils sail slam slim ail aim ala lam mil mis sal ai am as is la li ma mi si

aailmss salamis. *See* **aailss ailmss aailms**

aailmttu ultimata. *See* **aailm ailtt**

aailn lanai anal anil lain nail ail ala ana ani nil ai an in la li na

aailnnot national. *See* **ailnot ainnot**

aailnnpt plantain. *See* **aainpt ailnpt**

aailnnst annalist. *See* **aailns aalnst ailnst**

aailnort notarial rational. *See* **aailnr aailrt aainrt ailnot**

aailnotv lavation valiant. *See* **ailnot**

aailnqtu aliquant quantal quintal. *See* **aailqu aanqtu ainqtu**

aailnr narial lanai alar anal anil aria aril lain lair liar lira nail rail rain rani rial ail air ala ana ani lar nil ran ria ai an in la li na

aailns lanais salina alias anils lanai nails nasal slain snail ails alas anal anil lain nail nils sail sain ail ala ana ani nil sal sin ai an as in is la li na si

aailnss salinas. *See* **aailss aailns ailnss**

aailnssy analysis salinas. *See* **aailns aailss aalnsy ailnss**

aailnsty nasality analyst nastily saintly. *See* **aailns aalnst aalnsy ailnst**

aailntv valiant. *See* **ailnv aailv aainv**

aailors solaria. *See* **ailors aails aairs**

aailprst partials lariats partial spatial. *See* **aailrt aairst aalrst aaprst**

aailprsy airplays airplay parlays. *See* **aaipry aalpry aalpsy aalrsy**

aailprt partial. *See* **aailrt**

aailpry airplay. *See* **aaipry aalpry**

aailpst spatial. *See* **ailpst aails aalst**

aailqu qualia quail aqua ail ala qua ai la li

aailrrsv arrivals arrival. *See* **aailsv aalrsv ailrsv**

aailrrv arrival. *See* **aailv aalrv ailrv**

aailrst lariats. *See* **aalrst aairst aailrt ailrst**

aailrstv travails lariats travail. *See* **aailrt aailsv aairst aalrst**

aailrsvy salivary. *See* **aailsv aairvy aalrsv aalrsy**

aailrswy railways railway airways. *See* **aairwy aalrsy aalswy ailrsy**

aailrt atrial lariat latria altar atria riata tiara trail trial alar alit aria aril lair liar lira rail rial tail tali ail air ala alt art ita lar lit rat ria tar til ai at it la li ta ti

aailrtt rattail. *See* **aailrt**

aailrtv travail. *See* **aailrt**

aailrwy railway. *See* **aairwy ailrwy**

aails alias ails alas sail ail ala sal ai as is la li si

aailss assail alias assai sails salsa sisal ails alas lass sail sals ail ala ass sal sis ai as is la li si

aailsss assails. *See* **ailss aaisss aalsss ailsss**

aailsssw wassails assails wassail. *See* **ailss aaisss**

aailssv salivas salvias. *See* **aailss aailsv ailssv aalssv**

aailssw wassail. *See* **aailss ailsw**

aailsv avails saliva salvia alias avail silva vails vials ails alas lava sail vail vial visa ail ala sal via ai as is la li si v

aailv avail lava vail vial ail ala via ai la li

aailx axial axil ail ala lax ai ax la li xi

aaimmno ammonia. *See* **aaimn**

aaimmnos ammonias ammonia anosmia. *See* **aaimms aaimns aimmos immnos**

aaimmnst mainmast stamina. *See* **aaimms aaimns aamnst**

aaimms miasma imams maims mamas aims imam maim mama aim mim mis ai am as is ma mi si

aaimmss miasmas. *See* **aaimms aamss aimss**

aaimn amain anima mania main mana mina aim ana ani man nim ai am an in ma mi na

aaimnort animator tamarin. *See* **aaimnr aaimrt aainrt aamnrt**

aaimnos anosmia. *See* **aaimns**

aaimnoss anosmias anosmia. *See* **aaimns aamoss amnoss**

aaimnprz marzipan. *See* **aaimnr**

aaimnr airman marina amain anima mania maria amir aria main mana mina rain rami rani aim air ana ani arm man mar mir nim ram ran ria rim ai am an in ma mi na

aaimnrs marinas. *See* **aaimnr aaimns**

aaimnrst tamarins amritas antiars artisan mantras marinas martins stamina tamarin tsarina. *See* **aaimnr aaimns aaimrt aainrt**

aaimnrt tamarin. *See* **aaimnr aaimrt aainrt aamnrt aimnrt**

aaimns animas manias amain anima mains mania aims main mana mina

aahhlls hallahs. *See* **aahhll ahlls**

aahhlsv halvahs. *See* **aahhlv aahlsv**

aahhlv halvah halva lava aah aha ala hah ah ha la

aahhnpst naphthas naphtha. *See* **aahhpt**

aahhnpt naphtha. *See* **aahhpt**

aahhpt aphtha hath path tapa aah aha apt hah hap hat pah pat tap ah at ha pa ta

aahiimt himatia. *No 6s or 5s*

aahilnnt inhalant. *See* **aailn aalnt hinnt**

aahilnot halation. *See* **ailnot**

aahilsy aliyahs. *See* **aahily aails aahsy**

aahily aliyah ayah hail hyla aah aha ail ala hay lay yah ah ai ay ha hi la li

aahinop aphonia. *See* **aainp ainop**

aahinops aphonias aphonia paisano. *See* **ainops hinops**

aahinpr piranha. *See* **aahipr aainp**

aahinprs piranhas piranha pariahs. *See* **aahipr ahiprs ainprs**

aahipr pariah aria hair harp pair para aah aha air hap hip pah par rah rap ria rip ah ai ha hi pa pi

aahiprs pariahs. *See* **aahipr ahiprs**

aahipsxy asphyxia. *See* **ahips aahsy aahps**

aahirtv havarti. *See* **aairt**

aahjr rajah ajar raja aah aha jar rah raj ah ha

aahjrs rajahs rajah rajas ajar jars rahs raja rash aah aha ash has jar rah raj ah as ha sh

aahkllmr hallmark. *See* **aalmr aahlm aakmr**

aahkmssy yashmaks yashmak. *See* **aahmss aahssy**

aahkmsy yashmak. *See* **aahms aahsy aahks**

aahks kasha aah aha ash ask has kas ah as ha ka sh

aahllos halloas. *See* **aahlos ahllos**

aahllswy hallways hallway. *See* **aallsy aalswy**

aahllwy hallway. *See* **aally**

aahlm hamal amah lama aah aha ala ham lam ah am ha la ma

aahlmrs marshal. *See* **aalmrs aahlrs aahmrs aahlms**

aahlmrss marshals ashlars ashrams marshal. *See* **aahlms aahlrs aahmrs aahmss**

aahlms hamals amahs hamal lamas alas alms amah hams lama lams lash mash sham slam aah aha ala ash ham has lam sal ah am as ha la ma sh

aahlmst malthas. *See* **aahmst aahlms aahlmt**

aahlmstu thalamus malthas. *See* **aahlms aahmst**

aahlmt maltha hamal amah halt lama lath malt math aah aha ala alt ham hat lam mat tam ah am at ha la ma ta

aahlnpx phalanx. *See* **aahlp**

aahlnrsw narwhals narwhal narwals. *See* **aahlrs aalnrw**

aahlnrw narwhal. *See* **aalnrw**

aahlo aloha halo aah aha ala ah ha ho la lo oh

aahlos alohas aloha shoal alas also halo lash aah aha ala ash has los ohs sal sol ah as ha ho la lo oh os sh so

aahlp alpha aah aha ala alp hap lap pah pal ah ha la pa

aahlprs phrasal. *See* **aahlps aahlrs**

aahlps alphas alpha pasha plash salpa alas alps haps hasp laps lash pals slap aah aha ala alp ash asp hap has lap pah pal pas sal sap spa ah as ha la pa sh

aahlpsst asphalts asphalt. *See* **aahlps aahpss aalpss aapsst**

aahlpst asphalt. *See* **aahlps aalst ahlst**

aahlrs ashlar harls alar alas harl lash rahs rash aah aha ala ash has lar rah sal ah as ha la sh

aahlrss ashlars. *See* **aahlrs aahrss**

aahlsv halvas halva aahs alas lash lava aah aha ala ash has sal ah as ha la sh

aahlv halva lava aah aha ala ah ha la

aahm amah aah aha ham ah am ha ma

aahmnort marathon. *See* **aamnrt amnort**

aahmnpst phantasm. *See* **aahmns aahmst aamnps aamnst**

aahmns shaman amahs amah hams mana mash sham aah aha ana ash ham has man nah ah am an as ha ma na sh

aahmnss shamans. *See* **aahmns aahmss**

aahmopr amphora. *See* **aamopr hmopr**

aahmoprs amphoras amphora paramos. *See* **aahmrs aamopr aamors hmoprs**

aahmpy mayhap amah ayah maya aah aha amp ham hap hay map may pah pay pya yah yam yap ah am ay ha ma my pa

aahmqsu quamash. *See* **aahms aaqsu ahqsu**

aahmrs ashram amahs harms marsh amah arms hams harm mash rahs rams rash sham aah aha arm ash ham has mar rah ram ah am as ha ma sh

aahmrss ashrams. *See* **aahmrs aahrss aahmss**

aahms amahs amah hams mash sham aah aha ash ham has ah am as ha ma sh

aahmss shamas amahs amass shams smash amah hams mash mass sash sham aah aha ash ass ham has ah am as ha ma sh

aahmsst asthmas. *See* **aahmss aahmst**

aahmst asthma amahs aahs amah hams hast hats mash mast math mats sham tams aah aha ash ham has hat mat sat tam ah am as at ha ma sh ta

aahnnos hosanna. *No 6s or 5s*

aahnnstx xanthans xanthan. *See* **aanst ahnst**

aahnntx xanthan. *No 6s or 5s*

aahnsz hazans hazan azans aahs azan aah aha ana ash has nah ah an as ha na sh

aahnz hazan azan aah aha ana nah ah an ha na

aahoprtu autoharp. *See* **ahortu**

aahppr paraph harp papa para aah aha hap pah pap par rah rap ah ha pa

aahpprs paraphs. *See* **aahppr ahprs aapps**

aahprstw warpaths warpath. *See* **aaprst ahrstw**

aahprtw warpath. *See* **aaprt aprtw ahrtw**

aahps pasha haps hasp aah aha ash asp hap has pah pas sap spa ah as ha pa sh

aahpss pashas pasha hasps aahs asps haps hasp pass saps sash spas aah aha ash asp ass hap has pah pas sap spa ah as ha pa sh

aahpstwy pathways pathway. *See* **aahpty**

aahptwy pathway. *See* **aahpty**

aahpty apathy ayah path tapa aah aha apt hap hat hay pah pat pay pya tap thy yah yap ah at ay ha pa ta

aahrss harass aahs rahs rash sash aah aha ash ass has rah ah as ha sh

aahrssty ashtrays ashtray. *See* **aahrss aahssy aarsty ahrsty**

aahrsty ashtray. *See* **aarsty ahrsty**

aahrttw athwart. *See* **ahrttw aartt**

aahs aahs aah aha ash has ah as ha sh

aahsssy sashays. *See* **aahssy aassssy**

aahssy sashay ayahs assay aahs ashy ayah hays sash says shay aah aha ash ass has hay say shy yah ah as ay ha sh

aahsw awash aahs haws shaw wash aah aha ash has haw saw was ah as aw ha sh

aahsy ayahs aahs ashy ayah hays shay aah aha ash has hay say shy yah ah as ay ha sh

aahy ayah aah aha hay yah ah ay ha

aaiilmns mainsail animals. *See* **aailmn aailms aailns aaimns**

aaiilmr airmail. *See* **aalmr aailm aaimr**

aaiilmrs airmails airmail similar. *See* **aailms aalmrs**

aaiilnrz alizarin. *See* **aailnr**

aaiimnnt maintain. *See* **aimnnt**

aaiinotv aviation. *See* **aainv**

aaiinprr riparian. *See* **aainp**

aaiinrst intarsia antiars artisan tsarina. *See* **aainrt aairst aiinrs aiinst**

nims sain aim ana ani man mis nim sin ai am an as in is ma mi na si

aaimnsst mantissa stamina. *See* **aaimns aamnst aimnst ainsst**

aaimnst stamina. *See* **aaimns aamnst aimnst**

aaimnsty mainstay stamina. *See* **aaimns aamnst aimnst ainsty**

aaimprst pastrami amritas armpits imparts. *See* **aaimrt aairst aaprst aimprt**

aaimqruu aquarium. *See* **amruu aimqu aaimr**

aaimr maria amir aria rami aim air arm mar mir ram ria rim ai am ma mi

aaimrst amritas. *See* **aaimrt aairst**

aaimrsu samurai. *See* **aimrs aairs aarsu**

aaimrt amrita atria maria riata tiara amir aria mart rami tram trim aim air arm art ita mar mat mir ram rat ria rim tam tar ai am at it ma mi ta ti

aaimsstv atavisms atavism. *See* **aisstv**

aaimstv atavism. *See* **aastv aimsv aistv**

aaimz zamia aim ai am ma mi

aainnott natation. *See* **aaintt ainnot**

aainnrsv nirvanas nirvana. *See* **aainsv aanrsv**

aainnrv nirvana. *See* **aainv aanrv**

aainops paisano. *See* **ainops aainp**

aainopss paisanos paisano passion. *See* **ainops**

aainorrs rosarian. *See* **ainors**

aainosx anoxias. *See* **anosx**

aainottx taxation. *See* **aaintt**

aainp apian nipa pain ana ani nap nip pan pin ai an in na pa pi

aainprst aspirant partisan antiars artisan spirant tsarina. *See* **aainpt aainrt aairst aaprst**

aainpt patina apian inapt paint anta anti nipa pain pant pint pita tapa ana ani ant apt ita nap nip nit pan pat pin pit tan tap tin tip ai an at in it na pa pi ta ti

aainqrtu quatrain quartan. *See* **aainrt aainru aanqtu ainqtu**

aainqttu aquatint. *See* **aaintt aanqtu ainqtu**

aainrsst artisans tsarinas antiars artisan strains tsarina. *See* **aainrt aairst ainrst ainsst**

aainrssu saurians anurias saurian. *See* **aainru aanssu**

aainrst antiars artisan tsarina. *See* **aainrt aairst ainrst**

aainrstv variants antiars artisan variant. *See* **aainrt aainsv aairst aanrsv**

aainrsty sanitary antiars artisan tsarina. *See* **aainrt aairst aarsty ainrst**

aainrsu anurias saurian. *See* **aainru aairs aarsu**

aainrt antiar antra atria riant riata tiara train anta anti aria rain rani rant air ana ani ant art ita nit ran rat ria tan tar tin ai an at in it na ta ti

aainrtv variant. *See* **aainrt aainv aanrv**

aainrtw antiwar. *See* **aainrt aaitw aintw**

aainrtz tzarina. *See* **aainrt**

aainru anuria aria aura rain rani ruin air ana ani ran ria run urn ai an in na nu

aainssss assassin. *See* **aaisss**

aainstt attains. *See* **aaintt ainstt**

aainsttt attaints attains attaint. *See* **aaintt ainstt**

aainsv avians avian savin vinas sain vain vans vina visa ana ani sin van via ai an as in is na si

aaintt attain taint titan anta anti tint ana ani ant ita nit tan tat tin tit ai an at in it na ta ti

aainttt attaint. *See* **aaintt**

aainv avian vain vina ana ani van via ai an in na

aaiorstv aviators aviator travois. *See* **aairst aaorst aiorst aiorsv**

aaiortv aviator. *See* **aaort aairt aiort**

aaippstt pitapats pitapat. *See* **aippst**

aaipptt pitapat. *No 6s or 5s*

aaiprstt partitas partita. *See* **aairst aaprst aarstt aiprst**

aaiprtt partita. *See* **aaprt aartt aairt**

aaipry apiary airy aria pair para pray air par pay pry pya rap ray ria rip yap yar yip ai ay pa pi

aaipszz piazzas. *See* **aaipzz aipszz**

aaipzz piazza pizza zap zip ai pa pi

aaiqsssu quassias quassia. *See* **aaisss**

aaiqssu quassia. *See* **aaqsu aaiss aiqsu**

aaiqstuv aquavits aquavit. *See* **aaqsu aastv aiqsu**

aaiqtuv aquavit. *No 6s or 5s*

aair aria air ria ai

aairs arias airs aria rias sari air ria sir ai as is si

aairst arista atrias riatas tiaras arias astir atria riata sitar stair stria tarsi tiara airs aria arts rats rias sari star stir tars tsar air art ita its rat ria sat sir sit tar ai as at is it si ta ti

aairstwy stairway airways. *See* **aairst aairwy aaistw aarsty**

aairswy airways. *See* **aairwy aairs**

aairt atria riata tiara aria air art ita rat ria tar ai at it ta ti

aairvy aviary airy aria vair vara vary air ivy ray ria via yar ai ay

aairwy airway airy aria away awry wary wiry air raw ray ria war way yar yaw ai aw ay

aaiss assai ass sis ai as is si

aaisss assais assai sass ass sis ai as is si

aaistuy yautias. *See* **aaituy**

aaistw awaits await waist waits swat wait wast wits ita its sat saw sit was wis wit ai as at aw is it si ta ti

aaistwxy taxiways taxiway. *See* **aaistw**

aaituy yautia ita tau tui ai at ay it ta ti ut

aaitw await wait ita wit ai at aw it ta ti

aaitwxy taxiway. *See* **aaitw**

aajklswy jaywalks jaywalk. *See* **aalswy**

aajklwy jaywalk. *No 6s or 5s*

aajlp jalap ala alp lap pal la pa

aajlps jalaps jalap salpa alas alps laps pals slap ala alp asp lap pal pas sal sap spa as la pa

aajmmorr marjoram. *See* **amorr aamor ajmor**

aajmnzz jazzman. *No 6s or 5s*

aajmpsy pyjamas. *See* **aamsy**

aajnp japan ana nap pan an na pa

aajnps japans japan naps pans snap span ana asp nap pan pas sap spa an as na pa

aajr ajar raja jar raj

aajrs rajas ajar jars raja jar raj as

aajv java

aakk kaka ka

aakklp kalpak kaka ala alp kal lap pal ka la pa

aakklps kalpaks. *See* **aakklp aakks aalps**

aakklrsu karakuls karakul. *See* **aaklrs akklsu**

aakklru karakul. *See* **aalru aaklr akklu**

aakkmr markka karma arak kaka mark ark arm mar ram am ka ma

aakkop kakapo kapok kaka koa oak ka pa

aakkops kakapos. *See* **aakkop akkops**

aakks kakas kaka ask kas as ka

aakkstyz kazatsky. *See* **aakksy**

aakksy kayaks kakas kayak kyaks kaka kyak yaks ask kas say sky yak as ay ka

aakky kayak kaka kyak yak ka ay

aaklmry malarky. *See* **aalmr aalry aakmr**

aaklo koala kola ala kal koa oak ka la lo

aakloop palooka. *See* **aaklo aklop**

aakloops palookas palooka. *See* **aaklos aklops aloops**

aaklos koalas koala kolas skoal alas also koas kola oaks soak ala ask kal kas koa kos los oak sal sol as ka la lo os so

aaklr kraal alar arak lark ala ark kal lar ka la

aaklrs kraals araks kraal larks alar alas arak arks lark sark ala ark ask kal kas lar sal as ka la

aaklswwy walkways walkway. *See* **aalswy**

aaklwwy walkway. *No 6s or 5s*

aakmmnrs marksman. *See* **aakmrs**

aakmoruz mazourka mazurka. *See* amoru aamor aakmr

aakmossu moussaka. *See* aamoss akmosu

aakmr karma arak mark ark arm mar ram am ka ma

aakmrs karmas araks karma marks arak arks arms mark mask rams sark ark arm ask kas mar ram am as ka ma

aakmrsuz mazurkas mazurka. *See* aakmrs

aakmruz mazurka. *See* aakmr

aakmtu makuta auk kat mat tam tau am at ka ma mu ta um ut

aakn kana ana an ka na

aaknnstu nunataks nunatak. *See* aaknst annstu

aaknntu nunatak. *See* aaknt

aaknor anorak krona arak kana kaon knar koan nark okra rank roan ana ark koa kor nor oak oar ran an ka na no on or

aaknors anoraks. *See* aaknor aakrs anors

aakns kanas kana sank ana ask kas an as ka na

aaknst tankas antas kanas stank tanka tanks anta ants kana sank skat tank tans task ana ant ask kas kat sat tan tsk an as at ka na ta

aaknswz kwanzas. *See* aaknwz aansz aakns

aaknt tanka anta kana tank ana ant kat tan an at ka na ta

aaknwz kwanza kana azan ana awn wan an aw ka na

aakpp kappa papa pap ka pa

aakpps kappas kappa papas papa paps ask asp kas pap pas sap spa as ka pa

aakpr parka arak para park ark par rap ka pa

aakprs parkas araks paras parka parks spark arak arks para park pars raps rasp sark spar ark ask asp kas par pas rap sap spa as ka pa

aakprswy parkways parkway. *See* aakprs

aakprwy parkway. *See* aakpr akpwy

aakr arak ark ka

aakrs araks arak arks sark ark ask kas as ka

aakrst karats araks karat karst karts stark arak arks arts kart rats sark skat star tars task tsar ark art ask kas kat rat sat tar tsk as at ka ta

aakrt karat arak kart ark art kat rat tar at ka ta

aakrtuy autarky. *See* aakrt akrtu

aaksv kavas kava kvas ask kas as ka

aakv kava ka

aal ala la

aallm llama lama mall ala all lam am la ma

aallmnty tallyman. *See* aallny aalmny

aallmnuy manually. *See* aallny aalmnu aalmny

aallmpu ampulla. *See* aallu almpu aallm

aallms llamas lamas llama malls small alas alms lama lams mall slam ala all lam sal am as la ma

aallnnuy annually. *See* aallny aalnnu

aallnoty atonally tonally. *See* aallny

aallnsy nasally. *See* aallsy aallny aalnsy

aallny anally allay nyala anal ally ala all ana any lay nay an ay la na

aallorwy rollaway rollway. *See* allory

aallpp appall papal pall palp papa ala all alp lap pal pap la pa

aallpps appalls. *See* aallpp allps alpps

aallrv larval larva alar lava vara ala all lar la

aallsy allays allay sally alas ally lays slay ala all lay sal say sly as ay la

aallu alula ala all la

aally allay ally ala all lay la ay

aalmmm mammal mamma lama malm mama ala lam am la ma

aalmmms mammals. *See* aalmmm aammms

aalmmns almsman. *See* aalms almms aamms

aalmnoru monaural. *See* aalmnnu aalmor almnor

aalmnowy laywoman anomaly womanly. *See* aalmnw aalmny

aalmnoy anomaly. *See* aalmny aalmo almoy

aalmnp napalm anal lama lamp mana palm plan ala alp amp ana lam lap man map nap pal pan am an la ma na pa

aalmnps napalms. *See* aalmps aalmnp aamnps

aalmnsu manuals. *See* aalmnu

aalmnttu tantalum. *See* aalmnu aamntu amnttu

aalmntuu autumnal. *See* aalmnu aamntu almtuu

aalmnu alumna manual alum anal lama mana maul maun ulna ala ana lam lum man am an la ma mu na nu um

aalmnw lawman anal lama lawn mana ala ana awl awn lam law man maw wan am an aw la ma na

aalmny layman nyala manly amyl anal lama mana many maya myna ala ana any lam lay man may nay yam am an ay la ma my na

aalmo alamo lama loam mola ala lam moa am la lo ma mo om

aalmoppr malaprop. *See* aalmor aalmpr aamopr aloppr

aalmor amoral alamo alarm aroma malar molar moral alar lama loam marl mola mora oral roam ala arm lam lar mar moa mor oar ram am la lo ma mo om or

aalmory mayoral. *See* aalmor aalry almoy

aalmos alamos alamo lamas loams molas alas alms also lama lams loam moas mola slam soma ala lam los moa mos oms sal sol am as la lo ma mo om os so

aalmpr palmar alarm malar alar lama lamp marl palm para pram ramp ala alp amp arm lam lap lar map mar pal par ram rap am la ma pa

aalmprsy palmyras palmary palmyra parlays. *See* aalmpr aalmps aalmrs aalpry

aalmpry palmary palmyra. *See* aalmpr aalpry

aalmps lampas plasma lamas lamps palms psalm salpa alas alms alps amps lama lamp lams laps maps palm pals samp slam slap ala alp amp asp lam lap map pal pas sal sap spa am as la ma pa

aalmpss plasmas. *See* aalmps almpss aalpss

aalmr alarm malar alar lama marl ala arm lam lar mar ram am la ma

aalmrs alarms malars alarm lamas malar marls alar alas alms arms lama lams marl rams slam ala arm lam lar mar ram sal am as la ma

aalms lamas alas alms lama lams slam ala lam sal am as la ma

aaln anal ala ana an la na

aalnnru annular. *See* aalnnu aalru alnru

aalnns annals nasal anal alas ala ana sal an as la na

aalnnsu annuals. *See* aalnns aalnnu alnnsu

aalnnu annual annul anal ulna ala ana nun an la na nu

aalnoz azonal zonal anal azan loan ala ana azo zoa an la lo na no on

aalnpr planar alar anal para plan ala alp ana lap lar nap pal pan par ran rap an la na pa

aalnprt plantar. *See* aalnpr aalrt aanrt

aalnqtu quantal. *See* aanqtu aalnt

aalnrsw narwals. *See* aalnrw alnsw aalns

aalnrtu natural. *See* aalrt aanrt aalru

aalnrw narwal alar anal lawn warn ala ana awl awn lar law ran raw wan war an aw la na

aalns nasal anal alas ala ana sal an as la na

aalnssty   analysts analyst. *See* **aalnst aalnsy alnsst**

aalnst   aslant antas atlas nasal natal slant alas alts anal anta ants last salt slat tans ala alt ana ant sal sat tan an as at la na ta

aalnstt   saltant. *See* **aalnst**

aalnsty   analyst. *See* **aalnst aalnsy**

aalnsy   nyalas nasal nyala alas anal lays slay ala ana any lay nay sal say sly an as ay la na

aalnt   natal anal anta ala alt ana ant tan an at la na ta

aalnv   naval anal lava ala ana van an la na

aalny   nyala anal ala ana any lay nay an ay la na

aalopprv   approval. *See* **aloppr**

aaloprs   parasol. *See* **aloprs aaprs aalps**

aaloprss   parasols parasol. *See* **aalpss aloprs**

aaloprst   pastoral parasol patrols portals. *See* **aalrst aaorst aaprst aloprs**

aalopsy   payolas. *See* **aalopy aalpsy**

aalopszz   palazzos. *See* **aalpsz**

aalopy   payola playa opal paly play ploy ala alp lap lay lop pal pay ply pya yap ay la lo oy pa

aalorru   auroral. *See* **aaorru aalru alrru**

aalorssu   arousals arousal. *See* **aalru aarsu aloss**

aalorsu   arousal. *See* **aalru aarsu alors**

aalortvy   lavatory. *See* **aortvy**

aalosvw   avowals. *See* **aalovw aosvw alosv**

aalovw   avowal alow avow lava oval ala awl law low ova owl vow aw la lo ow

aalpp   papal papa palp ala alp lap pal pap la pa

aalprsy   parlays. *See* **aalpry aalpsy aalrsy**

aalpry   parlay playa alary alar aryl paly para play pray ala alp lap lar lay pal par pay ply pry pya rap ray yap yar ay la pa

aalps   salpa alas alps laps pals slap ala alp asp lap pal pas sal sap spa as la pa

aalpss   salpas salpa salsa slaps alas alps asps laps lass pals pass sals saps slap spas ala alp asp ass lap pal pas sal sap spa as la pa

aalpsstu   spatulas spatula assault. *See* **aalpss aapsst alpsst apsstu**

aalpstu   spatula. *See* **aalst aapst alpst**

aalpsy   playas palsy playa plays salpa splay alas alps laps lays pals paly pays play pyas slap slay spay yaps ala alp asp lap lay pal pas pay ply pya sal sap say sly spa spy yap as ay la pa

aalpsz   plazas salpa plaza alas alps laps pals slap spaz zaps ala alp asp lap pal pas sal sap spa zap as la pa

aalpy   playa paly play ala alp lap lay pal pay ply pya yap ay la pa

aalpz   plaza ala alp lap pal zap la pa

aalr   alar ala lar la

aalrsst   tarsals. *See* **aalrst**

aalrst   altars astral tarsal altar atlas alar alas alts arts last rats salt slat star tars tsar ala alt art lar rat sal sat tar as at la ta

aalrsttw   stalwart. *See* **aalrst aarstt alrstw**

aalrstu   austral. *See* **aalrst alrstu**

aalrstuy   salutary austral astylar. *See* **aalrst aalrsy aarsty alrstu**

aalrsty   astylar. *See* **aalrst aarsty aalrsy alrsty**

aalrsv   larvas larva varas alar alas lava vara ala lar sal as la

aalrsy   salary alary aryls alar alas aryl lays rays slay ala lar lay ray sal say sly yar as ay la

aalrsz   lazars lazar alar alas ala lar sal as la

aalrt   altar alar ala alt art lar rat tar at la ta

aalru   aural alar aura ala lar la

aalrv   larva alar lava vara ala lar la

aalry   alary alar aryl ala lar lay ray yar la ay

aalrz   lazar alar ala lar la

aals   alas ala sal as la

aalss   salsa alas lass sals ala ass sal as la

aalsss   salsas salsa alas lass sals sass ala ass sal as la

aalssstu   assaults assault. *See* **aalsss**

aalsssv   vassals. *See* **aalsss aalssv**

aalsstu   assault. *See* **aalst alsst lsstu**

aalssv   vassal salsa alas lass lava sals ala ass sal as la

aalst   atlas alas alts last salt slat ala alt sal sat as at la ta

aalswy   always yawls alas away awls laws lays slay sway ways yawl yaws ala awl law lay sal saw say sly was way yaw as aw ay la

aalswyy   waylays. *See* **aalswy aalwyy**

aalv   lava ala la

aalwyy   waylay away yawl ala awl law lay way yaw yay aw ay la

aamm   mama am ma

aammm   mamma mama am ma

aammmry   mammary. *See* **aammm ammmy**

aammms   mammas mamma mamas mama am as ma

aammoty   myomata. *See* **ammoy amoty**

aammrssu   marasmus. *See* **aamss aarsu aamms**

aamms   mamas mama am as ma

aammsuz   mazumas. *See* **aammuz aamms ammsu**

aammuz   mazuma mama mum am ma mu um

aamn   mana ana man am an ma na

aamnn   manna mana ana man am an ma na

aamnns   mannas manna mana ana man am an as ma na

aamnors   oarsman. *See* **aamors amnors**

aamnosz   amazons. *See* **aamnoz aansz amnos**

aamnoty   anatomy. *See* **aamnt amoty anoty**

aamnoz   amazon azan mana moan noma ana azo man moa mon zoa am an ma mo na no om on

aamnprt   rampant. *See* **aamnrt aaprt amprt**

aamnps   sampan amps mana maps naps pans samp snap span amp ana asp man map nap pan pas sap spa am an as ma na pa

aamnpss   sampans. *See* **aamnps aamss ampss**

aamnrst   mantras. *See* **aamnst aamnrt**

aamnrt   mantra antra atman manta anta mana mart rant tram ana ant arm art man mar mat ram ran rat tam tan tar am an at ma na ta

aamnst   atmans mantas antas atman manta anta ants mana mast mats tams tans ana ant man mat sat tam tan am an as at ma na ta

aamnstu   mantuas. *See* **aamnst aamntu**

aamnt   atman manta mana anta ana ant man mat tam tan am an at ma na ta

aamntu   mantua atman manta anta aunt mana maun tuna ana ant man mat nut tam tan tau tun am an at ma mu na nu ta um ut

aamopr   paramo aroma mora para pram proa prom ramp roam romp amp arm map mar moa mop mor oar par pro ram rap am ma mo om or pa

aamoprru   paramour. *See* **aamopr aaorru aoprru**

aamoprs   paramos. *See* **aamopr aamors**

aamor   aroma mora roam arm mar moa mor oar ram am ma mo om or

aamors   aromas aroma roams arms moas mora mors oars rams roam soar soma sora arm mar moa mor mos oar oms ram am as ma mo om or os so

aamorssv   samovars samovar. *See* **aamors amorss aamoss aorssv**

aamorsv   samovar. *See* **aamors aorsv aarsv**

aamorty   amatory. *See* **aaort aamor amoty**

aamoss samosa amass somas mass moas moss ossa soma ass moa mos oms am as ma mo om os so

aamosss samosas. *See* **aamoss**

aamost somata atoms moats stoma atom mast mats moas moat most mots oast oats soma stoa tams toms mat moa mos mot oat oms sat sot tam tom am as at ma mo om os so ta to

aamostt stomata. *See* **aamost aostt**

aamosttu automats stomata automat. *See* **aamost mosttu**

aamottu automat. *No 6s or 5s*

aampps pampas papas amps maps papa paps samp amp asp map pap pas sap spa am as ma pa

aamprrst ramparts rampart. *See* **aaprst amprst**

aamprrt rampart. *See* **aaprt amprt**

aamrssst smartass. *See* **amrsst arssst**

aamrstu traumas. *See* **aamrtu amrstu**

aamrstwy tramways tramway. *See* **aamrsw aarsty amrsty arstwy**

aamrsw aswarm swarm warms arms maws rams swam warm wars arm mar maw ram raw saw war was am as aw ma

aamrtu trauma aura mart tram arm art mar mat ram rat rum rut tam tar tau am at ma mu ta um ut

aamrtwy tramway. *See* **artwy**

aamss amass mass ass am as ma

aamsy mayas maya yams may say yam am as ay ma my

aamy maya may yam am ay ma my

aan ana an na

aannosst assonant sonatas sonants. *See* **aanost annost**

aannrsty stannary. *See* **aarsty**

aanntt natant anta ana ant tan tat an at na ta

aanorrrt narrator. *See* **aanrrt**

aanosst sonatas. *See* **aanost aosst nosst**

aanost sonata antas anta ants naos nota oast oats snot stoa tans tons ana ant not oat sat son sot tan ton an as at na no on os so ta to

aanpsst passant. *See* **aapsst aanst anpst**

aanpsv pavans pavan naps pans snap span vans ana asp nap pan pas sap spa van an as na pa

aanpv pavan ana nap pan van an na pa

aanqrstu quartans quartan. *See* **aanqst aanqrsu aaqrstu anqstu**

aanqrtu quartan. *See* **aanqtu aanrt aqrtu**

aanqst qanats qanat antas anta ants qats tans ana ant qat sat tan an as at na ta

aanqt qanat anta ana ant qat tan an at na ta

aanqtu quanta qanat quant anta aqua aunt tuna ana ant nut qat qua tan tau tun an at na nu ta ut

aanrrstw warrants warrant. *See* **aanrrt**

aanrrt arrant antra anta rant ana ant art ran rat tan tar an at na ta

aanrrtw warrant. *See* **aanrrt**

aanrrtwy warranty warrant. *See* **aanrrt**

aanrstt rattans tartans. *See* **aarstt aanrt**

aanrsuwy runaways runaway runways. *See* **anruwy**

aanrsv varnas varna varas vara vans ana ran van an as na

aanrt antra anta rant ana ant art ran rat tan tar an at na ta

aanrtt rattan tartan antra attar anta rant tart ana ant art ran rat tan tar tat an at na ta

aanruwy runaway. *See* **anruwy**

aanrv varna vara ana ran van an na

aansstv savants. *See* **aanstv**

aanssstz stanzas. *See* **aanstz**

aanssu saunas sauna anus suns ana ass sun an as na nu us

aanst antas anta ants tans ana ant sat tan an as at na ta

aanstv savant antas avast anta ants tans tavs vans vast vats ana ant sat tan tav van vat an as at na ta

aanstz stanza antas azans anta ants azan tans ana ant sat tan an as at na ta

aanswyy anyways. *See* **aanwyy answy**

aansz azans azan ana an as na

aant anta ana ant an at na ta

aantuv avaunt vaunt anta aunt tuna ana ant nut tan tau tav tun van vat an at na nu ta ut

aanwyy anyway away wany yawn ana any awn nay wan way yaw yay an aw ay na

aanz azan ana an na

aaopssty apostasy. *See* **aapsst**

aaorrsu auroras. *See* **aaorru aarrs aarsu**

aaorru aurora aura roar oar our or

aaorssvv vavasors vavasor. *See* **aorssv**

aaorst aortas aorta roast rotas taros toras arts oars oast oats orts rats rota rots soar sora sort star stoa taro tars tora tors tsar art oar oat ort rat rot sat sot tar tor as at or os so ta to

aaorsvv vavasor. *See* **aarsv aorsv**

aaort aorta rota taro tora art oar oat ort rat rot tar tor at or ta to

aapp papa pap pa

aapps papas papa paps asp pap pas sap spa as pa

aappsw papaws papas papaw papa paps paws swap waps wasp asp pap pas paw sap saw spa wap was as aw pa

aappsww pawpaws. *See* **aappsw aappwww**

aappw papaw papa pap paw wap pa aw

aappww pawpaw papaw papa pap paw wap pa aw

aapr para par rap pa

aaprrstt rattraps rattrap. *See* **aaprst aarrtt aarstt**

aaprrtt rattrap. *See* **aarrtt aaprt**

aaprs paras para pars raps rasp spar asp par pas rap sap spa as pa

aaprsst satraps. *See* **aapsst aaprst aprsst**

aaprst satrap apart paras parts pasta sprat strap tapas tarps traps arts para pars part past pats raps rapt rasp rats spar spat star tapa taps tarp tars trap tsar apt art asp par pas pat rap rat sap sat spa tap tar as at pa ta

aaprsty satrapy. *See* **aarsty aprsty aaprst**

aaprt apart para part rapt tapa tarp trap apt art par pat rap rat tap tar at pa ta

aaprtwy partway. *See* **aaprt aprty artwy**

aapsst pastas pasta pasts spats tapas asps pass past pats saps spas spat tapa taps tass apt asp ass pas pat sap sat spa tap as at pa ta

aapst pasta tapas past pats spat tapa taps apt asp pas pat sap sat spa tap as at pa ta

aapt tapa apt pat tap at pa ta

aapzzz pazazz zap pa

aaqrssu quasars. *See* **aaqrsu aqssu arssu**

aaqrsu quasar aquas auras aqua aura sura qua as us

aaqsu aquas aqua qua as us

aaqu aqua qua

aarrs arras as

aarrsy arrays arras array rays ray say yar as ay

aarrtt tartar attar tart art rat tar tat at ta

aarry array ray yar ay

aarstt attars strata attar start tarts arts rats star tars tart tats tsar art rat sat tar tat as at ta

aarsty astray artsy satyr stray trays arts arty rats rays star stay tars tray tsar art rat ray sat say sty tar try yar as at ay ta

aarsu auras aura sura as us

aarsv varas vara as

aartt attar tart art rat tar tat at ta

aaru aura

aarv vara

aasssy assays assay sassy sass says ass say as ay

aassy assay says ass say as ay

aastv avast tavs vast vats sat tav vat as at ta

aastzz tazzas tazza sat as at ta

aatzz tazza at ta
aawy away way yaw aw ay

---

ab

ab ba

abbbdel babbled blabbed. *See* **abbbel abbdel**

abbbeilr bribable babbler blabber. *See* **abbbel abbelr bbbeir bbeilr**

abbbel babble able babe bale blab bleb alb ale bel ebb lab lea ae ba be el la

abbbelr babbler blabber. *See* **abbbel abbelr**

abbbelrs babblers blabbers babbler babbles blabber rabbles slabber. *See* **abbbel abbelr abelrs**

abbbels babbles. *See* **abbbel abbes abels**

abbbgiln babbling blabbing. *See* **abgiln**

abbcde cabbed abed aced babe bade bead cade dace ace bad bed cab cad dab ebb ad ae ba be

abbcdekn backbend. *See* **abbcde abbden abcdek abdekn**

abbcdels scabbled dabbles scabbed scabble slabbed. *See* **abbcde abbdel abcdel abcels**

abbcder crabbed. *See* **abbder abcder abbcde**

abbcdes scabbed. *See* **abbcde abbes abdes**

abbceeru barbecue. *See* **abcer bceer**

abbcegir cribbage gabbier. *See* **abbcei acegir abceir abbegr**

abbcehoy beachboy. *See* **abbey abceh abbcy**

abbcei cabbie ceiba babe ace bib cab ebb ice ae ai ba be

abbceikt backbite backbit. *See* **abbcei**

abbceirr crabbier crabber. *See* **abbcei abberr abceir abcerr**

abbceirs scabbier ascribe cabbies caribes. *See* **abbcei abbeis abbirs abceir**

abbceis cabbies. *See* **abbeis abbcei abceis**

abbcekno backbone. *See* **abceno bcekno**

abbcelr clabber. *See* **abbelr abcer abcel**

abbcelrs clabbers scrabble clabber rabbles scabble slabber. *See* **abbelr abcels abcers abelrs**

abbcels scabble. *See* **abcels abbes abbls**

abbcelss scabbles scabble. *See* **abbess abcels abelss acelss**

abbcerr crabber. *See* **abberr abcerr**

abbcgin cabbing. *See* **abcin acgin**

abbcginr crabbing barbing bracing cabbing. *See* **abginr acginr**

abbcgins scabbing cabbing. *See* **abcins abgins acgins**

abbciill biblical bacilli. *See* **abiil aciil acill**

abbciinr rabbinic. *See* **abinr abcir abcin**

abbcikrt brickbat backbit. *See* **abbirt**

abbcikt backbit. *See* **abikt**

abbcilsy scabbily. *See* **abbcsy**

abbco cabob boa bob cab cob ba

abbcos cabobs cabob boas bobs cabs cobs scab boa bob cab cob sac sob as ba os so

abbcost bobcats. *See* **abbost abbcot abbcos**

abbcot bobcat cabob abbot boat coat taco act bat boa bob bot cab cat cob cot oat tab at ba ta to

abbcry crabby cabby baby barb bray crab racy aby arc bar bay bra cab car cay cry ray yar ay ba by

abbcryy crybaby. *See* **abbcry**

abbcsy scabby cabby baby bays cabs cays scab aby bay cab cay sac say as ay ba by

abbcy cabby baby aby bay cab cay ay ba by

abbdde dabbed abed babe bade bead dead add bad bed dab dad ebb ad ae ba be

abbddel dabbled. *See* **abddel abbdde abbdel**

abbddelr drabbled bladder dabbled drabbed drabble rabbled. *See* **abbdde abbdel abbder abbelr**

abbdder drabbed. *See* **abbder**

abbdeejr jabbered. *See* **abbder abdeer abbdej abbejr**

abbdeeln bendable enabled. *See* **abbdel abbden abdeel abdeen**

abbdeerr barbered drabber. *See* **abbder abberr abdeer adeerr**

abbdeery yabbered. *See* **abbder abbery abdeer abdery**

abbdeg gabbed badge abed aged babe bade bead egad gaed age bad bag bed beg dab dag ebb gab gad gae ad ae ba be

abbdegl gabbled. *See* **abbdel abbdeg abbegl abdegl**

abbdeglr grabbled drabble gabbled gabbler garbled grabbed grabble rabbled. *See* **abbdeg abbdel abbder abbegl**

abbdegr grabbed. *See* **abdegr abbder abbdeg abbegr**

abbdei babied abide abed aide babe bade bead bide idea aid bad bed bib bid dab die ebb ad ae ai ba be id

abbdeit tabbied. *See* **abbdei abdeit abbdet**

abbdej jabbed abed babe bade bead jade bad bed dab ebb jab ad ae ba be

abbdel dabble baled blade abed able babe bade bald bale bead blab bleb bled dale deal lade lead alb ale bad bed bel dab ebb eld lab lad lea led ad ae ba be el la

abbdelmr brambled bramble drabble marbled rabbled rambled. *See* **abbdel abbder abbelr abdelm**

abbdelr drabble rabbled. *See* **abdelr abbder abbdel abbelr**

abbdelrs drabbles dabbers dabbles drabble rabbled rabbles slabbed slabber. *See* **abbdel abbder abbelr abdelr**

abbdels dabbles slabbed. *See* **abbdel abdels**

abbden nabbed abed babe bade band bane bead bean bend dean and ane bad ban bed ben dab den ebb end nab nae neb ad ae an ba be en na ne

abbdeors absorbed dabbers dobbers. *See* **abbder abbors abdeos abders**

abbdeorx breadbox. *See* **abbder bbdeor**

abbder barbed dabber ardeb bared beard bread debar abed babe bade barb bard bare bead bear brad brae bred dare dear drab read are bad bar bed bra dab ear ebb era rad red ad ae ba be er re

abbderr drabber. *See* **abbder abberr abderr**

abbders dabbers. *See* **abders abbder**

abbderst drabbest barbets dabbers dabster rabbets stabbed. *See* **abbder abbdet abbert abders**

abbdest stabbed. *See* **abbdet abdest**

abbdesw swabbed. *See* **abbes abdes abdsw**

abbdet tabbed bated abed abet babe bade bate bead beat beta date debt aet ate bad bat bed bet dab eat ebb eta tab tad tea ted ad ae at ba be ta

abbdgiln dabbling dabbing balding. *See* **abgiln adgiln**

abbdgin dabbing. *No 6s or 5s*

abbdginr drabbing barbing brigand dabbing. *See* **abdinr abginr adginr**

abbdhirt birdbath. *See* **abbirt**

abbdhooy babyhood. *See* **bbooy bbhoy**

abbdmor bombard. *See* **abdor**

abbdmors bombards bombard. *See* **abbors abdors**

abbdnox bandbox. *See* **abbno**

abbe abbe babe ebb ae ba be

abbeejrr jabberer. *See* **abbejr abberr abeerr**

abbeejtt barbette abetter. *See* **abbert abeert abertt**

abbeesw bawbees. *See* **abbeew abbes**

abbeew bawbee babe awe bee ebb ewe web wee ae aw ba be we

abbefilr flabbier friable fribble. *See* **abbelr abeflr aefilr bbefir**

abbegir gabbier. *See* **abbegr bbegir**

abbegirr grabbier gabbier grabber. *See* **abbegr abberr bbegir bbeirr**

abbegist gabbiest tabbies gibbets. *See* **abbeis abegis bbegit**

abbegl gabble bagel gable able babe bale blab bleb gale age alb ale bag beg bel ebb gab gae gal gel lab lag lea leg ae ba be el la

abbeglr gabbler grabble. *See* **abbegr abbegl abeglr**

abbeglrs gabblers grabbles gabbers gabbler gabbles garbles grabble rabbles slabber. *See* **abbegl abbegr abbelr abeglr**

abbegls gabbles. *See* **abegls**

abbegnu bugbane. *See* **abegn begnu**

abbegr gabber barge ager babe barb bare bear berg brae brag garb gear grab rage age are bag bar beg bra ear ebb era erg gab gae gar rag reg ae ba be er re

abbegrr grabber. *See* **abberr abegrr abbegr**

abbegrrs grabbers barbers gabbers grabber. *See* **abbegr abberr abegrs aberrs**

abbegrs gabbers. *See* **abbegr abegrs**

abbegrsu bugbears gabbers bugbear. *See* **abbegr abegrs abersu aegrsu**

abbegru bugbear. *See* **abbegr aegru**

abbehirs shabbier bearish. *See* **abbeis abbirs abeirs aehirs**

abbehort bathrobe. *See* **abbert abehrt abeort behort**

abbeirrw barbwire. *See* **abberr bbeirr aeirrw**

abbeis babies babes babe base bias bibs bise ebbs bib ebb sea sib ae ai as ba be is si

abbeist tabbies. *See* **abbeis abest abist**

abbejr jabber babe barb bare bear brae are bar bra ear ebb era jab jar raj ae ba be er re

abbejrs jabbers. *See* **abbejr abbes abbrs**

abbek kebab babe bake beak kab ebb ae ba be ka

abbeks kebabs babes bakes beaks kebab babe bake base bask beak ebbs kabs sake ask ebb kab kas sea ae as ba be ka

abbellr barbell. *See* **abbelr abell**

abbellrs barbells barbell rabbles slabber. *See* **abbelr abells abelrs**

abbelmr bramble. *See* **abelmr abbelr**

abbelmrs brambles bramble marbles rabbles rambles slabber. *See* **abbelr abelmr abelms abelrs**

abbelnru burnable barbule nebular. *See* **abbelr abbelu abblru abelnu**

abbelopr probable belabor. *See* **abbelr abelor aelopr**

abbelor belabor. *See* **abbelr abelor**

abbelors belabors belabor rabbles slabber slobber. *See* **abbelr abbors abelor abelrs**

abbelqsu squabble baubles. *See* **abbelu abblsu abelsu abeqsu**

abbelr rabble abler blare blear able babe bale barb bare bear blab bleb brae earl rale real alb ale are bar bel bra ear ebb era lab lar lea ae ba be el er la re

abbelrs rabbles slabber. *See* **abelrs abbelr**

abbelrss slabbers braless rabbles slabber. *See* **abbelr abbess abelrs abelss**

abbelrsu barbules barbule baubles burbles lubbers rabbles rubbles slabber. *See* **abbelr abbelu abblru abblsu**

abbelru barbule. *See* **abbelu abblru bbelru**

abbelsu baubles. *See* **abblsu abbelu abelsu**

abbelu bauble babul able babe babu bale beau blab bleb blue bulb lube alb ale bel bub ebb lab leu ae ba be el la

abbeorrs reabsorb arbores barbers robbers. *See* **abberr abbors aberrs aborrs**

abbeortw browbeat. *See* **abbert abeort**

abberr barber barer barre babe barb bare bear brae rare rear are bar bra ear ebb era err ae ba be er re

abberrs barbers. *See* **abberr aberrs**

abberryy bayberry. *See* **abberr abbery aberry**

abberssw swabbers swabber. *See* **abbess aberss aerssw**

abberst barbets rabbets. *See* **abbert aberst**

abbersw swabber. *See* **abbes abbrs abers**

abbersy yabbers. *See* **abbery abbesy**

abbert barbet rabbet abet babe barb bare bate bear beat beta brae brat rate tare tear aet are art ate bar bat bet bra ear eat ebb era eta rat ret tab tar tea ae at ba be er re ta

abbery yabber abbey abye aery babe baby barb bare bear brae bray byre yare year aby are aye bar bay bey bra bye ear ebb era ray rye yar yea ae ay ba be by er re ye

abbes babes babe base ebbs sea ebb ae as ba be

abbess abbess babes bases babe base bass ebbs seas ass ebb ess sea ae as ba be

abbesy abbeys abbey babes abye ayes babe baby base bays beys byes easy ebbs eyas yeas aby aye bay bey bye ebb say sea yea yes ae as ay ba be by ye

abbey abbey abye babe baby aby aye bay bey bye ebb yea ae ay ba be by ye

abbfilly flabbily. *See* **abbfly**

abbfly flabby ably baby blab flab flay aby alb bay fay fly lab lay ay ba by fa la

abbggiln gabbling gabbing. *See* **abgiln**

abbggin gabbing. *See* **aggin**

abbgginr grabbing barbing barging gabbing garbing. *See* **abginr agginr**

abbgijn jabbing. *No 6s or 5s*

abbgilns slabbing. *See* **abgiln abgins abilns agilns**

abbginn nabbing. *No 6s or 5s*

abbginr barbing. *See* **abginr abbir**

abbginst stabbing tabbing basting. *See* **abgins abgint aginst**

abbginsw swabbing. *See* **abgins aginsw**

abbgint tabbing. *See* **abgint**

abbginty tabbying tabbing babying. *See* **abgint abginy**

abbginy babying. *See* **abginy abbgy**

abbgoosu bugaboos bugaboo. *See* **abbsu bgosu bboos**

abbgoou bugaboo. *No 6s or 5s*

abbgor gabbro barb boar bora brag garb grab ago bag bar boa bob bog bra gab gar goa gob oar orb rag rob ba go or

abbgors gabbros. *See* **abbgor abbors**

abbgry grabby gabby baby barb brag bray gaby garb grab gray aby bag bar bay bra gab gar gay rag ray yar ay ba by

abbgy gabby baby gaby aby bag bay gab gay ay ba by

abbhilsy shabbily babyish. *See* **abbhsy**

abbhisy babyish. *See* **abbhsy abhis**

abbhjsu jubbahs. *See* **abbhju abbsu**

abbhju jubbah babu juba bah bub hub jab ah ba ha

abbhrrsu rhubarbs rhubarb. *See* **abrrsu**

abbhrru rhubarb. *No 6s or 5s*

abbhsttu bathtubs bathtub. *See* **abstu abbsu abhst**

abbhsy shabby ashy baby bash bays hays shay aby ash bah bay has hay say shy yah ah as ay ba by ha sh

abbhttu bathtub. *No 6s or 5s*

abbilost bobtails bobtail. *See* **abbost ablost**

abbilot bobtail. *See* **abbot abilo bbilo**

abbimno bambino. *See* **abbno bbimo**

abbimnos bambinos bambino. *See* **abbnos abinos**

abbir rabbi barb air bar bib bra ria rib ba ai

abbirrty rabbitry. *See* **abbirt abirry airrty**

abbirs rabbis rabbi barbs airs barb bars bias bibs bras rias ribs sari air bar bib bra ria rib sib sir ai as ba is si

abbirst rabbits. *See* **abbirs abbirt**

abbirsuu suburbia. *See* **abbirs abirsu bbrsuu**

abbirt rabbit rabbi bait barb brat brit air art bar bat bib bit bra ita rat ria rib tab tar ai at ba it ta ti

abbkknoo bankbook. *See* **abbnoo**

abbko kabob boa bob kab koa kob oak ba ka

abbkos kabobs kabob bask boas bobs bosk kabs koas kobs oaks soak ask boa bob kab kas koa kob kos oak sob as ba ka os so

abbl blab alb lab ba la

abblmry brambly. *See* **ablmry**

abblopry probably. *See* **ablor abory bbloy**

abblru bulbar babul blurb babu barb blab blur bulb burl alb bar bra bub lab lar rub ba la

abbls blabs albs blab labs slab alb lab sal as ba la

abblsu babuls babul babus blabs bulbs albs babu blab bubs bulb labs slab slub alb bub bus lab sal sub as ba la us

abblu babul babu blab bulb alb bub lab ba la

abbmoo bamboo ambo bomb boob boom bam boa bob boo moa mob moo am ba ma mo om

abbmoos bamboos. *See* **abbmoo abmos bbmos**

---

abbmosst bombasts bombast. *See* **abbost abosst amosst**

abbmosst bombast. *See* **abbost abmos amost**

abbmostu bumboats bombast bumboat. *See* **abbost**

abbmotu bumboat. *See* **abbot abotu**

abbmox bombax ambo bomb moxa bam boa bob box moa mob am ax ba ma mo om ox

abbno nabob ban boa bob nab nob an ba na no on

abbnoo baboon nabob boob boon ban boa bob boo nab nob an ba na no on

abbnoos baboons. *See* **abbnoo abbnos**

abbnos nabobs nabob bans boas bobs nabs naos nobs snob ban boa bob nab nob sob son an as ba na no on os so

abbnrsuu suburban auburns. *See* **abnrsu bbrsuu**

abbors absorb barbs boars boras barb bars boar boas bobs bora bras oars orbs robs soar sora sorb bar boa bob bra oar orb rob sob as ba or os so

abborss absorbs. *See* **abbors abrss aorss**

abbost abbots abbot boast boats sabot bast bats boas boat bobs bots oast oats stab stoa stob tabs bat boa bob bot oat sat sob sot tab as at ba os so ta to

abbosty batboys. *See* **abbost abboty**

abbot abbot boat bat boa bob bot oat tab at ba ta to

abboty batboy abbot tabby baby boat aby bat bay boa bob bot boy oat tab toy yob at ay ba by oy ta to

abbqsuy squabby. *See* **abbsu bbsuy aqsuy**

abbr barb bar bra ba

abbrs barbs barb bars bras bar bra as ba

abbsu babus babu bubs bub bus sub as ba us

abbty tabby baby aby bat bay tab at ay ba by ta

abbu babu bub ba

abby baby aby bay ay ba by

abc cab ba

abcceelp peccable. *See* **abeel beelp abcel**

abcceily celibacy bicycle. *See* **abeily acceil cceily**

abcceir acerbic. *See* **abceir cceir accir**

abccekmo comeback. *See* **accko acemo bcemo**

abcchnoo cabochon. *See* **acchno**

abccilor carbolic caloric. *See* **accilo acilor**

abccilu cubical. *See* **abcclu bcciu**

abccimr cambric. *See* **abcir accir**

abccinor carbonic. *See* **abcnor**

abcciors ascorbic. *See* **abcios abcors abiors aciors**

---

abcckoot cockboat tobacco. *See* **accko accot accoo**

abcckstu cutbacks cutback sackbut. *See* **accstu**

abccktu cutback. *No 6s or 5s*

abcclu buccal caul club alb cab cub lab lac ba la

abccoost tobaccos tobacco. *See* **aboost accoos accost**

abccoot tobacco. *See* **accot accoo aboot**

abcddeor brocaded boarded brocade roadbed. *See* **abcder acdder addeor cddeor**

abcddetu abducted. *See* **abcdtu abddeu acddeu cddetu**

abcdeefk feedback. *See* **abcdek abdeek acdeef**

abcdeeh beached. *See* **abdeeh acdeh abceh**

abcdeehl bleached beached belched debacle leached. *See* **abcdel abcehl abdeeh abdeel**

abcdeehr breached beached reached. *See* **abcder abcehr abdeeh abdeer**

abcdeel debacle. *See* **abcdel abdeel**

abcdeelm becalmed debacle. *See* **abcdel abceem abcelm abdeel**

abcdeels debacles debacle beadles. *See* **abcdel abcels abdeel abdees**

abcdeelu educable debacle. *See* **abcdel abdeel acdelu**

abcdeemr cambered embraced embrace creamed. *See* **abcder abceem abcemr abdeem**

abcdeflo boldface. *See* **abcdel abdefl abdelo acdelo**

abcdehln blanched. *See* **abcdel abcehl abchln acdeln**

abcdehnr branched ranched. *See* **abcder abcehr abchnr acdehr**

abcdehor broached brocade. *See* **abcder abcehr abchor acdehr**

abcdeht batched. *See* **abdeht acdeht**

abcdehu debauch. *See* **acdeh abceh bcdeu**

abcdeiit diabetic. *See* **abdeit abeiit cdeiit**

abcdeiks backside sickbed. *See* **abcdek abceis abdeis abdeks**

abcdein cabined. *See* **abdei acden abcin**

abcdeip pedicab. *See* **abdei bdeip abcei**

abcdeips pedicabs pedicab. *See* **abceis abdeis acdeps aceips**

abcdeir carbide. *See* **abdeir abcder abceir**

abcdeirs ascribed carbides abiders ascribe braised carbide caribes radices scribed sidecar. *See* **abcder abceir abceis**

abcdeiss abscised abscise scabies. *See* **abceis abciss abdeis abeiss**

abcdek backed baked caked abed aced back bade bake bead beak beck cade cake dace deck ace bad bed cab cad dab kab ad ae ba be ka

abcdekl blacked. *See* **abcdek abdekl abcdel acdekl**

abcdeklo blockade blacked blocked cloaked. *See* **abcdek abcdel abdekl abdelo**

abcdeknn neckband. *See* **abcdek abdekn acdenn**

abcdeknu unbacked. *See* **abcdek abdekn bcdeku bdeknu**

abcdel cabled baled blade cable decal laced abed able aced bade bald bale bead bled cade clad dace dale deal lace lade lead ace alb ale bad bed bel cab cad dab eld lab lac lad lea led ad ae ba be el la

abcdeloo caboodle. *See* **abcdel abdelo acdelo bdeloo**

abcdemot combated. *See* **abcmot abdeot acdeot acemot**

abcdeor brocade. *See* **abcder abdeo adeor**

abcdeors brocades brocade. *See* **abcder abcers abcors abdeos**

abcder braced acerb acred arced ardeb bared beard brace bread caber cadre cared cedar debar raced abed aced acre bade bard bare bead bear brad brae bred cade card care crab dace dare dear drab race read ace arc are bad bar bed bra cab cad car dab ear era rad rec red ad ae ba be er re

abcderu cudbear. *See* **abcder bcderu abderu**

abcdhklo holdback. *See* **adhlo abckl bcklo**

abcdiilo diabolic. *See* **bdiilo**

abcdilr baldric. *See* **abdilr**

abcdilrs baldrics baldric scribal. *See* **abdilr abdirs abilrs**

abcdkoor backdoor cordoba. *See* **abdor bckor bdoor**

abcdkopr backdrop. *See* **abdor bckor abcor**

abcdnos abscond. *See* **abcno abdns bdnos**

abcdnoss absconds abscond. *See* **abcno abdns bdnos**

abcdoor cordoba. *See* **abdor bdoor abcor**

abcdoors cordobas cordoba. *See* **abcors abdors bdoors**

abcdopru cupboard. *See* **abdor abcor acopr**

abcdortu abductor. *See* **abcdtu abortu**

abcdstu abducts. *See* **abcdtu acdstu**

abcdtu abduct ducat abut baud daub duct tabu tuba act bad bat bud but cab cad cat cub cud cut dab dub tab tad tau tub ad at ba ta ut

abceehlm bechamel. *See* **abceem abcehl abcelm aceehl**

abceehlr bleacher leacher. *See* **abcehl abcehr abehlr aceehl**

abceehls bleaches beaches belches leaches. *See* **abcehl abcels abeels aceehl**

abceehrs breaches beaches reaches. *See* **abcehr abcers aceers acehrs**

abceehs beaches. *See* **acehs abceh bceeh**

abceeilt celibate. *See* **abeilt**

abceeimn ambience. *See* **abceem abcemn abeein aceemn**

abceeirr cerebral cerebra clearer. *See* **abcerr abeerr abelrr aceelr**

abceelrt bracelet treacle. *See* **abeert abelrt aceelr aceert**

abceem became acme beam bema came mace ace bam bee cab cam cee mac mae ae am ba be em ma me

abceemr embrace. *See* **aceemr abeemr abceem abcemr**

abceemrr embracer cerebra creamer embrace. *See* **abceem abcemr abcerr abeemr**

abceemrs embraces amerces beamers besmear cambers embrace racemes. *See* **abceem abcemr abcers abeemr**

abceens absence. *See* **aceens abens**

abceenss absences absence encases. *See* **aceens aceess ceenss**

abceerr cerebra. *See* **abeerr abcerr aceerr**

abceesu because. *See* **abesu acesu acees**

abcefiit beatific. *See* **abeiit**

abcefikr backfire. *See* **abceir abcekr abcfir acefir**

abceghin beaching. *See* **aceghn acghin**

abcegikv giveback. *See* **abcei**

abcegklo blockage backlog. *See* **abegl abckl abekl**

abcegkmu megabuck. *See* **abcegu**

abcegos boscage. *See* **acegos**

abcegoss boscages boscage socages. *See* **acegos**

abcegsu cubages. *See* **abcegu abesu aegsu**

abcegu cubage ague beau cage cube ace age bag beg bug cab cub cue gab gae ae ba be

abceh beach ache bach each ace bah cab hae ae ah ba be eh ha he

abcehko backhoe. *See* **abceh cehko abeho**

abcehkos backhoes backhoe. *See* **cehkos**

abcehl bleach beach belch cable chela leach able ache bach bale blah each hale heal lace lech ace alb ale bah bel cab hae lab lac lea ae ah ba be eh el ha he la

abcehlnr blancher charnel. *See* **abcehl abcehr abchln abchnr**

abcehlns blanches. *See* **abcehl abcels abchln**

abcehlor bachelor cholera chorale. *See* **abcehl abcehr abchor abehlr**

abcehlsu chasuble bascule. *See* **abcehl abcels abelsu acehls**

abcehmot hecatomb. *See* **abcmot acemot**

abcehmr chamber. *See* **abcehr abcemr**

abcehmrs chambers cambers chamber marches mesarch. *See* **abcehr abcemr abcers abemrs**

abcehnrs branches ranches. *See* **abcehr abcers abchnr acehrs**

abcehors broaches roaches. *See* **abcehr abcers abchor abcors**

abcehoru barouche. *See* **abcehr abchor acehor bcehor**

abcehr breach acerb beach brace brach caber chare reach rehab ache acre arch bach bare bear brae care char crab each hare hear herb race rhea ace arc are bah bar bra cab car ear era hae her rah rec ae ah ba be eh er ha he re

abcehst batches. *See* **abehst acehst**

abcei ceiba ace cab ice ae ai ba be

abceikwz zwieback. *See* **abcei abeiz**

abceilm alembic. *See* **abcelm aceilm**

abceilms alembics alembic becalms malices. *See* **abceis abcelm abcels abelms**

abceilnn binnacle. *See* **aceinn acelnn**

abceilor cabriole aerobic caliber calorie cariole corbeil loricae. *See* **abceir abelor aceilr acelor**

abceilos sociable. *See* **abceis abcels abcios acelos**

abceilr caliber. *See* **abceir aceilr**

abceilrs calibers ascribe caliber caribes claries eclairs scalier scribal. *See* **abceir abceis abcels abcers**

abceinr carbine. *See* **abceir aceinr**

abceinrs brisance carbines arsenic ascribe carbine caribes carnies. *See* **abceir abceis abcers abcins**

abceinst cabinets cabinet basinet. *See* **abceis abcins abeint abenst**

abceint cabinet. *See* **abeint acint abcin**

abceintu incubate cabinet. *See* **abeint abentu aeintu**

abceior aerobic. *See* **abceir bceior**

abceiors aerobics aerobic ascribe caribes corbies. *See* **abceir abceis abcers abcios**

abceiost iceboats iceboat. *See* **abceis abcios aceost aciost**

abceiot iceboat. *See* **abiot abcei aciot**

abceir caribe acerb baric brace caber ceiba ceria acre bare bear bier brae brie care crab crib race rice ace air arc are bar bra cab car ear era ice ire rec ria rib ae ai ba be er re

abceirs ascribe caribes. *See* **abcers abeirs abceir aceirs abceis**

abceirss ascribes abscise ascribe braises brassie caribes scabies scribes. *See* **abceir abceis abcers abciss**

abceirtt brattice battier biretta cattier citrate. *See* **abceir abeirt abertt aeirtt**

abceirty acerbity barytic. *See* **abceir abeirt aberty**

abceis ceibas ceiba basic aces asci base bias bise cabs case ices scab ace cab ice sac sea sib sic ae ai as ba be is si

abceiss abscise scabies. *See* **abciss abeiss abceis**

abcejlty abjectly. *See* **abcejt acelty**

abcejt abject abet bate beat beta cate ace act aet ate bat bet cab cat eat eta jab jet tab tea ae at ba be ta

abcekln blacken. *See* **aekln abckl abkln**

abceklns blackens blacken slacken. *See* **abcels abckls abklns**

abceklr blacker. *See* **abcekr abelr abckl**

abceklss backless. *See* **abcels abckls abelss acelss**

abceklst blackest setback tackles. *See* **abcels abckls abekst abelst**

abcekoos bookcase casebook caboose. *See* **abcks abeks bceks**

abcekr backer acerb baker brace brake break caber crake creak acre back bake bare bark beak bear beck brae cake care cark crab kerb race rack rake reck ace arc are ark bar bra cab car ear era kab rec ae ba be er ka re

abcekrs backers. *See* **abcekr abekrs abcers acekrs**

abcekrst backrest brackets backers bracket rackets setback. *See* **abcekr abcers abcrst abekrs**

abcekrt bracket. *See* **abcekr acekrt**

abceksst setbacks baskets caskets setback. *See* **abekst abesst acekst acesst**

abcekst setback. *See* **abekst acekst**

abcekstw wetbacks setback wetback. *See* **abekst acekst aekstw**

abcektw wetback. *See* **aektw**

abcel cable able bale lace ace alb ale bel cab lab lac lea ae ba be el la

abcellpu culpable. *See* **abellu**

abcelm becalm amble blame cable camel able acme bale balm beam bema calm came clam lace lamb lame mace male meal ace alb ale bam bel cab cam elm lab lac lam lea mac mae mel ae am ba be el em la ma me

abcelmo cembalo. *See* **abcelm aelmo acemo**

abcelmos cembalos cembalo becalms. *See* **abcelm abcels abelms acelms**

abcelmr clamber. *See* **abcelm acelmr abcemr abelmr**

abcelmrs clambers scramble becalms cambers clamber marbles marcels rambles. *See* **abcelm abcels abcemr abcers**

abcelms becalms. *See* **abelms abcelm abcels acelms**

abcelop placebo. *See* **abcel bcelo aclop**

abcelops placebos placebo. *See* **abcels acelos acelps aelops**

abcelort brocatel bloater locater. *See* **abclot abelor abelot abelrt**

abcelost obstacle boatels lactose locates oblates. *See* **abcels abclot abelot abelst**

abcelotu bluecoat. *See* **abclot abelot acelot bcelou**

abcelov vocable. *See* **acelov**

abcelru curable. *See* **abelr abcer belru**

abcels cables bales cable laces sable scale able aces albs ales bale base bels cabs case labs lace leas sale scab seal slab ace alb ale bel cab els lab lac lea sac sal sea ae as ba be el la

abcelssu bascules bascule clauses. *See* **abcels abelss abelsu abessu**

abcelsu bascule. *See* **abcels acelsu abelsu**

abcemn cabmen acme acne amen bane beam bean bema came cane mace mane mean name ace ane bam ban ben cab cam can mac mae man men nab nae neb ae am an ba be em en ma me na ne

abcemr camber acerb amber brace bream caber cream acme acre bare barm beam bear bema berm brae came care crab cram mace marc mare race ream ace arc are arm bam bar bra cab cam car ear era mac mae mar ram rec rem ae am ba be em er ma me re

abcemrs cambers. *See* **abemrs abcers abcemr acemrs**

abceno beacon bacon canoe ocean acne aeon bane bean bone cane cone ebon once ace ane ban ben boa cab can cob con eon nab nae neb nob one ae an ba be en na ne no on

abcenos beacons. *See* **abceno acenos**

abcenosw cowbanes beacons cowbane. *See* **abceno acenos**

abcenow cowbane. *See* **abceno**

abceoos caboose. *See* **beoos**

abceooss cabooses caboose. *See* **abess acess aeoss**

abceorr bracero. *See* **abcerr aborr beorr**

abcer acerb brace caber acre bare bear brae care crab race ace arc are bar bra cab car ear era rec ae ba be er re

abcerr bracer acerb barer barre brace caber racer acre bare bear brae care crab race rare rear ace arc are bar bra cab car ear era err rec ae ba be er re

abcerrs bracers. *See* **aberrs abcerr abcers acerrs**

abcers braces cabers acerb acres bares baser bears brace caber cares crabs races saber sabre scare aces acre arcs arse bare bars base bear brae bras cabs care cars case crab ears eras race rase scab scar sear sera ace arc are bar bra cab car ear era rec res sac sea ae as ba be er re

abcesss abscess. *See* **aesss abess acess**

abcfikll backfill. *See* **abckl acfkl afill**

abcfilo bifocal. *See* **abilo abcio acflo**

abcfilos bifocals bifocal. *See* **abcios acfils acfios acilos**

abcfir fabric baric crab crib fair air arc arf bar bra cab car far fib fir ria rib rif ai ba fa if

abcfirs fabrics. *See* **abcfir abcis abcrs**

abcfkllu fullback. *See* **abckl abllu acklu**

abcfno confab bacon ban boa cab can cob con fan fob nab nob oaf an ba fa na no of on

abcfnos confabs. *See* **abcfno**

abcghint batching bathing. *See* **abgint acghin acgint achint**

abcghko hogback. *No 6s or 5s*

abcghkos hogbacks hogback. *See* **abcks achos achks**

abcgiinn cabining. *See* **acginn**

abcgikln blacking backing balking cabling lacking. *See* **abgikn abgiln acgikn acgiln**

abcgikn backing. *See* **abgikn acgikn**

abcgikns backings backing basking sacking. *See* **abcins abgikn abgins acgikn**

abcgiln cabling. *See* **abgiln acgiln**

abcginr bracing. *See* **acginr abginr**

abcgklo backlog. *See* **abckl bcklo acklo**

abcgklos backlogs backlog. *See* **abckls acklos bcklos**

abch bach cab bah ah ba ha

abchhii hibachi. *No 6s or 5s*

abchhiis hibachis hibachi. *See* **achiis**

abchikls blackish kiblahs. *See* **abckls abhikl achkls**

abchikrs brackish. *See* **achirs ahikrs bcikrs chikrs**

abchimru brachium. *See* **abhimr abhmru**

abchinor bronchia. *See* **abchnr abchor abcnor achinr**

abchkmpu humpback. *See* **abchpu abckpu**

abchkoop chapbook. *See* **ahkoo achop choop**

abchkoos cashbook. *See* **ahkoos**

abchkstu hackbuts hackbut sackbut. *See* **abstu abcks abhst**

abchktu hackbut. *See* **abcht bchtu**

abchlluu clubhaul. *See* **abllu**

abchln blanch bach blah clan alb bah ban cab can lab lac nab nah ah an ba ha la na

abchmotx matchbox. *See* **abcmot abhotx**

abchnr branch brach ranch arch bach barn bran char crab narc arc bah ban bar bra cab can car nab nah rah ran ah an ba ha na

abchor broach abhor brach carob cobra orach roach arch bach boar bora char crab hoar hora arc bah bar boa bra cab car cob cor hob oar orb orc rah rho rob roc ah ba ha ho oh or

abchpsu hubcaps. *See* **abchpu achps bchsu**

abchpu hubcap bach chap chub bah cab cap cub cup hap hub hup pah pub ah ba ha pa up

abchr brach arch bach char crab arc bah bar bra cab car rah ah ba ha

abcht batch bach baht bath chat tach act bah bat cab cat hat tab ah at ba ha ta

abciill bacilli. *See* **abiil aciil acill**

abciilot biotical abiotic. *See* **abclot abiilt aciilt bciiot**

abciils basilic. *See* **abiils aciils**

abciim iambic mica aim bam cab cam mac ai am ba ma mi

abciims iambics. *See* **abciim abcis acims**

abciior ciboria. *See* **abcir bcior abcor**

abciiors isobaric ciboria. *See* **abcios abcors abiors aciors**

abciiot abiotic. *See* **bciiot abiot aciot**

abciisty basicity. *See* **abiist**

abcikkll kickball. *See* **abckl abikl acill**

abciklst backlist. *See* **abckls abikst**

abcillsu bacillus. *See* **acills acllsu**

abcilnpu publican. *See* **acilnu bcilpu**

abcilrs scribal. *See* **abilrs abcir abcis**

abcimmu cambium. *No 6s or 5s*

abcimorr microbar. *See* **abcmor abiorr bcimor**

abcimsst cambists cambist mastics miscast. *See* **abciss abimst acimst**

abcimst cambist. *See* **abimst acimst**

abcin cabin bani ani ban bin cab can nab nib ai an ba in na

abcins cabins basic basin cabin sabin asci bani bans bias bins cabs cans nabs nibs sain scab scan ani ban bin cab can nab nib sac sib sic sin ai an as ba in is na si

abcio cobia boa cab cob obi ba ai

abciorsu caribous caribou carious curiosa. *See* **abcios abcors abiors abirsu**

abcioru caribou. *See* **aciru abcir bcior**

abcios cobias cobia basic asci bias boas cabs cobs obis scab boa cab cob obi sac sib sic sob ai as ba is os si so

abciossu scabious. *See* **abcios abciss**

abciosuv bivouacs bivouac. *See* **abcios aciosv**

abciouv bivouac. *See* **abcio**

abcir baric crab crib air arc bar bra cab car ria rib ba ai

abcirty barytic. *See* **abcir abcrt**

abcis basic asci bias cabs scab cab sac sib sic ai as ba is si

abciss basics basic basis scabs asci bass bias cabs sacs scab sibs ass cab sac sib sic sis ai as ba is si

abcjkoot bootjack jackboot. *See* **abjot cjkoo aboot**

abck back cab kab ba ka

abckkoor bookrack. *See* **bckor bkoor abcor**

abckl black back balk calk lack alb cab kab kal lab lac ba ka la

abckllor rollback. *See* **acllor**

abckllpu pullback. *See* **abckpu**

abcklly blackly. *See* **abkly ablly abckl**

abcklopt blacktop. *See* **abclot**

abcklotu blackout outback. *See* **abclot**

abckls blacks backs balks black calks lacks slack albs back balk bask cabs calk cask kabs labs lack sack scab slab alb ask cab kab kal kas lab lac sac sal as ba ka la

abckmoss mossback. *See* **ackmss ckmoss**

abckmrsu buckrams buckram buckras. *See* **abckru abmrsu acmrsu bcmrsu**

abckmru buckram. *See* **abckru ackmu bcmru**

abcknrsu runbacks runback buckras. *See* **abckru abknrs abnrsu acknrs**

abcknru runback. *See* **abckru abnru acknr**

abcknstu cutbanks sackbut. *See* **acnstu**

abckooru buckaroo. *See* **abckru**

abckopst backstop. *See* **acost abcks abost**

abckostu outbacks outback sackbut. *See* **abotu abstu acost**

abckotu outback. *See* **abotu bckou**

abckpu backup back buck pack puck auk cab cap cub cup kab pub ba ka pa up

abckrsu buckras. *See* **abckru abcks abkrs**

abckru buckra back bark buck cark crab curb rack ruck arc ark auk bar bra cab car cub cur kab rub ba ka

abcks backs back bask cabs cask kabs sack scab ask cab kab kas sac as ba ka

abcksstu sackbuts sackbut. *See* **acksst**

abckssuw bucksaws bucksaw. *See* **acssu abcks abkss**

abckstu sackbut. *See* **abstu bcksu abcsu**

abcksuw bucksaw. *See* **abcks**

abcllnor cornball. *See* **abcnor acllor**

abcllosy callboys callboy. *See* **abllsy acllos allosy**

abclloy callboy. *See* **alloy ablly clloy**

abclmsy cymbals. *See* **abclmy abmsy aclsy**

abclmy cymbal balmy ably amyl balm calm clam clay cyma lacy lamb aby alb bam bay cab cam cay lab lac lam lay mac may yam am ay ba by la ma my

abclnory carbonyl balcony. *See* **abcnor abcory abnory aclory**

abclnoy balcony. *See* **abcno blnoy**

abclorxy carboxyl. *See* **abcorx abcory aclory**

abclot cobalt bloat alto blat bloc blot boat bolt clot coal coat cola colt lota taco talc tola act alb alt bat boa bot cab cat cob col cot lab lac lob lot oat tab at ba la lo ta to

abclsssu subclass. *See* **acssu aclsu aclss**

abcmop mobcap campo ambo camp capo coma comb comp amp bam boa bop cab cam cap cob cop mac map moa mob mop am ba ma mo om pa

abcmops mobcaps. *See* **abcmop acmops**

abcmor crambo carob carom cobra macro ambo barm boar bora coma comb corm crab cram marc mora roam arc arm bam bar boa bra cab cam car cob cor mac mar moa mob mor oar orb orc ram rob roc am ba ma mo om or

abcmost combats. *See* **abcmot acmost**

abcmot combat ambo atom boat coat coma comb moat taco tomb act bam bat boa bot cab cam cat cob cot mac mat moa mob mot oat tab tam tom am at ba ma mo om ta to

abcno bacon ban boa cab can cob con nab nob an ba na no on

abcnor carbon acorn bacon baron carob cobra narco barn boar bora born bran corn crab narc roan arc ban bar boa bra cab can car cob con cor nab nob nor oar orb orc ran rob roc an ba na no on or

abcnors carbons. *See* **acnors abnors abcnor abcors**

abcnouyy buoyancy. *See* **bcnouy**

abcor carob cobra boar bora crab arc bar boa bra cab car cob cor oar orb orc rob roc ba or

abcorrss crossbar. *See* **abcors aborrs acorss**

abcorrsw crowbars crowbar barrows. *See* **abcors aborrs aborrw aorrsw**

abcorrw crowbar. *See* **aborrw abcor**

abcors carobs cobras boars boras carob cobra crabs arcs bars boar boas bora bras cabs cars cobs cors crab oars orbs orcs robs rocs scab scar soar sora sorb arc bar boa bra cab car cob cor oar orb orc rob roc sac sob as ba or os so

abcorssu scabrous sarcous. *See* **abcors abrssu acorss bcrssu**

abcorsx boxcars. *See* **abcorx abcors**

abcorsy carboys. *See* **aborsy abcory abcors**

abcorx boxcar borax carob cobra boar bora coax coxa crab arc bar boa box bra cab car cob cor cox oar orb orc rob roc ax ba or ox

abcory carboy boyar carob cobra boar bora bray crab orby racy aby arc bar bay boa boy bra cab car cay cob cor coy cry oar orb orc ray rob roc yar yob ay ba by or oy

abcr crab arc bar bra cab car ba

abcrs crabs arcs bars bras cabs cars crab scab scar arc bar bra cab car sac ba as

abcrst bracts bract brats carts crabs acts arcs arts bars bast bats bras brat cabs cars cart cats crab rats scab scar scat stab star tabs tars tsar act arc art bar bat bra cab car cat rat sac sat tab tar as at ba ta

abcrsttu subtract. *See* **abcrst acrstt**

abcrt bract brat cart crab act arc art bar bat bra cab car cat rat tab tar at ba ta

abcs cabs scab cab sac as ba

abcss scabs bass cabs sacs scab ass cab sac as ba

abcsu scuba cabs cubs scab bus cab cub sac sub as ba us

abd bad dab ba ad

abddee beaded abed bade bead dead deed add bad bed bee dab dad ad ae ba be

abddeeeh beheaded. *See* **abddee abdeeh addeeh**

abddeegr badgered bearded breaded degrade. *See* **abddee abdeer abdegr abeegr**

abddeeht deathbed debated. *See* **abddee abdeeh abdeet abdeht**

abddeekr debarked bearded breaded. *See* **abddee abdeek abdeer abdekr**

abddeer bearded breaded. *See* **abddee abdeer**

abddeerr debarred bearded breaded. *See* **abddee abdeer abderr adeerr**

abddees debased. *See* **abddee abdees**

abddeest bedstead debased debated debates sedated. *See* **abddee abdees abdeet abdest**

abddeet debated. *See* **abddee abdeet**

abddegir abridged brigaded abridge braided bridged brigade. *See* **abddei abdegr abdeir addegr**

abddehmo hebdomad. *See* **abdeo bddeo bdemo**

abddei abided abide aided bided abed aide bade bead bide dead died idea add aid bad bed bid dab dad did die ad ae ai ba be id

abddeil addible. *See* **abddei abdeil abddel addeil**

abddeils disabled addible baldies disable laddies. *See* **abddei abddel abdeil abdeis**

abddein bandied. *See* **abddei abdden bddein**

abddeinr brandied bandied braided brained branded dandier drained. *See* **abddei abdden abdeir abdinr**

abddeir braided. *See* **abddei abdeir bddeir addeir**

abddel bladed addle baled blade laded abed able bade bald bale bead bled dale dead deal lade lead add alb ale bad bed bel dab dad eld lab lad lea led ad ae ba be el la

abddelr bladder. *See* **abdelr abddel addelr**

abddelrs bladders bladder ladders raddles saddler. *See* **abddel abdelr abdels abders**

abdden banded abed bade band bane bead bean bend dead dean add and ane bad ban bed ben dab dad den end nab nae neb ad ae an ba be en na ne

abddenou abounded bounded. *See* **abdden abddeu abdnou bddeno**

abddenr branded. *See* **abdden addenr**

abddeor boarded roadbed. *See* **addeor**

abddeors roadbeds boarded deodars roadbed. *See* **abdeos abders abdors addeor**

abddeu daubed abed bade baud bead beau daub dead duad dude add bad bed bud dab dad dub dud due ad ae ba be

abddilry ladybird. *See* **abdilr adilry**

abddins disband. *See* **abdns abins bdins**

abddinss disbands disband. *See* **abinss**

abddirry yardbird. *See* **abirry**

abddllo oddball. *No 6s or 5s*

abddllos oddballs oddball. *See* **ablls ablos bllos**

abde abed bade bead bad bed dab ad ae ba be

abdeeerv bereaved bereave. *See* **abdeer abderv abeerv adeerv**

abdeefmr bedframe. *See* **abdeem abdeer abeemr abefmr**

abdeeh behead abed bade bead hade head heed bad bah bed bee dab edh had hae ad ae ah ba be eh ha he

abdeehno bonehead. *See* **abdeeh abdeen bdeeno**

abdeehrt breathed berated berthed breadth breathe rebated. *See* **abdeeh abdeer abdeet abdeht**

abdeehs beheads. *See* **abdehs abdeeh abdees**

abdeehv behaved. *See* **abeehv adeehv**

abdeeiln deniable enabled delaine. *See* **abdeel abdeen abdeil abeein**

abdeeilr rideable beadier bedrail leadier ridable. *See* **abdeel abdeer abdeil abdeir**

abdeeilw bewailed. *See* **abdeel abdeil abdelw abeilw**

abdeeir beadier. *See* **abdeer abdeir**

abdeeist beadiest diabetes beastie betides debates ideates. *See* **abdees abdeet abdeis abdeit**

abdeejt jetbead. *See* **abdeet**

abdeek beaked baked abed bade bake bead beak eked bad bed bee dab eke kab ad ae ba be ka**

abdeekmn embanked. *See* **abdeek abdeem abdeen abdekn**

abdeekmr embarked. *See* **abdeek abdeem abdeer abdekr**

abdeel beadle abele baled blade bleed abed able alee bade bald bale bead bled dale deal dele lade lead alb ale bad bed bee bel dab eel eld lab lad lea led lee ad ae ba be el la

abdeell labeled. *See* **abdell abdeel bdeell**

abdeelll labelled labeled. *See* **abdeel abdell bdeell**

abdeelln lendable labeled enabled. *See* **abdeel abdeen abdell abeeln**

abdeellw weldable labeled. *See* **abdeel abdell abdelw adellw**

abdeelmm embalmed. *See* **abdeel abdeem abdelm abdemm**

abdeelmn mendable enabled. *See* **abdeel abdeem abdeen abdelm**

abdeelmz emblazed emblaze. *See* **abdeel abdeem abdelm abdelz**

abdeeln enabled. *See* **abeeln abdeen bdeeln adeeln**

abdeelor leeboard labored. *See* **abdeel abdeer abdelo abdelr**

abdeelrr barreled. *See* **abdeel abdeer abdelr abderr**

abdeels beadles. *See* **abeels abdeel abdels bdeels abdees**

abdeelt belated bleated. *See* **abdeel bdeelt abdeet adeelt abdelt**

abdeely belayed. *See* **abdeel abdly abdey**

abdeem beamed edema embed abed bade bead beam bema dame deem deme made mead meed bad bam bed bee dab dam mad mae ad ae am ba be em ma me

abdeemno bemoaned abdomen. *See* **abdeem abdeen abdemn abemno**

abdeemy embayed. *See* **abdeem abdey abemy**

abdeen beaned abed bade band bane bead bean been bend dean dene need and ane bad ban bed bee ben dab den end nab nae neb nee ad ae an ba be en na ne

abdeenrt bantered bartend berated rebated. *See* **abdeen abdeer abdeet abeent**

abdeenst absented debates. *See* **abdeen abdees abdeet abdest**

abdeentt battened abetted dentate. *See* **abdeen abdeet abdett abeent**

abdeer beader ardeb bared beard bread breed debar eared abed bade bard bare bead bear beer brad brae bred bree dare dear deer drab dree read reed are bad bar bed bee bra dab ear era ere rad red ad ae ba be er re

abdeerrt bartered berated rebated retread. *See* **abdeer abdeet abderr abeert**

abdeers sabered. *See* **abders abdeer bdeers abdees adeers**

abdeerst breasted beaters berated berates dabster dearest debates rebated rebates sabered. *See* **abdeer abdees abdeet abders**

abdeert berated rebated. *See* **abdeer abeert abdeet**

abdeertt battered abetted abetter berated rebated treated. *See* **abdeer abdeet abdett abeert**

abdeertw waterbed berated bewared rebated watered. *See* **abdeer abdeet abeert abeerw**

abdeerty betrayed berated rebated. *See* **abdeer abdeet abdery abeert**

abdeerw bewared. *See* **abdeer abeerw bdeerw**

abdees debase seabed based beads eased abed bade base bead beds bees dabs ease seed ads bad bed bee dab sad sea see ad ae as ba be

abdeess debases seabeds. *See* **abdees**

abdeest debates. *See* **abdest bdeest abdees abdeet adeest**

abdeet debate bated abed abet bade bate bead beat beet beta date debt teed aet ate bad bat bed bee bet dab eat eta tab tad tea ted tee ad ae at ba be ta

abdeett abetted. *See* **abdett bdeett abdeet**

abdeffl baffled. *See* **abdefl abeffl**

abdefiis basified. *See* **abdeis**

abdefl fabled baled blade fable abed able bade bald bale bead bled dale deaf deal delf fade flab flea fled lade lead leaf alb ale bad bed bel dab eld elf fad fed lab lad lea led ad ae ba be el fa la

abdeflor fordable forbade labored. *See* **abdefl abdelo abdelr abdfor**

abdeflst flatbeds baldest bedfast blasted flatbed stabled. *See* **abdefl abdels abdelt abdest**

abdeflt flatbed. *See* **abdefl abdelt**

abdefor forbade. *See* **abdfor adefor**

abdefst bedfast. *See* **abdest adefst**

abdeg badge abed aged bade bead egad gaed age bad bag bed beg dab dag gab gad gae ad ae ba be

abdegg bagged badge gaged abed aged bade bead egad gaed gage age bad bag bed beg dab dag egg gab gad gae gag ad ae ba be

abdeggr bragged. *See* **abdegr abdegg abeggr adeggr**

abdegin beading. *See* **abdegn adegin**

abdeginr breading abridge beading bearing brained brigade brigand grained reading. *See* **abdegn abdegr abdeir abdinr**

abdegins debasing beading bandies. *See* **abdegn abdegs abdeis abegis**

abdegint debating beading beating dingbat. *See* **abdegn abdeit abdint abeint**

abdegir abridge brigade. *See* **abdeir abdegr bdegir**

abdegirs abridges brigades abiders abridge badgers braised bridges brigade. *See* **abdegr abdegs abdeir abdeis**

abdegl gabled badge bagel baled blade gable glade abed able aged bade bald bale bead bled dale deal egad gaed gale geld glad lade lead age alb ale bad bag bed beg bel dab dag eld gab gad gae gal gel lab lad lag lea led leg ad ae ba be el la

abdeglm gambled. *See* **abdelm abdegl abeglm**

abdeglmo gamboled gambled. *See* **abdegl abdego abdelm abdelo**

abdeglr garbled. *See* **abdegr abdelr abdegl abeglr adeglr**

abdegn banged badge began abed aged bade band bane bang bead bean bend dean egad gaed age and ane bad bag ban bed beg ben dab dag den end gab gad gae gan nab nae nag neb ad ae an ba be en na ne

abdegno bondage dogbane. *See* **abdgno abdegn abdego**

abdegnos dogbanes bandogs bodegas bondage dogbane. *See* **abdegn abdego abdegs abdeos**

abdego bodega abode adobe badge abed aged bade bead bode doge egad gaed goad ado age ago bad bag bed beg boa bog dab dag doe dog ego gab gad gae goa gob god ode ad ae ba be do go od

abdegopr pegboard. *See* **abdego abdegr abegor bdeopr**

abdegos bodegas. *See* **abdeos abdegs adegos**

abdegr badger barged garbed ardeb badge bared barge beard bread debar grade raged abed aged ager bade bard bare bead bear berg brad brae brag bred dare dear drab drag egad gaed garb gear grab grad rage read age are bad bag bar bed beg bra dab dag ear era erg gab gad gae gar rad rag red reg ad ae ba be er re

abdegrs badgers. *See* **abders abdegr abdegs abegrs adegrs**

abdegs badges badge based beads degas abed aged ages bade bags base bead beds begs dabs dags egad gabs gads gaed sage ads age bad bag bed beg dab dag gab gad gae gas sad sag sea ad ae as ba be

abdehins banished bandies. *See* **abdehs abdeis abhins adhins**

abdehitu habitude. *See* **abdeht abdeit**

abdehklu bulkhead. *See* **abdekl adehlu bdeklu dehklu**

abdehllu bullhead. *See* **abdell abellu adehlu adellu**

abdehlms shambled shamble. *See* **abdehs abdelm abdels abelms**

abdehlr halberd. *See* **abdelr adehlr abehlr**

abdehlrs halberds halberd heralds. *See* **abdehs abdelr abdels abders**

abdehmsu ambushed subhead. *See* **abdehs abdesu abhmsu adehms**

abdehorr abhorred harbored arbored boarder broader hoarder. *See* **abderr abhorr adehrr adeorr**

abdehosw bowheads bowhead. *See* **abdehs abdeos adehsw adhosw**

abdehow bowhead. *See* **abdeo bdeow adehw**

abdehrst breadths bathers breadth breaths dabster hardest threads trashed. *See* **abdehs abdeht abders abdest**

abdehrt breadth. *See* **abdeht abehrt adehrt**

abdehs bashed based beads hades heads sadhe shade abed bade base bash bead beds dabs dash hade head shad shed ads ash bad bah bed dab edh had hae has sad sea she ad ae ah as ba be eh ha he sh

abdehssu   subheads subhead. *See* **abdehs abdesu abehss abessu**

abdehsu   subhead. *See* **abdesu abdehs bdehsu**

abdeht   bathed bated bathe death hated abed abet bade baht bate bath bead beat beta beth date debt hade hate head heat aet ate bad bah bat bed bet dab eat edh eta eth had hae hat het tab tad tea ted the ad ae ah at ba be eh ha he ta

abdei   abide abed aide bade bead bide idea aid bad bed bid dab die ad ae ai ba be id

abdeiirt   diatribe. *See* **abdeir abdeit abeiit abeirt**

abdeiknu   baudekin. *See* **abdekn bdeknu**

abdeil   bailed abide ailed baled bield blade ideal abed able aide bade bail bald bale bead bide bile bled dale deal deil deli dial idea idle lade laid lead lied aid ail alb ale bad bed bel bid dab die eld lab lad lea led lei lid lie ad ae ai ba be el id la li

abdeilmn   mandible. *See* **abdeil abdelm abdemn adeilm**

abdeilp   bipedal piebald. *See* **abdeil adeilp**

abdeilps   piebalds alipeds baldies bipedal disable palsied piebald. *See* **abdeil abdeis abdels adeilp**

abdeilr   bedrail ridable. *See* **abdeir abdeil abdelr bdeilr abdilr**

abdeilrs   bedrails abiders baldies bedrail braised bridles derails disable ridable. *See* **abdeil abdeir abdeis abdelr**

abdeilrt   librated bedrail driblet librate ridable trailed. *See* **abdeil abdeir abdeit abdelr**

abdeils   baldies disable. *See* **abdeis adeils abdeil bdeils abdels**

abdeilsu   audibles audible baldies disable. *See* **abdeil abdeis abdels abdesu**

abdeilu   audible. *See* **abdeil adeilu**

abdeilvv   bivalved bivalve. *See* **abdeil abeilv adeilv**

abdeinnr   endbrain brained. *See* **abdeir abdenn abdinr abennr**

abdeinor   debonair bandore brained broaden inboard. *See* **abdeir abdinr adeinr adinor**

abdeinot   obtained. *See* **abdeit abdeot abdint abeint**

abdeinr   brained. *See* **abdeir bdeinr adeinr abdinr**

abdeinrs   brandies abiders bandies binders brained braised randies ribands

---

sandier sardine. *See* **abdeir abdeis abders abdinr**

abdeins   bandies. *See* **abdeis**

abdeinsu   unbiased bandies. *See* **abdeis abdesu adeisu adensu**

abdeiotv   obviated obviate. *See* **abdeit abdeot adeitv**

abdeiptz   baptized baptize. *See* **abdeit**

abdeir   abider abide aired ardeb bared beard braid bread bride debar rabid abed aide arid bade bard bare bead bear bide bier bird brad brae bred brie dare dear dire drab drib idea raid read ride aid air are bad bar bed bid bra dab die ear era ire rad red ria rib rid ad ae ai ba be er id re

abdeirs   abiders braised. *See* **abdeir abdeis abders abdirs abeirs**

abdeirtv   vibrated vibrate. *See* **abdeir abdeit abderv abeirt**

abdeirw   bawdier. *See* **abdeir aderw deirw**

abdeis   abides biassed abide aides aside based beads bides ideas abed aide aids bade base bead beds bias bide bids bise dabs dais dibs dies idea ides said side ads aid bad bed bid dab die ids sad sea sib ad ae ai as ba be id is si

abdeissu   disabuse subside. *See* **abdeis abdesu abeiss abessu**

abdeistw   bawdiest. *See* **abdeis abdeit abdest adeisw**

abdeit   baited abide bated bidet debit abed abet adit aide bade bait bate bead beat beta bide bite date debt diet edit idea tide tied aet ait ate bad bat bed bet bid bit dab die dit eat eta ita tab tad tea ted tie ad ae ai at ba be id it ta ti

abdejnow   jawboned jawbone. *See* **abdeo adeno abjno**

abdek   baked abed bade bake bead beak bad bed dab kab ad ae ba be ka

abdekl   balked baked baled blade bleak abed able bade bake bald bale balk bead beak bled dale deal kale lade lake lead leak alb ale bad bed bel dab eld elk kab kal lab lad lea led lek ad ae ba be el ka la

abdekln   blanked. *See* **abdekl abdekn**

abdekn   banked baked knead naked abed bade bake band bane bank bead beak bean bend dank dean and ane bad ban bed ben dab den end kab ken nab nae neb ad ae an ba be en ka na ne

abdekorw   beadwork. *See* **abdekr dekorw**

abdekory   keyboard. *See* **abdekr abdery abdory abekry**

abdekr   barked braked debark ardeb baked baker bared beard brake bread break debar drake raked abed bade bake bard bare bark bead beak bear

---

brad brae bred dare dark dear drab kerb rake read are ark bad bar bed bra dab ear era kab rad red ad ae ba be er ka re

abdekrs   debarks. *See* **abders abekrs abdekr abdeks adekrs**

abdeks   basked asked baked bakes based beads beaks abed bade bake base bask bead beak beds dabs desk kabs sake ads ask bad bed dab kab kas sad sea ad ae as ba be ka

abdel   baled blade abed able bade bald bale bead bled dale deal lade lead alb ale bad bed bel dab eld lab lad lea led ad ae ba be el la

abdell   balled baled blade label ladle abed able bade bald bale ball bead bell bled dale deal dell lade lead leal alb ale all bad bed bel dab eld ell lab lad lea led ad ae ba be el la

abdellmo   moldable. *See* **abdell abdelm abdelo adelmo**

abdellot   balloted bloated. *See* **abdell abdelo abdelt abdeot**

abdelm   ambled bedlam blamed amble baled blade blame lamed medal abed able bade bald bale balm bead beam bema bled dale dame deal lade lamb lame lead made male mead meal meld alb ale bad bam bed bel dab dam eld elm lab lad lam lea led mad mae mel ad ae am ba be el em la ma me

abdelmr   marbled rambled. *See* **abdelm abdelr adelmr abelmr**

abdelmw   wambled. *See* **abdelm abdelw abelmw**

abdelnoz   blazoned. *See* **abdelo abdelz ablnoz adelno**

abdelnss   baldness badness sendals. *See* **abdels abelss adelns adenss**

abdelo   albedo abode adobe baled blade lobed abed able aloe bade bald bale bead bled bode bold bole dale deal dole lade lead load lobe lode ado alb ale bad bed bel boa dab doe eld lab lad lea led lob ode old ad ae ba be do el la lo od

abdelor   labored. *See* **abdelo abdelr bdelor abelor adelor**

abdeloru   laboured boulder durable labored roulade. *See* **abdelo abdelr abderu abelor**

abdelos   albedos. *See* **abdeos abdelo abdels**

abdelosv   absolved albedos absolve. *See* **abdelo abdels abdeos adelsv**

abdelot   bloated. *See* **abdelo abdeot abelot bdelot abdelt**

abdelpu   dupable. *See* **abdel bdelu delpu**

abdelr balder blared abler alder ardeb baled bared beard blade blare blear bread debar abed able bade bald bale bard bare bead bear bled brad brae bred dale dare deal dear drab earl lade lard lead rale read real alb ale are bad bar bed bel bra dab ear eld era lab lad lar lea led rad red ad ae ba be el er la re

abdelrsu durables durable. *See* **abdelr abdels abders abderu**

abdelru durable. *See* **abdelr bdelru abderu**

abdelrw brawled warbled. *See* **abdelr abdelw abelrw**

abdels blades baled bales based beads blade dales deals lades leads sable abed able albs ales bade bald bale base bead beds bels bled dabs dale deal labs lade lads lead leas sale seal slab sled ads alb ale bad bed bel dab eld els lab lad lea led sad sal sea ad ae as ba be el la

abdelst baldest blasted stabled. *See* **abelst abdest abdels adelst**

abdelstu sublated baldest blasted bustled saluted stabled sublate. *See* **abdels abdelt abdest abdesu**

abdelt tabled baled bated blade bleat dealt delta lated table abed abet able bade bald bale bate bead beat belt beta blat bled dale date deal debt lade late lead tael tale teal aet alb ale alt ate bad bat bed bel bet dab eat eld eta lab lad lea led let tab tad tea ted ad ae at ba be el la ta

abdeltt battled blatted. *See* **abdett abeltt abdelt**

abdelw bawled baled blade waled weald abed able awed bade bald bale bawd bawl bead bled blew dale deal lade lead lewd wade wale weal weld alb ale awe awl bad bed bel dab dew eld lab lad law lea led wad web wed ad ae aw ba be el la we

abdelz blazed baled blade blaze lazed abed able adze bade bald bale bead bled dale daze deal lade laze lead zeal adz alb ale bad bed bel dab eld lab lad lea led zed ad ae ba be el la

abdemm bammed abed bade bead beam bema dame made mead bad bam bed dab dam mad mae mem ad ae am ba be em ma me

abdemn badmen admen amend maned menad named abed amen bade band bane bead beam bean bema bend dame damn dean made mane mead mean mend name and ane bad bam ban bed ben dab dam den end mad

mae man men nab nae neb ad ae am an ba be em en ma me na ne

abdemnns bandsmen sandmen. *See* **abdemn ademns**

abdemno abdomen. *See* **abdemn abemno ademno**

abdemnos abdomens abdomen bemoans daemons. *See* **abdemn abdeos abemno ademno**

abdemrtu drumbeat matured. *See* **abderu abemru ademrt aemrtu**

abdenn banned abed bade band bane bead bean bend dean and ane bad ban bed ben dab den end nab nae neb ad ae an ba be en na ne

abdennos noseband. *See* **abdenn abdeos adenos**

abdenor bandore broaden. *See* **abdeo adeor adnor**

abdenors bandores broadens bandore broaden. *See* **abdeos abders abdnrs abdors**

abdenorw rawboned bandore broaden browned. *See* **adenrw adnorw denorw**

abdenotw downbeat. *See* **abdeot adenot adentw denotw**

abdenp bedpan abed aped bade band bane bead bean bend dean nape neap pane pean pend and ane ape bad ban bed ben dab dap den end nab nae nap neb pad pan pea pen ad ae an ba be en na ne pa pe

abdenps bedpans. *See* **abdenp aenps abdns**

abdenrst bartends banters bartend dabster. *See* **abders abdest abdnrs abenrt**

abdenrt bartend. *See* **adenrt abenrt**

abdenss badness. *See* **adenss abdns abdes**

abdenttu debutant abutted attuned taunted. *See* **abdett abentt abentu abettu**

abdeo abode adobe abed bade bead bode ado bad bed boa dab doe ode ad ae ba be do od

abdeoorw bearwood. *See* **abdeo adeor abder**

abdeoot tabooed. *See* **abdeot bdeoot**

abdeoprt probated aborted probate. *See* **abdeot abeort adeort adeprt**

abdeorr arbored boarder broader. *See* **adeorr abderr bdeorr**

abdeorrs boarders adorers arbored arbores boarder borders broader. *See* **abdeos abderr abders abdors**

abdeorrw wardrobe arbored boarder broader. *See* **abderr aborrw adeorr aderrw**

abdeorst broadest aborted boasted boaster boaters borates dabster debt-

ors roasted torsade. *See* **abdeos abdeot abders abdest**

abdeort aborted. *See* **abdeot abeort bdeort adeort**

abdeortu obdurate aborted doubter obtrude readout redoubt. *See* **abdeot abderu abeort abortu**

abdeos abodes adobes abode adobe based beads bodes abed ados bade base bead beds boas bode dabs does dose odes soda ado ads bad bed boa dab doe dos ode sad sea sob sod ad ae as ba be do od os so

abdeost boasted. *See* **abdeos abdest abdeot**

abdeot boated abode adobe bated abed abet bade bate bead beat beta boat bode date debt dote toad toed ado aet ate bad bat bed bet boa bot dab doe dot eat eta oat ode tab tad tea ted tod toe ad ae at ba be do od ta to

abdepssy bypassed. *See* **abpssy adepss adepsy**

abder ardeb bared beard bread debar abed bade bard bare bead bear brad brae bred dare dear drab read are bad bar bed bra dab ear era rad red ad ae ba be er re

abderr barred ardeb bared barer barre beard bread debar abed bade bard bare bead bear brad brae bred dare dear drab rare read rear are bad bar bed bra dab ear era err rad red ad ae ba be er re

abders ardebs beards breads debars sabred ardeb bards bared bares based baser beads beard bears brads bread dares dears debar drabs rased reads saber sabre abed arse bade bard bare bars base bead bear beds brad brae bras bred dabs dare dear drab ears eras rads rase read reds sard sear sera ads are bad bar bed bra dab ear era rad red res sad sea ad ae as ba be er re

abdersst dabsters dabster breasts. *See* **abders abdest aberss aberst**

abderst dabster. *See* **abders aberst abdest aderst**

abdersv adverbs. *See* **abderv abders abersv**

abderu dauber ardeb bared beard bread debar abed bade bard bare baud bead bear beau brad brae bred dare daub dear drab drub dura read rube rude rued urea are bad bar bed bra bud dab dub due ear era rad red rub rue urd ad ae ba be er re

abderv adverb braved ardeb bared beard brave bread debar raved abed aver bade bard bare bead bear brad brae bred dare dear deva drab rave read verb are ave bad bar bed bra dab ear era rad red rev ad ae ba be er re

abdery brayed ardeb bared bayed beady beard bread deary debar derby rayed ready abed abye aery bade bard bare bead bear brad brae bray bred byre dare dear drab dray dyer read yard yare year aby are aye bad bar bay bed bey bra bye dab day dey dry dye ear era rad ray red rye yar yea ad ae ay ba be by er re ye

abderz brazed ardeb bared beard braze bread debar razed zebra abed adze bade bard bare bead bear brad brae bred dare daze dear drab raze read adz are bad bar bed bra dab ear era rad red zed ad ae ba be er re

abdes based beads abed bade base bead beds dabs ads bad bed dab sad sea ad ae as ba be

abdest basted abets based baste bated bates beads beast beats betas dates debts sated stead tabes abed abet bade base bast bate bats bead beat beds best beta bets dabs date debt east eats etas seat seta stab tabs tads teas teds ads aet ate bad bat bed bet dab eat eta sad sat sea set tab tad tea ted ad ae as at ba be ta

abdesu abused abuse based beads beaus bused daubs abed bade base baud bead beau beds buds dabs daub dubs dues sued used ads bad bed bud bus dab dub due sad sea sub sue use ad ae as ba be us

abdet bated abed abet bade bate bead beat beta date debt aet ate bad bat bed bet dab eat eta tab tad tea ted ad ae at ba be ta

abdett batted bated betta abed abet bade bate bead beat beta date debt teat aet ate bad bat bed bet dab eat eta tab tad tat tea ted ad ae at ba be ta

abdettu abutted. *See* **abdett abettu bdettu**

abdey bayed beady abed abye bade bead aby aye bad bay bed bey bye dab day dey dye yea ad ae ay ba be by ye

abdfor forbad forbad board broad dobra bard boar bora brad drab faro fora forb ford orad road ado arf bad bar boa bra dab dor fad far fob for fro oaf oar orb rad rob rod ad ba do fa od of or

abdggin badging. *See* **aggin**

abdghinr hangbird brigand. *See* **abdinr abginr adghin adginr**

abdgiin abiding. *See* **adgiin bdgiin**

abdgiinr braiding abiding birding brigand raiding. *See* **abdinr abginr adgiin adginr**

abdgiln balding. *See* **abgiln adgiln**

abdginn banding. *No 6s or 5s*

abdginnr branding banding brigand darning. *See* **abdinr abginr adginr**

abdginny bandying banding. *See* **abginy**

abdginor boarding adoring brigand inboard. *See* **abdgno abdinr abgino abginr**

abdginr brigand. *See* **abginr adginr abdinr**

abdginrs brigands brigand gradins ribands sabring. *See* **abdinr abdirs abdnrs abginr**

abdginst dingbats bandits basting dingbat. *See* **abdint abgins abgint adgint**

abdginsw windbags windbag. *See* **abgins adginw aginsw**

abdgint dingbat. *See* **abdint abgint adgint**

abdginu daubing. *No 6s or 5s*

abdginw windbag. *See* **adginw**

abdglsuy ladybugs ladybug. *See* **dglsuy**

abdgluy ladybug. *See* **abdly bgluy adguy**

abdgno bandog donga gonad agon band bang bond bong dong goad ado ago and bad bag ban boa bog dab dag dog don gab gad gan goa gob god nab nag nob nod nog ad an ba do go na no od on

abdgnos bandogs. *See* **abdgno adgnos**

abdhiist adhibits adhibit. *See* **abhist abiist**

abdhiit adhibit. *See* **abhit abiit**

abdhilln handbill. *See* **abiln abdln bdiln**

abdhilns blandish. *See* **abhins abilns adhins adilns**

abdhinrs brandish ribands. *See* **abdinr abdirs abdnrs abhins**

abdhirty birthday. *See* **bdhiry**

abdhknoo handbook. *See* **ahkoo**

abdhlorw blowhard. *See* **abhor adhlo abdor**

abdhnssu husbands husband. *See* **adhssu**

abdhnsu husband. *See* **abdns abdsu adhns**

abdiijlr jailbird. *See* **abdilr**

abdiimnr midbrain birdman. *See* **abdinr adiimr**

abdiinos obsidian. *See* **abinos adinos**

abdiintt banditti. *See* **abdint bdiitt**

abdijrsy jaybirds jaybird. *See* **abdirs**

abdijry jaybird. *See* **abdir adiry**

abdilost tabloids tabloid. *See* **ablost adilst dilost**

abdilot tabloid. *See* **abilo abiot ablot**

abdilr bridal ribald braid brail laird libra rabid arid aril bail bald bard bird birl brad dial dirl drab drib laid lair lard liar lira raid rail rial aid ail air alb bad bar bid bra dab lab lad lar lid rad ria rib rid ad ai ba id la li

abdilrry ribaldry library. *See* **abdilr abirry adilry**

abdilrzz blizzard. *See* **abdilr adilrz adirzz**

abdiluy audibly. *See* **abdly abily bdilu**

abdimnr birdman. *See* **abdinr**

abdinor inboard. *See* **adinor abdinr**

abdinoty antibody. *See* **abdint abinot abnoty adinty**

abdinr riband bairn braid brain brand dinar drain nadir rabid arid band bani bard barn bind bird brad bran darn drab drib nard raid rain rand rani rind aid air and ani bad ban bar bid bin bra dab din nab nib rad ran ria rib rid ad ai an ba id in na

abdinrs ribands. *See* **abinrs abdirs abdnrs adinrs abdinr**

abdinst bandits. *See* **abdint adist ainst**

abdint bandit adit anti bait band bani bind aid and ani ant bad ban bat bid bin bit dab din dit ita nab nib nit tab tad tan tin ad ai an at ba id in it na ta ti

abdiprsu upbraids upbraid. *See* **abdirs abdrsu adiprs**

abdipru upbraid. *See* **abdir adipr**

abdir braid rabid arid bard bird brad drab drib raid aid air bad bar bid bra dab rad ria rib rid ad ai ba id

abdirs braids disbar bards birds brads braid drabs dribs rabid raids aids airs arid bard bars bias bids bird brad bras dabs dais dibs drab drib rads raid rias ribs rids said sard sari ads aid air bad bar bid bra dab ids rad ria rib rid sad sib sir ad ai as ba id is si

abdirss disbars. *See* **abdirs**

abdjmoor doorjamb. *See* **abdor bdoor bmoor**

abdkoosy daybooks daybook. *See* **bkoos akosy**

abdkooy daybook. *No 6s or 5s*

abdl bald alb bad dab lab lad ad ba la

abdllny blandly. *See* **abdlly abdny abdln**

abdllor bollard. *See* **adllor abdor ablor**

abdllors bollards bollard dollars. *See* **abdors ablors adllor adlors**

abdlly baldly badly baldy bally dally ably ally bald ball lady aby alb all bad bay dab day lab lad lay ad ay ba by la

abdln bland bald band land alb and bad ban dab lab lad nab ad an ba la na

abdlory broadly. *See* **abdory abdly adlry**

abdlrsuy absurdly durably. *See* **abdrsu ablrsu**

abdlruy durably. *See* **abdly blruy adlru**

abdly badly baldy ably bald lady aby alb bad bay dab day lab lad lay ad ay ba by la

abdmnnos bondsman. *See* **admnos**

abdn band and bad ban dab nab ad an ba na

abdnoruy boundary. *See* **abdnou abdnry abdory abnory**

abdnosu abounds. *See* **abdnou bdnosu**

abdnosx sandbox. *See* **anosx abdns bdnos**

abdnou abound bound band baud bond daub undo ado and bad ban boa bud bun dab don dub dun duo nab nob nod nub oud udo ad an ba do na no nu od on

abdnoyy anybody. *See* **abdny**

abdnr brand band bard barn brad bran darn drab nard rand and bad ban bar bra dab nab rad ran ad an ba na

abdnrs brands bands bards barns brads brand brans darns drabs nards rands band bans bard barn bars brad bran bras dabs darn drab nabs nard rads rand sand sard ads and bad ban bar bra dab nab rad ran sad ad an as ba na

abdnrssu sandburs sandbur. *See* **abdnrs abdrsu abnrsu abrssu**

abdnrsu sandbur. *See* **abdrsu abdnrs abnrsu**

abdnry brandy bandy brand randy band bard barn brad bran bray darn drab dray nard nary rand yard yarn aby and any bad ban bar bay bra dab day dry nab nay rad ran ray yar ad an ay by na

abdns bands band bans dabs nabs sand ads and bad ban dab nab sad ad an as ba na

abdnssty standbys standby dynasts. *See* **adnsst adnsty**

abdnsty standby. *See* **adnsty abdns abdny**

abdny bandy band aby and any bad ban bay dab day nab nay ad an ay ba by na

abdoortu outboard. *See* **abortu**

abdoossw basswood. *See* **abdsw adoss abssw**

abdor board broad dobra bard boar bora brad drab orad road ado bad bar boa bra dab dor oar orb rad rob rod ad ba do od or

abdors adsorb boards broads dobras bards board boars boras brads broad dobra dorsa drabs roads ados bard bars boar boas bora brad bras dabs drab oars orad orbs rads road robs rods sard soar soda sora sorb ado ads bad bar boa bra dab dor dos oar orb rad rob rod sad sob sod ad as ba do od or os so

abdorss adsorbs. *See* **abdors**

abdorsy byroads. *See* **abdors aborsy abdory**

abdory byroad board boyar broad dobra bard boar body bora brad bray dory drab dray orad orby road yard aby ado bad bar bay boa boy bra dab day dor dry oar orb rad ray rob rod yar yob yod ad ay ba by do od or oy

abdr bard brad drab bad bar bra dab rad ba ad

abdrrsu durbars. *See* **abdrsu abrrsu abdrru**

abdrru durbar bard baud brad burr daub drab drub dura bad bar bra bud dab dub rad rub urd ba ad

abdrs bards brads drabs bard bars brad bras dabs drab rads sard ads bad bar bra dab rad sad ad as ba

abdrsu absurd bards brads bursa daubs drabs drubs duras bard bars baud brad bras buds dabs daub drab drub dubs dura rads rubs sard sura surd urds ads bad bar bra bud bus dab dub rad rub sad sub urd ad as ba us

abdrsuzz buzzards buzzard. *See* **abdrsu**

abdruzz buzzard. *See* **abuzz**

abdrwy bawdry bawdy awry bard bawd brad braw bray drab draw dray ward wary yard aby bad bar bay bra dab day dry rad raw ray wad war way yar yaw ad aw ay ba by

abds dabs ads bad dab sad ad as ba

abdsu bauds daubs baud buds dabs daub dubs ads bad bud bus dab dub sad sub ad as ba us

abdsw bawds bawd dabs swab wads ads bad dab sad saw wad was ad as aw ba

abdu daub baud bad bud dab dub ba ad

abdw bawd bad dab wad ad aw ba

abdwy bawdy bawd aby bad bay dab day wad way yaw ad aw ay ba by

abeeegrv beverage bereave. *See* **abeegr abeerv aeegrv**

abeeels seeable. *See* **abeels**

abeeenst absentee. *See* **abeent abenst aeenst**

abeeersv bereaves bereave beavers. *See* **abeerv abersv aeersv beeesv**

abeeerv bereave. *See* **abeerv eeerv**

abeefils feasible beliefs. *See* **abeels abefls beefil beeils**

abeefilt fleabite. *See* **abeilt beefil**

abeeflll fellable. *See* **abefll aeelll beefll**

abeefflln befallen. *See* **abeeln abefll aeflln beefll**

abeeforr forebear forbear. *See* **abeeor abeerr beefor**

abeeghr herbage. *See* **abeegr aeghr abehr**

abeegirv verbiage. *See* **abeegr abeerv aeegrv aegirv**

abeegl beagle abele bagel eagle gable glebe able agee alee bale gale glee age

abeegls beagles. *See* **abeels abegls abeegl aeegls beegls**

abeeglt getable. *See* **abeegl aeeglt**

abeegmnr bargemen germane. *See* **abeegr abeemr abegmn abegnr**

abeegmty megabyte. *See* **aeegmt**

abeegr barege agree barge eager grebe agee ager bare bear beer berg brae brag bree garb gear grab gree rage age are bag bar bee beg bra ear era ere erg gab gae gar gee rag reg ae ba be er re

abeegrs bareges bargees. *See* **aeegrs abeegr abegrs beegrs**

abeegrw brewage agree. *See* **abeegr abeerw**

abeegttu baguette. *See* **abettu aegttu**

abeehllr harebell labeler. *See* **abehlr aeehlr eehllr**

abeehnn henbane. *See* **aehnn beenn**

abeehnns henbanes henbane banshee. *See* **aehnns beenns**

abeehns banshee. *See* **aehns abens eehns**

abeehnss banshees banshee. *See* **abehss eehnss**

abeehnt beneath. *See* **abeent aeehnt**

abeehqtu bequeath. *See* **aeeqtu**

abeehrrt breather breathe. *See* **abeerr abeert abehrt aeehrr**

abeehrst breathes bathers beaters berates breathe breaths heaters rebates reheats sherbet. *See* **abeert abehrt abehst aberst**

abeehrt breathe. *See* **abehrt abeert aeehrt**

abeehsv behaves. *See* **abeehv aeehsv**

abeehv behave heave eave have ave bah bee eve hae vee ae ah ba be eh ha he

abeeikrs bakeries beakers. *See* **abeekr abeirs abekrs aeeirs**

abeeillr reliable labeler libeler liberal. *See* **abeill beillr**

abeeillv liveable livable. *See* **abeill abeilv**

abeeilnp plebeian biplane. *See* **abeein abeeln aeilnp**

abeeilnv enviable. *See* **abeein abeeln abeilv aeelnv**

abeeilpx expiable. *See* **abeel aeilx beeil**

abeeilrt liberate librate. *See* **abeert abeilt abeirt abelrt**

abeeilsz sizeable sizable. *See* **abeels abeisz abelsz aeelsz**

abeeimr beamier. *See* **abeemr beeimr**

abeeimst beamiest beastie betimes. *See* **abimst aeimst**

abeein beanie bane bani bean been bine ane ani ban bee ben bin nab nae neb nee nib ae ai an ba be en in na ne

abeeins beanies. *See* **abeein aeins abins**

abeeisst beasties beastie easiest. *See* abeiss abesst aeesst aeisst

abeeist beastie. *See* abest abist beest

abeeistu beauties beastie. *See* abestu

abeejmor jamboree. *See* abeemr abeeor abejor

abeeklot keelboat. *See* abeekt abelot

abeeklr bleaker. *See* abeekr aeeklr

abeeklst bleakest betakes. *See* abeekt abeels abekst abelst

abeekmnr brakemen. *See* abeekr abeemr abekmn abekmr

abeekmrr reembark breaker. *See* abeekr abeemr abeerr abekmr

abeeknt betaken. *See* abeekt abeent

abeekoop peekaboo. *See* eekop

abeekps bespeak. *See* abeks beeps eekps

abeekpss bespeaks bespeak. *See* aeepss aekpss

abeekr beaker baker brake break rakee bake bare bark beak bear beer brae bree kerb rake reek are ark bar bee bra ear eke era ere kab ae ba be er ka re

abeekrr breaker. *See* abekrr abeekr abeerr

abeekrrs breakers barkers beakers bearers berserk breaker. *See* abeekr abeerr abekrs aberrs

abeekrs beakers. *See* abekrs aeekrs

abeekst betakes. *See* abeekt abekst

abeekt betake abet bake bate beak beat beet beta keet take teak aet ate bat bee bet eat eke eta kab kat tab tea tee ae at ba be ka ta

abeel abele able alee bale alb ale bee bel eel lab lea lee ae ba be el la

abeelllr labeller labeler. *See* aeelll

abeellmt meltable. *See* abellt aeellm aellmt

abeellov loveable lovable. *See* abeel abeov beell

abeellr labeler. *See* abeel abelr beell

abeellrs labelers labeler. *See* abeels abells abelrs aeelrs

abeellsy eyeballs eyeball. *See* abeels abells abelsy abllsy

abeelly eyeball. *See* abeel aelly ablly

abeelmmr embalmer. *See* abeemr abelmm abelmr beelmm

abeelmov moveable movable. *See* abeel abeov abelm

abeelmpr preamble. *See* abeemr abelmr aeelmp aeelpr

abeelmrt atremble lambert tremble. *See* abeemr abeert abelmr abelrt

abeelmss assemble measles. *See* abeels abelms abelss aeelss

abeelmsz emblazes emblaze. *See* abeels abelms abelsz aeelsz

abeelmtt embattle. *See* abellt eelmtt

abeelmz emblaze. *See* abeel abelm beelz

abeeln baleen enable abele able alee bale bane bean been lane lean alb ale ane ban bee bel ben eel lab lea lee nab nae neb nee ae an ba be el en la na ne

abeelnop beanpole. *See* abeeln

abeelnr enabler. *See* abeeln aeelnr

abeelnrs enablers baleens enabler enables leaners. *See* abeeln abeels abelrs aeelnr

abeelns baleens enables. *See* abeels abeeln

abeelnt tenable. *See* abeeln abeent aeelnt

abeelnu nebulae. *See* abeeln abelnu

abeelopr operable parolee. *See* abeeor abelor aeelor aeelpr

abeelorx exorable. *See* abeeor abelor aeelor

abeelqu equable. *See* abeel aelqu

abeelrsu reusable useable. *See* abeels abelrs abelsu abersu

abeels abeles abele bales easel lease sable able albs alee ales bale base bees bels ease eels else labs leas lees sale seal seel slab alb ale bee bel eel els lab lea lee sal sea see ae as ba be el la

abeelsss baseless. *See* abeels abelss aeelss aelsss

abeelssu sublease useable. *See* abeels abelss abelsu abessu

abeelsu useable. *See* abeels abelsu

abeelttw wettable. *See* abeltt aelttw

abeemmnr membrane. *See* abeemr aeemnr aemmnr beemmnr

abeemns basemen. *See* aeemns

abeemnst basement basemen batsmen meanest. *See* abeent abenst aeemns aeenst

abeemr beamer amber ameer bream ember bare barm beam bear beer bema berm brae bree mare mere ream are arm bam bar bee bra ear era ere mae mar ram rem ae am ba be em er ma me re

abeemrs beamers besmear. *See* abemrs aeemrs abeemr beemrs

abeemrss besmears beamers besmear. *See* abeemr abemrs aberss aeemrs

abeennrt banneret. *See* abeent abeert abennr abenrt

abeenntu unbeaten uneaten. *See* abeent abentu aeennt benntu

abeenors seaborne aerobes. *See* abeeor abnors aenors benors

abeenrrt banterer terrane. *See* abeent abeerr abeert abenrr

abeenrss bareness. *See* aberss aeerss aenrss eenrss

abeenrsv verbenas verbena beavers. *See* abeerv abersv aeersv aenrsv

abeenrv verbena. *See* abeerv eenrv aenrv

abeenry beanery. *See* aenry beery

abeensss baseness. *See* eensss

abeent beaten eaten abet ante bane bate bean beat been beet bent beta neat teen aet ane ant ate ban bat bee ben bet eat eta nab nae neb nee net tab tan tea tee ten ae an at ba be en na ne ta

abeeor aerobe aero bare bear beer boar bora bore brae bree robe are bar bee boa bra ear era ere oar orb ore rob roe ae ba be er or re

abeeorrv overbear. *See* abeeor abeerr abeerv

abeeors aerobes. *See* abeeor aeors abers

abeerr bearer barer barre bare bear beer brae bree rare rear are bar bee bra ear era ere err ae ba be er re

abeerrrt barterer. *See* aberrt abeerr abeert aeerrt

abeerrs bearers. *See* aberrs abeerr aeerrs

abeerrtt barrette berretta abetter retreat. *See* abeerr abeert abertt

abeerrtv vertebra. *See* abeerr abeert abeerv beertv

abeerrty betrayer. *See* abeerr abeert aberry aberty

abeerst beaters berates rebates. *See* aberst abeert beerst aeerst

abeersv beavers. *See* aeersv abeerv abersv beersv

abeersw bewares. *See* abeerw abers beers

abeert beater berate rebate beret eater abet bare bate bear beat beer beta brae brat bree rate rete tare tear tree aet are art ate bar bat bee bet bra ear eat era ere eta rat ret tab tar tea tee ae at ba be er re ta

abeertt abetter. *See* abertt abeert beertt

abeerv beaver brave breve aver bare bear beer brae bree eave ever rave veer verb are ave bar bee bra ear era ere eve rev vee ae ba be er re

abeerw beware bare bear beer brae braw bree brew ewer ware wear are awe bar bee bra ear era ere ewe raw war web wee ae aw ba be er re we

abeeswx beeswax. *See* aeswx

abeffl baffle fable able bale flab flea leaf alb ale bel elf lab lea ae ba be el fa la

abefflr baffler. *See* abeffl abeflr aefflr

abefflrs bafflers baffler baffles fablers raffles. *See* abeffl abeflr abefls abelrs

abeffls baffles. *See* abeffl abefls

abeffot offbeat. *No 6s or 5s*

abefgsst gabfests gabfest. *See* abesst aefsst aegsst

abefgst gabfest. *See* abest abegt aefst

abefhl behalf fable able bale blah flab flea hale half heal leaf alb ale bah bel

elf feh hae lab lea ae ah ba be eh el fa
ha he la

abefhoot   hoofbeat. *See* **afoot abeht bhoot**

abefilll   fallible. *See* **abefll abeill aefill**

abefillr   fireball friable liberal. *See* **abefll abeflr abeill aefill**

abefiln   finable. *See* **aefiln abiln abefl**

abefilot   lifeboat foliate. *See* **abeilt abelot befilo**

abefilr   friable. *See* **abeflr aefilr**

abefilrs   barflies friable fablers. *See* **abeflr abefls abeirs abelrs**

abefilsy   feasibly. *See* **abefls abeily abelsy abfisy**

abefilu   fibulae. *See* **abfilu abefl**

abefilx   fixable. *See* **abefl aeilx**

abefiort   fireboat. *See* **abeirt abeort**

abefituy   beautify beatify. *See* **abetuy**

abefity   beatify. *See* **befit**

abefl   fable able bale flab flea leaf alb ale bel elf lab lea ae ba be el fa la

abefll   befall fable fella label able bale ball bell fall fell flab flea leaf leal alb ale all bel elf ell lab lea ae ba be el fa la

abeflls   befalls. *See* **abefll abefls aeflls abells**

abefllu   baleful. *See* **abefll abellu**

abeflnu   baneful. *See* **abelnu**

abeflr   fabler abler blare blear fable feral flare able bale bare bear brae earl fare fear flab flea leaf rale real alb ale are arf bar bel bra ear elf era far lab lar lea ref ae ba be el er fa la re

abeflrs   fablers. *See* **abelrs abeflr abefls aeflrs**

abefls   fables bales fable false flabs fleas leafs sable able albs ales bale base bels flab flea labs leaf leas safe sale seal self slab alb ale bel elf els fas lab lea sal sea ae as ba be el fa la

abefmr   ferbam amber bream frame bare barm beam bear bema berm brae fame fare farm fear mare ream are arf arm bam bar bra ear era far mae mar ram ref rem ae am ba be em er fa ma me re

abefmrs   ferbams. *See* **abemrs abefmr aefmrs**

abefoort   barefoot. *See* **abeort**

abeforr   forbear. *See* **aefor aborr aberr**

abeforrs   forbears forbear arbores. *See* **aberrs aborrs beorrs**

abefpr   prefab bare bear brae fare fear frap pare pear rape reap ape are arf bar bra ear era far par pea per rap ref rep ae ba be er fa pa pe re

abegghlu   huggable. *See* **abeglu aegghl**

abeggir   baggier. *See* **abeggr beggir**

abeggist   baggiest baggits biggest. *See* **abegis**

abegglry   beggarly beggary. *See* **abeggr abeglr abelry aeglry**

abeggr   bagger beggar barge ager bare bear berg brae brag gage garb gear grab rage age are bag bar beg bra ear egg era erg gab gae gag gar rag reg ae ba be er re

abeggrr   bragger. *See* **abeggr**

abeggrrs   braggers baggers beggars bragger. *See* **abeggr abegrs aberrs**

abeggrs   baggers beggars. *See* **abeggr abegrs**

abeggrsu   burgages baggers beggars buggers burgage. *See* **abeggr abegrs abersu aeggsu**

abeggru   burgage. *See* **abeggr beggru**

abeggry   beggary. *See* **abeggr**

abeghinv   behaving heaving. *See* **aghinv**

abeghns   shebang. *See* **abghns aehns abens**

abeghnss   shebangs shebang gnashes. *See* **abehss abghns aeghss**

abeghrsu   bearhugs bearhug. *See* **abegrs abersu aeghrs aegrsu**

abeghru   bearhug. *See* **aegru abegr bghru**

abegijtu   bijugate. *See* **aegjtu**

abegiknr   breaking barking bearing braking. *See* **abegnr abeknr abgikn abginr**

abegiknt   betaking beating beatnik. *See* **abeint abgikn abgint aegint**

abegilln   labeling balling belling gallein. *See* **abegln abeill abgiln aegiln**

abegilnn   enabling beaning leaning. *See* **abegln abgiln aegiln beginn**

abegilnt   bleating tangible atingle beating belting elating gelatin genital tabling. *See* **abegln abeilt abeint abgiln**

abegilny   belaying belying. *See* **abegln abeily abgiln abginy**

abegilot   obligate. *See* **abeilt abelot aegilo aegilt**

abegimn   beaming. *See* **abegmn aegimn**

abegimny   embaying beaming. *See* **abegmn abgimy abginy aegimn**

abeginn   beaning. *See* **beginn abegn aeinn**

abegino   begonia. *See* **abgino**

abeginos   begonias agonies bagnios begonia gabions. *See* **abegis abgino abgins abinos**

abeginr   bearing. *See* **abegnr abginr aeginr**

abeginrs   bearings sabering bangers bearing earings erasing gainers regains sabring searing. *See* **abegis abegnr abegrs abeirs**

abeginrt   berating rebating bearing beating granite ingrate tangier tearing. *See* **abegnr abeint abeirt abenrt**

abeginrw   bewaring bearing brewing wearing. *See* **abegnr abginr aeginr aegirw**

abeginst   beatings basinet basting beating besting easting ingesta seating teasing. *See* **abegis abeint abenst abgins**

abegint   beating. *See* **abgint abeint aegint**

abegintt   abetting batting beating betting. *See* **abeint abentt abgint aegint**

abegipp   bagpipe. *See* **aegipp**

abegippr   bagpiper bagpipe. *See* **aegipp egippr**

abegipps   bagpipes bagpipe pipages. *See* **abegis aegipp**

abegis   gabies aegis gibes ages bags base begs bias bise egis gabs gibe gibs gies sage age bag beg big gab gae gas gib gie sag sea sib ae ai as ba be is si

abegl   bagel gable able bale gale age alb ale bag beg bel gab gae gal gel lab lag lea leg ae ba be el la

abeglm   gamble amble bagel blame gable gleam able bale balm beam bema gale gamb game lamb lame mage male meal age alb ale bag bam beg bel elm gab gae gal gam gel gem lab lag lam lea leg mae mag mel ae am ba be el em la ma me

abeglmr   gambler gambrel. *See* **abeglm abeglr abelmr**

abeglmrs   gamblers gambrels gambler gambles gambrel garbles marbles rambles. *See* **abeglm abeglr abegls abegrs**

abeglms   gambles. *See* **abelms abegls abeglm aeglms**

abeglmuy   mealybug. *See* **abeglm abeglu aeglmy aegmuy**

abegln   bangle angel angle bagel began gable glean able bale bane bang bean gale glen lane lean age alb ale ane bag ban beg bel ben gab gae gal gan gel lab lag lea leg nab nae nag neb ae an ba be el en la na ne

abeglns   bangles. *See* **aeglns abegln abegls**

abeglr   garble abler bagel barge blare blear gable glare lager large regal able ager bale bare bear berg brae brag earl gale garb gear grab rage rale real age alb ale are bag bar beg bel bra ear era erg gab gae gal gar gel lab lag lar lea leg rag reg ae ba be el er la re

abeglrr   garbler. *See* **abelrr abeglr aeglrr**

abeglrrs   garblers barrels garbler garbles. *See* **abeglr abegls abegrs**

abeglrs   garbles. *See* **abegls abegrs abelrs abeglr aeglrs**

abegls   bagels gables bagel bales gable gales sable able ages albs ales bags bale base begs bels gabs gale gals gels labs lags leas legs sage sale seal slab slag age alb ale bag beg bel els gab gae gal gas gel lab lag lea leg sag sal sea ae as ba be el la

abeglsu belugas. *See* **abegls abeglu beglsu abelsu**

abeglu beluga bagel bugle bulge gable able ague bale beau blue gale glue lube luge age alb ale bag beg bel bug gab gae gal gel lab lag lea leg leu lug ae ba be el la

abegmn bagmen began mange amen bane bang beam bean bema gamb game mage mane mean name age ane bag bam ban beg ben gab gae gam gan gem mae mag man men nab nae nag neb ae am an ba be em en ma me na ne

abegmnos gambeson bemoans mangoes. *See* **abegmn abemno aegmns aegmos**

abegmnoy bogeyman moneybag. *See* **abegmn abemno aemnoy begnoy**

abegmor embargo. *See* **abegor abemr aegmr**

abegmort bergamot embargo bromate. *See* **abegor abeort aegort**

abegmrsu umbrages umbrage. *See* **abegrs abemrs abemru abersu**

abegmru umbrage. *See* **abemru aegmru**

abegn began bane bang bean age ane bag ban beg ben gab gae gan nab nae nag neb ae an ba be en na ne

abegnr banger anger barge began range ager bane bang bare barn bean bear berg brae brag bran earn garb gear gnar grab near rage rang age ane are bag ban bar beg ben bra ear era erg gab gae gan gar nab nae nag neb rag ran reg ae an ba be en er na ne re

abegnrs bangers. *See* **aegnrs abegnr abegrs**

abegopsy pageboys pageboy. *See* **begosy**

abegopy pageboy. *See* **begoy**

abegor borage barge aero ager bare bear berg boar bora bore brae brag garb gear goer gore grab ogre rage robe age ago are bag bar beg boa bog bra ear ego era erg gab gae gar goa gob oar orb ore rag rob roe ae ba be er go or re

abegors borages. *See* **abegor abegrs**

abegorx gearbox. *See* **abegor aborx beorx**

abegosz gazebos. *See* **abegoz aegsz aeosz**

abegoz gazebo gaze zoea age ago azo bag beg boa bog ego gab gae goa gob zag zoa ae ba be go

abegr barge ager bare bear berg brae brag garb gear grab rage age are bag bar beg bra ear era erg gab gae gar rag reg ae ba be er re

---

abegrs barges bares barge baser bears bergs brags garbs gears grabs rages saber sabre sager ager ages arse bags bare bars base bear begs berg brae brag bras ears eras ergs gabs garb gars gear grab rage rags rase regs sage sear sera age are bag bar beg bra ear era erg gab gae gar gas rag reg res sag sea ae as ba be er re

abegt begat abet bate beat beta gate aet age ate bag bat beg bet eat eta gab gae gat get tab tag tea ae at ba be ta

abehikls bleakish kiblahs. *See* **abehil abhikl**

abehil habile able bail bale bile blah hail hale heal ail alb ale bah bel hae hie lab lea lei lie ae ah ai ba be eh el ha he hi la li

abehilnr hibernal hernial inhaler. *See* **abehil abehlr aehiln aehilr**

abehiltt tithable. *See* **abehil abeilt abeltt aehilt**

abehinrs banisher bearish hernias. *See* **abeirs abhins abinrs aehinr**

abehinss banishes. *See* **abehss abeiss abhins abhiss**

abehinst absinthe basinet. *See* **abehst abeint abenst abhins**

abehiorv behavior. *See* **abhor abeov aberv**

abehirs bearish. *See* **aehirs abeirs**

abehkrsu hauberks hauberk. *See* **abekrs abersu aehkrs bekrsu**

abehkru hauberk. *See* **abekr bekru abehr**

abehlms shamble. *See* **abelms**

abehlmss shambles shamble. *See* **abehss abelms abelss aehlss**

abehlr herbal abler blare blear haler rehab able bale bare bear blah brae earl hale hare harl heal hear herb herl rale real rhea alb ale are bah bar bel bra ear era hae her lab lar lea rah ae ah ba be eh el er ha he la re

abehlrst blathers bathers blather breaths halters labrets lathers slather thalers. *See* **abehlr abehrt abehst abelrs**

abehlrt blather. *See* **abehrt aehlrt abehlr abelrt**

abehmno hambone. *See* **abemno abeho**

abehmnor hornbeam hambone menorah. *See* **abemno aemnor behmor**

abehmnos hambones hambone bemoans. *See* **abemno ahmnos**

abehmssu ambushes. *See* **abehss abessu abhmsu aehmss**

abehnstu sunbathe butanes. *See* **abehst abenst abentu abestu**

abeho obeah bah boa hae hob hoe ae ah ba be eh ha he ho oh

abehorrr harborer. *See* **abhorr aeorrr**

---

abehostx hatboxes. *See* **abehst abhost abhotx aehosx**

abehr rehab bare bear brae hare hear herb rhea are bah bar bra ear era hae her rah ae ah ba be eh er ha he re

abehrrs brasher. *See* **aberrs aehrrs**

abehrsst brashest bathers breasts breaths rashest trashes. *See* **abehrt abehss abehst aberss**

abehrst bathers breaths. *See* **aberst abehrt abehst behrst aehrst**

abehrt bather bertha breath bathe berth earth hater heart rehab abet baht bare bate bath bear beat beta beth brae brat hare hart hate hear heat herb rate rath rhea tare tear aet are art ate bah bar bat bet bra ear eat era eta eth hae hat her het rah rat ret tab tar tea the ae ah at ba be eh er ha he re ta

abehrty breathy. *See* **abehrt aberty aehrty**

abehss bashes bases ashes base bash bass sash seas ash ass bah ess hae has sea she ae ah as ba be eh ha he sh

abehst bathes abets bahts baste bates bathe baths beast beats betas beths haste hates heats tabes abet baht base bash bast bate bath bats beat best beta beth bets east eats etas hast hate hats heat hest seat seta stab tabs teas aet ash ate bah bat bet eat eta eth hae has hat het sat sea set she tab tea the ae ah as at ba be eh ha he sh ta

abeht bathe abet baht bate bath beat beta beth hate heat aet ate bah bat bet eat eta eth hae hat het tab tea the ae ah at ba be eh ha he ta

abeiil bailie alibi able bail bale bile ilia ail alb ale bel lab lea lei lie ae ai ba be el la li

abeiilmt imitable limbate timbale. *See* **abeiil abeiit abeilt abilmt**

abeiilnn biennial aniline. *See* **abeiil**

abeiilpt pitiable. *See* **abeiil abeiit abeilt**

abeiils bailies. *See* **abeiil abiils**

abeiilst sibilate bailies bestial blastie laities stabile. *See* **abeiil abeiit abeilt abelst**

abeiinrs binaries. *See* **abeirs abinrs aeinrs aiinrs**

abeiit tibiae tibia abet bait bate beat beta bite aet ate bat bet bit eat eta ita tab tea tie ae ai at ba be it ta ti

abeijlno joinable. *See* **abilno**

abeijltu jubilate. *See* **abeilt**

abeijmnn benjamin. *See* **aeimn aeinn aijnn**

abeikll likable. *See* **abeill**

abeikllm lamblike likable. *See* **abeill**

abeiklln balkline likable. *See* **abeill aeilln**

abeiklss   kissable. *See* **abeiss abelss abilss aeilss**

abeiknrs   bearskin bankers snakier. *See* **abeirs abeknr abekrs abinrs**

abeiknst   beatniks basinet beatnik intakes. *See* **abeint abekst abenst abikst**

abeiknt   beatnik. *See* **abeint aeiknt**

abeikswy   bikeways bikeway. *See* **aeksw abeks beiks**

abeikwy   bikeway. *No 6s or 5s*

abeill   labile liable label libel able bail bale ball bell bile bill leal ail alb ale all bel ell ill lab lea lei lie ae ai ba be el la li

abeillov   violable alveoli livable lovable. *See* **abeill abeilv**

abeillp   pliable. *See* **abeill**

abeillr   liberal. *See* **abeill beillr**

abeillrs   liberals liberal rallies rebills. *See* **abeill abeirs abells abelrs**

abeillry   blearily reliably liberal. *See* **abeill abeily abelry aellry**

abeillst   bastille ballets bestial billets blastie stabile tailles tallies. *See* **abeill abeilt abells abellt**

abeillv   livable. *See* **abeill abeilv**

abeilmr   balmier. *See* **beilmr aeilmr abelmr**

abeilmst   balmiest timbales bestial blastie limbate stabile timbale timbals. *See* **abeilt abelms abelst abilmt**

abeilmt   limbate timbale. *See* **abeilt abilmt**

abeilmx   mixable. *See* **abelm aeilx**

abeilmy   beamily. *See* **abeily beilmy**

abeilnot   tailbone elation notable toenail. *See* **abeilt abeint abelot abilno**

abeilnp   biplane. *See* **aeilnp**

abeilnps   biplanes biplane lesbian spaniel. *See* **abilns aeilnp aeilns aeilps**

abeilns   lesbian. *See* **aeilns abilns**

abeilnss   lesbians lesbian. *See* **abeiss abelss abilns abilss**

abeilntv   bivalent. *See* **abeilt abeilv abeint aeilnt**

abeilnvy   enviably naively. *See* **abeilv abeily aeilnv ailnvy**

abeilprt   partible librate. *See* **abeilt abeirt abelrt abilrt**

abeilpss   passible espials palsies. *See* **abeiss abelss abilss aeilps**

abeilrst   librates baiters barites bestial blastie blister bristle labrets librate realist retails saltier saltire stabile terbias. *See* **abeilt abeirs abeirt abelrs**

abeilrt   librate. *See* **abeilt abeirt abelrt aeilrt abilrt**

abeilsst   blasties stabiles bestial blastie stabile stables. *See* **abeilt abeiss abelss abelst**

abeilst   bestial blastie stabile. *See* **abelst abeilt**

abeilstu   suitable bestial blastie stabile sublate subtile. *See* **abeilt abelst abelsu abestu**

abeilsux   bisexual. *See* **abelsu aelsux**

abeilsvv   bivalves bivalve. *See* **abeilv aeilsv aelsvv**

abeilsw   bewails. *See* **abeilw aeils abils**

abeilsz   sizable. *See* **abeisz abelsz**

abeilt   albeit bleat table abet able alit bail bait bale bate beat belt beta bile bite blat late tael tail tale tali teal tile aet ail alb ale alt ate bat bel bet bit eat eta ita lab lea lei let lie lit tab tea tie til ae ai at ba be el it la li ta ti

abeilv   viable alive able bail bale bile evil lave leva live vail vale veal veil vial vile ail alb ale ave bel lab lea lei lev lie via vie ae ai ba be el la li

abeilvv   bivalve. *See* **abeilv aelvv**

abeilw   bewail able bail bale bawl bile blew wail wale weal wile ail alb ale awe awl bel lab law lea lei lie web ae ai aw ba be el la li we

abeily   bailey belay bialy able ably abye bail bale bile aby ail alb ale aye bay bel bey bye lab lay lea lei lie lye yea ae ai ay ba be by el la li ye

abeimnt   ambient. *See* **abeint aeimnt**

abeimrr   barmier. *See* **abemr aberr abirr**

abeimrs   ambries. *See* **abemrs aeimrs abeirs**

abeimrst   barmiest ambries baiters barites imarets terbias timbers timbres. *See* **abeirs abeirt abemrs aberst**

abeimrtv   verbatim vibrate. *See* **abeirt aeimrt beimrt**

abeimssu   iambuses. *See* **abeiss abessu abimsu aemssu**

abeinnrr   brannier. *See* **abennr abenrr aeinnr**

abeinorr   airborne. *See* **abenrr abiorr beinor benorr**

abeinors   baronies erasion. *See* **abeirs abinos abinrs abiors**

abeinort   baritone baronet. *See* **abeint abeirt abenrt abeort**

abeinrrw   brawnier. *See* **abennr aeirrw aenrrw**

abeinrst   banister baiters banters barites basinet nastier retains retinas stainer terbias. *See* **abeint abeirs abeirt abenrt**

abeinrtu   urbanite ruinate taurine tribune turbine urinate. *See* **abeint abeirt abenrt abenru**

abeinruz   urbanize. *See* **abenru abenrz aeinrz**

abeinsst   basinets bassinet absents basinet entasis tansies. *See* **abeint abeiss abenst abesst**

abeinst   basinet. *See* **abeint abenst**

abeint   binate tenia tinea abet ante anti bait bane bani bate bean beat bent beta bine bite neat tine aet ane ani ant ate ban bat ben bet bin bit eat eta ita nab nae neb net nib nit tab tan tea ten tie tin ae ai an at ba be en in it na ne ta ti

abeinttu   intubate. *See* **abeint abentt abentu abettu**

abeiortv   abortive obviate vibrate vibrato. *See* **abeirt abeort beortv**

abeiostv   obviates obviate. *See* **eiostv**

abeiotv   obviate. *See* **abeov abiot aeotv**

abeiprrs   sparerib parries praiser rapiers repairs. *See* **abeirs aberrs abirrs aeiprr**

abeiprtz   baptizer baptize. *See* **abeirt aeiprt**

abeipstz   baptizes baptize. *See* **abeisz**

abeiptz   baptize. *See* **abeiz**

abeirr   barrier. *See* **aberr abirr beirr**

abeirrrs   barriers barrier. *See* **abeirs aberrs abirrs aeirrs**

abeirrss   brassier braises brassie sierras. *See* **abeirs abeiss aberrs aberss**

abeirrst   arbiters rarebits arbiter baiters barites barters rarebit tarries tarsier terbias. *See* **abeirs abeirt aberrs aberst**

abeirrsz   braziers bizarre brazers brazier. *See* **abeirs abeisz aberrs aberrz**

abeirrt   arbiter rarebit. *See* **abeirt aberrt**

abeirrtt   brattier arbiter battier biretta rarebit rattier. *See* **abeirt aberrt abertt aeirtt**

abeirrvy   breviary bravery. *See* **aberrv aberry abirry aeirrv**

abeirrz   bizarre brazier. *See* **aberrz abeiz abirr**

abeirs   braise rabies arise bares baser bears biers raise saber sabre serai airs arse bare bars base bear bias bier bise brae bras brie ears eras rase reis rias ribs rise sari sear sera sire air are bar bra ear era ire res ria rib sea sib sir ae ai as ba be er is re si

abeirss   braises brassie. *See* **aeirss abeiss abeirs aberss**

abeirst   baiters barites terbias. *See* **abeirt aberst beirst abeirs aeirst**

abeirstt   birettas artiste attires baiters barites batiste batters battier biretta bitters ratites striate tastier terbias. *See* **abeirs abeirt aberst abertt**

abeirstv   vibrates baiters barites bravest terbias vibrate. *See* **abeirs abeirt aberst abersv**

abeirsty bestiary baiters barites betrays terbias. *See* abeirs abeirt aberst aberty

abeirsx braxies. *See* abeirs

abeirt baiter barite terbia biter irate retia tribe abet bait bare bate bear beat beta bier bite brae brat brie brit rate rite tare tear tier tire aet air are art ate bar bat bet bit bra ear eat era eta ire ita rat ret ria rib tab tar tea tie ae ai at ba be er it re ta ti

abeirtt battier biretta. *See* aeirtt abeirt abertt beirtt

abeirtv vibrate. *See* abeirt

abeirux exurbia. *See* berux

abeiss biases bases basis bises base bass bias bise seas sibs ass ess sea sib sis ae ai as ba be is si

abeistt batiste. *See* abestt abist beist

abeisttt battiest batiste. *See* abestt

abeistux bauxites bauxite. *See* abestu

abeisuv abusive. *See* abesu aesuv beisv

abeisz baizes baize base bias bise size sea sib ae ai as ba be is si

abeitux bauxite. *See* abetu

abeiz baize ae ai ba be

abejmno jambone. *See* abemno abjno

abejnos banjoes. *See* abjnos aenos abens

abejnosw jawbones banjoes jawbone. *See* abjnos

abejnow jawbone. *See* abjno

abejor jerboa aero bare bear boar bora bore brae robe are bar boa bra ear era jab jar job joe oar orb ore raj rob roe ae ba be er jo or re

abek bake beak kab ae ba be ka

abekl bleak able bake bale balk beak kale lake leak alb ale bel elk kab kal lab lea lek ae ba be el ka la

abeklly bleakly. *See* aelly abkly ablly

abeklnow knowable. *See* aelno aekln aekow

abeklnst blankets blanket anklets. *See* abekst abelst abenst abklns

abeklnt blanket. *See* aeklnt abkln abekl

abeklorw workable. *See* abelor abelrw aeklrw belorw

abekmn embank amen bake bane bank beak beam bean bema kame make mane mean name ane bam ban ben kab ken mae man men nab nae neb ae am an ba be em en ka ma me na ne

abekmns embanks. *See* abekmn abeks abkns

abekmr embark amber baker brake break bream maker bake bare bark barm beak beam bear bema berm brae kame kerb make mare mark rake ream are ark arm bam bar bra ear era kab mae mar ram rem ae am ba be em er ka ma me re

abekmrs embarks. *See* abemrs abekrs abekmr aekmrs

abeknr banker baker brake break bake bane bank bare bark barn beak bean bear brae bran earn kerb kern knar nark near rake rank ane are ark ban bar ben bra ear era kab ken nab nae neb ran ae an ba be en er ka na ne re

abeknrs bankers. *See* abekrs abeknr abknrs

abekoory yearbook. *See* abekry

abekortu breakout outbreak. *See* abeort abortu

abekprsu breakups breakup. *See* abekrs abersu aeprsu bekrsu

abekpru breakup. *See* abekr bekru aepru

abekr baker brake break bake bare bark beak bear brae kerb rake are ark bar bra ear era kab ae ba be er ka re

abekrr barker baker barer barre brake break bake bare bark beak bear brae kerb rake rare rear are ark bar bra ear era err kab ae ba be er ka re

abekrrs barkers. *See* abekrs abekrr aberrs

abekrs bakers brakes breaks baker bakes bares barks baser beaks bears brake break eskar kerbs rakes saber sabre saker arks arse bake bare bark bars base bask beak bear brae bras ears eras kabs kerb rake rase sake sark sear sera are ark ask bar bra ear era kab kas res sea ae as ba be er ka re

abekrsty basketry betrays streaky. *See* abekrs abekry abekst aberst

abekry bakery baker brake break abye aery bake bare bark beak bear brae bray byre kerb rake yare year aby are ark aye bar bay bey bra bye ear era kab key ray rye yak yar yea ae ay ba be by er ka re ye

abeks bakes beaks bake base bask beak kabs sake ask kab kas sea ae as ba be ka

abeksst baskets. *See* abesst abekst aeksst

abekst basket abets bakes baste bates beaks beast beats betas skate stake steak tabes takes teaks abet bake base bask bast bate bats beak beat best beta bets east eats etas kabs sake seat seta skat stab tabs take task teak teas aet ask ate bat bet eat eta kab kas kat sat sea set tab tea tsk ae as at ba be ka ta

abel able bale alb ale bel lab lea ae ba be el la

abell label able bale ball bell leal alb ale all bel ell lab lea ae ba be el la

abelllsy syllable. *See* abells abelsy abllsy aellly

abellmru umbrella rubella. *See* abellu abelmr abemru ablmru

abellnot ballonet notable. *See* abellt abelot abllot

abellort balloter bloater. *See* abellt abelor abelot abelrt

abellosv solvable lovable absolve. *See* abells aelosv

abellov lovable. *See* abell abeov

abellrsu rubellas allures laurels rubella. *See* abells abellu abelrs abelsu

abellru rubella. *See* aellru abellu

abellrvy verbally bravely. *See* abelrv abelry aellry aellvy

abells labels bales balls bells label sable able albs ales bale ball base bell bels ells labs leal leas sale seal sell slab alb ale all bel ell els lab lea sal sea ae as ba be el la

abellst ballets. *See* abelst abellt abells aellst

abellt ballet bleat label table abet able bale ball bate beat bell belt beta blat late leal tael tale tall teal tell aet alb ale all alt ate bat bel bet eat ell eta lab lea let tab tea ae at ba be el la ta

abelltu bullate. *See* abellt abellu belltu

abellu bullae label bulla able bale ball beau bell blue bull leal lube alb ale all bel ell lab lea leu ae ba be el la

abelm amble blame able bale balm beam bema lamb lame male meal alb ale bam bel elm lab lam lea mae mel ae am ba be el em la ma me

abelmm embalm amble blame lemma able bale balm beam bema lamb lame male malm meal alb ale bam bel elm lab lam lea mae mel mem ae am ba be el em la ma me

abelmms embalms. *See* abelms abelmm aelmms

abelmnno nobleman. *See* abemno

abelmnoz emblazon. *See* abemno ablnoz belnoz

abelmnt lambent. *See* aelmnt

abelmnu albumen. *See* abelnu

abelmosv movables movable absolve. *See* abelms aelmos aelosv aemosv

abelmov movable. *See* abeov abelm aelmo

abelmr marble ramble abler amber amble blame blare blear bream lamer realm able bale balm bare barm beam bear bema berm brae earl lamb lame male mare marl meal merl rale real ream alb ale are arm bam bar bel bra ear elm era lab lam lar lea mae mar mel ram rem ae am ba be el em er la ma me re

abelmrr rambler. *See* abelrr abelmr

abelmrrs ramblers barrels marbles rambler rambles. *See* **abelmr abelms abelrr abelrs**

abelmrs marbles rambles. *See* **abemrs abelms abelrs abelmr aelmrs**

abelmrst lamberts armlets labrets lambert marbles rambles. *See* **abelmr abelms abelrs abelrt**

abelmrt lambert. *See* **aelmrt abelrt abelmr**

abelms ambles blames amble bales balms beams bemas blame lambs lames males meals sable able albs ales alms bale balm bams base beam bels bema elms labs lamb lame lams leas male meal mels mesa sale same seal seam slab slam alb ale bam bel elm els lab lam lea mae mel sal sea ae am as ba be el em la ma me

abelmssy assembly embassy. *See* **abelms abelss abelsy abemsy**

abelmsw wambles. *See* **abelms abelmw**

abelmtu mutable. *See* **aelmtu belmtu**

abelmw wamble amble blame able bale balm bawl beam bema blew lamb lame male meal mewl wale weal alb ale awe awl bam bel elm lab lam law lea mae maw mel mew web ae am aw ba be el em la ma me we

abelnost notables boatels notable oblates. *See* **abelot abelst abenst ablost**

abelnot notable. *See* **abelot**

abelnoy baloney. *See* **aelno abely benoy**

abelnrry barrenly blarney. *See* **abelrr abelry abenrr aberry**

abelnrsy blarneys blarney. *See* **abelrs abelry abelsy aelnrs**

abelnru nebular. *See* **abelnu aelnru abenru**

abelnruy urbanely nebular blarney. *See* **abelnu abelry abenru**

abelnry blarney. *See* **abelry aelnry**

abelnryz brazenly blarney. *See* **abelry abelrz abenrz aelnry**

abelnstu unstable butanes sublate tunable. *See* **abelnu abelst abelsu abenst**

abelnsty absently tenably beastly. *See* **abelst abelsy abenst aelnsy**

abelntu tunable. *See* **abentu aelntu abelnu**

abelnty tenably. *See* **aelnty abely abelt**

abelnu nebula unable ulnae able bale bane bean beau blue lane lean lube lune ulna alb ale ane ban bel ben bun lab lea leu nab nae neb nub ae an ba be el en la na ne nu

abeloprt portable bloater potable probate prolate. *See* **abelor abelot abelrt abeort**

abeloprv provable overlap. *See* **abelor abelrv aelopr eloprv**

abelopry operably. *See* **abelor abelry aelopr aelpry**

abelopst potables apostle boatels oblates pelotas potable. *See* **abelot abelst ablost aelops**

abelopt potable. *See* **abelot aelopt**

abeloqtu quotable. *See* **abelot aloqtu**

abelor boreal abler blare blear boral labor lobar roble able aero aloe bale bare bear boar bole bora bore brae earl lobe lore oral orle rale real robe role alb ale are bar bel boa bra ear era lab lar lea lob oar orb ore rob roe ae ba be el er la lo or re

abelorr laborer. *See* **abelor abelrr**

abelorrs laborers arbores barrels laborer. *See* **abelor abelrr abelrs aberrs**

abelorst bloaters sortable storable bloater boaster boatels boaters bolster bolters borates labrets lobster oblates. *See* **abelor abelot abelrs abelrt**

abelorsv absolver absolve. *See* **abelor abelrs abelrv abersv**

abelort bloater. *See* **abelot abeort belort abelor abelrt**

abelossv absolves absolve salvoes. *See* **abelss aelosv aelssv alossv**

abelost boatels oblates. *See* **abelst ablost abelot aelost**

abelostu absolute boatels boletus oblates sublate. *See* **abelot abelst abelsu abestu**

abelostw bestowal boatels oblates. *See* **abelot abelst ablost aelost**

abelosv absolve. *See* **aelosv abeov abels**

abelot boatel lobate oblate bleat bloat table abet able aloe alto bale bate beat belt beta blat blot boat bole bolt late lobe lota tael tale teal tola aet alb ale alt ate bat bel bet boa bot eat eta lab lea let lob lot oat tab tea toe ae at ba be el la lo ta to

abelotv votable. *See* **abelot**

abelquy equably. *See* **abely aelqu**

abelr abler blare blear able bale bare bear brae earl rale real alb ale are bar bel bra ear era lab lar lea ae ba be el er la re

abelrr barrel abler barer barre blare blear able bale bare bear brae earl rale rare real rear alb ale are bar bel bra ear era err lab lar lea ae ba be el er la re

abelrrs barrels. *See* **abelrr aberrs abelrs**

abelrrsw brawlers warblers barrels brawler warbler warbles. *See* **abelrr abelrs abelrw aberrs**

abelrrw brawler warbler. *See* **abelrr abelrw**

abelrs blares blears abler bales bares baser bears blare blear earls lares laser rales saber sable sabre able albs ales arse bale bare bars base bear bels brae bras earl ears eras labs leas rale rase real sale seal sear sera slab alb ale are bar bel bra ear els era lab lar lea res sal sea ae as ba be el er la re

abelrss braless. *See* **abelrs aelrss aberss abelss**

abelrst labrets. *See* **abelst aelrst aberst abelrs**

abelrstt battlers batters battler battles labrets rattles starlet startle tablets. *See* **abelrs abelrt abelst abeltt**

abelrstu baluster bluster butlers labrets saluter sublate. *See* **abelrs abelrt abelst abelsu**

abelrsw warbles. *See* **abelrs ablrsw abelrw**

abelrsz blazers. *See* **abelrs abelrz abelsz abersz**

abelrt labret abler alert alter blare blear bleat later table taler abet able bale bare bate bear beat belt beta blat brae brat earl late rale rate real tael tale tare teal tear aet alb ale alt are art ate bar bat bel bet bra ear eat era eta lab lar lea let rat ret tab tar tea ae at ba be el er la re ta

abelrtt battler. *See* **abertt abeltt abelrt aelrtt**

abelrttu rebuttal battler abutter. *See* **abelrt abeltt abertt abettu**

abelrv verbal abler blare blear brave laver ravel velar able aver bale bare bear brae earl lave leva rale rave real vale veal verb alb ale are ave bar bel bra ear era lab lar lea lev rev ae ba be el er la re

abelrvy bravely. *See* **abelry abelrv**

abelrw warble abler blare blear brawl able bale bare bawl bear blew brae braw brew earl rale real wale ware weal wear alb ale are awe awl bar bel bra ear era lab lar law lea raw war web ae aw ba be el er la re we

abelry barely barley bleary abler belay beryl blare blear early layer relay able ably abye aery aryl bale bare bear brae bray byre earl lyre rale real rely yare year aby alb ale are aye bar bay bel bey bra bye ear era lab lar lay lea lye ray rye yar yea ae ay ba be by el er la re ye

abelrz blazer abler blare blaze blear braze zebra able bale bare bear brae earl laze rale raze real zeal alb ale are bar bel bra ear era lab lar lea ae ba be el er la re

abels   bales sable able albs ales bale base bels labs leas sale seal slab alb ale bel els lab lea sal sea ae as ba be el la

abelss   sables bales bases bless sable sales seals slabs able albs ales bale base bass bels labs lass leas less sale sals seal seas slab alb ale ass bel els ess lab lea sal sea ae as ba be el la

abelsst   stables. *See* **abelst abesst ablsst abelss aelsst**

abelsstu   sublates bustles salutes stables sublate sublets taluses. *See* **abelss abelst abelsu abesst**

abelst   ablest bleats stable tables abets bales baste bates beast beats belts betas blast blats bleat blest least sable slate stale steal tabes table taels tales abet able albs ales alts bale base bast bate bats beat bels belt best beta bets blat east eats etas labs last late leas lest lets sale salt seal seat seta slab slat stab tabs tael tale teal teas aet alb ale alt ate bat bel bet eat els eta lab lea let sal sat sea set tab tea ae as at ba be el la ta

abelstt   battles tablets. *See* **abelst abeltt abestt aelstt**

abelstu   sublate. *See* **abelst abestu belstu aelstu abelsu**

abelstwy   beltways beastly beltway. *See* **abelst abelsy ablswy aestwy**

abelsty   beastly. *See* **abelst abelsy**

abelsu   suable usable abuse bales beaus blues lubes sable able albs ales bale base beau bels blue labs leas lube lues sale seal slab slub slue alb ale bel bus els lab lea leu sal sea sub sue use ae as ba be el la us

abelsy   basely belays bales belay sable able ably abye albs ales ayes bale base bays bels beys byes easy eyas labs lays leas lyes lyse sale seal slab slay yeas aby alb ale aye bay bel bey bye els lab lay lea lye sal say sea sly yea yes ae as ay ba be by el la ye

abelsz   blazes bales blaze lazes sable zeals able albs ales bale base bels labs laze leas sale seal slab zeal alb ale bel els lab lea sal sea ae as ba be el la

abelt   bleat table abet able bale bate beat belt beta blat late tael tale teal aet alb ale alt ate bat bel bet eat eta lab lea let tab tea ae at ba be el la ta

abeltt   battle tablet betta bleat table abet able bale bate beat belt beta blat late tael tale teal teat aet alb ale alt ate bat bel bet eat eta lab lea let tab tat tea ae at ba be el la ta

abeltwy   beltway. *See* **abely abelt ablwy**

abely   belay able ably abye bale aby alb ale aye bay bel bey bye lab lay lea lye yea ae ay ba be by el la ye

abelz   blaze able bale laze zeal alb ale bel lab lea ae ba be el la

abem   beam bema bam mae ae am ba be em ma me

abemmnoo   moonbeam. *See* **abemno**

abemno   bemoan aeon ambo amen bane beam bean bema bone ebon mane mean moan name noma nome omen ane bam ban ben boa eon mae man men moa mob mon nab nae neb nob one ae am an ba be em en ma me mo na ne no om on

abemnos   bemoans. *See* **abemno aenos abmos**

abemnot   boatmen. *See* **abemno bemnot**

abemnpru   penumbra. *See* **abemru abenru aemnpu aemnru**

abemnssu   sunbeams sunbeam. *See* **abessu abmnsu aemnss aemssu**

abemnst   batsmen. *See* **abenst aemnst**

abemnsu   sunbeam. *See* **abmnsu bemnsu**

abemnttu   abutment nutmeat. *See* **abentt abentu abettu aemttu**

abemorst   bromates boaster boaters borates bromate maestro mobster. *See* **abemrs abeort aberst aborst**

abemort   bromate. *See* **abeort**

abemr   amber bream bare barm beam bear bema berm brae mare ream are arm bam bar bra ear era mae mar ram rem ae am ba be em er ma me re

abemrs   ambers breams amber bares baser beams bears bemas berms bream mares maser reams saber sabre smear arms arse bams bare barm bars base beam bear bema berm brae bras ears eras mare mesa rams rase ream same seam sear sera are arm bam bar bra ear era mae mar ram rem res sea ae am as ba be em er ma me re

abemru   umbrae amber bream brume rumba umber umbra bare barm beam bear beau bema berm brae mare ream rube urea are arm bam bar bra bum ear emu era mae mar ram rem rub rue rum ae am ba be em er ma me mu re um

abems   beams bemas bams base beam bema mesa same seam bam mae sea ae am as ba be em ma me

abemssy   embassy. *See* **abemsy abmssy**

abemsy   embays abysm beams beamy bemas embay maybe seamy abye ayes bams base bays beam bema beys byes easy eyas mesa same seam yams yeas aby aye bam bay bey bye mae may say

sea yam yea yes ae am as ay ba be by em ma me my ye

abemy   beamy embay maybe abye beam bema aby aye bam bay bey bye mae may yam yea ae am ay ba be by em ma me my ye

aben   bane bean ane ban ben nab nae neb ae an ba be en na ne

abennr   banner bane bare barn bean bear brae bran earn near ane are ban bar ben bra ear era nab nae neb ran ae an ba be en er na ne re

abennrs   banners. *See* **abennr abnns abers**

abenopsu   subpoena subpena. *See* **aenops**

abenorss   baroness reasons. *See* **aberss abnors aenors aenoss**

abenorst   baronets atoners banters baronet boaster boaters borates senator treason. *See* **abenrt abenst abeort aberst**

abenort   baronet. *See* **aenort abenrt abeort**

abenortt   betatron abettor baronet taboret. *See* **abenrt abentt abeort abertt**

abenorty   barytone baronet bayonet. *See* **abenrt abeort aberty abnory**

abenossw   sawbones. *See* **aenoss**

abenossy   soybeans soybean. *See* **aenoss**

abenosty   bayonets soybean bayonet. *See* **abenst abnost abnoty aenost**

abenosy   soybean. *See* **aenos abens benos**

abenoty   bayonet. *See* **abnoty aenot benoy**

abenpsu   subpena. *See* **abesu aenps abens**

abenqstu   banquets banquet butanes. *See* **abenst abentu abeqsu abestu**

abenqtu   banquet. *See* **abentu anqtu aenqu**

abenrr   barren barer barre reran bane bare barn bean bear brae bran earn near rare rear ane are ban bar ben bra ear era err nab nae neb ran ae an ba be en er na ne re

abenrst   banters. *See* **abenst aenrst abenrt aberst**

abenrsz   brazens. *See* **abenrz abersz**

abenrt   banter abet ante bane bare barn bate bean bear beat bent beta brae bran brat earn near neat rant rate rent tare tear tern aet ane ant are art ate ban bar bat ben bet bra ear eat era eta nab nae neb net ran rat ret tab tan tar tea ten ae an at ba be en er na ne re ta

abenru   urbane buran urban bane bare barn bean bear beau brae bran burn earn near rube rune urea ane are ban bar ben bra bun ear era nab nae neb nub ran rub rue run urn ae an ba be en er na ne nu re

abenrux   exurban. *See* **abenru berux**

abenrz brazen braze zebra bane bare barn bean bear brae bran earn near raze ane are ban bar ben bra ear era nab nae neb ran ae an ba be en er na ne re

abens beans bane bans base bean bens nabs nebs sane ane ban ben ens nab nae neb sea sen ae an as ba be en na ne

abensst absents. *See* **abenst aensst abesst**

abenst absent abets antes baste bates beans beast beats betas nates tabes abet ante ants bane bans base bast bate bats bean beat bens bent best beta bets east eats etas nabs neat nebs nest nets sane seat sent seta stab tabs tans teas tens aet ane ant ate ban bat ben bet eat ens eta nab nae neb net sat sea sen set tab tan tea ten ae an as at ba be en na ne ta

abenstu butanes. *See* **abenst abestu abentu aenstu**

abenstz bezants. *See* **abenst abentz**

abentt batten betta abet ante bane bate bean beat bent beta neat teat tent aet ane ant ate ban bat ben bet eat eta nab nae neb net tab tan tat tea ten ae an at ba be en na ne ta

abentu butane beaut abet abut ante aunt bane bate bean beat beau bent beta bunt neat tabu tuba tube tuna tune aet ane ant ate ban bat ben bet bun but eat eta nab nae neb net nub nut tab tan tau tea ten tub tun ae an at ba be en na ne nu ta ut

abentz bezant abet ante bane bate bean beat bent beta neat zeta aet ane ant ate ban bat ben bet eat eta nab nae neb net tab tan tea ten ae an at ba be en na ne ta

abeootv obovate. *See* **abeov aeotv aboot**

abeoppry paperboy. *See* **aeppry**

abeoprst probates boaster boaters borates probate seaport. *See* **abeort aberst aborst aeoprs**

abeoprt probate. *See* **abeort**

abeoqru baroque. *See* **abeqru eoqru**

abeorrs arbores. *See* **aborrs aberrs beorrs**

abeorsst boasters boaster boaters borates breasts sorbets strobes. *See* **abeort aberss aberst abesst**

abeorst boaster boaters borates. *See* **aborst aberst abeort aeorst beorst**

abeorstt taborets abettor batters bettors boaster boaters borates rotates taboret toaster. *See* **abeort aberst abertt abestt**

abeorstu saboteur boaster boaters borates rubatos tabours. *See* **abeort aberst abersu abestu**

abeorsx boraxes. *See* **beorsx aeors abers**

abeorsz bezoars. *See* **abeorz abersz**

abeort boater borate abort orate tabor abet aero bare bate bear beat beta boar boat bora bore bort brae brat rate robe rota rote tare taro tear tora tore aet are art ate bar bat bet boa bot bra ear eat era eta oar oat orb ore ort rat ret rob roe rot tab tar tea toe tor ae at ba be er or re ta to

abeortt abettor taboret. *See* **abertt beortt abeort aeortt**

abeorttu obturate tabouret abettor abutter taboret. *See* **abeort abertt abettu abortu**

abeortz bezoar braze zebra aero bare bear boar bora bore brae raze robe zero zoea are azo bar boa bra ear era oar orb ore rob roe zoa ae ba be er or re

abeossst asbestos bassets. *See* **abesst abosst aessst beosst**

abeostwx sweatbox. *See* **beostw**

abeov above ave boa ova ae ba be

abeprssy passerby pessary. *See* **aberss abpssy abrssy aeprss**

abepsssy bypasses abysses. *See* **abpssy aepsss aesssy**

abeptu upbeat beaut taupe abet abut bate beat beau beta pate peat tabu tape tuba tube aet ape apt ate bat bet but eat eta pat pea pet pub put tab tap tau tea tub tup ae at ba be pa pe ta up ut

abeqrsu barques. *See* **abersu abeqru abeqsu aeqrsu**

abeqrsuu arquebus barques brusque bureaus. *See* **abeqru abeqsu abersu aersuu**

abeqru barque bare bear beau brae rube urea are bar bra ear era qua rub rue ae ba be er re

abeqssu basques. *See* **abessu abeqsu abqssu**

abeqsu basque abuse beaus squab base beau bus qua sea sub sue use ae as ba be us

aber bare bear brae are bar bra ear era ae ba be er re

aberr barer barre bare bear brae rare rear are bar bra ear era err ae ba be er re

aberrs barres barer bares barre baser bears rears saber sabre arse bare bars base bear brae bras ears eras errs rare rase rear sear sera are bar bra ear era err res sea ae as ba be er re

aberrst barters. *See* **aerrst aberst aberrs aberrt**

aberrsy bbarres. *See* **abberr abers berry**

aberrsz brazers. *See* **aberrs aberrz abersz**

aberrt barter barer barre abet bare bate bear beat beta brae brat rare rate rear tare tear aet are art ate bar bat bet bra ear eat era eta rat ret tab tar tea ae at ba be er re ta

aberrv braver barer barre brave aver bare bear brae rare rave rear verb ave bar bra ear era err rev ae ba be er re

aberrvy bravery. *See* **aberrv abberr**

aberry brayer barer barre berry abye aery bare bear brae bray byre rare rear yare year aby are aye bar bay bey bra bye ear era err ray rye yar yea ae ay ba be by er re ye

aberrz brazer barer barre braze zebra bare bear brae rare raze rear are bar bra ear era err ae ba be er re

abers bares baser bears saber sabre arse bare bars base bear brae bras ears eras rase sear sera are bar bra ear era res sea ae as ba be er re

aberss sabers sabres arses bares baser bases bears brass rases saber sabre sears arse bare bars base bass bear brae bras ears eras rase sear seas seas are ass bar bra ear era ess res sea ae as ba be er re

abersst breasts. *See* **aersst aberst abesst aberss**

abersstu abstruse abusers breasts busters. *See* **abersst abersu abesst**

aberssu abusers. *See* **abersu abessu aerssu abrssu berssu**

aberst barest breast abets aster bares baser baste bates bears beast beats betas brats rates saber sabre stare tabes tares tears abet arse arts bare bars base bast bate bats bear beat bens best bets brae bras brat ears east eats eras erst etas rase rate rats rest rets sear seat sera seta stab star tabs tare tars tear teas tsar aet are art ate bar bat bet bra ear eat era eta rat res ret sat sea set tab tar tea ae as at ba be er re ta

aberstt batters. *See* **aberst abertt abestt aerstt**

abersttu abutters abutter batters battues butters stature. *See* **aberst abersu abertt abestt**

aberstv bravest. *See* **aerstv aberst abersv**

abersty betrays. *See* **aberst aberty aersty**

abersu abuser bursae abuse bares baser bears beaus bursa burse rebus rubes saber sabre ureas arse bare bars base bear beau brae bras ears eras rase rube rubs rues ruse sear sera sura sure urea user are bar bra bus ear era res rub rue sea sub sue use ae as ba be er re us

abersuu bureaus. *See* **abersu aberuu aersuu**

abersv braves avers bares baser bears brave raves saber sabre saver verbs arse aver aves bare bars base bear brae bras ears eras rase rave revs save sear sera vase verb are ave bar bra ear era res rev sea ae as ba be er re

abersz brazes zebras bares baser bears braze razes saber sabre zebra arse bare bars base bear brae bras ears eras rase raze sear sera are bar bra ear era res sea ae as ba be er re

abertt batter betta tater tetra treat abet bare bate bear beat beta brae brat rate tare tart tear teat tret aet are art ate bar bat bet bra ear eat era eta rat ret tab tar tat tea ae at ba be er re ta

aberttu abutter. *See* **abertt abettu berttu**

abertty battery. *See* **abertt aberty abrtty aertty**

aberty betray teary abet abye aery arty bare bate bear beat beta brae brat bray byre byte rate tare tear tray yare year aby aet are art ate aye bar bat bay bet bey bra bye ear eat era eta rat ray ret rye tab tar tea try yar yea yet ae at ay ba be by er re ta ye

aberuu bureau bare bear beau brae rube urea are bar bra ear era rub rue ae ba be er re

aberv brave aver bare bear brae rave verb are ave bar bra ear era rev ae ba be er re

aberz braze zebra bare bear brae raze are bar bra ear era ae ba be er re

abes base sea ae as ba be

abess bases base bass seas ass ess sea ae as ba be

abessst bassets. *See* **aessst abesst**

abesssy abysses. *See* **aesssy abssy abess**

abesst basest basset bastes beasts abets asset bases baste basts bates beast beats bests betas sates seats stabs tabes tasse abet base bass bast bate bats beat best beta bets east eats etas seas seat seta sets stab tabs tass teas aet ass ate bat bet eat ess eta sat sea set tab tea ae as at ba be ta

abessu abuses abuse bases beaus buses base bass beau buss seas subs sues uses ass bus ess sea sub sue use ae as ba be us

abest abets baste bates beast beats betas tabes abet base bast bate bats beat best beta bets east eats etas seat seta stab tabs teas aet ate bat bet eat eta sat sea set tab tea ae as at ba be ta

abestt bettas abets baste bates beast beats betas betta state tabes taste teats testa abet base bast bate bats beat best beta bets east eats etas seat seta stab stet tabs tats teas teat test aet ate bat bet eat eta sat sea set tab tat tea ae as at ba be ta

abesttu battues. *See* **aesttu abettu abestu abestt**

abestu beauts abets abuse abuts baste bates beast beats beaus beaut betas tabes tubas tubes abet abut base bast bate bats beat beau best beta bets bust buts east eats etas seat seta stab stub suet tabs tabu teas tuba tube tubs aet ate bat bet bus but eat eta sat sea set sub sue tab tau tea tub use ae as at ba be ta us ut

abesu abuse beaus base beau bus sea sub sue use ae as ba be us

abet abet bate beat beta aet ate bat bet eat eta tab tea ae at ba be ta

abett betta abet bate beat beta teat aet ate bat bet eat eta tab tat tea ae at ba be ta

abettu battue betta beaut abet abut bate beat beau betta butt tabu taut teat tuba tube aet ate bat bet but eat eta tab tau tea tub tut ae at ba be ta ut

abetu beaut abet abut bate beat beau beta tabu tuba tube aet ate bat bet but eat eta tab tau tea tub ae at ba be ta ut

abetuy beauty beaut abet abut abye bate beat beau beta byte tabu tuba tube aby aet ate aye bat bay bet bey but buy bye eat eta tab tau tea tub yea yet ae at ay ba be by ta ut ye

abeu beau ae ba be

abey abye aby aye bay bey bye yea ae ay ba be by ye

abezzz bezazz ae ba be

abffgiln baffling fabling. *See* **abgiln**

abffiil bailiff. *See* **abiil**

abffiils bailiffs bailiff. *See* **abiils**

abffllpu puffball. *See* **afllpu**

abfflost blastoff. *See* **ablost afflos aflost**

abfflou buffalo. *See* **aflou bfflu afflu**

abffnotu bouffant. *See* **abotu abnot fnotu**

abfgiln fabling. *See* **abgiln afiln fgiln**

abfglloo goofball. *See* **abgllo**

abfglsu bagfuls. *See* **abfglu abfls afgls**

abfglu bagful fugal flab flag flub gulf alb bag bug fag flu fug gab gal lab lag lug ba fa la

abfhist batfish. *See* **abhist afhist**

abfhlsu bashful. *See* **abhls bhlsu abfls**

abfiilr bifilar. *See* **bfiilr abiil abilr**

abfillly fallibly. *See* **ablly abily billy**

abfilru fibular. *See* **abfilu abilru**

abfilstu fabulist fibulas fistula. *See* **abfilu aflstu**

abfilsu fibulas. *See* **abfilu afils abils**

abfilu fibula alif bail fail fila flab flub ail alb fib flu lab ai ba fa if la li

abfisy basify bays bias fays fibs aby bay fas fay fib ifs say sib ai as ay ba by fa if is si

abfl flab alb lab ba fa la

abflloot football. *See* **abllot**

abfllost softball ballots. *See* **abllot ablost aflost allost**

abflostu boastful. *See* **ablost aflost aflstu flostu**

abflosuu fabulous. *See* **aflou ablos blosu**

abflry barfly ably aryl bray flab flay fray aby alb arf bar bay bra far fay fly fry lab lar lay ray yar ay ba by fa la

abfls flabs albs flab labs slab alb fas lab sal as ba fa la

abfnortu turbofan. *See* **abnrtu abortu anortu bnortu**

abg bag gab ba

abgggin bagging. *See* **aggin**

abggginr bragging bagging barging garbing ragging raging.. *See* **abginr**

abggilmn gambling ambling blaming. *See* **abgiln aggimn agilmn**

abggilnr garbling barging blaring garbing glaring. *See* **abgiln abginr agginr**

abgginn banging. *See* **aggin**

abgginr barging garbing. *See* **abginr agginr**

abggnnuy gunnybag. *See* **abggy bgguy bnnuy**

abggnoot toboggan. *See* **abnot bgnoo aboot**

abggy baggy gaby aby bag bay gab gag gay ay ba by

abghhill highball. *See* **aghil**

abghins bashing. *See* **abhins abgins abghns**

abghint bathing. *See* **abgint aghint**

abghmoo goombah. *See* **aghmo**

abghmoos goombahs goombah. *See* **aghmos**

abghmoru brougham hamburg homburg. *See* **abhmru**

abghmrsu hamburgs hamburg rhumbas. *See* **abhmru abhmsu abmrsu bghrsu**

abghmru hamburg. *See* **abhmru bghru**

abghn bhang bang hang bag bah ban gab gan hag nab nag nah ah an ba ha na

abghnor hagborn. *See* **abgnor**

abghns bhangs bangs bhang gnash hangs bags bang bans bash gabs gash hags hang nabs nags sang shag snag ash bag bah ban gab gan gas hag has nab nag nah sag ah an as ba ha na sh

abghstu hagbuts. *See* **abghtu aghstu**

abghtu hagbut aught abut baht bath ghat tabu thug tuba bag bah bat bug but gab gat gut hag hat hub hug hut tab tag tau tub tug ugh ah at ba ha ta ut

abgiiln bailing. *See* **agiiln abgiln**

abgiimst bigamist gambits imagist. *See* **abgimt abiist abimst agimst**

abgiinnr braining brining ingrain raining. *See* **abginr**

abgiinrs braising arising biasing raising sabring. *See* **abginr abgins abinrs aginrs**

abgiins biasing. *See* **abgins**

abgiint baiting. *See* **abgint bgiint**

abgikln balking. *See* **abgikn abgiln**

abgiklnn blanking balking banking. *See* **abgikn abgiln**

abgikn baking kiang akin bang bani bank gain gink kina king ani bag ban big bin gab gan gib gin ink kab kin nab nag nib ai an ba in ka na

abgiknn banking. *See* **abgikn**

abgiknr barking braking. *See* **abgikn abginr agiknr**

abgikns basking. *See* **agikns abgikn abgins**

abgilln balling. *See* **abgiln**

abgilmn ambling blaming. *See* **abgiln agilmn**

abgilmnr marbling rambling ambling blaming blaring. *See* **abgiln abginr agilmn agimnr**

abgilmnw wambling ambling bawling blaming. *See* **abgiln agilmn agilnw**

abgilms gimbals. *See* **abils ablms abgms**

abgiln baling align blain ligan linga anil bail bang bani gain glib lain ling nail ail alb ani bag ban big bin gab gal gan gib gin lab lag nab nag nib nil ai an ba in la li na

abgilnnt bantling tabling. *See* **abgiln abgint**

abgilnor laboring blaring. *See* **abgiln abgino abginr abgnor**

abgilnot bloating boating bolting tabling. *See* **abgiln abgino abgint abilno**

abgilnr blaring. *See* **abgiln abginr**

abgilnrw brawling warbling blaring bawling. *See* **abgiln abginr agilnw aginrw**

abgilnst blasting stabling basting lasting salting slating staling tabling. *See* **abgiln abgins abgint abilns**

abgilnt tabling. *See* **abgiln abgint**

abgilntt battling blatting tabling batting. *See* **abgiln abgint**

abgilnty tangibly tabling. *See* **abgiln abgint abginy agilny**

abgilnw bawling. *See* **abgiln agilnw**

abgilnz blazing. *See* **abgiln agilnz**

abgiloot obligato. *See* **agilot agloot**

abgimmn bamming. *See* **agimn**

abgimosu bigamous. *See* **abimsu agimos bgmosu**

abgimst gambits. *See* **abimst abgimt agimst**

abgimt gambit ambit bait gait gamb iamb aim bag bam bat big bit gab gam gat gib ita mag mat tab tag tam ai am at ba it ma mi ta ti

abgimy bigamy gaby gamb gamy iamb aby aim bag bam bay big gab gam gay gib gym mag may yam ai am ay ba by ma mi my

abginnn banning. *No 6s or 5s*

abgino bagnio gabion bingo agio agon bang bani bong gain ago ani bag ban big bin boa bog gab gan gib gin goa gob ion nab nag nib nob nog obi ai an ba go in na no on

abginoot tabooing boating booting. *See* **abgino abgint abinot bginoo**

abginort aborting boating orating. *See* **abgino abginr abgint abgnor**

abginos bagnios gabions. *See* **abgino abgins bginos abinos**

abginost boasting agonist bagnios basting bastion boating gabions obtains. *See* **abgino abgins abgint abinos**

abginot boating. *See* **abgino abgint abinot**

abginr baring bairn brain bring grain bang bani barn brag bran brig gain garb gnar grab grin rain rang rani ring air ani bag ban bar big bin bra gab gan gar gib gin nab nag nib rag ran ria rib rig ai an ba in na

abginrr barring. *See* **abginr abirr**

abginrs sabring. *See* **abinrs abginr abgins bginrs aginrs**

abginrv braving. *See* **abginr aginrv**

abginry braying. *See* **abginr abginy abinry aginry**

abginrz brazing. *See* **abginr aginrz**

abgins basing bangs basin gains sabin bags bang bani bans bias bins gabs gain gibs gins nabs nags nibs sain sang sign sing snag ani bag ban big bin gab gan gas gib gin nab nag nib sag sib sin ai an as ba in is na si

abginsst bastings basting. *See* **abgins abgint abinss aginss**

abginst basting. *See* **abgins abgint aginst**

abginsu abusing. *See* **abgins bginsu**

abgint bating giant anti bait bang bani gain gait gnat tang ting ani ant bag ban bat big bin bit gab gan gat gib gin ita nab nag nib nit tab tag tan tin ai an at ba in it na ta ti

abgintt batting. *See* **abgint aintt**

abginttu abutting batting butting. *See* **abgint bgintu**

abginy baying ayin bang bani gaby gain yang aby ani any bag ban bay big bin gab gan gay gib gin nab nag nay nib yin ai an ay ba by in na

abgiopst pigboats pigboat. *See* **aiopst bgiost giopst**

abgiopt pigboat. *See* **bgiot abiot aiopt**

abglloy globally. *See* **abgllo**

abgllo global ball boll gall gaol glob goal olla ago alb all bag boa bog gab gal goa gob lab lag lob log ba go la lo

abglloru globular. *See* **abgllo abloru**

abglmo gambol ambo balm gamb gaol glob goal lamb loam mola ago alb bag bam boa bog gab gal gam goa gob lab lag lam lob log mag moa mob mog am ba go la lo ma mo om

abglmos gambols. *See* **abglmo abmos ablms**

abglmou lumbago. *See* **abglmo ablmu aglmu**

abglnoo bologna. *See* **aglnoo bglnoo**

abglnoos bolognas bologna lagoons oblongs. *See* **aglnoo aglnos alnoos bglnoo**

abglnoot longboat bologna. *See* **aglnoo agloot bglnoo**

abglnouw bungalow blowgun. *See* **aglow aglno blnow**

abglorsu glabrous labours. *See* **ablors abloru ablrsu aglors**

abglrrsu burglars burglary. *See* **ablrsu abrrsu**

abglrru burglar. *See* **alrru**

abglrruy burglary burglar. *See* **blrruy**

abgm gamb bag bam gab gam mag am ba ma

abgms gambs bags bams gabs gamb gams mags bag bam gab gam gas mag sag am as ba ma

abgn bang bag ban gab gan nab nag an ba na

abgnor barong brogan argon baron groan organ agon bang barn boar bong bora born brag bran garb gnar grab rang roan ago bag ban bar boa bog bra gab gan gar goa gob nab nag nob nog nor oar orb rag ran rob an ba go na no on or

abgnors barongs brogans. *See* **agnors abgnor abnors**

abgnorsu osnaburg barongs brogans. *See* **abgnor abnors abnrsu agnors**

abgnostu gunboats gunboat nougats. *See* **abnost agnost agnosu agnotu**

abgnotu gunboat. *See* **agnotu abotu abnot**

abgns bangs bags bang bans gabs nabs nags sang snag bag ban gab gan gas nab nag sag an as ba na

abgosttu tugboats tugboat. *See* **abotu abstu aostu**

abgottu tugboat. *See* **abotu agttu**

abgr brag garb grab bag bar bra gab gar rag ba

abgrs brags garbs grabs bags bars brag bras gabs garb gars grab rags bag bar bra gab gar gas rag sag ba as

abgs bags gabs bag gab gas sag as ba

abgy gaby aby bag bay gab gay ay ba by

abh bah ah ba ha

abhhsuy hushaby. *See* **bhsuy**

abhiinst inhabits inhabit. *See* **abhins abhist abiist aiinst**

abhiint inhabit. *See* **abhit abiit**

abhikl kiblah bail balk bilk blah haik hail kail lakh ail alb bah ilk kab kal lab ah ai ba ha hi ka la li

abhikllw hawkbill. *See* **abhikl**

abhiklor kohlrabi kilobar. *See* **abhikl**

abhikls kiblahs. *See* **abhikl abils abkls**

abhikst bhaktis. *See* **abikst abhikt abhist**

abhikt bhakti habit batik baht bait bath haik kith bah bat bit hat hit ita kab kat kit tab ah ai at ba ha hi i ka ta ti

abhilno hobnail. *See* **abilno**

abhilnos hobnails abolish albinos hobnail. *See* **abhins abilno abilns abinos**

abhilos abolish. *See* **abilo abils abhls**

abhilstu halibuts halibut. *See* **abhist ahilst ahistu bhilsu**

abhiltu halibut. *See* **biltu abhit abltu**

abhimr mihrab ihram amir barm brim hair harm rami aim air arm bah bam bar bra ham him mar mir rah ram ria rib rim ah ai am ba ha hi ma mi

abhimrs mihrabs. *See* **ahimrs abhimr**

abhins banish basin sabin sahib bani bans bash bias bins hins nabs nibs sain shin ani ash bah ban bin has hin his nab nah nib sib sin ah ai an as ba ha hi in is na sh si

abhiop phobia opah bah boa bop hap hip hob hop obi pah poi ah ai ba ha hi ho oh pa pi

abhiops phobias. *See* **abhiop bhiops**

abhiors boarish. *See* **abhors abiors**

abhiosst isobaths isobath. *See* **abhiss abhist abhost abosst**

abhiost isobath. *See* **abhist abhost**

abhirrsu airbrush. *See* **abirrs abirsu abrrsu ahirrs**

abhis sahib bash bias ash bah has his sib ah ai as ba ha hi is sh si

abhiss sahibs sahib basis bash bass bias hiss sash sibs ash ass bah has his sib sis ah ai as ba ha hi is sh si

abhist habits bahts baits baths habit sahib saith baht bait bash bast bath bats bias bits hast hats hist hits sith stab tabs this ash bah bat bit has hat his hit ita its sat sib sit tab ah ai as at ba ha hi is it sh si ta ti

abhit habit baht bait bath bah bat bit hat hit ita tab ah ai at ba ha hi it ta ti

abhkooot boathook. *See* **bhoot ahkoo aboot**

abhl blah alb bah lab ah ba ha la

abhllmot mothball. *See* **abllot**

abhllooy ballyhoo. *See* **ahlloo**

abhlosww washbowl. *See* **ablsw abhls blosw**

abhls blahs albs bash blah labs lash slab alb ash bah has lab sal ah as ba ha la sh

abhmnsu bushman. *See* **abhmsu abmnsu ahmnsu**

abhmnsuu subhuman bushman. *See* **abhmsu abmnsu ahmnsu**

abhmoort bathroom. *See* **abhor abort bhoot**

abhmrsu rhumbas. *See* **abhmsu abhmru bhmrsu abmrsu**

abhmru rhumba rhumb rumba umbra barm harm arm bah bam bar bra bum ham hub hum mar rah ram rub rum ah am ba ha ma mu um

abhmsu ambush bams bash bums bush hams hubs hums mash mush sham ash bah bam bum bus ham has hub hum mus sub sum ah am as ba ha ma mu sh um us

abhoorst tarboosh. *See* **abhors abhost aboost aborst**

abhoostw showboat. *See* **abhost aboost ahoosw bhoost**

abhor abhor boar bora hoar hora bah bar boa bra hob oar orb rah rho rob ah ba ha ho oh or

abhorr harbor abhor arbor boar bora hoar hora roar bah bar boa bra hob oar orb rah rho rob ah ba ha ho oh or

abhorrs harbors. *See* **abhors aborrs abhorr**

abhorrsu harbours harbors harbour. *See* **abhorr abhors aborrs abrrsu**

abhorru harbour. *See* **abhorr borru**

abhors abhors abhor boars boras brash horas bars bash boar boas bora bosh bras hoar hobs hora oars orbs rahs rash rhos robs soar sora sorb ash bah bar boa bra has hob oar ohs orb rah rho rob sob ah as ba ha ho oh or os sh so

abhost bathos bahts baths boast boats hosta oaths sabot shoat baht bash bast bath bats boas boat bosh both bots hast hats hobs host hots oast oath oats shot stab stoa stob tabs tosh ash bah bat boa bot has hat hob hot oat ohs sat sob sot tab tho ah as at ba ha ho oh os sh so ta to

abhostuy hautboys hautboy. *See* **abhost abosuy hostuy**

abhotuy hautboy. *See* **abotu abouy hotuy**

abhotx hatbox baht bath boat both hoax oath bah bat boa bot box hat hob hot oat tab tax tho ah at ax ba ha ho oh ox ta to

abhrs brash bars bash bras rahs rash ash bah bar bra has rah ah as ba ha sh

abhrsy brashy brash brays ashy bars bash bays bras bray hays rahs rash rays shay aby ash bah bar bay bra has hay rah ray say shy yah ah as ay ba by ha sh

abhs bash ash bah has ah as ba ha sh

abhsstuw washtubs washtub. *See* **ahsstw**

abhst bahts baths baht bash bast bath bats hast hats stab tabs ash bah bat has hat sat tab ah as at ba ha sh ta

abhstuw washtub. *See* **abstu abhst ahstw**

abht baht bath bah bat hat tab ah at ba ha ta

abiiklss basilisk. *See* **abiils abilss**

abiil alibi bail ilia ail alb lab ai ba la li

abiillmr millibar. *See* **abiil abilr**

abiilmno binomial. *See* **abilno aiilmn ailmno**

abiilmns albinism. *See* **abiils abilns aiilmn aiimns**

abiilmsu bulimias bulimia. *See* **abiils abilmu abimsu ablmsu**

abiilmu bulimia. *See* **abilmu abiil iilmu**

abiilnot libation. *See* **abiilt abilno abinot ailnot**

abiils alibis alibi bails basil ails albs bail bias ibis ilia labs sail slab ail alb lab sal sib ai as ba is la li si

abiilt tibial alibi alit bail bait blat ilia tail tali ail alb alt bat bit ita lab lit tab til ai at ba it la li ta ti

abiilty ability. *See* **abiilt abily ailty**

abiimnot ambition. *See* **abinot**

abiist tibias tibia baits bait bast bats bias bits ibis stab tabs bat bit ita its sat sib sit tab ai as at ba is it si ta ti

abiit tibia bait bat bit ita tab ai at ba it ta ti

abijlntu jubilant. *See* **abiln blntu biltu**

abijnost banjoist bastion obtains. *See* **abinos abinot abjnos abjost**

abijrsu jabirus. *See* **abijru abirsu**

abijru jabiru juba jura air bar bra jab jar jib raj ria rib rub ba ai

abiklmn lambkin. *See* **aiklmn abiln abkln**

abiklmns lambkins lambskin lambkin malkins. *See* **abilns abklns aiklmn aikmns**

abiklor kilobar. *See* **abilo ablor abilr**

abiklors kilobars kilobar kolbasi. *See* **abilrs abiors ablors ailors**

abiklos kolbasi. *See* **abilo abils abkls**

abikmo akimbo ambo amok iamb kami mako aim bam boa kab koa kob moa mob oak obi ai am ba ka ma mi mo om

abiknorr ironbark. *See* **abiorr**

abikrsst britskas britska. *See* **abikst aikrst airsst akrsst**

abikrst britska. *See* **abikst aikrst**

abikst batiks batik baits bait bask bast bats bias bits kabs kist kits saki skat skit stab tabs task ask bat bit ita its kab kas kat kit sat sib sit ski tab tsk ai as at ba is it ka si ta ti

abikt batik bait bat bit ita kab kat kit tab ai at ba it ka ta ti

abil bail ail alb lab ai ba la li

abilllpy playbill pliably. *See* **ablly abily billy**

abillmy balmily. *See* **ablly ablmy abily**

abillpst spitball. *See* **ailpst**

abillpy pliably. *See* **ablly abily billy**

abillssw sawbills sawbill. *See* **abilss illssw**

abillsw sawbill. *See* **abils ablls ablsw**

abilmnu albumin. *See* **ailmnu abilmu**

abilmox mailbox. *See* **abilo aimox bilmo**

abilmst timbals. *See* **abilmt abimst**

abilmt timbal ambit alit bail bait balm blat iamb lamb limb mail malt milt tail tali ail aim alb alt bam bat bit ita lab lam lit mat mil tab tam til ai am at ba it la li ma mi ta ti

abilmu labium album alum bail balm iamb lamb limb mail maul ail aim alb bam bum lab lam lum mil ai am ba la li ma mi mu um

abiln blain anil bail bani lain nail ail alb ani ban bin lab nab nib nil ai an ba in la li na

abilno albino blain aboil anil bail bani boil lain lion loan loin nail noil ail alb ani ban bin boa ion lab lob nab nib nil nob obi oil ai an ba in la li lo na no on

abilnoot oblation. *See* **abilno abinot ailnot binoot**

abilnopr panbroil bipolar parboil. *See* **abilno alnopr**

abilnos albinos. *See* **abilno abilns abinos**

abilnotu ablution bailout. *See* **abilno abilnot ailnot**

abilnrtu tribunal. *See* **abilrt abilru ablrtu abnrtu**

abilns blains anils bails basil basin blain nails sabin slain snail ails albs anil bail bani bans bias bins labs lain nabs nail nibs nils sail sain slab ail alb ani ban bin lab nab nib nil sal sib sin ai an as ba in is la li na si

abilo aboil bail boil ail alb boa lab lob obi oil ai ba la li lo

abilopr bipolar parboil. *See* **abilo ablor abilr**

abiloprs parboils bipolar parboil. *See* **abilrs abiors ablors ailors**

abilorsv bolivars bolivar. *See* **abilrs abiors ablors aborsv**

abilort orbital. *See* **ailort abilrt**

abilorv bolivar. *See* **abilo ablor aborv**

abilostu bailouts bailout. *See* **ablost biostu**

abilotu bailout. *See* **abilo abotu abiot**

abilr brail libra aril bail birl lair liar lira rail rial ail air alb bar bra lab lar ria rib ai ba la li

abilrry library. *See* **abirry abily abilr**

abilrs brails arils bails basil birls brail lairs liars libra liras rails rials ails airs albs aril bail bars bias birl bras labs lair liar lira rail rial rias ribs sail sari slab ail air alb bar bra lab lar ria rib sal sib sir ai as ba is la li si

abilrsu burials. *See* **abirsu abilrs abilru ablrsu**

abilrsz brazils. *See* **abilrs abilrz**

abilrt tribal brail libra trail trial alit aril bail bait birl blat brat brit lair liar lira rail rial tail tali ail air alb alt art bar bat bit bra ita lab lar lit rat ria rib tab tar til ai at ba it la li ta ti

abilru burial brail libra aril bail birl blur burl lair liar lira rail rial ail air alb bar bra lab lar ria rib rub ai ba la li

abilrz brazil brail libra aril bail birl lair liar lira rail rial ail air alb bar bra lab lar ria rib ai ba la li

abils bails basil ails albs bail bias labs sail slab ail alb lab sal sib ai as ba is la li si

abilss basils bails basil basis bliss sails sisal slabs ails albs bail bass bias labs lass sail sals sibs slab ail alb ass lab sal sib sis ai as ba is la li si

abilstuy suitably. *See* **bilsuy blstuy**

abilsyz sizably. *See* **abils abily bilsy**

abily bialy bail ably aby ail alb bay lab lay ai ay ba by la li

abim iamb aim bam ai am ba ma mi

abimnrsu urbanism. *See* **abimru abimsu abinrs abirsu**

abimpsst baptisms baptism. *See* **abimst ampsst**

abimpst baptism. *See* **abimst aipst ampst**

abimru barium rumba umbra amir barm brim iamb rami aim air arm bam bar bra bum mar mir ram ria rib rim rub rum ai am ba ma mi mu um

abims iambs aims bams bias aim bam mis sib ai am as ba is ma mi si

abimst ambits ambit baits iambs aims bait bams bast bats bias bits iamb mast mats mist stab tabs tams aim

bam bat bit ita its mat mis sat sib sit tab tam ai am as at ba is it ma mi si ta ti

abimsu iambus iambs aims bams bias bums iamb aim bam bum bus mis mus sib sub sum ai am as ba is ma mi mu si um us

abimt ambit bait iamb aim bam bat bit ita mat tab tam ai am at ba it ma mi ta ti

abin bani ani ban bin nab nib ai an ba in na

abinoort abortion oration. *See* **abinot ainort anoort binoot**

abinorsw rainbows rainbow warison. *See* **abinos abinrs abiors abnors**

abinorw rainbow. *See* **abinr abnor abnrw**

abinos bonsai basin bison sabin bani bans bias bins boas ions nabs naos nibs nobs obis sain snob ani ban bin boa ion nab nib nob obi sib sin sob son ai an as ba in is na no on os si so

abinosst bastions bastion obtains. *See* **abinos abinot abinss abnost**

abinost bastion obtains. *See* **abnost abinos abinot**

abinostt botanist bastion obtains station. *See* **abinos abinot abnost ainstt**

abinot obtain biota baton anti bait bani boat into iota nota obit ani ant ban bat bin bit boa bot ion ita nab nib nit nob not oat obi tab tan tin ton ai an at ba in it na no on ta ti to

abinr bairn brain bani barn bran rain rani air ani ban bar bin bra nab nib ran ria rib ai an ba in na

abinrs bairns brains bairn barns basin brain brans naris rains ranis sabin airs bani bans barn bars bias bins bran bras nabs nibs rain rani rias ribs sain sari air ani ban bar bin bra nab nib ran ria rib sib sin sir ai an as ba in is na si

abinrstu urbanist turbans nutrias. *See* **abinrs abirsu abnrsu abnrtu**

abinrtuy urbanity unitary. *See* **abinry abnrtu ainrtu**

abinrtv vibrant. *See* **abinr ainrt**

abinry binary brainy bairn brain briny rainy airy ayin bani barn bran bray nary rain rani yarn aby air ani any ban bar bay bin bra nab nay nib ran ray ria rib yar yin ai an ay ba by in na

abins basin sabin bani bans bias bins nabs nibs sain sani ban bin nab nib sib sin ai an as ba in is na si

abinss basins sabins basin basis sabin bani bans bass bias bins nabs nibs sain sibs sins ani ass ban bin nab nib sib sin sis ai an as ba in is na si

abiorr　barrio briar arbor birr boar bora roar air bar boa bra oar obi orb ria rib rob ai ba or

abiorrs　barrios. *See* aborrs abiorr abirrs abiors

abiorrst　arborist barrios. *See* abiorr abiors abirrs aborrs

abiorrtv　vibrator vibrato. *See* abiorr

abiors　isobar boars boras airs bars bias boar boas bora bras oars obis orbs rias ribs robs sari soar sora sorb sori air bar boa bra oar obi orb ria rib rob sib sir sob ai as ba is or os si so

abiorss　isobars. *See* abiors airss abiss

abiorstv　vibratos vibrato travois. *See* abiors aborst aborsv aiorst

abiortuy　obituary. *See* abortu

abiortv　vibrato. *See* abort abiot aborv

abiot　biota bait boat iota obit bat bit boa bot ita oat obi tab ai at ba it ta ti to

abipsstt　baptists baptist. *See* aipss abist abiss

abipstt　baptist. *See* abist bistt aipst

abirr　briar birr air bar bra ria rib ba ai

abirrs　briars arris birrs briar airs bars bias birr bras rias ribs sari air bar bra ria rib sib sir ai as ba is si

abirrstu　airburst. *See* abirrs abirsu abrrsu birstu

abirry　briary briar airy birr bray aby air bar bay bra ray ria rib yar ai ay ba by

abirsu　airbus bursa airs bars bias bras rias ribs rubs sari sura air bar bra bus ria rib rub sib sir sub ai as ba is si us

abis　bias sib ai as ba is si

abiss　basis bass bias sibs ass sib sis ai as ba is si

abisssst　bassists bassist assists. *See* aissst

abissst　bassist. *See* aissst

abist　baits bait bast bats bias bits stab tabs bat bit ita its sat sib sit tab ai as at ba is it si ta ti

abit　bait bat bit ita tab ai at ba it ta ti

abj　jab ba

abjlmsu　jumbals. *See* abjlmu ablmsu

abjlmu　jumbal album alum balm jamb juba lamb maul alb bam bum jab jam lab lam lum am ba la ma mu um

abjm　jamb bam jab jam am ba ma

abjms　jambs bams jabs jamb jams bam jab jam am as ba ma

abjno　banjo ban boa jab job nab nob an ba jo na no on

abjnos　banjos banjo bans boas jabs jobs nabs naos nobs snob ban boa jab job nab nob sob son an as ba jo na no on os so

abjost　jabots boast boats jabot jatos jotas sabot bast bats boas boat bots jabs jato jobs jota jots oast oats stab stoa stob tabs bat boa bot jab job jot oat sat sob sot tab as at ba jo os so ta to

abjot　jabot boat jato jota bat boa bot jab job jot oat tab at ba jo ta to

abjs　jabs jab as ba

abju　juba jab ba

abk　kab ba ka

abkkmoor　bookmark. *See* bkoor bmoor akoor

abkl　balk alb kab kal lab ba ka la

abkllnor　bankroll. *See* abnor abkln ablor

abkllny　blankly. *See* akllny abkly ablly

abkln　blank balk bank lank alb ban kab kal lab nab an ba ka la na

abklns　blanks balks banks blank albs balk bank bans bask kabs labs lank nabs sank slab alb ask ban kab kal kas lab nab sal an as ba ka la na

abkloopy　playbook. *See* abkly blooy loopy

abkloosw　lawbooks lawbook. *See* abkls ablsw blosw

abkloow　lawbook. *No 6s or 5s*

abklrsuw　bulwarks bulwark. *See* ablrsu ablrsw

abklruw　bulwark. *See* ablrw

abkls　balks albs balk bask kabs labs slab alb ask kab kal kas lab sal as ba ka la

abkly　balky ably balk laky aby alb bay kab kal lab lay yak ay ba by ka la

abkmnoo　bookman. *No 6s or 5s*

abkn　bank ban kab nab an ba ka na

abknnosw　snowbank. *See* abkns abnns bknos

abknprtu　bankrupt. *See* abnrtu abprtu

abknrs　branks banks barks barns brans knars narks ranks snark arks bank bans bark barn bars bask bran bras kabs knar nabs nark rank sank sark ark ask ban bar bra kab kas nab ran an as ba ka na

abkns　banks bank bans bask kabs nabs sank ask ban kab kas nab an as ba ka na

abkoopss　passbook. *See* koopss

abkr　bark ark bar bra kab ba ka

abkrs　barks arks bark bars bask bras kabs sark ark ask bar bra kab kas as ba ka

abks　bask kabs ask kab kas as ba ka

abkss　basks asks bask bass kabs ask ass kab kas as ba ka

abl　alb lab ba la

abll　ball alb all lab ba la

ablllluy　lullaby. *See* ablly abllu blluy

abllmoor　ballroom. *See* ablmoo

abllnoo　balloon. *See* allno

abllnoos　balloons balloon. *See* allnos alnoos

abllnosw　snowball. *See* allnos allosw

abllorsu　sourball labours. *See* ablors abloru ablrsu

abllost　ballots. *See* allost abllot ablost

abllosty　tallboys ballots tallboy. *See* abllot abllsy ablost allost

abllot　ballot allot atoll bloat alto ball blat blot boat boll bolt lota olla tall tola toll alb all alt bat boa bot lab lob lot oat tab at ba la lo ta to

ablloty　tallboy. *See* abllot alloy ablly

abllovy　lovably. *See* alloy ablly

abllrtuy　brutally. *See* ablrtu

ablls　balls albs ball labs slab alb all lab sal as ba la

abllssuy　syllabus. *See* abllsy

abllsy　ballsy balls bally sally ably albs ally ball bays labs lays slab slay aby alb all bay lab lay sal say sly as ay ba by la

abllu　bulla ball bull alb all lab ba la

ablly　bally ably ally ball aby alb all bay lab lay ay ba by la

ablm　balm lamb alb bam lab lam am ba la ma

ablmoo　abloom moola bloom ambo balm bolo boom lamb loam lobo loom mola alb bam boa boo lab lam lob loo moa mob moo am ba la lo ma mo om

ablmop　aplomb ambo balm lamb lamp loam mola opal palm alb alp amp bam boa bop lab lam lap lob lop map moa mob mop pal am ba la lo ma mo om pa

ablmpsuu　pabulums pabulum. *See* ablmsu almpsu blmpsu

ablmpuu　pabulum. *See* ablmu almpu blmpu

ablmru　brumal labrum lumbar album mural rumba umbra alum balm barm blur burl lamb marl maul alb arm bam bar bra bum lab lam lar lum mar ram rub rum am ba la ma mu um

ablmry　marbly ambry balmy barmy marly ably amyl army aryl balm barm bray lamb marl aby alb arm bam bar bay bra lab lam lar lay mar may ram ray yam yar am ay ba by la ma my

ablms　balms lambs albs alms balm bams labs lamb lams slab slam alb bam lab lam sal am as ba la ma

ablmsu　albums album alums balms lambs mauls albs alms alum balm bams bums labs lamb lams maul slab slam slub slum alb bam bum bus lab lam lum mus sal sub sum am as ba la ma mu um us

ablmtuy　mutably. *See* ablmu ablmy bltuy

ablmu　album alum balm lamb maul alb bam bum lab lam lum am ba la ma mu um

ablmy   balmy ably amyl balm lamb aby alb bam bay lab lam lay may yam am ay ba by la ma my

ablnoryz   blazonry. *See* ablnoz abnory anoryz

ablnosz   blazons. *See* ablnoz alnosz

ablnoty   notably. *See* abnoty ablot blnoty

ablnoz   blazon zonal loan alb azo ban boa lab lob nab nob zoa an ba la lo na no on

abloorst   barstool. *See* ablors ablost aboost aborst

abloprvy   provably. *See* aoprvy

ablopsyy   playboys playboy. *See* ablos alops alpsy

ablopyy   playboy. *No 6s or 5s*

abloqtuy   quotably. *See* aloqtu alotuy

ablor   boral labor lobar boar bora oral alb bar boa bra lab lar lob oar orb rob ba la lo or

ablors   borals labors boars bolas boral boras labor lobar orals solar albs also bars boar boas bora bras labs lobs oars oral orbs robs slab slob soar sora sorb alb bar boa bra lab lar lob los oar orb rob sal sob sol as ba la lo or os so

ablorsu   labours. *See* ablors ablrsu abloru

abloru   labour boral labor lobar blur boar bora burl oral alb bar boa bra lab lar lob oar orb our rob rub ba la lo or

ablos   bolas albs also boas labs lobs slab slob alb boa lab lob los sal sob sol as ba la lo os so

ablosst   oblasts. *See* ablsst ablost abosst

ablost   bloats oblast altos blast blats bloat blots boast boats bolas bolts lotas sabot tolas albs also alto alts bast bats blat blot boas boat bolt bots labs last lobs lost lota lots oast oats salt slab slat slob slot stab stoa stob tabs tola alb alt bat boa bot lab lob los lot oat sal sat sob sol sot tab as at ba la lo os so ta to

ablosttu   subtotal outlast. *See* ablost alostt

ablot   bloat alto blat blot boat bolt lota tola alb alt bat boa bot lab lob lot oat tab at ba la lo ta to

ablprsu   burlaps. *See* ablpru ablrsu alprsu

ablprtuy   abruptly. *See* ablpru ablrtu abprtu alprty

ablpru   burlap blur burl burp purl alb alp bar bra lab lap lar pal par pub pul rap rub ba la pa up

ablrsu   bursal blurs burls bursa slurb albs bars blur bras burl labs rubs slab slub slur sura alb bar bra bus lab lar rub sal sub as ba la us

ablrsw   brawls bawls brawl albs awls bars bawl bras braw labs laws slab swab wars alb awl bar bra lab lar law raw sal saw war was as aw ba la

ablrtu   brutal blurt tubal ultra abut blat blur brat burl tabu tuba alb alt art bar bat bra but lab lar rat rub rut tab tar tau tub at ba la ta ut

ablrtuu   tubular. *See* ablrtu

ablrw   brawl bawl braw alb awl bar bra lab lar law raw war aw ba la

abls   albs labs slab alb lab sal as ba la

ablss   slabs albs bass labs lass sals slab alb ass lab sal as ba la

ablsst   blasts basts blast blats lasts salts slabs slats stabs albs alts bass bast bats blat labs lass last sals salt slab slat stab tabs tass alb alt ass bat lab sal sat tab as at ba la ta

ablst   blast blats albs alts bast bats blat labs last salt slab slat stab tabs alb alt bat lab sal sat tab as at ba la ta

ablsw   bawls albs awls bawl labs laws slab swab alb awl lab law sal saw was as aw ba la

ablswy   bylaws bawls bylaw yawls ably albs awls bawl bays labs laws lays slab slay swab sway ways yawl yaws aby alb awl bay lab law lay sal saw say sly was way yaw as aw ay ba by la

ablt   blat alb alt bat lab tab at ba la ta

abltu   tubal abut blat tabu tuba alb alt bat but lab tab tau tub at ba la ta ut

ablw   bawl alb awl law aw ba la

ablwy   bylaw ably bawl yawl aby alb awl bay lab law lay way yaw aw ay ba by la

ably   ably aby alb bay lab lay ay ba by la

abm   bam am ba ma

abmmo   mambo ambo ammo bam boa moa mob mom am ba ma mo om

abmmos   mambos mambo ambos ambo ammo bams boas moas mobs moms soma bam boa moa mob mom mos oms sob am as ba ma mo om os so

abmnow   bowman woman ambo moan mown noma womb awn bam ban boa bow man maw moa mob mon mow nab nob now own wan won am an aw ba ma mo na no om on ow

abmnsu   busman manus numbs anus bams bans bums buns maun nabs nubs numb snub bam ban bam bum bun bus man mus nab nub sub sum sun am an as ba ma mu na nu um us

abmo   ambo bam boa moa mob am ba ma mo om

abmoorr   barroom. *See* aborr amorr bmoor

abmoorrs   barrooms barroom. *See* aborrs amorrs bmoors moorrs

abmorstu   tambours rubatos tabours tambour. *See* abmrsu aborst abortu amorsu

abmortu   tambour. *See* abortu

abmos   ambos ambo bams boas moas mobs soma bam boa moa mob mos oms sob am as ba ma mo om os so

abmostw   wombats. *See* abmotw abmos amost

abmotw   wombat ambo atom boat moat tomb womb bam bat boa bot bow mat maw moa mob mot mow oat tab tam tom tow two am at aw ba ma mo om ow ta to

abmr   barm arm bam bar bra mar ram am ba ma

abmrsu   rumbas umbras bursa ramus rumba umbra arms bams barm bars bras bums rams rubs rums sura arm bam bar bra bum bus mar mus ram rub rum sub sum am as ba ma mu um us

abmru   rumba umbra barm arm bam bar bra bum mar ram rub rum am ba ma mu um

abmry   ambry barmy army barm bray aby arm bam bar bay bra mar may ram ray yam yar am ay ba by ma my

abms   bams bam am as ba ma

abmssy   abysms abysm abyss massy bams bass bays mass says yams aby ass bam bay may say yam am as ay ba by ma my

abmsy   abysm bams bays yams aby bam bay may say yam am as ay ba by ma my

abn   ban nab an ba na

abnnry   branny barn bran bray nary yarn aby any ban bar bay bra nab nay ran ray yar an ay ba by na

abnns   banns bans nabs ban nab an as ba na

abnooss   bassoon. *See* bnoos bnoss

abnor   baron barn boar bora born bran roan ban bar boa bra nab nob nor oar orb ran rob an ba na no on or

abnors   barons arson barns baron boars boras brans roans sonar bans barn bars boar boas bora born bran bras nabs naos nobs oars orbs roan robs snob soar sora sorb ban bar boa bra nab nob nor oar orb ran rob sob son an as ba na no or os so

abnorsy   baryons. *See* abnors abnory aborsy anorsy

abnortuu   runabout burnout. *See* abnrtu abortu anortu bnortu

abnory   barony baryon baron boyar rayon barn boar bony bora born bran bray nary orby roan yarn aby any ban bar bay boa boy bra nab nay nob nor oar orb ran ray rob yar yob yon an ay ba by na no on or oy

abnost   batons baton boast boats sabot ants bans bast bats boas boat bots nabs naos nobs nota oast oats snob snot stab stoa stob tabs tans tons ant ban bat boa bot nab nob not oat sat sob son sot tab tan ton an as at ba na no on os so ta to

abnot   baton boat nota ant ban bat boa bot nab nob not oat tab tan ton an at ba na no on ta to

abnotuy   buoyant. *See* **abnoty bnotuy**

abnoty   botany baton atony boat bony nota tony aby ant any ban bat bay boa bot boy nab nay nob not oat tab tan ton toy yob yon an at ay ba by na no on oy ta to

abnr   barn bran ban bar bra nab ran an ba na

abnrs   barns brans bans barn bars bran bras nabs ban bar bra nab ran an as ba na

abnrstu   turbans. *See* **bnrstu abnrsu abnrtu**

abnrsu   burans barns brans buran burns bursa urban anus bans barn bars bran bras buns burn nabs nubs rubs runs snub sura urns ban bar bra bun bus nab nub ran rub run sub sun urn an as ba na nu us

abnrsuu   auburns. *See* **abnrsu abnruu**

abnrtu   turban brunt buran burnt urban abut aunt barn bran brat bunt burn rant runt tabu tuba tuna turn ant art ban bar bat bra bun but nab nub nut ran rat rub run rut tab tan tar tau tub tun urn an at ba na nu ta ut

abnru   buran urban barn bran burn ban bar bra bun nab nub rub run urn an ba na nu

abnruu   auburn buran urban barn bran burn ban bar bra bun nab nub ran rub run urn an ba na nu

abnrw   brawn barn bran braw warn awn ban bar bra nab ran raw wan war an aw ba na

abnrwy   brawny brawn awry barn bran braw bray nary wany warn wary yarn yawn aby any awn ban bar bay bra nab nay ran raw ray wan war way yar yaw an aw ay ba by na

abns   bans nabs ban nab an as ba na

abo   boa ba

aboopsx   soapbox. *No 6s or 5s*

aboorstw   rowboats rowboat. *See* **aboost aborst boorst**

aboortw   rowboat. *See* **abort aboot**

aboost   taboos boast boats boost boots sabot taboo bast bats boas boat boos boot bots oast oats soot stab stoa stob tabs bat boa boo bot oat sat sob sot tab too as at ba os so ta to

aboosttw   towboats towboat. *See* **aboost**

aboosz   bazoos bazoo bozos boas boos bozo zoos azo boa boo sob zoa zoo as ba os so

aboot   taboo boat boot bat boa boo bot oat tab too at ba ta to

aboottw   towboat. *See* **aboot**

abooz   bazoo bozo azo boa boo zoa zoo ba

abor   boar bora bar boa bra oar orb rob ba or

aborr   arbor boar bora roar bar boa bra oar orb rob ba or

aborrs   arbors arbor boars boras roars bars boar boas bora bras oars orbs roar robs soar sora sorb bar boa bra oar orb rob sob as ba or os so

aborrsw   barrows. *See* **aborrs aorrsw aborrw**

aborrw   barrow arbor arrow boar bora braw brow roar bar boa bow bra oar orb raw rob row war aw ba or ow

abors   boars boras bars boar boas bora bras oars orbs robs soar sora sorb bar boa bra oar orb rob sob as ba or os so

aborst   aborts tabors abort boars boast boats boras borts brats roast rotas sabot tabor taros toras arts bars bast bats boar boas boat bora bort bots bras brat oars oast oats orbs orts rats robs rota rots soar sora sorb sort stab star stoa stob tabs taro tars tora tors tsar art bar bat boa bot bra oar oat orb ort rat rob rot sat sob sot tab tar tor as at ba or os so ta to

aborstu   rubatos tabours. *See* **aborst borstu abortu**

aborsv   bravos boars boras bravo savor bars boar boas bora bras oars orbs robs soar sora sorb bar boa bra oar orb ova rob sob as ba or os so

aborsy   boyars boars boras boyar brays bars bays boar boas bora boys bras bray oars orbs orby rays robs rosy soar sora sorb yobs aby bar bay boa boy bra oar orb ray rob say sob soy yar yob as ay ba by or os oy so

abort   abort tabor boar boat bora bort brat rota taro tora art bar bat boa bot bra oar oat orb ort rat rob rot tab tar tor at ba or ta to

abortu   rubato tabour abort about tabor abut auto boar boat bora bort bout brat rota rout tabu taro tora tour tuba art bar bat boa bot bra but oar oat orb

ort our out rat rob rot rub rut tab tar tau tor tub at ba or ta to ut

aborv   bravo boar bora bar boa bra oar orb ova rob ba or

aborx   borax boar bora bar boa box bra oar orb rob ax ba or ox

abory   boyar boar bora bray orby aby bar bay boa boy bra oar orb ray rob yar yob ay ba by or oy

abos   boas boa sob as ba os so

abosst   boasts sabots basts boast boats oasts sabot stabs stoas stobs bass bast bats boas boat boss bots oast oats ossa sobs sots stab stoa stob tabs tass toss ass bat boa bot oat sat sob sot tab as at ba os so ta to

abost   boast boats sabot bast bats boas boat bots oast oats stab stoa stob tabs bat boa bot oat sat sob sot tab as at ba os so ta to

abostuu   autobus. *See* **abotu abstu aostu**

abosuy   bayous bayou buoys bays boas boys buoy busy buys yobs aby bay boa boy bus buy say sob sou soy sub yob you as ay ba by os oy so us

abot   boat bat boa bot oat tab at ba ta to

abotu   about abut auto boat bout tabu tuba bat boa bot but oat out tab tau tub at ba ta to ut

abouy   bayou buoy aby bay boa boy buy yob you ay ba by oy

abprtu   abrupt abut brat burp part rapt tabu tarp trap tuba apt art bar bat bra but par pat pub put rap rat rub rut tab tap tar tau tub tup at ba pa ta up ut

abpssy   bypass abyss spays asps bass bays pass pays pyas saps says spas spay yaps aby asp ass bay pas pay pya sap say spa spy yap as ay ba by pa

abqssu   squabs squab quass bass buss subs ass bus qua sub as ba us

abqsu   squab bus qua sub as ba us

abr   bar bra ba

abrrssu   bursars. *See* **abrrsu abrssu**

abrrsu   bursar bursa burrs bars bras burr rubs sura bra bus rub sub as ba us

abrrsuy   bursary. *See* **abrrsu abrsy arsuy**

abrs   bars bras bar bra as ba

abrss   brass bars bass bras ass bar bra as ba

abrssu   bursas brass bursa suras bars bass bras buss rubs subs sura ass bar bra bus rub sub as ba us

abrssy   brassy abyss brass brays bars bass bays bras bray rays says aby ass bar bay bra ray say yar as ay ba by

abrst   brats arts bars bast bats bras brat rats stab star tabs tars tsar art bar bat bra rat sat tab tar as at ba ta

abrsu bursa bars bras rubs sura bar bra bus rub sub as ba us

abrsy brays bars bays bras bray rays aby bar bay bra ray say yar as ay ba by

abrt brat art bar bat bra rat tab tar at ba ta

abrtty bratty batty ratty arty brat bray tart tray aby art bar bat bay bra rat ray tab tar tat try yar at ay ba by ta

abrw braw bar bra raw war ba aw

abrxy braxy bray aby bar bay bra ray yar ax ay ba by

abry bray aby bar bay bra ray yar ay ba by

abss bass ass as ba

absst basts stabs bass bast bats stab tabs tass ass bat sat tab as at ba ta

abssuwy subways. *See* **absuwy abssy abssw**

abssw swabs bass saws swab ass saw was as aw ba

abssy abyss bass bays says aby ass bay say as ay ba by

abst bast bats stab tabs bat sat tab as at ba ta

abstu abuts tubas abut bast bats bust buts stab stub tabs tabu tuba tubs bat bus but sat sub tab tau tub as at ba ta us ut

absuwy subway bays busy buys swab sway ways yaws aby bay bus buy saw say sub was way yaw as aw ba by us

absw swab saw was as aw ba

abswyy byways byway bays swab sway ways yaws aby bay saw say was way yaw yay as aw ay ba by

absy bays aby bay say as ay ba by

abt bat tab at ba ta

abtty batty aby bat bay tab tat at ay ba by ta

abtu abut tabu tuba bat but tab tau tub at ba ta ut

abuzz abuzz buzz ba

abwyy byway aby bay way yaw yay aw ay ba by

aby aby bay ay ba by

---

acccil calcic laic lac ail ai la li

acccily acyclic. *See* **acccil cccily**

accddee acceded. *See* **accdee acddee**

accddeen cadenced acceded cadence. *See* **accdee acddee acdden addeen**

accddeor accorded. *See* **accdor addeor acdder cddeor**

accddiit didactic. *See* **accdii acddit**

accdee accede aced cade ceca cede dace ace cad cee ad ae

accdeeln canceled cadence cenacle cleaned. *See* **accdee acceln acdeln adeeln**

accdeen cadence. *See* **accdee acden**

accdeens cadences accedes cadence encased. *See* **accdee acdees acdens aceens**

accdeent accented cadence enacted. *See* **accdee accent acdent aceent**

accdeept accepted. *See* **accdee accept acdeep adeept**

accdeert accreted accrete catered cerated created reacted. *See* **accdee acdert aceert**

accdees accedes. *See* **accdee acdees**

accdeess accessed accedes. *See* **accdee access acdees aceess**

accdegin acceding. *See* **adegin cdegin**

accdeh cached cache ached aced ache cade ceca dace each hade head ace cad edh had hae ad ae ah eh ha he

accdehil chaliced chalice. *See* **accdeh acceil adehil ccehil**

accdehin chicaned chained chanced chicane cinched. *See* **accdeh accehn cdehin**

accdehn chanced. *See* **accdeh accehn**

accdeho coached. *See* **accdeh accho**

accdeily delicacy. *See* **acceil acdily ccdely**

accdeint accident. *See* **acceit accent acdent adeint**

accdeirt accredit. *See* **acceit accirt acdert adeirt**

accdeisu caudices accused. *See* **accesu acdesu adeisu**

accdekl cackled clacked. *See* **accekl acdekl**

accdeklr crackled cackled clacked cracked crackle. *See* **accekl acdekl acdekr acdelr**

accdeko cockade. *See* **ccdeko accko acdek**

accdekos cockades cockade seacock. *See* **acdeks adekos ccdeko cdekos**

accdekr cracked. *See* **acdekr**

accdenov concaved concave. *See* **acdeno**

accdeny cadency. *See* **acden acdny accdy**

accdeost accosted coacted coasted decocts. *See* **accost acdeot acdest acdost**

accdeot coacted. *See* **acdeot ccdeot**

accderu accrued. *See* **acceru acder cderu**

accdesu accused. *See* **accesu acdesu**

accdesuu caduceus caucused accused. *See* **accesu acdesu**

accdfil flaccid. *No 6s or 5s*

accdii acidic acid cadi cad aid ad ai id

accdils scaldic. *See* **acdis adils acdls**

accdilty dactylic. *See* **accilt acdily acdlty**

accdioor coracoid. *See* **accdor**

accdor accord card coca coda cord orad road ado arc cad car cod cor doc dor oar orc rad roc rod ad do od or

accdors accords. *See* **accdor acdrs accos**

accdsy cycads cycad cads cays days scad ads cad cay day sac sad say ad as ay

accdy cycad cad cay day ad ay

acce ceca ace ae

acceehlo cochleae cochlea. *See* **aceehl ccehlo**

acceeils ecclesia calices. *See* **acceil accels**

acceekln necklace cenacle. *See* **accekl acceln**

acceeln cenacle. *See* **acceln**

acceelnr canceler clarence cenacle cleaner. *See* **acceln accenr aceelr aceenr**

acceelns cenacles cancels cenacle cleanse scalene. *See* **acceln accels aceens acelns**

acceelos coalesce. *See* **accels acelos**

acceerst accretes accrete creates. *See* **accers aceers aceert acerst**

acceert accrete. *See* **aceert**

acceesss accesses. *See* **access aceess**

accefils fascicle calices. *See* **acceil accels acefil acefis**

acceflsu feluccas felucca saccule. *See* **accels accesu acefsu acelsu**

acceflu felucca. *See* **acefl**

accegkmo gamecock. *See* **accko acemo cegko**

acceh   cache ache ceca each ace hae ae ah eh ha he

accehhkt   hatcheck. *See* **acceent acehht**

accehikp   chickpea. *See* **acceip acehik**

accehil   chalice. *See* **acceil ccehil**

accehilm   chemical chalice. *See* **acceil aceilm aehilm ccehil**

accehilp   cephalic chalice. *See* **acceil acceip acehlp aceilp**

accehils   chalices chalice calices. *See* **accehs acceil accels acehis**

accehimn   mechanic chicane machine. *See* **accehn aceimn ccehim**

accehin   chicane. *See* **accehn achin cehin**

accehins   chicanes chances chicane cinches. *See* **accehn accehs acehis aceins**

accehirt   catchier catcher. *See* **acceht acceit acchrt accirt**

accehkpy   paycheck. *See* **acehpy**

accehln   chancel. *See* **acceln accehn ccehln**

accehlns   chancels cancels chancel chances. *See* **accehn accehs acceln accels**

accehlo   cochlea. *See* **ccehlo acceh acehl**

accehmno   coachmen conchae. *See* **accehn acchno**

accehn   chance cache ache acne cane ceca each ace ane can hae hen nae nah ae ah an eh en ha he na ne

accehno   conchae. *See* **accehn acchno**

accehnor   encroach caroche chancre conchae. *See* **accehn accenr acchno acehor**

accehnr   chancre. *See* **accehn accenr**

accehnrs   chancres cancers chances chancre ranches. *See* **accehn accehs accenr accers**

accehnry   chancery chancre. *See* **accehn accenr acchny acenry**

accehns   chances. *See* **accehn accehs**

accehopt   cachepot. *See* **acceht accept acehop acehpt**

accehor   caroche. *See* **acehor acceh accho**

accehors   caroches caroche coaches roaches. *See* **accehs accers acehor acehrs**

accehos   coaches. *See* **accehs achos cehos**

accehpsu   capuches capuche. *See* **accehs accesu acehps**

accehpu   capuche. *See* **acceh acehp**

accehrst   catchers cratches cachets catcher catches scratch. *See* **accehs acceht accers acchrt**

accehrt   catcher. *See* **acceht acchrt**

accehs   caches aches cache chase aces ache case cash ceca each ace ash hae has sac sea she ae ah as eh ha he sh

accehst   cachets catches. *See* **accehs acceht acehst**

acceht   cachet cache catch cheat tache teach theca ache cate ceca chat each etch hate heat tach tech ace act aet ate cat eat eta eth hae hat het tea the ae ah at eh ha he ta

accehtu   catechu. *See* **acceht acetu cehtu**

accehxy   cachexy. *See* **acceh**

acceil   celiac ileac ceca ceil lace laic lice ace ail ale ice lac lea lei lie ae ai el la li

acceillr   clerical. *See* **acceil aceilr acellr cceilr**

acceillv   clavicle. *See* **acceil**

acceilnt   canticle calcite. *See* **acceil acceit acceln accent**

acceilrv   cervical caviler clavier. *See* **acceil aceilr acelrv cceilr**

acceils   calices. *See* **acceil accels**

acceilt   calcite. *See* **acceit acceil accilt**

acceimr   ceramic. *See* **aceim aceir cceir**

acceimrs   ceramics ceramic. *See* **accers aceims aceirs acemrs**

acceino   cocaine oceanic. *See* **aceno ccino**

acceinsv   vaccines vaccine. *See* **aceins aceisv aeinsv cceins**

acceinv   vaccine. *See* **aeinv**

acceiotv   coactive. *See* **acceit aceitv aceotv**

acceip   icecap ipecac cape ceca epic pace pica pice ace ape cap cep ice pea pie ae ai pa pe pi

acceipr   caprice. *See* **acceip**

acceiprs   caprices caprice icecaps. *See* **acceip accers aceips**

acceiprt   practice caprice. *See* **acceip acceit accept**

acceips   icecaps. *See* **aceips acceip**

acceiqsu   caciques cacique caiques. *See* **accesu aceiqu**

acceiqu   cacique. *See* **aceiqu**

acceirsu   curacies accrues accuser saucier. *See* **accers acceru accesu aceirs**

acceirtu   cruciate. *See* **acceit acceru accirt aceiru**

acceisst   ascetics ascetic. *See* **acceit access acesst aeisst**

acceist   ascetic. *See* **acceit acest ceist**

acceistt   ecstatic ascetic tactics. *See* **acceit accitt acesst acistt**

acceit   acetic cacti cate ceca cite ace act aet ate cat eat eta ice ita tea tic tie ae ai at it ta ti

accekl   cackle clack cake calk ceca kale lace lack lake leak ace ale elkkal lac lea lek ae el ka la

acceklnr   cracknel crackle. *See* **accekl acceln accenr acek
nr**

acceklr   crackle. *See* **accekl acelr ceklr**

acceklrs   crackles cackles crackle slacker. *See* **accekl accels accers acckls**

acceklss   cackles. *See* **acceckl accels acckls**

accekop   peacock. *See* **ccekop accko**

accekops   peacocks copecks peacock seacock. *See* **ccekop**

accekos   seacock. *See* **accko aceks accos**

accekoss   seacocks seacock cassock. *See* **access**

accekpsu   cupcakes cupcake. *See* **accesu**

accekpu   cupcake. *No 6s or 5s*

accekrr   cracker. *See* **acckr acekr acerr**

accekrrs   crackers cracker scarcer. *See* **accers acckrs acekrs acerrs**

acceln   cancel clean lance acne cane ceca clan lace lane lean ace ale ane can lac lea nae ae an el en la na ne

accelno   conceal. *See* **acceln aelno aceno**

accelnos   conceals conceal cancels. *See* **acceln accels acelns acelos**

accelnov   conclave conceal concave. *See* **acceln acelov celnov**

accelnru   caruncle lucarne nuclear unclear. *See* **acceln accenr acceru acelnr**

accelns   cancels. *See* **accels acceln acelns**

accelor   coracle. *See* **acelor**

accelors   coracles coalers coracle oracles. *See* **accels accers acelor acelos**

accelrsy   scarcely. *See* **accels accers acelrs acersy**

accelrtu   clearcut. *See* **acceru acelrt acertu celrtu**

accels   calces laces scale aces ales case ceca lace leas sale seal ace ale els lac lea sac sal sea ae as el la

accelssu   saccules accuses clauses saccule. *See* **accels access accesu acelss**

accelsu   saccule. *See* **accesu accels acelsu**

accennsy   nascency. *See* **acens acnny aenns**

accenost   cosecant accents octanes. *See* **accent accost acenos acenot**

accenosv   concaves concave. *See* **acenos cenosv**

accenov   concave. *See* **aceno cenov aenov**

accenpt   peccant. *See* **accent accept**

accenr   cancer caner crane nacre acne acre cane care ceca earn narc nearrace ace ane arc are can car ear era nae ran rec ae an en er na ne re

accenrs   cancers. *See* **accenr acenrs accers**

accenst   accents. *See* **accent acenst**

accent   accent enact acne ante cane cant cate ceca cent neat ace act aetane ant ate can cat eat eta nae net tan tea ten ae an at en na ne ta

accepry   peccary. *See* **aepry acepr**

accepst   accepts. *See* **accept acepst**

accept   accept epact cape cate ceca pace pact pate peat tape ace act aetape apt ate cap cat cep eat eta pat pea pet tap tea ae at pa pe ta

accerrs scarcer. *See* **accers acerrs**

accers scarce acres cares races scare aces acre arcs arse care cars case ceca ears eras race rase scar sear sera ace arc are car ear era rec res sac sea ae as er re

accersst scarcest actress casters recasts. *See* **accers access acerss acerst**

accerssu accusers accrues accuser accuses causers saucers. *See* **accers acceru access accesu**

accersu accrues accuser. *See* **acceru accesu acersu ccersu accers**

acceru accrue acre care ceca cure ecru race urea ace arc are car cue cur ear era rec rue ae er re

access access cases aces case ceca cess sacs seas ace ass ess sac sea ae as

accesstu cactuses accuses. *See* **access accesu accstu acesst**

accessu accuses. *See* **access acessu ccessu**

accessuu caucuses accuses. *See* **access accesu acessu**

accesu accuse cause cusec sauce aces case ceca cues ace cue sac sea sueuse ae as us

accfiip pacific. *No 6s or 5s*

accfily calcify. *No 6s or 5s*

accflnoo confocal. *See* **acflno**

accghin caching. *See* **acghin cchin**

accghinn chancing caching. *See* **acghin acginn**

accghino coaching caching. *See* **accgno acchno acghin acgino**

accghint catching caching. *See* **acghin acgint achint aghint**

accgikln cackling clacking lacking. *See* **acgikn acgiln**

accgikmr gimcrack. *See* **acikmr**

accgiknr cracking carking racking. *See* **acgikn acginr agiknr**

accgilox coxalgic. *See* **accilo**

accginot coacting coating. *See* **accgno acgino acgint acinot**

accginru accruing. *See* **acginr acinru cginru**

accginsu accusing causing saucing. *See* **acgins acinsu**

accgno cognac conga coca agon ago can cog con gan goa nag nog an go na no on

accgnos cognacs. *See* **accgno acgnos**

acchhitt chitchat. *See* **accitt achtt**

acchilot catholic chaotic. *See* **accilo accilt achilo**

acchinpu capuchin. *See* **achnpu cchipu**

acchiort thoracic chaotic chariot haricot. *See* **acchrt accirt aciort cchior**

acchiot chaotic. *See* **achit accit accht**

acchklor charlock. *See* **achlor**

acchkosy haycocks haycock. *See* **cchkos**

acchkoy haycock. *See* **accko cchko chkoy**

acchno concha coach conch coca can con hon nah ah an ha ho na no oh on

acchnotu couchant account. *See* **acchno acchou achntu acnotu**

acchny chancy achy any can cay hay nah nay yah ah an ay ha na

accho coach coca ah ha ho oh

acchosu cachous. *See* **acchou achos accos**

acchou cachou coach couch coca ouch ah ha ho oh

acchptu catchup. *See* **accht cchtu achpt**

acchrru currach. *See* **chrru acrru cchru**

acchrst scratch. *See* **achrst acchrt**

acchrsty scratchy scratch starchy. *See* **acchrt acchty achrst achsty**

acchrt cratch catch chart arch cart char chat hart rath tach act arc art car cat hat rah rat tar ah at ha ta

accht catch chat tach act cat hat ah at ha ta

acchty catchy catch yacht achy chat tach act cat cay hat hay thy yah ah at ay ha ta

acciilln clinical. *See* **cciiln**

acciilmt climatic. *See* **accilt aciilt**

acciilrt critical lactic.. *See* **accirt acilrt cciirt aciirt**

acciint actinic. *See* **accit acint**

acciirtx cicatrix. *See* **accirt cciirt aciirt**

acciist sciatic. *See* **accit**

accikknn nicknack. *See* **ackkn**

accikkrr rickrack. *See* **accir acckr ccikr**

acciklot cocktail. *See* **accilo accilt**

accikrs carsick. *See* **acckrs ccikrs**

accillu calculi. *See* **acill**

accilmo comical. *See* **accilo acilm ccimo**

accilmsu calciums calcium musical. *See* **acilms**

accilmu calcium. *See* **acilm**

accilno conical laconic. *See* **accilo ccilno acilno**

accilnov volcanic conical laconic. *See* **accilo acilno ccilno**

accilny cynical. *See* **acciny ailny**

accilo calico colic coal coca coil cola laic loci ail col lac oil ai la li lo

accilor caloric. *See* **accilo acilor**

accilort cortical caloric. *See* **accilo accilt accirt acilor**

accilos calicos. *See* **accilo acilos**

accilrru circular crucial. *See* **acilru acirru aclrru**

accilrsy acrylics acrylic. *See* **acilry ailrsy cilrsy**

accilru crucial. *See* **acilru accir**

accilry acrylic. *See* **acilry accir**

accilss classic. *See* **aclss ailss**

accilsss classics classic classis. *See* **acisss ailsss**

accilst clastic. *See* **accilt ailst aclst**

accilt lactic cacti alit laic tail talc tali act ail alt cat ita lac lit tic til ai at it la li ta ti

acciltuu cuticula. *See* **accilt**

accimnos moccasin camions maniocs masonic. *See* **acimno acimos acinos acmnos**

accinoos occasion. *See* **accoos acinos ccinos**

accinoot coaction. *See* **acinot**

accinort narcotic carotin. *See* **accirt acinot aciort acnort**

acciny cyanic cynic ayin ani any can cay icy nay yin ai an ay in na

acciorst acrostic arctics. *See* **accirt accost aciors aciort**

acciostu acoustic caustic. *See* **accost accstu aciost ccostu**

accir circa air arc car ria ai

accirst arctics. *See* **accirt acirst**

accirsty scarcity arctics satyric. *See* **accirt acirst ccisty**

accirt arctic circa cacti cart act air arc art car cat ita rat ria tar tic ai at it ta ti

accisstu caustics caustic casuist. *See* **accstu**

accistt tactics. *See* **acistt accitt**

accistu caustic. *See* **accstu accit cistu**

accit cacti act cat ita tic ai at it ta ti

accitt tactic attic cacti tact tact act cat ita tat tic tit ai at it ta ti

acckkrsu rucksack. *See* **acckrs**

acckl clack calk lack lac kal ka la

accklry crackly. *See* **acckry acckl aclry**

acckls clacks calks clack lacks slack calk cask lack sack ask kal kas lac sac sal as ka la

accko acock coca cock koa oak ka

acckooot cockatoo. *See* **accko accot accoo**

acckoprt crackpot. *See* **acoprt**

acckoss cassock. *See* **accko ackss accos**

acckosss cassocks cassock. *See* **accko ackss accos**

acckprsu crackups crackup. *See* **acckrs acprsu**

acckpru crackup. *See* **acckr**

acckr crack cark rack arc ark car ka

acckrs cracks carks crack racks arcs arks cark cars cask rack sack sarkscar arc ark ask car kas sac ka as

acckry cracky crack cark rack racy yack arc ark car cay cry ray yak yarka ay

accllosu occlusal callous. *See* **acllos acllsu**

accllsuu calculus. *See* **accsuu acllsu**

accmopst compacts compact. *See* **accost acmops acmost**

accmopt compact. *See* **accot acmop**

accmostu accustom. *See* **accost accstu acmost acmstu**

accnoor raccoon. *See* **acnoor**

accnoors raccoons raccoon racoons. *See* **accoos acnoor acnors cnoors**

accnootu cocoanut account coconut. *See* **acnotu**

accnoptu occupant account. *See* **acnotu**

accnortt contract contact. *See* **acnort acnott anortt**

accnostt contacts contact octants. *See* **accost acnost acnott acostt**

accnostu accounts account conatus toucans. *See* **accost accstu acnost acnotu**

accnott contact. *See* **acnott accot**

accnotu account. *See* **acnotu accot**

acco coca

accoo cocoa coca coco coo

accoos cocoas cocas cocoa cocos coca coco coos sac coo as os so

accopsty copycats copycat. *See* **accost**

accopty copycat. *See* **accot**

accos cocas coca sac as os so

accosst accosts. *See* **accost acosst**

accost accost coacts ascot coact coast coats cocas costa tacos acts cast cats coat coca cost cots oast oats scat scot stoa taco act cat cot oat sac sat sot as at os so ta to

accot coact coat coca taco act cat cot oat at ta to

accruy curacy yucca racy arc car cay cry cur ray yar ay

accstu cactus scuta acts cast cats cuts scat scut act cat cut sac sat tau as at ta us ut

accsuu caucus sac as us

accsuy yuccas yucca saucy cays cay sac say as ay us

accuy yucca cay ay

acd cad ad

acdddei caddied. *See* **acddei addde**

acdddeit addicted caddied. *See* **acddei acddit**

acdddeu adduced. *See* **acddeu addde**

acddee decade ceded aced cade cede dace dead deed ace add cad cee dad ad ae

acddeees deceased decades decease seceded. *See* **acddee acdees ddeees**

acddeef defaced. *See* **acddee acdeef**

acddeeht detached cheated. *See* **acddee acdeht cdeeht addeeh**

acddeeit dedicate ideated. *See* **acddee acddei acddit adeeit**

acddeelr declared cleared cradled declare. *See* **acddee acdder acdelr aceelr**

acddeemp decamped. *See* **acdemp acddee acdeep**

acddeens ascended deadens decades descend encased scended. *See* **acddee acdden acdees acdens**

acddeent decadent decanted enacted. *See* **acddee acdden acdent aceent**

acddees decades. *See* **acddee acdees**

acddeetu educated educate. *See* **acddee acddeu acddtu cddeeu**

acddeey decayed. *See* **acddee acddy acdey**

acddeg cadged cadge caged aced aged cade cage dace dead egad gaed ace add age cad dad dag gad gae ad ae

acddei caddie aided diced aced acid aide cade cadi dace dead dice died iced idea ace add aid cad dad did die ice ad ae ai id

acddeiim medicaid. *See* **acddei addeim**

acddein candied. *See* **acddei acddin acdden**

acddeinr riddance cairned candied dandier drained. *See* **acddei acdden acdder acddin**

acddeis caddies. *See* **acddei acddis**

acddeitt dictated dictate. *See* **acddei acddit acdett**

acddeklo deadlock cloaked. *See* **acdekl acdelo addelo cddeko**

acddeln candled. *See* **acdeln acdden addeln**

acddelr cradled. *See* **acdder acdelr addelr**

acddels scalded. *See* **acdels addels**

acdden danced acned caned dance aced acne cade cane dace dead dean ace add and ane cad can dad den end nae ad ae an en na ne

acddeop decapod. *See* **cddeo cdeop ddeop**

acddeops decapods decapod. *See* **acdeps addeos adeops**

acddeorr corraded corrade. *See* **acdder acderr addeor adeorr**

acdder carded acred adder arced cadre cared cedar dared dread raced aced acre cade card care dace dare dead dear race read redd ace add arc are cad car dad ear era rad rec red ad ae er re

acddersu crusaded adduces crusade. *See* **acdder acddeu acders acdesu**

acddertu traduced traduce. *See* **acdder acddeu acddtu acdert**

acddesu adduces. *See* **acddeu acdesu**

acddeu adduce adduced cade cued dace dead duad dude ace add cad cud cue dad dud due ad ae

acddgiln cladding addling. *See* **acddin acgiln addgin adgiln**

acddginu adducing. *See* **acddin addgin**

acddginy caddying. *See* **acddin acddiy addgin**

acddhis caddish. *See* **acddis**

acddhko haddock. *No 6s or 5s*

acddhkos haddocks shaddock haddock. *See* **achos acdos cdkos**

acddiior cardioid. *See* **acdir acior cdiio**

acddiksz zaddicks zaddick. *See* **acddis**

acddikz zaddick. *No 6s or 5s*

acddilny candidly. *See* **acddin acddiy acdily**

acddin candid acid cadi add aid and ani cad can dad did din ad ai an id in na

acddins candids. *See* **acddin acddis**

acddirs discard. *See* **acddis acdirs**

acddirss discards discard. *See* **acddis acdirs**

acddiry dryadic. *See* **acddiy acdir adiry**

acddis caddis acids cadis acid adds aids asci cadi cads dads dais disc said scad add ads aid cad dad did ids sac sad sic ad ai as id is si

acddist addicts. *See* **acddit acddis acdist**

acddit addict dicta acid adit cadi act add aid cad cat dad did dit ita tad tic ad ai at id it ta ti

acddiy dyadic caddy acidy acid cadi dyad add aid cad cay dad day did icy ad ai ay id

acddkop paddock. *No 6s or 5s*

acddkops paddocks paddock. *See* **acops acdos cdkos**

acddkory dockyard. *See* **ackory**

acddortu adductor. *See* **acddtu addort**

acddstu adducts. *See* **acddtu acdstu**

acddtu adduct ducat duad duct act add cad cat cud cut dad dud tad tau ad at ta ut

acddy caddy dyad add cad cay dad day ad ay

acde aced cade dace cad ace ad ae

acdeeeft defecate faceted. *See* **acdeef adeeft**

acdeeeks seedcake decease. *See* **acdees acdeks**

acdeeenr careened. *See* **acdenr aceenr adeenr cdeeer**

acdeeers decrease creased decease decrees recedes seceder. *See* **acdees acders aceers adeers**

acdeees decease. *See* **acdees cdeees**

acdeeess deceases seedcase decease secedes. *See* **acdees aceess**

acdeef deface faced aced cade cafe cede dace deaf face fade feed ace cad cee fad fed fee ad ae fa

acdeeff effaced. *See* **acdeef aceeff**

acdeefft affected effaced faceted. *See* **acdeef acefft adeeft**

acdeefis casefied defaces. *See* **acdeef acdees aceefs acefis**

acdeefn enfaced. *See* **adeefn acdeef aceefn cdeefn**

acdeefpr prefaced capered preface. *See* **acdeef acdeep acdepr adeefr**

acdeefs defaces. *See* **acdees aceefs**

acdeeft faceted. *See* **acdeef adeeft cdeeft**

acdeegn encaged. *See* **aceegn acden acdeg**

acdeehiv achieved achieve chevied. *See* **acdeiv adeehv cdeeiv**

acdeehl leached. *See* **aceehl adeehl cdeehl**

acdeehlp pleached leached. *See* **acdeep acdelp aceehl acehlp**

acdeehnn enhanced enhance. *See* **acdenn adeenn**

acdeehns enchased encased enchase. *See* **acdees acdehs acdens aceens**

acdeehpr preached capered cheaper parched perched reached. *See* **acdeep acdehr acdepr acehpr**

acdeehr reached. *See* **adeehr acdehr**

acdeehrs searched adheres crashed creased headers reached reaches sheared. *See* **acdees acdehr acdehs acders**

acdeehst detaches cheated escheat headset scathed teaches. *See* **acdees acdehs acdeht acdest**

acdeeht cheated. *See* **acdeht cdeeht adeeht**

acdeeilt delicate citadel cleated deltaic dialect edictal. *See* **adeeil adeeit adeelt adeilt**

acdeeimr medicare creamed. *See* **aceemr adeemr adeimr**

acdeeimt decimate medicate mediate. *See* **adeeit adeemt cdeeit ceeimt**

acdeeinu audience. *See* **cdeinu**

acdeeinv deviance evinced. *See* **acdeiv adeinv cdeeiv ceeinv**

acdeejkt jacketed. *See* **acdejk acdekt aceejt cdeejt**

acdeeknr cankered cranked creaked kneader redneck. *See* **acdekr acdenr aceenr aceknr**

acdeekpr repacked creaked capered. *See* **acdeep acdekp acdekr acdepr**

acdeekpt packeted. *See* **acdeep acdekp acdekt acekpt**

acdeekr creaked. *See* **acdekr cdeekr**

acdeekrs screaked creaked creased. *See* **acdees acdekr acdeks acders**

acdeekrt racketed catered cerated creaked created reacted tracked. *See* **acdekr acdekt acdert aceert**

acdeell cadelle. *See* **acdell aceell cdeell**

acdeellr cellared recalled cadelle cleared declare. *See* **acdell acdelr aceell aceelr**

acdeells cadelles cadelle allseed. *See* **acdees acdell acdels aceell**

acdeelmp emplaced clamped empaled emplace. *See* **acdeep acdelm acdelp acdemp**

acdeeln cleaned. *See* **acdeln adeeln**

acdeelnr calender cleaned cleaner cleared declare learned. *See* **acdeln acdelr acdenr aceelr**

acdeelns cleansed calends candles cleaned cleanse encased scalene. *See* **acdees acdeln acdels acdens**

acdeelpr parceled replaced capered cleared declare pearled percale replace. *See* **acdeep acdelp acdelr acdepr**

acdeelr cleared declare. *See* **aceelr acdelr adeelr**

acdeelrs declares cereals cleared cradles creased dealers declare leaders. *See* **acdees acdelr acdels acders**

acdeelt cleated. *See* **adeelt**

acdeelv cleaved. *See* **acdelv aceelv adeelv**

acdeemn menaced. *See* **aceemn adeemn**

acdeemnp encamped menaced. *See* **acdeep acdemp aceemn acemnp**

acdeemr creamed. *See* **aceemr adeemr**

acdeemrs screamed amerces creamed creased racemes smeared. *See* **acdees acders aceemr aceers**

acdeemrt cremated catered cerated creamed created cremate reacted. *See* **acdert aceemr aceert adeemr**

acdeemsv medevacs medevac. *See* **acdees adeems adeesv**

acdeemv medevac. *See* **acdev adeem adeev**

acdeennp penanced penance. *See* **acdeep acdenn adeenn adeenp**

acdeenot anecdote enacted acetone. *See* **acdeno acdent acdeot aceent**

acdeenrt cantered decanter recanted catered centred cerated created crenate enacted reacted reenact. *See* **acdenr acdent acdert aceenr**

acdeenrv caverned ravened. *See* **acdenr acderv aceenr acenrv**

acdeenrz credenza. *See* **acdenr acderz aceenr adeenr**

acdeens encased. *See* **acdens acdees cdeens aceens**

acdeent enacted. *See* **adeent acdent aceent cdeent**

acdeeort decorate catered cerated cordate created reacted redcoat. *See* **acdeot acdert aceert adeort**

acdeep peaced paced peace aced aped cade cape cede dace deep pace peed ace ape cad cap cee cep dap pad pea pee ad ae pa pe

acdeeppr recapped capered crapped papered. *See* **acdeep acdepp acdepr aceppr**

acdeepr capered. *See* **acdepr acdeep adeepr**

acdeeprs escarped capered creased escaped escaper redcaps scarped scraped speared. *See* **acdeep acdees acdepr acdeps**

acdeeprt carpeted capered catered cerated created predate reacted tapered. *See* **acdeep acdepr acdert aceert**

acdeeps escaped. *See* **acdees aceeps acdeep adeeps acdeps**

acdeerrt retraced terraced catered caterer cerated created reacted retrace retread terrace. *See* **acderr acdert aceerr aceert**

acdeers creased. *See* **acders acdees aceers cdeers adeers**

acdeerss caressed creased creases. *See* **acdees acders aceers aceess**

acdeert catered cerated created reacted. *See* **acdert aceert**

acdees ceased cades cased cease cedes daces eased aced aces cade cads case cede cees dace ease scad seed ace ads cad cee sac sad sea see ad ae as

acdeestu educates educate. *See* **acdees acdest acdesu acdstu**

acdeesux caudexes excused. *See* **acdees acdesu acdeux cdeesu**

acdeetu educate. *See* **acdet acetu cdeeu**

acdeetx exacted. *See* **acdet acetx adetx**

acdef faced aced cade cafe dace deaf face fade ace cad fad fed ad ae fa

acdeffh chaffed. *See* **acdefh acffh**

acdefgin defacing fancied. *See* **acefin acfgin adefgn adegin**

acdefgo dogface. *See* **acdeg defgo acdef**

acdefgos dogfaces dogface. *See* **acdegs acegos adegos defgos**

acdefh chafed ached chafe faced aced ache cade cafe chef dace deaf each face fade hade head ace cad edh fad fed feh had hae ad ae ah eh fa ha he

acdefiip pacified. *See* **cdefii**

acdefiln canfield fancied. *See* **acdeln acefil acefin adefil**

acdefin fancied. *See* **acefin acden defin**

acdefinn financed fancied finance. *See* **acdenn acefin aceinn adefnn**

acdefort factored cordate crafted fracted redcoat. *See* **acdeot acdert acfort adefor**

acdefrs scarfed. *See* **acders acefrs**

acdefrsu surfaced crusade scarfed surface. *See* **acders acdesu acefrs acefsu**

acdefrt crafted fracted. *See* **acdert adefrt**

acdefrtu furcated crafted facture fracted furcate traduce. *See* **acdert aceftu acertu adefrt**

acdeg cadge caged aced aged cade cage dace egad gaed ace age cad dag gad gae ad ae

acdeggr cragged. *See* **adeggr acdegr**

acdeghn changed. *See* **aceghn adeghn**

acdeghr charged. *See* **acdehr aceghr acdegr**

acdegimr decigram grimaced grimace. *See* **acdegr acegir adegim adeimr**

acdeginu guidance educing. *See* **adegin aeginu cdegin cdeinu**

acdeginy decaying cyanide. *See* **acegny adegin cdegin deginy**

acdegirs disgrace radices sidecar. *See* **acdegr acdegs acders acdirs**

acdegko dockage. *See* **acdeg acdek cdeko**

acdegkos dockages dockage. *See* **acdegs acdeks acegos adegos**

acdegln clanged glanced. *See* **adegln acdeln aceglm**

acdegno decagon. *See* **acdeno**

acdegnos decagons decagon deacons. *See* **acdegs acdeno acdens acegos**

acdegor cordage. *See* **acdegr cdegor**

acdegors cordages cargoes codgers cordage corsage. *See* **acdegr acdegs acders acegos**

acdegr graced acred arced cadge cadre caged cared cedar grace grade raced raged aced acre aged ager cade cage card care crag dace dare dear drag egad gaed gear grad race rage read ace age arc are cad car dag ear era erg gad gae gar rad rag rec red reg ad ae er re

acdegs cadges cades cadge caged cages cased daces degas aced aces aged ages cade cads cage case dace dags egad gads gaed sage scad scag ace ads age cad dag gad gae gas sac sad sag sea ad ae as

acdeh ached aced ache cade dace each hade head ace cad edh had hae ad ae ah eh ha he

acdehht hatched. *See* **acdeht acehht**

acdehhtt thatched chatted hatched hatchet. *See* **acdeht acdett acehht achhtt**

acdehijk hijacked. *See* **acdehk acdejk acehik achijk**

acdehilr heraldic chaired radicle. *See* **acdehr acdeil acehir aceilr**

acdehimn machined chained machine. *See* **aceimn adeimn cdehim cdehin**

acdehin chained. *See* **cdehin**

acdehir chaired. *See* **acdehr acehir cdehir**

acdehirv archived chaired archive. *See* **acdehr acdeiv acderv acehir**

acdehk hacked ached caked aced ache cade cake dace deck each hack hade hake head heck ace cad edh had hae ad ae ah eh ha he ka

acdehkl chalked. *See* **acdehk acehkl acdekl**

acdehklo headlock chalked cloaked. *See* **acdehk acdekl acdelo acehkl**

acdehkls shackled chalked clashed hackles shackle slacked. *See* **acdehk acdehs acdekl acdeks**

acdehkov havocked. *See* **acdehk cdehko**

acdehkru archduke. *See* **acdehk acdehr acdekr acehkr**

acdehktw thwacked whacked watched. *See* **acdehk acdeht acdehw acdekt**

acdehkw whacked. *See* **acdehw acdehk adehkw**

acdehlnr chandler charnel handler ranched. *See* **acdehr acdeln acdelr acdenr**

acdehlnu launched unlaced lunched. *See* **acdeln acdelu acdlnu acehnu**

acdehls clashed. *See* **acdehs acdels acehls adehls**

acdehlt latched. *See* **acehlt adehlt acdeht**

acdehmp champed. *See* **acdemp**

acdehmr charmed marched. *See* **acdehr acdhmr adehmr**

acdehms chasmed. *See* **acdehs adehms acehms**

acdehmt matched. *See* **acdeht acdem achmt**

acdehnor anchored ranched. *See* **acdehr acdeno acdenr acdnor**

acdehnr ranched. *See* **acdehr acdenr cdehnr adehnr**

acdehnst snatched chanted chasten decants descant handset scanted scathed. *See* **acdehs acdeht acdens acdent**

acdehnt chanted. *See* **acdent acdeht**

acdehop poached. *See* **acehop acdeh cdeop**

acdehost cathodes cathode coasted scathed. *See* **acdehs acdeht acdeot acdest**

acdehot cathode. *See* **acdeht acdeot**

acdehpp chapped. *See* **acdepp adehpp**

acdehpr parched. *See* **acdehr acdepr acehpr adehpr**

acdehpst despatch hepcats heptads patched patches scathed. *See* **acdehs acdeht acdeps acdest**

acdehpt patched. *See* **acdeht acehpt adehpt**

acdehr arched ached acred arced cadre cared cedar chard chare heard raced reach aced ache acre arch cade card care char dace dare dear each hade hard hare head hear herd race read rhea ace arc are cad car ear edh era had hae her rad rah rec red ad ae ah eh er ha he re

acdehrr charred. *See* **acdehr acehrr acderr adehrr**

acdehrs crashed. *See* **acdehr acders acdehs acdhrs acehrs**

acdehrst starched charted crashed hardest redacts scathed threads trashed. *See* **acdehr acdehs acdeht acders**

acdehrt charted. *See* **acdehr acdert adehrt acdeht**

acdehs cashed chased ached aches cades cased chase daces hades heads sadhe shade aced aces ache cade cads case cash dace dash each hade head scad shad shed ace ads ash cad edh had hae has sac sad sea she ad ae ah as eh ha he sh

acdehst scathed. *See* **acdest acdehs acehst adehst acdeht**

acdeht detach ached acted cadet cheat death hated tache teach theca aced ache cade cate chat dace date each etch hade hate head heat tach tech ace act aet ate cad cat eat edh eta eth had hae hat het tad tea ted the ad ae ah at eh ha he ta

acdehtt chatted. *See* **acdett acdeht adehtt**

acdehtw watched. *See* **acdehw adehtw**

acdehty yachted. *See* **acdeht acdey adehy**

acdehw chawed ached hawed aced ache awed cade chaw chew dace each hade head wade ace awe cad caw dew edh had hae haw hew wad wed ad ae ah aw eh ha he we

acdeiint indicate incited. *See* **acdent adeint cdeiit cdiint**

acdeijnu jaundice. *See* **cdeiju cdeinu**

acdeiknp panicked. *See* **acdekp adeinp adiknp cdeikn**

acdeikpx pickaxed. *See* **acdekp acikpx cdeikp**

acdeill cedilla. *See* **acdell adeill**

acdeills cedillas cedilla dallies sallied. *See* **acdell acdels acills adeill**

acdeilm claimed decimal declaim medical. *See* **acdelm adeilm aceilm**

acdeilms decimals declaims claimed decimal declaim malices medical misdeal mislead. *See* **acdelm acdels aceilm aceims**

acdeilmt maledict citadel claimed climate decimal declaim deltaic dialect edictal medical. *See* **acdelm aceilm acelmt adeilm**

acdeilmx climaxed claimed decimal declaim exclaim medical. *See* **acdelm aceilm acilmx adeilm**

acdeilps displace alipeds clasped palsied scalped special spliced. *See* **acdelp acdels acdeps acdilp**

acdeilr radicle. *See* **acdelr adeilr aceilr**

acdeilrs radicles claries cradles derails eclairs radices radicle scalier sidecar. *See* **acdelr acdels acders acdirs**

acdeilrt articled article citadel deltaic dialect edictal radicle recital trailed. *See* **acdelr acdert aceilr acelrt**

acdeilst citadels dialects castled citadel delicts deltaic details dialect dilates edictal elastic laciest. *See* **acdels acdest acdist acelst**

acdeilt citadel deltaic dialect edictal. *See* **cdeilt adeilt**

acdeiltt latticed citadel deltaic dialect dictate edictal lattice tactile. *See* **acdett aceltt adeilt cdeilt**

acdeimno comedian demoniac demonic encomia nomadic. *See* **acdeno aceimn acimno adeimn**

acdeimnp pandemic. *See* **acdemp aceimn acemnp adeimn**

acdeimpt impacted. *See* **acdemp acimpt adempt cdeipt**

acdeimrt timecard readmit. *See* **acdert adeimr adeirt ademrt**

acdeinos diocesan candies deacons incased. *See* **acdeno acdens aceins acenos**

acdeinpt pedantic pandect painted. *See* **acdent acinpt adeinp adeint**

acdeinr cairned. *See* **aceinr cdeinr acdenr adeinr acdinr**

acdeins candies incased. *See* **acdens aceins**

acdeinss acidness ascends candies incased incases. *See* **acdens aceins adeiss adenss**

acdeinst distance candies decants descant detains discant incased instead sainted scanted stained. *See* **acdens acdent acdest acdist**

acdeinsy cyanides candies cyanide incased. *See* **acdens acdesy aceins cdinsy**

acdeintt nictated dictate nictate tainted. *See* **acdent acdett acintt adeint**

acdeinvy deviancy cyanide. *See* **acdeiv adeinv**

acdeiny cyanide. *See* **acdiy acden acdny**

acdeiort ceratoid carotid cordate cordite erotica redcoat. *See* **acdeot acdert acdiot aciort**

acdeiosu edacious. *See* **acdesu adeisu cdeosu**

acdeipsz capsized capsize. *See* **acdeps aceips adeisz cdeips**

acdeiqru acquired quadric acquire. *See* **aceiqu aceiru ceiqru deiqru**

acdeirr carried. *See* **acderr aceirr adeirr**

acdeirs radices sidecar. *See* **acders acdirs aceirs cdeirs adeirs**

acdeirss sidecars radices sidecar. *See* **acders acdirs aceirs acerss**

acdeistt dictates dictate scatted. *See* **acdest acdett acdist acestt**

acdeisv advices. *See* **acdeiv adeisv aceisv**

acdeitt dictate. *See* **acdett acitt cdeit**

acdeity edacity. *See* **acdiy acdet acdey**

acdeiv advice caved aced acid aide avid cade cadi cave dace deva dice diva dive iced idea vice vied ace aid ave cad die ice vac via vie ad ae ai id

acdejk jacked caked aced cade cake dace deck jack jade jake cad ace ad ae ka

acdejlo cajoled. *See* **acdelo acejlo**

acdek caked aced cade cake dace deck cad ace ad ae ka

acdekl lacked caked decal laced aced cade cake calk clad dace dale deal deck kale lace lack lade lake lead leak ace ale cad eld elk kal lac lad lea led lek ad ae el ka la

acdeklm mackled. *See* **acdelm acdekl aceklm**

acdekln clanked. *See* **acdeln**

acdeklo cloaked. *See* **acdelo cdeklo**

acdeklps spackled clasped scalped slacked spackle. *See* **acdekl acdekp acdeks acdelp**

acdekls slacked. *See* **acdels acdekl acdeks adekls**

acdeklt tackled talcked. *See* **acdekl acdekt aceklt adeklt**

acdeklu caulked. *See* **acdelu acdekl cdeklu**

acdekms smacked. *See* **acdeks adekms**

acdeknpu unpacked. *See* **acdekp acknpu**

acdeknr cranked. *See* **aceknr acdekr acdenr adeknr**

acdekns snacked. *See* **acdens adekns acdeks**

acdekor croaked. *See* **acdekr cdekor**

acdekost stockade coasted dockets stacked stocked. *See* **acdeks acdekt acdeot acdest**

acdekp packed caked paced aced aped cade cake cape dace deck pace pack peak peck ace ape cad cap cep dap pad pea ad ae ka pa pe

acdekqu quacked. *See* **adekqu acdek ackqu**

acdekr carked racked acred arced cadre caked cared cedar crake creak drake raced raked aced acre cade cake card care cark dace dare dark dear deck race rack rake read reck ace arc are ark

cad car ear era rad rec red ad ae er ka re

acdekrt tracked. *See* **acdekr acdert acekrt acdekt**

acdeks sacked asked cades caked cakes cased daces decks aced aces cade cads cake case cask dace deck desk sack sake scad ace ads ask cad kas sac sad sea ad ae as ka

acdekst stacked. *See* **acdest acekst acdeks adekst acdekt**

acdekt tacked acted cadet caked aced cade cake cate dace date deck tack take teak ace act aet ate cad cat eat eta kat tad tea ted ad ae at ka ta

acdeky yacked caked decay aced cade cake dace deck dyke yack ace aye cad cay day dey dye key yak yea ad ae ay ka ye

acdel decal laced aced cade clad dace dale deal lace lade lead ace ale cad eld lac lad lea led ad ae el la

acdell called cella decal laced ladle aced cade call cell clad dace dale deal dell lace lade lead leal ace ale all cad eld ell lac lad lea led ad ae el la

acdellor collared caroled collard. *See* **acdell acdelo acdelr acello**

acdellot collated located collate. *See* **acdell acdelo acdeot acello**

acdellsu callused alludes aludels caudles cedulas sculled. *See* **acdell acdels acdelu acdesu**

acdelm calmed camel decal laced lamed maced medal aced acme cade calm came clad clam dace dale dame deal lace lade lame lead mace made male mead meal meld ace ale cad cam dam eld elm lac lad lam lea led mac mad mae mel ad ae am el em la ma me

acdelmm clammed. *See* **acdelm adelmm**

acdelmor clamored caroled caromed comrade earldom. *See* **acdelm acdelo acdelr acelmr**

acdelmp clamped. *See* **acdelm acdemp adelmp acdelp**

acdeln candle lanced acned caned clean dance decal eland laced laden lance aced acne cade cane clad clan dace dale deal dean elan lace lade land lane lead lean lend ace ale and ane cad can den eld end lac lad lea led nae ad ae an el en la na ne

acdelno celadon. *See* **acdeln acdeno cdelno acdelo adelno**

acdelnor colander caldron caroled celadon corneal. *See* **acdeln acdelo acdelr acdeno**

acdelns calends candles. *See* **acdens acdeln acelns acdels adelns**

acdelnu unlaced. *See* **acdeln acdelu acelnu acdlnu**

acdelo coaled decal laced aced aloe cade clad clod coal coda code coed cola cold cole dace dale deal dole lace lade lead load lode ace ado ale cad cod col doc doe eld lac lad lea led ode old ad ae do el la lo od

acdelor caroled. *See* **acdelo acelor cdelor acdelr adelor**

acdelot located. *See* **acdelo acdeot acelot**

acdelp placed decal laced paced paled pedal place plead aced aped cade cape clad clap dace dale deal lace lade lead leap pace pale peal plea pled ace ale alp ape cad cap cep dap eld lac lad lap lea led pad pal pea ad ae el la pa pe

acdelpp clapped. *See* **acdepp adelpp acdelp**

acdelps clasped scalped. *See* **acdels adelps acelps acdeps**

acdelpsu capsuled capsule caudles cedulas clasped scalped specula. *See* **acdelp acdels acdelu acdeps**

acdelr cradle acred alder arced cadre cared cedar clear decal laced raced aced acre cade card care carl clad dace dale dare deal dear earl lace lade lard lead race rale read real ace ale arc are cad car ear eld era lac lad lar lea led rec red ad ae el er la re

acdelrs cradles. *See* **adelrs acders acelrs acdelr acdels**

acdelrsw scrawled cradles crawled. *See* **acdelr acdels acdelw acders**

acdelrsy sacredly cradles. *See* **acdelr acdels acders acdesy**

acdelrw crawled. *See* **acdelr acdelw**

acdels decals scaled cades cased daces dales deals decal laced laces lades leads scald scale aced aces ales cade cads case clad dace dale deal lace lade lads lead leas sale scad seal sled ace ads ale cad eld els lac lad lea led sac sad sal sea ad ae as el la

acdelss classed. *See* **acdels acdlss acelss**

acdelst castled. *See* **acdest acelst acdels adelst**

acdelsu caudles cedulas. *See* **acdelu acdesu acelsu**

acdelu caudle cedula clued decal ducal laced aced auld cade caul clad clue cued dace dale deal dual duel lace lade laud lead luce ace ale cad cud cue due eld lac lad lea led leu ad ae el la

acdelv calved calve caved clave decal laced laved aced cade cave clad dace dale deal deva lace lade lave lead leva vale veal veld ace ale ave cad eld lac lad lea led lev vac ad ae el la

acdelw clawed decal laced waled weald aced awed cade clad claw clew dace dale deal lace lade lead lewd wade wale weal weld ace ale awe awl cad caw dew eld lac lad law lea led wad wed ad ae aw el la we

acdem maced aced acme cade came dace dame mace made mead ace cad cam dam mac mad mae ad ae am em ma me

acdemmr crammed. *See* **ademmr acder acemr**

acdemmrs scrammed crammed. *See* **acders acemrs ademmr ademrs**

acdemnor romanced caromed comrade madrone romance. *See* **acdeno acdenr acdnor acemnr**

acdemopr compadre compared caromed compare comrade cramped. *See* **acdemp acdepr acemop acempr**

acdemor caromed comrade. *See* **ademor**

acdemors comrades caromed comrade radomes. *See* **acders acemos acemrs aceors**

acdemort democrat caromed comrade cordate redcoat. *See* **acdeot acdert acemot ademor**

acdemp camped decamp maced paced aced acme aped cade came camp cape dace dame damp mace made mead pace ace amp ape cad cam cap cep dam dap mac mad mae map pad pea ad ae am em ma me pa pe

acdempr cramped. *See* **acdemp acempr acdepr acempr**

acdemps decamps scamped. *See* **acdemp acdeps**

acdemuuv vacuumed. *See* **acmuuv**

acden acned caned dance aced acne cade cane dace dean ace and ane cad can den end nae ad ae an en na ne

acdenn canned acned caned dance aced acne cade cane dace dean ace and ane cad can den end nae ad ae an en na ne

acdennor ordnance. *See* **acdenn acdeno acdenr acdnor**

acdennot cantoned connate contend. *See* **acdenn acdeno acdent acdeot**

acdenns scanned. *See* **acdens acdenn**

acdeno canoed deacon acned anode caned canoe coned dance ocean aced acne aeon cade cane coda code coed cone dace dean done node once ace ado and ane cad can cod con den doc doe don end eon nae nod ode one ad ae an do en na ne no od on

acdenory crayoned ardency. *See* **acdeno acdenr acdnor acenor**

acdenos deacons. *See* **adenos acdens acdeno acenos cdenos**

acdenppu uncapped. *See* **acdepp adenpp cdeppu**

acdenpr pranced. *See* **acdepr acdenr adenpr acenpr**

acdenpst pandects decants descant pandect pedants pentads scanted. *See* **acdens acdent acdeps acdest**

acdenpt pandect. *See* **acdent adenpt**

acdenr craned dancer acned acred arced cadre caned caner cared cedar crane dance nacre raced aced acne acre cade cane card care dace dare darn dean dear earn narc nard near nerd race rand read rend ace and ane arc are cad can car den ear end era nae rad ran rec red ad ae an en er na ne re

acdenrs dancers. *See* **acdens acders acenrs acdenr adenrs**

acdenrsu durances asunder crusade dancers danseur durance. *See* **acdenr acdens acders acdesu**

acdenru durance. *See* **acdenr adenru**

acdenrvy verdancy ardency. *See* **acdenr acderv acenrv acenry**

acdenry ardency. *See* **acenry acdenr adenry**

acdens ascend dances acned cades caned canes cased daces dance deans scend sedan aced aces acne cade cads cane cans case dace dean dens ends sand sane scad scan send ace ads and ane cad can den end ens nae sac sad sea sen ad ae an as en na ne

acdenss ascends. *See* **acdens adenss**

acdensst descants ascends ascents decants descant scanted secants stances. *See* **acdens acdent acdest acenst**

acdenst decants descant scanted. *See* **acdens acenst acdent acdest**

acdent cadent canted decant acned acted cadet caned dance enact aced acne ante cade cane cant cate cent dace date dean dent neat tend ace act aet and ane ant ate cad can cat den eat end eta nae net tad tan tea ted ten ad ae an at en na ne ta

acdeorr corrade. *See* **adeorr acderr cdeorr**

acdeorrs corrades adorers carders coarser corrade records scarred. *See* **acderr acders aceors acerrs**

acdeorst redcoats coasted coaster cordate costard redacts redcoat roasted torsade. *See* **acdeot acders acdert acdest**

acdeorsu caroused aroused carouse coursed crusade crusado scoured. *See* **acders acdesu aceors acersu**

acdeort cordate redcoat. *See* **acdert acdeot adeort**

acdeortu educator cordate courted readout redcoat traduce. *See* **acdeot acdert acertu adeort**

acdeortv cavorted cordate overact redcoat. *See* **acdeot acdert acderv aceotv**

acdeost coasted. *See* **acdest aceost acdost**

acdeot coated acted cadet octad aced cade cate coat coda code coed cote dace date dote taco toad toed ace act ado aet ate cad cat cod cot doc doe dot eat eta oat ode tad tea ted tod toe ad ae at do od ta to

acdeouv couvade. *See* **acdev cdeov cdeou**

acdeox coaxed coxae codex aced axed cade coax coda code coed coxa dace ace ado axe cad cod cox doc doe ode ad ae ax do ex od ox

acdep caped paced aced aped cade cape dace pace ace ape cad cap cep dap pad pea ad ae pa pe

acdepp capped caped paced aced aped cade cape dace pace ace ape cad cap cep dap pad pap pea pep ad ae pa pe

acdeppr crapped. *See* **acdepp aceppr acdepr adeppr**

acdepprs scrapped cappers crapped redcaps scarped scraped. *See* **acdepp acdepr acdeps acders**

acdepr carped craped redcap acred arced cadre caped caper cared cedar crape drape paced pacer padre pared raced raped recap aced acre aped cade cape card care carp crap dace dare dear pace pard pare pear race rape read reap ace ape arc are cad cap car cep dap ear era pad par pea per rad rap rec red rep ad ae er pa pe re

acdeprs redcaps scarped scraped. *See* **acders acdepr acdeps**

acdeprtu captured traduce capture. *See* **acdepr acdert aceprt aceptu**

acdeps scaped spaced cades caped capes cased daces paced paces scape space spade aced aces aped apes apse cade cads cape caps case ceps dace daps pace pads peas scad sped ace ads ape asp cap cap cep dap pad pas pea sac sad sap sea spa ad ae as pa pe

acdeqtuu aqueduct. *See* **acdet acetu acdtu**

acder acred arced cadre cared cedar raced aced acre cade card care dace dare dear race read ace arc are cad car ear era rad rec red ad ae er re

acderr carder arced arced cadre cared cedar raced racer aced acre cade card care dace dare dear race rare read rear ace arc are cad car ear era err rad rec red ad ae er re

acderrs carders scarred. *See* **acders acderr acerrs**

acderrsu crusader carders crusade curares scarred. *See* **acderr acders acdesu acerrs**

acderrtu traducer traduce. *See* **acderr acdert acerru acertu**

acders cadres cedars sacred scared acred acres arced cades cadre cards cared cares cased cedar daces dares dears raced races rased reads scare aced aces acre arcs arse cade cads card care cars case dace dare dear ears eras race rads rase read reds sard scad scar sear sera ace ads arc are cad car ear era rad rec red res sac sad sea ad ae as er re

acderssu crusades assured causers crusade saucers. *See* **acders acdesu acerss acersu**

acderst redacts. *See* **acdest acders acdert aderst**

acderstt detracts detract redacts scatted started tetrads. *See* **acders acdert acdest acdett**

acderstu traduces crudest crusade crusted curates custard redacts traduce. *See* **acders acdert acdest acdesu**

acdersu crusade. *See* **acders acdesu acersu cdersu**

acdert carted crated redact traced acred acted arced cadet cadre cared caret carte cater cedar crate raced rated react tared trace trade tread aced acre cade card care cart cate dace dare dart date dear drat race rate read tare tear ace act aet arc are art ate cad car cat ear eat era eta rad rat rec red ret tad tar tea ted ad ae at er re ta

acdertt detract. *See* **acdert acdett adertt**

acdertu traduce. *See* **acdert acertu**

acderv carved craved acred arced cadre cared carve caved cedar crave raced raved aced acre aver cade card care cave dace dare dear deva race rave read ace arc are ave cad car ear era rad rec red rev vac ad ae er re

acderz crazed acred arced cadre cared cedar craze raced razed aced acre adze cade card care czar dace dare daze dear race raze read ace adz arc are cad car ear era rad rec red zed ad ae er re

acdes cades cased daces aced aces cade cads case dace scad ace ads cad sac sad sea ad ae as

acdest cadets acted cades cadet cased caste cates daces dates sated stead aced aces acts cade cads case cast cate cats dace date east eats etas scad scat seat sect seta tads teas teds ace act ads aet ate cad cat eat eta sac sad sat sea set tad tea ted ad ae as at ta

acdestt scatted. *See* **acdest acdett acestt adestt**

acdesu caused sauced cades cased cause daces sauce aced aces cade cads case cuds cued cues dace dues scad scud sued used ace ads cad cud cue due sac sad sea sue use ad ae as us

acdesy decays cades cased daces decay aced aces ayes cade cads case cays dace days deys dyes easy eyas scad syce yeas ace ads aye cad cay day dey dye sac sad say sea yea yes ad ae as ay ye

acdet acted cadet aced cade cate dace date ace act aet ate cad cat eat eta tad tea ted ad ae at ta

acdett catted acted cadet tacet aced cade cate dace date tact teat ace act aet ate cad cat eat eta tad tat tea ted ad ae at ta

acdeux caudex aced axed cade cued dace ace axe cad cud cue due ad ae ax ex

acdev caved aced cade cave dace deva ace ave cad vac ad ae

acdey decay aced cade dace ace aye cad cay day dey dye yea ad ae ay ye

acdffhnu handcuff. *See* **acffh cffhu achnu**

acdffirt diffract traffic. *See* **adfirt affirt**

acdfflos scaffold. *See* **acffls afflos**

acdfiit fatidic. *See* **acdit**

acdfiiy acidify. *See* **acdiy**

acdggin cadging. *See* **acggin**

acdghotw watchdog. *See* **acdot achtw**

acdgiilo dialogic. *See* **adgil aciil cdiio**

acdgilnn candling dancing lancing landing. *See* **acgiln acginn adgiln adilnn**

acdgilnr cradling carding darling larding. *See* **acdinr acgiln acgilr acginr**

acdgilns scalding lacings ladings scaling. *See* **acgiln acgils acgins acglns**

acdgimot dogmatic. *See* **acdiot acimot adimot**

acdginn dancing. *See* **acginn**

acdginny candying dancing. *See* **acginn**

acdginr carding. *See* **acginr adginr acdinr**

acdgorst dogcarts dogcart costard. *See* **acdost acgors acorst agorst**

acdgort dogcart. *See* **acort agort acgor**

acdhiil chiliad. *See* **cdhil chiil aciil**

acdhiknp handpick. *See* **adiknp**

acdhinsw sandwich. *See* **achins adhins**

acdhiops scaphoid. *See* **achips adhips**

acdhipst dispatch. *See* **acdist achips adhips**

acdhlnor chaldron caldron. *See* **acdnor achlor achnor adlnor**

acdhmr drachm chard charm march arch card cham char cram dram hard harm marc arc arm cad cam car dam had ham mac mad mar rad rah ram ad ah am ha ma

acdhmrs drachms. *See* **acdhrs achmrs acdhmr**

acdhnosw cowhands cowhand. *See* **achnos adhosw**

acdhnow cowhand. *No 6s or 5s*

acdhopr pochard. *See* **achopr acdhr cdhor**

acdhoprs pochards pochard carhops. *See* **acdhrs achopr adhors**

acdhorr orchard. *See* **adorr adhor achor**

acdhorrs orchards orchard. *See* **acdhrs adhors adorrs**

acdhr chard arch card char hard arc cad car had rad rah ad ah ha

acdhrs chards cards chard chars crash hards shard arch arcs cads card cars cash char dash hard rads rahs rash sard scad scar shad ads arc ash cad car had has rad rah sac sad ad ah as ha sh

acdhryy dyarchy. *See* **acdhr achry adhry**

acdi acid cadi cad aid ad ai id

acdiijlu judicial. *See* **aciil acdlu cdilu**

acdiilms disclaim mislaid. *See* **aciils acilms adilms**

acdiilsu suicidal. *See* **aciils**

acdiilty dialytic acidity. *See* **acdily acdlty aciilt**

acdiinot actinoid diatonic diction. *See* **acdiot acinot cdiint**

acdiirst carditis drastic diarist. *See* **acdirs acdist acdiit acirst**

acdiirty acridity acidity aridity. *See* **aciirt**

acdiisst sadistic dicasts. *See* **acdist adisst**

acdiity acidity. *See* **acdit acdiy**

acdikltu ducktail. *See* **aikltu**

acdilmo domical. *See* **acilm adlmo**

acdilno nodical. *See* **acilno adino adlno**

acdilnoo conoidal nodical. *See* **acilno cdinoo**

acdilnor ironclad caldron clarion cordial nodical ordinal. *See* **acdinr acdnor acilno acilnr**

acdilop placoid. *See* **acdilp aclop**

acdilor cordial. *See* **acilor acdir adilr**

acdilors cordials cordial. *See* **acdirs acilor acilos aciors**

acdilot cotidal. *See* **acdiot adlot adilt**

acdilp placid plica plaid acid cadi clad clap clip dial laic laid paid pail pica aid ail alp cad cap dap dip lac lad lap lid lip pad pal ad ai id la li pa pi

acdilry acridly. *See* **acdily adilry acilry**

acdilstw wildcats wildcat. *See* **acdist adilst**

acdiltw wildcat. *See* **acdit adilt**

acdily acidly acidy daily acid cadi clad clay dial idly idyl lacy lady laic laid aid

ail cad cay day icy lac lad lay lid ad ai ay id la li

acdimmu cadmium. *See* **cdimu**

acdimno nomadic. *See* **acimno adimno**

acdimnsu scandium. *See* **acinsu adinsu admnsu aimnsu**

acdimnsy dynamics dynamic. *See* **adimsy cdinsy**

acdimny dynamic. *See* **acdiy acdny acimn**

acdinors sardonic inroads ordains sadiron. *See* **acdinr acdirs acdnor acinos**

acdinorw cordwain. *See* **acdinr acdnor acdorw adinor**

acdinr rancid acrid caird cairn dinar drain nadir acid arid cadi card darn narc nard raid rain rand rani rind aid air and ani arc cad can car din rad ran ria rid ad ai an id in na

acdinsst discants discant dicasts. *See* **acdist acinst acnsst adisst**

acdinst discant. *See* **acinst acdist**

acdinsty dynastic discant. *See* **acdist acinst acnsty adinty**

acdiopr picador. *See* **aciopr acdir adior**

acdioprs picadors sporadic picador picaros. *See* **acdirs aciopr aciors adiors**

acdiorst carotids carotid costard dacoits drastic. *See* **acdiot acdirs acdist acdost**

acdiort carotid. *See* **adiort aciort acdiot**

acdiortt dictator carotid citator ricotta. *See* **acdiot aciort adiort ciortt**

acdiost dacoits. *See* **aciost acdiot acdist cdiost acdost**

acdiosz zodiacs. *See* **acdioz acdis adios**

acdiot dacoit coati dicot dicta octad acid adit cadi coat coda doit iota odic otic taco toad act ado aid cad cat cod cot dit doc dot ita oat tad tic tod ad ai at do id it od ta ti to

acdioty dacoity. *See* **acdiot acdiy adoty**

acdioz zodiac azoic acid cadi coda odic ado adz aid azo cad cod coz doc zoa ad ai do id od

acdiprst adscript drastic. *See* **acdirs acdist acirst adiprs**

acdiqrsu quadrics quadric. *See* **acdirs adirsu**

acdiqru quadric. *See* **acdir aciru**

acdir acrid caird acid arid cadi card raid aid air arc cad car rad ria rid ad ai id

acdirs cairds acids acrid cadis caird cards raids acid aids airs arcs arid asci cadi cads card cars dais disc rads raid rias rids said sard sari scad scar ads aid air arc cad car ids rad ria rid sac sad sic sir ad ai as id is si

acdirst drastic. *See* **acdirs acdist acirst adirst**

acdirstt distract drastic. *See* **acdirs acdist acirst acistt**

acdis acids cadis acid aids asci cadi cads dais disc said scad ads aid cad ids sac sad sic ad ai as id is si

acdisst dicasts. *See* **acdist adisst**

acdist dicast acids adits cadis dicta staid tsadi acid acts adit aids asci cadi cads cast cats cist dais disc dits said scad scat tads tics act ads aid cad cat dit ids ita its sac sad sat sic sit tad tic ad ai as at id is it si ta ti

acdistuv viaducts viaduct. *See* **acdist acdstu adistu adistv**

acdit dicta acid adit cadi act aid cad cat dit ita tad tic ad ai at id it ta ti

acdituv viaduct. *See* **aditu aditv acdit**

acdiy acidy acid cadi aid cad cay day icy ad ai ay id

acdjnstu adjuncts adjunct. *See* **acdstu acnstu adjstu adnstu**

acdjntu adjunct. *See* **adntu acdtu ajntu**

acdklop padlock. *See* **acklo aclop aklop**

acdklops padlocks padlock. *See* **acklos aklops**

acdkmpsu mudpacks mudpack. *See* **acmpsu**

acdkmpu mudpack. *See* **ackmu**

acdl clad cad lac lad ad la

acdllor collard. *See* **acllor adllor**

acdllors collards collard collars dollars. *See* **acllor acllos aclors adllor**

acdlnor caldron. *See* **acdnor adlnor**

acdlnors caldrons caldron lardons. *See* **acdnor aclors acnors adlnor**

acdlnoru cauldron caldron nodular. *See* **acdlnu acdnor acloru acnoru**

acdlnu unclad ducal auld caul clad clan dual land laud ulna and cad can cud dun lac lad ad an la na nu

acdloort doctoral. *See* **cdoort**

acdlorwy cowardly. *See* **acdorw aclory aclrwy**

acdls scald cads clad lads scad ads cad lac lad sac sad sal ad as la

acdlss scalds class scads scald cads clad lads lass sacs sals scad ads ass cad lac lad sac sad sal ad as la

acdlsty dactyls. *See* **acdlty aclsy adlsy**

acdlty dactyl clad clay lacy lady talc act alt cad cat cay day lac lad lay tad ad at ay la ta

acdlu ducal auld caul clad dual laud cad cud lac lad ad la

acdmmno command. *See* **acmmo admno**

acdmmnoo commando command. *See* **cdmnoo cmmnoo**

acdmmnos commands command. *See* **acmmos admnos**

acdmnory dormancy acronym. *See* **acdnor acmnor acnory admnor**

acdnoor cardoon. *See* **acdnor cdnoor acnoor**

acdnoors cardoons cardoon cordons racoons. *See* **acdnor acnoor acnors adnors**

acdnoorv cordovan cardoon. *See* **acdnor acnoor cdnoor**

acdnor candor acorn adorn narco radon card coda cord corn darn narc nard orad rand road roan ado and arc cad can car cod con cor doc don dor nod nor oar orc rad ran roc rod ad an do na no od on or

acdnostw downcast. *See* **acdost acnost**

acdny candy and any cad can cay day nay ad an ay na

acdo coda ado cad cod doc ad do od

acdoprst postcard costard captors. *See* **acdost acoprt acorst adopst**

acdorssu crusados crusado sarcous. *See* **acorss cdorss corssu**

acdorst costard. *See* **acorst acdost**

acdorsu crusado. *See* **acdrs acdos cdors**

acdorsuz cruzados crusado cruzado. *See* **acdrs acdos cdors**

acdorsw cowards. *See* **acdorw cdorsw**

acdoruz cruzado. *No 6s or 5s*

acdorw coward crowd card coda cord craw crow draw orad road ward word ado arc cad car caw cod cor cow doc dor oar orc rad raw roc rod row wad war ad aw do od or ow

acdos codas ados cads coda cods docs scad soda ado ads cad cod doc dos sac sad sod ad as do od os so

acdost octads ascot coast coats codas costa octad tacos toads acts ados cads cast cats coat coda cods cost cots docs dots oast oats scad scat scot soda stoa taco tads toad act ado ads cad cat cod cot doc dos dot oat sac sad sat sod sot tad tod ad as at do od os so ta to

acdot octad coat coda taco toad act ado cad cat cod cot doc dot oat tad tod ad at do od ta to

acdr card arc cad car rad ad

acdrs cards arcs cads card cars rads sard scad scar ads arc cad car rad sac sad ad as

acdrsstu custards custard. *See* **acdstu arsstu crsstu**

acdrstu custard. *See* **acdstu acdrs acrst**

acds cads scad ads cad sac sad ad as

acdss scads cads sacs scad ads ass cad sac sad ad as

acdstu ducats adust ducat ducts scuta acts cads cast cats cuds cuts duct dust scad scat scud scut stud tads act ads cad cat cud cut sac sad sat tad tau ad as at ta us ut

acdtu ducat duct act cad cat cud cut tad tau ad at ta ut

ace ace ae

aceeefrr carefree. *See* **aceerr eeefrr**

aceeegln elegance. *See* **aceegn acegln**

aceeeipr earpiece. *See* **aceeip ceeipr**

aceeelmr cameleer. *See* **aceelr aceemr acelmr**

aceeensv evanesce. *See* **aceens**

aceeeps escapee. *See* **aceeps eeeps**

aceeepss escapees escapee escapes. *See* **aceeps aceess acepss aeepss**

aceeerrt recreate caterer retrace terrace. *See* **aceerr aceert**

aceeesuv evacuees evacuee. *See* **acesu acesv acees**

aceeeuv evacuee. *No 6s or 5s*

aceeff efface cafe face ace cee fee ae fa

aceeffin caffeine caffein faience fiancee. *See* **aceeff aceefn acefin**

aceeffr effacer. *See* **aceeff acefr**

aceeffrs effacers effacer effaces. *See* **aceeff aceefs aceers acefrs**

aceeffs effaces. *See* **aceeff aceefs**

aceefin faience fiancee. *See* **aceefn acefin**

aceefins faiences fiancees enfaces faience fancies fascine fiancee fiances. *See* **aceefn aceefs aceens acefin**

aceeflpu peaceful. *See* **acflpu**

aceeflss faceless. *See* **aceefs aceess acefss acelss**

aceefn enface fence acne cafe cane face fane ace ane can cee fan fee fen nae nee ae an en fa na ne

aceefns enfaces. *See* **aceens aceefn aceefs ceefns**

aceefpr preface. *See* **acepr ceepr acefr**

aceefprs prefaces preface escaper. *See* **aceefs aceeps aceers acefrs**

aceefprt perfecta perfect preface prefect. *See* **aceert aceprt aeefrt aeeprt**

aceefpty typeface. *See* **ceepty eefpty**

aceefs faeces cafes cease faces feces aces cafe case cees ease face fees safe ace cee fas fee sac sea see ae as fa

aceeghnx exchange. *See* **aceegn aceghn aeehnx**

aceeghrr recharge charger. *See* **aceerr aceghr aeehrr**

aceegil elegiac. *See* **aegil aeegl aceil**

aceegils legacies elegiac. *See* **acegls acgils aeegls aegils**

aceegins agencies encages ceasing. *See* **aceegn aceens aceins acgins**

aceegkrw wreckage. *See* **aeekrw**

aceegn encage acne agee cage cane gene ace age ane can cee gae gan gee nae nag nee ae an en na ne

aceegnoz cozenage. *See* **aceegn ceegno**

aceegns encages. *See* **aceegn aceens aeegns**

aceegnsv scavenge encages avenges. *See* **aceegn aceens aeegns aeegnv**

aceegorv coverage overage. *See* **aeegrv**

aceehhst cheetahs cheetah chetahs escheat hatches sheathe teaches. *See* **acehht acehst aehhst ceehst**

aceehht cheetah. *See* **acehht**

aceehint echinate. *See* **aceent achint aeehnt ceehnt**

aceehip cheapie. *See* **aceeip acehp ceehp**

aceehipr peachier cheapie cheaper. *See* **aceeip acehir acehpr ceeipr**

aceehips cheapies cheapie peaches. *See* **aceeip aceeps acehis acehps**

aceehirv achiever achieve archive heavier. *See* **acehir**

aceehisv achieves achieve chevies. *See* **acehis aceisv aeehsv ceehis**

aceehiv achieve. *See* **aeehv**

aceehko hoecake. *See* **aceek ceehk cehko**

aceehkos hoecakes hoecake. *See* **ceehks ceehos cehkos**

aceehl chelae chela leach leech ache alee each hale heal heel lace lech ace ale cee eel hae lac lea lee ae ah eh el ha he la

aceehlos shoelace leaches loaches. *See* **aceehl acehls acelos aehlos**

aceehlps pleaches chapels leaches peaches. *See* **aceehl aceeps acehlp acehls**

aceehlr leacher. *See* **aceelr aceehl aeehlr ceehlr**

aceehlrs leachers cereals healers larches leacher leaches lechers reaches. *See* **aceehl aceelr aceers acehls**

aceehls leaches. *See* **aceehl acehls ceehls**

aceehmnr menarche machree. *See* **aceemn aceemr aceenr aeehmr**

aceehmr machree. *See* **aceemr aeehmr**

aceehmrs cashmere machrees marchese amerces machree marches mesarch racemes reaches schemer. *See* **aceemr aceers acehms acehrs**

aceehmt machete. *See* **aceht achmt eehmt**

aceehnn enhance. *See* **aehnn ceehn**

aceehnns enhances enhance enchase. *See* **aceens aehnns**

aceehnp cheapen. *See* **aeehnp acehp ceehp**

aceehnps cheapens cheapen enchase peaches peahens. *See* **aceens aceeps acehps acenps**

aceehns enchase. *See* **aceens acehs aehns**

aceehnss enchases enchase encases. *See* **aceens aceess acehss ceenss**

aceehpr cheaper. *See* **acehpr**

aceehprr preacher cheaper. *See* **aceerr acehpr aceprr aeehrr**

aceehprs preaches cheaper eparchs escaper parches peaches perches reaches reshape. *See* **aceeps aceers acehpr acehps**

aceehps peaches. *See* **acehps ceehps aceeps**

aceehpst cheapest escheat hepcats patches peaches teaches. *See* **aceeps acehps acehpt acehst**

aceehrrs research searcher archers careers hearers reaches. *See* **aceerr aceers acehrr acehrs**

aceehrs reaches. *See* **acehrs ceehrs aceers aeehrs**

aceehrss searches crashes creases eschars hearses reaches. *See* **aceers aceess acehrs acehss**

aceehrst cheaters hectares teachers cheater creates escheat heaters hectare reaches reheats retches teacher teaches. *See* **aceers aceert acehrs acehst**

aceehrt cheater hectare teacher. *See* **aceert aeehrt**

aceehrtt catheter chatter cheater hectare ratchet teacher theater theatre. *See* **aceert aeehrt aehrtt eehrtt**

aceehsst escheats escheat sachets scathes teaches. *See* **aceess acehss acehst acesst**

aceehst escheat teaches. *See* **acehst ceehst**

aceeiknp peacenik kneecap. *See* **aceeip**

aceeikrr creakier. *See* **aceerr aceirr aeikrr**

aceeilnr reliance carline cleaner recline. *See* **aceelr aceenr aceilr aceinr**

aceeilns salience cleanse license sanicle scalene silence. *See* **aceens aceins acelns aeilns**

aceeilp calipee. *See* **aceeip aceilp**

aceeilps especial calipee eclipse special. *See* **aceeip aceeps aceilp aceips**

aceeimrr creamier creamer. *See* **aceemr aceerr aceirr aeemrr**

aceeimrs casimere amerces mercies racemes seamier. *See* **aceemr aceers aceims aceirs**

aceeinpt patience. *See* **aceeip aceent acinpt ceeint**

aceeinrs increase arsenic careens carnies sincere. *See* **aceenr aceens aceers aceinr**

aceeintv enactive. *See* **aceent aceitv aeintv ceeint**

aceeip apiece peace piece cape epic pace pica pice ace ape cap cee cep ice pea pee pie ae ai pa pe pi

aceeirsw wiseacre. *See* **aceers aceirs aeeirs**

aceeirtv creative reactive. *See* **aceert aceitv ceeirt**

aceejt ejecta eject cate ace act aet ate cat cee eat eta jet tea tee ae at ta

aceek ackee cake ace cee eke ae ka

aceeklmr mackerel. *See* **aceelr aceemr aceklm acelmr**

aceeknp kneecap. *See* **aceek aceep acenp**

aceeknps kneecaps kneecap. *See* **aceens aceeps acenps ceenps**

aceeknrw neckwear. *See* **aceenr aceknr aeeknw aeekrw**

aceell cellae cella alee call cell lace leal ace ale all cee eel ell lac lea lee ae el la

aceellmt cellmate. *See* **aceell acelmt aeellm aellmt**

aceelln nacelle. *See* **aceell aceln**

aceellns nacelles cleanse nacelle scalene. *See* **aceell aceens acelns**

aceellnt lancelet nacelle. *See* **aceell aceent acelnt aeelnt**

aceellrr cellarer clearer. *See* **aceell aceelr aceerr**

aceellrt cellaret treacle. *See* **aceell aceelr aceert acelrt**

aceelmp emplace. *See* **aeelmp acelm aclmp**

aceelmps emplaces emplace empales. *See* **aceeps acelms acelps aclmps**

aceelnpt pentacle. *See* **aceent acelnt acelpt aeelnt**

aceelnr cleaner. *See* **aceenr aceelr ceelnr acelnr aeelnr**

aceelnrs cleaners cleanser careens cereals cleaner cleanse crenels lancers leaners scalene. *See* **aceelr aceenr aceens aceers**

aceelnru cerulean cleaner lucarne nuclear unclear. *See* **aceelr aceenr acelnr acelnu**

aceelns cleanse scalene. *See* **acelns aceens**

aceelnss cleanses cleanse encases scalene. *See* **aceens aceess acelns acelss**

aceelnst cleanest cantles celesta centals cleanse lancets lateens leanest scalene tenaces. *See* **aceens aceent acelns acelnt**

aceelnsv enclaves valences cleanse cleaves enclave enslave leavens scalene valence. *See* **aceelv aceens acelns acelsv**

aceelntt tentacle. *See* **aceent acelnt aceltt aeelnt**

aceelntu nucleate cuneate. *See* **aceent acelnt acelnu aeelnt**

aceelnv enclave valence. *See* **aceelv aeelnv**

aceelops opalesce. *See* **aceeps acelos acelps aeelps**

aceelors escarole areoles cereals coalers creoles oracles. *See* **aceelr aceers acelor acelos**

aceelort relocate elector electro locater treacle. *See* **aceelr aceert acelor acelot**

aceelpr percale replace. *See* **acelpr aceelr aeelpr**

aceelprs percales replaces carpels cereals escaper leapers parcels percale placers relapse repeals replace scalper. *See* **aceelr aceeps aceers acelpr**

aceelptu peculate epaulet. *See* **acelpt aceptu**

aceelr cereal clear creel acre alee care carl cere earl lace leer race rale real reel ace ale arc are car cee ear eel era ere lac lar lea lee rec ae el er la re

aceelrr clearer. *See* **aceerr acelrr aceelr**

aceelrrs clearers careers carrels cereals clearer. *See* **aceelr aceerr aceers acelrs**

aceelrs cereals. *See* **aceelr acelrs aceers ceelrs aeelrs**

aceelrss careless cereals creases earless leasers resales reseals scalers scleras sealers. *See* **aceelr aceers aceess acelrs**

aceelrst clearest treacles cartels celesta cereals clarets creates elaters relates scarlet stealer tercels treacle. *See* **aceelr aceers aceert acelrs**

aceelrsv cleavers carvels cereals cleaver cleaves reveals several. *See* **aceelr aceelv aceers acelrs**

aceelrt treacle. *See* **acelrt aceert aceelr aeelrt ceelrt**

aceelrtu ulcerate treacle lecture. *See* **aceelr aceert acelrt acertu**

aceelrv cleaver. *See* **acelrv aceelr aceelv ceelrv aeelrv**

aceelsst celestas castles celesta selects teasels. *See* **aceess acelss acelst acesst**

aceelst celesta. *See* **acelst aeelst ceelst**

aceelstt telecast celesta. *See* **acelst aceltt acestt aeelst**

aceelsv cleaves. *See* **acelsv aceelv aeelsv**

aceelv cleave calve clave leave alee cave eave lace lave leva vale veal ace ale ave cee eel eve lac lea lee lev vac vee ae el la

aceemn menace enema acme acne amen came cane mace mane mean name ace ane cam can cee mac mae man men nae nee ae am an em en ma me na ne

aceemns menaces. *See* **aceens aeemns aceemn**

aceemnst casement cements meanest menaces tenaces. *See* **aceemn aceens aceent acenst**

aceemopr camporee compare compeer. *See* **aceemr acemop acempr aeempr**

aceemorv overcame. *See* **aceemr eemorv**

aceemr amerce raceme cream ameer acme acre came care cere cram mace marc mare mere race ream ace arc are arm cam car cee ear era ere mac mae mar ram rec rem ae am em er ma me re

aceemrr creamer. *See* **aceemr aceerr ceemrr aeemrr**

aceemrrs creamers screamer amerces careers creamer mercers racemes reamers. *See* **aceemr aceerr aceers acemrs**

aceemrry creamery creamer. *See* **aceemr aceerr acemry aeemrr**

aceemrs amerces racemes. *See* **aeemrs aceemr acemrs aceers**

aceemrst cremates amerces creates cremate racemes steamer. *See* **aceemr aceers aceert acemrs**

aceemrt cremate. *See* **aceemr aceert ceemrt**

aceemz eczema acme came mace maze ace cam cee mac mae zee ae am em ma me

aceennp penance. *See* **aeennp aceep acenp**

aceennps penances penance. *See* **aceens aceeps acenps aeennp**

aceennrt entrance canteen centner crenate reenact. *See* **aceenr aceent aceert acenrt**

aceennst canteens canteen nascent neatens tenaces. *See* **aceens aceent acenst aeennt**

aceennsy cayennes cayenne. *See* **aceens**

aceennt canteen. *See* **aceent aeennt**

aceenny cayenne. *See* **acnny**

aceenort carotene acetone crenate enactor reenact. *See* **aceenr aceent aceert acenor**

aceenost acetones acetone cenotes octanes tenaces. *See* **aceens aceent acenos acenot**

aceenot acetone. *See* **ceenot aceent acenot**

aceenprr parcener prancer. *See* **aceenr aceerr acenpr aceprr**

aceenr careen caner crane nacre acne acre cane care cere earn erne narc near race ace ane arc are can car cee ear era ere nae nee ran rec ae an en er na ne re

aceenrrt recreant caterer crenate reenact retrace terrace terrane. *See* **aceenr aceent aceerr aceert**

aceenrs careens. *See* **acenrs aceenr aceens ceenrs**

aceenrst reenacts sarcenet canters careens centers centres creates crenate earnest eastern nearest nectars recants reenact tenaces trances. *See* **aceenr aceens aceent aceers**

aceenrt crenate reenact. *See* **acenrt ceenrt aceert aceent aeenrt**

aceens encase canes cease cense scene aces acne cane cans case cees ease sane scan seen ace ane can cee ens nae nee sac sea see sen ae an as en na ne

aceenss encases. *See* **aceess ceenss aceens**

aceenst tenaces. *See* **acenst aceent aeenst**

aceent cetane tenace enact eaten acne ante cane cant cate cent neat teen ace act aet ane ant ate can cat cee eat eta nae nee net tan tea tee ten ae an at en na ne ta

aceentu cuneate. *See* **aceent**

aceep peace cape pace ace ape cap cee cep pea pee ae pa pe

aceeprs escaper. *See* **aceers ceeprs aceeps aeeprs**

aceeprss escapers asperse creases escaper escapes escarps parsecs precess scrapes serapes. *See* **aceeps aceers aceess aceprs**

aceeps escape capes cease paces peace pease scape space aces apes apse cape caps case cees ceps ease pace peas pees seep ace ape asp cap cee cep pas pea pee sac sap sea see spa ae as pa pe

aceepss escapes. *See* **aceess aceeps aeepss acepss**

aceerr career racer acre care cere race rare rear ace arc are car cee ear era ere err rec ae er re

aceerrs careers. *See* **aceerr aceers aeerrs acerrs**

aceerrst caterers retraces terraces careers carters caterer craters creates retrace serrate terrace tracers. *See* **aceerr aceers aceert acerrs**

aceerrt caterer retrace terrace. *See* **aceerr acerrt aceert aeerrt ceerrt**

aceerrtu creature caterer retrace terrace. *See* **aceerr aceert acerru acertu**

aceers crease acres cares cease erase races scare scree aces acre arcs arse care cars case cees cere ears ease eras race rase scar sear seer sera sere ace arc are car cee ear era ere rec res sac sea see ae as er re

aceerss creases. *See* **acerss aceess aceers aeerss ceerss**

aceersss caresses creases cresses. *See* **aceers aceess acerss aeerss**

aceerssv crevasse creases scarves. *See* **aceers aceess acerss acersv**

aceerst creates. *See* **aceert ceerst aeerst**

aceerstx exacters creates exacter excreta. *See* **aceers aceert acerst acestx**

aceersu cesurae. *See* **acersu ceersu aceers**

aceert cerate create caret carte cater crate eater erect react terce trace acre care cart cate cere race rate rete tare tear tree ace act aet arc are art ate car cat cee ear eat era ere eta rat rec ret tar tea tee ae at er re ta

aceerttu eructate curette. *See* **aceert acertu ceertt certtu**

aceertx exacter excreta. *See* **aceert**

acees cease aces case cees ease ace cee sac sea see ae as

aceess ceases cases cease eases aces case cees cess ease sacs seas sees ace ass cee ess sac sea see ae as

aceessst cassette stactes estates. *See* **aceess acesst acestt aeesst**

acef cafe face ace ae fa

aceffgin effacing caffein. *See* **acefin acfgin**

aceffhir chaffier chaffer. *See* **acefir acehir**

aceffhr chaffer. *See* **acefh acffh acehr**

aceffhrs chaffers chaffer. *See* **acefhs acefrs acehrs acffhs**

aceffin caffein. *See* **acefin**

aceffins caffeins caffein fancies fascine fiances. *See* **acefin acefis aceins**

aceffst affects. *See* **acefft acefst**

acefft affect facet cafe cate face fact fate feat ace act aet aft ate cat eat eft eta fat tea ae at fa ta

acefginn enfacing finance fencing. *See* **acefin aceinn acfgin**

acefgint faceting. *See* **acefin acfgin acgint aegint**

acefglru graceful careful rageful. *See* **acflru aeflru afglru**

acefh chafe ache cafe chef each face ace feh hae ae ah eh fa ha he

acefhmr chamfer. *See* **acefh acehr achmr**

acefhmrs chamfers chamfer marches mesarch. *See* **acefhs acefrs acehms acehrs**

acefhs chafes aches cafes chafe chase chefs faces sheaf aces ache cafe case cash chef each face fash safe ace ash fas feh hae has sac sea she ae ah as eh fa ha he sh

aceiipr pacifier. *See* **acefir**

acefiips pacifies. *See* **acefis aceips**

aceffirt artifice. *See* **acefir aciirt**

acefil facile fecal ileac alif cafe calf ceil clef face fail fila file flea lace laic leaf lice lief life ace ail ale elf fie ice lac lea lei lie ae ai el fa if la li

acefill icefall. *See* **acefil aefill**

acefills icefalls icefall failles. *See* **acefil acefis acfils acills**

acefilm malefic. *See* **acefil aceilm**

acefimpr campfire campier. *See* **acefir acempr**

acefin fiance acne cafe cane face fain fane fine naif nice ace ane ani can fan fen fie fin ice nae ae ai an en fa if in na ne

acefinn finance. *See* **acefin aceinn**

acefinns finances canines fancies fannies fascine fiances finance. *See* **acefin acefis aceinn aceins**

acefinr fancier. *See* **aceinr acefir acefin**

acefinrs fanciers arsenic carnies fancier fancies fascine fiacres fiances. *See* **acefin acefir acefis acefrs**

acefins fancies fascine fiances. *See* **aceins acefis**

acefinss fascines fancies fascine fiances incases. *See* **acefin acefis acefss aceins**

acefinst fanciest fancies fascine fiances infects. *See* **acefin acefis acefst aceins**

acefioss fiascoes fiascos. *See* **acefis acefss acfios aefoss**

acefir fiacre afire ceria facer farce feria acre cafe care face fair fare fear fire race rice rife ace air arc are arf car ear era far fie fir ice ire rec ref ria rif ae ai er fa if re

acefirrt craftier cirrate erratic refract. *See* **acefir aceirr aceirrt aefirr**

acefirs fiacres. *See* **aceirs acefrs acefis aefirs acefir**

acefirtt trifecta cattier citrate. *See* **acefir aefrtt aeirtt efirtt**

acefis facies cafes faces aces asci cafe case face fies fisc ices safe ace fas fie ice ifs sac sea sic ae ai as fa if is si

acefity acetify. *See* **aceft**

acefl fecal cafe calf clef face flea lace leaf ace ale elf lac lea ae el fa la

aceflmno flamenco. *See* **acflno aeflmn aefmno**

aceflnor falconer corneal. *See* **acelnr acelor acenor acflno**

aceflnot conflate falconet. *See* **acelnt acelot acenot acflno**

aceflru careful. *See* **acflru aeflru**

aceflruu furculae careful furcula. *See* **acflru aeflru celruu**

acefnorv conferva. *See* **acenor acenrv cefnor**

acefnrsu furnaces furnace surface. *See* **acefrs acefsu acenrs acensu**

acefnru furnace. *See* **acenr acefr acfnr**

aceforst forecast coaster factors. *See* **acefrs acefst aceors aceost**

acefr facer farce acre cafe care face fare fear race ace arc are arf car ear era far rec ref ae er fa re

acefrrst refracts carters craters rafters refract tracers. *See* **acefrs acefst acerrs acerrt**

acefrrt refract. *See* **acerrt aefrrt**

acefrrtu fracture facture furcate refract. *See* **aceftu acerrt acerru acertu**

acefrs facers farces acres cafes cares facer faces farce fares fears races safer scare scarf aces acre arcs arfs arse cafe care cars case ears eras face fare fear race rase refs safe scar sear sera serf ace arc are arf car ear era far fas rec ref res sac sea ae as er fa re

acefrssu surfaces causers saucers surface. *See* **acefrs acefss acefsu acerss**

acefrstu factures furcates curates facture faucets furcate surface. *See* **acefrs acefst acefsu aceftu**

acefrsu surface. *See* **acersu acefrs acefsu**

acefrtu facture furcate. *See* **aceftu acertu**

acefs cafes faces aces cafe case face safe ace fas sac sea ae as fa

acefss fasces cafes cases faces aces cafe case cess face fess sacs safe seas ace ass ess fas sac sea ae as fa

acefst facets faces caste cates faces facet facts fates feast feats feats aces acts cafe case cast cate cats east eats efts etas face fact fast fate fats feat safe scat seat sect seta teas ace act aet aft ate cat eat eft eta fas fat sac sat sea set tea ae as at fa ta

acefstu faucets. *See* **acefst acefsu aceftu**

acefsu fauces cafes cause faces sauce aces cafe case cues face feus fuse safe ace cue fas feu sac sea sue use ae as fa us

acefsy casefy cafes faces fyces aces ayes cafe case cays easy eyas face fays fyce safe syce yeas ace aye cay fas fay fey sac say sea yea yes ae as ay fa ye

aceft facet cafe cate face fact fate feat ace act aet aft ate cat eat eft eta fat tea ae at fa ta

aceftu faucet facet acute cafe cate cute face fact fate feat tufa ace act aet aft ate cat cue cut eat eft eta fat feu tau tea ae at fa ta ut

aceg cage ace age gae ae

acegginn encaging. *See* **aceinn acggin aeggin**

aceggirr craggier. *See* **acegir aceirr eggirr**

aceghiln leaching angelic healing leching. *See* **aceghn acegln acghin acgiln**

aceghinr reaching arching chagrin changer hearing. *See* **aceghn aceghr acegir acehir**

aceghint cheating teaching heating etching. *See* **aceghn acghin acgint achint**

aceghn change ache acne cage cane each hang ace age ane can gae gan hae hag hen nae nag nah ae ah an eh en ha he na ne

aceghnr changer. *See* **aceghn aceghr aeghnr**

aceghnrs changers changer changes charges hangers ranches. *See* **aceghn aceghr acegrs acehrs**

aceghns changes. *See* **aceghn acehs aehns**

aceghosu gouaches gouache gauchos. *See* **aceghu acegos acghou cehosu**

aceghou gouache. *See* **aceghu acghou**

aceghr charge chare gerah grace reach ache acre ager arch cage care char crag each gear hare hear race rage rhea ace age arc are car ear era erg gae gar hae hag her rag rah rec reg ae ah eh er ha he re

aceghrr charger. *See* **aceghr acehrr**

aceghrrs chargers archers charger charges. *See* **aceghr acegrs acehrr acehrs**

aceghrs charges. *See* **acehrs aceghr aeghrs acegrs**

aceghu gauche ache ague cage chug each huge ace age cue gae hae hag hue hug ugh ae ah eh ha he

acegiinv vicinage. *See* **acginv**

acegiknr creaking carking racking recking. *See* **acegir aceinr aceknr acgikn**

acegillr allergic glacier gracile. *See* **acegir aceilr acellr acgill**

acegilmu mucilage. *See* **aceilm**

acegiln angelic. *See* **aegiln acegln acgiln**

acegilnn cleaning angelic lancing leaning. *See* **acegln aceinn acgiln aegiln**

acegilnr clearing angelic carline clinger cringle glacier gracile realign. *See* **acegir acegln aceilr aceinr**

acegilnt cleating angelic atingle elating gelatin genital. *See* **acegln acelnt acgiln acgint**

acegilnv cleaving angelic calving leaving. *See* **acegln acgiln acginv aegiln**

acegilp pelagic. *See* **aceilp**

acegilr glacier gracile. *See* **acegir aceilr acgilr**

acegilrs glaciers claries eclairs garlics glacier gracile scalier. *See* **acegir acegls acegrs aceilr**

acegimnn menacing meaning. *See* **aceimn aceinn acgimn aegimn**

acegimnr creaming carmine grimace mangier reaming. *See* **acegir aceimn aceinr acemnr**

acegimnt magnetic mintage teaming tegmina. *See* **aceimn acgimn acgint acimnt**

acegimr grimace. *See* **acegir aegimr**

acegimrs grimaces grimace mirages. *See* **acegir acegrs aceims aceirs**

aceginno canoeing coinage. *See* **aceinn acginn acgino aegnno**

aceginns   encasing canines ceasing censing. *See* aceinn aceins acginn acgins

aceginnt   enacting ancient anteing antigen canting gentian. *See* aceinn acginn acgint aegint

acegino   coinage. *See* acgino aceno aegno

aceginos   coinages agonies ceasing coinage. *See* acegos aceins acenos acgino

aceginpr   capering carping craping reaping. *See* acegir aceinr acenpr acginp

aceginps   escaping ceasing scaping spacing. *See* aceins aceips acenps acginp

aceginrs   creasing arsenic carnies ceasing cringes earings erasing gainers regains sacring scaring searing. *See* acegir acegrs aceinr aceins

aceginrt   argentic catering creating reacting carting certain crating granite ingrate tangier tearing tracing. *See* acegir aceinr acenrt acginr

acegins   ceasing. *See* aceins acgins aegins

aceginss   caginess casings ceasing incases. *See* aceins acgins aegins aeinss

acegintx   exacting inexact. *See* acgint aegint agintx

acegiott   cogitate cottage. *See* acitt aciot acott

acegir   cagier ceria cigar grace acre ager cage care crag gear race rage rice ace age air arc are car ear era erg gae gar gie ice ire rag rec reg ria rig ae ai er re

acegist   cagiest. *See* cegist aegis acegs

acegjkl   jackleg. *No 6s or 5s*

acegjkls   jacklegs jackleg. *See* acegls

acegklr   grackle. *See* acelr ceklr acekr

acegklrs   grackles grackle slacker. *See* acegls acegrs acekrs acelrs

acegkor   corkage. *See* acgor acekr ackor

acegllno   collagen collage congeal galleon. *See* acegln acello agllno

acegllo   collage. *See* acello aegll

acegllos   collages collage locales. *See* acegls acegos acello acelos

acegln   glance angel angle canel clang clean glean lance acne cage cane clan gale glen lace lane lean ace age ale ane can gae gal gan gel lac lag lea leg nae nag ae an el en la na ne

aceglno   congeal. *See* acegln aelno aglno

aceglnos   congeals congeal glances. *See* acegln acegls acegos acelns

aceglns   glances. *See* aeglns acelns acglns acegls acegln

acegls   glaces cages gales laces scale aces ages ales cage case gale gals gels lace lags leas legs sage sale scag seal slag ace age ale els gae gal gas gel lac lag lea leg sac sag sal sea ae as el la

acegly   legacy cagey cage cagy clay gale lace lacy ace age ale aye cay gae gal gay

gel gey lac lag lay lea leg lye yea ae ay el la ye

acegmnoy   geomancy. *See* acegny aemnoy

acegnnty   tangency tenancy. *See* acegny aegnnt cegnty

acegnost   cognates cognate congest octanes onstage. *See* acegos acenos acenot acenst

acegnot   cognate. *See* acenot cegnot

acegny   agency cagey acne cage cagy cane yang yean ace age ane any aye can cay gae gan gay gey nae nag nay yea yen ae an ay en na ne ye

acegors   cargoes corsage. *See* acgors aceors acegrs acegos

acegorss   corsages cargoes corsage socages. *See* acegos acegrs aceors acerss

acegortt   cottager cottage garotte. *See* aegort aegrtt aeortt ceortt

acegorty   category. *See* aegort aegrty

acegoru   courage. *See* acgoru aegru acegr

acegos   socage cages aces ages cage case cogs egos goas goes sage sago scag sego ace age ago cog ego gae gas goa sac sag sea ae as go os so

acegoss   socages. *See* acegos acess aegss

acegostt   cottages cottage costate. *See* acegos aceost acestt acostt

acegott   cottage. *See* acott ceott acett

acegr   grace acre ager cage care crag gear race rage ace age arc are car ear era erg gae gar rag rec reg ae er re

acegrs   graces acres cages cares crags gears grace races rages sager scare scrag aces acre ager ages arcs arse cage care cars case crag ears eras ergs gars gear race rage rags rase regs sage scag scar sear sera ace age arc are car ear era erg gae gar gas rag rec reg res sac sag sea ae as er re

acegs   cages aces ages cage case sage scag ace age gae gas sac sag sea ae as

acegsstu   scutages scutage. *See* acesst acessu aegsst aegssu

acegstu   scutage. *See* acetu aegsu acegs

acegy   cagey cage cagy ace age aye cay gae gay gey yea ae ay ye

aceh   ache each ace hae ae ah eh ha he

acehhirr   hierarch charier. *See* acehir acehrr aceirr cehirr

acehhmnn   henchman. *See* aehnn

acehhnsu   haunches hunches. *See* acehnu acensu achhnu

acehhrst   hatchers chetahs hatcher hatches hearths. *See* acehht acehrs acehst acerst

acehhrsu   hachures hachure. *See* acehrs acersu aehhrs cehrsu

acehhrt   hatcher. *See* acehht aehhrt

acehhrty   hatchery hatcher. *See* acehht aehhrt aehhty aehrty

acehhru   hachure. *See* acehr cehru

acehhst   chetahs hatches. *See* acehst acehht aehhst

acehhstt   hatchets thatches chetahs hatches hatchet. *See* acehht acehst acestt achhtt

acehht   chetah cheat hatch heath tache teach theca ache cate chat each etch hate hath heat tach tech ace act aet ate cat eat eta eth hae hah hat heh het tea the ae ah at eh ha he ta

acehhtt   hatchet. *See* acehht achhtt

acehiirt   hieratic itchier. *See* acehir aciirt cehirt

acehijkr   hijacker. *See* acehik acehir acehkr achijk

acehik   hackie ache cake each hack haik hake heck hick hike ace chi hae hie ice ae ah ai eh ha he hi ka

acehiklr   chalkier. *See* acehik acehir acehkl acehkr

acehikrw   whackier wackier. *See* acehik acehir acehkr aehkrw

acehiks   hackies. *See* acehik acehis

acehill   challie helical. *See* acell acehl chill

acehilnt   ethnical ethical. *See* acehlt acelnt achint acilnt

acehilt   ethical. *See* acehlt aehilt

acehiltt   athletic chattel ethical latchet lattice tactile. *See* acehlt aceltt aehilt cehitt

acehimms   chammies. *See* acehis acehms aceims aehims

acehimn   machine. *See* aceimn

acehimnr   chairmen carmine chimera machine. *See* acehir aceimn aceinr acemnr

acehimns   machines amnesic cinemas machine. *See* acehis acehms aceimn aceims

acehimp   impeach. *See* aceim achmp acehp

acehimpt   empathic emphatic aphetic hematic hepatic impeach. *See* acehpt acimpt

acehimr   chimera. *See* acehir aehimr

acehimrs   chimeras marchesi cahiers cashier charism chimera chrisma marches mesarch. *See* acehir acehis acehms acehrs

acehimt   hematic. *See* achit aceim aceht

acehimtt   thematic hematic. *See* cehitt

acehinn   enchain. *See* aceinn achin cehin

acehinns   enchains enchain canines. *See* acehis aceinn aceins achins

acehinot   inchoate. *See* acenot achint acinot cehint

acehinrs inarches arsenic cahiers carnies cashier hernias ranches. *See* **acehir acehis acehrs aceinr**

acehinss achiness chaises incases. *See* **acehis acehss aceins achins**

acehinst asthenic chasten ethnics. *See* **acehis acehst acein acenst**

acehiprs seraphic cahiers cashier ciphers eparchs harpies parches sharpie spheric. *See* **acehir acehis acehpr acehps**

acehiprt patchier aphetic chapter hepatic patcher pitcher. *See* **acehir acehpr acehpt aceprt**

acehipst pastiche aphetic aseptic hepatic hepcats patches pitches. *See* **acehis acehps acehpt acehst**

acehipt aphetic hepatic. *See* **acehpt achit cehit**

acehiptt pathetic aphetic hepatic. *See* **acehpt cehitt**

acehiptw whitecap aphetic hepatic. *See* **acehpt**

acehir cahier ceria chair chare reach ache acre arch care char each hair hare hear heir hire race rhea rice rich ace air arc are car chi ear era hae her hie ice ire rah rec ria ae ah ai eh er ha he hi re

acehirr charier. *See* **acehrr acehir aceirr cehirr**

acehirs cahiers cashier. *See* **aehirs aceirs achirs acehis acehrs**

acehirss cashiers cahiers cashier chaises crashes eschars. *See* **acehir acehis acehrs acehss**

acehirst chariest cahiers cashier cithers hastier raciest richest stearic. *See* **acehir acehis acehrs acehst**

acehirsv archives archive cahiers cashier viscera. *See* **acehir acehis acehrs aceirs**

acehirtt chattier theatric cattier chatter chitter citrate ratchet. *See* **acehir aehrtt aeirtt cehirt**

acehirv archive. *See* **acehir acerv acirv**

acehis chaise aches chase aces ache asci case cash each hies ices ace ash chi hae has hie his ice sac sea she sic ae ah ai as eh ha he hi is sh si

acehiss chaises. *See* **acehss acehis**

acehisst chastise ashiest chaises sachets scathes. *See* **acehis acehss acehst acesst**

acehistx cathexis. *See* **acehis acehst acestx cehist**

acehkl hackle chalk chela leach ache cake calk each hack hake hale heal heck kale lace lack lake lakh leak lech ace ale elk hae kal lac lea lek ae ah eh el ha he ka la

acehklov havelock. *See* **acehkl acelov**

---

acehklpr kreplach. *See* **acehkl acehkr acehlp acehpr**

acehkls hackles shackle. *See* **achkls acehkl acehls**

acehklss shackles clashes hackles shackle. *See* **acehkl acehls acehss acelss**

acehklty latchkey. *See* **acehkl acehlt acehly aceklt**

acehkmn hackmen. *See* **cehkn**

acehknsy hackneys hackney. *See* **aehkns aehnsy aeknsy**

acehkny hackney. *See* **aehny cehkn**

acehkr hacker chare crake creak reach ache acre arch cake care cark char each hack hake hare hark hear heck race rack rake reck rhea ace arc are ark car ear era hae her rah rec ae ah eh er ha he ka re

acehkrs hackers. *See* **acehrs acekrs acehkr aehkrs**

acehl chela leach ache each hale heal lace lech ace ale hae lac lea ae ah eh el ha he la

acehlls shellac. *See* **acehls aclls acell**

acehllss shellacs shellac clashes. *See* **acehls acehss acelss acllss**

acehllst hellcats chalets hellcat latches satchel shellac. *See* **acehls acehlt acehst acelst**

acehllt hellcat. *See* **acehlt aehllt**

acehlmy alchemy. *See* **acehly acelm cehmy**

acehlnn channel. *See* **acelnn acehl aehnn**

acehlnns channels channel cannels. *See* **acehls acelnn acelns aehlns**

acehlnpt planchet chaplet. *See* **acehlp acehlt acehpt acelnt**

acehlnr charnel. *See* **acelnr acehr acehl**

acehlnrs charnels charnel lancers larches ranches. *See* **acehls acehrs acelnr acelns**

acehlnru launcher charnel lucarne nuclear unclear. *See* **acehnu acelnr acelnu achlnu**

acehlnsu launches launces lunches unlaces unleash. *See* **acehls acehnu acelns acelnu**

acehlop epochal. *See* **acehlp acehop**

acehlor cholera chorale. *See* **cehlor achlor acehor acelor**

acehlors choleras chorales cholera chorale chorals coalers larches loaches oracles roaches scholar. *See* **acehls acehor acehrs acelor**

acehlort chlorate cholera chorale chortle locater trochal. *See* **acehlt acehor acelor acelot**

acehlos loaches. *See* **aehlos acehls acelos**

---

acehlost eschalot chalets clothes lactose latches loaches loathes locates satchel. *See* **acehls acehlt acehst acelos**

acehlp chapel pleach aleph chape cheap chela leach peach place ache cape chap clap each hale heal heap help lace leap lech pace pale peal plea ace ale alp ape cap cep hae hap hep lac lap lea pah pal pea ae ah eh el ha he la pa pe

acehlps chapels. *See* **aehlps acehlp acehps acehls acelps**

acehlpst chaplets chalets chapels chaplet hepcats latches patches placets satchel. *See* **acehlp acehls acehlt acehps**

acehlpt chaplet. *See* **acehlt acehpt acelpt acehlp**

acehlpy cheaply. *See* **acehlp acehly acehpy aehlpy**

acehlrs larches. *See* **acehrs acelrs acehls aehlrs**

acehls laches aches chase chela clash hales heals laces leach leash scale selah shale aces ache ales case cash each hale heal lace lash leas lech sale seal ace ale ash els hae has lac lea sac sal sea she ae ah as eh el ha he la sh

acehlss clashes. *See* **acehss aehlss acelss**

acehlsst satchels castles chalets clashes latches sachets satchel scathes. *See* **acehls acehlt acehss acehst**

acehlst chalets latches satchel. *See* **acelst acehlt acehst aehlst acehls**

acehlstt chattels latchets chalets chattel latches latchet satchel stealth. *See* **acehls acehlt acehst acelst**

acehlsty chastely acetyls chalets latches satchel. *See* **acehls acehlt acehly acehst**

acehlt chalet cheat chela cleat eclat latch lathe leach letch tache teach theca ache cate celt chat each etch hale halt hate heal heat lace late lath lech tach tael talc tale teal tech ace act aet ale alt ate cat eat eta eth hae hat het lac lea let tea the ae ah at eh el ha he la ta

acehltt chattel latchet. *See* **acehlt aceltt**

acehly leachy chela chyle leach ache achy clay each hale heal hyla lace lacy lech yeah yech ace ale aye cay hae hay hey lac lay lea lye yah yea ae ah ay eh el ha he la ye

acehmnrt merchant chanter manchet rematch. *See* **acemnr acenrt aehmnt aehnrt**

acehmnss chessman sachems. *See* **acehss acehss achmss aehmss**

acehmnst manchets anthems chasten manchet matches. *See* **acehms acehst acenst achnst**

acehmnt manchet. *See* **aehmnt**

acehmntw watchmen manchet. *See* **aehmnt**

acehmny achemny. *See* **cehmy aehny ehmny**

acehmort chromate rematch. *See* **acehor acemot achmor cehmor**

acehmrr marcher. *See* **acehrr aehmrr**

acehmrrs marchers archers marcher marches mesarch. *See* **acehms acehrr acehrs acemrs**

acehmrs marches mesarch. *See* **acehrs achmrs acemrs aehmrs acehms**

acehmrt rematch. *See* **acert acehr achmr**

acehms sachem schema aches acmes cames chase chasm hames maces shame aces ache acme ahem came cams case cash cham each hame hams hems mace macs mash mesa mesh same scam seam sham ace ash cam hae ham has hem mac mae sac sea she ae ah am as eh em ha he ma me sh

acehmss sachems. *See* **acehss achmss aehmss**

acehmst matches. *See* **acehst acehms**

acehmstu mustache matches. *See* **acehms acehst acemtu achmsu**

acehnnpt penchant enchant. *See* **acehpt**

acehnnst enchants chasten enchant nascent. *See* **acehst acenst achnst aehnns**

acehnnt enchant. *See* **aennt achnt aceht**

acehnopr canephor chaperon poacher. *See* **acehop acehor acehpr acenor**

acehnopt cenotaph phaeton phonate. *See* **acehop acehpt acenot aceopt**

acehnorr ranchero rancher. *See* **acehor acehrr acenor achnor**

acehnpsu paunches punches. *See* **acehnu acehps acenps acensu**

acehnrr rancher. *See* **acehrr acenr achnr**

acehnrrs ranchers archers rancher ranches. *See* **acehrr acehrs acenrs acerrs**

acehnrs ranches. *See* **acenrs acehrs**

acehnrss archness caserns crashes eschars harness ranches. *See* **acehrs acehss acenrs acerss**

acehnrst chanters anthers canters chanter chasten nectars ranches recants thenars trances. *See* **acehrs acehst acenrs acenrt**

acehnrt chanter. *See* **aehnrt acenrt cehnrt**

acehnsst chastens snatches stanches ascents chasten hastens sachets scathes secants stances. *See* **acehss acehst acenst acesst**

acehnst chasten. *See* **acenst achnst acehst aehnst cehnst**

acehnstu nautches canthus chasten staunch. *See* **acehnu acehst acenst acensu**

acehnty chantey. *See* **achnt aceht acent**

acehnu nuchae nucha ache acne cane each ace ane can cue hae hen hue nae nah ae ah an eh en ha he na ne nu

acehop cheapo chape cheap epoch peach poach ache cape capo chap chop cope each echo heap hope opah pace ace ape cap cep cop hae hap hep hoe hop ope pah pea ae ah eh ha he ho oh pa pe

acehopr poacher. *See* **achopr acehop acehor acehpr**

acehoprr reproach poacher. *See* **acehop acehor acehpr acehrr**

acehops cheapos poaches. *See* **acehps cehops**

acehor chorea chare chore ocher ochre ocrea orach reach roach ache acre aero arch care cero char core each echo hare hear hero hoar hoer hora race rhea ace arc are car cor ear era hae her hoe oar orc ore rah rec rho roc roe ae ah eh er ha he ho oh or re

acehors roaches. *See* **aehors acehrs cehors aceors**

acehortt theocrat chatter ratchet. *See* **acehor aehrtt aeortt ahortt**

acehortu outreach retouch. *See* **acehor acertu ahortu cehort**

acehossw showcase cashews. *See* **acehss acehsw achssw aehssw**

acehostu cathouse acetous touches. *See* **acehst aceost cehosu cehstu**

acehp chape cheap peach ache cape chap each heap pace ace ape cap cep hae hap hep pah pea ae ah eh ha he pa pe

acehpr eparch preach caper chape chare cheap crape pacer parch peach perch reach recap ache acre arch cape care carp chap char crap each hare harp heap hear pace pare pear race rape reap rhea ace ape arc are cap car cep ear era hae hap hep her pah par pea per rah rap rec rep ae ah eh er ha he pa pe re

acehprs eparchs parches. *See* **acehps acehpr acehrs aehprs**

acehprst chapters patchers carpets chapter eparchs hepcats parches patcher patches spectra threaps. *See* **acehpr acehps acehpt acehrs**

acehprsu purchase eparchs parches. *See* **acehpr acehps acehrs aceprs**

acehprt chapter patcher. *See* **aceprt acehpt acehpr aehprt**

acehpry eparchy. *See* **cehpry acehpr acehpy**

acehps chapes aches capes chape chaps chase cheap heaps paces peach phase scape shape space aces ache apes apse cape caps case cash ceps chap each haps hasp heap pace peas ace ape ash asp cap cep hae hap has hep pah pas pea sac sap sea she spa ae ah as eh ha he pa pe sh

acehpst hepcats patches. *See* **acepst acehps acehst acehpt**

acehpt hepcat chape cheap cheat epact patch peach tache teach theca ache cape cate chap chat each etch hate heap heat pace pact path peat tach tape tech ace act aet ape apt ate cap cat cep eat eta eth hae hap hat hep het pah pat pea pet tap tea the ae ah at eh ha he pa pe ta

acehpy peachy chape cheap peach ache achy cape chap each heap hype pace yeah yech ace ape aye cap cay cep hae hap hay hep hey pah pay pea pya yah yap yea yep ae ah ay eh ha he pa pe ye

acehr chare reach ache acre arch care char each hare hear race rhea ace arc are car ear era hae her rah rec ae ah eh er ha he re

acehrr archer chare racer reach ache acre arch care char each hare hear race rare rear rhea ace arc are car ear era err hae her rah rec ae ah eh er ha he re

acehrrs archers. *See* **acehrr acehrs acerrs aehrrs**

acehrst charters archers carters charter craters tracers. *See* **acehrr acehrs acehst acerrs**

acehrrt charter. *See* **acehrr acerrt aehrrt**

acehrrtt tetrarch charter chatter ratchet retract. *See* **acehrr acerrt aehrrt aehrtt**

acehrrx xerarch. *See* **acehrr acehrx**

acehrry archery. *See* **acehrr achrry cehrry**

acehrs chares eschar search aches acres cares chare chars chase crash hares hears races reach rheas scare share shear aces ache acre arch arcs arse care cars case cash char each ears eras hare hear hers race rahs rase rash resh rhea scar sear sera ace arc are ash car ear era hae has her rah rec res sac sea she ae ah as eh er ha he re sh

acehrss crashes eschars. *See* **acerss acehss acehrs aehrss**

acehrsst starches actress casters crashes eschars rashest recasts sachets scathes trashes. *See* **acehrs acehss acehst acerss**

acehrssu chasseur causers crashes crushes eschars saucers. *See* **acehrs acehss acerss acersu**

72

acehrstt chatters ratchets chatter hatters ratchet shatter stretch. *See* **acehrs acehst acerst acestt**

acehrstw watchers watcher watches wreaths. *See* **acehrs acehst acehsw acerst**

acehrsx exarchs. *See* **acehrs acehrx**

acehrsy hyraces. *See* **acehrs acersy**

acehrtt chatter ratchet. *See* **aehrtt acert acehr**

acehrtw watcher. *See* **aehrtw cehrtw**

acehrx exarch chare reach ache acre arch care char each hare hear race rhea ace arc are axe car ear era hae her hex rah rec rex ae ah ax eh er ex ha he re

acehs aches chase aces ache case cash each ace ash hae has sac sea she ae ah as eh ha he sh

acehss cashes chases aches ashes cases chase chess aces ache case cash cess each sacs sash seas ace ash ass ess hae has sac sea she ae ah as eh ha he sh

acehsssu chausses. *See* **acehss acessu aehsss chsssu**

acehsst sachets scathes. *See* **acehss acesst acehst cehsst**

acehsstw swatches cashews sachets scathes swathes watches. *See* **acehss acehst acehsw acesst**

acehssw cashews. *See* **acehss acehsw aehssw achssw**

acehst chaste cheats sachet scathe aches caste cates chase chats cheat chest haste hates heats tache teach techs theca aces ache acts case cash cast cate cats chat each east eats etas etch hast hate hats heat hest scat seat sect seta tach teas tech ace act aet ash ate cat eat eta eth hae has hat het sac sat sea set she tea the ae ah as at eh ha he sh ta

acehstw watches. *See* **acehsw acehst achstw aehstw**

acehsw cashew aches chase chaws chews hawse schwa aces ache awes case cash caws chaw chew each haws hews shaw shew wash ace ash awe caw hae has haw hew sac saw sea sew she was ae ah as aw eh ha he sh we

aceht cheat tache teach theca ache cate chat each etch hate heat tach tech ace act aet ate cat eat eta eth hae hat het tea the ae ah at eh ha he ta

aceiilst ciliates silicate ciliate elastic elicits italics laciest laities. *See* **acelst aciils aciilt ceiilt**

aceiilt ciliate. *See* **aciilt ceiilt**

aceiimrs casimire. *See* **aceims aceirs acemrs acimrs**

aceiintv inactive. *See* **aceitv aeintv ceiint**

aceiiprs piracies spicier. *See* **aceips aceirs aceprs aeiprs**

aceiirrt criteria cirrate erratic. *See* **aceirr acerrt aciirt**

aceiistv cavities. *See* **aceisv aceitv ceiist ceiisv**

aceijmst majestic sematic. *See* **aceims acimst aeimst aejmst**

aceijnrr jerrican. *See* **aceinr aceirr**

aceiklt catlike. *See* **aceklt ceiklt**

aceikmnn nickname. *See* **aceimn aceinn**

aceikmr keramic. *See* **acikmr aceim aceir**

aceikmrv maverick keramic. *See* **acikmr**

aceiknrr crankier. *See* **aceinr aceirr aceknr aeikrr**

aceikpsx pickaxes. *See* **aceips acikpx**

aceikrt tackier. *See* **acekrt ceikrt**

aceikrw wackier. *See* **ceikrw aceir acekr**

aceikss seasick. *See* **aceks acess ackss**

aceikstt tackiest tickets. *See* **acekst acestt acistt ceiktt**

aceikstw wackiest wickets. *See* **acekst aekstw ceiktw eikstw**

aceil ileac ceil lace laic lice ace ail ale ice lac lea lei lie ae ai el la li

aceillmr millrace miracle reclaim. *See* **aceilm aceilr acellr acelmr**

aceillmt metallic climate. *See* **aceilm acelmt aeillt aellmt**

aceillnt cliental. *See* **acelnt acilnt aeilln aeillt**

aceillop calliope. *See* **aceilp acello ceillo ceilop**

aceilloz localize. *See* **acello ceillo**

aceillps allspice special scalpel. *See* **aceilp aceips acelps acills**

aceillx lexical. *See* **aeilx acilx acell**

aceilm malice amice camel claim clime ileac melic acme calm came ceil clam lace laic lame lice lime mace mail male meal mica mice mile ace ail aim ale cam elm ice lac lam lea lei lie mac mae mel mil ae ai am el em la li ma me mi

aceilmmo camomile. *See* **aceilm**

aceilmmr clammier clammer miracle reclaim. *See* **aceilm aceilr acelmr aeilmr**

aceilmnp maniple capelin impanel maniple pelican. *See* **aceilm aceilp aceimn acemnp**

aceilmos camisole malices. *See* **aceilm aceims acelms acelos**

aceilmps misplace impales malices special. *See* **aceilm aceilp aceims aceips**

aceilmr miracle reclaim. *See* **acelmr aceilr aeilmr aceilm**

aceilmrs miracles reclaims claries eclairs mailers malices marcels miracle realism reclaim scalier. *See* **aceilm aceilr aceims aceirs**

aceilmrt metrical article climate maltier miracle recital reclaim. *See* **aceilm aceilr acelmr acelmt**

aceilms malices. *See* **aceims acelms acilms ceilms aceilm**

aceilmst climates calmest camlets climate elastic laciest malices sematic. *See* **aceilm aceims acelms acelmt**

aceilmsx climaxes exclaims malices exclaim. *See* **aceilm aceims acelms acelsx**

aceilmt climate. *See* **aceilm acelmt**

aceilmx exclaim. *See* **aceilm acilmx**

aceilmy mycelia. *See* **aceilm eilmy aelmy**

aceilnnp pinnacle capelin pelican. *See* **aceilp aceinn acelnn aeilnp**

aceilnp capelin pelican. *See* **aeilnp aceilp ceilnp**

aceilnps capelins pelicans capelin enclasp pelican pencils sanicle spancel spaniel special. *See* **aceilp aceins aceips acelns**

aceilnr carline. *See* **acilnr aceinr aceilr acelnr aeilnr**

aceilnrs carlines arsenic carline carlins carnies claries eclairs lancers sanicle scalier. *See* **aceilr aceinr aceins aceirs**

aceilnrt clarinet article carline central certain latrine ratline recital reliant retinal. *See* **aceilr aceinr acelnr acelnt**

aceilns sanicle. *See* **aeilns acelns aceins ceilns**

aceilnss laciness sanicles sanicle incases. *See* **aceins acelns acelss aeilns**

aceilnsu lunacies launces sanicle unlaces. *See* **aceins acelns acelnu acelsu**

aceilnsy saliency sanicle. *See* **aceins acelns aeilns aeilsy**

aceilopr capriole caliper calorie cariole loricae replica. *See* **aceilp aceilr acelor acelpr**

aceilopt poetical capitol ectopia optical plicate polecat topical. *See* **aceilp acelot acelpt aceopt**

aceilor calorie cariole loricae. *See* **acelor aceilr acilor ceilor**

aceilorr carriole calorie cariole caroler loricae. *See* **aceilr aceirr acelor acilor**

aceilors calories carioles calorie cariole claries coalers eclairs loricae oracles recoils scalier. *See* **aceilr aceirs acelor acelos**

aceilort loricate article calorie cariole erotica locater loricae recital. *See* **aceilr acelor acelot acelrt**

aceilotv locative violate. *See* **aceitv acelot acelov aceotv**

aceilovz vocalize. *See* **acelov**

aceilp epical plicae ileac place plica cape ceil clap clip epic lace laic leap lice pace pail pale peal pica pice pile plea ace ail ale alp ape cap cep ice lac lap lea lei lie lip pal pea pie ae ai el la li pa pe pi

aceilpr caliper replica. *See* **acelpr aceilp aceilr**

aceilprs calipers replicas spiracle caliper carpels claries eclairs parcels placers replica scalier scalper special splicer. *See* **aceilp aceilr aceips aceirs**

aceilprt particle article caliper plectra plicate recital replica. *See* **aceilp aceilr acelpr acelpt**

aceilpru peculiar auricle caliper replica. *See* **aceilp aceilr aceiru acelpr**

aceilps special. *See* **aceips aeilps acelps aceilp ceilps**

aceilpss slipcase specials espials palsies special splices. *See* **aceilp aceips acelps acelss**

aceilpt plicate. *See* **aceilp acelpt**

aceilr eclair lacier ceria clear ileac relic acre aril care carl ceil earl lace laic lair liar lice lira lire race rail rale real rial rice riel rile ace ail air ale arc are car ear era ice ire lac lar lea lei lie rec ria ae ai el er la li re

aceilrs claries eclairs scalier. *See* **aceirs acelrs aceilr ceilrs aeilrs**

aceilrss classier airless claries eclairs sailers scalers scalier scleras serials slicers. *See* **aceilr aceirs acelrs acelss**

aceilrst articles recitals article cartels clarets claries eclairs elastic laciest raciest realist recital relicts retails saltier saltire scalier scarlet stearic. *See* **aceilr aceirs acelrs acelrt**

aceilrsu auricles auricle claries eclairs saucier scalier secular. *See* **aceilr aceirs aceiru acelrs**

aceilrsv cavilers visceral carvels caviler claries clavier eclairs revisal scalier viscera. *See* **aceilr aceirs aceisv acelrs**

aceilrt article recital. *See* **acelrt acilrt ceilrt aeilrt**

aceilrtt tractile article cattier citrate clatter lattice recital tactile tertial. *See* **aceilr acelrt aceltt acilrt**

aceilrtv vertical article caviler clavier recital. *See* **aceilr aceitv acelrt acelrv**

aceilrty literacy article clarity irately reality recital. *See* **aceilr acelrt acelty acilrt**

aceilru auricle. *See* **aceiru acilru aceilr**

aceilrv caviler clavier. *See* **acelrv aceilr**

aceilsst scaliest castles elastic laciest. *See* **acelss acelst acesst aeilss**

aceilst elastic laciest. *See* **acelst**

aceilstt lattices elastic laciest lattice tactile. *See* **acelst aceltt acestt acistt**

aceiltt lattice tactile. *See* **aceltt ailtt acitt**

aceiltvy actively. *See* **aceitv acelty acitvy eiltvy**

aceim amice acme came mace mica mice ace aim cam ice mac mae ae ai am em ma me mi

aceimn anemic cinema iceman amice amine anime manic minae mince acme acne amen came cane mace main mane mean mica mice mien mina mine name nice ace aim ane ani cam can ice mac mae man men nae nim ae ai am an em en in ma me mi na ne

aceimno encomia. *See* **aceimn aeimno acimno ceimno**

aceimnr carmine. *See* **aeimnr aceimn acemnr aceinr ceimnr**

aceimnrs carmines amnesic arsenic carmine carnies cinemas marines mincers remains seminar. *See* **aceimn aceims aceinr aceins**

aceimnru manicure carmine cranium. *See* **aceimn aceinr aceiru acemnr**

aceimns amnesic cinemas. *See* **aceims aeimns aceimn aceins ceimns**

aceimnss amnesics amnesic cinemas incases inseams samisen. *See* **aceimn aceims aceins aeimns**

aceimnst semantic amnesic cinemas inmates sematic. *See* **aceimn aceims aceins acenst**

aceimnntu neumatic. *See* **aceimn acemnu acemtu acimnt**

aceimpr campier. *See* **acempr aceim aceir**

aceimpss escapism impasse. *See* **aceims aceips acepss acimps**

aceimpst campiest campsite aseptic impacts pastime sematic. *See* **aceims aceips acepst acimps**

aceimrst matrices imarets metrics raciest sematic stearic. *See* **aceims aceirs acemrs acerst**

aceimrtu muricate muriate. *See* **aceiru acemtu acertu aeimrt**

aceims amices acmes amice cames maces mesic micas aces acme aims asci came cams case ices mace macs mesa mica mice mise same scam seam semi ace aim cam ice mac mae mis sac sea sic ae ai am as em is ma me mi si

aceimst sematic. *See* **aceims acimst aeimst**

aceinn canine inane acne cane nice nine ace ane ani can ice inn nae ae ai an en in na ne

aceinnoz canonize canzone. *See* **aceinn aeinno**

aceinnr cannier. *See* **aceinn aceinr aeinnr**

aceinnrs crannies arsenic canines cannier carnies scanner. *See* **aceinn aceinr aceins aceirs**

aceinns canines. *See* **aceinn aceins aeinns**

aceinnst ancients canniest instance ancient canines nascent. *See* **aceinn aceins acenst acinnt**

aceinnsu nuisance canines nuances. *See* **aceinn aceins acennu acensu**

aceinnt ancient. *See* **aceinn aeinnt acinnt**

aceinntu uncinate ancient. *See* **aceinn acennu acinnt aeinnt**

aceinops canopies. *See* **aceins aceips acenos acenps**

aceinopz caponize. *See* **aeinz acioz aceno**

aceinors scenario arsenic carnies coarsen corneas cronies erasion. *See* **aceinr aceins aceirs acenor**

aceinort creation reaction carotin certain enactor erotica. *See* **aceinr acenor acenot acenrt**

aceinorv veronica corvine. *See* **aceinr acenor acenrv aeinrv**

aceinorx anorexic. *See* **aceinr acenor aceorx**

aceinost canoeist actions cations notices octanes section. *See* **aceins acenos acenot acenst**

aceinotx exaction inexact exotica. *See* **acenot acinot ceinot ceiotx**

aceinptt pittance nictate patient. *See* **acinpt acintt aenptt ceinpt**

aceinpuy picayune. *See* **acinp acenp einpy**

aceinr carnie cairn caner ceria crane nacre nicer acne acre cane care earn narc near nice race rain rani rein rice ace air ane ani arc are can car ear era ice ire nae ran rec ria ae ai an en er in na ne re

aceinrry cinerary errancy. *See* **aceinr aceirr acenry**

aceinrs arsenic carnies. *See* **aeinrs acinrs acenrs aceirs aceinr**

aceinrss arsenics arsenic arsines carnies caserns incases. *See* **aceinr aceins aceirs acenrs**

aceinrst canister scantier arsenic canters carnies certain cistern cretins nastier nectars raciest recants retains retinas stainer stearic trances. *See* **aceinr aceins aceirs acenrs**

aceinrt certain. *See* **acenrt aceinr ceinrt aeinrt**

aceinrtt interact cattier certain citrate cittern iterant nattier nictate nitrate tertian. *See* **aceinr acenrt acintt aeinrt**

aceins casein incase anise canes since aces acne asci cane cans case ices nice sain sane scan sine ace ane ani can ens ice nae sac sea sen sic sin ae ai an as en in is na ne si

aceinss incases. *See* **aeinss aceins**

aceinssu issuance incases incuses usances. *See* **aceins acensu acessu acinsu**

aceinstt nictates nictate satinet. *See* **aceins acenst acestt acinst**

aceintt nictate. *See* **acintt acent acett**

aceinttx excitant extinct inexact nictate. *See* **acintt aenttx**

aceintty tenacity nictate. *See* **acintt ceinty eintty**

aceintx inexact. *See* **acint acetx aeint**

aceioprt operatic apricot ectopia erotica parotic. *See* **aceopt aceprt aciopr aciort**

aceiopst ectopias aseptic capotes ectopia opiates poetics. *See* **aceips aceopt aceost acepst**

aceiopt ectopia. *See* **aceopt aeiopt ceiopt**

aceiorsv varicose viscera ovaries. *See* **aceirs aceisv aceors acersv**

aceiort erotica. *See* **aciort ceiort**

aceiotvv vocative. *See* **aceitv aceotv**

aceiotx exotica. *See* **ceiotx aciot aceox**

aceippr crappie epicarp. *See* **aceppr aceir eippr**

aceipprr crappier crappie epicarp. *See* **aceirr aceppr aceprr aeiprr**

aceipprs crappies epicarps apprise cappers crappie epicarp sappier. *See* **aceips aceirs aceppr aceprs**

aceiprst practise aseptic carpets parties pastier piaster pirates raciest spectra stearic traipse. *See* **aceips aceirs aceprs aceprt**

aceips apices spicae aspic capes epics paces scape sepia space spica spice aces apes apse asci cape caps case ceps epic ices pace peas pica pice pies ace ape asp cap cep ice pas pea pie sac sap sea sic sip spa ae ai as is pa pe pi si

aceipsst escapist aseptic aspects pasties patsies spastic. *See* **aceips acepss acepst acesst**

aceipssu auspices auspice. *See* **aceips acepss acessu acipss**

aceipssz capsizes capsize. *See* **aceips acepss acipss aeissz**

aceipst aseptic. *See* **aceips acepst ceipst**

aceipstv captives aseptic captive. *See* **aceips aceisv aceitv acepst**

aceipsu auspice. *See* **aceips**

aceipsz capsize. *See* **aceips**

aceiptv captive. *See* **aceitv acept**

aceiqrsu acquires acquire caiques cirques saucier. *See* **aceiqu aceirs aceiru aceqsu**

aceiqru acquire. *See* **aceiqu ceiqru aceiru**

aceiqsu caiques. *See* **aceiqu aceqsu**

aceiqu caique ace cue ice qua ae ai

aceir ceria acre care race rice ace air arc are car ear era ice ire rec ria ae ai er re

aceirr racier ceria crier racer ricer acre care race rare rear rice ace air arc are car ear era err ice ire rec ria ae ai er re

aceirrr carrier. *See* **aceirr aerrr**

aceirrrs carriers carrier carries scarier. *See* **aceirr aceirs acerrs aeirrs**

aceirrs carries scarier. *See* **aceirs ceirrs acerrs aceirr aeirrs**

aceirrst erratics carries carters cirrate craters erratic raciest scarier stearic tarries tarsier tracers. *See* **aceirr aceirs acerrs acerrt**

aceirrt cirrate erratic. *See* **acerrt aceirr**

aceirs caries acres arise cares ceria cries races raise rices scare serai aces acre airs arcs arse asci care cars case ears eras ices race rase reis rias rice rise sari scar sear sera sire ace air arc are car ear era ice ire rec res ria sac sea sic sir ae ai as er is re si

aceirsst scariest actress casters raciest racists recasts satires stearic. *See* **aceirs acerss acerst acesst**

aceirst raciest stearic. *See* **aceirs acirst aeirst ceirst**

aceirstz craziest crazies czarist raciest stearic. *See* **aceirs acerst acersz acirst**

aceirsu saucier. *See* **aceirs acersu ceirsu aceiru**

aceirsv viscera. *See* **aceirs acersv aceisv aeirsv acirsv**

aceirsz crazies. *See* **aceirs acersz**

aceirtt cattier citrate. *See* **aeirtt**

aceirtuv curative. *See* **aceiru aceitv acertu ceirtu**

aceirtvy veracity variety. *See* **aceitv acitvy eirtvy**

aceiru curiae auric ceria curia curie acre care cure ecru race rice urea uric ace air arc are car cue cur ear era ice ire rec ria rue ae ai er re

aceisstu sauciest suitcase casuist ictuses. *See* **acesst acessu aeisst ceissu**

aceisttt cattiest. *See* **acestt acistt**

aceisv cavies caves vices aces asci aves case cave ices save vacs vase vice vies visa vase ace vie ice sac sea sic vac via vie ae ai as is si

aceitux auxetic. *See* **acetu ceitu acetx**

aceitv active civet evict vatic cate cave cite vice ace act aet ate ave cat eat eta ice ita tav tea tic tie vac vat vet via vie ae ai at it ta ti

aceivv vivace cave vice ace ave ice vac via vie ae ai

acejkst jackets. *See* **acejkt aceks**

acejkt jacket cake cate jack jake tack take teak ace act aet ate cat eat eta jet kat tea ae at ka ta

acejlo cajole aloe coal cola cole lace ace ale col joe lac lea ae el jo la lo

acejlor cajoler. *See* **acejlo acelor**

acejlors cajolers cajoler cajoles coalers oracles. *See* **acejlo acelor acelrs**

acejlory cajolery cajoler caloyer. *See* **acejlo acelor aclory**

acejlos cajoles. *See* **acejlo acelos**

acejnost jaconets jaconet octanes. *See* **acenos acenot acenst aceost**

acejnot jaconet. *See* **acenot**

acejnoy joyance. *See* **aceno cenoy ejnoy**

acejnrry jerrycan errancy. *See* **acenry**

acek cake ace ae ka

aceklmn knacker. *See* **aceknr aekknr**

aceklm mackle camel acme cake calk calm came clam kale kame lace lack lake lame leak mace mack make male meal ace ale cam elk elm kal lac lam lea lek mac mae mel ae am el em ka la ma me

aceklms mackles. *See* **acelms acelkm**

aceklns slacken. *See* **aeklns acelns acklns**

aceklnss slackens slacken. *See* **acelns acelss acklns acklss**

aceklorw lacework warlock. *See* **acelor aeklrw ceklor**

aceklps spackle. *See* **acelps aceks ackls**

aceklpss spackles spackle. *See* **acelps acelss acepss acklss**

aceklpst plackets packets placets placket spackle tackles. *See* **aceklt acekpt acekst acelps**

aceklpt placket. *See* **acekpt acelpt aceklt**

aceklrs slacker. *See* **acelrs ceklrs acekrs aeklrs**

aceklrss slackers sackers scalers scleras screaks slacker. *See* **acekrs acelrs acelss acerss**

aceklst tackles. *See* **acekst acelst aeklst aceklt**

aceklsy lackeys. *See* **acekly aclsy aceks**

aceklt tackle cleat eclat latke cake calk cate celt kale lace lack lake late leak tack tael take talc tale talk teak teal ace act aet ale alt ate cat eat elk eta kal kat lac lea lek let tea ae at el ka la ta

acekly lackey leaky cake calk clay kale lace lack lacy lake laky leak yack ace ale aye cay elk kal key lac lay lea lek lye yak yea ae ay el ka la ye

acekmnp packmen. *See* **acemnp**

acekmor comaker. *See* **cekmor acemo acmor**

acekmors comakers comaker mockers. *See* **acekrs acemos acemrs aceors**

aceknr canker caner crake crane crank creak nacre acne acre cake cane care cark earn kern knar narc nark near neck race rack rake rank reck ace ane arc are ark can car ear era ken nae ran rec ae an en er ka na ne re

acekrnrs cankers. *See* **acenrs aceknr acekrs acknrs**

acekoorw cookware. *See* **cekoor**

acekorr croaker. *See* **cekorr**

acekorrs croakers coarser corkers croaker rockers. *See* **acekrs aceors acerrs ackors**

acekorsw casework. *See* **acekrs aceors ackors ackosw**

acekpr packer repack caper crake crape creak pacer recap acre cake cape care cark carp crap pace pack pare park peak pear peck perk race rack rake rape reap reck ace ape arc are ark cap car cep ear era par pea per rap rec rep ae er ka pa pe re

acekprs packers repacks. *See* **acekrs acekpr**

acekpst packets. *See* **acepst acekst acekpt**

acekpt packet epact cake cape cate kept pace pack pact pate peak peat peck tack take tape teak ace act aet ape apt ate cap cat cep eat eta kat pat pea pet tap tea ae at ka pa pe ta

acekqruy quackery. *See* **acekry**

acekr crake creak acre cake care cark race rack rake reck ace arc are ark car ear era rec ae er ka re

acekrrst trackers carters craters kraters rackets tracers tracker. *See* **acekrs acekrt acekst acerrs**

acekrrt tracker. *See* **acerrt aekrrt acekrt**

acekrs crakes creaks sacker screak acres cakes cares carks crake creak eskar races racks rakes recks saker scare aces acre arcs arks arse cake care cark cars case cask ears eras race rack rake rase reck recs sack sake sark scar sear sera ace arc are ark ask car ear era kas rec res sac sea ae as er ka re

acekrss sackers screaks. *See* **aekrss acerss acekrs**

acekrst rackets. *See* **acekst acekrs acekrt aekrst ackrst**

acekrt racket caret carte cater crake crate creak react taker trace track acre cake care cark cart cate kart race rack rake rate reck tack take tare teak tear trek ace act aet arc are ark art ate car cat ear eat era eta kat rat rec ret tar tea ae at er ka re ta

acekry creaky crake creak acre aery cake care cark race rack racy rake reck yack yare year ace arc are ark aye car cay cry ear era key ray rec rye yak yar yea ae ay er ka re ye

---

aceks cakes aces cake case cask sack sake ace ask kas sac sea ae as ka

aceksst caskets. *See* **acekst acesst aeksst acksst**

acekst casket cakes caste cates skate stack stake steak tacks takes teaks aces acts cake case cask cast cate cats east eats etas sack sake scat seat sect seta skat tack take task teak teas ace act aet ask ate cat eat eta kas kat sac sat sea set tea tsk ae as at ka ta

acel lace ace ale lac lea ae el la

acell cella call cell lace leal ace ale all ell lac lea ae el la

acelllru cellular. *See* **acellr aellru**

acellmo calomel. *See* **acello aelmo acelm**

acellny cleanly. *See* **aelly aceln acell**

acello locale cella cello local aloe call cell coal cola cole lace leal olla ace ale all col ell lac lea ae el la lo

acellops collapse escallop locales scallop scalpel. *See* **acello acelos acelps acllos**

acellorv coverall overall. *See* **acello acellr acelor acelov**

acellos locales. *See* **cellos acello acllos acelos**

acellost collates collate lactose locales locates. *See* **acello acelos acelot acelst**

acellosw coleslaw locales. *See* **acello acelos acllos acllow**

acellot collate. *See* **acello acelot**

acellps scalpel. *See* **acelps aellps**

acellpss scalpels scalpel. *See* **acelps acelss acepss aclss**

acellr caller cellar recall cella clear acre call care carl cell earl lace leal race rale real ace ale all arc are car ear ell era lac lar lea rec ae el er la re

acellrs callers cellars recalls. *See* **acellr acelrs**

acellry clearly. *See* **acellr aellry**

acellssu calluses clauses. *See* **acelss acelsu acessu acllss**

acelm camel acme calm came clam lace lame mace male meal ace ale cam elm lac lam lea mac mae mel ae am el em la ma me

acelmmr clammer. *See* **acelmr**

acelmmrs clammers clammer marcels. *See* **acelmr acelms acelrs acemrs**

acelmnns clansmen cannels. *See* **acelms acelnn acelns aelmns**

acelmnor cornmeal corneal romance. *See* **acelmr acelnr acelor acemnr**

acelmnss calmness mescals manless. *See* **acelms acelns acelss aelmns**

acelmory claymore caloyer. *See* **acelmr acelor acemry aclmor**

acelmr calmer marcel camel clear cream lamer realm acme acre calm came care

---

carl clam cram earl lace lame mace male marc mare marl meal merl race rale real ream ace ale arc are arm cam car ear elm era lac lam lar lea mac mae mar mel ram rec rem ae am el em er la ma me re

acelmrs marcels. *See* **acelmr acelms acelrs acemrs aelmrs**

acelms camels mescal acmes calms camel cames clams laces lames maces males meals scale aces acme ales alms calm came cams case clam elms lace lame lams leas mace macs male meal mels mesa sale same scam seal seam slam ace ale cam elm els lac lam lea mac mae mel sac sal sea ae am as el acel la ma me

acelmss mescals. *See* **acelms acelss**

acelmst calmest camlets. *See* **acelms acelmt acelst aelmst**

acelmstu calumets muscatel amulets calmest calumet camlets muletas sulcate. *See* **acelms acelmt acelst acelsu**

acelmt camlet camel cleat eclat metal acme calm came cate celt clam lace lame late mace male malt mate meal meat melt tael talc tale tame teal team ace act aet ale alt ate cam cat eat elm eta lac lam lea let mac mae mat mel met tam tea ae am at el em la ma me ta

acelmtu calumet. *See* **acemtu aelmtu acelmt aclmtu**

acelmtuu cumulate calumet. *See* **acelmt acemtu aclmtu aelmtu**

aceln clean lance acne cane clan lace lane lean ace ale ane can lac lea nae ae an el en la na ne

acelnn cannel clean lance acne cane clan lace lane lean ace ale ane can lac lea nae ae an el en la na ne

acelnnrs scrannel cannels lancers lanners scanner. *See* **acelnn acelnr acelns acelrs**

acelnns cannels. *See* **acelns acelnn**

acelnnu unclean. *See* **acelnn acelnu acennu**

acelnny lyncean. *See* **acelnn acnny**

acelnor corneal. *See* **acelor acenor celnor acelnr aelnor**

acelnotv covalent centavo. *See* **acelnt acelot acelov acenot**

acelnps enclasp spancel. *See* **acelns aelnps acenps acelps**

acelnpss enclasps spancels enclasp napless spancel. *See* **acelns acelps acelss acenps**

acelnpsu cleanups capsule cleanup enclasp launces spancel specula unclasp unlaces. *See* **acelns acelnu acelps acelsu**

acelnpu   cleanup. *See* **acelnu**

acelnr   lancer caner clean clear crane lance learn nacre renal acne acre cane care carl clan earl earn lace lane lean narc near race rale real ace ale ane arc are can car ear era lac lar lea nae ran rec ae an el en er la na ne re

acelnrs   lancers. *See* **acelns acenrs acelrs acelnr aelnrs**

acelnrsu   lucarnes lancers launces lucarne lucerns nuclear secular unclear unlaces. *See* **acelnr acelns acelnu acelrs**

acelnrt   central. *See* **aelnrt acenrt acelnt acelrt acelnr**

acelnru   lucarne nuclear unclear. *See* **acelnu acelnr celnru aelnru**

acelnry   larceny. *See* **acenry aelnry**

acelns   cleans lances canes clans clean laces lance lanes leans scale aces acne ales cane cans case clan lace lane lean leas lens sale sane scan seal ace ale ane can els ens lac lea nae sac sal sea sen ae an as el en la na ne

acelnst   cantles centals lancets. *See* **acenst acelns acelnt acelst**

acelnsu   launces unlaces. *See* **acelns acelsu acelnu celnsu acensu**

acelnt   cantle cental lancet clean cleat eclat enact lance leant acne ante cane cant cate celt cent clan lace lane late lean lent neat tael talc tale teal ace act aet ale alt ane ant ate can cat eat eta lac lea let nae net tan tea ten ae an at el en la na ne ta

acelnty   latency. *See* **acelty acelnt aelnty**

acelnu   cuneal launce unlace clean lance ulnae uncle acne cane caul clan clue lace lane lean luce lune ulna ace ale ane can cue lac lea leu nae ae an el en la na ne nu

aceloppu   populace. *See* **aclopu aelppu celopu**

aceloprt   pectoral caltrop locater plectra polecat prolate. *See* **acelor acelot acelpr acelpt**

acelopst   polecats apostle capotes lactose locates pelotas placets polecat. *See* **acelos acelot acelps acelpt**

acelopt   polecat. *See* **aceopt acelot aelopt acelpt**

aceloptu   copulate polecat couplet. *See* **acelot acelpt aceopt aceptu**

aceloqsu   coequals coequal claques. *See* **acelos acelqu acelsu celosu**

aceloqu   coequal. *See* **acelqu**

acelor   coaler oracle carol ceorl claro clear coral ocrea acre aero aloe care carl cero coal cola cole core earl lace lore oral orle race rale real role ace ale

arc are car col cor ear era lac lar lea oar orc ore rec roc roe ae el er la lo or re

acelorr   caroler. *See* **acelrr acelor aclorr**

acelorrs   carolers caroler carrels coalers coarser corrals oracles. *See* **acelor acelos acelrr acelrs**

acelors   coalers oracles. *See* **aclors celors acelrs acelor aceors**

acelorss   lacrosse closers coalers cresols lassoer oarless oracles scalers scleras solaces. *See* **acelor acelos acelrs acelss**

acelorst   locaters cartels clarets coalers coaster colters costrel lactose lectors locater locates oracles scarlet scrotal. *See* **acelor acelos acelot acelrs**

acelorsu   carousel carouse closure coalers colures oculars oracles oscular secular. *See* **acelor acelos acelrs acelsu**

acelorsy   coarsely caloyer coalers oracles. *See* **acelor acelos acelrs aceors**

acelort   locater. *See* **acelrt acelor celort acelot**

acelory   caloyer. *See* **aclory**

acelos   solace aloes close coals colas coles laces scale socle aces ales aloe also case coal cola cole cols lace leas lose sale seal sloe sole ace ale col els lac lea los sac sal sea sol ae as el la lo os so

aceloss   solaces. *See* **celoss acelss acelos**

acelost   lactose locates. *See* **acelst celost aceost aclost acelot**

acelostt   calottes calotte costate lactose locates. *See* **acelos acelot acelst aceltt**

acelostu   osculate acetous lactose locates sulcate. *See* **acelos acelot acelst acelsu**

acelosty   acolytes acetyls acolyte lactose locates. *See* **acelos acelot acelst acelty**

acelosuv   vacuoles alcoves vacuole. *See* **acelos acelov acelsu acelsv**

acelosv   alcoves. *See* **acelov acelsv celosv aelosv acelos**

acelot   locate cleat eclat aloe alto cate celt clot coal coat cola cole colt cote lace late lota taco tael talc tale teal tola ace act aet ale alt ate cat col cot eat eta lac lea let lot oat tea toe ae at el la lo ta to

acelott   calotte. *See* **acelot aceltt**

aceloty   acolyte. *See* **acelot acelty**

acelouv   vacuole. *See* **acelov**

acelov   alcove coeval calve clave clove vocal aloe cave coal cola cole cove lace lave leva love oval vale veal vole ace ale ave col lac lea lev ova vac ae el la lo

acelp   place cape clap lace leap pace pale peal plea ace ale alp ape cap cep lac lap lea pal pea ae el la pa pe

acelppr   clapper. *See* **aceppr acelpr aelppr**

acelpprs   clappers scrapple cappers carpels clapper parcels placers rappels scalper. *See* **acelpr acelps acelrs aceppr**

acelpr   carpel parcel placer caper clear crape pacer paler pearl place recap acre cape care carl carp clap crap earl lace leap pace pale pare peal pear plea race rale rape real reap ace ale alp ape arc are cap car cep ear era lac lap lar lea pal par pea per rap rec rep ae el er la pa pe re

acelprs   carpels parcels placers scalper. *See* **acelpr acelrs aelprs acelps**

acelprss   scalpers carpels escarps parcels parsecs placers scalers scalper scleras scrapes. *See* **acelpr acelps acelrs acelss**

acelprst   spectral carpels carpets cartels clarets palters parcels placers placets plaster platers plectra psalter scalper scarlet spectra stapler. *See* **acelpr acelps acelpt acelrs**

acelprsu   specular capsule carpels parcels perusal placers scalper scruple secular specula. *See* **acelpr acelps acelrs acelsu**

acelprt   plectra. *See* **acelpr aceprt acelrt aelprt acelpt**

acelpry   prelacy. *See* **acelpr aelpry**

acelps   places capes claps clasp laces lapse leaps paces pales peals place pleas salep scale scalp scape sepal space aces ales alps apes apse cape caps case ceps clap lace laps leap leas pace pale pals peal peas plea sale seal slap ace ale alp ape asp cap cep els lac lap lea pal pas pea sac sal sap sea spa ae as el la pa pe

acelpssu   capsules capsule clauses specula. *See* **acelps acelss acelsu acepss**

acelpst   placets. *See* **acepst acelst aelpst acelps**

acelpsu   capsule specula. *See* **acelsu celpsu acelps**

acelpt   placet clapt cleat eclat epact petal place plate pleat cape cate celt clap lace late leap lept pace pact pale pate peal peat pelt plat plea tael talc tale tape teal ace act aet ale alp alt ape apt ate cap cat cep eat eta lac lap lea let pal pat pea pet tap tea ae at el la pa pe ta

acelqrsu   lacquers claques lacquer secular. *See* **acelqu acelrs acelsu acersu**

acelqru   lacquer. *See* **acelqu acelr celru**

acelqsu   claques. *See* **aceqsu acelqu acelsu aelqsu**

acelqu   claque equal quale caul clue lace luce ace ale cue lac lea leu qua ae el la

acelr   clear acre care carl earl lace race rale real ace ale arc are car ear era lac lar lea rec ae el er la re

acelrr   carrel clear racer acre care carl earl lace race rale rare real rear ace ale arc are car ear era err lac lar lea rec ae el er la re

acelrrs   carrels. *See* **acelrr acelrs acerrs**

acelrrsw   scrawler carrels crawler. *See* **acelrr acelrs acerrs aclrsw**

acelrrw   crawler. *See* **acelrr aclrw aerrw**

acelrs   clears scaler sclera acres cares carls clear earls laces lares laser races rales scale scare aces acre ales arcs arse care carl cars case earl ears eras lace leas race rale rase real sale scar seal sear sera ace ale arc are car ear els era lac lar lea rec res sac sal sea ae as el er la re

acelrss   scalers scleras. *See* **acerss acelrs aelrss acelss**

acelrsss   scarless classes rassles scalers scleras. *See* **acelrs acelss acerss aelsss**

acelrsst   scarlets actress artless cartels casters castles clarets recasts scalers scarlet scleras slaters. *See* **acelrs acelrt acelss acelst**

acelrst   cartels clarets scarlet. *See* **aelrst acelrt acelst acelrs**

acelrstt   clatters cartels clarets clatter rattles scarlet starlet startle. *See* **acelrs acelrt acelst aceltt**

acelrsu   secular. *See* **acersu acelsu aelrsu celrsu**

acelrsv   carvels. *See* **acelsv acelrv acersv acelrs aelrsv**

acelrt   cartel claret rectal alert alter caret carte cater clear cleat crate eclat later react taler trace acre care carl cart cate celt earl lace late race rale rate real tael talc tale tare teal tear ace act aet ale alt arc are art ate car cat ear eat era eta lac lar lea let rat rec ret tar tea ae at el er la re ta

acelrtt   clatter. *See* **acelrt aceltt aelrtt**

acelrttu   cultrate clatter clutter. *See* **acelrt aceltt acertu aelrtt**

acelrv   carvel calve carve clave clear crave laver ravel velar acre aver care carl cave earl lace lave leva race rale rave real vale veal ace ale arc are ave car ear era lac lar lea lev rec rev vac ae el er la re

acels   laces scale aces ales case lace leas sale seal ace ale els lac lea sac sal sea ae as el la

acelss   scales cases class laces sales scale seals aces ales case cess lace lass leas less sacs sale sals seal seas ace ale ass els ess lac lea sac sal sea ae as el la

acelsss   classes. *See* **acelss aelsss**

acelsst   castles. *See* **acesst acelst acelss aelsst**

acelsstt   tactless castles stactes stalest. *See* **acelss acelst aceltt acesst**

acelssu   clauses. *See* **acessu acelsu**

acelst   castle cleats eclats caste cates celts cleat eclat laces least scale slate stale steal taels talcs tales aces acts ales alts case cast cate cats celt east eats etas lace last late leas lest lets sale salt scat seal seat sect seta slat tael talc tale teal teas ace act aet ale alt ate cat eat els eta lac lea let sac sal sat sea set tea ae as at el la ta

acelstu   sulcate. *See* **acelst celstu aclstu aelstu**

acelsty   acetyls. *See* **acelty acelst**

acelsu   clause cauls cause clues laces luces sauce scale aces ales case caul clue cues lace leas luce lues sale seal slue ace ale cue els lac lea leu sac sal sea sue use ae as el la us

acelsv   calves claves calve caves clave laces laves salve scale slave vales veals aces ales aves case cave lace lave leas leva sale save seal vacs vale vase veal ace ale ave els lac lea lev sac sal sea vac ae as el la

acelsx   calxes axels axles laces scale aces ales axes axle calx case lace leas sale seal ace ale axe els lac lax lea sac sal sax sea sex ae as ax el ex la

acelsxy   calyxes. *See* **acelsx aclxy**

acelt   cleat eclat cate celt lace late tael talc tale teal ace act aet ale alt ate cat eat eta lac lea let tea ae at el la ta

aceltt   cattle cleat eclat tacet cate celt lace late tact tael talc tale teal teat ace act aet ale alt ate cat eat eta lac lea let tat tea ae at el la ta

aceltuy   acutely. *See* **acelty celtuy**

aceltxy   exactly. *See* **acelty aclxy acetx**

acelty   acetyl cleat eclat cate celt clay lace lacy late tael talc tale teal ace act aet ale alt ate aye cat cay eat eta lac lay lea let lye tea yea yet ae at ay el la ta ye

acelv   calve clave cave lace lave leva vale veal ace ale ave lac lea lev vac ae el la

acelyy   clayey clay lace lacy ace ale aye cay lac lay lea lye yay yea ae ay el la ye

acem   acme came mace ace cam mac mae ae am em ma me

acemnor   romance. *See* **acemnr acenor aemnor acmnor**

acemnorr   romancer romance. *See* **acemnr acenor acmnor acnorr**

acemnors   romances coarsen corneas enamors macrons oarsmen romance. *See* **acemnr acemos acemrs acenor**

acemnp   encamp pecan acme acne amen came camp cane cape mace mane mean name nape neap pace pane pean ace amp ane ape cam can cap cep mac mae man map men nae nap pan pea pen ae am an em en ma me na ne pa pe

acemnps   encamps. *See* **acemnp acenps**

acemnr   carmen caner crane cream nacre acme acne acre amen came cane care cram earn mace mane marc mare mean name narc near race ream ace ane arc are arm cam can car ear era mac mae man mar men nae ram ran rec rem ae am an em en er ma me na ne re

acemnu   acumen acme acne amen came cane mace mane maun mean menu name ace ane cam can cue cum emu mac mae man men nae ae am an em en ma me mu na ne nu um

acemo   cameo acme came coma come mace ace cam mac mae moa ae am em ma me mo om

acemoost   comatose comates. *See* **acemos acemot aceost acmost**

acemop   pomace cameo campo acme came camp cape capo coma come comp cope mace mope pace poem pome ace amp ape cam cap cep cop mac mae map moa mop ope pea ae am em ma me mo om pa pe

acemopr   compare. *See* **acemop acempr**

acemoprs   compares campers compare pomaces scamper. *See* **acemop acemos acempr acemrs**

acemops   pomaces. *See* **acemos acmops acemop**

acemorsy   sycamore. *See* **acemos acemrs acemry aceors**

acemos   cameos acmes cameo cames comes maces aces acme came cams case coma come mace macs mesa moas same scam seam soma some ace cam mac mae moa mos oms sac sea ae am as em ma me mo om os so

acemost   comates. *See* **acemos acemot cemost aceost acmost**

acemot   comate cameo comet acme atom came cate coat coma come cote mace mate meat moat mote taco tame team tome ace act aet ate cam cat cot eat eta mac mae mat met moa mot oat tam tea toe tom ae am at em ma me mo om ta to

acempr   camper caper cramp crape cream pacer recap acme acre came camp cape care carp cram crap mace marc mare pace pare pear perm pram race ramp rape ream reap ace amp ape arc are arm cam cap car cep ear era mac mae map mar par pea per ram rap rec rem rep ae am em er ma me pa pe re

acemprs   campers scamper. *See* **acempr acmprs acemrs**

acemprss   scampers campers escarps parsecs scamper scrapes screams. *See* **acempr acemrs aceprs acepss**

acempssu campuses. *See* **acepss acessu acmpss acmpsu**

acemr cream acme acre came care cram mace marc mare race ream ace arc are arm cam car ear era mac mae mar ram rec rem ae am em er ma me re

acemrs creams scream acmes acres cames cares crams cream maces marcs mares maser races reams scare scram smear aces acme acre arcs arms arse came cams care cars case cram ears eras mace macs marc mare mesa race rams rase ream same scam scar seam sear sera ace arc are arm cam car ear era mac mae mar ram rec rem res sac sea ae am as em er ma me re

acemrss screams. *See* **acerss acemrs aemrss acmrss**

acemry creamy cream mercy acme acre aery army came care cram cyma cyme mace marc mare race racy ream yare year ace arc are arm aye cam car cay cry ear era mac mae mar may ram ray rec rem rye yam yar yea ae am ay em er ma me my re ye

acems acmes cames maces aces acme came cams case mace macs mesa same scam seam ace cam mac mae sac sea ae am as em ma me

acemtu acetum acute acme came cate cute mace mate meat mute tame team ace act aet ate cam cat cue cum cut eat emu eta mac mae mat met tam tau tea ae am at em ma me mu ta um ut

acen acne cane ace ane can nae ae an en na ne

acennnou announce. *See* **acennu acnnno**

acennos ancones. *See* **acenos acnnos**

acennoss canoness ancones. *See* **acenos acnnos aennss aenoss**

acennot connate. *See* **acnnot acenot**

acennott cotenant connate content. *See* **acenot acnnot acnott aenntt**

acennotv covenant centavo connate convent. *See* **acenot aceotv acnnot aennov**

acennoz canzone. *See* **acnno aceno cenoz**

acennrs scanner. *See* **acenrs**

acennrss scanners scanner caserns. *See* **acenrs acerss aennss**

acennry cannery. *See* **acenry acnnry**

acennst nascent. *See* **acenst**

acennsu nuances. *See* **acennu acensu**

acennty tenancy. *See* **aennt acnny acent**

acennu nuance acne cane ace ane can cue nae nun ae an en na ne nu

aceno canoe ocean acne aeon cane cone once ace ane can con eon nae one ae an en na ne no on

acenoor coronae. *See* **acenor acnoor**

acenopst capstone octanes capotes. *See* **acenos acenot acenps acenst**

acenoqtu cotquean. *See* **acenot acnotu ceoqtu**

acenor cornea acorn caner canoe crane crone nacre narco ocean ocrea recon acne acre aeon aero cane care cero cone core corn earn narc near once race roan ace ane arc are can car con cor ear eon era nae nor oar one orc ore ran rec roc roe ae an en na ne no on or re

acenorrw careworn. *See* **acenor acnorr aenrrw anorrw**

acenors coarsen corneas. *See* **acnors acenrs acenos cenors aceors**

acenorss coarsens caserns censors coarsen corneas reasons. *See* **acenor acenos acenrs aceors**

acenorst ancestor enactors atoners canters cantors cartons coarsen coaster contras corneas cornets enactor nectars octanes recants senator trances treason. *See* **acenor acenos acenot acenrs**

acenorsu nacreous carouse coarsen corneas. *See* **acenor acenos acenrs acensu**

acenort enactor. *See* **aenort acenrt acnort acenor cenort**

acenortu courante centaur counter courant enactor recount trounce. *See* **acenor acenot acenrt acertu**

acenos canoes oceans aeons canes canoe cones ocean scone aces acne aeon cane cans case cone cons eons naos noes nose once ones sane scan ace ane can con ens eon nae one sac sea sen son ae an as en na ne no on os so

acenost octanes. *See* **acenst aenost acenos acnost cenost**

acenostv centavos avocets centavo octanes octaves. *See* **acenos acenot acenst aceost**

acenot octane atone canoe canto cento enact oaten ocean acne aeon ante cane cant cate cent coat cone cote neat nota note once taco tone ace act aet ane ant ate can cat con cot eat eon eta nae net not oat one tan tea ten toe ton ae an at en na ne no on ta to

acenotv centavo. *See* **aceotv acenot**

acenp pecan acne cane cape nape neap pace pane pean ace ane ape can cap cep nae nap pan pea pen ae an en na ne pa pe

acenpr prance caner caper crane crape nacre pacer pecan recap acne acre cane cape care carp crap earn nape narc neap near pace pane pare pean pear race rape reap ace ane ape arc are can

cap car cep ear era nae nap pan par pea pen per ran rap rec rep ae an en er na ne pa pe re

acenprr prancer. *See* **acenpr aceprr**

acenprrs prancers carpers prancer prances scarper scraper. *See* **acenpr acenps acenrs aceprr**

acenprs prances. *See* **acenrs acenps acenpr**

acenps pecans aspen canes capes napes neaps paces panes peans pecan scape space aces acne apes apse cane cans cape caps case ceps nape naps neap pace pane pans pean peas pens sane scan snap span ace ane ape asp can cap cep ens nae nap pan pas pea pen sac sap sea sen spa ae an as en na ne pa pe

acenpttu punctate. *See* **aceptu aenptt aenptu aenttu**

acenpty patency. *See* **acent acept anpty**

acenr caner crane nacre acne acre cane care earn narc near race ace ane arc are can car ear era nae ran rec ae an en er na ne re

acenrry errancy. *See* **acenry acrry acerr**

acenrs caners casern cranes nacres acres caner canes cares crane earns nacre narcs nares nears races saner scare snare aces acne acre arcs arse cane cans care cars case earn ears eras narc near race rase recs sane scan scar sear sera ace ane arc are can car ear ens era nae ran rec res sac sea sen ae an as en er na ne re

acenrss caserns. *See* **acenrs acerss aenrss**

acenrst canters nectars recants trances. *See* **acenst aenrst acenrs acenrt**

acenrstu centaurs canters centaur curates encrust natures nectars recants saunter trances. *See* **acenrs acenrt acenst acensu**

acenrsty ancestry canters nectars nectary recants sectary trances. *See* **acenrs acenrt acenry acenst**

acenrsv caverns. *See* **acenrs acenrv acersv aenrsv**

acenrt canter centra nectar recant trance caner caret carte cater crane crate enact nacre react trace acne acre ante cane cant care cart cate cent earn narc near neat race rant rate rent tare tear tern ace act aet ane ant arc are art ate can car cat ear eat era eta nae net ran rat rec ret tan tar tea ten ae an at en er na ne re ta

acenrttu truncate centaur taunter. *See* **acenrt acertu aenrtt aenrtu**

acenrtu centaur. *See* **acenrt acertu aenrtu**

acenrty nectary. *See* **acenrt acenry**

acenrv carven cavern craven caner carve crane crave nacre raven acne acre aver cane care cave earn narc nave near race rave vane ace ane arc are ave can car ear era nae ran rec rev vac van ae an en er na ne re

acenry carney caner carny crane nacre yearn acne acre aery cane care earn narc nary near race racy yare yarn yean year ace ane any arc are aye can car cay cry ear era nay ran ray rec rye yar yea yen ae an ay en er na ne re ye

acens canes aces acne cane cans case sane scan ace ane can ens nae sac sea sen ae an as en na ne

acensst ascents secants stances. *See* **acenst aensst acesst acnsst censst**

acensstw newscast ascents secants stances. *See* **acenst acesst acnsst aensst**

acenssu usances. *See* **aenssu acessu censsu acensu**

acenst ascent enacts secant stance antes canes cants caste cates cents enact nates scant scent aces acne acts ante ants cane cans cant case cast cate cats cent east eats etas neat nest nets sane scan scat seat sect sent seta tans teas tens ace act ante act ane ant ate can cat eat ens eta nae net sac sat sea sen set tan tea ten ae an as at en na ne ta

acensu usance canes cause sauce aces acne anus cane cans case cues sane scan ace ane can cue ens nae sac sea sen sue use ae an as en na ne nu us

acent enact acne ante cane cant cate cent neat ace act aet ane ant ate can cat eat eta nae net tan tea ten ae an at en na ne ta

aceoopp apocope. *No 6s or 5s*

aceoopps apocopes apocope papoose. *See* **aeopps eoopps**

aceoortv overcoat overact. *See* **aceotv acootv acortv ceortv**

aceopprs copperas cappers coppers. *See* **aceors aceppr aceprs aeopps**

aceoprsx exocarps exocarp coaxers. *See* **aceors aceorx aceosx aceprs**

aceoprx exocarp. *See* **aceorx acepr acopr**

aceopst capotes. *See* **acepst aceopt aceost**

aceopt capote epact atop cape capo cate coat cope cote pace pact pate peat poet taco tape tope ace act aet ape apt ate cap cat cep cop cot eat eta oat ope pat pea pet pot tap tea toe top ae at pa pe ta to

aceor ocrea acre aero care cero core race ace arc are car cor ear era oar orc ore rec roc roe ae er or re

aceorrs coarser. *See* **aceors ceorrs acerrs**

aceorrst creators reactors carrots carters coarser coaster craters creator reactor rectors roaster tracers. *See* **aceors aceost acerrs acerrt**

aceorrsu carouser carouse coarser courser curares scourer. *See* **aceors acerrs acerru acersu**

aceorrt creator reactor. *See* **acorrt acerrt ceorrt**

aceorrtt retroact creator reactor retract tractor. *See* **acerrt acorrt aeortt ceorrt**

aceors coarse acres arose cares ceros cores corse ocrea races scare score aces acre aero arcs arse care cars case cero core cors ears eras oars orcs ores race rase rocs roes rose scar sear sera soar sora sore ace arc are car cor ear era oar orc ore rec res roc roe sac sea ae as er or os re so

aceorsst coarsest coasters actress casters castors coaster corsets costars costers escorts recasts sectors. *See* **aceors aceost acerss acerst**

aceorssu carouses arouses carouse caseous causers courses sarcous saucers sources sucrose. *See* **aceors acerss acersu acessu**

aceorst coaster. *See* **acorst aceors ceorst aceost aeorst**

aceorstv overacts overcast avocets cavorts coaster octaves overact vectors. *See* **aceors aceost aceotv acerst**

aceorsu carouse. *See* **aeorsu acersu ceorsu aceors**

aceorsx coaxers. *See* **aceors aceorx aceosx**

aceortv overact. *See* **aceotv acortv ceortv**

aceorx coaxer ocrea coxae acre aero care cero coax core coxa race ace arc are axe car cor cox ear era oar orc ore rec rex roc roe ae ax er ex or ox re

aceossu caseous. *See* **acessu ceossu**

aceost costae ascot caste cates coast coats costa cotes stoae tacos aces acts case cast cate cats coat cost cote cots east eats etas oast oats scat scot seat sect seta stoa taco teas toes ace act aet ate cat cot eat eta oat sac sat sea set sot tea toe ae as at os so ta to

aceostt costate. *See* **aceost acostt ceostt acestt**

aceosttu outcaste acetous costate outcast. *See* **aceost acestt acostt aesttu**

aceosttv cavettos avocets cavetto costate octaves. *See* **aceost aceotv acestt acostt**

aceostu acetous. *See* **aceost acetu aostu**

aceostv avocets octaves. *See* **aceotv aceost ceostv**

aceosx coaxes coxae coxes aces axes case coax coxa ace axe cox sac sax sea sex sox ae as ax ex os ox so

aceottv cavetto. *See* **aceotv**

aceotv avocet octave ovate covet cate cave coat cote cove taco veto vote ace act aet ate ave cat cot eat eta oat ova tav tea toe vac vat vet ae at ta to

aceox coxae coax coxa ace axe cox ae ax ex ox

acep cape pace ace ape cap cep pea ae pa pe

aceppr capper caper crape pacer paper recap acre cape care carp crap pace pare pear prep race rape reap repp ace ape arc are cap car cep ear era pap par pea pep per rap rec rep ae er pa pe re

acepprs cappers. *See* **aceppr aepprs**

acepr caper crape pacer recap acre cape care carp crap pace pare pear race rape reap ace ape arc are cap car cep ear era par pea per rap rec rep ae er pa pe re

aceprr carper caper crape pacer racer recap acre cape care carp crap pace pare parr pear race rape rare reap rear ace ape arc are cap car cep ear era err par pea per rap rec rep ae er pa pe re

aceprrs carpers scarper scraper. *See* **aceprr acerrs aeprrs**

aceprrss scrapers carpers crasser escarps parsecs raspers scarper scraper scrapes sparers sparser. *See* **aceprr aceprs acepss acerrs**

aceprs crapes escarp pacers recaps scrape acres caper capes cares carps crape craps pacer paces pares parse pears races rapes reaps recap scape scare scarp scrap space spare spear aces acre apes apse arcs arse cape caps care carp cars case ceps crap ears eras pace pare pars pear peas race rape raps rase rasp reap reps scar sear sera spar ace ape arc are asp cap car cep ear era par pas pea per rap rec rep res sac sap sea spa ae as er pa pe re

aceprss escarps parsecs scrapes. *See* **acerss aeprss acepss acprss**

aceprst carpets spectra. *See* **aceprt acepst aeprst**

aceprstu captures capture carpets curates pasture spectra teacups. *See* **aceprs aceprt acepst aceptu**

aceprt carpet caper caret carte cater crape crate crept epact pacer pater peart prate react recap taper trace acre cape care carp cart cate crap pace pact pare part pate pear peat pert race rape rapt rate reap tape tare tarp tear trap ace act aet ape apt arc are art ate cap car cat cep ear eat era eta par pat pea

per pet rap rat rec rep ret tap tar tea ae
at er pa pe re ta

aceprtu capture. *See* **aceprt acertu aceptu**

aceps capes paces scape space aces apes
apse cape caps case ceps pace peas ace
ape asp cap cep pas pea sac sap sea spa
ae as pa pe

acepss scapes spaces apses capes cases
paces scape space specs aces apes apse
asps cape caps case ceps cess pace pass
peas sacs saps seas spas ace ape asp ass
cap cep ess pas pea sac sap sea spa ae
as pa pe

acepsst aspects. *See* **acepst acesst aepsst
acepss**

acepst aspect epacts capes caste cates
epact paces pacts paste pates scape
septa space spate tapes aces acts apes
apse cape caps case cast cate cats ceps
east eats etas pace pact past pate pats
peas peat pest pets scat seat sect sept
seta spat step tape taps teas ace act aet
ape apt asp ate cap cat cep eat eta pas
pat pea pet sac sap sat sea set spa tap
tea ae as at pa pe ta

acepstty typecast. *See* **acepst acepsy
acestt**

acepstu teacups. *See* **acepst acpstu aepstu aceptu**

acepsy spacey capes paces scape space
spacy aces apes apse ayes cape caps
case cays ceps easy espy eyas pace pays
peas pyas spay syce yaps yeas ace ape
asp aye cap cay cep pas pay pea pya
sac say say sea spa spy yap yea yep yes
ae as ay pa pe ye

acept epact cape cate pace pact pate peat
tape ace act aet ape apt ate cap cat cep
eat eta pat pea pet tap tea ae at pa pe ta

aceptu teacup acute epact taupe cape
cate cute pace pact pate peat puce tape
ace act aet ape apt ate cap cat cep cue
cup cut eat eta pat pea pet put tap tau
tea tup ae at pa pe ta up ut

aceqrstu racquets curates quartes
racquet. *See* **aceqsu acerst acersu
acertu**

aceqrtu racquet. *See* **acertu aeqrtu**

aceqssu casques. *See* **aceqsu acessu**

aceqsu casque cause sauce aces case cues
ace cue qua sac sea sue use ae as us

acer acre care race ace arc are car ear era
rec ae er re

acerr racer acre care race rare rear ace
arc are car ear era err rec ae er re

acerrs racers acres cares racer races rears
scare aces acre arcs arse care cars case
ears eras errs race rare rase rear scar
sear sera ace arc are car ear era err rec
res sac sea ae as er re

acerrss crasser. *See* **acerss acerrs**

acerrst carters craters tracers. *See* **aerrst
acerrt acerrs**

acerrstt retracts carters craters ratters
restart retract starter tracers. *See*
acerrs acerrt acerst acestt

acerrsu curares. *See* **acerrsu acerru cerrsu**

acerrsv carvers. *See* **acerrv acersv acerrs
aerrsv**

acerrt carter crater tracer caret carte cater crate racer react trace acre care cart
cate race rare rate rear tare tear ace act
aet arc are art ate car cat ear eat era err
eta rat rec ret tar tea ae at er re ta

acerrtt retract. *See* **acerrt aerrtt**

acerrty tracery. *See* **aerrty acerrt**

acerru curare crura racer recur acre care
cure ecru race rare rear urea ace arc are
car cue cur ear era err rec rue ae er re

acerrv carver carve crave racer acre aver
care cave race rave rear acre arc are
ave car ear era err rec rev vac ae er re

acers acres cares races scare aces acre
arcs arse care cars case ears eras race
rase scar sear sera ace arc are car ear
era rec res sac sea ae as er re

acerss caress scares acres arses cares
cases crass cress races rases scare scars
sears aces acre arcs arse care cars case
cess ears eras race rase sacs scar sear
seas sera ace arc are ass car ear era ess
rec res sac sea ae as er re

acerssst crassest actress asserts casters
recasts. *See* **acerss acerst acesst aersst**

acersst actress casters recasts. *See* **aersst
acerss acesst cersst**

acersstt scatters actress casters recasts
stactes tasters. *See* **acerss acerst acesst
acestt**

acerssu causers saucers. *See* **aerssu
acersu acessu cerssu acerss**

acerssv scarves. *See* **acerss acersv aerssv**

acerst carets caters crates reacts recast
traces acres aster cares caret carte carts
caste cater cates crate crest races rates
react scare stare tares tears trace aces
acre acts arcs arse arts care cars cart
case cast cate cats ears east eats eras
erst etas race rase rate rats rest rets scar
scat sear seat sect sera seta star tare
tars tear teas tsar ace act aet arc are art
ate car cat ear eat era eta rat rec res ret
sac sat sea set tar tea ae as at er re ta

acersttx extracts extract. *See* **acerst
acestt acestx acrstt**

acerstu curates. *See* **acersu cerstu acertu**

acersty sectary. *See* **acersy aersty**

acersu causer cesura saucer acres cares
cause cruse cures curse races sauce
scare ureas aces acre arcs arse care cars

case crus cues cure curs ears ecru eras
race rase rues ruse scar sear sera sura
sure urea user ace arc are car cue cur
ear era rec res rue sac sea sue use ae as
er re us

acersv carves craves acres avers cares
carve caves crave races raves saver
scare aces acre arcs arse aver aves care
cars case cave ears eras race rase rave
revs save scar sear sera vacs vase ace
arc are ave car ear era rec res rev sac
sea vac ae as er re

acersy creasy acres cares races sayer
scare scary years aces acre aery arcs
arse ayes care cars case cays ears easy
eras eyas race racy rase rays ryes scar
sear sera syce yare year yeas ace arc are
aye car cay cry ear era ray rec res rye
sac say sea yar yea yes ae as ay er re ye

acersz crazes acres cares craze czars
races razes scare aces acre arcs arse
care cars case czar ears eras race rase
raze scar sear sera ace arc are car ear
era rec res sac sea ae as er re

acert caret carte cater crate react trace
acre care cart cate race rate tare tear
ace act aet arc are art ate car cat ear eat
era eta rat rec ret tar tea ae at er re ta

acerttuw cutwater. *See* **acertu certtu**

acerttx extract. *See* **acert acetx aertx**

acertu curate acute caret carte cater
crate cruet curet cuter eruct react trace
truce acre care cart cate cure curt cute
ecru race rate tare tear true urea ace act
aet arc are art ate car cat cue cur cut
ear eat era eta rat rec ret rue rut tar tau
tea ae at er re ta ut

acerv carve crave acre aver care cave
race rave ace arc are ave car ear era rec
rev vac ae er re

acerz craze acre care czar race raze ace
arc are car ear era rec ae er re

aces aces case ace sac sea ae as

acess cases aces case cess sacs seas ace
ass ess sac sea ae as

acesst castes asset cases caste casts cates
sates scats seats sects tasse aces acts
case cast cate cats cess east eats etas
sacs scat seas seat sect seta sets tass
teas ace act aet ass ate cat eat ess eta
sac sat sea set tea ae as at ta

acesstt stactes. *See* **acesst acestt aesstt**

acessty ecstasy. *See* **acesst aessty**

acessu causes sauces ascus cases cause
sauce aces case cess cues cuss sacs seas
sues uses ace ass cue ess sac sea sue use
ae as us

acest caste cates aces acts case cast cate
cats east eats etas scat seat sect seta

teas ace act aet ate cat eat eta sac sat sea set tea ae as at ta

acestt stacte caste cates state tacet taste teats testa aces acts case cast cate cats east eats etas scat seat sect seta stet tact tats teas teat test ace act aet ate cat eat eta sac sat sea set tat tea ae as at ta

acestx exacts caste cates exact taxes aces acts axes case cast cate cats east eats etas scat seat sect seta sext teas ace act aet ate axe cat eat eta sac sat sax sea set sex tax tea ae as at ax ex ta

acesu cause sauce aces case cues ace cue sac sea sue use ae as us

acesv caves aces aves case cave save vacs vase ace ave sac sea vac ae as

acet cate ace act aet ate cat eat eta tea ae at ta

acett tacet cate tact teat ace act aet ate cat eat eta tat tea ae at ta

acetu acute cate cute ace act aet ate cat cue cut eat eta tau tea ae at ta ut

acetx exact cate ace act aet ate axe cat eat eta tax tea ae at ax ex ta

acev cave ace ave vac ae

acffghin chaffing chafing. *See* acfgin acghin

acffh chaff ah fa ha

acffhs chaffs chaff cash fash ash fas has sac ah as fa ha sh

acffhy chaffy chaff achy cay fay hay yah ah ay fa ha

acffiilo official. *See* aciil cffil acflo

acffiist caitiffs caitiff. *See* cfiist

acffiit caitiff. *No 6s or 5s*

acffilnu fanciful. *See* acilnu

acffilst afflicts afflict. *See* acffls acfils cffils

acffilt afflict. *See* cffil

acffirst traffics traffic tariffs. *See* acfrst acirst affirt

acffirt traffic. *See* affirt acfrt

acfflosw scofflaw. *See* acffls afflos

acffls sclaff calf fas lac sac sal as fa la

acfflss sclaffs. *See* acffls aclss

acffosst castoffs castoff. *See* acosst affsst cffoss

acffost castoff. *See* acost acfcst cffos

acfghin chafing. *See* acfgin acghin

acfgiipr caprifig. *See* acgir

acfgin facing acing fain fang gain naif ani can fag fan fig fin gan gin nag ai an fa if in na

acfginny fancying infancy. *See* acfgin acginn

acfginrs scarfing facings sacring scaring. *See* acfgin acfnrs acginr acgins

acfginrt crafting carting crating farting frantic infarct infract rafting tracing. *See* acfgin acginr acgint acgirt

acfgins facings. *See* acfgin acgins

acfhijks jackfish hijacks. *See* achijk

acfhilno falchion. *See* acflno achilo acilno cfhiln

acfhilos coalfish scholia. *See* acfils acfios achilo acilos

acfhirsw crawfish. *See* achirs

acfhirsy crayfish scarify. *See* achirs

acfhissu fuchsias fuchsia. *See* achisu cfhisu

acfhist catfish. *See* afhist achit achst

acfhisu fuchsia. *See* achisu cfhisu

acfhltuw watchful. *See* afluw afltu achlt

acfhmnor chamfron monarch. *See* achmor achnor acmnor

acfiiln finical. *See* afiiln aciil

acfiilty facility. *See* aciilt

acfiimps pacifism. *See* acimps

acfiipst pacifist. *See* cfiist

acfiklns calfskin. *See* acfils acklns afikls afilns

acfillsy fiscally. *See* acfils acills afills afilsy

acfilrty craftily clarify clarity frailty. *See* acfrty acilrt acilry afilry

acfilry clarify. *See* acilry afilry

acfils fiscal alifs fails ails alif asci calf fail fila fils fisc laic sail ail fas ifs lac sac sal sic ai as fa if is la li si

acfilss fiscals. *See* acfils aclss cfiss

acfilssy classify fiscals salsify. *See* acfils aclssy afilsy

acfimss fascism. *See* afimss cfiss acims

acfinny infancy. *See* acnny acfny afnny

acfinort fraction carotin faction frantic infarct infract. *See* acfort acinot aciort acnort

acfinost factions actions cations faction. *See* acfios acinos acinot acinst

acfinot faction. *See* acinot

acfinrst infarcts frantic infarct infract. *See* acfnrs acfrst acinrs acinst

acfinrt frantic infarct infract. *See* afirt acint acinr

acfinsty sanctify. *See* acinst acnsty afinst ainsty

acfios fiasco coifs asci coif fico fisc foci oafs sofa fas ifs oaf sac sic ai as fa if is of os si so

acfioss fiascos. *See* acfios cfiss afoss

acfiostu factious. *See* acfios aciost cfistu ciostu

acfipy pacify pica cap cay fay icy pay pya yap yip ai ay fa if pa pi

acfirsy scarify. *See* afirs afiry afrsy

acfissst fascists fascist. *See* acisss aissst

acfisst fascist. *See* acsst cisst acfst

acfkl flack calf calk flak lack kaf kal lac fa ka la

acfl calf lac fa la

acflno falcon focal calf clan coal cola flan floc foal loaf loan can col con fan lac oaf an fa la lo na no of on

acflnory falconry. *See* acflno aclory acnory

acflnos falcons. *See* acflno aclns aclos

acflo focal calf coal cola floc foal loaf col lac oaf fa la lo of

acfloops foolscap. *See* aloops

acflpsu capfuls. *See* acflpu aclsu aclps

acflpu capful calf caul clap flap alp cap cup flu lac lap pal pul fa la pa up

acflrsu carfuls. *See* acflru

acflru carful fulcra calf carl caul curl furl arc arf car cur far flu fur lac lar fa la

acflruu furcula. *See* acflru

acflttu tactful. *See* afltu

acfltuy faculty. *See* afltuy

acfmottu factotum. *See* acmott

acfnr franc narc arc arf can car fan far ran an fa na

acfnrs francs franc narcs scarf arcs arfs cans cars fans narc scan scar arc arf can car fan far fas ran sac an as fa na

acfny fancy any can cay fan fay nay an ay fa na

acforst factors. *See* acorst acfrst cforst acfort

acfort factor actor craft croft cart coat corf fact faro fart fora fort frat raft rota taco taro tora act aft arc arf art car cat cor cot far fat for fro oaf oar oat oft orc ort rat roc rot tar tor at fa of or ta to

acforty factory. *See* acfort acfrty

acfrs scarf arcs arfs cars scar arc arf car far fas sac as fa

acfrss scarfs crass scarf scars arcs arfs cars sacs scar arc arf ass car far fas sac fa as

acfrst crafts carts craft facts farts frats rafts scarf acts arcs arfs arts cars cart cast cats fact fart fast fats frat raft rats scar scat star tars tsar act aft arc arf art car cat far fas fat rat sac sat tar as at fa ta

acfrt craft cart fact fart frat raft act aft arc arf art car cat far fat rat tar at fa ta

acfrty crafty craft arty cart fact fart frat fray racy raft tray act aft arc arf art car cat cay cry far fat fay fry rat ray tar try yar at ay fa ta

acfst facts acts cast cats fact fast fats scat act aft cat fas fat sac sat as at fa ta

acft fact act aft cat fat at fa ta

acgghinn changing hanging. *See* acggin acghin acginn

acgghinr charging arching chagrin gracing. *See* acggin acghin acginr achinr

acggiint gigantic. *See* acggin acgint cgiint

acggiios isagogic. *See* agios

acggilnn clanging glancing lancing angling. *See* **acggin acgiln acginn**

acggin caging acing aging gang gain ani can gag gan gig gin nag ai an in na

acgginr gracing. *See* **acginr acggin agginr**

acgglrsy scraggly scraggy. *See* **acggry**

acggrsy scraggy. *See* **acggry acgrs agrsy**

acggry craggy cagy crag gray racy arc car cay cry gag gar gay rag ray yar ay

acghhint hatching. *See* **acghin acgint achint aghint**

acghiinn chaining inching niching. *See* **acghin acginn**

acghiinr chairing arching chagrin. *See* **acghin acginr achinr cgiinr**

acghikln chalking hackling hacking lacking. *See* **acghin acgikn acgiln aghiln**

acghikn hacking. *See* **acghin acgikn**

acghiknw whacking chawing hacking hawking. *See* **acghin acgikn aghinw agiknw**

acghilns clashing cashing chasing lacings lashing scaling. *See* **acghin acgiln acgils acgins**

acghilnt latching halting lathing. *See* **acghin acgiln acgint achint**

acghilny achingly. *See* **acghin acgiln acgily aghiln**

acghilor oligarch. *See* **acgilr achilo achilr achlor**

acghimnr charming marching arching chagrin harming. *See* **acghin acgimn acginr achinr**

acghimnt matching. *See* **acghin acgimn acgint achint**

acghin aching acing chain china chin gain hang inch nigh ani can chi gan gin hag hin nag nah ah ai an ha hi in na

acghinnr ranching arching chagrin craning. *See* **acghin acginn acginr achinr**

acghinnt chanting canting. *See* **acghin acginn acgint achint**

acghinop poaching aphonic. *See* **acghin acgino acginp cginop**

acghinpp chapping capping. *See* **acghin acginp**

acghinpr parching arching carping chagrin craping graphic harping. *See* **acghin acginp acginr achinr**

acghinpt nightcap patching. *See* **acghin acginp acgint achint**

acghinr arching chagrin. *See* **acghin acginr achinr**

acghinrr charring arching chagrin. *See* **acghin acginr achinr**

acghinrs chagrins crashing arching cashing chagrin chasing garnish sacring scaring sharing. *See* **acghin acginr acgins acgirs**

acghinrt charting arching carting chagrin crating tracing. *See* **acghin acginr acgint acgirt**

acghins cashing chasing. *See* **acghin acgins achins**

acghinst scathing cashing casting chasing hasting. *See* **acghin acgins acgint achins**

acghintt chatting catting hatting. *See* **acghin acgint achint acintt**

acghintw watching chawing thawing. *See* **acghin acgint achint aghint**

acghinty yachting. *See* **acghin acgint achint aghint**

acghinw chawing. *See* **acghin aghinw**

acghipr graphic. *See* **achir chipr acgir**

acghiprs graphics graphic. *See* **acgirs achips achirs aghirs**

acghnryy gynarchy. *See* **agnry acnry achry**

acghosu gauchos. *See* **acghou cghosu**

acghou gaucho cough chug ouch ago cog goa hag hog hug ugh ah go ha ho oh

acghtu caught aught chat chug ghat tach thug act cat cut gat gut hag hat hug hut tag tau tug ugh ah at ha ta ut

acgiilmn claiming calming mailing. *See* **acgiln acgimn agiiln agilmn**

acgiilno logician coaling coiling. *See* **acgiln acgino acilno agiiln**

acgiilnv caviling calving vailing vicinal. *See* **acgiln acginv agiiln agilnv**

acgiinns incasing niacins. *See* **acginn acgins cgiins**

acgiinrt granitic carting crating tracing tricing. *See* **acginr acgint acgirt aginrt**

acgijkn jacking. *See* **acgikn aijkn**

acgijlno cajoling coaling. *See* **acgiln acgino acilno**

acgiklmn mackling lacking calming. *See* **acgikn acgiln acgimn agikmn**

acgikln lacking. *See* **acgikn acgiln**

acgiklnn clanking lacking lancing. *See* **acgikn acgiln acginn**

acgiklno cloaking coaling lacking locking. *See* **acgikn acgiln acgino acilno**

acgiklns slacking lacings lacking sacking scaling slaking. *See* **acgikn acgiln acgils acgins**

acgiklnt tackling talcking lacking tacking talking. *See* **acgikn acgiln acgint aciknt**

acgiklnu caulking lacking lucking. *See* **acgikn acgiln acilnu agilnu**

acgiklry garlicky. *See* **acgilr acgily acilry agilry**

acgikmns smacking sacking masking. *See* **acgikn acgimn acgins agikmn**

acgikn caking acing kiang akin gain gink kina king nick ani can gan gin ink kin nag ai an in ka na

acgiknnr cranking carking craning racking ranking. *See* **acgikn acginn acginr agiknr**

acgiknns snacking sacking snaking. *See* **acgikn acginn acgins agikns**

acgiknor croaking carking corking organic racking rocking. *See* **acgikn acgino acginr agiknr**

acgiknp packing. *See* **acgikn acginp**

acgiknps packings packing sacking scaping spacing. *See* **acgikn acginp acgins acinps**

acgiknqu quacking quaking. *See* **acgikn**

acgiknr carking racking. *See* **acginr acgikn agiknr**

acgiknrt tracking carking carting crating racking tacking tracing. *See* **acgikn acginr acgint acgirt**

acgikns sacking. *See* **agikns acgins**

acgiknst stacking casting catkins sacking skating staking tacking tasking. *See* **acgikn acgins acgint aciknt**

acgiknt tacking. *See* **acgint acgikn aciknt agiknt**

acgikny yacking. *See* **acgikn**

acgikprs gripsack. *See* **acgirs cikprs**

acgill gallic lilac call gall gill laic ail all gal ill lac lag ai la li

acgilln calling. *See* **acgill acgiln**

acgillns callings calling lacings scaling. *See* **acgill acgiln acgils acgins**

acgillo logical. *See* **acgill acllo cgilo**

acgilmmn clamming calming lamming. *See* **acgiln acgimn agilmm agilmn**

acgilmn calming. *See* **acgiln agilmn acgimn**

acgilmy myalgic. *See* **acgily acilm acgim**

acgiln lacing acing align clang cling ligan linga anil clan gain laic lain ling nail ail ani can gal gan gin lac lag nag nil ai an in la li na

acgilnn lancing. *See* **acgiln acginn**

acgilnnu unlacing lancing. *See* **acgiln acginn acilnu agilnu**

acgilno coaling. *See* **acgino acgiln acilno**

acgilnor caroling clangor clarion coaling organic. *See* **acgiln acgilr acgino acginr**

acgilnot locating coaling coating. *See* **acgiln acgino acgint acilno**

acgilnp placing. *See* **acgiln acginp agilnp**

acgilnpp clapping capping lapping placing. *See* **acgiln acginp agilnp**

acgilnps clasping scalping lacings lapsing placing sapling scaling scaping spacing. *See* **acgiln acgils acginp acgins**

acgilnrw crawling clawing. *See* **acgiln acgilr acginr agilnw**

acgilns lacings scaling. *See* **agilns acgins acglns cgilns acgils**

acgilnss classing casings lacings scaling signals. *See* **acgiln acgils acgins acglns**

acgilnst castling casting lacings lasting salting scaling slating staling tincals. *See* **acgiln acgils acgins acgint**

acgilnv calving. *See* **acginv acgiln agilnv**

acgilnw clawing. *See* **acgiln agilnw**

acgilr garlic cigar glair aril carl crag girl laic lair liar lira rail rial ail air arc car gal gar lac lag lar rag ria rig ai la li

acgilrs garlics. *See* **acgirs acgilr acgils agilrs**

acgilrsu surgical garlics. *See* **acgilr acgils acgirs acilru**

acgils glacis ails asci gals lags laic sail scag slag ail gal gas lac lag sac sag sal sic ai as is la li si

acgily cagily gaily cagy clay lacy laic ail cay gal gay icy lac lag lay ai ay la li

acgim gamic magic mica aim cam gam mac mag ai am ma mi

acgimmnr cramming ramming. *See* **acgimn acginr agimnr**

acgimn macing acing gamic gamin magic manic gain main mica mina aim ani cam can gam gan gin mac mag man nag nim ai am an in ma mi na

acgimno coaming. *See* **acgino acimno cgimno acgimn**

acgimnor caroming coaming organic roaming. *See* **acgimn acgino acginr acimno**

acgimnos coamings camions coaming comings maniocs masonic. *See* **acgimn acgino acgins acgnos**

acgimnp camping. *See* **acgimn acginp**

acgimnpr cramping camping carping craping ramping. *See* **acgimn acginp acginr agimnr**

acgimnps scamping camping scaping spacing. *See* **acgimn acginp acgins acimps**

acgimors orgasmic. *See* **acgirs acgors acimos acimrs**

acgin acing gain ani can gan gin nag ai an in na

acginn caning acing gain ani can gan gin inn nag ai an in na

acginnn canning. *See* **acginn**

acginnns scanning canning. *See* **acginn acgins**

acginnpr prancing carping craning craping. *See* **acginn acginp acginr aginpr**

acginnr craning. *See* **acginr acginn**

acginnru uncaring craning. *See* **acginn acginr acinru cginru**

acginnst scanting canting casting. *See* **acginn acgins acgint acinst**

acginnt canting. *See* **acgint acinnt**

acgino agonic acing conga agio agon cion coin gain icon ago ani can cog con gan gin goa ion nag nog ai an go in na no on

acginor organic. *See* **acgino acginr cginor aginor**

acginost agnostic coasting coatings actions agonist casting cations coating costing gnostic. *See* **acgino acgins acgint acgnos**

acginot coating. *See* **acgint acinot acgino**

acginox coaxing. *See* **acgino aginx**

acginp pacing acing aping panic gain nipa pain pang pica ping ani can cap gan gap gin gip nag nap nip pan pig pin ai an in na pa pi

acginpp capping. *See* **acginp**

acginppr crapping capping carping craping rapping. *See* **acginp acginr aginpr**

acginpr carping craping. *See* **acginr acginp aginpr**

acginprs scarping scraping carping craping parings parsing rasping sacring scaping scaring spacing sparing. *See* **acginp acginr acgins acgirs**

acginps scaping spacing. *See* **acgins acinps**

acginr arcing caring racing acing cairn cigar grain crag gain gnar grin narc rain rang rani ring air ani arc can car gan gar gin nag rag ran ria rig ai an in na

acginrrs scarring sacring scaring. *See* **acginr acgins acgirs acinrs**

acginrry carrying. *See* **acginr aginry cginry**

acginrs sacring scaring. *See* **acginr acinrs acgins acgirs aginrs**

acginrsv carvings cravings carving craving sacring scaring. *See* **acginr acgins acginv acgirs**

acginrt carting crating tracing. *See* **acgint acginr aginrt acgirt**

acginrv carving craving. *See* **acginr acginv aginrv**

acginrz crazing. *See* **acginr aginrz**

acgins casing acing gains asci cans gain gins nags sain sang scag scan sign sing snag ani can gan gas gin nag sac sag sic sin ai an as in is na si

acginss casings. *See* **acgins aginss**

acginsst castings casings casting. *See* **acgins acgint acinst acnsst**

acginst casting. *See* **acgint acinst acgins aginst**

acginstt scatting casting catting stating tasting. *See* **acgins acgint acinst acintt**

acginsu causing saucing. *See* **acgins acinsu**

acgint acting acing antic giant anti cant gain gait gnat tang ting act ani ant can cat gan gat gin ita nag nit tag tan tic tin ai an at in it na ta ti

acgintt catting. *See* **acgint acintt**

acginv caving acing gain vain vang vina ani can gan gin nag vac van via ai an in na

acgioors gracioso. *See* **acgirs acgors aciors cgiors**

acgiorst orgastic gastric. *See* **acgirs acgirt acgors aciors**

acgiorsu gracious carious cougars curiosa giaours. *See* **acgirs acgors acgoru aciors**

acgir cigar crag air arc car gar rag ria rig ai

acgirs cigars cigar crags scrag airs arcs asci cars crag gars rags rias rigs sari scag scar air arc car gar gas rag ria rig sac sag sic sir ai as is si

acgirst gastric. *See* **acgirs agirst acirst acgirt**

acgirt tragic cigar cart crag gait girt grit trig act air arc art car cat gar gat ita rag rat ria rig tag tar tic ai at it ta ti

acgjlnou conjugal. *See* **cglnou**

acgln clang clan can gal gan lac lag nag an la na

acglnor clangor. *See* **acnor aglno aglor**

acglnors clangors clangor. *See* **acglns acgnos acgors aclors**

acglns clangs clang clans glans slang cans clan gals lags nags sang scag scan slag snag can gal gan gas lac lag nag sac sag sal an as la na

acglosuu glaucous. *See* **aclsu cglos aclos**

acgnnor crannog. *See* **acnor acnno agnor**

acgnnors crannogs crannog. *See* **acgnos acgors acnnos acnors**

acgno conga agon ago can cog con gan goa nag nog an go na no on on

acgnoost octagons octagon. *See* **acgnos acnost agnost cgnoos**

acgnoot octagon. *See* **acnot cgnoo acgno**

acgnorst congrats cantors cartons contras. *See* **acgnos acgors acnors acnort**

acgnos congas conga agon cans cogs cons goas nags naos nogs sago sang scag scan snag song ago can cog con gan gas goa nag nog sac sag son an as go na no on os so

acgor cargo crag ago arc car cog cor gar goa oar orc rag roc go or

acgors cargos cargo crags scrag arcs cars cogs cors crag gars goas oars orcs rags rocs sago scag scar soar sora ago arc car cog cor gar gas goa oar orc rag roc sac sag as go or os so

acgorsu cougars. *See* **acgors acgoru**

acgoru cougar cargo crag gaur ruga ago arc car cog cor cur gar goa oar orc our rag roc rug go or

acgr crag arc car gar rag

acgrs crags scrag arcs cars crag gars rags scag scar arc car gar gas rag sac sag as

acgrss scrags crags crass grass scars scrag arcs cars crag gars rags sacs sags scag scar arc ass car gar gas rag sac sag as

acgs scag gas sac sag as

acgsttu catguts. *See* **acgttu acstu**

acgttu catgut gutta tact taut act cat cut gat gut tag tat tau tug tut at ta ut

acgy cagy cay gay ay

achhinty hyacinth. *See* **achint**

achhippr hipparch. *See* **achir chipr achpr**

achhirs rhachis. *See* **achirs ahhrs**

achhnttu nuthatch. *See* **achhnu achhtt achntu**

achhnu haunch nucha hunch can hah huh nah ah an ha na nu

achhptuz chutzpah chutzpa hutzpah. *See* **achht chhtu achpt**

achht hatch chat hath tach act cat hah hat ah at ha ta

achhtt thatch hatch chat hath tach tact that act cat hah hat tat ah at ha ta

achiips pachisi. *See* **achiis achips**

achiipss pachisis pachisi. *See* **achiis achips acipss ahipss**

achiirst rachitis. *See* **achiis achirs achrst aciirt**

achiis ischia cash asci ash chi has his sac sic ah ai as ha hi is sh si

achijk hijack hack haik haji hick jack chi ah ai ha hi ka

achijks hijacks. *See* **achijk achks ahiks**

achijnst jacinths jacinth. *See* **achins achint achnst acinst**

achijnt jacinth. *See* **achint**

achikksw kickshaw. *See* **achksw ahikks**

achikqsu quackish. *See* **achisu ackqsu**

achikrsw rickshaw. *See* **achirs achksw ackrsw ahikrs**

achillp phallic. *See* **achilp ahillp**

achills challis. *See* **chills acills**

achilmty mythical. *See* **chimty**

achilnns clannish. *See* **achins**

achilo lochia loach coal coil cola hail halo laic loch loci ail chi col lac oil ah ai ha hi ho la li lo oh

achilos scholia. *See* **achilo acilos**

achilp caliph plica phial chap chip clap clip hail laic pail pica ail alp cap chi hap hip lac lap lip pah pal ah ai ha hi la li pa pi

achilps caliphs. *See* **achilp ahilps achips**

achilpsy physical apishly caliphs clayish. *See* **achilp achips ahilps chipsy**

achilr archil chair larch arch aril carl char hail hair harl laic lair liar lira rail rial rich ail air arc car chi lac lar rah ria ah ai ha hi la li

achilrs archils. *See* **achilr achirs**

achilrvy chivalry charily. *See* **achilr achlry acilry**

achilry charily. *See* **achilr achlry acilry**

achilsy clayish. *See* **aclsy achls ahils**

achimmos machismo chamois. *See* **acimos acmmos aimmos**

achimmst mismatch. *See* **acimst**

achimnop champion aphonic. *See* **acimno chinop**

achimnor harmonic monarch. *See* **achinr achmor achnor acimno**

achimnpt pitchman. *See* **achint acimnt acimpt acinpt**

achimos chamois. *See* **acimos achos achms**

achimpss scampish mishaps. *See* **achips achmps achmss acimps**

achimrs charism chrisma. *See* **achirs achmrs chimrs ahimrs acimrs**

achin chain china chin inch ani can chi hin nah ah ai an ha hi in na

achinnu unchain. *See* **achin achnu**

achinop aphonic. *See* **chinop acnop achin**

achinps spinach. *See* **achins acinps achips**

achinr inarch cairn chain chair china ranch arch char chin hair inch narc rain rani rich air ani arc can car chi hin nah rah ran ria ah ai an ha hi in na

achins chains chain china chins asci cans cash chin hins inch sain scan shin ani ash can chi has hin his nah sac sic sin ah ai an as ha hi in is na sh si

achint canthi aitch antic chain chant china natch anti cant chat chin chit hant hint inch itch tach than thin act ani ant can cat chi hat hin hit ita nah nit tan tic tin ah ai an at ha hi in it na ta ti

achintx xanthic. *See* **achint**

achioprt atrophic aphotic apricot chariot haricot parotic trophic. *See* **achopr aciopr aciort acoprt**

achiopt aphotic. *See* **achit aciot ciopt**

achiorst chariots haricots chariot haricot ostrich shortia. *See* **achirs achrst aciors**

achiort chariot haricot. *See* **aciort achit achir**

achips phasic aphis apish aspic chaps chips spahi spica asci caps cash chap chip haps hasp hips pica pish ship ash asp cap chi hap has hip his pah pas sac sap sic sip spa ah ai as ha hi is pa pi sh si

achiqru charqui. *See* **aciru achir**

achir chair arch char hair rich air arc car chi rah ria ah ai ha hi

achirs chairs chair chars crash hairs airs arch arcs asci cars cash char hair rahs rash rias rich sari scar air arc ash car chi has his rah ria sac sic sir ah ai as ha hi is sh si

achirstt chartist cattish athirst. *See* **achirs achrst acirst acistt**

achirstu haircuts haircut. *See* **achirs achisu achrst acirst**

achirtu haircut. *See* **achit aciru achrt**

achirty charity. *See* **achit achir achry**

achisss chassis. *See* **acisss**

achistt cattish. *See* **acistt chistt**

achistty chastity cattish. *See* **achsty achtty acistt chistt**

achisu chiaus asci cash such ash chi has his sac sic ah ai as ha hi is sh si us

achit aitch chat chit itch tach act cat chi hat hit ita tic ah ai at ha hi it ta ti

achk hack ah ha ka

achkl chalk calk hack lack lakh lac kal ah ha ka la

achkls chalks calks chalk clash hacks lacks lakhs shack slack calk cash cask hack lack lakh lash sack ash ask has kal kas lac sac sal ah as ha ka la sh

achkly chalky chalk achy calk clay hack hyla lack lacy lakh laky yack cay hay kal lac lay yah yak ah ay ha ka la

achkmmo hammock. *See* **acmmo achmo**

achkmmos hammocks hammock. *See* **acmmos**

achkmors shamrock. *See* **achmor achmrs ackors**

achkoss hassock. *See* **achkss ahkoss chkoss**

achkosss hassocks hassock. *See* **achkss ahkoss chkoss**

achkosw whackos. *See* **ackosw achkow achksw**

achkow whacko whack wacko chaw hack hawk hock whoa caw cow haw how koa oak who wok ah aw ha ho ka oh ow

achks hacks shack cash cask hack sack ash ask has kas sac ah as ha ka sh

achkss shacks casks hacks sacks shack asks cash cask hack sack sacs sash ash ask ass has kas sac ah as ha ka sh

achkstw thwacks. *See* **achstw achktw**

achksw whacks chaws hacks hawks schwa shack whack cash cask caws chaw hack hawk haws sack shaw wash ash ask caw has haw kas sac saw was ah as aw ha ka sh

achktw thwack whack watch chat chaw hack hawk tach tack thaw what act cat caw hat haw kat ah at aw ha ka ta

achkw   whack chaw hack hawk caw haw ah aw ha ka

achkwy   whacky whack wacky achy chaw hack hawk yack caw cay haw hay way why yah yak yaw ah aw ay ha ka

achllo   cholla hallo loach local call coal cola hall halo loch olla all col lac ah ha ho la lo oh

achlloo   alcohol. *See* **achllo ahlloo**

achlloos   alcohols alcohol chollas halloos. *See* **achllo acllos ahlloo ahllos**

achllor   chloral. *See* **achllo achlor acllor**

achllory   chorally chloral. *See* **achllo achlor achlry acllor**

achllos   chollas. *See* **achllo ahllos acllos**

achlmstz   schmaltz schmalz. *See* **aclms achms achst**

achlmsy   chlamys. *See* **aclsy almsy aclms**

achlmsz   schmalz. *See* **aclms achms achls**

achlnosy   halcyons halcyon. *See* **achnos ahlosy**

achlnoy   halcyon. *See* **achlo chlny**

achlntu   unlatch. *See* **achlnu achntu**

achlnu   launch nuchal lunch nucha uhlan caul clan haul hula ulna can lac nah ah an ha la na nu

achlo   loach coal cola halo loch lac col ah ha ho la lo oh

achloptt   potlatch. *See* **aclpt chlot aclop**

achlor   choral carol claro coral larch loach orach roach arch carl char coal cola halo harl hoar hora loch oral arc car col cor lac lar oar orc rah rho roc ah ha ho la lo oh or

achlors   chorals scholar. *See* **aclors achlor chlors**

achlorss   scholars chorals scholar schorls. *See* **achlor aclors acorss**

achlort   trochal. *See* **achlor ahlort**

achlr   larch arch carl char harl arc car lac lar rah ah ha la

achlry   archly chary clary larch achy arch aryl carl char clay harl hyla lacy racy arc car cay cry hay lac lar lay rah ray yah yar ah ay ha la

achls   clash cash lash ash has lac sac sal ah as ha la sh

achlt   latch chat halt lath tach talc act alt cat hat lac ah at ha la ta

achm   cham cam ham mac ah am ha ma

achmmy   chammy hammy achy cham cyma cam cay ham hay mac may yah yam ah am ay ha ma my

achmnor   monarch. *See* **achnor achmor acmnor**

achmnors   monarchs anchors archons macrons monarch ranchos. *See* **achmor achmrs achnor achnos**

achmnory   monarchy acronym harmony monarch. *See* **achmor achnor acmnor acnory**

achmo   macho mocha cham coma cam ham mac mho moa ohm ah am ha ho ma mo oh om

achmopr   camphor. *See* **achmor achopr**

achmoprs   camphors camphor carhops. *See* **achmor achmps achmrs achopr**

achmor   chroma carom charm macho macro march mocha orach roach arch cham char coma corm cram harm hoar hora marc mora roam arc arm cam car cor ham mac mar mho moa mor oar ohm orc rah ram rho roc ah am ha ho ma mo oh om or

achmosst   stomachs stomach mascots. *See* **achmss acmost acosst ahosst**

achmost   stomach. *See* **acmost achos achms**

achmp   champ camp cham chap amp cam cap ham hap mac map pah ah am ha ma pa

achmps   champs camps champ chaps chasm scamp amps camp cams caps cash cham chap hams haps hasp macs maps mash samp scam sham amp ash asp cam cap ham hap has mac map pah pas sac sap spa ah am as ha ma pa sh

achmpstu   matchups matchup. *See* **achmps achmsu acmpsu acmstu**

achmptu   matchup. *See* **achmp chmpu achmt**

achmr   charm march arch cham char cram harm marc arc arm cam car ham mac mar rah ram ah am ha ma

achmrs   charms charm chars chasm crams crash harms march marcs marsh scram arch arcs arms cams cars cash cham char cram hams harm macs marc mash rahs rams rash scam scar sham arc arm ash cam car ham has mac mar rah ram sac ah am as ha ma sh

achms   chasm cams cash cham hams macs mash scam sham ash cam ham has mac sac ah am as ha ma sh

achmss   chasms chasm scams shams smash cams cash cham hams macs mash mass sacs sash scam sham ash ass cam ham has mac sac ah am as ha ma sh

achmsu   sumach chasm chums sumac cams cash cham chum hams hums macs mash much mush scam scum sham such ash cam cum ham has hum mac mus sac sum ah am as ha ma mu sh um us

achmt   match cham chat math tach act cam cat ham hat mac mat tam ah am at ha ma ta

achnor   anchor archon rancho acorn narco orach ranch roach arch char corn hoar hora horn narc roan arc can car con cor hon nah nor oar orc rah ran rho roc ah an ha ho na no oh on or

achnors   anchors archons ranchos. *See* **acnors achnor achnos ahnors**

achnos   nachos chaos cans cash cons cosh naos nosh scan ash can con has hon nah ohs sac son ah an as ha ho na no oh on os sh so

achnovy   anchovy. *See* **achov**

achnppss   schnapps. *See* **achps ahpss acnss**

achnpu   paunch nucha punch chap can cap cup hap hup nah nap pah pan pun ah an ha na nu pa up

achnpuy   paunchy. *See* **achnpu chnpuy**

achnr   ranch arch char narc arc can car nah rah ran ah an ha na

achnrty   chantry. *See* **acnry achnt achrt**

achnruy   raunchy. *See* **acnry achry chnru**

achnst   chants snatch stanch cants chant chats hants natch scant snath acts ants cans cant cash cast cats chat hant hast hats scan scat tach tans than act ant ash can cat has hat nah sac sat tan ah an as at ha na sh ta

achnstu   canthus staunch. *See* **acnstu achnst ahnstu achntu**

achnt   chant natch cant chat hant tach than act ant can cat hat nah tan ah an at ha na ta

achntu   nautch chant haunt natch nucha aunt cant chat hant hunt tach than tuna act ant can cat cut hat hut nah nut tan tau tun ah an at ha na nu ta ut

achnu   nucha can nah ah an ha na nu

achoortu   coauthor. *See* **ahortu**

achoost   cahoots. *See* **acost achos achst**

achop   poach capo chap chop opah cap cop hap hop pah ah ha ho oh pa

achopr   carhop copra orach parch poach porch roach arch capo carp chap char chop crap crop harp hoar hora opah proa arc cap car cop cor hap hop oar orc pah par pro rah rap rho roc ah ha ho oh or pa

achoprs   carhops. *See* **achopr**

achor   orach roach arch char hoar hora arc car cor oar orc rah rho roc ah ha ho oh or

achos   chaos cash cosh ash has ohs sac ah as ha ho oh os sh so

achouv   avouch havoc vouch ouch vac ova ah ha ho oh

achov   havoc vac ova ah ha ho oh

achp   chap cap hap pah ah ha pa

achpr   parch arch carp chap char crap harp arc cap car hap pah par rah rap ah ha pa

achprstu   pushcart. *See* **achrst acprsu acpstu**

achps   chaps caps cash chap haps hasp ash asp cap hap has pah pas sac sap spa ah as ha pa sh

achpstuz   chutzpas chutzpa. *See* **acpstu**

achpt   patch chap chat pact path tach act apt cap cat hap hat pah pat tap ah at ha pa ta

achptuz   chutzpa. *See* **achpt**

achpty   patchy patch yacht achy chap chat pact path tach act apt cap cat cay hap hat hay pah pat pay pya tap thy yah yap ah at ay ha pa ta

achr   arch char arc car rah ah ha

achrry   charry carry chary harry achy arch char racy arc car cay cry hay rah ray yah yar ah ay ha

achrs   chars crash arch arcs cars cash char rahs rash scar arc ash car has rah sac ah as ha sh

achrst   charts starch carts chars chart chats crash harts trash acts arch arcs arts cars cart cash cast cats char chat hart hast hats rahs rash rath rats scar scat star tach tars tsar act arc art ash car cat has hat rah rat sac sat tar ah as at ha sh ta

achrsty   starchy. *See* **achrst ahrsty achsty**

achrt   chart char cart char chat hart rath tach act arc art car cat hat rah rat tar ah at ha ta

achry   chary achy arch char racy arc car cay cry hay rah ray yah yar ah ay ha

achs   cash ash has sac ah as ha sh

achssuw   cushaws. *See* **achssw achsuw**

achssw   schwas chaws schwa shaws swash cash caws chaw haws sacs sash saws shaw wash ash ass caw has haw sac saw was ah as aw ha sh

achst   chats acts cash cast cats chat hast hats scat tach act ash cat has hat sac sat ah as at ha sh ta

achstw   swatch chats chaws schwa swath thaws watch acts cash cast cats caws chat chaw hast hats haws scat shaw swat tach thaw wash wast what act ash cat caw has hat haw sac sat saw was ah as at aw ha sh ta

achsty   yachts chats hasty yacht achy acts ashy cash cast cats cays chat cyst hast hats hays scat shay stay tach act ash cat cay has hat hay sac sat say shy sty thy yah as at ay ha sh ta

achsuw   cushaw chaws schwa cash caws chaw haws shaw such wash ash caw has haw sac saw was ah as aw ha sh us

achsw   chaws schwa cash caws chaw haws shaw wash ash caw has haw sac saw was ah as aw ha sh

acht   chat tach act cat hat ah at ha ta

achtty   chatty yacht catty achy chat tach tact that act cat cay hat hay tat thy yah ah at ay ha ta

achtw   watch chat chaw tach thaw what act cat caw hat haw ah at aw ha ta

achty   yacht achy chat tach act cat cay hat hay thy yah ah at ay ha ta

achw   chaw caw haw ah aw ha

achy   achy cay hay yah ah ay ha

aciiilmn   inimical. *See* **aiilmn**

aciiilnv   civilian vicinal. *See* **ailnv acilv aciil**

aciiknnn   cannikin. *See* **aciinn aiknnn**

aciikrs   airsick. *See* **ackrs aikrs cikrs**

aciil   cilia iliac laic ilia lac ail ai la li

aciilltv   villatic. *See* **aciilt**

aciilmnr   criminal. *See* **acilnr aiilmn ailmnr**

aciilmot   comitial comitia. *See* **aciilt acimot**

aciilnor   ironical clarion. *See* **acilno acilnr acilor ciinor**

aciilnv   vicinal. *See* **ailnv acilv aciil**

aciilry   ciliary. *See* **acilry aiilry**

aciils   silica cilia iliac ails asci ilia laic sail ail lac sac sal sic ai as is la li si

aciilss   silicas. *See* **aciils aclss ailss**

aciilst   italics. *See* **aciils aciilt**

aciilt   italic cilia iliac licit alit ilia laic tail talc tali act ail alt cat ita lac lit tic til ai at it la li ta ti

aciimmn   minicam. *See* **acimn ciimm iimmn**

aciimmns   minicams minicam animism. *See* **aiimns ciimms iimmns**

aciimnno   amnionic. *See* **aciinn acimno aimnno iimnno**

aciimnot   amniotic comitia. *See* **acimno acimnt acimot acinot**

aciimnst   actinism animist intimas. *See* **acimnt acimst acinst aiimns**

aciimnsu   musician. *See* **acinsu aiimns aimnsu cimnsu**

aciimnty   intimacy. *See* **acimnt**

aciimot   comitia. *See* **acimot ciimot**

aciimrst   scimitar. *See* **aciirt acimrs acimst acirst**

aciimstv   activism victims. *See* **acimst ciimtv**

aciimtuv   viaticum. *See* **ciimtv**

aciinn   niacin ani can inn ai an in na

aciinnot   inaction actinon contain. *See* **aciinn acinnt acinot acnnot**

aciinns   niacins. *See* **aciinn**

aciinopt   optician caption. *See* **acinot acinpt**

aciinorz   zirconia. *See* **ciinor cinorz**

aciinosv   avionics avionic. *See* **acinos aciosv iinosv**

aciinott   citation titanic taction. *See* **acinot acintt acnott**

aciinov   avionic. *See* **ciino ciinv**

aciinps   piscina. *See* **acinps**

aciinpss   piscinas piscina. *See* **acinps acipss**

aciinrss   narcissi raisins. *See* **acinrs aiinrs ciinrs ciirss**

aciintt   titanic. *See* **acintt**

aciirstt   artistic. *See* **aciirt acirst acistt acrstt**

aciirt   iatric cart act air arc art car cat ita rat ria tar tic ai at it ta ti

aciisttu   autistic. *See* **acistt**

aciisttv   activist. *See* **acistt**

aciittvy   activity. *See* **acitvy**

aciitvvy   vivacity. *See* **acitvy**

acijkkps   skipjack. *See* **acips acjks aikks**

aciklwy   wackily. *See* **ackwy**

acikmr   karmic amir cark cram kami mack marc mark mica rack raki rami rick aim air arc ark arm cam car irk kir mac mar mir ram ria rim ai am ka ma mi

aciknpy   panicky. *See* **acinp cikpy iknpy**

aciknst   catkins. *See* **acinst aciknt**

aciknt   catkin antic akin anti cant kina knit nick tack tank tick act ani ant can cat ink ita kat kin kit nit tan tic tin ai an at in it ka na ta ti

acikpx   pickax pack pica pick pika cap kip pax pix ai ax ka pa pi xi

acil   laic lac ail ai la li

acill   lilac laic call ail all ill lac ai la li

acillmos   localism. *See* **acills acilms acilos acimos**

acillnoo   colonial. *See* **acilno**

acillnor   carillon clarion. *See* **acilno acilnr acilor acllor**

acillnos   scallion oilcans. *See* **acills acilno acilos acinos**

acillosy   socially. *See* **acills acilos acllos allosy**

acilloty   locality. *See* **allot alloy aciot**

acillry   lyrical. *See* **acilry acill allry**

acills   lilacs scilla calls lilac scall ails asci call laic sail sill ail all ill lac sac sal sic ai as is la li si

acillss   scillas. *See* **acills acllss**

acilm   claim calm clam laic mail mica ail aim cam lac lam mac mil ai am la li ma mi

acilmnop   complain complin. *See* **acilno acimno aclmop ailmno**

acilmopr proclaim. *See* **acilor aciopr acilmop aclmor**

acilmosv vocalism. *See* **acilms acilos acilsv acimos**

acilms claims calms claim clams mails micas salmi ails aims alms asci calm cams clam laic lams macs mail mica mils sail scam slam slim ail aim cam lac lam mac mil mis sac sal sic ai am as is la li ma mi si

acilmssu musicals musical. *See* **acilms acmssu ailmss**

acilmsty mystical. *See* **acilms acimst ailmsy cimsty**

acilmsu musical. *See* **acilms almsu aclsu**

acilmx climax claim calix axil calm calx clam laic mail maxi mica ail aim cam lac lam lax mac mil mix ai am ax la li ma mi xi

acilnny cannily. *See* **acnny ailny**

acilno oilcan colin anil cion clan coal coil coin cola icon laic lain lion loan loci loin nail noil ail ani can col con ion lac nil oil ai an in la li lo na no on

acilnoot location coolant. *See* **acilno acilnt acinot ailnot**

acilnor clarion. *See* **acilnr acilor acilno**

acilnors clarions carlins clarion oilcans. *See* **acilno acilnr acilor acilos**

acilnort cilantro contrail clarion carotin. *See* **acilno acilnr acilnt acilor**

acilnos oilcans. *See* **acinos cilnos acilos**

acilnosu unsocial acinous oilcans uncoils. *See* **acilno acilnu acilos acinos**

acilnpy pliancy. *See* **ailny ailnp acinp**

acilnr carlin cairn anil aril carl clan laic lain lair liar lira nail narc rail rain rani rial ail air ani arc can car lac lar nil ran ria ai an in la li na

acilnrs carlins. *See* **acilnr acinrs**

acilnruy culinary. *See* **acilnr acilnu acilru acilry**

acilnst tincals. *See* **acinst ailnst acilnt**

acilnstu lunatics tincals lunatic. *See* **acilnt acilnu acinst acinsu**

acilnsty scantily nastily saintly scantly tincals. *See* **acilnt acinst acnsty ailnst**

acilnt tincal antic alit anil anti cant clan laic lain lint nail tail talc tali act ail alt ani ant can cat ita lac lit nil nit tan tic til tin ai an at in it la li na ta ti

acilntu lunatic. *See* **cilntu acilnt acilnu**

acilnu uncial anil caul clan laic lain nail ulna ail ani can lac nil ai an in la li na nu

aciloprt tropical apricot caltrop capitol optical parotic topical.*See* **acilor acilrt aciopr aciort**

acilopst capitols apostil capitol optical plastic stoical topical topsail. *See* **acilos aciost aclost ailpst**

acilopt capitol optical topical. *See* **aclpt aciot aclop**

acilor lorica carol claro coral coria aril carl coal coil coir cola laic lair liar lira loci oral rail rial roil ail air arc car col cor lac lar oar oil orc ria roc ai la li lo or

acilorrv corrival. *See* **acilor aclorr**

acilos social coals coils colas ails also asci coal coil cola cols laic loci oils sail silo soil ail col lac los oil sac sal sic sol ai as is la li lo os si so

aciloss socials. *See* **acilos aclss aloss**

acilost stoical. *See* **aciost aclost acilos**

acilostv vocalist stoical. *See* **acilos acilsv aciost aciosv**

acilp plica clap clip laic pail pica ail alp cap lac lap lip pal ai la li pa pi

acilpsst plastics plastic spastic. *See* **acipss aclpss ailpst alpsst**

acilpst plastic. *See* **ailpst acips aclps**

acilpty typical. *See* **acipty alpty aclpt**

acilrstu curtails curtail rituals. *See* **acilrt acilru acirst aclstu**

acilrt citral trail trial alit aril carl cart laic lair liar lira rail rial tail talc tali act ail air alt arc art car cat ita lac lar lit rat ria tar tic til ai at it la li ta ti

acilrtu curtail. *See* **acilrt acilru ailrtu**

acilrty clarity. *See* **acilrt acilry**

acilru curial auric curia aril carl caul curl laic lair liar lira rail rial uric ail air arc car cur lac lar ria ai la li

acilry racily clary lyric riyal airy aril aryl carl clay lacy laic lair liar lira racy rail rial ail air arc car cay cry icy lac lar lay ray ria yar ai ay la li

acilryz crazily. *See* **acilry acryz**

acilsss classis. *See* **acisss ailsss**

acilstuv victuals victual. *See* **acilsv aclstu ailstv ailsuv**

acilsuy saucily. *See* **aclsy aclsu acsuy**

acilsv cavils cavil silva vails vials ails asci laic sail vacs vail vial visa ail lac sac sal sic vac via ai as is la li si

aciltty tacitly. *See* **ailtt acitt actty**

aciltuv victual. *See* **acilv acitv altuv**

acilv cavil laic vail vial ail lac vac via ai la li

acilx calix axil calx laic ail lac lax ai ax la li xi

acim mica aim cam mac ai am ma mi

acimn manic main mica mina aim ani cam can mac man nim ai am an in ma mi na

acimnnno cinnamon. *See* **acimno acnnno aimnno**

acimno camion manioc manic cion coin coma icon main mica mina moan noma aim ani cam can con ion mac man moa mon nim ai am an in ma mi mo na no om on

acimnort romantic carotin. *See* **acimno acimnt acimot**

acimnory acrimony acronym. *See* **acimno acmnor acnory cimnor**

acimnos camions maniocs masonic. *See* **acimno acinos acmnos acimos**

acimnost monastic actions camions cations maniocs masonic somatic. *See* **acimno acimnt acimos acimot**

acimnrsu craniums cranium. *See* **acimrs acinrs acinru acinsu**

acimnru cranium. *See* **acinru cimnu acimn**

acimnt mantic antic manic matin anti cant main mica mina mint act aim ani ant cam can cat ita mac man mat nim nit tam tan tic tin ai am an at in it ma mi na ta ti

acimos mosaic micas osmic aims asci cams coma macs mica moas scam soma aim cam mac mis moa mos oms sac sic ai am as is ma mi mo om os si so

acimoss mosaics. *See* **acimos cimoss**

acimost somatic. *See* **acimot aciost acmost acimst acimos**

acimot atomic coati atom coat coma iota mica moat omit otic taco act aim cam cat cot ita mac mat moa mot oat tam tic tom ai am at it ma mi mo om ta ti to

acimpry primacy. *See* **acipry cimpry**

acimps scampi aspic camps micas scamp spica aims amps asci camp cams caps imps macs maps mica pica samp scam simp aim amp asp cam cap imp mac map mis pas sac sap sic sip spa ai am as is ma mi pa pi si

acimpst impacts. *See* **acimpt acimst acimps**

acimpt impact camp mica pact pica pita tamp act aim amp apt cam cap cat imp ita mac map mat pat pit tam tap tic tip ai am at it ma mi pa pi ta ti

acimrrsy miscarry. *See* **acimrs**

acimrs racism amirs crams marcs micas scram scrim simar aims airs amir arcs arms asci cams cars cram macs marc mica mirs rami rams rias rims sari scam scar aim air arc arm cam car mac mar mir mis ram ria rim sac sic sir ai am as is ma mi si

acimrss racisms. *See* **acimrs acmrss cimrss aimrss**

acimrsz czarism. *See* **aimrsz acimrs**

acims micas aims asci cams macs mica scam aim cam mac mis sac sic ai am as is ma mi si

acimsst mastics miscast. *See* **acimst aimss acsst**

acimst mastic micas acts aims asci cams cast cats cist macs mast mats mica mist scam scat tams tics act aim cam cat ita its mac mat mis sac sat sic sit tam tic ai am as at is it ma mi si ta ti

acinnoot conation actinon contain. *See* **acinnt acinot acnnot ainnot**

acinnoss scansion caisson casinos. *See* **acinos acnnos ainnos cinoss**

acinnost actinons canonist contains sanction actinon actions anoints cantons cations contain nations. *See* **acinnt acinos acinot acinst**

acinnot actinon contain. *See* **acinot ainnot acnnot acinnt**

acinnt tannic antic cant anti act ani ant can cat inn ita nit tan tic tin ai an at in it na ta ti

acinoopr picaroon. *See* **aciopr acnoor**

acinootv vocation ovation. *See* **acinot acootv**

acinoppt panoptic caption appoint. *See* **acinot acinpt**

acinopst captions actions caption cations. *See* **acinos acinot acinps acinpt**

acinopt caption. *See* **acinot acinpt**

acinoqsu coquinas coquina acinous. *See* **acinos acinsu ainoqu cinosu**

acinoqu coquina. *See* **ainoqu**

acinorr carrion. *See* **acnorr acinr acior**

acinorrs carrions carrion corsair rancors. *See* **acinos acinrs aciors acnorr**

acinorss narcosis caisson casinos. *See* **acinos acinrs aciors acnors**

acinorst carotins actions cantors carotin cartons cations citrons contras rations. *See* **acinos acinot acinrs acinst**

acinort carotin. *See* **acinot aciort acnort cinort ainort**

acinortt traction carotin citator ricotta taction. *See* **acinot acintt aciort acnort**

acinos casino cions coins icons scion sonic asci cans cion coin cons icon ions naos sain scan ani can con ion sac sic sin son ai an as in is na no on os si so

acinoss caisson casinos. *See* **acinos cinoss**

acinosss caissons caisson casinos. *See* **acinos acisss cinoss**

acinossy cyanosis caisson casinos. *See* **acinos cinoss**

acinost actions cations. *See* **acinot acinst acnost acinos aciost**

acinostt tactions actions cations octants station taction. *See* **acinos acinot acinst acintt**

acinostu auctions cautions acinous actions auction cations caution conatus suction toucans. *See* **acinos acinot acinst acinsu**

acinostw wainscot actions cations. *See* **acinos acinot acinst aciost**

acinosu acinous. *See* **acinsu acinos cinosu**

acinoswx coxswain. *See* **acinos**

acinot action atonic cation antic canto coati tonic anti cant cion coat coin icon into iota nota otic taco act ani ant can cat con cot ion ita nit not oat tan tic tin ton ai an at in it na no on ta ti to

acinott taction. *See* **acinot acintt acnott**

acinottx toxicant taction. *See* **acinot acintt acnott**

acinotu auction caution. *See* **acinot acnotu**

acinp panic nipa pain pica ani can cap nap nip pan pin ai an in na pa pi

acinpquy piquancy. *See* **acinp**

acinprst cantrips cantrip spirant. *See* **acinps acinpt acinrs acinst**

acinprt cantrip. *See* **acinpt acinr inprt**

acinps panics aspic nipas pains panic spica asci cans caps naps nipa nips pain pans pica pins sain scan snap snip span spin ani asp can cap nap nip pan pas pin sac sap sic sin sip spa ai an as in is na pa pi si

acinpt catnip antic inapt paint panic anti cant nipa pact pain pant pica pint pita act ani ant apt can cap cat ita nap nip nit pan pat pin pit tan tap tic tin tip ai an at in it na pa pi ta ti

acinqstu quantics acquits asquint quantic. *See* **acinst acinsu aciqtu acnstu**

acinqtu quantic. *See* **aciqtu ainqtu**

acinr cairn narc rain rani air ani arc can car ran ria ai an in na

acinrs cairns cairn narcs naris rains ranis airs arcs asci cans cars narc rain rani rias sain sari scan scar air ani arc can car ran ria sac sic sin sir ai an as in is na si

acinrstu curtains curtain incrust nutrias. *See* **acinrs acinru acinst acinsu**

acinrttu taciturn curtain. *See* **acinru acintt ainrtu anrttu**

acinrtu curtain. *See* **acinru ainrtu**

acinru uranic auric cairn curia incur runic narc rain rani ruin uric air ani arc can car cur ran ria run urn ai an in na nu

acinst antics nastic antic antis cants saint satin scant stain acts anti ants asci cans cant cast cats cist nits sain scan scat snit tans tics tins act ani ant can cat ita its nit sac sat sic sin sit tan tic tin ai an as at in is it na si ta ti

acinstty sanctity. *See* **acinst acintt acistt acnsty**

acinsu acinus incus anus asci cans sain scan ani can sac sic sin sun ai an as in is na nu si us

acint antic cant anti act ani ant can cat ita nit tan tic tin ai an at in it na ta ti

acintt intact antic attic tacit taint tinct titan anti cant tact tint act ani ant can cat ita nit tan tat tic tin tit ai an at in it na ta ti

aciopr picaro coria copra capo carp coir crap crop pair pica proa air arc cap car cop cor oar orc par poi pro rap ria rip roc ai or pa pi

acioprs picaros. *See* **aciopr aciors**

acioprst apricots apricot captors parotic picaros tropics. *See* **aciopr aciors aciort aciost**

acioprt apricot parotic. *See* **aciort acoprt aciopr cioprt**

aciopssu spacious. *See* **acipss acpssu**

aciopstu captious. *See* **aciost acpstu aiopst ciopst**

aciopty opacity. *See* **acipty aciot ciopt**

acior coria coir air arc car cor oar orc ria roc ai or

aciorrs corsair. *See* **aciors airrs iorrs**

aciorrss corsairs corsair. *See* **aciors acorss**

aciors scoria coria coirs airs arcs asci cars coir cors oars orcs rias rocs sari scar soar sora sori air arc car cor oar orc ria roc sac sic sir ai as is or os si so

aciorssu scarious carious cuirass curiosa sarcous. *See* **aciors acorss ciorsu corssu**

aciorstt citators ricottas citator ricotta tricots. *See* **aciors aciort aciost acirst**

aciorsu carious curiosa. *See* **aciors ciorsu**

aciort aortic actor coati coria ratio toric cart coat coir iota otic riot rota taco taro tiro tora tori trio act air arc art car cat cor cot ita oar oat orc ort rat ria roc rot tar tic tor ai at it or ta ti to

aciortt citator ricotta. *See* **aciort ciortt**

aciortty atrocity citatory citator ricotta. *See* **aciort airtty ciortt cirtty**

aciortvy voracity victory. *See* **aciort acitvy acortv aortvy**

aciosst scotias. *See* **acosst aciost ciosst**

aciossv ovisacs. *See* **aciosv aioss aissv**

aciost coatis scotia ascot coast coati coats costa iotas stoic tacos acts asci cast cats cist coat cost cots iota oast oats otic scat scot stoa taco tics act cat cot ita its oat sac sat sic sit sot tic ai as at is it os si so ta ti to

aciostuu cautious. *See* **aciost ciostu**

aciosv ovisac asci vacs visa ova sac sic vac via ai as is os si so

aciot coati coat iota otic taco act cat cot ita oat tic ai at it ta ti to

acioz azoic azo coz zoa ai

acip pica cap ai pa pi

aciprsy piscary. *See* **acipry ciprsy**

aciprvy privacy. *See* **acipry acirv iprvy**

acipry piracy airy carp crap pair pica pray racy air arc cap car cay cry icy par pay pry pya rap ray ria rip yap yar yip ai ay pa pi

acips aspic spica asci caps pica asp cap pas sac sap sic sip spa ai as is pa pi si

acipss aspics apsis aspic spica asci asps caps pass pica sacs saps sips spas asp ass cap pas sac sap sic sip sis spa ai as is pa pi si

acipssst spastics spastic. *See* **acipss acisss aissst**

acipsst spastic. *See* **acipss acsst cisst**

aciptuy paucity. *See* **acipty acituy**

acipty atypic city pact pica pita pity act apt cap cat cay icy ita pat pay pit pya tap tic tip yap yip ai at ay it pa pi ta ti

aciqrstu quartics quartic acquits. *See* **aciqtu acirst aqrstu cirstu**

aciqrtu quartic. *See* **aciqtu aciru aqrtu**

aciqstu acquits. *See* **aciqtu cistu aiqsu**

aciqtu acquit quit act cat cut ita qat qua tau tic tui ai at it ta ti ut

acirru curari auric crura curia uric air arc car cur ria ai

acirsst racists. *See* **acirst airsst**

acirsstz czarists racists czarist. *See* **acirst airsst airssz**

acirssu cuirass. *See* **airss acssu aciru**

acirst racist astir carts sitar stair stria tarsi acts airs arcs arts asci cars cart cast cats cist rats rias sari scar scat star stir tars tics tsar act air arc art car cat ita its rat ria sac sat sic sir sit tar tic ai as at is it si ta ti

acirsty satyric. *See* **acirst arsty acrsy**

acirstz czarist. *See* **acirst acrsz airsz**

acirsv vicars vicar vairs airs arcs asci cars rias sari scar vacs vair visa air arc car ria sac sic sir vac via ai as is si

aciru auric curia uric air arc car cur ria ai

acirv vicar vair air arc car ria vac via ai

acis asci sac sic ai as is si

acisss cassis asci sacs sass ass sac sic sis ai as is si

acissstu casuists casuist. *See* **acisss aissst issstu**

acisstu casuist. *See* **acssu acsst cisst**

acistt attics static attic tacit acts asci cast cats cist scat tact tats tics tits act cat ita its sac sat sic sit tat tic tit ai as at is it si ta ti

acitt attic tacit tact act cat ita tat tic tit ai at it ta ti

acituy acuity city act cat cay cut icy ita tau tic tui ai at ay it ta ti ut

acitv vatic act cat ita tav tic vac vat via ai at it ta ti

acitvy cavity vatic cavy city act cat cay icy ita ivy tav tic vac vat via ai at ay it ta ti

acjk jack ka

acjkkssy skyjacks skyjack. *See* **ackksy**

acjkksy skyjack. *See* **ackksy acjks**

acjklow lockjaw. *See* **acklo ackow**

acjkopst jackpots jackpot. *See* **acost acops acjks**

acjkopt jackpot. *No 6s or 5s*

acjks jacks cask jack sack ask kas sac as ka

acjloru jocular. *See* **acloru ajlru**

acjmnstu muntjacs muntjac sanctum. *See* **acmstu acnstu ajnstu**

acjmntu muntjac. *See* **ajntu**

ackkmopr pockmark. *See* **acmop acmor acopr**

ackkn knack can an ka na

ackkns knacks knack snack cans cask sack sank scan ask can kas sac an as ka na

ackksy kyacks kyack kyaks yacks cask cays kyak sack yack yaks ask cay kas sac say sky yak as ay ka

ackky kyack yack kyak cay yak ka ay

ackl calk lack lac kal ka la

ackllpsu skullcap. *See* **acklsu acllsu cklpsu**

ackllsy slackly. *See* **aclsy ackls aclls**

acklmor armlock. *See* **aclmor acklo ackor**

acklmors armlocks armlock clamors. *See* **acklos ackors aclmor aclors**

ackln clank calk clan lack lank can kal lac an ka la na

acklns clanks calks clank clans lacks slack snack calk cans cask clan lack lank sack sank scan ask can kal kas lac sac sal an as ka la na

acklo cloak calk coal cola kola lack lock col kal koa lac oak ka la lo

ackloor oarlock. *See* **aclor cloor ckoor**

ackloors oarlocks oarlock. *See* **acklos ackors aclors akoors**

acklorsw warlocks warlock. *See* **acklos ackors ackosw ackrsw**

acklorw warlock. *See* **aclor acklo aclrw**

acklos cloaks calks cloak coals colas kolas lacks locks skoal slack also calk

cask coal cola cols koas kola lack lock oaks sack soak sock ask col kal kas koa kos lac los oak sac sal sol as ka la lo os so

ackls calks lacks slack calk cask lack sack ask kal kas lac sac sal as ka la

acklss slacks calks casks class lacks sacks slack asks calk cask lack lass sack sacs sals ask ass kal kas lac sac sal as ka la

acklsu caulks calks caulk cauls lacks lucks slack auks calk cask caul cusk lack luck sack suck sulk ask auk kal kas lac sac sal as ka la us

acklu caulk calk caul lack luck auk kal lac ka la

ackm mack cam mac am ka ma

ackmmmo mammock. *See* **acmmo**

ackmmmos mammocks mammock. *See* **acmmos**

ackmnost stockman. *See* **acmost acnost**

ackmostt mattocks mattock tomcats. *See* **acmost acmott acostt**

ackmott mattock. *See* **acmott**

ackms macks smack cams cask mack macs mask scam ask cam kas mac sac am as ka ma

ackmss smacks casks macks masks sacks scams smack asks cams cask mack macs mask mass sack sacs scam ask ass cam kas mac sac am as ka ma

ackmu amuck mack muck auk cam cum mac am ka ma mu um

acknpsu unpacks. *See* **acknpu aknpsu**

acknpu unpack punka knap pack puck punk auk can cap cup nap pan pun an ka na nu pa up

acknr crank cark knar narc nark rack rank arc ark can car ran an ka na

acknrs cranks carks crank knars narcs narks racks ranks snack snark arcs arks cans cark cars cask knar narc nark rack rank sack sank sark scan scar arc ark ask can car kas ran sac an as ka na

acknry cranky crank carny cark knar narc nark nary rack racy rank yack yank yarn any arc ark can car cay cry nay ran ray yak yar an ay ka na

ackns snack cans cask sack sank scan ask can kas sac an as ka na

acknss snacks casks sacks scans snack asks cans cask sack sans sank scan ask ass can kas sac an as ka na

ackopsy yapocks. *See* **ackpsy ackopy akopsy**

ackopy yapock yapok capo copy kayo okay pack pock poky yack yock cap cay cop coy koa oak pay pya yak yap ay ka oy pa

ackor croak cark cork okra rack rock arc ark car cor koa kor oak oar orc roc ka or

ackors croaks carks corks croak okras racks rocks arcs arks cark cars cask cork cors koas oaks oars okra orcs rack rock rocs sack sark scar soak soar sock sora arc ark ask car cor kas koa kor kos oak oar orc roc sac as ka or os so

ackory croaky corky croak rocky cark cork kayo okay okra rack racy rock yack yock arc ark car cay cor coy cry koa kor oak oar orc ray roc yak yar ay ka or oy

ackosw wackos wacko cask caws cows koas oaks sack scow soak sock woks ask caw cow kas koa kos oak sac saw sow was wok as aw ka os ow so

ackow wacko caw cow koa oak wok aw ka ow

ackp pack cap ka pa

ackps packs caps cask pack sack ask asp cap kas pas sac sap spa as ka pa

ackpssy skycaps. *See* **ackpsy ackss apssy**

ackpsy skycap packs spacy yacks caps cask cays pack pays pyas sack spay yack yaks yaps ask asp cap cay kas pas pay pya sac sap say sky spa spy yak yap as ay ka pa

ackqsu quacks quack auks cask cusk sack suck ask auk kas qua sac as ka us

ackqu quack auk qua ka

ackr cark rack arc ark car ka

ackrs carks racks arcs arks cark cars cask rack sack sark scar arc ark ask car kas sac ka as

ackrst tracks carks carts karst karts racks stack stark tacks track acts arcs arks arts cark cars cart cask cast cats kart rack rats sack sark scar scat skat star tack tars task tsar act arc ark art ask car cat kas kat rat sac sat tar tsk as at ka ta

ackrsw wracks carks craws racks wrack arcs arks cark cars cask caws craw rack sack sark scar wars arc ark ask car caw kas raw sac saw war was as aw ka

ackrt track cark cart kart rack tack act arc ark art car cat kat rat tar at ka ta

ackrw wrack cark craw rack arc ark car caw raw war ka aw

acks cask sack ask kas sac as ka

ackss casks sacks asks cask sack sacs ask ass kas sac as ka

acksst stacks casks casts sacks scats skats stack tacks tasks acts asks cask cast cats sack sacs scat skat tack task tass act ask ass cat kas kat sac sat tsk as at ka ta

ackst stack tacks acts cask cast cats sack scat skat tack task act ask cat kas kat sac sat tsk as at ka ta

acksy yacks cask cays sack yack yaks ask cay kas sac say sky yak as ay ka

ackt tack act cat kat at ka ta

ackty tacky kyat tack yack act cat cay kat yak at ay ka ta

ackwy wacky yack caw cay way yak yaw aw ay ka

acky yack cay yak ka ay

acl lac la

acll call lac all la

acllloy locally. *See* **alloy clloy acllo**

acllmy calmly ally amyl call calm clam clay cyma lacy mall all cam cay lac lam lay mac may yam am ay la ma my

acllo local call coal cola olla all col lac la lo

aclloor corolla. *See* **acllor cloor**

aclloors corollas corolla collars. *See* **acllor acllos aclors cllors**

aclloort collator corolla. *See* **acllor**

acllooss colossal. *See* **acllos acllss**

acllops scallop. *See* **acllos acops aclps**

acllopss scallops scallop. *See* **acllos acllss aclpss allpss**

acllor collar carol claro coral local call carl coal cola olla oral roll all arc car col cor lac lar oar orc roc la lo or

acllors collars. *See* **aclors acllor acllos cllors**

acllos locals calls coals colas local ollas scall also call coal cola cols olla all col lac los sac sal sol as la lo os so

acllosu callous. *See* **acllos acllsu**

acllovy vocally. *See* **alloy clloy acllo**

acllow callow local allow alow call claw coal cola cowl olla wall all awl caw col cow lac law low owl aw la lo ow

acllrtuu cultural. *See* **alrtu llrtu**

aclls calls scall call all lac sac sal as la

acllss scalls calls class scall call lass sacs sals all ass lac sac sal la as

acllsu callus calls cauls culls scall scull call caul cull all lac sac sal as la us

aclm calm clam cam lac lam mac am la ma

aclmmnou communal. *See* **clmnou**

aclmmy clammy amyl calm clam clay cyma lacy malm cam cay lac lam lay mac may yam am ay la ma my

aclmnoru columnar clamour. *See* **aclmor acloru acmnor acnoru**

aclmnory normalcy acronym. *See* **aclmor aclory acmnor acnory**

aclmnuy calumny. *See* **aclnuy almny**

aclmop copalm campo clamp clomp copal calm camp capo clam clap coal cola coma comp lamp loam mola opal palm alp amp cam cap col cop lac lam lap lop mac map moa mop pal am la lo ma mo om pa

aclmops copalms. *See* **acmops aclmps clmops aclmop**

aclmor clamor carol carom claro coral macro molar moral calm carl clam coal cola coma corm cram loam marc marl mola mora oral roam arc arm cam car col cor lac lam lar mac mar moa mor oar orc ram roc am la lo ma mo om or

aclmors clamors. *See* **aclors acmors aclmor almors**

aclmorsu clamours clamors clamour oculars oscular. *See* **aclmor aclors acloru acmors**

aclmoru clamour. *See* **aclmor acloru**

aclmp clamp calm camp clam clap lamp palm alp amp cam cap lac lam lap mac map pal am la ma pa

aclmps clamps calms camps clamp clams claps clasp lamps palms psalm scalp scamp alms alps amps calm camp cams caps clam clap lamp lams laps macs maps palm pals samp scam slam slap alp amp asp cam cap lac lam lap mac map pal pas sac sal sap spa am as la ma pa

aclmrsuu muscular. *See* **acmrsu almrsu amrsuu**

aclms calms clams alms calm cams clam lams macs scam slam cam lac lam mac sac sal am as la ma

aclmtu talcum mulct alum calm caul clam culm cult malt maul talc act alt cam cat cum cut lac lam lum mac mat tam tau am at la ma mu ta um ut

acln clan lac can an la na

aclnoor coronal. *See* **acnoor**

aclnoort colorant cartoon control coolant coronal ortolan. *See* **acnoor acnort anoort cnoort**

aclnoost coolants coolant. *See* **aclost acnost alnoos alnost**

aclnoosv volcanos volcano. *See* **aclosv alnoos clnoos**

aclnoot coolant. *See* **acnot clnoo cnoot**

aclnoov volcano. *See* **aclov**

aclnorsu consular oculars oscular. *See* **aclors acloru acnors acnoru**

aclnortu calutron courant. *See* **acloru acnort acnoru acnotu**

aclnpsu unclasp. *See* **aclsu aclns aclps**

aclnptuu punctual. *See* **aclpt cptuu alnpt**

aclns clans cans clan scan can lac sac sal an as la na

aclnsty scantly. *See* **acnsty aclsy aclns**

aclnuy lunacy caul clan clay lacy ulna yuan any can cay lac lay nay an ay la na nu

aclooprr corporal corpora. *See* **aclorr aloprr**

aclop copal capo clap coal cola opal alp cap col cop lac lap lop pal la lo pa

acloprst caltrops caltrop captors patrols portals scrotal. *See* **aclors aclost acoprt acorst**

acloprt caltrop. *See* **acoprt aloprt**

aclopssu scopulas copulas cupolas scopula spousal. *See* **aclopu aclpss acpssu clpssu**

aclopssy calypsos calypso. *See* **aclpss aclssy alpssy**

aclopsu copulas cupolas scopula. *See* **aclopu**

aclopsy calypso. *See* **aclsy acops aclps**

aclopu copula cupola copal capo caul clap coal cola coup opal alp cap col cop cup lac lap lop pal pul la lo pa up

aclor carol claro coral carl coal cola oral arc car col cor lac lar oar orc roc la lo or

aclorr corral carol claro coral carl coal cola oral roar arc car col cor lac lar oar orc roc la lo or

aclorrs corrals. *See* **aclors aclorr**

aclors carols claros corals carls carol claro coals colas coral orals solar also arcs carl cars coal cola cols cors oars oral orcs rocs scar soar sora arc car col cor lac lar los oar orc roc sac sal sol as la lo or os so

aclorst scrotal. *See* **acorst aclors aclost**

aclorsu oculars oscular. *See* **aclors acloru**

acloru ocular carol claro coral carl caul coal cola curl oral arc car col cor cur lac lar oar orc our roc la lo or

aclory calory carol claro clary coral royal aryl carl clay cloy coal cola lacy lory oral racy arc car cay col cor coy cry lac lar lay oar orc ray roc yar ay la lo or oy

aclos coals colas also coal cola cols col lac los sac sal sol as la lo os so

aclosstu outclass cutlass locusts. *See* **aclost aclstu acosst clostu**

aclost costal altos ascot clots coals coast coats colas colts costa lotas tacos talcs tolas acts also alto alts cast cats clot coal coat cola cols colt cost cots last lost lota lots oast oats salt scat scot slat slot stoa taco talc tola act alt cat col cot lac los lot oat sac sal sat sol sot as at la lo os so ta to

aclosv vocals coals colas ovals salvo vocal also coal cola cols oval vacs col lac los ova sac sal sol vac as la lo os so

aclosz colzas coals colas colza also coal cola cols azo col coz lac los sac sal sol zoa as la lo os so

aclov vocal coal cola oval col lac ova vac la lo

aclox coxal calx coal coax cola coxa col cox lac lax lox ax la lo ox

acloz colza coal cola azo col coz lac zoa la lo

aclp clap alp cap lac lap pal la pa

aclps claps clasp scalp alps caps clap laps pals slap alp asp cap lac lap pal pas sac sal sap spa as la pa

aclpss clasps scalps claps clasp class scalp slaps alps asps caps clap laps lass pals pass sacs sals saps slap spas alp asp ass cap lac lap pal pas sac sal sap spa as la pa

aclpt clapt clap pact plat talc act alp alt apt cap cat lac lap pal pat tap at la pa ta

aclr carl arc car lac lar la

aclrru crural crura rural carl caul curl arc car cur lac lar la

aclrs carls arcs carl cars scar arc car lac lar sac sal as la

aclrssty crystals crassly crystal. *See* **aclssy alrsty arssty**

aclrssw scrawls. *See* **aclrsw**

aclrssy crassly. *See* **aclssy alrsy aclrs**

aclrsty crystal. *See* **alrsty aclsy aclrs**

aclrsw crawls scrawl carls claws crawl craws arcs awls carl cars caws claw craw laws scar wars arc awl car caw lac lar law raw sac sal saw war was as aw la

aclrswy scrawly. *See* **aclrsw aclrwy**

aclrw crawl carl claw craw arc awl car caw lac lar law raw war la aw

aclrwy crawly crawl clary aryl awry carl claw clay craw lacy racy wary yawl arc awl car caw cay cry lac lar law lay raw ray war way yar yaw aw ay la

aclry clary aryl carl clay lacy racy arc car cay cry lac lar lay ray yar la ay

aclss class lass sacs sals ass lac sac sal as la

aclsstu cutlass. *See* **aclstu acssu acsst**

aclssy classy acyls class clays scaly slays cays clay lacy lass lays sacs sals says slay ass cay lac lay sac sal say sly as ay la

aclst talcs acts alts cast cats last salt scat slat talc act alt cat lac sac sal sat as at la ta

aclstu cutlas cauls cults scuta talcs talus acts alts cast cats caul cult cuts last lust salt scat scut slat slut talc act alt cat cut lac sac sal sat tau as at la ta us ut

aclsu cauls caul lac sac sal as la us

aclsw claws awls caws claw laws awl caw lac law sac sal saw was as aw la

aclsy acyls clays scaly cays clay lacy lays slay cay lac lay sac sal say sly as ay la

aclt talc act alt cat lac at la ta

aclu caul lac la

aclw claw awl caw lac law la aw

aclx calx lac lax la ax

aclxy calyx calx clay lacy cay lac lax lay ax ay la

acly clay lacy cay lac lay la ay

acm cam mac am ma

acmmo comma coma ammo cam mac moa mom am ma mo om

acmmos commas comma ammo cams coma macs moas moms scam soma cam mac moa mom mos oms sac am as ma mo om os so

acmnoort monocrat cartoon. *See* **acmnor acnoor acnort amnoor**

acmnopr crampon. *See* **acmnor anopr acmop**

acmnoprs corpsman crampons crampon macrons. *See* **acmnor acmops acmors**

acmnopy company. *See* **acnopy acmop acmpy**

acmnor macron acorn carom macro manor narco coma corm corn cram marc moan mora morn narc noma norm roam roan arc arm cam can car con cor mac man mar moa mon mor nor oar orc ram ran roc am an ma mo na no om on or

acmnors macrons. *See* **acnors acmors acmnor amnors acmnos**

acmnorsy acronyms acronym crayons macrons masonry. *See* **acmnor acmors acnors**

acmnory acronym. *See* **acmnor acnory**

acmnos mascon socman mason moans nomas cams cans coma cons macs moan moas mons naos noma scam scan soma cam can con mac man moa mon mos oms sac son am an as ma mo na no om on os so

acmnoss mascons. *See* **acmnos amnoss**

acmnsstu sanctums sanctum muscats. *See* **acmssu acmstu acnsst acnstu**

acmnstu sanctum. *See* **acmstu acnstu**

acmo coma cam mac moa am ma mo om

acmop campo camp capo coma comp amp cam cap cop mac map moa mop am ma mo om pa

acmops campos campo camps capos comps scamp amps camp cams capo caps coma comp cops macs maps moas mops samp scam scop soap soma amp asp cam cap cop mac map moa mop mos oms pas sac sap sop spa am as ma mo om os pa so

acmopss compass. *See* **acmops acmpss**

acmor carom macro coma corm cram marc mora roam arc arm cam car cor

mac mar moa mor oar orc ram roc am
ma mo om or

acmors caroms macros carom corms
crams macro marcs roams scram arcs
arms cams cars coma corm cors cram
macs marc moas mora mors oars orcs
rams roam rocs scam scar soar soma
sora arc arm cam car cor mac mar moa
mor mos oar oms orc ram roc sac am
as ma mo om or os so

acmorsty costmary. *See* **acmors acmost
acorst amorsy**

acmosst mascots. *See* **acosst acmost
amosst**

acmost mascot ascot atoms coast coats
costa moats stoma tacos acts atom
cams cast cats coat coma cost cots
macs mast mats moas moat most mots
oast oats scam scat scot soma stoa taco
tams toms act cam cat cot mac mat
moa mos mot oat oms sac sat sot tam
tom am as at ma mo om os so ta to

acmostt tomcats. *See* **acosstt acmott**

acmott tomcat cotta atom coat coma
moat taco tact act cam cat cot mac mat
moa mot oat tam tat tom tot am at ma
mo om ta to

acmp camp amp cam cap mac map am
ma pa

acmpr cramp camp carp cram crap marc
pram ramp amp arc arm cam cap car
mac map mar par ram rap am ma pa

acmprs cramps camps carps cramp
crams craps marcs prams ramps scamp
scarp scram scrap amps arcs arms
camp cams caps carp cars cram crap
macs maps marc pars pram ramp rams
raps rasp samp scam scar spar amp arc
arm asp cam cap car mac map mar par
pas ram rap sac sap spa am as ma pa

acmps camps scamp amps camp cams
caps macs maps samp scam amp asp
cam cap mac map pas sac sap spa am
as ma pa

acmpss scamps camps samps scamp
scams spasm amps asps camp cams
caps macs maps mass pass sacs samp
saps scam spas amp asp ass cam cap
mac map pas sac sap spa am as ma pa

acmpsu campus camps pumas scamp
scaup sumac amps camp cams caps
cups cusp macs maps puma samp scam
scum scup sump umps upas amp asp
cam cap cum cup mac map mus pas
pus sac sap spa sum sup ump am as ma
mu pa um up us

acmpy campy camp cyma amp cam cap
cay mac map may pay pya yam yap am
ay ma my pa

acmqstuu cumquats cumquat. *See* **acmstu cmstuu**

acmqtuu cumquat. *No 6s or 5s*

acmr cram marc arc arm cam car mac
mar ram am ma

acmrs crams marcs scram arcs arms
cams cars cram macs marc rams scam
scar arc arm cam car mac mar ram sac
am as ma

acmrss scrams crams crass marcs scams
scars scram arcs arms cams cars cram
macs marc mass rams sacs scam scar
arc arm ass cam car mac mar ram sac
am as ma

acmrssu sacrums. *See* **acmrsu acmrss
cmrssu acmssu**

acmrsu sacrum crams marcs ramus
scram scrum sumac arcs arms cams
cars cram crus curs macs marc rams
rums scam scar scum sura arc arm cam
car cum cur mac mar mus ram rum sac
sum am as ma mu um us

acms cams macs scam cam mac sac am
as ma

acmss scams cams macs mass sacs scam
ass cam mac sac am as ma

acmsstu muscats. *See* **acmssu acmstu**

acmssu sumacs ascus scams scums sumac cams cuss macs mass muss sacs
scam scum sums ass cam cum mac mus
sac sum am as ma mu um us

acmstu muscat scuta sumac acts cams
cast cats cuts macs mast mats must
scam scat scum scut smut stum tams
act cam cat cum cut mac mat mus sac
sat sum tam tau am as at ma mu ta um
us ut

acmsu sumac cams macs scam scum cam
cum mac mus sac sum am as ma mu
um us

acmsuuv vacuums. *See* **acmuuv cmsuu
acmsu**

acmuuv vacuum cam cum mac vac am
ma mu um

acmy cyma cam cay mac may yam am ay
ma my

acn can an na

acnnno cannon ancon canon anon can
con an na no on

acnnnory cannonry. *See* **acnnno acnnoy
acnnry acnory**

acnnnos cannons. *See* **acnnno acnnos**

acnnnuy uncanny. *See* **acnny annny**

acnno ancon canon anon can con an na
no on

acnnos canons ancon canon anon cans
cons naos scan can con sac son an as
na no on os so

acnnost cantons. *See* **acnnot acnnos acnost annost**

acnnostt constant cantons octants. *See*
acnnos acnnot acnost acnott

acnnosy canyons. *See* **annosy acnnoy**

acnnot cannot canton ancon canon
canto anon cant coat nota taco act ant
can cat con cot not oat tan ton an at na
no on ta to

acnnoy canyon ancon annoy canny canon anon cony any can cay con coy
nay yon an ay na no on oy

acnnry cranny canny carny narc nary
racy yarn any arc can car cay cry nay
ran ray yar an ay na

acnny canny any can cay nay an ay na

acnoor corona racoon acorn croon narco
coon corn narc roan arc can car con
coo cor nor oar orc ran roc an na no on
or

acnoorry coronary. *See* **acnoor acnorr
acnory**

acnoors racoons. *See* **acnors acnoor
cnoors**

acnoorst cartoons cantors cartons cartoon consort contras crotons racoons
ratoons. *See* **acnoor acnors acnort acnost**

acnoort cartoon. *See* **acnort cnoort acnoor anoort**

acnop capon capo can cap con cop nap
pan an na no on pa

acnops capons capon capos cans capo
caps cons cops naos naps pans pons
scan scop snap soap span asp can cap
con cop nap pan pas sac sap son sop
spa an as na no on os pa so

acnopssw snowcaps. *See* **acnops anpssw**

acnopy canopy capon capo cony copy
pony any can cap cay con cop coy nap
nay pan pay pya yap yon an ay na no
on oy pa

acnor acorn narco corn narc roan arc
can car con cor nor oar orc ran roc an
na no on or

acnorr rancor acorn narco corn narc
roan roar arc can car con cor nor oar
orc ran roc an na no on or

acnorrs rancors. *See* **acnors acnorr**

acnorrty contrary carroty. *See* **acnorr acnort acnory acorrt**

acnors acorns narcos acorn arson corns
narco narcs roans scorn sonar arcs
cans cars cons corn cors naos narc oars
orcs roan rocs scan scar soar sora arc
can car con cor nor oar orc ran roc sac
son an as na no on or os so

acnorst cantors cartons contras. *See* **acnors acorst acnort acnost**

acnorstt contrast attorns cantors cartons
contras octants. *See* **acnors acnort acnost acnott**

acnorsy crayons. *See* **acnors acnory anorsy**

acnort cantor carton contra acorn actor canto narco cant cart coat corn narc nota rant roan rota taco taro tora torn act ant arc art can car cat con cor cot nor not oar oat orc ort ran rat roc rot tan tar ton tor an at na no on or ta to

acnorttu turncoat courant. *See* **acnort acnoru acnott acnotu**

acnortu courant. *See* **acnort acnoru anortu acnotu**

acnoru cornua acorn cornu narco corn narc roan unco arc can car con cor cur nor oar orc our ran roc run urn an na no nu on or

acnory crayon acorn carny corny crony narco rayon cony corn narc nary racy roan yarn any arc can car cay con cor coy cry nay nor oar orc ran ray roc yar yon an ay na no on or oy

acnost ascot ascno canto cants coast coats costa scant tacos acts ants cans cant cast cats coat cons cost cots naos nota oast oats scan scat scot snot stoa taco tans tons act ant can cat con cot not oat sac sat son sot tan ton an as at na no on os so ta to

acnostt octants. *See* **acnost acostt acnott**

acnostu conatus toucans. *See* **acnost acnstu cnostu**

acnot canto cant coat nota taco act ant can cat con cot not oat tan ton an at na no on ta to

acnott octant canto cotta cant coat nota taco tact act ant can cat con cot not oat tan tat ton tot an at na no on ta to

acnotu toucan canto count aunt auto cant coat nota taco tuna unco unto act ant can cat con cot cut not nut oat out tan tau ton tun an at na no nu on ta to ut

acnr narc arc can car ran an na

acnrrstu currants currant. *See* **acnstu**

acnrrtu currant. *See* **acrru**

acnrs narcs arcs cans cars narc scan scar arc can car ran sac an as na

acnrswy scrawny. *See* **acnry acrsw acnrs**

acnrtuy truancy. *See* **antuy acnry nrtuy**

acnry carny narc nary racy yarn any arc can car cay cry nay ran ray yar an ay na

acns cans scan can sac an as na

acnss scans cans sacs scan ass can sac an as na

acnsst scants cants casts scans scant scats acts ants cans cant cast cats sacs scan scat tans tass act ant ass can cat sac sat tan an as at na ta

acnst cants scant acts ants cans cant cast cats scan scat tans act ant can cat sac sat tan an as at na ta

acnstu cantus aunts cants scant scuta tunas acts ants anus aunt cans cant cast cats cuts nuts scan scat scut stun tans tuna tuns act ant can cat cut nut sac sat sun tan tau tun an as at na nu ta us ut

acnsty scanty antsy cants nasty scant tansy acts ants cans cant cast cats cays cyst scan scat stay sync tans act ant any can cat cay nay sac sat say sty tan an as at ay na ta

acnt cant act ant can cat tan an at na ta

acooprr corpora. *See* **acopr**

acoopstt topcoats topcoat. *See* **acostt aooptt**

acooptt topcoat. *See* **aooptt acott**

acoostv octavos. *See* **acootv acost coost**

acootv octavo coat coot taco act cat coo cot oat ova tav too vac vat at ta to

acop capo cap cop pa

acopr copra capo carp crap crop proa arc cap car cop cor oar orc par pro rap roc pa or

acoprrst carports captors carport carrots parrots. *See* **acoprt acorrt acorst aoprrt**

acoprrt carport. *See* **acoprt acorrt aoprrt**

acoprrtt protract carport tractor. *See* **acoprt acorrt aoprrt**

acoprst captors. *See* **acorst acoprt aoprst**

acoprt captor actor aport copra atop capo carp cart coat crap crop pact part port proa rapt rota taco taro tarp tora trap act apt arc art cap car cat cop cor cot oar oat orc ort par pat pot pro rap rat roc rot tap tar top tor at or pa ta to

acops capos capo caps cops scop soap asp cap cop pas sac sap sop spa as os pa so

acorrst carrots. *See* **acorst acorrt aorrst**

acorrstt tractors carrots tractor. *See* **acorrt acorst acostt acrstt**

acorrstu curators carrots curator surcoat. *See* **acorrt acorst aorrst corrsu**

acorrt carrot actor cart coat roar rota taco taro tora torr act arc art car cat cor cot oar oat orc ort rat roc rot tar tor at or ta to

acorrtt tractor. *See* **acorrt acott aortt**

acorrtu curator. *See* **acorrt cortu acrru**

acorrty carroty. *See* **acorrt aorrty**

acorss across crass cross saros scars soars soras arcs cars cors oars orcs ossa rocs sacs scar soar sora arc ass car cor oar orc roc sac as or os so

acorsst castors costars. *See* **acorss acorst acosst aorsst**

acorsstu surcoats castors costars sarcous surcoat. *See* **acorss acorst acosst aorsst**

acorssu sarcous. *See* **acorss corssu**

acorst actors castor costar scrota actor ascot carts coast coats costa roast rotas tacos taros toras acts arcs arts cars cart cast cats coat cors cost cots oars oast oats orcs orts rats rocs rota rots scar scat scot soar sora sort star stoa taco taro tars tora tors tsar act arc art car cat cor cot oar oat orc ort rat roc rot sac sat sot tar tor as at or os so ta to

acorstu surcoat. *See* **acorst corstu**

acorstv cavorts. *See* **acorst acortv**

acorsuu raucous. *See* **aorsuu corsu**

acorsyz coryzas. *See* **acoryz acrsz acrsy**

acort actor cart coat rota taco taro tora act arc art car cat cor cot oar oat orc ort rat roc rot tar tor at or ta to

acortv cavort actor cart coat rota taco taro tora act arc art car cat cor cot oar oat orc ort ova rat roc rot tar tav tor vac vat at or ta to

acoryz coryza crazy cozy czar racy arc azo car cay cor coy coz cry oar orc ray roc yar zoa ay or oy

acosst ascots coasts ascot casts coast coats costa costs oasts scats stoas tacos acts cast cats coat cost cots oast oats ossa sacs scat scot sots stoa taco tass toss act ass cat cot oat sac sat sot as at os so ta to

acossttu outcasts outcast. *See* **acosst acostt aosstt assttu**

acost ascot coast coats costa tacos acts cast cats coat cost cots oast oats scat scot stoa taco act cat cot oat sac sat sot as at os so ta to

acostt cottas ascot coast coats costa cotta stoat tacos toast acts cast cats coat cost cots oast oats scat scot stoa taco tact tats tost tots act cat cot oat sac sat sot tat tot as at os so ta to

acosttu outcast. *See* **acostt aostu costu**

acosuuv vacuous. *No 6s or 5s*

acot coat taco act cat cot oat at ta to

acott cotta coat taco tact act cat cot oat tat tot at ta to

acox coax coxa cox ax ox

acp cap pa

acpprsy scrappy. *See* **acppry acprs aprsy**

acppry crappy carp crap pray racy arc cap car cay cry pap par pay pry pya rap ray yap yar pa ay

acpr carp crap arc cap car par rap pa

acprs carps craps scarp scrap arcs caps carp cars crap pars raps rasp scar spar arc asp cap car par pas rap sac sap spa pa as

acprss scarps scraps carps craps crass rasps scarp scars scrap spars arcs asps caps carp cars crap pars pass raps rasp sacs saps scar spar spas arc asp ass cap car par pas rap sac sap spa pa as

acprsu carpus carps craps scarp scaup scrap arcs caps carp cars crap crus cups curs cusp pars raps rasp scar scup spar spur sura upas arc asp cap car cup cur par pas pus rap sac sap spa sup as pa up us

acps caps asp cap pas sac sap spa as pa

acpsstu upcasts. *See* **acpstu acpssu apsstu**

acpsstuy pussycat upcasts. *See* **acpssu acpstu apsstu**

acpssu scaups ascus cusps scaup scups asps caps cups cusp cuss pass puss sacs saps scup spas sups upas asp ass cap cup pas pus sac sap spa sup as pa up us

acpst pacts acts caps cast cats pact past pats scat spat taps act apt asp cap cat pas pat sac sap sat spa tap as at pa ta

acpstu catsup upcast pacts scaup scuta stupa acts caps cast cats cups cusp cuts pact past pats puts scat scup scut spat taps tups upas act apt asp cap cat cup cut pas pat pus put sac sap sat spa sup tap tau tup as at pa ta up us ut

acpsu scaup caps cups cusp scup upas asp cap cup pas pus sac sap spa sup as pa up us

acpsy spacy caps cays pays pyas spay yaps asp cap cay pas pay pya sac sap say spa spy yap as ay pa

acpt pact act apt cap cat pat tap at pa ta

acr arc car

acrru crura arc car cur

acrry carry racy arc car cay cry ray yar ay

acrs arcs cars scar arc car sac as

acrss crass scars arcs cars sacs scar arc ass car sac as

acrst carts acts arcs arts cars cart cast cats rats scar scat star tars tsar act arc art car cat rat sac sat tar as at ta

acrstt tracts carts start tarts tract acts arcs arts cars cart cast cats rats scar scat star tact tars tart tats tsar act arc art car cat rat sac sat tar tat as at ta

acrsw craws arcs cars caws craw scar wars arc car caw raw sac saw war was as aw

acrsy scary arcs cars cays racy rays scar arc car cay cry ray sac say yar as ay

acrsz czars arcs cars czar scar arc car sac as

acrt cart act arc art car cat rat tar at ta

acrtt tract cart tact tart act arc art car cat rat tar tat at ta

acrw craw arc car caw raw war aw

acry racy arc car cay cry ray yar ay

acryz crazy racy czar arc car cay cry ray yar ay

acrz czar arc car

acs sac as

acss sacs sac ass as

acsst casts scats acts cast cats sacs scat tass act ass cat sac sat as at ta

acssu ascus sacs cuss sac ass as us

acst acts cast cats scat act cat sac sat as at ta

acstu scuta acts cast cats cuts scat scut act cat cut sac sat tau as at ta us ut

acsuy saucy cays cay sac say as ay us

acsv vacs sac vac as

acsw caws caw sac saw was as aw

acsy cays cay sac say as ay

act act cat at ta

actt tact act cat tat at ta

actty catty tact act cat cay tat at ay ta

acv vac

acvy cavy vac cay ay

acw caw aw

acy cay ay

---

ad ad

add add dad ad

addde added dead add dad ad ae

adddeegr degraded degrade dreaded dredged. *See* **adddeg addegr adeegr dddeer**

adddeeim diademed. *See* **addeim dddeei**

adddeemn demanded amended. *See* **addden addeen addemn adeemn**

adddeens saddened addends deadens. *See* **addden addeen addens**

adddeer dreaded. *See* **dddeer addde adder**

adddeg gadded added aged dead egad gaed add age dad dag gad gae ad ae

adddegju adjudged adjudge. *See* **adddeg ddegju**

adddeis daddies. *See* **addde addei adeis**

adddel addled added addle laded dale dead deal lade lead add ale dad eld lad lea led ad ae el la

adddelp paddled. *See* **adddel adddep addelp**

adddelr raddled. *See* **adddel addelr**

adddels saddled. *See* **adddel addels**

adddelsw swaddled dawdled dawdles saddled swaddle waddled waddles. *See* **adddel adddew addels addelw**

adddeltw twaddled dawdled twaddle waddled. *See* **adddel adddew addelw**

adddelw dawdled waddled. *See* **adddel addelw adddew**

adddemnu addendum. *See* **addden addemn dddemu**

addden addend added dead dean add and ane dad den end nae ad ae an en na ne

adddeno deodand. *See* **addden dddeno**

adddenos deodands deodand addends. *See* **addden addens addeos adenos**

adddens addends. *See* **addden addens**

adddep padded added dead aped add ape dad dap pad pea ad ae pa pe

adddequ quadded. *See* **addde**

adddew wadded added waded awed dead wade add awe dad dew wad wed ad ae aw we

adddoo doodad dado dodo add ado dad odd ad do od

adddoos doodads. *See* **adddoo ddoos**

adddy daddy dyad add dad day ad ay

adde dead add dad ad ae

addeeefn deafened. *See* **addeen adeefn**

addeeeft defeated. *See* **adeeft**

addeeemn demeaned amended emended. *See* **addeen addemn adeemn**

addeeenr endeared. *See* **addeen addenr adeenr ddeeer**

addeeesy deadeyes deadeye. *See* **ddeees**

addeeey deadeye. *No 6s or 5s*

addeeflt deflated delated deflate. *See* **addeel adeefl adeeft adeelt**

addeefm defamed. *See* **adeefm addef**

addeefry defrayed. *See* **addery adeefr adefry**

addeeggr daggered degrade dragged. *See* **addegr adeegr adeggr ddeegr**

addeegnr deranged gardened angered degrade derange enraged grandee grenade. *See* **addeen addegr addenr adeegr**

addeegr degrade. *See* **adeegr ddeegr addegr**

addeegrr regarded degrade. *See* **addegr adeegr adeerr ddeegr**

addeegrs degrades degrade dredges greased. *See* **addegr adders adeegr adeers**

addeegss degassed. *See* **adegss deegss**

addeeh headed haded dead deed hade head heed add dad edh had hae ad ae ah eh ha he

addeehlr heralded adhered redhead. *See* **addeeh addeel addelr adeehl**

addeehnr hardened adhered redhead. *See* **addeeh addeen addehn addenr**

addeehr adhered redhead. *See* **adeehr addeeh ddeehr**

addeehrs redheads adhered adheres headers redhead sheared shedder. *See* **addeeh addehs adders adeehr**

addeehrt threaded adhered redhead treaded. *See* **addeeh addert adeehr adeeht**

addeeiln deadline delaine. *See* **addeel addeen addeil addeln**

addeeilr deadlier derailed dreidel leadier readied. *See* **addeel addeil addeir addelr**

addeeilt detailed delated dilated ideated. *See* **addeel addeil adeeil adeeit**

addeeimt mediated ideated mediate. *See* **addeim adeeit adeeemt ddeeit**

addeeint detained ideated. *See* **addeen adeeit adeent adeint**

addeeipr diapered readied. *See* **addeir addepr adeepr adeipr**

addeeir readied. *See* **addeir ddeeir**

addeeiss diseased disease seaside. *See* **adeiss ddeeis deeiss**

addeeist steadied ideated ideates sedated teddies. *See* **adeeit adeest ddeeis ddeeit**

addeeit ideated. *See* **ddeeit adeeit**

addeeitv deviated ideated deviate. *See* **addeev adeeit adeitv ddeeit**

addeekn kneaded. *See* **addeen adekn deekn**

addeeknr darkened kneaded kneader. *See* **addeen addenr adeenr adeknr**

addeel leaded addle deled laded alee dale dead deal deed dele lade lead add ale dad eel eld lad lea led lee ad ae el la

addeellp pedalled pedaled pleaded. *See* **addeel addell addelp adeelp**

addeelnu unleaded. *See* **addeel addeen addeln addelu**

addeelor reloaded. *See* **addeel addelo addelr addeor**

addeelp pedaled pleaded. *See* **addeel adeelp addelp ddeelp**

addeelrt treadled alerted altered delated related treaded treadle. *See* **addeel addelr addert adeelr**

addeelt delated. *See* **adeelt addeel**

addeeluv devalued devalue. *See* **addeel addeev addelu adeelv**

addeely delayed. *See* **addeel addely**

addeemn amended. *See* **addemn addeen adeemn ddeemn**

addeemnr remanded amended amender dreamed meander renamed. *See* **addeen addemn addemr addenr**

addeemr dreamed. *See* **addemr adeemr**

addeen deaden ended dead dean deed dene need add and ane dad den end nae nee ad ae an en na ne

addeenpp appended. *See* **addeen addepp adeenp**

addeenpr pandered. *See* **addeen addenr addepr adeenp**

addeenpx expanded. *See* **addeen adeenp adenpx**

addeenrw wandered. *See* **addeen addenr addenw adderw**

addeens deadens. *See* **addeen addens**

addeenss deadness deadens saddens. *See* **addeen addens adenss deenss**

addeentt attended dentate. *See* **addeen adeent adentt deentt**

addeeprt departed predated predate tapered treaded. *See* **addepr addert adeepr adeept**

addeeprv depraved pervaded deprave pervade repaved. *See* **addeev addepr adeepr adeerv**

addeerrt retarded treaded retread. *See* **addert adeerr aeerrt ddeerr**

addeerrw rewarded. *See* **adderw adeerr aderrw aeerrw**

addeert treaded. *See* **addert**

addeertv adverted treaded averted. *See* **addeev addert adeerv adertv**

addeest sedated. *See* **adeest**

addeev evaded evade dead deed deva eave add ave dad eve vee ad ae

addef faded dead deaf fade add dad fad fed ad ae fa

addeff daffed faded daff dead deaf fade add dad fad fed ad ae fa

addeffor afforded. *See* **addeff addeor adefor adffor**

addeflru dreadful defraud. *See* **addelr addelu adeflr adeflu**

addefrsu defrauds defraud. *See* **adders adfrsu ddersu defrsu**

addefrt drafted. *See* **adefrt addert**

addefru defraud. *See* **adder addef adefr**

addefrw dwarfed. *See* **adderw adfrw addef**

addeggl daggled. *See* **adeggl**

addegglr draggled daggled dragged draggle gargled gladder. *See* **addegr addelr adeggl adeglr**

addeggr dragged. *See* **adeggr addegr**

addegho godhead. *See* **addego addeh**

addeginr dreading dandier drained grained reading redding. *See* **addegr addeir addenr addgin**

addegjsu adjudges adjudge. *See* **ddegju degjsu**

addegju adjudge. *See* **ddegju addej**

addegln dangled gladden. *See* **adegln addeln**

addeglns gladdens dangled dangles gladden. *See* **addeln addels addens adegln**

addeglr gladder. *See* **adeglr addegr addelr**

addeglst gladdest staddle. *See* **addels adegls adegst adelst**

addego goaded dodge aged dado dead doge egad gaed goad add ado age ago dad dag doe dog ego gad gae goa god odd ode ad ae do go od

addegpru upgraded guarded upgrade. *See* **addegr addepr adegru ddegru**

addegr graded adder dared dread grade raged aged ager dare dead dear drag egad gaed gear grad rage read redd add age are dad dag ear era erg gad gae gar rad rag red reg ad ae er re

addegru guarded. *See* **adegru ddegru addegr**

addeh haded dead hade head add dad edh had hae ad ae ah eh ha he

addehilr dihedral diehard. *See* **addeil addeir addelr adehil**

addehinw headwind. *See* **addehn addenw ddehin ddeinw**

addehir diehard. *See* **addeir addeh adehr**

addehirs diehards dashier diehard reddish shadier. *See* **addehs addeir adders adehrs**

addehln handled. *See* **addehn adehln addeln**

addehmru drumhead. *See* **addemr adehmr ddemru**

addehn handed haded dead dean hade hand head add and ane dad den edh end had hae hen nae nah ad ae ah an eh en ha he na ne

addehor hoarded. *See* **addeor ddehor**

addehosw shadowed. *See* **addehs addeos adehsw adhosw**

addehs dashed shaded haded hades heads sadhe shade adds dads dash dead hade head shad shed add ads ash dad edh had hae has sad sea she ad ae ah as eh ha he sh

addei　aided aide dead died idea add aid dad did die ad ae ai id

addeiitv　additive. *See* **adeiitv ddeiiv ddeiit**

addeijno　adjoined adenoid. *See* **adijno deijno**

addeil　dialed laddie addle aided ailed ideal idled laded aide dale dead deal deil deli dial died idea idle lade laid lead lied add aid ail ale dad did die eld lad lea led lei lid lie ad ae ai el id la li

addeill　dallied. *See* **adeill addeil addell**

addeilns　landside dandies denials laddies. *See* **addeil addeln addels addens**

addeilnt　tideland dilated. *See* **addeil addeln adeiln adeilt**

addeils　laddies. *See* **adeils addels ddeils**

addeilt　dilated. *See* **adeilt addeil**

addeilyz　dialyzed dialyze. *See* **addeil addely**

addeim　diadem aided aimed amide media aide amid dame dead died dime idea made maid mead add aid aim dad dam did die dim mad mae mid ad ae ai am em id ma me mi

addeimr　admired. *See* **adeimr addeim addemr addeir**

addeimrs　disarmed admired admires diadems misread sidearm. *See* **addeim addeir addemr adders**

addeims　diadems. *See* **adeims ddeims addeim**

addeimsy　dismayed diadems. *See* **addeim addimy adeims adimsy**

addeimtt　admitted. *See* **addeim ademtt**

addeimx　admixed. *See* **addeim adimx deimx**

addeino　adenoid. *See* **addei adeno adino**

addeinor　ordained adenoid adorned android dandier drained radioed. *See* **addeir addenr addeor adeinr**

addeinos　adenoids adenoid dandies noddies. *See* **addens addeos adenos adinos**

addeinp　pandied. *See* **adeinp addei ddein**

addeinr　dandier drained. *See* **addenr addeir adeinr ddeinr**

addeins　dandies. *See* **addens**

addeinst　dandiest dandies detains distend instead sainted stained. *See* **addens adeint ddeint**

addeinu　unaided. *See* **ddeinu adeiu addei**

addeinv　invaded. *See* **adeinv addei ddein**

addeiopr　parodied radioed. *See* **addeir addeor addepr adeipr**

addeior　radioed. *See* **addeor addeir**

addeiors　roadside deodars radioed roadies. *See* **addeir addeor addeos adders**

addeiot　toadied. *See* **addei addet ddeio**

addeiov　avoided. *See* **ddeiov**

addeips　paddies. *See* **addeps addei adeis**

addeir　raided adder aided aired dared dread dried redid aide arid dare dead dear died dire idea raid read redd ride add aid air are dad did die ear era ire rad red ria rid ad ae ai er id re

addeissu　dissuade disused. *See* **adeiss adeisu deissu**

addeisv　advised. *See* **adeisv**

addeisw　waddies. *See* **adeisw addei ddeis**

addeitu　audited. *See* **adeiu aditu addet**

addej　jaded dead jade add dad ad ae

addejly　jadedly. *See* **addely addej**

addejstu　adjusted. *See* **adjstu ddestu**

addeklr　darkled. *See* **adeklr addelr**

addel　addle laded dale dead deal lade lead add ale dad eld lad lea led ad ae el la

addell　ladled addle laded ladle dale dead deal dell lade lead leal add ale all dad eld ell lad lea led ad ae el la

addellu　alluded. *See* **adellu ddellu addell addelu**

addeln　landed addle eland laded laden dale dead deal dean lade land lane lead lean lend add ale and ane dad den eld end lad lea led nae ad ae an el en la na ne

addelnou　duodenal unloaded. *See* **addeln addelo addelu adelno**

addelnsu　unsaddle. *See* **addeln addels addelu addens**

addelo　loaded addle doled laded aloe dado dale dead deal dole lade lead load lode add ado ale dad doe eld lad lea led odd ode old ad ae do el la lo od

addelp　paddle addle laded paled pedal plead aped dale dead deal lade lead leap pale peal plea pled add ale alp ape dad dap eld lad lap lea led pad pal pea ad ae el la pa pe

addelpp　dappled. *See* **addepp adelpp addelp**

addelpr　paddler. *See* **addepr addelr**

addelprs　paddlers ladders paddler paddles raddles saddler. *See* **addelp addelr addels addepr**

addelps　paddles. *See* **adelps addelp addels addeps**

addelr　ladder larded raddle adder addle alder dared dread laded dale dare dead deal dear earl lade lard lead rale read real redd add ale are dad ear eld era lad lar lea led rad red ad ae el er la re

addelrs　ladders raddles saddler. *See* **adders adelrs addelr addels**

addelrst　straddle ladders raddles saddler staddle. *See* **addelr addels adders addert**

addelrsw　dawdlers dawdles drawled ladders raddles saddler swaddle waddles. *See* **addelr addels addelw adders**

addelrsy　saddlery ladders raddles saddler. *See* **addelr addels addely adders**

addelrtw　twaddler drawled trawled twaddle. *See* **addelr addelw addert adderw**

addelrw　drawled. *See* **addelw addelr adderw**

addels　saddle addle dales deals laded lades leads adds ales dads dale dead deal lade lads lead leas sale seal sled add ads ale dad eld els lad lea led sad sal sea ad ae as el la

addelss　saddles. *See* **addels aelss delss**

addelsst　staddles saddest saddles staddle. *See* **addels adelst aelsst**

addelssw　swaddles dawdles saddles swaddle waddles. *See* **addels addelw adelsw aelssw**

addelst　staddle. *See* **adelst addels**

addelstw　twaddles dawdles staddle swaddle twaddle waddles. *See* **addels addelw adelst adelsw**

addelsw　dawdles swaddle waddles. *See* **addelw adelsw**

addeltw　twaddle. *See* **addelw**

addelu　lauded addle laded auld dale dead deal duad dual dude duel lade laud lead add ale dad dud due eld lad lea led leu ad ae el la

addelw　dawdle waddle addle laded waded waled weald awed dale dead deal lade lead lewd wade wale weal weld add ale awe awl dad dew eld lad law lea led wad wed ad ae aw el la we

addely　deadly addle delay laded leady dale dead deal dyad dyed eddy lade lady lead add ale aye dad day dey dye eld lad lay lea led lye yea ad ae ay el la ye

addelzz　dazzled. *See* **adelzz addel addez**

addemm　dammed dame dead made mead add dad dam mad mae mem ad ae am em ma me

addemn　damned demand madden admen amend maned menad named amen dame damn dead dean made mane mead mean mend name add and ane dad dam den end mad mae man men nae ad ae am an em en ma me na ne

addemns　demands. *See* **ademns addemn addens**

addemop　pomaded. *See* **ademop ddemo ddeop**

addemr　madder adder armed dared derma dread dream dame dare dead dear dram made mare mead read ream redd add are arm dad dam ear era mad mae mar rad ram red rem ad ae am em er ma me re

addemst maddest. *See* **ademst addet**

addenopr pardoned adorned padrone. *See* **addenr addeor addepr adenpr**

addenor adorned. *See* **addeor addenr ddenor**

addenot donated. *See* **adenot**

addenpu pudenda. *See* **ddepu denpu**

addenr dander darned adder dared dread dare darn dead dean dear earn nard near nerd rand read redd rend add and ane are dad den ear end era nae rad ran red ad ae an en er na ne re

addenrs danders. *See* **adders addenr addens adenrs**

addenrst stranded danders. *See* **addenr addens adders addert**

addens dedans sadden sanded deans sedan adds dads dead dean dens ends sand sane send add ads and ane dad den end ens nae sad sea sen ad ae an as en na ne

addenss saddens. *See* **addens adenss**

addentu daunted undated. *See* **addet adntu dentu**

addenw dawned dewan waded waned anew awed dawn dead dean wade wand wane wean wend add and ane awe awn dad den dew end nae new wad wan wed wen ad ae an aw en na ne we

addeopt adopted. *See* **adept adopt addet**

addeor adored deodar adder adore dared dread oared oread aero dado dare dead dear doer orad read redd redo road rode add ado are dad doe dor ear era oar odd ode ore rad red rod roe ad ae do er od or re

addeors deodars. *See* **adders addeor adeors addeos**

addeos dadoes dosed adds ados dado dads dead does dose odds odes soda add ado ads dad doe dos odd ode sad sea sod ad ae as do od os so

addeottu outdated. *See* **ddeott deottu**

addepp dapped dead aped add ape dad dap pad pap pea pep ad ae pa pe

addepr draped adder dared drape dread padre pared raped aped dare dead dear pard pare pear rape read reap redd add ape are dad dap ear era pad par pea per rad rap red rep ad ae er pa pe re

addeps spaded spade adds aped apes apse dads daps dead pads peas sped add ads ape asp dad dap pad pas pea sad sap sea spa ad ae as pa pe

addeptu updated. *See* **adeptu addet ddepu**

adder adder dared dread dare dead dear read redd add are dad ear era rad red ad ae er re

adders adders dreads sadder adder dared dares dears dread rased reads redds adds arse dads dare dead dear ears eras rads rase read redd reds sard sear sera add ads are dad ear era rad red res sad sea sad ae as er re

adderss address. *See* **adders**

addert darted traded adder dared dated dread rated tared trade tread dare dart date dead dear drat rate read redd tare tear add aet are art ate dad ear eat era eta rad rat red ret tad tar tea ted ad ae at er re ta

addertt dratted. *See* **addert adertt**

adderw warded adder dared dread waded wader wared awed dare dead dear draw drew read redd wade ward ware wear add are awe dad dew ear era rad raw red wad war wed ad ae aw er re we

addery drayed yarded adder dared deary dread dryad rayed ready aery dare dead dear dray dyad dyed dyer eddy read redd yard yare year add are aye dad day dey dry dye ear era rad ray red rye yar yea ad ae ay er re ye

addesst saddest. *See* **aesst addet adest**

addet dated dead date add aet ate dad eat eta tad tea ted ad ae at ta

addew waded awed dead wade add awe dad dew wad wed ad ae aw we

addez dazed adze daze dead add adz dad zed ad ae

addffilo daffodil. *See* **afflo afilo**

addffnru dandruff. *See* **adffr adfru**

addfhis faddish. *No 6s or 5s*

addfims faddism. *See* **adims**

addfiny dandify. *See* **addfy addny**

addfisst faddists faddist. *See* **adisst**

addfist faddist. *See* **adist afist**

addfy faddy dyad add dad day fad fay ad ay fa

addggin gadding. *See* **addgin aggin**

addgiln addling. *See* **addgin adgiln**

addgilnp paddling addling padding. *See* **addgin adgiln agilnp**

addgilnr raddling addling darling larding. *See* **addgin adgiln adginr ddilnr**

addgilns saddling addling ladings. *See* **addgin adgiln adglns adilns**

addgilnw dawdling waddling addling wadding. *See* **addgin adgiln adginw agilnw**

addgimn madding. *See* **addgin agimn**

addgin adding gain ding add aid and ani dad dag did dig din gad gan gid gin nag ad ai an id in na

addginp padding. *See* **addgin aginp**

addginqu quadding. *See* **addgin**

addginw wadding. *See* **addgin adginw**

addgmno goddamn. *See* **agmno adgmo adgno**

addgmruu mudguard. *See* **agruu amruu adgru**

addgoo ogdoad dado dodo goad good add ado ago dad dag dog gad goa god goo odd ad do go od

addgoos ogdoads. *See* **addgoo ddoos adgos**

addhhlno handhold. *See* **adhlo adlno**

addhiks kaddish. *See* **adhiks**

addhims maddish. *See* **adims**

addhisty hydatids hydatid. *See* **adist adisy disty**

addhity hydatid. *No 6s or 5s*

addhoorw hardwood. *See* **adhor ahoow**

addiinot addition. *See* **adino diiot**

addiins disdain. *No 6s or 5s*

addiinss disdains disdain. *See* **adnss**

addiksty katydids katydid. *See* **ddiksy**

addikty katydid. *See* **ddiky**

addilmn midland. *No 6s or 5s*

addilmns midlands midland. *See* **adilms adilns**

addimno diamond. *See* **adimno**

addimnos diamonds daimons diamond domains. *See* **adimno adinos admnos**

addimy midday middy amid dyad maid add aid aim dad dam day did dim mad may mid yam ad ai am ay id ma mi my

addinor android. *See* **adinor**

addinors androids android inroads ordains sadiron. *See* **adinor adinos adinrs adiors**

addinrww windward. *See* **adinrw**

addknrru drunkard. *See* **adknr dknru**

addllnor landlord. *See* **adllor adlnor**

addllrsu dullards dullard. *See* **addsu adlsu dllsu**

addllru dullard. *See* **adlru**

addlnoow woodland. *See* **adlno**

addmoosy doomsday. *See* **dmoos**

addnopwy pandowdy. *See* **addny ddowy dnowy**

addnorww downward. *See* **adnorw**

addny dandy dyad add and any dad day nay ad an ay na

addo dado add ado dad odd ad do od

addorst dotards. *See* **addort adrst adors**

addort dotard dado dart drat orad road rota taro toad tora trod add ado art dad dor dot oar oat odd ort rad rat rod rot tad tar tod tor ad at do od or ta to addpy paddy dyad add dad dap day pad pay pya yap ad ay pa

addrsy dryads drays dryad dyads yards adds dads days dray dyad rads rays sard yard add ads dad day dry rad ray sad say yar ad as ay

addry dryad dray dyad yard add dad day dry rad ray yar ad ay

adds adds dads add ads dad sad ad as

addsu duads dads dads duad duds sudd add ads dad dud sad ad as us

addsy dyads adds dads days dyad add ads dad day sad say ad as ay

addu duad add dad dud ad

addwy waddy dyad add dad day wad way yaw ad aw ay

addy dyad add dad day ad ay

adeeefny fedayeen. *See* adeefn adeeny

adeeefrt federate draftee. *See* adeefr adeeft adefrt aeefrt

adeeeglt delegate legatee. *See* adeelt aeeglt

adeeegnr renegade angered derange enraged grandee greened grenade reneged. *See* adeegr adeenr adegnr aeegnr

adeeegnt teenaged teenage. *See* adeent aeegnt

adeeegrs degrease greased degrees. *See* adeegr adeers adegrs aeegrs

adeeehhw heehawed. *See* aeehhw

adeeehrt reheated. *See* adeehr adeeht adehrt aeehrt

adeeeknw weakened wakened weekend. *See* adeenw aeeknw deeekn

adeeeelmn enameled. *See* adeeln adeemn aeelmn

adeeelnv leavened. *See* adeeln adeelv aeelnv deeelv

adeeelpr repealed pearled. *See* adeelp adeelr adeepr aeelpr

adeeelrs released resealed dealers leaders release. *See* adeelr adeels adeers adelrs

adeeelrv revealed levered raveled reveled. *See* adeelr adeelv adeerv aeelrv

adeeelsw weaseled seaweed. *See* adeels adelsw aeelsw

adeeeltv elevated elevate. *See* adeelt adeelv aeeltv deeelv

adeeenrs serenade endears sneered. *See* adeenr adeers adenrs deenrs

adeeentt edentate dentate detente. *See* adeent adentt deentt

adeeeprt departee repeated petered predate tapered. *See* adeepr adeept adeprt aeeprt

adeeessw seaweeds seesawed seaweed. *See* aeessw

adeeesw seaweed. *See* adees adesw deesw

adeefgln fenagled fenagle flanged gleaned. *See* adeefl adeefn adeeln adefgn

adeefhnr freehand. *See* adeefn adeefr adeehr adeenr

adeefhor forehead. *See* adeefr adeehr adefor eefhor

adeefhrt fathered draftee feather. *See* adeefr adeeft adeehr adeeht

adeefirr rarefied ferried refried. *See* adeefr adeerr adefir adeirr

adeefkr freaked. *See* adeefr deefkr

adeefl leafed alee dale deaf deal dele delf fade feed feel flea fled flee lade lead leaf ale eel eld elf fad fed fee lad lea led lee ad ae el fa la

adeeflor freeload federal. *See* adeefl adeefr adeelr adeflo

adeeflr federal. *See* adeefr adeelr adeflr adeefl

adeeflrr deferral federal. *See* adeefl adeefr adeelr adeerr

adeeflrs federals dealers federal leaders. *See* adeefl adeefr adeelr adeels

adeeflrt faltered alerted altered deflate draftee federal related treadle. *See* adeefl adeefr adeeft adeelr

adeeflst deflates deafest defeats deflate delates feasted. *See* adeefl adeeft adeels adeelt

adeeflsx flaxseed. *See* adeefl adeels aeflsx eeflsx

adeeflt deflate. *See* adeeft adeelt deeflt

adeefm defame edema famed dame deaf deem deme fade fame feed feme made mead meed dam fad fed fee mad mae ad ae am em fa ma me

adeefmnr freedman amender freeman meander renamed. *See* adeefm adeefn adeefr adeemn

adeefms defames. *See* adeefm adeems

adeefn deafen deaf dean dene fade fane feed fend need and ane den end fad fan fed fee fen nae nee ad ae an en fa na ne

adeefns deafens. *See* adeefn adens deens

adeefnss deafness deafens. *See* adeefn adenss deenss

adeefnst fastened deafens deafest defeats feasted. *See* adeefn adeeft adeent adeest

adeefntt fattened dentate. *See* adeefn adeeft adeent adeftt

adeefr deafer feared defer eared fared freed dare deaf dear deer dree fade fare fear feed fere free read reed reef are arf ear era ere fad far fed fee rad red ref ad ae er fa re

adeefrst draftees deafest dearest defeats draftee feasted feaster strafed. *See* adeefr adeeft adeers adeest

adeefrt draftee. *See* aeefrt adefrt adeefr adeeft

adeefrtu featured draftee feature refuted. *See* adeefr adeeft adefrt aeefrt

adeefrw wafered. *See* adeefr

adeefst deafest defeats feasted. *See* adeeft adefst adeest

adeeft defeat fated feted daft date deaf deft fade fate feat feed feet fete teed aet aft ate eat eft eta fad fat fed fee tad tea ted tee ad ae at fa ta

adeeggh egghead. *See* adeggh deegg deegh

adeegghs eggheads egghead shagged. *See* adeggh adeggs adeghs deeghs

adeeggn engaged. *See* aeeggn adeggn

adeeghrt gathered. *See* adeegr adeehr adeeht adegrt

adeeginr regained angered derange dreeing enraged grained grandee grenade reading reeding reigned. *See* adeegr adeenr adegin adegnr

adeegirs disagree dearies greased readies. *See* adeegr adeers adegrs adeirs

adeegll alleged. *See* aeegll adegll deegll

adeegllt galleted alleged. *See* adeelt adegll aeegll aeeglt

adeeglm gleamed. *See* aeegl adeem adegm

adeegln gleaned. *See* adegln adeeln deegln

adeeglnr enlarged angered derange enlarge enraged general gleaned gleaner gnarled grandee grenade learned. *See* adeegr adeeln adeelr adeenr

adeeglrv graveled gaveled raveled. *See* adeegr adeelr adeelv adeerv

adeeglv gaveled. *See* adeelv aeegl aeglv

adeegmn endgame. *See* adeemn aeegmn

adeegmnr gendarme amender angered derange endgame enraged germane grandee grenade meander renamed. *See* adeegr adeemn adeemr adeenr

adeegmos megadose. *See* adeems adegos adgmos aegmos

adeegmss messaged message. *See* adeems adegss ademss aeemss

adeegnnr endanger angered derange enraged grandee grenade. *See* adeegr adeenn adeenr adegnr

adeegnr angered derange enraged grandee grenade. *See* adeegr adegnr adeenr aeegnr deegnr

adeegnrr gardener garnered angered derange enraged gnarred grandee grander grenade. *See* **adeegr adeenr adeerr adegnr**

adeegnrs deranges grandees grenades angered dangers derange endears enraged enrages ganders gardens genders grandee greased grenade. *See* **adeegr adeenr adeers adegnr**

adeegnru dungaree angered derange enraged grandee grenade. *See* **adeegr adeenr adegnr adegru**

adeegnrv engraved angered avenged avenger derange engrave enraged grandee grenade ravened. *See* **adeegr adeenr adeerv adegnr**

adeegnt negated. *See* **adeent aeegnt adegnt**

adeegnv avenged. *See* **aeegnv adeev**

adeegort derogate. *See* **adeegr adegot adegrt adeort**

adeegprs presaged grasped greased presage sparged speared. *See* **adeegr adeepr adeeps adeers**

adeegprt pargeted predate tapered. *See* **adeegr adeepr adeept adegrt**

adeegr agreed geared agree eager eared edger grade greed raged aged agee ager dare dear deer drag dree edge egad gaed gear geed grad gree rage read reed age are dag ear era ere erg gad gae gar gee rad rag red reg ad ae er re

adeegrrt gartered retread greater. *See* **adeegr adeerr adegrt aeerrt**

adeegrs greased. *See* **adeegr aeegrs deegrs adeers adegrs**

adeegrss dressage grassed greased greases. *See* **adeegr adeers adegrs adegss**

adeegrsw ragweeds greased ragweed wagered. *See* **adeegr adeers adegrs adersw**

adeegrtt targeted treated. *See* **adeegr adegrt adertt deertt**

adeegrw ragweed wagered. *See* **adeegr**

adeegswy edgeways. *See* **adeswy aeegsw deegsw**

adeegttz gazetted gazette. *See* **adegt adegz**

adeehhrs rehashed adheres headers sheared. *See* **adeehr adeers adehhs adehrs**

adeehhst sheathed headset sheathe. *See* **adeeht adeest adehhs adehst**

adeehiln headline delaine inhaled. *See* **adeehl adeeil adeeln adehil**

adeehir headier. *See* **adeehr**

adeehist headiest headset heisted ideates. *See* **adeeht adeeit adeest adehst**

adeehisv adhesive sheaved advisee. *See* **adeehv adeesv adehsv adeisv**

adeehknr hankered harkened kneader hearken. *See* **adeehr adeenr adehkr adehnr**

adeehkww hawkweed. *See* **adehkw**

adeehl healed haled alee dale deal dele hade hale head heal heed heel held lade lead ale edh eel eld had hae lad lea led lee ad ae ah eh el ha he la

adeehllw wellhead. *See* **adeehl adehlw adellw**

adeehlrt lathered alerted altered leather related treadle. *See* **adeehl adeehr adeeht adeelr**

adeehls leashed. *See* **adeehl adehls adeels**

adeehlss headless hassled leashed leashes slashed. *See* **adeehl adeels adehls adehss**

adeehlty heatedly. *See* **adeehl adeeht adeelt adehlt**

adeehlx exhaled. *See* **adeehl aeehlx**

adeehmmo homemade. *See* **adehmm deehmm**

adeehmmr hammered. *See* **adeehr adeemr adehmm adehmr**

adeehmn headmen. *See* **adeemn**

adeehmns headsmen headmen demeans. *See* **adeemn adeems adehms ademns**

adeehmpr hampered. *See* **adeehp adeehr adeemr adeepr**

adeehnot headnote. *See* **adeeht adeent adenot aeehnt**

adeehnpp happened. *See* **adeehp adeenp adehpp aeehnp**

adeehnrr hardener. *See* **adeehr adeenr adeerr adehnr**

adeehnrt adherent neatherd earthen hearten. *See* **adeehr adeeht adeenr adeent**

adeehnst hastened headset handset. *See* **adeeht adeent adeest adehst**

adeehors sorehead adheres headers sheared. *See* **adeehr adeers adehrs adeors**

adeehorv overhead hovered. *See* **adeehr adeehv adeerv**

adeehp heaped aped deep hade head heap heed peed ape dap edh had hae hap hep pad pah pea pee ad ae ah eh ha he pa pe

adeehprs reshaped adheres headers phrased reshape sharped sheared speared sphered. *See* **adeehp adeehr adeepr adeeps**

adeehr adhere header eared heard dare dear deer dree hade hard hare head hear heed herd here read reed rhea are ear edh era ere had hae her rad rah red ad ae ah eh er ha he re

adeehrrt threader retread. *See* **adeeht adeerr adehrt**

adeehrs adheres headers sheared. *See* **adeehr adehrs adeers aeehrs**

adeehrst headrest adheres dearest hardest headers headset heaters reheats sheared threads trashed. *See* **adeehr adeeht adeers adeest**

adeehrtw wreathed watered weather wreathe. *See* **adeehr adeeht adehrt adehtw**

adeehsst headsets headset sedates stashed. *See* **adeeht adeest adehss adehst**

adeehssy hayseeds hayseed essayed. *See* **adehss deessy**

adeehst headset. *See* **adehst adeeht adeest**

adeehsv sheaved. *See* **adeesv adeehv aeehsv adehsv**

adeehsy hayseed. *See* **adees adehs adehy**

adeeht heated death hated date hade hate head heat heed teed thee aet ate eat edh eta eth had hae hat het tad tea ted tee the ad ae ah at eh ha he ta

adeehv heaved evade heave deva eave hade have head heed ave edh eve had hae vee ad ae ah eh ha he

adeeiilz idealize. *See* **adeeil**

adeeijmr jeremiad. *See* **adeemr adeimr**

adeeijst jadeites jadeite ideates. *See* **adeeit adeest deejst**

adeeijt jadeite. *See* **adeeit**

adeeil aedile ailed edile elide ideal aide alee dale deal deil dele deli dial idea idle lade laid lead lied aid ail ale die eel eld lad lea led lee lei lid lie ad ae ai el id la li

adeeilm limeade. *See* **adeeil adeilm aeeilm**

adeeilmr remedial emerald leadier limeade mealier. *See* **adeeil adeelr adeemr adeilm**

adeeilms limeades aediles limeade misdeal mislead. *See* **adeeil adeels adeems adeilm**

adeeilmv medieval limeade. *See* **adeeil adeelv adeilm adeilv**

adeeiln delaine. *See* **adeeil adeiln adeeln**

adeeilns delaines aediles aniseed delaine denials linseed. *See* **adeeil adeeln adeels adeiln**

adeeilnt entailed delaine lineate. *See* **adeeil adeeit adeeln adeelt**

adeeilpt depilate petaled pileate plaited pleated. *See* **adeeil adeeit adeelp adeelt**

adeeilr leadier. *See* **adeeil adeelr adeilr deeilr**

adeeilrs sidereal aediles dealers dearies derails leaders leadier readies. *See* **adeeil adeelr adeels adeers**

adeeilrt retailed alerted altered leadier related trailed treadle. *See* **adeeil adeeit adeelr adeelt**

adeeilrz realized leadier realize. *See* **adeeil adeelr adeilr adilrz**

adeeils aediles. *See* **adeeil adeils deeils adeels**

adeeilst leadiest aediles delates details dilates ideates. *See* **adeeil adeeit adeels adeelt**

adeeimnr remained amender meander renamed. *See* **adeemn adeemr adeenr adeimn**

adeeimnt dementia matinee mediant mediate. *See* **adeeit adeemn adeemt adeent**

adeeimnx examined examine. *See* **adeemn adeimn aeemnx**

adeeimrr dreamier admirer dreamer married rearmed. *See* **adeemr adeerr adeimr adeirr**

adeeimrt diameter demerit dimeter emirate meatier mediate merited mitered readmit. *See* **adeeit adeemr adeemt adeimr**

adeeimst mediates ideates mediate steamed. *See* **adeeit adeems adeemt adeest**

adeeimt mediate. *See* **adeeit deeimt adeemt**

adeeimtt meditate emitted mediate teatime. *See* **adeeit adeemt ademtt deeimt**

adeeinrt retained retinae trained trainee. *See* **adeeit adeenr adeent adeinr**

adeeins aniseed. *See* **deeins**

adeeinss aniseeds aniseed disease seaside. *See* **adeiss adenss aeinss deeins**

adeeiprr repaired parried. *See* **adeepr adeerr adeipr adeirr**

adeeiptx expiated expiate. *See* **adeeit adeept adeitx**

adeeirrr drearier. *See* **adeerr adeirr**

adeeirst steadier astride dearest dearies diaster ideates readies reedits seriate tirades. *See* **adeeit adeers adeest adeirs**

adeeirtt iterated ariette attired iterate treated. *See* **adeeit adeirt adertt aeirtt**

adeeirw wearied. *See* **aeeir adeir adeer**

adeeiss disease seaside. *See* **adeiss deeiss**

adeeisss diseases disease seaside. *See* **adeiss adesss deeiss**

adeeisst steadies disease easiest ideates seaside sedates. *See* **adeeit adeest adeiss adisst**

adeeissv advisees advisee advises devises disease seaside. *See* **adeesv adeiss adeisv deeiss**

adeeist ideates. *See* **adeeit adeest**

adeeistv deviates sedative advisee deviate ideates. *See* **adeeit adeest adeesv adeisv**

adeeisv advisee. *See* **adeisv deeisv adeesv**

adeeit ideate adit aide date diet edit idea teed tide tied aet aid ate die dit eat eta ita tad tea ted tee tie ad ae ai at id it ta ti

adeeitv deviate. *See* **adeeit adeitv**

adeejsy deejays. *See* **adeejy adees adejs**

adeejy deejay jade eyed aye day dey dye eye jay yea ad ae ay ye

adeekl leaked alee dale deal dele eked kale keel lade lake lead leak leek ale eel eke eld elk kal lad lea led lee lek ad ae el ka la

adeekmrr remarked dreamer rearmed. *See* **adeemr adeerr adekmr ademrr**

adeekmrt marketed. *See* **adeemr adeemt adekmr ademrt**

adeeknp kneepad. *See* **adeekp adeenp**

adeeknps kneepads kneepad sneaked spanked. *See* **adeekp adeenp adeeps adekns**

adeeknpw knapweed kneepad wakened. *See* **adeekp adeenp adeenw adenpw**

adeeknr kneader. *See* **adeknr adeenr deeknr**

adeeknrs kneaders darkens endears kneader sneaked sneaker. *See* **adeenr adeers adeknr adekns**

adeekns sneaked. *See* **adekns**

adeeknw wakened. *See* **adeenw aeeknw**

adeekp peaked aped deep eked keep peak peed peek ape dap eke pad pea pee ad ae ka pa pe

adeekqsu squeaked. *See* **adekqu aekqsu**

adeekrst streaked darkest dearest retakes. *See* **adeers adeest adekrs adekst**

adeekrw wreaked. *See* **aeekrw adekr adeer**

adeekswy weekdays weekday. *See* **adeswy deeksw**

adeektw tweaked. *See* **aektw deetw adekw**

adeekwy weekday. *See* **deeky adekw deewy**

adeellmu medullae medulla. *See* **adellu adelmu aeellm dellmu**

adeellqu equalled equaled quelled. *See* **adellu**

adeellru laureled allured. *See* **adeelr adellu aellru deelru**

adeells allseed. *See* **adells adeels**

adeellss allseeds allseed. *See* **adeels adells aeelss**

adeellty elatedly. *See* **adeelt aellty deelly**

adeellwy walleyed walleye. *See* **adellw adelwy aeelwy deelly**

adeelmno lemonade. *See* **adeeln adeemn adelmo adelno**

adeelmnr aldermen amender emerald learned mandrel meander renamed. *See* **adeeln adeelr adeemn adeemr**

adeelmns leadsmen demeans enamels. *See* **adeeln adeels adeemn adeems**

adeelmnt lamented metaled mantled. *See* **adeeln adeelt adeemn adeemt**

adeelmp empaled. *See* **aeelmp adeelp adelmp**

adeelmr emerald. *See* **adeelr adelmr adeemr**

adeelmrs emeralds dealers emerald leaders medlars smeared. *See* **adeelr adeels adeemr adeems**

adeelmrt trameled alerted altered emerald metaled related treadle. *See* **adeelr adeelt adeemr adeemt**

adeelmrv marveled emerald raveled. *See* **adeelr adeelv adeemr adeerv**

adeelmt metaled. *See* **adeelt adelmt deelmt adeemt**

adeelmtu emulated metaled emulate. *See* **adeelt adeemt adelmt adelmu**

adeeln leaden leaned eland laden alee dale deal dean dele dene lade land lane lead lean lend need ale and ane den eel eld end lad lea led lee nae nee ad ae an el en la na ne

adeelnor oleander learned. *See* **adeeln adeenr adelno**

adeelnp deplane paneled. *See* **adeeln adeelp adeenp adelnp**

adeelnps deplanes deplane elapsed paneled pleased. *See* **adeeln adeelp adeels adeenp**

adeelnr learned. *See* **adelnr adeelr adeenr adeeln aeelnr**

adeelnrt antlered alerted altered enteral eternal learned related teleran treadle. *See* **adeeln adeelr adeelt adeenr**

adeelnrv lavender learned raveled ravened. *See* **adeeln adeelr adeelv adeenr**

adeelnsu unleased. *See* **adeeln adeels adelns adensu**

adeelnsv enslaved enslave leavens. *See* **adeeln adeels adeelv adeesv**

adeelntt talented dentate nettled. *See* **adeeln adeelt adeent adelnt**

adeelost desolate delates. *See* **adeels adeelt adeest adelst**

adeelp leaped pealed paled pedal plead alee aped dale deal deep dele lade lead leap pale peal peed peel plea pled ale alp ape dap eel eld lad lap lea led lee pad pal pea pee ad ae el la pa pe

adeelpr pearled. *See* **adeelr adeelp aeelpr adeepr**

adeelprs relapsed dealers elapsed leaders leapers pearled pleased relapse repeals speared. *See* **adeelp adeelr adeels adeepr**

adeelprt paltered alerted altered pearled petaled pleated predate prelate related tapered treadle. *See* **adeelp adeelr adeelt adeepr**

adeelpry parleyed replayed pearled relayed. *See* **adeelp adeelr adeepr adelpy**

adeelps elapsed pleased. *See* **aeelps adelps adeelp adeels adeeps**

adeelpst pedestal delates elapsed pestled petaled pleased pleated stapled. *See* **adeelp adeels adeelt adeeps**

adeelpt petaled pleated. *See* **adeelt adeept deelpt adelpt**

adeelqsu squealed equaled sequela. *See* **adeels aelqsu deelsu**

adeelqu equaled. *See* **deelu aelqu**

adeelr dealer leader alder eared elder alee dale dare deal dear deer dele dree earl lade lard lead leer rale read real reed reel ale are ear eel eld era ere lad lar lea led lee rad red ad ae el er la re

adeelrs dealers leaders. *See* **adelrs adeelr deelrs adeers adeels**

adeelrst treadles alerted altered dealers dearest delates elaters leaders related relates stealer treadle. *See* **adeelr adeels adeelt adeers**

adeelrsw leewards dealers leaders leeward welders. *See* **adeelr adeels adeers adelrs**

adeelrt alerted altered related treadle. *See* **adeelr adeelt aeelrt**

adeelrtv traveled alerted altered averted raveled related treadle. *See* **adeelr adeelt adeelv adeerv**

adeelruv revalued devalue raveled revalue. *See* **adeelr adeelv adeerv adeluv**

adeelrv raveled. *See* **adeelr adeerv adeelv aeelrv**

adeelrw leeward. *See* **adeelr deelrw**

adeelrx relaxed. *See* **adeelr adeerx**

adeelry relayed. *See* **adeelr adelry**

adeels leased sealed dales deals deles eased easel lades leads lease alee ales dale deal dele ease eels else lade lads lead leas lees sale seal seed seel sled ads ale eel eld els lad lea led lee sad sal sea see ad ae as el la

adeelsst dateless tasseled delates sedates teasels. *See* **adeels adeelt adeest adelst**

adeelst delates. *See* **adeelt adelst aeelst deelst adeest**

adeelsty sedately delates yeasted. *See* **adeels adeelt adeest adelst**

adeelsuv devalues devalue. *See* **adeels adeelv adeesv adelsv**

adeelt delate elated dealt delta elate lated alee dale date deal dele lade late lead leet tael tale teal teed aet ale alt ate eat eel eld eta lad lea led lee let tad tea ted tee ad ae at el la ta

adeeltx exalted. *See* **adeelt**

adeeluv devalue. *See* **adeelv adeluv**

adeelv leaved delve evade laved leave alee dale deal dele deva eave lade lave lead leva vale veal veld ale ave eel eld eve lad lea led lee lev vee ad ae el la

adeem edema dame deem deme made mead meed dam mad mae ad ae am em ma me

adeemmry yammered. *See* **ademry ademmr adeemr deemry**

adeemmss mesdames. *See* **adeems ademss aeemss deemss**

adeemn demean admen amend edema emend enema maned menad named amen dame damn dean deem deme dene made mane mead mean meed mend name need and ane dam den end mad mae man men nae nee ad ae am an em en ma me na ne

adeemnnr mannered amender meander renamed. *See* **adeemn adeemr adeenr**

adeemnor demeanor amender madrone meander renamed. *See* **adeemn adeemr adeenr ademno**

adeemnot nematode. *See* **adeemn adeemt adeent ademno**

adeemnr amender meander renamed. *See* **adeemn adeenr aeemnr deemnr adeemr**

adeemnrs amenders meanders amender demeans endears meander menders remands renamed renames smeared. *See* **adeemn adeemr adeems adeenr**

adeemns demeans. *See* **ademns adeemn adeems deemns aeemns**

adeemort moderate. *See* **adeemr adeemt ademor ademrt**

adeemppr pampered papered. *See* **adeemr adeepr adempp adempr**

adeemprt tampered predate tapered tempera tramped. *See* **adeemr adeemt adeepr adeept**

adeemprv revamped deprave pervade repaved. *See* **adeemr adeepr adeerv adempr**

adeempst stampede dampest stamped steamed. *See* **adeems adeemt adeeps adeept**

adeemr reamed remade ameer armed derma dream eared edema dame dare dear deem deer deme dram dree made mare mead meed mere read ream reed are arm dam ear era ere mad mae mar

rad ram red rem ad ae am em er ma me re

adeemrr dreamer rearmed. *See* **adeerr ademrr adeemr aeemrr**

adeemrrs dreamers dreamer readers reamers rearmed rereads smeared. *See* **adeemr adeems adeerr adeers**

adeemrs smeared. *See* **aeemrs ademrs adeems adeers adeemr**

adeemrst mastered streamed dearest smarted smeared steamed steamer. *See* **adeemr adeems adeemt adeers**

adeemrsu measured demures measure medusae resumed smeared. *See* **adeemr adeems adeers ademrs**

adeemrtt mattered treated. *See* **adeemr adeemt ademrt ademtt**

adeems edemas seamed dames deems demes eased edema meads meeds dame dams deem deme ease made mead meed mesa same seam seed seem ads dam mad mae sad sea see ad ae am as em ma me

adeemst steamed. *See* **adeems ademst adeest adeemt**

adeemsu medusae. *See* **ademsu adeems**

adeemt teamed edema mated meted tamed dame date deem deme made mate mead meat meed meet mete tame team teed teem aet ate dam eat eta mad mae mat met tad tam tea ted tee ad ae am at em ma me ta

adeenn ennead dean dene need and ane den end nae nee ad ae an en na ne

adeennrs ensnared endears enneads ensnare. *See* **adeenn adeenr adeers adenrs**

adeennru unearned. *See* **adeenn adeenr adennu adenru**

adeenns enneads. *See* **adeenn adees adens**

adeennx annexed. *See* **adeenn aennx**

adeenors reasoned endears endorse. *See* **adeenr adeers adenos adenrs**

adeenorv endeavor ravened. *See* **adeenr adeerv deenor deenrv**

adeenoss seasoned. *See* **adenos adenss aenoss deenss**

adeenott detonate dentate notated. *See* **adeent adenot adentt aenott**

adeenp neaped aped dean deep dene nape neap need neep pane pean peed peen pend and ane ape dap den end nae nap nee pad pan pea pee pen ad ae an en na ne pa pe

adeenppr endpaper papered. *See* **adeenp adeenr adeepr adenpp**

adeenprt parented predate pretend tapered. *See* **adeenp adeenr adeent adeepr**

adeenprx expander. *See* **adeenp adeenr adeepr adeerx**

adeenptt patented dentate. *See* **adeenp adeent adeept adenpt**

adeenr earned endear neared eared dare darn dean dear deer dene dree earn erne nard near need nerd rand read reed rend and ane are den ear end era ere nae nee rad ran red ad ae an en er na ne re

adeenrrw wanderer redrawn. *See* **adeenr adeenw adeerr adenrr**

adeenrs endears. *See* **deenrs adeenr adeers adenrs**

adeenrss dearness endears sanders senders. *See* **adeenr adeers adenrs adenss**

adeenrsu undersea asunder danseur endears endures ensured. *See* **adeenr adeers adenrs adenru**

adeenrsw answered endears wanders wardens. *See* **adeenr adeenw adeers adenrs**

adeenrtt nattered dentate entreat ternate treated. *See* **adeenr adeent adenrt adentt**

adeenrtu denature denture tenured. *See* **adeenr adeent adenrt adenru**

adeenrv ravened. *See* **adeenr adeerv deenrv**

adeenry deanery yearned. *See* **adenry adeenr adeeny**

adeensst assented densest sateens sedates senates sensate. *See* **adeent adeest adenss adnsst**

adeenssu danseuse sundaes. *See* **adenss adensu aenssu deenss**

adeenstu unseated. *See* **adeent adeest adensu adnstu**

adeent anteed eaten ante date dean dene dent neat need teed teen tend aet and ane ant ate den eat end eta nae nee net tad tan tea ted tee ten ad ae an at en na ne ta

adeentt dentate. *See* **adeent adentt deentt**

adeenttv vendetta dentate. *See* **adeent adentt adentv deentt**

adeenw weaned dewan waned anew awed dawn dean dene need wade wand wane wean weed wend and ane awe awn den dew end ewe nae nee new wad wan wed wee wen ad ae an aw en na ne we

adeeny yeaned needy dean dene deny dyne eyed need yean and ane any aye day den dey dye end eye nae nay nee yea yen ad ae an ay en na ne ye

adeeooprt operated operate predate tapered. *See* **adeepr adeept adeort adeprt**

adeeorvw overawed overawe. *See* **adeerv adeovw aeervw**

adeeppr papered. *See* **adeppr adeepr**

adeepprr prepared papered prepare. *See* **adeepr adeerr adeppr adeprr**

adeepr reaped drape eared padre pared raped aped dare dear deep deer dree pard pare pear peed peer rape read reap reed rape are dap ear era ere pad par pea pee per rad rap red rep ad ae er pa pe re

adeeprrs spreader drapers readers reapers rereads sparred speared. *See* **adeepr adeeps adeerr adeers**

adeeprs speared. *See* **adeers adeeps adeepr aeeprs**

adeeprss aspersed asperse depress pesades pressed serapes spaders speared spreads. *See* **adeepr adeeps adeers adeprs**

adeeprst pederast predates dearest departs petards predate repeats speared tapered. *See* **adeepr adeeps adeept adeers**

adeeprsu persuade speared perused. *See* **adeepr adeeps adeers adeprs**

adeeprsv depraves pervades adverse deprave pervade repaved repaves speared. *See* **adeepr adeeps adeers adeerv**

adeeprt predate tapered. *See* **adeprt adeept aeeprt**

adeeprtt pattered predate tapered treated. *See* **adeepr adeept adeprt adeptt**

adeeprtu depurate erupted predate reputed tapered. *See* **adeepr adeept adeprt adeptu**

adeeprv deprave pervade repaved. *See* **adeerv aeeprv adeepr**

adeeps pesade eased pease spade speed aped apes apse daps deep ease pads peas peed pees seed seep sped ads ape asp dap pad pas pea pee sad sap sea see spa ad ae as pa pe

adeepss pesades. *See* **adepss aeepss adeeps deepss**

adeepswy speedway. *See* **adeeps adepsy adeswy aeepsy**

adeept pedate adept taped aped date deep pate peat peed tape teed aet ape apt ate dap eat eta pad pat pea pee pet tad tap tea ted tee ad ae at pa pe ta

adeeqruv quavered. *See* **adeerv aeqruv**

adeeqtu equated. *See* **aeeqtu deetu**

adeer eared dare dear deer dree read reed are ear era ere rad red ad ae er re

adeerr dearer reader reared reread eared erred dare dear deer dree rare read rear

reed are ear era ere err rad red ad ae er re

adeerrs readers rereads. *See* **adeerr adeers aeerrs**

adeerrst arrested retreads serrated darters dearest readers rereads retards retread serrate starred traders. *See* **adeerr adeers adeest aderrt**

adeerrt retread. *See* **aderrt adeerr aeerrt**

adeerrv averred. *See* **adeerr adeerv**

adeers erased seared dares dears deers drees eared eased erase rased reads reeds arse dare dear deer dree ears ease eras rads rase read reds reed sard sear seed seer sera sere ads are ear era ere rad red res sad sea sed ae as er re

adeerrsst asserted dearest deserts dessert sedates teasers. *See* **adeers adeest aderst aeerss**

adeerst dearest. *See* **deerst aeerst adeers adeest aderst**

adeerstt restated dearest estreat restate started tetrads treated. *See* **adeers adeest aderst adertt**

adeersv adverse. *See* **aeersv adeers adeerv adeesv deersv**

adeertt treated. *See* **adertt deertt**

adeerttt tattered treated. *See* **adertt deertt**

adeertty yattered treated. *See* **adertt aeerty aertty deertt**

adeertv averted. *See* **adertv adeerv**

adeertw watered. *See* **deert adeer aeert**

adeerv evader reaved eared evade raved aver dare dear deer deva dree eave ever rave read reed veer are ave ear era ere eve rad red rev vee ad ae er re

adeervyy everyday. *See* **adeerv**

adeerx exedra eared axed dare dear deer dree read reed are axe ear era ere rad red rex ad ae ax er ex re

adees eased ease seed ads sad sea see ad ae as

adeessss assessed. *See* **adesss**

adeesst sedates. *See* **adeest deesst aeesst**

adeessx axseeds. *See* **adees deesx aeess**

adeessy essayed. *See* **deessy adees aessy**

adeest seated sedate teased dates eased sated setae stead steed tease date ease east eats etas seat seed seta tads teas teds teed tees ads aet ate eat eta sad sat sea see set tad tea ted tee ad ae as at ta

adeesttt attested testate. *See* **adeest adestt**

adeestw sweated. *See* **adeest deestw adestw**

adeesty yeasted. *See* **adeest adesty**

adeesv evades devas eased eaves evade saved aves deva ease eave eves save seed vase vees ads ave eve sad sea see vee ad ae as

adeeswwx waxweeds waxweed. *See* **adees deesx adesw**

adeev evade deva eave ave eve vee ad ae

adeewwx waxweed. *See* **adewx**

adef deaf fade fad fed ad ae fa

adeffg gaffed gaffe aged daff deaf egad fade gaed gaff age dag fad fag fed gad gae ad ae fa

adeffimr affirmed daffier. *See* **adefir adefmr adeimr affimr**

adeffip piaffed. *See* **aeffip deffi**

adeffir daffier. *See* **deffir adefir**

adeffist daffiest distaff staffed stiffed taffies. *See* **adefst aefist deffit defist**

adeffix affixed. *See* **affix deffi defix**

adefflns snaffled snaffle. *See* **adelns**

adefflo leadoff. *See* **adeflo**

adefflos leadoffs leadoff. *See* **adeflo afflos**

adefflr raffled. *See* **adeflr aefflr**

adefflw waffled. *See* **adeflw aefflw**

adeffqu quaffed. *See* **affqu**

adeffst staffed. *See* **adefst affst**

adefgg fagged gaged aged deaf egad fade gaed gage age dag egg fad fag fed gad gae gag ad ae fa

adefggl flagged. *See* **adeggl adefgg**

adefggr fragged. *See* **adeggr**

adefgiis gasified. *See* **aegis adeis adegs**

adefgiln finagled aligned dealing finagle flanged leading leafing. *See* **adefgn adefil adegin adegln**

adefgils gadflies. *See* **adefil adegls adeils aegils**

adefgimn defaming. *See* **adefgn adegim adegin adeimn**

adefgitu fatigued fatigue. *See* **defgit**

adefgln flanged. *See* **adegln adefgn aefgln**

adefglot gatefold floated gloated. *See* **adeflo adegot aeglot defglo**

adefgn fanged ganef agape deaf dean egad fade fane fang fend gaed age and ane dag den end fad fag fan fed fen gad gae gan nae nag ad ae an en fa na ne

adefgor foraged. *See* **adefor aefgor defgor**

adefgrt grafted. *See* **adefrt adegrt**

adefhily hayfield headily. *See* **adefil adefly adehil**

adefhims famished. *See* **adefhs adehms adeims aehims**

adefhls flashed. *See* **adefhs adehls**

adefhltu deathful default faulted hateful. *See* **adefht adeflu adehlt adehlu**

adefhmot fathomed. *See* **adefht adefmo afhmot dehmot**

adefhnor forehand. *See* **adefor adehnr dehnor**

adefhs fashed fades hades heads sadhe shade sheaf dash deaf fade fads fash feds hade head safe shad shed ads ash edh fad fas fed feh had hae has sad sea she ad ae ah as eh fa ha he sh

adefhst shafted. *See* **adehst adefhs adefst adefht**

adefht hafted death fated hated daft date deaf deft fade fate feat hade haft hate head heat heft aet aft ate edh eft eta eth fad fat fed feh had hae hat het tad tea ted the ad ae ah at eh fa ha he ta

adefiilr airfield deliria. *See* **adefil adefir adeflr adeilr**

adefiils salified dailies sedilia. *See* **adefil adeils defils**

adefiimr ramified. *See* **adeimr adefir adefmr defimr**

adefiirt ratified. *See* **adefir adefrt adeirt adfirt**

adefil afield failed ailed felid field filed flied ideal aide alif dale deaf deal deil delf deli dial fade fail fila file flea fled idea idle lade laid lead leaf lied lief life aid ail ale die eld elf fad fed fid fie lad lea led lei lid lie ad ae ai el fa id if la li

adefill flailed. *See* **adefil adeill aefill defill**

adefilmn inflamed inflame. *See* **adefil adeflm adeilm adeiln**

adefilnt inflated defiant fainted inflate. *See* **adefil adeiln adeilt adeint**

adefilot foliated floated foliate. *See* **adefil adeflo adeilo adeilt**

adefinrr infrared drainer refrain. *See* **adefir adeinr adeirr adenrr**

adefint defiant fainted. *See* **adeint afint adeft**

adefiors foresaid fedoras roadies. *See* **adefir adefor adeirs adeors**

adefir faired afire aired fared feria fired fried aide arid dare deaf dear dire fade fair fare fear fire idea raid read ride rife aid air are arf die ear era fad far fed fid fie fir ire rad red ref ria rid rif ad ae ai er fa id if re

adefirrt draftier drifter tardier tarried. *See* **adefir adefrt adeirr adeirt**

adefitx fixated. *See* **adeitx aefitx**

adefk faked deaf fade fake fad fed kaf kef ad ae fa ka

adefkl flaked faked flake dale deaf deal delf fade fake flak flea fled kale lade lake lead leaf leak ale eld elk fad fed kaf kal kef lad lea led lek ad ae el fa ka la

adefkln flanked. *See* **adefkl aekln adeln**

adefknr franked. *See* **adeknr**

adeflllu ladleful. *See* **adellu adeflu delllu**

adefllsw dewfalls dewfall. *See* **adeflw adells adellw adelsw**

adeflluy feudally. *See* **adeflu adefly adellu**

adefllw dewfall. *See* **adeflw adellw**

adeflm flamed famed flame fleam lamed medal dale dame deaf deal delf fade fame flam flea fled lade lame lead leaf made male mead meal meld ale dam eld elf elm fad fed lad lam lea led mad mae mel ad ae am el em fa la ma me

adeflnor foreland. *See* **adeflo adeflr adefor adelno**

adeflntu flaunted default faulted. *See* **adeflu adelnt aelntu aflntu**

adeflo foaled loafed aloe dale deaf deal delf dole fade flea fled floe foal fold lade lead leaf load loaf lode ado ale doe eld elf fad fed foe lad lea led oaf ode old ad ae do el fa la lo od of

adeflorv flavored favored. *See* **adeflo adeflr adefor adelor**

adeflot floated. *See* **adeflo deflot**

adeflpp flapped. *See* **adelpp**

adeflprs feldspar felspar. *See* **adeflr adelps adelrs adeprs**

adeflr flared alder fared feral flare dale dare deaf deal dear delf earl fade fare fear flea fled lade lard lead leaf rale read real ale are arf ear eld elf era fad far fed lad lar lea led rad red ref ad ae el er fa la re

adeflrsw selfward. *See* **adeflr adeflw adelrs adelsw**

adeflrtw leftward trawled. *See* **adeflr adeflw adefrt adeftw**

adeflrzz frazzled frazzle. *See* **adelzz adeflr aderzz**

adeflstu defaults default faulted saluted sulfate. *See* **adeflu adefst adelst adlstu**

adefltu default faulted. *See* **adeflu defltu**

adeflu feudal auld dale deaf deal delf dual duel fade feud flea fled flue fuel lade laud lead leaf ale due eld elf fad fed feu flu lad lea led leu ad ae el fa la

adeflw flawed waled weald awed dale deaf deal delf fade flaw flea fled flew lade lead leaf lewd wade wale weal weld ale awe awl dew eld elf fad fed few lad law lea led wad wed ad ae aw el fa la we

adefly deafly flayed delay leady leafy dale deaf deal defy delf fade flay flea fled lade lady lead leaf ale aye day dey dye eld elf fad fay fed fey fly lad lay lea led lye yea ad ae ay el fa la ye

adefm famed dame deaf fade fame made mead dam fad fed mad mae ad ae am em fa ma me

adefmo foamed famed dame deaf demo dome fade fame foam made mead mode ado dam doe fad fed foe mad mae moa mod oaf ode ad ae am do em fa ma me mo od of om

adefmr farmed framed armed derma dream famed fared frame dame dare deaf dear dram fade fame fare farm fear made mare mead read ream are arf arm dam ear era fad far fed mad mae mar rad ram red ref rem ad ae am em er fa ma me re

adefnn fanned deaf dean fade fane fend and ane den end fad fan fed fen nae ad ae an en fa na ne

adefnopr profaned padrone profane. *See* **adefor adenpr adnopr denopr**

adefnsst daftness fastens fatness. *See* **adefst adenss adnsst aefnst**

adefnsu snafued. *See* **adensu aefnsu**

adefnw fawned dewan waned anew awed dawn deaf dean fade fane fawn fend wade wand wane wean wend and ane awe awn den dew end fad fan fed fen few nae new wad wan wed wen ad ae an aw en fa na ne we

adefoos seafood. *See* **adefs dfoos**

adefooss seafoods seafood. *See* **aefoss**

adefor fedora adore afore fared oared oread aero dare deaf dear doer fade fare faro fear fora ford fore froe orad read redo road rode ado are arf doe dor ear era fad far fed foe for fro oaf oar ode ore rad red ref rod roe ad ae do er fa od of or re

adefors fedoras. *See* **adeors adefor**

adeforv favored. *See* **adefor deorv aforv**

adefory forayed. *See* **adefry adefor**

adefr fared deaf dear deaf dare fade fare fear read are arf ear era fad far fed rad red ref ad ae er fa re

adefrst strafed. *See* **adefrt adfrst adefst aefrst aderst**

adefrsy defrays. *See* **adefry**

adefrt dafter farted rafted after draft fared fated rated trade tread daft dare dart date deaf dear deft drat fade fare fart fate fear feat frat fret raft rate read reft tare tear aet aft are arf art ate ear eat eft era eta fad far fat fed rad rat red ref ret tad tar tea ted ad ae at er fa re ta

adefry defray frayed deary faery fared rayed ready aery dare deaf dear defy dray dyer fade fare fear fray read yard yare year are arf aye day dey dry dye ear era fad far fay fed fey fry rad ray red ref rye yar yea ad ae ay er fa re ye

adefs fades deaf fade fads feds safe ads fad fas fed sad sea ad ae as fa

adefst fasted dates fades fated fates feast feats sated stead daft date deaf deft

east eats efts etas fade fads fast fate fats feat feds safe seat seta tads teas teds ads aet aft ate eat eft eta fad fas fat fed sad sat sea set tad tea ted ad ae as at fa ta

adefstt daftest. *See* **adefst adeftt adestt**

adeft fated daft date deaf deft fade fate feat aet aft ate eat eft eta fad fat fed tad tea ted ad ae at fa ta

adeftt fatted fated daft date deaf deft fade fate feat teat aet aft ate eat eft eta fad fat fed tad tat tea ted ad ae at fa ta

adeftw wafted fated awed daft date deaf deft fade fate feat wade waft weft aet aft ate awe dew eat eft eta fad fat fed few tad tea ted wad wed wet ad ae at aw fa ta we

adefz fazed adze daze deaf fade faze adz fad fed fez zed ad ae fa

adeg aged egad gaed age dag gad gae ad ae

adegg gaged aged egad gaed gage age dag egg gad gae gag ad ae

adeggg gagged gaged aged egad gaed gage age dag egg gad gae gag ad ae

adeggh hagged gaged aged egad gaed gage hade head age dag edh egg gad gae gag had hae hag ad ae ah eh ha he

adegghl haggled. *See* **adeggl adeggh aegghl**

adegghs shagged. *See* **adeghs adeggs**

adeggj jagged gaged aged egad gaed gage jade age dag egg gad gae gag jag ad ae

adeggjly jaggedly. *See* **adegly adeggl adeggj**

adeggl daggle lagged gaged glade aged dale deal egad gaed gage gale geld glad lade lead age ale dag egg eld gad gae gag gal gel lad lag lea led leg ad ae el la

adegglr gargled. *See* **adeggr aegglr adeglr adeggl**

adegglrs draggles daggers draggle gargled gargles laggers slagged. *See* **adeggl adeggr adeggs adeglr**

adegglry raggedly draggle gargled raggedy. *See* **adeggl adeggr adeglr adegly**

adeggls slagged. *See* **adeggl adegls adeggs**

adegglw waggled. *See* **adeggl adeggw aegglw**

adeggmo demagog. *See* **adgmo adegg adegm**

adeggmoy demagogy demagog. *See* **dggoy adgmo adegg**

adeggn ganged nagged gaged aged dean egad gaed gage gang age and ane dag den egg end gad gae gag gan nae nag ad ae an en na ne

adeggns snagged. *See* **adeggn adeggs**

adeggopy pedagogy. *See* **dggoy deopy adegg**

adeggr dagger ragged gaged grade raged aged ager dare dear drag egad gaed gage gear grad rage read age are dag ear egg era erg gad gae gag gar rad rag red reg ad ae er re

adeggrs daggers. *See* **adeggr adegrs adeggs**

adeggrty gadgetry gadgety gyrated raggedy tragedy. *See* **adeggr adeggt adegrt adegry**

adeggry raggedy. *See* **adeggr deggry adegry**

adeggs sagged degas gaged gages aged ages dags egad eggs gads gaed gage gags sage ads age dag egg gad gae gag gas sad sag sea ad ae as

adeggst gadgets stagged. *See* **adeggt adeggs adegst**

adeggt gadget tagged gaged gated aged date egad gaed gage gate aet age ate dag eat egg eta gad gae gag gat get tad tag tea ted ad ae at ta

adeggty gadgety. *See* **adeggt**

adeggu gauged gaged gauge ague egad gaed gage gaud age dag due dug egg gad gae gag ad ae

adeggw wagged gaged waged aged awed egad gaed gage wade wage age awe dag dew egg gad gae gag wad wag wed ad ae aw we

adeghhos hogshead. *See* **adeghs adegos adehhs**

adeghilt alighted delight ligated lighted. *See* **adehil adehlt adeilt aegilt**

adeghin heading. *See* **adegin adghin adeghn deghin**

adeghinr adhering grained handier heading hearing herding reading. *See* **adeghn adegin adegnr adehnr**

adeghju jughead. *See* **adehj degju**

adeghlno headlong halogen. *See* **adeghn adegln adehln adehlo**

adeghlu laughed. *See* **adehlu adegl deglu**

adeghn hanged aged dean egad gaed hade hand hang head age and ane dag den edh end gad gae gan had hae hag hen nae nag nah ad ae ah an en ha he na ne

adeghns gnashed. *See* **adeghn adeghs**

adeghort goatherd. *See* **adegot adegrt adehrt adeort**

adeghpr graphed. *See* **adehpr adegp aegpr**

adeghrtu daughter draught. *See* **adegrt adegru adehrt aeghrt**

adeghs gashed degas hades heads sadhe shade aged ages dags dash egad gads gaed gash hade hags head sage shad shag shed ads age ash dag edh gad gae gas had hae hag has sad sag sea she ad ae ah as eh ha he sh

adegiilp　diplegia. *See* **adeilp**

adegiimn　imagined imagine. *See* **adegim adegin adeimn adgiin**

adegiint　ideating dieting editing ignited. *See* **adegin adegnt adeint adgiin**

adegiitt　digitate. *See* **adegt dgiit**

adegijsw　jigsawed. *See* **adeisw agijsw**

adegiknn　kneading. *See* **adegin deginn**

adegillp　pillaged pillage. *See* **adegll adeill adeilp adellp**

adegilmn　maligned aligned dealing leading mangled melding mingled. *See* **adegim adegin adegln adeilm**

adegiln　aligned dealing leading. *See* **adeiln adegln degiln adegin aegiln**

adegilnp　pedaling pleading aligned dealing leading leaping pealing. *See* **adegin adegln adeiln adeilp**

adegilnr　dragline aligned darling dealing gnarled grained larding leading reading realign. *See* **adegin adegln adeglr adegnr**

adegilns　dealings signaled aligned dangles dealing denials dingles ladings leading leasing linages sealing singled. *See* **adegin adegln adegls adeiln**

adegilnt　delating aligned atingle dealing elating gelatin genital glinted leading ligated tangled tingled. *See* **adegin adegln adegnt adeiln**

adegilny　delaying aligned dealing leading. *See* **adegin adegln adegly adeiln**

adegilou　dialogue eulogia. *See* **adeilo adeilu aegilo**

adegilss　glissade glassed silages. *See* **adegls adegss adeils adeiss**

adegilt　ligated. *See* **adeilt aegilt**

adegim　imaged aimed amide gamed image media midge aged aide amid dame dime egad gaed game gied idea made mage maid mead age aid aim dag dam die dig dim gad gae gam gem gid gie mad mae mag mid ad ae ai am em id ma me mi

adegimnn　amending damning meaning mending. *See* **adegim adegin adeimn aegimn**

adegimnr　dreaming grained mangier reading reaming. *See* **adegim adegin adegnr adeimn**

adegimrt　migrated migrate ragtime readmit. *See* **adegim adegrt adeimr adeirt**

adegin　gained deign aged aide dean dine ding egad gaed gain gied idea nide age aid and ane ani dag den die dig din end

gad gae gan gid gie gin nae nag ad ae ai an en id in na ne

adeginos　diagnose agonies dingoes ganoids. *See* **adegin adegos adenos adgino**

adeginoz　agonized agonize. *See* **adegin adgino adginz deginz**

adeginr　grained reading. *See* **adegnr adginr aeginr deginr adegin**

adeginrs　readings dangers earings engirds erasing gainers ganders gardens gradins grained randies reading regains sandier sardine searing. *See* **adegin adegnr adegrs adeinr**

adeginrt　gradient treading darting dragnet grained granite granted ingrate reading tangier tearing trading trained. *See* **adegin adegnr adegnt adegrt**

adeginry　readying draying grained reading yarding. *See* **adegin adegnr adegry adeinr**

adeginss　assigned designs. *See* **adegin adegss adeiss adenss**

adeginst　sedating detains easting ingesta instead sainted seating stained teasing. *See* **adegin adegnt adegst adeint**

adeginsw　windages windage swinged. *See* **adegin adegnw adeisw adensw**

adeginv　evading. *See* **adegin adeinv**

adeginw　windage. *See* **deginw adegin adegnw adginw**

adegiru　gaudier. *See* **adegru adeiu adeir**

adegistu　gaudiest. *See* **adegst adeisu adistu degist**

adegjln　jangled. *See* **adegln aegjln**

adegkw　gawked waged waked aged awed egad gaed gawk wade wage wake weak weka age awe dag dew gad gae keg wad wag wed ad ae aw ka we

adegl　glade aged dale deal egad gaed gale geld glad lade lead age ale dag eld gad gae gal gel lad lag lea led leg ad ae el la

adegll　galled glade ladle legal aged dale deal dell egad gaed gale gall geld glad lade lead leal age ale all dag eld ell gad gae gal gel lad lag lea led leg ad ae el la

adegllop　galloped. *See* **adegll adellp agllop dellop**

adeglmn　mangled. *See* **adegln aeglmn**

adegln　angled dangle angel angle eland glade gland glean laden aged dale deal dean egad gaed gale geld glad glen lade land lane lead lean lend age ale and ane dag den eld end gad gae gal gan gel lad lag lea led leg nae nag ad ae an el en la na ne

adeglnps　spangled dangles spangle. *See* **adegln adegls adegps adelnp**

adeglnr　gnarled. *See* **adegln aeglnr adegnr adelnr adeglr**

adeglnrw　wrangled gnarled wangled wrangle. *See* **adegln adeglr adegnr adegnw**

adeglns　dangles. *See* **aeglns adegln adelns adegls adglns**

adeglnss　gladness dangles glassed sendals. *See* **adegln adegls adegss adelns**

adeglnt　tangled. *See* **adegln adelnt adegnt aeglnt**

adeglnw　wangled. *See* **adegln adegnw aeglnw**

adeglot　gloated. *See* **adegot aeglot**

adeglppr　grappled grapple. *See* **adeglr adegpp adelpp adeppr**

adeglpu　plagued. *See* **aeglpu deglpu**

adeglr　glared alder glade glare grade lager large raged regal aged ager dale dare deal dear drag earl egad gaed gale gear geld glad grad lade lard lead rage rale read real age ale are dag ear eld era erg gad gae gal gar gel lad lag lar lea led leg rad rag red reg ad ae el er la re

adegls　glades dales deals degas gales gelds glade lades leads aged ages ales dags dale deal egad gads gaed gale gals geld gels glad lade lads lags lead leas legs sage sale seal slag sled ads age ale dag eld els gad gae gal gas gel lad lag lea led leg sad sag sal sea ad ae as el la

adeglss　glassed. *See* **adegls adegss**

adegly　agedly delay glade leady ledgy aged dale deal edgy egad gaed gale geld glad lade lady lead age ale aye dag day dey dye eld gad gae gal gay gel gey lad lag lay lea led leg lye yea ad ae ay el la ye

adeglz　glazed gazed glade glaze lazed adze aged dale daze deal egad gaed gale gaze geld glad lade laze lead zeal adz age ale dag eld gad gae gal gel lad lag lea led leg zag zed ad ae el la

adegm　gamed aged dame egad gaed game made mage mead age dag dam gad gae gam gem mad mae mag ad ae am em ma me

adegmm　gammed gamed gemma aged dame egad gaed game made mage mead age dag dam gad gae gam gem mad mae mag mem ad ae am em ma me

adegmmru　rummaged rummage. *See* **adegmm adegru ademmr aegmmr**

adegmnsu　agendums agendum medusan. *See* **ademns ademsu adensu admnsu**

adegmnu　agendum. *See* **ademn adegm aegmn**

adegmop　megapod. *See* **ademop adgmo adegm**

adegmops megapods megapod pomades. *See* **adegos adegps ademop adeops**

adegnnsu dunnages dunnage duennas. *See* **adennu adensu degnnu degnsu**

adegnnu dunnage. *See* **adennu degnnu**

adegnor groaned. *See* **adegnr adgnor aegnor**

adegnot tangoed. *See* **adenot adegot adegnt degnot**

adegnpu unpaged. *See* **adegp degnu denpu**

adegnr danger gander garden ranged anger grade grand raged range aged ager dare darn dean dear drag earn egad gaed gear gnar grad nard near nerd rage rand rang read rend age and ane are dag den ear end era erg gad gae gan gar nae nag rad rag ran red reg ad ae an en er na ne re

adegnrr gnarred grander. *See* **adegnr adenrr aegnrr adegrr**

adegnrru grandeur gnarred grander. *See* **adegnr adegrr adegru adenrr**

adegnrs dangers ganders gardens. *See* **aegnrs adegnr adegrs adgnrs adenrs**

adegnrst dragnets grandest argents dangers dragnet ganders gardens garnets granted strange. *See* **adegnr adegnt adegrs adegrt**

adegnrt dragnet granted. *See* **adenrt aegnrt adegnr adegrt adegnt**

adegnt tanged gated agent aged ante date dean dent egad gaed gate gent gnat neat tang tend aet age and ane ant ate dag den eat end eta gad gae gan gat get nae nag net tad tag tan tea ted ten ad ae an at en na ne ta

adegntw twanged. *See* **adegnw adegnt adentw**

adegnw gnawed dewan waged waned aged anew awed dawn dean egad gaed gnaw wade wage wand wane wean wend age and ane awe awn dag den dew end gad gae gan nae nag new wad wag wan wed wen ad ae an aw en na ne we

adegoprt portaged portage. *See* **adegot adegrt adeort adeprt**

adegorrt garroted garrote. *See* **adegot adegrr adegrt adeorr**

adegorsw dowagers dowager. *See* **adegos adegrs adeors adersw**

adegortt garotted rotated garotte. *See* **adegot adegrt adeort adertt**

adegortu outraged grouted outrage readout. *See* **adegot adegrt adegru adeort**

adegorw dowager. *See* **adeor deorw degor**

adegos dosage degas doges goads ados aged ages dags does doge dogs dose egad egos gads gaed goad goas gods goes odes sage sago sego soda ado ads age ago dag doe dog dos ego gad gae gas goa god ode sad sag sea sod ad ae as do go od os so

adegoss dosages. *See* **adegos adegss**

adegot dotage gated aged date doge dote egad gaed gate goad goat toad toed toga ado aet age ago ate dag doe dog dot eat ego eta gad gae gat get goa god got oat ode tad tag tea ted tod toe tog ad ae at do go od ta to

adegovy voyaged. *See* **aegovy degvy**

adegp gaped paged aged aped egad gaed gape page peag age ape dag dap gad gae gap pad pea peg ad ae pa pe

adegpp gapped gaped paged aged aped egad gaed gape page peag age ape dag dap gad gae gap pad pap pea peg pep ad ae pa pe

adegprs grasped sparged. *See* **aegprs adegps adegrs**

adegprsu upgrades grasped sparged sugared upgrade. *See* **adegps adegrs adegru adeprs**

adegpru upgrade. *See* **adegru degpru**

adegps gasped degas gaped gapes paged pages peags spade aged ages aped apes apse dags daps egad gads gaed gape gaps gasp pads page peag peas pegs sage sped ads age ape asp dag dap gad gae gap gas pad pas pea peg sad sag sap sea spa ad ae as pa pe

adegpstu upstaged updates upstage. *See* **adegps adegst adepst adepsu**

adegr grade raged aged ager dare dear drag egad gaed gear grad rage read age are dag ear era erg gad gae gar rad rag red reg ad ae er re

adegrr grader regard grade raged aged ager dare dear drag egad gaed gear grad rage rare read rear age are dag ear era erg err gad gae gar rad rag red reg ad ae er re

adegrrs graders regards. *See* **adegrr adegrs**

adegrs grades dares dears degas drags dregs gears grade grads raged rages rased reads sager aged ager ages arse dags dare dear drag ears egad eras ergs gads gaed gars gear grad rads rage rags rase read reds regs sage sard sear sera ads age are dag ear era erg gad gae gar gas rad rag red reg res sad sag sea ad ae as er re

adegrss grassed. *See* **adegss aegrss**

adegrssu graduses assured grassed saugers sugared. *See* **adegrs adegru adegss adgrsu**

adegrsu sugared. *See* **adegru aegrsu adgrsu degrsu**

adegrt grated gated grade grate great raged rated tared targe terga trade tread aged ager dare dart date dear drag drat egad gaed gate gear grad rage rate read tare tear aet age are art ate dag ear eat era erg eta gad gae gar gat get rad rag rat red reg ret tad tag tar tea ted ad ae at er re ta

adegrty gyrated tragedy. *See* **adegrt adegry aegrty**

adegru argued argue auger grade guard raged rugae urged aged ager ague dare dear drag drug dura egad gaed gaud gaur gear grad grue rage read rude rued ruga urea urge age are dag due dug ear era erg gad gae gar rad rag red reg rue rug urd ad ae er re

adegruu augured. *See* **adegru agruu**

adegrv graved grade grave raged raved aged ager aver dare dear deva drag egad gaed gave gear grad rage rave read age are ave dag ear era erg gad gae gar rad rag red reg rev ad ae er re

adegry grayed deary gayer grade gyred raged rayed ready aery aged ager dare dear drag dray dyer edgy egad gaed gear grad gray grey gyre rage read yard yare year age are aye dag day dey dry dye ear era erg gad gae gar gay gey rad rag ray red reg rye yar yea ad ae ay er re ye

adegrz grazed gazed gazer grade graze raged razed adze aged ager dare daze dear drag egad gaed gaze gear grad rage raze read adz age are dag ear era erg gad gae gar rad rag red reg zag zed ad ae er re

adegs degas aged ages dags egad gads gaed sage ads age dag gad gae gas sad sag sea ad ae as

adegss gassed degas gases sages aged ages dags egad gads gaed sage sags seas ads age ass dag ess gad gae gas sad sag sea ad ae as

adegst staged dates degas gated gates sated stage stead aged ages dags date east eats egad etas gads gaed gate gats gest gets sage seat seta stag tads tags teas teds ads aet age ate dag eat eta gad gae gas gat get sad sag sat sea set tad tag tea ted ad ae as at ta

adegt gated aged date egad gaed gate aet age ate dag eat eta gad gae gat get tad tag tea ted ad ae at ta

adegw waged aged awed egad gaed wade wage age awe dag dew gad gae wad wag wed ad ae aw we

adegz gazed adze aged daze egad gaed gaze adz age dag gad gae zag zed ad ae

adeh hade head edh had hae ad ae ah eh ha he

adehhop hophead. *See* **aehhp dehop**

adehhops hopheads hophead. *See* **adehhs adehps adeops aehhps**

adehhost hotheads hothead. *See* **adehhs adehst aehhst dehost**

adehhot hothead. *See* **adeht aehht**

adehhrst thrashed hardest hearths threads trashed. *See* **adehhs adehrs adehrt adehst**

adehhs hashed hades heads sadhe shade dash hade hahs hash head shad shah shed ads ash edh had hae hah has heh sad sea she ad ae ah as eh ha he sh

adehikns skinhead shanked hankies. *See* **adekns adhiks adhins aehikn**

adehil hailed halide ailed haled ideal aide dale deal deil deli dial hade hail hale head heal held hide hied idea idle lade laid lead lied aid ail ale die edh eld had hae hid hie lad lea led lei lid lie ad ae ah ai el ha he hi id la li

adehiln inhaled. *See* **adeiln adehil adehln aehiln**

adehilp helipad. *See* **adeilp**

adehilps helipads alipeds halides helipad palsied plashed. *See* **adehil adehls adehps adeilp**

adehils halides. *See* **adeils adehls dehils**

adehilsv lavished halides devisal. *See* **adehil adehls adehlv adehsv**

adehily headily. *See* **adehil**

adehimms shammied shammed shimmed. *See* **adehmm adehms adeimm adeims**

adehinop diaphone headpin pinhead. *See* **adeinp dehino dehnop deinop**

adehinos adhesion. *See* **adenos adhins adinos dehino**

adehinp headpin pinhead. *See* **adeinp adhip**

adehinps headpins pinheads dishpan headpin pandies pinhead. *See* **adehps adeinp adhins adhips**

adehinr handier. *See* **adehnr aehinr dehinr adeinr**

adehinst handiest detains handset instead sainted stained. *See* **adehst adeint adhins aehnst**

adehinsv vanished invades. *See* **adehsv adeinv adeisv adhins**

adehirr hardier harried. *See* **adehrr adeirr**

adehirs dashier shadier. *See* **aehirs adehrs dehirs adhirs adeirs**

adehirss radishes dashers dashier shadier. *See* **adehrs adehss adeirs adeiss**

adehirst hardiest astride dashier diaster dithers hardest hastier shadier threads tirades trashed. *See* **adehrs adehrt adehst adeirs**

adehirsv ravished adviser dashier dervish shadier shrived. *See* **adehrs adehsv adeirs adeirv**

adehirsw rawhides dashier rawhide shadier washier. *See* **adehrs adehsw adeirs adeisw**

adehirsy hayrides dashier hayride shadier. *See* **adehrs adehry adeirs adhirs**

adehirw rawhide. *See* **adeir adehw adehr**

adehiry hayride. *See* **adehry adeir adiry**

adehisst dashiest shadiest stashed ashiest. *See* **adehss adeiss adisst**

adehj jehad hade hadj head jade edh had hae ad ae ah eh ha he

adehklnu lunkhead. *See* **adehln adehlu dehklu**

adehkns shanked. *See* **adekns aehkns**

adehknt thanked. *See* **adeknt adeht aehnt**

adehkot kathode. *See* **adeht dekot**

adehkr harked drake heard raked dare dark dear hade hake hard hare hark head hear herd rake read rhea are ark ear edh era had hae her rad rah red ad ae ah eh er ha he ka re

adehkrs sharked. *See* **adehrs adekrs adehkr aehkrs**

adehkw hawked hawed waked awed hade hake hawk head wade wake weak weka awe dew edh had hae haw hew wad wed ad ae ah aw eh ha he ka we

adehl haled dale deal hade hale head heal held lade lead ale edh eld had hae lad lea led ad ae ah eh el ha he la

adehllow hallowed allowed. *See* **adehlo adehlw adellw ahllow**

adehlmno homeland manhole. *See* **adehln adehlo adelmo adelno**

adehln handle eland haled laden dale deal dean hade hale hand head heal held lade land lane lead lean lend ale and ane den edh eld end had hae hen lad lea led nae nah ad ae ah an eh el en ha he la na ne

adehlnr handler. *See* **adelnr adehln adehnr adehlr**

adehlnrs handlers darnels handler handles handsel hardens heralds landers slander snarled. *See* **adehln adehlr adehls adehnr**

adehlns handles handsel. *See* **adelns aehlns adehls**

adehlnss handless handsels handles handsel hansels hassled sendals slashed. *See* **adehln adehls adehss adelns**

adehlnsu unlashed handles handsel unleash. *See* **adehln adehls adehlu adelns**

adehlo haloed ahold dhole haled holed aloe dale deal dole hade hale halo head heal held hoed hold hole lade lead load lode ado ale doe edh eld had hae hod hoe lad lea led ode old ad ae ah do eh el ha he ho la lo od oh

adehlops asphodel deposal plashed shoaled. *See* **adehlo adehls adehps adelps**

adehlos shoaled. *See* **adhlos dehlos adehlo aehlos adehls**

adehlot loathed. *See* **adehlt adehlo aehlot dehlot**

adehlps plashed. *See* **aehlps adehps adelps adehls**

adehlpss splashed hapless hassled plashed plashes slashed. *See* **adehls adehps adehss adelps**

adehlr herald alder haled haler heard dale dare deal dear earl hade hale hard hare harl head heal hear held herd herl lade lard lead rale read real rhea als are ear edh eld era had hae her lad lar lea led rad rah red ad ae ah el er ha he la re

adehlrry heraldry. *See* **adehlr adehrr adehry adelry**

adehlrs heralds. *See* **adelrs adehrs adehlr aehlrs**

adehls lashed dales deals hades haled hales heads heals lades leads leash sadhe selah shade shale ales dale dash deal hade hale head heal held lade lads lash lead leas sale seal shad shed sled ads ale ash edh eld els had hae has lad lea led sad sal sea she ad ae ah as eh el ha he la sh

adehlss hassled slashed. *See* **adehss aehlss adehls**

adehlst daleths. *See* **adehlt adehst adelst aehlst**

adehlt daleth halted lathed dealt death delta haled hated lated lathe dale date deal hade hale halt hate head heal heat held lade late lath lead tael tale teal aet ale alt ate eat edh eld eta eth had hae hat het lad lea led let tad tea ted the ad ae ah at el ha he la ta

adehlu hauled haled lehua auld dale deal dual duel hade hale haul head heal held hued hula lade laud lead ale due edh eld had hae hue lad lea led leu ad ae ah eh el ha he la

adehlv halved haled halve laved dale deal deva hade hale have head heal held lade lave lead leva vale veal veld ale ave edh eld had hae lad lea led lev ad ae ah eh el ha he la

adehlw whaled haled hawed waled weald whale wheal awed dale deal hade hale head heal held lade lead lewd wade wale weal weld ale awe awl dew edh eld had hae haw hew lad law lea led wad wed ad ae ah aw eh el ha he la we

adehmm hammed ahem dame hade hame head made mead dam edh had hae ham hem mad mae mem ad ae ah am eh em ha he ma me

adehmms shammed. *See* **adehmm adehms**

adehmnny handymen. *See* **ademnn dehmny**

adehmnos handsome daemons. *See* **adehms ademno ademns adenos**

adehmnrs herdsman hardens remands. *See* **adehmr adehms adehnr adehrs**

adehmnru unharmed manured maunder unarmed unheard. *See* **adehmr adehnr ademnr adenru**

adehmoor headroom. *See* **adehmr ademor demoor**

adehmorw homeward. *See* **adehmr ademor ademow ademrw**

adehmost headmost methods. *See* **adehms adehst ademst dehmot**

adehmosu madhouse. *See* **adehms ademsu dehmsu dehosu**

adehmr harmed armed derma dream harem heard herma ahem dame dare dear dram hade hame hard hare harm head hear herd herm made mare mead read ream rhea are arm dam ear edh era had hae ham hem her mad mae mar rad rah ram red rem ad ae ah am eh em er ha he ma me re

adehms mashed shamed dames hades hames heads meads sadhe shade shame ahem dame dams dash hade hame hams head hems made mash mead mesa mesh same seam shad sham shed ads ash dam edh had hae ham has hem mad mae sad sea she ad ae ah am as eh em ha he ma me sh

adehmss smashed. *See* **adehss aehmss ademss adehms**

adehnopr orphaned padrone. *See* **adehnr adehpr adenpr adnopr**

adehnopt phonated phaeton phonate pothead. *See* **adehpt adenot adenpt dehnop**

adehnors hardnose hardens hoarsen. *See* **adehnr adehrs adenos adenrs**

adehnorv overhand. *See* **adehnr dehnor denorv**

adehnr harden heard dare darn dean dear earn hade hand hard hare head hear herd hern nard near nerd rand read rend rhea and ane are den ear edh end era had hae hen her nae nah rad rah ran red ad ae ah an eh en er ha he na ne re

adehnrs hardens. *See* **adehrs adehnr adenrs**

adehnrss hardness dashers hardens harness sanders. *See* **adehnr adehrs adehss adenrs**

adehnrtu unthread haunted haunter thunder unearth unheard. *See* **adehnr adehrt adenrt adenru**

adehnru unheard. *See* **adehnr adenru**

adehnsst handsets handset hastens stashed. *See* **adehss adehst adenss adnsst**

adehnssu sunshade sundaes. *See* **adehss adenss adensu adhssu**

adehnst handset. *See* **adehst aehnst**

adehnsuw unwashed. *See* **adehsw adensu adensw densuw**

adehntu haunted. *See* **dehntu adntu adeht**

adehoory hoorayed. *See* **adehry ahoory**

adehopst potheads pothead heptads. *See* **adehps adehpt adehst adeops**

adehopsx hexapods hexapod. *See* **adehox adehps adehsx adeops**

adehopt pothead. *See* **adehpt adopt deopt**

adehopx hexapod. *See* **adehox dehop**

adehorr hoarder. *See* **adeorr adehrr**

adehorrs hoarders adorers hoarder hoarser. *See* **adehrr adehrs adeorr adeors**

adehorrw harrowed hoarder. *See* **adehrr adeorr aderrw ahorrw**

adehostw towheads towhead swathed. *See* **adehst adehsw adehtw adestw**

adehotw towhead. *See* **adehtw deotw**

adehox hoaxed hexad axed hade head hoax hoed ado axe doe edh had hae hex hod hoe ode ad ae ah ax do eh ex ha he ho od oh ox

adehpp happed aped hade head heap ape dap edh had hae hap hep pad pah pap pea pep ad ae ah eh ha he pa pe

adehppw whapped. *See* **adehpp adeppw**

adehpr harped drape heard padre pared raped aped dare dear hade hard hare harp head heap hear herd pard pare pear rape read reap rhea ape are dap ear edh era had hae hap hep her pad pah par pea per rad rah rap red rep ad ae ah eh er ha he pa pe re

adehprs phrased sharped. *See* **adehrs adehpr adehps aehprs**

adehps hasped phased shaped hades heads heaps phase sadhe shade shape spade aped apes apse daps dash hade haps hasp head heap pads peas shad shed sped ads ape ash asp dap edh had hae hap has hep pad pah pas pea sad sap sea she spa ad ae ah as eh ha he pa pe sh

adehpst heptads. *See* **adehst dehpst adehpt adepst adehps**

adehpt heptad adept death depth hated taped aped date hade hate head heap heat pate path peat tape aet ape apt ate dap eat edh eta eth had hae hap hat hep het pad pah pat pea pet tad tap tea ted the ad ae ah at eh ha he pa pe ta

adehqssu squashed quashed quashes. *See* **adehss adhssu adqssu ahqssu**

adehqsu quashed. *See* **adehs adqsu ahqsu**

adehr heard dare dear hade hard hare head hear herd read rhea are ear edh era had hae her rad rah red ad ae ah eh er ha he re

adehrr harder heard dare dear hade hard hare head hear herd rare read rear rhea are ear edh era err had hae her rad rah red ad ae ah eh er ha he re

adehrs dasher shared dares dears hades hards hares heads heard hears herds rased reads rheas sadhe shade shard share shear sherd shred arse dare dash dear ears eras hade hard hare head hear herd hers rads rahs rase rash read reds resh rhea sard sear sera shad shed ads are ash ear edh era had hae has her rad rah red res sad sea she ad ae ah as eh er ha he re sh

adehrss dashers. *See* **adehrs adehss aehrss adhrss dehrss**

adehrst hardest threads trashed. *See* **adehrs adehrt adehst aehrst aderst**

adehrsty hydrates hardest hydrate strayed threads thready trashed. *See* **adehrs adehrt adehry adehst**

adehrt dearth hatred thread death earth hated hater heard heart rated tared trade tread dare dart date dear drat hade hard hare hart hate head hear heat herd rate rath read rhea tare tear aet are art ate ear eat edh era eta eth had hae hat her het rad rah rat red ret tad tar tea ted the ad ae ah at eh er ha he re ta

adehrttw thwarted. *See* **adehrt adehtt adehtw adertt**

adehrty hydrate thready. *See* **adehrt aehrty adehry**

adehry hydrae deary hardy hayed heady heard hydra rayed ready aery dare dear dray dyer hade hard hare head hear herd read rhea yard yare yeah year are aye day dey dry dye ear edh era had hae hay her hey rad rah ray red rye yah yar yea ad ae ah ay eh er ha he re ye

adehs hades heads sadhe shade dash hade head shad shed ads ash edh had hae has sad sea she ad ae ah as eh ha he sh

adehss dashes sadhes sashed shades ashes hades heads sadhe shade sheds dash hade head sash seas shad shed ads ash ass edh ess had hae has sad sea she ad ae ah as eh ha he ss

adehsst stashed. *See* **adehss adehst**

adehssw swashed. *See* **adehss aehssw adehsw**

adehst deaths hasted dates death hades hadst haste hated hates heads heats sadhe sated shade stead dash date east eats etas hade hast hate hats head heat hest seat seta shad shed tads teas teds ads aet ash ate eat edh eta eth had hae has hat het sad sat sea set she tad tea ted the ad ae ah as at eh ha he sh ta

adehstw swathed. *See* **adehst aehstw adehtw adehsw adestw**

adehsv shaved devas hades heads sadhe saved shade shave aves dash deva hade have head save shad shed vase ads ash ave edh had hae has sad sea she ad ae ah as eh ha he sh

adehsw washed hades hawed hawse heads sadhe sawed shade wades awed awes dash dews hade haws head hews shad shaw shed shew wade wads wash weds ads ash awe dew edh had hae has haw hew sad saw sea sew she wad was wed ad ae ah as aw eh ha he sh we

adehsx hexads hades heads hexad sadhe shade axed axes dash hade head shad shed ads ash axe edh had hae has hex sad sax sea sex she ad ae ah as ax eh ex ha he sh

adehsyy heydays. *See* **adehyy adehs adhsy**

adeht death hated date hade hate head heat aet ate eat edh eta eth had hae hat het tad tea ted the ad ae ah at eh ha he ta

adehtt hatted death hated theta date hade hate head heat teat teth that aet ate eat edh eta eth had hae hat het tad tat tea ted the ad ae ah at eh ha he ta

adehtw thawed death hated hawed wheat awed date hade hate head heat thaw thew wade what whet aet ate awe

dew eat edh eta eth had hae hat haw het hew tad tea ted the wad wed wet ad ae ah at aw eh ha he ta we

adehw hawed awed hade head wade awe dew edh had hae haw hew wad wed ad ae ah aw eh ha he we

adehx hexad axed hade head axe edh had hae hex ad ae ah ax eh ex ha he

adehy hayed heady hade head yeah aye day dey dye edh had hae hay hey yah yea ad ae ah ay eh ha he ye

adehyy heyday hayed heady hade head yeah aye day dey dye edh had hae hay hey yah yay yea ad ae ah ay eh ha he ye

adehz hazed adze daze hade haze head adz edh had hae zed ad ae ah eh ha he

adei aide idea aid die ad ae ai id

adeiilms idealism dailies misdeal mislaid mislead sedilia. *See* **adeilm adeils adeims adelms**

adeiilr deliria. *See* **adeilr**

adeiils dailies sedilia. *See* **adeils**

adeiilst idealist dailies details dilates laities sedilia. *See* **adeils adeilt adelst adilst**

adeiimnr meridian denarii. *See* **adeimn adeimr adeinr adiimr**

adeiimpr impaired. *See* **adeimr adeipr adempr adiimr**

adeiimrs semiarid admires dairies diaries misread sidearm. *See* **adeimr adeims adeirs ademrs**

adeiimtt imitated imitate. *See* **ademtt**

adeiinot ideation edition. *See* **adeint adenot deiino**

adeiinr denarii. *See* **adeinr diinr adiir**

adeiinrt daintier denarii inditer inertia nitride trained. *See* **adeinr adeint adeirt adenrt**

adeiinst dainties detains distain indites instead sainted stained tineids. *See* **adeint aiinst deiins deiist**

adeiirs dairies diaries. *See* **adeirs deiirs**

adeiiss daisies. *See* **adeiss deiiss**

adeiittv vitiated vitiate. *See* **adeitv adettv aeittv**

adeijl jailed ailed ideal aide dale deal deil deli dial idea idle jade jail lade laid lead lied aid ail ale die eld lad lea led lei lid lie ad ae ai el id la li

adeikllo keloidal. *See* **adeill adeilo deikll deiklo**

adeiklly ladylike ideally. *See* **adeill deikll eiklly**

adeiklsw sidewalk. *See* **adeils adeilw adeisw adekls**

adeiknyz kyanized kyanize. *See* **adekny deikny**

adeil ailed ideal aide dale deal deil deli dial idea idle lade laid lead lied aid ail

ale die eld lad lea led lei lid lie ad ae ai el id la li

adeill allied ailed ideal ladle aide dale deal deil deli dell dial dill idea idle lade laid lead leal lied aid ail ale all die eld ell ill lad lea led lei lid lie ad ae ai el id la li

adeillpr pillared dallier predial rallied. *See* **adeill adeilp adeilr adeipr**

adeillr dallier rallied. *See* **adeill adeilr**

adeills dallies sallied. *See* **adeils adeill aeills adells**

adeillsw sidewall dallies sallied swilled. *See* **adeill adeils adeilw adeisw**

adeillt tallied. *See* **adeill adeilt deillt aeillt**

adeilly ideally. *See* **adeill aelly adily**

adeilm mailed medial ailed aimed amide ideal lamed limed medal media aide amid dale dame deal deil deli dial dime idea idle lade laid lame lead lied lime made maid mail male mead meal meld mild mile aid ail aim ale dam die dim eld elm lad lam lea led lei lid lie mad mae mel mid mil ad ae ai am el em id la li ma me mi

adeilmm dilemma. *See* **adelmm adeilm adeimm**

adeilmms dilemmas dilemma melisma misdeal mislead slammed slimmed. *See* **adeilm adeils adeimm adeims**

adeilmno melanoid. *See* **adeilm adeiln adeilo adeimn**

adeilmny maidenly. *See* **adeilm adeiln adeimn adilmy**

adeilmp impaled implead. *See* **adeilp deilmp aeilmp adeilm adelmp**

adeilmry dreamily readily midyear. *See* **adeilm adeilr adeimr adelmr**

adeilms misdeal mislead. *See* **adeils adeims adelms adilms adeilm**

adeilmss misdeals misleads aimless damsels misdeal mislead. *See* **adeilm adeils adeims adeiss**

adeilmst medalist misdealt details dilates mildest misdeal mislead. *See* **adeilm adeils adeilt adeims**

adeiln alined denial nailed ailed alien aline anile eland ideal laden liane lined aide anil dale deal dean deil deli dial dine idea idle lade laid lain land lane lead lean lend lied lien line nail nide aid ail ale and ane ani den die din eld end lad lea led lei lid lie nae nil ad ae ai an el en id in la li na ne

adeilnn annelid. *See* **adeiln adilnn deilnn**

adeilnnr inlander annelid. *See* **adeiln adeilr adeinr adelnr**

adeilnns annelids annelid denials lindens. *See* **adeiln adeils adelns adilnn**

adeilnrs islander darnels denials derails landers randies sandier sardine slander snarled. *See* **adeiln adeilr adeils adeinr**

adeilns denials. *See* **adeils aeilns adeiln adelns adilns**

adeilnu aliunde. *See* **adeiln adeilu**

adeilo eidola ailed ideal oiled oldie aide aloe dale deal deil deli dial dole idea idle idol lade laid lead lied load lode ado aid ail ale die doe eld lad lea led lei lid lie ode oil old ad ae ai do el id la li lo od

adeilop oedipal. *See* **adeilp deilop adeilo**

adeilort idolater tailored delator dilator leotard trailed. *See* **adeilo adeilr adeilt adeirt**

adeilorv overlaid rivaled avoider. *See* **adeilo adeilr adeilv adeirv**

adeilost diastole isolated details dilates isolate toadies. *See* **adeilo adeils adeilt adelst**

adeilotv dovetail violated violate. *See* **adeilo adeilt adeilv adeitv**

adeilp aliped ailed ideal paled pedal piled plaid plead plied aide aped dale deal deil deli dial idea idle lade laid lead leap lied paid pail pale peal pied pile plea pled aid ail ale alp ape dap die dip eld lad lap lea led lei lid lie lip pad pal pea pie ad ae ai el id la li pa pe pi

adeilpp applied. *See* **adeilp adelpp deilpp**

adeilpr predial. *See* **adeilp adeilr adeipr**

adeilprs spiraled alipeds aspired derails despair diapers palsied praised predial. *See* **adeilp adeilr adeils adeipr**

adeilprt dipteral partied pirated plaited predial trailed tripled. *See* **adeilp adeilr adeilt adeipr**

adeilps alipeds palsied. *See* **adeils adeilp deilps aeilps adelps**

adeilpt plaited. *See* **adeilp adeilt adelpt**

adeilqtu liquated liquate quailed quilted tequila. *See* **adeilt adeilu deiltu**

adeilqu quailed. *See* **adeilu aelqu ailqu**

adeilr derail railed relaid ailed aired alder ideal idler laird riled aide arid aril dale dare deal dear deil deli dial dire dirl earl idea idle lade laid lair lard lead liar lied lira lire raid rail rale read real rial ride riel rile aid ail air ale are die ear eld era ire lad lar lea led lei lid lie rad red ria rid ad ae ai el er id la li re

adeilrr lardier. *See* **adeilr adelrr adeirr aeilrr**

adeilrry drearily lardier readily. *See* **adeilr adeirr adelry aderry**

adeilrs derails. *See* **aelrs ailrs deilr said**

adeilrst lardiest astride derails details diaster dilates realist retails saltier saltire

tirades trailed. *See* **adeilr adeils adeilt adeirs**

adeilrsu residual derails. *See* **adeilr adeils adeilu adeirs**

adeilrt trailed. *See* **adeilr adeilt aeilrt adeirt**

adeilrtt detrital attired rattled tertial trailed. *See* **adeilr adeilt adeirt adertt**

adeilrv rivaled. *See* **adeilr deilrv adeilv adeirv**

adeilry readily. *See* **adilry adelry adeilr deilry**

adeils aisled ideals ladies sailed aides ailed aisle aside dales deals deils delis dials ideal ideas idles lades leads sidle slide aide aids ails ales dais dale deal deil deli dial dies idea ides idle isle lade lads laid lead leas leis lids lied lies said sail sale seal side sled slid ads aid ail ale die eld els ids lad lea led lei lid lie sad sal sea ad ae ai as el id is la li si

adeilssv devisals advises devisal valises. *See* **adeils adeilv adeiss adeisv**

adeilst details dilates. *See* **aeils aelst ailst**

adeilsv devisal. *See* **adeisv adeils deilsv adelsv adeilv**

adeilsxy dyslexia. *See* **adeils adelsy deilsy**

adeilsyz dialyzes dialyze. *See* **adeils adeisz adelsy aelsyz**

adeilt detail dilate tailed ailed dealt delta ideal lated tidal tilde tiled adit aide alit dale date deal deil deli dial diet edit idea idle lade laid late lead lied tael tail tale tali teal tide tied tile aet aid ail ale alt ate die dit eat eld eta ita lad lea led lei let lid lie lit tad tea ted tie til ad ae ai at el id it la li ta ti

adeilttu altitude latitude. *See* **adeilt adeilu deiltt deiltu**

adeilu audile adieu ailed ideal aide auld dale deal deil deli dial dual duel idea idle lade laid laud lead lied lieu aid ail ale die due eld lad lea led lei leu lid lie ad ae ai el id la li

adeilv vailed ailed alive devil ideal laved lived valid aide avid dale deal deil deli deva dial diva dive evil idea idle lade laid lave lead leva lied live vail vale veal veil veld vial vied vile aid ail ale ave die eld lad lea led lei lev lid lie via vie ad ae ai el id la li

adeilw wailed ailed ideal waled weald wield wiled aide awed dale deal deil deli dial idea idle lade laid lead lewd lied wade wadi wail wale weal weld wide wild wile aid ail ale awe awl dew die eld lad law lea led lei lid lie wad wed ad ae ai aw el id la li we

adeilyz dialyze. *See* **adeil adeiz adily**

adeim aimed amide media aide amid dame dime idea made maid mead aid aim dam die dim mad mae mid ad ae ai am em id ma me mi

adeimm maimed aimed amide media mimed aide amid dame dime idea imam made maid maim mead mime aid aim dam die dim mad mae mem mid mim ad ae ai am em id ma me mi

adeimmr mermaid. *See* **adeimr deimmr adeimm aeimmr ademmr**

adeimmrs mermaids admires dimmers mermaid misread sidearm. *See* **adeimm adeimr adeims adeirs**

adeimn maiden median admen aimed amend amide amine anime denim maned media menad minae mined named aide amen amid dame damn dean dime dine idea made maid main mane mead mean mend mien mina mind mine name nide aid aim and ane ani dam den die dim din end mad mae man men mid nae nim ad ae ai am an em en id in ma me mi na ne

adeimnot dominate mediant. *See* **adeimn adeint ademno ademnt**

adeimnry dairymen draymen midyear yardmen. *See* **adeimn adeimr adeinr ademry**

adeimnrz zemindar. *See* **adeimn adeimr adeinr aeimnr**

adeimns maidens medians sideman. *See* **ademns adeims aeimns deimns adeimn**

adeimnt mediant. *See* **adeint aeimnt adeimn deimnt ademnt**

adeimnty dynamite amenity daytime mediant. *See* **adeimn adeint ademnt adinty**

adeimort mediator readmit. *See* **adeimr adeirt ademor ademrt**

adeimotz atomized atomize. *See* **adimot**

adeimow miaowed. *See* **ademow adeim aimow**

adeimprt imparted partied pirated primate readmit tramped. *See* **adeimr adeipr adeirt adempr**

adeimr admire aimed aired amide armed derma dimer dream media mired rimed aide amid amir arid dame dare dear dime dire dram emir idea made maid mare mead mire raid rami read ream ride rime aid aim air are arm dam die dim ear era ire mad mae mar mid mir rad ram red rem ria rid rim ad ae ai am em er id ma me mi re

adeimrr admirer married. *See* **adeimr ademrr adeirr**

adeimrrs admirers marrieds admirer admires married marries misread raiders sidearm. *See* **adeimr adeims adeirr adeirs**

adeimrs admires misread sidearm. *See* **adeimr adeims aeimrs ademrs deimrs**

adeimrss misreads sidearms admires disarms misread sidearm. *See* **adeimr adeims adeirs adeiss**

adeimrst readmits admires astride diaster imarets misread readmit sidearm smarted tirades. *See* **adeimr adeims adeirs adeirt**

adeimrsy midyears admires midyear misread myriads sidearm. *See* **adeimr adeims adeirs ademrs**

adeimrt readmit. *See* **adeimr ademrt aeimrt deimrt adeirt**

adeimry midyear. *See* **adeimr ademry adimry**

adeims amides aides aimed amide aside dames deism dimes ideas maids meads media aide aids aims amid dais dame dams dies dime dims idea ides made maid mead mesa mise said same seam semi side ads aid aim dam die dim ids mad mae mid mis sad sea ad ae ai am as em id is ma me mi si

adeimsty daytimes daytime stymied. *See* **adeims ademst adesty adimst**

adeimty daytime. *See* **adimt adeim aimty**

adeinnot anointed antinode intoned. *See* **adeint adennt adenot aeinno**

adeinntu inundate. *See* **adeint adennt adennu aeinnt**

adeinopt antipode opiated painted pointed. *See* **adeinp adeint adenot adenpt**

adeinorr ordainer drainer. *See* **adeinr adeirr adenrr adeorr**

adeinort ordinate rationed trained. *See* **adeinr adeint adeirt adenot**

adeinost sedation detains donates instead sainted stained toadies. *See* **adeint adenos adenot adinos**

adeinott antidote tainted notated. *See* **adeint adenot adentt aenott**

adeinp pained pined aide aped dean dine idea nape neap nide nipa paid pain pane pean pend pied pine aid and ane ani ape dap den die din dip end nae nap nip pad pan pea pen pie pin ad ae ai an en id in na ne pa pe pi

adeinppx appendix. *See* **adeinp adenpp adenpx deinpp**

adeinprs sprained aspired despair diapers panders pandies praised randies rapines sandier sardine. *See* **adeinp adeinr adeipr adeirs**

adeinps pandies. *See* **adeinp deinps**

adeinpt painted. *See* **adeint adeinp adinpt adenpt**

adeinqtu antiqued antique quanted quinate. *See* **adeint aeintu ainqtu deintu**

adeinr rained aired dinar diner drain nadir aide arid dare darn dean dear dine dire earn idea nard near nerd nide raid rain rand rani read rein rend ride rind aid air and ane ani are den die din ear end era ire nae rad ran red ria rid ad ae ai an en er id in na ne re

adeinrr drainer. *See* **adenrr adeirr adeinr**

adeinrrs drainers drainer errands raiders randies sandier sardine. *See* **adeinr adeirr adeirs adenrr**

adeinrs randies sandier sardine. *See* **aeinrs adinrs deinrs adeinr adeirs**

adeinrss aridness sardines arsines randies sanders sandier sardine. *See* **adeinr adeirs adeiss adenrs**

adeinrst strained astride detains diaster instead nastier randies retains retinas sainted sandier sardine stained stainer tirades trained. *See* **adeinr adeint adeirs adeirt**

adeinrsu denarius asunder danseur insured randies sandier sardine. *See* **adeinr adeirs adeisu adenrs**

adeinrsv invaders adviser invader invades randies ravines sandier sardine verdins. *See* **adeinr adeinv adeirs adeirv**

adeinrt trained. *See* **adenrt adeint adeinr aeinrt deinrt**

adeinrtt nitrated attired iterant nattier nitrate tainted tertian trained trident. *See* **adeinr adeint adeirt adenrt**

adeinrtu indurate ruinated urinated intrude ruinate taurine trained untried urinate. *See* **adeinr adeint adeirt adenrt**

adeinrv invader. *See* **deinrv adeinv aeinrv adeirv**

adeinrvy vineyard invader. *See* **adeinr adeinv adeirv adenry**

adeinsst sandiest detains dissent entasis instead sainted stained tansies. *See* **adeint adeiss adenss adisst**

adeinst detains instead sainted stained. *See* **adeint adist adeis**

adeinstu sinuated aunties detains instead sainted sinuate stained. *See* **adeint adeisu adensu adinsu**

adeinstv deviants advents detains deviant instead invades natives sainted stained. *See* **adeint adeinv adeisv adeitv**

adeinsv invades. *See* **adeisv adinsv adeinv aeinsv**

adeint detain tenia tinea adit aide ante anti date dean dent diet dine edit idea neat nide tend tide tied tine aet aid and ane ani ant ate den die din dit eat end eta ita nae net nit tad tan tea ted ten tie tin ad ae ai an at en id in it na ne ta ti

adeintt tainted. *See* **adentt adeint deintt**

adeintv deviant. *See* **adentv adeitv adeint adeinv aeintv**

adeinv invade divan naive viand aide avid dean deva dine diva dive idea nave nevi nide vain vane vein vend vied vina vine aid and ane ani ave den die din end nae van via vie ad ae ai an en id in na ne

adeioprs parodies adipose aspired despair diapers periods praised roadies soapier. *See* **adeipr adeirs adeops adeors**

adeioprv overpaid avoider provide. *See* **adeipr adeirv deiopr deiorv**

adeiops adipose. *See* **adeops deiops**

adeiopss adiposes adipose apsides dispose. *See* **adeiss adeops adepss deiops**

adeiopt opiated. *See* **aeiopt adept adopt**

adeioptv adoptive opiated pivoted. *See* **adeitv aeiopt**

adeiors roadies. *See* **adeors deiors adiors adeirs**

adeiorst asteroid astride diaster editors roadies roasted steroid storied tirades toadies torsade triodes. *See* **adeirs adeirt adeors adeort**

adeiorsv avoiders adviser avoider devisor ovaries roadies savored. *See* **adeirs adeirv adeisv adeors**

adeiortt teratoid attired dottier rotated. *See* **adeirt adeort adertt adiort**

adeiorv avoider. *See* **adeirv deiorv**

adeiorx exordia. *See* **adeor adeir aiorx**

adeiost toadies. *See* **deiost adios adist**

adeiosx oxidase. *See* **deiosx**

adeiotzz azotized azotize. *See* **adeiz aeotz**

adeippr prepaid. *See* **adeppr adeipr deippr**

adeipprs apprised apprise aspired despair diapers dippers praised prepaid sappier. *See* **adeipr adeirs adeppr adepps**

adeipr diaper paired repaid aired drape padre pared pride pried raped rapid aide aped arid dare dear dire drip idea paid pair pard pare pear peri pied pier raid rape read reap ride ripe aid air ape are dap die dip ear era ire pad par pea per pie rad rap red rep ria rid rip ad ae ai er id pa pe pi re

adeiprr parried. *See* **adeipr adeprr adeirr aeiprr**

adeiprs aspired despair diapers praised. *See* **aeiprs adeipr deiprs adeirs adiprs**

adeiprss despairs apsides aspired aspires despair diapers paresis praised praises spaders spiders spreads. *See* **adeipr adeirs adeiss adeprs**

adeiprst traipsed aspired astride departs despair diapers diaster partied parties pastier petards piaster pirated pirates praised striped tirades traipse. *See* **adeipr adeirs adeirt adeprs**

adeiprsu upraised aspired despair diapers praised upraise. *See* **adeipr adeirs adeisu adeprs**

adeiprt partied pirated. *See* **adeprt aeiprt adeipr adeirt**

adeipss apsides. *See* **adeiss adepss**

adeipssx spadixes apsides. *See* **adeiss adepss adipsx**

adeipttu aptitude puttied. *See* **adeptt adeptu deiptt**

adeiqrru quarried. *See* **adeirr deiqru**

adeir aired aide arid dare dear dire idea raid read ride aid air are die ear era ire rad red ria rid ad ae ai er id re

adeirr raider aired direr drier rider aide arid dare dear dire idea raid rare read rear ride aid air are die ear era err ire rad red ria rid ad ae ai er id re

adeirrs raiders. *See* **deirrs adeirr adeirs aeirrs adirrs**

adeirrt tardier tarried. *See* **aderrt adeirt**

adeirrv arrived. *See* **aeirrv deirrv adeirr adeirv**

adeirs raised aides aired arise aside dares dears dries ideas raids raise rased reads rides serai sired aide aids airs arid arse dais dare dear dies dire ears eras idea ides rads raid rase read reds reis rias ride rids rise said sard sari sear sera side sire ads aid air are die ear era ids ire rad red res ria rid sad sea sir ad ae ai as er id is re si

adeirsst diasters disaster astride diaster satires strides tirades. *See* **adeirs adeirt adeiss aderst**

adeirssu radiuses assured sauries. *See* **adeirs adeiss adeisu adirsu**

adeirssv advisers adviser advises. *See* **adeirs adeirv adeiss adeisv**

adeirst astride diaster tirades. *See* **deirst adeirs aeirst aderst adeirt**

adeirstt striated tardiest artiste astride attired attires diaster ratites started striate tastier tetrads tirades. *See* **adeirs adeirt aderst adertt**

adeirsv adviser. *See* **adeisv deirsv adeirs adeirv aeirsv**

adeirsx radixes. *See* **adeirs adirsx**

adeirt tirade aired irate rated retia tared tired trade tread triad tried adit aide arid dare dart date dear diet dire dirt drat edit idea iter raid rate read ride rite tare tear tide tied tier tire aet aid air are art ate die dit ear eat era eta ire

ita rad rat red ret ria rid tad tar tea ted tie ad ae ai at er id it re ta ti

adeirtt attired. *See* **aeirtt adertt adeirt**

adeirty dietary. *See* **adeirt adiry adery**

adeirv varied aired diver drive raved rived aide arid aver avid dare dear deva dire diva dive idea raid rave read ride rive vair vied aid air are ave die ear era ire rad red rev ria rid via vie ad ae ai er id re

adeirvwy driveway. *See* **adeirv adeivw aeirvw aervwy**

adeis aides aside ideas aide aids dais dies idea ides said side ads aid die ids sad sea ad ae ai as id is si

adeiss asides aides aside ideas sides aide aids dais dies idea ides said seas side ads aid ass die ess ids sad sea sis ad ae ai as id is si

adeissst assisted desists sadists siestas. *See* **adeiss adesss adisst aeisst**

adeisstt distaste. *See* **adeiss adestt adisst aeisst**

adeissv advises. *See* **adeisv adeiss**

adeisswy sideways waysides wayside. *See* **adeiss adeisw adeswy**

adeisttu situated statued situate. *See* **adeisu adestt adistu aesttu**

adeisu adieus adieu aides aside ideas aide aids dais dies dues idea ides said side sued used ads aid die due ids sad sea sue use ad ae ai as id is si us

adeisv advise visaed aides aside devas divas dives ideas saved vised aide aids aves avid dais deva dies diva dive idea ides said save side vase vied vies visa vise ads aid ave die ids sad sea via vie ad ae ai as id is si

adeisvv savvied. *See* **adeisv**

adeisw wadies aides aside ideas sawed wades wadis aide aids awed awes dais dews dies idea ides said side wade wadi wads weds wide wise ads aid awe dew die ids sad saw sea sew wad was wed wis ad ae ai as aw id is si we

adeiswy wayside. *See* **adeisw adeswy**

adeisz azides adzes aides aside azide dazes ideas sized adze aide aids dais daze dies idea ides said side size zeds ads adz aid die ids sad sea zed ad ae ai as id is si

adeitu attitude. *See* **adettt dettu**

adeitv dative davit adit aide avid date deva diet diva dive edit idea tide tied vied aet aid ate ave die dit eat eta ita tad tav tea ted tie vat vet via vie ad ae ai at id it ta ti

adeitw waited wited adit aide awed date diet edit idea tide tied wade wadi wait wide wite aet aid ate awe dew die dit

eat eta ita tad tea ted tie wad wed wet wit ad ae ai at aw id it ta ti we

adeitx taxied taxed adit aide axed date diet edit exit idea taxi tide tied aet aid ate axe die dit eat eta ita tad tax tea ted tie ad ae ai at ax ex id it ta ti xi

adeiu adieu aide idea aid die due ad ae ai id

adeiux adieux adieu aide axed idea aid axe die due ad ae ai ax ex id xi

adeivw waived waive waved wived aide avid awed deva diva dive idea vied view wade wadi wave wide wive aid ave awe dew die via vie wad wed ad ae ai aw id we

adeiz azide adze aide daze idea adz aid die zed ad ae ai id

adej jade ad ae

adejmm jammed dame jade made mead dam jam mad mae mem ad ae am em ma me

adejmor majored. *See* **ademor**

adejntu jaunted. *See* **adntu ajntu dentu**

adejopr jeopard. *See* **adeor deopr adepr**

adejoprs jeopards jeopard. *See* **adeops adeors adeprs aejprs**

adejopry jeopardy jeopard. *See* **adepry adopry**

adejp japed aped jade jape ape dap pad pea ad ae pa pe

adejrr jarred dare dear jade rare read rear are ear era err jar rad raj red ad ae er re

adejrstu adjuster readjust adjures. *See* **adejru aderst adjstu ajrstu**

adejrsu adjures. *See* **adejru aders dersu**

adejru adjure dare dear dura jade jura read rude rued urea are due ear era jar rad raj red rue urd ad ae er re

adejs jades jade ads sad sea ad ae as

adejw jawed awed jade wade awe dew jaw wad wed ad ae aw we

adejzz jazzed adze daze jade jazz adz zed ad ae

adekky yakked kyak dyke aye day dey dye key yak yea ad ae ay ka ye

adeklmry markedly. *See* **adeklr adekmr adelmr adelry**

adeklnp planked. *See* **adelnp aekln adekn**

adeklnr rankled. *See* **adeknr adeklr adelnr aeklnr**

adeklns kalends. *See* **aeklns adelns adekns adekls**

adeklny nakedly. *See* **adekny adklny**

adeklop polkaed. *See* **delop adelp dekop**

adeklprs sparkled sparked sparkle. *See* **adeklr adekls adekpr adekrs**

adeklr darkle larked alder drake laker raked dale dare dark deal dear earl kale lade lake lard lark lead leak rake

rale read real ale are ark ear eld elk era
kal lad lar lea led lek rad red ad ae el er
ka la re

adekls slaked asked dales deals lades
lakes leads leaks skald slake ales dale
deal desk elks kale lade lads lake lead
leak leas leks sake sale seal sled ads ale
ask eld elk els kal kas lad lea led lek sad
sal sea ad ae as el ka la

adeklst stalked. *See* **adelst aeklst adekst
adeklt**

adeklt talked dealt delta lated latke dale
date deal kale lade lake late lead leak
tael take tale talk teak teal aet ale alt
ate eat eld elk eta kal kat lad lea led lek
let tad tea ted ad ae at el ka la ta

adeklw walked waked waled weald awed
dale deal kale lade lake lead leak lewd
wade wake wale walk weak weal weka
weld ale awe awl dew eld elk kal lad
law lea led lek wad wed ad ae aw el ka
la we

adekmnru unmarked manured maunder
unarmed. *See* **adekmr adeknr ademnr
adenru**

adekmnsu unmasked unasked medusan.
See **adekms adekns ademns ademsu**

adekmr marked armed derma drake
dream maker raked dame dare dark
dear dram kame made make mare
mark mead rake read ream are ark arm
dam ear era mad mae mar rad ram red
rem ad ae am em er ka ma me re

adekms masked asked dames kames
makes meads dame dams desk kame
made make mask mead mesa sake
same seam ads ask dam kas mad mae
sad sea ad ae am as em ka ma me

adekn knead naked dean dank and ane
den end ken nae ad ae an en ka na ne

adeknnss dankness. *See* **adekns adenss
aeknss aennss**

adeknpp knapped. *See* **adenpp**

adeknps spanked. *See* **adekns**

adeknr danker darken ranked drake
drank knead naked raked dank dare
dark darn dean dear earn kern knar
nard nark near nerd rake rand rank
read rend and ane are ark den ear end
era ken nae rad ran red ad ae an en er
ka na ne re

adeknrr knarred. *See* **adeknr adekrr
adenrr aeknrr**

adeknrs darkens. *See* **adeknr adekrs
adekns adenrs**

adeknrss darkness darkens sanders. *See*
adeknr adekns adekrs adenrs

adekns kneads snaked asked deans
knead naked sedan skean snake sneak
dank dean dens desk ends kens sake

sand sane sank send ads and ane ask
den end ens kas ken nae sad sea sen ad
ae an as en ka na ne

adeknst dankest. *See* **adekns adekst
adeknt**

adeknsu unasked. *See* **adekns adensu**

adeknt tanked knead naked taken ante
dank date dean dent neat take tank
teak tend aet and ane ant ate den eat
end eta kat ken nae net tad tan tea ted
ten ad ae an at en ka na ne ta

adekny yanked knead naked dank dean
deny dyke dyne yank yean and ane any
aye day den dey dye end ken key nae
nay yak yea yen ad ae an ay en ka na ne
ye

adekootw teakwood. *See* **aekow dekot
deotw**

adekos soaked asked ados desk does
dose koas oaks odes okes sake soak
soda soke ado ads ask doe dos kas koa
kos oak ode oke sad sea sod ad ae as do
ka od os so

adekoy kayoed okayed yoked dyke kayo
okay yoke ado aye day dey doe dye key
koa oak ode oke yak yea yod ad ae ay
do ka od oy ye

adekpr parked drake drape padre pared
raked raped aped dare dark dear pard
pare park peak pear perk rake rape
read reap ape are ark dap ear era pad
par pea per rad rap red rep ad ae er ka
pa pe re

adekprs sparked. *See* **adekpr adekrs**

adekqsuw squawked. *See* **adekqu aekqsu
akqsuw**

adekqu quaked quake quad duke auk
due qua ad ae ka

adekr drake raked dare dark dear rake
read are ark ear era rad red ad ae er ka
re

adekrr darker drake raked dare dark
dear rake rare read rear are ark ear era
err rad red ad ae er ka re

adekrs drakes asked dares dears drake
eskar raked rakes rased reads saker
arks arse dare dark dear desk ears eras
rads rake rase read reds sake sard sark
sear sera ads are ark ask ear era kas rad
red res sad sea ad ae as er ka re

adekrst darkest. *See* **adekrs adekst aekrst
aderst**

adeks asked sake desk ads ask kas sad
sea ad ae as ka

adekst skated staked tasked asked dates
sated skate stake stead steak takes
teaks date desk east eats etas sake seat
seta skat tads take task teak teas teds
ads aet ask ate eat eta kas kat sad sat
sea set tad tea ted tsk ad ae as at ka ta

adekw waked awed wade wake weak
weka awe dew wad wed ad ae aw ka we

adel dale deal lade lead ale eld lad lea led
ad ae el la

adell ladle dale deal dell lade lead leal ale
all eld ell lad lea led ad ae el la

adellmsu medullas alludes aludels malleus medulla. *See* **adells adellu adelms
adelmu**

adellmu medulla. *See* **adellu adelmu
dellmu**

adellnnu annulled. *See* **adellu adennu**

adellnss landless sendals. *See* **adells
adelns adenss ellnss**

adellopw walloped allowed. *See* **adellp
adellw adelpw allopw**

adellott allotted totaled. *See* **dellot delott**

adellotw tallowed allowed. *See* **adellw
aelltw allotw dellot**

adellow allowed. *See* **adellw allow delow**

adelloww wallowed allowed. *See* **adellw
alloww**

adelloy alloyed. *See* **aelly alloy adlly**

adellp palled ladle lapel paled pedal
plead aped dale deal dell lade lead leal
leap pale pall peal plea pled ale all alp
ape dap eld ell lad lap lea led pad pal
pea ad ae el la pa pe

adellqsu squalled alludes aludels. *See*
adells adellu aelqsu ellqsu

adellru allured. *See* **adellu aellru dellru**

adells dalles ladles dales deals dells lades
ladle leads ales dale deal dell ells lade
lads lead leal leas sale seal sell sled ads
ale all eld ell els lad lea led sad sal sea
ad ae as el la

adellst stalled. *See* **adells adelst aellst**

adellsu alludes aludels. *See* **adellu adells**

adelltuu ululated ululate. *See* **adellu**

adellu allude aludel ladle auld dale deal
dell dual duel dull lade laud lead leal
ale all due eld ell lad lea led leu ad ae el
la

adellw walled dwell ladle waled weald
awed dale deal dell lade lead leal lewd
wade wale wall weal weld well ale all
awe awl dew eld ell lad law lea led wad
wed ad ae aw el la we

adelm lamed medal dale dame deal lade
lame lead made male mead meal meld
ale dam eld elm lad lam lea led mad
mae mel ad ae am el em la ma me

adelmm lammed lamed lemma medal
dale dame deal lade lame lead made
male malm mead meal meld ale dam
eld elm lad lam lea led mad mae mel
mem ad ae am el em la ma me

adelmms slammed. *See* **adelms adelmm
aelmms**

adelmnns landsmen sandmen. *See* **adelms adelns ademnn ademns**

adelmnr mandrel. *See* **adelnr adelmr ademnr**

adelmnrs mandrels darnels landers mandrel medlars remands slander snarled. *See* **adelmr adelms adelnr adelns**

adelmnt mantled. *See* **adelnt aelmnt adelmt ademnt**

adelmo loamed amole dolma lamed medal modal model aloe dale dame deal demo dole dome lade lame lead load loam lode made male mead meal meld mode mola mold mole ado ale dam doe eld elm lad lam lea led mad mae mel moa mod ode old ad ae am do el em la lo ma me mo od om

adelmor earldom. *See* **adelmr adelor adelmo delmor aelmor**

adelmors earldoms earldom loaders medlars molders morales ordeals radomes reloads smolder. *See* **adelmo adelmr adelms adelor**

adelmotu modulate moulted. *See* **adelmo adelmt adelmu aelmtu**

adelmp palmed ample lamed maple medal paled pedal plead aped dale dame damp deal lade lame lamp lead leap made male mead meal meld pale palm peal plea pled ale alp amp ape dam dap eld elm lad lam lap lea led mad mae map mel pad pal pea ad ae am el em la ma me pa pe

adelmprt trampled tramped trample. *See* **adelmp adelmr adelmt adelpt**

adelmps sampled. *See* **adelms adelps aelmps adelmp**

adelmr dermal marled medlar alder armed derma dream lamed lamer medal realm dale dame dare deal dear dram earl lade lame lard lead made male mare marl mead meal meld merl rale read real ream ale are arm dam ear eld elm era lad lam lar lea led mad mae mar mel rad ram red rem ad ae am el em er la ma me re

adelmrs medlars. *See* **adelrs adelms adelmr ademrs aelmrs**

adelms damsel medals dales dames deals lades lamed lames leads males meads meals medal melds ales alms dale dame dams deal elms lade lads lame lams lead leas made male mead meal meld mels mesa sale same seal seam slam sled ads ale dam eld elm els lad lam lea led mad mae mel sad sal sea ad ae am as el em la ma me

adelmss damsels. *See* **adelms ademss**

adelmt malted dealt delta lamed lated mated medal metal tamed dale dame

date deal lade lame late lead made male malt mate mead meal meat meld melt tael tale tame teal team aet ale alt ate dam eat eld elm eta lad lam lea led let mad mae mat mel met tad tam tea ted ad ae am at el em la ma me ta

adelmu mauled lamed medal ulema alum auld dale dame deal dual duel lade lame laud lead made male maud maul mead meal meld mule ale dam due eld elm emu lad lam lea led leu lum mad mae mel mud ad ae am el em la ma me mu um

adeln eland laden dale deal dean lade land lane lead lean lend ale and ane den eld end lad lea led nae ad ae an el en la na ne

adelnnp planned. *See* **adelnp adennp**

adelno loaned alone anode eland laden loden nodal olden aeon aloe dale deal dean dole done enol lade land lane lead lean lend leno load loan lode lone node noel ado ale and ane den doe don eld end eon lad lea led nae nod ode old one ad ae an do el en la lo na ne no od on

adelnors solander darnels landers lardons loaders loaners ordeals reloads rondels slander snarled. *See* **adelno adelnr adelns adelor**

adelnot taloned. *See* **adenot adlnot adelnt adelno**

adelnp planed eland laden paled panel pedal penal plane plead aped dale deal dean lade land lane lead lean leap lend nape neap pale pane peal pean pend plan plea pled ale alp and ane ape dap den eld end lad lap lea led nae nap pad pal pan pea pen ad ae an el en la na ne pa pe

adelnprs spandrel darnels landers panders planers slander snarled. *See* **adelnp adelnr adelns adelps**

adelnpru pendular launder plunder. *See* **adelnp adelnr adenpr adenru**

adelnpt planted. *See* **adelnt adenpt adelnp aelnpt adelpt**

adelnr darnel lander alder eland laden learn renal dale dare darn deal dean dear earl earn lade land lane lard lead lean lend nard near nerd rale rand read real rend ale and ane are den ear eld end era lad lar lea led nae rad ran red ad ae an el en er la na ne r

adelnrs darnels landers slander snarled. *See* **adelrs adelnr adelns aelnrs adenrs**

adelnrss slanders darnels landers rassled sanders sendals slander snarled. *See* **adelnr adelns adelrs adenrs**

adelnrsu launders asunder danseur darnels landers launder lurdans rundles slander snarled. *See* **adelnr adelns adelrs adenrs**

adelnrty ardently lyrated. *See* **adelnr adelnt adelry adenrt**

adelnru launder. *See* **adelnr adlnru aelnru delnru adenru**

adelnruy underlay launder laundry unready. *See* **adelnr adelry adenru adenry**

adelns elands sendal dales deals deans eland laden lades lands lanes leads leans lends sedan ales dale deal dean dens ends lade lads land lane lead lean leas lend lens sale sand sane seal send sled ads ale and ane den eld els end ens lad lea led nae sad sal sea sen ad ae an as el en la na ne

adelnss sendals. *See* **adelns adenss**

adelnst dentals slanted. *See* **adelst adelnt adelns**

adelnstu unsalted dentals saluted slanted. *See* **adelns adelnt adelst adensu**

adelnt dental dealt delta eland laden lated leant ante dale date deal dean dent lade land lane late lead lean lend lent neat tael tale teal tend aet ale alt and ane ant ate den eat eld end eta lad lea led let nae net tad tan tea ted ten ad ae an at el en la na ne ta

adelntuu undulate. *See* **adelnt aelntu**

adelntw wetland. *See* **adelnt adentw**

adeloorv overload. *See* **adelor deoorv**

adelopr leopard paroled. *See* **adelor aelopr delopr**

adeloprs leopards deposal leopard loaders ordeals paroled paroles polders reloads. *See* **adelor adelps adelrs adeops**

adelops deposal. *See* **aelops adelps delops adeops**

adelopss deposals deposal lassoed. *See* **adelps adeops adepss adloss**

adelopst tadpoles apostle deposal pelotas stapled tadpole. *See* **adelps adelpt adelst adeops**

adelopt tadpole. *See* **adelpt aelopt**

adelor loader ordeal reload adore alder oared older oread aero aloe dale dare deal dear doer dole earl lade lard lead load lode lord lore orad oral orle rale read real redo road rode role ado ale are doe dor earl era lad lar lea led oar ode old ore rad red rod roe ad ae do el er la lo od or re

adelors loaders ordeals reloads. *See* **adeors adelrs adlors adelor delors**

adelorst delators leotards lodestar delator leotard loaders oldster ordeals reloads roasted torsade. *See* **adelor adelrs adelst adeors**

adelorsu roulades aroused loaders ordeals reloads roulade. *See* **adelor adelrs adeors adlors**

adelort delator leotard. *See* **adelor adeort delort**

adeloru roulade. *See* **adelor deloru**

adeloss lassoed. *See* **adloss aelos adels**

adelott totaled. *See* **delott**

adelotuv ovulated ovulate vaulted voluted. *See* **adeluv deotuv elotuv**

adelovwy avowedly. *See* **adelwy adeovw delowy**

adelp paled pedal plead aped dale deal lade lead leap pale peal plea pled ale alp ape dap eld lad lap lea led pad pal pea ad ae el la pa pe

adelpp dapple lapped apple paled pedal pepla plead aped dale deal lade lead leap pale palp peal plea pled ale alp ape dap eld lad lap lea led pad pal pap pea pep ad ae el la pa pe

adelpps dapples slapped. *See* **aelpps adelpp adelps adepps**

adelprsw sprawled dewlaps. *See* **adelps adelpw adelrs adelsw**

adelprtt prattled partlet platted platter prattle rattled. *See* **adelpt adeprt adeptt adertt**

adelps lapsed pedals pleads deals lades lapse leads leaps paled pales peals pedal plead pleas salep sepal spade ales alps aped apes apse dale daps deal lade lads laps lead leap leas pads pale pals peal peas plea pled sale seal slap sled sped ads ale alp ape asp dap eld els lad lap lea led pad pal pas pea sad sal sap sea spa ad ae as el la pa pe

adelpst stapled. *See* **adelst adelps aelpst adepst adelpt**

adelpstu pulsated pulsate saluted stapled updates. *See* **adelps adelpt adelst adepst**

adelpsw dewlaps. *See* **adelpw adelsw**

adelpsy splayed. *See* **adelsy adelps adelpy adepsy**

adelpt plated adept dealt delta lated paled pedal petal plate plead pleat taped aped dale date deal lade late lead leap lept pale pate peal peat pelt plat plea pled tael tale tape teal aet ale alp alt a,ce apt ate dap eat eld eta lad lap lea led let pad pal pat pea pet tad tap tea ted ad ae at el la pa pe ta

adelptt platted. *See* **adelpt adeptt**

adelpty adeptly. *See* **adelpt adelpy**

adelpw dewlap paled pawed pedal plead waled weald aped awed dale deal lade

lead leap lewd pale pawl peal plea pled wade wale weal weld ale alp ape awe awl dap dew eld lad lap law lea led pad pal paw pea pew wad wap wed ad ae aw el la pa pe we

adelpy played delay leady paled payed pedal plead aped dale deal lade lady lead leap pale paly peal play plea pled yelp ale alp ape aye dap day dey dye eld lad lap lay lea led lye pad pal pay pea ply pya yap yea yep ad ae ay el la pa pe ye

adelr alder dale dare deal dear earl lade lard lead rale read real ale are ear eld era lad lar lea led rad red ad ae el er la re

adelrr larder alder dale dare deal dear earl lade lard lead rale rare read real rear ale are ear eld era err lad lar lea led rad red ad ae el er la re

adelrrs larders. *See* **adelrr adelrs**

adelrrsu ruderals larders ruderal slurred. *See* **adelrr adelrs aelrrsu elrrsu**

adelrrtu ultrared ruderal. *See* **adelrr aderrt**

adelrru ruderal. *See* **adelrr adlru delru**

adelrs alders alder dales dares deals dears earls lades lards lares laser leads rales rased reads ales arse dale dare deal dear earl ears eras lade lads lard lead leas rads rale rase read real reds sale sard seal sear sera sled ads ale are ear eld els era lad lar lea led rad red res sad sal sea ad ae as el er la re

adelrss rassled. *See* **adelrs aelrss**

adelrstt startled rattled rattles slatted starlet started startle tetrads. *See* **adelrs adelst aderst adertt**

adelrtt rattled. *See* **aelrtt adertt**

adelrtuy adultery lyrated. *See* **adelry aelrty delruy**

adelrtw trawled. *See* **adelr aelrt adelt**

adelrtx dextral. *See* **adelr aeltx aertx**

adelrty lyrated. *See* **adelry aelrty**

adelry dearly alder deary delay early lardy layer leady rayed ready relay aery aryl dale dare deal dear dray dyer earl lade lady lard lead lyre rale read real rely yard yare year ale are aye day dey dry dye ear eld era lad lar lay lea led lye rad ray red rye yar yea ad ae ay el er la re ye

adels dales deals lades leads ales dale deal lade lads lead leas sale seal sled ads ale eld els lad lea led sad sal sea ad ae as el la

adelst deltas lasted salted slated staled dales dates deals dealt delta lades lated leads least sated slate stale stead steal taels tales ales alts dale date deal east

eats etas lade lads last late lead leas lest lets sale salt seal seat seta slat sled tads tael tale teal teas teds ads aet ale alt ate eat eld els eta lad lea led let sad sal sat sea set tad tea ted ad ae as at el la ta

adelstt slatted. *See* **adelst aelstt adestt**

adelstu saluted. *See* **adlstu adelst delstu aelstu**

adelsv salved slaved dales deals devas lades laved laves leads salve saved slave vales veals velds ales aves dale deal deva lade lads lave lead leas leva sale save seal sled vale vase veal veld ads ale ave eld els lad lea led lev sad sal sea ad ae as el la

adelsw wealds dales deals lades leads sawed swale wades waled wales weald weals welds ales awed awes awls dale deal dews lade lads laws lead leas lewd sale seal sled slew wade wads wale weal weds weld ads ale awe awl dew eld els lad law lea led sad sal saw sea sew wad was wed ad ae as aw el la we

adelsy delays slayed dales deals delay lades leads leady lysed sadly ales ayes dale days deal deys dyes easy eyas lade lads lady lays lead leas lyes lyse sale seal slay sled yeas ads ale aye day dey dye eld els lad lay lea led lye sad sal say sea sly yea yes ad ae as ay el la ye

adelszz dazzles. *See* **adelzz adesz adels**

adelt dealt delta lated dale date deal lade late lead tael tale teal aet ale alt ate eat eld eta lad lea led let tad tea ted ad ae at el la ta

adelttt tattled. *See* **adettt aelttt**

adeltttw twattled tattled twattle wattled. *See* **adettt aelttt aelttw**

adelttw wattled. *See* **aelttw adelt deltw**

adeltuv vaulted. *See* **adeluv adltu adelt**

adeltux luxated. *See* **aeltux adltu adelt**

adeltwz waltzed. *See* **adelt deltw adelz**

adeluv valued laved value auld dale deal deva dual duel lade laud lave lead leva uvea vale veal veld ale ave due eld lad lea led leu lev luv ad ae el la

adelv laved dale deal deva lade lave lead leva vale veal veld ale ave eld lad lea led lev ad ae el la

adelw waled weald awed dale deal lade lead lewd wade wale weal weld ale awe awl dew eld lad law lea led wad wed ad ae aw el la we

adelwy yawled delay leady waled weald yawed awed dale deal dewy lade lady lead lewd wade wale weal weld yawl ale awe awl aye day dew dey dye eld lad law lay lea led lye wad way wed wye yaw yea yew ad ae aw ay el la we ye

adely delay leady dale deal lade lady lead ale aye day dey dye eld lad lay lea led lye yea ad ae ay el la ye

adelz lazed adze dale daze deal lade laze lead zeal adz ale eld lad lea led zed ad ae el la

adelzz dazzle lazed adze dale daze deal lade laze lead zeal adz ale eld lad lea led zed ad ae el la

adem dame made mead dam mad mae ad ae am em ma me

ademmn madmen admen amend maned menad named amen dame damn dean made mane mead mean mend name and ane dam den end mad mae man mem men nae ad ae am an em en ma me na ne

ademmnow madwomen. *See* **ademmn ademno ademow**

ademmr rammed armed derma dream dame dare dear dram made mare mead read ream are arm dam ear era mad mae mar mem rad ram red rem ad ae am em er ma me re

ademn admen amend maned menad named amen dame damn dean made mane mead mean mend name and ane dam den end mad mae man men nae ad ae am an em en ma me na ne

ademnn manned admen amend maned menad named amen dame damn dean made mane mead mean mend name and ane dam den end mad mae man men nae ad ae am an em en ma me na ne

ademnnnu unmanned mundane unnamed. *See* **ademnn adennu**

ademnns sandmen. *See* **ademns ademnn**

ademnnu mundane unnamed. *See* **ademnn adennu**

ademno daemon moaned admen amend anode demon maned menad monad named nomad aeon amen dame damn dean demo dome done made mane mead mean mend moan mode name node noma nome omen ado and ane dam den doe don end eon mad mae man men moa mod mon nae nod ode one ad ae am an do em en ma me mo na ne no od om on

ademnoor marooned doorman doormen madrone. *See* **ademno ademnr ademor admnor**

ademnopr pomander madrone padrone. *See* **ademno ademnp ademnr ademop**

ademnor madrone. *See* **ademno aemnor demnor ademor admnor**

ademnors madrones ransomed daemons enamors madrone moderns oarsmen radomes remands. *See* **ademno ademnr ademns ademor**

ademnos daemons. *See* **ademns adenos ademno admnos demnos**

ademnotu amounted mounted. *See* **ademno ademnt adenot amnotu**

ademnp dampen admen amend maned menad named amen aped dame damn damp dean made mane mead mean mend name nape neap pane pean pend amp and ane ape dam dap den end mad mae man map men nae nap pad pan pea pen ad ae am an em en ma me na ne pa pe

ademnps dampens. *See* **ademns ademnp**

ademnpss dampness dampens madness. *See* **ademnp ademns ademss adenss**

ademnr remand admen amend armed derma dream maned menad named amen dame damn dare darn dean dear dram earn made mane mare mead mean mend name nard near nerd rand read ream rend and ane are arm dam den ear end era mad mae man mar men nae rad ram ran red rem ad ae am an em en er ma me na ne re

ademnrru underarm eardrum manured maunder unarmed. *See* **ademnr ademrr adenrr adenru**

ademnrs remands. *See* **ademns ademrs ademnr adenrs**

ademnrsu maunders asunder danseur manured manures maunder medusan remands surname unarmed. *See* **ademnr ademns ademrs ademsu**

ademnru manured maunder unarmed. *See* **aemnru ademnr adenru**

ademnruw unwarmed manured maunder unarmed. *See* **ademnr ademrw adenru adenrw**

ademnry draymen yardmen. *See* **adenry ademry ademnr**

ademns amends desman menads admen amend dames damns deans maned manes manse meads means menad mends named names sedan amen dame damn dams dean dens ends made mane mead mean mend mesa name same sand sane seam send ads and ane dam den end ens mad mae man men nae sad sea sen ad ae am an as em en ma me na ne

ademnss madness. *See* **ademns aemnss ademss adenss**

ademnsu medusan. *See* **ademns ademsu admnsu adensu**

ademnt tandem admen amend maned mated meant menad named tamed amen ante dame damn date dean dent made mane mate mead mean meat

mend name neat tame team tend aet and ane ant ate dam den eat end eta mad mae man mat men met nae net tad tam tan tea ted ten ad ae am an at em en ma me na ta

ademoort moderato doormat motored tearoom. *See* **ademor ademrt adeort demoor**

ademoosv vamoosed vamosed vamoose. *See* **adeosv aemosv**

ademop pomade moped aped dame damp demo dome dope made mead mode mope oped poem pome ado amp ape dam dap doe mad mae map moa mod mop ode ope pad pea pod ad ae am do em ma me mo od om pa pe

ademops pomades. *See* **ademop adeops**

ademor radome roamed adore armed derma dream morae oared oread aero dame dare dear demo doer dome dorm dram made mare mead mode mora more omer orad read ream redo road roam rode ado are arm dam doe dor ear era mad mae mar moa mod mor oar ode ore rad ram red rem rod roe ad ae am do em er ma me mo od om or re

ademorr armored. *See* **adeorr demorr ademrr ademor admorr**

ademorrt mortared armored. *See* **ademor ademrr ademrt adeorr**

ademors radomes. *See* **adeors ademrs**

ademosv vamosed. *See* **adeosv aemosv**

ademosw meadows. *See* **ademow adems demos**

ademosy someday. *See* **adems demos amosy**

ademow meadow mowed awed dame demo dome made mead meow mode owed wade ado awe dam dew doe mad mae maw mew moa mod mow ode owe wad wed woe ad ae am aw do em ma me mo od om ow we

ademowy meadowy. *See* **ademow adewy**

adempp mapped aped dame damp made mead amp ape dam dap mad mae map pad pap pea pep ad ae am em ma me pa pe

adempr damper ramped armed derma drape dream padre pared raped aped dame damp dare dear dram made mare mead pard pare pear perm pram ramp rape read ream reap amp ape are arm dam dap ear era mad mae map mar pad par pea per rad ram rap red rem rep ad ae am em er ma me pa pe re

ademprs dampers. *See* **adempr ademrs**

ademprt tramped. *See* **adempr adeprt ademrt adempt aemprt**

adempst dampest stamped. *See* **ademst adepst adempt**

adempsw swamped. *See* **adems adepw adesw**

adempt tamped adept mated tamed taped aped dame damp date made mate mead meat pate peat tame tamp tape team aet amp ape apt ate dam dap eat eta mad mae map mat met pad pat pea pet tad tam tap tea ted ad ae am at em ma me pa pe ta

adempv vamped paved aped dame damp deva made mead pave vamp amp ape ave dam dap mad mae map pad pea ad ae am em ma me pa pe

ademr armed derma dream dame dare dear dram made mare mead read ream are arm dam ear era mad mae mar rad ram red rem ad ae am em er ma me re

ademrr marred armed derma dream re-arm dame dare dear dram made mare mead rare read ream rear are arm dam ear era err mad mae mar rad ram red rem ad ae am em er ma me re

ademrrsu eardrums armures eardrum murders. *See* **ademrr ademrs ademsu aemrrs**

ademrrty martyred. *See* **ademrr ademrt ademry aderry**

ademrru eardrum. *See* **aemrru ademrr demrru**

ademrs dermas dreams armed dames dares dears derma drams dream mares maser meads rased reads reams smear arms arse dame dams dare dear dram ears eras made mare mead mesa rads rams rase read ream reds same sard seam sear sera ads are arm dam ear era mad mae mar rad ram red rem res sad sea ad ae am as em er ma me re

ademrst smarted. *See* **ademrs ademrt ademst aemrst aderst**

ademrsw swarmed. *See* **ademrs adersw ademrw**

ademrt dreamt armed derma dream mated rated tamed tamer tared trade tread dame dare dart date dear dram drat made mare mart mate mead meat rate read ream tame tare team tear term tram aet are arm art ate dam ear eat era eta mad mae mar mat met rad ram rat red rem ret tad tam tar tea ted ad ae am at em er ma me re ta

ademrtu matured. *See* **ademrt aemrtu**

ademrw warmed armed derma dream wader wared awed dame dare dear dram draw drew made mare mead read ream wade ward ware warm wear are arm awe dam dew ear era mad mae mar maw mew rad ram raw red rem wad war wed ad ae am aw em er ma me re we

ademry dreamy armed deary derma dream rayed ready aery army dame dare dear demy dram dray dyer made mare mead read ream yard yare year are arm aye dam day dey dry dye ear era mad mae mar may rad ram ray red rem rye yam yar yea ad ae am ay em er ma me my re ye

adems dames meads dame dams made mead mesa same seam ads dam mad mae sad sea ad ae am as em ma me

ademss massed dames meads mesas seams dame dams made mass mead mesa mess same seam seas ads ass dam ess mad mae sad sea ad ae am as em ma me

ademssu assumed medusas. *See* **ademsu aemssu ademss demssu**

ademst masted dames dates mated mates meads meats sated satem stead steam tamed tames teams dame dams date east eats etas made mast mate mats mead meat mesa same seam seat seta stem tads tame tams team teas teds ads aet ate dam eat eta mad mae mat met sad sat sea set tad tam tea ted ad ae am as at em ma me ta

ademsu amused medusa amuse dames mauds meads mused sedum dame dams dues emus made maud mead mesa muds muse same seam sued used ads dam due emu mad mae mud mus sad sea sue sum use ad ae am as em ma me mu um us

ademt mated tamed dame date made mate mead meat tame team aet ate dam eat eta mad mae mat met tad tam tea ted ad ae am at em ma me ta

ademtt matted mated matte tamed dame date made mate mead meat tame team teat aet ate dam eat eta mad mae mat met tad tam tat tea ted ad ae am at em ma me ta

ademttu mutated. *See* **ademtt aemttu**

ademz mazed adze dame daze made maze mead adz dam mad mae zed ad ae am em ma me

aden dean and ane den end nae ad ae an en na ne

adennntu untanned. *See* **adennt adennu denntu**

adennoy annoyed anodyne. *See* **adenoy aennoy**

adennp panned panne penna aped dean nape neap pane pean pend and ane ape dap den end nae nap pad pan pea pen ad ae an en na ne pa pe

adennps spanned. *See* **adennp aennps**

adennpst pendants pedants pendant pentads spanned. *See* **adennp adennt adenpt adepst**

adennpt pendant. *See* **adennp adenpt adennt**

adennsu duennas. *See* **adennu adensu dennsu**

adennt tanned anent ante date dean dent neat tend aet and ane ant ate den eat end eta nae net tad tan tea ted ten ad ae an at en na ne ta

adenntuw unwanted. *See* **adennt adennu adennw adentw**

adennu duenna dean dune nude and ane den due dun end nae nun ad ae an en na ne nu

adennw wanned dewan waned anew awed dawn dean wade wand wane wean wend and ane awe awn den dew end nae new wad wan wed wen ad ae an aw en na ne we

adeno anode aeon dean done node ado and ane den doe don end eon nae nod ode one ad ae an do en na ne no od on

adenoort ratooned donator odorant tornado. *See* **adenot adenrt adeort aenort**

adenopr padrone. *See* **adenpr adnopr denopr**

adenoprr pardoner padrone pardner. *See* **adenpr adenrr adeorr adeprr**

adenoprs padrones padrone panders pardons persona ponders respond. *See* **adenos adenpr adenrs adeops**

adenorrw narrowed redrawn. *See* **adenrr adenrw adeorr aderrw**

adenortt attorned notated rotated. *See* **adenot adenrt adentt adeort**

adenoru rondeau. *See* **adenru adnoru**

adenorux rondeaux rondeau. *See* **adenru adnoru**

adenos anodes aeons anode deans nodes nosed sedan sonde ados aeon dean dens does done dons dose ends eons naos node nods noes nose odes ones sand sane send soda ado ads and ane den doe don dos end ens eon nae nod ode one sad sea sen sod son ad ae an as do en na ne no od on os so

adenost donates. *See* **adenos adenot aenost denost**

adenot atoned donate anode atone noted oaten toned aeon ante date dean dent done dote neat node nota note tend toad toed tone ado aet and ane ant ate den doe don dot eat end eon eta nae net nod not oat ode one tad tan tea ted ten tod toe ton ad ae an at do en na ne no od on ta to

adenott notated. *See* **adenot adentt aenott**

adenoy noyade anode doyen aeon dean deny done dyne node yean yond ado and ane any aye day den dey doe don dye end eon nae nay nod ode one yea yen yod yon ad ae an ay do en na ne no od on oy ye

adenpp append napped aped dean nape neap pane pean pend and ane ape dap den end nae nap pad pan pap pea pen pep ad ae an en na ne pa pe

adenpps appends snapped. *See* **adenpp adepps**

adenpr pander drape padre pared raped aped dare darn dean dear earn nape nard neap near nerd pane pard pare pean pear pend rand rape read reap rend and ane ape are dap den ear end era nae nap pad pan par pea pen per rad ran rap red rep ad ae an en er na ne pa pe re

adenprr pardner. *See* **adeprr adenrr adenpr**

adenprrs pardners drapers errands panders pardner sparred. *See* **adenpr adenrr adenrs adeprr**

adenprs panders. *See* **adenpr adenrs**

adenprty pedantry. *See* **adenpr adenpt adenrt adenry**

adenpruy underpay unready. *See* **adenpr adenru adenry adepry**

adenpst pedants pentads. *See* **adenpt adepst aenpst**

adenpsw spawned. *See* **adenpw adensw**

adenpsx expands spandex. *See* **adenpx aenps adens**

adenpt panted pedant pentad adept paten taped ante aped date dean dent nape neap neat pane pant pate pean peat pend pent tape tend aet and ane ant ape apt ate dap den eat end eta nae nap net pad pan pat pea pen pet tad tan tap tea ted ten ad ae an at en na ne pa pe ta

adenpuv unpaved. *See* **adepv denpu**

adenpw pawned dewan pawed waned anew aped awed dawn dean nape neap pane pawn pean pend wade wand wane wean wend and ane ape awe awn dap den dew end nae nap new pad pan paw pea pen pew wad wan wap wed wen ad ae an aw en na ne pa pe we

adenpx expand aped apex axed dean nape neap pane pean pend and ane ape axe dap den end nae nap pad pan pax pea pen ad ae an ax en ex na ne pa pe

adenqrsu squander asunder danseur squared. *See* **adenrs adenru adensu aenqsu**

adenqtu quanted. *See* **adntu anqtu aenqu**

adenrr errand reran dare darn dean dear earn nard near nerd rand rare read rear rend and ane are den ear end era err nae rad ran red ad ae an en er na ne re

adenrrs errands. *See* **adenrr adenrs**

adenrrw redrawn. *See* **aderrw adenrr adenrw aenrrw**

adenrs sander snared dares darns deans dears earns nards nares nears nerds rands rased reads rends saner sedan snare arse dare darn dean dear dens earn ears ends eras nard near nerd rads rand rase read reds rend sand sane sard sear send sera ads and ane are den ear end ens era nae rad ran red res sad sea sen ad ae an as en er na ne re

adenrss sanders. *See* **adenrs adenss aenrss**

adenrssu danseurs assured asunder danseur sanders sundaes sunders undress. *See* **adenrs adenru adenss adensu**

adenrsu asunder danseur. *See* **denrsu adenrs adensu adenru**

adenrsw wanders wardens. *See* **aenrsw adensw adenrs adersw adenrw**

adenrt ardent ranted rated tared trade tread trend ante dare darn dart date dean dear dent drat earn nard near neat nerd rand rant rate read rend rent tare tear tend tern aet and ane ant are art ate den ear eat end era eta nae net rad ran rat red ret tad tan tar tea ted ten ad ae an at en er na ne re ta

adenrtv verdant. *See* **adentv adertv adenrt aenrtv**

adenru unread under dare darn dean dear dune dura earn nard near nerd nude rand read rend rude rued rune urea and ane are den due dun ear end era nae rad ran red rue run urd urn ad ae an en er na ne nu re

adenruy unready. *See* **adenry adenru**

adenrw wander warden warned dewan drawn wader waned wared anew awed dare darn dawn dean dear draw drew earn nard near nerd rand read rend wade wand wane ward ware warn wean wear wend wren and ane are awe awn den dew ear end era nae new rad ran raw red wad wan war wed wen ad ae an aw en er na ne re we

adenry denary yarned deary nerdy randy rayed ready yearn aery dare darn dean dear deny dray dyer dyne earn nard nary near nerd rand read rend yard yare yarn yean year and ane any are aye day den dey dry dye ear end era nae nay rad ran ray red rye yar yea yen ad ae an ay en er na ne re ye

adens deans sedan dean dens ends sand sane send ads and ane den end ens nae sad sea sen ad ae an as en na ne

adenss sedans deans sands sedan sends dean dens ends sand sane seas send ads and ane ass den end ens ess nae sad sea sen ad ae an as en na ne

adensss sadness. *See* **adenss adesss**

adenssu sundaes. *See* **aenssu adenss adensu**

adenstt attends. *See* **adentt adestt**

adenstuy unsteady. *See* **adensu adesty adnstu adnsty**

adenstv advents. *See* **adentv adestv**

adensu sundae deans dunes nudes sedan anus dean dens dues dune duns ends nude sand sane send sued used ads and ane den due dun end ens nae sad sea sen sue sun use ad ae an as en na ne nu us

adensuwy unswayed endways. *See* **adensu adensw adenwy adeswy**

adensw dewans dawns deans dewan sawed sedan wades wands waned wanes weans wends anew awed awes awns dawn dean dens dews ends news sand sane sawn send sewn swan wade wads wand wane wean weds wend wens ads and ane awe awn den dew end ens nae new sad saw sea sen sew wad wan was wed wen ad ae an as aw en na ne we

adenswy endways. *See* **adensw adeswy adenwy**

adentt attend ante date dean dent neat teat tend tent aet and ane ant ate den eat end eta nae net tad tan tat tea ted ten ad ae an at en na ne ta

adenttu attuned taunted. *See* **adentt aenttu denttu**

adentuv vaunted. *See* **adentv adntu detuv**

adentv advent ante date dean dent deva nave neat tend vane vend vent aet and ane ant ate ave den eat end eta nae net tad tan tav tea ted ten van vat vet ad ae an at en na ne ta

adentw wanted dewan waned anew ante awed date dawn dean dent neat newt tend wade wand wane want wean wend aet and ane ant ate awe awn den dew eat end eta nae net new tad tan tea ted ten wad wan wed wen wet ad ae an at aw en na ne ta we

adenw dewan waned anew awed dawn dean wade wand wane wean wend and ane awe awn den dew end nae new wad wan wed wen ad ae an aw en na ne we

adenwy yawned dewan waned yawed anew awed dawn dean deny dewy dyne wade wand wane wany wean wend wynd yawn yean and ane any awe awn aye day den dew dey dye end nae nay new wad wan way wed wen wye yaw yea yen yew ad ae an aw ay en na ne we ye

adeoorrt toreador. *See* **adeorr adeort aoorrt deoort**

adeoottt tattooed. *See* **adettt aoottt deoott**

adeopprv approved approve. *See* **adeppr deoprv**

adeopps apposed. *See* **aeopps adepps adeops deopps**

adeopqu opaqued. *See* **aeopqu**

adeoprrt parroted predator prorated teardrop praetor prorate. *See* **adeorr adeort adeprr adeprt**

adeops soaped dopes posed spade ados aped apes apse daps does dope dose epos odes oped opes pads peas peso pods pose soap soda sped ado ads ape asp dap doe dos ode ope pad pas pea pod sad sap sea sod sop spa ad ae as do od os pa pe so

adeopstt postdate spatted spotted teapots toasted. *See* **adeops adepst adeptt adestt**

adeor adore oared oread aero dare dear doer orad read redo road rode ado are doe dor ear era oar ode ore rad red rod roe ad ae do er od or re

adeorr adorer roared adore ardor oared order oread aero dare dear doer orad rare read rear redo road roar rode ado are doe dor ear era err oar ode ore rad red rod roe ad ae do er od or re

adeorrs adorers. *See* **adeorr adeors adorrs deorrs**

adeorrst roadster adorers darters retards roasted roaster starred torsade traders. *See* **adeorr adeors adeort aderrt**

adeorrvw overdraw. *See* **adeorr adeovw aderrw deorrv**

adeors adores oreads soared adore arose dares dears doers dorsa oared oread rased reads roads rosed ados aero arse dare dear doer does dose ears eras oars odes orad ores rads rase read redo reds road rode rods roes rose sard sear sera soar soda sora sore ado ads are doe dor dos ear era oar ode ore rad red res rod roe sad sea sod ad ae as do er od or os re so

adeorsst assorted torsades roasted torsade. *See* **adeors adeort aderst aeorst**

adeorst roasted torsade. *See* **adeors deorst adeort aeorst aderst**

adeorstu readouts aroused detours readout roasted rousted torsade. *See* **adeors adeort aderst aeorst**

---

adeorstx extrados roasted torsade. *See* **adeors adeort aderst aeorst**

adeorsu aroused. *See* **adeors aeorsu deorsu**

adeorsuv savoured aroused devours savored. *See* **adeors adeosv aeorsu aorsuv**

adeorsv savored. *See* **adeors deorsv adeosv**

adeort orated adore doter oared orate oread rated tared trade tread aero dare dart date dear doer dote drat orad rate read redo road rode rota rote tare taro tear toad toed tora tore trod ado aet are art ate doe dor dot ear eat era eta oar oat ode ore ort rad rat red ret rod roe rot tad tar tea ted tod toe tor ad ae at do er od or re ta to

adeortt rotated. *See* **adeort adertt aeortt deortt**

adeortu readout. *See* **deortu adeort**

adeoryz zedoary. *See* **adeor adery aderz**

adeostt toasted. *See* **deostt adestt**

adeosv vadose devas doves saved ados aves deva does dose dove odes save soda vase ado ads ave doe dos ode ova sad sea sod ad ae as do od os so

adeovw avowed waved vowed avow awed deva dove owed wade wave wove ado ave awe dew doe ode ova owe vow wad wed woe ad ae aw do od ow we

adep aped ape dap pad pea ad ae pa pe

adeppr dapper rapped drape padre paper pared raped aped dare dear pard pare pear prep rape read reap repp ape are dap ear era pad pap par pea pep per rad rap red rep ad ae er pa pe re

adepprst strapped departs petards trapped. *See* **adeppr adepps adeppt adeprs**

adepprt trapped. *See* **adeppr adeprt adeppt**

adepprw wrapped. *See* **adeppr adeppw adeprw**

adepps sapped spade aped apes apse daps pads paps peas peps sped ads ape asp dap pad pap pas pea pep sad sap sea spa ad ae as pa pe

adeppsw swapped. *See* **adepps**

adeppt tapped adept taped aped date pate peat tape aet ape apt ate dap eat eta pad pap pat pea pep pet tad tap tea ted ad ae at pa pe ta

adepptu pupated. *See* **aepptu adeppt adeptu**

adeppw wapped pawed aped awed wade ape awe dap dew pad pap paw pea pep pew wad wap wed ad ae aw pa pe we

adeppy yapped payed aped ape aye dap day dey dye pad pap pay pea pep pya yap yea yep ad ae ay pa pe ye

---

adeppz zapped adze aped daze adz ape dap pad pap pea pep zap zed ad ae pa pe

adepr drape padre pared raped aped dare dear pard pare pear rape read reap ape are dap ear era pad par pea per rad rap red rep ad ae er pa pe re

adeprr draper parred drape padre pared raped aped dare dear pard pare parr pear rape rare read reap rear ape are dap ear era err pad par pea per rad rap red rep ad ae er pa pe re

adeprrs drapers sparred. *See* **adeprr aeprrs**

adeprrtu raptured rapture. *See* **adeprr adeprt adeptu aeprru**

adeprry drapery. *See* **adeprr aderry adeppr adepry**

adeprs drapes padres parsed rasped spader spared dares dears drape padre pards pared pares parse pears raped rapes rased reads reaps spade spare spear aped apes apse arse daps dare dear ears eras pads pard pare pars pear peas rads rape raps rase rasp read reap reds reps sard sear sera spar sped ads ape are asp dap ear era pad par pas pea per rad rap red rep res sad sap sea spa ad ae as er pa pe re

adeprss spaders spreads. *See* **aeprss adepss**

adeprst departs petards. *See* **adeprt adepst aeprst**

adeprstu pastured departs pasture petards spurted updates. *See* **adeprs adeprt adepst adepsu**

adeprsy sprayed. *See* **aeprsy adepry adepsy**

adeprt depart parted petard prated adept drape padre pared pater peart prate raped rated taped taper tared trade tread aped dare dart date dear drat pard pare part pate pear peat pert rape rapt rate read reap tape tare tarp tear trap aet ape apt are art ate dap ear eat era eta pad par pat pea per pet rad rap rat red rep ret tad tap tar tea ted ad ae at er pa pe re ta

adeprw warped drape padre pared pawed raped wader wared aped awed dare dear draw drew pard pare pear rape read reap wade ward ware warp wear wrap ape are awe dap dew ear era pad par paw pea per pew rad rap raw red rep wad wap war wed ad ae aw er pa pe re we

adepry prayed apery deary drape padre pared payed payer raped rayed ready repay aery aped dare dear dray dyer pard pare pear pray prey pyre rape read reap yard yare year ape are aye dap day dey dry dye ear era pad par pay pea per pry pya rad rap ray red rep rye yap yar yea yep ad ae ay er pa pe re ye

adeps spade aped apes apse daps pads peas sped ads ape asp dap pad pas pea sad sap sea spa ad ae as pa pe

adepss passed spades spade apses aped apes apse asps daps pads pass peas saps seas spas sped ads ape asp ass dap ess pad pas pea sad sap sea spa ad ae as pa pe

adepst pasted adept dates paste pates sated septa spade spate stead taped tapes aped apes apse daps date east eats etas pads past pate pats peas peat pest pets seat sept seta spat sped step tads tape taps teas teds ads aet ape apt asp ate dap eat eta pad pas pat pea pet sad sap sat sea set spa tad tap tea ted ad ae as at pa pe ta

adepstt spatted. *See* **adepst adeptt adestt**

adepstu updates. *See* **adepst adepsu aepstu adeptu**

adepsu paused spade pause aped apes apse daps dues pads peas sped spud spue sued upas used ads ape asp dap due pad pas pea pus sad sap sea spa sue sup use ad ae as pa pe up us

adepsy spayed spade payed aped apes apse ayes daps days deys dyes easy espy eyas pads pays peas pyas spay sped yaps yeas ads ape asp aye dap day dey dye pad pas pay pea pya sad sap say sea spa spy yap yea yep yes ad ae as ay pa pe ye

adept adept taped aped date pate peat tape aet ape apt ate dap eat eta pad pat pea pet tad tap tea ted ad ae at pa pe ta

adeptt patted adept taped aped date pate peat tape teat aet ape apt ate dap eat eta pad pat pea pet tad tap tat tea ted ad ae at pa pe ta

adeptu update adept taped taupe aped date duet pate peat tape aet ape apt ate dap due eat eta pad pat pea pet put tad tap tau tea ted tup ad ae at pa pe ta up ut

adepv paved aped deva pave ape ave dap pad pea ad ae pa pe

adepw pawed aped awed wade ape awe dap dew pad paw pea pew wad wap wed ad ae aw pa pe we

adepy payed aped ape aye dap day dey dye pad pay pea pya yap yea yep ad ae ay pa pe ye

adeqrsu squared. *See* **aeqrsu aders dersu**

adeqsttu squatted statued. *See* **adestt aesttu**

ader dare dear read are ear era rad red ad ae er re

aderrst darters retards starred traders. *See* **aerrst aderrt**

aderrsw drawers redraws rewards warders. *See* **aderrw adersw**

aderrt darter retard trader rated tared trade tread dare dart date dear drat rare rate read rear tare tear aet are art ate ear eat era err eta rad rat red ret tad tar tea ted ad ae at er re ta

aderrw drawer redraw reward warder warred rawer wader wared awed dare dear draw drew rare read rear wade ward ware wear are awe dew ear era err rad raw red wad war wed ad ae aw er re we

aderry dreary deary dryer rayed ready aery dare dear dray dyer rare read rear yard yare year are aye day dey dry dye ear era err rad ray red rye yar yea ad ae ay er re ye

aders dares dears rased reads arse dare dear ears eras rads rase read reds sard sear sera ads are ear era rad red res sad sea ad ae as er re

adersstw stewards steward wasters. *See* **aderst adersw adestw adrssw**

aderssu assured. *See* **aerssu derssu**

aderst stared trades treads aster dares darts dates dears rased rated rates reads sated stare stead tared tares tears trade tread arse arts dare dart date dear drat ears east eats eras erst etas rads rase rate rats read reds rest rets sard sear seat sera seta star tads tare tars tear teas teds tsar ads aet are art ate ear eat era eta rad rat red res ret sad sat sea set tad tar tea ted ad ae as at er re ta

aderstt started tetrads. *See* **adertt aderst adestt aerstt**

aderstux surtaxed. *See* **aderst aerstx arstux derstu**

aderstv adverts starved. *See* **adertv aerstv aderst adestv**

aderstw steward. *See* **aerstw aderst adersw adestw**

aderstww westward steward. *See* **aderst adersw adestw aerstw**

adersty strayed. *See* **aersty adesty**

adersw waders dares dears draws rased reads sawed sward swear wader wades wards wared wares wears arse awed awes dare dear dews draw drew ears eras rads rase read reds sard sear sera wade wads ward ware wars wear weds ads are awe dew ear era rad raw red res sad saw sea sew wad war was wed ad ae as aw er re we

adert rated tared trade tread dare dart date dear drat rate read tare tear aet are art ate ear eat era eta rad rat red ret tad tar tea ted ad ae at er re ta

adertt ratted tetrad rated tared tater tetra trade tread treat dare dart date dear drat rate read tare tart tear teat tret aet are art ate ear eat era eta rad rat red ret tad tar tat tea ted ad ae at er re ta

adertv advert avert rated raved tared trade trave tread aver dare dart date dear deva drat rate rave read tare tear vert aet are art ate ave ear eat era eta rad rat red ret rev tad tar tav tea ted vat vet ad ae at er re ta

aderv raved aver dare dear deva rave read are ave ear era rad red rev ad ae er re

aderw wader wared awed dare dear draw drew read wade ward ware wear are awe dew ear era rad raw red wad war wed ad ae aw er re we

adery deary rayed ready aery dare dear dray dyer read yard yare year are aye day dey dry dye ear era rad ray red rye yar yea ad ae ay er re ye

aderz razed adze dare daze dear raze read adz are ear era rad red zed ad ae er re

aderzz razzed razed adze dare daze dear raze razz read adz are ear era rad red zed ad ae er re

adesss sassed asses seas sass ads ass ess sad sea ad ae as

adest dates sated stead date east eats etas seat seta tads teas teds ads aet ate eat eta sad sat sea set tad tea ted ad ae as at ta

adestt stated tasted dates sated state stead taste teats testa date east eats etas seat seta stet tads tats teas teat teds test ads aet ate eat eta sad sat sea set tad tat tea ted ad ae as at ta

adesttu statued. *See* **aesttu adestt**

adesttw swatted. *See* **adestt adestw**

adestv staved dates devas sated saved stave stead aves date deva east eats etas save seat seta tads tavs teas teds vase vast vats vest vets ads aet ate ave eat eta sad sat sea set tad tav tea ted vat vet ad ae as at ta

adestw wasted dates sated sawed stead sweat wades waste awed awes date dews east eats etas seat seta stew swat tads teas teds wade wads wast weds west wets ads aet ate awe dew eat eta sad sat saw sea set sew tad tea ted wad was wed wet ad ae as at aw ta we

adesty stayed steady dates sated stead yeast ayes date days deys dyes east easy eats etas eyas seat seta stay tads teas teds yeas ads aet ate aye day dey dye eat eta sad sat say sea set sty tad tea ted yea yes yet ad ae as at ay ta ye

adesv devas saved aves deva save vase ads ave sad sea ad ae as

adesw sawed wades awed awes dews wade wads weds ads awe dew sad saw sea sew wad was wed ad ae as aw we

adeswy swayed sawed wades yawed awed awes ayes days dews dewy deys dyes easy eyas sway wade wads ways weds wyes yaws yeas yews ads awe aye day dew dey dye sad saw say sea sew wad was way wed wye yaw yea yes yew ad ae as aw ay we ye

adesz adzes dazes adze daze zeds ads adz sad sea zed ad ae as

adet date aet ate eat eta tad tea ted ad ae at ta

adettt tatted date teat aet ate eat eta tad tat tea ted ad ae at ta

adettv vatted date deva teat aet ate ave eat eta tad tat tav tea ted vat vet ad ae at ta

adetx taxed date axed aet axe ate eat eta tad tax tea ted ad ae at ax ex ta

adev deva ave ad ae

adevw waved awed deva wade wave ave awe dew wad wed ad ae aw we

adew awed wade awe dew wad wed ad ae aw we

adewx waxed awed axed wade awe axe dew wad wax wed ad ae aw ax ex we

adewy yawed awed dewy wade awe aye day dew dey dye wad way wed wye yaw yea yew ad ae aw ay we ye

adex axed axe ad ae ax ex

adez adze daze adz zed ad ae

adf fad ad fa

adff daff fad ad fa

adffgin daffing. *See* **adfgin**

adffhno handoff offhand

adffhnos handoffs handoff offhand. *See* **adhns dffos**

adffisst distaffs distaff. *See* **adisst affsst ffisst**

adffist distaff. *See* **adist afist affst**

adffnost standoff. *See* **dffos fnost affst**

adffor afford draff daff doff faro fora ford orad raff road ado arf dor fad far for fro oaf oar off rad rod ad do fa od of or

adffors affords. *See* **adffor adffrs**

adffr draff daff raff arf fad far rad ad fa

adffrs draffs draff raffs arfs daff fads rads raff sard ads arf fad far fas rad sad ad as fa

adffy daffy daff day fad fay ad ay fa

adfgin fading ding fain fang find gain naif aid and ani dag dig din fad fag fan fid fig fin gad gan gid gin nag ad ai an fa id if in na

adfginrt drafting darting farting indraft rafting trading. *See* **adfgin adfirt adginr adgint**

adfginrw dwarfing drawing. *See* **adfgin adginr adginw adinrw**

adfgly gadfly flag flay glad lady dag day fad fag fay fly gad gal gay lad lag lay ad ay fa la

adfhirsw dwarfish. *See* **adfrsw adhirs**

adfhlnsu handfuls handful. *See* **ahlnsu**

adfhlnu handful. *See* **ahlnu**

adfhlost holdfast. *See* **adhlos aflost ahlost**

adfhoos shadoof. *See* **dfoos dhoos fhoos**

adfhooss shadoofs shadoof. *See* **dfoos afoss dhoos**

adfillln landfill. *See* **afill afiln**

adfillnw windfall. *See* **afill afiln**

adfilmno manifold. *See* **adimno adlmno ailmno dfilno**

adfinrt indraft. *See* **adfirt adinr afint**

adfiorsv disfavor. *See* **adiors adiosv aforsv aiorsv**

adfirt adrift afrit draft drift triad adit arid daft dart dirt drat fair fart fiat frat frit raft raid rift aft aid air arf art dit fad far fat fid fir fit ita rad rat ria rid rif tad tar ad ai at fa id if it ta ti

adfllnow downfall lowland. *See* **afllow**

adflmnor landform. *See* **adlmno adlnor admnor aflmor**

adflorsu foulards foulard. *See* **adfrsu adlors aflors florsu**

adfloru foulard. *See* **aflou adlou adlru**

adflty daftly fatly daft flat flay lady aft alt day fad fat fay fly lad lay tad ad at ay fa la ta

adfoopst footpads footpad. *See* **adopst**

adfoopt footpad. *See* **adopt afoot**

adforrsw forwards forward farrows. *See* **adfrsw adorrs aforrw aorrsw**

adforrw forward. *See* **aforrw adorr adfrw**

adfprstu updrafts updraft. *See* **adfrst adfrsu**

adfprtu updraft. *See* **adfrt adfru**

adfrst drafts darts draft farts frats rafts arfs arts daft dart drat fads fart fast fats frat rads raft rats sard star tads tars tsar ads aft arf art fad far fas fat rad rat sad sat tad tar ad as at fa ta

adfrsu frauds fraud duras arfs dura fads furs rads sard sura surd surf urds ads arf fad far fas fur rad sad urd ad as fa us

adfrsw dwarfs draws dwarf sward wards arfs draw fads rads sard wads ward wars ads arf fad far fas rad raw sad saw wad war was ad as aw fa

adfrt draft daft dart drat fart frat raft aft arf art fad far fat rad rat tad tar ad at fa ta

adfrty drafty draft tardy arty daft dart drat dray fart frat fray raft tray yard aft arf art day dry fad far fat fay fry rad rat ray tad tar try yar ad at ay fa ta

adfru fraud dura arf fad far fur rad urd ad fa

adfrw dwarf draw ward arf fad far rad raw wad war ad aw fa

adfs fads ads fad fas sad ad as fa

adft daft aft fad fat tad ad at fa ta

adg dag gad ad

adgggiln daggling lagging. *See* **adgiln**

adggginr dragging grading niggard ragging. *See* **adginr agginr**

adgghno hangdog. *See* **adgno aghno**

adggilnn dangling landing angling. *See* **adgiln adilnn**

adggino goading. *See* **adgino aggin ggino**

adgginr grading niggard. *See* **adginr agginr**

adggirs gradings niggards grading gradins niggard. *See* **adginr adgnrs adinrs agginr**

adgginru guarding arguing grading niggard. *See* **adginr agginr dginru**

adghhiln highland. *See* **adghin adgiln aghiln**

adghhior highroad. *See* **adhior**

adghilnn handling handing landing. *See* **adghin adgiln adilnn aghiln**

adghilo hidalgo. *See* **adhilo adgil aghil**

adghilos hidalgos hidalgo. *See* **adhilo adhlos aghlos dhilos**

adghilty daylight. *See* **aghilt**

adghin hading ding gain hand hang hind nigh aid and ani dag dig din gad gan gid gin had hag hid hin nag nah ad ah ai an ha hi id in na

adghinn handing. *See* **adghin**

adghinor hoarding adoring hording. *See* **adghin adgino adginr adgnor**

adghinpr handgrip draping harping. *See* **adghin adginp aginpr**

adghins dashing shading. *See* **adghin adhins**

adghinss shadings dashing sandhis sashing shading. *See* **adghin adhins aginss**

adghirs dishrag. *See* **adhirs aghirs**

adghirss dishrags dishrag. *See* **adhirs adhrss aghirs**

adghittw tightwad. *See* **ghitt dhitw ghitw**

adghlnno longhand. *See* **aglnno**

adghnnsu handguns handgun unhands. *See* **adhnnu**

adghnnu handgun. *See* **adhnnu**

adghnos   sandhog. *See* **adgnos aghnos**

adghnoss   sandhogs sandhog. *See* **adgnos aghnos**

adghrstu   draughts draught. *See* **adgrsu aghrst aghstu agrstu**

adghrtu   draught. *See* **aghtu aghrt adgru**

adgiillo   gladioli. *See* **adgil**

adgiiln   dialing. *See* **adgiin agiiln dgiiln adiiln adgiln**

adgiilnt   dilating dialing digital tailing. *See* **adgiin adgiln adgint adiiln**

adgiilst   digitals digital. *See* **adilst dgiist**

adgiilt   digital. *See* **adgil dgiit adilt**

adgiimnr   admiring raiding. *See* **adgiin adginr adiimr agiimn**

adgiimnx   admixing. *See* **adgiin agiimn giimnx**

adgiin   aiding ding gain nidi aid and ani dag dig din gad gan gid gin nag ad ai an id in na

adgiinnr   draining darning ingrain raiding raining. *See* **adgiin adginr dgiinn dgiinr**

adgiinnv   invading. *See* **adgiin dgiinn**

adgiinor   radioing raiding adoring. *See* **adgiin adgino adginr adgnor**

adgiinov   avoiding voiding. *See* **adgiin adgino**

adgiinr   raiding. *See* **adgiin agiinr adginr dgiinr**

adgiinry   dairying draying raiding yarding. *See* **adgiin adginr aginry dgiinr**

adgiinsv   advising visaing. *See* **adgiin adinsv aginsv dgiins**

adgiintu   auditing. *See* **adgiin adgint**

adgiijn   jading gain ding aid and ani dag dig din gad gan gid gin jag jig nag ad ai an id in na

adgiklnr   darkling darling larding larking. *See* **adgiln adginr agiknr**

adgil   algid dial gild glad laid ail dag dig gad gal gid lad lag lid ad ai id la li

adgilln   ladling. *See* **adgiln**

adgillnu   alluding dulling ladling languid lauding lingual. *See* **adgiln agillu agilnu**

adgillny   dallying ladling allying. *See* **adgiln agilny**

adgilmor   marigold goliard. *See* **agilor dilmor**

adgiln   lading algid align gland ligan linga anil dial ding gain gild glad laid lain land ling nail aid ail and ani dag dig din gad gal gan gid gin lad lag lid nag nil ad ai an id in la li na

adgilnn   landing. *See* **adgiln adilnn**

adgilnns   landings ladings landing linsang sanding. *See* **adgiln adglns adilnn adilns**

adgilno   loading. *See* **dgilno adgino adgiln**

adgilnpp   dappling dapping lapping. *See* **adgiln agilnp**

adgilnr   darling larding. *See* **adginr**

adgilnrs   darlings darling gradins ladings larding. *See* **adgiln adginr adglns adgnrs**

adgilnrw   drawling darling drawing larding. *See* **adgiln adginr adginw adinrw**

adgilns   ladings. *See* **agilns adglns adilns adgiln**

adgilnu   languid lauding. *See* **adgiln agilnu**

adgilnzz   dazzling. *See* **adgiln adginz**

adgilopr   prodigal goliard dipolar. *See* **agilor**

adgilor   goliard. *See* **agilor adgil adilr**

adgilors   goliards girasol glorias goliard. *See* **adilrs adiors adlors agilor**

adgiluy   gaudily. *See* **adgil adily agily**

adgimmn   damming. *See* **agimn**

adgimnn   damning. *See* **agimnn**

adgimnop   pomading. *See* **adgino adimno dgimno dginop**

adgimny   digamy amid gamy maid aid aim dag dam day dig dim gad gam gay gid gym mad mag may mid yam ad ai am ay id ma mi my

adginnor   adorning adoring andiron darning droning. *See* **adgino adginr adgnor adinor**

adginnot   donating atoning. *See* **adgino adgint ainnot dginot**

adginnr   darning. *See* **adginr**

adginns   sanding. *See* **agins dgins**

adginnst   standing sanding. *See* **adgint aginst**

adginnsw   dawnings awnings dawning sanding. *See* **adginw aginnw aginsw**

adginntu   daunting. *See* **adgint ginntu**

adginnw   dawning. *See* **aginnw adginw**

adgino   ganoid danio dingo doing donga gonad agio agon ding dong gain goad ado ago aid and ani dag dig din dog don gad gan gid gin goa god ion nag nod nog ad ai an do go id in na no od on

adginoor   rigadoon adoring dragoon. *See* **adgino adginr adgnor adinor**

adginopt   adopting. *See* **adgino adgint adinpt aginpt**

adginor   adoring. *See* **adginr adgnor adgino adinor aginor**

adginos   ganoids. *See* **adinos dginos adgnos adgino**

adginoty   toadying. *See* **adgino adgint adinty dginot**

adginpp   dapping. *See* **aginp**

adginpr   draping. *See* **adginr aginpr**

adginps   spading. *See* **aginp dgins agins**

adginptu   updating. *See* **adgint adinpt adinpu aginpt**

adginr   daring gradin dinar drain grain grand grind nadir arid darn ding drag gain gird gnar grad grid grin nard raid rain rand rang rani rind ring aid air and ani dag dig din gad gan gar gid gin nag rad rag ran ria rid rig ad ai an id in na

adginrs   gradins. *See* **adginr adinrs aginrs adgnrs dginrs**

adginrsw   drawings drawing gradins inwards. *See* **adginr adginw adgnrs adinrs**

adginrt   darting trading. *See* **adginr adgint aginrt**

adginrw   drawing. *See* **adginr adinrw adginw aginrw**

adginry   draying yarding. *See* **adginr dginry aginry**

adgint   dating giant adit anti ding gain gait gnat tang ting aid and ani ant dag dig din dit gad gan gat gid gin ita nag nit tad tag tan tin ad ai an at id in it na ta ti

adginw   wading awing wigan dawn ding gain gnaw wadi wain wand wind wing aid and ani awn dag dig din gad gan gid gin nag wad wag wan wig win ad ai an aw id in na

adginz   dazing ding gain zing adz aid and ani dag dig din gad gan gid gin nag zag zig ad ai an id in na

adgirszz   gizzards gizzard izzards. *See* **adirzz**

adgirv   gravid virga arid avid diva drag gird grad grid raid vair aid air dag dig gad gar gid rad rag ria rid rig via ad ai id

adgirzz   gizzard. *See* **adirzz**

adgl   glad dag gad gal lad lag ad la

adgln   gland glad land and dag gad gal gan lad lag nag ad an la na

adglnoo   gondola. *See* **aglnoo adgno adgln**

adglnoos   gondolas gondola lagoons. *See* **adglns adgnos aglnoo aglnos**

adglnoy   daylong. *See* **agnoy aglno adgno**

adglnry   grandly. *See* **agnry adgln aglry**

adglns   glands gland glans lands slang dags gads gals glad lads lags land nags sand sang slag snag ads and dag gad gal gan gas lad lag nag sad sag sal ad an as la na

adgmnoo   goodman. *See* **agmno adgmo adgno**

adgmnor   gormand. *See* **adgnor admnor**

adgmnors   gormands gormand dragons. *See* **adgmos adgnor adgnos adgnrs**

adgmnoru   gourmand aground gormand organum. *See* **adgnor admnor admoru adnoru**

adgmo   dogma goad ado ago dag dam dog gad gam goa god mad mag moa mod mog ad am do go ma mo od om

adgmos   dogmas dogma goads ados dags dams dogs gads gams goad goas gods mags moas mods mogs sago smog soda soma ado ads ago dag dam dog dos gad gam gas goa god mad mag moa mod mog mos oms sad sag sod ad am as do go ma mo od om os so

adgnnors   grandson dragons. *See* **adgnor adgnos adgnrs adnors**

adgno   donga gonad agon dong goad ado ago and dag dog don gad gan goa god nag nod nog ad an do go na no od on

adgnoor   dragoon. *See* **adgnor dnoor**

adgnoors   dragoons dragoon dragons. *See* **adgnor adgnos adgnrs adnors**

adgnor   dragon adorn argon donga gonad grand groan organ radon agon darn dong drag gnar goad grad nard orad rand rang road roan ado ago and dag dog don dor gad gan gar goa god nag nod nog nor oar rad rag ran rod ad an do go na no od on or

adgnors   dragons. *See* **adnors agnors adgnos adgnor adgnrs**

adgnoru   aground. *See* **adnoru adgnor dgnoru**

adgnory   organdy. *See* **adgnor agnory**

adgnos   dongas gonads donga dongs goads gonad ados agon dags dogs dong dons gads goad goas gods nags naos nods nogs sago sand sang snag soda song ado ads ago and dag dog don dos gad gan gas goa god nag nod nog sad sag sod son ad an as do go na no od on os so

adgnr   grand darn drag gnar grad nard rand rang and dag gad gan gar nag rad rag ran ad an na

adgnrs   grands darns drags gnars grads grand nards rands dags darn drag gads gars gnar grad nags nard rads rags rand rang sand sang sard snag ads and dag gad gan gar gas nag rad rag ran sad sag ad an as na

adgo   goad ado ago dag dog gad goa god ad do go od

adgos   goads ados dags dogs gads goad goas gods sago soda ado ads ago dag dog dos gad gas goa god sad sag sod ad as do go od os so

adgr   drag grad dag gad gar rad rag ad

adgrs   drags grads dags drag gads gars grad rads rags sard ads dag gad gar gas rad rag sad sag ad as

adgrsu   gradus guards drags drugs duras gauds gaurs grads guard sugar dags drag drug dura gads gars gaud gaur

grad rads rags ruga rugs sard sura surd urds ads dag dug gad gar gas rad rag rug sad sag urd ad as us

adgru   guard drag drug dura gaud gaur grad ruga dag dug gad gar rad rag rug urd ad

adgs   dags gads ads dag gad gas sad sag ad as

adgsu   gauds dags gads gaud ads dag dug gad gas sad sag ad as us

adgu   gaud dag dug gad ad

adguy   gaudy gaud dag day dug gad gay guy ad ay

adh   had ad ah ha

adhhiprs   hardship. *See* **adhips adhirs adiprs ahiprs**

adhhosw   howdahs. *See* **adhhow adhosw**

adhhow   howdah whoa dhow ado had hah haw hod how wad who ad ah aw do ha ho od oh ow

adhiiks   dashiki. *See* **adhiks**

adhiinop   ophidian. *See* **adhip adino ainop**

adhij   hadji jihad hadj haji aid had hid ad ah ai ha hi id

adhijs   hadjis jadish jihads hadji hajis jihad aids dais dash dish hadj haji said shad ads aid ash had has hid his ids sad ad ah ai as ha hi id is sh si

adhik   khadi kadi haik aid had hid kid ad ah ai ha hi id ka

adhiks   khadis khadi haiks aids dais dash dish disk haik kadi kids said saki shad skid ads aid ask had has hid his ids kas kid sad ski ad ah ai as ha hi id is ka sh si

adhilmo   halidom. *See* **adhilo adlmo**

adhilmos   halidoms halidom. *See* **adhilo adhlos adilms adlmos**

adhilny   handily. *See* **adily adhny ailny**

adhilo   haloid ahold dial hail halo hold idol laid load ado aid ail had hid hod lad lid oil old ad ah ai do ha hi ho id la li lo od oh

adhilop   haploid. *See* **adhilo adhip ahilp**

adhilops   haploids shipload haploid. *See* **adhilo adhips adhlos adilps**

adhiloy   holidays holiday hyaloid shadily. *See* **adhilo adhlos ahlosy dhilos**

adhiloy   holiday hyaloid. *See* **adhilo adily diloy**

adhilpsy   ladyship apishly display shadily sylphid. *See* **adhips adilps ahilps**

adhilry   hardily. *See* **adhlry adilry**

adhilsy   shadily. *See* **adily adisy adils**

adhimnos   admonish daimons domains. *See* **adhins adimno adinos admnos**

adhimopp   amphipod. *See* **adhip hiopp**

adhimr   dirham ihram amid amir arid dram hair hard harm maid raid rami aid aim air arm dam dim had ham hid

him mad mar mid mir rad rah ram ria rid rim ad ah ai am ha hi id ma mi

adhimrs   dirhams. *See* **adhimr adimrs ahimrs adhirs**

adhinps   dishpan. *See* **adhins adhips**

adhinpss   dishpans dishpan sandhis. *See* **adhins adhips ahipss**

adhinpsu   dauphins dishpan dauphin. *See* **adhins adhips adinpu adinsu**

adhinpu   dauphin. *See* **adinpu adhip**

adhins   sandhi hands hinds aids dais dash dins dish hand hind hins said sain sand shad shin ads aid and ani ash din had has hid hin his ids nah sad sin ad ah ai an as ha hi id in is na sh si

adhinss   sandhis. *See* **adhins adnss hinss**

adhinsst   standish sandhis. *See* **adhins adisst adnsst ahnsst**

adhior   hairdo hoard radio arid hair hard hoar hora orad raid road ado aid air dor had hid hod oar rad rah rho ria rid rod ad ah ai do ha hi ho id od oh or

adhiors   hairdos. *See* **adhior adhors adiors**

adhip   aphid paid aid dap dip had hap hid hip pad pah ad ah ai ha hi id pa pi

adhiprsy   shipyard. *See* **adhips adhirs adhrsy adiprs**

adhips   aphids aphid aphis apish sapid spahi aids dais daps dash dips dish haps hasp hips pads paid pish said shad ship ads aid ash asp dap dip had hap has hid hip his ids pad pah pas sad sap sip spa ad ah ai as ha hi id is pa pi sh si

adhirs   radish hairs hards raids shard aids airs arid dais dash dish hair hard rads rahs raid rash rias rids said sard sari shad ads aid air ash had has hid his ids rad rah ria rid sad sir ad ah ai as ha hi id is sh si

adhirtww   withdraw. *See* **ahirtw**

adhj   hadj had ad ah ha

adhknorw   handwork. *See* **adnorw**

adhlnouw   downhaul. *See* **adlnou**

adhlo   ahold halo hold load ado had hod lad old ad ah do ha ho la lo od oh

adhlos   aholds ahold holds loads shoal ados also dash halo hods hold lads lash load shad shod soda sold ado ads ash dos had has hod lad los ohs old sad sal sod sol ad ah as do ha ho la lo od oh os sh so

adhlry   hardly hardy hydra lardy aryl dray hard harl hyla lady lard yard day dry had hay lad lar lay rad rah ray yah yar ad ah ay ha la

adhmnoo   manhood. *See* **admno**

adhn   hand and had nah ad ah an ha na

adhnnsu   unhands. *See* **adhnnu adhns adhsu**

adhnnu unhand hand and dun had nah nun ad ah an ha na nu

adhnostu handouts thousand handout astound. *See* **adnstu ahnstu dhnosu dnostu**

adhnotu handout. *See* **adntu dnotu ahntu**

adhnrsty hydrants hydrant. *See* **adhrsy adnrst adnsty ahnsty**

adhnrty hydrant. *See* **adhny adhry adnry**

adhns hands dash hand sand shad ads and ash had has nah sad ad ah an as ha na sh

adhny handy hand and any day had hay nah nay yah ad ah an ay ha na

adhoorsw roadshow. *See* **adhors adhosw ahoosw**

adhoprst hardtops hardtop. *See* **adhors adopst ahopst ahorst**

adhoprsy rhapsody. *See* **adhors adhrsy adopry dhorsy**

adhoprt hardtop. *See* **adopt aoprt adhor**

adhor hoard hard hoar hora orad road ado dor had hod oar rad rah rho rod ad ah do ha ho od oh or

adhors hoards dorsa hards hoard horas roads shard ados dash hard hoar hods hora oars orad rads rahs rash rhos road rods sard shad shod soar soda sora ado ads ash dor dos had has hod oar ohs rad rah rho rod sad sod ad ah as do ha ho od oh or os sh so

adhossw shadows. *See* **adhosw ahssw hossw**

adhosw shadow dhows ados dash dhow haws hods shad shaw shod show soda wads wash whoa ado ads ash dos had has haw hod how ohs sad saw sod sow wad was who ad ah as aw do ha ho od oh os ow sh so

adhoswy shadowy. *See* **adhosw dhowy adhsy**

adhprsu purdahs. *See* **adhpru adrsu adhrs**

adhpru purdah dura hard harp pard dap had hap hup pad pah par rad rah rap urd ad ah ha pa up

adhr hard had rad rah ad ah ha

adhrs hards shard dash hard rads rahs rash sard shad ads ash had has rad rah sad ad ah as ha sh

adhrss shards hards shard dash hard rads rahs rash sard sash shad ads ash ass had has rad rah sad ad ah as ha sh

adhrsy hydras drays hards hardy hydra shady shard yards ashy dash days dray hard hays rads rahs rash rays sard shad shay yard ads ash day dry had has hay rad rah ray sad say shy yah yar ad ah as ay ha sh

adhry hardy hydra dray hard yard day dry had hay rad rah ray yah yar ad ah ay ha

adhs dash shad ads ash had has sad ad ah as ha sh

adhssu sadhus sadhu dash sash shad suds ads ash ass had has sad ad ah as ha sh us

adhst hadst dash hast hats shad tads ads ash had has hat sad sat tad ad ah as at ha sh ta

adhsu sadhu dash shad ads ash had has sad ad ah as ha sh us

adhsy shady ashy dash days hays shad shay ads ash day had has hay sad say shy yah ad ah as ay ha sh

adi aid ad ai id

adiiiqru daiquiri. *See* **adiir**

adiiklmm milkmaid. *See* **iiklm**

adiiko aikido kadi ado aid kid koa oak ad ai do id ka od

adiikos aikidos. *See* **adiiko adios**

adiillmr milliard. *See* **adiimr**

adiilluv diluvial. *See* **diilv adilv aillv**

adiilms mislaid. *See* **adilms**

adiiln inlaid anil dial ilia laid lain land nail nidi aid ail and ani din lad lid nil ad ai an id in la li na

adiilnot dilation. *See* **adiiln adlnot ailnot**

adiilnsv invalids invalid. *See* **adiiln adilns adinsv ailnsv**

adiilnty daintily. *See* **adiiln adinty ailnty**

adiilnv invalid. *See* **adiiln ailnv adinv**

adiilssy dialysis. *See* **adily adisy adils**

adiiltvy validity avidity. *See* **adilvy**

adiimr midair radii amid amir arid dram maid raid rami aid aim air arm dam dim mad mar mid mir rad ram ria rid rim ad ai am id ma mi

adiinotu audition. *See* **adiou aditu adino**

adiinsst distains distain. *See* **adisst adnsst aiinst ainsst**

adiinst distain. *See* **aiinst adist adnst**

adiiprty rapidity aridity. *See* **aiprty**

adiipsty sapidity. *See* **adist adisy disty**

adiir radii arid raid aid air rad ria rid ad ai id

adiirsst diarists diarist. *See* **adirst adisst airsst**

adiirst diarist. *See* **adirst adiir**

adiirty aridity. *See* **adiry dirty adiir**

adiitvy avidity. *See* **aditv**

adijms masjid maids aids aims amid dais dams dims jams maid said ads aid aim dam dim ids jam mad mid mis sad ad ai am as id is ma mi si

adijmss masjids. *See* **adijss adijms adimss**

adijno adjoin danio join ado aid and ani din don ion nod ad ai an do id in jo na no od on

adijnos adjoins. *See* **adijno adinos**

adijss jassid aids dais said ads aid ass ids sad sis ad ai as id is si

adijsss jassids. *See* **adijss**

adik kadi aid kid ad ai id ka

adiklos odalisk. *See* **adios adils dilos**

adikloss odalisks odalisk. *See* **adklss adloss akloss diloss**

adikmnn mankind. *No 6s or 5s*

adikmo mikado amid amok kadi kami maid mako ado aid aim dam dim kid koa mad mid moa mod oak ad ai am do id ka ma mi mo od om

adikmos mikados. *See* **adikmo adios adims**

adiknnst inkstand. *See* **adist ainst dikns**

adiknp kidnap akin dank dink kadi kina kind knap nipa paid pain pika pink aid and ani dap din dip ink kid kin kip nap nip pad pan pin ad ai an id in ka na pa pi

adiknps kidnaps. *See* **adiknp dikns aknps**

adil dial laid aid ail lad lid ad ai id la li

adilllpy pallidly. *See* **adillp**

adillmnr mandrill mandril. *See* **ailmnr**

adillmsy dismally. *See* **adilms adilmy adimsy ailmsy**

adillnps landslip. *See* **adillp adilns adilps ailnps**

adillosw disallow. *See* **allosw**

adillosy disloyal solidly. *See* **allosy dillsy**

adillp pallid plaid dial dill laid paid pail pall pill aid ail all alp dap dip ill lad lap lid lip pad pal ad ai id la li pa pi

adillsty distally saltily. *See* **adilst allsty dillsy illsty**

adilmnno mandolin nominal. *See* **adilnn adimno adlmno ailmno**

adilmnr mandril. *See* **ailmnr adinr adilr**

adilmnrs mandrils mandril marlins. *See* **adilms adilns adilrs adimrs**

adilmnu maudlin. *See* **ailmnu**

adilmop diploma. *See* **ailmop adlmo adilp**

adilmops diplomas diploma lipomas. *See* **adilms adilps adlmos ailmop**

adilmopt diplomat diploma optimal. *See* **adimot ailmop**

adilmopy olympiad diploma. *See* **adilmy adimoy adlmpy ailmop**

adilmoty modality. *See* **adilmy adimot adimoy**

adilms dismal dials maids mails salmi aids ails aims alms amid dais dams dial dims lads laid lams lids maid mail mild mils said sail slam slid slim ads aid ail aim dam dim ids lad lam lid mad mid mil mis sad sal ad ai am as id is la li ma mi si

adilmssu dualisms dualism. *See* **adilms adimss ailmss**

adilmsu   dualism. *See* **adilms almsu adlsu**

adilmy   milady daily dimly madly amid amyl dial idly idyl lady laid limy maid mail mild aid ail aim dam day dim lad lam lay lid mad may mid mil yam ad ai am ay id la li ma mi my

adilnn   inland anil dial laid lain land linn nail aid ail and ani din inn lad lid nil ad ai an id in la li na

adilnor   ordinal. *See* **adinor adlnor**

adilnors   ordinals inroads lardons ordains ordinal sadiron. *See* **adilns adilrs adinor adinos**

adilnrwy   inwardly. *See* **adilry adinrw ailrwy**

adilns   island anils dials lands nails slain snail aids ails anil dais dial dins lads laid lain land lids nail nils said sail sain sand slid ads aid ail and ani din ids lad lid nil sad sal sin ad ai an as id in is la li na si

adilnss   islands. *See* **adilns ailnss**

adilnssu   sundials islands sundial. *See* **adilns adinsu ailnss**

adilnssw   windlass islands. *See* **adilns ailnss ainssw**

adilnsu   sundial. *See* **adilns adinsu**

adilooz   zooidal. *See* **diooz**

adilopr   dipolar. *See* **adilr alopr adilp**

adilopss   disposal. *See* **adilps adloss diloss ilopss**

adilorst   dilators dilator rialtos tailors. *See* **adilrs adilst adiors adiort**

adilort   dilator. *See* **adiort ailort**

adilorty   adroitly dilatory idolatry dilator tardily. *See* **adilry adiort ailort**

adilosty   sodality styloid. *See* **adilst adosty dilost**

adilp   plaid dial laid paid pail aid ail alp dap dip lad lap lid lip pad pal ad ai id la li pa pi

adilpry   rapidly. *See* **adilry adilp adipr**

adilps   plaids dials pails plaid sapid aids ails alps dais daps dial dips lads laid laps lids lips lisp pads paid pail pals said sail slap slid slip ads aid ail alp asp dap dip ids lad lap lid lip pad pal pas sad sal sap sip spa ad ai as id is la li pa pi si

adilpsst   plastids plastid. *See* **adilps adilst adisst ailpst**

adilpssy   displays display. *See* **adilps alpssy**

adilpst   plastid. *See* **adilst adilps ailpst**

adilpstu   plaudits dualist plastid plaudit. *See* **adilps adilst adistu adlstu**

adilpsy   display. *See* **adilps adily adisy**

adilptu   plaudit. *See* **adltu aditu ailpu**

adilpvy   vapidly. *See* **adilvy adilp adipv**

adilqsu   squalid. *See* **ailqsu adils adlsu**

adilr   laird arid aril dial dirl laid lair lard liar lira raid rail rial aid ail air lad lar lid rad ria rid ad ai id la li

adilrs   lairds arils dials dirls laird lairs lards liars liras raids rails rials aids ails airs arid aril dais dial dirl lads laid lair lard liar lids lira rads raid rail rial rias rids said sail sard sari slid ads aid ail air ids lad lar lid rad ria rid sad sal sir ad ai as id is la li si

adilrsz   lizards. *See* **adilrs adilrz**

adilrty   tardily. *See* **adilry dirty ailty**

adilry   aridly daily dairy diary laird lardy riyal airy arid aril aryl dial dirl dray idly idyl lady laid lair lard liar lira raid rail rial yard aid ail air day dry lad lar lay lid rad ray ria rid yar ad ai ay id la li

adilrz   lizard laird arid aril dial dirl laid lair lard liar lira raid rail rial adz aid ail air lad lar lid rad ria rid ad ai id la li

adils   dials aids ails dais dial lads laid lids said sail slid ads aid ail ids lad lid sad sal ad ai as id is la li si

adilsstu   dualists dualist. *See* **adilst adisst adistu adlstu**

adilst   distal adits dials staid tails tidal tsadi adit aids ails alit alts dais dial dits lads laid last lids list said sail salt silt slat slid slit tads tail tali tils ads aid ail alt dit ids ita its lad lid lit sad sal sat sit tad til ad ai as at id is it la li si ta ti

adilstu   dualist. *See* **adlstu adistu adilst**

adilt   tidal adit alit dial laid tail tali aid ail alt dit ita lad lid lit tad til ad ai at id it la li ta ti

adiltuy   duality. *See* **adltu aditu adily**

adilv   valid avid dial diva laid vail vial aid ail lad lid via ad ai id la li

adilvy   avidly valid daily avid dial diva idly idyl lady laid vail vial aid ail day ivy lad lay lid via ad ai ay id la li

adily   daily dial idly idyl lady laid aid ail day lad lay lid ad ai ay id la li

adim   amid maid aid aim dam dim mad mid ad ai am id ma mi

adimmnos   nomadism daimons domains. *See* **adimno adinos admnos aimmos**

adimnnsy   dynamism. *See* **adimsy**

adimnnot   dominant tinman.. *See* **aimnno ainnot adimno adimot**

adimno   daimon domain danio monad nomad amid damn maid main mina mind moan noma ado aid aim and ani dam dim din don ion mad man mid moa mod mon nim nod ad ai am an do id in ma mi mo na no od om on

adimnos   daimons domains. *See* **adimno admnos adinos**

adimopry   myriapod pyramid. *See* **adimoy adimry adopry aimopy**

adimorr   mirador. *See* **admorr adior**

adimorrs   miradors mirador ramrods. *See* **adimrs adiors adirrs admorr**

adimosst   mastoids diatoms mastoid. *See* **adimot adimss adimst adisst**

adimost   diatoms mastoid. *See* **adimst adimot**

adimostt   mattoids atomist diatoms mastoid mattoid. *See* **adimot adimst diostt**

adimosy   daimyos. *See* **adimoy adimsy**

adimot   diatom admit adit amid atom doit iota maid moat omit toad ado aid aim dam dim dit dot ita mad mat mid moa mod mot oat tad tam tod tom ad ai am at do id it ma mi mo od om ta ti to

adimott   mattoid. *See* **adimot diott**

adimoy   daimyo amid maid mayo ado aid aim dam day dim mad may mid moa mod yam yod ad ai am ay do id ma mi mo my od om oy

adimprsy   pyramids pyramid myriads. *See* **adimrs adimry adimsy adiprs**

adimpry   pyramid. *See* **adimry adipr**

adimrs   disarm amirs drams maids raids simar aids aims airs amid amir arid arms dais dams dims dram maid mirs rads raid rami rams rias rids rims said sard sari ads aid aim air arm dam dim ids mad mar mid mir mis rad ram ria rid rim sad sir ad ai am as id is ma mi si

adimrss   disarms. *See* **adimrs adimss aimrss**

adimrsu   radiums. *See* **adimrs adimru adirsu**

adimrsy   myriads. *See* **adimrs adimsy adimry**

adimru   radium amid amir arid dram drum dura maid maud raid rami aid aim air arm dam dim mad mar mid mir mud rad ram ria rid rim rum urd ad ai am id ma mi mu um

adimry   myriad dairy diary airy amid amir arid army dram dray maid miry raid rami rimy yard aid aim air arm dam day dim dry mad mar may mid mir rad ram ray ria rid rim yam yar ad ai am ay id ma mi my

adims   maids aids amid dais dams dims maid said ads aid aim dam dim ids mad mid mis sad ad ai am as id is ma mi si

adimss   sadism maids amiss aids aims amid dais dams dims maid mass miss said ads aid aim ass dam dim ids mad mid mis sad sis ad ai am as id is ma mi si

adimsss   sadisms. *See* **adimss**

adimsstu   stadiums stadium. *See* **adimss adimst adisst adistu**

adimssy dismays. *See* **adimsy dimssy adimss**

adimst admits amidst adits admit maids midst staid tsadi adit aids aims amid dais dams dims dits maid mast mats mist said tads tams ads aid aim dam dim dit ids ita its mad mat mid mis sad sat sit tad tam ad ai am as at id is it ma mi si ta ti

adimstu stadium. *See* **adimst adistu aimstu admstu**

adimsy dismay daisy maids mysid sayid aids aims amid dais dams days dims maid said yams ads aid aim dam day dim ids mad may mid mis sad say yam ad ai am as ay id is ma mi my si

adimt admit adit amid maid aid aim dam dim dit ita mad mat mid tad tam ad ai am at id it ma mi ta ti

adimwy midway amid maid wadi aid aim dam day dim mad maw may mid wad way yam yaw ad ai am aw ay id ma mi my

adimx admix amid maid maxi aid aim dam dim mad mid mix ad ai am ax id ma mi xi

adinnoot donation. *See* **ainnot innoot**

adinnor andiron. *See* **adinor**

adinnors andirons andiron innards inroads ordains sadiron. *See* **adinor adinos adinrs adiors**

adinnory nondairy andiron. *See* **adinor**

adinnrs innards. *See* **adinrs**

adinnrw indrawn. *See* **adinrw**

adino danio ado aid and ani din don ion nod ad ai an do id in na no od on

adinoopt adoption. *See* **adinpt inoopt**

adinoott dotation. *See* **adino diott aintt**

adinopp oppidan. *See* **adino ainop**

adinopps oppidans oppidan. *See* **adinos ainops**

adinopr padroni. *See* **adinor adnopr**

adinoprr raindrop padroni airdrop. *See* **adinor adnopr**

adinor inroad ordain adorn danio dinar drain nadir noria radio radon arid darn iron nard orad raid rain rand rani rind road roan ado aid air and ani din don dor ion nod nor oar rad ran ria rid rod ad ai an do id in na no od on or

adinorry ordinary. *See* **adinor**

adinors inroads ordains sadiron. *See* **adnors adinos adinrs adinor ainors**

adinorss sadirons inroads ordains sadiron. *See* **adinor adinos adinrs adiors**

adinorst intrados inroads ordains rations sadiron. *See* **adinor adinos adinrs adiors**

adinorsu dinosaur inroads ordains sadiron. *See* **adinor adinos adinrs adinsu**

adinortu duration auditor rainout rotunda. *See* **adinor adiort adnoru adnrtu**

adinos danios danio adios ados aids dais dins dons ions naos nods said sain sand soda ado ads aid and ani din don dos ids ion nod sad sin sod son ad ai an as do id in is na no od on os si so

adinotx oxidant. *See* **adino inotx**

adinpst pandits. *See* **ainpst adinpt**

adinpt pandit inapt paint adit anti nipa paid pain pant pint pita aid and ani ant apt dap din dip dit ita nap nip nit pad pan pat pin pit tad tan tap tin tip ad ai an at id in it na pa pi ta ti

adinpu unpaid nipa paid pain aid and ani dap din dip dun nap nip pad pan pin pun ad ai an id in na nu pa pi up

adinr dinar drain nadir arid darn nard raid rain rand rani rind aid air and ani din rad ran ria rid ad ai an id in na

adinrs dinars drains nadirs darns dinar drain nadir nards naris raids rains rands ranis rinds aids airs arid dais darn dins nard rads raid rain rand rani rias rids rind said sain sand sard sari ads aid air and ani din ids rad ran ria rid sad sin sir ad ai an as id in is na si

adinrsw inwards. *See* **adinrs adinrw**

adinrw inward dinar drain drawn nadir arid darn dawn draw nard raid rain rand rani rind wadi wain wand ward warn wind aid air and ani awn din rad ran raw ria rid wad wan war win ad ai an aw id in na

adinstt distant. *See* **ainstt**

adinsu unsaid nidus aids anus dais dins duns said sain sand ads aid and ani din dun ids sad sin sun ad ai an as id in is na nu si us

adinsv divans viands divan divas savin viand vinas aids avid dais dins diva said sain sand vain vans vina visa ads aid and ani din ids sad sin van via ad ai an as id in is na si

adintty dittany. *See* **adinty ditty antty**

adinty dainty adit anti ayin tidy tiny aid and ani ant any day din dit ita nay nit tad tan tin yin ad ai an at ay id in it na ta ti

adinv divan viand avid diva vain vina aid and ani din van via ad ai an id in na

adioppst postpaid. *See* **adopst aiopst aippst**

adioprr airdrop. *See* **adorr ioprr adior**

adioprrs airdrops airdrop. *See* **adiors adiprs adirrs adorrs**

adioprst parotids parotid. *See* **adiors adiort adiprs adirst**

adioprt parotid. *See* **adiort dioprt**

adior radio arid orad raid road ado aid air dor oar rad ria rid rod ad ai do id od or

adiors radios adios dorsa radio raids roads ados aids airs arid dais oars orad rads raid rias rids road rods said sard sari soar soda sora sori ado ads aid air dor dos ids oar rad ria rid rod sad sir sod ad ai as do id is od or os si so

adiorstu auditors auditor. *See* **adiors adiort adirst adirsu**

adiorsvy advisory. *See* **adiors adiosv aiorsv aorsvy**

adiort adroit droit radio ratio triad adit arid dart dirt doit drat iota orad raid riot road rota taro tiro toad tora tori trio trod ado aid air art dit dor dot ita oar oat ort rad rat ria rid rod rot tad tar tod tor ad ai at do id it od or ta ti to

adiortu auditor. *See* **adiort adiou aditu**

adiortuy auditory auditor. *See* **adiort**

adios adios ados aids dais said soda ado ads aid dos ids sad sod ad ai as do id is od os si so

adiossvw disavows disavow. *See* **adiosv**

adiosv avoids adios avoid divas voids ados aids avid dais diva said soda visa void ado ads aid dos ids ova sad sod via ad ai as do id is od os si so

adiosvw disavow. *See* **adiosv aosvw adisw**

adiou audio ado aid duo oud udo ad ai do id od

adiov avoid avid diva void ado aid ova via ad ai do id od

adip paid aid dap dip pad ad ai id pa pi

adipr rapid arid drip paid pair pard raid aid air dap dip pad par rad rap ria rid rip ad ai id pa pi

adiprs rapids drips pairs pards raids rapid sapid aids airs arid dais daps dips drip pads paid pair pard pars rads raid raps rasp rias rids rips said sard sari spar ads aid air asp dap dip ids pad par pas rad rap ria rid rip sad sap sip sir spa ad ai as id is pa pi si

adips sapid aids dais daps dips pads paid said ads aid asp dap dip ids pad pas sad sap sip spa ad ai as id is pa pi si

adipsx spadix sapid aids axis dais daps dips pads paid said ads aid asp dap dip ids pad pas pax pix sad sap sax sip six spa ad ai as ax id is pa pi si xi

adipv vapid avid diva paid aid dap dip pad via ad ai id pa pi

adir arid raid aid air rad ria rid ad ai id

adirrs sirdar arris raids aids airs arid dais rads raid rias rids said sard sari ads aid air ids rad ria rid sad sir ad ai as id is si

adirrss sirdars. *See* **adirrs airss**

adirrwyz wizardry. *See* **adirwz**

adirs raids aids airs arid dais rads raid rias rids said sard sari ads aid air ids rad ria rid sad sir ad ai as id si si

adirst triads adits astir darts raids sitar staid stair stria tarsi triad tsadi adit aids airs arid arts dais dart dirt dits drat rads raid rats rias rids said sard sari star stir tads tars tsar ads aid air art dit ids ita its rad rat ria rid sad sat sir sit tad tar ad ai as at id is it si ta ti

adirsu radius duras raids aids airs arid dais dura rads raid rias rids said sard sari sura surd urds ads aid air ids rad ria rid sad sir urd ad ai as id is si us

adirsvz vizards. *See* **adirvz adirs adisv**

adirswz wizards. *See* **adirwz adirs adrsw**

adirszz izzards. *See* **adirzz adirs airsz**

adirt triad adit arid dart dirt drat raid aid air art dit ita rad rat ria rid tad tar ad ai at id it ta ti

adirvz vizard arid avid diva raid vair adz aid air rad ria rid via ad ai id

adirwz wizard arid draw raid wadi ward adz aid air rad raw ria rid wad war ad ai aw id

adirx radix arid raid aid air rad ria rid ad ai ax id xi

adiry dairy diary airy arid dray raid yard aid air day dry rad ray ria rid yar ad ai ay id

adirzz izzard arid raid razz adz aid air rad ria rid ad ai id

adis aids dais said ads aid ids sad ad ai as id is si

adissst sadists. *See* **aissst adisst**

adisst sadist adits staid tsadi adit aids dais dits said sits tads tass ads aid ass dit ids ita its sad sat sis sit tad ad ai as at id is it si ta ti

adissyy sayyids. *See* **adisyy**

adist adits staid tsadi adit aids dais dits said tads ads aid dit ids ita its sad sat sit tad ad ai as at id is it si ta ti

adistu audits adits adust audit staid tsadi adit aids dais dits dust said stud suit tads tuis ads aid dit ids ita its sad sat sit tad tau tui ad ai as at id is it si ta ti us ut

adistv davits adits davit divas staid tsadi vista adit aids avid dais dits diva said tads tavs vast vats visa ads aid dit ids ita its sad sat sit tad tav vat via ad ai as at id is it si ta ti

adisv divas aids avid dais diva said visa ads aid ids sad via ad ai as id is si

adisw wadis aids dais said wadi wads ads aid ids sad saw wad was wis ad ai as aw id is si

adisy daisy sayid aids dais days said ads aid day ids sad say ad ai as ay id is si

adisyy sayyid daisy sayid aids dais days said ads aid day ids sad say yay ad ai as ay id is si

adit adit aid dit ita tad ad ai at id it ta ti

aditu audit adit aid dit ita tad tau tui ad ai at id it ta ti ut

aditv davit adit avid diva aid dit ita tad tav vat via ad ai at id it ta ti

adiv avid diva via ad ai id

adiw wadi aid wad ad ai aw id

adjknruy junkyard. *See* **adknr dknru jknuy**

adjkosu judokas. *See* **adjkou dkosu**

adjkou judoka judo ado auk duo koa oak oud udo ad do jo ka od

adjnorsu adjourns adjourn. *See* **adnors adnoru dnorsu**

adjnoru adjourn. *See* **adnoru**

adjorstu adjustor. *See* **adjstu ajrstu**

adjsstu adjusts. *See* **adjstu dsstu jsstu**

adjstu adjust adust dust just juts stud tads ads jus jut sad sat tad tau ad as at ta us ut

adklny dankly lanky dank lady laky land lank yank and any day kal lad lay nay yak ad an ay ka la na

adkloorw workload. *See* **dloor adlrw akoor**

adklry darkly lardy larky aryl dark dray lady laky lard lark yard ark day dry kal lad lar lay rad ray yak yar ad ay ka la

adkls skald lads ads ask kal kas lad sad sal ad as ka la

adklss skalds skald asks lads lass sals ads ask ass kal kas lad sad sal ad as ka la

adklsy alkyds sadly skald days lads lady laky lays slay yaks ads ask day kal kas lad lay sad sal say sky sly yak ad as ay ka la

adkmoorr darkroom. *See* **admorr**

adkn dank and ad an ka na

adknr drank dank dark darn knar nard nark rand rank and ark rad ran ad an ka na

adkoorrw roadwork. *See* **adorr aorrw akoor**

adkorrwy yardwork workday. *See* **aorrwy**

adkorswy workdays workday skyward. *See* **dorswy**

adkorwy workday. *See* **dkory dorwy**

adkosv vodkas vodka ados koas kvas oaks soak soda ado ads ask dos kas koa kos oak ova sad sod ad as do ka od os so

adkov vodka ado koa oak ova ad do ka od

adkr dark rad ark ad ka

adkrssw skywards skyward. *See* **adrssw**

adkrswy skyward. *See* **adrsw adrsy**

adl lad ad la

adllmoy modally. *See* **alloy adlly dlloy**

adllnosw lowlands lowland. *See* **allnos allosw**

adllnow lowland. *See* **allow allno adlno**

adllopr pollard. *See* **adllor allopr**

adlloprs pollards dollars pallors pollard. *See* **adllor adlors allopr aloprs**

adllor dollar droll doll lard load lord olla orad oral road roll ado all dor lad lar oar old rad rod ad do la lo od or

adllors dollars. *See* **adllor adlors dllors**

adllorsy dorsally dollars. *See* **adllor adlors allory allosy**

adllrswy drywalls drywall. *See* **adlrsw**

adllrwy drywall. *See* **adlly adlrw adlry**

adlly dally lady ally all day lad lay ad ay la

adlmno almond dolman dolma modal monad nodal nomad damn land load loam loan moan mola mold noma ado and dam don lad lam mad man moa mod mon nod old ad am an do la lo ma mo na no od om on

adlmnoor moorland doorman lardoon malodor. *See* **adlmno adlnor admnor almnor**

adlmnory randomly. *See* **adlmno adlnor admnor admnoy**

adlmnos almonds. *See* **adlmno admnos adlmos almnos**

adlmo dolma modal load loam mola mold ado dam lad lam mad moa mod old ad am do la lo ma mo od om

adlmoor malodor. *See* **adlmo dloor almor**

adlmoors malodors malodor. *See* **adlmos adlors almoos almors**

adlmopsy psalmody. *See* **adlmos adlmpy**

adlmoru modular. *See* **admoru adlou adlmo**

adlmos dolmas modals dolma loads loams modal molas molds ados alms also dams lads lams load loam moas mods mola mold slam soda sold soma ado ads dam dos lad lam los mad moa mod mos old oms sad sal sod sol ad am as do la lo ma mo od om os so

adlmpy damply amply madly palmy amyl damp lady lamp palm paly play alp amp dam dap day lad lam lap lay mad map may pad pal pay ply pya yam yap ad am ay la ma my pa

adlmy madly lady amyl dam day lad lam lay mad may yam ad am ay la ma my

adln land lad and ad an la na

adlnnttuu undulant. *See* **adltu alnnu adntu**

adlno nodal land load loan ado and don lad nod old ad an do la lo na no od on

adlnoor lardoon. *See* **adlnor dloor dnoor**

adlnoors lardoons lardoon lardons. *See* **adlnor adlors adnors alnoos**

adlnopru pauldron nodular poulard. *See* **adlnor adlnou adlnpu adlnru**

adlnopwy downplay. *See* **dnowy alnwy adlno**

adlnor lardon adorn nodal radon darn land lard load loan lord lorn nard orad oral rand road roan ado and don dor lad lar nod nor oar old rad ran rod ad an do la lo na no od on or

adlnors lardons. *See* **adnors adlors adlnor alnors**

adlnoru nodular. *See* **adnoru adlnor adlnru adlnou**

adlnosst sandlots daltons sandlot. *See* **adlnot adloss adnsst alnoss**

adlnost daltons sandlot. *See* **adlnot alnost**

adlnostu outlands astound daltons outland sandlot unloads. *See* **adlnot adlnou adlstu adnstu**

adlnosu unloads. *See* **adlnou adlsu adlns**

adlnosy synodal. *See* **adlns adlos alnos**

adlnot dalton dotal nodal talon tonal alto dolt land load loan lota nota toad tola told ado alt and ant don dot lad lot nod not oat old tad tan tod ton ad an at do la lo na no od on ta to

adlnotu outland. *See* **adlnot adlnou dlnotu**

adlnou unload nodal aloud auld dual land laud load loan loud ulna undo ado and don dun duo lad nod old oud udo ad an do la lo na no nu od on

adlnpsu uplands. *See* **adlnpu adlsu adlns**

adlnpu upland auld dual land laud plan ulna alp and dap dun lad lap nap pad pal pan pul pun ad an la na nu pa up

adlnrsu lurdans. *See* **adlnru adnrs adlsu**

adlnru lurdan dural lunar auld darn dual dura land lard laud nard rand ulna and dun lad lar rad ran run urd urn ad an la na nu

adlnruy laundry. *See* **adlnru adlry adnry**

adlns lands lads land sand ads and lad sad sal ad an as la na

adlo load ado lad old ad do la lo od

adloprsu poulards poulard parlous. *See* **adlors aloprs alprsu**

adlopru poulard. *See* **adlou adlru alopr**

adloprwy wordplay. *See* **adopry**

adlorrsw warlords warlord. *See* **adorrs aorrsw adlors adlrsw**

adlorrw warlord. *See* **adorr aorrsw adlrw**

adlors dorsal dorsa lards loads lords orals roads solar ados also lads lard load lord oars orad oral rads road rods sard soar soda sold sora ado ads dor

dos lad lar los oar old rad rod sad sal sod sol ad as do la lo od or os so

adlorss dorsals. *See* **adlors adloss**

adlos loads ados also lads load soda sold ado ads dos lad los old sad sal sod sol ad as do la lo od os so

adloss dossal lasso loads sodas ados also doss lads lass load loss ossa sals soda sods sold sols ado ads ass dos lad los old sad sal sod sol ad as do la lo od os so

adlot dotal alto dolt load lota toad tola told ado alt dot lad lot oat old tad tod ad at do la lo od ta to

adlou aloud auld dual laud load loud ado duo lad old oud udo ad do la lo od

adlpruwy upwardly. *See* **adpruw alpruw**

adlr lard lad lar rad ad la

adlrs lards lads lard rads sard ads lad lar rad sad sal ad as la

adlrsw drawls drawl draws lards sward wards awls draw lads lard laws rads sard wads ward wars ads awl lad lar law rad raw sad sal saw wad war was ad as aw la

adlru dural auld dual dura lard laud lad lar rad urd ad la

adlrw drawl draw lard ward awl lad lar law rad raw wad war ad aw la

adlry lardy aryl dray lady lard yard day dry lad lar lay rad ray yar ad ay la

adls lads ads lad sad sal ad as la

adlstu adults adult adust duals lauds talus alts auld dual dust lads last laud lust salt slat slut stud tads ads alt lad sad sal sat tad tau ad as at la ta us ut

adlsu duals lauds auld dual lads laud ads lad sad sal ad as la us

adlsy sadly days lads lady lays slay ads day lad lay sad sal say sly ad as ay la

adltu adult auld dual laud alt lad tad tau ad at la ta ut

adlu auld dual laud lad ad la

adluy yauld auld dual duly lady laud day lad lay ad ay la

adly lady day lad lay ad ay la

adm dam mad ad am ma

admn damn and dam mad man ad am an ma na

admnnory monandry. *See* **admnor admnoy amnnoy**

admno monad nomad damn moan noma ado and dam don mad man moa mod mon nod ad am an do ma mo na no od om on

admnoor doorman. *See* **admnor amnoor**

admnoost mastodon. *See* **admnos**

admnoosw woodsman woodman. *See* **admnos**

admnoow woodman. *See* **admno amnow**

admnor random adorn manor monad nomad radon damn darn dorm dram moan mora morn nard noma norm orad rand road roam roan ado and arm dam don dor mad man mar moa mod mon mor nod nor oar rad ram ran rod ad am an do ma mo na no od om on or

admnorst mordants dormant matrons mordant stardom transom. *See* **admnor admnos adnors adnrst**

admnort dormant mordant. *See* **admnor amnort**

admnos damson monads nomads damns mason moans monad nomad nomas ados damn dams dons moan moas mods mons naos nods noma sand soda soma ado ads and dam don dos mad man moa mod mon mos nod oms sad sod son ad am an as do ma mo na no od om on os so

admnoss damsons. *See* **admnos amnoss**

admnosy dynamos. *See* **admnos admnoy**

admnoy dynamo monad nomad damn many mayo moan myna noma yond ado and any dam day don mad man may moa mod mon nay nod yam yod yon ad am an ay do ma mo my na no od om on oy

admns damns damn dams sand ads and dam mad man sad ad am an as ma na

admnstu dustman. *See* **admstu adnstu admnsu**

admnsu maunds damns manus mauds maund anus damn dams duns maud maun muds sand ads and dam dun mad man mud mus sad sum sun ad am an as ma mu na nu um us

admnu maund damn maud maun and dam dun mad man mud ad am an ma mu na nu um

admoorrw wardroom. *See* **admorr amorrw moorrw**

admoorst doormats doormat stardom. *See* **moorst**

admoort doormat. *See* **moort**

admorr ramrod ardor armor dorm dram mora orad road roam roar ado arm dam dor mad mar moa mod mor oar rad ram rod ad am do ma mo od om or

admorrs ramrods. *See* **adorrs amorrs admorr**

admorsst stardoms stardom. *See* **amorss amosst amrsst aorsst**

admorst stardom. *See* **amost adrst dmors**

admorsu maduros. *See* **amorsu dmorsu admoru**

admoru maduro amour dorm dour dram drum dura duro maud mora orad road roam ado arm dam dor duo mad mar moa mod mor mud oar oud our rad ram rod rum udo urd ad am do ma mo mu od om or um

admp   damp amp dam dap mad map pad ad am ma pa

admr   dram arm dam mad mar rad ram ad am ma

admrs   drams arms dams dram rads rams sard ads arm dam mad mar rad ram sad ad am as ma

admrsstu   mustards mustard. *See* **admstu amrsst amrstu arsstu**

admrstu   mustard. *See* **admstu amrstu**

adms   dams ads dam mad sad ad am as ma

admstu   datums adust datum mauds dams dust mast mats maud muds must smut stud stum tads tams ads dam mad mat mud mus sad sat sum tad tam tau ad am as at ma mu ta um us ut

admsu   mauds dams maud muds ads dam mad mud mus sad sum ad am as ma mu um us

admtu   datum maud dam mad mat mud tad tam tau ad am at ma mu ta um ut

admtuy   adytum datum maud duty dam day mad mat may mud tad tam tau yam yum ad am at ay ma mu my ta um ut

admu   maud dam mad mud ad am ma mu um

adn   and ad an na

adnnoosy   noondays noonday. *See* **annosy**

adnnooy   noonday. *See* **annoy**

adnnorty   dynatron. *See* **anorty**

adnooqru   quadroon. *See* **adnoru**

adnoorst   donators odorants donator odorant ratoons tornado. *See* **adnors adnrst anoort dnoors**

adnoort   donator odorant tornado. *See* **anoort adnor dnoor**

adnopr   pardon adorn apron radon darn drop nard orad pard pond proa prod rand road roan ado and dap don dor nap nod nor oar pad pan par pod pro rad ran rap rod ad an do na no od on or pa

adnoprs   pardons. *See* **adnors anoprs adnopr**

adnoqrsu   squadron. *See* **adnors adnoru dnorsu**

adnor   adorn radon darn nard orad rand road roan ado and don dor nod nor oar rad ran rod ad an do na no od on or

adnors   adorns radons adorn arson darns dorsa nards radon rands roads roans sonar ados darn dons naos nard nods oars orad rads rand road roan rods sand sard soar soda sora ado ads and

don dor dos nod nor oar rad ran rod sad sod son ad an as do na no od on or os so

adnorstu   rotundas astound rotunda tundras. *See* **adnors adnoru adnrst adnrtu**

adnorstw   sandwort onwards towards. *See* **adnors adnorw adnrst adortw**

adnorsw   onwards. *See* **adnors dnorsw adnorw anorsw**

adnorsxy   sardonyx. *See* **adnors anorsy**

adnortu   rotunda. *See* **adnoru anortu dnortu adnrtu**

adnortuw   untoward rotunda outward. *See* **adnoru adnorw adnrtu adortw**

adnoru   around adorn radon round darn dour dura duro nard orad rand road roan undo ado and don dor dun duo nod nor oar oud our rad ran rod run udo urd urn ad an do na no nu od on or

adnorw   onward adorn drawn drown radon rowan darn dawn down draw nard orad rand road roan wand ward warn word worn ado and awn don dor nod nor now oar own rad ran raw rod row wad wan war won ad an aw do na no od on or ow

adnosstu   astounds astound. *See* **adnsst adnstu dnossu dnostu**

adnosttu   standout astound. *See* **adnstu ansttu dnostu**

adnostu   astound. *See* **adnstu dnostu**

adnpsstu   dustpans dustpan. *See* **adnsst adnstu apsstu**

adnpstu   dustpan. *See* **adnstu anpst npstu**

adnpy   pandy and any dap day nap nay pad pan pay pya yap ad an ay na pa

adnr   darn nard rand and rad ran ad an na

adnrs   darns nards rands darn nard rads rand sand sard ads and rad ran sad ad an as na

adnrsst   strands. *See* **adnrst adnsst**

adnrst   strand darns darts nards rands rants stand ants arts darn dart drat nard rads rand rant rats sand sard star tads tans tars tsar ads and ant art rad ran rat sad sat tad tan tar ad an as at na ta

adnrstu   tundras. *See* **adnstu adnrst adnrtu**

adnrtu   tundra daunt aunt darn dart drat dura nard rand rant runt tuna turd turn and ant art dun nut rad ran rat run rut tad tan tar tau tun urd urn ad an at na nu ta ut

adnrw   drawn darn dawn draw nard rand wand ward warn and awn rad ran raw wad wan war ad an aw na

adnry   randy darn dray nard nary rand yard yarn and any day dry nay rad ran ray yar ad an ay na

adns   sand ads and sad ad an as na

adnss   sands sand ads and ass sad ad an as na

adnsst   stands sands stand ants sand tads tans tass ads and ant ass sad sat tad tan ad an as at na ta

adnssty   dynasts. *See* **adnsst adnsty**

adnst   stand ants sand tads tans ads and ant sad sat tad tan ad an as at na ta

adnstu   daunts adust aunts daunt stand tunas ants anus aunt duns dust nuts sand stud stun tads tans tuna tuns ads and ant dun nut sad sat sun tad tan tau tun ad an as at na nu ta us ut

adnsty   dynast antsy nasty sandy stand tansy ants days sand stay tads tans ads and ant any day nay sad sat say sty tad tan ad an as at ay na ta

adnstyy   dynasty. *See* **adnsty**

adnsw   dawns wands awns dawn sand sawn swan wads wand ads and awn sad saw wad wan was ad an as aw na

adnsy   sandy sand days ads and any day nay sad say ad an as ay na

adntu   daunt aunt tuna and ant dun nut tad tan tau tun ad an at na nu ta ut

adnw   dawn wand and awn wad wan ad an aw na

ado   ado ad do od

adooprrt   trapdoor. *See* **aoorrt aoprrt ooprrt**

adoopsu   apodous. *No 6s or 5s*

adoorswy   doorways doorway. *See* **dooswy dorswy**

adoorwy   doorway. *See* **dorwy doowy**

adoosstt   tostados tostado. *See* **aosstt**

adoostt   tostado. *See* **aostt doost adost**

adoprssw   password. *See* **adrssw dorssw**

adopry   parody dory dray drop orad pard pray proa prod road ropy yard ado dap day dor dry oar pad par pay pod pro pry pya rad rap ray rod yap yar yod ad ay do od or oy pa

adopsssu   soapsuds. *See* **aopss adoss opssu**

adopst   adopts adopt toads ados atop daps dots oast oats pads past pats pods post pots soap soda spat spot stoa stop tads taps toad tops ado ads apt asp dap dos dot oat pad pas pat pod pot sad sap sat sod sop sot spa tad tap tod top ad as at do od os pa so ta to

adopt   adopt toad atop ado apt dap dot oat pad pat pod pot tad tap tod top ad at do od pa ta to

ador   orad road ado dor oar rad rod ad do od or

adorr ardor orad road roar ado dor oar rad rod ad do od or

adorrs ardors ardor dorsa roads roars ados oars orad rads road roar rods sard soar soda sora ado ads dor dos oar rad rod sad sod ad as do od or os so

adors dorsa roads ados oars orad rads road rods sard soar soda sora ado ads dor dos oar rad rod sad sod ad as do od or os so

adorstuw outwards towards outward. *See* **adortw**

adorstw towards. *See* **adortw adrst adors**

adorsuu arduous. *See* **aorsuu adors adrsu**

adortuw outward. *See* **adortw**

adortw toward dart drat draw orad road rota taro toad tora trod trow ward wart word ado art dor dot oar oat ort rad rat raw rod rot row tad tar tod tor tow two wad war ad at aw do od or ow ta to

ados ados soda ado ads dos sad sod ad as do od os so

adoss sodas ados doss ossa soda sods ado ads ass dos sad sod ad as do od os so

adost toads ados dots oast oats soda stoa tads toad ado ads dos dot oat sad sat sod sot tad tod ad as at do od os so ta to

adosty todays toads toady today ados days dots oast oats soda stay stoa tads toad tody toys yods ado ads day dos dot oat sad sat say sod sot soy sty tad

tod toy yod ad as at ay do od os oy so ta to

adot toad ado dot oat tad tod ad at do od ta to

adoty toady today toad tody ado day dot oat tad tod toy yod ad at ay do od oy ta to

adp dap pad ad pa

adpr pard dap pad par rad rap ad pa

adprs pards daps pads pard pars rads raps rasp sard spar ads asp dap pad par pas rad rap sad sap spa ad as pa

adprsuw upwards. *See* **adpruw adrsw adrsu**

adpruw upward draw dura pard ward warp wrap dap pad par paw rad rap raw urd wad wap war ad aw pa up

adps daps pads ads asp dap pad pas sad sap spa ad as pa

adqssu squads quads quass squad quad suds ads ass qua sad ad as us

adqsu quads squad quad ads qua sad ad as us

adqu quad qua ad

adr rad ad

adrs rads sard ads rad sad ad as

adrssw swards draws sward wards draw rads sard saws wads ward wars ads ass rad raw sad saw wad war was ad as aw

adrst darts arts dart drat rads rats sard star tads tars tsar ads art rad rat sad sat tad tar ad as at ta

adrsu duras dura rads sard sura surd urds ads rad sad urd ad as us

adrsw draws sward wards draw rads sard wads ward wars ads rad raw sad saw wad war was ad as aw

adrsy drays yards days dray rads rays sard yard ads day dry rad ray sad say yar ad as ay

adrt dart drat art rad rat tad tar ad at ta

adrtwy tawdry tardy warty arty awry dart drat draw dray tray ward wart wary yard art day dry rad rat raw ray tad tar try wad war way yar yaw ad at aw ay ta

adrty tardy arty dart drat dray tray yard art day dry rad rat ray tad tar try yar ad at ay ta

adru dura rad urd ad

adrw draw ward rad raw wad war ad aw

adry dray yard day dry rad ray yar ad ay

ads ads sad ad as

adsstuw sawdust. *See* **adstu dsstu asstw**

adst tads ads sad sat tad ad as at ta

adstu adust dust stud tads ads sad sat tad tau ad as at ta us ut

adsw wads ads sad saw wad was ad as aw

adsy days ads day sad say ad as ay

adt tad ad at ta

adw wad ad aw

ady day ad ay

adz adz ad

ae

ae ae

aeeeglls legalese alleges. *See* **aeegll aeegls**

aeeeglrt relegate legatee. *See* **aeeglr aeeglt aeelrt eeglrt**

aeeeglst legatees eaglets legatee legates. *See* **aeegls aeeglt aeegst aeelst**

aeeeglt legatee. *See* **aeeglt**

aeeegnrt generate teenager grantee greaten reagent teenage. *See* **aeegnr aeegnt aeenrt aegnrt**

aeeegnt teenage. *See* **aeegnt**

aeeegpr peerage. *See* **aeegr aegpr**

aeeegprs peerages peerage presage seepage. *See* **aeegrs aeeprs aegprs**

aeeegps seepage. *See* **eeeps aegps eeegs**

aeeegpss seepages seepage. *See* **aeepss**

aeeegrst steerage. *See* **aeegrs aeegst aegrst**

aeeegrsw sewerage. *See* **aeegrs aeegsw aegrsw**

aeeehlrt ethereal leather. *See* **aeehlr aeehrt aeelrt aehlrt**

aeeehmpr ephemera. *See* **aeehmr aeempr aehmpr**

aeeehrrs rehearse hearers. *See* **aeehrr aeehrs aeerrs**

aeeehstt aesthete esthete. *See* **aehstt eeehst eeehtt**

aeeeimnx examinee examine. *See* **aeemnx**

aeeeirst eateries seriate eeriest. *See* **aeeirs aeirst eeirst**

aeeekkps keepsake. *See* **eeeps eekks eekps**

aeeelmnr enameler. *See* **aeelmn aeelnr aeemnr**

aeeelnrv venereal. *See* **aeelnr aeelnv aeelrv aelnrv**

aeeelqsu sequelae sequela. *See* **aelqsu eelqsu**

aeeelrs release. *See* **aeelrs**

aeeelrss releases earless leasers release resales reseals sealers. *See* **aeelrs aeelss aeerss**

aeeelrtx axletree exalter. *See* **aeelrt**

aeeelstv elevates elevate. *See* **aeelst aeelsv aeeltv aelstv**

aeeeltv elevate. *See* **aeeltv eeelv**

aeeemnst easement meanest. *See* **aeemns aeenst aemnst eeemst**

aeeemprt permeate tempera. *See* **aeempr aeeprt aemprt eemprt**

aeeenrtv enervate venerate veteran. *See* **aeenrt aenrtv eeenrv eenrtv**

aeeeprrt repartee repeater. *See* **aeeprr aeeprt**

aeefgirt figeater frigate. *See* **aeefir aeefrt aegirt**

aeefgln fenagle. *See* **aefgln aeegl**

aeefglns fenagles fenagle flanges. *See* **aeegls aeegns aefgln aefgns**

aeefglsu fuselage easeful leagues. *See* **aeegls aeeglu**

aeefhrst feathers fathers feaster feather freshet heaters reheats. *See* **aeefrt aeehrs aeehrt aeerst**

aeefhrt feather. *See* **aeefrt aefhrt aeehrt**

aeefhrty feathery feather. *See* **aeefrt aeehrt aeerty aefhrt**

aeefikll leaflike. *See* **aefill**

aeefikrs fakeries faeries. *See* **aeefir aeeirs aeekrs aefirs**

aeefilr leafier. *See* **aeefir aefilr eefilr**

aeefilst fealties leafiest felsite lefties. *See* **aeelst aefist aeflst eeflst**

aeefilw alewife. *No 6s or 5s*

aeefir faerie feriae aerie afire feria fair fare fear fere fire free reef rife air are arf ear era ere far fee fie fir ire ref ria rif ae ai er fa if re

aeefirrs rarefies faeries ferries refries. *See* **aeefir aeeirs aeerrs aefirr**

aeefirs faeries. *See* **aeeirs aeefir aefirs**

aeefisst safeties easiest fiestas. *See* **aeesst aefist aefsst aeisst**

aeefkopr forepeak. *See* **aefor aefkr eekpr**

aeefllrw farewell welfare. *See* **aefllr eefllr**

aeefllss leafless. *See* **aeelss aeflls**

aeefllst leaflets leaflet. *See* **aeelst aeflls aeflst aellst**

aeefllt leaflet. *See* **aeelt aefll aeflt**

aeeflm female flame fleam alee fame feel feme flam flea flee lame leaf male meal ale eel elf elm fee lam lea lee mae mel ae am el em fa la ma me

aeeflms females. *See* **aeeflm aeflms**

aeeflmss fameless selfsame females measles. *See* **aeeflm aeelss aeemss aeflms**

aeeflnru funereal funeral. *See* **aeelnr aeflru aelnru eeflru**

aeeflorv overleaf. *See* **aeefov aeelor aeelrv aeflor**

aeeflrrr referral. *See* **aeflr eeflr eefrr**

aeeflrrt falterer. *See* **aeefrt aeelrt aeerrt aeflrt**

aeeflrss fearless earless leasers resales reseals sealers. *See* **aeelrs aeelss aeerss aeflrs**

aeeflrsw welfares welfare. *See* **aeelrs aeelsw aeflrs aefrsw**

aeeflrw welfare. *See* **aeflr eefrw eeflr**

aeeflsu easeful. *See* **aeels aefls eefls**

aeefmnor forename foramen foreman foremen freeman. *See* **aeemnr aefmno aemnor**

aeefmnr freeman. *See* **aeemnr**

aeefmors fearsome. *See* **aeemrs aefmrs**

aeefnrst fastener earnest eastern feaster nearest. *See* **aeefrt aeenrt aeenst aeerst**

aeefnrtt fattener entreat ternate. *See* **aeefrt aeenrt aefntt aefrtt**

aeefnsss safeness. *See* **eefsss eensss**

aeefov foveae fovea eave ave eve fee foe oaf ova vee ae fa of

aeefrsst feasters feaster festers strafes teasers. *See* **aeefrt aeerss aeesst**

aeefrst feaster. *See* **aeefrt aeerst aefrst eefrst**

aeefrstu features austere feaster feature refutes. *See* **aeefrt aefrst eefrst**

aeefrswy freeways freeway. *See* **aefrsw aefrwy aerswy**

aeefrt afreet after eater fare fart fate fear feat feet fere fete frat free fret raft rate reef reft rete tare tear tree aet aft are arf art ate ear eat eft era ere eta far fat fee rat ref ret tar tea tee ae at er fa re ta

aeefrtu feature. *See* **aeefrt eefrtu**

aeefrwy freeway. *See* **aefrwy eefrw**

aeefsz feazes feaze fazes ease faze fees safe zees fas fee fez sea see zee ae as fa

aeefz feaze faze fee fez zee ae fa

aeeg agee age gae gee ae

aeegginr agreeing gearing. *See* **aeeggn aeegnr aeggin aeginr**

aeeggirv aggrieve. *See* **aeegrv aegirv eeggiv**

aeegglt gateleg. *See* **aeeglt**

aeeggn engage agee gage gang gene age ane egg gae gag gan gee nae nag nee ae an en na ne

aeeggnnr gangrene. *See* **aeeggn aeegnr**

aeeggns engages. *See* **aeeggn aeegns**

aeeghirt heritage. *See* **aeehrt aeghir aeghrt aegirt**

aeeghnrs shagreen enrages hangers. *See* **aeegnr aeegns aeegrs aeehrs**

aeeghrrt gatherer greater. *See* **aeehrr aeehrt aeghrr eegrrt**

aeegiist gaieties. *See* **aeegst**

aeegill galilee. *See* **aeegll aegil eegil**

aeegills galilees galilee alleges. *See* **aeegll aeegls aegils aeills**

aeegillz legalize galilee gazelle. *See* **aeegll**

aeegilm mileage. *See* **aeeilm aegil aeegl**

aeegilms mileages mileage. *See* **aeegls aeeilm aegils aegims**

aeegiln lineage. *See* **aegiln**

aeegilns lineages leasing linages lineage sealing. *See* **aeegls aeegns aegiln aegils**

aeegilp epigeal. *See* **aeeglp aegil eegil**

aeegiltv levigate vegetal. *See* **aeeglt aeeltv aegilt aegilv**

aeegimnt geminate gatemen matinee meeting mintage teaming teeming tegmina. *See* **aeegmn aeegmt aeegnt aegimn**

aeegimrt emigrate emirate meatier migrate ragtime. *See* **aeegmr aeegmt aegimr aegirt**

aeeginss agenesis assignee senegas genesis. *See* **aeegns aegins aeinss aginss**

aeeginsv envisage avenges. *See* **aeegns aeegnv aegins aegisv**

aeegintv negative ventage vintage. *See* **aeegnt aeegnv aegint aeintv**

aeegipqu equipage. *See* **eipqu**

aeegirrs greasier greaser. *See* **aeegrs aeeirs aeerrs aeirrs**

aeegjr jaeger agree eager agee ager gear gree jeer rage age are ear era erg gae gar gee jag jar rag raj reg ae er re

aeegjrs jaegers. *See* **aeegrs aeegjr**

aeegl eagle agee alee gale glee age ale eel gae gal gee gel lag lea lee leg ae el la

aeegll allege eagle legal agee alee gale gall glee leal age ale all eel ell gae gal gee gel lag lea lee leg ae el la

aeegllnr allergen enlarge general gleaner. *See* **aeegll aeeglr aeegnr aeelnr**

aeeglls alleges. *See* **aeegll aeegls**

aeegllsz gazelles alleges gazelle. *See* **aeegll aeegls aeelsz aeglsz**

aeegllz gazelle. *See* **aeegll aeglz**

aeeglmn gleeman. *See* **aeelmn aeglmn eeglmn aeegmn**

aeeglmrt telegram. *See* **aeeglr aeeglt aeegmr aeegmt**

aeeglmry meagerly eagerly. *See* **aeeglr aeegmr aeglmy aeglry**

aeeglnnt entangle elegant. *See* **aeeglt aeegnt aeelnt aeennt**

aeeglnot elongate elegant tangelo. *See* **aeeglt aeegnt aeegot aeelnt**

aeeglnr enlarge general gleaner. *See* **aeglnr aeegnr aeelnr aeeglr**

aeeglnrr enlarger enlarge general gleaner learner. *See* **aeeglr aeegnr aeelnr aeennr**

aeeglnrs enlarges generals gleaners anglers enlarge enrages general gleaner leaners regales. *See* **aeeglr aeegls aeegnr aeegns**

aeeglnsv evangels avenges enslave evangel leavens selvage. *See* **aeegls aeegns aeegnv aeelnv**

aeeglnt elegant. *See* **aeeglt eeglnt aeelnt aeegnt aeglnt**

aeeglnv   evangel. *See* **aeegnv aeelnv**

aeeglp   pelage eagle plage agee alee gale gape glee leap page pale peag peal peel plea age ale alp ape eel gae gal gap gee gel lag lap lea lee leg pal pea pee peg ae el la pa pe

aeeglps   pelages. *See* **aeelps aeegls aeeglp aeglps**

aeeglr   regale agree eager eagle glare lager large regal agee ager alee earl gale gear glee gree leer rage rale real reel age ale are ear eel era ere erg gae gal gar gee gel lag lar lea lee leg rag reg ae el er la re

aeeglrs   regales. *See* **aeegrs aeglrs aeelrs aeeglr**

aeeglrss   eelgrass ageless earless greases largess leasers regales resales reseals sealers. *See* **aeeglr aeegls aeegrs aeelrs**

aeeglrsu   leaguers leaguer leagues regales reglues. *See* **aeeglr aeegls aeeglu aeegrs**

aeeglrtu   regulate leaguer. *See* **aeeglr aeeglt aeeglu aeelrt**

aeeglru   leaguer. *See* **aeeglu aeeglr eeglru**

aeeglry   eagerly. *See* **aeeglr aeglry**

aeegls   eagles eagle easel gales glees lease agee ages alee ales ease eels else gale gals gees gels glee lags leas lees legs sage sale seal seel slag age ale eel els gae gal gas gee gel lag lea lee leg sag sal sea see ae as el la

aeeglss   ageless. *See* **aeegls aeelss**

aeeglsst   gateless ageless eaglets legates teasels. *See* **aeegls aeeglt aeegst aeelss**

aeeglssv   selvages ageless selvage sleaves. *See* **aeegls aeelss aeelsv aeglsv**

aeeglst   eaglets legates. *See* **aeglst aeegls aeeglt aeegst aeelst**

aeeglsu   leagues. *See* **aeegls aeeglu**

aeeglsv   selvage. *See* **aeegls aeglsv aeelsv**

aeeglt   eaglet legate aglet eagle elate gleet agee alee gale agee glee late leet tael tale teal aet age ale alt ate eat eel eta gae gal gat gee gel get lag lea lee leg let tag tea tee ae at el la ta

aeeglttu   tutelage. *See* **aeeglt aegttu aeeglu**

aeegltv   vegetal. *See* **aeeglt aeeltv**

aeeglu   league eagle agee ague alee gale glee glue luge age ale eel gae gal gee gel lag lea lee leg leu lug ae el la

aeegmm   gemmae gemma agee game mage age gae gam gee gem mae mag mem ae am em ma me

aeegmn   manege menage enema mange agee amen game gene mage mane mean name age ane gae gam gan gee gem mae mag man men nae nag nee ae am an em en ma me na ne

aeegmnr   germane. *See* **aeegnr aegmnr aeegmn aeegmr aeemnr**

aeegmns   maneges menages. *See* **aeemns aegmns aeegns**

aeegmnss   gameness maneges menages message senegas. *See* **aeegmn aeegns aeemns aeemss**

aeegmnt   gatemen. *See* **aeegmt aegmnt aeegmn aeegnt eegmnt**

aeegmr   meager agree ameer eager marge merge agee ager game gear germ gram gree mage mare mere rage ream age are arm ear era ere erg gae gam gar gee gem mae mag mar rag ram reg rem ae am em er ma me re

aeegmrst   gamester gametes metages steamer. *See* **aeegmr aeegmt aeegrs aeegst**

aeegmss   message. *See* **aeemss aegms aegss**

aeegmsss   messages message. *See* **aeemss aemsss eemsss**

aeegmssu   messuage message. *See* **aeemss aegssu aemssu eegssu**

aeegmst   gametes metages. *See* **aeegst aeegmt**

aeegmt   gamete metage agee game gate mage mate meat meet mete tame team teem aet age ate eat eta gae gam gat gee gem get mae mag mat met tag tam tea tee ae am at em ma me ta

aeegnop   peonage. *See* **aeegop eegnop**

aeegnops   peonages apogees peonage pongees. *See* **aeegns aeegop aegnos aenops**

aeegnr   enrage genera agree anger eager genre green range agee ager earn erne gear gene gnar gree near rage rang age ane are ear era ere erg gae gan gar gee nae nag nee rag ran reg ae an en er na ne re

aeegnrs   enrages. *See* **aeegrs aegnrs aeegnr eegnrs aeegns**

aeegnrst   estrange greatens reagents sergeant argents earnest eastern enrages garnets grantee greaten nearest negates reagent regents strange. *See* **aeegnr aeegns aeegnt aeegns**

aeegnrsv   avengers engraves avenger avenges engrave enrages greaves. *See* **aeegnr aeegns aeegnv aeegrs**

aeegnrt   grantee greaten reagent. *See* **aegnrt aeegnr aeenrt aeegnt eegnrt**

aeegnrv   avenger engrave. *See* **aeegnv aegnrv aeegrv**

aeegns   senega genes agee ages ease gees gene gens nags sage sane sang seen snag age ane ens gae gan gas gee nae nag nee sag sea see sen ae an as en na ne

aeegnss   senegas. *See* **aeegns**

aeegnsss   sageness senegas. *See* **aeegns eensss**

aeegnst   negates. *See* **aegnst aeegst eegnst aeegns aeenst**

aeegnstv   ventages avenges negates ventage. *See* **aeegns aeegnt aeegnv aeegst**

aeegnsv   avenges. *See* **aeegnv aeegns**

aeegnt   negate agent eaten genet agee ante gate gene gent gnat neat tang teen aet age ane ant ate eat eta gae gan gat gee get nae nag nee net tag tan tea tee ten ae an at en na ne ta

aeegntv   ventage. *See* **aeegnt aeegnv**

aeegnv   avenge agee eave even gave gene nave vane vang age ane ave eve gae gan gee nae nag nee van vee ae an en na ne

aeegop   apogee agee gape ogee page peag age ago ape ego gae gap gee goa ope pea pee peg ae go pa pe

aeegops   apogees. *See* **aeegop aegps eegos**

aeegorsv   overages overage greaves. *See* **aeegrs aeegrv aeersv eeorsv**

aeegorv   overage. *See* **aeegrv egorv**

aeegost   goatees. *See* **aeegot aeegst**

aeegot   goatee agee gate goat ogee toga aet age ago ate eat ego eta gae gat gee get goa got oat tag tea tee toe tog ae at go ta to

aeegprs   presage. *See* **aeegrs aegprs aeeprs**

aeegprss   presages asperse greases presage serapes sparges. *See* **aeegrs aeeprs aeepss aeerss**

aeegr   agree eager agee ager gear gree rage age are ear era ere erg gae gar gee rag reg ae er re

aeegrrs   greaser. *See* **aeegrs aeerrs**

aeegrrss   greasers erasers greaser greases regress. *See* **aeegrs aeerrs aeerss aegrss**

aeegrrt   greater. *See* **aegrrt eegrrt aeerrt**

aeegrs   agrees grease agree eager erase gears grees rages sager serge agee ager ages arse ears ease eras ergs gars gear gees gree rage rags rase regs sage sear seer sera sere age are ear era ere erg gae gar gas gee rag reg res sag sea see ae as er re

aeegrss   greases. *See* **aeegrs eegrss aeerss aegrss**

aeegrstt   greatest estreat getters restate targets. *See* **aeegrs aeegst aeestt**

aeegrsv   greaves. *See* **aeegrs aeersv aegrsv aeegrv eegrsv**

aeegrv   greave agree eager grave verge agee ager aver eave ever gave gear gree rage rave veer age are ave ear era ere erg eve gae gar gee rag reg rev vee ae er re

aeegsstt gestates estates. *See* **aeegst aeesst aeestt aegsst**

aeegssw sewages. *See* **aeegsw aeessw**

aeegst egesta egest gates setae stage tease agee ages ease east eats etas gate gats gees gest gets sage seat seta stag tags teas tees aet age ate eat eta gae gas gat gee get sag sat sea see set tag tea tee ae as at ta

aeegsttz gazettes gazette. *See* **aeegst aeestt**

aeegsw sewage wages agee ages awes ease ewes gees sage swag wage wags age awe ewe gae gas gee sag saw sea see sew wag was wee ae as aw we

aeegttz gazette. *No 6s or 5s*

aeehhnst heathens heathen sheathe. *See* **aeehnt aeenst aehhst aehnst**

aeehhnt heathen. *See* **aeehnt aehht**

aeehhrss rehashes hearses. *See* **aeehrs aeerss aehhrs aehhss**

aeehhrst heathers hearths heaters heather reheats sheathe. *See* **aeehrs aeehrt aehhrs**

aeehhrt heather. *See* **aehhrt aeehrt**

aeehhrty heathery heather. *See* **aeehrt aeerty aehhrt aehhty**

aeehhsst sheathes sheathe sheaths. *See* **aeesst aehhss aehhst eehsst**

aeehhst sheathe. *See* **aehhst**

aeehhsw heehaws. *See* **aeehhw aehsw**

aeehhw heehaw awe ewe hae hah haw heh hew wee ae ah aw eh ha he we

aeehinr herniae. *See* **eehinr aehinr**

aeehirrt earthier heartier. *See* **aeehrr aeehrt eehirr eehirt**

aeehirsv shivaree heavier. *See* **aeehrs aeehsv aeeirs aeersv**

aeehirv heavier. *See* **aeehv aeeir**

aeehisst esthesia ashiest easiest hessite. *See* **aeesst aeisst eehsst ehisst**

aeehistt hesitate atheist. *See* **aeesst aehstt ehistt**

aeehistv heaviest thieves. *See* **aeehsv eehitv**

aeehkllu keelhaul. *See* **aehlu**

aeehknr hearken. *See* **aehknr**

aeehknrs hearkens hankers harkens hearken sneaker. *See* **aeehrs aeekrs aehknr aehkns**

aeehkwy hawkeye. *No 6s or 5s*

aeehllss seashell leashes. *See* **aeelss aehlss ehllss**

aeehlmny hymeneal. *See* **aeelmn aelmny ahlmny**

aeehlmpt helpmate heeltap. *See* **aeelmp aehlmt eehlmt eehmpt**

aeehlnpt elephant heeltap heptane. *See* **aeehnp aeehnt aeelnt aelnpt**

aeehlnrt leathern earthen enteral eternal hearten leather teleran. *See* **aeehlr aeehnt aeehrt aeelnr**

aeehlnvy heavenly. *See* **aeehnv aeelnv eelnvy**

aeehlosu alehouse. *See* **aehlos aehlsu ehlosu**

aeehlpst heeltaps heeltap. *See* **aeelps aeelst aeepst aehlps**

aeehlpt heeltap. *See* **aehlp aeelt aehlt**

aeehlptt telepath athlete heeltap palette. *See* **aehlp aeelt aehlt**

aeehlr healer haler alee earl hale hare harl heal hear heel here herl leer rale real reel rhea ale are ear eel era ere hae her lar lea lee rah ae ah eh el er ha he la re

aeehlrs healers. *See* **aeehlr aeehrs aehlrs aeelrs**

aeehlrst halteres leathers elaters halters healers heaters lathers leather reheats relates shelter slather stealer thalers. *See* **aeehlr aeehrs aeehrt aeelrs**

aeehlrt leather. *See* **aeelrt aehlrt aeehlr aeehrt**

aeehlrty leathery earthly lathery leather. *See* **aeehlr aeehrt aeelrt aeerty**

aeehlss leashes. *See* **aeelss aehlss**

aeehlsst heatless leashes teasels. *See* **aeelss aeelst aeesst aehlss**

aeehlstt athletes athlete stealth. *See* **aeelst aeestt aehlst aehstt**

aeehlsx exhales. *See* **aeehlx aelsx aeels**

aeehlsy eyelash. *See* **aeels aehls eehls**

aeehltt athlete. *See* **aeelt aehlt eehtt**

aeehlx exhale alee axle hale heal heel ale axe eel hae hex lax lea lee ae ah ax eh el ex ha he la

aeehmmrr hammerer reamer.. *See* **aehmmr aehmrr aeehrr eehmmr**

aeehmnps sheepman peahens. *See* **aeehnp aeemns eehmnp eehmns**

aeehmnrt earthmen earthen hearten methane thermae. *See* **aeehmr aeehnt aeehrt aeemnr**

aeehmnst methanes anthems meanest methane. *See* **aeehnt aeemns aeenst aehmnt**

aeehmnt methane. *See* **aehmnt aeehnt**

aeehmpss emphases. *See* **aeemss aeepss aehmss aehpss**

aeehmr hermae ameer harem herma ahem hame hare harm hear heme here herm mare mere ream rhea are arm ear era ere hae ham hem her mae mar rah ram rem ae ah am eh em er ha he ma me re

aeehmrt thermae. *See* **aeehrt aeehmr**

aeehmu heaume ahem emeu hame heme emu hae ham hem hue hum mae ae ah am eh em ha he ma me mu um

aeehnntx xanthene. *See* **aeehnt aeehnx aeennt**

aeehnopr earphone. *See* **aeehnp ahnopr eehnor eenopr**

aeehnp peahen heap nape neap neep pane pean peen ane ape hae hap hen hep nae nah nap nee pah pan pea pee pen ae ah an eh en ha he na ne pa pe

aeehnps peahens. *See* **aeehnp aehns aenps**

aeehnpt heptane. *See* **aeehnp aeehnt**

aeehnrst heartens anthers earnest earthen eastern hearten heaters nearest reheats thenars. *See* **aeehnt aeehrs aeehrt aeenrt**

aeehnrt earthen hearten. *See* **aehnrt aeehrt aeenrt eehnrt**

aeehnrtt threaten earthen entreat hearten ternate theater theatre. *See* **aeehnt aeehrt aeenrt aehnrt**

aeehnrtu urethane earthen haunter hearten unearth. *See* **aeehnt aeehrt aeenrt aehnrt**

aeehnrwy anywhere. *See* **aenrwy**

aeehnsx hexanes. *See* **aeehnx aehns eehsx**

aeehnt ethane eaten neath thane ante hant hate heat hent neat teen than thee then aet ane ant ate eat eta eth hae hat hen het nae nah nee net tan tea tee ten the ae ah an at eh en ha he na ne ta

aeehntw wheaten. *See* **aeehnt aehtw**

aeehnv heaven heave haven eave even have nave vane ane ave eve hae hen nae nah nee van vee ae ah an eh en ha he na ne

aeehnx hexane ane axe hae hen hex nae nah nee ae ah an ax eh en ex ha he na ne

aeehorrv overhear hoverer. *See* **aeehrr**

aeehorss seashore hearses. *See* **aeehrs aeerss aehors aehrss**

aeehortv overheat overate overeat. *See* **aeehrt eehort ehortv**

aeehostu teahouse. *See* **aostu ehost aehst**

aeehprrs rephrase harpers hearers reapers reshape sharper. *See* **aeehrr aeehrs aeeprr aeeprs**

aeehprs reshape. *See* **aeehrs eehprs aehprs aeeprs**

aeehprss reshapes asperse hearses phrases reshape serapes seraphs sherpas spheres. *See* **aeehrs aeeprs aeepss aeerss**

aeehprst preheats heaters preheat reheats repeats reshape threaps. *See* **aeehrs aeehrt aeeprs aeeprt**

aeehprt preheat. *See* **aeehrt aeeprt aehprt**

aeehrr hearer hare hear here rare rear rhea are ear era ere err hae her rah ae ah eh er ha he re

aeehrrs hearers. *See* **aeerrs aeehr aeehrs aehrss**

aeehrs hearse erase hares hears rheas share shear sheer arse ears ease eras hare hear here hers rahs rase rash resh rhea sear seer sera sere are ash ear era ere hae has her rah res sea see she ae ah as eh er ha he re sh

aeehrss hearses. *See* **aeerss aeehrs aehrss eehrss**

aeehrst heaters reheats. *See* **aehrst aeerst eehrst aeehrs aeehrt**

aeehrstt theaters theatres estreat hatters heaters reheats restate shatter tethers theater theatre. *See* **aeehrs aeehrt aeestt**

aeehrstw weathers wreathes heaters reheats sweater weather wethers whereas wreathe wreaths. *See* **aeehrs aeehrt aehrst**

aeehrsw whereas. *See* **aehrsw aeehrs eehrsw**

aeehrt heater hereat reheat earth eater ether hater heart there three hare hart hate hear heat here rate rath rete rhea tare tear thee tree aet are art ate ear eat era ere eta eth hae hat her het rah rat ret tar tea tee the ae ah at eh er ha he re ta

aeehrtt theater theatre. *See* **aehrtt aeehrt eehrtt**

aeehrtvw whatever weather wreathe. *See* **aeehrt aeervw aehrtw eehrtw**

aeehrtw weather wreathe. *See* **aeehrt eehrtw aehrtw**

aeehssv sheaves. *See* **aeehsv aehssv**

aeehsttw sawteeth. *See* **aeestt aehstt aehstw eesttw**

aeehstvy heavyset. *See* **aeehsv**

aeehsv heaves eaves heave shave aves ease eave eves have save vase vees ash ave eve hae has sea see she vee ae ah as eh ha he sh

aeehswy eyewash. *See* **aehsw ahswy ehswy**

aeehv heave eave have ave eve hae vee ae ah eh ha he

aeeijprs japeries. *See* **aeeirs aeeprs aeiprs aejprs**

aeeiklmu leukemia. *See* **aeeilm**

aeeiklr leakier. *See* **aeeklr aeeir aeikl**

aeeiklrw weaklier leakier warlike. *See* **aeeklr aeekrw aeklrw**

aeeiklst leakiest. *See* **aeelst aeklst eeilst**

aeeiklvw wavelike. *See* **eeilvw**

aeeiknrs sneakier sneaker snakier. *See* **aeeirs aeekrs aeikrs aeinrs**

aeeillrt laetrile literal. *See* **aeelrt aeillt aeilrt eillrt**

aeeilm mealie elemi alee lame lime mail male meal mile ail aim ale eel elm lam lea lee lei lie mae mel mil ae ai am el em la li ma me mi

aeeilmmt mealtime. *See* **aeeilm**

aeeilmr mealier. *See* **aeeilm aeilmr**

aeeilmrt materiel emirate maltier mealier meatier. *See* **aeeilm aeelrt aeilmr aeilrt**

aeeilmst mealiest. *See* **aeeilm aeelst aeilms aeimst**

aeeilmtz metalize. *See* **aeeilm aeeltz**

aeeilnpz penalize. *See* **aeilnp**

aeeillnt lineate. *See* **aeilnt aeelnt**

aeeilort aerolite. *See* **aeelor aeelrt aeilrt ailort**

aeeilprr pearlier earlier. *See* **aeelpr aeeprr aeilrr aeiprr**

aeeilprs espalier leapers relapse repeals replies spieler. *See* **aeeirs aeelpr aeelps aeelrs**

aeeilpt pileate. *See* **aeelt eeilt aelpt**

aeeilquz equalize. *See* **aelquz**

aeeilrr earlier. *See* **aeilrr aeeir**

aeeilrrt retailer earlier retrial trailer. *See* **aeelrt aeerrt aeilrr aeilrt**

aeeilrst earliest realties elaters leister realist relates retails saltier saltire seriate stealer sterile. *See* **aeeirs aeelrs aeelrt aeelst**

aeeilrsz realizes sleazier realize. *See* **aeeirs aeelrs aeelsz aeersz**

aeeilrtt literate ariette iterate tertial. *See* **aeelrt aeilrt aeirtt eilrtt**

aeeilrtv levirate relative. *See* **aeelrt aeelrv aeeltv aeilrt**

aeeilrz realize. *See* **aeilrz aeeir aeerz**

aeeilsvw alewives weevils. *See* **aeelsv aeelsw aeesvw aeilsv**

aeeilttv levitate. *See* **aeeltv aeittv**

aeeimmnt meantime matinee. *See* **aeimnt**

aeeimnrx examiner examine. *See* **aeemnr aeemnx aeimnr**

aeeimns meanies. *See* **aeimns aeemns**

aeeimnst matinees etesian inmates matinee meanest meanies. *See* **aeemns aeenst aeimnt**

aeeimnsx examines examens examine meanies. *See* **aeemns aeemnx aeinsx**

aeeimnt matinee. *See* **aeimnt aeent aeemn**

aeeimnx examine. *See* **aeemnx aeimn aeinx**

aeeimrrs smearier marries reamers seamier. *See* **aeeirs aeemrr aeemrs aeerrs**

aeeimrs seamier. *See* **aeeirs aeemrs aeimrs eeimrs**

aeeimrst emirates steamier emirate imarets meatier seamier seriate steamer. *See* **aeeirs aeemrs aeimrs**

aeeimrt emirate meatier. *See* **aeimrt aeeir aeemr**

aeeimsst seamiest easiest samites. *See* **aeemss aeesst aeimst aeisst**

aeeimstt estimate meatiest teatime. *See* **aeestt aeimst aemstt**

aeeimtt teatime. *See* **aemtt**

aeeinnrs anserine ensnare. *See* **aeeirs aeinnr aeinns aeinrs**

aeeinprs naperies rapines. *See* **aeeirs aeeprs aeinpr aeinrs**

aeeinprt aperient painter peatier pertain repaint retinae trainee. *See* **aeenrt aeeprt aeinpr aeinrt**

aeeinrrt retainer retinae retrain terrain terrane terrine trainee trainer. *See* **aeenrr aeenrt aeinrt eeinrt**

aeeinrst trainees earnest eastern entries etesian nastier nearest retains retinae retinas seriate stainer trainee. *See* **aeeirs aeenrt aeenst aeerst**

aeeinrt retinae trainee. *See* **eeinrt aeenrt aeinrt**

aeeinsss easiness. *See* **aeinss eeinss eensss**

aeeinst etesian. *See* **aeenst**

aeeinstt anisette etesian neatest satinet. *See* **aeenst aeestt ainstt eenstt**

aeeinsvw inweaves inweave. *See* **aeesvw aeinsv aeisvw eeinsv**

aeeinvw inweave. *See* **aeinv aeivw aeevw**

aeeipptt appetite pipette. *See* **eeiptt aeppt eipptt**

aeeiprst parietes parties pastier peatier piaster pirates repeats respite seriate traipse. *See* **aeeirs aeeprs aeeprt aeepst**

aeeiprt peatier. *See* **aeeprt aeiprt**

aeeipstt peatiest septate patties. *See* **aeepst aeestt eeiptt**

aeeipstx expiates expiate. *See* **aeepst aeepsx**

aeeipsv peavies. *See* **aeesv aepsv aipsv**

aeeiptx expiate. *No 6s or 5s*

aeeiqrsu queasier esquire queries. *See* **aeeirs aeqrsu eeqrsu eiqrsu**

aeeir aerie air are ear era ere ire ria ae ai er re

aeeirrst arteries retires retries seriate serrate tarries tarsier terries. *See* **aeeirs aeerrs aeerrt aeerst**

aeeirrw wearier. *See* **eeirrw aeirrw aeerrw**

aeeirs aeries easier aerie arise erase raise serai airs arse ears ease eras rase reis rias rise sari sear seer sera sere sire air are ear era ere ire res ria sea see sir ae ai as er is re si

aeeirsst seriates easiest satires seriate teasers. *See* **aeeirs aeerss aeesst**

aeeirst seriate. *See* **aeeirs aeerst eeirst aeirst**

aeeirstt iterates treaties treatise ariette artiste attires estreat iterate ratites re- state seriate striate tastier. *See* **aeeirs aeestt aeirst**

aeeirstw sweatier weariest seriate sweater waiters wariest. *See* **aeeirs aeirst aeirtw**

aeeirsty yeastier seriate. *See* **aeeirs aeerty aeirst**

aeeirtt ariette iterate. *See* **aeirtt**

aeeisst easiest. *See* **aeesst aeisst**

aeeisttv estivate. *See* **aeesstt aeittv**

aeeisvv evasive. *See* **aeesv eeisv**

aeekkno kokanee. *See* **aekno**

aeekknos kokanees kokanee. *See* **aenos aknos eekks**

aeekllst skeletal. *See* **aeelst aeklst aellst**

aeeklmrt telemark. *See* **aeeklr aeekmr aeekrt aeelrt**

aeeklr leaker rakee laker alee earl kale keel lake lark leak leek leer rake rale real reek reel ale are ark ear eel eke elk era ere kal lar lea lee lek ae el er ka la re

aeeklrs leakers. *See* **aeklrs aeeklr aeelrs aeekrs**

aeekmns kamseen. *See* **aeemns**

aeekmnss kamseens kamseen. *See* **aeemns aeemss aeknss eemnss**

aeekmr remake ameer maker rakee kame make mare mark meek mere rake ream reek are ark arm ear eke era ere mae mar ram rem ae am em er ka ma me re

aeekmrrt marketer. *See* **aeekmr aeekrt aeemrr aekmrt**

aeekmrs remakes. *See* **aeemrs eekmrs aekmrs aeekmr**

aeeknnn nankeen. *No 6s or 5s*

aeeknnns nankeens nankeen. *See* **eekns aenns aekns**

aeeknnp kneepan. *See* **aeennp**

aeeknrs sneaker. *See* **aeekrs aenrs eenrs**

aeeknrss sneakers sneaker. *See* **aeekrs aeerss aeknss aekrss**

aeeknrt retaken. *See* **aeenrt aeekrt aeknrt**

aeeknssw weakness weakens. *See* **aeeknw aeessw aeknss aeknsw**

aeeknsw weakens. *See* **aeeknw aeknsw**

aeeknw weaken waken anew keen knee knew wake wane weak wean week weka ane awe awn eke ewe ken nae nee new wan wee wen ae an aw en ka na ne we

aeekortv overtake takeover overate over- eat. *See* **aeekrt eekorv**

aeekprs speaker. *See* **eekprs aeekrs aeeprs**

aeekprss speakers asperse serapes speaker. *See* **aeekrs aeeprs aeepss aeerss**

aeekqrsu squeaker squeak.. *See* **aeekru aekqsu akqrsu eeqrsu**

aeekr rakee rake reek are ark ear eke era ere ae er ka re

aeekrrst streaker kraters retakes serrate. *See* **aeekrs aeekrt aeerrs aeerst**

aeekrrsw wreakers wearers. *See* **aeekrs aeekrw aeerrs aeerrw**

aeekrs rakees erase eskar esker rakee rakes reeks saker arks arse ears ease ekes eras rake rase reek sake sark sear seek seer sera sere skee are ark ask ear eke era ere kas res sea see ae as er ka re

aeekrst retakes. *See* **aeerst aeekrt aekrst**

aeekrt retake eater rakee taker kart keet rake rate reek rete take tare teak tear tree trek aet are ark art ate ear eat eke era ere eta kat rat ret tar tea tee ae at er ka re ta

aeekru eureka rakee rake reek urea are ark auk ear eke era ere rue ae er ka re

aeekrw weaker rakee wreak ewer rake reek wake ware weak wear week weka are ark awe ear eke era ere ewe raw war wee ae aw er ka re we

aeekstw weakest. *See* **aekstw eekst aeest**

aeel alee ale eel lea lee ae el la

aeelll allele alee leal ale all eel ell lea lee ae el la

aeellls alleles. *See* **aeelll aeels**

aeellltt telltale. *See* **aeelll**

aeellm mallee alee lame leal male mall meal mell ale all eel ell elm lam lea lee mae mel ae am el em la ma me

aeellms mallees. *See* **aeellm aeels aelms**

aeellptt platelet palette. *See* **aellpt eellpt**

aeellpty teleplay. *See* **aellpt aellpy aellty eellpt**

aeellswy walleyes walleye leeways. *See* **aeelsw aeelwy aellsy**

aeellwy walleye. *See* **aeelwy aelly**

aeelmmtu malemute emulate. *See* **aelmtu**

aeelmn enamel enema leman alee amen lame lane lean male mane meal mean name ale ane eel elm lam lea lee mae man mel men nae nee ae am an el em en la ma me na ne

aeelmnp empanel. *See* **aeelmn aeelmp**

aeelmnps empanels empales empanel enamels. *See* **aeelmn aeelmp aeelps aeemns**

aeelmns enamels. *See* **aeelmn aeemns aelmns**

aeelmnss lameness maleness nameless salesmen enamels manless measles. *See* **aeelmn aeelss aeemns aeemss**

aeelmnst talesmen enamels laments lateens leanest mantels mantles meanest. *See* **aeelmn aeelnt aeelst aeemns**

aeelmott matelote. *See* **eelmot elmott**

aeelmp empale ample maple alee lame lamp leap male meal pale palm peal peel plea ale alp amp ape eel elm lam lap lea lee mae map mel pal pea pee ae am el em la ma me pa pe

aeelmprx exemplar example exempla. *See* **aeelmp aeelpr aeempr aelmpr**

aeelmpry empyreal lamprey. *See* **aeelmp aeelpr aeempr aelmpr**

aeelmps empales. *See* **aeelps aeelmp aelmps**

aeelmpsx examples empales example ex- empla. *See* **aeelmp aeelps aeepsx aelmps**

aeelmptt template palette templet. *See* **aeelmp eelmpt**

aeelmpx example exempla. *See* **aeelmp eelpx**

aeelmss measles. *See* **aeelss aeemss**

aeelmsss seamless measles. *See* **aeelss aeemss aelsss eemss**

aeelmsst meatless measles samlets tea- sels. *See* **aeelss aeelst aeemss aeesst**

aeelmstu emulates amulets emulate muletas. *See* **aeelst aelmst aelmtu ael- stu**

aeelmtu emulate. *See* **aelmtu**

aeelnnrt lanneret enteral eternal lantern teleran. *See* **aeelnr aeelnt aeelrt aeennt**

aeelnopt antelope polenta. *See* **aeelnt aelnpt aelopt eenopt**

aeelnpss paleness elapses napless pleases spleens. *See* **aeelps aeelss aeepss aelnps**

aeelnr leaner learn renal alee earl earn erne lane lean leer near rale real reel ale ane are ear eel era ere lar lea lee nae nee ran ae an el en er la na ne re

aeelnrr learner. *See* **aeenrr aeelnr**

aeelnrrs learners earners leaners learner. *See* **aeelnr aeelrs aeenrr aeerrs**

aeelnrs leaners. *See* **aeelnr aelnrs aeelrs**

aeelnrst telerans antlers earnest eastern elaters enteral eternal lateens leaners leanest nearest nestler relates relents rentals saltern stealer sternal teleran. *See* **aeelnr aeelnt aeelrs aeelrt**

aeelnrsw renewals leaners renewal. *See* **aeelnr aeelrs aeelsw aelnrs**

aeelnrt enteral eternal teleran. *See* **aelnrt aeelrt aeelnt aeelnr aeenrt**

aeelnrtv relevant enteral eternal teleran ventral veteran. *See* **aeelnr aeelnt aeelnv aeelrt**

aeelnrtx external enteral eternal exalter teleran. *See* **aeelnr aeelnt aeelrt aeenrt**

aeelnrw renewal. *See* **aeelnr eelnw eenrw**

aeelnsst lateness lateens leanest nestles sateens senates sensate teasels. *See* **aeelnt aeelss aeelst aeenst**

aeelnssv enslaves enslave leavens sleaves. *See* **aeelnv aeelss aeelsv aelnsv**

aeelnst lateens leanest. *See* **aeelst aeelnt eelnst aeenst**

aeelnsv enslave leavens. *See* **aeelnv aeelsv aelnsv**

aeelnt lateen eaten elate leant alee ante lane late lean leet lent neat tael tale teal teen aet ale alt ane ant ate eat eel eta lea lee let nae nee net tan tea tee ten ae an at el en la na ne ta

aeelntuv eventual. *See* **aeelnt aeelnv aeeltv aeenuv**

aeelnv leaven leave navel venal alee eave even lane lave lean leva nave vale vane veal ale ane ave eel eve lea lee lev nae nee van vee ae an el en la na ne

aeelopr parolee. *See* **aeelor eelopr aeelpr aelopr**

aeeloprs parolees areoles elopers leapers leprose parolee paroles relapse repeals. *See* **aeelor aeelpr aeelps aeelrs**

aeelopsx poleaxes. *See* **aeelps aeepsx aelops aelopx**

aeelor areole aero alee aloe earl leer lore oral orle rale real reel role ale are ear eel era ere lar lea lee oar ore roe ae el er la lo or re

aeelors areoles. *See* **aeelor aeelrs eelors**

aeelortt tolerate. *See* **aeelor aeelrt aelrtt aeortt**

aeelortv elevator levator overate overeat. *See* **aeelor aeelrt aeelrv aeeltv**

aeeloru aureole. *See* **aeelor**

aeelpr leaper repeal leper paler pearl repel alee earl leap leer pale pare peal pear peel peer plea rale rape real reap reel ale alp ape are ear eel era ere lap lar lea lee pal par pea pee per rap rep ae el er la pa pe re

aeelprs leapers relapse repeals. *See* **aeelps aeelpr aeelrs eelprs aelprs**

aeelprss relapses asperse earless elapses leapers leasers pleases relapse repeals resales reseals sealers serapes. *See* **aeelpr aeelps aeelrs aeelss**

aeelprst prelates elaters leapers palters pelters petrels plaster platers prelate psalter relapse relates repeals repeats stapler stealer. *See* **aeelpr aeelps aeelrs aeelrt**

aeelprsu pleasure leapers perusal pleurae relapse repeals repulse. *See* **aeelpr aeelps aeelrs aeeprs**

aeelprsv vesperal leapers relapse repaves repeals reveals several. *See* **aeelpr aeelps aeelrs aeelrv**

aeelprt prelate. *See* **aeelrt aelprt eelprt aeelpr aeeprt**

aeelpru pleurae. *See* **aeelpr aelpru**

aeelps asleep elapse please easel lapse leaps lease pales peals pease peels pleas salep sepal sleep alee ales alps apes apse ease eels else laps leap leas lees pale pals peal peas peel pees plea sale seal seel seep slap ale alp ape asp eel els lap lea lee pal pas pea pee sal sap sea see spa ae as el la pa pe

aeelpss elapses pleases. *See* **aeelps aeelss aelpss aeepss eelpss**

aeelpstt palettes palette septate. *See* **aeelps aeelst aeepst aeestt**

aeelpstu epaulets epaulet pulsate. *See* **aeelps aeelst aeepst aelpst**

aeelptt palette. *See* **aeelt aelpt**

aeelptu epaulet. *See* **aeelt eeltu aelpt**

aeelqrsu squealer sequela. *See* **aeelrs aelqsu aelrsu eeqrsu**

aeelqsu sequela. *See* **aelqsu eelqsu**

aeelrrsv reversal reveals several. *See* **aeelrs aeelrv aeelsv aeerrs**

aeelrrtv traveler. *See* **aeelrt aeelrv aeeltv aeerrt**

aeelrrx relaxer. *See* **aelrx**

aeelrs leaser resale reseal sealer earls easel erase lares laser lease leers rales reels alee ales arse earl ears ease eels else eras leas leer lees rale rase real reel sale seal sear seel seer sera sere ale are ear eel els era ere lar lea lee res sal sea see ae as el er la re

aeelrss earless leasers resales reseals sealers. *See* **aeelss aeerss aelrss aeelrs eelrss**

aeelrsst stealers tearless artless earless elaters leasers relates resales reseals sealers slaters stealer teasels teasers. *See* **aeelrs aeelrt aeelss aeelst**

aeelrst elaters relates stealer. *See* **aelrst aeerst aeelrt aeelst aeelrs**

aeelrstx exalters elaters exalter latexes relates relaxes stealer. *See* **aeelrs aeelrt aeelst aeerst**

aeelrsty easterly elaters relates sealery stealer tersely. *See* **aeelrs aeelrt aeelst aeerst**

aeelrsuv revalues revalue reveals several velures. *See* **aeelrs aeelrv aeelsv aeersv**

aeelrsv reveals several. *See* **aeersv eelrsv aelrsv aeelrs aeelsv**

aeelrsvy aversely reveals sealery several slavery. *See* **aeelrs aeelrv aeelsv aeersv**

aeelrsx relaxes. *See* **aeelrs**

aeelrsy sealery. *See* **aelrsy aeelrs**

aeelrt elater relate alert alter eater elate later taler alee earl late leer leet rale rate real reel rete tael tale tare teal tear tree aet ale alt are art ate ear eat eel era ere eta lar lea lee let rat ret tar tea tee ae at el er la re ta

aeelrtx exalter. *See* **aeelrt**

aeelruv revalue. *See* **aeelrv eelruv**

aeelrv reveal elver laver leave lever ravel revel velar alee aver earl eave ever lave leer leva rale rave real reel vale veal veer ale are ave ear eel era ere eve lar lea lee lev rev vee ae el er la re

aeels easel lease alee ales ease eels else leas lees sale seal seel ale eel els lea lee sal sea see ae as el la

aeelss easels leases easel eases lease sales seals seels alee ales ease eels else lass leas lees less sale sals seal seas seel sees ale ass eel els ess lea lee sal sea see ae as el la

aeelsst teasels. *See* **aeelss aeelst aelsst eelsst aeesst**

aeelssv sleaves. *See* **aeelss aeelsv aelssv eelssv**

aeelssvw waveless aweless sleaves weasels. *See* **aeelss aeelsv aeelsw aeessw**

aeelssw aweless weasels. *See* **aeelss aeessw aelssw aeelsw**

aeelssz sleazes. *See* **aeelss aeelsz**

aeelst elates teasel easel elate lease least leets setae slate sleet stale steal steel stele taels tales tease alee ales alts ease east eats eels else etas last late leas lees leet lest lets sale salt seal seat seel seta slat tael tale teal teas tees aet ale alt ate eat eel els eta lea lee let sal sat sea see set tea tee ae as at el la ta

aeelstty layettes layette stately. *See* **aeelst aeestt aeltty eelsty**

aeelstx latexes. *See* **aeelst aelstx**

aeelstz teazels. *See* **aeelst aeelsz aeeltz**

aeelsv leaves sleave easel eaves elves laves lease leave salve slave vales veals alee ales aves ease eave eels else eves lave leas lees leva sale save seal seel vale vase veal vees ale ave eel els eve lea lee lev sal sea see vee ae as el la

aeelsw weasel easel lease swale wales weals alee ales awes awls ease eels else ewes laws leas lees sale seal seel slew wale weal ale awe awl eel els ewe law lea lee sal saw sea see sew was wee ae as aw el la we

aeelswy leeways. *See* **aeelsw aeelwy**

aeelsz sleaze easel lazes lease zeals alee ales ease eels else laze leas lees sale seal seel zeal zees ale eel els lea lee sal sea see zee ae as el la

aeelt elate alee late leet tael tale teal aet ale alt ate eat eel eta lea lee let tea tee ae at el la ta

aeeltty layette. *See* **aeltty aeelt**

aeeltv velate elate leave valet alee eave late lave leet leva tael tale teal vale veal aet ale alt ate ave eat eel eta eve lea lee let lev tav tea tee vat vee vet ae at el la ta

aeeltz teazel teazle elate alee late laze leet tael tale teal zeal zeta aet ale alt ate eat eel eta lea lee let tea tee zee ae at el la ta

aeelv leave alee eave lave leva vale veal ale ave eel eve lea lee lev vee ae el la

aeelwy leeway alee eely wale weal yawl ale awe awl aye eel ewe eye law lay lea lee lye way wee wye yaw yea yew ae aw ay el la we ye

aeemmrry yammerer. *See* **aeemrr aemmrr aemmry**

aeemmrst ammeters ammeter stammer steamer stemmer. *See* **aeemrs aemmst aemrst**

aeemmrt ammeter. *See* **aeemr aeert eemmr**

aeemn enema amen mane mean name ane mae man men nae nee ae am an em en ma me na ne

aeemnno anemone. *See* **aeemn emnno**

aeemnnos anemones anemone. *See* **aeemns**

aeemnnss meanness. *See* **aeemns aeemss aennss eemnss**

aeemnptv pavement. *See* **aeent aeemn eentv**

aeemnr meaner rename enema ameer amen earn erne mane mare mean mere name near ream ane are arm ear era ere mae man mar men nae nee ram ran rem ae am an em en er ma me na ne re

aeemnrs renames. *See* **aeemrs aeemns aeemnr**

aeemnrsw menswear renames. *See* **aeemnr aeemns aeemrs aenrsw**

aeemnrtv averment veteran. *See* **aeemnr aeenrt aemnrt aenrtv**

aeemnruv maneuver. *See* **aeemnr aeenuv aemnru**

aeemns enemas seamen enema manes manse means mesne names semen amen ease mane mean mesa name same sane seam seem seen ane ens mae man men nae nee sea see sen ae am an as em en ma me na ne

aeemnsss sameness. *See* **aeemns aeemss aemsss eemnss**

aeemnsst tameness meanest sateens senates sensate stamens. *See* **aeemns aeemss aeenst aeesst**

aeemnst meanest. *See* **aeemns aeenst aemnst**

aeemnsx examens. *See* **aeemns aeemnx**

aeemnx examen enema amen exam mane mean name ane axe mae man men nae nee ae am an ax em en ex ma me na ne

aeemosw awesome. *See* **emosw**

aeempprr pamperer prepare. *See* **aeempr aeemrr aeeprr aemppr**

aeempr ampere ameer mare mere pare pear peer perm pram ramp rape ream reap amp ape are arm ear era ere mae map mar par pea pee per ram rap rem rep ae am em er ma me pa pe re

aeemprrt tamperer tempera. *See* **aeempr aeemrr aeeprr aeeprt**

aeemprs amperes. *See* **aeemrs aeempr eemprs aeeprs**

aeemprst temperas amperes repeats stamper steamer tampers tempera tempers. *See* **aeempr aeemrs aeeprs aeeprt**

aeemprt tempera. *See* **aeempr aeeprt aemprt eemprt**

aeempstu amputees amputee. *See* **aeepst aepstu empstu**

aeemptu amputee. *See* **aeptu**

aeemqrsu marquees marquee marques masquer measure. *See* **aeemrs aemqru aemqsu aeqrsu**

aeemqru marquee. *See* **aemqru aeemr eeqru**

aeemr ameer mare mere ream are arm ear era ere mae mar ram rem ae am em er ma me re

aeemrr reamer ameer rearm mare mere rare ream rear are arm ear era ere err mae mar ram rem ae am em er ma me re

aeemrrs reamers. *See* **aeemrs aeerrs aeemrr aemrrs**

aeemrrst streamer armrest reamers serrate smarter steamer termers. *See* **aeemrr aeemrs aeerrs aeerrt**

aeemrrsu measurer armures erasure measure reamers. *See* **aeemrr aeemrs aeerrs aemrsu**

aeemrs ameers ameer erase mares maser meres reams smear arms arse ears ease eras mare mere mesa rams rase ream same seam sear seem seer sera sere are arm ear era ere mae mar ram rem res sea see ae am as em er ma me re

aeemrsst masseter steamers masters steamer streams teasers. *See* **aeemrs aeemss aeerss aeerst**

aeemrssu measures masseur measure resumes. *See* **aeemrs aeemss aeerss aemssu**

aeemrst steamer. *See* **aeemrs aeerst aemrst eemrst**

aeemrstt teamster estreat matters restate smatter steamer. *See* **aeemrs aeestt aemrst**

aeemrstw stemware steamer sweater warmest. *See* **aeemrs aemrst aerstw**

aeemrsu measure. *See* **aeemrs eemrsu**

aeemss sesame eases mesas seams seems ease mass mesa mess same seam seas seem sees ass ess mae sea see ae am as em ma me

aeemsssu masseuse assumes. *See* **aeemss aemsss aemssu eemsss**

aeennp pennae panne penna nape neap neep pane pean peen ane ape nae nap nee pan pea pee pen ae an en na ne pa pe

aeennrs ensnare. *See* **aenrs aeers eenrs**

aeennrss ensnares nearness ensnare. *See* **aeerss aennss aenrss eenrss**

aeennrx reannex. *See* **aennx**

aeennsss saneness. *See* **aennss eensss**

aeennsst neatness neatens sateens senates sennets sensate. *See* **aeennt aeenst aeesst aennss**

aeennst neatens. *See* **aeennt aeenst eennst**

aeennsx annexes. *See* **aenns aennx**

aeennt neaten eaten anent ante neat teen aet ane ant ate eat eta nae nee net tan tea tee ten ae an at en na ne ta

aeenntu uneaten. *See* **aeennt**

aeenoprs personae openers persona reopens. *See* **aeeprs aenops aenors aeoprs**

aeenorss seasoner reasons. *See* **aeerss aenors aenoss anorss**

aeenorst resonate atoners earnest eastern nearest roseate senator treason. *See* **aeenrt aeenst aenors**

aeenortv renovate overate overeat veteran. *See* **aeenrt aenort aenrtv eenrtv**

aeenpssx expanses expanse. *See* **aeepss aeepsx aenpss**

aeenpst penates. *See* **aenpst aeepst aeenst**

aeenpsx expanse. *See* **aeepsx aenps eenps**

aeenptty antetype. *See* **aenptt**

aeenrr earner nearer reran earn erne near rare rear ane are ear era ere err nae nee ran ae an en er na ne re

aeenrrs earners. *See* **aeenrr aeerrs**

aeenrrss rareness earners erasers. *See* **aeenrr aeerrs aeerss aenrss**

aeenrrst terranes earners earnest eastern nearest renters serrate sterner terrane. *See* **aeenrt aeenrt aeenst aeerrs**

aeenrrsy yearners earners yearner. *See* **aeenrr aeerrs aenrsy**

aeenrrt terrane. *See* **aeenrr aenrrt aeenrt eenrrt aeerrt**

aeenrry yearner. *See* **aeenrr**

aeenrst earnest eastern nearest. *See* **aenrst aeerst eenrst aeenrt aeenst**

aeenrstt entreats earnest eastern entreat estreat natters nearest neatest restate tenters ternate. *See* **aeenrt aeenst aeestt**

aeenrstu sauterne austere earnest eastern natures nearest neuters saunter tenures tureens. *See* **aeenrt aeenst aenrst**

aeenrstv veterans earnest eastern nearest servant taverns venters versant veteran. *See* **aeenrt aeenst aeersv**

aeenrt neater eaten eater enter ante earn erne near neat rant rate rent rete tare tear teen tern tree aet an ant are art ate ear eat era ere eta nae nee net ran rat ret tan tar tea tee ten ae an at en er na ne re ta

aeenrtt entreat ternate. *See* **aenrtt aeenrt eenrtt**

aeenrttv antevert entreat ternate veteran. *See* **aeenrt aenrtt aenrtv eenrtt**

aeenrtty entreaty entreat ternate. *See* **aeenrt aeerty aenrtt aertty**

aeenrtv veteran. *See* **aeenrt aenrtv eenrtv**

aeensst sateens senates sensate. *See* **aensst aeenst aeesst eensst**

aeenst sateen senate antes eaten nates setae tease teens tense ante ants ease east eats etas neat nest nets sane seat seen sent seta tans teas teen tees tens aet ane ant ate eat ens eta nae nee net sat sea see sen set tan tea tee ten ae an as at en na ne ta

aeenstt neatest. *See* **aeestt eenstt**

aeensuv avenues. *See* **aeenuv eensuv**

aeent eaten ante neat teen aet ane ant ate eat eta nae nee net tan tea tee ten ae an at en na ne ta

aeenuv avenue venue eave even nave uvea vane ane ave eve nae nee van vee ae an en na ne nu

aeeoprst operates operate repeats roseate seaport. *See* **aeeprs aeeprt aeepst aeerst**

aeeoprt operate. *See* **aeeprt aoprt aeopr**

aeeoprtt operetta operate treetop. *See* **aeeprt aeoptt aeortt eoprtt**

aeeorrtv overrate overate overeat. *See* **aeerrt eerrtv eorrtv**

aeeorssv overseas. *See* **aeerss aeersv aerssv aorssv**

aeeorst roseate. *See* **aeerst aeorst eeorst**

aeeorstv overeats overate overeat roseate. *See* **aeersv aeorst aerstv**

aeeorsvw overawes overawe oversaw weavers. *See* **aeersv aeervw aeesvw aersvw**

aeeortv overate overeat. *See* **aertv aeert eertv**

aeeorvw overawe. *See* **aeervw**

aeeoz zoeae zoea azo zee zoa ae

aeepprr prepare. *See* **aeeprr aepprr**

aeepprrs prepares prepare rappers reapers. *See* **aeeprr aeeprs aeerrs aepprr**

aeeprr reaper pare parr pear peer rape rare reap rear ape are ear era ere err par pea pee per rap rep ae er pa pe re

aeeprrrt parterre. *See* **aeeprr aeeprt**

aeeprrs reapers. *See* **aeerrs aeprrs aeeprr aeeprs**

aeeprrtu aperture rapture. *See* **aeeprr aeeprt aeprru eeprtu**

aeeprs serape erase pares parse pears pease peers perse rapes reaps spare spear spree apes apse arse ears ease eras pare pars pear peas peer pees rape raps rase rasp reap reps sear seep seer sera sere spar ape are asp ear era ere par pas pea pee per rap rep res sap sea see spa ae as er pa pe re

aeeprss asperse serapes. *See* **aeerss aeprss aeepss eeprss aeeprs**

aeeprsss asperses asperse passers presses serapes. *See* **aeeprs aeepss aeerss aeprss**

aeeprst repeats. *See* **aeerst aeprst aeepst eeprst aeeprt**

aeeprstz trapezes repeats trapeze. *See* **aeeprs aeeprt aeepst**

aeeprsv repaves. *See* **aeersv aeeprv aeprsv aeeprs eeprsv**

aeeprt repeat eater pater peart peter prate taper pare part pate pear peat peer pert rape rapt rate reap rete tape tare tarp tear trap tree aet ape apt are art ate ear eat era ere eta par pat pea pee per pet rap rat rep ret tap tar tea tee ae at er pa pe re ta

aeeprtz trapeze. *See* **aeeprt aeerz**

aeeprv pareve repave parve paver aver eave ever pare pave pear peer rape rave reap veep veer ape are ave ear era ere eve par pea pee per rap rep rev vee ae er pa pe re

aeeps pease apes apse ease peas pees seep ape asp pas pea pee sap sea see spa ae as pa pe

aeepss peases apses eases pease seeps apes apse asps ease pass peas pees saps seas seep sees spas ape asp ass ess pas pea pee sap sea see spa ae as pa pe

aeepsst pesetas. *See* **aepsst aeepss aeepst eepsst aeesst**

aeepst peseta paste pates pease septa setae spate steep tapes tease apes apse ease east eats etas past pate pats peas peat pees pest pets seat seep sept seta spat step tape taps teas tees aet ape apt asp ate eat eta pas pat pea pee pet sap sat sea see set spa tap tea tee ae as at pa pe ta

aeepstt septate. *See* **aeestt aeepst eepstt**

aeepsx apexes pease paxes apes apex apse axes ease exes peas pees seep ape asp axe pas pax pea pee sap sax sea see sex spa ae as ax ex pa pe

aeepsy payees payee pease seepy apes apse ayes ease easy espy eyas eyes pays peas pees pyas seep spay yaps yeas ape asp aye eye pas pay pea pee pya sap say sea see spa spy yap yea yep yes ae as ay pa pe ye

aeepvy peavey payee peavy eave pave veep ape ave aye eve eye pay pea pee pya vee yap yea yep ae ay pa pe ye

aeepy payee ape aye eye pay pea pee pya yap yea yep ae ay pa pe ye

aeeqrruv quaverer. *See* **aeqruv**

aeeqstu equates. *See* **aeeqtu eqstu aeest**

aeeqtu equate aet ate eat eta qat qua tau tea tee ae at ta ut

aeerrrst arrester serrate. *See* **aeerrs aeerrt**

aeerrs eraser erase rears arse ears ease eras errs rare rase rear sear seer sera sere are ear era ere err res sea see ae as er re

aeerrss erasers. *See* **aeerrs aeerss**

aeerrsst reassert serrates arrests erasers serrate teasers. *See* **aeerrs aeerrt aeerss aeerst**

aeerrssu erasures reassure erasers erasure. *See* **aeerrs aeerss aerssu eerssu**

aeerrst serrate. *See* **aerrst aeerst aeerrs aeerrt eerrst**

aeerrstt retreats estreat ratters restart restate retreat serrate starter terrets. *See* **aeerrs aeerrt aeestt**

aeerrstu treasure austere erasure serrate ureters. *See* **aeerrs aeerrt eerrtu**

aeerrstv traverse serrate reverts. *See* **aeerrs aeerrt aeersv**

aeerrsu erasure. *See* **aeerrs eersu errsu**

aeerrsw wearers. *See* **aeerrs aeerrw**

aeerrt tearer eater rare rate rear rete tare tear tree aet are art ate ear eat era ere err eta rat ret tar tea tee ae at er re ta

aeerrtt retreat. *See* **aerrtt aeerrt eerrtt**

aeerrvw waverer. *See* **aeerrw aeervw**

aeerrw wearer rawer ewer rare rear ware wear are awe ear era ere err ewe raw war wee ae aw er re we

aeers erase arse ears ease eras rase sear seer sera sere are ear era ere res sea see ae as er re

aeerss erases arses eases erase rases sears seers seres arse ears ease eras rase sear seas seer sees sera sere are ass ear era ere ess res sea see ae as er re

aeerssss reassess. *See* **aeerss aessss**

aeerssssy essayers essayer. *See* **aeerss aerssy aesssy eesssy**

aeerssst teasers. *See* **aerssst aeerst aeerss eerssst aeessst**

aeerssstt estreats restates estates estreat restate setters streets tasters teasers tersest testers. *See* **aeerss aeessst aeessstt**

aeerssstw sweaters sweater teasers wasters westers. *See* **aeerss aeessst aeesssw**

aeerssy essayer. *See* **aeerss aerssy**

aeersst eaters teaser aster eater erase ester rates reset setae stare steer stere tares tears tease terse trees arse arts ears ease east eats eras erst etas rase rate rats rest rete rets sear seat seer sera sere seta star tare tars tear teas tees tree tsar aet are art ate ear eat era ere eta rat res ret sat sea see set tar tea tee ae as at er re ta

aeersstt estreat restate. *See* **aeerst aeessst eerssstt aersstt**

aeerssttt attester estreat restate tatters testate tetters. *See* **aeessst aersstt**

aeerstu austere. *See* **aeerst**

aeerstw sweater. *See* **aeerst aerstw eerstw**

aeersv averse avers eaves erase raves saver serve sever veers verse arse aver aves ears ease eave eras ever eves rase rave revs save sear seer sera sere vase veer vees are ave ear era ere eve res rev sea see vee ae as er re

aeersvw weavers. *See* **aeersv eersvw aersvw aeervw aeesvw**

aeersz razees erase razee razes arse ears ease eras rase raze sear seer sera sere zees are ear era ere res sea see zee ae as er re

aeert eater rate rete tare tear tree aet are art ate ear eat era ere eta rat ret tar tea tee ae at er re ta

aeerty eatery eater teary aery arty eery eyre rate rete tare tear tray tree yare year aet are art ate aye ear eat era ere eta eye rat ray ret rye tar tea tee try yar yea yet ae at ay er re ta ye

aeervw weaver weave waver aver eave ever ewer rave veer ware wave wear are ave awe ear era ere eve ewe raw rev vee war wee ae aw er re we

aeerz razee raze are ear era ere zee ae er re

aees ease sea see ae as

aeess eases ease seas sees ass ess sea see ae as

aeesssss assesses. *See* **aessss**

aeessssw seesaws. *See* **aeessw aesss eesss**

aeessst teases asset eases sates seats setae tasse tease ease east eats etas seas seat sees seta sets tass teas tees aet ass ate eat ess eta sat sea see set tea tee ae as at ta

aeesssstt estates. *See* **aeessst eessstt aessstt aeessst**

aeessssw seesaw eases awes ease ewes saws seas sees sews ass awe ess ewe saw sea see sew was wee ae as aw we

aeesst setae tease ease east eats etas seat seta teas tees aet ate eat eta sat sea see set tea tee ae as at ta

aeesstt estate testae setae state taste tease teats testa ease east eats etas seat seta stet tats teas teat tees test aet ate eat eta sat sea see set tat tea tee ae as at ta

aeessstt testate. *See* **aessstt aeessst**

aeesv eaves aves ease eave eves save vase vees ave eve sea see vee ae as

aeesvw weaves eaves waves weave aves awes ease eave eves ewes save vase vees wave ave awe eve ewe saw sea see sew vee was wee ae as aw we

aeev eave ave eve vee ae

aeevw weave eave wave ave awe eve ewe vee wee ae aw we

aeffg gaffe gaff age fag gae ae fa

aeffgir giraffe. *See* **aeffgr effgir**

aeffgirs giraffes gaffers giraffe griffes. *See* **aeffgr aeffgs aefirs effgir**

aeffgost offstage. *See* **aeffgs afgost effost**

aeffgr gaffer gaffe ager fare fear frag gaff gear raff rage age are arf ear era erg fag far gae gar rag ref reg ae er fa re

aeffgrs gaffers. *See* **aeffgr aeffgs**

aeffgrsu suffrage gaffers. *See* **aeffgr aeffgs aegrsu effrsu**

aeffgs gaffes gaffe gaffs ages fags gaff safe sage age fag fas gae gas sag sea ae as fa

aeffimrr reaffirm firearm. *See* **aefirr aefmrr affimr efimrr**

aeffip piaffe fief fife ape fie pea pie ae ai fa if pa pe pi

aeffips piaffes. *See* **aeffip effis aeips**

aeffist taffies. *See* **aefist effis affst**

aeffisx affixes. *See* **affix aefsx effis**

aeffkost takeoffs takeoff. *See* **effost**

aeffkot takeoff. *No 6s or 5s*

aefflly flyleaf. *See* **aelly aefll efly**

aefflns snaffle. *See* **aefls aefns afns**

aefflnss snaffles snaffle. *See* **aefls aefns aflns**

aefflntu affluent fateful. *See* **aelntu aflntu eflntu**

aefflr raffle feral flare earl fare fear flea leaf raff rale real ale are arf ear elf era far lar lea ref ae el er fa la re

aefflrs raffles. *See* **aeflrs aefflr**

aefflru fearful. *See* **aeflru efflru**

aefflsux affluxes. *See* **aeflsx aelsux afflsu afflux**

aefflsw waffles. *See* **aefflw aefls aflsw**

aeffltu fateful. *See* **afltu aeflt efltu**

aefflw waffle flaw flea flew leaf waff wale weal ale awe awl elf few law lea ae aw el fa la we

aeffmrsu earmuffs. *See* **aefmrs effrsu efmrsu**

aeffrrsu staffers staffer strafes. *See* **aefrst aefsst aersst affsst**

aeffrst staffer. *See* **aefrst**

aeffrsz zaffers. *See* **aeffrz aefrs aefsz**

aeffrz zaffer fare faze fear raff raze zarf are arf ear era far fez ref ae er fa re

aefgglr flagger. *See* **aegglr**

aefgglrs flaggers flagger gargles laggers raggles. *See* **aeflrs aeglrs**

aefgiss gasifies. *See* **aegis aegss**

aefgiknr freaking fearing kerfing. *See* **aeginr afgikn afginr agiknr**

aefgiln finagle leafing. *See* **aefiln aefgln aegiln**

aefgilnr finagler fearing finagle flaring fragile leafing realign. *See* **aefgln aefiln aefilr aegiln**

aefgilns finagles finagle finales flanges leafing leasing linages sealing. *See* **aefgln aefgns aefiln aegiln**

aefgilo foliage. *See* **aegilo afilo**

aefgilr fragile. *See* **aefilr aegil agilr**

aefgimtu fumigate fatigue. *See* **agmtu aegim fimtu**

aefginr fearing. *See* **aeginr afginr efginr**

aefginrw wafering fearing wearing. *See* **aefnrw aeginr aegirw afginr**

aefginst feasting easting fasting ingesta seating teasing. *See* **aefgns aefist aefnst aegins**

aefgirst frigates fairest frigate gaiters seagirt triages. *See* **aefirs aefist aefrst aegirt**

aefgirt frigate. *See* **aegirt**

aefgistu fatigues fatigue. *See* **aefist**

aefgitu fatigue. *No 6s or 5s*

aefgllop flagpole. *See* **agllop**

aefglmn flagmen. *See* **aeflmn aefgln aeglmn**

aefglmnu fugleman flagmen. *See* **aefgln aeflmn aeglmn afglnu**

aefgln flange angel angle ganef glean fane fang flag flan flea gale glen lane leaf lean age ale ane elf fag fan fen gae gal gan gel lag lea leg nae nag ae an el en fa la na ne

aefglns flanges. *See* **aeglns aefgns**

aefglopr leapfrog pergola. *See* **aefgor aeflor aeglor aelopr**

aefglrtu grateful rageful tearful. *See* **aeflrt aeflru afglru aflrtu**

aefglru rageful. *See* **aeflru afglru**

aefgmnrt fragment garment. *See* **aegmnr aegmnt aegnrt aemnrt**

aefgn ganef fane fang age ane fag fan fen gae gan nae nag ae an en fa na ne

aefgnort frontage negator. *See* **aefgor aegnor aegnrt aegort**

aefgns ganefs fanes fangs ganef ages fags fane fang fans fens gens nags safe sage sane sang snag age ane ens fag fan fas fen gae gan gas nae nag sag sea sen ae an as en fa na ne

aefgoort footgear footage. *See* **aefgor aegort efgoor efgort**

aefgoot footage. *See* **afgot afoot**

aefgor forage afore forge gofer aero ager fare faro fear fora fore frag froe frog gear goer gore ogre rage age ago are arf ear ego era erg fag far foe fog for fro gae gar goa oaf oar ore rag ref reg roe ae er fa go of or re

aefgorr forager. *See* **aefgor efgorr**

aefgorrs foragers forager forages forgers. *See* **aefgor efgorr efgors**

aefgors forages. *See* **aefgor efgors**

aefgorv forgave. *See* **aefgor aforv aefov**

aefgrrst grafters garrets garters grafter graters rafters. *See* **aefrrt aefrst aegrrt aegrst**

aefgrrt grafter. *See* **aegrrt aefrrt**

aefhikrs freakish shakier. *See* **aefhrs aefirs aefkrs**

aefhilrs flashier flasher hailers. *See* **aefhrs aefilr aefirs aeflrs**

aefhimss famishes mashies messiah. *See* **aefhss aehims aehmss afhims**

aefhll fellah fella fall fell flea hale half hall heal hell leaf leal ale all elf ell feh hae lea ae ah eh el fa ha he la

aefhlls fellahs. *See* **aefhll aeflls**

aefhlmsu shameful. *See* **aeflms aehlsu eflmsu**

aefhlnot halftone ethanol. *See* **aehlot aflnot**

aefhlrs flasher. *See* **aefhrs aeflrs aehlrs**

aefhlrss flashers flasher flashes lashers slasher. *See* **aefhrs aefhss aeflrs aehlrs**

aefhlrty fatherly earthly lathery. *See* **aefhrt aeflrt aeflty aehlrt**

aefhlss flashes. *See* **aefhss aehlss**

aefhltu hateful. *See* **afltu aeflt efltu**

aefhmnrs freshman. *See* **aefhrs aefmrs aehmrs**

aefhrrt farther. *See* **aefhrt aefrrt aehrrt**

aefhrs afresh fares fears fresh hares hears rheas safer share sheaf shear arfs arse ears eras fare fash fear hare hear hers rahs rase rash refs resh rhea safe sear sera serf are arf ash ear era far fas feh hae has her rah ref res sea she ae ah as eh er fa ha he re sh

aefhrst fathers. *See* **aefhrs aehrst aefrst aefhrt**

aefhrstt farthest fathers hatters shatter. *See* **aefhrs aefhrt aefrst aefrtt**

aefhrt father after earth hater heart fare fart fate fear feat frat fret haft hare hart hate hear heat heft raft rate rath reft rhea tare tear aet aft are arf art ate ear eat eft era eta eth far fat feh hae hat her het rah rat ref ret tar tea the ae ah at eh er fa ha he re ta

aefhs sheaf safe fash ash fas feh hae has sea she ae ah as eh fa ha he sh

aefhss fashes sheaf ashes fash fess safe sash seas ash ass ess fas feh hae has sea she ae ah as eh fa ha he sh

aefiilms families misfile. *See* **aeflms aeilms**

aefiilnz finalize. *See* **aefiln afiiln**

aefiilss salifies falsies silesia. *See* **aeilss**

aefiimns infamies famines. *See* **aefimn aiimns eiimns**

aefiimrs ramifies fairies misfire. *See* **aefirs aefmrs aeimrs efimrs**

aefiinrv vinifera. *See* **aeinrv**

aefiiprt aperitif. *See* **aeiprt**

aefiirr friaries fairies. *See* **aefirr aefirs aeirrs**

aefiirs fairies. *See* **aefirs**

aefiirst ratifies airiest fairest fairies. *See* **aefirs aefist aefrst aeirst**

aefiitvx fixative. *See* **aefitx**

aefiklr flakier. *See* **aefilr aeikl aefkr**

aefiklst flakiest. *See* **aefist aefkls aeflst aeklst**

aefill faille fella flail alif fail fall fell fila file fill flea leaf leal lief life ail ale all elf ell fie ill lea lei lie ae ai el fa if la li

aefills failles. *See* **aeills aefill aeflls afills**

aefilmn inflame. *See* **aefimn aefiln aeflmn aeilmn**

aefilmnr inflamer rifleman fireman inflame manlier marline mineral. *See* **aefiln aefilr aefimn aeflmn**

aefilmns inflames famines finales flamens inflame malines menials seminal. *See* **aefiln aefimn aeflmn aeflms**

aefilmnt filament ailment aliment inflame inflate. *See* **aefiln aefimn aeflmn aeilmn**

aefilmsy mayflies. *See* **aeflms aeflsy aeilms aelmsy**

aefiln finale alien aline anile elfin final liane alif anil fail fain fane fila file fine flan flea lain lane leaf lean lief lien life line naif nail ail ale ane ani elf fan fen fie fin lea lei lie nae nil ae ai an el en fa if in la li na ne

aefilnnr infernal. *See* **aefiln aefilr aefnnr aeilnr**

aefilnrt inflater fainter inflate latrine ratline reliant retinal. *See* **aefiln aefilr aeflrt aeilnr**

aefilns finales. *See* **aeilns afilns**

aefilnst inflates elastin entails finales inflate salient saltine tenails. *See* **aefiln aefist aeflst aefnst**

aefilnt inflate. *See* **aeilnt aefiln**

aefilors foresail loafers safrole. *See* **aefilr aefirs aeflor aeflrs**

aefilost foliates foliate isolate. *See* **aefist aeflst aelost aflost**

aefilot foliate. *See* **aflot aeflt efilt**

aefilr ferial afire feral feria filar filer flair flare flier frail lifer rifle alif aril earl fail fair fare fear fila file fire flea lair leaf liar lief life lira lire rail rale real rial riel rife rile ail air ale are arf ear elf era far fie fir ire lar lea lei lie ref ria rif ae ai el er fa if la li re

aefilrsu failures earfuls failure refusal. *See* **aefilr aefirs aeflrs aeflru**

aefilrtt filtrate flatter flitter tertial. *See* **aefilr aeflrt aefrtt aeilrt**

aefilrtu faultier failure tearful. *See* **aefilr aeflrt aeflru aeilrt**

aefilru failure. *See* **aeflru aefilr efilru**

aefilss falsies. *See* **aeilss**

aefilssw sawflies falsies. *See* **aeilss aelssw**

aefilstu fistulae sulfate fistula. *See* **aefist aeflst aelstu aflstu**

aefilstv festival estival. *See* **aefist aeflst aeilsv aelstv**

aefimn famine amine anime minae amen fain fame fane fine main mane mean mien mina mine naif name aim ane ani fan fen fie fin mae man men nae nim ae ai am an em en fa if in ma me mi na ne

aefimnr fireman. *See* **aeimnr aefimn afimnr**

aefimns famines. *See* **aeimns**

aefimnst manifest famines inmates. *See* **aefimn aefist aefnst**

aefimor foamier. *See* **aefir aefor efimr**

aefimost foamiest atomies. *See* **aefist aeimst efiost eimost**

aefimrr firearm. *See* **aefirr aefmrr efimrr**

aefimrrs firearms farmers firearm framers marries. *See* **aefirr aefirs aefmrr aeimrs**

aefinns fannies. *See* **aeinns**

aefinnst infantes fannies infante infants. *See* **aefist aefnst aeinns aeinnt**

aefinnt infante. *See* **aeinnt afinnt**

aefinopr pinafore profane. *See* **aeinpr einopr**

aefinott fetation. *See* **aefntt aenott**

aefinrr refrain. *See* **aefirr efinr aenrr**

aefinrrs refrains refrain. *See* **aefirr aefirs aeinrs aeirrs**

aefinrss fairness fraises arsines. *See* **aefirs aeinrs aeinss aeirss**

aefinrt fainter. *See* **aeinrt**

aefinstt faintest fattens satinet. *See* **aefist aefnst aefntt afinst**

aefinsw fanwise. *See* **aeins aefns afnsw**

aefintx antefix. *See* **aefitx afint efint**

aefiortv favorite. *See* **aefir aefor afirt**

aefiprrt firetrap. *See* **aefirr aefrrt aeiprr aeiprt**

aefiqrsu aquifers aquifer. *See* **aefirs aeqrsu efirsu eiqrsu**

aefiqru aquifer. *See* **aefir eiqru**

aefir afire feria fair fare fear fire rife air are arf ear era far fie fir ire ref ria rif ae ai er fa if re

aefirr fairer afire feria friar frier fair fare fear fire rare rear rife air are arf ear era err far fie fir ire ref ria rif ae ai er fa if re

aefirrr farrier. *See* **aefirr aerrr**

aefirrrs farriers farrier. *See* **aefirr aefirs aeirrs**

aefirs ferias fraise afire arise fairs fares fears feria fires fries raise safer serai serif airs arfs arse ears eras fair fare fear fies fire firs rase refs reis rias rife rifs rise safe sari sear sera serf sire air are arf ear era far fas fie fir ifs ire ref res ria rif sea sir ae ai as er fa if is re si

aefirss fraises. *See* **aeirss aefirs efirss**

aefirst fairest. *See* **aefrst aefist aefirs efirst aeirst**

aefisst fiestas. *See* **aefsst efisst aefist aeisst**

aefist fiesta fates feast feats feist fiats east eats efts etas fast fate fats feat fiat fies fist fits safe seat seta sift site teas ties aet aft ate eat eft eta fas fat fie fit ifs ita its sat sea set sit tea tie ae ai as at fa if is it si ta ti

aefistx fixates. *See* **aefist aefitx**

aefitx fixate exit fate feat fiat fixt taxi aet aft ate axe eat eft eta fat fax fie fit fix ita tax tea tie ae ai at ax ex fa if it ta ti xi

aefjnst fanjets. *See* **aefjnt aefnst aejnst**

aefjnt fanjet ante fane fate fate feat jean neat aet aft ane ant ate eat eft eta fan fat fen jet nae net tan tea ten ae an at en fa na ne ta

aefk fake kaf kef ae fa ka

aefkl flake fake flak flea kale lake leaf leak ale elf elk kaf kal kef lea lek ae el fa ka la

aefklnr flanker. *See* **aeklnr aefkr aeflr**

aefklnrs flankers flanker rankles. *See* **aefkls aefkns aefkrs aeflrs**

aefkls flakes fakes false flake flaks flask fleas lakes leafs leaks slake ales elks fake flak flea kafs kale kefs lake leaf leak leas leks safe sake sale seal self ale ask elf elk els fas kaf kal kas kef lea lek sal sea ae as el fa ka la

aefkluw wakeful. *See* **afluw aefkl efklu**

aefkn kenaf fake fane ane fan fen kaf kef ken nae ae an en fa ka na ne

aefknors forsaken forsake. *See* **aefkns aefkrs aekors aenors**

aefkns kenafs fakes fanes kenaf skean snake sneak fake fane fans fens kafs kefs kens safe sake sane sank ane ask ens fan fas fen kaf kas kef ken nae sea sen ae an as en fa ka na ne

aefkors forsake. *See* **aekors aefkrs**

aefkorss forsakes forsake soakers. *See* **aefkrs aefoss aekors aekrss**

aefkortu freakout. *See* **aefor aefrt aefkr**

aefkr faker freak fake fare fear kerf rake are arf ark ear era far kaf kef ref ae er fa ka re

aefkrs fakers freaks eskar faker fakes fares fears freak kerfs rakes safer saker arfs arks arse ears eras fake fare fear kafs kefs kerf rake rase refs safe sake sark sear sera serf are arf ark ask ear era far fas kaf kas kef ref res sea ae as er fa ka re

aefkry fakery freaky faery faker freak aery fake fare fear fray fyke kerf rake yare year are arf ark aye ear era far fay fey fry kaf kef key ray ref rye yak yar yea ae ay er fa ka re ye

aefks fakes fake kafs kefs safe sake ask fas kaf kas kef sea ae as fa ka

aefl flea leaf ale elf lea ae el fa la

aefll fella fall fell flea leaf leal ale all elf ell lea ae el fa la

aefllln fallen fella fall fane fell flan flea lane leaf leal lean ale all ane elf ell fan fen lea nae ae an el en fa la na ne

aefllnn flannel. *See* **aeflln**

aefllnns flannels flannel. *See* **aefllln aeflls**

aefllptu plateful. *See* **aellpt afllpu ellptu**

aefllr faller fella feral flare earl fall fare fear fell flea leaf leal rale real ale all are

arf ear elf ell era far lar lea ref ae el er fa la re

aefllrs fallers. *See* **aefllr aeflrs aeflls**

aeflls fellas falls false fella fells fleas leafs ales ells fall fell flea leaf leal leas safe sale seal self sell ale all elf ell els fas lea sal sea ae as el fa la

aefllssw flawless lawless. *See* **aeflls aelssw ellssw**

aefllsty festally falsely. *See* **aeflls aeflst aeflsy aeflty**

aefllsy falsely. *See* **aellsy aeflls aeflsy**

aeflm flame fleam fame flam flea lame leaf male meal ale elf elm lam lea mae mel ae am el em fa la ma me

aeflmn flamen flame fleam leman amen fame fane flam flan flea lame lane leaf lean male mane meal mean name ale ane elf elm fan fen lam lea mae man mel men nae ae am an el em en fa la ma me na ne

aeflmns flamens. *See* **aeflmn aeflms aelmns**

aeflmoru formulae formula. *See* **aeflor aeflru aelmor aelmru**

aeflms flames fleams false fames flame flams fleam fleas lames leafs males meals ales alms elms fame flam flea lame lams leaf leas male meal mels mesa safe sale same seal seam self slam ale elf elm els fas lam lea mae mel sal sea ae am as el em fa la ma me

aeflnopt pantofle polenta. *See* **aelnpt aelopt aflnot elnopt**

aeflnrsu funerals earfuls funeral refusal. *See* **aeflrs aeflru aefnsu aelnrs**

aeflnru funeral. *See* **aeflru aelnru**

aeflnsst flatness falsest fastens fatness. *See* **aeflst aefnst aefsst aelsst**

aeflnstt flattens fattens flatten lattens talents. *See* **aeflst aefnst aefntt aelntt**

aeflntt flatten. *See* **aefntt aelntt**

aeflnx flaxen axle fane flan flax flea flex lane leaf lean ale ane axe elf fan fax fen lax lea nae ae an ax el en ex fa la na ne

aeflopry foreplay palfrey. *See* **aeflor aelopr aelpry**

aeflopsw peafowls peafowl seafowl. *See* **aelops**

aeflopw peafowl. *No 6s or 5s*

aeflor loafer afore feral flare flora aero aloe earl fare faro fear flea floe foal fora fore froe leaf loaf lore oral orle rale real role ale are arf ear elf era far foe for fro lar lea oaf oar ore ref roe ae el er fa la lo of or re

aeflors loafers safrole. *See* **aeflrs aflors aeflor**

aeflorss safroles lassoer loafers oarless safrole. *See* **aeflor aeflrs aefoss aelrss**

aeflorst floaters refloats falters floater florets loafers refloat safrole. *See* **aeflor aeflrs aeflrt aeflst**

aeflort floater refloat. *See* **aeflrt eflort**

aeflostt falsetto. *See* **aeflst aelost aelstt aflost**

aeflosw seafowl. *See* **aelos aefls aflsw**

aeflppr flapper. *See* **aelppr aeflr**

aeflpprs flappers felspar flapper rappels. *See* **aeflrs aelppr aelpps aelprs**

aeflppry flypaper flapper palfrey reapply. *See* **aelppr aelpry**

aeflprs felspar. *See* **aeflrs aelprs**

aeflprss felspars felspar. *See* **aeflrs aelprs aelpss aelrss**

aeflprsy palfreys felspar palfrey parleys parsley players replays sparely. *See* **aeflrs aeflsy aelprs aelpry**

aeflpry palfrey. *See* **aelpry**

aeflr feral flare earl fare fear flea leaf rale real ale are arf ear elf era far lar lea ref ae el er fa la re

aeflrs falser flares earls false fares fears feral flare fleas lares laser leafs rales safer ales arfs arse earl ears eras fare fear flea leaf leas rale rase real refs safe sale seal sear self sera serf ale are arf ear elf els era far fas lar lea ref res sal sea ae as el er fa la re

aeflrssu refusals earfuls refusal saurels. *See* **aeflrs aeflru aelrss aelrsu**

aeflrst falters. *See* **aelrst aeflrs aeflrt aefrst aeflst**

aeflrstt flatters falters flatter rattles starlet startle. *See* **aeflrs aeflrt aeflst aefrst**

aeflrsu earfuls refusal. *See* **aeflru aelrsu**

aeflrszz frazzles frazzle. *See* **aeflrs aerszz**

aeflrt falter after alert alter feral fetal flare later taler earl fare fart fate fear feat felt flat flea frat fret late leaf left raft rale rate real reft tael tale tare teal tear aet aft ale alt are arf art ate ear eat eft elf era eta far fat lar lea let rat ref ret tar tea ae at el er fa la re ta

aeflrtt flatter. *See* **aeflrt aefrtt aelrtt**

aeflrttu aflutter flatter flutter tearful. *See* **aeflrt aeflru aefrtt aflrtu**

aeflrtty flattery flatter. *See* **aeflrt aeflty aefrtt aelrty**

aeflrtu tearful. *See* **aflrtu aeflru aeflrt**

aeflru earful feral flare earl fare fear flea flue fuel furl leaf lure rale real rule urea ale are arf ear elf era far feu flu fur lar lea leu ref rue ae el er fa la re

aeflrzz frazzle. *See* **aeflr**

aefls false fleas leafs ales flea leaf leas safe sale seal self ale elf els fas lea sal sea ae as el fa la

aeflsst falsest. *See* **aefsst aeflst aelsst**

aeflsstu sulfates falsest salutes sulfate taluses. *See* **aeflst aefsst aelsst aelstu**

aeflst festal false fates feast feats felts fetal flats fleas leafs least slate stale steal taels tales ales alts east eats efts etas fast fate fats feat felt flat flea last late leaf leas left lest lets safe sale salt seal seat self seta slat tael tale teal teas aet aft ale alt ate eat eft elf els eta fas fat lea let sal sat sea set tea ae as at el fa la ta

aeflsttt flattest fattest tattles. *See* **aeflst aelstt**

aeflsttu tasteful sulfate. *See* **aeflst aelstt aelstu aesttu**

aeflstu sulfate. *See* **aflstu eflstu aelstu**

aeflstuw wasteful sulfate. *See* **aeflst aelstu aflstu eflstu**

aeflsx flaxes axels axles false faxes fleas leafs ales axes axle flax flea flex leaf leas safe sale seal self ale axe elf els fas fax lax lea sal sax sea sex ae as ax el ex fa la

aeflsy safely false flays fleas leafs leafy ales ayes easy eyas fays flay flea lays leaf leas lyes lyse safe sale seal self slay yeas ale aye elf els fas fay fey fly lay lea lye sal say sea sly yea yes ae as ay el fa la ye

aeflt fetal fate feat felt flat flea late leaf left tael tale teal aet aft ale alt ate eat eft elf eta fat lea let tea ae at el fa la ta

aeflty fealty featly fatly fetal leafy lefty fate feat felt flat flay flea late leaf left tael tale teal aet aft ale alt ate aye eat eft elf eta fat fay fey fly lay lea let lye tea yea yet ae at ay el fa la ta ye

aefly leafy flay flea leaf ale aye elf fay fey fly lay lea lye yea ae ay el fa la ye

aefm fame mae ae am em fa ma me

aefmno foeman aeon amen fame fane foam mane mean moan name noma nome omen ane eon fan fen foe mae man men moa mon nae oaf one ae am an em en fa ma me mo na ne no of om on

aefmnor foramen foreman. *See* **aemnor aefmno**

aefmnrry ferryman. *See* **aefmrr aefrry**

aefmorr forearm. *See* **aefmrr efmorr aemorr**

aefmorrs forearms farmers forearm framers reforms remoras roamers. *See* **aefmrr aefmrs aemorr aemrrs**

aefmorst foremast farmost formats maestro. *See* **aefmrs aefrst aemrst aeorst**

aefmr frame fame fare farm fear mare ream are arf arm ear era far mae mar ram ref rem ae am em er fa ma me re

aefmrr farmer framer frame rearm fame fare farm fear mare rare ream rear are arf arm ear era err far mae mar ram ref rem ae am em er fa ma me re

aefmrrs farmers framers. *See* **aefmrr aefmrs aemrrs**

aefmrs frames fames fares farms fears frame mares maser reams safer smear arfs arms arse ears eras fame fare farm fear mare mesa rams rase ream refs safe same seam sear sera serf are arf arm ear era far fas mae mar ram ref rem res sea ae am as em er fa ma me re

aefms fames fame mesa safe same seam fas mae sea ae am as em fa ma me

aefn fane ane fan fen nae ae an en fa na ne

aefnnr fanner earn fane fare fear fern near ane are arf ear era fan far fen nae ran ref ae an en er fa na ne re

aefnnrs fanners. *See* **aefnnr aenrs aefns**

aefnnstu unfasten. *See* **aefnst aefnsu aenstu annstu**

aefnopr profane. *See* **aefor anopr aeopr**

aefnoprs profanes profane persona. *See* **aenops aenors aeoprs anoprs**

aefnorrw forewarn frowner. *See* **aefnrw aenrrw aforrw anorrw**

aefnrrst transfer rafters. *See* **aefnst aefrrt aefrst aenrrt**

aefnrruy funerary. *See* **aefrry**

aefnrsw fawners. *See* **aenrsw aefnrw aefrsw**

aefnrw fawner wafer anew earn fane fare fawn fear fern near wane ware warn wean wear wren ane are arf awe awn ear era fan far fen few nae new ran raw ref wan war wen ae an aw en er fa na ne re we

aefns fanes fane fans fens safe sane ane ens fan fas fen nae sea sen ae an as en fa na ne

aefnssst fastness assents fastens fatness. *See* **aefnst aefsst aensst aessst**

aefnsst fastens fatness. *See* **aensst aefnst aefsst**

aefnst fasten antes fanes fates feast feats nates ante ants east eats efts etas fane fans fast fate fats feat fens neat nest nets safe sane seat sent seta tans teas tens aet aft ane ant ate eat eft ens eta fan fas fat fen nae net sat sea sen set tan tea ten ae an as at en fa na ne ta

aefnstt fattens. *See* **aefnst aefntt**

aefnsu unsafe fanes fauns snafu anus fane fans faun fens feus fuse safe sane ane ens fan fas fen feu fun nae sea sen sue sun use ae an as en fa na ne nu us

aefntt fatten ante fane fate feat neat teat tent aet aft ane ant ate eat eft eta fan fat fen nae net tan tat tea ten ae an at en fa na ne ta

aefoprsw forepaws forepaw foresaw. *See* **aefrsw aeoprs eoprsw**

aefoprw forepaw. *See* **aefor aeopr eoprw**

aefor afore aero fare faro fear fora fore froe are arf ear era far foe for fro oaf oar ore ref roe ae er fa of or re

aeforrsv favorers favorer fervors savorer. *See* **aerrsv aforsv eforrv eorrsv**

aeforrsw forswear foresaw farrows. *See* **aefrsw aforrw aorrsw eorrsw**

aeforrv favorer. *See* **eforrv aefor aforv**

aeforstw software foresaw twofers. *See* **aefrst aefrsw aeorst aerstw**

aeforsty forestay. *See* **aefrst aefsty aeorst aersty**

aeforsw foresaw. *See* **aefrsw aefor aeors**

aefoss fossae fossa fosse oases sofas fess foes foss oafs ossa safe seas sofa ass ess fas foe oaf sea ae as fa of os so

aefov fovea ave foe oaf ova ae fa of

aefr fare fear are arf ear era far ref ae er fa re

aefrrst rafters. *See* **aerrst aefrst aefrrt**

aefrrt rafter after fare fart fate fear feat frat fret raft rare rate rear reft tare tear aet aft are arf art ate ear eat eft era err eta far fat rat ref ret tar tea ae at er fa re ta

aefrry rarefy faery ferry fryer refry aery fare fear fray rare rear yare year are arf aye ear era err far fay fey fry ray ref rye yar yea ae ay er fa re ye

aefrs fares fears safer arfs arse ears eras fare fear rase refs safe sear sera serf are arf ear era far fas ref res sea ae as er fa re

aefrsst strafes. *See* **aersst aefsst**

aefrst faster strafe after aster fares farts fates fears feast feats frats frets rafts rates safer stare tares tears arfs arse arts ears east eats efts eras erst etas fare fart fast fate fats fear feat frat fret raft rase rate rats refs reft rest rets safe scar seat sera serf seta star tare tars tear teas tsar aet aft are arf art ate ear eat eft era eta far fas fat rat ref res ret sat sea set tar tea ae as at er fa re ta

aefrsw wafers fares fears safer swear wafer wares wears arfs arse awes ears eras fare fear rase refs safe sear sera serf ware wars wear are arf awe ear era far fas few raw ref res saw sea sew war was ae as aw er fa re we

aefrt after fare fart fate fear feat frat fret raft rate reft tare tear aet aft are arf art ate ear eat eft era eta far fat rat ref ret tar tea ae at er fa re ta

aefrtt fatter after tater tetra treat fare fart fate fear feat frat fret raft rate reft tare tart tear teat tret aet aft are arf art ate ear eat eft era eta far fat rat ref ret tar tat tea ae at er fa re ta

aefrw wafer fare fear ware wear are arf awe ear era far few raw ref war ae aw er fa re we

aefrwy wafery faery wafer weary aery awry fare fear fray ware wary wear yare year are arf awe aye ear era far fay few fey fry raw ray ref rye war way wye yar yaw yea yew ae aw ay er fa re we ye

aefry faery aery fare fear fray yare year are arf aye ear era far fay fey fry ray ref rye yar yea ae ay er fa re ye

aefs safe sea fas ae as fa

aefsst feasts safest asset fasts fates feast feats sates seats tasse east eats efts etas fast fate fats feat fess safe seas seat seta sets tass teas aet aft ass ate eat eft ess eta fas fat sat sea set tea ae as at fa ta

aefsstt fastest. *See* **aefsst aesstt**

aefst fates feast feats east eats efts etas fast fate fats feat safe seat seta teas aet aft ate eat eft eta fas fat sat sea set tea ae as at fa ta

aefsttt fattest. *See* **aesttt aefst**

aefsty safety fates feast feats yeast ayes east easy eats efts etas eyas fast fate fats fays feat safe seat seta stay teas yeas aet aft ate aye eat eft eta fas fat fay fey sat say sea set sty tea yea yes yet ae as at ay fa ta ye

aefsx faxes axes safe axe fas fax sax sea sex ae as ax ex fa

aefsz fazes safe faze fas fez sea ae as fa

aeft fate feat aet aft ate eat eft eta fat tea ae at fa ta

aefz faze fez ae fa

aeg age gae ae

aegg gage age egg gae gag ae

aeggginn engaging ganging nagging. *See* **aeggin**

aegggl gaggle gage gale age ale egg gae gag gal gel lag lea leg ae el la

aeggglu gaggles. *See* **aegggl aeggs aegls**

aeggglu luggage. *See* **aegggl egglu**

aegghirs shaggier hegaris. *See* **aeghir aeghis aeghrs aehirs**

aegghl haggle gage gale hale heal age ale egg gae gag gal gel hae hag lag lea leg ae ah eh el ha he la

aegghlr haggler. *See* **aegglr aegghl**

aegghlrs hagglers gargles haggler haggles laggers raggles. *See* **aegghl aeghrs aeglrs**

aegghls haggles. *See* **aegghl aeggs aegls**

aegghoru roughage. *See* **egghru eggoru**

aeggi aggie gage age egg gae gag gie gig ae ai

aeggijr jaggier. *See* **eggijr aeggi**

aeggijst jaggiest. *See* **aegis aeggi**

aeggilln alleging gallein galling gelling. *See* **aeggin aeggln aegiln aeillln**

aeggillr grillage. *See* **egillr**

aeggilmn gleaming. *See* **aeggin aeggln aeggmn aegiln**

aeggilnn gleaning leaning angling. *See* **aeggin aeggln aegiln**

aeggin gaeing aggie aging gage gain gang age ane ani egg gae gag gan gie gig gin nae nag ae ai an en in na ne

aegginnr angering enraging earning gearing nearing ranging. *See* **aeggin aeggnr aeginr aeinnr**

aegginnt negating anteing antigen gentian tanging. *See* **aeggin aegint aeggnnt aeinnt**

aegginnv avenging. *See* **aeggin**

aegginos seagoing isagoge agonies. *See* **aeggin aegins aegnos**

aegginr gearing. *See* **aeginr aeggin aeggnr egginr agginr**

aegginrs greasing earings erasing gainers gangers gearing gingers granges naggers regains searing snigger. *See* **aeggin aeggnr aeginr aegins**

aegginrw wagering gearing wearing. *See* **aeggin aeggnr aeginr aegirw**

aeggiopr arpeggio. *See* **aeggi aegpr eggor**

aeggios isagoge. *See* **aegis aeggi agios**

aeggioss isagoges isagoge. *See* **aegis aeggi agios**

aeggiqru quaggier. *See* **aeggi aegru aeggu**

aeggjry jaggery. *See* **aegry aggjy**

aeggln naggle angel angle glean gage gale gang glen lane lean age ale ane egg gae gag gal gan gel lag lea leg nae nag ae an el en la na ne

aegglnpt eggplant. *See* **aeggln aeglnt aelnpt**

aegglnr gangrel. *See* **aeglnr aeggnr aegglr aeggln**

aegglnrs gangrels anglers gangers gangrel gargles granges laggers naggers raggles. *See* **aegglln aeggnr aeglnr**

aegglory gargoyle. *See* **aeglor aeglry egglor**

aegglr gargle lagger glare lager large regal ager earl gage gale gear rage rale real age ale are ear egg era erg gae gag gal gar gel lag lar lea leg rag reg ae el er la re

aegglrs gargles laggers. *See* **aegglr aeglrs**

aegglrst straggle gagster gargets gargles laggers largest stagger taggers. *See* **aeggrt aeglrs aeglst**

aegglsw waggles. *See* **aegglw aeggs aegls**

aegglw waggle gage gale wage wale weal age ale awe awl egg gae gag gal gel lag law lea leg wag ae aw el la we

aeggmn gagmen mange amen gage game gang mage mane mean name age ane egg gae gag gam gan gem mae mag man men nae nag ae am an em en ma me na ne

aeggmort mortgage. *See* **aeggrt aegort aggmot eggort**

aeggnr ganger grange nagger anger range ager earn gage gang gear gnar near rage rang age ane are ear egg era erg gae gag gan gar nae nag rag ran reg ae an en er na ne re

aeggnrr granger. *See* **aeggnr aegnrr**

aeggnrrs grangers gangers garners granger granges naggers rangers. *See* **aeggnr aegnrr aegnrs**

aeggnrs gangers granges naggers. *See* **aegnrs aeggnr**

aeggnrst gangster argents gagster gangers gargets garnets granges naggers stagger strange taggers. *See* **aeggnr aeggrt aegnrs aegnrt**

aeggnsu gangues. *See* **aeggnu aeggsu**

aeggnu gangue gauge ague gage gang guan age ane egg gae gag gan gnu gun nae nag ae an en na ne nu

aeggrss aggress. *See* **aegrss aeggs**

aeggrsst staggers aggress gagster gargets stagers stagger taggers. *See* **aeggrt aegrss aegrst aegsst**

aeggrssw swaggers aggress swagger. *See* **aegrss aegrsw aerssw**

aeggrst gagster gargets stagger taggers. *See* **aeggrt aegrst**

aeggrsw swagger. *See* **aegrsw aeggs**

aeggrt garget tagger grate great targe terga ager gage gate gear rage rate tare tear aet age are art ate ear eat egg era erg eta gae gag gar gat get rag rat reg ret tag tar tea ae at er re ta

aeggrwy waggery. *See* **aegry aegrw aerwy**

aeggs gages ages eggs gage gags sage age egg gae gag gas sag sea ae as

aeggsu gauges agues gages gauge usage ages ague eggs gage gags sage age egg gae gag gas sag sea sue use ae as us

aeggsww gewgaws. *See* **aeggww aeggs aegsw**

aeggu gauge gage ague age egg gae gag ae

aeggww gewgaw gage wage age awe egg gae gag wag ae aw we

aeghilmt megalith. *See* **aegilt aehilm aehilt aehlmt**

aeghiln healing. *See* **aegiln aghiln aehiln**

aeghilns leashing healing inhales lashing leasing linages sealing shingle. *See* **aeghis aegiln aegins aeglns**

aeghilnx exhaling healing. *See* **aegiln aehiln aghiln eghinx**

aeghinp heaping. *See* **aginp eghin**

aeghinr hearing. *See* **aeginr aeghnr aeghir aehinr eghinr**

aeghinrs hearings shearing earings erasing gainers garnish hangers hearing hegaris hernias hingers regains searing sharing. *See* **aeghir aeghis aeghnr aeghrs**

aeghinsv sheaving heaving shaving. *See* **aeghis aegins aegisv aehnsv**

aeghint heating. *See* **aegint aghint**

aeghinv heaving. *See* **aghinv eginv aehnv**

aeghio hoagie agio age ago ego gae gie goa hae hag hie hoe hog ae ah ai eh go ha he hi ho oh

aeghiops esophagi hoagies. *See* **aeghio aeghis**

aeghios hoagies. *See* **aeghio aeghis**

aeghippr epigraph happier. *See* **aeghir aegipp egippr ehippr**

aeghiprt graphite. *See* **aeghir aeghrt aegirt aegprt**

aeghir hegari gerah ager gear hair hare hear heir hire rage rhea age air are ear era erg gae gar gie hae hag her hie ire rag rah reg ria rig ae ah ai eh er ha he hi re

aeghirrs gharries hegaris harries. *See* **aeghir aeghis aeghrs aehirs**

aeghirs hegaris. *See* **aehirs aghirs aeghis aeghrs aeghir**

aeghis geisha aegis ages egis gash gies hags hies sage shag sigh age ash gae gas gie hae hag has hie his sag sea she ae ah ai as eh ha he hi is sh si

aeghiss geishas. *See* **aeghis aeghss**

aeghiw aweigh weigh wage age awe gae gie hae hag haw hew hie wag wig ae ah ai aw eh ha he hi we

aeghlno halogen. *See* **aelno aglno aegln**

aeghlnos halogens halogen. *See* **aeglns aegnos aehlns aehlos**

aeghlopy hypogeal. *See* **aehlpy**

aeghloss galoshes glossae. *See* **aeghss aehlos aehlss aghlos**

aeghlrsu laughers laugher haulers. *See* **aeghrs aegirs aegrsu aehlrs**

aeghlrtu laughter laugher. *See* **aeghrt aehlrt aehlru ehlrtu**

aeghlrty lethargy earthly greatly lathery. *See* **aeghrt aeglry aegrty aehlrt**

aeghlru laugher. *See* **aehlru aegru aeghr**

aeghmnn hangmen. *See* **aegmn aehnn**

aeghmo homage ohmage omega ogham ahem game hame home mage age ago ego gae gam gem goa hae hag ham hem hoe hog mae mag mho moa mog ohm ae ah am eh em go ha he ho ma me mo oh om

aeghmopt apothegm apothem. *See* **aeghmo**

aeghmor homager. *See* **aeghmo**

aeghmors homagers homager ohmages. *See* **aeghmo aeghrs aegmos aegmrs**

aeghmos ohmages. *See* **aeghmo aghmos aegmos**

aeghnopt heptagon pathogen phaeton phonate. *See* **aegnt aenot aegno**

aeghnorv hangover overhang. *See* **aeghnr aegnor aegnrv egnorv**

aeghnosx hexagons hexagon hexosan. *See* **aegnos aehosx aghnos**

aeghnox hexagon. *See* **aegno aghno**

aeghnr hanger anger gerah range ager earn gear gnar hang hare hear hern near rage rang rhea age ane are ear era erg gae gan gar hae hag hen

aeghnrs hangers. *See* **aegnrs aeghrs aeghnr**

aeghnss gnashes. *See* **aeghss aehns aghns**

aeghorst shortage earshot gathers hostage orgeats storage. *See* **aeghrs aeghrt aegort aegrst**

aeghosst hostages hostage. *See* **aeghss aegsst ahosst ehosst**

aeghossu gashouse gaseous. *See* **aeghss aegssu eghssu ehossu**

aeghost hostage. *See* **ehost aegst aghst**

aeghr gerah ager gear hare hear rage rhea age are ear era erg gae gar hae hag her rag rah reg ae ah eh er ha he re

aeghrs gerahs gears gerah hares hears rages rheas sager share shear ager ages arse ears eras ergs gars gash gear hags hare hear hers rage rags rahs rase rash regs resh rhea rage sear sera shag age are ash ear era erg gae gar gas hae hag has her rag rah reg res sag sea she ae ah as eh er ha he re sh

aeghrst gathers. *See* **aehrst aghrst aeghrt aegrst**

aeghrt gather earth garth gerah grate great hater heart targe terga ager gate gear ghat hare hart hate hear heat rage rate rath rhea tare tear aet age are art ate ear eat era erg eta eth gae gar gat get hae hag hat her het rag rah rat reg ret tag tar tea the ae ah at eh er ha he re ta

aeghss gashes ashes gases sages shags ages gash hags sage sags sash seas shag age ash ass ess gae gas hae hag has sag sea she ae ah as eh ha he sh

aegiillu aiguille. *See* **agillu egillu**

aegiiltt litigate. *See* **aegilt**

aegiimn imagine. *See* **aegimn agiimn**

aegiimnr migraine imagine mangier reaming. *See* **aegimn aegimr aeginr aeimnr**

aegiimns imagines enigmas imagine seaming. *See* **aegimn aegims aegins aegmns**

aegiimtt mitigate imitate. *See* **aegim aemtt**

aegiinrr grainier angrier earring rainier rearing. *See* **aeginr aegnrr**

aegiirrt irrigate. *See* **aegirt aegrrt**

aegikln leaking linkage. *See* **aegiln**

aegiklns linkages leaking leasing linages linkage sealing sinkage slaking. *See* **aegiln aegils aegins aeglns**

aegiklnw weakling leaking linkage walking. *See* **aegiln aeglnw agiknw agilnw**

aegikmnr remaking mangier marking reaming. *See* **aegimn aegimr aeginr aeimnr**

aegiknns sneaking sinkage snaking. *See* **aegins aeinns agikns**

aegiknnw wakening weaning. *See* **agiknw aginnw**

aegiknp peaking. *See* **aginp egikn agikn**

aegiknps speaking peaking sinkage. *See* **aegins agikns**

aegiknrt retaking granite ingrate keratin tangier tearing. *See* **aeginr aegint aegirt aegnrt**

aegiknrw wreaking gawkier wearing. *See* **aeginr aegirw agiknr agiknw**

aegikns sinkage. *See* **agikns aegins**

aegiknss sinkages sinkage gaskins. *See* **aegins aeinss aeknss agikns**

aegikntw tweaking. *See* **aegint aeiknt agiknt agiknw**

aegikrw gawkier. *See* **aegirw aekrw**

aegikstw gawkiest. *See* **aegkst aekstw eikstw**

aegil agile gale age ail ale gae gal gel gie lag lea leg lei lie ae ai el la li

aegilll illegal. *See* **aegil aegll**

aegillms legalism. *See* **aegils aegims aeglms aeills**

aegilln gallein. *See* **aegiln aeilln**

aegillns galleins gallein leasing linages sealing selling. *See* **aegiln aegils aegins aeglns**

aegillny genially agilely allying gallein yelling. *See* **aegiln aeglly aeilln agilny**

aegillp pillage. *See* **aegil aellp aegll**

aegillps pillages spillage pillage. *See* **aegils aeglps aeills aeilps**

aegillrv villager village. *See* **aegilv aegirv aeglrv egillr**

aegillst legalist gallets ligates tailles tallies tillage. *See* **aegils aegilt aeglt aeglst**

aegillsv villages village glaives. *See* **aegils aegilv aegisv aeglsv**

aegillt tillage. *See* **aegllt aegilt aeillt**

aegillty legality tillage agilely. *See* **aegilt aegity aegllt aeglly**

aegillv village. *See* **aegilv aegll aillv**

aegilly agilely. *See* **aeglly aegil agily**

aegilmnp empaling impanel leaping maniple palming pealing. *See* **aegiln aegimn aegimp aeglmn**

aegilmnr germinal maligner malinger gremial gremlin mangier mangler manlier marline mineral mingler realign reaming. *See* **aegiln aegimn aegimr aeginr**

aegilmnt ligament metaling ailment aliment atingle elating gelatin genital malting melting mintage teaming tegmina. *See* **aegiln aegilt aegimn aegint**

aegilmr gremial. *See* **aegimr aeilmr**

aegilmrs gremials gremial mailers mirages realism. *See* **aegils aegimr aegims aeglms**

aegiln genial linage agile alien align aline angel angle anile glean ingle liane ligan linga anil gain gale glen lain lane lean lien line ling nail age ail ale ane ani gae gal gan gel gie gin lag lea leg lei lie nae nag nil ae ai an el en in la li na ne

aegilnn leaning. *See* **aegiln**

aegilnnp paneling leaning leaping pealing planing. *See* **aegiln aeilnp aeinnp agilnp**

aegilnnr learning earning leaning nearing realign. *See* **aegiln aeginr aeglnr aeilnr**

aegilnnt gantline anteing antigen atingle elating gelatin genital gentian leaning. *See* **aegiln aegilt aegint aeglnt**

aegilnny yeanling inanely leaning yeaning. *See* **aegiln agilny**

aegilnor regional aileron alienor realign. *See* **aegiln aegilo aeginr aeglnr**

aegilnos gasoline agonies eloigns goalies leasing legions linages lingoes sealing. *See* **aegiln aegilo aegils aegins**

aegilnot legation atingle elating elation gelatin genital lentigo tangelo toenail. *See* **aegiln aegilo aegilt aegint**

aegilnp leaping pealing. *See* **aeilnp aegiln agilnp**

aegilnpr pearling grapnel leaping pealing plainer praline realign reaping. *See* **aegiln aeginr aeglnr aeilnp**

aegilnps elapsing pleasing lapsing leaping leasing linages pealing sapling sealing spangle spaniel. *See* **aegiln aegils aegins aeglns**

aegilnpt pleating atingle elating gelatin genital leaping pantile pealing pelting plating. *See* **aegiln aegilt aegint aeglnt**

aegilnqu equaling linguae. *See* **aegiln aeginu agilnu**

aegilnr realign. *See* **aeglnr aeginr aegiln aeilnr egilnr**

aegilnrs realigns signaler anglers earings erasing gainers leasing linages lingers realign regains sealing searing. *See* **aegiln aegils aeginr aegins**

aegilnrt altering integral relating triangle atingle elating gelatin granite ingrate latrine ratline realign reliant retinal ringlet tangier tangler tearing tingler. *See* **aegiln aegilt aeginr aegint**

aegilnrv raveling leaving realign reaving vinegar. *See* **aegiln aegilv aeginr aegirv**

aegilnrx relaxing realign. *See* **aegiln aeginr aeglnr aeilnr**

aegilnry relaying yearling angrily realign relying. *See* **aegiln aeginr aeglnr aeglry**

aegilns leasing linages sealing. *See* **aeilns agilns aeglns aegins aegiln**

aegilnst gelatins genitals stealing atingle easting elastin elating entails gelatin genital glisten ingesta lasting leasing ligates linages salient saltine salting sealing seating singlet slating staling tangles teasing tenails tingles. *See* **aegiln aegils aegilt aegins**

aegilnsv leavings glaives leasing leaving linages salving sealing slaving. *See* **aegiln aegils aegilv aegins**

aegilnt atingle elating gelatin genital. *See* **aegint aeilnt aegiln aegilt aeglnt**

aegilntx exalting atingle elating gelatin genital. *See* **aegiln aegilt aegint aeglnt**

aegilnu linguae. *See* **aegiln aeginu agilnu**

aegilnv leaving. *See* **aegiln aegilv agilnv aeilnv**

aegilo goalie agile agio aloe gale gaol goal loge ogle age ago ail ale ego gae gal gel gie goa lag lea leg lei lie log oil ae ai el go la li lo**

aegilops spoilage goalies. *See* **aegilo aegils aeglps aeilps**

aegilors seraglio gaolers girasol glorias glories goalies. *See* **aegilo aegils aeglor aeglrs**

aegilos goalies. *See* **aegilo aegils**

aegilou eulogia. *See* **aegilo egilu**

aegilpps slippage pipages applies. *See* **aegils aegipp aeglps aeilps**

aegilppu pupilage. *See* **aegipp aeglpu aelppu**

aegilrsy greasily argyles. *See* **aegils aeglrs aeglry aeglsy**

aegilrsz glaziers glazier. *See* **aegils aeglrs aeglsz aegrsz**

aegilrtt aglitter tertial glitter. *See* **aegilt aegirt aegrtt aeilrt**

aegilrtu ligature. *See* **aegilt aegirt aeilrt agirtu**

aegilrvw lawgiver. *See* **aegilv aegirv aegirw aeglrv**

aegilrz glazier. *See* **aeilrz aegil aegrz**

aegils silage aegis agile aisle gales ages ails ales egis gale gals gels gies isle lags leas legs leis lies sage sail sale seal slag age ail ale els gae gal gas gel gie lag lea leg lei lie sag sal sea ae ai as el is la li si

aegilss silages. *See* **aeilss aegils**

aegilst ligates. *See* **aeglst egilst aegilt aegils**

aegilsv glaives. *See* **aeglsv aegilv aegils aeilsv aegisv**

aegilt ligate agile aglet legit alit gait gale gate gilt late tael tail tale tali teal tile aet age ail ale alt ate eat eta gae gal gat gel get gie ita lag lea leg lei lie lit tag tea tie til ae ai at el it la li ta ti

aegilv glaive agile alive gavel evil gale gave give lave leva live vail vale veal veil vial vile age ail ale ave gae gal gel gie lag lea leg lei lev lie via vie ae ai el la li

aegim image game mage age aim gae gam gem gie mae mag ae ai am em ma me mi

aegimn enigma amine anime gamin image mange minae amen gain game mage main mane mean mien mina mine name age aim ane ani gae gam gan gem gie gin mae mag man men nae nag nim ae ai am an em en in ma me mi na ne

aegimnn meaning. *See* **aegimn agimnn**

aegimnnr renaming earning mangier meaning nearing reaming. *See* **aegimn aegimr aeginr aeimnr**

aegimnns meanings enigmas meaning seaming. *See* **aegimn aegims aegins aegmns**

aegimnr mangier reaming. *See* **aeimnr agimnr aeginr aegimn aegimr**

aegimnrr rearming angrier armiger earring mangier mariner marring reaming rearing. *See* **aegimn aegimr aeginr aegnrr**

aegimnrs smearing earings enigmas erasing gainers mangers mangier margins marines mirages reaming regains remains seaming searing seminar. *See* **aegimn aegimr aegims aeginr**

aegimnrt emigrant garment granite ingrate mangier migrant migrate minaret mintage ragtime raiment reaming tangier teaming tearing tegmina terming. *See* **aegimn aegimr aeginr aegint**

aegimnru geranium mangier reaming. *See* **aegimn aegimr aeginr aeginu**

aegimns enigmas seaming. *See* **aegims aeimns aegins agimns aegmns**

aegimnst mangiest mintages steaming easting enigmas gamiest ingesta inmates magnets matings mintage seaming seating teaming teasing tegmina. *See* **aegimn aegims aegins aegint**

aegimnt mintage teaming tegmina. *See* **aegint aegimn aeimnt aegmnt agimnt**

aegimos imagoes. *See* **aegims agimos egimos aegmos**

aegimp magpie image game gamp gape gimp mage page peag age aim amp ape gae gam gap gem gie gip imp mae mag map pea peg pie pig ae ai am em ma me mi pa pe pi

aegimpr epigram. *See* **aegimr aegimp**

aegimprs epigrams epigram impresa magpies mirages. *See* **aegimp aegimr aegims aegmrs**

aegimpru umpirage epigram. *See* **aegimp aegimr aegmru egimpu**

aegimps magpies. *See* **aegims**

aegimqru quagmire. *See* **aegimr aegmru aemqru**

aegimr gamier mirage grime image marge ager amir emir game gear germ gram grim mage mare mire rage rami ream rime age aim air are arm ear era erg gae gam gar gem gie ire mae mag mar mir rag ram reg rem ria rig rim ae ai am em er ma me mi re

aegimrr armiger. *See* **aegimr**

aegimrrs armigers armiger marries mirages. *See* **aegimr aegims aegmrs aeimrs**

aegimrs mirages. *See* **aegims aeimrs aegimr egimrs aegmrs**

aegimrst migrates ragtimes gaiters gamiest imarets migrate mirages ragtime seagirt triages. *See* **aegimr aegims aegirt aegmrs**

aegimrt migrate ragtime. *See* **aegirt aegimr aeimrt**

aegimry imagery. *See* **aegimr**

aegims ageism images aegis games image mages sigma ages aims egis game gams gems gies mage mags mesa mise sage same seam semi age aim gae gam gas gem gie mae mag mis sag sea ae ai am as em is ma me mi si

aegimss ageisms. *See* **aegims agimss**

aegimst gamiest. *See* **aegims aeimst agimst**

aeginnnx annexing. *See* **aennx aginx aeinn**

aeginnot negation anteing antigen atoning gentian tonnage. *See* **aegint aegnno aegnnt aeinno**

aeginnpt patening anteing antigen gentian panting pinnate. *See* **aegint aegnnt aeinnp aginpt**

aeginnr earning nearing. *See* **aeginr aeinnr**

aeginnrs earnings grannies earings earning erasing gainers nearing regains searing. *See* **aeginr aegins aegnrs aeinnr**

aeginnrv ravening earning nearing nerving reaving vinegar. *See* **aeginr aegirv aegnrv aeinnr**

aeginnry yearning earning nearing yarning yeaning. *See* **aeginr aeinnr aginry**

aeginnst antigens gentians anteing antigen easting gannets gentian ingesta nesting seating teasing tensing. *See* **aegins aegint aegnnt aegnst**

aeginnsu sanguine ensuing guineas gunnies. *See* **aegins aeginu aeinns eginsu**

aeginnt anteing antigen gentian. *See* **aegint aegnnt aeinnt**

aeginnw weaning. *See* **aginnw**

aeginny yeaning. *See* **aeinn eginy**

aeginorz organize agonize zeroing. *See* **aeginr aegnor aeinrz aginor**

aeginos agonies. *See* **aegnos aegins**

aeginosz agonizes agonies agonize. *See* **aegins aegnos aeinsz**

aeginoz agonize. *See* **aegno aeinz**

aeginppr papering nappier rapping reaping. *See* **aeginr aegipp aeinpr aenppr**

aeginpr reaping. *See* **aeginr aginpr aeinpr**

aeginprs spearing earings erasing gainers parings parsing rapines rasping reaping regains searing sparing springe. *See* **aeginr aegins aegnrs aegprs**

aeginprt tapering granite ingrate painter parting pertain prating reaping repaint tangier tearing. *See* **aeginr aegint aegirt aegnrt**

aeginprv repaving reaping reaving vinegar. *See* **aeginr aegirv aegnrv aeinpr**

aeginpry repaying praying preying reaping. *See* **aeginr aeinpr aenpry aginpr**

aeginqtu equating antique quinate. *See* **aegint aeginu aeintu ainqtu**

aeginr earing gainer regain regina anger grain range reign ager earn gain gear gnar grin near rage rain rang rani rein ring age air ane ani are ear era erg gae gan gar gie gin ire nae nag rag ran reg ria rig ae ai an en er in na ne re

aeginrr angrier earring rearing. *See* **aeginr eginrr aegnrr**

aeginrrs earrings angrier earings earring erasing gainers garners rangers rearing regains ringers searing. *See* **aeginr aegins aegnrr aegnrs**

aeginrrv   averring angrier earring rearing reaving vinegar. *See* **aeginr aegirv aegnrr aegnrv**

aeginrs   earings erasing gainers regains searing. *See* **aegnrs aeinrs aeginr aegins aginrs**

aeginrss   assigner arsines earings erasing gainers gassier ingress regains resigns searing singers. *See* **aeginr aegins aegnrs aegrss**

aeginrst   angriest gantries granites ingrates argents earings easting erasing gainers gaiters garnets granite ingesta ingrate nastier ratings regains resting retains retinas seagirt searing seating stainer staring stinger strange tangier tearing teasing triages. *See* **aeginr aegins aegint aegirt**

aeginrsv   vinegars earings erasing gainers gravies ravines reaving regains rivages searing serving versing vinegar. *See* **aeginr aegins aegirv aegisv**

aeginrsw   swearing earings earwigs erasing gainers regains searing swinger wearing. *See* **aeginr aegins aegirw aegnrs**

aeginrt   granite ingrate tangier tearing. *See* **aegnrt aeginr aegint aegirt aginrt**

aeginrtt   treating gittern granite ingrate iterant nattier nitrate ratting retting tangier tearing tertian. *See* **aeginr aegint aegirt aegnrt**

aeginrtv   averting granite ingrate reaving tangier tearing vinegar vintage virgate. *See* **aeginr aegint aegirt aegirv**

aeginrtw   watering granite ingrate tangier tawnier tearing tinware wearing. *See* **aeginr aegint aegirt aegirw**

aeginrv   reaving vinegar. *See* **aeginr aegnrv aeinrv aginrv aegirv**

aeginrvy   vinegary reaving varying vinegar. *See* **aeginr aegirv aegnrv aeinrv**

aeginrw   wearing. *See* **aeginr aegirw aginrw**

aeginrwy   wearying wearing. *See* **aeginr aegirw aenrwy aginrw**

aegins   easing aegis anise gains segni singe ages egis gain gens gies gins nags sage sain sane sang sign sine sing snag age ane ani ens gae gan gas gie gin nae nag sag sea sen sin ae ai an as en in is na ne si

aeginsst   giantess easting entasis ingesta ingests seating signets tansies teasing. *See* **aegins aegint aegnst aegsst**

aeginssy   essaying gayness sayings yessing. *See* **aegins aeinss aginss aginsy**

aeginst   easting ingesta seating teasing. *See* **aegnst aegins aegint aginst eginst**

aeginstt   tangiest easting ingesta satinet seating setting stating tasting teasing testing. *See* **aegins aegint aegnst aginst**

aeginstv   vintages easting ingesta natives seating staving teasing vesting vintage. *See* **aegins aegint aegisv aegnst**

aeginstw   sweating easting ingesta seating stewing teasing twinges wasting westing. *See* **aegins aegint aegnst aginst**

aeginsty   yeasting easting ingesta seating staying teasing. *See* **aegins aegint aegity aegnst**

aeginsu   guineas. *See* **aegins eginsu aeginu**

aegint   eating agent giant tenia tinea tinge ante anti gain gait gate gent gnat neat tang tine ting aet age ane ani ant ate eat eta gae gan gat get gie gin ita nae nag net nit tag tan tea ten tie tin ae ai an at en in it na ne ta ti

aegintv   vintage. *See* **aegint aeintv**

aeginu   guinea ague gain guan age ane ani gae gan gie gin gnu gun nae nag ae ai an en in na ne nu

aeginvw   weaving. *See* **aginvw eginv aeinv**

aegiorss   argosies gassier. *See* **aegrss aeirss egiors egorss**

aegiorsv   viragoes gravies ovaries rivages viragos. *See* **aegirv aegisv aegrsv aeirsv**

aegipp   pipage gape page peag pipe age ape gae gap gie gip pap pea peg pep pie pig pip ae ai pa pe pi

aegipps   pipages. *See* **aegipp aegis aegps**

aegirrss   grassier gassier sierras. *See* **aegrss aeirrs aeirss**

aegirrz   grazier. *See* **aegrrz aeirz**

aegirss   gassier. *See* **aeirss aegrss**

aegirst   gaiters seagirt triages. *See* **aegirt aegrst agirst aeirst egirst**

aegirstv   virgates gaiters gravest gravies grivets rivages seagirt triages virgate. *See* **aegirt aegirv aegisv aegrst**

aegirsuu   auguries. *See* **aegrsu aersuu agrsuu egirsu**

aegirsv   gravies rivages. *See* **egirsv aegrsv aegirv aeirsv agirsv**

aegirsw   earwigs. *See* **aegirw aegrsw**

aegirt   gaiter triage grate great irate retia targe terga tiger ager gait gate gear girt grit rage rate rite tare tear tier tire trig aet age air are art ate ear eat era erg eta gae gar gat get gie ire ita rag rat reg ret ria rig tag tar tea tie ae ai at er it re ta ti

aegirtv   virgate. *See* **aegirt egirtv**

aegiruz   gauzier. *See* **aegru aeruz aeguz**

aegirv   rivage giver grave virga ager aver gave gear give rage rave rive vair age

air are ave ear era erg gae gar gie ire rag reg rev ria rig via vie ae ai er re

aegirw   earwig wager ager gear grew rage wage ware wear weir wire age air are awe ear era erg gae gar gie ire rag raw reg ria rig wag war wig ae ai aw er re we

aegis   aegis ages egis gies sage age gae gas gie sag sea ae ai as is si

aegissst   gassiest siestas. *See* **aegsst aeisst agisst**

aegissv   visages. *See* **aegisv aegss aessv**

aegistuz   gauziest. *See* **aegsuz**

aegisv   visage aegis gives ages aves egis gave gies give sage save vase vies visa vise age ave gae gas gie sag sea via vie ae ai as is si

aegity   gaiety gait gate yeti aet age ate aye eat eta gae gat gay get gey gie ita tag tea tie yea yet ae ai at ay it ta ti ye

aegjln   jangle angel angle glean gale glen jean lane lean age ale ane gae gal gan gel jag lag lea leg nae nag ae an el en la na ne

aegjlnr   jangler. *See* **aeglnr aegjln**

aegjlnrs   janglers anglers jangler jangles. *See* **aegjln aeglnr aeglns aeglrs**

aegjlns   jangles. *See* **aeglns**

aegjltuu   jugulate. *See* **aegjtu**

aegjtu   jugate ague gate juga jute aet age ate eat eta gae gat get gut jag jet jug jut tag tau tea tug ae at ta ut

aegkmry   kerygma. *See* **aegry aekmr aegmr**

aegksst   gaskets. *See* **aegkst aegsst aeksst**

aegkst   gasket gates skate stage stake steak takes teaks ages east eats etas gate gats gest gets kegs sage sake seat seta skat skeg stag tags take task teak teas aet age ask ate eat eta gae gas gat get kas kat keg sag sat sea set tag tea tsk ae as at ka ta

aegl   gale age ale gae gal gel lag lea leg ae el la

aegll   legal gale gall leal age ale all ell gae gal gel lag lea leg ae el la

aegllly   legally. *See* **aeglly aellly**

aegllno   galleon. *See* **agllno aelno aegln**

aegllnos   galleons galleon gallons. *See* **aeglns aegnos aelnos agllno**

aegllopr   galloper allegro pergola. *See* **aeglor aelopr agllop allopr**

aegllor   allegro. *See* **aeglor aegll**

aegllors   allegros allegro gaolers. *See* **aeglor aeglrs aglors eglors**

aegllory   allegory allegro allergy gallery largely. *See* **aeglly aeglor aeglry aellry**

aegllost   tollages tollage gallets. *See* **aegllt aeglot aeglst aellst**

aegllot   tollage. *See* **aegllt aeglot**

aegllott tollgate tollage glottal. *See* **aegllt aeglot**

aegllrvy gravelly allergy gallery largely. *See* **aeglly aeglrv aeglry aellry**

aegllry allergy gallery largely. *See* **aeglry aeglly aellry**

aegllssu galluses. *See* **aegssu**

aegllst gallets. *See* **aeglst aegllt aellst**

aegllsy galleys. *See* **aellsy aeglly aeglsy**

aegllt gallet legal aglet gale gall gate late leal tael tale tall teal tell aet age ale all alt ate eat ell eta gae gal gat gel get lag lea leg let tag tea ae at el la ta

aeglly galley legal alley ally gale gall leal yell age ale all aye ell gae gal gay gel gey lag lay lea leg lye yea ae ay el la ye

aeglm gleam gale game lame mage male meal age ale elm gae gal gam gel gem lag lam lea leg mae mag mel ae am el em la ma me

aeglmn legman mangle angel angle gleam glean leman mange amen gale game glen lame lane lean mage male mane meal mean name age ale ane elm gae gal gam gan gel gem lag lam lea leg mae mag man mel men nae nag ae am an el em en la ma me na ne

aeglmnno mangonel. *See* **aeglmn aegnno aglmno**

aeglmnr mangler. *See* **aeglnr aegmnr aeglmn**

aeglmns mangles. *See* **aeglns aegmns aeglms aeglmn aelmns**

aeglmosu moulages moulage. *See* **aeglms aegmos aelmos aglmsu**

aeglmou moulage. *See* **aglmu aelmo aeglm**

aeglmpsu plumages ampules plagues plumage. *See* **aeglms aeglps aeglpu aelmps**

aeglmpu plumage. *See* **aeglpu aelmpu**

aeglms gleams gales games gleam lames mages males meals ages ales alms elms gale gals game gams gels gems lags lame lams leas legs mage mags male meal mels mesa sage sale same seal seam slag slam sage sale ale elm els gae gal gam gas gel gem lag lam lea leg mae mag mel sag sal sea ae am as el em la ma me

aeglmy gamely gleam mealy amyl gale game gamy lame mage male meal ylem age ale aye elm gae gal gam gay gel gem gey gym lag lam lay lea leg lye mae mag may mel yam yea ae am ay el em la ma me my ye

aegln angel angle glean gale glen lane lean age ale ane gae gal gan gel lag lea leg nae nag ae an el en la na ne

aeglnnsy langsyne. *See* **aeglns aeglsy aelnsy aglnsy**

aeglnntu untangle tunnage annulet. *See* **aeglnt aegnnt aelntu eglnnu**

aeglnory yearlong orangey. *See* **aeglnr aeglor aeglry aegnor**

aeglnost tangelos longest onstage tangelo tangles. *See* **aeglns aeglnt aeglot aeglst**

aeglnot tangelo. *See* **aeglnt aeglot**

aeglnpr grapnel. *See* **aeglnr aelnpr**

aeglnprs grapnels anglers grapnel planers spangle. *See* **aeglnr aeglns aeglps aeglrs**

aeglnps spangle. *See* **aeglns aelnps aeglps**

aeglnpss spangles spangle napless. *See* **aeglns aeglps aelnps aelpss**

aeglnr angler regnal angel anger angle glare glean gnarl lager large learn range regal renal ager earl earn gale gear glen gnar lane lean near rage rale rang real age ale ane are ear era erg gae gal gan gar gel lag lar lea leg nae nag rag ran reg ae an el en er la na ne re

aeglnrrw wrangler wrangle. *See* **aeglnr aeglnw aeglrr aegnrr**

aeglnrs anglers. *See* **aeglns aegnrs aeglnr aeglrs aglnrs**

aeglnrst strangle tanglers anglers antlers argents garnets largest rentals saltern sternal strange tangler tangles. *See* **aeglnr aeglns aeglnt aeglrs**

aeglnrsu granules anglers granule langurs lungers. *See* **aeglnr aeglns aeglrs aegnrs**

aeglnrsw wrangles anglers wangles wrangle. *See* **aeglnr aeglns aeglnw aeglrs**

aeglnrsy larynges anglers argyles. *See* **aeglnr aeglns aeglrs aeglry**

aeglnrt tangler. *See* **aelnrt aeglnr aegnrt aeglnt**

aeglnru granule. *See* **aeglnr aglnru aelnru**

aeglnrw wrangle. *See* **aeglnr aeglnw**

aeglns angels angles gleans angel angle gales glans glean glens lanes leans slang ages ales gale gals gels gens glen lags lane lean leas legs lens nags sage sale sane sang seal slag snag age ale ane els ens gae gal gan gas gel lag lea leg nae nag sag sal sea sen ae an as el en la na ne

aeglnst tangles. *See* **aegnst aeglst aeglns**

aeglnstt gantlets gantlet gestalt lattens talents tangles. *See* **aeglns aeglnt aeglst aegnst**

aeglnsuw gunwales wangles gunwale. *See* **aeglns aeglnw eglnsu**

aeglnsw wangles. *See* **aeglns aeglnw**

aeglnt tangle agent aglet angel angle glean leant ante gale gate gent glen gnat lane late lean lent neat tael tale tang teal aet age ale alt ane ant ate eat eta gae gal gan gat gel get lag lea leg let nae nag net tag tan tea ten ae an at el en la na ne ta

aeglntt gantlet. *See* **aelntt**

aeglnttu gauntlet gantlet. *See* **aeglnt aegttu aelntt aelntu**

aeglntuu ungulate ungulae. *See* **aeglnt aelntu aglnuu eglntu**

aeglnuu ungulae. *See* **eglnuu aglnuu**

aeglnuw gunwale. *See* **aeglnw eglnu aelnu**

aeglnw wangle angel angle glean anew gale glen gnaw lane lawn lean wage wale wane weal wean age ale ane awe awl awn gae gal gan gel lag law lea leg nae nag new wag wan wen ae an aw el en la na ne we

aegloooz zoogloea. *See* **aeloz aeglz egloz**

aegloopu apologue. *See* **aeglpu**

aeglopr pergola. *See* **aeglor aelopr eglopr**

aegloprs pergolas gaolers paroles pergola prolegs. *See* **aeglor aeglps aeglrs aegprs**

aeglopry playgoer pergola. *See* **aeglor aeglry aelopr aelpry**

aeglor galore argol glare goral lager large largo ogler regal aero ager aloe earl gale gaol gear goal goer gore loge lore ogle ogre oral orle rage rale real role age ago ale are ear ego era erg gae gal gar gel goa lag lar lea leg log oar ore rag reg roe ae el er go la lo or re

aeglors gaolers. *See* **aglors aeglor aeglrs eglors**

aeglorst legators gaolers largest legator orgeats storage. *See* **aeglor aeglot aeglrs aeglst**

aeglort legator. *See* **aeglor aeglot aegort**

aeglortv travelog legator levator voltage. *See* **aeglor aeglot aeglov aeglrv**

aegloss glossae. *See* **aelos aegls aglos**

aeglostv voltages voltage solvate. *See* **aeglot aeglov aeglst aeglsv**

aeglot legato aglet gloat aloe alto gale gaol gate goal goat late loge lota ogle tael tale teal toga tola aet age ago ale alt ate eat ego eta gae gal gat gel get goa got lag lea leg let log lot oat tag tea toe tog ae at el go la lo ta to

aeglotv voltage. *See* **aeglot aeglov**

aeglov lovage gavel glove aloe gale gaol gave goal lave leva loge love ogle oval vale veal vole age ago ale ave ego gae gal gel goa lag lea leg lev log ova ae el go la lo

aeglp plage gale gape leap page pale peag peal plea age ale alp ape gae gal gap gel lag lap lea leg pal pea peg ae el la pa pe

aeglppr grapple. *See* **aelppr aegpr aeglr**

aeglpprr grappler grapple. *See* **aeglrr aelppr aelprr**

aeglpprs grapples grapple rappels. *See* **aeglps aeglrs aegprs aelppr**

aeglprsu earplugs earplug perusal plagues splurge. *See* **aeglps aeglpu aeglrs aegprs**

aeglpru earplug. *See* **aeglpu aelpru**

aeglps plages gales gapes lapse leaps pages pales peags peals plage pleas salep sepal ages ales alps apes apse gale gals gape gaps gasp gels lags laps leap leas legs page pale pals peag peal peas pegs plea sage sale seal slag slap age ale alp ape asp els gae gal gap gas gel lag lap lea leg pal pas pea peg sag sal sap sea spa ae as el la pa pe

aeglpsu plagues. *See* **aeglps aeglpu**

aeglpu plague plage ague gale gape glue gulp leap luge page pale peag peal plea plug pule age ale alp ape gae gal gap gel lag lap lea leg leu lug pal pea peg pug pul ae el la pa pe up

aeglr glare lager large regal ager earl gale gear rage rale real age ale are ear era erg gae gal gar gel lag lar lea leg rag reg ae el er la re

aeglrr larger glare lager large regal ager earl gale gear rage rale rare real rear age ale are ear era erg err gae gal gar gel lag lar lea leg rag reg ae el er la re

aeglrrsu regulars regular arguers. *See* **aeglrr aeglrs aegrru aegrsu**

aeglrru regular. *See* **aeglrr aegrru**

aeglrs glares earls gales gears glare lager lares large laser rages rales regal sager ager ages ales arse earl ears eras ergs gale gals gars gear gels lags leas legs rage rags rale rase real regs sage sale seal sear sera slag age ale are ear els era erg gae gal gar gas gel lag lar lea leg rag reg res sag sal sea ae as el er la re

aeglrss largess. *See* **aegrss aeglrs aelrss**

aeglrst largest. *See* **aeglst aelrst aeglrs aegrst**

aeglrsv gravels. *See* **aeglsv aeglrs aeglrv aegrsv aelrsv**

aeglrsy argyles. *See* **aeglry aegrsy aelrsy aeglsy**

aeglrty greatly. *See* **aeglry aegrty aelrty**

aeglrv gravel gavel glare grave lager large laver ravel regal velar ager aver earl gale gave gear lave leva rage rale rave real vale veal age ale are ave ear era erg

gae gal gar gel lag lar lea leg lev rag reg rev ae el er la re

aeglry argyle early gayer glare glary gyral lager large layer regal relay aery ager aryl earl gale gear gray grey gyre lyre rage rale real rely yare year age ale are aye ear era erg gae gal gar gay gel gey lag lar lay lea leg lye rag ray reg rye yar yea ae ay el er la re ye

aegls gales ages ales gale gals gels lags leas legs sage sale seal slag age ale els gae gal gas gel lag lea leg sag sal sea ae as el la

aeglsss glasses. *See* **aelsss aegls aegss**

aeglst aglets aglet gales gates least slate stage stale steal taels tales ages ales alts east eats etas gale gals gate gats gels gest gets lags last late leas legs lest lets sage sale salt seal seat seta slag slat stag tael tags tale teal teas aet age ale alt ate eat eats eta gae gal gas gat get lag lea leg let sag sal sat sea set tag tea ae as at el la ta

aeglstt gestalt. *See* **aeglst aelstt**

aeglsv gavels gales gavel laves salve slave vales veals ages ales aves gale gals gave gels lags lave leas legs leva sage sale save seal slag vale vase veal age ale ave els gae gal gas gel lag lea leg lev sag sal sea ae as el la

aeglsy sagely gales ages ales ayes easy eyas gale gals gays gels lags lays leas legs lyes lyse sage sale seal slag slay yeas age ale aye els gae gal gas gay gel gey lag lay lea leg lye sag sal say sea sly yea yes ae as ay el la ye

aeglsz glazes gales gazes glaze lazes zeals ages ales gale gals gaze gels lags laze leas legs sage sale seal slag zags zeal age ale els gae gal gas gel lag lea leg sag sal sea zag ae as el la

aeglt aglet gale gate late tael tale teal aet age ale alt ate eat eta gae gal gat gel get lag lea leg let tag tea ae at el la ta

aegluuy guayule. *See* **egluy**

aegluvy vaguely. *See* **aeglv egluy aelvy**

aeglv gavel gale gave lave leva vale veal age ale ave gae gal gel lag lea leg lev ae el la

aeglz glaze gale gaze laze zeal age ale gae gal gel lag lea leg zag ae el la

aegm game mage age gae gam gem mae mag ae am em ma me

aegmm gemma game mage age gae gam gem mae mag mem ae am em ma me

aegmmr gammer gemma marge ager game gear germ gram mage mare rage ream age are arm ear era erg gae gam gar gem mae mag mar mem rag ram reg rem ae am em er ma me re

aegmmrs gammers. *See* **aegmmr aegmrs aegmms**

aegmmrsu rummages gammers rummage. *See* **aegmmr aegmms aegmrs aegmru**

aegmmru rummage. *See* **aegmmr aegmru**

aegmms smegma games gemma mages ages game gams gems mage mags mems mesa sage same seam age gae gam gas gem mae mag mem sag sea ae am as em ma me

aegmmss smegmas. *See* **aegmms aegss aemss**

aegmn mange amen game mage mane mean name age ane gae gam gan gem mae mag man men nae nag ae am an em en ma me na ne

aegmnnot magneton megaton montage montane tonnage. *See* **aegmnt aegnno aegnnt**

aegmnorv mangrove. *See* **aegmnr aegnor aegnrv aemnor**

aegmnos mangoes. *See* **aegnos aegmns egmnos agmnos aegmos**

aegmnost magnetos megatons montages amongst magnets mangoes megaton montage onstage. *See* **aegmns aegmnt aegmos aegnos**

aegmnot megaton montage. *See* **aegmnt agmno aenot**

aegmnr german manger anger mange marge range ager amen earn game gear germ gnar gram mage mane mare mean name near rage rang ream age ane are arm ear era erg gae gam gan gar gem mae mag man mar men nae nag rag ram ran reg rem ae am an em en er ma me na ne re

aegmnrs mangers. *See* **aegnrs aegmns aegmnr aegmrs**

aegmnrst garments argents garment garnets magnets mangers martens smarten strange. *See* **aegmnr aegmns aegmnt aegmrs**

aegmnrt garment. *See* **aegnrt aegmnt aemnrt**

aegmnrtu argument garment augment. *See* **aegmnr aegmnt aegmru aegnrt**

aegmns gasmen manges games mages manes mange manse means names ages amen game gams gems gens mage mags mane mean mesa nags name sage same sane sang seam snag age ane ens gae gam gan gas gem mae mag man men nae nag sag sea sen ae am an as em en ma me na ne

aegmnst magnets. *See* **aegnst aegmns aegmnt aemnst**

aegmnstu augments augment magnets mustang nutmegs. *See* **aegmns aegmnt aegnst aemnst**

aegmnt magnet agent mange meant amen ante game gate gent gnat mage mane mate mean meat name neat tame tang team aet age ane ant ate eat eta gae gam gan gat gem get mae mag man mat men met nae nag net tag tam tan tea ten ae am an at em en ma me na ne ta

aegmntu augment. *See* **aegmnt egmntu**

aegmo omega game mage age ago ego gae gam gem goa mae mag moa mog ae am em go ma me mo om

aegmoor moorage. *See* **gmoor aegmr aemor**

aegmoors moorages moorage. *See* **aegmos aegmrs agmors emoors**

aegmorss gossamer orgasms. *See* **aegmos aegmrs aegrss aemrss**

aegmos omegas games mages omega ages egos game gams gems goas goes mage mags mesa moas mogs sage sago same seam sego smog soma some age ago ego gae gam gas gem goa mae mag moa mog mos oms sag sea ae am as em go ma me mo om os so

aegmoxy exogamy. *See* **aegmo**

aegmpstu stumpage upstage. *See* **aepstu agmstu empstu**

aegmr marge ager game gear germ gram mage mare rage ream age are arm ear era erg gae gam gar gem mae mag mar rag ram reg rem ae am em er ma me re

aegmrs marges games gears germs grams mages mares marge maser rages reams sager smear ager ages arms arse ears eras ergs game gams gars gear gems germ gram mage mags mare mesa rage rags rams rase ream regs sage same seam sear sera age are arm ear era erg gae gam gar gas gem mae mag mar rag ram reg rem res sag sea ae am as em er ma me re

aegmru maugre argue auger grume marge rugae ager ague game gaur gear germ geum gram grue grum mage mare rage ream ruga urea urge age are arm ear emu era erg gae gam gar gem gum mae mag mar mug rag ram reg rem rue rug rum ae am em er ma me mu re um

aegms games mages ages game gams gems mage mags mesa sage same seam age gae gam gas gem mae mag sag sea ae am as em ma me

aegmsuy magueys. *See* **aegmuy aegsu aemsu**

aegmsuz zeugmas. *See* **aegmuz aegsuz**

aegmuy maguey ague game gamy geum mage age aye emu gae gam gay gem gey gum guy gym mae mag may mug yam yea yum ae am ay em ma me mu my um ye

aegmuz zeugma gauze ague game gaze geum mage maze age emu gae gam gem gum mae mag mug zag ae am em ma me mu um

aegnno nonage genoa aeon agon anon gone neon none age ago ane ego eon gae gan goa nae nag nog one ae an en go na ne no on

aegnnopt pentagon tonnage. *See* **aegnno aegnnt**

aegnnost tonnages gannets onstage tonnage. *See* **aegnno aegnnt aegnos aegnst**

aegnnot tonnage. *See* **aegnno aegnnt**

aegnnprt pregnant regnant. *See* **aegnnt aegprt aenprt**

aegnnrt regnant. *See* **aegnrt aennrt**

aegnnst gannets. *See* **aegnnt aegnst**

aegnnstt tangents gannets tangent tenants. *See* **aegnnt aegnst aenntt**

aegnnt gannet agent anent ante gate gent gnat neat tang aet age ane ant ate eat eta gae gan gat get nae nag net tag tan tea ten ae an at en na ne ta

aegnntt tangent. *See* **aegnnt aenntt**

aegnntu tunnage. *See* **aegnnt agntu**

aegno genoa aeon agon gone age ago ane ego eon gae gan goa nae nag nog one ae an en go na ne no on

aegnoor oregano. *See* **aegnor**

aegnoors oreganos onagers oranges oregano. *See* **aegnor aegnos aegnrs aenors**

aegnoprr parergon groaner. *See* **aegnor aegnrr egoprr enoprr**

aegnor onager orange anger argon genoa genro goner groan organ range aeon aero ager agon earn gear gnar goer gone gore near ogre rage rang roan age ago ane are ear ego eon era erg gae gan gar goa nae nag nog nor oar one ore rag ran reg roe ae an en er go na ne no on or re

aegnorr groaner. *See* **aegnrr aegnor**

aegnorrs groaners garners groaner onagers oranges rangers. *See* **aegnor aegnos aegnrr aegnrs**

aegnors onagers oranges. *See* **aegnos aegnrs agnors egnors aegnor**

aegnorst negators argents atoners garnets negator onagers onstage oranges orgeats senator storage strange treason. *See* **aegnor aegnos aegnrs aegnrt**

aegnorsw wagoners onagers oranges wagoner. *See* **aegnor aegnos aegnrs aegrsw**

aegnort negator. *See* **aegnrt aenort aegnor aegort**

aegnortt tetragon negator garotte. *See* **aegnor aegnrt aegort aegrtt**

aegnorw wagoner. *See* **aegnor**

aegnory orangey. *See* **aegnor agnory**

aegnos agones genoas aeons genoa segno aeon ages agon egos eons gens goas goes gone nags naos noes nogs nose ones sage sago sane sang sego snag song age ago ane ego ens eon gae gan gas goa nae nag nog one sag sea sen son ae an as en go na ne no on os so

aegnossy nosegays nosegay gayness. *See* **aegnos aenoss**

aegnost onstage. *See* **aegnst aegnos aenost agnost**

aegnosy nosegay. *See* **aegnos**

aegnotuy autogeny. *See* **aegotu agnotu egnotu**

aegnr anger range ager earn gear gnar near rage rang age ane are ear era erg gae gan gar nae nag rag ran reg ae an en er na ne re

aegnrr garner ranger anger range reran ager earn gear gnar near rage rang rare rear age ane are ear era err gae gan gar nae nag rag ran reg ae an en er na ne re

aegnrrs garners rangers. *See* **aegnrs aegnrr**

aegnrrst granters stranger argents garners garnets garrets garters granter graters rangers strange. *See* **aegnrr aegnrs aegnrt aegnst**

aegnrrt granter. *See* **aegnrt aenrrt aegnrr aegrrt**

aegnrs angers ranges anger earns gears gnars nares nears rages range sager saner snare ager ages arse earn ears eras ergs gars gear gens gnar nags near rage rags rang rase regs sage sane sang sear sera snag age ane are ear ens era erg gae gan gar gas nae nag rag ran reg res sag sea sen ae an as en er na ne re

aegnrssy grayness gayness. *See* **aegnrs aegrss aegrsy aenrsy**

aegnrst argents garnets strange. *See* **aegnst aegnrs aegnrt aenrst agnrst**

aegnrt argent garnet agent anger grant grate great range targe terga ager ante earn gate gear gent gnar gnat near neat rage rang rant rate rent tang tare tear tern aet age ane ant are art ate ear eat era erg eta gae gan gar gat get nae nag net rag ran rat reg ret tag tan tar tea ten ae an at en er na ne re ta

aegnrv graven anger grave range raven ager aver earn gave gear gnar nave near rage rang rave vane vang age ane are ave ear era erg gae gan gar nae nag rag ran reg rev van ae an en er na ne re

aegnssu   sangsue. *See* **aegssu aenssu**

aegnssy   gayness. *See* **aessy aegss agssy**

aegnst   agents agent antes gates gents gnats nates stage stang tangs ages ante ants east eats etas gate gats gens gent gest gets gnat nags neat nest nets sage sane sang seat sent seta snag stag tags tang tans teas tens aet age ane ant ate eat ens eta gae gan gas gat get nae nag net sag sat sea sen set tag tan tea ten ae an as at en na ne ta

aegnt   agent ante gate gent gnat neat tang aet age ane ant ate eat eta gae gan gat get nae nag net tag tan tea ten ae an at en na ne ta

aegoppst   stoppage postage stopgap. *See* **aeopps**

aegoprst   portages orgeats pargets portage postage ragtops seaport storage. *See* **aegort aegprs aegprt aegrst**

aegoprt   portage. *See* **aegort aegprt agoprt**

aegopst   postage. *See* **eopst aegps aegst**

aegopstt   gatepost pottages postage pottage teapots. *See* **aeoptt**

aegoptt   pottage. *See* **aeoptt**

aegorrst   garrotes garrets garrote garters graters orgeats roaster storage. *See* **aegort aegrrt aegrst aeorst**

aegorrt   garrote. *See* **aegrrt aegort**

aegorsst   storages orgeats stagers storage. *See* **aegort aegrss aegrst aegsst**

aegorst   orgeats storage. *See* **agorst egorst aegrst aeorst aegort**

aegorstt   garottes garotte orgeats rotates storage targets toaster. *See* **aegort aegrst aegrtt aeorst**

aegorstu   outrages orgeats outages outrage storage. *See* **aegort aegotu aegrst aegrsu**

aegorsvy   voyagers voyager voyages. *See* **aegovy aegrsv aegrsy agorsy**

aegort   orgeat argot ergot grate great groat orate terga aero ager gate gear goat goer gore grot ogre rage rate rota rote tare taro tear toga tora tore aet age ago are art ate ear eat ego era erg eta gae gar gat get goa got oar oat ore ort rag rat reg ret roe rot tag tar tea toe tog tor ae at er go or re ta to

aegortt   garotte. *See* **aegort aeortt aegrtt**

aegortu   outrage. *See* **aegort aegotu**

aegorvy   voyager. *See* **aegovy aegry aegrv**

aegosstw   stowages stowage towages. *See* **aegotw aegsst aesstw**

aegossu   gaseous. *See* **aegssu egoss aeoss**

aegostu   outages. *See* **aegotu aegsu aostu**

aegostw   stowage towages. *See* **aegotw aegst agost**

aegosvy   voyages. *See* **aegovy egsvy aosvy**

aegotu   outage ague auto gate goat gout toga aet age ago ate eat ego eta gae gat get goa got gut oat out tag tau tea toe tog tug ae at go ta to ut

aegotw   towage gate goat toga wage aet age ago ate awe eat ego eta gae gat get goa got oat owe tag tea toe tog tow two wag wet woe ae at aw go ow ta to we

aegovy   voyage gave gyve yoga age ago ave aye ego gae gay gey goa goy ova yea ae ay go oy ye

aegp   gape page peag age ape gae gap pea peg ae pa pe

aegpr   gaper grape pager ager gape gear page pare peag pear rage rape reap age ape are ear era erg gae gap gar par pea peg per rag rap reg rep ae er pa pe re

aegprrs   grasper. *See* **aegprs aeprrs**

aegprrss   graspers grasper raspers sparers sparges sparser. *See* **aegprs aegrss aeprrs aeprss**

aegprry   grapery gpgaper. *See* **aepry aegry aegpr**

aegprs   gapers grapes pagers sparge gaper gapes gears grape grasp pager pages pares parse peags pears rages rapes reaps sager spare spear sprag ager ages apes apse arse ears eras ergs gape gaps gars gasp gear page pare pars peag pear peas pegs rage rags rape raps rase rasp reap regs reps sage sear sera spar age ape are asp ear era erg gae gap gar gas par pas pea peg per rag rap reg rep res sag sap sea spa ae as er pa pe re

aegprss   sparges. *See* **aegprs aegrss agprss aeprss**

aegprst   pargets. *See* **aegprs aegrst aegprt aeprst**

aegprt   parget gaper grape grate great pager pater peart prate taper targe terga ager gape gate gear page pare part pate peag pear peat pert rage rape rapt rate reap tape tare tarp tear trap aet age ape apt are art ate ear eat era erg eta gae gap gar gat get par pat pea peg per pet rag rap rat reg rep ret tag tap tar tea ae at er pa pe re ta

aegps   gapes pages peags ages apes apse gape gaps gasp page peag peas pegs sage age ape asp gae gap gas pas pea peg sag sap sea spa ae as pa pe

aegpsstu   upstages upstage petasus. *See* **aegsst aegssu aepsst aepssu**

aegpstu   upstage. *See* **aepstu aegsu aegps**

aegr   ager gear rage age are ear era erg gae gar rag reg ae er re

aegrrst   garrets garters graters. *See* **aerrst aegrrt aegrst**

aegrrsu   arguers. *See* **aegrru aegrsu**

aegrrsuv   gravures arguers gravure. *See* **aegrru aegrrv aegrsu aegrsv**

aegrrsz   grazers. *See* **aegrsz aegrrz**

aegrrt   garret garter grater grate great targe terga ager gate gear rage rare rate rear tare tear aet age are art ate ear eat era erg err eta gae gar gat get rag rat reg ret tag tar tea ae at er re ta

aegrru   arguer argue auger rugae ager ague gaur gear grue rage rare rear ruga urea urge age are ear era erg err gae gar rag reg rue rug ae er re

aegrruv   gravure. *See* **aegrru aegrrv aegruv**

aegrrv   graver grave ager aver gave gear rage rare rave rear age are ave ear era erg err gae gar rag reg rev ae er re

aegrry   grayer gayer aery ager gear gray grey gyre rage rare rear yare year age are aye ear era erg err gae gar gay gey rag ray reg rye yar yea ae ay er re ye

aegrrz   grazer gazer graze ager gaze gear rage rare raze rear age are ear era erg err gae gar rag reg zag ae er re

aegrs   gears rages sager ager ages arse ears eras ergs gars gear rage rags rase regs sage sear sera age are ear era erg gae gar gas rag reg res sag sea ae as er re

aegrss   gasser arses gases gears grass rages rases sager sages sears ager ages arse ears eras ergs gars gear rage rags rase regs sage sags sear seas sera age are ass ear era erg ess gae gar gas rag reg res sag sea ae as er re

aegrsss   gassers grasses. *See* **aegrss aesss**

aegrsst   stagers. *See* **aersst aegrss aegrst aegsst**

aegrssu   saugers. *See* **aegrsu aerssu aegrss agrssu egrssu**

aegrst   grates greats stager targes aster gates gears grate great rages rates sager stage stare tares targe tears terga ager ages arse arts ears east eats eras ergs erst etas gars gate gats gear gest gets rage rags rase rate rats regs rest rets sage sear seat sera seta stag star tags tare tars tear teas tsar aet age are art ate ear eat era erg eta gae gar gas gat get rag rat reg res ret sag sat sea set tag tar tea ae as at er re ta

aegrstt   targets. *See* **aegrst aegrtt aerstt**

aegrstty   strategy grayest gyrates targets yatters. *See* **aegrst aegrsy aegrtt aegrty**

aegrstv   gravest. *See* **aerstv aegrst aegrsv**

aegrsty   grayest gyrates. *See* **aersty aegsty aegrst aegrsy aegrty**

aegrsu argues augers sauger agues argue auger gaurs gears grues rages rugae sager sugar surge ureas urges usage ager ages ague arse ears eras ergs gars gaur gear grue rage rags rase regs rues ruga rugs ruse sage sear sera sura sure urea urge user age are ear era erg gae gar gas rag reg res rue rug sag sea sue use ae as er re us

aegrsv graves avers gears grave rages raves sager saver ager ages arse aver aves ears eras ergs gars gave gear rage rags rase rave regs revs sage save sear sera vase age are ave ear era erg gae gar gas rag reg res rev sag sea ae as er re

aegrsw wagers gears rages sager swear wager wages wares wears ager ages arse awes ears eras ergs gars gear grew rage rags rase regs sage sear sera swag wage wags ware wars wear age are awe ear era erg gae gar gas rag raw reg res sag saw sea sew wag war was ae as aw er re we

aegrsy greasy gayer gears grays greys gyres rages sager sayer years aery ager ages arse ayes ears easy eras ergs eyas gars gays gear gray grey gyre rage rags rase rays regs ryes sage sear sera yare year yeas age are aye ear era erg gae gar gas gay gey rag ray reg res rye sag say sea yar yea yes ae as ay er re ye

aegrsz gazers grazes gazer gazes gears graze rages razes sager ager ages arse ears eras ergs gars gaze gear rage rags rase raze regs sage sear sera zags age are ear era erg gae gar gas rag reg res sag sea zag ae as er re

aegrt grate great targe terga ager gate gear rage rate tare tear aet age are art ate ear eat era erg eta gae gar gat get rag rat reg ret tag tar tea ae at er re ta

aegrtt target grate great targe tater terga tetra treat ager gate gear rage rate tare tart tear teat tret aet age are art ate ear eat era erg eta gae gar gat get rag rat reg ret tag tar tat tea ae at er re ta

aegrty gyrate gayer grate great targe teary terga aery ager arty gate gear gray grey gyre rage rate tare tear tray yare year aet age are art ate aye ear eat era erg eta gae gar gat gay get gey rag rat ray reg ret rye tag tar tea try yar yea yet ae at ay er re ta ye

aegru argue auger rugae ager ague gaur gear grue rage ruga urea urge age are ear era erg gae gar rag reg rue rug ae er re

aegruv vaguer argue auger grave rugae vague ager ague aver gaur gave gear grue rage rave ruga urea urge uvea age

are ave ear era erg gae gar rag reg rev rue rug vug ae er re

aegrv grave ager aver gave gear rage rave age are ave ear era erg gae gar rag reg rev ae er re

aegrw wager ager gear grew rage wage ware wear age are awe ear era erg gae gar rag raw reg wag war ae aw er re we

aegry gayer aery ager gear gray grey gyre rage yare year age are aye ear era erg gae gar gay gey rag ray reg rye yar yea ae ay er re ye

aegrz gazer graze ager gaze gear rage raze age are ear era erg gae gar rag reg zag ae er re

aegs ages sage age gae gas sag sea ae as

aegss gases sages ages sage sags seas age ass ess gae gas sag sea ae as

aegsst sagest stages asset gases gates gests sages sates seats stage stags tasse ages east eats etas gate gats gest gets sage sags seas seat seta sets stag tags tass teas aet age ass ate eat ess eta gae gas gat get sag sat sea set tag tea ae as at ta

aegssu usages agues gases gauss guess sages usage ages ague sage sags seas sues uses age ass ess gae gas sag sea sue use ae as us

aegst gates stage ages east eats etas gate gats gest gets sage seat seta stag tags teas aet age ate eat eta gae gas gat get sag sat sea set tag tea ae as at ta

aegstuv vaguest. *See* aegsu aegst egstu

aegsty gayest stagey gates stage stagy yeast ages ayes east easy eats etas eyas gate gats gays gest gets sage seat seta stag stay tags teas yeas aet age ate aye eat eta gae gas gat gay get gey sag sat say sea set sty tag tea yea yes yet ae as at ay ta ye

aegsu agues usage ages ague sage age gas sag sea sue use ae as us

aegsuz gauzes agues gauze gazes usage ages ague gaze sage zags age gae gas sag sea sue use zag ae as us

aegsw wages ages awes sage swag wage wags age awe gae gas sag saw sea sew wag was ae as aw we

aegsz gazes ages gaze sage zags age gae gas sag sea zag ae as

aegt gate aet age ate eat eta gae gat get tag tea ae at ta

aegttu guttae gutta ague gate taut teat aet age ate eat eta gae gat get gut tag tat tau tea tug tut ae at ta ut

aegtyy gayety gate aet age ate aye eat eta gae gat gay get gey tag tea yay yea yet ae at ay ta ye

aegu ague age gae ae

aeguv vague ague gave uvea age ave gae vug ae

aeguz gauze ague gaze age gae zag ae

aegv gave age ave gae ae

aegw wage age awe gae wag ae aw we

aegz gaze age gae zag ae

aeh hae ae ah eh ha he

aehhlt health heath lathe hale halt hate hath heal heat late lath tael tale teal aet ale alt ate eat eta eth hae hah hat heh het lea let tea the ae ah at eh el ha he la

aehhlty healthy. *See* aehhlt aehhty

aehhp ephah heap ape hae hah hap heh hep pah pea ae ah eh ha he pa pe

aehhps ephahs ephah heaps phase shape apes apse hahs haps hash hasp heap peas shah ape ash asp hae hah hap has heh hep pah pas pea sap sea she spa ae ah as eh ha he pa pe sh

aehhpy hyphae ephah hypha heap hype yeah ape aye hae hah hap hay heh hep hey pah pay pea pya yah yap yea yep ae ah ay eh ha he pa pe ye

aehhrrs harsher. *See* aehrrs aehhrs

aehhrs rehash hares harsh hears rheas share shear arse ears eras hahs hare hash hear hers rahs rase rash resh rhea sear sera shah are ash ear era hae hah has heh her rah res sea she ae ah as eh er ha he re sh

aehhrsst harshest thrashes hearths rashest sheaths trashes. *See* aehhrs aehhrt aehhss aehhst

aehhrst hearths. *See* aehrst aehhrt aehhst aehhrs ahhrst

aehhrt hearth earth hater heart heath hare hart hate hath hear heat rate rath rhea tare tear aet are art ate ear eat era eta eth hae hah hat heh her het rah rat ret tar tea the ae ah at eh er ha he re ta

aehhss hashes ashes hahs hash sash seas shah ash ass ess hae hah has heh sea she ae ah as eh ha he sh

aehhsst sheaths. *See* aehhss aehhst

aehhst heaths sheath haste hates heath heats east eats etas hahs hash hast hate hath hats heat hest seat seta shah teas aet ash ate eat eta eth hae hah has hat heh het sat sea set she tea the ae ah as at eh ha he sh ta

aehht heath hate hath heat aet ate eat eta eth hae hah hat heh het tea the ae ah at eh ha he ta

aehhty heathy heath hate hath heat they yeah aet ate aye eat eta eth hae hah hat hay heh het hey tea the thy yah yea yet ae ah ay eh ha he ta ye

aehiiklr hairlike. *See* aehilr

aehiilnr hairline airline hernial inhaler. *See* **aehiln aehilr aehinr aeilnr**

aehiimnt thiamine intimae. *See* **aehmnt aeimnt**

aehiirr hairier. *See* **aeiirr ehirr**

aehiirrw wirehair hairier. *See* **aeiirr aeirrw**

aehiirst hairiest hastier airiest. *See* **aehirs aehrst aeirst ehirst**

aehijr hejira hair haji hare hear heir hire rhea air are ear era hae her hie ire jar rah raj ria ae ah ai eh er ha he hi re

aehijrs hejiras. *See* **aehijr aehirs**

aehikklw hawklike. *See* **aehilw**

aehikn hankie akin ankh haik hake hank hike khan kina kine ane ani hae hen hie hin ink ken kin nae nah ae ah ai an eh en ha he hi in ka na ne

aehikns hankies. *See* **aehikn aehkns**

aehikrs shakier. *See* **aehirs aeikrs aehkrs ahikrs ehikrs**

aehiksst shakiest ashiest. *See* **aehkss aeisst aeksst**

aehilm hiemal hemal ahem hail hale hame heal helm lame lime mail male meal mile ail aim ale elm hae ham hem hie him lam lea lei lie mae mel mil ae ah ai am eh el em ha he hi la li ma me mi

aehiln inhale alien aline anile liane anil hail hale heal lain lane lean lien line nail ail ale ane ani hae hen hie hin lea lei lie nae nah nil ae ah ai an eh el en ha he hi in la li na ne

aehilnop aphelion opaline pinhole. *See* **aehiln aeilnp ehlnop eilnop**

aehilnr hernial inhaler. *See* **aehilr aehinr aehiln aeilnr ahilnr**

aehilnrs inhalers hailers hernial hernias inhaler inhales. *See* **aehiln aehilr aehinr aehirs**

aehilns inhales. *See* **aeilns aehlns**

aehilny hyaline. *See* **aehiln aehny ailny**

aehilors shoalier hailers. *See* **aehilr aehirs aehlos aehlrs**

aehilpr harelip. *See* **aehilr aehlp aelpr**

aehilprs harelips hailers harelip harpies sharpie spheral. *See* **aehilr aehirs aehlps aehlrs**

aehilr hailer haler aril earl hail hair hale hare harl heal hear heir herl hire lair liar lira lire rail rale real rhea rial riel rile ail are ale are ear era hae her hie ire lar lea lei lie rah ria ae ah ai eh el er ha he hi la li re

aehilrs hailers. *See* **aehirs aehilr aehlrs ehilrs aeilrs**

aehilrss hairless airless hailers lashers sailers serials slasher. *See* **aehilr aehirs aehlrs aehlss**

aehilrsv shrieval hailers revisal shrivel. *See* **aehilr aehirs aehlrs aehlsv**

aehilrt lathier. *See* **aehilr aehilt aehlrt ehilrt aeilrt**

aehilrty heartily earthly hyalite irately lathery lathier reality. *See* **aehilr aehilt aehlrt aehrty**

aehilssv lavishes valises slavish. *See* **aehlss aehlsv aehssv aeilss**

aehilst halites. *See* **aehlst ahilst**

aehilstt lathiest atheist halites lithest stealth thistle. *See* **aehilt aehlst aehstt ahilst**

aehilsty hyalites halites hastily hyalite. *See* **aehilt aehlst aeilsy ahilst**

aehilt halite lathe lithe alit hail hale halt hate heal heat hilt late lath tael tail tale tali teal tile aet ail ale alt ate eat eta eth hae hat het hie hit ita lea lei let lie lit tea the tie til ae ah ai at eh el ha he hi it la li ta ti

aehilty hyalite. *See* **aehilt ehlty ailty**

aehilvy heavily. *See* **aeilv aehlv aehvy**

aehilw awhile whale wheal while hail hale heal wail wale weal wile ail ale awe awl hae haw hew hie law lea lei lie ae ah ai aw eh el ha he hi la li we

aehimmr hammier. *See* **aehmmr aehimr aeimmr**

aehimmss shammies mashies messiah. *See* **aehims aehmss**

aehimmst hammiest atheism. *See* **aehims aeimst aemmst ehimst**

aehimmsw whammies. *See* **aehims**

aehimnnu inhumane inhuman. *See* **aehmnu aimnnu ehimnu**

aehimnuz humanize. *See* **aehmnu ehimnu**

aehimprs samphire seraphim hampers harpies impresa sharpie. *See* **aehimr aehims aehirs aehmpr**

aehimprt teraphim primate. *See* **aehimr aehmpr aehprt aeimrt**

aehimpss emphasis misshape aphesis impasse mashies messiah mishaps. *See* **aehims aehmss aehpss ahimps**

aehimpst shipmate atheism pastime. *See* **aehims aeimst ahimps ehimst**

aehimr hermai harem herma ihram ahem amir emir hair hame hare harm hear heir herm hire mare mire rami ream rhea rime aim air are arm ear era hae ham hem her hie him ire mae mar mir rah ram rem ria rim ae ah ai am eh em er ha he hi ma me mi re

aehimrrs marshier harries marries. *See* **aehimr aehims aehirs aehmrr**

aehims mashie hames shame ahem aims hame hams hems hies mash mesa mesh mise same seam semi sham shim aim

ash hae ham has hem hie him his mae mis sea she ae ah ai am as eh em ha he hi is ma me mi sh si

aehimss mashies messiah. *See* **aehmss aehims**

aehimsss messiahs mashies messiah smashes. *See* **aehims aehmss aehsss ehisss**

aehimst atheism. *See* **aehims aeimst ehimst**

aehinntx xanthein xanthine. *See* **aeinnt**

aehinort antihero hairnet another. *See* **aehinr aehnrt aeinrt aenort**

aehinpst thespian hatpins panties sapient. *See* **aehnst aenpst ahinpt ainpst**

aehinr hernia earn hair hare hear heir hern hire near rain rani rein rhea air ane ani are ear era hae hen her hie hin ire nae nah rah ran ria ae ah ai an eh en er ha he hi in na ne re

aehinrs hernias. *See* **aeinrs aehirs aehinr ehinrs**

aehinrst hairnets anthers hairnet hastier hernias hinters nastier retains retinas stainer tarnish thenars. *See* **aehinr aehirs aehnrt aehnst**

aehinrt hairnet. *See* **aehnrt aehinr ehinrt aeinrt**

aehinsst anthesis ashiest entasis hastens tansies. *See* **aehnst aeinss aeisst aensst**

aehinssv vanishes. *See* **aehnsv aehssv aeinss aeinsv**

aehinssz haziness. *See* **aeinss aeinsz aeissz ehinss**

aehinstt hesitant atheist satinet. *See* **aehnst aehstt ainstt ehistt**

aehiopru euphoria. *See* **ahipru ehiopr**

aehioprz aphorize. *See* **aehirz ehiopr**

aehiorr hoarier. *See* **ehirr**

aehiorst hoariest earshot hastier heriots shortia shortie. *See* **aehirs aehors aehrst aeirst**

aehippr happier. *See* **ehippr aeppr**

aehipprs sapphire apprise happier harpies perhaps sappier sharpie shipper. *See* **aehirs aehprs aeiprs aepprs**

aehippst epitaphs happiest epitaph hippest. *See* **aippst eippst**

aehippt epitaph. *No 6s or 5s*

aehiprs harpies sharpie. *See* **aehirs aeiprs ahiprs ehiprs aehprs**

aehiprss parishes sharpies aphesis aspires harpies paresis phrases praises seraphs sharpie sherpas. *See* **aehprs aehpss aehrss**

aehipss aphesis. *See* **ahipss aehpss ehipss**

aehirrr harrier. *See* **aerrr ehirr**

aehirrrs harriers harrier harries. *See* **aehirs aehrrs aeirrs ahirrs**

aehirrs   harries. *See* **aehirs ehirrs aehrrs aeirrs ahirrs**

aehirrst   trashier harries hastier tarries tarsier. *See* **aehirs aehrrs aehrrt aehrst**

aehirrsv   ravisher harries arrives. *See* **aehirs aehrrs aehrsv aeirrs**

aehirs   ashier arise hairs hares hears heirs hires raise rheas serai share shear shire airs arse ears eras hair hare hear heir hers hies hire rahs rase rash reis resh rhea rias rise sari sear sera sire air are ash ear era hae has her hie his ire rah res ria sea she sir ae ah ai as eh er ha he hi is re sh si

aehirssv   ravishes shavers shivers shrives. *See* **aehirs aehrss aehrsv aehssv**

aehirst   hastier. *See* **aehirs aehrst aeirst ehirst**

aehirstu   thesauri hastier hirsute. *See* **aehirs aehrst aeirst ahistu**

aehirstw   waterish hastier waiters wariest washier withers wraiths wreaths writhes. *See* **aehirs aehrst aehrsw aehrtw**

aehirsty   hysteria hastier. *See* **aehirs aehrst aehrty aeirst**

aehirsw   washier. *See* **aehirs aehrsw ehirsw**

aehirtyz   yahrzeit. *See* **aehirz aehrty ehirtz**

aehirwy   haywire. *See* **aerwy ahiry**

aehirz   hazier zaire hair haze hear heir hire raze rhea air are ear era hae her hie ire rah ria ae ah ai eh er ha he hi re

aehisst   ashiest. *See* **ehisst aeisst**

aehisstt   atheists hastiest ashiest atheist theists. *See* **aehstt aeisst aesstt ehisst**

aehisstu   hiatuses ashiest. *See* **aeisst ahistu ehisst ehsstu**

aehisstw   washiest ashiest swathes. *See* **aehssw aehstw aeisst aesstw**

aehissvy   yeshivas yeshiva. *See* **aehssv ehissv**

aehistt   atheist. *See* **ehistt aehstt**

aehistz   haziest. *See* **aehst aehsz ehist**

aehisvy   yeshiva. *See* **aehvy ehisv aehsv**

aehjnnos   johannes. *See* **aehnns**

aehk   hake hae ae ah eh ha he ka

aehkms   samekh hakes hames kames makes shake shame ahem hake hame hams hems kame make mash mask mesa mesh sake same seam sham ash ask hae ham has hem kas mae sea she ae ah am as eh em ha he ka ma me sh

aehkmss   samekhs. *See* **aehmss aehkms aehkss**

aehknnsu   unshaken. *See* **aehkns aehnns**

aehknr   hanker harken ankh earn hake hank hare hark hear hern kern khan knar nark near rake rank rhea ane are ark ear era hae hen her ken nae nah rah ran ae ah an eh en er ha he ka na ne re

aehknrs   hankers harkens. *See* **aehknr aehkrs aehkns ahknrs**

aehkns   shaken ankhs ashen hakes hanks khans shake shank skean snake sneak ankh hake hank hens kens khan sake sane sank ane ash ask ens hae has hen kas ken nae nah sea sen she ae ah an as eh en ha he ka na ne sh

aehkrs   kasher shaker eskar hakes hares harks hears rakes rheas saker shake share shark shear arks arse ears eras hake hare hark hear hers rahs rake rase rash resh rhea sake sark sear sera are ark ash ask ear era hae has her kas rah res sea she ae ah as eh er ha he ka re sh

aehkrss   shakers. *See* **aekrss aehrss aehkrs aehkss ahkrss**

aehkrsw   hawkers. *See* **aehkrw aehrsw aekrsw**

aehkrw   hawker wreak hake hare hark hawk hear rake rhea wake ware weak wear weka are ark awe ear era hae haw her hew rah raw war ae ah aw eh er ha he ka re we

aehks   hakes shake hake sake ash ask hae has kas sea she ae ah as eh ha he ka sh

aehkss   shakes ashes hakes sakes shake asks hake sake sash seas ash ask ass ess hae has kas sea she ae ah as eh ha he ka sh

aehl   hale heal ale hae lea ae ah eh el ha he la

aehlllty   lethally. *See* **aehllt aellly aellty**

aehllnrt   enthrall. *See* **aehllt aehlrt aehnrt aelnrt**

aehllt   lethal lathe hale hall halt hate heal heat hell late lath leal tael tale tall teal tell aet ale all alt ate eat ell eta eth hae hat het lea let tea the ae ah at eh el ha he la ta

aehlluv   helluva. *See* **aehlv aehlu aeluv**

aehllyz   hazelly. *See* **aehlz aelly**

aehlm   hemal ahem hale hame heal helm lame male meal ale elm hae ham hem lam lea mae mel ae ah am eh el em ha he la ma me

aehlmmns   helmsman. *See* **aehlns aelmms aelmns**

aehlmno   manhole. *See* **aelno aelmo aehlm**

aehlmnos   manholes manhole. *See* **aehlns aehlos aelmns aelmos**

aehlmnot   methanol ethanol manhole menthol telamon. *See* **aehlmt aehlot aehmnt aelmnt**

aehlmnuy   humanely humanly. *See* **aehmnu aelmny ahlmny**

aehlmnw   whalmen. *See* **aelmnw aehlm aehlw**

aehlmor   armhole. *See* **aelmor aehlr aehmr**

aehlmors   armholes armhole morales. *See* **aehlos aehlrs aehmrs aehors**

aehlmppt   pamphlet. *See* **aehlmt aelppt**

aehlmrss   harmless armless lashers marshes mashers slasher smasher. *See* **aehlrs aehlss aehmrs aehmss**

aehlmrst   thermals armlets halters hamlets hamster lathers slather thalers thermal. *See* **aehlmt aehlrs aehlrt aehlst**

aehlmrt   thermal. *See* **aelmrt aehlrt aehlmt**

aehlmru   humeral. *See* **aehlru aelmru**

aehlmst   hamlets. *See* **aehlst aehlmt aelmst**

aehlmt   hamlet hemal lathe metal ahem hale halt hame hate heal heat helm lame late lath male malt mate math meal meat melt tael tale tame teal team them aet ale alt ate eat elm eta eth hae ham hat hem het lam lea let mae mat mel met tam tea the ae ah am at eh el em ha he la ma me ta

aehlnot   ethanol. *See* **aehlot aelno aenot**

aehlnprs   shrapnel planers sharpen spheral. *See* **aehlns aehlps aehlrs aehprs**

aehlns   hansel ashen hales heals lanes leans leash selah shale ales hale heal hens lane lash lean leas lens sale sane seal ale ane ash els ens hae has hen lea nae nah sal sea sen she ae ah an as eh el en ha he la na ne sh

aehlnss   hansels. *See* **aehlns aehlss**

aehlnssu   unlashes hansels sensual unleash. *See* **aehlns aehlss aehlsu aenssu**

aehlnsu   unleash. *See* **aehlns aehlsu ahlnsu**

aehlntuz   hazelnut. *See* **aelntu ahltuz**

aehloprt   plethora prolate. *See* **aehlot aehlrt aehprt aelopr**

aehlorsy   hoarsely. *See* **aehlos aehlrs aehors aelrsy**

aehloruv   overhaul. *See* **aehlru eloruv**

aehlos   haloes aloes hales heals holes leash selah shale shoal ales aloe also hale halo heal hoes hole hose lash leas lose sale seal shoe sloe sole ale ash els hae has hoe lea los ohs sal sea she sol ae ah as eh el ha he ho la lo oh os sh so

aehlost   loathes. *See* **aehlst aehlos ehlost aehlot ahlost**

aehlot   loathe hotel lathe loath lotah thole aloe alto hale halo halt hate heal heat hole holt late lath lota loth oath tael tale teal tola aet ale alt ate eat eta eth hae hat het hoe hot lea let lot oat tea the tho toe ae ah at eh el ha he ho la lo oh ta to

aehlp aleph hale heal heap help leap pale peal plea ale alp ape hae hap hep lap lea pah pal pea ae ah eh el ha he la pa pe

aehlprs spheral. *See* **aehlps aehlrs aelprs aehprs**

aehlps alephs aleph hales heals heaps helps lapse leaps leash pales peals phase plash pleas salep selah sepal shale shape shlep ales alps apes apse hale haps hasp heal heap help laps lash leap leas pale pals peal peas plea sale seal slap ale alp ape ash asp els hae hap has hep lap lea pah pal pas pea sal sap sea she spa ae ah as eh el ha he la pa pe sh

aehlpss hapless plashes. *See* **aehlps aehlss aelpss aehpss ehlpss**

aehlpsss splashes hapless hassles passels plashes sapless slashes. *See* **aehlps aehlss aehpss aehsss**

aehlpsst pathless hapless pastels plashes staples. *See* **aehlps aehlss aehlst aehpss**

aehlpsy shapely. *See* **aehlps aehlpy**

aehlpy phylae aleph haply phyla phyle hale heal heap help hyla hype leap pale paly peal play plea yeah yelp ale alp ape aye hae hap hay hep hey lap lay lea lye pah pal pay pea ply pya yah yap yea yep ae ah ay eh el ha he la pa pe ye

aehlr haler earl hale hare harl heal hear herl rale real rhea ale are ear era hae her lar lea rah ae ah eh el er ha he la re

aehlrs lasher earls haler hales hares harls heals hears herls lares laser leash rales rheas selah shale share shear ales arse earl ears eras hale hare harl heal hear herl hers lash leas rahs rale rase rash real resh rhea sale seal sear sera ale are ash ear els era hae has her lar lea rah res sal sea she ae ah as eh el er ha he la re sh

aehlrss lashers slasher. *See* **aehlss aelrss aehlrs aehrss**

aehlrsss slashers hassles lashers rassles slasher slashes. *See* **aehlrs aehlss aehrss aehsss**

aehlrsst slathers artless halters lashers lathers rashest slasher slaters slather thalers trashes. *See* **aehlrs aehlrt aehlss aehlst**

aehlrst halters lathers slather thalers. *See* **aelrst aehrst aehlst aehlrt aehlrs**

aehlrsu haulers. *See* **aehlru aehlrs aehlsu aelrsu**

aehlrsw whalers. *See* **aehrsw aehlrw aehlsw**

aehlrt halter lather thaler alert alter earth haler hater heart later lathe taler earl hale halt hare harl hart hate heal hear heat herl late lath rale rate rath real rhea tael tale tare teal tear aet ale alt are art ate ear eat era eta eth hae hat her het lar lea let rah rat ret tar tea the ae ah at eh el er ha he la re ta

aehlrty earthly lathery. *See* **aehrty aehlrt aelrty**

aehlru hauler haler lehua earl hale hare harl haul heal hear herl hula hurl lure rale real rhea rule urea ale are ear era hae her hue lar lea leu rah rue ae ah eh el er ha he la re

aehlrw whaler haler whale wheal earl hale hare harl heal hear herl rale real rhea wale ware weal wear ale are awe awl ear era hae haw her hew lar law lea rah raw war ae ah aw eh el er ha he la re we

aehls hales heals leash selah shale ales hale heal lash leas sale seal ale ash els hae has lea sal sea she ae ah as eh el ha he la sh

aehlss hassle lashes selahs shales ashes hales heals leash sales seals selah shale slash ales hale heal lash lass leas less sale sals sash seal seas ale ash ass els ess hae has lea sal sea she ae ah as eh el ha he la sh

aehlsss hassles slashes. *See* **aehlss aelsss aehsss**

aehlst halest haslet lathes hales halts haste hates heals heats lathe laths leash least selah shale shalt slate stale steal taels tales ales alts east eats etas hale halt hast hate hats heal heat hest lash last late lath leas lest lets sale salt seal seat seta slat tael tale teal teas aet ale alt ash ate eat els eta eth hae has hat het lea let sal sat sea set she tea the ae ah as at eh el ha he la sh ta

aehlstt stealth. *See* **aehlst aelstt aehstt**

aehlstty stealthy stealth stately. *See* **aehlst aehstt aeltty ehlsty**

aehlstw wealths. *See* **aehlst aehstw aehltw aehlsw**

aehlsu lehuas hales hauls heals hulas leash lehua selah shale ales hale haul heal hues hula lash leas lues lush sale seal slue ale ash els hae has hue lea leu sal sea she sue use ae ah as eh el ha he la sh us

aehlsv halves hales halve heals laves leash salve selah shale shave slave vales veals ales aves hale have heal lash lave leas leva sale save seal vale vase veal ale ash ave els hae has lea lev sal sea she ae ah as eh el ha he la sh

aehlsw whales wheals hales hawse heals leash selah shale shawl swale wales weals welsh whale wheal ales awes awls hale haws heal hews lash laws leas sale seal shaw shew slew wale wash weal ale ash awe awl els hae has haw hew law lea sal saw sea sew she was ae ah as aw eh el ha he la sh we

aehlsz hazels hales hazel hazes heals lazes leash selah shale zeals ales hale haze heal lash laze leas sale seal zeal ale ash els hae has lea sal sea she ae ah as eh el ha he la sh

aehlt lathe hale halt hate heal heat late lath tael tale teal aet ale alt ate eat eta eth hae hat het lea let tea the ae ah at eh el ha he la ta

aehltw wealth lathe whale wheal wheat hale halt hate heal heat late lath tael tale teal thaw thew wale weal welt what whet aet ale alt ate awe awl eat eta eth hae hat haw het hew law lea let tea the wet ae ah at aw eh el ha he la ta we

aehltwy wealthy. *See* **aehltw ehlty ahlty**

aehlu lehua hale haul heal hula ale hae hue lea leu ae ah eh el ha he la

aehlv halve hale have heal lave leva vale veal ale ave hae lea lev ae ah eh el ha he la

aehlw whale wheal hale heal wale weal ale awe awl hae haw hew law lea ae ah aw eh el ha he la we

aehlz hazel hale haze heal laze zeal ale hae lea ae ah eh el ha he la

aehm ahem hame hae ham hem mae ae ah am eh em ha he ma me

aehmmr hammer harem herma ahem hame hare harm hear herm mare ream rhea are arm ear era hae ham hem her mae mar mem rah ram rem ae ah am eh em er ha he ma me re

aehmmrs hammers shammer. *See* **aehmmr aehmrs**

aehmmrss shammers hammers marshes mashers shammer smasher. *See* **aehmmr aehmrs aehmss aehrss**

aehmmsy mayhems. *See* **aemmsy aehmmy ahmmsy**

aehmmy mayhem hammy ahem hame yeah aye hae ham hay hem hey mae may mem yah yam yea ae ah am ay eh em ha he ma me my ye

aehmnnpy nymphean. *See* **aemnnp**

aehmnor menorah. *See* **aemnor**

aehmnors horseman menorahs enamors hoarsen menorah oarsmen. *See* **aehmrs aehors aemnor aenors**

aehmnosu houseman. *See* **aehmnu ahmnos ahmnsu**

aehmnst anthems. *See* **aehmnt aehnst aemnst**

aehmnt anthem hetman meant neath thane ahem amen ante hame hant hate heat hent mane mate math mean meat name neat tame team than them then aet ane ant ate eat eta eth hae ham hat hem hen het mae man mat men met nae nah net tam tan tea ten the ae ah am an at eh em en ha he ma me na ne ta

aehmnu humane human ahem amen hame mane maun mean menu name ane emu hae ham hem hen hue hum mae man men nae nah ae ah am an eh em en ha he ma me mu na ne nu um

aehmoprt metaphor apothem. *See* **aehmpr aehprt aemprt ehmort**

aehmopst apothems apothem. *See* **ahopst emopst**

aehmopt apothem. *See* **emopt**

aehmostt hemostat. *See* **aehstt aemstt emostt**

aehmostw somewhat. *See* **aehstw**

aehmpr hamper harem herma ahem hame hare harm harp heap hear hemp herm mare pare pear perm pram ramp rape ream reap rhea amp ape are arm ear era hae ham hap hem hep her mae map mar pah par pea per rah ram rap rem rep ae ah am eh em er ha he ma me pa pe re

aehmprs hampers. *See* **aehmpr aehmrs aehprs**

aehmpty empathy. *See* **empty aemty aepty**

aehmr harem herma ahem hame hare harm hear herm mare ream rhea are arm ear era hae ham hem her mae mar rah ram rem ae ah am eh em er ha he ma me re

aehmrr harmer harem herma rearm ahem hame hare harm hear herm mare rare ream rear rhea are arm ear era err hae ham hem her mae mar rah ram rem ae ah am eh em er ha he ma me re

aehmrs harems masher hames harem hares harms hears herma herms mares marsh maser reams rheas shame share shear smear ahem arms arse ears eras hame hams hare harm hear hems herm hers mare mash mesa mesh rahs rams rase rash ream resh rhea same seam sear sera sham are arm ash ear era hae ham has hem her mae mar rah ram rem res sea she ae ah am as eh em er ha he ma me re sh

aehmrss marshes mashers smasher. *See* **aehmrs aemrss aehmss aehrss**

aehmrsss smashers marshes mashers smasher smashes. *See* **aehmrs aehmss aehrss aehsss**

aehmrsst hamsters hamster marshes mashers masters rashest smasher streams trashes. *See* **aehmrs aehmss aehrss aehrst**

aehmrst hamster. *See* **aehrst aehmrs aemrst**

aehms hames shame ahem hame hams hems mash mesa mesh same seam sham ash hae ham has hem mae sea she ae ah am as eh em ha he ma me sh

aehmss mashes shames ashes hames mesas seams shame shams smash ahem hame hams hems mash mass mesa mesh mess same sash seam seas sham ash ass ess hae ham has hem mae sea she ae ah am as eh em ha he ma me sh

aehmsss smashes. *See* **aehmss aemsss aehsss**

aehmsssu shamuses smashes assumes. *See* **aehmss aehsss aemssu ahmssu**

aehmstty amethyst. *See* **aehstt aemstt aemsty**

aehmsuzz mezuzahs mezuzah mezuzas. *See* **aemuzz**

aehmuzz mezuzah. *See* **aemuzz**

aehnn henna ane hae hen nae nah ae ah an eh en ha he na ne

aehnnopt pantheon phaeton phonate. *See* **aennt aenot aehnn**

aehnnotx xanthone. *See* **aennt aennx aenot**

aehnns hennas ashen henna senna sane hens ane ash ens hae has hen nae nah sea sen she ae ah an as eh en ha he na ne sh

aehnopst phaetons phonates stanhope phaeton phonate. *See* **aehnst aenops aenost aenpst**

aehnopt phaeton phonate. *See* **aenot aehnt aenop**

aehnors hoarsen. *See* **aehors ehnors aenors ahnors**

aehnorss hoarsens harness hoarsen reasons shorans. *See* **aehors aehrss aenors aenoss**

aehnort another. *See* **aehnrt aenort ehnort**

aehnosx hexosan. *See* **aehosx aenos aehns**

aehnpp happen heap nape neap pane pean ane ape hae hap hen hep nae nah nap pah pan pap pea pen pep ae ah an eh en ha he na ne pa pe

aehnpps happens. *See* **aehnpp aehns aenps**

aehnprs sharpen. *See* **aehprs**

aehnprss sharpens harness phrases seraphs sharpen sherpas. *See* **aehprs aehpss aehrss aenpss**

aehnprst panthers anthers arpents entraps panther parents pastern sharpen thenars threaps trepans. *See* **aehnrt aehnst aehprs aehprt**

aehnprt panther. *See* **aehnrt aenprt aehprt**

aehnrss harness. *See* **aehrss aenrss**

aehnrsss rashness harness. *See* **aehrss aehsss aenrss**

aehnrst anthers thenars. *See* **aehnrt aenrst aehrst aehnst**

aehnrstu haunters unearths anthers haunter hunters natures saunter thenars unearth. *See* **aehnrt aehnst aehrst aenrst**

aehnrt anther thenar earth hater heart neath thane ante earn hant hare hart hate hear heat hent hern near neat rant rate rath rent rhea tare tear tern than then aet ane ant are art ate ear eat era eta eth hae hat hen her het nae nah net rah ran rat ret tan tar tea ten the ae ah an at eh en er ha he na ne re ta

aehnrtu haunter unearth. *See* **aehnrt ehnrtu aenrtu**

aehnrtx narthex. *See* **aehnrt**

aehns ashen sane hens ane ash ens hae has hen nae nah sea sen she ae ah an as eh en ha he na ne sh

aehnsst hastens. *See* **aensst aehnst ahnsst**

aehnssty shanteys hastens shantey. *See* **aehnst aehnsy aensst aensty**

aehnst hasten thanes antes ashen hants haste hates heats hents nates neath snath thane ante ants east eats etas hant hast hate hats heat hens hent hest neat nest nets sane seat sent seta tans teas tens than then aet ane ant ash ate eat ens eta eth hae has hat hen het nae nah net sat sea sen set she tan tea ten the ae ah an as at eh en ha he na ne sh ta

aehnstuw unswathe. *See* **aehnst aehstw aenstu ahnstu**

aehnsty shantey. *See* **aehnst aehnsy ahnsty aensty**

aehnsv havens shaven ashen avens haven naves shave vanes aves have hens nave sane save vane vans vase ane ash ave ens hae has hen nae nah sea sen she van ae ah an as eh en ha he na ne sh

aehnsy hyenas ashen hyena yeans ashy ayes easy eyas hays hens sane shay yeah yean yeas yens ane any ash aye ens hae has hay hen hey nae nah nay say sea sen she shy yah yea yen yes ae ah an as ay eh en ha he na ne sh ye

aehnt neath thane ante hant hate heat hent neat than then aet ane ant ate eat eta eth hae hat hen het nae nah net tan tea ten the ae ah an at eh en ha he na ne ta

aehnv haven have nave vane ane ave hae hen nae nah van ae ah an eh en ha he na ne

aehny hyena yeah yean ane any aye hae hay hen hey nae nah nay yah yea yen ae ah an ay eh en ha he na ne ye

aehoprry pyorrhea orphrey. *See* **aehprr aeprry ahorry eoprry**

aehorrrw harrower. *See* **aeorrr ahorrw**

aehorrs hoarser. *See* **aehors aehrrs**

aehors ashore hoarse arose hares hears hoers horas horse rheas share shear shoer shore aero arse ears eras hare hear hero hers hoar hoer hoes hora hose oars ores rahs rase rash resh rhea rhos roes rose sear sera shoe soar sora sore are ash ear era hae has her hoe oar ohs ore rah res rho roe sea she ae ah as eh er ha he ho oh or os re sh so

aehorsst hoarsest earshot rashest trashes. *See* **aehors aehrss aehrst aeorst**

aehorssw sawhorse hawsers showers washers. *See* **aehors aehrss aehrsw aehssw**

aehorst earshot. *See* **aehors aehrst aeorst ehorst ahorst**

aehorstt rheostat earshot hatters rotates shatter throats toaster. *See* **aehors aehrst aehrtt aehstt**

aehorstx oxhearts thoraxes earshot exhorts hoaxers oxheart. *See* **aehors aehorx aehosx aehrst**

aehorsx hoaxers. *See* **aehors aehorx aehosx**

aehortx oxheart. *See* **ehortx ahortx**

aehorx hoaxer aero hare hear hero hoar hoax hoer hora rhea are axe ear era hae her hex hoe oar ore rah rex rho roe ae ah ax eh er ex ha he ho oh or ox re

aehosstu housesat. *See* **ahosst ehosst ehossu ehsstu**

aehosx hoaxes axes hoax hoes hose shoe ash axe hae has hex hoe ohs sax sea sex she sox ae ah as ax eh ex ha he ho oh os ox sh so

aehp heap ape hae hap hep pah pea ae ah eh ha he pa pe

aehpprs perhaps. *See* **aepprs aehprs**

aehprr harper hare harp heap hear pare parr pear rape rare reap rear rhea ape are ear era err hae hap hep her pah par pea per rah rap rep ae ah eh er ha he pa pe re

aehprrs harpers sharper. *See* **aehprr aehrrs aeprrs aehprs**

aehprs phrase seraph shaper sherpa hares harps heaps hears pares parse pears phase rapes reaps rheas shape share sharp shear spare spear apes apse arse ears eras haps hare harp hasp heap hear hers pare pars pear peas rahs rape raps rase rash rasp reap reps resh rhea sear sera spar ape are ash asp ear era hae hap has hep her pah par pas pea per rah rap rep res sap sea she spa ae ah as eh er ha he pa pe re sh

aehprss phrases seraphs sherpas. *See* **aeprss aehpss aehrss ahprss aehprs**

aehprsst sharpest pasters phrases rashest repasts seraphs sherpas sparest threaps trashes. *See* **aehprs aehprt aehpss aehrss**

aehprst threaps. *See* **aehprs aehprt aehrst aeprst**

aehprsux haruspex. *See* **aehprs aeprsu aepsux ehprsu**

aehprt teraph threap earth hater heart pater peart prate taper hare harp hart hate heap hear heat pare part pate path pear peat pert rape rapt rate rath reap rhea tape tare tarp tear trap aet ape apt are art ate ear eat era eta eth hae hap hat hep her het pah par pat pea per pet rah rap rat rep ret tap tar tea the ae ah at eh er ha he pa pe re ta

aehprty therapy. *See* **aehrty**

aehps heaps phase shape apes apse haps hasp heap peas ape ash asp hae hap has hep pah pas pea sap sea she spa ae ah as eh ha he pa pe sh

aehpss phases shapes apses ashes hasps heaps phase shape apes apse asps haps hasp heap pass peas saps sash seas spas ape ash asp ass ess hae hap has hep pah pas pea sap sea she spa ae ah as eh ha he pa pe sh

aehqrsu quasher. *See* **aeqrsu aehrs ahqsu**

aehqsssu squashes quashes quasses. *See* **aehsss ahqssu**

aehqssu quashes. *See* **ahqssu aehss**

aehr hare hear rhea are ear era hae her rah ae ah eh er ha he re

aehrrs rasher sharer hares hears rears rheas share shear arse ears eras errs hare hear hers rahs rare rase rash rear resh rhea sear sera are ash ear era err hae has her rah res sea she ae ah as eh er ha he re sh

aehrrss sharers. *See* **aehrrs aehrss**

aehrrstu urethras urethra. *See* **aehrrs aehrrt aehrst ehrrsu**

aehrrt rather earth hater heart hare hart hate hear heat rare rate rath rear rhea tare tear aet are art ate ear eat era err eta eth hae hat her het rah rat ret tar tea the ae ah at eh er ha he re ta

aehrrtu urethra. *See* **aehrrt errtu**

aehrs hares hears rheas share shear arse ears eras hare hear hers rahs rase rash resh rhea sear sera are ash ear era hae has her rah res sea she ae ah as eh er ha he re sh

aehrss rashes shares shears arses ashes hares hears rases rheas sears share shear arse ears eras hare hear hers rahs rase rash resh rhea sash sear seas sera are ash ass ear era ess hae has her rah res sea she ae ah as eh er ha he re sh

aehrsst rashest trashes. *See* **aersst aehrst aehrss**

aehrsstt shatters hatters rashest shatter tasters trashes. *See* **aehrss aehrst aehrtt aehstt**

aehrsstv harvests harvest rashest shavers starves trashes. *See* **aehrss aehrst aehrsv aehssv**

aehrssv shavers. *See* **aehrss aerssv aehrsv aehssv**

aehrssw hawsers washers. *See* **aehrsw aehssw aehrss ehrssw aerssw**

aehrst earths haters hearts aster earth hares harts haste hater hates hears heart heats rates rheas share shear stare tares tears trash arse arts ears east eats eras erst etas hare hart hast hate hats hear heat hers hest rahs rase rash rate rath rats resh rest rets rhea sear seat sera seta star tare tars tear teas tsar aet are art ash ate ear eat era eta eth hae has hat her het rah rat res ret sat sea set she tar tea the ae ah as at eh er ha he re sh ta

aehrstt hatters shatter. *See* **aehrst aehrtt aerstt aehstt**

aehrstv harvest. *See* **aerstv aehrst aehrsv**

aehrstw wreaths. *See* **aehrst aehrsw aerstw ahrstw aehstw**

aehrsv shaver avers hares hears raves rheas saver share shave shear arse aver aves ears eras hare have hear hers rahs rase rash rave resh revs rhea save sear sera vase are ash ave ear era hae has her rah res rev sea she ae ah as eh er ha he re sh

aehrsvw wharves. *See* **aehrsw aehrsv aersvw**

aehrsw hawser washer hares hawse hears rheas share shear shrew swear wares wears arse awes ears eras hare haws hear hers hews rahs rase rash resh rhea sear sera shaw shew ware wars wash wear are ash awe ear era hae has haw her hew rah raw res saw sea sew she war was ae ah as aw eh er ha he re sh we

aehrt earth hater heart hare hart hate hear heat rate rath rhea tare tear aet are art ate ear eat era eta eth hae hat her het rah rat ret tar tea the ae ah at eh er ha he re ta

aehrtt hatter earth hater heart tater tetra theta treat hare hart hate hear heat rate rath rhea tare tart tear teat teth that tret aet are art ate ear eat era eta eth hae hat her het rah rat ret tar tat tea the ae ah at eh er ha he re ta

aehrtuu hauteur. *See* **aertuu aehrt**

aehrtw wreath earth hater heart threw water wheat wrath hare hart hate hear heat rate rath rhea tare tear thaw thew ware wart wear what whet aet are art ate awe ear eat era eta eth hae hat haw her het hew rah rat raw ret tar tea the war wet ae ah at aw eh er ha he re ta we

aehrty earthy hearty earth hater heart teary aery arty hare hart hate hear heat rate rath rhea tare tear they tray yare yeah year aet are art ate aye ear eat era eta eth hae hat hay her het hey rah rat ray ret rye tar tea the thy try yah yar yea yet ae ah at ay eh er ha he re ta ye

aehss ashes seas sash ash ass ess hae has sea she ae ah as eh ha he sh

aehsss sashes ashes asses sash sass seas ash ass ess hae has sea she ae ah as eh ha he sh

aehssst stashes. *See* **aessst aehsss**

aehsssw swashes. *See* **aehssw**

aehsstux exhausts exhaust. *See* **ehsstu**

aehsstw swathes. *See* **aehssw aehstw ahsstw aesstw**

aehssv shaves ashes saves shave vases aves have sash save seas vase ash ass ave ess hae has sea she ae ah as eh ha he sh

aehssw hawses washes ashes hawse shaws shews swash awes haws hews sash saws seas sews shaw shew wash ash ass awe ess hae has haw hew saw sea sew she was ae ah as aw eh ha he sh we

aehst haste hates heats east eats etas hast hate hats heat hest seat seta teas aet ash ate eat eta eth hae has hat het sat sea set she tea the ae ah as at eh ha he sh ta

aehstt thetas haste hates heats state taste teats testa theta east eats etas hast hate hats heat hest seat seta stet tats teas teat test teth that aet ash ate eat eta eth hae has hat het sat sea set she tat tea the ae ah as at eh ha he sh ta

aehstux exhaust. *See* **aehst aestx estux**

aehstw swathe wheats haste hates hawse heats swath sweat thaws thews waste wheat whets awes east eats etas hast hate hats haws heat hest hews seat seta shaw shew stew swat teas thaw thew wash wast west wets what whet aet ash ate awe eat eta eth hae has hat haw het hew sat saw sea set sew she tea the was wet ae ah as at aw eh ha he sh ta we

aehsv shave aves have save vase ash ave hae has sea she ae ah as eh ha he sh

aehsw hawse awes haws hews shaw shew wash ash awe hae has haw hew saw sea sew she was ae ah as aw eh ha he sh we

aehsz hazes haze ash hae has sea she ae ah as eh ha he sh

aeht hate heat aet ate eat eta eth hae hat het tea the ae ah at eh ha he ta

aehtt theta hate heat teat teth that aet ate eat eta eth hae hat het tat tea the ae ah at eh ha he ta

aehtw wheat hate heat thaw thew what whet aet ate awe eat eta eth hae hat haw het hew tea the wet ae ah at aw eh ha he ta we

aehv have hae ave ae ah eh ha he

aehvy heavy have yeah ave aye hae hay hey yah yea ae ah ay eh ha he ye

aehy yeah aye hae hay hey yah yea ae ah ay eh ha he ye

aehz haze hae ae ah eh ha he

aeiiintt initiate. *See* **aintt aeint**

aeiikllt taillike. *See* **aeillt eiikll**

aeiiknt kainite. *See* **aeiknt**

aeiilltv illative. *See* **aeillt**

aeiilmns alienism malines menials seminal. *See* **aeilmn aeilms aeilns aeimns**

aeiilmpr imperial imperil lempira palmier. *See* **aeilmp aeilmr aelmpr aiimpr**

aeiilmtt militate imitate. *See* **ailtt iilmt**

aeiilnn aniline. *See* **aeiln aeinn**

aeiilnns anilines aniline asinine. *See* **aeilns aeinns eilnns**

aeiilnqu aquiline. *See* **aeiln aelqu**

aeiilnr airline. *See* **eiilnr aeilnr**

aeiilnrr airliner airline rainier. *See* **aeiirr aeilnr**

aeiilnrs airlines airline. *See* **aeilnr aeilns aeilrs aeinrs**

aeiilnrt inertial airline inertia latrine lintier ratline reliant retinal. *See* **aeilnr aeilnt aeilrt aeinrt**

aeiilnst alienist litanies elastin entails laities liniest salient saltine tenails. *See* **aeilns aeilnt aiinst ailnst**

aeiilppt tailpipe. *See* **aelppt eilppt**

aeiilrtt literati tertial. *See* **aeilrt aeirtt eilrtt**

aeiilss silesia. *See* **aeilss**

aeiilsss silesias silesia lassies. *See* **aeilss aelsss**

aeiilst laities. *See* **aeils eilst**

aeiiltvz vitalize. *See* **aeilv aeltv**

aeiimmrt maritime airtime. *See* **aeimmr aeimrt**

aeiimmxz maximize. *See* **iimmx aeimz aimmx**

aeiimnt intimae. *See* **aeimnt eiimn**

aeiimntt intimate intimae imitate. *See* **aeimnt eimntt**

aeiimntu minutiae intimae minutia. *See* **aeimnt aeintu aimntu eimntu**

aeiimrst airtimes airiest airtime imarets mistier. *See* **aeimrs aeimrt aeimst aeirst**

aeiimrt airtime. *See* **aeimrt**

aeiimstt imitates imitate. *See* **aeimst aemstt**

aeiimtt imitate. *See* **aemtt**

aeiinns asinine. *See* **aeinns**

aeiinrr rainier. *See* **aeiirr aenrr**

aeiinrrs airiness arsines raisins. *See* **aeinrs aeinss aeirss aiinrs**

aeiinrst rainiest airiest inertia nastier retains retinas stainer. *See* **aeinrs aeirst aenrst aiinrs**

aeiinrt inertia. *See* **aeinrt**

aeiinsst sanities entasis tansies. *See* **aeinss aeisst aensst aiinst**

aeiinstv vanities natives invites. *See* **aeinsv aeintv aiinst einstv**

aeiinsvv invasive navvies. *See* **aeinsv**

aeiiprr prairie. *See* **aeiirr aeiprr**

aeiiprrs prairies parries prairie praiser rapiers repairs. *See* **aeiirr aeiprr aeiprs aeirrs**

aeiiprst parities airiest parties pastier piaster pirates tipsier traipse. *See* **aeiprs aeiprt aeirst aeprst**

aeiiprzz pizzeria. *See* **aipzz eiprz aeirz**

aeiipsst epitasis pasties patsies. *See* **aeisst aepsst eiipst eipsst**

aeiirr airier rare rear air are ear era err ire ria ae ai er re

aeiirrst rarities airiest tarries tarsier. *See* **aeiirr aeirrs aeirst**

aeiirrtt irritate rattier. *See* **aeiirr aeirtt aerrtt eirrtt**

aeiirst airiest. *See* **aeirst**

aeiirstw wisteria airiest waiters wariest wiriest. *See* **aeirst aeirtw aerstw eirstw**

aeiirstz satirize airiest. *See* **aeirst aerstz**

aeiisttv vitiates vitiate. *See* **aeittv**

aeiittv vitiate. *See* **aeittv**

aeijlnsv javelins javelin. *See* **aeilns aeilnv aeilsv aeinsv**

aeijlnv javelin. *See* **aeilnv**

aeijlops jalopies. *See* **aeilps aelops eilops**

aeijlosu jalousie jealous. *See* **ejlosu**

aeijlr jailer aril earl jail jarl lair liar lira lire rail rale real rial riel rile ail air ale are ear era ire jar lar lea lei lie raj ria ae ai el er la li re

aeijlrs jailers. *See* aeijlr aeilrs

aeijmns jasmine. *See* aeimns aijmns

aeijmnss jasmines inseams jasmine samisen. *See* aeinss aemnss aijmns

aeijnrtu jauntier ruinate taurine urinate. *See* aeinrt aeintu aenrtu ainrtu

aeijrzz jazzier. *See* aeirz

aeijstzz jazziest. *See* aestz

aeikl alike kail kale lake leak like ail ale elk ilk kal lea lei lek lie ae ai el ka la li

aeiklmn manlike. *See* aeilmn aiklmn

aeiklmr armlike. *See* aeilmr eiklmr

aeiklnps skiplane spaniel. *See* aeilnp aeilns aeilps aeklns

aeiklnr lankier. *See* aeilnr eiklnr aeklnr

aeiklnss sealskin. *See* aeilns aeilss aeinss aeklns

aeiklnst lankiest anklets elastin entails intakes salient saltine tenails tinkles. *See* aeiknt aeilns aeilnt aeklns

aeiklrst starlike kilters kirtles realist retails saltier saltire talkers. *See* aeikrs aeilrs aeilrt aeirst

aeiklrw warlike. *See* aeklrw aeikl eiklr

aeikmnp pikeman. *See* aeimn

aeikmnst mistaken inmates intakes mistake. *See* aeiknt aeimnt aeimst

aeikmsst mistakes kismets mistake samites. *See* aeimst aeisst aeksst aemsst

aeikmst mistake. *See* eikmst aeimst

aeiknrs snakier. *See* aeinrs eiknrs aeikrs

aeiknrst keratins intakes keratin nastier rankest retains retinas snakier stainer stinker tankers tinkers. *See* aeiknt aeikrs aeinrs aeinrt

aeiknrt keratin. *See* aeiknt aeinrt aeknrt eiknrt

aeiknrtw knitwear keratin tawnier tinware. *See* aeiknt aeinrt aeirtw aeknrt

aeiknsst snakiest entasis intakes tansies. *See* aeiknt aeinss aeisst aeknss

aeiknst intakes. *See* aeiknt aeins aenst

aeiknsyz kyanizes kyanize. *See* aeinsz aeknsy ainsyz

aeiknt intake taken tenia tinea akin ante anti kina kine kite knit neat take tank teak tike tine aet ane ani ant ate eat eta ink ita kat ken kin kit nae net nit tan tea ten tie tin ae ai an at en in it ka na ne ta ti

aeiknyz kyanize. *See* aeinz ainyz iknyz

aeikprw pawkier. *See* eikpr eiprw aekrw

aeikpstw pawkiest. *See* aekstw eikstw

aeikqru quakier. *See* aikru aekqu akqru

aeikqstu quakiest. *See* aekqsu eiqstu

aeikrr kerria kier rake raki rare rear air are ark ear era err ire irk kir ria ae ai er ka re

aeikrs kaiser arise eskar kiers raise rakes rakis saker serai airs arks arse ears eras irks kier kris rake raki rase reis rias rise risk sake saki sari sark sear sera sire air are ark ask ear era ire irk kas kir res ria sea sir ski ae ai as er is ka re si

aeikrss kaisers. *See* aeirss aekrss aeikrs eikrss

aeikrsst asterisk kaisers satires skaters strakes streaks strikes. *See* aeikrs aeirss aeirst aeisst

aeilllmo malleoli. *See* aelmo allmo

aeilllny lineally. *See* aeilln aellly

aeilln lineal alien aline anile liane anil lain lane leal lean lien line nail nill ail ale all ane ani ell ill lea lei lie nae nil ae ai an el en in la li na ne

aeillnqu quinella. *See* aeilln

aeillnry linearly. *See* aeilln aeilnr aellry aelnry

aeillotv volatile alveoli violate. *See* aeillt eilotv

aeillov alveoli. *See* aeilv eilov aillv

aeillpst pastille pallets tailles talipes tallies. *See* aeills aeillt aeilps aellps

aeillrry raillery. *See* aeilrr aellry aelrry

aeillrs rallies. *See* aeills eillrs aeilrs

aeillrsy serially rallies. *See* aeills aeilrs aeilsy aellry

aeillrt literal. *See* aeilrt aeillt aellrt eillrt

aeills allies aisle lisle ails ales ells isle leal leas leis lies sail sale seal sell sill ail ale all ell els ill lea lei lie sal sea ae ai as el is la li si

aeillss sallies. *See* aeilss aeills eillss

aeillsst tailless sallets sallies tailles tallies. *See* aeills aeillt aeilss aeisst

aeillst tailles tallies. *See* aeills eillst aellst aeillt

aeillsuv allusive eluvial. *See* aeills aeilsv aelsuv aillsv

aeillt taille telial alit late leal lilt tael tail tale tali tall teal tell tile till aet ail ale all alt ate eat ell eta ill ita lea lei let lie lit tea tie til ae ai at el it la li ta ti

aeilluv eluvial. *See* aeilv aeluv aillv

aeilmmn mailmen. *See* aeilmn aelmm

aeilmmor memorial loamier immoral. *See* aeilmr aeimmr aelmor

aeilmmot immolate. *See* eilmot

aeilmms melisma. *See* aeilms aelmms

aeilmmss melismas melisma aimless. *See* aeilms aeilss aelmms ailmss

aeilmn menial alien aline amine anile anime leman liane limen minae amen anil lain lame lane lean lien lime limn line mail main male mane meal mean mien mile mina mine nail name ail aim ale ane ani elm lam lea lei lie mae man mel men mil nae nil nim ae ai am an el em en in la li ma me mi na ne

aeilmnn lineman. *See* aeilmn aeinn eilnn

aeilmnns linesman lineman malines menials seminal. *See* aeilmn aeilms aeilns aeimns

aeilmnos semolina anomies malines malison menials seminal. *See* aeilmn aeilms aeilns aeimno

aeilmnp impanel maniple. *See* aeilnp aeilmp aeilmn

aeilmnps impanels maniples impales impanel malines maniple menials seminal spaniel. *See* aeilmn aeilmp aeilms aeilnp

aeilmnr manlier marline mineral. *See* aeimnr eilmnr aeilnr aeilmr ailmnr

aeilmnrs minerals limners mailers malines manlier marines marline marlins menials merlins mineral realism remains seminal seminar. *See* aeilmn aeilmr aeilms aeilnr

aeilmnrt terminal ailment aliment latrine maltier manlier marline minaret mineral raiment ratline reliant retinal. *See* aeilmn aeilmr aeilnr aeilnt

aeilmns malines menials seminal. *See* aeilns aeimns aelmns aeilmn aeilms

aeilmnst ailments aliments manliest ailment aliment elastin entails inmates laments malines mantels mantles menials salient saltine seminal tenails. *See* aeilmn aeilms aeilns aeilnt

aeilmnt ailment aliment. *See* aeilnt aeimnt aelmnt

aeilmor loamier. *See* aeilmr aelmor

aeilmorz moralize loamier. *See* aeilmr aeilrz aeimrz aelmor

aeilmost loamiest atomies isolate maltose. *See* aeilms aeimst aelmos aelmst

aeilmp impale ample impel maple lame lamp leap lime limp mail male meal mile pail pale palm peal pile plea ail aim ale alp amp ape elm imp lam lap lea lei lie lip mae map mel mil pal pea pie ae ai am el em la li ma me mi pa pe pi

aeilmpr lempira palmier. *See* aelmpr aeilmp eilmpr aeilmr ailmpr

aeilmprs lempiras impales impresa lempira limpers mailers palmers palmier realism rimples sampler simpler. *See* aeilmp aeilmr aeilms aeilps

aeilmprv primeval lempira palmier prevail vampire. *See* aeilmp aeilmr aelmpr aelmrv

aeilmps impales. *See* aeilps eilmps aelmps aeilms

aeilmpst palmiest amplest impales limpest limpets palmist pastime talipes. *See* **aeilmp aeilms aeilps aeimst**

aeilmpty playtime emptily. *See* **aeilmp aelmty eilmpt eilmty**

aeilmr mailer lamer miler realm amir aril earl emir lair lame liar lime lira lire mail male mare marl meal merl mile mire rail rale rami real ream rial riel rile rime ail aim air ale are arm ear elm era ire lam lar lea lei lie mae mar mel mil mir ram rem ria rim ae ai am el em er la li ma me mi re

aeilmrs mailers realism. *See* **aeimrs aeilmr aeilms eilmrs aelmrs**

aeilmrss realisms aimless airless armless mailers realism rimless sailers serials smilers. *See* **aeilmr aeilms aeilrs aeilss**

aeilmrt maltier. *See* **aelmrt aeimrt aeilmr ailmrt aeilrt**

aeilmrtt remittal maltier martlet tertial. *See* **aeilmr aeilrt aeimrt aeirtt**

aeilmruv velarium. *See* **aeilmr aeimru aelmru aelmrv**

aeilms mesial aisle lames limes mails males meals miles salmi slime smile ails aims ales alms elms isle lame lams leas leis lies lime mail male meal mels mesa mile mils mise sail sale same seal seam semi slam slim ail aim ale elm els lam lea lei lie mae mel mil mis sal sea ae ai am as el em is la li ma me mi si

aeilmss aimless. *See* **aeilss aeilms ailmss eilmss**

aeilmssx smilaxes aimless. *See* **aeilms aeilss ailmss ailmsx**

aeilmstt maltiest. *See* **aeilms aeimst aelmst aelstt**

aeilmstu simulate amulets muletas. *See* **aeilms aeimst aelmst aelmtu**

aeilmttu mutilate ultimate. *See* **aelmtu aemttu**

aeiln alien aline anile liane anil lain lane lean lien line nail ail ale ane ani lea lei lie nae nil ae ai an el en in la li na ne

aeilnnrt internal lantern latrine ratline reliant retinal. *See* **aeilnr aeilnt aeilrt aeinnr**

aeilnnsy insanely inanely. *See* **aeilns aeilsy aeinns aelnsy**

aeilnnty innately inanely. *See* **aeilnt aeinnt aelnty ailnty**

aeilnny inanely. *See* **aeiln aeinn ailny**

aeilnop opaline. *See* **aeilnp eilnop**

aeilnops opalines epsilon opaline pinoles spaniel. *See* **aeilnp aeilns aeilps aelnos**

aeilnor aileron alienor. *See* **aeilnr aelnor**

aeilnors ailerons alienors aileron alienor erasion loaners. *See* **aeilnr aeilns aeilrs aeinrs**

aeilnort oriental relation aileron alienor elation latrine ratline reliant retinal toenail. *See* **aeilnr aeilnt aeilrt aeinrt**

aeilnost toenails elastin elation entails entoils isolate salient saltine talions tenails toenail. *See* **aeilns aeilnt aelnos aelost**

aeilnot elation toenail. *See* **aeilnt eilnot ailnot**

aeilnp alpine pineal alien aline anile lapin liane panel penal plain plane anil lain lane lean leap lien line nail nape neap nipa pail pain pale pane peal pean pile pine plan plea ail ale alp ane ani ape lap lea lei lie lip nae nap nil nip pal pan pea pen pie pin ae ai an el en in la li na ne pa pe pi

aeilnppt pieplant pantile. *See* **aeilnp aeilnt aelnpt aelppt**

aeilnpr plainer praline. *See* **aeilnp aeilnr aelnpr aeinpr**

aeilnprs pralines pilsner plainer planers praline rapines spaniel. *See* **aeilnp aeilnr aeilns aeilps**

aeilnps spaniel. *See* **aeilns aeilnp aeilps ailnps aelnps**

aeilnpss painless spaniels espials napless palsies pansies spaniel spinals splines. *See* **aeilnp aeilns aeilps aeilss**

aeilnpst panelist pantiles plainest elastin entails panties pantile plaints planets platens salient saltine sapient spaniel talipes tenails. *See* **aeilnp aeilns aeilnt aeilps**

aeilnpsx explains explain salpinx spaniel. *See* **aeilnp aeilns aeilps aeinsx**

aeilnpt pantile. *See* **aeilnp aeilnt eilnpt ailnpt aelnpt**

aeilnptt tinplate pantile patient. *See* **aeilnp aeilnt aelnpt aelntt**

aeilnpx explain. *See* **aeilnp**

aeilnqtu quantile antique liquate quinate quintal tequila. *See* **aeilnt aeintu aelntu ainqtu**

aeilnr linear alien aline anile learn liane liner renal anil aril earl earn lain lair lane lean liar lien line lira lire nail near rail rain rale rani real rein rial riel rile ail air ale ane ani are ear era ire lar lea lei lie nae nil ran ria ae ai an el en er in la li na ne re

aeilnrss rainless airless arsines sailers serials. *See* **aeilnr aeilns aeilrs aeilss**

aeilnrst entrails latrines ratlines antlers elastin entails latrine nastier ratline realist reliant rentals retails retains retinal retinas salient saltern saltier saltine saltire stainer sternal tenails. *See* **aeilnr aeilns aeilnt aeilrs**

aeilnrt latrine ratline reliant retinal. *See* **aelnrt aeilnr aeilrt aeinrt aeilnt**

aeilnrtv interval latrine ratline reliant retinal ventral. *See* **aeilnr aeilnt aeilnv aeilrt**

aeilns aliens alines lianes saline aisle alien aline anile anils anise lanes leans lenis liane liens lines nails slain snail ails ales anil isle lain lane lean leas leis lens lies line nail nils sail sain sale sane seal sine ail ale ane ani els ens lea lei lie nae nil sal sea sen sin ae ai an as el en in is la li na ne si

aeilnsst salients saltines elastin enlists entails entasis listens salient saltine tansies tenails tinsels. *See* **aeilns aeilnt aeilss aeinss**

aeilnssz laziness. *See* **aeilns aeilss aeinss aeinsz**

aeilnst elastin entails salient saltine tenails. *See* **aeilns eilnst aeilnt ailnst**

aeilnstu insulate aunties elastin entails salient saltine sinuate tenails. *See* **aeilns aeilnt aeintu aelntu**

aeilnsuy uneasily. *See* **aeilns aeilsy aelnsy aensuy**

aeilnt entail tenail alien aline anile inlet leant liane tenia tinea alit anil ante anti lain lane late lean lent lien line lint nail neat tael tail tale tali teal tile tine aet ail ale alt ane ani ant ate eat eta ita lea lei let lie lit nae net nil nit tan tea ten tie til tin ae ai an at el en in it la li na ne ta ti

aeilntvy natively venality naively naivety. *See* **aeilnt aeilnv aeintv aelntv**

aeilnv venial alien aline alive anile anvil levin liane liven naive navel nival venal anil evil lain lane lave lean leva lien line live nail nave nevi vail vain vale vane veal veil vein vial vile vina vine ail ale ane ani ave lea lei lev lie nae nil van via vie ae ai an el en in la li na ne

aeilnvy naively. *See* **aeilnv ailnvy**

aeiloppt oppilate. *See* **aeiopt aelopt aelppt eilopt**

aeiloprz polarize. *See* **aeilrz aelopr**

aeilopst spoliate apostil apostle isolate opiates pelotas pistole talipes topsail. *See* **aeilps aeiopt aelops aelopt**

aeilorsz solarize. *See* **aeilrs aeilrz aelosz ailors**

aeilosst isolates isolate. *See* **aeilss aeisst aelost aelsst**

aeilost isolate. *See* **aelost eilost**

aeilostv violates estival isolate solvate violate violets. *See* **aeilsv aelost aelosv aelstv**

aeilotv violate. *See* **eilotv aeilv aeotv**

aeilppqu applique. *See* **aelppu aelpqu**

aeilpps applies. *See* **aelpps aeilps ailpps**

aeilprrs reprisal parrels parries praiser railers rapiers repairs. *See* **aeilps aeilrr aeilrs aeiprr**

aeilprrt paltrier retrial trailer. *See* **aeilrr aeilrt aeiprr aeiprt**

aeilprsv prevails prevail revisal. *See* **aeilps aeilrs aeilsv aeiprs**

aeilprv prevail. *See* **aeilv aelrv eilrv**

aeilps espial aisle lapse leaps pails pales peals piles pleas salep sepal sepia spiel spile ails ales alps apes apse isle laps leap leas leis lies lips lisp pail pale pals peal peas pies pile plea sail sale seal slap slip ail ale alp ape asp els lap lea lei lie lip pal pas pea pie sal sap sea sip spa ae ai as el is la li pa pe pi si

aeilpss espials palsies. *See* **aeilss aeilps aelpss eilpss**

aeilpssy paisleys espials paisley palsies. *See* **aeilps aeilss aeilsy aelpss**

aeilpst talipes. *See* **aeilps aelpst ailpst eilpst**

aeilpsuv plausive. *See* **aeilps aeilsv aelsuv ailpsu**

aeilpsy paisley. *See* **aeilps aeilsy**

aeilqrtu quartile requital liquate quilter tequila. *See* **aeilrt aeqrtu ailrtu**

aeilqstu liquates tequilas liquate tequila. *See* **aelqsu aelstu ailqsu eiqstu**

aeilqsuy queasily. *See* **aeilsy aelqsu aeqsuy ailqsu**

aeilqtu liquate tequila. *See* **aelqu ailqu eiqtu**

aeilqtuy equality liquate quality quietly tequila. *See* **eiqtuy**

aeilrr railer aril earl lair liar lira lire rail rale rare real rear rial riel rile ail air ale are ear era err ire lar lea lei lie ria ae ai el er la li re

aeilrrs railers. *See* **aeilrr aeilrs aeirrs**

aeilrrst retrials trailers railers realist retails retrial saltier saltire tarries tarsier trailer. *See* **aeilrr aeilrs aeilrt aeirrs**

aeilrrt retrial trailer. *See* **aeilrr aeilrt aeilrt**

aeilrrty literary irately reality retrial trailer. *See* **aeilrr aeilrt aelrry aelrty**

aeilrruz ruralize. *See* **aeilrr aeilrz**

aeilrs sailer serial aisle arils arise earls lairs lares laser liars liras rails raise rales rials riels riles serai ails airs ales aril arse earl ears eras isle lair leas leis liar lies lira lire rail rale rase real reis rial rias riel rile rise sail sale sari seal sear sera sire ail air ale are ear els era ire lar lea lei lie res ria sal sea sir ae ai as el er is la li re si

aeilrss airless sailers serials. *See* **aeilss aeirss aelrss aeilrs**

aeilrsst realists saltires airless artless listers realist retails sailers saltier saltire

satires serials slaters. *See* **aeilrs aeilrt aeilss aeirss**

aeilrssv revisals airless revisal sailers serials silvers slavers slivers valises. *See* **aeilrs aeilss aeilsv aeirss**

aeilrst realist retails saltier saltire. *See* **aeilrs aeilrt aeirst aelrst ailrst**

aeilrstt tertials artiste attires litters ratites rattles realist retails saltier saltire starlet starlit startle striate tastier tertial. *See* **aeilrs aeilrt aeirst aeirtt**

aeilrsv revisal. *See* **aelrsv eilrsv ailrsv aeilrs aeilsv**

aeilrsvv revivals revisal revival. *See* **aeilrs aeilsv aeirsv aelrsv**

aeilrsvy virelays revisal silvery slavery virelay. *See* **aeilrs aeilsv aeilsy aeirsv**

aeilrt retail alert alter irate later liter litre retia taler tiler trail trial alit aril earl lair late liar lira lire rail rale rate real rial riel rile rite tael tail tale tali tare teal tear tier tile tire aet ail air ale alt are art ate ear eat era eta ire ita lar lea lei let lie lit rat ret ria tar tea tie til ae ai at el er it la li re ta ti

aeilrtt tertial. *See* **aeirtt aelrtt eilrtt aeilrt**

aeilrty irately reality. *See* **aelrty aeilrt**

aeilrvv revival. *See* **aeilv aelrv eilrv**

aeilrvy virelay. *See* **eilrvy**

aeilrwy wearily. *See* **aelrwy ailrwy**

aeilrz lazier zaire aril earl lair laze liar lira lire rail rale raze real rial riel rile zeal ail air ale are ear era ire lar lea lei lie ria ae ai el er la li re

aeils aisle ails ales isle leas leis lies sail sale seal ail ale els lea lei lie sal sea ae ai as el is la li si

aeilss aisles lassie aisle isles sails sales seals sisal ails ales isle lass leas leis less lies sail sale sals seal seas ail ale ass els ess lea lei lie sal sea sis ae ai as el is la li si

aeilsss lassies. *See* **aeilss aelsss ailsss**

aeilsstt saltiest stalest. *See* **aeilss aeisst aelsst aelstt**

aeilssv valises. *See* **aeilss aelssv ailssv**

aeilstv estival. *See* **aelstv aeilsv eilstv ailstv**

aeilstz laziest. *See* **aeils eilst aelsz**

aeilsv valise aisle alive evils laves lives salve silva slave vails vales veals veils vials ails ales aves evil isle lave leas leis leva lies live sail sale save seal vail vale vase veal veil vial vies vile visa vise ail ale ave els lea lei lev lie sal sea via vie ae ai as el is la li si

aeilsy easily aisle ails ales ayes easy eyas isle lays leas leis lies lyes lyse sail sale seal slay yeas ail ale aye els lay lea lei

lie lis lye sal say sea sly yea yes ae ai as ay el is la li si ye

aeilv alive evil lave leva live vail vale veal veil vial vile ail ale ave lea lei lev lie via vie ae ai el la li

aeilx axile axil axle ilex ail ale axe lax lea lei lie ae ai ax el ex la li xi

aeimmms mammies. *See* **aimms eimms**

aeimmnnt immanent. *See* **aeimnt aeinnt**

aeimmr maimer mimer amir emir imam maim mare mime mire rami ream rime aim air are arm ear era ire mae mar mem mim mir ram rem ria rim ae ai am em er ma me mi re

aeimmrtu immature muriate. *See* **aeimmr aeimrt aeimru aemrtu**

aeimn amine anime minae amen main mane mean mien mina mine name aim ane ani mae man men nae nim ae ai am an em en in ma me mi na ne

aeimnnot nominate montane mention. *See* **aeimno aeimnt aeinno aeinnt**

aeimno anomie amine anime minae aeon amen main mane mean mien mina mine moan name noma nome omen aim ane ani eon ion mae man men moa mon nae nim one ae ai am an em en in ma me mi moa na ne no om on

aeimnor moraine romaine. *See* **aeimnr aeimno aemnor eimnor**

aeimnors moraines romaines anomies enamors erasion marines merinos moraine oarsmen remains romaine seminar. *See* **aeimno aeimnr aeimrs**

aeimnos anomies. *See* **aeimns eimnos**

aeimnost masonite anomies atomies inmates moisten. *See* **aeimno aeimnt aeimst**

aeimnowz womanize. *See* **aeimno**

aeimnr airmen marine remain amine anime minae miner amen amir earn emir main mane mare mean mien mina mine mire name near rain rami rani ream rein rime aim air ane ani are arm ear era ire mae man mar men mir nae nim ram ran rem ria rim ae ai am an em en er in ma me mi na ne re

aeimnrr mariner. *See* **aeimnr**

aeimnrrs mariners mariner marines marries remains seminar. *See* **aeimnr aeimrs aeinrs**

aeimnrs marines remains seminar. *See* **aeimnr aeimns aeinrs aeimrs eimnrs**

aeimnrss seminars arsines inseams marines remains samisen seminar. *See* **aeimnr aeimrs aeinrs**

aeimnrst minarets raiments imarets inmates marines martens martins minaret minster nastier raiment remains retains retinas seminar smarten stainer. *See* **aeimnr aeimnt aeimrs**

aeimnrsu aneurism manures marines remains seminar surname uremias. *See* **aeimnr aeimrs aeimru**

aeimnrsy seminary marines remains seminar. *See* **aeimnr aeimrs aeinrs**

aeimnrt minaret raiment. *See* **aeimnr aeimrt aeimnt aemnrt aimnrt**

aeimnrtt martinet iterant minaret nattier nitrate raiment tertian. *See* **aeimnr aeimnt aeimrt aeinrt**

aeimnrtu ruminate minaret muriate raiment ruinate taurine urinate. *See* **aeimnr aeimnt aeimrt aeimru**

aeimns amines inseam semina amine anime anise mains manes manse means miens minae mines names aims amen main mane mean mesa mien mina mine mise name nims sain same sane seam semi sine aim ane ani ens mae man men mis nae nim sea sen sin ae ai am an as em en in is ma me mi na ne si

aeimnss inseams samisen. *See* **aeimns aeinss aemnss**

aeimnsss samisens inseams samisen. *See* **aeinss aemnss aemsss**

aeimnsst mantises entasis inmates inseams samisen samites stamens tansies. *See* **aeimnt aeimst aeinss**

aeimnst inmates. *See* **aeimns aeimnt aimnst aeimst aemnst**

aeimnt inmate amine anime matin meant minae tenia tinea amen ante anti emit item main mane mate mean meat mien mina mine mint mite name neat tame team time tine aet aim ane ani ant ate eat eta ita mae man mat men met nae net nim nit tam tan tea ten tie tin ae ai am an at em en in it ma me mi na ne ta ti

aeimnty amenity. *See* **aeimnt eimnty**

aeimopr emporia. *See* **aemor aeopr eimpr**

aeimorr armoire. *See* **aemorr**

aeimorrs armoires armories armoire marries remoras roamers. *See* **aeimrs aeirrs aemorr amorrs**

aeimortt amoretti. *See* **aeimrt aeirtt aemrtt aeortt**

aeimortz amortize atomizer atomize. *See* **aeimrt aeimrz**

aeimost atomies. *See* **aeimst eimost**

aeimostx toxemias atomies toxemia. *See* **aeimst aimosx eimost eimosx**

aeimostz atomizes atomies atomize mestizo. *See* **aeimst aeimsz aeostz**

aeimottv motivate. *See* **aeittv eimotv**

aeimotx toxemia. *See* **aimox eimox**

aeimotz atomize. *See* **aeotz aeimz amotz**

aeimprrt imparter primate. *See* **aeimrt aeiprr aeiprt aemprt**

aeimprs impresa. *See* **aeimrs aeiprs eimprs**

aeimprss impresas aspires impasse impresa impress paresis praises simpers. *See* **aeimrs aeiprs aeirss aemrss**

aeimprst primates armpits imarets imparts impresa imprest parties pastier pastime permits piaster pirates primate stamper tampers traipse. *See* **aeimrs aeimrt aeimst aeiprs**

aeimprsv vampires impresa revamps vampire. *See* **aeimrs aeiprs aeirsv aemprv**

aeimprt primate. *See* **aimprt aeimrt eimprt aeiprt aemprt**

aeimprtu apterium muriate primate tempura. *See* **aeimrt aeimru aeiprt aemprt**

aeimprv vampire. *See* **aemprv eimpr eiprv**

aeimpss impasse. *See* **aimss aepss aipss**

aeimpsss impasses impasse asepsis. *See* **aemsss aepsss ampsss eimsss**

aeimpsst pastimes impasse misstep pasties pastime patsies samites. *See* **aeimst aeisst aemsst aepsst**

aeimpst pastime. *See* **aeimst**

aeimqrsu marquise marques marquis masquer uremias. *See* **aeimrs aeimru aemqru aemqsu**

aeimrrs marries. *See* **aeimrs aemrrs aeirrs**

aeimrs armies amirs arise emirs mares maser mires miser raise reams rimes serai simar smear aims airs amir arms arse ears emir eras mare mesa mire mirs mise rami rams rase ream reis rias rime rims rise same sari seam sear semi sera sire aim air are arm ear era ire mae mar mir mis ram rem res ria rim sea sir ae ai am as em er is ma me mi re si

aeimrsst asterism smarties imarets masters misters samites satires smiters streams. *See* **aeimrs aeimrt aeimst aeirss**

aeimrssy emissary. *See* **aeimrs aeirss aemrss aemrsy**

aeimrst imarets. *See* **aeimrs aeimrt aeimst aeirst aemrst**

aeimrstt martites artiste attires imarets martite matters metrist ratites smatter striate tastier. *See* **aeimrs aeimrt aeimst aeirst**

aeimrstu muriates atriums imarets matures muriate strumae uremias. *See* **aeimrs aeimrt aeimru aeimst**

aeimrstw wartimes imarets waiters wariest warmest wartime. *See* **aeimrs aeimrt aeimst aeirst**

aeimrstx matrixes imarets. *See* **aeimrs aeimrt aeimst aeirst**

aeimrsu uremias. *See* **aeimrs aeimru**

aeimrsww swimwear. *See* **aeimrs**

aeimrt imaret irate merit miter mitre remit retia tamer timer amir emir emit item mare mart mate meat mire mite rami rate ream rime rite tame tare team tear term tier time tire tram trim aet aim air are arm art ate ear eat era eta ire ita mae mar mat met mir ram rat rem ret ria rim tam tar tea tie ae ai am at em er it ma me mi re ta ti

aeimrtu muriate. *See* **aimrtu aemrtu aeimru**

aeimrtw wartime. *See* **aeimrt aeirtw**

aeimru uremia amir emir mare mire rami ream rime urea aim air are arm ear emu era ire mae mar mir ram rem ria rim rue rum ae ai am em er ma me mi mu re um

aeimrz mazier maize mazer mirza zaire ziram amir emir mare maze mire rami raze ream rime aim air are arm ear era ire mae mar mir ram rem ria rim ae ai am em er ma me mi re

aeimss samites. *See* **aeimst aeisst eimsst aemsst**

aeimsstt misstate samites. *See* **aeimst aeisst aemsst aemstt**

aeimssv massive. *See* **aimss aimsv aemss**

aeimssw swamies. *See* **aimss aemss eimss**

aeimst samite emits items mates meats mites samen smite steam tames teams times aims east eats emit etas item mast mate mats meat mesa mise mist mite same seam seat semi seta site stem tame tams team teas ties time aet aim ate eat eta ita its mae mat met mis sat sea set sit tam tea tie ae ai am as at em is it ma me mi si ta ti

aeimsxx maxixes. *See* **aeimxx aemsx aimsx**

aeimsz maizes maize mazes smaze aims maze mesa mise same seam semi size aim mae mis sea ae ai am as em is ma me mi si

aeimxx maxixe exam maxi aim axe mae mix ae ai am ax em ex ma me mi xi

aeimz maize maze mae aim ae ai am em ma me mi

aeinn inane nine ane ani inn nae ae ai an en in na ne

aeinns nannies. *See* **aeinns**

aeinno eonian inane anion aeon anon neon nine none ane ani eon inn ion nae one ae ai an en in na ne no on

aeinnort anointer intoner ternion. *See* **aeinno aeinnr aeinnt aeinrt**

aeinnott intonate tontine. *See* **aeinno aeinnt aenntt aenott**

aeinnotv innovate. *See* **aeinno aeinnt aeintv aennov**

aeinnp pennia inane panne penna penni pinna nape neap nine nipa pain pane pean pine ane ani ape inn nae nap nip pan pea pen pie pin ae ai an en in na ne pa pe pi

aeinnpr pannier. *See* **aeinnr aeinnp aeinpr**

aeinnpt pinnate. *See* **aeinnp aeinnt**

aeinnr narine inane inner renin earn near nine rain rani rein air ane ani are ear era inn ire nae ran ria ae ai an en er in na ne re

aeinns insane sienna anise inane nines senna inns nine sain sane sine ane ani ens inn nae sea sen sin ae ai an as en in is na ne si

aeinnss siennas. *See* **aeinss aeinns aennss**

aeinnssv vainness siennas. *See* **aeinns aeinss aeinsv ainssv**

aeinnssz zaniness siennas. *See* **aeinns aeinss aeinsz aeissz**

aeinnt innate anent inane tenia tinea ante anti neat nine tine aet ane ani ant ate eat eta inn ita nae net nit tan tea ten tie tin ae ai an at en in it na ne ta ti

aeinoppt antipope appoint. *See* **aeiopt eioppt**

aeinoprt atropine operant painter pertain pointer protein repaint. *See* **aeinpr aeinrt aeiopt aeiprt**

aeinoqtu equation antique quinate. *See* **aeintu ainoqu ainqtu einqtu**

aeinorrt anterior retrain terrain trainer. *See* **aeinrt aenort aenrrt ainort**

aeinorrw ironware. *See* **aeirrw aenrrw anorrw einorr**

aeinors erasion. *See* **aeinrs ainors einors aenors**

aeinorss erasions arsines erasion reasons seniors. *See* **aeinrs aeinss aeirss aenors**

aeinorst notaries atoners erasion nastier orients rations retains retinas senator stainer stonier treason. *See* **aeinrs aeinrt aeirst aenors**

aeinorsv aversion erasion evasion ovaries ravines version. *See* **aeinrs aeinrv aeinsv aeirsv**

aeinortz notarize. *See* **aeinrt aeinrz aenort aenotz**

aeinossv evasions evasion. *See* **aeinss aeinsv aenoss ainssv**

aeinosv evasion. *See* **aeinsv aenos einos**

aeinotvx vexation. *See* **aeintv**

aeinoxz oxazine. *See* **aeinx aeinz**

aeinppp panpipe. *See* **aippp**

aeinppps panpipes nappies panpipe pinesap. *See* **einpps**

aeinppr nappier. *See* **aenppr einppr aeinpr**

aeinpprs snappier apprise nappers nappier nappies nippers parsnip pinesap rapines sappier snapper snipper. *See* **aeinpr aeinrs aeiprs aenppr**

aeinpps nappies pinesap. *See* **einpps aeins aenps**

aeinppst nappiest nappies panties pinesap sapient snippet. *See* **aenpst ainpst aippst einpps**

aeinpr rapine ripen earn nape neap near nipa pain pair pane pare pean pear peri pier pine pirn rain rani rape reap rein ripe air ane ani ape are ear era ire nae nap nip pan par pea pen per pie pin ran rap rep ria rip ae ai an en er in na ne pa pe pi re

aeinprrt terrapin painter partner pertain printer repaint reprint retrain terrain trainer. *See* **aeinpr aeinrt aeiprr aeiprt**

aeinprs rapines. *See* **aeinrs aeiprs aeinpr einprs ainprs**

aeinprst painters pantries pertains repaints arpents entraps nastier painter panties parents parties pastern pastier pertain piaster pirates rapines repaint retains retinas sapient spirant stainer traipse trepans. *See* **aeinpr aeinrs aeinrt aeiprs**

aeinprt painter pertain repaint. *See* **aenprt aeiprt aeinrt**

aeinpss pansies. *See* **aeinss aenpss einpss**

aeinpst panties sapient. *See* **einpst ainpst aenpst**

aeinpstt patients panties patents patient pattens patties sapient satinet. *See* **aenpst aenptt ainpst ainstt**

aeinpstu petunias aunties panties peanuts petunia punties sapient sinuate. *See* **aeintu aenpst aenptu aenstu**

aeinptt patient. *See* **aenptt**

aeinptty antitype patient tintype. *See* **aenptt ainpty eintty**

aeinptu petunia. *See* **aeintu aenptu**

aeinqrtu quainter antique quinate ruinate taurine urinate. *See* **aeinrt aeintu aenrtu aeqrtu**

aeinqstu antiques quinates antique asquint aunties inquest quinate quintes sinuate. *See* **aeintu aenqsu aenstu ainqtu**

aeinqttu equitant antique quinate quintet. *See* **aeintu aenttu ainqtu einqtu**

aeinqtu antique quinate. *See* **aeintu ainqtu einqtu**

aeinqtuz quantize antique quinate. *See* **aeintu ainqtu einqtu**

aeinrrst restrain retrains strainer trainers nastier retains retinas retrain stainer tarries tarsier terrain trainer. *See* **aeinrs aeinrt aeirrs aeirst**

aeinrrt retrain terrain trainer. *See* **aenrrt aeinrt**

aeinrs arisen arsine anise arise earns nares naris nears rains raise ranis reins resin rinse risen saner serai serin siren snare airs arse earn ears eras near rain rani rase rein reis rias rise sain sane sari sear sera sine sire air ane ani are ear ens era ire nae ran res ria sea sen sin sir ae ai an as en er in is na ne re si

aeinrss arsines. *See* **aeinss aeinrs aeirss einrss aenrss**

aeinrsst stainers arsines entasis inserts nastier retains retinas satires sinters stainer strains tansies. *See* **aeinrs aeinrt aeinss aeirss**

aeinrssw wariness arsines answers. *See* **aeinrs aeinss aeirss aenrsw**

aeinrst nastier retains retinas stainer. *See* **aeinrs aeinrt aeirst aenrst ainrst**

aeinrstt nitrates straiten artiste attires iterant nastier natters nattier nitrate ratites retains retinas satinet stainer striate tastier tertian transit. *See* **aeinrs aeinrt aeirst aeirtt**

aeinrstu ruinates taurines urinates aunties nastier natures nutrias retains retinas ruinate saunter sinuate stainer taurine triunes urinate. *See* **aeinrs aeinrt aeintu aeirst**

aeinrstw tinwares nastier retains retinas stainer tawnier tinware waiters wanters wariest winters. *See* **aeinrs aeinrt aeirst aeirtw**

aeinrsuz suzerain. *See* **aeinrs aeinrz aeinsz aersuz**

aeinrsv ravines. *See* **aeinrs aeinsv aenrsv aeinrv aeirsv**

aeinrt retain retina inert inter irate niter retia riant tenia tinea train trine ante anti earn near neat rain rani rant rate rein rent rite tare tear tern tier tine tire aet air ane ani ant are art ate ear eat era eta ire ita nae net nit ran rat ret ria tan tar tea ten tie tin ae ai an at en er in it na ne re ta ti

aeinrtt iterant nattier nitrate tertian. *See* **aeirtt aenrtt aeinrt einrtt**

aeinrtu ruinate taurine urinate. *See* **aeintu aenrtu ainrtu aeinrt einrtu**

aeinrtw tawnier tinware. *See* **aeinrt aeirtw aenrtw einrtw**

aeinrv ravine naive raven riven aver earn nave near nevi rain rani rave rein rive

vain vair vane vein vina vine air ane
ani are ave ear era ire nae ran rev ria
van via vie ae ai an en er in na ne re

aeinrz zanier azine zaire earn near rain
rani raze rein zein air ane ani are ear
era ire nae ran ria ae ai an en er in na
ne re

aeins anise sain sane sine ane ani ens nae
sea sen sin ae ai an as en in is na ne si

aeinss anises sanies anise sines sain sane
seas sine sins ane ani ass ens ess nae
sea sen sin sis ae ai an as en in is na ne
si

aeinsst entasis tansies. *See* **aeinss aensst
einsst ainsst aeisst**

aeinsstt nastiest satinets entasis satinet
tanists tansies. *See* **aeinss aeisst aensst
aesstt**

aeinsstu sinuates aunties entasis issuant
sinuate sustain tansies unseats. *See*
aeinss aeintu aeisst aensst

aeinssvw waviness. *See* **aeinss aeinsv
aeisvw ainssv**

aeinsswx waxiness. *See* **aeinss aeinsx
ainssw einssw**

aeinstt satinet. *See* **einstt ainstt**

aeinsttt nattiest satinet. *See* **aesttt ainstt
einstt**

aeinsttw tawniest satinet. *See* **ainstt
ainstw einstt einstw**

aeinstu aunties sinuate. *See* **aeintu einstu
aenstu**

aeinstv natives. *See* **einstv aeintv aeinsv**

aeinstz zaniest. *See* **aeinsz**

aeinsv navies anise avens naive naves
savin vanes veins vinas vines aves nave
nevi sain sane save sine vain vane vans
vase vein vies vina vine visa vise ane
ani ave ens nae sea sen sin van via vie
ae ai an as en in is na ne si

aeinsvv navvies. *See* **aeinsv**

aeinswy anywise. *See* **einswy aeins ainsy**

aeinsx xenias anise nixes xenia axes axis
nixe sain sane sine ane ani axe ens nae
nix sax sea sen sex sin six ae ai an as ax
en ex in is na ne si xi

aeinsz azines zanies anise azine sain sane
sine size zein ane ani ens nae sea sen
sin ae ai an as en in is na ne si

aeint tenia tinea ante anti neat tine aet
ane ani ant ate eat eta ita nae net nit
tan tea ten tie tin ae ai an at en in it na
ne ta ti

aeintu auntie tenia tinea unite untie ante
anti aunt etui neat tine tuna tune unit
aet ane ani ant ate eat eta ita nae net
nit nut tan tau tea ten tie tin tui tun ae
ai an at en in it na ne nu ta ti ut

aeintv native naive tenia tinea ante anti
nave neat nevi tine vain vane vein vent

vina vine aet ane ani ant ate ave eat eta
ita nae net nit tan tav tea ten tie tin van
vat vet via vie ae ai an at en in it na ne
ta ti

aeintvy naivety. *See* **aeintv aintvy**

aeintxy anxiety. *See* **aeint aeinx aenty**

aeinv naive nave nevi vain vane vein vina
vine ane ani ave nae van via vie ae ai an
en in na ne

aeinx xenia nixe ane ani axe nae nix ae ai
an ax en ex in na ne xi

aeinz azine zein ane ani nae ae ai an en in
na ne

aeioppst apposite opiates potpies. *See*
aeiopt aeopps aiopst aippst

aeioprrt priorate airport praetor prorate.
See **aeiopt aeiprr aeiprt aoprrt**

aeioprs soapier. *See* **aeiprs aeoprs**

aeioprvz vaporize. *See* **aeopr aeprv eiprz**

aeiopsst soapiest opiates pasties patsies.
See **aeiopt aeisst aepsst aiopst**

aeiopst opiates. *See* **aeiopt aiopst**

aeiopt opiate patio atop iota pate peat
pita poet tape tope aet ape apt ate eat
eta ita oat ope pat pea pet pie pit poi
pot tap tea tie tip toe top ae ai at it pa
pe pi ta ti to

aeiopttv optative. *See* **aeiopt aeittv aeoptt
eioptt**

aeioqssu sequoias sequoia. *See* **eissu
aeoss aioss**

aeioqsu sequoia. *See* **aiqsu**

aeiorrss rosaries sierras orrises. *See*
aeirrs aeirss eiorrs

aeiorrst rotaries rioters roaster tarries
tarsier. *See* **aeirrs aeirst aeorst aiorst**

aeiorrsv savorier arrives ovaries savorer.
See **aeirrs aeirrv aeirsv aiorsv**

aeiorstv votaries ovaries travois. *See*
aeirst aeirsv aeorst aerstv

aeiorsv ovaries. *See* **aiorsv aeirsv eiorsv**

aeiorttv rotative. *See* **aeirtt aeittv aeortt
eirttv**

aeiostzz azotizes azotize. *See* **aeostz**

aeiotzz azotize. *See* **aeotz**

aeipprs apprise sappier. *See* **aeiprs aepprs eipprs**

aeipprss apprises apprise aspires paresis
praises sappier sippers. *See* **aeiprs
aeirss aepprs aeprss**

aeippsst sappiest papists pasties patsies
sippets. *See* **aeisst aepsst aippst eippst**

aeipqrtu pratique parquet. *See* **aeiprt
aeqrtu eipqtu**

aeiprr rapier repair prier pair pare parr
pear peri pier rape rare reap rear ripe
air ape are ear era err ire par pea per
pie rap rep ria rip ae ai er pa pe pi re

aeiprrs parries praiser rapiers repairs.
See **aeiprs eiprrs aeiprr aeprrs aeirrs**

aeiprrss aspirers praisers aspires paresis
parries praiser praises rapiers raspers
repairs sierras sparers sparser. *See*
aeiprr aeiprs aeirrs aeirss

aeiprs aspire paries praise arise pairs
pares parse pears piers pries raise
rapes reaps sepia serai spare spear
spire airs apes apse arse ears eras pair
pare pars pear peas peri pier pies rape
raps rase rasp reap reis reps rias ripe
rips rise sari sear sera sire spar air ape
are asp ear era ire par pas pea per pie
rap rep res ria rip sap sea sip sir spa ae
ai as er is pa pe pi re si

aeiprss aspires paresis praises. *See* **aeirss
aeiprs aeprss eiprss**

aeiprsst pastries piasters raspiest
traipses aspires paresis parties pasters
pastier pasties patsies persist piaster
pirates praises priests rapists repasts
satires sparest sprites stripes traipse.
See **aeiprs aeiprt aeirss aeirst**

aeiprssu upraises aspires paresis praises
pussier sauries suspire upraise uprises.
See **aeiprs aeirss aeprss aeprsu**

aeiprssv parvises aspires paresis passive
pavises praises. *See* **aeiprs aeirss aeirsv
aeprss**

aeiprssx praxises aspires paresis praises.
See **aeiprs aeirss aeprss aiprsx**

aeiprst parties pastier piaster pirates
traipse. *See* **aeiprs aeiprt aeirst aeprst
aiprst**

aeiprstv privates parties pastier piaster
pirates private privets traipse. *See*
aeiprs aeiprt aeirst aeirsv

aeiprstw wiretaps parties pastier piaster
pirates traipse waiters wariest waspier
wiretap. *See* **aeiprs aeiprt aeirst aeirtw**

aeiprsty asperity parties pastier piaster
pirates pyrites traipse. *See* **aeiprs aeiprt
aeirst aeprst**

aeiprsu upraise. *See* **aeiprs aeprsu eiprsu**

aeiprsvy vespiary. *See* **aeiprs aeirsv
aeprsv aeprsy**

aeiprsw waspier. *See* **aeiprs aiprsw eiprsw**

aeiprt pirate irate pater peart prate retia
taper tapir tripe pair pare part pate
pear peat peri pert pier pita rape rapt
rate reap ripe rite tape tare tarp tear
tier tire trap trip aet air ape apt are art
ate ear eat era eta ire ita par pat pea per
pet pie pit rap rat rep ret ria rip tap tar
tea tie tip ae ai at er it pa pe pi re ta ti

aeiprtt partite. *See* **aeirtt aeprtt aeiprt**

aeiprtv private. *See* **aeiprt eiprtv**

aeiprtw wiretap. *See* **aeiprt aeirtw**

aeiprxy pyrexia. *See* **eiprxy aepry**

aeips sepia apes apse peas pies ape asp pas pea pie sap sea sip spa ae ai as is pa pe pi si

aeipsss asepsis. *See* **aepsss eipsss**

aeipsst pasties patsies. *See* **aepsst aeisst eipsst**

aeipsstt pastiest pasties patsies patties. *See* **aeisst aepsst aesstt eipsst**

aeipssw waspiest pasties patsies. *See* **aeisst aepsst aesstw aisstw**

aeipssv passive pavises. *See* **aepss aipss aepsv**

aeipstt patties. *See* **aepst eiptt aipst**

aeipttuv putative. *See* **aeittv**

aeiqrrru quarrier. *See* **aerrr eiqru**

aeiqrrsu quarries squarer. *See* **eiqrsu aeirrs aeqrsu .errsu**

aeirrrt tarrier. *See* **aeirt aerrr**

aeirrs sierra arise arris raise rears riser serai airs arse ears eras errs rare rase rear reis rias rise sari sear sera sire air are ear era err ire res ria sea sir ae ai as er is re si

aeirrss sierras. *See* **aeirss eirrss aeirrs**

aeirrst tarries tarsier. *See* **aerrst aeirst**

aeirrsv arrives. *See* **aeirrv aerrsv eirrsv aeirrs aeirsv**

aeirrtt rattier. *See* **aeirtt aerrtt eirrtt**

aeirrtty tertiary rattier. *See* **aeirtt aerrtt aerrty aertty**

aeirrtw wartier. *See* **aeirtw aeirrw eirrtw**

aeirrv arrive river aver rare rave rear rive vair air are ave ear era err ire rev ria via vie ae ai er re

aeirrw warier rawer wrier rare rear ware wear weir wire air are awe ear era err ire raw ria war ae ai aw er re we

aeirs arise raise serai airs arse ears eras rase reis rias rise sari sear sera sire air are ear era ire res ria sea sir ae ai as er is re si

aeirsss sassier. *See* **aeirss**

aeirsst satires. *See* **aeirss aersst eirsst aeirst aeisst**

aeirsstt artistes striates artiste artists attires ratites satires sitters straits striate tasters tastier tsarist. *See* **aeirss aeirst aeirtt aeisst**

aeirsstw waitress satires waiters wariest wasters. *See* **aeirss aeirst aeirtw aeisst**

aeirssu sauries. *See* **aeirss aerssu eirssu**

aeirst satire striae arise aster astir irate raise rates retia rites serai sitar stair stare stria tares tarsi tears tiers tires tries airs arse arts ears east eats eras

erst etas rase rate rats reis rest rets rias rise rite sari sear seat sera seta sire site star stir tare tars tear teas tier ties tire tsar aet air are art ate ear eat era ire ita its rat res ret ria sat sea set sir sit tar tea tie ae ai as at er is it re si ta ti

aeirstt artiste attires ratites striate tastier. *See* **airstt aeirtt eirstt aerstt**

aeirsttt rattiest titrates artiste attires ratites stretti striate tastier tatters titrate titters tritest. *See* **aeirst aeirtt aerstt airstt**

aeirsttw wartiest artiste attires ratites striate swatter tastier twister waiters wariest. *See* **aeirst aeirtt aeirtw aerstt**

aeirstuz azurites azurite. *See* **aeirst aerstz aersuz**

aeirstvy vestiary variety varsity. *See* **aeirst aeirsv aerstv aersty**

aeirstw waiters wariest. *See* **aerstw aeirst aeirtw eirstw**

aeirsv varies arise avers raise raves saver serai vairs airs arse aver aves ears eras rase rave reis revs rias rise rive sari save sear sera sire vair vase vies visa vise air are ave ear era ire res rev ria sea sir via vie ae ai as er is re si

aeirsvw waivers. *See* **aeirsv aeirvw aeisvw aersvw**

aeirt irate retia rate rite tare tear tier tire aet air are art ate ear eat era eta ire ita rat ret ria tar tea tie ae ai at er it re ta ti

aeirtt attire ratite irate retia tater tetra titter titre trait treat trite rate rite tare tart tear teat tier tire tret aet air are art ate ear eat era eta ire ita rat ret ria tar tat tea tie tit ae ai at er it re ta ti

aeirttt titrate. *See* **aeirtt aerttt eirttt**

aeirtttw atwitter titrate twitter. *See* **aeirtt aeirtw**

aeirtuz azurite. *See* **aeruz aeirt eirtu**

aeirtvy variety. *See* **eirtvy aertv aeirt**

aeirtw waiter irate retia water write rate rite tare tear tier tire wait ware wart wear weir wire wite writ aet air are art ate awe ear eat era eta ire ita rat raw ret ria tar tea tie war wet wit ae ai at aw er it re ta ti we

aeirvw waiver wavier waive waver aver rave rive vair view ware wave wear weir wire wive air are ave awe ear era ire raw rev ria via vie war ae ai aw er re we

aeirwx waxier waxer ware wear weir wire air are awe axe ear era ire raw rex ria war wax ae ai aw ax er ex re we xi

aeirz zaire raze air are ear era ire ria ae ai er re

aeissst sassiest siestas assists. *See* **aeisst aessss**

aeissst siestas. *See* **aessst aissst aeisst**

aeisssty essayist siestas. *See* **aeisst aessst aesssy aessty**

aeisssz assizes. *See* **aeissz aesss**

aeisst siesta asset sates seats sites tasse east eats etas seas seat seta sets site sits tass teas ties aet ass ate eat ess eta ita its sat sea set sis sit tea tie ae ai as at is it si ta ti

aeissttt tastiest attests. *See* **aeisst aesstt**

aeissttu situates situate statues. *See* **aeisst aesstt aesttu eisstu**

aeissuv suasive. *See* **eissu aessv aesuv**

aeissux auxesis. *See* **eissu aessx eissx**

aeissz assize sizes seas size ass ess sea sis ae ai as is si

aeisttu situate. *See* **aesttu**

aeistty satiety. *See* **aestt astty estty**

aeistvw waviest. *See* **aeisvw aestv aestw**

aeistwx waxiest. *See* **eistx aestx aistx**

aeisvw waives views waive waves wives aves awes save vase vies view visa vise wave wise wive ave awe saw sea sew via vie was wis ae ai as aw is si we

aeittv vittae vitta teat aet ate ave eat eta ita tat tav tea tie tit vat vet via vie ae ai at it ta ti

aeivw waive view wave wive ave awe via vie ae ai aw we

aejjlnu jejunal. *See* **aejjnu aelnu**

aejjnu jejuna jean ane nae ae an en na ne nu

aejk jake ae ka

aejks jakes jake sake ask kas sea ae as ka

aejlosu jealous. *See* **ejlosu aelos**

aejlosuy jealousy jealous. *See* **ejlosu**

aejmnzz jazzmen. *No 6s or 5s*

aejmrst ramjets. *See* **aejmst aemrst aejmrt**

aejmrt ramjet tamer mare mart mate meat rate ream tame tare team tear term tram aet are arm art ate ear eat era eta jam jar jet mae mar mat met raj ram rat rem ret tam tar tea ae am at em er ma me re ta

aejmst jetsam mates meats satem steam tames teams east eats etas jams jest jets mast mate mats meat mesa same seam seat seta stem tame tams team teas aet ate eat eta jam jet mae mat met sat sea set tam tea ae am as at em ma me ta

aejmsty majesty. *See* **aejmst aemsty**

aejn jean ane nae ae an en na ne

aejns jeans jean sane ane ens nae sea sen ae an as en na ne

aejnst sejant antes jeans nates ante ants east eats etas jean jest jets neat nest nets sane seat sent seta tans teas tens aet ane ant ate eat ens eta jet nae net sat sea sen set tan tea ten ae an as at en na ne ta

aejp   jape ape pea ae pa pe

aejpr   japer jape pare pear rape reap ape are ear era jar par pea per raj rap rep ae er pa pe re

aejprs   jasper japer japes pares parse pears rapes reaps spare spear apes apse arse ears eras jape jars pare pars pear peas rape raps rase rasp reap reps sear sera spar ape are asp ear era jar par pas pea per raj rap rep res sap sea spa ae as er pa pe re

aejprss   jaspers. *See* **aejprs aeprss**

aejps   japes apes apse jape peas ape asp pas pea sap sea spa ae as pa pe

aekkmnoo   kakemono. *See* **aekno**

aekknr   kraken earn kern knar nark near rake rank ane are ark ear era ken nae ran ae an en er ka na ne re

aekknrs   krakens. *See* **aekknr aenrs aekrs**

aekl   kale lake leak ale elk kal lea lek ae el ka la

aeklmruw   lukewarm. *See* **aeklrw aelmru**

aeklmruy   yarmulke. *See* **aelmru**

aekln   ankle kale lake lane lank leak lean ale ane elk kal ken lea lek nae ae an el en ka la na ne

aeklnnss   lankness. *See* **aeklns aeklss aennss**

aeklnr   rankle ankle laker learn renal earl earn kale kern knar lake lane lank lark leak lean nark near rake rale rank real ale ane are ark ear elk era kal ken lar lea lek nae ran ae an el en er ka la na ne re

aeklnrs   rankles. *See* **aeklns aeklrs aelnrs aeklnr**

aeklnrsv   klaverns klavern lekvars rankles. *See* **aeklnr aeklns aeklrs aeklrv**

aeklnrv   klavern. *See* **aeklrv aeklnr aelnrv**

aeklns   ankles ankle lakes lanes leaks leans skean slake snake sneak ales elks kale kens lake lane lank leak lean leas leks lens sake sale sane sank seal ale ane ask elk els ens kal kas ken lea lek nae sal sea sen ae an as el en ka la na ne

aeklnst   anklets. *See* **aeklns aeklnt aeklst**

aeklnsy   alkynes. *See* **aeklns aelnsy aeknsy**

aeklnt   anklet ankle knelt latke leant taken ante kale lake lane lank late leak lean lent neat tael take tale talk tank teak teal aet ale alt ane ant ate eat elk eta kal kat ken lea lek let nae net tan tea ten ae an at el en ka la na ne ta

aeklorvw   walkover. *See* **aeklrv aeklrw**

aeklprrs   sparkler parkers parrels sparker sparkle. *See* **aeklrr aeklrs aekprr aelprr**

aeklprs   sparkle. *See* **aeklrs aelprs**

aeklprss   sparkles sparkle. *See* **aeklrs aeklss aekpss aekrss**

aeklr   laker earl kale lake lark leak rake rale real ale are ark ear elk era kal lar lea lek ae el er ka la re

aeklrr   larker laker earl kale lake lark leak rake rale rare real rear ale are ark ear elk era err kal lar lea lek ae el er ka la re

aeklrs   lakers earls eskar laker lakes lares larks laser leaks rakes rales saker slake ales arks arse earl ears elks eras kale lake lark leak leas leks rake rale rase real sake sale sark seal sear sera ale are ark ask ear elk els era kal kas lar lea lek res sal sea ae as el er ka la re

aeklrst   talkers. *See* **aelrst aeklrs aeklst aekrst aeklrt**

aeklrsv   lekvars. *See* **aeklrs aelrsv aeklrv**

aeklrsw   walkers. *See* **aeklrs aeklrw aekrsw**

aeklrt   talker alert alter laker later latke taker taler earl kale kart lake lark late leak rake rale rate real tael take tale talk tare teak teal tear trek aet ale alt are ark art ate ear eat elk era eta kal kat lar lea lek let rat ret tar tea ae at el er ka la re ta

aeklrv   lekvar laker laver ravel velar aver earl kale lake lark lave leak leva rake rale rave real vale veal ale are ark ave ear elk era kal lar lea lek lev rev ae el er ka la re

aeklrw   walker laker wreak earl kale lake lark leak rake rale real wake wale walk ware weak weal wear weka ale are ark awe awl ear elk era kal lar law lea lek raw war ae aw el er ka la re we

aekls   lakes leaks slake ales elks kale lake leak leas leks sake sale seal ale ask elk els kal kas lea lek sal sea ae as el ka la

aeklss   slakes lakes leaks sakes sales seals slake ales asks elks kale lake lass leak leas leks less sake sals seal seas ale ask ass elk els ess kal kas lea lek sal sea ae as el ka la

aeklst   latkes lakes latke leaks least skate slake slate stake stale stalk steak steal taels takes tales talks teaks ales alts east eats elks etas kale lake last late leak leas leks lest lets sake sale salt seal seat seta skat slat tael take tale talk task teak teal teas aet ale alt ask ate eat elk els eta kal kas kat lea lek let sal sat sea set tea tsk ae as at el ka la ta

aeklstu   auklets. *See* **aekltu aeklst aelstu**

aeklt   latke kale lake late leak tael take tale talk teak teal aet ale alt ate eat elk eta kal kat lea lek let tea ae at el ka la ta

aekltu   auklet latke kale lake late leak lute tael take tale talk teak teal tule aet

ale alt ate auk eat elk eta kal kat lea lek let leu tau tea ae at el ka la ta ut

aeklwy   weakly leaky kale lake laky leak wake wale walk weak weal weka yawl ale awe awl aye elk kal key law lay lea lek lye way wye yak yaw yea yew ae aw ay el ka la we ye

aekly   leaky kale lake laky leak ale aye elk kal key lay lea lek lye yak yea ae ay el ka la ye

aekm   kame make mae ae am em ka ma me

aekmmnrs   marksmen. *See* **aekmrs aemmnr**

aekmortw   teamwork. *See* **aekmrt**

aekmr   maker kame make mare mark rake ream are ark arm ear era mae mar ram rem ae am em er ka ma me re

aekmrr   marker remark maker rearm kame make mare mark rake rare ream rear are ark arm ear era err mae mar ram rem ae am em er ka ma me re

aekmrrs   markers remarks. *See* **aekmrs aekmrr aemrrs**

aekmrs   makers maskers masker eskar kames maker makes mares marks maser merks rakes reams saker smear arks arms arse ears eras kame make mare mark mask mesa rake rams rase ream sake same sark seam sear sera are ark arm ask ear era kas mae mar ram rem res sea ae am as em er ka ma me re

aekmrss   maskers. *See* **aekrss aekmrs aemrss**

aekmrst   markets. *See* **aekmrs aekmrt aemrst**

aekmrt   market maker taker tamer kame kart make mare mark mart mate meat rake rate ream take tame tare teak team tear term tram trek aet are ark arm art ate ear eat era eta kat mae mar mat met ram rat rem ret tam tar tea ae am at em er ka ma me re ta

aekms   kames makes kame make mask mesa sake same seam ask kas mae sea ae am as em ka ma me

aeknnrss   rankness. *See* **aeknss aekrss aennss aenrss**

aekno   oaken aeon kaon keno koan ane eon ken koa nae oak oke one ae an en ka na ne no on

aeknprs   spanker. *See* **aknprs aenps aenrs**

aeknprss   spankers spanker. *See* **aeknss aekpss aekrss aenpss**

aeknrr   ranker reran earn kern knar nark near rake rank rare rear ane are ark ear era err ken nae ran ae an en er ka na ne re

aeknrrs   rankers. *See* **aeknrr aenrs aekrs**

aeknrst rankest tankers. *See* **aenrst aekrst aeknrt**

aeknrt tanker taken taker ante earn kart kern knar nark near neat rake rank rant rate rent take tank tare teak tear tern trek aet ane ant are ark art ate ear eat era eta kat ken nae net ran rat ret tan tar tea ten ae an at en er ka na ne re ta

aeknrvy knavery. *See* **aeknv enrvy aenrv**

aekns skean snake sneak kens sake sane sank ane ask ens kas ken nae sea sen ae an as en ka na ne

aeknss skeans snakes sneaks sakes skean snake sneak asks kens sake sane sank seas ane ask ass ens ess kas ken nae sea sen ae an as en ka na ne

aeknsv knaves avens knave naves skean snake sneak vanes aves kens kvas nave sake sane sank save vane vans vase ane ask ave ens kas ken nae sea sen van ae an as en ka na ne

aeknsw wakens askew skean snake sneak swank waken wakes wanes weans wekas anew awes awns kens knew news sake sane sank sawn sewn skew swan wake wane weak wean weka wens ane ask awe awn ens kas ken nae new saw sea sen sew wan was wen ae an as aw en ka na ne we

aeknsy sneaky skean snake snaky sneak yanks yeans ayes easy eyas kens keys sake sane sank yaks yank yean yeas yens ane any ask aye ens kas ken key nae nay say sea sen sky yak yea yen yes ae an as ay en ka na ne ye

aeknt taken ante neat take tank teak aet ane ant ate eat eta kat ken nae net tan tea ten ae an at en ka na ne ta

aeknv knave nave vane ane ave ken nae van ae an en ka na ne

aeknw waken anew knew wake wane weak wean weka ane awe awn ken nae new wan wen ae an aw en ka na ne we

aekors arkose soaker arose eskar okras rakes saker aero arks arse ears eras koas oaks oars okes okra ores rake rase roes rose sake sark sear sera soak soar soke sora sore are ark ask ear era kas koa kor kos oak oar oke ore res roe sea ae as er ka or os re so

aekorss soakers. *See* **aekors aekrss akorss**

aekorsss karosses soakers. *See* **aekors aekrss akorss**

aekosttu outtakes stakeout takeouts out-take takeout. *See* **aesttu eosttu**

aekottu outtake takeout

aekow awoke wake weak weka woke awe koa oak oke owe woe wok ae aw ka ow we

aekp peak ape pea ae ka pa pe

aekprr parker pare park parr peak pear perk rake rape rare reap rear ape are ark ear era err par pea per rap rep ae er ka pa pe re

aekprrs parkers sparker. *See* **aekprr aeprrs**

aekprrss sparkers parkers raspers spar-ers sparker sparser. *See* **aekprr aekpss aekrss aeprrs**

aekps peaks spake speak apes apse peak peas sake skep ape ask asp kas pas pea sap sea spa ae as ka pa pe

aekpss speaks apses peaks sakes spake speak apes apse asks asps pass peak peas sake saps seas skep spas ape ask asp ass ess kas pas pea sap sea spa ae as ka pa pe

aekpsssy passkeys passkey. *See* **aekpss aepsss aesssy**

aekpssy passkey. *See* **aekpss aessy ekpsy**

aekqssu squeaks. *See* **aekqsu aekssu**

aekqsu quakes squeak quake ukase sake auks ask auk kas qua sea sue use ae as ka us

aekqsuy squeaky. *See* **aekqsu aeqsuy**

aekqu quake auk qua ae ka

aekr rake are ark ear era ae er ka re

aekrrst kraters. *See* **aerrst aekrrt**

aekrrt krater taker kart rake rare rate rear take tare teak tear trek aet are ark art ate ear eat era err eta kat rat ret tar tea ae at er ka re ta

aekrs eskar rakes saker arks arse ears eras rake rase sake sark sear sera are ark ask ear era kas res sea ae as er ka re

aekrss askers eskars arses eskar rakes rases saker sakes sarks sears arks arse asks ears eras rake rase sake sark sear seas sera are ark ask ass ear era ess kas res sea ae as er ka re

aekrsst skaters strakes streaks. *See* **aekrss aersst akrsst aeksst aekrst**

aekrst skater strake streak takers aster eskar karst karts rakes rates saker skate stake stare stark steak taker takes tares teaks tears treks arks arse arts ears east eats eras erst etas kart rake rase rate rats rest rets sake sark sear seat sera seta skat star take tare tars task teak tear teas trek tsar aet are ark art ask ate ear eat era eta kas kat rat res ret sat sea set tar tea tsk ae as at er ka re ta

aekrsty streaky. *See* **aersty aekrst**

aekrsw wreaks askew eskar rakes saker swear wakes wares wears wekas wreak

arks arse awes ears eras rake rase sake sark sear sera skew wake ware wars weak wear weka are ark ask awe ear era kas raw res saw sea sew war was ae as aw er ka re we

aekrt taker kart rake rate take tare teak tear trek aet are ark art ate ear eat era eta kat rat ret tar tea ae at er ka re ta

aekrw wreak rake wake ware weak wear weka are ark awe ear era raw war ae aw er ka re we

aeks sake ask kas sea ae as ka

aekss sakes asks sake seas ask ass ess kas sea ae as ka

aeksssv kvasses. *See* **aesss akssv aekss**

aeksst skates stakes steaks asset sakes sates seats skate skats stake steak takes tasks tasse teaks asks east eats etas sake seas seat seta sets skat take task tass teak teas aet ask ass ate eat ess eta kas kat sat sea set tea tsk ae as at ka ta

aekssu ukases sakes ukase asks auks sake seas sues uses ask ass auk ess kas sea sue use ae as ka us

aekst skate stake steak takes teaks east eats etas sake seat seta skat take task teak teas aet ask ate eat eta kas kat sat sea set tea tsk ae as at ka ta

aekstw tweaks askew skate stake steak sweat takes teaks tweak wakes waste wekas awes east eats etas sake seat seta skat skew stew swat take task teak teas wake wast weak weka west wets aet ask ate awe eat eta kas kat sat saw sea set sew tea tsk was wet ae as at aw ka ta we

aeksu ukase sake auks ask auk kas sea sue use ae as ka us

aeksw askew wakes wekas awes sake skew wake weak weka ask awe kas saw sea sew was ae as aw ka we

aekswyy keyways. *See* **aekwyy akswyy**

aekt take teak aet ate eat eta kat tea ae at ka ta

aektw tweak take teak wake weak weka aet ate awe eat eta kat tea wet ae at aw ka ta we

aekw wake weak weka awe ae aw ka we

aekwyy keyway wake weak weka awe aye key way wye yak yaw yay yea yew ae aw ay ka we ye

ael ale lea ae el la

aell leal ale all ell lea ae el la

aellly leally alley ally leal yell ale all aye ell lay lea lye yea ae ay el la ye

aellmnty mentally. *See* **aellmt aellmy aellty aelmnt**

aellmrs smaller. *See* **aelmrs allms ellms**

aellmsst smallest mallets sallets samlets. *See* **aellmt aellst aelmst aelsst**

aellmst mallets. *See* **aelmst aellmt aellst**

aellmsu malleus. *See* **almsu aemsu aelms**

aellmswx maxwells maxwell. *See* **aelsx aemsx aelms**

aellmt mallet metal lame late leal male mall malt mate meal meat mell melt tael tale tall tame teal team tell aet ale all alt ate eat ell elm eta lam lea let mae mat mel met tam tea ae am at el em la ma me ta

aellmwx maxwell. *No 6s or 5s*

aellmy lamely alley mealy ally amyl lame leal male mall meal mell yell ylem ale all aye ell elm lam lay lea lye mae may mel yam yea ae am ay el em la ma me my ye

aellnosv novellas novella. *See* **aelnos aelnsv aelosv allnos**

aellnov novella. *See* **aelno allno aelnv**

aellnpru prunella pleural. *See* **aellru aelnpr aelnru aelpru**

aellnsst tallness sallets. *See* **aellst aelsst aensst alnsst**

aellntty latently. *See* **aellty aelntt aeltty aelnty**

aellnvy venally. *See* **aellvy aelnv**

aellorsv overalls overall. *See* **aelosv aelrsv alorsv elorsv**

aellorv overall. *See* **aelrv elorv alorv**

aellosuv alveolus. *See* **aelosv aelsuv elosuv**

aellp lapel leal leap pale pall peal plea ale all alp ape ell lap lea pal pea ae el la pa pe

aellpru pleural. *See* **aellru aelpru allpru**

aellps lapels lapel lapse leaps pales palls peals pleas salep sepal spall spell ales alps apes apse ells laps leal leap leas pale pall pals peal peas plea sale seal sell slap ale all alp ape asp ell els lap lea pal pas pea sal sap sea spa ae as el la pa pe

aellpst pallets. *See* **aellps aelpst aellpt aellst**

aellpt pallet lapel petal plate pleat late leal leap lept pale pall pate peal peat pelt plat plea tael tale tall tape teal tell aet ale all alp alt ape apt ate eat ell eta lap lea let pal pat pea pet tap tea ae at el la pa pe ta

aellpy palely alley lapel pally ally leal leap pale pall paly peal play plea yell yelp ale all alp ape aye ell lap lay lea lye pal pay pea ply pya yap yea yep ae ay el la pa pe ye

aellquy equally. *See* **aelly aelqu ellqu**

aellrst stellar. *See* **aelrst aellrt**

aellrsu allures laurels. *See* **aellru aelrsu**

aellrt taller alert alter later taler earl late leal rale rate real tael tale tall tare teal tear tell aet ale all alt are art ate ear eat

ell era eta lar lea let rat ret tar tea ae at el er la re ta

aellrty alertly. *See* **aellty aelrty aellry aellrt**

aellru allure laurel earl leal lure rale real rule urea ale all are ear ell era lar lea leu rue ae el er la re

aellry really alley early layer rally relay aery ally aryl earl leal lyre rale real rely yare year yell ale all are aye ear ell era lar lay lea lye ray rye yar yea ae ay el er la re ye

aellssst saltless sallets tassels. *See* **aellst aelsss aelsst**

aellsst sallets. *See* **aellst aelsst allsst**

aellssw lawless. *See* **aelssw ellssw**

aellst sallet least slate stale stall steal taels tales tells ales alts east eats ells etas last late leal leas lest lets sale salt seal seat sell seta slat tael tale tall teal teas tell aet ale all alt ate eat ell els eta lea let sal sat sea set tea ae as at el la ta

aellstt tallest. *See* **aellst aelstt**

aellstuu ululates ululate. *See* **aellst aelstu ellstu**

aellstw wallets. *See* **aellst aelltw**

aellsuxy sexually. *See* **aellsy aelsux**

aellsvy valleys. *See* **aellsy aelsvy aellvy**

aellsy alleys alley sally yells ales ally ayes easy ells eyas lays leal leas lyes lyse sale seal sell slay yeas yell ale all aye ell els lay lea lye sal say sea sly yea yes ae as ay el la ye

aelltuu ululate. *See* **elltu**

aelltw wallet late leal tael tale tall teal tell wale wall weal well welt aet ale all alt ate awe awl eat ell eta law lea let tea wet ae at aw el la ta we

aellty lately alley tally telly ally late leal tael tale tall teal tell yell aet ale all alt ate aye eat ell eta lay lea let lye tea yea yet ae at ay el la ta ye

aellvy valley alley leavy ally lave leal leva levy vale veal yell ale all ave aye ell lay lea lev lye yea ae ay el la ye

aelly alley ally leal yell ale all aye ell lay lea lye yea ae ay el la ye

aelm lame male meal ale elm lam lea mae mel ae am el em la ma me

aelmm lemma lame male malm meal ale elm lam lea mae mel mem ae am el em la ma me

aelmmorw mealworm. *See* **aelmor**

aelmmosy myelomas amylose malmsey myeloma. *See* **aelmms aelmos aelmsy aemmsy**

aelmmoy myeloma. *See* **aelmo aelmm almoy**

aelmmrst trammels armlets stammer trammel. *See* **aelmms aelmrs aelmrt**

aelmmrt trammel. *See* **aelmrt**

aelmms lemmas lames lemma males malms meals ales alms elms lame lams leas male malm meal mels mems mesa sale same seal seam slam ale elm els lam lea mae mel mem sal sea ae am as el em la ma me

aelmmssy malmseys malmsey. *See* **aelmms aelmsy aemmsy**

aelmmsy malmsey. *See* **aelmms aemmsy aelmsy**

aelmn leman amen lame lane lean male mane meal mean name ale ane elm lam lea mae man mel men nae ae am an el em en la ma me na ne

aelmnnry mannerly. *See* **aelmny aelnnr aelnry aemnnr**

aelmnops neoplasm. *See* **aelmns aelmos aelmps aelnos**

aelmnosu melanous. *See* **aelmns aelmos aelnos almnos**

aelmnot telamon. *See* **aelmnt elmnot**

aelmnowy laywomen womanly. *See* **aelmnw aelmny aemnoy elmnoy**

aelmnrsu numerals manures maulers numeral surname. *See* **aelmns aelmrs aelmru aelnrs**

aelmnru numeral. *See* **aemnru aelmru aelnru**

aelmns lemans mensal lames lanes leans leman males manes manse meals means names ales alms amen elms lame lams lane lean leas lens male mane meal mean mels mesa name sale same sane seal seam slam ale ane elm els ens lam lea mae man mel men nae sal sea sen ae am an as el em en la ma me na ne

aelmnss manless. *See* **aelmns aemnss**

aelmnst laments mantels mantles. *See* **aelmnt aelmst aelmns aemnst**

aelmnt lament mantel mantle mental leant leman meant metal amen ante lame lane late lean lent male malt mane mate meal mean meat melt name neat tael tale tame teal team aet ale alt ane ant ate eat elm eta lam lea let mae man mat mel men met nae net tam tan tea ten ae am an at el em en la ma me na ne ta

aelmnw lawmen leman amen anew lame lane lawn lean male mane meal mean mewl name wale wane weal wean ale ane awe awl awn elm lam law lea mae man maw mel men mew nae new wan wen ae am an aw el em en la ma me na ne we

aelmny laymen meanly namely leman manly mealy meany yamen amen amyl lame lane lean male mane many meal mean myna name yean ylem ale ane any aye elm lam lay lea lye mae man may mel men nae nay yam yea yen ae am an ay el em en la ma me my na ne ye

aelmo amole aloe lame loam male meal mola mole ale elm lam lea mae mel moa ae am el em la lo ma me mo om

aelmoprr premolar. *See* **aelmor aelmpr aelopr aelprr**

aelmoprt temporal marplot prolate trample. *See* **aelmor aelmpr aelmrt aelopr**

aelmopsy maypoles amylose employs maypole. *See* **aelmos aelmps aelmsy aelops**

aelmopy maypole. *See* **elmopy aelmo aelmp**

aelmor morale amole lamer molar morae moral morel realm aero aloe earl lame loam lore male mare marl meal merl mola mole mora more omer oral orle rale real ream roam role ale are arm ear elm era lam lar lea mae mar mel moa mor oar ore ram rem roe ae am el em er la lo ma me mo om or re

aelmors morales. *See* **aelmos almors aelmor elmors aelmrs**

aelmorsv removals marvels morales removal. *See* **aelmor aelmos aelmrs aelmrv**

aelmortu emulator. *See* **aelmor aelmrt aelmru aelmtu**

aelmorv removal. *See* **aelmor aelmrv**

aelmos amoles aloes amole lames loams males meals molas moles ales alms aloe also elms lame lams lea loam lose male meal mels mesa moas mola mole sale same seal seam slam sloe sole soma some ale elm els lam lea los mae mel moa mos oms sal sea sol ae am as el em la lo ma me mo om os so

aelmosss molasses lassoes. *See* **aelmos aelsss aemsss alosss**

aelmosst maltoses maltose molests samlets smaltos. *See* **aelmos aelmst aelost aelsst**

aelmossy amyloses amylose. *See* **aelmos aelmsy emossy**

aelmost maltose. *See* **almost aelmos aelmst elmost aelost**

aelmosy amylose. *See* **aelmos aelmsy**

aelmp ample maple lame lamp leap male meal pale palm peal plea ale alp amp ape elm lam lap lea mae map mel pal pea ae am el em la ma me pa pe

aelmpr ampler palmer ample lamer maple paler pearl realm earl lame lamp leap male mare marl meal merl pale palm pare peal pear perm plea pram

rale ramp rape real ream reap ale alp amp ape are arm ear elm era lam lap lar lea mae map mar mel pal par pea per ram rap rem rep ae am el em er la ma me pa pe re

aelmprs palmers sampler. *See* **aelmpr aelmps aelprs aelmrs**

aelmprss samplers armless palmers sampler samples. *See* **aelmpr aelmps aelmrs aelprs**

aelmprst tramples amplest armlets palmers palters plaster platers psalter sampler stamper stapler tampers trample. *See* **aelmpr aelmps aelmrs aelmrt**

aelmprsy lampreys lamprey palmers parleys parsley players replays sampler sparely. *See* **aelmpr aelmps aelmrs aelmsy**

aelmprt trample. *See* **aelmpr aelmrt aelprt aemprt**

aelmpry lamprey. *See* **aelmpr aelpry**

aelmps maples sample ample lames lamps lapse leaps males maple meals pales palms peals pleas psalm salep sepal ales alms alps amps apes apse elms lame lamp lams laps leap leas male maps meal mels mesa pale palm pals peal peas plea sale same samp seal seam slam slap ale alp amp ape asp elm els lam lap lea mae map mel pal pas pea sal sap sea spa ae am as el em la ma me pa pe

aelmpss samples. *See* **aelpss aelmps almpss**

aelmpst amplest. *See* **aelmps aelmst aelpst**

aelmpsu ampules. *See* **aelmpu almpsu aelmps elmpsu**

aelmpu ampule ample ampul maple plume ulema alum lame lamp leap lump male maul meal mule pale palm peal plea plum pule puma ale alp amp ape elm emu lam lap lea leu lum mae map mel pal pea pul ump ae am el em la ma me mu pa pe um up

aelmr lamer realm earl lame male mare marl meal merl rale real ream ale are arm ear elm era lam lar lea mae mar mel ram rem ae am el em er la ma me re

aelmrs realms earls lamer lames lares laser males mares marls maser meals merls rales realm reams smear ales alms arms arse earl ears elms eras lame lams leas male mare marl meal mels merl mesa rale rams rase real ream sale same seal seam sear sera slam ale are arm ear elm els era lam lar lea mae mar mel ram rem res sal sea ae am as el em er la ma me re

aelmrss armless. *See* **aelrss aemrss aelmrs**

aelmrst armlets. *See* **aelmrs aelmrt aelmst aelrst aemrst**

aelmrstt maltster martlets armlets martlet matters rattles smatter starlet startle. *See* **aelmrs aelmrt aelmst aelrst**

aelmrsty masterly armlets mastery myrtles smartly. *See* **aelmrs aelmrt aelmst aelmsy**

aelmrsu maulers. *See* **elmrsu aelmru almrsu aelmrs aelrsu**

aelmrsv marvels. *See* **aelrsv aelmrv**

aelmrt armlet alert alter lamer later metal realm taler tamer earl lame late male malt mare marl mart mate meal meat melt merl rale rate real ream tael tale tame tare teal team tear term tram aet ale alt are arm art ate ear eat elm era eta lam lar lea let mae mar mat mel met ram rat rem ret tam tar tea ae am at el em er la ma me re ta

aelmrtt martlet. *See* **aelmrt aelrtt aemrtt**

aelmrtuy maturely. *See* **aelmrt aelmru aelmtu aelmty**

aelmru mauler lamer lemur mural realm ulema alum earl lame lure male mare marl maul meal merl mule rale real ream rule urea ale are arm ear elm emu era lam lar lea leu lum mae mar mel ram rem rue rum ae am el em er la ma me mu re um

aelmrv marvel lamer laver ravel realm velar aver earl lame lave leva male mare marl meal merl rale rave real ream vale veal ale are arm ave ear elm era lam lar lea lev mae mar mel ram rem rev ae am el em er la ma me re

aelms lames males meals ales alms elms lame lams leas male meal mels mesa sale same seal seam slam ale elm els lam lea mae mel sal sea ae am as el em la ma me

aelmsss massless. *See* **aelsss aemsss**

aelmsst samlets. *See* **aelmst aelsst almsst elmsst aemsst**

aelmst lamest metals samlet lames least males malts mates meals meats melts metal satem slate smalt smelt stale steal steam taels tales tames teams ales alms alts east eats elms etas lame lams last late leas lest lets male malt mast mate mats meal meat mels melt mesa sale salt same seal seam seat seta slam slat stem tael tale tame tams teal team teas aet ale alt ate eat elm els eta lam lea let mae mat mel met sal sat sea set tam tea ae am as at el em la ma me ta

aelmstu amulets muletas. *See* **aelmtu aelmst aelstu**

aelmsy measly amyls lames males meals mealy seamy ales alms amyl ayes easy elms eyas lame lams lays leas lyes lyse male meal mels mesa sale same seal seam slam slay yams yeas ylem ale aye elm els lam lay lea lye mae may mel sal say sea sly yam yea yes ae am as ay el em la ma me my ye

aelmt metal lame late male malt mate meal meat melt tael tale tame teal team aet ale alt ate eat elm eta lam lea let mae mat mel met tam tea ae am at el em la ma me ta

aelmtu amulet muleta metal ulema alum lame late lute male malt mate maul meal meat melt mule mute tael tale tame teal team tule aet ale alt ate eat elm emu eta lam lea let leu lum mae mat mel met tam tau tea ae am at el em la ma me mu ta um ut

aelmty tamely etyma malty matey mealy meaty metal amyl lame late male malt mate meal meat melt tael tale tame teal team ylem aet ale alt ate aye eat elm eta lam lay lea let lye mae mat may mel met tam tea yam yea yet ae am at ay el em la ma me my ta ye

aelmu ulema alum lame male maul meal mule ale elm emu lam lea leu lum mae mel ae am el em la ma me mu um

aelmy mealy amyl lame male meal ylem ale aye elm lam lay lea lye mae may mel yam yea ae am ay el em la ma me my ye

aelnnoop napoleon. *See* **aelno alnop aenop**

aelnnpr planner. *See* **aelnnr aelnpr**

aelnnprs planners lanners planers planner spanner. *See* **aelnnr aelnpr aelnps aelnrs**

aelnnr lanner learn renal earl earn lane lean near rale real ale ane are ear era lar lea nae ran ae an el en er la na ne re

aelnnrs lanners. *See* **aelnnr aelnrs**

aelnnrst lanterns antlers lanners lantern rentals saltern sternal tanners. *See* **aelnnr aelnrs aelnrt aelrst**

aelnnrsu unlearns lanners runnels unlearn. *See* **aelnnr aelnrs aelnru aelrsu**

aelnnrt lantern. *See* **aelnrt aelnnr aennrt**

aelnnru unlearn. *See* **aelnnr aelnru elnnru**

aelnnstu annulets annulet tunnels. *See* **aelntu aelstu aenstu alnnsu**

aelnntu annulet. *See* **aelntu elnntu**

aelno alone aeon aloe enol lane lean leno loan lone noel ale ane eon lea nae one ae an el en la lo na ne no on

aelnoprs personal loaners paroles persona planers prolans. *See* **aelnor aelnos aelnpr aelnps**

aelnopst polentas apostle pelotas planets platens polenta. *See* **aelnos aelnps aelnpt aelops**

aelnopt polenta. *See* **elnopt aelopt aelnpt**

aelnor loaner alone learn loner renal aeon aero aloe earl earn enol lane lean leno loan lone lore lorn near noel oral orle rale real roan role ale ane are ear eon era lar lea nae nor oar one ore ran roe ae an el en er la lo na ne no on or re

aelnors loaners. *See* **aelnos aelnrs aelnor elnors alnors**

aelnortt tolerant. *See* **aelnor aelnrt aelntt aelrtt**

aelnorty ornately elytron. *See* **aelnor aelnrt aelnry aelnty**

aelnos lanose aeons aloes alone lanes leans loans noels salon solan aeon ales aloe also enol eons lane lean leas leno lens loan lone lose naos noel noes nose ones sale sane seal sloe sole ale ane els ens eon lea los nae one sal sea sen sol son ae an as el en la lo na ne no on os so

aelnp panel penal plane lane lean leap nape neap pale pane peal pean plan plea ale alp ane ape lap lea nae nap pal pan pea pen ae an el en la na ne pa pe

aelnppsy playpens playpen. *See* **aelnps aelnsy aelpps anppsy**

aelnppy playpen. *See* **aelpp alppy anppy**

aelnpr planer learn paler panel pearl penal plane renal earl earn lane lean leap nape neap near pale pane pare peal pean pear plan plea rale rape real reap ale alp ane ape are ear era lap lar lea nae nap pal pan par pea pen per ran rap rep ae an el en er la na ne pa pe re

aelnprs planers. *See* **aelnrs aelnps aelprs aelnpr**

aelnprst planters replants antlers arpents entraps palters parents pastern planers planets planter plaster platens platers psalter rentals replant saltern stapler sternal trepans. *See* **aelnpr aelnps aelnpt aelnrs**

aelnprsu purslane supernal planers perusal. *See* **aelnpr aelnps aelnrs aelnru**

aelnprt planter replant. *See* **aelnrt aenprt aelprt aelnpt**

aelnpry plenary. *See* **aenpry aelnry aelpry aelnpr**

aelnps panels planes aspen lanes lapse leans leaps napes neaps pales panel panes peals peans penal plane plans pleas salep sepal ales alps apes apse lane laps lean leap leas lens nape naps neap pale pals pane pans peal pean peas pens plan plea sale sane seal slap snap span ale alp ane ape asp els ens lap lea nae nap pal pan pas pea pen sal sap sea sen spa ae an as el en la na ne pa pe

aelnpss napless. *See* **aenpss aelpss aelnps**

aelnpst planets platens. *See* **aelpst aelnps aenpst aelnpt alnpst**

aelnpt planet platen leant panel paten penal petal plane plant plate pleat ante lane late lean leap lent lept nape neap neat pale pane pant pate peal pean peat pelt pent plan plat plea tael tale tape teal aet ale alp alt ane ant ape apt ate eat eta lap lea let nae nap net pal pan pat pea pen pet tan tap tea ten ae an at el en la na ne pa pe ta

aelnpttu petulant. *See* **aelnpt aelntt aelntu aenptu**

aelnpty aplenty penalty. *See* **aelnty aelnpt elnpty**

aelnqsuu unequals unequal. *See* **aelqsu aenqsu**

aelnquu unequal. *See* **aelqu aenqu aelnu**

aelnr learn renal earl earn lane lean near rale real ale ane are ear era lar lea nae ran ae an el en er la na ne re

aelnrrty errantly ternary. *See* **aelnrt aelnry aelnty aelrry**

aelnrs learns earls earns lanes lares laser leans learn nares nears rales renal saner snare snarl ales arse earl earn ears eras lane lean leas lens near rale rase real sale sane seal sear sera ale ane are ear els ens era lar lea nae ran res sal sea sen ae an as el en er la na ne re

aelnrsst salterns antlers artless rentals saltern slaters sternal. *See* **aelnrs aelnrt aelrss aelrst**

aelnrst antlers rentals saltern sternal. *See* **aelrst aelnrt aenrst aelnrs**

aelnrsuv unravels unravel. *See* **aelnrs aelnru aelnrv aelnsv**

aelnrsxy larynxes. *See* **aelnrs aelnry aelnsy aelrsy**

aelnrt antler learnt rental alert alter later leant learn renal taler ante earl earn lane late lean lent near neat rale rant rate real rent tael tale tare teal tear tern aet ale alt ane ant are art ate ear eat era eta lar lea let nae net ran rat ret tan tar tea ten ae an at el en er la na ne re ta

aelnrtu neutral. *See* **aelnrt aelntu aenrtu aelnru elnrtu**

aelnrtv ventral. *See* **aelnrt aelntv aenrtv aelrtv aelnrv**

aelnru neural unreal learn lunar renal ulnae earl earn lane lean lune lure near rale real rule rune ulna urea ale ane are ear era lar lea leu nae ran rue run urn ae an el en er la na ne nu re

aelnruv unravel. *See* **aelnru aelnrv**

aelnrv vernal laver learn navel ravel raven renal velar venal aver earl earn lane lave lean leva nave near rale rave real vale vane veal ale ane are ave ear era lar lea lev nae ran rev van ae an el en er la na ne re

aelnry nearly early layer learn relay renal yearn aery aryl earl earn lane lean lyre nary near rale real rely yare yarn yean year ale ane any are aye ear era lar lay lea lye nae nay ran ray rye yar yea yen ae an ay el en er la na ne re ye

aelns lanes leans ales lane lean leas lens sale sane seal ale ane els ens lea nae sal sea sen ae an as el en la na ne

aelnssst saltness tassels assents. *See* **aelsss aelsst aensst alnsst**

aelnssu sensual. *See* **aenssu elnssu**

aelnssx laxness. *See* **aelsx aelns aelss**

aelnstt lattens talents. *See* **aelntt aelstt**

aelnstv levants. *See* **aelntv aelnsv aelstv**

aelnsv navels avens lanes laves leans navel naves salve slave vales vanes veals venal ales aves lane lave lean leas lens leva nave sale sane save seal vale vane vans vase veal ale ane ave els ens lea lev nae sal sea sen van ae an as el en la na ne

aelnsy sanely lanes leans yeans ales ayes easy eyas lane lays lean leas lens lyes lyse sale sane seal slay yean yeas yens ale ane any aye els ens lay lea lye nae nay sal say sea sen sly yea yen yes ae an as ay el en la na ne ye

aelnt leant ante lane late lean lent neat tael tale teal aet ale alt ane ant ate eat eta lea let nae net tan tea ten ae an at el en la na ne ta

aelntt latent latten talent leant ante lane late lean lent neat tael tale teal teat tent aet ale alt ane ant ate eat eta lea let nae net tan tat tea ten ae an at el en la na ne ta

aelntu lunate leant ulnae ante aunt lane late lean lent lune lunt lute neat tael tale teal tule tuna tune ulna aet ale alt ane ant ate eat eta lea let leu nae net nut tan tau tea ten tun ae an at el en la na ne nu ta ut

aelntv levant leant navel valet venal ante lane late lave lean lent leva nave neat tael tale teal vale vane veal vent aet ale alt ane ant ate ave eat eta lea let lev nae net tan tav tea ten van vat vet ae an at el en la na ne ta

aelnty neatly leant yenta ante lane late lean lent neat tael tale teal yean aet ale

alt ane ant any ate aye eat eta lay lea let lye nae nay net tan tea ten yea yen yet ae an at ay el en la na ne ta ye

aelnu ulnae lane lean lune ulna ale ane lea leu nae ae an el en la na ne nu

aelnv navel venal lane lave lean leva nave vale vane veal ale ane ave lea lev nae van ae an el en la na ne

aelo aloe ale lea ae el la lo

aeloors aerosol roseola. *See* **eloors aelos aeors**

aeloorss aerosols roseolas aerosol lassoer oarless roseola. *See* **aelrss eloors elooss elorss**

aeloppprs prolapse loppers paroles poplars propels rappels. *See* **aelopr aelops aelppr aelpps**

aelopptu populate. *See* **aelppt aelppu aelopt aepptu**

aeloppxy apoplexy. *See* **aelopx**

aelopquy opaquely. *See* **aelpqu aeopqu**

aelopr parole loper opera paler parol pearl polar aero aloe earl leap lope lore opal oral orle pale pare peal pear plea pole pore proa rale rape real reap repo role rope ale alp ape are ear era lap lar lea lop oar ope ore pal par pea per pro rap rep roe ae el er la lo or pa pe re

aeloprs paroles. *See* **aelops eloprs aeoprs aelopr aloprs**

aeloprsv overlaps overlap paroles plovers. *See* **aelopr aelops aelosv aelprs**

aeloprt prolate. *See* **aelprt aelopr aloprt aelopt eloprt**

aeloprv overlap. *See* **aelopr eloprv**

aeloprvy overplay layover overlap overlay overpay. *See* **aelopr aelpry aoprvy eloprv**

aelops aslope aloes lapse leaps lopes opals pales peals pleas poles salep sepal slope ales aloe alps also apes apse epos laps leap leas lope lops lose opal opes pale pals peal peas peso plea pole pose sale seal slap sloe slop soap sole ale alp ape asp els lap lea lop los ope pal pas pea sal sap sea sol sop spa ae as el la lo os pa pe so

aelopsst apostles apostle pastels pelotas postals staples topless. *See* **aelops aelopt aelost aelpss**

aelopssu espousal spousal. *See* **aelops aelpss aepssu elopss**

aelopst apostle pelotas. *See* **aelops aelost aelpst alopst**

aelopstt paletots apostle paletot pelotas pottles teapots. *See* **aelops aelopt aelost aelpst**

aelopt pelota petal plate pleat aloe alto atop late leap lept lope lota opal pale pate peal peat pelt plat plea plot poet

pole tael tale tape teal tola tope aet ale alp alt ape apt ate eat eta lap lea let lop lot oat ope pal pat pea pet pot tap tea toe top ae at el la lo pa pe ta to

aeloptt paletot. *See* **aelopt eloptt aeoptt**

aelopx poleax aloe apex axle leap lope opal pale peal plea pole ale alp ape axe lap lax lea lop lox ope pal pax pea pox ae ax el ex la lo ox pa pe

aelorss lassoer oarless. *See* **aelrss elorss**

aelorsss lassoers lassoer lassoes lessors oarless rassles. *See* **aelrss aelssss alosss elorss**

aelorstv levators levator revolts solvate travels varlets. *See* **aelost aelosv aelrst aelrsv**

aelorsuu rouleaus rouleau. *See* **aelrsu aeorsu aersuu**

aelorsvy layovers overlays layover overlay slavery. *See* **aelosv aelrsv aelrsy aelsvy**

aelortv levator. *See* **elortv aelrtv**

aelortyz zealotry. *See* **aelotz aelrty**

aeloruu rouleau. *No 6s or 5s*

aelorvy layover overlay. *See* **elorvy aelry aelrv**

aelos aloes ales aloe also leas lose sale seal sloe sole ale els lea los sal sea sol ae as el la lo os so

aelosss lassoes. *See* **aelsss alosss elosss**

aelosstv solvates salvoes solvate. *See* **aelost aelosv aelsst aelssv**

aelossv salvoes. *See* **aelosv aelssv alossv elossv**

aelossz sleazos. *See* **aelosz**

aelost osteal aloes altos least lotas slate stale steal stoae stole taels tales tolas ales aloe also alto alts east eats etas last late leas lest lets lose lost lota lots oast oats sale salt seal seat seta slat sloe slot sole stoa tael tale teal teas toes tola aet ale alt ate eat els eta lea let los lot oat sal sat sea set sol sot tea toe ae as at el la lo os so ta to

aelostuv ovulates ovulate solvate volutes. *See* **aelost aelosv aelstu aelstv**

aelostv solvate. *See* **aelosv aelost aelstv**

aelostz zealots. *See* **aelosz aeostz aelost aelotz**

aelosuz zealous. *See* **aelosz elosuz**

aelosv loaves aloes laves loves ovals salve salvo slave solve vales veals voles ales aloe also aves lave leas leva lose love oval sale save seal sloe sole vale vase veal vole ale ave els lea lev los ova sal sea sol ae as el la lo os so

aelosz azoles sleazo aloes azole lazes zeals zoeal zoeas ales aloe also laze leas lose sale seal sloe sole zeal zoea ale azo

els lea los sal sea sol zoa ae as el la lo os
so

aelotuv ovulate. *See* **elotuv aeotv aeltv**

aelotz zealot azole azote zoeal aloe alto
late laze lota tael tale teal tola zeal zeta
zoea aet ale alt ate azo eat eta lea let lot
oat tea toe zoa ae at el la lo ta to

aeloz azole zoeal aloe laze zeal zoea ale
azo lea zoa ae el la lo

aelp leap pale peal plea ale alp ape lap
lea pal pea ae el la pa pe

aelpp apple pepla leap pale palp peal
plea ale alp ape lap lea pal pap pea pep
ae el la pa pe

aelppr rappel apple paler paper pearl
pepla earl leap pale palp pare peal pear
plea prep rale rape real reap repp ale
alp ape are ear era lap lar lea pal pap
par pea pep per rap rep ae el er la pa pe
re

aelpprs rappels. *See* **aelpps aepprs aelprs
aelppr**

aelppry reapply. *See* **aeppry aelpry**

aelpps apples apple lapse leaps pales
palps peals pepla pleas salep sepal ales
alps apes apse laps leap leas pale palp
pals paps peal peas peps plea sale seal
slap ale alp ape asp els lap lea pal pap
pas pea pep sal sap sea spa ae as el la
pa pe

aelppst lappets. *See* **aelpps aelppt aelpst**

aelppsu papules. *See* **aelpps alppsu
aelppu elppsu**

aelppt lappet apple pepla petal plate
pleat late leap lept pale palp pate peal
peat pelt plat plea tael tale tape teal aet
ale alp alt ape apt ate eat eta lap lea let
pal pap pat pea pep pet tap tea ae at el
la pa pe ta

aelppu papule apple pepla pupae pupal
leap pale palp peal plea pule pulp pupa
ale alp ape lap lea leu pal pap pea pep
pul pup ae el la pa pe up

aelpqsu plaques. *See* **aelqsu aelpqu**

aelpqu plaque equal quale leap pale peal
plea pule ale alp ape lap lea leu pal pea
pul qua ae el la pa pe up

aelpr paler pearl earl leap pale pare peal
pear plea rale rape real reap ale alp ape
are ear era lap lar lea pal par pea per
rap rep ae el er la pa pe re

aelprr parrel paler pearl earl leap pale
pare parr peal pear plea rale rape rare
real reap rear ale alp ape are ear era err
lap lar lea pal par pea per rap rep ae el
er la pa pe re

aelprrs parrels. *See* **aelprr aelprs aeprrs**

aelprrtt prattler partlet platter prattle
rattler. *See* **aelprr aelprt aelrtt**

aelprs pearls earls lapse lares laser leaps
paler pales pares parse peals pearl
pears pleas rales rapes reaps salep
sepal spare spear ales alps apes apse
arse earl ears eras laps leap leas pale
pals pare pars peal pear peas plea rale
rape raps rase rasp real reap reps sale
seal sear sera slap spar ale alp ape are
asp ear els era lap lar lea pal par pas
pea per rap rep res sal sap sea spa ae as
el er la pa pe re

aelprsst plasters psalters staplers artless
palters pastels pasters plaster platers
psalter repasts slaters sparest stapler
staples. *See* **aelprs aelprt aelpss aelpst**

aelprssu perusals perusal pulsars saurels.
See **aelprs aelpru aelpss aelrss**

aelprssy sparsely parleys parsley pessary
players rayless replays slayers sparely.
See **aelprs aelpry aelpss aelrss**

aelprst palters plaster platers psalter stapler. *See* **aelprs aelprt aelpst aelrst
aeprst**

aelprstt partlets platters prattles splatter
palters partlet patters plaster platers
platter prattle psalter rattles spatter
stapler starlet startle tapster. *See*
aelprs aelprt aelpst aelrst

aelprsu perusal. *See* **aeprsu aelprs aelpru
alprsu elprsu**

aelprsy parleys parsley players replays
sparely. *See* **aelrsy aelpry aeprsy aelprs**

aelprt palter plater alert alter later paler
pater pearl peart petal plate pleat prate
taler taper earl late leap lept pale pare
part pate peal pear peat pelt pert plat
plea rale rape rapt rate real reap tael
tale tape tare tarp teal tear trap aet ale
alp alt ape apt are art ate ear eat era eta
lap lar lea let pal par pat pea per pet
rap rat rep ret tap tar tea ae at el er la
pa pe re ta

aelprtt partlet platter prattle. *See* **aelrtt
aelprt aeprtt**

aelprty pteryla. *See* **aelrty alprty aelpry
elprty aelprt**

aelpru pleura paler pareu pearl earl leap
lure pale pare peal pear plea pule pure
purl rale rape real reap rule urea ale
alp ape are ear era lap lar lea leu pal
par pea per pul rap rep rue ae el er la
pa pe re up

aelpry parley pearly player replay apery
early layer paler payer pearl relay repay reply aery aryl earl leap lyre pale
paly pare peal pear play plea pray prey
pyre rale rape real reap rely yare year
yelp ale alp ape are aye ear era lap lar
lay lea lye pal par pay pea per ply pry

pya rap ray rep rye yap yar yea yep ae
ay el er la pa pe re ye

aelps lapse leaps pales peals pleas salep
sepal ales alps apes apse laps leap leas
pale pals peal peas plea sale seal slap
ale alp ape asp els lap lea pal pas pea
sal sap sea spa ae as el la pa pe

aelpss lapses passel saleps sepals apses
lapse leaps pales peals pleas salep sales
seals sepal slaps ales alps apes apse
asps laps lass leap leas less pale pals
pass peal peas plea sale sals saps seal
seas slap spas ale alp ape asp ass els ess
lap lea pal pas pea sal sap sea spa ae as
el la pa pe

aelpsss passels sapless. *See* **aelpss aelsss
aepsss**

aelpsst pastels staples. *See* **aelpss aelpst
aepsst aelsst alpsst**

aelpsstu pulsates pastels petasus pulsate
salutes staples taluses. *See* **aelpss
aelpst aelsst aelstu**

aelpst palest pastel petals plates pleats
staple lapse leaps least pales paste
pates peals pelts petal plate plats pleas
pleat salep sepal septa slate slept spate
spelt splat stale steal taels tales tapes
ales alps alts apes apse east eats etas
laps last late leap leas lept lest lets pale
pals past pate pats peal peas peat pelt
pest pets plat plea sale salt seal seat
sept seta slap slat spat step tael tale
tape taps teal teas aet ale alp alt ape
apt asp ate eat els eta lap lea let pal pas
pat pea pet sal sap sat sea set spa tap
tea ae as at el la pa pe ta

aelpstu pulsate. *See* **elpstu aelstu aelpst
aepstu**

aelpt petal plate pleat late leap lept pale
pate peal peat pelt plat plea tael tale
tape teal aet ale alp alt ape apt ate eat
eta lap lea let pal pat pea pet tap tea ae
at el la pa pe ta

aelqrrsu quarrels quarrel squarer. *See*
aelqsu aelrsu elrrsu

aelqrru quarrel. *See* **aelqu elrru alrru**

aelqrsuy squarely. *See* **aelqsu aelrsu
aelrsy aeqsuy**

aelqssu squeals. *See* **aelqsu**

aelqsu equals squeal equal quale ales
leas lues sale seal slue ale els lea leu
qua sal sea sue use ae as el la us

aelqtuz quetzal. *See* **aelquz**

aelqu equal quale ale lea leu qua ae el la

aelquz quezal equal quale laze zeal ale
lea leu qua ae el la

aelr earl rale real ale are ear era lar lea ae
el er la re

aelrrstt rattlers ratters rattler rattles restart starlet starter startle. *See* **aelrst aelrtt aelstt aerrst**

aelrrstw trawlers trawler wastrel. *See* **aelrst aerrst aerstw alrstw**

aelrrtt rattler. *See* **aelrtt aerrtt**

aelrrtw trawler. *See* **aelrt aerrw alrtw**

aelrry rarely early layer relay aery aryl earl lyre rale rare real rear rely yare year ale are aye ear era err lar lay lea lye ray rye yar yea ae ay el er la re ye

aelrs earls lares laser rales ales arse earl ears eras leas rale rase real sale seal sear sera ale are ear els era lar lea res sal sea ae as el er la re

aelrss lasers rassel arses earls lares laser rales rases sales seals sears ales arse earl ears eras lass leas less rale rase real sale sals seal sear seas sera ale are ass ear els era ess lar lea res sal sea ae as el er la re

aelrsss rassles. *See* **aelrss aelsss**

aelrssst starless artless asserts rassles slaters tassels. *See* **aelrss aelrst aelsss aelsst**

aelrssst artless slaters. *See* **aelrst aerssst aelrss aelsst**

aelrsstt starlets startles artless rattles slaters stalest starlet startle tasters. *See* **aelrss aelrst aelrtt aelsst**

aelrsstu saluters artless results rustles saluter salutes saurels slaters taluses ulsters. *See* **aelrss aelrst aelrsu aelsst**

aelrsstw wastrels artless slaters wasters wastrel. *See* **aelrss aelrst aelsst aelssw**

aelrssu saurels. *See* **aerssu aelrss aelrsu**

aelrssuw walruses saurels. *See* **aelrss aelrsu aelssw aerssu**

aelrssv slavers. *See* **aelrss aelrsv aelssv aerssv**

aelrssy rayless slayers. *See* **aelrss aelrsy aerssy**

aelrst alerts alters laster salter slater staler alert alter aster earls lares laser later least rales rates slate stale stare steal taels taler tales tares tears ales alts arse arts earl ears east eats eras erst etas last late leas lest lets rale rase rate rats real rest rets sale salt seal sear seat sera seta slat star steal tale tare tars teal tear teas tsar aet ale alt are art ate ear eat els era eta lar lea let rat res ret sal sat sea set tar tea ae as at el er la re ta

aelrstt rattles starlet startle. *See* **aelrst aelstt aelrtt aerstt**

aelrsttt tartlets tattlers rattles starlet startle tartlet tatters tattler tattles. *See* **aelrst aelrtt aelstt aerstt**

aelrsttu lustrate rattles saluter starlet startle stature turtles. *See* **aelrst aelrsu aelrtt aelstt**

aelrstu saluter. *See* **aelrst elrstu alrstu aelstu aelrsu**

aelrstuv vaulters saluter travels varlets vaulter. *See* **aelrst aelrsu aelrsv aelrtv**

aelrstv travels varlets. *See* **aelrst aerstv aelrsv aelrtv aelstv**

aelrstw wastrel. *See* **aelrst aerstw alrstw**

aelrstwz waltzers waltzer waltzes wastrel. *See* **aelrst aerstw aerstz alrstw**

aelrsu saurel earls lares laser lures rales rules ureas ales arse earl ears eras leas lues lure rale rase real rues rule ruse sale seal sear sera slue slur sura sure urea user ale are ear els era lar lea leu res rue sal sea sue use ae as el er la re us

aelrsv lavers ravels salver serval slaver avers earls lares laser laver laves rales ravel raves salve saver slave vales veals velar ales arse aver aves earl ears eras lave leas leva rale rase rave real revs sale save seal sear sera vale vase veal ale are ave ear els era lar lea lev res rev sal sea ae as el er la re

aelrsvy slavery. *See* **aelrsv aelrsy aelsvy**

aelrswy lawyers. *See* **aelrwy aerswy aelrsy**

aelrsy layers relays slayer aryls earls early lares laser layer lyres rales relay sayer slyer years aery ales arse aryl ayes earl ears easy eras eyas lays leas lyes lyre lyse rale rase rays real rely ryes sale seal sear sera slay yare year yeas ale are aye ear els era lar lay lea lye ray res rye sal say sea sly yar yea yes ae as ay el er la re ye

aelrt alert alter later taler earl late rale rate real tael tale tare teal tear aet ale alt are art ate ear eat era eta lar lea let rat ret tar tea ae at el er la re ta

aelrtt latter rattle alert alter later taler tater tetra treat earl late rale rate real tael tale tare tart teal tear teat tret aet ale alt are art ate ear eat era eta lar lea let rat ret tar tat tea ae at el er la re ta

aelrttt tartlet tattler. *See* **aelrtt aerttt aelttt**

aelrtuv vaulter. *See* **aelrtv**

aelrtv travel varlet alert alter avert later laver ravel taler trave valet velar aver earl late lave leva rale rate rave real tael tale tare teal tear vale veal vert aet ale alt are art ate ave ear eat era eta lar lea let lev rat ret rev tar tav tea vat vet ae at el er la re ta

aelrtwz waltzer. *See* **aelrt alrtw altwz**

aelrty lyrate realty alert alter early later layer relay taler teary aery arty aryl

earl late lyre rale rate real rely tael tale tare teal tear tray yare year aet ale alt are art ate aye ear eat era eta lar lay lea let lye rat ray ret rye tar tea try yar yea yet ae at ay el er la re ta ye

aelrv laver ravel velar aver earl lave leva rale rave real vale veal ale are ave ear era lar lea lev rev ae el er la re

aelrwy lawyer early layer relay weary aery aryl awry earl lyre rale real rely wale ware wary weal wear yare yawl year ale are awe awl aye ear era lar law lay lea lye raw ray rye war way wye yar yaw yea yew ae aw ay el er la re we ye

aelrx relax axle earl rale real ale are axe ear era lar lax lea rex ae ax el er ex la re

aelry early layer relay aery aryl earl lyre rale real rely yare year ale are aye ear era lar lay lea lye ray rye yar yea ae ay el er la re ye

aelryy yearly early layer relay aery aryl earl lyre rale real rely yare year ale are aye ear era lar lay lea lye ray rye yar yay yea ae ay el er la re ye

aels ales leas sale seal ale els lea sal sea ae as el la

aelss sales seals ales lass leas less sale sals seal seas ale ass els ess lea sal sea ae as el la

aelsss lasses asses sales seals ales lass leas less sale sals sass seal seas ale ass els ess lea sal sea ae as el la

aelssst tassels. *See* **aessst aelsss aelsst**

aelsst slates stales steals tassel asset lasts least sales salts sates seals seats slate slats stale steal taels tales tasse ales alts east eats etas lass last late leas less lest lets sale sals salt seal seas seat seta sets slat tael tale tass teal teas aet ale alt ass ate eat els ess eta lea let sal sat sea set tea ae as at el la ta

aelsstt stalest. *See* **aelstt aelsst aesstt**

aelsstu salutes taluses. *See* **aelstu elsstu**

aelssv salves slaves laves sales salve saves seals slave vales vases veals ales aves lass lave leas leva sale sals save seal seas vale vase veal ale ass ave els ess lea lev sal sea ae as el la

aelssw swales sales seals swale wales weals ales awes awls lass laws leas less sale sals saws seal seas sews slew wale weal ale ass awe awl els ess law lea sal saw sea sew was ae as aw el la we

aelst least slate stale steal taels tales ales alts east eats etas last late leas lest lets sale salt seal seat seta slat tael tale teal teas aet ale alt ate eat els eta lea let sal sat sea set tea ae as at el la ta

aelstt latest least slate stale state steal taels tales taste teats testa ales alts east eats etas last late leas lest lets sale salt seal seat seta slat stet tael tale tats teal teas teat test aet ale alt ate eat els eta lea let sal sat sea set tat tea ae as at el la ta

aelsttt tattles. *See* **aesttt aelstt aelttt**

aelstttw twattles tattles twattle wattles. *See* **aelstt aelttw**

aelsttuy astutely stately. *See* **aelstt aelstu aeltty aesttu**

aelsttw wattles. *See* **aelstt aelttw**

aelstty stately. *See* **aelstt aeltty elstty**

aelstu salute least lutes slate stale steal taels tales talus tules ales alts east eats etas last late leas lest lets lues lust lute sale salt seal seat seta slat slue slut suet tael tale teal teas tule aet ale alt ate eat els eta lea let leu sal sat sea set sue tau tea use ae as at el la ta us ut

aelstux luxates. *See* **aelstx elstux aeltux aelstu aelsux**

aelstv valets vestal laves least salve slate slave stale stave steal taels tales vales valet veals ales alts aves east eats etas last late lave leas lest lets leva sale salt save seal seat seta slat tael tale tavs teal teas vale vase vast vats veal vest vets aet ale alt ate ave eat els eta lea let lev sal sat sea set tav tea vat vet ae as at el la ta

aelstwz waltzes. *See* **aelsz aelst aelsw**

aelstx exalts axels axles exalt latex least slate stale steal taels tales taxes ales alts axes axle east eats etas last late leas lest lets sale salt seal seat seta sext slat tael tale teal teas aet ale alt ate axe eat els eta lax lea let sal sat sax sea set sex tax tea ae as at ax el ex la ta

aelsuv values laves salve slave uveas vales value veals ales aves lave leas leva lues sale save seal slue uvea vale vase veal ale ave els lea leu lev luv sal sea sue use ae as el la us

aelsuvy suavely. *See* **aelsuv aelsvy**

aelsux sexual axels axles luxes ales axes axle leas lues luxe sale seal slue ale axe els lax lea leu lux sal sax sea sex sue use ae as ax el ex la us

aelsv laves salve slave vales veals ales aves lave leas leva sale save seal vale vase veal ale ave els lea lev sal sea ae as el la

aelsvv valves laves salve slave vales valve veals ales aves lave leas leva sale save seal vale vase veal ale ave els lea lev sal sea ae as el la

aelsvy sylvae laves leavy salve slave sylva vales veals ales aves ayes easy eyas lave lays leas leva levy lyes lyse sale save seal slay vale vase veal yeas ale ave aye

els lay lea lev lye sal say sea sly yea yes ae as ay el la ye

aelsw swale wales weals ales awes awls laws leas sale seal slew wale weal ale awe awl els law lea sal saw sea sew was ae as aw el la we

aelsx axels axles ales axes axle leas sale seal ale axe els lax lea sal sax sea sex ae as ax el ex la

aelsyz sleazy lazes zeals ales ayes easy eyas lays laze lazy leas lyes lyse sale seal slay yeas zeal ale aye els lay lea lye sal say sea sly yea yes ae as ay el la ye

aelsz lazes zeals ales laze leas sale seal zeal ale els lea sal sea ae as el la

aelt late tael tale teal aet ale alt ate eat eta lea let tea ae at el la ta

aelttt tattle late tael tale teal teat aet ale alt ate eat eta lea let tat tea ae at el la ta

aeltttw twattle. *See* **aeltttt aelttw**

aelttux textual. *See* **aeltux**

aelttw wattle late tael tale teal welt wale watt weal welt aet ale alt ate awe awl eat eta law lea let tat tea wet ae at aw el la ta we

aeltty lyttae lytta late tael tale teal teat aet ale alt ate aye eat eta lay lea let lye tat tea yea yet ae at ay el la ta ye

aeltux luxate exalt exult latex axle late lute luxe tael tale teal tule aet ale alt ate axe eat eta lax lea let leu lux tau tax tea tux ae at ax el ex la ta ut

aeltv valet late lave leva tael tale teal vale veal aet ale alt ate ave eat eta lea let lev tav tea vat vet ae at el la ta

aeltx exalt latex axle late tael tale teal aet ale alt ate axe eat eta lax lea let tax tea ae at ax el ex la ta

aeluuv uvulae uvula lave leva luau uvea veal vale ale ave lea leu lev luv ulu ae el la

aeluv value lave leva uvea vale veal ale ave lea leu lev luv ae el la

aelv lave leva vale veal ale ave lea lev ae el la

aelvv valve lave leva vale veal ale ave lea lev ae el la

aelvy leavy lave leva levy vale veal ale ave aye lay lea lev lye yea ae ay el la ye

aelw wale weal ale awe awl law lea ae aw el la we

aelx axel axle ale axe lax lea ae ax el ex la

aelz laze zeal ale lea ae el la

aem mae ae am em ma me

aemmmsy mammeys. *See* **aemmmy aemmsy**

aemmmy mammey mammy aye mae may mem yam yea ae am ay em ma me my ye

aemmnot momenta. *See* **emmnot aenot aemnt**

aemmnr merman amen earn mane mare mean name near ream ane are arm ear era mae man mar mem men nae ram ran rem ae am an em en er ma me na ne re

aemmoort roommate tearoom. *See* **am-mort**

aemmorst marmoset maestro marmots stammer. *See* **aemmst aemrst aeorst ammort**

aemmrr rammer rearm mare rare ream rear are arm ear era err mae mar mem ram rem ae am em er ma me re

aemmrrs rammers. *See* **aemmrr aemrrs**

aemmrsst stammers masters stammer stemmas streams. *See* **aemmst aemrss aemrst aemsst**

aemmrst stammer. *See* **aemrst aemmst**

aemmrsy yammers. *See* **aemmsy ammrsy aemrsy aemmry**

aemmry yammer aery army mare ream yare year are arm aye ear era mae mar may mem ram ray rem rye yam yar yea ae am ay em er ma me my re ye

aemmsst stemmas. *See* **aemmst aemsst**

aemmst stemma mates meats satem steam tames teams east eats etas mast mate mats meat mems mesa same seam seat seta stem tame tams team teas aet ate eat eta mae mat mem met sat sea set tam tea ae am as at em ma me ta

aemmsu summae amuse summa emus mems mesa mums muse same seam emu mae mem mum mus sea sue sum use ae am as em ma me mu um us

aemmsy mameys seamy ayes easy eyas mems mesa same seam yams yeas aye mae may mem say sea yam yea yes ae am as ay em ma me my ye

aemn amen mane mean name ane mae man men nae ae am an em en ma me na ne

aemnnort ornament montane remnant. *See* **aemnnr aemnor aemnrt aennrt**

aemnnot montane. *See* **aennt aenot aemnt**

aemnnou noumena. *See* **emnno emnnu amnnu**

aemnnp penman panne penna amen mane mean name nape neap pane pean amp ane ape mae man map men nae nap pan pea pen ae am an em en ma me na ne pa pe

aemnnr manner amen earn mane mare mean name near ream ane are arm ear era mae man mar men nae ram ran rem ae am an em en er ma me na ne re

aemnnrs manners. *See* **aemnnr aenrs aemns**

aemnnrst remnants manners martens remnant smarten tanners. *See* **aemnnr aemnrt aemnst aemrst**

aemnnrt remnant. *See* **aemnnr aemnrt aennrt**

aemnnsw newsman. *See* **aemns aenns aensw**

aemnoort anteroom tearoom montero. *See* **aemnor aemnrt aenort amnoor**

aemnoprw manpower. *See* **aemnor aenopw**

aemnor enamor morae manor aeon aero amen earn mane mare mean moan mora more morn name near noma nome norm omen omer ream roam roan ane are arm ear eon era mae man mar men moa mon mor nae nor oar one ore ram ran rem roe ae am an em en er ma me mo na ne no om on or re

aemnors enamors oarsmen. *See* **aemnor amnors aenors emnors**

aemnorty monetary anymore. *See* **aemnor aemnoy aemnrt aenort**

aemnory anymore. *See* **aemnor aemnoy**

aemnoryy yeomanry anymore. *See* **aemnor aemnoy**

aemnostu seamount amounts. *See* **aemnst aenost aenstu amnotu**

aemnoy yeoman meany money yamen aeon amen mane many mayo mean moan myna name noma nome omen yean ane any aye eon mae man may men moa mon nae nay one yam yea yen yon ae am an ay em en ma me mo my na ne no om on oy ye

aemnprss pressman. *See* **aemnss aemrss aenpss aenrss**

aemnprsu superman manures pneumas surname. *See* **aemnpu aemnru aeprsu amnrsu**

aemnpsty payments amnesty payment. *See* **aemnst aemnsy aemsty aenpst**

aemnpsu pneumas. *See* **aemnpu aemsu aenps**

aemnpty payment. *See* **amnpty empty aemty**

aemnpu pneuma amen mane maun mean menu name nape neap pane pean puma amp ane ape emu mae man map men nae nap pan pea pen pun ump ae am an em en ma me mu na ne nu pa pe um up

aemnrsst smartens martens masters smarten stamens streams. *See* **aemnrt aemnss aemnst aemrss**

aemnrssu surnames manures masseur surname. *See* **aemnru aemnss aemrss aemssu**

aemnrst martens smarten. *See* **aenrst aemnrt aemrst aemnst**

aemnrsu manures surname. *See* **aemnru amnrsu**

aemnrt marten meant tamer amen ante earn mane mare mart mate mean meat name near neat rant rate ream rent tame tare team tear term tern tram aet ane ant are arm art ate ear eat era eta mae man mar mat men met nae net ram ran rat rem ret tam tan tar tea ten ae am an at em en er ma me na ne re ta

aemnru manure unarm rumen amen earn mane mare maun mean menu name near ream rune urea ane are arm ear emu era mae man mar men nae ram ran rem rue rum run urn ae am an em en er ma me mu na ne nu re um

aemns manes manse means names amen mane mean mesa name same sane seam ane ens mae man men nae sea sen ae am an as em en ma me na ne

aemnss manses manse means means mesas names seams amen mane mass mean mesa mess name same sane seam seas ane ass ens ess mae man men nae sea sen ae am an as em en ma me na ne

aemnsst stamens. *See* **aensst aemnss aemsst**

aemnst stamen antes manes manse mates means meant meats names nates satem steam tames teams amen ante ants east eats etas mane mast mate mats mean meat mesa name neat nest nets same sane seam seat sent seta stem tame tams tans team teas tens aet ane ant ate eat ens eta mae man mat men met nae net sat sea sen set tam tan tea ten ae am an as at em en ma me na ne ta

aemnsttu nutmeats attunes mutants mutates nutmeat tautens tetanus. *See* **aemnst aemstt aemttu aenstu**

aemnsty amnesty. *See* **aemsty aemnst aemnsy aensty**

aemnsv mavens avens manes manse maven means names naves vanes amen aves mane mean mesa name nave same sane save seam vane vans vase ane ave ens mae man men nae sea sen van ae am an as em en ma me na ne

aemnsy yamens manes manse means meany mynas names seamy yamen yeans amen ayes easy eyas mane many mean mesa myna name same sane seam yams yean yeas yens ane any aye ens mae man may men nae nay say sea sen sny yam yea yen yes ae am an as ay em en ma me my na ne ye

aemnt meant amen ante mane mate mean meat name neat tame team aet ane ant ate eat eta mae man mat men met nae net tam tan tea ten ae am an at em en ma me na ne ta

aemnttu nutmeat. *See* **aenttu amnttu aemttu**

aemnv maven amen mane mean name nave vane ave mae man men mean nae van ae am an em en ma me na ne

aemny meany yamen amen mane many mean myna name yean ane any aye mae man may men nae nay yam yea yen ae am an ay em en ma me my na ne ye

aemoorrw wareroom. *See* **aemorr aemrrw amorrw emoorr**

aemoorst tearooms tearoom maestro. *See* **aemrst aeorst emoors emorst**

aemoort tearoom. *See* **emort aemor moort**

aemoortt amoretto tearoom. *See* **aemrtt aeortt amoott**

aemoosst maestoso. *See* **aemsst amosst emooss**

aemoossv vamooses vamoose vamoses. *See* **aemosv emooss**

aemoostt tomatoes mottoes. *See* **aemstt amoott emostt moostt**

aemoosv vamoose. *See* **aemosv emoos**

aemoppr pampero. *See* **aemppr**

aemopprs pamperos mappers pampero pampers preamps. *See* **aemppr aeopps aeoprs aepprs**

aemoprtw tapeworm. *See* **aemprt**

aemor morae aero mare mora more omer ream roam are arm ear era mae mar moa mor oar ore ram rem roe ae am em er ma me mo om or re

aemorr remora roamer armor morae ormer rearm aero mara mora more omer rare ream rear roam roar are arm ear era err mae mar moa mor oar ore ram rem roe ae am em er ma me mo om or re

aemorrr armorer. *See* **aemorr aeorrr**

aemorrrs armorers armorer remoras roamers. *See* **aemorr aemrrs aeorrr amorrs**

aemorrs remoras roamers. *See* **amorrs emorrs aemrrs aemorr**

aemorrst rearmost armrest maestro mortars remoras roamers roaster smarter termors tremors. *See* **aemorr aemrrs aemrst aeorst**

aemorsss morasses. *See* **aemrss aemsss amorss emosss**

aemorsst maestros maestro masters streams. *See* **aemrss aemrst aemsst aeorst**

aemorssy mayoress. *See* **aemrss aemrsy aerssy amorss**

aemorst maestro. *See* **aemrst emorst aeorst**

aemossv vamoses. *See* **aemosv aemss aeoss**

aemosswy someways someway. *See* **emossy**

aemosv vamose moves aves mesa moas move same save seam soma some vase ave mae moa mos oms ova sea ae am as em ma me mo om os so

aemoswy someway. *See* **amosy emosw emosy**

aemottzz mozzetta. *See* **amottz**

aemppr pamper preamp paper mare pare pear perm pram prep ramp rape ream reap repp amp ape are arm ear era mae map mar pap par pea pep per ram rap rem rep ae am em er ma me pa pe re

aempprs mappers pampers preamps. *See* **aemppr aepprs**

aemprsst stampers masters pasters repasts sparest stamper streams tampers. *See* **aemprt aemrss aemrst aemsst**

aemprst stamper tampers. *See* **aemprt aemrst aeprst amprst**

aemprstu upstream matures pasture stamper strumae stumper sumpter tampers tempura. *See* **aemprt aemrst aemrtu aeprst**

aemprsv revamps. *See* **aemprv aeprsv**

aemprt tamper pater peart prate tamer taper tramp mare mart meat mae pare part pate pear peat perm pert pram ramp rape rapt rate ream reap tame tamp tape tare tarp team tear term tram trap aet amp ape apt are arm art ate ear eat era eta mae map mar mat met par pat pea per pet ram rap rat rem rep ret tam tap tar tea ae am at em er ma me pa pe re ta

aemprtu tempura. *See* **aemprt aemrtu**

aemprv revamp parve paver aver mare pare pave pear perm pram ramp rape rave ream reap vamp amp ape are arm ave ear era mae map mar par pea per ram rap rem rep rev ae am em er ma me pa pe re

aempsttt attempts attempt. *See* **aemstt empstt**

aempttt attempt. *See* **aemtt emptt**

aemqrssu marquess masquers marques masquer masques masseur squares. *See* **aemqru aemqsu aemrss aemssu**

aemqrsu marques masquer. *See* **aemqru aemqsu aeqrsu**

aemqru marque mare ream urea are arm ear emu era mae mar qua ram rem rue rum ae am em er ma me mu re um

aemqssu masques. *See* **aemssu**

aemqsu masque amuse emus mesa muse same seam emu mae mus qua sea sue sum use ae am as em ma me mu um us

aemr mare ream are arm ear era mae mar ram rem ae am em er ma me re

aemrr rearm mare rare ream rear are arm ear era err mae mar ram rem ae am em er ma me re

aemrrry remarry. *See* **amrry emrry aerrr**

aemrrs rearms mares maser reams rearm rears smear arms arse ears eras errs mare mesa rams rare rase ream rear same seam sear sera are arm ear era err mae mar ram rem res sea ae am as em er ma me re

aemrrsst armrests armrest arrests masters smarter streams. *See* **aemrrss aemrss aemrst aemsst**

aemrrst armrest smarter. *See* **aerrst aemrst aemrrs**

aemrrsu armures. *See* **aemrrss aemrru**

aemrrtu erratum. *See* **aemrru aemrtu**

aemrru armure rearm murre mare rare ream rear urea are arm ear emu era err mae mar ram rem rue rum ae am em er ma me mu re um

aemrrw warmer rearm rawer mare rare ream rear ware warm wear are arm awe ear era err mae mar maw mew ram raw rem war ae am aw em er ma me re we

aemrs mares maser reams smear arms arse ears eras mare mesa rams rase ream same seam sear sera are arm ear era mae mar ram rem res sea ae am as em er ma me re

aemrss masers smears arses mares maser mesas rases reams seams sears smear arms arse ears eras mare mass mesa mess rams rase ream same seam sear seas sera are arm ass ear era ess mae mar ram rem res sea ae am as em er ma me re

aemrsssu masseurs assumes assures masseur. *See* **aemrss aemsss aemssu aerssu**

aemrsst masters streams. *See* **aersst aemrss aemrst amrsst aemsst**

aemrsstt mattress smartest smatters masters matters smatter streams tasters. *See* **aemrss aemrst aemrtt aemsst**

aemrssu masseur. *See* **aemssu aerssu aemrss emrssu**

aemrst master stream aster mares marts maser mates meats rates reams satem smart smear stare steam tamer tames tares teams tears terms trams arms arse arts ears east eats eras erst etas mare mart mast mate mats meat mesa rams rase rate rats ream rest rets same seam sear seat sera seta star stem tame tams tare tars team tear teas term tram tsar aet are arm art ate ear eat era eta mae mar mat met ram rat rem res ret sat sea set tam tar tea ae am as at em er ma me re ta

aemrstt matters smatter. *See* **aemrst aemrtt aemstt aerstt**

aemrstu matures strumae. *See* **aemrst aemrtu emrstu amrstu**

aemrstw warmest. *See* **aemrst aerstw**

aemrsty mastery. *See* **aersty aemrst aemsty amrsty aemrsy**

aemrsy smeary mares maser reams sayer seamy smear years aery arms army arse ayes ears easy eras eyas mare mesa rams rase rays ream ryes same seam sear sera yams yare year yeas are arm aye ear era mae mar may ram ray rem res rye say sea yam yar yea yes ae am as ay em er ma me my re ye

aemrsz mazers mares maser mazer mazes razes reams smaze smear arms arse ears eras mare maze mesa rams rase raze ream same seam sear sera are arm ear era mae mar ram rem res sea ae am as em er ma me re

aemrt tamer mare mart mate meat rate ream tame tare team tear term tram aet are arm art ate ear eat era eta mae mar mat met ram rat rem ret tam tar tea ae am at em er ma me re ta

aemrtt matter matte tamer tater tetra treat mare mart mate meat rate ream tame tare tart team tear teat term tram tret aet are arm art ate ear eat era eta mae mar mat met ram rat rem ret tam tar tat tea ae am at em er ma me re ta

aemrtu mature tamer mare mart mate meat mute rate ream tame tare team tear term tram true urea aet are arm art ate ear eat emu era eta mae mar mat met ram rat rem ret rue rum rut tam tar tau tea ae am at em er ma me mu re ta um ut

aemrz mazer mare maze raze ream are arm ear era mae mar ram rem ae am em er ma me re

aems mesa same seam mae sea ae am as em ma me

aemss mesas seams mass mesa mess same seam seas ass ess mae sea ae am as em ma me

aemsss masses asses mesas seams mass mesa mess same sass seam seas ass ess mae sea ae am as em ma me

aemsssu assumes. *See* **aemssu aemsss emsssu**

aemsst steams asset masts mates meats mesas satem sates seams seats steam stems tames tasse teams east eats etas mass mast mate mats meat mesa mess same seam seas seat seta sets stem tame tams tass team teas aet ass ate eat ess eta mae mat met sat sea set tam tea ae am as at em ma me ta

aemssu amuses assume amuse mesas muses seams emus mass mesa mess muse muss same seam seas sues sums uses ass emu ess mae mus sea sue sum use ae am as em ma me mu um us

aemst mates meats satem steam tames teams east eats etas mast mate mats meat mesa same seam seat seta stem tame tams team teas aet ate eat eta mae mat met sat sea set tam tea ae am as at em ma me ta

aemstt mattes tamest mates matte meats satem state steam tames taste teams teats testa east eats etas mast mate mats meat mesa same seam seat seta stem stet tame tams tats team teas teat test aet ate eat eta mae mat met sat sea set tam tat tea ae am as at em ma me ta

aemsttu mutates. *See* **aesttu aemstt aemttu**

aemsty mateys mayest steamy etyma mates matey mayst meats meaty satem seamy steam tames teams yeast ayes east easy eats etas eyas mast mate mats meat mesa same seam seat seta stay stem tame tams team teas yams yeas aet ate aye eat eta mae mat may met sat say sea set sty tam tea yam yea yes yet ae am as at ay em ma me my ta ye

aemsu amuse emus mesa muse same seam emu mae mus sea sue sum use ae am as em ma me mu um us

aemsuv mauves amuse mauve uveas aves emus mesa muse same save seam uvea vase ave emu mae mus sea sue sum use ae am as em ma me mu um us

aemsuzz mezuzas. *See* **aemuzz aemsu aemsz**

aemsx exams axes exam mesa same seam axe mae sax sea sex ae am as ax em ex ma me

aemsy seamy ayes easy eyas mesa same seam yams yeas aye mae may say sea yam yea yes ae am as ay em ma me my ye

aemsyz zymase mazes seamy smaze zymes ayes easy eyas maze mazy mesa same seam yams yeas zyme aye mae may say sea yam yea yes ae am as ay em ma me my ye

aemsz mazes smaze maze mesa same seam mae sea ae am as em ma me

aemt mate meat tame team aet ate eat eta mae mat met tam tea ae am at em ma me ta

aemtt matte mate meat tame team teat aet ate eat eta mae mat met tam tat tea ae am at em ma me ta

aemttu mutate matte mate meat mute mutt tame taut team teat aet ate eat emu eta mae mat met tam tat tea tut ae am at em ma me mu ta um ut

aemty etyma matey meaty mate meat tame team aet ate aye eat eta mae mat may met tam tea yam yea yet ae am at ay em ma me my ta ye

aemuv mauve uvea ave emu mae ae am em ma me mu um

aemuzz mezuza maze mae emu ae am em ma me mu um

aemx exam mae ae am ax em ex ma me

aemz maze mae ae am em ma me

aen ane nae ae an en na ne

aennnpst pennants pennant. *See* **aennps aenpst**

aennnpt pennant. *See* **aennt aennp aenpt**

aennorst resonant atoners senator tanners treason. *See* **aennrt aenors aenort aenost**

aennorsu unreason neurons nonuser. *See* **aenors aeorsu ennoru**

aennostu tonneaus tonneau. *See* **aenost aenstu annost annstu**

aennosv novenas. *See* **aennov aenos aensv**

aennotu tonneau. *See* **aennt aenot ennot**

aennov novena novae aeon anon nave neon none nova oven vane ane ave eon nae one ova van ae an en na ne no on

aennoy anyone annoy aeon anon neon none yean ane any aye eon nae nay one yea yen yon ae an ay en na ne no on oy ye

aennp panne penna nape neap pane pean ane ape nae nap pan pea pen ae an en na ne pa pe

aennprs spanner. *See* **aennps aenrs aeprs**

aennprss spanners spanner. *See* **aennps aennss aenpss aenrss**

aennps pannes aspen napes neaps panes panne peans penna senna apes apse nape naps neap pane pans pean peas pens sane snap span ane ape asp ens nae nap pan pas pea pen sap sea sen spa ae an as en na ne pa pe

aennrst tanners. *See* **aenrst aennrt**

aennrstt entrants entrant natters tanners tenants. *See* **aennrt aenntt aenrst aenrtt**

aennrt tanner anent ante earn near neat rant rate rent tare tear tern aet ane ant are art ate ear eat era eta nae net ran rat ret tan tar tea ten ae an at en er na ne re ta

aennrtt entrant. *See* **aenrtt aenntt**

aennrty tannery. *See* **aennrt enrty aerty**

aennrw wanner anew earn near wane ware warn wean wear wren ane are awe awn ear era nae new ran raw wan war wen ae an aw en er na ne re we

aenns senna sane ane ens nae sea sen ae an as en na ne

aennss sennas senna sane seas ane ass ens ess nae sea sen ae an as en na ne

aennssw wanness. *See* **aennss anssw aensw**

aennstt tenants. *See* **aenntt aenst aenns**

aennstw wannest. *See* **aennt enstw aestw**

aennt anent ante neat aet ane ant ate eat eta nae net tan tea ten ae an at en na ne ta

aenntt tenant anent ante neat teat tent aet ane ant ate eat eta nae net tan tat tea ten ae an at en na ne ta

aennx annex ane axe nae ae an ax en na ne

aeno aeon ane eon nae one ae an en na ne no on

aenoopst teaspoon. *See* **aenops aenost aenpst enopst**

aenop paeon aeon nape neap nope open pane pean peon pone ane ape eon nae nap one ope pan pea pen ae an en na ne no on pa pe

aenoppr propane. *See* **aenppr anopr aeopr**

aenopprs propanes nappers persona propane snapper. *See* **aenops aenors aenppr aeopps**

aenoprs persona. *See* **anoprs aeoprs aenops enoprs aenors**

aenoprss personas parsons persona persons reasons. *See* **aenops aenors aenoss aenpss**

aenoprst operants arpents atoners entraps operant parents pastern patrons persona postern seaport senator tarpons treason trepans. *See* **aenops aenors aenort aenost**

aenoprt operant. *See* **aenprt aenort anoprt**

aenoprwy weaponry. *See* **aenopw aenpry aenrwy**

aenops paeons aeons aspen napes neaps opens paeon panes peans peons pones aeon apes apse eons epos naos nape naps neap noes nope nose ones open

opes pane pans pean peas pens peon
peso pone pons pose sane snap soap
span ane ape asp ens eon nae nap one
ope pan pas pea pen sap sea sen son
sop spa ae an as en na ne no on os pa
pe so

aenopsw weapons. *See* **aenops aenopw**

aenopw weapon paeon aeon anew enow
nape neap nope open pane pawn pean
peon pone wane wean ane ape awe
awn eon nae nap new now one ope owe
own pan paw pea pen pew wan wap
wen woe won ae an aw en na ne no on
ow pa pe we

aenorrrw narrower. *See* **aenrrw aeorrr anorrw**

aenors reason aeons arose arson earns
nares nears roans saner snare snore sonar aeon arse earn ears eons eras
naos near noes nose oars ones ores rase
roan roes rose sane sear sera soar sora
sore ane are ear ens eon era nae nor oar
one ore ran res roe sea sen son ae an as
en er na ne no on or os re so

aenorss reasons. *See* **anorss aenors ae-noss enorss aenrss**

aenorsst senators treasons atoners rea-
sons senator tensors treason. *See* **ae-nors aenort aenoss aenost**

aenorssu arsenous reasons arouses. *See*
aenors aenoss aenrss aenssu

aenorst atoners senator treason. *See*
aenrst aenort aenost enorst aeorst

aenorsuv ravenous nervous. *See* **aenors aenrsv aeorsu aorsuv**

aenort atoner ornate atone noter oaten
orate tenor toner aeon aero ante earn
near neat nota note rant rate rent roan
rota rote tare taro tear tern tone tora
tore torn aet ane ant are art ate ear eat
eon era eta nae net nor not oar oat one
ore ort ran rat ret roe rot tan tar tea ten
toe ton tor ae an at en er na ne no on or
re ta to

aenortty attorney. *See* **aenort aenott aenrtt aeortt**

aenos aeons aeon eons naos noes nose
ones sane ane ens eon nae one sea sen
son ae an as en na ne no on os so

aenoss season aeons noses oases aeon
eons naos noes nose ones ossa sane
seas sons ane ass ens eon ess nae one
sea sen son ae an as en na ne no on os
so

aenosss seasons. *See* **aenoss aesss**

aenossuu nauseous. *See* **aenoss aenssu enossu**

aenost atones aeons antes atone nates
notes oaten onset steno stoae stone
tones aeon ante ants east eats eons etas

naos neat nest nets noes nose nota note
oast oats ones sane seat sent seta snot
stoa tans teas tens toes tone tons aet
ane ant ate eat ens eon eta nae net not
oat one sat sea sen set son sot tan tea
ten toe ton ae an as at en na ne no on os
so ta to

aenostt notates. *See* **aenost aenott enostt**

aenot atone oaten aeon ante neat nota
note tone aet ane ant ate eat eon eta
nae net not oat one tan tea ten toe ton
ae an at en na ne no on ta to

aenott notate atone oaten aeon ante neat
nota note teat tent tone tote aet ane ant
ate eat eon eta nae net not oat one tan
tat tea ten toe ton tot ae an at en na ne
no on ta to

aenotz zonate atone azote oaten aeon
ante neat nota note tone zeta zoea zone
aet ane ant ate azo eat eon eta nae net
not oat one tan tea ten toe ton zoa ae
an at en na ne no on ta to

aenov novae aeon nave nova oven vane
ane ave eon nae one ova van ae an en
na ne no on

aenp nape neap pane pean ane ape nae
nap pan pea pen ae an en na ne pa pe

aenppr napper paper earn nape neap
near pane pare pean pear prep rape
reap repp ane ape are ear era nae nap
pan pap par pea pen pep per ran rap
rep ae an en er na ne pa pe re

aenpprs nappers snapper. *See* **aenppr aepprs**

aenprrst partners arpents entraps parents partner pastern trepans. *See*
aenprt aenpst aenrrt aenrst

aenprrt partner. *See* **aenprt aenrrt**

aenprsst pasterns aptness arpents entraps parents pastern pasters patness
repasts sparest trepans. *See* **aenprt aenpss aenpst aenrss**

aenprst arpents entraps parents pastern
trepans. *See* **aenprt aenpst aenrst aeprst**

aenprstt patterns transept arpents entraps natters parents pastern patents
pattens pattern patters spatter tapster
trepans. *See* **aenprt aenpst aenptt aenrst**

aenprsuv parvenus parvenu. *See* **aenrsv aeprsu aeprsv enprsu**

aenprsz panzers. *See* **aenprz aenps aenrs**

aenprt arpent enrapt entrap parent trepan paten pater peart prate taper ante
earn nape neap near neat pane pant
pare part pate pean pear peat pent pert
rant rape rapt rate reap rent tape tare
tarp tear tern trap aet ane ant ape apt
are art ate ear eat era eta nae nap net

pan par pat pea pen per pet ran rap rat
rep ret tan tap tar tea ten ae an at en er
na ne pa pe re ta

aenprtt pattern. *See* **aenprt aenrtt aenptt aeprtt**

aenpruv parvenu. *See* **aepru aeprv enpru**

aenpry napery apery payer repay yearn
aery earn nape nary neap near pane
pare pean pear pray prey pyre rape
reap yare yarn yean year ane any ape
are aye ear era nae nap nay pan par
pay pea pen per pry pya ran rap ray
rep rye yap yar yea yen yep ae an ay en
er na ne pa pe re ye

aenprz panzer earn nape neap near pane
pare pean pear rape raze reap ane ape
are ear era nae nap pan par pea pen per
ran rap rep zap ae an en er na ne pa pe
re

aenps aspen napes neaps panes peans
apes apse nape naps neap pane pans
pean peas pens sane snap span ane ape
asp ens nae nap pan pas pea pen sap
sea sen spa ae an as en na ne pa pe

aenpss aspens apses aspen napes neaps
panes peans snaps spans apes apse
asps nape naps neap pane pans pass
pean peas pens sane saps seas snap
span spas ane ape asp ass ens ess nae
nap pan pas pea pen sap sea sen spa ae
an as en na ne pa pe

aenpsssy synapses synapse. *See* **aenpss aepsss aesssy**

aenpsst aptness patness. *See* **aenpss aensst aepsst aenpst**

aenpsstw stewpans aptness patness
stewpan. *See* **aenpss aenpst aensst aepsst**

aenpssy synapse. *See* **aenpss aessy anpsy**

aenpst patens antes aspen napes nates
neaps panes pants paste paten pates
peans septa spate spent tapes ante ants
apes apse east eats etas nape naps neap
neat nest nets pane pans pant past pate
pats pean peas peat pens pent pest pets
sane seat sent sept seta snap span spat
step tans tape taps teas tens ante ant
ape apt asp ate eat ens eta nae nap net
pan pas pat pea pen pet sap sat sea sen
set spa tan tap tea ten ae an as at en na
ne pa pe ta

aenpstt patents pattens. *See* **aenpst aenptt**

aenpstu peanuts. *See* **aenpst aenptu aep-stu aenstu**

aenpstw stewpan. *See* **aenpst enstw anpsw**

aenpt paten ante nape neap neat pane
pant pate pean peat pent tape aet ane
ant ape apt ate eat eta nae nap net pan

pat pea pen pet tan tap tea ten ae an at en na ne pa pe ta

aenptt patent patten paten ante nape neap neat pane pant pate pean peat pent tape teat tent aet ane ant ape apt ate eat eta nae nap net pan pat pea pen pet tan tap tat tea ten ae an at en na ne pa pe ta

aenptu peanut paten taupe unapt ante aunt nape neap neat pane pant pate pean peat pent punt tape tuna tune aet ane ant ape apt ate eat eta nae nap net nut pan pat pea pen pet pun put tan tap tau tea ten tun tup ae an at en na ne nu pa pe ta up ut

aenqrrtu quartern quarter. *See* **aenrrt aenrtu aeqrtu enrrtu**

aenqsu queans quean sane anus ane ens nae qua sea sen sue sun use ae an as en na ne nu us

aenqu quean ane nae qua ae an en na ne nu

aenr earn near ane are ear era nae ran ae an en er na ne re

aenrr reran earn near rare rear ane are ear era err nae ran ae an en er na ne re

aenrrsw warrens. *See* **aenrrw aenrsw**

aenrrt errant ranter reran ante earn near neat rant rare rate rear rent tare tear tern aet ane ant are art ate ear eat era err eta nae net ran rat ret tan tar tea ten ae an at en er na ne re ta

aenrrty ternary. *See* **aerrty aenrrt**

aenrrw warren reran rawer anew earn near rare rear wane ware warn wean wear wren ane are awe awn ear era err nae new ran raw wan war wen ae an aw en er na ne re we

aenrs earns nares nears saner snare arse earn ears eras near rase sane sear sera ane are ear ens era nae ran res sea sen ae an as en er na ne re

aenrss snares arses earns nares nears rases saner sears snare arse earn ears eras near rase sane sear seas sera ane are ass ear ens era ess nae ran res sea sen ae an as en er na ne re

aenrsstt tartness natters tasters. *See* **aenrss aenrst aenrtt aensst**

aenrsstu saunters natures saunter unseats. *See* **aenrss aenrst aenrtu aensst**

aenrsstv servants versants servant starves taverns versant. *See* **aenrss aenrsv aenrtv**

aenrssw answers. *See* **aenrsw aenrss aerssw**

aenrst astern sterna antes aster earns nares nates nears rants rates rents saner snare stare stern tares tears terns ante ants arse arts earn ears east eats eras

erst etas near neat nest nets rant rase rate rats rent rest rets sane sear seat sent sera seta star tans tare tars tear teas tens tern tsar aet ane ant are art ate ear eat ens era eta nae net ran rat res ret sat sea sen set tan tar tea ten ae an as at en er na ne re ta

aenrstt natters. *See* **aenrst aenrtt aerstt**

aenrsttu taunters attunes entrust natters natures saunter stature taunter tautens tetanus truants. *See* **aenrst aenrtt aenrtu aenstu**

aenrstu natures saunter. *See* **aenrst aenrtu enrstu**

aenrstv servant taverns versant. *See* **aenrst aerstv aenrsv aenrtv**

aenrstw wanters. *See* **aenrsw aenrst aerstw enrstw aenrtw**

aenrstwy sternway wanters yawners. *See* **aenrst aenrsw aenrsy aenrtw**

aenrsv ravens avens avers earns nares naves nears raven raves saner saver snare vanes arse aver aves earn ears eras nave near rase rave revs sane save sear sera vane vans vase ane are ave ear ens era nae ran res rev sea sen van ae an as en er na ne re

aenrsw answer earns nares nears saner snare swear wanes wares warns weans wears wrens anew arse awes awns earn ears eras near news rase sane sawn sear sera sewn swan wane ware warn wars wean wear wens wren ane are awe awn ear ens era nae new ran raw res saw sea sen sew wan war was wen ae an as aw en er na ne re we

aenrswy yawners. *See* **aenrsw aerswy aenrsy aenrwy**

aenrsy senary yearns earns nares nears saner sayer snare yarns yeans yearn years aery arse ayes earn ears easy eras eyas nary near rase rays ryes sane sear sera yare yarn yean year yeas yens ane any are aye ear ens era nae nay ran ray res rye say sea sen yar yea yen yes ae an as ay en er na ne re ye

aenrtt natter tater tetra treat ante earn near neat rant rate rent tare tart tear teat tent tern tret aet ane ant are art ate ear eat era eta nae net ran rat ret tan tar tat tea ten ae an at en er na ne re ta

aenrttu taunter. *See* **aenttu aenrtt aenrtu anrttu**

aenrtu nature tuner ante aunt earn near neat rant rate rent rune runt tare tear tern true tuna tune turn urea aet ane ant are art ate ear eat era eta nae net nut ran rat ret rue run rut tan tar tau tea ten tun urn ae an at en er na ne nu re ta ut

aenrtv tavern avert raven trave ante aver earn nave near neat rant rate rave rent tare tear tern vane vent vert aet ane ant are art ate ave ear eat era eta nae net ran rat ret rev tan tar tav tea ten van vat vet ae an at en er na ne re ta

aenrtw wanter water anew ante earn near neat newt rant rate rent tare tear tern wane want ware warn wart wean wear wren aet ane ant are art ate awe awn ear eat era eta nae net new ran rat raw ret tan tar tea ten wan war wen wet ae an at aw en er na ne re ta we

aenrtwyy entryway. *See* **aenrtw aenrwy aertwy**

aenrv raven aver earn nave near rave vane ane are ave ear era nae ran rev van ae an en er na ne re

aenrwy yawner yearn weary aery anew awry earn nary near wane wany ware warn wary wean wear wren yare yarn yawn yean year ane any are awe awn aye ear era nae nay new ran raw ray rye wan war way wen wye yar yaw yea yen yew ae an aw ay en er na ne re we ye

aenry yearn aery earn nary near yare yarn yean year ane any are aye ear era nae nay ran ray rye yar yea yen ae an ay en er na ne re ye

aens sane ane ens nae sea sen ae an as en na ne

aenssst assents. *See* **aensst aessst**

aenssstv vastness assents. *See* **aensst aessst aesstv**

aensst assent sanest antes asset nates nests sates seats tasse ante ants east eats etas neat nest nets sane seas seat sent seta sets tans tass teas tens aet ane ant ass ate eat ens ess eta nae net sat sea sen set tan tea ten ae an as at en na ne ta

aenssttu tautness attunes statues tautens tetanus unseats. *See* **aensst aenssu aenstu aenttu**

aenssttx sextants sextant. *See* **aensst aenttx aesstt**

aenssu unseats. *See* **aenssu aensst ensstu aenstu**

aensstxy syntaxes. *See* **aensst aensty aessty anstxy**

aenssu anuses anus sane seas sues suns uses ane ass ens ess nae sea sen sue sun use ae an as en na ne nu us

aenst antes nates ante ants east eats etas neat nest nets sane seat sent seta tans teas tens aet ane ant ate eat ens eta nae net sat sea sen set tan tea ten ae an as at en na ne ta

aensttu attunes tautens tetanus. *See* **aesttu aenttu ansttu**

aensttx sextant. *See* **aenttx aenst aestt**

aenstu unseat antes aunts nates tunas tunes ante ants anus aunt east eats etas neat nest nets nuts sane seat sent seta stun suet tans teas tens tuna tune tuns aet ane ant ate eat ens eta nae net nut sat sea sen set sue sun tan tau tea ten tun use ae an as at en na ne nu ta us ut

aensty yentas antes antsy nasty nates tansy yeans yeast yenta ante ants ayes east easy eats etas eyas neat nest nets sane seat sent seta stay tans teas tens yean yeas yens ae an as ay ate aye eat ens eta nae nay net sat say sea sen set sty tan tea ten yea yen yes yet ae an as at ay en na ne ta ye

aensuy uneasy yeans yuans anus ayes easy eyas sane yean yeas yens yuan ane any aye ens nae nay say sea sen sue sun use yea yen yes ae an as ay en na ne nu us ye

aensv avens naves vanes aves nave sane save vane vans vase ane ave ens nae sea sen van ae an as en na ne

aensw wanes weans anew awes awns news sane sawn sewn swan wane wean wens ane awe awn ens nae new saw sea sen sew wan was wen ae an as aw en na ne we

aensy yeans ayes easy eyas sane yean yeas yens ane any aye ens nae nay say sea sen yea yen yes ae an as ay en na ne ye

aent ante neat aet ane ant ate eat eta nae net tan tea ten ae an at en na ne ta

aenttu attune tauten taunt ante aunt neat taut teat tent tuna tune aet ane ant ate eat eta nae net nut tan tat tau tea ten tun tut ae an at en na ne nu ta ut

aenttx extant ante neat next teat tent text aet ane ant ate axe eat eta nae net tan tat tax tea ten ae an at ax en ex na ne ta

aenty yenta ante neat yean aet ane ant any ate aye eat eta nae nay net tan tea ten yea yen yet ae an at ay en na ne ta ye

aenv nave vane ane ave nae van ae an en na ne

aenw anew wane wean ane awe awn nae new wan wen ae an aw en na ne we

aenwx waxen anew wane wean ane awe awn axe nae new wan wax wen ae an aw ax en ex na ne we

aeny yean ane any aye nae nay yea yen ae an ay en na ne ye

aeoopps papoose. *See* **aeopps eoopps**

aeooppss papooses apposes opposes papoose. *See* **aeopps eoopps**

aeooprrt operator praetor prorate trooper. *See* **aoorrt aoprrt eooprr eoorrt**

aeoopstt potatoes teapots. *See* **aeoptt aooptt**

aeoorttt tattooer. *See* **aeortt aoottt**

aeopprsv approves approve. *See* **aeopps aeoprs aeppps aeprsv**

aeopprv approve. *See* **aeopr aeppr aeprv**

aeopps appose popes apes apse epos opes paps peas peps peso pope pops pose soap ape asp ope pap pas pea pep pop sap sea sop spa ae as os pa pe so

aeoppss apposes. *See* **aeopps aepss aeoss**

aeopqsu opaques. *See* **aeopqu aepsu**

aeopqu opaque ape ope pea qua ae pa pe up

aeopr opera aero pare pear pore proa rape reap repo rope ape are ear era oar ope ore par pea per pro rap rep roe ae er or pa pe re

aeoprrst praetors prorates parrots porters praetor presort pretors prorate reports roaster seaport. *See* **aeoprs aeorst aeprrs aeprst**

aeoprrt praetor prorate. *See* **aoprrt eoprrt**

aeoprs operas arose opera pares parse pears pores poser proas prose rapes reaps repos ropes spare spear spore aero apes apse arse ears epos eras oars opes ores pare pars pear peas peso pore pose proa pros rape raps rase rasp reap repo reps roes rope rose sear sera soap soar sora sore spar ape are asp ear era oar ope ore par pas pea per pro rap rep res roe sap sea sop spa ae as er or os pa pe re so

aeoprsst seaports pasters pastors posters prestos repasts seaport sparest. *See* **aeoprs aeorst aeprss aeprst**

aeoprssv overpass. *See* **aeoprs aeprss aeprsv aerssv**

aeoprst seaport. *See* **aeoprs aeorst aeprst aoprst eoprst**

aeoprstt prostate patters potters protest rotates seaport spatter spotter tapster teapots toaster. *See* **aeoprs aeoptt aeorst aeortt**

aeoprstu apterous pasture petrous posture seaport troupes. *See* **aeoprs aeorst aeorsu aeprst**

aeoprsvy overpays overpay. *See* **aeoprs aeprsv aeprsy aoprsy**

aeoprvy overpay. *See* **aoprvy aepry aeopr**

aeopstt teapots. *See* **aeoptt eopst aepst**

aeopsty teapoys. *See* **aeopty eopst aepst**

aeopstz topazes. *See* **aeostz eopst aepst**

aeoptt teapot atop pate peat poet tape teat tope tote aet ape apt ate eat eta oat ope pat pea pet pot tap tat tea toe top tot ae at pa pe ta to

aeopty teapoy peaty atop pate peat poet tape tope type aet ape apt ate aye eat eta oat ope pat pay pea pet pot pya tap tea toe top toy yap yea yep yet ae at ay oy pa pe ta to ye

aeoqrstu quaestor equator quartes quartos questor quoters roquets torques. *See* **aeorst aeorsu aeqrsu aeqrtu**

aeoqrsuv vaqueros vaquero quavers. *See* **aeorsu aeqrsu aeqruv aorsuv**

aeoqrtu equator. *See* **aeqrtu aoqrtu eoqrtu**

aeoqruv vaquero. *See* **aeqruv eoqru**

aeoqsuu aqueous. *No 6s or 5s*

aeor aero are ear era oar ore roe ae er or re

aeorrr roarer rarer error aero rare rear roar are ear era err oar ore roe ae er or re

aeorrssv savorers savorer. *See* **aerrsv aerssv aorssv eorrsv**

aeorrst roaster. *See* **aerrst aeorst eorrst aorrst**

aeorrstt rostrate ratters restart retorts roaster rotates rotters starter stertor toaster. *See* **aeorst aeortt aerrst aerstt**

aeorrsv savorer. *See* **aerrsv eorrsv**

aeorrtzz terrazzo. *See* **eorrzz**

aeors arose aero arse ears eras oars ores rase roes rose sear sera soar sora sore are ear era oar ore res roe sea ae as er or os re so

aeorssss assessor. *See* **aessss**

aeorsstt toasters rotates stators tasters toaster. *See* **aeorst aeortt aersst aerstt**

aeorsstx storaxes. *See* **aeorst aersst aerstx aorsst**

aeorssu arouses. *See* **aeorsu aerssu eorssu**

aeorst orates arose aster orate rates roast rotas rotes stare stoae store tares taros tears toras aero arse arts ears east eats eras erst etas oars oast oats ores orts rase rate rats rest rets roes rose rota rote rots sear seat sera seta soar sora sore sort star stoa tare taro tars tear teas toes tora tore tors tsar aet are art ate ear eat era eta oar oat ore ort rat res ret roe rot sat sea set sot tar tea toe tor ae as at er or os re so ta to

aeorstt rotates toaster. *See* **aeorst eorstt aeortt aorstt aerstt**

aeorsttt attestor testator rotates stretto tatters toaster totters. *See* **aeorst aeortt aerstt aorstt**

aeorstuw outwears outwear. *See* **aeorst aeorsu aerstw eorstu**

aeorstvy overstay. *See* **aeorst aerstv aersty aorsvy**

aeorsu arouse arose rouse ureas aero arse ears eras oars ores ours rase roes rose rues ruse sear sera soar sora sore sour sura sure urea user are ear era oar ore our res roe rue sea sou sue use ae as er or os re so us

aeorsvw oversaw. *See* **aersvw aeors aosvw**

aeort orate aero rate rota rote tare taro tear tora tore aet are art ate ear eat era eta oar oat ore ort rat ret roe rot tar tea toe tor ae at er or re ta to

aeortt rotate orate otter tarot tater tetra torte toter treat aero rate rota rote tare taro tart tear teat tora tore tort tote tret trot aet are art ate ear eat era eta oar oat ore ort rat ret roe rot tar tat tea toe tor tot ae at er or re ta to

aeortuw outwear. *See* **aeort eortu eortw**

aeortvx overtax. *See* **eortvx aertv aertx**

aeoss oases seas ossa ass ess sea ae as os so

aeost stoae east eats etas oast oats seat seta stoa teas toes aet ate eat eta oat sat sea set sot tea toe ae as at os so ta to

aeostz azotes azote stoae zetas zoeas east eats etas oast oats seat seta stoa teas toes zest zeta zoea aet ate azo eat eta oat sat sea set sot tea toe zoa ae as at os so ta to

aeosz zoeas zoea azo sea zoa ae as os so

aeotv ovate veto vote aet ate ave eat eta oat ova tav tea toe vat vet ae at ta to

aeotz azote zoea zeta aet ate azo eat eta oat tea toe zoa ae at ta to

aeoz zoea azo zoa ae

aep ape pea ae pa pe

aeppr paper pare pear prep rape reap repp ape are ear era pap par pea pep per rap rep ae er pa pe re

aepprr rapper paper pare parr pear prep rape rare reap rear repp ape are ear era err pap par pea pep per rap rep ae er pa pe re

aepprrs rappers. *See* **aepprs aepprr aeprrs**

aepprrst strapper trappers rappers trapper. *See* **aepprr aepprs aeprrs aeprst**

aepprrsw wrappers rappers wrapper. *See* **aepprr aepprs aeprrs aeprrw**

aepprrt trapper. *See* **aepprr aeprt**

aepprrw wrapper. *See* **aepprr aeprrw**

aepprs papers sapper paper pares parse pears preps rapes reaps repps spare spear apes apse arse ears eras paps pare pars pear peas peps prep rape raps rase rasp reap repp reps sear sera spar ape are asp ear era pap par pas

aepprsu paupers. *See* **aepprs aeprsu aeppru epprsu**

aepprsy prepays yappers. *See* **aepprs aeppry aeprsy**

aeppru pauper paper pareu pupae upper pare pear prep pupa pure rape reap repp urea ape are ear era pap par pea pep per pup rap rep rue ae er pa pe re up

aeppry papery prepay yapper apery paper payer repay aery pare pear pray prep prey pyre rape reap repp yare year ape are aye ear era pap par pay pea pep per pry pya rap ray rep rye yap yar yea yep ae ay er pa pe re ye

aeppstt tappets. *See* **aeppttt aepst aesttt**

aeppstu pupates. *See* **aepptu aepstu**

aepptt tappet pate peat tape teat aet ape apt ate eat eta pap pat pea pep pet tap tat tea ae at pa pe ta

aepptu pupate pupae taupe pate peat pupa tape aet ape apt ate eat eta pap pat pea pep pet pup put tap tau tea tup ae at pa pe ta up ut

aeppu pupae pupa ape pap pea pep pup ae pa pe up

aepqrstu parquets parquet pasture quartes. *See* **aeprst aeprsu aepstu aeqrsu**

aepqrtu parquet. *See* **aeqrtu eprtu aepru**

aepr pare pear rape reap ape are ear era par pea per rap rep ae er pa pe re

aeprrs rasper sparer pares parrs parse pears rapes reaps rears spare spear apes apse arse ears eras errs pare parr pars pear peas rape raps rare rase rasp reap rear reps sear sera spar ape are asp ear era err par pas pea per rap rep res sap sea spa ae as er pa pe re

aeprrss raspers sparers sparser. *See* **aeprss aeprrs**

aeprrstu raptures parures pasture rapture. *See* **aeprrs aeprru aeprst aeprsu**

aeprrsu parures. *See* **aeprsu aeprru eprrsu aeprrs**

aeprrsy prasper ppayers. *See* **aeprsy aeprrs eprrsy**

aeprrtu rapture. *See* **aeprru eprtu aeprt**

aeprrty partyer partery. *See* **aepry aprry aprty**

aeprru parure pareu purer pare parr pear pure purr rape rare reap rear urea ape are ear era err par pea per rap rep rue ae er pa pe re up

aeprrw prewar rawer pare parr pear rape rare reap rear ware warp wear wrap ape are awe ear era err par paw pea per pew rap raw rep wap war ae aw er pa pe re we

aeprry prayer apery parry payer perry repay aery pare parr pear pray prey pyre rape rare reap rear yare year ape are aye ear era err par pay pea per pry pya rap ray rep rye yap yar yea yep ae ay er pa pe re ye

aeprs pares parse pears rapes reaps spare spear apes apse arse ears eras pare pars pear peas rape raps rase rasp reap reps sear sera spar ape are asp ear era par pas pea per rap rep res sap sea spa ae as er pa pe re

aeprss parses passer spares sparse spears apses arses pares parse pears press rapes rases rasps reaps sears spare spars spear apes apse arse asps ears eras pare pars pass pear peas rape raps rase rasp reap reps saps sear seas sera spar spas ape are asp ass ear era ess par pas pea per rap rep res sap sea spa ae as er pa pe re

aeprsss passers. *See* **aeprss aepsss**

aeprssst sparsest trespass asserts passers pasters repasts sparest. *See* **aeprss aeprst aepsss aepsst**

aeprsst pasters repasts sparest. *See* **aersst aeprss aeprst aepsst aprsst**

aeprsstt spatters tapsters pasters patters repasts sparest spatter tapster tasters. *See* **aeprss aeprst aeprtt aepsst**

aeprsstu pastures pasters pasture petasus repasts sparest. *See* **aeprss aeprst aeprsu aepsst**

aeprssy pessary. *See* **aeprss aeprsy aerssy aprssy**

aeprst paster paters prates repast tapers aster pares parse parts paste pater pates pears peart prate rapes rates reaps septa spare spate spear sprat stare strap strep taper tapes tares tarps tears traps apes apse arse arts ears east eats eras erst etas pare pars part past pate pats pear peas peat pert pest pets rape raps rapt rase rasp rate rats reap reps rest rets sear sept serat sera seta spar spat star step tape taps tare tarp tars tear teas trap tsar aet ape apt are art asp ate ear eat era eta par pas pat pea per pet rap rat rep res ret sap sat sea set spa tap tar tea ae as at er pa pe re ta

aeprstt patters spatter tapster. *See* **aeprst aeprtt aersttt**

aeprstty tapestry patters spatter tapster yatters. *See* **aeprst aeprsy aeprtt aersttt**

aeprstu pasture. *See* **eprstu aeprsu aeprst aepstu**

aeprsu pareus pares pareu parse pause pears purse rapes reaps spare spear sprue super ureas apes apse arse ears eras pare pars pear peas pure rape raps rase rasp reap reps rues ruse sear sera spar spue spur sura sure upas urea user ape are asp ear era par pas pea per pus rap rep res rue sap sea spa sue sup use ae as er pa pe re up us

aeprsv pavers avers pares parse parve paver paves pears rapes raves reaps saver spare spear apes apse arse aver aves ears eras pare pars pave pear peas rape raps rase rasp rave reap reps revs save sear sera spar vase ape are asp ave ear era par pas pea per rap rep res rev sap sea spa ae as er pa pe re

aeprsy payers repays apery pares parse payer pears prays preys pyres rapes raspy reaps repay sayer spare spear spray years aery apes apse arse ayes ears easy eras espy eyas pare pars pays pear peas pray prey pyas pyre rape raps rase rasp rays reap reps ryes sear sera spar spay spry yaps yare year yeas ape are asp aye ear era par pas pay pea per pry pya rap ray rep res rye sap say sea spa spy yap yar yea yep yes ae as ay er pa pe re ye

aeprt pater peart prate taper pare part pate pear peat pert rape rapt rate reap tape tare tarp tear trap aet ape apt are art ate eat era eta par pat pea per pet rap rat rep ret tap tar tea ae at er pa pe re ta

aeprtt patter pater peart prate taper tater tetra treat pare part pate pear peat pert rape rapt rate reap tape tare tarp tart tear teat trap tret aet ape apt are art ate ear eat era eta par pat pea per pet rap rat rep ret tap tar tat tea ae at er pa pe re ta

aeprtx pretax extra pater peart prate taper taxer apex pare part pate pear peat pert rape rapt rate reap tape tare tarp tear trap aet ape apt are art ate axe ear eat era eta par pat pax pea per pet rap rat rep ret rex tap tar tax tea ae at ax er ex pa pe re ta

aeprtxy apteryx. *See* **aeprtx aepry aprty**

aepru pareu pare pear pure rape reap urea ape are ear era par pea per rap rep rue ae er pa pe re up

aeprv parve paver aver pare pave pear rape rave reap ape are ave ear era par pea per rap rep rev ae er pa pe re

aepry apery payer repay aery pare pear pray prey pyre rape reap yare year ape are aye ear era par pay pea per pry pya

rap ray rep rye yap yar yea yep ae ay er pa pe re ye

aeps apes apse peas ape asp pas pea sap sea spa ae as pa pe

aepss apses apes apse asps pass peas saps seas spas ape asp ass ess pas pea sap sea spa ae as pa pe

aepsss passes apses asses apes apse asps pass peas saps sass seas spas ape asp ass ess pas pea sap sea spa ae as pa pe

aepsst pastes spates apses asset paste pasts pates pests sates seats septa spate spats steps tapes tasse apes apse asps east eats etas pass past pate pats peas peat pest pets saps seas seat sept seta sets spas spat step tape taps tass teas aet ape apt asp ass ate eat ess eta pas pat pea pet sap sat sea set spa tap tea ae as at pa pe ta

aepsstu petasus. *See* **aepsst aepssu epsstu apsstu aepstu**

aepssu pauses apses pause spues apes apse asps pass peas puss saps seas spas spue sues sups upas uses ape asp ass ess pas pea pus sap sea spa sue sup use ae as pa pe up us

aepssz spazes apses apes apse asps pass peas saps seas spas spaz zaps ape asp ass ess pas pea sap sea spa zap ae as pa pe

aepst paste pates septa spate tapes apes apse east eats etas past pate pats peas peat pest pets seat sept seta spat step tape taps teas aet ape apt asp ate eat eta pas pat pea pet sap sat sea set spa tap tea ae as at pa pe ta

aepstu taupes paste pates pause septa setup spate stupa stupe tapes taupe upset apes apse east eats etas past pate pats peas peat pest pets puts seat sept seta spat spue step suet tape taps teas tups upas aet ape apt asp ate eat eta pas pat pea pet pus put sap sat sea set spa sue sup tap tau tea tup use ae as at pa pe ta up us ut

aepsu pause apes apse peas spue upas ape asp pas pea pus sap sea spa sue sup use ae as pa pe up us

aepsux auspex pause paxes apes apex apse axes peas spue upas ape asp axe pas pax pea pus sap sax sea sex spa sue sup use ae as ax ex pa pe up us

aepsv paves apes apse aves pave peas save vase ape asp ave pas pea sap sea spa ae as pa pe

aepsx paxes apes apex apse axes peas ape asp axe pas pax pea sap sax sea sex spa ae as ax ex pa pe

aept pate peat tape aet ape apt ate eat eta pat pea pet tap tea ae at pa pe ta

aeptu taupe pate peat tape aet ape apt ate eat eta pat pea pet put tap tau tea tup ae at pa pe ta up ut

aepty peaty pate peat tape type aet ape apt ate aye eat eta pat pay pea pet pya tap tea yap yea yep yet ae at ay pa pe ta ye

aepv pave ape ave pea ae pa pe

aepvy peavy pave ape ave aye pay pea pya yap yea yep ae ay pa pe ye

aepx apex ape pax pea ae ax ex pa pe

aeqrrstu quarters quarter quartes squarer. *See* **aeqrsu aeqrtu aerrst aqrstu**

aeqrrsu squarer. *See* **aeqrsu aerrs errsu**

aeqrrtu quarter. *See* **aeqrtu errtu**

aeqrsstu squarest squares quartes. *See* **aeqrsu aeqrtu aersst aerssu**

aeqrssu squares. *See* **aeqrsu aerssu**

aeqrsttu quartets squatter quartes quartet stature. *See* **aeqrsu aeqrtu aerstt aesttu**

aeqrstu quartes. *See* **aeqrtu aqrstu aeqrsu**

aeqrstuz quartzes quartes. *See* **aeqrsu aeqrtu aerstz aersuz**

aeqrsu square ureas arse ears eras rase rues ruse sear sera sura sure urea user are ear era qua res rue sea sue use ae as er re us

aeqrsuv quavers. *See* **aeqrsu aeqruv**

aeqrttu quartet. *See* **aeqrtu aertt erttu**

aeqrtu quarte quart rate tare tear true urea aet are art ate ear eat era eta qat qua rat ret rue rut tar tau tea ae at er re ta ut

aeqruv quaver aver rave urea uvea are ave ear era qua rev rue ae er re

aeqruvy quavery. *See* **aeqruv eqruy**

aeqsssu quasses. *See* **aesss aqssu**

aeqsuy queasy quays ayes easy eyas quay yeas aye qua say sea sue use yea yes ae as ay us ye

aequyz queazy quay aye qua yea ae ay ye

aer are ear era ae er re

aerr rare rear are ear era err ae er re

aerrr rarer rare rear are ear era err ae er re

aerrs rears arse ears eras errs rare rase rear sear sera are ear era err res sea ae as er re

aerrsst arrests. *See* **aerrst aersst**

aerrsstt restarts starters arrests ratters restart starter tasters. *See* **aerrst aerrtt aersst aerstt**

aerrst arrest rarest aster rates rears stare tares tears arse arts ears east eats eras errs erst etas rare rase rate rats rear rest rets sear seat sera seta star tare tars tear teas tsar aet are art ate ear eat era err eta rat res ret sat sea set tar tea ae as at er re ta

aerrstt ratters restart starter. *See* **aerrst aerrtt aerstt**

aerrstuy treasury estuary. *See* **aerrst aerrty aersty**

aerrsv ravers avers raves rears saver arse aver aves ears eras errs rare rase rave rear revs save sear sera vase are ave ear era err res rev sea ae as er re

aerrtt ratter tater tetra treat rare rate rear tare tart tear teat tret aet are art ate ear eat era err eta rat ret tar tat tea ae at er re ta

aerrty artery retry tarry teary terry aery arty rare rate rear tare tear tray yare year aet are art ate aye ear eat era err eta rat ray ret rye tar tea try yar yea yet ae at ay er re ta ye

aerrw rawer rare rear ware wear are awe ear era err raw war ae aw er re we

aers arse ears eras rase sear sera are ear era res sea ae as er re

aerss arses rases sears arse ears eras rase sear seas sera are ass ear era ess res sea ae as er re

aerssst strasses asserts. *See* **aersst aessss**

aersssst asserts. *See* **aersst aessst arssst ersssst**

aerssssu assures. *See* **aerssu aesss**

aersst assert asters stares arses asset aster rases rates rests sates sears seats stare stars tares tasse tears trass tress tsars arse arts ears east eats eras erst etas rase rate rats rest rets sear seas seat sera seta sets star tare tars tass tear teas tsar aet are art ass ate ear eat era ess eta rat res ret sat sea set tar tea ae as at er re ta

aersstt tasters. *See* **aersst arsstt aesstt aerstt**

aerssttu statures statues stature stratus tasters. *See* **aersst aerssu aerstt aesstt**

aerssttw swatters swatter tasters wasters. *See* **aersst aerssw aerstt aerstw**

aersstux surtaxes. *See* **aersst aerssu aerstx arsstu**

aersstv starves. *See* **aersst aerstv aerssv aesstv ersstv**

aersstw wasters. *See* **aersst aerstw arsstw ersstw aerssw**

aerssu assure arses rases ruses sears suras ureas users arse ears eras rase rues ruse sear seas sera sues sura sure urea user uses are ass ear era ess res rue sea sue use ae as er re us

aerssv savers arses avers rases raves saver saves sears vases arse aver aves ears eras rase rave revs save sear seas

sera vase are ass ave ear era ess res rev sea ae as er re

aerssw swears arses rases sears swear wares wears arse awes ears eras rase saws sear seas sera sews ware wars wear are ass awe ear era ess raw res saw sea sew war was ae as aw er re we

aersswy sawyers. *See* **aerswy aerssy aerssw**

aerssy sayers arses essay rases sayer sears years aery arse ayes ears easy eras eyas rase rays ryes says sear seas sera yare year yeas are ass aye ear era ess ray res rye say sea yar yea yes ae as ay er re ye

aerst aster rates stare tares tears arse arts ears east eats eras erst etas rase rate rats rest rets sear seat sera seta star tare tars tear teas tsar aet are art ate ear eat era eta rat res ret sat sea set tar tea ae as at er re ta

aerstt taster taters tetras treats aster rates stare start state tares tarts taste tater tears teats testa tetra treat trets arse arts ears east eats eras erst etas rase rate rats rest rets sear seat sera seta star stet tare tars tart tats tear teas teat test tret tsar aet are art ate ear eat era eta rat res ret sat sea set tar tat tea ae as at er re ta

aersttt tatters. *See* **aesttt aerstt aerttt**

aersttu stature. *See* **aesttu ersttu**

aersttvy travesty yatters. *See* **aerstt aerstv aersty aertty**

aersttw swatter. *See* **aerstw aerstt**

aerstty yatters. *See* **aersty aertty**

aerstuu auteurs. *See* **aertuu erstuu aersuu**

aerstuy estuary. *See* **aersty erstuy**

aerstv averts starve traves aster avers avert rates raves saver stare stave tares tears trave verst verts arse arts aver aves ears east eats eras erst etas rase rate rats rave rest rets revs save sear seat sera seta star tare tars tavs tear teas tsar vase vast vats vert vest vets aet are art ate ave ear eat era eta rat res ret rev sat sea set tar tav tea vat vet ae as at er re ta

aerstw rawest waster waters aster rates stare straw strew swart swear sweat tares tears trews wares warts waste water wears wrest arse arts awes ears east eats eras erst etas rase rate rats rest rets sear seat sera seta star stew swat tare tars tear teas tsar ware wars wart wast wear west wets aet are art ate awe ear eat era eta rat raw res ret sat saw sea set sew tar tea war was wet ae as at aw er re ta we

aerstx extras taxers aster extra rates stare tares taxer taxes tears arse arts axes ears east eats eras erst etas rase rate rats rest rets sear seat sera seta sext star tare tars tear teas tsar aet are art ate axe ear eat era eta rat res ret rex sat sax sea set sex tar tax tea ae as at ax er ex re ta

aersty estray artsy aster rates satyr sayer stare stray tares tears teary trays years yeast aery arse arts arty ayes ears east easy eats eras erst etas eyas rase rate rats rays rest rets ryes sear seat sera seta star stay tare tars tear teas tray tsar yare year yeas aet are art ate aye ear eat era eta rat ray res ret rye sat say sea set sty tar tea try yar yea yes yet ae as at ay er re ta ye

aerstz ersatz aster rates razes stare tares tears zetas arse arts ears east eats eras erst etas rase rate rats raze rest rets sear seat sera seta star tare tars tear teas tsar tzar zest zeta aet are art ate ear eat era eta rat res ret sat sea set tar tea ae as at er re ta

aersu ureas arse ears eras rase rues ruse sear sera sura sure urea user are ear era res rue sea sue use ae as er re us

aersuu uraeus ureas arse ears eras rase rues ruse sear sera sura sure urea urus user are ear era res rue sea sue use ae as er re us

aersuz azures azure razes ureas arse ears eras rase raze rues ruse sear sera sura sure urea user are ear era res rue sea sue use ae as er re us

aersv avers raves saver arse aver aves ears eras rase rave revs save sear sera vase are ave ear era res rev sea ae as er re

aersvv varves avers raves saver varve arse aver aves ears eras rase rave revs save sear sera vase are ave ear era res rev sea ae as er re

aersvw wavers avers raves saver swear wares waver waves wears arse aver aves awes ears eras rase rave revs save sear sera vase ware wars wear are ave awe ear era raw res rev saw sea sew war was ae as aw er re we

aersw swear wares wears arse awes ears eras rase sear sera ware wars wear are awe ear era raw res saw sea sew war was ae as aw er re we

aerswx waxers swear wares waxer waxes wears arse awes axes ears eras rase sear sera ware wars wear are awe axe ear era raw res rex saw sax sea sew sex war was wax ae as aw ax er ex re we

aerswy sawyer sayer swear wares wears weary years aery arse awes awry ayes ears easy eras eyas rase rays ryes sear sera sway ware wars wary ways wear wyes yare yaws year yeas yews are awe aye ear era raw ray res rye saw say sea sew war was way wye yar yaw yea yes yew ae as aw ay er re we ye

aersy sayer years aery arse ayes ears easy eras eyas rase rays ryes sear sera yare year yeas are aye ear era ray res rye say sea yar yea yes ae as ay er re ye

aersz razes arse ears eras rase raze sear sera are ear era res sea ae as er re

aerszz razzes razes arse ears eras rase raze razz sear sera are ear era res sea ae as er re

aert rate tare tear aet are art ate ear eat era eta rat ret tar tea ae at er re ta

aertt tater tetra treat rate tare tart tear teat tret aet are art ate ear eat era eta rat ret tar tat tea ae at er re ta

aerttt tatter tater tetra treat rate tare tart tear teat tret aet are art ate ear eat era eta rat ret tar tat tea ae at er re ta

aertty treaty yatter ratty tater teary tetra treat aery arty rate tare tart tear teat tray tret yare year aet are art ate aye ear eat era eta rat ray ret rye tar tat tea try yar yea yet ae at ay er re ta ye

aertuu auteur rate tare tear true urea aet are art ate ear eat era eta rat ret rue rut tar tau tea ae at er re ta ut

aertv avert trave aver rate rave tare tear vert aet are art ate ave ear eat era eta rat ret rev tar tav tea vat vet ae at er re ta

aertw water rate tare tear ware wart wear aet are art ate awe ear eat era eta rat raw ret tar tea war wet ae at aw er re ta we

aertwy watery teary warty water weary aery arty awry rate tare tear tray ware wart wary wear yare year aet are art ate awe aye ear eat era eta rat raw ray ret rye tar tea try war way wet wye yar yaw yea yet yew ae at aw ay er re ta we ye

aertx extra taxer rate tare tear aet are art ate axe ear eat era eta rat ret rex tar tax tea ae at ax er ex re ta

aerty teary aery arty rate tare tear tray yare year aet are art ate aye ear eat era eta rat ray ret rye tar tea try yar yea yet ae at ay er re ta ye

aeru urea are ear era rue ae er re

aeruz azure urea raze are ear era rue ae er re

aerv aver rave are ave ear era rev ae er re

aervv varve aver rave are ave ear era rev ae er re

aervw waver aver rave ware wave wear are ave awe ear era raw rev war ae aw er re we

aervwy wavery waver weary aery aver awry rave vary very ware wary wave wavy wear yare year are ave awe aye ear era raw ray rev rye war way wye yar yaw yea yew ae av ay er re we ye

aerw ware wear are awe ear era raw war ae aw er re we

aerwx waxer ware wear are awe axe ear era raw rex war wax ae aw ax er ex re we

aerwy weary aery awry ware wary wear yare year are awe aye ear era raw ray rye war way wye yar yaw yea yew ae aw ay er re we ye

aery aery yare year are aye ear era ray rye yar yea ae ay er re ye

aerz raze are ear era ae er re

aes sea ae as

aess seas ass ess sea ae as

aesss asses seas sass ass ess sea ae as

aessss assess sasses asses seas sass ass ess sea ae as

aessst assets tasses asses asset sates seats tasse east eats etas sass seas seat seta sets tass teas aet ass ate eat ess eta sat sea set tea ae as at ta

aesssttu statuses statues. *See* **aessst aesstt aesttu**

aesssy essays asses essay sassy ayes easy eyas sass says seas yeas ass aye ess say sea yea yes ae as ay ye

aesst asset seats seas tasse east eats etas seas seat seta sets tass teas aet ass ate eat ess eta sat sea set tea ae as at ta

aesstt states tastes asset sates seats state stets tasse taste teats testa tests east eats etas seas seat seta sets stet tass tats teas teat test aet ass ate eat ess eta sat sea set tat tea ae as at ta

aessttt attests. *See* **aestt aesstt**

aesstttu statutes attests statues statute. *See* **aesstt aesttu**

aesstu statues. *See* **aesttu assttu aesstt**

aesstv staves asset sates saves seats stave tasse vases vests aves east eats etas save seas seat sets tass tavs teas vase vast vats vest vets aet ass ate ave eat ess eta sat sea set tav tea vat vet ae as at ta

aesstw sweats wastes asset sates seats stews swats sweat tasse waste wests awes east eats etas saws seas seat seta sets sews stew swat tass teas wast west wets aet ass ate awe eat ess eta sat saw sea set sew tea was wet ae as at aw ta we

aessty yeasts asset essay sates seats stays tasse yeast ayes east easy eats etas eyas

says seas seat seta sets stay tass teas yeas aet ass ate aye eat ess eta sat say sea set sty tea yea yes yet ae as at ay ta ye

aessv saves vases aves save seas vase ass ave ess sea ae as

aessx saxes axes seas ass axe ess sax sea sex ae as ax ex

aessy essay ayes easy eyas says seas yeas ass aye ess say sea yea yes ae as ay ye

aest east eats etas seat seta teas aet ate eat eta sat sea set tea ae as at ta

aestt state taste teats testa east eats etas seat seta stet tats teas teat test aet ate eat eta sat sea set tat tea ae as at ta

aesttt attest state taste teats testa east eats etas seat seta stet tats teas teat test aet ate eat eta sat sea set tat tea ae as at ta

aestttu statute. *See* **aesttu aesttt**

aesttu astute statue state taste teats testa east eats etas seat seta stet suet tats taut teas teat test tuts aet ate eat eta sat sea set sue tat tau tea tut use ae as at ta us ut

aestv stave aves east eats etas save seat seta tavs teas vase vast vats vest vets aet ate ave eat eta sat sea set tav tea vat vet ae as at ta

aestw sweat waste awes east eats etas seat seta stew swat teas wast west wets aet ate awe eat eta sat saw sea set sew tea was wet ae as at aw ta we

aestwy sweaty sweat waste yeast awes ayes east easy eats etas eyas seat seta stay stew swat sway teas wast ways west wets wyes yaws yeas yews aet ate awe aye eat eta sat saw say sea set sew sty tea was way wet wye yaw yea yes yet yew ae as at aw ay ta we ye

aestx taxes axes east eats etas seat seta sext teas aet ate axe eat eta sat sax sea set sex tax tea ae as at ax ex ta

aesty yeast ayes east easy eats etas eyas seat seta stay teas yeas aet ate aye eat eta sat say sea set sty tea yea yes yet ae as at ay ta ye

aestyy yeasty yeast ayes east easy eats etas eyas seat seta stay teas yeas aet ate aye eat eta sat say sea set sty tea yay yea yes yet ae as at ay ta ye

aestz zetas east eats etas seat seta teas zest zeta aet ate eat eta sat sea set tea ae as at ta

aesuv uveas aves save uvea vase ave sue use ae as us

aesv aves save vase sea ave ae as

aesvw waves aves awes save vase wave ave awe saw sea sew was ae as aw we

aesw awes awe saw sea sew was ae as aw we	**aesy** ayes easy eyas yeas aye say sea yea yes ae as ay ye	**aev** ave ae
aeswx waxes awes axes awe axe saw sax sea sew sex was wax ae as aw ax ex we	**aet** aet ate eat eta tea ae at ta	**aevw** wave ave awe ae aw we
aesx axes axe sax ae ax ex	**aett** teat aet ate eat eta tat tea ae at ta	**aew** awe ae aw we
aesxz zaxes axes axe sax sea sex zax ae as ax ex	**aetz** zeta aet ate eat eta tea ae at ta	**aex** axe ae ax ex
	aeuv uvea ave ae	**aey** aye yea ae ay ye

af

af fa

affffirr riffraff. *See* **afirr**

affg gaff fag fa

affggin gaffing. *See* **aggin**

affghirt affright. *See* **affirt aghirt fghirt**

affgiinp piaffing. *See* **ffgiin**

affgiinx affixing. *See* **ffgiin fgiinx**

affgiirt graffiti. *See* **affirt**

affgilnr raffling flaring. *See* **afginr**

affgilnw waffling flawing. *See* **agilnw**

affginqu quaffing. *See* **fginu affqu ffiqu**

affginst staffing fasting. *See* **afinst aginst**

affgiort graffito. *See* **affirt**

affgs gaffs gaff fags fag fas gas sag as fa

affgsuw guffaws. *See* **affguw affgs ffgsu**

affguw guffaw gaff guff waff fag fug wag fa aw

affhills fallfish. *See* **afills**

affhilst flatfish. *See* **afhist ahilst ffhist**

affhiltu faithful. *See* **ffiltu**

affhirs raffish. *See* **afirs ahirs affrs**

affiinty affinity tiffany. *See* **ffiint**

affillmm flimflam. *See* **afill**

affilp pilaff pilaf alif fail fila flap flip pail ail alp lap lip pal ai fa if la li pa pi

affilsy falsify. *See* **afilsy**

affimr affirm amir fair farm firm miff raff rami riff aim air arf arm far fir mar mir ram ria rif rim ai am fa if ma mi

affimrs affirms. *See* **affimr aimrs afirs**

affimsst mastiffs mastiff. *See* **affsst afimss ffisst**

affimst mastiff. *See* **afist ffims affst**

affinosu affusion. *See* **afinsu finosu**

affinrsu ruffians ruffian. *See* **afinru afinsu**

affinru ruffian. *See* **afinru**

affinty tiffany. *See* **afint ffity finty**

affipstt tipstaff. *See* **afist aipst ffips**

affirst tariffs. *See* **affirt airst afirs**

affirt tariff afrit fair fart fiat frat frit raff raft riff rift tiff aft air arf art far fat fir fit ita rat ria rif tar ai at fa if it ta ti

affix affix fax fix ai ax fa if xi

afflloot footfall. *See* **afoot allot aflot**

afflo offal foal loaf oaf off fa la lo of

affloott flatfoot. *See* **afoot aflot afloo**

afflopsy playoffs layoffs payoffs playoff. *See* **afflos affloy affopy**

afflopy playoff. *See* **affloy affopy**

afflos offals foals loafs offal also foal loaf oafs sofa fas los oaf off sal sol as fa la lo of os so

afflosy layoffs. *See* **afflos affloy**

affloy layoff offal flay foal loaf fay fly foy lay oaf off ay fa la lo of oy

afflsu luffas luffa luffs sluff sulfa luff flus fas flu sal as fa la us

afflu luffa luff flu fa la

afflux afflux luffa faux flax flux luff fax flu lax lux ax fa la

affnors saffron. *See* **anors afors fnors**

affnorss saffrons saffron. *See* **anorss**

affnorst affronts saffron affront. *See* **fnorst**

affnort affront. *See* **fnort**

affopsy payoffs. *See* **affopy aopsy**

affopy payoff fay fop foy oaf off pay pya yap ay fa of oy pa

affqsu quaffs quaff fas qua as fa us

affqu quaff qua fa

affr raff arf far fa

affrs raffs raff arfs arf far fas as fa

affsst staffs staff fasts fast fats tass aft ass fas fat sat as at fa ta

affst staff fast fats aft fas fat sat as at fa ta

affsw waffs waff fas saw was as aw fa

affty taffy aft fat fay at ay fa ta

affw waff fa aw

afg fag fa

afgggiln flagging fagging lagging. *See* **aggin agiln afiln**

afgggin fagging. *See* **aggin**

afggginr fragging fagging ragging. *See* **afginr agginr**

afggilnn flanging angling. *See* **aggin agiln afiln**

afgginor foraging forging. *See* **afginr agginr aginor gginor**

afgginot fagoting. *See* **afggot aggint**

afgginrt grafting farting grating rafting. *See* **afginr agginr aggint aginrt**

afggost faggots. *See* **afggot afgost**

afggot faggot fagot agog goat toga aft ago fag fat fog gag gat goa got oaf oat oft tag tog at fa go of ta to

afggy faggy fag fay gag gay fa ay

afghhis hagfish. *See* **ghhis**

afghilns flashing fashing lashing. *See* **afilns aghiln agilns fgilns**

afghilps flagship. *See* **afilps ahilps**

afghinrt farthing farting hafting rafting. *See* **afginr aghint aghirt aginrt**

afghins fashing. *See* **afgns agins aghns**

afghinst shafting fashing fasting hafting hasting. *See* **afhist afinst aghint aginst**

afghint hafting. *See* **aghint afint afhit**

afghirs garfish. *See* **aghirs afirs afgrs**

afghrtu fraught. *See* **aghtu afghu aghrt**

afghsu faughs faugh fags fash fugs gash gush hags hugs shag ash fag fas fug gas hag has hug sag ugh ah as fa ha sh us

afghu faugh fag fug hag hug ugh ah fa ha

afgiilln flailing failing falling filling. *See* **afiill afiiln agiiln fgiiln**

afgiiln failing. *See* **agiiln fgiiln afiiln**

afgiilns failings failing filings finials nilgais sailing. *See* **afiiln afilns agiiln agilns**

afgiinnt fainting. *See* **afinnt fgiinn**

afgiinr fairing. *See* **agiinr afginr fgiinr**

afgiinrs fairings arising fairing firings raising. *See* **afginr aginrs aiinrs**

afgiintx fixating taxiing. *See* **agintx fgiinx**

afgikln flaking. *See* **afgikn agiln afiln**

afgiklnn flanking flaking. *See* **afgikn**

afgikn faking kiang akin fain fang fink gain gink kina king naif ani fag fan fig fin gan gin ink kaf kif kin nag ai an fa if in ka na

afgiknnr franking ranking. *See* **afgikn afginr agiknr**

afgilln falling. *See* **agiln afiln afill**

afgilmn flaming. *See* **afgimn agilmn**

afgilmno flamingo flaming foaling foaming loafing loaming. *See* **afgimn afglno agilmn aglmno**

afgilno foaling loafing. *See* **afglno agiln afiln**

afgilnot floating fatling foaling loafing lofting. *See* **afglno aflnot agilot ailnot**

afgilnpp flapping lapping. *See* **agilnp**

afgilnr flaring. *See* **afginr agiln afilr**

afgilnst fatlings fasting fatling lasting salting slating staling. *See* **afilns afinst agilns aginst**

afgilnt fatling. *See* **agiln afint afiln**

afgilntu faulting fatling fluting gainful. *See* **afglnu aflntu agilnu fgilnu**

afgilnu gainful. *See* **afglnu fgilnu agilnu**

afgilnw flawing. *See* **agilnw afiln fgiln**

afgilny flaying. *See* **fgilny agilny**

afgimn faming gamin fain fang gain main mina naif aim ani fag fan fig fin gam gan gin mag man nag nim ai am an fa if in ma mi na

afgimno foaming. *See* **afgimn agimo agmno**

afgimnnr farming framing. *See* **agimnr afgimn afginr afimnr**

afgimny magnify. *See* **afgimn afimny agimny**

afginnn fanning. *No 6s or 5s*

afginnsu snafuing. *See* **afinsu fginsu**

afginnw fawning. *See* **aginnw**

afginorv favoring. *See* **afginr aginor aginrv agiorv**

afginory foraying fraying. *See* **afginr aginor aginry agnory**

afginppr frapping rapping. *See* **afginr aginpr**

afginr faring grain fain fair fang firn frag frig gain gnar grin naif rain rang rani ring air ani arf fag fan far fig fin fir gan gar gin nag rag ran ria rif rig ai an fa if in na

afginrst strafing farting fasting rafting ratings staring. *See* **afginr afgrst afinst aginrs**

afginrt farting rafting. *See* **afginr aginrt**

afginry fraying. *See* **afginr fginry aginry**

afginst fasting. *See* **afinst aginst**

afgintt fatting. *See* **afint agint aintt**

afgintw wafting. *See* **aginw afint agint**

afginz fazing fain fang gain naif zing ani fag fan fig fin gan gin nag zag zig ai an fa if in na

afgirty gratify. *See* **afirty afgrt**

afgisy gasify fags fays figs gays fag fas fay fig gas gay ifs sag say ai as ay fa if is si

afgitz zaftig fiat gait gift aft fag fat fig fit gat ita tag zag zig zit ai at fa if it ta ti

afgl flag fag gal lag fa la

afgllruy frugally. *See* **afglru**

afgllssu glassful. *See* **aflls afgls afglu**

afglnnoo gonfalon. *See* **afglno aglnno aglnoo**

afglno flagon along agon fang flag flan flog foal gaol goal golf loaf loan long ago fag fan fog gal gan goa lag log nag nog oaf an fa go la lo na no of on

afglnos flagons. *See* **afglno aglnos**

afglnu fungal fugal flung fang faun flag flan guan gulf lung ulna fag fan flu fug fun gal gan gnu gun lag lug nag an fa la na nu

afglru frugal fugal flag frag furl gaur gulf ruga arf fag far flu fug fur gal gar lag lar lug rag rug fa la

afgls flags fags flag gals lags slag fag fas gal gas lag sag sal as fa la

afglu fugal flag gulf fag flu fug gal lag lug fa la

afgmnor frogman. *See* **agmno agnor amnor**

afgn fang fag fan gan nag an fa na

afgns fangs fags fang fans nags sang snag fag fan fas gan gas nag sag an as fa na

afgost fagots fagot goats togas fags fast fats fogs gats goas goat oafs oast oats sago sofa soft stag stoa tags toga togs aft ago fag fas fat fog gas gat goa got oaf oat oft sag sat sot tag tog as at fa go of os so ta to

afgot fagot goat toga aft ago fag fat fog gat goa got oaf oat oft tag tog at fa go of ta to

afgr frag arf fag far gar rag fa

afgrs frags arfs fags frag gars rags arf fag far fas gar gas rag sag fa as

afgrst grafts farts frags frats graft rafts arfs arts fags fart fast fats frag frat gars gats raft rags rats stag star tags tars tsar aft arf art fag far fas fat gar gas gat rag rat sag tag tar as at fa ta

afgrt graft fart frag frat raft aft arf art fag far fat gar gat rag rat tag tar at fa ta

afgs fags fag fas gas sag as fa

afhiilss sailfish. *See* **afils afhls ahils**

afhiilst fishtail. *See* **afhist ahiilt ahilst**

afhiirs fairish. *See* **afirs ahirs**

afhikl khalif kalif alif fail fila flak haik hail half kail lakh ail ilk kaf kal kif ah ai fa ha hi if ka la li

afhikls khalifs. *See* **afhikl afikls**

afhillsy flashily. *See* **afhlsy afills**

afhilosy oafishly. *See* **afhios afhlsy afilsy ahlosy**

afhimnu hafnium. *See* **ahmnu**

afhims famish aims fash fish hams mash sham shim aim ash fas ham has him his ifs mis ah ai am as fa ha hi if is ma mi sh si

afhinos fashion. *See* **afhios afins**

afhinoss fashions fashion. *See* **afhios**

afhinps panfish. *See* **ahips ainps**

afhiors oarfish. *See* **afhios afhors**

afhios oafish fash fish oafs sofa ash fas foh has his ifs oaf ohs ah ai as fa ha hi ho if is of oh os sh si so

afhirsst starfish shrifts. *See* **afhist afhsst airsst fhirst**

afhissw sawfish. *See* **ahssw hissw afisw**

afhist faiths faith fiats hafts saith shaft shift fash fast fats fiat fish fist fits haft hast hats hist hits sift sith this aft ash fas fat fit has hat his hit ifs ita its sat sit ah ai as fa ha hi if is it sh si ta ti

afhistt fattish. *See* **afhist**

afhit faith haft fiat aft fat fit hat hit ita ah ai at fa ha hi if it ta ti

afhiz hafiz ah ai fa ha hi if

afhklntu thankful tankful. *See* **aflntu**

afhkorsy hayforks hayfork. *See* **afhors aforsy**

afhkory hayfork. *See* **afory ahory**

afhl half ah fa ha la

afhllotu loathful fallout. *See* **aflou allot aflot**

afhlmru harmful. *See* **aflmru**

afhloo loofah aloof foal fool half halo hoof loaf foh loo oaf oho ooh ah fa ha ho la lo of oh

afhloos loofahs. *See* **afhloo afhls aflos**

afhlosty haylofts hayloft. *See* **afhlsy aflost ahlost ahlosy**

afhloty hayloft. *See* **aflot aflty hloty**

afhlrtuw wrathful. *See* **aflrtu**

afhls flash fash half lash ash fas has sal ah as fa ha la sh

afhlsy flashy flash flays hylas ashy fash fays flay half hays hyla lash lays shay slay ash fas fay fly has hay lay sal say shy sly yah ah as ay fa ha la sh

afhmost fathoms. *See* **afhmot amost afmos**

afhmot fathom atom foam haft math moat moth oath aft fat foh ham hat hot mat mho moa mot oaf oat oft ohm tam tho tom ah am at fa ha ho ma mo of oh om ta to

afhooptt footpath. *See* **aooptt**

afhors shofar faros frosh horas arfs faro fash fora hoar hora oafs oars rahs rash rhos soar sofa sora arf ash far fas foh for fro has oaf oar ohs rah rho ah as fa ha ho of oh or os sh so

afhorss shofars. *See* **afhors afoss aorss**

afhrw wharf arf far haw rah raw war ah aw fa ha

afhs fash ash fas has ah as fa ha sh

afhsst shafts fasts hafts shaft stash fash fast fats haft hast hats sash tass aft ash ass fas fat has hat sat ah as at fa ha sh ta

afhst hafts shaft fash fast fats haft hast hats aft ash fas fat has hat sat ah as at fa ha sh ta

afht haft aft fat hat ah at fa ha ta

afiill filial flail alif fail fall fila fill ilia ail all ill ai fa if la li

afiiln finial final alif anil fail fain fila flan ilia lain naif nail ail ani fan fin nil ai an fa if in la li na

afiilns finials. *See* **afiiln afilns**

afiilnst finalist finials. *See* **afiiln afilns afinst aiinst**

afiilnty finality faintly. *See* **afiiln ailnty filnty**

afiilor airfoil. *See* **afilr aflor afilo**

afiilors airfoils airfoil. *See* **afilrs aflors ailors**

afiilrst airlifts airlift. *See* **afilrs ailrst filrst**

afiilrt airlift. *See* **afirt afilr filrt**

afiinotx fixation. *See* **afint fiinx inotx**

afikl kalif alif fail fila flak kail ail ilk kaf kal kif ai fa if ka la li

afiklnnr franklin. *See* **afikr afilr afiln**

afiklot flokati. *See* **aflot afilo afikl**

afikls kalifs alifs fails flaks flask kalif ails alif fail fila fils flak kafs kail kifs sail saki silk ail ask fas ifs ilk kaf kal kas kif sal ski ai as fa if is ka la li si

afikr fakir kafir fair raki air arf ark far fir irk kaf kif kir ria rif ai fa if ka

afikrs fakirs kafirs fairs fakir frisk kafir rakis airs arfs arks fair firs irks kafs kifs kris raki rias rifs risk saki sari sark air arf ark ask far fas fir ifs irk kaf kas kif kir ria rif sir ski ai as fa if is ka si

afil alif fail fila ail ai fa if la li

afill flail alif fail fall fila fill ail all ill ai fa if la li

afilllot flotilla. *See* **allot aflot afill**

afillny finally. *See* **filly afiln afill**

afillpst pitfalls pitfall. *See* **afills afilps ailpst**

afillpsu pailfuls pailful lapfuls. *See* **afills afilps afllpu ailpsu**

afillpt pitfall. *See* **afill afilp ailpt**

afillpu pailful. *See* **afllpu afill afilp**

afills flails alifs fails falls fills flail ails alif fail fall fila fill fils sail sill ail all fas ifs ill sal ai as fa if is la li si

afilltuy faultily. *See* **aflltv afltuy**

afilluv fluvial. *See* **afill aillv**

afilluw wailful. *See* **aflluw filluw**

afilmnor informal aliform. *See* **afimnr aflmor ailmno ailmnr**

afilmor aliform. *See* **aflmor afilr afilo**

afilmpy amplify. *See* **afilmy almpy ilmpy**

afilmu famuli filum alif alum fail fila film flam mail maul ail aim flu lam lum mil ai am fa if la li ma mi mu um

afilmy family filmy alif amyl fail fila film flam flay limy mail ail aim fay fly lam lay may mil yam ai am ay fa if la li ma mi my

afiln final alif anil fail fain fila flan lain naif nail ail ani fan fin nil ai an fa if in la li na

afilnort flatiron inflator frontal. *See* **aflnot ailnot ailnrt ailort**

afilnppt flippant. *See* **ailnpt**

afilnpu painful. *See* **afiln ailnp afilp**

afilnruy unfairly. *See* **afilry afinru ailnru**

afilns finals alifs anils fails final flans naifs nails slain snail ails alif anil fail fain fans fila fils fins flan lain naif nail nils sail sain ail ani fan fas fin ifs nil sal sin ai an as fa if in is la li na si

afilnty faintly. *See* **ailnty filnty**

afilo folia alif fail fila foal foil loaf ail oaf oil ai fa if la li lo of

afilorsw airflows airflow. *See* **afilrs aflors ailors**

afilorw airflow. *See* **afilr aflor afilo**

afilostx foxtails foxtail oxtails. *See* **aflost ailosx ailotx**

afilotx foxtail. *See* **ailotx aflot**

afilp pilaf alif fail fila flap flip pail ail alp lap lip pal ai fa if la li pa pi

afilps pilafs alifs fails flaps flips pails pilaf ails alif alps fail fila fils flap flip laps lips lisp pail pals sail slap slip ail alp asp fas ifs lap lip pal pas sal sap sip spa ai as fa if is la li pa pi si

afilquy qualify. *See* **ailqu**

afilr filar flair frail alif aril fail fair fila lair liar lira rail rial ail air arf far fir lar ria rif ai fa if la li

afilrs flairs alifs arils fails fairs filar flair frail lairs liars liras rails rials ails airs alif arfs aril fail fair fila fils firs lair liar lira rail rial rias rifs sail sari ail air arf far fas fir ifs lar ria rif sal sir ai as fa if is la li si

afilrstu fistular fistula rituals. *See* **afilrs aflrtu aflstu ailrst**

afilrty frailty. *See* **afilry filrty afirty**

afilry fairly fairy filar flair frail riyal airy alif aril aryl fail fair fila flay fray lair liar lira rail rial ail air arf far fay fir fly fry lar lay ray ria rif yar ai ay fa if la li

afils alifs fails ails alif fail fila fils sail ail fas ifs sal ai as fa if is la li si

afilsstu fistulas fistula. *See* **aflstu**

afilssy salsify. *See* **afilsy ilssy ailss**

afilsttu flautist fistula flutist. *See* **aflstu ilsttu**

afilstu fistula. *See* **aflstu**

afilsty falsity. *See* **afilsy aflty afist**

afilsy salify alifs fails flays ails alif fail fays fila fils flay lays sail slay ail fas fay fly ifs lay sal say sly ai as ay fa if is la li si

afimnopr napiform rampion. *See* **afimnr fimnor**

afimnosu infamous. *See* **afinsu afmosu aimnsu finosu**

afimnr firman amir fain fair farm firm firn main mina naif rain rami rani aim air ani arf arm fan far fin fir man mar mir nim ram ran ria rif rim ai am an fa if in ma mi na

afimny infamy ayin fain main many mina myna naif aim ani any fan fay fin man may nay nim yam yin ai am an ay fa if in ma mi my na

afimry ramify fairy airy amir army fair farm firm fray miry rami rimy aim air arf arm far fay fir fry mar may mir ram ray ria rif rim yam yar ai ay fa if ma mi my

afimss massif amiss aims mass miss aim ass fas ifs mis sis ai am as fa if is ma mi si

afimsss massifs. *See* **afimss**

afin fain naif ani fan fin ai an fa if in na

afinnost fontinas anoints fontina infants nations. *See* **afinnt afinst afnnos ainnos**

afinnot fontina. *See* **ainnot afinnt**

afinnotu fountain fontina. *See* **afinnt ainnot**

afinnrty infantry. *See* **afinnt afirty**

afinnst infants. *See* **afinnt afinst**

afinnt infant faint anti fain fiat naif aft ani ant fan fat fin fit inn ita nit tan tin ai an at fa if in it na ta ti

afinors insofar. *See* **ainors afirs afors**

afinqtuy quantify. *See* **ainqtu**

afinrstx transfix. *See* **afinst ainrst**

afinru unfair fain fair faun firn naif rain rani ruin air ani arf fan far fin fir fun fur ran ria rif run urn ai an fa if in na nu

afins naifs fain fans fins naif sain ani fan fas fin ifs sin ai an as fa if in is na si

afinssu fusains. *See* **afinsu afnssu**

afinst faints antis faint fiats naifs saint satin stain anti ants fain fans fast fats fiat fins fist fits naif nits sain sift snit tans tins aft ani ant fan fas fat fin fit ifs ita its nit sat sin sit tan tin ai an as at fa if in is it na si ta ti

afinstu fustian. *See* **afinst afinsu**

afinsu fusain fauns naifs snafu anus fain fans faun fins naif sain ani fan fas fin fun ifs sin sun ai an as fa if in is na nu si us

afint faint anti fain fiat naif aft ani ant fan fat fin fit ita nit tan tin ai an at fa if in it na ta ti

afir fair air arf far fir ria rif ai fa if

afirr friar fair air arf far fir ria rif ai fa if

afirrs friars arris fairs friar airs arfs fair firs rias rifs sari air arf far fas fir ifs ria rif sir ai as fa if is si

afirry friary fairy firry friar airy fair fray air arf far fay fir fry ray ria rif yar ai ay fa if

afirs fairs airs arfs fair firs rias rifs sari air arf far fas fir ifs ria rif sir ai as fa if is si

afirstty stratify. *See* **afirty airstt airtty**

afirt afrit fair fart fiat frat frit raft rift aft air arf art far fat fir fit ita rat ria rif tar ai at fa if it ta ti

afirty ratify afrit fairy airy arty fair fart fiat frat fray frit raft rift tray aft air arf art far fat fay fir fit fry ita rat ray ria rif tar try yar ai at ay fa if it ta ti

afiry fairy airy fair fray air arf far fay fir fry ray ria rif yar ai ay fa if

afissty satisfy. *See* **afsst afist fisst**

afist fiats fast fats fiat fist fits sift aft fas fat fit ifs ita its sat sit ai as at fa if is it si ta ti

afisw waifs waif fas ifs saw was wis ai as aw fa if is si

afit fiat aft fat fit ita ai at fa if it ta ti

afittuy fatuity. *See* **aftty fttuy**

afiw waif ai aw fa if

afk kaf fa ka

afkl flak kaf kal fa ka la

afkln flank flak flan lank fan kaf kal an fa ka la na

afklnotu outflank tankful. *See* **aflnot aflntu**

afklnry frankly. *See* **aklnry afkly afkln**

afklns flanks flaks flank flans flask fans flak flan kafs lank sank ask fan fas kaf kal kas sal an as fa ka la na

afklnstu tankfuls tankful flaunts. *See* **afklns aflntu aflstu alnstu**

afklntu tankful. *See* **aflntu afkln fklnu**

afkls flaks flask flak kafs ask fas kaf kal kas sal as fa ka la

afklss flasks flaks flask asks flak kafs lass sals ask ass fas kaf kal kas sal as fa ka la

afkly flaky flak flay laky fay fly kaf kal lay yak ay fa ka la

afkmoort footmark. *See* **afmort**

afknr frank knar nark rank arf ark fan far kaf ran an fa ka na

afknrs franks frank knars narks ranks snark arfs arks fans kafs knar nark rank sank sark arf ark ask fan far fas kaf kas ran an as fa ka na

afkrst krafts farts frats karst karts kraft rafts stark arfs arks arts fart fast fats frat kafs kart raft rats sark skat star tars task tsar aft arf ark art ask far fas fat kaf kas kat rat sat tar tsk as at fa ka ta

afkrt kraft fart frat kart raft aft arf ark art far fat kaf kat rat tar at fa ka ta

afks kafs ask fas kaf kas as fa ka

afll fall all fa la

aflluwy lawfully awfully. *See* **aflluw**

aflmnuy manfully. *See* **aflmnu**

aflmory formally morally. *See* **afllor aflmor allory**

afllnosw snowfall fallows. *See* **afllow allnos allosw**

afllnuuw unlawful. *See* **aflluw**

afllor floral flora fall faro foal fora loaf olla oral roll all arf far for fro lar oaf oar fa la lo of or

afllostu fallouts fallout. *See* **aflost aflstu allost flostu**

afllosw fallows. *See* **allosw afllow**

afllotu fallout. *See* **aflou allot aflot**

afllow fallow allow alow fall flaw flow foal fowl loaf olla wall wolf all awl law low oaf owl aw fa la lo of ow

afllpsu lapfuls. *See* **afllpu aflls aflps**

afllpu lapful fall flap full pall pull all alp flu lap pal pul fa la pa up

afllpuy playful. *See* **afllpu flluy alpuy**

afllrtuy artfully. *See* **afllty aflrtu**

aflls falls fall all fas sal as fa la

afllty flatly fatly tally ally fall flat flay tall aft all alt fat fay fly lay at ay fa la ta

aflluw lawful awful fall flaw full wall all awl flu law aw fa la

aflluwy awfully. *See* **aflluw flluy**

aflm flam lam am fa la ma

aflmnu manful alum faun flam flan maul maun ulna fan flu fun lam lum man am an fa la ma mu na nu um

aflmoprt platform marplot. *See* **aflmor afmort almort aloprt**

aflmor formal flora molar moral farm faro flam foal foam fora form from loaf loam marl mola mora oral roam arf arm far for fro lam lar mar moa mor oaf oar ram am fa la lo ma mo of om or

aflmors formals. *See* **aflors aflmor almors**

aflmorsu formulas armfuls formals formula fulmars. *See* **aflmor aflmru aflors afmosu**

aflmortw flatworm. *See* **aflmor afmort almort**

aflmoru formula. *See* **aflmru**

aflmosst flotsams flotsam smaltos. *See* **aflost almost almsst amosst**

aflmost flotsam. *See* **almost aflost**

aflmosuy famously. *See* **afmosu almsuy**

aflmrsu armfuls fulmars. *See* **aflmru almrsu**

aflmru armful fulmar mural alum farm flam furl marl maul arf arm far flu fur lam lar lum mar ram rum am fa la ma mu um

aflms flams alms flam lams slam fas lam sal am as fa la ma

aflmsuu famulus. *See* **almsu aflms alsuu**

aflmyy mayfly amyl flam flay fay fly lam lay may yam yay am ay fa la ma my

afln flan fan an fa la na

aflnorst frontals frontal. *See* **aflnot aflors aflost alnors**

aflnort frontal. *See* **aflnot aflor fnort**

aflnot fontal aloft float talon tonal alto flan flat foal font loaf loan loft lota nota tola aft alt ant fan fat lot not oaf oat oft tan ton an at fa la lo na no of on ta to

aflns flans flan fans fan fas sal an as fa la na

aflnstu flaunts. *See* **aflstu aflntu alnstu**

aflntu flaunt fault aunt faun flan flat lunt tufa tuna ulna aft alt ant fan fat flu fun nut tan tau tun an at fa la na nu ta ut

aflntuy flaunty. *See* **aflntu afltuy**

aflo foal loaf oaf fa la lo of

afloo aloof foal fool loaf oaf loo fa la lo of

aflopstt flattops flattop. *See* **aflost alopst alostt**

afloptt flattop. *See* **aflot alott**

aflor flora faro foal fora loaf oral arf far for fro lar oaf oar fa la lo of or

aflors floras faros flora foals loafs orals solar also arfs faro foal fora loaf oafs oars oral soar sofa sora arf far fas for fro lar los oaf oar sal sol as fa la lo of or os so

aflorsv flavors. *See* **aforsv aflorv aflors alorsv**

aflorv flavor favor flora valor volar faro foal fora loaf oral oval arf far for fro lar oaf oar ova fa la lo of or

aflos foals loafs also foal loaf oafs sofa fas los oaf sal sol as fa la lo of os so

aflost floats aloft altos flats float foals loafs lofts lotas tolas also alto alts fast fats flat foal last loaf loft lost lota lots oafs oast oats salt slat slot sofa soft stoa tola aft alt fas fat los lot oaf oat oft sal sat sol sot as at fa la lo of os so ta to

aflot   aloft float alto flat foal loaf loft lota tola aft alt fat lot oaf oat oft at fa la lo of ta to

aflou   afoul foal foul loaf oaf flu fa la lo of

aflp   flap alp lap pal fa la pa

aflprsty   flytraps flytrap. *See* **alprty alrsty aprsty**

aflprty   flytrap. *See* **alprty**

aflps   flaps alps flap laps pals slap alp asp fas lap pal pas sal sap spa as fa la pa

aflrtu   artful fault ultra fart flat frat furl raft tufa turf aft alt arf art fat fat flu fur lar rat rut tar tau at fa la ta ut

aflst   flats alts fast fats flat last salt slat aft alt fas fat sal sat as at fa la ta

aflstu   faults flatus fault flats sulfa talus tufas alts fast fats flat flus last lust salt slat slut tufa aft alt fas fat flu sal sat tau as at fa la ta us ut

aflsu   sulfa flus fas flu sal as fa la us

aflsw   flaws awls flaw laws awl fas law sal saw was as aw fa la

aflswy   sawfly flaws flays yawls awls fays flaw flay laws lays slay sway ways yawl yaws awl fas fay fly law lay sal saw say sly was way yaw as aw ay fa la

aflsy   flays fays flay lays slay fas fay fly lay sal say sly as ay fa la

aflt   flat aft alt fat at fa la ta

afltu   fault flat tufa aft alt fat flu tau at fa la ta ut

afltuy   faulty fault fatly flat flay tufa aft alt fat fay flu fly lay tau at ay fa la ta ut

aflty   fatly flat flay aft alt fat fay fly lay at ay fa la ta

afluw   awful flaw awl flu law aw fa la

aflw   flaw awl law aw fa la

aflx   flax fax lax ax fa la

aflxy   flaxy flax flay fax fay fly lax lay ax ay fa la

afly   flay fay fly lay ay fa la

afmnoot   footman. *See* **afoot**

afmo   foam oaf moa am fa ma mo of om

afmorst   farmost formats. *See* **afmort amost afmrs**

afmort   format atom farm faro fart foam fora form fort frat from mart moat mora mort raft roam rota taro tora tram aft arf arm art far fat for fro mar mat moa mor mot oaf oar oat oft ort

ram rat rot tam tar tom tor am at fa ma mo of om or ta to

afmos   foams foam moas oafs sofa soma fas moa mos oaf oms am as fa ma mo of om os so

afmosstu   sfumatos sfumato. *See* **afmosu amosst**

afmostu   sfumato. *See* **afmosu amost aostu**

afmosu   famous foams foam moas oafs sofa soma sumo fas moa mos mus oaf oms sou sum am as fa ma mo mu of om os so um us

afmoy   foamy foam mayo fay foy may moa oaf yam am ay fa ma mo my of om oy

afmr   farm arf arm far mar ram am fa ma

afmrs   farms arfs arms farm rams arf arm far fas mar ram am as fa ma

afn   fan an fa na

afnno   fanon anon fan oaf an fa na no of on

afnnos   fanons fanon anon fans naos oafs sofa fan fas oaf son an as fa na no of on os so

afnny   fanny any fan fay nay an ay fa na

afnprsy   frypans. *See* **afnpry afprs afrsy**

afnpry   frypan frap fray nary pray yarn any arf fan far fay fry nap nay pan par pay pry pya ran rap ray yap yar an ay fa na pa

afns   fans fan fas an as fa na

afnssu   snafus fauns snafu anus fans faun fuss suns ass fan fas fun sun an as fa na nu us

afnsu   fauns snafu anus fans faun fan fas fun sun an as fa na nu us

afnsw   fawns awns fans fawn sawn swan awn fan fas saw wan was an as aw fa na

afnu   faun fan fun an fa na nu

afnw   fawn awn fan wan an aw fa na

afo   oaf fa of

afoot   afoot foot aft fat oaf oat oft too at fa of ta to

afor   faro fora arf far for fro oaf oar fa of or

aforrsw   farrows. *See* **aforrw aorrsw**

aforrw   farrow arrow faro fora frow roar arf far for fro oaf oar raw row war aw fa of or ow

afors   faros arfs faro fora oafs oars soar sofa sora arf far fas for fro oaf oar as fa of or os so

aforsv   favors faros favor savor arfs faro fora oafs oars soar sofa sora arf far fas for fro oaf oar ova as fa of or os so

aforsy   forays faros foray frays arfs faro fays fora foys fray oafs oars rays rosy soar sofa sora arf far fas fay for foy fro fry oaf oar ray say soy yar as ay fa of or os oy so

aforv   favor faro fora arf far for fro oaf oar ova fa of or

afory   foray faro fora fray arf far fay for foy fro fry oaf oar ray yar ay fa of or oy

afos   oafs sofa oaf fas as fa of os so

afoss   fossa sofas foss oafs ossa sofa ass fas oaf as fa of os so

afostuu   fatuous. *See* **afstu aostu**

afpr   frap arf far par rap fa pa

afprs   fraps arfs frap pars raps rasp spar arf asp far fas par pas rap sap spa as fa pa

afr   arf far fa

afrs   arfs arf far fas as fa

afrst   farts frats rafts arfs arts fart fast fats frat raft rats star tars tsar aft arf art far fas fat rat sat tar as at fa ta

afrsy   frays arfs fays fray rays arf far fas fay fry ray say yar as ay fa

afrsz   zarfs arfs zarf arf far fas as fa

afrt   fart frat raft aft arf art far fat rat tar at fa ta

afry   fray arf far fay fry ray yar fa ay

afrz   zarf arf far fa

afs   fas fa as

afsst   fasts fast fats tass aft ass fas fat sat as at fa ta

afst   fast fats aft fas fat sat as at fa ta

afstu   tufas fast fats tufa aft fas fat sat tau as at fa ta us ut

afstw   wafts fast fats swat waft wast aft fas fat sat saw was as at aw fa ta

afsuv   favus fas as fa us

afsy   fays fas fay say as ay fa

aft   aft fat at fa ta

aftty   fatty aft fat fay tat at ay fa ta

aftu   tufa aft fat tau at fa ta ut

aftw   waft aft fat at aw fa ta

afux   faux fax fa ax

afx   fax fa ax

afy   fay fa ay

ag

agg gag

aggggin gagging. *See* **aggin**

aggghiln haggling lagging. *See* **aghiln**

aggghins shagging sagging gashing. *See* **agghis**

agggijn jagging. *See* **aggin**

agggiln lagging. *See* **aggin agiln**

agggilnn gangling angling ganging lagging nagging. *See* **aggin agiln**

agggilnr gargling glaring lagging ragging. *See* **agginr**

agggilns slagging lagging sagging. *See* **agilns**

agggilnw waggling lagging wagging. *See* **agginw agilnw**

aggginn ganging nagging. *See* **aggin**

aggginns snagging ganging nagging sagging. *See* **aggin agins aggns**

aggginr ragging. *See* **agginr**

agggins sagging. *See* **aggin agins aggns**

aggg016t staging sagging staging tagging. *See* **aggint aginst**

agggint tagging. *See* **aggint**

aggginu gauging. *See* **aggin**

aggginw wagging. *See* **agginw**

agghhis haggish. *See* **agghis ghhis**

agghilnu laughing hauling. *See* **aghiln agilnu ahilnu ggilnu**

agghilst gaslight alights. *See* **agghis aghilt ahilst ghilst**

agghimn gingham. *See* **aggimn**

agghimns ginghams gashing gingham mashing shaming. *See* **agghis aggimn agimns**

agghinn hanging. *See* **aggin**

agghinns gnashing hanging gashing. *See* **agghis**

agghinpr graphing harping. *See* **agginp agginr aginpr**

agghins gashing. *See* **agghis aggin agins**

agghis haggis gags gash gigs hags shag sigh ash gag gas gig hag has his sag ah ai as ha hi is sh si

agghsy shaggy saggy ashy gags gash gays hags hays shag shay ash gag gas gay hag has hay sag say shy yah ah as ay ha sh

aggiilnn aligning alining angling gaining nailing. *See* **agiiln giilnn**

aggiilnt ligating tailing. *See* **aggint agiiln giilnt**

aggiilnv gingival gingiva vailing. *See* **agiiln agilnv ggiinv giilnv**

aggiimn imaging. *See* **aggimn agiimn**

aggiinn gaining. *See* **aggin**

aggiinnr graining gaining ingrain raining ranging ringing. *See* **agginr**

aggiinv gingiva. *See* **ggiinv aggin**

aggijlnn jangling angling. *See* **aggin agiln aijnn**

aggiknw gawking. *See* **agginw agiknw**

aggilln galling. *See* **aggin agiln**

aggilmnn mangling angling. *See* **aggimn agilmn agimnn**

aggilmno gloaming loaming. *See* **aggilo aggimn agilmn aglmno**

aggilnn angling. *See* **aggin**

aggilnno ganglion angling loaning longing. *See* **aggilo aglnno ggilno gginno**

aggilnnr gnarling angling glaring ranging. *See* **agginr**

aggilnnt tangling angling tanging. *See* **aggint**

aggilnnw wangling angling gnawing. *See* **aginnw agginw agilnw**

aggilnot gloating. *See* **aggilo aggint agilot ailnot**

aggilnpu plaguing gulping. *See* **agginp agilnp agilnu ggilnu**

aggilnpy gapingly playing. *See* **agginp agglny agilnp agilny**

aggilnr glaring. *See* **agginr agiln agilr**

aggilnss glassing gassing signals. *See* **agilns aginss ailnss**

aggilnsz glazings glazing. *See* **agginz agilns**

aggilnz glazing. *See* **agginz agilnz**

aggilo loggia agio agog gaol goal ago ail gag gal gig goa lag log oil ai go la li lo

aggilos loggias. *See* **aggilo agios aglos**

aggimmn gamming. *See* **aggimn**

aggimn gaming aging gamin gain gang main mina aim ani gag gam gan gig gin mag man nag nim ai am an in ma mi na

aggin aging gang gain ani gag gan gig gin nag ai an in na

agginnor groaning ranging. *See* **agginr aginor gginno gginor**

agginnot tangoing atoning tanging tonging. *See* **aggint ainnot gginno ginnot**

agginnr ranging. *See* **agginr**

agginnrr gnarring ranging. *See* **agginr**

agginnrt granting grating ranging ranting tanging. *See* **agginr aggint aginrt**

agginnsw gnawings gnawing awnings. *See* **agginw aginnw aginsw**

agginnt tanging. *See* **aggint**

agginntw twanging gnawing tanging wanting. *See* **aggint agginw aginnw**

agginnw gnawing. *See* **aginnw agginw**

agginovy voyaging. *See* **gginvy**

agginp gaping paging aging aping gain gang nipa pain pang ping ani gag gan gap gig gin gip nag nap nip pan pig pin ai an in na pa pi

agginpp gapping. *See* **agginp**

agginprs grasping sparging gasping parings parsing rasping sparing. *See* **agginp agginr aginpr aginrs**

agginps gasping. *See* **agginp**

agginr raging aging grain gain gang gnar grig grin rain rang rani ring air ani gag gan gar gig gin nag rag ran ria rig ai an in na

agginrss grassing gassing. *See* **agginr aginrs aginss**

agginrst gratings grating ratings staging staring. *See* **agginr aggint aginrs aginrt**

agginrsu sugaring arguing surging. *See* **agginr aginrs gginru**

agginrt grating. *See* **aggint agginr aginrt**

agginrty gyrating grating graying. *See* **agginr aggint aginrt aginry**

agginru arguing. *See* **agginr gginru**

agginruu auguring arguing. *See* **agginr gginru**

agginrv graving. *See* **agginr aginrv**

agginry graying. *See* **aginry gginry agginr**

agginrz grazing. *See* **agginz agginr aginrz**

agginss gassing. *See* **aginss aggin aggns**

agginst staging. *See* **aggint aginst**

aggint gating aging giant anti gain gait gang gnat tang ting ani ant gag gan gat gig gin ita nag nit tag tan tin ai an at in it na ta ti

agginw waging aging awing wigan gain gang gnaw wain wing ani awn gag gan gig gin nag wag wan wig win ai an aw in na

agginz gazing aging gain gang zing ani gag gan gig gin nag zag zig ai an in na

aggirtuz ziggurat. *See* **agirtu**

aggisww wigwags. *See* **aggiww**

aggiszz zigzags. *See* **aggizz**

aggiww wigwag gag gig wag wig ai aw

aggizz zigzag gag gig zag zig ai

aggjy jaggy gag gay jag jay ay

aggllloy lollygag. *See* **alloy glloy llloy**

agglmoor logogram. *See* **aglor glmoo gmoor**

agglny gangly gang yang any gag gal gan gay lag lay nag nay an ay la na

agglrsty straggly. *See* **alrsty**

aggmost maggots. *See* **aggmot amost agost**

aggmot maggot agog atom goat moat toga ago gag gam gat goa got mag mat moa mog mot oat tag tam tog tom am at go ma mo om ta to

aggmoty maggoty. *See* **aggmot amoty**

aggn   gang gag gan nag an na

aggns   gangs gags gang nags sang snag gag gan gas nag sag an as na

aggnsy   snaggy gangs saggy yangs gags gang gays nags sang snag yang any gag gan gas gay nag nay sag say an as ay na

aggo   agog ago gag goa go

aggquy   quaggy quag quay gag gay guy qua ay

aggs   gags gag gas sag as

aggsy   saggy gags gays gag gas gay sag say as ay

agh   hag ah ha

aghhiilt   hightail. *See* **aghilt ahiilt**

aghhins   hashing. *See* **agins aghns ghhis**

aghhiswy   highways highway. *See* **ghhis ahswy hhisw**

aghhiwy   highway. *No 6s or 5s*

aghhlotu   although. *See* **ghhotu**

aghhosw   hogwash. *No 6s or 5s*

aghhtuy   haughty. *See* **aghtu**

aghiiln   hailing. *See* **agiiln aghiln**

aghiilnn   inhaling alining hailing nailing. *See* **aghiln agiiln giilnn**

aghiirtt   airtight. *See* **aghirt**

aghiknn   hanking. *See* **agikn**

aghiknns   shanking hanking shaking snaking. *See* **agikns**

aghiknnt   thanking hanking tanking. *See* **aghint agiknt ghiknt**

aghiknr   harking. *See* **agiknr**

aghiknrs   sharking garnish harking shaking sharing. *See* **aghirs agiknr agikns aginrs**

aghikns   shaking. *See* **agikns**

aghiknw   hawking. *See* **aghinw agiknw**

aghil   laigh hail ail gal hag lag ah ai ha hi la li

aghilmty   almighty. *See* **aghilt ghimty**

aghiln   haling align laigh ligan linga anil gain hail hang lain ling nail nigh ail ani gal gan gin hag hin lag nag nah nil ah ai an ha hi in la li na

aghilnoo   hooligan. *See* **aghiln aglnoo ghilno ghinoo**

aghilnor   longhair. *See* **aghiln agilor aginor ahilnr**

aghilnos   shoaling lashing longish. *See* **aghiln aghlos aghnos agilns**

aghilnot   loathing halting lathing tholing. *See* **aghiln aghilt aghint agilot**

aghilnps   plashing lapsing lashing phasing planish sapling shaping. *See* **aghiln agilnp agilns ahilps**

aghilns   lashing. *See* **agilns aghiln**

aghilnss   hassling lashings slashing lashing sashing signals. *See* **aghiln agilns aginss ailnss**

aghilnsu   languish anguish hauling in-hauls lashing. *See* **aghiln aghisu aghlsu agilns**

aghilnt   halting lathing. *See* **aghilt aghint**

aghilnu   hauling. *See* **aghiln ahilnu agilnu**

aghilnv   halving. *See* **aghiln aghinv agilnv**

aghilnw   whaling. *See* **aghiln aghinw agilnw**

aghilrs   largish. *See* **aghirs agilrs**

aghilrsy   garishly largish grayish. *See* **aghirs agilrs agilry ahlrsy**

aghilst   alights. *See* **aghilt ahilst ghilst**

aghilt   alight laigh light alit gait ghat gilt hail halt hilt lath tail tali ail alt gal gat hag hat hit ita lag lit tag til ah ai at ha hi it la li ta ti

aghimmn   hamming. *See* **agimn**

aghimmns   shamming hamming mashing shaming. *See* **agimns**

aghimmnw   whamming hamming. *See* **aghinw**

aghimnr   harming. *See* **agimnr**

aghimns   mashing shaming. *See* **agimns aghns**

aghimnss   smashing mashing massing sashing shaming. *See* **agimns agimss aginss**

aghinntu   haunting hunting. *See* **aghint aghntu ginntu**

aghinnty   anything. *See* **aghint aghiny ghinty**

aghinox   hoaxing. *See* **aghno aginx**

aghinppw   whapping wapping. *See* **aghinw aginpw**

aghinpr   harping. *See* **aginpr**

aghinprs   phrasing sharping garnish harping parings parsing phasing rasping shaping sharing sparing. *See* **aghirs aghprs aginpr aginrs**

aghinps   phasing shaping. *See* **ahips aginp agins**

aghinpsw   pshawing phasing shaping washing. *See* **aghinw aghnsw aginpw aginsw**

aghinqsu   quashing anguish. *See* **aghisu**

aghinrry   harrying. *See* **aghiny aghrry aginry**

aghinrs   garnish sharing. *See* **aghirs aginrs**

aghinrst   trashing garnish hasting ratings sharing staring tarnish. *See* **aghint aghirs aghirt aghrst**

aghinss   sashing. *See* **aginss aghns aghss**

aghinsst   stashing sashing hasting. *See* **aghint aginss aginst agisst**

aghinssv   shavings sashing savings shaving. *See* **aghinv aginss aginsv ahinsv**

aghinssw   swashing washings sashing washing. *See* **aghinw aghnsw aginss aginsw**

aghinst   hasting. *See* **aginst aghint ghinst**

aghinstw   swathing hasting thawing washing wasting. *See* **aghint aghinw aghnsw aginst**

aghinsu   anguish. *See* **aghisu agins aghns**

aghinsv   shaving. *See* **aghinv aginsv ahinsv**

aghinsw   washing. *See* **aghinw aginsw aghnsw**

aghinsz   hazings. *See* **aghinz aghisz**

aghint   hating giant night thing anti gain gait ghat gnat hang hant hint nigh tang than thin ting ani ant gan gat gin hag hat hin hit ita nag nah nit tag tan tin ah ai an at ha hi in it na ta ti

aghintt   hatting. *See* **aghint aintt ghitt**

aghintw   thawing. *See* **aghint aghinw**

aghinv   having gain hang nigh vain vang vina ani gan gin hag hin nag nah van via ah ai an ha hi in na

aghinw   hawing awing whang wigan gain gnaw hang nigh wain wing ani awn gan gin hag haw hin nag nah wag wan wig win ah ai an aw ha hi in na

aghiny   haying hying ayin gain hang nigh yang ani any gan gay gin hag hay hin nag nah nay yah yin ah ai an ay ha hi in na

aghinz   hazing ghazi gain hang nigh zing ani gan gin hag hin nag nah zag zig ah ai an ha hi in na

aghiost   goatish. *See* **agios agist aghst**

aghirs   garish hairs airs gars gash hags hair rags rahs rash rias rigs sari shag sigh air ash gar gas hag has his rag rah ria rig sag sir ah ai as ha hi is sh si

aghirstt   straight athirst. *See* **aghirs aghirt aghrst agirst**

aghirsy   grayish. *See* **aghirs agrsy ahiry**

aghirt   aright garth girth right gait ghat girt grit hair hart rath trig air art gar gat hag hat hit ita rag rah rat ria rig tag tar ah ai at ha hi it ta ti

aghisu   aguish gash gush hags hugs shag sigh ash gas hag has his hug sag ugh ah ai as ha hi is sh si us

aghisz   ghazis ghazi gash hags shag sigh zags zigs ash gas hag has his sag zag zig ah ai as ha hi is sh si

aghiz   ghazi hag zag zig ah ai ha hi

aghjmno   mahjong. *See* **agmno aghno aghmo**

aghjmnos   mahjongs mahjong. *See* **aghmos aghnos agmnos**

aghkossw   goshawks goshawk. *See* **ahkoss**

aghkosw   goshawk. *See* **agksw gkosw ahksw**

aghlmoor   hologram. *See* **ahlmoo**

aghlmpsu   galumphs galumph. *See* **aghlsu aglmsu almpsu**

aghlmpu   galumph. *See* **aglmu almpu ahlmu**

aghloos   gasohol. *See* **aghlos gloos**

aghlooss   gasohols gasohol. *See* **aghlos ahloss**

aghlos   galosh gaols goals shoal also gals gaol gash goal goas gosh hags halo hogs lags lash logs sago shag slag slog ago ash gal gas goa hag has hog lag log los ohs sag sal sol ah as go ha ho la lo oh os sh so

aghlosu   goulash. *See* **aghlos ghlosu aghlsu**

aghlsty   ghastly. *See* **aghst ahlst ahsty**

aghlsu   laughs hauls hulas laugh gals gash gush hags haul hugs hula lags lash lugs lush shag slag slug ash gal gas hag has hug lag lug sag sal ugh ah as ha la sh us

aghlu   laugh haul hula gal hag hug lag lug ugh ah ha la

aghmmooy   homogamy. *See* **agmooy**

aghmo   ogham ago gam goa hag ham hog mag mho moa mog ohm ah am go ha ho ma mo oh om

aghmos   oghams ogham gams gash goas gosh hags hams hogs mags mash mhos moas mogs ohms sago shag sham smog soma ago ash gam gas goa hag ham has hog mag mho moa mog mos ohm ohs oms sag ah am as go ha ho ma mo oh om os sh so

aghn   hang gan hag nag nah ah an ha na

aghno   hogan agon hang hong ago gan goa hag hog hon nag nah nog ah an go ha ho na no oh on

aghnos   hogans gnash hangs hogan hongs agon gash goas gosh hags hang hogs hong nags naos nogs nosh sago sang shag snag song ago ash gan gas goa hag has hog hon nag nah nog ohs sag son ah an as go ha ho na no oh on os sh so

aghnostu   hangouts gunshot hangout hognuts nougats shotgun. *See* **aghnos aghntu aghstu agnost**

aghnotu   hangout. *See* **ghnotu aghntu agnotu**

aghnpsu   hangups. *See* **aghns agnsu agnps**

aghns   gnash hangs gash hags hang nags sang shag snag ash gan gas hag has nag nah sag ah an as ha na sh

aghnsw   whangs gnash gnaws hangs swang whang awns gash gnaw hags hang haws nags sang sawn shag shaw snag swag swan wags wash ash awn gan gas hag has haw nag nah sag saw wag wan was ah an as aw ha na sh

aghntu   naught aught gaunt haunt aunt ghat gnat guan hang hant hung hunt tang than thug tuna ant gan gat gnu gun gut hag hat hug hut nag nah nut tag tan tau tug tun ugh ah an at ha na nu ta ut

aghntuy   naughty. *See* **aghntu antuy agnty**

aghnw   whang hang gnaw awn gan hag haw nag nah wag wan ah an aw ha na

aghoqsu   quahogs. *See* **aghoqu agqsu ahqsu**

aghoqu   quahog quag ago goa hag hog hug qua ugh ah go ha ho oh

aghoy   hoagy yoga ahoy ago gay goa goy hag hay hog hoy yah ah ay go ha ho oh oy

aghpr   graph harp gap gar hag hap pah par rag rah rap ah ha pa

aghprs   graphs graph grasp harps sharp sprag gaps gars gash gasp hags haps harp hasp pars rags rahs raps rash rasp shag spar ash asp gap gar gas hag hap has pah par pas rag rah rap sag sap spa ah as ha pa sh

aghrry   gharry harry gray gar gay hag hay rag rah ray yah yar ah ay ha

aghrst   garths garth ghats harts trash arts gars gash gats ghat hags hart hast hats rags rahs rash rath rats shag stag star tags tars tsar art ash gar gas gat hag has hat rag rah rat sag sat tag tar ah as at ha sh ta

aghrt   garth ghat hart rath art gar gat hag hat rag rah rat tag tar ah at ha ta

aghs   gash hags shag ash gas hag has sag ah as ha sh

aghss   shags gash hags sags sash shag ash ass gas hag has sag ah as ha sh

aghst   ghats gash gats ghat hags hast hats shag stag tags ash gas gat hag has hat sag sat tag ah as at ha sh ta

aghstu   aughts aught ghats thugs gash gats ghat gush gust guts hags hast hats hugs huts shag shut stag tags thug thus tugs tush ash gas gat gut hag has hat hug hut sag sat tag tau tug ugh ah as at ha sh ta us ut

aght   ghat gat hag hat tag ah at ha ta

aghttu   taught aught gutta ghat taut that thug gat gut hag hat hug hut tag tat tau tug tut ugh ah at ha ta ut

aghtu   aught ghat thug gat gut hag hat hug hut tag tau tug ugh ah at ha ta ut

agiiinns   insignia. *See* **agins**

agiijln   jailing. *See* **agiiln**

agiilmn   mailing. *See* **agiiln agiimn agilmn aiilmn giilmn**

agiilmnp   impaling limping mailing palming. *See* **agiiln agiimn agilmn agilnp**

agiilmns   mailings lingams mailing maligns nilgais sailing sliming smiling. *See* **agiiln agiimn agilmn agilns**

agiiln   ailing nilgai align ligan linga anil gain ilia lain ling nail ail ani gal gan gin lag nag nil ai an in la li na

agiilnn   alining nailing. *See* **agiiln giilnn**

agiilnnu   inguinal alining nailing. *See* **agiiln agilnu ailnnu giilnn**

agiilnny   inlaying alining nailing. *See* **agiiln agilny giilnn**

agiilnor   original ligroin railing roiling. *See* **agiiln agiinr agilor aginor**

agiilnot   intaglio ligation tailing toiling. *See* **agiiln agilot ailnot giilno**

agiilnpt   plaiting pigtail pintail plating tailing. *See* **agiiln agilnp aginpt ailnpt**

agiilnqu   quailing. *See* **agiiln agilnu**

agiilnr   railing. *See* **agiiln agiinr giilnr**

agiilnrt   trailing railing tailing. *See* **agiiln agiinr aginrt ailnrt**

agiilnrv   rivaling virginal railing vailing. *See* **agiiln agiinr agilnv aginrv**

agiilns   nilgais sailing. *See* **agiiln agilns**

agiilnt   tailing. *See* **agiiln giilnt**

agiilntt   litigant tailing tilting titling. *See* **agiiln giilnt**

agiilntv   vigilant tailing vailing. *See* **agiiln agilnv giilnt giilnv**

agiilnv   vailing. *See* **agiiln agilnv giilnv**

agiilnw   wailing. *See* **agiiln agilnw giilnw**

agiilpst   pigtails pigtail. *See* **ailpst iilpst**

agiilpt   pigtail. *See* **ailpt**

agiilty   agility. *See* **agily ailty**

agiimmn   maiming. *See* **agiimn giimmn**

agiimms   imagism. *See* **aimms agims**

agiimn   aiming gamin gain main mina aim ani gam gan gin mag man nag nim ai am an in ma mi na

agiimnow   miaowing. *See* **agiimn gimnow**

agiimor   origami. *See* **agimo**

agiimors   origamis origami. *See* **agimos agmors**

agiimsst   imagists imagist stigmas. *See* **agisst agimss agimst .imsst**

agiimst   imagist. *See* **agimst**

agiinnp   paining. *See* **giinnp aginp ainnp**

agiinnpt   painting paining panting. *See* **aginpt giinnp**

agiinnr   ingrain raining. *See* **agiinr**

agiinnrs   ingrains arising ingrain raining raising rinsing. *See* **agiinr aginrs aiinrs**

agiinnrt   training ingrain raining ranting. *See* **agiinr aginrt**

agiinnst   staining. *See* **aginst aiinst**

agiinntt   tainting tinting. *See* **agint aintt**

agiinopt   opiating. *See* **aginpt ginopt**

agiinort   rigatoni orating rioting. *See* **agiinr aginor aginrt ainort**

agiinpr   pairing. *See* **agiinr aginpr giinpr**

agiinprs aspiring pairings praising arising aspirin pairing parings parsing raising rasping sparing spiring. *See* **agiinr aginpr aginrs agnprs**

agiinprt pirating pairing parting prating. *See* **agiinr aginpr aginpt aginrt**

agiinr airing grain gain gnar grin rain rang rani ring air ani gan gar gin nag rag ran ria rig ai an in na

agiinrrv arriving. *See* **agiinr aginrv**

agiinrs arising raising. *See* **agiinr aginrs aiinrs giinrs**

agiinrtt attiring ratting. *See* **agiinr aginrt**

agiinsv visaing. *See* **aginsv giinsv**

agiintw waiting. *See* **giintw aginw agint**

agiintx taxiing. *See* **agintx**

agiinvw waiving. *See* **aginvw giinvw**

agijmmn jamming. *See* **agimn**

agijmnor majoring roaming. *See* **agimnr aginor agjnor**

agijnntu jaunting. *See* **ginntu**

agijnrr jarring. *See* **aginr**

agijnw jawing awing wigan gain gnaw wain wing ani awn gan gin jag jaw jig nag wag wan wig win ai in aw in na

agijnzz jazzing. *No 6s or 5s*

agijssw jigsaws. *See* **agijsw agssw gissw**

agijsw jigsaw jags jaws jigs swag swig wags wigs gas jag jaw jig sag saw wag was wig wis ai as aw is si

agikkny yakking. *See* **agikn ikkny**

agiklmor kilogram. *See* **agilor**

agiklnnp planking planing. *See* **agilnp aiknnp**

agiklnnr rankling larking ranking. *See* **agiknr**

agiklnop polkaing. *See* **agilnp agklno aiklno giknop**

agiklnr larking. *See* **agiknr agiln agilr**

agiklns slaking. *See* **agilns agikns**

agiklnst stalking lasting salting skating slaking slating staking staling talking tasking. *See* **agikns agiknt agilns aginst**

agiklnt talking. *See* **agiknt agiln gilnt**

agiklnw walking. *See* **agiknw agilnw**

agikmn making kiang gamin akin gain gink kami kina king main mina mink aim ani gam gan gin ink kin mag man nag nim ai am an in ka ma mi na

agikmnr marking. *See* **agimnr agikmn agiknr**

agikmnrs markings margins marking masking. *See* **agikmn agiknr agikns agimnr**

agikmns masking. *See* **agikns agimns aikmns agikmn**

agikn kiang akin gain gink kina king ani gan gin ink kin nag ai an in ka na

agiknnpp knapping napping. *See* **aiknnp**

agiknnps spanking snaking napkins. *See* **agikns aiknnp ainnps**

agiknnr ranking. *See* **agiknr**

agiknnrs rankings ranking snaking. *See* **agiknr agikns aginrs**

agiknns snaking. *See* **agikns**

agiknnt tanking. *See* **agiknt**

agiknny yanking. *See* **agikn**

agiknos soaking. *See* **agikns**

agiknost goatskin agonist skating soaking staking stoking tasking. *See* **agikns agiknt aginst agnost**

agiknoy kayoing okaying. *See* **giknoy agikn agnoy**

agiknpr parking. *See* **aginpr agiknr**

agiknprs sparking parings parking parsing rasping sparing. *See* **agiknr agikns aginpr aginrs**

agiknqu quaking. *See* **agikn**

agiknr raking kiang grain akin gain gink gnar grin kina king knar nark rain raki rang rani rank ring rink air ani ark gan gar gin ink irk kin kir nag rag ran ria rig ai an in ka na

agikns asking gaskin kiangs gains ginks kiang kings akin gain gink gins inks kina king nags sain saki sang sank sign sing sink skin snag ani ask gan gas gin ink kas kin nag sag sin ski ai an as in is ka na si

agiknss gaskins. *See* **agikns aginss**

agiknst skating staking tasking. *See* **agikns aginst agiknt**

agiknt taking kiang giant akin anti gain gait gink gnat kina king knit tang tank ting ani ant gan gat gin ink ita kat kin kit nag nit tag tan tin ai an at in it ka na ta ti**

agiknw waking awing kiang wigan akin gain gawk gink gnaw kina king wain wing wink ani awn gan gin ink kin nag wag wan wig win ai an aw in ka na

agillmnu mulligan gallium lingual mauling mulling. *See* **agillu agilmn agilnu ailmnu**

agillmsu galliums gallium ligulas. *See* **agillu aglmsu**

agillmu gallium. *See* **agillu aglmu**

agillnow allowing walling. *See* **agilnw agllno gilnow**

agillnoy alloying allying. *See* **agilny agllno gllnoy**

agillnp palling. *See* **agilnp**

agillnru alluring lingual. *See* **agillu agilnu aglnru ailnru**

agillnry rallying allying angrily. *See* **agilny agilry aginry**

agillnst stalling install lasting salting slating staling. *See* **agilns aginst ailnst gilnst**

agillnsy sallying signally allying slaying. *See* **agilns agilny aginsy aglnsy**

agillnty tallying allying. *See* **agilny aglnty ailnty**

agillnu lingual. *See* **agillu agilnu**

agillnw walling. *See* **agilnw**

agillny allying. *See* **agilny**

agillopt gallipot galliot. *See* **agilot agllop**

agillor gorilla. *See* **agilor gillr**

agillors gorillas girasol glorias gorilla. *See* **agilor agilrs aglors ailors**

agillost galliots galliot galiots. *See* **agilot aglost allost**

agillot galliot. *See* **agilot allot**

agillssy glassily. *See* **aglssy**

agillsu ligulas. *See* **agillu aglls gills**

agillu ligula gall gill gull ail all gal ill lag lug ai la li

agilmm gimmal glim imam mail maim malm ail aim gal gam lag lam mag mil mim ai am la li ma mi

agilmmn lamming. *See* **agilmm agilmn**

agilmmns slamming gimmals lamming lingams maligns. *See* **agilmm agilmn agilns agimns**

agilmms gimmals. *See* **agilmm aimms ailms**

agilmn laming lingam malign align gamin ligan linga anil gain glim lain limn ling mail main mina nail ail aim ani gal gam gan gin lag lam mag man mil nag nil nim ai am an in la li ma mi na

agilmnnt mantling malting. *See* **agilmn agimnn agimnt**

agilmno loaming. *See* **agilmn aglmno ailmno**

agilmnp palming. *See* **agilmn agilnp**

agilmnps sampling lapsing lingams maligns palming sapling. *See* **agilmn agilnp agilns agimns**

agilmns lingams maligns. *See* **agilns agimns agilmn**

agilmnt malting. *See* **agilmn agimnt**

agilmnu mauling. *See* **ailmnu agilmn agilnu**

agilmors algorism girasol glorias. *See* **agilor agilrs agimos aglors**

agiln align ligan linga anil gain lain ling nail ail ani gal gan gin lag nag nil ai an in la li na

agilnnnp planning planing panning. *See* **agilnp**

agilnno loaning. *See* **aglnno agiln ainno**

agilnnp planing. *See* **agilnp ainnp**

agilnnpt planting panting planing plating. *See* **agilnp aginpt ailnpt**

agilnnrs snarling linsang. *See* **agilns agilrs aginrs aglnrs**

agilnns linsang. *See* **agilns**

agilnnss linsangs linsang signals. *See* **agilns aginss ailnss**

agilnnst slanting lasting linsang salting slating staling. *See* **agilns aginst ailnst gilnst**

agilnnuy ungainly. *See* **ailnnu agilny agilnu**

agilnopr paroling. *See* **agilnp agilor aginor aginpr**

agilnort trigonal orating. *See* **agilor agilot aginor aginrt**

agilnoss lassoing signals slogans. *See* **agilns aginss aglnos ailnss**

agilnott totaling lotting. *See* **agilot ailnot ginott**

agilnp paling align aping lapin ligan linga plain anil gain lain ling nail nipa pail pain pang ping plan ail alp ani gal gan gap gin gip lag lap lip nag nap nil nip pal pan pig pin ai an in la li na pa pi

agilnpp lapping. *See* **agilnp ailpp**

agilnpps slapping lapping lapsing sapling sapping. *See* **agilnp agilns ailnps ailpps**

agilnppy applying lapping playing yapping. *See* **agilnp agilny aginpy gilnpy**

agilnps lapsing sapling. *See* **agilns ailnps agilnp**

agilnpss saplings lapsing passing sapling signals spinals. *See* **agilnp agilns aginss ailnps**

agilnpst stapling lapsing lasting pasting plaints plating salting sapling slating staling. *See* **agilnp agilns aginpt agintst**

agilnpsw lapwings lapsing lapwing sapling. *See* **agilnp agilns agilnw aginpw**

agilnpsy palsying splaying lapsing playing sapling slaying spangly spaying. *See* **agilnp agilns agilny aginpy**

agilnpt plating. *See* **agilnp ailnpt aginpt**

agilnptt platting plating patting. *See* **agilnp aginpt ailnpt**

agilnpw lapwing. *See* **agilnp aginpw agilnw**

agilnpy playing. *See* **agilny agilnp aginpy gilnpy**

agilnrss rassling signals. *See* **agilns agilrs aginrs aginss**

agilnrst starling lasting ratings salting slating staling staring. *See* **agilns agilrs aginrs aginrt**

agilnrsu singular insular langurs rulings urinals. *See* **agilns agilnu agilrs aginrs**

agilnrtt rattling ratting. *See* **aginrt ailnrt**

agilnrtw trawling. *See* **agilnw aginrt aginrw ailnrt**

agilnry angrily. *See* **agilny agilry aginry**

agilns aligns ligans lingas signal align anils gains glans ligan linga lings nails slain slang sling snail ails anil gain gals gins lags lain ling nags nail nils sail sain sang sign sing slag snag ail ani gal gan gas gin lag nag nil sag sal sin ai an as in is la li na si

agilnss signals. *See* **agilns aginss gilnss ailnss**

agilnst lasting salting slating staling. *See* **agilns aginst gilnst ailnst**

agilnstt slatting lasting salting slating staling stating tasting. *See* **agilns aginst ailnst ainstt**

agilnstu saluting lasting lusting salting slating staling. *See* **agilns agilnu aginst ailnst**

agilnsv salving slaving. *See* **agilns ailnsv agilnv aginsv**

agilnsy slaying. *See* **agilns agilny ailnsy gilnsy aginsy**

agilnttt tattling tatting. *See* **agiln ailtt agint**

agilnttw wattling. *See* **agilnw**

agilntuv vaulting valuing. *See* **agilnu agilnv gilntu**

agilntux luxating. *See* **agilnu agintx gilntu**

agilntwz waltzing. *See* **agilnw agilnz**

agilnu lingua align ligan linga lungi anil gain guan lain ling lung nail ulna ail ani gal gan gin gnu gun lag lug nag nil ai an in la li na nu

agilnuv valuing. *See* **agilnu agilnv**

agilnv laving align anvil ligan linga nival anil gain lain ling nail vail vain vang vial vina ail ani gal gan gin lag nag nil van via ai an in la li na

agilnw waling align awing ligan linga wigan anil gain gnaw lain lawn ling nail wail wain wing ail ani awl awn gal gan gin lag law nag nil wag wan wig win ai an aw in la li na

agilnwy yawling. *See* **agilny agilnw aginwy**

agilny gainly laying align gaily inlay ligan linga lying anil ayin gain inly lain ling liny nail yang ail ani any gal gan gay gin lag lay nag nay nil yin ai an ay in la li na

agilnz lazing align ligan linga anil gain lain ling nail zing ail ani gal gan gin lag nag nil zag zig ai an in la li na

agilor gloria argol glair goral largo agio aril gaol girl goal lair liar lira oral rail rial roil ago ail air gal gar goa lag lar log oar oil rag ria rig ai go la li lo or

agilors girasol glorias. *See* **aglors agilrs agilor ailors**

agilorss girasols girasol glorias sailors. *See* **agilor agilrs aglors ailors**

agilost galiots. *See* **agilot aglost**

agilot galiot gloat agio alit alto gait gaol gilt goal goat iota lota tail tali toga toil tola ago ail alt gal gat goa got ita lag lit log lot oat oil tag til tog ai at go it la li lo ta ti to

agilov ogival viola agio gaol goal oval vail vial viol ago ail gal goa lag log oil ova via ai go la li lo

agilr glair aril girl lair liar lira rail rial ail air gal gar lag lar rag ria rig ai la li

agilrs glairs arils girls glair lairs liars liras rails rials ails airs aril gals gars girl lags lair liar lira rags rail rial rias rigs sail sari slag ail air gal gar gas lag lar rag ria rig sag sal sir ai as is la li si

agilry glairy gaily glair glary gyral riyal airy aril aryl girl gray lair liar lira rail rial ail air gal gar gay lag lar lay rag ray ria rig yar ai ay la li

agiluyz gauzily. *See* **agily aguyz**

agily gaily ail gal gay lag lay ai ay la li

agimmnr ramming. *See* **agimnr**

agimmosy misogamy. *See* **agimos aimmos ammosy**

agimn gamin gain main mina aim ani gam gan gin mag man nag nim ai am an in ma mi na

agimnn naming gamin gain main mina aim ani gam gan gin inn mag man nag nim ai am an in ma mi na

agimnnn manning. *See* **agimnn**

agimnno moaning. *See* **aimnno gimnno agimnn**

agimnnru manuring unarming. *See* **agimnn agimnr agmnnu**

agimnnw wingman. *See* **aginnw agimnn**

agimnor roaming. *See* **agimnr aginor**

agimnors organism margins roaming signora soaring. *See* **agimnr agimns agimos aginor**

agimnosv vamosing. *See* **agimns agimos aginsv agmnos**

agimnpp mapping. *See* **agimn aginp**

agimnpr ramping. *See* **agimnr aginpr**

agimnprt tramping migrant parting prating ramping tamping. *See* **agimnr agimnt aginpr aginpt**

agimnpst stamping matings pasting tamping. *See* **agimns agimnt agimst aginpt**

agimnpsw swamping. *See* **agimns aginpw aginsw**

agimnpt tamping. *See* **agimnt aimnpt aginpt**

agimnpv vamping. *See* **aginpv agimn aimnv**

agimnr arming margin gamin grain amir gain gnar gram grim grin main mina rain rami rang rani ring aim air ani arm gam gan gar gin mag man mar mir nag nim rag ram ran ria rig rim ai am an in ma mi na

agimnrr marring. *See* **agimnr**

agimnrry _marrying marring. *See* **agimnr agimny aginry**

agimnrs margins. *See* **agimnr agimns aginrs**

agimnrst migrants smarting margins martins matings migrant ratings staring. *See* **agimnr agimns agimnt agimst**

agimnrsw swarming margins warming. *See* **agimnr agimns aginrs aginrw**

agimnrt migrant. *See* **agimnr aimnrt agimnt aginrt**

agimnrtu maturing migrant. *See* **agimnr agimnt aginrt agirtu**

agimnrw warming. *See* **agimnr aginrw**

agimns gamins gains gamin mains sigma aims gain gams gins mags main mina nags nims sain sang sign sing snag aim ani gam gan gas gin mag man mis nag nim sag sin ai am an as in is ma mi na si

agimnss massing. *See* **aginss agimns agimss**

agimnssu assuming amusing massing musings mussing. *See* **agimns agimss aginss aimnsu**

agimnst matings. *See* **agimns aginst aimnst agimnt agimst**

agimnsu amusing. *See* **aimnsu agimns gimnsu**

agimnt mating taming gamin giant matin anti gain gait gnat main mina mint tang ting aim ani ant gam gan gat gin ita mag man mat nag nim nit tag tam tan tin ai am an at in it ma mi na ta ti

agimntt matting. *See* **agimnt**

agimnttu mutating matting. *See* **agimnt aimntu amnttu gimntu**

agimny maying gamin mangy ayin gain gamy main many mina myna yang aim ani any gam gan gay gin gym mag man may nag nay nim yam yin ai am an ay in ma mi my na

agimnz mazing gamin gain main mina zing aim ani gam gan gin mag man nag nim zag zig ai am an in ma mi na

agimo amigo imago agio ago aim gam goa mag moa mog ai am go ma mi mo om

agimorrt migrator. *See* **amorrt**

agimorsu gouramis gourami giaours. *See* **agimos agioru agmors amorsu**

agimoru gourami. *See* **agioru agimo amoru**

agimos amigos agios amigo gismo imago sigma agio aims gams goas mags moas mogs sago smog soma ago aim gam gas

goa mag mis moa mog mos oms sag ai am as go is ma mi mo om os si so

agimqruy quagmiry. *See* **gimry aimqu**

agims sigma aims gams mags aim gam gas mag mis sag ai am as is ma mi si

agimss sigmas sigma amiss aims gams mags mass miss sags aim ass gam gas mag mis sag sis ai am as is ma mi si

agimsst stigmas. *See* **agisst agimss agimst**

agimst stigma gaits sigma aims gait gams gats gist mags mast mats mist stag tags tams aim gam gas gat ita its mag mat mis sag sat sit tag tam ai am as at is it ma mi si ta ti

agimsww wigwams. *See* **agimww agims aimsw**

agimww wigwam aim gam mag maw wag wig ai am aw ma mi

agin gain ani gan gin nag ai an in na

aginnnoy annoying. *See* **agnoy ainno annoy**

aginnnp panning. *See* **aginp ainnp**

aginnnps spanning panning. *See* **ainnps**

aginnnt tanning. *See* **ainnnt agint**

aginnnw wanning. *See* **aginnw**

aginnopt poignant atoning panting. *See* **aginpt ainnot ginnot ginopt**

aginnort ignorant atoning orating ranting. *See* **aginor aginrt ainnot ainort**

aginnot atoning. *See* **ainnot ginnot**

aginnott notating atoning. *See* **ainnot ginnot ginott**

aginnpp napping. *See* **aginp ainnp**

aginnpps snapping napping sapping. *See* **ainnps**

aginnpsw spawning wingspan pawning awnings. *See* **aginnw aginpw aginsw ainnps**

aginnpt panting. *See* **aginpt ainnp**

aginnpw pawning. *See* **aginnw aginpw**

aginnqtu quanting quintan. *See* **ainqtu ginntu**

aginnrsw warnings warning awnings. *See* **aginnw aginrs aginrw aginsw**

aginnrt ranting. *See* **aginrt**

aginnrw warning. *See* **aginnw aginrw**

aginnry yarning. *See* **aginry agnnry**

aginnsw awnings. *See* **aginnw aginsw**

aginnttu attuning taunting nutting. *See* **annttu ginntu**

aginntuv vaunting. *See* **ginntu**

aginntw wanting. *See* **aginnw**

aginnw awning waning awing wigan gain gnaw wain wing ani awn gan gin inn nag wag wan wig win ai an aw in na

aginnwy yawning. *See* **aginnw aginwy**

aginoort rogation orating oration rooting. *See* **aginor aginrt ainort anoort**

aginopps apposing sapping soaping sopping. *See* **ainops ginops**

aginopqu opaquing. *See* **agnoqu ainoqu**

aginops soaping. *See* **ginops ainops**

aginor oaring argon grain groan groin noria organ agio agon gain gnar grin iron rain rang rani ring roan ago air ani gan gar gin goa ion nag nog nor oar rag ran ria rig ai an go in na no on or

aginorr roaring. *See* **aginor giorr**

aginorrs garrison roaring signora soaring. *See* **aginor aginrs agnors ainors**

aginors signora soaring. *See* **agnors aginrs ginors ainors aginor**

aginorss assignor signoras sarongs signora signors soaring. *See* **aginor aginrs aginss agnors**

aginorst organist roasting agonist orating ratings rations signora soaring sorting staring orating trigons. *See* **aginor aginrs aginrt aginst**

aginorsu arousing giaours rousing signora soaring souring. *See* **aginor aginrs agioru agnors**

aginorsv savoring signora soaring viragos. *See* **aginor aginrs aginrv aginsv**

aginort orating. *See* **aginor aginrt ainort ginort**

aginortt rotating orating ratting rotting. *See* **aginor aginrt ainort anortt**

aginorty gyration orating. *See* **aginor aginrt aginry agnory**

aginosst agonists agonist tossing. *See* **aginss aginst agisst agnost**

aginost agonist. *See* **aginst ginost agnost**

aginostt toasting agonist stating station tasting. *See* **aginst agnost ainstt ginost**

aginovw avowing. *See* **aginvw ginovw**

aginp aping gain nipa pain pang ping ani gan gap gin gip nag nap nip pan pig pin ai an in na pa pi

aginppr rapping. *See* **aginpr**

aginpprw wrapping rapping wapping warping. *See* **aginpr aginpw aginrw**

aginpps sapping. *See* **aginp agins ainps**

aginppsw swapping sapping wapping. *See* **aginpw aginsw**

aginppt tapping. *See* **aginpt**

aginpptu pupating tapping. *See* **aginpt ginptu**

aginppw wapping. *See* **aginpw**

aginppy yapping. *See* **aginpy anppy inppy**

aginppz zapping. *See* **aginp**

aginpr paring raping aping grain gain gnar grin grip nipa pain pair pang ping pirn prig rain rang rani ring air ani gan gap gar gin gip nag nap nip pan par pig pin rag ran rap ria rig rip ai an in na pa pi

aginprr parring. *See* **aginpr**

aginprrs sparring parings parring parsing rasping sparing. *See* **aginpr aginrs agnprs ainprs**

aginprry parrying parring praying. *See* **aginpr aginpy aginry ginpry**

aginprs parings parsing rasping sparing. *See* **aginrs aginpr ainprs agnprs ginprs**

aginprst partings parings parsing parting pasting prating rasping ratings sparing spirant staring. *See* **aginpr aginpt aginrs aginrt**

aginprsy spraying parings parsing praying rasping sparing spaying springy. *See* **aginpr aginpy aginrs aginry**

aginprt parting prating. *See* **aginpr aginrt aginpt**

aginprty partying parting prating praying. *See* **aginpr aginpt aginpy aginrt**

aginprw warping. *See* **aginpr aginpw aginrw**

aginpry praying. *See* **aginry aginpr aginpy ginpry**

aginpss passing. *See* **aginss aginp aipss**

aginpst pasting. *See* **agnst ainpst aginpt**

aginpstt spatting pasting patting stating tasting. *See* **aginpt agnst ainpst ainstt**

aginpsu pausing. *See* **aginp agins agnsu**

aginpsy spaying. *See* **aginpy aginsy ginpsy**

aginpt taping aping giant inapt paint anti gain gait gnat nipa pain pang pant ping pint pita tang ting ani ant apt gan gap gat gin gip ita nag nap nip nit pan pat pig pin pit tag tan tap tin tip ai an at in it na pa pi ta ti

aginptt patting. *See* **aginpt aintt**

aginpv paving aping gain nipa pain pang ping vain vang vina ani gan gap gin gip nag nap nip pan pig pin van via ai an in na pa pi

aginpw pawing aping awing wigan gain gnaw nipa pain pang pawn ping wain wing ani awn gan gap gin gip nag nap nip pan paw pig pin wag wan wap wig win ai an aw in na pa pi

aginpy paying aping ayin gain nipa pain pang ping piny yang ani any gan gap gay gin gip gyp nag nap nay nip pan pay pig pin pya yap yin yip ai an ay in na pa pi

aginqrsu squaring. *See* **aginrs**

aginr grain gain gnar grin rain rang rani ring air ani gan gar gin nag rag ran ria rig ai an in na

aginrrst starring ratings staring. *See* **aginrs aginrt aginst agirst**

aginrrty tarrying trying.. *See* **agnrty aginry airrty aginrt**

aginrrw warring. *See* **aginrw**

aginrs grains rasing gains gnars grain grins naris rains ranis rings airs gain gars gins gnar grin nags rags rain rang rani rias rigs ring sain sang sari sign sing snag air ani gan gar gas gin nag rag ran ria rig sag sin sir ai an as in is na si

aginrssu assuring. *See* **aginrs aginss agrssu**

aginrst ratings staring. *See* **agnst aginrs agnrst agirst ainrst**

aginrstv starving ratings staring staving. *See* **aginrs aginrt aginrv agnst**

aginrsty stingray straying ratings staring staying stringy. *See* **aginrs aginrt aginry agnst**

aginrt rating taring giant grain grant riant train anti gain gait girt gnar gnat grin grit rain rang rani rant ring tang ting trig air ani ant art gan gar gat gin ita nag nit rag ran rat ria rig tag tan tar tin ai an at in it na ta ti

aginrtt ratting. *See* **aginrt**

aginrv raving grain virga gain gnar grin rain rang rani ring vain vair vang vina air ani gan gar gin nag rag ran ria rig van via ai an in na

aginrvy varying. *See* **aginry aginrv**

aginrw waring awing grain wigan wring gain gnar gnaw grin rain rang rani ring wain warn wing air ani awn gan gar gin nag rag ran raw ria rig wag wan war wig win ai an aw in na

aginry grainy raying angry grain rainy rangy airy ayin gain gnar gray grin nary rain rang rani ring yang yarn air ani any gan gar gay gin nag nay rag ran ray ria rig yar yin ai an ay in na

aginrz razing grain gain gnar grin rain rang rani ring zing air ani gan gar gin nag rag ran ria rig zag zig ai an in na

aginrzz razzing. *See* **aginrz**

agins gains gain gins nags sain sang sign sing snag ani gan gas gin nag sag sin ai an as in is na si

aginss assign gains signs sings snags gain gins nags sags sain sang sign sing sins snag ani ass gan gas gin nag sag sin sis ai an as in is na si

aginsss assigns sassing. *See* **aginss**

aginssv savings. *See* **aginss aginsv ainssv**

aginssy sayings. *See* **aginss aginsy**

aginst giants sating antis gains gaits giant gnats saint satin stain stang sting tangs tings anti ants gain gait gats gins gist gnat nags nits sain sang sign sing snag snit stag tags tang tans ting tins ani ant gan gas gat gin ita its nag nit sag sat sin sit tag tan tin ai an as at in is it na si ta ti

aginstt stating tasting. *See* **aginst ainstt**

aginsttt tattings stating tasting tatting. *See* **aginst ainstt**

aginsttw swatting stating tasting wasting. *See* **aginst aginsw agnstw ainstt**

aginstv staving. *See* **aginst aginsv**

aginstw wasting. *See* **aginst aginsw ainstw agnstw**

aginsty staying. *See* **aginst ainsty aginsy ginsty**

aginsv saving gains savin vangs vinas gain gins nags sain sang sign sing snag vain vang vans vina visa ani gan gas gin nag sag sin van via ai an as in is na si

aginsvvy savvying. *See* **aginsv aginsy**

aginsw sawing wigans awing gains gnaws swain swang swing wains wigan wings awns gain gins gnaw nags sain sang sawn sign sing snag swag swan swig wags wain wigs wing wins ani awn gan gas gin nag sag saw sin wag wan was wig win wis ai an as aw in is na si

aginswy swaying. *See* **aginsw aginsy ginswy aginwy**

aginsy saying ayins gains yangs ayin gain gays gins nags sain sang sign sing snag yang ani any gan gas gay gin nag nay sag say sin yin ai an as ay in is na si

agint giant anti gain gait gnat tang ting ani ant gan gat gin ita nag nit tag tan tin ai an at in it na ta ti

aginttt tatting. *See* **agint aintt**

aginttv vatting. *See* **agint aittv**

agintx taxing giant axing anti gain gait gnat tang taxi ting ani ant gan gat gin ita nag nit nix tag tan tax tin ai an at ax in it na ta ti xi

agintxy taxying. *See* **agintx agnty ginty**

aginvw waving awing wigan gain gnaw vain vang vina wain wing ani awn gan gin nag van via wag wan wig win ai an aw in na

aginw awing wigan gain gnaw wain wing ani awn gan gin nag wag wan wig win ai an aw in na

aginwx waxing awing axing wigan gain gnaw wain wing ani awn gan gin nag nix wag wan wax wig win ai an aw ax in na xi

aginwy yawing awing wigan ayin gain gnaw wain wany wing winy yang yawn ani any awn gan gay gin nag nay wag wan way wig win yaw yin ai an aw ay in na

aginx axing gain ani gan gin nag nix ai an ax in na xi

agio agio ago goa ai go

agiorsu giaours. *See* **agioru agios agrsu**

agiorsv   viragos. *See* **aiorsv giorsv agiorv agirsv**

agioru   giaour agio gaur ruga ago air gar goa oar our rag ria rig rug ai go or

agiorv   virago virga vigor agio vair ago air gar goa oar ova rag ria rig via ai go or

agios   agios agio goas sago ago gas goa sag ai as go is os si so

agiostu   agoutis. *See* **agiotu agios agist**

agiotu   agouti agio auto gait goat gout iota toga ago gat goa got gut ita oat out tag tau tog tug tui ai at go it ta ti to ut

agirst   gratis astir gaits girts grist grits sitar stair stria tarsi trigs airs arts gait gars gats girt gist grit rags rats rias rigs sari stag star stir tags tars trig tsar air art gar gas gat ita its rag rat ria rig sag sat sir sit tag tar ai as at is it si ta ti

agirstu   guitars. *See* **agirst agirtu agrstu**

agirsv   virgas virga vairs airs gars rags rias rigs sari vair visa air gar gas rag ria rig sag sir via ai as is si

agirttuy   gratuity. *See* **agirtu airtty girtty**

agirtu   guitar gait gaur girt grit ruga trig air art gar gat gut ita rag rat ria rig rug rut tag tar tau tug tui ai at it ta ti ut

agirtvy   gravity. *See* **agirv agrvy**

agirv   virga vair air gar rag ria rig via ai

agisst   agists gaits gists stags gait gats gist sags sits stag tags tass ass gas gat ita its sag sat sis sit tag ai as at is it si ta ti

agist   gaits gait gats gist stag tags gas gat ita its sag sat sit tag ai as at is it si ta ti

agit   gait gat ita tag ai at it ta ti

agj   jag

agjlmo   logjam gaol goal loam mola ago gal gam goa jag jam jog lag lam log mag moa mog am go jo la lo ma mo om

agjlmos   logjams. *See* **agjlmo aglos almos**

agjlrsuu   jugulars jugular. *See* **agrsuu**

agjlruu   jugular. *See* **agruu agjlu ajlru**

agjlu   jugal juga gal jug jug lag lug la

agjnor   jargon argon groan organ agon gnar rang roan ago gan gar goa jag jar jog nag nog nor oar rag raj ran an go jo na no on or

agjnors   jargons. *See* **agnors agjnor**

agjs   jags gas jag sag as

agju   juga jag jug

agklno   kalong along agon gaol goal kaon koan kola lank loan long ago gal gan goa kal koa lag log nag nog oak an go ka la lo na no on

agklnos   kalongs. *See* **agklno aglnos**

agkmmory   kymogram. *See* **agmmy amory ammoy**

agkmnop   kampong. *See* **agmno**

agkmnops   kampongs kampong. *See* **agmnos**

agkorssw   gasworks. *See* **akorss**

agksw   gawks gawk swag wags ask gas kas sag saw wag was as aw ka

agkw   gawk wag ka aw

agkwy   gawky gawk gay wag way yak yaw aw ay ka

agl   gal lag la

agll   gall all gal lag la

agllno   gallon along llano agon gall gaol goal loan long olla ago all gal gan goa lag log nag nog an go la lo na no on

agllnoo   galloon. *See* **agllno aglnoo**

agllnoos   galloons gallons galloon lagoons. *See* **agllno aglnoo aglnos allnos**

agllnos   gallons. *See* **agllno allnos aglnos**

agllnstu   gallnuts gallnut. *See* **alnstu**

agllntu   gallnut. *See* **agntu**

agllop   gallop galop gall gaol glop goal olla opal pall poll ago all alp gal gap goa lag lap log lop pal go la lo pa

agllops   gallops. *See* **agllop aglops**

aglloss   glossal. *See* **aglls aglos aglss**

agllosw   gallows. *See* **allosw**

agllott   glottal. *See* **allot aglot alott**

aglls   galls gall gals lags slag all gal gas lag sag sal as la

aglmno   logman along among mango agon gaol goal loam loan long moan mola noma ago gal gam gan goa lag lam log mag man moa mog mon nag nog am an go la lo ma mo na no om on

aglmopyy   polygamy. *See* **almpy aglop aglyy**

aglmoru   glamour. *See* **aglmu amoru aglor**

aglmsu   algums algum alums mauls alms alum gals gams glum gums lags lams lugs mags maul mugs slag slam slug slum smug gal gam gas gum lag lam lug lum mag mug mus sag sal sum am as la ma mu um us

aglmu   algum alum glum maul gal gam gum lag lam lug lum mag mug am la ma mu um

aglnno   longan along agon anon gaol goal loan long ago gal gan goa lag log nag nog an go la lo na no on

aglnnos   longans. *See* **aglnno aglnos**

aglno   along agon gaol goal loan long ago gal gan goa lag log nag nog an go la lo na no on

aglnoo   lagoon along agon gaol goal goon loan logo long loon ago gal gan goa goo lag log loo nag nog an go la lo na no on

aglnoos   lagoons. *See* **aglnoo alnoos aglnos**

aglnoru   languor. *See* **aglnru aglno aglor**

aglnos   slogan along gaols glans goals loans longs salon slang solan agon also gals gaol goal goas lags loan logs long nags naos nogs sago sang slag slog snag song ago gal gan gas goa lag log los nag nog sag sal sol son an as go la lo na no on os so

aglnoss   slogans. *See* **alnoss aglnos**

aglnoswy   longways. *See* **aglnos aglnsy agnosw**

aglnpsy   spangly. *See* **aglnsy alpsy agnps**

aglnpuy   gunplay. *See* **alpuy**

aglnr   gnarl gnar rang gal gan gar lag lar nag rag ran an la na

aglnrs   gnarls glans gnarl gnars slang snarl gals gars gnar lags nags rags rang sang slag snag gal gan gar gas lag lar nag rag ran sag sal an as la na

aglnrsu   langurs. *See* **aglnrs aglnru**

aglnru   langur gnarl lunar gaur gnar guan lung rang ruga rung ulna gal gan gar gnu gun lag lar lug nag rag ran rug run urn an la na nu

aglns   glans slang gals lags nags sang slag snag gal gan gas lag nag sag sal an as la na

aglnsssu   sunglass. *See* **agssu aglns aglss**

aglnsy   slangy glans slang yangs gals gays lags lays nags sang slag slay snag yang any gal gan gas gay lag lay nag nay sag sal say sly sny an as ay la na

aglntuy   gauntly. *See* **aglnty antuy**

aglnty   tangly tangy gnat tang yang alt ant any gal gan gat gay lag lay nag nay tag tan an at ay la na ta

aglnuu   ungual ungula guan luau lung ulna gal gan gnu gun lag lug nag ulu an la na nu

aglo   gaol goal ago gal goa lag log go la lo

agloopy   apology. *See* **aglop goopy loopy**

agloost   galoots. *See* **agloot aglost**

agloot   galoot gloat alto gaol goal goat logo loot lota toga tola tool ago alt gal gat goa goo got lag log loo lot oat tag tog too at go la lo ta to

aglop   galop gaol glop goal opal ago alp gal gap goa lag lap log lop pal go la lo pa

aglops   galops galop gaols glops goals opals alps also gals gaol gaps gasp glop goal goas lags laps logs lops opal pals sago slag slap slog slop soap ago alp asp gal gap gas goa lag lap log lop los pal pas sag sal sap sol sop spa as go la lo os pa so

aglor   argol goral largo gaol goal oral ago gal gar goa lag lar log oar rag go la lo or

aglors   argols gorals largos argol gaols goals goral largo orals solar also gals gaol gars goal goas lags logs oars oral rags sago slag slog soar sora ago gal gar gas goa lag lar log los oar rag sag sal sol as go la lo or os so

aglorssy   glossary grossly. *See* **aglors aglssy agorsy agrssy**

aglos   gaols goals also gals gaol goal goas lags logs sago slag slog ago gal gas goa lag log los sag sal sol as go la lo os so

aglost   gloats altos gaols gloat goals goats lotas togas tolas also alto alts gals gaol gats goal goas goat lags last logs lost lota lots oast oats sago salt slag slat slog slot stag stoa tags toga togs tola ago alt gal gas gat goa got lag log los lot oat sag sal sat sol sot tag tog as at go la lo os so ta to

aglot   gloat alto gaol goal goat lota toga tola ago alt gal gat goa got lag log lot oat tag tog at go la lo ta to

aglow   aglow alow gaol glow goal ago awl gal goa lag law log low owl wag aw go la lo ow

aglpsssy   spyglass. *See* **aglssy alpssy**

aglrttuu   guttural. *See* **agruu agttu alrtu**

aglruv   vulgar gaur ruga gal gar lag lar lug luv rag rug vug la

aglry   glary gyral gray aryl gal gar gay lag lar lay rag ray yar la ay

aglryy   grayly gayly glary gyral gray aryl gal gar gay lag lar lay rag ray yar yay la ay

agls   gals lags slag gal gas lag sag sal as la

aglss   glass slags gals lags lass sags sals slag ass gal gas lag sag sal la as

aglssy   glassy gassy glass slags slays gals gays lags lass lays sags sals says slag slay ass gal gas gay lag lay sag sal say sly as ay la

aglstuuy   augustly. *See* **agstuu**

aglyy   gayly gal gay lag lay yay la ay

agm   gam mag am ma

agmmno   gammon among mango agon ammo moan noma ago gam gan goa mag man moa mog mom mon nag nog am an go ma mo na no om on

agmmnoor   monogram. *See* **agmmno amnoor**

agmmnooy   monogamy. *See* **agmmno agmooy**

agmmnos   gammons. *See* **agmmno agmnos**

agmmnsu   magnums. *See* **agnsu amnsu ammsu**

agmmy   gammy gamy gam gay gym mag may yam am ay ma my

agmnnosw   gownsman snowman. *See* **agmnos agnosw**

agmnnu   gunman unman guan maun gam gan gnu gum gun mag man mug nag nun am an ma mu na nu um

agmno   among mango agon moan noma ago gam gan goa mag man moa mog

mon nag nog am an go ma mo na no om on

agmnorst   angstrom amongst matrons transom. *See* **agmnos agmors agnors agnost**

agmnorsu   organums organum. *See* **agmnos agmors agnors agnosu**

agmnoru   organum. *See* **agmno amoru agnor**

agmnos   mangos among mango mason moans nomas agon gams goas mags moan moas mogs mons nags naos nogs noma sago sang smog snag soma song ago gam gan gas goa mag man moa mog mon mos nag nog oms sag son am an as go ma mo na no om on os so

agmnost   amongst. *See* **agmnos gmnost agnost**

agmnsstu   mustangs mustang. *See* **agmstu agnsst**

agmnssty   gymnasts gymnast. *See* **agnsst**

agmnstu   mustang. *See* **agmstu anstu agntu**

agmnsty   gymnast. *See* **ansty agnst agmny**

agmny   mangy gamy many myna yang any gam gan gay gym mag man may nag nay yam am an ay ma my na

agmooy   oogamy gamy mayo yoga ago gam gay goa goo goy gym mag may moa mog moo yam am ay go ma mo my om oy

agmoprr   program. *See* **amorr**

agmoprrs   programs program. *See* **agmors agmprs amorrs**

agmors   orgasm grams roams arms gams gars goas gram mags moas mogs mora mors oars rags rams roam sago smog soar soma sora ago arm gam gar gas goa mag mar moa mog mor mos oar oms rag ram sag am as go ma mo om or os so

agmorss   orgasms. *See* **agmors amorss**

agmosyz   zygomas. *See* **agmoyz agosy amosy**

agmoyz   zygoma gamy mayo mazy yoga ago azo gam gay goa goy gym mag may moa mog yam zag zoa am ay go ma mo my om oy

agmp   gamp amp gam gap mag map am ma pa

agmprs   gramps gamps grams grasp prams ramps sprag amps arms gamp gams gaps gars gasp gram mags maps pars pram rags ramp rams raps rasp samp spar amp arm asp gam gap gar gas mag map mar par pas rag ram rap sag sap spa am as ma pa

agmps   gamps amps gamp gams gaps gasp mags maps samp amp asp gam

gap gas mag map pas sag sap spa am as ma pa

agmr   gram arm gam gar mag mar rag ram am ma

agmrs   grams arms gams gars gram mags rags rams arm gam gar gas mag mar rag ram sag am as ma

agms   gams mags gam gas mag sag am as ma

agmstu   gamuts gamut gams gats gums gust guts mags mast mats mugs must smug smut stag stum tags tams tugs gam gas gat gum gut mag mat mug mus sag sat sum tag tam tau tug am as at ma mu ta um us ut

agmtu   gamut gam gat gum gut mag mat mug tag tam tau tug am at ma mu ta um ut

agmy   gamy gam gay gym mag may yam am ay ma my

agn   gan nag an na

agnnnoo   nonagon. *No 6s or 5s*

agnnnoos   nonagons nonagon. *See* **gnoos nnoos**

agnnoor   organon. *See* **agnor**

agnnoors   organons organon. *See* **agnors**

agnnry   granny angry rangy gnar gray nary rang yang yarn any gan gar gay nag nay rag ran ray yar an ay na

agno   agon ago gan goa nag nog an go na no on

agnoqsu   quangos. *See* **agnoqu agnosu**

agnoqu   quango guano agon guan quag ago gan gnu goa gun nag nog qua an go na no nu on

agnor   argon groan organ agon gnar rang roan ago gan gar goa nag nog nor oar rag ran an go na no on or

agnorrst   grantors grantor. *See* **agnors agnost agnrst agorst**

agnorrt   grantor. *See* **agnor agort agnrt**

agnors   argons groans organs sarong argon arson gnars groan organ roans sonar agon gars gnar goas nags naos nogs oars rags rang roan sago sang snag soar song sora ago gan gar gas goa nag nog nor oar rag ran sag son an as go na no on or os so

agnorss   sarongs. *See* **agnors anorss**

agnortuy   nugatory. *See* **agnory agnotu agnrty anortu**

agnory   orangy agony angry argon groan organ rangy rayon agon gnar gory gray gyro nary orgy rang roan yang yarn yoga ago any gan gar gay goa goy nag nay nog nor oar rag ran ray yar yon an ay go na no on or oy

agnost   tangos tongas gnats goats stang tango tangs togas tonga tongs agon ants gats gnat goas goat nags naos nogs nota oast oats sago sang snag snot song stag stoa tags tang tans toga togs tong tons ago ant gan gas gat goa got nag nog not oat sag sat son sot tag tan tog ton an as at go na no on os so ta to

agnostu nougats. *See* **agnosu agnotu agnost**

agnosu guanos guano guans agon anus gnus goas guan guns nags naos nogs nous onus sago sang snag snug song sung ago gan gas gnu goa gun nag nog sag son sou sun an as go na no nu on os so us

agnosw gowans wagons gnaws gowan gowns swang wagon agon awns gnaw goas gown nags naos nogs owns sago sang sawn snag snow song sown swag swan wags ago awn gan gas goa nag nog now own sag saw son sow wag wan was won an as aw go na no on os ow so

agnot tango tonga agon gnat goat nota tang toga tong ago ant gan gat goa got nag nog not oat tag tan tog ton an at go na no on ta to

agnotu nougat gaunt guano tango tonga agon aunt auto gnat goat gout guan nota tang toga tong tuna unto ago ant gan gat gnu goa got gun gut nag nog not nut oat out tag tan tau tog ton tug tun an at go na no nu on ta to ut

agnou guano agon guan ago gan gnu goa gun nag nog an go na no nu on

agnow gowan wagon agon gnaw gown ago awn gan goa nag nog now own wag wan won an aw go na no on ow

agnoy agony agon yang yoga ago any gan gay goa goy nag nay nog yon an ay go na no on oy

agnp pang gan gap nag nap pan an na pa

agnprs sprang gnars grasp pangs spang sprag gaps gars gasp gnar nags naps pang pans pars rags rang raps rasp sang snag snap span spar asp gan gap gar gas nag nap pan par pas rag ran rap sag sap spa an as na pa

agnps pangs spang gaps gasp nags naps pang pans sang snag snap span asp gan gap gas nag nap pan pas sag sap spa an as na pa

agnr gnar rang gan gar nag rag ran an na

agnrs gnars gars gnar nags rags rang sang snag gan gar gas nag rag ran sag an as na

agnrst grants gnars gnats grant rants stang tangs ants arts gars gats gnar gnat nags rags rang rant rats sang snag stag star tags tang tans tars tsar ant art gan gar gas gat nag rag ran rat sag sat tag tan tar an as at na ta

agnrt grant gnar gnat rang rant tang ant art gan gar gat nag rag ran rat tag tan tar an at na ta

agnrty gantry angry grant rangy tangy arty gnar gnat gray nary rang rant tang tray yang yarn ant any art gan gar gat gay nag nay rag ran rat ray tag tan tar try yar an at ay na ta

agnry angry rangy gnar gray nary rang yang yarn any gan gar gay nag nay rag ran ray yar an ay na

agns nags sang snag gan gas nag sag an as na

agnss snags nags sags sang snag ass gan gas nag sag an as na

agnsst stangs gnats snags stags stang tangs ants gats gnat nags sags sang snag stag tags tang tans tass ant ass gan gas gat nag sag sat tag tan an as at na ta

agnst gnats stang tangs ants gats gnat nags sang snag stag tags tang tans ant gan gas gat nag sag sat tag tan an as at na ta

agnstw twangs gnats gnaws stang swang tangs twang wants ants awns gats gnat gnaw nags sang sawn snag stag swag swan swat tags tang tans wags want wast ant awn gan gas gat nag sag sat saw tag tan wag wan was an as at aw na ta

agnsu guans anus gnus guan guns nags sang snag snug sung gan gas gnu gun nag sag sun an as na nu us

agnsv vangs nags sang snag vang vans gan gas nag sag van an as na

agnsw gnaws swang awns gnaw nags sang sawn snag swag swan wags awn gan gas nag sag saw wag wan was an as aw na

agnsy yangs gays nags sang snag yang any gan gas gay nag nay sag say an as ay na

agnt gnat tang ant gan gat nag tag tan an at na ta

agntty gnatty tangy natty gnat tang yang ant any gan gat gay nag nay tag tan tat an at ay na ta

agntu gaunt aunt gnat guan tang tuna ant gan gat gnu gun gut nag nut tag tan tau tug tun an at na nu ta ut

agntw twang gnat gnaw tang want ant awn gan gat nag tag tan wag wan an at aw na ta

agnty tangy gnat tang yang ant any gan gat gay nag nay tag tan an at ay na ta

agnu guan gan gnu gun nag an na nu

agnv vang gan nag van an na

agnw gnaw awn gan nag wag wan an aw na

agnrt grant gnar gnat rang rant tang ant art gan gar gat nag rag ran rat tag tan tar an at na ta

agny yang any gan gay nag nay an ay na

ago ago goa go

agoortuy autogyro. *See* **gortuy**

agoppsst stopgaps stopgap. *See* **agpss agost aosst**

agoppst stopgap. *See* **agost**

agoprst ragtops. *See* **agorst aoprst agoprt**

agoprt ragtop aport argot groat atop goat grot part port proa rapt rota taro tarp toga tora trap ago apt art gap gar gat goa got oar oat ort par pat pot pro rag rap rat rot tag tap tar tog top tor at go or pa ta to

agorrstw ragworts ragwort. *See* **agorst aorrst aorrsw**

agorrsty gyrators gyrator. *See* **agorst agorsy aorrst aorrsy**

agorrtw ragwort. *See* **agort aorrw**

agorrty gyrator. *See* **aorrty agort**

agorst argots groats argot goats groat grots roast rotas taros togas toras arts gars gats goas goat grot oars oast oats orts rags rats rota rots sago soar sora sort stag star stoa tags taro tars toga togs tora tors tsar ago art gar gas gat goa got oar oat ort rag rat rot sag sat sot tag tar tog tor as at go or os so ta to

agorsy argosy grays gyros yogas gars gays goas gory goys gray gyro oars orgy rags rays rosy sago soar sora yoga ago gar gas gay goa goy oar rag ray sag say soy yar as ay go or os oy so

agort argot groat goat grot rota taro toga tora ago art gar gat goa got oar oat ort rag rat rot tag tar tog tor at go or ta to

agos goas sago ago gas goa sag as go os so

agoss sagos goas ossa sago sags ago ass gas goa sag as go os so

agost goats togas gats goas goat oast oats sago stag stoa tags toga togs ago gas gat goa got oat sag sat sot tag tog as at go os so ta to

agostv gavots gavot goats togas gats goas goat oast oats sago stag stoa tags tavs toga togs vast vats ago gas gat goa got oat ova sag sat sot tag tav tog vat as at go os so ta to

agosuyz azygous. *See* **agosy aguyz**

agosy yogas gays goas goys sago yoga ago gas gay goa goy sag say soy as ay go os oy so

agot goat toga ago gat goa got oat tag tog at go ta to

agotv gavot goat toga ago gat goa got oat ova tag tav tog vat at go ta to

agoy yoga ago gay goa goy ay go oy

agp gap pa

agprs grasp sprag gaps gars gasp pars rags raps rasp spar asp gap gar gas par pas rag rap sag sap spa pa as

agprss grasps sprags gasps grasp grass rasps spars sprag asps gaps gars gasp pars pass rags raps rasp sags saps spar spas asp ass gap gar gas par pas rag rap sag sap spa pa as

agpry grapy gray pray gap gar gay gyp par pay pry pya rag rap ray yap yar pa ay

agps gaps gasp asp gap gas pas sag sap spa as pa

agpss gasps asps gaps gasp pass sags saps spas asp ass gap gas pas sag sap spa pa as

agqsu quags quag gas qua sag as us

agqu quag qua

agr gar rag

agrs gars rags gar gas rag sag as

agrss grass gars rags sags ass gar gas rag sag as

agrssu sugars gaurs gauss grass sugar suras gars gaur rags ruga rugs sags sura ass gar gas rag rug sag as us

agrssy grassy gassy grass grays gars gays gray rags rays sags says ass gar gas gay rag ray sag say yar as ay

agrstu tragus gaurs sugar sutra arts gars gats gaur gust guts rags rats ruga rugs rust ruts stag star sura tags tars tsar tugs art gar gas gat gut rag rat rug rut sag sat tag tar tau tug as at ta us ut

agrsu gaurs sugar gars gaur rags ruga rugs sura gar gas rag rug sag as us

agrsuu augurs augur gaurs gurus sugar gars gaur guru rags ruga rugs sura urus gar gas rag rug sag as us

agrsuy sugary gaurs grays gyrus saury sugar gars gaur gray guys rags rays ruga rugs sura gar gas gay guy rag ray rug sag say yar as ay us

agrsy grays gars gays gray rags rays gar gas gay rag ray sag say yar as ay

agru gaur ruga gar rag rug

agruu augur gaur guru ruga gar rag rug

agruuy augury augur gaur gray guru ruga gar gay guy rag ray rug yar ay

agrvy gravy gray vary gar gay rag ray yar ay

agry gray gar gay rag ray yar ay

ags gas sag as

agss sags ass gas sag as

agsst stags gats sags stag tags tass ass gas gat sag sat tag as at ta

agssu gauss sags ass gas sag as us

agssw swags sags saws swag wags ass gas sag saw wag was as aw

agssy gassy gays sags says ass gas gay sag say as ay

agst gats stag tags gas gat sag sat tag as at ta

agstuu august gats gust guts stag tags tugs gas gat gut sag sat tag tau tug as at ta us ut

agsty stagy gats gays stag stay tags gas gat gay sag sat say sty tag as at ay ta

agsuv vagus vugs gas sag vug as us

agsw swag wags gas sag saw wag was as aw

agsy gays gas gay sag say as ay

agsz zags gas sag zag as

agt gat tag at ta

agttu gutta taut gat gut tag tat tau tug tut at ta ut

aguyz gauzy gay guy zag ay

agw wag aw

agy gay ay

agz zag

---

ah

ah ah ha

ahh hah ah ha

ahhhiss hashish. *No 6s or 5s*

ahhiksw hawkish. *See* **ahiks ahksw hhisw**

ahhilpsw whiplash. *See* **ahilps**

ahhimmss mishmash. *See* **aimss aimms ahmss**

ahhisstt shittahs shittah. *See* **ahist ahsst**

ahhistt shittah. *See* **ahist**

ahhkoo hookah hooka hook hah koa oak oho ooh ah ha ho ka oh

ahhkoos hookahs. *See* **ahhkoo ahkoos**

ahhlpy hyphal haply hypha phyla hyla paly play alp hah hap hay lap lay pah pal pay ply pya yah yap ah ay ha la pa

ahhlrsy harshly. *See* **ahlrsy ahhrs**

ahhmprru harrumph. *See* **ahhrru**

ahhnortw hawthorn. *See* **ahnrtw hnortw**

ahhoprs shophar. *See* **ahprs ahors ahops**

ahhoprss shophars shophar. *See* **ahprss**

ahhptuz hutzpah. *No 6s or 5s*

ahhpy hypha hah hap hay pah pay pya yah yap ah ay ha pa

ahhrrsu hurrahs. *See* **ahhrru ahhrs ahrsu**

ahhrru hurrah hah huh rah ah ha

ahhrs harsh hahs hash rahs rash shah ash hah has rah ah as ha sh

ahhrst thrash harsh harts trash arts hahs hart hash hast hath hats rahs rash rath rats shah star tars tsar art ash hah has hat rah rat sat tar ah as at ha sh ta

ahhs hahs hash shah ash hah has ah as ha sh

ahhsuzz huzzahs. *See* **ahhuzz**

ahht hath hah hat ah at ha ta

ahhuzz huzzah hah huh ah ha

ahiiilmn malihini. *See* **aiilmn**

ahiikrs shikari. *See* **ahikrs**

ahiikrss shikaris shikari shikars. *See* **ahikrs ahkrss hikrss**

ahiilrty hilarity. *See* **ahiilt aiilry**

ahiilt lithia alit hail halt hilt ilia lath tail tali ail alt hat hit ita lit til ah ai at ha hi it la li ta ti

ahiimnot himation. *See* **aimnt hmnot**

ahiimnst isthmian animist intimas. *See* **aiimns aiinst aimnst hiimns**

ahiinpr hairpin. *No 6s or 5s*

ahiinprs hairpins airship aspirin hairpin. *See* **ahiprs aiinrs ainprs**

ahiiprs airship. *See* **ahiprs**

ahiiprss airships airship. *See* **ahiprs ahipss ahprss**

ahij haji ah ai ha hi

ahijj hajji haji hajj ah ai ha hi

ahijjs hajjis hajji hajis haji hajj ash has his ah ai as ha hi is sh si

ahijs hajis haji ash has his ah ai as ha hi is sh si

ahik haik ah ai ha hi ka

ahikk khaki haik kaki ah ai ha hi ka

ahikks khakis kishka haiks kakis khaki haik kaki saki ash ask has his kas ski ah ai as ha hi is ka sh si

ahiklp kaliph phial haik hail kail kaph lakh pail pika ail alp hap hip ilk kal kip lap lip pah pal ah ai ha hi ka la li pa pi

ahiklps kaliphs. *See* **ahiklp ahilps**

ahiklrs larkish. *See* **ahikrs**

ahiklrsy rakishly larkish. *See* **ahikrs ahlrsy ailrsy**

ahikm hakim haik kami aim ham him ah ai am ha hi ka ma mi

ahikmns khamsin. *See* **ahikms aikmns**

ahikmnss khamsins khamsin kamsins. *See* **ahikms ahknss aikmns**

ahikms hakims hakim haiks aims haik hams kami mash mask saki sham shim skim aim ash ask ham has him his kas mis ski ah ai am as ha hi is ka ma mi sh si

ahikmsv mikvahs. *See* **ahikms ahikmv**

ahikmsw mawkish. *See* **ahikms ahksw aimsw**

ahikmv mikvah hakim haik kami kiva aim ham him via vim ah ai am ha hi ka ma mi

ahiknprs prankish. *See* **ahikrs ahiprs ahknrs ainprs**

ahiknsv knavish. *See* **ahinsv ahkns ahiks**

ahikrs rakish shikar haiks hairs harks rakis shark shirk airs arks haik hair hark irks kris rahs raki rash rias risk saki sari sark air ark ash ask has his irk kas kir rah ria sir ski ah ai as ha hi is ka sh si

ahikrss shikars. *See* **ahikrs ahkrss hikrss**

ahiks haiks haik saki ash ask has his kas ski ah ai as ha hi is ka sh si

ahiku haiku haik auk ah ai ha hi ka

ahil hail ail ah ai ha hi la li

ahillmss smallish. *See* **ailmss hillss**

ahillnst anthills anthill install tallish. *See* **ahilst ailnst hillst**

ahillnt anthill. *See* **hillt**

ahillp phalli phial hail hall hill pail pall pill ail all alp hap hip ill lap lip pah pal ah ai ha hi la li pa pi

ahillst tallish. *See* **ahilst hillst**

ahillsvy lavishly. *See* **ahilsv aillsv**

ahillsz zillahs. *See* **ahillz ahils ahlls**

ahilltt tallith. *See* **ailtt hillt hiltt**

ahillz zillah hail hall hill ail all ill ah ai ha hi la li

ahilmqsu qualmish. *See* **ahilmu ailqsu aimqsu almqsu**

ahilmu hamuli haulm hilum alum hail haul hula mail maul ail aim ham him hum lam lum mil ah ai am ha hi la li ma mi mu um

ahilnops siphonal planish. *See* **ahilps ailnps ainops alnops**

ahilnort horntail. *See* **ahilnr ahlort ailnot ailnrt**

ahilnps planish. *See* **ailnps ahilps**

ahilnr rhinal anil aril hail hair harl lain lair liar lira nail rail rain rani rial ail air ani hin lar nah nil rah ran ria ah ai an ha hi in la li na

ahilnsu inhauls. *See* **ahilnu ahlnsu**

ahilnu inhaul uhlan anil hail haul hula lain nail ulna ail ani hin nah nil ah ai an ha hi in la li na nu

ahilopst hospital apostil topsail. *See* **ahilps ahilst ahlost ahopst**

ahilp phial hail pail ail alp hap hip lap lip pah pal ah ai ha hi la li pa pi

ahilppy happily. *See* **alppy ahlpy ahppy**

ahilps palish phials aphis apish hails pails phial plash spahi ails alps hail haps hasp hips laps lash lips lisp pail pals pish sail ship slap slip ail alp ash asp hap has hip his lap lip pah pal pas sal sap sip spa ah ai as ha hi is la li pa pi sh si

ahilpsy apishly. *See* **ahilps**

ahilrw awhirl whirl aril hail hair harl lair liar lira rail rial wail whir ail air awl haw lar law rah raw ria war ah ai aw ha hi la li

ahils hails ails hail lash sail ail ash has his sal ah ai as ha hi is la li sh si

ahilsst saltish. *See* **ahilst alsst ilsst**

ahilssv slavish. *See* **ahilsv ailssv**

ahilst latish hails halts hilts laths saith shalt tails ails alit alts hail halt hast hats hilt hist hits lash last lath list sail salt silt sith slat slit tail tali this tils ail alt ash has hat his hit ita its lit sal sat sit til ah ai as at ha hi is it la li sh si ta ti

ahilsty hastily. *See* **ahilst ahsty ahlsy**

ahilsv lavish hails silva vails vials ails hail lash sail shiv vail vial visa ail ash has his sal via ah ai as ha hi is la li sh si

ahiltw withal alit hail halt hilt lath tail tali thaw wail wait what whit wilt with ail alt awl hat haw hit ita law lit til ah ai at aw ha hi it la li ta ti

ahimmnsu humanism. *See* **ahmnsu aimnsu**

ahimnns mannish. *See* **aimns**

ahimnnu inhuman. *See* **aimnnu ahmnu**

ahimnosw womanish showman. *See* **ahmnos aimosw**

ahimnps shipman. *See* **ahimps aimns ainps**

ahimnstu humanist tsunami. *See* **ahistu ahmnsu ahnstu aimnst**

ahimntuy humanity. *See* **aimntu imntuy**

ahimoprs aphorism mohairs. *See* **ahimor ahimps ahimrs ahiprs**

ahimor mohair ihram amir hair harm hoar hora mora rami roam aim air arm ham him mar mho mir moa mor oar ohm rah ram rho ria rim ah ai am ha hi ho ma mi mo oh om or

ahimorrw hairworm. *See* **ahorrw amorrw ahimor**

ahimors mohairs. *See* **ahimrs ahimor**

ahimppss sapphism mishaps. *See* **ahimps ahipss**

ahimps mishap aphis apish spahi aims amps hams haps hasp hips imps maps mash pish samp sham shim ship simp aim amp ash asp ham hap has him hip his imp map mis pah pas sap sip spa ah ai am as ha hi is ma mi pa pi sh si

ahimpss mishaps. *See* **ahipss ahimps**

ahimr ihram amir hair harm rami aim air arm ham him mar mir rah ram ria rim ah ai am ha hi ma mi

ahimrs ihrams marish amirs hairs harms ihram marsh simar aims airs amir arms hair hams harm mash mirs rahs rami rams rash rias rims sari sham shim aim air arm ash ham has him his mar mir mis rah ram ria rim sir ah ai am as ha hi is ma mi sh si

ahimrsw warmish. *See* **ahimrs**

ahimstuz azimuths azimuth. *See* **ahistu aimstu**

ahimtuz azimuth. *No 6s or 5s*

ahimtvz mitzvah. *No 6s or 5s*

ahinnopt antiphon. *See* **ahinpt ainnot**

ahinosst astonish. *See* **ahnsst ahosst ainsst hiosst**

ahinostz hoatzins hoatzin. *See* **ahostz**

ahinotz hoatzin. *See* **ahotz**

ahinppss snappish. *See* **ahipss**

ahinpst hatpins. *See* **ahinpt ainpst**

ahinpt hatpin inapt paint anti hant hint nipa pain pant path pint pita than thin ani ant apt hap hat hin hip hit ita nah nap nip nit pah pan pat pin pit tan tap tin tip ah ai an at ha hi in it na pa pi ta ti

ahinqsuv vanquish. *See* **ahinsv**

ahinrst tarnish. *See* **ainrst**

ahinrsv varnish. *See* **ahinsv ahirsv**

ahinsv vanish savin vinas hins sain shin shiv vain vans vina visa ani ash has hin his nah sin van via ah ai an as ha hi in is na sh si

ahioprst aphorist shortia harpist. *See* **ahiprs ahopst ahorst aiopst**

ahiopxy hypoxia. *No 6s or 5s*

ahiorsst shortias shortia. *See* **ahorst ahosst aiorst airsst**

ahiorst shortia. *See* **ahorst aiorst**

ahiprs parish aphis apish hairs harps pairs sharp spahi airs hair haps harp hasp hips pair pars pish rahs raps rash rasp rias rips sari ship spar air ash asp hap has hip his pah par pas rah rap ria rip sap sip sir spa ah ai as ha hi is pa pi sh si

ahiprsst   harpists harpist rapists. *See* **ahiprs ahipss ahprss ahpsst**

ahiprssw   warships ripsaws warship waspish. *See* **ahiprs ahipss ahprss ahpssw**

ahiprst   harpist. *See* **ahiprs aiprst**

ahiprsu   rupiahs. *See* **ahiprs ahipru**

ahiprsw   warship. *See* **ahiprs aiprsw**

ahipru   rupiah hair harp pair air hap hip hup pah par rah rap ria rip ah ai ha hi pa pi up

ahips   aphis apish spahi haps hasp hips pish ship ash asp hap has hip his pah pas sap sip spa ah ai as ha hi is pa pi sh si

ahipss   aspish spahis aphis apish apsis hasps ships spahi asps haps hasp hips hiss pass pish saps sash ship sips spas ash asp ass hap has hip his pah pas sap sip sis spa ah ai as ha hi is pa pi sh si

ahipssw   waspish. *See* **ahipss ahpssw**

ahipssww   whipsaws waspish whipsaw. *See* **ahipss ahpssw**

ahipsswy   shipways waspish shipway. *See* **ahipss ahpssw hisswy**

ahipsww   whipsaw. *See* **ahips ahpsw hipsw**

ahipswy   shipway. *See* **ahips ahswy apswy**

ahir   hair air rah ria ah ai ha hi

ahirrs   sirrah arris hairs shirr airs hair rahs rash rias sari air ash has his rah ria sir ah ai as ha hi is sh si

ahirrss   sirrahs. *See* **ahirrs hirrss**

ahirs   hairs airs hair rahs rash rias sari air ash has his rah ria sir ah ai as ha hi is sh si

ahirstt   athirst. *See* **airstt hirstt**

ahirstw   wraiths. *See* **ahrstw ahirtw**

ahirsv   ravish hairs vairs airs hair rahs rash rias sari shiv vair visa air ash has his rah ria sir via ah ai as ha hi is sh si

ahirtw   wraith wrath hair hart rath thaw wait wart what whir whit with writ air art hat haw hit ita rah rat raw ria tar war wit ah ai at aw ha hi it ta ti

ahiry   hairy hair airy air hay rah ray ria yah yar ah ai ay ha hi

ahist   saith hast hats hist hits sith this ash has hat his hit ita its sat sit ah ai as at ha hi is it sh si ta ti

ahistu   hiatus saith hast hats hist hits huts shut sith suit this thus tuis tush ash has hat his hit hut ita its sat sit tau tui ah ai as at ha hi is it sh si ta ti us ut

ahjj   hajj ah ha

ahjstu   thujas thuja hast hats huts just juts shut thus tush ash has hat hut jus jut sat tau ah as at ha sh ta us ut

ahjtu   thuja hat hut jut tau ah at ha ta ut

ahkkssu   sukkahs. *See* **ahkksu hkssu**

ahkksu   sukkah auks husk ash ask auk has kas ah as ha ka sh us

ahkl   lakh kal ah ha ka la

ahklopst   shoptalk. *See* **ahlost ahopst aklops alopst**

ahkls   lakhs lakh lash ash ask has kal kas sal ah as ha ka la sh

ahkn   ankh hank khan nah ah an ha ka na

ahknpsu   punkahs. *See* **ahknpu aknpsu**

ahknpu   punkah punka ankh hank hunk kaph khan knap punk auk hap hup nah nap pah pan pun ah an ha ka na nu pa up

ahknrs   shrank ankhs hanks harks khans knars narks ranks shank shark snark ankh arks hank hark khan knar nark rahs rank rash sank sark ark ash ask has kas nah rah ran ah an as ha ka na sh

ahkns   ankhs hanks khans shank ankh hank khan sank ash ask has kas nah ah an as ha ka na sh

ahknss   shanks ankhs hanks khans shank ankh asks hank khan sank sash ash ask ass has kas nah ah an as ha ka na sh

ahknst   thanks ankhs hanks hants khans shank snath stank tanks thank ankh ants hank hant hast hats khan sank skat tank tans task than ant ash ask has hat kas kat nah sat tan tsk ah an as at ha ka na sh ta

ahknt   thank ankh hank hant khan tank than ant hat kat nah tan ah an at ha ka na ta

ahkoo   hooka hook koa oak oho ooh ah ha ho ka oh

ahkoos   hookas hooka hooks shako shook hook koas oaks oohs shoo soak ash ask has kas koa kos oak oho ohs ooh ah as ha ho ka oh os sh so

ahkos   shako koas oaks soak ash ask has kas koa kos oak ohs ah as ha ho ka oh os sh so

ahkoss   shakos shako soaks asks koas oaks ossa sash soak ash ask ass has kas koa kos oak ohs ah as ha ho ka oh os sh so

ahkp   kaph hap pah ah ha ka pa

ahkps   kaphs haps hasp kaph ash ask asp hap has kas pah pas sap spa ah as ha ka pa sh

ahkr   hark rah ark ah ha ka

ahkrs   harks shark arks hark rahs rash sark ark ash ask has kas rah ah as ha ka sh

ahkrss   sharks harks sarks shark arks asks hark rahs rash sark sash ark ash ask ass has kas rah ah as ha ka sh

ahksw   hawks hawk haws shaw wash ash ask has haw kas saw was ah as aw ha ka sh

ahksy   shaky ashy hays shay yaks ash ask has hay kas say shy sky yah yak ah as ay ha ka sh

ahkw   hawk haw ah aw ha ka

ahll   hall all ah ha la

ahllmsu   mullahs. *See* **ahllmu almsu ahlls**

ahllmu   mullah haulm alum hall haul hula hull mall maul mull all ham hum lam lum ah am ha la ma mu um

ahllnoos   shalloon halloos. *See* **ahlloo ahllos allnos alnoos**

ahllnsu   nullahs. *See* **ahllnu ahlnsu**

ahllnu   nullah uhlan hall haul hula hull null ulna nah all ah an ha la na nu

ahllo   hallo hall halo olla all ah ha ho la lo oh

ahlloo   halloo hallo hollo hall halo olla all loo oho ooh ah ha ho la lo oh

ahlloos   halloos. *See* **ahlloo ahllos hlloos**

ahllops   shallop. *See* **ahllos ahops**

ahllopss   shallops shallop. *See* **ahllos ahloss ahlpss allpss**

ahllos   hallos hallo halls ollas shall shoal also hall halo lash olla all ash has los ohs sal sol ah as ha ho la lo oh os sh so

ahllosst   shallots shallot. *See* **ahllos ahloss ahlost ahosst**

ahllossw   shallows hallows sallows shallow. *See* **ahllos ahllow ahloss ahlssw**

ahllost   shallot. *See* **allost ahllos ahlost**

ahllosw   hallows shallow. *See* **allosw ahllow**

ahlloty   loathly tallyho. *See* **allot alloy ahllo**

ahllow   hallow hallo allow alow hall halo howl olla wall whoa all awl haw how law low owl who ah aw ha ho la lo oh ow

ahllrst   thralls. *See* **ahllrt ahlls ahlst**

ahllrt   thrall hall halt harl hart lath rath tall all alt art hat lar rah rat tar ah at ha la ta

ahlls   halls shall hall lash all ash has sal ah as ha la sh

ahllux   hallux hall haul hula hull all lax lux ah ax ha la

ahlmmopy   lymphoma. *See* **almpy ahmmy ahlpy**

ahlmnoor   hormonal. *See* **ahlmoo almnor amnoor**

ahlmnpy   nymphal. *See* **ahlmny almpy ahlpy**

ahlmnsy   hymnals. *See* **ahlmny ahmnsy**

ahlmnuy   humanly. *See* **ahlmny ahlmu ahmnu**

ahlmny   hymnal mynah manly amyl hyla hymn many myna any ham hay lam lay man may nah nay yah yam ah am an ay ha la ma my na

ahlmoo moolah moola halo holm homo loam loom mola ham lam loo mho moa moo ohm oho ooh ah am ha ho la lo ma mo oh om

ahlmoops omphalos shampoo. *See* **ahlmoo ahlmos ahloop ahmoop**

ahlmoru humoral. *See* **amoru hmoru almor**

ahlmos shalom holms loams molas shoal alms also halo hams holm lams lash loam mash mhos moas mola ohms sham slam soma ash ham has lam los mho moa mos ohm ohs oms sal sol ah am as ha ho la lo ma mo oh om os sh so

ahlmstyz shmaltzy. *See* **almsy ahlst ahsty**

ahlmsuu hamulus. *See* **almsu ahlmu ahlsu**

ahlmu haulm alum haul hula maul ham hum lam lum ah am ha la ma mu um

ahlnnort lanthorn. *See* **ahlort**

ahlnopr alphorn. *See* **ahnopr alnopr**

ahlnoprs alphorns alphorn orphans prolans. *See* **ahnopr ahnors alnopr alnops**

ahlnsu uhlans unlash hauls hulas uhlan ulnas anus haul hula lash lush shun ulna ash has nah sal sun ah an as ha la na nu sh us

ahlnu uhlan haul hula ulna nah ah an ha la na nu

ahlo halo ah ha ho la lo oh

ahloop hoopla halo holp hoop loop opah opal polo pooh pool alp hap hop lap loo lop oho ooh pah pal ah ha ho la lo oh pa

ahlorrty harlotry. *See* **ahlort ahorry aorrty**

ahlorst harlots. *See* **ahlort ahlost ahorst**

ahlort harlot loath lotah torah alto halo halt harl hart hoar holt hora lath lota loth oath oral rath rota rotl taro tola tora alt art hat hot lar lot oar oat ort rah rat rho rot tar tho tor ah at ha ho la lo oh or ta to

ahlos shoal also halo lash ash has los ohs sal sol ah as ha lo la lo oh os sh so

ahloss shoals lasso shoal slash slosh also halo lash lass loss ossa sals sash sols ash ass has los ohs sal sol ah as ha ho la lo oh os sh so

ahlost lotahs altos halts holts hosta laths loath lotah lotas oaths shalt shoal shoat sloth tolas also alto alts halo halt hast hats holt host hots lash last lath lost lota loth lots oast oath oats salt shot slat slot stoa tola tosh alt ash has hat hot los lot oat ohs sal sat sol sot tho ah as at ha ho la lo oh os sh so ta to

ahlosy shoaly shoal hylas ahoy also ashy halo hays holy hoys hyla lash lays shay

slay ash has hay hoy lay los ohs sal say shy sly sol soy yah ah as ay ha ho la lo oh os oy sh so

ahlot loath lotah alto halo halt holt lath lota loth oath tola alt hat hot lot oat tho ah at ha ho la lo oh ta to

ahlprsy sharply. *See* **ahlrsy ahlpy ahprs**

ahlps plash alps haps hasp laps lash pals slap alp ash asp hap has lap pah pal pas sal sap spa ah as ha la pa sh

ahlpss splash hasps plash slaps slash alps asps haps hasp laps lash lass pals pass sals saps sash slap spas alp ash asp ass hap has lap pah pal pas sal sap spa ah as ha la pa sh

ahlpssy splashy. *See* **ahlpss alpssy hlpssy**

ahlpy haply phyla hyla paly play alp hap hay lap lay pah pal pay ply pya yah yap ah ay ha la pa

ahlr harl rah lar ah ha la

ahlrs harls harl lash rahs rash ash has lar rah sal ah as ha la sh

ahlrsy rashly aryls harls hylas aryl ashy harl hays hyla lash lays rahs rash rays shay slay ash has hay lar lay rah ray sal say shy sly yah yar ah as ay ha la sh

ahls lash ash has sal ah as ha la sh

ahlss slash lash lass sals sash ash ass has sal ah as ha la sh

ahlssw shawls shawl shaws slash swash awls haws lash lass laws sals sash saws shaw wash ash ass awl has haw law sal saw was ah as aw ha la sh

ahlst halts laths shalt alts halt hast hats lash last lath salt slat alt ash has hat sal sat ah as at ha la sh ta

ahlsu hauls hulas haul hula lash lush ash has sal ah as ha la sh us

ahlsw shawl awls haws lash laws shaw wash ash awl has haw law sal saw was ah as aw ha la sh

ahlsy hylas ashy hays hyla lash lays shay slay ash has hay lay sal say shy sly yah ah as ay ha la sh

ahlt halt lath hat alt ah at ha la ta

ahltuz halutz halt haul hula lath alt hat hut tau ah at ha la ta ut

ahlty lathy halt hyla lath alt hat hay lay thy yah ah at ay ha la ta

ahlu haul hula ah ha la

ahly hyla hay lay yah ah ay ha la

ahm ham ah am ha ma

ahmmmost mammoths mammoth. *See* **amost ahost hmost**

ahmmmot mammoth. *No 6s or 5s*

ahmmow whammo ammo wham whoa whom ham haw how maw mho moa mom mow ohm who ah am aw ha ho ma mo oh om ow

ahmmsy shammy hammy ashy hams hays mash sham shay yams ash ham has hay may say shy yah yam ah am as ay ha ma my sh

ahmmwy whammy hammy wham ham haw hay maw may way why yah yam yaw ah am aw ay ha ma my

ahmmy hammy hammy hay may yah yam ah am ay ha ma my

ahmnnstu huntsman manhunts manhunt. *See* **ahmnsu ahnstu amnnsu**

ahmnntu manhunt. *See* **ahntu ahmnu amnnu**

ahmnopst phantoms phantom postman. *See* **ahmnos ahopst hmnost**

ahmnopt phantom. *See* **hmnot**

ahmnory harmony. *See* **ahory hnory amnor**

ahmnos hansom mason moans nomas hams mash mhos moan moas mons naos noma nosh ohms sham soma ash ham has hon man mho moa mon mos nah ohm ohs oms son ah am an as ha ho ma mo na no oh om on os sh so

ahmnoss hansoms. *See* **ahmnos amnoss**

ahmnosw showman. *See* **ahmnos hnosw ahmsw**

ahmnsu humans human manus anus hams hums mash maun mush sham shun ash ham has hum man mus nah sum sun ah am an as ha ma mu na nu sh um us

ahmnsy mynahs hymns mynah mynas ashy hams hays hymn many mash myna sham shay yams any ash ham has hay man may nah nay say shy yah yam ah am an as ay ha ma my na sh

ahmnu human maun ham hum man nah ah am an ha ma mu na nu um

ahmny mynah hymn many myna any ham hay man may nah nay yah yam ah am an ay ha ma my na

ahmoop oompah oomph homo hoop opah pooh amp ham hap hop map mho moa moo mop ohm oho ooh pah ah am ha ho ma mo oh om pa

ahmoops shampoo. *See* **ahmoop hoops ahops**

ahmoopss shampoos shampoo. *See* **ahmoop**

ahmoorsw washroom. *See* **ahoosw**

ahmoptyy myopathy. *See* **amoty hmoty**

ahmorsz mahzors. *See* **ahmorz ahmrs ahors**

ahmorz mahzor harm hoar hora mora roam arm azo ham mar mho moa mor oar ohm rah ram rho zoa ah am ha ho ma mo oh om or

ahmostu mahouts. *See* **ahmotu hmostu**

ahmoswy haymows. *See* **ahmowy amosy hoswy**

ahmottz matzoth. *See* **amottz ahotz**

ahmotu mahout mouth atom auto math moat moth oath thou ham hat hot hum hut mat mho moa mot oat ohm out tam tau tho tom ah am at ha ho ma mo mu oh om ta to um ut

ahmowy haymow ahoy homy mayo wham whoa whom ham haw hay how hoy maw may mho moa mow ohm way who why yah yam yaw yow ah am aw ay ha ho ma mo my oh om ow oy

ahmpssu smashup. *See* **ahmssu ahpss hmpsu**

ahmpstyy sympathy. *See* **ahsty amsty hmsty**

ahmr harm arm ham mar rah ram ah am ha ma

ahmrs harms marsh arms hams harm mash rahs rams rash sham arm ash ham has mar rah ram ah am as ha ma sh

ahmrsy marshy harms marsh arms army ashy hams harm hays mash rahs rams rash rays sham shay yams arm ash ham has hay mar may rah ram ray say shy yah yam yar ah am as ay ha ma my sh

ahmrtw warmth wrath harm hart mart math rath thaw tram warm wart wham what arm art ham hat haw mar mat maw rah ram rat raw tam tar war ah am at aw ha ma ta

ahms hams mash sham ash ham has ah am as ha ma sh

ahmss shams smash hams mash mass sash sham ash ass ham has ah am as ha ma sh

ahmssu shamus shams smash hams hums mash mass mush muss sash sham sums ash ass ham has hum mus sum ah am as ha ma mu sh um us

ahmsw whams hams haws mash maws sham shaw swam wash wham ash ham has haw maw saw was ah am as aw ha ma sh

ahmt math ham hat mat tam ah am at ha ma ta

ahmw wham ham haw maw ah am aw ha ma

ahn nah ah an ha na

ahnoopr harpoon. *See* **ahnopr hnoor noopr**

ahnooprs harpoons harpoon orphans soprano. *See* **ahnopr ahnors anoprs hnoors**

ahnoorry honorary. *See* **ahoory ahorry**

ahnoppsw pawnshop. *See* **ahops anpsw ahpsw**

ahnopr orphan apron harp hoar hora horn opah proa roan hap hon hop nah nap nor oar pah pan par pro rah ran rap rho ah an ha ho na no oh on or pa

ahnoprs orphans. *See* **anoprs ahnopr ahnors**

ahnopsst snapshot. *See* **ahnsst ahopst ahosst ahpsst**

ahnors shoran arson horas horns roans shorn sonar hoar hora horn naos nosh oars rahs rash rhos roan soar sora ash has hon nah nor oar ohs rah ran rho son ah an as ha ho na no oh on or os sh so

ahnorss shorans. *See* **anorss ahnors**

ahnorssx saxhorns shorans saxhorn. *See* **ahnors anorss**

ahnorsx saxhorn. *See* **ahnors anosx**

ahnosttw whatnots whatnot. *See* **ahnst ahost hnosw**

ahnostux xanthous. *See* **ahnstu**

ahnottw whatnot. *No 6s or 5s*

ahnowy anyhow noway ahoy wany whoa yawn any awn haw hay hon how hoy nah nay now own wan way who why won yah yaw yon yow ah an aw ay ha ho na no oh on ow oy

ahnppuy unhappy. *See* **ahppy anppy**

ahnprxy pharynx. *See* **ahpry ahrxy**

ahnrtw thrawn wrath hant hart rant rath than thaw want warn wart what ant art awn hat haw nah rah ran rat raw tan tar wan war ah an at aw ha na ta

ahnsst snaths hants snath stash ants hant hast hats sash tans tass than ant ash ass has hat nah sat tan ah an as at ha na sh ta

ahnst hants snath ants hant hast hats tans than ant ash has hat nah sat tan ah an as at ha na sh ta

ahnstu haunts aunts hants haunt hunts shunt snath tunas ants anus aunt hant hast hats hunt huts nuts shun shut stun tans than thus tuna tuns tush ant ash has hat hut nah nut sat sun tan tau tun ah an as at ha na nu sh ta us ut

ahnsty shanty antsy hants hasty nasty snath tansy ants ashy hant hast hats hays shay stay tans than ant any ash has hat hay nah nay sat say shy sty tan thy yah ah an as at ay ha na sh ta

ahnt hant than ant hat nah tan ah an at ha na ta

ahntu haunt aunt hant hunt than tuna ant hat hut nah nut tan tau tun ah an at ha na nu ta ut

ahoorsy hoorays. *See* **ahoory ahors horsy**

ahoory hooray hoary ahoy hoar hora hay hoy oar oho ooh rah ray rho yah yar ah ay ha ho oh or oy

ahoossty soothsay. *See* **ahosst hoossty**

ahoosttw sawtooth. *See* **ahoosw**

ahoosw wahoos wahoo woosh haws oohs shaw shoo show wash whoa woos ash has haw how oho ohs ooh saw sow was who woo ah as aw ha ho oh ow so

ahoow wahoo whoa haw how oho ooh who woo ah aw ha ho oh ow

ahop opah hap hop pah ah ha ho oh pa

ahoprty atrophy. *See* **hoprty aoprt ahpry**

ahops opahs haps hasp hops opah posh shop soap soph ash asp hap has hop ohs pah pas sap sop spa ah as ha ho oh os pa sh so

ahopst pathos potash hosta oaths opahs paths phots shoat staph atop haps hasp hast hats hops host hots oast oath oats opah past path pats phot posh post pots shop shot soap soph spat spot stoa stop taps tops tosh apt ash asp hap has hat hop hot oat ohs pah pas pat pot sap sat sop sot spa tap tho top ah as at ha ho oh os pa sh so ta to

ahopsttw towpaths towpath. *See* **ahopst**

ahopstuw southpaw washout. *See* **ahopst hopstu**

ahopttw towpath. *No 6s or 5s*

ahoqtu quotha quota quoth auto oath thou hat hot hut oat out qat qua tau tho ah at ha ho oh ta to ut

ahor hoar hora oar rah rho ah ha ho oh or

ahorrsw harrows. *See* **ahorrw aorrsw**

ahorrw harrow arrow hoar hora roar whoa haw how oar rah raw rho row war who ah aw ha ho oh or ow

ahorry horary hoary harry ahoy hoar hora roar hay hoy oar rah ray rho yah yar ah ay ha ho oh or oy

ahors horas hoar hora oars rahs rash rhos soar sora ash has oar ohs rah rho ah as ha ho oh or os sh so

ahorst torahs harts horas horst hosta oaths roast rotas shoat short taros torah toras trash arts hart hast hats hoar hora host hots oars oast oath oats orts rahs rash rath rats rhos rota rots shot soar sora sort star stoa taro tars tora tors tosh tsar art ash has hat hot oar oat ohs ort rah rat rho rot sat sot tar tho tor ah as at ha ho oh or os sh so ta to

ahorstt throats. *See* **aorstt ahortt ahorst horstt**

ahorstu authors. *See* **ahorst ahortu**

ahort torah hart hoar hora oath rath rota taro tora art hat hot oar oat ort rah rat rho rot tar tho tor ah at ha ho oh or ta to

ahortt　throat tarot torah troth hart hoar hora oath rath rota taro tart that tora tort trot art hat hot oar oat ort rah rat rho rot tar tat tho tor tot ah at ha ho oh or ta to

ahortty　throaty. *See* **ahortt ahory artty**

ahortu　author torah auto hart hoar hora hour hurt oath rath rota rout ruth taro thou thru tora tour art hat hot hut oar oat ort our out rah rat rho rot rut tar tau tho tor ah at ha ho oh or ta to ut

ahortx　thorax torah hart hoar hoax hora oath rath rota taro tora art hat hot oar oat ort rah rat rho rot tar tax tho tor ah at ax ha ho oh or ox ta to

ahory　hoary ahoy hoar hora hay hoy oar rah ray rho yah yar ah ay ha ho oh or oy

ahosst　hostas shoats hosta hosts oasts oaths shoat shots stash stoas hast hats host hots oast oath oats ossa sash shot sots stoa tass tosh toss ash ass has hat hot oat ohs sat sot tho ah as at ha ho oh os sh so ta to

ahosstuw　washouts washout. *See* **ahosst ahsstw hosstu**

ahost　hosta oaths shoat hast hats host hots oast oath oats shot stoa tosh ash has hat hot oat ohs sat sot tho ah as at ha ho oh os sh so ta to

ahostuw　washout. *See* **aostu ahost hostu**

ahostz　azoths azoth hosta oaths shoat hast hats host hots oast oath oats shot stoa tosh ash azo has hat hot oat ohs sat sot tho zoa ah as at ha ho oh os sh so ta to

ahot　oath hat hot oat tho ah at ha ho oh ta to

ahotz　azoth oath azo hat hot oat tho zoa ah at ha ho oh ta to

ahow　whoa haw how who ah aw ha ho oh ow

ahox　hoax ah ax ha ho oh ox

ahoy　ahoy hay hoy yah ah ay ha ho oh oy

ahp　hap pah ah ha pa

ahppy　happy hap hay pah pap pay pya yah yap ah ay ha pa

ahpr　harp hap pah par rah rap ah ha pa

ahpriy　phratry. *See* **ahpry ahrry aprry**

ahprs　harps sharp haps harp hasp pars rahs raps rash rasp spar ash asp hap has pah par pas rah rap sap spa ah as ha pa sh

ahprss　sharps harps hasps rasps sharp spars asps haps harp hasp pars pass rahs raps rash rasp saps sash spar spas ash asp ass hap has pah par pas rah rap sap spa ah as ha pa sh

ahpry　harpy harp pray hap hay pah par pay pry pya rah rap ray yah yap yar ah ay ha pa

ahps　haps hasp ash asp hap has pah pas sap spa ah as ha pa sh

ahpss　hasps asps haps hasp pass saps sash spas ash asp ass hap has pah pas sap spa ah as ha pa sh

ahpsst　staphs hasps pasts paths spats staph stash asps haps hasp hast hats pass past path pats saps sash spas spat taps tass apt ash asp ass hap has hat pah pas pat sap sat spa tap ah as at ha pa sh ta

ahpssw　pshaws hasps pshaw shaws swaps swash wasps whaps asps haps hasp haws paws pass saps sash saws shaw spas swap waps wash wasp whap ash asp ass hap has haw pah pas paw sap saw spa wap was ah as aw ha pa sh

ahpst　paths staph haps hasp hast hats past path pats spat taps apt ash asp hap has hat pah pas pat sap sat spa tap ah as at ha pa sh ta

ahpsw　pshaw whaps haps hasp haws paws shaw swap waps wash wasp whap ash asp hap has haw pah pas paw sap saw spa wap was ah as aw ha pa sh

ahpt　path apt hap hat pah pat tap ah at ha pa ta

ahpw　whap hap haw pah paw wap ah aw ha pa

ahqssu　squash quash quass sash ash ass has qua ah as ha sh us

ahqssuy　squashy. *See* **ahqssu hssuy aqsuy**

ahqsu　quash ash has qua ah as ha sh us

ahr　rah ah ha

ahrrsuy　hurrays. *See* **ahrruy hrsuy arsuy**

ahrruy　hurray harry hurry hay rah ray yah yar ah ay ha

ahrry　harry hay rah ray yah yar ah ay ha

ahrs　rahs rash ash has rah ah as ha sh

ahrsssu　hussars. *See* **ahrssu**

ahrssu　hussar surahs surah suras rahs rash rush sash sura ash ass has rah ah as ha sh us

ahrst　harts trash arts hart hast hats rahs rash rath rats star tars tsar art ash has hat rah rat sat tar ah as at ha sh ta

ahrsttw　thwarts. *See* **ahrstw ahrttw**

ahrstuwy　thruways swarthy thruway. *See* **ahrstw ahrsty ahrtwy arstwy**

ahrstw　swarth wraths harts straw swart swath thaws trash warts wrath arts hart hast hats haws rahs rash rath rats shaw star swat tars thaw tsar wars wart wash wast what art ash has hat haw rah rat raw sat saw tar war was ah as at aw ha sh ta

ahrstwy　swarthy. *See* **arstwy ahrstw ahrsty ahrtwy**

ahrsty　trashy artsy harts hasty satyr stray trash trays arts arty ashy hart hast hats hays rahs rash rath rats rays shay star stay tars tray tsar art ash has hat hay rah rat ray sat say shy sty tar thy try yah yar ah as at ay ha sh ta

ahrsu　surah rahs rash rush sura ash has rah ah as ha sh us

ahrt　hart rath art hat rah rat tar ah at ha ta

ahrttw　thwart wrath hart rath tart that thaw wart watt what art hat haw rah rat raw tar tat war ah at aw ha ta

ahrtuwy　thruway. *See* **ahrtwy**

ahrtw　wrath hart rath thaw wart what art hat haw rah rat raw tar war ah at aw ha ta

ahrtwy　wrathy wrath warty arty awry hart rath thaw tray wart wary what art hat haw hay rah rat raw ray tar thy try war way why yah yar yaw ah at aw ay ha ta

ahrxy　hyrax hay rah ray yah yar ah ax ay ha

ahs　ash has ah as ha sh

ahss　sash ash ass has ah as ha sh

ahsst　stash hast hats sash tass ash ass has hat sat ah as at ha sh ta

ahsstw　swaths shaws stash swash swath swats thaws hast hats haws sash saws shaw swat tass thaw wash wast what ash ass has hat haw sat saw was ah as at aw ha sh ta

ahssw　shaws swash haws sash saws shaw wash ash ass has haw saw was ah as aw ha sh

ahst　hast hats ash has hat sat ah as at ha sh ta

ahstw　swath thaws hast hats haws shaw swat thaw wash wast what ash has hat haw sat saw was ah as at aw ha sh ta

ahsty　hasty ashy hast hats hays shay stay ash has hat hay sat say shy sty thy yah ah as at ay ha sh ta

ahsw　haws shaw wash ash has haw saw was ah as aw ha sh

ahswy　washy ashy haws hays shaw shay sway wash ways yaws ash has haw hay saw say shy was way why yah yaw ah as aw ay ha sh

ahsy　ashy hays shay ash has hay say shy yah ah as ay ha sh

aht　hat ah at ha ta

ahtt　that hat tat ah at ha ta

ahtw　thaw what hat haw ah at aw ha ta

ahw　haw ah aw ha

ahy   hay yah ah ay ha
ahyz   hazy hay yah ah ay ha

ai

ai   ai
aiiilmst   militias militia. *See* iilmst
aiiilmt   militia. *See* iilmt
aiiilnst   initials initial. *See* aiinst ailnst
aiiilnt   initial. *No 6s or 5s*
aiikksuy   sukiyaki. *See* aikks akksy
aiikmnn   manikin. *See* iiknn
aiikmnnn   mannikin manikin. *See* aiknnn
aiikmnns   manikins manikin kinsman. *See* aiimns aikmns
aiiknnnp   pannikin. *See* aiknnn aiknnp
aiikorty   yakitori. *See* aikort
aiil   ilia ail ai la li
aiilllp   lapilli. *No 6s or 5s*
aiillmn   liminal. *See* aiilmn
aiillmry   milliary. *See* aiilry
aiillnnv   vanillin villain. *See* ailnv iilnn aillv
aiillnot   illation. *See* ailnot
aiillnsv   villains villain. *See* aillsv ailnsv
aiillnv   villain. *See* ailnv aillv
aiillnvy   villainy villain. *See* ailnvy
aiillqu   quillai. *See* ailqu illqu
aiilmmn   minimal. *See* aiilmn iimmn
aiilmn   limina anil ilia lain limn mail main mina nail ail aim ani lam man mil nil nim ai am an in la li ma mi na
aiilmntt   militant. *See* aiilmn
aiilmrs   similar. *See* aimrs ailrs ailms
aiilmrst   mistrial mistral mitrals similar. *See* ailmrt ailrst iilmst
aiilmrty   military. *See* aiilry ailmrt ilmrty
aiilmstv   vitalism. *See* ailstv iilmst
aiilnopv   pavilion. *See* iilnov
aiilnos   liaison. *See* ailns ilnos alnos
aiilnoss   liaisons liaison. *See* ailnss alnoss
aiilnpst   pintails tailspin pianist pintail plaints. *See* aiinst ailnps ailnpt ailnst
aiilnpt   pintail. *See* ailnpt
aiilntu   nautili. *See* ilntu
aiilorsv   raviolis ravioli. *See* ailors ailosv ailrsv aiorsv
aiilorv   ravioli. *See* ailrv alorv ailov
aiilrtv   trivial. *See* aiirtv ailrv ailrt
aiilry   airily riyal airy aril aryl ilia lair liar lira rail rial ail air lar lay ray ria yar ai ay la li
aiilttvy   vitality. *See* ailtt ailty altty
aiimmns   animism. *See* aiimns iimmns

aiimmnss   animisms animism simians. *See* aiimns iimmns
aiimnnos   insomnia amnions mansion minions onanism. *See* aiimns aimnno ainnos iimnno
aiimnpt   timpani. *See* aimnpt
aiimnrst   martinis animist intimas martini martins. *See* aiimns aiinrs aiinst aimnrt
aiimnrt   martini. *See* aimnrt
aiimns   simian mains aims main mina nims nisi sain aim ani man mis nim sin ai am an as in is ma mi na si
aiimnss   simians. *See* aiimns aimss
aiimnsst   animists animist intimas simians. *See* aiimns aiinst aimnst ainsst
aiimnst   animist intimas. *See* aiinst aimnst aiimns
aiimnstv   nativism vitamins animist intimas vitamin. *See* aiimns aiimnv aiinst aimnst
aiimnttu   titanium minutia. *See* iinttu aimntu amnttu
aiimntu   minutia. *See* aimntu
aiimntv   vitamin. *See* aiimnv aimnt
aiimnv   vimina mavin main mina vain vina aim ani man nim van via vim ai am an in ma mi na
aiimortt   imitator. *See* aiort aortt iiort
aiimpr   impair amir pair pram prim rami ramp aim air amp arm imp map mar mir par ram rap ria rim rip ai am ma mi pa pi
aiimprs   impairs. *See* aiimpr aimrs aiprs
aiimsstt   mastitis. *See* aimss amsst imsst
aiimssy   myiasis. *See* aimss amssy imssy
aiinnosv   invasion. *See* ainnos iinnos
aiinnqtu   quintain quintan. *See* ainqtu
aiinnsty   insanity inanity. *See* aiinst ainsty
aiinnsz   zinnias. *See* aiinnz
aiinnty   inanity. *See* innty
aiinnz   zinnia ani inn ai an in na
aiinprs   aspirin. *See* aiinrs ainprs
aiinprss   aspirins aspirin raisins sprains. *See* aiinrs ainprs
aiinpsst   pianists pianist ptisans. *See* aiinst ainpst ainsst
aiinpst   pianist. *See* aiinst ainpst

aiinrrtt   irritant. *See* ainrt aintt airtt
aiinrs   raisin naris rains ranis airs iris nisi rain rani rias sain sari air ani ran ria sin sir ai an as in is na si
aiinrss   raisins. *See* aiinrs airss
aiinst   isatin antis saint satin stain anti ants nisi nits sain snit tans tins ani ant ita its nit sat sin sit tan tin ai an as at in is it na si ta ti
aiinsttv   nativist visitant. *See* aiinst ainstt
aiinttvy   nativity tantivy. *See* aintvy
aiiprrst   airstrip. *See* aiprst iiprst
aiirsstt   satirist artists straits tsarist. *See* airsst airstt
aiirtv   trivia vair air art ita rat ria tar tav vat via ai at it ta ti
aiix   ixia ai ax xi
aijjmms   jimjams. *See* aimms
aijkknou   kinkajou. *See* aijkn
aijkn   kanji akin jink kina ani ink kin ai an in ka na
aijkns   kanjis kanji jinks akin inks jink kina sain saki sank sink skin ani ask ink kas kin sin ski ai an as in is ka na si
aijl   jail ail ai la li
aijllovy   jovially. *See* aijlov
aijlntuy   jauntily. *See* ailnty ajntuy
aijlor   jailor aril jail jarl lair liar lira oral rail rial roil ail air jar lar oar oil raj ria ai jo la li lo or
aijlors   jailors. *See* aijlor ailors
aijlov   jovial viola jail oval vail vial viol ail oil ova via ai jo la li lo
aijls   jails ails jail sail ail sal ai as is la li si
aijlyzz   jazzily. *See* ajyzz
aijmns   jasmin mains aims jams main mina nims sain aim ani jam man mis nim sin ai am an as in is ma mi na si
aijmorty   majority. *See* aimty amoty ajmor
aijnn   ninja jinn ani inn ai an in na
aijnns   ninjas jinns ninja inns jinn sain ani inn sin ai an as in is na si
aijnorst   janitors janitor rations. *See* ainors ainort ainrst aiorst
aijnort   janitor. *See* ainort ijnot
aikk   kaki ai ka
aikks   kakis kaki saki ask kas ski ai as is ka si

aikl kail ail ilk kal ai ka la li

aikllny lankily. *See* **akllny ailny**

aiklmmn milkman. *See* **aiklmn**

aiklmn malkin akin anil kail kami kiln kina lain lank limn link mail main milk mina mink nail ail aim ani ilk ink kal kin lam man mil nil nim ai am an in ka la li ma mi na

aiklmnn linkman. *See* **aiklmn**

aiklmns malkins. *See* **aiklmn aikmns**

aiklno kaolin akin anil ikon kail kaon kiln kilo kina kino koan kola lain lank link lion loan loin nail noil oink ail ani ilk ink ion kal kin koa nil oak oil ai an in ka la li lo na no on

aiklottw kilowatt. *See* **ailtt alott**

aiklquy quakily. *See* **ailqu akquy**

aiklsssy skysails skysail. *See* **ailsss**

aiklssy skysail. *See* **iksss ilssy**

aikltu likuta alit kail kilt tail tali talk ail alt auk ilk ita kal kat kit lit tau til tui ai at it ka la li ta ti ut

aikm kami aim ai am ka ma mi

aikmnns kinsman. *See* **aikmns**

aikmns kamsin mains minks aims akin inks kami kina main mask mina mink nims sain saki sank sink skim skin aim ani ask ink kas kin man mis nim sin ski ai am an as in is ka ma mi na si

aikmnss kamsins. *See* **aikmns aimss akmss**

aikmoo oomiak amok kami mako aim koa moa moo oak ai am ka ma mi mo om

aikmoos oomiaks. *See* **aikmoo**

aikmrstz sitzmark. *See* **aikrst aimrsz**

aikmsu umiaks umiak aims auks kami mask musk saki skim aim ask auk kas mis mus ski sum ai am as is ka ma mi mu si um us

aikmu umiak kami aim auk ai am ka ma mi mu um

aikn akin kina ani ink kin ai an in ka na

aiknnn nankin akin kina ani ink inn kin ai an in ka na

aiknnns nankins. *See* **aiknnn**

aiknnoos nainsook. *See* **ainnos innoos**

aiknnp napkin pinna akin kina knap nipa pain pika pink ani ink inn kin kip nap nip pan pin ai an in ka na pa pi

aiknnps napkins. *See* **aiknnp ainnps**

aiknnssw swanskin. *See* **ainssw**

aiknorty karyotin. *See* **aiknot aikort ainort aknory**

aiknostt stotinka station. *See* **aiknot ainstt iknost**

aiknot kation akin anti ikon into iota kaon kina kino knit knot koan nota oink tank ani ant ink ion ita kat kin kit

koa nit not oak oat tan tin ton ai an at in it ka na no on ta ti to

aikop okapi pika kip koa oak poi ai ka pa pi

aikops okapis okapi pikas kips koas oaks pika pois saki skip soak soap ask asp kas kip koa kos oak pas poi sap sip ski sop spa ai as is ka os pa pi si so

aikorst troikas. *See* **akorst aikrst aiorst aikort**

aikort troika korat krait ratio iota kart okra raki riot rota taro tiro tora tori trio air ark art irk ita kat kir kit koa kor oak oar oat ort rat ria rot tar tor ai at it ka or ta ti to

aikp pika kip ai ka pa pi

aikps pikas kips pika saki skip ask asp kas kip pas sap sip ski spa ai as is ka pa pi si

aikr raki air ark irk kir ria ai ka

aikrs rakis airs arks irks kris raki rias risk saki sari sark air ark ask irk kas kir ria sir ski ai as is ka si

aikrst kraits astir karst karts krait rakis sitar skirt stair stark stria tarsi airs arks arts irks kart kist kits kris raki rats rias risk saki sari sark skat skit star stir tars task tsar air ark art ask irk ita its kas kat kir kit rat ria sat sir sit ski tar tsk ai as at is it ka ta ti

aikrt krait raki kart air ark art irk ita kat kir kit rat ria tar ai at it ka ta ti

aikru kauri raki air ark auk irk kir ria ai ka

aiks saki ask kas ski ai as is ka si

aikss sakis asks kiss saki skis ask ass kas sis ski ai as is ka si

aiksv kivas kiva kvas saki visa ask kas ski via ai as is ka si

aikv kiva via ai ka

ail ail ai la li

ailllpsu lapillus. *See* **ailpsu**

ailllmost maillots maillot. *See* **allmos allost almost**

aillmot maillot. *See* **allot allmo**

aillmpsu palliums pallium. *See* **ailpsu almpsu**

aillmpu pallium. *See* **ailpu almpu**

aillmssw sawmills sawmill. *See* **ailmss illssw**

aillmsw sawmill. *See* **ailms allms illms**

aillmuuv alluvium. *See* **aillv aluuv**

aillnno lanolin. *See* **ainno allno**

aillnopp papillon. *See* **ilnopp**

aillnost stallion install talions. *See* **ailnot ailnst allnos allost**

aillnosu allusion. *See* **allnos**

aillnpy plainly. *See* **ailny ailnp allpy**

aillnsst installs install. *See* **ailnsst ainsst allsst**

aillnst install. *See* **ailnst illst illns**

aillortt littoral tortilla. *See* **ailort**

aillosty loyalist saltily. *See* **allost allosy allsty illsty**

aillpr pillar aril lair liar lira pail pair pall pill rail rial rill ail air all alp ill lap lar lip pal par rap ria rip ai la li pa pi

aillprs pillars. *See* **aillpr ailprs**

aillpswy spillway slipway. *See* **ailps allps allpy**

aillpuv pluvial. *See* **aillv ailpu**

aillrtuy ritually. *See* **ailrtu**

aillsty saltily. *See* **allsty illsty**

aillsuvy visually. *See* **aillsv ailsuv**

aillsv villas silva vails vials villa ails sail sill vail vial visa ail all ill sal via ai as is la li si

aillv villa vail vial ail all ill via ai la li

aillyz lazily ally illy lazy lily ail all ill lay ai ay la li

ailm mail ail aim lam mil ai am la li ma mi

ailmmnuu aluminum. *See* **ailmnu**

ailmmor immoral. *See* **almor**

ailmmors moralism immoral. *See* **ailors aimmos almors**

ailmmort immortal immoral. *See* **ailmrt ailort almort ammort**

ailmnno nominal. *See* **ailmno aimnno**

ailmnnos nominals amnions malison mansion nominal onanism. *See* **ailmno aimnno ainnos almnos**

ailmno oilman anil lain limn limo lion loam loan loin mail main milo mina moan moil mola nail noil noma ail aim ani ion lam man mil moa mon nil nim oil ai am an in la li lo ma mi mo na no om on

ailmnoop palomino lampoon. *See* **ailmno ailmop**

ailmnoor monorail. *See* **ailmno ailmnr almnor amnoor**

ailmnopy palimony alimony. *See* **ailmno ailmny ailmop aimnpy**

ailmnos malison. *See* **ailmno almnos**

ailmnoss malisons malison salmons. *See* **ailmno ailmss ailnss almnos**

ailmnoy alimony. *See* **ailmno ailmny**

ailmnpst implants implant palmist plaints. *See* **ailnps ailnpt ailnst ailpst**

ailmnpt implant. *See* **aimnpt ailnpt**

ailmnptu platinum implant nuptial. *See* **ailmnu ailnpt aimnpt aimntu**

ailmnr marlin amir anil aril lain lair liar limn lira mail main marl mina nail rail rain rami rani rial ail aim air ani arm lam lar man mar mil mir nil nim ram ran ria rim ai am an in la li ma mi na

ailmnrs marlins. *See* **ailmnr aimrs ailns**

ailmnruy luminary. *See* **ailmnr ailmnu ailmny ailnru**

ailmnu alumni lumina alum anil lain limn mail main maul maun mina nail ulna ail aim ani lam lum man mil nil nim ai am an in la li ma mi mu na nu um

ailmny mainly inlay manly amyl anil ayin inly lain limn limy liny mail main many mina myna nail ail aim ani any lam lay man may mil nay nil nim yam yin ai am an ay in la li ma mi my na

ailmop lipoma lamp limo limp loam mail milo moil mola opal pail palm ail aim alp amp imp lam lap lip lop map mil moa mop oil pal poi ai am la li lo ma mi mo om pa pi

ailmoprx proximal. *See* **ailmop ailmpr iloprx**

ailmops lipomas. *See* **ailmop almps ilmps**

ailmopt optimal. *See* **ailmop aiopt ilopt**

ailmorst moralist amorist mistral mitrals mortals rialtos tailors. *See* **ailmrt ailors ailort ailrst**

ailmorsu solarium. *See* **ailors almors almrsu amorsu**

ailmorty morality. *See* **ailmrt ailort almort ilmrty**

ailmostu solatium. *See* **aimstu almost ilmotu ilmstu**

ailmpr primal amir aril lair lamp liar limp lira mail marl pail pair palm pram prim rail rami ramp rial ail aim air alp amp arm imp lam lap lar lip map mar mil mir pal par ram rap ria rim rip ai am la li ma mi pa pi

ailmpsst palmists psalmist palmist. *See* **ailmss ailpst almpss almsst**

ailmpssy misplays misplay mislays. *See* **ailmss ailmsy almpss alpssy**

ailmpst palmist. *See* **ailpst almps ilmps**

ailmpsty ptyalism palmist misplay. *See* **ailmsy ailpst ilmpsy**

ailmpsy misplay. *See* **ailmsy ilmpsy**

ailmrrsu ruralism. *See* **almrsu**

ailmrsst mistrals mistral mitrals. *See* **ailmrt ailmss ailrst aimrss**

ailmrst mistral mitrals. *See* **ailmrt ailrst**

ailmrstu altruism atriums mistral mitrals rituals. *See* **ailmrt ailrst ailrtu aimrtu**

ailmrt mitral trail trial alit amir aril lair liar lira mail malt marl mart milt rail rami rial tail tali tram trim ail aim air alt arm art ita lam lar lit mar mat mil mir ram rat ria rim tam tar til ai am at it la li ma mi ta ti

ailms mails salmi ails aims alms lams mail mils sail slam slim ail aim lam mil mis sal ai am as is la li ma mi si

ailmss missal amiss mails sails salmi sisal slams ails aims alms lams lass mail mass mils miss sail sals slam slim ail aim ass lam mil mis sal sis ai am as is la li ma mi si

ailmsss missals. *See* **ailmss ailsss**

ailmssy mislays. *See* **ailmss ailmsy**

ailmsx smilax axils mails maxis salmi ails aims alms axil axis lams mail maxi mils sail slam slim ail aim lam lax mil mis mix sal sax six ai am as ax is la li ma mi si xi

ailmsy mislay amyls mails salmi slimy ails aims alms amyl lams lays limy mail mils sail slam slay slim yams ail aim lam lay may mil mis sal say sly yam ai am as ay is la li ma mi my si

ailn anil lain nail ail ani nil ai an in la li na

ailnnoot notional. *See* **ailnot ainnot ilnoot innoot**

ailnnu annuli annul anil lain linn nail ulna ail ani inn nil nun ai an in la li na nu

ailnoopt optional platoon. *See* **ailnot ailnpt ilnoot ilnopt**

ailnopty ponytail inaptly. *See* **ailnot ailnpt ailnty ainpty**

ailnost talions. *See* **ailnst ailnot alnost ilnost**

ailnosuv avulsion. *See* **ailnsv ailosv ailsuv inosuv**

ailnot talion talon tonal alit alto anil anti into iota lain lint lion loan loin lota nail noil nota tail tali toil tola ail alt ani ant ion ita lit lot nil nit not oat oil tan til tin ton ai an at in it la li lo na no on ta ti to

ailnotty tonality nattily. *See* **ailnot ailnty**

ailnotux luxation. *See* **ailnot ailotx**

ailnp lapin plain anil lain nail nipa pail pain plan ail alp ani lap lip nap nil nip pal pan pin ai an in la li na pa pi

ailnps lapins plains spinal anils lapin nails nipas pails pains plain plans slain snail ails alps anil lain laps lips lisp nail naps nils nipa nips pail pain pals pans pins plan sail sain slap slip snap snip span spin ail alp ani asp lap lip nap nil nip pal pan pas pin sal sap sin sip spa ai an as in is la li na pa pi si

ailnpss spinals. *See* **ailnps ailnss**

ailnpst plaints. *See* **ailnst ailnps ainpst ailnpt ailpst**

ailnpstu nuptials plaints nuptial. *See* **ailnps ailnpt ailnst ailpst**

ailnpsx salpinx. *See* **ailnps**

ailnpt plaint pliant inapt lapin paint plain plait plant alit anil anti lain lint nail nipa pail pain pant pint pita plan

plat tail tali ail alp alt ani ant apt ita lap lip lit nap nil nip nit pal pan pat pin pit tan tap til tin tip ai an at in it la li na pa pi ta ti

ailnptu nuptial. *See* **ailnpt**

ailnpty inaptly. *See* **ailnty ainpty ailnpt**

ailnqrtu tranquil quintal. *See* **ailnrt ailnru ailrtu ainqrt**

ailnqstu quintals quintal asquint. *See* **ailnst ailqsu ainqtu alnstu**

ailnqtu quintal. *See* **ainqtu ailqu ilqtu**

ailnqtuy quaintly quintal quality. *See* **ailnty ainqtu**

ailnrsu insular urinals. *See* **ailnru ailns ailrs**

ailnrt trinal riant trail train trial alit anil anti aril lain lair liar lint lira nail rail rain rani rant rial tail tali ail air alt ani ant art ita lar lit nil nit ran rat ria tan tar til tin ai an at in it la li na ta ti

ailnru urinal lunar anil aril lain lair liar lira nail rail rain rani rial ruin ulna ail air ani lar nil ran ria run urn ai an in la li na nu

ailns anils nails slain snail ails anil lain nail nils sail sain ail ani nil sal sin ai an as in is la li na si

ailnss snails anils nails sails sisal slain snail ails anil lain lass nail nils sail sain sals sins ail ani ass nil sal sin sis ai an as in is la li na si

ailnst instal anils antis lints nails saint satin slain slant snail stain tails ails alit alts anil anti ants lain last lint list nail nils nits sail sain salt silt slat slit snit tail tali tans tils tins ail alt ani ant ita its lit nil nit sal sat sin sit tan til tin ai an as at in is it la li na si ta ti

ailnstuu nautilus. *See* **ailnst ilnstu alnstu**

ailnsty nastily saintly. *See* **ailnsy ailnst ailnty ainsty**

ailnsv anvils silvan anils anvil nails nival savin silva slain snail vails vials vinas ails anil lain nail nils sail sain vail vain vans vial vina visa ail ani nil sal sin van via ai an as in is la li na si

ailnsy inlays anils ayins inlay lysin nails slain snail ails anil ayin inly lain lays liny nail nils sail sain slay ail ani any lay nay nil sal say sin sly yin ai an as ay in is la li na si

ailntty nattily. *See* **ailnty ailtt altty**

ailnty litany inlay laity linty alit anil anti ayin inly lain lint liny nail tail tali tiny ail alt ani ant any ita lay lit nay nil nit tan til tin yin ai an at ay in it la li na ta ti

ailnv anvil nival anil lain nail vail vain vial vina ail ani nil van via ai an in la li na

ailnvy   vainly anvil inlay nival vinyl anil ayin inly lain liny nail navy vail vain vial vina viny ail ani any ivy lay nay nil van via yin ai an ay in la li na

ailny   inlay anil ayin inly lain liny nail ail ani any lay nay nil yin ai an ay in la li na

ailnyz   zanily inlay zayin anil ayin inly lain lazy liny nail zany ail ani any lay nay nil yin ai an ay in la li na

ailoortv   violator. *See* **ailort**

ailoprty   polarity topiary. *See* **ailort aiprty aloprt alprty**

ailopsst   apostils topsails apostil pistols postals topsail. *See* **ailpst aiopst alopst alpsst**

ailopst   apostil topsail. *See* **aiopst ilopst alopst**

ailoptv   pivotal. *See* **aiopt ilopt ioptv**

ailoqtu   aliquot. *See* **aloqtu ailqu ilqtu**

ailors   sailor arils lairs liars liras loris orals rails rials roils solar ails airs also aril lair liar lira oars oils oral rail rial rias roil sail sari silo soar soil sora sori ail air lar los oar oil ria sal sir sol ai as is la li lo or os si so

ailorss   sailors. *See* **ailors airss aloss**

ailorst   rialtos tailors. *See* **aiorst ailort ailors ailrst**

ailorsty   royalist solitary ostiary rialtos tailors. *See* **ailors ailort ailrst ailrsy**

ailort   rialto tailor ratio trail trial alit alto aril iota lair liar lira lota oral rail rial riot roil rota rotl tail tali taro tiro toil tola tora tori trio ail air alt art ita lar lit lot oar oat oil ort rat ria rot tar til tor ai at it la li lo or ta ti to

ailorttu   tutorial titular. *See* **ailort ailrtu**

ailorux   uxorial. *See* **aiorx**

ailostx   oxtails. *See* **ailosx ailotx**

ailosv   violas ovals salvo silva vails vials viola viols ails also oils oval sail silo soil vail vial viol visa ail los oil ova sal sol via ai as is la li lo os si so

ailosx   oxalis axils ails also axil axis oils sail silo soil ail lax los lox oil sal sax six sol sox ai as ax is la li lo os ox si so xi

ailottty   totality. *See* **ailtt ailty altty**

ailotx   oxtail alit alto axil iota lota tail tali taxi toil tola ail alt ita lax lit lot lox oat oil tax til ai at ax it la li lo ox ta ti to xi

ailov   viola oval vail vial viol ail oil ova via ai la li lo

ailp   pail ail alp lap lip pal ai la li pa pi

ailpp   palpi pipal pail palp ail alp lap lip pal pap pip ai la li pa pi

ailpps   pipals pails palpi palps pipal ails alps laps lips lisp pail palp pals paps pips sail slap slip ail alp asp lap lip pal

pap pas pip sal sap sip spa ai as is la li pa pi si

ailppty   platypi. *See* **alppy alpty ailty**

ailpqssu   pasquils pasquil. *See* **ailpsu ailqsu**

ailpqsu   pasquil. *See* **ailpsu ailqsu**

ailprs   spiral arils lairs liars liras pails pairs rails rials ails airs alps aril lair laps liar lips lira lisp pail pair pals pars rail raps rasp rial rias rips sail sari slap slip spar ail air alp asp lap lar lip pal par pas rap ria rip sal sap sip sir spa ai as is la li pa pi si

ailps   pails ails alps laps lips lisp pail pals sail slap slip ail alp asp lap lip pal pas sal sap sip spa ai as is la li pa pi si

ailpsswy   slipways slipway. *See* **alpssy**

ailpst   plaits deils deism delis dimes idles limed limes melds miles sidle slide slime smile deil deli dies dime dims elms ides idle isle leis lids lied lies lime meld mels mild mile mils mise semi side sled slid slim apt die dim eld ids its led lei lid lie lip lit mid pat pit sat sip sit tap til tip ai as at is it la li pa pi si ta ti

ailpstuy   playsuit. *See* **ailpst ailpsu alpsuy ilpstu**

ailpsu   pilaus pails pilau pulis ails alps laps lips lisp pail pals plus puli puls sail slap slip upas ail alp asp lap lip pal pas pul pus sal sap sip spa sup ai as is la li pa pi si up us

ailpswy   slipway. *See* **ailps alpsy alpsw**

ailpt   plait alit pail pita plat tail tali ail alp alt apt ita lap lip lit pal pat pit tap til tip ai at it la li pa pi ta ti

ailpu   pilau pail puli ail alp lap lip pal pul ai la li pa pi up

ailqsu   quails quail quasi ails sail ail qua sal ai as is la li si us

ailqtuy   quality. *See* **ailty ailqu ilqtu**

ailqu   quail ail qua ai la li

ailr   aril lair liar lira rail rial ail air lar ria ai la li

ailrrstu   ruralist rituals. *See* **ailrst ailrtu alrstu**

ailrrvy   rivalry. *See* **ailrv ailry**

ailrs   arils lairs liars liras rails rials ails airs aril lair liar lira rail rial rias sail sari ail air lar ria sal sir ai as is la li si

ailrst   trails trials deist diets dries edits rides rites sired sited tides tiers tired tires tried tries dies diet dire dirt dits edit erst ides reds reis rest rets ride rids rise rite side sire site stir teds tide tied tier ties tire alt art die ita its lar lit rat red rid sat sat sir sit tar ted til ai as at is it la li si ta ti

ailrstt   starlit. *See* **airstt ailrst**

ailrsttu   altruist rituals starlit titular. *See* **ailrst ailrtu airstt alrstu**

ailrstty   straitly starlit tastily. *See* **ailrst ailrsy airstt airtty**

ailrstu   rituals. *See* **alrstu ailrtu ailrst**

ailrsuvv   survival. *See* **ailrsv ailsuv**

ailrsv   rivals arils lairs liars liras rails rials rival silva vails vairs vials viral ails airs aril lair liar lira rail rial rias sail sari vail vair vial visa ail air lar ria sal sir via ai as is la li si

ailrsy   riyals arils aryls lairs liars liras rails rials riyal ails airs airy aril aryl lair lays liar lira rail rays rial rias sail sari slay ail air lar lay ray ria sal say sir sly yar ai as ay is la li si

ailrt   trail trial alit aril lair liar lira rail rial tail tali ail air alt art ita lar lit rat ria tar til ai at it la li ta ti

ailrttu   titular. *See* **ailrtu ailtt airtt**

ailrtu   ritual trail trial ultra alit aril lair liar lira rail rial tail tali ail air alt art ita lar lit rat ria rut tar tau til tui ai at it la li ta ti ut

ailrtuv   virtual. *See* **ailrtu ailrv altuv**

ailrv   rival viral aril lair liar lira rail rial vail vair vial ail air lar ria via ai la li

ailrwy   warily riyal airy aril aryl awry lair liar lira rail rial wail wary wily wiry yawl ail air awl lar law lay raw ray ria war way yar yaw ai aw ay la li

ailry   riyal airy aril aryl lair liar lira rail rial ail air lar lay ray ria yar ai ay la li

ails   ails sail ail sal ai as is la li si

ailss   sails sisal ails lass sail sals ail ass sal sis ai as is la li si

ailsss   sisals sails sisal ails lass sail sals sass ail ass sal sis ai as is la li si

ailssstuw   lawsuits lawsuit. *See* **aisstw**

ailssuv   visuals. *See* **ailsssv ailsuv**

ailsssv   silvas sails silva sisal vails vials visas ails lass sail sals vail vial visa ail ass sal sis via ai as is la li si

ailst   tails ails alit alts last list sail salt silt slat slit tail tali tils ail alt ita its lit sal sat sit til ai as at is it la li si ta ti

ailstty   tastily. *See* **ailtt ailty altty**

ailstuw   lawsuit. *See* **ailst alstu ailsw**

ailstv   vitals silva tails vails vials vista vital ails alit alts last list sail salt silt slat slit tail tali tavs tils vail vast vats vial visa ail alt ita its lit sal sat sit tav til vat via ai as at is it la li si ta ti

ailsuv   visual silva vails vials ails sail vail vial visa ail luv sal via ai as is la li si us

ailsv   silva vails vials ails sail vail vial visa ail sal via ai as is la li si

ailsw   wails ails awls laws sail wail ail awl law sal saw was wis ai as aw is la li si

ailsx   axils ails axil axis sail ail lax sal sax six ai as ax is la li si xi

ailt   alit tail tali ail alt ita lit til ai at it la li ta ti

ailtt   atilt alit tail tali tilt ail alt ita lit tat til tit ai at it la li ta ti

ailtv   vital alit tail tali vail vial ail alt ita lit tav til vat via ai at it la li ta ti

ailtxy   laxity laity alit axil tail tali taxi ail alt ita lax lay lit tax til ai at ax ay it la li ta ti xi

ailty   laity alit tail tali ail alt ita lay lit til ai at ay it la li ta ti

ailv   vail vial ail via ai la li

ailw   wail ail awl law ai aw la li

ailx   axil ail lax ai ax la li xi

aim   aim ai am ma mi

aimm   imam maim aim mim ai am ma mi

aimmmsux   maximums maximum. *See* **aimmsx**

aimmmux   maximum. *See* **aimmx**

aimmnort   mortmain. *See* **aimnrt ainort ammort amnort**

aimmnstu   manumits manumit tsunami. *See* **aimnst aimnsu aimntu aimstu**

aimmntu   manumit. *See* **aimntu**

aimmos   mimosa imams maims aims ammo imam maim moas moms soma aim mim mis moa mom mos oms ai am as is ma mi mo om os si so

aimmoss   mimosas. *See* **aimmos aimss aioss**

aimmost   atomism. *See* **aimmos amost aiost**

aimms   imams maims aims imam maim aim mim mis ai am as is ma mi si

aimmsx   maxims imams maims maxim maxis aims axis imam maim maxi aim mim mis mix sax six ai am as ax is ma mi si xi

aimmx   maxim imam maim maxi aim mim mix ai am ax ma mi xi

aimn   main mina aim ani man nim ai am an in ma mi na

aimnno   amnion anion anon main mina moan noma aim ani inn ion man moa mon nim ai am an in ma mi mo na no om on

aimnnos   amnions mansion onanism. *See* **aimnno ainnos**

aimnnoss   mansions onanisms amnions mansion onanism. *See* **aimnno ainnos amnoss**

aimnnotu   mountain manitou tinamou. *See* **aimnno aimnnt aimnnu aimntu**

aimnnoty   antimony antinomy antonym. *See* **aimnno aimnnt aimnny ainnot**

aimnnrtu   ruminant. *See* **aimnnt aimnnu aimnrt aimntu**

aimnnsy   minyans. *See* **aimnny ainsy aimns**

aimnnt   tinman matin anti main mina mint aim ani ant inn ita man mat nim nit tam tan tin ai am an at in it ma mi na ta ti

aimnnu   numina unman main maun mina aim ani inn man nim nun ai am an in ma mi mu na nu um

aimnny   minyan minny ayin main many mina myna aim ani any inn man may nay nim yam yin ai am an ay in ma mi my na

aimnopr   rampion. *See* **anopr amnor imnor**

aimnoprs   rampions rampion. *See* **ainops ainors ainprs amnors**

aimnopst   maintops tampions impasto maintop postman tampion. *See* **aimnpt aimnst ainops ainpst**

aimnopt   maintop tampion. *See* **aimnpt aiopt ainop**

aimnorty   minatory. *See* **aimnrt ainort amnort anorty**

aimnostu   manitous amounts manitou tinamou tsunami. *See* **aimnst aimnsu aimntu aimstu**

aimnottu   mutation manitou tinamou. *See* **aimntu amnotu amnttu mnottu**

aimnotu   manitou tinamou. *See* **aimntu amnotu**

aimnpsy   paynims. *See* **aimnpy ainsy aimns**

aimnpt   pitman inapt matin paint anti main mina mint nipa pain pant pint pita tamp aim amp ani ant apt imp ita man map mat nap nim nip nit pan pat pin pit tam tan tap tin tip ai am an at in it ma mi na pa pi ta ti

aimnpty   tympani. *See* **ainpty aimnpy aimnpt amnpty**

aimnpy   paynim ayin main many mina myna nipa pain piny aim amp ani any imp man map may nap nay nim nip pan pay pin pya yam yap yin yip ai am an ay in ma mi my na pa pi

aimnrrsu   murrains murrain. *See* **aimnsu amnrsu**

aimnrru   murrain. *See* **amnru**

aimnrst   martins. *See* **ainrst aimnst aimnrt**

aimnrstt   transmit martins transit. *See* **aimnrt aimnst ainrst ainstt**

aimnrstv   varmints martins varmint. *See* **aimnrt aimnst aimnsv ainrst**

aimnrsuu   uraniums uranium. *See* **aimnsu amnrsu amrsuu**

aimnrt   martin matin riant train amir anti main mart mina mint rain rami rani rant tram trim aim air ani ant arm art

ita man mar mat mir nim nit ram ran rat ria rim tam tan tar tin ai am an at in it ma mi na ta ti

aimnrtv   varmint. *See* **aimnrt aimnv**

aimnruu   uranium. *See* **amnru amruu**

aimns   mains aims main mina nims sain aim ani man mis nim sin ai am an as in is ma mi na si

aimnsstu   tsunamis issuant sustain tsunami. *See* **aimnst aimnsu aimntu aimstu**

aimnst   mantis matins antis mains matin mints saint satin stain aims anti ants main mast mats mina mint mist nims nits sain snit tams tans tins aim ani ant ita its man mat mis nim nit sat sin sit tam tan tin ai am an as at in is it ma mi na si ta ti

aimnstu   tsunami. *See* **aimnsu aimstu aimntu aimnst**

aimnsu   animus mains manus minus aims anus main maun mina nims sain aim ani man mis mus nim sin sum sun ai am an as in is ma mi mu na nu si um us

aimnsv   mavins mains mavin mavis savin vinas aims main mina nims sain vain vans vims vina visa aim ani man mis nim sin van via vim ai am an as in is ma mi na si

aimnt   matin anti main mina mint aim ani ant ita man mat nim nit tam tan tin ai am an at in it ma mi na ta ti

aimntu   manitu matin anti aunt main maun mina mint tuna unit aim ani ant ita man mat nim nit nut tam tan tau tin tui tun ai am an at in it ma mi mu na nu ta ti um ut

aimnv   mavin main mina vain vina aim ani man nim van via vim ai am an in ma mi na

aimopsst   impastos impasto imposts. *See* **aiopst amosst ampsst imopst**

aimopst   impasto. *See* **imopst aiopst**

aimopsy   myopias. *See* **aimopy amosy aopsy**

aimopy   myopia mayo aim amp imp map may moa mop pay poi pya yam yap yip ai am ay ma mi mo my om oy pa pi

aimorsst   amorists amorist. *See* **aimrss aiorst airsst amorss**

aimorst   amorist. *See* **aiorst aimrs amost**

aimosstt   atomists atomist. *See* **amosst aossttt**

aimostt   atomist. *See* **amost aiost imstt**

aimosw   miaows miaow swami aims maws moas mows soma swam swim aim maw mis moa mos mow oms saw sow was wis ai am as aw is ma mi mo om os ow si so

aimosx   axioms axiom maxis moxas aims axis maxi moas moxa soma aim mis

mix moa mos oms sax six sox ai am as
ax is ma mi mo om os ox si so xi

aimow miaow aim maw moa mow ai am
aw ma mi mo om ow

aimox axiom maxi moxa aim mix moa ai
am ax ma mi mo om ox xi

aimprry primary. *See* **amrry aprry**

aimprst armpits imparts. *See* **aimprt
aiprst amprst**

aimprt armpit impart tapir tramp amir
mart pair part pita pram prim rami
ramp rapt tamp tarp tram trap trim
trip aim air amp apt arm art imp ita
map mar mat mir par pat pit ram rap
rat ria rim rip tam tap tar tip ai am at it
ma mi pa pi ta ti

aimqrsu marquis. *See* **aimqsu imqrsu**

aimqsu maquis maqui quasi umiaq aims
aim mis mus qua sum ai am as is ma mi
mu si um us

aimqu maqui umiaq aim qua ai am ma
mi mu um

aimr amir rami aim air arm mar mir ram
ria rim ai am ma mi

aimrs amirs simar aims airs amir arms
mirs rami rams rias rims sari aim air
arm mar mir mis ram ria rim sir ai am
as is ma mi si

aimrss simars amirs amiss arsis saris simar aims airs amir arms mass mirs
miss rami rams rias rims sari sirs aim
air arm ass mar mir mis ram ria rim sir
sis ai am as is ma mi si

aimrstu atriums. *See* **aimrtu aimstu amrstu imrstu**

aimrsz mirzas zirams amirs mirza simar
sizar ziram aims airs amir arms mirs
rami rams rias rims sari aim air arm
mar mir mis ram ria rim sir ai am as is
ma mi si

aimrttuy maturity yttrium. *See* **aimrtu
airtty**

aimrtu atrium amir mart rami tram trim
aim air arm art ita mar mat mir ram rat
ria rim rum rut tam tar tau tui ai am at
it ma mi mu ta ti um ut

aimrtx matrix amir mart maxi mixt rami
taxi tram trim aim air arm art ita mar
mat mir mix ram rat ria rim tam tar tax
ai am at ax it ma mi ta ti xi

aimrz mirza ziram amir rami aim air arm
mar mir ram ria rim ai am ma mi

aims aims aim mis ai am as is ma mi si

aimss amiss aims mass miss aim ass mis
sis ai am as is ma mi si

aimstu autism aims mast mats mist must
smut stum suit tams tuis aim ita its mat
mis mus sat sit sum tam tau tui ai am
as at is it ma mi mu si ta ti um us ut

aimsv mavis aims vims visa aim mis via
vim ai am as is ma mi si

aimsw swami aims maws swam swim
aim maw mis saw was wis ai am as aw
is ma mi si

aimsx maxis aims axis maxi aim mis mix
sax six ai am as ax is ma mi si xi

aimty amity aim ita mat may tam yam ai
am at ay it ma mi my ta ti

aimx maxi aim mix ai am ax ma mi xi

ain ani ai an in na

ainnnt tannin anti ani ant inn ita nit tan
tin ai an at in it na ta ti

ainno anion anon ani inn ion ai an in na
no on

ainnoott notation. *See* **ainnot innoot**

ainnootv novation ovation. *See* **ainnot
innoot**

ainnootz zonation. *See* **ainnot innoot**

ainnos anions anion anon inns ions naos
sain ani inn ion sin son ai an as in is na
no on os si so

ainnost anoints nations. *See* **ainnos ainnot annost**

ainnot anoint nation anion anon anti
into iota nota ani ant inn ion ita nit not
oat tan tin ton ai an at in it na no on ta
ti to

ainnp pinna nipa pain ani inn nap nip
pan pin ai an in na pa pi

ainnps pinnas nipas pains pinna inns
naps nipa nips pain pans pins sain
snap snip span spin ani asp inn nap
nip pan pas pin sap sin sip spa ai an as
in is na pa pi si

ainnqstu quintans quintan asquint. *See*
ainqtu annstu anqstu inqstu

ainnqtu quintan. *See* **ainqtu**

ainnsstt instants instant tanists. *See*
ainsst ainstt

ainnstt instant. *See* **ainstt**

ainntuy annuity. *See* **antuy innty intuy**

ainooptt potation. *See* **aooptt inoopt**

ainoorst orations oration rations ratoons
torsion. *See* **ainors ainort ainrst aiorst**

ainoort oration. *See* **ainort anoort**

ainoortt rotation oration tortoni. *See* **ainort anoort anortt inortt**

ainoostt ostinato station. *See* **ainstt**

ainoostv ovations ovation. *See* **ainst aiost
anosv**

ainootv ovation. *No 6s or 5s*

ainop piano nipa pain ani ion nap nip
pan pin poi ai an in na no on pa pi

ainoppst appoints appoint topspin. *See*
ainops aiopst aippst

ainoppt appoint. *See* **ainpt aiopt ainop**

ainopptu pupation appoint. *See* **ainpt
inptu aiopt**

ainops pianos nipas pains piano ions
naos naps nipa nips pain pans pins
pois pons sain snap snip soap span
spin ani asp ion nap nip pan pas pin
poi sap sin sip son sop spa ai an as in is
na no on os pa pi si so

ainopss passion. *See* **ainops aipss aioss**

ainopsss passions passion. *See* **ainops**

ainoqu quinoa quoin ani ion qua ai an in
na no nu on

ainor noria iron rain rani roan air ani ion
nor oar ran ria ai an in na no on or

ainors norias arson irons naris noria
rains ranis roans rosin sonar airs ions
iron naos oars rain rani rias roan sain
sari soar sora sori air ani ion nor oar
ran ria sin sir son ai an as in is na no on
or os si so

ainorsst arsonist rations strains. *See* **ainors ainort ainrst ainsst**

ainorssw warisons warison. *See* **ainors
ainssw anorss anorsw**

ainorst rations. *See* **ainrst ainors ainort
aiorst**

ainorstu rainouts nitrous nutrias rainout
rations. *See* **ainors ainort ainrst ainrtu**

ainorsw warison. *See* **ainors anorsw**

ainort ration noria ratio riant train anti
into iota iron nota rain rani rant riot
roan rota taro tiro tora tori torn trio air
ani ant art ion ita nit nor not oar oat
ort ran rat ria rot tan tar tin ton tor ai
an at in it na no on or ta ti to

ainortu rainout. *See* **ainrtu anortu**

ainosstt stations station tanists. *See*
ainsst ainstt aosstt

ainossu sanious suasion. *See* **inssu aioss**

ainostt station. *See* **ainstt**

ainosux anxious. *See* **ainsux anosx**

ainp nipa pain ani nap nip pan pin ai an
in na pa pi

ainpprs parsnip. *See* **ainprs**

ainpprss parsnips parsnip sprains. *See*
ainprs

ainpqtu piquant. *See* **ainqtu ainpt inptu**

ainprs sprain naris nipas pains pairs
pirns rains ranis airs naps nipa nips
pain pair pans pars pins pirn rain rani
raps rasp rias rips sain sari snap snip
span spar spin air ani asp nap nip pan
par pas pin ran rap ria rip sap sin sip
sir spa ai an as in is na pa pi si

ainprss sprains. *See* **ainprs aipss airss**

ainprsst spirants ptisans rapists spirant
sprains sprints strains. *See* **ainprs
ainpst ainrst ainsst**

ainprst spirant. *See* **ainrst ainpst inprst
aiprst ainprs**

ainprstu puritans nutrias puritan spirant
turnips. *See* **ainprs ainpst ainrst ainrtu**

ainprtu   puritan. *See* **ainrtu inprtu**

ainps   nipas pains naps nipa nips pain pans pins sain snap snip span spin ani asp nap nip pan pas pin sap sin sip spa ai an as in is na pa pi si

ainpsst   ptisans. *See* **ainpst ainsst**

ainpsstu   puissant issuant ptisans sustain. *See* **ainpst ainsst apsstu inpstu**

ainpssv   spavins. *See* **ainpsv ainssv**

ainpst   paints ptisan deils delis dirls dries idler idles rides riels riled riles sidle sired slide deil deli dies dire dirl ides idle isle leis lids lied lies lire reds reis ride rids riel rile rise side sire sled slid apt die eld ids ire its led lei lid lie nip nit pat pin pit red rid sat sin sip sit tap tin tip ai an as at in is it na pa pi si ta ti

ainpst   pantsuit. *See* **ainpst ainstt ansttu inpstu**

ainpsv   spavin nipas pains pavis savin vinas naps nipa nips pain pans pins sain snap snip span spin spiv vain vans vina visa ani asp nap nip pan pas pin sap sin sip spa van via ai an as in is na pa pi si

ainpt   inapt paint anti nipa pain pant pint pita ani ant apt ita nap nip nit pan pat pin pit tan tap tin tip ai an at in it na pa pi ta ti

ainpty   painty inapt paint panty anti ayin nipa pain pant pint piny pita pity tiny ani ant any apt ita nap nay nip nit pan pat pay pin pit pya tan tap tin tip yap yin yip ai an at ay in it na pa pi ta ti

ainqrst   qintars. *See* **ainrst ainqrt**

ainqrt   qintar riant train anti rain rani rant air ani ant art ita nit qat ran rat ria tan tar tin ai an at in it na ta ti

ainqruy   quinary. *See* **ainry**

ainqstu   asquint. *See* **ainqtu anqstu inqstu**

ainqttuy   quantity. *See* **ainqtu**

ainqtu   quaint quant quint anti aunt quit tuna unit ani ant ita nit nut qat qua tan tau tin tui tun ai an at in it na nu ta ti ut

ainr   rain rani air ani ran ria ai an in na

ainrruy   urinary. *See* **ainry**

ainrs   naris rains ranis airs rain rani rias sain sari air ani ran ria sin sir ai an as in is na si

ainrsst   strains. *See* **ainrst ainsst airsst**

ainrsstt   transits artists strains straits tanists transit tsarist. *See* **ainrst ainsst ainstt airsst**

ainrst   instar strain trains antis astir naris rains ranis rants riant saint satin sitar stain stair stria tarsi train airs anti ants arts nits rain rani rant rats rias sain sari snit star stir tans tars tins tsar air ani ant art ita its nit ran rat ria sat sin sir

sit tan tar tin ai an as at in is it na si ta ti

ainrstt   transit. *See* **airstt ainrst ainstt**

ainrstu   nutrias. *See* **ainrst ainrtu**

ainrt   riant train anti rain rani rant air ani ant art ita nit ran rat ria tan tar tin ai an at in it na ta ti

ainrtu   nutria riant train anti aunt rain rani rant ruin runt tuna turn unit air ani ant art ita nit nut ran rat ria run rut tan tar tau tin tui tun urn ai an at in it na nu ta ti ut

ainrtuy   unitary. *See* **ainrtu antuy ainry**

ainry   rainy airy ayin nary rain rani yarn air ani any nay ran ray ria yar yin ai an ay in na

ains   sain ani sin ai an as in is na si

ainssstu   sustains issuant sustain. *See* **ainsst aissst inssstu**

ainsst   saints satins stains antis saint satin snits stain anti ants nits sain sins sits snit tans tass tins ani ant ass ita its nit sat sin sis sit tan tin ai an as at in is it na si ta ti

ainsstt   tanists. *See* **ainsst insstt ainstt**

ainsstu   issuant sustain. *See* **ainsst insstu**

ainssv   savins savin vinas visas sain sins vain vans vina visa ani ass sin sis van via ai an as in is na si

ainssw   swains swain swans wains awns sain sawn saws sins swan wain wins ani ass awn saw sin sis wan was win wis ai an as aw in is na si

ainst   antis saint satin stain anti ants nits sain snit tans tins ani ant ita its nit sat sin sit tan tin ai an as at in is it na si ta ti

ainstt   taints tanist titans antis saint satin stain stint taint tints titan anti ants nits sain snit tans tats tins tint tits ani ant ita its nit sat sin sit tan tat tin tit ai an as at in is it na si ta ti

ainstw   twains witans antis saint satin stain swain twain twins wains waist waits wants witan anti ants awns nits sain sawn snit swan swat tans tins twin wain wait want wast wins wits ani ant awn ita its nit sat saw sin sit tan tin wan was win wis wit ai an as at aw in is it na si ta ti

ainsty   sanity satiny antis antsy ayins nasty saint satin stain tansy anti ants ayin nits sain snit stay tans tins tiny ani ant any ita its nay nit sat say sin sit sty tan tin yin ai an as at ay in is it na si ta ti

ainsux   auxins auxin anus axis sain ani nix sax sin six sun ai an as ax in is na nu si us xi

ainsv   savin vinas sain vain vans vina visa ani sin van via ai an as in is na si

ainsw   swain wains awns sain sawn swan wain wins ani awn saw sin wan was win wis ai an as aw in is na si

ainsy   ayins sain ayin ani any nay say sin yin ai an as ay in is na si

ainsyz   zayins ayins zayin ayin sain zany ani any nay say sin yin ai an as ay in is na si

aint   anti ani ant ita nit tan tin ai an at in it na ta ti

aintt   taint titan anti tint ani ant ita nit tan tat tin tit ai an at in it na ta ti

ainttvy   tantivy. *See* **aintvy antty intty**

aintvy   vanity anti ayin navy tiny vain vina viny ani ant any ita ivy nay nit tan tav tin van vat via yin ai an at ay in it na ta ti

aintw   twain witan anti twin wain wait want ani ant awn ita nit tan tin wan win wit ai an at aw in it na ta ti

ainux   auxin ani nix ai an ax in na nu xi

ainv   vain vina ani van via ai an in na

ainw   wain ani awn wan win ai an aw in na

ainy   ayin ani any nay yin ai an ay in na

ainyz   zayin ayin zany ani any nay yin ai an ay in na

aiooorrt   oratorio. *See* **aoorrt**

aioors   arioso airs oars rias sari soar sora sori air oar ria sir ai as is or os si so

aioprrst   airports airport parrots. *See* **aiopst aiorst aiprst aoprrt**

aioprrt   airport. *See* **aoprrt aiopt ioprr**

aioprrtt   portrait airport patriot traitor. *See* **aoprrt**

aioprsst   protasis rapists pastors. *See* **aiopst aiorst aiprst airsst**

aioprstt   patriots patriot. *See* **aiopst aiorst aiprst airstt**

aioprtt   patriot. *See* **aoprt aiort aiprt**

aioprty   topiary. *See* **aiprty aoprt aiopt**

aiopst   patios patois iotas patio pitas posit tapis atop iota oast oats past pats pita pits pois post pots soap spat spit spot stoa stop taps tips tops apt asp ita its oat pas pat pit poi pot sap sat sip sit sop sot spa tap tip top ai as at is it os pa pi si so ta ti to

aiopt   patio atop iota pita apt ita oat pat pit poi pot tap tip top ai at it pa pi ta ti to

aioptu   utopia patio atop auto iota pita pout topi apt ita oat out pat poi pot put tap tau top tup ai at it pi ta ti up ut

aiorrsw   warriors warrior. *See* **aorrsw**

aiorrrw   warrior. *See* **aorrw**

aiorrstt   traitors traitor. *See* **aiorst airstt aorrst aorstt**

aiorrtt   traitor. *See* **aiort aortt airtt**

aiorssuv   saviours saviors saviour savours various. *See* **aiorsv aorsuv**

aiorssv   saviors. *See* **aiorsv aorssv iorssv**

aiorst   ratios ceros codes coeds cords cored cores corse decor doers rosed score scrod cero code cods coed cord core cors docs doer does dose odes orcs ores redo reds rocs rode rods roes rose sore art cod cor doc doe dor ita its oar oat ode orc ort rat rec red roc rod rot sat sir sit sot tar tor ai as at is it or os si so ta ti to

aiorstv   travois. *See* **aiorst aiorsv**

aiorsty   ostiary. *See* **aiorst arsty orsty**

aiorsuv   saviour various. *See* **aiorsv aorsuv**

aiorsv   savior savor vairs visor airs oars rias sari soar sora sori vair visa air oar ova ria sir via ai as is or os si so

aiort   ratio iota riot rota taro tiro tora tori trio air art ita oar oat ort rat ria rot tar tor ai at it or ta ti to

aiorx   ixora air oar ria ai ax or ox xi

aioss   oasis ossa ass sis ai as is os si so

aiost   iotas iota oast oats stoa ita its oat sat sit sot ai as at is it os si so ta ti to

aiosyz   zoysia azo say soy zoa ai as ay is os oy si so

aiot   iota ita oat ai at it ta ti to

aippp   pappi pap pip ai pa pi

aippry   papyri airy pair pipy pray air pap par pay pip pry pya rap ray ria rip yap yar yip ai ay pa pi

aippsst   papists. *See* **aippst aipss apsst**

aippst   papist pitas tapis paps past pats pips pita pits spat spit taps tips apt asp ita its pap pas pat pip pit sap sat sip sit spa tap tip ai as at is it pa pi si ta ti

aipr   pair air par rap ria rip ai pa pi

aiprs   pairs airs pair pars raps rasp rias rips sari spar air asp par pas rap ria rip sap sip sir spa ai as is pa pi si

aiprsst   rapists. *See* **aiprst airsst aprsst iprsst**

aiprsstu   upstairs rapists purists. *See* **aiprst airsst aprsst apsstu**

aiprssty   sparsity rapists. *See* **aiprst aiprty airsst aprsst**

aiprssw   ripsaws. *See* **aiprsw aipss airss**

aiprst   rapist tapirs astir pairs parts pitas sitar sprat sprit stair strap stria strip tapir tapis tarps tarsi traps trips airs arts pair pars part past pats pita pits raps rapt rasp rats rias rips sari spar

spat spit star stir taps tarp tars tips trap trip tsar air apt art asp ita its par pas pat pit rap rat ria rip sap sat sip sir sit spa tap tar tip ai as at is it pa pi si ta ti

aiprsv   parvis pairs pavis vairs airs pair pars raps rasp rias rips sari spar spiv vair visa air asp par pas rap ria rip sap sip sir spa via ai as is pa pi si

aiprsw   ripsaw pairs warps wraps airs pair pars paws raps rasp rias rips sari spar swap waps warp wars wasp wisp wrap air asp par pas paw rap raw ria rip sap saw sip sir spa wap war was wis ai as aw is pa pi si

aiprsx   praxis pairs airs axis pair pars raps rasp rias rips sari spar air asp par pas pax pix rap ria rip sap sax sip sir six spa ai as ax is pa pi si xi

aiprt   tapir pair part pita rapt tarp trap trip air apt art ita par pat pit rap rat ria rip tap tar tip ai at it pa pi ta ti

aiprty   parity tapir party airy arty pair part pita pity pray rapt tarp trap tray trip air apt art ita par pat pay pit pry pya rap rat ray ria rip tap tar tip try yap yar yip ai at ay it pa pi ta ti

aipss   apsis asps pass saps sips spas asp ass pas sap sip sis spa ai as is pa pi si

aipst   pitas tapis past pats pita pits spat spit taps tips apt asp ita its pas pat pit sap sat sip sit spa tap tip ai as at is it pa pi si ta ti

aipsv   pavis visa spiv asp pas sap sip spa via ai as is pa pi si

aipszz   pizzas spaz zaps zips asp pas sap sip spa zap zip ai as is pa pi si

aipt   pita apt ita pat pit tap tip ai at it pa pi ta ti

aipzz   pizza zap zip ai pa pi

aipzzz   pizazz pizza zap zip ai pa pi

aiqsu   quasi qua ai as is si us

air   air ria ai

airrs   arris airs rias sari air ria sir ai as is si

airrstty   artistry. *See* **airrty airstt airtty arrsty**

airrty   rarity tarry airy arty tray air art ita rat ray ria tar try yar ai at ay it ta ti

airs   airs rias sari air ria sir ai as is si

airss   arsis saris airs rias sari sirs air ass ria sir sis ai as is si

airssstt   tsarists artists straits tsarist. *See* **airsst airstt aissst**

airsst   sistra sitars stairs arsis astir saris sitar stair stars stirs stria tarsi trass

tsars airs arts rats rias sari sirs sits star stir tars tass tsar air art ass ita its rat ria sat sir sis sit tar ai as at is it si ta ti

airsstt   artists straits tsarist. *See* **airstt airsst arsstt**

airssz   sizars arsis saris sizar airs rias sari sirs air ass ria sir sis ai as is si

airst   astir sitar stair stria tarsi airs arts rats rias sari star stir tars tsar air art ita its rat ria sat sir sit tar ai as at is it si ta ti

airstt   artist strait traits astir sitar stair start stria tarsi tarts trait airs arts rats rias sari star stir tars tart tats tits tsar air art ita its rat ria sat sir sit tar tat tit ai as at is it si ta ti

airstvy   varsity. *See* **arsty airst airsv**

airsv   vairs airs rias sari vair visa air ria sir via ai as is si

airsz   sizar airs rias sari air ria sir ai as is si

airtt   trait tart air art ita rat ria tar tat tit ai at it ta ti

airtty   yttria trait ratty airy arty tart tray air art ita rat ray ria tar tat tit try yar ai at ay it ta ti

airv   vair air ria via ai

airvx   varix vair air ria via ai ax xi

airy   airy air ray ria yar ai ay

aissst   assists. *See* **aissst**

aissst   assist stasis sass sits tass ass ita its sat sis sit ai as at is it si ta ti

aisstv   vistas visas vista sits tass tavs vast vats visa ass ita its sat sis sit tav vat via ai as at is it si ta ti

aisstw   waists swats waist waits saws sits swat tass wait wast wits ass ita its sat saw sis sit was wis wit ai as at aw is it si ta ti

aissv   visas visa ass sis via ai as is si

aistv   vista tavs vast vats visa ita its sat sit tav vat via ai as at is it si ta ti

aistw   waist waits swat wait wast wits ita its sat saw sit was wis wit ai as at aw is it si ta ti

aistx   taxis axis taxi ita its sat sax sit six tax ai as at ax is it si ta ti xi

aisv   visa via ai as is si

aisx   axis sax six ai as ax is si xi

ait   ita ai at it ta ti

aittv   vitta ita tat tav tit vat via ai at it ta ti

aitw   wait ita wit ai at aw it ta ti

aitx   taxi ita tax ai at ax it ta ti xi

aiv   via ai

aj

ajkmnnu   junkman. *See* **amnnu**
ajkmntu   muntjak. *See* **ajntu**
ajllruy   jurally. *See* **ajlru allry**
ajlnorsu   journals journal. *See* **alnors**
ajlnoru   journal. *See* **ajlru alnru**
ajlopy   jalopy opal paly play ploy alp jay joy lap lay lop pal pay ply pya yap ay jo la lo oy pa
ajlr   jarl jar lar raj la
ajlrs   jarls jarl jars jar lar raj sal as la
ajlru   jural jarl jura jar lar raj la
ajm   jam am ma
ajmor   major mora roam arm jam jar mar moa mor oar raj ram am jo ma mo om or
ajmors   majors major roams arms jams jars moas mora mors oars rams roam

soar soma sora arm jam jar mar moa mor mos oar oms raj ram am as jo ma mo om or os so
ajms   jams jam am as ma
ajnstu   jaunts aunts jaunt junta tunas ants anus aunt just juts nuts stun tans tuna tuns ant jus jut nut sat sun tan tau tun an as at na nu ta us ut
ajntu   jaunt junta aunt tuna ant jut nut tan tau tun an at na nu ta ut
ajntuy   jaunty aunty jaunt junta aunt tuna yuan ant any jay jut nay nut tan tau tun an at ay na nu ta ut
ajost   jatos jotas jato jota jots oast oats stoa jot oat sat sot as at jo os so ta to

ajot   jato jota oat jot at jo ta to
ajr   jar raj
ajrstu   jurats jurat sutra arts jars jura just juts rats rust ruts star sura tars tsar art jar jus jut raj rat rut sat tar tau as at ta us ut
ajrtu   jurat jura art jar jut raj rat rut tar tau at ta ut
ajru   jura jar raj
ajsw   jaws jaw saw was as aw
ajsy   jays jay say as ay
ajw   jaw aw
ajy   jay ay
ajyzz   jazzy jazz jay ay
ajzz   jazz

ak

ak   ka
akklrssy   skylarks skylark. *See* **alrsy akksy**
akklrsy   skylark. *See* **alrsy akksy**
akklsu   kulaks kulak skulk auks sulk ask auk kal kas sal as ka la us
akklu   kulak kal auk ka la
akkop   kapok koa oak ka pa
akkops   kapoks kapok koas oaks soak soap ask asp kas koa kos oak pas sap sop spa as ka os pa so
akksy   kyaks kyak yaks ask kas say sky yak as ay ka
akky   kyak yak ka ay
akl   kal ka la
akllny   lankly lanky ally laky lank yank all any kal lay nay yak an ay ka la na
aklmnoow   moonwalk. *See* **almoo amnow**
akln   lank kal an ka la na
aklnnopt   plankton. *See* **alnop aklnp alnpt**
aklnp   plank knap lank plan alp kal lap nap pal pan an ka la na pa
aklnps   planks knaps plank plans spank alps knap lank laps naps pals pans plan sank slap snap span alp ask asp kal kas lap nap pal pan pas sal sap spa an as ka la na pa
aklnry   rankly lanky larky aryl knar laky lank lark nark nary rank yank yarn any ark kal lar lay nay ran ray yak yar an ay ka la na

aklny   lanky laky lank yank any kal lay nay yak an ay ka la na
aklo   kola kal koa oak ka la lo
aklop   polka kola opal alp kal koa lap lop oak pal ka la lo pa
aklops   polkas kolas opals polka skoal alps also koas kola laps lops oaks opal pals slap slop soak soap alp ask asp kal kas koa kos lap lop los oak pal pas sal sap sol sop spa as ka la lo os pa so
aklos   kolas skoal also koas kola oaks soak ask kal kas koa kos los oak sal sol as ka la lo os so
akloss   skoals kolas lasso skoal soaks also asks koas kola lass loss oaks ossa sals soak sols ask ass kal kas koa kos los oak sal sol as ka la lo os so
aklostuw   walkouts walkout outlaws. *See* **alotuw**
aklotuw   walkout. *See* **alotuw**
aklprrsu   larkspur larrups. *See* **alprru alprsu**
aklr   lark ark kal lar ka la
aklrs   larks arks lark sark ark ask kal kas lar sal as ka la
aklrsty   starkly. *See* **aklsty alrsty**
aklry   larky aryl laky lark ark kal lar lay ray yak yar ay ka la
aklsst   stalks lasts salts skats slats stalk talks tasks alts asks lass last sals salt skat slat talk task tass alt ask ass kal kas kat sal sat tsk as at ka la ta

aklst   stalk talks alts last salt skat slat talk task alt ask kal kas kat sal sat tsk as at ka la ta
aklsty   stalky kyats salty slaty stalk talks talky alts kyat laky last lays salt skat slat slay stay talk task yaks alt ask kal kas kat lay sal sat say sky sly sty tsk yak as at ay ka la ta
aklsw   walks awls laws walk ask awl kal kas law sal saw was as aw ka la
aklt   talk alt kal kat at ka la ta
aklty   talky kyat laky talk alt kal kat lay yak at ay ka la ta
aklw   walk awl kal law aw ka la
akly   laky kal lay yak ay ka la
akmnorw   workman. *See* **aknor amnor anorw**
akmnssu   unmasks. *See* **akmnsu akmss**
akmnsu   unmask manus anus auks mask maun musk sank sunk ask auk kas man mus sum sun am an as ka ma mu na nu um us
akmo   amok mako koa moa oak am ka ma mo om
akmoprst   postmark. *See* **akorst amprst aoprst**
akmos   makos amok koas mako mask moas oaks soak soma ask kas koa kos moa mos oak oms am as ka ma mo om os so
akmosu   oakums makos oakum amok auks koas mako mask moas musk oaks

soak soma sumo ask auk kas koa kos moa mos mus oak oms sou sum am as ka ma mo mu om os so um us

akmou   oakum amok mako auk koa moa oak am ka ma mo mu om um

akmprsu   markups. *See* **akmpru akmrs kmrsu**

akmpru   markup mark murk park pram puma ramp rump amp ark arm auk map mar par ram rap rum ump am ka ma mu pa um up

akmqstuu   kumquats kumquat. *See* **aqstu**

akmqtuu   kumquat. *No 6s or 5s*

akmr   mark ark arm mar ram am ka ma

akmrs   marks arks arms mark mask rams sark ark arm ask kas mar ram am as ka ma

akmrsstu   muskrats muskrat. *See* **akrsst akrstu amrsst amrstu**

akmrstu   muskrat. *See* **akrstu amrstu**

akms   mask ask kas am as ka ma

akmss   masks asks mask mass ask ass kas am as ka ma

akno   kaon koan koa oak an ka na no on

aknor   krona kaon knar koan nark okra rank roan ark koa kor nor oak oar ran an ka na no on or

aknorstu   outranks korunas outrank. *See* **aknoru akorst akrstu anortu**

aknorsu   korunas. *See* **aknoru anors aknos**

aknorsy   ryokans. *See* **aknory anorsy**

aknortu   outrank. *See* **aknoru anortu**

aknoru   koruna krona korun kaon knar knur koan nark okra rank roan ark auk koa kor nor oak oar our ran run urn an ka na no nu on or

aknory   ryokan krona rayon kaon kayo knar koan nark nary okay okra rank roan yank yarn any ark koa kor nay nor oak oar ran ray yak yar yon an ay ka na no on or oy

aknos   kaons koans kaon koan koas naos oaks sank soak ask kas koa kos oak son an as ka na no on os so

aknp   knap nap pan an ka na pa

aknpr   prank knap knar nark park rank ark nap pan par ran rap an ka na pa

aknprs   pranks knaps knars narks parks prank ranks snark spank spark arks knap knar naps nark pans park pars rank raps rasp sank sark snap span spar ark ask asp kas nap pan par pas ran rap sap spa an as ka na pa

aknps   knaps spank knap naps pans sank snap span ask asp kas nap pan pas sap spa an as ka na pa

aknpss   spanks knaps snaps spank spans asks asps knap naps pans pass sank

saps snap span spas ask asp ass kas nap pan pas sap spa an as ka na pa

aknpsu   punkas knaps punka punks spank spunk anus auks knap naps pans punk puns sank snap span spun sunk upas ask asp auk kas nap pan pas pun pus sap spa sun sup an as ka na nu pa up us

aknpu   punka knap punk auk nap pan pun an ka na nu pa up

aknr   knar nark rank ark ran an ka na

aknrs   knars narks ranks snark arks knar nark rank sank sark ark ask kas ran an as ka na

aknrss   snarks knars narks ranks sarks snark arks asks knar nark rank sank sark ark ask ass kas ran an as ka na

akns   sank ask kas an as ka na

aknst   stank tanks ants sank skat tank tans task ant ask kas kat sat tan tsk an as at ka na ta

aknsw   swank awns sank sawn swan ask awn kas saw wan was an as aw ka na

aknswy   swanky snaky swank yanks yawns awns sank sawn swan sway wany ways yaks yank yawn yaws any ask awn kas nay saw say sky wan was way yak yaw an as aw ay ka na

aknsy   snaky yanks sank yaks yank any ask kas nay say sky yak an as ay ka na

aknt   tank ant kat tan an at ka na ta

akny   yank any nay yak an ay ka na

ako   koa oak ka

akooprt   partook. *See* **aoprt akoor akort**

akoor   karoo okra rook ark koa kor oak oar ka or

akoors   karoos karoo okras rooks arks koas oaks oars okra rook sark soak soar sora ark ask kas koa kor kos oak oar as ka or os so

akoosz   kazoos kazoo koas oaks soak zoos ask azo kas koa kos oak zoa zoo as ka os so

akooz   kazoo azo koa oak zoa zoo ka

akopsy   yapoks kayos okays soapy yapok kayo koas oaks okay pays poky posy pyas soak soap spay yaks yaps ask asp kas koa kos oak pas pay pya sap say sky sop soy spa spy yak yap as ay ka os oy pa so

akopy   yapok kayo okay poky koa oak pay pya yak yap ay ka oy pa

akor   okra ark koa kor oak oar ka or

akorrstw   artworks artwork. *See* **akorst aorrst aorrsw**

akorrtw   artwork. *See* **akort aorrw**

akors   okras arks koas oaks oars okra sark soak soar sora ark ask kas koa kor kos oak oar as ka or os so

akorss   kaross okras sarks saros soaks soars soras arks asks koas oaks oars okra ossa sark soak soar sora ark ask ass kas koa kor kos oak oar as ka or os so

akorst   korats doers drone nerds nodes nosed rends rosed snore sonde dens doer does done dons dose ends eons nerd node nods noes nose odes ones ores redo reds rend rode rods roes rose send sore den doe don dor dos end eon kor kos nod ode one ort red rod rot sat sod sot tor tsk as at ka or os so ta to

akorswwx   waxworks waxwork. *See* **akors korsw**

akort   korat kart okra rota taro tora ark art kat koa kor oak oar oat ort rat rot tar tor at ka or ta to

akorwwx   waxwork. *No 6s or 5s*

akos   koas oaks soak ask kas koa kos oak as ka os so

akoss   soaks asks koas oaks ossa soak ask ass kas koa kos oak as ka os so

akosy   kayos okays kayo koas oaks okay soak yaks ask kas koa kos oak say sky soy yak as ay ka os oy so

akoy   kayo okay koa oak yak ay ka oy

akpr   park ark par rap ka pa

akprs   parks spark arks park pars raps rasp sark spar ark ask asp kas par pas rap sap spa as ka pa

akprss   sparks parks rasps sarks spark spars arks asks asps park pars pass raps rasp saps sark spar spas ark ask asp ass kas par pas rap sap spa as ka pa

akptu   kaput apt auk kat pat put tap tau tup at ka pa ta up ut

akpwy   pawky yawp paw pay pya wap way yak yap yaw aw ay ka pa

akqrsu   quarks quark arks auks rusk sark sura ark ask auk kas qua as ka us

akqru   quark ark auk qua ka

akqssuu   squawks. *See* **akqsuw aqssuw**

akqsuw   squawk squaw auks ask auk kas qua saw was as aw ka us

akquy   quaky quay auk qua yak yuk ka ay

akr   ark ka

akrs   arks sark ark ask kas as ka

akrss   sarks arks asks sark ark ask ass kas as ka

akrsst   karsts karst karts sarks skats stark stars tasks trass tsars arks arts asks kart rats sark skat star tars task tass tsar ark art ask ass kas kat rat sat tar tsk as at ka ta

akrst   karst karts stark arks arts kart rats sark skat star tars task tsar ark art ask kas kat rat sat tar tsk as at ka ta

akrstu krauts kurtas karst karts kraut kurta stark sutra arks arts auks kart rats rusk rust ruts sark skat star sura tars task tsar tusk ark art ask auk kas kat rat rut sat tar tau tsk as at ka ta us ut

akrt kart ark art kat rat tar at ka ta

akrtu kraut kurta kart ark art auk kat rat rut tar tau at ka ta ut

aks ask kas ka as

akss asks ask ass kas as ka

aksst skats tasks asks skat task tass ask ass kas kat sat tsk as at ka ta

akssv kvass asks kvas ask ass kas as ka

aksswyy skyways. *See* **akswyy asswy**

akst skat task ask kas kat sat tsk as at ka ta

aksty kyats kyat skat stay task yaks ask kas kat sat say sky sty tsk yak as at ay ka ta

aksu auks ask auk kas as ka us

aksv kvas ask kas as ka

akswyy skyway sway ways yaks yaws ask kas saw say sky was way yak yaw yay as aw ay ka

aksy yaks ask kas say sky yak as ay ka

akt kat at ka ta

akty kyat kat yak at ay ka ta

aku auk ka

aky yak ka ay

---

al la

all all la

allloyy loyally. *See* **alloy llloy**

alllpruy plurally. *See* **allpru**

alllsy allyls sally ally lays slay all lay sal say sly as ay la

allm mall all lam am la ma

allmnory normally morally. *See* **allory almnor**

allmo molal loam mall mola moll olla all lam moa am la lo ma mo om

allmopsx smallpox. *See* **allmos**

allmorty mortally morally. *See* **allory almort**

allmory morally. *See* **allory almoy almry**

allmos slalom loams malls molal molas molls ollas small alms also lams loam mall moas mola moll olla slam soma all lam los moa mos oms sal sol am as la lo ma mo om os so

allmoss slaloms. *See* **allmos aloss almss**

allmosw mallows. *See* **allosw allmow allmos**

allmow mallow molal allow alow loam mall mola moll olla wall all awl lam law low maw moa mow owl am aw la lo ma mo om ow

allms malls small alms lams mall slam all lam sal am as la ma

allmtuuy mutually. *See* **almtuu**

allno llano olla loan all an la lo na no on

allnos llanos llano loans ollas salon solan also loan naos olla all los sal sol son an as la lo na no on os so

allnoty tonally. *See* **allot alloy anoty**

allnoyz zonally. *See* **alloy allno alnoz**

allnruu lunular. *See* **alnru**

allntuu ululant. *No 6s or 5s*

allo olla all la lo

alloostx axolotls axolotl. *See* **allost**

allootx axolotl. *See* **allot**

allopr pallor parol polar olla opal oral pall poll proa roll all alp lap lar lop oar pal par pro rap la lo or pa

alloprs pallors. *See* **allopr aloprs**

alloprsy payrolls pallors payroll. *See* **allopr allory allosy aloprs**

allopry payroll. *See* **allopr allory**

allopsw wallops. *See* **allosw allopw**

allopw wallop allow alow olla opal pall pawl plow poll wall all alp awl lap law lop low owl pal paw wap aw la lo ow pa

allorswy rollways rollway. *See* **allory allosw allosy alorsy**

allorwy rollway. *See* **allory allow llowy**

allory orally alloy loyal rally royal ally aryl lory olla oral roll all lar lay oar ray yar ay la lo or oy

alloryy royally. *See* **allory**

allos ollas olla also all los sal sol as la lo os so

allossw sallows. *See* **allosw**

allossww swallows sallows swallow wallows. *See* **allosw alloww**

allost allots atolls allot altos atoll lotas ollas stall tolas tolls also alto alts last lost lota lots oast oats olla salt slat slot stoa tall tola toll all alt los lot oat sal sat sol sot as at la lo os so ta to

allostw tallows. *See* **allost allosw allotw**

allosw allows sallow allow ollas walls alow also awls laws lows olla owls slow wall all awl law los low owl sal saw sol sow was as aw la lo os ow so

allossww swallow wallows. *See* **allosw alloww**

allosy alloys alloy loyal ollas sally ally also lays olla slay all lay los sal say sly sol soy as ay la lo os oy so

allot allot atoll alto lota olla tall tola toll all alt lot oat at la lo ta to

allotty totally. *See* **allot alloy altty**

allotw tallow allot allow atoll alow alto lota olla tall tola toll wall all alt awl law lot low oat owl tow two at aw la lo ow ta to

allotwy tallowy. *See* **allotw alloy llowy**

allotyy loyalty. *See* **allot allty**

allow allow alow olla wall all awl law low owl aw la lo ow

alloww wallow allow alow olla wall all awl law low owl wow aw la lo ow

alloy alloy loyal olla ally all lay ay la lo oy

allp pall all alp lap pal la pa

allprsu plurals. *See* **allpru alprsu**

allpru plural pall pull purl all alp lap lar pal par pul rap la pa up

allps palls spall alps laps pall pals slap all alp asp lap pal pas sal sap spa as la pa

allpss spalls palls slaps spall alps asps laps lass pall pals pass sals saps slap spas all alp asp ass lap pal pas sal sap spa as la pa

allpy pally ally pall paly play all alp lap lay pal pay ply pya yap ay la pa

allqssu squalls. *See* **allqsu aqssu**

allqsu squall all qua sal as la us

allqsuy squally. *See* **allqsu aqsuy allsy**

allrstu lustral. *See* **alrstu llrstu**

allry rally ally aryl all lar lay ray yar la ay

allsst stalls lasts salts slats stall alts lass last sals salt slat tall tass all alt ass sal sat as at la ta

allst stall alts last salt slat tall all alt sal sat as at la ta

allsty lastly sally salty slaty stall tally ally alts last lays salt slat slay stay tall all alt lay sal sat say sly sty as at ay la ta

allsuuy usually. *See* **alsuu llsuu llsuy**

allsw walls awls laws wall all awl law sal saw was as aw la

---

allsy   sally ally lays slay all lay sal say sly as ay la

allt   tall all alt at la ta

allty   tally tall ally all alt lay at ay la ta

allw   wall all awl law la aw

allxy   laxly ally all lax lay ax ay la

ally   ally all lay la ay

alm   lam am la ma

almm   malm lam am la ma

almms   malms alms lams malm slam lam sal am as la ma

almmsuy   amylums. *See* **almmuy almsuy**

almmuy   amylum alum amyl malm maul lam lay lum may mum yam yum am ay la ma mu my um

almnnuy   unmanly. *See* **alnnu almny amnnu**

almnoop   lampoon. *See* **almoo alnop**

almnoops   lampoons lampoon. *See* **almnos almoos alnoos alnops**

almnopw   plowman. *See* **alnop amnow**

almnor   normal manor molar moral loam loan lorn marl moan mola mora morn noma norm oral roam roan arm lam lar man mar moa mon mor nor oar ram ran am an la lo ma mo na no om on or

almnorty   matronly. *See* **almnor almort amnort anorty**

almnos   salmon loams loans mason moans molas nomas salon solan alms also lams loam loan moan moas mola mons naos noma slam soma lam los man moa mon mos oms sal sol son am an as la lo ma mo na no om on os so

almnoss   salmons. *See* **amnoss almnos alnoss**

almnowy   womanly. *See* **alnwy almoy almny**

almnpssu   sunlamps sunlamp. *See* **almpss almpsu lmpssu**

almnpsu   sunlamp. *See* **almpsu amnsu alnps**

almnsuu   alumnus. *See* **almsu alsuu amnsu**

almny   manly amyl many myna any lam lay man may nay yam am an ay la ma my na

almo   loam mola lam moa am la lo ma mo om

almoo   moola loam loom mola lam loo moa moo am la lo ma mo om

almoopry   playroom. *See* **loopry**

almoos   moolas loams looms molas moola alms also lams loam loom loos moas mola moos slam solo soma lam loo los moa moo mos oms sal sol am as la lo ma mo om os so

almoppst   lamppost. *See* **almost alopst**

almoprst   marplots marplot mortals patrols portals. *See* **almors almort almost aloprs**

almoprt   marplot. *See* **almort aloprt**

almor   molar moral loam marl mola mora oral roam arm lam lar mar moa mor oar ram am la lo ma mo om or

almors   molars morals loams marls molar molas moral orals roams solar alms also arms lams loam marl moas mola mora mors oars oral rams roam slam soar soma sora arm lam lar los mar moa mor mos oar oms ram sal sol am as la lo ma mo om or os so

almorst   mortals. *See* **almost almors almort**

almort   mortal molar moral alto atom loam lota malt marl mart moat mola molt mora mort oral roam rota rotl taro tola tora tram alt arm art lam lar lot mar mat moa mor mot oar oat ort ram rat rot tam tar tom tor am at la lo ma mo om or ta to

almos   loams molas alms also lams loam moas mola slam soma lam los moa mos oms sal sol am as la lo ma mo om os so

almosst   smaltos. *See* **almost almsst lmosst amosst**

almost   almost smalto doers herds hoers horde horse hosed rosed sherd shoed shoer shore shred doer does dose herd hero hers hods hoed hoer hoes hose odes ores redo reds resh rhos rode rods roes rose shed shod shoe sore alt doe dor dos edh hod los lot mat moa mos mot oat ode oms red rod sat sod sol sot tam tom am as at la lo ma mo om os so ta to

almosttu   mulattos mulatto outlast. *See* **almost alostt lmostu mosttu**

almottu   mulatto. *See* **alott lmotu**

almoy   loamy amyl loam mayo mola moly lam lay may moa yam am ay la lo ma mo my om oy

almp   lamp palm alp amp lam lap map pal am la ma pa

almps   lamps palms psalm alms alps amps lamp lams laps maps palm pals samp slam slap alp amp asp lam lap map pal pas sal sap spa am as la ma pa

almpss   psalms lamps palms psalm samps slams slaps spasm alms alps amps asps lamp lams laps lass maps mass palm pals pass sals samp saps slam slap spas alp amp asp ass lam lap map pal pas sal sap spa am as la ma pa

almpsu   ampuls alums ampul lamps lumps mauls palms plums psalm pumas slump alms alps alum amps

lamp lams laps lump maps maul palm pals plum plus puls puma samp slam slap slum sump umps upas alp amp asp lam lap lum map mus pal pas pul pus sal sap spa sum sup ump am as la ma mu pa um up us

almpu   ampul alum lamp lump maul palm plum puma alp amp lam lap lum map pal pul ump am la ma mu pa um up

almpy   amply palmy amyl lamp palm paly play alp amp lam lap lay map may pal pay ply pya yam yap am ay la ma my pa

almqsu   qualms alums mauls qualm alms alum lams maul slam slum lam lum mus qua sal sum am as la ma mu um us

almqu   qualm alum maul lam lum qua am la ma mu um

almr   marl arm lam lar mar ram am la ma

almrs   marls alms arms lams marl rams slam arm lam lar mar ram sal am as la ma

almrsty   smartly. *See* **amrsty alrsty**

almrsu   murals alums marls mauls mural ramus alms alum arms lams marl maul rams rums slam slum slur sura arm lam lar lum mar mus ram rum sal sum am as la ma mu um us

almru   mural alum marl maul arm lam lar lum mar ram rum am la ma mu um

almrwy   warmly marly amyl army aryl awry marl warm wary yawl arm awl lam lar law lay mar maw may ram raw ray war way yam yar yaw am aw ay la ma my

almry   marly amyl army aryl marl arm lam lar lay mar may ram ray yam yar am ay la ma my

alms   alms lams slam lam sal am as la ma

almss   slams alms lams lass mass sals slam ass lam sal am as la ma

almsssuy   alyssums alyssum asylums. *See* **almsuy**

almsst   smalts lasts malts masts salts slams slats smalt alms alts lams lass last malt mass mast mats sals salt slam slat tams tass alt ass lam mat sal sat tam am as at la ma ta

almssuy   alyssum asylums. *See* **almsuy amssy mssuy**

almst   malts smalt alms alts lams last malt mast mats salt slam slat tams alt lam mat sal sat tam am as at la ma ta

almstuu   umlauts. *See* **almtuu**

almsu   alums mauls alms alum lams maul slam slum lam lum mus sal sum am as la ma mu um us

almsuy   asylum alums amyls mauls alms alum amyl lams lays maul slam slay slum yams lam lay lum may mus sal say sly sum yam yum am as ay la ma mu my um us

almsy amyls alms amyl lams lays slam slay yams lam lay may sal say sly yam am as ay la ma my

almt malt alt lam mat tam am at la ma ta

almtuu mutual umlaut alum luau malt maul alt lam lum mat tam tau ulu am at la ma mu ta um ut

almty malty malt amyl alt lam lay mat may tam yam am at ay la ma my ta

almu alum maul lam lum am la ma mu um

almy amyl lam lay may yam am ay la ma my

alnnotwy wantonly. *See* **annotw**

alnnou nounal annul anon loan noun ulna nun an la lo na no nu on

alnnsu annuls annul ulnas anus nuns sunn ulna nun sal sun an as la na nu us

alnnsuu annulus. *See* **alnnsu alsuu**

alnnu annul ulna nun an la na nu

alno loan an la lo na no on

alnoopst platoons platoon. *See* **alnoos alnops alnost alnpst**

alnoopt platoon. *See* **alnop alnpt alnot**

alnoorst ortolans ortolan ratoons. *See* **alnoos alnors alnost anoort**

alnoort ortolan. *See* **anoort alnot**

alnoos saloon loans loons salon solan also loan loon loos naos solo soon loo los sal sol son an as la lo na no on os so

alnooss saloons. *See* **alnoss alnoos**

alnop nopal loan opal plan alp lap lop nap pal pan an la lo na no on pa

alnoppy panoply. *See* **alppy loppy anppy**

alnopr prolan apron nopal parol polar loan lorn opal oral plan proa roan alp lap lar lop nap nor oar pal pan par pro ran rap an la lo na no on or pa

alnoprs prolans. *See* **anoprs alnors alnops aloprs alnopr**

alnoprst plastron patrols patrons portals prolans tarpons. *See* **alnopr alnops alnors alnost**

alnops nopals loans nopal opals plans salon solan alps also laps loan lops naos naps opal pals pans plan pons slap slop snap soap span alp asp lap lop los nap pal pan pas sal sap sol son sop spa an as la lo na no on os pa so

alnorrwy narrowly. *See* **anorrw aorrwy**

alnors lorans arson loans orals roans salon snarl solan solar sonar also loan lorn naos oars oral roan soar sora lar los nor oar ran sal sol son an as la lo na no on or os so

alnoruz zonular. *See* **alnru alnoz**

alnos loans salon solan also loan naos los sal sol son an as la lo na no on os so

alnoss salons solans lasso loans salon solan also lass loan loss naos ossa sals sols sons ass los sal sol son an as la lo na no on os so

alnost talons altos loans lotas salon slant solan talon tolas tonal also alto alts ants last loan lost lota lots naos nota oast oats salt slat slot snot stoa tans tola tons alt ant los lot not oat sal sat sol son sot tan ton an as at la lo na no on os so ta to

alnosz azlons loans salon solan zonal also loan naos azo los sal sol son zoa an as la lo na no on os so

alnot talon tonal alto loan lota nota tola alt ant lot not oat tan ton an at la lo na no on ta to

alnoz zonal loan azo zoa an la lo na no on

alnp plan alp lap nap pal pan an la na pa

alnppstu supplant. *See* **alnpst alnstu alppsu**

alnps plans alps laps naps pals pans plan slap snap span alp asp lap nap pal pan pas sal sap spa an as la na pa

alnpst plants pants plans plant plats slant splat alps alts ants laps last naps pals pans pant past pats plan plat salt slap slat snap span spat tans taps alp alt ant apt asp lap nap pal pan pas pat sal sap sat spa tan tap an as at la na pa ta

alnpt plant pant plan plat alp alt ant apt lap nap pal pan pat tan tap an at la na pa ta

alnptuy unaptly. *See* **alpty antuy alpuy**

alnrs snarl lar ran sal an as la na

alnrss snarls snarl lass sals ass lar ran sal an as la na

alnru lunar ulna lar ran run urn an la na nu

alnrxy larynx xylan aryl lynx nary yarn any lar lax lay nay ran ray yar an ax ay la na

alnsst slants lasts salts slant slats alts ants lass last sals salt slat tans tass alt ant ass sal sat tan an as at la na ta

alnsstu sultans. *See* **alnsst alnstu**

alnst slant alts ants last salt slat tans alt ant sal sat tan an as at la na ta

alnstu sultan aunts lunts slant talus tunas ulnas alts ants anus aunt last lunt lust nuts salt slat slut stun tans tuna tuns ulna alt ant nut sal sat sun tan tau tun an as at la na nu ta us ut

alnstuw walnuts. *See* **alnstu alntuw**

alnsu ulnas ulna anus sal sun an as la na nu us

alnsuuu unusual. *See* **alsuu alnsu**

alnsvy sylvan sylva lays navy slay vans any lay nay sal say sly van an as ay la na

alnsw lawns awls awns lawn laws sawn swan awl awn law sal saw wan was an as aw la na

alnsxy xylans xylan lays lynx slay any lax lay nay sal sax say sly an as ax ay la na

alntuw walnut aunt lawn lunt tuna ulna want alt ant awl awn law nut tan tau tun wan an at aw la na nu ta ut

alnu ulna an la na nu

alnw lawn awl awn law wan an aw la na

alnwy lawny wanly lawn wany yawl yawn any awl awn law lay nay wan way yaw an aw ay la na

alnxy xylan lynx any lax lay nay an ax ay la na

aloopprs proposal poplars apropos. *See* **aloops aloppr aloprs looprs**

aloops saloop loops opals polos pools sloop spool alps also laps loop loos lops oops opal pals polo pool slap slop soap solo alp asp lap loo lop los pal pas sal sap sol sop spa as la lo os pa so

aloopss saloops. *See* **aloops loopss**

aloorsuv valorous. *See* **alorsv aorsuv**

aloortyz zoolatry. *See* **oorty alory lotyz**

alop opal alp lap lop pal la lo pa

aloppr poplar parol polar opal oral palp plop proa prop alp lap lar lop oar pal pap par pop pro rap la lo or pa

alopprs poplars. *See* **aloppr aloprs**

aloppru popular. *See* **aloppr alppu**

alopr parol polar opal oral proa alp lap lar lop oar pal par pro rap la lo or pa

aloprr parlor parol polar opal oral parr proa roar alp lap lar lop oar pal par pro rap la lo or pa

aloprrs parlors. *See* **aloprr aloprs**

aloprrsu parlours larrups parlors parlour parlous uproars. *See* **aloprr aloprs alprru alprsu**

aloprru parlour. *See* **alprru aloprr aoprru**

aloprs parols opals orals parol polar proas solar alps also laps lops oars opal oral pals pars proa pros raps rasp slap slop soap soar sora spar alp asp lap lar lop los oar pal par pas pro rap sal sap sol sop spa as la lo or os pa so

aloprst patrols portals. *See* **aloprs aoprst aloprt alopst**

aloprstu pulsator parlous patrols portals. *See* **aloprs aoprst aloprt alopst alprsu**

aloprsu parlous. *See* **aloprs alprsu**

aloprt patrol portal aport parol polar alto atop lota opal oral part plat plot port proa rapt rota rotl taro tarp tola tora trap alp alt apt art lap lar lop lot oar oat ort pal par pat pot pro rap rat rot tap tar top tor at la lo or pa ta to

alops opals alps also laps lops opal pals slap slop soap alp asp lap lop los pal pas sal sap sol sop spa as la lo os pa so

alopsst postals. *See* **alopst alpsst**

alopssu spousal. *See* **aloss alops alpss**

alopst postal doers douse druse duros rosed rouse uredo doer does dose dour dues duos duro odes ores ouds ours redo reds rode rods roes rose rude rued rues ruse sore sour sued surd sure udos urds used user apt asp doe dor dos due duo lop los lot ode oud pas pat pot red rod sap sat sod sol sop sot spa tap top udo as at la lo os pa so ta to

alopstuy outplays autopsy layouts outlays outplay payouts. *See* **alopst alotuy alpsuy aoptuy**

aloptuy outplay. *See* **alotuy aoptuy**

aloqrrsu rorquals rorqual squalor. *See* **alors aorrs alrru**

aloqrru rorqual. *See* **alrru**

aloqrssu squalors squalor. *See* **aloss alors aqssu**

aloqrsu squalor. *See* **alors**

aloqtu loquat quota alto auto lota lout tola tolu alt lot oat out qat qua tau at la lo ta to ut

alor oral lar oar la lo or

alorrst rostral. *See* **aorrst alost alors**

alors orals solar also oars oral soar sora lar los oar sal sol as la lo or os so

alorsttw saltwort. *See* **alostt alrstw aorstt**

alorsv salvor valors orals ovals salvo savor solar valor volar also oars oral oval soar sora lar los oar ova sal sol as la lo or os so

alorsy royals aryls orals royal solar also aryl lays lory oars oral rays rosy slay soar sora lar lay los oar ray sal say sly sol soy yar as ay la lo or os oy so

alortyy royalty. *See* **alory**

alorv valor volar oral oval lar oar ova la lo or

alory royal aryl lory oral lar lay oar ray yar ay la lo or oy

alos also los sal sol as la lo os so

aloss lasso also lass loss ossa sals sols ass los sal sol as la lo os so

alosss lassos lasso also lass loss ossa sals sass sols ass los sal sol as la lo os so

alossttu outlasts outlast. *See* **alostt aosstt assttu ossttu**

alossv salvos lasso ovals salvo also lass loss ossa oval sals sols ass los ova sal sol as la lo os so

alost altos lotas tolas also alto alts last lost lota lots oast oats salt slat slot stoa

tola alt los lot oat sal sat sol sot as at la lo os so ta to

alostt totals altos lotas stoat toast tolas total also alto alts last lost lota lots oast oats salt slat slot stoa tats tola tost tots alt los lot oat sal sat sol sot tat tot as at la lo os so ta to

alosttu outlast. *See* **alostt aostu lostu**

alostuw outlaws. *See* **alotuw alost aostu**

alostuy layouts outlays. *See* **alotuy**

alosv ovals salvo also oval los ova sal sol as la lo os so

alosvv volvas ovals salvo volva also oval los ova sal sol as la lo os so

alot alto lota tola alt lot oat at la lo ta to

alott total alto lota tola alt lot oat tat tot at la lo ta to

alotuw outlaw alow alto auto lota lout tola tolu alt awl law lot low oat out owl tau tow two at aw la lo ow ta to ut

alotuy layout outlay alto auto lota lout tola tolu alt lay lot oat out tau toy you at ay la lo oy ta to ut

alov oval ova la lo

alovv volva oval ova la lo

alow alow awl law low owl aw la lo ow

alp alp lap pal la pa

alpp palp alp lap pal pap la pa

alpps palps alps laps palp pals paps slap alp asp lap pal pap pas sal sap spa as la pa

alppstuy platypus. *See* **alppsu alpsuy lppsuy**

alppsu palpus palps pulps pupal alps laps palp pals paps plus pulp puls pupa pups slap upas alp asp lap pal pap pas pul pup pus sal sap spa sup as la pa up us

alppu pupal palp pulp pupa alp lap pal pap pul pup la pa up

alppy apply palp paly play alp lap lay pal pap pay ply pya yap ay la pa

alprrsu larrups. *See* **alprru alprsu**

alprru larrup rural parr purl purr alp lap lar pal par pul rap la pa up

alprssu pulsars. *See* **alprsu lprssu**

alprssw sprawls. *See* **alprsw aprss alpss**

alprsu pulsar purls slurp alps laps pals pars plus puls purl raps rasp slap slur spar spur sura upas alp asp lap lar pal par pas pul pus rap sal sap spa sup as la pa up us

alprsuw pulwars. *See* **alprsu alpruw alprsw alrsuw**

alprsw sprawl pawls warps wraps alps awls laps laws pals pars pawl paws raps rasp slap spar swap waps warp wars wasp wrap alp asp awl lap lar law pal par pas paw rap raw sal sap saw spa wap war was as aw la pa

alprty paltry partly aptly party platy typal arty aryl paly part plat play pray rapt tarp trap tray alp alt apt art lap lar lay pal par pat pay ply pry pya rap rat ray tap tar try yap yar at ay la pa ta

alpruw pulwar pawl purl warp wrap alp awl lap lar law pal par paw pul rap raw wap war aw la pa up

alps alps laps pals slap alp asp lap pal pas sal sap spa as la pa

alpss slaps alps asps laps lass pals pass sals saps slap spas alp asp ass lap pal pas sal sap spa as la pa

alpsst splats lasts pasts plats salts slaps slats spats splat alps alts asps laps lass last pals pass past pats plat sals salt saps slap slat spas spat taps tass alp alt apt asp ass lap pal pas pat sal sap sat spa tap as at la pa ta

alpssy splays palsy plays slaps slays spays splay alps asps laps lass lays pals paly pass pays play pyas sals saps says slap slay spas spay yaps alp asp ass lap lay pal pas pay ply pya sal sap say sly spa spy yap as ay la pa

alpst plats splat alps alts laps last pals past pats plat salt slap slat spat taps alp alt apt asp lap pal pas pat sal sap sat spa tap as at la pa ta

alpsuy layups layup palsy plays splay yaups alps laps lays pals paly pays play plus puls pyas slap slay spay upas yaps yaup yups alp asp lap lay pal pas pay ply pul pus pya sal sap say sly spa spy sup yap yup as ay la pa up us

alpsw pawls alps awls laps laws pals pawl paws slap swap waps wasp alp asp awl lap law pal pas paw sal sap saw spa wap was as aw la pa

alpsy palsy plays splay alps laps lays pals paly pays play pyas slap slay spay yaps alp asp lap lay pal pas pay ply pya sal sap say sly spa spy yap as ay la pa

alpt plat alp alt apt lap pal pat tap at la pa ta

alpty aptly platy typal paly plat play alp alt apt lap lay pal pat pay ply pya tap yap at ay la pa ta

alpuy layup paly play yaup alp lap lay pal pay ply pul pya yap yup ay la pa up

alpw pawl alp awl lap law pal paw wap aw la pa

alpy paly play alp lap lay pal pay ply pya yap ay la pa

alr lar la

alrru rural lar la

alrstu lustra sutra talus ultra alts arts last lust rats rust ruts salt slat slur slut star sura tars tsar alt art lar rat rut sal sat tar tau as at la ta us ut

alrstw   trawls straw swart trawl warts alts arts awls last laws rats salt slat star swat tars tsar wars wart wast alt art awl lar law rat raw sal sat saw tar war was as at aw la ta

alrsty   stylar artsy aryls salty satyr slaty stray trays alts arts arty aryl last lays rats rays salt slat slay star stay tars tray tsar alt art lar lay rat ray sal sat say sly sty tar try yar as at ay la ta

alrsuw   walrus awls laws slur sura wars awl lar law raw sal saw war was as aw la us

alrsy   aryls aryl lays rays slay lar lay ray sal say sly yar as ay la ya

alrtty   tartly lytta ratty arty aryl tart tray alt art lar lay rat ray tar tat try yar at ay la ta

alrtu   ultra alt art lar rat rut tar tau at la ta ut

alrtw   trawl wart alt art awl lar law rat raw tar war at aw la ta

alruuv   uvular uvula luau lar luv ulu la

alry   aryl lar lay ray yar la ay

als   sal la as

alss   lass sals sal ass as la

alsst   lasts salts slats alts lass last sals salt slat tass alt ass sal sat as at la ta

alssvy   sylvas slays sylva lass lays sals says slay ass lay sal say sly as ay la

alssy   slays lass lays sals says slay ass lay sal say sly as ay la

alst   alts last salt slat alt sal sat as at la ta

alstu   talus alts last lust salt slat slut alt sal sat tau as at la ta us ut

alstuv   vaults talus vault alts last lust salt slat slut tavs vast vats alt luv sal sat tau tav vat as at la ta us ut

alstvy   vastly salty slaty sylva alts last lays salt slat slay stay tavs vast vats alt lay sal sat say sly sty tav vat as at ay la ta

alsty   salty slaty alts last lays salt slat slay stay alt lay sal sat say sly sty as at ay la ta

alsuu   luaus usual luau ulus sal ulu as la us

alsuuv   uvulas luaus usual uvula luau ulus luv sal ulu as la us

alsvy   sylva lays slay lay sal say sly as ay la

alsw   awls laws awl law sal saw was as aw la

alswy   yawls awls laws lays slay sway ways yawl yaws awl law lay sal saw say sly was way yaw as aw ay la

alsy   lays slay lay sal say sly as ay la

alt   alt at la ta

alttuy   tautly lytta taut alt lay tat tau tut at ay la ta ut

altty   lytta alt lay tat at ay la ta

altuv   vault alt luv tau tav vat at la ta ut

altwz   waltz alt awl law at aw la ta

aluu   luau ulu la

aluuv   uvula luau ulu luv la

alw   awl law la aw

alwy   yawl awl law lay way yaw aw ay la

alx   lax la ax

aly   lay la ay

alyz   lazy lay la ay

---

am

am   am ma

ammmno   mammon ammo moan noma man moa mom mon am an ma mo na no om on

ammmnos   mammons. *See* **ammmno amnos**

ammmy   mammy may yam am ay ma my

ammnoort   motorman. *See* **ammort amnoor amnort anoort**

ammnptuy   tympanum. *See* **amnpty**

ammo   ammo moa mom am ma mo om

ammorst   marmots. *See* **ammort amost amrst**

ammort   marmot ammo atom mart moat mora mort roam rota taro tora tram arm art mar mat moa mom mor mot oar oat ort ram rat rot tam tar tom tor am at ma mo om or ta to

ammosxy   myxomas. *See* **ammosy ammoxy**

ammosy   myomas myoma mayos ammo mayo moas moms soma yams may moa mom mos oms say soy yam am as ay ma mo my om os oy so

ammoxy   myxoma myoma ammo mayo moxa may moa mom yam am ax ay ma mo my om ox oy

ammoy   myoma ammo mayo may moa mom yam am ay ma mo my om oy

ammpsuw   wampums. *See* **ammpuw mmpsu ampsu**

ammpuw   wampum puma amp map maw mum paw ump wap am aw ma mu pa um up

ammrsuy   summary. *See* **ammrsy amrsu mmruy**

ammrsy   smarmy arms army rams rays yams arm mar may ram ray say yam yar am as ay ma my

ammsu   summa mums mum mus sum am as ma mu um us

amn   man am an ma na

amnnostw   townsman snowman. *See* **annost annotw**

amnnosty   antonyms anonyms antonym. *See* **amnnoy annost annosy**

amnnosw   snowman. *See* **amnos amnow**

amnnosy   anonyms. *See* **amnnoy annosy**

amnnoty   antonym. *See* **amnnoy amoty anoty**

amnnoy   anonym annoy anon many mayo moan myna noma any man may moa mon nay yam yon am an ay ma mo my na no om on oy

amnnsttu   stuntman mutants. *See* **amnnsu amnttu annstu ansttu**

amnnsu   unmans manus unman anus maun nuns sunn man mus nun sum sun am an as ma mu na nu um us

amnnu   unman maun man nun am an ma mu na nu um

amno   moan noma man moa mon am an ma mo na no om on

amnoopp   pompano. *See* **mnoopp**

amnoopps   pompanos pompano. *See* **mnoopp**

amnoor   maroon manor moron moan mono moon moor mora morn noma norm roam roan room arm man mar moa mon moo mor nor oar ram ran am an ma mo na no om on or

amnoors   maroons. *See* **amnors amnoor mnoors**

amnoostt   ottomans ottoman. *See* **amoott moostt**

amnoott   ottoman. *See* **amoott**

amnootuy   autonomy. *See* **amnotu mnootu**

amnootxy   taxonomy. *See* **amoty anoty mnooy**

amnoppr   propman. *See* **amnor anopr**

amnoprsy paronyms paronym masonry. *See* **amnors amorsy anoprs anorsy**

amnopry paronym. *See* **anopr amnor amory**

amnopst postman. *See* **amost amnos anpst**

amnor manor moan mora morn noma norm roam roan arm man mar moa mon mor nor oar ram ran am an ma mo na no om on or

amnorr marron manor armor moan mora morn noma norm roam roan roar arm man mar moa mon mor nor oar ram ran am an ma mo na no om on or

amnorrs marrons. *See* **amorrs amnors amnorr**

amnors manors ransom arson manor mason moans morns nomas norms roams roans sonar arms moan moas mons mora morn mors naos noma norm oars rams roam roan soar soma sora arm man mar moa mon mor mos nor oar oms ram ran son am an as ma mo na no om on or os so

amnorss ransoms. *See* **anorss amnoss amorss amnors**

amnorsst transoms matrons ransoms transom. *See* **amnors amnort amnoss amorss**

amnorst matrons transom. *See* **amnors amnort**

amnorsy masonry. *See* **amnors amorsy anorsy**

amnort matron manor atom mart moan moat mora morn mort noma norm nota rant roam roan rota taro tora torn tram ant arm art man mar mat moa mon mor mot nor not oar oat ort ram ran rat rot tam tan tar tom ton tor am an at ma mo na no om on or ta to

amnos mason moans nomas moan moas mons naos noma soma man moa mon mos oms son am an as ma mo na no om on os so

amnoss masons mason moans nomas somas mass moan moas mons moss naos noma ossa soma sons ass man moa mon mos oms son am an as ma mo na no om on os so

amnostu amounts. *See* **amnotu mnostu**

amnotu amount mount notum atom aunt auto maun moan moat muon noma nota tuna unto ant man mat moa mon mot not nut oat out tam tan tau tom ton tun am an at ma mo mu na no nu om on ta to um ut

amnow woman moan mown noma awn man maw moa mon mow now own

wan won am an aw ma mo na no om on ow

amnpty tympan panty many myna pant tamp amp ant any apt man map mat may nap nay pan pat pay pya tam tan tap yam yap am an at ay ma my na pa ta

amnptyy tympany. *See* **amnpty**

amnqtuu quantum. *See* **amntuu anqtu**

amnrsttu tantrums mutants stratum tantrum truants. *See* **amnrsu amnrtu amnttu amrstu**

amnrsu unarms manus ramus unarm anus arms maun rams rums runs sura urns arm man mar mus ram ran rum run sum sun urn am an as ma mu na nu um us

amnrttu tantrum. *See* **amnrtu amnttu anrttu**

amnrtu antrum unarm aunt mart maun rant runt tram tuna turn ant arm art man mar mat nut ram ran rat rum run rut tam tan tar tau tun urn am an at ma mu na nu ta um ut

amnru unarm maun arm man mar ram ran rum run urn am an ma mu na nu um

amnsttu mutants. *See* **amnttu ansttu**

amnstuu autumns. *See* **amntuu anstu amnsu**

amnsu manus maun anus man mus sum sun am an as ma mu na nu um us

amnsy mynas many myna yams any man may nay say yam am an as ay ma my na

amnttu mutant taunt aunt maun mutt taut tuna ant man mat nut tam tan tat tau tun tut am an at ma mu na nu ta um ut

amntuu autumn aunt maun tuna ant man mat nut tam tan tau tun am an at ma mu na nu ta um ut

amnu maun man am an ma mu na nu um

amny many myna any man may nay yam am an ay ma my na

amo moa am ma mo om

amooprst taprooms taproom. *See* **amprst aoprst mooprs moorst**

amooprt taproom. *See* **aoprt moort moopr**

amoorsu amorous. *See* **amorsu**

amoorxy oxymora. *See* **amory moory**

amoott tomato motto atom moat moot toot mat moa moo mot oat tam tat tom too tot am at ma mo om ta to

amoottuy autotomy. *See* **amoott**

amoppsy maypops. *See* **amoppy amosy appsy**

amoppy maypop mayo pomp amp map may moa mop pap pay pop pya yam yap am ay ma mo my om oy pa

amoprsxy paroxysm. *See* **amorsy**

amopsstt topmasts topmast. *See* **amosst ampsst aosstt mopsst**

amopstt topmast. *See* **amost ampst aostt**

amor mora roam arm mar moa mor oar ram am ma mo om or

amorr armor mora roam roar arm mar moa mor oar ram am ma mo om or

amorrs armors armor roams roars arms moas mora mors oars rams roam roar soar soma sora arm mar moa mor mos oar oms ram am as ma mo om or os so

amorrst mortars. *See* **amorrs amorrt aorrst**

amorrsw marrows. *See* **amorrs aorrsw amorrw**

amorrt mortar armor atom mart moat mora mort roam roar rota taro tora torr tram arm art mar mat moa mor mot oar oat ort ram rat rot tam tar tom tor am at ma mo om or ta to

amorrtuy mortuary. *See* **amorrt amorry amrrty aorrty**

amorrw marrow armor arrow mora roam roar warm worm arm mar maw moa mor mow oar ram raw row war am aw ma mo om or ow

amorrwy marrowy. *See* **amorry amorrw aorrwy**

amorry armory armor marry mayor moray army mayo mora roam roar arm mar may moa mor oar ram ray yam yar am ay ma mo my om or oy

amors roams arms moas mora mors oars rams roam soar soma sora arm mar moa mor mos oar oms ram am as ma mo om or os so

amorss morass roams saros soars somas soras arms mass moas mora mors moss oars ossa rams roam soar soma sora arm ass mar moa mor mos oar oms ram am as ma mo om or os so

amorsttu outsmart stratum. *See* **amorsu amrstu aorstt morstu**

amorsu amours ramous amour ramus roams arms moas mora mors oars ours rams roam rums soar soma sora sour sumo sura arm mar moa mor mos mus oar oms our ram rum sou sum am as ma mo mu om or os so um us

amorsy mayors morays mayor mayos moray roams arms army mayo moas mora mors oars rams rays roam rosy soar soma sora yams arm mar may moa mor mos oar oms ram ray say soy yam yar am as ay ma mo my om or os oy so

amoru amour mora roam arm mar moa mor oar our ram rum am ma mo mu om or um

amory mayor moray army mayo mora roam arm mar may moa mor oar ram ray yam yar am ay ma mo my om or oy

amos moas soma moa mos oms am as ma mo om os so

amoss somas mass moas moss ossa soma ass moa mos oms am as ma mo om os so

amosst stomas atoms masts moats oasts somas stoas stoma atom mass mast mats moas moat moss most mots oast oats ossa soma sots stoa tams tass toms toss ass mat moa mos mot oat oms sat sot tam tom am as at ma mo om os so ta to

amost atoms moats stoma atom mast mats moas moat most mots oast oats soma stoa tams toms mat moa mos mot oat oms sat sot tam tom am as at ma mo om os so ta to

amostz matzos atoms matzo moats stoma atom mast mats moas moat most mots oast oats soma stoa tams toms azo mat moa mos mot oat oms sat sot tam tom zoa am as at ma mo om os so ta to

amosx moxas moas moxa soma moa mos oms sax sox am as ax ma mo om os ox so

amosy mayos mayo moas soma yams may moa mos oms say soy yam am as ay ma mo my om os oy so

amot atom moat mat moa mot oat tam tom am at ma mo om ta to

amottz matzot matzo atom moat azo mat moa mot oat tam tat tom tot zoa am at ma mo om ta to

amoty atomy atom mayo moat mat may moa mot oat tam tom toy yam am at ay ma mo my om oy ta to

amotz matzo atom moat azo mat moa mot oat tam tom zoa am at ma mo om ta to

amox moxa moa am ax ma mo om ox

amoy mayo may moa yam am ay ma mo my om oy

amp amp map am ma pa

ampr pram ramp amp arm map mar par ram rap am ma pa

amprs prams ramps amps arms maps pars pram ramp rams raps rasp samp spar amp arm asp map mar par pas ram rap sap spa am as ma pa

amprst tramps deils delis doles idles idols lodes oiled oldie sidle slide soled solid deil deli dies does dole dose ides idle idol isle leis lids lied lies lode lose odes oils side silo sled slid sloe soil sold sole apt arm art asp die doe dos eld ids led lid mar mat ode old par pas pat ram rap rat sap sat sod spa tam tap tar am as at ma pa ta

amprt tramp mart part pram ramp rapt tamp tarp tram trap amp apt arm art map mar mat par pat ram rap rat tam tap tar am at ma pa ta

amps amps maps samp amp asp map pas sap spa am as ma pa

ampss samps spasm amps asps maps mass pass samp saps spas amp asp ass map pas sap spa am as ma pa

ampsss spasms samps spasm amps asps maps mass pass samp saps sass spas amp asp ass map pas sap spa am as ma pa

ampsst stamps masts pasts samps spasm spats stamp tamps amps asps maps mass mast mats pass past pats samp saps spas spat tamp tams taps tass amp apt asp ass map mat pas pat sap sat spa tam tap am as at ma pa ta

ampssw swamps samps spasm swamp swaps wasps amps asps maps mass maws pass paws samp saps saws spas swam swap waps wasp amp asp ass map maw pas paw sap saw spa wap was am as aw ma pa

ampst stamp tamps amps maps mast mats past pats samp spat tamp tams taps amp apt asp map mat pas pat sap sat spa tam tap am as at ma pa ta

ampsu pumas amps maps puma samp sump umps upas amp asp map mus pas pus sap spa sum sup ump am as ma mu pa um up us

ampsv vamps amps maps samp vamp amp asp map pas sap spa am as ma pa

ampsw swamp amps maps maws paws samp swam swap waps wasp amp asp map maw pas paw sap saw spa wap was am as aw ma pa

ampswy swampy swamp swamy waspy yawps amps maps maws paws pays pyas samp spay swam swap sway waps wasp ways yams yaps yawp yaws amp asp map maw may pas paw pay pya sap saw say spa spy wap was way yam yap yaw am as aw ay ma py pa

ampt tamp amp apt map mat pat tam tap am at ma pa ta

ampu puma amp map ump am ma mu pa um up

ampv vamp amp map am ma pa

amr arm mar ram am ma

amrrsty martyrs. *See* **amrrty amrsty arrsty**

amrrty martyr marry tarry army arty mart tram tray arm art mar mat may ram rat ray tam tar try yam yar am at ay ma my ta

amrry marry army arm mar may ram ray yam yar am ay ma my

amrs arms rams arm mar ram am as ma

amrsst smarts marts masts smart stars trams trass tsars arms arts mart mass mast mats rams rats star tams tars tass tram tsar arm art ass mar mat ram rat sat tam tar am as at ma ta

amrssttu stratums stratum stratus. *See* **amrsst amrstu arsstu assttu**

amrssw swarms swarm warms arms mass maws rams saws swam warm wars arm ass mar maw ram raw saw war was am as aw ma

amrst marts smart trams arms arts mart mast mats rams rats star tams tars tram tsar arm art mar mat ram rat sat tam tar am as at ma ta

amrsttu stratum. *See* **amrstu msttu arstt**

amrstu struma marts ramus smart strum sutra trams arms arts mart mast mats must rams rats rums rust ruts smut star stum sura tams tars tram tsar arm art mar mat mus ram rat rum rut sat sum tam tar tau am as at ma mu ta um us ut

amrsty smarty artsy marts mayst satyr smart stray trams trays arms army arts arty mart mast mats rams rats rays star stay tams tars tram tray tsar yams arm art mar mat may ram rat ray sat say sty tam tar try yam yar am as at ay ma my ta

amrsu ramus arms rams rums sura arm mar mus ram rum sum am as ma mu um us

amrsuu aurums ramus aurum arms rams rums sura urus arm mar mus ram rum sum am as ma mu um us

amrsw swarm warms arms maws rams swam warm wars arm mar maw ram raw saw war was am as aw ma

amrt mart tram arm art mar mat ram rat tam tar am at ma ta

amruu aurum arm mar ram rum am ma mu um

amrvy marvy army vary arm mar may ram ray yam yar am ay ma my

amrw warm arm mar maw ram raw war am aw ma

amry army arm mar may ram ray yam yar am ay ma my

amss mass ass am as ma

amsst masts mass mast mats tams tass ass mat sat tam am as at ma ta

amssy massy mass says yams ass may say yam am as ay ma my

amst mast mats tams mat sat tam am as at ma ta

amsty mayst mast mats stay tams yams mat may sat say sty tam yam am as at ay ma my ta

amsw maws swam maw saw was am as aw ma

amswy swamy maws swam sway ways yams yaws maw may saw say was way yam yaw am as aw ay ma my

amsy yams may say yam am as ay ma my

amt mat tam am at ma ta

amw maw am aw ma

amy may yam am ay ma my

amyz mazy may yam am ay ma my

---

an

---

an an na

annny nanny any nay an ay na

anno anon an na no on

annosst sonants. *See* **annost aosst nosst**

annost sonant anon ants naos nota oast oats snot stoa tans tons ant not oat sat son sot tan ton an as at na no on os so ta to

annosy annoys annoy sonny anon naos nosy any nay say son soy yon an as ay na no on os oy so

annotw wanton anon nota nowt town want wont ant awn not now oat own tan ton tow two wan won an at aw na no on ow ta to

annoy annoy anon any nay yon an ay na no on oy

annpssu sannups. *See* **annpsu anpss**

annpsu sannup anus naps nuns pans puns snap span spun sunn upas asp nap nun pan pas pun pus sap spa sun sup an as na nu pa up us

annrtyy tyranny. *No 6s or 5s*

annsstu suntans. *See* **annstu nsstu**

annstu suntan aunts tunas ants anus aunt nuns nuts stun sunn tans tuna tuns ant nun nut sat sun tan tau tun an as at na nu ta us ut

annttu nutant taunt aunt taut tuna ant nun nut tan tat tau tun tut an at na nu ta ut

anooprs soprano. *See* **anoprs nooprs**

anooprss sopranos parsons soprano sponsor. *See* **anoprs anorss nooprs noopss**

anooprst patroons patrons patroon protons ratoons soprano tarpons. *See* **anoort anoprs anoprt aoprst**

anooprt patroon. *See* **anoprt nooprt anoort**

anoorst ratoons. *See* **anoort anors anrst**

anoort ratoon nota onto rant roan root rota roto taro toon tora torn ant art nor not oar oat ort ran rat rot tan tar ton too tor an at na no on or ta to

anopr apron roan proa nap nor oar pan par pro ran rap an na no on or pa

anoprs aprons parson apron arson proas roans sonar naos naps oars pans pars pons porn proa pros raps rasp roan snap soap soar sora span spar asp nap nor oar pan par pas pro ran rap sap son sop spa an as na no on or os pa so

anoprss parsons. *See* **anoprs anorss**

anoprst patrons tarpons. *See* **anoprs aoprst anoprt**

anoprt patron tarpon apron aport atop nota pant part porn port proa rant rapt roan rota taro tarp tora torn trap ant apt art nap nor not oar oat ort pan par pat pot pro ran rap rat rot tan tap tar ton top tor an at na no on or pa ta to

anopsuy yaupons. *See* **anopuy anpsy aopsy**

anopuy yaupon pony puny upon yaup yuan any nap nay pan pay pun pya yap yon you yup an ay na no nu on oy pa up

anor roan nor oar ran an na no on or

anorrsw narrows. *See* **aorrsw anorrw anorsw**

anorrw narrow rowan arrow roan roar warn worn awn nor now oar own ran raw row wan war won an aw na no on or ow

anors arson roans sonar naos oars roan soar sora nor oar ran son an as na no on or os so

anorss arsons sonars arson roans saros soars sonar soras naos oars ossa roan soar sors ass nor oar ran son an as na no on or os so

anorstt attorns. *See* **anortt aorstt**

anorsuv unsavory savoury. *See* **anorsy aorsuv aorsvy**

anorsw rowans arson roans rowan sonar sworn warns awns naos oars owns roan rows sawn snow soar sora sown swan warn wars worn awn nor now oar own ran raw row saw son sow wan war was won an as aw na no on or os ow so

anorsy rayons arson rayon roans sonar yarns naos nary nosy oars rays roan rosy soar sora yarn any nay nor oar ran ray say son soy yar yon an as ay na no on or os oy so

anortt attorn tarot nota rant roan rota taro tart tora torn tort trot ant art nor not oar oat ort ran rat rot tan tar ton tor tot an at na no on or ta to

anortu outran aunt auto nota rant roan rota rout runt taro tora torn tour tuna turn unto ant art nor not nut oar oat ort our out ran rat rot run rut tan tar tau ton tor tun urn an at na no nu on or ta to ut

anorty notary rayon atony arty nary nota rant roan rota ryot taro tony tora torn tray troy tyro yarn ant any art nay nor not oar oat ort ran rat ray rot tan tar ton tor toy try yar yon an at ay na no on or oy ta to

anorw rowan roan warn worn awn nor now oar own ran raw row wan war won an aw na no on or ow

anory rayon nary roan yarn any nay nor oar ran ray yar yon an ay na no on or oy

anoryz zonary rayon nary roan yarn zany any azo nay nor oar ran ray yar yon zoa an ay na no on or oy

anos naos son an as na no on os so

anosv novas naos nova vans ova son van an as na no on os so

anosx axons naos axon sax son sox an as ax na no on os ox so

anot nota ant not oat tan ton an at na no on ta to

anoty atony nota tony ant any nay not oat tan ton toy yon an at ay na no on oy ta to

anov nova van ova an na no on

anowy noway wany yawn any awn nay now own wan way won yaw yon yow an aw ay na no on ow oy

anox axon an ax na no on ox

anp nap pan an na pa

anppsy snappy nappy pansy sappy naps pans paps pays pyas snap span spay yaps any asp nap nay pan pap pas pay pya sap say spa spy yap an as ay na pa

anppy nappy any nap nay pan pap pay pya yap an ay na pa

anprstuu pursuant upturns. *See* **nprtuu**

anprsuw unwraps. *See* **anprsw anpruw**

anprsw prawns pawns prawn spawn warns warps wraps awns naps pans pars pawn paws raps rasp sawn snap span spar swan swap waps warn warp wars wasp wrap asp awn nap pan par pas paw ran rap raw sap saw spa wan wap war was an as aw na pa

anprty pantry panty party arty nary pant part pray rant rapt tarp trap tray yarn ant any apt art nap nay pan par pat pay pry pya ran rap rat ray tan tap tar try yap yar an at ay na pa ta

anpruw unwrap prawn pawn warn warp wrap awn nap pan par paw pun ran rap raw run urn wan wap war an aw na nu pa up

anprw prawn pawn warn warp wrap awn nap pan par paw ran rap raw wan wap war an aw na pa

anps naps pans snap span asp nap pan pas sap spa an as na pa

anpss snaps spans asps naps pans pass saps snap span spas asp ass nap pan pas sap spa an as na pa

anpssw spawns pawns snaps spans spawn swans swaps wasps asps awns naps pans pass pawn paws saps sawn saws snap span spas swan swap waps wasp asp ass awn nap pan pas paw sap saw spa wan wap was an as aw na pa

anpst pants ants naps pans pant past pats snap span spat tans taps ant apt asp nap pan pas pat sap sat spa tan tap an as at na pa ta

anpsw pawns spawn awns naps pans pawn paws sawn snap span swan swap waps wasp asp awn nap pan pas paw sap saw spa wan wap was an as aw na pa

anpsy pansy naps pans pays pyas snap span spay yaps any asp nap nay pan pas pay pya sap say spa spy yap an as ay na pa

anpt pant ant apt nap pan pat tan tap an at na pa ta

anptu unapt aunt pant punt tuna ant apt nap nut pan pat pun put tan tap tau tun tup an at na nu pa ta up ut

anpty panty pant ant any apt nap nay pan pat pay pya tan tap yap an at ay na pa ta

anpw pawn awn nap pan paw wan wap an aw na pa

anqstu quants aunts quant squat tunas ants anus aunt nuts qats stun tans tuna tuns ant nut qat qua sat sun tan tau tun an as at na nu ta us ut

anqtu quant aunt tuna ant nut qat qua tan tau tun an at na nu ta ut

anr ran an na

anrst rants ants arts rant rats star tans tars tsar ant art ran rat sat tan tar an as at na ta

anrsttu truants. *See* **anrttu ansttu**

anrstty tyrants. *See* **anrtty ansty arsty**

anrsuwy runways. *See* **anruwy**

anrsw warns awns sawn swan warn wars awn ran raw saw wan war was an as aw na

anrsy yarns nary rays yarn any nay ran ray say yar an as ay na

anrt rant ant art ran rat tan tar an at na ta

anrttu truant taunt aunt rant runt tart taut tuna turn ant art nut ran rat run rut tan tar tat tau tun tut urn an at na nu ta ut

anrtty tyrant natty ratty arty nary rant tart tray yarn ant any art nay ran rat ray tan tar tat try yar an at ay na ta

anruwy runway unwary awry nary wany warn wary yarn yawn yuan any awn nay ran raw ray run urn wan war way yar yaw an aw ay na nu

anrw warn awn ran raw wan war an aw na

anry nary yarn any nay ran ray yar an ay na

anssw swans awns sawn saws swan ass awn saw wan was an as aw na

anst ants tans ant sat tan an as at na ta

ansttu taunts aunts stunt taunt tunas ants anus aunt nuts stun tans tats taut tuna tuns tuts ant nut sat sun tan tat tau tun tut an as at na nu ta us ut

anstu aunts tunas ants anus aunt nuts stun tans tuna tuns ant nut sat sun tan tau tun an as at na nu ta us ut

anstuv vaunts aunts tunas vaunt ants anus aunt nuts stun tans tavs tuna tuns vans vast vats ant nut sat sun tan tau tav tun van vat an as at na nu ta us ut

anstw wants ants awns sawn swan swat tans want wast ant awn sat saw tan wan was an as at aw na ta

anstxy syntax antsy nasty tansy ants stay tans ant any nay sat sax say sny sty tan tax an as at ax ay na ta

ansty antsy nasty tansy ants stay tans ant any nay sat say sty tan an as at ay na ta

ansu anus sun an as na nu us

ansuy yuans anus yuan any nay say sun an as ay na nu us

ansv vans van an as na

answ awns sawn swan awn saw wan was an as aw na

answy yawns awns sawn swan sway wany ways yawn yaws any awn nay saw say wan was way yaw an as aw ay na

ansyzz snazzy zany any nay say an as ay na

ant ant tan an at na ta

anttu taunt aunt taut tuna ant nut tan tat tau tun tut an at na nu ta ut

antty natty ant any nay tan tat an at ay na ta

antu aunt tuna ant nut tan tau tun an at na nu ta ut

antuv vaunt aunt tuna ant nut tan tau tav tun van vat an at na nu ta ut

antuy aunty aunt tuna yuan ant any nay nut tan tau tun an at ay na nu ta ut

antw want ant awn tan wan an at aw na ta

antwy tawny want wany yawn ant any awn nay tan wan way yaw an at aw ay na ta

anuy yuan any nay an ay na nu

anv van an na

anvvy navvy navy any nay van an ay na

anvy navy any nay van an ay na

anw awn wan an aw na

anwy wany yawn any awn nay wan way yaw an aw ay na

any any nay an ay na

anyz zany any nay an ay na

aoopprs apropos. *See* **oopps aoprs opprs**

aooprssu saporous. *See* **ooprss ooprsu**

aooprstt taproots taproot. *See* **aoprst aoopt aorstt ooprst**

aooprsuv vaporous. *See* **aoprsv aorsuv ooprsu**

aooprtt taproot. *See* **aoopt aoprt aortt**

aoopt potato atop toot apt oat pat pot tap tat too top tot at pa ta to

aoorrst orators. *See* **aoorrt aorrst**

aoorrstt rotators orators rotator. *See* **aoorrt aorrst aorstt**

aoorrsy arroyos. *See* **aoorry aorrsy**

aoorrt orator roar root rota roto taro tora torr art oar oat ort rat rot tar too tor at or ta to

aoorrtt rotator. *See* **aoorrt aortt**

aoorrtty rotatory rotator oratory. *See* **aoorrt aoorry aorrty**

aoorrty oratory. *See* **aoorry aoorrt aorrty**

aoorry arroyo roar oar ray yar ay or oy

aoosttt tattoos. *See* **aoostt oostt**

aoottt tattoo toot oat tat too tot at ta to

aopprrst rapports rapport parrots. *See* **aoprrt aoprst aorrst**

aopprrt rapport. *See* **aoprrt**

aopprsst passport pastors. *See* **aoprst aorsst aprsst oprsst**

aopr proa oar par pro rap pa or

aoprrssw sparrows sparrow. *See* **aorrsw**

aoprrst parrots. *See* **aoprrt aoprst aorrst**

aoprrsty portrays parrots portray. *See* **aoprrt aoprst aorrst aorrsy**

aoprrsu uproars. *See* **aoprru aprrs oprsu**

aoprrsw sparrow. *See* **aorrsw aprrs aoprs**

aoprrt parrot aport atop parr part port proa rapt roar rota taro tarp tora torr trap apt art oar oat ort par pat pot pro rap rat rot tap tar top tor at or pa ta to

aoprrty portray. *See* **aoprrt aorrty**

aoprru uproar parr pour proa purr roar oar our par pro rap or pa up

aoprs proas oars pars proa pros raps rasp soap soar sora spar asp oar par pas pro rap sap sop spa as or os pa so

aoprsst pastors. *See* **aorsst aoprst oprsst aprsst**

aoprst pastor aport parts ports proas roast rotas sport sprat strap strop taros tarps toras traps arts atop oars oast oats orts pars part past pats port post pots proa pros raps rapt rasp rats rota rots soap soar sora sort spar spat spot star stoa stop taps taro tarp tars tops tora tors trap tsar apt art asp oar oat ort par pas pat pot pro rap rat rot sap

sat sop sot spa tap tar top tor as at or os pa so ta to

aoprstty pyrostat. *See* **aoprst aorstt aostty aprsty**

aoprstw postwar. *See* **aoprst oprsw arstw**

aoprsv vapors proas savor vapor oars pars proa pros raps rasp soap soar sora spar asp oar ova par pas pro rap sap sop spa as or os pa so

aoprt aport atop part port proa rapt rota taro tarp tora trap apt art oar oat ort par pat pot pro rap rat rot tap tar top tor at or pa ta to

aoprv vapor proa oar ova par pro rap pa or

aoprvy vapory vapor ovary pray proa ropy vary oar ova par pay pro pry pya rap ray yap yar ay or oy pa

aops soap asp pas sap sop spa as os pa so

aopss soaps asps ossa pass saps soap sops spas asp ass pas sap sop spa as os pa so

aopstuy autopsy payouts. *See* **aoptuy aostu apsty**

aopsy soapy pays posy pyas soap spay yaps asp pas pay pya sap say sop soy spa spy yap as ay os oy pa so

aopt atop apt oat pat pot tap top at pa ta to

aoptuy payout atop auto pout yaup apt oat out pat pay pot put pya tap tau top toy tup yap you yup at ay oy pa ta to up ut

aoptz topaz atop apt azo oat pat pot tap top zap zoa at pa ta to

aoqrstu quartos. *See* **aoqrtu aqrstu aoqstu**

aoqrtu quarto quota quart auto rota rout taro tora tour art oar oat ort our out qat qua rat rot rut tar tau tor at or ta to ut

aoqstu quotas autos quota squat auto oast oats oust outs qats stoa oat out qat qua sat sot sou tau as at os so ta to us ut

aoqtu quota auto oat out qat qua tau at ta to ut

aor oar or

aorr roar oar or

aorrs roars oars roar soar sora oar as or os so

aorrst rostra roars roast rotas taros toras arts oars oast oats orts rats roar rota rots soar sora sort star stoa taro tars tora torr tors tsar art oar oat ort rat rot sat sot tar tor as at or os so ta to

aorrsw arrows roars arrow oars roar rows soar sora wars oar raw row saw sow war was as aw or os ow so

aorrswy yarrows. *See* **aorrsw aorrsy aorrwy**

aorrsy rosary roars sorry oars rays roar rosy soar sora oar ray say soy yar as ay or os oy so

aorrsz razors roars razor oars roar soar sora azo oar zoa as or os so

aorrty rotary tarry arty roar rota ryot taro tora torr tray troy tyro art oar oat ort rat ray rot tar tor toy try yar at ay or oy ta to

aorrw arrow roar oar raw row war aw or ow

aorrwy yarrow arrow worry awry roar wary oar raw ray row war way yar yaw yow aw ay or ow oy

aorrz razor roar azo oar zoa or

aors oars soar sora oar as or os so

aorss saros soars soras oars ossa soar sora oar ass as or os so

aorsst assort roasts oasts roast rotas saros soars soras sorts stars stoas taros toras trass tsars arts oars oast oats orts ossa rats rota rots soar sora sort sots star stoa taro tars tass tora tors toss tsar art ass oar oat ort rat rot sat sot tar tor as at or os so ta to

aorsstt stators. *See* **aorsst arsstt aorstt aosstt**

aorssuv savours. *See* **aorssv aorsuv**

aorssuy ossuary. *See* **aorss arsuy orssu**

aorssv savors saros savor soars soras oars ossa soar sora ass oar ova as or os so

aorst roast rotas taros toras arts oars oast oats orts rats rota rots soar sora sort star stoa taro tars tora tors tsar art oar oat ort rat rot sat sot tar tor as at or os so ta to

aorstt stator roast rotas start stoat taros tarot tarts toast toras torts trots arts oars oast oats orts rats rota rots soar sora sort star stoa taro tars tart tats tora tors tort tost tots trot tsar art oar oat ort rat rot sat sot tar tat tor tot as at or os so ta to

aorstx storax roast rotas taros toras arts oars oast oats orts rats rota rots soar sora sort star stoa taro tars tora tors tsar art oar oat ort rat rot sat sax sot sox tar tax tor as at ax or os ox so ta to

aorsuu aurous oars ours soar sora sour sura urus oar our sou as or os so us

aorsuv savour savor varus oars ours soar sora sour sura oar our ova sou as or os so us

aorsuvy savoury. *See* **aorsuv aorsvy**

aorsv savor oars soar sora oar ova as or os so

aorsvy savory ovary savor savoy oars rays rosy soar sora vary oar ova ray say soy yar as ay or os oy so

aort rota taro tora art oar oat ort rat rot tar tor at or ta to

aortt tarot rota taro tart tora tort trot art oar oat ort rat rot tar tat tor tot at or ta to

aortvy votary ovary arty rota ryot taro tora tray troy tyro vary art oar oat ort

ova rat ray rot tar tav tor toy try vat yar at ay or oy ta to

aorvy ovary vary oar ova ray yar ay or oy

aoss ossa ass as os so

aosst oasts stoas oast oats ossa sots stoa tass toss ass oat sat sot as at os so ta to

aosstt stoats toasts oasts stoas stoat toast oast oats ossa sots stoa tass tats toss tost tots ass oat sat sot tat tot as at os so ta to

aosssvy savoys savoy ossa says soys ass ova say soy as ay os oy so

aost oast oats stoa oat sat sot as at os so ta to

aostt stoat toast oast oats stoa tats tost tots oat sat sot tat tot as at os so ta to

aostty toasty stoat tasty toast oast oats stay stoa tats tost tots toys oat sat say sot soy sty tat tot toy as at ay os oy so ta to

aostu autos auto oast oats oust outs stoa oat out sat sot sou tau as at os so ta to us ut

aosvw avows avow vows ova saw sow vow was as aw os ow so

aosvy savoy ova say soy as ay os oy so

aot oat at ta to

aotu auto oat out tau at ta to ut

aov ova

aovw avow ova vow aw ow

aoz azo zoa

ap pa

app pap pa

apppsu pappus paps pupa pups upas asp pap pas pup pus sap spa sup as pa up us

apprsuy papyrus. *See* **aprsy prsuy appsy**

apps paps asp pap pas sap spa as pa

appsy sappy paps pays pyas spay yaps asp pap pas pay pya sap say spa spy yap as ay pa

appu pupa pap pup pa up

apr par rap pa

aprr parr par rap pa

aprrs parrs parr pars raps rasp spar asp par pas rap sap spa as pa

aprry parry parr pray par pay pry pya rap ray yap yar pa ay

aprs pars raps rasp spar asp par pas rap sap spa as pa

aprss rasps spars asps pars pass raps rasp saps spar spas asp ass par pas rap sap spa pa as

aprsssu surpass. *See* **aprss prssu arssu**

aprsst sprats straps douse dunes nodes nodus nosed nudes sonde sound dens does done dons dose dues dune duns duos ends eons node nods noes nose nous nude odes ones onus ouds send sued udos undo used den doe don dos due dun duo end eon nod ode one oud sod udo as at pa ta

aprssttu upstarts upstart stratus. *See* **aprsst apsstu arsstt arsstu**

aprssy sprays prays rasps raspy spars spays spray asps pars pass pays pray

pyas raps rasp rays saps says spar spas spay spry yaps asp ass par pas pay pry pya rap ray sap say spa spy yap yar as ay pa

aprst parts sprat strap tarps traps arts pars part past pats raps rapt rasp rats spar spat star taps tarp tars trap tsar apt art asp par pas pat rap rat sap sat spa tap tar as at pa ta

aprsttu upstart. *See* **aprst psttu prstu**

aprsty pastry deils delfs delis felid field filed files flied flies idles sidle slide deil delf deli dies feds fids fies file fils fled ides idle isle leis lids lied lief lies life self side sled slid apt art die eld elf els fed fid fie ids led lei lid lie pat pay pry pya rat ray sat say spy sty tap tar try yap yar as at ay pa ta

aprsw warps wraps pars paws raps rasp spar swap waps warp wars wasp wrap asp par pas paw rap raw sap saw spa wap war was as aw pa

aprsy prays raspy spray pars pays pray pyas raps rasp rays spar spay spry yaps asp par pas pay pry pya rap ray sap say spa spy yap yar as ay pa

aprt part rapt tarp trap apt art par pat rap rat tap tar at pa ta

aprtw wrapt part rapt tarp trap warp wart wrap apt art par pat paw rap rat raw tap tar wap war at aw pa ta

aprty party arty part pray rapt tarp trap tray apt art par pat pay pry pya rap rat ray tap tar try yap yar at ay pa ta

aprw warp wrap par paw rap raw wap war pa aw

apry pray par pay pry pya rap ray yap yar pa ay

aps asp pas sap spa pa as

apss asps pass saps spas asp ass pas sap spa as pa

apsst pasts spats asps pass past pats saps spas spat taps tass apt asp ass pas pat sap sat spa tap as at pa ta

apsstu stupas pasts spats stupa asps pass past pats puss puts saps spas spat sups taps tass tups upas apt asp ass pas pat pus put sap sat spa sup tap tau tup as at pa ta up us ut

apssw swaps wasps asps pass paws saps saws spas swap waps wasp asp ass pas paw sap saw spa wap was as aw pa

apssy spays asps pass pays pyas saps says spas spay yaps asp ass pas pay pya sap say spa spy yap as ay pa

apst past pats spat taps apt asp pas pat sap sat spa tap as at pa ta

apstu stupa past pats puts spat taps tups upas apt asp pas pat pus put sap sat spa sup tap tau tup as at pa ta up us ut

apsty pasty patsy past pats pays pyas spat spay stay taps yaps apt asp pas pat pay pya sap sat say spa spy sty tap yap as at ay pa ta

apsu upas asp pas pus sap spa sup as pa up us

apsuy yaups pays pyas spay upas yaps yaup yups asp pas pay pus pya sap say spa spy sup yap yup as ay pa up us

apsw paws swap waps wasp asp pas paw sap saw spa wap was as aw pa

apswy waspy yawps paws pays pyas spay swap sway waps wasp ways yaps yawp yaws asp pas paw pay pya sap saw say spa spy wap was way yap yaw as aw ay pa

apsy pays pyas spay yaps asp pas pay pya sap say spa spy yap as ay pa

apsz spaz zaps asp pas sap spa zap as pa

apt apt pat tap at pa ta

aptty patty apt pat pay pya tap tat yap at ay pa ta

apuy yaup pay pya yap yup ay pa up

apw paw wap pa aw

apwy yawp paw pay pya wap way yap yaw aw ay pa

apx pax pa ax

apy pay pya yap pa ay

apz zap pa

---

aq

aqrruy quarry quay qua ray yar ay

aqrstu quarts quart squat sutra arts qats rats rust ruts star sura tars tsar art qat qua rat rut sat tar tau as at ta us ut

aqrtu quart art qat qua rat rut tar tau at ta ut

aqrtuz quartz quart tzar art qat qua rat rut tar tau at ta ut

aqsstu squats quass squat qats tass ass qat qua sat tau as at ta us ut

aqssu quass qua ass as us

aqssuw squaws quass squaw saws ass qua saw was as aw us

aqst qats qat sat as at ta

aqsttuy squatty. *See* **aqsuy aqstu astty**

aqstu squat qats qat qua sat tau as at ta us ut

aqsuw squaw qua saw was as aw us

aqsuy quays quay qua say as ay us

aqt qat at ta

aqu qua

aquy quay qua ay

---

ar

arrsty starry artsy satyr stray tarry trays arts arty rats rays star stay tars tray tsar art rat ray sat say sty tar try yar as at ay ta

arrty tarry arty tray art rat ray tar try yar at ay ta

arssst strass stars trass tsars arts rats sass star tars tass tsar art ass rat sat tar as at ta

arsst stars trass tsars arts rats star tars tass tsar art ass rat sat tar as at ta

arsstt starts stars start tarts trass tsars arts rats star tars tart tass tats tsar art ass rat sat tar tat as at ta

arssttu stratus. *See* **arsstt assttu rssttu arsstu**

arsstu sutras tarsus rusts stars suras sutra trass truss tsars arts rats rust ruts star sura tars tass tsar art ass rat rut sat tar tau as at ta us ut

arsstw straws stars straw swart swats trass tsars warts arts rats saws star swat tars tass tsar wars wart wast art ass rat raw sat saw tar war was as at aw ta

arssty satyrs strays artsy satyr stars stays stray trass trays tsars arts arty rats rays says star stay tars tass tray tsar art ass rat ray sat say sty tar try yar as at ay ta

arssu suras sura ass as us

arst arts rats star tars tsar art rat sat tar as at ta

arstt start tarts arts rats star tars tart tats tsar art rat sat tar tat as at ta

arstu sutra arts rats rust ruts star sura tars tsar art rat rut sat tar tau as at ta us ut

arstux surtax sutra arts rats rust ruts star sura tars tsar art rat rut sat sax tar tau tax tux as at ax ta us ut

arstw straw swart warts arts rats star swat tsar wars wart wast art rat raw sat saw tar war was as at aw ta

arstwy strawy artsy satyr straw stray swart trays warts warty arts arty awry rats rays star stay swat sway tars tray tsar wars wart wary wast ways yaws art rat raw ray sat saw say sty tar try war was way yar yaw as at aw ay ta

arsty artsy satyr stray trays arts arty rats rays star stay tars tray tsar art rat ray sat say sty tar try yar as at ay ta

arsu sura as us

arsuv varus sura as us

arsuy saury sura rays ray say yar as ay us

arsw wars raw saw war was as aw

arsy rays ray say yar as ay

art art rat tar at ta

artt tart art rat tar tat at ta

artty ratty arty tart tray art rat ray tar tat try yar at ay ta

artw wart art rat raw tar war at aw ta

artwy warty arty awry tray wart wary art rat raw ray tar try war way yar yaw at aw ay ta

arty arty tray art rat ray tar try yar at ay ta

artz tzar art rat tar at ta

arvy vary ray yar ay

arw raw war aw

arwy awry wary raw ray war way yar yaw aw ay

ary ray yar ay

arzz razz

as

as   as

ass   ass as

asss   sass ass as

asssy   sassy sass says ass say as ay

asst   tass ass sat as at ta

assttu   status tass tats taut tuts ass sat tat tau tut as at ta us ut

asstw   swats saws swat tass wast ass sat saw was as at aw ta

assty   stays says stay tass ass sat say sty as at ay ta

assw   saws ass saw was as aw

asswy   sways saws says sway ways yaws ass saw say was way yaw as aw ay

assy   says ass say as ay

ast   sat as at ta

astt   tats sat tat as at ta

asttw   watts swat tats wast watt sat saw tat was as at aw ta

astty   tasty tats stay sat say sty tat as at ay ta

astv   tavs vast vats sat tav vat as at ta

astw   swat wast sat saw was as at aw ta

asty   stay sat say sty as at ay ta

asvvy   savvy say as ay

asw   saw was as aw

aswy   sway ways yaws saw say was way yaw as aw ay

asx   sax as ax

asy   say as ay

at—ay

at   at ta

att   tat at ta

attty   tatty tat at ay ta

attu   taut tat tau tut at ta ut

attw   watt tat at aw ta

atu   tau at ta ut

atv   tav vat at ta

atx   tax at ax ta

avwy   wavy way yaw aw ay

aw   aw

awx   wax aw ax

awxy   waxy wax way yaw aw ax ay

awy   way yaw aw ay

ax   ax

axz   zax ax

ay   ay

ayy   yay ay

bb

bbbceowy cobwebby. *See* **bbceow**

bbbdei bibbed bibb bide bed bib bid die ebb be id

bbbdelo blobbed bobbled. *See* **bbbdeo bbbelo bbdelo**

bbbdelu bubbled. *See* **bbbelu bbdelu**

bbbdeo bobbed bode bed bob doe ebb ode be do od

bbbeilru bubblier blubber bubbler. *See* **bbbeir bbbelu bbeilr bbelru**

bbbeios bobbies. *See* **bbbis**

bbbeir bibber bribe bibb bier brie bib ebb ire rib be er re

bbbelo bobble bleb blob bole lobe bel bob ebb lob be el lo

bbbelos bobbles. *See* **bbbelo bbels bblos**

bbbelrsu blubbers bubblers blubber bubbler bubbles burbles lubbers rubbles. *See* **bbbelu bbelru bblrsu belrsu**

bbbelru blubber bubbler. *See* **bbbelu bbelru**

bbbelsu bubbles. *See* **bbbelu bbels belsu**

bbbelu bubble bleb blue bulb lube bel bub ebb leu be el

bbbely blebby bleb bel bey bye ebb lye be by el ye

bbbeor bobber bore robe bob ebb orb ore rob roe be er or re

bbbeors bobbers. *See* **bbbeor beors**

bbbgiin bibbing. *No 6s or 5s*

bbbgilno blobbing bobbling bobbing lobbing. *See* **bbbino bbgino bgilno**

bbbgilnu bubbling. *See* **bgilnu**

bbbgino bobbing. *See* **bbbino bbgino**

bbbhuu hubbub bub hub

bbbi bibb bib

bbbino bobbin bibb bib bin bob ion nib nob obi in no on

bbbinos bobbins. *See* **bbbino bbbis binos**

bbbis bibbs bibb bibs bib sib is si

bbbluy bubbly bulb bub buy by

bbboy bobby bob boy yob by oy

bbcciko bibcock. *See* **bccio**

bbccikos bibcocks bibcock. *See* **bccio ccios cckos**

bbcdeir cribbed. *See* **bbdeir**

bbcdelo cobbled. *See* **bbcelo bbdelo**

bbcdelu clubbed. *See* **bbdelu cdelu bcdeu**

bbcdersu scrubbed. *See* **bbderu bbdesu bcderu cdersu**

bbcehiru chubbier. *See* **bcehru**

bbceilrs scribble libbers. *See* **bbeilr bbeirs bceirs ceilrs**

bbceisu cubbies. *See* **bcesu**

bbcekko kebbock. *See* **bbeko**

bbcekku kebbuck. *No 6s or 5s*

bbcelo cobble coble bleb blob bloc bole cole lobe bel bob cob col ebb lob be el lo

bbcelor clobber cobbler. *See* **bbcelo bcelor**

bbcelors clobbers cobblers clobber cobbler cobbles corbels slobber. *See* **bbcelo bcelor bcelos belors**

bbcelos cobbles. *See* **bbcelo bcelos**

bbceosw cobwebs. *See* **bbceow**

bbceow cobweb bob bow cob cow ebb owe web woe be ow we

bbcerrsu scrubber rubbers. *See* **bberru cerrsu**

bbcgiinr cribbing bribing ribbing. *See* **cgiinr**

bbcgilno cobbling lobbing. *See* **bbgino bgilno**

bbcgilnu clubbing bulbing. *See* **bgilnu cgilnu bcginu**

bbchuy chubby cubby hubby chub bub buy cub hub by

bbcinou bubonic. *See* **bcnou**

bbcluy clubby cubby bulb club bub buy cub by

bbcrsuy scrubby. *See* **bbsuy bbcuy bcrsu**

bbcuy cubby bub buy cub by

bbddeemo demobbed. *See* **bbdemo**

bbddeil dibbled. *See* **bbdeil bddei ddeil**

bbddeilr dribbled bridled dibbled dribble. *See* **bbdeil bbdeir bbeilr bddeir**

bbdderu drubbed. *See* **bbddeu bdderu bbderu**

bbddeu dubbed dude bed bub bud dub dud due ebb be

bbdee ebbed bed bee ebb be

bbdeegir gibbered. *See* **bbdegi bbdeir bbegir bdegir**

bbdeegit gibbeted. *See* **bbdegi bbegit bdeeit**

bbdeelp pebbled. *See* **bbeelp bdeel bbdee**

bbdeemnu benumbed. *See* **bbemnu bdemnu**

bbdeew webbed ebbed weed bed bee dew ebb ewe web wed wee be we

bbdefi fibbed bide bed bib bid die ebb fed fib fid fie be id if

bbdefilr fribbled dribble fribble. *See* **bbdefi bbdeil bbdeir bbefir**

bbdeflu flubbed. *See* **bbdelu**

bbdefo fobbed bode bed bob doe ebb fed fob foe ode be do od of

bbdegi gibbed gibed bide gibe gied bed beg bib bid big die dig ebb gib gid gie be id

bbdeglo gobbled. *See* **bdeglo bbeglo bbdelo**

bbdegru grubbed. *See* **bbdegu bbderu**

bbdegsu bedbugs. *See* **bbdegu bdegsu bbdesu**

bbdegu bedbug budge debug bed beg bub bud bug dub due dug ebb be

bbdehlo hobbled. *See* **bdehlo bbehlo bbdelo**

bbdehort throbbed. *See* **behort bdeort bbdeor bdehot**

bbdeij jibbed jibed bide jibe bed bib bid die ebb jib be id

bbdeikl kibbled. *See* **bdeikl bbdeil bbeikl**

bbdeil dibble bield bide bile bleb bled deil deli idle lied bed bel bib bid die ebb eld led lei lid lie be el id li

bbdeiln nibbled. *See* **bdeiln bbdein bbeiln**

bbdeilo lobbied. *See* **bdeilo bbdeil bbdelo**

bbdeilqu quibbled quibble. *See* **bbdeil bbdelu**

bbdeilr dribble. *See* **bdeilr bbdeir bbdeil bbeilr**

bbdeilrs dribbles bridles dibbles dribble libbers. *See* **bbdeil bbdeir bbeilr bbeirs**

bbdeilru bluebird builder burbled dribble rebuild. *See* **bbdeil bbdeir bbdelu bbderu**

bbdeils dibbles. *See* **bbdeil bdeils**

bbdein nibbed bend bide bind bine dine nide bed ben bib bid bin den die din ebb end neb nib be en id in ne

bbdeinor ribboned nobbier. *See* **bbdein bbdeir bbdeno bbdeor**

bbdeiqsu squibbed. *See* **bbdesu bdeisu beiqsu**

bbdeir bribed ribbed bribe bride bide bier bird bred brie dire drib ride bed bib bid die ebb ire red rib rid be er id re

bbdejo jobbed bode bed bob doe ebb job joe ode be do jo od

bbdekno knobbed. *See* **bdekno**

bbdellmu dumbbell bumbled. *See* **bbdelu bbelmu bdellu dellmu**

bbdelmu bumbled. *See* **bbdelu bbelmu**

bbdelno nobbled. *See* **bdelno bbdelo bbelno**

bbdelo lobbed lobed bleb bled blob bode bold bole dole lobe lode bed bel bob doe ebb eld led lob ode old be do el lo od

bbdelos bobsled. *See* **bbdelo bbdeos**

bbdeloss bobsleds bobsled. *See* **bbdelo bbdeos bdeoss**

bbdelow wobbled. *See* **bdelow bbdelo bbelow**

bbdelru burbled. *See* **bbdelu bbelru bdelru bbderu**

bbdelsu slubbed. *See* **bbdelu bbdesu**

bbdelu bulbed blued bleb bled blue bulb duel lube bed bel bub bud dub due ebb eld led leu be el

bbdemo bombed mobbed demob bode bomb demo dome mode bed bob doe ebb mob mod ode be do em me mo od om

bbdensu snubbed. *See* **bbdesu**

bbdeor dobber robbed bored orbed robed bode bore bred doer redo robe rode bed bob doe dor ebb ode orb ore red rob rod roe be do er od or re

bbdeors dobbers. *See* **bbdeor bbdeos**

bbdeos sobbed bodes beds bobs bode does dose ebbs odes bed bob doe dos ebb ode sob sod be do od os so

bbderu rubbed bred drub rube rude rued bed bub bud dub due ebb red rub rue urd be er re

bbdessu subdebs. *See* **bdessu bbdesu**

bbdestu stubbed. *See* **bdestu**

bbdesu subbed subdeb bused beds bubs buds dubs dues ebbs sued used bed bub bud bus dub due ebb sub sue use be us

bbdgiiln dibbling. *See* **bdgiin dgiiln**

bbdginru drubbing dubbing rubbing. *See* **bbdinu dginru**

bbdginu dubbing. *See* **bbdinu**

bbdiksu dibbuks. *See* **bbdiku**

bbdiku dibbuk bib bid bub bud dub kid id

bbdino dobbin bind bond bib bid bin bob din don ion nib nob nod obi do id in no od on

bbdinos dobbins. *See* **bbdino bdins binos**

bbdinu dubbin bind bib bid bin bub bud bun din dub dun nib nub id in nu

bbdosuyy busybody. *See* **bbosuy**

bbe ebb be

bbeeiirr beriberi. *See* **bbeirr**

bbeeirw webbier. *See* **bbeir**

bbeeistw webbiest. *See* **beest beist eestw**

bbeelllu bluebell. *See* **beell**

bbeelp pebble bleep plebe beep bleb peel bee bel ebb eel lee pee be el pe

bbeelps pebbles. *See* **beelps bbeelp**

bbefilr fribble. *See* **bbefir bbeilr**

bbefilrs fribbles fibbers fribble libbers. *See* **bbefir bbeilr bbeirs befirs**

bbefimor firebomb. *See* **bbefir bbemor bfimor**

bbefir fibber bribe brief fiber bier brie fire rife bib ebb fib fie fir ire ref rib rif be er if re

bbefirs fibbers. *See* **bbeirs befirs bbefir**

bbegilnp pebbling. *See* **bbegin bbeiln**

bbegilr glibber gribble. *See* **begilr bbegir bbeilr**

bbegilrs gribbles gerbils gibbers glibber gribble libbers. *See* **bbegir bbeilr bbeirs begilr**

bbegilst glibbest gibbets giblets. *See* **bbegit begils begilt egilst**

bbegin ebbing begin being binge gibe bine beg ben bib big bin ebb gib gie gin neb nib be en in ne

bbeginw webbing. *See* **bbegin**

bbegir gibber bribe berg bier brie brig gibe beg bib big ebb erg gib gie ire reg rib rig be er re

bbegirru grubbier. *See* **bbegir bbeirr bberru begrru**

bbegirs gibbers. *See* **bbegir bbeirs**

bbegist gibbets. *See* **bbegit begis beist**

bbegit gibbet gibe bite beg bet bib big bit ebb get gib gie tie be it ti

bbeglo gobble globe bleb blob bole glob lobe loge ogle beg bel bob bog ebb ego gel gob leg lob log be el go lo

bbeglor gobbler. *See* **bbeglo eglor belor**

bbeglors gobblers gobbler gobbles slobber. *See* **bbeglo beglos belors eglors**

bbeglos gobbles. *See* **bbeglo beglos**

bbegost gobbets. *See* **bbegot beost**

bbegot gobbet begot beg bet bob bog bot ebb ego get gob got toe tog be go to

bbehik kibbeh bike hike kibe bib ebb hie be eh he hi

bbehins nebbish. *See* **beins ehins**

bbehios hobbies. *No 6s or 5s*

bbehiotw bobwhite howbeit. *See* **beiow ehitw**

bbehisu hubbies. *No 6s or 5s*

bbehlo hobble bleb blob bole hole lobe bel bob ebb hob hoe lob be eh el he ho lo oh

bbehlor hobbler. *See* **bbehlo belor**

bbehlors hobblers hobbler hobbles slobber. *See* **bbehlo belors**

bbehlos hobbles. *See* **bbehlo bbels bblos**

bbeiim imbibe ebb bib be em me mi

bbeiimr imbiber. *See* **bbeiim bbeir**

bbeiimrs imbibers imbiber imbibes. *See* **bbeiim bbeirs**

bbeiims imbibes. *See* **bbeiim**

bbeijr jibber bribe jiber bier brie jibe bib ebb ire jib rib be er re

bbeijrs jibbers. *See* **bbeirs bbeijr beijrs**

bbeikl kibble bike bile bilk bleb kibe like bel bib ebb elk ilk lei lek lie be el li

bbeikls kibbles. *See* **bbeikl beiks beils**

bbeiknor knobbier nobbier. *See* **bbinor beinor beknor**

bbeiln nibble bile bine bleb lien line bel ben bib bin ebb lei lie neb nib nil be el en in li ne

bbeilnr nibbler. *See* **beilnr bbeilr bbeiln**

bbeilnrs nibblers berlins libbers nibbler nibbles. *See* **bbeiln bbeilr bbeirs beilnr**

bbeilnru nubblier nibbler nubbier. *See* **bbeiln bbeilr bbelnu bbelru**

bbeilns nibbles. *See* **bbeiln beils beins**

bbeilos bilboes lobbies. *See* **beilos bbilo bbels**

bbeilost bibelots bibelot bilboes lobbies. *See* **beilos eilost**

bbeilot bibelot. *See* **bbilo eilot**

bbeilqru quibbler quibble. *See* **bbelru bbeilr**

bbeilqsu quibbles quibble. *See* **beiqsu**

bbeilqu quibble. *No 6s or 5s*

bbeilr libber bribe bier bile birl bleb brie lire riel rile bel bib ebb ire lei lie rib be el er li re

bbeilrry bilberry bribery. *See* **bbeirr beirry bbeilr**

bbeilrs libbers. *See* **bbeilr bbeirs**

bbeinor nobbier. *See* **bbinor beinor**

bbeinost nobbiest boniest. *See* **beost beins binos**

bbeinru nubbier. *See* **bbeir beinr binru**

bbeinstu nubbiest. *See* **einstu**

bbeioos boobies. *See* **bboos beoos**

bbeir bribe bier brie bib ebb ire rib be er re

bbeirr briber bribe brier bier birr brie bib ebb err ire rib be er re

bbeirrs bribers. *See* **bbeirr bbeirs beirrs**

bbeirry bribery. *See* **bbeirr beirry**

bbeirs bribes bribe biers bibs bier bise brie ebbs reis ribs rise sire bib ebb ire res rib sib sir be er is re si

bbeirstu stubbier tubbier. *See* **bbeirs beirst beirsu berstu**

bbeirtu tubbier. *See* **beirt bbeir birtu**

bbeissu busbies. *See* **beiss bessu eissu**

bbeisttu tubbiest. *See* **beist bistt bsttu**

bbejor jobber bore robe bob ebb job joe orb ore rob roe be er jo or re

bbejors jobbers. *See* **bbejor beors**

bbejory jobbery. *See* **bbejor**

bbeko kebob bob ebb kob oke be

bbekos kebobs kebob bobs bosk ebbs kobs okes soke bob ebb kob kos oke sob be os so

bbel bleb ebb bel be el

bbellosy bellboys bellboy. *See* **ellosy**

bbelloy bellboy. *See* **bbloy belly**

bbelmrsu bumblers bumbler bumbles burbles lubbers lumbers rubbles rumbles slumber. *See* **bbelmu bbelru bblrsu belmru**

bbelmru bumbler. *See* **bbelmu bbelru belmru**

bbelmsu bumbles. *See* **bbelmu belmsu**

bbelmu bumble umbel bleb blue bulb lube mule bel bub bum ebb elm emu leu lum mel be el em me mu um

bbelno nobble noble bleb blob bole bone ebon enol leno lobe lone noel bel ben bob ebb eon lob neb nob one be el en lo ne no on

bbelnor nobbler. *See* **bbelno benor elnor**

bbelnors nobblers nobbler nobbles slobber. *See* **bbelno belnos belors benors**

bbelnos nobbles. *See* **bbelno belnos**

bbelnsu nubbles. *See* **bbelnu bbels belsu**

bbelnu nubble bleb blue bulb lube lune bel ben bub bun ebb leu neb nub be el en ne nu

bbelors slobber. *See* **belors bbels bblos**

bbelorss slobbers slobber. *See* **belors beorss elorss**

bbelorsw wobblers blowers bowlers slobber wobbler wobbles. *See* **bbelow belors belorw belosw**

bbelorsy slobbery slobber soberly. *See* **belors belrsy elorsy**

bbelorw wobbler. *See* **belorw**

bbelorw wobbler. *See* **belorw bbelow**

bbelosw wobbles. *See* **belosw**

bbelow wobble below bowel elbow bleb blew blob blow bole bowl lobe bel bob bow ebb lob low owe owl web woe be el lo ow we

bbelpy pebbly bleb yelp bel bey bye ebb lye ply yep pe by el pe ye

bbelrsu burbles lubbers rubbles. *See* **bblrsu bbelru belrsu**

bbelru burble lubber rubble bluer blurb ruble bleb blue blur bulb burl lube lure rube rule bel bub ebb leu rub rue be el er re

bbels blebs bels bleb ebbs bel ebb els be el

bbelsstu stubbles bustles stubble sublets. *See* **belstu besstu elsstu**

bbelstu stubble. *See* **belstu**

bbemnsu benumbs. *See* **bbemnu bemnsu**

bbemnu benumb numb menu ben bub bum bun ebb emu men neb nub be em en me mu ne nu um

bbemor bomber omber ombre berm bomb bore more omer robe bob ebb mob mor orb ore rem rob roe be em er me mo om or re

bbemors bombers. *See* **bbemor bemors**

bbenorsy snobbery. *See* **bbnosy benors**

bbenrssu snubbers snubber. *See* **berssu enrssu**

bbenrsu snubber. *See* **bnrsu bersu enrsu**

---

bbeop bebop bob bop ebb ope be pe

bbeops bebops bebop bobs bops ebbs epos opes peso pose bob bop ebb ope sob sop be os pe so

bbeorr robber borer bore robe bob ebb err orb ore rob roe be er or re

bbeorrs robbers. *See* **beorrs bbeorr**

bbeorrxy boxberry robbery. *See* **bbeorr**

bbeorry robbery. *See* **bbeorr berry**

bbeosu buboes bouse bobs bubo bubs ebbs bob bub bus ebb sob sou sub sue use be os so us

bberrsu rubbers. *See* **bberru brrsu bersu**

bberru rubber rube burr bub ebb err rub rue be er re

bberruy rubbery. *See* **bberru berry beruy**

bbes ebbs ebb be

bbewy webby bey bye ebb web wye yew be by we ye

bbfgiin fibbing. *No 6s or 5s*

bbfgilnu flubbing. *See* **bgilnu fgilnu**

bbfgino fobbing. *See* **bbgino**

bbggiin gibbing. *See* **bggiin**

bbggilno gobbling lobbing globing. *See* **bbgino bgilno ggilno**

bbgginru grubbing rubbing. *See* **gginru**

bbghilno hobbling lobbing. *See* **bbgino bgilno ghilno**

bbgiiimn imbibing. *See* **biimn**

bbgiijn jibbing. *See* **bgiijn**

bbgiikln kibbling bilking. *See* **bgiikn giikln**

bbgiilnn nibbling nibbing. *See* **giilnn**

bbgiinn nibbing. *No 6s or 5s*

bbgiinr bribing ribbing. *See* **bginr**

bbgijno jobbing. *See* **bbgino gijno**

bbgiknno knobbing bonking. *See* **bbgino bginno**

bbgilmnu bumbling. *See* **bgilnu**

bbgilnno nobbling lobbing. *See* **bbgino bgilno bginno**

bbgilno lobbing. *See* **bbgino bgilno**

bbgilnow wobbling blowing bowling lobbing. *See* **bbgino bgilno bginow gilnow**

bbgilnoy lobbying ignobly lobbing nobbily. *See* **bbgino bgilno**

bbgilnru burbling burling rubbing. *See* **bgilnu gilnru**

bbgilnsu slubbing subbing. *See* **bgilnu bginsu gilnsu**

bbgimno bombing mobbing. *See* **bbgino bbimo**

bbgimnos bombings bombing gibbons mobbing sobbing. *See* **bbgino bginos**

bbginnsu snubbing subbing nubbins. *See* **bbinnu bginsu**

bbgino gibbon bingo bong bib big bin bob bog gib gin gob ion nib nob nog obi go in no on

---

bbginor robbing. *See* **bginor bbgino bbinor**

bbginos gibbons sobbing. *See* **bbgino bginos**

bbginru rubbing. *See* **bginr binru ginru**

bbginstu stubbing subbing. *See* **bginsu bgintu**

bbginsu subbing. *See* **bginsu**

bbgiosu gibbous. *See* **bgosu**

bbgruy grubby rugby burg bury grub ruby bub bug buy guy rub rug by

bbhinoss snobbish. *See* **binos hinss bnoss**

bbhiosty hobbyist. *See* **bhiosy**

bbhirsu rubbish. *See* **bhirsu**

bbhluy hubbly hubby bulb buhl bub buy hub by

bbhnoo hobnob boob boon hobo bob boo hob hon nob oho ooh ho no oh on

bbhnoos hobnobs. *See* **bbhnoo bboos bnoos**

bbhoy hobby bob boy hob hoy yob by ho oh oy

bbhrsuy shrubby. *See* **bhrsuy bbsuy bbhuy**

bbhuy hubby bub buy hub by

bbi bib

bbiiklnoo bobolink. *See* **bbilo bikln biloo**

bbiktuz kibbutz. *No 6s or 5s*

bbillsu bulbils. *See* **bbillu bills bblsu**

bbillu bulbil bill bulb bull bib bub ill li

bbilnoy nobbily. *See* **bbilo bbloy bbnoy**

bbilo bilbo blob boil bib bob lob obi oil li lo

bbilosty lobbyist. *See* **bbilo bblos blost**

bbilosuu bibulous bulbous. *See* **bbilo bblos bilos**

bbimnoss snobbism. *See* **bbimo binos bbmos**

bbimo bimbo bomb bib bob mob obi mi mo om

bbinnsu nubbins. *See* **bbinnu**

bbinnu nubbin bib bin bub bun inn nib nub nun in nu

bbinor ribbon robin born iron bib bin bob ion nib nob nor obi orb rib rob in no on or

bbinors ribbons. *See* **bbinor binors**

bbis bibs bib sib is si

bbknoy knobby nobby bonk bony knob bob boy kob nob yob yon by no on oy

bblluu bulbul bulb bull lulu bub ulu

bblnuy nubbly nubby bulb bub bun buy nub by nu

bblo blob bob lob lo

bblos blobs blob bobs lobs slob bob lob los sob sol lo os so

bblosuu bulbous. *See* **bblos blosu bblsu**

bblowy wobbly lobby blowy blob blow bowl yowl bob bow boy lob low owl yob yow by lo ow oy

bbloy   lobby blob bob boy lob yob by lo oy

bblrsu   blurbs blurb blurs bulbs burls slurb blur bubs bulb burl rubs slub slur bub bus rub sub us

bblru   blurb blur bulb burl bub rub

bblruy   rubbly blurb burly blur bulb burl bury ruby bub buy rub by

bblsu   bulbs bubs bulb slub bub bus sub us

bblu   bulb bub

bbmo   bomb bob mob mo om

bbmooox   boombox. *No 6s or 5s*

bbmos   bombs bobs bomb mobs bob mob mos oms sob mo om os so

bbnnoo   bonbon boob boon noon bob boo nob no on

bbnnoos   bonbons. *See* **bbnnoo bboos bnoos**

bbnoorsu   bourbons bourbon. *See* **bnoors bnorsu**

bbnooru   bourbon. *See* **bnoor bnoru**

bbnorstu   stubborn burbots burtons. *See* **bbortu bnorsu bnortu bnrstu**

bbnosy   snobby nobby bobs bony boys nobs nosy snob yobs bob boy nob sny sob son soy yob yon by no on os oy so

bbnoy   nobby bony bob boy nob yob yon by no on oy

bbnsuy   snubby nubby busby bubs buns busy buys nubs snub bub bun bus buy nub sub sun by nu us

bbnuy   nubby bub bun buy nub by nu

bbo   bob

bboo   boob bob boo

bboos   boobs bobs boob boos bob boo sob os so

bboosy   yobbos boobs booby yobbo bobs boob boos boyo boys yobs bob boo boy sob soy yob by os oy so

bbooy   booby yobbo boob boyo bob boo boy yob by oy

bborstu   burbots. *See* **bbortu borstu**

bbortu   burbot bort bout bubo rout tour bob bot bub but orb ort our out rob rot rub rut tor tub or to ut

bbos   bobs bob sob os so

bbossuy   busboys. *See* **bbosuy bossy**

bbosuy   busboy busby buoys bobs boys bubo bubs buoy busy buys yobs bob boy bub bus buy sob sou soy sub yob you by os oy so us

bbou   bubo bob bub

bbrssuu   suburbs. *See* **bbrsuu**

bbrsuu   suburb bubs rubs urus bub bus rub sub us

bbstuy   stubby busby busty tubby bubs bust busy buts buys stub tubs bub bus but buy sty sub tub by us ut

bbsu   bubs bub bus sub us

bbsuy   busby bubs busy buys bub bus buy sub by us

bbtuy   tubby bub but buy tub by ut

bbu   bub

bccdeily   bicycled bicycle. *See* **ccdely cceily**

bccehiru   cherubic. *See* **bcehru**

bcceilo   ecbolic. *See* **bcceio bcelo ccilo**

bcceilru   crucible cubicle. *See* **cceilr**

bcceilry   bicycler bicycle. *See* **cceilr cceily**

bcceilsu   cubicles cubicle. *See* **bccisu ceilsu**

bcceilsy   bicycles bicycle cylices. *See* **cceily ccelsy**

bcceilu   cubicle. *See* **bcciu**

bcceily   bicycle. *See* **cceily**

bcceio   boccie bocci cob ice obi be

bccemruu   cucumber. *See* **bcemru**

bcciimor   microbic. *See* **bcimor**

bcciloor   broccoli bicolor. *See* **bccio bcior bilor**

bccilosu   bucolics bucolic. *See* **bccisu**

bccilou   bucolic. *See* **bccio ccilo bcciu**

bccinoo   obconic. *See* **bccio ccino**

bccinorr   corncrib. *See* **bccio bcior ccino**

bccio   bocci cob obi

bccirtuu   cucurbit. *See* **birtu bcciu bcitu**

bccisu   cubics cubic cubs bus cub sib sic sub is si us

bccisuu   succubi. *See* **bccisu**

bcciu   cubic cub

bccmoosx   coxcombs coxcomb. *See* **bcmoos**

bccmoox   coxcomb. *See* **bcmoo**

bccmssuu   succumbs succumb. *See* **cmssu cmsuu**

bccmsuu   succumb. *See* **cmsuu**

bccnoor   corncob. *See* **bcnoor**

bccnoors   corncobs corncob broncos. *See* **bcnoor bnoors cnoors**

bcddeeek   bedecked. *See* **bcdeek cddeek**

bcddehil   childbed. *See* **cddehi cdehil**

bcddesuu   subduced subduce subdued. *See* **bdesuu**

bcdeeehr   breeched cheered. *See* **bceehr bdeehr cdeeer**

bcdeehl   belched. *See* **bdeehl cdeehl**

bcdeehn   benched. *See* **bceeh bcehn ceehn**

bcdeeikr   bickered bricked. *See* **bcdeek bceikr cdeekr cdeikr**

bcdeeil   decibel. *See* **bdeeil cdeeil**

bcdeeilr   credible decibel. *See* **bdeeil bdeilr cdeeil deeilr**

bcdeeils   decibels decibel deciles edibles. *See* **bdeeil bdeeis bdeels bdeils**

bcdeeilu   educible decibel. *See* **bdeeil cdeeil**

bcdeeint   benedict enticed. *See* **bdeeit cdeeit cdeent ceeint**

bcdeeirs   describe decries derbies scribed. *See* **bceers bceirs bdeeis bdeers**

bcdeejot   objected. *See* **bcejot cdeejt**

bcdeek   bedeck beck cede deck eked bed bee cee eke be

bcdeekno   beckoned nocked.. *See* **bcekno bcdeek bdekno bdeeno**

bcdeeks   bedecks. *See* **bcdeek bceks cdees**

bcdeektu   bucketed. *See* **bcdeek bcdeku bceekt bcektu**

bcdeelor   corbeled. *See* **bcelor bdelor cdelor ceelor**

bcdeemru   cumbered crumbed embrued umbered. *See* **bcderu bcemru bdemru beemru**

bcdeeorv   bedcover covered. *See* **bdeor bdeer beerv**

bcdehit   bitched. *See* **cdehit bdeit bchit**

bcdehlot   blotched botched clothed. *See* **bchlot bdehlo bdehot bdelot**

bcdehnu   bunched. *See* **bcehn bchnu bcdeu**

bcdehot   botched. *See* **bdehot bchot**

bcdehou   debouch. *See* **cdehou bcdeu**

bcdeikr   bricked. *See* **bceikr cdeikr**

bcdeiks   sickbed. *See* **cdeiks bceks bdeis**

bcdeikss sickbeds sickbed. *See* cdeiks deikss

bcdeilm climbed. *See* bdeilm bcilm ceilm

bcdeimno combined combine demonic. *See* bcdeio bcdemo cdeimn cdeino

bcdeinou icebound bounced buncoed. *See* bcdeio bcdiou bcenou cdeino

bcdeio bodice bide bode code coed dice iced odic bed bid cob cod die doc doe ice obi ode be do id od

bcdeios bodices. *See* bcdeio bdeios

bcdeirs scribed. *See* bdeirs cdeirs bceirs

bcdeklo blocked. *See* cdeklo bcklo beklo

bcdeklu buckled. *See* bcdeku bceklu bdeklu cdeklu

bcdekor bedrock. *See* cdekor

bcdeku bucked cubed beck buck cube cued deck duck duke bed bud cub cud cue dub due be

bcdelmru crumbled crumbed crumble rumbled. *See* bcderu bcemru bdelru bdemru

bcdelosu beclouds becloud bloused boucles doubles. *See* bcelos bcelou bdelou belosu

bcdelou becloud. *See* bcelou bdelou

bcdemo combed combe demob bode code coed comb come demo dome mode mod bed cob cod doc doe mob mod ode be do em me mo od om

bcdemru crumbed. *See* bcemru bcderu bdemru

bcdenou bounced buncoed. *See* bcenou bdeno bdnou

bcdeorsu obscured coursed obscure rosebud scoured. *See* bcderu beorsu cdeors cdeosu

bcderu curbed crude cubed cured bred crud cube cued curb curd cure drub ecru rube rude rued bed bud cub cud cue cur dub due rec red rub rue urd be er re

bcdessuu subduces subduce subdues. *See* bdessu cdessu

bcdesuu subduce. *See* bdesuu bcdeu bcesu

bcdeu cubed cube cued bed bud cub cud cue dub due be

bcdiipsu bicuspid. *See* cdipsu

bcdikllu duckbill. *See* bdilu cdilu

bcdinruu rubicund. *See* binru cinru

bcdiorsw cowbirds cowbird. *See* cdorsw

bcdiorw cowbird. *See* bcior cdorw

bcdiosu cuboids. *See* bcdiou cdios cdisu

bcdiou cuboid odic bid bud cob cod cub cud doc dub duo obi oud udo do id od

bcdkorsu burdocks burdock. *See* bckors

bcdkoru burdock. *See* bckor bckou

bcdsstuu subducts subduct. *See* bsstu cdstu dsstu

bcdstuu subduct. *See* cdstu

bceeefin benefice benefic. *See* ceefn ceein

bceeehrs breeches beeches beseech. *See* bceehr bceers ceeehs ceehrs

bceeehs beeches beseech. *See* ceeehs bceeh

bceefin benefic. *See* ceefn ceein

bceefltu clubfeet. *See* beelt beltu ceflt

bceegir iceberg. *See* beegi beegr bceer

bceegirs icebergs iceberg. *See* bceers bceirs beegis beegrs

bceeh beech bee cee be eh he

bceehls belches. *See* ceehls bceeh bcehl

bceehnr bencher. *See* bceehr bcehn ceehn

bceehnrs benchers bencher benches. *See* bceehr bceers ceehrs ceenrs

bceehns benches. *See* bceeh ceens eehns

bceehntu beechnut. *See* ceehnt

bceehr breech beech cheer rebec beer bree cere herb here bee cee ere her rec be eh er he re

bceeiilm imbecile. *See* bciilm

bceeikrr bickerer. *See* bceikr

bceeinot cenobite ebonite. *See* ceeint ceenot ceinot

bceeiosx iceboxes. *See* bceesx bceiox beeisx ceeisx

bceekst beckets. *See* bceekt bceks beest

bceeksuy buckeyes buckeye. *See* bceks bcksu bcesu

bceekt becket beck beet keet bee bet cee eke tee be

bceekuy buckeye. *No 6s or 5s*

bceemnru encumber cerumen. *See* bcemru beemru bemnru

bceemo become combe comb come bee cee cob mob be em me mo om

bceemos becomes. *See* bceemo bcemos

bceemrru cerebrum. *See* bcemru beemru ceemrr

bceenos obscene. *See* benos ceens cenos

bceer rebec beer bree cere bee cee ere rec be er re

bceers rebecs beers brees rebec scree beer bees bree cees cere seer sere bee cee ere rec res see be er re

bceesx xebecs xebec bees cees exes bee cee see sex be ex

bceesz zebecs zebec bees cees zees bee cee see zee be

bceex xebec bee cee be ex

bceez zebec bee cee zee be

bceffiir febrific. *See* befir effir ceiir

bcefilor forcible corbeil. *See* bceior bcelor befilo beilor

bceghiln belching leching. *See* bcehln cehiln

bcegimno becoming combine combing. *See* ceimno cgimno

bcehimrs besmirch birches. *See* bceirs cehims cehirs ceimrs

bcehimru cherubim. *See* bcehru bcemru beimru ceimru

bcehinru bunchier. *See* bcehru bchnru cehinr chinru

bcehior brioche. *See* bcehor cehior bceior

bcehiors brioches birches brioche co-heirs corbies heroics. *See* bcehor bceior bceirs

bcehiort botchier brioche botcher. *See* bcehor bceior behort cehior

bcehirs birches. *See* bceirs cehirs

bcehirst britches birches bitches cithers richest. *See* bceirs bceist behrst beirst

bcehist bitches. *See* bceist cehist

bcehitw bewitch. *See* bchit cehit ceitw

bcehl belch lech bel be eh el he

bcehln blench belch bench lech bel ben hen neb be eh el en he ne

bcehlost blotches botches clothes. *See* bcelos bchlot cehlot celost

bcehlrsu bluchers blucher blusher cherubs lurches. *See* bcehru behlsu belrsu cehrsu

bcehlru blucher. *See* bcehru bcehl belru

bcehn bench ben hen neb be eh en he ne

bcehnrsu brunches bunches cherubs. *See* bcehru bchnru cehrsu chnrsu

bcehnsu bunches. *See* bcehn bchnu bchsu

bcehoors brooches. *See* bcehor bchoor behoos cehoos

bcehor broche chore ocher ochre bore cero core echo herb hero hoer robe cob cor her hob hoe orb orc ore rec rho rob roc roe be eh er he ho oh or re

bcehorru brochure. *See* bcehor bcehru

bcehorst botchers borscht botcher botches bothers hectors rochets rotches torches troches. *See* bcehor behort behrst beorst

bcehort botcher. *See* behort bcehor cehort

bcehost botches. *See* beost behst bchot

bcehrstu butchers cherubs butcher. *See* bcehru behrst berstu cehrst

bcehrsu cherubs. *See* bcehru cehrsu

bcehrtu butcher. *See* bcehru behrt bertu

bcehrtuy butchery butcher. *See* bcehru

bcehru cherub ruche chub cube curb cure ecru herb rube cub cue cur her hub hue rec rub rue be eh er he re

bceiilms miscible. *See* bceiis bciilm bcilms ceilms

bceiilnv vincible. *See* ciilv ceiln eilnv

bceiinrs inscribe scribe.. *See* **beinrs bceiis ceiins ceiinr**

bceiis ibices bise ibis ices ice sib sic be is si

bceiklor blockier blocker brickle corbeil. *See* **bceikr bceior bcelor beilor**

bceiklr brickle. *See* **bceikr ceklr eiklr**

bceikr bicker brick -beck bier bike brie crib kerb kibe kier reck rice rick ice ire irk kir rec rib be er re

bceikrs bickers. *See* **bceikr bcikrs bceirs ceikrs**

bceilmo embolic. *See* **beilmo**

bceilmr climber. *See* **beilmr bcilm ceilm**

bceilmrs climbers climber. *See* **bceirs bcilms beilmr ceilms**

bceilor corbeil. *See* **beilor bcelor bceior ceilor**

bceilors corbeils boilers corbeil corbels corbies recoils. *See* **bceior bceirs bcelor beilor**

bceilpru republic. *See* **bcilpu**

bceimno combine. *See* **ceimno bcemo**

bceimnor combiner bromine combine microbe. *See* **bceior bcemor bcimor beinor**

bceimnos combines combine incomes. *See* **bcemos ceimno ceimns ceinos**

bceimor microbe. *See* **bcimor bcemor**

bceimors microbes combers corbies microbe. *See* **bceior bceirs bcemor bcemos**

bceinoru bouncier bouncer. *See* **bceior bcenou beinor**

bceinoz benzoic. *See* **benoz cenoz beinz**

bceior corbie boric bier bore brie cero coir core crib rice robe cob cor ice ire obi orb orc ore rec rib rob roc roe be er or re

bceiors corbies. *See* **bceior ceiors bceirs**

bceiorst bisector corbies. *See* **bceior bceirs bceist**

bceiox icebox ibex box cob cox ice obi be ex ox xi

bceips biceps epics spice bise ceps epic ices pice pies cep ice pie sib sic sip be is pe pi si

bceirrs scriber. *See* **beirrs ceirrs**

bceirs scribe biers cribs cries rices bier bise brie crib ices reis ribs rice rise sire ice ire rec res rib sib sic sir be er is re si

bceirss scribes. *See* **bceirs ceirss**

bceirtty ytterbic. *See* **beirtt cirtty**

bceisst bisects. *See* **bceist besst beiss**

bceist bisect bites cites best bets bise bite bits cist cite ices sect site tics ties bet bit ice its set sib sic sit tic tie be is it si ti

bcejoort objector. *See* **bcejot**

bcejost objects. *See* **bcejot beost ceost**

bcejot object cote bet bot cob cot jet job joe jot toe be jo to

bcejsstu subjects subject. *See* **besstu cesstu**

bcejstu subject. *See* **bcesu ejstu cestu**

bcek beck be

bceklnuu unbuckle. *See* **bceklu**

bceklor blocker. *See* **bcelor ceklor**

bceklors blockers blocker corbels lockers. *See* **bcelor bcelos bcklos bckors**

bceklsu buckles. *See* **bceklu ceklsu**

bceklu buckle beck blue buck bulk club clue cube lube luce luck bel cub cue elk lek leu be el

bcekno beckon beck bone bonk coke cone conk ebon keno knob neck nock once ben cob con eon ken kob neb nob oke one be en ne no on

bceknos beckons. *See* **bcekno bceks benos**

bcekorsu roebucks buckers buckoes obscure roebuck. *See* **bcekru bckors bekrsu beorsu**

bcekru roebuck. *See* **bcekru bckor bekor**

bcekosu buckoes. *See* **bceks beosu bckou**

bcekrsu buckers. *See* **bcekru bekrsu cekrsu**

bcekru bucker burke beck buck cube curb cure ecru kerb reck rube ruck cub cue cur rec rub rue be er re

bceks becks beck be

bcekstu buckets. *See* **bcektu bceks bcksu**

bcektu bucket beck buck cube cute tube tuck bet but cub cue cut tub be ut

bcellosw cowbells cowbell bellows. *See* **bcelos bellow belosw cellos**

bcellow cowbell. *See* **bellow cello bcelo**

bcelmrsu crumbles crumble cumbers lumbers rumbles slumber. *See* **bcemru bcmrsu belmru belmsu**

bcelmru crumble. *See* **bcemru belmru**

bcelo coble bloc bole cole lobe bel cob col lob be el lo

bcelor corbel ceorl coble roble bloc bole bore cero cole core lobe lore orle robe role bel cob col cor lob orb orc ore rec rob roc roe be el er lo or re

bcelors corbels. *See* **celors bcelos bcelor belors**

bcelos cobles blocs boles close coble coles lobes socle bels bloc bole cobs cole cols lobe lobs lose slob sloe sole bel cob col els lob los sob sol be el lo os so**

bcelosu boucles. *See* **belosu bcelou bcelos celosu**

bcelou boucle coble boule bloc blue bole club clue cole cube lobe lube luce bel cob col cub cue leu lob be el lo

bcemo combe comb come cob mob be em me mo om

bcemor comber combe comer omber ombre berm bore cero comb come core corm more omer robe cob cor mob mor orb orc ore rec rem rob roc roe be em er me mo om or re

bcemors combers. *See* **bcemor bcemos cemors bemors**

bcemos combes besom combe combs comes cobs comb come mobs some cob mob mos oms sob be em me mo om os so

bcemrsu cumbers. *See* **bemrsu bcmrsu bcemru**

bcemru cumber brume crumb umber berm cube curb cure ecru rube bum cub cue cum cur emu rec rem rub rue rum be em er me mu re um

bcenorsu bouncers bouncer bounces obscure. *See* **bcenou bcnosu benors beorsu**

bcenoru bouncer. *See* **bcenou benor bnoru**

bcenosu bounces. *See* **bcenou bcnosu cenosu**

bcenou bounce bunco ounce bone cone cube ebon once unco ben bun cob con cub cue eon neb nob nub one be en ne no nu on

bceorssu obscures bourses courses obscure sources sucrose. *See* **bcrssu beorss beorsu beossu**

bceorsu obscure. *See* **beorsu ceorsu**

bceott obtect octet bott cote tote bet bot cob cot toe tot be to

bcesu cubes cube cubs cues bus cub cue sub sue use be us

bceu cube cub cue be

bcfiimor morbific. *See* **bcimor bfimor cfimor**

bcfilory forcibly. *See* **cfilor**

bcfimoru cubiform. *See* **bcimor bfimor cfimor cimoru**

bcflootu clubfoot. *See* **clotu flotu**

bcghiint bitching itching. *See* **bgiint cgiint chiint**

bcghinnu bunching. *See* **bcginu**

bcghinot botching. *See* **chinot**

bcgiiknr bricking. *See* **bgiikn cgiinr giiknr**

bcgiilmn climbing. *See* **bciilm giilmn**

bcgiinrs scribing. *See* **bginrs cgiinr cgiins ciinrs**

bcgiklno blocking locking. *See* **bgilno cgikno**

bcgiklnu buckling bucking bulking lucking. *See* **bcginu bgilnu cgilnu**

bcgiknu bucking. *See* **bcginu**

bcgimno combing. *See* **cgimno**

bcgimnru crumbing curbing. *See* **bcginu cginru**

bcginnou bouncing buncoing. *See* **bcginu bginno binnou cginno**

bcginru curbing. *See* **bcginu cginru**

bcginu cubing cuing bung big bin bug bun cub gib gin gnu gun nib nub in nu

bcgorsy cyborgs. *See* **bcgory gorsy**

bcgory cyborg bogy goby gory gyro orby orgy bog boy cob cog cor coy cry gob goy orb orc rob roc yob by go or oy

bchiissu hibiscus. *See* **bchsu hissu**

bchiklos blockish. *See* **bcklos bhikos**

bchimor rhombic. *See* **bcimor bchir chior**

bchioory choirboy. *See* **bchoor**

bchiopr pibroch. *See* **bchir bcior chipr**

bchir birch crib rich rib chi hi

bchit bitch chit itch bit chi hit tic hi it ti

bchity bitchy bitch itchy chit city itch bit chi hit icy thy tic by hi it ti

bchkostu buckshot. *See* **bchot bostu bckou**

bchlot blotch botch cloth bloc blot bolt both clot colt holt loch loth bot cob col cot hob hot lob lot tho ho lo oh to

bchloty blotchy. *See* **bchlot bchoty**

bchnorsu bronchus. *See* **bchnru bcnosu bnorsu chnrsu**

bchnru brunch bunch churn burn chub curb bun cub cur hub nub rub run urn nu

bchnu bunch chub bun cub hub nub nu

bchnuy bunchy bunch chub bun buy cub hub nub by nu

bchoor brooch hobo boor boo cob coo cor hob oho ooh orb orc rho rob roc ho oh or

bchorsst borschts borscht. *See* **bhorst horsst**

bchorst borscht. *See* **bhorst**

bchot botch both bot cob cot hob hot tho ho oh to

bchoty botchy botch both bot boy cob cot coy hob hot hoy tho thy toy yob by ho oh oy to

bchsu chubs bush chub cubs hubs such bus cub hub sub sh us

bchtu butch chub but cub cut hub hut tub ut

bchu chub cub hub

bciikln niblick. *See* **bikln cikln**

bciiklns niblicks niblick. *See* **biklns ciklns**

bciilm limbic climb limb mil li mi

bciilmu bulimic. *See* **bciilm ciilmu**

bciimoru ciborium. *See* **bcimor cimoru**

bciino bionic ionic cion coin icon bin cob con ion nib nob obi in no on

bciinos bionics. *See* **bciino binos cinos**

bciinu incubi bin bun cub nib nub in nu

bciiot biotic obit otic bit bot cob cot obi tic it ti to

bciisstu biscuits biscuit. *See* **bcistu**

bciistu biscuit. *See* **bcistu**

bcikknsu buckskin. *See* **biknsu**

bcikr brick crib rick irk kir rib

bcikrs bricks brick brisk cribs ricks crib irks kris ribs rick risk sick irk kir rib sib sic sir ski is si

bcillpuy publicly. *See* **bcilpu**

bcilm climb limb mil li mi

bcilmosy symbolic. *See* **bcilms bilmos blmosy**

bcilms climbs climb limbs limb mils slim mil mis sib sic is li mi si

bciloor bicolor. *See* **bcior bilor cloor**

bcilpsu publics. *See* **bcilpu cilpsu**

bcilpu public pubic picul blip clip club puli cub cup lip pub pul li pi up

bcimor bromic boric micro brim coir comb corm crib cob cor mir mob mor obi orb orc rib rim rob roc mi mo om or

bcimsu cubism music bums cubs scum bum bus cub cum mis mus sib sic sub sum is mi mu si um us

bcinossu subsonic cousins. *See* **bcnosu bnossu cinoss cinosu**

bcinsuu incubus. *See* **cinsu cnsuu**

bcioorst robotics octrois. *See* **bioost biorst boorst cioort**

bciopstu subtopic. *See* **bcistu biostu ciopst ciostu**

bcior boric crib coir cob cor obi orb orc rib rob roc or

bcipu pubic cub cup pub pi up

bcir crib rib

bcirrsu rubrics. *See* **bcirru cirrsu**

bcirru rubric birr burr crib curb uric cub cur rib rub

bcirs cribs crib ribs rib sib sic sir is si

bcistu bustic cubits cubit cutis ictus bits bust buts cist cubs cuts scut stub suit tics tubs tuis bit bus but cub cut its sib sic sit sub tic tub tui is it si ti us ut

bcitu cubit bit but cub cut tic tub tui it ti ut

bckllosu bullocks bullock. *See* **bcklos**

bckllou bullock. *See* **bcklo bckou**

bcklo block bloc lock cob col kob lob lo

bckloox lockbox. *See* **bcklo**

bcklos blocks block blocs locks bloc bosk cobs cols kobs lobs lock slob sock cob col kob kos lob los sob sol lo os so

bckloy blocky block bloc cloy lock yock yolk boy cob col coy kob lob yob by lo oy

bckooopy copybook. *See* **ckooy**

bckor brock cork rock cob cor kob kor orb orc rob roc or

bckors brocks brock corks rocks bosk cobs cork cors kobs orbs orcs robs rock rocs sock sorb cob cor kob kor kos orb orc rob roc sob or os so

bckosttu buttocks buttock. *See* **bostt bostu bckou**

bckottu buttock. *See* **bckou**

bckou bucko buck cob cub kob

bcksu bucks buck cubs cusk suck bus cub sub us

bcku buck cub

bclmo clomb bloc comb cob col lob mob lo mo om

bclmoosu coulombs coulomb. *See* **bcmoos blmoos bloosu**

bclmoou coulomb. *See* **blmoo bclmo bcmoo**

bclmruy crumbly. *See* **bcmruy blmruy**

bclo bloc cob col lob lo

bclos blocs bloc cobs cols lobs slob cob col lob los sob sol lo os so

bclsu clubs club cubs slub bus cub sub us

bclu club cub

bcmo comb cob mob mo om

bcmoo combo comb boom boo cob coo mob moo mo om

bcmoos combos booms bosom combo combs boom boos cobs comb coos mobs moos boo cob coo mob moo mos oms sob mo om os so

bcmorsuu cumbrous brumous. *See* **bcmrsu cmosuu**

bcmorsy corymbs. *See* **bcmory bcmos cmors**

bcmory corymb comb corm orby boy cob cor coy cry mob mor orb orc rob roc yob by mo my om or oy

bcmos combs cobs comb mobs cob mob mos oms sob mo om os so

bcmosstu combusts combust customs. *See* **cmostu cosstu**

bcmostu combust. *See* **cmostu bostu bcmos**

bcmrsu crumbs crumb curbs scrub scrum bums crus cubs curb curs rubs rums scum bum bus cub cum cur mus rub rum sub sum mu um us

bcmru crumb curb bum cub cum cur rub rum mu um

bcmruy crumby crumb bury curb ruby bum buy cry cub cum cur rub rum yum by mu my um

bcnoor bronco boron croon boon boor born coon corn boo cob con coo cor nob nor orb orc rob roc no on or

bcnoors broncos. *See* **bnoors bcnoor cnoors**

bcnostu cobnuts. *See* **bcnosu bcnotu cnostu**

bcnosu buncos bonus bosun bunco buns cobs cons cubs nobs nous nubs onus snob snub unco bun bus cob con cub nob nub sob son sou sub sun no nu on os so us

bcnotu cobnut bunco count bout bunt unco unto bot bun but cob con cot cub cut nob not nub nut out ton tub tun no nu on to ut

bcnou bunco unco bun cob con cub nob nub no nu on

bcnouy bouncy bunco bony buoy cony unco boy bun buy cob con coy cub nob nub yob yon you by no nu on oy

bco cob

bcoorssw crossbow. *See* **boors borsw corss**

bcoostty boycotts boycott. *See* **oostty**

bcooswy cowboys. *See* **bcoowy**

bcootty boycott. *See* **booty**

bcoowy cowboy boyo boo bow boy cob coo cow coy woo yob yow by ow oy

bcorsttu obstruct turbots. *See* **borstu borttu corstu orsttu**

bcos cobs cob sob os so

bcrssu scrubs curbs scrub buss crus cubs curb curs cuss rubs subs bus cub cur rub sub us

bcrsu curbs scrub crus cubs curb curs rubs bus cub cur rub sub us

bcru curb cub cur rub

bcsu cubs bus cub sub us

bcu cub

---

bd

bdddee bedded deed bed bee be

bdddeeem embedded. *See* **bdddee ddeeem**

bdddeeim imbedded. *See* **bdddee dddeei**

bdddeu budded dude bed bud dub dud due be

bddeees seedbed. *See* **ddeees**

bddeeess seedbeds seedbed. *See* **ddeees**

bddeeflu befuddle deedful. *See* **bddelu ddeefu ddeelu ddeflu**

bddeeggu debugged. *See* **bddegu bdeegg**

bddeegtu budgeted. *See* **bddegu bdegtu**

bddeeimm bedimmed. *See* **ddeimm**

bddeeimo embodied. *See* **bddeio**

bddeeint indebted betided debited. *See* **bddein bdeeit ddeein ddeeit**

bddeeirs birdseed bedside bidders derbies derides desired resided. *See* **bddeir bdeeis bdeers bdeirs**

bddeeis bedside. *See* **bdeeis ddeeis**

bddeeit betided debited. *See* **bdeeit ddeeit**

bddeeln blended. *See* **bdeeln ddeel ddeen**

bddeeno deboned. *See* **bddeno bdeeno**

bddeenru burdened endured. *See* **bdderu bdeenr bdenru ddeenr**

bddeeorr bordered ordered. *See* **bdeorr ddeeor ddeerr**

bddegin bedding. *See* **bddein ddegin**

bddegir bridged. *See* **bddeir bdegir ddegir**

bddegu budged budge debug dude bed beg bud bug dub dud due dug be

bddei bided bide died bed bid did die be id

bddeiir birdied. *See* **bddeir bdeiir**

bddeiis biddies. *See* **bddei bdeis ddeis**

bddeiln blinded. *See* **bddein bdeiln**

bddeilnr brindled blinded blinder bridled brindle. *See* **bddein bddeir bdeiln bdeilr**

bddeiloo bloodied blooded. *See* **bddeio bdeilo bdeloo**

bddeilr bridled. *See* **bddeir bdeilr ddeilr**

bddein bidden bided dined bend bide bind bine died dine nide bed ben bid bin den did die din end neb nib be en id in ne

bddeinnu unbidden undine.. *See* **bddein bdeinn ddeinn ddennu**

bddeinru underbid. *See* **bddein bddeir bdderu bdeinr**

bddeio bodied bided boded diode bide bode dido died bed bid did die doe obi odd ode be do id od

bddeiors disrobed bidders borides disrobe. *See* **bddeio bddeir bdeior bdeios**

bddeir bidder bidded bride dried redid bide bier bird bred brie died dire drib redd ride bed bid did die ire red rib rid be er id re

bddeirrs redbirds bidders birders. *See* **bddeir bdeirr bdeirs beirrs**

bddeirs bidders. *See* **bddeir bdeirs**

bddeissu subsided buddies disused subside. *See* **bdeisu bdessu deissu**

bddeisu buddies. *See* **bdeisu bddei ddesu**

bddelnu bundled. *See* **bddelu bdelnu**

bddeloo blooded. *See* **bdeloo bddeo ddelo**

bddelou doubled. *See* **bddelu bdelou**

bddelsu buddles. *See* **bddelu belsu bdesu**

bddelu buddle blued bled blue dude duel lube bed bel bud dub dud due eld led leu be el

bddeno bonded boded boned bend bode bond bone done ebon node bed ben bon den doe don end eon neb nob nod odd ode one be do en ne no od on

bddenou bounded. *See* **bddeno bdnou**

bddeo boded bode bed doe odd ode be do od

bddeoor brooded. *See* **ddeoor bddeo bdeoo**

bddeortu obtruded doubted doubter obtrude redoubt. *See* **bdderu bdeort deortu**

bddeotu doubted. *See* **bddeo bdetu ddeot**

bddersu redbuds. *See* **bdderu ddersu**

bdderu redbud udder bred drub dude redd rube rudd rude rued bed bud dub dud due red rub rue urd be er re

bddesuu subdued. *See* **bdesuu ddesu**

bddgiin bidding. *See* **bdgiin**

bddginu budding. *See* **ddinu**

bddiy biddy bid did by id

bdduy buddy bud buy dub dud by

bde bed be

bdeeeems beseemed. *See* **bdeems**

bdeeef beefed beef feed bed bee fed fee be

bdeeegis besieged besiege. *See* **bdeeis beegis deegis**

bdeeehst bedsheet seethed sheeted. *See* **bdeeest beehst**

bdeeehtu hebetude. *See* **bdetu deetu**

bdeeeilv believed bedevil believe beveled. *See* **bdeeil deeelv deeilv**

bdeeellr rebelled bleeder. *See* **bdeell deeelr**

bdeeelmm emblemed. *See* **beelmm**

bdeeelr bleeder. *See* **deeelr**

bdeeelrs bleeders bleeder. *See* **bdeels bdeers beelrs deeelr**

bdeeelrt trebeled bleeder beetled. *See* **bdeelt beelrt deeelr**

bdeeelt beetled. *See* **beeelt bdeelt deeelt**

bdeeelv beveled. *See* **deeelv beelv bdeel**

bdeeerr breeder. *See* **bdeer deerr**

bdeeerrs breeders breeder. *See* **bdeers**

bdeeerz breezed. *See* **beeerz bdeer**

bdeeffru buffered rebuffed. *See* **bdeffu beffru deffru**

bdeefftu buffeted. *See* **bdeffu befftu**

bdeefggo befogged. *See* **bdeegg bdeggo defggo**

bdeefinr befriend briefed debrief inbreed refined. *See* **bdeenr bdeinr deefin deefir**

bdeefir briefed debrief. *See* **deefir bdeer bdeir**

bdeefirs debriefs briefed debrief derbies. *See* **bdeeis bdeers bdeirs befirs**

bdeefitt befitted. *See* **bdeeit defitt**

bdeeflou befouled. *See* **bdelou beflou deeflu deflou**

bdeefoor forebode. *See* **beefor defoor**

bdeegg begged egged edge geed bed bee beg egg gee be

bdeeggiw bewigged. *See* **bdeegg deggiw**

bdeeggru begrudge. *See* **bdeegg bdeggu beegru beggru**

bdeegiln bleeding deleing. *See* **bdeeil bdeeln bdegil bdeiln**

bdeegilu beguiled beguile. *See* **bdeeil bdegil bdegiu bdeglu**

bdeeginr breeding dreeing inbreed reeding reigned. *See* **bdeenr bdegir bdeinr deegir**

bdeeglno belonged. *See* **bdeeln bdeeno bdeglo bdelno**

bdeegoy bogeyed. *See* **bdeeoy begoy deego**

bdeehl beheld bleed bled dele heed heel held bed bee bel edh eel eld led lee be eh el he

bdeehlno beholden. *See* **bdeehl bdehlo bdeeln bdelno**

bdeehlor beholder. *See* **bdeehl bdeehr bdehlo bdelor**

bdeehlsu busheled blushed. *See* **bdeehl bdeels bdehsu behlsu**

bdeehmor homebred. *See* **bdeehr behmor**

bdeehoov behooved behoove. *See* **bdeoo dehoo**

bdeehort bothered berthed. *See* **bdeehr bdehot bdeort behort**

bdeehr herbed breed beer bred bree deer dree heed herb herd here reed bed bee edh eer her red be eh er he re

bdeehrt berthed. *See* **bdeehr beert behrt**

bdeeiiln inedible. *See* **bdeeil bdeeln bdeiln**

bdeeil belied edible belie bield bleed edile elide bide bile bled deil dele deli idle lied bed bee bel bid die eel eld led lee lei lid lie be el id li

bdeeill bellied libeled. *See* **bdeeil bdeell bdeill**

bdeeilll libelled bellied libeled. *See* **bdeeil bdeell bdeill**

bdeeillr rebilled bellied libeled libeler. *See* **bdeeil bdeell bdeill bdeilr**

bdeeillt billeted bellied libeled. *See* **bdeeil bdeeit bdeell bdeelt**

bdeeilmr limbered bemired. *See* **bdeeil bdeilm bdeilr beeimr**

bdeeilnv vendible bedevil livened. *See* **bdeeil bdeeln bdeiln deeilv**

bdeeiloz obelized obelize. *See* **bdeeil bdeilo**

bdeeilrw bewilder wielder. *See* **bdeeil bdeerw bdeilr deeilr**

bdeeils edibles. *See* **bdeeil beeils bdeeis bdeils bdeels**

bdeeilsv bedevils edibles bedevil. *See* **bdeeil bdeeis bdeels bdeils**

bdeeilv bedevil. *See* **bdeeil deeilv**

bdeeimos embodies. *See* **bdeeis bdeems bdeims bdeios**

bdeeimr bemired. *See* **beeimr**

bdeeimrt timbered bedtime bemired demerit dimeter merited mitered. *See* **bdeeit beeimr beimrt deeimt**

bdeeimt bedtime. *See* **bdeeit deeimt**

bdeeinot obedient ebonite. *See* **bdeeit bdeeno deenot**

bdeeinr inbreed. *See* **bdeenr bdeinr deeinr**

bdeeinrs inbreeds benders binders deniers derbies inbreed. *See* **bdeeis bdeenr bdeers bdeinr**

bdeeinsz bedizens bedizen. *See* **bdeeis deeins deeisz deinsz**

bdeeinz bedizen. *See* **beinz deinz**

bdeeirr berried. *See* **bdeirr bdeer deeir**

bdeeirrv riverbed berried. *See* **bdeirr bdeirv beerrv deeirv**

bdeeirs derbies. *See* **bdeeis bdeers bdeirs deeirs**

bdeeirtt bittered. *See* **bdeeit beertt beirtt deeirt**

bdeeis beside bides beds bees bide bids bise dibs dies ides seed side bed bee bid die ids see sib be id is si

bdeeiss besides. *See* **bdeeis deeiss**

bdeeist betides. *See* **bdeeis bdeest bdeeit bdeist**

bdeeit betide bidet debit beet bide bite debt diet edit teed tide tied bed bee bet bid bit die dit ted tee tie be id it ti

bdeekru rebuked. *See* **bdekru beekru**

bdeel bleed bled dele bed bee bel eel eld led lee be el

bdeell belled bleed belle bell bled dele dell bed bee bel eel eld ell led lee be el

bdeellow bellowed elbowed. *See* **bdeell bdelow bellow**

bdeelmno embolden. *See* **bdeeln bdeeno bdelno deemno**

bdeelmrt trembled tremble. *See* **bdeelt beelrt deelmt deemrt**

bdeelmru lumbered embrued rumbled umbered. *See* **bdelru bdemru beemru belmru**

bdeeln blende bleed blend been bend bled dele dene lend need bed bee bel ben den eel lend end led lee neb nee be el en ne

bdeelnno ennobled ennoble. *See* **bdeeln bdeeno bdelno**

bdeelnr blender. *See* **bdeenr bdeeln deelnr**

bdeelnrs blenders benders blender lenders slender. *See* **bdeeln bdeels bdeenr bdeers**

bdeeloru redouble boulder. *See* **bdelor bdelou bdelru beloru**

bdeelosv beloveds beloved. *See* **bdeels beelsv deelsv delosv**

bdeelov beloved. *See* **beelv bdeel deelv**

bdeelow elbowed. *See* **bdelow bdeel**

bdeels bleeds bleed deles beds bees bels bled dele eels else lees seed seel sled bed bee bel eel eld els led lee see be el

bdeelss bedless blessed. *See* **bdeels belss deess**

bdeelt belted bleed betel beet belt bled debt dele leet teed bed bee bel bet eel eld led lee let ted tee be el

bdeem embed deem deme meed bed bee be em me

bdeemnot entombed. *See* **bdeeno bemnot deemno deemnt**

bdeemnru numbered embrued umbered. *See* **bdeenr bdemnu bdemru bdenru**

bdeemoss embossed. *See* **bemoss bdeoss bdemos bdeems**

bdeemow embowed. *See* **bdeow bdemo bdeem**

bdeemru embrued umbered. *See* **deemru bdemru beemru**

bdeems embeds deems demes embed meeds beds bees deem deme meed seed seem bed bee see be em me

bdeemsu bemused. *See* **bdeems beemsu**

bdeennot bonneted. *See* **bdeeno bennot deenot**

bdeeno debone boned been bend bode bond bone dene done ebon need node bed bee ben den doe don end eon neb nee nob nod ode one be do en ne no od on

bdeenos debones. *See* **bdeeno bdens bdeos**

bdeenpr prebend. *See* **bdeenr eenpr**

bdeenprs prebends prebend benders. *See* **bdeenr bdeers deenrs eenprs**

bdeenr bender breed been beer bend bred bree deer dene dree erne need nerd reed rend bed bee ben den end ere neb nee red be en er ne re

bdeenrs benders. *See* **bdeenr bdeers deenrs**

bdeensuv subvened subvene vendues. *See* **deensu deenuv eensuv**

bdeeorrs resorbed bedsore borders reredos sobered. *See* **bdeers bdeorr beorrs deeors**

bdeeors bedsore sobered. *See* **bdeers deeors**

bdeeorss bedsores bedsore sobered. *See* **bdeers bdeoss beorss deeors**

bdeeorsv observed bedsore observe obverse sobered verbose. *See* **bdeers beersv deeors deorsv**

bdeeosss obsessed. *See* **bdeoss**

bdeeostt besotted. *See* **bdeest beostt deostt**

bdeeostw bestowed. *See* **bdeest beostw deestw deostw**

bdeeoy obeyed bode body eyed obey bed bee bey boy bye dey doe dye eye ode yob yod be by do od oy ye

bdeeprru purebred perdure. *See* **bdepru bderru deepru deprru**

bdeer breed beer bred bree deer dree reed bed bee ere red be er re

bdeerrwy dewberry brewery. *See* **bdeerw beerrw deerrw**

bdeers breeds beers breed brees deers drees reeds beds beer bees bred bree deer dree reds reed seed seer sere bed bee ere red res see be er re

bdeerttu buttered rebutted burette uttered. *See* **bdeett bdettu beertt berttu**

bdeerw brewed breed beer bred bree brew deer dree drew ewer reed weed bed bee dew ere ewe red web wed wee be er re we

bdeest bested beets beset debts steed beds bees beet best bets debt seed teds teed tees bed bee bet see set ted tee be

bdeett betted beet debt teed bed bee bet ted tee be

bdefflu bluffed. *See* **bdeffu defflu**

bdeffu buffed buff duff feud bed bud dub due fed feu be

bdefiirr firebird. *See* **bdeiir bdeirr**

bdeflmu fumbled. *See* **beflmu bdelu defmu**

bdegglo boggled. *See* **bdeggo begglo degglo bdeglo**

bdeggo bogged bode doge bed beg bog doe dog egg ego gob god ode be do go od

bdeggu bugged budge debug bed beg bud bug dub due dug egg be

bdeghhir highbred. *See* **bdegir eghhir**

bdeghilt blighted delight lighted. *See* **bdegil begilt behilt bghilt**

bdegi gibed bide gibe gied bed beg bid big die dig gib gid gie be id

bdegiint betiding debiting dieting editing ignited. *See* **bdgiin bgiint degint egiint**

bdegil bilged bield bilge gelid gibed glide bide bile bled deil deli geld gibe gied gild glib idle lied bed beg bel bid big die dig eld gel gib gid gie led leg lei lid lie be el id li

bdegilnn blending bending lending. *See* **bdegil bdeiln bdeinn beginn**

bdegilo obliged. *See* **bdegil bdeilo begilo**

bdeginn bending. *See* **beginn bdeinn deginn**

bdeginno deboning bending bonding. *See* **bdeinn bdgino beginn deginn**

bdegiot bigoted. *See* **begot bdeit bgiot**

bdegir bridge bride dirge gibed gride ridge berg bide bier bird bred brie brig dire drib gibe gied gird grid ride bed beg bid big die dig erg gib gid gie ire red reg rib rid rig be er id re

bdegirs bridges. *See* **bdeirs bdegir degirs**

bdegisu budgies. *See* **bdegsu bdegiu bdeisu degisu**

bdegiu budgie budge debug gibed guide bide gibe gied bed beg bid big bud bug die dig dub due dug gib gid gie be id

bdeglmru grumbled burgled grumble rumbled. *See* **bdeglu bdelru bdemru beglru**

bdeglnou bludgeon bungled lounged. *See* **bdeglo bdeglu bdegnu bdelno**

bdeglnu bungled. *See* **bdeglu bdelnu bdegnu beglnu deglnu**

bdeglo globed globe lobed lodge ogled bled bode bold bole doge dole geld glob gold lobe lode loge ogle bed beg bel bog doe dog ego eld gel gob god led leg lob log ode old be do el go lo od

bdeglru burgled. *See* **bdeglu beglru bdelru**

bdeglu bugled bulged blued budge bugle bulge debug glued luged bled blue duel geld glue lube luge bed beg bel bud bug dub due dug eld gel led leg leu lug be el

bdegnu bunged begun budge debug nudge bend bung dune dung nude bed beg ben bud bug bun den dub due dug dun end gnu gun neb nub be en ne nu

bdegorry dogberry. *See* **bdeorr**

bdegstu budgets. *See* **bdegsu bdegtu bdestu degstu**

bdegsu budges debugs budge bused debug beds begs buds bugs dubs dues sued used bed beg bud bug bus dub due dug sub sue use be us

bdegtu budget budge debug debut tubed debt duet tube bed beg bet bud bug but dub due dug get gut ted tub tug be ut

bdegu budge debug bed beg bud bug dub due dug be

bdehin behind bend bide bind bine dine hide hied hind nide bed ben bid bin den die din edh end hen hid hie hin neb nib be eh en he hi id in ne

bdehlmu humbled. *See* **behlmu bdelu**

bdehlo behold dhole holed lobed bled bode bold bole dole held hoed hold hole lobe lode bed bel doe edh eld hob hod hoe led lob ode old be do eh el he ho lo od oh

bdehlos beholds. *See* **bdehlo dehlos**

bdehlsu blushed. *See* **bdehsu behlsu**

bdehmooy homebody. *See* **bdemoo bdemoy**

bdehmtu thumbed. *See* **bdetu demtu bhmtu**

bdehoooo boohooed. *See* **bhoooo dhoooo**

bdehorsy herdboys herdboy. *See* **dehors dhorsy ehorsy**

bdehory herdboy. *See* **bdeor bdery behry**

bdehost hotbeds. *See* **bdehot dehost**

bdehot hotbed beth bode both debt dote hoed toed bed bet bot doe dot edh eth het hob hod hoe hot ode ted the tho tod toe be do eh he ho od oh to

bdehrsu brushed. *See* **bdehsu dehrsu**

bdehsu bushed bussed beds bush dubs dues hubs hued hues shed sued used bed bud bus dub due edh hub hue she sub sue use be eh he sh us

bdei bide bed bid die be id

bdeiiktz kibitzed. *See* **biiktz**

bdeiilty debility. *See* **bdeit bdeil deity**

bdeiir birdie bride bide bier bird bred brie dire drib ride bed bid die ire red rib rid be er id re

bdeiirs birdies. *See* **bdeiir bdeirs deiirs**

bdeij jibed bide jibe bed bid die jib be id

bdeik biked bide bike dike kibe bed bid die kid be id

bdeikl bilked bield biked liked bide bike bile bilk bled deil deli dike idle kibe lied like bed bel bid die eld elk ilk kid led lei lid lie be el id li

bdeikln blinked. *See* **bdeikl bdeiln deikln**

bdeiknsu buskined debunks. *See* **bdeisu bdekmu biknsu deinsu**

bdeil bield bide bile bled deil deli idle lied bed bel bid die eld led lei lid lie be el id li

bdeill billed bield libel bell bide bile bill bled deil deli dell dill idle lied bed bel bid die eld ell ill led lei lid lie be el id li

bdeillow billowed. *See* **bdeill bdeilo bdelow bellow**

bdeillox bollixed. *See* **bdeill bdeilo billox**

bdeillu bullied. *See* **bdeill bdeillu**

bdeilm limbed bedim bield imbed limed bide bile bled deil deli dime idle lied limb lime meld mild mile bed bel bid die dim eld elm led lei lid lie mel mid mil be el em id li me mi

bdeilmsu sublimed sublime. *See* **bdeilm bdeils bdeims bdeimu**

bdeilmw wimbled. *See* **bdeilm deilmw beilmw**

bdeiln bindle bield blend blind lined bend bide bile bind bine bled deil deli dine idle lend lied lien line nide bed bel ben bid bin den die din eld end led lei lid lie neb nib nil be el en id in li ne

bdeilnr blinder brindle. *See* **beilnr bdeinr bdeiln bdeilr**

bdeilnrs blinders brindles berlins binders bindles blinder bridles brindle. *See* **bdeiln bdeilr bdeils bdeinr**

bdeilnru unbridle blinder blunder brindle builder rebuild. *See* **bdeiln bdeilr bdeinr bdeiru**

bdeilns bindles. *See* **bdeils bdeiln bdelns bdilns**

bdeilo boiled bolide bield lobed oiled oldie bide bile bled bode boil bold bole deil deli dole idle idol lied lobe lode bed bel bid die doe eld led lei lid lie lob obi ode oil old be do el id li lo od

bdeiloor bloodier broiled. *See* **bdeilo bdeilr bdeior bdeloo**

bdeilor broiled. *See* **bdeilr bdeilo beilor bdelor bdeior**

bdeilorv lovebird broiled overbid. *See* **bdeilo bdeilr bdeior bdeirv**

bdeilos bolides. *See* **beilos bdeils bdeios bdeilo deilos**

bdeiloss bodiless bolides besoils. *See* **bdeilo bdeils bdeios bdeoss**

bdeilpp blipped. *See* **deilpp bdeil bdeip**

bdeilr birled bridle bield bride idler riled bide bier bile bird birl bled bred brie deil deli dire dirl drib idle lied lire ride riel rile bed bel bid die eld ire led lei lid lie red rib rid be el er id li re

bdeilrs bridles. *See* **bdeils bdeilr bdeirs deilrs**

bdeilrst bristled driblets blister bridles bristle driblet. *See* **bdeilr bdeils bdeirs bdeist**

bdeilrsu builders rebuilds bridles bruised builder rebuild. *See* **bdeilr bdeils bdeirs bdeiru**

bdeilrt driblet. *See* **bdeilr**

bdeilru builder rebuild. *See* **bdeilr bdeiru bdelru**

bdeils bields bides bield biles deils delis idles sidle slide beds bels bide bids bile bise bled deil deli dibs dies ides idle isle leis lids lied lies side sled slid bed bel bid die eld els ids led lei lid lie lis sib be el id is li si

bdeiltz blitzed. *See* **bdeit bdeil biltz**

bdeim bedim imbed bide dime bed bid die dim mid be em id me mi

bdeimmr brimmed. *See* **deimmr**

bdeimnr birdmen. *See* **bdeinr deimnr**

bdeimor bromide. *See* **bdeior bdimor**

bdeimors bromides borides bromide disrobe misdoer. *See* **bdeims bdeior bdeios bdeirs**

bdeimru imbrued. *See* **bdeiru bdemru beimru bdeimu**

bdeims bedims imbeds bedim bides deism dimes imbed beds bide bids bise dibs dies dime dims ides mise semi side bed bid die dim ids mid mis sib be em id is me mi si

bdeimu imbued bedim imbed imbue bide dime dumb bed bid bud bum die dim dub due emu mid mud be em id me mi mu um

bdeinn binned inned bend bide bind bine dine nide nine bed ben bid bin den die din end inn neb nib be en id in ne

bdeinoos nobodies boonies. *See* **bdeios deinos denoos**

bdeinoow woodbine. *See* **denoow**

bdeinr binder brined inbred bride brine diner bend bide bier bind bine bird bred brie dine dire drib nerd nide rein rend ride rind bed ben bid bin den die din end ire neb nib red rib rid be en er id in ne re

bdeinrs binders. *See* **bdeinr bdeirs beinrs deinrs**

bdeinry bindery. *See* **bdeinr**

bdeior boride bored bride orbed robed bide bier bird bode bore bred brie dire doer drib redo ride robe rode bed bid die doe dor ire obi ode orb ore red rib rid rob rod roe be do er id od or re

bdeiors borides disrobe. *See* **bdeios bdeior bdeirs deiors**

bdeiorss disrobes borides bossier disrobe dossier. *See* **bdeior bdeios bdeirs bdeoss**

bdeiorsv overbids borides devisor disrobe overbid verbids. *See* **bdeior bdeios bdeirs bdeirv**

bdeiort debitor orbited. *See* **bdeior bdeort deiort**

bdeiorv overbid. *See* **bdeior deiorv bdeirv**

bdeios bodies bides bodes beds bide bids bise bode dibs dies does dose ides obis odes side bed bid die doe dos ids obi ode sib sob sod be do id is od os si so

bdeiossy disobeys disobey. *See* **bdeios bdeoss**

bdeiosy disobey. *See* **bdeios beosy**

bdeip biped bide pied bed bid die dip pie be id pe pi

bdeips bipeds bides biped spied beds bide bids bise dibs dies dips ides pied pies side sped bed bid die dip ids pie sib sip be id is pe pi si

bdeir bride bide bier bird bred brie dire drib ride bed bid die ire red rib rid be er id re

bdeirr birder bride brier direr drier rider bide bier bird birr bred brie dire drib ride bed bid die err ire red rib rid be er id re

bdeirrs birders. *See* **bdeirr bdeirs beirrs deirrs**

bdeirs brides debris bides biers birds bride dribs dries rides sired beds bide bids bier bird bise bred brie dibs dies dire drib ides reds reis ribs ride rids rise side sire bed bid die ids ire red res rib rid sib sir be er id is re si

bdeirssu disburse bruised bruises subside. *See* **bdeirs bdeiru bdeisu bdessu**

bdeirsu bruised. *See* **bdeirs beirsu bdeiru bdeisu**

bdeirsv verbids. *See* **bdeirs deirsv bdeirv**

bdeirtu bruited. *See* **bdeiru bdirtu**

bdeiru buried rubied bride bide bier bird bred brie dire drib drub ride rube rude rued bed bid bud die dub due ire red rib rid rub rue urd be er id re

bdeirv verbid bride diver drive rived bide bier bird bred brie dire dive drib ride rive verb vied bed bid die ire red rev rib rid vie be er id re

bdeis bides beds bide bids bise dibs dies ides side bed bid die ids sib be id is si

bdeissu subsides subside disuses. *See* **bdeisu bdessu deissu**

bdeissu subside. *See* **bdeisu bdessu deissu**

bdeist bidets debits bides bidet bites debit debts deist diets edits sited tides beds best bets bide bids bise bite bits debt dibs dies diet dits edit ides side site teds tide tied ties bed bet bid bit die dit ids its set sib sit ted tie be id is it si ti

bdeisu busied bides bused beds bide bids bise buds dibs dies dubs dues ides side sued used bed bid bud bus die dub due ids sib sub sue use be id is si us

bdeit bidet debit bide bite debt diet edit tide tied bed bet bid bit die dit ted tie be id it ti

bdeituy dubiety. *See* **bdeit bdetu deity**

bdejlmu jumbled. *See* **bejlmu bdelu**

bdeklu bulked blued bled blue bulk duel duke lube bed bel bud dub due eld elk led lek leu be el

bdekno bonked boned kendo bend bode bond bone bonk done ebon keno knob node bed ben den doe don end eon ken kob neb nob nod ode oke one be do en ne no od on

bdeknoo bookend. *See* **bdekno bdekoo**

bdeknoos bookends bookend. *See* **bdekno bdekoo denoos**

bdeknsu debunks. *See* **bdeknu**

bdeknu bunked debunk nuked bend bunk duke dune dunk neuk nude nuke bed ben bud bun den dub due dun end ken neb nub be en ne nu

bdekoo booked booed bode book kobo oboe bed boo doe kob ode oke be do od

bdekoor brooked. *See* **bdekoo dekoor**

bdekru burked burke bred drub duke kerb rube rude rued bed bud dub due red rub rue urd be er re

bdel bled bed bel eld led be el

bdelloor bordello doorbell bedroll. *See* **bdeloo bdelor beloor dellor**

bdellor bedroll. *See* **bdelor dellor**

bdellors bedrolls bedroll bordels. *See* **bdelor belors dellor delors**

bdellouz bulldoze. *See* **bdellu bdelou**

bdellu bulled blued bell bled blue bull dell duel dull lube bed bel bud dub due eld ell led leu be el

bdelmmu mumbled. *See* **bdemmu belmmu**

bdelmoo bloomed. *See* **bdeloo bdemoo delmoo**

bdelmpu plumbed. *See* **bdempu delmpu**

bdelmru rumbled. *See* **bdelru bdemru belmru**

bdelmstu stumbled bustled dumbest stumble tumbled tumbles. *See* **bdestu belmsu belmtu belstu**

bdelmtu tumbled. *See* **belmtu bdelu bdetu**

bdeln blend bend bled lend bed bel ben den eld end led neb be el en ne

bdelno blonde blend blond boned lobed loden noble olden bend bled bode bold bole bond bone dole done ebon enol lend leno lobe lode lone node noel bed bel ben den doe don eld end eon led lob neb nob nod ode old one be do el en lo ne no od on

bdelnos blondes. *See* **bdelns bdelno bdlnos belnos**

bdelnoss boldness blondes oldness. *See* **bdelno bdelns bdeoss bdlnos**

bdelnotu unbolted blunted doublet. *See* **bdelno bdelnu bdelot bdelou**

bdelnrsu blunders blunder bundles burdens rundles. *See* **bdelns bdelnu bdelru bdenru**

bdelnru blunder. *See* **bdelnu bdenru bdelru delnru**

bdelns blends bends blend lends beds bels bend bens bled dens ends lend lens nebs send sled bed bel ben den eld els end ens led neb sen be el en ne

bdelnsu bundles. *See* **bdelns bdelnu**

bdelntu blunted. *See* **bdelnu bdentu**

bdelnu bundle blend blued bend bled blue duel dune lend lube lune nude bed bel ben bud bun den dub due dun eld end led leu neb nub be el en ne nu

bdelo lobed bled bode bold bole dole lobe lode bed bel doe eld led lob ode old be do el lo od

bdeloo boodle blood booed lobed looed bled bode bold bole bolo dole lobe lobo lode oboe oleo bed bel boo doe eld led lob loo ode old be do el lo od

bdeloos boodles. *See* **bdloos bdeloo deloos**

bdelor bolder bordel bored lobed older orbed robed roble bled bode bold bole bore bred doer dole lobe lode lord lore orle redo robe rode role bed bel doe dor eld led lob ode old orb ore red rob rod roe be do el er lo od or re

bdelors bordels. *See* **bdelor delors belors**

bdelorsu boulders bloused bordels boulder doubles rosebud roubles. *See* **bdelor bdelou bdelru belors**

bdelortu troubled blurted boulder doublet doubter obtrude redoubt trouble. *See* **bdelor bdelot bdelou bdelru**

bdeloru boulder. *See* **bdelor bdelru bdelou deloru beloru**

bdelost boldest. *See* **bdelot delost**

bdelostu doublets bloused boldest boletus bustled doubles doublet loudest tousled. *See* **bdelot bdelou bdestu bdostu**

bdelosu bloused doubles. *See* **belosu**

bdelot bolted lobed belt bled blot bode bold bole bolt debt dole dolt dote lobe lode toed told bed bel bet bot doe dot eld led let lob lot ode old ted tod toe be do el lo od to

bdelott blotted bottled. *See* **bdelot belott delott**

bdelotu doublet. *See* **bdelot bdelou**

bdelou double blued boule lobed bled blue bode bold bole dole duel lobe lode loud lube bed bel bud doe dub due duo eld led leu lob ode old oud udo be do el lo od

bdelow bowled below bowed bowel dowel elbow lobed lowed bled blew blow bode bold bole bowl dole lewd lobe lode owed weld wold bed bel bow dew doe eld led lob low ode old owe owl web wed woe be do el lo od ow we

bdelrru blurred. *See* **bdelru bderru**

bdelrtu blurted. *See* **bdelru belrtu**

bdelru burled blued bluer lured ruble ruled bled blue blur bred burl drub duel lube lure rube rude rued rule bed bel bud dub due eld led leu red rub rue urd be el er re

bdelssu budless. *See* **bdessu delssu**

bdelstu bustled. *See* **belstu bdestu delstu**

bdelu blued bled blue duel lube bed bel bud dub due eld led leu be el

bdemmu bummed dumb bed bud bum dub due emu mem mud mum be em me mu um

bdemnnos bondsmen. *See* **bdemos demnos**

bdemnssu dumbness. *See* **bdemnu bdessu bemnsu bemssu**

bdemnu numbed bend dumb dune mend menu nude numb bed ben bud bum bun den dub due dun emu end men mud neb nub be em en me mu ne nu um

bdemo demob bode demo dome mode bed doe mob mod ode be do em me mo od om

bdemoo boomed booed demob mooed bode boom demo dome doom mode mood oboe bed boo doe mob mod moo ode be do em me mo od om

bdemoor bedroom boredom. *See* **bdemoo bemoor demoor**

bdemoors bedrooms bedroom boomers boredom bosomed. *See* **bdemoo bdemos bdoors bemoor**

bdemoos bosomed. *See* **bdemoo bdemos**

bdemoosy somebody bosomed. *See* **bdemoo bdemos bdemoy bmoosy**

bdemoott bottomed. *See* **bdemoo bdeoot bmoott deoott**

bdemos demobs besom bodes demob demos domes modes beds bode demo does dome dose mobs mode mods odes some bed doe dos mob mod mos ode oms sob sod be do em me mo od om os so

bdemoy embody demob bode body demo demy dome mode obey bed bey boy bye dey doe dye mob mod ode yob yod be by do em me mo my od om oy ye

bdempu bumped umped bump dumb dump bed bud bum dub due emu mud pub ump be em me mu pe um up

bdemru dumber brume demur umber berm bred drub drum dumb rube rude rued bed bud bum dub due emu mud red rem rub rue rum urd be em er me mu re um

bdemstu dumbest. *See* **bdestu demsu demtu**

bden bend bed ben den end neb be en ne

bdennruu unburden. *See* **bdennu bdenru**

bdennsu unbends. *See* **bdennu dennsu**

bdennu unbend bend dune nude bed ben bud bun den dub due dun end neb nub nun be en ne nu

bdeno boned bend bode bond bone done ebon node bed ben den doe don end eon neb nob nod ode one be do en ne no od on

bdenootw bentwood. *See* **bdeoot denoow denotw**

bdenorsu bounders rebounds suborned bounder burdens rebound resound rosebud sounder. *See* **bdenru bdnosu benors beorsu**

bdenoru bounder rebound. *See* **bdenru**

bdenorw browned. *See* **denorw**

bdenorz bronzed. *See* **benorz bdeno bdeor**

bdenottu buttoned. *See* **bdentu bdettu bdnotu bnottu**

bdenoy beyond boned doyen ebony bend bode body bond bone bony deny done dyne ebon node obey yond bed ben bey boy bye den dey doe don dye end eon neb nob nod ode one yen yob yod yon be by do en ne no od on oy ye

bdenrsu burdens. *See* **bdenru denrsu**

bdenru burden burned under bend bred burn drub dune nerd nude rend rube rude rued rune bed ben bud bun den dub due dun end neb nub red rub rue run urd urn be en er ne nu re

bdenruuy underbuy. *See* **bdenru**

bdens bends beds bend bens dens ends nebs send bed ben den end ens neb sen be en ne

bdentu bunted bundt debut tubed tuned bend bent bunt debt dent duet dune nude tend tube tune bed ben bet bud bun but den dub due dun end neb net nub nut ted ten tub tun be en ne nu ut

bdeo bode bed doe ode be do od

bdeoo booed bode oboe bed boo doe ode be do od

bdeoorr brooder. *See* **bdeorr bdeoo bdoor**

bdeoorrs brooders brooder borders. *See* **bdeorr bdoors beorrs deoors**

bdeoorrw borrowed brooder. *See* **bdeorr boorrw deorrw**

bdeoost boosted. *See* **bdeoot deoost**

bdeoot booted booed bode boot debt dote oboe toed bed bet boo bot doe dot ode ted tod toe too be do od to

bdeooz boozed booed booze oozed bode bozo doze oboe ooze bed boo doe ode zed zoo be do od

bdeopp bopped bode dope oped pope bed bop bode ode ope pep pod pop be do od pe

bdeopr probed bored doper orbed pored probe robed roped bode bore bred doer dope drop oped pore prod redo repo robe rode rope bed bop doe dor ode ope orb ore per pod pro red rep rob rod roe be do er od or pe re

bdeopsst bedposts bedpost despots. *See* **bdeoss beosst deopst eopsst**

bdeopst bedpost. *See* **deopst**

bdeor bored orbed robed bode bore bred doer redo robe rode bed doe dor ode orb ore red rob rod roe be do er od or re

bdeorr border bored borer orbed order robed bode bore bred doer redo robe rode bed doe dor err ode orb ore red rob rod roe be do er od or re

bdeorrs borders. *See* **bdeorr beorrs deorrs**

bdeorrsu bordures borders bordure ordures rosebud. *See* **bdeorr bderru beorrs beorsu**

bdeorrtu obtruder bordure doubter obtrude redoubt. *See* **bdeorr bdeort bderru deorru**

bdeorru bordure. *See* **bdeorr bderru deorru**

bdeorruw burrowed bordure. *See* **bdeorr bderru borruw deorru**

bdeorssu rosebuds rosebud bourses. *See* **bdeoss bdessu beorss beorsu**

bdeorst debtors. *See* **bdeort deorst beorst**

bdeorstu doubters obtrudes redoubts debtors detours doubter obtrude redoubt rosebud rousted. *See* **bdeort bdestu bdostu beorst**

bdeorsu rosebud. *See* **beorsu deorsu**

bdeorsw browsed. *See* **beorsw deorsw**

bdeort debtor bored doter orbed robed bode bore bort bred debt doer dote redo robe rode rote toed tore trod bed bet bot doe dor dot ode orb ore ort red ret rob rod roe rot ted tod toe tor be do er od or re to

bdeortu doubter obtrude redoubt. *See* **bdeort deortu**

bdeos bodes beds bode does dose odes bed doe dos ode sob sod be do od os so

bdeoss bossed bodes doses beds bode boss does dose doss odes sobs sods bed doe dos ess ode sob sod be do od os so

bdeouy buoyed bode body buoy obey bed bey boy bud buy bye dey doe dub due duo dye ode oud udo yob yod you be by do od oy ye

bdeow bowed bode owed bed bow dew doe ode owe web wed woe be do od ow we

bdeox boxed bode bed box doe ode be do ex od ox

bdepru burped drupe duper perdu prude bred burp drub pure rube rude rued bed bud dub due per pub red rep rub rue urd be er pe re up

bder bred bed red be er re

bderru burred ruder bred burr drub rube rude rued bed bud dub due err red rub rue urd be er re

bdery derby bred byre dyer bed bey bye dey dry dye red rye be by er re ye

bdes beds bed be

bdessu bussed bused buses beds buds buss dubs dues subs suds sued sues used uses bed bud bus dub due ess sub sue use be us

bdessuu subdues. *See* **bdessu bdesuu**

bdest debts beds best bets debt teds bed bet set ted be

bdestu debuts bused debts debut duets tubed tubes beds best bets buds bust buts debt dubs dues duet dust stub stud sued suet teds tube tubs used bed bet bud bus but dub due set sub sue ted tub use be us ut

bdesu bused beds buds dubs dues sued used bed bud bus dub due sub sue use be us

bdesuu subdue bused beds buds dubs dues sued used bed bud bus dub due sub sue use be us

bdet debt bed bet ted be

bdettu butted debut tubed butt debt duet tube bed bet bud but dub due ted tub tut be ut

bdetu debut tubed debt duet tube bed bet bud but dub due ted tub be ut

bdfii bifid bid fib fid if if

bdfiior fibroid. *See* **bdfior bdfii biior**

bdfiiors fibroids fibroid forbids. *See* **bdfior biiors dfiors**

bdfilllo billfold. *See* **bdfilo**

bdfilo bifold boil bold foil fold idol bid fib fid fob lid lob obi oil old do id if li lo od of

bdfior forbid fiord bird drib forb ford bid dor fib fid fir fob for fro obi orb rib rid rif rob rod do id if od of or

bdfiors forbids. *See* **bdfior dfiors**

bdflotuu doubtful. *See* **bdotu flotu**

bdggiinr bridging birding girding griding ridging. *See* **bdgiin bggiin dgiinr**

bdgginu budging. *No 6s or 5s*

bdghoouy doughboy. *See* **dghouy**

bdgiiknr kingbird birding dirking. *See* **bdgiin bgiikn dgiikn dgiinr**

bdgiilnn blinding binding. *See* **bdgiin dgiiln dgiinn giilnn**

bdgiilnr bridling birding birling dirling. *See* **bdgiin dgiiln dgiinr giilnr**

bdgiilnu building. *See* **bdgiin bgilnu dgiiln**

bdgiin biding bind ding nidi bid big bin dig din gib gid gin nib id in

bdgiinn binding. *See* **bdgiin dgiinn**

bdgiinns bindings binding. *See* **bdgiin dgiinn dgiins**

bdgiinr birding. *See* **bdgiin dgiinr**

bdgilnnu bundling. *See* **bgilnu**

bdgilnou doubling. *See* **bdgino bgilno bgilnu dgilno**

bdgiloo globoid. *See* **bdloo giloo biloo**

bdginno bonding. *See* **bdgino bginno**

bdginnos bondings bonding bodings. *See* **bdgino bginno bginos dginos**

bdginnou bounding bonding inbound undoing. *See* **bdgino bginno binnou dginou**

bdgino boding bingo dingo doing bind bond bong ding dong bid big bin bog dig din dog don gib gid gin gob god ion nib nob nod nog obi do go id in no od on

bdginoor brooding bridoon. *See* **bdgino bginoo bginor dinoor**

bdginors songbird bodings borings. *See* **bdgino bginor bginos bginrs**

bdginos bodings. *See* **bginos bdgino dginos**

bdginotu doubting. *See* **bdgino bdiotu bdnotu bgintu**

bdginoy bodying. *See* **bdgino dginy**

bdginsuu subduing. *See* **bginsu dginsu**

bdgllosu bulldogs bulldog. *See* **bgosu bllos blosu**

bdgllou bulldog. *No 6s or 5s*

bdhimoor rhomboid. *See* **bdimor**

bdhirsy hybrids. *See* **bdhiry bdirs**

bdhiry hybrid bird drib bid dry hid rib rid by hi id

bdhoooy boyhood. *No 6s or 5s*

bdi bid id

bdiilo libido boil bold idol bid lid lob obi oil old do id li lo od

bdiilos libidos. *See* **bdiilo bilos dilos**

bdiistt tidbits. *See* **bdiitt bistt iistt**

bdiitt tidbit bitt titi bid bit dit tit id it ti

bdikno bodkin bind bond bonk dink ikon kind kino knob oink bid bin din don ink ion kid kin kob nib nob nod obi do id in no od on

bdiknos bodkins. *See* **bdikno bdins binos**

bdillny blindly. *See* **billy bdiln dilly**

bdillooy bloodily. *See* **bdiloy bdlloy bdlooy**

bdilmory morbidly. *See* **bdiloy bdimor dilmor**

bdiln blind bind bid bin din lid nib nil id in li

bdilnpru purblind. *See* **ilnpru**

bdilns blinds blind binds bids bind bins dibs dins lids nibs nils slid bid bin din ids lid nib nil sib sin id in is li si

bdiloy bodily doily body boil bold idly idol idyl oily bid boy lid lob obi oil old yob yod by do id li lo od oy

bdilpsuu buildups buildup. *See* **bdilsu**

bdilpuu buildup. *See* **bdilu**

bdilsu builds build bids buds dibs dubs lids slid slub bid bud bus dub ids lid sib sub id is li si us

bdilu build bid bud dub lid id li

bdimnoru moribund. *See* **bdimor**

bdimor morbid bird brim dorm drib bid dim dor mid mir mob mod mor obi orb rib rid rim rob rod do id mi mo od om or

bdin bind bid bin din nib id in

bdinnosu inbounds inbound bunions. *See* **bdnosu binnou innosu**

bdinnou inbound. *See* **binnou bdnou**

bdinoor bridoon. *See* **dinoor bnoor bdoor**

bdinoors bridoons bridoon indoors. *See* **bdoors binors bnoors dinoor**

bdinorsw snowbird. *See* **binors bnorsw dinosw dnorsw**

bdinrssu sunbirds sunbird. *See* **binrsu**

bdinrsu sunbird. *See* **binrsu bdins bdirs**

bdins binds bids bind bins dibs dins nibs bid bin din ids nib sib sin id in is si

bdinsstu dustbins dustbin nudists. *See* **bdnstu dinstu inssu**

bdinstu dustbin. *See* **bdnstu dinstu**

bdioorsu boudoirs boudoir. *See* **bdoors dioosu**

bdiooru boudoir. *See* **bdoor**

bdiop bipod bid bop dip obi pod poi do id od pi

bdiops bipods bipod bids bops dibs dips obis pods pois bid bop dip dos ids obi pod poi sib sip sob sod sop do id is od os pi si so

bdiostu outbids. *See* **bdostu bdiotu diostu biostu**

bdiostuy bodysuit outbids. *See* **bdiotu bdostu biostu diostu**

bdiosuu dubious. *No 6s or 5s*

bdiosv bovids bovid voids bids dibs obis void bid dos ids obi sib sob sod do id is od os si so

bdiotu outbid doubt bout doit obit bid bit bot bud but dit dot dub duo obi oud out tod tub tui udo do id it od ti to ut

bdiov bovid void bid obi do id od

bdir bird drib bid rib rid id

bdirs birds dribs bids bird dibs drib ribs rids bid ids rib rid sib sir id is si

bdirsstu disturbs disturb. *See* **bdirtu birstu brsstu**

bdirstu disturb. *See* **bdirtu birstu**

bdirtu turbid bruit bird brit dirt drib drub turd bid bit bud but dit dub rib rid rub rut tub tui urd id it ti ut

bdis bids dibs bid ids sib id is si

bdissuy subsidy. *See* **dssuy**

bdkloo kobold blood bold bolo book kobo kolo lobo look boo kob lob loo old do lo od

bdkloos kobolds. *See* **bdkloo bdloos**

bdknooor doorknob. *See* **bnoor bdoor bkoor**

bdkoooorw wordbook. *See* **bdoor bkoor**

bdlloy boldly dolly body bold boll doll boy lob old yob yod by do lo od oy

bdlmuy dumbly dumb duly bud bum buy dub lum mud yum by mu my um

bdlno blond blond bond don lob nob nod old do lo no od on

bdlnooou doubloon. *See* **bdlno bdloo bdnou**

bdlnos blonds blond bonds bold bond dons lobs nobs nods slob snob sold bon don dos lob los nob nod old sob sod sol son do lo no od on os so

bdlo bold lob old do lo od

bdloo blood bold bolo lobo boo lob loo old do lo od

bdlooosx oxbloods oxblood. *See* **bdloos**

bdlooox oxblood. *See* **bdloo**

bdloos bloods blood bolos lobos obols soldo bold bolo boos lobo lobs loos slob sold solo boo dos lob loo los old sob sod sol do lo od os so

bdlooy bloody blood looby body bold bolo boyo lobo boo boy lob loo old yob yod by do lo od oy

bdlouy doubly body bold buoy duly loud boy bud buy dub duo lob old oud udo yob you by do lo od oy

bdmu dumb bud bum dub mud mu um

bdno bond don nob nod do no od on

bdnoorsu bourdons bourdon. *See* **bdnosu bdoors bnoors bnorsu**

bdnooru bourdon. *See* **bnoor bdnou bnoru**

bdnootuu outbound. *See* **bdnotu**

bdnooy nobody body bond bony boon boyo yond boo boy don nob nod yob yod yon by do no od on oy

bdnorsuw rubdowns rubdown. *See* **bdnosu bnorsu bnorsw dnorsu**

bdnoruw rubdown. *See* **bdnou bnoru bnorw**

bdnos bonds bond dons nobs nods snob don dos nob nod sob sod son do no od on os so

bdnostu obtunds. *See* **bdnosu bdnstu dnostu bdnotu**

bdnosu bounds bonds bonus bosun bound nodus sound bond buds buns dons dubs duns duos nobs nods nous nubs onus ouds snob snub udos undo bon bud bun bus don dos dub dun duo nob nod nub oud sob sod son sou sub sun udo do no nu od on os so us

bdnotu obtund bound bundt donut doubt bond bout bunt undo unto bot bud bun but don dot dub dun duo nob nod not nub nut oud out tod ton tub tun udo do no nu od on to ut

bdnou bound bond undo bud bun don dub dun duo nob nod nub oud udo do no nu od on

bdnstu bundts bundt bunts buds buns bunt bust buts dubs duns dust nubs nuts snub stub stud stun tubs tuns bud bun bus but dub dun nub nut sub sun tub tun nu us ut

bdntu bundt bunt bud bun but dub dun nub nut tub tun nu ut

bdoooswx boxwoods boxwood. *See* **booswx**

bdooowx boxwood. *See* **boowx**

bdoor brood boor door odor ordo rood boo dor orb rob rod do od or

bdoors broods boors brood doors odors ordos roods boor boos door odor orbs ordo robs rods rood sorb boo dor dos orb rob rod sob sod do od or os so

bdoory broody brood body boor boyo door dory odor orby ordo rood boo boy dor dry orb rob rod yob yod by do od or oy

bdorswy bywords. *See* **bdorwy dorswy**

bdorwy byword dowry rowdy wordy body brow dory orby word bow boy dor dry orb rob rod row yob yod yow by do od or ow oy

bdostu doubts doubt bouts bots bout buds bust buts dots dubs duos dust ouds oust outs stob stub stud tubs udos bot bud bus but dos dot dub duo oud out sob sod sot sou sub tod tub udo do od os so to us ut

bdotu doubt bout bot bud but dot dub duo oud out tod tub udo do od to ut

bdoy body boy yob yod by do od oy

bdrsu drubs buds drub dubs rubs surd urds bud bus dub rub sub urd us

bdru drub bud dub rub urd

bdsu buds dubs bud bus dub sub us

bdu bud dub

---

be be

bee bee be

beeeefln enfeeble. *See* **beeefl**

beeeefr freebee. *No 6s or 5s*

beeeefrs freebees freebee. *See* **beefs beers eefrs**

beeefir beefier freebie. *See* **befir eeeir**

beeefirs freebies beefier freebie. *See* **befirs**

beeefist beefiest. *See* **befist**

beeefl feeble beef feel flee bee bel eel elf fee lee be el

beeeflr feebler. *See* **beeefl eeeflr**

beeeflst feeblest beetles. *See* **beeefl beeelt eeflst**

beeegis besiege. *See* **beegis eeegs**

beeegiss besieges besiege. *See* **beegis eegiss**

beeehisv beehives beehive. *See* **beeesv beeisv**

beeehiv beehive. *No 6s or 5s*

beeehnoy honeybee. *See* **benoy ehnoy**

beeehp ephebe beep epee bee hep pee be eh he pe

beeehps ephebes. *See* **beeehp beeps eeeps**

beeeiln beeline. *See* **beeil**

beeeilns beelines beeline. *See* **beeils eeilns**

beeeilrv believer believe relieve. *See* **eeilrv**

beeeilsv believes believe. *See* **beeesv beeils beeisv beelsv**

beeeilv believe. *See* **beeil beelv eeelv**

beeeirr beerier. *See* **eeeirr beirr**

beeeirrz breezier beerier. *See* **beeerz eeeirr**

beeeirst beeriest eeriest. *See* **beerst beirst eeirst**

beeejlsw bejewels bejewel. *See* **beejls eejlsw**

beeejlw bejewel. *See* **beejl eejlw**

beeelmns ensemble. *See* **beeems eeelms**

beeelmrs resemble. *See* **beeems beelrs beemrs eeelms**

beeelmzz embezzle. *See* **beelz eeelm**

beeelst beetles. *See* **beeelt beest belst**

beeelt beetle betel beet belt leet bee bel bet eel lee let tee be el

beeemmrr remember. *See* **beemmr**

beeems beseem bees seem bee see be em me

beeemss beseems. *See* **beeems eemss**

beeennsz benzenes benzene. *See* **beenns eeensz**

beeennz benzene. *See* **beenn**

beeentw between. *No 6s or 5s*

beeepr beeper beep beer bree epee peer bee ere pee per rep be er pe re

beeeprs beepers. *See* **beeepr beeps beers**

beeersz breezes. *See* **beeerz beers**

beeerz breeze beer bree bee ere zee be er re

beeesv beeves bees eves vees bee eve see vee be

beef beef bee fee be

beefgin beefing. *See* **eefgin begin beegi**

beefil belief belie beef bile feel file flee lief life bee bel eel elf fee fib fie lee lei lie be el if li

beefillx flexible flexile. *See* **beefil beefll**

beefilr febrile. *See* **beefil eefilr**

beefilrs belfries beliefs febrile refiles. *See* **beefil beeils beelrs befirs**

beefils beliefs. *See* **beefil beeils**

beefinst benefits benefit. *See* **befist efinst**

beefint benefit. *See* **befit efint**

beefll befell belle beef bell feel fell flee bee bel eel elf ell fee lee be el

beefly feebly beefy beef eely feel flee bee bel bey bye eel elf eye fee fey fly lee lye be by el ye

beefnorr freeborn. *See* **beefor benorr**

beefor before beef beer bore bree fere forb fore free froe reef robe bee ere fee fob foe for fro orb ore ref rob roe be er of or re

beefrt bereft beret beef beer beet bree feet fere fete free fret reef reft rete tree bee bet eft ere fee ref ret tee be er re

beefs beefs beef bees fees bee fee see be

beefy beefy beef bee bey bye eye fee fey be by ye

beegi beige gibe bee beg big gee gib gie be

beegiill eligible legible. *See* **beegi beeil beell**

beegill legible. *See* **beegi beeil beell**

beegilnt beetling beignet belting gentile. *See* **begilt eegilt eegint eeglnt**

beegilnv beveling. *See* **begin beegi beeil**

beegilru beguiler beguile. *See* **beegru begilr beglru eeglru**

beegilsu beguiles beguile. *See* **beegis beegls beeils begils**

beegilu beguile. *See* **beegi begil beglu**

beeginnr beginner. *See* **beginn eeginn**

beeginrz breezing zebrine. *See* **eginrz**

beeginst beignets beignet besting. *See* **beegis beegst begins eegins**

beeginsu beguines beguine. *See* **beegis begins bginsu eegins**

beeginsw beeswing. *See* **beegis begins eegins eginsw**

beegint beignet. *See* **eegint beegt begin**

beeginu beguine. *See* **begin begnu beegi**

beegis beiges beige gibes siege bees begs bise egis gees gibe gibs gies bee beg big gee gib gie see sib be is si

beegl glebe glee bee beg bel eel gee gel lee leg be el

beegls glebes glebe glees bees begs bels eels else gees gels glee lees legs seel bee beg bel eel els gee gel lee leg see be el

beegmnoy bogeymen. *See* **beegno begnoy eemnoy**

beegmrsu submerge burgees embrues. *See* **beegrs beegru beemrs beemru**

beegno begone been bone bong ebon gene gone ogee bee beg ben bog ego eon gee gob neb nee nob nog one be en go ne no on

beegnott begotten. *See* **beegno egnott**

beegr grebe beer berg bree gree bee beg ere erg gee reg be er re

beegrs grebes beers bergs brees grebe grees serge beer bees begs berg bree ergs gees gree regs seer sere bee beg ere erg gee reg res see be er re

beegrsu burgees. *See* **beegrs beegru**

beegru burgee grebe beer berg bree burg gree grub grue rube urge bee beg bug ere erg gee reg rub rue rug be er re

beegst begets beets beget beset egest bees beet begs best bets gees gest gets tees bee beg bet gee get see set tee be

beegt beget beet bee beg bet gee get tee be

beehhmot behemoth. *See* **eehmt eemot**

beehirr herbier. *See* **eehirr beirr**

beehirst herbiest sherbet heister. *See* **beehst beerst behrst beirst**

beehllnt hellbent. *See* **beehlt**

beehlrss herbless. *See* **beelrs eehrss eelrss**

beehlt bethel betel beet belt beth heel leet thee bee bel bet eel eth het lee let tee the be eh el he

beehnrt brethren. *See* **eehnrt eenrrt**

beehoosv behooves behoove. *See* **behoos ehoosv**

beehoov behoove. *No 6s or 5s*

beehop phoebe beep hope bee bop hep hob hoe hop ope pee be eh he ho oh pe

beehrsst sherbets sherbet. *See* **beehst beerst beesst behrst**

beehrssw beshrews beshrew. *See* **eehrss eehrsw eerssw ehrssw**

beehrst sherbet. *See* **beehst beerst behrst eehrst**

beehrsw beshrew. *See* **eehrsw beers bersw**

beehrty thereby. *See* **beehry beert behrt**

beehrwy whereby. *See* **beehry eehrw**

beehry hereby beery herby beer bree byre eery eyre herb here bee bey bye ere eye her hey rye be by eh er he re ye

beehst behest beets beset beths sheet these bees beet best beth bets hest tees thee bee bet eth het see set she tee the be eh he sh

beeiilnz zibeline. *See* **beeil beelz beinz**

beeijlsu jubilees jubilee. *See* **beeils beejls**

beeijlu jubilee. *See* **beeil beejl**

beeiklw weblike. *See* **beeil**

beeiklwy biweekly weblike. *See* **eeklwy**

beeil belie bile bee bel eel lee lei lie be el li

beeillr libeler. *See* **beillr beeil beell**

beeillrs libelers bellies libeler rebills. *See* **beeils beells beelrs beillr**

beeills bellies. *See* **beeils beells beills**

beeilltt belittle. *See* **beillt eilltt**

beeilnss sensible. *See* **beeils eeilns eeinss eelnss**

beeilnuz nebulize. *See* **beilnu**

beeilosz obelizes obelize. *See* **beeils beilos beelsz**

beeiloz obelize. *See* **beeil beelz**

beeilrrt terrible. *See* **beelrt eeirrt**

beeilryz breezily. *See* **beeryz eeilry**

beeils belies belie biles bees bels bile bise eels else isle lees leis lies seel bee bel eel els lee lei lie see sib be el is li si

beeimr bemire bireme ember beer berm bier bree brie brim emir mere mire rime bee ere ire mir rem rib rim be em er me mi re

beeimrs bemires biremes. *See* **beeimr beemrs eeimrs**

beeimrtt embitter emitter termite. *See* **beeimr beertt beimrt beirtt**

beeimst betimes. *See* **beest beist eimst**

beeinns bennies. *See* **beenns beins einns**

beeinnsz benzines bennies benzine. *See* **beenns**

beeinnz benzine. *See* **beenn beinz**

beeinos ebonies. *See* **beins binos benos**

beeinosz ebonizes ebonies ebonize. *See* **beins binos benos**

beeinot ebonite. *No 6s or 5s*

beeinoz ebonize. *See* **beinz benoz**

beeinrz zebrine. *See* **beinr beinz**

beeiorsw boweries. *See* **beirsw beorsw eeiors**

beeiortv overbite. *See* **beertv beortv**

beeiqsuz beziques bezique. *See* **beiqsu**

beeiquz bezique. *No 6s or 5s*

beeirrs berries. *See* **beirrs eeirrs**

beeisv bevies vibes sieve bees bise eves vees vies vise bee eve see sib vee vie be is si

beeisx ibexes bees bise exes ibex bee see sex sib six be ex is si xi

beejl jebel bee bel eel lee be el

beejls jebels jebel bees bels eels else lees seel bee bel eel els lee see be el

beeknot betoken. *See* **eeknot**

beekops bespoke. *See* **eekops beeps beeos**

beekrrs berserk. *See* **beers eekrs bekrs**

beekrsu rebukes. *See* **beekru bekrsu**

beekru rebuke burke beer bree kerb reek rube bee eke ere rub rue be er re

beell belle bell bee bel eel ell lee be el

beells belles belle bells bees bell bels eels ells else lees seel sell bee bel eel ell els lee see be el

beelmm emblem bee bel eel elm lee mel mem be el em me

beelmms emblems. *See* **beelmm**

beelmnno noblemen ennoble. *See* **beenn elmno eelno**

beelmrrt trembler tremble. *See* **beelrt eemrrt**

beelmrst trembles smelter trebles tremble. *See* **beelrs beelrt beemrs beerst**

beelmrt tremble. *See* **beelrt beemr eelmr**

beelnno ennoble. *See* **beenn eelno belno**

beelnnos ennobles ennoble. *See* **beenns belnos eelnos**

beelnoss boneless noblesse. *See* **belnos eelnos eelnss elnoss**

beelnosu bluenose nebulose. *See* **belnos belosu eelnos**

beelnssu blueness. *See* **eelnss eenssu elnssu**

beeloost obsolete bootees. *See* **beeoot**

beelp bleep plebe beep peel bee bel eel lee pee be el pe

beelps bleeps plebes beeps bleep peels plebe sleep beep bees bels eels else lees peel pees seel seep bee bel eel els lee pee see be el pe

beelr rebel beer bree leer reel bee bel eel ere lee be el er re

beelrs rebels beers brees leers rebel reels beer bees bels bree eels else leer lees reel seel seer sere bee bel eel els ere lee res see be el er re

beelrst trebles. *See* **beerst beelrs beelrt**

beelrt treble beret betel rebel beer beet belt bree leer leet reel rete tree bee bel bet eel ere lee let ret tee be el er le

beelsv bevels bevel elves bees bels eels else eves lees seel vees bee bel eel els eve lee lev see vee be el

beelsz bezels bezel bees bels eels else lees seel zees bee bel eel els lee see zee be el

beelt betel beet belt leet bee bel bet eel lee let tee be el

beelv bevel bee bel eel eve lee lev vee be el

beelz bezel bee bel eel lee zee be el

beemmr member ember emmer beer berm bree mere bee ere mem rem be em er me re

beemmrs members. *See* **beemrs eemmrs beemmr**

beemnrru numberer renumber. *See* **beemru bemnru benrru**

beemorss embosser. *See* **beemrs bemors bemoss beorss**

beemorsw embowers embower. *See* **beemrs bemors bemosw beorsw**

beemorw embower. *See* **beorw beemr bemow**

beemosss embosses. *See* **bemoss eemsss**

beemr ember beer berm bree mere bee ere rem be em er me re

beemrs embers beers berms brees ember meres beer bees berm bree mere seem seer sere bee ere rem res see be em er me re

beemrssu submerse bemuses embrues rebuses resumes. *See* **beemrs beemru beemsu bemrsu**

beemrsu embrues. *See* **beemsu bemrsu beemrs beemru eemrsu**

beemru embrue brume ember umber beer berm bree emeu mere rube bee bum emu ere rem rub rue rum be em er me mu re um

beemssu bemuses. *See* **beemsu bemssu**

beemsu bemuse sebum emeus bees bums emeu emus muse seem bee bum bus emu mus see sub sue sum use be em me mu um us

been been bee ben neb nee be en ne

beenn benne been bee ben neb nee be en ne

beenns bennes benne been bees bens nebs seen bee ben ens neb nee see sen be en ne

beenosst bonesets boneset. *See* **beesst beosst eensst enosst**

beenost boneset. *See* **beest beost benos**

beenrttu brunette burette. *See* **beertt benrtu berttu eenrtt**

beenssuv subvenes subvene. *See* **eenssu eenssv eensuv**

beensuv subvene. *See* **eensuv**

beeoost bootees. *See* **beeoot beest beost**

beeoot bootee beet boot oboe bee bet boo bot tee toe too be to

beeorrsu bourrees bourree. *See* **beorrs beorsu borrsu eorrsu**

beeorrsv observer observe obverse reverbs verbose. *See* **beerrv beersv beorrs eeorsv**

beeorru bourree. *See* **beorr borru**

beeorssv observes obverses observe obverse verbose. *See* **beersv beorss eeorsv**

beeorsv observe obverse verbose. *See* **beersv eeorsv**

beeorswy eyebrows bowyers eyebrow obeyers. *See* **beeory beorsw beorwy**

beeorsy obeyers. *See* **beeory beors beors**

beeorwy eyebrow. *See* **beorwy beeory**

beeory obeyer beery beer bore bree byre eery eyre obey orby robe yore bee bey boy bye ere eye orb ore rob roe rye yob be by er or oy re ye

beeos obese bees bee see sob be os so

beeossss obsesses. *See* **beosss**

beep beep bee pee be pe

beeps beeps beep bees pees seep bee pee see be pe

beeqsstu bequests bequest. *See* **beesst besstu eqsstu**

beeqstu bequest. *See* **beest eqstu bestu**

beer beer bree bee ere be er re

beerrsv reverbs. *See* **beersv beerrv eerrsv**

beerrsw brewers. *See* **beerrw beers bersw**

beerrv reverb breve beer bree ever veer verb bee ere err eve rev vee be er re

beerrw brewer beer bree brew ewer bee ere err ewe web wee be er re we

beerrwy brewery. *See* **beerrw beery berry**

beers beers brees beer bees bree seer sere bee ere res see be er re

beerssu rebuses. *See* **berssu eerssu**

beerssuv subserve rebuses. *See* **beersv berssu eerssu eersuv**

beerst berets beers beets beret beset brees ester reset steer stere terse trees beer bees beet best bets bree erst rest rete rets seer sere tees tree bee bet ere res ret see set tee be er re

beerstt betters. *See* **beerst beertt eerstt**

beersttu burettes betters burette butters trustee. *See* **beerst beertt berstu berttu**

beerstv brevets. *See* **beerst beersv beertv eerstv**

beersv breves beers brees breve serve sever veers verbs verse beer bees bree ever eves revs seer sere veer vees verb bee ere eve res rev see vee be er re

beert beret beer beet bree rete tree bee bet ere ret tee be er re

beertt better beret beer beet bree rete tree tret bee bet ere ret tee be er re

beerttu burette. *See* **beertt berttu**

beertv brevet beret breve evert beer beet bree ever rete tree veer verb vert bee bet ere eve ret rev tee vee vet be er re

beerv breve beer bree ever veer verb bee ere eve rev vee be er re

beery beery beer bree byre eery eyre bee bey bye ere eye rye be by er re ye

beeryz breezy beery beer bree byre eery eyre bee bey bye ere eye rye zee be by er re ye

bees bees bee see be

beesst besets beets beset bests bees beet best bets sees sets tees bee bet ess see set tee be

beest beets beset bees beet best bets tees bee bet see set tee be

beet beet bee bet tee be

beffllrsu bluffers bluffer buffers rebuffs ruffles. *See* **beffru belrsu bfflsu efflru**

beffllru bluffer. *See* **beffru effllru**

beffrsu buffers rebuffs. *See* **beffru effrsu**

beffru buffer rebuff buff rube ruff feu fur ref rub rue be er fu

beffstu buffets. *See* **befftu bffsu efstu**

befftu buffet buff tube tuff bet but eft feu tub be ut

befgiil filibeg. *See* **begil**

befgiils filibegs filibeg. *See* **begils**

befgiinr briefing. *See* **bfiinr efginr**

befgilnu fungible blueing fueling. *See* **beglnu beilnu bgilnu efglnu**

befgirsu firebugs firebug figures. *See* **befirs beirsu efgirs efgiru**

befgiru firebug. *See* **efgiru befir**

befgo befog beg bog ego fob foe fog gob be go of

befgos befogs befog begs bogs egos fobs foes fogs gobs goes sego beg bog ego fob foe fog gob sob be go of os so

befhilsu bluefish fusible. *See* **behlsu bhilsu efhils**

befilo foible bile boil bole file floe foil lief life lobe bel elf fib fie fob foe lei lie lob obi oil be el if li lo of

befilos foibles. *See* **beilos efilos befilo**

befilost botflies foibles. *See* **befilo befist beilos efilos**

befilrst filberts blister bristle filbert filters lifters trifles. *See* **befirs befist beirst efilrs**

befilrt filbert. *See* **efilrt**

befilry briefly. *See* **beflry befir efiry**

befilsu fusible. *See* **beils belsu efils**

befinor bonfire. *See* **beinor befir efinr**

befinors bonfires bonfire. *See* **befirs beinor beinrs**

befir brief fiber bier brie fire rife fib fie fir ire ref rib rif be er if re

befirs briefs fibers biers brief fiber fires fries serif bier bise brie fibs fies fire firs refs reis ribs rife rifs rise serf sire fib fie fir ifs ire ref res rib rif sib sir be er if is re si

befist befits befit bites feist best bets bise bite bits efts fibs fies fist fits sift site ties bet bit eft fib fie fit ifs its set sib sit tie be if is it si ti

befit befit bite bet bit eft fib fie fit tie be if it ti

befllluy bellyful. *See* **belluy**

beflmsu fumbles. *See* **eflmsu beflmu belmsu**

beflmu fumble umbel flume blue flub flue fuel fume lube mule bel bum elf elm emu feu flu leu lum mel be el em me mu um

befloruw furbelow. *See* **beflou beloru belorw eflorw**

beflosu befouls. *See* **beflou belosu**

beflou befoul boule blue bole floe flub flue foul fuel lobe lube bel elf feu flu fob foe leu lob be el lo of

beflry belfry beryl flyer byre lyre rely bel bey bye elf fey fly fry lye ref rye be by el er re ye

befnoorr forborne forbore. *See* **benorr efoorr**

befoorr forbore. *See* **efoorr beorr**

befootw webfoot. *No 6s or 5s*

beg beg be

begggin begging. *See* **egggin begin**

beggii biggie gibe beg big egg gib gie gig be

beggiis biggies. *See* **beggii begis**

begginoy bogeying obeying. *See* **begnoy**

beggir bigger berg bier brie brig gibe grig beg big egg erg gib gie gig ire reg rib rig be er re

beggiru buggier. *See* **beggir beggru**

beggist biggest. *See* **begis beist**

beggistu buggiest biggest buggies. *See* **eggisu**

beggisu buggies. *See* **eggisu begis**

begglo boggle globe bole glob lobe loge ogle beg bel bog egg ego gel gob leg lob log be el go lo

begglos boggles. *See* **begglo beglos**

beggrsu buggers. *See* **beggru eggrsu**

beggru bugger gurge berg burg grub grue rube urge beg bug egg erg reg rub rue rug be er re

beghinor neighbor bighorn. *See* **beinor bginor eghino eghinr**

beghinrt berthing brighten. *See* **bghirt eghinr ehinrt**

beghirrt brighter rebirth. *See* **bghirt**

beghnotu boughten toughen. *See* **bghotu eghnou egnotu ghnotu**

beghostu besought. *See* **beostu bghosu bghotu eghstu**

beghrrsu burghers burgher burgers. *See* **begrru bghrsu eghrsu ehrrsu**

beghrru burgher. *See* **begrru bghru eghru**

begi gibe beg big gib gie be

begiilln libeling belling billing. *See* **eiilln**

begiilly eligibly legibly. *See* **bgilly**

begiimnr bemiring. *See* **giimnr**

begiinn inbeing. *See* **beginn egiin**

begiintw bitewing. *See* **bgiint egiint egintw**

begiknru rebuking burking. *See* **beknru**

begil bilge bile gibe glib beg bel big gel gib gie leg lei lie be el li

begilllu bluegill gullible. *See* **egillu**

begilln belling. *See* **begin begil egiln**

begillny bellying belling belying legibly yelling. *See* **beilny bgilly**

begilly legibly. *See* **bgilly belly begil**

begilnny benignly belying. *See* **beginn beilny**

begilno ignoble. *See* **beglno egilno bgilno begilo**

begilnow elbowing blowing bowline bowling ignoble. *See* **begilo beglno bgilno bginow**

begilnrt trebling belting gilbert ringlet tingler. *See* **begilr begilt beilnr egilnr**

begilnss blessing glibness bigness singles. *See* **begils begins egilns eginss**

begilnt belting. *See* **begilt egilnt**

begilnu blueing. *See* **bgilnu beglnu beilnu**

begilny belying. *See* **beilny begin begil**

begilo oblige bilge bogie globe bile boil bole gibe glib glob lobe loge ogle beg bel big bog ego gel gib gie gob leg lei lie lob log obi oil be el go li lo

begilos obliges. *See* **beilos begils begios beglos begilo**

begilr gerbil bilge berg bier bile birl brie brig gibe girl glib lire riel rile beg bel big erg gel gib gie ire leg lei lie reg rib rig be el er li re

begilrs gerbils. *See* **begils begilr egilrs**

begilrst gilberts blister bristle gerbils giblets gilbert gristle. *See* **begilr begils begilt beirst**

begilrt gilbert. *See* **begilr begilt**

begils bilges biles bilge gibes glibs begs bels bile bise egis gels gibe gibs gies glib isle legs leis lies beg bel big els gel gib gie leg lei lie sib be el is li si

begilst giblets. *See* **begils egilst**

begilt giblet bilge legit belt bile bite gibe gilt glib tile beg bel bet big bit gel get gib gie leg lei let lie lit tie til be el it li ti

begimnow embowing. *See* **bemnow bginow egimnw gimnow**

begimnru embruing umbering. *See* **beimru bemnru eimnru**

begimnsu bemusing. *See* **begins begmsu beimsu bemnsu**

begin begin being binge gibe bine beg ben big bin gib gie gin neb nib be en in ne

beginn benign begin being binge bine gibe nine beg ben big bin gib gie gin inn neb nib be en in ne

beginors sobering borings ignores regions. *See* **begins begios beinor beinrs**

beginoy obeying. *See* **begnoy begin bgino**

beginrry berrying. *See* **beirry eginrr**

beginrw brewing. *See* **begin beinr bginr**

begins begins beings binges begin being bines binge gibes segni singe begs bens bine bins bise egis gens gibe gibs gies gins nebs nibs sign sine sing beg ben big bin ens gib gie gin neb nib sen sib sin be en in is ne si

beginss bigness. *See* **begins eginss**

beginst besting. *See* **begins eginst**

begintt betting. *See* **beintt begin egint**

begio bogie gibe beg big bog ego gib gie gob obi be go

begioo boogie bogie gibe oboe beg big bog boo ego gib gie gob goo obi be go

begioos boogies. *See* **begioo begios**

begios bogies bogie gibes begs bise bogs egis egos gibe gibs gies gobs goes obis sego beg big bog ego gib gie gob obi sib sob be go is os si so

begiosu bougies. *See* **begios begiou**

begiou bougie bogie gibe beg big bog bug ego gib gie gob obi be go

begis gibes begs bise egis gibe gibs gies beg big gib gie sib be is si

begkmos gemsbok. *See* **bemos ekmos**

begkmoss gemsboks gemsbok. *See* **bemoss ekmoss**

begllosu globules globule lobules soluble. *See* **beglos beglsu bellou belosu**

begllou globule. *See* **bellou beglu beglo**

beglmrru grumbler grumble. *See* **beglru begrru belmru**

beglmrsu grumbles buglers burgles grumble lumbers rumbles slumber. *See* **beglru beglsu begmsu belmru**

beglmru grumble. *See* **beglru belmru**

beglno belong globe longe noble bole bone bong ebon enol glen glob gone leno lobe loge lone long noel ogle beg bel ben bog ego eon gel gob leg lob log neb nob nog one be el en go lo ne no on

beglnos belongs. *See* **beglno beglos eglnos belnos**

beglnrsu bunglers buglers bungler bungles burgles lungers. *See* **beglnu beglru beglsu belrsu**

beglnru bungler. *See* **beglru beglnu**

beglnsu bungles. *See* **beglsu eglnsu**

beglnu bungle begun bugle bulge lunge blue bung glen glue lube luge lune lung beg bel ben bug bun gel gnu gun leg leu lug neb nub be el en ne nu

beglo globe bole glob lobe loge ogle beg bel bog ego gel gob leg lob log be el go lo

begloost bootlegs bootleg goblets. *See* **beglos beglot egoost**

begloot bootleg. *See* **beglot**

beglos globes boles globe globs lobes loges ogles begs bels bogs bole egos gels glob gobs goes legs lobe lobs loge logs lose ogle sego slob sloe slog sole beg bel bog ego els gel gob leg lob log los sob sol be el go lo os so

beglost goblets. *See* **beglos beglot**

beglosuv lovebugs lovebug. *See* **beglos beglsu belosu eglosv**

beglot goblet globe begot belt blot bole bolt glob lobe loge ogle beg bel bet bog bot ego gel get gob got leg let lob log lot toe tog be el go lo to

beglouv lovebug. *See* **belou beglu beglo**

beglrsu buglers burgles. *See* **beglru beglsu eglrsu belrsu**

beglru bugler burgle bluer bugle bulge gluer gruel ruble berg blue blur burg burl glue grub grue lube luge lure rube rule urge beg bel bug erg gel leg leu lug reg rub rue rug be el er re

beglsu bugles bulges blues bugle bulge glues gules lubes luges begs bels blue bugs gels glue legs lube lues luge lugs

slub slue slug beg bel bug bus els gel leg leu lug sub sue use be el us

beglu bugle bulge blue glue lube luge beg bel bug gel leg leu lug be el

begmsu begums begum geums sebum begs bugs bums emus gems geum gums mugs muse smug beg bug bum bus emu gem gum mug mus sub sue sum use be em me mu um us

begmu begum geum beg bug bum emu gem gum mug be em me mu um

begnorsu burgeons brogues burgeon surgeon. *See* **begoru benors beorsu bgorsu**

begnortu burgonet burgeon. *See* **begoru benrtu bnortu egnotu**

begnoru burgeon. *See* **begoru begnu benor**

begnosy bygones. *See* **begnoy begosy**

begnoy bygone bogey ebony bogy bone bong bony ebon goby gone gybe obey beg ben bey bog boy bye ego eon gey gob goy neb nob nog one yen yob yon be by en go ne no on oy ye

begnssuu subgenus. *See* **begnu bgnsu bessu**

begnu begun bung beg ben bug bun gnu gun neb nub be en ne nu

begoor goober berg boor bore goer gore oboe ogre robe beg bog boo ego erg gob goo orb ore reg rob roe be er go or re

begoors goobers. *See* **begoor begrs boors**

begorsu brogues. *See* **bgorsu beorsu begoru egorsu**

begoru brogue bourg rogue rouge berg bore burg goer gore grub grue ogre robe rube urge beg bog bug ego erg gob orb ore our reg rob roe rub rue rug be er go or re

begosy bogeys bogey gybes obeys begs beys bogs bogy boys byes egos gobs goby goes goys gybe obey oyes sego yobs beg bey bog boy ego gey gob goy sob soy yes yob be by go os oy so ye

begot begot beg bet bog bot ego get gob got toe tog be go to

begoy bogey bogy goby gybe obey beg bey bog boy bye ego gey gob goy yob be by go oy ye

begr berg beg erg reg be er re

begrrsu burgers. *See* **begrru begrs bgrsu**

begrru burger berg burg burr grub grue rube urge beg bug erg err reg rub rue rug be er re

begrs bergs begs berg ergs regs beg erg reg res be er re

begrssu burgess. *See* **berssu egrssu**

begs begs beg be

begsy gybes begs beys byes gybe beg bey bye gey yes be by ye

begy gybe beg bey bye gey be by ye

behiistx exhibits exhibit. *See* **behst beist eistx**

behiitx exhibit. *No 6s or 5s*

behikoss kiboshes. *See* **behoss bhikos ehikss**

behillty blithely lithely. *See* **behilt beillt**

behilmrw whimbrel. *See* **beilmr beilmw**

behilms blemish. *See* **beils ehlms bilms**

behilmst thimbles blemish thimble. *See* **behilt ehimst**

behilmt thimble. *See* **behilt**

behilorr horrible broiler. *See* **beilor ehilor**

behilrtu thurible rebuilt. *See* **behilt belrtu ehilrt ehlrtu**

behilt blithe lithe belt beth bile bite hilt tile bel bet bit eth het hie hit lei let lie lit the tie til be eh el he hi it li ti

behinnos shinbone. *See* **ehinos**

behinop hipbone. *See* **ehnop einop**

behinops hipbones hipbone phonies. *See* **bhiops ehinos ehnops einops**

behinosw wishbone. *See* **ehinos ehinsw einosw**

behiotw howbeit. *See* **beiow ehitw**

behirrst rebirths rebirth. *See* **behrst beirrs beirst bhirst**

behirrt rebirth. *See* **behrt bhirt beirt**

behirsu bushier. *See* **beirsu bhirsu**

behisstu bushiest busiest. *See* **behssu besstu ehisst ehsstu**

behkor rhebok broke bore herb hero hoer hoke kerb robe her hob hoe kob kor oke orb ore rho rob roe be eh er he ho oh or re

behkors rheboks. *See* **behkor ehkors**

behllop bellhop. *See* **ehllo**

behllops bellhops bellhop. *See* **ehllos**

behllox hellbox. *See* **ehllo**

behlmru humbler. *See* **behlmu belmru**

behlmstu humblest humbles stumble tumbles. *See* **behlmu behlsu belmsu belmtu**

behlmsu humbles. *See* **behlsu behlmu belmsu**

behlmu humble umbel blue buhl helm lube mule bel bum elm emu hem hub hue hum leu lum mel be eh el em he me mu um

behlorst brothels bolster bolters bothers brothel holster hostler lobster. *See* **behort behrst belors belort**

behlort brothel. *See* **behort belort**

behlrssu blushers blusher blushes brushes bushels. *See* **behlsu behssu belrsu berssu**

behlrsu blusher. *See* **behlsu belrsu**

behlssu blushes bushels. *See* **behlsu behssu ehlssu**

behlsu bushel blues blush buhls lubes bels blue buhl bush hubs hues lube lues lush slub slue bel bus els hub hue leu she sub sue use be eh el he sh us

behmnsu bushmen. *See* **bemnsu**

behmor hombre homer omber ombre rhomb berm bore herb herm hero hoer home more omer robe hem her hob hoe mho mob mor ohm orb ore rem rho rob roe be eh em er he ho me mo oh om or re

behmors hombres. *See* **behmor ehmors bemors bhmors**

behoorst theorbos booster bothers shooter theorbo. *See* **behoos behort behrst beorst**

behoort theorbo. *See* **behort ehoort**

behoos hoboes oboes hobos boos bosh hobo hobs hoes hose oboe oohs shoe shoo boo hob hoe oho ohs ooh she sob be eh he ho oh os sh so

behoostx hotboxes. *See* **behoos bhoost bhootx ehoost**

behoosuy houseboy. *See* **behoos**

behoprst potherbs bothers potherb strophe thorpes. *See* **behort behrst beoprs beorst**

behoprt potherb. *See* **behort ehoprt**

behorrst brothers bothers brother rhetors. *See* **behort behrst beorrs beorst**

behorrt brother. *See* **behort ehorrt**

behorssu rosebush brushes bourses. *See* **behoss behssu beorss beorsu**

behorst bothers. *See* **behrst behort bhorst ehorst beorst**

behorstt betroths betroth bettors bothers. *See* **behort behrst beorst beortt**

behort bother berth broth other throb throe beth bore bort both herb hero hoer robe rote tore bet bot eth her het hob hoe hot orb ore ort ret rho rob roe rot the tho toe tor be eh er he ho oh or re to

behortt betroth. *See* **beortt ehortt**

behoss boshes hoses shoes bosh boss hobs hoes hose shoe sobs ess hob hoe ohs she sob be eh he ho oh os sh so

behr herb her be eh er he re

behrs herbs herb hers resh her res she be eh er he re sh

behrssu brushes. *See* **berssu behssu ehrssu bhrssu**

behrst berths berth beths herbs best beth bets erst herb hers hest resh rest rets bet eth her het res ret set she the be eh er he re sh

behrt berth herb beth bet eth her het ret the be eh er he re

behry herby herb byre bey bye her hey rye be by eh er he re ye

behssu bushes buses bush buss hubs hues subs sues uses bus ess hub hue she sub sue use be eh he sh us

behst beths best beth bets hest bet eth het set she the be eh he sh

beht beth bet eth het the be eh he

beiiikmn minibike. *See* **biiikn**

beiik kibei bike kibe be

beiikrtz kibitzer. *See* **biiktz**

beiiks kibeis bikes kibei kibes bike bise ibis kibe sib ski be is si

beiikstz kibitzes. *See* **beiiks biiktz**

beiills billies. *See* **beills eiills**

beiilmmo immobile. *See* **beilmo**

beiilmoz mobilize. *See* **beilmo beimoz**

beiilrs risible. *See* **beirs beils bilrs**

beiilrst trilbies blister bristle risible siltier. *See* **beirst eilrst**

beiilrtt libretti brittle. *See* **beirtt eilrtt**

beiilsv visible. *See* **beils eilsv eiisv**

beiinors brionies ironies noisier. *See* **beinor beinrs benors**

beiinrr brinier. *See* **beinr beirr**

beiiopss biopsies. *See* **beiiss eiopss**

beiiss ibises bises bise ibis sibs ess sib sis be is si

beij jibe jib be

beijr jiber bier brie jibe ire jib rib be er re

beijrs jibers biers jiber jibes bier bise brie jibe jibs reis ribs rise sire ire jib res rib sib sir be er is re si

beijs jibes bise jibe jibs jib sib be is si

beik bike kibe be

beiklmot tomblike. *See* **beilmo eilmot**

beiklnr blinker. *See* **beilnr eiklnr**

beiklnrs blinkers blinker berlins. *See* **beilnr beinrs biklns biknrs**

beiklos obelisk. *See* **beklos beiks**

beikloty kilobyte. *See* **beklo eklot eilot**

beiklox boxlike. *See* **beklo**

beiklru bulkier. *See* **belru bekru eiklr**

beiklstu bulkiest subtile. *See* **belstu**

beikoo bookie bike book kibe kobo oboe boo kob obi oke be

beikoos bookies. *See* **beikoo beiks bkoos**

beikors boskier. *See* **beiks bikrs**

beikosst boskiest ketosis. *See* **beosst ekosst**

beikrsst briskets bestirs bisters brisket strikes. *See* **beirst eikrss eikrst eirsst**

beikrst brisket. *See* **beirst eikrst**

beiks bikes kibes bike bise kibe sib ski be is si

beil bile bel lei lie be el li

beill libel bell bile bill bel ell ill lei lie be el li

beillntu bulletin. *See* **beillt beilnu belltu eillnt**

beillosu libelous bullies lobules soluble. *See* **beills beilos bellou belosu**

beillosx bollixes. *See* **beills beilos billox**

beillr rebill libel rille bell bier bile bill birl brie lire riel rile rill bel ell ill ire lei lie rib be el er li re

beillrs rebills. *See* **billrs beills beillr eillrs**

beills libels bells biles bills libel lisle bell bels bile bill bise ells isle leis lies sell sill bel ell els ill lei lie sib be el is li si

beillst billets. *See* **beillt eillst**

beillsu bullies. *See* **beills belsu bllsu**

beillt billet libel bell belt bile bill bite lilt tell tile till bel bet bit ell ill lei let lie lit tie til be el it li ti

beilmmos embolism mobiles. *See* **beilmo beilos bilmos**

beilmn nimble limen bile bine lien limb lime limn line mien mile mine bel ben bin elm lei lie mel men mil neb nib nil nim be el em en in li me mi ne

beilmnou nobelium. *See* **beilmn beilmo beilnu eilmno**

beilmnr nimbler. *See* **beilnr beilmr eilmnr beilmn**

beilmnst nimblest. *See* **beilmn eilmns eilnst**

beilmo emboli mobile limbo bile boil bole limb lime limo lobe mile milo moil mole bel elm lei lie lob mel mil mob obi oil be el em li lo me mi mo om

beilmoor bloomier embroil bloomer. *See* **beilmo beilmr beilor beloor**

beilmor embroil. *See* **beilor beilmo beilmr**

beilmors embroils boilers embroil mobiles. *See* **beilmo beilmr beilor beilos**

beilmos mobiles. *See* **beilos bilmos beilmo**

beilmr limber miler berm bier bile birl brie brim emir limb lime lire merl mile mire riel rile rime bel elm ire lei lie mel mil mir rem rib rim be el em er li me mi re

beilmssu sublimes sublime. *See* **beimsu belmsu bemssu bilmsu**

beilmsu sublime. *See* **beimsu bilmsu belmsu**

beilmsw wimbles. *See* **beilmw beils eilsw**

beilmw wimble bile blew limb lime mewl mile wile bel elm lei lie mel mew mil web be el em li me mi we

beilmy blimey limey bile limb lime limy mile ylem bel bey bye elm lei lie lye mel mil be by el em li me mi my ye

beilnntu buntline. *See* **beilnu benntu eilnnt elnntu**

beilnops bonspiel epsilon pinoles. *See* **beilos belnos eilnop eilnos**

beilnosw bowlines bowline. *See* **beilos belnos belosw eilnos**

beilnow bowline. *See* **below blnow beiow**

beilnr berlin brine liner bier bile bine birl brie lien line lire rein riel rile bel ben bin ire lei lie neb nib nil rib be el en er in li ne re

beilnrs berlins. *See* **beilnr beinrs eilnrs**

beilnstz blintzes blintze blitzes. *See* **eilnst**

beilnsy bylines. *See* **beilny eilnsy**

beilntz blintze. *See* **belnt biltz eilnt**

beilnu nubile bile bine blue lien lieu line lube lune bel ben bin bun lei leu lie neb nib nil nub be el en in li ne nu

beilny byline bile bine inly lien line liny bel ben bey bin bye lei lie lye neb nib nil yen yin be by el en in li ne ye

beiloos loobies. *See* **beilos eiloos**

beiloppw blowpipe. *See* **below beiow**

beilopss possible besoils. *See* **beilos eilops eilpss eiopss**

beiloqu oblique. *See* **belou**

beilor boiler broil oiler oriel roble bier bile birl boil bole bore brie lire lobe lore orle riel rile robe roil role bel ire lei lie lob obi oil orb ore rib rob roe be el er li lo or re

beilorr broiler. *See* **beilor beorr beirr**

beilorrs broilers boilers broiler lorries. *See* **beilor beilos beirrs**

beilors boilers. *See* **beilos beilor bilors eilors**

beilorst strobile blister boilers bolster bolters bristle lobster loiters toilers. *See* **beilor beilos beirst**

beilorsu blousier boilers lousier roubles. *See* **beilor beilos beirsu**

beilorsw blowsier blowers boilers bowlers. *See* **beilor beilos beirsw**

beilortt libretto blotter bottler brittle tortile. *See* **beilor beirtt belort belott**

beilos besoil biles boils boles lobes bels bile bise boil bole isle leis lies lobe lobs lose obis oils silo slob sloe soil sole bel els lei lie lob los obi oil sib sob sol be el is li lo os si so

beiloss besoils. *See* **beilos beiss belss**

beilrrty terribly liberty. *See* **beirry bilrty**

beilrru burlier. *See* **beirru belru elrru**

beilrss ribless. *See* **beirs beils bilrs**

beilrsst blisters bristles bestirs bisters blister bristle listers ribless. *See* **beirst eilrst eilsst eirsst**

beilrst blister bristle. *See* **beirst eilrst**

beilrstt brittles bitters blister bristle brittle litters. *See* **beirst beirtt eilrst eilrtt**

beilrstu burliest blister bluster bristle butlers lustier rebuilt subtile. *See* **beirst beirsu belrsu belrtu**

beilrtt brittle. *See* **beirtt eilrtt**

beilrtty bitterly brittle liberty. *See* **beirtt bilrty eilrtt elrtty**

beilrtu rebuilt. *See* **belrtu beirt birtu**

beilrty liberty. *See* **bilrty belry beirt**

beils biles bile bise isle leis lies bel els lei lie sib be el is li si

beilsttu subtitle subtile. *See* **belstu eilstt ilsttu**

beilstu subtile. *See* **belstu**

beilstz blitzes. *See* **belst beils beist**

beimmrr brimmer. *See* **beirr eimmr**

beimnor bromine. *See* **beinor eimnor**

beimnors bromines bromine merinos. *See* **beinor beinrs bemors**

beimnssu nimbuses minuses. *See* **beimsu bemnsu bemssu bimnsu**

beimntu bitumen. *See* **eimntu**

beimorty biometry. *See* **beimrt bemory eimoty**

beimosz zombies. *See* **beimoz bimosz**

beimoz zombie zombi obi mob be em me mi mo om

beimpru bumpier. *See* **bempru beimru eimpru**

beimpstu bumpiest impetus imputes. *See* **beimsu bimstu eimptu empstu**

beimrst timbers timbres. *See* **beirst eimrst beimrt**

beimrstu resubmit imbrues timbers timbres. *See* **beimrt beimru beimsu beirst**

beimrsu imbrues. *See* **beirsu bemrsu beimru beimsu**

beimrt timber timbre biter merit miter mitre remit timer tribe berm bier bite brie brim brit emir emit item mire mite rime rite term tier time tire trim bet bit ire met mir rem ret rib rim tie be em er it me mi re ti

beimru imbrue brume imbue umber berm bier brie brim emir mire rime rube bum emu ire mir rem rib rim rub rue rum be em er me mi mu re um

beimsu imbues imbue sebum bise bums emus mise muse semi bum bus emu mis mus sib sub sue sum use be em is me mi mu si um us

beimu imbue bum emu be em me mi mu um

bein bine ben bin neb nib be en in ne

beinnor bonnier. *See* **beinor binnor**

beinnoss boniness. *See* **einoss**

beinnost bonniest boniest bonnets intones tension. *See* **bennot einnot einnst ennost**

beinnsu bunnies. *See* **beins einnu einns**

beinoos boonies. *See* **beins binos benos**

beinor bonier boner brine robin bier bine bone bore born brie ebon iron rein robe ben bin eon ion ire neb nib nob nor obi one orb ore rib rob roe be en er in ne no on or re

beinorsw brownies brownie snowier. *See* **beinor beinrs beirsw**

beinorw brownie. *See* **beinor beorw beiow**

beinost boniest. *See* **beost beins binos**

beinostu bounties boniest. *See* **beostu biostu einstu**

beinosv bovines. *See* **beinov beins binos**

beinov bovine ovine bine bone ebon nevi oven vein vine ben bin eon ion neb nib nob obi one vie be en in ne no on

beinr brine bier bine brie rein ben bin ire neb nib rib be en er in ne re

beinrs brines nebris biers bines brine reins resin rinse risen serin siren bens bier bine bins bise brie nebs nibs rein reis ribs rise sine sire ben bin ens ire neb nib res rib sen sib sin sir be en er in is ne re si

beinrstu tribunes turbines brunets burnets tribune triunes turbine. *See* **beinrs beirst beirsu benrtu**

beinrtt bittern. *See* **beintt beirtt einrtt**

beinrtu tribune turbine. *See* **benrtu einrtu**

beins bines bens bine bins bise nebs nibs sine ben bin ens neb nib sen sib sin be en in is ne si

beinssu business sinuses. *See* **besssu eisssu**

beintt bitten bent bine bite bitt tent tine tint ben bet bin bit neb net nib nit ten tie tin tit be en in it ne ti

beinz zineb bine zein ben bin neb nib be en in ne

beiooost booties. *See* **bioost eioost**

beioqtuu boutique bouquet. *See* **eiqtu ioqtu eoqtu**

beiorrst orbiters orbiter rioters. *See* **beirrs beirst beorrs**

beiorrt orbiter. *See* **eiorrt beirt beorr**

beiorss bossier. *See* **beorss**

beiorsty sobriety obesity. *See* **beirst beorst biorst**

beiorx boxier boxer bier bore brie ibex robe box ire obi orb ore rex rib rob roe be er ex or ox re xi

beiossst bossiest. *See* **beosss beosst eossst**

beiosssu soubises soubise. *See* **beosss beossu eisssu**

beiossu soubise. *See* **beossu beiss eissu**

beiostx boxiest. *See* **beost beist beosx**

beiosty obesity. *See* **beost besty beosy**

beiow   bowie bow obi owe web woe be ow we

beiqrstu   briquets briquet querist. *See* **beiqsu beirst beirsu berstu**

beiqrtu   briquet. *See* **beirt birtu bertu**

beiqssu   bisques. *See* **beiqsu biqssu**

beiqsu   bisque squib bise bus sib sub sue use be is si us

beir   bier brie rib ire be er re

beirr   brier bier birr brie err ire rib be er re

beirrs   briers biers birrs brier riser bier birr bise brie errs reis ribs rise sire err ire res rib sib sir be er is re si

beirrssu   bruisers bruiser bruises. *See* **beirrs beirru beirsu berssu**

beirrsu   bruiser. *See* **beirrs beirsu beirru**

beirru   burier brier bier birr brie burr rube err ire rib rub rue be er re

beirry   briery berry brier eyrir bier birr brie byre bey bye err ire rib rye be by er re ye

beirs   biers bier bise brie reis ribs rise sire ire res rib sib sir be er is re si

beirsst   bestirs bisters. *See* **beirst eirsst**

beirssu   bruises. *See* **beirsu berssu eirssu**

beirst   bestir bister biters tribes biers biter bites rites tiers tires tribe tries best bets bier bise bite bits brie brit erst reis rest rets ribs rise rite site stir tier ties tire bet bit ire its res ret rib set sib sir sit tie be er is it re si ti

beirstt   bitters. *See* **beirst beirtt eirstt**

beirsttu   tributes bitters butters tribute turbits. *See* **beirst beirsu beirtt berstu**

beirsu   bruise buries busier rubies biers burse rebus rubes bier bise brie reis ribs rise rube rubs rues ruse sire sure user bus ire res rib rub rue sib sir sub sue use be er is re si us

beirsw   brewis biers brews weirs wires wiser bier bise brew brie reis ribs rise sire webs weir wire wise ire res rib sew sib sir web wis be er is re si we

beirt   biter tribe bier bite brie brit rite tier tire bet bit ire ret rib tie be er it re ti

beirtt   bitter biter titer titre tribe trite bier bite bitt brie brit rite tier tire tret bet bit ire ret rib tie tit be er it re ti

beirttu   tribute. *See* **beirtt berttu birttu**

beirtvy   brevity. *See* **eirtvy beirt**

beis   bise sib be is si

beiss   bises bise sibs ess sib sis be is si

beisstu   busiest. *See* **besstu eisstu**

beist   bites best bets bise bite bits site ties bet bit its set sib sit tie be is it si ti

beisv   vibes bise vies vise sib vie be is si

beit   bite bet bit tie be it ti

beittwx   betwixt. *No 6s or 5s*

beix   ibex be ex xi

bejjsuu   jujubes. *See* **bejjuu jjsuu**

bejjuu   jujube juju be

bejkoux   jukebox. *No 6s or 5s*

bejlmsu   jumbles. *See* **bejlmu belmsu**

bejlmu   jumble umbel blue lube mule bel bum elm emu leu lum mel be el em me mu um

bejloss   jobless. *See* **belss belos eloss**

bejorttu   turbojet. *See* **beortt berttu borttu**

beklo   bloke bole koel lobe bel elk kob lek lob oke be el lo

bekloost   booklets booklet. *See* **beklos bekoot**

bekloot   booklet. *See* **bekoot beklo eklot**

beklos   blokes bloke boles koels lobes bels bole bosk elks kobs koel leks lobe lobs lose okes slob sloe soke sole bel elk els kob kos lek lob los oke sob sol be el lo os so

bekmnoo   bookmen. *No 6s or 5s*

beknnoru   unbroken. *See* **beknor beknru bnnoru ennoru**

beknooot   notebook. *See* **bekoot**

beknor   broken boner broke krone bone bonk bore born ebon keno kerb kern knob robe ben eon ken kob kor neb nob nor oke one orb ore rob roe be en er ne no on or re

beknors   bonkers. *See* **beknor benors**

beknrsu   bunkers. *See* **beknru bekrsu**

beknru   bunker burke bunk burn kerb kern knur neuk nuke rube rune ben bun ken neb nub rub rue run urn be en er ne nu re

bekoot   betook book boot kobo koto oboe toke took bet boo bot kob oke toe too be to

bekoottx   textbook. *See* **bekoot**

bekor   broke bore kerb robe kob kor oke orb ore rob roe be er or re

bekorr   broker broke borer bore kerb robe err kob kor oke orb ore rob roe be er or re

bekorrs   brokers. *See* **beorrs bekorr**

bekr   kerb be er re

bekrs   kerbs kerb res be er re

bekrsu   burkes brusk burke burse kerbs rebus rubes kerb rube rubs rues ruse rusk sure user bus res rub rue sub sue use be er re us

bekru   burke kerb rube rub rue be er re

bel   bel be el

bell   bell bel ell be el

bellnpsu   bullpens bullpen. *See* **ellnsu**

bellnpu   bullpen. *No 6s or 5s*

bellopty   potbelly. *See* **belly ellty**

bellortw   bellwort. *See* **bellow belort belorw elortw**

bellosu   lobules soluble. *See* **belosu bellou**

bellosw   bellows. *See* **bellow belosw**

bellou   lobule boule bell blue bole boll bull lobe lube bel ell leu lob be el lo

bellouv   voluble. *See* **bellou elouv**

bellow   bellow below bowel elbow bell blew blow bole boll bowl lobe well bel bow ell lob low owe owl web woe be el lo ow we

bells   bells bell bels ells sell bel ell els be el

bellstu   bullets. *See* **belstu belltu ellstu**

belltu   bullet bluet tulle bell belt blue bull lube lute tell tube tule bel bet but ell let leu tub be el ut

belluy   bluely belly bully bell blue bull lube yell yule bel bey buy bye ell leu lye be by el ye

belly   belly bell yell bel bey bye ell lye be by el ye

belmmrsu   mumblers bummers lumbers mumbler mumbles rumbles slumber. *See* **belmmu belmru belmsu belrsu**

belmmru   mumbler. *See* **bemmru belmru belmmu**

belmmsu   mumbles. *See* **belmmu belmsu**

belmmu   mumble umbel blue lube mule bel bum elm emu leu lum mel mem mum be el em me mu um

belmnsu   numbles. *See* **bemnsu elmnsu belmsu**

belmoor   bloomer. *See* **beloor bemoor**

belmoors   bloomers bloomer boleros boomers. *See* **beloor belors bemoor bemors**

belmoost   boomlets boomlet. *See* **blmoos elmost**

belmoot   boomlet. *See* **blmoo lmoot elmot**

belmopr   problem. *See* **elopr elmor bemor**

belmoprs   problems problem. *See* **belors bemors beoprs elmors**

belmorst   temblors bolster bolters lobster mobster temblor. *See* **belors belort bemors beorst**

belmorsy   somberly soberly embryos. *See* **belmoy belors belrsy bemors**

belmort   temblor. *See* **belort emort elmor**

belmosu   embolus. *See* **belosu belmsu**

belmoy   emboly bole lobe mole moly obey ylem bel bey boy bye elm lob lye mel mob yob be by el em lo me mo my om oy ye

belmprsu   plumbers bumpers lumbers plumber rumbles rumples slumber. *See* **belmru belmsu belrsu bempru**

belmpru   plumber. *See* **bempru belmru elmpru**

belmrruy   mulberry. *See* **belmru belruy blmruy blrruy**

belmrssu slumbers lumbers rumbles slumber. *See* **belmru belmsu belrsu bemrsu**

belmrstu tumblers tumbrels bluster butlers lumbers rumbles slumber stumble tumbler tumbles tumbrel. *See* **belmru belmsu belmtu belrsu**

belmrsu lumbers rumbles slumber. *See* **bemrsu elmrsu belmru belrsu belmsu**

belmrtu tumbler tumbrel. *See* **belrtu belmru belmtu**

belmrty trembly. *See* **elmrty belry**

belmru lumber rumble bluer brume lemur ruble umbel umber berm blue blur burl lube lure merl mule rube rule bel bum elm emu leu lum mel rem rub rue rum be el em er me mu re um

belmsstu stumbles bustles stumble sublets tumbles. *See* **belmsu belmtu belstu bemssu**

belmstu stumble tumbles. *See* **belstu**

belmsu umbels blues lubes mules sebum umbel bels blue bums elms emus lube lues mels mule muse slub slue slum bel bum bus elm els emu leu lum mel mus sub sue sum use be el em me mu um us

belmtu tumble umbel bluet belt blue lube lute melt mule mute tube tule bel bet bum but elm emu let leu lum mel met tub be el em me mu um ut

belmu umbel blue lube mule bel bum elm emu leu lum mel be el em me mu um

belno noble bole bone ebon enol leno lobe lone noel bel ben eon lob neb nob one be el en lo ne no on

belnoosy boloneys boloney. *See* **belnos elnoos**

belnooy boloney. *See* **benoy blooy lnooy**

belnos nobles boles bones lobes noble noels bels bens bole bone ebon enol eons leno lens lobe lobs lone lose nebs nobs noel noes nose ones slob sloe snob sole bel ben els ens eon lob los neb nob one sen sob sol son be el en lo ne no on os so

belnosuu nebulous. *See* **belnos belosu**

belnosyz benzoyls benzols benzoyl benzyls. *See* **belnos belnoz belnyz**

belnosz benzols. *See* **belnos belnoz**

belnoyz benzoyl. *See* **belnoz belnyz**

belnoz benzol noble bonze bole bone ebon enol leno lobe lone noel zone bel ben eon lob neb nob one be el en lo ne no on

belnsyz benzyls. *See* **belnyz**

belnt blent belt bent lent bel ben bet let neb net ten be el en ne

belnyz benzyl bel ben bey bye lye neb yen be by el en ne ye

belo bole lobe bel lob be el lo

beloopr blooper. *See* **beloor eloopr**

belooprs bloopers blooper boleros loopers. *See* **beloor belors beoprs eloopr**

beloor bolero roble bole bolo boor bore lobe lobo lore oboe oleo orle robe role bel boo lob loo orb ore rob roe be el er lo or re

beloors boleros. *See* **beloor eloors belors**

beloosst bootless loosest. *See* **beosst boosst elooss elosst**

belopsu pueblos. *See* **belosu belopu**

belopu pueblo boule blue bole lobe lope lube pole pule bel bop leu lob lop ope pub pul be el lo pe up

belor roble bole bore lobe lore orle robe role bel lob orb ore rob roe be el er lo or re

belors robles boles bores lobes lores loser orles robes roble roles sober bels bole bore lobe lobs lore lose orbs ores orle robe robs roes role rose slob sloe sole sorb sore bel els lob los orb ore res rob roe sob sol be el er lo or os re so

belorsst bolsters lobsters bolster bolters lobster ostlers sorbets sterols strobes. *See* **belors belort beorss beorst**

belorst bolster bolters lobster. *See* **belort elorst beorst**

belorstt blotters bottlers bettors blotter bolster bolters bottler bottles lobster. *See* **belors belort belott beorst**

belorstu troubles bluster boletus bolster bolters butlers lobster roubles trouble. *See* **belors belort beloru belosu**

belorsu roubles. *See* **belosu beorsu belors beloru belrsu**

belorsw blowers bowlers. *See* **belorw belosw beorsw elorsw belors**

belorsy soberly. *See* **belrsy belors elorsy**

belort bolter roble belt blot bole bolt bore bort lobe lore orle robe role rote rotl tore bel bet bot let lob lot orb ore ort ret rob roe rot toe tor be el er lo or re to

belortt blotter bottler. *See* **beortt belort belott**

belortu trouble. *See* **belort belrtu beloru**

beloru rouble bluer boule roble ruble blue blur bole bore burl lobe lore lube lure orle robe role rube rule bel leu lob orb ore our rob roe rub rue be el er lo or re

belorw blower bowler below bowel bower elbow lower roble rowel blew blow bole bore bowl brew brow lobe lore orle robe role wore bel bow lob low orb ore owe owl rob roe row web woe be el er lo or ow re we

belos boles lobes bels bole lobe lobs lose slob sloe sole bel els lob los sob sol be el lo os so

belossu blouses boluses. *See* **belosu beossu**

belostt bottles. *See* **belott beostt**

belostu boletus. *See* **belosu belstu beostu elostu**

belostuy obtusely boletus. *See* **belosu belstu beostu blosuy**

belosu blouse boules obelus blues boles bolus boule bouse lobes louse lubes bels blue bole lobe lobs lose lube lues slob sloe slub slue sole soul bel bus els leu lob los sob sol sou sub sue use be el lo os so us

belosw bowels elbows below blows boles bowel bowls elbow lobes bels blew blow bole bowl bows lobe lobs lose lows owes owls slew slob sloe slow sole webs woes bel bow els lob los low owe owl sew sob sol sow web woe be el lo os ow so we

belott bottle belt blot bole bolt bott lobe tote bel bet bot let lob lot toe tot be el lo to

belou boule blue bole lobe lube bel leu lob be el lo

below below bowel elbow blew blow bole bowl lobe bel bow lob low owe owl web woe be el lo ow we

belrsstu blusters bluster busters bustler bustles butlers results rustles sublets ulsters. *See* **belrsu belrtu belstu berssu**

belrstu bluster butlers. *See* **belstu blrstu berstu belrtu elrstu**

belrstuy blustery bluster burleys butlers butlery. *See* **belrsu belrsy belrtu belruy**

belrsu rubles bluer blues blurs burls burse lubes lures rebus rubes ruble rules slurb bels blue blur burl lube lues lure rube rubs rues rule ruse slub slue slur sure user bel bus els leu res rub rue sub sue use be el er re us

belrsuy burleys. *See* **belrsy belruy bersuy belrsu elrsuy**

belrsy beryls beryl byres lyres slyer bels beys byes byre lyes lyre lyse rely ryes bel bey bye els lye res rye sly yes be by el er re ye

belrtu butler bluer bluet blurt brute rebut ruble tuber belt blue blur burl lube lure lute rube rule true tube tule bel bet but let leu ret rub rue rut tub be el er re ut

belrtuy butlery. *See* **belrtu**

belru bluer ruble blue blur burl lube lure rube rule bel leu rub rue be el er re

belruy burley beryl bluer burly buyer ruble blue blur burl bury byre lube lure lyre rely rube ruby rule yule bel bey buy bye leu lye rub rue rye be by el er re ye

belry beryl byre lyre rely bel bey bye lye rye be by el er re ye

bels bels bel els be el

belss bless bels less bel els ess be el

belsstu bustles sublets. *See* **belstu besstu elsstu**

belst belts blest bels belt best bets lest lets bel bet els let set be el

belsttuy subtlety. *See* **belstu blstuy elstty**

belstu bluest bluets bustle sublet subtle belts blest blues bluet lubes lutes tubes tules bels belt best bets blue bust buts lest lets lube lues lust lute slub slue slut stub suet tube tubs tule bel bet bus but els let leu set sub sue tub use be el us ut

belsu blues blube bels blue lube lues slub slue bel bus els leu sub sue use be el us

belt belt bel bet let be el

beltu bluet belt blue lube lute tube tule bel bet but let leu tub be el ut

belu blue lube bel leu be el

belw blew bel web be el we

bemmoos embosom. *See* **bemos bmoos emmos**

bemmooss embosoms embosom. *See* **bemoss bmooss emooss**

bemmrsu bummers. *See* **bemrsu bemmru emmrsu**

bemmru bummer brume umber berm rube bum emu mem mum rem rub rue rum be em er me mu re um

bemnnssu numbness. *See* **bemnsu bemssu**

bemnoort trombone montero. *See* **bemnot bemoor emnort**

bemnost entombs. *See* **bemnot emnost**

bemnosu umbones. *See* **bemnsu bemos benos**

bemnot entomb monte bent bone ebon mote nome note omen tomb tome tone ben bet bot eon men met mob mon mot neb net nob not one ten toe tom ton be em en me mo ne no om on to

bemnow bowmen embow women bone ebon enow meow mown nome omen womb ben bon bow eon men mew mob mon mow neb new nob now one owe own web wen woe won be em en me mo ne no om on ow we

bemnrsu numbers. *See* **bemrsu bemnsu bemnru**

bemnru number brume rumen umber berm burn menu numb rube rune ben bum bun emu men neb nub rem rub rue rum run urn be em en er me mu ne nu re um

bemnstu numbest. *See* **bemnsu bnstu emstu**

bemnsu busmen menus numbs sebum bens bums buns emus menu muse nebs nubs numb snub ben bum bun bus emu ens men mus neb nub sen sub sue sum sun use be em en me mu ne nu um us

bemoor boomer broom omber ombre berm boom boor bore moor more oboe omer robe room boo mob moo mor orb ore rem rob roe be em er me mo om or re

bemoorrs sombrero boomers roomers. *See* **bemoor bemors beorrs bmoors**

bemoors boomers. *See* **bemoor bmoors emoors bemors**

bemor omber ombre berm bore more omer robe mob mor orb ore rem rob roe be em er me mo om or re

bemors ombers ombres somber berms besom bores mores omber ombre omers robes sober berm bore mobs more mors omer orbs ores robe robs roes rose some sorb sore mob mor mos oms orb ore rem res rob roe sob be em er me mo om or os re so

bemorsst mobsters mobster sorbets strobes. *See* **bemors bemoss beorss beorst**

bemorst mobster. *See* **emorst bemors beorst**

bemorsy embryos. *See* **bemory**

bemory embryo omber ombre berm bore byre more obey omer orby robe yore bey boy bye mob mor orb ore rem rob roe rye yob be by em er me mo my om or oy re ye

bemos besom mobs some mob mos oms sob be em me mo om os so

bemoss besoms emboss boss mess moss sobs some ess mob mos oms sob be em me mo om os so

bemosw embows besom embow meows wombs bows meow mews mobs mows owes smew some webs woes womb bow mew mob mos mow oms owe sew sob sow web woe be em me mo om os ow so we

bemow embow womb meow bow mew mob mow owe web woe be em me mo om ow we

bemprsu bumpers. *See* **bemrsu bempru beprsu**

bempru bumper brume umber berm bump burp perm pure rube rump bum emu per pub rem rep rub rue rum ump be em er me mu pe re um up

bemr berm rem be em er me re

bemrs berms berm rem res be em er me re

bemrsu brumes umbers berms brume burse rebus rubes sebum serum umber berm bums emus muse rube rubs rues rums ruse sure user bum bus emu mus rem res rub rue rum sub sue sum use be em er me mu re um us

bemru brume umber berm rube bum emu rem rub rue rum be em er me mu re um

bemssu sebums buses muses sebum bums buss emus mess muse muss subs sues sums uses bum bus emu ess mus sub sue sum use be em me mu um us

bemsu sebum bums emus muse bum bus emu mus sub sue sum use be em me mu um us

ben ben neb be en ne

bennorsw newborns newborn renowns. *See* **benors beorsw bnorsw ennorw**

bennorw newborn. *See* **ennorw benor beorw**

bennost bonnets. *See* **bennot ennost**

bennot bonnet nonet tenon tonne bent bone ebon neon none note tone ben bet bot eon neb net nob not one ten toe ton be en ne no on to

benntu unbent bent bunt tube tune ben bet bun but neb net nub nun nut ten tub tun be en ne nu ut

benny benny ben bey bye neb yen be by en ne ye

beno bone ebon ben eon neb nob one be en ne no on

benoorsu burnoose onerous. *See* **benors beorsu bnoors bnorsu**

benor boner bone bore born ebon robe ben eon neb nob nor one orb ore rob roe be en er ne no on or re

benorr reborn boner borer bone bore born ebon robe ben eon err neb nob nor one orb ore rob roe be en er ne no on or re

benorrw browner. *See* **benorr beorw bnorw**

benors boners boner bones bores robes snore sober bens bone bore born ebon eons nebs nobs noes nose ones orbs ores robe robs roes rose snob sorb sore ben ens eon neb nob nor one orb ore res rob roe sen sob son be en er ne no on or os re so

benorstw brownest. *See* **benors beorst beorsw beostw**

benorsz bronzes. *See* **benors benorz**

benorz bronze boner bonze bone bore born ebon robe zero zone ben eon neb nob nor one orb ore rob roe be en er ne no on or re

benos bones bens bone ebon eons nebs nobs noes nose ones snob ben ens eon neb nob one sen sob son be en ne no on os so

benossu bonuses. *See* **bnossu beossu enossu**

benosswy newsboys newsboy. *See* **benos bossy benoy**

benoswy newsboy. *See* **benos benoy enswy**

benoy ebony bone bony ebon obey ben bey boy bye eon neb nob one yen yob yon be by en ne no on oy ye

benoz bonze bone ebon zone ben eon neb nob one be en ne no on

benrrsu burners. *See* **benrru enrrsu**

benrru burner rerun burn burr rube rune ben bun err neb nub rub rue run urn be en er ne nu re

benrstu brunets burnets. *See* **benrtu bnrstu berstu enrstu**

benrtu brunet burnet brunt brute burnt rebut tuber tuner bent bunt burn rent rube rune runt tern true tube tune turn ben bet bun but neb net nub nut ret rub rue run rut ten tub tun urn be en er ne nu re ut

bens bens nebs ben ens neb sen be en ne

bensssuy busyness. *See* **besssu bsssuy**

bent bent ben bet neb net ten be en ne

beoo oboe boo be

beoorrrw borrower. *See* **boorrw**

beoorsst boosters booster sorbets strobes. *See* **beorss beorst beosst boorst**

beoorst booster. *See* **boorst beorst**

beoorsz boozers rebozos. *See* **beoorz beoosz**

beoorz boozer rebozo booze boor bore bozo oboe ooze orzo robe zero boo orb ore rob roe zoo be er or re

beoos oboes oboe boos boo sob be os so

beoosz boozes booze bozos oboes oozes boos bozo oboe ooze zoos boo sob zoo be os so

beooz booze bozo oboe ooze boo zoo be

beopr probe bore pore repo robe rope bop ope orb ore per pro rep rob roe be er or pe re

beoprr prober borer probe repro bore pore repo robe rope bop err ope orb ore per pro rep rob roe be er or pe re

beoprrs probers. *See* **beorrs beoprr beoprs eoprrs**

beoprrsv proverbs probers proverb. *See* **beoprr beoprs beorrs eoprsv**

beoprrv proverb. *See* **beoprr eoprv eorrv**

beoprs probes bores pores poser probe prose repos robes ropes sober spore bops bore epos opes orbs ores peso

---

pore pose pros repo reps robe robs roes rope rose sorb sore bop ope orb ore per pro rep res rob roe sob sop be er or os pe re so

beoqstuu bouquets bouquet. *See* **beostu eoqstu eqstuu**

beoqtuu bouquet. *See* **eoqtu eqstuu**

beor bore robe orb ore rob roe be er or re

beorr borer bore robe err orb ore rob roe be er or re

beorrruw burrower. *See* **borruw**

beorrs borers resorb borer bores robes sober sorer bore errs orbs ores robe robs roes rose sorb sore err orb ore res rob roe sob be er or os re so

beorrss resorbs. *See* **beorrs beorss**

beorrssw browsers browser browses resorbs. *See* **beorrs beorss beorsw eorrsw**

beorrsw browser. *See* **beorrs beorsw eorrsw**

beors bores robes sober bore orbs ores robe robs roes rose sorb sore orb ore res rob roe sob be er or os re so

beorss sobers bores robes roses sober sorbs sores bore boss orbs ores robe robs roes rose sobs sorb sore ess orb ore res rob roe sob be er or os re so

beorsst sorbets strobes. *See* **beosst beorst eorsst**

beorssu bourses. *See* **beorsu beossu berssu eorssu beorss**

beorssw browses. *See* **beorsw eorssw beorss**

beorst sorbet strobe besot bores borts robes rotes sober store best bets bore bort bots erst orbs ores orts rest rets robe robs roes rose rote rots sorb sore sort stob toes tore tors bet bot orb ore ort res ret rob roe rot set sob sot toe tor be er or os re so to

beorstt bettors. *See* **beortt beostt eorstt beorst**

beorstv obverts. *See* **beortv beorst eorstv**

beorsu bourse bores bouse burse rebus robes rouse rubes sober bore orbs ores ours robe robs roes rose rube rubs rues ruse sorb sore sour sure user bus orb ore our res rob roe rub rue sob sou sub sue use be er or os re so us

beorsuvy overbuys overbuy voyeurs. *See* **beorsu bersuy eoruvy ersuvy**

beorsw bowers browse bores bower brews brows robes serow sober sower swore worse bore bows brew brow orbs ores owes robe robs roes rose rows sorb sore webs woes wore bow orb ore owe res rob roe row sew sob sow web woe be er or os ow re so we

beorswy bowyers. *See* **beorsw beorwy**

---

beorsx boxers bores boxer boxes robes sober bore orbs ores robe robs roes rose sorb sore box orb ore res rex rob roe sex sob sox be er ex os ox re so

beortt bettor otter torte toter bore bort bott robe rote tore tort tote tret trot bet bot orb ore ort ret rob roe rot toe tor tot be er or re to

beortv obvert overt trove voter bore bort over robe rote rove tore verb vert veto vote bet bot orb ore ort ret rev rob roe rot toe tor vet be er or re to

beoruvy overbuy. *See* **eoruvy beruy**

beorw bower bore brew brow robe wore bow orb ore owe rob roe row web woe be er or ow re we

beorwy bowery bowyer bower bore brew brow byre obey orby robe wore yore bey bow boy bye orb ore owe rob roe row rye web woe wye yew yob yow be by er or ow oy re we ye

beorx boxer bore robe box orb ore rex rob roe be er ex or ox re

beosss bosses obsess boss sobs sob ess be os so

beosst besots besot bests stobs best bets boss bots sets sobs sots stob toes toss bet bot ess set sob sot toe be os so to

beosstt obtests. *See* **beosst beostt**

beosstw bestows. *See* **beosst beostw**

beossu bouses bouse buses souse boss buss sobs sous subs sues uses bus ess sob sou sub sue use be os so us

beost besot best bets bots stob toes bet bot set sob sot toe be os so to

beostt obtest besot botts totes best bets bots bott stet stob test toes tost tote tots bet bot set sob sot toe tot be os so to

beostu obtuse besot bouse bouts tubes best bets bots bout bust buts oust outs stob stub suet toes tube tubs bet bot bus but out set sob sot sou sub sue toe tub use be os so to us ut

beostw bestow besot best bets bots bows owes stew stob stow swot toes tows twos webs west wets woes bet bot bow owe set sew sob sot sow toe tow two web wet woe be os ow so to we

beosu bouse bus sob sou sub sue use be os so us

beosx boxes box sex sob sox be ex os ox so

beosy obeys beys boys byes obey oyes yobs bey boy bye sob soy yes yob be by os oy so ye

beoy obey bey boy bye yob be by oy ye

beprrstu perturbs perturb. *See* **beprsu berstu eprrsu eprstu**

beprrtu perturb. *See* **bertu eprtu eprru**

beprsu superb burps burse purse rebus rubes sprue super burp pubs pure reps rube rubs rues ruse spue spur sure user bus per pub pus rep res rub rue sub sue sup use be er pe re up us

beprtuy puberty. *See* **bertu beruy eprtu**

beqrsuu brusque. *See* **bersu**

berry berry byre bey bye err rye be by er re ye

bersttu buttress busters butters. *See* **berssu berstu berttu besstu**

bersstu busters. *See* **berstu berssu brsstu ersstu besstu**

bersstuv subverts busters subvert. *See* **berssu berstu besstu brsstu**

berssu burses burse buses rebus rubes ruses users buss rube rubs rues ruse subs sues sure user uses bus ess res rub rue sub sue use be er re us

bersttu butters. *See* **berstu berttu ersttu**

berstu brutes buster rebuts tubers brute burse burst rebus rebut rubes trues tuber tubes best bets bust buts erst rest rets rube rubs rues ruse rust ruts stub suet sure true tube tubs user bet bus but res ret rub rue rut set sub sue tub use be er re us ut

berstuv subvert. *See* **berstu**

bersu burse rebus rubes rube rubs rues ruse sure user bus res rub rue sub sue use be er re us

bersux exurbs burse exurb rebus rubes rube rubs rues ruse sure user bus res rex rub rue sex sub sue use be er ex re us

bersuy buyers burse buyer byres rebus rubes beys bury busy buys byes byre rube rubs ruby rues ruse ryes sure user bey bus buy bye res rub rue rye sub sue use yes be by er re us ye

bersuzz buzzers. *See* **beruzz besuzz**

bersv verbs verb revs res rev be er re

bersw brews brew webs res sew web be er re we

bersy byres beys byes byre ryes bey bye res rye yes be by er re ye

berttu butter brute rebut tuber utter butt rube tret true tube bet but ret rub rue rut tub tut be er re ut

berttuy buttery. *See* **berttu beruy rttuy**

bertu brute rebut tuber rube true tube bet but ret rub rue rut tub be er re ut

beru rube rub rue be er re

berux exurb rube rex rub rue be er ex re

beruy buyer bury byre rube ruby bey buy bye rub rue rye be by er re ye

beruzz buzzer buzz rube zebu rub rue be er re

berv verb rev be er re

berw brew web be er re we

bery byre bey bye rye be by er re ye

bessssuy byssuses. *See* **besssu bsssuy**

bessstu subsets. *See* **besssu besstu**

besssu busses buses buss subs sues uses bus ess sub sue use be us

besst bests best bets sets bet ess set be

bessttux subtexts subtext. *See* **besstu**

besstu subset bests buses busts stubs suets tubes best bets buss bust buts sets stub subs sues suet tube tubs uses bet bus but ess set sub sue tub use be us ut

bessu buses buss subs sues uses bus ess sub sue use be us

best best bets bet set be

besttux subtext. *See* **bsttu esttx bestu**

bestu tubes best bets bust buts stub suet tube tubs bet bus but set sub sue tub use be us ut

besty bytes best bets beys byes byte bet bey bye set sty yes yet be by ye

besuz zebus zebu bus sub sue use be us

besuzz buzzes zebus zebu buzz bus sub sue use be us

besw webs web sew be we

besy beys byes bey bye yes be by ye

bet bet be

betu tube bet but tub be ut

bety byte bet bey bye yet be by ye

beuz zebu be

bevy bevy bey bye be by ye

bew web be we

bey bey bye be by ye

---

bffgilnu bluffing buffing luffing. *See* **bgilnu fgilnu**

bffginu buffing. *See* **fginu**

bffhorsu brushoff. *See* **ffhors**

bffi biff fib if

bffis biffs biff fibs fib ifs sib if is si

bfflsu bluffs bluff buffs flubs luffs sluff buff flub flus luff slub bus flu sub us

bfflu bluff buff flub luff flu

bffnoosu buffoons buffoon. *See* **bffoo bnosu bnoos**

bffnoou buffoon. *See* **bffoo**

bffnosux snuffbox. *See* **bnosu bffsu ffnsu**

bffoo boffo boo fob off of

bffsu buffs buff bus sub us

bffu buff

bfgilmnu fumbling. *See* **bgilnu fgilnu fgimnu**

bfglloru bullfrog. *See* **bgoru floru**

bfgoosw fogbows. *See* **bfgoow fgoos foosw**

bfgoow fogbow goof woof bog boo bow fob fog gob goo woo go of ow

bfhilosw blowfish fishbowl wolfish. *See* **hilosw**

bfhimnsu numbfish. *See* **bimnsu**

bfhirsu furbish. *See* **bhirsu**

bfi fib if

bfiilr fibril birl fib fir rib rif if li

bfiinr fibrin firn bin fib fin fir nib rib rif if in

bfiinrs fibrins. *See* **bfiinr fiins finrs**

bfiiorss fibrosis. *See* **biiors**

bfillssu blissful. *See* **bills bilss bllsu**

bfilmru brimful. *See* **filmu**

bfimor biform brim firm forb form from fib fir fob for fro mir mob mor obi orb rib rif rim rob if mi mo of om or

bfinosw bowfins. *See* **bfinow inosw**

bfinow bowfin wino bin bow fib fin fob ion nib nob now obi own win won if in no of on ow

bfiorstt frostbit. *See* **biorst fiorst**

bfiorsu fibrous. *See* **bfors forsu**

bfis fibs fib ifs sib if is si

bfllnowy flyblown. *See* **blnow blowy flnow**

bfloorsu subfloor. *See* **bloosu floors florsu**

bfloty botfly lofty blot bolt loft bot boy fly fob foy lob lot oft toy yob by lo of oy to

bflsu flubs flub flus slub bus flu sub us

bflu flub flu

bfo fob of

bfooosty footboys footboy. *See* **boost booty fosty**

bfoooty footboy. *See* **booty**

bfor forb fob for fro orb rob of or

bfors   forbs fobs forb orbs robs sorb fob for fro orb rob sob of or os so

bfory   forby forb orby boy fob for foy fro fry orb rob yob by of or oy

bfos   fobs fob sob of os so

---

bg

bgggilno   boggling bogging globing logging. *See* **bgilno ggilno**

bgggino   bogging. *See* **bgino ggino**

bggginu   bugging. *No 6s or 5s*

bgghiis   biggish. *No 6s or 5s*

bggiiln   bilging. *See* **bggiin**

bggiilno   obliging bilging boiling globing. *See* **bggiin bgilno ggilno**

bggiin   biggin gibing big bin gib gig gin nib in

bggiinnr   bringing brining ringing. *See* **bggiin**

bggiins   biggins. *See* **bggiin**

bggiisw   bigwigs. *See* **bggiiw**

bggiiw   bigwig big gib gig wig

bggilnnu   bungling bugling bulging bunging lunging. *See* **bgilnu ggilnu**

bggilno   globing. *See* **bgilno ggilno**

bggilnru   burgling bugling bulging burling. *See* **bgilnu ggilnu gginru gilnru**

bggilnu   bugling bulging. *See* **bgilnu ggilnu**

bgginnu   bunging. *No 6s or 5s*

bgguy   buggy bug buy guy by

bghhinor   highborn bighorn. *See* **bginor**

bghhiosy   highboys highboy. *See* **bhiosy**

bghhioy   highboy. *No 6s or 5s*

bghilmnu   humbling. *See* **bgilnu**

bghilnsu   blushing bushing. *See* **bgilnu bginsu bhilsu gilnsu**

bghilrty   brightly rightly. *See* **bghilt bghirt bilrty**

bghilst   blights. *See* **bghist bghilt ghilst**

bghilt   blight bight light gilt glib hilt big bit gib hit lit til hi it li ti

bghimntu   thumbing. *See* **bgintu gimntu**

bghimotu   bigmouth. *See* **bghotu**

bghinor   bighorn. *See* **bginor**

bghinors   bighorns bighorn borings horsing shoring. *See* **bginor bginos bginrs binors**

bghinrsu   brushing burnish bushing rushing. *See* **bghrsu bginrs bginsu bhirsu**

bghinssu   bushings bushing busings bussing. *See* **bginsu**

bghinsu   bushing. *See* **bginsu**

bghirt   bright bight birth girth right brig brit girt grit trig big bit gib hit rib rig hi it ti

bghist   bights bight sight bits gibs gist hist hits sigh sith this big bit gib his hit its sib sit hi is it sh si ti

bghit   bight big bit gib hit hi it ti

bghmorsu   homburgs homburg rhombus sorghum. *See* **bghosu bghrsu bgmosu bgorsu**

bghmoru   homburg. *See* **bghou bgoru bghru**

bghmsuu   humbugs. *See* **bghmuu hmsuu**

bghmuu   humbug bug bum gum hub hug hum mug ugh mu um

bghoorsu   boroughs borough burgoos. *See* **bghosu bghrsu bgooru bgorsu**

bghooru   borough. *See* **bgooru bghou bghru**

bghortu   brought. *See* **bghotu ghortu**

bghosu   boughs bough bogus bogs bosh bugs bush gobs gosh gush hobs hogs hubs hugs bog bug bus gob hob hog hub hug ohs sob sou sub ugh go ho oh os sh so us

bghotu   bought bough ought tough both bout gout thou thug bog bot bug but gob got gut hob hog hot hub hug hut out tho tog tub tug ugh go ho oh to ut

bghou   bough bog bug gob hob hog hub hug ugh go ho oh

bghrsu   burghs brush burgh burgs grubs shrub shrug bugs burg bush grub gush hubs hugs rubs rugs rush bug bus hub hug rub rug sub ugh sh us

bghru   burgh burg grub bug hub hug rub rug ugh

bgi   big gib

bgiijn   jibing big bin gib gin jib jig nib in

bgiijns   jibings. *See* **bgiijn**

bgiikln   bilking. *See* **bgiikn giikln**

bgiiklnn   blinking bilking inkling linking. *See* **bgiikn giikln giiknn giilnn**

bgiikn   biking gink king big bin gib gin ink kin nib in

bgiilln   billing. *No 6s or 5s*

bgiillns   billings billing sibling. *See* **bills gills bgils**

bgiilmnw   wimbling. *See* **giilmn giilnw**

bgiilno   boiling. *See* **bgilno giilno**

bgiilnor   broiling birling boiling ligroin roiling. *See* **bgilno bginor giilnr**

bgiilnpp   blipping lipping. *See* **giilnp giinpp**

bgiilnr   birling. *See* **giilnr bginr**

bgiilnrs   brisling birling sibling. *See* **bginrs giilnr giinrs**

bgiilns   sibling. *See* **bgils gilns giils**

bgiilnss   siblings sibling. *See* **giilss gilnss**

bgiilnty   bitingly. *See* **bgiint giilnt iilnty**

bgiilntz   blitzing. *See* **bgiint giilnt**

bgiimmnr   brimming rimming. *See* **giimmn giimnr**

bgiimnru   imbruing imbuing. *See* **giimnr**

bgiimnu   imbuing. *See* **biimn**

bgiinnn   binning. *See* **giinnn**

bgiinnr   brining. *See* **bginr**

bgiinort   orbiting rioting. *See* **bgiint bginor giinrt ginort**

bgiinrtu   bruiting. *See* **bgiint bgintu giinrt ginrtu**

bgiint   biting ting big bin bit gib gin nib nit tin in it ti

bgijlmnu   jumbling. *See* **bgilnu**

bgijosuu   bijugous. *See* **bgosu bijou**

bgiklnot   kingbolt bolting inkblot. *See* **bgilno giknot**

bgiklnu   bulking. *See* **bgilnu bikln**

bgiknno   bonking. *See* **bginno**

bgiknnu   bunking. *See* **giknnu**

bgiknoo   booking. *See* **bginoo**

bgiknoor   brooking booking rooking. *See* **bginoo bginor**

bgiknoos   bookings booking. *See* **bginoo bginos bgnoos**

bgiknru   burking. *See* **bginr biknr binru**

bgil   glib big gib li

bgillnru   bullring bulling burling. *See* **bgilnu gilnru**

bgillnu   bulling. *See* **bgilnu**

bgillnuy   bullying bulling. *See* **bgilly bgilnu bginuy gilluy**

bgilly   glibly bilgy billy bill gill glib illy lily big gib ill by li

bgilmmnu   mumbling bumming. *See* **bgilnu**

bgilmnoo blooming booming looming. *See* **bgilno bginoo bglnoo gilnoo**

bgilmnpu plumbing bumping lumping pluming. *See* **bgilnu gilnpu gimnpu**

bgilmnru rumbling burling. *See* **bgilnu gilnru**

bgilmntu tumbling. *See* **bgilnu bgintu gilntu gimntu**

bgilnntu blunting bunting. *See* **bgilnu bgintu gilntu ginntu**

bgilno globin goblin bingo lingo boil bong glib glob ling lion loin long noil big bin bog gib gin gob ion lob log nib nil nob nog obi oil go in li lo no on

bgilnos globins goblins. *See* **bginos bgilno gilnos**

bgilnosu blousing bousing globins goblins. *See* **bgilno bgilnu bginos bginsu**

bgilnot bolting. *See* **bgilno**

bgilnott blotting bottling bolting lotting. *See* **bgilno ginott**

bgilnow blowing bowling. *See* **bginow gilnow**

bgilnoy ignobly. *See* **bgilno**

bgilnrru blurring burling burring. *See* **bgilnu gilnru**

bgilnrtu blurting burling. *See* **bgilnu bgintu gilnru gilntu**

bgilnru burling. *See* **bgilnu gilnru**

bgilnstu bustling lusting. *See* **bgilnu bginsu bgintu blnstu**

bgilnu bluing lungi bung glib ling lung big bin bug bun gib gin gnu gun lug nib nil nub in li nu

bgilooy biology. *See* **bgily giloo blooy**

bgils glibs glib gibs big gib sib is li si

bgily bilgy glib big gib by li

bgimmnu bumming. *No 6s or 5s*

bgimnnu numbing. *No 6s or 5s*

bgimnoo booming. *See* **bginoo gimnoo**

bgimnpu bumping. *See* **gimnpu**

bginno boning bingo bong big bin bog gib gin gob inn ion nib nob nog obi go in no on

bginnorw browning ingrown. *See* **bginno bginor bginow ginorw**

bginnorz bronzing. *See* **bginno bginor binnor ginnoz**

bginnru burning. *See* **bginr binru innru**

bginnstu buntings bunting. *See* **bginsu bgintu ginntu**

bginntu bunting. *See* **bgintu ginntu**

bgino bingo bong big bin bog gib gin gob ion nib nob nog obi go in no on

bginoo booing bingo bongo bong boon goon big bin bog boo gib gin gob goo ion nib nob nog obi go in no on

bginoost boosting bonitos booting sooting. *See* **bginoo bginos bgiost bgnoos**

bginoot booting. *See* **bginoo binoot**

bginooz boozing. *See* **bginoo ginooz**

bginopp bopping. *See* **bgino ginop**

bginopr probing. *See* **bginor ginopr**

bginor boring orbing robing bingo bring groin robin bong born brig grin iron ring big bin bog gib gin gob ion nib nob nog nor obi orb rib rig rob go in no on or

bginors borings. *See* **bginos bginor bginrs ginors binors**

bginorsw browsing borings bowings. *See* **bginor bginos bginow bginrs**

bginos bingos bingo bison bongs bins bogs bong gibs gins gobs ions nibs nobs nogs obis sign sing snob song big bin bog gib gin gob ion nib nob nog obi sib sin sob son go in is no on os si so

bginoss bossing. *See* **bginos ginoss**

bginosu bousing. *See* **bginos bginsu**

bginosw bowings. *See* **bginos bginow ginosw**

bginouy buoying. *See* **bginuy bgino gnouy**

bginow bowing bingo owing bong gown wing wino big bin bog bow gib gin gob ion nib nob nog now obi own wig win won go in no on ow

bginox boxing bingo bong big bin bog box gib gin gob ion nib nix nob nog obi go in no on ox xi

bginpru burping. *See* **bginr binru ginru**

bginr bring brig grin ring big bin bog gin nib rib rig in

bginrru burring. *See* **bginr**

bginrs brings brigs bring grins rings bins brig gibs gins grin nibs ribs rigs ring sign sing big bin bog gin nib rib rig sib sin sir in is si

bginrstu bursting rusting. *See* **bginrs bginsu bgintu binrsu**

bginruy burying. *See* **bginuy bginr binry**

bginssu busings bussing. *See* **bginsu inssu ginss**

bginsu busing bungs suing using bins bugs bung buns gibs gins gnus guns nibs nubs sign sing snub snug sung big bin bug bun bus gib gin gnu gun nib nub sib sin sub sun in is nu si us

bginsuy busying. *See* **bginsu bginuy**

bginttu butting. *See* **bgintu**

bgintu tubing bung bunt ting unit big bin bit bug bun but gib gin gnu gun gut nib nit nub nut tin tub tug tui tun in it nu ti ut

bginuy buying bung big bin bug bun buy gib gin gnu gun guy nib nub yin by in nu

bginuzz buzzing. *No 6s or 5s*

bgiorty bigotry. *See* **bgiot biort**

bgiost bigots bigot obits bits bogs bots gibs gist gobs obis obit stob togs big bit bog bot gib gob got its obi sib sit sob sot tog go is it os si so ti to

bgiot bigot obit big bit bog bot gib gob got obi tog go it ti to

bgir brig big gib rib rig

bgirs brigs brig gibs ribs rigs big gib rib rig sib sir is si

bgis gibs big gib sib is si

bgklooo logbook. *No 6s or 5s*

bgklooos logbooks logbook. *See* **bloos bkoos bglos**

bglmruy grumbly. *See* **blmruy bgluy bgruy**

bglnoo oblong bongo bolo bong boon glob goon lobo logo long loon bog boo gob goo lob log loo nob nog go lo no on

bglnoos oblongs. *See* **bglnoo bgnoos**

bglnoosw longbows oblongs longbow. *See* **bglnoo bgnoos**

bglnoow longbow. *See* **bglnoo blnow**

bglnosuw blowguns blowgun. *See* **bnosuw**

bglnouw blowgun. *See* **blnow**

bglo glob bog gob lob log go lo

bglooyy bryology. *See* **blooy glory**

bglos globs bogs glob gobs lobs logs slob slog bog gob lob log los sob sol go lo os so

bglrsuu bulgurs. *See* **bglruu blrsu bgrsu**

bglruu bulgur blur burg burl grub guru bug lug rub rug ulu

bgluy bulgy ugly bug buy guy lug by

bgmoostu gumboots gumboot. *See* **bgmosu**

bgmootu gumboot. *See* **bgmou gootu**

bgmosu gumbos bogus gumbo umbos bogs bugs bums gobs gums mobs mogs mugs smog smug sumo umbo bog bug bum bus gob gum mob mog mos mug mus oms sob sou sub sum go mo mu om os so um us

bgmou gumbo umbo bog bug bum gob gum mob mog mug go mo mu om um

bgno bong bog gob nob nog go no on

bgnoo bongo bong boon goon bog boo gob goo nob nog go no on

bgnoos bongos bongo bongs boons goons bogs bong boon boos gobs goon goos nobs nogs snob song soon bog boo gob goo nob nog sob son go no on os so

bgnos bongs bogs bong gobs nobs nogs snob song bog gob nob nog sob son go no on os so

bgnsu bungs bugs bung buns gnus guns nubs snub snug sung bug bun bus gnu gun nub sub sun nu us

bgnu bung bug bun gnu gun nub nu
bgo bog gob go
bgoorsu burgoos. *See* **bgooru bgorsu**
bgooru burgoo bourg boor burg grub bog boo bug gob goo orb our rob rub rug go or
bgorsu bourgs bogus bourg burgs grubs bogs bugs burg gobs grub orbs ours robs rubs rugs sorb sour bog bug bus

gob orb our rob rub rug sob sou sub go or os so us
bgoru bourg burg grub bog bug gob orb our rob rub rug go or
bgos bogs gobs bog gob sob go os so
bgosu bogus bogs bugs gobs bog bug bus gob sob sou sub go os so us
bgoy bogy goby bog boy gob goy yob by go oy

bgrsu burgs grubs bugs burg grub rubs rugs bug bus rub rug sub us
bgru burg grub bug rub rug
bgruy rugby burg bury grub ruby bug buy guy rub rug by
bgsu bugs bug bus sub us
bgu bug

---

bh

bhiiinst inhibits inhibit. *See* **hinst**
bhiiint inhibit. *No 6s or 5s*
bhiilmps blimpish. *See* **bilmps hiimps**
bhiioprt prohibit. *See* **bhirt bhort biort**
bhikoos bookish. *See* **bhikos bkoos bhoos**
bhikos kibosh bosh bosk hobs kobs obis his hob kob kos obi ohs sib ski sob hi ho is oh os sh si so
bhillnor hornbill. *See* **billno**
bhillsu bullish. *See* **bhilsu bills bllsu**
bhilorry horribly. *See* **bilor lorry ilory**
bhilosyy boyishly. *See* **bhiosy**
bhilpsu publish. *See* **bhilsu bilps hlpsu**
bhilsu bluish blush buhls buhl bush hubs lush slub bus his hub sib sub hi is li sh si us
bhimsstu bismuths bismuth isthmus submits. *See* **bhmstu bimstu himsst**
bhimstu bismuth. *See* **bhmstu bimstu**
bhinorsw brownish. *See* **binors bnorsw hinors**
bhinrsu burnish. *See* **binrsu bhirsu hinrsu**
bhioors boorish. *See* **bhoos boors**
bhiops bishop bops bosh hips hobs hops obis pish pois posh ship shop soph bop hip his hob hop obi ohs poi sib sip sob sop hi ho is oh os pi sh si so
bhiopss bishops. *See* **bhiops hipss hopss**
bhiosy boyish bosh boys hobs hoys obis yobs boy his hob hoy obi ohs shy sib sob soy yob by hi ho is oh os oy sh si so
bhirst births birth shirt bits brit hist hits ribs sith stir this bit his hit its rib sib sir sit hi is it sh si ti
bhirstu brutish. *See* **bhirst birstu bhirsu**
bhirsu hubris brush shrub bush hubs ribs rubs rush bus his hub rib rub sib sir sub hi is sh si us

bhirt birth brit bit hit rib hi it ti
bhknoor hornbook. *See* **bnoor bkoor hnoor**
bhllnoru bullhorn. *See* **bnoru hllou**
bhllrsuu bullrush bulrush. *See* **blrsu bhlsu bhrsu**
bhlmuy humbly buhl bum buy hub hum lum yum by mu my um
bhlrsuu bulrush. *See* **blrsu bhlsu bhrsu**
bhlsu blush buhls buhl bush hubs lush slub bus hub sub sh us
bhlu buhl hub
bhmor rhomb hob mho mob mor ohm orb rho rob ho mo oh om or
bhmors rhombs rhomb bosh hobs mhos mobs mors ohms orbs rhos robs sorb hob mho mob mor mos ohm ohs oms orb rho rob sob ho mo oh om or os sh so
bhmorsu rhombus. *See* **hmorsu bhmors bhmrsu**
bhmrsu rhumbs brush rhumb shrub bums bush hubs hums mush rubs rums rush bum bus hub hum mus rub rum sub sum mu sh um us
bhmru rhumb bum hub hum rub rum mu um
bhmstu thumbs thumb bums bush bust buts hubs hums huts mush must shut smut stub stum thus tubs tush bum bus but hub hum hut mus sub sum tub mu sh um us ut
bhmtu thumb bum but hub hum hut tub mu um ut
bhnoortx boxthorn. *See* **bhootx**
bho hob ho oh
bhoo hobo boo hob oho ooh ho oh
bhoooo boohoo hobo boo hob oho ooh ho oh

bhooos boohoos. *See* **bhoooo bhoos**
bhoos hobos boos bosh hobo hobs oohs shoo boo hob oho ohs ooh sob ho oh os sh so
bhoost booths boost booth boots hobos hoots shoot sooth boos boot bosh both bots hobo hobs hoot host hots oohs shoo shot soot stob tosh boo bot hob hot oho ohs ooh sob sot tho too ho oh os sh so to
bhoot booth boot both hobo hoot boo bot hob hot oho ooh tho too ho oh to
bhootx hotbox booth boot both hobo hoot boo bot box hob hot oho ooh tho too ho oh ox to
bhorst broths throbs borts broth horst short throb bort bosh both bots hobs host hots orbs orts rhos robs rots shot sorb sort stob tors tosh bot hob hot ohs orb ort rho rob rot sob sot tho tor ho oh or os sh so to
bhort broth throb both bort bot hob hot orb ort rho rob rot tho tor ho oh or to
bhos bosh hobs hob ohs sob ho oh os sh so
bhot both bot hob hot tho ho oh to
bhrssu shrubs brush shrub bush buss hubs rubs rush subs bus hub rub sub sh us
bhrsu brush shrub bush hubs rubs rush bus hub rub sub sh us
bhrsuy brushy brush bushy rushy shrub bury bush busy buys hubs rubs ruby rush bus buy hub rub shy sub by sh us
bhsu bush hubs bus hub sub sh us
bhsuy bushy bush busy buys hubs bus buy hub shy sub by sh us
bhu hub

biiikn bikini bin ink kin nib in

biiikns bikinis. *See* **biiikn**

biiktz kibitz tiki ziti bit kit zit it ti

biillno billion. *See* **billno**

biillnos billions billion billons. *See* **billno**

biilmoty mobility. *See* **bilmo iilmt**

biilnoov oblivion. *See* **iilnov**

biilosu bilious. *See* **bilos blosu ilosu**

biilsvy visibly. *See* **bilsy**

biimn nimbi bin nib nim mi in

biimnosu niobiums minibus niobium omnibus. *See* **bimnsu iimnou**

biimnou niobium. *See* **iimnou biimn**

biimnsu minibus. *See* **bimnsu biimn**

biior oribi obi orb rib rob or

biiors oribis oribi ibis iris obis orbs ribs robs sorb sori obi orb rib rob sib sir sob is or os si so

biirsstu bursitis. *See* **birstu brsstu**

biis ibis sib is si

biisttt titbits. *See* **biittt bistt iistt**

biittt titbit bitt titi bit tit it ti

bij jib

bijnossu subjoins subjoin. *See* **bnossu**

bijnosu subjoin. *See* **bijou binos bnosu**

bijou bijou jib job obi jo

bijoux bijoux bijou box jib job obi jo ox xi

bijs jibs jib sib is si

bikl bilk ilk li

bikln blink bilk kiln link bin ilk ink kin nib nil li in

biklnost inkblots inkblot. *See* **biklns iknost ilnost**

biklnosy linkboys linkboy. *See* **biklns iklnsy ilnosy**

biklnot inkblot. *See* **bikln**

biklnoy linkboy. *See* **bikln blnoy**

biklns blinks bilks blink kilns links slink bilk bins inks kiln link nibs nils silk sink skin bin ilk ink kin nib nil sib sin ski in is li si

biklrsy briskly. *See* **bikls bilrs bikrs**

bikls bilks bilk silk ilk sib ski is li si

bikmnpsu bumpkins bumpkin. *See* **biknsu bimnsu**

bikmnpu bumpkin. *No 6s or 5s*

biknr brink rink bin ink irk kin kir nib rib in

biknrs brinks brink brisk rinks bins inks irks kris nibs ribs rink risk sink skin bin ink irk kin kir nib rib sib sin sir ski in is si

biknssu buskins. *See* **biknsu inssu iknss**

biknsu buskin bunks bins bunk buns inks nibs nubs sink skin snub sunk bin bun bus ink kin nib nub sib sin ski sub sun in is nu si us

bikrs brisk irks kris ribs risk irk kir rib sib sir ski is si

bill bill ill li

billno billon bill boil boll lion loin nill noil bin ill ion lob nib nil nob obi oil in li lo no on

billnoou bouillon bullion. *See* **billno**

billnos billons. *See* **billno bills binos**

billnosu bullions billons bullion. *See* **billno**

billnou bullion. *See* **billno**

billopx pillbox. *See* **billox ilopx**

billosw billows. *See* **billow bills blosw**

billow billow bill blow boil boll bowl will bow ill lob low obi oil owl li lo ow

billowy billowy. *See* **billow billy blowy**

billox bollix bill boil boll box ill lob lox obi oil li lo ox xi

billrs brills bills birls rills bill birl ribs rill sill ill rib sib sir is li si

bills bills bill sill ill sib is li si

billy billy bill illy lily ill by li

bilm limb mil li mi

bilmnor nombril. *See* **bilor bilmo imnor**

bilmnors nombrils nombril. *See* **bilmos bilors binors imnors**

bilmny nimbly inly limb limn limy liny bin mil nib nil nim yin by in li mi my

bilmo limbo boil limb limo milo moil lob mil mob obi oil li lo mi mo om

bilmos limbos boils limbo limbs limos moils boil limb limo lobs milo mils mobs moil obis oils silo slim slob soil lob los mil mis mob mos obi oil oms sib sob sol is li lo mi mo om os si so

bilmostu botulism ultimos. *See* **bilmos bilmsu bimstu biostu**

bilmp blimp blip limb limp imp lip mil li mi pi

bilmps blimps blimp blips limbs limps blip imps limb limp lips lisp mils simp slim slip imp lip mil mis sib sip is li mi pi si

bilms limbs limb mils slim mil mis sib is li mi si

bilmsu limbus limbs bums limb mils slim slub slum bum bus lum mil mis mus sib sub sum is li mi mu si um us

bilo boil lob obi oil li lo

biloo oboli boil bolo lobo olio boo lob loo obi oil li lo

bilopssy possibly. *See* **bilssy biopsy ilopss**

bilor broil birl boil roil lob obi oil orb rib rob li lo or

bilors broils birls boils broil loris roils birl boil lobs obis oils orbs ribs robs roil silo slob soil sorb sori lob los obi oil orb rib rob sib sir sob sol is li lo or os si so

bilos boils boil lobs obis oils silo slob soil lob los obi oil sib sob sol is li lo os si so

bilosssu subsoils subsoil. *See* **bilss bilos blosu**

bilossu subsoil. *See* **bilss bilos blosu**

bilp blip lip li pi

bilps blips blip lips lisp slip lip sib sip is li pi si

bilr birl rib li

bilrs birls birl ribs rib sib sir is li si

bilrsty bristly. *See* **bilrty ilrsty**

bilrtuy tilbury. *See* **bilrty blrtu birtu**

bilrty trilby birl brit bit lit rib til try by it li ti

bilss bliss sibs sib sis is li si

bilssy sibyls bliss lysis sibyl sibs sib sis sly by is li si

bilsuy busily sibyl busy buys slub bus buy sib sly sub by is li si us

bilsy sibyl sib sly by is li si

biltu built bit but lit til tub tui it li ti ut

biltz blitz bit lit til zit it li ti

bimnosu omnibus. *See* **bimnsu binos bnosu**

bimnsu nimbus numbs minus bins bums buns nibs nims nubs numb snub bin bum bun bus mis mus nib nim nub sib sin sub sum sun in is mi mu nu si um us

bimosss bossism. *No 6s or 5s*

bimosz zombis zombi obis mobs mis mob mos obi oms sib sob is mi mo om os si so

bimoz zombi obi mob mi mo om

bimr brim mir rib rim mi

bimrs brims brim mirs ribs rims mir mis rib rim sib sir is mi si

bimrssux bruxisms bruxism. *See* **bimrs**

bimrsux bruxism. *See* **bimrs**

bimsstu submits. *See* **bimstu bsstu imsst**

bimstu submit bits bums bust buts mist must smut stub stum suit tubs tuis bit bum bus but its mis mus sib sit sub sum tub tui is it mi mu si ti um us ut

bin bin nib in

binnor inborn robin born iron bin inn ion nib nob nor obi orb rib rob in no on or

binnortw twinborn. *See* **binnor**

binnosu bunions. *See* **binnou innosu**

binnou bunion union noun bin bun inn ion nib nob nub nun obi in no nu on

binoost bonitos. *See* **binoot bioost**

binoot bonito boon boot into obit onto toon bin bit boo bot ion nib nit nob not obi tin ton too in it no on ti to

binor robin born iron bin ion nib nob nor obi orb rib rob in no on or

binors robins bison irons robin rosin bins born ions iron nibs nobs obis orbs ribs robs snob sorb sori bin ion nib nob nor obi orb rib rob sib sin sir sob son in is no on or os si so

binory briony briny irony robin bony born iron orby yoni bin boy ion nib nob nor obi orb rib rob yin yob yon by in no on or oy

binos bison bins ions nibs nobs obis snob bin ion nib nob obi sib sin sob son in is no on os si so

binrsu burins burin burns ruins bins buns burn nibs nubs ribs rubs ruin runs snub urns bin bun bus nib nub rib rub run sib sin sir sub sun urn in is nu si us

binru burin burn ruin bin bun nib nub rib rub run urn in nu

binry briny bin nib rib yin by in

bins bins nibs bin nib sib sin in is si

bio obi

bioorsz borzois. *See* **bioorz boors boosz**

bioorz borzoi boor bozo orzo zori boo obi orb rib rob zoo or

bioosst oboists. *See* **bioost boosst**

bioost oboist boost boots obits bits boos boot bots obis obit soot stob bit boo bot its obi sib sit sob sot too is it os si so ti to

bioosuv obvious. *No 6s or 5s*

bioprstw bowsprit. *See* **biorst ioprst**

bioprty probity. *See* **biort**

biopsy biopsy bops boys obis pois posy yips yobs bop boy obi poi sib sip sob sop soy spy yip yob by is os oy pi si so

biorrstu burritos burrito. *See* **biorst biostu birstu borrsu**

biorrtu burrito. *See* **birtu borru biort**

biorsst bistros. *See* **biorst**

biorst bistro orbits borts obits orbit riots tiros torsi trios bits bort bots brit obis obit orbs orts ribs riot robs rots sorb sori sort stir stob tiro tori tors trio bit bot its obi orb ort rib rob rot sib sir sit sob sot tor is it or os si so ti to

biorstuy bistoury. *See* **biorst biostu birstu borstu**

biort orbit bort brit obit riot tiro tori trio bit bot obi orb ort rib rob rot tor it or ti to

bios obis obi sib sob is os si so

biost obits bits bots obis obit stob bit bot its obi sib sit sob sot is it os si so ti to

biostu subito obits bouts bits bots bout bust buts obis obit oust outs stob stub suit tubs tuis bit bot bus but its obi out

sib sit sob sot sou sub tub tui is it os si so ti to us ut

biot obit bit bot obi it ti to

biqssu squibs squib buss sibs subs bus sib sis sub is si us

biqsu squib bus sib sub is si us

bir rib

birr birr rib

birrs birrs birr ribs rib sib sir is si

birs ribs rib sib sir is si

birsttu turbits. *See* **birstu birttu**

birstu bruits bruit burst bits brit bust buts ribs rubs rust ruts stir stub suit tubs tuis bit bus but its rib rub rut sib sir sit sub tub tui is it si ti us ut

birt brit rib bit it ti

birttu turbit bruit bitt brit butt bit but rib rub rut tit tub tui tut it ti ut

birtu bruit brit bit but rib rub rut tub tui it ti ut

bis sib is si

biss sibs sib sis is si

bisssstu subsists subsist. *See* **issstu**

bissstu subsist. *See* **issstu bsstu**

bist bits bit its sib sit is it si ti

bistt bitts bits bitt tits bit its sib sit tit is it si ti

bit bit it ti

bitt bitt bit tit it ti

bitty bitty bitt bit tit by it ti

---

bjmosu jumbos jumbo umbos bums jobs mobs sumo umbo bum bus job jus mob mos mus oms sob sou sub sum jo mo mu om os so um us

bjmou jumbo umbo bum job mob jo mo mu om um

bjo job jo

bjos jobs job sob jo os so

---

bkkooorw workbook. *See* **bkoor**

bklsu bulks bulk slub sulk bus sub us

bklu bulk

bkluy bulky bulk buy yuk by

bkmnsuu bunkums. *See* **bkmnuu bknsu bmnsu**

bkmnuu bunkum bunk numb bum bun nub mu nu um

bkmooorw bookworm. *See* **bkoor bmoor**

bkno bonk knob kob nob no on

bknoostw bowknots bowknot. *See* **bknos bkoos bnoos**

bknootw bowknot. *No 6s or 5s*

bknos bonks knobs bonk bosk knob kobs nobs snob kob kos nob sob son no on os so

bknosu bunkos bonks bonus bosun bunko bunks knobs bonk bosk bunk buns knob kobs nobs nous nubs onus snob snub sunk bun bus kob kos nob nub sob son sou sub sun no nu on os so us

bknou bunko bonk bunk knob bun kob nob nub no nu on

bknsu   bunks bunk buns nubs snub sunk bun bus nub sub sun nu us

bknu   bunk bun nub nu

bko   kob

bkoo   book kobo kob boo

bkoor   brook book boor kobo rook boo kob kor orb rob or

bkoors   brooks books boors brook rooks book boor boos bosk kobo kobs orbs robs rook sorb boo kob kor kos orb rob sob or os so

bkoos   books book boos bosk kobo kobs boo kob kos sob os so

bkorsuwy   busywork. *See* **borsw bkrsu bosuy**

bkos   bosk kobs kob kos sob os so

bkoss   bosks bosk boss kobs sobs kob kos sob os so

bkrsu   brusk rubs rusk bus rub sub us

---

bl

---

bllntuy   bluntly. *See* **blntu blluy bltuy**

bllo   boll lob lo

bllos   bolls boll lobs slob lob los sob sol lo os so

bllosuy   solubly. *See* **blosuy bllos bllsu**

bllouvy   volubly. *See* **blluy**

bllsu   bulls bull slub bus sub us

bllu   bull

blluy   bully bull buy by

blmnuy   numbly numb bum bun buy lum nub yum by mu my nu um

blmoo   bloom bolo boom lobo loom boo lob loo mob moo lo mo om

blmoooty   lobotomy. *See* **blmooy bmooty**

blmoos   blooms bloom bolos booms bosom lobos looms obols bolo boom boos lobo lobs loom loos mobs moos slob solo boo lob loo los mob moo mos oms sob sol lo mo om os so

blmooss   blossom. *See* **blmoos bmooss**

blmoosss   blossoms blossom. *See* **blmoos bmooss**

blmoossy   blossomy blossom symbols. *See* **blmoos blmooy blmosy bmooss**

blmooy   bloomy bloom looby bolo boom boyo lobo loom moly boo boy lob loo mob moo yob by lo mo my om oy

blmossy   symbols. *See* **blmosy bossy mossy**

blmosy   symbol boys lobs mobs moly slob yobs boy lob los mob mos oms sly sob sol soy yob by lo mo my om os oy so

blmouxy   buxomly. *See* **bmoux**

blmpsu   plumbs bumps lumps plumb plums slump bump bums lump plum plus pubs puls slub slum sump umps bum bus lum mus pub pul pus sub sum sup ump mu um up us

blmpu   plumb bump lump plum bum lum pub pul ump mu um up

blmruy   rumbly burly blur burl bury ruby bum buy lum rub rum yum by mu my um

blnoorw   lowborn. *See* **blnow bnoor bnorw**

blnow   blown blow bowl bow lob low nob now owl own won lo no on ow

blnoy   nobly bony only boy lob nob yob yon by lo no on oy

blnstu   blunts blunt bunts lunts buns bunt bust buts lunt lust nubs nuts slub slut snub stub stun tubs tuns bun bus but nub nut sub sun tub tun nu us ut

blntu   blunt bunt lunt bun but nub nut tub tun nu ut

blo   lob lo

bloootx   toolbox. *No 6s or 5s*

bloopswy   plowboys plowboy lowboys. *See* **bloowy bloswy**

bloopwy   plowboy. *See* **bloowy loopy**

blooquy   obloquy. *See* **blooy**

bloorsww   lowbrows lowbrow. *See* **blosw bloos boors**

bloorww   lowbrow. *No 6s or 5s*

bloos   bolos lobos obols bolo boos lobo lobs loos slob solo boo lob loo los sob sol lo os so

bloostuw   blowouts blowout. *See* **bloosu**

bloosu   obolus bolos bolus lobos obols bolo boos lobo lobs loos slob slub solo soul boo bus lob loo los sob sol sou sub lo os so us

blooswy   lowboys. *See* **bloowy bloswy**

bloott   blotto lotto blot bolo bolt boot bott lobo loot tool toot boo bot lob loo lot too tot lo to

blootuw   blowout. *No 6s or 5s*

bloowy   lowboy looby blowy blow bolo bowl boyo lobo wool yowl boo bow boy lob loo low owl woo yob yow by lo ow oy

blooy   looby bolo boyo lobo boo boy lob loo yob by lo oy

blopsstu   subplots subplot. *See* **lopstu opsstu**

blopstu   subplot. *See* **lopstu blost blosu**

blopsuw   blowups. *See* **blopuw blosw blosu**

blopuw   blowup blow bowl plow bop bow lob lop low owl pub pul lo ow up

blorstuy   robustly. *See* **blosuy blrstu blstuy borstu**

blos   lobs slob lob los sob sol lo os so

bloss   slobs boss lobs loss slob sobs sols lob los sob sol lo os so

blost   blots bolts blot bolt bots lobs lost lots slob slot stob bot lob los lot sob sol sot lo os so to

blosu   bolus lobs slob slub soul bus lob los sob sol sou sub lo os so us

blosuy   blousy bolus buoys lousy boys buoy busy buys lobs slob slub soul yobs boy bus buy lob los sly sob sol sou soy sub yob you by lo os oy so us

blosw   blows bowls blow bowl bows lobs lows owls slob slow bow lob los low owl sob sol sow lo os ow so

bloswy   blowsy blows blowy bowls yowls blow bowl bows boys lobs lows owls slob slow yobs yowl bow boy lob los low owl sly sob sol sow soy yob yow by lo os ow oy so

blot   blot bolt bot lob lot lo to

blow   blow bowl bow lob low owl lo ow

blowy   blowy blow bowl yowl bow boy lob low owl yob yow by lo ow oy

blowyz   blowzy blowy blow bowl yowl bow boy lob low owl yob yow by lo ow oy

blrruy   blurry burly blur burl burr bury ruby rub buy by

blrssu   slurbs blurs burls slurb slurs blur burl buss rubs slub slur subs bus rub sub us

blrstu   blurts blurs blurt burls burst slurb blur burl bust buts lust rubs rust ruts slub slur slut stub tubs bus but rub rut sub tub us ut

blrsu   blurs burls slurb blur burl rubs slub slur bus rub sub us

blrtu blurt blur burl but rub rut tub ut	**blstuy** butyls subtly busty butyl lusty	**blsu** slub bus sub us
blru blur burl rub	bust busy buts buys lust slub slut stub	**bltuy** butyl but buy tub by ut
blruy burly blur burl bury ruby rub buy by	tubs bus but buy sly sty sub tub by us ut	

---

bm

bmnsu numbs bums buns nubs numb snub bum bun bus mus nub sub sum sun mu nu um us

bmnu numb bum bun nub mu nu um

bmo mob mo om

bmoo boom boo mob moo mo om

bmoor broom boom boor moor room boo mob moo mor orb rob mo om or

bmoors brooms booms boors bosom broom moors rooms boom boor boos mobs moor moos mors orbs robs room sorb boo mob moo mor mos oms orb rob sob mo om or os so

bmoorstu motorbus. *See* **bmoors boorst borstu moorst**

bmoos booms bosom boom boos mobs moos boo mob moo mos oms sob mo om os so

bmooss bosoms booms bosom boom boos boss mobs moos moss sobs boo mob moo mos oms sob mo om os so

bmoostt bottoms. *See* **bmoott moostt**

bmoosty tomboys. *See* **bmoosy bmooty**

bmoosy bosomy booms bosom boom boos boyo boys mobs moos yobs boo boy mob moo mos oms sob soy yob by mo my om os oy so

bmoott bottom motto boom boot bott moot tomb toot boo bot mob moo mot tom too tot mo om to

bmooty tomboy booty boom boot boyo moot tomb boo bot boy mob moo mot tom too toy yob by mo my om oy to

bmorsuu brumous. *See* **bmosu**

bmos mobs mob mos oms sob mo om os so

bmost tombs bots mobs most mots stob tomb toms bot mob mos mot oms sob sot tom mo om os to to

bmosu umbos bums mobs sumo umbo bum bus mob mos mus oms sob sou sub sum mo mu om os so um us

bmosw wombs bows mobs mows womb bow mob mos mow oms sob sow mo om os ow so

bmot tomb bot mob mot tom mo om to

bmou umbo mob bum mo mu om um

bmoux buxom umbo box bum mob mo mu om ox um

bmow womb bow mob mow mo om ow

bmpsu bumps bump bums pubs sump umps bum bus mus pub pus sub sum sup ump mu um up us

bmpu bump bum pub ump mu um up

bmpuy bumpy bump bum buy pub ump yum yup by mu my um up

bmsu bums bum bus mus sub sum mu um us

bmu bum mu um

---

bn

bnnoru unborn bourn born burn noun bun nob nor nub nun orb our rob rub run urn no nu on or

bnnottuu unbutton. *See* **bnottu**

bnnoy bonny bony boy nob yob yon by no on oy

bnnrssuu sunburns sunburn. *See* **bnrsu bnssu**

bnnrstuu sunburnt sunburn. *See* **bnrstu**

bnnrsuu sunburn. *See* **bnrsu**

bnnuy bunny bun buy nub nun by nu

bno nob no on

bnoo boon boo nob no on

bnoor boron boon boor born boo nob nor orb rob no on or

bnoors borons boons boors boron boon boor boos born nobs orbs robs snob soon sorb boo nob nor orb rob sob son no on or os so

bnoortuw brownout outworn. *See* **bnortu**

bnoos boons boon boos nobs snob soon boo nob son no on os so

bnor born nob nor orb rob no on or

bnorssu suborns. *See* **bnorsu bnossu**

bnorstu burtons. *See* **bnrstu bnortu borstu bnorsu**

bnorstuu burnouts burnous burnout burtons outruns. *See* **bnorsu bnortu bnrstu borstu**

bnorsu suborn bonus bosun bourn burns born buns burn nobs nous nubs onus orbs ours robs rubs runs snob snub sorb sour urns bun bus nob nor nub orb our rob rub run sob son sou sub sun urn no nu on or os so us

bnorsuu burnous. *See* **bnorsu**

bnorsw browns brown brows sworn born bows brow nobs orbs owns robs rows snob snow sorb sown worn bow nob nor now orb own rob row sob son sow won no on or os ow so

bnortu burton bourn brunt burnt born bort bout bunt burn rout runt torn tour turn unto bot bun but nob nor not nub nut orb ort our out rob rot rub run rut ton tor tub tun urn no nu on or to ut

bnortuu burnout. *See* **bnortu nortuu**

bnoru bourn born burn bun nob nor nub orb our rob rub run urn no nu on or

bnorw brown born brow worn bow nob nor now orb own rob row won no on or ow

bnos   nobs snob nob sob son no on os so

bnoss   snobs boss nobs snob sobs sons nob sob son no on os so

bnossu   bosuns bonus bosun snobs snubs boss buns buss nobs nous nubs onus snob snub sobs sons sous subs suns bun bus nob nub sob son sou sub sun no nu on os so us

bnossuw   sunbows. *See* **bnossu bnosuw**

bnosttu   buttons. *See* **bnottu bnosu bostt**

bnosu   bonus bosun buns nobs nous nubs onus snob snub bun bus nob nub sob son sou sub sun no nu on os so us

bnosuw   sunbow bonus bosun bows buns nobs nous nubs onus owns snob snow snub sown bow bun bus nob now nub own sob son sou sow sub sun won no nu on os ow so us

bnottu   button bott bout bunt butt tout unto bot bun but nob not nub nut out ton tot tub tun tut no nu on to ut

bnotuy   bounty bony bout bunt buoy tony unto bot boy bun but buy nob not nub nut out ton toy tub tun yob yon you by no nu on oy to ut

bnoy   bony boy nob yob yon by no on oy

bnrsstuu   sunburst. *See* **bnrstu brsstu**

bnrstu   brunts brunt bunts burns burnt burst runts turns buns bunt burn bust buts nubs nuts rubs runs runt rust ruts snub stub stun tubs tuns turn urns bun bus but nut rub run rut sub sun tub tun urn nu us ut

bnrsu   burns buns burn nubs rubs runs snub urns bun bus nub rub run sub sun urn nu us

bnrtu   brunt burnt bunt burn runt turn bun but nub nut rub run rut tub tun urn nu ut

bnru   burn bun nub rub run urn nu

bnssu   snubs buns buss nubs snub subs suns bun bus nub sub sun nu us

bnstu   bunts buns bunt bust buts nubs nuts snub stub stun tubs tuns bun bus but nub nut sub sun tub tun nu us ut

bnsu   buns nubs snub bun bus nub sub sun nu us

bntu   bunt bun but nub nut tub tun nu ut

bnu   bun nub nu

boo   boo

boopstx   postbox. *See* **boost oopst**

boor   boor boo orb rob or

boorrsw   borrows. *See* **boorrw oorrsw**

boorrw   borrow boor brow boo bow orb rob row woo or ow

boors   boors boor boos orbs robs sorb boo orb rob sob or os so

boorst   robots robot boors boost boots borts roost roots rotos torso boor boos boot bort bots orbs orts robs root roto rots soot sorb sort stob tors boo bot orb ort rob rot sob sot too tor or os so to

boort   robot boor boot bort root roto boo bot orb ort rob rot too tor or to

boos   boos boo sob os so

boosst   boosts boost boots soots stobs boos boot boss bots sobs soot sots stob toss boo bot sob sot too os so to

boost   boost boots boos boot bots soot stob boo bot sob sot too os so to

booswww   bowwows. *See* **boowww**

booswx   oxbows oxbow boos bows woos boo bow box sob sow sox woo os ow ox so

boosz   bozos boos bozo zoos boo sob zoo os so

boot   boot boo bot too to

booty   booty boot boyo boo bot boy too toy yob by oy to

boowww   bowwow boo bow woo wow ow

boowx   oxbow boo bow box woo ow ox

booy   boyo boo boy yob by oy

booyz   boozy boyo bozo oozy boo boy yob zoo by oy

booz   bozo boo zoo

bop   bop

bops   bops bop sob sop os so

bor   orb rob or

borrsu   burros burro burrs burr orbs ours robs rubs sorb sour bus orb our rob rub sob sou sub or os so us

borrsuw   burrows. *See* **borrsu borruw**

borru   burro burr orb our rob rub or

borruw   burrow burro brow burr bow orb our rob row rub or ow

bors   orbs robs sorb orb rob sob or os so

borss   sorbs boss orbs robs sobs sorb orb rob sob or os so

borst   borts bort bots orbs orts robs rots sorb sort stob tors bot orb ort rob rot sob sot tor or os so to

borsttu   turbots. *See* **borstu orsttu borttu**

borsttuu   outburst turbots surtout. *See* **borstu borttu orsttu**

borstu   robust borts bouts burst roust routs stour torus tours bort bots bout bust buts orbs orts ours oust outs robs rots rout rubs rust ruts sorb sort sour stob stub tors tour tubs bot bus but orb ort our out rob rot rub rut sob sot sou sub tor tub or os so to us ut

borsw   brows bows brow orbs robs rows sorb bow orb rob row sob sow or os ow so

bort   bort bot orb ort rob rot tor or to

borttu   turbot trout tutor bort bott bout butt rout tort tour tout trot bot but orb ort our out rob rot rub rut tor tot tub tut or to ut

borw   brow bow orb rob row or ow

bory   orby boy orb rob yob by or oy

bos   sob os so

boss   boss sobs sob os so

bosst   stobs boss bots sobs sots stob toss bot sob sot os so to

bossy   bossy boss boys sobs soys yobs boy sob soy yob by os oy so

bost   bots stob bot sob sot os so to

bostt   botts bots bott stob tost tots bot sob sot tot os so to

bostu   bouts bots bout bust buts oust outs stob stub tubs bot bus but out sob sot sou sub tub os so to us ut

bostuuy   buyouts. *See* **botuuy bostu bosuy**

bosuy   buoys boys buoy busy buys yobs boy bus buy sob sou soy sub yob you by os oy so us

bosw   bows bow sob sow os ow so

bosy   boys yobs boy sob soy yob by os oy so

bot   bot to

bott   bott bot tot to

botu   bout bot but out tub to ut

botuuy   buyout bout buoy bot boy but buy out toy tub yob you by oy to ut

bouy   buoy boy buy yob you by oy

bow   bow ow

box   box ox
boxy   boxy box boy yob by ox oy
boy   boy yob by oy

---

bp

bprsu   burps burp pubs rubs spur bus
pub pus rub sub sup up us
bpru   burp pub rub up

bpsu   pubs bus pub pus sub sup up us
bpu   pub up

---

br

brrsu   burrs burr rubs bus rub sub us
brru   burr rub
brsstu   bursts burst busts rusts stubs
truss buss bust buts rubs rust ruts stub
subs tubs bus but rub rut sub tub us ut

brstu   burst bust buts rubs rust ruts stub
tubs bus but rub rut sub tub us ut
brsu   rubs bus rub sub us

bru   rub
bruy   bury ruby rub buy by

---

bs

bsssuy   byssus buss busy buys subs bus
buy sub by us
bsstu   busts stubs buss bust buts stub
subs tubs bus but sub tub us ut
bssu   buss subs bus sub us

bsttu   butts bust buts butt stub tubs tuts
bus but sub tub tut us ut
bstu   bust buts stub tubs bus but sub tub
us ut

bstuy   busty bust busy buts buys stub
tubs bus but buy sty sub tub by us ut
bsu   bus sub us
bsuy   busy buys bus buy sub by us

---

bt—by

bttu   butt but tub tut ut
btu   but tub ut
buy   buy by

buzz   buzz
by   by

cc

cccceeilt   eclectic. *See* **ceelt eeilt ceilt**

cccceilny   encyclic. *See* **cccily cceily ceilny**

cccilnoy   cyclonic. *See* **cccily ccilno**

cccily   cyclic icy li

cccinstu   succinct. *See* **cinstu**

cccio   cocci

cccnoost   concocts concoct. *See* **cnoost**

cccnoot   concoct. *See* **cnoot**

cccosu   coccus sou os so us

cccoxy   coccyx cox coy ox oy

ccddeeno   conceded concede encoded. *See* **cddeeo cdeeno**

ccddeeot   decocted. *See* **ccdeot cddeeo**

ccddelou   occluded occlude clouded. *See* **cddelo cddelu**

ccddenou   conduced conduce. *See* **cddeo cdeno cdeou**

ccdeeenr   credence. *See* **cdeeer deeenr**

ccdeehk   checked. *See* **ccehk ceehk**

ccdeehln   clenched. *See* **ccehln cdeehl**

ccdeeiop   codpiece. *See* **cdeeip cdeiop**

ccdeeirv   creviced crevice. *See* **cdeirv deeirv cdeeiv**

ccdeeekor   cockered coerced crocked. *See* **ccdeko cceeor ccekor cdeekr**

ccdeekoy   cockeyed cockeye. *See* **ccdeko**

ccdeelry   recycled recycle. *See* **ccdely ceelry**

ccdeeno   concede. *See* **cdeeno**

ccdeenos   concedes concede encodes sconced. *See* **ccenos cdeeno cdeens cdenos**

ccdeeny   decency. *See* **deeny**

ccdeeor   coerced. *See* **cceeor cdeor cdeer**

ccdeessu   succeeds succeed seduces. *See* **ccessu cdessu deessu**

ccdeesu   succeed. *See* **cdeesu**

ccdehhru   churched. *See* **cchhru**

ccdehin   cinched. *See* **cdehin**

ccdehipu   hiccuped. *See* **cchipu**

ccdehklu   chuckled chucked chuckle clucked. *See* **cdeklu cehklu dehklu**

ccdehko   chocked. *See* **cdehko ccdeko**

ccdehku   chucked. *See* **ccehk cchku**

ccdehltu   clutched. *See* **cchltu cdeltu**

ccdehnru   crunched churned. *See* **cchnru cdehnr**

ccdehors   scorched. *See* **cceors cchors cdehos cdeors**

ccdehort   crotched crochet torched. *See* **ccdeot cchort cehort**

ccdehoru   crouched couched. *See* **cchoru cdehou**

ccdehost   scotched decocts. *See* **ccdeot cchost cdehos dehost**

ccdehou   couched. *See* **cdehou cchou**

ccdehrtu   crutched. *See* **cchrtu**

ccdeiil   icicled. *See* **cceiil**

ccdeiino   coincide. *See* **cciino cdeino deiino**

ccdeiit   deictic. *See* **cdeiit**

ccdeikl   clicked. *See* **cdeikl ccikl**

ccdeikr   cricked. *See* **cdeikr cceir ccikr**

ccdeilr   circled. *See* **cceilr**

ccdeinor   corniced cornice. *See* **cdeino cdeinr cdenor deinor**

ccdeinot   occident conceit ctenoid noticed. *See* **ccdeot cdeino cdenot ceinot**

ccdeiopu   occupied. *See* **cdeiop**

ccdeios   codices. *See* **ccios cdeos cdeis**

ccdeklo   clocked cockled. *See* **ccdeko cceklo cdeklo**

ccdeklu   clucked. *See* **cdeklu ccklu**

ccdeko   cocked coked cock code coed coke deck dock cod doc doe ode oke do od

ccdekoou   cuckooed. *See* **ccdeko cckoou cdekoo**

ccdekor   crocked. *See* **ccdeko ccekor cdekor**

ccdelnou   conclude occlude conduce. *See* **cdelno delnou**

ccdelosu   occludes occlude. *See* **cdelos cdeosu cdlosu celosu**

ccdelou   occlude. *See* **cdlou cdelu cdeou**

ccdely   cycled cycle dey dye eld led lye el ye

ccdenooo   cocooned. *See* **ccnooo**

ccdenos   sconced. *See* **ccenos cdenos**

ccdenosu   conduces sconced conduce. *See* **ccenos cdenos cdensu cdeosu**

ccdenou   conduce. *See* **cdeno cdeou cdenu**

ccdeorru   occurred reoccur. *See* **cdeorr cderru deorru**

ccdeorsu   succored coursed scoured. *See* **cceors ccersu ccorsu cdeors**

ccdeost   decocts. *See* **ccdeot cdeos ceost**

ccdeot   decoct code coed cote dote toed cod cot doc doe dot ode ted tod toe do od to

ccdhinoo   conchoid. *See* **cdinoo**

ccdiilo   codicil. *See* **ccilo cdiio**

ccdiilos   codicils codicil. *See* **ccios cdlos cilos**

ccdiior   cricoid. *See* **cdiio**

ccdilosy   cycloids cycloid. *See* **ccios cdlos closy**

ccdiloy   cycloid. *See* **ccilo diloy**

ccdklosu   cuckolds cuckold. *See* **ccklos ccklsu cdlosu**

ccdklou   cuckold. *See* **ccklo cdlou ccklu**

ccdnoor   concord. *See* **cdnoor**

ccdnoors   concords concord cordons. *See* **cdnoor cnoors dnoors**

ccdnostu   conducts conduct. *See* **ccostu cnostu dnostu**

ccdnotu   conduct. *See* **cnotu dnotu**

cceehik   chickee. *See* **ccehk ceehk cchik**

cceehiks   chickees chickee. *See* **ccehks cchiks ceehis ceehks**

cceehkr   checker recheck. *See* **ccehk ceehr ceekr**

cceehkrs   checkers rechecks checker recheck screech. *See* **ccehks ceehks ceehrs ceekrs**

cceehlns   clenches. *See* **ccehln ceehls**

cceehrs   screech. *See* **ceehrs**

cceehrsy   screechy screech secrecy. *See* **ceehrs ceehry ceehsy eehrsy**

cceeiils   cicelies icicles. *See* **cceiil**

cceeilnr   encircle recline. *See* **cceilr ceelnr eeilnr**

cceeilnt   elenctic. *See* **ceeint ceilnt**

cceeilpy   epicycle. *See* **cceily ceilpy**

cceeilrt   electric circlet reticle tiercel. *See* **cceilr ceeirt ceelrt ceilrt**

cceeinor   cicerone cornice. *See* **cceeor ceenor**

cceeinov   conceive. *See* **ceeinv ceinov**

cceeins   science. *See* **ccins ceeins**

cceeinss   sciences science. *See* **ccins ceeins ceeiss ceenss**

cceeiorv   coercive crevice. *See* **cceeor ceiorv**

cceeirsv   cervices crescive crevices crevice service. *See* **ceeirs eeirsv**

cceeirv   crevice. *See* **cceir**

cceeittu   eutectic. *See* **ceitu**

cceeklor   cockerel. *See* **cceeor cceklo ccekor ceelor**

cceekoy   cockeye. *See* **cckoy**

cceelmny   clemency. *See* **ccely eemny**

cceelrsy   recycles recycle secrecy. *See* **ccelsy ceelrs ceelry**

cceelry   recycle. *See* **ceelry ccely**

cceemmor   commerce. *See* **cceeor**

cceennos   ensconce. *See* **ccenos**

cceenort   concrete concert. *See* **cceeor ceenor ceenot ceenrt**

cceenrst   crescent centers centres. *See* **ceenrs ceenrt ceerst eenrst**

cceeor   coerce cere cero core cee cor ere orc ore rec roc roe er or re cceeors   coerces. *See* **cceeor cceors**

cceersy   secrecy. *See* **eersy ceers ceesy**

cceffhko   checkoff. *See* **ccehk cchko cehko**

ccefiips   specific. *See* **ceips**

ccefirru   crucifer. *See* **cefirr**

ccefloos   floccose. *See* **cefls celos ccoos**

ccefnost   confects confect. *See* **ccenos cenost efnost**

ccefnot   confect. *See* **cenot efnot**

cceghikn   checking chicken. *See* **ccehk cchik cehin**

cceginor   coercing cornice. *See* **ceginr cegnor cginor**

ccehhins   chinches cinches. *See* **cchhin cehins cceins**

ccehhrsu   churches curches. *See* **ccersu cchhru cehrsu**

ccehiimr   chimeric. *See* **ccehim**

ccehikn   chicken. *See* **ccehk cchik cehin**

ccehikns   chickens chicken cinches. *See* **ccehks cceins cchiks cehins**

ccehil   chicle ceil chic lech lice chi hie ice lei lie eh el he hi li

ccehilnr   clincher. *See* **ccehil ccehln cceilr cchiln**

ccehilns   clinches cinches lichens. *See* **ccehil ccehln cceins cchiln**

ccehiloy   choicely. *See* **ccehil ccehio ccehlo cceily**

ccehim   chemic chime hemic chic mice chi hem hie him ice eh em he hi me mi

ccehins   cinches. *See* **cehins cceins**

ccehinst   technics cinches ethnics technic. *See* **ccehit cceins cehins cehint**

ccehint   technic. *See* **ccehit cehint**

ccehio   choice echoic chico chic echo chi hie hoe ice eh he hi ho oh

ccehior   choicer. *See* **ccehio cchior cehior**

ccehiort   ricochet choicer crochet. *See* **ccehio ccehit cchior cchort**

ccehios   choices. *See* **cchios ccehio**

ccehiost   choicest choices. *See* **ccehio ccehit cchios cchost**

ccehit   hectic ethic chic chit cite etch itch tech chi eth het hie hit ice the tic tie eh he hi it ti

ccehk   check heck eh he

ccehklru   chuckler chuckle. *See* **cehklu ceklru**

ccehklsu   chuckles chuckle culches huckles. *See* **ccehks cchksu ccklsu cehklu**

ccehklu   chuckle. *See* **cehklu ccehk cchku**

ccehkotu   checkout. *See* **ccehk cchko cehko**

ccehkpsu   checkups checkup. *See* **ccehks cchksu**

ccehkpu   checkup. *See* **ccehk cchku**

ccehks   checks check hecks heck she eh he sh

ccehlmor   cromlech. *See* **ccehlo cehlor cehmor**

ccehln   clench lech hen eh el en he ne

ccehlnnu   unclench. *See* **ccehln**

ccehlo   cloche cole echo hole lech loch col hoe eh el he ho lo oh

ccehlos   cloches. *See* **ccehlo cehos celos**

ccehlstu   clutches cultches culches cutches. *See* **cchltu cchstu cehstu celstu**

ccehlsu   culches. *See* **celsu cchlu ccesu**

ccehnos   conches. *See* **ccenos cehnos**

ccehnrsu   crunches curches scrunch. *See* **ccersu cchnru cehrsu chnrsu**

ccehorrs   scorcher. *See* **cceors cchors cehors ceorrs**

ccehorss   scorches soccers coshers. *See* **cceors cchors cehors cehoss**

ccehorst   crochets crotches crochet hectors rochets rotches torches troches. *See* **cceors cchors cchost cehors**

ccehorsu   crouches couches curches. *See* **cceors ccersu cchors cchoru**

ccehort   crochet. *See* **cchort cehort**

ccehortt   crotchet crochet. *See* **cchort cehort ceortt ehortt**

ccehosst   scotches. *See* **cchost cehoss cehsst ceosst**

ccehosu   couches. *See* **cehosu**

ccehrstu   crutches curches cutches. *See* **ccersu cchrtu cchstu cehrst**

ccehrsu   curches. *See* **ccersu cehrsu**

ccehsstu   scutches cutches. *See* **ccessu cchstu cehsst cehstu**

ccehstu   cutches. *See* **cchstu cehstu**

cceiil   cilice icicle ceil lice ice lei lie el li

cceiilnt   enclitic. *See* **cceiil cciiln ceiilt ceiint**

cceiilor   licorice. *See* **cceiil cceilr ceilor**

cceiilpt   ecliptic. *See* **cceiil cceipt ceiilt**

cceiils   icicles. *See* **cceiil**

cceiirt   icteric. *See* **cciirt**

cceiiklr   clicker. *See* **cceilr**

cceiiklrs   clickers circles clerics clicker slicker. *See* **cceilr ccikls ccikrs ceikls**

cceikor   cockier. *See* **ccekor cceir ccikr**

cceikost   cockiest. *See* **cekost**

cceikrst   crickets cricket rickets sticker tickers. *See* **ccikrs ceikrs ceikrt ceirst**

cceikrt   cricket. *See* **ceikrt cceir ccikr**

cceilnuy   unicycle. *See* **cceily ceilnu ceilny**

cceilr   circle cleric ceric relic ceil lice lire rice riel rile ice ire lei lie rec el er li re

cceilrru   curricle. *See* **cceilr celrru**

cceilrs   circles clerics. *See* **cceilr ceilrs**

cceilrst   circlets circles circlet clerics relicts. *See* **cceilr ceilrs ceilrt ceirst**

cceilrt   circlet. *See* **cceilr ceilrt**

cceilrty   tricycle circlet. *See* **cceilr cceily ceilrt**

cceilruu   curlicue. *See* **cceilr celruu**

cceilstu   cuticles cuticle. *See* **ceilsu ceiltu ceistu celstu**

cceilsy   cylices. *See* **cceily ccelsy**

cceiltu   cuticle. *See* **ceiltu**

cceily   cicely cycle ceil lice ice icy lei lie lye el li ye

cceimnoo   economic. *See* **ceimno**

cceimost   cosmetic. *See* **ccimos cemost cimost eimost**

cceimrru   mercuric. *See* **ceimru**

cceinnov   convince connive. *See* **ceinov**

cceinoor   coercion cornice. *See* **cceir ccino cenor**

cceinor   cornice. *See* **cceir ccino cenor**

cceinors   cornices concise cornice cronies. *See* **cceins ccenos cceors ccinos**

cceinort   necrotic centric conceit concert cornice. *See* **ceinot ceinrt ceiort cenort**

cceinos   concise. *See* **ccinos ceinos cceins ccenos**

cceinost   conceits conceit concise notices section. *See* **cceins ccenos ccinos ceinos**

cceinot   conceit. *See* **ceinot**

cceinprt   precinct centric. *See* **cceipt ceinpr ceinpt ceinrt**

cceinrt   centric. *See* **ceinrt cceir**

cceinrtu   cincture centric. *See* **ceinrt ceirtu einrtu**

cceins   scenic since ices nice sine ens ice sen sic sin en in is ne si

cceiopp   coppice. *No 6s or 5s*

cceiopps   coppices coppice. *See* **ceiops**

cceiopsu   occupies piceous. *See* **ceiops ceopsu**

cceiopt   ectopic. *See* **cceipt ceiopt**

cceiopty   ecotypic ectopic. *See* **cceipt ceiopt**

cceiorst   cortices. *See* **cceors ceiors ceiort ceirst**

cceipt   pectic cite epic pice cep ice pet pie pit tic tie tip it pe pi ti

cceir   ceric rice ice ire rec er re

cceirssu   circuses cruises. *See* **ccersu ccessu ccirsu ceirss**

cceklo   cockle clock cock coke cole koel lock col elk lek oke el lo

cceklos   cockles. *See* **cceklo ccklos**

cceknosy   cockneys cockney. *See* **ccenos cenosy**

cceknoy   cockney. *See* **cckoy cenoy**

ccekop   copeck cock coke cope peck pock poke cep cop oke ope pe

ccekops   copecks. *See* **ccekop cckos cekos**

ccekopst   petcocks copecks petcock pockets. *See* **ccekop cekopt cekost**

ccekopt petcock. *See* **ccekop cekopt**

ccekor cocker crock cero cock coke core cork reck rock cor kor oke orc ore rec roc roe er or re

ccekorry crockery. *See* **ccekor cekorr**

ccekors cockers. *See* **ccekor cckors cekors cceors**

ccekorst crockets cockers crocket restock rockets. *See* **ccekor cceors cckors cekors**

ccekorsu cocksure cockers. *See* **ccekor cceors ccersu cckors**

ccekort crocket. *See* **ccekor cekort**

ccellost collects collect. *See* **cellos celost**

ccellot collect. *See* **cello**

ccelnosy cyclones cyclone. *See* **ccelsy ccenos celnos cenosy**

ccelnoy cyclone. *See* **celno cenoy ccely**

ccelsy cycles cycle lyes lyse syce els lye sly yes el ye

ccely cycle lye el ye

ccemu cecum cue cum emu em me mu um

ccennor concern. *See* **cenor cenno**

ccennors concerns concern. *See* **ccenos cceors cenors**

ccennost concents connects concent connect consent. *See* **ccenos cenost ennost**

ccennot concent connect. *See* **cenot ennot**

ccenoort concerto concert coronet. *See* **cenort cnoort**

ccenopst concepts concept. *See* **ccenos cenost enopst**

ccenopt concept. *See* **cenot**

ccenorst concerts concert cornets. *See* **ccenos cceors cenors cenort**

ccenort concert. *See* **cenort**

ccenos sconce cones scone cone cons eons noes nose once ones con ens eon one sen son en ne no on os so

ccenoss sconces. *See* **ccenos cenoss**

ccenrruy currency. *See* **crruy cerru enrru**

cceoostt cocottes cocotte. *See* **ceostt**

cceoott cocotte. *See* **ceott**

cceopruy reoccupy. *See* **ccopuy ceopru ceopry copruy**

cceorrst corrects correct rectors. *See* **cceors ceorrs ceorrt ceorst**

cceorrsu reoccurs courser reoccur scourer. *See* **cceors ccersu ccorsu ceorrs**

cceorrt correct. *See* **ceorrt**

cceorru reoccur. *See* **ceorr ccoru cerru**

cceors soccer ceros cores corse score cero core cors orcs ores rocs roes rose sore cor orc ore rec res roc roe er or os re so

cceorss soccers. *See* **ceorss**

cceorssu crocuses courses soccers sources succors sucrose. *See* **cceors ccersu ccessu ccorsu**

ccersu cruces cruse cures curse cusec crus cues cure curs ecru rues ruse sure user cue cur rec res rue us

ccesssu success. *See* **ccessu cesssu**

ccessu cusecs cusec cess cues cuss sues uses cue ess sue use us

ccesu cusec cues cue sue use us

ccfilnot conflict. *See* **ccilno**

ccfiruy crucify. *No 6s or 5s*

ccfkloot cockloft. *See* **ccklo cfklo**

ccflosu floccus. *See* **cflos cfosu flosu**

ccghhiou hiccough. *See* **cghhou**

ccghiinn cinching inching niching. *See* **cchin cgiin**

ccghikno chocking choking cocking hocking. *See* **cgikno ghikno**

ccghiknu chucking. *See* **cchik chikn cchku**

ccghinou couching. *See* **cchio chino cchin**

ccgiikln clicking licking. *See* **cciiln giikln**

ccgiiknr cricking. *See* **cgiinr giiknr**

ccgiilnr circling. *See* **cciiln cgiinr giilnr**

ccgiklno clocking cockling cocking locking. *See* **cciilno cgikno**

ccgiklnu clucking lucking. *See* **cgilnu**

ccgikno cocking. *See* **cgikno ccino**

ccgiknor crocking cocking corking rocking. *See* **cgikno cginor**

ccgilny cycling. *See* **cgiln cciny gilny**

ccginnos sconcing consign. *See* **ccinos cginno ginnos**

cchhii chichi chic chi hi

cchhiis chichis. *See* **cchhii**

cchhiity ichthyic. *See* **cchhii**

cchhin chinch cinch chic chin inch chi hin hi in

cchhlruy churchly. *See* **cchhru**

cchhru church curch cur huh

cchi chic chi hi

cchiinuz zucchini. *See* **cchin**

cchik chick chic hick chi hi

cchiks chicks chick hicks chic hick sick chi his sic ski hi is sh si

cchiksst schticks schtick shticks. *See* **cchiks chikst chisst ciksst**

cchikst schtick. *See* **cchiks chikst**

cchiln clinch cinch chic chin inch chi hin nil hi in li

cchilor chloric. *See* **cchior chilor**

cchimor chromic. *See* **cchior ccimo cimor**

cchin cinch chic chin inch chi hin hi in

cchinor chronic. *See* **cchior chino cchin**

cchinors chronics chronic. *See* **cchior cchios cchors ccinos**

cchio chico chic chi hi ho oh

cchior choric chico choir ichor chic coir rich chi cor orc rho roc hi ho oh or

cchiory chicory. *See* **cchior**

cchios chicos chico cisco chic cosh chi his ohs sic hi ho is oh os sh si so

cchipssy psychics psychic physics. *See* **chipsy**

cchipsu hiccups. *See* **cchipu chips**

cchipsy psychic. *See* **chipsy**

cchipu hiccup chic chip chi cup hip hup hi pi up

cchklos schlock. *See* **cchkos ccklos**

cchkloss schlocks schlock. *See* **cchkos ccklos chkoss**

cchklosy schlocky schlock. *See* **cchkos ccklos**

cchkmssu schmucks schmuck shmucks. *See* **cchksu chkmsu chkssu**

cchkmsu schmuck. *See* **cchksu chkmsu**

cchko chock cock hock ho oh

cchkos chocks chock cocks hocks shock cock cosh hock sock ohs kos ho oh os sh so

cchkpsuu upchucks upchuck. *See* **cchksu**

cchkpuu upchuck. *See* **cchku**

cchksu chucks chuck shuck cusk husk such suck sh us

cchku chuck

cchltu clutch cultch culch cutch cult cut hut ut

cchlu culch

cchno conch con hon ho no oh on

cchnrsu scrunch. *See* **cchnru chnrsu**

cchnru crunch curch churn cur run urn nu

cchnruy crunchy. *See* **cchnru**

cchors scorch cors cosh orcs rhos rocs cor ohs orc rho roc ho oh or os sh so

cchort crotch torch cor cot hot orc ort rho roc rot tho tor ho oh or to

cchoru crouch couch curch occur ouch hour cor cur orc our rho roc ho oh or

cchost scotch cosh cost cots host hots scot shot tosh cot hot ohs sot tho ho oh os sh so to

cchou couch ouch ho oh

cchrtu crutch curch cutch curt hurt ruth thru cur cut hut rut ut

cchru curch cur

cchstu scutch cutch cuts huts scut shut such thus tush cut hut sh us ut

cchtu cutch cut hut ut

cciiln clinic nil li in

cciilns clinics. *See* **cciiln**

cciimnsy cynicism. *See* **ccinsy**

cciino iconic conic ionic cion coin icon con ion in no on

cciinorz zirconic. *See* **cciino ciinor cinorz**

cciinp picnic nip pin in pi

cciinps picnics. *See* **cciinp**

cciirst critics. *See* cciirt

cciirstu circuits critics circuit. *See* cciirt ccirsu cirstu

cciirt citric critic tic it ti

cciirtu circuit. *See* cciirt

cciirtuy circuity circuit. *See* cciirt

cciisv civics civic sic is si

cciiv civic

ccikklop picklock. *See* ccikl ccklo ccilo

ccikkott ticktock. *See* cciott

ccikl click lick ilk li

cciklosw cowlicks cowlick. *See* ccikls ccklos

cciklow cowlick. *See* ccikl ccklo ccilo

cciklov colicky. *See* ccikl cckoy

ccikls clicks click licks slick lick sick silk ilk sic ski is li si

ccikopst cockpits cockpit. *See* ciopst

ccikopt cockpit. *See* ciopt

ccikr crick rick irk kir

ccikrs cricks crick ricks irks kris rick risk sick irk kir sic sir ski is si

ccilno clonic colic colin conic cion coil coin icon lion loci loin noil col con ion nil oil in li lo no on

ccilnosu councils council uncoils. *See* ccilno ccinos cilnos cilnou

ccilnou council. *See* ccilno cilnou

ccilo colic coil loci col oil li lo

cciloop piccolo. *See* ccilo

cciloops piccolos piccolo. *See* ccios cilps clops

ccilssty cyclists cyclist. *See* ccisty

ccilsty cyclist. *See* ccisty cilty ilsty

ccimo comic mi mo om

ccimos comics cosmic cisco comic osmic mis mos oms sic is mi mo om os si so

ccino conic cion coin icon con ion in no on

ccinorsy cryonics. *See* ccinos ccinsy inorsy

ccinos conics cions cisco coins conic icons scion sonic cion coin cons icon ions con ion sic sin son in is no on os si so

ccinostv convicts convict. *See* ccinos cinost

ccinotv convict. *See* ccino cinot

ccinsy cynics cynic sync icy sic sin yin in is si

cciny cynic icy yin in

ccioors sirocco. *See* ccios ccoos ciors

ccioorss siroccos sirocco. *See* ccioss

cciopstu occiputs occiput. *See* ccostu ciopst ciostu

ccioptu occiput. *See* ciopt

ccios cisco sic is os si so

ccioss ciscos cisco sic sis is os si so

cciostt tictocs. *See* cciott ccios ciost

cciott tictoc otic cot tic tit tot it ti to

cciprty cryptic. *See* cprty

ccipru cupric uric cup cur rip pi up

ccirsu circus crus curs uric cur sic sir is si us

ccisty cystic cist city cyst tics icy its sic sit sty tic is it si ti

ccjnnotu conjunct. *See* cnotu cjnou jnotu

ccklo clock cock lock col lo

ccklos clocks clock cocks locks cock cols lock sock col kos los sol lo os so

ccklsu clucks cluck lucks cusk luck suck sulk us

ccklu cluck luck

cckо cock

cckoosu cuckoos. *See* cckoou cckos ccoos

cckoou cuckoo cock coco cook coo

cckor crock cock cork rock cor kor orc roc or

cckors crocks cocks corks crock rocks cock cork cors orcs rock rocs sock cor kor kos orc roc or os so

cckos cocks cock sock kos os so

cckoy cocky cock yock coy oy

cclotu occult clout clot colt cult lout tolu col cot cut lot out lo to ut

ccnooo cocoon coco coon con coo no on

ccnooos cocoons. *See* ccnooo ccoos cnoos

ccnoostu coconuts coconut. *See* cnoost cnostu ccostu

ccnootu coconut. *See* cnoot cnotu

ccnorsu concurs. *See* ccnoru ccorsu

ccnoru concur occur cornu corn unco con cor cur nor orc our roc run urn no nu on or

ccoo coco coo

ccooor rococo coco coo cor orc roc or

ccooors rococos. *See* ccooor ccoos

ccoos cocos coco coos coo os so

ccoossuu couscous. *See* ccoos

ccopuy occupy coypu coup copy cop coy cup you yup oy up

ccorsstu crosscut succors stuccos. *See* ccorsu ccostu corssu corstu

ccorssu succors. *See* ccorsu corssu

ccorsu crocus occurs succor occur scour cors crus curs orcs ours rocs sour cor cur orc our roc sou or os so us

ccoru occur cor cur orc our roc or

ccosstu stuccos. *See* ccostu cosstu

ccostu stucco scout cost cots cuts oust outs scot scut cot cut out sot sou os so to us ut

---

cd

---

cdddeeo decoded. *See* cdddeo cddeeo

cdddeetu deducted deduced. *See* cddeeu cddetu dddeet .deetu

cdddeeu deduced. *See* cddeeu

cdddelo coddled. *See* cdddeo cddelo

cdddelu cuddled. *See* cddelu

cdddeo codded coded code coed cod doc doe odd ode do od

cdddeors scrodded dodders. *See* cdddeo cddeor cdeors dddeos

cddderu crudded. *See* cdderu

cdddesu scudded. *See* ddesu

cddee ceded cede deed cee

cddeeeex exceeded. *See* cdeeex

cddeeeft defected. *See* cdeeft

cddeeeiv deceived deceive. *See* cddeei cdeeiv

cddeeejt dejected ejected. *See* cdeejt

cddeeent decedent. *See* cdeent ddeen

cddeeepr preceded decreed precede receded. *See* cdeeer ddeeer deeepr

cddeeer decreed receded. *See* cdeeer ddeeer

cddeees seceded. *See* cdeees ddeees

cddeeett detected. *See* cdeett

cddeefor deforced deforce. *See* cddeeo cddeor cdefor ddeeor

cddeeglu cudgeled deluged. *See* cddeeu cddelu cdeglu ddeegl

cddeehnr drenched. *See* cdehnr ddeehr ddeenr

cddeei decide ceded diced cede deed dice died iced cee did die ice id

cddeeii deicide. *See* cddeei

cddeeikr dickered decried. *See* cddeei cddeek cdeekr cdeikr

cddeeiln declined decline. *See* **cddeei cdeeil ddeeil ddeein**

cddeeinr cindered decried. *See* **cddeei cdeinr ddeein ddeeir**

cddeeipt depicted. *See* **cddeei cdeeip cdeeit cdeipt**

cddeeir decried. *See* **cddeei ddeeir**

cddeeirt credited directed decried recited. *See* **cddeei cdeeit cdeirt ceeirt**

cddeeis decides. *See* **cddeei ddeeis**

cddeeix excided. *See* **cddeei cdeeix**

cddeek decked ceded cede deck deed eked cee eke

cddeekot docketed. *See* **cddeek cddeeo cddeko cdekot**

cddeelsu secluded cuddles deduces deludes seclude seduced. *See* **cddeeu cddelu cdeesu ddeelu**

cddeelux excluded exclude. *See* **cddeeu cddelu ddeelu ddeeux**

cddeeno encoded. *See* **cddeeo cdeeno**

cddeenos seconded decodes descend encoded encodes scended. *See* **cddeeo cdeeno cdeens cdenos**

cddeens descend scended. *See* **cdeens cddee ddees**

cddeenss descends descend scended. *See* **cdeens ceenss deenss**

cddeeo decode ceded coded cede code coed deed cee cod doc doe odd ode do od

cddeeorr recorded ordered. *See* **cddeeo cddeor cdeorr ddeeor**

cddeeos decodes. *See* **cddeeo cdees cdeos**

cddeeoy decoyed. *See* **cddeeo cdeoy**

cddeeru reduced. *See* **cdderu cddeeu cdeeru**

cddeeruv decurved reduced. *See* **cddeeu cdderu cdeeru cderuv**

cddeesu deduces seduced. *See* **cddeeu cdeesu**

cddeeu deduce deuced educed ceded deuce educe cede cued deed dude cee cud cue dud due

cddefiio codified. *See* **cdefii ddeiio**

cddefino confided confide. *See* **cdeino**

cddegiin deciding. *See* **cdegin cdgiin ddegin**

cddegino decoding codding. *See* **cdegin cdeino cdgino ddegin**

cddeginu deducing induced educing. *See* **cdegin cdeinu ceginu ddegin**

cddehi chided diced chide chid dice died hide hied iced chi did die edh hid hie ice eh he hi id

cddehin chidden. *See* **cddehi ddehin cdehin**

cddehit ditched. *See* **cddehi cdehit**

cddehor chorded. *See* **cddeor ddehor**

cddehou douched. *See* **cdehou cddeo**

cddei diced dice died iced did die ice id

cddeiint indicted incited indited. *See* **cdeiit cdiint ceiint ddeiit**

cddeillo collided collide collied. *See* **cddelo cdeilo ceillo**

cddeilnu included include induced nuclide. *See* **cddelu cdeinu ceilnu ddeinu**

cddeintu inducted induced. *See* **cddetu cdeinu cdintu ddeint**

cddeinu induced. *See* **cdeinu ddeinu**

cddeiorv divorced divorce. *See* **cddeor cdeiov cdeirv ceiorv**

cddeisu cuddies. *See* **cddei cdeis ddesu**

cddeko docked coded coked code coed coke deck dock cod doc doe odd ode oke do od

cddeku ducked cued deck duck dude duke cud cue dud due

cddellou colluded clouded collude. *See* **cddelo cddelu cddellu**

cddelnoo condoled condole noodled. *See* **cddelo cdelno cdeloo delnoo**

cddelo coddle coded doled clod code coed cold cole dole lode cod col doc doe eld led odd ode old do el lo od

cddelos coddles scolded. *See* **cddelo cdelos**

cddelou clouded. *See* **cddelo cddelu**

cddelru curdled. *See* **cddelu cdderu cdelru**

cddelsu cuddles. *See* **cddelu celsu ddesu**

cddelu cuddle clued clue cued dude duel luce cud cue dud due eld led leu el

cddennoo condoned condone. *See* **cdenno**

cddeo coded code coed cod doc doe odd ode do od

cddeoorr corroded corrode. *See* **cddeor cdeorr ddeoor**

cddeoort doctored. *See* **cddeor cdoort ddeoor deoort**

cddeopru produced produce. *See* **cddeor cdderu ceopru deopru**

cddeor corded coded cored decor cero code coed cord core doer redd redo rode cod cor doc doe dor odd ode orc ore rec red roc rod roe do er od or re

cddeorw crowded. *See* **cddeor cdeorw ddeorw**

cdderu curded crude cured udder crud cued curd cure dude ecru redd rudd rude rued cud cue cur dud due rec red rue urd er re

cddestu deducts. *See* **cddetu ddestu cdestu**

cddetu deduct educt cued cute duct dude duet cud cue cut dud due ted ut

cddghilo godchild. *See* **cdhil cgilo**

cddgilno coddling codding codling. *See* **cdgino dgilno**

cddgilnu cuddling. *See* **cgilnu**

cddgino codding. *See* **cdgino**

cddginru crudding curding. *See* **cginru dginru**

cddginsu scudding. *See* **dginsu**

cddhilos cloddish. *See* **dhilos**

cddiios discoid. *See* **cdiio cdios**

cddiioss discoids discoid cissoid. *See* **cdioss**

cddiors discord. *See* **ddiors ciors cdors**

cddiorss discords discord. *See* **cdioss cdorss ddiors**

cddkorsu ruddocks ruddock. *See* **cdors ckors cdrsu**

cddkoru ruddock. *No 6s or 5s*

cddloy cloddy oddly clod cloy cold cod col coy doc odd old yod do lo od oy

cddluy cuddly cuddy duly cud dud

cddooorw cordwood. *See* **cdorw**

cddruy cruddy cuddy ruddy crud curd rudd cry cud cur dry dud urd

cdduy cuddy cud dud

cdee cede cee

cdeeefft effected. *See* **cdeeft**

cdeeefl fleeced. *See* **ceeefl**

cdeeehk cheeked. *See* **ceehk**

cdeeehl leeched. *See* **cdeehl deeehl**

cdeeehp cheeped. *See* **ceehp**

cdeeehr cheered. *See* **cdeeer**

cdeeehrw rechewed cheered. *See* **cdeeer cdeehw cdeerw ceehrw**

cdeeehsw eschewed. *See* **cdeees cdeehw ceeehs ceehsw**

cdeeeinv evidence deceive evinced. *See* **cdeeiv ceeinv deeenv deeinv**

cdeeeirv received deceive receive. *See* **cdeeer cdeeiv cdeirv deeerv**

cdeeeisv deceives deceive devices. *See* **cdeees cdeeiv deeisv**

cdeeeiv deceive. *See* **cdeeiv**

cdeeejrt rejected ejected erected. *See* **cdeeer cdeejt ceejrt**

cdeeejt ejected. *See* **cdeejt**

cdeeellx excelled. *See* **cdeeex cdeell**

cdeeelst selected celeste deletes elected sleeted steeled. *See* **cdeees ceelst deeelt deelst**

cdeeelt elected. *See* **deeelt ceelt**

cdeeem emceed emcee cede deem deme meed cee em me

cdeeemnt cemented. *See* **cdeeem cdeent ceemnt deeemt**

cdeeenrs screened secerned decrees recedes seceder sneered. *See* **cdeeer cdeees cdeens cdeers**

cdeeenrt centered centred entered erected. *See* **cdeeer cdeent ceenrt deeenr**

cdeeepr precede. *See* **cdeeer deeepr**

cdeeeprs precedes decrees precede recedes seceder speeder. *See* **cdeeer cdeees cdeers ceeprs**

cdeeeptx excepted expected. *See* **cdeeex ceeptx**

cdeeer decree recede creed cede cere deer dree reed cee ere rec red er re

cdeeers decrees recedes seceder. *See* **cdeers ceeers cdeeer cdeees deeers**

cdeeerss recessed seceders decrees recedes seceder secedes seeders. *See* **cdeeer cdeees cdeers ceerss**

cdeeert erected. *See* **cdeeer**

cdeeertx excreted erected excrete exerted. *See* **cdeeer cdeeex deertx**

cdeees secede cedes cede cees seed cee see

cdeeess secedes. *See* **cdeees deess**

cdeeesx exceeds. *See* **cdeees cdeeex**

cdeeetux executed execute. *See* **cdeeex cdeeex** exceed cede cee ex

cdeefht fetched. *See* **cdeeft cdeeht deefht**

cdeefii edifice. *See* **cdefii**

cdeefiis edifices deifies edifice edifies. *See* **cdefii deefis**

cdeefiit feticide deficit edifice eidetic. *See* **cdeeft cdeeit cdefii**

cdeefint infected enticed feinted. *See* **cdeefn cdeeft cdeeit cdeent**

cdeefkl flecked. *See* **cdeekl cefkl**

cdeefklr freckled clerked flecked freckle. *See* **cdeekl cdeekr deefkr**

cdeeflst deflects deflect defects. *See* **cdeeft ceelst ceflst deeflt**

cdeeflt deflect. *See* **cdeeft deeflt**

cdeefn fenced fence cede dene feed fend need cee den end fed fee fen nee en ne

cdeefnor enforced cornfed deforce encoder encored enforce. *See* **cdeefn cdeeno cdefor cdenor**

cdeefor deforce. *See* **cdefor cdeer deefr**

cdeefors deforces deforce. *See* **cdeers cdefor cdeors cefors**

cdeefort defector deforce. *See* **cdeeft cdefor deeort**

cdeefst defects. *See* **cdeeft cdees ceefs**

cdeeft defect feted cede deft feed feet fete teed cee eft fed fee ted tee

cdeegiir regicide. *See* **cdeiir deegir**

cdeegino genocide codeine. *See* **cdeeno cdegin cdeino cdgino**

cdeeginr receding cringed dreeing generic reeding reigned. *See* **cdegin cdeinr ceginr deegir**

cdeegins seceding seeding. *See* **cdeens cdegin ceeins deegis**

cdeegios geodesic diocese. *See* **deegis deegos degios**

cdeehils chiseled deciles helices lichees. *See* **cdeehl cdeeil cdehil cdehis**

cdeehinr enriched inhered. *See* **cdehin cdehir cdehnr cdeinr**

cdeehip cepheid. *See* **cdeeip ceehp cdehi**

cdeehipr ciphered decipher cepheid chirped perched pierced. *See* **cdeeip cdehir cdeipr ceeipr**

cdeehips cepheids cepheid. *See* **cdeeip cdehis cdeips ceehis**

cdeehiv chevied. *See* **cdeeiv cdehi dehiv**

cdeehkl heckled. *See* **cdeekl ceehkl cdeehl**

cdeehkst sketched ketches. *See* **cdeeht ceehks ceehst cehkst**

cdeehktv kvetched. *See* **cdeeht cehktv**

cdeehl leched leech cede dele heed heel held lech cee edh eel eld led lee eh el he

cdeehlsu schedule seclude. *See* **cdeehl cdeesu ceehls deelsu**

cdeehlt letched. *See* **cdeehl cdeeht**

cdeehms schemed. *See* **ceehms deehms**

cdeehnqu quenched. *See* **ceehqu cehnqu**

cdeehnrs drenches. *See* **cdeens cdeers cdehnr ceehrs**

cdeehnrt trenched retched centred. *See* **cdeeht cdeent cdehnr ceehnt**

cdeehnrw wrenched wenched wencher. *See* **cdeehw cdeerw cdehnr ceehnw**

cdeehnw wenched. *See* **cdeehw ceehnw**

cdeeho echoed cede code coed echo heed hoed cee cod doc doe edh hod hoe ode do eh he ho od oh

cdeehor cohered. *See* **cdeeho ceehor**

cdeehort hectored cohered retched torched trochee. *See* **cdeeho cdeeht ceehor cehort**

cdeehpr perched. *See* **ceehp ceehr cdeer**

cdeehrt retched. *See* **cdeeht ceehr cehrt**

cdeehrtw wretched retched. *See* **cdeeht cdeehw cdeerw ceehrw**

cdeeht etched cede etch heed tech teed thee cee edh eth het ted tee the eh he

cdeehtt tetched. *See* **cdeeht cdeett**

cdeehw chewed hewed cede chew heed weed cee dew edh ewe hew wed wee eh he we

cdeeiilt elicited eidetic. *See* **cdeeil cdeeit cdeilt ceiilt**

cdeeiimn medicine endemic. *See* **cdeimn ceeimn**

cdeeiimp epidemic. *See* **cdeeip deeimp**

cdeeiirt dieretic eidetic recited. *See* **cdeeit cdeeir cdeirt ceeirt**

cdeeiisv decisive devices. *See* **cdeeiv cdiisv ceiisv deeisv**

cdeeiit eidetic. *See* **cdeeit cdeiit**

cdeeiitt dietetic eidetic. *See* **cdeeit**

cdeeijnt injected enticed. *See* **cdeeit cdeejt cdeent ceeint**

cdeeijor rejoiced rejoice. *See* **cdeir cdeor cdeer**

cdeeikln nickeled clinked decline likened. *See* **cdeeil cdeekl cdeekn cdeikl**

cdeeikns sickened dickens snicked. *See* **cdeekn cdeens cdeikn cdeiks**

cdeeikpt picketed. *See* **cdeeip cdeeit cdeekp cdeikp**

cdeeiktt ticketed. *See* **cdeeit cdeikt ceiktt**

cdeeil ceiled decile edile elide cede ceil deil dele deli dice iced idle lice lied cee die eel eld ice led lee lei lid lie el id li

cdeeiln decline. *See* **cdeeil**

cdeeilnp penciled decline. *See* **cdeeil cdeeip ceilnp**

cdeeilnr reclined decline recline. *See* **cdeeil cdeinr ceelnr deeilr**

cdeeilns declines licensed silenced deciles decline license linseed silence. *See* **cdeeil cdeens cdeils ceeins**

cdeeilnt denticle decline enticed. *See* **cdeeil cdeent cdeent cdeilt**

cdeeilor recoiled. *See* **cdeeil cdeilo cdelor ceelor**

cdeeilps eclipsed deciles eclipse spliced. *See* **cdeeil cdeeip cdeils cdeips**

cdeeilrt derelict recited reticle tiercel. *See* **cdeeil cdeeit cdeilt cdeirt**

cdeeils deciles. *See* **cdeeil deeils cdeils**

cdeeimn endemic. *See* **cdeimn ceeimn**

cdeeimnr endermic endemic. *See* **cdeimn cdeinr ceeimn ceimnr**

cdeeimns endemics endemic sidemen. *See* **cdeens cdeimn cdeims ceeimn**

cdeeimor mediocre dormice. *See* **cdeir cemor cdeor**

cdeeimos comedies diocese. *See* **cdeims deeims**

cdeeimrv decemvir. *See* **cdeeiv cdeirv deeirv**

cdeeinns incensed incense. *See* **cdeens ceeins deeinn deeins**

cdeeinnt indecent enticed. *See* **cdeeit cdeent ceeint deeinn**

cdeeino codeine. *See* **cdeeno cdeino**

cdeeint enticed. *See* **cdeeit cdeent ceeint**

cdeeintu inductee enticed detinue. *See* **cdeeit cdeent cdeinu cdintu**

cdeeinv evinced. *See* **deeinv cdeeiv ceeinv**

cdeeiopr recopied pierced proceed. *See* **cdeeip cdeiop cdeipr ceeipr**

cdeeiorv divorcee covered divorce. *See* **cdeeiv cdeiov cdeirv ceiorv**

cdeeios diocese. *See* **cdees cdeos cdeis**

cdeeioss dioceses diocese. *See* **cdioss ceeiss deeiss**

cdeeip pieced piece cede deep dice epic iced peed pice pied cee cep die dip ice pee pie id pe pi

cdeeipr pierced. *See* **cdeeip ceeipr cdeipr**

cdeeiprt decrepit pierced predict receipt recited. *See* **cdeeip cdeeit cdeipr cdeipt**

cdeeipru pedicure pierced epicure. *See* **cdeeip cdeeru cdeipr ceeipr**

cdeeirrt redirect recited retired retried. *See* **cdeeit cdeirt ceeirt ceerrt**

cdeeirs decries. *See* **ceeirs cdeirs cdeers deeirs**

cdeeirst discreet discrete credits crested decries directs recited recites reedits tierces. *See* **cdeeit cdeers cdeirs cdeirt**

cdeeirsv serviced decries derives devices diverse revised service. *See* **cdeeiv cdeers cdeirs cdeirv**

cdeeirt recited. *See* **cdeirt cdeeit ceeirt deeirt**

cdeeisv devices. *See* **cdeeiv deeisv**

cdeeisx excides excised. *See* **deeisx cdeeix ceeisx**

cdeeit deceit cited edict cede cite dice diet edit iced teed tide tied cee die dit ice ted tee tic tie id it ti

cdeeitv evicted. *See* **cdeeit cdeeiv**

cdeeitx excited. *See* **cdeeit cdeeix ceeitx deeitx**

cdeeiv device cede dice dive iced vice vied cee die eve ice vee vie id

cdeeix excide cede dice iced cee die ice ex id xi

cdeejkoy jockeyed. *See* **cejkoy**

cdeejst dejects. *See* **cdeejt ceejst deejst**

cdeejt deject eject cede teed cee jet ted tee

cdeekk kecked cede deck eked keck keek cee eke

cdeekl deckle cleek cede deck dele eked keel leek cee eel eke eld elk led lee lek el

cdeeklps speckled deckles skelped specked speckle. *See* **cdeekl cdeekp ceekls**

cdeeklr clerked. *See* **cdeekl cdeekr**

cdeekls deckles. *See* **cdeekl ceekls**

cdeekn necked kneed cede deck dene eked keen knee neck need cee den eke end ken nee en ne

cdeeknor reckoned encoder encored redneck. *See* **cdeekn cdeekr cdeeno cdekno**

cdeeknr redneck. *See* **deeknr cdeekn ceeknr cdeekr**

cdeeknrs rednecks redneck neckers. *See* **cdeekn cdeekr cdeens cdeers**

cdeekoor recooked crooked. *See* **cdeekr cdekoo cdekor cekoor**

cdeekopt pocketed. *See* **cdeekp cdekot cekopt**

cdeekort rocketed. *See* **cdeekr cdekor cdekot cekort**

cdeekorw rockweed wrecked cowered. *See* **cdeekr cdeerw cdekor cdeorw**

cdeekp pecked cede deck deep eked keep peck peed peek cee cep eke pee pe

cdeekpru puckered. *See* **cdeekp cdeekr cdeeru cdekru**

cdeekps specked. *See* **cdeekp cdees cdeks**

cdeekr recked creed creek cede cere deck deer dree eked reck reed reek cee eke ere rec red er re

cdeekrw wrecked. *See* **cdeekr cdeerw**

cdeell celled cede cell dele dell cee eel eld ell led lee el

cdeellor cordelle. *See* **cdeell cdelor ceelor dellor**

cdeelmow welcomed welcome. *See* **cdeelw cdelow ceelmo**

cdeelnos enclosed encodes enclose. *See* **cdeeno cdeens cdelno cdelos**

cdeelnpu peduncle cupeled. *See* **cdelu celpu cdeeu**

cdeelnty decently. *See* **cdeent**

cdeeloow locoweed. *See* **cdeelw cdeloo cdelow**

cdeelost closeted coldest. *See* **cdelos ceelst celost deelst**

cdeelpru preclude cupeled prelude. *See* **cdeeru cdelru deelru deepru**

cdeelpu cupeled. *See* **cdelu celpu cdeeu**

cdeelpy ycleped. *See* **deelpy**

cdeelrtu lectured lecture. *See* **cdeeru cdelru cdeltu ceelrt**

cdeelrux excluder exclude. *See* **cdeeru cdelru deelru deelux**

cdeelssu secludes seclude seduces. *See* **cdeesu cdessu deelsu deessu**

cdeelsu seclude. *See* **cdeesu deelsu**

cdeelsux excludes exclude excused seclude. *See* **cdeesu ceelsx deelsu deelux**

cdeelux exclude. *See* **deelux cdelu celux**

cdeelw clewed cede clew dele lewd weed weld cee dew eel eld ewe led lee wed wee el we

cdeemopt competed compete. *See* **cdemop deemot eemopt**

cdeemort ectoderm. *See* **ceemrt deemot deemrt deeort**

cdeennos condense encodes. *See* **cdeeno cdeens cdenno cdenos**

cdeennou denounce. *See* **cdeeno cdenno dennou**

cdeennov convened convene. *See* **cdeeno cdenno**

cdeennpy pendency. *See* **deennp deenny**

cdeennty tendency. *See* **cdeent deenny**

cdeeno encode coned cede code coed cone dene done need node once cee cod con den doc doe don end eon nee nod ode one do en ne no od on

cdeenor encoder encored. *See* **cdenor cdeeno ceenor deenor**

cdeenorr cornered encoder encored. *See* **cdeeno cdenor cdeorr ceenor**

cdeenors censored encoders necrosed encoder encodes encored encores endorse necrose scorned. *See* **cdeeno cdeens cdeers cdenor**

cdeenos encodes. *See* **cdeens cdenos**

cdeenovy conveyed. *See* **cdeeno cenovy**

cdeenoz cozened. *See* **cdeeno cenoz denoz**

cdeenpru prudence. *See* **cdeeru deenru deepru denpru**

cdeenrsu censured censure endures ensured recused reduces rescued secured seducer. *See* **cdeens cdeers cdeeru cdeesu**

cdeenrt centred. *See* **ceenrt cdeent deenrt**

cdeens censed cedes cense denes dense needs scend scene cede cees dene dens ends need seed seen cee den end ens nee see sen en ne

cdeensst descents densest descent scented. *See* **cdeens cdeent ceenss censst**

cdeenst descent scented. *See* **cdeens deenst**

cdeensty encysted descent scented. *See* **cdeens cdeent censty deenst**

cdeent decent cede cent dene dent need teed teen tend cee den end nee net ted tee ten en ne

cdeeoopr coopered proceed. *See* **cdeoop ceoopr**

cdeeootv dovecote coveted. *See* **deeotv**

cdeeoppr coppered proceed cropped. *See* **cdeopp ceoppr**

cdeeopr proceed. *See* **cdeop cdeor cdeer**

cdeeoprs proceeds proceed reposed. *See* **cdeers cdeors ceeprs ceoprs**

cdeeopru recouped proceed produce. *See* **cdeeru ceopru deepru deopru**

cdeeorrr recorder rerecord orderer reorder. *See* **cdeorr**

cdeeorst corseted escorted crested oersted teredos. *See* **cdeers cdeors ceerst ceorst**

cdeeorv covered. *See* **cdeor cdeov ceorv**

cdeeorw cowered. *See* **cdeerw cdeorw**

cdeeosst cosseted. *See* **ceosst deesst deosst**

cdeeotv coveted. *See* **deeotv**

cdeer creed cede cere deer dree reed cee ere rec red er re

cdeerrru recurred reducer. *See* **cdeeru cderru**

cdeerrsu reducers recused reducer reduces rescued rescuer secured securer seducer. *See* **cdeers cdeeru cdeesu cderru**

cdeerru reducer. *See* **cdeeru cderru**

cdeers creeds screed cedes creed deers drees reeds scree cede cees cere deer dree reds reed seed seer sere cee ere rec red res see er re

cdeerssu seducers recused reduces rescued rescues secured secures seducer seduces. *See* **cdeers cdeeru cdeesu cdersu**

cdeerst crested. *See* **ceerst cdeers deerst**

cdeersu recused reduces rescued secured seducer. *See* **ceersu cdersu cdeesu cdeeru deersu**

cdeersw screwed. *See* **cdeers cdeerw**

cdeeru reduce creed crude cured deuce educe cede cere crud cued curd cure deer dree ecru reed rude rued cee cud cue cur due ere rec red rue urd er re

cdeerw crewed creed cede cere crew deer dree drew ewer reed weed cede dew ere ewe rec red wed wee er re we

cdees cedes cede cees seed cee see

cdeessu seduces. *See* **cdessu cdeesu deessu**

cdeestt detects. *See* **cdeett deestt**

cdeesu deuces educes seduce cedes deuce educe suede cede cees cuds cued cues dues scud seed sued used cee cud cue due see sue use us

cdeesux excused. *See* **cdeesu ceesux deesux**

cdeett detect cede teed cee ted tee

cdeeu deuce educe cede cued cee cud cue due

cdeffhu chuffed. *See* **cdeffu defffhu**

cdeffio coiffed. *See* **ceffio deffi deffo**

cdeffisu sufficed diffuse scuffed suffice. *See* **cdeffu**

cdefflsu scuffled duffels duffles scuffed scuffle sluffed. *See* **cdeffu defflu**

cdeffos scoffed. *See* **cdeos dffos cffos**

cdeffsu scuffed. *See* **cdeffu dffsu defsu**

cdeffu cuffed cued cuff duff feud cud cue due fed feu

cdefhil filched. *See* **cdehil cefhi defil**

cdefhiln flinched filched. *See* **cdehil cdehin cehiln cfhiln**

cdefhimo chiefdom. *See* **cdehim**

cdefii deific dice iced die fed fid fie ice id if

cdefiiit citified deficit. *See* **cdefii cdeiit**

cdefiior codifier orifice. *See* **cdefii cdefor cdeiir**

cdefiios codifies. *See* **cdefii cefios**

cdefiist deficits deficit deistic diciest. *See* **cdefii cdeiit cdeist cfiist**

cdefiit deficit. *See* **cdefii cdeiit**

cdefikl flicked. *See* **cdeikl cefikl**

cdefinno confined confide confine. *See* **cdeino cdenno definn**

cdefino confide. *See* **cdeino defin**

cdefinor confider confide conifer cornfed. *See* **cdefor cdeino cdeinr cdenor**

cdefinos confides confide. *See* **cdeino cdenos cefios ceinos**

cdefklo flocked. *See* **cdeklo cefkl cfklo**

cdefkor defrock frocked. *See* **cdekor cdefor defkor**

cdefkors defrocks defrock frocked. *See* **cdefor cdekor cdekos cdeors**

cdeflnou flounced flounce. *See* **cdefnu cdelno deflno deflou**

cdefnor cornfed. *See* **cefnor cdenor cdefor**

cdefnoru frounced cornfed founder frounce. *See* **cdefnu cdefor cdenor cefnor**

cdefnosu confused confuse focused fondues. *See* **cdefnu cdenos cdensu cdeosu**

cdefnotu confuted confute counted defunct. *See* **cdefnu cdenot defnot**

cdefntu defunct. *See* **cdefnu cdetu dentu**

cdefnu fecund dunce unfed cued dune fend feud fund nude cud cue den due dun end fed fen feu fun en ne nu

cdefor forced cored decor force cero code coed cord core corf doer ford fore froe redo rode cod cor doc doe dor fed foe for fro ode orc ore rec red ref roc rod roe do er od of or re

cdefossu focussed escudos focused focuses. *See* **cdeosu cdessu ceossu defssu**

cdefosu focused. *See* **cdeosu defsu cfosu**

cdegghu chugged. *See* **degghu**

cdegglo clogged. *See* **cdeggo degglo**

cdeggo cogged code coed doge cod cog doc doe dog egg ego god ode do go od

cdeghoru grouched coughed roughed. *See* **cdegor cdehou cghoru degoru**

cdeghou coughed. *See* **cdehou cghou dghou**

cdegiinx exciding. *See* **cdegin cdgiin**

cdegikn decking. *See* **cdegin cdeikn**

cdegin ceding deign dice dine ding gied iced nice nide den die dig din end gid gie gin ice en id in ne

cdeginno encoding condign. *See* **cdegin cdeino cdenno cdgino**

cdeginns scending censing endings sending. *See* **cdegin deginn degins deinns**

cdeginos cosigned dingoes. *See* **cdegin cdeino cdenos cdgino**

cdeginoy decoying. *See* **cdegin cdeino cdgino cginoy**

cdeginoz cognized cognize. *See* **cdegin cdeino cdeinz cdgino**

cdeginr cringed. *See* **cdegin cdeinr ceginr deginr**

cdeginru reducing cringed curding educing. *See* **cdegin cdeinr cdeinu ceginr**

cdeginry decrying cringed cindery. *See* **cdegin cdeinr ceginr cginry**

cdeginsu seducing educing incudes induces. *See* **cdegin cdeinu cdensu ceginu**

cdeginu educing. *See* **cdegin ceginu cdeinu**

cdeglsu cudgels. *See* **cdeglu deglsu**

cdeglu cudgel clued glued luged clue cued duel geld glue luce luge cud cue due dug eld gel led leg leu lug el

cdegor codger cored decor gored cero code coed cord core doer doge goer gore ogre redo rode cod cog cor doc doe dog dor ego erg god ode orc ore rec red reg roc rod roe do er go od or re

cdegors codgers. *See* **cdegor cdeors**

cdegorsu scourged codgers coursed drogues gourdes groused scoured scourge. *See* **cdegor cdeors cdeosu cdersu**

cdehhit hitched. *See* **cdehit chhit**

cdehhnu hunched. *See* **cdenu chhnu**

cdehi chide chid dice hide hied iced chi die edh hid hie ice eh he hi id

cdehiilo helicoid. *See* **cdehil cdeilo**

cdehiimo homicide. *See* **cdehim**

cdehikn chinked. *See* **cdehin cdeikn**

cdehil chield chide child ceil chid deil deli dice held hide hied iced idle lech lice lied chi die edh eld hid hie ice led lei lid lie eh el he hi id li

cdehill chilled. *See* **cdehil dehill**

cdehilnr children. *See* **cdehil cdehin cdehir cdehnr**

cdehilor chloride choired. *See* **cdehil cdehir cdeilo cdelor**

cdehilrt eldritch thirled. *See* **cdehil cdehir cdehit cdeilt**

cdehim chimed chide chime hemic medic chid dice dime hide hied iced mice chi die dim edh hem hid hie him ice mid eh em he hi id me mi

cdehimot methodic demotic. *See* **cdehim cdehit dehmot**

cdehimrs smirched. *See* **cdehim cdehir cdehis cdeims**

cdehin inched niched chide chine niche chid chin dice dine hide hied hind iced inch nice nide chi den die din edh end hen hid hie hin ice eh en he hi id in ne

cdehinn chinned. *See* **cdehin**

cdehinp pinched. *See* **cdehin**

cdehinst snitched ditches ethnics. *See* **cdehin cdehis cdehit cdeist**

cdehinw winched. *See* **cdehin dehinw cdeinw**

cdehior choired. *See* **cehior cdehir cdhior**

cdehiosw cowhides cowhide. *See* **cdehis cdehos dehisw dehosw**

cdehioty theodicy. *See* **cdehit**

cdehiow cowhide. *See* **cdehi**

cdehipp chipped. *See* **dehipp cdehi**

cdehipr chirped. *See* **cehipr cdehir cdeipr**

cdehipt pitched. *See* **cdehit cdeipt**

cdehir herdic chide cider cried hider hired riced chid dice dire heir herd hide hied hire iced rice rich ride chi die edh her hid hie ice ire rec red rid eh er he hi id re

cdehis chides chide dices hides shied chid dice dies disc dish hide hied hies iced ices ides shed side chi die edh hid hie his ice ids she sic eh hi id is sh si

cdehist ditches. *See* **cdehis cdeist cehist cdehit**

cdehistt stitched ditches. *See* **cdehis cdehit cdeist cehist**

cdehistw switched ditches witches. *See* **cdehis cdehit cdeist cehist**

cdehisu duchies. *See* **cdehis cdisu**

cdehit itched chide cited ditch edict ethic chid chit cite dice diet edit etch hide hied iced itch tech tide tied chi die dit edh eth het hid hie hit ice ted the tic tie eh he hi id it ti

cdehittw twitched. *See* **cdehit cehitt chittw dehitw**

cdehko choked hocked coked choke code coed coke deck dock echo heck hock hoed hoke cod doc doe edh hod hoe ode oke do eh he ho od oh

cdehkos shocked. *See* **cdehko cehkos cdehos cdekos**

cdehksu shucked. *See* **cdeksu dehksu**

cdehlmu mulched. *See* **cdelmu chlmu**

cdehlnu lunched. *See* **cdelu cdenu chlnu**

cdehlny lynched. *See* **cehly chlny**

cdehloos schooled. *See* **cdehos cdeloo cdelos cehoos**

cdehlort chortled chortle clothed torched. *See* **cdelor cehlor cehlot cehort**

cdehlosu slouched choused douches hocused. *See* **cdehos cdehou cdelos cdeosu**

cdehlot clothed. *See* **cehlot dehlot**

cdehlru lurched. *See* **cdelru dehlru**

cdehmmu chummed. *See* **dehmmu**

cdehmnu munched. *See* **cdenu chmnu**

cdehmoo mooched. *See* **cdeoo dehmo chmoo**

cdehmoos smooched mooched mooches. *See* **cdehos cehoos cemoos chmoos**

cdehmop chomped. *See* **cdemop chmop dehop**

cdehmor chromed. *See* **cehmor cdhor cdeor**

cdehmstu smutched. *See* **cdestu cehstu chmstu dehmsu**

cdehnot notched. *See* **cdenot dehno chnot**

cdehnpu punched. *See* **cdenu chnpu denpu**

cdehnr drench herd hern nerd rend den edh end hen her rec red eh en er he ne re

cdehnru churned. *See* **cdehnr chnru cderu**

cdehopp chopped. *See* **cdeopp dehopp**

cdehopu pouched. *See* **cdehou cdeop ceopu**

cdehorsu chorused choused coursed crushed douches hocused scoured. *See* **cdehos cdehou cdeors cdeosu**

cdehorsw chowders cowherds chowder cowherd. *See* **cdehos cdeors cdeorw cdhors**

cdehorw chowder cowherd. *See* **cdeorw dehorw**

cdehos coshed chose codes coeds hosed shoed code cods coed cosh docs does dose echo hods hoed hoes hose odes shed shod shoe cod doc doe dos edh hod hoe ode ohs she sod do eh he ho od oh os sh so

cdehosu choused douches hocused. *See* **cehosu cdehos cdehou cdeosu dehosu**

cdehotu touched. *See* **cdehou cehtu chotu**

cdehou douche douce code coed cued echo hoed hued ouch cod cud cue doc doe due duo edh hod hoe hue ode oud udo do eh he ho od oh

cdehouv vouched. *See* **cdehou cdeov chouv**

cdehpsy psyched. *See* **dehpy ehpsy chpsy**

cdehrsu crushed. *See* **cdersu cehrsu dehrsu**

cdehsssu schussed duchess. *See* **cdessu chsssu**

cdehssu duchess. *See* **cdessu cehss dehss**

cdehsty scythed. *See* **cehsty**

cdei dice iced ice die id

cdeiiios idiocies. *See* **cdeos cdeis cdios**

cdeiikks sidekick. *See* **cdeikk cdeiks**

cdeiikmm mimicked. *See* **deiim cdeim deikm**

cdeiilmo domicile melodic. *See* **cdeilo deilmo**

cdeiilnn inclined incline. *See* **deilnn**

cdeiilno indocile. *See* **cdeilo cdeino cdelno deiino**

cdeiilps disciple spliced. *See* **cdeils cdeips ceilps deilps**

cdeiilru ridicule. *See* **cdeiir cdelru**

cdeiinnt incident incited. *See* **cdeiit cdiint ceiint deiint**

cdeiinos decision incised indices. *See* **cdeino cdenos ceiins ceinos**

cdeiinrt indirect citrine crinite incited inciter inditer neritic nitride. *See* **cdeiir cdeiit cdeinr cdeirt**

cdeiins incised indices. *See* **ceiins deiins**

cdeiint incited. *See* **cdeiit ceiint cdiint deiint**

cdeiiopr periodic. *See* **cdeiir cdeiop cdeipr ceiopr**

cdeiiops episodic. *See* **cdeiop cdeips ceiops deiops**

cdeiir dicier cider cried icier riced dice dire iced rice ride die ice ire rec red rid er id re

cdeiirtu diuretic. *See* **cdeiir cdeiit cdeirt ceirtu**

cdeiissu suicides suicide. *See* **cdessu cdissu ceissu deiiss**

cdeiist deistic diciest. *See* **cdeiit ceiist cdeist deiist**

cdeiisu suicide. *See* **cdeis cdisu**

cdeiit cited cited edict cite dice diet edit iced tide tied die dit ice ted tic tie id it ti

cdeiju juiced juice cued dice iced cud cue die due ice id

cdeikk kicked deck dice dike iced keck kick die ice kid id

cdeikl licked liked ceil deck deil deli dice dike iced idle lice lick lied like die eld elk ice ilk kid led lei lek lid lie el id li

cdeikln clinked. *See* **deikln cdeikl cdeikn ceikln**

cdeiklnr crinkled clinked clinker crinkle kindler. *See* **cdeikl cdeikn cdeikr cdeinr**

cdeiklp pickled. *See* **cdeikl cdeikp ceiklp**

cdeiklpr prickled pickled pricked prickle. *See* **cdeikl cdeikp cdeikr cdeipr**

cdeiklrt trickled tickled tickler tricked trickle. *See* **cdeikl cdeikr cdeikt cdeilt**

cdeiklst stickled delicts sticked stickle tickled tickles. *See* **cdeikl cdeiks cdeikt cdeils**

cdeiklt tickled. *See* **cdeilt deiklt cdeikl cdeikt ceiklt**

cdeiklwy wickedly. *See* **cdeikl cdeikw cdeiky deilwy**

cdeikn nicked inked deck dice dike dine dink iced kind kine neck nice nick nide den die din end ice ink ken kid kin en id in ne

cdeikns dickens snicked. *See* **cdeikn cdeiks ceikns**

cdeiknz zincked. *See* **cdeikn cdeinz**

cdeikp picked piked deck dice dike epic iced kepi peck pice pick pied pike cep die dip ice kid kip pie id pe pi

cdeikpr pricked. *See* **cdeikr cdeikp ceikpr cdeipr**

cdeikr dicker cider cried irked riced deck dice dike dire dirk iced kier reck rice rick ride die ice ire irk kid kir rec red rid er id re

cdeikrr derrick. *See* **cdeikr ceirr deirr**

cdeikrrs derricks derrick dickers skirred. *See* **cdeikr cdeiks cdeirs ceikrs**

cdeikrs dickers. *See* **cdeirs cdeikr deikrs cdeiks ceikrs**

cdeikrt tricked. *See* **cdeirt cdeikt ceikrt**

cdeikru duckier. *See* **cdeikr cdekru**

cdeiks sicked decks dices dikes skied deck desk dice dies dike disc disk iced ices ides kids sick side skid die ice ids kid sic ski id is si

cdeikst sticked. *See* **cdeist cdeiks cdeikt**

cdeikstu duckiest sticked. *See* **cdeiks cdeikt cdeist cdeksu**

cdeikt ticked cited edict kited cite deck dice diet dike edit iced kite tick tide tied tike die dit ice kid kit ted tic tie id it ti

cdeikw wicked deck dice dike iced wick wide dew die ice kid wed id we

cdeiky dickey dicey dicky deck dice dike dyke iced icky dey die dye ice icy key kid id ye

cdeillo collide collied. *See* **cdeilo ceillo**

cdeillos collides collide collied collies dollies. *See* **cdeilo cdeils cdelos ceillo**

cdeillpu pellucid cullied. *See* **cdellu deillp dellpu**

cdeillu cullied. *See* **cdellu cdilu**

cdeilmo melodic. *See* **cdeilo deilmo**

cdeilmop compiled complied clomped compile implode melodic polemic policed. *See* **cdeilo cdeiop cdemop ceilop**

cdeilmru dulcimer. *See* **cdelmu cdelru ceimru deilmr**

cdeilnou uncoiled include nuclide. *See* **cdeilo cdeino cdeinu cdelno**

cdeilnry cylinder cindery. *See* **cdeinr ceilny deilry**

cdeilnsu includes include incudes induces nuclide sluiced. *See* **cdeils cdeinu cdensu ceilns**

cdeilnu include nuclide. *See* **cdeinu ceilnu**

cdeilo coiled docile oiled oldie oleic ceil clod code coed coil cold cole deil deli dice dole iced idle idol lice lied loci lode odic cod col die doc doe eld ice led lei lid lie ode oil old do el id li lo od

cdeilop policed. *See* **cdeilo cdeiop deilop ceilop**

cdeiloru cloudier. *See* **cdeilo cdelor cdeilru ceilor**

cdeiloss disclose ossicle. *See* **cdeilo cdeils cdelos cdioss**

cdeilpp clipped. *See* **deilpp**

cdeilppr crippled clipped clipper cripple rippled. *See* **cdeipr deilpp deippr eilppr**

cdeilps spliced. *See* **deilps cdeils cdeips ceilps**

cdeilrty directly. *See* **cdeilt cdeirt ceilrt deilry**

cdeils sliced ceils deils delis dices idles sidle slice slide ceil deil deli dice dies disc iced ices ides idle isle leis lice lids lied lies side sled slid die eld els ice ids led lei lid lie sic el id is li si

cdeilst delicts. *See* **cdeilt cdeist deilst cdeils**

cdeilsu sluiced. *See* **cdeils ceilsu**

cdeilsxy dyslexic. *See* **cdeils deilsy**

cdeilt delict cited edict telic tilde tiled ceil celt cite deil deli dice diet edit iced idle lice lied tide tied tile die dit eld ice led lei let lid lie lit ted tic tie til el id it li ti

cdeiltu ductile. *See* **cdeilt deiltu cdeltu ceiltu**

cdeim medic dice dime iced mice die dim ice mid em id me mi

cdeimn minced denim medic mince mined dice dime dine iced mend mice mien mind mine nice nide den die dim din end ice men mid nim em en id in me mi ne

cdeimno demonic. *See* **cdeino ceimno cdeimn**

cdeimor dormice. *See* **cdeir cemor cdeor**

cdeimost domestic demotic modiste. *See* **cdeims cdeist cdiost cemost**

cdeimot demotic. *See* **cdeit cemot deimt**

cdeimpr crimped. *See* **cdeipr deimpr**

cdeimprs scrimped crimped crisped. *See* **cdeims cdeipr cdeips cdeirs**

cdeimpu pumiced. *See* **ceimpu cdeim cdimu**

cdeims medics deism dices dimes medic mesic dice dies dime dims disc iced ices ides mice mise semi side die dim ice ids mid mis sic em id is me mi si

cdeimsu miscued. *See* **ceimsu cdeims**

cdeinnov connived connive. *See* **cdeino cdeiov cdenno ceinov**

cdeino coined coned cion code coed coin cone dice dine done iced icon nice nide node odic once cod con den die din doc doe don end eon ice ion nod ode one do en id in ne no od on

cdeinors consider cinders cronies discern indorse rescind rosined scorned. *See* **cdeino cdeinr cdeirs cdenor**

cdeinort doctrine cordite ctenoid noticed. *See* **cdeino cdeinr cdeirt cdenor**

cdeinoru decurion. *See* **cdeino cdeinr cdeinu cdenor**

cdeinot ctenoid noticed. *See* **cdeino cdenot ceinot**

cdeinotu eduction conduit counted ctenoid noctuid noticed. *See* **cdeino cdeinu cdenot cdintu**

cdeinr cinder cider cried diner nicer riced dice dine dire iced nerd nice nide rein rend rice ride rind den die din end ice ire rec red rid en er id in ne re

cdeinrru incurred curried. *See* **cdeinr cdeinu cderru deinru**

cdeinrs cinders discern rescind. *See* **cdeirs cdeinr deinrs**

cdeinrss discerns rescinds cinders discern rescind. *See* **cdeinr cdeirs ceirss deinrs**

cdeinrsu inducers cinders cruised discern incudes induces insured rescind. *See* **cdeinr cdeinu cdeirs cdensu**

cdeinry cindery. *See* **cdeinr cdery cdeiy**

cdeinssx exscinds exscind. *See* **cdeis deins cdiss**

cdeinsu incudes induces. *See* **cdensu ceinsu cdeinu deinsu**

cdeinsx exscind. *See* **cdeis deins deinx**

cdeinu induce dunce indue nudie cued dice dine dune iced nice nide nude cud cue den die din due dun end ice en id in ne nu

cdeinw winced widen wince wined dice dine iced nice nide wend wide wind wine den dew die din end ice new wed wen win en id in ne we

cdeinz zinced dizen dice dine iced nice nide zein zinc den die din end ice zed en id in ne

cdeiop copied coped code coed cope dice dope epic iced odic oped pice pied cep cod cop die dip doc doe ice ode ope pie pod poi do id od pe pi

cdeiopst despotic depicts deposit dopiest poetics posited topside. *See* **cdeiop cdeips cdeipt cdeist**

cdeiorrt creditor director cordite. *See* **cdeirt cdeorr ceiorr ceiort**

cdeiorsv discover divorces divorce devisor. *See* **cdeiov cdeirs cdeirv cdeors**

cdeiort cordite. *See* **cdeirt deiort ceiort**

cdeiorv divorce. *See* **cdeirv deiorv ceiorv**

cdeiov voiced coved video voice code coed cove dice dive dove iced odic vice vied void cod die doc doe ice ode vie do id od

cdeipr priced cider cried price pride pried riced dice dire drip epic iced peri

pice pied pier rice ride ripe cep die dip
ice ire per pie rec red rep rid rip er id pe
pi re

cdeiprs crisped. *See* **cdeirs cdeipr ceiprs
deiprs cdeips**

cdeiprst predicts scripted credits crisped
depicts directs predict striped. *See*
cdeipr cdeips cdeipt cdeirs

cdeiprt predict. *See* **cdeirt cdeipt cdeipr**

cdeiprtu pictured predict picture. *See*
cdeipr cdeipt cdeirt ceirtu

cdeips spiced dices epics spice spied ceps
dice dies dips disc epic iced ices ides
pice pied pies side sped cep die dip ice
ids pie sic sip id is pe pi si

cdeipst depicts. *See* **cdeipt cdeist ceipst
cdeips deipst**

cdeipt depict cited edict tepid cite dice
diet edit epic iced pice pied tide tied
cep die dip dit ice pet pie pit ted tic tie
tip id it pe pi ti

cdeir cider cried riced dice dire iced rice
ride die ice ire rec red rid er id re

cdeirrsu scurried cruised cruiser curried
curries. *See* **cdeirs cderru cdersu ceirrs**

cdeirru curried. *See* **cderru cdeir ceirr**

cdeirs ciders cider cried cries dices dries
riced rices rides sired dice dies dire disc
iced ices ides reds reis rice ride rids rise
side sire die ice ids ire rec red res rid sic
sir er id is re si

cdeirst credits directs. *See* **cdeirs cdeirt
deirst cdeist ceirst**

cdeirstu curtsied credits crudest cruised
crusted directs dustier icterus. *See*
cdeirs cdeirt cdeist cdersu

cdeirstv verdicts credits directs diverts
verdict. *See* **cdeirs cdeirt cdeirv cdeist**

cdeirsu cruised. *See* **cdeirs ceirsu cdersu**

cdeirt credit direct triced cider cited
cried edict riced tired trice tried cite
dice diet dire dirt edit iced rice ride rite
tide tied tier tire die dit ice ire rec red
ret rid ted tic tie er id it re ti

cdeirtv verdict. *See* **cdeirv cdeirt deirtv**

cdeirv cervid cider cried diver drive riced
rived dice dire dive iced rice ride rive
vice vied die ice ire rec red rev rid vie er
id re

cdeis dices dice dies disc iced ices ides
side die ice ids sic id is si

cdeissst dissects dissect desists. *See*
cdeist deisst

cdeisssu discuses cuisses discuss disuses.
See **cdessu cdissu ceissu deissu**

cdeisst dissect. *See* **deisst cdeist**

cdeist edicts cited cites deist dices diets
edict edits sited tides cist cite dice dies
diet disc dits edit iced ices ides sect

side site teds tics tide tied ties die dit
ice ids its set sic sit ted tic tie id is it si ti

cdeit cited edict cite dice diet edit iced
tide tied die dit ice ted tic tie id it ti

cdeiy dicey dice iced dey die dye ice icy
id ye

cdejnoru conjured jounced conjure. *See*
cdenor cdjnou cejnou

cdejnou jounced. *See* **cdjnou cejnou**

cdek deck

cdekklnu knuckled clunked knuckle. *See*
cdeklu

cdekkno knocked. *See* **cdekno ckkno**

cdeklno clonked. *See* **cdelno cdeklo
cdekno**

cdeklnou unlocked clonked clunked. *See*
cdeklo cdeklu cdekno cdelno

cdeklnu clunked. *See* **cdeklu cklnu cdenu**

cdeklo locked coked clod code coed coke
cold cole deck dock dole koel lock lode
cod col doc doe eld elk led lek ode oke
old do el lo od

cdeklow wedlock. *See* **cdeklo cdelow**

cdeklpu plucked. *See* **cdeklu celpu delpu**

cdeklrtu truckled trucked truckle. *See*
cdeklu cdekru cdektu cdelru

cdeklsu suckled. *See* **cdeklu cdeksu
ceklsu deklsu**

cdeklu lucked clued clue cued deck duck
duel duke luce luck cud cue due eld elk
led lek leu el

cdekmo mocked coked code coed coke
come deck demo dock dome mock
mode moke cod doc doe mod ode oke
do em me mo od om

cdekmos smocked. *See* **cdekmo dekmos
cdekos**

cdekmu mucked cued deck duck duke
muck cud cue cum due emu mud em
me mu um

cdekno nocked coked coned kendo code
coed coke cone conk deck dock done
keno neck nock node once cod con den
doc doe don end eon ken nod ode oke
one do en ne no od on

cdeknoou uncooked. *See* **cdekno cdekoo**

cdeknoov convoked convoke. *See*
cdekno cdekoo

cdeknoru uncorked. *See* **cdekno cdekor
cdekru cdenor**

cdeko coked code coed coke deck dock
cod doc doe ode oke do od

cdekoo cooked coked cooed code coed
coke cook deck dock cod coo doc doe
ode oke do od

cdekoor crooked. *See* **cdekoo cekoor
cdekor dekoor**

cdekor corked rocked coked cored decor
cero code coed coke cord core cork

deck dock doer reck redo rock rode
cod cor doc doe dor kor ode oke orc
ore rec red roc rod roe do er od or re

cdekos socked codes coeds coked cokes
decks docks code cods coed coke deck
desk dock docs does dose odes okes
sock soke cod doc doe dos kos ode oke
sod do od os so

cdekost dockets stocked. *See* **cdekot
cdekos cekost dekost**

cdekot docket coked toked code coed
coke cote deck dock dote toed toke cod
cot doc doe dot ode oke ted tod toe do
od to

cdekrtu trucked. *See* **cdekru cdektu**

cdekru rucked crude cured crud cued
curd cure deck duck duke ecru reck
ruck rude rued cud cue cur due rec red
rue urd er re

cdeks decks deck desk

cdeksu sucked decks ducks dukes cuds
cued cues cusk deck desk duck dues
duke dusk scud suck sued used cud cue
due sue use us

cdektu tucked educt cued cute deck duck
duct duet duke tuck cud cue cut due
ted ut

cdellors scrolled scolder. *See* **cdelor
cdelos cdeors cellos**

cdellosu colludes collude sculled. *See*
cdellu cdelos cdeosu cdlosu

cdellotu cloudlet collude clouted. *See*
cdellu cdeltu celltu dellot

cdellou collude. *See* **cdellu cello cdlou**

cdellsu sculled. *See* **cdellu cells celsu**

cdellu culled clued cell clue cued cull dell
duel dull luce cud cue due eld ell led
leu el

cdelmnou columned. *See* **cdelmu cdelno
clmnou delmno**

cdelmop clomped. *See* **cdemop celmop**

cdelmpru crumpled clumped crumped
crumple rumpled. *See* **cdelmu cdelru
delmpu delpru**

cdelmpu clumped. *See* **cdelmu delmpu**

cdelmsu muscled. *See* **cdelmu celmsu**

cdelmtu mulcted. *See* **cdelmu cdeltu**

cdelmu culmed clued clue cued culm
duel luce meld mule cud cue cum due
eld elm emu led leu lum mel mud el em
me mu um

cdelno cloned clone coned loden olden
clod code coed cold cole cone dole
done enol lend leno lode lone node
noel once cod col con den doc doe don
eld end eon led nod ode old one do el
en lo ne no od on

cdelnoo condole. *See* **cdelno cdeloo
delnoo**

cdelnoos condoles consoled condole console noodles. *See* **cdelno cdeloo cdelos cdenos**

cdelnoss coldness seconds oldness. *See* **cdelno cdelos cdenos cdloss**

cdelnosy condyles secondly condyle. *See* **cdelno cdelos cdeloy cdenos**

cdelnow clowned. *See* **cdelno cdelow**

cdelnoy condyle. *See* **cdelno cdeloy**

cdelnruu uncurled. *See* **cdelru celnru celruu delnru**

cdeloo cooled cooed looed clod code coed cold cole cool dole loco lode oleo cod col coo doc doe eld led loo ode old do el lo od

cdeloor colored. *See* **cdelor cdeloo celoor**

cdelooru coloured colored. *See* **cdeloo cdelor cdelru celoor**

cdelopp coppled. *See* **cdeopp delopp**

cdeloptu octupled clouted coupled couplet. *See* **cdeltu celopu deoptu eloptu**

cdelopu coupled. *See* **celopu cdlou cdelu**

cdelor colder ceorl cored decor older cero clod code coed cold cole cord core doer dole lord lore orle redo rode role cod col cor doc doe dor eld led ode old orc ore rec red roc rod roe do el er lo od or re

cdelors scolder. *See* **celors cdelos cdelor cdeors delors**

cdelorss cordless scolders closers cresols crossed scolder solders. *See* **cdelor cdelos cdeors cdloss**

cdelorsu closured closure colures coursed curdles scolder scoured. *See* **cdelor cdelos cdelru cdeors**

cdelos closed clods close codes coeds colds coles doles lodes scold socle soled clod code cods coed cold cole cols docs does dole dose lode lose odes sled sloe sold sole cod col doc doe dos eld els led los ode old sod sol do el lo od os so

cdelost coldest. *See* **cdelos celost delost**

cdelosw scowled. *See* **cdelos cdelow delosw**

cdelott clotted. *See* **delott**

cdelotu clouted. *See* **cdeltu cdlou clotu**

cdelow cowled dowel lowed clew clod code coed cold cole cowl dole lewd lode owed weld wold cod col cow dew doc doe eld led low ode old owe owl wed woe do el lo od ow we

cdeloy cloyed decoy yodel clod cloy code coed cold cole dole lode cod col coy dey doc doe dye eld led lye ode old yod do el lo od oy ye

cdelprsu scrupled curdles scruple slurped spruced. *See* **cdelru cdepsu cdersu celpsu**

cdelpstu sculpted. *See* **cdeltu cdepsu cdestu celpsu**

cdelrsu curdles. *See* **cdelru cdersu celrsu**

cdelrtuu cultured culture. *See* **cdelru cdeltu celrtu celruu**

cdelru curdle curled clued crude cruel cured lucre lured ruled ulcer clue crud cued curd cure curl duel ecru luce lure rude rued rule cud cue cur due eld led leu rec red rue urd el er re

cdelruy crudely. *See* **cdelru delruy**

cdelsstu ductless tussled. *See* **cdeltu cdessu cdestu celstu**

cdelsttu scuttled cutlets scuttle. *See* **cdeltu cdestu celstu celttu**

cdeltu dulcet clued culet educt luted celt clue cued cult cute duct duel duet luce lute tule cud cue cut due eld led let leu ted el ut

cdelu clued clue cued duel luce cud cue due eld led leu el

cdemmno commend. *See* **cdeno demmno demmo**

cdemmnos commends commend. *See* **cdenos demmos demnos**

cdemmnou commuted commend commune. *See* **cdeno demno cdeou**

cdemmoo commode. *See* **cdeoo demmo demoo**

cdemmoos commodes commode. *See* **cemoos demmos**

cdemmotu commuted commute. *See* **cemot cdeou cdetu**

cdemmsu scummed. *See* **demmsu**

cdemnno condemn. *See* **cdenno demno emnno**

cdemnnos condemns condemn. *See* **cdenno cdenos demnos**

cdemnoow comedown woodmen. *See* **cdmnoo demnoo denoow**

cdemnosu consumed consume. *See* **cdenos cdensu cdeosu cenosu**

cdemnotu document counted mounted. *See* **cdenot cemntu**

cdemoops composed scooped compose. *See* **cdemop cdeoop cemoos cmoops**

cdemop comped coped moped code coed come comp cope demo dome dope mode me mo od om pe

cdemoptu computed compute. *See* **cdemop deoptu**

cdemoru decorum. *See* **cemor cdeor cderu**

cdemostu costumed scouted costume. *See* **cdeosu cdestu cemost cmostu**

cdemoy comedy decoy code coed come cyme demo demy dome mode cod coy dey doc doe dye mod ode yod do em me mo my od om oy ye

cdempru crumped. *See* **dempru cderu cmpru**

cdenno conned coned nonce code coed cone done neon node none once cod con den doc doe don end eon nod ode one do en ne no od on

cdennoo condone. *See* **cdenno cdnoo cdeoo**

cdennoos condones condone. *See* **cdenno cdenos denoos**

cdennoot connoted condone connote contend. *See* **cdenno cdenot dennot**

cdennost contends consent contend docents tendons. *See* **cdenno cdenos cdenot cenost**

cdennot contend. *See* **cdenno cdenot dennot**

cdeno coned code coed cone done node once cod con den doc doe don end eon nod ode one do en ne no od on

cdenoor crooned. *See* **cdnoor cdenor**

cdenoott cottoned. *See* **cdenot cnoott deoott**

cdenoovy convoyed. *See* **cenovy cnoovy**

cdenopu pounced. *See* **cenopu cdeno cdeop**

cdenor corned coned cored crone decor drone recon cero code coed cone cord core corn doer done nerd node once redo rend rode cod con cor den doc doe don dor end eon nod nor ode one orc ore rec red roc rod roe do en er ne no od on or re

cdenors scorned. *See* **cenors cdenor denors cdenos**

cdenortu trounced counted counter courted recount trounce. *See* **cdenor cdenot cenort denort**

cdenorw crowned. *See* **cdenor cdeorw denorw**

cdenos second codes coeds coned cones nodes nosed scend scone sonde code cods coed cone cons dens docs does done dons dose ends eons node nods noes nose odes once ones send cod con den doc doe don dos end ens eon nod ode one sen sod son do en ne no od on os so

cdenoss seconds. *See* **cenoss cdenos denoss**

cdenost docents. *See* **cenost cdenot cdenos denost**

cdenostu contused contuse counted docents scouted. *See* **cdenos cdenot cdensu cdeosu**

cdenot docent cento coned noted toned cent code coed cone cote dent done dote node note once tend toed tone cod con cot den doc doe don dot end eon net nod not ode one ted ten tod toe ton do en ne no od on to

cdenotu counted. *See* **cdenot cnotu dnotu**

cdenrtuu undercut. *See* **denrtu**

cdens scend dens ends send den end ens sen en ne

cdensu dunces secund dunce dunes nudes scend cuds cued cues dens dues dune duns ends nude scud send sued used cud cue den due dun end ens sen sue sun use en ne nu us

cdenu dunce cued dune nude cud cue den due dun end en ne nu

cdeo code coed cod doc doe ode do od

cdeoo cooed code coed cod coo doc doe ode do od

cdeoop cooped cooed coped code coed coop cope dope oped cep cod coo cop doc doe ode ope pod do od pe

cdeoops scooped. *See* **cdeoop cdeos co-ops**

cdeoorr corrode. *See* **cdeorr cdeoo deoor**

cdeoorrs corrodes corrode records. *See* **cdeorr cdeors ceorrs deoors**

cdeoorsu decorous coursed scoured. *See* **cdeors cdeosu cdersu ceorsu**

cdeoost scooted. *See* **deoost cdeos cdeoo**

cdeop coped code coed cope dope oped cep cod cop doc doe ode ope pod do od pe

cdeopp copped coped code coed cope dope oped pope cep cod cop doc doe ode ope pep pod pop do od pe

cdeoppr cropped. *See* **cdeopp ceoppr**

cdeoprru procured producer produce procure. *See* **cdeorr cderru ceopru deopru**

cdeoprsu produces coursed produce recoups scoured spruced. *See* **cdeors cdeosu cdepsu cdersu**

cdeopru produce. *See* **ceopru deopru**

cdeor cored decor cero code coed cord core doer redo rode cod cor doc doe dor ode orc ore rec red roc rod roe do er od or re

cdeorr record cored corer crore decor order cero code coed cord core doer redo rode cod cor doc doe dor err ode orc ore rec red roc rod roe do er od or re

cdeorrs records. *See* **ceorrs cdeors deorrs cdeorr**

cdeors decors scored ceros codes coeds cords cored cores corse decor doers rosed score scrod cero code cods coed cord core orcs docs doer does dose odes orcs ores redo reds rocs rode rods roes rose sore cod cor doc doe dor dos ode orc ore rec red res roc rod roe sod do er od or os re so

cdeorss crossed. *See* **ceorss deorss cdeors cdorss**

cdeorsu coursed scoured. *See* **ceorsu cdersu cdeosu deorsu cdeors**

cdeortu courted. *See* **deortu**

cdeorw crowed cored cower crowd decor dower rowed cero code coed cord core crew crow doer drew owed redo rode word wore cod cor cow dew doc doe dor ode orc ore owe rec red roc rod roe row wed woe do er od or ow re we

cdeorz crozed cored croze decor cero code coed cord core doer doze redo rode zero cod cor coz doc doe dor ode orc ore rec red roc rod roe zed do er od or re

cdeos codes coeds code cods coed docs does dose odes cod doc doe dos ode sod do od os so

cdeossu escudos. *See* **cdessu deossu ce-ossu**

cdeost costed codes coeds cotes code cods coed cost cots docs does dose dote dots odes scot teds toed toes ale cod doc doe dos dot set sod sot tod toe do od os so

cdeostu scouted. *See* **cdestu cdeosu deostu**

cdeosu escudo codes coeds douce douse scudo code cods coed cuds cued cues docs does dose dues duos odes ouds scud sued udos used cod cud cue doc doe dos due duo ode oud sod sou sue udo use do od os so us

cdeosy decoys codes coeds decoy code cods coed cosy deys docs does dose dyes odes oyes syce yods cod coy dey doc doe dos dye ode sod soy yes yod do od os oy so ye

cdeou douce code coed cued cod cud cue doc doe due duo ode oud udo do od

cdeov coved code coed cove dove cod doc doe ode do od

cdeox codex code coed cod cox doc doe ode do ex od ox

cdeoy decoy code coed cod coy dey doc doe dye ode yod do od oy ye

cdeoyz zydeco decoy code coed cozy doze dozy oyez cod coy coz dey doc doe dye ode yod zed do od oy ye

cdeppu cupped cued puce cep cud cue cup due pep pup pe up

cdeprsu spruced. *See* **cdersu cdepsu deprsu ceprsu**

cdepsu cusped puces ceps cuds cued cues cups cusp dues puce scud scup sped spud spue sued used cep cud cue cup due pus sue sup use pe up us

cderru cruder crude cured recur ruder crud cued curd cure ecru rude rued cud cue cur due err rec red rue urd er re

cdersttu destruct crudest crusted cutters trusted. *See* **cdersu cdestu cerstu certtu**

cderstu crudest crusted. *See* **cerstu cdersu derstu cdestu**

cdersu cursed crude cruds cruse curds cured cures curse druse crud crus cuds cued cues curd cure curs dues ecru reds rude rued rues ruse scud sued surd sure urds used user cud cue cur due rec red res rue sue urd use er re us

cdersy descry decry dyers deys dyer dyes reds ryes syce cry dey dry dye rec red res rye yes er re ye

cderu crude cured crud cued curd cure ecru rude rued cud cue cur due rec red rue urd er re

cderuv curved crude cured curve crud cued curd cure ecru rude rued cud cue cur due rec red rev rue urd er re

cdery decry dyer cry dey dry dye rec red rye er re ye

cdessu cussed scuds cess cuds cued cues cuss dues scud suds sued sues used uses cud cue due ess sue use us

cdestu educts ducts duets educt scute cuds cued cues cute cuts duct dues duet dust scud scut sect stud sued suet teds used cud cue cut due set sue ted use us ut

cdetu educt cued cute duct duet cud cue cut due ted ut

cdeu cued cud cue due

cdfhios codfish. *See* **cfios cdios**

cdfiluy dulcify. *See* **cdilu dfilu**

cdfioy codify coif fico foci odic cod coy doc fid foy icy yod do id if od of oy

cdfnnoou confound. *See* **cdnoo dfnou**

cdghiin chiding. *See* **cdgiin dghiin**

cdghiint ditching chiding itching. *See* **cdgiin cdiint cgiint chiint**

cdghinor chording cording hording. *See* **cdgino cdhior cginor**

cdghinou douching. *See* **cdgino dginou**

cdgiin dicing icing ding nidi dig din gid gin id in

cdgiinnu inducing induing. *See* **cdgiin dgiinn**

cdgiklnu duckling ducking lucking. *See* **cgilnu**

cdgikno docking. *See* **cdgino cgikno**

cdgiknu ducking. *See* **cginu**

cdgilno codling. *See* **cdgino dgilno**

cdgilnos scolding codling closing. *See* **cdgino cgilns cgilos cilnos**

cdgilnou clouding codling. *See* **cdgino cgilnu cglnou cilnou**

cdgilnru curdling curding curling. *See* **cgilnu cginru dginru gilnru**

cdginno condign. *See* **cdgino cginno**

cdgino coding dingo doing cion coin ding dong icon odic cod cog con dig din doc dog don gid gin god ion nod nog do go id in no od on

cdginor cording. *See* **cdgino cginor**

cdginorw crowding cording crowing wording. *See* **cdgino cginor ginorw**

cdginru curding. *See* **cginru dginru**

cdhhiils childish. *See* **cdhil chiil**

cdhi chid chi hid id hi

cdhiiosz schizoid. *See* **cdios cdiio**

cdhiist distich. *See* **chist cdhit**

cdhil child chid chi hid lid hi id li

cdhilly childly. *See* **chilly cdhil dilly**

cdhior orchid rhodic choir chord ichor chid coir cord odic rich chi cod cor doc dor hid hod orc rho rid roc rod do hi ho id od oh or

cdhiors orchids. *See* **chiors cdhors cdhior**

cdhipty diptych. *See* **cdhit chity chipt**

cdhiry hydric chid rich chi cry dry hid icy rid id hi

cdhit ditch chid chit itch chi dit hid hit tic hi id it ti

cdhloopy copyhold. *See* **choop loopy**

cdhor chord cord cod cor doc dor hod orc rho roc rod do ho od oh or

cdhors chords chord cords scrod cods cord cors cosh docs hods orcs rhos rocs rods shod cod cor doc dor dos hod ohs orc rho roc rod sod do ho od oh or os sh so

cdhuy duchy cud

cdiiiot idiotic. *See* **cdiot diiot cdiio**

cdiiir iridic rid id

cdiijru juridic. *No 6s or 5s*

cdiikpst dipstick. *See* **cikps cikst iipst**

cdiilly idyllic. *See* **dilly ciily**

cdiiloty docility. *See* **cdiioy**

cdiiltuy lucidity. *See* **ciily ciilt cdilu**

cdiinor crinoid. *See* **ciinor diinr cdiio**

cdiinors crinoids cirsoid crinoid incisor. *See* **ciinor ciinrs diinrs**

cdiinot diction. *See* **cdiint cdiot diiot**

cdiinst indicts. *See* **cdiint**

cdiinstt distinct indicts. *See* **cdiint cinstt**

cdiint indict nidi din dit nit tic tin id in it ti

cdiio iodic odic cod doc do id od

cdiioprt dioptric. *See* **cioprt dioprt**

cdiiors cirsoid. *See* **ciors cdors cdios**

cdiioss cissoid. *See* **cdioss cdiio**

cdiiosss cissoids cissoid. *See* **cdioss**

cdiioy idiocy iodic odic cod coy doc icy yod do id od oy

cdiirstt district. *See* **cirstt**

cdiisv viscid disc sic ids id is si

cdijnstu disjunct inducts. *See* **cdintu cinstu dinstu**

cdiknor dornick. *See* **diknr**

cdiknors dornicks dornick. *See* **diknrs**

cdiknosw windsock. *See* **dinosw**

cdiknpsu duckpins. *See* **cdipsu**

cdiky dicky icky icy kid id

cdilloo colloid. *No 6s or 5s*

cdilloos colloids colloid. *See* **cdlos cilos cloos**

cdillouy cloudily lucidly. *See* **cdlloy cdlouy dllouy**

cdilluy lucidly. *See* **clluy dilly dlluy**

cdiloors discolor. *See* **cloors dloors**

cdilu lucid cud lid id li

cdimmosu modicums modicum. *See* **cimmos dimosu immosu**

cdimmou modicum. *See* **cdimu dimou**

cdimoort microdot. *See* **cdoort cioort**

cdimstu dictums. *See* **cdimtu cistu cdstu**

cdimtu dictum mucid tumid duct cud cum cut dim dit mid mud tic tui id it mi mu ti um ut

cdimu mucid cud cum dim mid mud id mi mu um

cdinoo conoid condo cion coin coon icon odic cod con coo din doc don ion nod do id in no od on

cdinoos conoids. *See* **cdinoo cinos cnoos**

cdinortu inductor conduit noctuid ruction. *See* **cdintu cinort dnortu**

cdinostu conduits discount noctuids conduit inducts noctuid suction. *See* **cdintu cdiost cinost cinosu**

cdinotu conduit noctuid. *See* **cdintu cnotu cdiot**

cdinstu inducts. *See* **cdintu dinstu cinstu**

cdinsy syndic dins disc sync din icy ids sic sin yin id in is si

cdintu induct cutin tunic duct unit cud cut din dit dun nit nut tic tin tui tun id in it nu ti ut

cdio odic cod doc do id od

cdioprsu cuspidor. *See* **cdipsu ciorsu coprsu**

cdios disco cods disc docs odic cod doc dos ids sic sod do id is od os si so

cdioss discos disco discs cods disc docs doss odic sods cod doc dos ids sic sis sod do id is od os si so

cdiossty cystoids cystoid. *See* **cdioss cdiost ciosst**

cdiost dicots dicot disco doits stoic cist cods cost cots disc dits docs doit dots odic otic scot tics cod cot dit doc dos dot ids its sic sit sod sot tic tod do id is it od os si so ti to

cdiostuv oviducts oviduct. *See* **cdiost ciostu diostu diostv**

cdiosty cystoid. *See* **cdiost disty**

cdiot dicot doit odic otic cod cot dit doc dot tic tod do id it od ti to

cdiotuv oviduct. *See* **cdiot diotv**

cdipssu cuspids. *See* **cdipsu cdissu**

cdipsu cuspid cupids scudi cuds cups cusp dips disc scud scup spud cud cup dip ids pus sic sip sup id is pi si up us

cdipu cupid cud cup dip id pi up

cdirtuy crudity. *See* **dirty**

cdis disc sic ids id is si

cdiss discs disc ids sic sis id is si

cdisssu discuss. *See* **cdissu**

cdissu discus discs scudi scuds cuds cuss disc scud suds cud ids sic sis id is si us

cdisu scudi cuds disc scud cud ids sic id is si us

cdjlnouy jocundly. *See* **cdjnou cdlouy cjnouy**

cdjnou jocund junco judo unco undo cod con cud doc don dun duo nod oud udo do jo no nu od on

cdko dock cod doc do od

cdkos docks cods dock docs sock cod doc dos kos sod do od os so

cdksu ducks cuds cusk duck dusk scud suck cud us

cdku duck cud

cdkuy ducky duck yuck cud yuk

cdllloop clodpoll. *See* **clloop dlloop llloop**

cdlloy coldly colly dolly clod cloy cold doll cod col coy doc old yod do lo od oy

cdlo clod cold cod col doc old do lo od

cdlos clods colds scold clod cods cold cols docs sold cod col doc dos los old sod sol do lo od os so

cdloss scolds clods colds scold clod cods cold cols docs doss loss sods sold sols cod col doc dos los old sod sol do lo od os so

cdlosu clouds clods cloud colds could locus scold scudo clod cods cold cols cuds docs duos loud ouds scud sold soul udos cod col cud doc dos duo los old oud sod sol sou udo do lo od os so us

cdlou cloud could clod cold loud cod col cud doc duo old oud udo do lo od

cdlouy cloudy cloud could clod cloy cold duly loud cod col coy cud doc duo old oud udo yod you do lo od oy

cdmnoo condom condo coon doom mono mood moon cod con coo doc don mod mon moo nod do mo no od om on

cdmnoopu compound. *See* **cdmnoo cnoopu**

cdmnoos condoms. *See* **cdmnoo cnoos dmoos**

cdmnoruu corundum. *See* **cnoru dmnou mnoru**

cdnoo condo coon cod con coo doc don nod do no od on

cdnoor condor cordon condo croon donor rondo coon cord corn door odor ordo rood cod con coo cor doc don dor nod nor orc roc rod do no od on or

cdnoors cordons. *See* **cdnoor cnoors dnoors**

cdo cod doc do od

cdooopst octopods octopod. *See* **coops coost doost**

cdooopt octopod. *No 6s or 5s*

cdoorruy corduroy. *See* **crruy**

cdoorst doctors. *See* **cdoort coost cdors**

cdoort doctor coot cord door odor ordo rood root roto trod cod coo cor cot doc dor dot orc ort roc rod rot tod too tor do od or to

cdoostuw woodcuts woodcut. *See* **coost cdstu dootu**

cdootuw woodcut. *See* **dootu**

cdoprstu products product. *See* **coprsu corstu oprstu**

cdoprtu product. *See* **cortu copru dopru**

cdor cord cod cor doc dor orc roc rod do od or

cdors cords scrod cods cord cors docs orcs rocs rods cod cor doc dor dos orc roc rod sod do od or os so

cdorss scrods cords cross dross scrod cods cord cors docs doss orcs rocs rods sods cod cor doc dor dos orc roc rod sod do od or os so

cdorsw crowds cords crowd crows scrod sword words cods cord cors cows crow docs orcs rocs rods rows scow word cod cor cow doc dor dos orc roc rod row sod sow do od or os ow so

cdorw crowd cord crow word cod cor cow doc dor orc roc rod row do od or ow

cdos cods docs cod doc dos sod do od os so

cdostuy custody. *See* **cdstu dstuy costu**

cdosu scudo cods cuds docs duos ouds scud udos cod cud doc dos duo oud sod sou udo do od os so us

cdrsu cruds curds crud crus cuds curd curs scud surd urds cud cur urd us

cdru crud curd cud cur urd

cdssu scuds cuds cuss scud suds cud us

cdstu ducts cuds cuts duct dust scud scut stud cud cut us ut

cdsu cuds scud cud us

cdtu duct cud cut ut

cdu cud

---

cee cee

ceeeeipy eyepiece. *See* **ceeip**

ceeeelst selectee celeste. *See* **ceelst**

ceeeffrt effecter. *See* **ceefft**

ceeefl fleece clef feel flee cee eel elf fee lee el

ceeeflrs fleecers fleeces feelers. *See* **ceeefl ceeers ceelrs eeeflr**

ceeefls fleeces. *See* **ceeefl cefls ceefs**

ceeefnor conferee enforce. *See* **ceefnr ceenor cefnor**

ceeegimn emceeing. *See* **ceeimn**

ceeehikr cheekier. *See* **ceehk ceehr chikr**

ceeehirs cheesier. *See* **ceeirs ceehrs ceeehs ceeers**

ceeehls leeches. *See* **ceeehs ceehls**

ceeehpss speeches cheeses. *See* **ceeehs ceehps**

ceeehs cheese cees cee see she eh he sh

ceeehss cheeses. *See* **ceeehs cehss**

ceeeijtv ejective. *See* **ceitv ceejt**

ceeeilnn lenience. *See* **ceiln eilnn ceein**

ceeeilns licensee license silence. *See* **ceeins ceilns eeilns**

ceeeilrt erectile reelect reticle tiercel. *See* **ceeirt ceelrt ceilrt**

ceeeiltv elective. *See* **ceitv ceelt eeilt**

ceeeimnn eminence. *See* **ceeimn**

ceeeinnt enceinte. *See* **ceeint**

ceeeinp epicene. *See* **ceein ceenp ceeip**

ceeeiprr creepier creeper piercer. *See* **ceeipr ceiprr eeeirr**

ceeeiprv perceive receive. *See* **ceeipr**

ceeeirrv receiver receive receive reverie. *See* **eeeirr eeerrv**

ceeeirsv receives receive service veeries. *See* **ceeers ceeirs eeersv eeirsv**

ceeeirsx exercise. *See* **ceeers ceeirs ceeisx eeirsx**

ceeeirv receive. *See* **eeeir eeerv**

ceeellnr crenelle. *See* **ceelnr**

ceeelrrv cleverer. *See* **ceelrv eeerrv**

ceeelrst reelects celeste reelect secrete tercels. *See* **ceeers ceelrs ceelrt ceelst**

ceeelrt reelect. *See* **ceelrt**

ceeelst celeste. *See* **ceelst**

ceeem emcee cee em me

ceeemnrt cerement. *See* **ceemnt ceemrt ceenrt**

ceeemrty cemetery. *See* **ceemrt**

ceeems emcees emcee cees seem cee see em me

ceeennst sentence. *See* **eennst**

ceeenprs presence spencer. *See* **ceeers ceenps ceenrs ceeprs**

ceeenprt pretence percent preteen. *See* **ceenrt eenprt**

ceeenqsu sequence. *See* **eenqsu**

ceeenrrs screener. *See* **ceeers ceenrs**

ceeenss essence. *See* **ceenss**

ceeensss essences essence. *See* **ceenss eensss**

ceeeprr creeper. *See* **ceepr**

ceeeprrs creepers creeper. *See* **ceeprs ceeers**

ceeers creese scree cees cere seer sere cee ere rec res see er re

ceeersss recesses cresses seeress. *See* **ceeers ceerss**

ceeersst secretes sesterce cresset secrete secrets. *See* **ceeers ceerss ceerst cersst**

ceeerssu cereuses rescues secures. *See* **ceeers ceerss ceersu cerssu**

ceeerst secrete. *See* **ceerst ceeers**

ceeerstx excretes secrete excrete. *See* **ceeers ceerst eerstx**

ceeertux executer excrete execute. *See* **certu ceert eertx**

ceeertx excrete. *See* **ceert eertx**

ceeesssx excesses. *See* **ceessx**

ceeestux executes execute. *See* **ceesux**

ceeetux execute. *No 6s or 5s*

ceeffno offence. *See* **ceeffo ceefn**

ceeffnos offences coffees offence offense. *See* **ceeffo ceefns**

ceeffo coffee cee fee foe off of

ceeffort effector. *See* **ceeffo ceefft ceffor eeffot**

ceeffos coffees. *See* **ceeffo ceefs cffos**

ceeffst effects. *See* **ceefft ceefs eefst**

ceefft effect feet fete cee eft fee tee

ceefgiln fleecing feeling fleeing. *See* **eefgin eefiln**

ceefhikr kerchief. *See* **ceefir eefhir**

ceefhist fetiches fetches fitches. *See* **ceehis ceehst cefhis cefhit**

ceefhlrt fletcher reflect. *See* **ceehlr ceelrt cefhlt**

ceefhlru cheerful. *See* **ceehlr ceehru eeflru**

ceefhlst fletches fetches letches. *See* **ceehls ceehst ceelst cefhlt**

ceefhst fetches. *See* **ceehst cefhs ceefs**

ceefilry fiercely. *See* **ceefir ceefly ceelry eefilr**

ceefinrt frenetic enteric. *See* **ceefir ceefnr ceeint ceeirt**

ceefir fierce cere fere fire free reef rice rife cee ere fee fie fir ice ire rec ref rif er if re

ceefirr fiercer. *See* **ceefir cefirr**

ceefirst fiercest recites tierces. *See* **ceefir ceeirs ceeirt ceerst**

ceefklr freckle. *See* **ceekl ceklr ceekr**

ceefklrs freckles freckle. *See* **ceekls ceekrs ceelrs cefkls**

ceefklss feckless. *See* **ceekls cefkls**

ceeflntu feculent. *See* **celntu eflntu**

ceeflrst reflects reflect tercels. *See* **ceelrs ceelrt ceelst ceerst**

ceeflrt reflect. *See* **ceelrt ceflt eeflr**

ceefly fleecy clef eely feel flee fyce cee eel elf eye fee fey fly lee lye el ye

ceefn fence cee fee fen nee en ne

ceefnn fennec fence cee fee fen nee en ne

ceefnns fennecs. *See* **ceefnn ceefns**

ceefnor enforce. *See* **cefnor ceenor ceefnr**

ceefnorr confrere enforcer enforce. *See* **ceefnr ceenor cefnor ceforr**

ceefnors enforces confers encores enforce fencers necrose. *See* **ceefnr ceefns ceenor ceenrs**

ceefnr fencer fence cere erne fere fern free reef cee ere fee fen nee rec ref en er ne re

ceefnrs fencers. *See* **ceefnr ceefns ceenrs**

ceefnrvy fervency. *See* **ceefnr eenrvy**

ceefns fences cense feces fence scene cees fees fens seen cee ens fee fen nee see sen en ne

ceefoprr perforce. *See* **ceforr eefprr**

ceeforss frescoes frescos. *See* **ceerss cefors ceorss**

ceefortw crowfeet. *See* **efortw**

ceefprst perfects prefects perfect prefect respect scepter sceptre specter. *See* **ceeprs ceerst eefrst eeprst**

ceefprt perfect prefect. *See* **ceepr ceprt ceert**

ceefs feces cees fees cee fee see

ceefssu fescues. *See* **ceefsu eefssu**

ceefsu fescue feces fusee cees cues fees feus fuse cee cue fee feu see sue use us

ceeghikn cheeking. *See* **ceehk cehin chikn**

ceeghiln leeching leching heeling. *See* **ceehil cehiln**

ceeghinp cheeping. *See* **eeginp**

ceeghinr cheering generic. *See* **ceginr cehinr eehinr eghinr**

ceeghlow cogwheel. *See* **ceehl eehlw ehlow**

ceegijnt ejecting genetic. *See* **ceeint ceijnt eegint**

ceegilnt electing genetic gentile neglect. *See* **ceeint ceilnt eegilt eegint**

ceegilrs clergies. *See* **ceeirs ceelrs ceilrs eegils**

ceeginpr creeping generic peering. *See* **ceeipr ceginr ceinpr eeginp**

ceeginr generic. *See* **ceginr eegin eegnr**

ceeginrs generics cringes generic sincere. *See* **ceeins ceeirs ceenrs ceginr**

ceeginrt erecting enteric generic genetic integer treeing. *See* **ceeint ceeirt ceenrt ceginr**

ceeginst genetics genetic entices. *See* **ceeins ceeint cegist ceinst**

ceeginsu eugenics eugenic. *See* **ceeins ceginu ceinsu eegins**

ceegint genetic. *See* **ceeint eegint**

ceeginu eugenic. *See* **ceginu eegin ceein**

ceeginxy exigency. *See* **eeginy**

ceegllo college. *See* **cello**

ceegllos colleges college. *See* **cellos**

ceeglnst neglects neglect. *See* **ceelst eeglnt eeglst eegnst**

ceeglnt neglect. *See* **eeglnt ceelt**

ceeglosu eclogues eclogue glucose. *See* **ceelou celosu**

ceeglou eclogue. *See* **ceelou**

ceegno congee cone gene gone ogee once cee cog con ego eon gee nee nog one en go ne no on

ceegnorv converge. *See* **ceegno ceenor cegnor egnorv**

ceegnos congees. *See* **ceegno ceens cenos**

ceegnry regency. *See* **eegnry**

ceegorst corteges cortege. *See* **ceerst ceorst eegrst eeorst**

ceegort cortege. *See* **eegrt ceert egort**

ceehhmnn henchmen. *See* **ceehn**

ceehikly cheekily. *See* **ceehky ceehkl cehiky ceehil**

ceehil lichee leech ceil heel lech lice cee chi eel hie ice lee lei lie eh el he hi li

ceehilln chenille. *See* **ceehil cehiln**

ceehilrs chiseler helices lechers lichees. *See* **ceehil ceehis ceehlr ceehls**

ceehilry cheerily lechery. *See* **ceehil ceehlr ceehly ceehry**

ceehils helices lichees. *See* **cehils ceehls ceehil ceehis**

ceehilsv vehicles chevies helices lichees vehicle vesicle. *See* **ceehil ceehis ceehls cehils**

ceehilv vehicle. *See* **ceehil eehlv**

ceehimr chimere. *See* **ceehr cehim ceimr**

ceehimrs chimeres chemise chimere mercies schemer. *See* **ceehis ceehms ceehrs ceeirs**

ceehimrt hermetic chimere heretic thermic. *See* **ceeimt ceeirt ceemrt cehirt**

ceehims chemise. *See* **cehims ceehis**

ceehimss chemises chemise schemes seiches. *See* **ceehis ceehms ceeiss cehims**

ceehinpr encipher phrenic. *See* **ceeipr cehinr cehipr ceinpr**

ceehinrs enriches henries inheres sincere. *See* **ceehis ceehrs ceeins ceeirs**

ceehior cheerio. *See* **cehior ceehor**

ceehiors cheerios cheerio coheirs heroics. *See* **ceehis ceehor ceehos ceehrs**

ceehiosu icehouse. *See* **ceehis ceehos cehosu**

ceehiosv cohesive chevies. *See* **ceehis ceehos cehisv ceiosv**

ceehirrs cherries rehires. *See* **ceehis ceehrs ceeirs cehirr**

ceehirst heretics cithers heister heretic recites retches richest tierces. *See* **ceehis ceehrs ceehst ceeirs**

ceehirt heretic. *See* **cehirt eehirt ceeirt**

ceehirw chewier. *See* **ceehrw**

ceehis seiche cees hies ices cee chi hie his ice see she sic eh he hi is sh si

ceehiss seiches. *See* **ceehis ceeiss**

ceehistt esthetic. *See* **ceehis ceehst cehist cehitt**

ceehistw chewiest witches. *See* **ceehis ceehst ceehsw cehist**

ceehisv chevies. *See* **ceehis cehisv**

ceehk cheek heck cee eke eh he

ceehkl heckle cheek cleek leech heck heel keel lech leek cee eel eke elk lee lek eh el he

ceehklr heckler. *See* **ceehkl ceehlr**

ceehklrs hecklers heckler heckles lechers. *See* **ceehkl ceehks ceehlr ceehls**

ceehkls heckles. *See* **ceehks ceekls ceehkl ceehls eehkls**

ceehknp henpeck. *See* **ceehk ceehp ceehn**

ceehknps henpecks henpeck kenches. *See* **ceehks ceehps ceenps**

ceehkns kenches. *See* **ceehks ceens ceehn**

ceehkrst sketcher ketches retches. *See* **ceehks ceehrs ceehst ceekrs**

ceehks cheeks cheek hecks cees ekes heck seek skee cee eke see she eh he sh

ceehksst sketches ketches. *See* **ceehks ceehst cehkst cehsst**

ceehkst ketches. *See* **ceehks ceehst cehkst**

ceehkstv kvetches ketches vetches. *See* **ceehks ceehst cehkst cehktv**

ceehky cheeky cheek heck yech cee eke eye hey key eh he ye

ceehl leech lech heel cee eel lee eh el he

ceehlno echelon. *See* **celno ceehn ceehl**

ceehlnos echelons echelon enclose. *See* **ceehls ceehos cehnos celnos**

ceehlnpu penuchle penuche. *See* **ceehp celpu ceehn**

ceehlnsu elenchus lunches. *See* **ceehls celnsu**

ceehlr lecher cheer creel leech cere heel here herl lech leer reel cee eel ere her lee rec eh el er he re

ceehlrs lechers. *See* **ceehrs ceelrs ceehlr**

ceehlry lechery. *See* **ceelry ceehry ceehly**

ceehls leches leech heels cees eels else heel lech lees seel cee eel els lee see she eh el he sh

ceehlst letches. *See* **ceelst ceehst ceehls**

ceehly lychee leech chyle eely heel lech yech cee eel eye hey lee lye eh el he ye

ceehmnss chessmen schemes. *See* **ceehms ceenss eehmns eehmss**

ceehmrs schemer. *See* **ceehms ceehrs**

ceehmrss schemers schemer schemes. *See* **ceehms ceehrs ceerss eehmss**

ceehms scheme cees heme hems mesh seem cee hem see she eh em he me sh

ceehmss schemes. *See* **ceehms eehmss**

ceehn hence cee hen nee eh en he ne

ceehnnrt entrench centner. *See* **ceehnt ceenrt cehnrt eehnrt**

ceehnort coherent trochee thereon. *See* **ceehnt ceehor ceenor ceenot**

ceehnpsu penuches penuche punches. *See* **ceehps ceenps**

ceehnpu penuche. *See* **ceehp ceehn ceenp**

ceehnqru quencher. *See* **ceehqu ceehru cehnqu**

ceehnqsu quenches cheques. *See* **ceehqu cehnqu eenqsu**

ceehnrrt retrench trencher. *See* **ceehnt ceenrt ceerrt cehnrt**

ceehnrst trenches centers centres retches tenches. *See* **ceehnt ceehrs ceehst ceenrs**

ceehnrsw wenchers wrenches chewers rechews wencher wenches. *See* **ceehnw ceehrs ceehrw ceehsw**

ceehnrw wencher. *See* **ceehrw ceehnw cehnrw**

ceehnsst stenches tenches. *See* **ceehnt ceehst ceenss cehnst**

ceehnst tenches. *See* **ceehst cehnst ceehnt**

ceehnsw wenches. *See* **ceehnw ceehsw**

ceehnt thence hence tench cent etch hent tech teen thee then cee eth hen het nee net tee ten the eh en he ne

ceehnw whence hence wench chew hewn when cee ewe hen hew nee new wee wen eh en he ne we

ceehor cohere cheer chore ocher ochre cere cero core echo here hero hoer cee cor ere her hoe orc ore rec rho roc roe eh er he ho oh or re

ceehorrt torchere trochee erector. *See* **ceehor ceerrt cehort ceorrt**

ceehorst trochees hectors retches rochets rotches torches trochee troches. *See* **ceehor ceehos ceehrs ceehst**

ceehort trochee. *See* **ceehor cehort eehort**

ceehos echoes chose cees cosh echo hoes hose shoe cee hoe ohs see she eh he ho oh os sh so

ceehp cheep cee cep hep pee eh he pe

ceehprs perches. *See* **ceehps ceehrs ceeprs eehprs**

ceehps cheeps speech cheep sheep cees ceps pees seep cee cep hep pee see she eh he pe sh

ceehqsu cheques. *See* **ceehqu**

ceehqu cheque cee cue hue eh he

ceehr cheer cere here cee ere her rec eh er he re

ceehrs cheers cheer scree sheer cees cere here hers resh seer sere cee ere her rec res see she eh er he re sh

ceehrst retches. *See* **ceerst cehrst ceehst eehrst**

ceehrstw wretches chewers rechews retches wethers. *See* **ceehrs ceehrw ceehst ceehsw**

ceehrsw chewers rechews. *See* **ceehrs ceehrw ceehsw eehrsw**

ceehru euchre cheer ruche cere cure ecru here cee cue cur ere her hue rec rue eh er he re

ceehrw chewer rechew cheer hewer where cere chew crew ewer here cee ere ewe her hew rec wee eh er he re we

ceehry cheery cheer cere eery eyre here yech cee cry ere eye her hey rec rye eh er he re ye

ceehssw eschews. *See* **ceehsw cehss ehssw**

ceehst etches chest sheet techs these cees etch hest sect tech tees thee cee eth het see set she tee the eh he sh

ceehstv vetches. *See* **ceehst cehtv**

ceehsw eschew chews cees chew ewes hews shew cee ewe hew see sew she wee eh he sh we

ceehsy cheesy sycee cees eyes syce yech cee eye hey see she shy yes eh he sh ye

ceeiinst niceties entices incites. *See* **ceeins ceeint ceiins ceiist**

ceeijnot ejection. *See* **ceeint ceenot ceijnt ceinot**

ceeijor rejoice. *No 6s or 5s*

ceeijors rejoices rejoice. *See* **ceeirs ceiors eeiors**

ceeijruv verjuice. *See* **ceiru ceruv ceiju**

ceeiklnn neckline. *See* **ceikln eeklnn**

ceeiklpr pickerel prickle. *See* **ceeipr ceiklp ceikpr eeiklp**

ceeiknst neckties necktie entices. *See* **ceeins ceeint ceikns ceinst**

ceeiknt necktie. *See* **ceeint**

ceeikprt picketer receipt pricket. *See* **ceeipr ceeirt ceikpr ceikpt**

ceeilllp pellicle. *See* **ceeip**

ceeillm micelle. *See* **ceilm eeilm**

ceeillms micelles micelle. *See* **ceilms eeilms**

ceeilmor comelier. *See* **ceelmo ceelor ceilor**

ceeilmps semplice eclipse. *See* **ceeips ceilms ceilps eeilms**

ceeilmx lexemic. *See* **ceimx ceilm eeilm**

ceeilnny leniency. *See* **ceilny**

ceeilno cineole. *See* **ceiln celno cilno**

ceeilnot election cineole lection. *See* **ceeint ceenot ceilnt ceinot**

ceeilnov violence cineole. *See* **ceeinv ceinov celnov eelnov**

ceeilnr recline. *See* **ceelnr eeilnr**

ceeilnrr recliner recline. *See* **ceelnr eeilnr**

ceeilnrs reclines silencer crenels license liernes recline silence sincere. *See* **ceeins ceeirs ceelnr ceelrs**

ceeilns license silence. *See* **ceilns ceeins eeilns**

ceeilnss licenses silences iceless license silence. *See* **ceeins ceeiss ceenss ceilns**

ceeilps eclipse. *See* **ceeips ceilps**

ceeilpss eclipses eclipse iceless pelisse species splices. *See* **ceeips ceeiss ceilps ceilss**

ceeilrst reticles tiercels leister recites relicts reticle sectile sterile tercels tiercel tierces. *See* **ceeirs ceeirt ceelrs ceelrt**

ceeilrt reticle tiercel. *See* **ceeirt ceilrt ceelrt**

ceeilrtu reticule lecture leucite reticle tiercel. *See* **ceeirt ceelrt ceilrt ceiltu**

ceeilrty celerity erectly reticle tiercel. *See* **ceeirt ceelrt ceelry ceilrt**

ceeilss iceless. *See* **ceeiss ceilss**

ceeilssv vesicles iceless vesicle. *See* **ceeiss ceilss ceilsv eeilsv**

ceeilst sectile. *See* **ceelst eeilst**

ceeilsv vesicle. *See* **ceilsv eeilsv**

ceeiltu leucite. *See* **ceiltu ceelt eeilt**

ceeimn icemen niece mince mice mien mine nice cee ice men nee nim em en in me mi ne

ceeimnny eminency. *See* **ceeimn**

ceeimnps specimen. *See* **ceeimn ceeins ceeips ceenps**

ceeimnst centimes cements centime emetics entices. *See* **ceeimn ceeimt ceeins ceeint**

ceeimnt centime. *See* **ceemnt ceeimt ceeint ceeimn**

ceeimort meteoric coterie. *See* **ceeimt ceeirt ceemrt ceimrt**

ceeimrs mercies. *See* **ceeirs ceimrs eeimrs**

ceeimst emetics. *See* **ceeimt ceist eimst**

ceeimt emetic cite emit item meet mete mice mite teem time cee ice met tee tic tie em it me mi ti

ceein niece nice cee ice nee en in ne

ceeinns incense. *See* **ceeins einns**

ceeinnss incenses niceness incense. *See* **ceeins ceeiss ceenss eeinss**

ceeinnst nescient entices incense intense. *See* **ceeins ceeint ceinst eennst**

ceeinort erection neoteric enteric coterie. *See* **ceeint ceeirt ceenor ceenot**

ceeinprt prentice enteric percent receipt. *See* **ceeint ceeipr ceeirt ceenrt**

ceeinpsx sixpence. *See* **ceeins ceeips ceeisx ceenps**

ceeinqru quercine enquire. *See* **ceinqu ceiqru eeinqu**

ceeinrrs sincerer sincere. *See* **ceeins ceeirs ceenrs ceirrs**

ceeinrs sincere. *See* **ceeirs ceeins ceenrs eeinrs**

ceeinrsu insecure sinecure sincere censure. *See* **ceeins ceeirs ceenrs ceersu**

ceeinrt enteric. *See* **ceenrt ceinrt ceeint eeinrt ceeirt**

ceeinrv cervine. *See* **ceeinv eeinrv**

ceeins nieces cense niece scene seine since cees ices nice seen sine cee ens ice nee see sen sic sin en in is ne si

ceeinst entices. *See* **ceeint ceinst ceeins**

ceeinsv evinces. *See* **eeinsv ceeinv**

ceeint entice niece cent cite nice teen tine cee ice nee net nit tee ten tic tie tin en in it ne ti

ceeinv evince niece even nevi nice vein vice vine cee eve ice nee vee vie en in ne

ceeioppr pericope. *See* **ceeipr ceiopr ce-oppr**

ceeioprs recopies copiers piecers pierces precise recipes. *See* **ceeipr ceeips ceeirs ceeprs**

ceeiopst picotees picotee poetics. *See* **ceeips ceiops ceiopt ceipst**

ceeiopt picotee. *See* **ceiopt ceeip eeopt**

ceeiorst coteries esoteric coterie recites tierces. *See* **ceeirs ceeirt ceerst ceiors**

ceeiorsx exorcise. *See* **ceeirs ceeisx ceiors eeiors**

ceeiort coterie. *See* **ceiort ceeirt**

ceeiortx exoteric coterie exciter. *See* **ceeirt ceeitx ceiort ceiotx**

ceeip piece epic pice cee cep ice pee pie pe pi

ceeipptu eupeptic. *See* **ceippt**

ceeipr piecer pierce recipe creep crepe piece price cere epic peer peri pice pier rice ripe cee pep ere ice ire pee per pie rec rep rip er pe pi re

ceeiprr piercer. *See* **ceeipr ceiprr**

ceeiprrs piercers crisper perries piecers piercer pierces precise pricers recipes reprise respire. *See* **ceeipr ceeips ceeirs ceeprs**

ceeiprs piecers pierces precise recipes. *See* **ceeirs ceeprs ceeipr ceeips ceiprs**

ceeiprst receipts piecers pierces precise receipt recipes recites respect respite scepter sceptre specter tierces. *See* **ceeipr ceeips ceeirs ceeirt**

ceeiprsu epicures epicure piecers pierces precise recipes. *See* **ceeipr ceeips ceeirs ceeprs**

ceeiprt receipt. *See* **ceeipr ceeirt**

ceeipru epicure. *See* **ceeipr**

ceeips pieces specie epics piece spice cees ceps epic ices pees pice pies seep cee cep ice pee pie see sic sip is pe pi si

ceeipss species. *See* **ceeiss eeipss ceeips ceipss**

ceeirrsw screwier rewires. *See* **ceeirs ceirrs eeirrw**

ceeirs cerise cries rices scree cees cere ices reis rice rise seer sere sire cee ere ice ire rec res see sic sir er is re si

ceeirssv services service revises. *See* **ceeirs ceeiss ceerss ceirss**

ceeirst recites tierces. *See* **ceeirs ceerst ceeirt eeirst ceirst**

ceeirstv vertices recites restive service tierces veriest. *See* **ceeirs ceeirt ceerst ceirst**

ceeirstx exciters exciter excites recites tierces. *See* **ceeirs ceeirt ceeisx ceeitx**

ceeirsv service. *See* **ceeirs eeirsv**

ceeirsvx cervixes service. *See* **ceeirs ceeisx ceirvx eeirsv**

ceeirt recite tierce erect retie terce trice cere cite rete rice rite tier tire tree cee ere ice ire rec ret tee tic tie er it re ti

ceeirtx exciter. *See* **ceeitx ceeirt**

ceeiss ecesis cees cess ices sees cee ess ice see sic sis is si

ceeissx excises. *See* **ceeiss ceessx ceeisx**

ceeistx excites. *See* **ceeisx ceeitx**

ceeisx excise cees exes ices cee ice see sex sic six ex is si xi

ceeitx excite cite exit cee ice tee tic tie ex it ti xi

ceejorst ejectors ejector rejects. *See* **ceejrt ceejst ceerst ceorst**

ceejort ejector. *See* **ceejrt ceort**

ceejrst rejects. *See* **ceerst ceejst eejrst ceejrt**

ceejrt reject eject erect terce cere jeer rete tree cee ere jet rec ret tee er re

ceejst ejects eject cees jest jets sect tees cee jet see set tee

ceejt eject cee jet tee

ceekl cleek keel leek cee eel eke elk lee lek el

ceeklnss neckless. *See* **ceekls ceenss eeklns**

ceeklps speckle. *See* **ceekls eekps eeklp**

ceeklpss speckles speckle. *See* **ceekls cekpss eelpss**

ceeklrss reckless. *See* **ceekls ceekrs ceelrs ceerss**

ceekls cleeks cleek keels leeks sleek cees eels ekes elks else keel leek lees leks seek seel skee cee eel eke elk els lee lek see el

ceeknr necker creek cere erne keen kern knee neck reck reek cee eke ere ken nee rec en er ne re

ceeknrs neckers. *See* **ceekrs ceeknr ceenrs**

ceekr creek cere reck reek cee eke ere rec er re

ceekrrsw wreckers wrecker. *See* **ceekrs cekrsw eekrsw**

ceekrrw wrecker. *See* **ceekr cekrw**

ceekrs creeks creek esker recks reeks scree cees cere ekes reck reek seek seer sere skee cee eke ere rec res see er re

ceelllsu cellules cellule. *See* **cells celsu cllsu**

ceelllu cellule. *No 6s or 5s*

ceellmou molecule. *See* **ceelmo ceelou**

ceellno colleen. *See* **cello celno eelno**

ceellnos colleens colleen enclose. *See* **cellos celnos eelnos**

ceellrvy cleverly. *See* **ceelrv ceelry eellry**

ceelmnt clement. *See* **ceemnt ceelt**

ceelmo cleome cole come mole cee col eel elm lee mel el em lo me mo om**

ceelmopt complete compete. *See* **ceelmo celmop eelmot eelmpt**

ceelmos cleomes. *See* **ceelmo celos cemos**

ceelmosw welcomes cleomes welcome. *See* **ceelmo**

ceelmow welcome. *See* **ceelmo**

ceelmrtu electrum lecture. *See* **ceelrt ceemrt celrtu cemrtu**

ceelnopu opulence. *See* **ceelou celopu cenopu**

ceelnort electron elector electro lectern. *See* **ceelnr ceelor ceelrt ceenor**

ceelnos enclose. *See* **celnos eelnos**

ceelnoss encloses enclose. *See* **ceenss celnos celoss cenoss**

ceelnr crenel creel cere erne leer reel cee eel ere lee nee rec el en er ne re

ceelnrs crenels. *See* **ceelrs ceelnr ceenrs**

ceelnrst lecterns centers centres crenels lectern nestler relents tercels. *See* **ceelnr ceelrs ceelrt ceelst**

ceelnrt lectern. *See* **ceenrt eelnrt ceelrt**

ceelnrty recently lectern erectly. *See* **ceelnr ceelrt ceelry ceenrt**

ceelor creole creel ceorl cere cero cole core leer lore orle reel role cee col cor eel ere lee orc ore rec roc roe el er lo or re

ceelors creoles. *See* **celors ceelrs ceelor eelors**

ceelorst corselet electors electros selector colters costrel creoles elector electro lectors tercels. *See* **ceelor ceelrs ceelrt ceelst**

ceelort elector electro. *See* **celort ceelor ceelrt**

ceelortv coverlet elector electro. *See* **ceelor ceelrt ceelrv celort**

ceelou coulee clue cole luce cee col cue eel lee leu el lo

ceelprst prelects pelters petrels prelect respect scepter sceptre specter tercels. *See* **ceelrs ceelrt ceelst ceeprs**

ceelprt prelect. *See* **eelprt**

ceelr creel cere leer reel cee eel ere lee rec el er re

ceelrrtu lecturer crueler lecture. *See* **ceelrt ceerrt celrru celrtu**

ceelrru crueler. *See* **celrru ceelr**

ceelrs creels creel leers reels scree cees cere eels else leer lees reel seel seer sere cee eel els ere lee rec res see el er re

ceelrssu recluses recluse rescues secures. *See* **ceelrs ceerss ceersu celrsu**

ceelrst tercels. *See* **ceerst ceelrs ceelst ceelrt**

ceelrstu cruelest lectures cluster cutlers lecture recluse tercels. *See* **ceelrs ceelrt ceelst ceerst**

ceelrsty secretly erectly tercels tersely. *See* **ceelrs ceelrt ceelry ceelst**

ceelrsu recluse. *See* **ceersu celrsu**

ceelrsuy securely recluse. *See* **ceelrs ceelry ceersu celrsu**

ceelrt tercel creel elect erect terce celt cere leer leet reel rete tree cee eel ere lee let rec ret tee el er re

ceelrtu lecture. *See* **ceelrt celrtu**

ceelrty erectly. *See* **ceelrt ceelry**

ceelrv clever creel elver lever revel cere ever leer reel veer cee eel ere eve lee lev rec rev vee el er re

ceelrw crewel creel cere clew crew ewer leer reel cee eel ere ewe lee rec wee el er re we

ceelry celery creel leery cere eely eery eyre leer lyre reel rely cee cry eel ere eye lee lye rec rye el er re ye

ceelsst selects. *See* **ceelst eelsst**

ceelst elects select celts elect leets sleet steel stele cees celt eels else lees leet lest lets sect seel tees cee eel els lee let see set tee el

ceelsttu lettuces cutlets lettuce scuttle. *See* **ceelst celstu celttu cesttu**

ceelsx excels excel cees eels else exes lees seel cee eel els lee see sex el ex

ceelt elect celt leet cee eel lee let tee el

ceelttu lettuce. *See* **celttu ceelt eeltu**

ceelx excel cee eel lee el ex

ceemnorw newcomer. *See* **ceenor eemnor eenorw**

ceemnory ceremony. *See* **ceenor eemnor eemnoy**

ceemnru cerumen. *See* **eemnu emnru**

ceemnst cements. *See* **ceemnt ceens censt**

ceemnt cement cent meet mete teem teen cee men met nee net tee ten em en me ne**

ceemoorv overcome. *See* **eemorv**

ceemopr compeer. *See* **cemor ceepr emopr**

ceemoprs compeers compeer. *See* **ceeprs cemors ceoprs eemprs**

ceemopt compete. *See* **eemopt cemot**

ceemrr mercer cere mere cee ere err rec rem em er me re

ceemrrs mercers. *See* **ceemrr ceers eemrs**

ceemrt cermet erect meter metre retem terce cere meet mere mete rete teem term tree cee ere met rec rem ret tee em er me re

ceennort cretonne centner. *See* **ceenor ceenot ceenrt cenort**

ceennoru renounce. *See* **ceenor cennru ennoru**

ceennosv convenes convene. *See* **cenosv**

ceennov convene. *See* **cenno cenov**

ceennrst centners centers centner centres rennets. *See* **ceenrs ceenrt ceerst eennst**

ceennrt centner. *See* **ceenrt eennrt**

ceenoptw twopence. *See* **ceenot eenopt**

ceenor encore crone recon cere cero cone core corn erne once cee con cor eon ere nee nor one orc ore rec roc roe en er ne no on or re

ceenors encores necrose. *See* **cenors ceenor ceenrs**

ceenorss necroses censors encores necrose screens secerns. *See* **ceenor ceenrs ceenss ceerss**

ceenorsv conserve converse encores necrose. *See* **ceenor ceenrs cenors cenosv**

ceenorvy conveyer. *See* **ceenor cenovy eenrvy**

ceenost cenotes. *See* **ceenot cenost**

ceenosvx convexes. *See* **cenosv cenovx**

ceenot cenote cento cent cone cote note once teen tone cee con cot eon nee net not one tee ten toe ton en ne no on to

ceenp pence neep peen cee cep nee pee pen en ne pe

ceenprs spencer. *See* **ceeprs ceenps eenprs ceenrs**

ceenprss spencers precess screens secerns spencer. *See* **ceenps ceenrs ceenss ceeprs**

ceenprst percents centers centres percent present repents respect scepter sceptre serpent specter spencer. *See* **ceenps ceenrs ceenrt ceeprs**

ceenprt percent. *See* **ceenrt eenprt**

ceenps pences cense neeps peens pence scene cees ceps neep peen pees pens seen seep cee cep ens nee pee pen see sen en ne pe

ceenrs screen secern cense ernes scene scree sneer cees cere erne seen seer sere cee ens ere nee rec res see sen en er ne re

ceenrss screens secerns. *See* **ceenss ceerss eenrss**

ceenrssu censures censure ensures rescues screens secerns secures. *See* **ceenrs ceenss ceerss ceersu**

ceenrst centers centres. *See* **ceenrt ceerst eennrst**

ceenrsu censure. *See* **ceersu eenrsu**

ceenrsy scenery. *See* **ceenrs**

ceenrt center centre recent tenrec enter erect terce cent cere erne rent rete teen tern tree cee ere nee net rec ret tee ten en er ne re

ceens cense scene cees seen cee ens nee see sen en ne

ceenss censes scenes cense scene sense cees cess seen sees cee ens ess nee see sen en ne

ceensstu cuteness. *See* ceenss censst censsu cesstu

ceeoorst creosote scooter. *See* ceerst ceorst eeorst

ceeopsty ecotypes ecotype ectypes peyotes. *See* ceepty ceosty eeopst

ceeopty ecotype. *See* ceepty eeopty

ceeoqttu coquette. *See* ceoqtu

ceeorrrs sorcerer. *See* ceorrs eorrrs

ceeorrst erectors erector rectors restore. *See* ceerrt ceerst ceorrs ceorrt

ceeorrsu recourse resource courser rescuer scourer securer. *See* ceersu ceorrs ceorsu cerrsu

ceeorrsv recovers recover. *See* ceorrs ceorsv eeorsv eorrsv

ceeorrt erector. *See* ceerrt ceorrt

ceeorrv recover. *See* ceorr ceorv eorrv

ceeorrvy recovery recover. *See* eerrvy

ceeorttv corvette. *See* ceertt ceortt ceortv

ceeortux executor. *See* ceortx

ceepprst percepts precepts percept precept respect scepter sceptre specter stepper. *See* ceeprs ceerst eeppst eeprst

ceepprt percept precept. *See* ceepr ceprt ceert

ceepr creep crepe cere peer cee cep ere pee per rec rep er pe re

ceeprs creeps crepes creep crepe peers perse scree spree cees ceps cere peer pees reps seep seer sere cee cep ere pee per rec rep res see er pe re

ceeprss precess. *See* ceeprs eeprss ceerss

ceeprsst respects scepters specters spectres cresset pesters precess presets respect sceptre secrets specter. *See* ceeprs ceerss ceerst cersst

ceeprst respect scepter sceptre specter. *See* ceerst ceeprs eeprst

ceeprstx excerpts excepts excerpt expects experts respect scepter sceptre specter. *See* ceeprs ceeptx ceerst eeprst

ceeprtx excerpt. *See* ceeptx eeprtx

ceepry creepy creep crepe cere eery eyre peer prey pyre cee cep cry ere eye pee per pry rec rep rye yep er pe re ye

ceepstx excepts expects. *See* ceeptx

ceepsty ectypes. *See* ceepty eepsy eepst

ceepsuy eyecups. *See* ceepuy cepsu eepsy

ceeptx except expect cee cep pee pet tee pe ex

ceepty ectype type cee cep eye pee pet tee yep yet pe ye

ceepuy eyecup puce cee cep cue cup eye pee yep yup pe up ye

ceer cere cee ere rec er re

ceerrssu rescuers securers rescuer rescues securer secures. *See* ceerss ceersu cerrsu cerssu

ceerrsu rescuer securer. *See* ceersu cerrsu

ceerrt tercer erect terce cere rete tree cee ere err rec ret tee er re

ceers scree cees cere seer sere cee ere rec res see er re

ceerss recess screes cress scree seers seres cees cere cess seer sees sere cee ere ess rec res see er re

ceerssst cresses. *See* ceerss

ceerssst cressets cresses cresset secrets tresses. *See* ceerss ceerst cersst

ceerssst cresset secrets. *See* ceerst cersst ceerss eersst

ceerssstw setscrew cresset secrets westers. *See* ceerss ceerst cersst cerssw

ceerssu rescues secures. *See* ceersu cerssu eerssu ceerss

ceerst certes erects secret crest erect ester reset scree steer stere terce terse trees cees cere erst rest rete rets sect seer sere tees tree cee ere rec res ret see set tee er re

ceerstt tercets. *See* ceerst eerstt ceertt

ceersttu curettes curette cutters tercets trustee. *See* ceerst ceersu ceertt cerstu

ceersu cereus ceruse recuse rescue secure cruse cures curse reuse scree cees cere crus cues cure curs ecru rues ruse seer sere sure user cee cue cur ere rec res rue see sue use er us

ceert erect terce cere rete tree cee ere rec ret tee er re

ceertt tercet erect terce cere rete tree tret cee ere rec ret tee er re

ceerttu curette. *See* ceertt certtu

cees cees cee see

ceessux excuses. *See* ceessx ceesux

ceessx excess sexes cees cess exes sees cee ess see sex ex

ceessy sycees sycee syces yeses cees cess eyes sees syce cee ess eye see yes ye

ceesttuv cuvettes cuvette. *See* cesttu eesttu

ceesux excuse cees cues exes cee cue see sex sue use ex us

ceesy sycee cees eyes syce cee eye see yes ye

ceettuv cuvette. *No 6s or 5s*

ceffio office coif fico fief fife foci fie foe ice off if of

ceffior officer. *See* ceffio ceffor

ceffiors officers coffers officer offices scoffer. *See* ceffio ceffor cefios cefors

ceffioru coiffeur coiffure officer. *See* ceffio ceffor

ceffios offices. *See* ceffio cefios

ceffissu suffices suffice. *See* ceissu cffssu

ceffisu suffice. *See* effis cffsu

cefflo coffle clef cole floc floe col elf foe off el lo of

ceffloru forceful. *See* cefflo ceffor celoru efflru

cefflos coffles. *See* cefflo cefls celos

cefflssu scuffles scuffle. *See* cffssu fflssu

cefflsu scuffle. *See* cefls celsu eflsu

ceffor coffer force offer cero core corf fore froe cor foe for fro off orc ore rec ref roc roe er of or re

ceffors coffers scoffer. *See* ceffor cefors effors

cefforss scoffers coffers frescos scoffer. *See* ceffor cefors ceorss cffoss

cefghint fetching etching hefting. *See* cefhit cefint cehint efgint

cefgikln flecking. *See* cefikl ceikln

cefginn fencing. *See* efgin

cefh chef feh eh he

cefhi chief fiche chef chi feh fie hie ice eh he hi if

cefhiims mischief. *See* cefhis cehims

cefhilns flinches filches finches lichens. *See* cefhis cehiln cehils cehins

cefhils filches. *See* cefhis cehils efhils

cefhily chiefly. *See* cefhi cehly cfhil

cefhins finches. *See* cefhis cehins

cefhis chiefs fiches chefs chief fiche chef fies fisc fish hies ices chi feh fie hie his ice ifs she sic eh he hi if is sh si

cefhist fitches. *See* cefhis cehist cefhit efhist

cefhistw fitchews fitches fitchew witches. *See* cefhis cefhit cehist chistw

cefhit fetich chief ethic fetch fiche fitch thief chef chit cite etch heft itch tech chi eft eth feh fie fit het hie hit ice the tic tie eh he hi if it ti

cefhitw fitchew. *See* cefhit ceitw ehitw

cefhlt fletch cleft fetch letch celt chef clef etch felt heft lech left tech eft elf eth feh het let the eh el he

cefhs chefs chef feh she eh he sh

cefht fetch chef etch heft tech eft eth feh het the eh he

cefiilt fictile. *See* ceiilt ceflt efilt

cefiilty felicity fictile. *See* ceiilt

cefiior orifice. *See* cefor ceiir

cefiiors orifices orifice. *See* cefios cefors ceiors

cefiirrt terrific. *See* cefirr

cefiitv fictive. *See* ceitv

cefikl fickle fleck flick ceil clef file lice lick lief life like elf elk fie ice ilk kef kif lei lek lie el if li

cefiklr flicker. *See* cefikl ceklr efilr

cefiklrs flickers flicker slicker. *See* cefikl cefkls ceikls ceikrs

cefilllo follicle. *See* **ceillo**

cefilmru merciful. *See* **ceimru efilru**

cefilnot flection inflect lection. *See* **cefint ceilnt ceinot efilno**

cefilnst inflects clients infects inflect lectins stencil. *See* **cefint ceflst ceilns ceilnt**

cefilnsu funicles funicle. *See* **ceilns ceilnu ceilsu ceinsu**

cefilnt inflect. *See* **ceilnt cefint**

cefilnu funicle. *See* **ceilnu efiln**

cefimor comfier. *See* **cfimor cemor ceimr**

cefimost comfiest comfits. *See* **cefios cemost cfimot cimost**

cefinno confine. *See* **cenno**

cefinnos confines confine. *See* **cefios ceinos**

cefinor conifer. *See* **cefnor efinr ceinr**

cefinors conifers forensic confers conifer cronies. *See* **cefios cefnor cefors ceinos**

cefinort infector conifer. *See* **cefint cefnor ceinot ceinrt**

cefinott confetti. *See* **cefint ceinot**

cefinst infects. *See* **efinst ceinst cefint**

cefint infect feint cent cite fine nice tine eft fen fie fin fit ice net nit ten tic tie tin en if in it ne ti

cefiorty ferocity certify rectify. *See* **ceiort efirty**

cefios ficoes coifs coif fico fies fisc foci foes ices fie foe ice ifs sic if is of os si so

cefipsy specify. *See* **ceips cefsy cipsy**

cefirr ferric crier frier ricer fire rice rife err fie fir ice ire rec ref rif er if re

cefirty certify rectify. *See* **efirty ceirt**

cefkl fleck clef elf elk kef lek el

cefkllo elflock. *See* **cello cefkl cfklo**

cefkllos elflocks elflock. *See* **cefkls cellos cfklos**

cefkloor forelock. *See* **ceklor cekoor celoor ekloor**

cefklost fetlocks fetlock lockets. *See* **cefkls ceflst ceklot cekost**

cefklot fetlock. *See* **ceklot ceflt cefkl**

cefklpsy flyspeck. *See* **cefkls**

cefklry freckly. *See* **ceklr cefkl eflry**

cefkls flecks fleck clefs clef elks kefs leks self elf elk els kef lek el

cefl clef elf el

ceflnosu flounces confuse counsel flounce. *See* **celnos celnsu celosu cenosu**

ceflnou flounce. *See* **celno eflno cenou**

ceflnuy fluency. *See* **celnu**

cefls clefs clef self elf els el

ceflst clefts celts clefs cleft felts celt clef efts felt left lest lets sect self eft elf els let set el

ceflt cleft celt clef felt left eft elf let el

cefmory comfrey. *See* **cemor cfmoy ceory**

cefnor confer crone force recon cero cone core corf corn fern fore froe once con cor eon fen foe for fro nor one orc ore rec ref roc roe en er ne no of on or re

cefnors confers. *See* **cenors cefnor cefors**

cefnorsu frounces confers confuse frounce. *See* **cefnor cefors cenors cenosu**

cefnoru frounce. *See* **cefnor cnoru cenou**

cefnoss confess. *See* **cenoss efoss**

cefnossu confuses confess confuse focuses. *See* **cenoss cenosu censsu ceossu**

cefnostu confutes confuse confute contuse. *See* **cenost cenosu cnostu efnost**

cefnosu confuse. *See* **cenosu cfosu**

cefnotu confute. *See* **cenot cnotu fnotu**

cefoprs forceps. *See* **ceoprs cefors**

cefor force cero core corf fore froe cor foe for fro orc ore rec ref roc roe er of or re

ceforr forcer corer crore force cero core corf fore froe cor err foe for fro orc ore rec ref roc roe er of or re

ceforrs forcers. *See* **ceorrs ceforr cefors**

ceforrst crofters crofter forcers rectors. *See* **ceforr cefors ceorrs ceorrt**

ceforrt crofter. *See* **ceforr ceorrt**

cefors forces fresco ceros cores corse force fores froes score cero core corf cors foes fore froe orcs ores refs rocs roes rose serf sore cor foe for fro orc ore rec ref res roc roe er of or os re so

ceforss frescos. *See* **ceorss**

ceforstu fructose scouter. *See* **cefors ceorst ceorsu cerstu**

cefossu focuses. *See* **ceossu cfosu efoss**

cefrsuw curfews. *See* **cefruw cersw cersu**

cefruw curfew crew cure ecru cue cur feu few fur rec ref rue er re we

cefsy fyces fyce syce fey yes ye

cefy fyce fey ye

cegghir chigger. *No 6s or 5s*

cegghirs chiggers chigger. *See* **cehirs eghirs**

ceggiloo geologic. *See* **ceiloo eggilo ggiloo**

ceggior georgic. *See* **cgior eggor**

ceggiors georgics georgic soggier. *See* **ceiors cgiors eggors egiors**

ceghiiny hygienic. *See* **eghiin**

ceghikln heckling leching. *See* **cehiln ceikln**

ceghiln leching. *See* **cehiln cgiln eghin**

ceghilnt letching etching leching lighten. *See* **cehiln cehint ceilnt cghilt**

ceghilst glitches sleight. *See* **cegist cehils cehist cghilt**

ceghimns scheming meshing. *See* **cehims cehins ceimns eghins**

ceghinnw wenching chewing. *See* **eghinw**

ceghino echoing. *See* **eghino cehin chino**

ceghinor cohering echoing. *See* **ceginr cegnor cehinr cehior**

ceghinpr perching phrenic. *See* **ceginr cehinr cehipr ceinpr**

ceghinrt retching etching cithern. *See* **ceginr cehinr cehint cehirt**

ceghinst etchings etching ethnics nighest. *See* **cegist cehins cehint cehist**

ceghint etching. *See* **cehint eghit eghin**

ceghinvy chevying. *See* **cehvy cehin eginy**

ceghinw chewing. *See* **eghinw cehin cehnw**

ceghlsu gulches. *See* **cghsu celsu eglsu**

ceghnors groschen congers. *See* **cegnor cehnos cehors cenors**

ceghorsu grouches scourge. *See* **cehors cehosu cehrsu ceorsu**

cegiiln ceiling. *See* **ceiln cgiln egiin**

cegiilns ceilings ceiling slicing. *See* **ceiins ceilns cgiins cgilns**

cegiinnt enticing. *See* **ceiint cgiint egiint**

cegiinnv evincing. *See* **egiin eginv cgiin**

cegiinp piecing. *See* **egiinp cgiin**

cegiinpr piercing piecing pricing. *See* **ceginr ceiinp ceinpr cgiinr**

cegiinrt reciting citrine crinite igniter inciter neritic tricing. *See* **ceginr ceiint ceiint ceinrt**

cegiinsx excising. *See* **ceiins cgiins eginsx eiinsx**

cegiintv evicting. *See* **ceiint cgiint egiint eiintv**

cegiintx exciting exiting. *See* **ceiint cgiint egiint**

cegiiost egoistic. *See* **cegist egiost**

cegikkln keckling kecking. *See* **ceikln**

cegikkn kecking. *See* **egikn**

cegiklnr clerking clinger clinker cringle crinkle erlking recking. *See* **ceginr ceikln ceiknr egilnr**

cegiknn necking. *See* **egikn**

cegiknnr ringneck kerning necking recking. *See* **ceginr ceiknr**

cegiknp pecking. *See* **egikn**

cegiknps specking pecking. *See* **ceikns**

cegiknr recking. *See* **ceginr ceiknr**

cegiknrw wrecking recking crewing. *See* **ceginr ceiknr ceikrw**

cegilnpu cupeling. *See* **ceginu ceilnp ceilnu cgilnu**

cegilnr clinger cringle. *See* **ceginr egilnr**

cegilnrs cringles clinger cringes cringle lingers. *See* **ceginr ceilns ceilrs cgilns**

cegilnry glycerin clinger cringle glycine relying. *See* **ceginr ceglry ceilny cginry**

cegilnsy glycines glycine. *See* **ceilns ceilny cgilns egilns**

cegilnw clewing. *See* **ceiln cgiln egiln**

cegilny   glycine. *See* ceilny cgiln eginy

ceginnor   encoring corning. *See* ceginr cegnor cginno cginor

ceginnoz   cozening cognize. *See* cginno ginnoz

ceginnrt   centring renting. *See* ceginr ceinrt einnrt

ceginns   censing. *See* eginns ceins

ceginnst   scenting censing nesting tensing. *See* cegist ceinst eginns eginst

ceginoop   geoponic cooping. *See* cginoo cginop eginop

ceginooz   zoogenic cognize. *See* cginoo ginooz

ceginors   cosigner congers cringes cronies ignores regions scoring. *See* ceginr cegnor ceinos ceiors

ceginorv   covering corvine. *See* ceginr cegnor ceinov ceiorv

ceginorw   cowering crewing crowing. *See* ceginr cegnor ceiorw cginor

ceginosz   cognizes cognize. *See* ceinos cenosz

ceginotv   coveting vetoing. *See* cegnot ceinot ceinov cginov

ceginoz   cognize. *See* cenoz

ceginr   cringe nicer reign grin nice rein rice ring erg gie gin ice ire rec reg rig en er in ne re

ceginrs   cringes. *See* ceginr eginrs

ceginrst   cresting cistern cretins cringes resting stinger. *See* ceginr cegist ceinrt ceinst

ceginrsu   recusing rescuing securing cringes cursing reusing. *See* ceginr ceginu ceinsu ceirsu

ceginrsw   screwing crewing cringes swinger. *See* ceginr ceinsw eginrs eginsw

ceginrw   crewing. *See* ceginr ceinw ginrw

ceginsux   excusing. *See* ceginu ceinsu eginsu eginsx

ceginu   cueing cuing nice cue gie gin gnu gun ice en in ne nu

cegist   gestic cites cist cite egis gest gets gies gist ices sect site tics ties get gie ice its set sic sit tic tie is it si ti

cegko   gecko coke cog ego keg oke go

cegkos   geckos gecko cokes cogs coke egos goes kegs okes sego skeg sock soke cog ego keg kos oke go os so

cegllory   glycerol. *See* ceglry cglloy

ceglnoo   cologne. *See* celno cgnoo clnoo

ceglnoos   colognes cologne console. *See* celnos cgnoos clnoos eglnos

ceglnoty   cogently. *See* cegnot cegnty eglnty

ceglooty   cetology ecology. *See* celoot ceooty

ceglooy   ecology. *See* egooy

ceglossu   glucoses glucose. *See* celoss celosu ceossu

ceglosu   glucose. *See* celosu cglos eglsu

ceglry   clergy grey gyre lyre rely cry erg gel gey leg lye rec reg rye el er re ye

cegnnpuy   pungency. *See* ennpy gnnuy

cegnor   conger crone genro goner recon cero cone core corn goer gone gore ogre once cog con cor ego eon erg nog nor one orc ore rec reg roc roe en er go ne no on or re

cegnors   congers. *See* cenors cegnor egnors

cegnorss   congress censors congers engross. *See* cegnor cenors cenoss ceorss

cegnorsu   scrounge congers scourge surgeon. *See* cegnor cenors cenosu ceorsu

cegnorsy   cryogens congers cryogen. *See* cegnor cenors cenosy egnors

cegnory   cryogen. *See* cegnor cenoy cnory

cegnosst   congests congest. *See* cegnot cenoss cenost censst

cegnost   congest. *See* cegnot cenost

cegnot   cogent cento cent cone cote gent gone note once tone tong cog con cot ego eon get got net nog not one ten toe tog ton en go ne no on to

cegnruy   urgency. *See* egnruy

cegnsty   cygnets. *See* cegnty censty

cegnty   cygnet cent gent get gey net ten yen yet en ne ye

cegorr   grocer corer crore roger cero core goer gore ogre cog cor ego erg err orc ore rec reg roc roe er go or re

cegorrs   grocers. *See* ceorrs cegorr

cegorry   grocery. *See* cegorr ceory

cegorssu   scourges courses grouses scourge sources sucrose. *See* ceorss ceorsu ceossu cerssu

cegorsu   scourge. *See* ceorsu egorsu

cehhirs   cherish. *See* cehirs

cehhist   hitches. *See* cehist

cehhnsu   hunches. *See* chhnu

cehhoos   hooches. *See* cehoos chhoo

cehhstu   hutches. *See* cehstu chhtu

cehiillr   chillier chiller hillier. *See* chiill

cehiilnt   lecithin ichnite. *See* cehiln cehint ceiilt ceilnt

cehiilot   eolithic. *See* cehlot ceiilt chiilt ehilot

cehiils   chilies. *See* cehils chiil

cehiimpt   mephitic. *See* cehim chimp cehit

cehiinr   hircine. *See* cehinr ceiinr

cehiinst   ichnites ethnics ichnite incites. *See* cehins cehint cehist cehnst

cehiint   ichnite. *See* chiint cehint ceiint

cehiipps   chippies hippies. *See* ehiipp

cehiiprr   chirpier. *See* cehipr cehirr ceiprr

cehiirt   itchier. *See* cehirt

cehiistt   ethicist itchiest theistic. *See* cehist cehitt chistt ehistt

cehikmos   homesick echoism. *See* cehims cehkos

cehiknru   chunkier. *See* cehinr cehknu ceiknr chinru

cehiknst   kitchens thickens ethnics kitchen thicken. *See* cehins cehint cehist cehkst

cehiknsw   chewinks chewink winches. *See* cehins ceikns ceinsw chikns

cehiknt   kitchen thicken. *See* cehint chikn cehkn

cehiknw   chewink. *See* cehin cehnw ehinw

cehikrt   thicker. *See* cehirt ceikrt

cehikstt   thickest thickets thicket tickets. *See* cehist cehitt cehkst ceiktt

cehiksy   hickeys. *See* cehiky cehks chiks

cehiktt   thicket. *See* cehitt ceiktt

cehiky   hickey heck hick hike icky yech chi hey hie ice icy key eh he hi ye

cehillr   chiller. *See* chill ceilr eillr

cehillrs   chillers schiller chiller. *See* cehils cehirs ceilrs chills

cehillsy   chiselly. *See* cehils chills chilly ehllsy

cehiln   lichen chine cline niche ceil chin inch lech lice lien line nice chi hen hie hin ice lei lie nil eh el en he hi in li ne

cehilno   choline helicon. *See* cehiln chino celno

cehilnop   pinochle choline chopine helicon pinhole. *See* cehiln ceilnp ceilop chinop

cehilnor   chlorine choline helicon. *See* cehiln cehinr cehior cehlor

cehilnos   helicons choline helicon inclose lichens. *See* cehiln cehils cehins cehnos

cehilns   lichens. *See* cehins cehils ceilns cehiln

cehilort   clothier chortle. *See* cehior cehirt cehlor cehlot

cehilpty   phyletic. *See* ceilpy celpty

cehilrsv   chervils chervil shrivel. *See* cehils cehirs cehisv ceilrs

cehilrv   chervil. *See* eilrv ceilr

cehils   chisel ceils slice ceil hies ices isle lech leis lice lies chi els hie his ice lei lie she sic eh el he hi is li sh si

cehilss   chisels. *See* cehils ceilss

cehilsz   zilches. *See* cehils chilz

cehim   chime hemic mice chi hem hie him ice eh em he hi me mi

cehimmru   chummier. *See* ceimru cemmru ehimru eimmru

cehimnpt   pitchmen. *See* cehint ceinpt eimnpt

cehimnsu   munchies munches inhumes. *See* cehims cehins ceimns ceimsu

cehimnsy chimneys chimney. *See* **cehims cehins ceimns ehmnsy**

cehimny chimney. *See* **cehim cehin cehmy**

cehimos echoism. *See* **cehims cehos cemos**

cehimoss echoisms echoism schmoes. *See* **cehims cehoss ceioss chimss**

cehimrss smirches chrisms. *See* **cehims cehirs ceimrs ceirss**

cehimrt thermic. *See* **cehirt ehimrt ceimrt**

cehims chimes chime hemic mesic hems hies ices mesh mice mise semi shim chi hem hie him his ice mis she sic eh em he hi is me mi sh si

cehimsst chemists chemist theisms. *See* **cehims cehist cehsst chimss**

cehimst chemist. *See* **cehims cehist ehimst**

cehin chine niche chin inch nice chi hen hie hin ice eh en he hi in ne

cehinnrt intrench cithern thinner. *See* **cehinr cehint cehirt cehnrt**

cehinoos cohesion. *See* **cehins cehnos cehoos ceinos**

cehinop chopine. *See* **chinop cehin cehop**

cehinopt phonetic chopine. *See* **cehint ceinot ceinpt ceiopt**

cehinopu euphonic chopine. *See* **cenopu chinop**

cehinpr phrenic. *See* **cehipr cehinr ceinpr**

cehinprs pinchers ciphers phrenic pincers pinches princes spheric. *See* **cehinr cehins cehipr cehirs**

cehinpru punchier phrenic puncher. *See* **cehinr cehipr ceinpr chinru**

cehinps pinches. *See* **cehins**

cehinr enrich chine nicer niche chin heir hern hire inch nice rein rice rich chi hen her hie hin ice ire rec eh en er he hi in ne re

cehinrss richness shiners shrines. *See* **cehinr cehins cehirs ceirss**

cehinrst christen citherns cistern cithern cithers cretins ethnics hinters richest. *See* **cehinr cehins cehint cehirs**

cehinrt cithern. *See* **cehirt ceinrt cehinr cehint ehinrt**

cehins chines inches niches chine chins niche shine since chin hens hies hins ices inch nice shin sine chi ens hen hie hin his ice sen she sic sin eh en he hi in is ne sh si

cehinsst snitches ethnics insects. *See* **cehins cehint cehist cehnst**

cehinst ethnics. *See* **cehins cehist cehint ceinst chinst**

cehinstz chintzes ethnics zechins zeniths. *See* **cehins cehint cehinz cehist**

cehinsw winches. *See* **cehins ehinsw ceinsw**

cehinsz zechins. *See* **cehins cehinz**

cehint ethnic chine ethic niche tench thine cent chin chit cite etch hent hint inch itch nice tech then thin tine chi eth hen het hie hin hit ice net nit ten the tic tie tin eh en he hi in it ne ti

cehinz zechin chine niche chin inch nice zein zinc chi hen hie hin ice eh en he hi in ne

cehioors choosier coheirs heroics. *See* **cehior cehirs cehoos cehors**

cehioppr choppier chipper chopper. *See* **cehior cehipr ceiopr ceoppr**

cehiopru euphoric. *See* **cehior cehipr ceiopr ceopru**

cehiops hospice. *See* **cehops ceiops**

cehiopss hospices hospice. *See* **cehops cehoss ceiops ceioss**

cehior coheir heroic choir chore ichor ocher ochre cero coir core echo heir hero hire hoer rice rich chi cor her hie hoe ice ire orc ore rec rho roc roe eh er he hi ho oh or re

cehiorrt rhetoric heritor. *See* **cehior cehirr cehirt cehort**

cehiors coheirs heroics. *See* **chiors cehors cehior ceiors ehiors**

cehiortu touchier retouch. *See* **cehior cehirt cehort ceiort**

cehippr chipper. *See* **cehipr ehippr**

cehipprs chippers chipper ciphers shipper spheric. *See* **cehipr cehirs ceiprs chiprs**

cehipr cipher chirp perch price chip epic heir hire peri pice pier rice rich ripe cep chi hep her hie hip ice ire per pie rec rep rip eh er he hi pe pi re

cehiprs ciphers spheric. *See* **chiprs cehipr ehiprs ceiprs cehirs**

cehiprst pitchers ciphers cithers hipster pitcher pitches richest spheric. *See* **cehipr cehirs cehirt cehist**

cehiprt pitcher. *See* **cehipr cehirt**

cehipst pitches. *See* **cehist ceipst**

cehiqstu quitches quiches. *See* **cehiqu cehist cehstu ceistu**

cehiqsu quiches. *See* **cehiqu**

cehiqu quiche chi cue hie hue ice eh he hi

cehirr richer chirr crier hirer ricer heir hire rice rich chi err her hie ice ire rec eh er he hi re

cehirs riches cries heirs hires rices shire heir hers hies hire ices reis resh rice rich rise sire chi her hie his ice ire rec res she sic sir eh er he hi is re sh si

cehirst cithers richest. *See* **cehrst cehirt cehist ceirst ehirst**

cehirstt chitters chitter cithers hitters richest stretch. *See* **cehirs cehirt cehist cehitt**

cehirsty hysteric cithers richest. *See* **cehirs cehirt cehist cehrst**

cehirsu cushier. *See* **ceirsu cehirs cehrsu**

cehirsz scherzi. *See* **cehirs**

cehirt cither thrice chert ethic retch their trice chit cite etch heir hire itch rice rich rite tech tier tire chi eth her het hie hit ice ire rec ret the tic tie eh er he hi it re ti

cehirtt chitter. *See* **cehirt ehirtt cehitt**

cehirtwy witchery. *See* **cehirt cehrtw ehirtw ehitwy**

cehisstt stitches theists. *See* **cehist cehitt cehsst chisst**

cehisstu cushiest ictuses. *See* **cehist cehsst cehstu ceissu**

cehisstw switches witches. *See* **cehist cehsst chisst chistw**

cehist ethics itches chest chits cites ethic heist stich techs chit cist cite etch hest hies hist hits ices itch sect site sith tech this tics ties chi eth het hie his hit ice its set she sic sit the tic tie eh he hi is it sh si ti

cehisttw twitches wettish whitest witches. *See* **cehist cehitt chistt chistw**

cehistw witches. *See* **cehist chistw ehistw**

cehisv chives hives shive vices hies hive ices shiv vice vies vise chi hie his ice she sic vie eh he hi is sh si

cehit ethic chit cite etch itch tech chi eth het hie hit ice the tic tie he hi it ti

cehitt thetic ethic tithe chit cite etch itch tech teth chi eth het hie hit ice the tic tie tit eh he hi it ti

cehk heck eh he

cehkkru chukker. *See* **cehru**

cehklmo hemlock. *See* **cehko**

cehklmos hemlocks hemlock. *See* **cehkos**

cehklsu huckles. *See* **cehklu ceklsu**

cehklu huckle clue heck hulk lech luce luck cue elk hue lek leu eh el he

cehkn kench heck neck hen ken eh en he ne

cehknpuy keypunch. *See* **cehknu chknuy chnpuy**

cehknu kuchen kench chunk heck hunk neck neuk nuke cue hen hue ken eh en he ne nu

cehko choke coke echo heck hock hoke hoe oke eh he ho oh

cehkor choker choke chore ocher ochre cero coke core cork echo heck hero hock hoer hoke reck rock cor her hoe kor oke orc ore rec rho roc roe eh er he ho oh or re

cehkors chokers shocker. *See* **cehkor cehkos cehors ehkors cekors**

cehkorss shockers chokers coshers shocker. *See* **cehkor cehkos cehors cehoss**

cehkos chokes choke chose cokes hecks hocks hokes shock coke cosh echo heck hock hoes hoke hose okes shoe sock soke hoe kos ohs oke she eh he ho oh os sh so

cehkoy chokey hockey choke choky hokey coke echo heck hock hoke yech yock yoke coy hey hoe hoy key oke eh he ho oh oy ye

cehkpstu ketchups ketchup. *See* **cehkst cehstu**

cehkptu ketchup. *See* **cehkt cehtu**

cehkrssu shuckers crushes huskers shucker suckers. *See* **cehrsu cekrsu cerssu chkssu**

cehkrstu huckster shucker. *See* **cehkst cehrst cehrsu cehstu**

cehkrsu shucker. *See* **ehkrsu cehrsu cekrsu**

cehks hecks heck she eh he sh

cehkst sketch chest hecks ketch techs etch heck hest khet sect tech eth het set she the tsk eh he sh

cehksty sketchy. *See* **cehsty cehkst**

cehkt ketch etch heck khet tech eth het the eh he

cehktv kvetch ketch vetch etch heck khet tech eth het the vet eh he

cehl lech eh el he

cehlmsu mulches. *See* **celmsu chmsu ehlms**

cehlnnou luncheon nucleon. *See* **celno chlnu cenno**

cehlnrsy lynchers lyncher lynches. *See* **cehly ehnry ehlrs**

cehlnry lyncher. *See* **cehly ehnry chlny**

cehlnsu lunches. *See* **celnsu chlnu**

cehlnsy lynches. *See* **cehly chlny chnsy**

cehlor choler ceorl chore ocher ochre cero cole core echo herl hero hoer hole lech loch lore orle role col cor her hoe orc ore rec rho roc roe eh el er he ho lo oh or re

cehlorst chortles chortle clothes colters costrel hectors holster hostler lectors rochets rotches torches troches. *See* **cehlor cehlot cehors cehort**

cehlort chortle. *See* **cehlor cehlot celort cehort**

cehlossu slouches chouses housels. *See* **cehoss cehosu celoss celosu**

cehlost clothes. *See* **celost chlost ehlost**

cehlot clothe cloth hotel letch thole celt clot cole colt cote echo etch hole holt lech loch loth tech col cot eth het hoe

hot let lot the tho toe eh el he ho lo oh to

cehlpps schlepp. *See* **ehlpps**

cehlppss schlepps schlepp shlepps. *See* **ehlpps ehlpss**

cehlqsu squelch. *See* **celsu**

cehlrsu lurches. *See* **chlrsu cehrsu celrsu**

cehlt letch celt etch lech tech eth het let the eh el he

cehly chyle lech yech hey lye eh el he ye

cehmnsu munches. *See* **chmsu emnsu chmnu**

cehmoor moocher. *See* **cehmor chmoo**

cehmoors moochers chromes moocher mooches. *See* **cehmor cehoos cehors cemoos**

cehmoos mooches. *See* **cehoos cemoos chmoos**

cehmooss smooches chooses mooches schmoes schmoos. *See* **cehoos cehoss cemoos chmoos**

cehmoosz schmooze mooches. *See* **cehoos cemoos chmoos**

cehmoprs chompers chromes porches. *See* **cehmor cehops cehors cemors**

cehmor chrome chore comer homer ocher ochre cero come core corm echo herm hero hoer home more omer cor hem her hoe mho mor ohm orc ore rec rem rho roc roe eh em er he ho me mo oh om or re

cehmors chromes. *See* **cehors cehmor cemors ehmors**

cehmoss schmoes. *See* **cehoss cemos ehmos**

cehmsstu smutches. *See* **cehsst cehstu cesstu chmstu**

cehmy chyme yech cyme hem hey eh em he me my ye

cehnnopu puncheon. *See* **cenopu**

cehnnosu nonesuch. *See* **cehnos cehosu cenosu**

cehnoors schooner onshore. *See* **cehnos cehoos cehors cenors**

cehnorsv chevrons chevron. *See* **cehnos cehors cenors cenosv**

cehnorv chevron. *See* **cehor cenov ceorv**

cehnos chosen chose cones hones hosen scone shone cone cons cosh echo eons hens hoes hone hose noes nose nosh once ones shoe con ens eon hen hoe hon ohs one sen she son eh en he ho ne no oh on os sh so

cehnost notches. *See* **cenost cehnos ehnost cehnst**

cehnprsu punchers puncher punches. *See* **cehrsu ceprsu chnrsu ehprsu**

cehnpru puncher. *See* **chnru cehpr enpru**

cehnpsu punches. *See* **cepsu chnpu**

cehnqu quench cue hen hue eh en he ne nu

cehnrt trench chert retch tench cent etch hent hern rent tech tern then eth her het net rec ret ten the eh en er he ne re

cehnrw wrench wench chew crew hern hewn when wren hen her hew new rec wen eh en er he ne re we

cehnst stench cents chest hents scent techs tench cent etch hens hent hest nest nets sect sent tech tens then ens eth hen het net sen set she ten the eh en he ne sh

cehnsttu chestnut. *See* **cehnst cehstu cesttu ehnstt**

cehnstuy chutneys chutney. *See* **cehnst cehstu cehsty censty**

cehnsuu eunuchs. *See* **cehnuu cnsuu**

cehnt tench cent etch hent tech then eth hen het net ten the eh en he ne

cehntuy chutney. *See* **cehtu cetuy cehty**

cehnuu eunuch cue hen hue eh en he ne nu

cehnw wench chew hewn when hen hew new wen eh en he ne we

ceho echo hoe eh he ho oh

cehoops pooches. *See* **cehoos cehops**

cehoorst cheroots cheroot cohorts hectors rochets rotches scooter shooter torches troches. *See* **cehoos cehors cehort cehrst**

cehoort cheroot. *See* **cehort ehoort**

cehoos choose chose coos cosh echo hoes hose oohs shoe shoo coo hoe oho ohs ooh she eh he ho oh os sh so

cehooss chooses. *See* **cehoos cehoss**

cehop epoch chop cope echo hope cep cop hep hoe hop ope eh he ho oh pe

cehoppr chopper. *See* **ceoppr ehoppr**

cehopprs choppers chopper coppers hoppers porches shopper. *See* **cehops cehors ceoppr ceoprs**

cehoppry prophecy chopper. *See* **cehpry ceoppr ceopry choppy**

cehoprs porches. *See* **cehors ceoprs ehoprs cehops**

cehops epochs chops chose copes copse epoch hopes scope ceps chop cope cops cosh echo epos hoes hope hops hose opes peso pose posh scop shoe shop soph cep cop hep hoe hop ohs ope she sop eh he ho oh os pe sh so

cehopsu pouches. *See* **cehosu ceopsu cehops ehopsu**

cehor chore ocher ochre cero core echo hero hoer cor her hoe orc ore rec rho roc roe eh er he ho oh or re

cehors chores cosher ochers ochres ceros chore chose cores corse hoers horse ocher ochre score shoer shore cero core cors cosh echo hero hers hoer hoes hose orcs ores resh rhos rocs roes rose shoe sore cor her hoe ohs orc ore rec res rho roc roe she eh er he ho oh or os re sh so

cehorss coshers. *See* **cehors ceorss cehoss ehorss**

cehorssu choruses chouses coshers courses crushes sources sucrose. *See* **cehors cehoss cehosu cehrsu**

cehorssz scherzos coshers scherzo. *See* **cehors cehoss ceorss ceorsz**

cehorst hectors rochets rotches torches troches. *See* **cehrst cehors ceorst cehort ehorst**

cehorsuv vouchers voucher vouches. *See* **cehors cehosu cehrsu ceorsu**

cehorsz scherzo. *See* **cehors ceorsz**

cehort hector rochet rotche troche chert chore ocher ochre other recto retch throe torch cero core cote echo etch hero hoer rote tech tore cor cot eth her het hoe hot orc ore ort rec ret rho roc roe rot the tho toe tor eh er he ho oh or re to

cehortu retouch. *See* **cehort**

cehoruv voucher. *See* **cehor ceorv ceruv**

cehos chose cosh echo hoes hose shoe hoe ohs she eh he ho oh os sh so

cehoss coshes chess chose hoses shoes cess cosh echo hoes hose shoe ess hoe ohs she eh he ho oh os sh so

cehossu chouses. *See* **cehosu cehoss ehossu ceossu**

cehostu touches. *See* **cehosu cehstu**

cehosu chouse ouches chose hocus house cosh cues echo hoes hose hues ouch shoe such cue hoe hue ohs she sou sue use eh he ho oh os sh so us

cehosuv vouches. *See* **cehosu**

cehpr perch cep hep her per rec rep eh er he pe re

cehprsy cyphers. *See* **cehpry ehprsy**

cehpry cypher perch hyper hype prey pyre yech cep cry hep her hey per pry rec rep rye yep eh er he pe re ye

cehpssy psyches. *See* **cehss ehpsy chpsy**

cehrrssu crushers crusher crushes rushers. *See* **cehrsu cerrsu cerssu chrrsu**

cehrrsu crusher. *See* **chrrsu cerrsu cehrsu ehrrsu**

cehrry cherry yech cry err her hey rec rye eh er he re ye

cehrssu crushes. *See* **cerssu ehrssu**

cehrst cherts chert chest crest retch techs erst etch hers hest resh rest rets sect tech eth her het rec res ret set she eh er he re sh

cehrstt stretch. *See* **cehrst erstt**

cehrstty stretchy stretch. *See* **cehrst cehsty cehtty**

cehrsu ruches cruse crush cures curse ruche usher crus cues cure curs ecru hers hues resh rues ruse rush such sure user cue cur her hue rec res rue she sue use eh er he re sh us

cehrt chert retch etch tech eth her het rec ret the eh er he re

cehrtw wretch chert crwth retch threw chew crew etch tech thew whet eth her het hew rec ret the wet eh er he re we

cehru ruche cure ecru cue cur her hue rec rue eh er he re

cehss chess cess she ess eh he sh

cehsst chests chess chest hests sects techs cess etch hest sect sets tech ess eth het set she the eh he sh

cehssty scythes. *See* **cehsst cehsty ehssty**

cehst chest techs etch hest sect tech eth het set she the eh he sh

cehstu chutes chest chute scute techs cues cute cuts etch hest hues huts scut sect shut such suet tech thus tush cue cut eth het hue hut set she sue the use eh he sh us ut

cehsty chesty scythe chest techs techy cyst etch hest sect syce tech they yech eth het hey set she shy sty the thy yes yet eh he sh ye

cehsw chews chew hews shew hew sew she eh he sh we

ceht etch tech eth het the eh he

cehtty tetchy techy etch tech teth they yech eth het hey the thy yet eh he ye

cehtu chute cute etch tech cue cut eth het hue hut the eh he ut

cehtv vetch etch tech eth het the vet eh he

cehty techy etch tech they yech eth het hey the thy yet eh he ye

cehvy chevy yech hey eh he ye

cehw chew hew eh he we

cehwy chewy chew whey yech hew hey why wye yew eh he we ye

cehy yech hey eh he ye

cei ice

ceiiilvz civilize. *See* **ciilv**

ceiiinsv incisive. *See* **ceiins ceiisv**

ceiijru juicier. *See* **ceiru ceiir ceiju**

ceiijstu juiciest justice. *See* **ceiist ceijsu ceistu**

ceiikkr kicker. *See* **ceiikr ceikkr**

ceiikkst kickiest ickiest. *See* **ceiiks ceiist**

ceiiklmr limerick milkier. *See* **ceiikr ceiklm eiilmr eiklmr**

ceiiklrs sicklier slicker silkier. *See* **ceiikr ceiiks ceikls ceikrs**

ceiikmmr mimicker. *See* **ceiikr**

ceiikms mickies. *See* **ceiiks ceims eikms**

ceiikns kinesic. *See* **ceiins ceikns ceiiks**

ceiiknss ickiness kinesics iciness incises kinesic sickens. *See* **ceiiks ceiins ceikns ciknss**

ceiiknst kinetics ickiest incites inkiest kinesic kinetic. *See* **ceiiks ceiins ceiint ceiist**

ceiiknt kinetic. *See* **ceiint**

ceiikpr pickier. *See* **ceiikr ceikpr**

ceiikpst pickiest ickiest pickets skeptic. *See* **ceiiks ceiist ceikpt ceipst**

ceiikqsu quickies quickie. *See* **ceiiks**

ceiikqu quickie. *See* **cikqu**

ceiikr ickier icier kier reck rice rick ice ire irk kir rec er re

ceiikrrt trickier tricker. *See* **ceiikr ceikrt**

ceiikrst stickier eristic ickiest rickets sticker tickers. *See* **ceiikr ceiiks ceiist ceikrs**

ceiiks sickie ices sick ice sic ski is si

ceiikst ickiest. *See* **ceiist**

ceiillpt elliptic. *See* **ceiilt**

ceiilnn incline. *See* **ceiln eilnn iilnn**

ceiilnnr incliner incline. *See* **ceiinr eiilnr**

ceiilnns inclines incline. *See* **ceiins ceilns eilnns**

ceiilnos isocline silicone elision inclose silicon. *See* **ceiins ceilns ceinos celnos**

ceiilops policies polices. *See* **ceilop ceilps ceiops eilops**

ceiilotz zeolitic. *See* **ceiilt eiilot**

ceiilptx explicit. *See* **ceiilt ceiilx**

ceiilsss scissile. *See* **ceilss**

ceiilst elicits. *See* **ceiist ceiilt**

ceiilt elicit telic licit ceil celt cite lice tile ice lei let lie lit tic tie til el it li ti

ceiilx exilic ceil ilex lice ice lei lie el ex li xi

ceiimns menisci. *See* **eiimns ceiins ceimns**

ceiimost comities semiotic. *See* **ceiist cemost ciimot cimost**

ceiimpr empiric. *See* **ceimr cimpr ceiir**

ceiimprs empirics empiric spicier. *See* **ceimrs ceiprs cimprs eimprs**

ceiimss seismic. *See* **ceims eimss**

ceiimtt titmice. *No 6s or 5s*

ceiinnot nicotine. *See* **ceiint einnot ceinot .cenno**

ceiinor oneiric. *See* **ceiinr ciinor**

ceiinors recision cronies incisor ironies noisier oneiric. *See* **ceiinr ceiins ceinos ceiors**

ceiinosv invoices invoice novices. *See* **ceiins ceiisv ceinos ceinov**

ceiinosx excision. *See* **ceiins ceinos eiinsx**

ceiinotv eviction invoice. *See* **ceiint ceinot ceinov eiintv**

ceiinov invoice. *See* **ceinov ciino ciinv**

ceiinr irenic icier nicer ricin nice rein rice ice ire rec en er in ne re

ceiinrst citrines inciters cistern citrine cretins crinite eristic inciter incites neritic. *See* **ceiinr ceiins ceiint ceiist**

ceiinrt citrine crinite inciter neritic. *See* **ceinrt ceiint ceiinr ciinrt**

ceiins incise since ices nice nisi sine ens ice sen sic sin en in is ne si

ceiinss iciness incises. *See* **ceiins einss**

ceiinssu cuisines cuisine iciness incises incuses. *See* **ceiins ceinsu ceissu censsu**

ceiinst incites. *See* **ceiist ceinst ceiins ceiint**

ceiinstz citizens zincites citizen incites zincite. *See* **ceiins ceiint ceiist ceinst**

ceiinsu cuisine. *See* **ceiins ceinsu**

ceiint incite cent cite nice tine ice net nit ten tic tie tin en in it ne ti

ceiintz citizen zincite. *See* **ceiint**

ceiiopz epizoic. *No 6s or 5s*

ceiiprrs crispier crisper pricers spicier. *See* **ceiiprr ceiprs ceiirrs**

ceiiprs spicier. *See* **ceiprs ceiir**

ceiipsst spiciest. *See* **ceiist ceipss ceipst eiipst**

ceiiqrtu critique. *See* **ceiqru ceirtu**

ceiir icier rice ice ire rec er re

ceiirsst eristics eristic. *See* **ceiist ceirss ceirst cersst**

ceiirst eristic. *See* **ceiist ceirst**

ceiist cities iciest cites cist cite ices sect site tics ties ice its set sic sit tic tie is it si ti

ceiistvv vivisect civvies. *See* **ceiist ceistv ceiisv .iistv**

ceiisv civies vices ivies ices vice vies vise ice sic vie is si

ceiisvv civvies. *See* **ceiisv**

ceijnort injector. *See* **ceijnt ceinot ceinrt ceiort**

ceijnst injects. *See* **ceinst ceijnt**

ceijnt inject cent cite nice tine ice jet net nit ten tic tie tin en in it ne ti

ceijsstu justices justice ictuses. *See* **ceijsu ceissu ceistu cesstu**

ceijstu justice. *See* **ceijsu ceistu**

ceijsu juices juice ices cues cue ice jus sic sue use is si us

ceiju juice ice cue

ceikknrs knickers kickers nickers snicker. *See* **ceikkr ceiknr ceikns ceikrs**

ceikkr kicker keck kick kier kirk reck rice rick ice ire irk kir rec er re

ceikkrs kickers. *See* **ceikkr ceikrs**

ceiklm mickle clime melic ceil lice lick like lime mice mike mile milk elk elm ice ilk lei lek lie mel mil el em li me mi

ceiklms mickles. *See* **ceilms ceiklm ceikls**

ceikln nickel cline clink inkle liken ceil kiln kine lice lick lien like line link neck nice nick elk ice ilk ink ken kin lei lek lie nil el en in li ne

ceiklnr clinker crinkle. *See* **eiklnr ceikln ceiknr**

ceiklnrs clinkers crinkles clinker crinkle nickels nickers slicker snicker. *See* **ceikln ceikls ceiknr ceikns**

ceiklns nickels. *See* **ceilns ciklns eiklns ceikln ceikns**

ceiklosv lovesick. *See* **ceikls ceilsv ceiosv celosv**

ceiklp pickle ceil clip epic kelp kepi lice lick like peck pice pick pike pile cep elk ice ilk kip lei lek lie lip pie el li pe pi

ceiklpr prickle. *See* **ceiklp ceikpr**

ceiklprs prickles pickers pickles prickle slicker splicer. *See* **ceiklp ceikls ceikpr ceikrs**

ceiklpru pluckier luckier plucker prickle. *See* **ceiklp ceikpr ceklru cekpru**

ceiklps pickles. *See* **ceiklp ceikls ceilps**

ceiklrs slicker. *See* **ceklrs ceilrs ceikrs ceikls**

ceiklrss slickers sickles slicers slicker. *See* **ceikls ceikrs ceilrs ceilss**

ceiklrst stickler strickle ticklers trickles kilters kirtles relicts rickets slicker sticker stickle tickers tickler tickles trickle. *See* **ceikls ceiklt ceikrs ceikrt**

ceiklrt tickler trickle. *See* **eiklrt ceilrt ceikrt ceiklt**

ceiklru luckier. *See* **ceklru ceiru**

ceikls sickle ceils licks likes slice slick ceil elks ices isle leis leks lice lick lies like sick silk elk els ice ilk lei lek lie lis sic ski el is li si

ceiklss sickles. *See* **ceikls ceilss ciklss**

ceiklsst slickest stickles sickest sickles stickle tickles. *See* **ceikls ceiklt ceilss ciklss**

ceiklst stickle tickles. *See* **ceikls ceiklt**

ceiklstu luckiest stickle tickles. *See* **ceikls ceiklt ceilsu ceiltu**

ceiklt tickle telic ceil celt cite kilt kite lice lick like tick tike tile elk ice ilk kit lei lek let lie lit tic tie til el it li ti

ceikmnor monicker moniker. *See* **ceiknr ceimno ceimnr cekmor**

ceikmru muckier. *See* **ceimru cekmru**

ceikmstu muckiest. *See* **ceimsu ceistu eikmst eikmsu**

ceikmy mickey micky cyme icky mice mike ice icy key em me mi my ye

ceiknqsu quickens quicken quinces. *See* **ceikns ceinqu ceinsu**

ceiknqu quicken. *See* **ceinqu cikqu**

ceiknr nicker inker nicer kern kier kine neck nice nick reck rein rice rick rink ice ink ire irk ken kin kir rec en er in ne re

ceiknrs nickers snicker. *See* **eiknrs ceiknr ceikns ceikrs**

ceiknrss snickers nickers sickens sinkers snicker. *See* **ceiknr ceikns ceikrs ceirss**

ceiknrst stricken cistern cretins nickers rickets snicker sticker stinker tickers tinkers. *See* **ceiknr ceikns ceikrs ceikrt**

ceikns sicken necks nicks since skein snick ices inks kens kine neck nice nick sick sine sink skin ens ice ink ken kin sen sic sin ski en in is ne si

ceiknss sickens. *See* **ceikns eiknss ciknss**

ceiknsss sickness sickens. *See* **ceikns ciknss eiknss**

ceikoo cookie coke cook coo ice oke

ceikoos cookies. *See* **ceikoo cekos ckoos**

ceikorr corkier rockier. *See* **cekorr ceiorr**

ceikorst corkiest rockiest stockier restock rickets rockets sticker tickers. *See* **ceikrs ceikrt ceiors ceiort**

ceikpr picker piker price prick epic kepi kier peck peri perk pice pick pier pike reck rice rick ripe cep ice ire irk kip kir per pie rec rep rip er pe pi re

ceikprs pickers. *See* **ceikpr eikprs ceiprs cikprs ceikrs**

ceikprst prickets pickers pickets pricket rickets skeptic sticker tickers. *See* **ceikpr ceikpt ceikrs ceikrt**

ceikprt pricket. *See* **ceikpr ceikpt ceikrt**

ceikpsst skeptics pickets sickest skeptic. *See* **ceikpt ceipss ceipst cekpss**

ceikpst pickets skeptic. *See* **ceikpt ceipst**

ceikpt picket cite epic kepi kept kite peck pice pick pike tick tike cep ice kip kit pet pie pit tic tie tip it pe pi ti

ceikqru quicker. *See* **ceiqru cikqu**

ceikqstu quickest quickset. *See* **ceistu eiqstu**

ceikrrst trickers rickets sticker striker tickers tricker. *See* **ceikrs ceikrt ceirrs ceirst**

ceikrrt tricker. *See* **ceikrt ceirr**

ceikrrty trickery tricker rickety. *See* **ceikrt ceikry cikrty**

ceikrs sicker cries kiers recks rices ricks ices irks kier kris reck reis rice rick rise risk sick sire ice ire irk kir rec res sic sir ski er is re si

ceikrsst stickers rickets sickest sticker strikes tickers. *See* **ceikrs ceikrt ceirss ceirst**

ceikrst rickets sticker tickers. *See* **eikrst ceikrs ceirst cikrst ceikrt**

ceikrsw wickers. *See* **ceikrs ceikrw cekrsw**

ceikrsy rickeys. *See* **ceikrs ceikry**

ceikrt ticker kiter trice trick cite kier kite reck rice rick rite tick tier tike tire trek ice ire irk kir kit rec ret tic tie er it re ti

ceikrty rickety. *See* **ceikry ceikrt cikrty**

ceikruy yuckier. *See* **ceikry ceiru**

ceikrw wicker wreck crew kier reck rice rick weir wick wire ice ire irk kir rec er re we

ceikry rickey icky kier reck rice rick cry ice icy ire irk key kir rec rye er re ye

ceiksst sickest. *See* **ciksst ceist eikst**

ceikstt tickets. *See* **ceiktt ceist eikst**

ceikstuy yuckiest. *See* **ceistu cestuy ciksty**

ceikstw wickets. *See* **ceiktw eikstw**

ceiktt ticket cite kite tick tike ice kit tic tie tit it ti

ceiktw wicket twice cite kite tick tike wick wite ice kit tic tie wet wit it ti we

ceil ceil lice ice lei lie el li

ceillnou nucleoli. *See* **ceillo ceilnu cilnou eillno**

ceillo collie oleic cello ceil cell coil cole lice loci col ell ice ill lei lie oil el li lo

ceilloqu coquille. *See* **ceillo ceilqu**

ceillor collier. *See* **ceillo ceilor**

ceillors colliers collier collies recoils. *See* **ceillo ceilor ceilrs ceiors**

ceillory colliery collier. *See* **ceillo ceilor**

ceillos collies. *See* **ceillo cellos**

ceillsst cellists cellist. *See* **ceilss eillss eillst eilsst**

ceillst cellist. *See* **eillst ceils cells**

ceillsu cullies. *See* **ceilsu cillsu**

ceilm clime melic ceil lice lime mice mile elm ice lei lie mel mil el em li me mi

ceilmop compile polemic. *See* **ceilop celmop**

ceilmopr compiler compile crimple implore polemic. *See* **ceilop ceilor ceiopr celmop**

ceilmops compiles complies polemics compels compile polemic polices. *See* **ceilms ceilop ceilps ceiops**

ceilmoss solecism ossicle lissome. *See* **ceilms ceilss ceioss celoss**

ceilmpr crimple. *See* **eilmpr**

ceilmprs crimples crimple limpers rimples simpler splicer. *See* **ceilms ceilps ceilrs ceimrs**

ceilmrsu clumsier misrule. *See* **ceilms ceilrs ceilsu ceimrs**

ceilms climes ceils clime limes melic mesic miles slice slime smile ceil elms ices isle leis lice lies lime mels mice mile mils mise semi slim elm els ice lei lie mel mil mis sic el em is li me mi si

ceiln cline ceil lice lien line nice ice lei lie nil el en in li ne

ceilnoos colonies console coolies inclose. *See* **ceilns ceiloo ceinos celnos**

ceilnooz colonize. *See* **ceiloo**

ceilnos inclose. *See* **ceilns celnos cilnos ceinos eilnos**

ceilnoss incloses cession cosines inclose insoles lesions lioness oscines ossicle. *See* **ceilns ceilss ceinos celnos**

ceilnost lections clients entoils inclose lectins lection notices section stencil. *See* **ceilns ceilnt ceinos ceinot**

ceilnosx lexicons inclose lexicon. *See* **ceilns ceinos celnos celosx**

ceilnot lection. *See* **ceilnt eilnot ceinot**

ceilnox lexicon. *See* **ceiln celno cilno**

ceilnp pencil cline ceil clip epic lice lien line nice pice pile pine cep ice lei lie lip nil nip pen pie pin el en in li ne pe pi

ceilnpry princely. *See* **ceilnp ceilny ceilpy ceinpr**

ceilnps pencils. *See* **ceilns ceilnp eilnps ceilps**

ceilnruv culverin. *See* **ceilnu celnru celruv eilnuv**

ceilns clines ceils cline lenis liens lines since slice ceil ices isle leis lens lice lien lies line nice nils sine els ens ice lei lie lis nil sen sic sin el en in is li ne si

ceilnsst stencils clients enlists insects lectins listens stencil tinsels. *See* **ceilns ceilnt ceilss ceinst**

ceilnst clients lectins stencil. *See* **ceilnt ceilns eilnst ceinst**

ceilnt client lectin lentic cline inlet telic ceil celt cent cite lent lice lien line lint nice tile tine ice lei let lie lit net nil nit ten tic tie til tin el en in it li ne ti

ceilnu nuclei cline uncle ceil clue lice lien lieu line luce lune nice cue ice lei leu lie nil el en in li ne nu

ceilny nicely cline ceil inly lice lien line liny nice ice icy lei lie lye nil yen yin el en in li ne ye

ceilo oleic ceil coil cole lice loci col ice lei lie oil el li lo

ceiloo coolie oleic looie ceil coil cole cool lice loci loco oleo olio col coo ice lei lie loo oil el li lo

ceiloos coolies. *See* **ceiloo eiloos**

ceilop police oleic ceil clip coil cole cope epic lice loci lope pice pile pole cep col cop ice lei lie lip lop oil ope pie poi el li lo pe pi

ceilopps popsicle polices. *See* **ceilop ceilps ceiops eilops**

ceilops polices. *See* **ceiops eilops ceilop ceilps**

ceiloptu poultice couplet. *See* **ceilop ceiltu ceiopt celopu**

ceilor recoil ceorl oiler oleic oriel relic ceil cero coil coir cole core lice lire loci lore orle rice riel rile roil role col cor ice ire lei lie oil orc ore rec roc roe el er li lo or re

ceilors recoils. *See* **celors ceiors eilors ceilor ceilrs**

ceilorst cloister coistrel costlier colters costrel lectors lictors loiters recoils relicts toilers. *See* **ceilor ceilrs ceilrt ceiors**

ceiloss ossicle. *See* **celoss ceioss ceilss**

ceilosss ossicles ossicle. *See* **ceilss ceioss celoss**

ceilosst solecist solstice closest closets cosiest ossicle. *See* **ceilss ceioss celoss celost**

ceilossu coulisse ossicle sluices. *See* **ceilss ceilsu ceioss ceissu**

ceilotvy velocity. *See* **eilotv eiltvy**

ceilppr clipper cripple. *See* **eilppr ceipr ceilr**

ceilpprs clippers cripples clipper cripple ripples slipper splicer. *See* **ceilps ceilrs ceiprs eilppr**

ceilprs splicer. *See* **eilprs ceiprs ceilps**

ceilprss splicers lispers slicers splicer splices. *See* **ceilps ceilrs ceilss ceiprs**

ceilprsu surplice splicer scruple. *See* **ceilps ceilrs ceilsu ceiprs**

ceilps splice ceils clips epics piles slice spice spiel spile ceil ceps clip epic ices isle leis lice lies lips lisp pice pies pile slip cep els ice lei lie lip pie sic sip el is li pe pi si

ceilpss splices. *See* **ceilss ceipss eilpss ceilps**

ceilpv pelvic ceil clip epic evil lice live pice pile veil vice vile cep ice lei lev lie lip pie vie el li pe pi

ceilpy clypei ceil clip epic lice pice pile yelp yipe cep ice icy lei lie lip lye pie ply yep yip el li pe pi ye

ceilqsu cliques. *See* **ceilqu ceilsu**

ceilqu clique ceil clue lice lieu luce cue ice lei leu lie el li

ceilr relic ceil lice lire rice riel rile ice ire lei lie rec el er li re

ceilrs slicer ceils ceilr ceils cries relic rices riels riles slice ceil ices isle leis lice lies lire reis rice riel rile rise sire els ice ire lei lie rec res sic sir el er is li re si

ceilrss slicers. *See* **ceirss ceilrs ceilss**

ceilrst relicts. *See* **eilrst ceilrt ceirst**

ceilrsy clerisy. *See* **cilrsy ceilrs**

ceilrt relict liter litre relic telic tiler trice ceil celt cite lice lire rice riel rile rite tier tile tire ice ire lei let lie lit rec ret tic tie til el er it li re ti

ceils ceils slice ceil ices isle leis lice lies els ice lei lie sic el is li si

ceilss slices ceils isles slice ceil cess ices isle leis less lice lies els ess ice lei lie sic sis el is li si

ceilssu sluices. *See* **ceissu ceilss ceilsu**

ceilsu sluice ceils clues ileus luces slice ceil clue cues ices isle leis lice lies lieu luce lues slue cue els ice lei leu lie sic sue use el is li si us

ceilsv clevis ceils evils lives slice veils vices ceil evil ices isle leis lice lies live veil vice vies vile vise els ice lei lev lie lis sic vie el is li si

ceilt telic ceil celt cite lice tile ice lei let lie lit tic tie til el it li ti

ceiltu luetic culet cutie telic utile ceil celt cite clue cult cute etui lice lieu luce lute tile tule cue cut ice lei let leu lie lit tic tie til tui el it li ti ut

ceim mice ice em me mi

ceimmnno mnemonic. *See* **ceimno**

ceimmnou encomium meconium commune. *See* **ceimno cimmnu cimnou eimmnu**

ceimmosx commixes. *See* **cimmos cimmox eimosx**

ceimmrru crummier. *See* **ceimru cemmru eimmru emmru**

ceimmrsu scummier cummers immures rummies. *See* **ceimrs ceimru ceimsu ceirsu**

ceimn mince mice mien mine nice ice men nim em en in me mi ne

ceimnnoy neomycin. *See* **ceimno**

ceimno income mince cion coin come cone icon mice mien mine nice nome omen once con eon ice ion men mon nim one em en in me mi mo ne no om on

ceimnopy eponymic. *See* **ceimno cimopy emnopy**

ceimnors sermonic crimson cronies incomes merinos microns mincers. *See* **ceimno ceimnr ceimns ceimrs**

ceimnort intercom centimo. *See* **ceimno ceimnr ceimrt ceinot**

ceimnos incomes. *See* **ceinos ceimno ceimns eimnos**

ceimnost centimos centimo incomes moisten notices section. *See* **ceimno ceimns ceinos ceinot**

ceimnot centimo. *See* **ceimno ceinot**

ceimnr mincer crime mince miner nicer emir mice mien mine mire nice rein rice rime ice ire men mir nim rec rem rim em en er in me mi ne re

ceimnrs mincers. *See* **ceimrs ceimnr eimnrs**

ceimns minces mesic miens mince mines since ices mice mien mine mise nice

nims semi sine ens ice men mis nim sen sic sin em en in is me mi ne si

ceimnssu meniscus incuses minuses miscues. *See* **ceimns ceimsu ceinsu ceissu**

ceimoprs comprise copiers imposer promise semipro. *See* **ceimrs ceiopr ceiops ceiors**

ceimopt metopic. *See* **ceiopt cemot eimpt**

ceimorsx exorcism. *See* **ceimrs ceiors cemors eimosx**

ceimostv vicomtes costive motives vicomte. *See* **ceiosv ceistv cemost ceostv**

ceimott totemic. *See* **cemot emott ceott**

ceimotv vicomte. *See* **eimotv ceitv cemot**

ceimpsu pumices. *See* **ceimsu ceimpu**

ceimpu pumice epic mice pice puce cep cue cum cup emu ice imp pie ump em me mi mu pe pi um up

ceimr crime emir mice mire rice rime ice ire mir rec rem rim em er me mi re

ceimrs crimes cries crime emirs mesic mires miser rices rimes scrim emir ices mice mire mirs mise reis rice rime rims rise semi sire ice ire mir mis rec rem res rim sic sir em er is me mi re si

ceimrst metrics. *See* **ceimrs eimrst ceimrt ceirst**

ceimrt metric crime merit miter mitre remit timer trice cite emir emit item mice mire mite rice rime rite term tier time tire trim ice ire met mir rec rem ret rim tic tie em er it me mi re ti

ceimru cerium crime curie cure ecru emir mice mire rice rime uric cue cum cur emu ice ire mir rec rem rim rue rum em er me mi mu re um

ceims mesic ices mice mise semi ice mis sic em is me mi si

ceimssty systemic mystics stymies. *See* **cimsty eimsst eimsty emssty**

ceimssu miscues. *See* **ceimsu ceissu eimssu**

ceimsu cesium miscue mesic music cues emus ices mice mise muse scum semi cue cum emu ice mis mus sic sue sum use em is me mi mu si um us

ceimx cimex mice ice mix em ex me mi xi

cein nice ice en in ne

ceinnnot innocent. *See* **ceinot einnot**

ceinnorv conniver connive corvine environ. *See* **ceinov ceiorv**

ceinnosv connives connive novices venison. *See* **ceinos ceinov ceiosv cenosv**

ceinnotu continue unction. *See* **ceinot cinnou einnot**

ceinnov connive. *See* **ceinov cenno einnv**

ceinopr porcine. *See* **ceiopr einopr ceinpr**

ceinoprs conspire copiers cronies orpines pincers porcine princes. *See* **ceinos ceinpr ceiopr ceiops**

ceinoprv province porcine corvine. *See* **ceinov ceinpr ceiopr ceiorv**

ceinorr cornier. *See* **cenorr ceiorr einorr**

ceinors cronies. *See* **cenors ceinos ceiors einors**

ceinorss necrosis censors cession cosines cronies oscines seniors. *See* **ceinos ceiors ceioss ceirss**

ceinorst corniest cistern citrons cornets cretins cronies notices orients section stonier. *See* **ceinos ceinot ceinrt ceinst**

ceinorsu coinsure cronies. *See* **ceinos ceinsu ceiors ceirsu**

ceinortt contrite cittern cottier. *See* **ceinot ceinrt ceiort cenort**

ceinortu neurotic counter recount routine ruction trounce. *See* **ceinot ceinrt ceiort ceirtu**

ceinortv contrive corvine convert. *See* **ceinot ceinov ceinrt ceiort**

ceinorv corvine. *See* **ceinov ceiorv**

ceinos conies cosine oscine cions coins cones eosin icons noise scion scone since sonic cion coin cone cons eons ices icon ions nice noes nose once ones sine con ens eon scion one sen sic sin son en in is ne no on os si so

ceinoss cession cosines oscines. *See* **ceinos ceioss einoss cinoss cenoss**

ceinosss cessions cosiness cession cosines oscines session. *See* **ceinos ceioss cenoss cinoss**

ceinosst sections cession consist cosiest cosines insects nosiest notices oscines section tocsins. *See* **ceinos ceinot ceinst ceioss**

ceinost notices section. *See* **cenost ceinos ceinst ceinot cinost**

ceinostu counties contuse notices section suction. *See* **ceinos ceinot ceinst ceinsu**

ceinosv novices. *See* **ceinos cenosv ceinov ceiosv**

ceinot noetic notice cento tonic cent cion cite coin cone cote icon into nice note once otic tine tone con cot eon ice ion net nit not one ten tic tie tin toe ton en in it ne no on ti to

ceinov novice coven ovine voice cion coin cone cove icon nevi nice once oven vein vice vine con eon ice ion one vie en in ne no on

ceinpr prince nicer price ripen epic nice peri pice pier pine pirn rein rice ripe cep ice ire nip pen per pie pin rec rep rip en er in ne pe pi re

ceinprs pincers princes. *See* **ceiprs ceinpr einprs**

ceinprss princess pincers princes snipers. *See* **ceinpr ceiprs ceipss ceirss**

ceinpsst inspects incepts insects inspect insteps pectins spinets. *See* **ceinpt ceinst ceipss ceipst**

ceinpst incepts inspect pectins. *See* **ceinpt ceinst einpst ceipst**

ceinpt incept pectin inept cent cite epic nice pent pice pine pint tine cep ice net nip nit pen pet pie pin pit ten tic tie tin tip en in it ne pe pi ti

ceinqsu quinces. *See* **ceinsu ceinqu einqsu**

ceinqu quince nice ice cue en in ne nu

ceinr nicer nice rein rice ice ire rec en er in ne re

ceinrsst cisterns cistern cretins insects inserts sinters. *See* **ceinrt ceinst ceirss ceirst**

ceinrst cistern cretins. *See* **ceinrt ceinst einrst ceirst**

ceinrstt centrist citterns cistern cittern cretins. *See* **ceinrt ceinst ceirst cinstt**

ceinrt cretin inert inter nicer niter trice trine cent cite nice rein rent rice rite tern tier tine tire ice ire net nit rec ret ten tic tie tin en er in it ne re ti

ceinrtt cittern. *See* **ceinrt einrtt**

ceinrttu tincture cittern nuttier. *See* **ceinrt ceirtu certtu einrtt**

ceins since ices nice sine ens ice sen sic sin en in is ne si

ceinsst insects. *See* **ceinst einsst censst**

ceinssu incuses. *See* **censsu ceissu ceinsu**

ceinst incest insect nicest cents cites inset scent since stein tines cent cist cite ices nest nets nice nits sect sent sine site snit tens tics ties tine tins ens ice its net nit sen set sic sin sit ten tic tie tin en in is it ne si ti

ceinsty cystine. *See* **censty ceinst ceinty**

ceinsu incuse since incus cues ices nice sine cue ens ice sen sic sin sue sun use en in is ne nu si us

ceinsw winces since sinew swine wince wines ices news nice sewn sine wens wine wins wise ens ice new sen sew sic sin wen win wis en in is ne si we

ceinttx extinct. *See* **cintt**

ceinty nicety cent cite city nice tine tiny yeti ice icy net nit ten tic tie tin yen yet yin en in it ne ti ye

ceinw wince nice wine ice new wen win en in ne we

ceioost cooties. *See* **ceioot eioost**

ceioot cootie cootie cite coot cote otic coo cot ice tic tie toe too it ti to

ceiopprs croppies copiers coppers. *See* **ceiopr ceiops ceiors ceiprs**

ceiopr copier price cero coir cope core crop epic peri pice pier pore repo rice ripe rope cep cop cor ice ire ope orc ore per pie poi pro rec rep rip roc roe er or pe pi re

ceioprru croupier courier procure. *See* **ceiopr ceiorr ceiprr ceopru**

ceioprs copiers. *See* **ceiopr ceiops ceoprs ceiors ceiprs**

ceioprsu precious copiers piceous recoups soupier. *See* **ceiopr ceiops ceiors ceiprs**

ceiops copies copes copse epics poise scope spice ceps cope cops epic epos ices opes peso pice pies pois pose scop cep cop ice ope pie poi sic sip sop is os pe pi si so

ceiopssu specious piceous. *See* **ceiops ceioss ceipss ceissu**

ceiopst poetics. *See* **ceiops ciopst ceiopt ceipst**

ceiopsu piceous. *See* **ceiops ceopsu**

ceiopsw cowpies. *See* **ceiops ceiopw**

ceiopt poetic optic picot topic cite cope cote epic otic pice poet tope cep cop cot ice ope pet pie pit poi pot tic tie tip toe top it pe pi ti to

ceiopw cowpie cope epic pice wipe cep cop cow ice ope owe pew pie poi woe ow pe pi we

ceiorr corrie corer crier crore ricer cero coir core rice cor err ice ire orc ore rec roc roe er or re

ceiorrs cirrose corries crosier. *See* **ceorrs ceiorr ceiors ceirrs eiorrs**

ceiorrsu couriers cirrose corries courier courser crosier cruiser curries scourer. *See* **ceiorr ceiors ceirrs ceirsu**

ceiorrtu courtier courier recruit. *See* **ceiorr ceiort ceirtu ceorrt**

ceiorru courier. *See* **ceiorr ceiru cioru**

ceiorruz cruzeiro courier crozier. *See* **ceiorr ceiorz**

ceiorrz crozier. *See* **ceiorr ceiorz**

ceiors cosier ceros coirs cores corse cries osier rices score cero coir core cors ices orcs ores reis rice rise rocs roes rose sire sore sori cor ice ire orc ore rec res roc roe sic sir er is or os re si so

ceiorstu outcries icterus scouter. *See* **ceiors ceiort ceirst ceirsu**

ceiorstv vortices costive vectors victors. *See* **ceiors ceiort ceiorv ceiosv**

ceiorstx exorcist coexist exotics. *See* **ceiors ceiort ceiotx ceirst**

ceiorsvy viceroys viceroy. *See* **ceiors ceiorv ceiosv ceorsv**

ceiorsw cowries. *See* **ceiors ceorsw ceiorw**

ceiort erotic recto toric trice cero cite coir core cote otic rice riot rite rote tier tire tiro tore tori trio cor cot ice ire orc ore ort rec ret roc roe rot tic tie toe tor er it or re ti to

ceiortt cottier. *See* **ceortt ceiort ciortt**

ceiorv voicer cover vireo voice cero coir core cove over rice rive rove vice cor ice ire orc ore rec rev roc roe vie er or re

ceiorvy viceroy. *See* **ceiorv ceovy ceory**

ceiorw cowrie cower cero coir core crew crow rice weir wire wore cor cow ice ire orc ore owe rec roc roe row woe er or ow re we

ceiorz cozier croze cero coir core rice zero zori cor coz ice ire orc ore rec roc roe er or re

ceioss cosies cess ices ess ice sic sis is os si so

ceiosst cosiest. *See* **ceioss ceosst ciosst**

ceiosstx coexists coexist cosiest exotics. *See* **ceioss ceiotx ceosst ciosst**

ceiostv costive. *See* **ceistv ceostv eiostv ceiosv**

ceiostx coexist exotics. *See* **ceiotx ceist ceost**

ceiosty society. *See* **ceosty ceist ciost**

ceiostz coziest. *See* **ceist ceost**

ceiosv voices coves vices voice cove ices vice vies vise ice sic vie is os si so

ceiotx exotic toxic cite cote exit otic cot cox ice tic tie toe ex it ox ti to xi

ceiov voice vice cove ice vie

ceip epic pice cep ice pie pe pi

ceippt peptic pice epic pice pipe cep ice pep pet pie pip pit tic tie tip it pe pi ti

ceipr price epic peri pice pier rice ripe cep ice ire per pie rec rep rip er pe pi re

ceiprr pricer crier price prier ricer epic peri pice pier rice ripe cep err ice ire per pie rec rep rip er pe pi re

ceiprrs crisper pricers. *See* **ceirrs ceiprr ceiprs eiprrs**

ceiprrss crispers crisper pricers. *See* **ceiprr ceiprs ceipss ceirrs**

ceiprs prices cries crisp epics piers price pries rices scrip spice spire ceps epic ices peri pice pier pies reis reps rice ripe rips rise sire cep ice ire per pie rec rep res rip sic sip sir er is pe pi re si

ceiprst triceps. *See* **ceiprs ceipst ceirst ciprst**

ceiprstu pictures picture icterus. *See* **ceiprs ceipst ceirst ceirsu**

ceiprsy spicery. *See* **ceiprs ciprsy**

ceiprtu picture. *See* **ceirtu ceprt eprtu**

ceips epics spice ceps epic ices pice pies cep ice pie sic sip is pe pi si

ceipss spices epics specs spice spies ceps cess epic ices pice pies sips cep ess ice pie sic sip sis is pe pi si

ceipst septic cites epics spice spite stipe ceps cist cite epic ices pest pets pice pies pits sect sept site spit step tics ties tips cep ice its pet pie pit set sic sip sit tic tie tip is it pe pi si ti

ceiqrsu cirques. *See* **ceiqru ceirsu eiqrsu**

ceiqru cirque curie quire cure ecru rice uric cue cur ice ire rec rue er re

ceir rice ice ire rec er re

ceirr crier ricer rice err ice ire rec er re

ceirrrsu curriers cruiser currier curries. *See* **ceirrs ceirsu cerrsu**

ceirrru currier. *See* **ceirr ceiru cerru**

ceirrs criers ricers crier cries ricer rices riser errs ices reis rice rise sire err ice ire rec res sic sir er is re si

ceirrssu cruisers cruiser cruises curries. *See* **ceirrs ceirss ceirsu ceissu**

ceirrstt critters restrict critter. *See* **ceirrs ceirst cirstt eirrtt**

ceirrstu crustier recruits cruiser curries icterus recruit rustier. *See* **ceirrs ceirst ceirsu ceirtu**

ceirrsu cruiser curries. *See* **cirrsu ceirrs ceirsu cerrsu**

ceirrtt critter. *See* **eirrtt ceirr ceirt**

ceirrtu recruit. *See* **ceirtu ceirr cerru**

ceirruv curvier. *See* **ceirr ceiru ceruv**

ceirs cries rices ices reis rice rise sire ice ire rec res sic sir er is re si

ceirss crises cress cries rices rises sires cess ices reis rice rise sire sirs ess ice ire rec res sic sir sis er is re si

ceirsssu scissure cruises cuisses issuers. *See* **ceirss ceirsu ceissu cerssu**

ceirsstu citruses curtsies cruises icterus ictuses rustics. *See* **ceirss ceirst ceirsu ceirtu**

ceirssu cruises. *See* **ceirss ceirsu cerssu ceissu eirssu**

ceirssuv cursives cruises cursive viruses. *See* **ceirss ceirsu ceissu cerssu**

ceirst steric trices cites crest cries rices rites tiers tires trice tries cist cite erst ices reis rest rets rice rise rite sect sire site stir tics tier ties tire ice ire its rec res ret set sic sir sit tic tie er is it re si ti

ceirstu icterus. *See* **cirstu cerstu ceirsu ceistu ceirst**

ceirstuv curviest cursive curvets icterus virtues. *See* **ceirst ceirsu ceirtu ceistu**

ceirstuy security icterus curtsey. *See* **ceirst ceirsu ceirtu ceistu**

ceirsu cruise curies cries cruse cures curie curse rices crus cues cure curs ecru ices reis rice rise rues ruse sire sure uric

user cue cur ice ire rec res rue sic sir sue use er is re si us

ceirsuv cursive. *See* **ceirsu cersuv**

ceirsuzz scuzzier. *See* **ceirsu**

ceirt trice cite rice rite tier tire ice ire rec ret tic tie er it re ti

ceirtu uretic cruet curet curie cuter cutie eruct trice truce uteri cite cure curt cute ecru etui rice rite tier tire true uric cue cur cut ice ire rec ret rue rut tic tie tui er it re ti ut

ceiru curie cure ecru rice uric cue cur ice ire rec rue er re

ceirvx cervix xeric rice rive vice ice ire rec rev rex vex vie er ex re xi

ceirx xeric rice ice ire rec rex er ex re xi

ceis ices ice sic is si

ceisssu cuisses. *See* **ceissu cesssu eisssu**

ceisstu ictuses. *See* **cesstu ceissu ceistu eisstu**

ceissu cuisse issue cess cues cuss ices sues uses cue ess ice sic sis sue use is si us

ceist cites cist cite ices sect site tics ties ice its set sic sit tic tie is it si ti

ceistu cuties cites cutie cutis etuis ictus scute suite cist cite cues cute cuts etui ices scut sect site suet suit tics ties tuis cue cut ice its set sic sit sue tic tie tui use is it si ti us ut

ceistv civets evicts cites civet evict vices cist cite ices sect site tics ties vest vets vice vies vise ice its set sic sit tic tie vet vie is it si ti

ceisv vices ices vice vies vise ice sic vie is si

ceit cite ice tic tie it ti

ceitu cutie cite cute etui cue cut ice tic tie tui it ti ut

ceitv civet evict cite vice ice tic tie vet vie it ti

ceitw twice cite wite ice tic tie wet wit it ti we

ceiv vice ice vie

cejkosy jockeys. *See* **cejkoy cekos cjkos**

cejkoy jockey jokey coke jock joey joke joky yock yoke coy joe joy key oke jo oy ye

cejloosy jocosely. *See* **cejoos**

cejnorru conjurer conjure. *See* **cejnou cenorr**

cejnorsu conjures conjure jounces. *See* **cejnou cenors cenosu ceorsu**

cejnoru conjure. *See* **cejnou cnoru cenor**

cejnosu jounces. *See* **cejnou cjnosu cenosu**

cejnou jounce ounce junco cone jeon once unco con cue eon joe one en jo ne no nu on

cejnrtuu juncture. *See* **enrtuu**

cejoos jocose coos joes coo joe jo os so

cejoprst projects project copters. *See* **ceoprs ceoprt ceorst eoprst**

cejoprt project. *See* **ceoprt**

cekk keck

cekklnru knuckler knuckle. *See* **ceklru celnru eklnru**

cekklnsu knuckles knuckle. *See* **ceklsu celnsu cklnsu**

cekklnu knuckle. *See* **celnu cklnu**

cekknor knocker. *See* **ceknor ckkno**

cekknors knockers knocker reckons. *See* **ceknor cekors cenors ckknos**

cekkop kopeck coke cope keck peck pock poke cep cop oke ope pe

cekkops kopecks. *See* **cekkop cekos ceops**

cekks kecks keck

ceklloov lovelock. *See* **cello celov**

cekllry clerkly. *See* **ceklr**

ceklssu luckless suckles. *See* **ceklsu cllssu kllssu**

ceklmsu muckles. *See* **ceklmu celmsu ceklsu**

ceklmu muckle clue culm luce luck muck mule cue cum elk elm emu lek leu lum mel el em me mu um

ceklnrsu clunkers ruckles lucerns. *See* **ceklrs ceklru ceklsu cekrsu**

ceklor locker clerk ceorl cero coke cole core cork koel lock lore orle reck rock role col cor elk kor lek oke orc ore rec roc roe el er lo or re

ceklors lockers. *See* **celors ceklrs ceklor cekors**

ceklorss rockless closers cresols lockers. *See* **ceklor ceklrs cekors celors**

ceklost lockets. *See* **celost ceklot cekost**

ceklot locket ketol celt clot coke cole colt cote koel lock toke col cot elk lek let lot oke toe el lo to

ceklpru plucker. *See* **ceklru cekpru**

ceklr clerk reck elk lek rec el er re

ceklrs clerks clerk recks elks leks reck elk els lek rec res el er re

ceklrstu truckles cluster cutlers ruckles truckle. *See* **ceklrs ceklru ceklsu cekrsu**

ceklrsu ruckles. *See* **ceklrs ceklru cekrsu ceklsu celrsu**

ceklrtu truckle. *See* **ceklru celrtu**

ceklru ruckle clerk cruel lucre ulcer clue cure curl ecru luce luck lure lurk reck ruck rule cue cur elk lek leu rec rue el er re

ceklssu suckles. *See* **ceklsu ckssu elssu**

ceklsu suckle clues luces lucks clue cues cusk elks leks luce luck lues slue suck sulk cue elk els lek leu sue use el us

cekmnost stockmen. *See* **cekost cemost cenost eknost**

cekmor mocker comer cero coke come core cork corm mock moke more omer reck rock cor kor mor oke orc ore rec rem roc roe em er me mo om or re

cekmors mockers. *See* **cemors cekmor cekors ekmors**

cekmory mockery. *See* **cekmor ckory ceory**

cekmrsu muckers. *See* **cekmru cekrsu**

cekmru mucker cure ecru muck murk reck ruck cue cum cur emu rec rem rue rum em er me mu re um

cekn neck ken en ne

ceknoosv convokes convoke. *See* **cenosv**

ceknoov convoke. *See* **cenov**

ceknor reckon crone krone recon cero coke cone conk core cork corn keno kern neck nock once reck rock con cor eon ken kor nor oke one orc ore rec roc roe en er ne no on or re

ceknors reckons. *See* **cenors cekors ceknor**

cekns necks neck kens ens ken sen en ne

ceko coke oke

cekoopr precook. *See* **cekoor ceoopr**

cekooprs precooks cookers coopers precook recooks. *See* **cekoor cekors ceoopr ceoprs**

cekoopsw cowpokes cowpoke. *See* **cekos ckoos coops**

cekoopw cowpoke. *No 6s or 5s*

cekoor cooker recook crook cero coke cook core cork reck rock rook coo cor kor oke orc ore rec roc roe er or re

cekoors cookers recooks. *See* **cekoor ckoors cekors**

cekoory cookery. *See* **cekoor**

cekoprst sprocket copters pockets restock rockets. *See* **cekopt cekors cekort cekost**

cekopst pockets. *See* **cekopt cekost**

cekopt pocket coke cope cote kept peck pock poet poke toke tope cep cop cot oke ope pet pot toe top pe to

cekorr corker rocker corer crore cero coke core cork reck rock cor err kor oke orc ore rec roc roe er or re

cekorrs corkers rockers. *See* **ceorrs cekorr**

cekorrty rocketry rectory. *See* **cekorr cekort ceorrt**

cekors ockers ceros cokes cores corks corse recks rocks score cero coke core cork cors okes orcs ores reck rock rocs roes rose sock soke sore cor kor kos oke orc ore rec res roc roe er or os re so

cekorsst restocks corsets costers escorts restock rockets sectors sockets stokers strokes. *See* **cekors cekort cekost ceorss**

cekorst restock rockets. *See* **ceorst cekort cekost ekorst**

cekort rocket recto cero coke core cork cote reck rock rote toke tore trek cor cot kor oke orc ore ort rec ret roc roe rot toe tor er or re to

cekos cokes coke okes sock soke oke kos os so

cekosst sockets. *See* **ceosst cekost ckosst ekosst**

cekost socket cokes cotes stock stoke tokes coke cost cote cots okes scot sect sock soke toes toke cot kos oke set sot toe tsk os so to

cekp peck cep pe

cekprsu puckers. *See* **cekpru ceprsu cekrsu**

cekpru pucker cure ecru peck perk puce puck puke pure reck ruck cep cue cup cur per rec rep rue er pe re up

cekpruy puckery. *See* **cekpru ekpry**

cekps pecks speck ceps peck skep cep pe

cekpss specks pecks speck specs ceps cess peck skep cep ess pe

cekr reck rec er re

cekrrstu truckers trucker. *See* **cekrsu cerrsu cerstu ckrstu**

cekrrtu trucker. *See* **certu cerru ckrtu**

cekrs recks reck rec res er re

cekrssu suckers. *See* **cerssu cekrsu**

cekrssuu ruckuses suckers. *See* **cekrsu cerssu ckrsuu**

cekrsu sucker cruse cures curse recks rucks crus cues cure curs cusk ecru reck ruck rues ruse rusk suck sure user cue cur rec res rue sue use er re us

cekrsw wrecks crews recks screw wreck crew reck skew rec res sew er re we

cekrw wreck reck crew rec er re we

ceksttu tuckets. *See* **cekttu cesttu**

cekttu tucket cute tuck cue cut tut ut

cell cell ell el

cellnoo colonel. *See* **cello celno clnoo**

cellnoos colonels colonel console. *See* **cellos celnos clnoos elnoos**

cellnsuu nucellus nucleus. *See* **celnsu ellnsu**

cellntuu luculent. *See* **celltu celntu**

cello cello cell cole col ell el lo

cellos cellos cello cells close coles losel socle cell cole cols ells lose sell sloe sole col ell els los sol el lo os so

cellosy closely. *See* **cellos ellosy**

cellrrsu crullers cruller curlers. *See* **cellrru celrsu cerrsu**

cellrru cruller. *See* **celrru**

cellrsuy scullery cruelly. *See* **celrsu elrsuy**

cellruy cruelly. *See* **celru clluy clruy**

cells cells cell ells sell ell els el

cellstu cullets. *See* **celstu celtu ellstu**

celltu cullet culet tulle cell celt clue cull cult cute luce lute tell tule cue cut ell let leu el ut

celmnoo monocle. *See* **celno clnoo elmno**

celmnoos monocles monocle console. *See* **celnos cemoos clnoos elmnos**

celmop compel clomp cole come comp cope lope mole mope poem pole pome cep col cop elm lop mel mop ope el em lo me mo om pe

celmops compels. *See* **celmop clmops**

celmopx complex. *See* **celmop**

celmoy comely cloy cole come cyme mole moly ylem col coy elm lye mel el em lo me mo my om oy ye

celmprsu crumples crumple rumples scruple. *See* **celmsu celpsu celrsu ceprsu**

celmprtu plectrum crumple crumpet. *See* **celrtu cemrtu elmpru**

celmpru crumple. *See* **elmpru clmpu celru**

celmpsuu speculum cupules. *See* **celmsu celpsu celpuu clmpsu**

celmssu muscles. *See* **celmsu elmssu**

celmsu muscle clues culms luces mules clue cues culm elms emus luce lues mels mule muse scum slue slum cue cum elm els emu leu lum mel mus sue sum use el em me mu um us

celmsuy lyceums. *See* **clmsuy celmuy elmsuy celmsu**

celmuy lyceum muley clue culm cyme luce mule ylem yule cue cum elm emu leu lum lye mel yum el em me mu my um ye

celnnou nucleon. *See* **celno cenno cenou**

celno clone cole cone enol leno lone noel once col con eon one el en lo ne no on

celnos console. *See* **celnos clnoos elnoos**

celnooss consoles coolness console consols loosens. *See* **celnos celoss cenoss clnoos**

celnoovv convolve. *See* **celnov**

celnopuu uncouple. *See* **celopu celpuu cenopu**

celnor cornel ceorl clone crone loner recon cero cole cone core corn enol leno lone lore lorn noel once orle role col con cor eon nor one orc ore rec roc roe el en er lo ne no on or re

celnors cornels. *See* **cenors celors celnos celnor elnors**

celnorwy clownery. *See* **celnor elorwy**

celnos clones clone close coles cones noels scone socle cole cols cone cons enol eons leno lens lone lose noel noes nose once ones sloe sole col con els ens eon los one sen sol son el en lo ne no on os so

celnossu counsels counsel consuls. *See* **celnos celnsu celoss celosu**

celnosu counsel. *See* **celnos clnosu celosu cenosu celnsu**

celnosuv convulse counsel. *See* **celnos celnov celnsu celosu**

celnosvy solvency conveys. *See* **celnos celnov celosv cenosv**

celnov cloven clone clove coven novel cole cone cove enol leno lone love noel once oven vole col con eon lev one el en lo ne no on

celnovxy convexly. *See* **celnov cenovx cenovy**

celnrsu lucerns. *See* **celnru celrsu celnsu**

celnru lucern cruel lucre ulcer uncle clue cure curl ecru luce lune lure rule rune cue cur leu rec rue run urn el en er ne nu re

celnsu uncles clues luces lunes uncle clue cues lens luce lues lune slue cue els ens leu sen sue sun use el en ne nu us

celnsuu nucleus. *See* **celnsu cnsuu**

celntu lucent uncle culet celt cent clue cult cute lent luce lune lunt lute tule tune cue cut let leu net nut ten tun el en ne nu ut

celnu uncle clue luce lune cue leu el en ne nu

celo cole col el lo

celoopr precool. *See* **celoor ceoopr eloopr**

celooprs precools coolers coopers loopers precool. *See* **celoor celors ceoopr ceoprs**

celoopss cesspool. *See* **celoss ceopss coopss elooss**

celoor cooler ceorl color cero cole cool core loco lore oleo orle col coo cor loo orc ore rec roc roe el er lo or re

celoorr recolor. *See* **celoor ceorr**

celoorrs recolors recolor coolers. *See* **celoor celors ceorrs cloors**

celoors coolers. *See* **celors cloors celoor eloors**

celoost coolest ocelots. *See* **celoot celost**

celoot ocelot celt clot cole colt cool coot cote loco loot oleo tool col coo cot let loo lot toe too el lo to

celoprsu couplers closure colures coupler couples leprous recoups scruple. *See* **celopu celors celoru celosu**

celopru coupler. *See* **celoru celopu ceopru**

celopstu couplets couples couplet tupelos. *See* **celopu celost celosu celpsu**

celopsu couples. *See* **celosu ceopsu celopu celpsu**

celopttu octuplet couplet. *See* **celopu celttu eloptt eloptu**

celoptu couplet. *See* **celopu eloptu**

celopu couple cupel coupe clue cole cope coup lope luce pole puce pule cep col cop cue cup leu lop ope pul el lo pe up

celor ceorl cero cole core lore orle role col cor orc ore rec roc roe el er lo or re

celors ceorls closer cresol ceorl ceros close coles cores corse lores loser orles roles score socle cero cole cols core cors lore lose orcs ores orle rocs roes role rose sloe sole sore col cor els los orc ore rec res roc roe sol el er lo or os re so

celorss closers cresols. *See* **celors celoss ceorss elorss**

celorsst costrels crosslet closers closest closets colters corsets costers costrel cresols escorts lectors ostlers sectors sterols. *See* **celors celort celoss celost**

celorssu closures closers closure colures courses cresols sources sucrose. *See* **celors celoru celoss celosu**

celorst colters costrel lectors. *See* **celors celost celort ceorst elorst**

celorstu coulters closure cloture cluster colters colures costrel coulter cutlers lectors scouter. *See* **celors celort celoru celost**

celorsu closure colures. *See* **celors ceorsu celosu celoru celrsu**

celorsuu ulcerous urceolus closure colures. *See* **celors celoru celosu celrsu**

celorsv clovers. *See* **celors celorv celosv ceorsv elorsv**

celort colter lector ceorl recto celt cero clot cole colt core cote lore orle role rote rotl tore col cor cot let lot orc ore ort rec ret roc roe rot toe tor el er lo or re to

celortu cloture coulter. *See* **celort celoru celrtu**

celortvy covertly overtly. *See* **celort celorv ceortv elortv**

celoru colure ceorl cruel lucre ulcer cero clue cole cure cure curl ecru lore luce lure orle role rule col cor cue cur leu orc ore our rec roc roe rue el er lo or re

celorv clover ceorl clove cover lover cero cole core cove lore love orle over role rove vole col cor lev orc ore rec rev roc roe el er lo or re

celos close coles socle cole cols lose sloe sole col els los sol el lo os so

celoss closes close coles loess loses sloes socle soles cess cole cols less lose loss sloe sole sols col els ess los sol el lo os so

celosst closest closets. *See* **celoss celost ceosst elosst**

celost closet celts close clots coles colts cotes socle stole celt clot cole cols colt cost cote cots lest lets lose lost lots scot sect sloe slot sole toes col cot els let los lot set sol sot toe el lo os so to

celosttu culottes cutlets outlets scuttle. *See* **celost celosu celstu celttu**

celosu coleus close clues coles locus louse luces socle clue cole cols cues lose luce lues sloe slue sole soul col cue els leu los sol sou sue use el lo os so us

celosv cloves close clove coles coves loves socle solve voles cole cols cove lose love sloe sole vole col els lev los sol el lo os so

celosx scolex close coles coxes socle cole cols lose sloe sole col cox els los lox sex sol sox el ex lo os ox so

celov clove cole cove love vole col lev el lo

celoz cloze cole col coz el lo

celprssu scruples percuss scruple spruces. *See* **celpsu celrsu ceprsu cerssu**

celprsu scruple. *See* **celpsu elprsu ceprsu celrsu**

celpsu cupels clues cupel luces puces pules pulse sculp ceps clue cues cups cusp luce lues plus puce pule puls scup slue spue cep cue cup els leu pul pus sue sup use el pe up us

celpsuu cupules. *See* **celpsu celpuu**

celpsuy clypeus. *See* **celpsu elpsy elsuy**

celpty yclept celt lept pelt type yelp cep let lye pet ply yep yet el pe ye

celpu cupel clue luce puce pule cep cue cup leu pul el pe up

celpuu cupule cupel clue luce puce pule cep cue cup leu pul ulu el pe up

celrrsu curlers. *See* **celrru cerrsu elrrsu**

celrru curler cruel lucre recur ruler ulcer clue cure curl ecru luce lure rule cue cur err leu rec rue el er re

celrsstu clusters cluster cutlers results rustles ulsters. *See* **celrsu celrtu celstu cersst**

celrstu clutters cluster clutter cutlers cutlets cutters scuttle turtles. *See* **celrsu celrtu celstu celttu**

celrstu cluster cutlers. *See* **cerstu celstu celrtu elrstu celrsu**

celrstuu cultures cluster culture cutlers. *See* **celrsu celrtu celruu celstu**

celrstuv culverts cluster culvers culvert curvets cutlers. *See* **celrsu celrtu celruv celstu**

celrstuy clustery cluster cruelty curtsey cutlers cutlery. *See* **celrsu celrtu celstu celtuy**

celrsu ulcers clues cruel cruse cures curls curse luces lucre lures rules ulcer clue crus cues cure curl curs ecru luce lues lure rues rule ruse slue slur sure user cue cur els leu rec res rue sue use el er re us

celrsuv culvers. *See* celruv cersuv celrsu

celrsuw curlews. *See* celrsu celruw

celrttu clutter. *See* celrtu celttu certtu elrttu

celrtu cutler cruel cruet culet curet cuter eruct lucre truce ulcer celt clue cult cure curl curt cute ecru luce lure lute rule true tule cue cur cut let leu rec ret rue rut el er re ut

celrtuu culture. *See* celrtu celruu

celrtuv culvert. *See* celruv certuv celrtu

celrtuy cruelty cutlery. *See* clrtuy celtuy

celru cruel lucre ulcer clue cure curl ecru luce lure rule cue cur leu rec rue el er re

celruu curule cruel lucre ulcer clue cure curl ecru luce lure rule cue cur leu rec rue ulu el er re

celruv culver cruel curve lucre ulcer clue cure curl ecru luce lure rule cue cur leu lev luv rec rev rue el er re

celruw curlew cruel lucre ulcer clew clue crew cure curl ecru luce lure rule cue cur leu rec rue el er re we

celssttu scuttles cutlets scuttle. *See* celstu celttu cesstu cesttu

celsstuu cultuses. *See* celstu cesstu clstuu elsstu

celst celts celt lest lets sect els let set el

celsttu cutlets scuttle. *See* celstu cesttu celttu

celstu culets celts clues culet cults luces lutes scute tules celt clue cues cult cute cuts lest lets luce lues lust lute scut sect slue slut suet tule cue cut els let leu set sue use el us ut

celsu clues luces clue cues luce lues slue cue els leu sue use el us

celsw clews clew slew els sew el we

celt celt let el

celttu cutlet culet celt clue cult cute luce lute tule cue cut let leu tut el ut

celtu culet celt clue cult cute luce lute tule cue cut let leu el ut

celtuy cutely culet cutey celt clue cult cute luce lute tule yule cue cut let leu lye yet el ut ye

celu clue luce cue leu el

celux culex clue luce luxe cue leu lux el ex

celw clew el we

cemmnoor commoner. *See* cmmnoo

cemmnost comments comment moments. *See* cemost cenost emmnot emnost

cemmnosu communes commune consume. *See* cenosu mmnosu

cemmnot comment. *See* emmnot cenot cemot

cemmnou commune. *See* cenou

cemmortu commuter commute. *See* cemmru cemrtu

cemmostu commutes commute costume. *See* cemost cmostu

cemmotu commute. *See* cemot

cemmrsu cummers. *See* cemmru emmrsu

cemmru cummer cure ecru cue cum cur emu mem mum rec rem rue rum em er me mu re um

cemmnost contemns contemn consent. *See* cemost cenost emnost ennost

cemmnot contemn. *See* cenot cemot emnot

cemnooy economy. *See* cenoy emnoy mnooy

cemnoprs corpsmen. *See* cemors cenors ceoprs emnors

cemnoptt contempt. *See* enoptt

cemnorsu consumer consume. *See* cemors cenors cenosu ceorsu

cemnossu consumes consume. *See* cenoss cenosu censsu ceossu

cemnosu consume. *See* cenosu cemos emnsu

cemnrtu centrum. *See* cemntu cemrtu

cemntu centum cent cute menu mute tune cue cum cut emu men met net nut ten tun em en me mu ne nu um ut

cemo come em me mo om

cemooprs composer compose coopers. *See* cemoos cemors ceoopr ceoprs

cemoops compose. *See* cemoos cmoops

cemoopss composes compose. *See* cemoos ceopss cmoops cmooss

cemoopst compotes compose compost compote. *See* cemoos cemost cmoops emopst

cemoopt compote. *See* cemot cmoop emopt

cemoos comose comes moose come coos moos some coo moo mos oms em me mo om os so

cemoostu outcomes outcome costume. *See* cemoos cemost cmostu

cemootu outcome. *See* cemot

cemoprss compress corpses process. *See* cemors ceoprs ceopss ceorss

cemoprtu computer compute crumpet. *See* cemrtu ceoprt ceopru eoprtu

cemopstu computes compute costume. *See* cemost ceopsu cmostu emopst

cemoptu compute. *See* cemot ceopu

cemor comer cero come core corm more omer cor mor orc ore rec rem roc roe em er me mo om or re

cemors comers ceros comer comes cores corms corse mores omers score cero come core corm cors more mors omer orcs ores rocs roes rose some sore cor mor mos oms orc ore rec rem res roc roe em er me mo om or os re so

cemorstu customer costume rectums scouter scrotum. *See* cemors cemost cemrtu ceorst

cemos comes come some mos oms em me mo om os so

cemosstu costumes costume customs. *See* cemost ceosst ceossu cesstu

cemossy mycoses. *See* emossy cemos cemsy

cemost comets comes comet cotes motes smote tomes come cost cote cots most mote mots scot sect some stem toes tome toms cot met mos mot oms set sot toe tom em me mo om os so to

cemostu costume. *See* cemost cmostu

cemot comet come cote mote tome cot met mot toe tom em me mo om to

cemprstu crumpets spectrum crumpet rectums stumper sumpter. *See* cemrtu ceprsu cerstu cmprsu

cemprtu crumpet. *See* cemrtu ceprt cmpru

cemrruy mercury. *See* emrruy crruy cemry

cemrstu rectums. *See* cerstu emrstu cemrtu

cemrtu rectum cruet curet cuter eruct truce cure curt cute ecru mute term true cue cum cur cut emu met rec rem ret rue rum rut em er me mu re um ut

cemry mercy cyme cry rec rem rye em er me my re ye

cemsy cymes cyme syce yes em me my ye

cemy cyme em me my ye

cenno nonce cone neon none once con eon one en ne no on

cennoost connotes connote consent. *See* cenost cnoost ennost

cennoot connote. *See* cenot cnoot cenno

cennortu nocturne counter neutron nocturn recount trounce. *See* cennru cenort ennoru

cennosst consents consent sonnets. *See* cenoss cenost censst ceosst

cennost consent. *See* cenost ennost

cennostt contents consent content contest. *See* cenost ceostt ennost enostt

cennostv convents consent convent. *See* cenost cenosv ceostv ennost

cennott content. *See* cenot cenno ennot

cennotv convent. *See* cenot cenov ceotv

cennrssu scunners scunner. *See* cennru censsu cerssu enrssu

cennrsu scunner. *See* cennru cersu enrsu

cennru cunner cure ecru rune cue cur nun rec rue run urn en er ne nu re

ceno cone once con eon one en ne no on

cenoorr coroner. *See* **cenorr cnoor**

cenoorrs coroners corners coroner scorner. *See* **cenorr cenors ceorrs cnoors**

cenoorst coronets consort cornets coronet crotons scooter. *See* **cenors cenort cenost ceorst**

cenoorsu corneous onerous. *See* **cenors cenosu ceorsu cnoors**

cenoort coronet. *See* **cenort cnoort**

cenoorvy conveyor. *See* **cenovy cnoovy**

cenoprsy necropsy syncope. *See* **cenors cenosy ceoprs ceopry**

cenopssy syncopes syncope coyness. *See* **cenoss cenosy ceopss eopssy**

cenopsu pounces. *See* **ceopsu cenosu cenopu**

cenopsy syncope. *See* **cenosy ceops enops**

cenopty potency. *See* **cenot cenoy enopy**

cenopu pounce ounce coupe cone cope coup nope once open peon pone puce unco upon cep con cop cue cup eon one ope pen pun en ne no nu on pe up

cenoqrsu conquers conquer. *See* **cenors cenosu ceorsu enqrsu**

cenoqru conquer. *See* **cnoru cenor cenou**

cenoqstu conquest contuse coquets. *See* **cenost cenosu ceoqtu cnostu**

cenor crone recon cero cone core corn once con cor eon nor one orc ore rec roc roe en er ne no on or re

cenorr corner corer crone crore recon cero cone core corn once con cor eon err nor one orc ore rec roc roe en er ne no on or re

cenorrs corners scorner. *See* **cenors ceorrs cenorr enorrs**

cenorrss scorners censors corners crosser scorers scorner snorers. *See* **cenorr cenors cenoss ceorrs**

cenors censor crones recons ceros cones cores corns corse crone recon scone score scorn snore cero cone cons core corn cors eons noes nose once ones orcs ores rocs roes rose sore con cor ens eon nor one orc ore rec res roc roe sen son en er ne no on or os re so

cenorss censors. *See* **cenors ceorss cenoss cnorss enorss**

cenorst cornets. *See* **cenors cenost cenort ceorst enorst**

cenorstu construe counters recounts trounces contuse cornets counter encrust recount scouter tonsure trounce. *See* **cenors cenort cenost cenosu**

cenorstv converts convert cornets vectors. *See* **cenors cenort cenost cenosv**

cenorsuv uncovers uncover nervous. *See* **cenors cenosu cenosv ceorsu**

cenort cornet cento crone noter recon recto tenor toner cent cero cone core corn cote note once rent rote tern tone tore torn con cor cot eon net nor not one orc ore ort rec ret roc roe rot ten toe ton tor en er ne no on or re to

cenortu counter recount trounce. *See* **cenort cnoru cnotu**

cenortv convert. *See* **cenort ceortv**

cenoruv uncover. *See* **cnoru cenov ceorv**

cenos cones scone cone cons eons noes nose once ones con ens eon one sen son en ne no on os so

cenoss scones cones noses scone cess cone cons eons noes nose once ones sons con ens eon ess one sen son en ne no on os so

cenosstt contests contest stetson testons. *See* **cenoss cenost censst ceosst**

cenosstu contuses countess contuse. *See* **cenoss cenost cenosu censst**

cenossy coyness. *See* **cenoss cenosy**

cenost centos cento cents cones cotes notes onset scent scone steno stone tones cent cone cons cost cote cots eons nest nets noes nose note once ones scot sect sent snot tens toes tone tons con cot ens eon net not one sen set son sot ten toe ton en ne no on os so to

cenostt contest. *See* **cenost ceostt enostt**

cenostu contuse. *See* **cenost cnostu cenosu**

cenosu ounces cones ounce scone cone cons cues eons noes nose nous once ones onus unco con cue ens eon one sen son sou sue sun use en ne no nu on os so us

cenosv covens cones coven coves ovens scone cone cons cove eons noes nose once ones oven con ens eon one sen son en ne no on os so

cenosvy conveys. *See* **cenosy cenovy cenosv ceosvy enosvy**

cenosy coneys cones coney nosey scone cone cons cony cosy eons noes nose nosy once ones oyes syce sync yens con coy ens eon one sen son soy yen yes yon en ne no on os oy so ye

cenosz cozens cones cozen scone zones cone cons eons noes nose once ones zone con coz ens eon one sen son en ne no on os so

cenot cento cent cone cote note once tone con cot eon net not one ten toe ton en ne no on to

cenottx context. *See* **cenot ceott**

cenou ounce cone once unco con cue eon one en ne no nu on

cenov coven cone cove once oven con eon one en ne no on

cenovx convex coven cone cove exon once oven con cox eon one vex en ex ne no on ox

cenovy convey coney coven covey envoy cone cony cove envy once oven con coy eon one yen yon en ne no on oy ye

cenoy coney cone cony once con coy eon one yen yon en ne no on oy ye

cenoz cozen cone once zone con coz eon one en ne no on

cenprtuu puncture. *See* **enprtu**

cenrrstu currents current encrust returns. *See* **cerrsu cerstu enrrsu enrrtu**

cenrrtu current. *See* **enrrtu certu cerru**

cenrsstu encrusts encrust. *See* **censst censsu cersst cerssu**

cenrssuw unscrews unscrew. *See* **censsu cerssu cerssw enrssu**

cenrstu encrust. *See* **cerstu enrstu**

cenrsuw unscrew. *See* **cersw cersu enrsu**

cenrtuy century. *See* **certu cetuy enrty**

censst scents cents nests scent sects cent cess nest nets sect sent sets tens ens ess net sen set ten en ne

censsty encysts. *See* **censst censty**

censsu census cess cues cuss sues suns uses cue ens ess sen sue sun use en ne nu us

censt cents scent cent nest nets sect sent tens ens net sen set ten en ne

censty encyst cents scent cent cyst nest nets sect sent syce sync tens yens ens net sen set sty ten yen yes yet en ne ye

cent cent net ten en ne

ceoopr cooper cero coop cope core crop poor pore repo rope cep coo cop cor ope orc ore per pro rec rep roc roe er or pe re

ceooprs coopers. *See* **ceoopr ceoprs**

ceoopry coopery. *See* **ceoopr ceopry**

ceoorsst scooters corsets costers escorts scooter sectors. *See* **ceorss ceorst ceosst cersst**

ceoorst scooter. *See* **ceorst**

ceoostuv covetous. *See* **ceostv**

ceoosty coyotes oocytes. *See* **ceosty ceooty**

ceooty coyote oocyte cote coot coo cot coy toe too toy yet oy to ye

ceop cope cep cop ope pe

ceoppr copper cero cope core crop pope pore prep prop repo repp rope cep cop cor ope orc ore pep per pop pro rec rep roc roe er or pe re

ceopprr cropper. *See* **ceoppr eopprr**

ceopprrs croppers coppers cropper prosper. *See* **ceoppr ceoprs ceorrs eopprr**

ceopprs coppers. *See* **ceoppr ceoprs**

ceopprst prospect coppers copters stopper toppers. *See* **ceoppr ceoprs ceoprt ceorst**

ceoprrru procurer procure. *See* **ceopru**

ceoprrsu procures courser procure recoups scourer sprucer. *See* **ceoprs ceopru ceopsu ceorrs**

ceoprru procure. *See* **ceopru ceorr eprru**

ceoprs corpse ceros copes copse cores corps corse crops pores poser prose repos ropes scope score spore ceps cero cope cops core cors crop epos opes orcs ores peso pore pose pros repo reps rocs roes rope rose scop sore cep cop cor ope orc ore per pro rec rep res roc roe sop er or os pe re so

ceoprss corpses process. *See* **ceopss ceoprs ceorss eoprss**

ceoprst copters. *See* **ceoprt ceorst eoprst**

ceoprstt protects copters cotters potters protect protest spotter. *See* **ceoprs ceoprt ceorst ceortt**

ceoprsu recoups. *See* **ceorsu ceoprs coprsu ceopsu eoprsu**

ceoprsuu cupreous recoups cuprous. *See* **ceoprs ceopru ceopsu ceorsu**

ceoprt copter crept recto repot toper trope cero cope core cote crop pert poet pore port repo rope rote tope tore cep cop cor cot ope orc ore ort per pet pot pro rec rep ret roc roe rot toe top tor er or pe re to

ceoprtt protect. *See* **ceoprt ceortt eoprtt**

ceopru recoup coupe croup cero cope core coup crop cure ecru pore pour puce pure repo rope cep cop cor cue cup cur ope orc ore our per pro rec rep roc roe rue er or pe re up

ceopruv coverup. *See* **ceopru ceorv ceruv**

ceopry recopy coyer cero cope copy core crop pore prey pyre repo rope ropy yore cep cop cor coy cry ope orc ore per pro pry rec rep roc roe rye yep er or oy pe re ye

ceops copes copse scope ceps cope cops epos opes peso pose scop cep cop ope sop os pe so

ceopss copses scopes copes copse pesos poses posse scope scops specs ceps cope cops epos opes peso pose scop sops cep cop ess ope sop os pe so

ceopsu coupes copes copse coupe coups puces scope ceps cope cops coup cues cups cusp epos opes opus peso pose puce scop scup soup spue cep cop cue cup ope pus sop sou sue sup use os pe so up us

ceopu coupe cope coup puce cep cop cue cup ope pe up

ceoqrstu croquets coquets croquet questor quoters roquets scouter torques. *See* **ceoqtu ceorst ceorsu cerstu**

ceoqrtu croquet. *See* **ceoqtu eoqrtu**

ceoqrtuy coquetry croquet. *See* **ceoqtu cortuy eoqrtu**

ceoqstu coquets. *See* **ceoqtu eoqstu**

ceoqtu coquet quote toque cote cute cot cue cut out toe to ut

ceor cero core cor orc ore rec roc roe er or re

ceorr corer crore cero core cor err orc ore rec roc roe er or re

ceorrs corers crores scorer ceros corer cores corse crore score sorer cero core cors errs orcs ores rocs roes rose sore cor err orc ore rec res roc roe er or os re so

ceorrss crosser scorers. *See* **ceorrs ceorss**

ceorrssu scourers courser courses crosser cursors scorers scourer sources sucrose. *See* **ceorrs ceorss ceorsu ceossu**

ceorrst rectors. *See* **ceorrs ceorst ceorrt eorrst**

ceorrsu courser scourer. *See* **ceorsu ceorrs corrsu cerrsu eorrsu**

ceorrsy sorcery. *See* **ceorrs eorrsy**

ceorrt rector corer crore recto retro cero core cote rote tore torr cor cot err orc ore ort rec ret roc roe rot toe tor er or re to

ceorrty rectory. *See* **ceorrt ceory errty**

ceors ceros cores corse score cero core cors orcs ores rocs roes rose sore cor orc ore rec res roc roe er or os re so

ceorss corses crosse scores ceros cores corse cress cross roses score sores cero cess core cors orcs ores rocs roes rose sore cor ess orc ore rec res roc roe er or os re so

ceorsss crosses. *See* **ceorss**

ceorssst crossest corsets cossets costers crosses escorts sectors. *See* **ceorss ceorst ceosst cersst**

ceorsssu sucroses courses crosses sources sucrose. *See* **ceorss ceorsu ceossu cerssu**

ceorsst corsets costers escorts sectors. *See* **ceorss ceorst ceosst cersst eorsst**

ceorsstu scouters corsets costers courses escorts oestrus ousters scouter sectors sources sourest sucrose. *See* **ceorss ceorst ceorsu ceosst**

ceorssu courses sources sucrose. *See* **ceorsu ceorss cerssu eorssu corssu**

ceorssw escrows. *See* **ceorss ceorsw cerssw eorssw**

ceorst corset coster escort rectos scoter sector ceros cores corse cotes crest recto rotes score store cero core cors cost cote cots erst orcs ores orts rest rets rocs roes rose rote rots scot sect sore sort toes tore tors cor cot orc ore ort rec res ret roc roe rot set sot toe tor er or os re so to

ceorstt cotters. *See* **ceorst ceortt ceostt eorstt**

ceorstu scouter. *See* **ceorsu ceorst corstu cerstu eorstu**

ceorstuy courtesy scouter curtsey. *See* **ceorst ceorsu ceosty cerstu**

ceorstv vectors. *See* **ceorst ceorsv ceortv ceostv eorstv**

ceorsu cerous course source ceros cores corse cruse cures curse rouse score scour cero core cors crus cues cure curs ecru orcs ores ours rocs roes rose rues ruse sore sour sure user cor cue cur orc ore our rec res roc roe rue sou sue use er or os re so us

ceorsv corves covers ceros cores corse cover coves roves score servo verso cero core cors cove orcs ores over revs rocs roes rose rove sore cor orc ore rec res rev roc roe er or os re so

ceorsw cowers escrow ceros cores corse cower crews crows score screw serow sower swore worse cero core cors cows crew crow orcs ores owes rocs roes rose rows scow sore woes wore cor cow orc ore owe rec res roc roe row sew sow woe er or os ow re so we

ceorsz crozes ceros cores corse croze score zeros cero core cors orcs ores rocs roes rose zero coz orc ore rec res roc roe er or os re so

ceort recto cero core cote rote tore cor cot orc ore ort rec ret roc roe rot toe tor er or re to

ceortt cotter octet otter recto torte toter cero core cote rote tore tort tote tret trot cor cot orc ore ort rec ret roc roe rot toe tor tot er or re to

ceortuu couture. *See* **cortu certu eortu**

ceortv covert vector cover covet overt recto trove voter cero core cote cove over rote rove tore vert veto vote cor cot orc ore ort rec ret rev roc roe rot toe tor vet er or re to

ceortx cortex recto cero core cote rote tore cor cot cox orc ore ort rec ret rex roc roe rot toe tor er ex or ox re to

ceorv cover cero core cove over rove cor orc ore rec rev roc roe er or re

ceorw cower cero core crew crow wore cor cow orc ore owe rec roc roe row woe er or ow re we

ceory　coyer cero core yore cor coy cry orc ore rec roc roe rye er or oy re ye

ceorz　croze cero core zero cor coz orc ore rec roc roe er or re

ceossst　cossets. *See* **ceosst eossst**

ceosst　cosset costs cotes sects cess cost cote cots scot sect sets sots toes toss cot ess set sot toe os so to

ceossu　scouse souse cess cues cuss sous sues uses cue ess sou sue use os so us

ceost　cotes cost cote cots scot sect toes cot set sot toe os so to

ceostt　octets cotes octet totes cost cote cots scot sect stet test toes tost tote tots cot set sot toe tot os so to

ceostv　covets cotes coves covet stove votes cost cote cots cove scot sect toes vest veto vets vote cot set sot toe vet os so to

ceosty　coyest cotes cost cosy cote cots cyst oyes scot sect syce toes toys cot coy set sot soy sty toe toy yes yet os oy so to ye

ceosv　coves cove os so

ceosvy　coveys coves covey cosy cove oyes syce coy soy yes os oy so ye

ceosx　coxes cox sex sox ex os ox so

ceot　cote cot toe to

ceott　octet cote tote cot toe tot to

ceotv　covet cote cove veto vote cot toe vet to

ceov　cove

ceovy　covey cove coy ye oy

cep　cep pe

cepprrsu　cruppers crupper cuppers scupper sprucer. *See* **ceppru ceprsu cerrsu epprsu**

cepprru　crupper. *See* **ceppru eprru cerru**

cepprrssu　scuppers cuppers percuss scupper spruces suppers. *See* **ceppru ceprsu cerssu epprsu**

cepprsu　cuppers scupper. *See* **ceppru ceprsu epprsu**

cepprtuu　uppercut. *See* **ceppru**

ceppru　cupper upper cure ecru prep puce pure repp cep cue cup cur pep per pup rec rep rue er pe re up

ceprrsu　sprucer. *See* **eprrsu cerrsu ceprsu**

ceprrssu　percuss spruces. *See* **cerssu eprssu**

ceprssy　cypress. *See* **cerss eprss eprsy**

ceprstuu　cutpurse. *See* **ceprsu cerstu cpstuu eprstu**

ceprsu　spruce cruse cures curse puces purse sprue super ceps crus cues cups cure curs cusp ecru puce pure reps rues ruse scup spue spur sure user cep cue cup cur per pus rec rep res rue sue sup use er pe re up us

ceprt　crept pert cep per pet rec rep ret er pe re

ceps　ceps cep pe

cepss　specs ceps cess cep ess pe

cepssstu　suspects suspect. *See* **cesssu cesstu epsssu epsstu**

cepsstu　suspect. *See* **cesstu epsstu**

cepsu　puces ceps cues cups cusp puce scup spue cep cue cup pus sue sup use pe up us

cepu　puce cep cue cup pe up

cer　rec er re

cerrsu　recurs cruse cures curse recur surer crus cues cure curs ecru errs rues ruse sure user cue cur err rec res rue sue use er re us

cerru　recur cure ecru cue cur err rec rue er re

cerss　cress cess ess rec res er re

cersst　crests cress crest rests sects tress cess erst rest rets sect sets ess rec res ret set er re

cerssu　cruses curses cress cruse cures curse ruses users cess crus cues cure curs cuss ecru rues ruse sues sure user uses cue cur ess rec res rue sue use er re us

cerssw　screws cress crews screw cess crew sews ess rec res sew er re we

cerst　crest erst rest rets sect rec res ret set er re

cersttu　cutters. *See* **cerstu cesttu certtu ersttu**

cerstu　cruets curets eructs rectus truces crest cruet cruse crust cures curet curse curst cuter eruct scute truce trues crus cues cure curs curt cute cuts ecru erst rest rets rues ruse rust ruts scut sect suet sure true user cue cur cut rec res ret rue rut set sue use er re us ut

cerstuv　curvets. *See* **cerstu cersuv certuv**

cerstuy　curtsey. *See* **cerstu crstuy cestuy erstuy**

cersu　cruse cures curse crus cues cure curs ecru rues ruse sure user cue cur rec res rue sue use er re us

cersuv　curves cruse cures curse curve crus cues cure curs ecru revs rues ruse sure user cue cur rec res rev rue sue use er re us

cersux　cruxes cruse cures curse crus crux cues cure curs ecru rues ruse sure user cue cur rec res rex rue sex sue use er ex re us

cersw　crews screw crew rec res sew er re we

cerswy　screwy crews screw crew ryes syce wyes yews cry rec res rye sew wye yes yew er re we ye

certtu　cutter cruet curet cuter eruct truce utter cure curt cute ecru tret true cue cur cut rec ret rue rut tut er re ut

certu　cruet curet cuter eruct truce cure curt cute ecru true cue cur cut rec ret rue rut er re ut

certuv　curvet cruet curet curve cuter eruct truce cure curt cute ecru true vert cue cur cut rec ret rev rue rut vet er re ut

ceru　cure ecru cue cur rec rue er re

ceruv　curve cure ecru cue cur rec rev rue er re

cerw　crew rec er re we

cess　cess ess

cesssu　cusses cess cues cuss sues uses cue ess sue use us

cesst　sects cess sect sets ess set

cesstu　cestus scutes scute scuts sects suets cess cues cuss cute cuts scut sect sets sues suet uses cue cut ess set sue use us ut

cessy　syces cess syce ess yes ye

cest　sect set

cesttu　cutest scute cues cute cuts scut sect stet suet test tuts cue cut set sue tut use us ut

cestu　scute cues cute cuts scut sect suet cue cut set sue use us ut

cestuy　cutesy scute cutey cues cute cuts cyst scut sect suet syce cue cut set sty sue use yes yet us ut ye

cesu　cues cue sue use us

cesy　syce yes ye

cetu　cute cue cut ut

cetuy　cutey cute cue cut yet ye ut

ceu　cue

cffghinu chuffing cuffing huffing. *See* **cf-fhu cginu cfhiu**

cffginos scoffing coffins offings. *See* **cffino ffgino**

cffginsu scuffing cuffing. *See* **fginsu**

cffginu cuffing. *See* **cginu fginu**

cffhino chiffon. *See* **cffino cfhin chino**

cffhinos chiffons chiffon coffins. *See* **cffino chinos ffhios**

cffhsu chuffs chuff huffs scuff cuff huff such sh us

cffhu chuff cuff huff

cffhuy chuffy chuff huffy cuff huff

cffikko kickoff. *No 6s or 5s*

cffikkos kickoffs kickoff. *See* **cfios cikks ikkos**

cffil cliff if li

cffils cliffs cliff fisc fils ifs sic if is li si

cffino coffin cion coif coin fico foci icon con fin ion off if in no of on

cffinos coffins. *See* **cffino cinos cfios**

cffirtuy fructify. *See* **firtuy**

cffkknoo knockoff. *See* **ckkno**

cffos scoff off of os so

cffoss scoffs scoff foss off of os so

cffostu cutoffs. *See* **cffotu cfosu cffos**

cffotu cutoff cuff toff tofu tuff cot cut off oft out of to ut

cffrssu scruffs. *See* **cffrsu cffssu cfrssu**

cffrsu scruff ruffs scuff scurf crus cuff curs furs ruff surf cur fur us

cffrsuy scruffy. *See* **cffrsu cfrsuy**

cffssu scuffs scuff cuff cuss fuss us

cffsu scuff cuffs cuff us

cffu cuff

cfghiiln filching. *See* **cfhiln fgiiln**

cfgiikln flicking licking. *See* **fgiiln giikln**

cfgiklno flocking locking. *See* **cgikno**

cfgiknor frocking corking forcing forking rocking. *See* **cgikno cginor**

cfginor forcing. *See* **cginor**

cfginosu focusing congius. *See* **cinosu fginsu finosu**

cfhiiorr horrific. *See* **chirr chior ciirr**

cfhikors rockfish. *See* **cfkors chikrs chiors**

cfhil filch chi hi if li

cfhiln flinch filch finch chin inch chi fin hin nil hi if in li

cfhin finch chin inch chi fin hin hi if in

cfhisu fichus fichu fisc fish such chi his ifs sic hi if is sh si us

cfhit fitch chit itch chi fit hit tic hi if it ti

cfhiu fichu chi if hi

cfiiknny finnicky finicky. *See* **finny iiknn**

cfiikny finicky. *No 6s or 5s*

cfiilnst inflicts inflict. *See* **cfiist filnst iilnst**

cfiilnt inflict. *See* **ciilt filnt**

cfiilopr prolific. *See* **cfilor**

cfiinort friction fiction. *See* **ciinor ciinrt cinort finort**

cfinot fiction. *See* **ciino cinot**

cfiist fistic cist fisc fist fits sift tics fit ifs its sic sit tic if is it si ti

cfikl flick lick kif ilk if li

cfiklory frolicky. *See* **cfilor**

cfikls flicks flick licks slick fils fisc kifs lick sick silk ifs ilk kif sic ski if is li si

cfiklstu stickful. *See* **cfikls cfistu**

cfilor frolic coif coil coir corf fico floc foci foil loci roil col cor fir for fro oil orc rif roc if li lo of or

cfilors frolics. *See* **cfilor cfios cilos**

cfilrsuu sulfuric. *See* **flrsuu**

cfimnor confirm. *See* **cfimor fimnor cimnor**

cfimnors confirms confirm crimson informs microns. *See* **cfimor cimnor fimnor imnors**

cfimnoru unciform confirm uniform. *See* **cfimor cimnor cimnou cimoru**

cfimor formic micro coif coir corf fico firm foci form from cor fir for fro mir mor orc rif rim roc if mi mo of om or

cfimost comfits. *See* **cfimot fimost cimost**

cfimot comfit motif coif fico foci omit otic cot fit mot oft tic tom if it mi mo of om ti to

cfinnotu function unction. *See* **cinnou**

cfio coif fico foci if of

cfios coifs coif fico fisc foci sic ifs if is of os si so

cfis fisc sic ifs if is si

cfiss fiscs fisc ifs sic sis if is si

cfistu fustic cutis ictus cist cuts fisc fist fits scut sift suit tics tuis cut fit ifs its sic sit tic tui if is it si ti us ut

cfklo flock floc folk lock col of lo

cfklos flocks flock flocs folks locks cols floc folk lock sock col kos los sol lo of os so

cfkor frock corf cork fork rock cor for fro kor orc roc of or

cfkors frocks corks forks frock rocks corf cork cors fork orcs rock rocs sock cor for fro kor kos orc roc of or os so

cfkosttu futtocks futtock. *See* **cfosu costu ckost**

cfkottu futtock. *No 6s or 5s*

cfllooru colorful. *See* **clooru**

cflmrsuu fulcrums fulcrum. *See* **flrsuu**

cflmruu fulcrum. *No 6s or 5s*

cflnorsu scornful. *See* **clnosu florsu**

cflnoux conflux. *No 6s or 5s*

cflnouy flouncy. *No 6s or 5s*

cflo floc col of lo

cfloopsu scoopful. *See* **clops cloos coops**

cflos flocs floc cols col los sol lo of os so

cflpsuu cupfuls. *See* **cflpuu cfsuu lpsuu**

cflpuu cupful cup flu pul ulu up

cfmnoor conform. *See* **cnoor mnoor**

cfmnoors conforms conform. *See* **cnoors mnoors**

cfmoorst comforts comfort. *See* **cforst moorst**

cfmoort comfort. *See* **cfort moort**

cfmoy comfy coy foy mo my of om oy

cfnnoort confront. *See* **cnoort**

cfooortw crowfoot. *See* **cfort**

cfor corf cor for fro orc roc of or

cforst crofts croft forts frost corf cors cost cots fort orcs orts rocs rots scot soft sort tors cor cot for fro oft orc ort roc rot sot tor of or os so to

cfort croft corf fort cor cot for fro oft orc ort roc rot tor of or to

cfossuu fuscous. *See* **cfosu cfsuu**

cfosu focus sou of os so us

cfrssu scurfs scurf surfs crus curs cuss furs fuss surf cur fur us

cfrstuuu usufruct. *See* **crstu cfsuu cfrsu**

cfrsu scurf crus curs furs surf cur fur us

cfrsuy scurfy scurf surfy crus curs furs fury surf cry cur fry fur us

cfsuu fucus us

cggghinu chugging hugging. *See* **cginu**

cgggilno clogging cogging logging. *See* **ggilno**

cgggino cogging. *See* **ggino**

cgghinou coughing. *See* **chino cghou cginu**

cggiilnn clinging. *See* **giilnn**

cggiinnr cringing ringing. *See* **cgiinr**

cggloy cloggy clog cloy logy cog col coy goy log go lo oy

cghhiint hitching itching. *See* **cgiint chiint**

cghhinnu hunching. *See* **cginu chhnu**

cghhou chough cough chug ouch cog hog hug huh ugh go ho oh

cghiiknn chinking inching niching nicking. *See* **ghiikn giiknn**

cghiilln chilling hilling. *See* **chiill**

cghiimn chiming. *See* **cgiin**

cghiinn inching niching. *See* **cgiin**

cghiinnn chinning inching niching. *See* **giinnn**

cghiinnp pinching inching niching. *See* **giinnp**

cghiinnw winching inching niching whining wincing. *See* **giinnw**

cghiinor choiring. *See* **cgiino cgiinr cginor ghiinr**

cghiinpp chipping hipping. *See* **giinpp**

cghiinpr chirping pricing. *See* **cgiinr ghiinr giinpr**

cghiinpt pitching itching. *See* **cgiint chiint**

cghiint itching. *See* **cgiint chiint**

cghiintw witching itching whiting withing. *See* **cgiint chiint giintw hiintw**

cghikno choking hocking. *See* **cgikno ghikno**

cghiknos shocking choking coshing hocking hogskin socking. *See* **cgikno chikns chinos ghikno**

cghiknsu shucking sucking husking. *See* **chikns chknsu**

cghilmnnu mulching. *See* **cgilnu**

cghilnnu lunching. *See* **cgilnu**

cghilnny lynching. *See* **cgiln hinny ghiny**

cghilnot clothing tholing. *See* **cghilt chinot ghilno**

cghilnru lurching curling hurling. *See* **cgilnu cginru chinru gilnru**

cghilpy glyphic. *See* **ghlpy**

cghilt glitch licht light chit gilt hilt itch chi hit lit tic til hi it li ti

cghimmnu chumming humming. *See* **cimmnu**

cghimnnu munching. *See* **cginu cimnu chimu**

cghimnoo mooching. *See* **cgimno cginoo ghimno ghinoo**

cghimnop chomping comping. *See* **cgimno cginop chinop ghimno**

cghimnor chroming. *See* **cgimno cginor cimnor ghimno**

cghinno chignon. *See* **cginno ghinno**

cghinnos chignons chignon consign coshing noshing. *See* **cginno chinos ghinno ghinos**

cghinnot notching chignon nothing. *See* **cginno chinot ghinno ginnot**

cghinnpu punching. *See* **cginu chinp chnpu**

cghinnru churning. *See* **cginru chinru**

cghinoos choosing coshing shooing. *See* **cginoo cgnoos chinos ghinoo**

cghinopp chopping copping hopping. *See* **cginop chinop ghinop**

cghinopu pouching. *See* **cginop chinop ghinop**

cghinort torching. *See* **cginor chinot cinort ghiort**

cghinos coshing. *See* **chinos ghinos**

cghinosu chousing hocusing congius coshing cushion housing. *See* **cghosu chinos cinosu ghinos**

cghinotu touching. *See* **chinot ghnotu ginotu**

cghinouv vouching. *See* **cginov**

cghinpsy psyching. *See* **chipsy ghinpy ghinsy ginpsy**

cghinrsu crushing cursing rushing urchins. *See* **cginru chinru chnrsu cinrsu**

cghinsty scything. *See* **chinst ghinst ghinsy ghinty**

cghlosu cloughs. *See* **cghlou cghosu ghlosu chlosu**

cghlou clough cough ghoul gulch lough chug clog loch ouch cog col hog hug log lug ugh go ho lo oh

cghlu gulch chug hug lug ugh

cghoru grouch cough rough chug hour ouch cog cor cur hog hug orc our rho roc rug ugh go ho oh or

cghoruy grouchy. *See* **cghoru**

cghosu coughs chugs cough hocus chug cogs cosh gosh gush hogs hugs ouch such cog hog hug ohs sou ugh go ho oh os sh so us

cghou cough chug ouch cog hog hug ugh go ho oh

cghsu chugs chug gush hugs such hug ugh sh us

cghu chug hug ugh

cgiiinns incising. *See* **cgiins**

cgiiinnt inciting. *See* **cgiint**

cgiijnu juicing. *See* **cgiin cginu**

cgiikkn kicking. *See* **cgiin**

cgiikln licking. *See* **giikln cgiln cikln**

cgiiklnn clinking inkling licking linking nicking. *See* **giikln giiknn giilnn**

cgiiklnp pickling licking picking. *See* **giikln giiknp giilnp**

cgiiklns lickings licking sicking slicing. *See* **cgiins cgilns cikuns giikln**

cgiiklnt tickling kilting licking ticking. *See* **cgiint giikln giiknt giilnt**

cgiikmm gimmick. *See* **ciimm**

cgiikmms gimmicks gimmick. *See* **ciimms**

cgiikmmy gimmicky gimmick. *See* **ciimm cikmy**

cgiiknn nicking. *See* **giiknn cgiin**

cgiiknns snicking nicking sicking sinking. *See* **cgiins giiknn giikns**

cgiiknnz zincking nicking zincing. *See* **giiknn**

cgiiknp picking. *See* **giiknp cgiin**

cgiiknpr pricking picking pricing. *See* **cgiinr giiknp giiknr giinpr**

cgiiknps pickings picking pigskin sicking spicing spiking. *See* **cgiins giiknp giikns**

cgiiknrt tricking ticking tricing. *See* **cgiinr cgiint giiknr giiknt**

cgiikns sicking. *See* **cgiins giikns**

cgiiknst sticking sicking ticking. *See* **cgiins cgiint giikns giiknt**

cgiiknt ticking. *See* **cgiint giiknt**

cgiillo illogic. *See* **cgilo**

cgiilno coiling. *See* **cgiino giilno**

cgiilnop policing coiling. *See* **cgiino cginop giilno giilnp**

cgiilnpp clipping lipping. *See* **giilnp giinpp**

cgiilnps splicing lisping pilings slicing spicing. *See* **cgiins cgilns giilnp**

cgiilns slicing. *See* **cgiins cgilns**

cgiilnsu sluicing slicing. *See* **cgiins cgilns cgilnu gilnsu**

cgiilost logistic colitis solicit. *See* **cgilos**

cgiimnn mincing. *See* **giimnn cgiin**

cgiimnno incoming mincing coining. *See* **cgiino cgimno cginno iimnno**

cgiimnpr crimping pricing priming. *See* **cgiinr giimnr giinpr**

cgiimnpu pumicing. *See* **gimnpu**

cgiimnsu miscuing. *See* **cgiins cimnsu gimnsu**

cgiin icing gin in

cgiinno coining. *See* **cgiino cginno**

cgiinnot noticing coining. *See* **cgiino cgiint cginno ginnot**

cgiinnw wincing. *See* **giinnw cgiin**

cgiinnz zincing. *See* **cgiin**

cgiino congii icing ionic cion coin icon cog con gin ion nog go in no on

cgiinoos isogonic. *See* **cgiino cgiins cginoo cgnoos**

cgiinov voicing. *See* **cgiino cginov**

cgiinpr pricing. *See* **cgiinr giinpr**

cgiinprs crisping pricing spicing spiring. *See* **cgiinr cgiins ciinrs giinpr**

cgiinps spicing. *See* **cgiins ginps**

cgiinr ricing icing ricin grin ring gin rig in

cgiinrsu cruising cursing. *See* **cgiinr cgiins cginru ciinrs**

cgiinrt tricing. *See* **cgiint ciinrt cgiinr giinrt**

cgiins icings icing gins nisi sign sing gin sic sin in is si

cgiint citing icing ting gin nit tic tin in it ti

cgijnnou jouncing. *See* **cginno cinnou**

cgikknno knocking nocking. *See* **cgikno cginno**

cgiklnno clonking cloning locking nocking. *See* **cgikno cginno**

cgiklnnu clunking lucking. *See* **cgilnu giknnu**

cgiklno locking. *See* **cgikno cgiln cikln**

cgiklnpu plucking lucking kingcup. *See* **cgilnu giknpu gilnpu iklnpu**

cgiklnsu suckling lucking sucking sulking. *See* **cgilns cgilnu ciklns cklnsu**

cgiklnu lucking. *See* **cgilnu cikln cklnu**

cgikmno mocking. *See* **cgikno cgimno**

cgikmnos smocking comings mocking smoking socking. *See* **cgikno cgimno**

cgikmnu mucking. *See* **cginu cimnu**

cgiknno nocking. *See* **cgikno cginno**

cgikno coking cion coin conk gink icon ikon king kino nick nock oink cog con gin ink ion kin nog go in no on

cgiknoo cooking. *See* **cgikno cginoo**

cgiknoor crooking cooking corking rocking rooking. *See* **cgikno cginoo cginor**

cgiknor corking rocking. *See* **cgikno cginor**

cgiknos socking. *See* **cgikno cinos cknos**

cgiknost stocking costing gnostic socking stoking. *See* **cgikno cinost giknot ginost**

cgiknpsu kingcups kingcup sucking. *See* **giknpu**

cgiknpu kingcup. *See* **giknpu cginu**

cgiknrtu trucking rucking tucking. *See* **cginru ginrtu**

cgiknru rucking. *See* **cginru**

cgiknsu sucking. *See* **cginu gikns cgksu**

cgikntu tucking. *See* **cginu cintu**

cgillnoy collying cloying. *See* **cginoy cglloy gllnoy**

cgillnsu sculling culling. *See* **cgilns cgilnu cillsu gilnsu**

cgillnu culling. *See* **cgilnu**

cgillnuy cullying culling. *See* **cgilnu gilluy**

cgilmnop clomping comping complin. *See* **cgimno cginop gilnop gimnop**

cgilmnpu clumping lumping pluming. *See* **cgilnu gilnpu gimnpu**

cgilmnsu muscling. *See* **cgilns cgilnu cimnsu gilnsu**

cgilmntu mulcting. *See* **cgilnu cilntu gilntu gimntu**

cgiln cling ling gin nil li in

cgilnno cloning. *See* **cginno cgiln cilno**

cgilnnow clowning cloning cowling. *See* **cginno gilnow**

cgilnoo cooling. *See* **cginoo gilnoo**

cgilnoor coloring cooling. *See* **cginoo cginor gilnoo**

cgilnopu coupling. *See* **cgilnu cginop cglnou cilnou**

cgilnos closing. *See* **cgilns cilnos cgilos gilnos**

cgilnoss closings closing cosigns. *See* **cgilns cgilos cilnos cinoss**

cgilnosw scowling closing cowling slowing. *See* **cgilns cgilos cilnos clnosw**

cgilnott clotting lotting. *See* **ginott**

cgilnotu clouting linocut. *See* **cgilnu cglnou cilnou cilntu**

cgilnow cowling. *See* **gilnow cgiln clnow**

cgilnoy cloying. *See* **cginoy cgiln cilno**

cgilnru curling. *See* **cgilnu cginru gilnru**

cgilns clings cling lings sling gins ling nils sign sing gin nil sic sin in is li si

cgilnu cluing cling clung cuing lungi ling lung gin gnu gun lug nil in li nu

cgilo logic clog coil loci cog col log oil go li lo

cgiloooz zoologic. *See* **cgilo giloo**

cgilorsw cowgirls cowgirl. *See* **cgilos cgiors glorsw**

cgilorw cowgirl. *See* **cgior glorw cgilo**

cgilos logics clogs coils logic clog cogs coil cols loci logs oils silo slog soil cog col log los oil sic sol go is li lo os si so

cgilpsty glyptics glyptic. *See* **gipsty**

cgilpty glyptic. *See* **cilty**

cgimmnsu scumming summing. *See* **cimmnu cimnsu gimnsu**

cgimnnoo oncoming. *See* **cgimno cginno cginoo cmnnoo**

cgimno coming gnomic cion coin icon cog con gin ion mog mon nim nog go in mi mo no om on

cgimnop comping. *See* **cgimno cginop gimnop**

cgimnopu upcoming comping. *See* **cgimno cginop cimnou gimnop**

cgimnos comings. *See* **cgimno**

cgimnpru crumping. *See* **cginru gimnpu**

cginnno conning. *See* **cginno innno**

cginnnu cunning. *See* **cginu**

cginno coning cion coin icon cog con gin inn ion nog go in no on

cginnoor crooning corning. *See* **cginno cginoo cginor**

cginnopu pouncing. *See* **cginno cginop cinnou**

cginnor corning. *See* **cginno cginor**

cginnors scorning consign corning scoring snoring. *See* **cginno cginor cgiors ginnos**

cginnorw crowning corning crowing ingrown. *See* **cginno cginor ginnow ginorw**

cginnos consign. *See* **cginno ginnos**

cginnoss consigns consign cosigns. *See* **cginno ginoss ginnos cinoss**

cginnotu counting unction. *See* **cginno cinnou ginnot ginntu**

cginoo cooing cogon congo cion coin coon goon icon cog con coo gin goo ion nog go in no on

cginoop cooping. *See* **cginoo cginop**

cginoops scooping cooping. *See* **cginoo cginop cgnoos ginops**

cginoost scooting costing gnostic sooting. *See* **cginoo cgnoos cinost cnoost**

cginop coping gipon oping cion coin icon ping cog con cop gin gip ion nip nog pig pin poi go in no on pi

cginopp copping. *See* **cginop**

cginoppr cropping copping. *See* **cginop cginor ginopr**

cginopy copying. *See* **cginop cginoy**

cginor coring corgi groin cion coin coir corn grin icon iron ring cog con cor gin ion nog nor orc rig roc go in no or

cginors scoring. *See* **cgiors cginor ginors**

cginorss crossing cosigns scoring signors. *See* **cginor cgiors cinoss cnorss**

cginorsu coursing scouring congius cursing rousing scoring souring. *See* **cginor cginru cgiors cinosu**

cginortu courting routing ruction touring. *See* **cginor cginru cinort ginort**

cginorw crowing. *See* **cginor ginorw**

cginoss cosigns. *See* **cinoss ginoss**

cginosst gnostics consist cosigns costing gnostic tocsins tossing. *See* **cinoss cinost ciosst ginoss**

cginost costing gnostic. *See* **ginost cinost**

cginostu scouting congius costing gnostic outings suction. *See* **cinost cinosu cinstu ciostu**

cginosu congius. *See* **cinosu cginu ginsu**

cginosv   covings. See **cginov cinos**

cginov   coving cion coin icon cog con gin ion nog go in no on

cginoy   coying yogic cion coin cony icon yogi yoni cog con coy gin goy icy ion nog yin yon go in no on oy

cginppu   cupping. See **cginu inppu**

cginprsu   sprucing cursing pursing. See **cginru cinrsu ginprs gnprsu**

cginrruy   currying. See **cginru cginry**

cginrstu   crusting cursing incrust rusting. See **cginru cinrsu cinstu cirstu**

cginrsu   cursing. See **cginru cinrsu**

cginru   curing cuing incur ruing runic grin ring ruin rung uric cur gin gnu gun rig rug run urn in nu

cginruv   curving. See **cginru**

cginry   crying grin ring cry gin icy rig yin in

cginssu   cussing. See **cginu cinsu inssu**

cginsttu   cuttings cutting. See **cinstt cinstu**

cginttu   cutting. See **cginu cintu cintt**

cginu   cuing gin gnu gun in nu

cgior   corgi coir cog cor orc rig roc go or

cgiors   corgis corgi coirs cogs coir cors orcs rigs rocs sori cog cor orc rig roc sic sir go is or os si so

cgiotyz   zygotic. See **cgioy**

cgioy   yogic yogi cog coy goy icy go oy

cgklnosu   gunlocks unclogs unlocks. See **cglnou cklnos cklnou cklnsu**

cgknostu   gunstock. See **cnostu knostu**

cgksu   gucks cusk guck suck us

cgku   guck

cgllosy   glycols. See **cglloy cglos closy**

cglloy   glycol colly golly clog cloy logy cog col coy goy log go lo oy

cglnoooy   oncology. See **clnooy glnooo gloooy**

cglnosu   unclogs. See **clnosu cglnou**

cglnou   unclog clung clog long lung unco cog col con gnu gun log lug nog go lo no nu on

cglnu   clung lung gnu gun lug nu

cglo   clog cog col log go lo

cglootyy   cytology. See **cloyy**

cglos   clogs clog cogs cols logs slog cog col log los sol go lo os so

cgnoo   cogon congo coon goon cog con coo goo nog go no on

cgnoos   cogons cogon congo coons goons cogs cons coon coos goon goos nogs song soon cog con coo goo nog son go no on os so

cgnoou   congou cogon congo coon goon unco cog con coo gnu goo gun nog go no nu on

cgo   cog go

cgos   cogs cog go os so

---

chhiinpt   pinchhit. See **chiint**

chhiipst   phthisic. See **chips chist chhit**

chhilrsu   churlish. See **chlrsu**

chhimrty   rhythmic. See **chimty hhmrty**

chhit   hitch chit itch chi hit tic hi it ti

chhiw   which chi hi

chhnoo   honcho hooch coon con coo hon oho ooh ho no oh on

chhnoos   honchos. See **chhnoo cnoos**

chhnu   hunch huh nu

chhoo   hooch coo oho ooh ho oh

chhooptt   hotchpot. See **chhoo hoopt choop**

chhtu   hutch cut huh hut ut

chi   chi hi

chiiklst   ticklish litchis. See **chiilt chikst chilst**

chiikm   kimchi hick chi him hi mi

chiikss   sickish. See **chiks**

chiill   chili chi hi li

chiill   chilli chili chill hill chi ill hi li

chiilnnp   linchpin. See **chiil iilnn chinp**

chiilnst   chitlins litchis. See **chiilt chiint chilst chinst**

chiilost   holistic colitis coltish litchis solicit. See **chiilt chilst chlost hilost**

chiilqsu   cliquish. See **chiil**

chiilst   litchis. See **chilst chiilt**

chiilt   litchi lithic chili licht licit chit hilt itch chi hit lit tic til hi it li ti

chiimsu   ischium. See **chmsu chimu cimsu**

chiinops   siphonic phonics. See **chinop chinos hinops**

chiinort   ornithic. See **chiint chinot ciinor cinort**

chiint   chitin chin chit hint inch itch thin chi hin hit nit tic tin hi in it ti

chiiorst   historic ostrich. See **chiors**

chik   hick chi hi

chikllo   hillock. See **chill**

chikllos   hillocks hillock. See **chills**

chiklty   thickly. See **chity chilt cilty**

chikmnnu   munchkin. See **chikn chknu cimnu**

chikmnpu   chipmunk. See **chimp chikn chmpu**

chikn   chink chin hick inch nick chi hin ink kin hi in

chikns   chinks chink chins hicks knish nicks snick chin hick hins inch inks nick shin sick sink skin chi hin his ink kin sic sin ski hi in is sh si

chikory   hickory. See **chikr chior chkoy**

chikr   chirk hick rich rick chi irk kir hi

chikrs   chirks kirsch chirk hicks ricks shirk hick irks kris rich rick risk sick chi his irk kir sic sir ski hi is sh si

chiks   hicks hick sick chi his sic ski hi is sh si

chiksst   shticks. See **chikst chisst ciksst**

chikst   kitsch schtik shtick chits hicks stich stick thick ticks chit cist hick hist hits itch kist kith kits sick sith skit this tick tics chi his hit its kit sic sit ski tic tsk hi is it sh si ti

chikt   thick chit hick itch kith tick chi hit kit tic hi it ti

chill   chill hill chi ill hi li

chilloot   oilcloth. See **chill chlot hlloo**

chills   chills chill hills shill hill sill chi his ill sic hi is li sh si

chilly   chilly chill hilly hill illy lily chi icy ill hi li

chilm   milch chi him mil hi li mi

chilmosu   scholium. See **chlosu hilmos hilmsu**

chilnosw   clownish. See **chinos cilnos clnosw hilosw**

chilnsy   lychnis. See **chins chlny ilnsy**

chiloooz   holozoic. See **chilz**

chilor   orchil choir ichor coil coir loch loci rich roil chi col cor oil orc rho roc hi ho li lo oh or

chilors   orchils. See **chiors chilor chlors**

chilost   coltish. See **chlost hilost chilst**

chilst   lichts chits hilts licht stich chit cist hilt hist hits itch list silt sith slit this tics tils chi his hit its lit sic sit tic til hi is it li sh si ti

chilt   licht chit hilt itch chi hit lit tic til hi it li ti

chilz   zilch chi hi li

chimmoru   chromium. See **cimoru**

chimnorw inchworm. *See* **cimnor**

chimnosu insomuch cushion coniums. *See* **chinos cimnou cimnsu cinosu**

chimo ohmic chi him mho ohm hi ho mi mo oh om

chimors chrisom. *See* **chiors chimrs**

chimp chimp chip chi him hip imp hi mi pi

chimps chimps chimp chips chip hips imps pish shim ship simp chi him hip his imp mis sic sip hi is mi pi sh si

chimrs chrism smirch scrim mirs rich rims shim chi him his mir mis rim sic sir hi is mi sh si

chimrss chrisms. *See* **chimrs chimss cimrss**

chimss schism shims hiss miss shim chi him his mis sic sis hi is mi sh si

chimsss schisms. *See* **chimss**

chimty mythic itchy chit city itch myth chi him hit icy thy tic hi it mi my ti

chimu humic chum much chi cum him hum hi mi mu um

chin chin inch chi hin hi in

chino chino chin cion coin icon inch chi con hin hon ion hi ho in no oh on

chinop phonic chino pinch chin chip chop cion coin icon inch chi con cop hin hip hon hop ion nip pin poi hi ho in no oh on pi

chinops phonics. *See* **chinos chinop hinops**

chinopty hypnotic pythonic. *See* **chinop chinot inopty**

chinos chinos chino chins cions coins icons scion sonic chin cion coin cons cosh hins icon inch ions nosh shin chi con hin his hon ion ohs sic sin son hi ho in is no oh on os sh si so

chinossu cushions cushion cousins. *See* **chinos cinoss cinosu**

chinost chitons. *See* **chinos chinot chinst cinost**

chinosu cushion. *See* **chinos cinosu**

chinot chiton chino notch tonic chin chit cion coin hint icon inch into itch otic thin chi con cot hin hit hon hot ion nit not tho tic tin ton hi ho in it no oh on ti to

chinp pinch chin chip inch chi hin hip nip pin hi in pi

chinrsu urchins. *See* **chnrsu cinrsu hinrsu chinru**

chinru urchin churn incur runic chin inch rich ruin uric chi cur hin run urn hi in nu

chins chins chin hins inch shin chi hin his sic sin hi in is sh si

chinst snitch chins chits hints stich chin chit cist hins hint hist hits inch itch nits

shin sith snit thin this tics tins chi hin his hit its nit sic sin sit tic tin hi in is it sh si ti

chintyz chintzy. *See* **chintz chity cinyz**

chintz chintz chin chit hint inch itch thin zinc chi hin hit nit tic tin zit hi in it ti

chinw winch chin inch chi hin win hi in

chioorsu ichorous. *See* **chiors chorsu ciorsu hiorsu**

chioorsz chorizos chorizo. *See* **chiors**

chioorz chorizo. *See* **chior**

chioprt trophic. *See* **cioprt chipr chior**

chiopttu pitchout. *See* **chotu ciopt chipt**

chiopxy hypoxic. *No 6s or 5s*

chior choir ichor rich coir chi cor orc rho roc hi ho oh or

chiors choirs orchis choir coirs ichor coir cors cosh orcs rhos rich rocs sori chi cor his ohs orc rho roc sic sir hi ho is oh or os sh si so

chiorst ostrich. *See* **chiors**

chip chip chi hip hi pi

chippy chippy hippy chip pipy chi hip icy pip yip hi pi

chipr chirp chip rich chi hip rip hi pi

chiprrsu chirrups chirrup. *See* **chiprs chirrs chrrsu cirrsu**

chiprrsy pyrrhics pyrrhic. *See* **chiprs chipry chipsy chirrs**

chiprru chirrup. *See* **chipr chirr chrru**

chiprry pyrrhic. *See* **chipry chirr**

chiprs chirps chips chirp crisp scrip chip hips pish rich rips ship chi hip his rip sic sip sir hi is pi sh si

chipry chirpy chirp chip rich chi cry hip icy pry rip yip hi pi

chips chips chip hips pish ship chi hip his sic sip hi is pi sh si

chipssy physics. *See* **chipsy hipss**

chipsy physic chips psych spicy chip hips pish ship yips chi hip his icy shy sic sip spy yip hi is pi sh si

chipt pitch chip chit itch chi hip hit pit tic tip hi it pi ti

chiqtu quitch chit itch quit chi cut hit hut tic tui hi it ti ut

chir rich chi hi

chirr chirr rich chi hi

chirrs chirrs chirr shirr rich chi his sic sir hi is sh si

chissst schists. *See* **chisst**

chisst schist chits cists stich chit cist hiss hist hits itch sith sits this tics chi his hit its sic sis sit tic hi is it sh si ti

chist chits stich chit cist hist hits itch sith this tics chi his hit its sic sit tic hi is it sh si ti

chistt stitch chits stich chit cist hist hits itch sith this tics tits chi his hit its sic sit tic tit hi is it sh si ti

chistw switch chits stich whist whits witch chit cist hist hits itch sith this tics whit wish with wits chi his hit its sic sit tic wis wit hi is it sh si ti

chisyz schizy chi his icy shy sic hi is sh si

chisyzz schizzy. *See* **chisyz**

chit chit itch chi hit tic hi it ti

chittw twitch witch chit itch twit whit with chi hit tic tit wit hi it ti

chitw witch chit itch whit with chi hit tic wit hi it ti

chity itchy chit city itch chi hit icy thy tic hi it ti

chkmmosu hummocks hummock. *See* **chkmsu hkmosu**

chkmmou hummock. *See* **hkmou**

chkmmouy hummocky hummock. *See* **chmmuy**

chkmssu shmucks. *See* **chkmsu chkssu**

chkmsu shmuck chums mucks shuck chum cusk hums husk much muck mush musk scum such suck cum hum mus sum mu sh um us

chknoos schnook. *See* **hknoos cknos ckoos**

chknooss schnooks schnook shnooks. *See* **chkoss hknoos**

chknsu chunks chunk hunks shuck cusk hunk husk shun such suck sunk sun nu sh us

chknu chunk hunk nu

chknuy chunky chunk yuck hunk yuk nu

chko hock ho oh

chkos hocks shock cosh hock sock ohs kos ho oh os sh so

chkoss shocks hocks shock socks cosh hock sock ohs kos ho oh os sh so

chkoy choky hock yock coy hoy ho oh oy

chkssu shucks cusks husks shuck sucks cusk cuss husk such suck sh us

chksu shuck cusk husk such suck sh us

chlmu mulch chum culm much cum hum lum mu um

chlmuy muchly mulch chum culm much cum hum lum yum mu my um

chlnooop colophon. *See* **chnoop**

chlnu lunch nu

chlny lynch

chlo loch col ho lo oh

chloorsu chlorous colours. *See* **chloos chlors chlosu chlrsu**

chloos school cools locos cols cool coos cosh loch loco loos oohs shoo solo col coo loo los oho ohs ooh sol ho lo oh os sh so

chlooss schools. *See* **chloos hooss hloss**

chlopst splotch. *See* **chlost chops clops**

chlopsty splotchy splotch. *See* **chlost chopsy closty hlopsy**

chlors   schorl cols cors cosh loch orcs rhos rocs col cor los ohs orc rho roc sol ho lo oh or os sh so

chlorss   schorls. *See* **chlors corss hloss**

chlost   cloths cloth clots colts holts sloth clot cols colt cosh cost cots holt host hots loch lost lots scot shot slot tosh col cot hot los lot ohs sol sot tho ho lo oh os sh so to

chlosu   slouch hocus locus cols cosh loch lush ouch soul such col los ohs sol sou ho lo oh os sh so us

chlosuy   slouchy. *See* **chlosu closy chsuy**

chlot   cloth clot colt holt loch loth col cot hot lot tho ho lo oh to

chlrsu   churls churl crush curls hurls lurch crus curl curs hurl lush rush slur such cur sh us

chlru   churl lurch curl hurl cur

chmmuy   chummy chum much cum hum mum yum mu my um

chmnu   munch chum much cum hum mu nu um

chmoo   mooch homo coo mho moo ohm oho ooh ho mo oh om

chmoos   smooch mooch schmo coos cosh homo mhos moos ohms oohs shoo coo mho moo mos ohm oho ohs oms ooh ho mo oh om os sh so

chmooss   schmoos. *See* **chmoos cmooss**

chmop   chomp chop comp cop hop mho mop ohm ho mo oh om

chmops   chomps chomp chops comps schmo chop comp cops cosh hops mhos mops ohms posh scop shop soph cop hop mho mop mos ohm ohs oms sop ho mo oh om os sh so

chmos   schmo cosh mhos ohms mho mos ohm ohs oms ho mo oh om os sh so

chmpsu   chumps chump chums humps chum cups cusp hump hums much mush push scum scup such sump umps cum cup hum hup mus pus sum sup ump mu sh um up us

chmpu   chump chum hump much cum cup hum hup ump mu um up

chmstu   smutch chums chum cuts hums huts much mush must scum scut shut smut stum such thus tush cum cut hum hut mus sum mu sh um us ut

chmsu   chums chum hums much mush scum such cum hum mus sum mu sh um us

chmu   chum much cum hum mu um

chnoop   poncho pooch chop coon coop hoop pooh poon con coo cop hon hop oho ooh ho no oh on

chnoops   ponchos. *See* **chnoop chops cnoos**

chnot   notch con cot hon hot not tho ho no oh on to

chnotuu   uncouth. *See* **cnotu chotu chnot**

chnpu   punch cup hup pun nu up

chnpuy   punchy punch puny cup hup pun yup nu up

chnrsu   churns churn crush crus curs runs rush shun such urns cur run sun urn nu sh us

chnru   churn cur run urn nu

chnsy   synch sync shy sh

choop   pooch chop coop hoop pooh coo cop hop oho ooh ho oh

choorst   cohorts. *See* **coost hoost horst**

choosy   choosy coos cosh cosy hoys oohs shoo coo coy hoy oho ohs ooh shy soy ho oh os oy sh so

chop   chop cop hop ho oh

choppy   choppy chop copy hypo cop coy hop hoy pop ho oh oy

chopr   porch chop crop cop cor hop orc pro rho roc ho oh or

chops   chops chop cops cosh hops posh scop shop soph cop hop ohs sop ho oh os sh so

chopssy   psychos. *See* **chopsy hopssy**

chopsy   psycho chops hypos psych chop cops copy cosh cosy hops hoys hypo posh posy scop shop soph cop coy hop hoy ohs shy sop soy spy ho oh os oy sh so

chopu   pouch chop coup ouch cop cup hop hup ho oh up

chopuy   pouchy pouch coypu chop copy coup hypo ouch cop coy cup hop hoy hup you yup ho oh oy up

chorsttu   shortcut. *See* **chorsu corstu horstt hrsttu**

chorsu   chorus crush hocus hours scour cors cosh crus curs hour orcs ouch ours rhos rocs rush sour such cor cur ohs orc our rho roc sou ho oh or os sh so us

chort   torch cor cot hot orc ort rho roc rot tho tor ho oh or to

chos   cosh ohs ho oh os sh so

chosu   hocus cosh ouch such ohs sou ho oh os sh so us

chosw   chows chow cosh cows scow show cow how ohs sow who ho oh ow sh

chotu   couth touch ouch thou cot cut hot hut out tho ho oh to ut

chotuy   touchy couth touch youth ouch thou cot coy cut hot hoy hut out tho thy toy you ho oh oy to ut

chou   ouch ho oh

chouv   vouch ouch ho oh

chow   chow cow how who ho ow

chpssuy   scyphus. *See* **chsuy cpssu hssuy**

chpsy   psych shy spy sh

chrrsu   churrs churr crush crus curs rush such cur sh us

chrru   churr cur

chrstw   crwths crwth sh

chrsu   crush crus curs rush such cur sh us

chrtw   crwth

chsssu   schuss such cuss sh us

chsu   such sh us

chsuy   cushy such shy sh us

---

ciiillt   illicit. *See* **ciilt**

ciiilmpt   implicit. *See* **ciilt iilmt**

ciiiltvy   civility. *See* **ciilv ciily ciilt**

ciiinnos   incision. *See* **iinnos**

ciiintvy   vicinity. *See* **ciinv**

ciijluy   juicily. *See* **ciily cijuy**

ciikkll   killick. *No 6s or 5s*

ciikklls   killicks killick. *See* **cikks iklls cikls**

ciiklpst   lipstick. *See* **iilpst**

ciiknppr   pinprick. *See* **iiknpp**

ciiknpst   nitpicks stickpin nitpick. *See* **iknst cikns cikps**

ciiknpt   nitpick. *No 6s or 5s*

ciillty   licitly. *See* **ciily ciilt cilty**

ciillvy   civilly. *See* **ciilv ciily**

ciilmopy   impolicy. *See* **cilopy cimopy clmopy**

ciilmoss   sciolism. *See* **cimoss**

ciilmrsy   lyricism. *See* **cilrsy ilmrsy**

ciilmu cilium ilium culm cum lum mil li mi mu um

ciilnos silicon. *See* **cilnos ciino**

ciilnoss silicons silicon. *See* **cilnos cinoss**

ciilnuv uncivil. *See* **ciilv ciinv**

ciiloopt politico politic copilot. *See* **cioopt**

ciilopst politics colitis politic solicit. *See* **ciopst iilpst ilopst**

ciilopt politic. *See* **ciilt ciopt ilopt**

ciilosst solicits colitis solicit. *See* **ciosst**

ciilost colitis solicit. *See* **clost cilos ciilt**

ciilrsty lyricist. *See* **cilrsy ilrsty**

ciilt licit lit tic til it li ti

ciilv civil li

ciily icily icy li

ciimm mimic mim mi

ciimmry mimicry. *See* **ciimm**

ciimms mimics mimic mim mis sic is mi si

ciimnost monistic. *See* **ciimot cimost cinost imnost**

ciimot miotic otic omit cot mot tic tom it mi mo om ti to

ciimstv victims. *See* **ciimtv iistv**

ciimtv victim tic vim it mi ti

ciinnstt instinct. *See* **cinstt**

ciino ionic cion coin icon con ion in no on

ciinoot coition. *See* **cnoot ciino cinot**

ciinor ironic ionic ricin cion coin coir corn icon iron con cor ion nor orc roc in no on or

ciinors incisor. *See* **ciinor ciinrs**

ciinorss incisors incisor. *See* **ciinor ciinrs ciirss cinoss**

ciinosss scission. *See* **cinoss**

ciinpstu sinciput. *See* **cinstu inpstu**

ciinr ricin in

ciinrs ricins ricin nisi iris sic sin sir in is si

ciinrt nitric ricin nit tic tin in it ti

ciinv vinic in

ciioqtux quixotic. *See* **ciotx ioqtu**

ciiosuv vicious. *No 6s or 5s*

ciiottxy toxicity. *See* **ciotx**

ciiprty pyritic. *See* **cprty**

ciirr cirri

ciirss crisis iris sirs sic sir sis is si

ciirtv vitric tic it ti

ciisstty cystitis. *See* **cisst cssty iistt**

cijkosty joystick. *See* **cikosy ciksty ckosty**

cijnnoo conjoin. *See* **innoo**

cijnnoos conjoins conjoin. *See* **innoos**

cijnnoot conjoint conjoin. *See* **innoot**

cijnnotu junction unction. *See* **cinnou**

cijoosty jocosity. *See* **coost ijost oosty**

cijuy juicy icy

cikk kick

cikkllo killock. *No 6s or 5s*

cikkllos killocks killock. *See* **cilos cikks ikllo**

cikkpu kickup kick pick puck cup kip pi up

cikks kicks kick sick sic ski is si

cikky kicky kick icky icy

cikl lick ilk li

cikllor rollick. *See* **ikllr**

cikllors rollicks rollick. *See* **cllors**

ciklluy luckily. *See* **ckluy clluy**

cikln clink kiln lick link nick ilk ink kin nil li in

ciklnry crinkly. *See* **cikln cilry**

ciklns clinks clink kilns licks links nicks slick slink snick inks kiln lick link nick nils sick silk sink skin ilk ink kin nil sic sin ski in is li si

ciklpry prickly. *See* **cilry cikpy cikpr**

ciklquy quickly. *See* **cikqu ckluy**

cikls licks slick lick sick silk ilk sic ski is li si

ciklss slicks licks silks slick kiss lick sick silk skis ilk sic sis ski is li si

ciklsy sickly licks silky slick icky lick sick silk icy ilk sic ski sky sly is li si

cikmoors sickroom. *See* **ckoors**

cikmy micky icky icy mi my

cikn nick ink kin in

ciknnoos coonskin. *See* **innoos**

ciknptu nutpick. *See* **cintu inptu**

cikns nicks snick inks nick sick sink skin ink kin sic sin ski in is si

ciknss snicks nicks sinks skins snick inks kiss nick sick sink sins skin skis ink kin sic sin sis ski in is si

ciknsstu unsticks unstick. *See* **ciknss ciksst cinstu iknsst**

ciknstu unstick. *See* **cinstu iknst cikns**

ciknyz zincky zincy zinky icky inky nick zinc icy ink kin yin in

cikos sicko sick sock kos sic ski is os si so

cikoss sickos sicko socks kiss sick skis sock kos sic sis ski is os si so

cikosy yoicks sicko yocks cosy icky sick sock yock coy icy kos sic ski sky soy is os oy si so

cikp pick kip pi

cikppsu pickups. *See* **cikppu cikps ckpsu**

cikppu pickup pick puck cup kip pip pup pi up

cikpr prick pick rick irk kip kir rip pi

cikprs pricks crisp picks prick ricks scrip irks kips kris pick rick rips risk sick skip irk kip kir rip sic sip sir ski is pi si

cikps picks kips pick sick skip kip sic sip ski is pi si

cikpsstu stickups stickup. *See* **ciksst ipsstu**

cikpstu stickup. *See* **cistu ipstu cikst**

cikpy picky pick icky icy kip yip pi

cikqu quick

cikr rick irk kir

cikrs ricks irks kris rick risk sick irk kir sic sir ski is si

cikrst strick tricks ricks skirt stick ticks trick cist irks kist kits kris rick risk sick skit stir tick tics irk its kir kit sic sir sit ski tic tsk is it si ti

cikrt trick rick tick irk kir kit tic it ti

cikrty tricky trick city icky rick tick cry icy irk kir kit tic try it ti

ciks sick sic ski is si

cikssst sticks cists kists skits stick ticks cist kiss kist kits sick sits skis skit tick tics its kit sic sis sit ski tic tsk is it si ti

cikst stick ticks cist kist kits sick skit tick tics its kit sic sit ski tic tsk is it si ti

ciksty sticky stick ticks cist city cyst icky kist kits sick skit tick tics icy its kit sic sit ski sky sty tic tsk is it si ti

ciksw wicks sick wick sic ski wis is si

cikt tick tic kit it ti

cikw wick

ciky icky icy

cillmsuy clumsily. *See* **cillsu clmsuy**

cillnosu scullion uncoils. *See* **cillsu cilnos cilnou cinosu**

cillsu cullis culls scull cull sill ill sic is li si us

cilmnop complin. *See* **cilno clmop**

cilmnops complins complin. *See* **cilnos clmops**

cilmnuuv vinculum. *See* **cimnu**

cilmstu cultism. *See* **clmstu ilmstu**

cilno colin cion coil coin icon lion loci loin noil col con ion nil oil in li lo no on

cilnoost colonist lotions. *See* **cilnos cinost clnoos cnoost**

cilnootu locution linocut. *See* **cilnou cilntu ilnoot**

cilnos colins cions coils coins colin icons lions loins noils scion sonic cion coil coin cols cons icon ions lion loci loin nils noil oils silo soil col con ion los nil oil sic sin sol son in is li lo no on os si so

cilnostu linocuts consult linocut oculist suction uncoils. *See* **cilnos cilnou cilntu cinost**

cilnosu uncoils. *See* **clnosu cilnos cinosu cilnou**

cilnotu linocut. *See* **cilnou cilntu**

cilnou uncoil colin cion coil coin icon lion loci loin noil unco col con ion nil oil in li lo no nu on

cilntu incult cutin tunic until cult lint lunt unit cut lit nil nit nut tic til tin tui tun in it li nu ti ut

cilo coil loci col oil li lo

ciloopst copilots copilot topsoil. *See* **cioopt ciopst ilopst**

ciloopt copilot. *See* **cioopt ilopt**

ciloorrt tricolor. *See* **cilort cioort**

ciloorst colorist lictors octrois. *See* **cilort cioort cloors**

ciloorsu couloirs couloir colours. *See* **ciorsu cloors clooru**

cilooru couloir. *See* **clooru cioru**

cilooss colossi. *See* **cilos cloos iloos**

cilopry pyloric. *See* **cilopy cilry ilory**

cilopssw cowslips cowslip. *See* **clossw ilopss**

cilopsu oilcups. *See* **cilopu cilpsu ilopsu**

cilopsw cowslip. *See* **cilps clops cilos**

cilopu oilcup picul poilu clip coil coup loci puli col cop cup lip lop oil poi pul li lo pi up

cilopy policy clip cloy coil copy loci oily ploy col cop coy icy lip lop oil ply poi yip li lo oy pi

cilorst lictors. *See* **cilort clost cilos**

cilort lictor toric clot coil coir colt loci otic riot roil rotl tiro toil tori trio col cor cot lit lot oil orc ort roc rot tic til tor it li lo or ti to

cilos coils coil cols loci oils silo soil col los oil sic sol is li lo os si so

cilossttu oculists oculist locusts. *See* **ciosst ciostu clostu cosstu**

cilossty systolic. *See* **ciosst closty**

cilossuu luscious. *See* **cilos closu ilosu**

cilostu oculist. *See* **clostu ciostu**

cilow wilco coil cowl loci col cow low oil owl li lo ow

ciloyz cozily cloy coil cozy loci oily col coy coz icy oil li lo oy

cilp clip lip li pi

cilprstu culprits culprit. *See* **cilpsu ciprst cirstu clpstu**

cilprsy crisply. *See* **cilrsy ciprsy**

cilprtu culprit. *See* **cilpu ilptu**

cilps clips clip lips lisp slip lip sic sip is li pi si

cilpsu piculs clips picul pulis sculp clip cups cusp lips lisp plus puli puls scup slip cup lip pul pus sic sip sup is li pi si up us

cilpu picul clip puli cup lip pul li pi up

cilrrsu scurril. *See* **cirrsu clrsu**

cilrstty strictly. *See* **cilrsy cirstt cirtty ilrsty**

cilrstuy rusticly rustily. *See* **cilrsy cirstu clrtuy crstuy**

cilrsy lyrics lyric cry icy sic sir sly is li si

cilry lyric icy cry li

cilssttu cultists cultist lutists. *See* **ilsstt ilsttu**

cilsttu cultist. *See* **ilsttu clstu cistu**

cilty lytic city icy lit tic til it li ti

cilxy cylix icy li xi

cimmnu cummin cumin cum mim mum nim in mi mu nu um

cimmos commis osmic moms mim mis mom mos oms sic is mi mo om os si so

cimmost commits. *See* **cimmos cimmot cimost**

cimmot commit otic omit cot mim mom mot tic tom it mi mo om ti to

cimmox commix comix cox mim mix mom mi mo om ox xi

cimnoor moronic omicron. *See* **cimnor imnoor**

cimnoors omicrons crimson microns morions moronic omicron. *See* **cimnor cnoors imnoor imnoos**

cimnor micron micro minor cion coin coir corm corn icon iron morn norm con cor ion mir mon mor nim nor orc rim roc in mi mo no om on or

cimnors crimson microns. *See* **cimnor imnors**

cimnorss crimsons crimson microns. *See* **cimnor cimoss cimrss cinoss**

cimnostu miscount coniums suction. *See* **cimnou cimnsu cimost cinost**

cimnosu coniums. *See* **cimnou cinosu cimnsu**

cimnou conium cumin cion coin icon muon unco con cum ion mon nim in mi mo mu no nu om on um

cimnsu cumins cumin incus minus music scum nims cum mis mus nim sic sin sum sun in is mi mu nu si um us

cimnu cumin cum nim in mi mu nu um

cimoost osmotic. *See* **cimost coost moost**

cimopy myopic comp copy cop coy icy imp mop poi yip mi mo my om oy pi

cimor micro coir corm cor mir mor orc rim roc mi mo om or

cimoru corium micro curio coir corm uric cor cum cur mir mor orc our rim roc rum mi mo mu om or um

cimos osmic mis mos oms sic is mi mo om os si so

cimoss osmics osmic miss moss mis mos oms sic sis is mi mo om os si so

cimosst sitcoms. *See* **cimoss cimost ciosst**

cimossy mycosis. *See* **cimoss imssy mossy**

cimost sitcom moist omits osmic stoic cist cost cots mist most mots omit otic scot tics toms cot its mis mos mot oms sic sit sot tic tom is it mi mo om os si so ti to

cimoty comity city omit otic cot coy icy mot tic tom toy it mi mo my om oy ti to

cimotyz zymotic. *See* **cimoty**

cimox comix cox mix mi mo om ox xi

cimpr crimp prim imp mir rim rip mi pi

cimprs crimps scrimp crimp crisp prism scrim scrip imps mirs prim rims rips simp imp mir mis rim rip sic sip sir is mi pi si

cimprss scrimps. *See* **cimprs ciprss imprss cimrss**

cimprsy scrimpy. *See* **cimprs cimpry ciprsy**

cimpry crimpy crimp miry prim rimy cry icy imp mir pry rim rip yip mi my pi

cimrs scrim mirs rims mir mis rim sic sir is mi si

cimrss scrims scrim mirs miss rims sirs mir mis rim sic sir sis is mi si

cimruu curium uric cum cur mir rim rum mi mu um

cimssty mystics. *See* **cimsty cisst cssty**

cimsty mystic misty cist city cyst mist tics icy its mis sic sit sty tic is it mi my si ti

cimsu music scum cum mis mus sic sum is mi mu si um us

cinnootu continuo unction. *See* **cinnou innoot**

cinnootx nontoxic. *See* **innoot**

cinnorsu unicorns unicorn nuncios. *See* **cinnou cinosu cinrsu ciorsu**

cinnoru unicorn. *See* **cinnou cnoru cioru**

cinnostu unctions nonsuit nuncios suction unction. *See* **cinnou cinost cinosu cinstu**

cinnosu nuncios. *See* **cinosu cinnou innosu**

cinnotu unction. *See* **cinnou cnotu cintu**

cinnou nuncio union cion coin icon noun unco con inn ion nun in no nu on

cino cion coin icon con ion in no on

cinooprs scorpion. *See* **cnoors inoops inoors inoprs**

cinopsty synoptic copyist. *See* **cinost ciopst inopst inopty**

cinorrst tricorns tricorn citrons. *See* **cinort cinost**

cinorrt tricorn. *See* **cinort**

cinorst citrons. *See* **cinort cinost**

cinorstu ructions citrons incrust nitrous ruction suction. *See* **cinort cinost cinosu cinrsu**

cinorsuy cousinry. *See* **cinosu cinrsu ciorsu inorsy**

cinorsz zircons. *See* **cinorz cinos ciors**

cinort citron tonic toric cion coin coir corn icon into iron otic riot tiro tori torn trio con cor cot ion nit nor not orc ort roc rot tic tin ton tor in it no on or ti to

cinortu ruction. *See* **cinort cnoru cnotu**

cinorz zircon cion coin coir corn icon iron zinc zori con cor coz ion nor orc roc in no on or

cinos cions coins icons scion sonic cion coin cons icon ions con ion sic sin son in is no on os si so

cinoss scions cions coins icons scion sonic cion coin cons icon ions sins sons con ion sic sin sis son in is no on os si so

cinossst consists consist tocsins. *See* **cinoss cinost ciosst**

cinosst consist tocsins. *See* **cinoss ciosst cinost**

cinosstu suctions consist cousins suction tocsins. *See* **cinoss cinost cinosu cinstu**

cinossu cousins. *See* **cinoss cinosu**

cinost tocsin tonics cions coins icons scion sonic stoic tonic cion cist coin cons cost cots icon into ions nits otic scot snit snot tics tins tons con cot ion its nit not sic sin sit son sot tic tin ton in is it no on os si so ti to

cinostu suction. *See* **ciostu cnostu cinosu cinost cinstu**

cinostuv viscount suction. *See* **cinost cinosu cinstu ciostu**

cinosu cousin cions coins icons incus scion sonic cion coin cons icon ions nous onus unco con ion sic sin son sou sun in is no nu on os si so us

cinot tonic cion coin icon into otic con cot ion nit not tic tin ton in it no on ti to

cinrsstu incrusts incrust rustics. *See* **cinrsu cinstu cirstu crsstu**

cinrsttu instruct incrust. *See* **cinrsu cinstt cinstu cirstt**

cinrstu incrust. *See* **cirstu cinrsu cinstu**

cinrstuy scrutiny incrust. *See* **cinrsu cinstu cirstu crstuy**

cinrsu incurs incur incus ruins runic crus curs ruin runs uric urns cur run sic sin sir sun urn in is nu si us

cinru incur runic uric ruin cur run urn in nu

cinstt tincts stint tinct tints cist nits snit tics tins tint tits its nit sic sin sit tic tin tit in is it si ti

cinstu tunics cutin cutis ictus incus suint tunic units cist cuts nits nuts scut snit stun suit tics tins tuis tuns unit cut its nit nut sic sin sit sun tic tin tui tun in is it nu si ti us ut

cinsu incus sic sin sun in is nu si us

cinsz zincs zinc sic sin in is si

cintt tinct tint nit tic tin tit in it ti

cintu cutin tunic unit cut nit nut tic tin tui tun in it nu ti ut

cinyz zincy zinc icy yin in

cinz zinc in

ciooprst porticos octrois portico tropics. *See* **cioopt cioort cioprt ciopst**

ciooprt portico. *See* **cioopt cioort cioprt**

cioopsu copious. *See* **coops copsu iopsu**

cioopt octopi optic picot topic coop coot otic coo cop cot pit poi pot tic tip too top it pi ti to

ciooqstu coquitos coquito. *See* **ciostu ioqstu**

ciooqtu coquito. *See* **ioqtu**

cioorst octrois. *See* **cioort ciors coost**

cioort octroi toric coir coot otic riot root roto tiro tori trio coo cor cot orc ort roc rot tic too tor it or ti to

cioprst tropics. *See* **ciopst ciprst ioprst cioprt**

cioprt tropic optic picot topic toric coir crop otic port riot tiro tori trio trip cop cor cot orc ort pit poi pot pro rip roc rot tic tip top tor it or pi ti to

ciopssty copyists copyist. *See* **ciopst ciosst iopsst**

ciopst optics picots topics optic picot posit stoic topic cist cops cost cots otic pits pois post pots scop scot spit spot stop tics tips tops cop cot its pit poi pot sic sip sit sop sot tic tip top is it os pi si so ti to

ciopsty copyist. *See* **ciopst**

ciopt optic picot topic otic cop cot pit poi pot tic tip top it pi ti to

cioqrsu croquis. *See* **ciorsu**

cior coir cor orc roc or

ciors coirs coir cors orcs rocs sori cor orc roc sic sir is or os si so

ciorsss scissor. *See* **ciors corss**

ciorssss scissors scissor. *See* **ciors corss**

ciorstt tricots. *See* **ciortt cirstt**

ciorstv victors. *See* **ciortv ciors iorst**

ciorsu curios coirs curio scour coir cors crus curs orcs ours rocs sori sour uric cor cur orc our roc sic sir sou is or os si so us

ciorsuu curious. *See* **ciorsu**

ciort toric coir otic riot tiro tori trio cor cot orc ort roc rot tic tor it or ti to

ciortt tricot toric coir otic riot tiro tori tort trio trot cor cot orc ort roc rot tic tit tor tot it or ti to

ciortv victor toric coir otic riot tiro tori trio cor cot orc ort roc rot tic tor it or ti to

ciortvy victory. *See* **ciortv iorvy**

cioru curio coir uric cor cur orc our roc or

ciosst stoics cists costs stoic cist cost cots otic scot sits sots tics toss cot its sic sis sit sot tic is it os si so ti to

ciossuv viscous. *See* **cissuv**

ciost stoic cist cost cots otic scot tics cot its sic sit sot tic is it os si so ti to

ciostu coitus cutis ictus scout stoic cist cost cots cuts otic oust outs scot scut suit tics tuis cot cut its out sic sit sot sou tic tui is it os si so ti to us ut

ciot otic tic cot it ti to

ciotx toxic otic cot cox tic it ox ti to xi

ciprs crisp scrip rips rip sic sip sir is pi si

ciprss crisps scrips crisp priss scrip rips sips sirs rip sic sip sir sis is pi si

ciprsst scripts. *See* **ciprss ciprst iprsst**

ciprst script crisp scrip sprit strip trips cist pits rips spit stir tics tips trip its pit rip sic sip sir sit tic tip is it pi si ti

ciprsy crispy crisp scrip spicy spiry rips spry yips cry icy pry rip sic sip sir spy yip is pi si

cipstty styptic. *See* **ipstty cipsy**

cipsy spicy yips icy sic sip spy yip is pi si

cirrsu cirrus crus curs uric cur sic sir is si us

cirsstu rustics. *See* **cirstu crsstu**

cirstt strict cist stir tics tits its sic sir sit tic tit is it si ti

cirstu citrus rustic crust curst cutis ictus cist crus curs curt cuts rust ruts scut stir suit tics tuis uric cur cut its rut sic sir sit tic tui is it si ti us ut

cirtty yttric city cry icy tic tit try it ti

ciru uric cur

cis sic is si

cisst cists cist sits tics its sic sis sit tic is it si ti

cissuv viscus cuss sic sis is si us

cist cist tics its sic sit tic is it si ti

cistu cutis ictus cist cuts scut suit tics tuis cut its sic sit tic tui is it si ti us ut

cit tic it ti

city city tic icy it ti

ciy icy

cj

cjko jock jo
cjkoo jocko jock cook coo jo
cjkos jocks jock sock kos jo os so
cjnoorru conjuror. *See* **cnoru cnoor cjnou**

cjnosu juncos junco cons nous onus unco con jus son sou sun jo no no on os so us

cjnou junco unco con jo no nu on on
cjnouy jouncy junco unco cony con coy joy yon you jo no nu on oy

ck

ckkno knock conk konk nock con no on
ckknootu knockout. *See* **cnoot cnotu ckkno**
ckknos knocks conks knock nocks conk cons konk nock sock con kos son no on os so
cklloop pollock. *See* **clloop**
cklloops pollocks collops pollock scollop. *See* **clloop**
cklnos clonks conks locks nocks cols conk cons lock nock sock col con kos los sol son lo no on on os so
cklnostu locknuts consult locknut unlocks. *See* **cklnos cklnou cklnsu clnosu**
cklnosu unlocks. *See* **cklnos clnosu cklnsu cklnou**
cklnotu locknut. *See* **cklnou clotu cnotu**
cklnou unlock clunk conk lock luck nock unco col con lo no nu on
cklnsu clunks clunk lucks slunk cusk luck suck sulk sunk sun nu us
cklnu clunk luck nu
cklnuuy unlucky. *See* **cklnuy**
cklnuy clunky clunk lucky luck yuck yuk nu
cklo lock col lo
ckloorsw rowlocks rowlock. *See* **ckoors cloors**
ckloorw rowlock. *See* **ckoor cloor**
ckloostu lockouts lockout. *See* **clostu**
cklootu lockout. *See* **clotu**
cklopstu potlucks lockups potluck. *See* **cklopu cklpsu clostu clpstu**
cklopsu lockups. *See* **cklopu cklpsu**
ckloptu potluck. *See* **cklopu clotu loptu**
cklopu lockup pluck coup lock luck pock puck col cop cup lop pul lo up
cklos locks cols lock sock col kos los sol lo os so
cklpsu plucks lucks pluck pucks sculp cups cusk cusp luck plus puck puls scup suck sulk cup pul pus sup up us
cklpu pluck luck puck cup pul up

cklpuy plucky pluck lucky luck puck yuck cup ply pul yuk yup up
cklsu lucks cusk luck suck sulk us
cklu luck
ckluy lucky luck yuck yuk
ckmo mock mo om
ckmos mocks smock mock sock kos mos oms mo om os so
ckmoss smocks mocks smock socks mock moss sock kos mos oms mo om os so
ckmsu mucks cusk muck musk scum suck cum mus sum mu um us
ckmu muck cum mu um
ckmuy mucky muck yuck cum yuk yum mu my um
ckno conk nock con no on
cknorsu uncorks. *See* **cknoru cknos ckors**
cknoru uncork cornu korun conk cork corn knur nock rock ruck unco con cor cur kor nor orc our roc run urn no nu on or
cknos conks nocks conk cons nock sock con kos son no on os so
cknstuu unstuck. *See* **ckstu knstu cnsuu**
ckoo cook coo
ckooostu cookouts cookout. *See* **ckoos coost costu**
ckoootu cookout. *No 6s or 5s*
ckoor crook cook cork rock rook coo cor kor orc roc or
ckoors crooks cooks corks crook rocks rooks cook coos cork cors orcs rock rocs rook sock coo cor kor kos orc roc or os so
ckoos cooks cook coos sock coo kos os so
ckooy cooky cook yock coo coy oy
ckop pock cop
ckops pocks cops pock scop sock cop kos sop os so
ckor cork rock cor kor orc roc or

ckors corks rocks cork cors orcs rock rocs sock cor kor kos orc roc or os so
ckorstuw cutworks cutwork. *See* **ckrstu corstu**
ckortuw cutwork. *See* **ckrtu cortu**
ckory corky rocky cork rock yock cor coy cry kor orc roc or oy
ckos sock kos os so
ckoss socks sock kos os so
ckossstu tussocks tussock. *See* **ckosst cosstu**
ckosst stocks costs socks stock cost cots scot sock sots toss cot kos sot tsk os so to
ckosstu tussock. *See* **ckosst cosstu**
ckost stock cost cots scot sock cot kos sot tsk os so to
ckosty stocky stock yocks cost cosy cots cyst scot sock toys yock cot coy kos sky sot soy sty toy tsk os oy so to
ckosy yocks cosy sock yock coy kos sky soy os oy so
ckoy yock coy oy
ckpsu pucks cups cusk cusp puck scup suck cup pus sup up us
ckpu puck cup up
ckrstu struck trucks crust curst rucks stuck truck tucks crus curs curt cusk cuts ruck rusk rust ruts scut suck tusk cur cut rut tsk us ut
ckrsu rucks crus curs cusk ruck rusk suck cur us
ckrsuu ruckus rucks crus curs cusk kuru ruck rusk suck urus cur us
ckrtu truck curt ruck tuck cur cut rut ut
ckru ruck cur
ckssu cusks sucks cusk cuss suck us
ckstu stuck tucks cusk cuts scut suck tuck tusk cut tsk us ut
cksu cusk suck us
cksuy yucks cusk suck yuck yuks sky yuk us
cktu tuck cut ut

ckuy   yuck yuk
ckuyy   yucky yuck yuk

---

clloop   collop cool coop loco loop poll polo pool col coo cop loo lop lo

clloops   collops scollop. *See* clloop clops cloos

clloopss   scollops collops scollop. *See* clloop coopss loopss

cllooquy   colloquy. *See* cllooy

cllooy   coolly colly cloy cool loco col coo coy loo lo oy

cllors   scroll rolls cols cors orcs rocs roll col cor los orc roc sol lo or os so

cllorss   scrolls. *See* cllors corss

clloy   colly cloy col coy lo oy

cllssu   sculls culls scull cull cuss us

cllsu   culls scull cull us

cllu   cull

clluy   cully cull

clmmnooy   commonly. *See* clnooy cmmnoo

clmnosu   columns. *See* clnosu clmnou

clmnou   column culm muon unco col con cum lum mon lo mo mu no nu om on um

clmoopst   complots complot compost. *See* clmops cmoops

clmoopt   complot. *See* clmop cmoop lmoot

clmop   clomp comp col cop lop mop lo mo om

clmops   clomps clomp clops comps cols comp cops lops mops scop slop col cop lop los mop mos oms sol sop lo mo om os so

clmopy   comply clomp cloy comp copy moly ploy col cop coy lop mop ply lo mo my om oy

clmosuuu   cumulous cumulus. *See* cmosuu

clmpsu   clumps clump culms lumps plums sculp slump culm cups cusp lump plum plus puls scum scup slum sump umps cum cup lum mus pul pus sum sup ump mu um up us

clmpu   clump culm lump plum cum cup lum pul ump mu um up

clmpuy   clumpy clump lumpy culm lump plum cum cup lum ply pul ump yum yup mu my um up

clmstu   mulcts culms cults mulct culm cult cuts lust must scum scut slum slut smut stum cum cut lum mus sum mu um us ut

clmsu   culms culm scum slum cum lum mus sum mu um us

clmsuuu   cumulus. *See* clmsu cmsuu

clmsuy   clumsy culms culm scum slum cum lum mus sly sum yum mu my um us

clmtu   mulct culm cult cum cut lum mu um ut

clmu   culm cum lum mu um

clnoo   colon cool coon loco loon col con coo loo lo no on

clnoorst   controls consort control crotons. *See* clnoos cloors cnoors cnoort

clnoort   control. *See* cnoort clnoo cloor

clnoos   colons colon cools coons locos loons cols cons cool coon coos loco loon loos solo soon col con coo loo los sol son lo no on os so

clnooss   consols. *See* clnoos looss

clnooy   colony colon loony cloy cony cool coon loco loon only col con coo coy loo yon lo no on oy

clnosstu   consults consuls consult locusts. *See* clnosu clostu cnostu cosstu

clnossu   consuls. *See* clnosu

clnostu   consult. *See* clnosu clostu cnostu

clnosu   clonus consul locus cols cons nous onus soul unco col con los sol son sou sun lo no nu on os so us

clnosw   clowns clown cowls scowl cols cons cowl cows lows owls owns scow slow snow sown col con cow los low now owl own sol son sow won lo no on os ow so

clnow   clown cowl col con cow low now owl own won lo no on ow

clnrsuu   uncurls. *See* clnruu clrsu cnsuu

clnruu   uncurl curl cur run ulu urn nu

clo   col lo

cloo   cool loco col coo loo lo

cloooprt   protocol. *See* cloor loopr ooprt

cloor   color cool loco col coo cor loo orc roc lo or

cloors   colors color cools locos cols cool coos cors loco loos orcs rocs solo col coo cor loo los orc roc sol lo or os so

cloorsu   colours. *See* cloors clooru

clooru   colour color cool curl loco col coo cor cur loo orc our roc lo or

cloos   cools locos cols cool coos loco loos solo col coo loo los sol lo os so

cloosssu   colossus. *See* cloos closu looss

cloprstu   sculptor. *See* clostu clpstu coprsu corstu

clops   clops cols cops lops scop slop col cop lop los sol sop lo os so

clorssy   crossly. *See* closy corss

clortuy   courtly. *See* clrtuy cortuy

clos   cols col los sol lo os so

closstu   locusts. *See* clostu cosstu

clossw   scowls cowls scowl scows slows cols cowl cows loss lows owls scow slow sols sows col cow los low owl sol sow lo os ow so

clost   clots colts clot cols colt cost cots lost lots scot slot col cot los lot sol sot lo os so to

clostu   clouts locust clots clout colts cults locus lotus louts scout clot cols colt cost cots cult cuts lost lots lout lust oust outs scot scut slot slut soul tolu col cot cut los lot out sol sot sou lo os so to us ut

closty   costly clots cloys colts clot cloy cols colt cost cosy cots cyst lost lots scot slot toys col cot coy los lot sly sol sot soy sty toy lo os oy so to

closu   locus cols soul col los sol sou lo os so us

closw   cowls scowl cols cowl cows lows owls scow slow col cow los low owl sol sow lo os ow so

closy   cloys cloy cols cosy col coy los sly sol soy lo os oy so

clot   clot colt col cot lot lo to

clotu   clout clot colt cult lout tolu col cot cut lot out lo to ut

clow   cowl col cow low owl lo ow

cloy   cloy col coy lo oy

cloyy   coyly cloy col coy lo oy

clpsstu   sculpts. *See* clpssu clpstu

clpssu sculps cusps sculp scups cups cusp cuss plus puls puss scup sups cup pul pus sup up us

clpstu sculpt sculp cults cult cups cusp cuts lust plus puls puts scup scut slut tups cup cut pul pus put sup tup up us ut

clpsu sculp cups cusp plus puls scup cup pul pus sup up us

clrsu curls crus curl curs slur cur us

clrtuy curtly curly truly cult curl curt yurt cry cur cut rut try ut

clru curl cur

clruy curly curl cur cry

clstu cults cult cuts lust scut slut cut us ut

clstuu cultus cults cult cuts lust scut slut ulus cut ulu us ut

cltu cult cut ut

---

cm

cmmnnoou uncommon. *See* **cmmnoo cmnnoo**

cmmnoo common coon mono moon con coo mom mon moo mo no om on

cmmnoos commons. *See* **cmmnoo cnoos mnoos**

cmmruy crummy rummy cry cum cur mum rum yum mu my um

cmmsuy scummy scum mums cum mum mus sum yum mu my um us

cmnnoo noncom coon mono moon noon con coo mon moo mo no om on

cmnnoos noncoms. *See* **cmnnoo cnoos mnoos**

cmoop compo comp coop coo cop moo mop mo om

cmooprst comports comport compost. *See* **cmoops mooprs moorst ooprst**

cmooprt comport. *See* **cmoop moort moopr**

cmoops compos compo comps coops scoop comp coop coos cops moos mops oops scop coo cop moo mop mos oms sop mo om os so

cmoopsst composts compost. *See* **cmoops cmooss coopss coosst**

cmoopst compost. *See* **cmoops coost moost**

cmooss cosmos coos moos moss coo moo mos oms mo om os so

cmop comp cop mop mo om

cmops comps comp cops mops scop cop mop mos oms sop mo om os so

cmor corm cor mor orc roc mo om or

cmors corms corm cors mors orcs rocs cor mor mos oms orc roc mo om or os so

cmorsstu scrotums scrotum customs. *See* **cmostu cmrssu corssu corstu**

cmorstu scrotum. *See* **corstu cmostu morstu**

cmorstuw cutworms scrotum cutworm. *See* **cmostu corstu morstu**

cmortuw cutworm. *See* **cortu mortu**

cmosstu customs. *See* **cmostu cosstu**

cmostu custom scout cost cots cuts most mots must oust outs scot scum scut smut stum sumo toms cot cum cut mos mot mus oms out sot sou sum tom mo mu om os so to um us ut

cmosuu mucous mucus scum sumo cum mos mus oms sou sum mo mu om os so um us

cmprsu crumps crump rumps scrum crus cups curs cusp rump rums scum scup spur sump umps cum cup cur mus pus rum sum sup ump mu um up us

cmpru crump rump cum cup cur rum ump mu um up

cmrssu scrums scrum scums crus curs cuss muss rums scum sums cum cur mus rum sum mu um us

cmrsu scrum crus curs rums scum cum cur mus rum sum mu um us

cmssu scums cuss muss scum sums cum mus sum mu um us

cmstuu scutum mucus cuts must scum scut smut stum cum cut mus sum mu um us ut

cmsu scum cum mus sum mu um us

cmsuu mucus scum cum mus sum mu um us

cmu cum mu um

---

cn

cnnorstu nocturns nocturn. *See* **cnostu corstu**

cnnortu nocturn. *See* **cnoru cnotu cortu**

cno con no on

cnoo coon con coo no on

cnoooort octoroon. *See* **cnoort**

cnooppr popcorn. *See* **cnoor noopr**

cnoopsu coupons. *See* **cnoopu cnoos co-ops**

cnoopu coupon coon coop coup poon unco upon con coo cop cup pun no nu on up

cnoor croon coon corn con coo cor nor orc roc no on or

cnoorrsw cornrows cornrow. *See* **cnoors cnorsw oorrsw**

cnoorrw cornrow. *See* **cnoor cnorw**

cnoors croons coons corns croon scorn cons coon coos corn cors orcs rocs soon con coo cor nor orc roc son no on or os so

cnoorsst consorts consort crotons nostocs tonsors. *See* **cnoors cnoort cnoost cnorss**

cnoorst consort crotons. *See* **cnoost cnoors cnoort**

cnoorstt contorts consort contort cottons crotons. *See* **cnoors cnoort cnoost cnoott**

cnoorstu contours croutons consort contour crotons crouton. *See* **cnoors cnoort cnoost cnostu**

cnoort croton croon conto coon coot corn onto root roto toon torn con coo cor cot nor not orc ort roc rot ton too tor no on or to

cnoortt contort. *See* **cnoort cnoott**

cnoortu contour crouton. *See* **cnoort cnoru cnotu**

cnoos coons cons coon coos soon con coo son no on os so

cnoosst nostocs. *See* **cnoost coosst noosst**

cnoost contos nostoc conto coons coots scoot snoot toons cons coon coos coot cost cots onto scot snot soon soot tons toon con coo cot not son sot ton too no on os so to

cnoostt cottons. *See* **cnoost cnoott**

cnoosty tycoons. *See* **cnoost noosty cnooty**

cnoosuu nocuous. *See* **cnoos cnsuu**

cnoosvy convoys. *See* **cnoovy cnoos**

cnoot conto coon coot onto toon con coo cot not ton too no on to

cnoott cotton conto coon coot onto toon toot con coo cot not ton too tot no on to

cnootty cottony. *See* **cnoott cnooty**

cnooty tycoon conto toyon cony coon coot onto tony toon con coo cot coy not ton too toy yon no on oy to

cnoovy convoy coon cony con coo coy yon no on oy

cnor corn con cor nor orc roc no on or

cnors corns scorn cons corn cors orcs rocs con cor nor orc roc son no on or os so

cnorss scorns corns cross scorn cons corn cors orcs rocs sons con cor nor orc roc son no on or os so

cnorsw crowns corns crown crows scorn sworn cons corn cors cows crow orcs owns rocs rows scow snow sown worn con cor cow nor now orc own roc row son sow won no on or os ow so

cnortuy country. *See* **cnotuy cortuy**

cnoru cornu corn unco con cor cur nor orc our roc run urn no nu on or

cnorw crown corn crow worn con cor cow nor now orc own roc row won no on or ow

cnory corny crony corn cony con cor coy cry nor orc roc yon no on or oy

cnos cons con son no on os so

cnostu counts count scout snout tonus cons cost cots cuts nous nuts onus oust outs scot scut snot stun tons tuns unco unto con cot cut not nut out son sot sou sun ton tun no nu on os so to us ut

cnostuuu unctuous. *See* **cnostu**

cnotu count unco unto con cot cut not nut out ton tun no nu on to ut

cnotuy county count cony tony unco unto con cot coy cut not nut out ton toy tun yon you no nu on oy to ut

cnou unco con no nu on

cnoy cony con coy yon no on oy

cnssy syncs sync

cnsuu uncus sun nu us

cnsy sync

cntuu uncut cut nut tun nu ut

coo coo

coop coop coo cop

cooprrst proctors proctor torpors. *See* **ooprrt ooprst**

cooprrt proctor. *See* **ooprrt**

cooprstu outcrops octopus outcrop uproots. *See* **coprsu corstu ooprst ooprtu**

cooprtu outcrop. *See* **ooprtu cortu copru**

coops coops scoop coop coos cops oops scop coo cop sop os so

coopss scoops coops scoop scops coop coos cops oops scop sops coo cop sop os so

coopstu octopus. *See* **coops coost copsu**

coopwx cowpox coop coo cop cow cox pox woo ow ox

coos coos coo os so

coosst scoots coots costs scoot soots coos coot cost cots scot soot sots toss coo cot sot too os so to

coost coots scoot coos coot cost cots scot soot coo cot sot too os so to

coot coot coo cot too to

cop cop

copr crop cop cor orc pro roc or

coprrstu corrupts corrupt. *See* **coprsu corstu oprstu**

coprrtu corrupt. *See* **copru cortu**

coprs corps crops cops cors crop orcs pros rocs scop cop cor orc pro roc sop or os so

coprsu corpus corps coups crops croup pours scour cops cors coup crop crus cups curs cusp opus orcs ours pour pros rocs scop scup soup sour spur cop cor cup cur orc our pro pus roc sop sou sup or os so up us

coprsuu cuprous. *See* **coprsu prsuu**

copru croup coup crop pour cop cor cup cur orc our pro roc or up

copruy croupy croup coypu copy coup crop pour ropy your cop cor coy cry cup cur orc our pro pry roc you yup or oy up

cops cops scop cop sop os so

copss scops cops scop sops cop sop os so

copsu coups cops coup cups cusp opus scop scup soup cop cup pus sop sou sup os so up us

copsuy coypus coups coypu soupy cops copy cosy coup cups cusp opus posy scop scup soup yups cop coy cup pus sop sou soy spy sup you yup os oy so up us

copu coup cop cup up

copuy coypu coup copy cop coy cup you yup oy up

copy copy cop coy oy

cor cor orc roc or

corrssu cursors. *See* **corrsu corssu**

corrsu cursor scour cors crus curs orcs ours rocs sour cor cur orc our roc sou or os so us

corrsuy cursory. *See* **corrsu crrsuy**

cors cors orcs rocs cor orc roc or os so

corss cross cors orcs rocs cor orc roc or os so

corssu scours cross scour sorus sours cors crus curs cuss orcs ours rocs sour sous cor cur orc our roc sou or os so us

corstu courts court crust curst roust routs scour scout stour torus tours cors cost cots crus curs curt cuts orcs orts ours oust outs rocs rots rout rust ruts scot scut sort sour tors tour cor cot cur cut orc ort our out roc rot rut sot sou tor or os so to us ut

corsu scour cors crus curs orcs ours rocs sour cor cur orc our roc sou or os so us

corsw crows cors cows crow orcs rocs rows scow cor cow orc roc row sow or os ow so

cortu court curt rout tour cor cot cur cut orc ort our out roc rot rut tor or to ut

cortuy outcry court curt rout ryot tour troy tyro your yurt cor cot coy cry cur cut orc ort our out roc rot rut tor toy try you or oy to ut

corw crow cor cow orc roc row or ow

corwy cowry crow cor cow coy cry orc roc row yow or ow oy

cosst costs cost cots scot sots toss cot sot os so to

cosstu scouts costs ousts scout scuts cost cots cuss cuts oust outs scot scut sots sous toss cot cut out sot sou os so to us ut

cossw scows cows scow sows cow sow os ow so

cost cost cots scot cot sot os so to

costtuu cutouts. *See* **cottuu costu osttu**

costu scout cost cots cuts oust outs scot scut cot cut out sot sou os so to us ut

cosw cows scow cow sow os ow so

cosy cosy coy soy os oy so

cot cot to

cottuu cutout tout tutu cot cut out tot tut to ut

cow cow ow

cox cox ox

coy coy oy

coyz cozy coy coz oy

coz coz

---

cp

cprsty crypts crypt cyst spry cry pry spy sty try

cprty crypt cry pry try

cpssu cusps scups cups cusp cuss puss scup sups cup pus sup up us

cpstuu cutups cutup cups cusp cuts puts scup scut tups cup cut pus put sup tup up us ut

cpsu cups cusp scup cup pus sup up us

cptuu cutup cup cut put tup up ut

cpu cup up

---

cr

crrsuy scurry curry crus curs cur cry us

crruy curry cur cry

crsstu crusts crust curst rusts scuts truss crus curs curt cuss cuts rust ruts scut cur cut rut us ut

crstu crust curst crus curs curt cuts rust ruts scut cur cut rut us ut

crstuy crusty curtsy crust curst rusty yurts crus curs curt cuts cyst rust ruts scut yurt cry cur cut rut sty try us ut

crsu crus curs cur us

crsuvy scurvy curvy crus curs cur cry us

crtu curt cur cut rut ut

cru cur

cruvy curvy cur cry

crux crux cur

cry cry

cs

csstu scuts cuss cuts scut cut us ut	**cssu** cuss us	**csty** cyst sty
cssty cysts cyst sty	**cstu** cuts scut cut us ut	**csuyzz** scuzzy us

ct

ctu cut ut		

dd

ddddeeor doddered. *See* **dddeer dddeor ddeeor**

ddddeil diddled. *See* **dddeil**

dddeee deeded deed

dddeeefn defended. *See* **dddeee ddeeen ddeefn**

dddeeenp depended. *See* **dddeee ddeeen ddeenp deeenp**

dddeeenr reddened. *See* **dddeee dddeer ddeeen ddeenr**

dddeefor foddered. *See* **dddeer dddeor ddeeor ddefor**

dddeegr dredged. *See* **dddeer ddeegr**

dddeehrs shredded shedder. *See* **dddeer ddeehr**

dddeei eddied deed died did die id

dddeeir derided. *See* **ddeeir dddeei dddeer dddeir**

dddeejru juddered. *See* **dddeer ddejru**

dddeelm meddled. *See* **ddeelm**

dddeelp peddled. *See* **ddeelp**

dddeels sledded. *See* **ddees ddeel deels**

dddeelu deluded. *See* **ddeelu**

dddeenos soddened. *See* **dddeno dddeos ddenos**

dddeenu denuded. *See* **ddeenu**

dddeer redded dreed deed deer dree redd reed red ere er re

dddeertu detruded detrude. *See* **dddeer dddeet**

dddeet tedded deed teed ted tee

dddeew wedded dewed deed weed dew ewe wed wee we

dddefil fiddled. *See* **dddeil ddefil**

dddeflu fuddled. *See* **ddeflu**

dddegilr griddled girdled griddle riddled. *See* **dddeil dddeir ddegil ddegir**

dddego dodged dodge doge dog ego god odd ode do go od

dddegru drudged. *See* **ddegru**

dddehlu huddled. *See* **ddehlu**

dddehtu thudded. *No 6s or 5s*

dddeiinv dividend divided divined. *See* **ddeiiv deiinv**

dddeiiv divided. *See* **ddeiiv**

dddeik kidded diked died dike did die kid id

dddeiks skidded. *See* **dddeik deiks ddeis**

dddeil diddle lidded idled deil deli died idle lied did die eld led lei lid lie el id li

dddeilm middled. *See* **dddeil ddeilm**

dddeilnw dwindled dwindle. *See* **dddeil ddeinw**

dddeilp piddled. *See* **dddeil deilp**

dddeilr riddled. *See* **dddeil ddeilr**

dddeils diddles. *See* **dddeil ddeils**

dddeiltw twiddled twiddle. *See* **dddeil deiltw**

dddeimu muddied. *See* **dddemu**

dddeinor dendroid. *See* **dddeir dddeno dddeor ddeinr**

dddeinru underdid. *See* **dddeir ddeinr ddeinu deinru**

dddeir ridded dried redid died dire redd ride did die ire red rid er id re

dddeloo doodled. *See* **ddelo deloo**

dddelop plodded. *See* **dddeop ddelo delop**

dddelot toddled. *See* **ddelot**

dddelpu puddled. *See* **ddelpu**

dddemu mudded dude dud due emu mud em me mu um

dddeno nodded done node den doe don end eon nod odd ode one do en ne no od on

dddeop podded doped dope oped doe odd ode ope pod do od pe

dddeopr prodded. *See* **dddeor dddeop**

dddeor dodder rodded doer redd redo rode doe dor odd ode ore red rod roe do er od or re

dddeors dodders. *See* **dddeor dddeos**

dddeos sodded dosed does dose odds odes doe dos odd ode sod do od os so

dddepsu spudded. *See* **ddepu ddesu**

dddestu studded. *See* **ddestu**

dddgiiln diddling. *See* **dgiiln**

ddee deed

ddeeeemr redeemed. *See* **ddeeem ddeeer deeemr**

ddeeeflx deflexed. *See* **deeflx**

ddeeefnr defender. *See* **ddeeen ddeeer ddeefn ddeenr**

ddeeefrr deferred. *See* **ddeeer ddeerr deeefr eeefrr**

ddeeegrt deterged deterge greeted. *See* **ddeeer ddeegr**

ddeeeh heeded deed heed edh eh he

ddeeehlw wheedled wheedle. *See* **ddeeeh ddeeew ddeehl ddeelw**

ddeeehnu unheeded. *See* **ddeeeh ddeeen ddeenu**

ddeeeimr remedied. *See* **ddeeem ddeeer ddeeir deeemr**

ddeeeirt reedited. *See* **ddeeir ddeeit ddeeer deeirt**

ddeeeln needled. *See* **ddeeen deeeln**

ddeeelpt depleted deleted deplete. *See* **ddeelp deeelp deeelt deelpt**

ddeeelss deedless. *See* **ddeees eeelss**

ddeeelt deleted. *See* **deeelt ddeel**

ddeeeltw tweedled deleted tweedle. *See* **ddeeew ddeelw deeelt deeltw**

ddeeem deemed deed deem deme meed em me

ddeeemn emended. *See* **ddeeem ddeemn ddeeen**

ddeeemnt demented emended. *See* **ddeeem ddeeen ddeemn ddeent**

ddeeen needed ended deed dene need den end nee en ne

ddeeennu unneeded. *See* **ddeeen ddeenu ddennu**

ddeeenpx expended. *See* **ddeeen ddeenp deeenp deenpx**

ddeeenrr rendered. *See* **ddeeen ddeeer ddeenr ddeerr**

ddeeenrt tendered entered. *See* **ddeeen ddeeer ddeenr ddeent**

ddeeentx extended. *See* **ddeeen ddeent deentx**

ddeeeps speeded. *See* **ddeees deeeps**

ddeeer reeded dreed deed deer dree redd reed red ere er re

ddeeerrt deterred. *See* **ddeeer ddeerr**

ddeeerst deserted reddest steered. *See* **ddeeer ddeees deeers deerst**

ddeeersv deserved deserve. *See* **ddeeer ddeees deeers deeerv**

ddeees seeded deeds deed seed see

ddeeestt detested. *See* **ddeees deestt**

ddeeestv devested. *See* **ddeees deestv**

ddeeew weeded dewed deed weed dew ewe wed wee we

ddeeffir differed. *See* **ddeefi ddeeir deefir deffir**

ddeeffno offended. *See* **ddeefn ddeffo deffno**

ddeefggo defogged. *See* **ddeggo defggo**

ddeefgit fidgeted. *See* **ddeefi ddeeit defgit**

ddeefgl fledged. *See* **ddeegl deefgl**

ddeefi defied deed died feed did die fed fee fid fie id if

ddeefii deified edified. *See* **ddeefi**

ddeefil defiled fielded. *See* **ddeefi ddeefil ddeeil ddefil**

ddeefin defined. *See* **ddeefn ddeefi deefin ddeein**

ddeeflu deedful. *See* **ddeelu ddeefu ddeflu deeflu**

ddeefmor deformed freedom. *See* **ddeeor ddefor defmor**

ddeefn defend fended ended deed dene feed fend need den end fed fee fen nee en ne**

ddeefnru refunded underfed endured. *See* **ddeefn ddeefu ddeenr ddeenu**

ddeefns defends. *See* **ddeefn**

ddeefsu defused. *See* **ddeefu deefsu**

ddeefu feuded deed dude feed feud dud due fed fee feu

ddeeg edged deed edge geed gee

ddeegh hedged edged hedge deed edge geed ghee heed edh gee eh he

ddeegin deeding deigned. *See* **ddeein ddegin**

ddeeginr engirded deeding deigned dreeing redding reeding reigned. *See* **ddeegr ddeein ddeeir ddeenr**

ddeegins designed deeding deigned seeding. *See* **ddeein ddeeis ddegin deegis**

ddeegirv diverged derived diverge grieved. *See* **ddeegr ddeeir ddegir deegrv**

ddeegist digested teddies edgiest. *See* **ddeeis ddeeit deegis degist**

ddeegk kedged kedge deed edge eked geed geek eke gee keg

ddeegl gelded deled edged glede gleed ledge deed dele edge geed geld glee eel eld gee gel led lee leg el

ddeeglp pledged. *See* **ddeegl ddeelp deeglp**

ddeegls sledged. *See* **ddeegl deegls**

ddeeglu deluged. *See* **ddeelu deeglu ddeegl**

ddeegr dredge dreed edged edger greed deed deer dree edge geed gree redd reed ere erg gee red reg er re

ddeegrs dredges. *See* **ddeegr deegrs**

ddeegw wedged dewed edged wedge deed edge geed weed dew ewe gee wed wee we

ddeehils shielded heddles. *See* **ddeehl ddeeil ddeeis ddehis**

ddeehinr hindered inhered. *See* **ddeehr ddeein ddeeir ddeenr**

ddeehl heddle deled deed dele heed heel held edh eel eld led lee eh el he

ddeehls heddles. *See* **ddeehl ddees deels**

ddeehr herded dreed deed deer dree heed herd here redd reed edh ere her red eh er he re

ddeehrrs shredder shedder herders. *See* **ddeehr ddeerr**

ddeehrs shedder. *See* **ddeehr ddees deers**

ddeehrss shedders shedder dressed. *See* **ddeehr dehrss eehrss**

ddeeil elided deled edile elide idled deed deil dele deli died idle lied did die eel eld led lee lei lid lie el id li

ddeeilmw mildewed wielded. *See* **ddeeil ddeelm ddeelw ddeilm**

ddeeilr dreidel. *See* **ddeeir ddeilr ddeeil deeilr**

ddeeilrs dreidels derides desired dreidel resided riddles sledder. *See* **ddeeil ddeeir ddeeis ddeilr**

ddeeilrv driveled deliver derived deviled dreidel relived reviled. *See* **ddeeil ddeeir ddeelv ddeilr**

ddeeilrw wildered dreidel wielded wielder. *See* **ddeeil ddeeir ddeelw ddeilr**

ddeeilv deviled. *See* **ddeelv ddeeil deeilv**

ddeeilw wielded. *See* **ddeeil ddeelw**

ddeeily yielded. *See* **ddeeil deeily**

ddeeimnp impended impeded. *See* **ddeein ddeemn ddeenp ddeimn**

ddeeimnr reminded. *See* **ddeein ddeeir ddeemn ddeenr**

ddeeimp impeded. *See* **deeimp**

ddeeims demised misdeed. *See* **deeims ddeims ddeeis**

ddeeimss misdeeds demised demises misdeed. *See* **ddeeis ddeims deeims deeiss**

ddeeimtt demitted emitted. *See* **ddeeit deeimt**

ddeein denied indeed ended dined deed dene died dine need nide den did die din end nee en id in ne

ddeeinnt indented intended. *See* **ddeein ddeeit ddeent ddeinn**

ddeeinrt dendrite. *See* **ddeein ddeeir ddeeit ddeenr**

ddeeinst destined destine distend teddies. *See* **ddeein ddeeis ddeeit ddeent**

ddeeintu unedited detinue. *See* **ddeein ddeeit ddeent ddeenu**

ddeeinw widened. *See* **ddeein ddeenw ddeinw**

ddeeinx indexed. *See* **ddeein**

ddeeinz dizened. *See* **ddeein**

ddeeiprs presided derides desired preside resided. *See* **ddeeir ddeeis ddeipr deeips**

ddeeipss despised despise. *See* **ddeeis deeips deeiss deepss**

ddeeipst despited teddies despite. *See* **ddeeis ddeeit deeips deipst**

ddeeir deride dreed dried eider redid deed deer died dire dree redd reed ride did die ere ire red rid er id re

ddeeirs derides desired resided. *See* **ddeeir deeirs ddeeis**

ddeeirtv diverted derived riveted. *See* **ddeeir ddeeit deeirt deeirv**

ddeeirv derived. *See* **ddeeir deeirv**

ddeeis eddies deeds sided deed died dies ides seed side did die ids see id is si

ddeeisst desisted teddies. *See* **ddeeis ddeeit deeiss deesst**

ddeeist teddies. *See* **ddeeit ddeeis**

ddeeistv divested teddies devised. *See* **ddeeis ddeeit deeisv deestv**

ddeeisv devised. *See* **deeisv**

ddeeit dieted edited tided deed died diet edit teed tide tied did die dit ted tee tie id it ti

ddeel deled deed dele eel eld led lee el

ddeelloy yodelled yodeled. *See* **deelly**

ddeellu duelled. *See* **ddeelu ddellu**

ddeellw dwelled. *See* **ddeelw dellw**

ddeelm meddle melded deled deed deem dele deme meed meld eel eld elm led lee mel el em me

ddeelmo modeled. *See* **ddeelm ddelmo**

ddeelmr meddler. *See* **ddeelm**

ddeelmrs meddlers meddler meddles sledder. *See* **ddeelm deelrs eelmrs**

ddeelms meddles. *See* **ddeelm**

ddeelopr deplored peddler deplore. *See* **ddeelp ddeeor ddelor deelop**

ddeelopx exploded explode. *See* **ddeelp deelop**

ddeelopy deployed yodeled. *See* **ddeelp deelop deelpy delopy**

ddeelors soldered sledder resoled. *See* **ddeeor ddelor deelrs deeors**

ddeelosu deloused deludes delouse. *See* **ddeelu ddeosu deelsu**

ddeelow doweled. *See* **ddeelw ddelo delow**

ddeeloy yodeled. *See* **ddeel ddloy deloy**

ddeelp peddle deled deed deep dele peed peel pled eel eld led lee pee el pe

ddeelpr peddler. *See* **ddeelp ddeer deelr**

ddeelprs peddlers peddler peddles sledder. *See* **ddeelp deelrs eelprs**

ddeelpru preluded peddler prelude puddler. *See* **ddeelp ddeelu ddelpu deelru**

ddeelps peddles. *See* **ddeelp ddees deels**

ddeelrs sledder. *See* **deelrs ddees ddeel**

ddeelrss sledders sledder dressed. *See* **deelrs eelrss**

ddeelsu deludes. *See* **ddeelu deelsu**

ddeelu delude dueled eluded deled elude deed dele dude duel dud due eel eld led lee leu el

ddeelv delved deled delve deed dele veld eel eld eve led lee lev vee el

ddeelw welded deled dewed deed dele lewd weed weld dew eel eld ewe led lee wed wee el we

ddeemn mended ended emend deed deem deme dene meed mend need den end men nee em en me ne

ddeemot demoted. *See* **deemot**

ddeemrru demurred murdered demurer. *See* **ddeerr ddemru dderru deemru**

ddeen ended deed dene need den end nee en ne

ddeenn denned ended deed dene need den end nee en ne

ddeenop deponed. *See* **ddeenp deenop**

ddeenopr pondered deponed. *See* **ddeenp ddeenr ddeeor ddenor**

ddeenopw pondweed deponed endowed. *See* **ddeenp ddeenw ddenow deenop**

ddeenors endorsed endorse nodders reddens. *See* **ddeenr ddeeor ddenor ddenos**

ddeenorw wondered dowered drowned endowed. *See* **ddeenr ddeenw ddeeor ddenor**

ddeenot denoted. *See* **deenot ddeent**

ddeenow endowed. *See* **ddeenw ddenow**

ddeenp depend pended ended deed deep dene need neep peed peen pend den end nee pee pen en ne pe

ddeenps depends. *See* **ddeenp**

ddeenpu upended. *See* **ddeenu ddeenp**

ddeenr redden ended dreed deed deer dene dree erne need nerd redd reed rend den end ere nee red en er ne re

ddeenrs reddens. *See* **deenrs ddeenr**

ddeenrsu sundered denudes endured endures ensured reddens. *See* **ddeenr ddeenu ddensu ddersu**

ddeensu endured. *See* **ddeenu deenru ddeenr**

ddeensu denudes. *See* **ddeenu deensu ddensu**

ddeent dented tended ended deed dene dent need teed teen tend den end nee net ted tee ten en ne

ddeenu denude endued ended endue deed dene dude dune need nude den dud due dun end nee en nu

ddeenv vended ended deed dene even need vend den end eve nee vee en ne

ddeenw wended ended dewed deed dene need weed wend den dew end ewe nee new wed wee wen en ne we

ddeeoprt deported. *See* **ddeeor deeort deoprt**

ddeeoprw powdered dewdrop dowered powered. *See* **ddeeor ddeorw deoprw**

ddeeops deposed. *See* **deeops**

ddeeor eroded dreed erode deed deer doer dree redd redo reed rode doe dor ere odd ode ore red rod roe do er od or re

ddeeorr ordered. *See* **ddeeor ddeerr**

ddeeorrw reworded ordered dowered. *See* **ddeeor ddeerr ddeorw deerrw**

ddeeortu detoured detrude. *See* **ddeeor deeort deortu**

ddeeoruv devoured overdue. *See* **ddeeor ddeoruv deoruv**

ddeeorw dowered. *See* **ddeeor ddeorw**

ddeeotv devoted. *See* **deeotv**

ddeeprru perdured perdure. *See* **deepru deprru ddeerr dderru**

ddeeptu deputed. *See* **deeptu ddepu**

ddeer dreed deed deer dree redd reed red ere er re

ddeerr redder dreed erred deed deer dree redd reed ere err red er re

ddeerss dressed. *See* **ddees ddeers ddeer**

ddeerst reddest. *See* **deerst**

ddeerstu detrudes reddest detrude. *See* **ddersu ddestu deerst deersu**

ddeertu detrude. *See* **deert ddeer deetu**

ddeertux extruded detrude extrude. *See* **ddeeux deertx**

ddees deeds deed seed see

ddeeux exuded exude deed dude dud due ex

ddeew dewed deed weed dew ewe wed wee we

ddeffisu diffused diffuse. *See* **ddesu dffsu defsu**

ddeffo doffed offed doff doe fed foe odd ode off do od of

ddefgu fudged fudge dude feud dud due dug fed feu fug

ddefiiin nidified. *See* **ddein defin**

ddefiilm midfield midlife. *See* **ddefil ddeilm defilm**

ddefiimo modified. *See* **ddeiio**

ddefil fiddle felid field filed flied idled deil delf deli died file fled idle lied lief life did die eld elf fed fid fie led lei lid lie el id if li

ddefilr fiddler. *See* **ddeilr ddefil defilr**

ddefilrs fiddlers fiddler fiddles riddles. *See* **ddefil ddeilr ddeils defilr**

ddefils fiddles. *See* **defils ddeils**

ddeflno fondled. *See* **deflno ddeflo ddelno**

ddeflnou unfolded fondled founded. *See* **ddeflo ddeflu ddefnu ddelno**

ddeflo folded doled delf dole fled floe fold lode doe eld elf fed foe led odd ode old do el lo od of

ddefloo flooded. *See* **ddeflo defloo**

ddeflsu fuddles. *See* **ddeflu defls ddesu**

ddeflu fuddle delf dude duel feud fled flue fuel dud due eld elf fed feu flu led leu el

ddefnou founded. *See* **ddefnu defnou**

ddefnu funded unfed dude dune fend feud fund nude den dud due dun end fed fen feu fun en ne nu

ddefor fodder forded doer ford fore froe redd redo rode doe dor fed foe for fro odd ode ore red ref rod roe do er od of or re

ddefors fodders. *See* **ddefor**

ddegginr dredging redding. *See* **ddegin ddegir ddeinr deggin**

ddeggloy doggedly. *See* **ddeggo ddeglo**

ddeggnoo doggoned doggone. *See* **ddeggo deggno**

ddeggo dogged dodge doge doe dog egg ego god odd ode do go od

ddeggru drugged grudged. *See* **ddegru deggru**

ddeghins shedding. *See* **ddegin ddehin ddehis deghin**

ddegiinr deriding giddier redding ridding. *See* **ddegin ddegir ddeinr deginr**

ddegiir giddier. *See* **ddegir**

ddegiist giddiest. *See* **ddeiit degist dgiist**

ddegil gilded glided gelid glide idled deil deli died geld gied gild idle lied did die dig eld gel gid gie led leg lei lid lie el id li

ddegilmn meddling melding mingled. *See* **ddegil ddegin ddeilm ddeimn**

ddegilnp peddling. *See* **ddegil ddegin ddeilp degiln**

ddegilns sledding dingles singled. *See* **ddegil ddegin ddeils degiln**

ddegilnu deluding indulged dueling eluding indulge. *See* **ddegil ddegin ddegiu ddegnu**

ddegilos dislodge. *See* **ddegil ddeglo ddegos ddeils**

ddegilr girdled griddle. *See* **ddeilr ddegil degilr ddegir**

ddegilrs griddles gilders girdled girdles gliders griddle riddles. *See* **ddegil ddegir ddeilr ddeils**

ddegiluv divulged divulge. *See* **ddegil ddegiu**

ddegimo demigod. *See* **ddeio ddego degio**

ddegimos demigods demigod desmoid. *See* **ddegos ddeims ddeios degims**

ddegin dinged dined deign died dine ding gied nide den did die dig din end gid gie gin en id in ne

ddeginnu denuding enduing. *See* **ddegin ddegiu ddegnu ddeinn**

ddeginr redding. *See* **ddegin deginr ddegir ddeinr**

ddeginsw weddings wedding swinged. *See* **ddegin ddeinw degins deginw**

ddegint tedding. *See* **ddegin ddeint degint**

ddeginuu unguided. *See* **ddegin ddegiu ddegnu ddeinu**

ddeginw wedding. *See* **deginw ddegin ddeinw**

ddeginy eddying. *See* **ddegin deginy**

ddegir girded grided ridged dirge dried gride redid ridge died dire gied gird grid redd ride did die dig erg gid gie ire red reg rid rig er id re

ddegiu guided guide died dude gied did die dig dud due dug gid gie id

ddegju judged judge dude dud due dug jug

ddeglo lodged dodge doled lodge ogled doge dole geld gold lode loge ogle doe dog ego eld gel god led leg log odd ode old do el go lo od

ddegmsu smudged. *See* **degmsu ddesu**

ddegnoru grounded underdog dudgeon guerdon redound rounded underdo undergo. *See* **ddegnu ddegor ddegru ddenor**

ddegnos godsend. *See* **ddegos ddenos**

ddegnoss godsends goddess godsend oddness soddens. *See* **ddegos ddenos denoss**

ddegnosu dudgeons dudgeon godsend sounded. *See* **ddegnu ddegos ddenos ddensu**

ddegnou dudgeon. *See* **ddegnu**

ddegnu dunged nudged nudge dude dune dung nude den dud due dug dun end gnu gun en ne nu

ddego dodge doge doe dog ego god odd ode do go od

ddegor dodger dodge gored doer doge goer gore ogre redd redo rode doe dog dor ego erg god odd ode ore red reg rod roe do er go od or re

ddegors dodgers. *See* **ddegor ddegos**

ddegory dodgery. *See* **ddegor ddgoy degry**

ddegos dodges dodge doges dosed does doge dogs dose egos gods goes odds odes sego doe dog dos ego god ode sod do go od os so

ddegoss goddess. *See* **ddegos deoss egoss**

ddegrruy drudgery. *See* **ddegru dderru**

ddegrsu drudges. *See* **ddegru degrsu ddersu**

ddegrtu trudged. *See* **ddegru degrtu**

ddegru drudge udder urged drug dude grue redd rudd rude rued urge dud due dug erg red reg rue rug urd er re

ddehin hidden dined died dine hide hied hind nide den did die din edh end hen hid hie hin eh en he hi id in ne

ddehiors shoddier reddish. *See* **ddehis ddehor ddeios ddiors**

ddehirs reddish. *See* **ddehis dehirs**

ddehirsy hydrides reddish hydride. *See* **ddehis dehirs**

ddehiry hydride. *See* **ddeir dehir**

ddehis dished hides shied sided dies dish hide hied hies ides shed side did die edh hid hie his ids she eh he hi id is sh si

ddehlrsu huddlers huddler huddles hurdled hurdles shudder. *See* **ddehlu ddersu dehlru dehrsu**

ddehlru huddler hurdled. *See* **ddehlu dehlru**

ddehlsu huddles. *See* **ddehlu ddesu delsu**

ddehlu huddle dude duel held hued dud due edh eld hue led leu eh el he

ddehnos shodden. *See* **ddenos dehnos**

ddehnou hounded. *See* **dehno dhnou**

ddehnrsu hundreds hundred shudder. *See* **ddensu ddersu dehrsu denrsu**

ddehnru hundred. *See* **dderu denru**

ddehoo hooded oohed dodo hoed hood doe edh hod hoe odd ode oho ooh do eh he ho od oh

ddehoosw woodshed wooshed. *See* **ddehoo ddeoos ddeoow ddeosw**

ddehor horded horde doer herd hero hoed hoer redd redo rode doe dor edh her hod hoe odd ode ore red rho rod roe do eh er he ho od oh or re

ddehorsu shrouded shudder. *See* **ddehor ddeosu ddersu dehors**

ddehrssu shudders shudder. *See* **ddersu dehrss dehrsu derssu**

ddehrsu shudder. *See* **ddersu dehrsu**

ddehrsuy shuddery shudder. *See* **ddersu dehrsu**

ddei died did die id

ddeiik kiddie diked died dike did die kid id

ddeiikls disliked kiddies dislike. *See* **ddeiik ddeils**

ddeiiks kiddies. *See* **ddeiik deiks ddeis**

ddeiiloz idolized iodized idolize. *See* **ddeiio deiioz**

ddeiint indited. *See* **ddeint ddeiint ddeiit**

ddeiinv divined. *See* **ddeiiv deiinv**

ddeiio iodide diode died dido did die doe odd ode do id od

ddeiiops dipodies. *See* **ddeiio ddeios deiops**

ddeiiost oddities toddies. *See* **ddeiio ddeiit ddeios deiist**

ddeiiosx dioxides dioxide. *See* **ddeiio ddeios deiosx**

ddeiiox dioxide. *See* **ddeiio deiox**

ddeiioz iodized. *See* **ddeiio deiioz**

ddeiirsv dividers divider divides. *See* **ddeiiv deiirs deirsv**

ddeiirt dirtied. *See* **ddeiit deiirt**

ddeiirv divider. *See* **ddeiiv deirv ddeir**

ddeiisv divides. *See* **ddeiiv deisv eiisv**

ddeiit tidied tided diet edit tide tied did die dit ted tie id it ti

ddeiiv divide dived ivied died dive vied did die vie id

ddeiivv divvied. *See* **ddeiiv diivv**

ddeiizz dizzied. *No 6s or 5s*

ddeik diked died dike did die kid id

ddeikln kindled. *See* **deikln**

ddeiknr kindred. *See* **ddeikr deiknr**

ddeikr dirked kidder diked dried irked redid died dike dire dirk kier redd ride did die ire irk kid kir red rid er id re

ddeikrs kidders. *See* **ddeikr deikrs**

ddeil idled deil deli died idle lied did die eld led lei lid lie el id li

ddeillr drilled. *See* **ddeilr**

ddeilm middle idled limed deil deli died dime idle lied lime meld mild mile did die dim eld elm led lei lid lie mel mid mil el em id li me mi

ddeilmop imploded dimpled implode. *See* **ddeilm ddeilp ddelmo deilmo**

ddeilmp dimpled. *See* **deilmp ddeilm ddeilp**

ddeilms middles. *See* **ddeims deilms ddeils**

ddeilmsu mudslide middles muddles. *See* **ddeilm ddeils ddeims ddelmu**

ddeilnps spindled splendid piddles spindle splined. *See* **ddeilp ddeils deilps deinps**

ddeilnsw dwindles swindled dwindle swindle. *See* **ddeils ddeinw deilsw deinsw**

ddeilnw dwindle. *See* **ddeinw ddeil deiln**

ddeilops lopsided despoil dipoles piddles spoiled. *See* **ddeilp ddeils ddeios ddeilop**

ddeilost deltoids deltoid toddies toddles. *See* **ddeils ddeios ddelot deilos**

ddeilot deltoid. *See* **ddelot deilot**

ddeilp piddle idled piled plied deil deli died idle lied pied pile pled did die dip eld led lei lid lie lip pie el id li pe pi

ddeilps piddles. *See* **deilps ddeilp ddeils**

ddeilr dirled riddle dried idled idler redid riled deil deli died dire dirl idle lied lire redd ride riel rile did die eld ire led lei lid lie red rid el er id li re

ddeilrs riddles. *See* **ddeilr deilrs**

ddeilrzz drizzled drizzle. *See* **ddeilr**

ddeils sidled deils delis idled idles sided sidle slide deil died dies ides isle isle leis lids lied lies side sled slid did die eld els ids led lei lid lie el id is li si

ddeilstw twiddles twiddle wildest. *See* **ddeils deilst deilsw deiltw**

ddeiltu diluted. *See* **deiltu ddeil ddeit**

ddeiltw twiddle. *See* **deiltw ddeil ddeit**

ddeilty lyddite. *See* **ddilty deity ddeil**

ddeimm dimmed mimed died dime mime did die dim mem mid mim em id me mi

ddeimn midden minded denim dined mined died dime dine mend mien mind mine nide den did die dim din end men mid nim em en id in me mi ne

ddeimns middens. *See* **deimns ddeims ddeimn**

ddeimos desmoid. *See* **ddeims ddeios**

ddeimru muddier. *See* **ddemru deimr ddeir**

ddeims desmid deism dimes sided died dies dime dims ides mise semi side did die dim ids mid mis em id is me mi si

ddeimstu muddiest studied tediums. *See* **ddeims ddestu deimst deimtu**

ddein dined died dine nide den did die din end en id in ne

ddeinn dinned inned died dine nide nine den did die din end inn en id in ne

ddeinors indorsed indorse nodders noddies rosined. *See* **ddeinr ddeios ddenor ddenos**

ddeinos noddies. *See* **ddeios deinos ddenos**

ddeinosw disowned noddies dowdies. *See* **ddeinw ddeios ddenos ddenow**

ddeinot dentoid. *See* **ddeint ddeio ddeot**

ddeinr ridden dined diner dried redid died dine dire nerd nide redd rein rend ride rind den did die din end ire red rid en er id in ne re

ddeinrst stridden distend. *See* **ddeinr ddeint deinrs deinrt**

ddeinrtu intruded intrude untried. *See* **ddeinr ddeint ddeinu deinrt**

ddeinsst distends distend dissent. *See* **ddeint deisst einsst**

ddeinst distend. *See* **ddeint deist denst**

ddeint dinted dined tided dent died diet dine edit nide tend tide tied tine den did die din dit end net nit ted ten tie tin en id in it ne ti

ddeinu indued dined indue nudie undid died dine dude dune nide nude den did die din dud due dun end en id in ne nu

ddeinw winded dined widen wined died dine nide wend wide wind wine den dew did die din end new wed wen win en id in ne we

ddeio diode died dido did die doe odd ode do id od

ddeioprs dropsied periods. *See* **ddeios ddeipr ddiors deiopr**

ddeioprv provided provide. *See* **ddeiov ddeipr ddeorv deiopr**

ddeiopss disposed dispose. *See* **ddeios deiops eiopss**

ddeiorrs disorder. *See* **ddeios ddiors deiors deirrs**

ddeiorw dowdier. *See* **ddeorw deiorw**

ddeios didoes diodes diode dosed sided dido died dies does dose ides odds odes side did die doe dos ids odd ode sod do id is od os si so

ddeiost toddies. *See* **ddeios deiost**

ddeiostw dowdiest toddies dowdies. *See* **ddeios ddeosw deiost deistw**

ddeiosw dowdies. *See* **ddeios ddeosw**

ddeiott dittoed. *See* **ddeott ddeio diott**

ddeiov devoid voided diode dived video dido died dive dove vied void did die doe odd ode vie do id od

ddeioww widowed. *See* **ddeio dioww**

ddeipp dipped piped died pied pipe did die dip pep pie pip id pe pi

ddeippr dripped. *See* **ddeipp deippr ddeipr**

ddeipr prided dried pride pried redid died dire drip peri pied pier redd ride ripe did die dip ire per pie red rep rid rip er id pe pi re

ddeipstu disputed studied dispute. *See* **ddestu deipst deipsu deistu**

ddeir dried redid died dire redd ride did die ire red rid er id re

ddeirru ruddier. *See* **dderru deirr ddeir**

ddeirstu ruddiest studied dustier. *See* **ddersu ddestu ddirsu deirst**

ddeis sided died dies ides side did die ids id is si

ddeissu disused. *See* **deissu**

ddeistu studied. *See* **ddestu deistu**

ddeit tided died diet edit tide tied did die dit ted tie id it ti

ddeiv dived died dive vied did die vie id

ddejrsu judders. *See* **ddejru ddersu**

ddejru judder udder dude redd rudd rude rued dud due red rue urd er re

ddeky dyked dyed dyke eddy dey dye key ye

ddellor drolled. *See* **ddelor dellor**

ddellu dulled dell dude duel dull dud due eld ell led leu el

ddelmo molded doled domed model demo dole dome lode meld mode mold mole doe eld elm led mel mod odd ode old do el em lo me mo od om

ddelmrsu muddlers muddler muddles. *See* **ddelmu ddemru ddersu demrsu**

ddelmru muddler. *See* **ddelmu ddemru**

ddelmsu muddles. *See* **ddelmu ddesu delsu**

ddelmu muddle dude duel meld mule dud due eld elm emu led leu lum mel mud el em me mu um

ddelno noddle doled loden olden dole done enol lend leno lode lone node noel den doe don eld end eon led nod odd ode old one do el en lo ne no od on

ddelnoo noodled. *See* **ddelno delnoo**

ddelnos noddles. *See* **ddelno ddenos**

ddelnrtu trundled trundle. *See* **delnru denrtu elnrtu**

ddelnsuy suddenly. *See* **ddensu delnuy**

ddelo doled dole lode doe eld led odd ode old do el lo od

ddeloor drooled. *See* **ddelor ddeoor**

ddeloos doodles. *See* **ddeoos deloos**

ddelor lorded doled older doer dole lode lord lore orle redd redo rode role doe dor eld led odd ode old ore red rod roe do el er lo od or re

ddelorst toddlers oldster toddler toddles. *See* **ddelor ddelot delors delort**

ddelort toddler. *See* **ddelor delort ddelot**

ddelost toddles. *See* **ddelot delost**

ddelot toddle doled doted dole dolt dote lode toed told doe dot eld led let lot odd ode old ted tod toe do el lo od to

ddelprsu puddlers puddler puddles slurped. *See* **ddelpu ddersu delpru deprsu**

ddelpru puddler. *See* **ddelpu delpru**

ddelpsu puddles. *See* **ddelpu ddesu delsu**

ddelpu puddle duped duple puled dude duel pled pule dud due eld led leu pul el pe up

ddemmru drummed. *See* **ddemru**

ddemnost oddments oddment endmost. *See* **ddenos demnos demost denost**

ddemnot oddment. *See* **demno ddemo ddeot**

ddemnou mounded. *See* **demno dmnou**

ddemnouu duodenum mounded. *See* **demno ddemo dmnou**

ddemnpuu pudendum. *See* **ddempu**

ddemo domed demo dome mode doe mod odd ode do em me mo od om

ddemoo doomed domed mooed demo dodo dome doom mode mood doe mod moo odd ode do em me mo od om

ddemootu outmoded. *See* **ddemoo**

ddempu dumped duped umped dude dump dud due emu mud ump em me mu pe um up

ddemru mudder udder demur drum dude redd rudd rude rued dud due emu mud red rem rue rum urd em er me mu re um

ddennu dunned dude dune nude den dud due dun end nun en ne nu

ddenops despond. *See* **ddenos ddeop deops**

ddenopss desponds despond oddness soddens. *See* **ddenos denoss denpss**

ddenopu pounded. *See* **ddeop ddepu dnopu**

ddennor droned nodder drone doer done nerd node redd redo rend rode den doe don dor end eon nod nor odd ode one ore red rod roe do en er ne no od on or re

ddenors nodders. *See* **ddenor denors ddenos**

ddenorsu redounds nodders redound resound rounded sounded sounder underdo. *See* **ddenor ddenos ddensu ddeosu**

ddenort trodden. *See* **ddenor denort**

ddenoru redound rounded underdo. *See* **ddenor**

ddenorw drowned. *See* **ddenow denorw ddenor ddeorw**

ddenos sodden dosed nodes nosed sonde dens does done dons dose ends eons node nods noes nose odds odes ones send den doe don dos end ens eon nod odd ode one sen sod son do en ne no od on os so

ddenoss oddness soddens. *See* **ddenos denoss**

ddenosu sounded. *See* **ddeosu ddenos ddensu denosu**

ddenouw wounded. *See* **ddenow denuw dnouw**

ddenow downed endow owned done down enow node owed wend den dew doe don end eon new nod now odd ode one owe own wed wen woe won do en ne no od on ow we

ddensu sudden dudes dunes nudes dens dude duds dues dune duns ends nude send sudd sued used den dud due dun end ens sen sue sun use en ne nu us

ddeoopr drooped. *See* **ddeoor ddeop deopr**

ddeoor odored rodeo dodo doer door odor ordo redd redo rode rood doe dor odd ode ore red rod roe do er od or re

ddeoorsw redwoods redwood drowsed. *See* **ddeoor ddeoos ddeoow ddeorw**

ddeoorw redwood. *See* **ddeoor ddeoow ddeorw**

ddeoos dodoes dosed dodos dodo does dose odds odes doe dos odd ode sod do od os so

ddeoow wooded wooed dodo owed wood dew doe odd ode owe wed woe woo do od ow we

ddeop doped dope oped doe odd ode ope pod do od pe

ddeoppr dropped. *See* **ddeop deopr**

ddeoprsw dewdrops dewdrop drowsed powders. *See* **ddeorw ddeosw deoprs deoprw**

ddeoprw dewdrop. *See* **ddeorw deoprw**

ddeorsw drowsed. *See* **deorsw ddeosw**

ddeorv droved drove roved doer dove over redd redo rode rove doe dor odd ode ore red rev rod roe do er od or re

ddeorw worded dower rowed doer drew owed redd redo rode word wore dew doe dor odd ode ore owe red rod roe row wed woe do er od or ow re we

ddeos dosed does dose odds odes doe dos odd ode sod do od os so

ddeosu doused dosed douse dudes does dose dude duds dues duos odds odes ouds sudd sued udos used doe dos dud due duo odd ode oud sod sou sue udo use do od os so us

ddeosw dowsed dosed dowse sowed dews does dose odds odes owed owes weds woes dew doe dos odd ode owe sew sod sow wed woe do od os ow so we

ddeot doted dote toed doe dot odd ode ted tod toe do od to

ddeott dotted doted toted dote toed tote doe dot odd ode ted tod toe tot do od to

ddeoz dozed doze doe odd ode zed do od

ddepu duped dude dud due pe up

dder redd red er re

dderrsu rudders. *See* **dderru ddersu**

dderru rudder udder ruder dude redd rudd rude rued dud due err red rue urd er re

dders redds redd reds red res er re

ddersu udders druse dudes redds rudds udder dude duds dues redd reds rudd rude rued rues ruse sudd sued surd sure urds used user dud due red res rue sue urd use er re us

dderu udder dude redd rudd rude rued dud due red rue urd er re

ddestu dusted dudes duets dude duds dues duet dust stud sudd sued suet teds used dud due set sue ted use us ut

ddesu dudes dude duds dues sudd sued used dud due sue use us

ddety teddy dyed eddy dey dye ted yet ye

ddeu dude dud due

ddey dyed eddy dey dye ye

ddfgiiln fiddling. *See* **dgiiln fgiiln**

ddfgilnu fuddling. *See* **fgilnu**

ddfior fordid fiord dido ford did dor fid fir for fro odd rid rif rod do id if od of or

ddfmnouu dumfound. *See* **dfnou dmnou**

ddggino dodging. *See* **dgino ggino**

ddgginru drudging. *See* **dginru gginru**

ddghilnu huddling. *See* **dgilu gilnu ddinu**

ddghintu thudding hindgut. *See* **ghint ddinu**

ddgiiinv dividing. *See* **dgiinv**

ddgiikn kidding. *See* **dgiikn**

ddgiikns skidding kidding. *See* **dgiikn dgiins giikns**

ddgiilmn middling. *See* **dgiiln giilmn**

ddgiilnp piddling. *See* **dgiiln dgiinp giilnp**

ddgiilnr riddling ridding dirling. *See* **ddilnr dgiiln dgiinr giilnr**

ddgiily giddily. *See* **ddgiy**

ddgiinr ridding. *See* **dgiinr**

ddgilmnu muddling mudding. *See* **dgilu gilnu ddinu**

ddgilnoo doodling. *See* **dgilno gilnoo**

ddgilnop plodding podding. *See* **dgilno dginop gilnop**

ddgilnot toddling. *See* **dgilno dgilot dginot**

ddgilnpu puddling pudding. *See* **dginpu gilnpu**

ddgimnu mudding. *See* **ddinu**

ddgimnuy muddying mudding. *See* **dginy dgnuy ddgiy**

ddginno nodding. *See* **dgino**

ddginop podding. *See* **dginop**

ddginopr prodding podding. *See* **dginop ginopr**

ddginos sodding. *See* **dginos**

ddginpsu puddings spudding pudding. *See* **dginpu dginsu**

ddginpu pudding. *See* **dginpu ddinu**

ddginstu studding dusting. *See* **dginsu dinstu**

ddgipuy giddyup. *See* **ddgiy dgpuy**

ddgiy giddy did dig gid id

ddgooosw dogwoods dogwood. *See* **ddoos dgoos doosw**

ddgooow dogwood. *No 6s or 5s*

ddgoy dodgy dogy dog god goy odd yod do go od oy

ddhiiks kiddish. *No 6s or 5s*

ddhilosy shoddily. *See* **ddhosy dhilos**

ddhiorsy hydroids hydroid. *See* **ddhosy ddiors dhorsy**

ddhiory hydroid. *See* **dhioy dhory**

ddhisu dudish dish duds sudd did dud hid his ids hi id is sh si us

ddhosy shoddy yodhs hods hoys odds shod yodh yods dos hod hoy odd ohs shy sod soy yod do ho od oh os oy sh so

ddi did id

ddiilop diploid. *See* **diilp**

ddiilops diploids diploid. *See* **diilps**

ddiims misdid dims did dim ids mid mis id is mi si

ddikoos skiddoo. *See* **ddoos**

ddikooss skiddoos skiddoo. *See* **dikss ddoos**

ddiksy skiddy kiddy disk kids skid did ids kid ski sky id is si

ddiky kiddy did kid id

ddilnr dirndl dirl rind did din lid nil rid id in li

ddilnrs dirndls. *See* **ddilnr dilrs dinrs**

ddilowy dowdily. *See* **diloy ddowy ddloy**

ddilty tiddly idly idyl tidy did dit lid lit til id it li ti

ddimy middy did dim mid id mi my

ddinnoww downwind. *See* **dinoww innoww**

ddinooww woodwind. *See* **dinoww**

ddinu undid did din dud dun id in nu

ddio dido did odd do id od

ddiopy dipody dido did dip odd pod poi yip yod do id od oy pi

ddiors sordid dido odds rids rods sori did dor dos ids odd rid rod sir sod do id is od or os si so

ddiotu outdid dido doit did dit dot dud duo odd oud out tod tui udo do id it od ti to ut

ddioty oddity toddy dido doit tidy tody did dit dot odd tod toy yod do id it od oy ti to

ddirsu druids druid rudds duds rids rudd sudd surd urds did dud ids rid sir urd id is si us

ddiru druid rudd did dud rid urd id

ddlmorsu doldrums. *See* **dlmosu dmorsu**

ddloy oddly odd old yod do lo od oy

ddlpuy puddly duly dud ply pul yup up

ddmmuu dumdum dud mud mum mu um

ddmnoor dromond. *See* **dnoor mnoor**

ddmnoors dromonds dromond. *See* **dnoors mnoors**

ddmuy muddy dud mud yum mu my um

ddnoy noddy yond don nod odd yod yon do no od on oy

ddo odd do od

ddoo dodo odd do od

ddoos dodos dodo odds dos odd sod do od os so

ddos odds dos odd sod do od os so

ddoty toddy tody dot odd tod toy yod do od oy to

ddowy dowdy odd yod yow do od ow oy

ddrsu rudds duds rudd sudd surd urds dud urd us

ddru rudd dud urd

ddruy ruddy rudd dry dud urd

ddsu duds sudd dud us

ddu dud

---

deeeegkr kedgeree. *See* **deeegr deeekr**

deeeemrr redeemer. *See* **deeemr**

deeeemst esteemed. *See* **deeems deeemt eeemst**

deeeenrv veneered. *See* **deeenr deeenv deeerv deenrv**

deeeertt teetered. *See* **deertt**

deeefinr redefine needier refined. *See* **deeefr deeenr deefin deefir**

deeeflru refueled feruled. *See* **deeefr deeelr deeflu deelru**

deeeflrx reflexed reflex.. *See* **deeefr eeeflr deeflx deeelr**

deeefmnr freedmen freemen. *See* **deeefr deeemr deeenr deefnr**

deeefnrt deferent entered. *See* **deeefr deeenr deefnr deenrt**

deeefns defense. *See* **deens deefs defns**

deeefnss defenses defense. *See* **deenss**

deeefr feeder reefed defer freed deer dree feed fere free reed reef ere fed fee red ref er re

deeefrrr referred. *See* **deeefr eeefrr**

deeefrrt ferreted. *See* **deeefr eeefrr eefrrt**

deeefrs feeders. *See* **deefrs deeefr deeers**

deeefrst festered feeders steered. *See* **deeefr deeers deefrs deerst**

deeefrtt fettered fretted. *See* **deeefr deertt eefrtt**

deeefrv fevered. *See* **deeefr deeerv**

deeegilz elegized elegize. *See* **deeil degil deegl**

deeegins designee seeding. *See* **deegis deeins degins eegins**

deeegipr pedigree perigee. *See* **deeepr deeegr deegir degipr**

deeegirr greedier. *See* **deeegr deegir degirr eeeirr**

deeegisw edgewise. *See* **deegis deegsw**

deeegmr emerged. *See* **deeegr eeegmr deegmr deeemr**

deeegnnr engender greened reneged. *See* **deeegr deeenr deegnr**

deeegnr greened reneged. *See* **deeegr deegnr deeenr eeegnr**

deeegnrv revenged greened reneged revenge. *See* **deeegr deeenr deeenv deeerv**

deeegr degree edger greed deer dree edge geed gree reed ere erg gee red reg er re

deeegrs degrees. *See* **deeegr deegrs deeers**

deeegrst deterges degrees deterge egested greeted steered. *See* **deeegr deeers deegrs deerst**

deeegrt deterge greeted. *See* **deeegr deert eegrt**

deeegst egested. *See* **deegs eegst eeegs**

deeehl heeled dele heed heel held edh eel eld led lee eh el he

deeehlmt helmeted. *See* **deeelt deeehl deehlm eehlmt**

deeehlss heedless. *See* **deeehl eeelss**

deeehlsw wheedles wheedle welshed. *See* **deeehl deehsw eehlsw**

deeehlw wheedle. *See* **deeehl deehw eehlw**

deeehmns enmeshed sheened demesne. *See* **deeems deehms deemns eehmns**

deeehns sheened. *See* **deens deehs eehns**

deeehrs sheered. *See* **deeers deehs**

deeehrtt tethered teethed. *See* **deertt eeehtt eehrtt**

deeehst seethed sheeted. *See* **eeehst deehs deest**

deeehtt teethed. *See* **eeehtt**

deeehwz wheezed. *See* **eeehwz deehw**

deeeilrv relieved deliver levered relieve relived reveled reviled. *See* **deeelr deeelv deeerv deeilr**

deeeimrs remedies emersed redeems remised seedier. *See* **deeemr deeems deeers deeims**

deeeimst seedtime. *See* **deeems deeemt deeims deeimt**

deeeinr needier. *See* **deeinr deeenr**

deeeinrr reindeer needier. *See* **deeenr deeinr deenrr eeeirr**

deeeinst neediest destine. *See* **deeins deenst**

deeeintv eventide evident. *See* **deeenv deeinv deentv**

deeeiprs speedier preside seedier seepier speeder. *See* **deeepr deeeps deeers deeips**

deeeiptx expedite. *See* **deeitx**

deeeirs seedier. *See* **deeirs deeers**

deeeirss diereses desires resides seeders seedier. *See* **deeers deeirs deeiss eeirss**

deeeirvw reviewed weedier. *See* **deeerv deeerw deeirv deeivw**

deeeirw weedier. *See* **deeerw eeeir deeir**

deeeisst seediest. *See* **deeiss deesst deisst**

deeeistw weediest dewiest sweetie. *See* **deestw deistw**

deeejlw jeweled. *See* **eejlw**

deeejr jeered deer dree jeer reed red ere er re

deeekk keeked eked keek eke

deeekl keeled dele eked keel leek eel eke eld elk led lee lek el

deeekln kneeled. *See* **deeekl deeekn deeeln**

deeeklnn kenneled kneeled. *See* **deeekl deeekn deeeln eeklnn**

deeeklnr kerneled kneeled kneeler needler. *See* **deeekl deeekn deeekr deeeln**

deeekn keened kneed dene eked keen knee need den eke end ken nee en ne

deeeknsw weekends weekend. *See* **deeekn deeksw**

deeeknw weekend. *See* **deeekn**

deeekopw pokeweed. *See* **deeekp**

deeekp peeked deep eked epee keep peed peek eke pee pe

deeekr reeked deer dree eked reed reek eke ere red er re

deeelllv levelled leveled. *See* **deeelv**

deeellpr repelled. *See* **deeelp deeelr deeepr eeelpr**

deeellpt pelleted deplete. *See* **deeelt deeelp eellpt deelpt**

deeellpx expelled. *See* **deeelp**

deeellv leveled. *See* **deeelv eellv**

deeeln needle dele dene lend need den eel eld end led lee nee el en ne

deeelnr needler. *See* **deeelr deelnr deeenr deeeln**

deeelnrs needlers lenders needler needles slender sneered. *See* **deeeln deeelr deeenr deeers**

deeelnrt relented needler entered. *See* **deeeln deeelr deeelt deeenr**

deeelns needles. *See* **deeeln deels deens**

deeelnss lessened needless needles endless. *See* **deeeln deenss eeelss eelnss**

deeelp peeled deep dele epee peed peel pled eel eld led lee pee el pe

deeelpst depletes deepest deletes deplete pestled sleeted steeled steeped steeple. *See* **deeelp deeelt deeeps deelpt**

deeelpt deplete. *See* **deeelt deeelp deelpt**

deeelr leered reeled elder deer dele dree leer reed reel eel eld ere led lee red el er re

deeelrss reedless seeders. *See* **deeelr deeers deelrs eeelss**

deeelrtt lettered terete.. *See* **deeelt deeelr eelrtt deertt**

deeelrv levered reveled. *See* **deeelr deeelv deeerv**

deeelsss seedless lessees. *See* **eeelss**

deeelst deletes sleeted steeled. *See* **deeelt deelst**

deeelstw tweedles deletes sleeted steeled tweedle. *See* **deeelt deelst deeltw deestw**

deeelsv sleeved. *See* **deelsv deeelv eeelsv**

deeelt delete dele leet teed eel eld led lee let ted tee el

deeeltw tweedle. *See* **deeelt deeltw**

deeelv leveed delve levee dele veld eel eld eve led lee lev vee el

deeemns demesne. *See* **deeems deemns**

deeemnss demesnes demesne. *See* **deeems deemns deemss deenss**

deeemprt tempered metered petered. *See* **deeemr deeemt deeepr deempr**

deeemptx exempted. *See* **deeemt eemptx**

deeemr redeem emeer deem deer deme dree meed mere reed ere red rem em er me re

deeemrs emersed redeems. *See* **deeemr deeers deeems**

deeemrt metered. *See* **deeemr deeemt deemrt**

deeems seemed deems demes meeds deem deme meed seed seem see em me

deeemt teemed meted deem deme meed meet mete teed teem met ted tee em me

deeenopr reopened preened. *See* **deeenp deeenr deeepr deenop**

deeenp deepen peened deep dene epee need neep peed peen pend den end nee pee pen en ne pe

deeenpr preened. *See* **deeenp deeepr deeenr**

deeenprt repented entered petered preened preteen pretend. *See* **deeenp deeenr deeepr deenrt**

deeenps deepens. *See* **deeenp deeeps**

deeenpsx expensed deepens expends expense. *See* **deeenp deeeps deenpx**

deeenqu queened. *See* **deenu eenqu**

deeenr needer deer dene dree erne need nerd reed rend den end ere nee red en er ne re

deeenrrv reverend revered. *See* **deeenr deeenv deeerv deenrr**

deeenrs sneered. *See* **deenrs deeenr deeers eeenrs**

deeenrst resented entered entrees sneered steered tenders. *See* **deeenr deeers deenrs deenrt**

deeenrt entered. *See* **eeenrt deenrt**

deeenrtu neutered denture entered tenured. *See* **deeenr deenrt deenru denrtu**

deeenrtx extender entered exerted. *See* **deeenr deenrt deentx deertx**

deeenrw renewed. *See* **deeenr deeerw**

deeensv vendees. *See* **deeenv**

deeensz sneezed. *See* **eeensz deens**

deeentt detente. *See* **deentt**

deeenv evened vendee dene even need vend den end eve nee vee en ne

deeeostv devotees devotee devotes. *See* **deeotv deestv eeostv**

deeeotv devotee. *See* **deeotv**

deeepp peeped deep epee peed peep pee pep pe

deeepppr peppered prepped. *See* **deeepp deeepr eeeppr**

deeepr deeper peered deep deer dree epee peed peer reed ere pee per red rep er pe re

deeeprs speeder. *See* **deeepr deeeps**

deeeprss speeders depress peeress pressed seeders speeder. *See* **deeepr deeers deepss eeprss**

deeeprst pestered deepest petered speeder steeped steered. *See* **deeepr deeeps deeers deerst**

deeeprt petered. *See* **deeepr**

deeeps seeped speed epees deep epee peed pees seed seep sped pee see pe

deeepst deepest steeped. *See* **deeeps eeepst**

deeepv peeved peeve deep epee peed veep eve pee vee pe

deeeqsuz squeezed squeeze. *See* **deesu**

deeerrrv verderer revered. *See* **deeerv eeerrv**

deeerrsv reserved reversed deserve reserve revered reveres reverse severer. *See* **deeers deeerv deersv eeerrv**

deeerrtv reverted revered everted. *See* **deeerv eeerrv eerrtv**

deeerrv revered. *See* **deeerv eeerrv**

deeers seeder deers drees reeds deer dree reds reed seed seer sere ere red res see er re

deeerss seeders. *See* **deeers derss deess**

deeerssv deserves seeders deserve. *See* **deeers deeerv deersv eerssv**

deeerst steered. *See* **deerst deeers**

deeersv deserve. *See* **eeersv deersv deeerv**

deeersw sewered weeders. *See* **deeers deeerw**

deeersy redeyes. *See* **deeers deeery**

deeertv everted. *See* **deeerv deert eertv**

deeertx exerted. *See* **deertx**

deeerv veered reeve deer dree ever reed veer ere eve red rev vee er re

deeerw weeder deer dree drew ewer reed weed dew ere ewe red wed wee er re we

deeery redeye reedy deer dree dyer eery eyed eyre reed dey dry dye ere eye red rye er re ye

deeessx desexes. *See* **deesx deess eessx**

deeesttv vedettes vedette. *See* **deestt deestv**

deeettv vedette. *See* **deettv**

deeettw tweeted. *See* **deettw**

deeetwz tweezed. *See* **eeetwz deetw**

deef feed fed fee

deeffgor goffered offered. *See* **defgor effgor**

deeffin effendi. *See* **deefin deffi**

deeffinr niffered effendi refined. *See* **deefin deefir deefnr deeinr**

deeffins effendis defines effendi sniffed. *See* **deefin deefis deeins defins**

deeffnor forefend offender offered. *See* **deefnr deenor deffno**

deeffor offered. *See* **deefr deeor deffo**

deeffrsu suffered duffers effused refused. *See* **deefrs deefsu deersu deffru**

deeffsu effused. *See* **deefsu eeffsu**

deefggor defogger. *See* **defggo defgor deggor**

deefgin feeding feigned. *See* **deefin eefgin**

deefginr fingered dreeing feeding feigned feigner freeing fringed reeding reefing refined reigned. *See* **deefin deefir deefnr deegir**

deefgl fledge glede gleed ledge dele delf edge feed feel fled flee geed geld glee eel eld elf fed fee gee gel led lee leg el

deefglnu engulfed needful. *See* **deefgl deefiu deegln deeglu**

deefgls fledges. *See* **deefgl deegls**

deefgru refuged. *See* **eefgru deefr deegr**

deefhlor freehold. *See* **deflor dehlor eefhor**

deefhls fleshed. *See* **deels defls deefs**

deefhlu heedful. *See* **deeflu**

deefht hefted feted deft feed feet fete heed heft teed thee edh eft eth fed fee feh het ted tee the eh he

deefiint definite feinted. *See* **deefin deiint efiint**

deefiir reified. *See* **deefir**

deefiirs fireside deifies edifies reified reifies. *See* **deefir deefis deefrs deeirs**

deefiirv verified reified. *See* **deefir deeirv defirv**

deefiis deifies edifies. *See* **deefis**

deefil defile edile elide felid field filed flied deil dele delf deli feed feel file fled flee idle lied lief life die eel eld elf fed fee fid fie led lee lei lid lie el id if li

deefillr refilled defiler fielder frilled refiled. *See* **deefil deefir deefll deeilr**

deefillt filleted. *See* **deefil deefll deeflt defill**

deefilms medflies defiles. *See* **deefil deefis deeils deeims**

deefilpr pilfered defiler fielder periled refiled replied. *See* **deefil deefir deeilr defilr**

deefilr defiler fielder refiled. *See* **deefir deefil deeilr eefilr defilr**

deefilrs fielders defiler defiles fielder refiled refiles. *See* **deefil deefir deefis deefrs**

deefilrt filtered defiler fertile fielder flirted refiled trifled. *See* **deefil deefir deeflt deeilr**

deefils defiles. *See* **deefis deeils defils**

deefimtu tumefied. *See* **deeimt deimtu**

deefin define fiend fined dene dine feed fend find fine need nide den die din end fed fee fen fid fie fin nee en id if in ne

deefinr refined. *See* **deefir deefin deeinr deefnr eefinr**

deefinrr inferred ferried refined refiner refried. *See* **deefin deefir deefnr deeinr**

deefinrz frenzied refined. *See* **deefin deefir deefnr deeinr**

deefins defines. *See* **deefis deeins defins**

deefinss finessed defines finesse. *See* **deefin deefis deeins deeiss**

deefinst infested defines destine feinted. *See* **deefin deefis deeins deenst**

deefint feinted. *See* **deefin efint deeft**

deefiprx prefixed refixed expired. *See* **deefir eeiprx efiprx**

deefir defier defer eider fired freed fried deer dire dree feed fere fire free reed reef ride rife die ere fed fee fid fie fir ire red ref rid rif er id if re

deefirr ferried refried. *See* **deefir deirr deerr**

deefirtt refitted fretted. *See* **deefir deeirt deertt defirt**

deefirx refixed. *See* **deefir defix efirx**

deefis defies feeds dies feds feed fees fids fies ides seed side die fed fee fid fie ids ifs see id if is si

deefkr kerfed defer freed deer dree eked feed fere free keef kerf reed reef reek eke ere fed fee kef red ref er re

deefll felled dele delf dell feed feel fell fled flee eel eld elf ell fed fee led lee el

deefllu fuelled. *See* **deefll deeflu**

deeflnnu funneled needful. *See* **deeflu defnnu eeflnn eflnnu**

deeflns flensed. *See* **eeflns deels defls**

deeflnu needful. *See* **deeflu deenu defnu**

deeflorw deflower flowered lowered roweled. *See* **deelrw deflor deflow eflorw**

deeflost feedlots feedlot. *See* **deeflt deelst deflot deflst**

deeflot feedlot. *See* **deeflt deflot**

deeflpsu speedful. *See* **deefsu deelsu deeflu**

deeflrru ferruled feruled ferrule. *See* **deeflu deelru deflru defrru**

deeflru feruled. *See* **deelru eeflru deeflu deflru**

deefit felted delft feted fleet deft dele delf feed feel feet felt fete fled flee leet left teed eel eft eld elf fed fee led lee let ted tee el

deefltt fettled. *See* **deeflt eefltt**

deeflu fueled elude dele delf duel feed feel feud fled flee flue fuel due eel eld elf fed fee feu flu led lee leu el

deeflx flexed dele delf feed feel fled flee flex eel eld elf fed fee led lee el ex

deefmnot fomented. *See* **deemno deemnt deemot deenot**

deefmor freedom. *See* **defmor**

deefmorr reformed freedom. *See* **defmor demorr**

deefmors freedoms deforms freedom serfdom. *See* **deefrs deeors defmor**

deefmpru perfumed perfume. *See* **deempr deemru deepru dempru**

deefnost softened denotes. *See* **deenot deenst denost efnost**

deefnr fender defer freed deer dene dree erne feed fend fere fern free need nerd reed reef rend den end ere fed fee fen nee red ref en er ne re

deefnrs fenders. *See* **deefrs deenrs deefnr**

deefnsst deftness densest. *See* **deenss deenst deesst eensst**

deeforst forested fostered defrost frosted oersted teredos. *See* **deefrs deeors deeort deerst**

deefprsu perfused perfuse perused refused. *See* **deefrs deefsu deepru deersu**

deefr defer freed deer dree feed fere free reed reef ere fed fee red ref er re

deefrs defers deers defer drees feeds feres freed frees reeds reefs deer dree feds feed fees fere free reds reed reef refs seed seer sere serf ere fed fee red ref res see er re

deefrsu refused. *See* **deefrs deefsu eefrsu deersu defrsu**

deefrtt fretted. *See* **deertt eefrtt**

deefrtu refuted. *See* **eefrtu deefr deert**

deefs feeds feds feed fees seed fed fee see

deefssu defuses. *See* **deefsu eefssu defssu deessu**

deefsu defuse feeds feuds fused fusee suede dues feds feed fees feud feus fuse seed sued used due fed fee feu see sue use us

deeft feted deft feed feet fete teed eft fed fee ted tee

deeg edge geed gee

deegg egged edge geed gee egg

deegghho hedgehog. *See* **deggho**

deeggirr dreggier. *See* **deggir deegir degirr eggirr**

deeggl legged egged glede gleed ledge dele edge geed geld glee eel egg eld gee gel led lee leg el

deegglor doggerel. *See* **deeggl deeglr degglo deggor**

deeggnor engorged engorge. *See* **deegnr deenor deggno deggor**

deeggp pegged egged deep edge geed peed egg gee pee peg pe

deegh hedge edge geed ghee heed edh gee eh he

deeghils sleighed. *See* **deeghs deegis deegls deeils**

deeghin heeding neighed. *See* **deghin eegin deegh**

deeghitw weighted weighed. *See* **degitw dehitw eghitw**

deeghiw weighed. *See* **deegh deehw deegw**

deeghnru hungered. *See* **deegnu deenru deegnr degnru**

deeghops sheepdog. *See* **deeghs deegos deeops dehops**

deeghorw hedgerow hogweed. *See* **deeghr dehorw**

deeghosw hogweeds hogweed. *See* **deeghs deegos deegsw deehsw**

deeghow hogweed. *See* **deego deegh deehw**

deeghr hedger edger greed hedge deer dree edge geed ghee gree heed herd here reed edh ere erg gee her red reg eh er he re

deeghrs hedgers. *See* **deegrs deeghr deeghs**

deeghs hedges edges ghees hedge heeds sedge edge geed gees ghee heed seed shed edh gee see she eh he sh

deegiln deleing. *See* **deegln degiln**

deegilnn needling deleing lending needing. *See* **deegln deeinn degiln deilnn**

deegilnr engirdle lingered deleing dreeing leering reeding reeling reigned. *See* **deegir deegln deeglr deegnr**

deegilns seedling deleing dingles legends linseed seeding singled. *See* **deegis deegln deegls deeils**

deegilnt deleting deleing gentile gentled glinted tingled. *See* **deegln degiln degint deilnt**

deegilry greedily yielder. *See* **deegir deeglr deegry deeilr**

deegimn deeming. *See* **degin deimn deemn**

deegimnn emending deeming mending needing. *See* **deeinn deginn eeginn**

deegimru demiurge. *See* **deegir deegmr deemru degimr**

deeginn needing. *See* **deginn eeginn deeinn**

deeginps speeding seeding seeping. *See* **deegis deeins deeips deginp**

deeginr dreeing reeding reigned. *See* **deeinr deegir deginr deegnr**

deeginrs designer redesign resigned deniers dreeing engirds genders reeding reigned seeding. *See* **deegir deegis deegnr deegrs**

deegins seeding. *See* **degins deeins eegins deegis**

deeginst ingested destine edgiest seeding. *See* **deegis deeins deenst degins**

deeginw weeding. *See* **deginw**

deegipsw pigweeds pigweed. *See* **deegis deegsw deeips deepsw**

deegipw pigweed. *See* **deegw deipw**

deegir edgier dirge edger eider greed gride ridge deer dire dree edge geed gied gird gree grid reed ride die dig ere erg gee gid gie ire red reg rid rig er id re

deegirsv diverges derives diverge diverse grieved grieves revised. *See* **deegir deegis deegrs deegrv**

deegirv diverge grieved. *See* **deeirv deegir eegirv deegrv**

deegirw wedgier. *See* **deegir deegw deirw**

deegis sieged edges sedge siege dies digs edge egis geed gees gids gied gies ides seed side die dig gee gid gie ids see id is si

deegist edgiest. *See* **deegis degist**

deegistw wedgiest dewiest edgiest widgets. *See* **deegis deegsw deestw degist**

deegjpru prejudge. *See* **deepru degjru degpru**

deegk kedge edge eked geed geek eke gee keg

deegks kedges edges geeks kedge sedge desk edge eked ekes geed geek gees kegs seed seek skee skeg eke gee keg see

deegl glede gleed ledge dele edge geed geld glee eel eld gee gel led lee leg el

deegll gelled glede gleed ledge dele dell edge geed geld glee eel eld ell gee gel led lee leg el

deegln legend glede gleed ledge dele dene edge geed geld gene glee glen lend need den eel eld end gee gel led lee leg nee el en ne

deeglns legends. *See* **deegls deegln**

deeglnt gentled. *See* **deegln eeglnt**

deeglorv groveled. *See* **deeglr deegrv deglor deglov**

deeglp pledge glede gleed ledge deep dele edge geed geld glee peed peel pled eel eld gee gel led lee leg pee peg el pe

deeglpr pledger. *See* **deeglp deeglr**

deeglprs pledgers ledgers pledger pledges. *See* **deeglp deeglr deegls deegrs**

deeglps pledges. *See* **deegls deeglp**

deeglpst pledgets pestled pledges pledget. *See* **deeglp deegls deelpt deelst**

deeglpt pledget. *See* **deeglp deelpt**

deeglr ledger edger elder glede gleed greed ledge deer dele dree edge geed geld glee gree leer reed reel eel eld ere erg gee gel led lee leg red reg el er re

deeglrs ledgers. *See* **deegrs deelrs deegls deeglr**

deeglru reglued. *See* **deeglu deelru deeglr eeglru**

deegls gledes ledges sledge deles edges gelds glede gleed glees ledge sedge dele edge eels else geed gees geld gels glee lees legs seed seel sled eel eld els gee gel led lee leg see el

deeglss sledges. *See* **deegls deegss**

deeglsu deluges. *See* **deeglu deelsu deegls deegsu deglsu**

deeglu deluge elude glede gleed glued ledge luged dele duel edge geed geld glee glue luge due dug eel eld gee gel led lee leg leu lug el

deegmm gemmed deem deme edge geed meed gee gem mem em me

deegmr merged edger greed merge deem deer deme dree edge geed germ gree meed mere reed ere erg gee gem red reg rem em er me re

deegnorv governed. *See* **deegnr deegrv deenor deenrv**

deegnpux expunged expunge. *See* **deegnu deenpx**

deegnr gender edger genre greed green deer dene dree edge erne geed gene gree need nerd reed rend den end ere erg gee nee red reg en er ne re

deegnrs genders. *See* **deenrs deegrs deegnr eegnrs**

deegnsu dengues. *See* **deegnu deensu degnsu deegsu**

deegnu dengue endue nudge dene dune dung edge geed gene need nude den due dug dun end gee gnu gun nee en ne nu

deego geode doge edge geed ogee doe dog ego gee god ode do go od

deegos geodes doges edges geode ogees sedge does doge dogs dose edge egos geed gees gods goes odes ogee seed sego doe dog dos ego gee god ode see sod do go od os so

deegosy geodesy. *See* **deegos degsy deesy**

deegr edger greed deer dree edge geed gree reed ere erg gee red reg er re

deegrs edgers deers drees dregs edger edges greed grees reeds sedge serge deer dree edge ergs geed gees gree reds reed regs seed seer sere ere erg gee red reg res see er re

deegrstu gestured trudges gesture. *See* **deegrs deegsu deerst deersu**

deegrttu guttered uttered. *See* **deertt degrtu degttu derttu**

deegrv verged edger greed verge deer dree edge ever geed gree reed veer ere erg eve gee red reg rev vee er re

deegry greedy edger greed gyred reedy deer dree dyer edge edgy eery eyed eyre geed gree grey gyre reed dey dry dye ere erg eye gee gey red reg rye er re ye

deegs edges sedge edge geed gees seed gee see

deegss sedges edges sedge seeds edge geed gees seed sees ess gee see

deegsstu gusseted guessed. *See* **deegss deegsu deesst deessu**

deegssu guessed. *See* **deegss deegsu eegssu deessu**

deegsu segued edges sedge segue suede dues edge geed gees seed sued used due dug gee sue sue use us

deegsw wedges edges sedge sewed wedge weeds dews edge ewes geed gees seed weds weed dew ewe gee see sew wed wee we

deegw wedge edge geed weed dew ewe gee wed wee we

deeh heed edh eh he

deehhprs shepherd sphered. *See* **eehprs**

deehhrst threshed. *See* **deerst eehrst eh-hrst**

deehikrs shrieked shirked. *See* **deeirs dehirs deikrs ehikrs**

deehiksv khedives khedive. *See* **deeisv deiksv**

deehikv khedive. *See* **dehik dehiv**

deehilrs relished. *See* **deeilr deeils deeirs deelrs**

deehilss hideless diesels idlesse seidels shields. *See* **deeils deeiss dehils dehiss**

deehilsv dishevel shelved. *See* **deehlv deeils deeilv deeisv**

deehimns inmeshed sidemen. *See* **deehms deeims deeins deemns**

deehinr inhered. *See* **deeinr eehinr dehinr**

deehintw whitened. *See* **dehint dehinw dehitw deintw**

deehiprs perished sphered preside. *See* **deeips deeirs dehirs deiprs**

deehirr rehired. *See* **deehrr eehirr**

deehirrw wherried rehired rewired whirred. *See* **deehrr deerrw eehirr eeirrw**

deehirsv shivered derives dervish diverse revised shrived. *See* **deeirs deeirv deeisv deersv**

deehirtw withered. *See* **deeirt dehirt dehitw eehirt**

deehirty heredity. *See* **deeirt dehirt eehirt**

deehist heisted. *See* **deist deehs ehist**

deehitv thieved. *See* **eehitv dehiv**

deehknos keeshond. *See* **dehkno dehnos**

deehknru hunkered. *See* **deeknr deenru ehknru**

deehllo helloed. *See* **dehlo ehllo**

deehllor hollered helloed. *See* **dehlor dellor eehllr ehllor**

deehlls shelled. *See* **deels dells deehs**

deehlm helmed deem dele deme heed heel held helm heme meed meld edh eel eld elm hem led lee mel eh el em he me

deehlost hosteled. *See* **deelst dehlos dehlot dehost**

deehlosv shoveled hoveled shelved. *See* **deehlv deelsv dehlos dehosv**

deehlov hoveled. *See* **deehlv dehlo ehlov**

deehlp helped deep dele heed heel held help peed peel pled edh eel eld hep led lee pee eh el he pe

deehlpps shlepped. *See* **deehlp ehlpps**

deehlpw whelped. *See* **deehlp deehw eehlw**

deehlstu sleuthed hustled. *See* **deelst deelsu deeltu deestu**

deehlsv shelved. *See* **deelsv deehlv eehlsv**

deehlsw welshed. *See* **deehsw eehlsw**

deehlv helved delve helve dele heed heel held veld edh eel eld eve led lee lev vee eh el he

deehmm hemmed deem deme heed heme meed edh hem mem eh em he me

deehmnrs herdsmen menders. *See* **deehms deemnr deemns deenrs**

deehmort mothered theorem. *See* **deemot deemrt deeort dehmot**

deehms meshed deems demes heeds meeds deem deme heed heme hems meed mesh seed seem shed edh hem see she eh em he me sh

deehmux exhumed. *See* **eehmux deehx deeux**

deehnort dethrone throned thereon. *See* **deenor deenot deenrt deeort**

deehnowy honeydew honeyed. *See* **dehnoy**

deehnoy honeyed. *See* **dehnoy deeny**

deehorsw showered. *See* **deehsw deeors dehors dehorw**

deehortx exhorted. *See* **deeort deertx eehort ehortx**

deehorv hovered. *See* **deorv deeor**

deehprs sphered. *See* **eehprs**

deehrr herder erred deer dree heed herd here reed edh ere err her red eh er he re

deehrrs herders. *See* **deehrr deers deehs**

deehrrsw shrewder herders. *See* **deehrr deehsw deerrw eehrsw**

deehs heeds heed seed shed edh see she eh he sh

deehsw shewed heeds hewed sewed weeds dews ewes heed hews seed shed shew weds weed dew edh ewe hew see sew she wed wee eh he sh we

deehttw whetted. *See* **deettw deehw eehtt**

deehw hewed heed weed dew edh ewe hew wed wee eh he we

deehx hexed heed edh hex eh ex he

deeilns sideline linseed. *See* **deeils deeins deeins eeilns**

deeiilrv liveried deliver relived reviled. *See* **deeilr deeily deeirv deilrv**

deeiimtz itemized itemize. *See* **deeimt**

deeiirss dieresis desires resides. *See* **deeirs deeiss deiirs eeirss**

deeiirst siderite deities dirties reedits. *See* **deeirs deeirt deerst deiirs**

deeiirsv derisive derives diverse revised. *See* **deeirs deeirv deeisv deersv**

deeiissw sidewise. *See* **deeiss**

deeiist deities. *See* **deiist deest**

deeijll jellied. *See* **deejll deeil**

deeijnno enjoined. *See* **deeinn deijno eijnno**

deeijnor rejoined joinder. *See* **deeinr deenor deijno deinor**

deeijrtt jittered jettied jettier. *See* **deeirt deejtt deertt eijrtt**

deeijtt jettied. *See* **deejtt**

deeikll killdee. *See* **deikll deeil**

deeikllr killdeer killdee. *See* **deeilr deikll eikllr**

deeiklmw milkweed midweek. *See* **deiklm deilmw**

deeikln likened. *See* **deikln**

deeiklnr rekindle likened kindler. *See* **deeilr deeinr deeknr deelnr**

deeiklsw silkweed. *See* **deeils deeksw deilsw**

deeikmw midweek. *See* **deemw deikm**

deeiknrs deerskin deniers. *See* **deeinr deeins deeirs deeknr**

deeiknrt tinkered. *See* **deeinr deeirt deeknr deenrt**

deeikppr kippered. *See* **deekpr deippr eikppr**

deeikstt diskette. *See* **deestt**

deeil edile elide deil dele deli idle lied die eel eld led lee lei lid lie el id li

deeillmp impelled. *See* **deeimp deillm deillp deilmp**

deeillno nielloed. *See* **eillno**

deeilmos melodies. *See* **deeils deeims deilmo deilms**

deeilmoz melodize. *See* **deilmo**

deeilnot deletion. *See* **deenot deilnt deilot eilnot**

deeilnru underlie. *See* **deeilr deeinr deelnr deelru**

deeilns linseed. *See* **deeins deeils eeilns**

deeilnss idleness linseeds diesels endless idlesse linseed seidels. *See* **deeils deeins deeiss deenss**

deeilnst enlisted listened tinseled dentils destine linseed nestled tensile. *See* **deeils deeins deelst deenst**

deeilnsv sniveled deveins endives linseed livened. *See* **deeils deeilv deeins deeinv**

deeilntt entitled dinette entitle nettled. *See* **deentt deilnt deiltt deintt**

deeilnuv unveiled livened. *See* **deeilv deeinv deenuv eilnuv**

deeilnv livened. *See* **deeinv deeily**

deeilort dolerite loitered. *See* **deeilr deeirt deeort deilor**

deeilorv evildoer deliver overlie relived reviled. *See* **deeilr deeilv deeirv deilor**

deeilpr periled replied. *See* **deeilr**

deeilpsy speedily eyelids. *See* **deeils deeilv deeips deelpy**

deeilr lieder relied edile eider elder elide idler riled deer deil dele deli dire dirl dree idle leer lied lire reed reel ride riel rile die eel eld ere ire led lee lei lid lie red rid el er id li re

deeilrsv delivers silvered slivered deliver derives diverse drivels relived relives reviled reviles revised servile. *See* **deeilr deeils deeilv deeirs**

deeilrsw wielders swirled welders wielder. *See* **deeilr deeils deeirs deelrs**

deeilrsy yielders yielder eyelids. *See* **deeilr deeils deeily deeirs**

deeilrtt littered. *See* **deeilr deeirt deertt deiltt**

deeilrv deliver relived reviled. *See* **deeirv deilrv deeilv deeilr eeilrv**

deeilrvy delivery deliver devilry relived reviled yielder. *See* **deeilr deeilv deeily deeirv**

deeilrw wielder. *See* **deeilr deelrw deilrw**

deeilry yielder. *See* **deilry eeilry deeily**

deeils diesel elides sedile seidel deils deles delis edile elide idles sidle slide deil dele deli dies eels else ides idle isle lees leis lids lied lies seed seel side sled slid die eel eld els ids led lee lei lid lie see el id is li si

deeilss diesels idlesse seidels. *See* **deeils deeiss deilss**

deeilsuv delusive elusive. *See* **deeils deeilv deeisv deelsu**

deeilsvw swiveled weevils. *See* **deeils deeilv deeisv deeivw**

deeilsy eyelids. *See* **deeils deeily deilsy**

deeiltuy yuletide. *See* **deeily deeiltu deiltu**

deeilv levied veiled delve devil edile elide lived deil dele deli dive evil idle lied live veil veld vied vile die eel eld eve led lee lei lev lid lie vee vie el id li

deeilx exiled edile elide exile deil dele deli idle ilex lied die eel eld led lee lei lid lie el ex id li xi

deeily eyelid edile elide yield deil dele deli eely eyed idle idly idyl lied dey die dye eel eld eye led lee lei lid lie lye el id li ye

deeimmos semidome. *See* **deeims demmos**

deeimmrs immersed simmered dimmers immerse remised. *See* **deeims deeirs deimmr deimrs**

deeimnor domineer. *See* **deeinr deemno deemnr deenor**

deeimnoz demonize. *See* **deemno**

deeimnpt pediment emptied. *See* **deeimp deeimt deemnt deimnp**

deeimnrr reminder. *See* **deeinr deemnr deenrr deimnr**

deeimns sidemen. *See* **deeims deeins deimns deemns**

deeimnst sediment dements destine mindset sidemen. *See* **deeims deeimt deeins deemns**

deeimp impede deem deep deme dime meed peed pied die dim dip imp mid pee pie em id me mi pe pi

deeimpr demirep impeder. *See* **eeimpr deeimp deempr deimpr**

deeimprs demireps impeders simpered demirep empires emprise impeder impedes premise preside remised. *See* **deeimp deeims deeips deeirs**

deeimps impedes. *See* **deeims deeips deeimp**

deeimpt emptied. *See* **deeimp deeimt**

deeimrs remised. *See* **deeims deimrs deeirs eeimrs**

deeimrst demerits dimeters demerit dimeter merited mitered reedits remised. *See* **deeims deeimt deeirs deeirt**

deeimrt demerit dimeter merited mitered. *See* **deeimt deimrt deeirt deemrt**

deeimrtt remitted demerit dimeter emitted emitter merited mitered termite. *See* **deeimt deeirt deemrt deertt**

deeimrx remixed. *See* **deimr deeir eimrx**

deeims demise deems deism demes dimes meeds deem deme dies dime dims ides meed mise seed seem semi side die dim ids mid mis see em id is me mi si

deeimss demises. *See* **deimss deeims deeiss eeimss deemss**

deeimt itemed demit meted timed deem deme diet dime edit emit item meed meet mete mite teed teem tide tied time die dim dit met mid ted tee tie em id it me mi ti

deeimtt emitted. *See* **deeimt**

deeinn indene inned dene dine need nide nine den die din end inn nee en id in ne

deeinnrt interned interne. *See* **deeinn deeinr deeirt deenrt**

deeinnsz denizens denizen. *See* **deeinn deeins deeisz deinns**

deeinntv invented evident. *See* **deeinn deeinv deentv deinnt**

deeinntw entwined twinned entwine. *See* **deeinn deinnt deintw**

deeinnz denizen. *See* **deeinn deinz**

deeinort oriented. *See* **deeinr deeirt deenor deenot**

deeinorw ironweed widener downier. *See* **deeinr deenor deinor deinrw**

deeinpr ripened. *See* **deeinr**

deeinpss dispense despise. *See* **deeins deeips deeiss deenss**

deeinqru enquired queried enquire. *See* **deeinr deenru deinru deiqru**

deeinqsu sequined equines. *See* **deeins deensu deinsu eeinqu**

deeinr denier reined eider diner deer dene dire dree erne need nerd nide reed rein rend ride rind den die din end ere ire nee red rid en er id in ne re

deeinrrt interred trendier retired retried terrine. *See* **deeinr deeirt deenrr deenrt**

deeinrs deniers. *See* **deeinr deeins deenrs deeirs deinrs**

deeinrst inserted resident sintered trendies deniers destine entries reedits tenders. *See* **deeinr deeins deeirs deeirt**

deeinrsx indexers deniers indexer indexes. *See* **deeinr deeins deeirs deeisx**

deeinrtu reunited denture detinue erudite intrude retinue reunite tenured untried. *See* **deeinr deeirt deenrt deenru**

deeinrtv inverted evident riveted. *See* **deeinr deeinv deeirt deeirv**

deeinrtw wintered widener. *See* **deeinr deeirt deenrt deinrt**

deeinrw widener. *See* **deeinr deinrw eeinrw**

deeinrx indexer. *See* **deeinr**

deeins denies seined denes dense dines needs nides seine snide dene dens dies dine dins ends ides need nide seed seen

deeinssw   send side sine den die din end ens ids nee see sen sin en id in is ne si

deeinssw   wideness endwise sinewed. *See* **deeins deeiss deenss deinsw**

deeinst   destine. *See* **deeins deenst**

deeinstt   dinettes dentist destine dinette stinted. *See* **deeins deenst deentt deestt**

deeinstu   detinues destine detinue. *See* **deeins deenst deensu deestu**

deeinstv   invested destine deveins endives evident. *See* **deeins deeinv deeisv deenst**

deeinsv   deveins endives. *See* **deeins deeinv deeisv eeinsv**

deeinsw   endwise sinewed. *See* **deeins deinsw**

deeinsx   indexes. *See* **deeins deeisx**

deeintt   dinette. *See* **deentt deintt**

deeintu   detinue. *See* **deintu**

deeintv   evident. *See* **deeinv deentv**

deeinv   devein endive envied dene dine dive even need nevi nide vein vend vied vine den die din end eve nee vee vie en id in ne

deeinwz   wizened. *See* **deinz deinw einwz**

deeioprx   peroxide expired. *See* **deiopr eeiprx**

deeiops   episode. *See* **deeops deeips deiops**

deeiopss   episodes deposes despise dispose episode poesies. *See* **deeips deeiss deeops deepss**

deeiopt   epidote. *See* **deopt deeop deipt**

deeioptz   poetized epidote poetize. *See* **deopt deeop deipt**

deeiorrv   override. *See* **deeirv deiorv deirrv deorrv**

deeippqu   equipped quipped. *See* **deipqu**

deeippst   peptides despite peptide stepped. *See* **deeips deipps deippt deipst**

deeippt   peptide. *See* **deippt**

deeiprrs   presider respired perries preside reprise respire. *See* **deeips deeirs deiprs deirrs**

deeiprs   preside. *See* **deeirs deeips deiprs**

deeiprss   disperse presides depress desires despise preside pressed resides spiders. *See* **deeips deeirs deeiss deepss**

deeiprst   respited despite preside reedits respite striped. *See* **deeips deeirs deeirt deerst**

deeiprsu   duperies perused preside residue. *See* **deeips deeirs deepru deersu**

deeiprsv   deprives prevised deprive derives diverse preside previse revised. *See* **deeips deeirs deeirv deeisv**

deeiprtt   prettied pettier. *See* **deeirt deeptt deertt deiptt**

deeiprv   deprive. *See* **deeirv deipr eiprv**

deeiprx   expired. *See* **eeiprx deeir deipr**

deeips   espied speed spied deep dies dips ides peed pees pied pies seed seep side sped die dip ids pee pie see sip id is pe pi si

deeipss   despise. *See* **deeiss deeips eeipss deepss**

deeipsss   despises despise. *See* **deeips deeiss deepss eeipss**

deeipsst   sidestep despise despite. *See* **deeips deeiss deepss deesst**

deeipst   despite. *See* **deeips deipst**

deeipstu   deputies deputes despite dispute. *See* **deeips deeptu deestu deipst**

deeiptuz   deputize. *See* **deeptu**

deeiqrru   required queried require. *See* **deiqru**

deeiqru   queried. *See* **deiqru deeir eeqru**

deeiqruv   quivered queried. *See* **deeirv deiqru**

deeiqtu   quieted. *See* **deetu eiqtu**

deeiqtuu   quietude quieted. *See* **deequu**

deeir   eider deer dire dree reed ride die ere ire red rid er id re

deeirrss   dressier desires dresser redress resides sirrees. *See* **deeirs deeiss deirrs eeirss**

deeirrst   destrier reedits retired retires retried retries stirred terries. *See* **deeirs deeirt deerst deirrs**

deeirrt   retired retried. *See* **deeirt eeirrt**

deeirrw   rewired. *See* **deerrw eeirrw**

deeirs   desire eiders reside deers drees dries eider reeds rides sired deer dies dire dree ides reds reed reis ride rids rise seed seer sere side sire die ere ids ire red res rid see sir er id is re si

deeirss   desires resides. *See* **deeirs deeiss eeirss**

deeirsst   resisted deserts desires dessert reedits resides strides. *See* **deeirs deeirt deeiss deerst**

deeirssu   reissued residues desires reissue resides residue. *See* **deeirs deeiss deersu deessu**

deeirst   reedits. *See* **deerst deeirs deirst deeirt eeirst**

deeirsu   residue. *See* **deeirs deersu**

deeirsv   derives diverse revised. *See* **deeirv deeirs deeisv deirsv eeirsv**

deeirt   reedit retied deter eider retie tired treed tried deer diet dire dirt dree edit reed rete ride rite teed tide tied tier tire tree die dit ere ire red ret rid ted tee tie er id it re ti

deeirttt   tittered. *See* **deeirt deertt eirttt**

deeirtu   erudite. *See* **deeirt**

deeirtv   riveted. *See* **deeirv deirtv deeirt**

deeirv   derive diver drive eider rived deer dire dive dree ever reed ride rive veer

vied die ere eve ire red rev rid vee vie er id re

deeirvv   revived. *See* **deeirv eeirvv deervv**

deeiss   dieses seeds sides dies ides seed sees side die ess ids see sis id is si

deeissv   devises. *See* **deeisv deeiss eeissv**

deeistw   dewiest. *See* **deestw deistw**

deeistx   existed. *See* **deeisx deeitx**

deeisv   devise sieved dives sieve vised dies dive eves ides seed side vees vied vies vise die eve ids see vee vie id is si

deeisx   dexies desex sexed dies exes ides seed side die ids see sex six ex id is si xi

deeisz   seized sized seize dies ides seed side size zeds zees die ids see zed zee id is si

deeitx   exited diet edit exit teed tide tied die dit ted tee tie ex id it ti xi

deeivw   viewed wived dive vied view weed wide wive dew die eve ewe vee vie wed wee id we

deejkntu   junketed. *See* **dejknu ejkntu**

deejkr   jerked deer dree eked jeer jerk reed reek eke ere red er re

deejll   jelled dele dell jell eel eld ell led lee el

deejnoy   enjoyed. *See* **denoy ejnoy deeny**

deejprru   perjured perdure perjure. *See* **deepru deprru**

deejst   jested steed jest jets seed teds teed tees jet see set ted tee

deejtt   jetted teed jet ted tee

deek   eked eke

deekkrt   trekked. *See* **deert**

deeklln   knelled. *See* **deekn eekln eklln**

deeklps   skelped. *See* **deels eekls eekps**

deekmnoy   monkeyed moneyed. *See* **deemno deknoy eemnoy ekmnoy**

deekn   kneed dene eked keen knee need den eke end ken nee en ne

deeknn   kenned kneed dene eked keen knee need den eke end ken nee en ne

deeknotw   knotweed. *See* **deenot denotw eeknot**

deeknoty   keynoted keynote. *See* **deenot deknoy eeknot**

deeknr   kerned kneed deer dene dree eked erne keen kern knee need nerd reed reek rend den eke end ere ken nee red en er ne re

deekorv   revoked. *See* **deekov eekorv**

deekov   evoked evoke eked dove doe eke eve ode oke vee do od

deekpr   perked kreep deep deer dree eked keep peed peek peer perk reed reek eke ere pee per red rep er pe re

deeksw   skewed sewed weeds weeks desk dews eked ekes ewes seed seek skee skew weds weed week dew eke ewe see sew wed wee we

deeky keyed dyke eked eyed dey dye eke eye key ye

deel dele eel eld led lee el

deellmow mellowed. *See* **ellmow**

deellms smelled. *See* **deems deels dells**

deellnor enrolled. *See* **deelnr deenor dellor delnor**

deellotx extolled. *See* **dellot ellotx**

deellovy volleyed. *See* **deelly ellovy**

deellowy yellowed. *See* **deelly dellwy delowy ellowy**

deellps spelled. *See* **deels dells eelps**

deellqu quelled. *See* **deelu ellqu**

deellrsw dwellers dweller swelled welders. *See* **deelrs deelrw dellsw**

deellrw dweller. *See* **deelrw dellw**

deellry elderly. *See* **deelly eellry**

deellsw swelled. *See* **dellsw deels deesw**

deelly yelled dele dell eely eyed yell dey dye eel eld ell eye led lee lye el ye

deelmmop pommeled. *See* **deelop elmmop**

deelmnoo melodeon. *See* **deemno delmno delmoo delnoo**

deelmoos dolesome. *See* **delmoo delmos deloos**

deelmopy employed. *See* **deelmy deelop deelpy delmoy**

deelmor modeler remodel. *See* **delmor deelr deeor**

deelmors modelers remodels modeler molders remodel resoled smolder. *See* **deelrs deeors delmor delmos**

deelmost molested demotes omelets smelted. *See* **deelmt deelst deemot delmos**

deelmruy demurely. *See* **deelmy deelru deemru deemry**

deelmst smelted. *See* **deelmt deelst**

deelmsy medleys. *See* **deelmy eelmsy**

deelmt melted meted deem dele deme leet meed meet meld melt mete teed teem eel eld elm led lee let mel met ted tee el em me

deelmy medley deem dele deme demy eely eyed meed meld ylem dey dye eel eld elm eye led lee lye mel el em me my ye

deelnntu tunneled. *See* **deeltu denntu eelnnt elnntu**

deelnoos loosened noodles. *See* **delnoo deloos denoos eelnos**

deelnort redolent. *See* **deelnr deenor deenot deenrt**

deelnr lender elder deer dele dene dree erne leer lend need nerd reed reel rend den eel eld end ere led lee nee red el en er ne re

deelnrs lenders slender. *See* **deenrs deelrs deelnr**

deelnrty tenderly. *See* **deelnr deenrt denrty eelnrt**

deelnss endless. *See* **eelnss deenss**

deelnssw lewdness endless. *See* **deenss eelnss eelnsw**

deelnst nestled. *See* **deelst deenst eelnst**

deelnsy densely. *See* **deels deens densy**

deelntt nettled. *See* **deentt eelntt**

deelnwwy newlywed. *See* **deeny eelnw elnwy**

deelop eloped elope epode loped poled deep dele dole dope lode lope oped peed peel pled plod pole doe eel eld led lee lop ode old ope pee pod do el lo od pe

deelopp peopled. *See* **deelop delopp eelopp**

deelopr deplore. *See* **deelop eelopr delopr**

deeloprs deplores deplore elopers leprose polders reposed resoled. *See* **deelop deelrs deeops deeors**

deeloprx exploder explored deplore explode explore. *See* **deelop delopre elopr eloprx**

deelopsv develops develop. *See* **deelop deelsv deeops delops**

deelopsx explodes explode exposed. *See* **deelop deeops delops eelops**

deelopv develop. *See* **deelop deelv delov**

deelopx explode. *See* **deelop eelpx**

deelors resoled. *See* **deelrs deeors delors eelors**

deelorsv resolved resoled resolve. *See* **deelrs deelsv deeors deersv**

deelorsy yodelers resoled yodeler. *See* **deelrs deeors delors delosy**

deelortv revolted. *See* **deeort deeotv delort elortv**

deelortw troweled lowered roweled toweled towered. *See* **deelrw deeltw deeort delort**

deeloruv louvered overdue. *See* **deelru deloru deoruv eelruv**

deelorvv revolved evolved revolve. *See* **deervv eelovv**

deelorw lowered roweled. *See* **deelrw delow deorw**

deelory yodeler. *See* **deelr deeor eelry**

deelossu delouses delouse. *See* **deelsu deessu delssu deossu**

deelosu delouse. *See* **deelsu delos deosu**

deelosvv devolves evolved evolves. *See* **deelsv delosv**

deelotw toweled. *See* **deeltw delow elotw**

deelovv evolved. *See* **eelovv deelv delov**

deelprsu preludes repulsed duelers perused prelude repulse slurped. *See* **deelrs deelru deelsu deepru**

deelpru prelude. *See* **deelru deepru delpru**

deelpst pestled. *See* **deelst deelpt eelpst**

deelpsux duplexes. *See* **deelsu deelux deesux delpux**

deelpt pelted deep dele leet lept peed peel pelt pled teed eel eld led lee let pee pet ted tee el pe

deelpy deeply yelped deep dele eely eyed peed peel pled yelp dey dye eel eld eye led lee lye pee ply yep el pe ye

deelr elder deer dele dree leer reed reel eel eld ere led lee red el er re

deelrs elders deers deles drees elder leers reeds reels deer dele dree eels else leer lees reds reed reel seed seel seer sere sled eel eld els ere led lee red res see el er re

deelrstu resulted duelers rustled strudel. *See* **deelrs deelru deelst deelsu**

deelrstw wrestled strewed swelter welders welters wrested wrestle. *See* **deelrs deelrw deelst deeltw**

deelrsu duelers. *See* **deelru deelrs deelsu deersu**

deelrsw welders. *See* **deelrs deelrw**

deelru dueler elder elude lured ruled deer dele dree duel leer lure reed reel rude rued rule due eel eld ere led lee leu red rue urd el er re

deelrw welder elder deer dele dree drew ewer leer lewd reed reel weed weld dew eel eld ere ewe led lee red wed wee el er re we

deels deles dele eels else lees seed seel sled eel eld els led lee see el

deelst eldest deles leets sleet steed steel stele dele eels else lees leet lest lets seed seel sled teds teed tees eel eld els led lee let see set ted tee el

deelstt settled. *See* **deestt deelst eelstt**

deelsu eludes deles duels dulse elude suede dele duel dues eels else lees lues seed seel sled slue sued used due eel eld els led lee leu see sue use el us

deelsv delves deles delve elves velds dele eels else eves lees seed seel sled vees veld eel eld els eve led lee lev see vee el

deeltu eluted teledu elude elute etude luted dele duel duet leet lute teed tule due eel eld led lee let leu ted tee el ut

deeltux exulted. *See* **deelux deeltu**

deeltw welted tweed dwelt dele leet lewd teed weed weld welt dew eel eld ewe led lee let ted tee wed wee wet el we

deelu elude dele duel due eel eld led lee leu el

deelux deluxe elude exude dele duel luxe due eel eld lee leu lux el ex

deelv delve dele veld eel eld eve led lee lev vee el

deem deem deme meed em me

deemmors mesoderm. *See* **deeors demmos eemmrs**

deemmrsu summered demures resumed. *See* **deemru deersu demmsu demrsu**

deemmst stemmed. *See* **eemmst deems deemt**

deemn emend deem deme dene meed mend need den end men nee em en ne ne

deemno omened emend demon deem deme demo dene dome done meed mend mode need node nome omen den doe don end eon men mod mon nee nod ode one do em en me mo ne no od om on

deemnoqu queendom. *See* **deemno**

deemnoy moneyed. *See* **deemno eemnoy**

deemnr mender emend deem deer deme dene dree erne meed mend mere need nerd reed rend den end ere men nee red rem em en er me ne re

deemnrs menders. *See* **deenrs deemns deemnr**

deemns emends deems demes denes dense emend meeds mends mesne needs semen deem deme dene dens ends meed mend need seed seem seen send den end ens men nee see sen em en me ne

deemnst dements. *See* **deemnt deenst**

deemnt dement emend meted deem deme dene dent meed meet mend mete need teed teem teen tend den end men met nee net ted tee ten em en me ne

deemoort odometer motored. *See* **deemot deemrt deeort demoor**

deemorv removed. *See* **eemorv deorv deeor**

deemost demotes. *See* **deemot eemost demost**

deemosy moseyed. *See* **deems demos emosy**

deemot demote emoted meted emote deem deme demo dome dote meed meet mete mode mote teed teem toed tome doe dot met mod mot ode ted tee tod toe tom do em me mo od om to

deempr permed deem deep deer deme dree meed mere peed peer perm reed ere pee per red rem rep em er me pe re

deemprsu presumed demures dumpers perused presume resumed supreme. *See* **deempr deemru deepru deersu**

deemprtu permuted erupted permute reputed trumped. *See* **deempr deemrt deemru deepru**

deemptt tempted. *See* **deeptt deemt emptt**

deemrrru murderer demurer. *See* **deemru demrru**

deemrrsu demurers demurer demures murders resumed. *See* **deemru deersu demrru demrsu**

deemrstu mustered demures resumed. *See* **deemrt deemru deerst deersu**

deemrsu demures resumed. *See* **deemru demrsu eemrsu**

deemrt termed deter meted meter metre retem treed deem deer deme dree meed meet mere mete reed rete teed teem term tree ere met red rem ret ted tee em er me re

deemrttu muttered uttered. *See* **deemrt deemru deertt derttu**

deemru demure demur deem deer deme dree drum emeu meed mere reed rude rued due emu ere mud red rem rue rum urd em er me mu re um

deemry remedy reedy emery deem deer deme demy dree dyer eery eyed eyre meed mere reed dey dry dye ere eye red rem rye em er me my re ye

deems deems demes meeds deem deme meed seed seem see em me

deemss messed deems demes meeds seeds seems deem deme meed mess seed seem sees see ess em me

deemt metted deem deme meed meet mete teed teem met ted tee em me

deemw mewed deem deme meed weed dew ewe mew wed wee em me we

deen dene need den end nee en ne

deennopu unopened. *See* **deennp deenop dennou dennpu**

deennorw renowned. *See* **denorw eenorw deenor ennorw**

deennp penned deep dene need neep peed peen pend den end nee pee pen en ne pe

deennpst pendents pendent. *See* **deennp deenst**

deennpt pendent. *See* **deennp**

deennruv unnerved. *See* **deenru deenrv deenuv**

deennssu nudeness unseen.. *See* **deensu eenssu deenss deessu**

deenny yenned needy dene deny dyne eyed need den dey dye end eye nee yen en ne ye

deenoorv overdone. *See* **deenor deenrv denorv deoorv**

deenop depone opened epode deep dene done dope need neep node nope oped open peed peen pend peon pond pone den doe don end eon nee nod ode one ope pee pen pod do en ne no od on pe

deenops depones. *See* **deenop deeops**

deenor redone erode drone deer dene doer done dree erne need nerd node redo reed rend rode den doe don dor end eon ere nee nod nor ode one ore red rod roe do en er ne no od on or re

deenorrw wonderer wonder.. *See* **denorw eenorw deenor deerrw**

deenors endorse. *See* **deenrs denors deeors**

deenorss endorses endorse senders. *See* **deenor deenrs deenss deeors**

deenorsw worsened downers endorse wonders. *See* **deenor deenrs deeors denors**

deenortu deuteron denture tenured. *See* **deenor deenot deenrt deenru**

deenorz rezoned. *See* **deenor eenorz deeorz**

deenost denotes. *See* **deenot deenst denost**

deenot denote noted toned dene dent done dote need node note teed teen tend toed tone den doe don dot end eon nee net nod not ode one ted tee ten tod toe ton do en ne no od on to

deenprst pretends present pretend repents serpent tenders. *See* **deenrs deenrt deenst deerst**

deenprt pretend. *See* **deenrt eenprt**

deenpsx expends. *See* **deenpx deens deesx**

deenpx expend deep dene need neep peed peen pend den end nee pee pen en ex ne pe

deenrr render erred deer dene dree erne need nerd reed rend den end ere err nee red en er ne re

deenrrs renders. *See* **deenrs deenrr**

deenrrtu returned denture tenured. *See* **deenrr deenrt deenru denrtu**

deenrs denser sender deers denes dense drees ernes needs nerds reeds rends sneer deer dene dens dree ends erne need nerd reds reed rend seed seen seer send sere den end ens ere nee red res see sen en er ne re

deenrss senders. *See* **deenrs deenss eenrss**

deenrssu rudeness endures ensured ensures senders sunders undress. *See* **deenrs deenru deenss deensu**

deenrst tenders. *See* **deenrs deerst eenrst deenst deenrt**

deenrstu dentures denture endures ensured neuters tenders tenured tenures tureens. *See* **deenrs deenrt deenru deenst**

deenrsu endures ensured. *See* **deenrs deensu deenru eenrsu denrsu**

deenrsuv unversed endures ensured vendues. *See* **deenrs deenru deenrv deensu**

deenrt rented tender deter enter treed trend deer dene dent dree erne need nerd reed rend rent rete teed teen tend tern tree den end ere nee net red ret ted tee ten en er ne re

deenrtu denture tenured. *See* **deenru eenrtu deenrt denrtu**

deenrtuv ventured denture tenured venture. *See* **deenrt deenru deenrv deentv**

deenru endure endue under deer dene dree dune erne need nerd nude reed rend rude rued rune den due dun end ere nee red rue run urd urn en er ne nu re

deenrv nerved nerve never deer dene dree erne even ever need nerd reed rend veer vend ven end ere eve nee red rev vee en er ne re

deens denes dense needs dene dens ends need seed seen send den end ens nee see sen en ne

deenss sensed denes dense needs seeds sends sense dene dens ends need seed seen sees send den end ens ess nee see sen en ne

deensst densest. *See* **deenst deenss deesst eensst**

deenst nested tensed denes dense dents needs steed teens tends tense dene dens dent ends need nest nets seed seen send sent teds teed teen tees tend tens den end ens nee net see sen set ted tee ten en ne

deensttu untested student stunted. *See* **deenst deensu deentt deestt**

deenstx extends. *See* **deentx deenst**

deensu endues ensued denes dense dunes endue ensue needs nudes suede dene dens dues dune duns ends need nude seed seen send sued used den due dun end ens nee see sen sue sun use en ne nu us

deensuv vendues. *See* **deensu deenuv eensuv**

deentt detent netted tented tenet dene dent need teed teen tend tent den end nee net ted tee ten en ne

deentv vented event dene dent even need teed teen tend vend vent den end eve nee net ted tee ten vee vet en ne

deentx extend dene dent need next teed teen tend den end nee net ted tee ten en ex ne

deenu endue dene dune need nude den due dun end nee en ne nu

deenuv vendue endue venue dene dune even need nude vend den due dun end eve nee vee en ne nu

deenuvx unvexed. *See* **deenuv deeux deevx**

deeny needy dene deny dyne eyed need den dey dye end eye nee yen en ne ye

deeoorrv overrode. *See* **deoorv deorrv**

deeoorsv overdose. *See* **deeors deersv deoors deoorv**

deeop epode deep dope oped peed doe ode ope pee pod do od pe

deeoppst estopped stepped stopped. *See* **deeops deopps deoppt deopst**

deeoppy popeyed. *See* **deeop deopy**

deeoprrt reported. *See* **deeort deoprt eoprrt**

deeoprrv reproved reprove. *See* **deoprv deorrv**

deeoprs reposed. *See* **deeops deoprs deeors eeoprs**

deeoprst dopester deports oersted redtops reposed sported teredos. *See* **deeops deeors deeort deerst**

deeoprtt repotted tetrode treetop. *See* **deeort deeptt deertt deoprt**

deeoprtx exported. *See* **deeort deertx deoprt eeprtx**

deeoprw powered. *See* **deoprw deeop deeor**

deeops depose epodes dopes epode posed speed deep does dope dose epos odes oped opes peed pees peso pods pose seed seep sped doe dos ode ope pee pod see sod sop do od os pe so

deeopss deposes. *See* **deeops deepss**

deeopssu espoused deposes espouse pseudos. *See* **deeops deepss deessu deopsu**

deeopsx exposed. *See* **deeops eeopsx**

deeor erode deer doer dree redo reed rode doe dor ere ode ore red rod roe do er od or re

deeorrr orderer reorder. *See* **deeor deerr eorrr**

deeorrrs orderers reorders orderer reorder reredos. *See* **deeors deorrs eorrrs**

deeorrs reredos. *See* **deeors deorrs**

deeorrst resorted restored oersted reredos restore teredos. *See* **deeors deeort deerst deorrs**

deeorrtt retorted tetrode. *See* **deeort deertt deortt eerrtt**

deeorrtu rerouted reroute. *See* **deeort deorru deortu eerrtu**

deeorrvw overdrew. *See* **deerrw deorrv deorrw**

deeors erodes redoes deers doers drees erode erose reeds rosed deer doer does dose dree odes ores redo reds reed rode rods roes rose seed seer sere sore doe dor dos ere ode ore red res rod roe see sod do er od or os re so

deeorst oersted teredos. *See* **deerst deorst deeors eeorst deeort**

deeorstt tetrodes oersted rosette teredos tetrode. *See* **deeors deeort deerst deertt**

deeorstx dextrose oersted redoxes teredos. *See* **deeors deeort deerst deertx**

deeorsty oystered destroy oersted teredos. *See* **deeors deeort deerst deorst**

deeorsuv overused devours overdue overuse. *See* **deeors deersu deersv deorsu**

deeorsx redoxes. *See* **deeors**

deeort teredo deter doter erode treed deer doer dote dree redo reed rete rode rote teed toed tore tree trod doe dor dot ere ode ore ort red ret rod roe rot ted tee tod toe tor do er od or re to

deeortt tetrode. *See* **deertt deortt deeort**

deeorttt tottered tetrode trotted. *See* **deeort deertt deortt**

deeorttx extorted tetrode. *See* **deertx eorttx deertt deortt**

deeortw towered. *See* **deeort deortw**

deeoruv overdue. *See* **deoruv deeor eeruv**

deeorxx xeroxed. *See* **deeor deorx eorxx**

deeorz zeroed erode deer doer doze dree redo reed rode zero doe dor ere ode ore red rod roe zed zee do er od or re

deeostv devotes. *See* **deestv deeotv eeostv**

deeotv devote vetoed voted dote dove teed toed veto vote doe dot eve ode ted tee tod toe vee vet do od to

deep deep peed pee pe

deepppp pepped deep peed peep pee pep pe

deepppr prepped. *See* **deepppp eepppr**

deeppst stepped. *See* **eeppst deeps deest**

deeprrsu perdures perdure perused peruser spurred. *See* **deepru deersu deprru deprsu**

deeprru perdure. *See* **deepru deprru**

deeprss depress pressed. *See* **eeprss deepss**

deeprsu perused. *See* **deprsu deepru eeprsu deersu**

deeprtu erupted reputed. *See* **deeptu eeprtu**

deeprty retyped. *See* **deepry eeprty**

deepru perdue pureed drupe duper perdu prude puree rupee deep deer dree peed peer pure reed rude rued due ere pee per red rep rue urd er pe re up

deepruvy purveyed. *See* **deepru deepry depruy eepruv**

deepry preyed reedy deep deer dree dyer eery eyed eyre peed peer prey pyre reed dey dry dye ere eye pee per pry red rep rye yep er pe re ye

deeps speed deep peed pees seed seep sped pee see pe

deepss speeds seeds seeps speed deep peed pees seed seep sees sped ess pee see pe

deepstu deputes. *See* **deeptu deestu**

deepsw spewed sewed speed sweep weeds weeps deep dews ewes peed pees pews seed seep sped spew weds weed weep dew ewe pee pew see sew wed wee pe we

deepsy speedy seedy seepy speed deep deys dyes espy eyed eyes peed pees seed seep sped dey dye eye pee see spy yep yes pe ye

deeptt petted deep peed teed pee pet ted tee pe

deeptu depute etude deep duet peed teed due pee pet put ted tee tup pe up ut

deeqstu quested. *See* **deestu eqstu**

deequu queued queue due

deer deer dree reed red ere er re

deerr erred deer dree reed ere err red er re

deerrss dresser redress. *See* **deers derss deerr**

deerrsss dressers dresser dresses redress. *See* **deers derss deerr**

deerrsuv verdures verdure. *See* **deersu deersv eerrsv eersuv**

deerrttu turreted uttered utterer. *See* **deertt derttu eerrtt eerrtu**

deerrtux extruder extrude. *See* **deertx eerrtu**

deerruv verdure. *See* **deerr eeruv derru**

deerrw redrew erred deer dree drew ewer reed weed dew ere err ewe red wed wee er re we

deers deers drees reeds deer dree reds reed seed seer sere ere red res see er re

deersss dresses. *See* **deers derss eessss**

deerssst desserts stressed deserts dessert dresses tresses. *See* **deerst deesst eersst**

deerssst deserts dessert. *See* **deerst eersst deesst**

deerst desert deters rested deers deter drees ester reeds reset steed steer stere terse treed trees deer dree erst reds reed rest rete rets seed seer sere teds teed tees tree ere red res ret see set ted tee er re

deerstux extrudes extrude. *See* **deerst deersu deertx deestu**

deerstw strewed wrested. *See* **deerst deestw eerstw**

deersu reused deers drees druse reeds reuse suede deer dree dues reds reed rude rued rues ruse seed seer sere sued surd sure urds used user due ere red res rue see sue urd use er re us

deersuvy surveyed. *See* **deersu deersv eersuv ersuvy**

deersv served versed deers drees reeds serve sever veers verse deer dree ever eves reds reed revs seed seer sere veer vees ere eve red res rev see vee er re

deersvw swerved. *See* **deersv eersvw**

deert deter treed deer dree reed rete teed tree ere red ret ted tee er re

deertt retted deter treed deer dree reed rete teed tree tret ere red ret ted tee er re

deerttu uttered. *See* **deertt derttu**

deerttux textured extrude texture uttered. *See* **deertt deertx derttu**

deertux extrude. *See* **deertx deetu deeux**

deertx dexter deter exert treed deer dree reed rete teed tree ere red ret rex ted tee er ex re

deervv revved verve deer dree ever reed veer ere eve red rev vee er re

deery reedy deer dree dyer eery eyed eyre reed dey dry dye ere eye red rye er re ye

dees seed see

deess seeds seed sees see ess

deesst steeds seeds steed seed sees sets teds teed tees ess see set ted tee

deesstt detests. *See* **deestt eesstt deesst**

deesstv devests. *See* **deestv deesst**

deessu suedes seeds suede dues seed sees suds sued sues used uses due ess sue use us

deessy yessed seeds seedy yeses deys dyes eyed eyes seed sees dey dye ess eye see yes ye

deest steed seed teds teed tees see set ted tee

deestt detest tested steed seed stet teds teed tees test see set ted tee

deestu etudes duets etude steed suede dues duet dust seed stud sued suet teds teed tees used due see set sue ted tee use us ut

deestv devest vested steed eves seed teds teed tees vees vest vets eve see set ted tee vee vet

deestw stewed tweeds sewed steed sweet tweed weeds weest dews ewes seed stew teds teed tees weds weed west wets dew ewe see set sew ted tee wed wee wet we

deesu suede dues seed sued used due see sue use us

deesux exudes desex exude sexed suede dues exes seed sued used due see sex sue use ex us

deesw sewed weeds dews ewes seed weds weed dew ewe see sew wed wee wee we

deesx desex sexed seed exes see sex ex

deesy seedy deys dyes eyed eyes seed dey dye eye see yes ye

deet teed ted tee

deettv vetted teed eve ted tee vee vet

deettw wetted tweed tweet teed weed dew ewe ted tee wed wee wet we

deetu etude teed duet due ted tee ut

deetw tweed teed weed dew ewe ted tee wed wee wet we

deetwy tweedy tweed weedy dewy eyed teed weed dew dey dye ewe eye ted tee wed wee wet wye yet yew we ye

deeux exude due ex

deevx vexed eve vee vex ex

deew weed dew ewe wed wee we

deewy weedy dewy eyed weed dew dey dye ewe eye wed wee wye yew we ye

deey eyed dey dye eye ye

def fed

defflu fluffed. *See* **defflu**

deffhilw whiffled whiffed whiffle. *See* **dehilw**

deffhiw whiffed. *See* **deffi ffhiw**

deffhlsu shuffled duffels duffles flushed shuffle sluffed. *See* **deffhu defflu**

deffhu huffed duff feud hued huff due edh fed feh feu hue eh he

deffi fifed fief fife die fed fid fie id if

deffilns sniffled sniffed sniffle. *See* **defils defins**

deffilov fivefold. *See* **defilo**

deffilr riffled. *See* **deffir effilr defilr**

deffim miffed fifed dime fief fife miff die dim fed fid fie mid em id if me mi

deffimo fiefdom. *See* **deffim deffo**

deffimos fiefdoms fiefdom offside. *See* **deffim**

deffins sniffed. *See* **defins effis deffi**

deffios offside. *See* **dffos deffo**

deffioss offsides offside. *See* **dffos deoss effis**

deffips spiffed. *See* **effis deffi deips**

deffir differ riffed fifed fifer fired fried dire fief fife fire ride rife riff die fed fid fie fir ire red ref rid rif er id if re

deffirs differs. *See* **deffir effirs**

deffissu diffuses diffuse. *See* **defssu deissu**

deffist stiffed. *See* **defist deffit**

deffisu diffuse. *See* **dffsu defsu effis**

deffisux suffixed diffuse. *See* **ffisux**

deffit tiffed fifed fetid deft diet edit fief fife tide tied tiff die dit eft fed fid fie fit ted tie id if it ti

defflmu muffled. *See* **defflu deffmu efflmu**

defflnsu snuffled duffels duffles sluffed snuffed snuffle. *See* **defflu**

defflru ruffled. *See* **defflu deffru deflru efflru**

defflsu duffels duffles sluffed. *See* **defflu**

defflu duffel duffle luffed delf duel duff feud fled flue fuel luff due eld elf fed feu flu led leu el

deffmu muffed fumed duff feud fume muff due emu fed feu mud em me mu um

deffno offend offed doff done fend fond node den doe don end eon fed fen foe nod ode off one do en ne no od of on

deffnos offends. See **deffno dffos defns**

deffnsu snuffed. See **dffsu densu defsu**

deffo offed doff doe fed foe ode off do od of

deffpu puffed duff feud puff due fed feu pe up

deffrsu duffers. See **deffru effrsu defrsu**

deffru duffer ruffed duff feud rude rued ruff due fed feu fur red ref rue urd er re

deffssuu suffused suffuse. See **defssu**

deffstu stuffed. See **destu dffsu efstu**

deffstuy dyestuff stuffed. See **ffstuy**

defggi figged gied die dig egg fed fid fie fig gid gie gig id if

defggiln fledging gelding niggled. See **defggi deggin degiln**

defggir frigged. See **deggir defggi defgir**

defgglo flogged. See **degglo defggo defglo**

defggo fogged defog doge doe dog egg ego fed foe fog god ode do go od of

defgiiln defiling fielding infidel infield. See **degiln dgiiln fgiiln**

defgiilu uglified. See **defglu**

defgiinn defining fending finding indigen. See **definn deginn dgiinn fgiinn**

defgiiny deifying edifying defying dignify. See **deginy dfiiny**

defgilnu ingulfed dueling eluding feuding fueling indulge. See **defglu degiln deglnu efglnu**

defginn fending. See **deginn definn**

defginr fringed. See **deginr definr efginr defgir**

defginsu defusing feuding infused. See **defgsu defins degins degisu**

defginu feuding. See **degin efgin defin**

defginy defying. See **deginy**

defgioow goodwife. See **defgoo**

defgir fridge dirge fired fried gride grief ridge dire fire frig gied gird grid ride rife die dig erg fed fid fie fig fir gid gie ire red ref reg rid rif rig er id if re

defgirs fridges. See **degirs defgir efgirs**

defgiru figured. See **defgir efgiru**

defgist fidgets. See **degist defgit defist**

defgit fidget gifted fetid deft diet edit gied gift tide tied die dig dit eft fed fie fig fit get gid gie ted tie id if it ti

defgity fidgety. See **defgit**

defgjoru forjudge. See **defgor degjru degoru**

defglo golfed defog lodge ogled delf doge dole fled floe flog fold geld gold golf lode loge ogle doe dog ego eld elf fed foe fog gel god led leg log ode old do el go lo od of

defglu gulfed fudge glued luged delf duel feud fled flue fuel geld glue gulf luge due dug eld elf fed feu flu fug gel led leg leu lug el

defgo defog doge doe dog ego fed foe fog god ode do go od of

defgoo goofed defog doge food good goof doe dog ego fed foe fog god goo ode do go od of

defgor forged defog forge gofer gored doer doge ford fore froe frog goer gore ogre redo rode doe dog dor ego erg fed foe fog for fro god ode ore red ref reg rod roe do er go od of or re

defgos defogs defog doges does doge dogs dose egos feds foes fogs gods goes odes sego doe dog ego fed foe fog god ode sod do go od of os so

defgsu fudges feuds fudge fused dues feds feud feus fugs fuse sued used due dug fed feu fug sue use us

defgu fudge feud due dug fed feu fug

defhiins fiendish finished. See **defhis defns dehins deiins**

defhioow wifehood. See **defhoo**

defhis fished hides shied dies dish feds fids fies fish hide hied hies ides shed side die edh fed feh fid fie hid hie his ids ifs she eh he hi id if is sh si

defhist shifted. See **efhist defhis**

defhloos selfhood. See **defhoo defloo dehlos dehoos**

defhlsu flushed. See **defls delsu defsu**

defhoo hoofed oohed food hoed hood hoof doe edh fed feh foe foh hod hoe ode oho ooh do eh he ho od of oh

defhoors serfhood hoofers. See **defhoo defoor dehoos dehors**

defhort frothed. See **deort efort fhort**

defiiilv vilified. See **deilv defil deiiv**

defiiimn minified. See **deimn defin deiim**

defiiins nidifies. See **defins deiins**

defiiivv vivified. See **deiiv diivv**

defiillp filliped. See **defill deillp fiillp**

defiillw wildlife. See **defill deillw**

defiilm midlife. See **defilm deiim**

defiilms misfiled midlife misfile. See **defilm defils deiims deilms**

defiiln infidel infield. See **efiln defil defin**

defiilns infidels infidel infield. See **defils defins deiins**

defiilrw wildfire. See **defilr deilrw**

defiilty fidelity putting. See **ginptu ginpty**

defiimor modifier. See **defimr defmor**

defiimos modifies. See **deiims diimos**

defiimrs misfired misfire. See **defimr deiims deiirs deimrs**

defiimw midwife. See **deiim**

defiinot notified edition. See **deiino deiint efiint**

defiinty identify. See **deiint dfiiny efiint**

defiinu unified. See **defin dfinu deinu**

defiinx infixed. See **defin defix deinx**

defiioss ossified. See **deiiss**

defiipru purified. See **depru defir deipr**

defiipss fissiped. See **deiiss**

defiipty typified. See **deiipt**

defiirrt driftier drifter dirtier. See **defirt**

defikn finked knifed fiend fined inked knife dike dine dink fend find fine fink kind kine nide den die din end fed fen fid fie fin ink kef ken kid kif kin en id if in ne

defikrs frisked. See **deikrs efikrs**

defil felid field filed flied deil delf deli file fled idle lied lief life die eld elf fed fid fie led lei lid lie el id if li

defill filled felid field filed flied deil delf deli dell dill fell file fill fled idle lied lief life die eld elf ell fed fid fie ill led lei lid lie el id if li

defillnu unfilled. See **defill**

defillr frilled. See **defill efillr defilr**

defilm filmed felid field filed flied limed deil delf deli dime file film fled idle lied lief life lime meld mild mile die dim eld elf elm fed fid fie led lei lid lie mel mid mil el em id if li me mi

defilnno ninefold. See **defilo definn deflno deilnn**

defilnry friendly. See **defilr definr deilry efilny**

defilo foiled felid field filed flied oiled oldie deil delf deli dole file fled floe foil fold idle idol lied lief life lode die doe eld elf fed fid fie foe led lei lid lie ode oil old do el id if li lo od of

defilopr profiled profile. See **defilo defilr deflor deilop**

defiloru fluoride direful floured. See **defilo defilr deflor deflou**

defilotu outfield flouted. See **defilo defilt deflot deflou**

defilow oldwife. See **deflow defilo**

defilpp flipped. See **deilpp efilpp**

defilpru prideful direful purfled. See **defilr deflru delpru efilpr**

defilptu uplifted. See **defilt defltu deiltu eilptu**

defilr rifled felid field filed filer fired flied flier fried idler lifer rifle riled deil delf deli dirl file fire fled idle lied lief life lire ride riel rife rile die eld elf fed fid fie fir ire led lei lid lie red ref rid rif el er id if li re

defilrru flurried direful. *See* **defilr deflru defrru efilru**

defilrt flirted trifled. *See* **efilrt defilt defirt**

defilru direful. *See* **deflru efilru defilr**

defilrvy fervidly devilry. *See* **defilr defirv deilrv deilry**

defilrzz frizzled drizzle fizzled frizzed frizzle. *See* **defilr defizz**

defils felids fields deils delfs delis felid field filed files flied flies idles sidle slide deil delf deli dies feds fids fies file fils fled ides idle isle leis lids lied lief lies life self side sled slid die eld elf els fed fid fie ids ifs led lei lid lie el id if is li si

defilssu sulfides sulfide. *See* **defils defssu deilss deissu**

defilst stifled. *See* **deflst defils efilst defist deilst**

defilsu sulfide. *See* **defils dfilsu**

defilt lifted delft felid fetid field filed filet flied tilde tiled deft deil delf deli diet edit felt file fled flit idle left lied lief life lift tide tied tile die dit eft eld elf fed fid fie fit led lei let lid lie lit ted tie til el id if it li ti

defiltt flitted. *See* **defitt defilt deiltt**

defilty fetidly. *See* **defilt deflty**

defilxy fixedly. *See* **defiy defil defix**

defilzz fizzled. *See* **defizz efilzz**

defimnor informed. *See* **defimr definr defmor deimnr**

defimr firmed dimer fermi fired fried mired rimed dime dire emir fire firm mire ride rife rime die dim fed fid fie fir ire mid mir red ref rem rid rif rim em er id if me mi re

defimrru drumfire. *See* **defimr defrru demrru efimrr**

defin fiend fined dine fend find fine nide den die din end fed fen fid fie fin en id if in ne

definn finned fiend fined inned dine fend find fine nide nine den die din end fed fen fid fie fin inn en id if in ne

definr finder friend redfin diner fiend fined finer fired fried infer dine dire fend fern find fine fire firn nerd nide rein rend ride rife rind den die din end fed fen fid fie fin fir ire red ref rid rif en er id if in ne re

definrs finders friends redfins. *See* **deinrs defins definr efinrs**

defins fiends dines fends fiend finds fined fines nides snide dens dies dine dins ends feds fend fens fids fies find fine fins ides nide send side sine den die din end ens fed fen fid fie fin ids ifs sen sin en id if in is ne si

definsu infused. *See* **defins deinsu efinsu**

definux unfixed. *See* **defin defix dfinu**

defioorw firewood woodier. *See* **defoor deiorw efoorw**

defioprt profited diopter. *See* **defirt deiopr deiort deoprt**

defiost foisted. *See* **defist efiost deiost**

defiotxy detoxify. *See* **defiy deity defit**

defipry perfidy. *See* **defiy efiry defir**

defir fired fried drift dire fire ride rife die fed fid fie fir ire red ref rid rif er id if re

defirrst drifters drifter stirred. *See* **defirt defist deirrs deirst**

defirrt drifter. *See* **defirt deirr efirr**

defirssu fissured fissure fussier. *See* **defrsu defssu deissu derssu**

defirt rifted drift fetid fired fried refit tired tried deft dirt dire dirt edit fire fret frit reft ride rife rift rite tide tied tier tire die dit eft fed fid fie fir fit ire red ref ret rid rif ted tie er id if it re ti

defirtu fruited. *See* **defirt firtu dertu**

defirv fervid diver drive fired fiver fried rived dire dive fire five ride rife rive vied die fed fid fie fir ire red ref rev rid rif vie er id if re

defirzz frizzed. *See* **defizz defir**

defisstu feudists feudist studies. *See* **defist defssu deisst deissu**

defist fisted sifted deist diets edits feist fetid sited tides deft dies diet dits edit efts feds fids fies fist fits ides side sift site teds tide tied ties die dit eft fed fid fie fit ids ifs its set sit ted tie id if is it si ti

defistu feudist. *See* **deistu defist**

defit fetid deft diet edit tide tied die dit eft fed fid fie fit ted tie id if it ti

defitt fitted fetid deft diet edit tide tied die dit eft fed fid fie fit ted tie tit id if it ti

defix fixed die fed fid fie fix ex id if xi

defiy deify edify defy dey die dye fed fey fid fie id if ye

defizz fizzed fizz die fed fez fid fie zed id if

defklnu flunked. *See* **defklu defknu**

defklu fluked fluke delf duel duke feud fled flue fuel due eld elf elk fed feu flu kef led lek leu el

defknu funked unfed nuked duke dune dunk fend feud fund funk neuk nude nuke den due dun end fed fen feu fun kef ken en ne nu

defkor forked doer ford fore fork froe kerf redo rode doe dor fed foe for fro kef kor ode oke ore red ref rod roe do er od of or re

defl delf fled eld elf fed led el

deflloor folderol floored. *See* **defloo deflor defoor dellor**

deflloow followed. *See* **defloo deflow efllow flloow**

defllou doleful. *See* **deflou**

deflmy medfly defy delf demy fled meld ylem dey dye eld elf elm fed fey fly led lye mel el em me my ye

deflno enfold fondle felon loden olden delf dole done enol fend fled floe fold fond lend leno lode lone node noel den doe don eld elf end eon fed fen foe led nod ode old one do el en lo ne no od of on

deflnoru flounder floured founder roundel. *See* **deflno deflor deflou deflru**

deflnos enfolds fondles. *See* **deflno eflnos**

deflnot tenfold. *See* **deflno deflot**

deflnruu unfurled. *See* **deflru defnru delnru eflruu**

deflnssu fundless. *See* **defssu delssu elnssu**

defloo fooled looed flood delf dole fled floe fold food fool lode oleo doe eld elf fed foe led loo ode old do el lo od of

defloor floored. *See* **deflor defloo defoor**

defloort foretold floored. *See* **defloo deflor deflot defoor**

deflooss foodless flossed. *See* **defloo deloos dfloos eflooss**

deflooz foozled. *See* **defloo eflooz**

deflopp flopped. *See* **delopp**

deflor folder older delf doer dole fled floe fold ford fore froe lode lord lore orle redo rode role doe dor eld elf fed foe for fro led ode old ore red ref rod roe do el er lo od of or re

deflors folders. *See* **deflor delors**

defloru floured. *See* **deflor deflou deflru deloru**

defloss flossed. *See* **defls delos deoss**

deflot lofted delft deft delf dole dolt dote felt fled floe fold left lode loft toed told doe dot eft eld elf fed foe led let lot ode oft old ted tod toe do el lo od of to

deflotu flouted. *See* **defltu deflou deflot**

deflou fouled delf dole duel feud fled floe flue fold foul fuel lode loud doe due duo eld elf fed feu flu foe led leu ode old oud udo do el lo od of

deflow flowed fowled dowel lowed delf dole fled flew floe flow fold fowl lewd lode owed weld wold wolf dew doe eld elf fed few foe led low ode old owe owl wed woe do el lo od of ow we

deflpru purfled. *See* **deflru eflpru delpru**

deflru furled lured ruled delf duel feud fled flue fuel furl lure rude rued rule due eld elf fed feu flu fur led leu red ref rue urd el er re

defls delfs delf feds fled self sled eld elf els fed led el

deflst delfts delfs delft felts deft delf efts feds felt fled left lest lets self sled teds eft eld elf els fed led let set ted el

deflt delft deft delf felt fled left eft eld elf fed led let ted el

defltu fluted delft flute luted deft delf duel duet felt feud fled flue fuel left lute tule due eft eld elf fed feu flu led let leu ted el ut

deflty deftly delft lefty deft defy delf felt fled left dey dye eft eld elf fed fey fly led let lye ted yet el ye

deflux fluxed delf duel feud fled flex flue flux fuel luxe due eld elf fed feu flu led leu lux el ex

defmnoru unformed founder mourned. *See* **defmor defnou defnru demnor**

defmor deform formed demo doer dome dorm ford fore form froe from mode more omer redo rode doe dor fed foe for fro mod mor ode ore red ref rem rod roe do em er me mo od of om or re

defmors deforms serfdom. *See* **defmor**

defmorss serfdoms deforms serfdom. *See* **defmor deorss**

defmu fumed feud fume due emu fed feu mud em me mu um

defn fend den end fed fen en ne

defnnoss fondness. *See* **denoss**

defnnu funned unfed dune fend feud fund nude den due dun end fed fen feu fun nun en ne nu

defnoor fordone. *See* **defoor dnoor denor**

defnorsu founders fondues founder refunds resound sounder. *See* **defnou defnru defrsu denors**

defnort fronted. *See* **denort efort dfnor**

defnortu fortuned fortune founder fronted. *See* **defnou defnru denort denrtu**

defnoru founder. *See* **defnou defnru**

defnorw frowned. *See* **denorw**

defnosu fondues. *See* **defnou dfnosu denosu**

defnou fondue fondu found unfed done dune fend feud fond fund node nude undo den doe don due dun duo end eon fed fen feu foe fun nod ode one oud udo do en ne no nu od of on

defnrsu refunds. *See* **denrsu defnru defrsu**

defnru refund unfed under dune fend fern feud fund nerd nude rend rude rued rune den due dun end fed fen feu fun fur red ref rue run urd urn en er ne nu re

defns fends dens ends feds fend fens send den end ens fed fen sen en ne

defnu unfed dune fend feud fund nude den due dun end fed fen feu fun en ne nu

defoops spoofed. *See* **deops dfoos foops**

defoor roofed rodeo fordo doer door food ford fore froe odor ordo redo rode rood roof doe dor fed foe for fro ode ore red ref rod roe do er od of or re

defoorrw foreword. *See* **defoor deorrw efoorw**

defoot footed deft dote food foot toed doe dot eft fed foe ode oft ted tod toe too do od of to

defootux outfoxed. *See* **defoot deotux footux**

deforruw furrowed. *See* **defrru deorru deorrw eforru**

deforsst defrosts defrost forests fosters frosted. *See* **deorss deorst deosst eforst**

deforst defrost frosted. *See* **deorst eforst**

defrru furred ruder feud rude rued due err fed feu fur red ref rue urd er re

defrsu surfed druse feuds fused dues feds feud feus furs fuse reds refs rude rued rues ruse serf sued surd sure surf urds used user due fed feu fur red ref res rue sue urd use er re us

defs feds fed

defssu fussed feuds fused fuses dues feds fess feud feus fuse fuss suds sued sues used uses due ess fed feu sue use us

defsu feuds fused dues feds feud feus fuse sued used due fed feu sue use us

deft deft eft fed ted

defttu tufted deft duet feud tuft due eft fed feu ted tut ut

deftuz futzed fuzed deft duet feud futz fuze due eft fed feu fez ted zed ut

defu feud due fed feu

defuz fuzed feud fuze due fed feu fez zed

defuzz fuzzed fuzed feud fuze fuzz due fed feu fez zed

defy defy dey dye fed fey ye

degggi gigged gied die dig egg gid gie gig id

degggil giggled. *See* **degggi eggil**

deggglo goggled. *See* **degglo eggglo**

degggllu glugged guggled. *See* **degglu eggglu**

degghil higgled. *See* **egghil degil**

degghin hedging. *See* **deggin deghin**

deggho hogged doge hoed doe dog edh egg ego god hod hoe hog ode do eh go he ho od oh

degghrsu shrugged grudges huggers. *See* **degghu deggru deghsu degrsu**

degghu hugged hued huge due dug edh egg hue hug ugh eh he

deggij jigged gied die dig egg gid gie gig jig id

deggijl jiggled. *See* **deggij eggijl**

deggikn kedging. *See* **deggin egikn deikn**

deggiln gelding niggled. *See* **degiln deggin eggiln**

deggilnp pledging gelding niggled. *See* **deggin deggip degiln deginp**

deggilns geldings sledging dingles edgings gelding niggled niggles singled. *See* **deggin degiln degils degins**

deggilnu deluging dueling eluding gelding indulge lugeing niggled. *See* **deggin degglu degiln deglnu**

deggilrw wriggled wergild wiggled wriggle. *See* **deggir deggiw degilr deilrw**

deggilw wiggled. *See* **deggiw eggilw**

deggin edging deign dine ding gied nide den die dig din egg end gid gie gig gin en id in ne

deggins edgings. *See* **degins deggin**

degginw wedging. *See* **deginw deggiw**

deggior doggier. *See* **deggir deggor**

deggios doggies. *See* **degios**

deggiost doggiest doggies. *See* **deggot degios degist degost**

deggip pigged gied pied die dig dip egg gid gie gig gip peg pie pig id pe pi

deggipr prigged. *See* **deggir degipr deggip**

deggir digger rigged dirge gride ridge dire gied gird grid grig ride die dig egg erg gid gie gig ire red reg rid rig er id re

deggirs diggers. *See* **deggir degirs**

deggisw swigged. *See* **deggiw**

deggiw wigged gied wide dew die dig egg gid gie gig wed wig id we

deggiz zigged gied die dig egg gid gie gig zed zig id

deggjlo joggled. *See* **degglo deggjo eggjlo**

deggjlu juggled. *See* **deggju eggjlu degglu**

deggjo jogged doge doe dog egg ego god joe jog ode do go jo od

deggju jugged judge due dug egg jug

degglmsu smuggled slugged smuggle. *See* **degglu deggmu deglsu degmsu**

degglnsu snuggled guldens slugged snugged snuggle. *See* **degglu deglnu deglsu degnsu**

degglo dogleg logged lodge ogled doge dole geld gold lode loge ogle doe dog egg ego eld gel god led leg log ode old do el go lo od

degglos doglegs slogged. *See* **degglo deglos**

degglpu plugged. *See* **deglpu degglu deggpu**

degglru gurgled. *See* **deggru egglru degglu**

degglruy ruggedly gurgled. *See* **degglu deggru deggry delruy**

degglsu slugged. *See* **degglu deglsu**

degglu lugged glued luged duel geld glue glug luge due dug egg eld gel led leg leu lug el

deggmu mugged geum due dug egg emu gem gum mud mug em me mu um

deggno gonged doge done dong gone gong node nogg den doe dog don egg ego end eon god nod nog ode one do en go ne no od on

deggnoo doggone. *See* **deggno**

deggnoos doggones doggone. *See* **deggno degoos denoos dgnoos**

deggnosu gudgeons gudgeon snugged. *See* **deggno deggou degnsu denosu**

deggnou gudgeon. *See* **deggno deggou**

deggnsu snugged. *See* **degnsu**

deggopr progged. *See* **deggor degopr**

deggor gorged gored gorge doer doge goer gore grog ogre redo rode doe dog dor egg ego erg god ode ore red reg rod roe do er go od or re

deggot togged doge dote toed doe dog dot egg ego get god got ode ted tod toe tog do go od to

deggou gouged gouge doge doe dog due dug duo egg ego god ode oud udo do go od

deggpu pugged due dug egg peg pug pe up

deggrstu druggets drugget grudges trudges. *See* **deggru deggtu degrsu degrtu**

deggrsu grudges. *See* **deggru eggrsu degrsu**

deggrtu drugget. *See* **deggru degrtu deggtu**

deggru grudge rugged urged gurge drug grue rude rued urge due dug egg erg red reg rue rug urd er re

deggry dreggy gyred dyer edgy grey gyre yegg dey dry dye egg erg gey red reg rye er re ye

deggtu tugged duet due dug egg get gut ted tug ut

deghiins dinghies dishing. *See* **deghin deghis degins dehins**

deghiknt knighted. *See* **deghin degint dehikt dehint**

deghilns shingled dingles shingle singled. *See* **deghin deghis degiln degils**

deghilpt plighted delight lighted. *See* **dehilt egilpt ghilpt**

deghilst delights slighted delight lighted sighted sleight. *See* **deghis degils degist dehils**

deghilt delight lighted. *See* **dehilt eghilt degil**

deghin hinged deign hinge neigh dine ding gied hide hied hind nide nigh den

die dig din edh end gid gie gin hen hid hie hin eh en he hi id in ne

deghinr herding. *See* **deginr dehinr deghin eghinr**

deghioru doughier roughed. *See* **degoru**

deghiot hogtied. *See* **eghiot dhiot degio**

deghirt righted. *See* **dehirt degir eghit**

deghis sighed hides shied dies digs dish egis gids gied gies hide hied hies ides shed side sigh die dig edh gid gie hid hie his ids she eh he hi id is sh si

deghist sighted. *See* **degist eghist deghis**

deghnort thronged throned. *See* **degnot dehnor denort ehnort**

deghnory hydrogen. *See* **dehnor dehnoy denory**

deghoosu doghouse. *See* **deghsu degoos dehoos dehosu**

deghoru roughed. *See* **degoru**

deghost ghosted. *See* **degost dehost**

deghsu gushed dues gush hued hues huge hugs shed sued used due dug edh hue hug she sue ugh use eh he sh us

degi gied die dig gid gie id

degiilns sideling dingles sidling singled sliding. *See* **degiln degils degins deiins**

degiilnt diligent dieting editing glinted ignited lignite tingled. *See* **degiln degint deiint deilnt**

degiilnv deviling delving veiling. *See* **degiln deiinv giilnv**

degiilnw wielding welding. *See* **degiln deginw dgiiln**

degiilny yielding. *See* **degiln deginy dgiiln**

degiimnp impeding impinged impinge. *See* **degimp deginp deimnp dgiinp**

degiimns demising smidgen. *See* **degims degins deiims deiins**

degiinn indigen. *See* **dgiinn deginn**

degiinns indigens endings indigen insigne seining sending. *See* **deginn degins deiins deinns**

degiinnt indigent denting dieting dinting editing ignited indigen tending. *See* **deginn degint deiint egiint**

degiinnw widening indigen wending winding. *See* **deginn deginw dgiinn**

degiinnx indexing indigen. *See* **deginn dgiinn giinnx**

degiinnz dizening indigen. *See* **dgiinn deginn deginz .egiin**

degiinos indigoes dingoes. *See* **degins degios deiino deiins**

degiinrs desiring residing ringside engirds insider. *See* **deginr degins degirs deiins**

degiinrv deriving diviner driving. *See* **deginr deiinv deinrv dgiinr**

degiinst dingiest dieting editing ignited ignites indites tidings tineids. *See* **degins degint degist deiins**

degiinsv devising divines sieving. *See* **degins deiins deiinv eginsv**

degiint dieting editing ignited. *See* **egiint deiint degint**

degiirr ridgier. *See* **degirr dgiir**

degiirst ridgiest dirties. *See* **degirs degist deiirs deiirt**

degiissu disguise. *See* **degisu deiiss deissu egissu**

degijln jingled. *See* **degiln egijln**

degijmsu misjudge. *See* **degims degisu degjsu degmsu**

degiklo godlike. *See* **deiklo degio degil**

degil gelid glide deil deli geld gied gild idle lied die dig eld gel gid gie led leg lei lid lie el id li

degill gilled gelid glide deil deli dell dill geld gied gild gill idle lied die dig eld ell gel gid gie ill led leg lei lid lie el id li

degillnu duelling dueling dulling eluding indulge. *See* **degill degiln degllu deglnu**

degillnw dwelling welding indwell. *See* **degill degiln deginw deillw**

degillr grilled. *See* **degilr degill egillr**

degilm midleg gelid gimel glide limed midge deil deli dime geld gied gild glim idle lied lime meld mild mile die dig dim eld elm gel gem gid gie led leg lei lid lie mel mid mil el em id li me mi

degilmn melding mingled. *See* **degilm deilmn egilmn**

degilmno modeling melding mingled molding. *See* **degilm degiln deglno deilmn**

degilmps glimpsed dimples glimpse. *See* **degilm degils degimp degims**

degiln dingle deign gelid glide ingle lined deil deli dine ding geld gied gild glen idle lend lied lien line ling nide den die dig din eld end gel gid gie gin led leg lei lid lie nil el en id in li ne

degilnn lending. *See* **degiln deginn deilnn**

degilnos sidelong dingles dingoes eloigns legions lingoes singled. *See* **degiln degils degins degios**

degilnow doweling welding. *See* **degiln deginw deglno deglow**

degilnoy yodeling. *See* **degiln deginy deglno dgilno**

degilns dingles singled. *See* **degins degiln degils egilns**

degilnsu indulges dingles dueling eluding guldens indulge singled. *See* **degiln degils degins degisu**

degilnsw swingled dingles singled swindle swinged swingle welding. *See* **degiln degils degins deginw**

degilnt glinted tingled. *See* **deilnt degint egilnt**

degilnu dueling eluding indulge. *See* **degiln deglnu**

degilnv delving. *See* **degiln deilv eginv**

degilnw welding. *See* **deginw degiln**

degilooy ideology. *See* **dglooy**

degilor gloried godlier. *See* **degilr deglor egilor deilor**

degilost godliest diglots logiest. *See* **degils degios degist deglos**

degilr gilder girdle glider dirge gelid glide gride idler ridge riled deil deli dire dirl geld gied gild gird girl grid idle lied lire ride riel rile die dig eld erg gel gid gie ire led leg lei lid lie red reg rid rig el er id li re

degilrs gilders girdles gliders. *See* **degirs degilr degils egilrs deilrs**

degilrsu guilders gilders girdles gliders guilder ligures. *See* **degilr degils degirs degisu**

degilrsw wergilds gilders girdles gliders swirled wergild. *See* **degilr degils degirs deilrs**

degilru guilder. *See* **degilr egilru**

degilrw wergild. *See* **degilr deilrw**

degilrzz grizzled drizzle grizzle. *See* **degilr**

degils glides deils delis gelds gelid gilds glide idles sidle slide deil deli dies digs egis geld gels gids gied gies gild ides idle isle legs leis lids lied lies side sled slid die dig eld els gel gid gie ids led leg lei lid lie el id is li si

degilsuv divulges divulge. *See* **degils degisu deglsu deilsv**

degiluv divulge. *See* **deilv degil deglu**

degim midge gied dime die dig dim gem gid gie mid em id me mi

degimnn mending. *See* **deginn**

degimnot demoting emoting. *See* **degimt degint degnot deimnt**

degimnpu impugned dumping. *See* **degimp deginp deimnp dginpu**

degimns smidgen. *See* **degins deimns degims**

degimnss smidgens designs messing smidgen. *See* **degims degins deimns deimss**

degimp gimped midge dime gied gimp pied die dig dim dip gem gid gie gip imp mid peg pie pig em id me mi pe pi

degimr grimed dimer dirge gride grime midge mired ridge rimed dime dire emir germ gied gird grid grim mire ride rime die dig dim erg gem gid gie ire mid mir red reg rem rid rig rim em er id me mi re

degims midges deism dimes midge dies digs dime dims egis gems gids gied gies ides mise semi side die dig dim gem gid gie ids mid mis em id is me mi si

degimst midgets. *See* **deimst degist degimt**

degimt midget demit midge timed diet dime edit emit gied item mite tide tied time die dig dim dit gem get gid gie met mid ted tie em id it me mi ti

degin deign dine ding gied nide den die dig din end gid gie gin en id in ne

deginn ending ginned deign inned dine ding gied nide nine den die dig din end gid gie gin inn en id in ne

deginnn denning. *See* **deginn**

deginnnu unending denning dunning enduing. *See* **deginn degnnu deinnu**

deginnop deponing pending opening. *See* **deginn deginp deinnp deinop**

deginnot denoting denting intoned tending. *See* **deginn degint degnot dennot**

deginnow endowing wending downing. *See* **deginn deginw degnow dennow**

deginnp pending. *See* **deginn deginp deinnp**

deginnps spending endings pending sending. *See* **deginn deginp degins deinnp**

deginnpu upending enduing pending penguin. *See* **deginn deginp degnnu deinnp**

deginnr grinned rending. *See* **deinnr deginn deginr**

deginnru enduring enduing grinned inurned rending. *See* **deginn deginr degnnu degnru**

deginns endings sending. *See* **degins eginns deginn deinns**

deginnt denting tending. *See* **deinnt deginn degint**

deginntu untinged denting enduing tending. *See* **deginn degint degnnu deinnu**

deginnu enduing. *See* **deginn degnnu deinnu**

deginnv vending. *See* **deginn**

deginnw wending. *See* **deginw deginn**

deginny denying. *See* **deginy**

deginops deposing dingoes pigeons sponged. *See* **deginp degins degios deinop**

deginor eroding groined ignored redoing. *See* **deinor deginr eginor**

deginorr ordering eroding grinder groined ignored ignorer redoing. *See* **deginr degirr deinor eginor**

deginorw dowering downier eroding groined ignored redoing wording

wringed wronged. *See* **deginr deginw degnow deinor**

deginos dingoes. *See* **degins dginos degios deinos**

deginotv devoting vetoing. *See* **degint degnot dginot**

deginp pinged deign pined dine ding gied nide pend pied pine ping den die dig din dip end gid gie gin gip nip peg pen pie pig pin en id in ne pe pi

deginprs springed engirds springe. *See* **deginp deginr degins degipr**

deginptu deputing. *See* **deginp degint deintu denptu**

deginr engird deign diner dirge gride grind reign ridge dine ding dire gied gird grid grin nerd nide rein rend ride rind ring den die dig din end erg gid gie gin ire red reg rid rig en er id in ne re

deginrr grinder. *See* **deginr eginrr degirr**

deginrrs grinders engirds girders grinder ringers. *See* **deginr degins degirr deinrs**

deginrs engirds. *See* **degins deinrs degirs deginr dginrs**

deginrss dressing designs digress engirds ingress resigns singers. *See* **deginr degins degirs deinrs**

deginrw wringed. *See* **deginw deginr deinrw**

degins deigns design signed singed deign dines dings nides segni singe snide dens dies digs dine ding dins egis ends engs gens gids gied gies gins ides nide send side sign sine sing den die dig din end ens gid gie gin ids sen sin en id in is ne si

deginss designs. *See* **degins eginss**

deginssu dinguses designs. *See* **degins degisu degnsu deinsu**

deginsw swinged. *See* **degins deginw eginsw deinsw**

degint tinged deign tinge dent diet dine ding edit gent gied nide tend tide tied tine ting den die dig din dit end get gid gie gin net nit ted ten tie tin en id in it ne ti

degintw twinged. *See* **deginw degint deintw egintw degitw**

deginux exuding. *See* **degin degiu deinx**

deginw dewing winged deign widen wined dine ding gied nide wend wide wind wine wing den dew die dig din end gid gie gin new wed wen wig win en id in ne we

deginy dingey dyeing deign dingy dying eying deny dine ding dyne edgy gied nide den dey die dig din dye end gey gid gie gin yen yin en id in ne ye

deginz zinged deign dizen dine ding gied nide zein zing den die dig din end gid gie gin zed zig en id in ne

degio dogie geoid gied doge die dig doe dog ego gid gie god ode do go id od

degioos goodies. *See* **degios degoos**

degioprr porridge. *See* **degipr degirr degopr deiopr**

degiopss gossiped dispose. *See* **degios deiops eiopss giopss**

degios geoids doges dogie geoid dies digs does doge dogs dose egis egos gids gied gies gods goes ides odes sego side die dig doe dog dos ego gid gie god ids ode sod do go id is od os si so

degipp gipped piped gied pied pipe die dig dip gid gie gip peg pep pie pig pip id pe pi

degippr gripped. *See* **deippr degipp degipr egippr**

degipr griped dirge gride gripe pride pried ridge dire drip gied gird grid grip peri pied pier prig ride ripe die dig dip erg gid gie gip ire peg per pie pig red reg rep rid rig rip er id pe pi re

degipru pudgier. *See* **degipr degpru**

degipstu pudgiest dispute. *See* **degist degisu degstu deipst**

degir dirge gride ridge dire gied gird grid ride die dig erg gid gie ire red reg rid rig er id re

degirr girder direr dirge drier gride rider ridge dire gied gird grid ride die dig erg err gid gie ire red reg rid rig er id re

degirrs girders. *See* **deirrs degirs degirr**

degirs dirges grides ridges dirge dregs dries girds gride grids rides ridge sired dies digs dire egis ergs gids gied gies gird grid ides reds regs reis ride rids rigs rise side sire die dig erg gid gie ids ire red reg res rid rig sir er id is re si

degirss digress. *See* **degirs**

degirtt gritted. *See* **degir egirt deirt**

degisst digests. *See* **deisst degist**

degist digest deist diets edits sited tides dies diet digs dits edit egis gest gets gids gied gies gist ides side site teds tide tied ties die dig dit get gid gie ids its set sit ted tie id is it si ti

degistw widgets. *See* **degist deistw degitw**

degisu guides guide guise dies digs dues egis gids gied gies ides side sued used die dig due dug gid gie ids sue use id is si us

degitw widget wited diet edit gied tide tied twig wide wite dew die dig dit get gid gie ted tie wed wet wig wit id it ti we

degiu guide gied die dig due dug gid gie id

degjmntu judgment. *See* **egmntu**

degjrsu judgers. *See* **degjru degjsu degrsu**

degjru judger judge urged drug grue rude rued urge due dug erg jug red reg rue rug urd er re

degjsu judges judge dues jugs sued used due dug jug jus sue use us

degju judge due dug jug

degklu kludge glued kluge kugel luged duel duke geld glue luge due dug eld elk gel keg led leg lek leu lug el

degl geld eld gel led leg el

degllu gulled glued luged dell duel dull geld glue gull luge due dug eld ell gel led leg leu lug el

deglmoo gloomed. *See* **delmoo glmoo eglmo**

deglnno endlong. *See* **deglno**

deglno golden longed loden lodge longe ogled olden doge dole done dong enol geld glen gold gone lend leno lode loge lone long node noel ogle den doe dog don ego eld end eon gel god led leg log nod nog ode old one do el en go lo ne no od on

deglnou lounged. *See* **deglno deglnu delnou eglnou**

deglnpu plunged. *See* **deglnu deglpu eglnpu**

deglnsu guldens. *See* **deglnu eglnsu degnsu deglsu**

deglnu gulden lunged glued luged lunge nudge duel dune dung geld glen glue lend luge lune lung nude den due dug dun eld end gel gnu gun led leg leu lug el en ne nu

deglnuu unglued. *See* **deglnu eglnuu**

deglo lodge ogled doge dole geld gold lode loge ogle doe dog ego eld gel god led leg log ode old do el go lo od

deglor lodger gored lodge ogled ogler older doer doge dole geld goer gold gore lode loge lord lore ogle ogre orle redo rode role doe dog dor ego eld erg gel god led leg log ode old ore red reg rod roe do el er go lo od or re

deglors lodgers. *See* **deglor deglos eglors delors**

deglorw growled. *See* **deglow eglorw deglor**

deglos lodges doges doles gelds lodes lodge loges ogled ogles soled does doge dogs dole dose egos geld gels gods goes gold legs lode loge logs lose odes ogle sego sled sloe slog sold sole doe dog dos ego eld els gel god led leg log los ode old sod sol do el go lo od os so

degloss godless. *See* **deglos deoss egoss**

deglov gloved glove lodge loved ogled doge dole dove geld gold lode loge love

ogle veld vole doe dog ego eld gel god led leg lev log ode old do el go lo od

deglow glowed dowel lodge lowed ogled doge dole geld glow gold lewd lode loge ogle owed weld wold dew doe dog ego eld gel god led leg log low ode old owe owl wed woe do el go lo od ow we

degloz glozed gloze lodge ogled doge dole doze geld gold lode loge ogle doe dog ego eld gel god led leg log ode old zed do el go lo od

deglprsu splurged slurped splurge. *See* **deglpu deglsu degpru degrsu**

deglpu gulped duple glued luged puled duel geld glue gulp luge pled plug pule due dug eld gel led leg leu lug peg pug pul el pe up

degls gelds geld gels legs sled eld els gel led leg el

deglssu sludges. *See* **deglsu delssu**

deglsu sludge duels dulse gelds glued glues gules luged luges duel dues geld gels glue legs lues luge lugs sled slue slug sued used due dug eld els gel led leg leu lug sue use el us

deglttu glutted. *See* **degttu deglu deltu**

deglu glued luged duel geld glue luge due dug eld gel led leg leu lug el

degluzz guzzled. *See* **egluzz deglu**

degly ledgy geld edgy dey dye eld gel gey led leg lye el ye

degmmu gummed geum due dug emu gem gum mem mud mug mum em me mu um

degmnoo goodmen. *See* **demnoo egmno gmnoo**

degmoor groomed. *See* **demoor**

degmssu smudges. *See* **demssu degmsu**

degmsu smudge geums mused sedum dues emus gems geum gums muds mugs muse smug sued used due dug emu gem gum mud mug mus sue sum use em me mu um us

degnnosu dungeons dungeon. *See* **degnnu degnsu dennou dennsu**

degnnou dungeon. *See* **degnnu dennou**

degnnu gunned nudge dune dung nude den due dug dun end gnu gun nun en ne nu

degnooss goodness godsons. *See* **degoos denoos denoss dgnoos**

degnoppu oppugned. *See* **gnoppu**

degnopr pronged. *See* **degopr denopr**

degnops sponged. *See* **egnops degos dgnos**

degnorru grounder guerdon rounder undergo. *See* **degnru degoru deorru dgnoru**

degnorsu guerdons drogues gerunds gourdes grounds groused guerdon resound sounder surgeon undergo. *See* **degnru degnsu degoru degrsu**

degnoru guerdon undergo. *See* **degoru degnru dgnoru**

degnorw wronged. *See* **denorw degnow**

degnot tonged noted toned dent doge done dong dote gent gone node note tend toed tone tong den doe dog don dot ego end eon get god got net nod nog not ode one ted ten tod toe tog ton do en go ne no od on to

degnotu tongued. *See* **degnot egnotu**

degnow gowned endow owned doge done dong down enow gone gown node owed wend den dew doe dog don ego end eon god new nod nog now ode one owe own wed wen woe won do en go ne no od on ow we

degnrsu gerunds. *See* **degnru degnsu denrsu degrsu**

degnrtu grunted. *See* **degnru degrtu denrtu egnrtu**

degnru gerund nudge under urged drug dune dung grue nerd nude rend rude rued rune rung urge den due dug dun end erg gnu gun red reg rue rug run urd urn en er ne nu re

degnsu nudges dunes dungs genus negus nudes nudge dens dues dune dung duns ends engs gens gnus guns nude send snug sued sung used den due dug dun end ens gnu gun sen sue sun use en ne nu us

degnu nudge dune dung nude den due dug dun end gnu gun en ne nu

dego doge doe dog ego god ode do go od

degoorv grooved. *See* **deoorv egoorv**

degoos goosed doges goods goose does doge dogs dose egos gods goes good goos odes sego doe dog dos ego god goo ode sod do go od os so

degopr groped doper gored grope pored roped doer doge dope drop goer gore ogre oped pore prod prog redo repo rode rope doe dog dor ego erg god ode ope ore peg per pod pro red reg rep rod roe do er go od or pe re

degopru grouped. *See* **degoru degopr deopru degpru**

degor gored doer doge goer gore ogre redo rode doe dog dor ego erg god ode ore red reg rod roe do er go od or re

degorsu drogues gourdes groused. *See* **degoru dgorsu egorsu deorsu degrsu**

degortu grouted. *See* **deortu degoru degrtu**

degoru drogue gourde rouged gored gourd rogue rouge uredo urged doer doge dour drug duro goer gore grue ogre redo rode rude rued urge doe dog

dor due dug duo ego erg god ode ore oud our red reg rod roe rue rug udo urd do er go od or re

degos doges does doge dogs dose egos gods goes odes sego doe dog dos ego god ode sod do go od os so

degosst stodges. *See* **degost deosst**

degost stodge doges dotes does doge dogs dose dote dots egos gest gets gods goes odes sego teds toed toes togs doe dog dos dot ego get god got ode set sod sot ted tod toe tog do go od os so to

degppy gypped edgy dey dye gey gyp peg pep yep pe ye

degprsuu upsurged pursued upsurge. *See* **degpru degrsu deprsu egprsu**

degpru purged drupe duper perdu prude purge urged drug grue pure rude rued urge due dug erg peg per pug red reg rep rue rug urd er pe re up

degrs dregs ergs reds regs erg red reg res er re

degrstu trudges. *See* **derstu degstu**

degrsu surged dregs drugs druse grues surge urged urges drug dues ergs grue reds regs rude rued rues rugs ruse sued surd sure urds urge used user due dug erg red reg res rue rug sue urd use er re us

degrtu trudge urged trued drug duet grue rude rued true turd urge due dug erg get gut red reg ret rue rug rut ted tug urd er re ut

degru urged drug grue rude rued urge due dug erg red reg rue rug urd er re

degry gyred dyer edgy grey gyre dey dry dye erg gey red reg rye er re ye

degstu gusted duets guest dues duet dust gest gets gust guts stud sued suet teds tugs used due dug get gut set sue ted tug use us ut

degsy sedgy deys dyes edgy dey dye gey yes ye

degttu gutted duet due dug get gut ted tug tut ut

deguy guyed edgy dey due dug dye gey guy ye

degvy gyved edgy gyve dey dye gey ye

degwy wedgy edgy dewy dew dey dye gey wed wye yew we ye

degy edgy dey dye gey ye

deh edh eh he

dehhiltw withheld. *See* **dehilt dehilw dehitw deiltw**

dehhisw whished. *See* **dehisw hhisw**

dehhsu hushed dues hued hues hush shed sued used due edh heh hue huh she sue use eh he sh us

dehi hide hied die edh hid hie eh he hi id

dehiills hillside dillies. *See* **dehill dehils eiills**

dehiilsv devilish. *See* **dehils deilsv ehilsv**

dehiimms shimmied shimmed. *See* **deiims**

dehiimns minished shined.. *See* **deimns deiims eiimns ehimns**

dehiimst ditheism. *See* **deiims deiist deimst ehimst**

dehiinns shinnied shinned hinnies. *See* **dehins deiins deinns**

dehiinnw whinnied. *See* **dehinw**

dehiinss shindies. *See* **deiiss dehiss deiins dehins**

dehiipss shipside. *See* **dehiss dhiips ehipss**

dehijmno demijohn. *See* **dehino deijno**

dehik hiked dike hide hied hike die edh hid hie kid eh he hi id

dehikmos sheikdom. *See* **dekmos dhimos**

dehikrs shirked. *See* **dehirs deikrs ehikrs**

dehiksw whisked. *See* **dehisw deiks dehik**

dehikt kithed hiked kited kithe diet dike edit hide hied hike khet kite kith tide tied tike die dit edh eth het hid hie hit kid kit ted the tie eh he hi id it ti

dehill hilled deil deli dell dill held hell hide hied hill idle lied die edh eld ell hid hie ill led lei lid lie eh el he hi id li

dehillrs shrilled. *See* **dehill dehils dehirs deilrs**

dehillrt thrilled thirled trilled. *See* **dehill dehilt dehirt deillt**

dehilmos demolish. *See* **dehils dehlos deilmo deilms**

dehilops polished despoil dipoles spoiled. *See* **dehils dehlos dehops deilop**

dehiloty holytide. *See* **dehilt dehlot deilot ehilot**

dehilrt thirled. *See* **dehirt dehilt ehilrt**

dehilrw whirled. *See* **dehilw deilrw**

dehils shield deils delis hides idles shied sidle slide deil deli dies dish held hide hied hies ides idle isle leis lids lied lies shed side sled slid die edh eld els hid hie his ids led lei lid lie she eh el he hi id is li sh si

dehilss shields. *See* **dehiss dehils deilss**

dehilstw whistled wildest whistle. *See* **dehils dehilt dehilw dehisw**

dehilt hilted lithe tilde tiled deil deli diet edit held hide hied hilt idle lied tide tied tile die dit edh eld eth het hid hie hit led lei let lid lie lit ted the tie til eh el he hi id it li ti

dehilttw whittled whittle. *See* **dehilt dehilw dehitt dehitw**

dehilw whiled while wield wiled deil deli held hide hied idle lewd lied weld wide wild wile dew die edh eld hew hid hie led lei lid lie wed eh el he hi id li we

dehimms shimmed. *See* **deims dehis deimm**

dehimnos hedonism misdone. *See* **dehino dehins dehnos deimns**

dehimnu inhumed. *See* **ehimnu deimn dhimu**

dehimor heirdom. *See* **ehimor deimr dehir**

dehimors heirdoms heirdom heroism misdoer. *See* **dehirs dehors deimrs deiors**

dehinns shinned. *See* **dehins deinns**

dehinnt thinned. *See* **deinnt dehint**

dehino honied honed dine done hide hied hind hoed hone nide node den die din doe don edh end eon hen hid hie hin hod hoe hon ion nod ode one do eh en he hi ho id in ne no od oh on

dehinops siphoned sphenoid phonies. *See* **dehino dehins dehnop dehnos**

dehinost hedonist hoisted. *See* **dehino dehins dehint dehnos**

dehinpsu punished. *See* **dehins dehpsu deinps deinsu**

dehinr hinder diner hider hired dine dire heir herd hern hide hied hind hire nerd nide rein rend ride rind den die din edh end hen her hid hie hin ire red rid eh en er he hi id in ne re

dehinrs hinders shrined. *See* **deinrs dehirs dehinr dehins ehinrs**

dehins shined dines hides hinds nides shied shine snide dens dies dine dins dish ends hens hide hied hies hind hins ides nide send shed shin side sine den die din edh end ens hen hid hie hin his ids sen she sin eh en he hi id in is ne sh si

dehint hinted thine dent diet dine edit hent hide hied hind hint nide tend then thin tide tied tine den die din dit edh end eth hen het hid hie hin hit net nit ted ten the tie tin eh en he hi id in it ne ti

dehinw whined whine widen wined dine hewn hide hied hind nide wend when wide wind wine den dew die din edh end hen hew hid hie hin new wed wen win eh en he hi id in ne we

dehioprs spheroid periods. *See* **dehirs dehops dehors deiopr**

dehiort theroid. *See* **dehirt deiort ehiort**

dehiossw sideshow swished. *See* **dehiss dehisw dehosw deossw**

dehiost hoisted. *See* **dhiost dehost deiost**

dehiosu hideous. *See* **dehosu dehis**

dehipp hipped piped hide hied pied pipe die dip edh nep hid hie hip pep pie pip eh he hi id pe pi

dehipps shipped. *See* **dehipp deipps**

dehippw whipped. *See* **dehipp deipw**

dehiqssu squished. *See* **dehiss deissu diqssu hiqssu**

dehir hider hired dire heir herd hide hied hire ride die edh her hid hie ire red rid eh er he hi id re

dehirrs shirred. *See* **deirrs dehirs ehirrs**

dehirru hurried. *See* **deirr dehir ehirr**

dehirrw whirred. *See* **deirr deirw eirrw**

dehirs hiders dries heirs herds hider hides hired hides rides rides sherd shied shire shred sired dies dire dish heir herd hers hide hied hies hire ides reds reis resh ride rids rise shed side sire die edh her hid hie his ids ire red res rid she sir eh er he hi id is re sh si

dehirst dithers. *See* **deirst dehirt dehirs ehirst dhirst**

dehirstt thirsted dithers hitters. *See* **dehirs dehirt dehitt deirst**

dehirsv dervish shrived. *See* **deirsv ehirsv**

dehirt dither hider hired their third tired tried diet dire dirt edit heir herd hide hied hire ride rite tide tied tier tire die dit edh eth her het hid hie hit ire red ret rid ted the tie eh er he hi id it re ti

dehirtv thrived. *See* **dehirt deirtv ehirtv**

dehirtww withdrew. *See* **dehirt dehitw ehirtw**

dehis hides shied dies dish hide hied hies ides shed side die edh hid hie his ids she eh he hi id is sh si

dehiss dishes hissed hides sheds shied shies sides dies dish hide hied hies hiss ides shed side die edh ess hid hie his ids she sis eh he hi id is sh si

dehissw swished. *See* **dehiss dehisw ehissw**

dehisw wished hides shied dews dies dish hews hide hied hies ides shed shew side weds wide wise wish dew die edh hew hid hie his ids sew she wed wis eh he hi id is sh si we

dehitt tithed tithe diet edit hide hied teth tide tied die dit edh eth het hid hie hit ted the tie tit eh he hi id ti ti

dehitw whited withed white width wited withe diet edit hide hied thew tide tied whet whit wide wite with dew die dit edh eth het hew hid hie hit ted the tie wed wet wit eh he hi id it ti we

dehiv hived dive hide hied hive vied die edh hid hie vie eh he hi id

dehiwzz whizzed. *See* **hiwzz**

dehjos joshed hosed shoed does dose hods hoed hoes hose joes josh odes

shed shod shoe doe dos edh hod hoe joe ode ohs she sod do eh he ho jo od oh os sh so

dehklu hulked duel duke held hued hulk due edh eld elk hue led lek leu eh el he

dehkno honked honed kendo done hoed hoke hone honk keno node den doe don edh end eon hen hod hoe hon ken nod ode oke one do eh en he ho ne no od oh on

dehknoou unhooked. *See* **dehkno dehkoo hknoou**

dehkoo hooked oohed hoed hoke hood hook doe edh hod hoe ode oho oke ooh do eh he ho od oh

dehksu husked dukes desk dues duke dusk hued hues husk shed sued used due edh hue she sue use eh he sh us

dehl held edh eld led eh el he

dehlloow hollowed. *See* **dehlow hlloow**

dehllou hullooed. *See* **dehllu dehlo ehllo**

dehllu hulled dell duel dull held hell hued hull due edh eld ell hue led leu eh el he

dehlno holden dhole holed honed loden olden dole done enol held hoed hold hole hone lend leno lode lone node noel den doe don edh eld end eon hen hod hoe hon led nod odd old one do eh el en he ho lo ne no od oh on

dehlo dhole holed dole held hoed hold hole lode doe edh eld hod hoe led ode old do eh el he ho lo od oh

dehloorv holdover. *See* **dehlor deoorv**

dehloost toeholds toolshed soothed stooled toehold. *See* **dehlos dehlot dehoos dehoot**

dehloot toehold. *See* **dehoot deloot dehlot**

dehlopp hoppled. *See* **dehopp ehlopp delopp**

dehlor holder dhole holed horde older doer dole held herd herl hero hoed hoer hold hole lode lord lore orle redo rode role doe dor edh eld her hod hoe led ode old ore red rho rod roe do eh el er he ho lo od oh or re

dehlors holders. *See* **dehlos dehlor dehors delors**

dehlorsu shoulder holders hurdles. *See* **dehlor dehlos dehlru dehors**

dehlorw whorled. *See* **dehlor dehlow ehlorw dehorw**

dehlos dholes dhole doles holds holed holes hosed lodes shoed soled does dole dose held hods hoed hoes hold hole hose lode lose odes shed shod shoe sled sloe sold sole doe dos edh eld els hod hoe led los ode ohs old she sod sol do eh el he ho lo od oh os sh so

dehloss sloshed. *See* **dehlos deoss ehoss**

dehlot tholed dhole holed hotel thole dole dolt dote held hoed hold hole holt lode loth toed told doe dot edh eld eth het hod hoe hot led let lot ode old ted the tho tod toe do eh el he ho lo od oh to

dehlow howled dhole dowel holed lowed whole dhow dole held hoed hold hole howl lewd lode owed weld wold dew doe edh eld hew hod hoe how led low ode old owe owl wed who woe do eh el he ho lo od oh ow we

dehlpu upheld duple puled duel held help hued pled pule due edh eld hep hue hup led leu pul eh el he pe up

dehlrrsu hurdlers hurdler hurdles hurlers slurred. *See* **dehlru dehrsu ehlrru ehrrsu**

dehlrru hurdler. *See* **dehlru ehlrru**

dehlrsu hurdles. *See* **dehlru dehrsu**

dehlrswy shrewdly. *See* **dersy dehrs ehlrs**

dehlrtu hurtled. *See* **dehlru ehlrtu**

dehlru hurdle hurled lured ruled duel held herd herl hued hurl lure rude rued rule due edh eld her hue led leu red rue urd eh el er he re

dehlssu slushed. *See* **delssu ehlssu**

dehlsttu shuttled hustled shuttle. *See* **dehttu delstu ehlstu**

dehlstu hustled. *See* **ehlstu delstu**

dehmmu hummed hued due edh emu hem hue hum mem mud mum eh em he me mu um

dehmny hymned hymen demy deny dyne hymn mend den dey dye edh end hem hen hey men yen eh em en he me my ne ye

dehmo homed demo dome hoed home mode doe edh hem hod hoe mho mod ode ohm do eh em he ho me mo od oh om

dehmoost smoothed methods soothed. *See* **dehmot dehoos dehoot dehost**

dehmopry hypoderm. *See* **dehmry dehopy demopr**

dehmopw whomped. *See* **dehop dehmo demop**

dehmoru humored. *See* **demru ehmor dehor**

dehmost methods. *See* **dehost dehmot demost**

dehmot method homed demo dome dote hoed home mode mote moth them toed tome doe dot edh eth hem het hod hoe hot met mho mod mot ode ohm ted the tho tod toe tom do eh em he ho me mo od oh om to

dehmotu mouthed. *See* **dehmot hmotu demtu**

dehmptu thumped. *See* **dehmpu dehpt demtu**

dehmpu humped umped dump hemp hued hump due edh emu hem hep hue hum hup mud ump eh em he me mu pe um up

dehmpuw whumped. *See* **dehmpu hmpuw**

dehmry rhymed rhyme demy dyer herd herm dey dry dye edh hem her hey red rem rye eh em er he me my re ye

dehmsu mushed mused sedum dues emus hems hued hues hums mesh muds muse mush shed sued used due edh emu hem hue hum mud mus she sue sum use eh em he me mu sh um us

dehnnsu shunned. *See* **dennsu**

dehno honed done hoed hone node den doe don edh end eon hen hod hoe hon nod ode one do eh en he ho ne no od oh on

dehnoor honored. *See* **dehnor dnoor hnoor**

dehnooru honoured honored. *See* **dehnor hnooru**

dehnoosw hoedowns hoedown swooned wooshed. *See* **dehnos dehoos dehosw denoos**

dehnoow hoedown. *See* **denoow dehno hnoow**

dehnop phoned ephod honed hoped phone done dope hoed hone hope node nope oped open pend peon pond pone den doe don edh end eon hen hep hod hoe hon hop nod ode one ope pen pod do eh en he ho ne no od oh on pe

dehnopsy syphoned hoydens. *See* **dehnop dehnos dehnoy dehops**

dehnor horned drone heron honed horde doer done herd hern hero hoed hoer hone horn nerd node redo rend rode den doe don dor edh end eon hen her hod hoe hon nod nor ode one ore red rho rod roe do eh en er he ho ne no od oh on or re

dehnorsu enshroud resound sounder. *See* **dehnor dehnos dehors dehosu**

dehnort throned. *See* **dehnor ehnort denort**

dehnorty threnody throned. *See* **dehnor dehnoy denort denory**

dehnos noshed honed hones hosed hosen nodes nosed shoed shone sonde dens does done dons dose ends eons hens hods hoed hoes hone hose node nods noes nose nosh odes ones send shed shod shoe den doe don dos edh end ens eon hen hod hoe hon nod ode ohs one sen she sod son do eh en he ho ne no od oh on os sh so

dehnosy hoydens. *See* **denosy ehnosy dehnoy dehnos**

dehnoy hoyden doyen honed honey deny done dyne hoed hone node yodh yond den dey doe don dye edh end eon hen hey hod hoe hon hoy nod ode one yen yod yon do eh en he ho ne no od oh on oy ye

dehnrstu thunders hunters shunted thunder. *See* **dehntu dehrsu denrst denrsu**

dehnrtu thunder. *See* **dehntu ehnrtu denrtu**

dehnrtuy thundery thunder. *See* **dehntu denrtu denrty ehnrtu**

dehnstu shunted. *See* **dehntu denst destu**

dehntu hunted tuned dent duet dune hent hued hunt nude tend then thud tune den due dun edh end eth hen het hue hut net nut ted ten the tun eh en he ne nu ut

deho hoed doe edh hod hoe ode do eh he ho od oh

dehoo oohed hoed hood doe edh hod hoe ode oho ooh do eh he ho od oh

dehoop hooped ephod hoped oohed dope hoed hood hoop hope oped pooh doe edh hep hod hoe hop ode oho ooh ope pod do eh he ho od oh pe

dehooprt theropod torpedo trooped. *See* **dehoop dehoot deoort deoprt**

dehoopw whooped. *See* **dehoop hoopw deoow**

dehoos shooed hoods hosed oohed shoed does dose hods hoed hoes hood hose odes oohs shed shod shoe shoo doe dos edh hod hoe ode oho ohs ooh she sod do eh he ho od oh os sh so

dehoossw swooshed wooshed wooshes. *See* **dehoos dehosw deossw hoossw**

dehoost soothed. *See* **dehoot dehost dehoos deoost ehoost**

dehoosw wooshed. *See* **dehoos dehosw**

dehoot hooted oohed dote hoed hood hoot toed doe dot edh eth het hod hoe hot ode oho ooh ted the tho tod toe too do eh he ho od oh to

dehoott toothed. *See* **dehoot deoott**

dehop ephod hoped dope hoed hope oped doe edh hep hod hoe hop ode ope pod do eh he ho od oh pe

dehopp hopped ephod hoped dope hoed hope oped pope doe edh hep hod hoe hop ode ope pep pod pop do eh he ho od oh pe

dehopps shopped. *See* **dehops dehopp ehopps deopps**

dehoppw whopped. *See* **dehopp**

dehops ephods dopes ephod hoped hopes hosed posed shoed does dope dose epos hods hoed hoes hope hops hose odes oped opes peso pods pose posh shed shod shoe shop soph sped doe dos edh hep hod hoe hop ode ohs ope pod she sod sop do eh he ho od oh os pe sh so

dehopy hypoed dopey ephod hoped hyped dope hoed hope hype hypo oped yodh dey doe dye edh hep hey hod hoe hop hoy ode ope pod yep yod do eh he ho od oh oy pe ye

dehoqtu quothed. *See* **deoqtu hoqtu**

dehor horde doer herd hero hoed hoer redo rode doe dor edh her hod hoe ode ore red rho rod roe do eh er he ho od oh or re

dehors hordes horsed shored doers herds hoers horde horse hosed rosed sherd shoed shoer shore shred doer does dose herd hero hers hods hoed hoer hoes hose odes ores redo reds resh rhos rode rods roes rose shed shod shoe sore doe dor dos edh her hod hoe ode ohs ore red res rho rod roe she sod do eh er he ho od oh or os re sh so

dehorst shorted. *See* **deorst dehors dehost ehorst**

dehorw whored dower horde rowed whore dhow doer drew herd hero hoed hoer owed redo rode word wore dew doe dor edh her hew hod hoe how ode ore owe red rho rod roe row wed who woe do eh er he ho od oh or ow re we

dehos hosed shoed does dose hods hoed hoes hose odes shed shod shoe doe dos edh hod hoe ode ohs she sod do eh he ho od oh os sh so

dehost hosted dotes ethos hosed shoed shote those does dose dote dots hest hods hoed hoes hose host hots odes shed shod shoe shot teds toed toes tosh doe dos dot edh eth het hod hoe hot ode ohs set she sod sot ted the tho tod toe do eh he ho od oh os sh so to

dehostt shotted. *See* **dehost deostt**

dehostu shouted. *See* **dehost dehosu deostu**

dehosu housed douse hosed house shoed does dose dues duos hods hoed hoes hose hued hues odes ouds shed shod shoe sued udos used doe dos due duo edh hod hoe hue ode ohs oud she sod sou sue udo use do eh he ho od oh os sh so us

dehosv shoved doves hosed shoed shove does dose dove hods hoed hoes hose hove odes shed shod shoe doe dos edh hod hoe ode ohs she sod do eh he ho od oh os sh so

dehosw showed dhows dowse hosed shoed sowed whose dews dhow does dose hews hods hoed hoes hose odes owed owes shed shew shod shoe show weds woes dew doe dos edh hew hod hoe how ode ohs owe sew she sod sow wed who woe do eh he ho od oh os ow sh so we

dehpst depths depth hest pest pets sept shed sped step teds edh eth hep het pet set she ted the eh he pe sh

dehpsu pushed dues hued hues push shed sped spud spue sued used due edh hep hue hup pus she sue sup use eh he pe sh up us

dehpt depth edh eth hep het pet ted the eh he pe

dehpy hyped hype dey dye edh hep hey yep eh he pe ye

dehr herd edh her red eh er he re

dehrrstu druthers. *See* **dehrsu derstu ehrrsu**

dehrs herds sherd shred herd hers reds resh shed edh her red res she eh er he re sh

dehrss sherds shreds dress herds sheds sherd shred herd hers reds resh shed edh ess her red res she eh er he re sh

dehrsttu thrusted trusted shutter. *See* **dehrsu dehttu derstu derttu**

dehrsu rushed druse herds sherd shred usher dues herd hers hued hues reds resh rude rued rues ruse rush shed sued surd sure urds used user due edh her hue red res rue she sue urd use eh er he re sh us

dehrsw shrewd. *See* **edhrs ehrsw**

dehs shed edh she eh he sh

dehss sheds shed edh ess she eh he sh

dehttu hutted duet hued teth thud due edh eth het hue hut ted the tut eh he ut

dehu hued due edh hue eh he

dei die id

deiiimst dimities. *See* **deiims deiist deimst**

deiiisvv divisive. *See* **deisv deiiv eiisv**

deiijmm jimmied. *See* **deiim deimm**

deiikkl kidlike. *See* **deikl**

deiiklnr kindlier dinkier kindler. *See* **deikln deiknr eiilnr eiklnr**

deiikls dislike. *See* **deils deiks deikl**

deiiklss dislikes dislike. *See* **deiiss deikss deilss**

deiiknr dinkier. *See* **deiknr eiiknr**

deiikns dinkies. *See* **deiins deiks dikns**

deiiknst dinkiest dinkies indites inkiest kindest tineids. *See* **deiins deiint deiist**

deiill lilied deil deli dell dill idle lied die eld ell ill led lei lid lie el id li

deiills dillies. *See* **deiill eiills**

deiilmn midline. *See* **deilmn deiim eiimn**

deiilmns midlines midline. *See* **deiims deiins deilmn deilms**

deiilmp implied. *See* **deilmp diilmp**

deiilmru delirium. *See* **deilmr eiilmu**

deiilmst delimits delimit elitism limiest limited mildest. *See* **deiims deiist deilms deilst**

deiilmt delimit limited. *See* **deimt deiim deilm**

deiilnoz lionized idolize ionized lionize. *See* **deiino deiioz eiinoz**

deiilnpv vilipend. *See* **deiinv**

deiilnvy divinely. *See* **deiinv**

deiilnxy xylidine. *See* **deinx deiln eiinx**

deiilos doilies. *See* **deilos**

deiilosz idolizes doilies idolize iodizes. *See* **deiioz deilos**

deiiloz idolize. *See* **deiioz deilo**

deiilpss sideslip dispels. *See* **deiiss deilps deilss diilps**

deiiltuz utilized utilize. *See* **deiltu**

deiim imide dime die dim mid em id me mi

deiimmx immixed. *See* **deiim iimmx deimm**

deiimno dominie. *See* **deiino demno deimn**

deiimnos dominies dominie misdone. *See* **deiims deiino deiins deimns**

deiimnrt diriment inditer interim mintier nitride. *See* **deiint deiirt deimnr deimnt**

deiimntu mutinied. *See* **deiint deimnt deimtu deintu**

deiims imides deism dimes imide dies dime dims ides mise semi side die dim ids mid mis em id is me mi si

deiimsvw midwives. *See* **deiims**

deiimsz midsize. *See* **deiims deisz**

deiino iodine dine done nide nidi node den die din doe don end eon ion nod ode one do en id in ne no od on

deiinors derision indorse insider ironies noisier rosined. *See* **deiino deiins deiirs deinor**

deiinost editions sedition edition indites tineids. *See* **deiino deiins deiint deiist**

deiinot edition. *See* **deiint deiino**

deiinoz ionized. *See* **deiino deiioz eiinoz**

deiinppw windpipe. *See* **deinpp**

deiinprs inspired insider inspire spinier. *See* **deiins deiirs deinps deinrs**

deiinprt intrepid inditer nitride printed riptide. *See* **deiint deiipt deiirt deinrt**

deiinqru inquired inquire. *See* **deinru deiqru**

deiinrs insider. *See* **deinrs diinrs deiins deiirs**

deiinrss insiders insider. *See* **deiins deiirs deiiss deinrs**

deiinrst disinter inditers nitrides dirties inditer indites insider nitride tineids. *See* **deiins deiint deiirs deiirt**

deiinrsv diviners diviner divines insider verdins. *See* **deiins deiinv deiirs deinrs**

deiinrt inditer nitride. *See* **deiint deiirt deinrt**

deiinrtu untidier inditer intrude nitride untried. *See* **deiint deiirt deinrt deinru**

deiinrv diviner. *See* **deiinv deinrv**

deiinrw windier. *See* **deinrw eiinrw**

deiins inside dines nides snide dens dies dine dins ends ides nide nidi nisi send side sine den die din end ens ids sen sin en id in is ne si

deiinsst insisted tidiness dissent indites tineids. *See* **deiins deiint deiiss deiist**

deiinst indites tineids. *See* **deiint deiins deiist**

deiinstu disunite nudities indites tineids unities. *See* **deiins deiint deiist deinsu**

deiinstw windiest indites tineids winiest. *See* **deiins deiint deiist deinsw**

deiinsv divines. *See* **deiins deiinv**

deiint indite tineid dent diet dine edit nide nidi tend tide tied tine den die din dit end net nit ted ten tie tin en id in it ne ti

deiinttu intuited. *See* **deiint deintt deintu denttu**

deiintty identity. *See* **deiint deintt eintty**

deiintuz unitized unitize. *See* **deiint deintu**

deiintv invited. *See* **deiinv deiint eiintv**

deiinv divine ivied dine dive nevi nide nidi vein vend vied vine den die din end vie en id in ne

deiioprs presidio periods. *See* **deiirs deiopr deiops deiors**

deiiorst diorites diorite dirties editors steroid storied triodes. *See* **deiirs deiirt deiist deiors**

deiiort diorite. *See* **deiort deiirt**

deiiorxz oxidizer oxidize. *See* **deiioz deiorz**

deiiosxz oxidizes iodizes oxidize. *See* **deiioz deiosx**

deiiosz iodizes. *See* **deiioz deisz deosz**

deiioxz oxidize. *See* **deiioz deiox**

deiioz iodize doze die doe ode zed do id od

deiippr dippier. *See* **deippr eiippr**

deiipprr drippier dippier. *See* **deippr eipprr**

deiippst dippiest pipiest. *See* **deiipt deiist deipps deipst**

deiiprst riptides spirited dirties riptide striped tipsier. *See* **deiipt deiirs deiirt deiist**

deiiprt riptide. *See* **deiipt deiirt**

deiipt pitied tepid diet edit pied tide tied tipi die dip dit pet pie pit ted tie tip id it pe pi ti

deiiqstu disquiet. *See* **deiist deistu eiqstu**

deiirrt dirtier. *See* **deiirt deirr**

deiirs irides dries rides sired dies dire ides iris reds reis ride rids rise side sire die ids ire red res rid sir er id is re si

deiirst dirties. *See* **deirst deiirs deiirt deiist**

deiirt tidier tired tried diet dire dirt edit ride rite tide tied tier tire die dit ire red ret rid ted tie er id it re ti

deiirzz dizzier. *No 6s or 5s*

deiiss diesis sides dies ides side die ess ids sis id is si

deiist tidies deist diets edits sited tides dies diet dits edit ides side site teds tide tied ties die dit ids its set sit ted tie id is it si ti

deiistt ditties tidiest. *See* **deiist iistt**

deiistv visited. *See* **deiist deistv**

deiistzz dizziest dizzies tizzies. *See* **deiist**

deiiszz dizzies. *See* **deisz**

deiiv ivied dive vied die vie id

deijllo jollied. *See* **deilo**

deijlt jilted tilde tiled deil deli diet edit idle jilt lied tide tied tile die dit eld jet led lei let lid lie lit ted tie til el id it li ti

deijno joined dine done jeon join nide node den die din doe don end eon ion joe nod ode one do en id in jo ne no od on

deijnor joinder. *See* **deinor deijno eijnor**

deijnot jointed. *See* **deijno ijnot denot**

deijnru injured. *See* **eijnru deinru**

deijv jived dive jive vied die vie id

deik dike die kid id

deikkn kinked inked dike dine dink kind kine kink nide den die din end ink ken kid kin en id in ne

deikl liked deil deli dike idle lied like die eld elk ilk kid led lei lek lid lie el id li

deikll killed liked deil deli dell dike dill idle kill lied like die eld elk ell ilk ill kid led lei lek lid lie el id li

deiklls skilled. *See* **deikll deils dells**

deiklm milked liked limed miked deil deli dike dime idle lied like lime meld mike mild mile milk die dim eld elk elm ilk kid led lei lek lid lie mel mid mil el em id li me mi

deikln kindle linked inked inkle liked liken lined deil deli dike dine dink idle kiln kind kine lend lied lien like line link nide den die din eld elk end ilk ink ken kid kin led lei lid lie nil el en id in li ne

deiklnp plinked. *See* **deikln deiknp**

deiklnr kindler. *See* **deiknr deikln eiklnr**

deiklnrw wrinkled kindler winkled wrinkle. *See* **deikln deiknr deiknw deilrw**

deiklns kindles slinked. *See* **deikln eiklns**

deiklnt tinkled. *See* **deilnt deiklt deikln eiklnt**

deiklntw twinkled indwelt tinkled twinkle winkled. *See* **deikln deiklt deiknw**

deiklnw winkled. *See* **deikln eiklnw deiknw**

deiklo keloid liked oiled oldie deil deli dike dole idle idol kilo koel lied like lode die doe eld elk ilk kid led lei lek lid lie ode oil oke old do el id li lo od

deiklos keloids. *See* **deiklo deilos**

deiklrs skirled. *See* **deilrs deikrs**

deiklstt skittled kittled kittles skittle stilted. *See* **deiklt deilst deiltt eilstt**

deiklt kilted kited liked tilde tiled deil deli diet dike edit idle kilt kite lied like tide tied tile tile die dit eld elk ilk kid kit led lei lek let lid lie lit ted tie til el id it li ti

deikltt kittled. *See* **deiklt eikltt deiltt**

deikm miked dike dime mike die dim kid mid em id me mi

deikmms skimmed. *See* **deims deiks deikm**

deikmps skimped. *See* **deikps deims eikms**

deikmrs smirked. *See* **deimrs eikmrs deikrs**

deikn inked dike dine dink kind kine nide den die din end ink ken kid kin en id in ne

deiknns skinned. *See* **deinns deiks dikns**

deiknnss kindness skinned. *See* **deikss deinns eiknss**

deikno oinked eikon inked kendo koine dike dine dink done ikon keno kind kine kino nide node oink den die din doe don end eon ink ion ken kid kin nod ode oke one do en id in ne no od on

deiknos doeskin. *See* **eiknos deinos deikno**

deiknoss doeskins doeskin kenosis. *See* **deikno deikss deinos denoss**

deiknov invoked. *See* **deikno eiknov**

deiknp pinked inked piked pined dike dine dink kepi kind kine nide pend pied pike pine pink den die din dip end ink ken kid kin kip nip pen pie pin en id in ne pe pi

deiknr kinder diner drink inked inker irked dike dine dink dire dirk kern kier kind kine nerd nide rein rend ride rind rink den die din end ink ire irk ken kid kin kir red rid en er id in ne re

deiknrr drinker. *See* **deiknr deirr**

deiknst kindest. *See* **deist denst**

deiknsy kidneys. *See* **deikny**

deikntt knitted. *See* **eikntt deintt**

deiknw winked inked widen wined dike dine dink kind kine knew nide wend wide wind wine wink den dew die din end ink ken kid kin new wed wen win en id in ne we

deikny dinkey kidney inked dinky deny dike dine dink dyke dyne inky kind kine nide den dey die din dye end ink ken key kid kin yen yin en id in ne ye

deikp piked dike kepi pied pike die dip kid kip pie id pe pi

deikpps skipped. *See* **deikps deipps**

deikps spiked dikes kepis piked pikes skied spied spike desk dies dike dips disk ides kepi kids kips pied pies pike side skep skid skip sped die dip ids kid kip pie sip ski id is pe pi si

deikqru quirked. *See* **deiqru deikr ikqru**

deikr irked dike dire dirk kier ride die ire irk kid kir red rid er id re

deikrrs skirred. *See* **deirrs deikrs**

deikrs risked dikes dirks dries irked kiers rides sired skied desk dies dike dire dirk disk ides irks kids kier kris reds reis ride rids rise risk side sire skid die ids ire irk kid kir red res rid sir ski er id is re si

deikrst skirted. *See* **deirst eikrst deikrs**

deikrsu duskier. *See* **deikrs dersu deksu**

deiks dikes skied desk dies dike disk ides kids side skid die ids kid ski id is si

deikss kissed desks dikes disks sides skids skied skies desk dies dike disk ides kids kiss side skid skis die ess ids kid sis ski id is si

deiksstu duskiest studies. *See* **deikss deisst deissu deistu**

deiksv skived dikes dives skied skive vised desk dies dike disk dive ides kids side skid vied vies vise die ids kid ski vie id is si

deikt kited diet dike edit kite tide tied tike die dit kid kit ted tie id it ti

deil deil deli idle lied die eld led lei lid lie el id li

deillm milled limed deil deli dell dill dime idle lied lime meld mell mild mile mill die dim eld ell elm ill led lei lid lie mel mid mil el em id li me mi

deillmu illumed. *See* **eillmu deillm dellmu**

deillnsw indwells indwell swilled swindle. *See* **deillw deilsw deinsw dellsw**

deillnw indwell. *See* **deillw deiln deinw**

deillopw pillowed. *See* **deillp deillw deilop dellop**

deillorr lordlier. *See* **deilor dellor ellorr**

deillos dollies. *See* **deilos**

deillp pilled piled plied deil deli dell dill idle lied pied pile pill pled die dip eld ell ill led lei lid lie lip pie el id li pe pi

deillps spilled. *See* **deilps deillp**

deillqu quilled. *See* **ellqu illqu**

deillrt trilled. *See* **deillt eillrt**

deillss lidless. *See* **eillss deilss**

deillst stilled. *See* **deilst deillt eillst**

deillsu sullied. *See* **deils dells delsu**

deillsw swilled. *See* **dellsw deilsw deillw**

deillt lilted tilled tilde tiled deil deli dell diet dill edit idle lied lilt tell tide tied tile till die dit eld ell ill led lei let lid lie lit ted tie til el id it li ti

deilltw twilled. *See* **deillt deiltw**

deillw willed dwell wield wiled deil deli dell dill idle lewd lied weld well wide wild wile will dew die eld ell ill led lei lid lie wed el id li we

deilm limed deil deli dime idle lied lime meld mild mile die dim eld elm led lei lid lie mel mid mil el em id li me mi

deilmms slimmed. *See* **deilms**

deilmn milden denim limed limen lined mined deil deli dime dine idle lend lied lien lime limn line meld mend mien mild mile mind mine nide den die dim din eld elm end led lei lid lie mel men mid mil nil nim el em en id in li me mi ne

deilmnss mildness mindless simnels. *See* **deilmn deilms deilss deimns**

deilmo moiled limed model oiled oldie deil deli demo dime dole dome idle idol lied lime limo lode meld mild mile milo mode moil mold mole die dim doe eld elm led lei lid lie mel mid mil mod ode oil old do el em id li lo me mi mo od om

deilmoot dolomite. *See* **deilmo deilot delmoo delmot**

deilmop implode. *See* **deilmp deilop deilmo**

deilmopr implored implode implore moldier rimpled. *See* **deilmo deilmp deilmr deilop**

deilmops implodes despoil dimples dipoles implode imposed spoiled. *See* **deilmo deilmp deilms deilop**

deilmor moldier. *See* **deilmr dilmor delmor deilor**

deilmost melodist moldiest mildest modiste. *See* **deilmo deilms deilos deilot**

deilmoy myeloid. *See* **deilmo delmoy**

deilmp dimple limped impel limed piled plied deil deli dime idle lied lime limp meld mild mile pied pile pled die dim dip eld elm imp led lei lid lie lip mel mid mil pie el em id li me mi pe pi

deilmpr rimpled. *See* **deilmp eilmpr deilmr deimpr**

deilmps dimples. *See* **deilmp deilps eilmps deilms**

deilmpw wimpled. *See* **deilmp deilmw eilmpw**

deilmr milder dimer idler limed miler mired riled rimed deil deli dime dire dirl emir idle lied lime lire meld merl mild mile mire ride riel rile rime die dim eld elm ire led lei lid lie mel mid mil mir red rem rid rim el em er id li me mi re

deilmrsu misruled misrule. *See* **deilmr deilms deilrs deimrs**

deilms misled slimed smiled deils deism delis dimes idles limed limes melds miles sidle slide slime smile deil deli dies dime dims elms ides idle isle leis lids lied lies lime meld mels mild mile mils mise semi side sled slid slim die dim eld elm els ids led lei lid lie lis mel mid mil mis el em id is li me mi si

deilmst mildest. *See* **deimst deilst**

deilmsw mildews. *See* **deilmw deilms deilsw**

deilmw mildew limed wield wiled deil deli dime idle lewd lied lime meld mewl mild mile weld wide wild wile dew die dim eld elm led lei lid lie mel mew mid mil wed el em id li me mi we

deilmwy mildewy. *See* **deilmw deilwy**

deilmzz mizzled. *See* **eilmzz deilm**

deiln lined deil deli dine idle lend lied lien line nide den die din eld end led lei lid lie nil el en id in li ne

deilnn linden inned lined linen deil deli dine idle lend lied lien line linn nide nine den die din eld end inn led lei lid lie nil el en id in li ne

deilnnot indolent intoned. *See* **deilnn deilnt deilot dennot**

deilnns lindens. *See* **deilnn eilnns deinns**

deilnnu unlined. *See* **deilnn deinnu**

deilnoo eidolon. *See* **delnoo eilno deiln**

deilnoos eidolons solenoid doolies eidolon noodles. *See* **deilos deinos delnoo deloos**

deilnosu delusion nodules elusion. *See* **deilos deinos deinsu delnou**

deilnotu outlined diluent outline. *See* **deilnt deilot deiltu deintu**

deilnovv involved involve. *See* **deilv eilno eilnv**

deilnps spindle splined. *See* **deilps deinps eilnps**

deilnpss spindles dispels spindle splined splines. *See* **deilps deilss deinps denpss**

deilnpst splinted dentils spindle splined stipend. *See* **deilnt deilps deilst deinps**

deilnrst tendrils tendril dentils. *See* **deilnt deilrs deilst deinrs**

deilnrsw swindler rewinds swindle swirled winders. *See* **deilrs deilrw deilsw deinrs**

deilnrt tendril. *See* **deilnt deinrt**

deilnssw swindles wildness windless swindle. *See* **deilss deilsw deinsw einssw**

deilnst dentils. *See* **deilnt eilnst deilst**

deilnstu diluents insulted unlisted dentils diluent dilutes duelist indults. *See* **deilnt deilst deiltu deinsu**

deilnsw swindle. *See* **deilsw deinsw**

deilnt dentil linted inlet lined tilde tiled deil deli dent diet dine edit idle lend lent lied lien line lint nide tend tide tied tile tine den die din dit eld end led lei let lid lie lit net nil nit ted ten tie til tin el en id in it li ne ti

deilnttu untitled diluent. *See* **deilnt deiltt deiltu deintt**

deilntu diluent. *See* **deilnt deiltu dilntu deintu**

deilntw indwelt. *See* **deilnt deintw deiltw**

deilnuwy unwieldy. *See* **deilwy delnuy**

deilo oiled oldie deil deli dole idle idol lied lode die doe eld led lei lid lie ode oil old do el id li lo od

deiloopw woodpile. *See* **deilop deloop delopw**

deiloos doolies. *See* **eiloos deloos deilos**

deilop dipole loped oiled oldie piled plied poled deil deli dole dope idle idol lied lode lope oped pied pile pled plod pole die dip doe eld led lei lid lie lip lop ode oil old ope pie pod poi do el id li lo od pe pi

deilops despoil dipoles spoiled. *See* **deilop deilps eilops deiops delops**

deilopss despoils despoil dipoles dispels dispose spoiled. *See* **deilop deilos deilps deilss**

deilopst pistoled deposit despoil dipoles dopiest piloted pistole posited spoiled topside. *See* **deilop deilos deilot deilps**

deilopt piloted. *See* **deilop eilopt deilot**

deilor roiled idler oiled oiler older oldie oriel riled deil deli dire dirl doer dole idle idol lied lire lode lord lore orle redo ride riel rile rode roil role die doe dor eld ire led lei lid lie ode oil old ore red rid rod roe do el er id li lo od or re

deilors soldier. *See* **deiors deilrs eilors deilos delors**

deilorss soldiers dossier rissole sliders solders soldier. *See* **deilor deilos deilrs deilss**

deilorsy soldiery soldier. *See* **deilor deilos deilrs deilry**

deilos oldies soiled deils delis doles idles idols lodes oiled oldie sidle slide soled solid deil deli dies does dole dose ides idle idol isle leis lids lied lies lode lose odes oils side silo sled slid sloe soil sold sole die doe dos eld els ids led lei lid lie los ode oil old sod sol do el id is li lo od os si so

deilossv dissolve. *See* **deilos deilss deilsv deiosv**

deilosvw oldwives. *See* **deilos deilsv deilsw deiosv**

deilot toiled oiled oldie tilde tiled toile deil deli diet doit dole dolt dote edit idle idol lied lode tide tied tile toed toil told die dit doe dot eld led lei let lid lie lit lot ode oil old ted tie til tod toe do el id it li lo od ti to

deilotuv outlived voluted outlive. *See* **deilot deiltu deotuv eilotv**

deilp piled plied deil deli idle lied pied pile pled die dip eld led lei lid lie lip pie el id li pe pi

deilpp lipped piled piped plied deil deli idle lied pied pile pipe pled die dip eld led lei lid lie lip pep pie pip el id li pe pi

deilppr rippled. *See* **deippr deilpp eilppr**

deilpps slipped. *See* **deilps deipps**

deilppst stippled slipped stipple tippled tipples. *See* **deilpp deilps deilst deipps**

deilppsu supplied slipped suppled. *See* **deilpp deilps deipps deipsu**

deilppt tippled. *See* **deilpp deippt eilppt**

deilprt tripled. *See* **eilprt diprt deilr**

deilps dispel lisped deils delis idles piled piles plied side slide spied spiel spile deil deli dies dips ides idle isle leis lids lied lies lips lisp pied pies pile pled side sled slid slip sped die dip eld els ids led lei lid lie lip pie sip el id is li pe pi si

deilpss dispels. *See* **deilps deilss eilpss**

deilpty tepidly. *See* **deity eipty deilp**

deilpx diplex piled pixel plied deil deli idle ilex lied pile pled die dip eld led lei lid lie lip pie pix el ex id li pe pi xi

deilqtu quilted. *See* **deiltu eiqtu ilqtu**

deilr idler riled deil deli dire dirl idle lied lire ride riel rile die eld ire led lei lid lie red rid el er id li re

deilrs idlers slider deils delis dirls dries idler idles rides riels riled riles sidle sired slide deil deli dies dire dirl ides idle isle leis lids lied lies lire reds reis ride rids riel rile rise side sire sled slid die eld els ids ire led lei lid lie red res rid sir el er id is li re si

deilrss sliders. *See* **deilrs deilss**

deilrssy dressily sliders. *See* **deilrs deilry deilss deilsy**

deilrsv drivels. *See* **deilsv deirsv deilrv deilrs eilrsv**

deilrsw swirled. *See* **deilrs deilsw deilrw**

deilrszz drizzles drizzle sizzled. *See* **deilrs eilszz**

deilrtvy deviltry devilry. *See* **deilrv deilry deirtv eilrvy**

deilrtw twirled. *See* **deilrw deiltw**

deilrv drivel devil diver drive idler lived liver livre riled rived viler deil deli dire dirl dive evil idle lied lire live ride riel rile rive veil veld vied vile die eld ire led lei lev lid lie red rev rid vie el er id li re

deilrvy devilry. *See* **deilry deilrv eilrvy**

deilrw wilder idler riled weird wider wield wiled wired deil deli dire dirl drew idle lewd lied lire ride riel rile weir weld wide wild wile wire dew die eld ire led lei lid lie red rid wed el er id li re we

deilrwy weirdly. *See* **deilry deilwy deilrw**

deilry direly ridley idler riled yield deil deli dire dirl dyer idle idly idyl lied lire lyre rely ride riel rile dey die dry dye eld ire led lei lid lie lye red rid rye el er id li re ye

deilrzz drizzle. *See* **deilr**

deils deils delis idles sidle slide deil deli dies ides idle isle leis lids lied lies side sled slid die eld els ids led lei lid lie lis el id is li si

deilss sidles slides deils delis idles isles sides sidle sleds slide deil deli dies ides idle isle leis less lids lied lies side sled slid die eld els ess ids led lei lid lie sis el id is li si

deilsstu duelists dilutes duelist studies tussled. *See* **deilss deilst deiltu deisst**

deilst idlest listed silted tildes deils deist delis diets edits islet istle sidle sited slide stile tides tilde tiled tiles deil deli dies diet dits edit ides idle isle leis lest lets lids lied lies list side silt site sled slid slit teds tide tied ties tile tils die dit eld els ids its led lei let lid lie lit set sit ted tie til el id is it li si ti

deilstt stilted. *See* **deilst deiltt eilstt**

deilstu dilutes duelist. *See* **deiltu deistu deilst delstu**

deilstuy sedulity dilutes duelist. *See* **deilst deilsy deiltu deistu**

deilstw wildest. *See* **deilst deistw deilsw deiltw**

deilstyz stylized stylize. *See* **deilst deilsy delsty**

deilsv devils deils delis devil dives evils idles lived lives sidle slide veils velds vised deil deli dies dive evil ides idle isle leis lids lied lies live side sled slid veil veld vied vies vile vise die eld els ids led lei lev lid lie vie el id is li si

deilsw wields deils delis idles lewis sidle slide welds wield wilds wiled wiles deil deli dews dies ides idle isle leis lewd lids lied lies side sled slew slid weds weld wide wild wile wise dew die eld els ids led lei lid lie sew wed wis el id is li si we

deilsy yields deils delis idles idyls lysed sidle slide yield deil deli deys dies dyes ides idle idly idyl isle leis lids lied lies lyes lyse side sled slid dey die dye eld els ids led lei lid lie lye sly yes el id is li si ye

deilszz sizzled. *See* **eilszz deils deisz**

deilt tilde tiled deil deli diet edit idle lied tide tied tile die dit eld led lei let lid lie lit ted tie til el id it li ti

deiltt tilted titled tilde tiled title deil deli diet edit idle lied tide tied tile tilt die dit eld led lei let lid lie lit ted tie til tit el id it li ti

deiltu dilute luted tilde tiled utile deil deli diet duel duet edit etui idle lied lieu lute tide tied tile tule die dit due eld led lei let leu lid lie lit ted tie til tui el id it li ti ut

deiltw wilted dwelt tilde tiled wield wiled wited deil deli diet edit idle lewd lied tide tied tile weld welt wide wild wile wilt wite dew die dit eld led lei let lid lie lit ted tie til wed wet wit el id it li ti we

deilv devil lived deil deli dive evil idle lied live veil veld vied vile die eld led lei lev lid lie vie el id li

deilw wield wiled deil deli idle lewd lied weld wide wild wile dew die eld led lei lid lie wed el id li we

deilwy widely wield wiled yield deil deli dewy idle idly idyl lewd lied weld wide wild wile wily dew dey die dye eld led lei lid lie lye wed wye yew el id li we ye

deily yield deil deli idle idly idyl lied dey die dye eld led lei lid lie lye el id li ye

deim dime die dim mid em id me mi

deimm mimed dime mime die dim mem mid mim em id me mi

deimmnos demonism misdone. *See* **deimns deinos demmos demnos**

deimmost immodest dimmest midmost modiste. *See* **deimst deiost demmos demost**

deimmpr primmed. *See* **deimmr deimpr**

deimmr dimmer rimmed dimer mimed mimer mired rimed dime dire emir mime mire ride rime die dim ire mem mid mim mir red rem rid rim em er id me mi re

deimmrs dimmers. *See* **deimrs deimmr eimmrs**

deimmrst midterms dimmers dimmest midterm trimmed. *See* **deimmr deimrs deimrt deimst**

deimmrt midterm trimmed. *See* **deimmr deimrt**

deimmru immured. *See* **deimmr eimmru deimmu**

deimmst dimmest. *See* **deimst**

deimmsu dummies mediums. *See* **deimmu demmsu**

deimmu medium mimed dime mime die dim due emu mem mid mim mud mum em id me mi mu um

deimn denim mined dime dine mend mien mind mine nide den die dim din end men mid nim em en id in me mi ne

deimnnsu minuends minuend. *See* **deimns deinns deinnu deinsu**

deimnnu minuend. *See* **deinnu deimn emnnu**

deimnoos dominoes misdone noisome. *See* **deimns deinos demnoo demnos**

deimnoot demotion motioned emotion. *See* **deimnt demnoo dimnoo imnoot**

deimnoox monoxide. *See* **demnoo dimnoo**

deimnos misdone. *See* **demnos deimns eimnos deinos**

deimnp impend denim mined pined dime dine mend mien mind mine nide pend pied pine den die dim din dip end imp men mid nim nip pen pie pin em en id in me mi ne pe pi

deimnps impends. *See* **deimns deimnp deinps**

deimnptu impudent imputed pinetum. *See* **deimnp deimnt deimtu deintu**

deimnr remind denim dimer diner mined miner mired rimed dime dine dire emir mend mien mind mine mire nerd nide rein rend ride rime rind den die dim din end ire men mid mir nim red rem rid rim em en er id in me mi ne re

deimnrs reminds. *See* **deimns deimrs deinrs eimnrs deimnr**

deimnrtu rudiment intrude untried. *See* **deimnr deimnt deimrt deimtu**

deimns denims deism denim dimes dines mends miens minds mined mines nides snide dens dies dime dims dine dins ends ides mend mien mind mine mise nide nims semi send side sine den die dim din end ens ids men mid mis nim sen sin em en id in is me mi ne si

deimnst mindset. *See* **deimst deimns deimnt**

deimnt minted demit denim mined timed dent diet dime dine edit emit

item mend mien mind mine mint mite nide tend tide tied time tine den die dim din dit end men met mid net nim nit ted ten tie tin em en id in it me mi ne ti

deimnux unmixed. *See* **deimn deinx deinu**

deimoor moidore moodier. *See* **demoor eimoor**

deimoors moidores misdoer moidore moodier roomies. *See* **deimrs deiors demoor deoors**

deimoost moodiest modiste osteoid. *See* **deimst deiost demost deoost**

deimoprs promised imposed imposer misdoer periods promise semipro. *See* **deimpr deimrs deiopr deiops**

deimoprt imported diopter. *See* **deimpr deimrt deiopr deiort**

deimoprv improved provide improve. *See* **deimpr deiopr deiorv demopr**

deimops imposed. *See* **deiops eimops**

deimorrr mirrored. *See* **demorr imorrr**

deimors misdoer. *See* **deimrs deiors eimors**

deimorss misdoers dossier isomers misdoer mossier rimoses. *See* **deimrs deimss deiors deorss**

deimorst mortised editors misdoer modiste moister mortise steroid storied stormed triodes. *See* **deimrs deimrt deimst deiors**

deimorux exordium. *See* **demru deimr eimrx**

deimosst modistes modiste somites. *See* **deimss deimst deiost deisst**

deimost modiste. *See* **deimst demost eimost deiost**

deimott omitted. *See* **deimt diott emott**

deimotv vomited. *See* **eimotv deimt diotv**

deimpp pimped piped dime pied pimp pipe die dim dip imp mid pep pie pip em id me mi pe pi

deimppr primped. *See* **deippr deimpp deimpr**

deimpr primed dimer mired pride pried prime rimed dime dire drip emir mire peri perm pied pier prim ride rime ripe die dim dip imp ire mid mir per pie red rem rep rid rim rip em er id me mi pe pi re

deimpru dumpier umpired. *See* **dempru eimpru**

deimpstu dumpiest dispute impetus imputed imputes stumped tediums. *See* **deimst deimtu deipst deipsu**

deimptu imputed. *See* **deimtu eimptu**

deimqrsu squirmed squired. *See* **deimrs deiqru demrsu**

deimr dimer mired rimed dime dire emir mire ride rime die dim ire mid mir red rem rid rim em er id me mi re

deimrs dermis dimers deism dimer dimes dries emirs mired mires miser rides rimed rimes sired dies dime dims dire emir ides mire mirs mise reds reis ride rids rime rims rise semi side sire die dim ids ire mid mir mis red rem res rid rim sir em er id is me mi re si

deimrssu surmised misused surmise. *See* **deimrs deimss deissu demrsu**

deimrt mitred demit dimer merit mired miter mitre remit rimed timed timer tired tried diet dime dire dirt edit emir emit item mire mite ride rime rite term tide tied tier time tire trim die dim dit ire met mid mir red rem ret rid rim ted tie em er id it me mi re ti

deims deism dimes dies dime dims ides mise semi side die dim ids mid mis em id is me mi si

deimss deisms missed deism dimes semis sides dies dime dims ides mess mise miss semi side die dim ess ids mid mis sis em id is me mi si

deimssu misused. *See* **deimss deissu eimssu demssu**

deimst demits misted deism deist demit diets dimes edits emits items midst mites sited smite tides timed times dies diet dime dims dits edit emit ides item mise mist mite semi side site stem teds tide tied ties time die dim dit ids its met mid mis set sit ted tie em id is it me mi si ti

deimstu tediums. *See* **deimst deistu deimtu**

deimsty stymied. *See* **deimst eimsty**

deimt demit timed diet dime edit emit item mite tide tied time die dim dit met mid ted tie em id it me mi ti

deimtu tedium demit muted timed tumid diet dime duet edit emit etui item mite mute tide tied time die dim dit due emu met mid mud ted tie tui em id it me mi mu ti um ut

deimx mixed dime die dim mid mix em ex id me mi xi

dein dine nide den die din end en id in ne

deinn inned dine nide nine den die din end inn en id in ne

deinnnou innuendo. *See* **deinnu dennou**

deinnnpu unpinned. *See* **deinnp deinnu dennpu**

deinnoot noontide intoned. *See* **deinnt dennot einnot innoot**

deinnot intoned. *See* **deinnt einnot dennot**

deinnoww winnowed. *See* **dennow dinoww innoww**

deinnp pinned inned penni pined dine nide nine pend pied pine den die din dip end inn nip pen pie pin en id in ne pe pi

deinnpru underpin inurned. *See* **deinnp deinnr deinnu deinru**

deinnr dinner diner inned inner renin dine dire nerd nide nine rein rend ride rind den die din end inn ire red rid en er id in ne re

deinnrs dinners. *See* **deinrs deinnr einnrs deinns**

deinnru inurned. *See* **deinnr deinru deinnu**

deinns sinned dines inned nides nines snide dens dies dine dins ends ides inns nide nine send side sine den die din end ens ids inn sen sin en id in is ne si

deinnst dentins indents intends. *See* **deinnt einnst**

deinnt dentin indent intend tinned inned dent diet dine edit nide nine tend tide tied tine den die din dit end inn net nit ted ten tie tin en id in it ne ti

deinntw twinned. *See* **deinnt deintw**

deinnu undine ennui indue inned nudie dine dune nide nine nude den die din due dun end inn nun en id in ne nu

deinoops poisoned snooped spooned. *See* **deinop deinos deinps deiops**

deinootv devotion. *See* **diotv denot einov**

deinop opined pined opine dine done dope nide node nope oped open pend peon pied pine pond pone den die din dip doe don end eon ion nip nod ode one ope pen pie pin pod poi do en id in ne no od on pe pi

deinoprs prisoned indorse orpines periods ponders respond rosined. *See* **deinop deinor deinos deinps**

deinopsu unpoised. *See* **deinop deinos deinps deinsu**

deinopt pointed. *See* **deinop deopt einpt**

deinor dinero ironed diner drone dine dire doer done iron nerd nide node redo rein rend ride rind rode den die din doe don dor end eon ion ire nod nor ode one ore red rid rod roe do en er id in ne no od on or re

deinors indorse rosined. *See* **deinor deinrs deiors denors deinos**

deinorss indorses dossier indorse rosined seniors. *See* **deinor deinos deinrs deiors**

deinorvw overwind downier. *See* **deinor deinrv deinrw deiorv**

deinorw downier. *See* **deinor denorw deinrw deiorw**

deinos noised onside dines eosin nides nodes noise nosed snide sonde dens dies dine dins does done dons dose ends eons ides ions nide node nods noes nose odes ones send side sine den die din doe don dos end ens eon ids ion nod ode one sen sin sod son do en id in is ne no od on os si so

deinostw downiest townies. *See* **deinos deinsw deintw deiost**

deinp pined dine nide pend pied pine den die din dip end nip pen pie pin en id in ne pe pi

deinpp nipped pined piped dine nide pend pied pine pipe den die din dip end nip pen pep pie pin pip en id in ne pe pi

deinpps snipped. *See* **deinpp einpps deipps deinps**

deinppuz unzipped. *See* **deinpp deippz**

deinprst sprinted printed stipend striped. *See* **deinps deinrs deinrt deiprs**

deinprt printed. *See* **deinrt diprt einpt**

deinps sniped spined dines nides pends pined pines snide snipe spend spied spine dens dies dine dins dips ends ides nide nips pend pens pied pies pine pins send side sine snip sped spin den die din dip end ens ids nip pen pie pin sen sin sip en id in is ne pe pi si

deinpsst stipends dissent insteps spinets stipend. *See* **deinps deipst deisst denpss**

deinpst stipend. *See* **einpst deinps deipst**

deinqstu squinted inquest quintes. *See* **deinsu deintu deistu dinstu**

deinr diner dine dire nerd nide rein rend ride rind den die din end ire red rid en er id in ne re

deinrrtu intruder intrude runtier untried. *See* **deinrt deinru deintu denrtu**

deinrs diners rinsed diner dines dries nerds nides reins rends resin rides rinds rinse risen serin sired siren snide dens dies dine dins dire ends ides nerd nide reds rein reis rend ride rids rind rise send side sine sire den die din end ens ids ire red res rid sen sin sir en er id in is ne re si

deinrssu sundries insured insures sunders sunrise undress. *See* **deinrs deinru deinsu deissu**

deinrstt strident tridents dentist stinted trident. *See* **deinrs deinrt deintt deirst**

deinrstu intrudes dustier insured intrude triunes untried. *See* **deinrs deinrt deinru deinsu**

deinrsu insured. *See* **deinrs deinsu einrsu deinru denrsu**

deinrsv verdins. *See* **deinrs deirsv deinrv**

deinrsw rewinds winders. *See* **deinrs deinrw deinsw**

deinrt tinder diner inert inter niter tired trend tried trine dent diet dine dire dirt edit nerd nide rein rend rent ride rind rite tend tern tide tied tier tine tire den die din dit end ire net nit red ret rid ted ten tie tin en er id in it ne re ti

deinrtt trident. *See* **deinrt deintt einrtt**

deinrtu intrude untried. *See* **deinru deinrt einrtu denrtu deintu**

deinru inured ruined diner indue inure nudie under urine dine dire dune nerd nide nude rein rend ride rind rude rued ruin rune den die din due dun end ire red rid rue run urd urn en er id in ne nu re

deinrv driven verdin diner diver drive rived riven dine dire dive nerd nevi nide rein rend ride rind rive vein vend vied vine den die din end ire red rev rid vie en er id in ne re

deinrw rewind winder diner weird widen wider wined wired dine dire drew nerd nide rein rend ride rind weir wend wide wind wine wire wren den dew die din end ire new red rid wed wen win en er id in ne re we

deins dines snide dens dies dine dins ends ides nide send side sine den die din end ens ids sen sin en id in is ne si

deinssst dissents dissent desists. *See* **deisst einsst**

deinsst dissent. *See* **deisst einsst**

deinsstt dentists dentist dissent stinted. *See* **deintt deisst einsst einstt**

deinstt dentist stinted. *See* **deintt einstt**

deinstuu unsuited. *See* **deinsu deintu deistu densuu**

deinsty density destiny. *See* **deist deity denst**

deinsu indues nudies undies dines dunes indue nides nidus nudes nudie snide dens dies dine dins dues dune duns ends ides nide nude send side sine sued used den die din due dun end ens ids sen sin sue sun use en id in is ne nu si us

deinsw widens dines nides sinew snide swine wends widen winds wined wines dens dews dies dine dins ends ides news nide send sewn side sine weds wend wens wide wind wine wins wise den dew die din end ens ids new sen sew sin wed wen win wis en id in is ne si we

deinsz dizens dines dizen nides sized snide dens dies dine dins ends ides nide send side sine size zeds zein den

die din end ens ids sen sin zed en id in is ne si

deintt tinted dent diet dine edit nide tend tent tide tied tine tint den die din dit end net nit ted ten tie tin tit en id in it ne ti

deintu united untied indue nudie tuned unite untie dent diet dine duet dune edit etui nide nude tend tide tied tine tune unit den die din dit due dun end net nit nut ted ten tie tin tui tun en id in it ne nu ti ut

deintw twined twine widen wined wited dent diet dine edit newt nide tend tide tied tine twin wend wide wind wine wite den dew die din dit end net new nit ted ten tie tin wed wen wet win wit en id in it ne ti we

deinu indue nudie dine dune nide nude den die din due dun end en id in ne nu

deinw widen wined dine nide wend wide wind wine den dew die din dew end new wed wen win en id in ne we

deinx index nixed dine nide nixe den die din end nix en ex id in ne xi

deinz dizen dine nide zein den die din end zed en id in ne

deiooprr droopier. *See* **deiopr eooprr**

deioorsw woodsier dowries rowdies weirdos woodier. *See* **deiors deiorw deoors deorsw**

deioorw woodier. *See* **deiorw deoor deoow**

deioost osteoid. *See* **eioost deoost deiost**

deioostw woodiest osteoid. *See* **deiost deistw deoost deostw**

deiopr dopier period doper pored pride pried roped dire doer dope drip drop oped peri pied pier pore prod redo repo ride ripe rode rope die dip doe dor ire ode ope ore per pie pod poi pro red rep rid rip rod roe do er id od or pe pi re

deioprrv provider provide. *See* **deiopr deiorv deirrv deoprv**

deioprs periods. *See* **deoprs deiopr deiors deiops deiprs**

deioprst diopters deports deposit diopter dopiest editors periods posited redtops sported steroid storied topside triodes. *See* **deiopr deiops deiors deiort**

deioprsv disprove provides devisor periods provide. *See* **deiopr deiops deiors deiorv**

deioprt diopter. *See* **deoprt deiort deiopr dioprt**

deioprv provide. *See* **deiorv deiopr deoprv**

deiops poised dopes poise posed spied dies dips does dope dose epos ides

odes oped opes peso pied pies pods pois pose side sped die dip doe dos ids ode ope pie pod poi sip sod sop do id is od os pe pi si so

deiopss dispose. *See* **deiops eiopss**

deiopsss disposes dispose. *See* **deiops eiopss**

deiopsst deposits topsides deposit despots dispose dopiest posited topside. *See* **deiops deiost deipst deisst**

deiopst deposit dopiest posited topside. *See* **deopst deiops deipst deiost**

deioptt tiptoed. *See* **deiptt deoptt eioptt**

deioptv pivoted. *See* **deopt diotv ioptv**

deiorrss drossier dossier orrises. *See* **deiors deirrs deorrs deorss**

deiorrsw drowsier dowries rewords rowdier rowdies weirdos wordier worried worries. *See* **deiors deiorw deirrs deorrs**

deiorrsy derisory. *See* **deiors deirrs deorrs derrsy**

deiorrtu outrider outride. *See* **deiort deorru deortu diorrt**

deiorrw rowdier wordier worried. *See* **deiorw deorrw**

deiors dories doers dries osier rides rosed sired dies dire doer does dose ides odes ores redo reds reis ride rids rise rode rods roes rose side sire sore sori die doe dor dos ids ire ode ore red res rid rod roe sir sod do er id is od or os re si so

deiorss dossier. *See* **deiors deorss**

deiorsss dossiers dossier dossers. *See* **deiors deorss**

deiorsst steroids dossier editors rosiest sorites sorties steroid storied stories strides triodes. *See* **deiors deiort deiost deirst**

deiorssu desirous dossier serious. *See* **deiors deissu deorss deorsu**

deiorssv devisors dossier devisor. *See* **deiors deiorv deiosv deirsv**

deiorst editors steroid storied triodes. *See* **deirst deiors deorst diorst deiort**

deiorstu outrides outsider detours dustier editors outride outside rousted steroid storied tedious triodes. *See* **deiors deiort deiost deirst**

deiorstw rowdiest wordiest dowries editors rowdies steroid storied triodes weirdos worsted. *See* **deiors deiort deiorw deiost**

deiorsv devisor. *See* **deiorv deirsv deiors deorsv deiosv**

deiorsw dowries rowdies weirdos. *See* **deiors deorsw deiorw**

deiorsww widowers dowries rowdies weirdos widower. *See* **deiors deiorw deorsw diosww**

deiort editor rioted triode doter droit tired tried diet dire dirt doer doit dote edit redo ride riot rite rode rote tide tied tier tire tiro toed tore tori trio trod die dit doe dor dot ire ode ore ort red ret rid rod roe rot ted tie tod toe tor do er id it od or re ti to

deiortt dottier. *See* **deiort deortt**

deiortu outride. *See* **deortu deiort**

deiorv devoir diver drive drove rived roved video dire dive doer dove over redo ride rive rode rove vied void die doe dor ire ode ore red rev rid rod roe vie do er id od or re

deiorw weirdo dower rowed weird wider wired dire doer drew owed redo ride rode weir wide wire word wore dew die doe dor ire ode ore owe red rid rod roe row wed woe do er id od or ow re we

deiorww widower. *See* **deiorw dioww**

deiorz dozier dire doer doze redo ride rode zero zori die doe dor ire ode ore red rid rod roe zed do er id od or re

deiosstu outsides outside studies studios tedious. *See* **deiost deisst deissu deistu**

deiost todies deist diets doits dotes edits sited tides dies diet dits does doit dose dote dots edit ides odes side site teds tide tied ties toed toes die dit doe dos dot ids its ode set sit sod sot ted tie tod toe do id is it od os si so ti to

deiosttt dottiest. *See* **deiost deostt diostt**

deiostu outside tedious. *See* **deistu deostu diostu deiost**

deiostuz outsized doziest outside outsize tedious. *See* **deiost deistu deostu**

deiostz doziest. *See* **deiost deosz deisz**

deiosuv devious. *See* **deiosv deosu**

deiosv videos dives doves video vised voids dive does dose dove ides odes side vied vies vise void die doe dos ids ode sod vie do id is od os si so

deiosx doxies oxides oxide dies does dose ides odes side die doe dos ids ode sex six sod sox do ex id is od os ox si so xi

deiov video dive dove vied void die doe ode vie do id od

deiox oxide die doe ode do ex id od ox xi

deip pied die dip pie id pe pi

deipp piped pied pipe die dip pep pie pip id pe pi

deippp pipped piped pied pipe die dip pep pie pip id pe pi

deippqu quipped. *See* **deipqu deipp**

deippr dipper ripped piped piper pride pried dire drip peri pied pier pipe prep

deipprs dippers. *See* **deippr eipprs deiprs deipps**

deipprst stripped dippers striped tippers tripped. *See* **deippr deipps deippt deiprs**

deipprt tripped. *See* **deippr deippt eipprt**

deipps sipped piped pipes spied dies dips ides peps pied pies pipe pips side sped die dip ids pep pie pip sip id is pe pi si

deippt tipped piped tepid diet edit pied pipe tide tied die dip dit pep pet pie pip pit ted tie tip id it pe pi ti

deippy yipped piped dippy pied pipe pipy yipe dey die dip dye pep pie pip yep yip id pe pi ye

deippz zipped piped pied pipe die dip pep pie pip zed zip id pe pi

deippqu piqued equip pique pied quid quip die dip due pie id pe pi up

deipr pride dried drip peri pied pier ride ripe die dip ire per pie red rep rid rip er id pe pi re

deiprrtu irrupted. *See* **deprru diprtu**

deiprs prides spider spired dries drips piers pride pried pries rides sired spied spire dies dips dire drip ides peri pied pier pies reds reis reps ride rids ripe rips rise side sire sped die dip ids ire per pie red rep res rid rip sip sir er id is pe pi re si

deiprss spiders. *See* **deiprs eiprss**

deiprssu suspired pussier spiders suspire uprises upsides. *See* **deiprs deipsu deissu deprsu**

deiprst striped. *See* **deirst eiprst deiprs deipst**

deiprstz spritzed striped. *See* **deiprs deiprz deipst deirst**

deiprsy spidery. *See* **deiprs**

deiprz prized pride pried prize dire drip peri pied pier ride ripe die dip ire per pie red rep rid rip zed zip er id pe pi re

deips spied dies dips ides pied pies side sped die dip ids pie sip id is pe pi si

deipsstu disputes dispute studies upsides. *See* **deipst deipsu deisst deissu**

deipssu upsides. *See* **deissu deipsu**

deipst spited deist diets edits sited spied spite stipe tepid tides dies diet dips dits edit ides pest pets pied pies pits sept side site sped spit step teds tide tied ties tips die dip dit ids its pet pie pit set sip sit ted tie tip id is it pe pi si ti

deipstu dispute. *See* **deistu deipst dipstu deipsu**

deipsu upside spied dies dips dues ides pied pies side sped spud spue sued used die dip due ids pie pus sip sue sup use id is pe pi si up us

deipsw swiped spied swipe wiped wipes dews dies dips ides pews pied pies side sped spew weds wide wipe wise wisp dew die dip ids pew pie sew sip wed wis id is pe pi si we

deipsxy pyxides. *See* **eipsxy deips**

deipt tepid diet edit pied tide tied die dip dit pet pie pit ted tie tip id it pe pi ti

deiptt pitted tepid petit diet edit pied tide tied die dip dit pet pie pit ted tie tip tit id it pe pi ti

deipttu puttied. *See* **deiptt**

deipw wiped pied wide wipe dew die dip pew pie wed id pe pi we

deiqrstu squirted dustier querist quirted squired. *See* **deiqru deirst deistu derstu**

deiqrsu squired. *See* **deiqru eiqrsu**

deiqrtu quirted. *See* **deiqru eiqtu iqrtu**

deiqru quired quire dire quid ride rude rued die due ire red rid rue urd er id re

deiqttu quitted. *See* **eiqtu**

deiquzz quizzed. *No 6s or 5s*

deir dire ride die ire red rid er id re

deirr direr drier rider dire ride die err ire red rid er id re

deirrs derris riders sirred direr drier dries rider rides riser sired dies dire errs ides reds reis ride rids rise side sire die err ids ire red res rid sir er id is re si

deirrst stirred. *See* **deirrs deirst**

deirrstu sturdier dustier rustier stirred. *See* **deirrs deirst deistu derstu**

deirrsv drivers. *See* **deirrs deirsv deirrv eirrsv**

deirrv driver direr diver drier drive rider rived river dire dive ride rive vied die err ire red rev rid vie er id re

deirs dries rides sired dies dire ides reds reis ride rids rise side sire die ids ire red res rid sir er id is re si

deirssst distress desists resists sisters strides. *See* **deirst deisst eirsst**

deirsst strides. *See* **deisst deirst eirsst**

deirst direst driest stride deist diets dries edits rides rites sired sited tides tiers tired tires tried tries dies diet dire dirt dits edit erst ides reds reis rest rets ride rids rise rite side sire site stir teds tide tied tier ties tire die dit ids ire its red res ret rid set sir sit ted tie er id is it re si ti

deirstu dustier. *See* **deirst derstu deistu**

deirstv diverts. *See* **deirst deirsv deirtv deistv eirstv**

deirsuvv survived survive. *See* **deirsv**

deirsv divers drives diver dives dries drive rides rived sired vised dies dire dive ides reds reis revs ride rids rise rive side sire vied vies vise die ids ire red res rev rid sir vie er id is re si

deirt tired tried diet dire dirt edit ride rite tide tied tier tire die dit ire red ret rid ted tie er id it re ti

deirtv divert diver drive rived rivet tired tried diet dire dirt dive edit ride rite rive tide tied tier tire vert vied die dit ire red ret rev rid ted tie vet vie er id it re ti

deirv diver drive rived dire dive ride rive vied die ire red rev rid vie er id re

deirw weird wider wired dire drew ride weir wide wire dew die ire red rid wed er id re we

deis dies ides side die ids id is si

deiss sides dies ides side die ess ids sis id is si

deissst desists. *See* **deisst**

deisssu disuses. *See* **deissu eisssu**

deisst deists desist desit diets edits sides sited sites tides dies diet dits edit ides sets side site sits teds tide tied ties die dit ess ids its set sis sit ted tie id is it si ti

deissttu dustiest studies. *See* **deisst deissu deistu eisstu**

deisstu studies. *See* **deisst deissu deistu eisstu**

deisstv divests. *See* **deisst deistv**

deissu disuse issued sides issue dies dues ides side suds sued sues used uses die due ess ids sis sue use id is si us

deist deist diets edits sited tides dies diet dits edit ides side site teds tide tied ties die dit ids its set sit ted tie id is it si ti

deisttw twisted. *See* **deistw isttw**

deistu duties suited deist diets duets edits etuis sited suite tides dies diet dits dues duet dust edit etui ides side site stud sued suet suit teds tide tied ties tuis used die dit due ids its set sit sue ted tie tui use id is it si ti us ut

deistv divest deist diets dives edits sited tides vised dies diet dits dive edit ides side site teds tide tied ties vest vets vied vies vise die dit ids its set sit ted tie vet vie id it si ti

deistw widest deist diets edits sited tides wited wites dews dies diet dits edit ides side site stew teds tide tied ties weds west wets wide wise wite wits dew die dit ids its set sew sit ted tie wed wet wis wit id is it si ti we

deisv dives vised dies dive ides side vied vies vise die ids vie id is si

deisz sized dies ides side size zeds die ids zed id is si

deit diet edit tide tied die dit ted tie id it ti

deitttw twitted. *See* **deitw**

deitw wited diet edit tide tied wide wite dew die dit ted tie wed wet wit id it ti we

deity deity diet edit tide tidy tied yeti dey die dit dye ted tie yet id it ti ye

deiv dive vied die vie id

deivw wived dive vied view wide wive dew die vie wed id we

deiw wide dew die wed id we

dejknu junked juked nuked duke dune dunk juke junk neuk nude nuke den due dun end ken en ne nu

dejko joked joke doe joe ode oke do jo od

dejku juked duke juke due

dejlost jostled. *See* **dejlot ejlost delost**

dejlot jolted dole dolt dote jolt lode toed told doe dot eld jet joe jot led let lot ode old ted tod toe do el jo lo od to

dejlstu justled. *See* **delstu ejlstu**

dejmpu jumped umped dump jump due emu mud ump em me mu pe um up

dejostu jousted. *See* **deostu jostu ejstu**

dejott jotted toted dote toed tote doe dot jet joe jot ode ted tod toe tot do jo od to

dejttu jutted duet jute due jet jut ted tut ut

dekklsu skulked. *See* **deklsu kklsu**

dekknsu skunked. *See* **kknsu**

dekkuy yukked duke dyke dey due dye key yuk ye

dekllno knolled. *See* **dekno eklln kllno**

deklnpu plunked. *See* **delpu deknu klnpu**

deklnru knurled. *See* **eklnru deklru delnru**

dekloo looked looed dole koel kolo lode look oleo doe eld elk led lek loo ode oke old do el lo od

dekloy yolked yodel yoked yokel dole dyke koel lode yoke yolk dey doe dye eld elk key led lek lye ode oke old yod do el lo od oy ye

deklru lurked lured ruled duel duke lure lurk rude rued rule due eld elk led lek leu red rue urd el er re

deklsu sulked duels dukes dulse desk duel dues duke dusk elks leks lues sled slue sued sulk used due eld elk els led lek leu sue use el us

dekmos smoked demos domes modes mokes smoke demo desk does dome dose mode mods moke odes okes soke some doe dos kos mod mos ode oke oms sod do em me mo od om os so

deknnru drunken. *See* **dknru deknu denru**

dekno kendo done keno node den doe don end eon ken nod ode oke one do en ne no od on

deknosy donkeys. *See* **deknoy denosy**

deknott knotted. *See* **dekno denot dekot**

deknotu knouted. *See* **dnotu dekno knotu**

deknoy donkey doyen kendo yoked deny done dyke dyne keno node yoke yond den dey doe don dye end eon ken key nod ode oke one yen yod yon do en ne no od on oy ye

deknoz zonked dozen kendo zoned done doze keno node zone zonk den doe don end eon ken nod ode oke one zed do en ne no od on

deknu nuked duke dune dunk neuk nude nuke den due dun end ken en ne nu

dekooprv provoked provoke. *See* **dekoor deoorv deoprv**

dekoops spooked. *See* **dekops koops**

dekoor rooked rodeo doer door odor ordo redo rode rood rook doe dor kor ode oke ore red rod roe do er od or re

dekootww kowtowed. *See* **kootww**

dekop poked dope oped poke doe ode oke ope pod do od pe

dekops spooked dopes poked pokes posed spoke desk does dope dose epos odes okes oped opes peso pods poke pose skep soke sped doe dos kos ode oke ope pod sod sop do od os pe so

dekopst desktop. *See* **deopst dekops dekost**

dekorst stroked. *See* **deorst ekorst**

dekorw worked dower rowed doer drew owed redo rode woke word wore work dew doe dor kor ode oke ore owe red rod roe row wed woe wok do er od or ow re we

dekost stoked dotes stoke toked tokes desk does dose dote dots odes okes soke teds toed toes toke doe dos dot kos ode oke set sod sot ted tod toe tsk do od os so to

dekot toked dote toed toke doe dot ode oke ted tod toe do od to

dekoy yoked dyke yoke dey doe dye key ode oke yod do od oy ye

dekpu puked duke puke due pe up

deks desk

dekss desks desk ess

deksu dukes desk dues duke dusk sued used due sue use us

deksy dykes desk deys dyes dyke keys dey dye key sky yes ye

deku duke due

deky dyke dey dye key ye

del eld led el

dell dell ell dell led el

delllo lolled dell dole doll lode loll doe eld ell led ode old do el lo od

delllu lulled dell duel dull lull due eld ell led leu el

dellmu mulled dell duel dull meld mell mule mull due eld ell elm emu led leu lum mel mud el em me mu um

dellnssu dullness. *See* **delssu ellnss ellnsu elnssu**

dellop polled loped poled dell dole doll dope lode lope oped pled plod pole poll doe eld ell led lop ode old ope pod do el lo od pe

delloptu polluted pollute. *See* **dellop dellot dellpu deoptu**

dellor rolled older droll dell doer dole doll lode lord lore orle redo rode role roll doe dor eld ell led ode old ore red rod roe do el er lo od or re

dellorry drollery orderly. *See* **dellor dllory ellorr**

dellorst strolled trolled oldster. *See* **dellor dellot delors delort**

dellort trolled. *See* **delort dellor dellot**

dellot tolled dell dole doll dolt dote lode tell toed told toll doe dot eld ell led let lot ode old ted tod toe do el lo od to

dellpu pulled duple puled dell duel dull pled pule pull due eld ell led leu pul el pe up

dellru duller lured ruled dell duel dull lure rude rued rule due eld ell led leu red rue urd el er re

dells dells dell ells sell sled eld ell els led el

dellstu dullest. *See* **delstu ellstu**

dellsw dwells dells dwell swell welds wells dell dews ells lewd sell sled slew weds weld well dew eld ell els led sew wed el we

dellw dwell dell lewd weld well dew eld ell led wed el we

dellwy lewdly dwell dell dewy lewd weld well yell dew dey dye eld ell led lye wed wye yew el we ye

delm meld eld elm led mel el em me

delmmsu slummed. *See* **demmsu delsu delms**

delmno dolmen demon lemon loden melon model olden demo dole dome done enol lend leno lode lone meld mend mode mold mole node noel nome omen den doe don eld elm end eon led mel men mod mon nod ode old one do el em en lo me mo ne no od om on

delmnotw meltdown letdown. *See* **delmno delmot denotw elmnot**

delmnpuu pendulum. *See* **delmpu**

delmo model demo dole dome lode meld mode mold mole doe eld elm led mel mod ode old do el em lo me mo od om

delmoo loomed looed model mooed demo dole dome doom lode loom meld

mode mold mole mood oleo doe eld elm led loo mel mod moo ode old do el em lo me mo od om

delmor molder model morel older demo doer dole dome dorm lode lord lore meld merl mode mold mole more omer orle redo rode role doe dor eld elm led mel mod mor ode old ore red rem rod roe do el em er lo me mo od om or re

delmors molders smolder. *See* **delmos delmor elmors delors**

delmorss smolders molders morsels smolder solders. *See* **delmor delmos delors deorss**

delmorsu smoulder modules molders smolder. *See* **delmor delmos delmou delors**

delmos models seldom demos doles domes lodes melds model modes molds moles soled demo does dole dome dose elms lode lose meld mels mode mods mold mole odes sled sloe sold sole some doe dos eld elm els led los mel mod mos ode old oms sod sol do el em lo me mo od om os so

delmosty modestly modesty. *See* **delmos delmot delmoy delost**

delmosu modules. *See* **delmos delmou dlmosu demosu**

delmot molted model motel demo dole dolt dome dote lode meld melt mode mold mole molt mote toed told tome doe dot eld elm led let lot mel met mod mot ode old ted tod toe tom do el em lo me mo od om to

delmott mottled. *See* **delott delmot elmott**

delmotu moulted. *See* **delmot delmou**

delmou module model mould demo dole dome duel lode loud meld mode mold mole mule doe due duo eld elm emu led leu lum mel mod mud ode old oud udo do el em lo me mo mu od om um

delmoy melody model moldy yodel demo demy dole dome lode meld mode mold mole moly ylem dey doe dye eld elm led lye mel mod ode old yod do el em lo me mo my od om oy ye

delmppu plumped. *See* **delmpu elmppu delppu demppu**

delmpru rumpled. *See* **dempru delmpu delpru elmpru**

delmpsu slumped. *See* **delmpu elmpsu dempsu**

delmpu lumped plumed duple plume puled umped duel dump lump meld mule pled plum pule due eld elm emu led leu lum mel mud pul ump el em me mu pe um up

delms melds elms meld mels sled eld elm els led mel el em me

delmuzz muzzled. *See* **elmuzz**

deln lend den eld end led el en ne

delno loden olden dole done enol lend leno lode lone node noel den doe don eld end eon led nod ode old one do el en lo ne no od on

delnoo noodle loden looed olden dole done enol lend leno lode lone loon node noel oleo den doe don eld end eon led loo nod ode old one do el en lo ne no od on

delnoos noodles. *See* **deloos elnoos denoos delnoo**

delnoowy woodenly. *See* **delnoo delowy denoow elnoow**

delnoprs splendor polders ponders respond rondels. *See* **delnor delopr delops delors**

delnor rondel drone loden loner olden older doer dole done enol lend leno lode lone lord lore lorn nerd node noel orle redo rend rode role den doe don dor eld end eon led nod nor ode old one ore red rod roe do el en er lo ne no od on or re

delnors rondels. *See* **denors elnors delors delnor**

delnorsu roundels nodules resound rondels roundel rundles sounder. *See* **delnor delnou delnru delors**

delnortu roundlet roundel trundle. *See* **delnor delnou delnru delort**

delnoru roundel. *See* **delnou deloru delnru**

delnoss oldness. *See* **denoss elnoss**

delnossu loudness oldness nodules. *See* **delnou delssu denoss denosu**

delnostw letdowns letdown. *See* **delost delosw denost denosw**

delnosu nodules. *See* **delnou denosu**

delnosuv unsolved nodules unloved. *See* **delnou delosv denosu elnosv**

delnotw letdown. *See* **denotw delow deltw**

delnoty notedly. *See* **denoy elnot delno**

delnou louden nodule loden olden dole done enol lend leno lode lone loud lune node noel nude undo den doe don due dun duo eld end eon led leu nod ode old one oud udo do el en lo ne no nu od on

delnouv unloved. *See* **delnou**

delnprsu plunders plunder rundles slurped spurned. *See* **delnru delpru denpru denpsu**

delnpru plunder. *See* **denpru delpru delnru**

delnrstu trundles rundles runlets rustled strudel trundle. *See* **delnru delstu denrst denrsu**

delnrsu rundles. *See* **denrsu delnru**

delnrtu trundle. *See* **delnru elnrtu denrtu**

delnru rundle lured ruled under duel dune lend lune lure nerd nude rend rude rued rule rune den due dun eld end led leu red rue run urd urn el en er ne nu re

delns lends dens ends lend lens send sled den eld els end ens led sen el en ne

delnuy nudely deny duel duly dune dyne lend lune nude yule den dey due dun dye eld end led leu lye yen el en ne nu ye

delnuzz nuzzled. *See* **elnuzz**

delo dole lode doe eld led ode old do el lo od

deloo looed dole lode oleo doe eld led loo ode old do el lo od

deloop looped poodle pooled looed loped poled dole dope lode loop lope oleo oped pled plod pole polo pool doe eld led loo lop ode old ope pod do el lo od pe

deloops poodles spooled. *See* **deloop deloos dloops delops**

deloorrv overlord. *See* **deoorv deorrv**

deloorss odorless solders. *See* **deloos delors deoors deorss**

deloos loosed oodles soloed doles lodes looed loose oleos soloed does dole dose lode loos lose odes oleo sled sloe sold sole solo doe dos eld els led loo los ode old sod sol do el lo od os so

deloost stooled. *See* **deloos deloot delost deoost**

deloot looted tooled looed dole dolt dote lode loot oleo toed told tool doe dot eld led let loo lot ode old ted tod toe too do el lo od to

deloott tootled. *See* **delott deoott eloott**

delop loped poled dole dope lode lope oped pled plod pole doe eld led lop ode old ope pod do el lo od pe

delopp lopped loped poled dole dope lode lope oped pled plod plop pole pope doe eld led lop ode old ope pep pod pop do el lo od pe

deloppp plopped poppled. *See* **delopp deoppp eloppp**

delopps slopped. *See* **delopp elopps delops deopps**

deloppst stoppled slopped stopped stopple toppled topples. *See* **delopp delops delost deopps**

deloppt toppled. *See* **delopp deoppt eloppt**

delopr polder doper loped loper older poled pored roped doer dole dope drop lode lope lord lore oped orle pled plod pole pore prod redo repo rode role rope doe dor eld led lop ode old ope ore per pod pro red rep rod roe do el er lo od or pe re

deloprs polders. *See* **deoprs eloprs delopr delors delops**

deloprst droplets deports oldster petrols polders redtops sported. *See* **delopr delops delors delort**

deloprw prowled. *See* **delopw delopr deoprw**

delops sloped doles dopes lodes loped lopes plods poled poles posed slope soled does dole dope dose epos lode lope lops lose odes oped opes peso pled plod pods pole pose sled sloe slop sold sole sped doe dos eld els led lop los ode old ope pod sod sol sop do el lo od os pe so

delopstu postlude loudest spouted tousled tupelos. *See* **delops delost delstu deopst**

delopsy deploys. *See* **delopy delops delosy**

deloptt plotted. *See* **delott deoptt eloptt**

delopw plowed dowel loped lowed poled dole dope lewd lode lope oped owed pled plod plow pole weld wold dew doe eld led lop low ode old ope owe owl pew pod wed woe do el lo od ow pe we

delopy deploy dopey loped poled yodel dole dope lode lope oped pled plod ploy pole yelp dey doe dye eld led lop lye ode old ope ply pod yep yod do el lo od oy pe ye

delor older doer dole lode lord lore orle redo rode role doe dor eld led ode old ore red rod roe do el er lo od or re

delorrt realtor. *see* **aelrt aeort eorrt**

delorry orderly. *See* **derry lorry delor**

delors resold solder doers doles lodes lords lores loser older orles roles rosed soled doer does dole dose lode lord lore lose odes ores orle redo reds rode rods roes role rose sled sloe sold sole sore doe dor dos eld els led los ode old ore red res rod roe sod sol do el er lo od or os re so

delorss solders. *See* **deorss elorss**

delorsst oldsters oldster ostlers solders sterols. *See* **delors delort delost deorss**

delorssw wordless solders drowses. *See* **delors delosw deorss deorsw**

delorst oldster. *See* **deorst delost elorst delort delors**

delorsuy delusory elusory. *See* **delors deloru delosy delruy**

delort retold older doter doer dole dolt dote lode lord lore orle redo rode role rote rotl toed told tore trod doe dor dot eld led let lot ode old ore ort red ret rod roe rot ted tod toe tor do el er lo od or re to

deloru louder lured older ruled uredo doer dole dour duel duro lode lord lore loud lure orle redo rode role rude rued rule doe dor due duo eld led leu ode old ore oud our red rod roe rue udo urd do el er lo od or re

delos doles lodes soled does dole dose lode lose odes sled sloe sold sole doe dos eld els led los ode old sod sol do el lo od os so

delossuu sedulous. *See* **delssu deossu**

delost oldest doles dolts dotes lodes soled stole does dole dolt dose dote dots lest lets lode lose lost lots odes sled sloe slot sold sole teds toed toes told doe dos dot eld els led let los lot ode old set sod sol sot ted tod toe do el lo od os so to

delostt dottles slotted. *See* **delott deostt**

delostu loudest tousled. *See* **delstu delost deostu elostu**

delosv solved doles doves lodes loved loves soled solve velds voles does dole dose dove lode lose love odes sled sloe sold sole veld vole doe dos eld els led lev los ode old sod sol do el lo od os so

delosw dowels slowed doles dowel dowse lodes lowed soled sowed welds dews does dole dose lewd lode lose lows odes owed owes owls sled slew sloe slow sold sole weds weld woes wold dew doe dos eld els led los low ode old owe owl sew sod sol sow wed woe do el lo od os ow so we

delosy yodels doles lodes lysed soled yodel deys does dole dose dyes lode lose lyes lyse odes oyes sled sloe sold sole yods dey doe dos dye eld els led los lye ode old sly sod sol soy yes yod do el lo od os oy so ye

deloszz sozzled. *See* **delos deosz**

delott dottle lotted toted dole dolt dote lode toed told tote doe dot eld led let lot ode old ted tod toe tot do el lo od to

delotuv voluted. *See* **deotuv elotuv**

delotuvy devoutly voluted. *See* **deotuv elotuv**

delov loved dole dove lode love veld vole doe eld led lev ode old do el lo od

delow dowel lowed dole lewd lode owed weld wold dew doe eld led low ode old owe owl wed woe do el lo od ow we

delowy yowled dowel lowed yodel dewy dole lewd lode owed weld wold yowl dew dey doe dye eld led low lye ode old owe owl wed woe wye yew yod yow do el lo od ow oy we ye

deloy yodel dole lode dey doe dye eld led lye ode old yod do el lo od oy ye

delp pled eld led el pe

delppru purpled. *See* **delppu delpru elppru**

delppsu suppled. *See* **delppu deppsu elppsu**

delppu pulped duple puled duel pled pule pulp due eld led leu pep pul pup el pe up

delprsu slurped. *See* **deprsu elprsu delpru**

delpru purled drupe duper duple lured perdu prude puled ruled duel lure pled pule pure purl rude rued rule due eld led leu per pul red rep rue urd el er pe re up

delpu duple puled duel pled pule due eld led leu pul el pe up

delpux duplex duple puled duel luxe pled pule due eld led leu lux pul el ex pe up

delpuzz puzzled. *See* **elpuzz delpu**

delrrsu slurred. *See* **elrrsu dersu delsu**

delrsstu strudels dusters results rustled rustles strudel trussed tussled ulsters. *See* **delssu delstu derssu derstu**

delrstu rustled strudel. *See* **derstu delstu elrstu**

delru lured ruled duel lure rude rued rule due eld led leu red rue urd el er re

delruy rudely lured ruled duel duly dyer lure lyre rely rude rued rule yule dey dry due dye eld led leu lye red rue rye urd el er re ye

dels sled eld els led el

delss sleds sled less eld els ess led el

delssstu dustless tussled tussles. *See* **delssu delstu elsstu .dsstu**

delsstu tussled. *See* **delssu elsstu**

delssu dulses duels dulse sleds slues duel dues less lues sled slue suds sued sues used uses due eld els ess led leu sue use el us

delstu lusted duels duets dulse luted lutes tules duel dues duet dust lest lets lues lust lute sled slue slut stud sued suet teds tule used due eld els led let leu set sue ted use el us ut

delstv veldts velds veldt lest lets sled teds veld vest vets eld els led let lev set ted vet el

delsty styled lysed style deys dyes lest lets lyes lyse sled teds dey dye eld els led let lye set sly sty ted yes yet el ye

delsu duels dulse duel dues lues sled slue sued used due eld els led leu sue use el us

delsv velds sled veld eld els led lev el

delsw welds dews lewd sled slew weds weld dew eld els led sew wed el we

delsy lysed deys dyes lyes lyse sled dey dye eld els led lye sly yes el ye

deltu luted duel duet lute tule due eld led let leu ted el ut

deltv veldt veld eld led let lev ted vet el

deltw dwelt lewd weld welt dew eld led let ted wed wet el we

delu duel due eld led leu el

delv veld eld led lev el

delw lewd weld dew eld led wed el we

demmnosu summoned. *See* **demmos demmsu demnos demosu**

demmo modem demo dome memo mode mome doe mem mod mom ode do em me mo od om

demmos modems demos domes memos modem modes momes demo does dome dose memo mems mode mods mome moms odes some doe dos mem mod mom mos ode oms sod do em me mo od om os so

demmrrsu drummers drummer murders rummers. *See* **demmsu demrru demrsu**

demmrru drummer. *See* **demrru emmrru**

demmrruu murmured drummer. *See* **demrru emmrru**

demmrstu strummed stummed. *See* **demmsu demrsu derstu emrstu**

demmstu stummed. *See* **demmsu destu demtu**

demmsu summed mused sedum dues emus mems muds mums muse sued used due emu mem mud mum mus sue sum use em me mu um us

demn mend den end men em en me ne

demno demon demo dome done mend mode node nome omen den doe don end eon men mod mon nod ode one do em en me mo ne no od om on

demnoo mooned demon mooed demo dome done doom mend mode mono mood moon node nome omen den doe don end eon men mod mon moo nod ode one do em en me mo ne no od om on

demnooop monopode. *See* **demnoo**

demnoor doormen. *See* **demnor demnoo demoor**

demnoosw woodsmen woodmen swooned. *See* **demnoo demnos denoos denoow**

demnoow woodmen. *See* **demnoo denoow**

demnor modern demon drone demo doer dome done dorm mend mode more morn nerd node nome norm omen omer redo rend rode den doe don dor end eon men mod mon mor nod nor ode one ore red rem rod roe do em en er me mo ne no od om on or re

demnors moderns. *See* **demnos denors demnor emnors**

demnorst mordents endmost mentors moderns monster mordent rodents snorted stormed. *See* **demnor demnos demost denors**

demnorsy syndrome moderns. *See* **demnor demnos denors denory**

demnort mordent. *See* **emnort demnor denort**

demnoru mourned. *See* **demnor demru dmnou**

demnos demons demon demos domes mends meson modes nodes nomes nosed omens sonde demo dens does dome done dons dose ends eons mend mode mods mons node nods noes nome nose odes omen ones send some den doe don dos end ens eon men mod mon mos nod ode oms one sen sod son do em en me mo ne no od om on os so

demnost endmost. *See* **demnos demost emnost denost**

demnotu mounted. *See* **demno dnotu emnot**

demnouv unmoved. *See* **demno dmnou demov**

demns mends dens ends mend send den end ens men sen em en me ne

demnstu dustmen. *See* **denst destu densu**

demo demo dome mode doe mod ode do em me mo od om

demoo mooed demo dome doom mode mood doe mod moo ode do em me mo od om

demoopp popedom. *See* **demopp deoopp**

demoopps popedoms popedom opposed. *See* **demopp deoopp deopps eoopps**

demooprt promoted motored promote torpedo trooped. *See* **demoor demopr deoort deoprt**

demoor moored roomed mooed rodeo demo doer dome doom door dorm mode mood moor more odor omer ordo redo rode rood room doe dor mod moo mor ode ore red rem rod roe do em er me mo od om or re

demoorsu dormouse. *See* **demoor demosu demrsu deoors**

demoort motored. *See* **demoor deoort**

demooss osmosed. *See* **emooss demos dmoos**

demop moped demo dome dope mode mope oped poem pome doe mod mop ode ope pod do em me mo od om pe

demopp mopped moped demo dome dope mode mope oped poem pome pomp pope doe mod mop ode ope pep pod pop do em me mo od om pe

demopprt prompted. *See* **demopp demopr deoppt deoprt**

demopr romped doper moped pored proem roped demo doer dome dope dorm drop mode mope more omer oped perm poem pome pore prod prom redo repo rode romp rope doe dor mod mop mor ode ope ore per pod pro red rem rep rod roe do em er me mo od om or pe re

demopst stomped. *See* **deopst demost emopst**

demorr dormer order ormer demo doer dome dorm mode more omer redo rode doe dor err mod mor ode ore red rem rod roe do em er me mo od om or re

demorrs dormers. *See* **demorr deorrs emorrs**

demorru rumored. *See* **demorr demrru deorru**

demorst stormed. *See* **deorst emorst demost**

demorw wormed dower mowed mower rowed demo doer dome dorm drew meow mode more omer owed redo rode word wore worm dew doe dor mew mod mor mow ode ore owe red rem rod roe row wed woe do em er me mo od om or ow re we

demos demos domes modes demo does dome dose mode mods odes some doe dos mod mos ode oms sod do em me mo od om os so

demost modest demos domes dotes modes motes smote tomes demo does dome dose dote dots mode mods most mote mots odes some stem teds toed toes tome toms doe dos dot met mod mos mot ode oms set sod sot ted tod toe tom do em me mo od om os so to

demosty modesty. *See* **demost emosy deoty**

demosu moused demos domes douse modes mouse mused sedum demo does dome dose dues duos emus mode mods muds muse odes ouds some sued sumo udos used doe dos due duo emu mod mos mud mus ode oms oud sod sou sue sum udo use do em me mo mu od om os so um us

demov moved demo dome dove mode move doe mod ode do em me mo od om

demow mowed demo dome meow mode owed dew doe mew mod mow ode owe wed woe do em me mo od om ow we

demppu pumped umped dump pump due emu mud pep pup ump em me mu pe um up

demprsu dumpers. *See* **demrsu deprsu dempru dempsu**

demprtu trumped. *See* **dempru eprtu demtu**

dempru dumper demur drupe duper perdu prude umped drum dump perm pure rude rued rump due emu mud per red rem rep rue rum ump urd em er me mu pe re um up

dempstu stumped. *See* **dempsu empstu**

dempsu spumed dumps mused sedum spume umped dues dump emus muds muse sped spud spue sued sump umps used due emu mud mus pus sue sum sup ump use em me mu pe um up us

dempu umped dump due emu mud ump em me mu pe um up

demrrsu murders. *See* **demrru demrsu**

demrru murder demur murre ruder drum rude rued due emu err mud red rem rue rum urd em er me mu re um

demrsu demurs demur drums druse mused sedum serum drum dues emus muds muse reds rude rued rues rums ruse sued surd sure urds used user due emu mud mus red rem res rue rum sue sum urd use em er me mu re um us

demru demur drum rude rued due emu mud red rem rue rum urd em er me mu re um

demssu mussed sedums mused muses sedum dues emus mess muds muse muss suds sued sues sums used uses due emu ess mud mus sue sum use em me mu um us

demsttu smutted. *See* **destu demsu emstu**

demsu mused sedum dues emus muds muse sued used due emu mud mus sue sum use em me mu um us

demtu muted duet mute due emu met mud ted em me mu um ut

demy demy dey dye em me my ye

den den end en ne

dennost tendons. *See* **ennost denost dennot**

dennot tendon nonet noted tenon toned tonne dent done dote neon node none note tend toed tone den doe don dot end eon net nod not ode one ted ten tod toe ton do en ne no od on to

dennou undone done dune neon node none noun nude undo den doe don due dun duo end eon nod nun ode one oud udo do en ne no nu od on

dennow wonned endow owned done down enow neon node none owed wend den dew doe don end eon new nod now ode one own wed wen woe won do en ne no od on ow we

dennpu punned upend dune nude pend den due dun end nun pen pun en ne nu pe up

dennstu stunned. *See* **dennsu denntu**

dennsu sunned dunes nudes dens dues dune duns ends nude nuns send sued sunn used den due dun end ens nun sen sue sun use en ne nu us

denntu tunned tuned dent duet dune nude tend tune den due dun end net nun nut ted ten tun en ne nu ut

deno done node den doe don end eon nod ode one do en ne no od on

denooppr proponed propend propone. *See* **denopr deoopp**

denoops snooped spooned. *See* **denoos**

denoos nodose noosed nodes noose nosed snood sonde dens does done dons dose ends eons node nods noes nose odes ones send soon den doe don dos end ens eon nod ode one sen sod son do en ne no od on os so

denoosw swooned. *See* **denosw denoos denoow**

denoosz snoozed. *See* **denosz enoosz**

denootu outdone. *See* **dnotu denot dootu**

denoow wooden endow owned wooed done down enow node owed wend wood den dew doe don end eon new nod now ode one owe own wed wen woe won woo do en ne no od on ow we

denoppr propend. *See* **denopr**

denopprs propends ponders propend respond. *See* **denopr denors deopps deoprs**

denopr ponder doper drone pored prone roped doer done dope drop nerd node nope oped open pend peon pond pone pore prod redo rend repo rode rope den doe don dor end eon nod nor ode one ope ore pen per pod pro red rep rod roe do en er ne no od on or pe re

denoprs ponders respond. *See* **deoprs denors enoprs denopr**

denoprss responds persons ponders respond. *See* **denopr denors denoss denpss**

denoprst portends deports ponders portend postern redtops respond rodents snorted sported. *See* **denopr denors denort denost**

denoprsu pounders ponders pounder resound respond sounder spurned. *See* **denopr denors denosu denpru**

denoprt portend. *See* **deoprt denopr denort**

denopru pounder. *See* **denopr deopru denpru**

denopruv unproved pounder. *See* **denopr denorv denpru deopru**

denopsux expounds expound. *See* **denosu denpsu deopsu deosux**

denopux expound. *See* **denpu dnopu**

denor drone doer done nerd node redo rend rode den doe don dor end eon nod nor ode one ore red rod roe do en er ne no od on or re

denorrsu rounders ordures resound rounder sounder. *See* **denors denosu denrsu deorrs**

denorru rounder. *See* **deorru denor enrru**

denors drones snored doers drone nerds nodes nosed rends rosed snore sonde dens doer does done dons dose ends eons nerd node nods noes nose odes ones ores redo reds rend rode rods roes rose send sore den doe don dor dos end ens eon nod nor ode one ore red res rod roe sen sod son do en er ne no od on or os re so

denorssu resounds sounders resound sounder sunders undress. *See* **denors denoss denosu denrsu**

denorst rodents snorted. *See* **deorst denors enorst denort denost**

denorstu roundest tonsured detours resound rodents rousted snorted sounder tonsure. *See* **denors denort denost denosu**

denorsu resound sounder. *See* **denors denrsu dnorsu deorsu denosu**

denorsv vendors. *See* **denors deorsv denorv**

denorsw downers wonders. *See* **deorsw denorw denors dnorsw denosw**

denort rodent doter drone noted noter tenor toned toner trend dent doer done dote nerd node note redo rend rent rode rote tend tern toed tone tore torn trod den doe don dor dot end eon net nod nor not ode one ore ort red ret rod roe rot ted ten tod toe ton tor do en er ne no od on or re to

denortuw undertow rewound. *See* **denort denorw denotw denrtu**

denoruw rewound. *See* **denorw**

denorv vendor drone drove roved doer done dove nerd node oven over redo rend rode rove vend den doe don dor end eon nod nor ode one ore red rev rod roe do en er ne no od on or re

denorw downer wonder dower drone drown endow owned owner rowed rowen doer done down drew enow nerd node owed redo rend rode wend word wore worn wren den dew doe don dor end eon new nod nor now ode one ore owe own red rod roe row wed wen woe won do en er ne no od on or ow re we

denory yonder doyen drone nerdy deny doer done dory dyer dyne nerd node redo rend rode yond yore den dey doe don dor dry dye end eon nod nor ode one ore red rod roe rye yen yod yon do en er ne no od on or oy re ye

denos nodes nosed sonde dens does done dons dose ends eons node nods noes nose odes ones send den doe don dos end ens eon nod ode one sen sod son do en ne no od on os so

denoss sondes doses nodes nosed noses sends sonde dens does done dons dose doss ends eons node nods noes nose odes ones send sods sons den doe don dos end ens eon ess nod ode one sen sod son do en ne no od on os so

denost stoned downs dowse endow nodes nosed owned sonde sowed wends dens dews does done dons dose down ends enow eons news node nods noes nose odes ones owed owes owns send sewn snow sown weds wend wens woes den dew doe don don dos dos dot end ens eon net nod nod not ode one one sen set sod sod son sot ted ten tod toe ton wed do en ne no od on os so to

denosu undoes douse dunes nodes nodus nosed nudes sonde sound dens does done dons dose dues dune duns duos ends eons node nods nose nous nude odes ones onus ouds send sued udos undo used den doe don dos due dun duo end ens eon nod ode one oud sen sod son sou sue sun udo use do en ne no nu od on os so us

denosw endows snowed downs dowse endow nodes nosed owned sonde sowed wends dens dews does done dons dose down ends enow eons news node nods noes nose odes ones owed owes owns send sewn snow sown weds wend wens woes den dew doe don dos end ens eon new nod now ode one owe own sen sew sod son sow wed wen woe won do en ne no od on os ow so we

denosy doyens doyen dynes nodes nosed nosey sonde synod dens deny deys does done dons dose dyes dyne ends eons node nods noes nose nosy odes ones oyes send yens yods yond den dey doe don dos dye end ens eon nod ode one sen sod son soy yen yes yod yon do en ne no od on os oy so ye

denosz dozens dozen dozes nodes nosed sonde zoned zones dens does done dons dose doze ends eons node nods noes nose odes ones send zeds zone den doe don dos end ens eon nod ode one sen sod son zed do en ne no od on os so

denot noted toned dent done dote node note tend toed tone den doe don dot end eon net nod not ode one ted ten tod toe ton do en ne no od on to

denotw wonted endow noted owned toned towed dent done dote down enow newt node note nowt owed tend toed tone town wend wont den dew doe don dot end eon net new nod not now ode one owe own ted ten tod toe ton tow two wed wen wet woe won do en ne no od on ow to we

denow endow owned done down enow node owed wend den dew doe don end eon new nod now ode one owe own wed wen woe won do en ne no od on ow we

denoy doyen deny done dyne node yond den dey doe don dye end eon nod ode one yen yod yon do en ne no od on oy ye

denoz dozen zoned done doze node zone den doe don end eon nod ode one zed do en ne no od on

denp pend den end pen en ne pe

denprsu spurned. *See* **deprsu denrsu denpru enprsu denpsu**

denprtu prudent. *See* **denpru denptu enprtu denrtu**

denprtuu upturned prudent. *See* **denpru denptu denrtu enprtu**

denpru pruned drupe duper perdu prude prune under upend dune nerd nude pend pure rend rude rued rune den due dun end pen per pun red rep rue run urd urn en er ne nu pe re up

denps pends spend dens ends pend pens send sped den end ens pen sen en ne pe

denpss spends pends sends spend dens ends pend pens send sped den end ens ess pen sen en ne pe

denpsssu suspends suspend. *See* **denpss denpsu epsssu**

denpssu suspend. *See* **denpss denpsu**

denpsu upends dunes nudes pends spend upend dens dues dune duns ends nude pend pens puns send sped spud spue spun sued used den due dun end ens pen pun pus sen sue sun sup use en ne nu pe up us

denptu punted upend tuned dent duet dune nude pend pent punt tend tune den due dun end net nut pen pet pun put ted ten tun tup en ne nu pe up ut

denpu upend dune nude pend den due dun end pen pun en ne nu pe up

denr nerd rend den end red en er ne re

denrrtuu nurtured nurture. *See* **denrtu enrrtu**

denrs nerds rends dens ends nerd reds rend send den end ens red res sen en er ne re

denrssu sunders undress. *See* **derssu denrsu enrssu**

denrssy dryness. *See* **derssy densy denrs**

denrst trends dents nerds rends rents stern tends terns trend dens dent ends erst nerd nest nets reds rend rent rest rets send sent teds tend tens tern den end ens net red res ret sen set ted ten en er ne re

denrsu nursed sunder druse dunes nerds nudes nurse rends runes under dens dues dune duns ends nerd nude reds rend rude rued rues rune runs ruse send sued surd sure urds urns used user den due dun end ens red res rue run sen sue sun urd urn use en er ne nu re us

denrt trend dent nerd rend rent tend tern den end net red ret ted ten en er ne re

denrtu turned trend trued tuned tuner under dent duet dune nerd nude rend rent rude rued rune runt tend tern true tune turd turn den due dun end net nut red ret rue run rut ted ten tun urd urn en er ne nu re ut

denrty trendy entry nerdy trend dent deny dyer dyne nerd rend rent tend tern den dey dry dye end net red ret rye ted ten try yen yet en er ne re ye

denru under dune nerd nude rend rude rued rune den due dun end red rue run urd urn en er ne nu re

denry nerdy deny dyer dyne nerd rend den dey dry dye end red rye yen en er ne re ye

dens dens ends send den end ens sen en ne

denss sends dens ends send den end ens ess sen en ne

densttu students student stunted. *See* **denttu ensttu nssttu**

denssuw sundews. *See* **densuw denss**

denst dents tends dens dent ends nest nets send sent teds tend tens den end ens net sen set ted ten en ne

densttu student stunted. *See* **denttu denst destu**

densu dunes nudes dens dues dune duns ends nude send sued used den due dun end ens sen sue sun use en ne nu us

densuu unused dunes nudes undue dens dues dune duns ends nude send sued used den due dun end ens sen sue sun use en ne nu us

densuw sundew dunes nudes unwed wends dens dews dues dune duns ends news nude send sewn sued used weds wend wens den dew due dun end ens new sen sew sue sun use wed wen en ne nu us we

densv vends dens ends send vend den end ens sen en ne

densw wends dens dews ends news send sewn weds wend wens den dew end ens new sen sew wed wen en ne we

densy dynes dens deny deys dyes dyne ends send yens den dey dye end ens sen yen yes en ne ye

dent dent tend den end net ted ten en ne

denttu nutted tuned dent duet dune nude tend tent tune den due dun end net nut ted ten tun tut en ne nu ut

dentu tuned dent duet dune nude tend tune den due dun end net nut ted ten tun en ne nu ut

denu dune nude den due dun end en ne nu

denuu undue dune nude den due dun end en ne nu

denuw unwed dune nude wend den dew due dun end new wed wen en ne nu we

denv vend den end en ne

denw wend den dew end new wed wen en ne we

deny deny dyne den dey dye end yen en ne ye

deo doe ode do od

deooorsw rosewood. *See* **deoors deorsw eoorsw**

deoopp pooped dope oped poop pope doe ode ope pep pod pop do od pe

deoopprs proposed opposed opposer propose spoored. *See* **deoopp deoors deopps deoprs**

deoopprt pteropod torpedo trooped. *See* **deoopp deoort deoppt deoprt**

deoopps opposed. *See* **eoopps deoopp deopps**

deooprs spoored. *See* **deoprs dooprs deoors**

deooprst doorstep deports poorest redtops roosted spoored sported stooped torpedo trooped. *See* **deoors deoort deoost deoprs**

deooprt torpedo trooped. *See* **deoprt deoort**

deooprtu uprooted dropout outrode torpedo trooped trouped. *See* **deoort deoprt deopru deoptu**

deoopst stooped. *See* **deopst deoost**

deoopsw swooped. *See* **deops deosw oopsw**

deoor rodeo doer door odor ordo redo rode rood doe dor ode ore red rod roe do er od or re

deoors rodeos doers doors odors ordos rodeo roods rosed doer does door dose odes odor ores redo reds rode rods roes rood rose sore doe dor dos ode ore red res rod roe sod do er od or os re so

deoorst roosted. *See* **deorst deoors deoort deoost**

deoort rooted rodeo doter doer door dote odor ordo redo rode rood root rote roto toed tore trod doe dor dot ode ore ort red ret rod roe rot ted tod toe too tor do er od or re to

deoortu outrode. *See* **deortu deoort**

deoorv overdo drove rodeo roved doer door dove odor ordo over redo rode rood rove doe dor ode ore red rev rod roe do er od or re

deoost sooted dotes stood does dose dote dots odes soot teds toed toes doe dos dot ode set sod sot ted tod toe too do od os so to

deoostu outdoes. *See* **deoost deostu**

deoott tooted toted dote toed toot tote doe dot ode ted tod toe too tot do od to

deoow wooed owed wood dew doe ode owe wed woe woo do od ow we

deooz oozed doze ooze doe ode zed zoo do od

deop dope oped doe ode ope pod do od pe

deoppp popped dope oped pope doe ode ope pep pod pop do od pe

deopppr propped. *See* **deoppp eopppr**

deopprr dropper. *See* **eopprr deopr deorr**

deopprrs droppers dropper prosper. *See* **deopps deoprs deorrs eopprr**

deopprst stropped deports redtops sported stopped stopper toppers. *See* **deopps deoppt deoprs deoprt**

deopprsu purposed purpose. *See* **deopps deoprs deopru deopsu**

deopps sopped dopes popes posed does dope dosa epos odes oped opes peps peso pods pope pops pose sped doe dos ode ope pep pod pop sod sop do od os pe so

deoppssu supposed pseudos suppose. *See* **deopps deopsu deossu deppsu**

356

deoppst　stopped. *See* **deopst deopps de-oppt**

deoppsw　swopped. *See* **deopps deosw**

deoppt　topped depot toped dope dote oped poet pope toed tope doe dot ode ope pep pet pod pop pot ted tod toe top do od pe to

deopr　doper pored roped doer dope drop oped pore prod redo repo rode rope doe dor ode ope ore per pod pro red rep rod roe do er od or pe re

deoprrtu　protrude trouped trouper. *See* **deoprt deopru deoptu deorru**

deoprs　dopers prosed spored honed hones hosed hosen nodes nosed shoed shone sonde dens does done dons dose ends eons hens hods hoed hoes hone hose node nods noes nose nosh odes ones send shed shod shoe den doe don dor dos dos edh end ens eon hen hod hoe nod ode one ope ore per pod pro red rep res rod roe sen she sod sod sop do er od or os pe re so

deoprst　deports redtops sported. *See* **deoprt deopst deoprs deorst eoprst**

deoprstu　postured sprouted deports detours petrous posture redtops rousted sported spouted spurted trouped troupes. *See* **deoprs deoprt deopru deopst**

deoprsw　powders. *See* **deoprs deorsw deoprw eoprsw**

deoprt　deport ported redtop depot doper doter pored repot roped toped toper trope doer dope dote drop oped pert poet pore port prod redo repo rode rope rote toed tope tore trod doe dor dot ode ope ore ort per pet pod pot pro red rep ret rod roe rot ted tod toe top tor do er od or pe re to

deoprtu　trouped. *See* **deoprt deortu deopru deoptu eoprtu**

deopru　poured doper drupe duper perdu pored proud prude roped uredo doer dope dour drop duro oped pore pour prod pure redo repo rode rope rude rued doe dor due duo ode ope ore oud our per pod pro red rep rod roe rue udo urd do er od or pe re up

deoprv　proved doper drove pored prove roped roved doer dope dove drop oped over pore prod redo repo rode rope rove doe dor ode ope ore per pod pro red rep rev rod roe do er od or pe re

deoprw　powder doper dower pored power roped rowed doer dope drew drop oped owed pore prod prow redo repo rode rope word wore dew doe dor ode ope ore owe per pew pod pro red

rep rod roe row wed woe do er od or ow pe re we

deoprwy　powdery. *See* **deoprw deopy dorwy**

deops　dopes posed does dope dose epos odes oped opes peso pods pose sped doe dos ode ope pod sod sop do od os pe so

deopsst　despots. *See* **deopst eopsst deosst**

deopssu　pseudos. *See* **deossu eopssu deopsu**

deopst　depots despot posted stoped depot dopes dotes estop poets posed stope toped topes does dope dose dote dots epos odes oped opes peso pest pets pods poet pose post pots sept sped spot step stop teds toed toes tope tops doe dos dot ode ope pet pod pot set sod sop sot ted tod toe top do od os pe so to

deopstt　spotted. *See* **deopst deoptt deostt**

deopstu　spouted. *See* **deopst deostu deopsu**

deopsu　pseudo dopes douse posed does dope dose dues duos epos odes oped opes opus ouds peso pods pose soup sped spud spue sued udos used doe dos due duo ode ope oud pod pus sod sop sou sue sup udo use do od os pe so up us

deopt　depot toped dope dote oped poet toed tope doe dot ode ope pet pod pot ted tod toe top do od pe to

deoptt　potted depot toped toted dope dote oped poet toed tope tote doe dot ode ope pet pod pot ted tod toe top tot do od pe to

deoptu　pouted depot toped dope dote duet oped poet pout toed tope doe dot due duo ode ope oud out pet pod pot put ted tod toe top tup udo do od pe to up ut

deopy　dopey dope oped dey doe dye ode ope pod yep yod do od oy pe ye

deoqtu　quoted quote toque dote duet quod toed doe dot due duo ode oud out ted tod toe udo do od to ut

deor　doer redo rode doe dor ode ore red rod roe do er od or re

deorr　order doer redo rode doe dor err ode ore red rod roe do er od or re

deorrs　orders doers order rosed sorer doer does dose errs odes ores redo reds rode rods roes rose sore doe dor dos err ode ore red res rod roe sod do er od or os re so

deorrsu　ordures. *See* **deorrs deorru deorsu eorrsu**

deorrsv　drovers. *See* **deorrv deorsv deorrs eorrsv**

deorrsw　rewords. *See* **deorsw deorrw eorrsw**

deorrttu　tortured tutored torture. *See* **deorru deortt deortu deottu**

deorru　ordure order ruder uredo doer dour duro redo rode rude rued doe dor due duo err ode ore oud our red rod roe rue udo urd do er od or re

deorrv　drover drove order roved rover doer dove over redo rode rove doe dor err ode ore red rev rod roe do er od or re

deorrw　reword dower order rowed rower doer drew owed redo rode word wore dew doe dor err ode ore owe red rod roe row wed woe do er od or ow re we

deors　doers rosed doer does dose odes ores redo reds rode rods roes rose sore doe dor dos ode ore red res rod roe sod do er od or os re so

deorss　dosser doers doses dress dross rosed roses sores doer does dose doss odes ores redo reds rode rods roes rose sods sore doe dor dos ess ode ore red res rod roe sod do er od or os re so

deorsss　dossers. *See* **deorss**

deorssty　destroys destroy oysters. *See* **deorss deorst deosst derssy**

deorssw　drowses. *See* **deorss deorsw deossw eorssw dorssw**

deorst　doters sorted stored strode doers doter dotes rosed rotes store doer does dose dote dots erst odes ores orts redo reds rest rets rode rods roes rose rote rots sore sort teds toed toes tore tors trod doe dor dos dot ode ore ort red res ret rod roe rot set sod sot ted tod toe tor do er od or os re so to

deorstu　detours rousted. *See* **deortu deorst derstu deostu eorstu**

deorstux　dextrous detours rousted tuxedos. *See* **deorst deorsu deortu deostu**

deorstw　worsted. *See* **deorst deorsw deostw eorstw deortw**

deorsty　destroy. *See* **deorst eorsty**

deorsu　roused soured uredos doers douse druse duros rosed rouse uredo doer does dose dour dues duos duro odes ores ouds ours redo reds rode rods roes rose rude rued rues ruse sore sour sued surd sure udos urds used user doe dor dos due duo ode ore oud our red res rod roe rue sod sou sue udo urd use do er od or os re so us

deorsuv　devours. *See* **deoruv deorsv deorsu**

deorsv　droves doers doves drove rosed roved roves servo verso doer does dose

deor dove odes ores over redo reds revs rode rods roes rose rove sore doe dor dos ode ore red res rev rod roe sod do er od or os re so

deorsw dowers drowse doers dower dowse rosed rowed serow sowed sower sword swore words worse dews doer does dose drew odes ores owed owes redo reds rode rods roes rose rows sore weds woes word wore dew doe dor dos ode ore owe red res rod roe row sew sod sow wed woe do er od or os ow re so we

deort doter doer dote redo rode rote toed tore trod doe dor dot ode ore ort red ret rod roe rot ted tod toe tor do er od or re to

deortt rotted doter otter torte toted toter doer dote redo rode rote toed tore tort tote tret trod trot doe dor dot ode ore ort red ret rod roe rot ted tod toe tor tot do er od or re to

deorttt trotted. *See* **deortt deottt eorttt**

deorttu tutored. *See* **deortu deortt derttu deottu**

deortu detour routed toured doter outer route trued uredo doer dote dour duet duro redo rode rote rout rude rued toed tore tour trod true turd doe dor dot due duo ode ore ort oud our out red ret rod roe rot rue rut ted tod toe tor udo urd do er od or re to ut

deortw trowed doter dower rowed towed tower wrote doer dote drew owed redo rode rote toed tore trod trow word wore dew doe dor dot ode ore ort owe red ret rod roe rot row ted tod toe tor tow two wed wet woe do er od or ow re to we

deoru uredo doer dour duro redo rode rude rued doe dor due duo ode ore oud our red rod roe rue udo urd do er od or re

deoruv devour drove roved uredo doer dour dove duro over redo rode rove rude rued doe dor due duo ode ore oud our red rev rod roe rue udo urd do er od or re

deorv drove roved doer dove over redo rode rove doe dor ode ore red rev rod roe do er od or re

deorw dower rowed doer drew owed redo rode word wore dew doe dor ode ore owe red rod roe row wed woe do er od or ow re we

deorx redox doer redo rode doe dor ode ore red rex rod roe do er ex od or ox re

deos does dose odes doe dos ode sod do od os so

deoss doses does dose doss odes sods doe dos ess ode sod do od os so

deosst tossed doses dotes does dose doss dote dots odes sets sods sots teds toed toes toss doe dos dot ess ode set sod sot ted tod toe do od os so to

deossu douses soused doses douse souse does dose doss dues duos odes ouds sods sous suds sued sues udos used uses doe dos due duo ess ode oud sod sou sue udo use do od os so us

deossw dowses doses dowse sowed dews does dose doss odes owed owes sews sods sows weds woes dew doe dos ess ode owe sew sod sow wed woe do od os ow so we

deost dotes does dose dote dots odes teds toed toes doe dos dot ode set sod sot ted tod toe do od os so to

deostt sotted dotes toted totes does dose dote dots odes stet teds test toed toes tost tote tots doe dos dot ode set sod sot ted tod toe tot do od os so to

deosttu testudo. *See* **deostu eosttu deostt**

deosttw swotted. *See* **deostt deostw**

deostu ousted dotes douse duets does dose dote dots dues duet duos dust odes ouds oust outs stud sued suet teds toed toes udos used doe dos dot due duo ode oud out set sod sot sou sue ted tod toe udo use do od os so to us ut

deostuu duteous. *See* **deostu**

deostux tuxedos. *See* **deosux deostu deotux**

deostw stowed dotes dowse sowed towed dews does dose dote dots odes owed owes stew stow swot teds toed toes tows twos weds west wets woes dew doe dos dot ode owe set sew sod sot sow tod toe tow two wed wet woe do od os ow so to we

deosu douse does dose dues duos odes ouds sued udos used doe dos due duo ode oud sod sou sue udo use do od os so us

deosux exodus douse does dose dues duos odes ouds sued udos used doe dos due duo ode oud sex sod sou sox sue udo use do ex od os ox so us

deosv doves does dose dove odes doe dos ode sod do od os so

deosw dowse sowed dews does dose odes owed owes weds woes dew doe dos ode owe sew sod sow wed woe do od os ow so we

deosz dozes does dose doze odes zeds doe dos ode sod zed do od os so

deot dote toed doe dot ode ted tod toe do od to

deott toted dote toed tote doe dot ode ted tod toe tot do od to

deottt totted toted dote toed tote doe dot ode ted tod toe tot do od to

deottu touted toted dote duet toed tote tout doe dot due duo ode oud out ted tod toe tot tut udo do od to ut

deotuv devout voted duvet dote dove duet toed veto vote doe dot due duo ode oud out ted tod toe udo vet do od to ut

deotux tuxedo dote duet toed doe dot due duo ode oud out ted tod toe tux udo do ex od ox to ut

deotv voted dote dove toed veto vote doe dot ode ted tod toe vet do od to

deotw towed dote owed toed dew doe dot ode owe ted tod toe tow two wed wet woe do od ow to we

deoty toyed dote tody toed dey doe dot dye ode ted tod toe toy yet yod do od oy to ye

deov dove doe ode do od

deovw vowed dove owed wove dew doe ode owe vow wed woe do od ow we

deow owed dew doe ode owe wed woe do od ow we

deoz doze doe ode zed do od

depppu pupped due pep pup pe up

deppsu supped dues peps pups sped spud spue sued used due pep pup pus sue sup use pe up us

deprrsu spurred. *See* **deprsu deprru eprrsu**

deprrtuu ruptured rupture. *See* **deprru**

deprru purred drupe duper perdu prude purer ruder pure purr rude rued due err per red rep rue urd er pe re up

deprruy prudery. *See* **deprru depruy**

deprstu spurted. *See* **deprsu derstu eprstu**

deprsu drupes dupers prudes pursed drupe druse duper perdu prude purse sprue super dues pure reds reps rude rued rues ruse sped spud spue spur sued surd sure urds used user due per pus red rep res rue sue sup urd use er pe re up us

deprsuu pursued. *See* **deprsu eprsuu**

depru drupe duper perdu prude pure rude rued due per. red rep rue urd er pe re up

depruy dupery drupe duper perdu prude dyer prey pure pyre rude rued dey dry due dye per pry red rep rue rye urd yep yup er pe re up ye

deps sped pe

deptuy deputy typed duet duty type dey due dye pet put ted tup yep yet yup pe up ut ye

depty typed type dey dye pet ted yep yet pe ye

der red er re

derrsy dryers dryer dyers deys dyer dyes errs reds ryes dey dry dye err red res rye yes er re ye

derru ruder rude rued due err red rue urd er re

derry dryer dyer dey dry dye err red rye er re ye

ders reds red res er re

derss dress reds ess red res er re

dersstu dusters trussed. *See* **derssu der-stu ersstu**

derssu druses duress dress druse ruses users dues reds rude rued rues ruse suds sued sues surd sure urds used user uses due ess red res rue sue urd use er re us

derssy dressy dress dyers deys dyer dyes reds ryes dey dry dye ess red res rye yes er re ye

derstttu strutted trusted stutter. *See* **der-stu derttu ersttu**

dersttu trusted. *See* **derstu derttu ersttu**

derstty trysted. *See* **dersy estty erstt**

derstu duster rudest rusted druse duets durst trued trues turds dues duet dust erst reds rest rets rude rued rues ruse rust ruts stud sued suet surd sure teds true turd urds used user due red res ret rue rut set sue ted urd use er re us ut

derstuu sutured. *See* **derstu erstuu**

dersu druse dues reds rude rued rues ruse sued surd sure urds used user due red res rue sue urd use er re us

dersy dyers deys dyer dyes reds ryes dey dry dye red rye res rye yes er re ye

derttu rutted trued utter duet rude rued tret true turd due red ret rue rut ted tut urd er re ut

dertu trued duet rude rued true turd due red ret rue rut ted urd er re ut

deru rude rued due red rue urd er re

derux redux rude rued due red rex rue urd er ex re

derw drew dew red wed er re we

dery dyer dey dry dye red rye er re ye

dest teds ted set

destu duets dues duet dust stud sued suet teds used due set sue ted use us ut

destuv duvets duets duvet dues duet dust stud sued suet teds used vest vets due set sue ted use vet us ut

desu dues sued used due sue use us

desw dews weds dew sew wed we

desy deys dyes dey dye yes ye

desz zeds zed

det ted

dettu tutted duet due ted tut ut

detu duet ted due ut

detuv duvet duet due ted vet ut

deu due

dew dew wed we

dewy dewy dew dey dye wed wye yew we ye

dey dey dye ye

dez zed

---

dffgino doffing. *See* **ffgino dgino**

dffiimr midriff. *No 6s or 5s*

dffiimrs midriffs midriff. *See* **fimrs ffims ffirs**

dfflooru fourfold. *See* **dloor dfloo floor**

dffo doff off do od of

dffooruw woodruff. *See* **dfoor**

dffos doffs doff dos off sod do od of os so

dffsu duffs duff us

dffu duff

dfgghiot dogfight. *See* **dhiot fghit**

dfgginu fudging. *See* **dfinu fginu**

dfghilos goldfish dogfish. *See* **dhilos**

dfghios dogfish. *No 6s or 5s*

dfgiilry frigidly rigidly. *See* **dfgiir**

dfgiinn finding. *See* **dgiinn fgiinn**

dfgiinns findings finding finings. *See* **dgi-inn dgiins fgiinn**

dfgiiny dignify. *See* **dfiiny dginy**

dfgiir frigid rigid frig gird grid dig fid fig fir gid rid rif rig id if

dfgilno folding. *See* **dfilno dgilno**

dfgilnoo flooding folding fooling. *See* **dfilno dgilno gilnoo**

dfginnou founding funding fungoid un-doing. *See* **dginou**

dfginnu funding. *See* **dfinu fginu**

dfginoor fordoing fording roofing. *See* **dinoor**

dfginor fording. *See* **dgino dfior dfnor**

dfginou fungoid. *See* **dginou dfnou dfinu**

dfhiimuy humidify. *See* **dhimu**

dfhilssu dishfuls dishful. *See* **dfilsu**

dfhilsu dishful. *See* **dfilsu fhlsu**

dfhinops fishpond. *See* **hinops**

dfhlooot foothold. *See* **dfloo**

dfhnoous foxhound. *See* **dfnou dhnou**

dfi fid id if

dfiilosy solidify. *See* **diloy filos dflos**

dfiiltuy fluidity. *See* **dfilu filty**

dfiiny nidify find nidi din fid fin yin id if in

dfiirt trifid drift dirt frit rift dit fid fir fit rid rif id if it ti

dfilloot floodlit. *See* **dfloo filoo**

dfillory floridly. *See* **dfilor dllory fillry**

dfilloww wildfowl. *See* **illoww**

dfilluy fluidly. *See* **dilly dlluy filly**

dfilmnu mindful. *See* **filmu dfilu dfinu**

dfilno infold find foil fold fond idol lion loin noil din don fid fin ion lid nil nod oil old do id if in li lo no od of on

dfilnop pinfold. *See* **dfilno**

dfilnops pinfolds pinfold infolds. *See* **dfilno**

dfilnos infolds. *See* **dfilno dfins filos**

dfilor florid fiord dirl foil fold ford idol lord roil dor fid fir for fro lid oil old rid rif rod do id if li lo od of or

dfilosx sixfold. *See* **filos dflos dilos**

dfilsu fluids fluid fusil fids fils flus lids slid fid flu ids ifs lid id if is li si us

dfiltuu dutiful. *See* **dfilu**

dfilu fluid fid flu lid id if li

dfimoy modify dim fid foy mid mod yod do id if mi mo my od of om oy

dfin find din fid fin id if in

dfins finds dins fids find fins din fid fin ids ifs sin id if in is si

dfinu fundi find fund din dun fid fin fun id if in nu

dfiooprs disproof. *See* **dfiors dioops dooprs fooprs**

dfior fiord ford dor fid fir for fro rid rif rod do id if od of or

dfiors fiords fiord fords fids firs ford rids rifs rods sori dor dos fid fir for fro ids ifs rid rif rod sir sod do id if is od of or os si so

dfirst drifts drift first frits rifts rift dits fids firs fist fits frit rids rifs rift sift stir dit fid fir fit ids ifs its rid rif sir sit id if is it si ti

dfirt drift dirt frit rift dit fid fir fit rid rif id if it ti

dfirty drifty drift dirty dirt frit rift tidy dit dry fid fir fit fry rid rif try id if it ti

dfis fids fid ids ifs id if is si

dfjor fjord ford dor for fro rod do jo od of or

dfjors fjords fjord fords ford rods dor dos for fro rod sod do jo od of or os so

dflnosu unfolds. See **dfnosu dflnou**

dflnou unfold fondu found fold fond foul fund loud undo don dun duo flu fun nod old oud udo do lo no nu od of on

dflnoy fondly fold fond only yond don fly foy nod old yod yon do lo no od of on oy

dflo fold old do lo od of

dfloo flood fold food fool old loo do lo od of

dfloos floods flood folds foods fools soldo fold food fool loos sold solo dos loo los old sod sol do lo od of os so

dfloostu foldouts foldout outsold. See **dfloos flostu**

dflootu foldout. See **dfloo flotu dootu**

dflootw twofold. See **dfloo**

dflos folds fold sold dos los old sod sol do lo od of os so

dfno fond don nod do no od of on

dfnoopru profound. See **doopru**

dfnor frond fond ford don dor for fro nod nor rod do no od of on or

dfnors fronds fords frond frons dons fond ford nods rods don dor dos for fro nod nor rod sod son do no od of on or os so

dfnoruy foundry. See **dfnou dfnor dnoru**

dfnosu fondus founds fondu found funds nodus sound dons duns duos fond fund nods nous onus ouds udos undo don dos dun duo fun nod oud sod son sou sun udo do no nu od of on os so us

dfnou fondu found fond fund undo don dun duo fun nod oud udo do no nu od of on

dfnsu funds fund duns dun fun sun nu us

dfnsuu fundus funds fund duns dun fun sun nu us

dfnu fund dun fun nu

dfoo food do od of

dfoor fordo door food ford odor ordo rood roof dor for fro rod do od of or

dfoorsx oxfords. See **dfoorx doors dfoos**

dfoorx oxford fordo door food ford odor ordo rood roof dor for fox fro rod do od of or ox

dfoos foods food dos sod do od of os so

dfor ford dor for fro rod do od of or

dfors fords ford rods dor dos for fro rod sod do od of or os so

---

dg

dgggiin digging. No 6s or 5s

dgggino dogging. See **dgino ggino**

dggginru drugging grudging. See **dginru gginru**

dgghios doggish. No 6s or 5s

dggiiln gilding gliding. See **dgiiln**

dggiilnr girdling dirling gilding girding gliding griding ridging. See **dgiiln dgiinr giilnr**

dggiilns gildings gilding gliding sidling sliding. See **dgiiln dgiins**

dggiinn dinging. See **dgiinn**

dggiinnr grinding dinging girding griding ridging ringing. See **dgiinn dgiinr**

dggiinnw wingding dinging winding winging. See **dgiinn giinnw**

dggiinr girding griding ridging. See **dgiinr**

dggiinu guiding. No 6s or 5s

dggijnu judging. No 6s or 5s

dggilno godling lodging. See **dgilno ggilno**

dggilnos lodgings godling gosling lodging. See **dgilno dginos ggilno gginos**

dggimnsu smudging. See **dginsu dimnsu gimnsu**

dgginnu dunging nudging

dgginrtu trudging. See **dginru dgirtu gginru ginrtu**

dggirstu druggist. See **dgirtu**

dggoy doggy dogy dog god goy yod do go od oy

dghiiln hilding. See **dghiin dgiiln**

dghiimnt midnight. See **dghiin giimnt**

dghiin hiding ding hind nidi nigh dig din gid gin hid hin hi id in

dghiins dishing. See **dghiin dgiins**

dghilno holding. See **dgilno ghilno**

dghilnos holdings holding longish. See **dgilno dginos dhilos ghilno**

dghilnru hurdling hurling. See **dginru gilnru**

dghiloor girlhood. See **dloor giloo**

dghinnou hounding undoing. See **dginou ghinno**

dghinoo hooding. See **ghinoo dgino**

dghinor hording. See **dgino dginr ginor**

dghinstu hindguts hindgut dusting. See **dginsu dinstu ghinst**

dghintu hindgut. See **ghint**

dghiny dinghy dingy dying hying ding hind nigh dig din gid gin hid hin yin hi id in

dghioos goodish. See **dgoos dhoos**

dghnotuu doughnut. See **dgotuu ghnotu**

dghorstu droughts drought troughs. See **dghosu dgorsu dhorsu ghorsu**

dghortu drought. See **ghortu dghou dgoru**

dghortuy droughty doughty drought yoghurt. See **dghouy ghortu gortuy**

dghosu doughs dough dogs duos gods gosh gush hods hogs hugs ouds shod udos dog dos dug duo god hod hog hug ohs oud sod sou udo ugh do go ho od oh os sh so us

dghotuy doughty. See **dghouy gotuy ghotu**

dghou dough dog dug duo god hod hog hug oud udo ugh do go ho od oh

dghouy doughy dough dogy yodh dog dug duo god goy guy hod hog hoy hug oud udo ugh yod you do go ho od oh oy

dgi dig gid id

dgiiinnt inditing dinting. See **dgiinn**

dgiiinnv divining. See **dgiinn**

dgiiinoz iodizing. See **dgiino dginoz**

dgiiirty rigidity. See **dgiit dirty dgiry**

dgiiklnn kindling inkling linking. See **dgiikn dgiiln dgiinn giikln**

dgiikn diking ding dink gink kind king nidi dig din gid gin ink kid kin id in

dgiiknnr drinking dirking. See **dgiikn dgiinn dgiinr giiknn**

dgiiknr dirking. See **dgiikn giiknr dgiinr**

dgiillnr drilling dirling rilling. See **dgiiln dgiinr giilnr**

dgiilmnp dimpling limping. *See* **dgiiln dgiinp diilmp giilmn**

dgiiln idling ding gild ling nidi dig din gid gin lid nil id in li

dgiilnnp pindling. *See* **dgiiln dgiinn dgiinp giilnn**

dgiilnr dirling. *See* **dgiiln dgiinr giilnr**

dgiilns sidling sliding. *See* **dgiiln dgiins**

dgiilntu diluting. *See* **dgiiln dilntu gilntu giilnt**

dgiilry rigidly. *See* **dgiir dgiry**

dgiimmn dimming. *See* **giimmn**

dgiimnn minding. *See* **dgiinn giimnn**

dgiimnos misdoing. *See* **dgiino dgiins dgimno dginos**

dgiinn dining indign ding nidi dig din gid gin inn id in

dgiinnn dinning. *See* **dgiinn giinnn**

dgiinnt dinting. *See* **dgiinn**

dgiinnu induing. *See* **dgiinn**

dgiinnw winding. *See* **dgiinn giinnw**

dgiino indigo dingo doing ding dong nidi dig din dog don gid gin god ion nod nog do go id in no od on

dgiinorr gridiron. *See* **dgiino dgiinr giinor**

dgiinott dittoing dotting. *See* **dgiino dginot ginott**

dgiinov voiding. *See* **dgiino dgiinv**

dgiinoww widowing. *See* **dgiino dinoww**

dgiinp pidgin ding nidi ping dig din dip gid gin gip nip pig pin id in pi

dgiinpp dipping. *See* **dgiinp giinpp**

dgiinppr dripping dipping priding ripping. *See* **dgiinp dgiinr giinpp giinpr**

dgiinpps dippings dipping pidgins sipping. *See* **dgiinp dgiins giinpp**

dgiinpr priding. *See* **dgiinp dgiinr giinpr**

dgiinps pidgins. *See* **dgiinp dgiins**

dgiinpu pinguid. *See* **dgiinp dginpu**

dgiinr riding grind indri rigid ding gird grid grin nidi rind ring dig din gid gin rid rig id in

dgiinrst striding tidings. *See* **dgiinr dgiins dgiist dginrs**

dgiinrty dirtying dignity tidying. *See* **dgiinr dginry giinrt ginrty**

dgiinrv driving. *See* **dgiinv dgiinr giinrv**

dgiins siding dings digs ding dins gids gins nidi nisi sign sing dig din gin ids sin id in is si

dgiinss sidings. *See* **dgiins ginss**

dgiinssu disusing sidings issuing. *See* **dgiins dginsu**

dgiinst tidings. *See* **dgiist dgiins giinst**

dgiinty dignity tidying. *See* **dgiit dginy ginty**

dgiinv diving ding nidi dig din gid gin id in

dgiinvvy divvying. *See* **dgiinv**

dgiinyzz dizzying. *See* **dginy diyzz**

dgiir rigid gird grid dig gid rid rig id

dgiist digits digit digs dits gids gist dig dit gid ids its sit id is it si ti

dgiit digit dig dit gid id it ti

dgikmno kingdom. *See* **dgimno**

dgikmnos kingdoms kingdom smoking. *See* **dgimno dginos**

dgikny dyking dingy dinky dying ding dink gink inky kind king dig din gid gin ink kid kin yin id in

dgil gild dig gid lid id li

dgillnor drolling lording rolling. *See* **dgilno**

dgillnu dulling. *See* **dgilu gilnu**

dgilloow goodwill. *See* **giloo**

dgilmno molding. *See* **dgilno dgimno**

dgilmnos moldings molding. *See* **dgilno dgimno dginos gilnos**

dgilmnpu dumpling dumping lumping pluming. *See* **dginpu gilnpu gimnpu**

dgilnoo noodling. *See* **dgilno gilnoo**

dgilno doling dingo doing lingo ding dong gild gold idol ling lion loin long noil dig din dog don gid gin god ion lid log nil nod nog oil old do go id in li lo no od on

dgilnoor drooling lording. *See* **dgilno dinoor gilnoo**

dgilnor lording. *See* **dgilno dginr ginor**

dgilnoty dotingly. *See* **dgilno dgilot dginot ginoty**

dgilost diglots. *See* **dgilot dilost**

dgilot diglot doit dolt gild gilt gold idol toil told dig dit dog dot gid god got lid lit log lot oil old til tod tog do go id it li lo od ti to

dgilrtuy turgidly liturgy. *See* **dgirtu giltuy**

dgils gilds digs gids gild lids slid dig gid ids lid id is li si

dgilsu guilds gilds guild digs gids gild lids lugs slid slug dig dug gid ids lid lug id is li si us

dgilu guild gild dig dug gid lid lug id li

dgimmnru drumming. *See* **dginru**

dgimnnou mounding undoing. *See* **dgimno dginou gimnno**

dgimno doming dingo doing ding dong mind dig dim din dog don gid gin god ion mid mod mog mon nim nod nog do go id in mi mo no od om on

dgimnoo dooming. *See* **dgimno dimnoo gimnoo**

dgimnpu dumping. *See* **dginpu gimnpu**

dgin ding dig din gid gin id in

dginnno donning. *See* **dgino innno**

dginnnu dunning. *No 6s or 5s*

dginnopu pounding undoing. *See* **dginop dginou dginpu**

dginnor droning. *See* **dgino dginr ginor**

dginnoru rounding droning undoing. *See* **dginou dginru dgnoru**

dginnorw drowning downing droning ingrown wording. *See* **ginnow ginorw**

dginnosu sounding dousing guidons undoing. *See* **dginos dginou dginsu dgnosu**

dginnou undoing. *See* **dginou innou**

dginnouw wounding downing inwound undoing. *See* **dginou dinnuw ginnow**

dginnow downing. *See* **ginnow dgino**

dgino dingo doing ding dong dig din dog don gid gin god ion nod nog do go id in no od on

dginoopr drooping. *See* **dginop dinoor ginopr**

dginootu outdoing. *See* **dginot dginou ginotu**

dginop doping dingo doing gipon oping ding dong ping pond dig din dip dog don gid gin gip god ion nip nod nog pig pin pod poi do go id in no od on pi

dginoppr dropping. *See* **dginop ginopr**

dginorsw drowsing wording dowsing. *See* **dginos dginrs dinosw dnorsw**

dginorv droving. *See* **ginorv dgino dginr**

dginorw wording. *See* **ginorw dgino dnorw**

dginos doings dosing dingo dings doing dongs digs ding dins dogs dong dons gids gins gods ions nods nogs sign sing song dig din dog don dos gid gin god ids ion nod nog sin sod son do go id in is no od on os si so

dginosu dousing guidons. *See* **dginsu dginos dginou dgnosu**

dginosw dowsing. *See* **dinosw ginosw**

dginot doting dingo doing ingot ding doit dong into ting tong dig din dit dog don dot gid gin god got ion nit nod nog not tin tod tog ton do go id in it no od on ti to

dginott dotting. *See* **dginot ginott**

dginou guidon dingo doing ding dong dung undo dig din dog don dug dun duo gid gin gnu god gun ion nod nog oud udo do go id in no nu od on

dginoz dozing dingo doing ding dong zing dig din dog don gid gid god ion nod nog zig do go id in no od on

dginpu duping ding dung ping pung dig din dip dug dun gid gin gip gnu gun nip pig pin pug pun id in nu pi up

dginr grind ding gird grid grin rind ring dig din gid gin rid rig id in

dginrs grinds dings girds grids grind grins rinds rings digs ding dins gids gins gird grid grin rids rigs rind ring sign sing dig din gid gin ids rid rig sin sir id in is si

dginru   during grind ruing ding drug dung gird grid grin rind ring ruin rung dig din dug dun gid gin gnu gun rid rig rug run urd urn id in nu

dginry   drying dingy dying grind ridgy ding gird grid grin rind ring dig din dry gid gin rid rig yin id in

dgins   dings digs ding dins gids gins sign sing dig din gid gin ids sin id in is si

dginstu   dusting. *See* **dginsu dinstu**

dginstuy   studying dusting. *See* **dginsu dinstu dintuy ginsty**

dginsu   dingus dings dungs nidus suing using digs ding dins dung duns gids gins gnus guns sign sing snug sung dig din dug dun gid gin gnu gun ids sin sun id in is nu si us

dginy   dingy dying ding dig din gid gin yin id in

dgiopry   prodigy. *See* **dgiry gopry**

dgioyz   zygoid dogy dozy yogi dig dog gid god goy yod zig do go id od oy

dgir   gird grid dig gid rid rig id

dgirs   girds grids digs gids gird grid rids rigs dig gid ids rid rig sir id is si

dgirtu   turgid dirt drug gird girt grid grit trig turd dig dit dug gid gut rid rig rug rut tug tui urd id it ti ut

dgiry   ridgy gird grid dig dry gid rid rig id

dgis   digs gids dig gid ids id is si

dgissstu   disgusts. *See* **issstu**

dglnouy   ungodly. *See* **dgnuy dgloy gnouy**

dglo   gold dog god log old do go lo od

dglooosw   logwoods logwood. *See* **glosw dgoos gloos**

dglooow   logwood. *No 6s or 5s*

dgloooxy   doxology. *See* **dglooy**

dglooy   goodly godly goody dogy gold good logo logy dog god goo goy log loo old yod do go lo od oy

dgloy   godly dogy gold logy dog god goy log old yod do go lo od oy

dglsuy   sludgy duly guys lugs slug ugly dug guy lug sly us

dgmoprsu   gumdrops gumdrop. *See* **dgorsu dmorsu gmprsu goprsu**

dgmopru   gumdrop. *See* **dgoru gopru gmpru**

dgmsuy   smudgy gums guys gyms muds mugs smug dug gum guy gym mud mug mus sum yum mu my um us

dgno   dong dog don god nod nog do go no od on

dgnoos   godson dongs goods goons snood dogs dong dons gods good goon goos nods nogs song soon dog don dos god goo nod nog sod son do go no od on os so

dgnooss   godsons. *See* **dgnoos dnooss**

dgnoosw   godowns. *See* **dgnoos dgnoow**

dgnoow   godown dong down good goon gown wood dog don god goo nod nog now own won woo do go no od on ow

dgnorsu   grounds. *See* **dgorsu dgnoru dnorsu**

dgnoru   ground gourd round dong dour drug dung duro rung undo dog don dor dug dun duo gnu god gun nod nog nor oud our rod rug run udo urd urn do go no nu od on or

dgnos   dongs dogs dong dons gods nods nogs song dog don dos god nod nog sod son do go no od on os so

dgnossu   sundogs. *See* **dgnosu dnossu**

dgnosu   sundog dongs dungs nodus sound dogs dong dons dung duns duos gnus gods guns nods nogs nous onus ouds snug song sung udos undo dog don dos dug dun duo gnu god gun nod nog oud sod son sou sun udo do go no nu od on os so us

dgnsu   dungs dung duns gnus guns snug sung dug dun gnu gun sun nu us

dgnu   dung dug dun gnu gun nu

dgnuy   dungy dung dug dun gnu gun guy nu

dgo   dog god do go od

dgoo   good dog god goo do go od

dgoorstt   dogtrots dogtrot. *See* **goortt**

dgoortt   dogtrot. *See* **goortt**

dgoos   goods dogs gods good goos dog dos god goo sod do go od os so

dgooy   goody good dogy dog god goo goy yod do go od oy

dgorsu   gourds drugs duros gourd dogs dour drug duos duro gods ouds ours rods rugs sour surd udos urds dog dor dos dug duo god oud our rod rug sod sou udo urd do go od or os so us

dgoru   gourd dour drug duro dog dor dug duo god oud our rod rug udo urd do go od or

dgos   dogs gods dog dos god sod do go od os so

dgostuu   dugouts. *See* **dgotuu gostu**

dgosty   stodgy stogy dogs dogy dots gods goys tody togs toys yods dog dos dot god got goy sod sot soy sty tod tog toy yod do go od os oy so to

dgotuu   dugout gout dog dot dug duo god got gut oud out tod tog tug udo do go od to ut

dgoy   dogy dog god goy yod do go od oy

dgpuy   pudgy dug guy gyp pug yup up

dgrsu   drugs drug rugs surd urds dug rug urd us

dgru   drug dug rug urd

dgu   dug

---

dhhilotw   withhold. *See* **dhiot hilot dhitw**

dhi   hid id hi

dhiiimns   diminish. *See* **hiimns**

dhiilot   lithoid. *See* **dhiot diiot hilot**

dhiimno   hominid. *See* **diimo**

dhiimnos   hominids hominid. *See* **dhimos diimos hiimns**

dhiimpss   midships. *See* **dhiips hiimps**

dhiimtuy   humidity. *See* **diimty**

dhiiopx   xiphoid. *No 6s or 5s*

dhiiorsz   rhizoids rhizoid. *See* **iorsz**

dhiiorz   rhizoid. *No 6s or 5s*

dhiips   hispid dips dish hips pish ship dip hid hip his ids sip hi id is pi sh si

dhiknoow   hoodwink inkwood. *See* **hnoow**

dhikssu   duskish. *See* **dikss dkssu hkssu**

dhillsu   dullish. *See* **dllsu hills hllsu**

dhilmosy   modishly. *See* **dhilos dhimos hilmos hilmoy**

dhilnop   dolphin. *No 6s or 5s*

dhilnops   dolphins dolphin. *See* **dhilos hilops hinops**

dhiloprs   lordship. *See* **dhilos hilops**

dhilopss   slipshod. *See* **dhilos diloss hilops ilopss**

dhilorry   horridly. *See* **dhiorr**

dhilos   oldish holds idols solid dish hods hold idol lids oils shod silo slid soil sold dos hid his hod ids lid los ohs oil old sod sol do hi ho id is li lo od oh os sh si so

dhilosu   loudish. *See* **dhilos dhlosu**

dhilpssy   sylphids sylphid. *See* **hlpssy**

dhilpsy   sylphid. *See* **dilsy hlpsy**

dhilrty   thirdly. *See* **dirty dhirt hilrt**

dhimnost hindmost. *See* **dhimos dhiost hmnost imnost**

dhimorsu humidors rhodiums humidor rhodium. *See* **dhimos dhorsu dimosu dmorsu**

dhimoru humidor rhodium. *See* **hioru dhimu hmoru**

dhimos modish misdo dims dish hods mhos mods ohms shim shod dim dos hid him his hod ids mho mid mis mod mos ohm ohs oms sod do hi ho id is mi mo od oh om os sh si so

dhimpsu dumpish. *See* **dmpsu hmpsu**

dhimu humid dim hid him hum mid mud hi id mi mu um

dhin hind din hid hin hi id in

dhinnos donnish. *See* **dhins**

dhinoors dishonor indoors. *See* **dinoor dnoors hinors hnoors**

dhinorsu roundish nourish. *See* **dhnosu dhorsu dnorsu hinors**

dhinotuw whodunit. *See* **dhiot dnotu dhnou**

dhins hinds dins dish hind hins shin din hid hin his ids sin hi id in is sh si

dhinsy shindy hinds shiny dins dish hind hins shin din hid hin his ids shy sin yin hi id in is sh si

dhiopty typhoid. *See* **dhiot dhioy hipty**

dhiorr horrid dor hid hod rho rid rod do hi ho id od oh or

dhiorsty thyroids thyroid history. *See* **dhiost dhirst dhorsy diorst**

dhiorty thyroid. *See* **dhiot dirty diort**

dhiost dhotis dhoti doits hoist dish dits doit dots hist hits hods host hots shod shot sith this tosh dit dos dot hid his hit hod hot ids its ohs sit sod sot tho tod do hi ho id is it od oh os sh si so ti to

dhiot dhoti doit dit dot hid hit hod hot tho tod do hi ho id it od oh ti to

dhioy hyoid yodh hid hod hoy yod do hi ho id od oh oy

dhiprsu prudish. *See* **diprs**

dhirst thirds third shirt dirt dish dits hist hits rids sith stir this dit hid his hit ids its rid sir sit hi id is it sh si ti

dhirt third dirt dit hid hit rid hi id it ti

dhis dish hid his ids hi id is sh si

dhistw widths whist whits width dish dits hist hits sith this whit wish with wits dit hid his hit ids its sit wis wit hi id is it sh si ti

dhitw width whit with dit hid hit wit hi id it ti

dhjoprsu jodhpurs jodhpur. *See* **dhorsu**

dhjopru jodhpur. *See* **dopru**

dhkorsy droshky. *See* **dhorsy dkory**

dhlmoosu hoodlums hoodlum. *See* **dhlosu dlmosu hlmoos**

dhlmoou hoodlum. *See* **dlmou**

dhlo hold hod old do ho lo od oh

dhloostu holdouts holdout outsold. *See* **dhlosu**

dhlootu holdout. *See* **dootu**

dhlopsu holdups upholds. *See* **dhlopu dhlosu**

dhlopu holdup uphold hold holp loud plod duo hod hop hup lop old oud pod pul udo do ho lo od oh up

dhlorxyy hydroxyl. *See* **dhory dlryy**

dhlos holds hods hold shod sold dos hod los ohs old sod sol do ho lo od oh os sh so

dhlosstu shouldst. *See* **dhlosu hlosst hosstu**

dhlosu should holds duos hods hold loud lush ouds shod sold soul udos dos duo hod los ohs old oud sod sol sou udo do ho lo od oh os sh so us

dhmmruu humdrum. *No 6s or 5s*

dhmnoyy hymnody. *No 6s or 5s*

dhnoosww showdown. *See* **dhosw dnosw dhoos**

dhnostuw shutdown. *See* **dhnosu dnostu dnosuw**

dhnosu hounds hound nodus sound dons duns duos hods nods nosh nous onus ouds shod shun udos undo don dos dun duo hod hon nod ohs oud sod son sou sun udo do ho no nu od oh on os sh so us

dhnou hound undo don dun duo hod hon nod oud udo do ho no nu od oh on

dho hod do ho od oh

dhoo hood hod oho ooh do ho od oh

dhoooo hoodoo hood hod oho ooh do ho od oh

dhooooos hoodoos. *See* **dhoooo dhoos**

dhooortx orthodox. *See* **hoort**

dhoos hoods hods hood oohs shod shoo dos hod oho ohs ooh sod do ho od oh os sh so

dhorssu shrouds. *See* **dhorsu orssu**

dhorsu shroud duros hours dour duos duro hods hour ouds ours rhos rods rush shod sour surd udos urds dor dos duo hod ohs oud our rho rod sod sou udo urd do ho od oh or os sh so us

dhorsuy hydrous. *See* **dhorsu dhorsy**

dhorsy hydros horsy hydro yodhs dory hods hoys rhos rods rosy shod yodh yods dor dos dry hod hoy ohs rho rod shy sod soy yod do ho od oh or os oy sh so

dhory hydro yodh dory dor dry hod hoy rho rod yod do ho od oh or oy

dhos hods shod dos hod ohs sod do ho od oh os sh so

dhosw dhows dhow hods shod show dos hod how ohs sod sow who do ho od oh os ow sh so

dhosy yodhs hods hoys shod yodh yods dos hod hoy ohs shy sod soy yod do ho od oh os oy sh so

dhow dhow hod how who do ho od oh ow

dhowy howdy dhow yodh hod how hoy who why yod yow do ho od oh ow oy

dhoy yodh hod hoy yod do ho od oh oy

dhstu thuds dust huts shut stud thud thus tush hut sh us ut

dhtu thud hut ut

di id

diiiltvy lividity. *See* **diilv**

diiimru iridium. *No 6s or 5s*

diiimtty timidity. *See* **diimty**

diiinosv division. *See* **iinosv**

diiinps insipid. *No 6s or 5s*

diiirtvy viridity. *See* **dirty**

diijnos disjoin. *See* **ijnos**

diijnoss disjoins disjoin. *See* **ijnos**

diijnost disjoint disjoin. *See* **diiost ijnost**

diikkns kidskin. *See* **dikns ikkns**

diikknss kidskins kidskin. *See* **iiknss ikknss**

diillmpy limpidly. *See* **diilmp dillmy dilmpy illmpy**

diillquy liquidly. *See* **diilqu**

diillsst distills distill. *See* **illsst**

diillst distill. *See* illst

diillsty idyllist distill. *See* dillsy illsty

diilmp limpid lipid mild limp dim dip imp lid lip mid mil id li mi pi

diilmty timidly. *See* diimty dilmy iilmt

diilmuuv diluvium. *See* diilv iilmu

diilnotu dilution. *See* dilntu dlnotu

diilosty solidity styloid. *See* diiost dilost

diilp lipid dip lid lip id li pi

diilps lipids lipid dips lids lips lisp slid slip dip ids lid lip sip id is li pi si

diilqsu liquids. *See* diilqu diqsu

diilqu liquid quid lid id li

diilv livid lid id li

diilvvy vividly. *See* divvy diilv diivv

diilyzz dizzily. *See* diyzz

diimnnoo dominion. *See* dimnoo iimnno

diimnopt midpoint. *See* diimo diiot inopt

diimnor midiron. *See* diimo diinr imnor

diimnors midirons midiron. *See* diimos diinrs imnors

diimnnu indium nidi mind dim din dun mid mud nim id in mi mu nu um

diimo idiom dim mid mod do id mi mo od om

diimoprs prismoid. *See* diimos imoprs

diimos idioms idiom misdo dims mods dim dos ids mid mis mod mos oms sod do id is mi mo od om os si so

diimsss dismiss. *No 6s or 5s*

diimstw dimwits. *See* diimtw dimst

diimt timid dim dit mid id it mi ti

diimtw dimwit timid dim dit mid wit id it mi ti

diimty dimity timid tidy dim dit mid id it mi my ti

diin nidi din id in

diinnsw inwinds. *See* dinsw

diinoqsu quinoids quinoid. *See* inoqsu

diinoqu quinoid. *See* inoqu

diinr indri nidi rind din rid id in

diinrs indris indri rinds dins iris nidi nisi rids rind din ids rid sin sir id in is si

diinstuy disunity. *See* dinstu dintuy

diiorssv divisors divisor. *See* iorssv

diiorsv divisor. *See* diosv iorsv

diiost idiots idiot doits dits doit dots dit dos dot ids its sit sod sot tod do id is it od os si so ti to

diiot idiot doit dit dot tod do id it od ti to

diivv vivid id v

dijmssu musjids. *See* dijmsu

dijmsu musjid dims muds dim ids jus mid mis mud mus sum id is mi mu si um us

dik kid id

diklnnuy unkindly. *See* diklny diknnu

diklny kindly dinky dink idly idyl inky inly kiln kind link liny din ilk ink kid kin lid nil yin id in li

diklsuy duskily. *See* dksuy dilsy iklsy

dikmnnu dinkum dink dunk kind mind mink dim din dun ink kid kin mid mud nim id in mi mu nu um

dikn dink kind din ink kid kin id in

diknnos nonskid. *See* dikns iknos

diknnsu nudniks. *See* diknnu

diknnu nudnik unkind dink dunk kind din dun ink inn kid kin nun id in nu

diknoow inkwood. *No 6s or 5s*

diknr drink dink dirk kind rind rink din ink irk kid kin kir rid id in

diknrs drinks dinks dirks drink kinds rinds rinks dink dins dirk disk inks irks kids kind kris rids rind rink risk sink skid skin din ids ink irk kid kin kir rid sin sir ski id in is si

dikns dinks kinds dink dins disk inks kids kind sink skid skin din ids ink kid kin sin ski id in is si

dikny dinky dink inky kind din ink kid kin yin id in li

dikr dirk irk kid kir rid id

dikrs dirks dirk disk irks kids kris rids risk skid ids irk kid kir rid sir ski id is si

diks disk kids skid ids kid ski id is si

dikss disks skids disk kids kiss skid skis ids kid sis ski id is si

dil lid id li

dill dill lid ill id li

dillmy mildly dilly dimly idyll dill idly idyl illy lily limy mild mill dim ill lid mid mil id li mi my

dilloors doorsill. *See* dillrs dllors dloors

dillosty stolidly solidly styloid. *See* dillsy dilost illsty

dillosy solidly. *See* dillsy diloy dllos

dillr drill dill dirl rill ill lid rid id li

dillrs drills dirls drill rills dill dirl lids rids rill sill slid ids ill lid rid sir id is li si

dillruy luridly. *See* dilly dillr dlluy

dillsy idylls dilly idyll idyls silly dill idly idyl illy lids lily sill slid ids ill lid sly id is li si

dillwy wildly dilly idyll dill idly idyl illy lily wild will wily lid ill id li

dilly dilly idyll dill idly idyl illy lily lid ill id li

dilm mild dim lid mid mil id li mi

dilmnrsu drumlins drumlin. *See* dimnsu ilmnsu

dilmnru drumlin. *See* dilru

dilmooy moodily. *See* dilmy diloy dlmoy

dilmor milord dirl dorm idol limo lord mild milo moil mold roil dim dor lid mid mil mir mod mor oil old rid rim rod do id li lo mi mo od om or

dilmpy dimply dimly imply idly idyl limp limy mild dim dip imp lid lip mid mil ply yip id li mi my pi

dilmy dimly idly idyl limy mild dim lid mid mil id li mi my

dilnpsy spindly. *See* dilsy ilnsy inpsy

dilnstu indults. *See* dilntu ilnstu dinstu

dilntu indult until lint lunt unit din dit dun lid lit nil nit nut til tin tui tun id in it li nu ti ut

dilo idol lid oil old do id li lo od

diloorss lordosis. *See* diloss dloors

diloosuy odiously. *See* dioosu

diloprty torpidly. *See* dioprt ilopty ilprty loprty

dilorswy drowsily wordily. *See* dlorsw dorswy ilrswy

dilorwy wordily. *See* diloy dorwy ilory

dilos idols solid idol lids oils silo slid soil sold dos ids lid los oil old sod sol do id is li lo od os si so

diloss solids idols silos soils solid doss idol lids loss oils silo slid sods soil sold sols dos ids lid los oil old sis sod sol do id is li lo od os si so

dilost stolid doits dolts idols solid toils dits doit dolt dots idol lids list lost lots oils silo silt slid slit slot soil sold tils toil told dit dos dot ids its lid lit los lot oil old sit sod sol sot til tod do id is it li lo od os si so ti to

dilosty styloid. *See* dilost disty diloy

diloxy xyloid doily doxy idly idol idyl oily lid lox oil old yod do id li lo od ox oy xi

diloy doily idly idol idyl oily lid oil old yod do id li lo od oy

dilpstuy stupidly. *See* dipstu ilpstu

dilr dirl lid rid id li

dilrs dirls dirl lids rids slid ids lid rid sir id is li si

dilrstuy sturdily rustily. *See* drstuy ilrsty lrstuy

dilru lurid dirl lid rid urd id li

dilryzz drizzly. *See* diyzz

dils lids slid ids lid id is li si

dilsw wilds lids slid wild ids lid wis id is li si

dilsy idyls idly idyl lids slid ids lid sly id is li si

dilw wild lid id li

dily idly idyl lid id li

dim dim mid id mi

dimmost midmost. *See* diost dimst dimos

dimn mind dim din mid nim id in mi

dimnoo domino doom mind mono mood moon dim din don ion mid mod mon moo nim nod do id in mi mo no od om on

dimnopsu impounds impound. *See* dimnsu dimopu dimosu dmnosu

dimnopu impound. *See* dimopu dmnou dnopu

dimnostu dismount. *See* **dimnsu dimosu dinstu diostu**

dimnotw midtown. *No 6s or 5s*

dimns minds dims dins mind nims dim din ids mid mis nim sin id in is mi si

dimnssu nudisms. *See* **dimnsu inssu**

dimnsu nudism minds minus nidus dims dins duns mind muds nims dim din dun ids mid mis mud mus nim sin sum sun id in is mi mu nu si um us

dimopu podium odium opium dump dim dip duo imp mid mod mop mud oud pod poi udo ump do id mi mo mu od om pi um up

dimorswy rowdyism. *See* **dimosw dorswy**

dimos misdo dims mods dim dos ids mid mis mod mos oms sod do id is mi mo od om os si so

dimossu sodiums. *See* **dimosu**

dimossw wisdoms. *See* **dimosw imssw**

dimosu odiums sodium misdo odium dims duos mods muds ouds sumo udos dim dos duo ids mid mis mod mos mud mus oms oud sod sou sum udo do id is mi mo mu od om os si so um us

dimosw wisdom misdo dims mods mows swim dim dos ids mid mis mod mos mow oms sod sow wis do id is mi mo od om os ow si so

dimou odium dim duo mid mod mud oud udo do id mi mo mu od om um

dimrsuuv duumvirs duumvir. *See* **dmrsu irsuv**

dimrtuu triduum. *See* **dimtu**

dimruuv duumvir. *No 6s or 5s*

dims dims dim dis mid mis id is mi si

dimssy mysids mysid missy dims miss dim ids mid mis sis id is mi my si

dimst midst dims dits mist dim dit ids its mid mis sit id is it mi si ti

dimsy mysid dims dim ids mid mis id is mi my si

dimtu tumid dim dit mid mud tui id it mi mu ti um ut

din din id in

dinnouw inwound. *See* **dinnuw dnouw innou**

dinnsuw unwinds. *See* **dinnuw dinsu dinsw**

dinnuw unwind wind din dun inn nun win id in nu

dinooorw ironwood. *See* **dinoor**

dinoor indoor donor rondo door iron odor ordo rind rood din don dor ion nod nor rid rod do id in no od on or

dinoors indoors. *See* **dnoors dinoor inoors**

dinoosty nodosity. *See* **noosty**

dinorsww windrows windrow windows. *See* **dinosw dinoww diosww dnorsw**

dinorww windrow. *See* **dinoww dnorw**

dinossw disowns. *See* **dinosw nossw**

dinosw disown downs winds winos dins dons down ions nods owns snow sown wind wino wins din don dos ids ion nod now own sin sod son sow win wis won do id in is no od on os ow si so

dinosww windows. *See* **dinosw diosww dinoww**

dinoww window widow down wind wino din don ion nod now own win won wow do id in no od on ow

dinpstu pundits. *See* **inpstu dinstu dinptu dipstu**

dinpsuw windups. *See* **dinpuw**

dinptu pundit input pint punt unit din dip dit dun nip nit nut pin pit pun put tin tip tui tun tup id in it nu pi ti up ut

dinpuw upwind windup wind din dip dun nip pin pun win id in nu pi up

dinr rind din rid id in

dinrs rinds dins rids rind din ids rid sin sir id in is si

dinrstuy industry. *See* **dinstu dintuy dnrsuy drstuy**

dins dins din ids sin id in is si

dinsstu nudists. *See* **dinstu insstu**

dinstu nudist nidus suint units dins dits duns dust nits nuts snit stud stun suit tins tuis tuns unit din dit dun ids its nit nut sin sit sun tin tui tun id in is it nu si ti us ut

dinsu nidus dins duns din dun ids sin sun id in is nu si us

dinsw winds dins wind wins din ids sin win wis id in is si

dintuy nudity untidy unity duty tidy tiny unit din dit dun nit nut tin tui tun yin id in it nu ti ut

dinw wind din win id in

dinwy windy wind winy wynd din win yin id in

dioops isopod dips oops pods pois dip dos ids pod poi sip sod sop do id is od os pi si so

dioopss isopods. *See* **dioops**

dioorstt ridottos ridotto distort. *See* **diorst diostt**

dioortt ridotto. *See* **diort diott**

dioostx toxoids. *See* **diootx diost doost**

dioosu iodous odious duos ouds udos dos duo ids oud sod sou udo do id is od os si so us

dioosv ovoids ovoid voids void dos ids sod do id is od os si so

dioosz zooids zooid zoos dos ids sod zoo do id is od os si so

diootx toxoid doit dit dot tod too do id it od ox ti to xi

dioov ovoid void do id od

diooz zooid zoo do id od

dioprt torpid droit dript dirt doit drip drop port prod riot tiro trio trip trod dip dit dor dot ort pit pod poi pot pro rid rip rod rot tip tod top tor do id it od or pi ti to

diorrt torrid droit dirt doit riot tiro tori torr trio trod dit dor dot ort rid rod rot tod tor do id it od or ti to

diorsstt distorts distort. *See* **diorst diostt**

diorst droits doits droit riots tiros torsi trios dirt dits doit dots orts rids riot rods rots sori sort stir tiro tori tors trio trod dit dor dos dot ids its ort rid rod rot sir sit sod sot tod tor do id is it od or os si so ti to

diorstt distort. *See* **diorst diostt**

diort droit dirt doit riot tiro tori trio trod dit dor dot ort rid rod rot tod tor do id it od or ti to

diosstu studios. *See* **diostu dsstu osstu**

diosstuu studious studios. *See* **diostu**

diost doits dits doit dots dit dos dot ids its sit sod sot tod do id is it od os si so ti to

diostt dittos doits ditto dits doit dots tits tost tots dit dos dot ids its sit sod sot tit tod tot do id is it od os si so ti to

diostu studio doits dits doit dots duos dust ouds oust outs stud suit tuis udos dit dos dot duo ids its oud out sit sod sot sou tod tui udo do id is it od os si so ti to us ut

diostv divots divot doits voids dits doit dots void dit dos dot ids its sit sod sot tod do id is it od os si so ti to

diosv voids void dos ids sod do id is od os si so

diosww widows widow wows dos ids sod sow wis wow do id is od os ow si so

diot doit dit dot tod do id it od ti to

diott ditto doit dit dot tit tod tot do id it od ti to

diotv divot doit void dit dot tod do id it od ti to

diov void do id od

dioww widow wow do id od ow

dip dip id pi

dippry drippy dippy drip pipy dip dry pip pry rid rip yip id pi

dippy dippy pipy dip pip yip id pi

dipr drip dip rid rip id pi

diprs drips dips drip rids rips dip ids rid rip sip sir id is pi si

diprsstu disrupts disrupt purists. *See* **diprtu dipstu iprsst iprstu**

diprstu disrupt. *See* **iprstu diprtu dipstu**

diprt dript dirt drip trip dip dit pit rid rip tip id it pi ti

diprtu putrid dript dirt drip trip turd dip dit pit put rid rip rut tip tui tup urd id it pi ti up ut

dips dips dip ids sip id is pi si

dipstu stupid situp dips dits dust pits puts spit spud stud suit tips tuis tups dip dit ids its pit pus put sip sit sup tip tui tup id is it pi si ti up us ut

diqssu squids quids squid quid suds ids sis id is si us

diqsu quids squid quid ids id is si us

diqu quid id

dir rid id

dirs rids ids rid sir id is si

dirssttu distrust. *See* **rssttu**

dirt dirt rid dit id it ti

dirty dirty dirt tidy dit dry rid try id it ti

dis ids id is si

dist dits dit ids its sit id is it si ti

disty ditsy dits tidy dit ids its sit sty id is it si ti

dit dit id it ti

ditty ditty tidy dit tit id it ti

dity tidy dit id it ti

dityz ditzy tidy dit zit id it ti

divvy divvy ivy id

diyzz dizzy id

---

dj

djnnoo donjon dojo noon don nod do jo no od on

djnnoos donjons. *See* **djnnoo djoos nnoos**

djoo dojo do jo od

djoos dojos dojo dos sod do jo od os so

djou judo duo oud udo do jo od

---

dk

dkmnooor komondor. *See* **dnoor mnoor**

dknrsu drunks drunk dunks knurs dunk duns dusk knur runs rusk sunk surd urds urns dun run sun urd urn nu us

dknru drunk dunk knur dun run urd urn nu

dknsu dunks dunk duns dusk sunk dun sun nu us

dknu dunk dun nu

dkoooo koodoo do od

dkoooos koodoos. *See* **dkoooo**

dkory dorky dory dor dry kor rod yod do od or oy

dkosu kudos duos dusk ouds udos dos duo kos oud sod sou udo do od os so us

dkssu dusks dusk suds us

dksu dusk us

dksuu kudus dusk kudu us

dksuuz kudzus kudus kudzu dusk kudu us

dksuy dusky dusk yuks sky yuk us

dkuu kudu

dkuuz kudzu kudu

---

dl

dlmorsu slumlord. *See* **dllors dlmosu dmorsu**

dllo doll old do lo od

dlloop dollop doll loop plod poll polo pool loo lop old pod do lo od

dlloops dollops. *See* **dlloop dloops**

dllor droll doll lord roll dor old rod do lo od or

dllors drolls dolls droll lords rolls doll lord rods roll sold dor dos los old rod sod sol do lo od or os so

dllorwy worldly. *See* **dllory**

dllory drolly lordly droll dolly doll dory lord lory roll dor dry old rod yod do lo od or oy

dllos dolls doll sold dos los old sod sol do lo od os so

dllouy loudly dolly dully doll dull duly loud duo old oud udo yod you do lo od oy

dlloy dolly doll old yod do lo od oy

dllsu dulls dull us

dllu dull

dlluy dully dull duly

dlmo mold old mod do lo mo od om

dlmos molds mods mold sold dos los mod mos old oms sod sol do lo mo od om os so

dlmosu moulds molds mould duos loud mods mold muds ouds slum sold soul sumo udos dos duo los lum mod mos mud mus old oms oud sod sol sou sum udo do lo mo mu od om os so um us

dlmou mould mold loud duo lum mod mud old oud udo do lo mo mu od om um

dlmouy mouldy mould moldy duly loud mold moly duo lum mod mud old oud udo yod you yum do lo mo mu my od om oy um

dlmoy moldy mold moly mod old yod do lo mo my od om oy

dlnoosww slowdown lowdown. *See* **dnosw lnoos dnoos**

dlnooww lowdown. *No 6s or 5s*

dlnoruy roundly. *See* **dnoru**

dlnosuy soundly. *See* **losuy dnosu dnosy**

dlnotu untold donut dolt loud lout lunt told tolu undo unto don dot dun duo lot nod not nut old oud out tod ton tun udo do lo no nu od on to ut

dlnuuy unduly duly dun ulu nu

dlo old do lo od

dlooorsu dolorous odorous. *See* **dloors**

dlooppuw pulpwood. *See* **dlouw**

dloops podsol loops plods polos pools sloop soldo spool loop loos lops oops plod pods polo pool slop sold solo dos loo lop los old pod sod sol sop do lo od os so

dloopss podsols. *See* **dloops loopss**

dloopswy plywoods plywood. *See* **dloops dooswy**

dloopwy plywood. *See* **doowy loopy**

dloor dolor drool door lord odor ordo rood dor loo old rod do lo od or

dloors dolors drools dolor doors drool lords odors ordos roods soldo door loos lord odor ordo rods rood sold solo dor dos loo los old rod sod sol do lo od or os so

dloos soldo loos sold solo dos loo los old sod sol do lo od os so

dloostu outsold. *See* **dlost loost lostu**

dlop plod lop old pod do lo od

dlopruy proudly. *See* **dopru**

dlops plods lops plod pods slop sold dos lop los old pod sod sol sop do lo od os so

dlor lord dor old rod do lo od or

dlors lords lord rods sold dor dos los old rod sod sol do lo od or os so

dlorsw worlds lords sword words world lord lows owls rods rows slow sold wold word dor dos los low old owl rod row sod sol sow do lo od or os ow so

dlorw world lord wold word dor low old owl rod row do lo od or ow

dlos sold dos los old sod sol do lo od os so

dlost dolts dolt dots lost lots slot sold told dos dot los lot old sod sol sot tod do lo od os so to

dlot dolt told dot lot old tod do lo od to

dlou loud duo old oud udo do lo od

dlouw would loud wold duo low old oud owl udo do lo od ow

dlow wold low old owl do lo od ow

dlryy dryly dry

dluy duly

dmmoorsu mudrooms mudroom. *See* **dmorsu**

dmmooru mudroom. *No 6s or 5s*

dmmuy dummy mud mum yum mu my um

dmnooy monody moody moony doom mono mood moon yond don mod mon moo nod yod yon do mo my no od om on oy

dmnosu mounds mound muons nodus sound dons duns duos mods mons muds muon nods nous onus ouds sumo udos undo don dos dun duo mod mon mos mud mus nod oms oud sod son sou sum sun udo do mo mu no nu od om on os so sum us

dmnou mound undo muon don dun duo mod mon mud nod oud udo do mo mu no nu od om on um

dmo mod do mo od om

dmoo doom mood mod moo do mo od om

dmoos dooms moods doom mods mood moos dos mod moo mos oms sod do mo od om os so

dmooy moody doom mood mod moo yod do mo my od om oy

dmor dorm dor mod mor rod do mo od om or

dmors dorms dorm mods mors rods dor dos mod mor mos oms rod sod do mo od om or os so

dmorsu dorsum dorms drums duros dorm dour drum duos duro mods mors muds ouds ours rods rums sour sumo surd udos urds dor dos duo mod mor

mos mud mus oms oud our rod rum sod sou sum udo urd do mo mu od om or os so um us

dmos mods dos mod mos oms sod do mo od om os so

dmpsu dumps dump muds spud sump umps mud mus pus sum sup ump mu um up us

dmpu dump mud ump mu um up

dmpuy dumpy dump mud ump yum yup mu my um up

dmrsu drums drum muds rums surd urds mud mus rum sum urd mu um us

dmru drum mud rum urd mu um

dmsu muds mud mus sum mu um us

dmu mud mu um

dnnortuw turndown rundown. *See* **dnortu**

dnnoruw rundown. *See* **dnorw dnoru dnouw**

dnnossuw sundowns sundown. *See* **dnossu dnosuw**

dnnosuu   unsound. *See* **dnosu nnosu**

dnnosuw   sundown. *See* **dnosuw nnosu**

dnnouuw   unwound. *See* **dnouw**

dno   don nod do no od on

dnooppru   propound. *See* **doopru**

dnooprsw   snowdrop. *See* **dnoors dnorsw dooprs nooprs**

dnoopruw   downpour. *See* **doopru**

dnoor   donor rondo door odor ordo rood don dor nod nor rod do no od on or

dnoors   donors rondos donor doors odors ordos rondo roods snood dons door nods odor ordo rods rood soon don dor dos nod nor rod sod son do no od on or os so

dnoorsuw   wondrous. *See* **dnoors dnorsu dnorsw dnosuw**

dnoortu   orotund. *See* **dnortu dnoor dootu**

dnoos   snood dons nods soon don dos nod sod son do no od on os so

dnooss   snoods snood dons doss nods sods sons soon don dos nod sod son do no od on os so

dnop   pond don nod pod do no od on

dnoprsuu   roundups roundup. *See* **dnopsu dnorsu**

dnopruu   roundup. *See* **dnopu dopru dnoru**

dnops   ponds dons nods pods pond pons don dos nod pod sod son sop do no od on os so

dnopsu   pounds nodus ponds pound sound dons duns duos nods nous onus opus ouds pods pond pons puns soup spud spun udos undo upon don dos dun duo nod oud pod pun pus sod son sop sou sun sup udo do no nu od on os so up us

dnopu   pound pond undo upon don dun duo nod oud pod pun udo do no nu od on up

dnorrsuu   surround. *See* **dnorsu**

dnorsu   rounds duros nodus round sound dons dour duns duos duro nods nous onus ouds ours rods runs sour surd udos undo urds urns don dor dos dun duo nod nor oud our rod run sod son sou sun udo urd urn do no nu od on or os so us

dnorsw   drowns downs drown sword sworn words dons down nods owns rods rows snow sown word worn don dor dos nod nor now own rod row sod son sow won do no od on or os ow so

dnortu   rotund round donut dour duro rout runt torn tour trod turd turn undo unto don dor dot dun duo nod nor not nut ort oud our out rod rot run rut tod ton tor tun udo urd urn do no nu od on or to ut

dnoru   round dour duro undo don dor dun duo nod nor oud our rod run udo urd urn do no nu od on or

dnorw   drown down word worn don dor nod nor now own rod row won do no od on or ow

dnos   dons nods don dos nod sod son do no od on os so

dnossu   sounds nodus sound dons doss duns duos nods nous onus ouds sods sons sous suds suns udos undo don dos dun duo nod oud sod son sou sun udo do no nu od on os so us

dnossy   synods synod dons doss nods nosy sods sons soys yods yond don dos nod sod son soy yod yon do no od on os oy so

dnostu   donuts donut nodus snout sound tonus dons dots duns duos dust nods nous nuts onus ouds oust outs snot stud stun tons tuns udos undo unto don dos dot dun duo nod not nut oud out sod son sot sou sun tod ton tun udo do no nu od on os so to us ut

dnosu   nodus sound dons duns duos nods nous onus ouds udos undo don dos dun duo nod oud sod son sou sun udo do no nu od on os so us

dnosuw   wounds downs nodus sound wound dons down duns duos nods nous onus ouds owns snow sown udos undo don dos dun duo nod now oud own sod son sou sow sun udo won do no nu od on os ow so us

dnosuz   zounds nodus sound dons duns duos nods nous onus ouds udos undo don dos dun duo nod oud sod son sou sun udo do no nu od on os so us

dnosw   downs dons down nods owns snow sown don dos nod now own sod son sow won do no od on os ow so

dnosy   synod dons nods nosy yods yond don dos nod sod son soy yod yon do no od on os oy so

dnotu   donut undo unto don dot dun duo nod not nut oud out tod ton tun udo do no nu od on to ut

dnou   undo don dun duo nod oud udo do no nu od on

dnouw   wound undo down don dun duo nod now oud own udo won do no nu od on ow

dnow   down don nod now own won do no od on ow

dnowy   downy down wynd yond don nod now own won yod yon yow do no od on ow oy

dnoy   yond don nod yod yon do no od on oy

dnrsuy   sundry duns runs surd urds urns dry dun run sun urd urn nu us

dnsu   duns dun sun nu us

dnswy   wynds wynd

dnu   dun nu

dnwy   wynd

---

do

do   do od

doooosv   voodoos. *See* **dooooov**

dooooov   voodoo do od

doooprst   doorstop. *See* **dooprs ooprst**

dooorstu   outdoors odorous outdoor. *See* **oorstu**

dooorsu   odorous. *See* **doors dorsu**

dooortu   outdoor. *See* **dootu**

doopr   droop door drop odor ordo poor prod rood dor pod pro rod do od or

dooprs   droops doors droop drops odors ordos prods roods sopor spoor door drop odor oops ordo pods poor prod pros rods rood dor dos pod pro rod sod sop do od or os so

dooprstu   dropouts dropout uproots uropods. *See* **dooprs doopru ooprst ooprsu**

dooprsu   uropods. *See* **dooprs ooprsu doopru**

dooprsy   prosody. *See* **dooprs doopry doprsy**

dooprtu   dropout. *See* **doopru ooprtu**

doopru   uropod droop proud door dour drop duro odor ordo poor pour prod rood dor duo oud our pod pro rod udo urd do od or up

doopry droopy droop door dory drop odor ordo poor prod rood ropy dor dry pod pro pry rod yod do od or oy

door door odor ordo rood dor rod do od or

doors doors odors ordos roods door odor ordo rods rood dor dos rod sod do od or os so

doost stood dots soot dos dot sod sot tod too do od os so to

doosw woods wood woos dos sod sow woo do od os ow so

dooswy woodsy woods woody wood woos yods dos sod sow soy woo yod yow do od os ow oy so

dootu outdo dot duo oud out tod too udo do od to ut

doow wood woo do od ow

doowy woody wood woo yod yow do od ow oy

dop pod do od

dopr drop prod dor pod pro rod do od or

doprs drops prods drop pods prod pros rods dor dos pod pro rod sod sop do od or os so

doprsy dropsy drops prods prosy dory drop pods posy prod pros rods ropy rosy spry yods dor dos dry pod pro pry rod sod sop soy spy yod do od or os oy so

dopru proud dour drop duro pour prod dor duo oud our pod pro rod udo urd do od or up

dops pods dos pod sod sop do od os so

doqsu quods duos ouds quod udos dos duo oud sod sou udo do od os so us

doqu quod duo oud udo do od

dor dor rod do od or

dorss dross doss rods sods dor dos rod sod do od or os so

dorssw swords dross sword words doss rods rows sods sows word dor dos rod row sod sow do od or os ow so

dorssy drossy dross dory doss rods rosy sods soys yods dor dos dry rod sod soy yod do od or os oy so

dorsu duros dour duos duro ouds ours rods sour surd udos urds dor dos duo oud our rod sod sou udo urd do od or os so us

dorsw sword words rods rows word dor dos rod row sod sow do od or os ow so

dorswy drowsy dowry rowdy sword words wordy dory rods rosy rows word yods dor dos dry rod row sod sow soy yod yow do od or os ow oy so

dort trod dor dot ort rod rot tod tor do od or to

doru dour duro dor duo oud our rod udo urd do od or

dorw word dor rod row do od or ow

dorwy dowry rowdy wordy word dory dor dry rod row yod yow do od or ow oy

dory dory dor dry rod yod do od or oy

dos dos sod do od os so

doss doss sods dos sod do od os so

dost dots dos dot sod sot tod do od os so to

dosu duos ouds udos dos duo oud sou udo do od os so us

dosy yods dos sod soy yod do od os oy so

dot dot tod do od to

dotty dotty tody dot tod tot toy yod do od oy to

doty tody dot tod toy yod do od oy to

dou duo oud udo do od

doxy doxy yod do od ox oy

doy yod do od oy

doyz dozy yod do od oy

---

dpssu spuds puss spud suds sups pus sup up us

dpsu spud pus sup up us

---

drstu durst turds dust rust ruts stud surd turd urds urd rut us ut

drstuy sturdy durst dusty rusty study turds yurts dust duty rust ruts stud surd turd urds yurt dry rut sty try urd us ut

drsu surd urds urd us

drtu turd urd rut ut

dru urd

dry dry

ds

dsstu dusts studs dust stud suds us ut
dssu suds us

dssuy sudsy suds us
dstu dust stud us ut

dstuy dusty study dust duty stud sty us ut

dt

dtuy duty ut

ee

eeeefrr referee. *See* **eeefrr**

eeeefrrs referees referee reefers. *See* **eeefrr eefrrs**

eeeegmrr reemerge. *See* **eeegmr eegmrr**

eeeegqsu squeegee. *See* **eeegs eegsu**

eeeehtty eyeteeth. *See* **eeehtt**

eeeepst teepees. *See* **eeeept eeepst**

eeeepsw peewees. *See* **eeeepw eeepsw**

eeeept teepee tepee epee pee pet tee pe

eeeepw peewee pewee epee weep ewe pee pew wee pe we

eeeffnrt efferent. *See* **eeefft eeenrt**

eeeffort forefeet. *See* **eeefft eeffot effort**

eeeefft effete feet fete eft fee tee

eeefgrsu refugees refugee refuges. *See* **eefgru eefrsu**

eeefgru refugee. *See* **eefgru**

eeefipst tepefies epeeist. *See* **eeepst**

eeeeflr feeler fleer feel fere flee free leer reef reel eel elf ere fee lee ref el er re

eeeflrs feelers. *See* **eeeflr eeflrs**

eeeflrsx reflexes feelers. *See* **eeeflr eeflrs eeflrx eeflsx**

eeefmnr freemen. *See* **eeemr**

eeefnrss freeness. *See* **eeenrs eenrss**

eeeforrs foreseer foresee reefers. *See* **eeefrr eefrrs**

eeefors foresee. *See* **eeors eefrs efors**

eeeforss foresees foresee. *See* **eeors eefrs eefss**

eeeefrr reefer freer refer fere free reef ere err fee ref er re

eeefrrrt ferreter. *See* **eeefrr eefrrt**

eeefrrs reefers. *See* **eeefrr eefrrs**

eeefrrsz freezers freezer freezes reefers. *See* **eeefrr eeefrz eeefsz eefrrs**

eeefrrz freezer. *See* **eeefrr eeefrz**

eeefrsz freezes. *See* **eeefrz eeefsz**

eeefrz freeze feeze fere free reef ere fee fez ref zee er re

eeefsz feezes feeze fees zees fee fez see zee

eeefz feeze fee fez zee

eeeggiln negligee. *See* **eeggin eggiln**

eeeghint eighteen. *See* **eegint eehint**

eeegilnv leveeing. *See* **eeelnv**

eeegils elegies. *See* **eegils eeegs**

eeegilsz elegizes elegies elegize. *See* **eegils**

eeegilz elegize. *See* **eegil**

eeeginnr engineer. *See* **eeegnr eeginn**

eeeginrs energies greenies reneges. *See* **eeegnr eeenrs eegins eegnrs**

eeeginrz energize. *See* **eeegnr eginrz**

eeegipr perigee. *See* **eeeir egipr**

eeegiprs perigees perigee seepier. *See* **egiprs**

eeegissx exegesis. *See* **eegiss**

eeeglmn gleemen. *See* **eeglmn eeelm**

eeeglnt genteel. *See* **eeglnt**

eeegmnrt emergent. *See* **eeegmr eeegnr eeenrt eegmnt**

eeegmnru merengue. *See* **eeegmr eeegnr**

eeegmr emerge emeer merge germ gree mere ere erg gee gem reg rem em er me re

eeegmrs emerges. *See* **eeegmr eegmrs**

eeegnpr epergne. *See* **eeegnr eenpr**

eeegnprs epergnes epergne reneges. *See* **eeegnr eeenrs eegnrs eenprs**

eeeegnr renege genre green erne gene gree ere erg gee nee reg en er ne re

eeegnrry greenery. *See* **eeegnr eegnry**

eeegnrs reneges. *See* **eegnrs eeegnr eeenrs**

eeegnrst greenest entrees regents reneges. *See* **eeegnr eeenrs eeenrt eegnrs**

eeegnrsv revenges reneges revenge veneers. *See* **eeegnr eeenrs eeenrv eeersv**

eeegnrv revenge. *See* **eeegnr eeenrv**

eeegnss geneses. *See* **eeegs eegns eenss**

eeegrrst greeters greeter regrets. *See* **eegrrt eegrst eerrst**

eeegrrt greeter. *See* **eegrrt**

eeegrsux exergues exergue. *See* **eeegs eegrs egrsu**

eeegrsz geezers. *See* **eeegs eegrs**

eeegrux exergue. *No 6s or 5s*

eeegs geese gees gee see

eeehilrw erewhile wheelie. *See* **eeehlr**

eeehilsw wheelies wheelie. *See* **eehlsw**

eeehilw wheelie. *See* **eehlw ehilw**

eeehirss heresies heiress. *See* **ehirss eehrss eeirss .eeeir**

eeehirwz wheezier. *See* **eeehwz**

eeehlmpt helpmeet. *See* **eehlmt eehmpt eelmpt**

eeehlntv eleventh. *See* **eeelnv**

eeehlnty ethylene. *See* **eeelty**

eeehlopp peephole. *See* **eeeopp eelopp ehlopp**

eeehlosy eyeholes eyehole. *See* **eehls ehlos ehloy**

eeehloy eyehole. *See* **ehloy**

eeeehlr heeler heel here herl leer reel eel ere her lee eh el er he re

eeehlrs heelers. *See* **eeehlr eehls ehlrs**

eeehmnps sheepmen. *See* **eehmnp eehmns**

eeehmnss enmeshes. *See* **eehmns eehmss eehnss**

eeehmntv vehement. *See* **eehmt eentv**

eeehnnpt nepenthe. *See* **eeept**

eeehnrvw whenever. *See* **eeenrv eeervw**

eeehrrvw wherever. *See* **eeerrv eeervw**

eeehssst seethes. *See* **eeehst eehsst**

eeehst seethe sheet these hest tees thee eth het see set she tee the eh he sh

eeehstt esthete. *See* **eeehst eeestt eeehtt**

eeehswz wheezes. *See* **eeehwz**

eeehtt teethe teeth thee teth eth het tee the eh he

eeehwz wheeze ewe hew wee zee eh he we

eeeiklsw weeklies. *See* **eekls eilsw eikls**

eeeillrv reveille relieve leveler. *See* **eeilrv**

eeeilmrs seemlier. *See* **eeelms eeilms eeilrs eeimrs**

eeeilnry eyeliner. *See* **eeilnr eeilry**

eeeilnst enlistee tensile. *See* **eeilns eeilst eelnst eilnst**

eeeilprs sleepier peelers replies seepier sleeper spieler. *See* **eeelpr eeilrs eelprs eilprs**

eeeilrr leerier. *See* **eeeirr**

eeeilrst leeriest steelier eeriest leister sterile. *See* **eeilrs eeilst eirst eilrst**

eeeilrsv relieves relieve relives reviles servile veeries. *See* **eeelsv eeersv eeilrs eeilrv**

eeeilrv relieve. *See* **eeilrv**

eeeilstv televise velites. *See* **eeelsv eeestv eeilst eeilsv**

eeeimns enemies. *See* **eemns eimns eeins**

eeeimprr premiere premier. *See* **eeeirr eeimpr eimprr**

eeeimprs emperies empires emprise premise seepier. *See* **eeimpr eeimrs eemprs eimprs**

eeeimrrs miserere. *See* **eeeirr eeimrs eeirrs**

eeeimrst eremites eremite eeriest. *See* **eeemst eeimrs eeirst eemrst**

eeeimrt eremite. *See* **eeeir eeemr eimrt**

eeeinnrt internee teenier interne. *See* **eeenrt eeinrt einnrt**

eeeinrss eeriness serines. *See* **eeenrs eeinrs eeinss eeirss**

eeeinrsv veneries enviers inverse veeries veneers. *See* **eeenrs eeenrv eeersv eeinrs**

eeeinrt teenier. *See* **eeinrt eeenrt**

eeeinstt teeniest. *See* **eeestt eenstt einstt**

eeeinsw weenies. *See* **eeeinw eeins einsw**

eeeinw   weenie wine ewe nee new wee wen win en in ne we

eeeiprrv   reprieve reverie. *See* **eeeirr eeerrv**

eeeiprs   seepier. *See* **eeeir eeeps eeprs**

eeeiprw   weepier. *See* **eeeipw eeeprw**

eeeipsst   epeeists seepiest epeeist. *See* **eeepst eeipss eepsst eipsst**

eeeipst   epeeist. *See* **eeepst eipst**

eeeipstw   weepiest epeeist sweetie. *See* **eeeipw eeepst eeepsw**

eeeipw   weepie pewee epee weep wipe ewe pee pew pie wee pe pi we

eeeir   eerie ere ire er re

eeeirr   eerier eerie ere err ire er re

eeeirrst   retirees eeriest retiree retires retries terries. *See* **eeeirr eeirrs eeirrt eeirst**

eeeirrsv   reveries reserve reveres reverie reverse severer veeries. *See* **eeeirr eeerrv eeersv eeirrs**

eeeirrt   retiree. *See* **eeeirr eeirrt**

eeeirrtv   retrieve retiree reverie riveter. *See* **eeeirr eeerrv eeirrt eerrtv**

eeeirrv   reverie. *See* **eeeirr eeerrv**

eeeirrvw   reviewer reverie. *See* **eeeirr eeerrv eeervw eeirrw**

eeeirst   eeriest. *See* **eeirst eeeir**

eeeirsv   veeries. *See* **eeersv eeirsv**

eeeirtvx   exertive. *See* **eertvx**

eeeisstw   sweeties sweetie. *See* **eesstw eisstw**

eeeistw   sweetie. *See* **eestw eistw**

eeejlrsw   jewelers jeweler. *See* **eejlsw**

eeejlrw   jeweler. *See* **eejlw**

eeejprs   jeepers. *See* **eeeps eejps eejrs**

eeejrr   jeerer jeer ere err er re

eeeklnr   kneeler. *See* **eeklnr**

eeeklnrs   kneelers kernels kneeler sleeker. *See* **eeekrs eeenrs eeklnr eeklns**

eeeklrs   sleeker. *See* **eeekrs eekls eelrs**

eeeklsst   sleekest. *See* **eeelss eeksst eelsst**

eeekmnss   meekness. *See* **eemnss**

eeekmr   meeker emeer meek mere reek eke ere rem em er me re

eeekmst   meekest. *See* **eeemst eekst**

eeeknnss   keenness. *See* **eekns eekss eenss**

eeeknors   kerosene. *See* **eeekrs eeenrs**

eeeknt   ketene keen keet knee teen eke ken nee net tee ten en ne

eeekpr   keeper kreep epee keep peek peer perk reek eke ere pee per rep er pe re

eeekprs   keepers. *See* **eeekpr eekprs eeekrs**

eeekrs   seeker esker reeks ekes reek seek seer sere skee eke ere res see er re

eeekrss   seekers. *See* **eeekrs eekrss**

eeekrsst   keesters seekers keester. *See* **eeekrs eekrss eeksst eersst**

eeekrst   keester. *See* **eeekrs eerst eekst**

eeellnqu   quenelle. *See* **eenqu ellqu**

eeellrsv   levelers leveler. *See* **eeelsv eeersv eellrs eellsv**

eeellrv   leveler. *See* **eelrv eeelv eellv**

eeelm   melee eel elm lee mel el em me

eeelmnst   elements element. *See* **eeelms eeemst eelnst**

eeelmnt   element. *See* **eeelm**

eeelmopy   employee. *See* **elmopy**

eeelmrtu   muleteer. *See* **eeltu eeemr elmru**

eeelms   melees melee eels elms else lees mels seel seem eel elm els lee mel see el em me

eeelmsx   lexemes. *See* **eeelms eeelmx**

eeelmx   lexeme melee eel elm lee mel el em ex me

eeelnopv   envelope envelop. *See* **eeelnv eelnov**

eeelnrsw   newsreel. *See* **eeenrs eelnsw eenrsw**

eeelnrsy   serenely. *See* **eeenrs**

eeelnv   eleven levee even eel eve lee lev nee vee el en ne

eeelpr   peeler leper repel epee leer peel peer reel eel ere lee pee per rep el er pe re

eeelprs   peelers sleeper. *See* **eelprs eeelpr**

eeelprss   peerless sleepers peelers peeress sleeper. *See* **eeelpr eeelss eelprs eelpss**

eeelprst   repletes peelers pelters petrels replete sleeper steeple. *See* **eeelpr eeepst eelprs eelprt**

eeelprt   replete. *See* **eeelpr eelprt**

eeelpsst   steeples steeple pestles. *See* **eeelss eeepst eelpss eelpst**

eeelpst   steeple. *See* **eeepst eelpst**

eeelrrtt   letterer. *See* **eeertt eelrtt eerrtt**

eeelrstv   leverets leveret. *See* **eeelsv eeersv eeestv eelrsv**

eeelrsvy   severely. *See* **eeelsv eeersv eelrsv**

eeelrtv   leveret. *See* **eelrv eertv eeelv**

eeelss   lessee seels eels else lees less seel sees eel els ess lee see el

eeelsss   lessees. *See* **eeelss eesss**

eeelssv   sleeves. *See* **eeelss eeelsv eelssv**

eeelssy   eyeless. *See* **eeelss elssy eessy**

eeelsty   eyelets. *See* **eeelty eelsty**

eeelsv   levees sleeve levee elves eels else eves lees seel vees eel els eve lee lev see vee el

eeelty   eyelet leet eely eel eye lee let lye tee yet el ye

eeelv   levee eel eve lee lev vee el

eeemms   sememe seem mems see mem em me

eeemmss   sememes. *See* **eeemms eemss**

eeemnntt   tenement entente. *See* **eentt**

eeemorrv   evermore remover. *See* **eeerrv eemorv**

eeemr   emeer mere ere rem em er me re

eeemrsst   semester esteems. *See* **eeemst eemrst eersst**

eeemrstx   extremes extreme. *See* **eeemst eemrst eerstx**

eeemrtx   extreme. *See* **eeemr eertx eemrt**

eeemsst   esteems. *See* **eeemst eemss emsst**

eeemst   esteem meets metes teems meet mete seem stem teem tees met see set tee em me

eeennssv   evenness. *See* **eenssv**

eeennstt   ententes entente. *See* **eeestt eennst eenstt**

eeenntt   entente. *See* **eentt**

eeenorsv   overseen veneers oversee. *See* **eeenrs eeenrv eeersv eenrsv**

eeenorvy   everyone. *See* **eeenrv eenrvy**

eeenprrt   repenter preteen reenter terrene. *See* **eeenrt eenprt eenrrt**

eeenprst   preteens pretense entrees present preteen repents serpent steepen. *See* **eeenrs eeenrt eeepst eenprs**

eeenprt   preteen. *See* **eeenrt eenprt**

eeenpsst   steepens steepen. *See* **eeepst eensst eepsst**

eeenpssx   expenses expense. *See* **eeeps eenps eepss**

eeenpst   steepen. *See* **eeepst eenps enpst**

eeenpsx   expense. *See* **eeeps**

eeenrrst   reenters terrenes entrees reenter renters sterner terrene. *See* **eeenrs eeenrt eenrrt eenrst**

eeenrrt   reenter terrene. *See* **eeenrt eenrrt**

eeenrrtu   returnee reenter terrene. *See* **eeenrt eenrrt eenrtu eerrtu**

eeenrrtv   reverent reenter terrene. *See* **eeenrt eeenrv eeerrv eenrtv**

eeenrruv   revenuer revenue nervure. *See* **eeenrv eeerrv**

eeenrs   serene ernes sneer erne seen seer sere ens ere nee res see sen en er ne re

eeenrst   entrees. *See* **eenrst eeenrt eeenrs**

eeenrsty   yestreen entrees styrene. *See* **eeenrs eeenrt eenrst eensty**

eeenrsuv   revenues veneers revenue. *See* **eeenrs eeenrv eeersv eenrsu**

eeenrsv   veneers. *See* **eenrsv eeersv eeenrv**

eeenrt   entree eterne enter erne rent rete teen tern tree ere nee net ret tee ten en er ne re

eeenruv   revenue. *See* **eeenrv eeruv eenuv**

eeenrv   veneer nerve never reeve erne even ever veer ere eve nee rev vee en er ne re

eeensstw sweetens sweeten wetness. *See* **eensst eenstw eesstw**

eeenssz sneezes. *See* **eeensz eenss**

eeenstw sweeten. *See* **eenstw**

eeensz sneeze seen zees ens nee see sen zee en ne

eeeopp epopee epee peep pope ope pee pep pop pe

eeeorrsv overseer oversee reserve reveres reverse severer. *See* **eeerrv eeersv eeorsv eerrsv**

eeeorrsx xerosere. *See* **eeors eorrs**

eeeorssv oversees oversee. *See* **eeersv eeorsv eerssv eorssv**

eeeorssy eyesores eyesore. *See* **eeors eersy eorss**

eeeorsv oversee. *See* **eeersv eeorsv**

eeeorsy eyesore. *See* **eeors eersy eorsy**

eeep epee pee pe

eeeppr peeper epee peep peer prep repp ere pee pep per rep er pe re

eeepprs peepers. *See* **eeeppr eeeps eeprs**

eeeprrst pesterer. *See* **eeepst eeprst eerrst**

eeeprrsv perverse preserve reserve reveres reverse severer. *See* **eeepsv eeerrv eeersv eeprsv**

eeeprss peeress. *See* **eeprss**

eeeprssw sweepers peeress sweeper weepers. *See* **eeeprw eeepsw eeprss eepssw**

eeeprsw sweeper weepers. *See* **eeeprw eeepsw**

eeeprw weeper pewee epee ewer peer weep ere ewe pee per pew rep wee er pe re we

eeeps epees epee pees seep pee see pe

eeepst tepees epees steep tepee epee pees pest pets seep sept step tees pee pet see set tee pe

eeepsv peeves epees peeve veeps epee eves pees seep veep vees eve pee see vee pe

eeepsw pewees epees pewee sweep weeps epee ewes pees pews seep spew weep ewe pee pew see sew wee pe we

eeept tepee epee pee pet tee pe

eeepv peeve epee veep eve pee vee pe

eeepw pewee epee weep ewe pee pew wee pe we

eeeqrru queerer. *See* **eeqru**

eeeqrstu queerest quester request. *See* **eeqrsu**

eeeqsuz squeeze. *No 6s or 5s*

eeerrssv reserves reverses reserve reveres reverse servers severer. *See* **eeerrv eeersv eerrsv eerssv**

eeerrsv reserve reveres reverse severer. *See* **eeersv eeerrv eerrsv**

eeerrv revere reeve ever veer ere err eve rev vee er re

eeersss seeress. *See* **eesss eerss**

eeersstv severest steeves vestees. *See* **eeersv eeestv eersst eerstv**

eeerstt teeters. *See* **eeestt eerstt eeertt**

eeersttw tweeters sweeter teeters tweeter. *See* **eeertt eeestt eerstt eerstw**

eeerstvx vertexes. *See* **eeersv eeestv eerstv eerstx**

eeerstw sweeter. *See* **eerstw**

eeerstwz tweezers sweeter tweezes. *See* **eeetwz eerstw**

eeersv reeves severe reeve serve sever veers verse ever eves revs seer sere veer vees ere eve res rev see vee er re

eeersvw weevers. *See* **eeersv eersvw eeervw**

eeertt teeter terete rete tree tret ere ret tee er re

eeerttw tweeter. *See* **eeertt eerttw**

eeerv reeve ever veer ere eve rev vee er re

eeervw weever reeve ever ewer veer ere eve ewe rev vee wee er re we

eeesstt settees testees. *See* **eesstt eeestt**

eeessttw sweetest settees testees. *See* **eeestt eesstt eesstw eesttw**

eeesstv steeves vestees. *See* **eeestv**

eeestt settee testee stet tees test see set tee

eeestv steeve vestee eves tees vees vest vets eve see set tee vee vet

eeestwz tweezes. *See* **eeetwz eestw**

eeetwz tweeze ewe tee wee wet zee we

eef fee

eeffgiis effigies. *See* **effis eegis**

eeffint fifteen. *See* **efint**

eeffisuv effusive. *See* **eeffsu**

eefflntu effluent. *See* **eflntu**

eefflsux effluxes. *See* **eeffsu eeflsx efflux eflsux**

eeffnos offense. *No 6s or 5s*

eeffnoss offenses offense. *See* **eefss efoss enoss**

eeforr offerer. *See* **eefrr effor**

eefforrs offerers offerer. *See* **eefrrs effors**

eeffost toffees. *See* **effost eeffot**

eeffot toffee feet fete toff eft fee foe off oft tee toe of to

eeffrrsu sufferer. *See* **eeffsu eefrrs eefrsu effrsu**

eeffssu effuses. *See* **eeffsu eefssu**

eeffsu effuse fusee fees feus fuse fee feu see sue use us

eefgiilr filigree. *See* **eefilr egiilr**

eefgiln feeling fleeing. *See* **eefgin eefiln**

eefgilns feelings feeling felines fleeing. *See* **eefgin eefiln eeflns eegils**

eefgilnt fleeting feeling felting fleeing gentile. *See* **eefgin eefiln eegilt eegint**

eefgin feeing genie feign gene fine fee fen fie fig fin gee gie gin nee en if in ne

eefginr feigner freeing reefing. *See* **eefgin eefinr efginr**

eefginrs feigners feigner fingers freeing fringes reefing refines. *See* **eefgin eefinr eegins eegnrs**

eefginrz freezing feigner freeing reefing. *See* **eefgin eefinr eefirz efginr**

eefgllu gleeful. *No 6s or 5s*

eefglmnu fuglemen. *See* **eeglmn eeglmu efglnu**

eefglnuv vengeful. *See* **efglnu**

eefglor foreleg. *See* **efglor eeflr**

eefglors forelegs foreleg golfers. *See* **eeflrs eelors efglor efgors**

eefgnoor foregone forgone. *See* **efgoor**

eefgrsu refuges. *See* **eefgru eefrsu**

eefgru refuge fere free gree grue reef urge ere erg fee feu fug fur gee ref reg rue rug er re

eefhillr hellfire. *See* **eefhir eefilr eefllr eehllr**

eefhinw henwife. *See* **ehinw**

eefhir heifer fere fire free heir here hire reef rife ere fee feh fie fir her hie ire ref rif eh er he hi if re

eefhirs heifers. *See* **efhirs eefhir**

eefhirsv feverish heifers. *See* **eefhir eefrsv eeirsv efhirs**

eefhirt heftier. *See* **eefhir eehirt**

eefhisst fetishes hessite. *See* **eehsst efhiss efhist efisst**

eefhistt heftiest. *See* **efhist efhstt ehistt**

eefhllwy flywheel. *See* **eehlw eflly**

eefhlrs herself. *See* **eeflrs efhls efhrs**

eefhlss fleshes. *See* **eefls eefss efhls**

eefhmnrs freshmen freshen. *See* **eehmns**

eefhnrs freshen. *See* **eenrs eefrs efnrs**

eefhnrss freshens freshen. *See* **eehnss eehrss eenrss**

eefhor hereof fere fore free froe here hero hoer reef ere fee feh foe foh for fro her hoe ore ref rho roe eh er he ho of oh or re

eefhort thereof. *See* **eefhor eehort**

eefhorw whereof. *See* **eefhor eefrw eehrw**

eefhrrs fresher refresh. *See* **eefrrs efhrs eehrs**

eefhrsst freshest freshets freshet festers. *See* **eefrst eehrss eehrst eehsst**

eefhrst freshet. *See* **eehrst eefrst**

eefiikll lifelike. *See* **eiikll**

eefiilln lifeline. *See* **eefiln eiilln**

eefiilmt lifetime. *See* **eeilm eeilt efilt**

eefiimnn feminine. *See* **eiimn**

eefiimnz feminize. *See* **eiimn eimnz**

eefiinrs fineries reifies refines. *See* **eefinr eeinrs efinrs**

eefiirr fierier. *See* **eefrr efirr**

eefiirrv verifier fierier. *See* **eefrv efirv eefrr**

eefiirs reifies. *See* **eefrs efirs**

eefiirst ferities fieriest reifies. *See* **eefrst eeirst efirst**

eefiirsv verifies reifies. *See* **eefrsv eeirsv efirsv**

eefiknnp penknife. *See* **efikn einnp**

eefills fellies. *See* **eefls eflls efils**

eefillss lifeless fellies. *See* **eillss**

eefillx flexile. *See* **eeilx**

eefilmnr riflemen firemen. *See* **eefiln eefilr eefinr eeilnr**

eefiln feline elfin feel file fine flee lief lien life line eel elf fee fen fie fin lee lei lie nee nil el en if in li ne

eefilnos felonies felines olefins oneself. *See* **eefiln eeflns eeilns eelnos**

eefilns felines. *See* **eefiln eeflns eeilns**

eefilprr pilferer. *See* **eefilr eefprr efilpr**

eefilr refile relief filer fleer flier lifer rifle feel fere file fire flee free leer lief life lire reef reel riel rife rile eel elf ere fee fie fir ire lee lei lie ref rif el er if li re

eefilrs refiles. *See* **efilrs eeflrs eefilr eeilrs**

eefilrss fireless refiles. *See* **eefilr eeflrs eeilrs eeirss**

eefilrt fertile. *See* **efilrt**

eefilsst felsites felsite lefties stifles telesis. *See* **eeflst eeilst eelsst efilst**

eefilst felsite lefties. *See* **eeilst efilst eeflst**

eefimnr firemen. *See* **eeimnr eefinr**

eefimstu tumefies. *See* **fimstu**

eefinnss fineness finesse. *See* **eeinss**

eefinr ferine refine finer infer erne fere fern fine fire firn free reef rein rife ere fee fen fie fin fir ire nee ref rif en er if in ne re

eefinrr refiner. *See* **eefinr**

eefinrrr inferrer refiner. *See* **eefinr**

eefinrrs refiners ferries refiner refines refries. *See* **eefinr eefrrs eeinrs eeirrs**

eefinrry refinery refiner fernery. *See* **eefinr efinry**

eefinrs refines. *See* **eefinr efinrs eeinrs**

eefinrst infester entries refines snifter. *See* **eefinr eefrst eeinrs eeinrt**

eefinrsz frenzies refines friezes. *See* **eefinr eefizr eeinrs eeirsz**

eefinss finesse. *See* **eeinss eefss efins**

eefinssss finesses finesse. *See* **eefsss eeinss**

eefiprsx prefixes expires prexies refixes. *See* **eeiprx eeirsx efiprx efirsx**

eefirrs ferries refries. *See* **efirrs eefrrs eeirrs**

eefirrst ferrites ferrets ferries ferrite refries retires retries terries. *See* **eefrrs eefrrt eefrst eeirrs**

eefirrt ferrite. *See* **eefrrt eeirrt**

---

eefirstt frisette fetters fitters. *See* **eefrst eefrtt eeirst eerstt**

eefirsx refixes. *See* **eeirsx efirsx**

eefirsz friezes. *See* **eefirz eeirsz**

eefirttz frizette. *See* **eefirz eefrtt efirtt**

eefirz frieze fere fire free friz reef rife ere fee fez fie fir ire ref rif zee er if re

eefistv festive. *See* **efist eefst efisv**

eefk keef eke fee kef

eefks keefs ekes fees keef kefs seek skee eke fee kef see

eefl feel flee eel elf fee lee el

eefllnss fellness flenses. *See* **eeflns eelnss ellnss**

eefllort foretell. *See* **eefllr eellrt eflort**

eefllr feller fleer feel fell fere flee free leer reef reel eel elf ell ere fee lee ref el er re

eefllrs fellers. *See* **eefllr eeflrs eellrs**

eefllsss selfless. *See* **eefsss**

eefllty fleetly. *See* **eflly eeflt eflty**

eeflnn fennel feel flee eel elf fee fen lee nee el en ne

eeflnns fennels. *See* **eeflnn eeflns**

eeflnos oneself. *See* **eflnos eelnos**

eeflns flense feels flees eels else feel fees fens flee lees lens seel seen self eel elf els ens fee fen lee nee see sen el en ne

eeflnss flenses. *See* **eeflns eelnss**

eeflntuv eventful. *See* **eflntu**

eeflortv leftover. *See* **eflort elortv**

eeflortw floweret. *See* **eelrtw eflort eflorw efortw**

eeflorww werewolf. *See* **eflorw**

eeflr fleer feel fere flee free leer reef reel eel elf ere fee lee ref el er re

eeflrru ferrule. *See* **eeflru**

eeflrs fleers feels feres fleer flees frees leers reefs reels eels else feel fees fere flee free leer lees reef reel refs seel seer self sere serf eel elf els ere fee lee ref res see el er re

eeflrsu ferules refuels. *See* **eeflru eeflrs eefrsu**

eeflrsux flexures refluxes ferules flexure refuels. *See* **eeflrs eeflru eeflrx eeflsx**

eeflru ferule refuel fleer feel fere flee flue free fuel furl leer lure reef reel rule eel elf ere fee feu flu fur lee leu ref rue el er re

eeflrux flexure. *See* **eeflru eeflrx eflrux**

eeflrx reflex fleer feel fere flee flex free leer reef reel eel elf ere fee lee ref rex el er ex re

eeflry freely fleer flyer leery eely eery eyre feel fere flee free leer lyre reef reel rely eel elf ere eye fee fey fly fry lee lye ref rye el er re ye

eefls feels flees eels else feel fees flee lees seel self eel elf els fee lee see el

---

eeflst fleets feels felts fetes flees fleet leets sleet steel stele eels efts else feel fees feet felt fete flee lees leet left lest lets seel self tees eel eft elf els fee lee let see set tee el

eeflstt fettles. *See* **eefltt eeflst eelstt**

eeflsuy eyefuls. *See* **eefluy eefls eflsu**

eeflsx flexes feels flees eels else exes feel fees flee flex lees seel self eel elf els fee lee see sex el ex

eeflt fleet feel feet felt fete flee leet left eel eft elf fee lee let tee el

eefltt fettle fleet feel feet felt fete flee leet left eel eft elf fee lee let tee el

eefluy eyeful eely feel flee flue fuel yule eel elf eye fee feu fey flu fly lee leu lye el ye

eefm feme fee em me

eefmm femme feme fee mem em me

eefmms femmes femme femes fees feme mems seem fee mem see em me

eefmnor foremen. *See* **eemnor**

eefmnrry ferrymen fernery. *See* **eemry eemny efnry**

eefmnrst ferments ferment. *See* **eefrst eemrst eenrst**

eefmnrt ferment. *See* **eenrt eemrt**

eefmorrr reformer. *See* **efmorr**

eefmostt mofettes mofette. *See* **eemost emostt**

eefmott mofette. *See* **eemot emott**

eefmprru perfumer perfume. *See* **eefprr**

eefmprsu perfumes perfume perfuse presume supreme. *See* **eefrsu eemprs eemrsu eeprsu**

eefmpru perfume. *See* **efmru fmpru eepru**

eefms femes fees feme seem fee see em me

eefnorst softener. *See* **eefrst eenrst eeorst efnost**

eefnortu fourteen fortune. *See* **eefrtu eenrtu**

eefnortw forewent forwent. *See* **eenorw efortw**

eefnqrtu frequent. *See* **eefrtu eenrtu**

eefnrry fernery. *See* **efnry efrry eefrr**

eefnrtv fervent. *See* **eenrtv eefrv**

eefnssw fewness. *See* **eefss eenss**

eeforrst forester reforest ferrets restore. *See* **eefrrs eefrrt eefrst eeorst**

eeforrsu ferreous ferrous. *See* **eefrrs eefrsu eforru efrrsu**

eeforrv forever. *See* **eforrv eefrv eefrr**

eefprr prefer freer refer fere free peer reef ere err fee pee per ref rep er pe re

eefprrs prefers. *See* **eefprr eefrrs**

eefprssu perfuses perfuse peruses refuses. *See* **eefrsu eefssu eeprss eeprsu**

eefprsu perfuse. *See* **eeprsu eefrsu**

eefpty　tepefy feet fete type eft eye fee fey pee pet tee yep yet pe ye

eefr　fere free reef ere fee ref er re

eefrr　freer refer fere free reef ere err fee ref er re

eefrrs　refers feres freer frees reefs refer errs fees fere free reef refs seer sere serf ere err fee ref res see er re

eefrrst　ferrets. *See* **eefrrt eefrst eefrrs eerrst**

eefrrt　ferret freer refer feet fere fete free fret reef reft rete tree eft ere err fee ref ret tee er re

eefrs　feres frees reefs fees fere free reef refs seer sere serf ere fee ref res see er re

eefrsst　festers. *See* **eefrst eersst**

eefrssu　refuses. *See* **eefssu eefrsu eerssu**

eefrst　fester freest ester feres fetes frees frets reefs reset steer stere terse trees efts erst fees feet fere fete free fret reef refs reft rest rete rets seer sere serf tees tree eft ere fee ref res ret see set tee er re

eefrstt　fetters. *See* **eefrst eefrtt eerstt**

eefrstu　refutes. *See* **eefrst eefrsu eefrtu**

eefrsu　refuse feres frees fusee reefs reuse fees fere feus free furs fuse reef refs rues ruse seer sere serf sure surf user ere fee feu fur ref res rue see sue use er re us

eefrsv　fevers feres fever frees reefs serve sever veers verse ever eves fees fere free reef refs revs seer sere serf veer vees ere eve fee ref res rev see vee er re

eefrtt　fetter feet fere fete free fret reef reft rete tree tret eft ere fee ref ret tee er re

eefrtu　refute feet fere fete free fret reef reft rete tree true turf eft ere fee feu fur ref ret rue rut tee er re ut

eefrv　fever ever fere free reef veer ere eve fee ref rev vee er re

eefrw　fewer ewer fere free reef ere ewe fee few ref wee er re we

eefs　fees fee see

eefss　fesse fees fess sees ess fee see

eefsss　fesses fesse esses fees fess sees ess fee see

eefsstu　fetuses. *See* **eefssu eefst efstu**

eefssu　fusees fesse fusee fuses fees fess feus fuse fuss sees sues uses ess fee feu see sue use us

eefst　fetes efts fees feet fete tees eft fee see set tee

eefstw　fewest fetes sweet weest wefts efts ewes fees feet fete stew tees weft west wets eft ewe fee few see set sew tee wee wet we

eefsu　fusee fees feus fuse fee feu see sue use us

eefsuz　fuzees fusee fuzee fuzes fees feus fuse fuze zees fee feu fez see sue use zee us

eefszz　fezzes fees zees fee fez see zee

eeft　feet fete eft fee tee

eefuz　fuzee fuze fee feu fez zee

eeg　gee

eegghlls　eggshell. *See* **eeghs eegls eehls**

eegghstu　thuggees thuggee. *See* **eghstu**

eegghtu　thuggee. *No 6s or 5s*

eeggilr　leggier. *See* **eegil**

eeggilst　leggiest elegist elegits. *See* **eegils eegilt eeglst eeilst**

eeggimnr　emerging regimen merging. *See* **eeggin eegimr eeimnr egginr**

eeggin　geeing genie gene egg gee gie gig gin nee en in ne

eegginnr　greening reneging. *See* **eeggin eeginn egginr**

eegginrt　greeting integer treeing. *See* **eeggin eegint eegnrt eeinrt**

eegginst　egesting. *See* **eeggin eegins eegint eegnst**

eegginsu　segueing. *See* **eeggin eegins eginsu eggisu**

eeggirs　greiges. *See* **eegrs ggirs eegis**

eeggisv　veggies. *See* **eeggiv egisv eegis**

eeggiv　veggie give egg eve gee gie gig vee vie

eeggnor　engorge. *See* **eegnr egnor eggor**

eeggnors　engorges engorge. *See* **eegnrs eggors egnors**

eegh　ghee gee eh he

eeghhint　heighten. *See* **eegint eehint eghhit**

eeghiist　eighties. *See* **eghist**

eeghiln　heeling. *See* **eegin eghin egiln**

eeghinns　sheening engines. *See* **eeginn eegins eghins eginns**

eeghinrs　greenish sheering henries hingers inheres. *See* **eegins eegnrs eehinr eeinrs**

eeghinst　seething sheeting nighest. *See* **eegins eegint eegnst eehint**

eeghintt　teething tighten. *See* **eegint eehint**

eeghinwz　wheezing. *See* **eghinw**

eeghiny　hygiene. *See* **eeginy eghin ghiny**

eeghirsw　weighers weigher. *See* **eehrsw eghirs eghisw ehirsw**

eeghirw　weigher. *See* **eehrw eghiw**

eeghisty　eyesight. *See* **eghist eghity**

eeghlnnt　lengthen. *See* **eeglnt eghlnt**

eeghmnoy　hegemony. *See* **eemnoy**

eeghnops　phosgene pongees. *See* **eegnop egnops ehnops**

eeghnopy　hypogene. *See* **eegnop ehnopy**

eeghnssu　hugeness neguses. *See* **eegssu eehnss eenssu eghssu**

eeghortt　together thereto. *See* **eegrtt eehort eehrtt eghott**

eeghostt　ghettoes. *See* **eghott**

eeghs　ghees ghee gees gee see she eh he sh

eegiilnr　lingerie leering reeling. *See* **eeilnr egiilr egilnr**

eegiilnv　inveigle veiling. *See* **giilnv**

eegiintv　genitive invitee. *See* **eegint egiint eiintv**

eegijlnw　jeweling. *See* **egijln**

eegijnr　jeering. *See* **eegin eegnr eginr**

eegikkn　keeking. *See* **eegin egikn**

eegikln　keeling. *See* **egikn eegin egiln**

eegiklnn　kneeling keeling keening kneeing. *See* **eeginn eeklnn**

eegiknn　keening kneeing. *See* **eeginn egikn**

eegiknp　keeping peeking. *See* **eeginp egikn**

eegiknr　reeking. *See* **egikn eegin eegnr**

eegikns　seeking. *See* **eegins**

eegil　liege glee eel gee gel gie lee leg lei lie el li

eegillnv　leveling. *See* **eegin eginv egiln**

eegilnp　peeling. *See* **eeginp egiln eegil**

eegilnps　sleeping peeling pensile seeping. *See* **eegils eeginp eegins eeilns**

eegilnr　leering reeling. *See* **eeilnr egilnr**

eegilnrr　lingerer leering reeling. *See* **eeilnr egilnr eginrr**

eegilnrv　levering reveling leering livener reeling veering. *See* **eegirv eeilnr eeilrv eeinrv**

eegilnst　gentiles sleeting steeling elegist elegits gentile glisten singlet tensile tingles. *See* **eegils eegilt eegins eegint**

eegilnsv　sleeving. *See* **eegils eegins eeilns eeilsv**

eegilnt　gentile. *See* **eegilt eeglnt eegint egilnt**

eegilopu　epilogue. *See* **eelop egilu eegil**

eegilosu　eulogies. *See* **eegils egilsu**

eegilouz　eulogize. *See* **egloz egilu eegil**

eegils　lieges glees liege siege eels egis else gees gels gies glee isle lees legs leis lies seel eel els gee gel gie lee leg lei lie see el is li si

eegilsst　elegists elegist elegits legists telesis. *See* **eegils eegilt eegiss eeglst**

eegilst　elegist elegits. *See* **eegilt eeilst eeglst egilst eegils**

eegilt　elegit elite gleet legit liege gilt glee leet tile eel gee gel get gie lee leg lei let lie lit tee tie til el it li ti

eegimnr　regimen. *See* **eegimr eeimnr**

eegimnrs　regimens ermines regimen regimes remiges seeming. *See* **eegimr eegins eegmrs eegnrs**

eegimnrt metering regiment integer meeting regimen teeming terming tree-ing. *See* **eegimr eegint eegmnt eegnrt**

eegimnru meringue regimen. *See* **eegimr eeimnr eimnru**

eegimns seeming. *See* **eegins**

eegimnst meetings meeting seeming segment teeming. *See* **eegins eegint eegmnt eegnst**

eegimnt meeting teeming. *See* **egimnt eegint eegmnt**

eegimr regime merge grime emir germ gree grim mere mire rime ere erg gee gem gie ire mir reg rem rig rim em er me mi re

eegimrs regimes remiges. *See* **egimrs eegmrs eegimr eeimrs**

eegin genie gene gee gie gin nee en in ne

eeginn engine genie gene nine gee gie gin inn nee en in ne

eeginnp peening. *See* **eeginn eeginp**

eeginnpr preening peening peering. *See* **eeginn eeginp**

eeginnqu queening genuine ingenue. *See* **eeginn eeinqu**

eeginnrs sneering engines. *See* **eeginn eegins eegnrs eeinrs**

eeginnrt entering integer interne renting treeing. *See* **eeginn eegint eegnrt eeinrt**

eeginns engines. *See* **eeginn eginns eegins**

eeginnsu ingenues engines ensuing genu-ine gunnies ingenue. *See* **eeginn eegins eennsu eginns**

eeginnsv evenings engines evening. *See* **eeginn eegins eeinsv eginns**

eeginnsz sneezing engines. *See* **eeginn eegins eginns**

eeginnu genuine ingenue. *See* **eeginn einnu**

eeginnv evening. *See* **eeginn eginv einnv**

eeginop epigone. *See* **eeginp eginop eeg-nop**

eeginops epigones epigone peonies pi-geons pongees seeping. *See* **eeginp eegins eegnop eginop**

eeginost egestion. *See* **eegins eegint eegnst**

eeginp peeing genie gene neep peen pine ping gee gie gin gip nee nip pee peg pen pie pig pin en in ne pe pi

eeginpp peeping. *See* **eeginp eginpp**

eeginpr peering. *See* **eeginp eegnr egipr**

eeginprt petering integer peering treeing. *See* **eeginp eegint eegnrt eeinrt**

eeginpru pureeing peering. *See* **eeginp**

eeginps seeping. *See* **eegins eeginp**

eeginpst steeping seeping. *See* **eeginp eegins eegint eegnst**

eeginpsw sweeping seeping spewing weeping. *See* **eeginp eegins eginsw**

eeginpv peeving. *See* **eeginp eginv**

eeginpw weeping. *See* **eeginp**

eeginrrv revering griever nervier veering vernier. *See* **eegirv eegrrv eeinrv eginrr**

eeginrst integers steering entries integer regents resting stinger treeing. *See* **eegins eegint eegnrs eegnrt**

eeginrsu seigneur reusing. *See* **eegins eegnrs eeinrs eenrsu**

eeginrsv severing enviers grieves inverse serving veering versing. *See* **eegins eegirv eegnrs eegrsv**

eeginrsw sewering newsier swinger wie-ners. *See* **eegins eegnrs eeinrs eeinrw**

eeginrt integer treeing. *See* **eeinrt eegnrt eegint**

eeginrtv everting integer treeing veering. *See* **eegint eegirv eegnrt eeinrt**

eeginrtx exerting exigent integer treeing. *See* **eegint eegnrt eeinrt eenrtx**

eeginrv veering. *See* **eegirv eeinrv**

eegins genies seeing genes genie segni seine siege singe egis engs gees gene gens gies gins seen sign sine sing ens gee gie gin nee see sen sin en in is ne si

eeginss genesis. *See* **eegins eginss eeinss eegiss**

eeginssu geniuses genesis neguses. *See* **eegins eegiss eegssu eeinss**

eegint teeing genet genie tinge gene gent teen tine ting gee get gie gin nee net nit tee ten tie tin en in it ne ti

eeginttv vignette. *See* **eegint**

eeginttw tweeting wetting. *See* **eegint egintw**

eegintwz tweezing. *See* **eegint egintw**

eegintx exigent. *See* **eegint**

eeginy eyeing genie eying gene eye gee gey gie gin nee yen yin en in ne ye

eegiopsu epigeous. *See* **egisu eegos iopsu**

eegiprst prestige respite. *See* **eegrst eeirst eeprst egiprs**

eegirrst register regrets retires retries ter-ries. *See* **eegrrt eegrst eeirrs eeirrt**

eegirrsv grievers griever grieves vergers. *See* **eegirv eegrrv eegrsv eeirrs**

eegirrv griever. *See* **eegirv eegrrv**

eegirstt grisette getters. *See* **eegrst eegrtt eeirst eerstt**

eegirsv grieves. *See* **egirsv eegirv eeirsv eegrsv**

eegirv grieve verge giver ever give gree rive veer ere erg eve gee gie ire reg rev rig vee vie er re

eegis siege egis gees gies gee gie see is si

eegiss sieges siege egis gees gies sees ess gee gie see sis is si

eegisstv vestiges vestige. *See* **eegiss eegsst eeissv**

eegistv vestige. *See* **eegst egisv eegis**

eegk geek eke gee keg

eegklr kegler geek glee gree keel leek leer reek reel eel eke elk ere erg gee gel keg lee leg lek reg el er re

eegklrs keglers. *See* **eegklr eekrs eegks**

eegknor kerogen. *See* **eegnr egnor eknor**

eegks geeks ekes geek gees kegs seek skee skeg eke gee keg see

eegl glee eel gee gel lee leg el

eeglmmsu gemmules gemmule legumes. *See* **eeglmu**

eeglmmu gemmule. *See* **eeglmu**

eeglmn legmen gene glee glen eel elm gee gel gem lee leg mel men nee el em en me ne

eeglmsu legumes. *See* **eeglmu eemsu egmsu**

eeglmu legume emeu geum glee glue glum luge mule eel elm emu gee gel gem gum lee leg leu lug lum mel mug el em me mu um

eeglnor erelong. *See* **eglnor eegnr eelno**

eeglnosz lozenges lozenge. *See* **eelnos eglnos eglosz**

eeglnoz lozenge. *See* **egloz eelno eglno**

eeglnrt gentler. *See* **eeglnt eegnrt eeglrt eelnrt**

eeglnry greenly. *See* **eegnry**

eeglnstt gentlest nettles. *See* **eeglnt eeglst eegnst eelnst**

eeglnt gentle gleet genet gene gent glee glen leet lent teen eel gee gel get lee leg let nee net tee ten el en ne

eegloprs gospeler elopers leprose prolegs. *See* **eelopr eelops eelors eelprs**

eeglrst reglets. *See* **eegrst eeglst**

eeglrsu reglues. *See* **eglrsu eeglru**

eeglrt reglet egret gleet greet glee gree leer leet reel rete tree eel ere erg gee gel get lee leg let reg ret tee el er re

eeglru reglue gluer gruel glee glue gree grue leer luge lure reel rule urge eel ere erg gee gel lee leg leu lug reg rue rug el er re

eegls glees eels else gees gels glee lees legs seel eel els gee gel lee leg see el

eeglst gleets egest glees gleet leets sleet steel stele eels else gees gels gest gets glee lees leet legs lest lets seel tees eel els gee gel get lee leg let see set tee el

eeglt gleet glee leet eel gee gel get lee leg let tee el

eegly elegy glee eely eel eye gee gel gey lee leg lye el ye

eegmnost gemstone segment. *See* **eegmnt eegnst eemost egmnos**

eegmnsst segments segment. *See* **eegmnt eegnst eegsst eemnss**

eegmnst segment. *See* **eegnst eegmnt**

eegmnt tegmen genet gene gent meet mete teem teen gee gem get men met nee net tee ten em en me ne

eegmorsu gruesome morgues. *See* **eegmrs eemrsu egmoru egmrsu**

eegmorty geometry. *See* **eemort**

eegmr merge germ gree mere ere erg gee gem reg rem em er me re

eegmrr merger merge germ gree mere ere erg err gee gem reg rem em er me re

eegmrrs mergers. *See* **eegmrr eegmrs**

eegmrs merges germs grees meres merge serge ergs gees gems germ gree mere regs seem seer sere ere erg gee gem reg rem res see em er me re

eegn gene gee nee en ne

eegnnort roentgen. *See* **eegnrt**

eegnnosv evensong. *See* **eensv eegns ennos**

eegnop pongee gene gone neep nope ogee open peen peon pone ego eon gee nee nog one ope pee peg pen en go ne no on pe

eegnops pongees. *See* **eegnop egnops**

eegnorst estrogen regents. *See* **eegnrs eegnrt eegnst eegrst**

eegnorsu generous surgeon. *See* **eegnrs eenrsu egnors egorsu**

eegnosx exogens. *See* **eegnox enosx eegns**

eegnotyz zygotene. *See* **egotyz**

eegnox exogen exon gene gone ogee ego eon gee nee nog one en ex go ne no on ox

eegnpsux expunges expunge. *See* **eensu eegns egnsu**

eegnpux expunge. *No 6s or 5s*

eegnr genre green erne gene gree ere erg gee nee reg en er ne re

eegnrs genres greens ernes genes genre green grees serge sneer engs ergs erne gees gene gens gree regs seen seer sere ens ere erg gee nee reg res see sen en er ne re

eegnrst regents. *See* **eegrst eenrst eegnst eegnrs eegnrt**

eegnrsuy guernsey gurneys. *See* **eegnrs eegnry eegrsy eenrsu**

eegnrt regent egret enter genet genre green greet erne gene gent gree rent rete teen tern tree ere erg gee get nee net reg ret tee ten en er ne re

eegnry energy greeny gyrene genre green eery erne eyre gene gree grey gyre ere erg eye gee gey nee reg rye yen en er ne re ye

eegns genes gees gene gens seen ens gee nee see sen en ne

eegnssu neguses. *See* **eegssu eenssu**

eegnst genets gentes egest genes genet gents teens tense engs gees gene gens gent gest gets nest nets seen sent teen tees tens ens gee get nee net see sen set tee ten en ne

eegnt genet gene gent teen gee get nee net tee ten en ne

eego ogee gee ego go

eegoprsu superego. *See* **eeoprs eeprsu egoprs egorsu**

eegorrvw overgrew. *See* **eegrrv egorrw**

eegorsss ogresses grosses. *See* **eegrss egorss**

eegos ogees egos gees goes ogee sego ego gee see go os so

eegr gree ere erg gee reg er re

eegrrss regress. *See* **eegrss**

eegrrst regrets. *See* **eegrst eegrrt eerrst**

eegrrstu gesturer gesture regrets ureters. *See* **eegrrt eegrst eerrst eerrtu**

eegrrsv vergers. *See* **eerrsv eegrrv eegrsv**

eegrrt regret egret greet gree rete tree ere erg err gee get reg ret tee er re

eegrrv verger verge ever gree veer ere erg err eve gee reg rev vee er re

eegrs grees serge ergs gees gree regs seer sere ere erg gee reg res see er re

eegrss egress serges grees seers seres serge ergs gees gree regs seer sees sere ere erg ess gee reg res see er re

eegrsstu gestures gesture. *See* **eegrss eegrst eegsst eegssu**

eegrssy geysers. *See* **eegrss eegrsy**

eegrst egrets greets egest egret ester grees greet reset serge steer stere terse trees ergs erst gees gest gets gree regs rest rete rets seer sere tees tree ere erg gee get reg res ret see set tee er re

eegrstt getters. *See* **eegrst eegrtt eerstt**

eegrstu gesture. *See* **eegrst**

eegrsv verges grees serge serve sever veers verge verse ergs ever eves gees gree regs revs seer sere veer vees ere erg eve gee reg res rev see vee er re

eegrsy geyser eyres grees greys gyres serge eery ergs eyes eyre gees gree grey gyre regs ryes seer sere ere erg eye gee gey reg res rye see yes er re ye

eegrt egret greet gree rete tree ere erg gee get reg ret tee er re

eegrtt getter egret greet gree rete tree tret ere erg gee get reg ret tee er re

eegrv verge ever gree veer ere erg eve gee reg rev vee er re

eegs gees gee see

eegsssu guesses. *See* **eegssu**

eegsst egests egest gests gees gest gets sees sets tees ess gee get see set tee

eegssu segues segue guess gees sees sues uses ess gee see sue use us

eegst egest gees gest gets tees gee get see set tee

eegsu segue gees gee see sue use us

eehhipss sheepish. *See* **eeipss ehipss**

eehhirtw herewith whether whither. *See* **eehirt eehrtw ehhirt ehirtw**

eehhlllo hellhole. *See* **ehllo**

eehhnosu henhouse. *See* **eensu ehnos ehosu**

eehhrrst thresher. *See* **eehrst eerrst ehhrst**

eehhrsst threshes. *See* **eehrss eehrst eehsst eersst**

eehhrtw whether. *See* **eehrtw**

eehiin heinie hen hie hin nee eh en he hi in ne

eehiklmo homelike hoelike. *See* **eeilm**

eehikln henlike. *See* **eikln eekln**

eehiklo hoelike. *No 6s or 5s*

eehikrrs shrieker kerries rehires shirker. *See* **eehirr eeirrs ehikrs ehirrs**

eehillrs shellier hellers sheller. *See* **eehllr eeilrs eellrs ehilrs**

eehilmn hemline. *See* **eeilm eilmn**

eehilmns hemlines hemline. *See* **eehmns eeilms eeilns ehimns**

eehilmor homelier. *See* **ehilor ehimor**

eehilnpw pinwheel. *See* **eehnpw**

eehilort hotelier. *See* **eehirt eehort ehilor ehilot**

eehilrss heirless relishes heiress. *See* **eehrss eeilrs eeirss eelrss**

eehilsst shelties hessite hitless telesis. *See* **eehsst eeilst eelsst ehisst**

eehilsx helixes. *See* **eeilsx**

eehimnrt theremin neither therein. *See* **eehinr eehint eehirt eehnrt**

eehinnrs enshrine henries inheres. *See* **eehinr eeinrs ehinrs einnrs**

eehinnrt inherent interne neither therein thinner. *See* **eehinr eehint eehirt eehnrt**

eehinor heroine. *See* **eehinr eehnor ehinor**

eehinort hereinto heroine neither therein thereon. *See* **eehinr eehint eehirt eehnor**

eehinprt nephrite neither therein. *See* **eehinr eehint eehirt eehnrt**

eehinpsx phenixes. *See* **ehinpx hinpsx**

eehinr herein inhere erne heir here hern hire rein ere hen her hie hin ire nee eh en er he hi in ne re

eehinrs henries inheres. *See* **eehinr eeinrs ehinrs**

eehinrt neither therein. *See* **eehirt eeinrt eehinr ehinrt eehnrt**

eehinrtt thirteen neither therein. *See* **eehinr eehint eehirt eehnrt**

eehinrtw whitener neither therein wherein. *See* **eehinr eehint eehirt eehnrt**

eehinrw wherein. *See* **eehinr ehinrw eeinrw**

eehinsvw henwives. *See* **eeinsv ehinsw**

eehint theine thine hent hint teen thee then thin tine eth hen het hie hin hit nee net nit tee ten the tie tin eh en he hi in it ne ti

eehiorst theories heister heriots shortie. *See* **eehirt eehors eehort eehrst**

eehiortz theorize. *See* **eehirt eehort ehiort ehirtz**

eehiprss perishes heiress spheres. *See* **eehprs eehrss eeipss eeirss**

eehipstt epithets epithet pettish. *See* **eeiptt eepstt ehistt**

eehipsv peevish. *See* **ehisv eehps eeisv**

eehiptt epithet. *See* **eeiptt eehtt ehitt**

eehiqrsu queerish esquire queries. *See* **eehrsu eeqrsu eiqrsu**

eehirr rehire hirer heir here hire ere err her hie ire eh er he hi re

eehirrs rehires. *See* **ehirrs eehirr eeirrs**

eehirrss sherries heiress rehires sirrees. *See* **eehirr eehrss eeirrs eeirss**

eehirrsw wherries rehires rewires. *See* **eehirr eehrsw eeirrs eeirrw**

eehirss heiress. *See* **ehirss eehrss eeirss**

eehirsst heisters heiress heister hessite. *See* **eehirt eehrss eehrst eehsst**

eehirst heister. *See* **eehirt eehrst eeirst ehirst**

eehirt either ether retie their there three heir here hire rete rite thee tier tire tree ere eth her het hie hit ire ret tee the tie eh er he hi it re ti

eehirtvy thievery. *See* **eehirt eehitv ehirtv eirtvy**

eehisst hessite. *See* **ehisst eehsst**

eehistv thieves. *See* **eehitv ehist ehisv**

eehitv thieve thee hive eth eve het hie hit tee the tie vee vet vie eh he hi it ti

eehklosy keyholes keyhole. *See* **eehkls eklosy**

eehkloy keyhole. *See* **ehkoy ehloy ekloy**

eehkls shekel heels keels leeks sleek eels ekes elks else heel keel leek lees leks seek seel skee eel eke elk els lee lek see she eh el he sh

eehklss shekels. *See* **eehkls**

eehl heel eel lee eh el he

eehllmss helmless. *See* **eehmss ehllss ellmss**

eehlloss holeless. *See* **ehllos ehllss**

eehllpss helpless. *See* **eelpss ehllss ehlpss ellpss**

eehlllr heller heel hell here herl leer reel eel ell ere her lee eh el er he re

eehllrs hellers sheller. *See* **eehlllr eellrs**

eehllrss shellers hellers resells sellers sheller. *See* **eehlllr eehrss eellrs eelrss**

eehlmmns helmsmen. *See* **eehmns**

eehlmoss homeless. *See* **eehmss**

eehlmst helmets. *See* **eehlmt eehmst**

eehlmt helmet theme heel helm heme leet meet melt mete teem thee them eel elm eth hem het lee let mel met tee the eh el em he me

eehlnott telethon. *See* **eelntt**

eehlopss hopeless. *See* **eelops eelpss ehlpss elopss**

eehlorst hosteler holster hostler shelter. *See* **eehors eehort eehrst eelors**

eehlpr helper leper repel heel help here herl leer peel peer reel eel ere hep her lee pee per rep eh el er he pe re

eehlprs helpers. *See* **eehlpr eehprs eelprs**

eehlprst telphers helpers pelters petrels shelter telpher. *See* **eehlpr eehprs eehrst eelprs**

eehlprt telpher. *See* **eehlpr eelprt**

eehlrsst shelters shelter. *See* **eehrss eehrst eehsst eelrss**

eehlrssw welshers welsher welshes. *See* **eehlsw eehrss eehrsw eelrss**

eehlrst shelter. *See* **eehrst**

eehlrsw welsher. *See* **eehlsw eehrsw**

eehlrsy sheerly. *See* **eehrsy eehls ehlrs**

eehls heels eels else heel lees seel eel els lee see she eh el he sh

eehlssu hueless. *See* **ehlssu eehls eelss**

eehlssv shelves. *See* **eehlsv eelssv**

eehlssw welshes. *See* **eehlsw ehssw**

eehlsv helves shelve elves heels helve eels else eves heel lees seel vees eel els eve lee lev see she vee eh el he sh

eehlsw wheels heels welsh wheel eels else ewes heel hews lees seel shew slew eel els ewe hew lee see sew she wee eh el he sh we

eehlv helve heel eel eve lee lev vee eh el he

eehlw wheel heel eel ewe hew lee wee eh el he we

eehm heme hem eh em he me

eehmmort ohmmeter theorem. *See* **eehmmr eehort eemort ehmort**

eehmmr hemmer emmer heme here herm mere ere hem her mem rem eh em er he me re

eehmmrs hemmers. *See* **eehmmr eemmrs**

eehmnors horsemen moreens. *See* **eehmns eehnor eehors eemnor**

eehmnosu housemen. *See* **eehmns eemnsu**

eehmnp hempen heme hemp neep peen hem hen hep men nee pee pen eh em en he me ne pe

eehmns enmesh mesne semen sheen heme hems hens mesh seem seen ens hem hen men nee see sen she eh em en he me ne sh

eehmorst theorems meteors mothers smother theorem thermos. *See* **eehmst eehors eehort eehrst**

eehmort theorem. *See* **eehort eemort ehmort**

eehmorvw whomever however whoever. *See* **eemorv**

eehmpst tempehs. *See* **eehmpt eehmst**

eehmpt tempeh theme heme hemp meet mete teem thee them eth hem hep het met pee pet tee the eh em he me pe

eehmss meshes seems heme hems mesh mess seem sees ess hem see she eh em he me sh

eehmst themes meets metes sheet teems theme these heme hems hest meet mesh mete seem stem teem tees thee them eth hem het met see set she tee the eh em he me sh

eehmsux exhumes. *See* **eehmux eehsx eemsu**

eehmt theme heme meet mete teem thee them eth hem het met tee the eh em he me

eehmux exhume heme emeu emu hem hex hue hum eh em ex he me mu um

eehnnor enthrone thereon. *See* **eehnor eehnrt eehort ehnort**

eehnnry hennery. *See* **ehnry**

eehnoor honoree. *See* **eehnor hnoor**

eehnoors honorees honoree onshore. *See* **eehnor eehors ehnors enoors**

eehnopru hereupon. *See* **eehnor eenopr**

eehnopty neophyte. *See* **eenopt eeopty ehnopy**

eehnor hereon heron erne here hern hero hoer hone horn eon ere hen her hoe hon nee nor one ore rho roe eh en er he ho ne no oh on or re

eehnort thereon. *See* **eehnor eehort ehnort eehnrt**

eehnorw nowhere. *See* **eehnor eenorw**

eehnox hexone hone exon eon hen hex hoe hon nee one eh en ex he ho ne no oh on ox

eehnpsw nephews. *See* **eehnpw eenps eehns**

eehnpw nephew hewn neep peen phew weep when ewe hen hep hew nee new pee pen pew wee wen eh en he ne pe we

eehnrt nether enter ether there three erne hent here hern rent rete teen tern

thee then tree ere eth hen her het nee
net ret tee ten the eh en er he ne re

eehns sheen seen hens ens hen nee see
sen she eh en he ne sh

eehnss sheens sheen sense hens seen sees
ens ess hen nee see sen she eh en he ne
sh

eehnsstv sevenths seventh. *See* **eehnss
eehsst eensst eenssv**

eehnstv seventh. *See* **eenstv ehnst eehns**

eehoopw whoopee. *See* **hoopw**

eehoorsv overshoe. *See* **eehors eeorsv
ehoosv ehorsv**

eehootty eyetooth. *See* **hootty**

eehorrsv hoverers hoverer. *See* **eehors
eeorsv eerrsv ehorsv**

eehorrv hoverer. *See* **ehorv eorrv**

eehors heroes erose hoers horse sheer
shoer shore here hero hers hoer hoes
hose ores resh rhos roes rose seer sere
shoe sore ere her hoe ohs ore res rho
roe see she eh er he ho oh or os re sh so

eehort hereto ether other there three
throe here hero hoer rete rote thee tore
tree ere eth her het hoe hot ore ort ret
rho roe rot tee the tho toe tor eh er he
ho oh or re to

eehortt thereto. *See* **eehort ehortt eehrtt**

eehortw whereto. *See* **eehort eehrtw**

eehorvw however whoever. *See* **eehrw
ehorv ehorw**

eehossty eyeshots eyeshot. *See* **eehsst
eeosst ehosst ehssty**

eehosty eyeshot. *See* **ehost eehst**

eehosx hexose hexes exes hoes hose shoe
hex hoe ohs see sex she sox eh ex he ho
oh os ox sh so

eehprs herpes sphere peers perse sheep
sheer spree here hers peer pees reps
resh seep seer sere ere hep her pee per
rep res see she eh er he pe re sh

eehprss spheres. *See* **eehprs eeprss
eehrss**

eehps sheep pees seep hep pee see she eh
he pe sh

eehr here ere her eh er he re

eehrs sheer here hers resh seer sere ere
her res see she eh er he re sh

eehrss reshes sheers seers seres sheer
here hers resh seer sees sere ere ess her
res see she eh er he re sh

eehrssu rushees. *See* **eehrss eerssu ehrssu eehrsu**

eehrst ethers threes ester ether reset
sheer sheet steer stere terse there these
three trees erst here hers hest resh rest
rete rets seer sere tees thee tree ere eth
her het res ret see set she tee the eh er
he re sh

eehrstt tethers. *See* **eehrst eerstt eehrtt**

eehrstw wethers. *See* **eehrst eehrsw
eerstw eehrtw**

eehrsu rushee reuse sheer usher here hers
hues resh rues ruse rush seer sere sure
user ere her hue res rue see she sue use
eh er he re sh us

eehrsw hewers hewer sewer sheer shrew
where ewer ewes here hers hews resh
seer sere shew ere ewe her hew res see
sew she wee eh er he re sh we

eehrsx hexers hexer hexes sheer exes
here hers resh seer sere ere her hex res
rex see sex she eh er ex he re sh

eehrsy heresy eyres sheer shyer eery eyes
eyre here hers resh ryes seer sere ere
eye her hey res rye see she shy yes eh er
he re sh ye

eehrt ether there three here rete thee tree
ere eth her het ret tee the eh er he re

eehrtt tether ether teeth there three here
rete teth thee tree tret ere eth her het
ret tee the eh er he re

eehrtw wether ether hewer there three
threw where ewer here rete thee thew
tree whet ere eth ewe her het hew ret
tee the wee wet eh er he re we

eehrw hewer where ewer here ere ewe her
hew wee eh er he re we

eehrx hexer here ere her hex rex eh er ex
he re

eehsst sheets theses hests sheet these
hest sees sets tees thee ess eth het see
set she tee the eh he sh

eehst sheet these hest tees thee eth het
see set she tee the eh he sh

eehsx hexes exes hex see sex she eh ex he
sh

eeht thee eth het tee the eh he

eehtt teeth thee teth eth het tee the eh he

eehwyz wheezy whey ewe eye hew hey
wee why wye yew zee eh he we ye

eeiikllr likelier. *See* **eiikll eiikllr**

eeiikllv veillike. *See* **eiikll**

eeiiklsw likewise. *See* **eekls iiksw eilsw**

eeiillrv livelier. *See* **eeilrv eiilrv**

eeiilnpp pipeline. *See* **eilnpp**

eeiilntv lenitive invitee. *See* **eiintv**

eeiilrsv liveries relives reviles servile. *See*
eeilrs eeilrv eeilsv eeirsv

eeiilstv levities velites. *See* **eeilst eeilsv
eelstv eilstv**

eeiimnst enmities. *See* **eiimns**

eeiimost moieties. *See* **eemost eimost**

eeiimrss miseries messier remises. *See*
eeimrs eeimss eeirss eiirss

eeiimssv emissive missive. *See* **eeimss
eeissv**

eeiimstz itemizes itemize. *See* **eimst
eemst eeisz**

eeiimtz itemize. *No 6s or 5s*

eeiinnst nineties intense. *See* **eennst
einnst**

eeiinppr piperine nippier. *See* **eiinpr
eiippr**

eeiinprs pineries inspire spinier. *See*
eeinrs eenprs eiinpr einprs

eeiinrrv riverine nervier vernier. *See*
eeinrv

eeiinrsv vineries enviers inverse. *See*
eeinrs eeinrv eeinsv eeirsv

eeiinrsw wineries newsier wieners
wienies. *See* **eeiinw eeinrs eeinrw
eenrsw**

eeiinstt entities. *See* **eenstt einstt**

eeiinstv invitees invitee invites. *See*
eeinsv eenstv eiintv einstv

eeiinsw wienies. *See* **eeiinw eeins einsw**

eeiintv invitee. *See* **eiintv eentv**

eeiinw wienie wine ewe nee new wee wen
win en in ne we

eeiiprsx expiries expires prexies. *See*
eeiprx eeirsx

eeiipst pieties. *See* **eiipst eepst**

eeiiqstu equities equites. *See* **eiqstu**

eeiirstv verities restive revisit veriest. *See*
eeirst eeirsv eerstv eirstv

eeijkrr jerkier. *No 6s or 5s*

eeijkrst jerkiest keister. *See* **eeirst eejrst
eikrst**

eeijlls jellies. *See* **eills ejlls**

eeijlnrt jetliner. *See* **eeilnr eeinrt eelnrt**

eeijlnuv juvenile. *See* **eilnuv**

eeijmms jemmies. *See* **eimms**

eeijnns jennies. *See* **ijnns einns eeins**

eeijrtt jettier. *See* **eijrtt eeirt**

eeijstt jetties. *See* **eejst**

eeijsttt jettiest jetties. *See* **eejst**

eeiklnos noselike keelson. *See* **eeilns
eeklns eelnos eiklns**

eeiklnss likeness. *See* **eeilns eeinss
eeklns**

eeiklnst nestlike netlike tensile tinkles.
See **eeilns eeilst eeklns eelnst**

eeiklnt netlike. *See* **eiklnt eeilt eekln**

eeiklors roselike. *See* **eeilrs eeiors eelors
eilors**

eeiklp kelpie kelep keel keep kelp kepi
leek like peek peel pike pile eel eke elk
ilk kip lee lei lek lie lip pee pie el li pe pi

eeiklps kelpies. *See* **eeiklp eekls eekps**

eeikmnp pikemen. *No 6s or 5s*

eeiknpsy pinkeyes pinkeye pinkeys. *See*
eekns eekps eikps

eeiknpy pinkeye. *See* **einpy iknpy**

eeikprr perkier. *See* **eekpr eikpr eiprr**

eeikprs peskier. *See* **eekprs eikprs**

eeikprst perkiest keister peskier respite.
See **eeirst eekprs eeprst eikprs**

eeikpsst peskiest. *See* **eeipss eeksst
eepsst eikpss**

eeikrrs   kerries. *See* **eeirrs eekrs eikrs**

eeikrsst   keisters keister strikes. *See* **eeirss eeirst eekrss eeksst**

eeikrst   keister. *See* **eikrst eeirst**

eeiksttt   tektites tektite. *See* **eekst eikst**

eeikttt   tektite. *No 6s or 5s*

eeillmpr   impeller. *See* **eeimpr eillmr eilmpr**

eeillmrs   smellier millers. *See* **eeilms eeilrs eeimrs eellrs**

eeillnor   lonelier. *See* **eeilnr eillno ellnor**

eeillorv   lovelier overlie. *See* **eeilrv**

eeillps   ellipse. *See* **eills eelps eilps**

eeillpss   ellipses ellipse lipless pelisse. *See* **eeipss eelpss eillss eilpss**

eeillpsy   sleepily ellipse. *See* **eelpsy**

eeilm   elemi lime mile eel elm lee lei lie mel mil el em li me mi

eeilmnn   linemen. *See* **eeilm eilmn eilnn**

eeilmnns   linesmen linemen. *See* **eeilms eilnns eeilns eilmns**

eeilmnsu   selenium. *See* **eeilms eeilns eemnsu eilmns**

eeilmrsv   vermeils relives reviles servile vermeil. *See* **eeilms eeilrs eeilrv eeilsv**

eeilmrv   vermeil. *See* **eeilrv**

eeilms   elemis elemi limes miles slime smile eels elms else isle lees leis lies lime mels mile mils mise seel seem semi slim eel elm els lee lei lie mel mil mis see el em is li me mi si

eeilmsst   timeless telesis. *See* **eeilms eeilst eeimss eelsst**

eeilmsuv   emulsive elusive. *See* **eeilms eeilsv**

eeilnno   leonine. *See* **eilno eelno**

eeilnnst   sentinel intense lenient linnets tensile. *See* **eeilns eeilst eelnnt eelnst**

eeilnnsv   enlivens enliven. *See* **eeilns eeilsv eeinsv eilnns**

eeilnnt   lenient. *See* **eelnnt eilnnt**

eeilnnv   enliven. *See* **eilnv eilnn einnv**

eeilnopr   leporine pioneer. *See* **eeilnr eelopr eenopr eilnop**

eeilnovz   novelize. *See* **eelnov eenovz**

eeilnps   pensile. *See* **eeilns eilnps eelnps**

eeilnpt   penlite. *See* **eilnpt eeilt**

eeilnr   lierne liner erne leer lien line lire reel rein riel rile eel ere ire lee lei lie nee nil el en er in li ne re

eeilnrs   liernes. *See* **eeilnr eilnrs eeilrs eeilns eeinrs**

eeilnrst   listener reenlist entries leister liernes nestler relents sterile tensile. *See* **eeilnr eeilns eeilrs eeilst**

eeilnrty   entirely inertly. *See* **eeilnr eeilry eeinrt eelnrt**

eeilnrv   livener. *See* **eeinrv eeilnr eeilrv**

eeilns   senile lenis liens lines seine eels else isle lees leis lens lien lies line nils

---

seel seen sine eel els ens lee lei lie nee nil see sen sin el en in is li ne si

eeilnssv   evilness snivels. *See* **eeilns eeilsv eeinss eeinsv**

eeilnst   tensile. *See* **eeilst eilnst eelnst**

eeilnstt   entitles entitle nettles tensile. *See* **eeilns eeilst eelnst eelntt**

eeilntt   entitle. *See* **eelntt eeilt eilnt**

eeilopst   petioles epistle petiole pistole. *See* **eeilst eelops eelpst eeopst**

eeilopt   petiole. *See* **eilopt eeilt eelop**

eeilorrt   loiterer. *See* **eeirrt eilort eiorrt**

eeilorv   overlie. *See* **eeilrv**

eeilostz   zeolites zeolite. *See* **eeilst eilost**

eeilotz   zeolite. *See* **eeilt eilot**

eeilppsy   epilepsy. *See* **eelpsy ilppsy**

eeilprs   replies spieler. *See* **eelprs eilprs eeilrs**

eeilprss   spielers lispers pelisse replies spieler. *See* **eeilrs eeipss eeirss eelprs**

eeilprst   peltries perlites reptiles epistle leister pelters perlite petrels replies reptile respite spieler sterile triples. *See* **eeilrs eeilst eeirst eelprs**

eeilprt   perlite reptile. *See* **eelprt eilprt**

eeilpru   puerile. *See* **eelpr eilpr eepru**

eeilpss   pelisse. *See* **eeipss eelpss eilpss**

eeilpsss   pelisses pelisse sessile. *See* **eeipss eelpss eilpss**

eeilpsst   epistles epistle pelisse pestles stipels telesis. *See* **eeilst eeipss eelpss eelpst**

eeilpssv   pelvises pelisse. *See* **eeilsv eeipss eeissv eelpss**

eeilpst   epistle. *See* **eeilst eelpst eilpst**

eeilpsty   epistyle epistle steeply. *See* **eeilst eelpst eelpsy eelsty**

eeilrs   relies leers reels riels riles eels else isle leer lees leis lies lire reel reis riel rile rise seel seer sere sire eel els ere ire lee lei lie res see sir el er is li re si

eeilrsst   leisters tireless leister listers sterile telesis. *See* **eeilrs eeilst eeirss eeirst**

eeilrssw   wireless. *See* **eeilrs eeirss eelrss eerssw**

eeilrst   leister sterile. *See* **eeilst eilrst eeilrs eeirst**

eeilrsu   leisure. *See* **eeilrs eilsu elrsu**

eeilrsv   relives reviles servile. *See* **eelrsv eeilsv eilrsv eeilrs eeilrv**

eeilrv   relive revile elver lever liver livre revel viler ever evil leer lire live reel riel rile rive veer veil vile eel ere eve ire lee lei lev lie rev vee vie el er li re

eeilry   eerily leery eely eery eyre leer lire lyre reel rely riel rile eel ere eye ire lee lei lie lye rye el er li re ye

eeilsss   sessile. *See* **eesss eilss eelss**

eeilsst   telesis. *See* **eeilst eilsst eelsst**

---

eeilsstx   sextiles sexiest sextile telesis. *See* **eeilst eeilsx eelsst eilsst**

eeilssvw   viewless weevils swivels. *See* **eeilsv eeilvw eeissv eelssv**

eeilst   elites elite islet istle leets sleet steel stele stile tiles eels else isle lees leet leis lest lets lies list seel silt site slit tees ties tile tils eel els its lee lei let lie lit see set sit tee tie til el is it li si ti

eeilsttx   textiles sextile textile. *See* **eeilst eeilsx eelstt eesttx**

eeilstv   velites. *See* **eeilst eeilsv eelstv eilstv**

eeilstx   sextile. *See* **eeilst eeilsx**

eeilsuv   elusive. *See* **eeilsv eilsu**

eeilsv   levies elves evils lives sieve veils eels else eves evil isle lees leis lies live seel vees veil vies vile vise eel els eve lee lei lev lie see vee vie el is li si

eeilsvw   weevils. *See* **eeilsv eilsvw eeilvw**

eeilsx   exiles ilexes exile lexis eels else exes ilex isle lees leis lies seel eel els lee lei lie see sex six el ex is li si xi

eeilt   elite leet tile eel lee lei let lie lit tee tie til el it li ti

eeilttx   textile. *See* **eeilt eeilx eiltx**

eeilvw   weevil evil live veil view vile wile wive eel eve ewe lee lei lev lie vee vie wee el li we

eeilx   exile ilex eel lee lei lie el ex li xi

eeimmns   immense. *See* **eemns eimns eimms**

eeimmors   memories immerse memoirs. *See* **eeimrs eeiors eemmrs eimmor**

eeimmorz   memorize. *See* **eimmor emmorz**

eeimmost   sometime. *See* **eemmst eemost eimost**

eeimmrs   immerse. *See* **eemmrs eimmrs eeimrs**

eeimmrss   immerses immerse messier remises simmers. *See* **eeimrs eeimss eeirss eemmrs**

eeimnno   nominee. *See* **emnno**

eeimnnos   nominees nominee. *See* **eimnos**

eeimnnt   eminent. *See* **eimnnt**

eeimnors   emersion ermines merinos moreens. *See* **eeimnr eeimrs eeinrs eeiors**

eeimnost   semitone moisten. *See* **eemost eimnos eimost emnost**

eeimnr   ermine miner emir erne mere mien mine mire rein rime ere ire men mir nee nim rem rim em en er in me mi ne re

eeimnrs   ermines. *See* **eeimnr eimnrs eeinrs**

eeimnrtu   mutineer retinue reunite. *See* **eeimnr eeinrt eenrtu eimnru**

eeimnss nemesis. *See* **eeimss eemnss eeinss**

eeimoprs promisee empires emprise imposer premise promise semipro. *See* **eeimpr eeimrs eeiors eemprs**

eeimopst epitomes empties epitome metopes septime. *See* **eemopt eemost eeopst eimops**

eeimopt epitome. *See* **eemopt eimpt**

eeimorst tiresome meteors moister mortise. *See* **eeimrs eeiors eeirst eemort**

eeimortv overtime emotive. *See* **eemort eemorv eimotv**

eeimotv emotive. *See* **eimotv eemot**

eeimppst pipestem empties septime. *See* **eeppst eippst**

eeimpr empire prime emir mere mire peer peri perm pier prim rime ripe ere imp ire mir pee per pie rem rep rim rip em er me mi pe pi re

eeimprr premier. *See* **eeimpr eimprr**

eeimprrs premiers empires emprise perries premier premise primers reprise respire. *See* **eeimpr eeimrs eeirrs eemprs**

eeimprs empires emprise premise. *See* **eeimpr eimprs eeimrs eemprs**

eeimprss emprises premises empires empress emprise impress messier premise remises simpers. *See* **eeimpr eeimrs eeimss eeipss**

eeimprt emptier. *See* **eeimpr eimprt eemprt**

eeimpsst septimes empties misstep septime. *See* **eeimss eeipss eepsst eimsst**

eeimpst empties septime. *See* **eimst eemst eipst**

eeimpstt emptiest empties septime tempest. *See* **eeiptt eepstt empstt**

eeimqrsu requiems esquire queries requiem. *See* **eeimrs eemrsu eeqrsu eiqrsu**

eeimqru requiem. *See* **eeqru eiqru**

eeimqstu mesquite equites mesquit. *See* **eiqstu**

eeimrrr merrier. *No 6s or 5s*

eeimrrst merriest retires retries termers terries. *See* **eeimrs eeirrs eeirrt eeirst**

eeimrs remise emirs meres mires miser rimes emir mere mire mirs mise reis rime rims rise seem seer semi sere sire ere ire mir mis rem res rim see sir em er is me mi re si

eeimrss messier remises. *See* **eeimss eimrss eeimrs eeirss**

eeimrstt termites emitter metrist termite. *See* **eeimrs eeirst eemrst eerstt**

eeimrstu emeritus. *See* **eeimrs eeirst eemrst eemrsu**

eeimrsx remixes. *See* **eimrsx eeimrs eeirsx**

eeimrtt emitter termite. *See* **eimrt eemrt eeirt**

eeimrtty temerity emitter termite. *See* **eemry eimrt eemrt**

eeimss emesis seems semis mess mise miss seem sees semi ess mis see sis em is me mi si

eeimssst messiest. *See* **eeimss eemsss eimsst**

eeinnps pennies. *See* **einnps eenps eeins**

eeinnptt penitent. *See* **eeiptt einntt**

eeinnrst internes entries intense interne interns rennets tinners. *See* **eeinrs eeinrt eeirst eennst**

eeinnrt interne. *See* **eeinrt einnrt eennrt**

eeinnst intense. *See* **eennst einnst**

eeinnstt sentient intense. *See* **eennst eenstt einnst einntt**

eeinnstw entwines intense entwine. *See* **eennst eenstw einnst einstw**

eeinntw entwine. *See* **eintw**

eeinoppr peperoni pioneer. *See* **eenopr einoppr**

eeinopr pioneer. *See* **eenopr einopr**

eeinoprs pioneers openers orpines peonies pioneer reopens. *See* **eeinrs eeiors eenopr eenprs**

eeinops peonies. *See* **einops**

eeinorsv eversion enviers erosive inverse version. *See* **eeinrs eeinrv eeinsv eeiors**

eeinortx exertion. *See* **eeinrt eenrtx einort**

eeinprss ripeness serines snipers. *See* **eeinrs eeinss eeipss eeirss**

eeinprsu penuries uprisen. *See* **eeinrs eenprs eenrsu eeprsu**

eeinprtx inexpert. *See* **eeinrt eeiprx eenprt eenrtx**

eeinpsv pensive. *See* **eeinsv eenps einps**

eeinqrsu enquires squireen enquire equines esquire queries. *See* **eeinqu eeinrs eenqsu eenrsu**

eeinqru enquire. *See* **eeinqu einru eeqru**

eeinqstu quietens equines equites inquest quieten quintes sequent. *See* **eeinqu eenqsu eenstu einqsu**

eeinqsu equines. *See* **eeinqu eenqsu einqsu**

eeinqtu quieten. *See* **eeinqu einqtu**

eeinqu equine queen nee en in ne nu

eeinrrst terrines entries renters retires retries sterner terries terrine. *See* **eeinrs eeinrt eeirrs eeirst**

eeinrrt terrine. *See* **eeinrt eenrrt eeirrt**

eeinrrtx interrex terrine. *See* **eeinrt eeirrt eenrtx**

eeinrrv nervier vernier. *See* **eeinrv eirrv**

eeinrs serine ernes reins resin rinse risen seine serin siren sneer erne rein reis rise seen seer sere sine sire ens ere ire nee res see sen sin sir en er in is ne re si

eeinrss serines. *See* **einrss eeinss eeinrs eenrss**

eeinrsst sentries entries inserts nesters resents serines sinters. *See* **eeinrs eeinrt eeinss eeirss**

eeinrssu enuresis ensures insures reissue serines sunrise. *See* **eeinrs eeinss eeirss eenrsu**

eeinrst entries. *See* **eenrst eeinrt einrst eeirst eeinrs**

eeinrstt interest entries tenters. *See* **eeinrs eeinrt eeirst eenrst**

eeinrstu retinues reunites entries neuters retinue reunite tenures triunes tureens. *See* **eeinrs eeinrt eeirst eenrst**

eeinrstv nerviest reinvest sirvente entries enviers inverse inverts restive striven venters veriest. *See* **eeinrs eeinrt eeinrv eeinsv**

eeinrstx intersex entries externs sixteen. *See* **eeinrs eeinrt eeirst eeirsx**

eeinrsuv universe enviers inverse. *See* **eeinrs eeinrv eeinsv eeirsv**

eeinrsv enviers inverse. *See* **eeinrv eeinsv eenrsv eeirsv**

eeinrsw newsier wieners. *See* **eenrsw eeinrs eeinrw**

eeinrt entire enter inert inter niter retie trine erne rein rent rete rite teen tern tier tine tire tree ere ire nee net nit ret tee ten tie tin en er in it ne re ti

eeinrtty entirety eternity. *See* **eeinrt eenrtt einrtt eintty**

eeinrtu retinue reunite. *See* **eeinrt eenrtu einrtu**

eeinrv envier nerve never riven erne even ever nevi rein rive veer vein vine ere eve ire nee rev vee vie en er in ne re

eeinrw wiener newer renew erne ewer rein weir wine wire wren ere ewe ire nee new wee wen win en er in ne re we

eeins seine seen sine ens nee see sen sin en in is ne si

eeinss seines seine sense sines seen sees sine sins ens ess nee see sen sin sis en in is ne si

eeinsssx sexiness. *See* **eeinss eensss**

eeinsstw newsiest wetness wisents witness. *See* **eeinss eensst eenstw eesstw**

eeinsttw twenties. *See* **eenstt eenstw eesttw einstt**

eeinsttx existent sixteen extents. *See* **eenstt eenttx eesttx einstt**

eeinstx sixteen. *See* **eistx einst einsx**

eeinsv envies evens neves seine seven sieve veins vines even eves nevi seen sine vees vein vies vine vise ens eve nee see sen sin vee vie en in is ne si

eeioprrs roperies perries prosier reprise respire. *See* eeiors eeirrs eeoprs eiorrs

eeioprrt portiere. *See* eeirrt eiorrt eoprrt

eeiopss poesies. *See* eeipss eiopss

eeiopstz poetizes poetize. *See* eeopst

eeiopsx epoxies. *See* eeopsx eipsx eiops

eeioptz poetize. *See* eeopt

eeiorrrs orreries sorrier. *See* eeiors eeirrs eiorrs eorrrs

eeiorrtx exterior. *See* eeirrt eiorrt

eeiors soiree erose osier ores reis rise roes rose seer sere sire sore sori ere ire ore res roe see sir er is or os re si so

eeiorss soirees. *See* eeiors eeirss

eeiorsv erosive. *See* eeirsv eeorsv eeiors eiorsv

eeiorsvz oversize erosive. *See* eeiors eeirsv eeirsz eeorsv

eeiorvvw overview. *See* eeirvv eeirvw

eeipppr peppier preppie. *See* eepppr eippr

eeipppst peppiest. *See* eeppst eippst

eeipprrs perspire perries repise respire rippers. *See* eeirrs eipprr eipprs

eeippstt pipettes pipette tippets. *See* eeiptt eeppst eepstt eippst

eeipptt pipette. *See* eeiptt eipptt

eeipqrsu periques esquire perique queries. *See* eeprsu eeqrsu eipqsu eiprsu

eeipqru perique. *See* eipqu eepru eeqru

eeiprrs perries reprise respire. *See* eeirrs eiprrs

eeiprrss reprises respires perries presser repress reprise respire sirrees. *See* eeipss eeirrs eeirss eeprss

eeiprrtt preterit prettier pettier. *See* eeiptt eeirrt eerrtt eirrtt

eeiprsst respites persist pesters presets priests respite sprites stripes. *See* eeipss eeirss eeirst eeprss

eeiprssv previses previse revises vespers. *See* eeipss eeirss eeirsv eeissv

eeiprst respite. *See* eiprst eeprst eeirst

eeiprstt pretties pettier pretest respite spitter tipster. *See* eeiptt eeirst eeprst eepstt

eeiprstx preexist experts expires prexies respite. *See* eeiprx eeirst eeirsx eeprst

eeiprsv previse. *See* eeirsv eeprsv eiprsv

eeiprsvw previews preview previse reviews viewers. *See* eeirsv eeirvw eeprsv eersvw

eeiprsx expires prexies. *See* eeiprx eeirsx

eeiprtt pettier. *See* eeiptt eeprt eeirt

eeiprtuv eruptive. *See* eeprtu eepruv eiprtv eirtuv

eeiprvw preview. *See* eeirvw

eeiprx expire peer peri pier ripe ere ire pee per pie pix rep rex rip er ex pe pi re xi

eeipss espies seeps spies pees pies seep sees sips ess pee pie see sip sis is pe pi si

eeipsttt pettiest. *See* eeiptt eepstt

eeiptt petite petit pee pet pie pit tee tie tip tit it pe pi ti

eeiqrrsu requires esquire queries require. *See* eeirrs eeqrsu eiqrsu

eeiqrru require. *See* eeqru eiqru

eeiqrssu esquires esquire queries reissue squires. *See* eeirss eeqrsu eerssu eiqrsu

eeiqrstu quieters equites esquire queries querist quester quieter request. *See* eeirst eeqrsu eiqrsu eiqstu

eeiqrsu esquire queries. *See* eeqrsu eiqrsu

eeiqrtu quieter. *See* eeqru eiqtu eiqru

eeiqstu equites. *See* eiqstu

eeirrrst terriers retires retries terrier terries. *See* eeirrs eeirrt eeirst

eeirrrt terrier. *See* eeirrt

eeirrrtw rewriter terrier rewrite. *See* eeirrt eeirrw eirrtw

eeirrs sirree riser errs reis rise seer sere sire ere err ire res see sir er is re si

eeirrss sirrees. *See* eirrss eeirss eeirrs

eeirrsst resister retires retries sirrees terries. *See* eeirrs eeirrt eeirss eeirst

eeirrst retires retries terries. *See* eeirst eeirrt eerrst

eeirrstv riveters restive retires retries reverts riveter terries veriest. *See* eeirrs eeirrt eeirst eeirsv

eeirrsw rewires. *See* eeirrs eeirrw

eeirrt retire retie rete rite tier tire tree ere err ire ret tee tie er it re ti

eeirrtv riveter. *See* eeirrt eerrtv

eeirrtw rewrite. *See* eeirrt eeirrw eirrtw

eeirrw rewire wrier ewer weir wire ere err ewe ire wee er re we

eeirss series rises seers seres sires reis rise seer sees sere sire sirs ere ess ire res see sir sis er is re si

eeirsssu reissues reissue issuers. *See* eeirss eerssu eirssu

eeirsstu sureties reissue. *See* eeirss eeirst eersst eerssu

eeirsstv vestries restive revises stivers strives veriest. *See* eeirss eeirst eeirsv eeissv

eeirssu reissue. *See* eirssu eerssu eeirss

eeirssuz seizures reissue seizers seizure. *See* eeirss eeirsz eeissz eerssu

eeirssv revises. *See* eeirsv eeirss eerssv eeissv

eeirssz seizers. *See* eeirsz eeissz eeirss

eeirst reties ester reset retie rites steer stere terse tiers tires trees tries erst reis rest rete rets rise rite seer sere sire site stir tees tier ties tire tree ere ire its res ret see set sir sit tee tie er is it re si ti

eeirstv restive veriest. *See* eerstv eeirst eeirsv eirstv

eeirstvy severity restive veriest. *See* eeirst eeirsv eerstv eersty

eeirsuz seizure. *See* eeirsz eersu

eeirsv revise serve sever sieve veers verse ever eves reis revs rise rive seer sere sire veer vees vies vise ere eve ire res rev see sir vee vie er is re si

eeirsvv revives. *See* eeirsv eeirvv eersvv

eeirsvw reviews viewers. *See* eeirvw eeirsv eersvw

eeirsx sexier exes reis rise seer sere sire ere ire res rex see sex sir six er ex is re si xi

eeirsz seizer seize reis rise seer sere sire size zees ere ire res see sir zee er is re si

eeirt retie rete rite tier tire tree ere ire ret tee tie er it re ti

eeirvv revive verve ever rive veer ere eve ire rev vee vie er re

eeirvw review viewer ever ewer rive veer view weir wire wive ere eve ewe ire rev vee vie wee er re we

eeisstx sexiest. *See* eisstx

eeissv sieves sieve vises eves sees vees vies vise ess eve see sis vee vie is si

eeissz seizes seize sizes sees size zees ess see sis zee is si

eeisv sieve eves vees vies vise eve see vee vie is si

eeisz seize zees size see zee is si

eejjlnuy jejunely. *See* eejjnu

eejjnu jejune nee en ne nu

eejkorst jokester. *See* eejrst eekost eeorst ejkors

eejlrwy jewelry. *See* eejlw eelry

eejlsw jewels jewel eels else ewes lees seel slew eel els ewe lee see sew wee el we

eejlw jewel eel ewe lee wee el we

eejnnst jennets. *See* eejnnt eennst

eejnnt jennet teen jet nee net tee ten en ne

eejp jeep pee pe

eejprrru perjurer perjure. *See* eepru eprru

eejprrsu perjures perjure peruser. *See* eeprsu eprrsu

eejprru perjure. *See* eepru eprru

eejps jeeps jeep pees seep pee see pe

eejr jeer ere er re

eejrs jeers jeer seer sere ere res see er re

eejrsst jesters. *See* eejrst eersst

eejrssy jerseys. *See* eejrsy eejss eerss

eejrst jester ester jeers reset steer stere terse trees erst jeer jest jets rest rete rets seer sere tees tree ere jet res ret see set tee er re

eejrsy jersey jeers eyres eery eyes eyre jeer ryes seer sere ere eye res rye see yes er re ye

eejss jesse sees jess see ess

eejsss jesses jesse esses sees jess see ess

eejz jeez zee

eek eke

eekk keek eke

eekkrrst trekkers trekker. *See* **eerrst**

eekkrrt trekker. *No 6s or 5s*

eekks keeks ekes keek seek skee eke see

eekl keel leek eel eke elk lee lek el

eekllsuu ukuleles ukulele. *See* **eekls llsuu kllsu**

eeklluu ukulele. *No 6s or 5s*

eeklmrz klezmer. *See* **eelmr**

eeklmy meekly eely keel leek meek ylem eel eke elk elm eye key lee lek lye mel el em me my ye

eekln kneel keen knee leek eel eke elk ken lee lek nee el en ne

eeklnn kennel kneel keel keen knee leek eel eke elk ken lee lek nee el en ne

eeklnns kennels. *See* **eeklnn eeklns**

eeklnos keelson. *See* **eklnos eelnos**

eeklnoss keelsons keelson kelsons. *See* **eeklss eelnoss eelnss**

eeklnost skeleton keelson ketones. *See* **eeklns eeknot eekost eelnos**

eeklnr kernel kneel erne keel keen kern knee leek leer reek reel eel eke elk ere ken lee lek nee el en er ne re

eeklnrs kernels. *See* **eeklnr eeklns**

eeklns kneels keels keens kneel knees leeks sleek eels ekes elks else keel keen kens knee leek lees leks lens seek seel seen skee eel eke elk els ens ken lee lek nee see sen el en ne

eeklny keenly kneel eely keel keen knee leek eel eke elk eye ken key lee lek lye nee yen el en ne ye

eeklp kelep keel keep kelp leek peek peel eel eke elk lee lek pee el pe

eeklrsst kestrels kestrel. *See* **eekrss eeksst eelrss**

eeklrst kestrel. *See* **eekrs eerst eekls**

eekls keels leeks sleek eels ekes elks else keel leek lees seek seel skee eel eke elk els lee lek see el

eeklstt kettles. *See* **eekltt eelstt**

eeklsv kevels elves keels kevel leeks sleek eels ekes elks else eves keel leek lees leks seek seel skee vees eel eke elk els eve lee lek lev see vee el

eekltt kettle keel keet leek leet eel eke elk lee lek let tee el

eeklv kevel keel leek eel eke elk eve lee lek lev vee el

eeklwy weekly eely keel leek week eel eke elk ewe eye key lee lek lye wee wye yew el we ye

eekm meek eke em me

eekmrs kermes esker meres reeks ekes meek mere reek seek seem seer sere skee eke ere rem res see em er me re

eekmrss kermess. *See* **eekmrs eekrss**

eekn keen knee eke ken nee en ne

eeknorty keynoter keynote. *See* **eeknot**

eeknost ketones. *See* **eeknot eekost eknost**

eeknosty keynotes keystone ketones keynote. *See* **eeknot eekost eensty eknost**

eeknot ketone token keen keet keno knee knot note teen toke tone eke eon ken nee net not oke one tee ten toe ton en ne no on to

eeknoty keynote. *See* **eeknot eenty**

eekns keens knees ekes keen kens knee seek seen skee eke ens ken nee see sen en ne

eeknsstu netsukes netsuke. *See* **eeksst eensst eenssu eenstu**

eeknstu netsuke. *See* **eenstu eekns eekst**

eekop pekoe keep peek poke eke oke ope pee pe

eekops pekoes keeps peeks pekoe pokes spoke ekes epos keep okes opes peek pees peso poke pose seek seep skee skep soke eke kos oke ope pee see sop os pe so

eekorsv revokes. *See* **eekosv eekorv eeorsv**

eekorv revoke evoke ever over reek rove veer eke ere eve kor oke ore rev roe vee er or re

eekost ketose keets skeet stoke tokes ekes keet okes seek skee soke tees toes toke eke kos oke see set sot tee toe tsk os so to

eekosv evokes evoke ekes eves okes seek skee soke vees eke eve kos oke see vee os so

eekov evoke eke eve oke vee

eekp keep peek eke pee pe

eekppsu upkeeps. *See* **eekppu eekps eepps**

eekppu upkeep keep peek peep puke eke pee pep pup pe up

eekpr kreep keep peek peer perk reek eke ere pee per rep er pe re

eekprs kreeps esker keeps kreep peeks peers perks perse reeks spree ekes keep peek peer pees perk reek reps seek seep seer sere skee skep eke ere pee per rep res see er pe re

eekprsu perukes. *See* **eekprs eekpru eeprsu**

eekpru peruke kreep puree rupee keep peek peer perk puke pure reek eke ere pee per rep rue er pe re up

eekps keeps peeks ekes keep peek pees seek seep skee skep eke pee see pe

eekr reek eke ere er re

eekrrsuz kreuzers kreuzer. *See* **eekrs eersu errsu**

eekrrtuz kreutzer kreuzer. *See* **eerrtu**

eekrruz kreuzer. *No 6s or 5s*

eekrs esker reeks ekes reek seek seer sere skee eke ere res see er re

eekrss eskers esker reeks seeks seers seres skees ekes reek seek seer sees sere skee eke ere ess res see er re

eekrssw skewers. *See* **eekrss eerssw eekrsw**

eekrssy kerseys. *See* **eekrss eekrsy**

eekrsw skewer esker reeks sewer weeks ekes ewer ewes reek seek seer sere skee skew week eke ere ewe res see sew wee er re we

eekrsy kersey esker eyres reeks reeky eery ekes eyes eyre keys reek ryes seek seer sere skee eke ere eye key res rye see sky yes er re ye

eekry reeky eery eyre reek eke ere eye key rye er re ye

eeks ekes seek skee eke see

eekss seeks skees ekes seek sees skee eke ess see

eeksst skeets keets seeks skees skeet ekes keet seek sees sets skee tees eke ess see set tee tsk

eekst keets skeet ekes keet seek skee tees eke see set tee tsk

eeksw weeks ekes ewes seek skee skew week eke ewe see sew wee we

eekt keet eke tee

eekw week eke ewe wee we

eel eel lee el

eelllvy levelly. *See* **eellv**

eellnov novelle. *See* **eelnov eellv**

eellorst solleret retells tellers. *See* **eellrs eellrt eelors eeorst**

eellortx extoller. *See* **eellrt ellotx**

eellorwy yellower. *See* **eellry ellowy elorwy**

eellossv loveless. *See* **eellsv eelssv elossv**

eellprs speller. *See* **eelprs eellrs**

eellprss spellers resells sellers speller. *See* **eellrs eelprs eelpss eelrss**

eellpst pellets. *See* **eellpt eelpst**

eellpt pellet leet lept peel pelt tell eel ell lee let pee pet tee el pe

eellrs resell seller leers reels eels ells else leer lees reel seel seer sell sere eel ell els ere lee res see el er re

eellrss resells sellers. *See* **eelrss eellrs**

eellrst retells tellers. *See* **eellrs eellrt**

eellrsy   yellers. *See* **eellrs eellry**

eellrt   retell teller leer leet reel rete tell tree eel ell ere lee let ret tee el er re

eellry   yeller leery eely eery eyre leer lyre reel rely yell eel ell ere eye lee lye rye el er re ye

eellsv   levels level elves eels ells else eves lees seel sell vees eel ell els eve lee lev see vee el

eellv   level eel ell eve lee lev vee el

eelmmpux   exemplum. *See* **eelpx elmpu**

eelmnoos   lonesome someone. *See* **eelnos elmnos elnoos**

eelmnsuy   unseemly. *See* **elmnsu elmsuy eemnsu eelmsy**

eelmopry   employer polymer. *See* **eelmry eelopr eelpry eempry**

eelmorst   molester meteors omelets smelter. *See* **eelmot eelmrs eelors eemort**

eelmorsw   eelworms eelworm. *See* **eelmrs eelors elmors elorsw**

eelmorty   remotely. *See* **eelmot eelmry eemort elmoty**

eelmorw   eelworm. *See* **elorw eelmr elmor**

eelmost   omelets. *See* **eemost elmost eelmot**

eelmot   omelet emote motel leet meet melt mete mole molt mote teem tome eel elm lee let lot mel met mot tee toe tom el em lo me mo om to

eelmpst   temples. *See* **eelmpt eelpst**

eelmpstt   templets mettles tempest temples templet. *See* **eelmpt eelpst eelstt empstt**

eelmpt   temple leet lept meet melt mete peel pelt teem eel elm lee let mel met pee pet tee el em me pe

eelmptt   templet. *See* **eelmpt eelmtt**

eelmr   merle leer mere merl reel eel elm ere lee mel rem el em er me re

eelmrs   merles leers meres merle merls reels eels elms else leer lees mels mere merl reel seel seem seer sere eel elm els ere lee mel rem res see el em er me re

eelmrsst   smelters termless smelter. *See* **eelmrs eelrss eelsst eemrst**

eelmrst   smelter. *See* **eemrst eelmrs**

eelmrsty   smeltery myrtles smelter tersely. *See* **eelmrs eelmry eelmsy eelsty**

eelmrsu   lemures. *See* **elmrsu eemrsu**

eelmry   merely emery leery merle eely eery eyre leer lyre mere merl reel rely ylem eel elm ere eye lee lye mel rem rye el em er me my re ye

eelmstt   mettles. *See* **eelmtt eelstt**

eelmsy   seemly eels eely elms else eyes lees lyes lyse mels seel seem ylem eel

elm els eye lee lye mel see sly yes el em me my ye

eelmtt   mettle leet meet melt mete teem eel elm lee let mel met tee el em me

eelnnoss   loneness oneness. *See* **eelnos eelnss elnoss**

eelnnt   lenten leet lent teen eel lee let nee net tee ten el en ne

eelnnuvy   unevenly. *See* **eelnvy eennuv**

eelno   leone enol leno lone noel eel eon lee nee one el en lo ne no on

eelnoors   loosener. *See* **eelnos eelors elnoos elnors**

eelnoprt   petronel. *See* **eelnrt eelopr eelprt eenopr**

eelnopsv   envelops envelop elevons. *See* **eelnos eelnov eelnps eelops**

eelnopv   envelop. *See* **eelnov eelop**

eelnoqtu   eloquent. *See* **eeltu elnot eelno**

eelnorst   entresol nestler relents. *See* **eelnos eelnrt eelnst eelors**

eelnos   leones leone noels eels else enol eons lees leno lens lone lose noel noes nose ones seel seen sloe sole eel els ens eon lee los nee one see sen sol son el en lo ne no on os so

eelnosss   noseless lessens lessons. *See* **eelnos eelnss eensss elnoss**

eelnosst   noteless nestles toeless. *See* **eelnos eelnss eelnst eelsst**

eelnosv   elevons. *See* **eelnov eelnos elnosv**

eelnov   elevon leone novel enol even leno lone love noel oven vole eel eon eve lee lev nee one vee el en lo ne no on

eelnps   spleen neeps peels peens sleep eels else lees lens neep peel peen pees pens seel seen seep eel els ens lee nee pee pen see sen el en ne pe

eelnpss   spleens. *See* **eelnss eelpss eelnps**

eelnpsy   spleeny. *See* **eelnps eelpsy**

eelnquy   queenly. *See* **eenqu**

eelnrsst   nestlers nesters nestler nestles relents resents. *See* **eelnrt eelnss eelnst eelrss**

eelnrst   nestler relents. *See* **eenrst eelnst eelnrt**

eelnrt   relent enter erne leer leet lent reel rent rete teen tern tree eel ere lee let nee net ret tee ten el en er ne re

eelnss   lenses lessen seels sense eels else lees lens less seel seen sees eel els ens ess lee nee see sen el en ne

eelnsss   lessens. *See* **eelnss eensss**

eelnsst   nestles. *See* **eelnss eelnst eelsst eensst**

eelnst   nestle leets sleet steel stele teens tense eels else lees leet lens lent lest lets nest nets seel seen sent teen tees tens eel els ens lee let nee net see sen set tee ten el en ne

eelnstt   nettles. *See* **eelnst eelntt eelstt eenstt**

eelnsttu   lunettes unsettle nettles lunette. *See* **eelnst eelntt eelstt eelstu**

eelnsty   tensely. *See* **eelnst eelsty eensty**

eelnsw   newels newel eels else ewes lees lens news seel seen sewn slew wens eel els ens ewe lee nee new see sen sew wee wen el en ne we

eelnsxy   xylenes. *See* **eelnxy elnsxy**

eelntt   nettle tenet leet lent teen tent eel lee let nee net tee ten el en ne

eelnttu   lunette. *See* **eelntt elnttu**

eelnvy   evenly eely envy even levy eel eve eye lee lev lye nee vee yen el en ne ye

eelnw   newel eel ewe lee nee new wee wen el en ne we

eelnxy   xylene eely lynx eel eye lee lye nee yen el en ex ne ye

eelop   elope lope peel pole eel lee lop ope pee el lo pe

eelopp   people elope lope peel peep plop pole pope eel lee lop ope pee pep pop el lo pe

eelopps   peoples. *See* **eelops eelopp elopps**

eeloppss   peploses peoples. *See* **eelops eelopp elopps eelpss**

eelopr   eloper elope leper loper repel leer lope lore orle peel peer pole pore reel repo role rope eel ere lee lop ope ore pee per pro rep roe el er lo or pe re

eeloprrx   explorer explore. *See* **eelopr eloprx**

eeloprs   elopers leprose. *See* **eelopr eelops eelprs eloprs eeoprs**

eeloprsx   explores elopers explore leprose plexors. *See* **eelopr eelops eelors eelprs**

eeloprx   explore. *See* **eelopr eloprx**

eelops   elopes elope lopes peels poles sleep slope eels else epos lees lope lops lose opes peel pees peso pole pose seel seep sloe slop sole eel els lee lop los ope pee see sol sop el lo os pe so

eelopstu   eelpouts eelpout toupees tupelos. *See* **eelops eelpst eelstu eeopst**

eeloptu   eelpout. *See* **eeoptu eloptu**

eelorrvv   revolver revolve. *See* **eelovv**

eelors   resole erose leers lores loser orles reels roles eels else leer lees lore lose ores orle reel roes role rose seel seer sere sloe sole sore eel els ere lee los ore res roe see sol el er lo or os re so

eelorss   resoles. *See* **eelrss elorss eelors**

eelorssv   resolves resoles resolve solvers. *See* **eelors eelrss eelrsv eeorsv**

eelorstu   resolute. *See* **eelors eelstu eeorst elorst**

eelorsv   resolve. *See* **eelrsv elorsv eeorsv**

eelorsvv revolves evolves resolve revolve. *See* **eelors eelovv eelrsv eeorsv**

eelorttu roulette. *See* **eelrtt elottu elrttu**

eelorvv revolve. *See* **eelovv eelrv elorv**

eelosst toeless. *See* **eeosst eelsst elosst**

eelosvv evolves. *See* **eelovv eelsv elosv**

eelovv evolve love vole eel eve lee lev vee el lo

eelp peel eel lee pee el pe

eelpprx perplex. *See* **eelpx eelpr**

eelppstu septuple. *See* **eelpst eelstu eeppst elppsu**

eelpr leper repel leer peel peer reel eel ere lee pee per rep el er pe re

eelprs lepers repels leers leper peels peers perse reels repel sleep spree eels else leer lees peel peer pees reel reps seel seep seer sere eel els ere lee pee per rep res see el er pe re

eelprssu repulses repulse peruses. *See* **eelprs eelpss eelrss eeprss**

eelprst pelters petrels. *See* **eelprs eelprt eeprst eelpst**

eelprstz pretzels pelters petrels pretzel seltzer. *See* **eelprs eelprt eelpst eeprst**

eelprsu repulse. *See* **eelprs elprsu eeprsu**

eelprsy yelpers. *See* **eelprs eelpsy eelpry**

eelprt pelter petrel leper peter repel leer leet lept peel peer pelt pert reel rete tree eel ere lee let pee per pet rep ret tee el er pe re

eelprtxy expertly. *See* **eelprt eelpry eeprtx eeprty**

eelprtz pretzel. *See* **eelprt**

eelpry yelper leery leper repel reply eely eery eyre leer lyre peel peer prey pyre reel rely yelp eel ere eye lee lye pee per ply pry rep rye yep el er pe re ye

eelps peels sleep eels else lees peel pees seel seep eel els lee pee see el pe

eelpss sleeps peels seels seeps sleep eels else lees less peel pees seel seep sees eel els ess lee pee see el pe

eelpsst pestles. *See* **eelpst eelpss eelsst eepsst**

eelpssux plexuses. *See* **eelpss eelpsx elpssu elpsux**

eelpst pestle leets peels pelts sleep sleet slept spelt steel steep stele eels else lees leet lept lest lets peel pees pelt pest pets seel seep sept step tees eel els lee let pee pet see set tee el pe

eelpstux sextuple. *See* **eelpst eelpsx eelstu elpstu**

eelpsty steeply. *See* **eelpst eelpsy eelsty**

eelpsv pelves elves peels sleep veeps eels else eves lees peel pees seel seep veep vees eel els eve lee lev pee see vee el pe

eelpsx expels expel peels sleep eels else exes lees peel pees seel seep eel els lee pee see sex el ex pe

eelpsy sleepy peels seepy sleep yelps eels eely else espy eyes lees lyes lyse peel pees seel seep yelp eel els eye lee lye pee ply see sly spy yep yes el pe ye

eelpx expel peel eel lee pee el ex pe

eelqruy queerly. *See* **eelry eeqru eqruy**

eelqssu sequels. *See* **eelqsu eelss elssu**

eelqsu sequel eels else lees lues seel slue eel els lee leu see sue use el us

eelr leer reel eel ere lee el er re

eelrrstw wrestler swelter welters wrestle. *See* **eelrtw eerrst eerstw**

eelrrvy revelry. *See* **eerrvy eelrv eelry**

eelrs leers reels eels else leer lees reel seel seer sere eel els ere lee res see el er re

eelrss lesser leers reels seels seers seres eels else leer lees less reel seel seer sees sere eel els ere ess lee res see el er re

eelrssst restless tresses. *See* **eelrss eelsst eersst**

eelrsstt settlers trestles letters setters settler settles streets tersest testers trestle. *See* **eelrss eelrtt eelsst eelstt**

eelrsstw swelters wrestles swelter welters westers wrestle. *See* **eelrss eelrtw eelsst eersst**

eelrsstz seltzers seltzer. *See* **eelrss eelsst eersst**

eelrstt letters settler trestle. *See* **eelrtt eerstt eelstt**

eelrstw swelter welters wrestle. *See* **eelrtw eerstw**

eelrstwy westerly sweetly swelter tersely welters wrestle. *See* **eelrtw eelsty eerstw eersty**

eelrsty tersely. *See* **eelsty eersty**

eelrstz seltzer. *See* **eerst eelrs eelst**

eelrsuv velures. *See* **eelrsv eersuv eelruv**

eelrsv elvers levers revels elver elves leers lever reels revel serve sever veers verse eels else ever eves leer lees reel revs seel seer sere veer vees eel els ere eve lee lev res rev see vee el er re

eelrtt letter leer leet reel rete tree tret eel ere lee let ret tee el er re

eelrtw welter ewer leer leet reel rete tree welt eel ere ewe lee let ret tee wee wet el er re we

eelruv velure elver lever revel revue ever leer lure reel rule veer eel ere eve lee leu lev luv rev rue vee el er re

eelrv elver lever revel ever leer reel veer eel ere eve lee lev rev vee el er re

eelry leery eely eery eyre leer lyre reel rely eel ere eye lee lye rye el er re ye

eels eels else lees seel eel els lee see el

eelss seels eels else lees less seel sees eel els ess lee see el

eelsssu useless. *See* **eesss eelss elssu**

eelsssv vessels. *See* **eelssv**

eelsssx sexless. *See* **eesss eessx**

eelsst sleets steels steles leets seels sleet steel stele eels else lees leet less lest lets seel sees sets tees eel els ess lee let see set tee el

eelsstt settles. *See* **eesstt eelstt eelsst**

eelssv selves vessel seels elves eels else eves lees less seel sees vees eel els ess eve lee lev see vee el

eelst leets sleet steel stele eels else lees leet lest lets seel tees eel els lee let see set tee el

eelstt settle leets sleet steel stele eels else lees leet lest lets seel stet tees test eel els lee let see set tee el

eelstu elutes elute leets lutes sleet steel stele tules eels else lees leet lest lets lues lust lute seel slue slut suet tees tule eel els lee let leu see set sue tee use el us ut

eelstv svelte elves leets sleet steel stele eels else eves lees leet lest lets seel tees vees vest vets eel els eve lee let lev see set tee vee vet el

eelstvv velvets. *See* **eelstv eeltvv**

eelstvw twelves. *See* **eelstv eeltvw**

eelstwy sweetly. *See* **eelsty**

eelsty sleety steely leets sleet steel stele style eels eely else eyes lees leet lest lets lyes lyse seel tees eel els eye lee let lye see set sly sty tee yes yet el ye

eelsv elves eels else eves lees seel vees eel els eve lee lev see vee el

eelt leet eel lee let tee el

eeltu elute leet lute tule eel lee let leu tee el ut

eeltvv velvet leet eel eve lee lev tee vee vet el

eeltvvy velvety. *See* **eeltvv**

eeltvw twelve leet welt eel eve ewe lee let lev tee vee vet wee wet el we

eely eely eel eye lee lye el ye

eemmnost mementos memento moments. *See* **eemmst eemost emmnot emnost**

eemmnot memento. *See* **emmnot eemmt eemot**

eemmnotv movement memento. *See* **emmnot**

eemmnr mermen emmer mere erne ere mem men nee rem em en er me ne re

eemmr emmer mere ere mem rem em er me re

eemmrs emmers emmer meres mems mere seem seer sere ere mem rem res see em er me re

eemmrst stemmer. *See* **eemmrs eemmst eemrst**

eemmst emmets emmet meets metes teems meet mems mete seem stem teem tees mem met see set tee em me

eemmt emmet meet mete teem mem met tee em me

eemnnosv envenoms envenom. *See* **emnosv**

eemnnov envenom. *See* **emnno emnov**

eemnnp penmen neep peen men nee pee pen em en me ne pe

eemnnsw newsmen. *See* **eemns**

eemnoos someone. *See* **eemns emnos mnoos**

eemnor moreen erne mere more morn nome norm omen omer eon ere men mon mor nee nor one ore rem roe em en er me mo ne no om on or re

eemnors moreens. *See* **cemnor emnors**

eemnoy yeomen enemy money nome omen eon eye men mon nee one yen yon em en me mo my ne no om on oy ye

eemnprss pressmen empress. *See* **eemnss eemprs eenprs eenrss**

eemnptu umpteen. *See* **eemnu**

eemns mesne semen seem seen ens men nee see sen em en me ne

eemnss menses mesnes semens mesne seems semen sense mess seem seen sees ens ess men nee see sen em en me ne

eemnsttv vestment. *See* **eenstt eenstv**

eemnsu neumes emeus ensue menus mesne neume semen emeu emus menu muse seem seen emu ens men mus nee see sen sue sum sun use em en me mu ne nu um us

eemnsyz enzymes. *See* **eemnyz eemns emsyz**

eemnu neume emeu menu emu men nee em en me mu ne nu um

eemny enemy eye men nee yen em en me my ne ye

eemnyz enzyme enemy zyme eye men nee yen zee em en me my ne ye

eemoorrv moreover remover. *See* **eemorv emoorr**

eemoosw woesome. *See* **emoos emosw**

eemoprr emperor. *See* **emoprr**

eemoprrs emperors emperor remorse rompers. *See* **eemprs eeoprs emoprr emoprs**

eemoprsw empowers empower. *See* **eemprs eeoprs emoprs emorsw**

eemoprw empower. *See* **emorw eoprw emopr**

eemopst metopes. *See* **eemost eemopt emopst eeopst**

eemopt metope emote tempo topee meet mete mope mote poem poet pome teem tome tope met mop mot ope pee pet pot tee toe tom top em me mo om pe to

eemorrs remorse. *See* **emorrs eeors eemrs**

eemorrss remorses remorse. *See* **emorrs**

eemorrt remoter. *See* **eemort eemrrt emorrt**

eemorrv remover. *See* **eemorv emorr eorrv**

eemorst meteors. *See* **eemost eemrst eemort emorst eeorst**

eemorstt remotest meteors rosette. *See* **eemort eemost eemrst eeorst**

eemorsv removes. *See* **emorsv eemorv eeorsv**

eemort meteor remote emote meter metre metro retem meet mere mete more mort mote omer rete rote teem term tome tore tree ere met mor mot ore ort rem ret roe rot tee toe tom tor em er me mo om or re to

eemorv remove mover vomer ever mere more move omer over rove veer ere eve mor ore rem rev roe vee em er me mo om or re

eemost emotes emote meets metes motes smote teems tomes meet mete most mote mots seem some stem teem tees toes tome toms met mos mot oms set sot tee toe tom em me mo om os so to

eemot emote meet mete mote teem tome met mot tee toe tom em me mo om to

eempprst preempts preempt stepper tempers. *See* **eemprs eemprt eemrst eeppst**

eempprt preempt. *See* **eemprt**

eemprs sempre meres peers perms perse sperm spree mere peer pees perm reps seem seep seer sere ere pee per rem rep res see em er me pe re

eemprss empress. *See* **eeprss eemprs emprss**

eemprssu presumes empress peruses presume resumes supreme. *See* **eemprs eemrsu eeprss eeprsu**

eemprst tempers. *See* **eemrst eeprst eemprs eemprt**

eemprstt tempters pretest tempers tempest tempter. *See* **eemprs eemprt eemrst eeprst**

eemprstu permutes permute presume reputes stumper sumpter supreme tempers. *See* **eemprs eempprt eemrst eemrsu**

eemprsu presume supreme. *See* **eeprsu eemrsu**

eemprt temper meter metre peter retem meet mere mete peer perm pert rete teem term tree ere met pee per pet rem rep ret tee em er me pe re

eemprtt tempter. *See* **eemprt emptt**

eemprtu permute. *See* **eemprt eeprtu**

eempry empery emery eery eyre mere peer perm prey pyre ere eye pee per pry rem rep rye yep em er me my pe re ye

eempsstt tempests tempest septets. *See* **eepsst eepstt eesstt empstt**

eempstt tempest. *See* **eepstt empstt**

eempstx exempts. *See* **eemptx eemst eepst**

eemptx exempt meet mete teem met pee pet tee em ex me pe

eemr mere ere rem em er me re

eemrrst termers. *See* **eemrst eemrrt eerrst**

eemrrt termer meter metre retem meet mere mete rete teem term tree ere err met rem ret tee em er me re

eemrs meres mere seem seer sere ere rem res see em er me re

eemrssu resumes. *See* **eemrsu eerssu emrssu**

eemrst merest meters metres retems ester meets meres meter metes metre reset retem steer stere teems terms terse trees erst meet mere mete rest rete rets seem seer sere stem teem tees term tree ere met rem res ret see set tee em er me re

eemrsu resume emeus meres reuse serum emeu emus mere muse rues rums ruse seem seer sere sure user emu ere mus rem res rue rum see sue sum use em er me mu re um us

eemrsux murexes. *See* **eemrsu emrux**

eemrt meter metre retem meet mere mete rete teem term tree ere met rem ret tee em er me re

eemry emery eery eyre mere ere eye rem rye em er me my re ye

eems seem see em me

eemss seems mess seem sees see ess em me

eemsss messes seems esses mess seem sees see ess em me

eemsttu musettes musette suttees. *See* **eesstt eesttu**

eemst meets metes teems meet mete seem stem teem tees met see set tee em me

eemsttu musette. *See* **eesttu eemsu eemst**

eemsu emeus emeu emus muse seem emu mus see sue sum use em me mu um us

eemt meet mete teem tee met em me

eemu emeu emu em me mu um

een nee en ne

eennnoss nonsense oneness. *See* **ennos enoss eenss**

eennnotv nonevent. *See* **eentv ennot**

eennnpty tenpenny. *See* **ennpy eenty**

eennopss openness oneness. *See* **eenps ennos enoss**

eennoptx exponent. *See* **eenopt**

eennoss oneness. *See* **ennos enoss eenss**

eennrst rennets. *See* **eenrst eennrt eennst**

eennrsuv unnerves venues.. *See* **eenrsu eenrsv eersuv eennuv**

eennrt rennet enter erne rent rete teen tern tree ere nee net ret tee ten en er ne re

eennsst sennets. *See* **eennst eensst**

eennssw newness. *See* **eenss**

eennst sennet teens tense nest nets seen sent teen tees tens ens nee net see sen set tee ten en ne

eennsu unseen ensue nuns seen sunn ens nee nun see sen sue sun use en ne nu us

eennuv uneven venue even eve nee nun vee en ne nu

eenoortv overtone. *See* **eenrtv**

eenoppst peptones peptone poteens. *See* **eenopt eeopst eeppst enopst**

eenoppt peptone. *See* **eenopt**

eenopr opener reopen preen prone erne neep nope open peen peer peon pone pore repo rope eon ere nee nor one ope ore pee pen per pro rep roe en er ne no on or pe re

eenoprs openers reopens. *See* **eenopr enoprs eenprs eeoprs**

eenoprss response openers persons reopens reposes. *See* **eenopr eenprs eenrss eeoprs**

eenopst poteens. *See* **enopst eenopt eeopst**

eenopt poteen topee neep nope note open peen pent peon poet pone teen tone tope eon nee net not one ope pee pen pet pot tee ten toe ton top en ne no on pe to

eenorrtt rottener torrent. *See* **eenrrt eenrtt enortt eorrtt**

eenorsss soreness sensors. *See* **eenrss eensss enorss**

eenorssu neuroses ensures. *See* **eenrss eenrsu eenssu eerssu**

eenorstx extensor externs. *See* **eenrst eenrtx eeorst eerstx**

eenorsz rezones. *See* **eenorz eeorsz**

eenorw erenow newer owner renew rowen enow erne ewer wore worn wren eon ere ewe nee new nor now one ore owe own roe row wee wen woe won en er ne no on or ow re we

eenorz rezone erne zero zone eon ere nee nor one ore roe zee en er ne no on or re

eenosvz evzones. *See* **eenovz eensv enosv**

eenovz evzone even oven zone eon eve nee one vee zee en ne no on

eenp neep peen nee pee pen en ne pe

eenpr preen erne neep peen peer ere nee pee pen per rep en er ne pe re

eenprs preens ernes neeps peens peers perse preen sneer spree erne neep peen peer pees pens reps seen seep seer sere ens ere nee pee pen per rep res see sen en er ne pe re

eenprsst pertness presents serpents nesters pesters present presets repents resents serpent. *See* **eenprs eenprt eenrss eenrst**

eenprssu pureness ensures peruses. *See* **eenprs eenrss eenrsu eenssu**

eenprst present repents serpent. *See* **eenrst eeprst eenprs eenprt**

eenprstv prevents present prevent repents serpent venters. *See* **eenprs eenprt eenrst eenrsv**

eenprsy pyrenes. *See* **eenprs eenpry**

eenprt repent enter peter preen erne neep peen peer pent pert rent rete teen tern tree ere nee net pee pen per pet rep ret tee ten en er ne pe re

eenprtv prevent. *See* **eenprt eenrtv**

eenpry pyrene preen eery erne eyre neep peen peer prey pyre ere eye nee pee pen per pry rep rye yen yep en er ne pe re ye

eenps neeps peens neep peen pees pens seen seep ens nee pee pen see sen en ne pe

eenpsssu suspense. *See* **eensss eenssu epsssu**

eenqstu sequent. *See* **eenqsu eenstu**

eenqsu queens queen ensue seen ens nee see sen sue sun use en ne nu us

eenqu queen nee en ne nu

eenr erne nee ere en er ne re

eenrrst renters sterner. *See* **eenrst eenrrt eerrst**

eenrrsuv nervures nervure. *See* **eenrsu eenrsv eensuv eerrsv**

eenrrt renter enter erne rent rete teen tern tree ere err nee net ret tee ten en er ne re

eenrrtuv venturer nervure venture. *See* **eenrrt eenrtu eenrtv eerrtu**

eenrrty reentry. *See* **eenrrt enrty errty**

eenrruv nervure. *See* **eenrv enrru eeruv**

eenrs ernes sneer erne seen seer sere ens ere nee res see sen en er ne re

eenrss sneers ernes seers sense seres sneer erne seen seer sees sere ens ere ess nee res see sen en er ne re

eenrsssu sureness ensures. *See* **eenrss eenrsu eensss eenssu**

eenrsst nesters resents. *See* **eenrst eersst eenrss enrsst eensst**

eenrsstt sternest nesters resents setters streets tensest tenters tersest testers. *See* **eenrss eenrst eenrtt eensst**

eenrsstu trueness ensures nesters neuters resents tenures tureens. *See* **eenrss eenrst eenrsu eenrtu**

eenrsstw westerns nesters resents western westers wetness. *See* **eenrss eenrst eenrsw eensst**

eenrssty styrenes nesters resents styrene. *See* **eenrss eenrst eensst eensty**

eenrssu ensures. *See* **eenssu eenrsu enrssu eerssu eenrss**

eenrst enters nester resent tenser enter ernes ester rents reset sneer steer stere stern teens tense terse trees erne erst nest nets rent rest rete rets seen seer sent sere teen tees tens tern tree ens ere nee net res ret see sen set tee ten en er ne re

eenrstt tenters. *See* **eenrst eerstt eenstt eenrtt**

eenrstu neuters tenures tureens. *See* **eenrsu eenrst eenrtu eenstu enrstu**

eenrstuv ventures neuters tenures tureens venters venture vesture. *See* **eenrst eenrsu eenrsv eenrtu**

eenrstv venters. *See* **eenrst eenstv eerstv eenrsv eenrtv**

eenrstw western. *See* **eenrst eenstw eenrsw enrstw eerstw**

eenrstx externs. *See* **eenrst eerstx eenrtx**

eenrsty styrene. *See* **eenrst enrsty eensty eersty**

eenrsu ensure ensue ernes nurse reuse runes sneer erne rues rune runs ruse seen seer sere sure urns user ens ere nee res rue run see sen sue sun urn use en er ne nu re us

eenrsv nerves ernes evens nerve never neves serve seven sever sneer veers verse erne even ever eves revs seen seer sere veer vees ens ere eve nee res rev see sen vee en er ne re

eenrsw renews ernes newer renew sewer sneer wrens erne ewer ewes news seen seer sere sewn wens wren ens ere ewe nee new res see sen sew wee wen en er ne re we

eenrt enter erne rent rete teen tern tree ere nee net ret tee ten en er ne re

eenrtt tenter enter tenet erne rent rete teen tent tern tree tret ere nee net ret tee ten en er ne re

eenrtu neuter tenure tureen enter tuner erne rent rete rune runt teen tern tree true tune turn ere nee net nut ret rue run rut tee ten tun urn en er ne nu re ut

eenrtuv venture. *See* eenrtu eenrtv

eenrtv venter enter event evert nerve never erne even ever rent rete teen tern tree veer vent vert ere eve nee net ret rev tee ten vee vet en er ne re

eenrtx extern enter exert erne next rent rete teen tern tree ere nee net ret rex tee ten en er ex ne re

eenrv nerve never erne even ever veer ere eve nee rev vee en er ne re

eenrvy venery every nerve nervy never veery eery envy erne even ever eyre veer very ere eve eye nee rev rye vee yen en er ne re ye

eenrw newer renew erne ewer wren ere ewe nee new wee wen en er ne re we

eens seen ens nee see sen en ne

eenss sense seen sees ens ess nee see sen en ne

eensss senses sense esses seen sees ens ess nee see sen en ne

eensst tenses nests sense teens tense nest nets seen sees sent sets teen tees tens ens ess nee net see sen set tee ten en ne

eensstt tensest. *See* eesstt eenstt eensst

eensstw wetness. *See* eenstw eesstw

eenssu ensues sense ensue seen sees sues suns uses ens ess nee see sen sue sun use en ne nu us

eenssux nexuses. *See* eenssu ensux eessx

eenssv sevens evens neves sense seven even eves seen sees vees ens ess eve nee see sen vee en ne

eenst teens tense nest nets seen sent teen tees tens ens nee net see sen set tee ten en ne

eenstt tenets teens tenet tense tents nest nets seen sent stet teen tees tens tent test ens nee net see sen set tee ten en ne

eensttx extents. *See* eenttx eesttx eenstt

eenstu tenues ensue teens tense tunes nest nets nuts seen sent stun suet teen tees tens tune tuns ens nee net nut see sen set sue sun tee ten tun use en ne nu us ut

eenstv events evens event neves seven teens tense vents even eves nest nets seen sent teen tees tens vees vent vest vets ens eve nee net see sen set tee ten vee vet en ne

eenstvy seventy. *See* eenstv eensty

eenstw newest newts sweet teens tense weest ewes nest nets news newt seen sent sewn stew teen tees tens wens west wets ens ewe nee net new see sen set sew tee ten wee wen wet en ne we

eensty teensy yentes teens teeny tense yente eyes nest nets seen sent teen tees

tens yens ens eye nee net see sen set sty tee ten yen yes yet en ne ye

eensu ensue seen ens nee see sen sue sun use en ne nu us

eensuv venues ensue evens neves nevus seven venue even eves seen vees ens eve nee see sen sue sun use vee en ne nu us

eensv evens neves seven even eves seen vees ens eve nee see sen vee en ne

eent teen nee net tee ten en ne

eentt tenet teen tent nee net tee ten en ne

eenttx extent tenet next teen tent text nee net tee ten en ex ne

eentux exeunt next teen tune nee net nut tee ten tun tux en ex ne nu ut

eentv event even vent eve nee net tee ten vee vet en ne

eenty teeny yente teen eye nee net tee ten yen yet en ne ye

eenuv venue even eve nee vee en ne nu

eenv even eve nee vee en ne

eenwy weeny ewe eye nee new wee wen wye yen yew en ne we ye

eeooprs operose. *See* eeoprs ooprs

eeoprrrt reporter. *See* eoprrt eorrrt

eeoprrsv reproves reprove. *See* eeoprs eeorsv eeprsv eerrsv

eeoprrtx exporter reexport. *See* eeprtx eoprrt eoprtx

eeoprrv reprove. *See* eoprrv eoprr eorrv

eeoprs repose erose peers perse pores poser prose repos ropes spore spree epos opes ores peer pees peso pore pose pros repo reps roes rope rose seep seer sere sore ere ope ore pee per pro rep res roe see sop er or os pe re so

eeoprss reposes. *See* eeprss eoprss eeoprs

eeoprsss espresso reposes presses. *See* eeoprs eeprss eoprss

eeoprssu espouser espouse peruses poseurs reposes. *See* eeoprs eeprss eeprsu eerssu

eeoprssx expresso exposes express reposes. *See* eeoprs eeopsx eeprss eoprss

eeoprstt treetops potters pretest protest rosette spotter treetop. *See* eeoprs eeopst eeorst eeprst

eeoprstv overstep. *See* eeoprs eeopst eeorst eeorsv

eeoprsux exposure. *See* eeoprs eeopsx eeprsu eoprsu

eeoprtt treetop. *See* eoprtt eeprt eeopt

eeopsssu espouses espouse spouses. *See* eopsss eopssu

eeopsst poetess. *See* eopsst eeosst eepsst eeopst

eeopssu espouse. *See* eopssu

eeopssx exposes. *See* eeopsx eessx

eeopst topees estop poets steep stope topee topes epos opes pees peso pest pets poet pose post pots seep sept spot step stop tees toes tope tops ope pee pet pot see set sop sot tee toe top os pe so to

eeopstu toupees. *See* eeopst eeoptu

eeopsty peyotes. *See* eeopst eeopty

eeopsx expose poxes epos exes opes pees peso pose seep ope pee pox see sex sop sox ex os ox pe so

eeopt topee poet tope ope pee pet pot tee toe top pe to

eeoptu toupee topee poet pout tope ope out pee pet pot put tee toe top tup pe to up ut

eeopty peyote topee poet tope type eye ope pee pet pot tee toe top toy yep yet oy pe to ye

eeorrsst restores resorts restore rosters sorters stereos. *See* eeorst eeosst eerrst eersst

eeorrst restore. *See* eorrst eeorst eerrst

eeorrstu reroutes reroute restore routers ureters. *See* eeorst eerrst eerrtu eorrst

eeorrtu reroute. *See* eerrtu eorrtu

eeorrtuv overture reroute. *See* eerrtu eerrtv eorrtu eorrtv

eeorrtw rewrote. *See* eorrt eorrw eortw

eeors erose ores roes rose seer sere sore ere ore res roe see er or os re so

eeorsst stereos. *See* eersst eeosst eorsst eeorst

eeorsstt rosettes rosette setters stereos streets tersest testers. *See* eeorst eeosst eersst eerstt

eeorssuv overuses overuse. *See* eeorsv eerssu eersuv eorssu

eeorst stereo erose ester reset rotes steer stere store terse trees erst ores orts rest rete rets roes rose rote rots seer sere sore sort tees toes tore tors tree ere ore ort res ret roe rot see set sot tee toe tor er or os re so to

eeorstt rosette. *See* eorstt eerstt eeorst

eeorstvx vortexes. *See* eeorst eeorsv eeostv eerstv

eeorsuv overuse. *See* eeorsv eersuv

eeorsv soever erose roves serve servo sever veers verse verso ever eves ores over revs roes rose rove seer sere sore veer vees ere eve ore res rev roe see vee er or os re so

eeorsxx xeroxes. *See* eeors eorxx

eeorsz zeroes erose zeros ores roes rose seer sere sore zees zero ere ore res roe see zee er or os re so

eeosst setose sees sets sots tees toes toss ess see set sot tee toe os so to

eeostv vetoes stove votes eves tees toes vees vest veto vets vote eve see set sot tee toe vee vet os so to

eeosxy oxeyes oxeye exes eyes oyes sexy eye see sex sox soy yes ex os ox oy so ye

eeoxy oxeye eye ex ox oy ye

eep pee pe

eepp peep pee pep pe

eepppr pepper peep peer prep repp ere pee pep per rep er pe re

eeppprs peppers. *See* eepppr eepps eeprs

eepppry peppery. *See* eepppr epppy

eepprsst steppers pesters presets stepper steppes. *See* eeppst eeprss eeprst eepsst

eepprst stepper. *See* eeprst eeppst

eepps peeps peep pees peps seep pee pep see pe

eeppsst steppes. *See* eeppst eepsst

eeppst steppe peeps steep peep pees peps pest pets seep sept step tees pee pep pet see set tee pe

eepr peer ere pee per rep er pe re

eeprrss presser repress. *See* eeprss

eeprrsss pressers presser presses repress. *See* eeprss

eeprrssu perusers pressure peruser peruses pursers pursers repress. *See* eeprss eeprsu eerssu eprrsu

eeprrstv perverts pervert reverts. *See* eeprst eeprsv eerrst eerrtv

eeprrsu peruser. *See* eeprsu eprrsu

eeprrtv pervert. *See* eerrtv eeprt

eeprs peers perse spree peer pees reps seep seer sere ere pee per rep res see er pe re

eeprss perses sprees peers perse press seeps seers seres spree peer pees reps seep seer sees sere ere ess pee per rep res see er pe re

eeprsss presses. *See* eeprss

eeprsst pesters presets. *See* eeprss eeprst eersst eepsst eprsst

eeprsstt pretests pesters presets pretest septets setters streets tersest testers. *See* eeprss eeprst eepsst eepstt

eeprssu peruses. *See* eeprss eeprsu eprssu eerssu

eeprssv vespers. *See* eeprss eerssv eeprsv

eeprssx express. *See* eeprss

eeprst pester peters preset ester peers perse peter reset spree steep steer stere strep terse trees erst peer pees pert pest pets reps rest rete rets seep seer sept sere step tees tree ere pee per pet rep res ret see set tee er pe re

eeprstt pretest. *See* eeprst eepstt eersttt

eeprsttx pretexts experts pretest pretext. *See* eeprst eeprtx eepstt eersttt

eeprstu reputes. *See* eprstu eeprst eeprsu eeprtu

eeprstw pewters. *See* eeprst eeprtw eprstw eerstw

eeprstx experts. *See* eerstx eeprtx eeprst

eeprsty retypes. *See* eeprst eeprty eersty

eeprsu purees rupees peers perse puree purse reuse rupee spree sprue super peer pees pure reps rues ruse seep seer sere spue spur sure user ere pee per pus rep res rue see sue sup use er pe re up us

eeprsuv prevues. *See* eepruv eeprsu eersuv eeprsv

eeprsv vesper peers perse serve sever spree veeps veers verse ever eves peer pees reps revs seep seer sere veep veer vees ere eve pee per rep res rev see vee er pe re

eeprt peter peer pert rete tree ere pee per pet rep ret tee er pe re

eeprttx pretext. *See* eeprtx

eeprtu repute erupt peter puree rupee peer pert pure rete tree true ere pee per pet put rep ret rue rut tee tup er pe re up ut

eeprtw pewter peter twerp ewer peer pert rete tree weep wept ere ewe pee per pet pew rep ret tee wee wet er pe re we

eeprtx expert peter exert peer pert rete tree ere pee per pet rep ret rex tee er ex pe re

eeprty retype peter eery eyre peer pert prey pyre rete tree type ere eye pee per pet pry rep ret rye tee try yep yet er pe re ye

eepru puree rupee peer pure ere pee per rep rue er pe re up

eepruv prevue puree revue rupee ever peer pure veep veer ere eve pee per rep rev rue vee er pe re up

eeps pees seep pee see pe

eepss seeps pees seep sees ess pee see pe

eepsst steeps pests seeps steep steps pees pest pets seep sees sept sets step tees ess pee pet see set tee pe

eepstt septets. *See* eepstt eesstt eepsst

eepssw sweeps seeps spews sweep weeps ewes pees pews seep sees sews spew weep ess ewe pee pew see sew wee pe we

eepst steep pees pest pets seep sept step tees pee pet see set tee pe

eepstt septet steep pees pest pets seep sept step stet tees test pee pet see set tee pe

eepstty typeset. *See* eepstt eptty eepsy

eepsv veeps eves pees seep veep vees eve pee see vee pe

eepsw sweep weeps ewes pees pews seep spew weep ewe pee pew see sew wee pe we

eepsy seepy espy eyes pees seep eye pee see spy yep yes pe ye

eepv veep eve pee vee pe

eepw weep ewe pee pew wee pe we

eepwy weepy weep ewe eye pee pew wee wye yep yew pe we ye

eeqrruy equerry. *See* eeqru eqruy

eeqrsstu questers requests quester request. *See* eeqrsu eersst eerssu eqsstu

eeqrstu quester request. *See* eeqrsu eerst eqstu

eeqrsu queers queer reuse rues ruse seer sere sure user ere res rue see sue use er re us

eeqru queer ere rue er re

eeqsuu queues queue see sue use us

eequu queue

eer ere er re

eerrssv servers. *See* eerrsv eerssv

eerrst terser ester reset steer stere terse trees errs erst rest rete rets seer sere tees tree ere err res ret see set tee er re

eerrstt terrets. *See* eerstt eerrtt eerrst

eerrsttu utterers terrets trustee turrets ureters utterer. *See* eerrst eerrtt eerrtu eerstt

eerrstu ureters. *See* eerrst eerrtu

eerrstv reverts. *See* eerstv eerrsv eerrtv eerrst

eerrsv revers server serve sever veers verse errs ever eves revs seer sere veer vees ere err eve res rev see vee er re

eerrtt terret rete tree tret ere err ret tee er re

eerrttu utterer. *See* eerrtt errttu eerrtu

eerrtu ureter truer rete tree true ere err ret rue rut tee er re ut

eerrtv revert evert ever rete tree veer vert ere err eve ret rev tee vee vet er re

eerrvy revery every veery eery ever eyre veer very ere err eve eye rev rye vee er re ye

eers seer sere ere res see er re

eerss seers seres seer sees sere ere ess res see er re

eerssst stresses tresses. *See* eersst

eersst tresses. *See* eersst erssst

eersst resets steers steres ester reset rests seers seres steer stere terse trees tress erst rest rete rets seer sees sere sets tees tree ere ess res ret see set tee er re

eerssstt setters streets tersest testers. *See* eersst eesstt eerstt

eerssttu trustees setters streets suttees tersest testers trustee. *See* eersst eerssu eerstt eesstt

eersstuv vestures vesture. *See* eersst eerssu eerssv eerstv

eersstw westers. *See* eersst eerssw ersstw eesstw eerstw

eerssu reuses reuse ruses seers seres users rues ruse seer sees sere sues sure user uses ere ess res rue see sue use er re us

eerssv serves severs verses seers seres serve sever verry verse ever eves revs seer sees sere veer vees ere ess eve res rev see vee er re

eerssvw swerves. *See* **eerssv eersvw**

eerssw sewers seers seres sewer ewer ewes seer sees sere sews ere ess ewe res see sew wee er re we

eerst ester reset steer stere terse trees erst rete rets seer sere tees tree ere res ret see set er re

eerstt setter street tester ester reset steer stere terse trees trets erst rest rete rets seer sere stet tees test tree tret ere res ret see set tee er re

eersttt tetters. *See* **eerstt eerttt**

eersttu trustee. *See* **eerstt eesttu ersttu**

eersttux textures trustee texture. *See* **eerstt eerstx eesttu eesttx**

eerstuv vesture. *See* **eerstv eersuv**

eerstv everts ester evert reset serve sever steer stere terse trees veers verse verst verts erst ever eves rest rete rets revs seer sere tees tree veer vees vert vest vets ere eve res ret rev see set tee vee vet er re

eerstvv vervets. *See* **eerstv eersvv eertvv**

eerstw wester ester reset sewer steer stere strew sweet terse trees trews weest wrest erst ewer ewes rest rete rets seer sere stew tees tree west wets ere ewe res ret see set sew tee wee wet er re we

eerstx exerts ester exert reset steer stere terse trees erst exes rest rete rets seer sere sext tees tree ere res ret rex see set sex tee er ex re

eersty yester ester eyres reset steer stere terse trees eery erst eyes eyre rest rete

rets ryes seer sere tees tree ere eye res ret rye see set sty tee try yes yet er re ye

eersu reuse rues ruse seer sere sure user ere res rue see sue use er re us

eersuv revues reuse revue serve sever veers verse ever eves revs rues ruse seer sere sure user veer vees ere eve res rev rue see sue use vee er re us

eersv serve sever veers verse ever eves revs seer sere veer vees ere eve res rev see vee er re

eersvv verves serve sever veers verse verve ever eves revs seer sere veer vees ere eve res rev see vee er re

eersvw swerve serve sever sewer veers verse ever eves ewer ewes revs seer sere veer vees ere eve ewe res rev see sew vee wee er re we

eersw sewer ewer ewes seer sere ere ewe res see sew wee er re we

eersy eyres eery eyes eyre ryes seer sere ere eye res rye see yes er re ye

eert rete tree ere ret tee er re

eertt tetter rete tree tret ere ret tee er re

eerttux texture. *See* **eertx erttu**

eerttw wetter tweet ewer rete tree tret ere ewe ret tee wee wet er re we

eertv evert ever rete tree veer vert ere eve ret rev tee vee vet er re

eertvv vervet evert verve ever rete tree veer vert ere eve ret rev tee vee vet er re

eertvx vertex evert exert ever rete tree veer vert ere eve ret rev rex tee vee vet vex er ex re

eertx exert rete tree ere ret rex tee er ex re

eeruv revue ever veer ere eve rev rue vee er re

eerv ever veer ere eve rev vee er re

eervv verve ever veer ere eve rev vee er re

eervy every veery eery ever eyre veer very ere eve eye rev rye vee er re ye

eerw were ewer ere ewe wee er re we

eery eery eyre ere eye rye er re ye

ees see

eess sees see ess

eesss esses sees see ess

eessstt sestets. *See* **eesstt eesss**

eesssy yesses esses yeses sees eyes ess eye see yes ye

eesstt sestet stets tests sees sets stet tees test ess see set tee

eessttu suttees. *See* **eesstt eesttu**

eessttx sextets. *See* **eesstt eesttx**

eesstw sweets stews sweet weest wests ewes sees sets sews stew tees west wets ess ewe see set sew tee wee wet we

eessx sexes sees exes ess see sex ex

eessy yeses sees eyes ess eye see yes ye

eest tees see set tee

eestttw wettest. *See* **eesttw**

eesttu suttee stet suet tees test tuts see set sue tee tut use us ut

eesttw tweets sweet tweet weest ewes stet stew tees test west wets ewe see set sew tee wee wet we

eesttx sextet texts exes sext stet tees test text see set sex tee ex

eestw sweet weest ewes stew tees west wets ewe see set sew tee wee wet we

eesv eves vees eve see vee

eesvx vexes eves exes vees eve see sex vee vex ex

eesw ewes ewe see sew wee we

eesx exes see sex ex

eesy eyes eye see yes ye

eesz zees see zee

eet tee

eettw tweet ewe tee wee wet we

eev eve vee

eew ewe wee we

eey eye ye

eez zee

---

ef

efffilru fluffier. *See* **effilr efflru efilru**

efffo feoff foe off of

efffos feoffs feoff foes foe off of os so

effginor offering foreign. *See* **effgir effgor effinr efginr**

effgir griffe fifer grief fief fife fire frig rife riff erg fie fig fir gie ire ref reg rif rig er if re

effgirs griffes. *See* **effirs efgirs effgir**

effgiy effigy fief fife iffy fey fie fig gey gie ye if

effgor goffer forge gofer offer fore froe frog goer gore ogre ego erg foe fog for fro off ore ref reg roe er go of or re

effgors goffers. *See* **efgors effgor effors**

effhiils filefish. *See* **efhils**

effhiisw fishwife. *See* **ffhisw**

effhiitt fiftieth. *See* **ffhit efhtt efhit**

effhilrw whiffler whiffle. *See* **effilr**

effhilsw whiffles whiffle. *See* **efhils ffhisw**

effhilw whiffle. *See* **ehilw ffhiw**

effhirs sheriff. *See* **effirs efhirs**

effhirss sheriffs fishers sheriff sherifs. *See* **effirs efhirs efhiss efirss**

effhiru huffier. *See* **effir**

effhistu huffiest. *See* **efhist ffhist**

effhlrsu shuffler flusher ruffles shuffle. *See* **efflru effrsu**

effhlssu shuffles shuffle flushes. *See* **ehlssu fflssu**

effhlsu shuffle. *See* **efhls eflsu fhlsu**

effhoors offshore hoofers. *See* **efhors efhoor ffhors**

effi fief fife fie if

effiijs jiffies. *See* **effis**

effiiprs spiffier. *See* **effirs**

effiist fifties. *See* **efist effis ffist**

effikls skiffle. *See* **effis efils efiks**

effiklss skiffles skiffle. *See* **ffikss**

effilns sniffle. *See* **efiln effis efils**

effilnss sniffles sniffle finless. *See* **ffinss**

effilp piffle fief fife file flip lief life pelf pile elf fie lei lie lip pie el if li pe pi

effilps piffles. *See* **effilp effis filps**

effilr riffle fifer filer flier lifer rifle fief fife file fire lief life lire riel rife riff rile elf fie fir ire lei lie ref rif el er if li re

effilrs riffles. *See* **effirs efilrs effilr**

effilry firefly. *See* **effilr efiry eflry**

effinosu effusion. *See* **efinsu finosu**

effinr niffer fifer finer infer fern fief fife fine fire firn rein rife riff fen fie fin fir ire ref rif en er if in ne re

effinrs niffers. *See* **effirs efinrs effinr**

effinsst stiffens fitness infests stiffen. *See* **efinst efisst einsst ffinss**

effinst stiffen. *See* **efinst**

effiorst forfeits efforts forfeit forties stiffer. *See* **effirs effors effort effost**

effiort forfeit. *See* **effort effir efirt**

effipru puffier. *See* **effpru effir**

effipstu puffiest. *See* **eistu efist efstu**

effir fifer fief fife fire rife riff fie fir ire ref rif er if re

effirs fifers fiefs fifer fifes fires fries riffs serif fief fies fife fire firs refs reis rife riff rifs rise serf sire fie fir ifs ire ref res rif sir er if is re si

effirst stiffer. *See* **effirs efirst**

effirstu stuffier stiffer surfeit. *See* **effirs effrsu efirst firstu**

effis fiefs fifes fief fies fife fie ifs if is si

effisstt stiffest. *See* **efisst ffisst**

effissux suffixes. *See* **ffisux**

efflmrsu mufflers muffler muffles ruffles. *See* **efflmu efflru effrsu eflmsu**

efflmru muffler. *See* **efflmu efflru**

efflmsu muffles. *See* **efflmu eflmsu**

efflmu muffle flume flue fuel fume luff muff mule elf elm emu feu flu leu lum mel el em me mu um

efflnssu snuffles snuffle. *See* **elnssu fflssu ffnssu**

efflnsu snuffle. *See* **eflsu fflsu elnsu**

efflossu souffles souffle. *See* **fflssu**

efflosu souffle. *See* **eflos eflsu flosu**

effllrstu truffles fluster fretful restful ruffles truffle. *See* **efflru effrsu eflstu elrstu**

effllrsu ruffles. *See* **efflru effrsu**

effllrtu fretful truffle. *See* **efflru efltu**

effllru ruffle flue fuel furl luff lure ruff rule elf feu flu fur leu ref rue el er re

effllux efflux flex flue flux fuel luff luxe elf feu flu leu lux el ex

effnrsu snuffer. *See* **effrsu efnrs enrsu**

effooort forefoot. *See* **effort**

effoprr proffer. *See* **effor eoprr**

effoprrs proffers proffer. *See* **effors eoprrs**

effopsu pouffes. *See* **effopu ffpsu fopsu**

effopu pouffe puff pouf feu foe fop off ope of pe up

effor offer fore froe foe for fro off ore ref roe er of or re

effors offers fores froes offer foes fore froe ores refs roes rose serf sore foe for fro off ore ref res roe er of or os re so

efforst efforts. *See* **effort eforst effors effost**

effort effort fetor forte offer fore fort fret froe reft rote toff tore eft foe for fro off oft ore ort ref ret roe rot toe tor er of or re to

effosst offsets setoffs. *See* **effost**

effost offset setoff toffs efts foes soft toes toff eft foe off oft set sot toe of os so to

effprsu puffers. *See* **effpru effrsu**

effpru puffer puff pure ruff feu fur per ref rep rue er pe re up

effpruy puffery. *See* **effpru ffpuy**

effrrsuu furfures. *See* **effrsu effrsu errsuu**

effrssu suffers. *See* **effrsu efssu erssu**

effrsu suffer ruffs feus furs fuse refs rues ruff ruse serf sure surf user feu fur ref res rue sue use er re us

effssssuu suffuses suffuse. *See* **efsssu**

effsssuu suffuse. *See* **efssu**

efggiinn feigning. *See* **eggiin fgiinn**

efgginru refuging gunfire. *See* **efginr efgiru egginr gginru**

efggior foggier. *See* **efgor eggor efgir**

efggiost foggiest. *See* **efgios efiost egiost**

efgglor flogger. *See* **efglor egglor**

efgglors floggers flogger golfers loggers slogger. *See* **efglor efgors egglor eggors**

efghinrt frighten fighter freight hefting. *See* **efginr efgint eghinr ehinrt**

efghint hefting. *See* **efgint eghit fghit**

efghirst fighters freights fighter freight frights shifter. *See* **efgirs efhirs efhist efirst**

efghirt fighter freight. *See* **fghirt eghit efgir**

efgiilnr refiling rifling. *See* **efginr egiilr egilnr fgiiln**

efgiilsu uglifies. *See* **egilsu**

efgiinnr infringe refining reining. *See* **efginr fgiinn**

efgiinnt feinting. *See* **efgint egiint fgiinn**

efgiinru figurine gunfire. *See* **efginr efgiru**

efgiinrx refixing. *See* **efginr fgiinx**

efgiinry reifying. *See* **efginr efinry fginry**

efgiknr kerfing. *See* **efginr**

efgilln felling. *See* **efiln efgin fgiln**

efgillno lifelong felling. *See* **efilno egilno eillno**

efgillnu fuelling felling fueling. *See* **efglnu egillu fgilnu**

efgilluu guileful. *See* **egillu**

efgilmor filmgoer. *See* **efglor egilor**

efgilnns flensing. *See* **efgins egilns eginns eilnns**

efgilnru feruling fueling furling gunfire. *See* **efginr efgiru efglnu efilru**

efgilnt felting. *See* **efgint egilnt**

efgilntt fettling felting letting. *See* **efgint egilnt**

efgilnu fueling. *See* **efglnu fgilnu**

efgilnx flexing. *See* **efiln efgin egiln**

efgilpru fireplug. *See* **efgiru efilpr efilru eflpru**

efgimnst figments figment. *See* **efgins efgint efinst egimnt**

efgimnt figment. *See* **efgint egimnt**

efgin feign fine fen fie fig fin gie gin en if in ne

efginnp pfennig. *See* **efgin einnp**

efginor foreign. *See* **efginr eginor**

efginorv forgiven foreign forgive. *See* **efginr eginor egnorv ginorv**

efginr finger fringe feign finer grief infer reign fern fine fire firn frig grin rein rife ring erg fen fie fig fin fir gie gin ire ref reg rif rig en er if in ne re

efginrry ferrying refrying. *See* **efginr efinry eginrr fginry**

efginrs fingers fringes. *See* **efgins efginr efgirs efinrs eginrs**

efginrsu gunfires refusing figures fingers fringes gunfire infuser reusing surfing. *See* **efginr efgins efgirs efgiru**

efginrtt fretting gittern retting. *See* **efginr efgint efirtt einrtt**

efginrtu refuting gunfire. *See* **efginr efgint efgiru egnrtu**

efginru gunfire. *See* **efgiru**

efgins feigns feign fines segni singe egis engs fens fies figs fine fins gens gies gins sign sine sing ens fen fie fig fin gie gin ifs sen sin en if in is ne si

efgint feting feign feint tinge fine gent gift tine ting eft fen fie fig fin fit get gie gin net nit ten tie tin en if in it ne ti

efgioor goofier. *See* **efgoor egioor**

efgioost goofiest footies footsie. *See* **efgios efioot efiost egiost**

efgioptt pettifog. *See* **eioptt**

efgiorrv forgiver forgive. *See* **efgorr eforrv egiorr**

efgiorsv forgives forgive. *See* **efgios efgirs efgors efirsv**

efgiorv forgive. *See* **efirv efgor egirv**

efgios fogies egis egos fies figs foes fogs gies goes sego ego fie fig foe fog gie ifs go if is of os si so

efgir grief fire frig rife erg fie fig fir gie ire ref reg rif rig er if re

efgirrst grifters grifter. *See* **efgirs efirrs efirst egirst**

efgirrt grifter. *See* **efirr efgir efirt**

efgirs griefs fires fries frigs grief serif egis ergs fies figs fire firs frig gies refs regs reis rife rifs rigs rise serf sire erg fie fig fir gie ifs ire ref reg res rif rig sir er if is re si

efgirsu figures. *See* **efgiru efirsu efgirs egirsu**

efgiru figure grief fire frig grue rife urge erg feu fie fig fir fug fur gie ire ref reg rif rig rue rug er if re

efglnsu engulfs. *See* **efglnu eglnsu**

efglntu fulgent. *See* **efglnu eflntu eglntu**

efglnu engulf lunge flung flue fuel glen glue gulf luge lune lung elf fen feu flu fug fun gel gnu gun leg leu lug el en ne nu

efgloovx foxglove. *See* **eglov**

efglor golfer forge gofer ogler floe flog fore froe frog goer golf gore loge lore ogle ogre orle role ego elf erg foe fog for fro gel leg log ore ref reg roe el er go lo of or re

efglors golfers. *See* **efgors efglor eglors**

efgloss fogless. *See* **eflos fglos floss**

efglsstu slugfest gutless. *See* **eflstu egsstu elsstu**

efgmnor frogmen. *See* **egmnor**

efgnoor forgone. *See* **efgoor egnor fgnoo**

efgnosst songfest softens. *See* **efnost enosst**

efgnosu fungoes. *See* **fgnou egnsu egnos**

efgnssuu funguses. *See* **efgsuu fgnsuu**

efgoor forego forge forgo gofer fore froe frog goer goof gore ogre roof ego erg foe fog for fro goo ore ref reg roe er go of or re

efgoorr forgoer. *See* **efgoor efgorr efoorr**

efgoorrs forgoers foregos forgers forgoer roofers. *See* **efgoor efgorr efgors**

efgoors foregos. *See* **efgoor efgors**

efgor forge gofer fore froe frog goer gore ogre ego erg foe fog for fro ore ref reg roe er go of or re

efgorr forger forge gofer roger fore froe frog goer gore ogre ego erg err foe fog for fro ore ref reg roe er go of or re

efgorrs forgers. *See* **efgorr**

efgorry forgery. *See* **efgorr efrry efgoy**

efgors forges gofers fores forge froes frogs goers gofer gores gorse ogres egos ergs foes fogs fore froe frog goer goes gore ogre ores refs regs roes rose sego serf sore ego erg foe fog for fro ore ref reg res roe er go of or os re so

efgorst forgets. *See* **egorst eforst efgors efgort**

efgort forget ergot fetor forge forte gofer fore fort fret froe frog goer gore grot ogre reft rote tore eft ego erg foe fog for fro get got oft ore ort ref reg ret roe rot toe tog tor er go of or re to

efgosy fogeys fogey egos foes fogs fogy foys goes goys oyes sego ego fey foe fog foy gey goy soy yes go of os oy so ye

efgoy fogey fogy ego fey foe fog foy gey goy go of oy ye

efgsuu fugues fugue feus fugs fuse feu fug sue use us

efguu fugue feu fug

efh feh eh he

efhiikls fishlike. *See* **efhils**

efhiilrt filthier. *See* **efilrt ehilrt**

efhiinrs finisher refinish fishier shinier. *See* **efhirs efinrs ehinrs fhiins**

efhiinss finishes. *See* **efhiss ehinss fhiins**

efhiirs fishier. *See* **efhirs**

efhiirst shiftier fishier shifter. *See* **efhirs efhist efirst ehirst**

efhiisst fishiest. *See* **efhiss efhist efisst ehisst**

efhillsy elfishly. *See* **efhils efhlsy ehllsy**

efhilms himself. *See* **efhils films ehlms**

efhils elfish files flesh flies shelf fies file fils fish hies isle leis lief lies life self elf els feh fie hie his ifs lei lie she eh el he hi if is li sh si

efhilss selfish. *See* **efhils efhiss**

efhilst leftish. *See* **efhils efhist efilst**

efhiorrt frothier rotifer heritor. *See* **ehiort ehorrt**

efhiortt fortieth. *See* **efirtt ehiort ehirtt ehortt**

efhirrtu thurifer further. *See* **fhirt efirr firtu**

efhirs fisher sherif fires fresh fries heirs hires serif shire fies fire firs fish heir hers hies hire refs reis resh rife rifs rise serf sire feh fie fir her hie his ifs ire ref res rif she sir eh er he hi if is re sh si

efhirss fishers sherifs. *See* **efhirs efhiss ehirss efirss**

efhirsst shifters fishers sherifs shifter shrifts sifters strifes. *See* **efhirs efhiss efhist efirss**

efhirst shifter. *See* **efhist fhirst efhirs efirst ehirst**

efhirsy fishery. *See* **efhirs**

efhiss fishes shies fess fies fish hies hiss ess feh fie hie his ifs she sis eh he hi if is sh si

efhist fetish feist hefts heist shift thief efts fies fish fist fits heft hest hies hist hits sift site sith this ties eft eth feh fie fit het hie his hit ifs its set she sit the tie eh he hi if is it sh si ti

efhit thief heft eft eth feh fie fit het hie hit the tie eh he hi if it ti

efhllpu helpful. *No 6s or 5s*

efhlooss hoofless. *See* **elooss**

efhloosx foxholes. *See* **efhls eflos floos**

efhlopst fleshpot. *See* **ehlost**

efhlopsu hopefuls hopeful. *See* **ehlosu ehopsu**

efhlopu hopeful. *See* **ehopu**

efhlorsy horsefly freshly. *See* **efhlsy eflrsy eforsy ehorsy**

efhlosuu houseful. *See* **eflsuu ehlosu**

efhlosuy housefly. *See* **efhlsy ehlosu**

efhlrssu flushers flusher flushes. *See* **ehlssu ehrssu**

efhlrsu flusher. *See* **efhls eflsu fhlsu**

efhlrsy freshly. *See* **efhlsy eflrsy**

efhls flesh shelf self elf els feh she eh el he sh

efhlssu flushes. *See* **ehlssu efhls eflsu**

efhlsttw twelfths twelfth. *See* **efhstt**

efhlsty thyself. *See* **ehlsty efhlsy**

efhlsy fleshy flesh shelf lyes lyse self elf els feh fey fly hey lye she shy sly yes eh el he sh ye

efhlttw twelfth. *See* **efhtt**

efhoor hoofer fore froe hero hoer hoof roof feh foe foh for fro her hoe oho ooh ore ref rho roe eh er he ho of oh or re

efhoors hoofers. *See* **efhoor efors efhrs**

efhrrtu further. *See* **errtu**

efhrs fresh hers refs resh serf feh her ref res she eh er he re sh

efhrsttu furthest shutter. *See* **efhstt ersttu hrsttu**

efhrst hefts efts heft hest eft eth feh het set she the eh he sh

efhstt thefts hefts theft efts heft hest stet test teth eft eth feh het set she the eh he sh

efht heft eft eth feh het the eh he

efhtt theft heft teth eft eth feh het the eh he

efhty hefty heft they eft eth feh fey het hey the thy yet eh he ye

efi fie if

efiiilsv vilifies. *See* eiilsv efils efisv

efiiinnt infinite. *See* efiint

efiiistx fixities. *See* eistx efist efisx

efiiisvv vivifies. *See* efisv eiisv

efiikrrs friskier riskier. *See* efikrs efirrs

efiillrr frillier. *See* efillr

efiills fillies. *See* eiills eflls efils

efiilmr filmier. *See* eiilmr efimr efilr

efiilmrs flimsier filmier misfile misfire slimier. *See* efilrs efimrs eiilmr eiilms

efiilms misfile. *See* eiilms efils films

efiilmss flimsies misfiles misfile missile similes. *See* eiilms eilmss

efiilmst filmiest elitism limiest misfile. *See* efilst eiilms fiimst iilmst

efiilnty felinity finitely. *See* efiint efilny eilnty filnty

efiilrsu fusilier. *See* efilrs efilru efirsu

efiilry fierily. *See* efiry efilr eflry

efiimmns feminism. *See* eiimns iimmns

efiimnst feminist. *See* efiint efinst eiimns fiimst

efiimrr rimfire. *See* efimrr

efiimrs misfire. *See* efimrs

efiimrss misfires misfire. *See* efimrs efirss eiirss eimrss

efiinorr inferior. *See* einorr

efiinort notifier niftier. *See* efiint einort finort

efiinost notifies. *See* efiint efinst efiost efnost

efiinrt niftier. *See* efiint efinr einrt

efiinstt niftiest. *See* efiint efinst einstt

efiinsu unifies. *See* efinsu fiins

efiinsuv infusive unifies. *See* efinsu

efiinsx infixes. *See* eiinsx efins fiins

efiint finite feint fine tine eft fen fie fin fit net nit ten tie tin en if in it ne ti

efiiosss ossifies. *See* efoss

efiiprru purifier. *See* efirr eiprr eprru

efiiprst spitfire tipsier. *See* efirst eiipst eiprst iiprst

efiiprsu purifies. *See* efirsu eiprsu

efiipsty typifies. *See* efisty eiipst

efiirrtu fruitier. *See* efirr firtu efirt

efiirrzz frizzier fizzier. *See* efirr

efiirzz fizzier. *No 6s or 5s*

efiistzz fizziest tizzies. *See* efiszz

efijlly jellify. *See* eflly filly ejlly

efijlor frijole. *See* fijlor efilr eilor

efijlors frijoles frijole. *See* efilos efilrs eilors fijlor

efiklnsu flunkies skinful. *See* efinsu efklsu eiklns eiklnu

efiklorw lifework. *See* eflorw

efikn knife fine fink kine fen fie fin ink kef ken kif kin en if in ne

efiknors foreskin. *See* efikrs efinrs eiknos eiknrs

efiknru funkier. *See* efinr eiknr einru

efiknstu funkiest. *See* efinst efinsu einstu

efikorrw firework. *See* ekorrw

efikr kefir fire kerf kier rife fie fir ire irk kef kif kir ref rif er if re

efikrs kefirs fires fries frisk kefir kerfs kiefs kiers serif fies fire firs irks kefs kerf kier kifs kris refs reis rife rifs rise risk serf sire fie fir ifs ire irk kef kif kir ref res rif sir ski er if is re si

efiks kiefs fies kefs kifs fie ifs kef kif ski if is si

efil file lief life elf fie lei lie el if li

efillos follies. *See* efilos eflls fills

efillosw lowlifes fellows follies lowlife. *See* efilos eflow

efillow lowlife. *See* eflow

efillr filler refill filer flier frill lifer rifle rille fell file fill fire lief life lire riel rife rile rill elf ell fie fir ill ire lei lie ref rif el er if li re

efillrs fillers refills. *See* efilrs efillr fillrs eillrs

efillst fillets. *See* efilst efillt eillst

efillt fillet filet fell felt file fill flit left lief life lift lilt tell tile till eft elf ell fie fit ill lei let lie lit tie til el if it li ti

efilltuy futilely. *See* efillt efiltu eilltu

efilmsuy emulsify. *See* eflmsu eflmsy eilmsy elmsuy

efiln elfin file fine lief lien life line elf fen fie fin lei lie nil el en if in li ne

efilnntu influent. *See* efiltu eflnnu eflntu eilnnt

efilno olefin elfin eloin felon olein enol file fine floe foil leno lief lien life line lion loin lone noel noil elf eon fen fie fin foe ion lei lie nil oil one el en if in li lo ne no of on

efilnoru fluorine. *See* efilno efilru filnor

efilnos olefins. *See* eilnos eflnos efilos efilno

efilnosx flexions olefins flexion. *See* efilno efilos eflnos eilnos

efilnox flexion. *See* efilno

efilnss finless. *See* efiln efils efins

efilny finely elfin file fine inly lief lien life line liny elf fen fey fie fin fly lei lie lye nil yen yin el en if in li ne ye

efiloos foliose. *See* efilos filoos eiloos

efiloosz floozies floozie foliose foozles. *See* efilos eflooz eiloos filoos

efilooz floozie. *See* eflooz eiloo filoo

efiloppr floppier flipper loppier profile. *See* efilpp efilpr eilppr eloppr

efilopps floppies fipples. *See* efilos efilpp eilops elopps

efilopr profile. *See* efilpr elopr eilor

efiloprs profiles pilfers profile spoiler. *See* efilos efilpr efilrs eilops

efilorst trefoils filters florets florist forties lifters loftier loiters toilers trefoil trifles. *See* efilos efilrs efilrt efilst

efilort loftier trefoil. *See* efilrt eflort eilort

efilos filose files flies floes foils fies file fils floe foes foil isle leis lief lies life lose oils self silo sloe soil sole elf els fie foe ifs lei lie los oil sol el if is li lo of os si so

efilostt loftiest leftist litotes toilets. *See* efilos efilst efiost eilost

efilpp fipple file flip lief life pelf pile pipe elf fie lei lie lip pep pie pip el if li pe pi

efilppr flipper. *See* efilpp efilpr eilppr

efilpprs flippers fipples flipper pilfers ripples slipper. *See* efilpp efilpr efilrs eilppr

efilpps fipples. *See* efilpp efils filps

efilppsu pipefuls fipples pipeful. *See* efilpp eilpsu elppsu ilppsu

efilppu pipeful. *See* efilpp ilppu

efilpr pilfer filer flier lifer peril plier rifle file fire flip lief life lire pelf peri pier pile riel rife rile ripe elf fie fir ire lei lie lip per pie ref rep rif rip el er if li pe pi re

efilprs pilfers. *See* efilrs eilprs efilpr

efilpstu spiteful stipule uplifts. *See* efilst efiltu eflstu eilpst

efilquy liquefy. *No 6s or 5s*

efilr filer flier lifer rifle file fire lief life lire riel rife rile elf fie fir ire lei lie ref rif el er if li re

efilrrst triflers filters lifters trifler trifles. *See* efilrt efilst efirrs

efilrrsu flurries friseur surfier. *See* efilrs efilru efirrs efirsu

efilrrt trifler. *See* efilrt

efilrry riflery. *See* eirry efrry efiry

efilrs filers fliers lifers rifles filer files fires flier flies fries lifer riels rifle riles serif fies fils fire firs isle leis lief lies life lire refs reis riel rife rifs rile rise self serf sire elf els fie fir ifs ire lei lie ref res rif sir el er if is li re si

efilrst filters lifters trifles. *See* efilrs efilst efilrt filrst eilrst

efilrstt flitters filters fitters flitter leftist lifters litters trifles. *See* efilrs efilrt efilst efirst

efilrsvv flivvers flivver. *See* efilrs efirsv eilrsv

efilrszz frizzles frizzle fizzles. *See* efilrs efilzz efiszz

efilrt filter lifter trifle filer filet flier flirt lifer liter litre refit rifle tiler felt file fire flit fret frit left lief life lift lire reft riel rife rift rile rite tier tile tire eft elf fie fir fit ire lei let lie lit ref ret rif tie til el er if it li re ti

efilrtt flitter. *See* **efilrt efirtt eilrtt**

efilru ireful filer flier lifer rifle file fire flue fuel furl lief lieu life lire lure riel rife rile rule elf feu fie fir flu fur ire lei leu lie ref rif rue el er if li re

efilrvv flivver. *See* **efilr efirv eilrv**

efilrzz frizzle. *See* **efilzz efilr**

efils files flies fies file fils isle leis lief lies life self elf els fie ifs lei lie el if is li si

efilsst stifles. *See* **efisst efilst eilsst**

efilsstt leftists stifles leftist. *See* **efilst efisst eilsst eilstt**

efilst filets itself stifle feist felts files filet flies flits islet istle lifts stile tiles efts felt fies file fils fist flit isle left leis lest lets lief lies life lift list self sift silt site slit ties tile tils eft elf els fie fit ifs its lei let lie lit set sit tie til el if is it li si ti

efilstt leftist. *See* **efilst eilstt**

efilszz fizzles. *See* **efiszz efilzz eilszz**

efilt filet felt file flit left lief life lift tile eft elf fie fit lei let lie lit tie til el if it li ti

efiltu futile filet flute utile etui felt file flit flue fuel left lief lieu life lift lute tile tule eft elf feu fie fit flu lei let leu lie lit tie til tui el if it li ti ut

efilwy wifely file flew lief life wife wile wily elf few fey fie fly lei lie lye wye yew el if li we ye

efilzz fizzle file fizz lief life elf fez fie lei lie el if li

efimnorr informer. *See* **efimrr efmorr eimnor fimnor**

efimnrss firmness. *See* **efimrs efinrs efirss eimnrs**

efimprru frumpier. *See* **efimrr eimprr eimpru**

efimr fermi emir fire firm mire rife rime fie fir ire mir ref rem rif rim em er if me mi re

efimrr firmer fermi frier emir fire firm mire rife rime err fie fir ire mir ref rem rif rim em er if me mi re

efimrs fermis emirs fermi fires firms fries mires miser rimes serif emir fies fire firm firs mire mirs mise refs reis rife rifs rime rims rise semi serf sire fie fir ifs ire mir mis ref rem res rif rim sir em er if is me mi re si

efimrst firmest. *See* **efimrs eimrst efirst**

efin fine fen fie fin en if in ne

efinnor inferno. *See* **efinr einnr**

efinnors infernos inferno. *See* **efinrs einnrs einors**

efinnru funnier. *See* **einnu efinr einnr**

efinnstu funniest funnies. *See* **efinst efinsu einnst einstu**

efinnsu funnies. *See* **efinsu einnu einns**

efinoptx pontifex. *See* **efint einpt efnot**

efinorrt frontier rotifer. *See* **einorr einort eiorrt finort**

efinossx foxiness. *See* **einoss**

efinr finer infer fern fine fire firn rein rife fen fie fin fir ire ref rif en er if in ne re

efinrs infers ferns finer fines fires firns fries infer reins resin rinse risen serif serin siren fens fern fies fine fins fire firn firs refs rein reis rife rifs rise serf sine sire ens fen fie fin fir ifs ire ref res rif sen sin sir en er if in is ne re si

efinrsst snifters fitness infests inserts sifters sinters snifter strifes. *See* **efinrs efinst efirss efirst**

efinrssu infusers fissure fussier infuser infuses insures sunrise. *See* **efinrs efinsu efirss efirsu**

efinrst snifter. *See* **efinst efinrs einrst efirst**

efinrsu infuser. *See* **efirsu efinsu einrsu**

efinruy reunify. *See* **efinry einru finuy**

efinry finery ferny fiery finer infer reify fern fine fire firn rein rife fen fey fie fin fir fry ire ref rif rye yen yin en er if in ne re ye

efins fines fens fies fine fins sine ens fen fie fin ifs sen sin en if in is ne si

efinsst fitness infests. *See* **efinst efisst einsst**

efinssu infuses. *See* **efinsu efsssu eissu**

efinst feints finest infest feint feist fines inset stein tines efts fens fies fine fins fist fits nest nets nits sent sift sine site snit tens ties tine tins eft ens fen fie fin fit ifs its net nit sen set sin sit ten tie tin en if in is it ne si ti

efinsu infuse fines fens feus fies fine fins fuse sine ens fen feu fie fin fun ifs sen sin sue sun use en if in is ne nu si us

efinsux unfixes. *See* **efinsu einsux**

efint feint fine tine eft fen fie fin fit net nit ten tie tin en if in it ne ti

efioosst footsies footies footsie softies. *See* **efioot efiost efisst eioost**

efioost footies footsie. *See* **efioot eioost efiost**

efioot footie foot eft fie fit foe oft tie toe too if it of ti to

efiorrst frostier rotifers forties rioters rotifer. *See* **efiost efirrs efirst eforst**

efiorrt rotifer. *See* **eiorrt efort efirr**

efiorst forties. *See* **eforst fiorst efiost eiorst efirst**

efiorx foxier fixer refix fire fore froe rife fie fir fix foe for fox fro ire ore ref rex rif roe er ex if of or ox re xi

efiosst softies. *See* **efisst fiosst**

efiost softie feist foist efts fies fist fits foes sift site soft ties toes eft fie fit foe

ifs its oft set sit sot tie toe if is it of os si so ti to

efiostx foxiest. *See* **efiost eistx efisx**

efipprry frippery. *See* **eipprr**

efiprtty prettify petrify. *See* **efirtt efirty eiprty eprtty**

efiprty petrify. *See* **efirty eiprty**

efiprx prefix fixer refix fire peri pier rife ripe fie fir fix ire per pie pix ref rep rex rif rip er ex if pe pi re xi

efir fire rife fie fir ire ref rif er if re

efirr frier fire rife err fie fir ire ref rif er if re

efirrrsu furriers friseur furrier surfier. *See* **efirrs efirsu efrrsu**

efirrru furrier. *See* **efirr**

efirrruy furriery furrier. *See* **eirry efrry efiry**

efirrs friers fires frier fries riser serif errs fies fire firs refs reis rife rifs rise serf sire err fie fir ifs ire ref res rif sir er if is re si

efirrssu friseurs fissure friseur fussier surfers surfier. *See* **efirrs efirss efirsu efrrsu**

efirrstt fritters fritter fitters. *See* **efirrs efirst efirtt eirstt**

efirrstu furriest friseur rustier surfeit surfier. *See* **efirrs efirst efirsu efrrsu**

efirrsu friseur surfier. *See* **efirrs efirsu efrrsu**

efirrtt fritter. *See* **efirtt eirrtt**

efirrty terrify. *See* **efirty eirry efrry**

efirs fires fries serif fies fire firs refs reis rife rifs rise serf sire fie fir ifs ire ref res rif sir er if is re si

efirss serifs fires fries rises serfs serif sires fess fies fire firs refs reis rife rifs rise serf sire sirs ess fie fir ifs ire ref res rif sir sis er if is re si

efirssu fissures fissure fussier issuers. *See* **efirss efirsu efsssu eirssu**

efirsst sifters strifes. *See* **efisst firsst efirst eirsst efirss**

efirsstu surfeits surfiest fissure fussier sifters strifes surfeit. *See* **efirss efirst efirsu efisst**

efirssu fissure fussier. *See* **efirsu eirssu efirss**

efirst refits sifter strife feist fires first frets fries frits refit rifts rites serif tiers tires tries efts erst fies fire firs fist fits fret frit refs reft reis rest rets rife rifs rift rise rite serf sift sire site stir tier ties tire eft fie fir fit ifs ire its net res ret rif set sir sit tie er if is it re si ti

efirstt fitters. *See* **efirtt efirst eirstt**

efirstu surfeit. *See* **firstu efirsu efirst**

efirstux fixtures surfeit fixture. *See* **efirst efirsu efirsx firstu**

efirstw swifter. *See* **efirst eirstw**

efirsu furies fires fries serif feus fies fire firs furs fuse refs reis rife rifs rise rues ruse serf sire sure surf user feu fie fir fur ifs ire ref res rif rue sir sue use er if is re si us

efirsv fivers fires fiver fives fries serif fies fire firs five refs reis revs rife rifs rise rive serf sire vies vise fie fir ifs ire ref res rev rif sir vie er if is re si

efirsvy versify. *See* **efirsv efirvy**

efirsx fixers fires fixer fixes fries refix serif fies fire firs refs reis rife rifs rise serf sire fie fir fix ifs ire ref res rex rif sex sir six er ex if is re si xi

efirt refit fire fret frit reft rife rift rite tier tire eft fie fir fit ire ref ret rif tie er if it re ti

efirtt fitter refit titer titre trite fire fret frit reft rife rift rite tier tire tret eft fie fir fit ire ref ret rif tie tit er if it re ti

efirtuv furtive. *See* **eirtuv efirv firtu**

efirtux fixture. *See* **efirx firtu efirt**

efirty ferity fiery refit reify fire fret frit reft rife rift rite tier tire yeti eft fey fie fir fit fry ire ref ret rif rye tie try yet er if it re ti ye

efiruzz fuzzier. *See* **efruz**

efirv fiver fire five rife rive fie fir ire ref rev rif vie er if re

efirvy verify fiery fiver reify fire five rife rive very fey fie fir fry ire ivy ref rev rif rye vie er if re ye

efirx fixer refix fire rife fie fir fix ire ref rex rif er ex if re xi

efiry fiery reify fire rife fey fie fir fry ire ref rif rye er if re ye

efis fies fie ifs if is si

efissstu fussiest tissues. *See* **efisst efsssu eisssu eisstu**

efisst feists feist fists sifts sites efts fess fies fist fits sets sift site sits ties eft ess fie fit ifs its set sis sit tie if is it si ti

efissttw swiftest. *See* **efisst eisstw issttw**

efist feist efts fies fist fits sift site ties eft fie fit ifs its set sit tie if is it si ti

efisttt fittest. *See* **efist**

efistty testify. *See* **efist estty**

efistuzz fuzziest. *See* **efiszz efstuz efsuzz**

efisty feisty feist yetis efts fies fist fits sift site ties yeti eft fey fie fit ifs its set sit sty tie yes yet if is it si ti ye

efisv fives fies five vies vise fie ifs vie if is si

efisx fixes fies fie fix ifs sex six ex if is si xi

efiszz fizzes fies fizz size fez fie ifs if is si

efiv five fie vie if

efiw wife fie few we if

efk kef

efklloor folklore. *See* **ekloor**

efklmno menfolk. *See* **eflno elmno**

efklnsuy flunkeys. *See* **efklsu fklnsu fklnuy**

efklsu flukes flues fluke fuels elks feus flue flus fuel fuse kefs leks lues self slue sulk elf elk els feu flu kef lek leu sue use el us

efklu fluke flue fuel elf elk feu flu kef lek leu el

efkorrtw fretwork. *See* **efortw ekorrw**

efkr kerf kef ref er re

efkrs kerfs kefs kerf refs serf kef ref res er re

efks kefs kef

efksy fykes fyke kefs keys fey kef key sky yes ye

efky fyke fey kef key ye

efl elf el

efll fell elf ell el

eflllow woolfell. *See* **efllow flloow**

eflnssu fullness. *See* **ellnss ellnsu elnssu**

eflntuy fluently. *See* **eflntu**

eflloorw follower. *See* **efllow eflorw efoorw flloow**

efllosw fellows. *See* **efllow eflls eflsw**

efllow fellow fell flew floe flow fowl well wolf ell elf few foe low owe owl woe el lo of ow we

efllru fuller fell flue fuel full furl lure rule elf ell feu flu fur leu ref rue el er re

eflls fells ells fell self sell elf ell els el

efllstu fullest. *See* **eflstu ellstu**

efllsuuy usefully. *See* **eflsuu**

eflly felly fell yell elf ell fey fly lye el ye

eflmorry formerly. *See* **efmorr**

eflmorss formless morsels. *See* **elmors elorss**

eflmosu fulsome. *See* **eflmsu eflos flosu**

eflmsu flumes flues flume fuels fumes mules elms emus feus flue flus fuel fume fuse lues mels mule muse self slue slum elf elm els emu feu flu leu lum mel mus sue sum use el em me mu um us

eflmsy myself elms lyes lyse mels self ylem elf elm els fey fly lye mel sly yes el em me my ye

eflmu flume flue fuel fume mule elf elm emu feu flu leu lum mel el em me mu um

eflnnsu funnels. *See* **eflnnu eflsu elnsu**

eflnnu funnel flue fuel lune elf fen feu flu fun leu nun el en ne nu

eflno felon enol floe leno lone noel elf eon fen foe one el en lo ne no of on

eflnortt frontlet. *See* **eflort enortt**

eflnory felonry. *See* **eflnoy efnry eflry**

eflnos felons felon floes noels enol eons fens floe foes leno lens lone lose noel noes nose ones self sloe sole elf els ens eon fen foe los one sen sol son el en lo ne no of on os so

eflnossu foulness. *See* **eflnos elnoss elnssu enossu**

eflnoy felony felon enol floe leno lone noel only elf eon fen fey fly foe foy lye one yen yon el en lo ne no of on oy ye

eflntu fluent unfelt flute felt flue fuel left lent lune lunt lute tule tune eft elf fen feu flu fun let leu net nut ten tun el en ne nu ut

eflntuu tuneful. *See* **eflntu**

eflo floe elf foe el lo of

efloorss roofless. *See* **eloors elooss elorss floors**

efloorvw overflow. *See* **eflorw efoorw**

efloory foolery. *See* **eflooy floor eflry**

efloosst footless loosest. *See* **elooss elosst loosst**

eflooz foozles. *See* **eflooz eflos floos**

eflooy flooey floe fool oleo elf fey fly foe foy loo lye el lo of oy ye

eflooz foozle floe fool oleo ooze elf fez foe loo zoo el lo of

eflopruw powerful. *See* **eflorw eflouw eflpru**

eflorst florets. *See* **eforst eflort elorst**

eflorstu flouters florets flouter fluster ourself restful. *See* **eflort eflstu eforst elorst**

eflorsu ourself. *See* **florsu**

eflorsuy yourself ourself elusory. *See* **efirsy eforsy elorsy elrsuy**

eflorsw flowers fowlers. *See* **eflorw elorsw**

eflorsx flexors. *See* **eflorx eflos efors**

eflort floret fetor forte felt floe fore fort fret froe left loft lore orle reft role rote rotl tore eft elf foe for fro let lot oft ore ort ref ret roe rot toe tor el er lo of or re to

eflortu flouter. *See* **eflort floru flotu**

eflorw flower fowler lower rowel flew floe flow fore fowl froe frow lore orle role wolf wore elf few foe for fro low ore owe owl ref roe row woe el er lo of or ow re we

eflorwy flowery. *See* **eflorw elorwy**

eflorx flexor flex floe fore froe lore orle role elf foe for fox fro lox ore ref rex roe el er ex lo of or ox re

eflos floes floe foes lose self sloe sole elf els foe los sol el lo of os so

eflosss flosses. *See* **elosss eflos floss**

eflouw woeful flew floe flow flue foul fowl fuel wolf elf feu few flu foe leu low owe owl woe el lo of ow we

eflp pelf elf el pe

eflprsu purfles. *See* **eflpru elprsu**

eflpru purfle flue fuel furl lure pelf pule pure purl rule elf feu flu fur leu per pul ref rep rue el er pe re up

eflps pelfs pelf self elf els el pe

eflrsstu flusters fluster restful results rustles ulsters. *See* **eflstu elrstu elsstu ersstu**

eflrsttu flutters fluster flutter restful turtles. *See* **eflstu elrstu elrttu ersttu**

eflrstu fluster restful. *See* **eflstu elrstu**

eflrstuu frustule fluster futures restful. *See* **eflruu eflstu eflsuu efrtuu**

eflrsy flyers flyer lyres slyer lyes lyre lyse refs rely ryes self serf elf els fey fly fry lye ref res rye sly yes el er re ye

eflrttu flutter. *See* **elrttu efltu**

eflrttuy fluttery flutter utterly. *See* **elrttu elrtty**

eflruu rueful flue fuel furl lure rule elf feu flu fur leu ref rue ulu el er re

eflrux reflux flex flue flux fuel furl lure luxe rule elf feu flu fur leu lux ref rex rue el er ex re

eflry flyer lyre rely elf fey fly fry lye ref rye el er re ye

efls self elf els el

eflst felts efts felt left lest lets self eft elf els let set el

eflstu flutes felts fetus flues flute fuels lutes tules efts felt feus flue flus fuel fuse left lest lets lues lust lute self slue slut suet tule elf elf els feu flu let leu set sue use el us ut

eflstuz zestful. *See* **eflstu efstuz**

eflsu flues fuels feus flue flus fuel fuse lues self slue elf els feu flu leu sue use el us

eflsuu useful flues fuels feus flue flus fuel fuse lues self slue ulus elf els feu flu leu sue ulu use el us

eflsux fluxes flues fuels luxes feus flex flue flus flux fuel fuse lues luxe self slue elf els feu flu leu lux sex sue use el ex us

eflsw flews flew self slew elf els few sew el we

eflt felt left eft elf let el

efltu flute felt flue fuel left lute tule eft elf feu flu let leu el ut

eflty lefty felt left eft elf fey fly let lye yet el ye

eflu flue fuel elf feu flu leu el

eflw flew elf few el we

eflx flex elf el ex

efmnoot footmen. *See* **efmnot**

efmnost foments. *See* **efmnot efnost emnost**

efmnot foment often monte font mote nome note omen tome tone eft eon fen foe men met mon mot net not oft one

---

ten toe tom ton em en me mo ne no of om on to

efmnrsu frenums. *See* **efmnru efmrsu**

efmnru frenum femur rumen fern fume menu rune emu fen feu fun fur men ref rem rue rum run urn em en er me mu ne nu re um

efmoorst foremost footers. *See* **eforst emoors emorst moorst**

efmoorsu foursome. *See* **efmrsu emoors emorsu fmorsu**

efmoprr perform preform. *See* **efmorr emoprr**

efmoprrs performs preforms perform preform reforms rompers. *See* **efmorr emoprr emoprs emorrs**

efmorr former reform ormer fore form froe from more omer err foe for fro mor ore ref rem roe em er me mo of om or re

efmorrs reforms. *See* **efmorr emorrs**

efmpruy perfumy. *See* **fmpruy efmru**

efmrsu femurs femur fumes serum emus feus fume furs fuse muse refs rues rums ruse serf sure surf user emu feu fur mus ref rem res rue rum sue sum use em er me mu re um us

efmru femur fume emu feu fur ref rem rue rum em er me mu re um

efmsu fumes emus feus fume fuse muse emu feu mus sue sum use em me mu um us

efmtuy tumefy fume fumy mute eft emu feu fey met yet yum em me mu my um ut ye

efmu fume feu emu em me mu um

efn fen en ne

efnny fenny fen fey yen en ne ye

efnooott footnote. *See* **efnot**

efnoosst eftsoons festoons eftsoon festoon softens. *See* **efnost enooss enosst noosst**

efnoost eftsoon festoon. *See* **efnost**

efnorrsw frowners frowner. *See* **enorrs enorsw eorrsw fnorsw**

efnorrw frowner. *See* **fnorw enorw eorrw**

efnorstu fortunes fortune tonsure. *See* **efnost eforst enorst enrstu**

efnortu fortune. *See* **efort fnotu fnort**

efnortw forwent. *See* **efortw fnort fnorw**

efnorz frozen froze fern fore froe zero zone eon fen fez foe for fro nor one ore ref roe en er ne no of on or re

efnossst softness softens. *See* **efnost enosst eossst**

efnosst softens. *See* **efnost enosst**

efnost soften fonts notes often onset steno stone tones efts eons fens foes font nest nets noes nose note ones sent snot soft tens toes tone tons eft ens eon

---

fen foe net not oft one sen set son sot ten toe ton en ne no of on os so to

efnot often font note tone eft eon fen foe net not oft one ten toe ton en ne no of on to

efnr fern fen ref en er ne re

efnrs ferns fens fern refs serf ens fen ref res sen en er ne re

efnry ferny fern fen fey fry ref rye yen en er ne re ye

efnryz frenzy ferny fern fen fey fez fry ref rye yen en er ne re ye

efns fens ens fen sen en ne

efo foe of

efooorst footsore footers. *See* **eforst**

efooprr reproof. *See* **efoorr eooprr**

efooprrs reproofs reproof roofers. *See* **efoorr eooprr eoprrs fooprs**

efooprst foretops footers foretop poorest. *See* **eforst eoprst fooprs ooprst**

efooprt foretop. *See* **efort foopr eoprt**

efoopstt footstep. *See* **eopst foops oopst**

efoorr roofer fore froe roof err foe for fro ore ref roe er of or re

efoorrs roofers. *See* **efoorr efors foors**

efoorrsw forswore roofers woofers. *See* **efoorr efoorw eoorsw eorrsw**

efoorst footers. *See* **eforst**

efoorstt footrest footers. *See* **eforst eorstt**

efoorsw woofers. *See* **efoorw eoorsw**

efoorw woofer wooer fore froe frow roof woof wore few foe for fro ore owe ref roe row woe woo er of or ow re we

efoostux outfoxes. *See* **footux**

efoppry foppery. *See* **efory**

efoprss profess. *See* **eoprss**

efoprsu profuse. *See* **eoprsu**

efor fore froe foe for fro ore ref roe er of or re

eforrsst fortress forests fosters resorts rosters sorters. *See* **eforst eorrst eorsst forsst**

eforrsty forestry torrefy. *See* **eforst eforsy efrrsy eorrst**

eforrsu ferrous. *See* **eforru forrsu eorrsu efrrsu**

eforrsv fervors. *See* **eforrv eorrsv**

eforrty torrefy. *See* **efrry efort forty**

eforru furore furor fore four froe err feu foe for fro fur ore our ref roe rue er of or re

eforrv fervor rover fore froe over rove err foe for fro ore ref rev roe er of or re

efors fores froes foes fore froe ores refs roes rose serf sore foe for fro ore ref res roe er of or os re so

eforsst forests fosters. *See* **eforst forsst eorsst**

eforst fetors forest fortes foster softer fetor fores forte forts frets froes frost rotes store efts erst foes fore fort fret froe ores orts refs reft rest rets roes rose rote rots serf soft sore sort toes tore tors eft foe for fro oft ore ort ref res ret roe rot set sot toe tor er of or os re so to

eforstw twofers. *See* **eforst eorstw efortw**

eforsy foyers fores foyer froes yores foes fore foys froe ores oyes refs roes rose rosy ryes serf sore yore fey foe for foy fro fry ore ref res roe rye soy yes er of or os oy re so ye

efort fetor forte fore fort fret froe reft rote tore eft foe for fro oft ore ort ref ret roe rot toe tor er of or re to

efortw twofer fetor forte tower wrote fore fort fret froe frow reft rote tore trow weft wore eft few foe for fro oft ore ort owe ref ret roe rot row toe tor tow two wet woe er of or ow re to we

efory foyer fore froe yore fey foe for foy fro fry ore ref roe rye er of or oy re ye

eforz froze fore froe zero fez foe for fro ore ref roe er of or re

efos foes foe of os so

efoss fosse fess foes foss foe ess of os so

efosstt softest. *See* **efoss esstt fostt**

efosx foxes foes foe fox sex sox ex of os ox so

efprtuy putrefy. *See* **eprtu frtuy**

efpstuy stupefy. *See* **efstu fstuy epstu**

efr ref er re

efrrssu surfers. *See* **efrrsu efssu erssu**

efrrsu surfer surer errs feus furs fuse refs rues ruse serf sure surf user err feu fur ref res rue sue use er re us

efrrsy fryers ferry fryer refry errs refs ryes serf err fey fry ref res rye yes er re ye

efrry ferry fryer refry err fey fry ref rye er re ye

efrs refs serf ref res er re

efrss serfs fess refs serf ess ref res er re

efrst frets efts erst fret refs reft rest rets serf eft ref res ret set er re

efrstuu futures. *See* **efrtuu erstuu**

efrsuz furzes furze fuzes feus furs fuse fuze refs rues ruse serf sure surf user feu fez fur ref res rue sue use er re us

efrt fret reft eft ref ret er re

efrtuu future fret reft true turf eft feu fur ref ret rue rut er re ut

efruz furze fuze feu fez fur ref rue er re

efss fess ess

efsssu fusses fuses fess feus fuse fuss sues uses ess feu sue use us

efssu fuses fess feus fuse fuss sues uses ess feu sue use us

efst efts eft set

efstu fetus efts feus fuse suet eft feu set sue use us ut

efstuz futzes fetus fuzes efts feus fuse futz fuze suet zest eft feu fez set sue use us ut

efstw wefts efts stew weft west wets eft few set sew wet we

efsu feus fuse feu sue use us

efsuz fuzes feus fuse fuze feu fez sue use us

efsuzz fuzzes fuzes feus fuse fuze fuzz feu fez sue use us

eft eft

eftw weft eft few wet we

efu feu

efuz fuze feu fez

efw few we

efy fey ye

efz fez

---

egg egg

egggiilr gigglier giggler. *See* **egggil egiilr**

egggil giggle egg gel gie gig leg lei lie el li

egggiln legging. *See* **egggin egggil eggiln**

egggilns leggings giggles legging niggles. *See* **egggil egggin eggiln egilns**

egggilr giggler. *See* **egggil**

egggilrs gigglers giggler giggles. *See* **egggil egilrs**

egggils giggles. *See* **egggil**

egggin egging egg gie gig gin en in ne

egggimp pegging. *See* **egggin**

egggiorr groggier. *See* **eggirr egiorr**

eggglo goggle loge ogle egg ego gel leg log el go lo

eggglos goggles. *See* **egggglo eglos**

egggglsu guggles. *See* **egggglu eglsu gglsu**

egggglu guggle glue glug luge egg gel leg leu lug el

egggno eggnog gone gong nogg egg ego eon nog one en go ne no on

egggnos eggnogs. *See* **egggno egnos ggnos**

egghiinn neighing hinging. *See* **eggiin eghiin**

egghiinw weighing. *See* **eggiin eghiin eghinw**

egghil higgle egg gel gie gig hie leg lei lie eh el he hi li

egghilr higgler. *See* **egghil**

egghilrs higglers higgler higgles. *See* **egghil eghils eghirs egilrs**

egghils higgles. *See* **egghil eghils**

egghrsu huggers. *See* **eggrsu eghrsu egghru**

egghru hugger gurge huger grue huge urge egg erg her hue hug reg rue rug ugh eh er he re

eggiilrw wigglier wriggle. *See* **eggilw egiilr eiilrw**

eggiin gieing genii egg gie gig gin en in ne

eggiinnr reigning reining ringing. *See* **eggiin egginr**

eggiinns singeing ginseng insigne seining sieging signing singing. *See* **eggiin eginns**

eggiint tingeing tinging. *See* **eggiin egiint**

eggiinrv grieving verging. *See* **eggiin egginr**

eggiins sieging. *See* **eggiin egins**

eggiip piggie egg gie gig gip peg pie pig pe pi

eggiips piggies. *See* **eggiip**

eggijl jiggle egg gel gie gig jig leg lei lie el li

eggijls jiggles. *See* **eggijl**

eggijr jigger grig egg erg gie gig ire jig reg rig er re

eggijrs jiggers. *See* **eggijr ggirs**

eggiknos ginkgoes. *See* **eiknos ggikno gginos**

eggilln gelling. *See* **eggiln**

eggiln niggle ingle glen lien line ling egg gel gie gig gin leg lei lie nil el en in li ne

eggilnnt gentling. *See* **eggiln egilnt eilnnt**

eggilnr niggler. *See* **egginr egilnr eggiln**

eggilnrs nigglers gingers lingers niggler niggles snigger. *See* **eggiln egginr egilnr egilns**

eggilnru grueling regluing niggler lugeing. *See* **eggiln egginr egglru egilnr**

eggilnry gingerly gingery niggler relying. *See* **eggiln egginr egilnr gginry**

eggilns niggles. *See* **egilns eggiln**

eggilnu lugeing. *See* **eggiln ggilnu**

eggilo loggie loge ogle egg ego gel gie gig leg lei lie log oil el go li lo

eggilqsu squiggle. *See* **eggisu egilsu**

eggilrsw wriggles wriggle wiggles. *See* **eggilw egilrs**

eggilrw wriggle. *See* **eggilw**

eggilsw wiggles. *See* **eggilw eilsw**

eggilw wiggle wile egg gel gie gig leg lei lie wig el li we

eggimmn gemming. *See* **egimm**

eggimnr merging. *See* **egginr egimr eimnr**

egginns ginseng. *See* **eginns**

egginr ginger reign grig grin rein ring egg erg gie gig gin ire reg rig en er in ne re

egginrru grungier. *See* **egginr eggirr eggrru gginru**

egginrs gingers snigger. *See* **egginr eginrs**

egginrv verging. *See* **egginr eginv egirv**

egginry gingery. *See* **egginr gginry**

egginssu guessing. *See* **eggisu eginss eginsu egissu**

eggintt getting. *See* **egint**

eggiors soggier. *See* **eggors egiors**

eggiosst soggiest egoists stogies. *See* **egiost**

eggiprry priggery. *See* **eggirr egiprr**

eggirr rigger grig egg erg err gie gig ire reg rig er re

eggirrs riggers. *See* **eggirr eirrs ggirs**

eggirrst triggers riggers trigger. *See* **eggirr egirst**

eggirrt trigger. *See* **eggirr egirt**

eggisu gigues gigue guise eggs egis gies gigs egg gie gig sue use is si us

eggiu gigue egg gie gig

eggjlo joggle loge ogle egg ego gel joe jog leg log el go jo lo

eggjlos joggles. *See* **eggjlo eglos**

eggjlrsu jugglers gurgles juggler juggles luggers slugger. *See* **eggjlu egglru eggrsu eglrsu**

eggjlru juggler. *See* **egglru eggjlu**

eggjlsu juggles. *See* **eggjlu eglsu gglsu**

eggjlu juggle glue glug luge egg gel jug leg leu lug el

eggjor jogger gorge goer gore grog ogre egg ego erg joe jog ore reg roe er go jo or re

eggjors joggers. *See* **eggjor eggors**

egglmrsu smuggler gurgles luggers muggers slugger smuggle. *See* **egglru eggmru eggrsu eglrsu**

egglmssu smuggles smuggle. *See* **elmssu**

egglmsu smuggle. *See* **egmsu eglsu elmsu**

egglnssu snuggles snuggle. *See* **eglnsu elnssu**

egglnsu snuggle. *See* **eglnsu gglsu**

egglooy geology. *See* **gglooy eggly egooy**

egglor logger gorge ogler goer gore grog loge lore ogle ogre orle role egg ego erg gel leg log ore reg roe el er go lo or re

egglors loggers slogger. *See* **eggors egglor eglors**

egglorss sloggers loggers slogger. *See* **egglor eggors eglors egorss**

egglost goglets toggles. *See* **egglot**

egglot goglet toggle loge ogle egg ego gel get got leg let log lot toe tog el go lo to

egglrssu sluggers gurgles luggers slugger. *See* **egglru eggrsu eglrsu egrssu**

egglrstu gurglets struggle gurgles gurglet luggers slugger. *See* **egglru eggrsu eglrsu elrstu**

egglrsu gurgles luggers slugger. *See* **eglrsu eggrsu egglru**

egglrtu gurglet. *See* **egglru**

egglru gurgle lugger gluer gruel gurge glue glug grue luge lure rule urge egg erg gel leg leu lug reg rue rug el er re

eggly leggy yegg egg gel gey leg lye el ye

eggmrsu muggers. *See* **egmrsu eggmru**

eggmru mugger gurge grume germ geum grue grum urge egg emu erg gem gum mug reg rem rue rug rum em er me mu re um

eggnoosy geognosy. *See* **egoosy**

eggnrsu grunges snugger. *See* **eggrsu egnsu enrsu**

eggnsstu snuggest nuggets suggest. *See* **eggntu egsstu ensstu**

eggnstu nuggets. *See* **eggntu egnst egnsu**

eggntu nugget gent tune egg get gnu gun gut net nut ten tug tun en ne nu ut

eggoorsu gorgeous gougers. *See* **eggors eggoru eggosu eggrsu**

eggor gorge goer gore grog ogre egg ego erg ore reg roe er go or re

eggors gorges goers gores gorge gorse grogs ogres ogres egos ergs goer goes gore grog ogre ores regs roes rose sego sore egg ego erg ore reg res roe er go or os re so

eggorst gorgets. *See* **egorst eggors eggort**

eggorsu gougers. *See* **eggors eggoru eggosu egorsu eggrsu**

eggort gorget gorge ergot goer gore grog grot ogre rote tore egg ego erg get got ore ort reg ret roe rot toe tog tor er go or re to

eggoru gouger gorge gouge gurge rogue rouge goer gore grog grue ogre urge egg ego erg ore our reg roe rue rug er go or re

eggosu gouges gouge eggs egos goes sego egg ego sou sue use go os so us

eggou gouge egg ego go

eggrrsu ruggers. *See* **eggrru eggrsu**

eggrru rugger gurge grue urge egg erg err reg rue rug er re

eggrsu gurges grues gurge surge urges eggs ergs grue regs rues rugs ruse sure urge user egg erg reg res rue rug sue use er re us

eggru gurge grue urge egg erg reg rue rug er re

eggs eggs egg

eggssstu suggests suggest gussets. *See* **egsstu**

eggsstu suggest. *See* **egsstu**

eggsy yeggs eggs yegg egg gey yes ye

eggy yegg egg gey ye

eghhhit heighth. *See* **eghhit**

eghhi heigh high gie heh hie eh he hi

eghhinss highness. *See* **eghins eginss ehinss**

eghhir higher heigh heir high hire erg gie heh her hie ire reg rig eh er he hi re

eghhist eighths heights highest. *See* **eghhit eghist ghhist**

eghhit eighth height eight heigh hight thigh high eth get gie heh het hie hit the tie eh he hi it ti

eghiilnr hireling. *See* **eghiin eghinr egiilr egilnr**

eghiimrt mightier. *See* **ehimrt**

eghiin hieing genii hinge neigh nigh gie gin hen hie hin eh en he hi in ne

eghiinnr inhering reining. *See* **eghiin eghinr**

eghiinrr rehiring herring. *See* **eghiin eghinr eginrr**

eghiinst heisting nighties ignites insight nighest nightie. *See* **eghiin eghins eghist eghnst**

eghiinsv inveighs inveigh sieving. *See* **eghiin eghins eginsv giinsv**

eghiint nightie. *See* **eghiin egiint**

eghiintv thieving nightie inveigh. *See* **eghiin egiint eiintv**

eghiinv inveigh. *See* **eghiin ghiinv**

eghiirst tigerish. *See* **eghist ghirst eghirs ehirst**

eghiklo hoglike. *See* **egikl**

eghiknr gherkin. *See* **eghinr**

eghiknrs gherkins gherkin hingers. *See* **eghinr eghins eghirs eginrs**

eghillno helloing hellion. *See* **eghino egilno eillno**

eghillns shelling shingle selling. *See* **eghils eghins egilns**

eghilmn helming. *See* **egilmn eghin**

eghilnov hoveling helving. *See* **eghino egilno gilnov**

eghilnp helping. *See* **eghin egiln**

eghilnps helpings helping plenish shingle. *See* **eghils eghins egilns eilnps**

eghilnpt   penlight helping lighten pelting. *See* **eghlnt egilnt egilpt eilnpt**

eghilnpw   whelping helping. *See* **eghinw**

eghilns   shingle. *See* **eghins egilns eghils**

eghilnss   shingles shingle singles sleighs. *See* **eghils eghins egilns eginss**

eghilnst   lightens glisten lengths lighten nighest shingle singlet sleight tingles. *See* **eghils eghins eghist eghlnt**

eghilnsv   shelving shingle helving. *See* **eghils eghins egilns eginsv**

eghilnsw   welshing shewing shingle swingle. *See* **eghils eghins eghinw eghisw**

eghilnt   lighten. *See* **eghlnt egilnt**

eghilnv   helving. *See* **eginv eghin egiln**

eghilrst   lighters gristle lighter sleight slither. *See* **eghils eghirs eghist egilrs**

eghilrt   lighter. *See* **ehilrt eghit ghirt**

eghils   sleigh egis gels gies hies isle legs leis lies sigh els gel gie hie his leg lei lie she eh el he hi is li sh si

eghilss   sleighs. *See* **eghils eilss ehiss**

eghilsss   sighless sleighs. *See* **eghils ehisss**

eghilsst   sleights hitless legists sleighs sleight slights. *See* **eghils eghist egilst ehisst**

eghilst   sleight. *See* **eghist egilst ghilst eghils**

eghilstt   lightest lithest sleight thistle. *See* **eghils eghist egilst ehistt**

eghimmn   hemming. *See* **egimm eghin**

eghimns   meshing. *See* **eghins ehimns**

eghimnux   exhuming. *See* **eghinx ehimnu**

eghin   hinge neigh nigh gie gin hen hie hin eh en he hi in ne

eghinnoy   honeying. *See* **eghino ghinno**

eghinnst   sennight henting nesting nighest tensing. *See* **eghins eghist eghnst eginns**

eghinnt   henting. *See* **eghit eghin ghint**

eghino   hoeing hinge neigh gone hone hong nigh ego eon gie gin hen hie hin hoe hog hon ion nog one eh en go he hi ho in ne no oh on

eghinorv   hovering. *See* **eghino eghinr eginor egnorv**

eghinos   shoeing. *See* **eghins eghino ehinos ghinos**

eghinr   hinger nigher hinge neigh reign grin heir hern hire nigh rein ring erg gie gin hen her hie hin ire reg rig eh en er he hi in ne re

eghinrr   herring. *See* **eginrr eghinr**

eghinrrs   herrings herring hingers ringers. *See* **eghinr eghins eghirs eginrr**

eghinrru   hungrier herring. *See* **eghinr eghnru eginrr**

eghinrs   hingers. *See* **eghinr eghins eginrs ehinrs eghirs**

eghins   hinges neighs hinge neigh segni shine singe egis engs gens gies gins hens hies hins nigh shin sigh sign sine sing ens gie gin hen hie hin his sen she sin eh en he hi in is ne sh si

eghinst   nighest. *See* **eghist eginst eghins ghinst eghnst**

eghinstt   tightens nighest setting testing tighten. *See* **eghins eghist eghnst eginst**

eghinsw   shewing. *See* **eghinw eghins ehinsw eginsw eghisw**

eghintt   tighten. *See* **eghit eghin ghint**

eghinttw   whetting tighten wetting. *See* **eghinw eghitw egintw ehintw**

eghinw   hewing hinge neigh weigh whine hewn nigh when wine wing gie gin hen hew hie hin new wen wig win eh en he hi in ne we

eghinx   hexing hinge neigh nixe nigh gie gin hen hex hie hin nix eh en ex he hi in ne xi

eghiors   ogreish. *See* **ehiors ghiors egiors eghirs**

eghiost   hogties. *See* **egiost eghist eghiot**

eghiot   hogtie eight ego eth get gie got het hie hit hoe hog hot the tho tie toe tog eh go he hi ho it oh ti to

eghiotuw   outweigh. *See* **eghiot eghitw**

eghirs   sigher heirs hires shire egis gies gies heir hers hies hire regs reis resh rigs rise sigh sire erg gie her hie his ire reg res rig she sir eh er he hi is re sh si

eghirss   sighers. *See* **ehirss eghirs**

eghirtt   tighter. *See* **ehirtt eghit ghirt**

eghist   eights eight heist sight egis gest gets gies gist hest hies hist hits sigh site sith this ties eth get gie het hie his hit its set she sit the tie eh he hi is it sh si ti

eghistt   tightest. *See* **eghist ehistt ghistt**

eghistw   weights. *See* **eghist eghisw eghitw ehistw ghistw**

eghisw   weighs weigh egis gies hews hies shew sigh swig wigs wise wish gie hew hie his sew she wig wis eh he hi is sh si we

eghit   eight eth get gie het hie hit the tie eh he hi it ti

eghitw   weight eight weigh white wight withe thew twig whet whit wite with eth get gie het hew hie hit the tie wet wig wit eh he hi it ti we

eghitwy   weighty. *See* **eghity eghitw ehitwy**

eghity   eighty eight they yeti eth get gey gie het hey hie hit the thy tie yet eh he hi it ti ye

eghiw   weigh gie hew hie wig eh he hi we

eghlmp   phlegm helm help hemp elm gel gem hem hep leg mel peg eh el em he me pe

eghlmpy   phlegmy. *See* **eghlmp ghlpy hlmpy**

eghlnor   leghorn. *See* **eglnor ehnor**

eghlnors   leghorns leghorn. *See* **eglnor eglnos eglors egnors**

eghlnst   lengths. *See* **eghlnt eghnst**

eghlnt   length thegn gent glen hent lent then eth gel get hen het leg let net ten the eh el en he ne

eghlnty   lengthy. *See* **eghlnt eglnty**

eghlooor   horologe. *See* **eglor**

eghlooty   theology. *See* **ehlty egooy ehloy**

eghluy   hugely gluey glue huge luge ugly yule gel gey guy hey hue hug leg leu lug lye ugh eh el he ye

eghmopuy   hypogeum. *See* **ehmoy hmpuy emopy**

eghmossu   gumshoes gumshoe. *See* **eghssu ehmssu ehossu emossu**

eghmosu   gumshoe. *See* **egmsu ehmos ehosu**

eghnooty   theogony. *See* **egooy ehnoy ehooy**

eghnorsu   roughens hungers roughen surgeon. *See* **eghnou eghnru eghrsu egnors**

eghnoru   roughen. *See* **eghnou eghnru**

eghnoruv   overhung roughen. *See* **eghnou eghnru egnorv**

eghnostu   toughens gunshot hognuts shotgun tongues toughen. *See* **eghnou eghnst eghstu egnotu**

eghnotu   toughen. *See* **eghnou ghnotu egnotu**

eghnou   enough gone hone hong huge hung ego eon gnu gun hen hoe hog hon hue hug nog one ugh eh en go he ho ne no nu oh on

eghnrstt   strength. *See* **eghnst ehnstt**

eghnrsu   hungers. *See* **eghnru eghrsu**

eghnru   hunger huger grue hern huge hung rune rung urge erg gnu gun hen her hue hug reg rue rug run ugh urn eh en er he ne nu re

eghnst   thegns gents hents thegn engs gens gent gest gets hens hent hest nest nets sent tens then ens eth get hen het net sen set she ten the eh en he ne sh

eghnt   thegn gent hent then eth get hen het net ten the eh en he ne ne

eghooosw   hoosegow hoosgow. *See* **egoos ehosw hoosw**

eghopr   gopher ephor grope hoper goer gore hero hoer hope ogre pore prog repo rope ego erg hep her hoe hog hop ope ore peg per pro reg rep rho roe eh er go he ho oh or pe re

eghoprs   gophers. *See* **ehoprs eghopr egoprs**

eghorru   rougher. *See* **eghru egorr egoru**

eghorstu roughest shouter souther troughs. *See* **eghrsu eghstu egorst egorsu**

eghott ghetto teth tote ego eth get got het hoe hog hot the tho toe tog tot eh go he ho oh to

eghrssu gushers. *See* **eghrsu eghssu ehrssu ghrssu egrssu**

eghrsu gusher grues huger shrug surge urges usher ergs grue gush hers hues huge hugs regs resh rues rugs ruse rush sure urge user erg her hue hug reg res rue rug she sue ugh use eh er he re sh us

eghrtuy theurgy. *See* **eghru**

eghru huger grue huge urge erg her hue hug reg rue rug ugh eh er he re

eghssu gushes guess gush hues huge hugs sues uses ess hue hug she sue ugh use eh he sh us

eghstu hugest guest thugs gest gets gush gust guts hest hues huge hugs huts shut suet thug thus tugs tush eth get gut het hue hug hut set she sue the tug ugh use eh he sh us ut

eghu huge hue hug ugh eh he

egi gie

egiiklnn likening inkling linking. *See* **giiikln giiknn giilnn**

egiiklnr kinglier erlking. *See* **egiilr egilnr eiikinr eiklnr**

egiilnnv livening veiling. *See* **giilnn giilnv**

egiilnor religion ligroin roiling. *See* **egiilr egilno egilnr egilor**

egiilnpr periling. *See* **egiilr egiinp egilnr eiinpr**

egiilnrv reliving reviling veiling. *See* **egiilr egilnr eiilrv giilnv**

egiilnt lignite. *See* **egiint giilnt egilnt**

egiilnv veiling. *See* **giilnv egiin eginv**

egiilnx exiling. *See* **egiin egiln eiinx**

egiilr girlie girl lire riel rile erg gel gie ire leg lei lie reg rig el er li re

egiilrrs grislier girlies. *See* **egiilr egilrs**

egiilrs girlies. *See* **egiilr egilrs**

egiilrtu guiltier. *See* **egiilr egilru**

egiimm gimmie gimme mime gem gie mem mim em me mi

egiimms gimmies. *See* **egiimm eimms**

egiimnp impinge. *See* **egiinp eiimn**

egiimnps impinges impinge. *See* **egiinp eiimns**

egiimnrs remising. *See* **egimrs eginrs eiimns eimnrs**

egiimnrt meriting mitering igniter interim mintier mitring terming. *See* **egiint egimnt giimnr giinrt**

egiimnrx remixing. *See* **giimnr giimnx**

egiimntt emitting. *See* **egiint egimnt eimntt giimnt**

egiimopt impetigo. *See* **eimpt emopt**

egiimrr grimier. *See* **egimr**

egiimrst grimiest mistier. *See* **egimrs egirst eimrst**

egiin genii gie gin en in ne

egiinnpr ripening reining. *See* **egiinp eiinpr giinnp giinpr**

egiinnr reining. *See* **egiin einnr eginr**

egiinns insigne seining. *See* **eginns egiin**

egiinnsw sinewing insigne seining. *See* **eginns eginsw**

egiinntu untieing uniting. *See* **egiint ginntu**

egiinnwz wizening. *See* **einwz**

egiinopr peignoir. *See* **egiinp eginop egiinor eiinpr**

egiinors seignoir ignores ironies noisier origins regions signior. *See* **eginor eginrs egiors**

egiinp pieing genii pine ping gie gin gip nip peg pen pie pig pin en in ne pe pi

egiinprx expiring. *See* **egiinp eiinpr giinpr**

egiinqtu quieting. *See* **egiint einqtu**

egiinrrt retiring igniter. *See* **egiint egirr giinrt**

egiinrrw rewiring wringer. *See* **egiinrr eiinrw eiirrw giinrw**

egiinrst igniters stingier igniter ignites resting stinger. *See* **egiint eginrs eginst egirst**

egiinrsv revising serving sieving versing virgins. *See* **eginrs eginsv egirsv giinrs**

egiinrt igniter. *See* **egiint giinrt**

egiinrtu intrigue igniter. *See* **egiint egnrtu einrtu giinrt**

egiinrtv riveting igniter vitrine. *See* **egiint egirtv eiintv einrtv**

egiinrvv reviving revving. *See* **giinrv**

egiinst ignites. *See* **egiint eginst giinst**

egiinstx existing ignites exiting. *See* **egiint eginst eginsx eiinsx**

egiinsv sieving. *See* **eginsv giinsv**

egiinsz seizing. *See* **eiinsz giinsz**

egiint ignite tieing genii tinge gent tine ting get gie gin net nit ten tie tin en in it ne ti

egiintx exiting. *See* **egiint**

egiinvw viewing. *See* **giinvw egiin eginv**

egiiprsw periwigs periwig wispier. *See* **egiprs eiprsw**

egiiprw periwig. *See* **egipr eiprw**

egiipsst pigsties. *See* **eiipst eipsst**

egiirtt grittier. *See* **eirrtt**

egijknr jerking. *See* **eijknr egikn eginr**

egijlln jelling. *See* **egijln**

egijllny jellying jelling yelling. *See* **egijln gijlny**

egijln jingle ingle glen lien line ling gel gie gin jig leg lei lie nil el en in li ne

egijlns jingles. *See* **egilns egijln**

egijlnst jinglets glisten jesting jingles jinglet singlet tingles. *See* **egijln egilns egilnt egilst**

egijlnt jinglet. *See* **egijln egilnt**

egijnnoy enjoying. *See* **eijnno**

egijnos jingoes. *See* **gijno ijnos**

egijnst jesting. *See* **eginst**

egijntt jetting. *See* **egint**

egijntty jettying jetting. *See* **eijnty eintty**

egikknrt trekking. *See* **eiknrt**

egikl kleig like elk gel gie ilk keg leg lei lek lie el li

egikllnn knelling. *See* **egikn egiln eikln**

egikllnos songlike eloigns legions lingoes. *See* **egilno egilns eglnos**

egiklnps skelping. *See* **egilns eiklns eilnps iklnps**

egiklnr erlking. *See* **egilnr eiklnr**

egiklnrs erlkings erlking lingers. *See* **egilnr egilns egilrs eginrs**

egiklnst kinglets glisten kinglet singlet tingles tinkles. *See* **egilns egilnt egilst eginst**

egiklnt kinglet. *See* **egilnt eiklnt**

egikn eking gink kine king gie gin ink keg ken kin en in ne

egiknnn kenning. *See* **egikn**

egiknnr kerning. *See* **egikn eiknr einnr**

egiknorv revoking evoking invoker. *See* **eginor egnorv eiknov ginorv**

egiknov evoking. *See* **eiknov egikn eginv**

egiknpr perking. *See* **egikn egipr eiknr**

egikny keying eking eying gink inky kine king gey gie gin ink keg ken key kin yen yin en in ne ye

egillmns smelling selling mingles. *See* **egilmn egilms egilns eilmns**

egillnov livelong. *See* **egilno eillno gilnov**

egillnps spelling selling. *See* **egilns eilnps**

egillnqu quelling. *See* **egillu**

egillns selling. *See* **egilns**

egillnsw swelling selling swingle. *See* **egilns eginsw**

egillnt telling. *See* **eillnt egilnt**

egillny yelling. *See* **eginy egiln gilny**

egillr grille rille grill gill girl lire riel rile rill ell erg gel gie ill ire leg lei lie reg rig el er li re

egillrs grilles. *See* **egillr gillrs egilrs eillrs**

egillsu gullies ligules. *See* **egillu egilsu**

egillu ligule guile gill glue gull lieu luge ell gel gie ill leg lei leu lie lug el li

egilm gimel glim lime mile elm gel gem gie leg lei lie mel mil el em li me mi

egilmmn lemming. *See* **egilmn egimm**

egilmmns lemmings lemming mingles. *See* **egilmn egilms egilns eilmns**

egilmmr glimmer. *See* **egimmr egilm eilmr**

egilmmrs   glimmers glimmer megrims slimmer. *See* **egilms egilrs egimmr egimrs**

egilmn   mingle gimel ingle limen glen glim lien lime limn line ling mien mile mine elm gel gem gie gin leg lei lie mel men mil nil nim el em en in li me mi ne

egilmnot   longtime emoting lentigo melting molting. *See* **egilmn egilmt egilno egilnt**

egilmnr   gremlin mingler. *See* **eilmnr egilnr egilmn**

egilmnrs   gremlins minglers gremlin limners lingers merlins mingler mingles. *See* **egilmn egilms egilnr egilns**

egilmns   mingles. *See* **egilms egilns eilmns**

egilmnst   smelting gimlets glisten melting mingles singlet tingles. *See* **egilmn egilms egilmt egilns**

egilmnt   melting. *See* **egilmt egimnt egilmn egilnt**

egilmps   glimpse. *See* **egilms eilmps**

egilmpss   glimpses glimpse. *See* **egilms eilmps eilmss eilpss**

egilms   gimels gimel limes miles slime smile egis elms gels gems gies glim isle legs leis lies lime mels mile mils mise semi slim elm els gel gem gie leg lei lie mel mil mis el em is li me mi si

egilmst   gimlets. *See* **egilms egilmt egilst**

egilmt   gimlet gimel legit emit gilt glim item lime melt mile milt mite tile time elm gel gem get gie leg lei let lie lit mel met mil tie til el em it li me mi ti

egiln   ingle glen lien line ling gel gie gin leg lei lie nil el en in li ne

egilnnst   nestling glisten linnets nesting singlet tensing tingles. *See* **egilns egilnt egilst eginns**

egilnntt   nettling letting netting tenting. *See* **egilnt eilnnt einntt**

egilno   eloign legion eloin ingle lingo longe olein enol glen gone leno lien line ling lion loge loin lone long noel noil ogle ego eon gel gie gin ion leg lei lie log nil nog oil one el en go in li lo ne no on

egilnop   eloping. *See* **egilno gilnop eginop eilnop**

egilnopp   peopling eloping lopping. *See* **egilno eginop eginpp eilnop**

egilnors   resoling eloigns glories ignores legions lingers lingoes regions. *See* **egilno egilnr egilns egilor**

egilnorw   lowering roweling. *See* **egilno egilnr egilor eginor**

egilnos   eloigns legions lingoes. *See* **egilno eilnos egilns eglnos gilnos**

egilnosu   ligneous eloigns elusion igneous legions lingoes lounges. *See* **egilno egilns egilsu**

egilnot   lentigo. *See* **egilno eilnot egilnt eginot**

egilnotw   toweling lentigo welting. *See* **egilno egilnt eginot egintw**

egilnovv   evolving involve. *See* **egilno gilnov**

egilnpry   replying preying relying yelping. *See* **egilnr eilpry einpry gilnpy**

egilnpst   pestling glisten pelting piglets singlet tingles. *See* **egilns egilnt egilpt egilst**

egilnpt   pelting. *See* **egilpt eilnpt**

egilnpy   yelping. *See* **gilnpy eginy egiln**

egilnr   linger ingle liner reign girl glen grin lien line ling lire rein riel rile ring erg gel gie gin ire leg lei lie nil reg rig el en er in li ne re

egilnrry   erringly relying. *See* **egilnr eginrr**

egilnrs   lingers. *See* **egilrs egilns eilnrs egilnr eginrs**

egilnrst   ringlets sterling tinglers glisten gristle lingers resting ringlet singlet stinger tingler tingles. *See* **egilnr egilns egilnt egilrs**

egilnrt   ringlet tingler. *See* **egilnr egilnt**

egilnry   relying. *See* **egilnr eginy gilny**

egilns   ingles single glens ingle lenis liens lines lings segni singe sling egis engs gels gens gies gins glen isle legs leis lens lien lies line ling nils sign sine sing els ens gel gie gin leg lei lie nil sen sin el en in is li ne si

egilnss   singles. *See* **eginss egilns gilnss**

egilnsst   glistens singlets enlists glisten ingests legists listens signets singles singlet tingles tinsels. *See* **egilns egilnt egilst eginss**

egilnssu   ugliness singles. *See* **egilns egilsu eginss eginsu**

egilnssw   swingles wingless singles swingle wigless. *See* **egilns eginss eginsw einssw**

egilnst   glisten singlet tingles. *See* **eilnst gilnst eginst egilns egilst**

egilnstt   settling glisten letting setting singlet testing tingles. *See* **egilns egilnt egilst eginst**

egilnsw   swingle. *See* **egilns eginsw**

egilnt   tingle glint ingle inlet legit tinge gent gilt glen lent lien line ling lint tile tine ting gel get gie gin leg lei let lie lit net nil nit ten tie til tin el en in it li ne ti

egilntt   letting. *See* **egilnt eiltt**

egilntu   eluting. *See* **eglntu gilntu egilnt**

egilntux   exulting eluting. *See* **egilnt eglntu gilntu**

egilntw   welting. *See* **egilnt egintw**

egilnvxy   vexingly levying. *See* **eginvx**

egilnvy   levying. *See* **eginy eginv egiln**

egilor   logier ogler oiler oriel girl goer gore lire loge lore ogle ogre orle riel rile roil role ego erg gel gie ire leg lei lie log oil ore reg rig roe el er go li lo or re

egilors   glories. *See* **egilrs egilor eglors eilors egiors**

egilorss   glossier glories grilses rissole. *See* **egilor egilrs egiors eglors**

egilosss   glossies glosses. *See* **egosss elosss**

egilost   logiest. *See* **egiost egilst eilost**

egilostu   eulogist logiest ugliest. *See* **egilst egilsu egiost eilost**

egilpst   piglets. *See* **egilst egilpt eilpst**

egilpt   piglet legit gilt lept pelt pile tile gel get gie gip leg lei let lie lip lit peg pet pie pig pit tie til tip el it li pe pi ti

egilrs   grilse girls riels riles egis ergs gels gies girl isle legs leis lies lire regs reis riel rigs rile rise sire els erg gel gie ire leg lei lie reg res rig sir el er is li re si

egilrss   grilses. *See* **egilrs eilss eirss**

egilrst   gristle. *See* **egilrs egilst eilrst egirst**

egilrstt   glitters glitter gristle litters. *See* **egilrs egilst egirst eilrst**

egilrsu   ligures. *See* **eglrsu egilrs egilsu egilru egirsu**

egilrszz   grizzles grizzle. *See* **egilrs eilszz**

egilrtt   glitter. *See* **eilrtt egilt egirt**

egilrtty   glittery glitter. *See* **eilrtt elrtty girtty**

egilru   ligure uglier gluer gruel guile girl glue grue lieu lire luge lure riel rile rule urge erg gel gie ire leg lei leu lie lug reg rig rue rug el er li re

egilrzz   grizzle. *No 6s or 5s*

egilsst   legists. *See* **eilsst egilst**

egilssw   wigless. *See* **eilss eilsw gissw**

egilst   legist gilts islet istle legit stile tiles egis gels gest gets gies gilt gist isle legs leis lest lets lies list silt site slit ties tile tils els gel get gie its leg lei let lie lit set sit tie til el is it li si ti

egilstu   ugliest. *See* **egilst egilsu**

egilsu   guiles glues guile guise gules ileus luges egis gels gies glue isle legs leis lies lieu lues luge lugs slue slug els gel gie leg lei leu lie lug sue use el is li si us

egilt   legit tile gilt gel get gie leg lei let lie lit tie til el it li ti

egilu   guile glue lieu luge gel gie leg lei leu lie lug el li

egimm   gimme mime gem gie mem mim em me mi

egimmnst   stemming. *See* **egimnt eginst**

egimmr   megrim gimme grime mimer emir germ grim mime mire rime erg gem gie ire mem mim mir reg rem rig rim en er me mi re
egimmrr   grimmer. *See* egimmr
egimmrs   megrims. *See* egimrs egimmr eimmrs
egimmrst   grimmest megrims. *See* egimmr egimrs egirst eimmrs
egimmru   gummier. *See* egimmr eimmru
egimmstu   gummiest tummies. *See* immstu
egimnno   omening. *See* gimnno egmno emnno
egimnnw   wingmen. *See* egimnw
egimnorv   removing. *See* eginor egmnor egnorv eimnor
egimnosy   moseying isogeny. *See* egimos egmnos eimnos
egimnot   emoting. *See* egimnt eginot
egimnpr   perming. *See* egimr egipr eimnr
egimnpst   pigments pigment. *See* egimnt eginst eimnpt einpst
egimnpt   pigment. *See* egimnt eimnpt
egimnptt   tempting pigment petting. *See* egimnt eimnpt eimntt
egimnpty   emptying pigment. *See* egimnt eimnpt eimnty ginpty
egimnrsu   resuming reusing. *See* egimrs eginrs eginsu egirsu
egimnrt   terming. *See* egimnt egimr einrt
egimnss   messing. *See* eginss
egimnt   meting tinge emit gent item mien mine mint mite time tine ting gem get gie gin men met net nim nit ten tie tin em en in it me mi ne ti
egimnw   mewing mien mine wine wing gem gie gin men mew new nim wen wig win em en in me mi ne we
egimos   egoism gismo egis egos gems gies goes mise mogs sego semi smog some ego gem gie mis mog mos oms em go is me mi mo om os si so
egimost   egotism. *See* egimos egiost eimost
egimpsu   guimpes. *See* egimpu egmsu gimps
egimpsy   pygmies. *See* gimps gimpy
egimpu   guimpe geum gimp emu gem gie gip gum imp mug peg pie pig pug ump em me mi mu pe pi um up
egimr   grime emir germ grim mire rime erg gem gie ire mir reg rem rig rim em er me mi re
egimrs   grimes emirs germs grime mires miser rimes egis emir ergs gems germ gies grim mire mirs mise regs reis rigs rime rims rise semi sire erg gem gie ire mir mis reg rem res rig rim sir em er is me mi re si

eginnnp   penning. *See* einnp
eginnny   yenning. *See* eginy innny
eginnop   opening. *See* eginop einnp
eginnops   openings opening pension pigeons. *See* eginns eginop egnops
eginnort   nitrogen intoner renting ternion. *See* eginor eginot egiort einnot
eginnorz   rezoning zeroing. *See* eginor eginrz ginnoz
eginnpsu   penguins ensuing gunnies penguin. *See* eginns eginsu einnps einpsu
eginnpu   penguin. *See* einnu innpu
eginnrru   unerring runnier. *See* eginrr egnnru ennrru
eginnrsu   ensuring ensuing gunners gunnies nursing reusing sunnier. *See* eginns eginrs eginsu egirsu
eginnrt   renting. *See* einnrt
eginnrv   nerving. *See* eginv egirv einnr
eginns   ensign nines segni singe egis engs gens gies gins inns nine sign sine sing ens gie gin inn sen sin en in is ne si
eginnss   ensigns sensing. *See* eginns eginss
eginnst   nesting tensing. *See* eginns eginst einnst
eginnsu   ensuing gunnies. *See* eginns eginsu
eginntt   netting tenting. *See* einntt egint
eginntv   venting. *See* einntv eginv egint
eginnvy   envying. *See* eginy einvy einnv
eginop   pigeon gipon opine oping gone nope open peon pine ping pone ego eon gie gin gip ion nip nog one ope peg pen pie pig pin poi en go in ne no on pe pi
eginoprs   reposing spongier ignores orpines pigeons porgies prosing regions sponger sporing springe. *See* eginop eginor eginrs
eginoprw   powering. *See* eginop eginor einopr ginopr
eginops   pigeons. *See* ginops einops eginop egnops
eginopsx   exposing pigeons. *See* eginop eginsx egnops
eginor   ignore region genro goner groin reign goer gone gore grin iron ogre rein ring ego eon erg gie gin ion ire nog nor one ore reg rig roe en er go in ne no on or re
eginorr   ignorer. *See* eginrr egiorr eginor einorr
eginorrs   ignorers ignorer ignores ironers regions ringers. *See* eginor eginrr eginrs
eginors   ignores regions. *See* egnors ginors einors egiors eginor
eginortw   towering trowing. *See* eginor eginot egintw egiort

eginorxx   xeroxing. *See* eginor
eginorz   zeroing. *See* eginor eginrz
eginosu   igneous. *See* eginsu
eginosy   isogeny. *See* eginy inosy
eginot   toeing tinge ingot gent gone into note tine ting tone tong ego eon get gie gin got ion net nit nog not one ten tie tin toe tog ton en go in it ne no on ti to
eginotv   vetoing. *See* eginot ginotv
eginpp   pigpen pine ping pipe gie gin gip nip peg pen pep pie pig pin pip en in ne pe pi
eginppp   pepping. *See* eginpp
eginpppr   prepping pepping. *See* eginpp egippr einppr
eginpps   pigpens. *See* eginpp einpps
eginppst   stepping pigpens snippet. *See* eginpp eginst einpps einpst
eginprs   springe. *See* egiprs eginrs einprs ginprs
eginprss   pressing springes ingress resigns singers snipers springe springs. *See* eginrs eginss egiprs einprs
eginprsu   perusing pursing reusing springe uprisen. *See* eginrs eginsu egiprs egirsu
eginprtu   erupting reputing. *See* egnrtu einrtu enprtu ginptu
eginprty   retyping preying retying. *See* egnrty einpry eiprty ginpry
eginpry   preying. *See* einpry ginpry
eginpsw   spewing. *See* eginsw
eginpsy   espying. *See* ginpsy eginy einps
eginptt   petting. *See* einpt eiptt egint
eginqruy   querying enquiry. *See* egnruy
eginqstu   questing inquest quintes. *See* eginst eginsu einqtu einstu
eginquu   queuing. *No 6s or 5s*
eginr   reign grin rein ring erg gie gin ire reg rig en er in ne re
eginrr   erring ringer reign grin rein ring erg err gie gin ire reg rig en er in ne re
eginrrs   ringers. *See* eginrr eginrs einrrs
eginrrst   stringer resting ringers stinger. *See* eginrr eginrs eginst egirst
eginrrsw   wringers ringers swinger wringer. *See* eginrr eginrs eginsw einrrs
eginrrty   retrying retying. *See* eginrr egnrty ginrty
eginrrw   wringer. *See* eginrr
eginrs   reigns resign singer grins reign reins resin rings rinse risen segni serin singe siren egis engs ergs gens gies gins grin regs rein reis rigs ring rise sign sine sing sire ens erg gie gin ire reg res rig sen sin sir en er in is ne re si
eginrss   ingress resigns singers. *See* eginss einrss eginrs
eginrsst   stingers ingests ingress inserts resigns resting signets singers sinters

stinger strings tigress. *See* **eginrs eginss eginst egirst**

eginrssv servings ingress resigns serving singers versing. *See* **eginrs eginss eginsv egirsv**

eginrssw swingers ingress resigns singers swinger. *See* **eginrs eginss eginsw einrss**

eginrssy syringes ingress resigns singers syringe yessing. *See* **eginrs eginss einrss**

eginrst resting stinger. *See* **eginst einrst ginrst egirst**

eginrstt gitterns gittern resting retting setting stinger testing. *See* **eginrs eginst egirst einrst**

eginrstw strewing wresting resting stewing stinger swinger twinges westing winters. *See* **eginrs eginst eginsw egintw**

eginrsu reusing. *See* **eginsu einrsu egirsu eginrs**

eginrsv serving versing. *See* **eginsv egirsv eginrs**

eginrsvw swerving serving swinger versing. *See* **eginrs eginsv eginsw egirsv**

eginrsw swinger. *See* **eginrs eginsw ginrsw**

eginrsy syringe. *See* **eginrs**

eginrtt gittern retting. *See* **einrtt eginr egirt**

eginrttu uttering gittern nuttier retting rutting. *See* **egnrtu egrttu einrtt einrtu**

eginrty retying. *See* **egnrty ginrty**

eginrvv revving. *See* **eginv egirv eginr**

eginrz zinger reign grin rein ring zein zing erg gie gin ire reg rig zig en er in ne re

egins segni singe egis gens gies gins sign sine sing ens gie gin sen sin en in is ne si

eginss gneiss singes segni signs sines singe sings egis engs gens gies gins sign sine sing sins ens ess gie gin sen sin sis en in is ne si

eginsst ingests signets. *See* **eginss eginst einsst ginsst**

eginsstt settings ingests setting signets testing. *See* **eginss eginst einsst einstt**

eginssy yessing. *See* **eginss**

eginst ingest signet tinges gents inset segni singe stein sting tines tinge tings egis engs gens gent gest gets gies gins gist nest nets nits sent sign sine sing site snit tens ties tine ting tins ens get gie gin its net nit sen set sin sit ten tie tin en in is it ne si ti

eginstt setting testing. *See* **eginst einstt**

eginstv vesting. *See* **eginsv eginst einstv**

eginstw stewing twinges westing. *See* **eginst eginsw einstw egintw**

eginsu genius genus guise negus segni singe suing using egis engs gens gies gins gnus guns sign sine sing snug sung ens gie gin gnu gun sen sin sue sun use en in is ne nu si us

eginsv givens given gives segni singe veins vines egis engs gens gies gins give nevi sign sine sing vein vies vine vise ens gie gin sen sin vie en in is ne si

eginsw sewing swinge segni sinew singe swine swing wines wings egis engs gens gies gins news sewn sign sine sing swig wens wigs wine wing wins wise ens gie gin new sen sew sin wen wig win wis en in is ne si we

eginsx sexing nixes segni singe egis engs gens gies gins nixe sign sine sing ens gie gin nix sen sex sin six en ex in is ne si xi

egint tinge gent tine ting get gie gin net nit ten tie tin en in it ne ti

eginttw wetting. *See* **egintw**

egintw twinge tinge twine gent newt tine ting twig twin wine wing wite get gie gin net new nit ten tie tin wen wet wig win wit en in it ne ti we

eginv given give nevi vein vine gie gin vie en in ne

eginvx vexing given vixen give nevi nixe vein vine gie gin nix vex vie en ex in ne xi

eginy eying gey gie gin yen yin en in ne ye

egioopr goopier. *See* **egioor egipr egopr**

egioopst goopiest isotope. *See* **egiost egoost giopst**

egioor gooier goer gore ogre ego erg gie goo ire ore reg rig roe er go or re

egioprs porgies. *See* **egiprs egoprs egiors**

egioprss gossiper porgies. *See* **egiors egiprs egoprs egorss**

egioprsu groupies groupie porgies soupier. *See* **egiors egiprs egirsu egoprs**

egiopru groupie. *See* **egipr egopr gopru**

egiorr gorier roger rigor goer gore ogre ego erg err gie ire ore reg rig roe er go or re

egiors orgies goers gores gorse ogres osier egis egos ergs gies goer goes gore ogre ores regs reis rigs rise roes rose sego sire sore sori ego erg gie ire ore reg res rig roe sir er go is or os re si so

egiorst goiters goriest. *See* **egiost egorst egiort egiors eiorst**

egiorsuv grievous. *See* **egiors egiosv egirsu egirsv**

egiort goiter tiger ergot girt goer gore grit grot ogre riot rite rote tier tire tiro tore tori trig trio ego erg get gie got ire

ore ort reg ret rig roe rot tie toe tog tor er go it or re ti to

egiortv vertigo. *See* **egiort egirtv**

egiosst egoists stogies. *See* **egiost**

egiosstt egotists egoists egotist stogies. *See* **egiost**

egiost egoist stogie egis egos gest gets gies gist goes sego site ties toes togs ego get gie got its set sit sot tie toe tog go is it os si so ti to

egiostt egotist. *See* **egiost**

egiosuux exiguous. *See* **egisu**

egiosv ogives ogive gives egis egos gies give goes sego vies vise ego gie vie go is os si so

egiov ogive give ego gie vie go

egippr grippe gripe piper grip peri pier pipe prep prig repp ripe erg gie gip ire peg pep per pie pig pip reg rep rig rip er pe pi re

egipprr gripper. *See* **egiprr egippr eipprr**

egipprrs grippers gripers gripper grippes rippers. *See* **egippr egiprr egiprs eipprs**

egipprs grippes. *See* **egiprs eipprs**

egippsu guppies. *See* **egisu eipps**

egipr gripe grip peri pier prig ripe erg gie gip ire peg per pie pig reg rep rig rip er pe pi re

egiprr griper gripe prier grip peri pier prig ripe erg err gie gip ire peg per pie pig reg rep rig rip er pe pi re

egiprrs gripers. *See* **egiprr egiprs eiprrs**

egiprs gripes gripe grips piers pries prigs spire sprig egis ergs gies gips grip pegs peri pier pies pigs prig regs reis reps rigs ripe rips rise sire erg gie gip ire peg per pie pig reg rep res rig rip sip sir er is pe pi re si

egiprsuu guipures euripus guipure upsurge. *See* **egiprs egirsu egprsu eprsuu**

egipruu guipure. *See* **egipr egpru**

egipssy gypsies. *See* **eipss**

egirrsty registry. *See* **egirst**

egirsst tigress. *See* **girsst eirsst egirst**

egirst tigers girts grist grits rites tiers tiger tires tries trigs egis ergs erst gest gets gies girt gist grit regs reis rest rets rigs rise rite sire site stir tier ties tire trig erg get gie ire its reg res ret rig set sir sit tie er is it re si ti

egirstu gutsier. *See* **egirst egirsu**

egirstv grivets. *See* **egirsv egirtv eirstv egirst**

egirsu regius grues guise surge urges egis ergs gies grue regs reis rigs rise rues rugs ruse sire sure urge user erg gie ire reg res rig rue rug sir sue use er is re si us

egirsv givers giver gives egis ergs gies give regs reis revs rigs rise rive sire vies vise erg gie ire reg res rev rig sir vie er is re si

egirt tiger girt grit rite tier tire trig erg get gie ire reg ret rig tie er it re ti

egirtv grivet giver rivet tiger girt give grit rite rive tier tire trig vert erg get gie ire reg ret rev rig tie vet vie er it re ti

egirv giver give rive erg gie ire reg rev rig vie er re

egis egis gies gie is si

egisssu gussies. *See* **egissu eisssu**

egissttu gutsiest. *See* **egissu egsstu eisstu**

egissu guises guess guise issue egis gies sues uses ess gie sis sue use is si us

egissyyz syzygies. *See* **eissz**

egisu guise egis gies gie sue use is si us

egisv gives egis gies give vies vise gie vie is si

egiv give gie vie

egjlnoru jongleur lounger. *See* **egjlnu eglnor**

egjlnsu jungles. *See* **egjlnu eglnsu**

egjlnu jungle lunge glen glue luge lune lung gel gnu gun jug leg leu lug el en ne nu

egk keg

egklorw legwork. *See* **eglorw**

egklu kluge kugel glue luge elk gel keg leg lek leu lug el

egkmssu muskegs. *See* **egkmsu egssu emssu**

egkmsu muskeg geums emus gems geum gums kegs mugs muse musk skeg smug emu gem gum keg mug mus sue sum use em me mu um us

egks kegs skeg keg

egkss skegs kegs skeg keg ess

egl gel leg el

egllstu gullets. *See* **eglltu ellstu**

eglltu gullet tulle glue glut gull luge lute tell tule ell gel get gut leg let leu lug tug el ut

eglmmru glummer. *See* **eglru egmru elmru**

eglmmstu glummest. *See* **egmsu eglsu glstu**

eglmnooy menology neology. *See* **elmnoy glmooy**

eglmnor mongrel. *See* **eglnor elmnor egmnor**

eglmnors mongrels merlons mongers mongrel morgens. *See* **eglmos eglnor eglnos eglors**

eglmo golem loge mole ogle ego elm gel gem leg log mel mog el em go lo me mo om

eglmoor legroom. *See* **glmoo eglmo gmoor**

eglmopru promulge. *See* **eglopr egmoru elmpru**

eglmos golems golem loges moles ogles egos elms geis gems goes legs loge logs lose mels mogs mole ogle sego sloe slog smog sole some ego elm els gel gem leg log los mel mog mos oms sol el em go lo me mo om os so

egln glen gel leg el en ne

eglnnooy gunnels. *See* **eglnnu eglnsu**

eglnnu gunnel lunge glen glue luge lune lung gel gnu gun leg leu lug nun el en ne nu

eglno longe enol glen gone leno loge lone long noel ogle ego eon gel leg log nog one el en go lo ne no on

eglnoooy oenology neology. *See* **glnooo gloooy**

eglnoopy penology neology polygon. *See* **elnopy**

eglnooy neology. *See* **egooy eglno lnooy**

eglnor longer genro goner loner longe ogler enol glen goer gone gore leno loge lone long lorn noel ogle ogre orle role ego eon erg gel leg log nog nor one ore reg roe el en er go lo ne no on or re

eglnorsu loungers lounger lounges lungers surgeon. *See* **eglnor eglnos eglnou eglnsu**

eglnoru lounger. *See* **eglnor eglnou**

eglnos longes glens loges longe longs noels ogles segno egos engs enol eons gels gens glen goes gone legs leno lens loge logs lone long lose noel noes nogs nose ogle ones sego sloe slog sole song ego els ens eon gel leg log los nog one sen sol son el en go lo ne no on os so

eglnosss songless glosses lessons. *See* **eglnos egosss elnoss**

eglnost longest. *See* **eglnos elnost**

eglnosu lounges. *See* **eglnos eglnou eglnsu**

eglnou lounge longe lunge enol glen glue gone leno loge lone long luge lune lung noel ogle ego eon gel gnu gun leg leu log lug nog one el en go lo ne no nu on

eglnprsu plungers lungers plunger plunges splurge. *See* **eglnpu eglnsu eglrsu egprsu**

eglnpru plunger. *See* **eglnpu eglru enpru**

eglnpsu plunges. *See* **eglnpu eglnsu**

eglnpu plunge lunge glen glue gulp luge lune lung plug pule pung gel gnu gun leg leu lug peg pen pug pul pun el en ne nu pe up

eglnrsu lungers. *See* **eglrsu**

eglnrtuy urgently. *See* **eglntu eglnty egnrtu egnrty**

eglns glens gels gens glen legs lens els ens gel leg sen el en ne

eglnstu glutens. *See* **eglnsu eglntu**

eglnsu lunges genus glens glues gules luges lunes lunge lungs negus slung engs gels gens glen glue gnus guns legs lens lues luge lugs lune lung slue slug snug sung els ens gel gnu gun leg leu lug sen sue sun use el en ne nu us

eglnsuu unglues. *See* **eglnsu eglnuu**

eglntu gluten lunge gent glen glue glut lent luge lune lung lunt lute tule tune gel get gnu gun gut leg let leu lug net nut ten tug tun el en ne nu ut

eglnty gently gent glen lent gel get gey leg let lye net ten yen yet el en ne ye

eglnu lunge glen glue luge lune lung gel gnu gun leg leu lug el en ne nu

eglnuu unglue lunge glen glue luge lune lung gel gnu gun leg leu lug ulu el en ne nu

eglo loge ogle ego gel leg log el go lo

egloopru prologue. *See* **eglopr eloopr**

egloorsy serology. *See* **eglors egoosy eloors elorsy**

eglopr proleg grope loper ogler glop goer gore loge lope lore ogle ogre orle pole pore prog repo role rope ego erg gel leg log lop ope ore peg per pro reg rep roe el er go lo or pe re

egloprs prolegs. *See* **eglops egoprs eloprs eglors eglopr**

eglops gospel glops loges lopes ogles poles slope egos epos gels glop goes legs loge logs lope lops lose ogle opes pegs peso pole pose sego sloe slog slop sole ego els gel leg log lop los ope peg sol sop el go lo os pe so

eglopss gospels. *See* **eglops elopss**

eglopstu gluepots gluepot putlogs tupelos. *See* **eglops eloptu elostu elpstu**

egloptu gluepot. *See* **eloptu gloptu**

eglor ogler goer gore loge lore ogle ogre orle role ego erg gel leg log ore reg roe el er go lo or re

eglorrsw growlers glowers growers growler. *See* **eglors eglorw egorrw elorrs**

eglorrw growler. *See* **eglorw egorrw**

eglors oglers goers gores gorse loges lores loser ogler ogles ogres orles roles egos ergs gels goer goes gore legs loge logs lore lose ogle ogre ores orle regs roes role rose sego sloe slog sole sore ego els erg gel leg log los ore reg res roe sol el er go lo or os re so

eglorsv glovers grovels. *See* **eglorv eglosv egorsv elorsv eglors**

eglorsw glowers. *See* **eglorw glorsw elorsw eglors**

eglorv glover grovel glove grove lover ogler goer gore loge lore love ogle ogre orle over role rove vole ego erg gel leg lev log ore reg rev roe el er go lo or re

eglorw   glower growl lower ogler rowel glow goer gore grew grow loge lore ogle ogre orle role wore ego erg gel leg log low ore owe owl reg roe row woe el er go lo or ow re we

eglos   loges ogles egos gels goes legs loge logs lose ogle sego sloe slog sole ego els gel leg log los sol el go lo os so

eglosss   glosses. *See* **egosss elosss**

eglosv   gloves glove loges loves ogles solve voles egos gels goes legs loge logs lose love ogle sego sloe slog sole vole ego els gel leg lev log los sol el go lo os so

eglosz   glozes gloze loges ogles egos gels goes legs loge logs lose ogle sego sloe slog sole ego els gel leg log los sol el go lo os so

eglouy   eulogy gluey glue loge logy luge ogle ugly yule ego gel gey goy guy leg leu log lug lye you el go lo oy ye

eglov   glove loge love ogle vole ego gel leg lev log el go lo

egloz   gloze loge ogle ego gel leg log el go lo

eglprssu   splurges splurge. *See* **eglrsu egprsu egrssu elprsu**

eglprsu   splurge. *See* **eglrsu elprsu egprsu**

eglrsu   gluers gruels gluer glues gruel grues gules luges lures rules surge urges ergs gels glue grue legs lues luge lugs lure regs rues rugs rule ruse slue slug slur sure urge user els erg gel leg leu lug reg res rue rug sue use el er re us

eglrsuzz   guzzlers guzzler guzzles. *See* **eglrsu**

eglru   gluer gruel glue grue luge lure rule urge erg gel leg leu lug reg rue rug el er re

eglruzz   guzzler. *See* **egluzz eglru**

egls   gels legs els gel leg el

eglsstu   gutless. *See* **egsstu elsstu**

eglstuu   gluteus. *See* **eglsu glstu egstu**

eglsu   glues gules luges gels glue legs lues luge lugs slue slug els gel leg leu lug sue use el us

eglsuzz   guzzles. *See* **egluzz eglsu**

eglu   glue luge gel leg leu lug el

egluy   gluey glue luge ugly yule gel gey guy leg leu lug lye el ye

egluzz   guzzle glue luge gel leg leu lug el

egm   gem em me

egmmorst   grommets grommet. *See* **egorst emorst**

egmmort   grommet. *See* **egort emort**

egmmy   gemmy gem gey gym mem em me my ye

egmnnosw   gownsmen. *See* **egmnos**

egmnnu   gunmen numen geum menu emu gem gnu gum gun men mug nun em en me mu ne nu um

egmno   gnome gone nome omen ego eon gem men mog mon nog one em en go me mo ne no om on

egmnooos   mongoose. *See* **egmnos**

egmnor   monger morgen genro gnome goner germ goer gone gore more morn nome norm ogre omen omer ego eon erg gem men mog mon mor nog nor one ore reg rem roe em en er go me mo ne no om on or re

egmnors   mongers morgens. *See* **egmnos egnors egmnor emnors**

egmnos   gnomes gnome meson nomes omens segno egos engs eons gems gens goes gone mogs mons noes nogs nome nose omen ones sego smog some song ego ens eon gem men mog mon mos nog oms one sen son em en go me mo ne no om on os so

egmnosyz   zymogens zymogen. *See* **egmnos emnosy**

egmnoyz   zymogen. *See* **egmno emnoy**

egmnsssu   smugness. *See* **emsssu**

egmnstu   nutmegs. *See* **egmntu egnst egnsu**

egmntu   nutmeg gent geum menu mute tune emu gem get gnu gum gun gut men met mug net nut ten tug tun em en me mu ne nu um ut

egmorstu   gourmets morgues gourmet. *See* **egmoru egmrsu egmrtu egorst**

egmorsu   morgues. *See* **egorsu egmrsu egmoru emorsu**

egmortu   gourmet. *See* **egmoru egmrtu**

egmoru   morgue grume rogue rouge germ geum goer gore grue grum more ogre omer urge ego emu erg gem gum mog mor mug ore our reg rem roe rue rug rum em er go me mo mu om or re um

egmr   germ erg gem reg rem em er me re

egmrs   germs ergs gems germ regs erg gem reg rem res em er me re

egmrsu   grumes germs geums grues grume serum surge urges emus ergs gems germ geum grue grum gums mugs muse regs rues rugs rums ruse smug sure urge user emu erg gem gum mug mus reg rem res rue rug rum sue sum use em er me mu re um us

egmrtu   tergum grume germ geum grue grum mute term true urge emu erg gem get gum gut met mug reg rem ret rue rug rum rut tug em er me mu re um ut

egmru   grume germ geum grue grum urge emu erg gem gum mug reg rem rue rug rum em er me mu re um

egms   gems gem em me

egmsu   geums emus gems geum gums mugs muse smug emu gem gum mug mus sue sum use em me mu um us

egmu   geum emu gem gum mug em me mu um

egnnoo   nonego gone goon neon none noon ego eon goo nog one en go ne no on

egnnoos   nonegos. *See* **egnnoo gnoos egoos**

egnnooty   ontogeny. *See* **egnnoo**

egnnptu   pungent. *No 6s or 5s*

egnnrsu   gunners. *See* **egnnru egnsu egrsu**

egnnru   gunner grue rune rung urge erg gnu gun nun reg rue rug run urn en er ne nu re

egnnruy   gunnery. *See* **egnnru egnruy**

egnnsttu   tungsten. *See* **egnst egnsu egstu**

egnnstuu   unguents unguent. *See* **gnnsuu**

egnntuu   unguent. *No 6s or 5s*

egno   gone ego eon nog one en go ne no on

egnoorrv   governor. *See* **egnorv egoorv**

egnootux   oxtongue. *See* **egnotu**

egnoprs   sponger. *See* **egnors egoprs enoprs gnoprs egnops**

egnoprss   spongers engross persons sponger sponges. *See* **egnops egnors egoprs egorss**

egnopry   progeny. *See* **egnor egopr enopy**

egnops   sponge opens peons pones segno egos engs eons epos gens goes gone noes nogs nope nose ones open opes pegs pens peon peso pone pons pose sego song ego ens eon nog one ope peg pen sen son sop en go ne no on os pe so

egnopss   sponges. *See* **egnops egoss enoss**

egnor   genro goner goer gone gore ogre ego eon erg nog nor one ore reg roe en er go ne no on or re

egnorrst   stronger. *See* **egnors egorst enorrs enorst**

egnors   goners genro goers goner gores gorse ogres segno snore egos engs eons ergs gens goer goes gone gore noes nogs nose ogre ones ores regs roes rose sego song sore ego ens eon erg nog nor one ore reg res roe sen son en er go ne no on or os re so

egnorss   engross. *See* **egnors egorss enorss**

egnorsst   songster engross tensors. *See* **egnors egorss egorst enorss**

egnorssu   surgeons engross grouses surgeon. *See* **egnors egorss egorsu egrssu**

egnorstu   sturgeon surgeon tongues tonsure. *See* **egnors egnotu egnrtu egorst**

egnorsu   surgeon. *See* **egnors egorsu**

egnorsv   governs. *See* **egnors egnorv egorsv**

egnoruy younger. *See* **egnruy egnor egoru**

egnorv govern genro goner grove goer gone gore ogre oven over rove ego eon erg nog nor one ore reg rev roe en er go ne no on or re

egnos segno egos eons gens goes gone noes nogs nose ones sego song ego ens eon nog one sen son en go ne no on os so

egnostu tongues. *See* **egnotu egnst egnsu**

egnostuy youngest tongues. *See* **egnotu gostuy**

egnosxy oxygens. *See* **egnoxy enosxy**

egnott gotten gent gone note tent tone tong tote ego eon get got net nog not one ten toe tog ton tot en go ne no on to

egnotu tongue gent gone gout note tone tong tune unto ego eon get gnu got gun gut net nog not nut one out ten toe tog ton tug ton un go ne no nu on to ut

egnoxy oxygen exon gone onyx ego eon gey goy nog one yen yon en ex go ne no on ox oy ye

egnrrstu grunters grunter returns. *See* **egnrtu enrrsu enrrtu enrstu**

egnrrtu grunter. *See* **egnrtu enrrtu**

egnrsuy gurneys. *See* **egnruy egnsu egrsy**

egnrsyy synergy. *See* **egrsy**

egnrtu urgent tuner grunt gent grue rent rune rung runt tern true tune turn urge erg get gnu gun gut net nut reg ret rue rug run rut ten tug tun urn en er ne nu re ut

egnrty gentry entry gent grey gyre rent tern erg get gey net reg ret rye ten try yen yet en er ne re ye

egnruy gurney grey grue gyre rune rung urge erg gey gnu gun guy reg rue rug run rye urn yen en er ne nu re ye

egnst gents gens gent gest gets nest nets sent tens ens get net sen set ten en ne

egnsu genus negus gens gnus guns snug sung ens gnu gun sen sue sun use en ne nu us

egnt gent get net ten en ne

ego ego go

egoorrvw overgrow. *See* **egoorv egorrw**

egoorstt grottoes. *See* **egoost egorst eorstt goortt**

egoorsv grooves. *See* **egoorv egorsv**

egoorv groove grove goer gore ogre over rove ego erg goo ore reg rev roe er go or re

egoos goose egos goes goos sego ego goo go os so

egooss gooses gesso goose segos egos goes goos sego ego ess goo go os so

egoosst stooges. *See* **egooss egoost**

egoost stooge goose egos gest gets goes goos sego soot toes togs ego get goo got set sot toe tog too go os so to

egoostu outgoes. *See* **egoost gostu egstu**

egoosy goosey goose gooey egos goes goos goys oyes sego ego gey goo goy soy yes go os oy so ye

egooy gooey ego gey goo goy go oy ye

egopr grope goer gore ogre pore prog repo rope ego erg ope ore peg per pro reg rep roe er go or pe re

egoprr groper grope repro roger goer gore ogre pore prog repo rope ego erg err ope ore peg per pro reg rep roe er go or pe re

egoprrs gropers. *See* **egoprr egoprs eoprrs**

egoprrss progress gropers grosser pressor. *See* **egoprr egoprs egorss eoprrs**

egoprrsu groupers regroups gropers grouper purgers regroup. *See* **egoprr egoprs egorsu egprru**

egoprru grouper regroup. *See* **egoprr egprru**

egoprs gropes goers gores gorse grope ogres pores poser progs prose repos ropes spore egos epos ergs goer goes gore ogre opes ores pegs peso pore pose prog pros repo reps roes rope rose sego sore ego erg ope ore peg per pro reg rep res roe sop er go or os pe re so

egor goer gore ogre ego erg ore reg roe er go or re

egorr roger goer gore ogre ego erg err ore reg roe er go or re

egorrss grosser. *See* **egorss**

egorrstu grouters routers. *See* **egorst egorsu eorrst eorrsu**

egorrsw growers. *See* **egorrw eorrsw**

egorruy roguery. *See* **grruy egorr egoru**

egorrw grower roger rower goer gore grew grow ogre wore ego erg err ore owe reg roe row woe er go or ow re we

egors goers gores gorse ogres egos ergs goer goes gore ogre ores regs roes rose sego sore ego erg ore reg res roe er go or os re so

egorss gorses ogress gesso goers gores gorse gross ogres roses segos sores egos ergs goer goes gore ogre ores regs roes rose sego sore ego erg ess ore reg res roe er go or os re so

egorsss grosses. *See* **egosss egorss**

egorssst grossest grosses. *See* **egorss egorst eorsst eossst**

egorssu grouses. *See* **egorss egorsu eorssu egrssu**

egorst ergots ergot goers gores gorse grots ogres rotes store egos ergs erst gest gets goer goes gore grot ogre ores orts regs rest rets roes rose rote rots sego sore sort toes togs tore tors ego erg get got ore ort reg res ret roe rot set sot toe tog tor er go or os re so to

egorsu grouse rogues rouges rugose goers gores gorse grues ogres rogue rouge rouse surge urges egos ergs goer goes gore grue ogre ores ours regs roes rose rues rugs ruse sego sore sour sure urge user ego erg ore our reg res roe rue rug sou sue use er go or os re so us

egorsv groves goers gores gorse grove ogres roves servo verso egos ergs goer goes gore ogre ores over regs revs roes rose rove sego sore ego erg ore reg res rev roe er go or os re so

egort ergot goer gore grot ogre rote tore ego erg get got ore ort reg ret roe rot toe tog tor er go or re to

egortuw outgrew. *See* **egort gortu eortu**

egoru rogue rouge goer gore grue ogre urge ego erg ore our reg roe rue rug er go or re

egorv grove goer gore ogre over rove ego erg ore reg rev roe er go or re

egos egos goes sego ego go os so

egoss gesso segos egos goes sego ego ess go os so

egosss gessos gesso segos egos goes sego ego ess go os so

egostyz zygotes. *See* **egotyz estyz gosty**

egosuv vogues vogue egos goes sego vugs ego sou sue use vug go os so us

egotyz zygote oyez ego get gey got goy toe tog toy yet go oy to ye

egouv vogue ego vug go

egp peg pe

egprrsu purgers. *See* **egprru egprsu eprrsu**

egprru purger purge purer grue pure purr urge erg err peg per pug reg rep rue rug er pe re up

egprssuu upsurges upsurge pursues. *See* **egprsu egrssu eprssu eprsuu**

egprsu purges grues purge purse sprue super surge urges ergs grue pegs pugs pure regs reps rues rugs ruse spue spur sure urge user erg peg per pug pus reg rep res rue rug sue sup use er pe re up us

egprsuu upsurge. *See* **egprsu eprsuu**

egpru purge grue pure urge erg peg per pug reg rep rue rug er pe re up

egps pegs peg pe

egr erg reg er re

egrrsuy surgery. *See* **errsuy egrsy egrsu**

egrs ergs regs erg reg res er re

egrssu surges grues guess ruses surge urges users ergs grue regs rues rugs ruse sues sure urge user uses erg ess reg res rue rug sue use er re us

egrsttu gutters. *See* **egrttu ersttu**

egrsu grues surge urges ergs grue regs rues rugs ruse sure urge user erg reg res rue rug sue use er re us

egrsy greys gyres ergs grey gyre regs ryes erg gey reg res rye yes er re ye

egrttu gutter utter grue tret true urge erg get gut reg ret rue rug rut tug tut er re ut

egru grue urge erg reg rue rug er re

egrw grew erg reg er re we

egry grey gyre erg gey reg rye er re ye

egssstu gussets. *See* **egsstu**

egsst gests gest gets sets ess get set

egsstu guests gusset gests guess guest gusts suets gest gets gust guts sets sues suet tugs uses ess get gut set sue tug use us ut

egssu guess sues uses ess sue use us

egst gest gets get set

egstu guest gest gets gust guts suet tugs get gut set sue tug use us ut

egsvy gyves gyve gey yes ye

egt get

egvy gyve gey ye

egy gey ye

eh

eh eh he

ehh heh eh he

ehhiiprs heirship. *See* **ehiprs**

ehhiistv thievish. *See* **ehist ehisv eiisv**

ehhiks sheikh hikes sheik hike hies heh hie his she ski eh he hi is sh si

ehhills hellish. *See* **ehlls hills eills**

ehhilmnt helminth. *See* **eilnt eilmn ehilt**

ehhiortt hitherto thither. *See* **ehhirt ehiort ehirtt ehortt**

ehhirssw shrewish whishes wishers. *See* **ehirss ehirsw ehissw**

ehhirt hither their heir hire rite tier tire eth heh her het hie hit ire ret the tie eh er he hi it re ti

ehhirtt thither. *See* **ehhirt ehirtt**

ehhirtw whither. *See* **ehhirt ehirtw**

ehhissw whishes. *See* **ehissw hhisw**

ehhkt kheth khet eth heh het the eh he

ehhnoors shoehorn onshore. *See* **ehnors enoors hnoors**

ehhnpsy hyphens. *See* **ehhnpy ehpsy**

ehhnpy hyphen hype heh hen hep hey pen yen yep eh en he ne pe ye

ehhoossw whooshes wooshes. *See* **hhoosw hoossw**

ehhoostu hothouse. *See* **ehoost**

ehhrsstu thrushes. *See* **ehhrst ehhssu ehrssu**

ehhrst thresh erst hers hest resh rest rets eth heh her het res ret set she the eh er he re sh

ehhsssu shushes. *See* **ehhssu**

ehhssu hushes shush hues hush sues uses ess heh hue huh she sue use eh he sh us

ehi hie eh he hi

ehiiklp hiplike. *See* **eiilp**

ehiikssw whiskies. *See* **ehikss hikssw ehissw**

ehiillr hillier. *See* **eillr**

ehiillst hilliest. *See* **eiills eillst hillst**

ehiilmos homilies. *See* **ehilos eiilms hilmos**

ehiimmss shimmies mimesis. *See* **eimms eimss ehiss**

ehiimnss minishes. *See* **ehimns ehinss eiimns**

ehiimsst smithies theisms. *See* **ehimst ehisst eimsst himsst**

ehiimssw whimsies. *See* **ehissw**

ehiinnos inhesion hinnies. *See* **ehinos iinnos**

ehiinns hinnies. *See* **ehins einns**

ehiinnss shinnies hinnies. *See* **ehinss**

ehiinrs shinier. *See* **ehinrs**

ehiinrst inherits hinters inherit shinier. *See* **ehinrs ehinrt ehirst einrst**

ehiinrt inherit. *See* **ehinrt**

ehiinsst shiniest. *See* **ehinss ehisst einsst iinsst**

ehiinsvx vixenish. *See* **eiinsx einsvx**

ehiipp hippie pipe hep hie hip pep pie pip eh he hi pe pi

ehiipps hippies. *See* **ehiipp eipps**

ehiiprsv viperish privies. *See* **ehiprs ehirsv eiprsv**

ehiiprt pithier. *See* **ehirt eiprt**

ehiipstt pithiest pettish. *See* **ehistt eiipst**

ehiirstt thirties hitters. *See* **ehirst ehirtt ehistt eirstt**

ehiistw withies. *See* **ehistw**

ehijnnos johnnies enjoins. *See* **ehinos eijnno**

ehik hike hie eh he hi

ehikks kishke hikes sheik hike hies hie his she ski eh he hi is sh si

ehikkss kishkes. *See* **ehikks ehikss**

ehiklmny hymnlike. *See* **eilmny**

ehiklnor hornlike. *See* **ehilor ehinor ehknor eiklnr**

ehiklnos sinkhole honkies. *See* **ehilos ehinos eiklns eiknos**

ehiklru hulkiest. *See* **eiklr**

ehiklstu hulkiest. *See* **ehikst ehlstu**

ehikmnst methinks. *See* **ehikst ehimns ehimst eikmst**

ehiknos honkies. *See* **eiknos ehinos**

ehiknrst rethinks thinkers hinters rethink stinker thinker tinkers. *See* **ehikrs ehikst ehinrs ehinrt**

ehiknrt rethink thinker. *See* **ehinrt eiknrt**

ehiknss knishes. *See* **ehikss ehinss eiknss**

ehikrrs shirker. *See* **ehirrs ehikrs**

ehikrrss shirkers shirker shrieks shrikes. *See* **ehikrs ehikss ehirrs ehirss**

ehikrs shriek shrike heirs hikes hires kiers sheik shire shirk heir hers hies hike hire irks kier kris reis resh rise risk sire her hie his ire irk kir res she sir ski eh er he hi is re sh si

ehikrss shrieks shrikes. *See* **ehirrs eikrss ehikss hikrss ehikrs**

ehikrsu huskier. *See* **ehkrsu ehikrs**

ehiks hikes sheik hike hies hie his she ski eh he hi is sh si

ehikss sheiks hikes sheik shies skies hies hike hiss kiss skis ess hie his she sis ski eh he hi is sh si

ehiksstu huskiest huskies. *See* **ehikss ehikst ehisst ehsstu**

ehikssu huskies. *See* **ehikss hkssu eissu**

ehiksswy whiskeys whiskey. *See* **ehikss ehissw hikssw hikswy**

ehikst kithes heist hikes kites kithe sheik tikes hest hies hike hist hits khet kist kite kith kits site sith skit this ties tike eth het hie his hit its kit set she sit ski the tie tsk eh he hi is it sh si ti

ehikswy whiskey. *See* **hikswy ehiks eh-swy**

ehikt kithe hike khet kite kith tike eth het hie hit kit the tie eh he hi it ti

ehilllmo molehill. *See* **ehllo**

ehillmop philomel. *See* **ehlmop**

ehillno hellion. *See* **eillno ehllo**

ehillnos hellions hellion hollies niellos. *See* **ehilos ehinos ehllos eillno**

ehillos hollies. *See* **ehllos ehilos**

ehillrrt thriller. *See* **ehilrt eillrt hillrt**

ehillsvy elvishly. *See* **ehilsv ehllsy eillvy**

ehillty lithely. *See* **ehlty hilly ehilt**

ehilmoor heirloom. *See* **ehilor ehimor eiloor eimoor**

ehilmu helium ileum hilum helm lieu lime mile mule elm emu hem hie him hue hum lei leu lie lum mel mil eh el em he hi li me mi mu um

ehilnop pinhole. *See* **ehlnop eilnop**

ehilnops pinholes epsilon phenols phonies pinhole pinoles plenish. *See* **ehilos ehinos ehlnop ehnops**

ehilnoru unholier. *See* **ehilor ehinor**

ehilnoss holiness insoles isohels lesions lioness. *See* **ehilos ehinos ehinss ehnoss**

ehilnost neoliths entoils eoliths holiest hostile neolith. *See* **ehilos ehilot ehinos ehlost**

ehilnot neolith. *See* **ehilot eilnot**

ehilnotx xenolith neolith. *See* **ehilot eilnot**

ehilnps plenish. *See* **eilnps**

ehiloprs polisher spoiler. *See* **ehilor ehilos ehilrs ehiopr**

ehiloprt heliport hoplite philter. *See* **ehilor ehilot ehilrt ehiopr**

ehilopss polishes isohels hipless. *See* **ehilos ehipss ehlpss eilops**

ehilopst hoplites eoliths holiest hoplite hostile pistole. *See* **ehilos ehilot ehlost eilops**

ehilopt hoplite. *See* **ehilot eilopt**

ehilor holier oiler oriel heir herl hero hire hoer hole lire lore orle riel rile roil role her hie hoe ire lei lie oil ore rho roe eh el er he hi lo li lo oh or re

ehilorss sloshier isohels rissole. *See* **ehilor ehilos ehilrs ehiors**

ehilos holies isohel holes hies hoes hole hose isle leis lies lose oils shoe silo sloe soil sole els hie his hoe lei lie los ohs oil she sol eh el he hi ho is li lo oh os sh si so

ehiloss isohels. *See* **ehilos**

ehilost eoliths holiest hostile. *See* **ehilot ehilos hilost ehlost eilost**

ehilot eolith hotel lithe litho thole toile hilt hole holt loth tile toil eth het hie hit

hoe hot lei let lie lit lot oil the tho tie til toe eh el he hi ho it li lo oh ti to

ehilprst philters hipster philter slither triples. *See* **ehilrs ehilrt ehiprs ehirst**

ehilprt philter. *See* **ehilrt eilprt**

ehilpss hipless. *See* **ehipss ehlpss eilpss**

ehilrs relish heirs herls hires riels riles shire heir herl hers hies hire isle leis lies lire reis resh riel rile rise sire els her hie his ire lei lie res she sir eh el er he hi is li re sh si

ehilrsst slithers hitless listers slither. *See* **ehilrs ehilrt ehirss ehirst**

ehilrssu slushier. *See* **ehilrs ehirss ehlssu ehrssu**

ehilrssv shrivels shivers shrivel shrives silvers slivers. *See* **ehilrs ehilsv ehirss ehirsv**

ehilrst slither. *See* **eilrst ehilrt ehilrs ehirst hilrst**

ehilrstw whistler slither whistle withers writhes. *See* **ehilrs ehilrt ehirst ehirsw**

ehilrsv shrivel. *See* **ehilsv eilrsv ehirsv**

ehilrt lither liter lithe litre their thirl tiler heir herl hilt hire lire riel rile rite tier tile tire eth her het hie hit ire lei let lie lit ret the tie til eh el er he hi it li re ti

ehilsssw wishless swishes. *See* **ehisss ehissw**

ehilsst hitless. *See* **ehisst eilsst**

ehilsstt thistles hitless lithest theists thistle. *See* **ehisst ehistt eilsst eilstt**

ehilsstw whistles hitless whistle witless. *See* **ehisst ehissw ehistw eilsst**

ehilstt lithest thistle. *See* **ehistt hilstt eilstt**

ehilsttw whittles lithest thistle wettish whistle whitest whittle. *See* **ehistt ehistw eilstt hilstt**

ehilstw whistle. *See* **hilstw ehistw**

ehilsv elvish evils hives lives shive veils evil hies hive isle leis lies live shiv veil vies vile vise els hie his lei lev lie she vie eh el he hi is li sh si

ehilt lithe tile hilt eth het hie hit lei let lie lit the tie til eh el he hi it li ti

ehilttw whittle. *See* **ehilt hiltt ehitt**

ehiltwy whitely. *See* **ehitwy ehlty ehilt**

ehilw while wile hew hie lei lie eh el he hi li we

ehilx helix ilex hex hie lei lie eh el ex he hi li xi

ehimmrs shimmer. *See* **eimmrs**

ehimmrss shimmers shimmer simmers. *See* **ehirss eimmrs eimrss**

ehimmrsy shimmery shimmer. *See* **ehmrsy eimmrs eimrsy himmsy**

ehimnopr morphine phonier. *See* **ehimnr ehimor ehinor ehiopr**

ehimnort thermion. *See* **ehimnr ehimor ehimrt ehinor**

ehimnott monteith. *See* **eimntt**

ehimnpst shipment. *See* **ehimns ehimst eimnpt einpst**

ehimnr menhir miner emir heir herm hern hire mien mine mire rein rime hem hen her hie him hin ire men mir nim rem rim eh em en er he hi in me mi ne re

ehimnrs menhirs. *See* **ehimns ehimnr eimnrs ehinrs**

ehimns inmesh miens mines shine hems hens hies hins mesh mien mine mise nims semi shim shin sine ens hem hie him hin his men mis nim sen she sin eh em en he hi in is me mi ne sh si

ehimnsu inhumes. *See* **ehimns ehimnu**

ehimnu inhume menu mien mine emu hem hen hie him hin hue hum men nim eh em en he hi in me mi mu ne nu um

ehimoost smoothie homiest. *See* **ehimst ehoost eimost hmoost**

ehimor homier homer emir heir herm hero hire hoer home mire more omer rime hem her hie him hoe ire mho mir mor ohm ore rem rho rim roe eh em er he hi ho me mi mo oh om or re

ehimors heroism. *See* **ehmors ehimor ehiors eimors**

ehimorst isotherm heriots hermits heroism homiest mithers moister mortise mothers shortie smother thermos. *See* **ehimor ehimrt ehimst ehiors**

ehimorsz rhizomes heroism rhizome. *See* **ehimor ehimrs ehmors eimors**

ehimortu mouthier thorium. *See* **ehimor ehimrt ehimru ehiort**

ehimorz rhizome. *See* **ehimor**

ehimost homiest. *See* **ehimst eimost**

ehimprrs shrimper primers. *See* **ehiprs ehirrs eimprr eimprs**

ehimprsu murphies humpier mushier pushier umpires. *See* **ehimru ehiprs ehmrsu ehprsu**

ehimprsw whimpers whimper whisper. *See* **ehiprs ehirsw eimprs eiprsw**

ehimpru humpier. *See* **ehimru eimpru**

ehimprw whimper. *See* **eimpr eiprw**

ehimpstu humpiest impetus imputes. *See* **ehimst eimptu empstu hmpstu**

ehimpsuu euphuism. *See* **ehmps hmpsu hmsuu**

ehimrst hermits mithers. *See* **ehimrt eimrst ehirst ehimst**

ehimrsu mushier. *See* **ehimru ehmrsu**

ehimrt hermit merit mirth miter mitre remit their therm timer emir emit heir herm hire item mire mite rime rite term them tier time tire trim eth hem her het hie him hit ire met mir rem ret rim the tie eh em er he hi it me mi re ti

ehimru humeri rheum emir heir herm hire mire rime emu hem her hie him hue hum ire mir rem rim rue rum eh em er he hi me mi mu re um

ehimsst theisms. *See* **ehisst eimsst himsst**

ehimsstu mushiest theisms isthmus. *See* **ehimst ehisst ehmssu ehsstu**

ehimst theism emits heist items mites smite smith times emit hems hest hies hist hits item mesh mise mist mite semi shim site sith stem them this ties time eth hem het hie him his hit its met mis set she sit the tie eh em he hi is it me mi sh si ti

ehinnotw nonwhite. *See* **ehintw einnot einotw**

ehinnrst thinners hinters interns thinner tinners. *See* **ehinrs ehinrt ehirst einnrs**

ehinnrt thinner. *See* **ehinrt einnrt**

ehinnsst thinness sennits. *See* **ehinss ehisst einnst einsst**

ehinnssu sunshine. *See* **ehinss**

ehinnstt thinnest. *See* **ehistt ehnstt einnst einntt**

ehinoppr hornpipe phonier. *See* **ehinor ehiopr ehippr ehoppr**

ehinopr phonier. *See* **ehiopr ehinor einopr**

ehinops phonies. *See* **ehinos einops ehnops hinops**

ehinopst phoniest phonies. *See* **ehinos ehnops ehnost einops**

ehinopx phoenix. *See* **ehinpx ehnop einop**

ehinor heroin heron rhino heir hern hero hire hoer hone horn iron rein eon hen her hie hin hoe hon ion ire nor one ore rho roe eh en er he hi ho in ne no oh on or re

ehinorr hornier. *See* **ehinor einorr**

ehinorrt thornier heritor hornier norther. *See* **ehinor ehinrt ehiort ehnort**

ehinors inshore. *See* **ehinor ehnors ehinos ehiors einors**

ehinorst horniest heriots hinters hornets inshore orients shorten shortie stonier thrones. *See* **ehinor ehinos ehinrs ehinrt**

ehinos honies eosin hones hosen noise shine shone eons hens hies hins hoes hone hose ions noes nose nosh ones shin shoe sine ens eon hen hie hin his hoe hon ion ohs one sen she sin son eh en he hi ho in is ne no oh on os sh si so

ehinostu outshine heinous. *See* **ehinos ehnost einstu**

ehinosu heinous. *See* **ehinos ehosu**

ehinprsu punisher pushier uprisen. *See* **ehinrs ehiprs ehprsu einprs**

ehinpssu punishes puisnes supines. *See* **ehinss ehipss ehpssu einpss**

ehinpssx sphinxes. *See* **ehinpx ehinss ehipss einpss**

ehinpx phenix pine nixe hen hep hex hie hin hip nip nix pen pie pin pix eh en ex he hi in ne pe pi xi

ehinrs shiner shrine heirs herns hires reins resin rinse risen serin shine shire siren heir hens hern hers hies hins hire rein reis resh rise shin sine sire ens hen her hie hin his ire res sen she sin sir eh en er he hi in is ne re sh si

ehinrss shiners shrines. *See* **ehirss einrss ehinrs ehinss**

ehinrssu inrushes insures shiners shrines sunrise. *See* **ehinrs ehinss ehirss ehrssu**

ehinrst hinters. *See* **ehinrt einrst ehirst**

ehinrsv shriven. *See* **ehinrs ehirsv**

ehinrsw whiners. *See* **ehinsw ehinrs ehinrw ehirsw**

ehinrt hinter inert inter niter their thine trine heir hent hern hint hire rein rent rite tern then thin tier tine tire eth hen her het hie hin hit ire net nit ret ten the tie tin eh en er he hi in it ne re ti

ehinrtv thriven. *See* **ehinrt einrtv ehirtv**

ehinrw whiner whine heir hern hewn hire rein weir when whir wine wire wren hen her hew hie hin ire new wen win eh en er he hi in ne re we

ehins shine hens hies hins shin sine ens hen hie hin his sen she sin eh en he hi in is ne sh si

ehinss shines shies shine shins sines hens hies hins hiss shin sine sins ens ess hen hie hin his sen she sin sis eh en he hi in is ne sh si

ehinstw whitens. *See* **ehinsw einstw ehintw ehistw**

ehinstz zeniths. *See* **ehintz ehist ehnst**

ehinsw newish whines shewn shine sinew swine whine wines hens hewn hews hies hins news sewn shew shin sine wens when wine wins wise wish ens hen hew hie hin his new sen sew she sin wen win wis eh en he hi in is ne sh si we

ehint thine hent hint then thin tine eth hen het hie hin hit net nit ten the tie tin eh en he hi in it ne ti

ehintw whiten thine twine whine white withe hent hewn hint newt then thew thin tine twin when whet whit wine wite with eth hen het hew hie hin hit net new nit ten the tie tin wen wet win wit eh en he hi in it ne ti we

ehintz zenith thine hent hint then thin tine zein eth hen het hie hin hit net nit ten the tie tin zit eh en he hi in it ne ti

ehinw whine hewn when wine hen hew hie hin new wen win eh en he hi in ne we

ehioppsu eohippus. *See* **ehopps ehopsu hiopps hippsu**

ehiopr ephori ephor hoper heir hero hire hoer hope peri pier pore repo ripe rope hep her hie hip hoe hop ire ope ore per pie poi pro rep rho rip roe eh er he hi ho oh or pe pi re

ehioprst trophies heriots hipster shortie strophe thorpes. *See* **ehiopr ehiors ehiort ehiprs**

ehiorrs horsier. *See* **ehirrs ehiors eiorrs**

ehiorrt heritor. *See* **ehiort ehorrt eiorrt**

ehiorrtw worthier heritor. *See* **ehiort ehirtw ehorrt eirrtw**

ehiors hosier heirs hires hoers horse osier shire shoer shore heir hero hers hies hire hoer hoes hose ores reis resh rhos rise roes rose shoe sire sore sori her hie his hoe ire ohs ore res rho roe she sir eh er he hi ho is oh or os re sh si so

ehiorsst horsiest heriots rosiest shortie sorites sorties stories. *See* **ehiors ehiort ehirss ehirst**

ehiorst heriots shortie. *See* **ehiort ehiors ehorst eiorst ehirst**

ehiorstt theorist heriots hitters shortie. *See* **ehiors ehiort ehirst ehirtt**

ehiorstw worthies heriots shortie showier withers writhes. *See* **ehiors ehiort ehirst ehirsw**

ehiorsw showier. *See* **ehiors ehorsw ehirsw**

ehiorsy hosiery. *See* **ehiors ehorsy**

ehiort heriot other their throe heir hero hire hoer riot rite rote tier tire tiro tore tori trio eth her het hie hit hoe hot ire ore ort ret rho roe rot the tho tie toe tor eh er he hi ho it oh or re ti to

ehiortwz howitzer. *See* **ehiort ehirtw ehirtz**

ehiosstu housesit. *See* **ehisst ehosst ehossu ehsstu**

ehiosstw showiest. *See* **ehisst ehissw ehistw ehosst**

ehippr hipper piper heir hire peri pier pipe prep repp ripe hep her hie hip ire pep per pie pip rep rip eh er he hi pe pi re

ehipprs shipper. *See* **ehippr ehiprs eipprs**

ehipprss shippers shipper sippers. *See* **ehippr ehiprs ehipss ehirss**

ehippst hippest. *See* **eippst ehist**

ehippstw whippets hippest whippet. *See* **ehistw eippst**

ehipptw whippet. *See* **hiptw ehitw**

ehipqsuy physique. *See* **eipqsu**

ehiprs perish heirs hires piers pries shire spire heir hers hies hips hire peri pier pies pish reis reps resh ripe rips rise ship sire hep her hie hip his ire per pie rep res rip she sip sir eh er he hi is pe pi re sh si

ehiprsst hipsters hipster persist priests sprites stripes. *See* **ehiprs ehipss ehirss ehirst**

ehiprssw whispers whisper wishers. *See* **ehiprs ehipss ehirss ehirsw**

ehiprst hipster. *See* **eiprst ehiprs**

ehiprsu pushier. *See* **ehiprs ehprsu eiprsu**

ehiprsw whisper. *See* **ehiprs eiprsw ehirsw**

ehipss pishes shies ships spies hies hips hiss pies pish ship sips ess hep hie hip his pie she sip sis eh he hi is pe pi sh si

ehipsstu pushiest. *See* **ehipss ehisst ehpssu ehsstu**

ehipstt pettish. *See* **ehistt**

ehipstuu euphuist. *See* **eistu ehist epstu**

ehiqsssu squishes hussies. *See* **ehisss eisssu hiqssu**

ehir heir hire her hie ire eh er he hi re

ehirr hirer heir hire err her hie ire eh er he hi re

ehirrs hirers heirs hirer hires riser shire shirr errs heir hers hies hire reis resh rise sire err her hie his ire res she sir eh er he hi is re sh si

ehirrsu hurries rushier. *See* **ehirrs ehrrsu**

ehirs heirs hires shire heir hers hies hire reis resh rise sire her hie his ire res she sir eh er he hi is re sh si

ehirss hisser shires heirs hires rises shies shire sires heir hers hies hire hiss reis resh rise sire sirs ess her hie his ire res she sir sis eh er he hi is re sh si

ehirsss hissers. *See* **ehirss ehisss**

ehirsstu rushiest hirsute. *See* **ehirss ehirst ehisst ehrssu**

ehirssv shivers shrives. *See* **ehirss ehirsv ehissv**

ehirssw wishers. *See* **ehirss ehrssw ehirsw ehissw**

ehirst theirs heirs heist hires rites shire shirt their tiers tires tries erst heir hers hest hies hire hist hits reis resh rest rets rise rite sire site sith stir this tier ties tire eth her het hie his hit ire its res ret set she sir sit the tie eh er he hi is it re sh si ti

ehirstt hitters. *See* **ehirtt eirstt ehirst ehistt hirstt**

ehirstu hirsute. *See* **ehirst eistu hrstu**

ehirstv thrives. *See* **eirstv ehirsv ehirst ehirtv**

ehirstw withers writhes. *See* **ehirst ehirtw ehistw ehirsw eirstw**

ehirstz zithers. *See* **ehirst ehirtz**

ehirsv shiver shrive heirs hires hives shire shive heir hers hies hire hive reis resh revs rise rive shiv sire vies vise her hie his ire res rev she sir vie eh er he hi is re sh si

ehirsvy shivery. *See* **ehirsv**

ehirsw wisher heirs hires shire shrew weirs whirs wires wiser heir hers hews hies hire reis resh rise shew sire weir whir wire wise wish her hew hie his ire res sew she sir wis eh er he hi is re sh si we

ehirt their heir hire rite tier tire eth her het hie hit ire ret the tie eh er he hi it re ti

ehirtt hitter their titer tithe titre trite heir hire rite teth tier tire tret eth her het hit ire ret the tie tit eh er he hi it re ti

ehirtv thrive their rivet heir hire hive rite rive tier tire vert eth her het hie hit ire ret rev the tie vet vie eh er he hi it re ti

ehirtw whiter wither writhe their threw white withe write their rite thew tier tire weir whet whir whit wire wite with writ eth her het hew hie hit ire ret the tie wet wit eh er he hi it re ti we

ehirtz zither their hertz heir hire rite tier tire eth her het hie hit ire ret the tie zit eh er he hi it re ti

ehis hies hie his she eh he hi is sh si

ehiss shies hies hiss ess hie his she sis eh he hi is sh si

ehisss hisses shies hies hiss ess hie his she sis eh he hi is sh si

ehisssu hussies. *See* **ehisss eisssu**

ehisssw swishes. *See* **ehisss ehissw**

ehisst heists thesis heist hests shies sites hest hies hiss hist hits sets site sith sits this ties ess eth het hie his hit its set she sis sit the tie eh he hi is it sh si ti

ehisstt theists. *See* **ehisst ehistt**

ehissv shives hives shies shive shivs vises hies hiss hive shiv vies vise ess hie his she sis vie eh he hi is sh si

ehissw wishes shews shies swish hews hies hiss sews shew wise wish ess hew hie his sew she sis wis eh he hi is sh si we

ehist heist hest hies hist hits site sith this ties eth het hie his hit its set she sit the tie eh he hi is it sh si ti

ehistt theist tithes heist tithe hest hies hist hits site sith stet teth this ties tits eth het hie his hit its set she sit the tie tit eh he hi is it sh si ti

ehisttw wettish whitest. *See* **ehistt**

ehistw whites withes heist thews whets whist white whits wites withe hest hews hies hist hits shew site sith stew thew this ties west wets whet whit wise wish wite with wits eth het hew hie his hit its set sew she sit the tie wet wis wit eh he hi is it sh si ti we

ehisv hives shive hies hive shiv vies vise hie his she vie eh he hi is sh si

ehiswzz whizzes. *See* **hiwzz**

ehitt tithe teth eth het hie hit the tie tit eh he hi it ti

ehitw white withe thew whet whit wite with eth het hew hie hit the tie wet wit eh he hi it ti we

ehitwy whitey thewy white withe withy thew they whet whey whit wite with yeti eth het hew hey hie hit the thy tie wet why wit wye yet yew eh he hi it ti we ye

ehiv hive hie vie eh he hi

ehjors josher hoers horse shoer shore hero hers hoer hoes hose joes josh ores resh rhos roes rose shoe sore her hoe joe ohs ore res rho roe she eh er he ho jo oh or os re sh so

ehjorss joshers. *See* **ehorss ehjors ehjoss**

ehjoss joshes hoses shoes hoes hose jess joes josh joss shoe oss hoe joe ohs she eh he ho jo oh os sh so

ehklnoot knothole. *See* **ehlot eklot eklnt**

ehklpst klephts. *See* **ehklpt ehlps eklps**

ehklpt klepht help kelp kept khet lept pelt elk eth hep het lek let pet the eh el he pe

ehklsw whelks whelk welsh elks hews leks shew skew slew elk els hew lek sew she eh el he sh we

ehklw whelk elk hew lek eh el he we

ehkmoorw homework. *See* **ehkoor**

ehkmorsw meshwork. *See* **ehkors ehmors ehorsw ekmors**

ehknnrsu shrunken hunkers shunner. *See* **ehknru ehkrsu hknrsu**

ehknor honker heron krone hern hero hoer hoke hone honk horn keno kern eon hen her hoe hon ken kor nor oke one ore rho roe eh en er he ho ne no oh on or re

ehknors honkers. *See* **ehnors ehknor ehkors**

ehknrsu hunkers. *See* **ehknru ehkrsu hknrsu**

ehknru hunker hern hunk kern knur neuk nuke rune hen her hue ken rue run urn eh en er he ne nu re

ehko hoke hoe oke eh he ho oh

ehkoor hooker hero hoer hoke hook rook her hoe kor oho oke ooh ore rho roe eh er he ho oh or re

ehkoors hookers. *See* **ehkoor ehkors**

ehkooy hookey hokey hooey hooky hoke hook yoke hey hoe hoy key oho oke ooh eh he ho oh oy ye

ehkors kosher hoers hokes horse shoer shore hero hers hoer hoes hoke hose okes ores resh rhos roes rose shoe soke sore her hoe kor kos ohs oke ore res rho roe she eh er he ho oh or os re sh so

ehkos hokes hoes hoke hose okes shoe soke hoe kos ohs oke she eh he ho oh os sh so

ehkoy hokey hoke yoke hey hoe hoy key oke eh he ho oh oy ye

ehkrssu huskers. *See* **ehkrsu ehrssu**

ehkrsu husker usher hers hues husk resh rues ruse rush rusk sure user her hue res rue she sue use eh er he re sh us

ehkt khet eth het the eh he

ehll hell ell eh el he

ehllnstu nutshell. *See* **ehlstu ellnsu ellstu**

ehllo hello hell hole hoe ell eh el he ho lo oh

ehllooop loophole. *See* **ehooop**

ehllor holler hello hell herl hero hoer hole lore orle role roll ell her hoe ore rho roe eh el er he ho lo oh or re

ehllors hollers. *See* **ehllor ehllos**

ehllos hellos hello hells holes losel shell ells hell hoes hole hose lose sell shoe sloe sole ell els hoe los ohs she sol eh el he ho lo oh os sh so

ehllrsu hullers. *See* **ehllru ehlls ehlrs**

ehllru huller hell herl hull hurl lure rule ell her hue leu rue eh el er he re

ehlls hells shell ells hell sell ell els she eh el he sh

ehllss shells hells sells shell ells hell less sell ell els ess she eh el he sh

ehllsy shelly hells shell yells ells hell lyes lyse sell yell ell els hey lye she shy sly yes eh el he sh ye

ehlm helm elm hem mel eh el em he me

ehlmnost menthols menthol loments. *See* **ehlost ehnost elmnos elmnot**

ehlmnot menthol. *See* **elmnot**

ehlmop phloem helm help hemp hole holm holp home hope lope mole mope poem pole pome elm hem hep hoe hop lop mel mho mop ohm ope eh el em he ho lo me mo oh om pe

ehlmorty motherly helotry. *See* **ehlmoy ehlmty ehmort ehorty**

ehlmoy homely holey homey helm hole holm holy home homy mole moly ylem elm hem hey hoe hoy lye mel mho ohm eh el em he ho lo me mo my oh om oy ye

ehlms helms elms helm hems mels mesh elm els hem mel she eh el em he me sh

ehlmsty methyls. *See* **ehlsty ehlmty**

ehlmty methyl ethyl helm melt myth them they ylem elm eth hem het hey let lye mel met the thy yet eh el em he me my ye

ehlnop holpen phenol phone enol help hole holp hone hope leno lone lope noel nope open peon pole pone eon hen hep hoe hon hop lop one ope pen eh el en he ho lo ne no oh on pe

ehlnops phenols. *See* **ehlnop ehnops**

ehlnorss hornless. *See* **ehnors ehnoss ehorss elnors**

ehlnosty honestly honesty. *See* **ehlost ehlsty ehnost ehnosy**

ehlnpsy phenyls. *See* **ehlnpy ehlps ehpsy**

ehlnpy phenyl phyle help hype yelp hen hep hey lye pen ply yen yep eh el en he ne pe ye

ehlnsssu lushness slushes sunless. *See* **ehlssu elnssu**

ehlntty tenthly. *See* **ehlty ehntt**

ehlo hole hoe eh el he ho lo oh

ehlooprt porthole pothole. *See* **ehoort ehoprt eloopr eloort**

ehloopst potholes pothole. *See* **ehlost ehoost hoopst**

ehloopt pothole. *See* **ehlot hoopt**

ehloopty holotype pothole. *See* **ehoopy**

ehlopp hopple help hole holp hope lope plop pole pope hep hoe hop lop ope pep pop eh el he lo oh pe

ehlopps hopples. *See* **ehlopp elopps ehlpps ehopps**

ehlorsst holsters hostlers holster hostels hostler ostlers sterols. *See* **ehlost ehorss ehorst ehosst**

ehlorst holster hostler. *See* **ehlost elorst ehorst**

ehlorsty hostelry helotry holster hostler shortly. *See* **ehlost ehlsty ehorst ehorsy**

ehlorsw howlers. *See* **ehlorw elorsw ehorsw hlorsw**

ehlorttt throttle. *See* **ehortt**

ehlorty helotry. *See* **ehorty ehlty ehloy**

ehlorw howler lower rowel whole whore whorl herl hero hoer hole howl lore orle role wore her hew hoe how low ore owe owl rho roe row who woe eh el er he ho lo oh or ow re we

ehlos holes hoes hole hose lose shoe sloe sole els hoe los ohs she sol eh el he ho lo oh os sh so

ehlosss sloshes. *See* **elosss ehlos ehoss**

ehlosst hostels. *See* **ehlost ehosst hlosst elosst**

ehlossu housels. *See* **ehlosu ehossu ehlssu**

ehlossv shovels. *See* **ehlosv ehossv elossv**

ehlost hostel hotels tholes ethos holes holts hotel shote sloth stole thole those hest hoes hole holt hose host hots lest lets lose lost loth lots shoe shot sloe slot sole toes tosh els eth het hoe hot let los lot ohs set she sol sot the tho toe eh el he ho lo oh os sh so to

ehlosu housel holes house louse hoes hole hose hues hule lush shoe sloe slue sole soul els hoe hue leu los ohs she sol sou sue use eh el he ho lo oh os sh so us

ehlosv hovels shovel holes hovel loves shove solve voles hoes hole hose hove lose love shoe sloe sole vole els hoe lev los ohs she sol eh el he ho lo oh os sh so

ehlot hotel thole hole holt loth eth het hoe hot let lot the tho toe eh el he ho lo oh to

ehlov hovel hole hove love vole hoe lev eh el he ho lo oh

ehlow whole hole howl hew hoe how low owe owl who woe eh el he ho lo oh ow we

ehloy holey hole holy hey hoe hoy lye eh el he ho lo oh oy ye

ehlp help hep eh el he pe

ehlpps shlepp helps shlep help peps els hep pep she eh el he pe sh

ehlppss shlepps. *See* **ehlpps ehlpss**

ehlps helps shlep help els hep she eh el he pe sh

ehlpss shleps helps shlep help less els ess hep she eh el he pe sh

ehlpsw whelps helps shlep welsh whelp help hews pews phew shew slew spew els hep hew pew sew she eh el he pe sh we

ehlpw whelp help phew hep hew pew eh el he pe we

ehlpy phyle help hype yelp hep hey lye ply yep eh el he pe ye

ehlr herl her eh el er he re

ehlrrsu hurlers. *See* **ehlrru elrrsu ehrrsu**

ehlrru hurler ruler herl hurl lure rule err her hue leu rue eh el er he re

ehlrs herls herl hers resh els her res she eh el er he re sh

ehlrsstu hustlers ruthless hurtles hustler hustles results rustles sleuths ulsters. *See* **ehlrtu ehlssu ehlstu ehrssu**

ehlrstu hurtles hustler. *See* **ehlrtu ehlstu elrstu**

ehlrtu hurtle herl hurl hurt lure lute rule ruth thru true tule eth her het hue hut let leu ret rue rut the eh el er he re ut

ehlsssu slushes. *See* **ehlssu**

ehlssttu shuttles hustles shuttle sleuths. *See* **ehlssu ehlstu ehsstu elsstu**

ehlsstu hustles sleuths. *See* **ehlstu ehlssu ehsstu elsstu**

ehlssu lushes slues slush hues less lues lush slue sues uses els ess hue leu she sue use eh el he sh us

ehlsttu shuttle. *See* **ehlstu**

ehlstu hustle sleuth lutes tules hest hues huts lest lets lues lush lust lute shut slue slut suet thus tule tush els eth het hue hut let leu set she sue the use eh el he sh us ut

ehlsty ethyls shelty ethyl style hest lest lets lyes lyse they els eth het hey let lye set she shy sly sty the thy yes yet eh el he sh ye

ehlsw welsh hews shew slew els hew sew she eh el he sh we

ehlty ethyl they eth het hey let lye the thy yet eh el he ye

ehlxy hexyl hex hey lye eh el ex he ye

ehm hem eh em he me

ehmmooor homeroom. *See* **ehmor**

ehmmrsu hummers. *See* **ehmmru ehmrsu emmrsu**

ehmmru hummer rheum herm emu hem her hue hum mem mum rem rue rum eh em er he me mu re um

ehmnoor hormone. *See* **ehnor ehmor hnoor**

ehmnoors hormones hormone onshore. *See* **ehmors ehnors emnors emoors**

ehmnootw hometown. *See* **emnot hmnot hnoow**

ehmnopsu homespun spumone. *See* **ehnops ehopsu**

ehmnosw showmen. *See* **ehmos ehnos emosw**

ehmnpsty nymphets nymphet. *See* **ehmnsy hmnpsy**

ehmnpty nymphet. *See* **empty ehmny hmnpty**

ehmnsttu hutments hutment. *See* **ehnstt**

ehmnsy hymens hymen hymns meshy hems hens hymn mesh yens ens hem hen hey men sen she shy yen yes eh em en he me my ne sh ye

ehmnttu hutment. *See* **ehntt**

ehmny hymen hymn hem hen hey men yen eh em en he me my ne ye

ehmo home hem hoe mho ohm eh em he ho me mo oh om

ehmoorst smoother mothers shooter smother thermos. *See* **ehmors ehmort ehoort ehoost**

ehmoosw somehow. *See* **ehmos emosw emoos**

ehmor homer herm hero hoer home more omer hem her hoe mho mor ohm ore rem rho roe eh em er he ho me mo oh om or re

ehmors homers herms hoers homer homes horse mores omers shoer shore hems herm hero hers hoer hoes home hose mesh mhos more mors ohms omer ores resh rhos roes rose shoe some sore hem her hoe mho mor mos ohm ohs oms ore rem res rho roe she eh em er he ho me mo oh om or os re sh so

ehmorsst smothers mothers smother thermos. *See* **ehmors ehmort ehorss ehorst**

ehmorst mothers smother thermos. *See* **ehmors emorst ehmort ehorst**

ehmorsty smothery mothers smother thermos. *See* **ehmors ehmort ehmrsy ehorst**

ehmort mother homer metro other therm throe herm hero hoer home more mort mote moth omer rote term them tome tore eth hem her het hoe hot met mho mor mot ohm ore ort rem ret rho roe rot the tho toe tom tor eh em er he ho me mo oh om or re to

ehmortuv vermouth. *See* **ehmort ehortv**

ehmos homes hems hoes home hose mesh mhos ohms shoe some hem hoe mho mos ohm ohs oms she eh em he ho me mo oh om os sh so

ehmoy homey home homy hem hey hoe hoy mho ohm eh em he ho me mo my oh om oy ye

ehmp hemp hem hep eh em he me pe

ehmprstu thumpers stumper sumpter thumper. *See* **ehmrsu ehprsu empstu emrstu**

ehmprtu thumper. *See* **eprtu ehmru ehmrt**

ehmps hemps hemp hems mesh hem hep she eh em he me pe sh

ehmr herm hem her rem eh em er he me re

ehmrs herms hems herm hers mesh resh hem her rem res she eh em er he me re sh

ehmrsu rheums herms rheum serum usher emus hems herm hers hues hums mesh muse mush resh rues rums ruse rush sure user emu hem her hue hum mus rem res rue rum she sue sum use eh em er he me mu re sh um us

ehmrsuu humerus. *See* **ehmrsu hmsuu**

ehmrsy rhymes herms meshy rhyme shyer hems herm hers mesh resh ryes hem her hey rem res rye she shy yes eh em er he me my re sh ye

ehmrt therm herm term them eth hem her het met rem ret the eh em er he me re

ehmrtuyy eurythmy. *See* **ehmru ehmry ehmrt**

ehmru rheum herm emu hem her hue hum rem rue rum eh em er he me mu re um

ehmry rhyme herm hem her hey rem rye eh em er he me my re ye

ehms hems mesh hem she eh em he me sh

ehmsstuy thymuses. *See* **ehmssu ehsstu ehssty emssty**

ehmssu mushes muses emus hems hues hums mesh mess muse mush muss sues sums uses emu ess hem hue hum mus she sue sum use eh em he me mu sh um us

ehmsy meshy hems mesh hem hey she shy yes eh em he me my sh ye

ehmt them eth hem het met the eh em he me

ehmty thyme them they myth eth hem het hey met the thy yet eh em he me my ye

ehn hen eh en he ne

ehnnorrt northern norther. *See* **ehnort ehorrt**

ehnnrssu shunners shunner. *See* **ehrssu enrssu**

ehnnrsu shunner. *See* **ehnrs enrsu ehrsu**

ehno hone eon hen hoe hon one eh en he ho ne no oh on

ehnoorr honorer. *See* **ehnor hnoor**

ehnoorrs honorers honorer onshore. *See* **ehnors enoors enorrs hnoors**

ehnoors onshore. *See* **ehnors hnoors enoors**

ehnoossw snowshoe wooshes. *See* **ehnoss enooss hoossw noossw**

ehnoostu outshone. *See* **ehnost ehoost**

ehnop phone hone hope nope open peon pone eon hen hep hoe hon hop one ope pen eh en he ho ne no oh on pe

ehnoprsy hyperons hyperon. *See* **ehnops ehnopy ehnors ehnosy**

ehnopry hyperon. *See* **ehnopy ehopr ehnry**

ehnops phones hones hopes hosen opens peons phone pones shone eons epos hens hoes hone hope hops hose noes nope nose nosh ones open opes pens peon peso pone pons pose posh shoe shop soph ens eon hen hep hoe hon hop ohs one ope pen sen she son sop eh en he ho ne no oh on os pe sh so

ehnopsss poshness. *See* **ehnops ehnoss eopsss**

ehnopuy euphony. *See* **ehnopy ehopu**

ehnopy phoney honey peony phone phony hone hope hype hypo nope open peon pone pony eon hen hep hey hoe hon hop hoy one ope pen yen yep yon eh en he ho ne no oh on oy pe ye ehnor   heron hern hero hoer hone horn eon hen her hoe hon nor one ore rho roe eh en er he ho ne no oh on or re

ehnorrst   northers hornets norther rhetors shorten thrones. *See* **ehnors ehnort ehnost ehorrt**

ehnorrt   norther. *See* **ehnort ehorrt**

ehnors   herons herns heron hoers hones horns horse hosen shoer shone shore shorn snore eons hens hern hero hers hoer hoes hone horn hose noes nose nosh ones ores resh rhos roes rose shoe sore ens eon hen her hoe hon nor ohs one ore res rho roe sen she son eh en er he ho ne no oh on or os re sh so

ehnorsst   shortens hornets hotness shorten tensors thrones. *See* **ehnors ehnort ehnoss ehnost**

ehnorssu   onrushes. *See* **ehnors ehnoss ehorss ehossu**

ehnorst   hornets shorten thrones. *See* **ehnors ehnost ehnort hnorst enorst**

ehnorstu   southern hornets hunters shorten shouter souther thrones tonsure. *See* **ehnors ehnort ehnost ehnrtu**

ehnort   hornet throne heron north noter other tenor thorn throe toner hent hern hero hoer hone horn note rent rote tern then tone tore torn eon eth hen her het hoe hon hot net nor not one ore ort ret rho roe rot ten the tho toe ton tor eh en er he ho ne no oh on or re to

ehnos   hones hosen shone eons hens hoes hone hose noes nose nosh ones shoe ens eon hen hoe hon ohs one sen she son eh en he ho ne no oh on os sh so

ehnoss   noshes hones hosen hoses noses shoes shone eons hens hoes hone hose noes nose nosh ones shoe sons ens eon ess hen hoe hon ohs one sen she son eh en he ho ne no oh on os sh so

ehnosst   hotness. *See* **ehnost ehnoss enosst ehosst**

ehnost   honest ethos hents hones hosen notes onset shone shote steno stone those tones eons hens hent hest hoes hone hose host hots nest nets noes nose nosh note ones sent shoe shot snot tens then toes tone tons tosh ens eon eth hen het hoe hon hot net not ohs one sen set she son sot ten the tho toe ton eh en he ho ne no oh on os sh so to

ehnosty   honesty. *See* **ehnost ehnosy**

ehnosy   honeys hones honey hosen hyson nosey shone eons hens hoes hone hose hoys noes nose nosh nosy ones oyes shoe yens ens eon hen hey hoe hon hoy ohs one sen she shy son soy yen yes yon eh en he ho ne no oh on os oy sh so ye

ehnoy   honey hone eon hen hey hoe hon hoy one yen yon eh en he ho ne no oh on oy ye

ehnr   hern hen her eh en er he ne re

ehnrs   herns hens hern hers resh ens hen her res sen she eh en er he ne re sh

ehnrsstu   huntress hunters. *See* **ehnrtu ehrssu ehsstu enrsst**

ehnrstu   hunters. *See* **ehnrtu enrstu**

ehnrtu   hunter tuner hent hern hunt hurt rent rune runt ruth tern then thru true tune turn eth hen her het hue hut net nut ret rue run rut ten the tun urn eh en er he ne nu re ut

ehnry   henry hern hen her hey rye yen eh en er he ne re ye

ehns   hens ens hen sen she eh en he ne sh

ehnsssy   shyness. *No 6s or 5s*

ehnst   hents hens hent hest nest nets sent tens then ens eth hen het net sen set she ten the eh en he ne sh

ehnstt   tenths hents tenth tents hens hent hest nest nets sent stet tens tent test teth then ens eth hen het net sen set she ten the eh en he ne sh

ehnsw   shewn hens hewn hews news sewn shew wens when ens hen hew new sen sew she wen eh en he ne sh we

ehnt   hent then eth hen het net ten the eh en he ne

ehntt   tenth hent tent teth then eth hen het net ten the eh en he ne

ehnw   hewn when hen hew new wen eh en he ne we

eho   hoe eh he ho oh

ehooop   hoopoe hoop hope pooh hep hoe hop oho ooh ope eh he ho oh pe

ehooops   hoopoes. *See* **ehooop hoops ehops**

ehooprty   orthoepy. *See* **ehoopy ehoort ehoprt ehorty**

ehoopstu   housetop. *See* **ehoost ehopsu hoopst hopstu**

ehooptyz   zoophyte. *See* **ehoopy**

ehoopy   phooey hooey hoop hope hype hypo pooh hep hey hoe hop hoy oho ooh ope yep eh he ho oh oy pe ye

ehoorsst   shooters shooter soothes. *See* **ehoort ehoost ehorss ehorst**

ehoorst   shooter. *See* **ehoort ehorst ehoost**

ehoorstv   overshot shooter. *See* **ehoort ehoost ehoosv ehorst**

ehoort   hooter other thoro throe hero hoer hoot root rote roto tore eth her het hoe hot oho ooh ore ort ret rho roe rot tho toe too tor eh er he ho oh or re to

ehoosssw   swooshes wooshes. *See* **hoossw**

ehoosst   soothes. *See* **hoosst ehosst**

ehoossw   wooshes. *See* **hoossw ehoss ehssw**

ehoost   soothe ethos hoots shoot shote sooth those hest hoes hoot hose host hots oohs shoe shoo shot soot toes tosh eth het hoe hot oho ohs ooh set she sot the tho toe too eh he ho oh os sh so to

ehoostuu   outhouse. *See* **ehoost**

ehoosv   hooves shove hoes hose hove oohs shoe shoo hoe oho ohs ooh she eh he ho oh os sh so

ehooy   hooey hey hoe hoy oho ooh eh he ho oh oy ye

ehop   hope hep hoe hop ope eh he ho oh pe

ehoppr   hopper ephor hoper hero hoer hope pope pore prep prop repo repp rope hep her hoe hop ope ore pep per pop pro rep rho roe eh er he ho oh or pe re

ehopprs   hoppers shopper. *See* **ehoprs ehoppr ehopps**

ehopprss   shoppers hoppers oppress shopper shoppes. *See* **ehoppr ehopps ehoprs ehorss**

ehopprst   prophets hoppers prophet shopper stopper strophe thorpes toppers. *See* **ehoppr ehopps ehoprs ehoprt**

ehopprsw   whoppers hoppers shopper whopper. *See* **ehoppr ehopps ehoprs ehorsw**

ehopprsy   prophesy hoppers shopper. *See* **ehoppr ehopps ehoprs ehorsy**

ehopprt   prophet. *See* **ehoppr ehoprt eopprt**

ehopprw   whopper. *See* **ehoppr eoprw ehorw**

ehopps   shoppe hopes popes epos hoes hope hops hose opes peps peso pope pops pose posh shoe shop soph hep hoe hop ohs ope pep pop she sop eh he ho oh os pe sh so

ehoppss   shoppes. *See* **ehopps ehoss eopss**

ehopr   ephor hoper hero hoer hope pore repo rope hep her hoe hop ope ore per pro rep rho roe eh er he ho oh or pe re

ehoprrsy   orphreys orphrey. *See* **ehoprs ehorsy ehprsy ehrrsy**

ehoprry   orphrey. *See* **eoprry ehopr ehpry**

ehoprs   ephors hopers ephor hoers hoper hopes horse pores poser prose repos ropes shoer shore spore epos hero hers hoer hoes hope hops hose opes ores peso pore pose posh pros repo reps resh rhos roes rope rose shoe shop soph sore hep her hoe hop ohs ope ore per pro rep res rho roe she sop eh er he ho oh or os pe re sh so

ehoprsst strophes posters prestos strophe thorpes. *See* **ehoprs ehoprt ehorss ehorst**

ehoprst strophe thorpes. *See* **ehoprs ehorst eoprst ehoprt hoprst**

ehoprsuv pushover. *See* **ehoprs ehopsu ehorsv ehprsu**

ehoprt pother thorpe ephor hoper other repot thorp throe toper trope hero hoer hope pert phot poet pore port repo rope rote tope tore eth hep her het hoe hop hot ope ore ort per pet pot pro rep ret rho roe rot the tho toe top tor eh er he ho oh or pe re to

ehops hopes epos hoes hope hops hose opes peso pose posh shoe shop soph hep hoe hop ohs ope she sop eh he he oh os pe sh so

ehopsu ouphes hopes house ouphe epos hoes hope hops hose hues opes opus peso pose posh push shoe shop soph soup spue hep hoe hop hue hup ohs ope pus she sop sou sue sup use eh he ho oh os pe sh so up us

ehopu ouphe hope hope hoe hop hue hup ope eh he ho oh pe up

ehor hero hoer her hoe ore rho roe eh er he ho oh or re

ehorrst rhetors. *See* **ehorst eorrst ehorrt**

ehorrt rhetor other retro throe hero hoer rote tore torr err eth her het hoe hot ore ort ret rho roe rot the tho toe tor eh er he ho oh or re to

ehors hoers horse shoer shore hero hers hoer hoes hose ores resh rhos roes rose shoe sore her hoe ohs ore res rho roe she eh er he ho oh or os re sh so

ehorss horses shoers shores hoers horse hoses roses shoer shoes shore sores hero hers hoer hoes hose ores resh rhos roes rose shoe sore ess her hoe ohs ore res rho roe she eh er he ho oh or os re sh so

ehorsstu shouters southers oestrus ousters shouter sourest souther. *See* **ehorss ehorst ehosst ehossu**

ehorssv shovers. *See* **ehorss ehorsv eorssv ehossv**

ehorssw showers. *See* **ehorss eorssw ehorsw ehrssw**

ehorst others throes ethos hoers horse horst other rotes shoer shore short shote store those throe erst hero hers hest hoer hoes hose host hots ores orts resh rest rets rhos roes rose rote rots shoe shot sore sort toes tore tors tosh eth her het hoe hot ohs ore ort res ret rho roe rot set she sot the tho tor eh er he ho oh or os re sh so to

ehorstu shouter souther. *See* **ehorst eorstu**

ehorstx exhorts. *See* **ehortx ehorst eorstx**

ehorsv hovers shover shrove hoers horse hover roves servo shoer shore shove verso hero hers hoer hoes hose hove ores over resh revs rhos roes rose rove shoe sore her hoe ohs ore res rev rho roe she eh er he ho oh or os re sh so

ehorsw shower whores hoers horse serow shoer shore shrew sower swore whore whose worse hero hers hews hoer hoes hose ores owes resh rhos roes rose rows shew shoe show sore woes wore her hew hoe how ohs ore owe res rho roe row sew she sow who woe eh er he ho oh or os ow re sh so we

ehorswy showery. *See* **ehorsy ehorsw**

ehorsy horsey hoers horse horsy shoer shore shyer yores hero hers hoer hoes hose hoys ores oyes resh rhos roes rose rosy ryes shoe sore yore her hey hoe hoy ohs ore res rho roe rye she shy soy yes eh er he ho oh or os oy re sh so ye

ehort other throe hero hoer rote tore eth her het hoe hot ore ort ret rho roe rot the tho toe tor eh er he ho oh or re to

ehortt hotter other otter throe torte toter troth hero hoer rote teth tore tort tote tret trot eth her het hoe hot ore ort ret rho roe rot the tho toe tor tot eh er he ho oh or re to

ehortv throve hover other overt throe trove voter hero hoer hove over rote rove tore vert veto vote eth her het hoe hot ore ort ret rev rho roe rot the tho toe tor vet eh er he ho oh or re to

ehortx exhort other throe hero hoer rote tore eth her het hex hoe hot ore ort ret rex rho roe rot the tho toe tor eh er ex he ho oh or ox re to

ehorty theory other throe hero hoer rote ryot they tore troy tyro yore eth her het hey hoe hot hoy ore ort ret rho roe rot rye the tho thy toe tor toy try yet eh er he ho oh or oy re to ye

ehorv hover hero hoer hove over rove her hoe ore rev rho roe eh er he ho oh or re

ehorw whore hero hoer wore her hew hoe how ore owe rho roe row who woe eh er he ho oh or ow re we

ehos hoes hose shoe hoe ohs she eh he ho oh os sh so

ehoss hoses shoes hoes hose shoe ess hoe ohs she eh ho oh os sh so

ehossst hostess. *See* **ehosst eossst**

ehosst shotes ethos hests hoses hosts shoes shote shots those hest hoes hose host hots sets shoe shot sots toes tosh toss ess eth het hoe hot ohs set she sot the tho toe eh he ho oh os sh so to

ehossu houses hoses house shoes souse hoes hose hues shoe sous sues uses ess hoe hue ohs she sou sue use eh he ho oh os sh so us

ehossv shoves hoses shoes shove hoes hose hove shoe ess hoe ohs she eh he ho oh os sh so

ehost ethos shote those hest hoes hose host hots shoe shot toes tosh eth het hoe hot ohs set she sot the tho toe eh he ho oh os sh so to

ehosttt hottest. *See* **ehost eostt**

ehosu house hoes hose hues shoe hoe hue ohs she sou sue use eh he ho oh os sh so us

ehosv shove hoes hose hove shoe hoe ohs she eh he ho oh os sh so

ehosw whose hews hoes hose owes shew shoe show woes hew hoe how ohs owe sew she sow who woe eh he ho oh os ow sh so we

ehov hove hoe eh he ho oh

ehp hep eh he pe

ehprssu pushers. *See* **eprssu ehprsu ehpssu ehrssu**

ehprsu pusher purse sprue super usher hers hues pure push reps resh rues ruse rush spue spur sure user hep her hue hup per pus rep res rue she sue sup use eh er he pe re sh up us

ehprsy sphery hyper hypes preys pyres shyer espy hers hype prey pyre reps resh ryes spry hep her hey per pry rep res rye she shy spy yep yes eh er he pe re sh ye

ehprsyz zephyrs. *See* **ehprsy ehpryz**

ehpry hyper hype prey pyre hep her hey per pry rep rye yep eh er he pe re ye

ehpryz zephyr hyper hype prey pyre hep her hey per pry rep rye yep eh er he pe re ye

ehpssu pushes spues hues push puss spue sues sups uses ess hep hue hup pus she sue sup use eh he pe sh up us

ehpsy hypes hype espy hep hey she shy spy yep yes eh he pe sh ye

ehpw phew hep hew pew eh he pe we

ehpy hype hep hey yep eh he pe ye

ehr her eh er he re

ehrrssu rushers. *See* **ehrssu ehrrsu**

ehrrsu rusher usher surer errs hers hues resh rues ruse rush sure user err her hue res rue she sue use eh er he re sh us

ehrrsy sherry shyer errs hers resh ryes err her hey res rye she shy yes eh er he re sh ye

ehrrwy wherry whey err her hew hey rye why wye yew eh er he re we ye

ehrs hers resh her res she eh er he re sh

ehrsssty shysters shyster. *See* **ehssty erssst**

ehrssttu shutters shutter thrusts. *See* **ehrssu ehsstu ersstu ersttu**

ehrssty shyster. *See* **ehssty ersst ehrsy**

ehrssu rhesus rushes ushers ruses users usher hers hues resh rues ruse rush sues sure user uses ess her hue res rue she sue use eh er he re sh us

ehrssw shrews shrew shews hers hews resh sews shew ess her hew res sew she eh er he re sh we

ehrsttu shutter. *See* **hrsttu ersttu**

ehrsu usher hers hues resh rues ruse rush sure user her hue res rue she sue use eh er he re sh us

ehrsw shrew hers hews resh shew her hew res sew she eh er he re sh we

ehrsy shyer hers resh ryes her hey res rye she shy yes eh er he re sh ye

ehrtw threw thew whet eth her het hew ret the wet eh er he re we

ehrtz hertz eth her het ret the eh er he re

ehs she eh he sh

ehsst hests hest sets ess eth het set she the eh he sh

ehsstu tushes hests shuts suets hest hues huts sets shut sues suet thus tush uses ess eth het hue hut set she sue the use eh he sh us ut

ehssty shyest hests hest sets they ess eth het hey set she shy sty the thy yes yet eh he sh ye

ehssw shews hews sews shew ess hew sew she eh he sh we

ehst hest eth het set she the eh he sh

ehstw thews whets hest hews shew stew thew west wets whet eth het hew set sew she the wet eh he sh we

ehsu hues hue she sue use eh he sh us

ehsw hews shew hew sew she eh he sh we

ehswy wheys hews shew whey wyes yews hew hey sew she shy why wye yes yew eh he sh we ye

eht eth het the eh he

ehtt teth eth het the eh he

ehtw thew whet eth het hew the wet eh he we

ehtwy thewy thew they whet whey eth het hew hey the thy wet why wye yet yew eh he we ye

ehty they eth het hey the thy yet eh he ye

ehu hue eh he

ehw hew eh he we

ehww whew hew eh he we

ehwy whey hew hey why wye yew eh he we ye

ehx hex eh ex he

ehy hey eh he ye

eiiilppr liripipe. *See* **eiippr eilppr**

eiiilst ileitis. *See* **eilst**

eiiimmnz minimize. *See* **eiimn iimmn eimnz**

eiijmms jimmies. *See* **eimms**

eiijnrsu injuries injures. *See* **eijnru eijrsu einrsu**

eiikknr kinkier. *See* **eiiknr**

eiikknst kinkiest inkiest. *See* **einst ikkns eikst**

eiikll killie like kill elk ell ilk ill lei lek lie el li

eiikllmn limekiln milline. *See* **eiikll eiilln**

eiiklls killies. *See* **eiikll eiills**

eiiklmr milkier. *See* **eiilmr eiklmr**

eiiklmst milkiest elitism limiest. *See* **eiilms eikmst iiklms iilmst**

eiiklnor ironlike. *See* **eiiknr eiilnr eiilor eiklnr**

eiiklrs silkier. *See* **eikrs eiklr eikls**

eiiklsst silkiest. *See* **eilsst**

eiikmprs skimpier. *See* **eikmrs eikprs eimprs**

eiiknnrs skinnier skinner. *See* **eiiknr eiknrs einnrs**

eiiknnsw wineskin. *See* **iiknn iiksw einns**

eiiknnt kinetin. *See* **iiknn**

eiiknp pinkie kepi kine pike pine pink ink ken kin kip nip pen pie pin en in ne pe pi

eiiknps pinkies. *See* **eiiknp eikps einps**

eiiknr inkier inker kern kier kine rein rink ink ire irk ken kin kir en er in ne re

eiiknst inkiest. *See* **einst eikst iknst**

eiikqrru quirkier. *See* **eiqru ikqru**

eiikrrs riskier. *See* **eikrs eirrs ikrrs**

eiikrsst riskiest strikes. *See* **eiirss eikrss eikrst eirsst**

eiikssvv skivvies. *See* **eikssv**

eiikstt kitties. *See* **eikst iistt**

eiillmm millime. *No 6s or 5s*

eiillmmr millirem millime. *See* **eiilmr eillmr**

eiillmms millimes millime. *See* **eiills eiilms**

eiillmn milline. *See* **eiilln eiimn eilmn**

eiillmnr milliner milline. *See* **eiilln eiilmr eiilnr eillmr**

eiillmns millines milline. *See* **eiilln eiills eiilms eiimns**

eiillmnu illumine milline. *See* **eiilln eiilmu eillmu**

eiilln nielli lien line nill ell ill lei lie nil el en in li ne

eiillnsv villeins villein. *See* **eiilln eiills eillnsv**

eiillnv villein. *See* **eiilln eilnv**

eiillpss ellipsis sillies lipless. *See* **eiills eillss eilpss ellpss**

eiillrs sillier. *See* **eiills eillrs**

eiills lilies lisle ells isle leis lies sell sill ell els ill lei lie el is li si

eiillss sillies. *See* **eiills eillss**

eiillsst silliest sillies. *See* **eiills eillss eillst eilsst**

eiillsuv illusive. *See* **eiills**

eiillsw willies. *See* **eiills eilsw ellsw**

eiilmmot immotile. *See* **eiilot eilmot**

eiilmnnt liniment. *See* **eilnnt eimnnt**

eiilmopt impolite. *See* **eiilot eilmot eilmpt eilopt**

eiilmppr pimplier imperil. *See* **eiilmr eiippr eilmpp eilmpr**

eiilmpr imperil. *See* **eiilmr eilmpr**

eiilmprs imperils imperil implies limpers rimples simpler slimier. *See* **eiilmr eiilms eilmpr eilmps**

eiilmps implies. *See* **eilmps eiilms**

eiilmr limier miler emir lime lire merl mile mire riel rile rime elm ire lei lie mel mil mir rem rim el em er li me mi re

eiilmrs slimier. *See* **eiilmr eilmrs eiilms**

eiilmrt limiter. *See* **eiilmr iilmt eilrt**

eiilms simile limes miles slime smile elms isle leis lies lime mels mile mils mise semi slim elm els lei lie mel mil mis el em is li me mi si

eiilmss missile similes. *See* **eiilms eilmss**

eiilmsss missiles missies missile similes. *See* **eiilms eilmss**

eiilmsst slimiest elitism limiest missile similes. *See* **eiilms eilmss eilsst eimsst**

eiilmst elitism limiest. *See* **eiilms iilmst**

eiilmsty myelitis elitism limiest. *See* **eiilms eilmsy eilmty eimsty**

eiilmsu milieus. *See* **eiilms eiilmu**

eiilmu milieu ileum ilium lieu lime mile mule elm emu lei leu lie lum mel mil el em li me mi mu um

eiilnos elision. *See* **eilnos**

eiilnoss elisions oiliness elision insoles lesions lioness. *See* **eilnos einoss elnoss**

eiilnosz lionizes elision ionizes lionize. *See* **eiinoz eiinsz eilnos**

eiilnoz lionize. *See* **eiinoz eilno**

eiilnqtu quintile inutile. *See* **einqtu**

eiilnr inlier linier liner lien line lire rein riel rile ire lei lie nil el en er in li ne re

eiilnrt lintier. *See* **eiilnr**

eiilnssw wiliness. *See* **einssw**

eiilnst liniest. *See* **eilnst iilnst**

eiilnstt lintiest liniest elitist. *See* **eilnst eilstt einstt iilnst**

eiilnsty senility liniest. *See* **eilnst eilnsy eilnty iilnst**

eiilntu inutile. *See* **eilnt eintu ilntu**

eiilopst polities oiliest pistole. *See* **eiilot eiipst eilops eilopt**

eiilor oilier oiler oriel lire lore orle riel rile roil role ire lei lie oil ore roe el er li lo or re

eiilost oiliest. *See* **eiilot eilost**

eiilot iolite toile tile toil lei let lie lit lot oil tie til toe el it li lo ti to

eiilp pilei pile lei lie lip pie el li pe pi

eiilqssu siliques silique. *See* **eilsu eilss eissu**

eiilqsu silique. *See* **eilsu**

eiilrst siltier. *See* **eilrst**

eiilrsx elixirs. *See* **eiilrx eilsx eilrs**

eiilrtuz utilizer utilize. *See* **eilrt eirtu eiltu**

eiilrv virile liver livre viler evil lire live riel rile rive veil vile ire lei lev lie rev vie el er li re

eiilrw wilier lire riel rile weir wile wire ire lei lie el er li re we

eiilrx elixir ilex lire riel rile ire lei lie rex el er ex li re xi

eiilsstt elitists siltiest elitist. *See* **eilsst eilstt**

eiilstt elitist. *See* **eilstt iistt**

eiilstuz utilizes utilize. *See* **eistu eilsu eilst**

eiilstw wiliest. *See* **eilst eilsw elstw**

eiiltuz utilize. *See* **eiltu**

eiimmnnt imminent. *See* **eimnnt**

eiimmnnuz immunize. *See* **eimmnu iimmnu**

eiimmpru imperium premium. *See* **eimmru eimpru**

eiimmss mimesis. *See* **eimms eimss**

eiimmsx immixes. *See* **iimmx eimms eimsx**

eiimn imine mien mine men nim em en in me mi ne

eiimnoss emission meiosis mission. *See* **eiimns eimnos eimoss einoss**

eiimnrst minister interim minster mintier mistier. *See* **eiimns eimnrs eimrst einrst**

eiimnrsv minivers miniver. *See* **eiimns eimnrs eimnrv eimrsv**

eiimnrt interim mintier. *See* **eiimn einrt eimrt**

eiimnrtx intermix interim mintier. *See* **eiimn einrt eimrt**

eiimnrv miniver. *See* **eimnrv eiimn**

eiimns imines imine miens mines mien mine mise nims nisi semi sine ens men mis nim sen sin em en in is me mi ne si

eiimnstt mintiest mittens smitten. *See* **eiimns eimntt einstt**

eiimnstu mutinies minuets minutes unities. *See* **eiimns eimntu einstu**

eiimnty nimiety. *See* **eimnty eiimn**

eiimoptz optimize. *See* **eimpt emopt**

eiimoss meiosis. *See* **eimoss iimoss**

eiimpty impiety. *See* **empty eipty eimpt**

eiimqstu quietism mesquit. *See* **eiqstu**

eiimrst mistier. *See* **eimrst**

eiimsss missies. *See* **eimsss**

eiimsssv missives missies missive. *See* **eimsss**

eiimsstt mistiest. *See* **eimsst**

eiimssv missive. *See* **eiisv eimss eissv**

eiinnnps ninepins ninnies. *See* **einnps**

eiinnns ninnies. *See* **einns**

eiinnosv envision venison. *See* **einnsv iinnos**

eiinnouz unionize. *See* **eiinoz**

eiinnqsu quinines quinine. *See* **einqsu**

eiinnqu quinine. *See* **einnu**

eiinnrt tinnier. *See* **einnrt**

eiinnstt tinniest. *See* **einnst einntt einstt**

eiinoprt pointier pointer protein. *See* **eiinpr eiinpt einopr einort**

eiinoptt petition. *See* **eiinpt eioptt enoptt**

eiinorrt interior. *See* **einorr einort eiorrt**

eiinors ironies noisier. *See* **einors**

eiinorsv revision ironies ivories noisier version. *See* **einors eiorsv iinosv**

eiinorsz ionizers ionizer ionizes ironies noisier. *See* **eiinoz eiinsz einors eiorsz**

eiinorz ionizer. *See* **eiinoz**

eiinosst noisiest nosiest. *See* **einoss einsst enosst iinsst**

eiinosz ionizes. *See* **eiinoz eiinsz**

eiinoz ionize zein zone eon ion one en in ne no on

eiinppr nippier. *See* **einppr eiinpr eiippr**

eiinppst nippiest piniest pipiest snippet tiepins. *See* **eiinpt eiipst einpps eipst**

eiinpr pinier ripen peri pier pine pirn rein ripe ire nip pen per pie pin rep rip en er in ne pe pi re

eiinprs inspire spinier. *See* **eiinpr einprs**

eiinprss inspires inspire snipers spinier. *See* **eiinpr eiirss einprs einpss**

eiinprst pristine inspire piniest spinier tiepins tipsier. *See* **eiinpr eiinpt eiipst einprs**

eiinpsst spiniest insteps piniest spinets tiepins. *See* **eiinpt eiipst einpss einpst**

eiinpst piniest tiepins. *See* **einpst eiipst eiinpt**

eiinpt tiepin inept pent pine pint tine tipi net nip nit pen pet pie pin pit ten tie tin tip en in it ne pe pi ti

eiinptuv punitive. *See* **eiinpt eiintv**

eiinqrru inquirer inquire. *See* **einru enqru eiqru**

eiinqrsu inquires inquire. *See* **einqsu einrsu eiqrsu enqrsu**

eiinqru inquire. *See* **einru enqru eiqru**

eiinqssu quinsies sequins. *See* **einqsu**

eiinqtuy inequity. *See* **einqtu eiqtuy**

eiinrrtw wintrier. *See* **eiinrw eiirrw einrtw**

eiinrsst sinister inserts sinters. *See* **eiirss einrss einrst einsst**

eiinrssw wiriness. *See* **eiinrw eiirss einrss einssw**

eiinrstt nitrites nitrite. *See* **einrst einrtt einstt eirstt**

eiinrstu neuritis unities triunes. *See* **einrst einrsu einrtu einstu**

eiinrstv vitrines inverts invites revisit striven vitrine. *See* **eiintv einrst einrtv einstv**

eiinrtt nitrite. *See* **einrtt**

eiinrtv vitrine. *See* **eiintv einrtv**

eiinrw winier rein weir wine wire wren ire new wen win en er in ne re we

eiinstu unities. *See* **einstu**

eiinstuz unitizes unities unitize. *See* **eiinsz einstu**

eiinstv invites. *See* **eiintv einstv**

eiinstw winiest. *See* **einstw**

eiinsx nixies nixie nixes nisi nixe sine ens nix sen sex sin six en ex in is ne si xi

eiinsz seizin nisi sine size zein ens sen sin en in is ne si

eiintuz unitize. *See* **eintu**

eiintv invite nevi tine vein vent vine net nit ten tie tin vet vie en in it ne ti

eiinx nixie nixe nix en ex in ne xi

eiioprrs priories prosier. *See* **eiorrs eiprrs eoprrs**

eiiopstv positive. *See* **eiipst eiostv iopstv**

eiiorsv ivories. *See* **eiorsv eiisv**

eiiosstt osteitis. *See* **iiostt**

eiiostz   zoisite. *No 6s or 5s*

eiippr   pipier piper peri pier pipe prep repp ripe ire pep per pie pip rep rip er pe pi re

eiipprz   zippier. *See* **eiippr eipprz**

eiippst   pipiest. *See* **iippst eiipst eippst**

eiippstz   zippiest pipiest. *See* **eiipst eippst iippst**

eiippsy   yippies. *See* **eiippy eipps**

eiippy   yippie pipe pipy yipe pep pie pip yep yip pe pi ye

eiiprrss   prissier. *See* **eiirss eiprrs eiprss**

eiiprrtw   tripwire. *See* **eiirrw eirrtw**

eiiprst   tipsier. *See* **eiprst eiipst iiprst**

eiiprstu   purities tipsier. *See* **eiipst eiprst eiprsu eprstu**

eiiprsv   privies. *See* **eiprsv eiisv**

eiiprsw   wispier. *See* **eiprsw**

eiipsstt   tipsiest. *See* **eiipst eipsst**

eiipsstw   wispiest. *See* **eiipst eipsst eipssw eisstw**

eiipst   pities spite stipe tipis pest pets pies pits sept site spit step ties tipi tips its pet pie pit set sip sit tie tip is it pe pi si ti

eiipx   pixie pie pix ex pe pi xi

eiiqsttu   quietist. *See* **eiqstu**

eiirrtz   ritzier. *No 6s or 5s*

eiirrw   wirier wrier weir wire ire err er re we

eiirss   irises rises sires iris reis rise sire sirs ess ire res sir sis er is re si

eiirsstv   revisits revisit stivers strives. *See* **eiirss eirsst eirstv ersstv**

eiirsttz   ritziest. *See* **eirstt**

eiirstv   revisit. *See* **eirstv**

eiirstw   wiriest. *See* **eirstw**

eiirttw   wittier. *See* **eirtt eirtw**

eiirvz   vizier rive ire rev vie er re

eiissss   sissies. *No 6s or 5s*

eiisstx   sixties. *See* **eisstx**

eiistttw   wittiest. *See* **iistt isttw eistw**

eiistzz   tizzies. *See* **iitzz**

eiisv   ivies vies vise vie is si

eijklry   jerkily. *See* **eiklr ejkry**

eijknr   jerkin inker jerk jink kern kier kine rein rink ink ire irk ken kin kir en er in ne re

eijknrs   jerkins. *See* **eiknrs eijknr**

eijknru   junkier. *See* **eijnru ejknru eijknu**

eijknstu   junkiest junkies junkets. *See* **eijknt eijknu einstu ejkntu**

eijknsu   junkies. *See* **eijknu ijkns ejksu**

eijknt   inkjet jink kine kite knit tike tine ink jet ken kin kit net nit ten tie tin en in it ne ti

eijknu   junkie jink juke junk kine neuk nuke ink ken kin en in ne nu

eijllor   jollier. *See* **eilor eillr**

eijllos   jollies. *See* **ejlls eills ellos**

eijllost   jolliest jollies. *See* **eillst eilost ejlost**

eijlort   joltier. *See* **eilort**

eijlostt   joltiest litotes toilets. *See* **eilost eilott eilstt ejlost**

eijmpru   jumpier. *See* **eimpru ejmpru**

eijmpstu   jumpiest impetus imputes. *See* **eimptu empstu**

eijnno   enjoin jeon jinn join neon nine none eon inn ion joe one en in jo ne no on

eijnnos   enjoins. *See* **eijnno einos ijnns**

eijnor   joiner rejoin iron jeon join rein eon ion ire joe nor one ore roe en er in jo ne no on or re

eijnors   joiners rejoins. *See* **eijnor einors**

eijnortu   jointure routine. *See* **eijnor eijnru einort einrtu**

eijnory   joinery. *See* **eijnor**

eijnostt   jettison. *See* **einstt enostt ijnost**

eijnprsu   junipers injures juniper uprisen. *See* **eijnru eijrsu einprs einpsu**

eijnpru   juniper. *See* **eijnru enpru einpr**

eijnrrsu   injurers injurer injures insurer. *See* **eijnru eijrsu einrrs einrsu**

eijnrru   injurer. *See* **eijnru enrru**

eijnrsu   injures. *See* **eijnru einrsu eijrsu**

eijnru   injure inure urine rein ruin rune ire rue run urn en er in ne nu re ne si xi

eijnsty   jitneys. *See* **eijnty einst eisty**

eijnty   jitney tine tiny yeti jet net nit ten tie tin yen yet yin en in it ne ti ye

eijrstt   jitters. *See* **eijrtt eirstt**

eijrsu   juries reis rise rues ruse sire sure user ire jus res rue sir sue use er is re si us

eijrtt   jitter titer titre trite rite tier tire tret ire jet ret tie tit er it re ti

eijrtty   jittery. *See* **eijrtt ejtty**

eijssuv   jussive. *See* **eissu eijsv eissv**

eijsv   jives jive vies vise vie is si

eijv   jive vie

eikklsy   kylikes. *See* **eikls iklsy eiksy**

eikkoo   kookie kook oke

eikkoor   kookier. *See* **eikkoo eikoor**

eikkoost   kookiest. *See* **eikkoo eioost**

eikl   like elk ilk lei lek lie el li

eikllnsw   inkwells inkwell welkins winkles. *See* **eiklns eiklnw ekllns**

eikllnuy   unlikely. *See* **eiklly eiklnu**

eikllnw   inkwell. *See* **eiklnw**

eikllorv   overkill. *See* **eikllr**

eikllow   owllike. *No 6s or 5s*

eikllr   killer krill liker rille kier kill like lire riel rile rill elk ell ilk ill ire irk kir lei lek lie el er li re

eikllrs   killers. *See* **eikllr eillrs**

eikllsst   skillets skillet. *See* **eillss eillst eilsst ikllss**

eikllst   skillet. *See* **eillst iklls iklst**

eiklly   likely illy kill like lily yell elk ell ilk ill key lei lek lie lye el li ye

eiklmmn   milkmen. *See* **eikln eilmn**

eiklmnn   linkmen. *See* **eikln eilnn**

eiklmnos   moleskin. *See* **eiklns eiknos eilmno eilmns**

eiklmnr   kremlin. *See* **eilmnr eiklnr eiklmr**

eiklmnrs   kremlins kremlin limners merlins milkers. *See* **eiklmr eiklnr eiklns eikmrs**

eiklmr   milker liker miler emir kier like lime lire merl mike mile milk mire riel rile rime elk elm ilk ire irk kir lei lek lie mel mil mir rem rim el em er li me mi re

eiklmrs   milkers. *See* **eikmrs eilmrs**

eikln   inkle liken kiln kine lien like line link elk ilk ink ken kin lei lek lie nil el en in li ne

eiklnprs   sprinkle pilsner. *See* **eiklnr eiklns eiknrs eikprs**

eiklnr   linker inker inkle liken liker liner kern kier kiln kine lien like line link lire rein riel rile rink elk ilk ink ire irk ken kin kir lei lek lie nil el en er li ne re

eiklnrru   knurlier. *See* **eiklnr eiklnu eklnru**

eiklnrsw   wrinkles welkins winkles wrinkle. *See* **eiklnr eiklns eiklnw eiknrs**

eiklnrw   wrinkle. *See* **eiklnr eiklnw**

eiklns   likens silken inkle kilns lenis liens liken likes lines links skein slink elks inks isle kens kiln kine leis leks lens lien lies like line link nils silk sine sink skin elk els ens ilk ink ken kin lei lek lie nil sen sin ski el en in is li ne si

eiklnsss   skinless sinless. *See* **eiklns eiknss iklnss**

eiklnssy   skylines skyline linseys. *See* **eiklns eiknss eilnsy iklnss**

eiklnst   tinkles. *See* **eilnst eiklns eiklnt**

eiklnstw   twinkles tinkles twinkle welkins winkles. *See* **eiklns eiklnt eiklnw eikstw**

eiklnsw   welkins winkles. *See* **eiklns eiklnw**

eiklnsy   skyline. *See* **eiklns eilnsy iklnsy**

eiklnt   tinkle inkle inlet knelt liken kiln kilt kine kite knit lent lien like line link lint tike tile tine elk ilk ink ken kin kit lei lek lie lit net nil nit ten tie til tin el en in it li ne ti

eiklntw   twinkle. *See* **eiklnt eiklnw**

eiklnu   unlike inkle liken kiln kine lien lieu like line link lune neuk nuke elk ilk ink ken kin lei lek leu lie nil el en in li ne nu

eiklnw   welkin winkle inkle liken kiln kine knew lien like line link wile wine wink elk ilk ink ken kin lei lek lie new nil wen win el en in li ne we

eiklpry perkily. *See* **eilpry eklpy eiklr**

eiklr liker kier like lire riel rile elk ilk ire irk kir lei lek lie el er li re

eiklrst kilters kirtles. *See* **eiklrt eikrst eilrst**

eiklrsu sulkier. *See* **eilsu eikrs eiklr**

eiklrt kilter kirtle kiter liker liter litre tiler kier kilt kite like lire riel rile rite tier tike tile tire trek elk ilk ire irk kir kit lei lek let lie lit ret tie til el er it li re ti

eikls likes elks isle leis leks lies like silk elk els ilk lei lek lie ski el is li si

eiklsstt skittles kittles skittle. *See* **eikltt eilsst eilstt**

eiklssu sulkies. *See* **eilsu eilss eissu**

eiklstt kittles skittle. *See* **eikltt eilstt**

eikltt kittle title kilt kite like tike tile tilt elk ilk kit lei let lie lit tie til tit el it li ti

eikm mike em me mi

eikmmrr krimmer. *See* **eimmr**

eikmmrrs krimmers krimmer skimmer. *See* **eikmrs eimmrs**

eikmmrs skimmer. *See* **eikmrs eimmrs**

eikmmrss skimmers kirmess simmers skimmer. *See* **eikmrs eikrss eimmrs eimrss**

eikmnns kinsmen. *See* **eimns eikms ikmns**

eikmnor moniker. *See* **eimnor eikno eiknr**

eikmnors monikers irksome merinos moniker smokier. *See* **eikmrs eiknos eiknrs eimnor**

eikmnost tokenism moisten. *See* **eikmst eiknos eimnos eimost**

eikmopss misspoke imposes. *See* **eikops eikpss eimops eimoss**

eikmors irksome smokier. *See* **eimors eikmrs ekmors**

eikmosst smokiest ketosis kismets somites. *See* **eikmst eimoss eimost eimsst**

eikmrru murkier. *See* **emrru**

eikmrs kermis emirs kiers mikes mires miser rimes smirk emir irks kier kris mike mire mirs mise reis rime rims rise risk semi sire skim ire irk kir mir mis rem res rim sir ski em er is me mi re si

eikmrss kirmess. *See* **eikmrs eikrss eimrss ikmrss**

eikmrsu muskier. *See* **eikmrs eikmsu**

eikms mikes mike mise semi skim ski mis em is me mi si

eikmsst kismets. *See* **eikmst eimsst**

eikmst kismet emits items kites mikes mites smite tikes times emit item kist kite kits mike mise mist mite semi site skim skit stem ties tike time its kit met mis set sit ski tie tsk em is it me mi si ti

eikmsu muskie mikes emus mike mise muse musk semi skim emu mis mus ski sue sum use em is me mi mu si um us

eikn kine ink ken kin en in ne

eiknnrs skinner. *See* **eiknrs einnrs**

eiknnrss skinners sinkers sinners skinner. *See* **eiknrs eiknss eikrss einnrs**

eikno eikon koine ikon keno kine kino oink eon ink ion ken kin oke one en in ne no on

eiknorsv invokers invoker invokes version. *See* **eiknos eiknov eiknrs eiknsv**

eiknortt knottier knitter trinket. *See* **eiknrt eikntt einort einrtt**

eiknorv invoker. *See* **eiknov eiknr eknor**

eiknos eikons koines eikon eosin ikons kenos kinos koine noise oinks skein eons ikon inks ions keno kens kine kino noes nose oink okes ones sine sink skin soke ens eon ink ion ken kin kos oke one sen sin ski son en in is ne no on os si so

eiknoss kenosis. *See* **eiknos einoss eiknss**

eiknosv invokes. *See* **eiknos eiknov eiknsv**

eiknov invoke eikon koine ovine ikon keno kine kino nevi oink oven vein vine eon ink ion ken kin oke one vie en in ne no on

eiknprsu spunkier punkier uprisen. *See* **eiknpu eiknrs eikprs einprs**

eiknprtu turnpike punkier. *See* **eiknpu eiknrt einrtu enprtu**

eiknpru punkier. *See* **eiknpu eiknr einru**

eiknpstu punkiest punties sputnik. *See* **eiknpu einpst einpsu einstu**

eiknpsy pinkeys. *See* **eikps ekpsy einps**

eiknpu punkie kepi kine neuk nuke pike pine pink puke punk ink ken kin kip nip pen pie pin pun en in ne nu pe pi un

eiknr inker kern kier kine rein rink ink ire irk ken kin kir en er in ne re

eiknrs inkers sinker inker kerns kiers reins resin rinks rinse risen serin siren skein inks irks kens kern kier kine kris rein reis rink rise risk sine sink sire skin ens ink ire irk ken kin kir res sen sin sir ski en er in is ne re si

eiknrss sinkers. *See* **eiknrs eikrss einrss eiknss**

eiknrsst stinkers inserts sinkers sinters stinker strikes tinkers. *See* **eiknrs eiknrt eiknss eikrss**

eiknrst stinker tinkers. *See* **eiknrs einrst eikrst eiknrt**

eiknrstt knitters trinkets kittens knitter skitter stinker tinkers trinket. *See* **eiknrs eiknrt eikntt eikrst**

eiknrt tinker inert inker inter kiter niter trine kern kier kine kite knit rein rent rink rite tern tier tike tine tire trek ink ire irk ken kin kir kit net nit ret ten tie tin en er in it ne re ti

eiknrtt knitter trinket. *See* **eikntt eiknrt einrtt**

eikns skein inks kens kine sine sink skin ens ink ken kin sen sin ski en in is ne si

eiknss skeins sines sinks skein skies skins inks kens kine kiss sine sink sins skin skis ens ess ink ken kin sen sin sis ski en in is ne si

eiknstt kittens. *See* **eikntt einstt**

eiknsv knives skein skive veins vines inks kens kine nevi sine sink skin vein vies vine vise ens ink ken kin sen sin ski vie en in is ne si

eikntt kitten kine kite knit tent tike tine tint ink ken kin kit net nit ten tie tin tit en in it ne ti

eikntuz kunzite. *See* **eintu**

eikooprs spookier rookies. *See* **eikoor eikopr eikops eikprs**

eikoor rookie kier rook ire irk kir kor oke ore roe er or re

eikoors rookies. *See* **eikoor eikrs eiors**

eikoppr porkpie. *See* **eikopr eikppr**

eikopr pokier piker poker kepi kier peri perk pier pike poke pore pork repo ripe rope ire irk kip kir kor oke ope ore per pie poi pro rep rip roe er or pe pi re

eikoprr porkier. *See* **eikopr ekoprr**

eikoprst porkiest pokiest. *See* **eikopr eikops eikprs eikrst**

eikops pokies kepis pikes poise pokes spike spoke epos kepi kips okes opes peso pies pike pois poke pose skep soke kip kos oke ope pie poi sip ski sop is os pe pi si so

eikopst pokiest. *See* **eikops eopst eikst**

eikorrww wirework. *See* **ekorrw**

eikosst ketosis. *See* **ekosst iksst eikst**

eikp kepi pike pie kip pe pi

eikppr kipper piker piper kepi kier peri perk pier pike pipe prep repp ripe ire irk kip kir pep per pie pip rep rip er pe pi re

eikpprs kippers skipper. *See* **eikppr eikprs eipprs**

eikpprss skippers kippers sippers skipper. *See* **eikppr eikprs eikpss eikrss**

eikpr piker kepi kier peri perk pier pike ripe ire irk kip kir per pie rep rip er pe pi re

eikprs pikers kepis kiers perks piers piker pikes pries spike spire irks kepi kier kips kris peri perk pier pies pike reis reps ripe rips rise risk sire skep

skip ire irk kip kir per pie rep res rip sip
sir ski er is pe pi re si

eikps kepis pikes spike kepi kips pies
pike skep skip kip pie sip ski is pe pi si

eikpss spikes kepis pikes skies skips
spies spike kepi kips kiss pies pike sips
skep skip skis ess kip pie sip sis ski is
pe pi si

eikpsss skepsis. *See* **eiksss eipsss eikpss**

eikr kier ire irk kir er re

eikrrsst strikers striker strikes. *See* **eikrss
eikrst eirrss eirsst**

eikrrst striker. *See* **eikrst**

eikrs kiers irks kier kris reis rise risk sire
ire irk kir res sir ski er is re si

eikrss kisser kiers rises risks sires skies
irks kier kiss kris reis rise risk sire sirs
skis ess ire irk kir res sir sis ski er is re si

eikrsss kissers. *See* **eikrss eiksss**

eikrsst strikes. *See* **eikrss eikrst eirsst
ikrsst**

eikrsstt skitters sitters skitter strikes. *See*
eikrss eikrst eirsst eirstt

eikrssv skivers. *See* **eikrss eikrsv eikssv**

eikrst kiters strike kiers kiter kites rites
skirt tiers tikes tires treks tries erst irks
kier kist kite kits kris reis rest rets rise
risk rite sire site skit stir tier ties tike
tire trek ire irk its kir kit res ret set sir
sit ski tie tsk er is it re si ti

eikrstt skitter. *See* **eikrst eirstt**

eikrsv skiver kiers skive irks kier kris reis
revs rise risk rive sire vies vise ire irk
kir res rev sir ski vie er is re si

eikrt kiter kier kite rite tier tike tire trek
ire irk kir kit ret tie er it re ti

eikss skies kiss skis ess sis ski is si

eiksss kisses skies kiss skis ess sis ski is si

eiksstw weskits. *See* **eikstw eisstw**

eikssv skives skies skive vises kiss skis
vies vise ess sis ski vie is si

eikst kites tikes kist kite kits site skit ties
tike its kit set sit ski tie tsk is it si ti

eikstw weskit kites tikes wites kist kite
kits site skew skit stew ties tike west
wets wise wite wits its kit set sew sit ski
tie tsk wet wis wit is it si ti we

eiksv skive vies vise vie ski is si

eiksy yikes keys key ski sky yes is si ye

eikt kite tike tie kit it ti

eil lei lie el li

eilllos lollies. *See* **eills lllos ellos**

eillmnou linoleum mullion. *See* **eillmu
eillno eilmno**

eillmos mollies. *See* **eilms ilmos eills**

eillmost melilots melilot millets mollies.
See **eillmt eillst eilmot eilost**

eillmot melilot. *See* **eillmt eilmot**

eillmpss misspell lipless. *See* **eillss eilmps
eilmss eilpss**

eillmptu multiple. *See* **eillmt eillmu eilltu
eilmpt**

eillmr miller rille miler emir lime lire
mell merl mile mill mire riel rile rill
rime ell elm ill ire lei lie mel mil mir
rem rim el em er li me mi re

eillmrs millers. *See* **eilmrs eillmr eillrs**

eillmst millets. *See* **eillmt eillst**

eillmsu illumes. *See* **eillmu eilsu eilms**

eillmt millet emit item lilt lime mell melt
mile mill milt mite tell tile till time ell
elm ill lei let lie lit mel met mil tie til el
em it li me mi ti

eillmu illume ileum lieu lime mell mile
mill mule mull ell elm emu ill lei leu lie
lum mel mil el em li me mi mu um

eillmuvx vexillum. *See* **eillmu ellmuv**

eillno niello eloin olein enol leno lien
line lion loin lone nill noel noil ell eon
ill ion lei lie nil oil one el en in li lo ne
no on

eillnos niellos. *See* **eilnos eillno**

eillnss illness. *See* **eillss ellnss**

eillnst lentils lintels. *See* **eilnst eillnt eillst**

eillnsty silently lentils lintels. *See* **eillnt
eillst eilnst eilnsy**

eillnt lentil lintel inlet lent lien lilt line
lint nill tell tile till tine ell ill lei let lie
lit net nil nit ten tie til tin el en in it li
ne ti

eilloorw woollier lowlier. *See* **eiloor**

eilloosw woollies. *See* **eiloos**

eillopty politely. *See* **eilopt ilopty**

eillorsz zorilles zorille. *See* **eillrs eilors
eiorsz**

eillorw lowlier. *See* **elorw eilor eillr**

eillorz zorille. *See* **eilor**

eillostw lowliest. *See* **eillst eilost elostw
illstw**

eillpss lipless. *See* **eillss ellpss eilpss illpss**

eillr rille lire riel rile rill ell ill ire lei lie el
er li re

eillrs rilles lisle riels riles rille rills ells isle
leis lies lire reis riel rile rill rise sell sill
sire ell els ill ire lei lie lis res sir el er is li
re si

eillrst tillers trellis. *See* **eillst eilrst eillrs
eillrt illrst**

eillrt tiller liter litre rille tiler trill lilt lire
riel rile rill rite tell tier tile till tire ell ill
ire lei let lie lit ret tie til el er it li re ti

eillrtt littler. *See* **eilrtt eilltt eillrt**

eills lisle ells isle leis lies sell sill ell els ill
lei lie el is li si

eillss lisles isles lisle sells sills ells isle leis
less lies sell sill ell els ess ill lei lie sis el
is li si

eillssst listless. *See* **eillss eillst eilsst**

eillsstt stillest. *See* **eillss eillst eilltt eilsst**

eillssu sullies. *See* **eillss eilsu eissu**

eillst listel islet istle lilts lisle stile still
tells tiles tills ells isle leis lest lets lies
lilt list sell sill silt site slit tell ties tile
till tils ell els ill its lei let lie lit set sit tie
til el is it li si ti

eillsttt littlest tittles. *See* **eillst eilltt eilstt**

eillstu tuilles. *See* **eillst eilltu ellstu**

eilltt little title lilt tell tile till tilt ell ill lei
let lie lit tie til tit el it li ti

eilltu tuille utile tulle etui lieu lilt lute tell
tile till tule ell ill lei let leu lie lit tie til
tui el it li ti ut

eillvy evilly lively vilely evil illy levy lily
live veil vile yell ell ill ivy lei lev lie lye
vie el li ye

eilm lime mile elm lei lie mel mil el em li
me mi

eilmmrs slimmer. *See* **eilmrs eimmrs**

eilmmsst slimmest. *See* **eilmss eilsst
eimsst elmsst**

eilmn limen lien lime limn line mien mile
mine elm lei lie mel men mil nil nim el
em en in li me mi ne

eilmno lomein moline eloin lemon limen
melon olein enol leno lien lime limn
limo line lion loin lone mien mile milo
mine moil mole noel noil nome omen
elm eon ion lei lie mel men mil mon nil
nim oil one el em en in li lo me mi mo
ne no om on

eilmnosu emulsion elusion. *See* **eilmno
eilmns eilnos eimnos**

eilmnpss limpness simnels splines. *See*
eilmns eilmps eilmss eilnps

eilmnr limner merlin limen liner miler
miner emir lien lime limn line lire merl
mien mile mine mire rein riel rile rime
elm ire lei lie mel men mil mir nil nim
rem rim el em en er in li me mi ne re

eilmnrs limners merlins. *See* **eilmnr
eilnrs eilmrs eimnrs eilmns**

eilmnrst minstrel limners merlins minster. *See* **eilmnr eilmns eilmrs eilnrs**

eilmns simnel lenis liens limen limes
limns lines miens miles mines slime
smile elms isle leis lens lien lies lime
limn line mels mien mile mils mine
mise nils nims semi sine slim elm els
ens lei lie mel men mil mis nil nim sen
sin el em en in is li me mi ne si

eilmnss simnels. *See* **eilmns eilmss**

eilmnsy myelins. *See* **eilmsy eilnsy
eilmny eilmns**

eilmntuy minutely untimely. *See* **eilmny
eilmty eilnty eimntu**

eilmny myelin limen limey inly lien lime
limn limy line liny mien mile mine
ylem elm lei lie lye mel men mil nil nim
yen yin el em en in li me mi my ne ye**

eilmoost toilsome oolites ostiole stoolie. *See* **eilmot eiloos eiloot eilost**

eilmopr implore. *See* **eilmpr**

eilmoprs implores implore imposer limpers promise rimples semipro simpler spoiler. *See* **eilmpr eilmps eilmrs eilops**

eilmopst milepost limpest limpets pistole. *See* **eilmot eilmps eilmpt eilops**

eilmoss lissome. *See* **eimoss eilmss**

eilmot motile toile motel emit item lime limo melt mile milo milt mite moil mole molt mote omit tile time toil tome elm lei let lie lit lot mel met mil mot oil tie til toe tom el em it li lo me mi mo om ti to

eilmp impel lime limp mile pile elm imp lei lie lip mel mil pie el em li me mi pe pi

eilmpp pimple impel lime limp mile pile pimp pipe elm imp lei lie lip mel mil pep pie pip el em li me mi pe pi

eilmpps pimples. *See* **eilmps eilmpp**

eilmpr limper rimple impel miler peril plier prime emir lime limp lire merl mile mire peri perm pier pile prim riel rile rime ripe elm imp ire lei lie lip mel mil mir per pie rem rep rim rip el em er li me mi pe pi re

eilmprs limpers rimples simpler. *See* **eilmps eilmpr eilprs eilmrs eimprs**

eilmpru lumpier. *See* **eimpru elmpru**

eilmpry primely. *See* **eilmpr ilmpry eilpry**

eilmps impels simple impel limes limps miles piles slime smile spiel spile elms imps isle leis lies lime limp lips lisp mels mile mils mise pies pile semi simp slim slip elm els imp lei lie lip mel mil mis pie sip el em is li me mi pe pi si

eilmpsst simplest limpest limpets misstep stipels. *See* **eilmps eilmpt eilmss eilpss**

eilmpssu impulses impulse. *See* **eilmps eilmss eilpss eilpsu**

eilmpst limpest limpets. *See* **eilmps eilmpt eilpst**

eilmpstu lumpiest impetus impulse imputes limpest limpets stipule. *See* **eilmps eilmpt eilpst eilpsu**

eilmpsu impulse. *See* **eilmps eilpsu elmpsu**

eilmpsw wimples. *See* **eilmps eilmpw**

eilmpt limpet impel tempi emit item lept lime limp melt mile milt mite pelt pile tile time elm imp lei let lie lip lit mel met mil pet pie pit tie til tip el em it li me mi pe pi ti

eilmpty emptily. *See* **eilmpt eilmty**

eilmpw wimple impel lime limp mewl mile pile wile wimp wipe elm imp lei lie

lip mel mew mil pew pie el em li me mi pe pi we

eilmr miler emir lime lire merl mile mire riel rile rime elm ire lei lie mel mil mir rem rim el em er li me mi re

eilmrry merrily. *See* **eirry eilmy emrry**

eilmrs milers smiler emirs limes merls miler miles mires miser riels riles rimes slime smile elms emir isle leis lies lime lire mels merl mile mils mire mirs mise reis riel rile rime rims rise semi sire slim elm els ire lei lie mel mil mir mis rem res rim sir el em er is li me mi re si

eilmrss rimless smilers. *See* **eilmrs eimrss eilmss**

eilmrssu misrules misrule rimless smilers surmise. *See* **eilmrs eilmss eimrss eimssu**

eilmrssy remissly messily miserly rimless smilers. *See* **eilmrs eilmss eilmsy eimrss**

eilmrsu misrule. *See* **elmrsu eilmrs**

eilmrsy miserly. *See* **eilmsy ilmrsy eilmrs eimrsy**

eilms limes miles slime smile elms isle leis lies lime mels mile mils mise semi slim elm els lei lie mel mil mis el em is li me mi si

eilmss slimes smiles isles limes miles semis slime smile elms isle leis less lies lime mels mess mile mils mise miss semi slim elm els ess lei lie mel mil mis sis el em is li me mi si

eilmssy messily. *See* **eilmsy eilmss**

eilmsy limeys limes limey miles slime slimy smile elms isle leis lies lime limy lyes lyse mels mile mils mise semi slim ylem elm els lei lie lye mel mil mis sly yes el em is li me mi my si ye

eilmszz mizzles. *See* **eilmzz eilszz**

eilmty timely limey emit item lime limy melt mile milt mite tile time yeti ylem elm lei let lie lit lye mel met mil tie til yet el em it li me mi my ti ye

eilmu ileum lieu lime mile mule elm emu lei leu lie lum mel mil el em li me mi mu um

eilmuuv eluvium. *See* **eilmu elmuv**

eilmy limey lime limy mile ylem elm lei lie lye mel mil el em li me mi my ye

eilmzz mizzle lime mile elm lei lie mel mil el em li me mi

eiln lien line lei lie nil el en in li ne

eilnn linen lien line linn nine inn lei lie nil el en in li ne

eilnnost insolent entoils intones linnets tension. *See* **eilnns eilnnt eilnos eilnot**

eilnns linens lenis liens lines lines linns nines inns isle leis lens lien lies line linn nils nine sine els ens inn lei lie nil sen sin el en in is li ne si

eilnnst linnets. *See* **eilnst eilnns eilnnt einnst**

eilnnt linnet linen inlet lent lien line linn lint nine tile tine inn lei let lie lit net nil nit ten tie til tin el en in it li ne ti

eilnntty intently. *See* **eintty einntt eilnty eilnnt**

eilno eloin olein enol leno lien line lion loin lone noel noil eon ion lei lie nil oil one el en in li lo ne no on

eilnoor loonier. *See* **eiloor eilno eilnr**

eilnoost looniest oilstone entoils isotone lotions oolites ostiole stoolie. *See* **eilnos eilnot eilnst eiloos**

eilnop pinole eloin olein opine enol leno lien line lion loin lone lope noel noil nope open peon pile pine pole pone eon ion lei lie lip lop nil nip oil one ope pen pie pin poi el en in li lo ne no on pe pi

eilnops epsilon pinoles. *See* **eilnos einops eilops eilnop eilnps**

eilnopss epsilons epsilon insoles lesions lioness pinoles splines. *See* **eilnop eilnos eilnps eilops**

eilnopty linotype ineptly. *See* **eilnop eilnot eilnpt eilnty**

eilnortt trotline tortile. *See* **eilnot eilort eilott eilrtt**

eilnortu outliner outlier outline routine. *See* **eilnot eilort einort einrtu**

eilnos eloins insole lesion oleins eloin eosin lenis liens lines lions loins noels noils noise olein enol eons ions isle leis leno lens lien lies line lion loin lone lose nils noel noes noil nose oils ones silo sine sloe soil sole els ens eon ion lei lie los nil oil one sen sin sol son el en in is li lo ne no on os si so

eilnoss insoles lesions lioness. *See* **eilnos elnoss einoss**

eilnost entoils. *See* **eilnos eilnst eilnot elnost eilost**

eilnostu outlines elusion entoils outline. *See* **eilnos eilnot eilnst eilost**

eilnostv novelist entoils solvent violent violets. *See* **eilnos eilnot eilnst eilnsv**

eilnosu elusion. *See* **eilnos**

eilnosvv involves involve. *See* **eilnos eilnsv eilosv elnosv**

eilnot entoil eloin inlet lento olein toile enol into leno lent lien line lint lion loin lone noel noil note tile tine toil tone eon ion lei let lie lit lot net nil nit not oil one ten tie til tin toe ton el en in it li lo ne no on ti to

eilnotu outline. *See* **eilnot eintu ilntu**

eilnotuv involute outline outlive violent. *See* **eilnot eilnuv eilotv elotuv**

eilnotv violent. *See* **eilnot eilotv**

eilnovv involve. *See* **eilno eilnv elnov**

eilnpp nipple lien line pile pine pipe lei lie lip nil nip pen pep pie pin pip el en in li ne pe pi

eilnpps nipples. *See* **eilnpp einpps eilnps**

eilnprs pilsner. *See* **eilnrs eilprs einprs eilnps**

eilnprss pilsners lispers pilsner snipers splines. *See* **eilnps eilnrs eilprs eilpss**

eilnprst splinter pilsner triples. *See* **eilnps eilnpt eilnrs eilnst**

eilnps spinel spline lenis liens lines piles pines snipe spiel spile spine isle leis lens lien lies line lips lisp nils pens pies pile pine pins sine slip snip spin els ens lei lie lip nil nip pen pie pin sen sin sip el en in is li ne pe pi si

eilnpss splines. *See* **einpss eilpss**

eilnpsu lineups lupines. *See* **eilnpu eilpsu einpsu**

eilnpt pintle inlet inept lent lept lien line lint pelt pent pile pine pint tile tine lei let lie lip lit net nil nip nit pen pet pie pin pit ten tie til tin tip el en in it li ne pe pi ti

eilnpty ineptly. *See* **eilnty eilnpt elnpty**

eilnpu lineup lupine lien lieu line lune pile pine pule puli lei leu lie lip nil nip pen pie pin pul pun el en in li ne nu pe pi up

eilnpuv vulpine. *See* **eilnpu eilnuv**

eilnr liner lien line lire rein riel rile ire lei lie nil el en er in li ne re

eilnrs liners lenis liens liner lines reins resin riels riles rinse risen serin siren isle leis lens lien lies line lire nils rein reis riel rile rise sine sire els ens ire lei lie nil res sen sin sir el en er in is li ne re si

eilnrstu insulter lustier runlets triunes. *See* **eilnrs eilnst eilrst einrst**

eilnrsv silvern. *See* **eilnrs eilnsv eilrsv**

eilnrtuv virulent rivulet. *See* **eilnuv einrtu einrtv eirtuv**

eilnrty inertly. *See* **eilnty enrty einrt**

eilnrvy nervily. *See* **eilrvy einrvy**

eilns lenis liens lines isle leis lens lien lies line nils sine els ens lei lie nil sen sin el en in is li ne si

eilnsss sinless. *See* **eilss eilns einss**

eilnsst enlists listens tinsels. *See* **eilnst einsst eilsst**

eilnssv snivels. *See* **eilnsv**

eilnssy linseys. *See* **eilnsy ilnssy**

eilnst enlist inlets listen silent tinsel inlet inset islet istle lenis liens lines lints stein stile tiles tines isle leis lens lent lest lets lien lies line lint list nest nets nils nits sent silt sine site slit snit tens ties tile tils tine tins els ens its lei let lie

lis lit net nil nit sen set sin sit ten tie til tin el en in is it li ne si ti

eilnsuv unveils. *See* **eilnsv eilnuv**

eilnsuwy unwisely. *See* **eilnsy eilswy einsuw einswy**

eilnsv livens snivel evils lenis levin liens lines liven lives veils veins vines evil isle leis lens lien lies line live nevi nils sine veil vein vies vile vine vise els ens lei lev lie nil sen sin vie el en in is li ne si

eilnsy linsey lenis liens lines lysin inly isle leis lens lien lies line liny lyes lyse nils sine yens els ens lei lie lye nil sen sin sly yen yes yin el en in is li ne si ye

eilnt inlet lent lien line lint tile tine lei let lie lit net nil nit ten tie til tin el en in it li ne ti

eilnty lenity inlet linty inly lent lien line lint liny tile tine tiny yeti lei let lie lit lye net nil nit ten tie til tin yen yet yin el en in it li ne ti ye

eilnuv unveil levin liven evil lien lieu line live lune nevi veil vein vile vine lei leu lev lie luv nil vie el en in li ne nu

eilnv levin liven evil lien line live nevi veil vein vile vine lei lev lie nil vie el en in li ne

eiloo looie oleo olio lei lie loo oil el li lo

eiloor oriole looie oiler oriel lire lore oleo olio orle riel rile roil role ire lei lie loo oil ore roe el er li lo or re

eiloors orioles. *See* **eiloos eloors eilors eiloor**

eiloos looies looie loose oleos olios isle leis lies loos lose oils oleo olio silo sloe soil sole solo els lei lie loo los oil sol el is li lo os si so

eiloosst ostioles loosest oolites ostiole soloist stoolie. *See* **eiloos eiloot eilost eilsst**

eiloost oolites ostiole stoolie. *See* **eiloos eiloot eioost eilost**

eiloot oolite looie toile loot oleo olio tile toil tool lei let lie lit loo lot oil tie til toe too el it li lo ti to

eiloppr loppier. *See* **eloppr eilppr**

eilopprs sloppier loppers loppier propels ripples slipper spoiler. *See* **eilops eilors eilppr eilprs**

eiloppst loppiest pistole potpies stipple stopple tipples topples. *See* **eilops eilopt eilost eilppt**

eiloprrt portlier. *See* **eilopt eilort eilprt eiorrt**

eiloprs spoiler. *See* **eilprs eloprs eilors eilops**

eiloprss spoilers lispers rissole spoiler. *See* **eilops eilors eilprs eilpss**

eiloprsu perilous leprous lousier pileous soupier spoiler. *See* **eilops eilors eilprs eilpsu**

eiloprsv slipover spoiler plovers. *See* **eilops eilors eilosv eilprs**

eilops pilose poleis lopes piles poise poles polis slope spiel spile spoil epos isle leis lies lips lisp lope lops lose oils opes peso pies pile pois pole pose silo slip sloe slop soil sole els lei lie lip lop los oil ope pie poi sip sol sop el is li lo os pe pi si so

eilopsst pistoles pistole pistols stipels topless. *See* **eilops eilopt eilost eilpss**

eilopst pistole. *See* **eilops ilopst eilopt eilpst**

eilopstx exploits pistole exploit. *See* **eilops eilopt eilost eilpst**

eilopsu pileous. *See* **eilpsu eilops ilopsu**

eilopt polite toile pilot lept lope pelt pile plot poet pole tile toil tope lei let lie lip lit lop lot oil ope pet pie pit poi pot tie til tip toe top el it li lo pe pi ti to

eiloptx exploit. *See* **eilopt elotx eiltx**

eilor oiler oriel lire lore orle riel rile roil role ire lei lie oil ore roe el er li lo or re

eilorrs lorries. *See* **eilors eiorrs elorrs**

eilorrtu ulterior outlier. *See* **eilort eiorrt eorrtu**

eilors oilers oriels lores loris loser oiler oriel orles osier riels riles roils roles isle leis lies lire lore lose oils ores orle reis riel rile rise roes roil role rose silo sire sloe soil sole sore sori els ire lei lie los oil ore res roe sir sol el er is li lo or os re si so

eilorss rissole. *See* **elorss eilors**

eilorsss rissoles rissole lessors. *See* **eilors elorss**

eilorst loiters toilers. *See* **eilrst eilort eilors elorst eiorst**

eilorsu lousier. *See* **eilors**

eilort loiter toiler liter litre oiler oriel tiler toile lire lore orle riel rile riot rite roil role rote rotl tier tile tire tiro toil tore tori trio ire lei let lie lit lot oil ore ort ret roe rot tie til toe tor el er it li lo or re ti to

eilortt tortile. *See* **eilrtt eilott**

eilortty toiletry tortile lottery. *See* **eilort eilott eilrtt elrtty**

eilortu outlier. *See* **eilort**

eilosstu lousiest lotuses solutes tousles. *See* **eilost eilsst eisstu elosst**

eilost toiles islet istle stile stole tiles toile toils isle leis lest lets lies list lose lost lots oils silo silt site slit sloe slot soil sole ties tile tils toes toil els its lei let lie lit los lot oil set sit sol sot tie til toe el is it li lo os si so ti to

eilostt litotes toilets. *See* **eilstt eilost eilott**

eilosttt stiletto litotes tittles toilets. *See* **eilost eilott eilstt**

eilostuv outlives outlive violets volutes. *See* **eilost eilosv eilotv eilstv**

eilostv violets. *See* **eilosv eiostv eilost eilstv eilotv**

eilosv olives evils lives loves olive solve veils viols voles evil isle leis lies live lose love oils silo sloe soil sole veil vies vile viol vise vole els lei lev lie los oil sol vie el is li lo os si so

eilot toile tile toil lei let lie lit lot oil tie til toe el it li lo ti to

eilott toilet toile title tile tilt toil tote lei let lie lit lot oil tie til tit toe tot el it li lo ti to

eilotuv outlive. *See* **eilotv elotuv**

eilotv violet toile olive evil live love tile toil veil veto vile viol vole volt vote lei let lev lie lit lot oil tie til toe vet vie el it li lo ti to

eilov olive evil live love veil vile viol vole lei lev lie oil vie el li lo

eilp pile lei lie lip pie el li pe pi

eilppr ripple peril piper plier lire peri pier pile pipe prep repp riel rile ripe ire lei lie lip pep per pie pip rep rip el er li pe pi re

eilpprs ripples slipper. *See* **eilprs eipprs eilppr**

eilpprss slippers lispers ripples sippers slipper. *See* **eilppr eilprs eilpss eipprs**

eilpprst tipplers ripples slipper stipple tippers tippler tipples triples. *See* **eilppr eilppt eilprs eilprt**

eilpprsu supplier pulpier purples ripples slipper suppler. *See* **eilppr eilprs eilpsu eipprs**

eilpprsy slippery ripples slipper. *See* **eilppr eilprs eilpry eipprs**

eilpprt tippler. *See* **eilppr eipprt eilppt eilprt**

eilppru pulpier. *See* **eilppr elppru**

eilppsst stipples sippets stipels stipple tipples. *See* **eilppt eilpss eilpst eilsst**

eilppssu supplies supples. *See* **eilpss eilpsu elppsu elpssu**

eilppssw swipples swipple. *See* **eilpss eipssw**

eilppst stipple tipples. *See* **eippst eilpst**

eilppstu pulpiest pulpits stipple stipule tipples. *See* **eilppt eilpst eilpsu eilptu**

eilppsw swipple. *See* **eilsw eilps eipps**

eilppt tipple lept pelt pile pipe tile lei let lie lip lit pep pet pie pip pit tie til tip el it li pe pi ti

eilpr peril plier lire peri pier pile riel rile ripe ire lei lie lip per pie rep rip el er li pe pi re

eilprs lisper perils pliers peril piers piles plier pries riels riles spiel spile spire isle leis lies lips lire lisp peri pier pies pile reis reps riel rile ripe rips rise sire slip els ire lei lie lip per pie rep res rip sip sir el er is li pe pi re si

eilprss lispers. *See* **eilprs eilpss eiprss**

eilprst triples. *See* **eiprst eilprs eilrst eilpst eilprt**

eilprsty priestly triples pyrites. *See* **eilprs eilprt eilpry eilpst**

eilprsuu purlieus purlieu euripus. *See* **eilprs eilpsu eiprsu elprsu**

eilprsuy pleurisy. *See* **eilprs eilpry eilpsu eiprsu**

eilprt triple liter litre peril plier tiler tripe lept lire pelt peri pert pier pile riel rile ripe rite tier tile tire trip ire lei let lie lip lit per pet pie pit rep ret rip tie til tip el er it li pe pi re ti

eilprtty prettily. *See* **eilprt eilpry eilrtt eiprty**

eilpruu purlieu. *See* **eilpr**

eilpry ripely peril plier reply lire lyre peri pier pile prey pyre rely riel rile ripe yelp yipe ire lei lie lip lye per pie ply pry rep rip rye yep yip el er li pe pi re ye

eilps piles spiel spile isle leis lies lips lisp pies pile slip els lei lie lip pie sip el is li pe pi si

eilpss spiels spiles isles lisps piles slips spiel spies spile isle leis less lies lips lisp pies pile sips slip els ess lei lie lip pie sip sis el is li pe pi si

eilpsst stipels. *See* **eilsst eilpss ilpsst eipsst**

eilpsstt spittles stipels spittle. *See* **eilpss eilpst eilsst eilstt**

eilpsstu stipules stipels stipule. *See* **eilpss eilpst eilpsu eilptu**

eilpst stipel islet istle pelts piles slept spelt spiel spile spilt spite split stile stipe tiles tile leis lept lest lets lies lisp list pelt pest pets pies pile pits sept silt site slip slit spit step ties tile tils tips els its lei let lie lip lit pet pie pit set sip sit tie til tip el is it li pe pi si ti

eilpstt spittle. *See* **eilpst eilstt**

eilpstu stipule. *See* **elpstu eilpsu eilptu eilpst ilpstu**

eilpsu pileus ileus piles pules pulis pulse spiel spile isle leis lies lieu lips lisp lues pies pile plus pule puli puls slip slue spue els lei leu lie lip pie pul pus sip sue sup use el is li pe pi si up us

eilpsv pelvis evils lives piles spiel spile veils evil isle leis lies lips lisp live pies pile slip spiv veil vies vile vise els lei lev lie lip pie sip vie el is li pe pi si

eilpsx pixels lexis piles pixel pixes spiel spile ilex isle leis lies lips lisp pies pile slip els lei lie lip pie pix sex sip six el ex is li pe pi si xi

eilpsz pizzles. *See* **eilpzz eilszz**

eilptu plutei letup tulip utile etui lept lieu lute pelt pile pule puli tile tule lei let leu lie lip lit pet pie pit pul put tie til tip tui tup el it li pe pi ti up ut

eilpx pixel pile ilex lei lie lip pie pix el ex li pe pi xi

eilpzz pizzle pile lei lie lip pie zip el li pe pi

eilqrrsu squirrel. *See* **eiqrsu elrrsu**

eilqrstu quilters lustier querist quilter. *See* **eilrst eiqrsu eiqstu elrstu**

eilqrsuu liqueurs liqueur. *See* **eiqrsu**

eilqrtu quilter. *See* **eilrt eiqtu ilqtu**

eilqruu liqueur. *See* **eiqru**

eilqtuy quietly. *See* **eiqtuy ilqtu eiltu**

eilr lire riel rile ire lei lie el er li re

eilrrssu slurries. *See* **eirrss eirssu elrrsu**

eilrrstw twirlers twirler writers. *See* **eilrst eirrtw eirstw ilrstw**

eilrrtw twirler. *See* **eirrtw eilrt ilrtw**

eilrs riels riles isle leis lies lire reis riel rile rise sire els ire lei lie res sir el er is li re si

eilrsst listers. *See* **eilsst eilrst eirsst**

eilrssty sisterly listers. *See* **eilrst eilsst eirsst elssty**

eilrssv silvers slivers. *See* **eilrsv**

eilrst lister litres tilers islet istle liter litre riels riles rites stile tiers tiler tiles tires tries erst isle leis lest lets lies lire list reis rest rets riel rile rise rite sett stir sire site slit stir tier ties tile tils tire els ire its lei let lie lit res ret set sir sit tie til el er is it li re si ti

eilrstt litters. *See* **eilrst eilrtt eirstt eilstt**

eilrsttw wristlet litters twister. *See* **eilrst eilrtt eilstt eirstt**

eilrstu lustier. *See* **eilrst elrstu**

eilrstuv rivulets lustier rivulet virtues. *See* **eilrst eilrsv eilstv eirstv**

eilrsuux luxuries. *See* **eilsu eilsx elrsu**

eilrsv livers livres silver sliver evils liver lives livre riels riles veils viler evil isle leis lies lire live reis revs riel rile rise rive sire veil vies vile vise els ire lei lev lie res rev sir vie el er is li re si

eilrsvy silvery. *See* **eilrsv eilrvy**

eilrt liter litre tiler lire riel rile rite tier tile tire ire lei let lie lit ret tie til el er it li re ti

eilrtt   litter liter litre tiler titer title titre trite lire riel rile rite tier tile tilt tire tret ire lei let lie lit ret tie til tit el er it li re ti

eilrtuv   rivulet. *See* **eirtuv eilrt eilrv**

eilrv   liver livre viler evil lire live riel rile rive veil vile ire lei lev lie rev vie el er li re

eilrvy   livery verily liver livre viler evil levy lire live lyre rely riel rile rive veil very vile ire ivy lei lev lie lye rev rye vie el er li re ye

eils   isle leis lies els lei lie el is li si

eilss   isles isle leis less lies els ess lei lie sis el is li si

eilsst   islets istles stiles isles islet istle lists silts sites slits stile tiles isle leis less lest lets lies list sets silt site sits slit ties tile tils els ess its lei let lie lit set sis sit tie til el is it li si ti

eilssttu   lustiest lutists. *See* **eilsst eilstt eisstu elsstu**

eilsstty   stylites stylets stylist stylite testily. *See* **eilsst eilstt elssty elstty**

eilsstw   witless. *See* **eilsst eisstw**

eilsstyz   stylizes stylize. *See* **eilsst elssty**

eilssvw   swivels. *See* **eilsvw eilss eissv**

eilsswzz   swizzles sizzles swizzle. *See* **eilszz**

eilsszz   sizzles. *See* **eilszz eilss eissz**

eilst   islet istle stile tiles isle leis lest lets lies list silt site slit ties tile tils els its lei let lie lit set sit tie til el is it li si ti

eilstt   titles islet istle stile stilt tiles tilts title isle leis lest lets lies list silt site slit stet test ties tile tils tilt tits els its lei let lie lit set sit tie til tit el is it li si ti

eilsttt   tittles. *See* **eilstt eilttt**

eilstty   stylite testily. *See* **eilstt elstty**

eilstv   vilest evils islet istle lives stile tiles veils evil isle leis lest lets lies list live silt site slit ties tile tils veil vest vets vies vile vise els its lei let lev lie lit set sit tie til vet vie el is it li si ti

eilstyz   stylize. *See* **eilst ilsty elsty**

eilsu   ileus isle leis lies lieu lues slue els lei leu lie sue use el is li si us

eilsv   evils lives veils evil isle leis lies live veil vies vile vise els lei lev lie vie el is li si

eilsvw   swivel evils lewis lives veils views wiles wives evil isle leis lies live slew veil vies view vile vise wile wise wive els lei lev lie sew vie wis el is li si we

eilsw   lewis wiles isle leis lies slew wile wise els lei lie sew wis el is li si we

eilswy   wisely lewis wiles isle leis lies lyes lyse slew wile wily wise wyes yews els lei lie lye sew sly wis wye yes yew el is li si we ye

eilswzz   swizzle. *See* **eilszz eilsw**

eilsx   lexis ilex isle leis lies els lei lie sex six el ex is li si xi

eilszz   sizzle isle leis lies size els lei lie el is li si

eilt   tile lei let lie lit tie til el it li ti

eiltt   title tile tilt lei let lie lit tie til tit el it li ti

eilttt   tittle title tile tilt lei let lie lit tie til tit el it li ti

eiltu   utile etui lieu lute tile tule lei let leu lie lit tie til tui el it li ti ut

eiltvy   levity evil levy live tile veil vile yeti ivy lei let lev lie lit lye tie til vet vie yet el it li ti ye

eiltx   ixtle exit ilex tile lei let lie lit tie til el ex it li ti xi

eilu   lieu lei leu lie el li

eilv   evil live veil vile lei lev lie vie el li

eilw   wile lei lie el li we

eilx   ilex lei lie el ex li xi

eimm   mime mem mim em me mi

eimmmos   mommies. *See* **immmos emmos eimms**

eimmmsu   mummies. *See* **eimms**

eimmnors   misnomer memoirs merinos. *See* **eimmor eimmrs eimnor eimnos**

eimmnsu   immunes. *See* **eimmnu emnsu eimns**

eimmnu   immune menu mien mime mine emu mem men mim mum nim em en in me mi mu ne nu um

eimmopru   emporium premium. *See* **eimmor eimmru eimpru**

eimmor   memoir mimer emir memo mime mire mome more omer rime ire mem mim mir mom mor ore rem rim roe em er me mi mo om or re

eimmors   memoirs. *See* **eimors eimmor eimmrs**

eimmostt   totemism. *See* **eimost emostt**

eimmprr   primmer. *See* **eimprr eimmr**

eimmprst   primmest imprest permits. *See* **eimmrs eimprs eimprt eimrst**

eimmprsu   premiums immures premium rummies umpires. *See* **eimmrs eimmru eimprs eimpru**

eimmpru   premium. *See* **eimmru eimpru**

eimmr   mimer emir mime mire rime ire mem mim rem rim em er me mi re

eimmrrst   trimmers trimmer. *See* **eimmrs eimrst**

eimmrrt   trimmer. *See* **eimrt eimmr**

eimmrs   mimers simmer emirs mimer mimes mires miser rimes emir mems mime mire mirs mise reis rime rims rise semi sire ire mem mim mir mis rem res rim sir em er is me mi re si

eimmrss   simmers. *See* **eimmrs eimrss**

eimmrssw   swimmers simmers swimmer. *See* **eimmrs eimrss**

eimmrstt   trimmest metrist. *See* **eimmrs eimrst eirstt**

eimmrsu   immures rummies. *See* **eimmru eimmrs emmrsu**

eimmrsw   swimmer. *See* **eimmrs**

eimmru   immure mimer emir mime mire rime emu ire mem mim mir mum rem rim rue rum em er me mi mu re um

eimmruy   yummier. *See* **eimmru mmruy**

eimms   mimes mems mime mise semi mem mim mis em is me mi si

eimmstu   tummies. *See* **immstu eimst eistu**

eimmstuy   yummiest tummies. *See* **eimsty immstu**

eimn   mien mine men nim em en in me mi ne

eimnnoot   noontime mention emotion. *See* **eimnnt einnot imnoot innoot**

eimnnost   mentions intones mention moisten tension. *See* **eimnnt eimnos eimost einnot**

eimnnot   mention. *See* **eimnnt einnot**

eimnnott   ointment mention tontine. *See* **eimnnt eimntt einnot**

eimnnt   tinmen emit item mien mine mint mite nine time tine inn men met net nim nit ten tie tin em en in it me mi ne ti

eimnnx   meninx mien mine minx nine nixe inn men mix nim nix em en ex in me mi ne xi

eimnoos   noisome. *See* **eimnos imnoos**

eimnoost   emotions emotion isotone moisten motions noisome. *See* **eimnos eimost eioost emnost**

eimnoot   emotion. *See* **imnoot emnot**

eimnopst   nepotism pimentos moisten pimento postmen. *See* **eimnos eimnpt eimops eimost**

eimnopt   pimento. *See* **eimnpt emnot einop**

eimnoptt   impotent pimento. *See* **eimnpt eimntt eioptt enoptt**

eimnor   merino miner minor emir iron mien mine mire more morn nome norm omen omer rein rime eon ion ire men mir mon mor nim nor one ore rem rim roe em en er in me mi mo ne no om on or re

eimnors   merinos. *See* **eimors eimnor eimnrs imnors eimnos**

eimnorsu   monsieur merinos mousier. *See* **eimnor eimnos eimnrs eimnru**

eimnortw   timeworn. *See* **eimnor einort einotw einrtw**

eimnorty   enormity. *See* **eimnor eimnty eimoty einort**

eimnos   monies eosin meson miens mines noise nomes omens eons ions mien mine mise mons nims noes nome nose omen ones semi sine some ens eon ion men mis mon mos nim oms one sen sin son em en in is me mi mo ne no om on os si so

eimnosst moistens moisten monists nosiest somites. *See* **eimnos eimoss eimost eimsst**

eimnost moisten. *See* **imnost eimnos emnost eimost**

eimnosw winsome. *See* **eimnos einosw**

eimnprss primness impress simpers snipers. *See* **eimnrs eimprs eimrss einprs**

eimnpt pitmen tempi inept emit item mien mine mint mite pent pine pint time tine imp men met net nim nip nit pen pet pie pin pit ten tie tin tip em en in it me mi ne pe pi ti

eimnptu pinetum. *See* **eimptu eimntu eimnpt**

eimnr miner emir mien mine mire rein rime ire men mir nim rem rim em en er in me mi ne re

eimnrs miners emirs miens miner mines mires miser reins resin rimes rinse risen serin siren emir mien mine mire mirs mise nims rein reis rime rims rise semi sine sire ens ire men mir mis nim rem res rim sen sin sir em en er in is me mi ne re si

eimnrsst minsters trimness inserts minster misters sinters smiters. *See* **eimnrs eimrss eimrst eimsst**

eimnrst minster. *See* **einrst eimrst eimnrs**

eimnrstu terminus minster minuets minutes sternum triunes. *See* **eimnrs eimnru eimntu eimrst**

eimnru murine inure miner rumen urine emir menu mien mine mire rein rime ruin rune emu ire men mir nim rem rim rue rum run urn em en er in me mi mu ne nu re um

eimnrv vermin miner riven vimen emir mien mine mire nevi rein rime rive vein vine ire men mir nim rem rev rim vie vim em en er in me mi ne re

eimns miens mines mien mine mise nims semi sine ens men mis nim sen sin em en in is me mi ne si

eimnssu minuses. *See* **eimssu emnsu eimns**

eimnstt mittens smitten. *See* **eimntt einstt**

eimnstu minuets minutes. *See* **eimntu einstu**

eimnsuzz muezzins mizzens muezzin. *See* **eimnzz**

eimnsx minxes miens mines mixes nixes mien mine minx mise nims nixe semi

sine ens men mis mix nim nix sen sex sin six em en ex in is me mi ne si xi

eimnszz mizzens. *See* **eimnzz eimns**

eimntt mitten emit item mien mine mint mite mitt tent time tine tint men met net nim nit ten tie tin tit em en in it me mi ne ti

eimntu minuet minute unite untie emit etui item menu mien mine mint mite mute time tine tune unit emu men met net nim nit nut ten tie tin tui tun em en in it me mi mu ne nu ti um ut

eimnty enmity minty emit item mien mine mint mite time tine tiny yeti men met net nim nit ten tie tin yen yet yin em en in it me mi my ne ti ye

eimnuzz muezzin. *See* **eimnzz**

eimnv vimen mien mine nevi vein vine men nim vie vim em en in me mi ne

eimnz mizen mien mine zein men nim em en in me mi ne

eimnzz mizzen mizen mien mine zein men nim em en in me mi ne

eimoor roomie emir mire moor more omer rime room ire mir moo mor ore rem rim roe em er me mi mo om or re

eimoorr roomier. *See* **eimoor emoorr**

eimoors roomies. *See* **eimors emoors eimoor**

eimoorst roomiest moister mortise roomies sootier. *See* **eimoor eimors eimost eimrst**

eimoortz motorize. *See* **eimoor eioorz**

eimopprr improper. *See* **eimprr eipprr emoprr eopprr**

eimoprrs primrose promiser imposer primers promise prosier rompers semipro. *See* **eimops eimors eimprr eimprs**

eimoprrt importer. *See* **eimprr eimprt eiorrt emoprr**

eimoprrv improver improve. *See* **eimprr emoprr imoprv**

eimoprs imposer promise semipro. *See* **eimops eimors imoprs eimprs emoprs**

eimoprss imposers promises semipros imposer imposes impress isomers mossier porisms promise semipro simpers. *See* **eimops eimors eimoss eimprs**

eimoprst imposter imports imposer imprest moister mortise permits promise semipro tropism. *See* **eimops eimors eimost eimprs**

eimoprsv improves imposer improve improvs promise semipro. *See* **eimops eimors eimosv eimprs**

eimopruu europium. *See* **eimpru**

eimoprv improve. *See* **imoprv emorv eimov**

eimops impose mopes poems poise pomes epos imps mise mope mops opes peso pies poem pois pome pose semi simp some imp mis mop mos oms ope pie poi sip sop em is me mi mo om os pe pi si so

eimopss imposes. *See* **eimops eimoss eiopss**

eimoqstu misquote mesquit. *See* **eimost eiqstu emoqsu eoqstu**

eimorrst stormier moister mortise rioters termors tremors. *See* **eimors eimost eimrst eiorrs**

eimorrw wormier. *See* **emorw emorr eorrw**

eimors isomer emirs mires miser mores omers osier rimes emir mire mirs mise more mors omer ores reis rime rims rise roes rose semi sire some sore sori ire mir mis mor mos oms ore rem res rim roe sir em er is me mi mo om or os re si so

eimorss isomers mossier. *See* **eimors eimoss eimrss**

eimorsst mortises isomers misters moister mortise mossier rosiest smiters somites sorites sorties stories. *See* **eimors eimoss eimost eimrss**

eimorst moister mortise. *See* **eimors eimrst emorst eimost eiorst**

eimorstu moisture moister mortise mousier tourism. *See* **eimors eimost eimrst eiorst**

eimorsu mousier. *See* **eimors emorsu**

eimoss mioses semis mess mise miss moss semi some ess mis mos oms sis em is me mi mo om os si so

eimossst mossiest somites. *See* **eimoss eimost eimsst eosst**

eimosst somites. *See* **eimoss eimsst eimost**

eimosstt moistest somites mostest. *See* **eimoss eimost eimsst emostt**

eimosstu mousiest somites. *See* **eimoss eimost eimsst eimssu**

eimosstz mestizos somites mestizo. *See* **eimoss eimost emostz**

eimost somite emits items mites moist motes omits smite smote times tomes emit item mise mist mite most mote mots omit semi site some stem ties time toes tome toms its met mis mos mot oms set sit sot tie toe tom em is it me mi mo om os si so ti to

eimosttu timeouts titmouse timeout. *See* **eimost emostt eosttu mosttu**

eimostv motives. *See* **eimotv eimosv eiostv imostv**

eimostz mestizo. *See* **eimost**

eimosv movies movie moves mise move semi some vies vims vise mis mos oms vie vim em is me mi mo om os si so

eimosx oximes mixes moxie oxime mise semi some mis mix mos oms sex six sox em ex is me mi mo om os ox si so xi

eimosyz isozyme. *See* **emosy emsyz**

eimottu timeout. *See* **emott**

eimotv motive movie vomit emit item mite mote move omit time tome veto vote met mot tie toe tom vet vie vim em it me mi mo om ti to

eimoty moiety emit item mite mote omit time tome yeti met mot tie toe tom toy yet em it me mi mo my om oy ti to ye

eimov movie move vie vim em me mi mo om

eimox moxie oxime mix em ex me mi mo om ox xi

eimpr prime emir mire peri perm pier prim rime ripe imp ire mir per pie rem rep rim rip em er me mi pe pi re

eimprr primer prime prier emir mire peri perm pier prim rime ripe err imp ire mir per pie rem rep rim rip em er me mi pe pi re

eimprrs primers. *See* **eiprrs eimprr eimprs**

eimprs primes simper emirs mires miser perms piers pries prime prism rimes sperm spire emir imps mire mirs mise peri perm pier pies prim reis reps rime rims ripe rips rise semi simp sire imp ire mir mis per pie rem rep res rim rip sip sir em er is me mi pe pi re si

eimprss impress simpers. *See* **eimrss eimprs imprss emprss eiprss**

eimprst imprest permits. *See* **eiprst eimrst eimprt eimprs**

eimprsu umpires. *See* **eimpru eimprs imprsu eiprsu**

eimprt permit merit miter mitre prime remit tempi timer tripe emir emit item mire mite peri perm pert pier prim rime ripe rite term tier time tire trim trip imp ire met mir per pet pie pit rem rep ret rim rip tie tip em er it me mi pe pi re ti

eimpru impure umpire prime emir mire peri perm pier prim pure rime ripe rump emu imp ire mir per pie rem rep rim rip rue rum ump em er me mi mu pe pi re um up

eimpssst missteps misstep. *See* **eimsss eimsst eipsss eipsst**

eimpsst misstep. *See* **eimsst eipsst**

eimpstu impetus imputes. *See* **eimptu empstu**

eimpt tempi emit item mite time imp met pet pie pit tie tip em it me mi pe pi ti

eimptu impute tempi emit etui item mite mute time tump emu imp met pet pie pit put tie tip tui tup ump em it me mi mu pe pi ti um up ut

eimqstu mesquit. *See* **eiqstu eimst emstu**

eimqstuy mystique mesquit. *See* **eimsty eiqstu**

eimrs emirs mires miser rimes emir mire mirs mise reis rime rims rise semi sire ire mir mis rem res rim sir em er is me mi re si

eimrss misers remiss emirs mires miser rimes rises semis sires emir mess mire mirs mise miss reis rime rims rise semi sire sirs ess ire mir mis rem res rim sir sis em er is me mi re si

eimrssst mistress misters resists sisters smiters. *See* **eimrss eimrst eimsst eirsst**

eimrsssu surmises issuers misuses surmise. *See* **eimrss eimssu eirssu emrssu**

eimrsst misters smiters. *See* **eimrst eimrss eirsst eimsst**

eimrsstt metrists metrist misters sitters smiters. *See* **eimrss eimrst eimsst eirsst**

eimrssu surmise. *See* **eirssu eimssu eimrss emrssu**

eimrssv verisms. *See* **eimrss eimrsv**

eimrst merits mister miters mitres remits timers emirs emits items merit mires miser miter mites mitre remit rimes rites smite terms tiers timer times tires tries trims emir emit erst item mire mirs mise mist mite reis rest rets rime rims rise rite semi sire site stem stir term tier ties time tire trim ire its met mir mis rem res ret rim set sir sit tie em er is it me mi re si ti

eimrstt metrist. *See* **eimrst eirstt**

eimrstux mixtures mixture. *See* **eimrst eimrsx emrstu imrstu**

eimrsv verism emirs mires miser rimes emir mire mirs mise reis revs rime rims rise rive semi sire vies vims vise ire mir mis rem res rev rim sir vie vim em er is me mi re si

eimrsx mixers emirs mires mirex miser mixer mixes remix rimes emir mire mirs mise reis rime rims rise semi sire ire mir mis mix rem res rex rim sex sir six em er ex is me mi re si xi

eimrsy misery emirs mires miser rimes emir mire mirs miry mise reis rime rims rimy rise ryes semi sire ire mir mis rem res rim rye sir yes em er is me mi my re si ye

eimrt merit miter mitre remit timer emir emit item mire mite rime rite term tier time tire trim ire met mir rem ret rim tie em er it me mi re ti

eimrtux mixture. *See* **eimrt eimrx emrux**

eimruzz muzzier. *No 6s or 5s*

eimrx mirex mixer remix emir mire rime ire mir mix rem rex rim em er ex me mi re xi

eims mise semi mis em is me mi si

eimss semis mess mise miss semi ess mis sis em is me mi si

eimsss misses semis mess mise miss semi ess mis sis em is me mi si

eimsssu misuses. *See* **eisssu eimsss imsssu eimssu emsssu**

eimsst smites tmesis emits items mists mites semis sites smite stems times emit mess mise miss mist mite semi sets site sits stem ties time ess its met mis set sis sit tie em is it me mi si ti

eimssty stymies. *See* **eimsst eimsty emssty**

eimssu misuse issue muses semis emus mess mise miss muse muss semi sues sums uses emu ess mis mus sis sue sum use em is me mi mu si um us

eimssx sexism mixes semis sixes mess mise miss semi ess mis mix sex sis six em ex is me mi si xi

eimst emits items mites smite times emit item mise mist mite semi site stem ties time its met mis set sit tie em is it me mi si ti

eimsty stymie emits items misty mites smite times yetis emit item mise mist mite semi site stem ties time yeti its met mis set sit sty tie yes yet em is it me mi my si ti ye

eimsx mixes semi mis mix sex six em ex is me mi si xi

eimt emit item mite time tie met em it me mi ti

einn nine inn en in ne

einnnr rennin inner renin nine rein ire inn en er in ne re

einnnrs rennins. *See* **einnrs einnnr**

einnops pension. *See* **einops einnps**

einnopss pensions pension. *See* **einnps einops einoss einpss**

einnorst intoners ternions interns intoner intones orients stonier tension ternion tinners. *See* **einnot einnrs einnrt einnst**

einnorsu reunions neurons nonuser reunion sunnier. *See* **einnrs einors einrsu ennoru**

einnorsv environs environ venison version. *See* **einnrs einnsv einors eiorsv**

einnort intoner ternion. *See* **einnrt einnot einort**

einnortu neutrino intoner neutron reunion routine ternion. *See* **einnot einnrt einort einrtu**

einnortv inventor environ intoner ternion vintner. *See* **einnot einnrt einntv einort**

einnoru reunion. *See* **ennoru einnu einnr**

einnorv environ. *See* **einnr einov einrv**

einnorww winnower. *See* **einnrw ennorw innoww**

einnosss nosiness session. *See* **einoss**

einnosst tensions intones nosiest sennits sonnets tension. *See* **einnot einnst einoss einsst**

einnossv venisons venison. *See* **einnsv einoss**

einnost intones tension. *See* **einnot ennost einnst**

einnostt tontines intones tension tontine. *See* **einnot einnst einntt einstt**

einnosv venison. *See* **einnsv einos ennos**

einnot intone nonet tenon tonne into neon nine none note tine tone eon inn ion net nit not one ten tie tin toe ton en in it ne no on ti to

einnott tontine. *See* **einnot einntt**

einnovw inwoven. *See* **einovw einnv**

einnp penni nine pine inn nip pen pie pin en in ne pe pi

einnprs spinner. *See* **einnps einnrs einprs**

einnprss spinners sinners snipers spinner. *See* **einnps einnrs einprs einpss**

einnps pennis nines penni pines snipe spine inns nine nips pens pies pine pins sine snip spin ens inn nip pen pie pin sen sin sip en in is ne pe pi si

einnpssu puniness puisnes supines. *See* **einnps einpss einpsu innpsu**

einnpst tenpins. *See* **einpst einnps einnst**

einnpsy spinney. *See* **einnps ennpy einpy**

einnr inner renin nine rein ire inn en er in ne re

einnrru runnier. *See* **ennrru einnu einnr**

einnrs renins sinner inner nines reins renin resin rinse risen serin siren inns nine rein reis rise sine sire ens inn ire res sen sin sir en er in is ne re si

einnrss sinners. *See* **einnrs einrss**

einnrst interns tinners. *See* **einrst einnrt einnrs einnst**

einnrstu runniest interns stunner sunnier tinners triunes. *See* **einnrs einnrt einnst einrst**

einnrstv vintners interns invents inverts striven tinners vintner. *See* **einnrs einnrt einnst einnsv**

einnrsu sunnier. *See* **einrsu innrsu**

einnrt intern tinner inert inner inter niter renin trine nine rein rent rite tern tier tine tire inn ire net nit ret ten tie tin en er in it ne re ti

einnrttu nutrient nuttier. *See* **einnrt einntt einrtt einrtu**

einnrtv vintner. *See* **einnrt einntv einrtv**

einnrw winner inner renin nine rein weir wine wire wren inn ire new wen win en er in ne re we

einns nines inns nine sine ens inn sen sin en in is ne si

einnsst sennits. *See* **einsst einnst**

einnsstu sunniest sennits. *See* **einnst einsst einstu eisstu**

einnst sennit tennis inset nines stein tines inns nest nets nine nits sent sine site snit tens ties tine tins ens inn its net nit sen set sin sit ten tie tin en in is it ne si ti

einnstv invents. *See* **einntv einstv einnst einnsv**

einnsv venins nines veins venin vines inns nevi nine sine vein vies vine vise ens inn sen sin vie en in is ne si

einntt intent nine tent tine tint inn net nit ten tie tin tit en in it ne ti

einntv invent venin nevi nine tine vein vent vine inn net nit ten tie tin vet vie en in it ne ti

einnty ninety tinny nine tine tiny yeti inn net nit ten tie tin yen yet yin en in it ne ti ye

einnu ennui nine inn nun en in ne nu

einnv venin nevi nine vein vine vie inn en in ne

einooprs poisoner erosion orpines snooper. *See* **einopr einops einors einprs**

einoors erosion. *See* **einors inoors enoors**

einoosst isotones isotone nosiest. *See* **einoss einsst eioost enooss**

einoost isotone. *See* **eioost einos einst**

einop opine nope open peon pine pone eon ion nip one ope pen pie pin poi en in ne no on pe pi

einopr orpine opine prone ripen iron nope open peon peri pier pine pirn pone pore rein repo ripe rope eon ion ire nip nor one ope ore pen per pie pin poi pro rep rip roe en er in ne no on or pe pi re

einoprrs prisoner ironers orpines perrons prosier. *See* **einopr einops einorr einors**

einoprs orpines. *See* **einors einops einopr enoprs inoprs**

einoprst pointers proteins orients orpines pointer postern protein stonier. *See* **einopr einops einors einort**

einoprt pointer protein. *See* **einopr einort**

einoprtu eruption pointer protein routine. *See* **einopr einort einrtu enprtu**

einops opines ponies eosin noise opens opine peons pines poise pones snipe spine eons epos ions nips noes nope nose ones open opes pens peon peso pies pine pins pois pone pons pose sine snip spin ens eon ion nip one ope pen pie pin poi sen sin sip son sop en in is ne no on os pe pi si so

einopstt nepotist potties tiptoes. *See* **einops einpst einstt eioptt**

einoqstu question inquest quintes. *See* **einqsu einqtu einstu eiqstu**

einoqttu quotient quintet. *See* **einqtu einttu enottu**

einoqux equinox. *See* **inoqu**

einorr ironer rein iron eon err ion ire nor one ore roe en er in ne no on or re

einorrs ironers. *See* **einorr einors einrrs eiorrs enorrs**

einors nosier senior eosin irons noise osier reins resin rinse risen rosin serin siren snore eons ions iron noes nose ones ores rein reis rise roes rose sine sire sore sori ens eon ion ire nor one ore res roe sen sin sir son en er in is ne no on or os re si so

einorss seniors. *See* **einoss einrss inorss einors enorss**

einorsss rosiness seniors sensors session. *See* **einors einoss einrss enorss**

einorssu neurosis resinous insures seniors serious sunrise. *See* **einors einoss einrss einrsu**

einorssv versions seniors version. *See* **einors einoss einrss eiorsv**

einorst orients stonier. *See* **einrst einors enorst einort eiorst**

einorstu routines nitrous orients routine stonier tonsure triunes. *See* **einors einort einrst einrsu**

einorstv investor inverts orients stonier striven version. *See* **einors einort einrst einrtv**

einorsuv souvenir envious nervous niveous version. *See* **einors einrsu eiorsv enosuv**

einorsv version. *See* **einors eiorsv**

einorsw snowier. *See* **einors einosw enorsw**

einort orient inert inter niter noter tenor toner trine into iron note rein rent riot rite rote tern tier tine tire tiro tone tore tori torn trio eon ion ire net nit nor not one ore ort ret roe rot ten tie tin toe ton tor en er in it ne no on or re ti to

einortu routine. *See* **einort einrtu**

einos eosin noise eons ions noes nose ones sine ens eon ion one sen sin son en in is ne no on os si so

einoss noesis noises eosin noise noses sines eons ions noes nose ones sine sins sons ens eon ess ion one sen sin sis son en in is ne no on os si so

einosss session. *See* **einoss**

einossss sessions session. *See* **einoss**

einosst nosiest. *See* **einsst einoss enosst**

einosstt stoniest nosiest stetson testons. *See* **einoss einsst einstt enosst**

einosstw snowiest nosiest townies wisents witness. *See* **einoss einosw einotw einsst**

einostw townies. *See* **einosw einotw einstw**

einosuv envious niveous. *See* **enosuv inosuv**

einosw nowise eosin noise sinew swine wines winos enow eons ions news noes nose ones owes owns sewn sine snow sown wens wine wino wins wise woes ens eon ion new now one owe own sen sew sin son sow wen win wis woe won en in is ne no on os ow si so we

einotw townie twine enow into newt note nowt tine tone town twin wine wino wite wont eon ion net new nit not now one owe own ten tie tin toe ton tow two wen wet win wit woe won en in it ne no on ow ti to we

einov ovine nevi oven vein vine eon ion one vie en in ne no on

einovw inwove ovine woven enow nevi oven vein view vine wine wino wive wove eon ion new now one owe own vie vow wen win woe won en in ne no on ow we

einp pine nip pen pie pin en in ne pe pi

einppr nipper ripen piper peri pier pine pipe pirn prep rein repp ripe ire nip pen pep per pie pin pip rep rip en er in ne pe pi re

einpprs nippers snipper. *See* **einppr einpps eipprs einprs**

einpprss snippers nippers pepsins sippers snipers snipper. *See* **einppr einpps einprs einpss**

einpps pepsin pines pipes snipe spine nips pens peps pies pine pins pipe pips sine snip spin ens nip pen pep pie pin pip sen sin sip en in is ne pe pi si

einppss pepsins. *See* **einpps einpss**

einppsst snippets insteps pepsins sippets snippet spinets. *See* **einpps einpss einpst einsst**

einppst snippet. *See* **einpst einpps eippst**

einpr ripen peri pier pine pirn rein ripe ire nip pen per pie pin rep rip en er in ne pe pi re

einprrst printers reprints sprinter printer reprint striper. *See* **einprs einpst einrrs einrst**

einprrt printer reprint. *See* **einpt einrt eiprr**

einprrtu prurient printer reprint runtier. *See* **einrtu enprtu enrrtu inprtu**

einprrty printery printer reprint. *See* **einpry eiprty**

einprs ripens sniper piers pines pirns pries reins resin rinse ripen risen serin siren snipe spine spire nips pens peri pier pies pine pins pirn rein reis reps ripe rips rise sine sire snip spin ens ire nip pen per pie pin rep res rip sen sin sip sir en er in is ne pe pi re si

einprss snipers. *See* **einrss einprs einpss eiprss**

einprsst spinster inserts insteps persist priests sinters snipers spinets sprints sprites stripes. *See* **einprs einpss einpst einrss**

einprsu uprisen. *See* **einrsu enprsu einpsu einprs eiprsu**

einpry pinery ripen piney peri pier pine piny pirn prey pyre rein ripe yipe ire nip pen per pie pin pry rep rip rye yen yep yin yip en er in ne pe pi re ye

einps pines snipe spine nips pens pies pine pins sine snip spin ens nip pen pie pin sen sin sip en in is ne pe pi si

einpss snipes spines pines sines snipe snips spies spine spins nips pens pies pine pins sine sins sips snip spin ens ess nip pen pie pin sen sin sip sis en in is ne pe pi si

einpsst insteps spinets. *See* **einsst einpst einpss eipsst**

einpssu puisnes supines. *See* **einpsu einpss**

einpst instep spinet inept inset pines pints snipe spent spine spite stein stipe tines nest nets nips nits pens pent pest pets pies pine pins pint pits sent sept sine site snip snit spin spit step tens ties tine tins tips ens its net nip nit pen pet pie pin pit sen set sin sip sit ten tie tin tip en in is it ne pe pi si ti

einpstty tintypes tintype. *See* **einpst einstt eintty ipstty**

einpstu punties. *See* **inpstu einpst einpsu einstu**

einpsu puisne supine pines snipe spine nips pens pies pine pins puns sine snip spin spue spun ens nip pen pie pin pun pus sen sin sip sue sun sup use en in is ne nu pe pi si up us

einpt inept pent pine pint tine net nip nit pen pet pie pin pit ten tie tin tip en in it ne pe pi ti

einpty tintype. *See* **eintty einpt eiptt**

einpy piney pine piny yipe nip pen pie pin yen yep yin yip en in ne pe pi ye

einqrttu quitrent nuttier quintet quitter. *See* **einqtu einrtt einrtu einttu**

einqruy enquiry. *See* **einru enqru eqruy**

einqsstu inquests inquest quintes sequins squints. *See* **einqsu einqtu einsst einstu**

einqssu sequins. *See* **einqsu eissu inssu**

einqsttu quintets inquest quintes quintet. *See* **einqsu einqtu einstt einstu**

einqstu inquest quintes. *See* **eiqstu einqtu inqstu einqsu einstu**

einqsu sequin sine ens sen sin sue sun use en in is ne nu si us

einqttu quintet. *See* **einqtu einttu**

einqtu quinte quiet quint quite unite untie etui quit tine tune unit net nit nut ten tie tin tui tun en in it ne nu ti ut

einr rein ire en er in ne re

einrrs rinser reins resin rinse risen riser serin siren errs rein reis rise sine sire ens err ire res sen sin sir en er in is ne re si

einrrss rinsers. *See* **einrss einrrs eirrss**

einrrssu insurers insurer insures rinsers sunrise. *See* **einrrs einrss einrsu eirssu**

einrrsu insurer. *See* **einrsu enrrsu einrrs**

einrrtu runtier. *See* **einrtu enrrtu**

einrs reins resin rinse risen serin siren rein reis rise sine sire ens ire res sen sin sir en er in is ne re si

einrss resins rinses serins sirens reins resin rinse risen rises serin sines siren sires rein reis rise sine sins sire sirs ens ess ire res sen sin sir sis en er in is ne re si

einrsssu sunrises insures issuers sinuses sunrise. *See* **einrss einrsu eirssu enrssu**

einrsst inserts sinters. *See* **einrst einsst einrss eirsst enrsst**

einrssu insures sunrise. *See* **einrsu eirssu enrssu einrss**

einrssxy syrinxes. *See* **einrss inrsxy**

einrst insert inters sinter inert inset inter niter reins rents resin rinse risen rites serin siren stein stern terns tiers tines tires tries trine erst nest nets nits rein reis rent rest rets rise rite sent sine sire site snit stir tens tern tier ties tine tins tire ens ire its net nit res ret sen set sin sir sit ten tie tin en er in is it ne re si ti

einrsttu runtiest entrust nuttier triunes. *See* **einrst einrsu einrtt einrtu**

einrstu triunes. *See* **einrst einrsu einstu einrtu enrstu**

einrstv inverts striven. *See* **einrst einrtv einstv eirstv**

einrstw winters. *See* **einrst enrstw einstw einrtw eirstw**

einrsu insure inures ursine inure nurse reins resin rinse risen ruins runes serin siren urine rein reis rise rues ruin rune runs ruse sine sire sure urns user ens ire res rue run sen sin sir sue sun urn use en er in is ne nu re si us

einrt inert inter niter trine rein rent rite tern tier tine tire ire net nit ret ten tie tin en er in it ne re ti

einrtt tinter inert inter niter titer titre trine trite rein rent rite tent tern tier tine tint tire tret ire net nit ret ten tie tin tit en er in it ne re ti

einrttu nuttier. *See* **einttu einrtt einrtu**

einrttw written. *See* **einrtt einrtw**

einrtu triune inert inter inure niter trine tuner unite untie urine uteri etui rein rent rite ruin rune runt tern tier tine tire true tune turn unit ire net nit nut ret rue run rut ten tie tin tui tun urn en er in it ne nu re ti ut

einrtv invert inert inter niter riven rivet trine nevi rein rent rite rive tern tier tine tire vein vent vert vine ire net nit ret rev ten tie tin vet vie en er in it ne re ti

einrtw winter inert inter niter trine twine write newt rein rent rite tern tier tine tire twin weir wine wire wite wren writ ire net new nit ret ten tie tin wen wet win wit en er in it ne re ti we

einru inure urine rein ruin rune ire rue run urn en er in ne nu re

einrv riven nevi rein rive vein vine ire rev vie en er in ne re

einrvy vinery nervy riven veiny envy nevi rein rive vein very vine viny ire ivy rev rye vie yen yin en er in ne re ye

einrwy winery rein weir wine winy wire wiry wren ire new rye wen win wye yen yew yin en er in ne re we ye

eins sine ens sen sin en in is ne si

einss sines sine sins ens ess sen sin sis en in is ne si

einsssu sinuses. *See* **eisssu inssu einss**

einsst insets steins inset nests sines sites snits stein tines nest nets nits sent sets sine sins site sits snit tens ties tine tins ens ess its net nit sen set sin sis sit ten tie tin en in is it ne si ti

einsstv invests. *See* **einsst einstv**

einsstw wisents witness. *See* **einsst einssw einstw eisstw**

einssw sinews sines sinew swine wines news sewn sews sine sins wens wine wins wise ens ess new sen sew sin sis wen win wis en in is ne si we

einst inset stein tines nest nets nits sent sine site snit tens ties tine tins ens its net nit sen set sin sit ten tie tin en in is it ne si ti

einstt sitten inset stein stint tents tines tints nest nets nits sent sine site snit stet tens tent test ties tine tins tint tits ens its net nit sen set sin sit ten tie tin tit en in is it ne si ti

einsttu nuttiest. *See* **einstt einstu einttu istttu**

einstu tenuis unites unties etuis inset stein suint suite tines tunes unite units untie etui nest nets nits nuts sent sine site snit stun suet suit tens ties tine tins tuis tune tuns unit ens its net nit nut sen set sin sit sue sun ten tie tin tui tun use en in is it ne nu si ti us ut

einstv invest inset stein tines veins vents vines nest nets nevi nits sent sine site snit tens ties tine tins vein vent vest vets vies vine vise ens its net nit sen set sin sit ten tie tin vet vie en in is it ne si ti

einstw twines wisent inset newts sinew stein swine tines twine twins wines wites nest nets news newt nits sent sewn sine site snit stew tens ties tine tins twin wens west wets wine wins wise wite wits ens its net new nit sen set sew sin sit ten tie tin wen wet win wis wit en in is it ne si ti we

einsuw unwise sinew swine wines news sewn sine wens wine wins wise ens new sen sew sin sue sun use wen win wis en in is ne nu si us we

einsux unisex nixes nexus sine nixe ens nix sen sex sin six sue sun use en ex in is ne nu si us xi

einsv veins vines nevi sine vein vies vine vise ens sen sin vie en in is ne si

einsvx vixens nixes veins vines vixen nevi nixe sine vein vies vine vise ens nix sen sex sin six vex vie en ex in is ne si xi

einsw sinew swine wines news sewn sine wens wine wins wise ens new sen sew sin wen win wis en in is ne si we

einswy sinewy newsy sinew swine wines news sewn sine wens wine wins winy wise wyes yens yews ens new sen sew sin wen win wis wye yen yes yew yin en in is ne si we ye

einswz wizens sinew swine wines wizen news sewn sine size wens wine wins wise zein ens new sen sew sin wen win wis en in is ne si we

einsx nixes sine nixe ens nix sen sex sin six ex en ix in is ne si xi

eint tine net nit ten tie tin en in it ne ti

einttu tenuti unite untie etui tent tine tint tune unit net nit nut ten tie tin tit tui tun tut en in it ne nu ti ut

eintty entity nitty tent tine tint tiny yeti net nit ten tie tin tit yen yet yin en in it ne ti ye

eintu unite untie etui tine tune unit net nit nut ten tie tin tui tun en in it ne nu ti ut

eintw twine newt tine twin wine wite net new nit ten tie tin wen wet win wit en in it ne ti we

einv nevi vein vine vie en in ne

einvx vixen nevi nixe vein vine nix vex vie en ex in ne xi

einvy veiny envy nevi vein vine viny ivy vie yen yin en in ne ye

einw wine new wen win en in ne we

einwz wizen wine zein new wen win en in ne we

einx nixe nix en ex in ne xi

einz zein en in ne

eioopprs porpoise opposer propose. *See* **eipprs eoopps**

eiooppst opposite isotope potpies. *See* **eioost eioppt eippst eoopps**

eioopsst isotopes isotope. *See* **eioost eiopss eipsst eopsst**

eioopst isotope. *See* **eioost eopst eiops**

eioorrt rootier. *See* **eiorrt eoorrt**

eioorst sootier. *See* **eioost eiorst**

eioorstt rootiest tortoise sootier tootsie. *See* **eioost eiorst eirstt eorstt**

eioorwz woozier. *See* **eioorz eiowz eoorw**

eioorz oozier ooze orzo zero zori ire ore roe zoo er or re

eioosstt sootiest tootsies tootsie. *See* **eioost**

eioost otiose site soot ties toes its set sit sot tie toe too is it os si so ti to

eioostt tootsie. *See* **eioost eostt oostt**

eioostwz wooziest ooziest. *See* **eioost eioswz**

eioostz ooziest. *See* **eioost eoosz**

eioppps poppies. *See* **eipps eiops eopps**

eioppst potpies. *See* **eioppt eippst**

eioppt potpie pipe poet pope tope ope pep pet pie pip pit poi pop pot tie tip toe top it pe pi ti to

eiopqrsu piroques piroque soupier. *See* **eipqsu eiprsu eiqrsu eoprsu**

eiopqru piroque. *See* **eipqu eiqru eoqru**

eioprrs prosier. *See* **eiprrs eoprrs eiorrs**

eioprrss prioress orrises pressor prosier. *See* **eiopss eiorrs eiprrs eiprss**

eioprrst sportier porters presort pretors prosier reports rioters striper. *See* **eiorrs eiorrt eiorst eiprrs**

eioprrsu superior prosier pursier soupier. *See* **eiorrs eiprrs eiprsu eoprrs**

eioprsst prosiest persist posters prestos priests rosiest sorites sorties sprites stories stripes. *See* **eiopss eiorst eiprss eiprst**

eioprstt spottier potters potties protest spitter spotter tipster tiptoes. *See* **eioptt eiorst eiprst eirstt**

eioprstv sportive privets. *See* **eiorst eiorsv eiostv eiprst**

eioprsu soupier. *See* **eoprsu eiprsu**

eioprsuv pervious previous viperous soupier. *See* **eiorsv eiprsu eiprsv eoprsu**

eioprsx proxies. *See* **eiors eiprs eipsx**

eiops poise epos opes peso pies pois pose ope pie poi sip sop is os pe pi si so

eiopss poises posies pesos poise poses posse spies epos opes peso pies pois pose sips sops ess ope pie poi sip sis sop is os pe pi si so

eiopsstu soupiest piteous. *See* **eiopss eipsst eisstu eopsst**

eiopstt potties tiptoes. *See* **eioptt eopst eiops**

eiopstu piteous. *See* **eopst eistu iopsu**

eiopstuw wipeouts piteous wipeout. *See* **eopst eistu iopsu**

eioptt tiptoe petit poet tope tote ope pet pie pit poi pot tie tip tit toe top tot it pe pi ti to

eioptuw wipeout. *No 6s or 5s*

eiorrrs sorrier. *See* **eiors eorrrs**

eiorrrsw worriers sorrier worrier worries. *See* **eiors eorrrs eorrsw**

eiorrrtu roturier. *See* **eiorrt eorrrt eorrtu**

eiorrrw worrier. *See* **eorrr eorrw eirrw**

eiorrs rosier orris osier riser sorer errs ores reis rise roes rose sire sore sori err ire ore res roe sir er is or os re si so

eiorrss orrises. *See* **eiorrs eirrss**

eiorrsst resistor sorriest orrises resorts rioters rosiest rosters sorites sorters sorties stories. *See* **eiorrs eiorrt eiorst eirrss**

eiorrst rioters. *See* **eorrst eiorrt eiorrs eiorst**

eiorrstv servitor rioters trovers. *See* **eiorrs eiorrt eiorst eiorsv**

eiorrsw worries. *See* **eiorrs eorrsw**

eiorrt rioter retro riot rite rote tier tire tiro tore tori torr trio err ire ore ort ret roe rot tie toe tor er it or re ti to

eiors osier ores reis rise roes rose sire sore sori ire ore res roe sir er is or os re si so

eiorsst rosiest sorites sorties stories. *See* **eirsst eorsst**

eiorssu serious. *See* **eirssu eorssu**

eiorssx xerosis. *See* **eiors eirss eorss**

eiorssz seizors. *See* **eiorsz eissz**

eiorst sortie osier riots rites rotes store tiers tires tiros torsi tries trios erst ores orts reis rest rets riot rise rite roes rose

---

rote rots sire site sore sori sort stir tier ties tire tiro toes tore tori tors trio ire its ore ort res ret roe rot set sir sit sot tie toe tor er is it or os re si so ti to

eiorstuv vitreous virtues. *See* **eiorst eiorsv eiostv eirstv**

eiorsv vireos osier roves servo verso vireo visor ores over reis revs rise rive roes rose rove sire sore sori vies vise ire ore res rev roe sir vie er is or os re si so

eiorsz seizor osier zeros zoris ores reis rise roes rose sire size sore sori zero zori ire ore res roe sir er is or os re si so

eiorv vireo over rive rove ire ore rev roe vie er or re

eiosstuz outsizes outsize. *See* **eisstu**

eiosstv soviets. *See* **eiostv eosstv**

eiostuz outsize. *See* **eistu**

eiostv soviet stove votes site ties toes vest veto vets vies vise vote its set sit sot tie toe vet vie is it os si so ti to

eioswz zowies zowie owes size wise woes owe sew sow wis woe is os ow si so we

eiotvv votive veto vote tie toe vet vie it ti to

eiowz zowie owe woe we ow

eip pie pe pi

eipp pipe pep pie pip pe pi

eippppsu puppies. *See* **eipps**

eippr piper peri pier pipe prep repp ripe ire pep per pie pip rep rip er pe pi re

eipprr ripper piper prier peri pier pipe prep repp ripe err ire pep per pie pip rep rip er pe pi re

eipprrs rippers. *See* **eipprs eiprrs eipprr**

eipprrst stripper trippers rippers striper tippers tripper. *See* **eipprr eipprs eipprt eippst**

eipprrt tripper. *See* **eipprr eipprt**

eipprs pipers sipper piers piper pipes preps pries repps spire peps peri pier pies pipe pips prep reis repp reps ripe rips rise sire ire pep per pie pip rep res rip sip sir er is pe pi re si

eipprss sippers. *See* **eipprs eiprss**

eipprst tippers. *See* **eiprst eipprs eippst eipprt**

eipprsz zippers. *See* **eipprs eiprsz eipprz**

eipprt tipper piper tripe peri pert pier pipe prep repp ripe rite tier tire trip ire pep per pet pie pip pit rep ret rip tie tip er it pe pi re ti

eipprz zipper piper prize peri pier pipe prep repp ripe ire pep per pie pip rep rip zip er pe pi re

eipps pipes peps pies pipe pips pep pie pip sip is pe pi si

eippsst sippets. *See* **eippst eipsst**

eippst sippet pipes spite stipe peps pest pets pies pipe pips pits sept site spit

---

step ties tips its pep pet pie pip pit set sip sit tie tip is it pe pi si ti

eippstt tippets. *See* **eippst eipptt**

eippsuy yuppies. *See* **eippuy eipps**

eipptt tippet petit pipe pep pet pie pip pit tie tip tit it pe pi ti

eippuy yuppie pipe pipy yipe pep pie pip pup yep yip yup pe pi up ye

eipqrstu quipster piquets querist. *See* **eipqsu eipqtu eiprst eiprsu**

eipqstu piquets. *See* **eipqsu eipqtu eiqstu**

eipqsu equips piques equip pique quips pies quip spue pie pus sip sue sup use is pe pi si up us

eipqtu piquet equip pique quiet quite etui quip quit pet pie pit put tie tip tui tup it pe pi ti up ut

eipqu equip pique quip pie pe pi up

eipr peri pier ripe ire per pie rep rip er pe pi re

eiprr prier peri pier ripe err ire per pie rep rip er pe pi re

eiprrrsu spurrier pursier. *See* **eiprrs eiprsu eprrsu**

eiprrs priers piers prier pries riser spire errs peri pier pies reis reps ripe rips rise sire err ire per pie rep res rip sip sir er is pe pi re si

eiprrsst stripers persist priests sprites striper stripes. *See* **eiprrs eiprss eiprst eipsst**

eiprrssu surprise pursers pursier pussier suspire uprises. *See* **eiprrs eiprss eiprsu eirssu**

eiprrst striper. *See* **eiprst eiprrs**

eiprrstz spritzer striker. *See* **eiprrs eiprst eiprsz iprstz**

eiprrsu pursier. *See* **eiprrs eprrsu eiprsu**

eiprs piers pries spire peri pier pies reis reps ripe rips rise sire ire per pie rep res rip sip sir er is pe pi re si

eiprss spires piers press pries priss rises sires spies spire peri pier pies reis reps ripe rips rise sips sire sirs ess ire per pie rep res rip sip sir sis er is pe pi re si

eiprsss prisses. *See* **eipsss eiprss**

eiprssst persists persist priests prisses resists sisters sprites stripes. *See* **eiprss eiprst eipsst eirsst**

eiprsssu suspires issuers prisses pussier pussies suspire uprises. *See* **eiprss eiprsu eirssu eprssu**

eiprsst persist priests sprites stripes. *See* **eiprst eirsst eiprss iprsst eipsst**

eiprsstt spitters tipsters persist priests sitters spitter sprites stripes tipster. *See* **eiprss eiprst eipsst eirsst**

eiprsstu pursiest persist priests purists pussier sprites stripes suspire uprises. *See* **eiprss eiprst eiprsu eipsst**

eiprsstz spritzes persist priests spitzes sprites stripes. *See* **eiprss eiprst eiprsz eipsst**

eiprssu pussier suspire uprises. *See* **eirssu eprssu eiprsu**

eiprst esprit priest sprite stripe tripes piers pries rites spire spite sprit stipe strep strip tiers tires tries tripe trips erst iter peri pert pest pets pier pies pits reis reps rest rets ripe rips rise rite sept sire site spit step stir tier ties tips tire trip ire its per pet pie pit rep res ret rip set sip sir sit tie tip er is it pe pi re si ti

eiprstt spitter tipster. *See* **eiprst eirstt**

eiprstv privets. *See* **eiprst eiprtv eirstv eiprsv**

eiprsty pyrites. *See* **eiprst eiprty iprsty**

eiprsu uprise piers pries purse spire sprue super peri pier pies pure reis reps ripe rips rise rues ruse sire spue spur sure user ire per pie pus rep res rip rue sip sir sue sup use er is pe pi re si up us

eiprsuu euripus. *See* **eiprsu eprsuu**

eiprsuvw purviews purview. *See* **eiprsu eiprsv eiprsw**

eiprsv vipers piers pries spire viper peri pier pies reis reps revs ripe rips rise rive sire spiv vies vise ire per pie rep res rev rip sip sir vie er is pe pi re si

eiprsw wipers piers pries spire swipe weirs wiper wipes wires wiser peri pews pier pies reis reps ripe rips rise sire spew weir wipe wire wise wisp ire per pew pie rep res rip sew sip sir wis er is pe pi re si we

eiprsz prizes piers pries prize spire peri pier pies reis reps ripe rips rise sire size zips ire per pie rep res rip sip sir zip er is pe pi re si

eiprt tripe peri pert pier ripe rite tier tire trip ire per pet pie pit rep ret rip tie tip er it pe pi re ti

eiprtv privet rivet tripe viper peri pert pier ripe rite rive tier tire trip vert ire per pet pie pit rep ret rev rip tie tip vet vie er it pe pi re ti

eiprty pyrite tripe piety peri pert pier pity prey pyre ripe rite tier tire trip type yeti yipe ire per pet pie pit pry rep ret rip rye tie tip try yep yet yip er it pe pi re ti ye

eipruvw purview. *See* **eiprv eiprw**

eiprv viper peri pier ripe rive ire per pie rep rev rip vie er pe pi re

eiprw wiper peri pier ripe weir wipe wire ire per pew pie rep rip er pe pi re we

eiprxy expiry pyxie prexy peri pier pixy prey pyre ripe yipe ire per pie pix pry pyx rep rex rip rye yep yip er ex pe pi re xi ye

eiprz prize peri pier ripe ire per pie rep rip zip er pe pi re

eips pies pie sip is pe pi si

eipss spies pies sips ess pie sip sis is pe pi si

eipsss sepsis speiss spies pies sips ess pie sip sis is pe pi si

eipssstu pussiest pussies tissues. *See* **eipsss eipsst eisssu eisstu**

eipsssu pussies. *See* **eisssu epsssu eipsss**

eipsst stipes pests sites spies spite spits steps stipe pest pets pies pits sept sets sips site sits spit step ties tips ess its pet pie pit set sip sis sit tie tip is it pe pi si ti

eipsstz spitzes. *See* **eipsst eissz ipstz**

eipssw swipes spews spies swipe wipes wisps pews pies sews sips spew wipe wise wisp ess pew pie sew sip sis wis is pe pi si we

eipst spite stipe pest pets pies pits sept site spit step ties tips its pet pie pit set sip sit tie tip is it pe pi si ti

eipstu putties. *See* **eistu eiptt psttu**

eipsw swipe wipes pews pies spew wipe wise wisp pew pie sew pis wis is pe pi si we

eipsx pixes pies pie pix sex sip six ex is pe pi si xi

eipsxy pyxies pixes pyxes pyxie pyxis espy pies pixy sexy yipe yips pie pix pyx sex sip six spy yep yes yip ex is pe pi si xi ye

eiptt petit pet pie pit tie tip tit it pe pi ti

eipty piety pity type yeti yipe pet pie pit tie tip yep yet yip it pe pi ti ye

eipw wipe pie pew pe pi we

eipxy pyxie yipe pixy pie pix pyx yep yip ex pe pi xi ye

eipy yipe pie yep yip pe pi ye

eiqrsstu querists querist squires squirts. *See* **eiqrsu eiqstu eirsst eirssu**

eiqrssu squires. *See* **eirssu eiqrsu**

eiqrsttu quitters querist quitter. *See* **eiqrsu eiqstu eirstt ersttu**

eiqrstu querist. *See* **eiqstu iqrstu eiqrsu**

eiqrsu quires squire quire reis rise rues ruse sire sure user ire res rue sir sue use er is re si us

eiqrsuv quivers. *See* **eiqrsu eiqruv**

eiqrsuzz quizzers quizzer quizzes. *See* **eiqrsu**

eiqrttu quitter. *See* **eiqtu eiqru iqrtu**

eiqru quire ire rue er re

eiqruv quiver quire rive ire rev rue vie er re

eiqruvy quivery. *See* **eiqruv eqruy**

eiqruzz quizzer. *See* **eiqru**

eiqstu quiets etuis quest quiet quite quits suite etui quit site suet suit ties tuis its set sit sue tie tui use is it si ti us ut

eiqstuu quietus. *See* **eiqstu eqstuu**

eiqsuzz quizzes. *No 6s or 5s*

eiqtu quiet quite etui quit tie tui it ti ut

eiqtuy equity quiet quite etui quit yeti tie tui yet it ti ut ye

eir ire er re

eirrs riser errs reis rise sire err ire res sir er is re si

eirrss risers riser rises sires errs reis rise sire sirs err ess ire res sir sis er is re si

eirrstu rustier. *See* **eistu eirrs**

eirrstw writers. *See* **eirstw eirrtw**

eirrsv rivers riser river errs reis revs rise rive sire vies vise err ire res rev sir vie er is re si

eirrtt triter titer titre trite rite tier tire tret err ire ret tie tit er it re ti

eirrtw writer wrier write rite tier tire weir wire wite writ err ire ret tie wet wit er it re ti we

eirrv river rive err ire rev vie er re

eirrw wrier weir wire ire err er re we

eirry eyrir err ire rye er re ye

eirs reis rise sire ire res sir er is re si

eirss rises sires reis rise sire sirs ess ire res sir sis er is re si

eirssst resists sisters. *See* **eirsst erssst**

eirsssu issuers. *See* **eirssu eisssu**

eirsst resist sister rests rises rites sires sites stirs tiers tires tress tries erst reis rest rets rise rite sets sire sirs site sits stir tier ties tire ess ire its res ret set sir sis sit tie er is it re si ti

eirsstt sitters. *See* **eirsst eirstt**

eirssttu rustiest trusties sitters. *See* **eirsst eirssu eirstt eisstu**

eirssttw twisters sitters twister. *See* **eirsst eirstt eirstw eisstw**

eirsstv stivers strives. *See* **eirsst eirstv ersstv**

eirssu issuer issue rises ruses sires users reis rise rues ruse sire sirs sues sure user uses ess ire res rue sir sis sue use er is re si us

eirssuu usuries. *See* **eirssu erssuu**

eirssuv viruses. *See* **eirssu erssuv**

eirssuvv survives viruses survive. *See* **eirssu erssuv**

eirst rites tiers tires tries erst reis rest rets rise rite sire site stir tier ties tire ire its res ret set sir sit tie er is it re si ti

eirstt sitter titers titres rites tiers tires titer titre trets tries trite erst reis rest rets rise rite sire site stet stir test tier ties tire tits tret ire its res ret set sir sit tie tit er is it re si ti

eirsttt stretti titters tritest. *See* **eirstt eirttt**

eirstttw twitters stretti titters tritest twister twitter. *See* **eirstt eirstw**

eirsttv   trivets. *See* eirstv eirstt eirttv

eirsttw   twister. *See* eirstt eirstw

eirstuv   virtues. *See* eirstv eirtuv

eirstv   rivets stiver strive rites rivet tiers tires tries verst verts erst reis rest rets revs rise rite rive sire site stir tier ties tire vert vest vets vies vise ire its res ret rev set sir sit tie vet vie er is it re si ti

eirstw   wriest writes rites strew tiers tires trews tries weirs wires wiser wites wrest wrist write writs erst reis rest rets rise rite sire site stew stir tier ties tire weir west wets wire wise wite wits writ ire its res ret set sew sir sit tie wet wis wit er is it re si ti we

eirsuvv   survive. *See* irsuv

eirsw   weirs wires wiser reis rise sire weir wire wise ire res sew sir wis er is re si we

eirtt   titer titre trite rite tier tire tret ire ret tie tit er it re ti

eirttt   titter titer titre trite rite tier tire tret ire ret tie tit er it re ti

eirtttw   twitter. *See* eirtttt eirtw

eirttv   trivet rivet titer titre trite rite rive tier tire tret vert ire ret rev tie tit vet vie er it re ti

eirtu   uteri etui rite tier tire true ire ret rue rut tie tui er it re ti ut

eirtuv   virtue rivet uteri virtu etui rite rive tier tire true vert ire ret rev rue rut tie tui vet vie er it re ti ut

eirtv   rivet rite rive tier tire vert ire ret rev tie vet vie er it re ti

eirtvy   verity rivet rite rive tier tire vert very yeti ire ivy ret rev rye tie try vet vie yet er it re ti ye

eirtw   write rite tier tire weir wire wite writ ire ret tie wet wit er it re ti we

eirv   rive ire rev vie er re

eirw   weir wire ire er re we

eissstu   tissues. *See* eisssu eisstu issstu

eisssstx   sexists. *See* eissstx

eisssu   issues issue sues uses ess sis sue use is si us

eisst   sites sets site sits ties ess its set sis sit tie is it si ti

eisstu   suites tissue etuis issue sites situs suets suite suits etui sets site sits sues suet suit ties tuis uses ess its set sis sit sue tie tui use is it si ti us ut

eisstw   wisest sites stews wests wites sets sews site sits stew ties west wets wise wite wits ess its set sew sis sit tie wet wis wit is it si ti we

eisstx   exists sexist exist exits sexts sites sixes exit sets sext site sits ties ess its set sex sis sit six tie ex is it si ti xi

eissu   issue sues uses ess sis sue use is si us

eissv   vises vies vise ess sis vie is si

eissx   sixes ess sex sis six ex is si xi

eissz   sizes size ess sis is si

eist   site ties its set sit tie is it si ti

eistu   etuis suite etui site suet suit ties tuis its set sit sue tie tui use is it si ti us ut

eistw   wites site stew ties west wets wise wite wits its set sew sit tie wet wis wit is it si ti we

eistx   exist exits exit sext site ties its set sex sit six tie ex is it si ti xi

eisty   yetis site ties yeti its set sit sty tie yes yet is it si ti ye

eisv   vies vise vie is si

eisvw   views wives vies view vise wise wive sew vie wis is si we

eisw   wise sew wis is si we

eisz   size is si

eit   tie it ti

eitu   etui tie tui it ti ut

eitw   wite tie wet wit it ti we

eitx   exit tie ex it ti xi

eity   yeti tie yet it ti ye

eiv   vie

eivw   view wive vie we

ejjmnuu   jejunum. *No 6s or 5s*

ejkmnnu   junkmen. *See* emnnu

ejknrsu   junkers. *See* ejknru ejkrs ejksu

ejknru   junker jerk juke junk kern knur neuk nuke rune ken rue run urn en er ne nu re

ejknstu   junkets. *See* ejkntu ejksu

ejkntu   junket juke junk jute neuk nuke tune jet jut ken net nut ten tun en ne nu ut

ejko   joke joe oke jo

ejkor   joker joke jerk joe kor oke ore roe er jo or re

ejkors   jokers jerks joker jokes jerk joes joke okes ores roes rose soke sore joe kor kos oke ore res roe er jo or os re so

ejkos   jokes joes joke okes soke joe kos oke jo os so

ejkoy   jokey joey joke joky yoke joe joy key oke jo oy ye

ejkr   jerk er re

ejkrs   jerks jerk res er re

ejkry   jerky jerk key rye er re ye

ejksu   jukes juke jus sue use us

ejku   juke

ejll   jell ell el

ejlls   jells ells jell sell ell els el

ejlly   jelly jell yell ell lye el ye

ejlorsst   jostlers jostler jostles ostlers sterols. *See* ejlost elorss elorst elosst

ejlorst   jostler. *See* ejlost elorst

ejlosst   jostles. *See* ejlost elosst

ejlossy   joyless. *See* ejosy eloss elssy

ejlost   jostle stole jolts jest jets joes jolt jots lest lets lose lost lots sloe slot sole toes els jet joe jot let los lot set sol sot toe el jo lo os so to

ejlosu   joules joule louse joes lose lues sloe slue sole soul els joe jus leu los sol sou sue use el jo lo os so us

ejlou   joule joe leu el jo lo

ejlpsu   juleps julep pules pulse lues plus pule puls slue spue els jus leu pul pus sue sup use el pe up us

ejlpu   julep pule leu pul el pe up

ejlrsu   jurels jurel lures rules lues lure rues rule ruse slue slur sure user els jus leu res rue sue use el er re us

ejlru   jurel lure rule leu rue el er re

ejlsstu   justles. *See* ejlstu elsstu

ejlstu   justle jutes lutes tules jest jets just jute juts lest lets lues lust lute slue slut suet tule els jet jus jut let leu set sue use el us ut

ejmmy   jemmy mem em me my ye

ejmprsu   jumpers. *See* ejmpru jmpsu emprs

ejmpru   jumper jump perm pure rump emu per rem rep rue rum ump em er me mu pe re um up

ejnny   jenny yen en ne ye

ejno   jeon eon joe one en jo ne no on

ejnorsuy   journeys journey. *See* ejnosy

ejnoruy   journey. *See* ejnoy

ejnos jones eons jeon joes noes nose ones ens eon joe one sen son en jo ne no on os so

ejnosy enjoys enjoy joeys jones nosey eons jeon joes joey joys noes nose nosy ones oyes yens ens eon joe joy one sen son soy yen yes yon en jo ne no on os oy so ye

ejnoy enjoy jeon joey eon joe joy one yen yon en jo ne no on oy ye

ejnssstu justness sunsets. *See* **ensstu**

ejo joe jo

ejoorvy overjoy. *No 6s or 5s*

ejopprst propjets propjet stopper toppers. *See* **eopprt eoprst**

ejopprt propjet. *See* **eopprt**

ejoprstt jetports jetport potters protest spotter. *See* **eoprst eoprtt eorstt**

ejoprtt jetport. *See* **eoprtt**

ejos joes joe jo os so

ejosss josses jess joes joss joe ess jo os so

ejosy joeys joes joey joys oyes joe joy soy yes jo os oy so ye

ejoy joey joe joy jo oy ye

ejprruy perjury. *See* **eprru eprry**

ejss jess ess

ejsst jests jess jest jets sets ess jet set

ejst jest jets jet set

ejstu jutes jest jets just jute juts suet jet jus jut set sue use us ut

ejt jet

ejtty jetty jet yet ye

ejtu jute jet jut ut

---

ek

---

ekklnpru kerplunk. *See* **eklnru**

ekl elk lek el

eklln knell elk ell ken lek el en ne

ekllns knells knell snell elks ells kens leks lens sell elk ell els ens ken lek sen el en ne

ekllrrsu krullers kruller. *See* **elrrsu**

ekllrru kruller. *See* **elrru**

eklnooor onlooker. *See* **ekloor**

eklnors snorkel. *See* **eklnos elnors**

eklnorss snorkels snorkel kelsons. *See* **eklnos elnors elnoss elorss**

eklnos kelson kenos koels noels elks enol eons keno kens koel leks leno lens lone lose noel noes nose okes ones sloe soke sole elk els ens eon ken kos lek los oke one sen sol son el en lo ne no on os so

eklnoss kelsons. *See* **eklnos elnoss**

eklnru lunker knurl kern knur lune lure lurk neuk nuke rule rune elk ken lek leu rue run urn el en er ne nu re

eklnt knelt lent elk ken lek let net ten el en ne

eklo koel elk lek oke el lo

eklooorv overlook. *See* **ekloor**

ekloopsw slowpoke. *See* **eklps eklos kloos**

ekloor looker koel kolo look lore oleo orle role rook elk kor lek loo oke ore roe el er lo or re

ekloors lookers. *See* **ekloor eloors**

eklorssw workless. *See* **elorss elorsw eorssw**

eklos koels elks koel leks lose okes sloe soke sole elk els kos lek los oke sol el lo os so

eklosy yokels koels yokel yokes yolks elks keys koel leks lose lyes lyse okes oyes sloe soke sole yoke yolk elk els key kos lek los lye oke sky sly sol soy yes el lo os oy so ye

eklot ketol koel toke elk lek let lot oke toe el lo to

ekloy yokel koel yoke yolk elk key lek lye oke el lo oy ye

eklp kelp elk lek el pe

eklps kelps skelp elks kelp leks skep elk els lek el pe

eklpss skelps kelps skelp elks kelp leks less skep elk els ess lek el pe

eklpy kelpy kelp yelp elk key lek lye ply yep el pe ye

ekls elks leks elk els lek el

eklstuz klutzes. *See* **kltuz elstu**

ekmnorw workmen. *See* **eknorw emorw emnow**

ekmnosy monkeys. *See* **ekmnoy emnosy**

ekmnoy monkey money keno moke monk nome omen yoke eon ken key men mon oke one yen yon em en me mo my ne no om on oy ye

ekmnptu unkempt. *See* **ekmpt**

ekmo moke oke em me mo om

ekmors smoker mokes mores omers smoke moke more mors okes omer ores roes rose soke some sore kor kos mor mos oke ore rem res roe em er me mo om or os re so

ekmorss smokers. *See* **ekmors ekmoss**

ekmos mokes smoke moke okes soke some kos mos oke oms em me mo om os so

ekmoss smokes mokes smoke sokes mess moke moss okes soke some ess kos mos oke oms em me mo om os so

ekmpt kempt kept met pet em me pe

ekmrstuy musketry turkeys. *See* **ekmstu ekrtuy emrstu erstuy**

ekmsstu muskets. *See* **ekmstu emssu msstu**

ekmstu musket mutes emus muse musk must mute smut stem stum suet tusk emu met mus set sue sum tsk use em me mu um us ut

ekn ken en ne

eknnopsu unspoken. *See* **eknops**

eknnost nektons. *See* **eknnot ennost eknost**

eknnot nekton nonet tenon token tonne keno knot neon none note toke tone eon ken net not oke one ten toe ton en ne no on to

ekno keno eon ken oke one en ne no on

eknoors snooker. *See* **enoors eknos eknrs**

eknoorss snookers snooker. *See* **enoors enooss enorss**

eknops spoken kenos knops opens peons pokes pones spoke eons epos keno kens knop noes nope nose okes ones open opes pens peon peso poke pone pons pose skep soke ens eon ken kos oke one ope pen sen son sop en ne no on os pe so

eknor krone keno kern eon ken kor nor oke one ore roe en er ne no on or re

eknorr kroner krone keno kern eon err ken kor nor oke one ore roe en er ne no on or re

eknorstw networks knowers network. *See* **eknorw eknost ekorst enorst**

eknorsuy younkers younker. *See* **eknos eknrs knrsu**

eknorsw knowers. *See* **eknorw enorsw**

eknortw network. *See* **eknorw enort eknot**

eknoruy younker. *See* **eknor knoru**

eknorw knower krone owner rowen woken enow keno kern knew know woke wore work worn wren eon ken kor new nor now oke one ore owe own roe row wen woe wok won en er ne no on or ow re we

eknos kenos eons keno kens noes nose okes ones soke ens eon ken kos oke one sen son en ne no on os so

eknost tokens kenos knots notes onset steno stoke stone token tokes tones eons keno kens knot nest nets noes nose note okes ones sent snot soke tens toes toke tone tons ens eon ken kos net not oke one sen set son sot ten toe ton tsk en ne no on os so to

eknot token keno knot note toke tone eon ken net not oke one ten toe ton en ne no on to

eknow woken enow keno knew know woke eon ken new now oke one owe own wen woe wok won en ne no on ow we

eknr kern ken en er ne re

eknrs kerns kern kens ens ken res sen en er ne re

eknrstuy turnkeys turnkey turkeys. *See* **ekrtuy enrstu enrsty erstuy**

eknrtuy turnkey. *See* **ekrtuy enrty nrtuy**

ekns kens ens ken sen en ne

eknsu neuks nukes kens neuk nuke sunk ens ken sen sue sun use en ne nu us

eknu neuk nuke ken en ne nu

eknw knew ken new wen en ne we

eko oke

ekooortv overtook. *See* **ekoort**

ekooprrv provoker provoke. *See* **ekoprr eooprr**

ekooprsv provokes provoke. *See* **ekoprs eoprsv**

ekooprv provoke. *See* **ekopr eoprv**

ekoorrvw overwork. *See* **ekorrw**

ekoorry rookery. *See* **koory**

ekoort retook koto rook root rote roto toke took tore trek kor oke ore ort ret roe rot toe too tor er or re to

ekop poke oke ope pe

ekopr poker perk poke pore pork repo rope kor oke ope ore per pro rep roe er or pe re

ekoprr porker poker repro perk poke pore pork repo rope err kor oke ope ore per pro rep roe er or pe re

ekoprrs porkers. *See* **ekoprs ekoprr eoprrs**

ekoprs pokers perks poker pokes pores porks poser prose repos ropes spoke spore epos okes opes ores perk peso poke pore pork pose pros repo reps roes rope rose skep soke sore kor kos oke ope ore per pro rep res roe sop er or os pe re so

ekops pokes spoke epos okes opes peso poke pose skep soke kos oke ope sop os pe so

ekopss spokes pesos pokes poses posse sokes spoke epos okes opes peso poke pose skep soke sops ess kos oke ope sop os pe so

ekorrsw reworks workers. *See* **eorrsw ekorrw**

ekorrw worker rower woke wore work err kor oke ore owe roe row woe wok er or ow re we

ekorsst stokers strokes. *See* **eorsst ekorst ekosst korsst**

ekorst stoker stroke rotes stoke store stork tokes torsk treks erst okes ores orts rest rets roes rose rote rots soke sore sort toes toke tore tors trek kor kos oke ore ort res ret roe rot set sot toe tor tsk er or os re so to

ekos okes soke oke kos os so

ekoss sokes okes soke ess kos oke os so

ekosst stokes sokes stoke tokes okes sets soke sots toes toke toss ess kos oke set sot toe tsk os so to

ekost stoke tokes okes soke toes toke kos oke set sot toe tsk os so to

ekosy yokes keys okes oyes soke yoke key kos oke sky soy yes os oy so ye

ekot toke oke toe to

ekow woke oke owe woe wok we ow

ekoy yoke oke key ye oy

ekppssuu seppukus seppuku. *See* **ekpsu epssu**

ekppsuu seppuku. *See* **ekpsu**

ekpr perk per rep er pe re

ekprs perks perk reps skep per rep res er pe re

ekpry perky perk prey pyre key per pry rep rye yep er pe re ye

ekps skep pe

ekpsu pukes puke skep spue pus sue sup use pe up us

ekpsy pesky espy keys skep key sky spy yep yes pe ye

ekpt kept pet pe

ekpu puke pe up

ekrst treks erst rest rets trek res ret set tsk er re

ekrstuy turkeys. *See* **ekrtuy erstuy**

ekrt trek ret er re

ekrtuy turkey trek true tyke yurt key ret rue rut rye try yet yuk er re ut ye

ekssw skews skew sews ess sew we

eksty tykes keys tyke key set sky sty tsk yes yet ye

eksw skew sew we

eksy keys key sky yes ye

eksyy skyey keys key sky yes ye

ekty tyke key yet ye

eky key ye

---

el el

ell ell el

elllmowy mellowly. *See* **ellmow ellowy**

elllnsuy sullenly. *See* **ellnsu**

elllor loller loll lore orle role roll ell ore roe el er lo or re

elllors lollers. *See* **elllor lllos elors**

ellm mell ell elm mel el em me

ellmnosy solemnly. *See* **ellmsy ellnoy ellosy elmnos**

ellmoor morello. *See* **elmor**

ellmoors morellos morello. *See* **elmors eloors emoors**

ellmosw mellows. *See* **ellmow ellos ellms**

ellmow mellow mell meow mewl mole moll well ell elm low mel mew mow owe owl woe el em lo me mo om ow we

ellmpsuu plumules plumule. *See* **elmpsu**

ellmpuu plumule. *See* **elmpu**

ellms mells smell ells elms mell mels sell ell elm els mel el em me

ellmss smells mells sells smell ells elms less mell mels mess sell ell elm els ess mel el em me

ellmstu mullets. *See* **ellmtu ellstu**

ellmsuv vellums. *See* **ellmuv ellms elmsu**

ellmsy smelly mells smell yells ells elms lyes lyse mell mels sell yell ylem ell elm els lye mel sly yes el em me my ye

ellmtu mullet tulle lute mell melt mule mull mute tell tule ell elm emu let leu lum mel met el em me mu um ut

ellmuv vellum velum mell mule mull ell elm emu leu lev lum luv mel el em me mu um

ellnoorv lovelorn. *See* **ellnor**

ellnop pollen enol leno lone lope noel nope open peon pole poll pone ell eon lop one ope pen el en lo ne no on pe

ellnops pollens. *See* **ellnop elops ellos**

ellnor enroll loner enol leno lone lore lorn noel orle role roll ell eon nor one ore roe el en er lo ne no on or re

ellnors enrolls. *See* **ellnor elnors**

ellnosvy slovenly volleys. *See* **ellnoy ellosy ellovy elnosv**

ellnosw swollen. *See* **ellos elnos ellns**

ellnoy lonely enol leno lone noel only yell ell eon lye one yen yon el en lo ne no on oy ye

ellns snell ells lens sell ell els ens sen el en ne

ellnss snells snell sells ells lens less sell ell els ens ess sen el en ne

ellnsu sullen snell lunes ells lens lues lune null sell slue ell els ens leu sen sue sun use el en ne nu us

ellnuw unwell lune null well ell leu new wen el en ne nu we

elloosy loosely. *See* **ellosy eloos**

ellopr poller loper lope lore orle pole poll pore repo role roll rope ell lop ope ore per pro rep roe el er lo or pe re

elloprs pollers. *See* **ellopr eloprs**

elloprst pollster pollers petrols. *See* **ellopr eloprs eloprt elorst**

ellopruv pullover. *See* **ellopr eloprv eloruv**

ellopstu pollutes outsell pollute pullets sellout tupelos. *See* **ellptu ellstu eloptu elostu**

elloptu pollute. *See* **ellptu eloptu**

ellopx pollex lope pole poll ell lop lox ope pox el ex lo ox pe

ellorr roller lore orle role roll ell err ore roe el er lo or re

ellorrs rollers. *See* **ellorr elorrs**

ellorrst stroller rollers. *See* **ellorr elorrs elorst eorrst**

ellorsty trolleys trolley. *See* **ellosy elorst elorsy eorsty**

ellorty trolley. *See* **ellty llort**

ellorvy loverly. *See* **ellovy elorvy**

ellos losel ells lose sell sloe sole ell els los sol el lo os so

ellosssu soulless. *See* **elosss eosssu**

ellosstu outsells sellouts lotuses outsell sellout solutes tousles. *See* **ellstu elosst elostu elsstu**

ellostu outsell sellout. *See* **elostu ellstu**

ellostx extolls. *See* **ellotx elostx**

ellosvy volleys. *See* **ellovy ellosy**

elloswy yellows. *See* **lloswy ellowy**

ellosy solely losel yells ells lose lyes lyse oyes sell sloe sole yell ell els los lye sly sol soy yes el lo os oy so ye

ellotx extoll extol tell toll ell let lot lox toe el ex lo ox to

ellovy lovely volley levy love vole yell ell lev lye el lo oy ye

ellowy yellow lowly well yell yowl ell low lye owe owl woe wye yew yow el lo ow oy we ye

ellowyy yellowy. *See* **ellowy**

ellps spell ells sell ell els el pe

ellpss spells spell sells ells less sell ell els ess el pe

ellpstu pullets. *See* **elpstu ellptu ellstu**

ellpsuy pulleys. *See* **ellpuy elpsu llpsu**

ellptu pullet tulle letup lept lute pelt pule pull tell tule ell let leu pet pul put tup el pe up ut

ellpuy pulley pule pull yell yelp yule ell leu lye ply pul yep yup el pe up ye

ellqsu quells quell ells lues sell slue ell els leu sue use el us

ellqu quell ell leu el

ells ells sell ell els el

ellss sells ells less sell ell els ess el

ellssw swells sells swell wells ells less sell sews slew well ell els ess sew el we

ellst tells ells lest lets sell tell ell els let set el

ellstu tulles lutes stull tells tules tulle ells lest lets lues lust lute sell slue slut suet tell tule ell els let leu set sue use el us ut

ellsw swell wells ells sell slew well ell els sew el we

ellsy yells ells lyes lyse sell yell ell els lye sly yes el ye

ellt tell ell let el

elltu tulle lute tell tule ell let leu el ut

ellty telly tell yell ell let lye yet el ye

ellw well ell el we

elly yell ell lye el ye

elm elm mel el em me

elmmop pommel lope memo mole mome mope poem pole pome elm lop mel mem mom mop ope el em lo me mo om pe

elmmops pommels. *See* **elmmop elops emops**

elmmosux lummoxes. *See* **lmmoux**

elmmpstu plummets plummet. *See* **elmpsu elpstu empstu**

elmmptu plummet. *See* **elmpu elptu**

elmno lemon melon enol leno lone mole noel nome omen elm eon mel men mon one el em en lo me mo ne no om on

elmnooss moonless loosens. *See* **elmnos elnoos elnoss elooss**

elmnoost moonlets moonlet loments. *See* **elmnos elmnot elmost elnoos**

elmnoot moonlet. *See* **elmnot**

elmnor merlon lemon loner melon morel enol leno lone lore lorn merl mole more morn noel nome norm omen omer orle role elm eon mel men mon mor nor one ore rem roe el em en er lo me mo ne no om on or re

elmnors merlons. *See* **elmnos elnors elmnor elmors emnors**

elmnos lemons melons solemn lemon melon meson moles noels nomes omens elms enol eons leno lens lone lose mels mole mons noel noes nome nose omen ones sloe sole some elm els ens eon los mel men mon mos oms one sen sol son el em en lo me mo ne no om on os so

elmnost loments. *See* **elmnos elmnot elmost emnost elnost**

elmnot loment molten lemon lento melon monte motel enol leno lent lone melt mole molt mote noel nome note omen tome tone elm eon let lot mel men met mon mot net not one ten toe tom ton el em en lo me mo ne no om on to

elmnoy lemony lemon melon money enol leno lone mole moly noel nome omen only ylem elm eon lye mel men mon one yen yon el em en lo me mo my ne no om on oy ye

elmnsu lumens lumen lunes menus mules elms emus lens lues lune mels menu mule muse slue slum elm els emu ens leu lum mel men mus sen sue sum sun use el em en me mu ne nu um us

elmnu lumen lune menu mule elm emu leu lum mel men el em en me mu ne nu um

elmo mole elm mel el em lo me mo om

elmoop pomelo loom loop lope mole mope oleo poem pole polo pome pool elm loo lop mel moo mop ope el em lo me mo om pe

elmoops pomelos. *See* **elmoop lmoos loops**

elmoorst tremolos tremolo looters. *See* **elmors elmost eloors eloort**

elmoorsy morosely. *See* **elmors eloors elorsy emoors**

elmoort tremolo. *See* **eloort emort lmoot**

elmoprsy polymers employs leprosy polymer. *See* **elmopy elmors eloprs elorsy**

elmopry polymer. *See* **elmopy elopr elmor**

elmopsy employs. *See* **elmopy emopsy**

elmopy employ myope lope mole moly mope ploy poem pole pome yelp ylem elm lop lye mel mop ope ply yep el em lo me mo my om oy pe ye

elmor morel lore merl mole more omer orle role elm mel mor ore rem roe el em er lo me mo om or re

elmors morels morsel lores loser merls moles morel mores omers orles roles elms lore lose mels merl mole more mors omer ores orle roes role rose sloe sole some sore elm els los mel mor mos oms ore rem res roe sol el em er lo me mo om or os re so

elmorss morsels. *See* **elorss elmors**

elmos moles elms lose mels mole sloe sole some elm els los mel mos oms sol el em lo me mo om os so

elmosst molests. *See* **elmost elmsst lmosst elosst**

elmost molest motels melts moles molts motel motes smelt smolt smote stole tomes elms lest lets lose lost lots mels melt mole molt most mote mots sloe slot sole some stem toes tome toms elm els let los lot mel met mos mot oms set sol sot toe tom el em lo me mo om os so to

elmostt mottles. *See* **elmost emostt elmott**

elmosuu emulous. *See* **elosu elmos emosu**

elmosuv volumes. *See* **elmouv elosuv**

elmot motel melt mole molt mote tome elm let lot mel met mot toe tom el em lo me mo om to

elmott mottle motel motet totem melt mole molt mote tome tote elm let lot mel met mot toe tom tot el em lo me mo om to

elmoty motley motel melt mole molt moly mote tome ylem elm let lot lye mel met mot toe tom toy yet el em lo me mo my om oy to ye

elmouv volume velum ovule love mole move mule ovum vole elm emu leu lev lum luv mel el em lo me mo mu om um

elmpprsu plumpers peplums plumper pumpers purples rumples suppler. *See* **elmppu elmpru elmpsu elmrsu**

elmppru plumper. *See* **elmppu emppru elppru elmpru**

elmppsu peplums. *See* **elmppu elmpsu lmppsu elppsu**

elmppu peplum plume plump lump mule plum pule pulp pump elm emu leu lum mel pep pul pup ump el em me mu pe um up

elmprsu rumples. *See* **elmrsu elprsu elmpru**

elmpru rumple plume lemur lump lure merl mule perm plum pule pure purl rule rump elm emu leu lum mel per pul rem rep rue rum ump el em er me mu pe re um up

elmpruy plumery. *See* **elpruy elmpru lmpruy**

elmpsu plumes lumps mules plume plums pules pulse slump spume elms emus lues lump mels mule muse plum plus pule puls slue slum spue sump umps elm els emu leu lum mel mus pul pus sue sum sup ump use el em me mu pe um up us

elmpu plume lump mule plum pule elm emu leu lum mel pul ump el em me mu pe um up

elmr merl elm mel rem el em er me re

elmrs merls elms mels merl elm els mel rem res el em er me re

elmrsty myrtles. *See* **elmrty elrsy elmst**

elmrsu lemurs lemur lures merls mules rules serum elms emus lues lure mels merl mule muse rues rule rums ruse slue slum slur sure els emu leu lum mel mus rem res rue rum sue sum use el em er me mu re um us

elmrsuzz muzzlers muzzler muzzles. *See* **elmrsu**

elmrty myrtle lyre melt merl rely term ylem elm let lye mel met rem ret rye try yet el em er me my re ye

elmru lemur lure merl mule rule elm emu leu lum mel rem rue rum el em er me mu re um

elmruzz muzzler. *See* **elmuzz elmru**

elms elms mels elm els mel el em me

elmsssu mussels. *See* **elmssu emsssu**

elmsst smelts melts smelt stems elms less lest lets mels melt mess sets stem elm els ess let mel met set el em me

elmssu mussel mules muses slues slums elms emus less lues mels mess mule muse muss slue slum sues sums uses elm els emu ess leu lum mel mus sue sum use el em me mu um us

elmst melts smelt elms lest lets mels melt stem elm els let mel met set el em me

elmstuu mutuels mutules. *See* **elmtuu**

elmsu mules elms emus lues mels mule muse slue slum elm els emu leu lum mel mus sue sum use el em me mu um us

elmsuy muleys mules muley yules elms emus lues lyes lyse mels mule muse slue slum ylem yule elm els emu leu lum lye mel mus sly sue sum use yes yum el em me mu my um us ye

elmsuzz muzzles. *See* **elmuzz elmsu**

elmsw mewls elms mels mewl mews slew smew elm els mel mew sew el em me we

elmsxy xylems xylem elms lyes lyse mels sexy ylem elm els lye mel sex sly yes el em ex me my ye

elmt melt elm let mel met el em me

elmtuu mutuel mutule lute melt mule mute tule elm emu let leu lum mel met ulu el em me mu um ut

elmtuy mutely muley lute melt mule mute tule ylem yule elm emu let leu lum lye mel met yet yum el em me mu my um ut ye

elmu mule elm emu leu lum mel el em me mu um

elmuv velum mule elm emu leu lev lum luv mel el em me mu um

elmuy muley mule ylem yule elm emu leu lum lye mel yum el em me mu my um ye

elmuzz muzzle mule elm emu leu lum mel el em me mu um

elmw mewl elm mel mew el em me we

elmxy xylem ylem elm lye mel el em ex me my ye

elmy ylem elm lye mel el em me my ye

elnnrsu runnels. *See* **elnnru elnsu elrsu**

elnnru runnel lune lure rule rune leu nun rue run urn el en er ne nu re

elnnstu tunnels. *See* **elnntu elnsu lnstu**

elnntu tunnel lent lune lunt lute tule tune let leu net nun nut ten tun el en ne nu ut

elno enol leno lone noel eon one el en lo ne no on

elnoos loosen loons loose noels noose oleos enol eons leno lens lone loon loos lose noel noes nose oleo ones sloe sole solo soon els ens eon loo los one sen sol son el en lo ne no on os so

elnooss loosens. *See* **elnoss elnoos elooss enooss**

elnoosw woolens. *See* **elnoos elnoow**

elnoow woolen enol enow leno lone loon noel oleo wool eon loo low new now one owe owl own wen woe won woo el en lo ne no on ow we

elnopt lepton lento enol leno lent lept lone lope noel nope note open pelt pent peon plot poet pole pone tone tope eon let lop lot net not one ope pen pet pot ten toe ton top el en lo ne no on pe to

elnoptty potently. *See* **elnopt elnopy elnpty eloptt**

elnoptu opulent. *See* **elnopt elnptu eloptu**

elnopy openly peony pylon enol leno lone lope noel nope only open peon ploy pole pone pony yelp eon lop lye one ope pen ply yen yep yon el en lo ne no on oy pe ye

elnor loner enol leno lone lore lorn noel orle role eon nor one ore roe el en er lo ne no on or re

elnors loners loner lores loser noels orles roles snore enol eons leno lens lone lore lorn lose noel noes nose ones ores orle roes role rose sloe sole sore els ens eon los nor one ore res roe sen sol son el en er lo ne no on or os re so

elnorty elytron. *See* **enrty elnot elnor**

elnos noels enol eons leno lens lone lose noel noes nose ones sloe sole els ens eon los one sen sol son el en lo ne no on os so

elnoss lesson loess loses noels noses sloes soles enol eons leno lens less lone lose loss noel noes nose ones sloe sole sols sons els ens eon ess los one sen sol son el en lo ne no on os so

elnosss lessons. *See* **elnoss elosss**

elnosstv solvents solvent. *See* **elnoss elnost elnosv elosst**

elnossw lowness. *See* **elnoss lossw nossw**

elnost stolen lento noels notes onset steno stole stone tones enol eons leno lens lent lest lets lone lose lost lots nest nets noel noes nose note ones sent sloe slot snot sole tens toes tone tons els ens eon let los lot net not one sen set sol son sot ten toe ton el en lo ne no on os so to

elnostv solvent. *See* **elnosv elnost**

elnosuz zonules. *See* **elnouz elosuz**

elnosv novels sloven loves noels novel ovens solve voles enol eons leno lens lone lose love noel noes nose ones oven sloe sole vole els ens eon lev los one sen sol son el en lo ne no on os so

elnot lento enol leno lent lone noel note tone eon let lot net not one ten toe ton el en lo ne no on to

elnotvy novelty. *See* **enovy elnot elnov**

elnouz zonule ouzel enol leno lone lune noel zone eon leu one el en lo ne no nu on

elnov novel enol leno lone love noel oven vole eon lev one el en lo ne no on

elnpstu penults. *See* **elnptu elpstu**

elnptu penult letup lent lept lune lunt lute pelt pent pule punt tule tune let leu net nut pen pet pul pun put ten tun tup el en ne nu pe up ut

elnpty plenty lent lept pelt pent type yelp let lye net pen pet ply ten yen yep yet el en ne pe ye

elnrstu runlets. *See* **elrstu elnrtu enrstu**

elnrsty sternly. *See* **enrsty elrsy elsty**

elnrsuzz nuzzlers nuzzler nuzzles. *See* **elnuzz**

elnrtu runlet tuner lent lune lunt lure lute rent rule rune runt tern true tule tune turn let leu net nut ret rue run rut ten tun urn el en er ne nu re ut

elnruzz nuzzler. *See* **elnuzz**

elns lens els ens sen el en ne

elnsssu sunless. *See* **elnssu**

elnsssy slyness. *See* **elsssy**

elnssu unless lunes slues lens less lues lune slue sues suns uses els ens ess leu sen sue sun use el en ne nu us

elnsu lens luns lues lune slue els ens lune sen sue sun use el en ne nu us

elnsuzz nuzzles. *See* **elnuzz elnsu**

elnsxy lynxes lens lyes lynx lyse sexy yens els ens lye sen sex sly yen yes el en ex ne ye

elnt lent let net ten el en ne

elnttu nutlet lent lune lunt lute tent tule tune let leu net nut ten tun tut el en ne nu ut

elnu lune leu el en ne nu

elnuzz nuzzle lune leu el en ne nu

elnwy newly lye new wen wye yen yew el en ne we ye

eloo oleo loo el lo

eloopr looper loper orlop loop lope lore oleo orle pole polo pool poor pore repo role rope loo lop ope ore per pro rep roe el er lo or pe re

elooprs loopers. *See* **eloopr eloors elopprs looprs**

eloors looser loose lores loser oleos orles roles loos lore lose oleo ores orle roes role rose sloe sole solo sore els loo los ore res roe sol el er lo or os re so

eloorsst rootless loosest looters ostlers sterols. *See* **eloors elooss elorss elorst**

eloorst looters. *See* **eloors eloort elorst**

eloorstt rootlets looters rootlet tootles. *See* **eloors eloort eloott elorst**

eloorsuv oversoul louvers louvres velours. *See* **eloors elorsv eloruv elosuv**

eloort looter loot lore oleo orle role root rote rotl roto tool tore let loo lot ore ort ret roe rot toe too tor el er lo or re to

eloortt rootlet. *See* **eloort eloott**

eloos loose oleos loos lose oleo sloe sole solo els loo los sol el lo os so

eloosss looses loess loose loses oleos sloes soles solos less loos lose loss oleo sloe sole solo sols els ess loo los sol el lo os so

eloosst loosest. *See* **elooss loosst elosst**

eloostt tootles. *See* **eloott eloos loost**

eloosvvx volvoxes. *See* **loovvx**

eloott tootle lotto loot oleo tool toot tote let loo lot toe too tot el lo to

elop lope pole ope lop el lo pe

eloppp popple lope plop pole pope lop ope pep pop el lo pe

eloppps popples. *See* **eloppp elopps**

eloppr lopper propel loper lope lore orle plop pole pope pore prep prop repo repp role rope lop ope ore pep per pop pro rep roe el er lo or pe re

elopprry properly. *See* **eloppr eopprr eoprry loppry**

elopprs loppers propels. *See* **eloprs eloppr elopps**

elopps peplos lopes plops poles popes slope epos lope lops lose opes peps peso plop pole pope pops pose sloe slop sole els lop los ope pep pop sol sop el lo os pe so

eloppsst stopples stopple topless topples. *See* **elopps eloppt elopss elosst**

eloppst stopple topples. *See* **elopps eloppt**

eloppt topple lept lope pelt plop plot poet pole pope tope let lop lot ope pep pet top pot toe top el lo pe to

elopr loper lope lore orle pole pore repo role rope lop ope ore per pro rep roe el er lo or pe re

eloprrsw prowlers prowler. *See* **eloprs elorrs elorsw eoprrs**

eloprrw prowler. *See* **elopr elorw eoprw**

eloprs lopers loper lopes lores loser orles poles pores poser prose repos roles ropes slope spore epos lope lops lore lose opes ores orle peso pole pore pose pros repo reps roes role rope rose sloe slop sole sore els lop los ope ore per pro rep res roe sol sop el er lo or os pe re so

eloprst petrols. *See* **eloprs elorst eloprt eoprst**

eloprsty prostyle petrols leprosy. *See* **eloprs eloprt elorst elorsy**

eloprsu leprous. *See* **eloprs eoprsu elprsu**

eloprsv plovers. *See* **eloprs elorsv eloprv eoprsv**

eloprsx plexors. *See* **eloprs eloprx**

eloprsy leprosy. *See* **eloprs eoprsy elorsy**

eloprt petrol loper repot toper trope lept lope lore orle pelt pert plot poet pole pore port repo role rope rote rotl tope tore let lop lot ope ore ort per pet pot pro rep ret roe rot toe top tor el er lo or pe re to

eloprv plover loper lover prove lope lore love orle over pole pore repo role rope rove vole lev lop ope ore per pro rep rev roe el er lo or pe re

eloprx plexor loper lope lore orle pole pore repo role rope lop lox ope ore per pox pro rep rex roe el er ex lo or ox pe re

elops lopes poles slope epos lope lops lose opes peso pole pose sloe slop sole els lop los ope sol sop el lo os pe so

elopss slopes loess lopes loses pesos poles poses posse sloes slope slops soles epos less lope lops lose loss opes peso pole pose sloe slop sole sols sops els ess lop los ope sol sop el lo os pe so

elopssst spotless topless possets. *See* **elopss elosst eopsst eossst**

elopsst topless. *See* **eopsst elopss elosst**

elopstt pottles. *See* **eloptt eopst elops**

elopstu tupelos. *See* **elpstu lopstu elostu eloptu**

eloptt pottle lept lope pelt plot poet pole tope tote let lop lot ope pet pot tot el lo pe to

eloptu tupelo letup poult lept lope lout lute pelt plot poet pole pout pule tolu tope tule let leu lop lot ope out pet pot pul put toe top tup el lo pe to up ut

elor lore orle role ore roe el er lo or re

elorrs sorrel lores loser orles roles sorer errs lore lose ores orle roes role rose sloe sole sore els err los ore res roe sol el er lo or os re so

elorrss sorrels. *See* **elorss elorrs**

elors lores loser orles roles lore lose ores orle roes role rose sloe sole sore els los ore res roe sol el er lo or os re so

elorss lessor losers loess lores loser loses orles roles roses sloes soles sores less lore lose loss ores orle roes role rose sloe sole sols sore els ess los ore res roe sol el er lo or os re so

elorsss lessors. *See* **elorss elosss**

elorsst ostlers sterols. *See* **elorss elorst eorsst elosst**

elorssv solvers. *See* **elorss elorsv eorssv elossv**

elorst ostler sterol lores loser orles roles rotes stole store erst lest lets lore lose lost lots ores orle orts rest rets roes role rose rote rotl rots sloe slot sole sore sort toes tore tors els let los lot ore ort res ret roe rot set sol sot toe tor el er lo or os re so to

elorstv revolts. *See* **elorsv elorst elortv eorstv**

elorstw trowels. *See* **elorsw elostw elorst eorstw elortw**

elorsuv louvers louvres velours. *See* **eloruv elorsv elosuv**

elorsuy elusory. *See* **elorsy lorsuy elrsuy**

elorsv lovers solver lores loser lover loves orles roles roves servo solve verso voles lore lose love ores orle over revs roes

role rose rove sloe sole sore vole els lev los ore res rev roe sol el er lo or os re so

elorsw lowers rowels slower lores loser lower orles roles rowel serow sower swore worse lore lose lows ores orle owes owls roes role rose rows slew sloe slow sole sore woes wore els los low ore owe owl res roe row sew sol sow woe el er lo or os ow re so ow

elorsy sorely lores loser lyres orles roles slyer yores lore lory lose lyes lyre lyse ores orle oyes rely roes role rose rosy ryes sloe sole sore yore els los lye ore res roe rye sly sol soy yes el er lo or os oy re so ye

elortty lottery. *See* **elrtty eortt**

elortv revolt lover overt trove voter lore love orle over role rote rotl rove tore vert veto vole volt vote let lev lot ore ort ret rev roe rot toe tor vet el er lo or re to

elortvy overtly. *See* **elortv elorvy**

elortw trowel lower owlet rowel towel tower wrote lore orle role rote rotl tore trow welt wore let lot low ore ort owe owl ret roe rot row toe tor tow two wet woe el er lo or ow re to we

eloruv louver louvre velour lover ovule lore love lure orle over role rove rule vole leu lev luv ore our rev roe rue el er lo or re

elorv lover lore love orle over role rove vole lev ore rev roe el er lo or re

elorvy overly lover levy lore lory love lyre orle over rely role rove very vole yore lev lye ore rev roe rye el er lo or oy re ye

elorw lower rowel lore orle role wore low ore owe owl roe row woe el er lo or ow re we

elorwy lowery lower rowel lore lory lyre orle rely role wore yore yowl low lye ore owe owl roe row rye woe wye yew yow el er lo or ow oy re we ye

elos lose sloe sole els los sol el lo os so

eloss loess loses sloes soles less lose loss sloe sole sols els ess los sol el lo os so

elosss losses loess loses sloes soles less lose loss sloe sole sols els ess los sol el lo os so

elosssty systoles systole. *See* **elosss elosst elssty eossst**

elosst stoles loess loses sloes slots soles stole less lest lets lose loss lost lots sets sloe slot sole sols sots toes toss els ess let los lot set sol sot toe el lo os so to

elosstu lotuses solutes tousles. *See* **elostu elosst elsstu**

elosstw slowest. *See* **elostw**

elossty systole. *See* **elssty**

elossv solves loess loses loves sloes soles solve voles less lose loss love sloe sole sols vole els ess lev los sol el lo os so

elost stole lest lets lose lost lots sloe slot sole toes els let los lot set sol sot toe el lo os so to

elosttu outlets. *See* **elottu eosttu elostu**

elostu solute tousle lotus louse louts lutes stole tules lest lets lose lost lots lout lues lust lute oust outs sloe slot slue slut sole soul suet toes tolu tule els let leu los lot out set sol sot sou sue toe use el lo os so to us ut

elostuv volutes. *See* **elosuv elostu elotuv**

elostw lowest owlets towels owlet stole towel welts lest lets lose lost lots lows owes owls slew sloe slot slow sole stew stow swot toes tows twos welt west wets woes els let los lot low owe owl set sew sol sot sow toe tow two wet woe el lo os ow so to we

elostx extols stole extol lest lets lose lost lots sext sloe slot sole toes els let los lot lox set sex sol sot sox toe el ex lo os ox so to

elosu louse lose lues sloe slue sole soul els leu los sol sou sue use el lo os so us

elosuv ovules louse loves ovule solve voles lose love lues sloe slue sole soul vole els leu lev los luv sol sou sue use el lo os so us

elosuz ouzels louse ouzel lose lues sloe slue sole soul els leu los sol sou sue use el lo os so us

elosv loves solve voles lose love sloe sole vole els lev los sol el lo os so

elosvw vowels wolves loves solve voles vowel lose love lows owes owls slew sloe slow sole vole vows woes wove els lev los low owe owl sew sol sow vow woe el lo os ow so we

elosxy xylose lose lyes lyse oyes sexy sloe sole els los lox lye sex sly sol sox soy yes el ex lo os ox oy so ye

elottu outlet lout lute tolu tote tout tule let leu lot out toe tot tut el lo to ut

elotuv volute ovule lout love lute tolu tule veto volt vote let leu lev lot luv out toe vet el lo to ut

elotw owlet towel welt let lot low owe owl toe tow two wet woe el lo ow to we

elotx extol let lot lox toe el ex lo ox to

elouv ovule love vole leu lev luv el lo

elouz ouzel leu el lo

elov love vole lev el lo

elovw vowel love vole wove lev low owe owl vow woe el lo ow we

elpprsu purples suppler. *See* **elprsu elppru epprsu elppsu**

elpprsuy resupply purples suppler. *See* **elppru elppsu elprsu elpruy**

elppru purple upper lure prep pule pulp pure purl repp rule leu pep per pul pup rep rue el er pe re up

elppsstu supplest supples. *See* **elppsu elppssu elpstu elsstu**

elppssu supples. *See* **elppsu elppsu**

elppsu supple pules pulps pulse lues peps plus pule pulp pul puls pups slue spue els leu pep pul pup pus sue sup use el pe up us

elpqsuu pulques. *See* **elpquu lpsuu elpsu**

elpquu pulque pule leu pul ulu el pe up

elprsttu splutter putters sputter turtles. *See* **elprsu elpstu elrstu elrttu**

elprsu pulser lures pules pulse purls purse rules slurp sprue super lues lure plus pule puls pure purl reps rues rule ruse slue slur spue spur sure user els leu per pul pus rep res rue sue sup use el er pe re up us

elprsuzz puzzlers puzzler puzzles. *See* **elprsu**

elprty peltry pertly reply lept lyre pelt pert prey pyre rely type yelp let lye per pet ply pry rep ret rye try yep yet el er pe re ye

elpruy purely reply lure lyre prey pule pure purl pyre rely rule yelp yule leu lye per ply pry pul rep rue rye yep yup el er pe re up ye

elpruzz puzzler. *See* **elpuzz**

elpry reply lyre prey pyre rely yelp lye per ply pry rep rye yep el er pe re ye

elpsssu plusses. *See* **elpssu epsssu**

elpsstuu pustules pluteus pustule. *See* **elpssu elpstu elsstu epsstu**

elpssu pluses pulses pules pulse slues spues less lues plus pule puls puss slue spue sues sups uses els ess leu pul pus sue sup use el pe up us

elpst pelts slept spelt lept lest lets pelt pest pets sept step els let pet set el pe

elpstu letups letup lutes pelts pules pulse setup slept spelt stupe tules upset lept lest lets lues lust lute pelt pest pets plus pule puls puts sept slue slut spue step suet tule tups els let leu pet pul pus put set sue sup tup use el pe up us ut

elpstuu pluteus pustule. *See* **elpstu lpsuu**

elpsu pules pulse lues plus pule puls slue spue els leu pul pus sue sup use el pe up us

elpsux plexus luxes pules pulse lues luxe plus pule puls slue spue els leu lux pul pus sex sue sup use el ex pe up us

elpsuzz puzzles. *See* **elpuzz elpsu**

elpsy yelps espy lyes lyse yelp els lye ply sly spy yep yes el pe ye

elpt lept pelt let pet el pe

elptu letup lept lute pelt pule tule let leu pet pul put tup el pe up ut

elpu pule leu pul el pe up

elpuzz puzzle pule leu pul el pe up

elpy yelp lye ply yep el pe ye

elrrsstu rustlers results rustler rustles ulsters. *See* **elrrsu elrstu elsstu**

elrrstu rustler. *See* **elrstu elrrsu**

elrrsu rulers lures ruler rules surer errs lues lure rues rule ruse slue slur sure user els err leu res rue sue use el er re us

elrru ruler lure rule err leu rue el er re

elrsstu results rustles ulsters. *See* **ersstu elrstu elsstu**

elrsttu turtles. *See* **elrstu ersttu elrttu**

elrstu luster lustre result rustle sutler ulster lures lutes rules trues tules erst lest lets lues lure lust lute rest rets rues rule ruse rust ruts slue slur slut suet sure true tule user els let leu res ret rue rut set sue use el er re us ut

elrstuuv vultures vulture. *See* **elrstu erstuu**

elrsu lures rules lues lure rues rule ruse slue slur sure user els leu res rue sue use el er re us

elrsuy surely lures lyres rules slyer surly yules lues lure lyes lyre lyse rely rues rule ruse ryes slue slur sure user yule els leu lye res rue rye sly sue use yes el er re us ye

elrsy lyres slyer lyes lyre lyse rely ryes els lye res rye sly yes el er re ye

elrttu turtle utter lure lute rule tret true tule let leu ret rue rut tut el er re ut

elrttuy utterly. *See* **elrttu elrtty**

elrtty tetryl lyre rely tret let lye ret rye try yet el er re ye

elrtuuv vulture. *No 6s or 5s*

elru lure rule leu rue el er re

elry lyre rely lye rye el er re ye

els els el

elss less els ess el

elssstu tussles. *See* **elsstu**

elssstuy styluses tussles. *See* **elssty lsstuy elsstu**

elsstty stylets. *See* **elssty elstty**

elsstu tussle lusts lutes slues sluts suets tules less lest lets lues lust lute sets slue slut sues suet tule uses els ess let leu set sue use el us ut

elssty slyest styles lyses style less lest lets lyes lyse sets els ess let lye set sly sty yes yet el ye

elssu slues less lues slue sues uses els ess leu sue use el us

elssy lyses less lyes lyse els ess lye sly yes el ye

elst lest lets els let set el

elstty stylet style testy lest lets lyes lyse stet test els let lye set sly sty yes yet el ye

elstu lutes tules lest lets lues lust lute slue slut suet tule els let leu set sue use el us ut

elstux exults exult lutes luxes tules tuxes lest lets lues lust lute luxe sext slue slut suet tule els let leu lux set sex sue tux use el ex us ut

elstw welts lest lets slew stew welt west wets els let set sew wet el we

elsty style lest lets lyes lyse els let lye set sly sty yes yet el ye

elsu lues slue els leu sue use el us

elsux luxes lues luxe slue els leu lux sex sue use el ex us

elsuy yules lues lyes lyse slue yule els leu lye sly sue use yes el us ye

elsw slew els sew el we

elsy lyes lyse els lye sly yes el ye

elt let el

eltu lute tule let leu el ut

eltux exult lute luxe tule let leu lux tux el ex ut

eltw welt let wet el we

eltwy wetly welt let lye wet wye yet yew el we ye

elu leu el

elux luxe leu lux el ex

eluy yule leu lye el ye

elv lev el

elvy levy lev lye el ye

ely lye el ye

em

em   em me

emm   mem em me

emmmnotu   momentum. *See* **emmnot**

emmmrsu   mummers. *See* **emmmru emmrsu**

emmmru   mummer emu mem mum rem rue rum em er me mu re um

emmnnotu   monument. *See* **emmnot**

emmnoost   momentos momento moments. *See* **emmnot emnost**

emmnoot   momento. *See* **emmnot**

emmnost   moments. *See* **emmnot emnost**

emmnosty   metonyms etymons metonym moments. *See* **emmnot emnost emnosy emnoty**

emmnot   moment monte memo mome mote nome note omen tome tone eon mem men met mom mon mot net not one ten toe tom ton em en me mo ne no om on to

emmnoty   metonym. *See* **emmnot emnoty**

emmnotyy   metonymy metonym. *See* **emmnot emnoty**

emmo   memo mome mem mom em me mo om

emmooty   myotome. *No 6s or 5s*

emmory   memory memo mome more omer yore mem mom mor ore rem roe rye em er me mo my om or oy re ye

emmorz   momzer memo mome more omer zero mem mom mor ore rem roe em er me mo om or re

emmos   memos momes memo mems mome moms some mem mom mos oms em me mo om os so

emmrrsu   rummers. *See* **emmrru emmrsu**

emmrru   rummer murre emu err mem mum rem rue rum em er me mu re um

emmrssu   summers. *See* **emmrsu emrssu**

emmrstyy   symmetry mystery. *See* **emrst mstyy**

emmrsu   summer serum emus mems mums muse rues rums ruse sure user emu mem mum mus rem res rue rum sue sum use em er me mu re um us

emmrsuy   summery. *See* **emmrsu mmruy**

emms   mems mem em me

emmssuu   museums. *See* **emmsuu emssu**

emmsuu   museum emus mems mums muse emu mem mum mus sue sum use em me mu um us

emn   men em en me ne

emmnnnoou   noumenon. *See* **emnno emnnu**

emnno   nomen neon nome none omen eon men mon one em en me mo ne no om on

emnnooot   monotone. *See* **emnot emnno ennot**

emnnostw   townsmen newtons. *See* **emnost ennost ennotw**

emnnsttu   stuntmen. *See* **emnsu emstu msttu**

emnnu   numen menu emu men nun em en me mu ne nu um

emno   nome omen eon men mon one em en me mo ne no om on on

emnoorst   monteros mentors monster montero. *See* **emnors emnort emnost emoors**

emnoorsu   enormous onerous. *See* **emnors emoors emorsu enoors**

emnoorsw   newsroom. *See* **emnors emoors emorsw enoors**

emnoort   montero. *See* **emnort mnoor moort**

emnoosuv   venomous. *See* **emnosv enosuv**

emnoppr   propmen. *See* **emopr enopr**

emnopssu   spumones spumone. *See* **emnoss emossu empssu enossu**

emnopst   postmen. *See* **emnost enopst emopst**

emnopsu   spumone. *See* **emnsu emnos emops**

emnopsy   eponyms. *See* **emnopy emnosy emopsy**

emnopy   eponym money myope peony mope nome nope omen open peon poem pome pone pony eon men mon mop one ope pen yen yep yon em en me mo my ne no om on oy pe ye

emnorrsu   mourners mourner. *See* **emnors emorrs emorsu enrrsu**

emnorru   mourner. *See* **mnoru emrru emorr**

emnors   sermon meson mores morns nomes norms omens omers snore eons mons more morn mors noes nome norm nose omen omer ones ores roes rose some sore ens eon men mon mor mos nor oms one ore rem res roe sen son em en er me mo ne no om on or os re so

emnorss   sermons. *See* **emnoss enorss emnors**

emnorsst   monsters mentors monster sermons tensors. *See* **emnors emnort emnoss emnost**

emnorst   mentors monster. *See* **emnort emorst emnost enorst emnors**

emnorstt   torments mentors monster stentor torment. *See* **emnors emnort emnost emorst**

emnorstu   remounts mentors monster nostrum remount sternum tonsure. *See* **emnors emnort emnost emorst**

emnorsuu   numerous. *See* **emnors emorsu mnorsu**

emnort   mentor metro monte noter tenor toner more morn mort mote nome norm note omen omer rent rote term tern tome tone tore torn eon men met mon mor mot net nor not one ore ort rem ret roe rot ten toe tom ton tor em en er me mo ne no om on or re to

emnortt   torment. *See* **emnort enortt**

emnortu   remount. *See* **emnort mnotu mnoru**

emnos   meson nomes omens eons mons noes nome nose omen ones some ens eon men mon mos oms one sen son em en me mo ne no om on os so

emnoss   mesons meson nomes noses omens eons mess mons moss noes nome nose omen ones some sons ens eon ess men mon mos oms one sen son em en me mo ne no om on os so

emnost   montes meson monte motes nomes notes omens onset smote steno stone tomes tones eons mons most mote mots nest nets noes nome nose note omen ones sent snot some stem tens toes tome tons tone tons ens eon men met mon mos mot net not oms one sen set son sot ten toe tom ton em en me mo ne no om on os so to

emnosty   etymons. *See* **emnoty emnosy emnost**

emnosv   venoms meson moves nomes omens ovens venom eons mons move noes nome nose omen ones oven some ens eon men mon mos oms one sen son em en me mo ne no om on os so

emnosy   moneys meson money mosey nomes nosey omens eons mons noes nome nose nosy omen ones oyes some yens ens eon men mon mos oms one sen son soy yen yes yon em en me mo my ne no om on os oy so ye

emnot   monte mote nome note omen tome tone eon men met mon mot net not one ten toe tom ton em en me mo ne no om on to

emnoty   etymon monte money mote nome note omen tome tone tony eon men met mon mot net not one ten toe tom ton toy yen yet yon em en me mo my ne no om on oy to ye

emnov venom move nome omen oven eon men mon one em en me mo ne no om on

emnow women enow meow mown nome omen eon men mew mon mow new now one owe own wen woe won em en me mo ne no om on ow we

emnoy money nome omen eon men mon one yen yon em en me mo my ne no om on oy ye

emnrsstu sternums sternum musters. *See* **emrssu emrstu enrsst enrssu**

emnrstu sternum. *See* **emrstu enrstu**

emnru rumen menu rune emu men rem rue rum run urn em en er me mu ne nu re um

emnsu menus emus menu muse emu ens men mus sen sue sum sun use em en me mu ne nu um us

emnu menu men emu em en me mu ne nu um

emooprrt promoter promote trooper. *See* **emoorr emoprr emorrt eooprr**

emooprst promotes promote poorest. *See* **emoors emoprs emopst emorst**

emooprt promote. *See* **emort moort emopr**

emoorr roomer ormer morro moor more omer room err moo mor ore rem roe em er me mo om or re

emoorrs roomers. *See* **emoors moorrs emorrs emoorr**

emoorrst restroom roomers rooster rooters termors toreros tremors. *See* **emoorr emoors emorrs emorrt**

emoors morose moors moose mores omers rooms moor moos more mors omer ores roes room rose some sore moo mor mos oms ore rem res roe em er me mo om or os re so

emoortyz zoometry. *See* **emort moort moory**

emoos moose some moos moo mos oms em me mo om os so

emooss osmose moose mess moos moss some ess moo mos oms em me mo om os so

emoosss osmoses. *See* **emooss emosss**

emoosstw twosomes twosome. *See* **emooss**

emoostt mottoes. *See* **emostt moostt**

emoostw twosome. *See* **emosw emoos moost**

emop mope poem pome ope mop em me mo om pe

emopprrt prompter. *See* **emoppt emoprr emorrt eopprr**

emoppst moppets. *See* **emoppt emopst**

emoppt moppet tempo mope mote poem poet pome pomp pope tome tope met mop mot ope pep pet pop pot toe tom top em me mo om pe to

emopr proem mope more omer perm poem pome pore prom repo romp rope mop mor ope ore per pro rem rep roe em er me mo om or pe re

emoprr romper ormer proem repro mope more omer perm poem pome pore prom repo romp rope err mop mor ope ore per pro rem rep roe em er me mo om or pe re

emoprrs rompers. *See* **emorrs emoprs eoprrs emoprr**

emoprs proems mopes mores omers perms poems pomes pores poser proem proms prose repos romps ropes sperm spore epos mope mops more mors omer opes ores perm peso poem pome pore pose prom pros repo reps roes romp rope rose some sore mop mor mos oms ope ore per pro rem rep res roe sop em er me mo om or os pe re so

emops mopes poems pomes epos mope mops opes peso poem pome pose some mop mos oms ope sop em me mo om os pe so

emopst tempos estop mopes motes poems poets pomes smote stomp stope tempo tomes topes epos mope mops most mote mots opes peso pest pets poem poet pome pose post pots sept some spot stem step stop toes tome toms tope tops met mop mos mot oms ope pet pot set sop sot toe tom top em me mo om os pe so to

emopsy myopes mopes mosey myope poems poesy pomes sepoy epos espy mope mops opes oyes peso poem pome pose posy some mop mos oms ope sop soy spy yep yes em me mo om my om os oy pe so ye

emopt tempo mope mote poem poet pome tome tope met mop mot ope pet pot toe tom top em me mo om pe to

emopy myope mope poem pome mop ope yep em me mo my om oy pe ye

emoqssu mosques. *See* **emoqsu emossu**

emoqsu mosque mouse emus muse some sumo emu mos mus oms sou sue sum use em me mo mu om os so um us

emor more omer mor ore rem roe em er me mo om or re

emorr ormer more omer err mor ore rem roe em er me mo om or re

emorrs ormers mores omers ormer sorer errs more mors omer ores roes rose some sore err mor mos oms ore rem res roe em er me mo om or os re so

emorrst termors tremors. *See* **emorst emorrs eorrst emorrt**

emorrt termor tremor metro ormer retro more mort mote omer rote term tome tore torr err met mor mot ore ort rem ret roe rot toe tom tor em er me mo om or re to

emors mores omers more mors omer ores roes rose some sore mor mos oms ore rem res roe em er me mo om or os re so

emorssu mousers. *See* **emorsu emossu eorssu emrssu**

emorst metros metro mores morts motes omers rotes smote store storm terms tomes erst more mors mort most mote mots omer ores orts rest rets roes rose rote rots some sore sort stem term toes tome toms tore tors met mor mos mot oms ore ort rem res ret roe rot set sot toe tom tor em er me mo om or os re so to

emorsu mouser mores mouse omers rouse serum emus more mors muse omer ores ours roes rose rues rums ruse some sore sour sumo sure user emu mor mos mus oms ore our rem res roe rue rum sou sue sum use em er me mo mu om or os re so um us

emorsv movers vomers mores mover moves omers roves servo verso vomer more mors move omer ores over revs roes rose rove some sore mor mos oms ore rem res rev roe em er me mo om or os re so

emorsw mowers meows mores mower omers serow sower swore worms worse meow mews more mors mows omer ores owes roes rose rows smew some sore woes wore worm mew mor mos mow oms ore owe rem res roe row sew sow woe em er me mo om or os ow re so we

emort metro more mort mote omer rote term tome tore met mor mot ore ort rem ret roe rot toe tom tor em er me mo om or re to

emorv mover vomer more move omer over rove mor ore rem rev roe em er me mo om or re

emorw mower meow more omer wore worm mew mor mow ore owe rem roe row woe em er me mo om or ow re we

emos some mos oms em me mo om os so

emosss mosses mess moss some ess mos oms em me mo om os so

emosssu mousses. *See* **emosss emsssu eosssu**

emosstt mostest. *See* **emostt**

emossttw westmost mostest. *See* **emostt**

emosstvz   zemstvos zemstvo. *See* **eosstv**

emossu   mousse mouse muses souse sumos emus mess moss muse muss some sous sues sumo sums uses emu ess mos mus oms sou sue sum use em me mo mu om os so um us

emossy   moseys messy mosey mossy mess moss oyes some soys ess mos oms soy yes em me mo my om os oy so ye

emossyz   zymoses. *See* **emossy emsyz**

emost   motes smote tomes most mote mots some stem toes tome toms met mos mot oms set sot toe tom em me mo om os so to

emostt   motets totems motes motet smote tomes totem totes most mote mots some stem stet test toes tome toms tost tote tots met mos mot oms set sot toe tom tot em me mo om os so to

emostvz   zemstvo. *See* **emost emosv eostv**

emosu   mouse emus mouse muse some emu mos mus oms sou sue sum use em me mo mu om os so um us

emosuy   mousey mosey mouse mousy emus muse oyes some sumo emu mos mus oms sou soy sue sum use yes you yum em me mo mu my om os oy so um us ye

emosv   moves some move mos oms em me mo om os so

emosw   meows meow mews mows owes smew some woes mew mos mow oms owe sew sow woe em me mo om os ow so we

emosy   mosey some oyes mos oms soy yes em me mo my om os oy so ye

emoszz   mezzos mezzo some mos oms em me mo om os so

emot   mote tome met mot toe tom em me mo om to

emott   motet totem mote tome tote met mot toe tom tot em me mo om to

emov   move em me mo om

emow   meow mew mow owe woe em me mo om ow we

emozz   mezzo em me mo om

empprsu   pumpers. *See* **emppru epprsu**

emppru   pumper upper perm prep pump pure repp rump emu pep per pup rem rep rue rum ump em er me mu pe re um up

empr   perm per rem rep em er me pe re

emprrtuy   trumpery. *See* **emrruy**

emprs   perms sperm perm reps per rem rep res em er me pe re

emprss   sperms perms press sperm mess perm reps ess per rem rep res em er me pe re

emprsstu   stumpers sumpters musters septums stumper sumpter. *See* **emprss empssu empstu emrssu**

emprssuu   rumpuses pursues. *See* **emprss empssu emrssu eprssu**

emprsttu   strumpet trumpets mutters putters sputter stumper sumpter trumpet. *See* **empstt empstu emrstu emrttu**

emprstu   stumper sumpter. *See* **eprstu emrstu empstu mprstu**

emprttu   trumpet. *See* **emrttu eprttu**

empsstu   septums. *See* **empstu epsstu empssu mpsstu**

empssu   spumes muses spues spume sumps emus mess muse muss puss spue sues sump sums sups umps uses emu ess mus pus sue sum sup ump use em me mu pe um up us

empstt   tempts tempt pest pets sept stem step stet test met pet set em me pe

empstu   septum mutes setup spume stump stupe tumps upset emus muse must mute pest pets puts sept smut spue stem step stum suet sump tump tups umps emu met mus pet pus put set sue sum sup tup ump use em me mu pe um up us ut

empsu   spume emus muse spue sump umps emu mus pus sue sum sup ump use em me mu pe um up us

emptt   tempt met pet em me pe

empty   empty type met pet yep yet em me my pe ye

emr   rem em er me re

emrrsuy   murreys. *See* **emrruy errsuy**

emrru   murre emu err rem rue rum em er me mu re um

emrruy   murrey murre merry emu err rem rue rum rye yum em er me mu my re um ye

emrry   merry err rem rye em er me my re ye

emrsstu   musters. *See* **ersstu emrstu emrssu mrsstu**

emrssu   serums muses ruses serum users emus mess muse muss rues rums ruse sues sums sure user uses emu ess mus rem res rue rum sue sum use em er me mu re um us

emrst   terms erst rest rets stem term met rem res ret set em er me re

emrsttu   mutters. *See* **emrstu emrttu ersttu**

emrstu   muster mutes serum strum terms trues emus erst muse must mute rest rets rues rums ruse rust ruts smut stem stum suet sure term true user emu met mus rem res ret rue rum rut set sue sum use em er me mu re um us ut

emrstyy   mystery. *See* **emrst mstyy**

emrsu   serum emus muse rues rums ruse sure user emu mus rem res rue rum sue sum use em er me mu re um us

emrt   term met rem ret em er me re

emrttu   mutter utter mute mutt term tret true emu met rem ret rue rum rut tut em er me mu re um ut

emrux   murex emu rem rex rue rum em er ex me mu re um

emss   mess ess em me

emsssty   systems. *See* **emssty**

emsssu   musses muses emus mess muse muss sues sums uses emu ess mus sue sum use em me mu um us

emsst   stems mess sets stem ess met set em me

emssty   system stems messy mess sets stem ess met set sty yes yet em me my ye

emssu   muses emus mess muse muss sues sums uses emu ess mus sue sum use em me mu um us

emssw   smews mess mews sews smew ess mew sew em me we

emssy   messy mess ess yes em me my ye

emst   stem met set em me

emstu   mutes emus muse must mute smut stem stum suet emu met mus set sue sum use em me mu um us ut

emsu   emus muse emu mus sue sum use em me mu um us

emsw   mews smew mew sew em me we

emsyz   zymes zyme yes em me my ye

emt   met em me

emtu   mute met emu em me mu um ut

emu   emu em me mu um

emw   mew em me we

emyz   zyme em me my ye

en   en ne

ennnop   pennon neon none nope open peon pone eon one ope pen en ne no on pe

ennnops   pennons. *See* **ennnop ennos enops**

ennnruy   nunnery. *See* **nnruy**

enno   neon none eon one en ne no on

ennooootz   entozoon. *See* **ennot enooz**

ennnooppt   opponent. *See* **ennot**

ennoortv   nonvoter. *See* **ennot enort eortv**

ennorssu   nonusers neurons nonuser. *See* **ennoru enorss enossu enrssu**

ennorstu   neutrons neurons neutron non-user stunner tonsure. *See* **ennoru ennost enorst enrstu**

ennorsu   neurons nonuser. *See* **ennoru ennos nnosu**

ennorsw   renowns. *See* **enorsw ennorw**

ennortu   neutron. *See* **ennoru ennot enort**

ennoru   neuron neon none noun rune eon nor nun one ore our roe rue run urn en er ne no nu on or re

ennorw   renown owner rowen enow neon none wore worn wren eon new nor now one ore owe own roe row wen woe won en er ne no on or ow re we

ennos   neons eons neon noes none nose ones ens eon one sen son en ne no on os so

ennosst   sonnets. *See* **ennost enosst**

ennost   nonets sonnet tenons tonnes ne-ons nonet notes onset steno stone tenon tones tonne eons neon nest nets noes none nose note ones sent snot tens toes tone tons ens eon net not one sen set son sot ten toe ton en ne no on os so to

ennostw   newtons. *See* **ennotw ennost**

ennosx   xenons exons neons xenon eons exon neon noes none nose ones ens eon one sen sex son sox en ex ne no on os ox so

ennot   nonet tenon tonne neon none note tone eon net not one ten toe ton en ne no on to

ennotw   newton nonet tenon tonne enow neon newt none note nowt tone town wont eon net new not now one owe own ten toe ton tow two wen wet woe won en ne no on ow to we

ennox   xenon exon neon none eon one en ex ne no on ox

ennpy   penny pen yen yep en ne pe ye

ennrrsu   runners. *See* **ennrru enrrsu**

ennrru   runner rerun rune err nun rue run urn en er ne nu re

ennrstu   stunner. *See* **enrstu**

eno   eon one en ne no on

enooossz   zoonoses snoozes. *See* **enooss enoosz**

enooppr   propone. *See* **enopr noopr**

enoopprs   propones opposer propone propose snooper. *See* **enoors enoprs eoopps nooprs**

enooppst   postpone. *See* **enopst eoopps**

enooprs   snooper. *See* **enoprs nooprs enoors**

enooprss   poorness snoopers persons snooper sponsor. *See* **enoors enooss enoprs enorss**

enoors   sooner noose snore eons noes nose ones ores roes rose soon sore ens eon nor one ore res roe sen son en er ne no on or os re so

enoorsu   onerous. *See* **enoors enrsu eorsu**

enooss   noose eons noes nose ones soon ens eon one sen son en ne no on os so

enooss   nooses noose noses eons noes nose ones sons soon ens eon ess one sen son en ne no on os so

enoossz   snoozes. *See* **enooss enoosz**

enoosz   ozones snooze noose oozes ozone zones eons noes nose ones ooze soon zone zoon zoos ens eon one sen son zoo en ne no on os so

enootxy   oxytone. *See* **nooty**

enooz   ozone ooze zone zoon eon one zoo en ne no on

enop   nope open peon pone eon one ope pen en ne no on pe

enopr   prone nope open peon pone pore repo rope eon nor one ope ore pen per pro rep roe en er ne no on or pe re

enoprr   perron prone repro nope open peon pone porn pore repo rope eon err nor one ope ore pen per pro rep roe en er ne no on or pe re

enoprrs   perrons. *See* **enoprr enoprs eoprrs enorrs**

enoprs   person opens peons pones pores poser prone prose repos ropes snore spore eons epos noes nope nose ones open opes ores pens peon peso pone pons pore porn pose pros repo reps roes rope rose sore ens eon nor one ope ore pen per pro rep res roe sen son sop en er ne no on or os pe re so

enoprss   persons. *See* **enoprs eoprss enorss**

enoprsst   posterns persons postern pos-ters prestos stepson tensors. *See* **enoprs enopst enorss enorst**

enoprst   postern. *See* **enorst enoprs enopst eoprst**

enoprstt   portents portent postern pot-ters protest spotter stentor. *See* **enoprs enopst enoptt enorst**

enoprtt   portent. *See* **enoptt eoprtt enortt**

enoprty   entropy. *See* **eoprty enrty enort**

enoprv   proven prone prove nope open oven over peon pone pore porn repo rope rove eon nor one ope ore pen per pro rep rev roe en er ne no on or pe re

enops   opens peons pones eons epos noes nope nose ones open opes pens peon peso pone pons pose ens eon one ope pen sen son sop en ne no on os pe so

enopsst   stepsons stepson possets. *See* **enopst enosst eopsss eopsst**

enopsssy   synopses. *See* **eopsss eopssy**

enopsst   stepson. *See* **eopsst enosst enopst**

enopst   pontes estop notes onset opens peons poets pones spent steno stone stope tones topes eons epos nest nets noes nope nose note ones open opes pens pent peon peso pest pets poet pone pons pose post pots sent sept snot spot step stop tens toes tone tons tope tops ens eon net not one ope pen pet pot sen set son sop sot ten toe ton top en ne no on os pe so to

enoptt   potent nope note open pent peon poet pone tent tone tope tote eon net not one ope pen pet pot ten toe ton top tot en ne no on pe to

enopy   peony nope open peon pone pony eon one ope pen yen yep yon en ne no on oy pe ye

enoqtuu   unquote. *See* **eoqtu eqtuu**

enorrs   snorer snore sorer eons errs noes nose ones ores roes rose sore ens eon err nor one ore res roe sen son en er ne no on or os re so

enorrss   snorers. *See* **enorss enorrs**

enorrstt   torrents retorts rotters stentor stertor torrent. *See* **enorrs enorst enortt enostt**

enorrsuv   overruns overrun nervous. *See* **enorrs enosuv enrrsu eorrsu**

enorrtt   torrent. *See* **eorrtt enortt**

enorrtuv   overturn turnover overrun. *See* **enrrtu eorrtu eorrtv**

enorruv   overrun. *See* **enrru eorrv**

enorry   ornery yore eon err nor one ore roe rye yen yon en er ne no on or oy re ye**

enors snore eons noes nose ones ores roes rose sore ens eon nor one ore res roe sen son en er ne no on or os re so

enorss sensor snores noses roses snore sores eons noes nose ones ores roes rose sons sore ens eon ess nor one ore res roe sen son en er ne no on or os re so

enorsss sensors. *See* **enorss**

enorsssu sourness sensors. *See* **enorss enossu enrssu eorssu**

enorsst tensors. *See* **enorst enosst enorss norsst eorsst**

enorsstt stentors stentor stetson tensors testons. *See* **enorss enorst enortt enosst**

enorsstu tonsures oestrus ousters sourest tensors tonsure. *See* **enorss enorst enosst enossu**

enorssw worsens. *See* **enorsw eorssw**

enorssy sensory. *See* **enorss**

enorst noters tenors tensor toners noter notes onset rents rotes snore snort steno stern stone store tenor terns toner tones eons erst nest nets noes nose note ones ores orts rent rest rets roes rose rote rots sent snot sore sort tens tern toes tone tons tore torn tors ens eon net nor not one ore ort res ret roe rot sen set son sot ten toe ton tor en er ne no on or os re so to

enorstt stentor. *See* **enorst eorstt enortt enostt**

enorstu tonsure. *See* **enorst eorstu enrstu**

enorstuy tourneys tonsure tourney. *See* **enorst enrstu enrsty eorstu**

enorsuv nervous. *See* **enosuv enrsu eorsu**

enorsw owners rowens worsen owner rowen serow snore sower swore sworn worse wrens enow eons news noes nose ones ores owes owns roes rose rows sewn snow sore sown wens woes wore worn wren ens eon new nor now one ore owe own res roe row sen sew son sow wen woe won en er ne no on or os ow re so we

enort noter tenor toner note rent rote tern tone tore torn eon net nor not one ore ort ret roe rot ten toe ton tor en er ne no on or re to

enortt rotten noter otter tenor toner torte toter note rent rote tent tern tone tore torn tort tote tret trot eon net nor not one ore ort ret roe rot ten toe ton tor tot en er ne no on or re to

enortuy tourney. *See* **enrty enort eortu**

enorw owner rowen enow wore worn wren eon new nor now one ore owe own roe row wen woe won en er ne no on or ow re we

enos eons noes nose ones ens eon one sen son en ne no on os so

enoss noses eons noes nose ones sons ens eon ess one sen son en ne no on os so

enossstt stetsons stetson testons. *See* **enosst enostt eossst**

enosssuu sensuous. *See* **enossu**

enosst onsets stenos stones nests noses notes onset snots steno stone tones eons nest nets noes nose note ones sent sets snot sons sots tens toes tone tons toss ens eon ess net not one sen set son sot ten toe ton en ne no on os so to

enosstt stetson testons. *See* **enosst**

enosstx sextons. *See* **enosst enostx**

enossu onuses noses souse eons noes nose nous ones onus sons sous sues suns uses ens eon ess one sen son sou sue sun use en ne no nu on os so us

enost notes onset steno stone tones eons nest nets noes nose note ones sent snot tens toes tone tons ens eon net not one sen set son sot ten toe ton en ne no on os so to

enostt teston notes onset steno stone tents tones totes eons nest nets noes nose note ones sent snot stet tens tent test toes tone tons tost tote tots ens eon net not one set sen son sot ten toe ton tot en ne no on os so to

enostuu tenuous. *See* **enost nostu enstu**

enostx sexton exons notes onset steno stone tones eons exon nest nets next noes nose note ones sent sext snot tens toes tone tons ens eon net not one sen set sex son sot sox ten toe ton en ex ne no on os ox so to

enosuv venous ovens nevus eons noes nose nous ones onus oven ens eon one sen son sou sue sun use en ne no nu on os so us

enosv ovens eons noes nose ones oven ens eon one sen son en ne no on os so

enosvy envoys envoy nosey ovens envy eons noes nose nosy ones oven oyes yens ens eon one sen son soy yen yes yon en ne no on os oy so ye

enosx exons eons exon noes nose ones ens eon one sen sex son sox en ex ne no on os ox so

enosxy onyxes exons nosey eons exon noes nose nosy ones onyx oxen oyes sexy yens ens eon one sen sex son sox soy yen yes yon en ex ne no on os ox oy so ye

enosy nosey eons noes nose nosy ones oyes yens ens eon one sen son soy yen yes yon en ne no on os oy so ye

enosz zones eons noes nose ones zone ens eon one sen son en ne no on os so

enot note tone eon net not one ten toe ton en ne no on to

enottu tenuto note tent tone tote tout tune unto eon net not nut one out ten toe ton tot tun tut en ne no nu on to ut

enov oven eon one en ne no on

enovw woven enow oven wove eon new now one owe own vow wen woe won en ne no on ow we

enovy envoy oven envy eon one yen yon en ne no on oy ye

enow enow eon new now one owe own wen woe won en ne no on ow we

enox exon oxen eon one en ex ne no on ox

enoz zone eon one en ne no on

enp pen en ne pe

enprsstu punsters punster punters. *See* **enprsu enprtu enrsst enrssu**

enprstu punster punters. *See* **eprstu enprsu enprtu enrstu**

enprsu prunes nurse prune purse runes sprue spurn super pens puns pure reps rues rune runs ruse spue spun spur sure urns user ens pen per pun pus rep res rue run sen sue sun sup urn use en er ne nu pe re up us

enprtu punter erupt prune tuner pent pert punt pure rent rune runt tern true tune turn net nut pen per pet pun put rep ret rue run rut ten tun tup urn en er ne nu pe re up ut

enpru prune rune pure pen per pun rep rue run urn en er ne nu pe re up

enpruy penury prune prey puny pure pyre rune pen per pry pun rep rue run rye urn yen yep yup en er ne nu pe re up ye

enps pens ens pen sen en ne pe

enpst spent nest nets pens pent pest pets sent sept step tens ens net pen pet sen set ten en ne pe

enpstuu tuneups. *See* **enptuu npstu epstu**

enpt pent net pen pet ten en ne pe

enptuu tuneup pent punt tune net nut pen pet pun put ten tun tup en ne nu pe up ut

enqrsu querns nurse quern runes rues rune runs ruse sure urns user ens res rue run sen sue sun urn use en er ne nu re us

enqru quern rune rue run urn en er ne nu re

enrrstu returns. *See* **enrrsu enrrtu errstu**

enrrstuu nurtures returns nurture. *See* **enrrsu enrrtu enrstu errsuu**

enrrsu reruns nurse rerun runes surer errs rues rune runs ruse sure urns user ens err res rue run sen sue sun urn use en er ne nu re us

enrrsuy　nursery. *See* **enrrsu errsuy**

enrrtu　return rerun truer tuner rent rune runt tern true tune turn err net nut ret rue run rut ten tun urn en er ne nu re ut

enrrtuu　nurture. *See* **enrrtu enrtuu**

enrru　rerun rune err rue run urn en er ne nu re

enrsst　sterns nests rents rests stern terns tress erst nest nets rent rest rets sent sets tens tern ens ess net res ret sen set ten en er ne re

enrssttu　entrusts entrust. *See* **enrsst enrssu enrstu enssttu**

enrssu　nurses nurse runes ruses users rues rune runs ruse sues suns sure urns user uses ens ess res rue run sen sue sun urn use en er ne nu re us

enrsswy　wryness. *See* **enrsw enswy**

enrst　rents stern terns erst nest nets rent rest rets sent tens tern ens net res ret sen set ten en er ne re

enrsttu　entrust. *See* **ersttu enrstu**

enrstu　tuners unrest nurse rents runes runts stern terns trues tuner tunes turns erst nest nets nuts rent rest rets rues rune runs runt ruse rust ruts sent stun suet sure tens tern true tune tuns turn urns user ens net nut res ret rue run rut sen set sue sun ten tun urn use en er ne nu re us ut

enrstw　strewn newts rents stern strew terns trews wrens wrest erst nest nets news newt rent rest rets sent sewn stew tens tern wens west wets wren ens net new res ret sen set sew ten wen wet en er ne re we

enrsty　sentry entry rents stern terns erst nest nets rent rest rets ryes sent tens tern yens ens net res ret rye sen set sty ten try yen yes yet en er ne re ye

enrsu　nurse runes rues rune runs ruse sure urns user ens res rue run sen sue sun urn use en er ne nu re us

enrsw　wrens news sewn wens wren ens new res sen sew wen en er ne re we

enrt　rent tern net ret ten en er ne re

enrtu　tuner rent rune runt tern true tune turn net nut ret rue run rut ten tun urn en er ne nu re ut

enrtuu　untrue tuner rent rune runt tern true tune turn net nut ret rue run rut ten tun urn en er ne nu re ut

enrty　entry rent tern net ret rye ten try yen yet en er ne re ye

enru　rune rue run urn en er ne nu re

enrvwy　wyvern nervy envy very wren new rev rye wen wye yen yew en er ne re we ye

enrvy　nervy envy very rev rye yen en er ne re ye

enrw　wren new wen en er ne re we

ens　ens sen en ne

enssstu　sunsets. *See* **enssttu**

ensst　nests nest nets sent sets tens ens ess net sen set ten en ne

ensstu　sunset nests stuns suets tunes nest nets nuts sent sets stun sues suet suns tens tune tuns uses ens ess net nut sen set sue sun ten tun use en ne nu us ut

enst　nest nets sent tens ens net sen set ten en ne

enstt　tents nest nets sent stet tens tent test ens net sen set ten en ne

enstu　tunes nest nets nuts sent stun suet tens tune tuns ens net nut sen set sue sun ten tun use en ne nu us ut

enstv　vents nest nets sent tens vent vest vets ens net sen set ten vet en ne

enstw　newts nest nets news newt sent sewn stew tens wens west wets ens net new sen set sew ten wen wet en ne we

ensuv　nevus ens sen sue sun use en ne nu us

ensux　nexus ens sen sex sue sun use en ex ne nu us

ensw　news sewn wens ens new sen sew wen en ne we

enswy　newsy news sewn wens wyes yens yews ens new sen sew wen wye yen yes yew en ne we ye

ensy　yens ens sen yen yes en ne ye

ent　net ten en ne

entt　tent net ten en ne

enttwy　twenty tent newt went net new ten wen wet wye yen yet yew en ne we ye

entu　tune net nut ten tun en ne nu ut

entv　vent net ten vet en ne

entw　newt went net new ten wen wet en ne we

entx　next net ten en ex ne

envy　envy yen en ne ye

enw　new wen en ne we

eny　yen en ne ye

---

eo

---

eoooprsz　zoospore. *See* **eoosz oorsz eoprs**

eooorrst　roseroot rooster rooters toreros. *See* **eoorrt eorrst**

eoopprrs　proposer opposer propose prosper. *See* **eoopps eooprr eopprr eoprrs**

eooppprs　opposer propose. *See* **eoopps eoprs epprs**

eoopprss　opposers proposes opposer opposes oppress propose. *See* **eoopps eoprss ooprss**

eoopprsv　popovers opposer popover propose. *See* **eoopps eoprsv**

eoopprv　popover. *See* **eoprv**

eoopps　oppose popes poops epos oops opes peps peso poop pope pops pose ope pep pop sop os pe so

eoopss　opposes. *See* **eoopps eopss**

eooprr　poorer repro poor pore repo rope err ope ore per pro rep roe er or pe re

eooprrst　troopers poorest porters presort pretors reports rooster rooters toreros torpors trooper. *See* **eooprr eoorrt eoprrs eoprrt**

eooprrt　trooper. *See* **eooprr eoprrt eoorrt ooprrt**

eooprst　poorest. *See* **eoprst ooprst**

eooprstv　stopover overtop poorest provost. *See* **eoprst eoprsv eorstv ooprst**

eooprstw　towropes poorest towrope. *See* **eoorsw eoprst eoprsw eorstw**

eooprtv　overtop. *See* **eortv eoprv eoprt**

eooprtw　towrope. *See* **eoprw eoprt eortw**

eoorrsst　roosters resorts rooster rooters rosters sorters toreros. *See* **eoorrt eorrst eorsst oorsst**

eoorrst　rooster rooters toreros. *See* **eorrst eoorrt**

eoorrt　rooter torero retro root rote roto tore torr err ore ort ret roe rot toe too tor er or re to

eoorsw wooers serow sower swore wooer worse ores owes roes rose rows sore woes woos wore ore owe res roe row sew sow woe woo er or os ow re so we

eoortuw outwore. *See* **eortu eoorw**

eoorw wooer wore ore owe roe row woe woo er or ow re we

eoosttuv outvotes outvote. *See* **eosttu**

eoosz oozes ooze zoos zoo os so

eoottuv outvote. *No 6s or 5s*

eooz ooze zoo

eop ope pe

eopp pope ope pep pop pe

eopppr popper pope pore prep prop repo repp rope ope ore pep per pop pro rep roe er or pe re

eoppprs poppers. *See* **eopppr eopps eoprs**

eopprr proper repro pope pore prep prop repo repp rope err ope ore pep per pop pro rep roe er or pe re

eopprrs prosper. *See* **eopprr eoprrs**

eopprrss prospers oppress pressor prosper. *See* **eopprr eoprrs eoprss**

eopprrty property. *See* **eopprr eoprrt eoprrt eoprry**

eopprss oppress. *See* **eoprss**

eopprsst stoppers oppress posters prestos stopper toppers. *See* **eopprt eoprss eoprst eopsst**

eopprssu purposes oppress poseurs purpose suppers suppose. *See* **eoprss eoprsu eopssu eorssu**

eopprst stopper toppers. *See* **eoprst eopprt**

eopprsu purpose. *See* **eoprsu epprsu**

eopprt topper repot toper trope pert poet pope pore port prep prop repo repp rope rote tope tore ope ore ort pep per pet pop pot pro rep ret roe rot toe top tor er or pe re to

eopps popes epos opes peps peso pope pops pose ope pep pop sop os pe so

eoppsssu supposes suppose spouses. *See* **eopsss eopssu**

eoppssu suppose. *See* **eopssu**

eopr pore repo rope ope ore per pro rep roe er or pe re

eoprr repro pore repo rope err ope ore per pro rep roe er or pe re

eoprrs repros pores poser prose repos repro ropes sorer spore epos errs opes ores peso pore pose pros repo reps roes rope rose sore err ope ore per pro rep res roe sop er or os pe re so

eoprrss pressor. *See* **eoprss eoprrs**

eoprrsss pressors pressor. *See* **eoprrs eoprss**

eoprrsst presorts porters posters presort pressor prestos pretors reports resorts rosters sorters. *See* **eoprrs eoprrt eoprss eoprst**

eoprrst porters presort pretors reports. *See* **eoprrt eoprst eoprrs eorrst**

eoprrstu posturer troupers petrous porters posture presort pretors reports routers trouper troupes. *See* **eoprrs eoprrt eoprst eoprtu**

eoprrt porter pretor report repot repro retro toper trope pert poet pore port repo rope rote tope tore torr err ope ore ort per pet pot pro rep ret roe rot toe top tor er or pe re to

eoprrtu trouper. *See* **eoprrt eorrtu eoprtu**

eoprruvy purveyor. *See* **epruvy eoprry eoruvy**

eoprry ropery repro perry pore prey pyre repo rope ropy yore err ope ore per pro pry rep roe rye yep er or oy pe re ye

eoprs pores poser prose repos ropes spore epos opes ores peso pore pose pros repo reps roes rope rose sore ope ore per pro rep res roe sop er or os pe re so

eoprss posers proses spores pesos pores poser poses posse press prose repos ropes roses sores spore epos opes ores peso pore pose pros repo reps roes rope rose sops sore ess ope ore per pro rep res roe sop er or os pe re so

eoprsst posters prestos. *See* **eopsst eoprss eoprst oprsst eprsst**

eoprsstt protests spotters posters potters prestos protest spotter. *See* **eoprss eoprst eoprtt eopsst**

eoprsstu postures oestrus ousters petrous poseurs posters posture prestos sourest sprouts stupors troupes. *See* **eoprss eoprst eoprsu eoprtu**

eoprssu poseurs. *See* **eopssu eoprsu eoprss eprssu eorssu**

eoprssw prowess. *See* **eoprss eoprsw eorssw**

eoprssy ospreys. *See* **eoprsy eoprss eopssy**

eoprst poster presto repots topers tropes estop poets pores ports poser prose repos repot ropes rotes spore sport stope store strep strop toper topes trope epos erst opes ores orts pert peso pest pets poet pore port pose post pots pros repo reps rest rets roes rope rose rote rots sept sore sort spot step stop toes tope tops tore tors ope ore ort per pet pot pro rep res ret roe rot set sop sot toe top tor er or os pe re so to

eoprstt potters protest spotter. *See* **eorstt eoprst eoprtt**

eoprstu petrous posture troupes. *See* **eprstu eorstu eoprsu eoprst oprstu**

eoprstx exports. *See* **eoprtx eorstx eoprst eopstx**

eoprsu poseur uprose pores poser pours prose purse repos ropes rouse spore sprue super epos opes opus ores ours peso pore pose pour pros pure repo reps roes rope rose rues ruse sore soup sour spue spur sure user ope ore our per pro pus rep res roe rue sop sou sue sup use er or os pe re so up us

eoprsv proves pores poser prose prove repos ropes roves servo spore verso epos opes ores over peso pore pose pros repo reps revs roes rope rose rove sore ope ore per pro rep res rev roe sop er or os pe re so

eoprsw powers pores poser power prose prows repos ropes serow sower spore swore worse epos opes ores owes peso pews pore pose pros prow repo reps roes rope rose rows sore spew swop woes wore ope ore owe per pew pro rep res roe row sew sop sow woe er or os ow pe re so we

eoprsy osprey poesy pores poser preys prose prosy pyres repos ropes sepoy spore yores epos espy opes ores oyes peso pore pose posy prey pros pyre repo reps roes rope ropy rose rosy ryes sore spry yore ope ore per pro pry rep res roe rye sop soy spy yep yes er or os oy pe re so ye

eoprt repot toper trope pert poet pore port repo rope rote tope tore ope ore ort per pet pot pro rep ret roe rot toe top tor er or pe re to

eoprtt potter otter repot toper torte toter trope pert poet pore port repo rope rote tope tore tort tote tret trot ope ore ort per pet pot pro rep ret roe rot toe top tor tot er or pe re to

eoprtty pottery. *See* **eoprty eoprtt eprtty**

eoprtu troupe erupt outer repot route toper trope pert poet pore port pour pout pure repo rope rote rout tope tore tour true ope ore ort our out per pet pot pro put rep ret roe rot rue rut toe top tor tup er or pe re to up ut

eoprtvy poverty. *See* **eoprty eortv eoprv**

eoprtx export repot toper trope pert poet pore port repo rope rote tope tore ope ore ort per pet pot pox pro rep ret rex roe rot toe top tor er ex or ox pe re to

eoprty poetry repot toper trope pert poet pore port prey pyre repo rope ropy rote ryot tope tore troy type tyro yore ope ore ort per pet pot pro pry rep ret roe rot rye toe top tor toy try yep yet er or oy pe re to ye

eoprv prove over pore repo rope rove ope ore per pro rep rev roe er or pe re

eoprw power pore prow repo rope wore ope ore owe per pew pro rep roe row woe er or ow pe re we

eops epos opes peso pose ope sop os pe so

eopss pesos poses posse epos opes peso pose sops ess ope sop os pe so

eopsss posses pesos poses posse epos opes peso pose sops ess ope sop os pe so

eopssss possess. *See* **eopsss**

eopssst possets. *See* **eopsst eopsss eossst**

eopsssu spouses. *See* **eopssu epsssu eosssu**

eopsst estops posset stopes estop pesos pests poets poses posse posts spots steps stope stops topes epos opes peso pest pets poet pose post pots sept sets sops sots spot step stop toes tope tops toss ess ope pet pot set sop sot toe top os pe so to

eopsstx sexpots. *See* **eopsst eopstx**

eopssu opuses spouse pesos poses posse soups souse spues epos opes opus peso pose puss sops soup sous spue sues sups uses ess ope pus sop sou sue sup use os pe so up us

eopssy sepoys pesos poesy poses posse sepoy epos espy opes oyes peso pose posy sops soys ess ope sop soy spy yep yes os oy pe so ye

eopst estop poets stope topes epos opes peso pest pets poet pose post pots sept spot step stop toes tope tops ope pet pot set sop sot toe top os pe so to

eopstx sexpot estop poets poxes stope topes epos opes peso pest pets poet pose post pots sept sext spot step stop toes tope tops ope pet pot pox set sex sop sot sox toe top ex os ox pe so to

eopsx poxes epos opes peso pose ope pox sex sop sox ex os ox pe so

eopsy poesy sepoy epos espy opes oyes peso pose posy ope sop soy spy yep yes os oy pe so ye

eopt poet tope ope pet pot toe top pe to

eopxy epoxy ope pox pyx yep ex ox oy pe ye

eoqrsstu questors oestrus ousters questor quoters roquets sourest torques. *See* **eoqrsu eoqrtu eoqstu eorsst**

eoqrstu questor quoters roquets torques. *See* **eorstu eoqrtu eoqstu eoqrsu**

eoqrsu roques roque rouse rouse ores ours roes rose rues ruse sore sour sure user ore our res roe rue sou sue use er or os re so us

eoqrtu quoter roquet torque outer quote roque route toque rote rout tore tour true ore ort our out ret roe rot rue rut toe tor er or re to ut

eoqru roque ore our roe rue er or re

eoqstu quotes toques quest quote toque oust outs suet toes out set sot sou sue toe use os so to us ut

eoqtu quote toque toe out to ut

eor ore roe er or re

eorr error err ore roe er or re

eorrs errors error sorer errs ores roes rose sore err ore res roe er or os re so

eorrst terrors. *See* **eorrrs eorrst eorrrt**

eorrrt terror error retro rote tore torr err ore ort ret roe rot toe tor er or re to

eorrrttu torturer torture. *See* **eorrtt eorrtu errttu**

eorrry orrery error yore err ore roe rye er or oy re ye

eorrs sorer errs ores roes rose sore err ore res roe er or os re so

eorrsst resorts rosters sorters. *See* **eorrst eorsst**

eorrsstt stertors resorts retorts rosters rotters sorters stertor. *See* **eorrst eorrtt eorrsst eorstt**

eorrsstu trousers oestrus ousters resorts rosters routers sorters sourest. *See* **eorrst eorrsu eorrtu eorsst**

eorrst resort roster sorter retro rotes sorer store errs erst ores orts rest rets roes rose rote rots sore sort toes tore torr tors err ore ort res ret roe rot set sot toe tor er or os re so to

eorrstt retorts rotters stertor. *See* **eorstt eorrst eorrtt**

eorrsttt trotters retorts rotters stertor stretto totters trotter. *See* **eorrst eorrtt eorstt**

eorrsttu tortures retorts rotters routers stertor torture turrets. *See* **eorrst eorrsu eorrtt eorrtu**

eorrstu routers. *See* **eorstu eorrtu eorrst eorrsu**

eorrstv trovers. *See* **eorrst eorrsv eorstv eorrtv**

eorrsu sourer rouse sorer surer errs ores ours roes rose rues ruse sore sour sure user err ore our res roe rue sou sue use er or os re so us

eorrsuvy surveyor voyeurs. *See* **eorrsu eorrsv eorrsy eoruvy**

eorrsv rovers rover roves servo sorer verso errs ores over revs roes rose rove sore err ore res rev roe er or os re so

eorrsw rowers worser rower serow sorer sower swore worse errs ores owes roes rose rows sews sore sows woes wore err ore owe

res roe row sew sow woe er or os ow re so we

eorrsy rosery sorer sorry yores errs ores oyes roes rose rosy ryes sore yore err ore res rye soy yes er or os oy re so ye

eorrszz rozzers. *See* **eorrzz eorrs eorsz**

eorrt retro rote tore torr err ore ort ret roe rot toe tor er or re to

eorrtt retort rotter otter retro torte toter rote tore torr tort tote tret trot err ore ort ret roe rot toe tor tot er or re to

eorrttt trotter. *See* **eorrtt eorstt**

eorrttu torture. *See* **eorrtt eorrtu errttu**

eorrtu router outer retro route truer rote rout tore torr tour true err ore ort our out ret roe rot rue rut toe tor er or re to ut

eorrtv trover overt retro rover trove voter over rote rove tore torr vert veto vote err ore ort ret rev roe rot toe tor vet er or re to

eorrv rover over rove err ore rev roe er or re

eorrw rower wore err ore owe roe row woe er or ow re we

eorrzz rozzer zero err ore roe er or re

eors ores roes rose sore ore res roe er or os re so

eorss roses sores ores roes rose sore ess ore res roe er or os re so

eorsst sorest stores rests roses rotes sores sorts store tress erst ores orts rest rets roes rose rote rots sets sore sort sots toes tore tors toss ess ore ort res ret roe rot set sot toe tor er or os re so to

eorssttt strettos stretto totters. *See* **eorsst eorstt**

eorsstu oestrus ousters sourest. *See* **ersstu eorstu eorssu orsstu eorsst**

eorsstv stovers. *See* **eorssv eorsst eorstv eosstv ersstv**

eorssty oysters. *See* **eorsty**

eorssu rouses serous roses rouse ruses sores sorus sours souse users ores ours roes rose rues ruse sore sour sous sues sure user uses ess ore our res roe rue sou sue use er or os re so us

eorssv servos versos roses roves servo sores verso ores over revs roes rose rove sore ess ore res rev roe er or os re so

eorssw serows sowers roses serow sores sower swore worse ores owes roes rose rows sews sore sows woes wore ess ore owe res roe row sew sow woe er or os ow re so we

eorst rotes store erst ores orts rest rets roes rose rote rots sore sort toes tore

tors ore ort res ret roe rot set sot toe tor er or os re so to

eorstt otters tortes otter rotes store torte torts toter totes trets trots erst ores orts rest rets roes rose rote rots sore sort stet test toes tore tors tort tost tote tots tret trot ore ort res ret roe rot set sot toe tor tot er or os re so to

eorsttt stretto totters. *See* **eorstt eorttt**

eorsttx extorts. *See* **eorttx eorstt eorstx**

eorstu ouster routes outer rotes rouse roust route routs store stour torus tours trues erst ores orts ours oust outs rest rets roes rose rote rots rout rues ruse rust ruts sore sort sour suet sure toes tore tors tour true user ore ort our out res ret roe rot rue rut set sot sou sue toe tor use er or os re so to us ut

eorstv stover strove troves voters overt rotes roves servo store stove trove verso verst verts voter votes erst ores orts over rest rets revs roes rose rote rots rove sore sort toes tore tors vert vest veto vets vote ore ort res ret rev roe rot set sot toe tor vet er or os re so to

eorstw towers rotes serow sower store strew swore tower trews trows worse worst wrest wrote erst ores orts owes rest rets roes rose rote rots rows sore sort skew stew swot toes tore tors tows trow twos west wets woes wore ore ort owe res ret roe rot row set sew sot sow toe tor tow two wet woe er or os ow re so to we

eorstx oxters rotes store erst ores orts rest rets roes rose rote rots sext sore sort toes tore tors ore ort res ret rex roe rot set sex sot sox toe tor er ex or os ox re so to

eorsty oyster rotes ryots store story tyros yores erst ores orts oyes rest rets roes rose rosy rote rots ryes ryot sore sort

toes tore tors toys troy tyro yore ore ort res ret roe rot rye set sot soy sty toe tor toy try yes yet er or os oy re so to ye

eorsu rouse ores ours roes rose rues ruse sore sour sure user ore our res roe rue sou sue use er or os re so us

eorsuvy voyeurs. *See* **eoruvy ersuvy**

eorsv roves servo verso ores over revs roes rose rove sore ore res rev roe er or os re so

eorsw serow sower swore worse ores owes roes rose rows sore woes wore ore owe res roe row sew sow woe er or os ow re so we

eorsxy oryxes yores ores oryx oyes roes rose rosy ryes sexy sore yore ore res rex roe rye sex sox soy yes er ex or os ox oy re so ye

eorsy yores ores oyes roes rose rosy ryes sore yore ore res roe rye soy yes er or os oy re so ye

eorsz zeros ores roes rose sore zero ore res roe er or os re so

eort rote tore ore ort ret roe rot toe tor er or re to

eortt otter torte toter rote tore tort tote tret trot ore ort ret roe rot toe tor tot er or re to

eorttt totter otter torte toter rote tore tort tote tret trot ore ort ret roe rot toe tor tot er or re to

eorttx extort otter torte toter rote text tore tort tote tret trot ore ort ret rex roe rot toe tor tot er ex or ox re to

eortu outer route rote rout tore tour true ore ort our out ret roe rot rue rut toe tor er or re to ut

eortv overt trove voter over rote rove tore vert veto vote ore ort ret rev roe rot toe tor vet er or re to

eortvx vortex overt trove voter over rote rove tore vert veto vote ore ort ret rev

rex roe rot toe tor vet vex er ex or ox re to

eortw tower wrote rote tore trow wore ore ort owe ret roe rot row toe tor tow two wet woe er or ow re to we

eoruvy voyeur over rove very yore your ore our rev roe rue rye you er or oy re ye

eorv over rove ore rev roe er or re

eorw wore ore owe roe row woe er or ow re we

eorxx xerox ore rex roe er ex or ox re

eory yore ore roe rye er or oy re ye

eorz zero ore roe er or re

eossst tosses stoss sets sots toes toss ess set sot toe os so to

eosssu souses souse sous sues uses ess sou sue use os so us

eossttu outsets. *See* **eosttu ossttu**

eosstv stoves stove vests votes sets sots toes toss vest veto vets vote ess set sot toe vet os so to

eossu souse sous sues uses ess sou sue use os so us

eost toes set sot toe os so to

eostt totes stet test toes tost tote tots set sot toe tot os so to

eosttu outset stout totes touts oust outs stet suet test toes tost tote tots tout tuts out set sot sou sue toe tot tut use os so to us ut

eostv stove votes toes vest veto vets vote set sot toe vet os so to

eosw owes woes owe sew sow woe os ow so we

eosy oyes yes soy os oy so ye

eot toe to

eott tote toe tot to

eotv veto vote toe vet to

eovw wove owe vow woe we ow

eow owe woe we ow

eoyz oyez ye oy

---

ep pe

epp pep pe

eppprtuy puppetry. *See* **eppptu**

epppstu puppets. *See* **eppptu epstu**

eppptu puppet pep pet pup put tup pe up ut

epppy peppy pep yep pe ye

eppr prep repp pep per rep er pe re

epprs preps repps peps prep repp reps pep per rep res er pe re

epprsssu suppress suppers. *See* **epprsu eprssu**

epprssu suppers. *See* **eprssu epprsu**

epprsu supper uppers preps purse repps sprue super upper peps prep pups pure repp reps rues ruse spue spur sure user

pep per pup pus rep res rue sue sup use er pe re up us

eppru upper prep pure repp pep per pup rep rue er pe re up

epps peps pep pe

eppstuw upswept. *See* **epstu epstw**

epr per rep er pe re

eprrssu pursers. *See* **eprrsu eprssu**

eprrstuu ruptures rupture. *See* **eprrsu eprstu eprsuu**

eprrsu purser purer purrs purse sprue super surer errs pure purr reps rues ruse spue spur sure user err per pus rep res rue sue sup use er pe re up us

eprrsy spryer perry preys pyres errs espy prey pyre reps ryes spry err per pry rep res rye spy yep yes er pe re ye

eprrtuu rupture. *See* **eprtu eprru errtu**

eprru purer pure purr err per rep rue er pe re up

eprry perry prey pyre err per pry rep rye yep er pe re ye

eprs reps per rep res er pe re

eprss press reps ess per rep res er pe re

eprsst streps pests press rests steps strep tress erst pert pest pets reps rest rets sept sets step ess per pet rep res ret set er pe re

eprssttu sputters putters sputter. *See* **eprsst eprssu eprstu eprttu**

eprssu purses sprues supers press purse ruses sprue spues spurs super users pure puss reps rues ruse spue spur sues sups sure user uses ess per pus rep res rue sue sup use er pe re up us

eprssuu pursues. *See* **eprssu eprsuu er-ssuu prssuu**

eprst strep erst pert pest pets reps rest rets sept step per pet rep res ret set er pe re

eprsttu putters sputter. *See* **eprstu eprttu ersttu**

eprstu erupts purest erupt purse setup sprue spurt strep stupe super trues up-set erst pert pest pets pure puts reps rest rets rues ruse rust ruts sept spue spur step suet sure true tups user per pet pus put rep res ret rue rut set sue sup tup use er pe re up us ut

eprstw twerps strep strew swept trews twerp wrest erst pert pest pets pews reps rest rets sept spew step stew wept west wets per pet pew rep res ret set sew wet er pe re we

eprsu purse sprue super pure reps rues ruse spue spur sure user per pus rep res rue sue sup use er pe re up us

eprsuu pursue purse sprue super usurp pure reps rues ruse spue spur sure urus user per pus rep res rue sue sup use er pe re up us

eprsuvy purveys. *See* **epruvy ersuvy**

eprsy preys pyres espy prey pyre reps ryes spry per pry rep res rye spy yep yes er pe re ye

eprt pert per pet rep ret er pe re

eprttu putter erupt utter pert pure putt tret true per pet put rep ret rue rut tup tut er pe re up ut

eprtty pretty petty pert prey pyre tret type per pet pry rep ret rye try yep yet er pe re ye

eprtu erupt pert pure true per pet put rep ret rue rut tup er pe re up ut

eprtw twerp pert wept per pet pew rep ret wet er pe re we

epru pure per rep rue er pe re up

epruvy purvey prey pure pyre very per pry rep rev rue rye yep yup er pe re up ye

eprxy prexy prey pyre per pry pyx rep rex rye yep er ex pe re ye

epry prey pyre per pry rep rye yep er pe re ye

epsssu pusses spues puss spue sues sups uses ess pus sue sup use pe up us

epsst pests steps pest pets sept sets step ess pet set pe

epsstu setups upsets pests setup spues steps stupe suets upset pest pets puss puts sept sets spue step sues suet sups tups uses ess pet pus put set sue sup tup use pe up us ut

epssu spues puss spue sues sups uses ess pus sue sup use pe up us

epssw spews pews sews spew ess pew sew pe we

epst pest pets sept step pet set pe

epstu setup stupe upset pest pets puts sept spue step suet tups pet pus put set sue sup tup use pe up us ut

epstw swept pest pets pews sept spew step stew wept west wets pet pew set sew wet pe we

epsty types espy pest pets sept step type pet set spy sty yep yes yet pe ye

epsu spue pus sue sup use pe up us

epsw pews spew pew sew pe we

epsxy pyxes espy sexy pyx sex spy yep yes ex pe ye

epsy espy spy yep yes pe ye

ept pet pe

eptty petty type pet yep yet pe ye

eptw wept pet pew wet pe we

epty type pet yep yet pe ye

epw pew pe we

epy yep pe ye

---

eqruy query rue rye er re ye

eqsstu quests quest suets sets sues suet uses ess set sue use us ut

eqstu quest suet set sue use us ut

eqstuu tuques quest tuque suet set sue use us ut

eqtuu tuque ut

---

er er re

err err er re

errs errs err res er re

errssuu usurers. *See* **errsuu erssuu**

errssuy surreys. *See* **errsuy erssu**

errsttu turrets. *See* **ersttu errttu**

errsu surer errs rues ruse sure user err res rue sue use er re us

errsuu usurer surer errs rues ruse sure urus user err res rue sue use er re us

errsuy surrey surer errs rues ruse ryes sure user err res rue rye sue use yes er re us ye

errttu turret truer utter tret true err ret rue rut tut er re ut

errtu truer true err ret rue rut er re ut

errty retry terry err ret rye try yet er re ye

ers res er re

erssst stress rests tress erst rest rets sets ess res ret set er re

erssstu russets trusses. *See* ersstu erssst

ersst rests tress erst rest rets sets ess res ret set er re

ersstttu stutters stutter. *See* ersstu ersttu

ersstu estrus russet surest rests ruses rusts suets tress trues truss users erst rest rets rues ruse rust ruts sets sues suet sure true user uses ess res ret rue rut set sue use er re us ut

ersstuu sutures. *See* ersstu erstuu erssuu

ersstv versts rests tress verst verts vests erst rest rets revs sets vert vest vets ess res ret rev set vet er re

ersstw strews wrests rests stews strew tress trews wests wrest erst rest rets

sets sews stew west wets ess res ret set sew wet er re we

ersstxy xysters. *See* erstxy ersst esstx

erssu ruses users rues ruse sues sure user uses ess res rue sue use er re us

erssuu uruses ruses users rues ruse sues sure urus user uses ess res rue sue use er re us

erssuv versus ruses users revs rues ruse sues sure user uses ess res rev rue sue use er re us

erssuvy surveys. *See* erssuv ersuvy

erst erst rest rets res ret set er re

erstt trets erst rest rets stet test tret res ret set er re

erstttu stutter. *See* ersttu

ersttu truest utters strut trets trues trust utter erst rest rets rues ruse rust ruts stet suet sure test tret true tuts user res ret rue rut set sue tut use er re us ut

erstu trues erst rest rets rues ruse rust ruts suet sure true user res ret rue rut set sue use er re us ut

erstuu suture uterus trues erst rest rets rues ruse rust ruts suet sure true urus user res ret rue rut set sue use er re us ut

erstuy surety rusty trues yurts erst rest rets rues ruse rust ruts ryes suet sure

true user yurt res ret rue rut rye set sty sue try use yes yet er re us ut ye

erstv verst verts erst rest rets revs vert vest vets res ret rev set vet er re

erstvy vestry verst verts erst rest rets revs ryes vert very vest vets res ret rev rye set sty try vet yes yet er re ye

erstw strew trews wrest erst rest rets stew west wets res ret set sew wet er re we

erstxy xyster erst rest rets ryes sext sexy res ret rex rye set sex sty try yes yet er ex re ye

ersu rues ruse sure user res rue sue use er re us

ersuvy survey revs rues ruse ryes sure user very res rev rue rye use yes er re us ye

ersv revs res rev er re

ersy ryes res rye yes er re ye

ert ret er re

ertt tret ret er re

erttu utter tret true ret rue rut tut er re ut

ertu true ret rue rut er re ut

ertv vert ret rev vet er re

eru rue er re

erv rev er re

ervy very rev rye er re ye

erx rex er ex re

ery rye er re ye

---

es

ess ess

esst sets ess set

esstt stets tests sets stet test ess set

esstu suets sets sues suet uses ess set sue use us ut

esstv vests sets vest vets ess set vet

esstw stews wests sets sews stew west wets ess set sew wet we

esstx sexts sets sext ess set sex ex

esstz zests sets zest ess set

essu sues uses ess sue use us

essw sews ess sew we

est set

estt stet test set

esttx texts sext stet test text set sex ex

estty testy stet test set sty yes yet ye

estu suet set sue use us ut

estux tuxes suet sext set sex sue tux use ex us ut

estv vest vets set vet

estw stew west wets set sew wet we

estx sext set sex ex

estyz zesty zest set sty yes yet ye

estz zest set

esu sue use us

esw sew we

eswy wyes yews sew wye yes yew we ye

esx sex ex

esxy sexy sex yes ex ye

esy yes ye

---

et

ettx text ex

etv vet

etw wet we

ety yet ye

ev—ey

evx vex ex	**ex** ex
ew we	**ey** ye
ewy wye yew we ye	

ff

fffgilnu   fluffing luffing. *See* **fgilnu**
fffilost   liftoffs liftoff. *See* **ffiost**
fffilot   liftoff. *No 6s or 5s*
ffflsu   fluffs fluff luffs sluff luff flus flu us
ffflu   fluff luff flu
fffluy   fluffy fluff luff flu fly
ffghiinw   whiffing. *See* **ffgiin**
ffghinu   huffing. *See* **fginu**
ffgiilnr   riffling griffin riffing rifling. *See* **ffgiin fgiiln fgiinr giilnr**
ffgiimn   miffing. *See* **ffgiin**
ffgiin   fifing fig fin gin if in
ffgiinns   sniffing finings. *See* **ffgiin fgiinn**
ffgiinps   spiffing. *See* **ffgiin**
ffgiinr   griffin riffing. *See* **ffgiin fgiinr**
ffgiinrs   griffins firings griffin riffing. *See* **ffgiin fgiinr giinrs**
ffgiinst   stiffing sifting tiffing tiffins. *See* **ffgiin ffiint giinst**
ffgiint   tiffing. *See* **ffgiin ffiint**
ffgilmnu   muffling luffing muffing. *See* **ffimnu fgilnu fgimnu**
ffgilnru   ruffling luffing furling. *See* **fgilnu gilnru**
ffgilnsu   sluffing luffing ingulfs. *See* **fgilns fgilnu fginsu filnsu**
ffgilnu   luffing. *See* **fgilnu**
ffgimnu   muffing. *See* **ffimnu fgimnu**
ffginnsu   snuffing. *See* **fginsu**
ffgino   offing fig fin fog gin ion nog off go if in no of on
ffginos   offings. *See* **ffgino ffins**
ffginpu   puffing. *See* **ffinpu fginu**
ffginstu   stuffing. *See* **fginsu**
ffglruy   gruffly. *See* **ffgru**
ffgru   gruff guff ruff fug fur rug
ffgsu   guffs guff fugs fug us
ffgu   guff fug
ffhhisu   huffish. *See* **ffhsu**
ffhios   offish fish foh his ifs off ohs hi ho if is of oh os sh si so
ffhist   fifths fifth shift stiff tiffs fish fist fits hist hits sift sith this tiff fit his hit ifs its sit hi if is it sh si ti
ffhisw   whiffs whiff fish wish his ifs wis hi if is sh si
ffhit   fifth tiff fit hit hi if it ti
ffhiw   whiff if hi
ffhoooost   offshoot. *See* **fhoos hoost ffost**
ffhoossw   showoffs showoff. *See* **hoossw**
ffhoosw   showoff. *See* **fhoos foosw hoosw**

ffhors   shroff frosh rhos foh for fro off ohs rho ho of oh or os sh so
ffhorss   shroffs. *See* **ffhors**
ffhsu   huffs huff sh us
ffhu   huff
ffhuy   huffy huff
ffiinst   tiffins. *See* **ffiint fiins ffins**
ffiint   tiffin tiff fin fit nit tin if in it ti
ffij   jiff if
ffijy   jiffy jiff iffy if
ffiklort   forklift. *See* **filrt**
ffiks   skiff kifs ifs kif ski if is si
ffikss   skiffs skiff kifs kiss skis ifs kif sis ski if is si
ffilllsu   fulfills fulfill fulfils. *See* **ffillu**
ffilllu   fulfill. *See* **ffillu**
ffillsu   fulfils. *See* **ffillu fills filsu**
ffilltuy   fitfully. *See* **ffillu ffiltu**
ffillu   fulfil fill full luff flu ill if li
ffilpuy   puffily. *See* **ffpuy**
ffilrtuu   fruitful. *See* **ffiltu**
ffilsstu   fistfuls fistful. *See* **ffiltu ffisst ffl-ssu ffsstu**
ffilstu   fistful. *See* **ffiltu filst filsu**
ffilsty   stiffly. *See* **ffity filty filst**
ffiltu   fitful flit lift luff tiff tuff fit flu lit til tui if it li ti ut
ffim   miff if mi
ffimnsu   muffins. *See* **ffimnu ffims imnsu**
ffimnu   muffin miff muff fin fun nim if in mi mu nu um
ffims   miffs miff ifs mis if is mi si
ffinoprt   offprint pontiff. *See* **finort fioprt**
ffinops   spinoff. *See* **ffins ffips**
ffinopss   spinoffs spinoff. *See* **ffinss ffipss**
ffinopst   pontiffs spinoff pontiff. *See* **ffiost inopst**
ffinopt   pontiff. *See* **inopt**
ffinpsu   puffins. *See* **ffinpu ffpsu ffins**
ffinpu   puffin puff fin fun nip pin pun if in nu pi up
ffins   sniff fins fin ifs sin if in is si
ffinss   sniffs sniff fins sins fin ifs sin sis if in is si
ffinsy   sniffy sniff iffy fins fin ifs sin yin if in is si
ffiorty   fortify. *See* **ffity forty**
ffiosst   soffits. *See* **fiosst ffiost ffisst**
ffiost   soffit foist stiff tiffs toffs fist fits sift soft tiff toff fit ifs its off oft sit sot if is it of os si so ti to

ffips   spiff ifs sip if is pi si
ffipss   spiffs spiff sips ifs sip sis if is pi si
ffipsy   spiffy spiff iffy yips ifs sip spy yip if is pi si
ffiqsu   quiffs quiff ifs if is si us
ffiqu   quiff if
ffir   riff fir rif if
ffirs   riffs firs riff rifs fir ifs rif sir if is si
ffisst   stiffs fists sifts stiff tiffs fist fits sift sits tiff fit ifs its sis sit if is it si ti
ffist   stiff tiffs fist fits sift tiff fit ifs its sit if is it si ti
ffisux   suffix fix ifs six if is si us xi
ffit   tiff fit if it ti
ffity   fifty tiff iffy fit if it ti
ffiy   iffy if
ffklorsu   forkfuls forkful. *See* **florsu**
ffkloru   forkful. *See* **floru**
ffllosty   fylflots fylflot. *See* **flosty**
fflloty   fylflot. *See* **flloy floty**
fflssu   sluffs luffs sluff flus fuss luff flu us
fflsu   luffs sluff luff flus flu us
fflu   luff flu
ffmsu   muffs muff mus sum mu um us
ffmu   muff mu um
ffnorstu   turnoffs runoffs turnoff. *See* **ffnoru fnorst fnostu**
ffnorsu   runoffs. *See* **ffnoru forsu fnors**
ffnortu   turnoff. *See* **ffnoru fnotu fnort**
ffnoru   runoff ruff four for fro fun fur nor off our run urn no nu of on or
ffnssu   snuffs snuff fuss suns fun sun nu us
ffnsu   snuff fun sun nu us
ffnsuy   snuffy snuff fun sun nu us
ffo   off of
ffoorruu   froufrou. *See* **ffrruu**
ffost   toffs toff soft off oft sot of os so to
ffot   toff off oft of to
ffpsu   puffs puff pus sup up us
ffpu   puff up
ffpuy   puffy puff yup up
ffrruu   furfur ruff fur
ffrsu   ruffs furs ruff surf fur us
ffru   ruff fur
ffsstu   stuffs stuff tuffs tuff fuss us ut
ffstu   stuff tuffs tuff us ut
ffstuy   stuffy fusty stuff tuffs tuff sty us ut
fftu   tuff ut

fg

fgggiin figging. *No 6s or 5s*

fgggiinr frigging figging rigging. *See* **fgiinr**

fgggilno flogging fogging golfing logging. *See* **gglno**

fgggino fogging. *See* **ggino**

fgghiint fighting. *See* **fghit ghint**

fgghintu gunfight. *See* **fghit fginu ghint**

fggiilnn flinging. *See* **fgiiln fgiinn giilnn**

fggiinnr fringing ringing. *See* **fgiinn fgiinr**

fggiinru figuring. *See* **fgiinr gginru**

fggilno golfing. *See* **gglno fgiln**

fggilnu gulfing. *See* **fgilnu ggilnu**

fggiloy foggily. *See* **fggoy**

fgginoo goofing. *See* **fgnoo ggino**

fgginoor forgoing forging goofing roofing. *See* **gginor ggnoor**

fgginor forging. *See* **gginor**

fggory froggy foggy fogy frog gory grog gyro orgy fog for foy fro fry goy go of or oy

fggoy foggy fogy fog foy goy go of oy

fghhios hogfish. *See* **ghhis**

fghiikns kingfish fishing. *See* **fhiins ghiikn giikns**

fghiins fishing. *See* **fhiins**

fghiinst shifting fishing insight sifting. *See* **fghist fhiins ghinst**

fghilnsu flushing lungfish ingulfs. *See* **fgilns fgilnu fginsu filnsu**

fghilrtu rightful. *See* **fghist fghirt**

fghilst flights. *See* **fghist fghilt ghilst**

fghilt flight fight filth light flit gift gilt hilt lift fig fit hit lit til hi if it li ti

fghilty flighty. *See* **fghilt fhilty**

fghinoo hoofing. *See* **ghinoo fgnoo**

fghinort frothing. *See* **fghirt finort ghiort ghnort**

fghirst frights. *See* **fghist fhirst fghirt ghirst**

fghirt fright fight firth frith girth right frig frit gift girt grit rift trig fig fir fit hit rif rig hi if it ti

fghist fights fight gifts shift sight figs fish fist fits gift gist hist hits sift sigh sith this fig fit his hit ifs its sit hi if is it sh si ti

fghit fight gift fig fit hit hi if it ti

fghloruu furlough. *See* **floru ghlou ghoru**

fghnoor foghorn. *See* **fgoor fgnoo hnoor**

fghnoors foghorns foghorn. *See* **fgnoos hnoors**

fghotu fought ought tough gout thou thug tofu fog foh fug got gut hog hot hug hut oft out tho tog tug ugh go ho of oh to ut

fgi fig if

fgiiinnx infixing. *See* **fgiinn fgiinx**

fgiiknn finking knifing. *See* **fgiinn giiknn**

fgiiknrs frisking firings firkins risking. *See* **fgiinr fiiknr giiknr giikns**

fgiilln filling. *See* **fgiiln**

fgiillnr frilling filling rifling rilling. *See* **fgiiln fgiinr giilnr**

fgiillns fillings filling filings. *See* **fgiiln fgilns**

fgiilmn filming. *See* **fgiiln giilmn**

fgiiln filing fling ling fig fin gin nil if in li

fgiilno foiling. *See* **fgiiln giilno**

fgiilnpp flipping lipping. *See* **fgiiln giilnp giinpp**

fgiilnr rifling. *See* **fgiiln fgiinr giilnr**

fgiilnrt flirting trifling lifting rifling rifting. *See* **fgiiln fgiinr giilnr giilnt**

fgiilns filings. *See* **fgiiln fgilns**

fgiilnst stifling filings lifting listing sifting silting. *See* **fgiiln fgilns filnst giilnt**

fgiilnt lifting. *See* **fgiiln giilnt**

fgiilntt flitting fitting lifting tilting titling. *See* **fgiiln giilnt**

fgiilny lignify. *See* **fgiiln fgilny**

fgiilnzz fizzling fizzing. *See* **fgiiln**

fgiimnr firming. *See* **fgiinr fiimnr giimnr**

fgiinn fining fig fin gin inn if in

fgiinns finings. *See* **fgiinn fiins**

fgiinnsu infusing finings. *See* **fgiinn fginsu**

fgiinnux unfixing. *See* **fgiinn fgiinx**

fgiinnuy unifying. *See* **fgiinn**

fgiinost foisting sifting. *See* **giinst ginost**

fgiinr firing firn frig grin ring fig fin fir gin rif rig if in

fgiinrs firings. *See* **fgiinr giinrs**

fgiinrt rifting. *See* **fgiinr giinrt**

fgiinrzz frizzing fizzing. *See* **fgiinr**

fgiinst sifting. *See* **giinst fiins fgist**

fgiinstt fittings fitting sifting sitting. *See* **giinst**

fgiinsx fixings. *See* **fgiinx fiins**

fgiinsy signify. *See* **fiins**

fgiintt fitting. *No 6s or 5s*

fgiinx fixing infix fig fin fix gin nix if in xi

fgiinzz fizzing. *No 6s or 5s*

fgiklnnu flunking funking. *See* **fgilnu giknnu**

fgiknnu funking. *See* **giknnu fginu**

fgiknor forking. *See* **ginor**

fgiln fling ling fig fin gin nil if in li

fgilnoo fooling. *See* **gilnoo fgiln filoo**

fgilnoor flooring fooling roofing. *See* **filnor gilnoo**

fgilnooz foozling fooling. *See* **gilnoo ginooz**

fgilnopp flopping lopping. *See* **gilnop ilnopp**

fgilnoru flouring fouling furling furlong. *See* **fgilnu filnor gilnru**

fgilnoss flossing. *See* **fgilns filoss gilnos gilnss**

fgilnot lofting. *See* **fgiln filnt gilnt**

fgilnotu flouting fluting fouling lofting. *See* **fgilnu gilntu ginotu**

fgilnou fouling. *See* **fgilnu fgnou gilno**

fgilnow flowing fowling. *See* **filnow gilnow**

fgilnpru purfling furling purling. *See* **fgilnu gilnpu gilnru ilnpru**

fgilnru furling. *See* **fgilnu gilnru**

fgilns flings fling lings sling figs fils fins gins ling nils sign sing fig fin gin ifs nil sin if in is li si

fgilnsu ingulfs. *See* **fgilns fginsu fgilnu gilnsu filnsu**

fgilntu fluting. *See* **fgilnu gilntu**

fgilnu ingulf fling flung fungi lungi gulf ling lung fig fin flu fug fun gin gnu gun lug nil if in li nu

fgilnux fluxing. *See* **fgilnu filnux**

fgilny flying fling lying inly ling liny fig fin fly gin nil yin if in li

fgilory glorify. *See* **glory ilory**

fgiluy uglify gulf ugly fig flu fly fug guy lug if li

fgimnor forming. *See* **fimnor ginor**

fgimnu fuming fungi fig fin fug fun gin gnu gum gun mug nim if in mi mu nu um

fginnnu funning. *See* **fginu**

fginnort fronting. *See* **finort ginnot ginort**

fginnorw frowning ingrown. *See* **ginnow ginorw**

fginoops spoofing. *See* **fgnoos ginops inoops**

fginoor roofing. *See* **fgoor fgnoo ginor**

fginoost footings footing sooting. *See* **fgnoos ginost**

fginoot footing. *See* **fgnoo ginot**

fginorst frosting forints sorting storing trigons. *See* **finort fiorst fnorst ginors**

fginox foxing fig fin fix fog fox gin ion nix nog go if in no of on ox xi

fginrru furring. *See* **fginu ginru**

fginrsu surfing. *See* **fginsu finrs fgirs**

fginry frying firn frig grin ring fig fin fir fry gin rif rig yin if in

fginssu fussing. *See* **fginsu inssu ginss**

fginsu fusing fungi suing using figs fins fugs gins gnus guns sign sing snug sung fig fin fug fun gin gnu gun ifs sin sun if in is nu si us

fginttu tufting. *See* **fginu fintu**
fgintuz futzing. *See* **fginuz fintu**
fginu fungi fig fin fug fun gin gnu gun if in nu
fginuz fuzing fungi zing fig fin fug fun gin gnu gun zig if in nu
fginuzz fuzzing. *See* **fginuz**
fgir frig fig fir rif rig if
fgirs frigs figs firs frig rifs rigs fig fir ifs rif rig sir if is si
fgis figs fig ifs if is si
fgist gifts figs fist fits gift gist sift fig fit ifs its sit if is it si ti
fgit gift fig fit if it ti
fgjlsuu jugfuls. *See* **fgjluu fglsu**
fgjluu jugful gulf flu fug jug lug ulu
fglnorsu furlongs furlong. *See* **florsu**
fglnoru furlong. *See* **floru fglnu fgnou**
fglnoruw wrongful furlong. *See* **floru flnow fglnu**

fglnu flung gulf lung flu fug fun gnu gun lug nu
fglo flog golf fog log go lo of
fglos flogs golfs flog fogs golf logs slog fog log los sol go lo of os so
fglsu gulfs flus fugs gulf lugs slug flu fug lug us
fglu gulf flu fug lug
fgnoo gonof goof goon fog goo nog go no of on
fgnoos gonofs gonof goofs goons fogs goof goon goos nogs song soon fog goo nog son go no of on os so
fgnosuu fungous. *See* **fgnsuu fgnou**
fgnou fungo fog fug fun gnu gun nog go no nu of on
fgnsuu fungus fugs gnus guns snug sung fug fun gnu gun sun nu us

fgo fog of go
fgoo goof fog goo of go
fgoor forgo frog goof roof fog for fro goo go of or
fgoort forgot forgo foot fort frog goof grot roof root roto fog for fro goo got oft ort rot tog too tor go of or to
fgoos goofs fogs goof goos fog goo go of os so
fgooy goofy goof fogy fog foy goo goy go of oy
fgor frog fog for fro go of or
fgors frogs frog fogs fog for fro go of or os so
fgos fogs fog go of os so
fgoy fogy fog foy goy go of oy
fgsu fugs fug us
fgu fug

fhhikoos fishhook. *See* **fhoos hkoos**
fhiilsty shiftily fishily. *See* **fhilty fhisty**
fhiilsy fishily. *See* **fhisy**
fhiinps pinfish. *See* **fhiins**
fhiins finish finis fins fish hins nisi shin fin hin his ifs sin hi if in is sh si
fhikmnos monkfish monkish. *See* **fikns hknos iknos**
fhilloot foothill. *See* **fhilt filoo hlloo**
fhilmrtu mirthful. *See* **fhilt filmu fhirt**
fhiloos foolish. *See* **filoos fhoos**
fhilorsu flourish. *See* **florsu hiorsu**
fhilorty frothily. *See* **fhilty fhorty filrty**
fhilosw wolfish. *See* **hilosw flosw filos**
fhilsuw wishful. *See* **fhlsu filsu**
fhilt filth flit hilt lift fit hit lit til hi if it li ti
fhilty filthy filth fitly flit hilt lift fit fly hit lit thy til hi if it li ti
fhimorsw fishworm. *See* **fimrs fmors fhors**
fhimprsu frumpish. *See* **fmprsu himprs**
fhinrsu furnish. *See* **hinrsu finrs**
fhinssu sunfish. *See* **inssu hinss hnssu**
fhiopps foppish. *See* **hiopps**
fhiorry horrify. *See* **firry**
fhirsst shrifts. *See* **firsst fhirst fhisst hirsst**
fhirst firths friths shrift first firth frith frits rifts shift shirt firs fish fist fits frit

hist hits rifs rift sift sith stir this fir fit his hit ifs its rif sir sit hi if is it sh si ti
fhirt firth frith frit rift fir fit hit rif hi if it ti
fhirtt thrift firth frith frit rift fir fit hit rif tit hi if it ti
fhirtty thrifty. *See* **fhirtt hirtty**
fhis fish ifs his hi if is sh si
fhisst shifts fists shift sifts fish fist fits hiss hist hits sift sith sits this fit his hit ifs its sis sit hi if is it sh si ti
fhist shift fish fist fits hist hits sift sith this fit his hit ifs its sit hi if is it sh si ti
fhisty shifty shift fishy fish fist fits hist hits sift sith this fit his hit ifs its shy sit sty thy hi if is it sh si ti
fhisy fishy fish his ifs shy hi if is sh si
fhlmotuu mouthful. *See* **flotu lmotu hmotu**
fhloosy shoofly. *See* **fhoos floos**
fhlortuy fourthly. *See* **fhortu fhorty floruy hloruy**
fhlotuuy youthful. *See* **flotu hloty floty**
fhlrttuu truthful hurtful ruthful. *See* **hrttu**
fhlrtuu hurtful ruthful
fhlsu flush flus lush flu sh us

fho foh ho of oh
fhoo hoof foh oho ooh ho of oh
fhooorst forsooth. *See* **fhorst**
fhooostt hotfoots hotfoot. *See* **fhoos hoost fostt**
fhooott hotfoot. *See* **hoott**
fhoos hoofs hoof oohs shoo foh oho ohs ooh ho of oh os sh so
fhors frosh rhos foh for fro ohs rho ho of oh or os sh so
fhorst froths forth forts frosh frost froth horst short fort host hots orts rhos rots shot soft sort tors tosh foh for fro hot oft ohs ort rho rot sot tho tor ho of oh or os sh so to
fhorstu fourths. *See* **fhorst fhortu**
fhort forth froth fort foh for fro hot oft ort rho rot tho tor ho of oh or to
fhortu fourth forth froth fort four hour hurt rout ruth thou thru tofu tour turf foh for fro fur hot hut oft ort our out rho rot rut tho tor ho of oh or to ut
fhorty frothy forth forty froth fort ryot troy tyro foh for foy fro fry hot hoy oft ort rho rot tho thy tor toy try ho of oh or oy to

fi

fi   if
fiiinnty   infinity. *See* **finny finty innty**
fiiklrsy   friskily riskily. *See* **fikrsy**
fiiknr   firkin fink firn rink fin fir ink irk kif kin kir rif if in
fiiknrs   firkins. *See* **fiiknr fiins fikns**
fiillmo   milfoil. *No 6s or 5s*
fiillmos   milfoils milfoil. *See* **fills films filos**
fiillmsy   flimsily slimily. *See* **filmsy**
fiillp   fillip fill flip pill ill lip if li pi
fiillps   fillips. *See* **fiillp filps illps**
fiilmpsy   simplify. *See* **filmsy ilmpsy**
fiilnost   tinfoils tinfoil. *See* **filnst iilnst ilnost**
fiilnot   tinfoil. *See* **filnt**
fiilptu   pitiful. *See* **filptu**
fiilttuy   futility utility. *See* **filty fttuy**
fiilvy   vilify fly ivy if li
fiimnr   infirm firm firn fin fir mir nim rif rim if in mi
fiimny   minify fin nim yin if in mi my
fiimsst   misfits. *See* **fiimst fisst imsst**
fiimst   misfit fist fits mist sift fit ifs its mis sit if is it mi si ti
fiinnosu   infusion. *See* **finosu iinnos innosu**
fiinortu   fruition. *See* **finort**
fiinoss   fission. *See* **fiins**
fiinosss   fissions fission. *See* **fiins**
fiinrty   nitrify. *See* **finty**
fiins   finis fins nisi fin ifs sin if in is si
fiinx   infix fin fix nix if in xi
fiirtvy   vitrify. *No 6s or 5s*
fiitxy   fixity fixt fit fix if it ti xi
fiivvy   vivify ivy if
fijlloy   jollify. *See* **filly flloy jlloy**
fijlor   frijol foil roil fir for fro oil rif if jo li lo of or
fijstuy   justify. *See* **fstuy**
fik   kif if
fikklno   kinfolk. *No 6s or 5s*
fikklnos   kinfolks kinfolk. *See* **fikns filos fklos**
fikllsu   skillful skilful. *See* **fills filsu iklls**
fikllsu   skilful. *See* **fills filsu iklls**
fiklnssu   skinfuls skinful. *See* **filnsu fklnsu iklnss**
fiklnsu   skinful. *See* **filnsu fklnsu**
fiklrsù   riskful. *See* **fikrs flrsu filsu**
fikn   fink fin ink kif kin if in
fikns   finks fink fins inks kifs sink skin fin ifs ink kif kin sin ski if in is si
fikrs   frisk firs irks kifs kris rifs risk fir ifs irk kif kir rif sir ski if is si

fikrss   frisks frisk risks firs irks kifs kiss kris rifs risk sirs skis fir ifs irk kif kir rif sir sis ski if is si
fikrsy   frisky frisk risky firs irks kifs kris rifs risk fir fry ifs irk kif kir rif sir ski sky if is si
fiks   kifs ifs kif ski if is si
fill   fill ill if li
fillluw   willful. *See* **filluw**
fillluwy   wilfully willful. *See* **filluw**
fillmoy   mollify. *See* **filly filmy flloy**
fillnuy   nullify. *See* **filly flluy finuy**
filloppy   floppily. *See* **floppy**
filloty   loftily. *See* **filly filty flloy**
fillr   frill fill rill fir ill rif if li
fillrs   frills fills frill rills fill fils firs rifs rill sill fir ifs ill rif sir if is li si
fillry   frilly frill filly fill illy lily rill fir fly fry ill rif if li
fills   fills fill fils sill ifs ill if is li si
fillstu   listful. *See* **fills filst filsu**
filluw   wilful fill full will flu ill if li
filly   filly fill illy lily fly ill if li
film   film mil if li mi
filmosu   foliums. *See* **filmou films filos**
filmou   folium filum film foil foul limo milo moil flu lum mil oil if li lo mi mo mu of om um
filmry   firmly filmy film firm limy miry rimy fir fly fry mil mir rif rim if li mi my
films   films film fils mils slim ifs mil mis if is li mi si
filmsy   flimsy films filmy slimy film fils limy mils slim fly ifs mil mis sly if is li mi my si
filmu   filum film flu lum mil if li mi mu um
filmy   filmy film limy fly mil if li mi my
filnnuy   funnily. *See* **finny fnnuy finuy**
filnor   florin firn foil iron lion loin lorn noil roil fin fir for fro ion nil nor oil rif if in li lo no of on or
filnors   florins. *See* **filnor finrs fnors**
filnosux   fluxions fluxion. *See* **filnsu filnux finosu**
filnosw   inflows. *See* **filnow flosw filos**
filnoux   fluxion. *See* **filnux**
filnow   inflow flown flow foil fowl lion loin noil wino wolf fin ion low nil now oil owl own win won if in li lo no of on ow
filnst   flints flint flits lifts lints fils fins fist fits flit lift lint list nils nits sift silt slit snit tils tins fin fit ifs its lit nil nit sin sit til tin if in is it li si ti

filnsu   sinful fusil fils fins flus nils fin flu fun ifs nil sin sun if in is li nu si us
filnt   flint flit lift lint fin fit lit nil nit til tin if in it li ti
filnty   flinty fitly flint linty nifty flit inly lift lint liny tiny fin fit fly lit nil nit til tin yin if in it li ti
filnux   influx unfix flux fin fix flu fun lux nil nix if in li nu xi
filo   foil oil if li lo of
filoo   folio foil fool olio oil loo if li lo of
filoos   folios foils folio fools olios fils foil fool loos oils olio silo soil solo ifs loo los oil sol if is li lo of os si so
filorsst   florists florist. *See* **filoss filrst fiorst fiosst**
filorst   florist. *See* **filrst fiorst**
filorsty   frostily florist firstly. *See* **filrst filrty fiorst flosty**
filorwyz   frowzily. *See* **forwyz**
filos   foils fils foil oils silo soil ifs los oil sol if is li lo of os si so
filoss   fossil floss foils silos soils fils foil foss loss oils silo soil sols ifs los oil sis sol if is li lo of os si so
filosss   fossils. *See* **filoss**
filp   flip lip if li pi
filppuy   pulpify. *See* **ilppu lppuy**
filps   flips fils flip lips lisp slip ifs lip sip if is li pi si
filpstu   uplifts. *See* **filptu ilpstu**
filptu   uplift tulip flip flit lift puli fit flu lip lit pit pul put til tip tui tup if it li pi ti up ut
filrst   flirts first flirt flits frits lifts rifts fils firs fist fits flit frit lift list rifs rift sift silt slit stir tils fir fit ifs its lit rif sir sit til if is it li si ti
filrsty   firstly. *See* **filrst filrty ilrsty**
filrt   flirt flit frit lift rift fir fit lit rif til if it li ti
filrty   flirty flirt fitly flit frit lift rift fir fit fly fry lit rif til try if it li ti
fils   fils ifs if is li si
filssttu   flutists flutist lutists. *See* **ilssttt ilsttu**
filssuy   fussily. *See* **filsu fssuy ilssy**
filst   flits lifts fils fist fits flit lift list sift silt slit tils fit ifs its lit sit til if is it li si ti
filsttu   flutist. *See* **ilsttu filst filsu**
filstuw   wistful. *See* **filst filsu fistw**
filstwy   swiftly. *See* **filty filst ilsty**
filsu   fusil fils flus flu ifs if is li si us
filt   flit lift fit lit til if it li ti
filty   fitly flit lift fit fly lit til if it li ti
filuyzz   fuzzily. *See* **fiyzz fuyzz**
fimmmuy   mummify. *See* **mmmuy**

fimnor inform minor firm firn form from iron morn norm fin fir for fro ion mir mon mor nim nor rif rim if in mi mo no of om on or

fimnors informs. *See* **fimnor imnors**

fimnorsu uniforms informs uniform. *See* **fimnor finosu fmorsu imnors**

fimnoru uniform. *See* **fimnor fmoru mnoru**

fimoorrt rotiform. *See* **moorr fimot moort**

fimorty mortify. *See* **fimot forty**

fimost motifs foist moist motif omits fist fits mist most mots omit sift soft toms fit ifs its mis mos mot oft oms sit sot tom if is it mi mo of om os si so ti to

fimot motif omit fit mot oft tom if it mi mo of om ti to

fimr firm fir mir rif rim if mi

fimrs firms firm firs mirs rifs rims fir ifs mir mis rif rim sir if is mi si

fimrstuu futurism frustum. *See* **fimstu firstu imrstu**

fimstu muftis mufti fist fits mist must sift smut stum suit tuis fit ifs its mis mus sit sum tui if is it mi mu si ti um us ut

fimstyy mystify. *See* **imsty mstyy**

fimtu mufti fit tui if it mi mu ti um ut

fin fin if in

finny finny fin inn yin if in

finorst forints. *See* **finort fiorst fnorst**

finort forint front firn font fort frit into iron rift riot tiro tori torn trio fin fir fit for fro ion nit nor not oft ort rif rot tin ton tor if in it no of on or ti to

finorx fornix firn iron fin fir fix for fox fro ion nix nor rif if in no of on or ox xi

finossu fusions. *See* **finosu inssu**

finosu fusion fins ions nous onus fin fun ifs ion sin son sou sun if in is no nu of on os si so us

finoty notify nifty font into tiny tony yoni fin fit foy ion nit not oft tin ton toy yin yon if in it no of on oy ti to

finr firn fin fir rif if in

finrs firns fins firn firs rifs fin fir ifs rif sin sir if in is si

fins fins fin ifs sin if in is si

fintu unfit unit fin fit fun nit nut tin tui tun if in it nu ti ut

finty nifty tiny fin fit nit tin yin if in it ti

finux unfix fin fix fun nix if in nu xi

finuy unify fin fun yin if in nu

fioprst profits. *See* **fiorst fioprt ioprst**

fioprt profit fort frit port prof rift riot tiro tori trio trip fir fit fop for fro oft ort pit poi pot pro rif rip rot tip top tor if it of or pi ti to

fiopstx postfix. *See* **fiost iopst**

fiorst fortis first foist forts frits frost rifs riots tiros torsi trios firs fist fits fort frit orts rifs rift riot rots sift soft sori sort stir tiro tori tors trio fir fit for fro ifs its oft ort rif rot sir sit sot tor if is it of or os si so ti to

fiorsuu furious. *See* **forsuu**

fiorttuy fortuity. *See* **fiottu firtuy orttuy**

fiosst foists fists foist sifts fist fits foss sift sits soft sots toss fit ifs its oft sis sit sot if is it of os si so ti to

fiossy ossify foss foys soys foy ifs sis soy if is of os oy si so

fiost foist fist fits sift soft fit ifs its oft sit sot if is it of os si so ti to

fiosttu outfits. *See* **fiottu fiost osttu**

fiottu outfit toft tofu tout tuft fit oft out tit tot tui tut if it of ti to ut

fipruy purify fury fir fry fur pry rif rip yip yup if pi up

fiptyy typify pity fit pit tip yip if it pi ti

fir fir rif if

firry firry fir fry rif if

firs firs rifs fir ifs rif sir if is si

firsst firsts first fists frits rifts sifts stirs firs fist fits frit rifs rift sift sirs sits stir fir fit ifs its rif sir sis sit if is it si ti

first first frits rifts firs fist fits frit rifs rift sift stir fir fit ifs its rif sir sit if is it si ti

firsttuu futurist. *See* **firstu**

firstu fruits first frits fruit rifts turfs firs fist fits frit furs rifs rift rust ruts sift stir suit surf tuis turf fir fit fur ifs its rif rut sir sit tui if is it si ti us ut

firt frit rift fir fit rif if it ti

firttuuy futurity. *See* **firtuy**

firtu fruit frit rift turf fir fit fur rif rut tui if it ti ut

firtuy fruity fruit turfy frit fury rift turf yurt fir fit fry fur rif rut try tui if it ti ut

firtz fritz frit friz rift fir fit rif zit if it ti

firyzz frizzy fizzy friz fizz fir fry rif if

firz friz fir rif if

fis ifs if is si

fisst fists sifts fist fits sift sits fit ifs its sis sit if is it si ti

fist fist fits sift fit ifs its sit if is it si ti

fistw swift fist fits sift wits fit ifs its sit wis wit if is it si ti

fit fit if it ti

fitx fixt fit fix if it ti xi

fix fix if xi

fiyzz fizzy fizz if

fizz fizz if

fj

fjllouyy joyfully. *See* **fjlouy fllouy**

fjlouy joyful foul flu fly foy joy you jo lo of oy

fk

fklnsu flunks flunk funks slunk flus funk sulk sunk flu fun sun nu us
fklnu flunk funk flu fun nu
fklnuy flunky fluky flunk funky funk flu fly fun yuk nu
fklo folk of lo

fklos folks folk kos los sol lo of os so
fklosy folksy folks yolks folk foys yolk fly foy kos los sky sly sol soy lo of os oy so
fkluy fluky flu fly yuk
fknsu funks funk sunk fun sun nu us

fknu funk fun nu
fknuy funky funk fun yuk nu
fkooors forsook. *See* **fkors foors koors**
fkor fork for fro kor of or
fkors forks fork for fro kor kos of or os so

fl

flloosw follows. *See* **flloow flosw foosw**
flloow follow flow fool fowl wolf woof wool loo low owl woo lo of ow
fllosuu soulful. *See* **flosu llsuu**
fllouy foully folly fully full foul flu fly foy you lo of oy
flloy folly fly foy lo of oy
fllstuu lustful. *See* **llstu**
fllu full flu
flluy fully full flu fly
flmmoux flummox. *See* **lmmoux**
flmnoruu mournful. *See* **flnruu**
flmooru roomful. *See* **lmooru floor floru**
flnoopsu spoonful. *See* **flops floos flosu**
flnoorr forlorn. *See* **floor**
flnow flown flow fowl wolf low now owl own won lo no of on ow
flnrsuu unfurls. *See* **flnruu flrsuu**
flnruu unfurl furl flu fun fur run ulu urn nu
floo fool loo of lo
floor floor fool roof for fro loo lo of or
floors floors floor fools roofs fool loos roof solo for fro loo los sol lo of or os so
floos fools fool loos solo loo los sol lo of os so
floostuw outflows outflow. *See* **flostu**
flootuw outflow. *See* **flotu**
flooyz floozy fool oozy fly foy loo zoo lo of oy

flop flop fop lop of lo
floppy floppy loppy polyp flop plop ploy fly fop foy lop ply pop lo of oy
floprstu sportful potfuls. *See* **floptu florsu flostu lopstu**
flops flops flop fops lops slop fop lop los sol sop lo of os so
flopstu potfuls. *See* **flostu floptu lopstu**
floptu potful flout poult flop foul loft lout plot pouf pout tofu tolu flu fop lop lot oft out pot pul put top tup lo of to up ut
florsu flours fluors flour fluor fouls fours furls flus foul four furl furs ours slur soul sour surf flu for fro fur los our sol sou lo of or os so us
floru flour fluor foul four furl flu for fro fur our lo of or
floruy floury flour fluor foul four furl fury lory your flu fly for foy fro fry fur our you lo of or oy
floss floss foss loss sols los sol lo of os so
flossy flossy floss foss foys loss sols soys fly foy los sly sol soy lo of os oy so
flost lofts loft lost lots slot soft los lot oft sol sot lo of os so to
flostu flouts flout fouls lofts lotus louts flus foul loft lost lots lout lust oust outs slot slut soft soul tofu tolu flu los lot oft out sol sot sou lo of os so to us ut

flosty softly lofts lofty softy foys loft lost lots slot soft toys fly foy los lot oft sly sol sot soy sty toy lo of os oy so to
flosu fouls flus foul soul flu los sol sou lo of os so us
flosuuv fulvous. *See* **flosu**
flosw flows fowls flow fowl lows owls slow wolf los low owl sol sow lo of os ow so
flot loft oft lot lo of to
flotu flout foul loft lout tofu tolu flu lot oft out lo of to ut
floty lofty loft fly foy lot oft toy lo of oy to
flou foul flu of lo
flow flow fowl wolf low owl lo of ow
flrruy flurry furry furl fury flu fly fry fur
flrssuu sulfurs. *See* **flrsuu lrssu frssu**
flrsttuu trustful. *See* **flrsuu**
flrsu furls flus furl furs slur surf flu fur us
flrsuu sulfur furls flus furl furs slur surf ulus urus flu fur ulu us
flru furl flu fur
flsu flus flu us
flu flu
flux flux flu lux
fly fly

fm

fmor form from for fro mor mo of om or
fmors forms form from mors for fro mor mos oms mo of om or os so

fmorsu forums forms forum fours form four from furs mors ours rums sour sumo surf for fro fur mor mos mus oms our rum sou sum mo mu of om or os so um us
fmoru forum form four from for fro fur mor our rum mo mu of om or um

fmprsu   frumps frump rumps furs rump rums spur sump surf umps fur mus pus rum sum sup ump mu um up us

fmpru   frump rump fur rum ump mu um up

fmpruy   frumpy frump fumy fury rump fry fur pry rum ump yum yup mu my um up

fmrsstuu   frustums frustum. *See* **mrsstu**

fmrstuu   frustum. *See* **frstu mrstu**

fmuy   fumy yum mu my um

---

fn

fnnuy   funny fun nun nu

fnoorrsw   forsworn. *See* **fnorsw oorrsw**

fnoorssu   sunroofs sunroof. *See* **forsu fnors foors**

fnoorsu   sunroof. *See* **forsu fnors foors**

fnors   frons for fro nor son no of on or os so

fnorst   fronts fonts forts frons front frost snort font fort orts rots snot soft sort tons torn tors for fro nor not oft ort rot son sot ton tor no of on or os so to

fnorsw   frowns frons frown frows sworn frow owns rows snow sown worn for fro nor now own row son sow won no of on or os ow so

fnort   front font fort torn for fro nor not oft ort rot ton tor no of on or to

fnorw   frown frow worn for fro nor now own row won no of on or ow

fnost   fonts font snot soft tons not oft son sot ton no of on os so to

fnostu   founts futons fonts fount futon snout tonus font nous nuts onus oust outs snot soft stun tofu tons tuns unto fun not nut oft out son sot sou sun ton tun no nu of on os so to us ut

fnot   font not oft ton no of on to

fnotu   fount futon font tofu unto fun not nut oft out ton tun no nu of on to ut

fnu   fun nu

---

fo

fo   of

foooprst   rooftops rooftop. *See* **fooprs ooprst**

foooprt   rooftop. *See* **foopr ooprt**

foop   poof fop of

foopr   proof poof poor prof roof fop for fro pro of or

fooprs   proofs profs proof roofs sopor spoof spoor fops oops poof poor prof pros roof fop for fro pro sop of or os so

foops   spoof fops oops poof fop sop of os so

foopss   spoofs spoof fops foss oops poof sops fop sop of os so

foor   roof for fro of or

foors   roofs roof for fro of or os so

foosw   woofs woof woos woo sow of os ow so

foot   foot oft too of to

footux   outfox foot tofu fox oft out too tux of ox to ut

foow   woof woo of ow

fop   fop of

fopr   prof fop for fro pro of or

foprs   profs fops prof pros fop for fro pro sop of or os so

fops   fops fop sop of os so

fopsu   poufs fops opus pouf soup fop pus sop sou sup of os so up us

fopu   pouf fop of up

for   for fro of or

forrsu   furors furor fours four furs ours sour surf for fro fur our sou of or os so us

forrsuw   furrows. *See* **forrsu forruw**

forru   furor four for fro fur our of or

forruw   furrow furor four frow for fro fur our row of or ow

forsst   frosts forts frost sorts fort foss orts rots soft sort sots tors toss for fro oft ort rot sot tor of or os so to

forst   forts frost fort orts rots soft sort tors for fro oft ort rot sot tor of or os so to

forsty   frosty forts forty frost ryots softy story tyros fort foys orts rosy rots ryot soft sort tors toys troy tyro for foy fro fry oft ort rot sot soy sty tor toy try of or os oy so to

forsu   fours four furs ours sour surf for fro fur our sou of or os so us

forsuu   rufous fours four furs ours sour surf urus for fro fur our sou of or os so us

forsw   frows frow rows for fro row sow of or os ow so

forswy   frowsy frows foys frow rosy rows for foy fro fry row sow soy yow of or os ow oy so

fort   fort for fro oft ort rot tor of or to

forty   forty fort ryot troy tyro for foy fro fry oft ort rot tor toy try of or oy to

foru   four for fro fur our of or

forw   frow for fro row of or ow

forwyz   frowzy frow for foy fro fry row wry yow of or ow oy

foss   foss of os so

fost   soft oft sot of os so to

fostt   tofts soft toft tost tots oft sot tot of os so to

fosty   softy foys soft toys foy oft sot soy sty toy of os oy so to

fosy   foys foy soy of os oy so

fot   oft of to

fott   toft oft tot of to

fotu   tofu oft out of to ut

fox   fox of ox

foxy　foxy fox foy of ox oy
foy　foy of oy

──────────────── **fr** ────────────────

frruy　furry fury fur fry
frssu　surfs furs fuss surf fur us
frstu　turfs furs rust ruts surf turf fur rut
　　us ut

frsu　furs surf fur us
frsuy　surfy furs fury surf fur fry us
frtu　turf fur rut ut
frtuy　turfy fury turf yurt fry fur rut try ut

fru　fur
fruy　fury fur fry
fruyz　furzy fury fur fry
fry　fry

──────────────── **fs** ────────────────

fssu　fuss us
fssuy　fussy fuss us

fsttu　tufts tuft tuts tut us ut
fstuy　fusty sty us ut

──────────────── **ft** ────────────────

fttu　tuft tut ut
fttuy　tufty tuft tut ut
ftuz　futz ut

──────────────── **fu** ────────────────

fuyzz　fuzzy fuzz
fuzz　fuzz

ggggiin gigging. *No 6s or 5s*
ggggilno goggling logging. *See* **ggilno**
ggggilnu glugging guggling lugging. *See* **ggilnu**
ggghino hogging. *See* **ggino**
ggghinu hugging. *No 6s or 5s*
gggiijn jigging. *No 6s or 5s*
gggiilnn niggling. *See* **giilnn**
gggiilnw wiggling wigging. *See* **giilnw**
gggiinp pigging. *No 6s or 5s*
gggiinpr prigging griping pigging rigging. *See* **giinpr**
gggiinr rigging. *No 6s or 5s*
gggiinsw swigging wigging. *See* **ginsw**
gggiinw wigging. *No 6s or 5s*
gggiinz zigging. *No 6s or 5s*
gggijlno joggling jogging logging. *See* **ggilno**
gggijlnu juggling jugging lugging. *See* **ggilnu**
gggijno jogging. *See* **ggino gijno**
gggijnu jugging. *No 6s or 5s*
gggilno logging. *See* **ggilno**
gggilnos slogging logging gosling. *See* **ggilno gginos gilnos**
gggilnpu plugging gulping lugging pugging. *See* **ggilnu gilnpu**
gggilnru gurgling lugging. *See* **ggilnu gginru gilnru**
gggilnsu slugging lugging. *See* **ggilnu gilnsu**
gggilnu lugging. *See* **ggilnu**
gggily giggly gig li
gggimnu mugging. *No 6s or 5s*
ggginno gonging nogging. *See* **gginno**
ggginnsu snugging. *See* **ginsu**
ggginopr progging gorging groping. *See* **gginor ginopr**
ggginor gorging. *See* **gginor**
ggginot togging. *See* **ggino ginot**
ggginou gouging. *See* **ggino**
ggginpu pugging. *No 6s or 5s*
gggintu tugging. *No 6s or 5s*
gggory groggy gory grog gyro orgy goy go or oy
gghhios hoggish. *See* **ghhis**
gghiilnt lighting hilting. *See* **giilnt**
gghiinn hinging. *No 6s or 5s*
gghiinrt righting. *See* **ghiinr giinrt**
gghiins sighing. *No 6s or 5s*
gghiinst sighting sighing insight. *See* **ghinst giinst**
gghiiprs priggish piggish. *See* **ggirs giprs**
gghiips piggish. *No 6s or 5s*
gghilssu sluggish. *See* **gglsu ghiss glssu**

gghinoru roughing rouging. *See* **gginor gginru**
gghinost ghosting hosting. *See* **gginos ghinos ghinst ghnost**
gghinoty hogtying. *See* **ghinty ginoty**
gghinsu gushing. *See* **ginsu**
gghooprs grogshop. *See* **goops ggors hoops**
ggi gig
ggiijlnn jingling. *See* **giilnn**
ggiillnr grilling rilling. *See* **giilnr**
ggiilmnn mingling. *See* **giilmn giilnn**
ggiilnns singling slinging linings signing singing. *See* **giilnn**
ggiilnnt glinting tingling tinging linting. *See* **giilnn giilnt**
ggiimnp gimping. *No 6s or 5s*
ggiimnr griming. *See* **giimnr**
ggiinnn ginning. *See* **giinnn**
ggiinnnr grinning ginning ringing. *See* **giinnn**
ggiinno ingoing. *See* **gginno iinno**
ggiinnor groining ignoring ingoing ironing ringing. *See* **gginno gginor**
ggiinnp pinging. *See* **giinnp**
ggiinnr ringing. *No 6s or 5s*
ggiinnrw wringing ringing winging. *See* **giinnw giinrw**
ggiinns signing singing
ggiinnst stinging signing singing tinging. *See* **giinst**
ggiinnsw swinging signing singing winging. *See* **giinnw**
ggiinnt tinging. *No 6s or 5s*
ggiinntw twinging tinging twining winging. *See* **giinnw giintw**
ggiinnw winging. *See* **giinnw**
ggiinnz zinging. *No 6s or 5s*
ggiinpp gipping. *See* **giinpp**
ggiinppr gripping gipping griping ripping. *See* **giinpp giinpr**
ggiinpr griping. *See* **giinpr**
ggiinrtt gritting. *See* **giinrt**
ggiinv giving gig gin in
ggiijly jiggly gig jig li
ggikno ginkgo going gink gong ikon king kino nogg oink gig gin ink ion kin nog go in no on
ggillnu gulling. *See* **ggilnu**
ggilmnoo glooming looming. *See* **ggilno ggiloo gilnoo gimnoo**
ggilnno longing. *See* **ggilno gginno**
ggilnnos longings gosling longing noggins. *See* **ggilno gginno gginos gilnos**

ggilnnou lounging longing lunging. *See* **ggilno ggilnu gginno**
ggilnnpu plunging lunging gulping. *See* **ggilnu gilnpu**
ggilnnu lunging. *See* **ggilnu**
ggilnnuu ungluing lunging. *See* **ggilnu**
ggilno ogling going lingo gong ling lion loin long nogg noil gig gin ion log nil nog oil go in li lo no on
ggilnorw growling glowing growing. *See* **ggilno gginor gilnow ginorw**
ggilnory glorying. *See* **ggilno gginor gginry**
ggilnos gosling. *See* **gginos gilnos ggilno**
ggilnoss goslings gosling. *See* **ggilno gginos gilnos gilnss**
ggilnov gloving. *See* **ggilno gilnov**
ggilnow glowing. *See* **ggilno gilnow**
ggilnoz glozing. *See* **ggilno**
ggilnpu gulping. *See* **ggilnu gilnpu**
ggilnttu glutting gutting. *See* **ggilnu gilntu**
ggilnu gluing lungi glug ling lung gig gin gnu gun lug nil in li nu
ggilnuzz guzzling. *See* **ggilnu**
ggiloo gigolo igloo logo olio gig goo log loo oil go li lo
ggiloos gigolos. *See* **ggiloo giloos**
ggilrwy wriggly. *See* **ggilwy**
ggilwy wiggly wily gig wig li
ggimmnu gumming. *No 6s or 5s*
ggimnoor grooming mooring rooming. *See* **gginor ggnoor gimnoo imnoor**
gginnnu gunning. *No 6s or 5s*
gginno noggin going gong nogg gig gin inn ion nog go in no on
gginnoo ongoing. *See* **gginno innoo**
gginnopr pronging groping. *See* **gginno gginor ginopr**
gginnops sponging noggins. *See* **gginno gginos ginnos ginops**
gginnorw wronging gowning growing ingrown. *See* **gginno gginor ginnow ginorw**
gginnos noggins. *See* **gginos gginno ginnos**
gginnoss singsong noggins. *See* **gginno gginos ginnos ginoss**
gginnot tonging. *See* **gginno ginnot**
gginnotu tonguing tonging. *See* **gginno ginnot ginntu ginotu**
gginnow gowning. *See* **gginno ginnow**
gginnrtu grunting turning. *See* **gginru ginntu ginrtu**

ggino   going gong nogg gig gin ion nog go in no on

gginoorv   grooving. *See* **gginor ggnoor giinorv**

gginoos   goosing. *See* **gginos gnoos**

gginootu   outgoing. *See* **ginotu**

gginopr   groping. *See* **gginor ginopr**

gginopru   grouping groping ingroup pouring purging rouging. *See* **gginor gginru ginopr**

gginor   goring gringo going groin gong grig grin grog iron nogg ring gig gin ion nog nor rig go in no on or

gginors   gringos. *See* **gginos gginor ginors**

gginorsu   grousing gringos rouging rousing souring surging. *See* **gginor gginos gginru ginors**

gginortu   grouting rouging routing touring. *See* **gginor gginru ginort ginotu**

gginoru   rouging. *See* **gginor gginru**

gginorw   growing. *See* **gginor ginorw**

gginos   goings going gongs gigs gins gong ions nogg nogs sign sing song gig gin ion nog sin son go in is no on os si so

gginppy   gypping. *See* **ggipy inppy**

gginpru   purging. *See* **gginru**

gginrsu   surging. *See* **gginru ggirs ginrs**

gginru   urging ruing grig grin ring ruin rung gig gin gnu gun rig rug run urn in nu

gginry   gyring grig grin ring gig gin rig yin in

gginstu   gusting. *See* **ginst gnstu ginsu**

gginttu   gutting. *No 6s or 5s*

gginuy   guying gig gin gnu gun guy yin in nu

gginvy   gyving vying viny gig gin ivy yin in

ggiprsy   spriggy. *See* **ggirs giprs ggipy**

ggipy   piggy gig gip gyp pig yip pi

ggir   grig gig rig

ggirs   grigs gigs grig rigs gig rig sir is si

ggis   gigs gig is si

ggitwy   twiggy twig gig wig wit it ti

gglooo   googol logo goo log loo go lo

gglooos   googols. *See* **gglooo gloos**

gglooy   googly logo logy goo goy log loo go lo oy

gglsu   glugs glug lugs slug lug us

gglu   glug lug

ggmuy   muggy gum guy gym mug yum mu my um

ggno   gong nogg nog go no on

ggnoor   gorgon gong goon grog nogg goo nog nor go no on or

ggnoors   gorgons. *See* **ggnoor ggnos gnoos**

ggnos   gongs gong nogg nogs song nog son go no on os so

ggnruy   grungy rung gnu gun guy rug run urn nu

ggor   grog go or

ggors   grogs grog go or os so

ggosy   soggy goys goy soy go os oy so

ghhi   high hi

ghhiilst   lightish. *See* **ghhist ghilst**

ghhiinsw   whishing wishing. *See* **ghhis ginsw hhisw**

ghhilosu   ghoulish. *See* **ghlosu**

ghhily   highly high hi li

ghhinsu   hushing. *See* **ghhis ginsu**

ghhis   highs high sigh his hi is sh si

ghhist   hights thighs highs hight sight thigh gist high hist hits sigh sith this his hit its sit hi is it sh si ti

ghhit   hight thigh high hit hi it ti

ghhoortu   thorough through. *See* **ghhotu ghortu**

ghhortu   through. *See* **ghhotu ghortu**

ghhosttu   thoughts thought. *See* **ghhotu ghostu**

ghhottu   thought. *See* **ghhotu**

ghhotu   though ought tough gout thou thug got gut hog hot hug huh hut out tho tog tug ugh go ho oh to ut

ghiikn   hiking gink king nigh gin hin ink kin hi in

ghiiknnt   thinking hinting kithing. *See* **ghiikn ghiknt giiknn**

ghiiknps   kingship kinship pigskin pinkish spiking. *See* **ghiikn giiknp giikns**

ghiiknrs   shirking risking. *See* **ghiikn ghiinr giiknr giikns**

ghiiknsw   whisking wishing. *See* **ghiikn giikns**

ghiiknt   kithing. *See* **ghiikn giiknt ghiknt**

ghiilln   hilling. *No 6s or 5s*

ghiillns   shilling hilling. *See* **gills hills gilns**

ghiilmty   mightily. *See* **ghimty**

ghiilnrt   thirling hilting. *See* **ghiinr giilnr giilnt giinrt**

ghiilnrw   whirling whiling. *See* **ghiinr giilnr giilnw giinrw**

ghiilnt   hilting. *See* **giilnt ghilt ghint**

ghiilnw   whiling. *See* **giilnw**

ghiilrs   girlish. *See* **gills gilrs**

ghiilttw   twilight. *See* **ghilt ghitt hiltt**

ghiimmns   shimming. *See* **giimmn iimmns hiimns**

ghiimnnu   inhuming. *See* **giimnn**

ghiinnns   shinning innings shining sinning. *See* **giinnn**

ghiinnnt   thinning hinting tinning. *See* **giinnn**

ghiinnrs   shrining shining rinsing. *See* **ghiinr giinrs**

ghiinns   shining. *No 6s or 5s*

ghiinnt   hinting. *See* **ghint hinnt**

ghiinnw   whining. *See* **giinnw**

ghiinost   hoisting insight hosting. *See* **ghinos ghinst ghnost giinst**

ghiinpp   hipping. *See* **giinpp**

ghiinpps   shipping hipping sipping. *See* **giinpp**

ghiinppw   whipping hipping. *See* **giinpp giinpw**

ghiinr   hiring grin nigh ring gin hin rig hi in

ghiinrrs   shirring sirring. *See* **ghiinr giinrs**

ghiinrrw   whirring. *See* **ghiinr giinrw**

ghiinrst   shirting insight. *See* **ghiinr ghinst ghirst giinrs**

ghiinrsv   shriving virgins. *See* **ghiinr giinrs**

ghiinrtv   thriving. *See* **ghiinr giinrt**

ghiinrtw   writhing whiting withing writing. *See* **ghiinr ghirtw giinrt giinrw**

ghiinss   hissing. *See* **hinss ghiss ginss**

ghiinsst   insights hissing insight. *See* **ghinst ghisst giinst ginsst**

ghiinssw   swishing hissing swinish wishing. *See* **ginssw**

ghiinst   insight. *See* **ghinst giinst**

ghiinstw   whitings insight whiting wishing withing. *See* **ghinst ghistw giinst giintw**

ghiinsw wishing. *See* **ginsw**

ghiintt hitting tithing. *See* **ghint ghitt**

ghiinttw twinight hitting tithing whiting withing witting. *See* **giintw hiintw iinttw**

ghiintw whiting withing. *See* **giintw hiintw**

ghiinv hiving nigh gin hin hi in

ghiinwzz whizzing. *See* **hiwzz**

ghiiorsv vigorish. *See* **ghiors giorsv**

ghiirstt rightist. *See* **ghirst ghistt**

ghijnos joshing. *See* **ghinos gijno hjnos**

ghiklnty knightly nightly. *See* **ghiknt ghinty giklny hilnty**

ghiklnu hulking. *See* **gilnu**

ghiklsty skylight sightly. *See* **ghilst**

ghiknno honking. *See* **ghikno ghinno**

ghikno hoking gink hong honk ikon king kino nigh oink gin hin hog hon ink ion kin nog go hi ho in no oh on

ghiknoo hooking. *See* **ghikno ghinoo**

ghiknos hogskin. *See* **ghikno ghinos**

ghiknoss hogskins hogskin. *See* **ghikno ghinos ginoss**

ghiknst knights. *See* **ghiknt ghinst hiknst**

ghiknsu husking. *See* **gikns gknsu hknsu**

ghiknt knight night thing think gink hint king kith knit nigh thin ting gin hin hit ink kin kit nit tin hi in it ti

ghillnou hulloing hulling. *See* **ghilno**

ghillnu hulling. *See* **gilnu**

ghillsty slightly lightly sightly. *See* **ghilst hillst illsty**

ghillty lightly. *See* **hilly ghilt hillt**

ghilno holing lingo hong ling lion loin long nigh noil gin hin hog hon ion log nil nog oil go hi ho in li lo no oh on

ghilnopp hoppling hopping lopping. *See* **ghilno ghinop gilnop ilnopp**

ghilnos longish. *See* **ghilno ghinos gilnos**

ghilnoss sloshing longish. *See* **ghilno ghinos gilnos gilnss**

ghilnot tholing. *See* **ghilno gilnt ginot**

ghilnow howling. *See* **ghilno gilnow**

ghilnrtu hurtling hurling hurting. *See* **gilnru gilntu ginrtu**

ghilnru hurling. *See* **gilnru**

ghilnruy hungrily hurling. *See* **ghnruy gilnru**

ghilnssu slushing. *See* **gilnss gilnsu**

ghilnstu hustling sunlight lusting. *See* **ghilst ghinst gilnst gilnsu**

ghilnty nightly. *See* **ghinty hilnty**

ghiloprs shopgirl. *See* **ghiors hilops**

ghilorsw showgirl. *See* **ghiors glorsw hilosw hilrsw**

ghilprty triglyph rightly. *See* **ghilpt ilprty**

ghilpst plights. *See* **ghilst ghilpt hilpst**

ghilpt plight light gilt hilt gip hip hit lip lit pig pit til tip hi it li pi ti

ghilrty rightly. *See* **ghirt ghilt hilrt**

ghilsst slights. *See* **ghilst ghisst**

ghilst lights slight gilts hilts light sight gilt gist hilt hist hits list sigh silt sith slit this tils his hit its lit sit til hi is it li sh si ti

ghilsty sightly. *See* **ghilst**

ghilt light gilt hilt hit lit til hi it li ti

ghiltty tightly. *See* **ghilt ghitt hiltt**

ghimmnu humming. *No 6s or 5s*

ghimnny hymning. *See* **hinny ghiny imnny**

ghimno homing nigh hong gin him hin hog hon ion mho mog mon nim nog ohm go hi ho in mi mo no oh om on

ghimnopw whomping. *See* **ghimno ghinop gimnop gimnow**

ghimnoru humoring. *See* **ghimno**

ghimnos gnomish. *See* **ghimno ghinos**

ghimnotu mouthing. *See* **ghimno ghnotu gimntu ginotu**

ghimnptu thumping humping. *See* **gimnpu gimntu ginptu**

ghimnpu humping. *See* **gimnpu**

ghimnpuw whumping humping. *See* **gimnpu**

ghimnry rhyming. *See* **ghiny gimry**

ghimnstu gunsmith mushing. *See* **ghimst ghinst gimnsu gimntu**

ghimnsu mushing. *See* **gimnsu**

ghimprsu grumpish. *See* **gmprsu himprs**

ghimst mights might sight smith gist hist hits mist shim sigh sith this him his hit its mis sit hi is it mi sh si ti

ghimt might him hit hi it mi ti

ghimty mighty might myth gym him hit thy hi it mi my ti

ghin nigh gin hin hi in

ghinnnsu shunning sunning nunnish. *See* **ginsu**

ghinno honing nigh hong gin hin hog hon inn ion nog go hi ho in no oh on

ghinnoor honoring horning. *See* **ghinno ghinoo**

ghinnop phoning. *See* **ghinno ghinop**

ghinnor horning. *See* **ghinno ginor hinor**

ghinnort northing throning horning nothing tinhorn. *See* **ghinno ghiort ghnort ginnot**

ghinnos noshing. *See* **ghinno ghinos ginnos**

ghinnot nothing. *See* **ghinno ginnot**

ghinnstu shunting hunting. *See* **ghinst ginntu hinnst**

ghinntu hunting. *See* **ginntu ghint hinnt**

ghinoo oohing goon hong nigh gin goo hin hog hon ion nog oho ooh go hi ho in no oh on

ghinoop hooping. *See* **ghinoo ghinop**

ghinoopw whooping hooping. *See* **ghinoo ghinop ginoow**

ghinoos shooing. *See* **ghinoo ghinos**

ghinoost shooting soothing hooting hosting shooing sooting. *See* **ghinoo ghinos ghinst ghnost**

ghinoosw wooshing shooing showing. *See* **ghinoo ghinos ginoow ginosw**

ghinoot hooting. *See* **ghinoo ginot ghint**

ghinop hoping gipon oping hong nigh ping gin gip hin hip hog hon hop ion nip nog pig pin poi go hi ho in no oh on pi

ghinopp hopping. *See* **ghinop hiopp**

ghinopps shopping hopping sopping. *See* **ghinop ghinos ginops hinops**

ghinoppw whopping hopping. *See* **ghinop**

ghinopy hypoing. *See* **ghinop ghinpy**

ghinoqtu quothing quoting. *See* **ghnotu ginotu**

ghinors horsing shoring. *See* **ginors ghinos ghiors hinors**

ghinorss shorings horsing shoring signors. *See* **ghinos ghiors ginors ginoss**

ghinorst shorting horsing hosting shoring sorting storing throngs trigons. *See* **ghinos ghinst ghiors ghiort**

ghinortw throwing whoring trowing. *See* **ghiort ghirtw ghnort ghortw**

ghinorw whoring. *See* **ginorw hinor**

ghinos hosing hongs gins gosh hins hogs hong ions nigh nogs nosh shin sigh sign sing song gin hin his hog hon ion nog ohs sin son go hi ho in is no oh on os sh si so

ghinossw showings showing. *See* **ghinos ginoss ginosw ginssw**

ghinost hosting. *See* **ghinos ginost ghinst ghnost**

ghinostu shouting gunshot hognuts hosting housing outings shotgun. *See* **ghinos ghinst ghnost ghnosu**

ghinosu housing. *See* **ghinos ghnosu**

ghinosuy youngish housing. *See* **ghinos ghinsy ghnosu**

ghinosv shoving. *See* **ghinos**

ghinosw showing. *See* **ghinos ginosw**

ghinott tonight. *See* **ginott ghint ghnot**

ghinpssu gunships gunship pushing. *See* **hinpsu**

ghinpsu gunship pushing. *See* **hinpsu ginps gnpsu**

ghinpy hyping hying nigh ping piny gin gip gyp hin hip nip pig pin yin yip hi in pi

ghinrruy hurrying. *See* **ghnruy**

ghinrsu rushing. *See* **hinrsu ginrs ginru**

ghinrtu hurting. *See* **ginrtu ghirt ghint**

ghinsstu hustings. *See* **ghinst ghisst ginsst hnsstu**

ghinst nights things hints night sight sting thing tings gins gist hins hint hist hits nigh nits shin sigh sign sing sith snit thin this ting tins gin hin his hit its nit sin sit tin hi in is it sh si ti

ghinsttu shutting hutting. *See* **ghinst ghistt**

ghinsy shying hying shiny gins hins nigh shin sigh sign sing gin hin his shy sin yin hi in is sh si

ghint night thing hint nigh thin ting gin hin hit nit tin hi in it ti

ghinttu hutting. *See* **ghint ghitt**

ghinty nighty hying night thing tying hint nigh thin ting tiny gin hin hit nit thy tin yin hi in it ti

ghiny hying nigh gin hin yin hi in

ghiors ogrish gosh hogs rhos rigs sigh sori his hog ohs rho rig sir go hi ho is oh or os sh si so

ghiorsu roguish. *See* **hiorsu ghiors ghorsu**

ghiort righto girth right girt grit grot riot tiro tori trig trio got hit hog hot ort rho rig rot tho tog tor go hi ho it oh or ti to

ghiorttu outright. *See* **ghiort ghortu gorttu**

ghiprstu uprights upright. *See* **ghirst iprstu**

ghiprtu upright. *See* **ghirt**

ghipttu uptight. *See* **ghitt**

ghirst girths rights girth girts grist grits right shirt sight trigs girt gist grit hist hits rigs sigh sith stir this trig his hit its rig sir sit hi is it sh si ti

ghirstw wrights. *See* **ghirst ghistw ghirtw**

ghirt girth right girt grit trig rig hit hi it ti

ghirtw wright girth right wight girt grit trig twig whir whit with writ hit rig wig wit hi it ti

ghis sigh his hi is sh si

ghiss sighs sigh hiss his sis hi is sh si

ghisst sights gists sighs sight gist hiss hist hits sigh sith sits this his hit its sis sit hi is it sh si ti

ghist sight gist hist hits sigh sith this his hit its sit hi is it sh si ti

ghistt tights sight tight gist hist hits sigh sith this tits his hit its sit tit hi is it sh si ti

ghistw wights sight twigs whist whits wight gist hist hits sigh sith swig this twig whit wigs wish with wits his hit its sit wig wis wit hi is it sh si ti

ghitt tight hit tit hi it ti

ghitw wight twig whit with hit wig wit hi it ti

ghlmooy homology. *See* **glmooy**

ghlnnoor longhorn. *See* **hnoor**

ghloooory horology orology. *See* **gloooy**

ghloruy roughly. *See* **hloruy ghlou glory**

ghlossu sloughs. *See* **ghlosu**

ghlosty ghostly. *See* **ghost hlost hloty**

ghlosu ghouls loughs slough ghoul lough gosh gush hogs hugs lugs lush slog slug soul hog hug log los lug ohs sol sou ugh go ho lo oh os sh so us

ghlou ghoul lough hog hug log lug ugh go ho lo oh

ghlpsy glyphs glyph sylph gyps gyp ply shy sly spy sh

ghlpy glyph gyp ply

ghmorssu sorghums sorghum. *See* **ghorsu hmorsu**

ghmorsu sorghum. *See* **hmorsu ghorsu**

ghno hong hog hon nog go ho no oh on

ghnorst throngs. *See* **hnorst gnorst ghnost ghnort**

ghnort throng north thong thorn grot hong horn tong torn got hog hon hot nog nor not ort rho rot tho tog ton tor go ho no oh on or to

ghnos hongs gosh hogs hong nogs nosh song hog hon nog ohs son go ho no oh on os sh so

ghnosstu gunshots shotguns gunshot hognuts shoguns shotgun. *See* **ghnost ghnosu ghnotu ghosst**

ghnossu shoguns. *See* **ghnosu hnssu gnoss**

ghnost thongs ghost hongs thong tongs gosh hogs hong host hots nogs nosh shot snot song togs tong tons tosh got hog hon hot nog not ohs son sot tho tog ton go ho no oh on os sh so to

ghnostu gunshot hognuts shotgun. *See* **ghnotu ghnosu ghostu ghnost**

ghnostuu unsought gunshot hognuts shotgun. *See* **ghnost ghnosu ghnotu ghostu**

ghnosu shogun hongs gnus gosh guns gush hogs hong hugs hung nogs nosh nous onus shun snug song sung gnu gun hog hon hug nog ohs son sou sun ugh go ho no nu oh on os sh so us

ghnot thong hong tong got hog hon hot nog not tho tog ton go ho no oh on to

ghnotu hognut nought ought thong tough gout hong hung hunt thou thug tong unto gnu got gun gut hog hon hot hug hut nog not nut out tho tog ton tug tun ugh go ho no nu oh on to ut

ghnruy hungry hung rung gnu gun guy hug rug run ugh urn nu

ghnu hung gnu gun hug ugh nu

gho hog go ho oh

ghooossw hoosgows hoosgow. *See* **hoossw**

ghoooosw hoosgow. *See* **hoosw**

ghorstu troughs. *See* **gorstu ghorsu ghortu**

ghorstuy yoghurts troughs yoghurt yogurts. *See* **ghorsu ghortu ghostu gorstu**

ghorstw growths. *See* **ghortw horstw**

ghorsu roughs hours rough shrug gosh gush hogs hour hugs ours rhos rugs rush sour hog hug ohs our rho rug sou ugh go ho oh or os sh so us

ghortu trough grout ought rough tough gout grot hour hurt rout ruth thou thru thug tour got gut hog hot hug hut ort our out rho rot rug rut tho tog tor tug ugh go ho oh or to ut

ghortuw wrought. *See* **ghortu ghortw**

ghortuy yoghurt. *See* **ghortu gortuy**

ghortw growth throw worth grot grow trow got hog hot how ort rho rot row tho tog tor tow two who go ho oh or ow to

ghoru rough hour hog hug our rho rug ugh go ho oh or

ghos gosh hogs hog ohs go ho oh os sh so

ghosst ghosts ghost hosts shots gosh hogs host hots shot sots togs tosh toss got hog hot ohs sot tho tog go ho oh os sh so to

ghost ghost gosh hogs host hots shot togs tosh got hog hot ohs sot tho tog go ho oh os sh so to

ghostu sought toughs ghost gouts gusto ought shout south thugs tough gosh gout gush gust guts hogs host hots hugs huts oust outs shot shut thou thug thus togs tosh tugs tush got gut hog hot hug hut ohs out sot sou tho tog tug ugh go ho oh os sh so to us ut

ghotu ought tough gout thou thug got hog hot hug hut out tho tog tug ugh go ho oh to ut

ghpu pugh hug hup pug ugh up

ghrssu shrugs shrug gush hugs rugs rush hug rug ugh sh us

ghrsu shrug gush hugs rugs rush hug rug ugh sh us

ghstu thugs gush gust guts hugs huts shut thug thus tugs tush gut hug hut tug ugh sh us ut

ghsu gush hugs hug ugh sh us

ghsuy gushy gush guys hugs guy hug shy ugh sh us

ghtu thug gut hug hut tug ugh ut

ghu hug ugh

gi

giiilmnt limiting. *See* **giilmn giilnt giimnt**

giiilnnu linguini. *See* **giilnn iilnnu**

giiimmnx immixing. *See* **giimmn giimnx**

giiinnot ignition. *See* **ginnot**

giiinnoz ionizing. *See* **ginnoz**

giiinstv visiting. *See* **giinst**

giijlnt jilting. *See* **giilnt**

giijmmny jimmying. *See* **giimmn**

giijmnos jingoism. *See* **gimos gijno ijnos**

giijnno joining. *See* **iinno gijno iijnn**

giijnnru injuring inuring ruining. *See* **innru iijnn ginru**

giijnost jingoist. *See* **giinst ginost ijnost**

giijnv jiving jig gin in

giikknn kinking. *See* **giiknn**

giiklln killing. *See* **giikln**

giikllns killings skilling killing. *See* **giikln giikns**

giiklmn milking. *See* **giikln giilmn giikmn**

giikln liking gink kiln king ling link gin ilk ink kin nil li in

giiklnn inkling linking. *See* **giiknn giilnn giikln**

giiklnnp plinking inkling kingpin linking pinking. *See* **giikln giiknn giiknp giilnn**

giiklnns inklings slinking inkling linings linking sinking. *See* **giikln giiknn giikns giilnn**

giiklnnt tinkling inkling kilting linking linting. *See* **giikln giiknn giiknt giilnn**

giiklnnw winkling inkling linking winking. *See* **giikln giiknn giilnn giilnw**

giiklnrs skirling risking. *See* **giikln giiknr giikns giilnr**

giiklnt kilting. *See* **giiknt giikln giilnt**

giiklntt kittling kilting tilting titling. *See* **giikln giiknt giilnt**

giikmmns skimming. *See* **giikmn giikns giimmn iimmns**

giikmn miking gink king mink gin ink kin nim mi in

giikmnps skimping pigskin spiking. *See* **giikmn giiknp giikns**

giikmnrs smirking risking. *See* **giikmn giiknr giikns giimnr**

giiknn inking kinin gink king gin ink inn kin in

giiknns skinning innings sinking sinning. *See* **giiknn giikns**

giiknno oinking. *See* **giiknn iinno**

giiknnov invoking oinking. *See* **giiknn**

giiknnp kingpin pinking. *See* **giiknn giiknp giinnp**

giiknnps kingpins kingpin pigskin pinking sinking sniping spiking. *See* **giiknn giiknp giikns**

giiknns sinking. *See* **giiknn giikns**

giiknnst stinking sinking. *See* **giiknn giikns giiknt giinst**

giiknntt knitting tinting. *See* **giiknn giiknt**

giiknnw winking. *See* **giiknn giinnw**

giiknp piking gink king ping pink gin gip ink kin kip nip pig pin in pi

giiknpps skipping pigskin pipkins sipping spiking. *See* **giiknp giikns giinpp**

giiknps pigskin spiking. *See* **giiknp giikns**

giiknpss pigskins kissing pigskin spiking. *See* **giiknp giikns iiknss**

giiknr irking gink grin king ring rink gin ink irk kin kir rig in

giiknrrs skirring risking sirring. *See* **giiknr giikns giinrs**

giiknrs risking. *See* **giiknr giinrs giikns**

giiknrst skirting striking risking. *See* **giiknr giikns giiknt giinrs**

giikns skiing ginks kings gink gins inks king nisi sign sing sink skin gin ink kin sin ski in is si

giiknss kissing. *See* **giikns iiknss**

giiknsv skiving vikings. *See* **giikns giiknv giinsv**

giiknt kiting gink king knit ting gin ink kin kit nit tin in it ti

giiknv viking gink king gin ink kin in

giillmn milling. *See* **giilmn**

giillmnu illuming milling mulling. *See* **giilmn**

giillnp pilling. *See* **giilnp**

giillnps spilling lisping pilings pilling. *See* **giilnp**

giillnqu quilling. *See* **gilnu illqu**

giillnr rilling. *See* **giilnr gillr**

giillnrt trilling lilting rilling tilling. *See* **giilnr giilnt giinrt**

giillnst stilling instill lilting listing silting tilling. *See* **giilnt giinst gilnst**

giillnsw swilling willing. *See* **giilnw**

giillnt lilting tilling. *See* **giilnt**

giillntw twilling lilting tilling willing wilting. *See* **giilnt giilnw giintw**

giillnw willing. *See* **giilnw**

giilmmns slimming sliming smiling. *See* **giilmn giimmn iimmns**

giilmn liming glim limn ling gil mil nil nim in li mi

giilmno moiling. *See* **giilmn giilno**

giilmnp limping. *See* **giilmn giilnp**

giilmnpp pimpling limping lipping pimping. *See* **giilmn giilnp giinpp**

giilmnpw wimpling limping. *See* **giilmn giilnp giilnw**

giilmnpy implying limping. *See* **giilmn giilnp gilnpy**

giilmns sliming smiling. *See* **giilmn ilmns gilns**

giilmnzz mizzling. *See* **giilmn**

giilmpr pilgrim. *No 6s or 5s*

giilmprs pilgrims pilgrim. *See* **gimps gilrs giprs**

giilmpsu pugilism. *See* **gimps glpsu iilmu**

giilnn lignin lining linin ling linn gin inn nil li in

giilnns linings. *See* **giilnn**

giilnnt linting. *See* **giilnn giilnt**

giilno oiling lingo ling lion loin long noil gin ion log nil nog oil go in li lo no on

giilnops spoiling lisping pilings poising sloping soiling. *See* **giilno giilnp gilnop gilnos**

giilnopt piloting toiling. *See* **giilno giilnp giilnt gilnop**

giilnor ligroin roiling. *See* **giilno giinor giilnr**

giilnos soiling. *See* **gilnos giilno**

giilnot toiling. *See* **giilno giilnt**

giilnp piling ling ping gin gip lip nil nip pig pin in li pi

giilnpp lipping. *See* **giilnp giinpp**

giilnppr rippling lipping ripping. *See* **giilnp giilnr giinpp giinpr**

giilnpps slipping lipping lisping pilings sipping. *See* **giilnp giinpp**

giilnppt tippling lipping tipping. *See* **giilnp giilnt giinpp**

giilnprt tripling. *See* **giilnp giilnr giilnt giinpr**

giilnps lisping pilings. *See* **giilnp gilns ginps**

giilnqsu quisling. *See* **gilnsu**

giilnqtu quilting. *See* **giilnt gilntu**

giilnr riling girl grin ling ring gin nil rig li in

giilnrsw swirling. *See* **giilnr giilnw giinrs giinrw**

giilnrtw twirling wilting writing. *See* **giilnr giilnt giilnw giinrt**

giilnsst listings instils listing silting. *See* **giilnt giilss giinst gilnss**

giilnst listing silting. *See* **gilnst iilnst giinst giilnt**

giilnstt slitting listing silting sitting tilting titling. *See* **giilnt giinst gilnst**

giilnstu linguist listing lusting silting suiting. *See* **giilnt giinst gilnst gilnsu**

giilnszz sizzling. *See* **giinsz**

giilnt tiling glint gilt ling lint ting gin lit nil nit til tin in it li ti

giilntt tilting titling. *See* **giilnt**

giilntw wilting. *See* **giilnt giilnw giintw**

giilnv living vigil ling gin nil li in

giilnw   wiling ling wing gin nil wig win li
in

giilpstu   pugilist. *See* iilpst ilpstu

giils   sigil is li si

giilss   sigils sigil sis is li si

giilsv   vigils sigil vigil is li si

giilv   vigil li

giimmn   miming minim gin mim nim mi
in

giimmnpr   primming rimming priming.
See giimmn giimnr giinpr

giimmnr   rimming. *See* giimmn giimnr

giimmnrt   trimming rimming mitring.
See giimmn giimnr giimnt giinrt

giimmnru   immuring rimming. *See* giimmn giimnr iimmnu

giimmnsw   swimming. *See* giimmn
iimmns

giimnn   mining gin inn nim mi in

giimnnoy   ignominy. *See* gimnno giimnn
iimnno giinoy

giimnnt   minting. *See* giimnn giimnt

giimnops   imposing poising. *See* gimnop
ginops

giimnott   omitting. *See* giimnt ginott

giimnotv   vomiting. *See* giimnt gimnov ginotv

giimnpp   pimping. *See* giinpp

giimnppr   primping pimping priming ripping. *See* giimnr giinpp giinpr

giimnpr   priming. *See* giimnr giinpr

giimnpru   umpiring priming. *See* giimnr
giinpr gimnpu

giimnptu   imputing. *See* giimnt gimnpu
gimntu ginptu

giimnr   miring riming grim grin ring gin
mir nim rig rim mi in

giimnrt   mitring. *See* giimnr giimnt giinrt

giimnss   missing. *See* ginss

giimnssu   misusing issuing missing musings mussing. *See* gimnsu

giimnst   misting smiting. *See* giimnt giinst

giimnt   timing ting mint gin nim nit tin in
it mi ti

giimnx   mixing minx gin mix nim nix in
mi xi

giimorrs   rigorism. *See* giorrs

giinnn   inning gin inn in

giinnnot   intoning tinning. *See* giinnn
ginnot

giinnnp   pinning. *See* giinnn giinnp

giinnnps   spinning innings pinning sinning sniping. *See* giinnn giinnp

giinnnru   inurning inuring ruining running. *See* giinnn

giinnns   innings sinning. *See* giinnn

giinnnsw   winnings innings sinning winning. *See* giinnn giinnw

giinnnt   tinning. *See* giinnn

giinnntw   twinning tinning twining winning. *See* giinnn giinnw giintw

giinnnw   winning. *See* giinnn giinnw

giinnop   opining. *See* giinnp iinnop

giinnopt   pointing opining. *See* ginnot giinnp iinnop ginopt

giinnor   ironing. *See* giinor iinno

giinnos   noising. *See* ginnos iinnos

giinnp   pining ping gin gip inn nip pig pin
in pi

giinnpp   nipping. *See* giinnp giinpp

giinnpps   snipping nipping sipping sniping. *See* giinnp giinpp

giinnprt   printing. *See* giinnp giinpr giinrt

giinnps   sniping. *See* giinnp ginps

giinnrs   rinsing. *See* giinrs

giinnrsu   insuring inuring nursing rinsing
ruining. *See* giinrs innrsu

giinnrtu   untiring inuring ruining turning
uniting. *See* giinrt ginntu ginrtu

giinnru   inuring ruining. *See* ginru innru

giinnstt   stinting tinting sitting. *See* giinst

giinntt   tinting. *No 6s or 5s*

giinntu   uniting. *See* ginntu

giinntw   twining. *See* giinnw giintw

giinnw   wining wing gin inn wig win in

giinnx   nixing gin inn nix in xi

giinops   poising. *See* ginops

giinopst   positing poising posting spiting
stoping. *See* giinst ginops ginopt ginost

giinoptv   pivoting. *See* ginopt

giinoqtu   quoiting quoting. *See* ginotu

giinor   origin groin grin iron ring gin ion
nog nor rig go in no on or

giinors   origins signior. *See* ginors giinor
giinrs

giinorss   signiors origins signior signors.
See giinor giinrs ginors ginoss

giinort   rioting. *See* giinor giinrt ginort

giinosy   yoginis. *See* giinoy inosy giosy

giinoy   yogini yogi yoni gin goy ion nog
yin yon go in no on oy

giinpp   piping ping gin gip nip pig pin pip
in pi

giinppp   pipping. *See* giinpp iinppp

giinppqu   quipping piquing. *See* giinpp

giinppr   ripping. *See* giinpp giinpr

giinpprt   tripping ripping tipping. *See* giinpp giinpr giinrt

giinpps   sipping. *See* giinpp ginps

giinppt   tipping. *See* giinpp iippt

giinppy   yipping. *See* giinpp inppy

giinppz   zipping. *See* giinpp

giinpqu   piquing. *No 6s or 5s*

giinpr   riping grin grip ping pirn prig ring
gin gip nip pig pin rig rip in pi

giinprs   spiring. *See* giinpr giinrs ginprs

giinprst   striping spiring spiting. *See* giinpr giinrs giinrt giinst

giinprsu   uprising spiring pursing. *See* giinpr giinrs ginprs gnprsu

giinprz   prizing. *See* giinpr

giinpst   spiting. *See* giinst ginps inpst

giinpstt   spitting pitting sitting spiting.
See giinst

giinpstw   wingtips spiting swiping wingtip. *See* giinpw giinst giintw

giinpsw   swiping. *See* giinpw ginps ginsw

giinptt   pitting. *No 6s or 5s*

giinptw   wingtip. *See* giinpw giintw

giinpty   pitying. *See* ginpty

giinpw   wiping ping wing gin gip nip pig
pin wig win in pi

giinqrsu   squiring quiring. *See* giinrs

giinqrtu   quirting quiring. *See* giinrt
ginrtu

giinqru   quiring. *See* ginru

giinqttu   quitting. *See* iinttu

giinrrs   sirring. *See* giinrs

giinrrst   stirring sirring. *See* giinrs giinrt
giinst ginrst

giinrs   rising siring grins rings gins grin
iris nisi rigs ring sign sing gin rig sin sir
in is si

giinrstv   striving virgins. *See* giinrs giinrt
giinst ginrst

giinrstw   writings writing. *See* giinrs giinrt giinrw giinst

giinrsv   virgins. *See* giinrs giinrv giinsv

giinrt   tiring girt grin girt ring ting trig gin
nit rig tin in it ti

giinrtw   writing. *See* giinrt giinrw giintw

giinrv   riving virgin grin ring gin rig in

giinrw   wiring wring grin ring wing gin rig
wig win in

giinsstt   sittings sitting. *See* iinsstt giinst
ginsst insstt

giinsstu   tissuing issuing suiting. *See* giinst ginsst insstu

giinssu   issuing. *See* inssu ginss ginsu

giinssz   sizings. *See* giinsz ginss

giinst   siting sting tings gins gist nisi nits
sign sing snit ting tins gin its nit sin sit
tin in is it si ti

giinstt   sitting. *See* giinst instt iistt

giinsttw   twisting nitwits sitting witting.
See giinst giintw iinttw

giinstu   suiting. *See* giinst gnstu ginsu

giinsv   vising gins nisi sign sing gin sin in
is si

giinsz   sizing zings gins nisi sign sing zigs
zing gin sin zig in is si

giintttw   twitting witting. *See* giintw
iinttw

giinttw   witting. *See* giintw iinttw

giintw   witing ting twig twin wing gin nit
tin wig win wit in it ti

giinvw   wiving wing gin wig win in

gij   jig

gijklnoy jokingly yolking. *See* **gijkno gijlny giklny giknoy**

gijknnu junking. *See* **giknnu**

gijkno joking jingo gink ikon jink join king kino oink gin ink ion jig jog kin nog go in jo no on

gijllnoy jollying. *See* **gijlny gllnoy**

gijlnost jostling jolting. *See* **gilnos gilnst ginost ijnost**

gijlnot jolting. *See* **gilnt ginot gijno**

gijlnstu justling lusting. *See* **gilnst gilnsu gilntu ilnstu**

gijlny jingly lying inly ling liny gin jig nil yin li in

gijmnpu jumping. *See* **gimnpu**

gijno jingo join gin ion jig jog nog go in jo no on

gijnostt jottings jotting. *See* **ginost ginott ijnost**

gijnostu jousting outings. *See* **ginost ginotu ijnost jnostu**

gijnott jotting. *See* **ginott gijno ijnot**

gijnttu jutting. *No 6s or 5s*

gijs jigs jig is si

gikklnsu skulking sulking. *See* **gilnsu**

gikknnsu skunking. *See* **giknnu**

gikknuy yukking. *See* **gknuy ikkny**

gikllnno knolling. *See* **gilno kllno**

giklnnpu plunking. *See* **giknnu giknpu gilnpu iklnpu**

giklnnru knurling lurking. *See* **giknnu gilnru**

giklnoo looking. *See* **gilnoo**

giklnoy yolking. *See* **giklny giknoy**

giklnru lurking. *See* **gilnru**

giklnsu sulking. *See* **gilnsu**

giklny kingly lying gink inky inly kiln king ling link liny gin ilk ink kin nil yin li in

gikmnos smoking. *See* **gikns gimos iknos**

gikn gink king gin ink kin in

giknnott knotting. *See* **giknot ginnot ginott**

giknnotu knouting. *See* **giknnu giknot ginntu ginotu**

giknnow knowing. *See* **ginnow knnow**

giknnoz zonking. *See* **ginnoz**

giknnu nuking gink gunk king gin gnu gun ink inn kin nun in nu

giknoops spooking spoking. *See* **giknop ginops iknops inoops**

giknoor rooking. *See* **ginor**

giknop poking gipon oping pinko gink ikon king kino knop oink ping pink gin gip ink ion kin kip nip nog pig pin poi go in no on pi

giknops spoking. *See* **ginops iknops giknop**

giknorst stroking sorting stoking storing trigons. *See* **giknot ginors ginort ginost**

giknorsw workings working. *See* **ginors ginorw ginosw gnorsw**

giknorw working. *See* **ginorw**

giknost stoking. *See* **ginost iknost giknot**

giknot toking ingot gink ikon into king kino knit knot oink ting tong gin got ink ion kin kit nit nog not tin tog ton go in it no on ti to

giknoy yoking gink ikon inky king kino oink yogi yoni gin goy ink ion kin nog yin yon go in no on oy

giknpu puking gink gunk king ping pink pung punk gin gip gnu gun ink kin kip nip pig pin pug pun in nu pi up

gikns ginks kings gink gins inks king sign sing sink skin gin ink kin sin ski in is si

gill gill ill li

gilllno lolling. *See* **gilno**

gilllnu lulling. *See* **gilnu**

gillmnu mulling. *See* **gilnu**

gillmooy gloomily. *See* **glmooy**

gillnop polling. *See* **gilnop**

gillnor rolling. *See* **gillr ginor gilno**

gillnort trolling rolling tolling. *See* **ginort**

gillnot tolling. *See* **gilnt ginot**

gillnovy lovingly. *See* **gilnov gllnoy**

gillnpu pulling. *See* **gilnpu**

gillnpuy pulingly pulling. *See* **gilluy gilnpu gilnpy**

gillnsuy sullying. *See* **gilluy gilnsu gilnsy glnsuy**

gillr grill gill girl rill rig ill li

gillrs grills gills girls grill rills gill girl rigs rill sill ill rig sir is li si

gilluy uglily gully gill gull illy lily ugly guy ill lug li

gilm glim mil li mi

gilmmnsu slumming summing. *See* **gilnsu gimnsu ilmnsu**

gilmnoo looming. *See* **gilnoo gimnoo**

gilmnot molting. *See* **gilnt ginot**

gilmnott mottling molting lotting. *See* **ginott**

gilmnotu moulting molting. *See* **gilntu gimntu ginotu ilmotu**

gilmnovy movingly. *See* **gilnov gimnov**

gilmnppu plumping lumping pluming pulping pumping. *See* **gilnpu gimnpu**

gilmnpru rumpling lumping pluming purling. *See* **gilnpu gilnru gimnpu ilnpru**

gilmnpsu slumping impugns lumping pluming spuming. *See* **gilnpu gilnsu gimnpu gimnsu**

gilmnpu lumping pluming. *See* **gimnpu gilnpu**

gilmnuzz muzzling. *See* **gilnu**

gilmoosy misology. *See* **giloos glmoos glmooy**

gilmpruy grumpily. *See* **gilmry gmpruy ilmpry lmpruy**

gilmry grimly grimy girl glim grim limy miry rimy gym mil mir rig rim li mi my

giln ling gin nil li in

gilnnouv unloving. *See* **gilnov**

gilnnrsu nursling rulings nursing. *See* **gilnru gilnsu innrsu**

gilnnuzz nuzzling. *See* **gilnu**

gilno lingo ling lion loin long noil gin ion log nil nog oil go in li lo no on

gilnoo looing lingo igloo goon ling lion logo loin long loon noil olio gin goo ion log loo nil nog oil go in li lo no on

gilnoop looping pooling. *See* **gilnoo gilnop**

gilnoops spooling looping loosing pooling sloping soloing. *See* **gilnoo gilnop gilnos giloos**

gilnoos loosing soloing. *See* **giloos gilnoo gilnos**

gilnoost stooling loosing looting lotions soloing sooting tooling. *See* **gilnoo gilnos gilnst giloos**

gilnoot looting tooling. *See* **gilnoo ilnoot**

gilnoott tootling looting lotting tooling tooting. *See* **gilnoo ginott ilnoot**

gilnoowy wooingly yowling. *See* **gilnoo gilnow ginoow**

gilnop loping poling gipon lingo oping glop ling lion loin long noil ping gin gip ion lip log lop nil nip nog oil pig pin poi go in li lo no on pi

gilnopp lopping. *See* **gilnop ilnopp**

gilnoppp plopping poppling lopping popping poplin.. *See* **gilnop**

gilnopps slopping lopping poplins sloping sopping. *See* **gilnop gilnos ginops ilnopp**

gilnoppt toppling lopping topping. *See* **gilnop ginopt ilnopp ilnopt**

gilnoprw prowling plowing. *See* **gilnop gilnow ginopr ginorw**

gilnops sloping. *See* **ginops gilnop**

gilnoptt plotting lotting potting. *See* **gilnop ginopt ginott ilnopt**

gilnopw plowing. *See* **gilnop gilnow**

gilnos losing soling lingo lings lions loins longs noils sling gins ions ling lion logs loin long nils nogs noil oils sign silo sing slog soil song gin ion log los nil nog oil sin sol son go in is li lo no on os si so

gilnostt slotting lotting glottis. *See* **gilnos gilnst ginost ginott**

gilnostu tousling lusting outings. *See* **gilnos gilnst gilnsu gilntu**

gilnosv solving. *See* **gilnos gilnov**

gilnosw slowing. *See* **gilnos gilnow ginosw**

gilnott lotting. *See* **ginott gilnt gilno**

gilnotuy outlying. *See* **gilntu giltuy ginotu ginoty**

gilnov loving lingo ling lion loin long noil viol gin ion log nil nog oil go in li lo no on

gilnow lowing lingo owing glow gown ling lion loin long noil wing wino gin ion log low nil nog now oil owl own wig win won go in li lo no on ow

gilnowy yowling. *See* **gilnow gilny**

gilnppru purpling pulping purling. *See* **gilnpu gilnru ilnpru**

gilnppsu suppling pulping supping. *See* **gilnpu gilnsu ilppsu inppsu**

gilnppu pulping. *See* **gilnpu inppu ilppu**

gilnprsu slurping purling purlins pursing rulings. *See* **gilnpu gilnru gilnsu ginprs**

gilnpru purling. *See* **gilnru gilnpu ilnpru**

gilnpryy pryingly. *See* **gilnpy ginpry**

gilnpu puling lungi gulp ling lung ping plug puli pung gin gip gnu gun lip lug nil nip pig pin pug pul pun in li nu pi up

gilnpuzz puzzling. *See* **gilnpu**

gilnpy plying lying inly ling liny ping piny gin gip gyp lip nil nip pig pin ply yin yip in li pi

gilnrrsu slurring rulings. *See* **gilnru gilnsu**

gilnrstu rustling lusting rulings rusting. *See* **gilnru gilnst gilnsu gilntu**

gilnrsu rulings. *See* **gilnsu gilnru**

gilnru luring ruling lungi ruing girl grin ling lung ring ruin rung gin gnu gun lug nil rig rug run urn in li nu

gilns lings sling gins ling nils sign sing gin nil sin in is li si

gilnss slings lings signs sings sling gins ling nils sign sing sins gin nil sin sis in is li si

gilnsstu tussling lusting insults. *See* **gilnss gilnst gilnsu gilntu**

gilnst glints gilts glint lings lints sling sting tings gilt gins gist ling lint list nils nits sign silt sing slit snit tils ting tins gin its lit nil nit sin sit til tin in is it li si ti

gilnstu lusting. *See* **gilnst ilnstu gilnsu gilntu**

gilnsty styling. *See* **gilnst gilnsy ginsty**

gilnsu lungis sluing lings lungi lungs sling slung suing using gins gnus guns ling lugs lung nils sign sing slug snug sung gin gnu gun lis lug nil sin sun in is li nu si us

gilnsy lysing singly lings lying lysin sling gins inly ling liny nils sign sing gin nil sin sly yin in is li si

gilnt glint gilt ling lint ting gin lit nil nit til tin in it li ti

gilntu luting glint guilt lungi until gilt glut ling lint lung lunt ting unit gin gnu gun gut lit lug nil nit nut til tin tug tui tun in it li nu ti ut

gilnu lungi ling lung gin gnu gun lug nil in li nu

gilny lying inly ling liny gin nil yin li in

giloo igloo logo olio goo log loo oil go li lo

giloorsu glorious. *See* **giloos**

giloos igloos igloo logos olios goos logo logs loos oils olio silo slog soil solo goo log loo los oil sol go is li lo os si so

gilorty trilogy. *See* **glory ilory**

gilostt glottis. *See* **gilst ilstt ilost**

gilr girl rig li

gilrs girls girl rigs rig sir is li si

gilrsty gristly. *See* **gilrsy ilrsty**

gilrsy grisly girls girl rigs rig sir sly is li si

gilrtuy liturgy. *See* **giltuy lrtuy**

gilst gilts gilt gist list silt slit tils its lit sit til is it li si ti

gilt gilt lit til it li ti

giltu guilt gilt glut gut lit lug til tug tui it li ti ut

giltuy guilty guilt gilt glut ugly gut guy lit lug til tug tui it li ti ut

giltyz glitzy glitz gilt lit til zig zit it li ti

giltz glitz gilt lit til zig zit it li ti

gimmnstu stumming summing. *See* **gimnsu gimntu immstu**

gimmnsu summing. *See* **gimnsu**

gimnno mignon gin inn ion mog mon nim nog go in mi mo no om on

gimnnor morning. *See* **gimnno ginor imnor**

gimnnors mornings morning snoring. *See* **gimnno ginnos ginors imnors**

gimnnoru mourning morning. *See* **gimnno**

gimnnotu mounting. *See* **gimnno gimntu ginnot ginntu**

gimnnouv unmoving. *See* **gimnno gimnov**

gimnoo mooing mongo goon mono moon gin goo ion mog mon moo nim nog go in mi mo no om on

gimnoor mooring rooming. *See* **gimnoo imnoor**

gimnoors moorings mooring morions rooming. *See* **gimnoo ginors gmoors imnoor**

gimnoort motoring monitor mooring rooming rooting. *See* **gimnoo ginort imnoor imnoot**

gimnooss osmosing. *See* **gimnoo gimoss ginoss imnoos**

gimnop moping gipon oping gimp ping gin gip imp ion mog mon mop nim nip nog pig pin poi go in mi mo no om on pi

gimnopp mopping. *See* **gimnop**

gimnopr romping. *See* **gimnop ginopr**

gimnopst stomping posting stoping. *See* **gimnop ginops ginopt ginost**

gimnoptu gumption pouting. *See* **gimnop gimnpu gimntu ginopt**

gimnorru rumoring. *See* **ginor imnor mnoru**

gimnorrw ringworm worming. *See* **gimnow ginorw**

gimnorst storming sorting storing trigons. *See* **ginors ginort ginost ginrst**

gimnorw worming. *See* **gimnow ginorw**

gimnosu mousing. *See* **gimnsu gmnosu**

gimnosw mowings. *See* **gimnow ginosw**

gimnosyy misogyny. *See* **imnosy**

gimnov moving gin ion mog mon nim nog vim go in mi mo no om on

gimnow mowing owing gown mown wing wino gin ion mog mon mow nim nog now own wig win won go in mi mo no om on ow

gimnppu pumping. *See* **gimnpu**

gimnprtu trumping. *See* **gimnpu gimntu ginptu ginrtu**

gimnpstu stumping impugns pignuts spuming. *See* **gimnpu gimnsu gimntu ginptu**

gimnpsu impugns spuming. *See* **gimnpu gimnsu**

gimnpu impugn umping gimp ping pung gin gip gnu gum gun imp mug nim nip pig pin pug pun ump in mi mu nu pi um up

gimnssu musings mussing. *See* **gimnsu inssu ginss**

gimnsttu smutting. *See* **gimnsu gimntu**

gimnstyy stymying. *See* **ginsty**

gimnsu musing minus suing using gins gnus gums guns mugs nims sign sing smug snug sung gin gnu gum gun mis mug mus nim sin sum sun in is mi mu nu si um us

gimntu muting mint ting unit gin gnu gum gun gut mug nim nit nut tin tug tui tun in it mi mu nu ti um ut

gimos gismo mogs smog mis mog mos oms go is mi mo om os si so

gimoss gismos gismo smogs miss mogs moss smog mis mog mos oms sis go is mi mo om os si so

gimosz gizmos gismo gizmo mogs smog zigs mis mog mos oms zig go is mi mo om os si so

gimoy goyim yogi goy gym mog go mi mo my om oy

gimoz gizmo zig mog go mi mo om

gimp gimp gip imp pig mi pi

gimps gimps gimp gips imps pigs simp gip imp mis pig sip is mi pi si

gimpy gimpy gimp gip gym gyp imp pig yip mi my pi

gimr grim mir rig rim mi

gimry grimy grim miry rimy gym mir rig rim mi my

gin gin in

ginnnoo nooning. *See* **innno innoo**

ginnnow wonning. *See* **ginnow innno**

ginnnpu punning. *See* **innpu**

ginnnru running. *See* **ginru innru**

ginnnstu stunning sunning tunning. *See* **ginntu**

ginnnsu sunning. *See* **ginsu**

ginnntu tunning. *See* **ginntu**

ginnoops snooping spooning noosing. *See* **ginnos ginops innoos inoops**

ginnoos noosing. *See* **ginnos innoos**

ginnoosw swooning noosing snowing. *See* **ginnos ginnow ginoow ginosw**

ginnoosz snoozing noosing. *See* **ginnos ginnoz ginooz innoos**

ginnoptu gunpoint punting pouting. *See* **ginnot ginntu ginopt ginotu**

ginnors snoring. *See* **ginors ginnos**

ginnorst snorting snoring sorting stoning storing trigons. *See* **ginnos ginnot ginors ginort**

ginnorw ingrown. *See* **ginnow ginorw**

ginnos nosing gins inns ions nogs sign sing song gin inn ion nog sin son go in is no on os si so

ginnost stoning. *See* **ginost ginnos ginnot**

ginnosw snowing. *See* **ginnos ginnow ginosw**

ginnot noting toning ingot into ting tong gin got inn ion nit nog not tin tog ton go in it no on ti to

ginnotw wonting. *See* **ginnot ginotw**

ginnow owning owing gown wing wino gin inn ion nog now own wig win won go in no on ow

ginnoz zoning zing gin inn ion nog zig go in no on

ginnprsu spurning nursing pruning pursing. *See* **ginprs gnprsu innpsu innrsu**

ginnpru pruning. *See* **innru ginru innpu**

ginnptu punting. *See* **ginntu ginptu**

ginnrsu nursing. *See* **innrsu ginrs ginru**

ginnrtu turning. *See* **ginntu ginrtu**

ginnsttu stunting nutting. *See* **ginntu**

ginnttu nutting. *See* **ginntu**

ginntu tuning ting unit gin gnu gun gut inn nit nun nut tin tug tui tun in it nu ti ut

ginoopp pogonip pooping. *See* **ginop**

ginoopps opposing pogonips pogonip pooping sopping. *See* **ginops inoops**

ginooprs spooring prosing sporing. *See* **ginopr ginops ginors ginprs**

ginooprt trooping porting portion rooting. *See* **ginopr ginopt ginort inoopt**

ginoopst stooping options posting potions sooting stoping. *See* **ginops ginopt ginost giopst**

ginoopsw swooping. *See* **ginoow ginops ginosw inoops**

ginoorst roosting rooting sooting sorting storing torsion trigons. *See* **ginors ginort ginost ginrst**

ginoort rooting. *See* **ginort**

ginoost sooting. *See* **ginost gnoos noost**

ginoott tooting. *See* **ginott**

ginoow wooing wooing goon gown wing wino gin goo ion nog now own wig win won woo go in no on ow

ginooz oozing goon zing zoon gin goo ion nog zig zoo go in no on

ginop gipon oping ping gin gip ion nip nog pig pin poi go in no on pi

ginoppp popping. *See* **ginop**

ginopppr propping popping. *See* **ginopr**

ginopps sopping. *See* **ginops**

ginoppst stopping toppings posting sopping stoping topping topspin. *See* **ginops ginopt ginost giopst**

ginoppsw swopping sopping. *See* **ginops ginosw**

ginoppt topping. *See* **ginopt**

ginopr poring roping gipon groin oping prong grin grip iron ping pirn prig prog ring gin gip ion nip nog nor pig pin poi pro rig rip go in no on or pi

ginoprs prosing sporing. *See* **ginops ginors ginopr inoprs gnoprs**

ginoprst sporting porting posting prosing sorting sporing stoping storing trigons. *See* **ginopr ginops ginopt ginors**

ginoprsu ingroups ingroup pouring prosing pursing rousing souring sporing. *See* **ginopr ginops ginors ginprs**

ginoprt porting. *See* **ginopr ginopt ginort**

ginoprtu trouping ingroup porting pouring pouting routing touring. *See* **ginopr ginopt ginort ginotu**

ginopru ingroup pouring. *See* **ginopr**

ginoprv proving. *See* **ginopr ginorv**

ginops gipons posing gipon oping pings gins gips ions nips nogs pigs ping pins pois pons sign sing snip song spin gin gip ion nip nog pig pin poi sin sip son sop go in is no on os pi si so

ginopsst signpost pistons posting spigots stoping tossing. *See* **ginops ginopt ginoss ginost**

ginopst posting stoping. *See* **ginops ginost inopst giopst ginopt**

ginopstt spotting posting potting stoping. *See* **ginops ginopt ginost ginott**

ginopstu spouting outings pignuts pigouts posting pouting stoping. *See* **ginops ginopt ginost ginotu**

ginopt toping gipon ingot oping pinto piton point into ping pint ting tong gin gip got ion nip nit nog not pig pin pit poi pot tin tip tog ton top go in it no on pi ti to

ginoptt potting. *See* **ginopt ginott**

ginoptu pouting. *See* **ginotu ginptu gioptu ginopt**

ginoqtu quoting. *See* **ginotu inqtu inoqu**

ginor groin grin iron ring gin ion nog nor rig go in no on or

ginorrwy worrying. *See* **ginorw**

ginors groins rosing signor grins groin irons rings rosin gins grin ions iron nogs rigs ring sign sing song sori gin ion nog nor rig sin sir son go in is no on or os si so

ginorss signors. *See* **ginoss ginors inorss**

ginorsst ringtoss signors sorting storing strings tossing trigons. *See* **ginors ginort ginoss ginost**

ginorst sorting storing trigons. *See* **ginors ginost ginrst gnorst ginort**

ginorstu rousting nitrous outings rousing routing rusting sorting souring storing touring trigons. *See* **ginors ginort ginost ginotu**

ginorsty storying sorting storing stringy trigons. *See* **ginors ginort ginost ginoty**

ginorsu rousing souring. *See* **ginors**

ginort trigon groin ingot girt grin grit grot into iron ring riot ting tiro tong tori torn trig trio gin got ion nit nog nor not ort rig rot tin tog ton tor go in it no on or ti to

ginortt rotting. *See* **ginott ginort inortt**

ginorttt trotting rotting totting. *See* **ginort ginott inortt**

ginorttu tutoring rotting routing rutting touring touting. *See* **ginort ginott ginotu ginrtu**

ginortu routing touring. *See* **ginotu ginrtu**

ginortw trowing. *See* **ginorw ginotw ginort**

ginorv roving groin vigor grin iron ring gin ion nog nor rig go in no on or

ginorw rowing groin grown owing wring wrong gown grin grow iron ring wing wino worn gin ion nog nor now own rig row wig win won go in no on or ow

ginoss gnosis signs sings songs gins ions nogs sign sing sins song sons gin ion nog sin sis son go in is no on os si so

ginosst tossing. *See* **ginoss ginost ginsst**

ginossu sousing. *See* **ginoss inssu ginsu**

ginost ingots ingot sting tings tongs gins gist into ions nits nogs sign sing snit snot song ting tins togs tong tons gin got ion its nit nog not sin sit son sot tin tog ton go in is it no on os si so ti to

ginosttw swotting stowing. *See* **ginost ginosw ginott ginotw**

ginostu outings. *See* **ginost ginotu**

ginostw stowing. *See* **ginost ginosw ginotw**

ginosw sowing gowns owing swing wings winos gins gown ions nogs owns sign sing snow song sown swig wigs wing wino wins gin ion nog now own sin son sow wig win wis won go in is no on os ow si so

ginot ingot into ting tong gin got ion nit nog not tin tog ton go in it no on ti to

ginott toting ingot into ting tint tong gin got ion nit nog not tin tit tog ton tot go in it no on ti to

ginottt totting. *See* **ginott**

ginottu touting. *See* **ginott ginotu**

ginotu outing ingot gout into ting tong unit unto gin gnu got gun gut ion nit nog not nut out tin tog ton tug tui tun go in it no nu on ti to ut

ginotv voting ingot into ting tong gin got ion nit nog not tin tog ton go in it no on ti to

ginotw towing ingot owing gown into nowt ting tong town twig twin wing wino wont gin got ion nit nog not now own tin tog ton tow two wig win wit won go in it no on ow ti to

ginoty toying ingot tying into ting tiny tong tony yogi yoni gin got goy ion nit nog not tin tog ton toy yin yon go in it no on oy ti to

ginovw vowing owing gown wing wino gin ion nog now own vow wig win won go in no on ow

ginow owing gown wing wino gin ion nog now own wig win won go in no on ow

ginp ping gin gip nip pig pin in pi

ginpppu pupping. *See* **inppu**

ginppsu supping. *See* **inppsu ginps gnpsu**

ginprrsu spurring purring pursing. *See* **ginprs gnprsu**

ginprru purring. *See* **ginru**

ginprs spring grins grips pings pirns prigs rings sprig gins gips grin grip nips pigs ping pins pirn prig rigs ring rips

sign sing snip spin gin gip nip pig pin rig rip sin sip sir in is pi si

ginprss springs. *See* **ginprs giprss**

ginprstu spurting pignuts pursing rusting turnips. *See* **ginprs ginptu ginrst ginrtu**

ginprsu pursing. *See* **ginprs gnprsu**

ginprsuu pursuing pursing. *See* **ginprs ginsuu gnprsu**

ginprsy springy. *See* **ginpry ginprs ginpsy**

ginpry prying grin grip ping piny pirn prig ring gin gip gyp nip pig pin pry rig rip yin yip in pi

ginps pings gins gips nips pigs ping pins sign sing snip spin gin gip nip pig pin sin sip in is pi si

ginpssuw upswings upswing. *See* **ginssw**

ginpstu pignuts. *See* **ginptu inpstu**

ginpsuw upswing. *See* **ginps gnpsu ginsu**

ginpsy spying pings spiny gins gips gyps nips pigs ping pins piny sign sing snip spin yips gin gip gyp nip pig pin sin sip spy yin yip in is pi si

ginpttu putting. *See* **ginptu**

ginpttuy puttying putting. *See* **ginptu ginpty**

ginptu pignut input ping pint pung punt ting unit gin gip gnu gun gut nip nit nut pig pin pit pug pun put tin tip tug tui tun tup in it nu pi ti up ut

ginpty typing tying ping pint piny pity ting tiny gin gip gyp nip nit pig pin pit tin tip yin yip in it pi ti

ginr grin ring gin rig in

ginrs grins rings gins grin rigs ring sign sing gin rig sin sir in is si

ginrsst strings. *See* **girsst ginsst ginrst**

ginrsstu trussing strings rusting. *See* **ginrst ginrtu ginsst girsst**

ginrst string girts grins grist grits rings sting tings trigs gins girt gist grin grit nits rigs ring sign sing snit stir ting tins trig gin its nit rig sin sir sit tin in is it si ti

ginrsttu trusting rusting rutting. *See* **ginrst ginrtu gnrstu**

ginrstty trysting stringy. *See* **ginrst ginrty ginsty girtty**

ginrstu rusting. *See* **gnrstu ginrst ginrtu**

ginrstuu suturing rusting. *See* **ginrst ginrtu ginsuu gnrstu**

ginrsty stringy. *See* **ginsty ginrty**

ginrsw wrings grins rings swing wings wring gins grin rigs ring sign sing swig wigs wing wins gin rig sin sir wig win wis in is si

ginrttu rutting. *See* **ginrtu**

ginrtu truing ruing grunt girt grin grit ring ruin rung runt ting trig turn unit

gin gnu gun gut nit nut rig rug run rut tin tug tui tun urn in it nu ti nu it ut

ginrty trying tying girt grin grit ring ting tiny trig gin nit rig tin try yin in it ti

ginru ruing grin ring ruin rung gin gnu gun rig rug run urn in nu

ginrw wring grin ring wing gin rig wig win in

gins gins sign sing gin sin in is si

ginss signs sings gins sign sing sins gin sin sis in is si

ginsst stings gists signs sings snits sting tings gins gist nits sign sing sins sits snit ting tins gin its nit sin sis sit tin in is it si ti

ginssw swings signs sings swigs swing wings gins sign sing sins swig wigs wing wins gin sin sis wig win wis in is si

ginst sting tings gins gist nits sign sing snit ting tins gin its nit sin sit tin in is it si ti

ginsty stingy sting tings tying gins gist nits sign sing snit ting tins tiny gin its nit sin sit sty tin yin in is it si ti

ginsu suing using gins gnus guns sign sing snug sung gin gnu gun sin sun in is nu si us

ginsuu unguis suing using gins gnus guns sign sing snug sung gin gnu gun sin sun in is nu si us

ginsw swing wings gins sign sing swig wigs wing wins gin sin wig win wis in is si

ginswy swingy swing wings gins sign sing swig wigs wing wins winy gin sin wig win wis yin in is si

ginsz zings gins sign sing zigs zing gin sin zig in is si

gint ting gin nit tin in it ti

ginttu tutting. *See* **itttu**

ginty tying ting tiny gin nit tin yin in it ti

ginvy vying viny gin ivy yin in

ginw wing gin wig win in

ginz zing gin zig in

giooorsv vigoroso. *See* **giorsv**

gioorrsu rigorous. *See* **giorrs**

gioorsuv vigorous. *See* **giorsv**

gioprrsu prurigos prurigo. *See* **giorrs goprsu**

gioprru prurigo. *See* **gopru ioprr giorr**

giopss gossip gips pigs pois sips sops gip pig poi sip sis sop go is os pi si so

giopsss gossips. *See* **giopss**

giopsst spigots. *See* **giopss iopsst giopst**

giopssy gossipy. *See* **giopss giosy**

giopst spigot posit gips gist pigs pits pois post pots spit spot stop tips togs tops gip got its pig pit poi pot sip sit sop sot tip tog top go is it os pi si so ti to

giopstu pigouts. *See* **giopst gioptu**

gioptu pigout gout pout gip got gut out pig pit poi pot pug put tip tog top tug tui tup go it pi ti to up ut

giorr rigor rig go or

giorrs rigors rigor orris rigs sori rig sir go is or os si so

giorsv vigors vigor visor rigs sori rig sir go is or os si so

giorv vigor rig go or

giosy yogis yogi goys goy soy go is os oy si so

gioy yogi goy go oy

gip gip pig pi

gipr grip prig gip pig rig rip pi

giprs grips prigs sprig gips grip pigs prig rigs rips gip pig rig rip sip sir is pi si

giprss sprigs grips prigs priss sprig gips grip pigs prig rigs rips sips sirs gip pig rig rip sip sir sis is pi si

gips gips pigs gip pig sip is pi si

gipsty pigsty tipsy gips gist gyps pigs pits pity spit tips yips gip gyp its pig pit sip sit spy sty tip yip is it pi si ti

gir rig

girs rigs rig sir is si

girsst grists girts gists grist grits stirs trigs girt gist grit rigs sirs sits stir trig its rig sir sis sit is it si ti

girst girts grist grits trigs girt gist grit rigs stir trig its rig sir sit is it si ti

girt girt grit trig rig it ti

girtty gritty girt grit trig rig tit try it ti

gisst gists gist sits its sis sit is it si ti

gissw swigs swig wigs sis wig wis is si

gist gist its sit is it si ti

gistw twigs gist swig twig wigs wits its sit wig wis wit is it si ti

gisw swig wigs wig wis is si

gisz zigs zig is si

gitw twig wig wit it ti

giw wig

giz zig

---

gj

gjlnuy jungly lung ugly gnu gun guy jug lug nu

gjmsuu jugums jugum gums jugs mugs smug gum jug jus mug mus sum mu um us

gjmuu jugum gum jug mug mu um

gjo jog go jo

gjos jogs jog go jo os so

gjsu jugs jug jus us

gju jug

---

gk

gknsu gunks gnus gunk guns snug sung sunk gnu gun sun nu us

gknu gunk gnu gun nu

gknuy gunky gunk gnu gun guy yuk nu

gkoo gook goo go

gkoos gooks gook goos goo kos go os so

gkosw gowks gowk woks kos sow wok go os ow so

gkow gowk wok go ow

---

gl

gllloor logroll. *No 6s or 5s*

gllloors logrolls logroll. *See* **gloos lllos llors**

gllmuy glumly gully glum gull mull ugly gum guy gym lug lum mug yum mu my um

gllnoy longly golly logy long only goy log nog yon go lo no on oy

glloopty polyglot. *See* **glloy goopy loopy**

glloopwy pollywog. *See* **lloowy**

glloy golly logy log goy go lo oy

gllsu gulls gull lugs slug lug us

gllu gull lug

glluy gully gull ugly lug guy

glmnooo monolog. *See* **glnooo glmoo gmnoo**

glmnooos monologs monolog oolongs. *See* **glmoos glnooo**

glmnooot monoglot monolog. *See* **glnooo**

glmoo gloom logo loom goo log loo mog moo go lo mo om

glmoooopy pomology. *See* **glmooy**

glmoorww glowworm. *See* **glmoo gmoor glorw**

glmoos glooms gloom logos looms goos logo logs loom loos mogs moos slog smog solo goo log loo los mog moo mos oms sol go lo mo om os so

glmooy gloomy gloom logo logy loom moly goo goy gym log loo mog moo go lo mo my om oy

glmooyyz zymology. *See* **glmooy**

glmosu moguls mogul glum gums logs lugs mogs mugs slog slug slum smog smug soul sumo gum log los lug lum mog mos mug mus oms sol sou sum go lo mo mu om os so um us

glmou mogul glum gum log lug lum mog mug go lo mo mu om um

glmsuy smugly glum gums guys gyms lugs mugs slug slum smug ugly gum guy gym lug lum mug mus sly sum yum mu my um us

glmu glum gum lug lum mug mu um

glno long log nog go lo no on

glnooo oolong goon logo long loon goo log loo nog go lo no on

glnooos oolongs. *See* **glnooo gnoos gloos**

glnooosy nosology oolongs. *See* **glnooo gloooy**

glnoooty ontology. *See* **glnooo gloooy**

glnoopr prolong. *See* **loopr noopr gnopr**

glnooprs prolongs prolong. *See* **gnoprs looprs nooprs**

glnoopsy polygons polygon. *See* **gnopsy lnopsy noopsy**

glnoopy polygon. *See* **goopy lnooy loopy**

glnoprsu longspur. *See* **gnoprs gnprsu goprsu**

glnorsty strongly. *See* **gnorst**

glnorwy wrongly. *See* **glory glorw gnorw**

glnos longs logs long nogs slog song log los nog sol son go lo no on os so

glnosttu gluttons glutton. *See* **glstu gostu glnos**

glnottu glutton. *No 6s or 5s*

glnottuy gluttony glutton. *See* **gotuy nttuy gnouy**

glnpsuu unplugs. *See* **glnpuu glpsu glnsu**

glnpuu unplug gulp lung plug pung gnu gun lug pug pul pun ulu nu up

glnsu lungs slung gnus guns lugs lung slug snug sung gnu gun lug sun nu us

glnsuy snugly lungs slung gnus guns guys lugs lung slug snug sung ugly gnu gun guy lug sly sun nu us

glnu lung gnu gun lug nu

glo log go lo

gloo logo goo log loo go lo

gloopsy posology. *See* **gloooy**

glooopty topology. *See* **gloooy**

glooory orology. *See* **gloooy glory**

gloooy oology logo logy goo goy log loo go lo oy

gloooyz zoology. *See* **gloooy**

glooruy urology. *See* **glory**

gloos logos goos logo logs loos slog solo goo log loo los sol go lo os so

glop glop log lop go lo

gloppy gloppy loppy polyp glop logy plop ploy pogy goy gyp log lop ply pop go lo oy

glops glops glop logs lops slog slop log lop los sol sop go lo os so

glopstu putlogs. *See* **gloptu lopstu**

gloptu putlog poult glop glut gout gulp lout plot plug pout tolu got gut log lop lot lug out pot pug pul put tog top tug tup go lo to up ut

glorssy grossly. *See* **glossy glory gorss**

glorsw growls glows growl grows glow grow logs lows owls rows slog slow log los low owl row sol sow go lo or os ow so

glorw growl glow grow log low owl row go lo or ow

glory glory gory gyro logy lory orgy log goy go lo or oy

glos logs slog log los sol go lo os so

gloss gloss slogs logs loss slog sols log los sol go lo os so

glossy glossy gloss slogs goys logs logy loss slog sols soys goy log los sly sol soy go lo os oy so

glosw glows glow logs lows owls slog slow log los low owl sol sow go lo os ow so

glow glow log low owl go lo ow

gloy logy log goy go lo oy

glpsu gulps plugs gulp lugs plug plus pugs puls slug lug pug pul pus sup up us

glpu gulp plug lug pug pul up

glssu slugs lugs slug lug us

glstu gluts glut gust guts lugs lust slug slut tugs gut lug tug us ut

glsu lugs slug lug us

gltu glut gut lug tug ut

glu lug

gluy ugly lug guy

gmmpsuuw mugwumps mugwump. *See* **mmpsu**

gmmpuuw mugwump. *No 6s or 5s*

gmmuy gummy gum guy gym mug mum yum mu my um

gmnnoo gnomon mongo goon mono moon noon goo mog mon moo nog go mo no om on

gmnnoos gnomons. *See* **gmnnoo gnoos mnoos**

gmnoo mongo goon mono moon goo mog mon moo nog go mo no om on

gmnost mongst tongs mogs mons most mots nogs smog snot song togs toms tong tons got mog mon mos mot nog not oms son sot tog tom ton go mo no om on os so to

gmnosu mungos mungo muons gnus gums guns mogs mons mugs muon nogs nous onus smog smug snug song sumo sung gnu gum gun mog mon mos mug mus nog oms son sou sum sun go mo mu no nu om on os so um us

gmnou mungo muon gnu gum gun mog mon mug nog go mo mu no nu om on um

gmo mog go mo om

gmoopr pogrom groom promo goop moor poor prog prom romp room goo mog moo mop mor pro go mo om or

gmooprs pogroms. *See* **gmoors gmoopr mooprs**

gmoor groom moor room goo mog moo mor go mo om or

gmoors grooms groom moors rooms sorgo goos mogs moor moos mors room smog goo mog moo mor mos oms go mo om or os so

gmos mogs smog mog mos oms go mo om os so

gmoss smogs mogs moss smog mog mos oms go mo om os so

gmprsu grumps grump rumps grum gums mugs pugs rugs rump rums smug spur sump umps gum mug mus pug pus rug rum sum sup ump mu um up us

gmpru grump grum rump gum mug pug rug rum ump mu um up

gmpruy grumpy grump grum rump gum guy gym gyp mug pry pug rug rum ump yum yup mu my um up

gmpssuy gypsums. *See* **gmpsuy gssuy mssuy**

gmpsuy gypsum spumy gums guys gyms gyps mugs pugs smug sump umps yups gum guy gym gyp mug mus pug pus spy sum sup ump yum yup mu my um up us

gmpyy pygmy gym gyp my

gmru grum gum mug rug rum mu um
gmruyyz zymurgy. *No 6s or 5s*
gmsu gums mugs smug gum mug mus sum mu um us

gmsy gyms gym my
gmu gum mug mu um
gmy gym my

---

gn

gnnsuu unsung gnus guns nuns snug sung sunn gnu gun nun sun nu us
gnnuy gunny gnu gun guy nun nu
gno nog go no on
gnoo goon nog goo go no on
gnooss gossoon. *See* **gnoos gnoss**
gnoosss gossoons gossoon. *See* **gnoos gnoss**
gnoortuw outgrown outgrow outworn. *See* **gortu gnorw gnrtu**
gnoos goons goon goos nogs song soon goo nog son go no on os so
gnoppsu oppugns popguns. *See* **gnoppu**
gnoppu oppugn popgun pung upon gnu gun nog pop pug pun pup go no nu on up
gnopr prong prog nog nor pro go no on or
gnoprs prongs prong progs nogs pons porh prog pros song nog nor pro son sop go no on or os so
gnoprsuw grownups grownup. *See* **gnoprs gnorsw gnprsu goprsu**
gnopruw grownup. *See* **gopru gnorw gnopr**
gnopsy spongy goys gyps nogs nosy pogy pons pony posy song goy gyp nog son sop soy spy yon go no on os oy so

gnorst strong grots snort tongs grot nogs orts rots snot song sort togs tong tons torn tors got nog nor not ort rot son sot tog ton tor go no on or os so to
gnorsw wrongs gowns grown grows sworn wrong gown grow nogs owns rows snow song sown worn nog nor now own row son sow won go no on or os ow so
gnorw grown wrong gown grow worn nog nor now own row won go no on or ow
gnos nogs song nog son go no on os so
gnoss songs nogs song sons nog son go no on os so
gnost tongs nogs snot song togs tong tons got nog not son sot tog ton go no on os so to
gnosw gowns gown nogs owns snow song sown nog now own son sow won go no on os ow so
gnot tong got nog not tog ton go no on to
gnouy young gnu goy gun guy nog yon you go no nu on oy
gnow gown nog now own won go no on ow
gnprsu sprung pungs rungs spurn gnus guns pugs pung puns rugs rung runs

snug spun spur sung urns gnu gun pug pun pus rug run sun sup urn nu up us
gnpsu pungs gnus guns pugs pung puns snug spun sung gnu gun pug pun pus sun sup nu up us
gnpu pung gnu gun pug pun nu up
gnrstu grunts strung grunt rungs runts stung turns gnus guns gust guts nuts rugs rung runs runt rust ruts snug stun sung tugs tuns turn urns gnu gun gut nut rug run rut sun tug tun urn nu us ut
gnrsu rungs gnus guns rugs rung runs snug sung urns gnu gun rug run sun urn nu us
gnrtu grunt rung runt turn gnu gun gut nut rug run rut tug tun urn nu ut
gnru rung gnu gun rug run urn nu
gnruw wrung rung gnu gun rug run urn nu
gnstu stung gnus guns gust guts nuts snug stun sung tugs tuns gnu gun gut nut sun tug tun nu us ut
gnsu gnus guns snug sung gnu gun sun nu us
gnsuw swung gnus guns snug sung gnu gun sun nu us
gnu gnu gun nu

---

go

go go
goo goo go
goop goop goo go
goops goops goop goos oops goo sop go os so
goopy goopy goop pogy goo goy gyp go oy
goors sorgo goos goo go or os so
goorss sorgos sorgo gross goos goo go or os so

goorstuw outgrows outgrow. *See* **gorstu oorstu**
goortt grotto grot root roto toot tort trot goo got ort rot tog too tor tot go or to
goortuw outgrow. *See* **gootu gortu**
goorvy groovy gory gyro orgy goo goy go or oy
goos goos goo go os so
gootu outgo gout goo got gut out tog too tug go to ut
gopr prog pro go or

goprs progs prog pros pro sop go or os so
goprsu groups group pours progs opus ours pour prog pros pugs rugs soup sour spur our pro pug pus rug sop sou sup go or os so up us
gopru group prog pour our pro pug rug go or up
gopry porgy gory gyro orgy pogy prog ropy goy gyp pro pry go or oy
gopy pogy goy gyp go oy
gorss gross go or os so

471

gorst grots grot orts rots sort togs tors got ort rot sot tog tor go or os so to

gorsttu rotguts. *See* **gorstu gorttu orsttu**

gorstu grouts gouts grots grout gusto roust routs stour torus tours gout grot gust guts orts ours oust outs rots rout rugs rust ruts sort sour togs tors tour tugs got gut ort our out rot rug rut sot sou tog tor tug go or os so to us ut

gorstuy yogurts. *See* **gorstu gostuy gortuy**

gorsw grows grow rows row sow go or os ow so

gorsy gyros gory goys gyro orgy rosy goy soy go or os oy so

gorsz grosz go or os so

gort grot got ort rot tog tor go or to

gorttu rotgut grout trout tutor gout grot rout tort tour tout trot got gut ort our out rot rug rut tog tor tot tug tut go or to ut

gortu grout gout grot rout tour got gut ort our out rot rug rut tog tor tug go or to ut

gortuy yogurt gouty grout guyot gory gout grot gyro orgy rout ryot tour troy tyro your yurt got goy gut guy ort our out rot rug rut tog tor toy try tug you go or oy to ut

gorw grow row go or ow

gory gory gyro orgy goy go or oy

gost togs got sot tog go os so to

gostu gouts gusto gout gust guts oust outs togs tugs got gut out sot sou tog tug go os so to us ut

gostuy guyots gouts gouty gusto gusty gutsy guyot stogy gout goys gust guts guys oust outs togs toys tugs got goy gut guy out sot sou soy sty tog toy tug you go os oy so to us ut

gosty stogy goys togs toys got goy sot soy sty tog toy go os oy so to

gosy goys goy soy go os oy so

got got tog go to

gotu gout got gut out tog tug go to ut

gotuy gouty guyot gout got goy gut guy out tog toy tug you go oy to ut

goy goy go oy

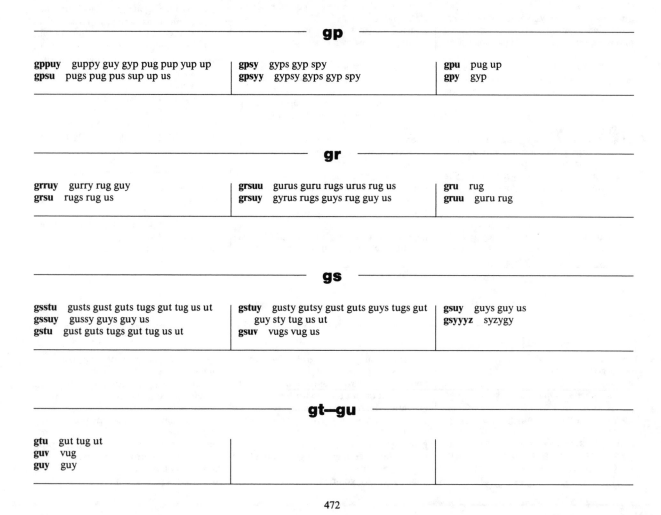

gp

gppuy guppy guy gyp pug pup yup up
gpsu pugs pug pus sup up us

gpsy gyps gyp spy
gpsyy gypsy gyps gyp spy

gpu pug up
gpy gyp

gr

grruy gurry rug guy
grsu rugs rug us

grsuu gurus guru rugs urus rug us
grsuy gyrus rugs guys rug guy us

gru rug
gruu guru rug

gs

gsstu gusts gust guts tugs gut tug us ut
gssuy gussy guys guy us
gstu gust guts tugs gut tug us ut

gstuy gusty gutsy gust guts guys tugs gut guy sty tug us ut
gsuv vugs vug us

gsuy guys guy us
gsyyyz syzygy

gt—gu

gtu gut tug ut
guv vug
guy guy

hh

hhiipsst phthisis. *See* **hipss ipsst iipst**
hhiistw whitish. *See* **hhisw histw**
hhimmoss mishmosh. *See* **himss**
hhiopst hipshot. *See* **hiost hopst iopst**
hhiorsst shortish. *See* **hiosst hirsst horsst**
hhisw whish wish his wis hi is sh si
hhmpu humph hump huh hum hup ump mu um up

hhmrsty rhythms. *See* **hhmrty hmsty**
hhmrty rhythm myth thy try my
hhoosstt hotshots hotshot. *See* **hoosst**
hhoostt hotshot. *See* **hoost hoott oostt**
hhoosw whoosh woosh oohs shoo show woos how oho ohs ooh sow who woo ho oh os ow sh so

hhrstu thrush hurst hurts hurt hush huts rush rust ruth ruts shut thru thus tush huh hut rut sh us ut
hhssu shush hush huh sh us
hhsu hush huh sh us
hhu huh

hi

hi hi
hiiilmns nihilism. *See* **hiimns**
hiiilnst nihilist. *See* **iilnst**
hiiilnty nihility. *See* **hilnty**
hiijkns hijinks. *See* **hikns ijkns**
hiikmrss skirmish. *See* **hikrss ikmrss**
hiiknps kinship pinkish. *See* **hikns iknps**
hiikoprs piroshki. *See* **hkops koprs hikrs**
hiiksstt skittish. *See* **iksst iistt**
hiilmost homilist. *See* **hiimst hilmos hilost iilmst**
hiilmpsy impishly. *See* **hiimps hlmpsy ilmpsy**
hiilmtuy humility. *See* **hilmu iilmu iilmt**
hiilpssy syphilis. *See* **hlpssy**
hiilpty pithily. *See* **hipty**
hiimns minish hins nims nisi shim shin him hin his mis nim sin hi in is mi sh si
hiimnstt tinsmith shittim. *See* **hiimns hi-imst**
hiimps impish hips imps pish shim ship simp him hip his imp mis sip hi is mi pi sh si
hiimpsw wimpish. *See* **hiimps himsw hipsw**
hiimst isthmi smith hist hits mist shim sith this him his hit its mis sit hi is it mi sh si ti
hiimstt shittim. *See* **hiimst imstt iistt**
hiinssw swinish. *See* **hinss hissw**
hiintw within hint thin twin whit with hin hit nit tin win wit hi in it ti
hiitzz zizith zizit ziti hit zit hi it ti
hijos shoji josh his ohs hi ho is jo oh os sh si so
hijoss shojis shoji hiss josh joss his ohs sis hi ho is jo oh os sh si so
hiklsuy huskily. *See* **hklsu hkluy hksuy**
hikmnos monkish. *See* **hknos iknos hikns**

hiknnor inkhorn. *See* **hinor**
hiknnors inkhorns inkhorn. *See* **hiknrs hinors**
hiknottu outthink. *See* **hiknt knotu**
hiknrs shrink knish rinks shirk hins inks irks kris rink risk shin sink skin hin his ink irk kin kir sin sir ski hi in is sh si
hiknrss shrinks. *See* **hiknrs hikrss**
hikns knish hins inks shin sink skin hin his ink kin sin ski hi in is sh si
hiknst thinks hints knish knits stink think hins hint hist hits inks kist kith kits knit nits shin sink sith skin skit snit thin this tink tins hin his hit ink its kin kit nit sin sit ski tin tsk hi in is it sh si ti
hiknt think hint kith knit thin hin hit ink kin kit nit tin hi in it ti
hikopssy kyphosis. *See* **hopssy**
hikrs shirk irks kris risk his irk kir sir ski hi is sh si
hikrss shirks shirk risks hiss irks kiss kris risk sirs skis his irk kir sir sis ski hi is sh si
hikssw whisks whisk swish hiss kiss skis wish his sis ski wis hi is sh si
hiksw whisk wish his ski wis hi is sh si
hikswy whisky whisk wish shy ski sky why wis hi is sh si
hikt kith hit kit hi it ti
hill hill ill hi li
hillmsuy mulishly mushily. *See* **hilmsu hllsuy**
hillopst hilltops hilltop. *See* **hillst hilops hilost hilpst**
hillopt hilltop. *See* **hilot ilopt hillt**
hilloy holily hilly holly hill holy illy lily oily hoy ill oil hi ho li lo oh oy

hillrs shrill hills rills shill hill rill sill his ill sir hi is li sh si
hillrss shrills. *See* **hillrs hillss**
hillrst thrills. *See* **hillrs hillst hilrst hillrt illrst**
hillrsy shrilly. *See* **hillrs hilly illsy**
hillrt thrill thill thirl trill hill hilt lilt rill till hit ill lit til hi it li ti
hills hills shill hill sill his ill hi is li sh si
hillss shills hills shill sills hill hiss sill his ill sis hi is li sh si
hillst thills hills hilts lilts shill still thill tills hill hilt hist hits lilt list sill silt sith slit this till tils his hit ill its lit ist til hi is it li sh si ti
hillt thill hill hilt lilt till hit ill lit til hi it li ti
hilly hilly hill illy lily ill hi li
hilmnoot monolith moonlit. *See* **ilnoot imnoot**
hilmos holism holms limos moils holm limo mhos milo mils moil ohms oils shim silo slim soil him his los mho mil mis mos ohm ohs oil oms sol hi ho is li lo mi mo oh om os sh si so
hilmosw wholism. *See* **hilmos hilosw**
hilmoy homily holm holy homy limo limy milo moil moly oily him hoy mho mil ohm oil hi ho li lo mi mo my oh om oy
hilmprtu philtrum triumph. *See* **hilmu himrt hilrt**
hilmpsu lumpish. *See* **hilmsu hmpsu ilmps**
hilmstuu thuliums thulium. *See* **hilmsu ilmstu**
hilmsu mulish hilum hums lush mils mush shim slim slum him his hum lum

mil mis mus sum hi is li mi mu sh si um us

hilmsuy mushily. *See* **hilmsu hmsuy ilmsy**

hilmtuu thulium. *See* **hilmu**

hilmu hilum him hum lum mil hi li mi mu um

hilnnty ninthly. *See* **hilnty hinny hinnt**

hilnory hornily. *See* **hnory inory hinor**

hilnpt plinth hilt hint lint pint thin hin hip hit lip lit nil nip nit pin pit til tin tip hi in it li pi ti

hilnty thinly linty hilt hint inly lint liny thin tiny hin hit lit nil nit thy til tin yin hi in it li ti

hiloopyz zoophily. *See* **ilooyz**

hilops polish polis spoil hips holp hops lips lisp lops oils pish pois posh ship shop silo slip slop soil soph hip his hop lip lop los ohs oil poi sip sol sop hi ho is li lo oh os pi sh si so

hilopxy oxyphil. *See* **hlopx ilopx**

hilosst holists. *See* **hiosst hilost hlosst**

hilost holist lithos hilts hoist holts litho sloth toils hilt hist hits holt host hots list lost loth lots oils shot silo silt sith slit slot soil this tils toil tosh his hit hot its lit los lot ohs oil sit sol sot tho til hi ho is it li lo oh os sh si so ti to

hilostu loutish. *See* **hilost**

hilosw owlish howls howl lows oils owls show silo slow soil wish his how los low ohs oil owl sol sow who wis hi ho is li lo oh os ow sh si so

hilot litho hilt holt loth toil hit hot lit lot oil tho til hi ho it li lo oh ti to

hilpprsu purplish. *See* **hippsu ilppsu**

hilpsst spilths. *See* **hilpst ilpsst**

hilpst spilth hilts spilt split hilt hips hist hits lips lisp list pish pits ship silt sith slip slit spit this tils tips hip his hit its lip lit pit sip sit til tip hi is it li pi sh si ti

hilrst thirls hilts shirt thirl hilt hist hits list silt sith slit stir this tils his hit its lit sir sit til hi is it li sh si ti

hilrsw whirls swirl whirl whirs whir wish his sir wis hi is li sh si

hilrt thirl hilt hit lit til hi it li ti

hilrw whirl whir hi li

hilssttu sluttish lutists. *See* **hilstt ilsstt ilsttu**

hilssty stylish. *See* **hilst ilsst ilssy**

hilst hilts hilt hist hits list silt sith slit this tils his hit its lit sit til hi is it li sh si ti

hilstt tilths hilts stilt tilth tilts hilt hist hits list sith slit this tils tilt tits his hit its lit sit til tit hi is it li sh si ti

hilstw whilst hilts whist whits wilts hilt hist hits list silt sith slit this tils whit wilt wish with wits his hit its lit sit til wis wit hi is it li sh si ti

hilt hilt hit lit til hi it li ti

hiltt tilth hilt tilt hit lit til tit hi it li ti

him him hi mi

himmsy shimmy shim him his mim mis shy hi is mi my sh si

himnoy hominy homy hymn yoni him hin hon hoy ion mho mon nim ohm yin yon hi ho in mi mo my no oh om on oy

himnssty hymnists hymnist. *See* **himsst himsty**

himnsty hymnist. *See* **himsty hinst hmnsy**

himops mopish hips hops imps mhos mops ohms pish pois posh shim ship shop simp soph him hip his hop imp mho mis mop mos ohm ohs oms poi sip sop hi ho is mi mo oh om os pi sh si so

himopss sophism. *See* **himops himss hipss**

himopsss sophisms sophism. *See* **himops**

himorstu humorist thoriums thorium tourism. *See* **hiorsu hmorsu hmostu hmrstu**

himortu thorium. *See* **hioru hmoru himrt**

himotty timothy. *See* **hmoty**

himprs shrimp prism hips imps mirs pish prim rims rips shim ship simp him hip his imp mir mis rim rip sip sir hi is mi pi sh si

himprss shrimps. *See* **himprs imprss**

himprstu triumphs triumph. *See* **himprs hmpstu hmrstu imprsu**

himprtu triumph. *See* **himrt hmrtu hmptu**

himrt mirth trim him hit mir rim hi it mi ti

hims shim him his mis hi is mi sh si

himss shims hiss miss shim him his mis sis hi is mi sh si

himsst smiths mists shims smith hiss hist hits miss mist shim sith sits this him his hit its mis sis sit hi is it mi sh si ti

himsstu isthmus. *See* **himsst msstu hsstu**

himst smith hist hits mist shim sith this him his hit its mis sit hi is it mi sh si ti

himsty smithy misty myths smith hist hits mist myth shim sith this him his hit its mis shy sit sty thy hi is it mi my sh si ti

himsw whims shim swim whim wish him his mis wis hi is mi sh si

himswy whimsy whims shim swim whim wish him his mis shy why wis hi is mi my sh si

himw whim him hi mi

hin hin hi in

hinnnsu nunnish. *No 6s or 5s*

hinnorst tinhorns tinhorn. *See* **hinnst hinors hnorst**

hinnort tinhorn. *See* **hinnt hnort hinor**

hinnssuy sunshiny. *See* **hinnsy**

hinnst ninths ninth hints hins hint hist hits inns nits shin sith snit thin this tins hin his hit inn its nit sin sit tin hi in is it sh si ti

hinnsy shinny hinny shiny hins inns shin hin his inn shy sin yin hi in is sh si

hinnt ninth hint thin hin hit inn nit tin hi in it ti

hinnwy whinny hinny whiny winy hin inn why win yin hi in

hinny hinny hin inn yin hi in

hinoorst hornitos hornito torsion. *See* **hinors hnoors hnorst**

hinoorsz horizons horizon. *See* **hinors hnoors**

hinoort hornito. *See* **hnoor hoort**

hinoorz horizon. *See* **hinor hnoor**

hinops siphon hins hips hops ions nips nosh pins pish pois pons posh shin ship shop snip soph spin hin hip his hon hop ion nip ohs pin poi sin sip son sop hi ho in is no oh on os pi sh si so

hinopss siphons. *See* **hinops hinss hipss**

hinopssy hypnosis siphons syphons. *See* **hinops hnopsy hopssy**

hinopstw township. *See* **hinops inopst**

hinor rhino horn iron hin hon ion nor rho hi ho in no oh on or

hinors rhinos horns irons rhino rosin shorn hins horn ions iron nosh rhos shin sori hin his hon ion nor ohs rho sin sir son hi ho in is no oh on or os sh si so

hinorsu nourish. *See* **hiorsu hinrsu hnorsu hinors**

hinppssu pushpins pushpin. *See* **hinpsu hippsu inppsu**

hinppsu pushpin. *See* **inppsu hinpsu hippsu**

hinpsu punish hins hips nips pins pish puns push shin ship shun snip spin spun hin hip his hup nip pin pun pus sin sip sun sup hi in is nu pi sh si up us

hinpsx sphinx hins hips nips pins pish shin ship snip spin hin hip his nip nix pin pix sin sip six hi in is pi sh si xi

hinrsu inrush ruins hins ruin runs rush shin shun urns hin his run sin sir sun urn hi in is nu sh si us

hins hins shin hin his sin hi in is sh si

hinss shins hins hiss shin sins hin his sin sis hi in is sh si

hinst hints hins hint hist hits nits shin sith snit thin this tins hin his hit its nit sin sit tin hi in is it sh si ti

hinsy shiny hins shin hin his shy sin yin hi in is sh si

hint hint thin hin hit nit tin hi in it ti

hinwy whiny winy hin why win yin hi in

hiopp hippo hip hop pip poi pop hi ho oh pi

hiopps hippos hippo hips hops pips pish pois pops posh ship shop soph hip his hop ohs pip poi pop sip sop hi ho is oh os pi sh si so

hioprssw worships worship. *See* **iprss oprsw hipss**

hioprsw worship. *See* **oprsw hipsw hirsw**

hiopssst sophists sophist. *See* **hiosst iopsst**

hiopsst sophist. *See* **hiosst iopsst**

hiorsty history. *See* **horsty hiost iorst**

hiorsu houris houri hours hour ours rhos rush sori sour his ohs our rho sir sou hi ho is oh or os sh si so us

hioru houri hour rho our hi ho oh or

hiosst hoists hoist hosts shots hiss hist hits host hots shot sith sits sots this tosh toss his hit hot its ohs sis sit sot tho hi ho is it oh os sh si so ti to

hiosstt sottish. *See* **hiosst**

hiost hoist hist hits host hots shot sith this tosh his hit hot its ohs sit sot tho hi ho is it oh os sh si so ti to

hiottuw without. *See* **iottuw**

hip hip hi pi

hippsu uppish hips pips pish pups push ship hip his hup pip pup pus sip sup hi is pi sh si up us

hippy hippy pipy hip pip yip hi pi

hips hips pish ship hip his sip hi is pi sh si

hipss ships hips hiss pish ship sips hip his sip sis hi is pi sh si

hipsw whips hips pish ship whip wish wisp hip his sip wis hi is pi sh si

hiptw whipt whip whit with hip hit pit tip wit hi it pi ti

hipty pithy pity hip hit pit thy tip yip hi it pi ti

hipw whip hip hi pi

hiqssu squish sushi hiss his sis hi is sh si us

hiqssuy squishy. *See* **hiqssu hssuy**

hirrs shirr hiss hir hi is sh si

hirrss shirrs shirr hiss sirs his sir sis hi is sh si

hirsst shirts shirt stirs hiss hist hits sirs sith sits stir this his hit its sir sis sit hi is it sh si ti

hirsstt thirsts. *See* **hirsst hirstt**

hirst shirt hist hits sith stir this his hit its sir sit hi is it sh si ti

hirstt thirst shirt hist hits sith stir this tits his hit its sir sit tit hi is it sh si ti

hirsttu ruttish. *See* **hirstt hrsttu**

hirstty thirsty. *See* **histty hirstt hirtty**

hirsw whirs whir wish his sir wis hi is sh si

hirtty thirty hit thy tit try hi it ti

hirw whir hi

his his hi is sh si

hiss hiss his sis hi is sh si

hisstw whists swish whist whits hiss hist hits sith sits this whit wish with wits his hit its sis sit wis wit hi is it sh si ti

hisstx sixths sixth hiss hist hits sith sits this his hit its sis sit six hi is it sh si ti xi

hissu sushi hiss his sis hi is sh si us

hissv shivs hiss shiv his sis hi is sh si

hissw swish hiss wish his sis wis hi is sh si

hisswy swishy swish hiss wish his shy sis why wis hi is sh si

hist hist hits sith this his hit its sit hi is it sh si ti

histty stithy hist hits sith this tits his hit its shy sit sty thy tit hi is it sh si ti

histw whist whits hist hits sith this whit wish with wits his hit its sit wis wit hi is it sh si ti

histx sixth hist hits sith this his hit its sit six hi is it sh si ti xi

hisv shiv his hi is sh si

hisw wish his wis hi is sh si

hit hit hi it ti

hitw whit with hit wit hi it ti

hitwy withy whit with hit thy why wit hi it ti

hiwz whiz hi

hiwzz whizz whiz hi

---

hj

hjnnoy johnny john hon hoy joy yon ho jo no oh on oy

hjno john hon ho jo no oh on

hjnos johns john josh nosh hon ohs son ho jo no oh on os sh so

hjos josh ohs ho jo oh os sh so

---

hk

hkklooz kolkhoz. *No 6s or 5s*

hkkou hokku ho oh

hklo kohl ho lo oh

hklos kohls kohl kos los ohs sol ho lo oh os sh so

hklsu hulks hulk husk lush sulk sh us

hklu hulk

hkluy hulky hulk yuk

hkmosu khoums hokum hums husk mhos mush musk ohms sumo hum kos mho mos mus ohm ohs oms sou sum ho mo mu oh om os sh so um us

hkmou hokum hum mho ohm ho mo mu oh om um

hkno honk hon ho no oh on

hknoos shnook honks hooks nooks shook honk hook nook nosh oohs shoo soon hon kos oho ohs ooh son ho no oh on os sh so

hknooss shnooks. *See* **hknoos hooss**

hknoosu unhooks. *See* **hknoos hknoou**

hknoou unhook honk hook hunk nook hon oho ooh ho no nu oh on

hknos honks honk nosh hon kos ohs son ho no oh on os sh so

hknoy honky honk hon hoy yon ho no oh on oy

hknrsu shrunk hunks knurs hunk husk knur runs rush rusk shun sunk urns run sun urn nu sh us

hknsu hunks hunk husk shun sunk sun nu sh us
hknu hunk nu
hkoo hook oho ooh ho oh
hkooopst pothooks pothook. *See* **hoopst**
hkooopt pothook. *See* **hoopt**
hkooprsw workshop. *See* **hoopsw**

hkoopsu hookups. *See* **hkoopu hkoos hoops**
hkoopu hookup hook hoop koph pooh hop hup oho ooh ho oh up
hkoos hooks shook hook oohs shoo kos oho ohs ooh ho oh os sh so
hkooy hooky hook hoy oho ooh ho oh oy

hkop koph hop ho oh
hkops kophs hops koph posh shop soph hop kos ohs sop ho oh os sh so
hkssu husks husk sh us
hksu husk sh us
hksuy husky husk yuks shy sky yuk sh us

---

hl

hllloowy hollowly. *See* **hlloow hllowy**
hlloo hollo loo oho ooh ho lo oh
hlloos hollos hollo loos oohs shoo solo loo los oho ohs ooh sol ho lo oh os sh so
hlloosw hollows. *See* **hlloos hlloow**
hlloow hollow hollo howl wool how loo low oho ooh owl who woo ho lo oh ow
hllosu hullos hullo hulls hull lush soul los ohs sol sou ho lo oh os sh so us
hllou hullo hull ho lo oh
hllowy wholly holly lowly holy howl yowl how hoy low owl who why yow ho lo oh ow oy
hlloy holly holy hoy ho lo oh oy
hllsu hulls hull lush sh us
hllsuy lushly hulls sully hull lush shy sly sh us
hllu hull
hlmnoty monthly. *See* **hlmoty hmnot**
hlmo holm mho ohm ho lo mo oh om
hlmoos sholom holms looms holm homo loom loos mhos moos ohms oohs shoo solo loo los mho moo mos ohm oho ohs oms ooh sol ho lo mo oh om os sh so
hlmoosty smoothly. *See* **hlmoos hlmoty hmoost hmosty**
hlmos holms holm mhos ohms los mho mos ohm ohs oms sol ho lo mo oh om os sh so
hlmoty thymol hotly mothy holm holt holy homy loth molt moly moth myth

hot hoy lot mho mot ohm tho thy tom toy ho lo mo my oh om oy to
hlmpsy lymphs lymph sylph ply shy sly spy sh my
hlmpuy phylum humpy lumpy lymph hump lump plum hum hup lum ply pul ump yum yup mu my um up
hlmpy lymph ply my
hlnouy unholy holy only hon hoy yon you ho lo no nu oh on oy
hlop holp hop lop ho lo oh
hlopsy poshly hypos ploys sylph holp holy hops hoys hypo lops ploy posh posy shop slop soph hop hoy lop los ohs ply shy sly sol sop soy spy ho lo oh os oy sh so
hlopx phlox holp hop lop lox pox ho lo oh ox
hlorsty shortly. *See* **horsty hlost hloty**
hlorsw whorls whorl howls howl lows owls rhos rows show slow how los low ohs owl rho row sol sow who ho lo oh or os ow sh so
hloruy hourly hurly holy hour hurl lory your hoy our rho you ho lo oh or oy
hlorw whorl howl how low owl rho row who ho lo oh or ow
hloss slosh loss sols los ohs sol ho lo oh os sh so
hlosst sloths holts hosts shots slosh sloth slots holt host hots loss lost loth lots shot slot sols sots tosh toss hot los lot ohs sol sot tho ho lo oh os sh so to

hlossy sloshy slosh holy hoys loss sols soys hoy los ohs shy sly sol soy ho lo oh os oy sh so
hlost holts sloth holt host hots lost loth lots shot slot tosh hot los lot ohs sol sot tho ho lo oh os sh so to
hlosw howls howl lows owls show slow how los low ohs owl sol sow who ho lo oh os ow sh so
hlot holt loth hot lot tho ho lo oh to
hloty hotly holt holy loth hot hoy lot tho thy toy ho lo oh oy to
hlow howl how low owl who ho lo oh ow
hloy holy hoy ho lo oh oy
hlprssuu sulphurs sulphur surplus. *See* **lprssu prssuu**
hlprsuu sulphur. *See* **hlrsu lpsuu hlpsu**
hlpssy sylphs sylph ply shy sly spy sh
hlpsu plush lush plus puls push hup pul pus sup sh up us
hlpsy sylph ply shy sly spy sh
hlrsu hurls hurl lush rush slur sh us
hlru hurl
hlruy hurly hurl
hlssu slush lush sh us
hlssuy slushy slush hussy lush shy sly sh us
hlstuy thusly lusty huts lush lust shut slut thus tush hut shy sly sty thy sh us ut
hlsu lush sh us
hlsyy shyly shy sly sh

---

hm

hmmnoosy homonyms homonym. *See* **hmnsy hnosy mnoos**
hmmnooy homonym. *See* **mnooy**

hmmoorsu mushroom. *See* **hmorsu**
hmmsuu hummus humus hums mums mush hum mum mus sum mu sh um us

hmnooost moonshot. *See* **hmnost hmoost**
hmnopsy nymphos. *See* **hmnopy hmnpsy hnopsy**

hmnopsyy symphony nymphos. *See* **hmnopy hmnpsy hnopsy**

hmnopy nympho nymph phony homy hymn hypo pony hon hop hoy mho mon mop ohm yon ho mo my no oh om on oy

hmnost months month moths host hots mhos mons most moth mots nosh ohms shot snot toms tons tosh hon hot mho mon mos mot not ohm ohs oms son sot tho tom ton ho mo no oh om on os sh so to

hmnot month moth hon hot mho mon mot not ohm tho tom ton ho mo no oh om on to

hmnpsy nymphs nymph hymns hymn shy spy sh my

hmnpy nymph hymn my

hmnsy hymns hymn shy sh my

hmny hymn my

hmo mho ohm ho mo oh om

hmoo homo mho moo ohm oho ooh ho mo oh om

hmooorsw showroom. *See* **moors hoosw morsw**

hmoop oomph homo hoop pooh hop mho moo mop ohm oho ooh ho mo oh om

hmoorsuu humorous. *See* **hmorsu**

hmoosst smooths. *See* **hmoost hoosst**

hmoost smooth hoots moots moths shoot sooth homo hoot host hots mhos moos moot most moth mots ohms oohs shoo shot soot toms tosh hot mho moo mos mot ohm oho ohs oms ooh sot tho tom too ho mo oh om os sh so to

hmopr morph prom romp hop mho mop mor ohm pro rho ho mo oh om or

hmoprs morphs morph proms romps hops mhos mops mors ohms posh prom pros rhos romp shop soph hop mho mop mor mos ohm ohs oms pro rho sop ho mo oh om or os sh so

hmopsw whomps whomp whops hops mhos mops mows ohms posh shop show soph swop whom whop hop how mho mop mos mow ohm ohs oms sop sow who ho mo oh om os ow sh so

hmopw whomp whom whop hop how mho mop mow ohm who ho mo oh om ow

hmorsu humors mohurs hours humor mohur hour hums mhos mors mush ohms ours rhos rums rush sour sumo hum mho mor mos mus ohm ohs oms our rho rum sou sum ho mo mu oh om or os sh so um us

hmoru humor mohur hour hum mho mor ohm our rho rum ho mo mu oh om or um

hmos mhos ohms mho mos ohm ohs oms ho mo oh om os sh so

hmost moths host hots mhos most moth mots ohms shot toms tosh hot mho mos mot ohm ohs oms sot tho tom ho mo oh om os sh so to

hmostu mouths moths mouth shout south host hots hums huts mhos most moth mots mush must ohms oust outs shot shut smut stum sumo thou thus toms tosh tush hot hum hut mho mos mot mus ohm ohs oms out sot sou sum tho tom ho mo mu oh om os sh so to um us ut

hmosty mythos moths mothy myths homy host hots hoys mhos most moth mots myth ohms shot toms tosh toys hot hoy mho mos mot ohm ohs oms shy sot soy sty tho thy tom toy ho mo my oh om os oy sh so to

hmot moth hot mho mot ohm tho tom ho mo oh om to

hmotu mouth moth thou hot hum hut mho mot ohm out tho tom ho mo mu oh om to um ut

hmotuy mouthy mothy mouth youth homy moth myth thou hot hoy hum hut mho mot ohm out tho thy tom toy you yum ho mo mu my oh om oy to um ut

hmoty mothy homy moth myth hot hoy mho mot ohm tho thy tom toy ho mo my oh om oy to

hmow whom how mho mow ohm who ho mo oh om ow

hmoy homy hoy mho ohm ho mo my oh om oy

hmpruy murphy humpy hump rump hum hup pry rum ump yum yup mu my um up

hmpstu thumps humps stump thump tumps hump hums huts mush must push puts shut smut stum sump thus tump tups tush umps hum hup hut mus pus put sum sup tup ump mu sh um up us ut

hmpsu humps hump hums mush push sump umps hum hup mus pus sum sup ump mu sh um up us

hmpsuw whumps humps whump hump hums mush push sump swum umps hum hup mus pus sum sup ump mu sh um up us

hmptu thump hump tump hum hup hut put tup ump mu um up ut

hmpu hump hum hup ump mu um up

hmpuw whump hump hum hup ump mu um up

hmpuy humpy hump hum hup ump yum yup mu my um up

hmrrsy myrrhs myrrh shy sh my

hmrry myrrh my

hmrstu thrums hurst hurts strum thrum hums hurt huts mush must rums rush rust ruth ruts shut smut stum thru thus tush hum hut mus rum rut sum mu sh um us ut

hmrtu thrum hurt ruth thru hum hut rum rut mu um ut

hmstuy thymus mushy musty myths hums huts mush must myth shut smut stum thus tush hum hut mus shy sty sum thy yum mu my sh um us ut

hmsty myths myth shy sty thy sh my

hmsu hums mush hum mus sum mu sh um us

hmsuu humus hums mush hum mus sum mu sh um us

hmsuy mushy hums mush hum mus shy sum yum mu my sh um us

hmty myth thy my

hmu hum mu um

hn

hno   hon ho no oh on

hnoopst   photons. *See* **hnoopt hoopst**

hnoopsty   typhoons photons toyshop typhoon. *See* **hnoopt hnopsy hoopst noopsy**

hnoopt   photon photo hoop hoot onto phot pooh poon toon hon hop hot not oho ooh pot tho ton too top ho no oh on to

hnoopty   typhoon. *See* **hnoopt hnopy nooty**

hnoor   honor horn hon nor oho ooh rho ho no oh on or

hnoorrtw   hornwort. *See* **hnortw**

hnoors   honors honor horns shorn horn nosh oohs rhos shoo soon hon nor oho ohs ooh rho son ho no oh on or os sh so

hnoorsu   honours. *See* **hnoors hnooru hnorsu**

hnooru   honour honor horn hour hon nor oho ooh our rho run urn ho no nu oh on or

hnoow   nohow hon how now oho ooh own who won woo ho no oh on ow

hnopssy   syphons. *See* **hnopsy hopssy**

hnopsy   syphon hypos hyson phony hops hoys hypo nosh nosy pons pony posh posy shop soph hon hop hoy ohs shy son sop soy spy yon ho no oh on os oy sh so

hnopy   phony hypo pony hon hop hoy yon ho no oh on oy

hnor   horn hon nor rho ho no oh on or

hnors   horns shorn horn nosh rhos hon nor ohs rho son ho no oh on or os sh so

hnorst   norths thorns horns horst north shorn short snort thorn horn host hots nosh orts rhos rots shot snot sort tons torn tors tosh hon hot nor not ohs ort rho rot son sot tho ton tor ho no oh on or os sh so to

hnorsty   rhytons. *See* **hnorst hnorty horsty**

hnorsu   onrush horns hours shorn horn hour nosh nous onus ours rhos runs rush shun sour urns hon nor ohs our rho run son sou sun urn ho no nu oh on or os sh so us

hnort   north thorn horn torn hon hot nor not ort rho rot tho ton tor ho no oh on or to

hnortuwy   unworthy. *See* **hnortw hnorty hortwy**

hnortw   thrown north thorn throw worth horn nowt torn town trow wont worn son sop soy spy yon ho no oh on os oy sh so

hnopy   phony hypo pony hon hop hoy yon ho no oh on oy

hnor   horn hon nor rho ho no oh on or

hon hot how nor not now ort own rho rot row tho ton tor tow two who won ho no oh on or ow to

hnorty   rhyton thorny horny north thorn horn ryot tony torn troy tyro hon hot hoy nor not ort rho rot tho thy ton tor toy try yon ho no oh on or oy to

hnory   horny horn hon hoy nor rho yon ho no oh on or oy

hnos   nosh hon ohs son ho no oh on os sh so

hnosw   shown nosh owns show snow sown hon how now ohs own son sow who won ho no oh on os ow sh so

hnosy   hyson hoys nosh nosy hon hoy ohs shy son soy yon ho no oh on os oy sh so

hnsstu   shunts hunts shuns shunt shuts stuns hunt huts nuts shun shut stun suns thus tuns tush hut nut sun tun nu sh us ut

hnssu   shuns shun suns sun nu sh us

hnstu   hunts shunt hunt huts nuts shun shut stun thus tuns tush hut nut sun tun nu sh us ut

hnsu   shun sun nu sh us

hntu   hunt hut nut tun nu ut

ho

ho   ho oh

hoo   oho ooh ho oh

hoop   hoop pooh hop oho ooh ho oh

hoops   hoops poohs hoop hops oohs oops pooh posh shoo shop soph hop oho ohs ooh sop ho oh os sh so

hoopsstt   potshots potshot. *See* **hoopst hoosst oopsst**

hoopssty   toyshops toyshop. *See* **hoopst hoosst hopssy oopsst**

hoopst   photos hoops hoots photo phots poohs shoot sooth stoop hoop hoot hops host hots oohs oops phot pooh posh post pots shoo shop shot soot soph spot stop tops tosh hop hot oho ohs ooh pot sop sot tho too top ho oh os sh so to

hoopstt   potshot. *See* **hoopst opstt hoott**

hoopsty   toyshop. *See* **hoopst hopsy opsty**

hoopsw   whoops hoops poohs swoop whoop whops woosh hoop hops oohs

oops pooh posh shoo shop show soph swop whop woos hop how oho ohs ooh sop sow who woo ho oh os ow sh so

hoopt   photo hoop hoot phot pooh hop hot oho ooh pot tho too top ho oh to

hoopw   whoop hoop pooh whop hop how oho ooh who woo ho oh ow

hoorrr   horror oho ooh rho ho oh or

hoorrrs   horrors. *See* **hoorrr**

hoort   thoro hoot root roto hot oho ooh ort rho rot tho too tor ho oh or to

hoos   oohs shoo oho ohs ooh ho oh os sh so

hooss   shoos oohs shoo oho ohs ooh ho oh os sh so

hoosst   shoots hoots hosts shoos shoot shots sooth soots hoot host hots oohs shoo shot soot sots tosh toss hot oho ohs ooh sot tho too ho oh os sh so to

hoossw   swoosh shoos shows woosh oohs shoo show sows woos how oho ohs ooh sow who woo ho oh os ow sh so

hoost   hoots shoot sooth hoot host hots oohs shoo shot soot tosh hot oho ohs ooh sot tho too ho oh os sh so to

hoosw   woosh oohs shoo show woos how oho ohs ooh sow who woo ho oh os ow sh so

hoot   hoot hot oho ooh tho too ho oh to

hoott   tooth hoot toot hot oho ooh tho too tot ho oh to

hootty   toothy tooth hoot toot hot hoy oho ooh tho thy too tot toy ho oh oy to

hop   hop ho oh

hoprsstu   hotspurs hotspur sprouts stupors upshots. *See* **hoprst hopstu horsst hosstu**

hoprst   thorps horst phots ports short sport strop thorp hops host hots orts phot port posh post pots pros rhos rots shop shot soph sort spot stop tops tors tosh hop hot ohs ort pot pro rho rot sop sot tho top tor ho oh or os sh so to

hoprstu hotspur. *See* **oprstu hoprst hopstu**

hoprt thorp phot port hop hot ort pot pro rho rot tho top tor ho oh or to

hoprty trophy thorp hypo phot port ropy ryot troy tyro hop hot hoy ort pot pro pry rho rot tho thy top tor toy try ho oh or oy to

hops hops posh shop soph hop ohs sop ho oh os sh so

hopss shops hops posh shop soph sops hop ohs sop ho oh os sh so

hopsssy hyssops. *See* **hopssy**

hopsstu upshots. *See* **hosstu opsstu**

hopssy hyssop shops hypos hops hoys hypo posh posy shop soph sops soys hop hoy ohs shy sop soy spy ho oh os oy sh so

hopst phots hops host hots phot posh post pots shop shot soph spot stop tops tosh hop hot ohs pot sop sot tho top ho oh os sh so to

hopstu upshot phots pouts shout south spout stoup hops host hots huts opus oust outs phot posh post pots pout push puts shop shot shut soph soup spot stop thou thus tops tosh tups tush hop hot hup hut ohs out pot pus put sop sot sou sup tho top tup ho oh os sh so to up us ut

hopsw whops hops posh shop show soph swop whop hop how ohs sop sow who ho oh os ow sh so

hopsy hypos hops hoys hypo posh posy shop soph hop hoy ohs shy sop soy spy ho oh os oy sh so

hopt phot hop hot pot tho top ho oh to

hopw whop hop how who ho oh ow

hopy hypo hop hoy ho oh oy

hoqstu quoths quoth shout south host hots huts oust outs shot shut thou thus tosh tush hot hut ohs out sot sou tho ho oh os sh so to us ut

hoqtu quoth thou hot hut out tho ho oh to ut

hor rho ho oh or

hors rhos rho ohs ho oh or os sh so

horsst horsts shorts horst hosts short shots sorts host hots orts rhos rots shot sort sots tors tosh toss hot ohs ort rho rot sot tho tor ho oh or os sh so to

horst horst short host hots orts rhos rots shot sort tors tosh hot ohs ort rho rot sot tho tor ho oh or os sh so to

horstt troths horst short torts troth trots host hots orts rhos rots shot sort tors tort tosh tost tots trot hot ohs ort rho rot sot tho tor tot ho oh or os sh so to

horstw throws worths horst short throw trows worst worth host hots orts rhos rots rows shot show sort stow swot tors tosh tows trow twos hot how ohs ort rho rot row sot sow tho tor tow two who ho oh or os ow sh so to

horsty shorty horst horsy ryots short story tyros host hots hoys orts rhos rosy rots ryot shot sort tors tosh toys troy tyro hot hoy ohs ort rho rot shy sot soy sty tho thy tor toy try ho oh or os oy sh so to

horsu hours hour ours rhos rush sour ohs our rho sou ho oh or os sh so us

horsy horsy hoys rhos rosy hoy ohs rho shy soy ho oh or os oy sh so

hortt troth tort trot hot ort rho rot tho tor tot ho oh or to

hortw throw worth trow hot how ort rho rot row tho tor tow two who ho oh or ow to

hortwy worthy throw worth ryot trow troy tyro hot how hoy ort rho rot row

tho thy tor tow toy try two who why yow ho oh or ow oy to

horu hour rho our ho oh or

hos ohs ho oh os sh so

hosst hosts shots host hots shot sots tosh toss hot ohs sot tho ho oh os sh so to

hossttuu shutouts shutout. *See* **hosstu ossttu**

hosstu shouts hosts ousts shots shout shuts south host hots huts oust outs shot shut sots sous thou thus tosh toss tush hot hut ohs out sot sou tho ho oh os sh so to us ut

hossw shows show sows how ohs sow who ho oh os ow sh so

host host hots shot tosh hot ohs sot tho ho oh os sh so to

hosttuu shutout. *See* **hostu ossttu sttuu**

hostu shout south host hots huts oust outs shot shut thou thus tosh tush hot hut ohs out sot sou tho ho oh os sh so to us ut

hostuy youths shout south youth host hots hoys huts oust outs shot shut thou thus tosh toys tush hot hoy hut ohs out shy sot sou soy sty tho thy toy you ho oh os oy sh so to us ut

hosw show how ohs sow who ho oh os ow sh so

hoswy showy show hoys how hoy ohs shy sow soy who why yow ho oh os ow oy sh so

hosy hoys hoy ohs shy soy ho oh os oy sh so

hot hot tho ho oh to

hotu thou hot hut out tho ho oh to ut

hotuy youth thou hot hoy hut out tho thy toy you ho oh oy to ut

how how who ho oh ow

hoy hoy ho oh oy

hpstuy typhus pushy huts push puts shut thus tups tush yups hup hut pus put shy spy sty sup thy tup yup sh up us ut

hpsu push hup pus sup sh up us

hpsuy pushy push yups hup pus shy spy sup yup sh up us

hpu hup up

hr

hrruy   hurry

hrssttu   thrusts. *See* **hrsstu rssttu hrsttu**

hrsstu   hursts hurst hurts rusts shuts truss hurt huts rush rust ruth ruts shut thru thus tush hut rut sh us ut

hrsttu   thrust truths hurst hurts strut trust truth hurt huts rush rust ruth ruts shut thru thus tush tuts hut rut tut sh us ut

hrstu   hurst hurts hurt huts rush rust ruth ruts shut thru thus tush hut rut sh us ut

hrsu   rush sh us

hrsuy   rushy rush shy sh us

hrttu   truth hurt ruth thru hut rut tut ut

hrtu   hurt ruth thru hut rut ut

hs

hs   sh

hsstu   shuts huts shut thus tush hut sh us ut

hssuy   hussy shy sh us

hstu   huts shut thus tush hut sh us ut

hsy   shy sh

ht—hw

htu   hut ut

hty   thy

hwy   why

---

ii

---

iiimmprs imprimis. *See* **imprs**
iiinqtuy iniquity. *See* **inqtu intuy**
iiirst iritis iris stir its sir sit is it si ti
iijjstuu jiujitsu jujitsu. *See* **jjsuu**
iijllno jillion. *No 6s or 5s*
iijllnos jillions jillion. *See* **ijnos ilnos illns**
iijnn jinni jinn inn in
iiklm kilim milk ilk mil li mi
iiklmnp limpkin. *See* **iiklm iklnp**
iiklmnps limpkins limpkin. *See* **iiklms iklnps**
iiklms kilims kilim milks milk mils silk skim slim ilk mil mis ski is li mi si
iiklnos oilskin. *See* **iknos iklns iklos**
iiklnoss oilskins oilskin. *See* **iiknss iklnss**
iiklqruy quirkily. *See* **ikqruy**
iiklrsy riskily. *See* **ikrsy iklsy iklrs**
iiknn kinin ink inn kin in
iiknostt stotinki. *See* **iiostt iknost**
iiknpp pipkin pink ink kin kip nip pin pip in pi
iiknpps pipkins. *See* **iiknpp iknps**
iiknss siskin sinks skins inks kiss nisi sink sins skin skis ink kin sin sis ski in is si
iiknsss siskins. *See* **iiknss**
iikst tikis kist kits skit its kit sit ski tsk is it ti
iiksw kiwis kiwi iwis ski wis is si
iikt tiki kit it ti
iikw kiwi
iillmno million. *No 6s or 5s*
iillmnos millions million. *See* **ilmns ilmos ilnos**
iillmsy slimily. *See* **illms illsy ilmsy**
iillnop pillion. *No 6s or 5s*
iillnops pillions pillion. *See* **ilnos illns illps**
iillnort trillion. *See* **iiort illrt llort**
iillnosu illusion. *See* **ilnos ilosu illns**
iillnosz zillions zillion. *See* **ilnos illns**
iillnoz zillion. *No 6s or 5s*
iillnsst instills instill instils. *See* **iinsst iilnst illsst**
iillnst instill. *See* **iilnst illst illns**
iilmmu milium ilium lum mil mim mum li mi mu um
iilmotty motility. *See* **iilmt**
iilmst limits limit milts list mils milt mist silt slim slit tils its lit mil mis sit til is it li mi si ti
iilmstu stimuli. *See* **iilmst ilmstu**
iilmt limit milt lit mil til it li mi ti
iilmu ilium mil lum li mi mu um
iilnn linin linn nil inn li in

iilnnsu insulin inulins. *See* **iilnnu ilnns**
iilnnu inulin linin linn inn nil nun in li nu
iilnootv volition. *See* **iilnov ilnoot**
iilnors sirloin. *See* **inors ilnos ilors**
iilnorss sirloins sirloin. *See* **inorss**
iilnosv violins. *See* **iilnov iinosv**
iilnosy noisily. *See* **ilnosy**
iilnov violin lion loin noil viol ion nil oil in li lo no on
iilnsst instils. *See* **iilnst iinsst**
iilnst instil lints lint list nils nisi nits silt slit snit tils tins its lit nil nit sin sit til tin in is it li si ti
iilnty tinily linty inly lint liny tiny lit nil nit til tin yin in it li ti
iilopsty pilosity. *See* **iilpst ilopst ilopty**
iilorstv vitriols violist visitor vitriol. *See* **ilors iorst ilost**
iilortv vitriol. *See* **iiort**
iilosstv violists violist. *See* **iisstv**
iilostv violist. *See* **ilost ilosv iistv**
iilprssy prissily. *See* **iprssy**
iilprvy privily. *See* **iprvy**
iilpsst pistils. *See* **iilpst ilpsst**
iilpst pistil spilt split tipis lips lisp list pits silt slip slit spit tils tipi tips its lip lit pit sip sit til tip is it li pi si ti
iilpswy wispily. *See* **ipswy**
iilrwy wirily wily wiry li
iilsttt titlist. *See* **ilstt iistt**
iilttuy utility. *No 6s or 5s*
iilttwy wittily. *See* **ittwy**
iimmmnsu minimums minimum miniums. *See* **iimmns iimmnu**
iimmmnu minimum. *See* **iimmnu**
iimmn minim mim nim mi in
iimmns minims minim nisi nims mim mis nim sin in is mi si
iimmnsu miniums. *See* **iimmns iimmnu**
iimmntuy immunity. *See* **iimmnu imntuy**
iimmnu minium minim mim mum nim in mi mu nu um
iimmopst optimism. *See* **imopst**
iimmsttu mittimus. *See* **immstu**
iimmx immix mim mix mi xi
iimnno minion inion inn ion mon nim in mi mo no om on
iimnnoot monition. *See* **iimnno imnoot innoot**
iimnnos minions. *See* **iimnno iinnos**
iimnnosu unionism minions. *See* **iimnno iimnou iinnos innosu**
iimnnotu munition. *See* **iimnno iimnou imnntu**

iimnooss omission mission. *See* **iimoss imnoos**
iimnoprs imprison. *See* **imnors imoprs inoprs**
iimnorty minority. *See* **inory imnor imnty**
iimnoss mission. *See* **iimoss**
iimnosss missions mission. *See* **iimoss**
iimnou ionium muon ion mon nim in mi mo mu no nu om on um
iimnprst imprints misprint imprint. *See* **iiprst inprst**
iimnprt imprint. *See* **inprt**
iimnptuy impunity. *See* **imntuy**
iimnrsty ministry. *See* **imnst imnty imsty**
iimopstt optimist. *See* **iiostt imopst**
iimopsu impious. *See* **imopsu**
iimoss miosis miss moss mis mos oms sis is mi mo om os si so
iimosst mitosis. *See* **iimoss imsst imost**
iimprtuy impurity. *See* **iprtuy**
iimrrtuv triumvir. *See* **irtuv**
iimsstuw swimsuit. *See* **imsst msstu isstu**
iinno inion inn ion in no on
iinnoop opinion. *See* **iinnop innoo**
iinnoops opinions opinion pinions. *See* **iinnop iinnos innoos inoops**
iinnop pinion inion inn ion nip pin poi in no on pi
iinnoppt pinpoint. *See* **iinnop**
iinnops pinions. *See* **iinnop iinnos**
iinnos inions inion inns ions nisi inn ion sin son in is no on os si so
iinnsttu tinnitus intuits. *See* **iinttu**
iinoopst position options potions. *See* **inoops inoopt inopst**
iinorst ironist. *See* **inors iorst norst**
iinortt introit. *See* **inortt iiort**
iinossv visions. *See* **iinosv**
iinosttu tuitions tuition intuits. *See* **iinttu iiostt**
iinosv vision nisi ions ion sin son in is no on os si so
iinottu tuition. *See* **iinttu**
iinppp pippin nip pin pip in pi
iinqruy inquiry. *No 6s or 5s*
iinrtty trinity. *See* **intty**
iins nisi sin in is si
iinssst insists. *See* **iinsst**
iinsst insist snits nisi nits sins sits snit tins its nit sin sis sit tin in is it si ti
iinsttu intuits. *See* **iinttu instt nsttu**
iinsttw nitwits. *See* **iinttw instt iistt**
iinttu intuit tint titi unit nit nut tin tit tui tun tut in it nu ti ut

iinttw nitwit tint titi twin twit nit tin tit win wit in it ti

iioostty otiosity. *See* **iiostt oostty**

iioprrty priority. *See* **ioprry**

iiorsstv visitors visitor. *See* **iisstv iorssv**

iiorstuv virtuosi visitor. *See* **iorstu**

iiorstv visitor. *See* **iorst iiort iistv**

iiort torii riot tiro tori trio ort rot tor it or ti to

iiostt otitis titis titi tits tost tots its sit sot tit tot is it os si so ti to

iippst pipits pipit tipis pips pits spit tipi tips its pip pit sip sit tip is it pi si ti

iippt pipit tipi pip pit tip it pi ti

iiprsst spirits. *See* **iiprst iprsst**

iiprst spirit sprit strip tipis trips iris pits rips spit stir tipi tips trip its pit rip sip sir sit tip is it pi si ti

iipst tipis pits spit tipi tips its pit sip sit tip is it pi si ti

iipt tipi pit tip it pi ti

iiqstuv qiviuts. *See* **iiqtuv iistv iqstu**

iiqtuv qiviut quit tui it ti ut

iirs iris sir is si

iisstv visits visit sits its sis sit is it si ti

iistt titis titi tits its sit tit is it si ti

iistv visit its sit is it si ti

iisw iwis wis is si

iitt titi tit it ti

iitz ziti zit it ti

iitzz zizit ziti zit it ti

---

ij

ijjstuu jujitsu. *See* **jjsuu**

ijkllosy killjoys killjoy. *See* **jlloy iklls iklos**

ijklloy killjoy. *See* **jlloy**

ijkmou moujik jo mi mo mu om um

ijkn jink ink kin in

ijkns jinks inks jink sink skin ink kin sin ski in is si

ijlloy jollily. *See* **jlloy llloy**

ijlloty jollity. *See* **jlloy jloty**

ijlmpuy jumpily. *See* **ilmpy jmpuy lmpuy**

ijlnoqsu jonquils jonquil. *See* **inoqsu**

ijlnoqu jonquil. *See* **inoqu**

ijlnoty jointly. *See* **ijnot jloty ilnty**

ijlst jilts jilt list silt slit tils its lit sit til is it li si ti

ijlt jilt lit til it li ti

ijmmy jimmy mim mi my

ijnn jinn inn in

ijnns jinns jinn inns inn sin in is si

ijno join ion in jo no on

ijnorsu juniors. *See* **ijnoru inors ijnos**

ijnoru junior iron join ruin ion nor our run urn in jo no nu on or

ijnos joins join ions ion sin son in is jo no on os si so

ijnost joints joins joint joist into ions join jots nits snit snot tins tons ion its jot nit not sin sit son sot tin ton in is it jo no on os si so ti to

ijnot joint join into ion jot nit not tin ton in it jo no on ti to

ijnruy injury ruin jury run urn yin in nu

ijnx jinx nix in xi

ijosst joists joist joss jots sits sots toss its jot sis sit sot is it jo os si so ti to

ijost joist jots its jot sit sot is it jo os si so ti to

ijrsstu jurists. *See* **ijrstu jsstu rsstu**

ijrstu jurist just juts rust ruts stir suit tuis its jus jut rut sir sit tui is it si ti us ut

---

ik

ikkn kink ink kin in

ikkns kinks skink inks kink sink skin ink kin sin ski in is si

ikknss skinks kinks sinks skink skins inks kink kiss sink sins skin skis ink kin sin sis ski in is si

ikkny kinky kink inky ink kin yin in

ikkos kiosk ski kos is os si so

ikkoss kiosks kiosk kiss skis kos sis ski is os si so

ikkr kirk irk kir

ikkru kukri kirk irk kir

ikl ilk li

ikll kill ilk ill li

ikllr krill kill rill ilk ill irk kir li

iklls kills skill kill silk sill ilk ill ski is li si

ikllss skills kills silks sills skill kill kiss silk sill skis ilk ill sis ski is li si

iklm milk ilk mil li mi

iklmops milksop. *See* **iklos ilmos ilmps**

iklmopss milksops milksop. *See* **ikmpss ilopss**

iklmorsw silkworm. *See* **iklos ilmos ilors**

iklms milks milk mils silk skim slim ilk mil mis ski is li mi si

iklmy milky milk limy ilk mil li mi my

ikln kiln link ilk ink kin nil li in

iklnoost kilotons kiloton lotions. *See* **iknost ilnoot ilnost**

iklnoot kiloton. *See* **ilnoot**

iklnopst slipknot pontils. *See* **iklnps iknops iknost ilnopt**

iklnp plink kiln link pink ilk ink kin kip lip nil nip pin in li pi

iklnps plinks kilns links pinks plink slink inks kiln kips link lips lisp nils nips pink pins silk sink skin skip slip snip spin ilk ink kin kip lip nil nip pin sin sip ski in is li pi si

iklnpsu linkups. *See* **iklnpu iklnps klnpsu**

iklnpu linkup plink plunk pulik kiln link pink puli punk ilk ink kin kip lip nil nip pin pul pun in li nu pi up

iklnrwy wrinkly. *No 6s or 5s*

iklns kilns links slink inks kiln link nils silk sink skin ilk ink kin nil sin ski in is li si

iklnss slinks kilns links silks sinks skins slink inks kiln kiss link nils silk sink sins skin skis ilk ink kin nil sin sis ski in is li si

iklnsy slinky kilns links lysin silky slink inks inky inly kiln link liny nils silk sink skin ilk kin nil sin ski sky sly yin in is li si

iklnty tinkly linty inky inly kiln kilt knit link lint liny tiny ilk ink kin kit lit nil nit til tin yin in it li ti

iklo kilo ilk oil li lo

iklos kilos kilo oils silk silo soil ilk kos los oil ski sol is li lo os si so

iklpu pulik puli ilk kip lip pul li pi up

iklrs skirl irks kris risk silk ilk irk kir sir ski is li si

iklrss skirls risks silks skirl irks kiss kris risk silk sirs skis ilk irk kir sir sis ski is li si

ikls silk ilk ski is li si

iklss silks kiss silk skis ilk sis ski is li si

iklst kilts kilt kist kits list silk silt skit slit tils ilk its kit lit sit ski til tsk is it li si ti

iklsy silky silk ilk ski sky sly is li si

iklt kilt ilk kit lit til it li ti

iklxy kylix ilk li xi

ikmn mink ink kin nim mi in

ikmnoo kimono ikon kino mink monk mono moon nook oink ink ion kin mon moo nim in mi mo no om on

ikmnoor omikron. *See* **ikmnoo imnoor**

ikmnoos kimonos. *See* **ikmnoo imnoos**

ikmnppsu pumpkins pumpkin. *See* **inppsu**

ikmnppu pumpkin. *See* **inppu**

ikmns minks inks mink nims sink skim skin ink kin mis nim sin ski in is mi si

ikmoost mistook. *See* **imost moost koost**

ikmps skimp imps kips simp skim skip imp kip mis sip ski is mi pi si

ikmpss skimps simps skimp skims skips imps kips kiss miss simp sips skim skip skis imp kip mis sip sis ski is mi pi si

ikmpsy skimpy skimp spiky imps kips simp skim skip yips imp kip mis sip ski sky spy yip is mi my pi si

ikmrs smirk irks kris mirs rims risk skim irk kir mir mis rim sir ski is mi si

ikmrss smirks risks skims smirk irks kiss kris mirs miss rims risk sirs skim skis irk kir mir mis rim sir sis ski is mi si

ikms skim ski mis is mi si

ikmss skims kiss miss skim skis mis sis ski is mi si

ikmssu kumiss skims kiss miss musk muss skim skis sums mis mus sis ski sum is mi mu si um us

ikn ink kin in

iknnsy skinny inks inky inns sink skin ink inn kin sin ski sky yin in is si

ikno ikon kino oink ink ion kin in no on

iknoorrw ironwork. *See* **knoorr**

iknop pinko ikon kino knop oink pink ink ion kin kip nip pin poi in no on pi

iknops pinkos ikons kinos knops oinks pinko pinks ikon inks ions kino kips knop nips oink pink pins pois pons sink skin skip snip spin ink ion kin kip kos nip pin poi sin sip ski son sop in is no on os pi si so

iknopstt stinkpot. *See* **iknops iknost inopst**

iknorstw tinworks tinwork. *See* **iknost**

iknortw tinwork. *No 6s or 5s*

iknos ikons kinos oinks ikon inks ions kino oink sink skin ink ion kin kos sin ski son in is no on os si so

iknost stinko ikons kinos knits knots oinks stink ikon inks into ions kino kist kits knit knot nits oink sink skin skit snit snot tins tons ink ion its kin kit kos nit not sin sit ski son sot tin ton tsk in is it no on os si so ti to

iknp pink ink kin kip nip pin in pi

iknpr prink pink pirn rink ink irk kin kip kir nip pin rip in pi

iknprs prinks pinks pirns prink rinks inks irks kips kris nips pink pins pirn rink rips risk sink skin skip snip spin ink irk kin kip kir nip pin rip sin sip sir ski in is pi si

iknps pinks inks kips nips pink pins sink skin skip snip spin ink kin kip nip pin sin sip ski in is pi si

iknpsstu sputniks sputnik. *See* **iknsst inpstu insstu ipsstu**

iknpstu sputnik. *See* **inpstu iknst iknps**

iknpy pinky inky pink piny ink kin kip nip pin yin yip in pi

iknr rink ink irk kin kir in

iknrs rinks inks irks kris rink risk sink skin ink irk kin kir sin sir ski in is si

ikns inks sink skin ink kin sin ski in is si

iknss sinks skins inks kiss sink sins skin skis ink kin sin sis ski in is si

iknsst stinks kists knits sinks skins skits snits stink inks kiss kist kits knit nits sink sins sits skin skis skit snit tins ink

its kin kit nit sin sis sit ski tin tsk in is it si ti

iknst knits stink inks kist kits knit nits sink skin skit snit tins ink its kin kit nit sin sit ski tin tsk in is it si ti

iknsty stinky knits stink inks inky kist kits knit nits sink skin skit snit tins tiny ink its kin kit nit sin sit ski sky sty tin tsk yin in is it si ti

iknsw winks inks sink skin wink wins ink kin sin ski win wis in is si

iknw wink ink kin win in

ikny inky ink kin yin in

iknyz zinky inky ink kin yin in

ikorsstu kurtosis suitors. *See* **ikrsst iorstu korsst orsstu**

ikorsttu outskirt tourist. *See* **iorstu orsttu**

ikp kip pi

ikps kips skip kip sip ski is pi si

ikpss skips kips kiss sips skip skis kip sip sis ski is pi si

ikpsy spiky kips skip yips kip sip ski sky spy yip is pi si

ikqrsu quirks quirk irks kris risk rusk irk kir sir ski is si us

ikqru quirk irk kir

ikqruy quirky quirk irk kir yuk

ikr irk kir

ikrrs skirr irks kris risk irk kir sir ski is si

ikrrss skirrs skirr risks irks kiss kris risk sirs skis irk kir sir sis ski is si

ikrs irks kris risk irk kir sir ski is si

ikrss risks irks kiss kris risk sirs skis irk kir sir sis ski is si

ikrsst skirts kists risks skirt skits stirs irks kiss kist kits kris risk sirs sits skis skit stir irk its kir kit sir sis sit ski tsk is it si ti

ikrst skirt irks kist kits kris risk skit stir irk its kir kit sir sit ski tsk is it si ti

ikrsy risky irks kris risk irk kir sir ski sky is si

iks ski is si

ikss kiss skis ski sis is si

iksst kists skits kiss kist kits sits skis skit its kit sis sit ski tsk is it si ti

ikssy kissy kiss skis sis ski sky is si

ikst kist kits skit its kit sit ski tsk is it si ti

iksvvy skivvy ivy ski sky is si

ikt kit it ti

iktty kitty kit tit it ti

---

il

---

il　li

ill　ill li

illloopp　lollipop. *See* **llloop**

illm　mill ill mil li mi

illmnosu　mullions mullion. *See* **ilmnsu**

illmnou　mullion. *No 6s or 5s*

illmptuy　multiply. *See* **illmpy**

illmpy　limply imply illy lily limp limy mill pill ill imp lip mil ply yip li mi my pi

illms　mills mill mils sill slim ill mil mis is li mi si

illn　nill ill nil li in

illnoqsu　quillons quillon. *See* **illqsu inoqsu**

illnoqu　quillon. *See* **illqu inoqu**

illns　nills nill nils sill ill nil sin in is li si

illntuy　nullity. *See* **ilnty intuy ilntu**

illoppss　slipslop. *See* **illpss ilopss**

illopry　pillory. *See* **ilory**

illopsw　pillows. *See* **illopw illps lopsw**

illopw　pillow pill plow poll will ill lip lop low oil owl poi li lo ow pi

illopwy　pillowy. *See* **illopw llowy**

illorsuy　illusory lousily. *See* **lorsuy**

illosuy　lousily. *See* **ilosu losuy illsy**

illosww　willows. *See* **illoww illsw**

illotxy　xylitol. *See* **lloxy**

illoww　willow will ill low oil owl wow li lo ow

illp　pill ill lip li pi

illps　pills spill lips lisp pill sill slip ill lip sip is li pi si

illpss　spills lisps pills sills slips spill lips lisp pill sill sips slip ill lip sip sis is li pi si

illqssu　squills. *See* **illqsu**

illqsu　quills squill quill sill ill is li si us

illqu　quill ill li

illr　rill ill li

illrs　rills rill sill ill sir is li si

illrst　trills lilts rills still tills trill lilt list rill sill silt sirt stir till tils ill its lit sir sit til is it li si ti

illrt　trill lilt rill till ill lit til it li ti

ills　sill ill is li si

illss　sills sill ill sis is li si

illsst　stills lilts lists sills silts slits still tills lilt list sill silt sits slit till tils ill its lit sis sit til is it li si ti

illssw　swills sills swill wills sill will ill sis wis is li si

illst　lilts still tills lilt list sill silt slit till tils ill its lit sit til is it li si ti

illstuy　lustily. *See* **illsty lstuy llstu**

illstw　twills lilts still swill tills twill wills wilts lilt list sill silt slit till tils will wilt wits ill its lit sit til wis wit is it li si ti

illsty　stilly lilts silly silty still styli tills illy lilt lily list sill silt slit till tils ill its lit sit sly sty til is it li si ti

illsw　swill wills sill will ill wis is li si

illsy　silly illy lily sill ill sly is li si

illt　lilt till ill lit til it li ti

illtw　twill lilt till will wilt ill lit til wit it li ti

illw　will ill li

illy　illy lily ill li

ilm　mil li mi

ilmn　limn mil nil nim in li mi

ilmnoot　moonlit. *See* **ilnoot imnoot**

ilmnosuu　luminous. *See* **ilmnsu**

ilmns　limns limn mils nils nims slim mil mis nil nim sin in is li mi si

ilmnssu　muslins. *See* **ilmnsu inssu lmssu**

ilmnsu　muslin limns minus limn mils nils nims slim slum lum mil mis mus nil nim sin sum sun in is li mi mu nu si um us

ilmo　limo milo moil mil oil li lo mi mo om

ilmortu　turmoil. *See* **ilmotu mortu**

ilmos　limos moils limo milo mils moil oils silo slim soil los mil mis mos oil oms sol is li lo mi mo om os si so

ilmosty　moistly. *See* **lmosty ilmos ilmst**

ilmotu　ultimo moult limo lout milo milt moil molt omit toil tolu lit lot lum mil mot oil out til tom tui it li lo mi mo mu om ti to um ut

ilmp　limp imp lip mil li mi pi

ilmppy　pimply imply limp limy pimp pipy imp lip mil pip ply yip li mi my pi

ilmpry　primly imply limp limy miry prim rimy imp lip mil mir ply pry rim rip yip li mi my pi

ilmps　limps imps limp lips lisp mils simp slim slip imp lip mil mis sip is li mi pi si

ilmpsy　simply imply limps slimy imps limp limy lips lisp mils simp slim slip yips imp lip mil mis ply sip sly spy yip is li mi my pi si

ilmpy　imply limp limy imp lip mil ply yip li mi my pi

ilmrsy　lyrism slimy limy mils mirs miry rims rimy slim mil mir mis rim sir sly is li mi my si

ilmrty　trimly limy milt miry rimy trim lit mil mir rim til try it li mi my ti

ilms　mils slim mil mis is li mi si

ilmss　slims mils miss slim mil mis sis li mi is si

ilmsstuu　stimulus. *See* **ilmstu**

ilmst　milts list mils milt mist silt slim slit tils its lit mil mis sit til is it li mi si ti

ilmstu　litmus milts list lust mils milt mist must silt slim slit slum slut smut stum suit tils tuis its lit lum mil mis mus sit sum til tui is it li mi mu si ti um us ut

ilmsy　slimy limy mils slim mil mis sly is li mi my si

ilmt　milt lit mil til it li mi ti

ilmy　limy mil li mi my

ilmyzz　mizzly limy mil li mi my

iln　nil li in

ilnn　linn nil inn li in

ilnns　linns inns linn nils inn nil sin in is li si

ilno　lion loin noil ion nil oil in li lo no on

ilnoost　lotions. *See* **ilnoot ilnost**

ilnoostu　solution lotions. *See* **ilnoot ilnost ilnstu**

ilnoot　lotion into lint lion loin loon loot noil olio onto toil tool toon ion lit loo lot nil nit not oil til tin ton too in it li lo no on ti to

ilnootuv　volution. *See* **ilnoot**

ilnopp　poplin lion loin noil plop ion lip lop nil nip oil pin pip poi pop in li lo no on pi

ilnopps　poplins. *See* **ilnopp ilnos lopps**

ilnoprsu　purloins purlins purloin upsilon. *See* **ilnpru ilopsu inoprs**

ilnopru　purloin. *See* **ilnpru ilopu**

ilnopssu　upsilons upsilon spinous. *See* **ilopss ilopsu**

ilnopst　pontils. *See* **ilopst inopst ilnopt ilnpst ilnost**

ilnopsu　upsilon. *See* **ilopsu ilnos**

ilnopt　pontil pilot pinto piton point into lint lion loin noil pint plot toil ion lip lit lop lot nil nip nit not oil pin pit poi pot til tin tip ton top in it li lo no on pi ti to

ilnorsst　nostrils nostril tonsils. *See* **ilnost inorss norsst**

ilnorst　nostril. *See* **ilnost inors ilors**

ilnos　lions loins noils ions lion loin nils noil oils silo soil ion los nil oil sin sol son in is li lo no on os si so

ilnosst　tonsils. *See* **ilnost ilsst iloss**

ilnost　tonsil lints lions loins noils toils into ions lint lion list loin lost lots nils nits noil oils silo silt slit slot snit snot soil tils tins toil tons ion its lit los lot nil nit not oil sin sit sol son sot til tin ton in is it li lo no on os si so ti to

ilnosty　stonily. *See* **ilnost ilnosy**

ilnosy nosily lions loins lysin noils noisy yonis inly ions liny lion loin nils noil nosy oils oily only silo soil yoni ion los nil oil sin sly sol son soy yin yon in is li lo no on os oy si so

ilnprsu purlins. *See* **ilnpru inprs ilpsu**

ilnpru purlin pirn puli purl ruin lip nil nip pin pul pun rip run urn in li nu pi up

ilnpsst splints. *See* **ilnpst ilpsst**

ilnpst splint lints pints spilt split lint lips lisp list nils nips nits pins pint pits silt slip slit snip snit spin spit tils tins tips its lip lit nil nip nit pin pit sin sip sit til tin tip in is it li pi si ti

ilns nils nil sin in is li si

ilnsstu insults. *See* **ilnstu insstu**

ilnssy lysins lysin lysis inly liny nils sins nil sin sis sly yin in is li si

ilnst lints lint list nils nits silt slit snit tils tins its lit nil nit sin sit til tin in is it li si ti

ilnstu insult lints lunts suint units until lint list lunt lust nils nits nuts silt slit slut snit stun suit tils tins tuis tuns unit its lit nil nit nut sin sit sun til tin tui tun in is it li nu si ti us ut

ilnsvy vinyls lysin vinyl inly liny nils viny ivy nil sin sly yin in is li si

ilnsy lysin inly liny nils nil sin sly yin in is li si

ilnt lint lit nil nit til tin in it li ti

ilnttuy nuttily. *See* **ilnty intty nttuy**

ilntu until lint lunt unit lit nil nit nut til tin tui tun in it li nu ti ut

ilnty linty inly lint liny tiny lit nil nit tin yin in it li ti

ilnvy vinyl inly liny viny ivy nil yin li in

ilny inly liny nil yin li in

ilo oil li lo

iloo olio oil loo li lo

iloop polio loop olio polo pool lip loo lop oil poi li lo pi

iloopsst topsoils pistols soloist topsoil. *See* **ilopss ilopst ilpsst iopsst**

iloopst topsoil. *See* **ilopst**

iloos olios loos oils olio silo soil solo loo los oil sol is li lo os si so

iloossst soloists soloist ostosis. *See* **loosst**

iloosst soloist. *See* **loosst**

ilooyz oozily oily olio oozy loo oil zoo li lo oy

iloprx prolix oxlip roil lip lop lox oil pix poi pox pro rip li lo or ox pi xi

ilops polis spoil lips lisp lops oils pois silo slip slop soil lip lop los oil poi sip sol sop is li lo os pi si so

ilopss spoils lisps polis silos slips slops soils spoil lips lisp lops loss oils pois silo sips slip slop soil sols sops lip lop los oil poi sip sis sol sop is li lo os pi si so

ilopsst pistols. *See* **ilopst iopsst ilpsst ilopss**

ilopst pilots pistol spoilt pilot plots polis posit spilt split spoil toils lips lisp list lops lost lots oils pits plot pois post pots silo silt slip slit slop slot soil spit spot stop tils tips toil tops its lip lit lop los lot oil pit poi pot sip sit sol sop sot til tip top is it li lo os pi si so ti to

ilopsu poilus louis pious poilu polis pulis spoil lips lisp lops oils opus plus pois puli puls silo slip slop soil soul soup lip lop los oil poi pul pus sip sol sop sou sup is li lo os pi si so up us

ilopsx oxlips oxlip polis spoil lips lisp lops oils pois silo slip slop soil lip lop los lox oil pix poi pox sip six sol sop sox is li lo os ox pi si so xi

ilopt pilot plot toil lip lit lop lot oil pit poi pot til tip top it li lo pi ti to

ilopty polity pilot oily plot ploy toil lip lit lop lot oil pit ply poi pot til tip top toy yip it li lo oy pi ti to

ilopu poilu puli lip lop oil poi pul li lo pi up

ilopx oxlip lip lop lox oil pix poi pox li lo ox pi xi

iloqrsu liquors. *See* **iloqru ilors ilosu**

iloqru liquor roil oil our li lo or

ilor roil oil li lo or

ilorrsy sorrily. *See* **ilors lorry iorrs**

ilors loris roils oils roil silo soil sori los oil sir sol is li lo or os si so

ilory roily lory oily roil oil li lo or oy

ilos oils silo soil los oil sol is li lo os si so

iloss silos soils loss oils silo soil sols los oil sis sol is li lo os si so

ilost toils list lost lots oils silo silt slit slot soil tils toil its lit los lot oil sit sol sot til is it li lo os si so ti to

ilosu louis oils silo soil soul los oil sol sou is li lo os si so us

ilosv viols oils silo soil viol los oil sol is li lo os si so

ilot toil lit lot oil til it li lo ti to

ilov viol oil li lo

iloy oily oil li lo oy

ilp lip li pi

ilppry ripply pipy lip pip ply pry rip yip li pi

ilppstu pulpits. *See* **ilppsu ilpstu**

ilppsu pupils pulis pulps pupil lips lisp pips plus puli pulp puls pups slip lip pip pul pup pus sip sup is li pi si up us

ilppsy slippy lips lisp pips pipy slip yips lip pip ply sip sly spy yip is li pi si

ilppu pupil puli pulp lip pip pul pup li pi up

ilprty triply trip pity lip lit pit ply pry rip til tip try yip it li pi ti

ilps lips lisp slip lip sip is li pi si

ilpss lisps slips lips lisp sips slip lip sip sis is li pi si

ilpsst splits lisps lists silts slips slits spilt spits split lips lisp list pits silt sips sits slip slit spit tils tips its lip lit pit sip sis sit til tip is it li pi si si

ilpst spilt split lips lisp list pits silt slip slit spit tils tips its lip lit pit sip sit til tip is it li pi si ti

ilpsttu uptilts. *See* **ilsttu ilpttu**

ilpstu tulips pulis situp spilt split tulip lips lisp list lust pits plus puli puls puts silt slip slut spit suit tils tips tuis tups its lip lit pit pul pus put sip sit sup til tip tui tup is it li pi si ti up us ut

ilpsu pulis lips lisp plus puli puls slip lip pul pus sip sup is li pi si up us

ilpttu uptilt tulip puli putt tilt lip lit pit pul put til tip tit tui tup tut it li pi ti up ut

ilptu tulip puli lip lit pit pul put til tip tui tup it li pi ti up ut

ilpu puli lip pul li pi up

ilqstu quilts quilt quits list lust quit silt slit slut suit tils tuis its lit sit til tui is it li si ti us ut

ilqtu quilt quit lit til tui it li ti ut

ilrssw swirls swirl sirs sir sis wis is li si

ilrstuy rustily. *See* **ilrsty lrstuy**

ilrstw twirls swirl twirl wilts wrist writs list silt slit stir tils wilt wits writ its lit sir sit til wis wit is it li si ti

ilrsty lyrist silty styli list silt stir tils its lit sir sit sly sty til try is it li si ti

ilrsw swirl sir wis is li si

ilrswy swirly swirl wily wiry sir sly wis is li si

ilrtw twirl wilt writ lit til wit it li ti

ilssstty stylists stylist. *See* **ilsstt**

ilsst lists silts slits list silt sits slit tils its lit sis sit til is it li si ti

ilsstt stilts lists silts slits stilt tilts list silt sits slit tils tilt tits its lit sis sit til tit is it li si ti

ilssttu lutists. *See* **ilsstt ilsttu**

ilsstty stylist. *See* **ilsstt ilssy ilsty**

ilssy lysis sis sly is li si

ilst list silt slit tils its lit sit til is it li si ti

ilstt stilt tilts list silt slit tils tilt tits its lit sit til tit is it li si ti

ilsttu lutist stilt tilts list lust silt slit slut suit tils tilt tits tuis tuts its lit sit til tit tui tut is it li si ti us ut

ilstw wilts list silt slit tils wilt wits its lit til wis wit is it li si ti

ilsty silty styli list silt slit tils its lit sit sly sty til is it li si ti

485

ilt   lit til it li ti   **iltw**   wilt lit til wit it li ti
iltt   tilt lit til tit it li ti   **ilwy**   wily li

---

im

im   mi

imm   mim mi

immmos   momism moms mim mis mom mos oms is mi mo om os si so

immmoss   momisms. *See* **immmos**

immnos   monism ions moms mons nims ion mim mis mom mon mos nim oms sin sin is mi mo no om on os si so

immnoss   monisms. *See* **immnos**

immoos   simoom moms moos mim mis mom moo mos oms is mi mo om os si so

immooss   simooms. *See* **immoos**

immopstu   optimums optimum. *See* **immosu immstu imopst imopsu**

immoptu   optimum. *See* **imopu**

immossu   osmiums. *See* **immosu mossu**

immosu   osmium moms mums sumo mim mis mom mos mum mus oms sou sum is mi mo mu om os si so um us

immsstu   summits. *See* **immstu imsst msstu**

immstu   summit mist mums must smut stum suit tuis its mim mis mum mus sit sum tui is it mi mu si ti um us ut

imn   nim mi in

imnnosuu   numinous. *See* **innosu**

imnnosw   minnows. *See* **imnnow inosw**

imnnow   minnow wino mown inn ion mon mow nim now own win won in mi mo no om on ow

imnnstu   muntins. *See* **imnntu imnst imnsu**

imnntu   muntin mint unit inn nim nit nun nut tin tui tun in it mi mu nu ti um ut

imnny   minny inn nim yin in mi my

imnoor   morion minor moron iron mono moon moor morn norm room ion mir mon moo mor nim nor rim in mi mo no om on or

imnoors   morions. *See* **imnors imnoor mnoors inoors imnoos**

imnoorst   monitors monitor morions motions torsion. *See* **imnoor imnoos imnoot imnors**

imnoort   monitor. *See* **imnoor imnoot**

imnoos   simoon moons ions mono mons moon moos nims soon ion mis mon moo mos nim oms sin son in is mi mo no om on os si so

imnoost   motions. *See* **imnost imnoos**

imnoosu   ominous. *See* **imnoos imnsu mnosu**

imnoot   motion into mint mono moon moot omit onto toon ion mon moo mot nim nit not tin tom ton too in it mi mo no om on ti to

imnoprsw   pinworms pinworm. *See* **imnors imoprs inoprs**

imnoprw   pinworm. *See* **imnor**

imnor   minor iron morn norm ion mir mon mor nim nor rim in mi mo no om on or

imnors   minors irons minor morns norms rosin ions iron mirs mons morn mors nims norm rims sori ion mir mis mon mor mos nim nor oms rim sin sir son in is mi mo no om on or os si so

imnosst   monists. *See* **imnost**

imnossy   myosins. *See* **imnosy**

imnost   inmost monist mints moist omits into ions mint mist mons most mots nims nits omit snit snot tins toms tons ion its mis mon mos mot nim nit not oms sin sit son sot tin tom ton in is it mi mo no om on os si so ti to

imnostuu   mutinous. *See* **imnost mnostu**

imnosy   myosin simony noisy yonis ions mons nims nosy yoni ion mis mon mos nim oms sin son soy yin yon in is mi mo my no om on os oy si so

imns   nims mis nim sin in is mi si

imnst   mints mint mist nims nits snit tins its mis nim nit sin sit tin in is it mi si ti

imnsu   minus nims mis mus nim sin sum sun in is mi mu nu si um us

imnt   mint nim nit tin in it mi ti

imntuy   mutiny minty unity mint tiny unit nim nit nut tin tui tun yin yum in it mi mu my nu ti um ut

imnty   minty mint tiny nim nit tin yin in it mi my ti

imnx   minx mix nim nix in mi xi

imooprst   impostor imports tropism. *See* **imoprs imoprt imopst ioprst**

imooprx   proximo. *See* **moopr**

imooqstu   mosquito. *See* **ioqstu**

imoorstt   motorist. *See* **moorst moostt**

imoorstu   timorous tourism riotous. *See* **imrstu iorstu moorst morstu**

imoosss   osmosis. *No 6s or 5s*

imoprs   porism prism proms romps imps mirs mops mors pois prim prom pros rims rips romp simp sori imp mir mis mop mor mos oms poi pro rim rip sip sir sop is mi mo om or os pi si so

imoprss   porisms. *See* **imoprs imprss**

imoprsst   tropisms imports imposts porisms tropism. *See* **imoprs imoprt imopst imprss**

imoprst   imports tropism. *See* **imoprt imopst imoprs ioprst**

imoprsv   improvs. *See* **imoprs imoprv**

imoprt   import mort omit port prim prom riot romp tiro tori trim trio trip imp mir mop mor mot ort pit poi pot pro rim rip rot tip tom top tor it mi mo om or pi ti to

imoprv   improv prim prom romp imp mir mop mor poi pro rim rip vim mi mo om or pi

imopsst   imposts. *See* **imopst iopsst mopsst**

imopst   impost moist omits posit stomp imps mist mops most mots omit pits pois post pots simp spit spot stop tips toms tops imp its mis mop mos mot oms pit poi pot sip sit sop sot tip tom top is it mi mo om os pi si so ti to

imopsu   opiums opium pious imps mops opus pois simp soup sumo sump umps imp mis mop mos mus oms poi pus sip sop sou sum sup ump is mi mo mu om os pi si so um up us

imopu   opium imp mop poi ump mi mo mu om pi um up

imorrr   mirror mir mor rim mi mo om or

imorrrs   mirrors. *See* **imorrr iorrs**

imorstu   tourism. *See* **iorstu imrstu morstu**

imossyz   zymosis. *See* **imssy mossy**

imost   moist omits mist most mots omit toms its mis mos mot oms sit sot tom is it mi mo om os si so ti to

imostv   vomits moist omits vomit mist most mots omit toms vims its mis mos mot oms sit sot tom vim is it mi mo om os si so ti to

imot   omit mot tom it mi mo om ti to

imotv   vomit omit mot tom vim it mi mo om ti to

imp   imp mi pi

impp   pimp imp pip mi pi

imppr   primp pimp prim imp mir pip rim rip mi pi

impprs   primps pimps primp prism imps mirs pimp pips prim rims rips simp imp mir mis pip rim rip sip sir is mi pi si

impps   pimps imps pimp pips simp imp mis pip sip is mi pi si

impr   prim imp mir rim rip mi pi

imprs   prism imps mirs prim rims rips simp imp mir mis rim rip sip sir is mi pi si

imprss   prisms prism priss simps imps mirs miss prim rims rips simp sips sirs imp mir mis rim rip sip sir sis is mi pi si

imprssu   purisms. *See* **imprss imprsu**

imprsu   purism prism rumps imps mirs prim rims rips rump rums simp spur sump umps imp mir mis mus pus rim

rip rum sip sir sum sup ump is mi mu pi si um up us

imps   imps simp imp mis sip is mi pi si

impss   simps imps miss simp sips imp mis sip sis is mi pi si

impsw   wimps imps simp swim wimp wisp imp mis sip wis is mi pi si

impw   wimp imp mi pi

impwy   wimpy wimp imp yip mi my pi

imqrssu   squirms. *See* **imqrsu**

imqrsu   squirm mirs rims rums mir mis mus rim rum sir sum is mi mu si um us

imr   mir rim mi

imrs   mirs rims mir mis rim sir is mi si

imrssstu   sistrums sistrum truisms. *See* **imrstu imsssu issstu mrsstu**

imrssttu   mistrust sistrum truisms. *See* **imrstu mrsstu rsttu**

imrsstu   sistrum truisms. *See* **imrstu mrsstu**

imrst   trims mirs mist rims stir trim its mir mis rim sir sit is it mi si ti

imrsttuy   yttriums yttrium. *See* **imrstu msttuy rsttuy**

imrstu   truism trims strum mirs mist must rims rums rust ruts smut stir

stum suit trim tuis its mir mis mus rim rum rut sir sit sum tui is it mi mu si ti um us ut

imrt   trim mir rim it mi ti

imrttuy   yttrium. *See* **rttuy**

imry   miry rimy mir rim mi my

ims   mis is mi si

imss   miss mis sis is mi si

imsssu   missus miss muss sums mis mus sis sum is mi mu si um us

imsst   mists miss mist sits its mis sis sit is it mi si ti

imssw   swims miss swim mis sis wis is mi si

imssy   missy miss mis sis is mi my si

imst   mist its mis sit is it mi si ti

imstt   mitts mist mitt tits its mis sit tit is it mi si ti

imsty   misty mist its mis sit sty is it mi my si ti

imsv   vims mis vim is mi si

imsw   swim mis wis is mi si

imtt   mitt tit it mi ti

imtx   mixt mix it mi ti xi

imv   vim mi

imx   mix mi xi

in   in

inn   inn in

innnnoou   nonunion. *See* **innno innoo innou**

innno   ninon inn ion in no on

innnortu   trunnion. *See* **innru innno innou**

innnos   ninons ninon inns ions inn ion sin son in is no on os si so

innny   ninny inn yin in

innoo   onion noon inn ion in no on

innoos   onions onion noons inns ions noon soon inn ion sin son in is no on os si so

innoost   notions. *See* **innoos innoot**

innoot   notion onion into noon onto toon inn ion nit not tin ton too in it no on ti to

innosstu   nonsuits nonsuit. *See* **innosu insstu nosstu**

innostu   nonsuit. *See* **innosu**

innosu   unions unison union nouns inns ions noun nous nuns onus sunn inn ion nun sin son sou sun in is no nu on os si so us

innosww   winnows. *See* **innoww inosw**

innou   union noun inn ion nun in no nu on

innoww   winnow wino inn ion now own win won wow in no on ow

innpsu   unpins unpin inns nips nuns pins puns snip spin spun sunn inn nip nun pin pun pus sin sip sun sup in is nu pi si up us

innpu   unpin inn nip nun pin pun in nu pi up

innrsu   inurns inurn ruins inns nuns ruin runs sunn urns inn nun run sin sir sun urn in is nu si us

innru   inurn ruin inn nun run urn in nu

inns   inns inn sin in is si

innty   tinny tiny inn nit tin yin in it ti

ino   ion in no on

inooprst   portions positron options portion potions protons torsion. *See* **inoops inoopt inoors inoprs**

inooprt   portion. *See* **inoopt nooprt**

inoops   poison poons snoop spoon ions nips oops pins pois pons poon snip soon spin ion nip pin poi sin sip son sop in is no on os pi si so

inoopss   poisons. *See* **inoops noopss**

inoopst   options potions. *See* **inoopt inopst inoops**

inoopstt   spittoon options potions. *See* **inoops inoopt inopst**

inoopt   option potion pinto piton point into onto pint poon toon ion nip nit not pin pit poi pot tin tip ton too top in it no on pi ti to

inoors   orison irons rosin ions iron soon sori ion nor sin sir son in is no on or os si so

inoorss   orisons. *See* **inoors inorss**

inoorsst   torsions orisons torsion. *See* **inoors inorss noosst norsst**

inoorst   torsion. *See* **inoors iorst oorst**

inoorstt   tortonis torsion tortoni tritons. *See* **inoors inortt**

inoortt   tortoni. *See* **inortt**

inoosux   noxious. *No 6s or 5s*

inoppsst   topspins topspin pistons. *See* **inopst iopsst**

inoppst   topspin. *See* **inopst**

inoprs   prison irons pirns rosin ions iron nips pins pirn pois pons porn pros rips snip sori spin ion nip nor pin poi pro rip sin sip sir son sop in is no on or os pi si so

inoprss prisons. *See* **inoprs inorss**

inoprttu printout. *See* **inortt inprtu**

inoprtuy punitory. *See* **inopty inprtu iprtuy**

inopsssy synopsis. *See* **inosy issssy inpss**

inopsst pistons. *See* **inopst iopsst**

inopssu spinous. *See* **inssu iopsu inpss**

inopst pintos piston pitons points pinto pints piton point posit into ions nips nits pins pint pits pois pons post pots snip snit snot spin spit spot stop tins tips tons tops ion its nip nit not pin pit poi pot sin sip sit son sop sot tin tip ton top in is it no on os pi si so ti to

inopt pinto piton point into pint ion nip nit not pin pit poi pot tin tip ton top in it no on pi ti to

inopty pointy pinto piton point into pint piny pity pony tiny tony yoni ion nip nit not pin pit poi pot tin tip ton top toy yin yip yon in it no on oy pi ti to

inoqsu quoins quoin ions nous onus ion sin son sou sun in is no nu on os si so us

inoqu quoin ion in no nu on

inor iron ion nor in no on or

inors irons rosin ions iron sori ion nor sin sir son in is no on or os si so

inorss rosins irons rosin ions iron sins sirs sons sori ion nor sin sir sis son in is no on or os si so

inorstt tritons. *See* **inortt inors iorst**

inorstu nitrous. *See* **iorstu inors inrsu**

inorsuu ruinous. *See* **inors**

inorsy rosiny irons irony noisy rosin yonis ions iron nosy rosy sori yoni ion nor sin sir son soy yin yon in is no on or os oy si so

inortt triton into iron riot tint tiro tori torn tort trio trot ion nit nor not ort rot tin tit ton tor tot in it no on or ti to

inory irony iron yoni ion nor yin yon in no on or oy

inos ions ion sin son in is no on os si so

inosstuw snowsuit. *See* **insstu nosstu**

inossuu sinuous. *See* **inssu**

inostx toxins toxin into ions nits snit snot tins tons ion its nit nix not sin sit six son sot sox tin ton in is it no on os ox si so ti to xi

inosuv vinous ions nous onus ion sin son sou sun in is no nu on os si so us

inosw winos ions owns snow sown wino wins ion now own sin son sow win wis won in is no on os ow si so

inosy noisy yonis ions nosy yoni ion sin son soy yin yon in is no on os oy si so

inot into ion nit not tin ton in it no on ti to

inotx toxin into ion nit nix not tin ton in it no on ox ti to xi

inow wino ion now own win won in no on ow

inoy yoni ion yin yon in no on oy

inp nip pin in pi

inppsu pinups pinup nips pins pips puns pups snip spin spun nip pin pip pun pup pus sin sip sun sup in is nu pi si up us

inppsy snippy nippy spiny nips pins piny pips pipy snip spin yips nip pin pip sin sip spy yin yip in is pi si

inppu pinup nip pin pip pun pup in nu pi up

inppy nippy piny pipy nip pin pip yin yip in pi

inpr pirn nip pin rip in pi

inprrstu surprint irrupts stirrup turnips. *See* **inprst inprtu inpstu iprrtu**

inprs pirns nips pins pirn rips snip spin nip pin rip sin sip sir in is pi si

inprsst sprints. *See* **inprst iprsst**

inprst prints sprint pints pirns print sprit strip trips nips nits pins pint pirn pits rips snip snit spin spit stir tins tips trip its nip nit pin pit rip sin sip sir sit tin tip in is it pi si ti

inprstu turnips. *See* **inpstu inprst iprstu inprtu**

inprt print pint pirn trip nip nit pin pit rip tin tip in it pi ti

inprtu turnip print input pint pirn punt ruin runt trip turn unit nip nit nut pin pit pun put rip run rut tin tip tui tun tup urn in it nu pi ti up ut

inps nips pins snip spin nip pin sin sip in is pi si

inpss snips spins nips pins sins sips snip spin nip pin sin sip sis in is pi si

inpst pints nips nits pins pint pits snip snit spin spit tins tips its nip nit pin pit sin sip sit tin tip in is it pi si ti

inpstu inputs input pints punts situp suint units nips nits nuts pins pint pits puns punt puts snip snit spin spit spun stun suit tins tips tuis tuns tups unit its nip nit nut pin pit pun pus put sin sip sit sun sup tin tip tui tun tup in is it nu pi si ti up us ut

inpsuz unzips unzip nips pins puns snip spin spun zips nip pin pun pus sin sip sun sup zip in is nu pi si up us

inpsy spiny nips pins piny snip spin yips nip pin sin sip spy yin yip in is pi si

inpt pint nip nit pin pit tin tip in it pi ti

inptu input pint punt unit nip nit nut pin pit pun put tin tip tui tun tup in it nu pi ti up ut

inpuz unzip nip pin pun zip in nu pi up

inpy piny nip pin yin yip in pi

inqsstu squints. *See* **inqstu insstu**

inqstu quints squint quint quits suint units nits nuts quit snit stun suit tins tuis tuns unit its nit nut sin sit sun tin tui tun in is it nu si ti us ut

inqstuy squinty. *See* **inqsuy inqstu**

inqsuy quinsy sin sun yin in is nu si us

inqtu quint unit quit nit nut tin tui tun in it nu ti ut

inrsu ruins ruin runs urns run sin sir sun urn in is nu si us

inrsxy syrinx nix sin sir six yin in is si xi

inrtwy wintry tiny twin winy wiry writ nit tin try win wit yin in it ti

inru ruin run urn in in nu

ins sin in is si

inss sins sin sis in is si

insst snits nits sins sits snit tins its nit sin sis sit tin in is it si ti

insstt stints snits stint tints nits sins sits snit tins tint tits its nit sin sis sit tin tit in is it si ti

insstu suints nisus sinus situs snits stuns suint suits units nits nuts sins sits snit stun suit suns tins tuis tuns unit its nit nut sin sis sit sun tin tui tun in is it nu si ti us ut

inssu nisus sinus sins suns sin sis sun in is nu si us

inst nits snit tins its nit sin sit tin in is it si ti

instt stint tints nits snit tins tint tits its nit sin sit tin tit in is it si ti

instu suint units nits nuts snit stun suit tins tuis tuns unit its nit nut sin sit sun tin tui tun in is it nu si ti us ut

instw twins nits snit tins twin wins wits its nit sin sit tin win wis wit in is it si ti

insw wins sin win wis in is si

int nit tin in it ti

intt tint nit tin tit in it ti

intty nitty tint tiny nit tin tit yin in it ti

intu unit nit nut tin tui tun in it nu ti ut

intuy unity unit tiny nit nut tin tui tun yin in it nu ti ut

intw twin nit tin win wit in it ti

inty tiny nit tin yin in it ti

invy viny yin ivy in

inw win in

inwy winy win yin in

inx nix in xi
iny yin in

---

io

iooprssv provisos proviso. *See* **iorssv ooprss**

iooprsv proviso. *See* **ooprs iorsv**

ioorrsty sorority. *See* **iorrs iorst oorst**

ioorssuv voussoir. *See* **iorssv**

ioorstu riotous. *See* **iorstu oorstu**

ioorstuv virtuoso riotous. *See* **iorstu oorstu**

ioossst ostosis. *See* **oosst ossst**

iop poi pi

ioppstt tiptops. *See* **iopptt iopst opstt**

iopptt tiptop pip pit poi pop pot tip tit top tot it pi ti to

ioprr prior poi pro rip pi or

ioprry priory prior ropy poi pro pry rip yip or oy pi

ioprssuu spurious. *See* **prssuu**

ioprst tripos ports posit riots sport sprit strip strop tiros torsi trios trips orts pits pois port post pots pros riot rips rots sori sort spit spot stir stop tips tiro tops tori tors trio trip its ort pit poi pot pro rip rot sip sir sit sop sot tip top tor is it or os pi si so ti to

ioprsttu outstrip tourist. *See* **ioprst iorstu iprstu oprstu**

iops pois poi sip sop is os pi si so

iopsst posits ptosis posit posts spits spots stops pits pois post pots sips sits sops sots spit spot stop tips tops toss its pit poi pot sip sis sit sop sot tip top is it os pi si so ti to

iopst posit pits pois post pots spit spot stop tips tops its pit poi pot sip sit sop sot tip top is it os pi si so ti to

iopstv pivots pivot posit pits pois post pots spit spiv spot stop tips tops its pit poi pot sip sit sop sot tip top is it os pi si so ti to

iopsu pious opus pois soup poi pus sip sop sou sup is os pi si so up us

ioptv pivot pit poi pot tip top it pi ti to

ioqrsttu quittors quittor tourist. *See* **ioqstu iorstu iqrstu orsttu**

ioqrttu quittor. *See* **iqrtu ioqtu orttu**

ioqrtuxy quixotry. *See* **ioqtu iqrtu**

ioqstu quoits quoit quits oust outs quit suit tuis its out sit sot sou tui is it os si so ti to us ut

ioqtu quoit quit tui out it ti to ut

iorrs orris sori sir is or os si so

iorrsuvv survivor. *See* **iorrs irsuv iorsv**

iors sori sir is or os si so

iorssttu tourists suitors tourist. *See* **iorstu orsstu orsttu ossttu**

iorsstu suitors. *See* **orsstu iorstu**

iorssuuu usurious. *See* **orssu**

iorssv visors visor sori sirs sir sis is or os si so

iorst riots tiros torsi trios orts riot rots sori sort stir tiro tori tors trio its ort rot sir sit sot tor is it or os si so ti to

iorsttu tourist. *See* **iorstu orsttu**

iorsttuy touristy tourist tryouts. *See* **iorstu orsttu orttuy rsttuy**

iorstu suitor riots roust routs stour tiros torsi torus tours trios orts ours oust outs riot rots rout rust ruts sori sort sour stir suit tiro tori tors tour trio tuis its ort our out rot rut sir sit sot sou tor tui is it or os si so ti to us ut

iorstuuv virtuous. *See* **iorstu**

iorsv visor sori sir is or os si so

iorsvz vizors visor vizor zoris sori zori sir is or os si so

iorsz zoris sori zori sir is or os si so

iort riot tiro tori trio ort rot tor it or ti to

iorvy ivory ivy or oy

iorvz vizor zori or

iorz zori or

iosttuw outwits. *See* **iottuw osttu isttw**

iottuw outwit twit tout out tit tot tow tui tut two wit it ow ti to ut

---

ip

ip pi

ipp pip pi

ipps pips pip sip is pi si

ipptuy uppity pipy pity pip pit pup put tip tui tup yip yup it pi ti up ut

ippy pipy pip yip pi

ippyz zippy pipy pip yip zip pi

ipqsu quips quip pus sip sup is pi si up us

ipqsuu quipus quips quipu quip pus sip sup is pi si up us

ipqu quip pi up

ipquu quipu quip pi up

ipr rip pi

iprrsstu stirrups irrupts purists stirrup. *See* **iprrtu iprsst iprstu ipsstu**

iprrstu irrupts stirrup. *See* **iprrtu iprstu**

iprrtu irrupt trip purr pit put rip rut tui tup it pi ti up ut

iprs rips rip sip sir is pi si

iprss priss rips sips sirs rip sip sir sis is pi si

iprsst sprits stirps strips priss spits sprit stirs strip trips pits rips sips sirs sits spit stir tips trip its pit rip sip sir sis sit pi si ti

iprsstu purists. *See* **iprstu ipsstu iprsst prsstu**

iprsstuu pursuits purists pursuit. *See* **iprsst iprstu ipsstu prsstu**

iprssy prissy priss spiry rips sips sirs spry yips pry rip sip sir sis spy yip is pi si

iprst sprit strip trips pits rips spit stir tips trip its pit rip sip sir sit tip is it pi si ti

iprstu purist situp sprit spurt strip trips pits puts rips rust ruts spit spur stir suit

---

tips trip tuis tups its pit pus put rip rut sip sir sit sup tip tui tup is it pi si ti up us ut

iprstuu pursuit. *See* **iprstu prsuu**

iprsty stripy spiry sprit strip tipsy trips pits pity rips spit spry stir tips trip yips its pit pry rip sip sir sit spy sty tip try yip is it pi si ti

iprstz spritz spitz sprit strip trips pits rips spit stir tips trip zips zits its pit rip sip sir sit tip zip zit is it pi si ti

iprsy spiry rips spry yips pry rip sip sir spy yip is pi si

iprt trip pit rip tip it pi ti

iprtuy purity pity trip yurt pit pry put rip rut tip try tui tup yip yup it pi ti up ut

iprvy privy ivy pry rip yip pi

ips sip is pi si

ipss sips sip sis is pi si

ipsst spits pits sips sits spit tips its pit sip sis sit tip is it pi si ti

ipsstty typists. *See* **ipstty ipsst**

ipsstu situps situp situs spits suits pits puss puts sips sits spit suit sups tips tuis tups its pit pus put sip sis sit sup tip tui tup is it pi si ti up us ut

ipssv spivs sips spiv sip sis is pi si

ipssw wisps sips wisp sip sis wis is pi si

ipst pits spit tips its pit sip sit tip is it pi si ti

ipstttu tittups. *See* **iptttu istttu**

ipstty typist tipsy pits pity spit tips tits yips its pit sip sit spy sty tip tit yip is it pi si ti

ipstu situp pits puts spit suit tips tuis tups its pit pus put sip sit sup tip tui tup is it pi si ti up us ut

ipsty tipsy pits pity spit tips yips its pit sip sit spy sty tip yip is it pi si ti

ipstz spitz pits spit tips zips zits its pit sip sit tip zip zit is it pi si ti

ipsv spiv sip is pi si

ipsw wisp sip wis is pi si

ipswy wispy wisp yips sip spy wis yip is pi si

ipsxy pyxis yips pixy pix pyx sip six spy yip is pi si xi

ipsy yips sip spy yip is pi si

ipsz zips sip zip is pi si

ipt pit tip it pi ti

iptttu tittup tutti putt pit put tip tit tui tup tut it pi ti up ut

ipty pity pit tip yip it pi ti

ipx pix pi xi

ipxy pixy pix pyx yip pi xi

ipy yip pi

ipz zip pi

---

iq

iqrsstu squirts. *See* **iqrstu**

iqrstu quirts squirt quirt quits quit rust ruts stir suit tuis its rut sir sit tui is it si ti us ut

iqrtu quirt quit tui rut it ti ut

iqstu quits quit suit tuis its sit tui is it si ti us ut

iqtu quit tui it ti ut

iquz quiz

---

ir

irs sir is si

irss sirs sir sis is si

irsst stirs sirs sits stir its sir sis sit is it si ti

irsstw wrists stirs wrist writs sirs sits stir wits writ its sir sis sit wis wit is it si ti

irst stir its sir sit is it si ti

irstw wrist writs stir wits writ its sir sit wis wit is it si ti

irsuv virus sir is si us

irtuv virtu tui rut it ti ut

irtw writ wit it ti

irtyz ritzy zit try it ti

irwy wiry

---

is

is is si

iss sis is si

issstu tussis situs suits sits suit tuis its sis sit tui is it si ti us ut

isssy sissy sis is si

isst sits its sis sit is it si ti

issttw twists twist twits sits tits twit wits its sis sit tit wis wit is it si ti

isstu situs suits sits suit tuis its sis sit tui is it si ti us ut

ist its sit is it si ti

istt tits its sit tit is it si ti

istttu tuttis tutti suit tits tuis tuts its sit tit tui tut is it si ti us ut

isttw twist twits tits twit wits its sit tit wis wit is it si ti
istu suit tuis its sit tui is it si ti us ut

istw wits its sit wis wit is it si ti
istxy sixty its sit six sty is it si ti xi
istz zits its sit zit is it si ti

isw wis is si
isx six is si xi

it

it it ti
itt tit it ti
itttu tutti tit tui tut it ti ut
ittty titty tit it ti

ittw twit tit wit it ti
ittwy witty twit tit wit it ti
itu tui it ti ut

itw wit it ti
ityzz tizzy zit it ti
itz zit it ti

iv—ix

ivy ivy
ix xi

j

jjsuu jujus juju jus us

jjuu juju

jknsu junks junk sunk jus nu us

jknu junk nu

jknuy junky junk yuk nu

jkoy joky joy jo oy

jlloy jolly joy jo lo oy

jlnstuuy unjustly. *See* **jnstuu**

jloosuyy joyously. *See* **joosuy**

jlost jolts jolt jots lost lots slot jot los lot sol sot jo lo os so to

jlosw jowls jowl lows owls slow los low owl sol sow jo lo os ow so

jlot jolt jot lot jo lo to

jloty jolty jolt jot joy lot toy jo lo oy to

jlow jowl low owl jo lo ow

jlowy jowly jowl yowl joy low owl yow jo lo ow oy

jmoo mojo moo jo mo om

jmoos mojos mojo moos moo mos oms jo mo om os so

jmorsu jorums jorum mors ours rums sour sumo jus mor mos mus oms our rum sou sum jo mo mu om or os so um us

jmoru jorum mor our rum jo mo mu om or um

jmpsu jumps jump sump umps jus mus pus sum sup ump mu um up us

jmpu jump ump mu um up

jmpuy jumpy jump ump yum yup mu my um up

jnnoorru nonjuror. *See* **jorru**

jnoorssu sojourns sojourn. *See* **orssu**

jnoorsu sojourn. *No 6s or 5s*

jnopsu jupons jupon nous onus opus pons puns soup spun upon jus pun pus son sop sou sun sup jo no nu on os so up us

jnopu jupon upon pun jo no nu on up

jnostu juntos joust junto snout tonus jots just juts nous nuts onus oust outs snot stun tons tuns unto jot jus jut not nut out son sot sou sun ton tun jo no nu on os so to us ut

jnotu junto unto jot jut not nut out ton tun jo no nu on to ut

jnstuu unjust just juts nuts stun tuns jus jut nut sun tun nu us ut

jo jo

joosuy joyous joys joy jus sou soy you jo os oy so us

jorrsu jurors juror ours sour jus our sou jo or os so us

jorru juror our jo or

joss joss jo os so

josstu jousts joust justs ousts joss jots just juts oust outs sots sous toss jot jus jut out sot sou jo os so to us ut

jost jots jot sot jo os so to

jostu joust jots just juts oust outs jot jus jut out sot sou jo os so to us ut

josy joys joy soy jo os oy so

jot jot jo to

joy joy jo oy

jruy jury

jsstu justs just juts jus jut us ut

jstu just juts jus jut us ut

jsu jus us

jtu jut ut

kk

kklmsuu mukluks. *See* **kklmuu kklsu**
kklmuu mukluk lum ulu mu um
kklssu skulks skulk sulks sulk us
kklsu skulk sulk us
kkmstuu muktuks. *See* **kkmtuu**

kkmtuu muktuk mu um ut
kkno konk no on
kknssu skunks skunk sunk suns sun nu us
kknsu skunk sunk sun nu us

kkoo kook
kkoos kooks kook kos os so
kkooy kooky kook oy
kkostu sukkot oust outs tusk kos out sot sou tsk os so to us ut

kl

kllmnsuu numskull. *See* **llsuu llmsu kllsu**
kllmossu mollusks mollusk. *See* **kllssu**
kllmosu mollusk. *See* **llmos llmsu kllsu**
kllno knoll lo no on
kllnos knolls knoll kos los sol son lo no on os so
kllssu skulls skull sulks sulk us
kllsu skull sulk us
klnorsty klystron. *See* **knost orsty norst**
klnpsu plunks plunk punks slunk spunk plus puls punk puns spun sulk sunk pul pun pus sun sup nu up us

klnpu plunk punk pul pun nu up
klnrsu knurls knurl knurs lurks slunk knur lurk runs rusk slur sulk sunk urns run sun urn nu us
klnru knurl lurk knur run urn nu
klnruy knurly knurl lurk knur run urn yuk nu
klnsu slunk sulk sunk sun nu us
kloo kolo look loo lo
klooostu lookouts outlooks lookout outlook. *See* **kloos loost lostu**
kloootu lookout outlook

kloos kolos looks kolo look loos solo kos loo los sol lo os so
klosy yolks yolk kos los sky sly sol soy lo os oy so
kloy yolk lo oy
kloyy yolky yolk lo oy
klrsu lurks lurk rusk slur sulk us
klru lurk
klssu sulks sulk us
klsu sulk us
kltuyz klutzy klutz yuk ut
kltuz klutz ut

km

kmno monk mon mo no om on
kmnos monks monk mons kos mon mos oms son mo no om on os so
kmosy smoky kos mos oms sky soy mo my om os oy so

kmrsu murks murk musk rums rusk mus rum sum mu um us
kmru murk rum mu um
kmruy murky murk rum yuk yum mu my um

kmsu musk mus sum mu um us
kmsuy musky musk yuks mus sky sum yuk yum mu my um us

kn

knnnosuw unknowns unknown. *See* **knnow knosw nnosu**
knnnouw unknown. *See* **knnow**
knnow known know now own wok won no on ow
knoo nook no on
knoopstt topknots topknot. *See* **knops knost knoos**

knooptt topknot. *No 6s or 5s*
knoorr kronor nook rook kor nor no on or
knoos nooks nook soon kos son no on os so
knooy nooky nook yon no on oy
knop knop no on
knoprty krypton. *See* **kopry**

knops knops knop pons kos son sop no on os so
knoru korun knur kor nor our run urn no nu on or
knost knots knot snot tons kos not son sot ton tsk no on os so to
knostu knouts knots knout snout stunk tonus knot nous nuts onus oust outs

snot stun sunk tons tuns tusk unto kos not nut out son sot sou sun ton tsk tun no nu on os so to us ut

knosw knows know owns snow sown woks kos now own son sow wok won no on os ow so

knosz zonks zonk kos son no on os so

knot knot not ton no on to

knotty knotty knot tony not ton tot toy yon no on oy to

knotu knout knot unto not nut out ton tun no nu on to ut

know know now own wok won no on ow

knowy wonky know now own wok won yon yow no on ow oy

knoz zonk no on

knpssu spunks punks spunk punk puns puss spun sunk suns sups pun pus sun sup nu up us

knpsu punks spunk punk puns spun sunk pun pus sun sup nu up us

knpsuy spunky punks punky spunk punk puns puny spun sunk yuks yups pun pus sky spy sun sup yuk yup nu up us

knpu punk pun nu up

knpuy punky punk puny pun yuk yup nu up

knrstu trunks knurs runts stunk trunk turns knur nuts runs runt rusk rust ruts stun sunk tuns turn tusk urns nut run rut sun tsk tun urn nu us ut

knrsu knurs knur runs rusk sunk urns run sun urn nu us

knrtu trunk knur runt turn nut run rut tun urn nu ut

knru knur run urn nu

knstu stunk nuts stun sunk tuns tusk nut sun tsk tun nu us ut

knsu sunk sun nu us

---

ko

koops spook oops kos sop os so

koopss spooks spook oops sops kos sop os so

koopsy spooky spook oops poky posy kos sky sop soy spy os oy so

koor rook kor or

koors rooks rook kor kos or os so

koorstuw workouts workout. *See* **oorstu**

koortuw workout. *No 6s or 5s*

koory rooky rook kor or oy

koost stook koto soot took kos sot too tsk os so to

koostww kowtows. *See* **kootww koost**

koot koto took too to

kootww kowtow koto took too tow two wok woo wow to ow

kopr pork kor pro or

koprs porks pork pros kor kos pro sop or os so

kopry porky poky pork ropy kor pro pry or oy

kopy poky oy

kor kor or

korsst storks torsks sorts stork torsk orts rots sort sots tors toss kor kos ort rot sot tor tsk or os so to

korst stork torsk orts rots sort tors kor kos ort rot sot tor tsk or os so to

korsw works rows woks work kor kos row sow wok or os ow so

korw work kor row wok or ow

kos kos os so

kosw woks kos sow wok os ow so

kow wok ow

---

kr

krssu rusks rusk us
krsu rusk us
kruu kuru

---

ks—ku

ksstu tusks tusk tsk us ut
kst tsk

kstu tusk tsk us ut
ksuy yuks sky yuk us

ksy sky
kuy yuk

ll

lllo loll lo
llloop lollop loll loop poll polo pool loo lop lo
lllooppy lollypop. *See* **llloop**
llloops lollops. *See* **llloop lllos loops**
lllos lolls loll los sol lo os so
llloy lolly loll lo oy
lllsu lulls lull us
lllu lull
llmo moll lo mo om
llmos molls moll los mos oms sol lo mo om os so
llmoy molly moll moly lo mo my om oy
llmppuy plumply. *See* **lmpuy lmppu lppuy**
llmsu mulls mull slum lum mus sum mu um us
llmu mull lum mu um
llnu null nu
llooprst trollops trollop. *See* **llorst looprs ooprst**
llooprt trollop. *See* **loopr llort ooprt**

lloowy woolly lowly wool yowl loo low owl woo yow lo ow oy
llop poll lop lo
llops polls lops poll slop lop los sol sop lo os so
llopstuu pullouts pullout. *See* **lopstu**
lloptuu pullout. *See* **loptu**
llor roll lo or
llors rolls roll los sol lo or os so
llorsst strolls. *See* **llorst**
llorst stroll trolls rolls tolls troll lost lots orts roll rotl rots slot sort toll tors los lot ort rot sol sot tor lo or os so to
llort troll roll rotl toll lot ort rot tor lo or to
llost tolls lost lots slot toll los lot sol sot lo os so to
lloswy slowly lowly yowls lows owls slow yowl los low owl sly sol sow soy yow lo os ow oy so

llot toll lot lo to
llowy lowly yowl low owl yow lo ow oy
lloxy xylol lox lo ox oy
llppsuu pullups. *See* **llppuu llsuu lpsuu**
llppuu pullup lulu pull pulp pul pup ulu up
llpsu pulls plus pull puls pul pus sup up us
llpu pull pul up
llrstu trulls trull stull lust rust ruts slur slut rut us ut
llrtu trull rut ut
llsstu stulls lusts sluts stull lust slut us ut
llstu stull lust slut us ut
llsuu lulus lulu ulus ulu us
llsuy sully sly us
llsyy slyly sly
lluu lulu ulu

fm

lmmoux lummox lox lum lux mom mum lo mo mu om ox um
lmnooopy monopoly. *See* **lnooy loopy mnooy**
lmoo loom loo moo lo mo om
lmooopr poolroom. *See* **loopr moopr**
lmoooort toolroom. *See* **lmoot moort**
lmoorsu ormolus. *See* **lmooru lmoos moors**
lmooru ormolu loom moor room loo lum moo mor our rum lo mo mu om or um
lmoos looms loom loos moos solo loo los moo mos oms sol lo mo om os so
lmoot molto loom loot molt moot tool loo lot moo mot tom too lo mo om to
lmootxyy xylotomy. *See* **lmoot**
lmoopprty promptly. *See* **loppry loprty mopprt**
lmosst smolts molts slots smolt loss lost lots molt moss most mots slot sols sots toms toss los lot mos mot oms sol sot tom lo mo om os so to
lmost molts smolt lost lots molt most mots slot toms los lot mos mot oms sol sot tom lo mo om os so to

lmostu moults lotus louts molts moult smolt lost lots lout lust molt most mots must oust outs slot slum slut smut soul stum sumo tolu toms los lot lum mos mot mus oms out sol sot sou sum tom lo mo mu om os so to um us ut
lmosty mostly molts smolt lost lots molt moly most mots slot toms toys los lot mos mot oms sly sol sot soy sty tom toy lo mo my om os oy so to
lmot molt lot mot tom lo mo om to
lmotu moult lout molt tolu lum mot out tom lo mo mu om to um ut
lmoy moly lo mo my om oy
lmppsu plumps lumps plump plums pulps pumps slump lump plum plus pulp puls pump pups slum sump umps lum mus pul pup pus sum sup ump mu um up us
lmppu plump lump plum pulp pump lum pul pup ump mu um up

lmpruy rumply lumpy lump plum purl rump lum ply pry pul rum ump yum yup mu my um up
lmpssu slumps lumps plums slump slums sumps lump muss plum plus puss slum sump sums sups umps lum mus pul pus sum sup ump mu um up us
lmpsu lumps plums slump lump plum plus puls slum sump umps lum mus pul pus sum sup ump mu um up us
lmpu lump plum lum pul ump mu um up
lmpuy lumpy lump plum lum ply pul ump yum yup mu my um up
lmrsstuu lustrums lustrum. *See* **mrsstu**
lmrstuu lustrum. *See* **mrstu**
lmssu slums muss slum sums lum mus sum mu um us
lmsttuu tumults. *See* **lmttuu msttu sttuu**
lmstuuu tumulus. *No 6s or 5s*
lmsu slum lum mus sum mu um us

lmttuu tumult mutt tutu lum tut ulu mu
 um ut
lmu lum mu um

---

ln

lnnopsu nonplus. *See* **nnosu**
lnnosy nonyls nylons nonyl nylon sonny
 only nosy los sly sol son soy yon lo no
 on os oy so
lnnoy nonyl nylon only yon lo no on oy
lnoo loon loo lo no on
lnoooprt poltroon. *See* **nooprt**
lnoopsww snowplow. *See* **lnoos loops
 lopsw**

lnoos loons loon loos solo soon loo los
 sol son lo no on os so
lnooy loony loon only loo yon lo no on
 oy
lnopsy pylons pylon ploys lops nosy
 only ploy pons pony posy slop lop los
 ply sly sol son sop soy spy yon lo no on
 os oy so
lnopy pylon only ploy pony lop ply yon
 lo no on oy

lnor lorn nor lo no on or
lnoy only yon lo no on oy
lnruuy unruly run ulu urn nu
lnstu lunts lunt lust nuts slut stun tuns
 nut sun tun nu us ut
lntu lunt nut tun nu ut
lnxy lynx

---

lo

lo lo
loo loo lo
looov ovolo loo lo
loop loop polo pool loo lop lo
looppsuu populous pulpous. *See* **loops
 lpsuu lopps**
loopr orlop loop polo pool poor loo lop
 pro lo or
looprs orlops loops orlop polos pools
 sloop sopor spool spoor loop loos lops
 oops polo pool poor pros slop solo loo
 lop los pro sol sop lo or os so
loopry poorly orlop loopy loop lory ploy
 polo pool poor ropy loo lop ply pro pry
 lo or oy
loops loops polos pools sloop spool loop
 loos lops oops polo pool slop solo loo
 lop los sol sop lo os so
loopss sloops spools loops polos pools
 sloop slops solos spool loop loos lops
 loss oops polo pool slop solo sols sops
 loo lop los sol sop lo os so
loopy loopy loop ploy polo pool loo lop
 ply lo oy
loos loos solo loo los sol lo os so
looss solos loos loss solo sols loo los sol
 lo os so
loosst sotols stools loots slots solos soots
 sotol stool tools loos loot loss lost lots

slot solo sols soot sots tool toss loo los
 lot sol sot too lo os so to
loosstv volosts. *See* **loosst loostv**
loost loots sotol stool tools loos loot lost
 lots slot solo soot tool loo los lot sol sot
 too lo os so to
loostv volost loots sotol stool tools volts
 loos loot lots slot solo soot tool
 volt loo los lot sol sot too lo os so to
loosw wools loos lows owls slow solo
 wool woos loo los low owl sol sow woo
 lo os ow so
loot loot tool loo lot too lo to
loott lotto loot tool toot loo lot too tot lo
 to
loovvx volvox loo lox lo ox
loow wool loo low owl woo lo ow
lop lop lo
lopp plop lop pop lo
lopprsy propyls. *See* **loppsy loppry**
loppry propyl loppy polyp lory plop ploy
 prop ropy lop ply pop pro pry lo or oy
lopps plops lops plop pops slop lop los
 pop sol sop lo os so
loppsuu pulpous. *See* **lpsuu lopps lppsu**
loppsy polyps sloppy loppy plops ploys
 polyp soppy lops plop ploy pops posy
 slop lop los ply pop sly sol sop soy spy
 lo os oy so

loppy loppy polyp plop ploy lop ply pop
 lo oy
loprsuy pylorus. *See* **lorsuy lopsy oprsu**
loprsw prowls plows prowl prows lops
 lows owls plow pros prow rows slop
 slow swop lop los low owl pro row sol
 sop sow lo or os ow so
loprtuy poultry. *See* **loprty loptu lrtuy**
loprty portly lory plot ploy port ropy rotl
 ryot troy tyro lop lot ort ply pot pro
 pry rot top tor toy try lo or oy to
loprw prowl plow prow lop low owl pro
 row lo or ow
lops lops slop lop los sol sop lo os so
lopss slops lops loss slop sols sops lop los
 sol sop lo os so
lopst plots lops lost lots plot post pots
 slop slot spot stop tops slop lop los lot pot
 sol sop sot top lo os so to
lopstu poults lotus louts plots poult
 pouts spout stoup lops lost lots lout
 lust opus oust outs plot plus post pots
 pout puls puts slop slot slut soul soup
 spot stop tolu tops tups lop los lot out
 pot pul pus put sol sop sot sou sup top
 tup lo os so to up us ut
lopsw plows lops lows owls plow slop
 slow swop lop los low owl sol sop sow
 lo os ow so

lopsy   ploys lops ploy posy slop lop los ply sly sol sop soy spy lo os oy so

lopt   plot lop lot pot top lo to

loptu   poult lout plot pout tolu lop lot out pot pul put top tup lo to up ut

lopw   plow lop low owl lo ow

lopy   ploy lop ply lo oy

lorry   lorry lory lo or oy

lorsstuu   lustrous. *See* **orsstu**

lorsuy   sourly lousy surly yours lory ours rosy slur soul sour your los our sly sol sou soy you lo or os oy so us

lort   rotl lot ort rot tor lo or to

lory   lory lo or oy

los   los sol lo os so

loss   loss sols los sol lo os so

losst   slots loss lost lots slot sols sots toss los lot sol sot lo os so to

lossu   souls loss sols soul sous los sol sou lo os so us

lossw   slows loss lows owls slow sols sows los low owl sol sow lo os ow so

lost   lost lots slot los lot sol sot lo os so to

losttuy   stoutly. *See* **lostu losuy lstuy**

lostu   lotus louts lost lots lout lust oust outs slot slut soul tolu los lot out sol sot sou lo os so to us ut

lostv   volts lost lots slot volt los lot sol sot lo os so to

lostyz   zlotys zloty lost lots slot toys los lot sly sol sot soy sty toy lo os oy so to

losu   soul los sol sou lo os so us

losuy   lousy soul los sly sol sou soy you lo os oy so us

losw   lows owls slow los low owl sol sow lo os ow so

loswy   yowls lows owls slow yowl los low owl sly sol sow soy yow lo os ow oy so

lot   lot lo to

lotu   lout tolu lot out lo to ut

lotv   volt lot lo to

lotyz   zloty lot toy lo oy to

low   low owl lo ow

lowy   yowl low owl yow lo ow oy

lox   lox lo ox

lppsu   pulps plus pulp puls pups pul pup pus sup up us

lppsuy   supply pulps pulpy plus pulp puls pups yups ply pul pup pus sly spy sup yup up us

lppu   pulp pul pup up

lppuy   pulpy pulp ply pul pup yup up

lprssu   slurps purls slurp slurs spurs plus puls purl puss slur spur sups pul pus sup up us

lprssuu   surplus. *See* **lprssu prssuu**

lprsu   purls slurp plus puls purl slur spur pul pus sup up us

lprsyy   spryly spry ply pry sly spy

lpru   purl pul up

lpsu   plus puls pul pus sup up us

lpsuu   lupus plus puls ulus pul pus sup ulu up us

lpu   pul up

lpy   ply

lrrsuy   slurry surly slur sly us

lrssu   slurs slur us

lrstuy   sultry lusty rusty surly truly yurts lust rust ruts slur slut yurt rut sly sty try us ut

lrsu   slur us

lrsuy   surly slur sly us

lrtuy   truly yurt rut try ut

lruuxy   luxury ulu lux

lrwyy   wryly wry

lsstu   lusts sluts lust slut us ut

lsstuy   stylus lusts lusty sluts lust slut sly sty us ut

lstu   lust slut us ut

lstuy   lusty lust slut sly sty us ut

lsuu   ulus ulu us

lsy   sly

---

lu

luu ulu
luv luv
lux lux

---

mm

mmmoy mommy mom mo my om oy
mmmuy mummy mum yum mu my um
mmnossu summons. *See* **mmnosu mossu**
mmnosu summon muons moms mons
   mums muon nous onus sumo mom
   mon mos mum mus oms son sou sum
   sun mo mu no nu om on os so um us
mmo mom mo om
mmoopp pompom pomp poop mom
   moo mop pop mo om

mmoopps pompoms. *See* **mmoopp oopps**
mmoostt motmots. *See* **mmoott moostt**
mmoott motmot motto moot toot mom
   moo mot tom too tot mo om to
mmopssty symptoms symptom. *See*
   mopsst
mmopsty symptom. *See* **mopst opsty**
mmos moms mom mos oms mo om os so
mmpsu mumps mums sump umps mum
   mus pus sum sup ump mu um up us

mmrrsuu murmurs. *See* **mmrruu**
mmrruu murmur mum rum mu um
mmruy rummy mum rum yum mu my
   um
mmsu mums mum mus sum mu um us
mmsuuuu muumuus. *See* **mmuuuu**
mmtuy tummy mum yum mu my um ut
mmu mum mu um
mmuuuu muumuu mum mu um
mmuyy yummy mum yum mu my um

---

mn

mnnooos monsoon. *See* **mnoos nnoos**
mnnoooss monsoons monsoon. *See*
   mnoos nnoos
mnnoooty monotony. *See* **mnooy nooty**
mnnossyy synonyms synonym. *See*
   mossy nnosy
mnnosyy synonym. *See* **nnosy**
mnnosyyy synonymy synonym. *See*
   nnosy
mnnouw unmown mown muon noun
   mon mow now nun own won mo mu
   no nu om on ow um
mno mon mo no om on
mnoo mono moon mon moo mo no om
   on
mnooorxy oxymoron. *See* **mnooy mnoor**
   moory
mnoopp pompon mono moon pomp
   poon poop mon moo mop pop mo no
   om on
mnoor moron mono moon moor morn
   norm room mon moo mor nor mo no
   om on or
mnoors morons moons moors morns
   moron norms rooms mono mons
   moon moor moos morn mors norm
   room soon mon moo mor mos nor oms
   son mo no om on or os so

mnoos moons mono mons moon moos
   soon mon moo mos oms son mo no om
   on os so
mnoostu moutons. *See* **mnostu mnootu**
mnootu mouton mount notum mono
   moon moot muon onto toon unto mon
   moo mot not nut out tom ton too tun
   mo mu no nu om on to um ut
mnooy moony mono moon mon moo
   yon mo my no om on oy
mnor morn norm mon mor nor mo no
   om on or
mnors morns norms mons morn mors
   norm mon mor mos nor oms son mo
   no om on or os so
mnorsstu nostrums nostrum. *See* **mnorsu**
   mnostu morsst morstu
mnorstu nostrum. *See* **mnostu mnorsu**
   morstu
mnorstuu surmount nostrum outruns.
   See **mnorsu mnostu morstu nortuu**
mnorsu mourns morns mourn muons
   norms mons morn mors muon norm
   nous onus ours rums runs sour sumo
   urns mon mor mos mus nor oms our
   rum run son sou sum sun urn mo mu
   no nu om on or os so um us

mnoru mourn morn muon norm mon
   mor nor our rum run urn mo mu no nu
   om on or um
mnos mons mon mos oms son mo no om
   on os so
mnosttu muttons. *See* **mnostu mnottu**
   mosttu
mnostu mounts mutons mount muons
   notum snout tonus mons most mots
   muon must nous nuts onus oust outs
   smut snot stum stun sumo toms tons
   tuns unto mon mos mot mus not nut
   oms out son sot sou sum sun tom ton
   tun mo mu no nu om on os so to um us
   ut
mnosu muons mons muon nous onus
   sumo mon mos mus oms son sou sum
   sun mo mu no nu om on os so um us
mnottu mutton mount notum muon
   mutt tout unto mon mot not nut out
   tom ton tot tun tut mo mu no nu om
   on to um ut
mnotu mount notum muon unto mon
   mot not nut out tom ton tun mo mu no
   nu om on to um ut
mnou muon mon mo mu no nu om on
   um

mnow mown mon mow now own won mo no om on ow

---

mo

mo mo om

moo moo mo om

mooorrtw tomorrow. *See* **moorrw**

moootyz zootomy. *No 6s or 5s*

mooppsu pompous. *See* **mppsu oopps**

moopr promo moor poor prom romp room moo mop mor pro mo om or

mooprs promos moors promo proms romps rooms sopor spoor moor moos mops mors oops poor prom pros romp room moo mop mor mos oms pro sop mo om or os so

moopsssu opossums opossum possums. *See* **mopssu**

moopssu opossum. *See* **mopssu**

moopstt topmost. *See* **moostt mopst oopst**

moor moor room moo mor mo om or

moorr morro moor room moo mor mo om or

moorrs morros moors morro rooms moor moos mors room moo mor mos oms mo om or os so

moorrsw morrows. *See* **moorrs moorrw oorrsw**

moorrw morrow morro moor room worm moo mor mow row woo mo om or ow

moors moors rooms moor moos mors room moo mor mos oms mo om or os so

moorst motors moors moots morts motor rooms roost roots rotos storm torso moor moos moot mors mort most mots orts room root roto rots soot sort toms tors moo mor mos mot oms ort rot sot tom too tor mo om or os so to

moort motor moor moot mort room root roto moo mor mot ort rot tom too tor mo om or to

moory roomy moor room moo mor mo my om or oy

moos moos moo mos oms mo om os so

moost moots moos moot most mots soot toms moo mos mot oms sot tom too mo om os so to

moostt mottos moots motto toots moos moot most mots soot toms toot tost tots moo mos mot oms sot tom too tot mo om os so to

moosttu outmost. *See* **moostt mosttu**

moot moot moo mot tom too mo om to

moott motto moot toot moo mot tom too tot mo om to

mooz zoom zoo mo om

mop mop mo om

mopp pomp mop pop mo om

mopprst prompts. *See* **mopprt morst oprst**

mopprt prompt mort pomp port prom prop romp mop mor mot ort pop pot pro rot tom top tor mo om or to

mopr prom romp mop mor pro mo om or

moprs proms romps mops mors prom pros romp mop mor mos oms pro sop mo om or os so

mops mops mop mos oms sop mo om os so

mopsssu possums. *See* **mopssu**

mopsst stomps posts spots stomp stops mops moss most mots post pots sops sots spot stop toms tops toss mop mos mot oms pot sop sot tom top mo om os so to

mopssu possum soups sumos sumps mops moss muss opus puss sops soup sous sumo sump sums sups umps mop mos mus oms pus sop sou sum sup ump mo mu om os so um up us

mopssuu spumous. *See* **mopssu**

mopst stomp mops most mots post pots spot stop toms tops mop mos mot oms pot sop sot tom top mo om os so to

mopstu upmost pouts spout stomp stoup stump tumps mops most mots must opus oust outs post pots pout puts smut soup spot stop stum sumo sump toms tops tump tups umps mop mos mot mus oms out pot pus put sop sot sou sum sup tom top tup ump mo mu om os so to um up us ut

moqrsuu quorums. *See* **moqruu**

moqruu quorum mor our rum mo mu om or um

mor mor mo om or

morrsstu rostrums rostrum. *See* **morrsu morsst morstu mrsstu**

morrstu rostrum. *See* **morrsu morstu**

morrsu rumors rumor mors ours rums sour sumo mor mos mus oms our rum sou sum mo mu om or os so um us

morru rumor mor our rum mo mu om or um

mors mors mor mos oms mo om or os so

morsst storms morts sorts storm mors mort moss most mots orts rots sort sots toms tors toss mor mos mot oms ort rot sot tom tor mo om or os so to

morst morts storm mors mort most mots orts rots sort toms tors mor mos mot oms ort rot sot tom tor mo om or os so to

morstu tumors morts roust routs storm stour strum torus tours tumor mors mort most mots must orts ours oust outs rots rout rums rust ruts smut sort sour stum sumo toms tors tour mor mos mot mus oms ort our out rot rum rut sot sou sum tom tor mo mu om or os so to um us ut

morsty stormy morts ryots storm story tyros mors mort most mots orts rosy rots ryot sort toms tors toys troy tyro mor mos mot oms ort rot sot soy sty tom tor toy try mo my om or os oy so to

morsw worms mors mows rows worm mor mos mow oms row sow mo om or os ow so

mort mort mor mot ort rot tom tor mo om or to

mortu tumor mort rout tour mor mot ort our out rot rum rut tom tor mo mu om or to um ut

morw worm mor mow row mo om or ow

morwy wormy worm mor mow row yow mo my om or ow oy

mos mos oms mo om os so

moss moss mos oms mo om os so

mossu sumos moss muss sous sumo sums mos mus oms sou sum mo mu om os so um us

mossy mossy moss soys mos oms soy mo my om os oy so

most most mots toms mos mot oms sot tom mo om os so to

mosttu utmost mutts stout touts most mots must mutt oust outs smut stum sumo toms tost tots tout tuts mos mot mus oms out sot sou sum tom tot tut mo mu om os so to um us ut

mosu sumo mos mus oms sou sum mo mu om os so um us

mosuy mousy sumo mos mus oms sou soy sum you yum mo mu my om os oy so um us

mosw mows mos mow oms sow mo om os ow so

mot mot tom mo om to

mouv ovum mo mu om um

mow mow mo om ow

---

mp

mppsu pumps pump pups sump umps mus pup pus sum sup ump mu um up us

mppu pump ump pup mu um up

mprstu trumps rumps spurt strum stump trump tumps must puts rump rums rust ruts smut spur stum sump tump tups umps mus pus put rum rut sum sup tup ump mu um up us ut

mprsu rumps rump rums spur sump umps mus pus rum sum sup ump mu um up us

mprsuu rumpus rumps usurp rump rums spur sump umps urus mus pus rum sum sup ump mu um up us

mprtu trump rump tump put rum rut tup ump mu um up ut

mpru rump ump rum mu um up

mpsstu stumps musts smuts stump stums sumps tumps muss must puss puts smut stum sump sums sups tump tups umps mus pus put sum sup tup ump mu um up us ut

mpssu sumps muss puss sump sums sups umps mus pus sum sup ump mu um up us

mpstu stump tumps must puts smut stum sump tump tups umps mus pus put sum sup tup ump mu um up us ut

mpstuu sputum stump tumps must puts smut stum sump tump tups umps mus

pus put sum sup tup ump mu um up us ut

mpstuy stumpy musty spumy stump tumps must puts smut stum sump tump tups umps yups mus pus put spy sty sum sup tup ump yum yup mu my um up us ut

mpsu sump umps mus pus sum sup ump mu um up us

mpsuy spumy sump umps yups mus pus spy sum sup ump yum yup mu my um up us

mptu tump put tup ump mu um up ut

mpu ump mu um up

---

mr

mrsstu strums musts rusts smuts strum stums truss muss must rums rust ruts smut stum sums mus rum rut sum mu um us ut

mrstu strum must rums rust ruts smut stum mus rum rut sum mu um us ut

mrsu rums mus rum sum mu um us

mru rum mu um

---

ms

msstu musts smuts stums muss must smut stum sums mus sum mu um us ut

mssu muss sums mus sum mu um us

mssuy mussy muss sums mus sum yum mu my um us

msttu mutts must mutt smut stum tuts mus sum tut mu um us ut

msttuy smutty mutts musty must mutt smut stum tuts mus sty sum tut yum mu my um us ut

mstu must smut stum mus sum mu um us ut

mstuy musty must smut stum mus sty sum yum mu my um us ut

mstyy stymy sty my

msu   mus sum mu um us
msuw   swum mus sum mu um us

---

mt—my

mttu   mutt tut mu um ut   **muyzz**   muzzy yum mu my um
mu   mu um   **my**   my
muy   yum mu my um

nn

nnoo noon no on
nnooopst pontoons pontoon nonstop. *See* **nnoos noops noost**
nnoopt pontoon. *No 6s or 5s*
nnooprsu pronouns pronoun. *See* **nooprs ooprsu**
nnoopru pronoun. *See* **noopr**
nnoopss sponson. *See* **noopss**

nnoopsss sponsons sponson. *See* **noopss**
nnoopst nonstop. *See* **nnoos noops noost**
nnoos noons noon soon son no on os so
nnosu nouns noun nous nuns onus sunn nun son sou sun no nu on os so us
nnosy sonny nosy son soy yon no on os oy so

nnou noun nun no nu on
nnruy runny nun run urn nu
nnsu nuns sunn nun sun nu us
nnsuy sunny nuns sunn nun sun nu us
nnu nun nu

no

no no on
nooorssu sonorous. *See* **orssu**
noop poon no on
noopr porno poon poor nor pro no on or
nooprs pornos poons porno snoop sopor spoon oops pons poon poor porn pros soon nor pro son sop no on or os so
nooprss sponsor. *See* **nooprs noopss ooprss**
nooprsss sponsors sponsor. *See* **nooprs noopss**
nooprst protons. *See* **nooprs nooprt ooprst**
nooprt pronto proton porno troop onto poon poor porn port root roto toon torn nor not ort pot pro rot ton too top tor no on or to
noops poons snoop spoon oops pons poon soon son sop no on os so
noopss snoops spoons poons snoop spoon oops pons poon sons soon sops son sop no on os so
noopsy snoopy spoony poons snoop spoon nosy oops pons pony poon posy soon son sop soy spy yon no on os oy so
noortuw outworn. *No 6s or 5s*
noos soon son no on os so
noosst snoots snoot snots soots toons onto snot sons soon soot sots tons toon toss not son sot ton too no on os so to
noossw swoons swoon snows owns snow sons soon sown sows woos now own son sow won woo no on os so ow so
noost snoot toons onto snot soon soot tons toon not son sot ton too no on os so to

noosty snooty toyons snoot sooty stony toons toyon nosy onto snot soon soot tons tony toon toys not son sot soy sty ton too toy yon no on os oy so to
noosw swoon owns snow soon sown woos now own son sow won woo no on os ow so
noot onto toon not ton too no on to
nooty toyon onto tony toon not ton too toy yon no on oy to
nooz zoon zoo no on
nopr porn nor pro no on or
nops pons son sop no on os so
nopssstu sunspots sunspot tossups. *See* **nosstu opsstu**
nopsstu sunspot. *See* **nosstu opsstu**
noptuw uptown nowt pout punt town unto upon wont not now nut out own pot pun put ton top tow tun tup two won no nu on ow to up ut
nopu upon pun no nu on up
nopy pony yon no on oy
nor nor no on or
norsst snorts snort snots sorts orts rots snot sons sort sots tons torn tors toss nor not ort rot son sot ton tor no on or os so to
norst snort orts rots snot sort tons torn tors nor not ort rot son sot ton tor no on or os so to
norsttuu turnouts outruns surtout turnout. *See* **nortuu orsttu**
norstuu outruns. *See* **nortuu orstu nrstu**
norsw sworn owns rows snow sown worn nor now own row son sow won no on or os ow so
nort torn nor not ort rot ton tor no on or to
norttuu turnout. *See* **nortuu orttu**

nortuu outrun rout runt torn tour turn unto nor not nut ort our out rot run rut ton tor tun urn no nu on or to ut
norw worn nor now own row won no on or ow
nos son no on os so
noss sons son no on os so
nosst snots snot sons sots tons toss not son sot ton no on os so to
nosstu snouts ousts snots snout stuns tonus nous nuts onus oust outs snot sons sots sous stun suns tons toss tuns unto not nut out son sot sou sun ton tun no nu on os so to us ut
nossw snows owns snow sons sown sows now own son sow won no on os ow so
nost snot tons not son sot ton no on os so to
nostty snotty stony nosy snot tons tony tost tots toys not son sot soy sty ton tot toy yon no on os oy so to
nostu snout tonus nous nuts onus oust outs snot stun tons tuns unto not nut out son sot sou sun ton tun no nu on os so to us ut
nostw towns wonts nowt owns snot snow sown stow swot tons town tows twos wont not now own son sot sow ton tow two won no on os ow so to
nosty stony nosy snot tons tony toys not son sot soy sty ton toy yon no on os oy so to
nosu nous onus son sou sun no nu on os so us
nosw owns snow sown now own son sow won no on os ow so
noswy snowy nosy owns snow sown now own son sow soy won yon yow no on os ow oy so

nosy nosy son soy yon no on os oy so
not not ton no on to
notu unto not nut out ton tun no nu on to ut

notw nowt town wont not now own ton tow two won no on ow to
noty tony not ton toy yon no on oy to

now now own won no on ow
noxy onyx yon no on ox oy
noy yon no on oy

---

np

nprssu spurns spurn spurs puns puss runs spun spur suns sups urns pun pus run sun sup urn nu up us
nprstuu upturns. *See* **nprtuu npstu nrstu**
nprsu spurn puns runs spun spur urns pun pus run sun sup urn nu up us
nprtuu upturn punt runt turn nut pun put run rut tun tup urn nu up ut

npssuu sunups sunup puns puss spun suns sups pun pus sun sup nu up us
npstu punts nuts puns punt puts spun stun tuns tups nut pun pus put sun sup tun tup nu up us ut
npsu puns spun pun pus sun sup nu up us

npsuu sunup puns spun pun pus sun sup nu up us
nptu punt nut pun put tun tup nu up ut
nptuy punty punt puny nut pun put tun tup yup nu up ut
npu pun nu up
npuy puny pun yup nu up

---

nr

nrstu runts turns nuts runs runt rust ruts stun tuns turn urns nut run rut sun tun urn nu us ut
nrsu runs urns run sun urn nu us

nrtu runt turn nut run rut tun urn nu ut
nrtuy runty runt turn yurt nut run rut try tun urn nu ut
nru run urn nu

---

ns

nssttu stunts stuns stunt nuts stun suns tuns tuts nut sun tun tut nu us ut
nsstu stuns nuts stun suns tuns nut sun tun nu us ut

nssu suns sun nu us
nsttu stunt nuts stun tuns tuts nut sun tun tut nu us ut
nstu nuts stun tuns nut sun tun nu us ut

nstuy nutsy nuts stun tuns nut sty sun tun nu us ut
nsu sun nu us

---

nt—nu

nttuy nutty nut tun tut nu ut
ntu nut tun nu ut
nu nu

oo

oopp poop pop

oopps poops oops poop pops pop sop os so

oopr poor pro or

ooprrst torpors. *See* **ooprrt ooprst**

ooprrt torpor troop poor port root roto torr ort pot pro rot too top tor or to

ooprs sopor spoor oops poor pros pro sop or os so

ooprss sopors spoors sopor spoor oops poor pros sops pro sop or os so

ooprsstv provosts provost. *See* **ooprss ooprst oopsst oorsst**

ooprst troops ports roost roots rotos sopor spoor sport stoop strop torso troop oops orts poor port post pots pros root roto rots soot sort spot stop tors ort pot pro rot sop sot too top tor or os so to

ooprstu uproots. *See* **ooprsu oprstu oorstu ooprst ooprtu**

ooprstv provost. *See* **ooprst**

ooprsu porous pours sopor spoor oops opus ours poor pour pros soup sour spur our pro pus sop sou sup or os so up us

ooprt troop poor port root roto ort pot pro rot too top tor or to

ooprtu uproot troop poor port pour pout root roto rout tour ort our out pot pro put rot rut too top tor tup or to up ut

oops oops sop os so

oopsst stoops posts soots spots stoop stops oops post pots soot sops sots spot stop tops toss pot sop sot too top os so to

oopssttu outposts outpost. *See* **oopsst opsstu ossttu**

oopssw swoops swoop swops oops sops sows swop woos sop sow woo os ow so

oopst stoop oops post pots soot spot stop tops pot sop sot too top os so to

oopsttu outpost. *See* **opstu psttu oopst**

oopsw swoop oops swop woos sop sow woo os ow so

oopswww powwows. *See* **oopwww oopsw**

oopwww powwow woo wow ow

oorrssw sorrows. *See* **oorrsw**

oorrsw sorrow woos rows row sow woo or os ow so

oorsst roosts torsos roost roots rotos soots sorts torso orts root roto rots soot sort sots tors toss ort rot sot too tor or os so to

oorst roost roots rotos torso orts root roto rots soot sort tors ort rot sot too tor or os so to

oorsttuu tortuous surtout. *See* **oorstu orsttu**

oorstu torous roost roots rotos roust routs stour torso torus tours orts ours oust outs root roto rots rout rust ruts soot sort sour tors tour ort our out rot rut sot sou too tor or os so to us ut

oorsz orzos orzo zoos zoo or os so

oort root roto ort rot too tor or to

oorty rooty root roto ryot troy tyro ort rot too tor toy try or oy to

oorz orzo zoo or

oosst soots soot sots toss too sot os so to

oost soot too sot os so to

oostt toots soot toot tost tots sot too tot os so to

oostty tootsy toots sooty soot toot tost tots toys sot soy sty too tot toy os oy so to

oosty sooty soot toys sot soy sty too toy os oy so to

oosuz ouzos zoos ouzo zoo sou os so us

oosw woos woo sow os ow so

oosz zoos zoo os so

oot too to

oott toot too tot to

oouz ouzo zoo

oow woo ow

oowyz woozy oozy woo yow zoo ow oy

ooyz oozy zoo oy

ooz zoo

op

opp pop

opppy poppy pop oy

oppr prop pop pro or

opprrstu purports purport support. *See* **oprstu**

opprrtu purport. *No 6s or 5s*

opprs props pops prop pros pop pro sop or os so

opprsstu supports sprouts stupors support. *See* **oprsst oprstu opsstu orsstu**

opprstu support. *See* **oprstu**

opps pops pop sop os so

oppsy soppy pops posy pop sop soy spy os oy so

opr pro or

oprs pros pro sop or os so

oprsssuu sourpuss. *See* **prssuu**

oprsst sports strops ports posts sorts sport spots stops strop orts port post pots pros rots sops sort sots spot stop tops tors toss ort pot pro rot sop sot top tor or os so to

oprsstu sprouts stupors. *See* **orsstu oprsst opsstu oprstu prsstu**

oprst ports sport strop orts port post pots pros rots sort spot stop tops tors ort pot pro rot sop sot top tor or os so to

oprstu sprout stupor ports pours pouts roust routs sport spout spurt stoup stour strop torus tours opus orts ours oust outs port post pots pour pout pros puts rots rout rust ruts sort soup sour spot spur stop tops tors tour tups ort our out pot pro pus put rot rut sop sot sou sup top tor tup or os so to up us ut

oprsty sporty ports potsy prosy ryots sport story strop tyros orts port post posy pots pros ropy rosy rots ryot sort spot spry stop tops tors toys troy tyro ort pot pro pry rot sop sot soy spy sty top tor toy try or os oy so to

oprsu pours opus ours pour pros soup sour spur our pro pus sop sou sup or os so up us

oprsw prows pros prow rows swop pro row sop sow or os ow so

oprsy prosy posy pros ropy rosy spry pro pry sop soy spy or os oy so

oprt port ort pot pro rot top tor or to

opru pour pro our or up

oprw prow pro row or ow

oprxy proxy ropy oryx pox pro pry pyx or ox oy

opry ropy pro pry or oy

ops sop os so

opss sops sop os so

opssstu tossups. *See* **opsstu**

opsst posts spots stops post pots sops sots spot stop tops toss pot sop sot top os so to

opsstu spouts stoups tossup ousts posts pouts soups spots spout stops stoup opus oust outs post pots pout puss puts sops sots soup sous spot stop sups tops toss tups out pot pus put sop sot sou sup top tup os so to up us ut

opssu soups opus puss sops soup sous sups pus sop sou sup os so up us

opssw swops sops sows swop sop sow os ow so

opst post pots spot stop tops pot sop sot top os so to

opstt stopt post pots spot stop tops tost tots pot sop sot top tot os so to

opsttuu putouts. *See* **opttuu opstu psttu**

opstty spotty potsy potty stopt post posy pots spot stop tops tost tots toys pot sop sot soy spy sty top tot toy os oy so to

opstu pouts spout stoup opus oust outs post pots pout puts soup spot stop tops tups out pot pus put sop sot sou sup top tup os so to up us ut

opsty potsy post posy pots spot stop tops toys pot sop sot soy spy sty top toy os oy so to

opsu opus soup pus sop sou sup os so up us

opsuy soupy opus posy soup yups pus sop sou soy spy sup you yup os oy so up us

opsw swop sop sow os ow so

opsy posy sop soy spy os oy so

opt pot top to

opttuu putout pout putt tout tutu out pot put top tot tup tut to up ut

optty potty pot top tot toy to oy

optu pout out pot put top tup to up ut

opx pox ox

or or

orrsy sorry rosy soy or os oy so

orrt torr ort rot tor or to

orrwy worry row yow or ow oy

orsst sorts orts rots sort sots tors toss ort rot sot tor or os so to

orsstu rousts stours ousts roust routs rusts sorts sorus sours stour torus tours truss orts ours oust outs rots rout rust ruts sort sots sour sous tors toss tour ort our out rot rut sot sou tor or os so to us ut

orssu sorus sours ours sour sous our sou or os so us

orst orts rots sort tors ort rot sot tor or os so to

orstt torts trots orts rots sort tors tort tost tots trot ort rot sot tor tot or os so to

orsttu trouts tutors roust routs stour stout strut torts torus tours touts trots trout trust tutor orts ours oust outs rots rout rust ruts sort sour tors tort tost tots tour tout trot tuts ort our out rot rut sot sou tor tot tut or os so to us ut

orstu roust routs stour torus tours orts ours oust outs rots rout rust ruts sort sour tors tour ort our out rot rut sot sou tor or os so to us ut

orstw trows worst orts rots rows sort stow swot tors tows trow twos ort rot row sot sow tor tow two or os ow so to

orsty ryots story tyros orts rosy rots ryot sort tors toys troy tyro ort rot sot soy sty tor toy try or os oy so to

orsu ours sour our sou or os so us

orsuy yours ours rosy sour your our sou soy you or os oy so us

orsw rows row sow or os ow so

orsy rosy soy or os oy so

ort ort rot tor or to

ortt tort trot ort rot tor tot or to

orttu trout tutor rout tort tour tout trot ort our out rot rut tor tot tut or to ut

orttuy tryout rutty trout tutor rout ryot tort tour tout trot troy tyro your yurt ort our out rot rut tor tot toy try tut you or oy to ut

ortu rout tour ort our out rot rut tor or to ut

ortw trow ort rot row tor tow two or ow to

orty ryot troy tyro ort rot tor toy try or oy to

oru our or

orux roux our or ox

oruy your our you or oy

orw row or ow

orxy oryx or ox oy

os os so

ossst stoss sots toss sot os so to

osst sots toss sot os so to

ossttu stouts ousts stout touts oust outs sots sous toss tost tots tout tuts out sot sou tot tut os so to us ut

osstu ousts oust outs sots sous toss out sot sou os so to us ut

osstw stows swots sots sows stow swot toss tows twos sot sow tow two os ow so to

ossu sous sou os so us

ossw sows sow os ow so

ossy soys soy os oy so

ost sot os so to

ostt tost tots sot tot os so to

osttu stout touts oust outs tost tots tout tuts out sot sou tot tut os so to us ut

ostu oust outs out sot sou os so to us ut

ostw stow swot tows twos sot sow tow two os ow so to

osty toys sot soy sty toy os oy so to

osu sou os so us

osvw vows sow vow os ow so

osw sow os ow so

osww wows sow wow os ow so

osx sox os ox so

osy soy os oy so

---

ot

ot to

ott tot to

ottu tout out tot tut to ut

otu out to ut

otw tow two to ow

oty toy to oy

---

ou—oy

ouy you oy

ovw vow ow

ow ow

oww wow ow

owy yow ow oy

ox ox

oy oy

─────────────────────────────────── **pp** ───────────────────────────────────

pppuy puppy pup yup up
ppsu pups pup pus sup up us
ppu pup up

─────────────────────────────────── **pr** ───────────────────────────────────

prrsu purrs purr spur pus sup up us
prrsuy spurry purrs pursy syrup purr
  spry spur yups pry pus spy sup yup up
  us
prru purr up
prsstu spurts rusts spurs spurt truss puss
  puts rust ruts spur sups tups pus put
  rut sup tup up us ut

prssu spurs puss spur sups pus sup up us
prssuu usurps spurs usurp puss spur
  sups urus pus sup up us
prssuy syrups pursy pussy spurs syrup
  puss spry spur sups yups pry pus spy
  sup yup up us
prstu spurt puts rust ruts spur tups pus
  put rut sup tup up us ut

prsu spur pus sup up us
prsuu usurp spur urus pus sup up us
prsuy pursy syrup spry spur yups pry
  pus spy sup yup up us
prsuyy syrupy pursy syrup spry spur
  yups pry pus spy sup yup up us
prsy spry pry spy
pry pry

─────────────────────────────────── **ps** ───────────────────────────────────

pssu puss sups pus sup up us
pssuy pussy puss sups yups pus spy sup
  yup up us

psttu putts puts putt tups tuts pus put
  sup tup tut up us ut
pstu puts tups pus put sup tup up us ut

psu pus sup up us
psuy yups pus spy sup yup up us
psy spy

─────────────────────────────────── **pt—px** ───────────────────────────────────

pttu putt put tup tut up ut
pttuy putty putt put tup tut yup up ut

ptu put tup up ut
pu up

puy yup up
pxy pyx

---

rs

---

rssttu struts trusts rusts strut truss trust rust ruts tuts rut tut us ut
rsstty trysts tryst try sty
rsstu rusts truss rust ruts rut us ut
rsstuw wursts rusts truss wurst rust ruts rut us ut

rsttu strut trust rust ruts tuts rut tut us ut
rsttuy trusty rusty rutty strut trust tryst yurts rust ruts tuts yurt rut sty try tut us ut
rstty tryst try sty
rstu rust ruts rut us ut

rstuw wurst rust ruts rut us ut
rstuy rusty yurts rust ruts yurt rut sty try us ut
rsuu urus us
rsuuy usury urus us

---

rt

---

rttuy rutty yurt rut try tut ut
rtu rut ut
rtuy yurt rut try ut

rty try
rwy wry

sttu tuts tut us ut	**sty** sty	
sttuu tutus tuts tutu us ut	**su** us	

---

tt

---

ttu tut ut	**tu** ut	
ttuu tutu tut ut	**tux** tux ut	

II. THE WORD BUILDER

One sure way to boost your score in board games is to add letters to the beginning or end of a word already on the board. That way you get points for letters on the board, plus any you add, and the total can be substantial.

In the past, finding opportunities to build on a word invovled some work, however. After all, you had only trial and error methods to identify what longer word could be built using letters on the board and those you had on hand.

Not any more! This first-ever Word Builder section makes the job unbelievably simple. Just look up the word on the board that you want to build on. It takes only a second because entry words are in simple alphabetical order. Once you've located the word, say it's *fling*, check the list of answer words to see if you have the letters needed to spell one of them. If so, just add your letters to *fling* on the board (say, baf + fling), and the points are yours.

If you don't have the letters needed, don't worry. Pick another likely looking word on the board and look that one up. The Word Builder makes this process so quick that you can check out the possibilities during every turn if you want.

Suppose you look up a word and find it isn't listed in the Word Builder. That will happen sometimes, and there are four possible reasons why: the base word (the one you looked up) is too long; the longer answer words are too long to be included; there are no longer answer words; or the base word isn't eligible for play in most word games. For reasons of length, the Word Builder covers only those base words that are from 2 to 5 letters long. For the same reason, it includes only those answer words that are from 1 to 3 letters longer than the base word. And, as always in this book, words that cannot be played in word games are not included.

Despite these limits, you will have no problem finding plenty of answers from among the almost 60,000 longer words included in these pages. Plural forms, verb forms, prefixes, suffixes, and combinations of letters you might never suspect are among the answer words. All you need are the word to build on and the required extra letters. The Word Builder does the rest.

aah aahs aahed

aba baba abaci aback abaft abase abash abate babas cabal kabab rabat abacus abased abases abated abater abates abatis abator cabala cabals cabana casaba kababs kabala labara rabato rabats tabard

abase abased abases diabase diabases

abash abashed abashes calabash

abate abated abater abates abaters

abba abbacy cabbage kabbala

abbey abbeys

abbot abbots

abed seabed seabeds

abele abeles labeled labeler labelers

abet abets abetted abetter abettor

abhor abhors abhorred

abide abided abider abides abiders

able abler cable fable gable sable table ablest arable cabled cables enable fabled fabler fables gabled gables liable sables stable suable tabled tables tablet unable usable viable actable addable affable amiable arables capable curable disable dupable durable eatable enabled enabler enables equable fablers finable fixable friable getable likable livable lovable makable mixable movable mutable namable notable parable payable pliable potable ratable ridable salable seeable sizable stabled stables tableau tablets taxable tenable tunable useable vocable votable

abler fabler enabler fablers enablers

ably affably amiably capably durably equably lovably mutably notably pliably sizably tenably

abode abodes

abort aborts aborted aborting abortion abortive

about gadabout runabout

abuse abused abuser abuses abusers disabuse

abut abuts abutted abutter

aby abye baby gaby abysm abyss abysms

abysm abysms abysmal

abyss abyssal abysses

ace aced aces dace face lace mace pace race acerb apace brace daces faced facer faces facet glace grace laced laces maced maces paced pacer paces peace place raced racer races space tacet trace acetic acetum acetyl braced bracer braces deface efface enface facers facets glaces graced graces menace pacers palace peaced placed placer places placet pomace raceme racers solace spaced spaces spacey tenace traced tracer traces unlace vivace

aced faced laced maced paced raced braced graced peaced placed spaced traced defaced effaced enfaced menaced unlaced

acerb acerbic acerbate acerbity

aces daces faces laces maces paces races braces glaces graces places spaces traces defaces effaces enfaces hyraces menaces palaces pomaces solaces tenaces unlaces

ache ached aches cache tache apache cached caches cachet laches sachem sachet achemny apaches attache beached beaches cachets cachexy coached coaches earache gouache leached leacher leaches loaches machete panache peaches poached poacher poaches reached reaches roaches sachems sachets teacher teaches trachea

ached cached beached coached leached poached reached attached bleached breached broached detached pleached preached

aches caches laches apaches beaches coaches leaches loaches peaches poaches reaches roaches teaches attaches bleaches breaches broaches detaches earaches gouaches panaches pleaches preaches

achy leachy peachy

acid acids acidy acidic acidly placid acidify acidity antacid

acids antacids

acing facing lacing macing pacing racing bracing facings gracing lacings placing spacing tracing defacing effacing enfacing menacing unlacing

acme acmes

acne acned

acock peacock seacock peacocks seacocks

acorn acorns

acre acred acres nacre fiacre nacres sacred acreage fiacres

acred sacred sacredly

acres nacres fiacres

acrid acridly acridity

act acts fact pact tact acted actor bract cacti coact enact epact exact facts pacts react tract acting action active actors actual bracts cactus coacts dactyl enacts epacts exacta exacts factor impact intact lactic reacts redact stacte tactic tracts

acted coacted enacted exacted fracted reacted impacted

actor actors factor enactor factors factory reactor tractor enactors factored reactors tractors

acts facts pacts bracts coacts enacts epacts exacts reacts tracts impacts redacts

acute acutely

ad add ado ads adz bad cad dad fad gad had lad mad pad rad sad tad wad adds adit ados adze bade bead brad cade cadi cads clad dado dads dead duad dyad egad fade fads gads glad goad grad hade hadj head jade kadi lade lads lady lead load made mead orad pads quad rads read road scad shad tads toad wade wadi wads adage adapt addax added adder addle adept adieu adios adits adman admen admit admix adobe adopt adore adorn adult adust adyta adzes ahead badge badly beads beady blade brads bread broad caddy cades cadet cadge cadis cadre cycad daddy dread dryad duads dyads evade faddy faded fades farad glade goads gonad grade grads haded hades hadji hadst heads heady hexad jaded jades jehad jihad khadi knead laded laden lades ladle leads leady loads madam madly meads menad monad nadir naiad nomad octad oread paddy padre plead quads radar radii radio radix radon reads ready roads sadhe sadhu sadly salad scads shade shady spade squad stead toads toady trade tread triad tsadi waddy waded wader wades wadis

adage adages

adapt adapts adapted adapter adapters adapting adaption adaptive

add adds addax added adder addle caddy daddy faddy paddy waddy addend adders addict adding addled adduce adduct caddie caddis gadded ladder laddie madden madder padded paddle raddle sadden sadder saddle wadded waddle

added gadded padded wadded quadded

adder adders ladder madder sadder bladder gladder ladders bladders

addle addled paddle raddle saddle waddle paddled paddler paddles raddled raddles saddled saddler saddles staddle swaddle twaddle waddled waddles paddlers saddlery staddles straddle swaddled swaddles twaddled twaddler twaddles unsaddle

adept adeptly

adieu adieus adieux

adios radios

adit adits

adman badman madman headman

admen badmen madmen headmen

admit admits readmit admitted readmits

admix admixed admixing

ado ados dado adobe adopt adore adorn radon adobes adopts adored adorer adores adorns dadoes meadow mikado radome radons shadow vadose

adobe adobes

adopt adopts adopted adopting adoption adoptive

adore adored adorer adores adorers

adorn adorns adorned adorning

ados vadose mikados parados

ads cads dads fads gads lads pads rads tads wads beads brads duads dyads goads grads hadst heads leads loads meads quads reads roads scads toads adsorb breads broads cycads dreads dryads farads gonads hexads jihads kneads menads monads naiads nomads octads oreads pleads salads squads treads triads

adult adults adultery

adz adze adzes

adze adzes

ae aet gae hae mae nae aeon aero aery brae gaed tael aegis aeons aerie algae antae aquae aurae coxae faery minae morae novae paean paeon pupae rugae setae stoae taels ulnae zoeae

aeon aeons paeon paeons

aeons paeons

aerie aeries faerie faeries

aero aerobe aerobes aerobic aerosol

aery faery

aet chaeta

afar safari safaris

affix affixal affixed affixes affixing

afore pinafore

aft daft haft raft waft abaft after craft draft graft hafts kraft rafts shaft wafts caftan crafts crafty dafter daftly drafts drafty grafts hafted kaftan krafts rafted rafter shafts wafted zaftig

after dafter rafter grafter rafters grafters

aga agar agas gaga raga saga again agama agamy agape agars agate agave agaze lagan pagan ragas sagas vagal agamas agaric agates agaves lagans nagana pagans plagal vagary

again against

agama agamas

agar agars agaric vagary agarics

agas ragas sagas

agate agates runagate

agave agaves

age aged agee ager ages cage gage mage page rage sage wage adage agent bagel caged cages cagey eager gaged gages image lager mages paged pager pages plage raged rages sager sages stage usage waged wager wages adages agedly ageism agency agenda agents ambage bagels borage cubage damage dosage dotage encage engage enrage forage garage homage imaged images laager lavage linage lovage manage meager menage metage mirage nonage ohmage onager outage pagers pelage pipage plages ravage rivage sagely sagest savage sewage silage socage staged stager stages stagey towage triage usages visage voyage wagers

aged caged gaged paged raged waged agedly imaged staged damaged encaged engaged enraged foraged managed ravaged savaged tragedy unpaged voyaged

agent agents magenta reagent magentas reagents

ager eager lager pager sager wager laager meager onager pagers stager wagers dowager eagerly forager homager imagery laagers manager onagers stagers tanager voyager wagered

ages cages gages mages pages rages sages wages adages images plages sagest stages usages ambages borages cubages damages dosages encages engages enrages forages garages linages manages menages metages mirages ohmages outages pelages pipages ravages rivages savages sewages silages socages towages triages visages voyages

aggie baggier jaggier baggiest craggier jaggiest quaggier shaggier

agile agilely fragile

aging caging paging raging waging imaging staging damaging encaging engaging enraging foraging managing ravaging savaging voyaging

agio agios adagio

aglet aglets eaglet eaglets

ago agog agon sago agony agora fagot imago sagos wagon agones agonic agorae agouti dragon fagots flagon lagoon pagoda virago wagons

agog anagoge demagog isagoge

agon agony wagon agones agonic dragon flagon wagons agonies agonist agonize decagon dragons flagons hexagon nonagon octagon paragon wagoner

agora agorae

agree agreed agrees agreeing disagree shagreen

ague agues vague league maguey plague vaguer leaguer leagues magueys plagued plagues vaguely vaguest

agues leagues plagues vaguest

ah aah aha bah hah nah pah rah yah ahem ahoy amah ayah baht blah hahs opah rahs shah yeah aahed ahead ahold amahs ayahs bahts blahs ephah gerah lotah mynah obeah opahs rajah sahib selah spahi surah torah wahoo

aha graham

ahold aholds

ai aid ail aim air aide aids ails aims airs airy bail bait dais fail fain fair gain gait haik hail hair jail kail laic laid lain lair maid mail maim main naif nail paid pail pain pair raid rail rain said sail sain tail vail vain vair waif wail wain wait again aided aides ailed aimed aired aisle aitch amain assai avail await bails bairn baits baize blain braid brail brain caird cairn chain chair claim daily dairy daisy drain fails faint fairs fairy faith flail flair frail gaily gains gaits glair grain haiks haiku hails hairs hairy jails krait laigh laird lairs laity lanai maids mails maims mains maize naiad naifs nails naive pails pains paint pairs plaid plain plait quail raids rails rains rainy raise saiga sails saint saith serai slain snail staid stain stair swain taiga tails taint trail train trait twain vails vairs waifs wails wains waist waits waive zaire

aid aide aids laid maid paid raid said aided aides braid maids plaid raids staid afraid aiding braids inlaid maiden plaids raided raider relaid repaid unpaid unsaid

aide aided aides maiden raided raider braided maidens raiders unaided

aided raided braided unaided

aids maids raids braids plaids

ail ails bail fail hail jail kail mail nail pail rail sail tail vail wail ailed avail bails brail daily fails flail frail gaily hails jails mails nails pails quail rails sails snail tails trail vails wails ailing assail avails bailed bailey bailie bewail brails derail detail entail failed faille flails hailed hailer jailed jailer jailor mailed mailer nailed oxtail quails railed railer retail sailed sailer sailor snails tailed taille tailor tenail vailed wailed

ailed   bailed failed hailed jailed mailed nailed railed sailed tailed vailed wailed availed flailed quailed trailed assailed bewailed derailed detailed entailed retailed

ails   bails fails hails jails mails nails pails rails sails tails vails wails avails brails flails quails snails assails bewails entails oxtails tenails

aim   aims maim aimed claim maims aiming caiman claims daimon daimyo maimed maimer

aimed   maimed claimed

aims   maims claims

air   airs airy fair hair lair pair vair aired bairn caird cairn chair dairy fairs fairy flair glair hairs hairy laird lairs pairs stair vairs zaire affair airbus airier airily airing airman airmen airway bairns cairds cairns chairs eclair faired fairer fairly flairs glairs glairy hairdo impair lairds midair mohair paired repair stairs unfair

aired   faired paired chaired impaired repaired

airs   fairs hairs lairs pairs vairs chairs flairs glairs stairs affairs airship airsick eclairs impairs mohairs repairs

airy   dairy fairy hairy glairy

aisle   aisled aisles paisley paisleys

ajuga   ajugas

akin   baking caking faking making raking taking waking awaking braking flaking leaking manakin peaking quaking shaking slaking snaking soaking staking

ala   alar alas gala alack alamo alarm alary alate balas galas galax jalap koala malar nyala salad alamos alarms alated balata cabala calami calash dalasi galaxy impala jalaps kabala kamala koalas malady malars malate nyalas palace palate salaam salads salami salary scalar

alamo   alamos alamode alamodes

alar   alarm alary malar alarms malars salary scalar alarmed malaria malarky scalars talaria

alarm   alarms alarmed alarming alarmism alarmist

alary   salary

alas   balas galas calash dalasi koalas nyalas cabalas impalas kabalas kamalas

alate   alated malate palate galatea malates oxalate palated palates escalate galateas oxalates

alb   alba albs albas album albedo albeit albino albums

alba   albas

album   albums albumen albumin

alder   alders balder caldera alderman aldermen calderas falderal

ale   alee ales bale dale gale hale kale male pale rale sale tale vale wale aleph alert baled bales dales galea gales haled haler hales males palea paled paler pales quale rales salep sales scale shale stale swale taler tales vales valet waled wales whale alephs alerts alexia azalea baleen chalet coaled coaler daleth dealer dialed empale exhale female finale foaled galeae galena halest healed healer impale inhale locale morale paleae palely palest pealed regale resale saleps scaled scaler scales sealed sealer shales staled staler stales swales talent tamale thaler valets whaled whaler whales

alee   baleen baleens

aleph   alephs

alert   alerts alerted alertly

ales   bales dales gales hales males pales rales sales tales vales wales halest palest scales shales stales swales whales braless empales exhales females finales impales inhales locales morales regales resales stalest tamales

alga   algae algal amalgam

algum   algums

alias   aliases

alibi   alibis

alien   aliens alienor salient alienate alienism alienist alienors salience saliency salients

alif   alifs kalif kalifs khalif salify aliform khalifs qualify

alifs   kalifs khalifs

align   aligns malign aligned maligns realign aligning maligned maligner realigns

aline   alined alines saline hyaline malines opaline praline alkaline opalines pralines

alit   halite duality halites hyalite quality reality

all   ally ball call fall gall hall mall pall tall wall allay alley allot allow alloy balls bally calla calls dally falls galls hallo halls malls palls pally rally sally scall shall small spall stall tally walls allays allege allele alleys allied allies allots allows alloys allude allure allyls anally appall ballad balled ballet ballot ballsy

befall callas called caller callow callus dalles fallal fallen faller fallow galled gallet galley gallic gallon gallop hallah halloo hallos hallow hallux leally mallee mallet mallow orally palled pallet pallid pallor phalli really recall sallet sallow scalls spalls squall stalls taller tallow thrall valley walled wallet wallop wallow

allay   allays allayed allaying

alley   alleys galley valley galleys valleys walleye alleyway walleyed walleyes

allot   allots ballot ballots shallot allotted balloted balloter shallots

allow   allows callow fallow hallow mallow sallow tallow wallow allowed fallows gallows hallows mallows sallows shallow swallow tallows tallowy wallows allowing disallow hallowed shallows swallows tallowed wallowed

alloy   alloys alloyed alloying

ally   bally dally pally rally sally tally allyls anally leally orally really allying axially equally fatally finally ideally jurally legally locally loyally modally morally nasally royally squally tallyho tonally totally usually venally vocally zonally

alms   balms calms malms palms psalms qualms realms almsman becalms copalms embalms malmsey napalms

aloe   aloes haloed haloes

aloes   haloes

aloha   alohas

alone   abalone baloney taloned

along   kalong kalongs

alp   alps palp alpha palpi palps salpa scalp alpaca alphas alpine calpac kalpak kalpis palpus salpae salpas scalps

alpha   alphas alphabet

alps   palps scalps

alt   alto alts halt malt salt altar alter altos dealt exalt halts malts malty salts salty shalt smalt waltz altars alters basalt cobalt dalton exalts falter fealty halted halter health malted maltha palter paltry realty rialto salted salter smalto smalts wealth

altar   altars

alter   alters falter halter palter salter altered exalter falters halters saltern altering exalters faltered falterer halteres paltered psalters salterns

alto   altos dalton rialto daltons maltose rialtos smaltos

altos   maltose rialtos smaltos maltoses

alts   halts malts salts exalts smalts basalts

alula   alulae

alum alums alumna alumni alumnae alumnus calumet calumny galumph

am amp bam cam dam gam ham jam lam ram tam yam amah ambo amen amid amir ammo amok amps amyl bams beam came camp cams cham clam cram dame damn damp dams dram exam fame flam foam gamb game gamp gams gamy gram hame hams imam jamb jams kame kami lama lamb lame lamp lams loam mama name pram rami ramp rams ream roam same samp scam seam sham slam swam tame tamp tams team tram vamp wham yams abeam agama alamo amahs amain amass amaze amber ambit amble ambos ambry ameba ameer amend amice amide amigo amine amirs amiss amity amole among amour ample amply ampul amuck amuse amyls beams beamy blame bream camas camel cameo cames campo camps campy champ clamp clams cramp crams cream dames damns drama drams dream exams famed fames flame flams fleam foams foamy frame gamay gambs gamed games gamic gamin gamma gammy gamps gamut gleam grams hamal hames hammy ihram imams jambs kames lamas lambs lamed lamer lames lamia lamps llama loams loamy madam mamas mamba mambo mamma mammy named names ogham prams ramps ramus reams roams samba samps scamp scams scram seams seamy shame shams slams stamp steam swami swamp swamy tamed tamer tames tamps teams tramp trams vamps whams yamen zamia ziram

amah amahs

amass amassed amasses amassing

amaze amazed amazes amazedly

amber ambers camber cambers chamber clamber lambert cambered chambers clambers lamberts

ambit ambits gambit gambits ambition

amble ambled ambles gamble ramble wamble bramble gambled gambler gambles rambled rambler rambles shamble wambled wambles brambled brambles gamblers preamble ramblers scramble shambled shambles

ambo ambos mambo bamboo crambo gambol mambos bamboos gambols hambone jambone tambour

ambos mambos

ameba amebae amebas

ameer ameers

amen amend yamen amends examen flamen lament seamen stamen yamens amended amender amenity examens flamens foramen laments stamens

amend amends amended amender amenders amending

amice amices

amid amide amides amidst pyramid

amide amides

amigo amigos

amine amines famine examine famines calamine examined examinee examiner examines thiamine

amir amirs

amity calamity

ammo gammon mammon whammo ammonia gammons hammock mammock mammons mammoth

amole amoles

among amongst

amour amours clamour glamour clamours paramour

amp amps camp damp gamp lamp ramp samp tamp vamp ample amply ampul campo camps campy champ clamp cramp gamps lamps ramps samps scamp stamp swamp tamps tramp vamps ampere ampler ampule ampuls camped camper campos campus champs clamps cramps dampen damper damply decamp encamp gramps hamper lampas pampas pamper preamp ramped revamp sampan sample scampi scamps stamps swamps swampy tamped tamper vamped wampum

ample ampler sample example sampled sampler samples trample examples samplers trampled tramples

amply damply

amps camps gamps lamps ramps samps tamps vamps champs clamps cramps gramps scamps stamps swamps decamps encamps preamps revamps

ampul ampule ampuls ampules ampulla ampullae

amuse amused amuses shamuses

amyl amyls amylum amylose amylums

an ana and ane ani ant any ban can fan gan man pan ran tan van wan anal anew anil ankh anon anta ante anti ants anus azan band bane bang bani bank bans bean bran cane cans cant clan dank dean fane fang fans flan gang guan hand hang hank hant jean kana khan koan land lane lank lean loan mana mane many mean moan pane pang pans pant pean plan rand rang rani rank rant roan sand sane sang sank scan span swan tang tank tans than vane vang vans wand wane want wany wean yang yank yean yuan zany adman ancon anear anent angel anger angle angry anile anils anima anime anion anise ankhs ankle annex annoy annul anode antae antas antes antic antis antra antsy anvil apian atman avian azans banal bands bandy bangs banjo banks banns beans began bhang blanc bland blank brand brans buran bwana canal candy caned caner canes canny canoe canon canto cants chant clang clank clans clean crane crank dance dandy danio deans dewan divan drank eland fancy fanes fangs fanny fanon flank flans franc frank ganef gangs giant gland glans glean gowan grand grant groan guano guans hands handy hangs hanks hants hazan hogan human inane japan jeans kanas kanji khans kiang koans lagan lanai lance lands lanes lanky leans leant leman liane ligan llano loans maned manes mange mango mangy mania manic manly manna manor manse manta manus means meant meany moans nanny ocean organ paean pagan panda pandy panel panes panga pangs panic panne pansy pants panty pavan peans pecan piano plane plank plans plant prank qanat quant quean ranch rands randy range rangy ranis ranks rants reran riant roans rowan sands sandy saner scans scant sedan shank skean slang slant solan spang spank spans stand stang stank swang swank swans tango tangs tangy tanka tanks tansy thane thank titan twang uhlan unman urban vanda vanes vangs viand wands waned wanes wanly wants weans whang wigan witan woman xylan yangs yanks yeans yuans

ana anal kana mana banal bwana canal kanas lanai qanat anadem anally analog banana bwanas cabana canada canals canape canard canary iguana jacana lanais lanate manage nagana planar qanats zenana

anal banal canal anally analog canals analogs analogy analyst analyze

ancon ancones

and band hand land rand sand wand bands bandy bland brand candy dandy eland gland grand hands handy lands panda pandy rands randy sands sandy stand vanda viand wands banded bandit bandog brands brandy candid candle candor dander demand elands errand expand gander glands grands handed handle inland island landau landed lander pandas pander pandit random remand riband sandal sanded sander sandhi stands strand tandem unhand upland vandas viands wander

ane anew bane cane fane lane mane pane sane vane wane anear anent caned caner canes crane fanes ganef inane lanes liane maned manes panel panes plane saner thane vanes waned wanes anemia anemic arcane beaned butane caners cetane craned cranes ethane ganefs hexane humane insane leaned leaner lianes loaned loaner manege meaner moaned octane panels pavane planed planer planes planet sanely sanest thanes urbane weaned yeaned

anent immanent

angel angels angelic evangel tangelo evangels tangelos

anger angers banger danger ganger hanger manger ranger angered bangers changer dangers gangers granger hangers mangers rangers angering changers endanger grangers stranger

angle angled angler angles bangle dangle jangle mangle tangle wangle anglers bangles dangled dangles jangled jangler jangles mangled mangler mangles spangle tangled tangler tangles wangled wangles wrangle entangle janglers spangled spangles strangle tanglers triangle untangle wrangled wrangler wrangles

ani anil bani rani anile anils anima anime anion anise danio mania manic panic ranis animal animas animes animus anions anises banian banish beanie canine caning crania cyanic danios maniac manias manioc manitu panics sanies sanity tanist uranic vanish vanity waning zanier zanies zanily

anil anile anils zanily aniline vanilla

anima animal animas animals animate animated animates animator

anion anions

anise anises aniseed aniseeds anisette

ankh ankhs

ankle ankles anklet rankle anklets rankled rankles

annex annexed annexes reannex annexing

annoy annoys annoyed annoying

annul annuli annuls annular annulet annulus cannula annulate annulets annulled cannulas

anode anodes

anon canon fanon anonym canons fanons anonyms organon

ant anta ante anti ants cant hant pant rant want antae antas antes antic antis antra antsy canto cants chant giant grant hants leant manta meant pants panty plant quant rants riant scant slant wants anteed anthem anther antiar antics antler antrum arrant aslant bantam banter bezant canted canter canthi cantle canton cantor cantos cantus chants decant errant extant gantry giants grants infant levant mantas mantel mantic mantis mantle mantra mantua mutant natant nutant octant panted pantry pedant plants pliant quanta quants ranted ranter recant savant scants scanty secant sejant shanty slants sonant tenant truant tyrant vacant wanted wanter wanton

anta antae antas manta bantam mantas quanta antacid bantams cantata fantail fantasm fantast fantasy infanta plantar quantal tantara vantage

antis mantas fantasm fantast fantasy fantasia fantasms fantasts infantas phantasm

ante antes anteed banter canted canter mantel panted ranted ranter wanted wanter andante antefix anteing antenna banters canteen canters chanted chanter chantey granted grantee granter infante lantern manteau mantels planted planter quanted scanted shantey slanted wanters

antes andantes atlantes giantess infantes

anti antic antis antiar antics mantic mantis antiars antigen antique antiwar cantina canting frantic panties pantile panting quantic ranting tantivy wanting

antic antics mantic frantic quantic canticle gigantic pedantic quantics romantic semantic

antis mantis mantises mantissa

antra mantra mantras

ants antsy cants hants pants rants wants chants giants grants plants quants scants slants bezants decants infants levants mutants octants pedants recants savants secants sonants tenants truants tyrants

anus manus anuses tetanus

anvil anvils

any many wany zany meany anyhow anyone anyway banyan botany canyon litany

aorta aortae aortas

apace carapace

ape aped apes apex cape gape jape nape rape tape agape apeak apery caper capes chape crape drape gaped gaper

gapes grape japed japer japes lapel napes paper raped rapes scape shape taped taper tapes apexes canape chapel chapes craped crapes diaper draped draper drapes escape gapers grapes heaped lapels leaped leaper napery neaped papers papery reaped reaper sarape scaped scapes scrape serape shaped shaper shapes soaped tapers

aped gaped japed raped taped craped draped heaped leaped neaped reaped scaped shaped soaped escaped scraped

apery napery papery drapery grapery

apes capes gapes japes napes rapes tapes chapes crapes drapes grapes scapes shapes anapest canapes escapes scrapes serapes

apex apexes

aphid aphids

aping gaping raping taping craping draping heaping leaping reaping scaping shaping soaping escaping gapingly scraping

apish apishly

apnea apneas

aport seaports

apple apples dapple dappled dapples grapple grappled grappler grapples scrapple

apply reapply applying

apron aprons

apse apses lapse elapse lapsed lapses elapsed elapses relapse synapse

apses lapses elapses relapses synapses

apt rapt adapt aptly clapt inapt unapt wrapt adapts captor enrapt

aptly inaptly unaptly

aqua aquae aquas aquaria aquatic aquavit

arak araks karakul

arbor arbors harbor arbored arbores harbors arboreal arborist harbored harborer

arc arca arch arcs marc narc arced farce larch march marcs narco narcs parch arcade arcane arched archer archil archly archon arcing arctic eparch exarch farces inarch marcel narcos parcel scarce search starch

arch larch march parch arched archer archil archly archon eparch exarch inarch search starch anarchy archaic archers archery archils arching archive archons archway dyarchy eparchs eparchy exarchs larches marched marcher marches mesarch monarch parched parches starchy xerarch

arcs marcs narcs

ardeb ardebs

ardor ardors

are area bare care dare fare hare mare pare rare tare ware yare areas areca arena arete aware bared barer bares blare cared cares caret chare dared dares eared fared fares flare glare harem hares lares mares nares oared pared pares pareu parer scare share snare spare stare tared tares wared wares arecas arenas areola areole aretes barege barely barest bearer beware blared blares careen career caress carets chares claret curare dearer feared flared flares geared glared glares harems hearer imaret neared nearer parent pareus pareve rarefy rarely rarest reared roared roarer scared scares seared shared sharer shares snared snares soared spared sparer spares square stared stares tearer wearer zareba

area areas

areca arecas

arena arenas

arf arfs zarf dwarf scarf wharf zarfs barfly carful dwarfs earful scarfs

arfs zarfs dwarfs scarfs

argol argols

argon argons jargon jargons

argot argots

argue argued arguer argues arguers

aria arias maria lariat narial pariah aquaria lariats malaria pariahs solaria talaria variant

arid acarid aridly acarids aridity

aril arils warily charily wearily

arise arisen arises

ark arks bark cark dark hark lark mark nark park sark barks carks harks larks larky marks narks parka parks quark sarks shark snark spark stark arkose barked barker carked charka darken darker darkle darkly debark embark harked harken larked larker marked marker market markka markup parkas parked parker quarks remark sharks snarks sparks

arks barks carks harks larks marks narks parks sarks quarks sharks snarks sparks debarks embarks remarks

arm arms army barm farm harm warm alarm armed armor barmy charm farms harms karma rearm swarm unarm warms alarms armada armful armies arming armlet armors armory armpit armure aswarm carman carmen charms dharma disarm farmed farmer harmed harmer karmas karmic marmot rearms smarmy swarms unarms warmed warmer warmly warmth

armed farmed harmed warmed alarmed charmed rearmed swarmed unarmed disarmed unharmed unwarmed

armor armors armory armored armorer armorers armorial armories

arms farms harms warms alarms charms rearms swarms unarms disarms

army barmy smarmy

aroma aromas aromatic

array arrays arrayed arraying disarray

arris garrison

arrow arrows barrow farrow harrow marrow narrow yarrow barrows farrows harrows marrows marrowy narrows sparrow yarrows harrowed harrower narrowed narrower narrowly sparrows

arse arses parse coarse hearse hoarse parsed parses sparse arsenal arsenic coarsen coarser hearses hoarsen hoarser parsecs sparser

arses parses hearses coarsest hoarsest sparsest

arson arsons parson parsons arsonist

art arts arty cart dart fart hart kart mart part tart wart apart artsy carte carts chart darts earth farts garth harts heart karts marts parts party peart quart smart start swart tarts warts warty artery artful artist barter carted cartel carter carton charts darted darter dearth depart earths earthy farted garter garths hearth hearts hearty impart marten martin martyr parted partly quarte quarto quarts quartz smarts smarty starts swarth tartan tartar tartly thwart

arts artsy carts darts farts harts karts marts parts tarts warts charts hearts quarts smarts starts departs imparts thwarts

arty party warty hearty martyr smarty martyrs partyer

aryl aryls

as ash ask asp ass fas gas has kas pas was agas alas asci ashy asks asps baas base bash bask bass bast bias boas bras case cash cask cast dash ease east easy eras etas eyas fash fast gash gasp goas hash hasp hast koas kvas lash lass last leas mash mask mass mast moas oast pass past peas pyas rase rash rasp rias sash sass seas spas task tass teas upas vase vast wash wasp wast yeas abase abash albas alias almas amass antas aquas areas arias arras ascot ascus ashen ashes aside asked askew aspen aspic assai assay asses asset aster astir atlas auras avast awash babas balas basal based baser bases basic basil basin basis

basks baste basts beast bemas betas blast boast bolas boras brash brass camas cased cases casks caste casts cease chase chasm clash clasp class coast cocas codas colas crash crass degas devas divas duras eased easel eases erase fasts feast flash flask fleas galas gases gasps gassy glass gnash grasp grass hasps haste hasty horas hulas hylas ideas iotas jotas kakas kanas kasha kavas kivas kolas kvass lamas laser lasso lasts lease leash least liras lotas mamas maser masks mason massy masts mayas mesas micas mola moxas mynas nasal nasty nipas nomas novas oases oasis oasts okras ollas pacas papas paras pasha pasta paste pasts pasty pease phase pikas pitas plash pleas proas pumas quash quasi quass ragas rajas rased rases rasps raspy rheas roast rotas sagas sassy slash smash sodas sofas somas soras spasm stash stoas suras swash tapas tasks tasse taste tasty tease toast togas tolas toras trash trass tubas tufas tunas ukase ulnas ureas uveas varas vases vinas visas washy wasps waspy waste wekas yeast yogas zetas zoeas

asci fascia fasciae fascias fascine fascism fascist

ascot ascots mascot mascots

ash ashy bash cash dash fash gash hash lash mash rash sash wash abash ashen ashes awash brash clash crash flash gnash kasha leash pasha plash quash slash smash stash swash trash washy ashcan ashier ashlar ashore ashram bashaw bashed bashes brashy calash cashaw cashed cashes cashew dashed dasher dashes fashed fashes flashy gashed gashes hashed hashes kasher lashed lasher lashes mashed masher mashes mashie pashas potash rasher rashes rashly rehash sashay sashed sashes splash squash thrash trashy unlash washed washer washes

ashes bashes cashes dashes fashes gashes hashes lashes mashes rashes sashes washes abashes clashes crashes flashes gnashes leashes plashes quashes rashest slashes smashes stashes swashes trashes brashest calashes rehashes splashes squashes thrashes unlashes

ashy washy brashy flashy trashy splashy squashy

aside asides seaside

ask asks bask cask mask task asked askew basks casks flask masks tasks askers asking basked basket casket damask flasks gasket gaskin masked masker tasked unmask

asked basked masked tasked unasked unmasked

asks basks casks masks tasks flasks damasks unmasks

asp asps gasp hasp rasp wasp aspen aspic clasp gasps grasp hasps rasps raspy wasps waspy aspect aspens aspics aspire aspish clasps gasped grasps hasped jasper rasped rasper

aspen aspens

aspic aspics

asps gasps hasps rasps wasps clasps grasps

ass bass lass mass pass sass tass amass assai assay asses asset brass class crass gassy glass grass kvass lasso massy quass sassy tasse trass assail assais assays assent assert assess assets assign assist assize assort assume assure basset brassy bypass cassia cassis classy gassed gasser glassy grassy harass hassle jassid lasses lassie lassos massed masses massif morass passed passel passer passes rassel sassed sasses strass tassel tasses vassal

assai assail assais assails wassail assailed assailer wassails

assay assays assayed assayer assayers assaying

asses assess lasses masses passes sasses tasses amasses classes glasses grasses kvasses quasses assessed assesses assessor bypasses crassest harasses impasses molasses morasses reassess strasses

asset assets basset bassets cassette masseter

aster astern asters faster laster master paster taster waster boaster casters coaster diaster eastern feaster masters mastery pasters roaster tasters toaster wasters asterisk asterism asternal asteroid boasters cadaster coasters diasters disaster easterly feasters mastered masterly pasterns piasters plasters toasters

at ate bat cat eat fat gat hat kat mat oat pat qat rat sat tat vat atom atop bate bath bats beat blat boat brat cate cats chat coat data date drat eats fate fats feat fiat flat frat gate gats ghat gnat goat hate hath hats heat jato kyat late lath mate math mats meat moat neat oath oats pate path pats peat plat qats rate rath rats scat seat skat slat spat swat tats teat that vats watt what abate agate alate atilt atlas atman atoll atoms atomy atone atony atria attar attic

batch bated bates bathe baths batik baton batty beats begat blats bleat bloat boats brats carat catch cater cates catty chats cheat cleat coati coats crate dated dates datum death ducat eaten eater eclat elate fatal fated fates fatly fatty feats fiats flats float frats gated gates ghats gloat gnats goats grate great groat hatch hated hater hates heath heats irate jatos jurat karat korat kyats latch lated later latex lathe laths lathy latke loath match mated mates matey matin matte matzo meats meaty moats natal natch nates natty neath oaten oaths orate ovate patch paten pater pates paths patio patly patsy peaty plate plats platy pleat prate qanat rabat rated rates ratio ratty reata riata sated satem sates satin satyr scats seats shoat skate skats slate slats slaty snath spate spats splat sprat squat state stoat swath swats sweat tater tatty teats treat vatic watch water watts wheat wrath

ate bate cate date fate gate hate late mate pate rate abate agate alate bated bates cater cates crate dated dates eaten eater elate fated fates gated gates grate hated hater hates irate lated later latex mated mates matey nates oaten orate ovate paten pater pates plate prate rated rates sated satem sates skate slate spate state tater water abated abater abates acuate aerate agates agnate alated ansate bateau beaten beater berate binate boated boatel boater borate catena caters cerate coated comate crated crater crates create curate debate delate dilate donate eaters eatery elated elater elates equate estate fixate gateau goatee grated grater grates gyrate haters heated heater ideate inmate innate jugate karate krater lanate lateen lately latent latest legate ligate lobate locate lunate luxate lyrate malate mateys mutate neaten neater negate notate oblate opiate orated orates ornate palate patens patent paters pedate pirate plated platen plater plates prated prates pupate rebate relate rotate sateen savate seated sedate senate skated skater skates slated slater slates spates stated states taters update vacate velate watery zonate

atlas atlases

atman atmans batman boatman

atoll atolls

atom atoms atomy atomic diatom anatomy atomies atomism atomist atomize diatoms

atoms diatoms

atomy anatomy

atone atoned atoner atones atoners

atria atrial atrias latria

attar attars

attic attics lattice brattice latticed lattices

audit audits audited auditor plaudit auditing audition auditors auditory plaudits

auger augers sauger saugers

aught aughts caught naught taught draught fraught haughty naughty daughter draughts laughter

augur augurs augury augured auguries auguring

auk auks auklet

auld yauld

aunt aunts aunty daunt gaunt haunt jaunt taunt vaunt auntie avaunt daunts flaunt haunts jaunts jaunty taunts vaunts aunties daunted flaunts flaunty gauntly haunted haunter jaunted saunter taunted taunter vaunted

aunts daunts haunts jaunts taunts vaunts flaunts

aunty jaunty flaunty

aura aurae aural auras

aural monaural

auric auricle auricles

aurum aurums

auto autos autobus automat autopsy

auxin auxins

avail avails availed travail availing travails

ave aver aves cave eave gave have lave nave pave rave save wave agave avens avers avert brave caved caves clave crave eaves gavel grave haven heave knave laved laver laves leave maven navel naves paved paver paves raved ravel raven raves saved saver saves shave slave stave trave waved waver waves weave agaves avenge avenue averse averts beaver behave braved braver braves caveat cavern claves cleave craved craven craves gavels graved gravel graven graver graves greave havens heaved heaven heaves knaves lavers leaved leaven leaves loaves mavens navels octave pavers peavey quaver ravels ravens ravers reaved repave savely savers shaved shaven shaver shaves slaved slaver slaves sleave staved staves tavern travel traves wavers wavery weaver weaves

avens havens mavens ravens leavens

aver avers avert laver paver saver waver averse averts beaver braver cavern graver lavers pavers quaver ravers savers shaver slaver tavern wavers wavery weaver average averred averted beavers bravery cadaver caverns cleaver klavern knavery palaver quavers quavery shavers slavers slavery taverns waverer weavers

avers averse lavers pavers ravers savers wavers beavers quavers shavers slavers weavers aversely aversion cadavers cleavers palavers traverse

avert averts averted averting

aves caves eaves laves naves paves raves saves waves agaves braves claves craves graves heaves knaves leaves loaves shaves slaves staves traves weaves behaves bravest cleaves gravest greaves octaves repaves sheaves sleaves

avian avians

avid avidly gravid avidity

avoid avoids avoided avoider avoiders avoiding

avow avows avowal avowed avowals avowing disavow

avows disavows

aw awe awl awn caw haw jaw law maw paw raw saw yaw away awed awes awls awns awry bawd bawl braw caws chaw claw craw dawn draw fawn flaw gawk gnaw hawk haws jaws lawn laws maws pawl pawn paws sawn saws shaw thaw yawl yawn yawp yaws await awake award aware awash awful awing awoke bawds bawdy bawls brawl brawn bylaw chaws claws crawl craws dawns drawl drawn draws fawns flaws gawks gawky gnaws hawed hawks hawse jawed lawns lawny macaw nawab papaw pawed pawky pawls pawns prawn pshaw rawer sawed shawl shaws spawn squaw straw tawny thaws trawl yawed yawls yawns yawps

await awaits awaited awaiting

awake awaked awaken awakes awakens awakened reawaken

award awards awarded awarding

aware unaware unawares

away seaway caraway cutaway faraway getaway layaway runaway seaways

awe awed awes hawed jawed pawed rawer sawed yawed aweigh chawed clawed drawer flawed gnawed rawest thawed

awed hawed jawed pawed sawed yawed chawed clawed flawed gnawed thawed

awes rawest awesome

awful lawful awfully lawfully unlawful

awing hawing jawing pawing sawing yawing chawing clawing drawing flawing gnawing thawing drawings gnawings pshawing

awl awls bawl pawl yawl bawls brawl crawl drawl pawls shawl trawl yawls bawled brawls crawls crawly drawls scrawl shawls sprawl trawls yawled

awls bawls pawls yawls brawls crawls drawls shawls trawls scrawls sprawls

awn awns dawn fawn lawn pawn sawn yawn brawn dawns drawn fawns lawns lawny pawns prawn spawn tawny yawns awning brawny dawned fawned fawner pawned prawns spawns thrawn yawned yawner

awns dawns fawns lawns pawns yawns prawns spawns

ax fax lax pax sax tax wax zax axed axes axil axis axle axon coax flax hoax maxi taxi waxy addax axels axial axile axils axing axiom axles axons borax braxy faxes flaxy galax hyrax laxly maxim maxis paxes relax saxes taxed taxer taxes taxis waxed waxen waxer waxes zaxes

axed taxed waxed coaxed hoaxed relaxed

axel axels

axes faxes paxes saxes taxes waxes zaxes coaxes flaxes hoaxes boraxes relaxes

axial axially biaxial coaxial preaxial

axil axile axils axilla axillae axillar maxilla

axing taxing waxing coaxing hoaxing relaxing

axiom axioms

axis maxis taxis praxis

axle axles

axon axons

ay aye bay cay day fay gay hay jay lay may nay pay ray say way yay away ayah ayes ayin bays bray cays clay days dray fays flay fray gays gray hays jays kayo lays maya mayo okay pays play pray quay rays says shay slay spay stay sway tray ways allay array assay ayahs ayins bayed bayou belay brays byway clays decay delay drays embay essay flays foray frays gamay gayer gayly grays hayed inlay kayak kayos layer layup mayas maybe mayor mayos mayst moray noway okays payed payee payer playa plays prays quays rayed rayer rayon relay repay sayer sayid slays spays splay spray stays stray sways today trays zayin

ayah ayahs

aye ayes bayed gayer hayed layer payed payee payer rayed rayer sayer brayed brayer clayey drayed flayed frayed gayest gayety grayed grayer layers mayest okayed payees payers played player prayed prayer rayers sayers slayed slayer spayed stayed swayed

ayes gayest mayest grayest

ayin ayins zayin baying haying laying maying paying raying saying zayins braying draying flaying fraying graying okaying playing praying sayings slaying spaying staying swaying

ayins zayins

azan azans hazan hazans

azans hazans

azide azides

azine azines oxazine haziness laziness magazine

azo azoic azole azote azoth bazoo kazoo razor amazon azoles azonal azotes azoths bazoos blazon kazoos razors sleazo

azole azoles

azote azotes

azoth azoths

azure azures

b

ba   aba baa bad bag bah bam ban bar bat bay abba alba baas baba babe babu baby bach back bade bags baht bail bait bake bald bale balk ball balm bams band bane bang bani bank bans barb bard bare bark barm barn bars base bash bask bass bast bate bath bats bawd bawl bays juba tuba abaci aback abaft abase abash abate albas ameba babas babes babul babus backs bacon badge badly bagel baggy bahts bails bairn baits baize baked baker bakes balas baldy baled bales balks balky balls bally balms balmy balsa banal bands bandy bangs banjo banks banns barbs bards bared barer bares barge baric barks barmy barns baron barre basal based baser bases basic basil basin basis basks baste basts batch bated bates bathe baths batik baton batty bawds bawdy bawls bayed bayou bazoo cabal ceiba debar embay kabab kebab lobar mamba rabat rumba samba scuba tubal tubas urban

baa   baas
baba   babas
babe   babes
babu   babul babus babuls
babul   babuls
baby   babying babyish crybaby
bach   hibachi
back   aback backs backed backer backup backbit backers backhoe backing backlog cutback fatback hogback outback runback setback wetback
backs   backside backstay backstop cutbacks fatbacks hogbacks outbacks runbacks setbacks wetbacks
bad   bade badge badly badger badges badman badmen forbad
bade   forbade
badge   badger badges badgers badgered
bag   bags bagel baggy ambage bagels bagful bagged bagger baggit bagman bagmen bagnio cubage gasbag ragbag
bagel   bagels
bags   gasbags ragbags
bah   baht bahts casbah jubbah kasbah
baht   bahts
bail   bails bailed bailey bailie bailies bailiff bailing bailout
bairn   bairns
bait   baits baited baiter baiters baiting
baize   baizes
bake   baked baker bakes bakers bakery

baker   bakers bakery bakeries
balas   cabalas kabalas kabbalas
bald   baldy balder baldly ribald baldest baldies balding baldric piebald
bale   baled bales baleen baleens baleful timbale
bales   timbales
balk   balks balky balked balking
ball   balls bally ballad balled ballet ballot ballsy ballads ballast ballets balling balloon ballots eyeball oddball
balls   ballsy eyeballs oddballs
bally   ballyhoo globally verbally
balm   balms balmy embalm balmier balmily embalms
balms   embalms
balsa   balsam balsams
bam   bams bamboo bammed ferbam
bams   ferbams
ban   band bane bang bani bank bans banal bands bandy bangs banjo banks banns urban banana banded bandit bandog banged banger bangle banian banish banjos banked banker banned banner bantam banter banyan banzai cabana embank riband turban urbane
banal   banality
band   bands bandy banded bandit bandog riband abandon armband bandage bandana bandbox bandeau bandied bandies banding bandits bandogs bandore disband hatband husband ribands
bands   ribands armbands bandsman bandsmen disbands hatbands husbands
bandy   bandying
bane   urbane baneful bugbane cowbane dogbane henbane
bang   bangs banged banger bangle bangers banging bangles shebang
bangs   shebangs
bani   banian banish banians
banjo   banjos banjoes banjoist
bank   banks banked banker embank bankers banking embanks
banks   embanks cutbanks
bans   banshee turbans
bar   barb bard bare bark barm barn bars barbs bards bared barer bares barge baric barks barmy barns baron barre debar lobar barbed barber barbet bardic barege barely barest barfly barged barges baring barite barium barked barker barley barong barons

barony   barque barred barrel barren barres barrio barrow barter baryon baryta bulbar debark debars disbar durbar embark isobar labara lumbar sambar tabard
barb   barbs barbed barber barbet barbell barbers barbets barbing barbule rhubarb
barbs   rhubarbs
bard   bards tabard bombard tabards
bards   tabards bombards
bare   bared barer bares barege barely barest bareges cabaret
bares   barest
barge   barged barges bargees bargeman bargemen
baric   barbaric isobaric
bark   barks barked barker debark embark barkers barking debarks embarks tanbark
barks   debarks embarks tanbarks
barm   barmy barmaid barmier
barn   barns
baron   barong barons barony baronet barongs baronage baroness baronets baronial baronies
barre   barred barrel barren barres barrels bbarres barreled barrenly barrette debarred
bars   debars disbars durbars isobars sambars
basal   basalt basalts basaltic
base   abase based baser bases abased abases basely basest debase baseman basemen debased debases diabase
based   abased debased
bases   abases basest debases diabases
bash   abash bashaw bashed bashes abashed abashes bashaws bashful bashing
basic   basics basicity
basil   basils basilar basilic basilica basilisk
basin   basing basins abasing basinet basinets debasing
bask   basks basked basket baskets basking
bass   basset bassets bassist bassoon embassy
bast   baste basts basted bastes bastard basting bastion bombast lambast
baste   basted bastes lambaste
basts   bombasts lambasts
bat   bate bath bats abate batch bated bates bathe baths batik baton batty

rabat abated abater abates abatis abator batboy bateau bathed bather bathes bathos batiks bating batman batons batted batten batter battle battue combat debate lobate rabato rabats rebate rubato wombat

batch batched batches batching

bate abate bated bates abated abater abates bateau debate lobate rebate abaters bateaux debated debates limbate probate rebated rebates

bated abated debated rebated combated probated

bates abates debates rebates probates

bath bathe baths bathed bather bathes bathos bathers bathing bathtub bathyal isobath

bathe bathed bather bathes bathers sunbathe

baths isobaths

batik batiks

baton batons

bats rabats batsman batsmen combats wombats

bawd bawds bawdy bawdry bawdier

bawl bawls bawled bawling

bay bays bayed bayou embay baying bayous embays

bayed embayed

bayou bayous

bays embays

bazoo bazoos bazooka bazookas

be bed bee beg bel ben bet bey abed abet babe bead beak beam bean bear beat beau beck beds beef been beep beer bees beet begs bell bels belt bema bend bens bent berg berm best beta beth bets bevy beys cube gibe gybe ibex jibe kibe lobe lube obey robe rube tube abbey abeam abele abets adobe amber babes beach beads beady beaks beams beamy beans beard bears beast beats beaus beaut bebop becks bedim beech beefs beefy beeps beers beery beets befit befog began begat beget begin begot begum begun beige being belay belch belie belle bells belly below belts bemas bench bends benne benny beret bergs berms berry berth beryl beset besom besot bests betas betel beths betta bevel bezel bribe caber combe cubed cubes ebbed embed ember fiber gibed gibes glebe globe grebe gybes imbed jebel jibed jiber jibes kibei kibes label libel lobed lobes lubes maybe obeah obese obeys omber orbed plebe probe rebec rebel robed robes rube saber sober tabes tribe tubed tuber tubes umbel umber vibes xebec zebec

beach beached beaches beachboy beaching

bead beads beady beaded beader beadle beaders beadier beading beadles jetbead

beak beaks beaked beaker beakers

beam abeam beams beamy beamed beamer beamers beamier beamily beaming sunbeam

beams sunbeams

bean beans beaned beanie beanbag beanery beanies beaning soybean

beans soybeans

bear beard bears beards bearer bearded bearers bearhug bearing bearish bugbear cudbear forbear

beard beards bearded

bears bearskin bugbears forbears

beast beasts beastie beastly beasties

beat beats beaten beater upbeat beaters beatify beating beatnik offbeat

beau beaus beaut beauts beauty jambeau

beaut beauts beauty beauties beautify

bebop bebops

beck becks becket beckon beckets beckons

bed abed beds bedim cubed ebbed embed gibed imbed jibed lobed orbed robed tubed albedo barbed bedbug bedded bedeck bedims bedlam bedpan bibbed bobbed bombed bribed bulbed cabbed combed curbed dabbed daubed dubbed embeds fibbed fobbed gabbed garbed gibbed globed herbed hotbed imbeds jabbed jibbed jobbed limbed lobbed mobbed nabbed nibbed numbed probed ribbed robbed rubbed seabed sobbed subbed tabbed webbed

bedim bedims bedimmed

beds embeds imbeds bedside bedsore hotbeds seabeds

bee beef been beep beer bees beet beech beefs beefy beeps beers beery beets bawbee beefed beeper beetle beeves

beech beeches beechnut

beef beefs beefy beefed beefier beefing

beep beeps beeper beepers

beer beers beery beerier

bees bawbees beeswax

beet beets beetle beetled beetles

befit befits befitted

befog befogs befogged

beg begs began begat beget begin begot begum begun begets beggar begged begins begone begums

beget begets

begin begins beginner

begot begotten

begum begums

beige beiges

being beings inbeing

bel bell bels belt abele belay belch belie belle bells belly below belts jebel label libel rebel umbel abeles belays belfry belied belief belies belled belles bellow belong belted beluga corbel jebels labels libels obelus rebels umbels

belay belays belayed belaying

belch belched belches belching

belie belied belief belies beliefs believe believed believer believes

bell belle bells belly belled belles bellow barbell bellboy bellhop bellied bellies belling bellows cowbell rubella

belle belled belles labelled labeller libelled rebelled

bells barbells cowbells

belly bellyful bellying potbelly

below furbelow

bels jebels labels libels rebels umbels corbels

belt belts belted belting beltway

bema bemas bemata

ben bend bens bent bench bends benne benny bender benign bennes benumb benzol benzyl unbend unbent

bench benched bencher benches benchers

bend bends bender unbend benders bending prebend unbends

bends unbends prebends

benne bennes

bent unbent lambent

beret berets

berg bergs iceberg

bergs icebergs

berm berms

berry bayberry berrying bilberry boxberry dewberry dogberry mulberry

berth bertha berths berthed berthing

beryl beryls

beset besets

besom besoms

besot besots besotted

best bests bested bestir bestow bestial besting bestirs bestows dumbest numbest

bet abet beta beth bets abets betas betel beths betta barbet betake bethel betide betook betray bettas betted better bettor gibbet gobbet rabbet sorbet

beta betas betake betaken betakes

beth beths bethel

bets abets barbets gibbets gobbets rabbets sorbets

betta bettas

bevel bevels beveled beveling

bey beys obey abbey obeys abbeys beyond obeyed obeyer

beys   obeys abbeys
bezel   bezels
bhang   bhangs
bias   biased biases cobias tibias biasing phobias terbias
bib   bibb bibs bibbs bibbed bibber imbibe
bibb   bibbs bibbed bibber bibbing
bid   bide bids abide biddy bided bides bidet rabid abided abider abides bidden bidder bidets biding forbid ibidem libido morbid outbid turbid verbid
bide   abide bided bides bidet abided abider abides bidets abiders carbide
bided   abided
bides   abides carbides
bidet   bidets
bids   forbids outbids verbids
bield   bields
bier   biers gabbier herbier nobbier nubbier tubbier webbier
biff   biffs
big   bight bigot bigamy bigger biggie biggin bights bigots bigwig
bight   bights
bigot   bigots bigoted bigotry
bijou   bijoux
bike   biked bikes bikeway
bilbo   bilboes
bile   biles habile labile mobile nubile jubilee mobiles stabile
biles   mobiles stabiles
bilge   bilged bilges
bilk   bilks bilked bilking
bill   bills billy billed billet billon billow rebill billets billies billing billion billons billows billowy rebills sawbill
bills   rebills sawbills
bin   bind bine bins binds bines binge bingo cabin robin sabin albino binary binate binder bindle binges bingos binned bobbin cabins cubing dobbin dubbin ebbing gibing globin jibing nubbin orbing robing robins sabins tubing
bind   binds binder bindle binders bindery binding bindles
bine   bines cabined cabinet carbine combine turbine
bines   carbines combines turbines
binge   binges
bingo   bingos
bins   cabins robins sabins bobbins dobbins globins nubbins
biped   bipeds bipedal
bipod   bipods
birch   birches
bird   birds birder birdie birders birdied birdies birding birdman birdmen cowbird jaybird sunbird

birds   birdseed cowbirds jaybirds redbirds sunbirds
birl   birls birled birling
birr   birrs
birth   births rebirth birthday rebirths
bise   bises bisect ibises bisects soubise
bises   ibises soubises
bit   bite bits bitt obit ambit bitch biter bites bitts bitty cubit debit habit obits orbit ambits bitchy biters biting bitten bitter cubits debits gambit habits kibitz orbits rabbit subito tidbit titbit turbit
bitch   bitchy bitched bitches bitching
bite   biter bites biters arbiter debited orbited orbiter
biter   biters arbiter orbiter arbiters orbiters
bits   obits ambits cubits debits habits orbits gambits rabbits tidbits titbits turbits
bitt   bitts bitty bitten bitter bittern bitters
blab   blabs blabbed blabber
black   blacks blacked blacken blacker blackly blackcap blackens blackest blacking blackish blackout blacktop
blade   bladed blades
blah   blahs kiblah kiblahs
blahs   kiblahs
blain   blains
blame   blamed blames
bland   blandly blandish
blank   blanks blanked blanket blankly blankets blanking
blare   blared blares
blast   blasts oblast blasted blastie oblasts blastema blasties blasting blastoff blastula
blat   blats oblate blatant blather blatted oblates sublate
blaze   ablaze blazed blazer blazes blazers emblaze emblazed emblazes
bleak   bleaker bleakly bleakest bleakish
blear   blears bleary blearily
bleat   bleats bleated bleating
bleb   blebs blebby
bled   ambled cabled fabled gabled tabled babbled bobbled bubbled bumbled burbled cobbled dabbled dibbled doubled enabled fumbled gabbled gambled garbled gobbled hobbled humbled jumbled kibbled marbled mumbled nibbled nobbled pebbled rabbled rambled rumbled stabled tumbled wambled warbled wimbled wobbled
bleed   bleeds bleeder bleeders bleeding
bleep   bleeps
blend   blende blends blended blender blenders blending

bless   blessed jobless ribless blessing herbless noblesse
blest   ablest feeblest humblest nimblest
blimp   blimps blimpish
blind   blinds blinded blinder blindly blinders blinding blindman blindmen purblind
blink   blinks blinked blinker blinkers blinking
blip   blips blipped
bliss   blissful
blitz   blitzed blitzes blitzing
bloat   bloats bloated bloater bloaters bloating
blob   blobs blobbed
bloc   block blocs blocks blocky blocked blocker
block   blocks blocky blocked blocker blockade blockage blockers blockier blocking blockish
bloke   blokes
blond   blonde blonds blondes
blood   bloods bloody blooded oxblood bloodied bloodier bloodily oxbloods
bloom   abloom blooms bloomy bloomed bloomer bloomers bloomier blooming
blot   blots blotch blotto blotchy blotted blotter inkblot
blots   inkblots
blow   blown blows blowy blower blowsy blowup blowzy blowers blowgun blowing blowout blowups
blown   flyblown
blows   blowsy blowsier
blue   blued bluer blues bluet bluely bluest bluets blueing
blues   bluest
bluet   bluets
bluff   bluffs bluffed bluffer bluffers bluffing
blunt   blunts blunted bluntly blunting
blur   blurb blurs blurt blurbs blurry blurts blurred blurted
blurb   blurbs
blurt   blurts blurted blurting
blush   blushed blusher blushes blushers blushing
boa   boar boas boat board boars boast boats aboard boards boasts boated boatel boater jerboa
boar   board boars aboard boards boarded boarder boarish inboard
board   aboard boards boarded boarder inboard boarders boarding cupboard keyboard lapboard larboard leeboard outboard pegboard seaboard
boas   boast boasts boasted boaster
boast   boasts boasted boaster boasters boastful boasting

boat boats boated boatel boater boatels boaters boating boatman boatmen bumboat catboat gunboat iceboat pigboat rowboat towboat tugboat

boats bumboats catboats gunboats iceboats pigboats rowboats towboats tugboats

bob bobs bobby cabob kabob kebob nabob bobbed bobber bobbin bobble bobcat cabobs kabobs kebobs nabobs

bobs cabobs kabobs kebobs nabobs bobsled

bocci boccie

bode abode boded bodes abodes bodega bodegas

bodes abodes

body embody nobody anybody bodying

bog bogs bogy bogey bogie bogus bogeys bogged boggle bogies

bogey bogeys bogeyed bogeying bogeyman bogeymen

bogie bogies

boil aboil boils boiled boiler boilers boiling parboil

boils parboils

bold bolder boldly kobold boldest kobolds

bole boles bolero boleros boletus

boll bolls bollix bollard

bolo bolos bologna boloney

bolt bolts bolted bolter bolters bolting

bolus obolus boluses embolus

bomb bombs bombax bombed bomber bombard bombast bombers bombing

bon bona bond bone bong bonk bony ebon bonds boned boner bones bongo bongs bonks bonny bonus bonze ebony bonbon bonded boners bongos bonier boning bonito bonked bonnet bonsai carbon debone gibbon ribbon

bond bonds bonded bondage bonding

bonds bondsman bondsmen

bone boned boner bones boners debone boneset deboned debones hambone hipbone jambone jawbone umbones

boned deboned jawboned rawboned ribboned

boner boners

bones boneset debones umbones bonesets hambones hipbones jawbones sawbones

bong bongo bongs bongos

bongo bongos

bonk bonks bonked bonkers bonking

bonus bonuses

bony ebony

boo boob book boom boon boor boos boot boobs booby booed books booms boons boors boost booth boots booty booze boozy taboo baboon bamboo boodle boogie boohoo booing booked bookie boomed boomer boosts booted bootee booths boozed boozer boozes taboos

boob boobs booby boobies

booed tabooed

book books booked bookie bookend bookies booking bookish booklet bookman bookmen daybook lawbook logbook

books daybooks lawbooks logbooks

boom booms boomed boomer boombox boomers booming boomlet

boon boons baboon baboons boonies

boons baboons

boor boors boorish

boos boost boosts taboos bamboos boosted booster caboose

boost boosts boosted booster boosters boosting

boot booth boots booty booted bootee booths bootees booties booting bootleg gumboot

booth booths

boots gumboots

booze boozed boozer boozes boozers

bop bops bebop bebops bopped

bops bebops

bora boral boras borax borage borals borate borages borates boraxes

boral borals

borax boraxes

bore bored borer bores boreal borers arbored arbores boredom forbore labored laborer taboret

bored arbored boredom labored harbored

borer borers laborer harborer laborers

bores arbores

born inborn reborn suborn unborn hagborn lowborn newborn suborns

boron borons

bort abort borts aborts aborted

borts aborts

bosh boshes kibosh

bosk bosks boskier

bosom bosoms bosomy bosomed embosom embosoms

boss bossy bossed bosses emboss bossier bossing bossism

bosun bosuns

bot both bots bott abbot botch botts jabot sabot abbots botany botchy botfly bother bottle bottom burbot jabots robots sabots turbot

botch botchy botched botcher botches botchers botchier botching

both bother bothers

bots abbots jabots robots sabots burbots turbots

bott botts bottle bottom bottled bottler bottles bottoms

bough boughs bought boughten

boule boules

bound abound bounds abounds bounded bounder inbound rebound abounded boundary bounders bounding icebound inbounds outbound rebounds

bourg bourgs

bouse bouses

bout about bouts

bovid bovids

bow bowl bows bowed bowel bower bowie bowls elbow embow oxbow bowels bowers bowery bowfin bowing bowled bowler bowman bowmen bowwow bowyer elbows embows fogbow oxbows sunbow

bowed elbowed embowed

bowel bowels

bower bowers bowery embower boweries embowers

bowl bowls bowled bowler bowlers bowline bowling

bows elbows embows oxbows fogbows sunbows

box boxy boxed boxer boxes boxcar boxers boxier boxing hatbox hotbox icebox

boxer boxers

boxes hatboxes hotboxes iceboxes

boy boyo boys boyar batboy boyars boyish busboy carboy cowboy lowboy tomboy

boyar boyars

boys batboys busboys carboys cowboys lowboys tomboys

bozo bozos rebozo rebozos

bozos rebozos

bra brad brae brag bran bras brat braw bray brace brach bract brads brags braid brail brain brake brand brans brash brass brats brave bravo brawl brawn braws braxy brays braze cobra dobra labra libra sabra umbra zebra abrade braced bracer braces bracts braids brails brains brainy braise braked brakes branch brands brandy branks branny brashy brassy bratty braved braver braves bravos brawls brawny brayed brayer brazed brazen brazer brazes brazil cobras dobras sabras umbrae umbras zebras

brace braced bracer braces bracero bracers embrace bracelet embraced embracer embraces

brach brachial brachium

bract bracts

brad brads abrade abraded abrades bradawl

brae umbrae

brag brags bragged bragger umbrage

braid braids braided upbraid braiding upbraids

brail brails

brain brains brainy brained braining brainpan endbrain midbrain

brake braked brakes brakeman brakemen

bran brand brans branch brands brandy branks branny branded vibrant

brand brands brandy branded brandied brandies branding brandish

bras brash brass brashy brassy cobras dobras sabras umbras zebras brasher brassie

brash brashy brasher brashest

brass brassy brassie brassart brassier

brat brats bratty librate vibrate vibrato

brave braved braver braves bravely bravery bravest

bravo bravos

braw brawl brawn brawls brawny brawled brawler

brawl brawls brawled brawler brawlers brawling

brawn brawny brawnier

bray brays brayed brayer braying

braze brazed brazen brazer brazes brazens brazers brazenly

bread breads breaded breadth breadbox breading breadths

break breaks breaker breakup breakage breakers breaking breakout breakups daybreak outbreak

bream breams

bred inbred sabred

bree breed brees breech breeds breeze breezy breeder breezed breezes inbreed

breed breeds breeder inbreed breeders breeding inbreeds

breve breves brevet brevets

brew brews brewed brewer brewis brewage brewers brewery brewing

briar briars briary

bribe bribed briber bribes bribers bribery

brick bricks bricked brickle brickbat bricking

bride brides

brie brief brier briefs briers briery ambries briefed briefly debrief

brief briefs briefed briefly debrief briefing debriefs

brier briers briery

brig brigs bright brigade brigand

brim brims brimful brimmed brimmer

brine brined brines zebrine

bring brings sabring bringing

brink brinks

brisk brisket briskly briskets

brit britska brittle

broad abroad broads broadax broaden broader broadly broadens broadest

brock brocks

broil broils broiled broiler embroil broilers broiling embroils panbroil

broke broken broker brokers unbroken

brood broods broody brooded brooder brooders brooding

brook brooks brooked brooking

broom brooms

broth broths brothel brother brothels brothers

brow brown brows browns browse browned browner brownie browsed browser browses eyebrow lowbrow

brown browns browned browner brownie brownest brownies browning brownish brownout

brows browse browsed browser browses browsers browsing eyebrows lowbrows

bruit bruits bruited bruiting

brume brumes

brunt brunts

brush brushy brushed brushes airbrush brushing brushoff

brute brutes

bub bubo bubs bubble bubbly buboes hubbub

bubo buboes bubonic

buck bucko bucks bucked bucker bucket buckle buckra buckers buckets buckeye bucking buckled buckles buckoes buckram buckras bucksaw kebbuck roebuck

bucko buckoes

bucks bucksaw bucksaws buckshot buckskin roebucks

bud buds buddy budge budded buddle budged budges budget budgie redbud

budge budged budges budget budgets budgeted

buds redbuds

buff buffs buffed buffer buffet rebuff buffalo buffers buffets buffing buffoon rebuffs

buffs rebuffs

bug bugs buggy bugle debug bedbug bugged bugger bugled bugler bugles debugs humbug

bugle bugled bugler bugles buglers

bugs debugs bedbugs humbugs

buhl buhls

build builds builder buildup rebuild builders building buildups rebuilds

built rebuilt

bulb bulbs bulbar bulbed bulbil bulbul bulbils bulbous

bulge bulged bulges

bulk bulks bulky bulked bulkier bulking

bull bulla bulls bully bullae bulled bullet bullate bulldog bullets bullied bullies bulling bullion bullish bullock bullpen

bulla bullae bullate

bully bullying

bum bump bums album bumps bumpy sebum albums bumble bummed bummer bumped bumper sebums

bump bumps bumpy bumped bumper bumpers bumpier bumping bumpkin

bums albums sebums

bun bung bunk buns bunt bunch bunco bundt bungs bunko bunks bunny bunts bunchy buncos bundle bundts bunged bungle bunion bunked bunker bunkos bunkum bunted debunk

bunch bunchy bunched bunches bunchier bunching

bunco buncos buncoed buncoing

bundt bundts

bung bungs bunged bungle bunging bungled bungler bungles

bunk bunko bunks bunked bunker bunkos bunkum debunk bunkers bunking bunkums debunks

bunko bunkos

bunks debunks

bunt bunts bunted bunting

buoy buoys buoyed buoyant buoying

buran burans

burg burgh burgs burgee burger burghs burgle burgoo burgage burgees burgeon burgers burgess burgher burglar burgled burgles burgoos hamburg homburg

burgh burghs burgher burghers

burgs hamburgs homburgs

burin burins

burke burked burkes

burl burls burly burlap burled burley burlaps burleys burlier burling

burn burns burnt auburn burned burner burnet auburns burners burnets burning burnish burnous burnout sunburn

burns auburns sunburns

burnt sunburnt

burp burps burped burping

burr burro burrs burred burros burrow burring burrito burrows

burro burros burrow burrows burrowed burrower

bursa bursae bursal bursar bursas bursars bursary

burse burses disburse

burst bursts airburst bursting outburst sunburst

bury burying tilbury

bus bush buss bust busy abuse babus busby bused buses bushy busts busty rebus zebus abused abuser abuses airbus ambush busboy bushed bushel bushes busied busier busily busing buskin busman busmen bussed busses buster bustic bustle iambus limbus nimbus robust

bused abused

buses abuses rebuses iambuses nimbuses

bush bushy ambush bushed bushel bushes bushels bushier bushing bushman bushmen

buss bussed busses bussing

bust busts busty buster bustic bustle robust busters bustled bustler bustles combust

busts combusts

busy busying

but abut buts butt abuts butch butts butyl debut rebut butane butler butted butter button butyls debuts hagbut rebuts

butch butcher butchers butchery

buts abuts debuts rebuts hagbuts

butt butts butted butter button abutted abutter butters buttery butting buttock buttons

butyl butyls

buxom buxomly

buy buys buyer buyers buying buyout

buyer buyers

buzz abuzz buzzer buzzes buzzard buzzers buzzing

bwana bwanas

by aby bye abye baby byes byre byte gaby goby orby ruby abysm abyss bobby booby busby bylaw byres bytes byway cabby cubby derby forby gabby herby hobby hubby lobby looby nobby nubby rugby sibyl tabby tubby webby

bye abye byes

bylaw bylaws

byre byres

byte bytes

byway byways

c

cab cabs scab cabal cabby caber cabin cable cabob scabs cabala cabals cabana cabbed cabbie cabers cabins cabled cables cabman cabmen cabobs scabby

cabal cabala cabals cabalas cabalism cabalist caballed

cabby scabby

caber cabers macaber

cabin cabins cabined cabinet cabinets cabining

cable cabled cables vocable amicable educable peccable placable

cabob cabobs

cabs scabs

cacao cacaos

cache cached caches cachet cachets cachexy cachepot

cad cade cadi cads scad caddy cades cadet cadge cadis cadre cycad scads arcade caddie caddis cadent cadets cadged cadges cadres cicada cycads decade facade

caddy caddying

cade cades cadet arcade cadent cadets decade facade academe academy arcades brocade cadelle cadence cadency cadenza cascade decades facades saccade

cades arcades decades facades brocades cascades saccades

cadet cadets

cadge cadged cadges

cadi cadis

cadre cadres

cads scads cycads

cafe cafes

cage caged cages cagey encage socage boscage encaged encages socages

caged encaged

cages encages socages boscages

caird cairds

cairn cairns cairned

cake caked cakes cupcake hoecake oatcake pancake

caked pancaked

cakes cupcakes hoecakes oatcakes pancakes

calk calks

call calla calls scall callas called caller callow callus recall scalls callboy callers calling callous catcall locally recalls scallop vocally

calla callas

calls scalls recalls catcalls

calm calms becalm calmed calmer calmly becalms calmest calming

calms becalms

calve calved calves

calx calxes

calyx calyxes

cam came camp cams scam camas camel cameo cames campo camps campy camus scamp scams became camber cambia camels cameos camera camion camlet camped camper campos campus decamp encamp jicama scampi scamps

came camel cameo cames became camels cameos camera cameral cameras

camel camels cameleer

cameo cameos

camp campo camps campy scamp camped camper campos campus decamp encamp scampi scamps campers camphor campier camping decamps encamps scamped scamper

campo campos camporee

camps scamps decamps encamps campsite

cams scams

can cane cans cant scan canal candy caned caner canes canny canoe canon canto cants pecan scans scant arcane ashcan canada canals canape canard canary cancan cancel cancer candid candle candor caners canine caning canker canned cannel cannon cannot canoed canoes canons canopy canted canter canthi cantle canton cantor cantos cantus canvas canyon decant jacana oilcan pecans recant scants scanty secant toucan vacant

canal canals canalize canalled

candy candying

cane caned caner canes arcane caners chicane

caned chicaned

caner caners

canes chicanes

canny uncanny

canoe canoed canoes canoeing canoeist

canon canons canoness canonist canonize

cans scans pecans ashcans cancans oilcans toucans

cant canto cants scant canted canter canthi cantle canton cantor cantos cantus decant recant scants scanty secant vacant cantata canteen canters canthus cantina canting cantles cantons cantors cantrip decants descant discant peccant recants scanted scantly secants

canto canton cantor cantos cantons cantors cantoned

cants scants decants recants secants descants discants

cap cape capo caps caped caper capes capon capos recap scape capful capias capons capote capped capper capric captor escape hubcap icecap madcap mobcap recaps redcap scaped scapes skycap

cape caper capes scape escape scaped scapes capelin capered escaped escapee escaper escapes

caped scaped escaped

caper capered escaper capering escapers

capes scapes escapes

capo capon capos capons capote capotes decapod

capon capons caponize

caps recaps capsize capstan capsule hubcaps icecaps madcaps mobcaps redcaps skycaps

car card care cark carl carp cars cart scar carat cards cared cares caret cargo carks carls carny carob carol carom carps carry carte carts carve scare scarf scarp scars scary vicar acarid boxcar calcar carafe carats carbon carboy carded carder careen career caress carets carful cargos carhop caribe caries carina caring carked carlin carman carmen carnal carney carnie carobs carols caroms carpal carped carpel carper carpet carpus carrel carrot carted cartel carter carton carved carvel carven carver carves escarp lascar picaro scarab scarce scared scares scarfs scarps vicars

carat carats baccarat

card cards carded carder carders cardiac carding cardoon discard placard

cards discards placards

care cared cares caret scare careen career caress carets scared scares careens careers careful

cared scared

cares caress scares caressed caresses

caret carets

cargo cargos cargoes

cark carks carked carking

carl carls carlin carline carlins carload scarlet

carob carobs

carol carols caroled caroler carolers caroling escarole

carom caroms caromed caroming

carp carps scarp carpal carped carpel carper carpet carpus escarp scarps carpals carpels carpers carping carport epicarp escarps exocarp scarped scarper

carps scarps escarps epicarps exocarps

carry carryall carrying miscarry

cars scars vicars boxcars carsick lascars

cart carte carts carted cartel carter carton cartage cartels carters carting cartons cartoon dogcart

carte carted cartel carter cartels carters

carts dogcarts

carve carved carvel carven carver carves carvels carvers scarves

case cased cases casefy casein casern encase incase caseate caseous caserns encased encases incased incases

cased encased incased

cases encases incases fracases

cash cashaw cashed cashes cashew cashews cashier cashing

cask casks casket caskets

cast caste casts castes castle castor dicast recast upcast casters casting castled castles castoff castors dicasts miscast outcast recasts upcasts

caste castes casters outcaste

casts dicasts recasts upcasts outcasts

cat cate cats scat catch cater cates catty ducat scats bobcat catchy catena caters catgut cation catkin catnap catnip catsup catted cattle ducats hepcat locate muscat scathe tomcat vacate

catch catchy catcher catches catchup catchall catchers catchier catching

cate cater cates catena caters locate vacate baccate catechu catenae catered caterer educate falcate furcate located locater locates placate plicate saccate sulcate vacated vacates

cater caters catered caterer locater caterers catering locaters

cates locates vacates educates furcates placates

cats scats catsup ducats bobcats hepcats muscats tomcats

caul caulk cauls caulks caulked

caulk caulks caulked caulking

cause caused causer causes because causers causeway

cave caved caves caveat cavern caveats caverns cavetto concave

caved concaved

caves concaves

cavil cavils caviler cavilers caviling

caw caws macaw

cay cays decay cayman decays

cays decays

cease ceased ceases decease deceased deceases

ceca icecap icecaps

cedar cedars

cede ceded cedes accede recede secede acceded accedes concede precede receded recedes seceded seceder secedes

ceded acceded receded seceded conceded preceded

cedes accedes recedes secedes concedes precedes

cee cees emcee sycee emceed emcees exceed sycees

cees emcees sycees

ceiba ceibas

ceil ceils ceiled ceiling

cell cella cello cells cellae cellar celled cellos cellars cellist cellule micelle nacelle

cella cellae cellar cellars cellared cellarer cellaret

cello cellos

celt celts

cense censed censes incense license incensed incenses licensed licensee licenses

cent cento cents scent accent ascent cental center centos centra centre centum decent docent lucent recent scents accents ascents centals centaur centavo centers centime centimo centner central centred centres centric centrum century concent descent docents nascent percent scented

cento centos

cents scents accents ascents docents concents descents percents

ceorl ceorls

cep ceps accept biceps except incept

ceps biceps forceps

cere cereal cereus cereals cerebra sincere

cero ceros cerous bracero viceroy

cess access excess recess abscess cession precess process success

chafe chafed chafes

chaff chaffs chaffy chaffed chaffer chaffers chaffier chaffing

chain chains chained enchain unchain chaining chainman enchains

chair chairs chaired armchair chairing chairman chairmen

chalk chalks chalky chalked chalkier chalking

cham champ chammy champs chamade chamber chamfer chamois champed

champ champs champed champion

chant chants chanted chanter chantey chantry enchant chanters chanting couchant enchants merchant penchant

chap chape chaps chapel chapes chapeau chapels chaplet chapped chapter

chape chapel chapes chapeau chapels chaperon

char chard chare charm chars chart chary chards chares charge charka charms charry charts eschar charade charged charger charges charier charily chariot charism charity charkas charmed charnel charqui charred charted charter eschars orchard pochard

chard chards orchard pochard orchards pochards

chare chares

charm charms charmed charming

chars eschars

chart charts charted charter charters charting chartist

chase chased chases enchase enchased enchases purchase

chasm chasms chasmed

chat chats chatty chatted chattel chatter

chaw chaws chawed chawing

cheap cheapo cheapen cheaper cheapie cheaply cheapos cheapens cheapest cheapies

cheat cheats cheated cheater escheat cheaters cheating escheats

check checks checked checker checkup recheck checkers checking checkoff checkout checkups hatcheck paycheck rechecks

cheek cheeks cheeky cheeked cheekier cheekily cheeking

cheep cheeps cheeped cheeping

cheer cheers cheery cheered cheerio cheerful cheerily cheering cheerios

chef chefs

chela chelae

chert cherts

chess duchess chessman chessmen

chest chests chesty richest chestnut

chevy chevying

chew chews chewy chewed chewer eschew rechew chewers chewier chewing chewink eschews fitchew rechews

chews eschews rechews fitchews

chi chic chid chin chip chit chick chico chide chids chief child chili chill chime chimp china chine chink chino chins chips chirk chirp chirr chits aching archil chiaus chichi chicks chicle chicos chided chides chiefs chield chilli chills chilly chimed chimes chimps chinch chines chinks chinos chintz chippy chirks chirps chirpy chirrs chisel chitin chiton chives ischia kimchi litchi lochia orchid orchil orchis schism schist schizy urchin zechin

chic chick chico chichi chicks chicle chicos chicane chichis chickee chicken chicory psychic

chick chicks chickee chicken chickees chickens chickpea

chico chicos chicory

chid chide chided chides orchid chidden chiding orchids

chide chided chides

chief chiefs chiefly chiefdom kerchief mischief

child childly childbed childish children godchild

chili chiliad chilies

chill chilli chills chilly chilled chiller chillers chillier chilling schiller

chime chimed chimes chimera chimere chimeras chimeres chimeric

chimp chimps

chin china chine chink chino chins aching chinch chines chinks chinos chintz urchin zechin arching caching chinked chinned chintzy etching inching itching kachina leching machine niching urchins zechins

china kachina echinate kachinas

chine chines machine achiness machined machines

chink chinks chinked chinking

chino chinos

chins urchins zechins

chip chips chippy chipped chipper

chirk chirks

chirp chirps chirpy chirped chirpier chirping

chirr chirrs chirrup chirrups

chit chits chitin chiton chitons chitter

chock chocks chocked chocking

choir choirs choired choirboy choiring

choke choked choker chokes chokey chokers

chomp chomps chomped chompers chomping

chop chops choppy chopine chopped chopper

chord chords chorded chording

chore chorea chores anchored

chose chosen

chub chubs chubby

chuck chucks chucked chuckle upchuck chucking chuckled chuckler chuckles upchucks

chow chows

chuff chuffs chuffy chuffed chuffing

chug chugs chugged

chum chump chums chummy chumps chummed

chump chumps

chunk chunks chunky chunkier

churl churls churlish

churn churns churned churning

churr churrs

chute chutes

cider ciders

cigar cigars

cilia ciliary ciliate ciliates

cinch cinched cinches cinching

cion cions scion scions

cions scions

cisco ciscos

cist cists racist cistern fascist racists

cists racists fascists

cite cited cites excite incite recite calcite excited exciter excites incited inciter incites leucite recited recites zincite

cited excited incited recited elicited

cites excites incites recites zincites

city edacity opacity paucity

civet civets

civic civics

civil civilly uncivil civilian civility civilize

clack clacks clacked clacking

clad unclad

claim claims acclaim claimed declaim exclaim reclaim acclaims claimant claiming declaims disclaim exclaims proclaim reclaims

clam clamp clams clammy clamor clamps clamant clamber clammed clammer clamors clamour clamped

clamp clamps clamped

clan clang clank clans clangs clanks clanged clangor clanked

clang clangs clanged clangor clanging clangors

clank clanks clanked clanking

clans clansman clansmen

clap claps clapt clapped clapper

clapt claptrap

claro claros

clash clashed clashes clashing

clasp clasps clasped enclasp unclasp clasping enclasps

class classy classed classes classic classis classics classier classify classing outclass subclass

clave claves enclave conclave enclaves

claw claws clawed clawing

clay clays clayey clayish

clean cleans cleaned cleaner cleanly cleanse cleanup unclean cleaners cleanest cleaning cleansed cleanser cleanses cleanups

clear clears cleared clearer clearly nuclear unclear clearage clearcut clearers clearest clearing

cleat cleats cleated cleating nucleate

cleek cleeks

clef clefs cleft clefts

cleft clefts

clerk clerks clerked clerkly clerking

clew clews clewed clewing

click clicks clicked clicker clickers clicking

cliff cliffs

climb climbs climbed climber climbers climbing

clime climes

cline clines decline incline recline declined declines inclined incliner inclines isocline reclined recliner reclines

cling clings clinger cycling circling clinging muscling

clink clinks clinked clinker clinkers clinking

clip clips clipped clipper eclipse

clips eclipse eclipsed eclipses

cloak cloaks cloaked cloaking

clock clocks clocked clocking

clod clods cloddy

clog clogs cloggy unclog clogged eclogue unclogs

clogs unclogs

clomp clomps clomped clomping

clone cloned clones cyclone cyclones

close closed closer closes closet closely closers closest closets enclose inclose closeted disclose enclosed encloses incloses

clot cloth clots clothe cloths clothed clothes clotted cloture

cloth clothe cloths clothed clothes clothier clothing oilcloth

cloud clouds cloudy becloud clouded beclouds cloudier cloudily clouding cloudlet

clout clouts clouted clouting

clove cloven clover cloves clovers

clown clowns clowned clownery clowning clownish

cloy cloys cloyed cloying

club clubs clubby clubbed

cluck clucks clucked clucking

clue clued clues

clump clumps clumpy clumped clumping

clunk clunks clunky clunked clunkers clunking

coach coached coaches coaching coachman coachmen

coact coacts coacted coacting coaction coactive

coal coals coaled coaler coalers coaling

coast coasts coastal coasted coaster coasters coasting seacoast

coat coati coats coated coatis coating peacoat redcoat surcoat topcoat

coati coatis coating coatings

coats peacoats redcoats surcoats topcoats

coax coaxal coaxed coaxer coaxes coaxers coaxial coaxing

cob cobs cobia coble cobra cobalt cobble cobias cobles cobnut cobras cobweb

cobia cobias

coble cobles

cobra cobras

coca cocas cocaine

cock acock cocks cocky cocked cocker cockle bibcock cockade cockers cockeye cockier cocking cockled cockles cockney cockpit haycock peacock petcock seacock

cocks bibcocks cocksure haycocks peacocks petcocks seacocks

coco cocoa cocos cocoas cocoon rococo coconut cocoons cocotte rococos

cocoa cocoas cocoanut

cocos rococos

cod coda code cods codas coded codes codex codded coddle codger codify coding decode encode

coda codas

code coded codes codex decode encode codeine decoded decodes encoded encoder encodes

coded decoded encoded

codes decodes encodes

coed coeds buncoed

cog cogs cogon cogent cogged cognac cogons

cogon cogons

coif coifs coiffed

coil coils coiled recoil uncoil coiling recoils uncoils

coils recoils uncoils

coin coins coined coinage coining

coins coinsure

coir coirs

coke coked cokes

col cola cold cole cols colt colas colds coles colic colin colly colon color colts colza scold colder coldly coleus colins collar collie collop colons colony colors colour colter column colure colzas glycol scolds scolex

cola colas

cold colds scold colder coldly scolds coldest scolded scolder

colds scolds

cole coles coleus scolex

coles coleslaw

colic bucolic colicky bucolics

colin colins

colly collying

colon colons colony colonel colonels colonial colonies colonist colonize

color colors bicolor colored recolor colorant colorful coloring colorist discolor recolors tricolor

cols glycols

colt colts colter colters coltish

colza colzas

coma comate comaker comates sarcoma

comb combe combo combs combat combed comber combes combos combats combers combine combing combust coxcomb

combe combed comber combes combers

combo combos

combs coxcombs

come comer comes comet become comedy comely comers comets income becomes incomes outcome welcome

comer comers newcomer

comes becomes incomes outcomes welcomes

comet comets

comic comics comical

comma commas command commando commands

comp compo comps comped compel comply compos compact company compare compass compeer compels compete compile comping complex complin complot comport compose compost compote compute

compo compos comport compose compost compote comports composed composer composes composts compotes compound

con cone conk cons cony icon ancon bacon conch condo coned cones coney conga congo conic conks conto icons recon scone beacon concha concur condom condor coneys confab confer congas congee conger congii congou conics conies coning conium conned conoid consul contos contra convex convey convoy deacon falcon iconic mascon recons sconce scones second zircon

conch concha conchae conches conchoid

condo condom condor condole condoms condone condoled condoles condoned condones

cone coned cones coney scone coneys scones ancones jaconet

cones scones ancones

coney coneys

conga congas

congo congou

conic conics iconic conical laconic obconic zirconic

conk conks

cons icons consul recons beacons consent consign consist console consols consort consuls consult consume deacons falcons mascons zircons

conto contos contort contour contorts contours

cony balcony

coo cook cool coon coop coos coot cooed cooks cooky cools coons coops coots scoop scoot cocoon cooing cooked cooker cookie cooled cooler coolie coolly cooped cooper cootie racoon recook scoops scoots tycoon

cook cooks cooky cooked cooker cookie recook cookers cookery cookies cooking cookout precook recooks

cooks recooks precooks

cool cools cooled cooler coolie coolly coolant coolers coolest coolies cooling precool

cools precools

coon coons cocoon racoon tycoon cocoons raccoon racoons tycoons

coons cocoons racoons tycoons coonskin raccoons

coop coops scoop cooped cooper scoops coopers coopery cooping scooped

coops scoops

coot coots scoot cootie scoots cooties scooted scooter

coots scoots

cop cope cops copy scop copal coped copes copra copse scope scops copalm copeck copied copier copies coping copped copper copses copter copula recopy scopes

copal copalm copalms

cope coped copes scope copeck scopes apocope copecks syncope

copes scopes apocopes syncopes

cops copse scops copses

copse copses

copy recopy copycat copying copyist

cor cord core corf cork corm corn cors acorn coral cords cored corer cores corgi coria corks corky corms corns cornu corny corps corse decor score scorn accord acorns corals corbel corbie corded cordon corers corgis coring corium corked corker cornea corned cornel corner cornet cornua corona corpse corpus corral corrie corses corset cortex corves corymb coryza decors encore escort rancor record scorch scored scorer scores scoria scorns succor uncork

coral corals

cord cords accord corded cordon record accords concord cordage cordate cordial cording cordite cordoba cordons discord records

cords accords records concords discords

core cored corer cores score corers encore scored scorer scores encored encores scorers

cored scored encored succored

corer corers scorer scorers

cores scores encores

corgi corgis

coria scoria

cork corks corky corked corker uncork corkage corkers corkier corking uncorks

corks uncorks

corm corms

corn acorn corns cornu corny scorn acorns cornea corned cornel corner cornet cornua scorns corncob corneal corneas cornels corners cornets cornfed cornice cornier corning cornrow popcorn scorned scorner tricorn unicorn

corns acorns scorns tricorns unicorns

cornu cornua

corps corpse corpses corpsman corpsmen

cors corse corses corset decors corsage corsair corsets rancors succors

corse corses corset corsets corselet corseted

cosh coshed cosher coshes coshers coshing

cost costa costs accost costae costed costal costar coster costly accosts costard costars costate costers costing costive costrel costume

costa costae costal costar costard costars costate

costs accosts

cot cote cots scot ascot cotes cotta dicot picot ascots cottas cotter cotton dicots mascot picots scotch scoter scotia tricot

cote cotes scoter coterie picotee

cots ascots dicots picots mascots tricots

cotta cottas cottage ricotta cottager cottages ricottas

couch couched couches couchant couching

cough coughs coughed coughing hiccough

count counts county account counted counter country recount accounts counters countess counties counting discount miscount recounts viscount

coup coupe coups coupes couple coupon recoup coupled coupler couples couplet coupons recoups

coupe coupes recouped

coups recoups

court courts courted courtly courtesy courtier courting

couth uncouth

cove coved coven cover coves covet covey alcove covens covers covert covets coveys alcoves covered coverup coveted recover uncover

coven covens covenant

cover covers covert covered coverup recover uncover bedcover coverage coverall covering coverlet covertly discover recovers recovery uncovers

coves alcoves

covet covets coveted coveting covetous

covey coveys

cow cowl cows scow cower cowls cowry scowl scows coward cowboy cowers cowled cowpie cowpox cowrie scowls

cower cowers cowered cowering

cowl cowls scowl cowled scowls cowlick cowling scowled

cowls scowls

cows scows cowslip

cox coxa coxae coxal coxes

coxa coxae coxal

coxal coxalgia coxalgic

coy coyed coyer coyly coypu decoy coyest coying coyote coypus decoys

coypu coypus

coz cozy cozen cozens cozier cozily

cozen cozens cozened cozenage cozening

crab crabs crabby crabbed crabber

crack cracks cracky cracked cracker crackle crackly crackup crackers cracking crackled crackles cracknel crackpot crackups gimcrack

craft crafts crafty crafted aircraft craftier craftily crafting

crag crags scrag craggy scrags cragged scraggy

crags scrags

crake crakes

cram cramp crams scram crambo cramps scrams crammed cramped crampon

cramp cramps cramped crampon cramping crampons

crams scrams

crane craned cranes

crank cranks cranky cranked crankier cranking

crap crape craps scrap craped crapes crappy scrape scraps craping crapped crappie scraped scraper scrapes scrappy

crape craped crapes scrape scraped scraper scrapes scrapers

craps scraps

crash crashed crashes crashing

crass crasser crassly crassest

crate crated crater crates craters

crave craved craven craves

craw crawl craws crawls crawly scrawl crawdad crawled crawler scrawls scrawly scrawny

crawl crawls crawly scrawl crawled crawler scrawls scrawly crawling scrawled scrawler

craze crazed crazes

creak creaks creaky screak creaked screaks creakier creaking screaked

cream creams creamy scream creamed creamer screams creamers creamery creamier creaming screamed screamer

creed creeds screed decreed

creek creeks

creel creels

creep creeps creepy creeper creepers creepier creeping

crepe crepes

cress cresses cresset cressets

crest crests crested cresting

crew crews screw crewed crewel screws screwy crewing screwed unscrew

crews screws unscrews

crib cribs scribe ascribe cribbed scribal scribed scriber scribes

crick cricks cricked cricket crickets cricking

cried decried

crier criers

cries decries outcries

crime crimes

crimp crimps crimpy scrimp crimped crimple scrimps scrimpy crimping crimples scrimped

crisp crisps crispy crisped crisper crisply crispers crispier crisping

croak croaks croaky croaked croaker croakers croaking

crock crocks crocked crocket crockery crockets crocking

croft crofts crofter crofters

crone crones

crony acronym acronyms

crook crooks crooked crooking

croon croons crooned crooning

crop crops cropped cropper outcrop

crops necropsy outcrops

crore crores

cross across crosse crossed crosser crosses crossly crossbar crossbow crosscut crossest crossing crosslet lacrosse

croup croupy croupier
crow crowd crown crows crowds crowed crowns escrow crowbar crowded crowing crowned escrows
crowd crowds crowded crowding
crown crowns crowned crowning
crows escrows
croze crozed crozes
crud crude cruds cruddy cruder crudded crudely crudest crudity
crude cruder crudely crudest
cruel crueler cruelly cruelty cruelest
cruet cruets
crumb crumbs crumby crumbed crumble crumbly crumbing crumbled crumbles
crump crumps crumped crumpet crumple crumpets crumping crumpled crumples
crura crural
crus cruse crush crust cruses crusts crusty crusade crusado crushed crusher crushes crusted encrust incrust
cruse cruses
crush crushed crusher crushes crushers crushing
crust crusts crusty crusted encrust incrust crustier crusting encrusts incrusts
crux cruxes
crwth crwths
cry crypt decry crying crypts descry outcry
crypt crypts cryptic
cub cube cubs cubby cubed cubes cubic cubit scuba cubage cubics cubing cubism cubits cuboid incubi
cube cubed cubes
cubic cubics cubical cubicle cubicles
cubit cubits
cud cuds scud cuddy scudi scudo scuds cuddle cuddly cudgel escudo
cuds scuds
cue cued cues cueing fescue miscue rescue
cued miscued rescued

cues fescues miscues rescues
cuff cuffs scuff cuffed scuffs cuffing scuffed scuffle
cuffs scuffs
cuing miscuing rescuing
culch culches
culet culets
cull culls cully scull culled cullet cullis sculls cullets cullied cullies culling sculled
culls sculls
cully cullying
culm culms culmed
cult cults cultch cultus incult occult cultism cultist culture faculty
cum scum cecum cumin scums acumen cumber cumins cummer cummin scummy talcum
cumin cumins
cup cups scup cupel scups cupels cupful cupola cupped cupper cupric cupule eyecup hiccup occupy oilcup teacup
cupel cupels cupeled cupeling
cupid cupids
cups scups eyecups hiccups oilcups teacups
cur curb curd cure curl curs curt curbs curch curds cured cures curet curia curie curio curls curly curry curse curst curve curvy incur occur recur scurf concur curacy curare curari curate curbed curded curdle curets curfew curiae curial curies curing curios curium curled curler curlew cursed curses cursor curtly curtsy curule curved curves curvet incurs occurs recurs scurfs scurfy scurry scurvy secure uncurl
curb curbs curbed curbing
curch curches
curd curds curded curdle curding curdled curdles
cure cured cures curet curets secure curette epicure obscure procure secured securer secures
cured secured obscured procured

cures secures epicures obscures procures
curet curets curette curettes
curia curiae curial
curie curies
curio curios curiosa curious decurion
curl curls curly curled curler curlew uncurl curlers curlews curling uncurls
curls uncurls
curry scurry currying
curs curse curst cursed curses cursor incurs occurs recurs concurs cursing cursive cursors cursory
curse cursed curses
curt curtly curtsy curtail curtain curtsey
curve curved curves curvet curvets decurved
curvy scurvy
cusec cusecs
cusk cusks
cusp cusps cusped cuspid cuspids
cuss cussed cusses cussing discuss percuss
cut cute cuts scut acute cutch cuter cutey cutie cutin cutis cutup scuta scute scuts uncut cutely cutest cutesy cuties cutlas cutler cutlet cutoff cutout cutter cutups scutch scutes scutum
cutch scutch cutches scutches
cute acute cuter cutey scute cutely cutest cutesy scutes acutely execute
cuter executer
cutie cuties
cuts scuts
cutup cutups
cycad cycads
cycle cycled cycles bicycle recycle bicycled bicycler bicycles epicycle recycled recycles tricycle unicycle
cyme cymes
cynic cynics cynical cynicism
cyst cysts cystic encyst cystine cystoid encysts
cysts encysts
czar czars czardas czarina czarism czarist

d

dab dabs dabbed dabber dabble
dabs dabster
dace daces
dad dado dads daddy aoudad caudad dadoes doodad
dado dadoes
dads aoudads doodads
daff daffy daffed daffier daffing
daft dafter daftly daftest
dag dags adage adages adagio dagger daggle
dairy dairying dairyman dairymen nondairy
dais daisy daisies
dale dales daleth daleths pedaled
dally modally dallying feudally
dam dame damn damp dams dames damns madam damage damask dammed damned dampen damper damply damsel damson madame madams
dame dames madame
dames mesdames
damn damns damned damning goddamn
damp dampen damper damply dampens dampers dampest
dams damsel damson madams damsels damsons
dance danced dancer dances dancers abidance guidance riddance
danio danios
dank danker dankly dankest
dap daps adapt adapts dapped dapper dapple
dare dared dares
dark darken darker darkle darkly darkens darkest darkled
darn darns darned darnel darnels darning
dart darts darted darter darters darting
dash dashed dasher dashes dashers dashier dashiki dashing
data datary
date dated dates pedate sedate update caudate cordate gradate mandate predate sedated sedates undated updated updates
dated sedated undated updated caudated gradated mandated outdated predated
dates sedates updates gradates mandates predates
datum datums
daub daubs daubed dauber daubing

daunt daunts daunted daunting
davit davits
dawn dawns dawned dawning
day days today heyday midday payday todays
days todays daysman daystar heydays paydays
daze dazed dazes
dead deaden deadly deadens deadeye deadpan
deaf deafen deafer deafly deafens deafest
deal deals dealt ideal dealer ideals ordeal dealers dealing ideally misdeal ordeals
deals ideals ordeals misdeals
dealt misdealt
dean deans deanery
dear dears deary dearer dearly dearth endear dearest dearies endears sidearm
dears endears
death deaths deathbed deathful
debar debark debars debarks debarked debarred
debit debits debited debitor debiting
debt debts debtor debtors
debug debugs debugged
debut debuts debutant
decal decals
decay decays decayed decaying
deck decks bedeck decked deckle bedecks decking deckles
decks bedecks
decor decors decorum decorate decorous
decoy decoys decoyed decoying
decry decrying
deed deeds deeded indeed deedful deeding misdeed
deeds misdeeds
deem deems deemed redeem deeming redeems
deems redeems
deep deepen deeper deeply deepens deepest
deer deers
deers deerskin
defer defers deferent deferral deferred
defog defogs defogged defogger
deft deftly
defy defying
degas bodegas degassed
deify deifying
deign deigns deigned
deil deils

deism deisms
deist deists deistic
delay delays delayed delaying
dele deled deles delete deleing deleted deletes modeled modeler yodeled yodeler
deled modeled yodeled
deles hideless
delf delfs delft delfts
delft delfts
deli delis delict delicts delight delimit deliria deliver
dell dells cadelle
delta deltas deltaic
delve delved delves
deme demes demean dement academe demeans dements demerit demesne sidemen
demes demesne academes demesnes
demit demits demitted
demo demob demon demos demobs demons demote demonic demoted demotes demotic
demob demobs demobbed
demon demons demonic demoniac demonism demonize
demur demure demurs demurer demurely demurred
demy academy
den dene dens dent deny denes denim dense dents laden loden olden widen addend ardent bidden burden cadent deaden denary dengue denial denied denier denies denims denned denote denser dental dented dentil dentin denude garden golden gulden harden hidden holden hoyden indene indent leaden linden louden madden maiden midden milden redden ridden rodent sadden sodden sudden warden widens wooden
dene denes indene widened widener
denes nudeness rudeness wideness
denim denims
dens dense denser widens burdens deadens densely densest density gardens guldens hardens hoydens lindens maidens middens reddens saddens soddens wardens
dense denser densely densest condense
dent dents ardent cadent dental dented dentil dentin indent rodent dentals dentate dentils denting dentins dentist dentoid denture evident indents mor-

dent pendent prudent rodents student trident

dents indents rodents mordents pendents students tridents

deny denying

depot depots

depth depths

derma dermal dermas alderman

desex desexes

desk desks desktop

deter deters deterge deterged deterges deterred

deuce deuced deuces

deva devas devalue medevac

devil devils bedevil deviled devilry bedevils deviling devilish deviltry

dew dews dewy dewan dewed dewans dewing dewlap mildew sundew

dewan dewans

dewed mildewed

dews mildews sundews

dewy mildewy

dey deys redeye

dhole dholes

dhoti dhotis

dhow dhows

dial dials dialed medial radial cordial dialect dialing dialyze predial radials sundial

dials radials cordials sundials

dice diced dices dicey bodice bodices codices indices radices

dices bodices codices indices radices caudices

dicot dicots

dicta dictate edictal dictated dictates dictator

did dido redid undid candid diddle didoes fordid iodide misdid outdid sordid

dido didoes

die died dies diet adieu diets nudie oldie adieus adieux birdie bodied bodies caddie diesel dieses diesis dieted eddied eddies kiddie laddie ladies nudies oldies tidied tidier tidies todies undies wadies

died bodied eddied tidied bandied birdied caddied candied muddied pandied readied studied toadied

dies bodies diesel dieses diesis eddies ladies nudies oldies tidies todies undies wadies baldies bandies biddies birdies buddies caddies candies cuddies daddies dandies diesels dowdies goodies kiddies laddies noddies paddies pandies randies readies roadies rowdies studies teddies tidiest toadies toddies waddies

diet diets dieted dietary dieting

dig digs digit digamy digest digger digits diglot indign indigo

digit digits digital digitals digitate

dike diked dikes

dill dilly cedilla dillies

dim dime dims bedim dimer dimes dimly bedims dimers dimity dimmed dimmer dimple dimply dimwit

dime dimer dimes dimers dimeter

dimer dimers

dims bedims

din dine ding dink dins dinar dined diner dines dingo dings dingy dinks dinky adding aiding biding boding ceding coding dinars dinero diners dinged dingey dinghy dingle dingus dining dinkey dinkum dinned dinner dinted ending fading gradin hading hiding iodine jading lading riding siding undine verdin wading

dinar dinars ordinary

dine dined diner dines dinero diners iodine undine dinette sardine

diner dinero diners

dines sardines tidiness

ding dingo dings dingy adding aiding biding boding ceding coding dinged dingey dinghy dingle dingus ending fading hading hiding jading lading riding siding wading abiding balding banding beading bedding bending bidding binding birding bodings bonding budding carding chiding codding cording curding deeding dingbat dinging dingles dingoes eluding endings eroding evading exuding feeding fending feuding finding folding fording funding gadding gelding gilding girding gliding goading grading griding guiding handing heading heeding herding hilding holding hooding hording kidding ladings landing larding lauding leading lending loading lording madding melding mending minding molding mudding needing nodding padding pending podding priding pudding raiding reading redding reeding rending ridding sanding seeding sending shading sidings sliding sodding spading tedding tending tidings trading vending voiding wadding wedding weeding welding wending winding wording yarding

dingo dingoes

dings bodings endings ladings sidings tidings bindings bondings findings geldings gildings gradings holdings landings moldings puddings readings shadings weddings

dink dinks dinky dinkey dinkum dinkier dinkies

dins gradins verdins

diode diodes

dip dips dippy diplex dipody dipole dipped dipper

dire direr direct direly direst directs direful

dirge dirges

dirk dirks dirked dirking

dirl dirls dirled dirling

dirt dirty dirtied dirtier dirties

dirty dirtying

disc disco discs discos discus discant discard discern discoid discord discuss

disco discos discoid discord discoids discolor discords discount discover

dish dished dishes dudish jadish modish oldish radish caddish dishful dishing dishpan dishrag faddish goodish kaddish kiddish loudish maddish prudish reddish

disk disks

dit adit dits edit adits audit ditch ditsy ditto ditty ditzy edits audits bandit credit dither dittos edited editor indite nudity oddity pandit pundit reedit

ditch ditched ditches ditching

dits adits ditsy edits audits bandits credits pandits pundits reedits

ditto dittos dittoed dittoing

diva divan divas divans

divan divans

dive dived diver dives divers divert divest endive diverge diverse diverts divests endives khedive

diver divers divert diverge diverse diverts diverged diverges diverted

dives divest divests endives divested khedives

divot divots

divvy divvying

dizen dizens bedizen dizened bedizens dizening

dizzy dizzying

do ado doc doe dog don dor dos dot udo ados dado dido dock docs dodo doer does doff doge dogs dogy doit dojo dole doll dolt dome done dong dons doom door dope dorm dory dose doss dote dots dour dove down doxy doze dozy idol judo odor ordo redo udos undo adobe adopt adore adorn ardor condo dobra docks dodge dodgy dodos doers doffs doges doggy dogie dogma doily doing doits dojos doled doles dolls dolly dolma dolor dolts domed domes donga dongs donor donut dooms doors doped doper dopes dopey dorky dorms dorsa dosed doses dotal doted doter dotes dotty doubt douce dough douse doves dowdy dowel dower downs downy dowry dowse doyen dozed dozen dozes endow fordo idols kendo kudos misdo odors ordos outdo radon redox rondo scudo soldo uredo widow

dobra dobras

doc dock docs docks docent docile docked docket doctor

dock docks docked docket burdock dockage dockets docking haddock paddock ruddock

docks burdocks haddocks paddocks ruddocks

dodge dodged dodger dodges dodgers dodgery

dodo dodos dodoes

doe doer does doers dadoes didoes dodoes redoes undoes

doer doers misdoer

doers misdoers

does dadoes didoes dodoes redoes undoes doeskin outdoes

doff doffs doffed doffing handoff leadoff

doffs handoffs leadoffs

dog doge dogs dogy doges doggy dogie dogma bandog dogged dogleg dogmas sundog

doge doges

dogma dogmas dogmata dogmatic

dogs bandogs sundogs

doing doings redoing undoing fordoing misdoing outdoing

doit doits

dojo dojos

dole doled doles condole doleful

doled condoled

doles condoles dolesome

doll dolls dolly dollar dollop dollars dollies dollops

dolma dolman dolmas

dolor dolors dolorous

dolt dolts

dome domed domes radome abdomen radomes

domes radomes domestic

don done dong dons donga dongs donor donut radon cordon donate dongas donjon donkey donors donuts guidon lardon pardon radons redone tendon undone

done redone undone condone fordone misdone outdone

dong donga dongs dongas

donga dongas

donor donors

dons radons cordons guidons lardons pardons tendons

donut donuts

doom dooms doomed dooming

dooms doomsday

door doors indoor doorman doormat doormen doorway indoors outdoor

doors indoors doorsill doorstep doorstop outdoors

dope doped doper dopes dopey

dopes dopester

dor dorm dors dory odor adore adorn ardor dorky dorms dorsa odors adored adorer adores adorns ardors candor condor dories dormer dorsal dorsum fedora odored vendor

dorm dorms dormer dormant dormers dormice

dorsa dorsal dorsals dorsally

dos ados dose doss udos dodos dosed doses kudos ordos dosage dosing dossal dosser nodose rondos uredos vadose

dose dosed doses nodose vadose

doss dossal dosser dossers dossier

dot dote dots dotal doted doter dotes dotty dotage dotard doters doting dotted dottle

dote doted doter dotes doters epidote

doter doters

doubt doubts doubted doubter redoubt doubters doubtful doubting redoubts

dough doughs doughy doughty doughboy doughier doughnut

douse doused douses

dove doves

dowdy pandowdy

dowel dowels doweled doweling

dower dowers dowered widower dowering widowers

down downs downy downed downer godown downers downier downing godowns hoedown letdown lowdown rubdown rundown sundown

downs godowns hoedowns letdowns rubdowns sundowns

dowse dowsed dowses

doyen doyens

doze dozed dozen dozes dozens

dozen dozens

drab drabs drabbed drabber drabble

draff draffs

draft drafts drafty drafted draftee indraft updraft draftees draftier drafting updrafts

drag drags dragon dragged dragnet dragons dragoon

drain drains drained drainer drainage drainers draining

drake drakes mandrake

dram drama drams dramas

drama dramas dramatic

drape draped draper drapes drapers

drat dratted hydrate quadrat

draw drawl drawn draws drawer drawls redraw drawers drawing drawled indrawn redrawn redraws

drawl drawls drawled drawling

drawn indrawn redrawn

draws redraws

dray drays drayed drayage draying drayman draymen

dread dreads dreaded dreadful dreading

dream dreams dreamt dreamy dreamed dreamer daydream dreamers dreamier dreamily dreaming

dree dreed drees dreeing

dress dressy address dressed dresser dresses redress undress dressage dressers dressier dressily dressing

drew redrew

drib dribs dribble driblet

dries driest sundries

drift adrift drifts drifty drifter drifters driftier

drill drills drilled drilling mandrill

drink drinks drinker drinking

drip drips dript drippy dripped

drive drivel driven driver drives drivels drivers driveled driveway

droit adroit droits adroitly

droll drolls drolly bedroll drolled bedrolls drollery drolling

drone droned drones madrone padrone madrones padrones

drool drools drooled drooling

droop droops droopy drooped droopier drooping

drop drops dropsy airdrop dewdrop dropout dropped dropper gumdrop

drops dropsy airdrops dewdrops dropsied gumdrops

dross drossy drossier

drove droved drover droves drovers

drown drowns drowned drowning

drub drubs drubbed

drug drugs drugged drugget

druid druids

drum drums drumlin drummed drummer eardrum humdrum

drums doldrums eardrums

drunk drunks drunken drunkard

drupe drupes

druse druses

dry dryad dryer dryly bawdry dryads dryers drying sundry tawdry

dryad dryads dryadic

dryer dryers

duad duads

dual duals dualism dualist duality gradual

dub dubs dubbed dubbin

ducat ducats educate educated educates educator

duck ducks ducky ducked duckier ducking

duct ducts educt abduct adduct deduct educts induct abducts adducts conduct deducts ductile inducts oviduct product subduct viaduct

ducts educts abducts adducts deducts inducts conducts oviducts products subducts viaducts

dud dude duds dudes dudish

dude dudes

due duel dues duet duels duets endue indue undue dueled dueler duenna endued endues fondue indued indues perdue subdue vendue

duel duels dueled dueler duelers dueling duelist duelled

dues endues indues fondues subdues vendues

duet duets

duff duffs duffel duffer duffle duffels duffers duffles

dug dugout

duke dukes

dull dulls dully dulled duller dullard dullest dulling dullish medulla

dulse dulses

duly unduly

dumb dumber dumbly dumbest

dump dumps dumpy dumped dumper dumpers dumpier dumping dumpish

dun dune dung dunk duns dunce dunes dungs dungy dunks dunces dunged dunned

dunce dunces

dune dunes

dung dungs dungy dunged dungeon dunging

dunk dunks

duo duos

duper dupers dupery duperies

duple duplex duplexes

dura dural duras durable durably durance

duro duros maduro maduros

duros maduros

dusk dusks dusky duskier duskily duskish

dust adust dusts dusty dusted duster dustbin dusters dustier dusting dustman dustmen dustpan sawdust

duvet duvets

dwarf dwarfs dwarfed dwarfing dwarfish

dwell dwells dwelled dweller indwell dwellers dwelling indwells

dwelt indwelt

dyad dyads dyadic

dye dyed dyer dyes dyers dyeing

dyer dyers

dying bodying eddying tidying bandying caddying candying muddying readying studying toadying

dyke dyked dykes

dyne dynes anodyne

e

each beach leach peach reach teach bleach breach leachy peachy pleach preach beached beaches impeach leached leacher leaches peaches reached reaches teacher teaches

eager meager eagerly meagerly

eagle beagle eagles eaglet beagles eaglets

ear bear dear earl earn ears fear gear hear near pear rear sear tear wear year anear beard bears blear clear dears deary eared earls early earns earth fears gears heard hears heart learn nears pearl pears peart rearm rears sears shear smear spear swear tears teary wears weary yearn years afeard appear beards bearer blears bleary clears dearer dearly dearth dreary earful earing earned earner earths earthy earwax earwig endear feared geared hearer hearse hearth hearts hearty learns learnt linear neared nearer nearly pearls pearly reared rearms search seared shears smears smeary spears swears tearer wearer yearly yearns

eared feared geared neared reared seared cleared sheared smeared speared appeared endeared

earl earls early pearl dearly nearly pearls pearly yearly clearly earldom earless earlier pearled

earls pearls

early dearly nearly pearly yearly clearly linearly

earn earns learn yearn earned earner learns learnt yearns earners earnest earning learned learner unlearn yearned yearner

earns learns yearns unlearns

ears bears dears fears gears hears nears pears rears sears tears wears years blears clears hearse shears smears spears swears arrears earshot endears hearsay hearses

earth dearth earths earthy hearth earthen earthly hearths unearth earthier earthman earthmen unearths

ease cease eased easel eases lease pease tease ceased ceases crease easels grease leased leaser leases peases please teased teasel teaser teases weasel appease creased creases decease disease easeful greased greaser greases leasers pleased pleases release teasels teasers weasels

eased ceased leased teased creased greased pleased appeased deceased diseased released unleased

easel easels teasel weasel teasels weasels weaseled

eases ceases leases peases teases creases greases pleases appeases deceases diseases releases

east beast feast least yeast beasts breast feasts yeasts yeasty abreast beastie beastly breasts eastern easting feasted feaster yeasted

easy creasy greasy queasy uneasy

eat beat eats feat heat meat neat peat seat teat beats bleat cheat cleat death eaten eater feats great heath heats meats meaty neath peaty pleat reata seats sweat teats treat wheat beaten beater bleats breath caveat cheats cleats create deaths defeat eaters eatery eating featly greats heated heater heaths heathy hereat ideate neaten neater neatly orgeat pleats reatas reheat repeat seated sheath sweats sweaty treats treaty unseat upbeat wheats wreath

eaten beaten neaten greaten neatens uneaten wheaten greatens threaten unbeaten

eater beater eaters eatery heater neater beaters cheater greater heaters sweater theater anteater cheaters eateries figeater repeater sweaters theaters

eats beats feats heats meats seats teats bleats cheats cleats greats pleats sweats treats wheats caveats defeats orgeats reheats repeats unseats

eave eaves heave leave weave beaver cleave greave heaved heaven heaves leaved leaven leaves peavey reaved sleave weaver weaves beavers bereave cleaved cleaver cleaves greaves inweave leavens sheaved sheaves sleaves weavers

eaves heaves leaves weaves cleaves greaves sheaves sleaves bereaves inweaves

ebb ebbs ebbed webby blebby ebbing pebble pebbly webbed

ebbed webbed

ebon ebony debone deboned debones ebonies ebonite ebonize

echo echoed echoes echoic echoing echoism

eclat eclats

ecru recruit

eddy teddy eddying

edema edemas edemata

edge edged edger edges hedge kedge ledge sedge wedge dredge edgers fledge hedged hedger hedges kedged kedges ledger ledges pledge sedges sledge wedged wedges dredged dredges fledged fledges hedgers ledgers pledged pledger pledges pledget sledged sledges

edged hedged kedged wedged dredged fledged pledged sledged

edger edgers hedger ledger hedgers ledgers pledger hedgerow kedgeree pledgers

edges hedges kedges ledges sedges wedges dredges fledges pledges sledges

edgy ledgy sedgy wedgy

edict edicts edictal predict benedict maledict predicts

edify edifying

edile aedile sedile aediles

edit edits credit edited editor reedit credits editing edition editors reedits

edits credits reedits

educe deduce educed educes reduce seduce deduced deduces reduced reducer reduces seduced seducer seduces reducers seducers

educt deduct educts deducts aqueduct deducted eduction

eel eels eely feel heel keel peel reel seel creel feels heels keels kneel peels reels seels steel wheel creels feeler freely heeled heeler keeled kneels peeled peeler reeled steels steely wheels

eels feels heels keels peels reels seels creels kneels steels wheels keelson

eely freely steely

eerie eerier beerier eeriest leerier veeries beeriest leeriest

eery beery leery veery cheery

eft deft efts heft left reft weft cleft hefts hefty lefty theft wefts bereft clefts deftly hefted thefts

efts hefts wefts clefts thefts eftsoon

egest egesta egests egested egesting egestion

egg eggs yegg egged leggy yeggs beggar begged dreggy egging eggnog legged pegged veggie

egged begged legged pegged

eggs yeggs

egis aegis legist elegist legists

ego egos sego begot segos begone egoism egoist forego nonego

egos segos foregos nonegos

egret egrets regret regrets

eh feh heh jehad lehua rehab

eider eiders

eight eighth eights eighty height weight eighteen eighties freights heighten sleights weighted

eikon eikons

eject deject ejecta ejects reject dejects ejected ejector rejects dejected ejecting ejection ejective ejectors rejected

eke eked ekes keeked meeker peeked reeked seeker shekel

eked keeked peeked reeked cheeked

ekes meekest

eking keeking peeking reeking seeking cheeking

el bel eel eld elf elk ell elm els gel mel bell bels belt cell celt dele delf deli dell duel eels eely elks ells elms else feel fell felt fuel geld gels heel held hell helm help jell keel kelp koel meld mell mels melt noel peel pelf pelt reel rely riel seel self sell tael tell veld weld well welt yell yelp abele angel axels bagel belay belch belie belle bells belly below belts betel bevel bezel bield bowel camel cella cello cells celts chela creel cruel cupel delay deled deles delfs delft delis dells delta delve dowel duels dwell dwelt easel eland elate elbow elder elect elegy elemi elfin elide elite eloin elope elude elute elver elves excel expel feels felid fella fells felly felon felts field fuels gavel gelds gelid gimel gruel hazel heels helix hello hells helms helps helve hotel hovel impel jebel jells jelly jewel jurel keels kelep kelps kelpy kevel kneel knell knelt koels kugel label lapel level libel losel melds melee melic mells melon melts model morel motel navel newel noels novel oriel ouzel panel peels pelfs pelts pixel quell ravel rebel reels relax relay relic repel revel riels rowel seels selah sells shelf shell skelp smell smelt snell spell spelt spiel steel stele swell taels telic tells telly towel umbel velar velds veldt velum vowel welds wells welsh welts wheel whelk whelp wield yells yelps yield yodel yokel

eland elands foreland homeland tideland

elate delate elated elater elates relate velate belated delated delates elaters prelate related relates elatedly prelates

elbow elbows elbowed elbowing

eld geld held meld veld weld bield elder field gelds melds velds veldt welds wield yield afield beheld bields chield elders eldest fields gelded melded seldom shield upheld veldts welded welder wields yields

elder elders welder elderly fielder welders wielder yielder fielders wielders yielders

elect elects select elected elector electro prelect reelect selects electing election elective electors electric electron electros electrum prelects reelects selected selectee selector

elemi elemis

elf delf pelf self delfs delft elfin pelfs shelf belfry delfts elfish itself myself

elide elided elides

elite elites velites

elk elks whelk welkin whelks

elks whelks

ell bell cell dell ells fell hell jell mell sell tell well yell belle bells belly cella cello cells dells dwell fella fells felly hello hells jells jelly knell mells quell sells shell smell snell spell swell tells telly wells yells befell belled belles bellow cellae cellar celled cellos dwells fellah fellas felled feller fellow gelled heller hellos jelled knells mellow nielli niello paella pellet quells resell retell seller shells shelly smells smelly snells spells swells teller unwell vellum yelled yeller yellow

ells bells cells dells fells hells jells mells sells tells wells yells dwells knells quells shells smells snells spells swells resells retells

elm elms helm helms helmed helmet

elms helms

eloin eloins

elope eloped eloper elopes antelope envelope

els bels eels else gels mels axels duels feels fuels heels keels koels noels peels reels riels seels taels welsh angels bagels bevels bezels bowels camels creels cupels dowels easels excels expels gavels gimels gruels hazels hotels hovels impels jebels jewels jurels kelson kevels kneels labels lapels levels libels models morels motels navels newels novels oriels ouzels panels pixels ravels rebels repels revels rowels spiels steels towels umbels vowels wheels yodels yokels

elude delude eluded eludes deluded deludes prelude preluded preludes

elute eluted elutes

elver elvers

elves delves helves pelves selves shelves

em emu gem hem mem rem ahem bema deem deme demo demy emeu emir emit emus feme gems heme hemp hems item memo mems poem seem semi stem teem them ylem bemas deems demes demit demob demon demos demur edema elemi embay embed ember embow emcee emeer emend emery emeus emirs emits emmer emmet emote empty enema enemy femes femme femur gemma gemmy golem harem hemal hemic hemps items jemmy kempt leman lemma lemon lemur memos modem poems proem remit remix retem satem seems semen semis stems teems tempi tempo tempt theme totem ulema xylem

embay embays embayed embaying

embed embeds embedded

ember embers member members remember

embow embows embowed embower embowers embowing

emcee emceed emcees emceeing

emend emends emended emending

emeu emeus

emir emirs bemire bemired bemires demirep emirate

emit demit emits remit demits remits emitted emitter eremite

emits demits remits

emmer emmers hemmer hemmers

emmet emmets

emote demote emoted emotes remote demoted demotes remotely remotest

empty emptying

emu emus demur femur lemur bemuse demure demurs femurs lemurs

emus bemuse bemused bemuses

en ben den end ens fen hen ken men pen sen ten wen yen amen been bend bens bent cent dene dens dent deny ends enol enow envy even fend fens gene gens gent glen hens hent keen keno kens lend leno lens lent lien mend menu mien omen open oven peen pend pens pent rend rent seen send sent teen tend tens tent then vend vent wend wens when wren yens admen agent alien amend anent arena ashen aspen avens bench bends benne benny blend blent cense cento cents coven cozen denes denim dense dents dizen doyen dozen eaten emend enact ended endow endue enema enemy enjoy ennui ensue enter entry envoy evens event fence fends fenny fiend genes genet genie genii genoa genre genro gents genus given glens green haven hence henna henry hents hosen hyena hymen jenny keens kenaf kench kendo kenos laden lends lenis lento liens liken limen linen liven loden lumen maven menad mends menus miens mizen nomen numen oaken oaten often olden omens opens ovens paten peens penal pence pends penna penni penny preen queen raven renal rends renew renin rents ripen risen riven rowen rumen scend scene scent semen sends senna sense seven sheen siren spend spent steno taken teens teeny tench tends tenet tenia tenon tenor tense tenth tents token trend upend venal vends venin venom vents venue vimen vixen waken waxen weeny wench wends widen wizen woken women woven wrens xenia xenon yamen yenta yente

enact   enacts enacted enactor reenact enacting enactive enactors reenacts

end   bend ends fend lend mend pend rend send tend vend wend amend bends blend emend ended endow endue fends fiend kendo lends mends pends rends scend sends spend tends trend upend vends wends addend agenda amends append ascend attend bender blende blends defend depend emends endear ending endive endows endued endues endure expend extend fended fender fiends friend gender impend intend legend lender mended mender offend pended render sendal sender spends tended tender tendon trends trendy unbend upends vended vendee vendor vendue wended

ended   fended mended pended tended vended wended amended blended emended scended upended appended ascended attended defended depended expended extended impended intended offended

endow   endows endowed endowing

ends   bends fends lends mends pends rends sends tends vends wends amends blends emends fiends spends trends upends addends appends ascends attends calends defends depends expends extends friends impends intends kalends legends offends unbends

endue   endued endues vendue vendues

enema   enemas

enjoy   enjoys enjoyed enjoying

enol   phenol phenols

enow   erenow renown renowns

ens   bens dens fens gens hens kens lens pens tens wens yens avens cense dense ensue evens glens keens liens miens omens opens ovens peens sense teens

tense wrens aliens aspens censed censes censor census covens cozens denser dizens doyens dozens ensign ensued ensues ensure flense givens greens havens hymens lenses likens linens livens lumens mavens mensal menses patens preens queens ravens ripens rowens semens sensed senses sensor sevens sheens sirens teensy tensed tenser tenses tensor tokens vixens wakens widens wizens yamens

ensue   ensued ensues

enter   center enters renter tenter venter centers enteral entered enteric reenter centered entering reenters repenter

entry   gentry sentry entryway

envoy   envoys

envy   envying

eon   aeon eons jeon neon peon aeons leone neons paeon peons peony eonian hereon leones paeons pigeon

eons   aeons neons peons paeons pigeons

epact   epacts

epee   epees tepee teepee tepees epeeist teepees

epees   tepees teepees

ephah   ephahs

ephod   ephods

ephor   ephori ephors canephor

epic   epics depict epical depicts epicarp epicene epicure

epoch   epochs epochal

epode   epodes

epos   repos depose repose deposal deposed deposes deposit reposed reposes

equal   equals coequal equaled equally unequal coequals equaling equality equalize equalled unequals

equip   equips equipage equipped

er   era ere erg err her per aero aery ager aver beer berg berm bier cere cero deer doer dyer eery eras ergs erne errs erst ever ewer fere fern germ goer herb herd here herl herm hern hero hers hoer jeer jerk kerb kerf kern kier leer mere merl nerd omer over peer peri perk perm pert pier seer sera sere serf term tern tier user veer verb vert very zero abler acerb adder aerie after alder alert alter amber ameer anger apery aster auger avers avert baker barer baser beers beery beret bergs berms berry berth beryl biers biter bluer boner borer bower boxer brier buyer caber caner caper cater ceria ceric ceros cheer chert cider clerk comer corer cover cower coyer crier cuter deers defer derby derma deter dimer diner direr diver doers doper doter dower drier dryer duper dyers eager eater edger eerie ei-

der elder elver ember emeer emery emmer enter erase erect ergot ernes erode erose erred error eruct erupt esker ester ether evert every exert facer faery faker feral feres feria fermi ferns ferny ferry fever fewer fiber fiery fifer filer finer fiver fixer fleer flier flyer foyer freer frier fryer gaper gayer gazer gerah germs giver gluer goers gofer goner haler hater herbs herby herds herls herma herms herns heron hertz hewer hexer hider hirer hoers homer hoper hover huger hyper icier idler infer inker inner japer jeers jerks jerky jiber joker kerbs kerfs kerns kiers kiter lager laker lamer laser later laver layer leers leery leper lever lifer liker liner liter liver loner loper loser lover lower maker maser mazer mercy meres merge merit merle merls merry meter miler mimer miner miser miter mixer mover mower nerds nerdy nerve nervy never newer nicer noter ocher offer ogler oiler older omber omers opera order ormer osier other otter outer overt owner oxter pacer pager paler paper pater paver payer peers perch perdu peril perks perky perms perry perse peter piers piker piper plier poker poser power prier purer queer quern query racer rarer rawer rayer refer reran rerun ricer rider riser river roger rover rower ruder ruler saber safer sager saker saner saver sayer seers serai seres serfs serge serif serin serow serum serve servo sever sewer sheer sherd shoer shyer slyer sneer sober sorer sower sperm steer stere stern super surer taker taler tamer taper tater taxer terce terga terms terns terry terse there therm tiers tiger tiler timer titer toner toper toter tower truer tuber tuner twerp udder ulcer umber under upper users usher uteri utter veers veery verbs verge verse verso verst verts verve viler viper vomer voter wader wafer wager water waver waxer where wider wiper wiser wooer wrier xeric xerox zeros

era   eras sera erase feral gerah opera reran serai aerate berate camera cerate derail erased eraser erases genera gerahs herald operas sclera serais serape seraph teraph

eras   erase erased eraser erases operas cameras erasers erasing erasion erasure scleras

erase   erased eraser erases erasers

ere   cere fere here mere sere beret erect feres meres seres stere there where adhere ampere bereft berets cereal cereus cohere erects erenow hereat hereby herein hereof hereon heresy hereto inhere jeered jeerer leered merely merest peered reread revere serene severe sphere stereo steres teredo terete veered

erect erects erected erectly erector erectile erecting erection erectors

erg berg ergs bergs ergot merge serge terga verge clergy emerge energy ergots merged merger merges serges tergum verged verger verges

ergot ergots

ergs bergs

erne ernes eterne kerned kernel lierne fernery interne kernels liernes sterner

ernes liernes internes sternest

erode eroded erodes

erose kerosene xerosere

err errs berry erred error ferry merry perry terry cherry derris errand errant errata erring errors ferret ferric kerria perron sherry sierra terret terror wherry

erred averred deferred deterred inferred interred referred

error errors terror

erst verst versts oersted

eruct eructs eructate

erupt erupts erupted erupting eruption eruptive

eskar eskars

esker eskers

espy espying

ess cess fess jess less mess bless chess cress dress essay esses fesse gesso guess jesse loess messy press tress abbess access assess caress dressy duress egress essays excess fesses gessos jesses lessee lessen lesser lesson lessor messed messes obsess ogress recess stress unless vessel yessed yesses

essay essays essayed essayer essayers essaying essayist

esses fesses jesses messes yesses cresses dresses guesses accesses assesses caresses excesses finesses obsesses ogresses recesses stresses

ester fester jester nester pester tester wester yester festers keester arrester attester dopester festered forester gamester infester jokester keesters molester pestered pesterer questers semester sesterce westerly westerns

estop estops estopped

eta beta etas seta zeta betas fetal metal petal setae theta zetas betake cetane

chaeta chetah detach detail detain metage metals muleta peseta petals petard pretax retail retain retake retard thetas

etas betas zetas thetas muletas pesetas petasus

etch fetch ketch letch retch vetch etched etches fletch kvetch sketch tetchy wretch etching fetched fetches ketches ketchup letched letches retched retches sketchy stretch tetched vetches

eth beth teth beths ether ethic ethos ethyl kheth sheth teeth bethel daleth ethane ethers ethics ethnic ethyls lethal method methyl nether seethe sheths teethe tether wether

ether ethers nether tether wether tethers wethers whether ethereal tethered together

ethic ethics ethical ethicist

ethyl ethyls methyl ethylene

etude etudes hebetude quietude

etui etuis

evade evaded evader evades

eve even ever eves bevel breve evens event evert every fever kevel levee level lever never neves peeve reeve revel seven sever sieve beeves bevels breves brevet clever devein devest eleven evened evenly events everts fevers grieve kevels leveed levees levels levers pareve peeved peeves reeves reveal revels reverb revere revers revert revery sevens severe severs sieved sieves sleeve soever steeve thieve uneven weever

even evens event seven eleven evened evenly events sevens uneven evening prevent revenge revenue seventh seventy

evens sevens evensong

event events seventh eleventh eventful eventide eventual nonevent prevents sevenths

ever evert every fever lever never sever clever everts fevers levers reverb revere revers revert revery severe severs soever weever everted fevered forever griever however levered leveret reverbs revered reveres reverie reverse reverts several severer weevers whoever

evert everts revert everted antevert everting reverted

every revery everyday everyone thievery

eves neves beeves breves devest peeves reeves sieves devests grieves sleeves steeves thieves

evict evicts evicted evicting eviction

evil devil evils devils evilly revile weevil bedevil deviled devilry reviled reviles weevils

evils devils weevils bedevils

evoke evoked evokes revoke revoked

ewe ewer ewes dewed fewer hewed hewer jewel mewed newel newer pewee sewed sewer brewed brewer chewed chewer clewed crewed crewel fewest hewers jewels newels newest peewee pewees sewers shewed skewed skewer spewed stewed viewed viewer

ewer fewer hewer newer sewer brewer chewer hewers sewers skewer viewer brewers brewery chewers sewered skewers viewers

ewes fewest newest

ex hex rex sex vex apex exam exes exit exon flex ibex ilex next sext sexy text annex cimex codex culex desex exact exalt exams excel exert exile exist exits exons expel extol extra exude exult exurb hexad hexed hexer hexes hexyl index latex lexis mirex murex nexus prexy sexed sexes sexts texts vexed vexes

exact exacta exacts exacted exacter exactly inexact exacters exacting exaction

exalt exalts exalted exalter exalters exalting

exam exams examen examens examine example

excel excels excelled

exert exerts exerted exerting exertion exertive

exes hexes sexes vexes apexes flexes ibexes ilexes annexes desexes indexes latexes murexes

exile exiled exiles flexile

exist exists sexist coexist existed coexists existent existing preexist

exit exits exited exiting

exon exons hexone

expel expels expelled

extol extoll extols extolled extoller

extra extras dextral extract extracts extrados

exude exuded exudes

exult exults exulted exulting

exurb exurbs exurban exurbia

eye eyed eyes keyed oxeye eyecup eyeful eyeing eyelet eyelid obeyed obeyer oxeyes preyed redeye

eyed keyed obeyed preyed bogeyed honeyed moneyed moseyed popeyed

eyes oxeyes eyeshot eyesore redeyes

eying   keying obeying bogeying honeying
    moseying
eyre   eyres

f

fa fad fag fan far fas fat fax fay afar face fact fade fads fags fail fain fair fake fall fame fane fang fans fare farm faro fart fash fast fate fats faun faux fawn fays faze sofa tufa fable faced facer faces facet facts faddy faded fades faery faggy fagot fails faint fairs fairy faith faked faker fakes fakir falls false famed fames fancy fanes fangs fanny fanon farad farce fared fares farms faros farts fasts fatal fated fates fatly fatty faugh fault fauna fauns favor favus fawns faxes fazed fazes luffa offal sofas sulfa tufas

fable fabled fabler fables affable fablers

face faced facer faces facet deface efface enface facers facets defaced defaces dogface effaced effacer effaces enfaced enfaces faceted preface surface

faced defaced effaced enfaced prefaced surfaced

facer facers effacer effacers

faces defaces effaces enfaces dogfaces prefaces surfaces

facet facets faceted faceting

fact facts factor faction factors factory factual facture

fad fade fads faddy faded fades fading

fade faded fades

fag fags faggy fagot fagged faggot fagots

fagot fagots fagoting

fail fails failed faille failing failles failure

fain faint faints fainted fainter faintly

faint faints fainted fainter faintly faintest fainting

fair fairs fairy affair faired fairer fairly unfair affairs fairest fairies fairing fairish fairway

fairs affairs

faith faiths faithful

fake faked faker fakes fakers fakery

faker fakers fakery fakeries

fakir fakirs

fall falls befall fallal fallen faller fallow befalls dewfall fallacy fallals fallers falling fallout fallows icefall pitfall

falls befalls dewfalls icefalls pitfalls

false falser falsely falsest falsetto

fame famed fames defame defamed defames

famed defamed

fames defames

fan fane fang fans fancy fanes fangs fanny fanon fanged fanjet fanned fanner fanons infant

fancy infancy fancying

fane fanes profane

fanes profanes

fang fangs fanged

fanon fanons

far afar fare farm faro fart farad farce fared fares farms faros farts farads farces farina faring farmed farmer farrow farted safari shofar

farad farads faradize

farce farces

fare fared fares carfare fanfare warfare welfare

fares carfares fanfares warfares welfares

farm farms farmed farmer farmers farming farmost

faro faros

fart farts farted farther farting

fas fash fast fasts sofas tufas fasces fascia fashed fashes fasted fasten faster luffas

fash fashed fashes fashing fashion

fast fasts fasted fasten faster bedfast fastens fastest fasting

fat fate fats fatal fated fates fatly fatty father fathom fatted fatten fatter

fatal fatally fatalism fatalist fatality

fate fated fates fateful sulfate

fates sulfates

faugh faughs

fault faults faulty default faulted defaults faultier faultily faulting

faun fauna fauns faunae faunal faunas

fauna faunae faunal faunas

favor favors favored favorer disfavor favorers favoring favorite

fawn fawns fawned fawner fawners fawning

fax faxes

fay fays

faze fazed fazes

fear fears afeard feared fearful fearing

fears fearsome

feast feasts feasted feaster feasters feasting

feat feats defeat featly defeats feather feature

feats defeats

feaze feazes

fed feds fifed offed unfed beefed buffed chafed cuffed daffed doffed fedora gaffed golfed goofed gulfed hoofed huffed kerfed knifed leafed loafed luffed miffed muffed puffed reefed riffed roofed ruffed surfed tiffed

fee feed feel fees feet feeds feels feeze coffee feeble feebly feeder feeing feeler feezes toffee

feed feeds feeder feeders feeding feedlot

feel feels feeler feelers feeling

fees coffees toffees

feeze feezes

feign feigns feigned feigner feigners feigning

feint feints feinted feinting

feist feists feisty

felid felids

fell fella fells felly befell fellah fellas felled feller fellow fellahs fellers fellies felling fellows

fella fellah fellas fellahs fellable

felon felons felony felonies lifelong

felt felts felted unfelt felting

feme femes

femme femmes

femur femurs

fen fend fens fence fends fenny deafen defend fenced fencer fences fended fender fennec fennel offend

fence fenced fencer fences fencers offence offences

fend fends defend fended fender offend defends effendi fenders fending offends

fends defends offends

fens deafens defense offense

feoff feoffs

fere feres offered offerer referee wafered

feria feriae ferial ferias

fermi fermis

fern ferns ferny fernery inferno

ferry ferrying ferryman ferrymen

fess fesse fesses confess profess

fesse fesses

fetch fetched fetches fetching

fete feted fetes effete

feted buffeted

fetid fetidly

fetor fetors

fetus fetuses

feu feud feus feuds feudal feuded

feud feuds feudal feuded feuding feudist

fever fevers fevered feverish

few fewer curfew fewest

fez fezzes

fiat fiats

fib fibs fiber fibbed fibber fibers fibril fibrin fibula

fiber fibers

fiche fiches

fichu fichus

fico ficoes

fid fids bifid fiddle fidget trifid

fie fief fies fiefs field fiend fiery afield defied defier defies fields fiends fierce fiesta

fief fiefs fiefdom

field afield fields fielded fielder infield airfield canfield fielders fielding hayfield midfield outfield

fiend fiends fiendish

fies defies fiesta deifies edifies fiestas jiffies reifies taffies unifies

fife fifed fifer fifes fifers

fifer fifers

fifth fifths

fig figs fight effigy figged fights figure

fight fights dogfight fighters fighting gunfight

fila filar bifilar

filar bifilar

filch filched filches filching

file filed filer files filet defile filers filets refile defiled defiler defiles misfile profile refiled refiles

filed defiled refiled misfiled profiled

filer filers defiler

files defiles refiles misfiles profiles

filet filets

fill fills filly filled filler fillet fillip refill fillers fillets fillies filling fillips fulfill refills

fills fulfills

film films filmy filmed filmier filming

fils fulfils

filth filthy filthier

fin find fine fink fins elfin final finch finds fined finer fines finis finks finny bowfin coffin define fifing finale finals finder finely finery finest finger finial fining finish finite finked finned muffin offing olefin puffin redfin refine tiffin

final finale finals affinal finales finally finalist finality finalize

finch finches

find finds finder finders finding

fine fined finer fines define finely finery finest refine confine defined defines finesse refined refiner refines

fined defined refined confined

finer finery refiner fineries refiners refinery

fines finest defines finesse refines confines finessed finesses

finis finish finished finisher finishes refinish

fink finks finked finking

fins bowfins coffins muffins olefins puffins redfins tiffins

fiord fiords

fir fire firm firn firs afire fired fires firms firns firry first firth kafir kefir affirm firing firkin firman firmed firmer firmly firsts firths infirm kafirs kefirs

fire afire fired fires bonfire firearm firebug firefly fireman firemen gunfire misfire rimfire

fired misfired

fires bonfires fireside gunfires misfires

firm firms affirm firman firmed firmer firmly infirm affirms confirm firmest firming

firms affirms confirms

firn firns

firs first firsts kafirs kefirs firstly

first firsts

firth firths

fisc fiscs fiscal fiscals

fish fishy elfish fished fisher fishes oafish offish batfish catfish codfish dogfish fishers fishery fishier fishily fishing garfish hagfish hogfish huffish oarfish panfish pinfish raffish sawfish selfish sunfish wolfish

fist fists fisted fistic fistful fistula

fit fits befit fitch fitly refit unfit befits comfit fitful fitted fitter misfit outfit profit refits soffit

fitch fitches fitchew fitchews

fits befits refits comfits misfits outfits profits soffits

five fiver fives fivers

fiver fivers

fix fixt affix fixed fixer fixes infix refix unfix fixate fixers fixing fixity prefix suffix

fixed affixed fixedly infixed refixed unfixed prefixed suffixed

fixer fixers

fixes affixes refixes prefixes suffixes

fixt fixture

fizz fizzy fizzed fizzes fizzle fizzier fizzing fizzled fizzles

fjord fjords

flab flabs flabby

flag flags flagon flagged flagger flagman flagmen flagons

flags flagship

flail flails flailed flailing

flair flairs

flak flake flaks flaky flaked flakes flakier flaking

flake flaked flakes

flam flame flams aflame flamed flamen flames flamens flaming inflame

flame aflame flamed flamen flames flamens inflame flamenco inflamed inflamer inflames

flan flank flans flange flanks flanged flanges flanked flanker flannel

flank flanks flanked flanker flankers flanking outflank

flap flaps flapped flapper

flare flared flares

flash flashy flashed flasher flashes flashers flashier flashily flashing

flask flasks

flat flats flatly flatus deflate flatbed flatcar flatten flatter flattop inflate

flaw flaws flawed flawing

flax flaxy flaxen flaxes

flay flays flayed flaying

flea fleam fleas fleams fleabag

fleam fleams

fleck flecks flecked flecking

fled fledge rifled baffled fledged fledges muffled purfled raffled riffled ruffled stifled trifled waffled

flee fleer flees fleet fleece fleecy fleers fleets fleeced fleeces fleeing fleetly

fleer fleers

fleet fleets fleetly fleeting

flesh fleshy fleshed fleshes fleshpot

flew flews

flex flexed flexes flexor reflex flexile flexing flexion flexors flexure

flick flicks flicked flicker flickers flicking

flier fliers

flies barflies botflies gadflies mayflies medflies sawflies

fling flings baffling flinging muffling purfling raffling riffling ruffling stifling trifling waffling

flint flints flinty

flip flips flipped flipper

flirt flirts flirty flirted flirting

flit flits flitted flitter

float afloat floats floated floater refloat floaters floating refloats

floc flock flocs flocks elflock floccus flocked

flock flocks elflock flocked elflocks flocking

floe floes

flog flogs flogged flogger

flood floods flooded flooding floodlit

floor floors floored flooring subfloor

flop flops floppy flopped

flora floral floras

floss flossy flossed flossing

flour flours floury floured flouring flourish

flout flouts flouted flouters flouting

flow flown flows flowed flower inflow airflow flowers flowery flowing inflows outflow

flows airflows outflows

flu flub flue flus flux flubs flues fluff fluid fluke fluky flume flung flunk fluor flush flute afflux efflux fluent fluffs fluffy fluids fluked flukes flumes flunks flunky fluors flurry fluted flutes fluxed fluxes influx reflux

flub flubs flubbed

flue flues fluent fluency

fluff fluffs fluffy fluffed fluffier fluffing

fluid fluids fluidly fluidity

fluke fluked flukes

flume flumes

flunk flunks flunky flunked flunkeys flunkies flunking

fluor fluors fluoride fluorine

flus flush flushed flusher flushes fluster

flush flushed flushers flushing

flute fluted flutes

flux afflux efflux fluxed fluxes influx reflux conflux fluxing fluxion

fly flyer barfly botfly deafly flyers flying gadfly mayfly medfly sawfly

flyer flyers

foal foals foaled foaling

foam foams foamy foamed foamier foaming

fob fobs fobbed

focal bifocal bifocals confocal

focus focused focuses focusing focussed

foe foes foeman

fog fogs fogy befog defog fogey foggy befogs defogs fogbow fogeys fogged fogies

fogey fogeys

fogs befogs defogs

foil foils foiled airfoil foiling milfoil tinfoil trefoil

foils airfoils milfoils tinfoils trefoils

foist foists foisted foisting

fold folds bifold enfold folded folder infold unfold enfolds folders folding foldout infolds pinfold sixfold tenfold twofold unfolds

folds enfolds infolds unfolds pinfolds

folia foliage foliate foliated foliates

folio folios

folk folks folksy kinfolk menfolk

folks folksy kinfolks

fond fondu fondle fondly fondue fondus fondled fondles fondues

fondu fondue fondus fondues

font fonts fontal fontina

food foods seafood

foods seafoods

fool fools fooled foolery fooling foolish

fools foolscap

foot afoot footed footie footage footboy footers footies footing footman footmen footpad footsie hotfoot webfoot

fop fops

for fora forb ford fore fork form fort afore foray forbs forby force fordo fords fores forge forgo forks forms forte forth forts forty forum afford before biform deform effort forage forays forbad forbid forced forcer forces forded fordid forego forest forged forger forges forget forgot forint forked formal format formed former formic fornix fortes fortis forums inform oxford reform

fora foray forage forays foraged forager forages foramen forayed

foray forays forayed foraying

forb forbs forby forbad forbid forbade forbear forbids forbore

force forced forcer forces deforce enforce forceps forcers deforced deforces enforced enforcer enforces forceful perforce

ford fordo fords afford forded fordid oxford affords fording fordone oxfords

fordo fordone fordoing

fords affords oxfords

fore afore fores before forego forest forearm foregos foreign foreleg foreman foremen forepaw foresaw foresee forests foretop forever

fores forest foresee foresaid foresail foresaw foresees foreskin forestay forested forester forestry reforest

forge forged forger forges forget

forgo forgot forgoers forgoing

fork forks forked forkful forking hayfork

forks hayforks

form forms biform deform formal format formed former formic inform reform aliform conform deforms formals formats forming formula informs perform preform reforms uniform

forms deforms conforms performs preforms uniforms

fort forte forth forts forty effort fortes fortis comfort efforts forties fortify fortune

forte fortes

forts comforts

forum forums

foss fossa fosse fossae fossil fossils

fossa fossae

foul afoul fouls befoul fouled foully befouls foulard fouling

fouls befouls

found founds founded founder foundry confound dumfound founders founding profound

fount founts fountain

four fours fourth fourths

fours foursome

fovea foveae

fowl fowls fowled fowler fowlers fowling peafowl seafowl

fowls peafowls

fox foxy foxes foxier foxing outfox

foxes outfoxes

foy foys foyer foyers

foyer foyers

frag frags fragged fragile

frail frailty taffrail

frame framed framer frames framers airframe bedframe

franc francs

frank franks franked frankly franking franklin

frap fraps

frat frats

fraud frauds defraud defrauds

fray frays affray defray frayed affrays defrays fraying

frays affrays defrays

freak freaks freaky freaked freaking freakish freakout

free freed freer frees afreet freely freest freeze freebee freebie freedom freeing freeman freemen freeway freezer freezes

freed freedom freedman freedmen freedoms

frees freest

fresh afresh freshen fresher freshet refresh freshens freshest freshets freshman freshmen

fret frets fretful fretted

friar friars friary friaries

fried refried

frier friers

fries refries belfries

frig frigs fright frigid frigate frigged frights

frill frills frilly frilled frillier frilling

frisk frisks frisky frisked friskier friskily frisking

frit afrit frith frits fritz friths fritter

frith friths

friz frizzy frizzed frizzle

fro froe frog from frow frock froes frogs frond frons front frosh frost froth frown frows froze frocks froggy frolic fronds frosts frosty froths frothy frowns frowsy frowzy frozen

frock frocks defrock frocked defrocks frocking

froe froes

frog frogs froggy frogman frogmen

frond fronds

frons saffrons

front fronts affront frontal fronted affronts confront frontage frontals frontier fronting frontlet

frost frosts frosty defrost frosted defrosts frostbit frostier frostily frosting
froth froths frothy frothed frothier frothily frothing
frow frown frows frowns frowsy frowzy frowned frowner
frown frowns frowned frowners frowning
frows frowsy
froze frozen
fruit fruits fruity fruited fruitful fruitier fruition
frump frumps frumpy frumpier frumpish
fry fryer refry belfry fryers frying frypan
fryer fryers
fudge fudged fudges
fuel fuels fueled refuel fueling fuelled refuels
fuels refuels
fug fugs fugal fugue fugues refuge
fugue fugues
full fully fuller awfully fullest
fully awfully artfully fitfully joyfully lawfully manfully usefully wilfully

fume fumed fumes perfume
fumed perfumed
fumes perfumes
fumy perfumy
fun fund funk fundi funds fungi fungo funks funky funny funded fundus fungal fungus funked funned funnel refund
fund fundi funds funded fundus refund funding refunds
fundi funding
funds refunds
fungi fungible
fungo fungoid
funk funks funky funked funkier funking
fur furl furs fury furls furor furry furze furzy furfur furies furled furore furors furred furrow furzes sulfur unfurl
furl furls furled unfurl furling furlong unfurls
furor furore furors
furs sulfurs

furze furzes
fuse fused fusee fuses defuse effuse fusees infuse refuse confuse defused defuses diffuse effused effuses infused infuser infuses perfuse profuse refused refuses suffuse
fused defused effused infused refused confused diffused perfused suffused
fusee fusees
fuses defuses effuses refuses confuses diffuses perfuses suffuses
fusil fusilier
fuss fussy fussed fusses fussier fussily fussing
futon futons
futz futzed futzes futzing
fuze fuzed fuzee fuzes fuzees
fuzee fuzees
fuzz fuzzy fuzzed fuzzes fuzzier fuzzily fuzzing
fyce fyces
fyke fykes

g

gab   gabs gaby gabby gable gabbed gabber gabble gabbro gabies gabion gabled gables

gable   gabled gables hangable huggable

gad   egad gads gadded gadfly gadget

gae   gaed algae rugae gaeing

gaff   gaffe gaffs gaffed gaffer gaffes gaffers gaffing

gaffe   gaffed gaffer gaffes gaffers

gag   gaga gage gags gaged gages engage gagged gaggle gagman gagmen

gage   gaged gages engage baggage burgage engaged engages luggage

gaged   engaged

gages   engages burgages

gags   gagster

gain   again gains gained gainer gainly regain against bargain gainers gainful gaining gainsay regains

gains   against gainsay regains bargains gainsaid gainsays

gait   gaits gaiter gaiters

gal   gala gale gall gals algal fugal galas galax galea gales galls galop jugal legal regal vagal argali frugal fungal galaxy galeae galena galiot galled gallet galley gallic gallon gallop galoot galops galore galosh galyak plagal regale

gala   galas galax galaxy galatea

galax   galaxy galaxies

gale   galea gales galeae galena regale galenas regales

galea   galeae galeated

gales   regales legalese

gall   galls galled gallet galley gallic gallon gallop gallant gallein galleon gallery gallets galleys galling galliot gallium gallnut gallons galloon gallops gallows legally

galop   galops

gam   gamb game gamp gams gamy agama agamy gamay gambs gamed games gamic gamin gamma gammy gamps gamut agamas bigamy digamy gambit gamble gambol gamely gamete gamier gaming gamins gammas gammed gammer gammon gamuts lingam oogamy

gamb   gambs gambit gamble gambol gambits gambled gambler gambles gambols gambrel

game   gamed games gamely gamete endgame gametes

games   gamester

gamin   gaming gamins

gamma   gammas

gamp   gamps

gams   lingams

gamut   gamuts

gamy   bigamy digamy oogamy apogamy exogamy

gan   gang began ganef gangs hogan lagan ligan organ pagan wigan brogan gander ganefs ganged ganger gangly gangue ganjah gannet ganoid gantry hogans lagans ligans longan nagana organs pagans slogan wigans

ganef   ganefs

gang   gangs ganged ganger gangly gangue gangers ganging ganglia gangrel gangues gangway

gangs   gangster

gaol   gaols gaolers

gap   gape gaps agape gaped gaper gapes gapers gaping gapped

gape   agape gaped gaper gapes gapers gpgaper

gaper   gapers

gaps

gar   agar garb gars agars cigar garbs garth sugar agaric angary beggar cigars cougar garage garbed garble garden garget gargle garish garlic garner garnet garret garter garths hangar hegari regard saggar sugars sugary vagary vulgar

garb   garbs garbed garble garbage garbing garbled garbler garbles

gars   agars cigars sugars beggars cougars hangars saggars

garth   garths

gas   agas gash gasp degas gases gasps gassy ragas sagas togas yogas ajugas amigas congas dongas gasbag gashed gashes gasify gasket gaskin gasmen gasped gassed gasser lingas omegas orgasm pangas saigas taigas tongas virgas

gash   gashed gashes gashing

gasp   gasps gasped gasping

gat   gate gats agate begat gated gates agates gateau gather gating jugate legate legato ligate negate nougat

gate   agate gated gates agates gateau jugate legate ligate negate frigate gateaux gateleg gateman gatemen gateway legatee legates ligated ligates negated negates virgate

gated   ligated negated

gamma   gammas

gamp   gamps

gams   lingams

gamut   gamuts

gamy   bigamy digamy oogamy apogamy exogamy

gates   agates legates ligates negates frigates virgates

gats   nougats

gaud   gauds gaudy gaudier gaudily

gauge   gauged gauges

gaunt   gauntly gauntlet

gaur   gaurs

gauze   gauzes

gave   agave gavel agaves gavels forgave gaveled

gavel   gavels gaveled

gavot   gavots

gawk   gawks gawky gawked gawkier gawking

gay   gays gayer gayly gayest gayety margay

gays   margays

gaze   agaze gazed gazer gazes gazebo gazers gazebos gazelle gazette

gazer   gazers

gear   gears geared gearbox gearing

gecko   geckos

gee   agee geed geek gees ogee geeks geese ogees apogee burgee congee geeing pongee

geek   geeks

gees   geese ogees apogees bargees burgees congees pongees

gel   geld gels angel bagel gelds gelid kugel angels bagels cudgel gelada gelded gelled hugely sagely

geld   gelds gelded gelding

gels   angels bagels cudgels

gem   gems gemma gemmy gemmae gemmed

gemma   gemmae

gems   gemsbok

gene   genes genet genera genets general generic geneses genesis genetic

genes   geneses genesis agenesis hugeness sageness

genet   genets genetic genetics

genie   genies

genoa   genoas

genre   genres

gens   exogens morgens oxygens

gent   agent gents agents argent cogent gentes gentle gently gentry regent urgent argents exigent fulgent genteel gentian gentile gentled gentler magenta pungent reagent regents tangent

gents   agents argents regents reagents tangents

genus   subgenus

geode   geodes geodesy geodesic

geoid   geoids
gerah   gerahs
germ   germs german germane
gesso   gessos
gest   egest gests digest egesta egests gestic hugest ingest sagest biggest congest digests egested gestalt gesture ingesta ingests largest longest suggest
gests   egests digests congests suggests
get   gets beget begets budget fidget forget gadget garget getter gorget midget nugget parget target widget
gets   begets budgets fidgets forgets gadgets gargets gorgets midgets nuggets pargets targets widgets
geum   geums
gey   bogey cagey fogey bogeys dingey fogeys geyser stagey
ghat   ghats
ghazi   ghazis
ghee   ghees
ghost   ghosts ghosted ghosting
ghoul   ghouls ghoulish
giant   giants giantess
gib   gibe gibs gibed gibes gibbed gibber gibbet gibbon gibing giblet
gibe   gibed gibes
gid   gids algid giddy rigid frigid turgid
giddy   giddyup
gie   gied gies aggie bogie dogie biggie bogies boogie bougie budgie cagier edgier fogies gieing hoagie loggie logier orgies piggie stogie veggie
gies   bogies fogies orgies biggies boogies bougies budgies buggies cagiest doggies edgiest elegies hoagies logiest piggies porgies stogies veggies
gift   gifts gifted
gig   gigs gigue gigged giggle giggly gigolo gigues
gigue   gigues
gild   gilds gilded gilder gilders gilding wergild
gilds   wergilds
gill   gills gilled
gilt   gilts
gimel   gimels
gimp   gimps gimpy gimped gimping
gin   gink gins aging begin ginks angina begins biggin caging edging egging engine ginger ginkgo ginned margin noggin origin paging pidgin raging regina urging virgin waging yogini
gink   ginks ginkgo
gins   begins biggins ginseng margins noggins origins pidgins virgins
gip   gips gipon gipons gipped
gipon   gipons
gird   girds engird girded girder girdle engirds girders girding girdled girdles

girds   engirds
girl   girls girlie cowgirl girlies girlish
girls   cowgirls
girt   girth girts girths seagirt
girth   girths
gismo   gismos
gist   gists agists legist elegist imagist legists
gists   agists elegists imagists
give   given giver gives ogive givens givers ogives forgive
given   givens forgiven
giver   givers forgiver lawgiver
gives   ogives forgives
gizmo   gizmos
glad   glade glades gladden gladder
glade   glades
glair   glairs glairy
gland   glands gangland
glans   raglans
glare   glared glares
glary   burglary
glass   glassy glassed glasses glassful glassily glassing spyglass sunglass
glaze   glazed glazes
gleam   agleam gleams gleamed gleaming
glean   gleans gleaned gleaner gleaners gleaning
glebe   glebes
glede   gledes
glee   gleed glees gleet gleets gleeful gleeman gleemen
gleet   gleets
glen   glens
glib   glibs glibly glibber
glide   glided glider glides gliders
glim   glimmer glimpse
glint   glints glinted glinting
glitz   glitzy
gloat   gloats gloated gloating
glob   globe globs global globed globes globin globing globins globoid globule
globe   globed globes
gloom   glooms gloomy gloomed gloomily glooming
glop   glops gloppy
glory   glorying
gloss   glossy glossae glossal glossary glossier glossies
glove   gloved glover gloves foxglove
glow   aglow glows glowed glower glowers glowing
gloze   glozed glozes
glue   glued gluer glues gluey gluers reglue unglue gluepot reglued reglues unglued unglues
glued   reglued unglued
gluer   gluers
glues   reglues
glug   glugs glugged

glum   glumly glummer
glut   gluts gluten glutens gluteus glutted glutton
glyph   glyphs glyphic anaglyph triglyph
gnar   gnarl gnars gnarls gnarled gnarred
gnarl   gnarls gnarled gnarling
gnash   gnashed gnashes gnashing
gnat   gnats agnate gnatty agnates cognate magnate
gnaw   gnaws gnawed gnawing
gnome   gnomes
gnu   gnus hognut pignut
go   ago ego goa gob god goo got goy agog agon egos goad goal goas goat gobs goby gods goer goes gold golf gone gong good goof gook goon goop goos gore gory gosh gout gowk gown goys logo sago sego agony agora amigo argol argon argot begot bigot bingo bongo cargo cogon congo dingo ergot fagot forgo fungo goads goals goats godly goers gofer going golem golfs golly gonad goner gongs gonof goods goody gooey goofs goofy gooks goons goops goopy goose goral gored gores gorge gorse gouge gourd gouts gouty gowan gowks gowns goyim imago ingot jingo largo lingo logos mango mongo mungo outgo rigor sagos segos sorgo tango vigor wagon
goa   goad goal goas goat goads goals goats goaded goalie goatee
goad   goads goaded goading
goal   goals goalie goalies
goat   goats goatee goatees goatish
goats   goatskin
gob   gobs goby gobbet gobble goblet goblin
god   gods godly godown godson pagoda
godly   ungodly
gods   godson godsend godsons
goer   goers forgoer
goers   forgoers
goes   cargoes dingoes fungoes imagoes jingoes lingoes mangoes outgoes
gofer   gofers
going   goings forgoing outgoing seagoing tangoing
gold   golden
golem   golems
golf   golfs golfed golfer golfers golfing
gonad   gonads
gone   goner agones begone bygone goners bygones doggone epigone forgone wagoner
goner   goners wagoner wagoners
gong   gongs gonged gonging
gonof   gonofs
goo   good goof gook goon goop goos goods goody gooey goofs goofy gooks

goons goops goopy goose burgoo goober goodly goofed googly googol gooier goosed gooses goosey lagoon

good goods goody goodly goodies goodish goodman goodmen

goof goofs goofy goofed goofier goofing

gook gooks

goon goons lagoon dragoon lagoons

goons lagoons dragoons

goop goops goopy goopier

goos goose goosed gooses goosey burgoos goosing

goose goosed gooses goosey mongoose

goral gorals

gore gored gores

gorge gorged gorges gorget engorge engorged engorges gorgeous

gorse gorses

gosh goshawk

got argot begot bigot ergot fagot ingot argots bigots ergots faggot fagots forgot gotten ingots maggot spigot zygote

gouge gouged gouger gouges

gourd gourde gourds gourdes

gout gouts gouty agouti dugout pigout agoutis dugouts hangout pigouts

gouts dugouts hangouts

gowan gowans

gowk gowks

gown gowns gowned gowning

gowns gownsman gownsmen

goy goys goyim

grab grabs grabby grabbed grabber grabble

grace graced graces disgrace graceful

grad grade grads graded grader grades gradin gradus degrade gradate graders grading gradins gradual upgrade

grade graded grader grades degrade graders upgrade degraded degrades paygrade upgraded upgrades

graft grafts grafted grafter grafters grafting

grain grains grainy grained ingrain grainier graining ingrains migraine

gram grams gramps anagram diagram epigram grammar program

grams anagrams diagrams epigrams programs

grand grands grandam grandee grander grandly grandma grandpa grandams granddad grandees grandest grandeur grandmas grandpas grandson

grant grants granted grantee granter grantor migrant vagrant emigrant flagrant fragrant granters granting grantors migrants vagrants

grape grapes grapery

graph graphs agrapha graphed graphic epigraph graphics graphing graphite

grasp grasps grasped grasper graspers grasping

grass grassy grassed grasses eelgrass grassier grassing

grate grated grater grates graters ingrate migrate emigrate grateful ingrates migrated migrates

grave graved gravel graven graver graves engrave gravels gravest engraved engraver engraves graveled gravelly margrave

gray grays grayed grayer grayly grayest graying grayish

graze grazed grazer grazes grazers

great greats greaten greater greatly greatens greatest

grebe grebes

gree agree greed green grees greet agreed agrees degree greedy greens greeny greets degrees greened greenly greeted greeter

greed agreed greedy greedier greedily

green greens greeny greened greenly greenery greenest greenies greening greenish shagreen

grees agrees degrees

greet greets greeted greeter greeters greeting

grew outgrew

grey greys

grid gride grids grided grides griddle griding

gride grided grides

grief griefs

grig grigs

grill grille grills grilled grillage grilling

grim grime grimy grimed grimes grimly megrim grimace grimier griming grimmer megrims pilgrim

grime grimed grimes

grin grind grins grinds gringo chagrin grinder gringos grinned

grind grinds grinder grinders grinding

grins chagrins

grip gripe grips griped griper gripes grippe gripers griping gripped gripper grippes

gripe griped griper gripes

grips gripsack

grist grists

grit grits gritty gritted

groan groans groaned groaner groaners groaning

groat groats

grog grogs groggy

grogs grogshop

groin groins groined groining

groom grooms groomed grooming

grope groped groper gropes

gross grossest

grot grots grotto

group groups grouped groupers groupies grouping ingroups regroups

grout grouts grouted grouters grouting

grove grovel groves groveled mangrove

grow growl grown grows grower growls growth growers growing growled growler grownup growths ingrown outgrow

growl growls growled growlers growling

grown grownups outgrown

grows outgrows

grub grubs grubby grubbed

grue gruel grues gruels

gruel gruels grueling

grues gruesome

grum grume grump grumes grumps grumpy grumble grumbly

grume grumes

grump grumps grumpy grumpily grumpish

grunt grunts grunted grunters grunting

guan guano guans guanos iguana guanaco iguanas

guano guanos

guard guards guarded guardian guarding mudguard vanguard

guava guavas

guck gucks

guess guessed guesses guessing

guest guests vaguest

guff guffs guffaw guffaws

guide guided guides unguided

guild guilds guilder guilders

guile guiles beguile beguiled beguiler beguiles guileful

guilt guilty guiltier

guise guises disguise

gulch gulches

gulf gulfs engulf gulfed ingulf engulfs gulfing ingulfs

gull gulls gully gulled gullet gullets gullies gulling

gulp gulps gulped gulping

gum gums algum begum gumbo gummy jugum algums begums gumbos gummed jugums legume tergum

gumbo gumbos gumboot gumboots

gums algums begums jugums gumshoe

gun gunk guns begun gunks gunky gunny gunman gunmen gunned gunnel gunner popgun shogun

gunk gunks gunky

gunny gunnybag

guns gunship gunshot popguns shoguns

gurge gurges

guru gurus

gush gushy gushed gusher gushes gushers gushing

gust gusto gusts gusty august gusted gusting

gusts disgusts

gut guts gutsy gutta catgut guttae gutted gutter rotgut

guts gutsy catguts gutsier rotguts

gutta guttae

guy guys guyed guyot guying guyots

guyot guyots

gybe gybes

gym gyms

gyp gyps gypsy gypped gypsum

gyps gypsy gypsum gypsies gypsums

gyre gyred gyres gyrene

gyro gyros

gyve gyved gyves

ha　aha had hae hag hah ham hap has hat haw hay cham chap char chat chaw ghat hack hade hadj haft hags hahs haik hail hair haji hajj hake hale half hall halo halt hame hams hand hang hank hant haps hard hare hark harl harm harp hart hash hasp hast hate hath hats haul have hawk haws hays haze hazy khan shad shag shah sham shaw shay than that thaw wham whap what aloha alpha bhang chafe chaff chain chair chalk champ chant chaos chape chaps chard chare charm chars chart chary chase chasm chats chaws ephah ghats ghazi habit hacks haded hades hadji hadst hafiz hafts haiks haiku hails hairs hairy hajis hajji hakes hakim haled haler hales hallo halls halts halva halve hamal hames hammy hands handy hangs hanks hants haply happy hards hardy harem hares harks harls harms harps harpy harry harsh harts hasps haste hasty hatch hated hater hates haulm hauls haunt haven havoc hawed hawks hawse hayed hazan hazed hazel hazes hypha jehad jihad kasha khadi khaki khans mocha nucha ogham pasha phase pshaw rehab shack shade shady shaft shags shake shako shaky shale shall shalt shame shams shank shape shard share shark sharp shave shawl shaws thane thank thaws whack whale whams whang whaps wharf

habit　habits habitan habitat inhabit habitans habitant habitats habitual habitude inhabits

hack　hacks shack whack hacked hacker hackie hackle shacks whacko whacks whacky hackbut hackers hackies hacking hackles hackman hackmen hackney hacksaw shackle whacked whackos

hacks　shacks whacks hacksaw hacksaws

had　hade hadj shad haded hades hadji hadst jehad jihad khadi shade shady hading hadjis jihads khadis shaded shades shadow

hade　haded hades shade shaded shades

haded　shaded

hades　shades

hadj　hadji hadjis

hadji　hadjis

hae　chaeta hyphae nuchae

haft　hafts shaft hafted shafts hafting shafted

hafts　shafts

hag　hags shag shags hagbut hagged haggis haggle shaggy

hags　shags

hah　hahs shah ephah ephahs

hahs　ephahs

haik　haiks haiku

hail　hails hailed hailer hailers hailing

hair　chair hairs hairy chairs hairdo mohair chaired haircut hairdos hairier hairnet hairpin mohairs

hairs　chairs mohairs

haji　hajis

hajj　hajji hajjis

hajji　hajjis

hake　hakes shake shaken shaker shakes shakers

hakes　shakes

hakim　hakims

hale　haled haler hales shale whale chalet exhale halest inhale shales thaler whaled whaler whales chalets exhaled exhales inhaled inhaler inhales thalers whalers

haled　whaled exhaled inhaled

haler　thaler whaler inhaler thalers whalers inhalers

hales　halest shales whales exhales inhales

half　behalf halfway

hall　hallo halls shall hallah halloo hallos hallow hallux phalli challie challis hallahs halloas halloos hallows hallway phallic shallop shallot shallow

hallo　halloo hallos hallow halloas halloos hallows shallop shallot shallow hallowed shalloon shallops shallots shallows

halo　haloed haloes haloid shalom halogen

halt　halts shalt halted halter asphalt halters halting

halts　asphalts

halva　halvah halvas halvahs

halve　halved halves

ham　cham hame hams sham wham champ hamal hames hammy ogham shame shams whams chammy champs dirham graham hamals hamlet hammed hammer hamper hamuli oghams shaman shamas shamed shames shammy shamus whammo whammy

hamal　hamals

hame　hames shame shamed shames ashamed

hames　shames

hammy　chammy shammy whammy

hams　shams whams oghams dirhams hamster khamsin

hand　hands handy handed handle unhand cowhand handbag handcar handful handgun handier handily handing handled handler handles handoff handout handsaw handsel handset offhand unhands

hands　handsaw handsel handset unhands cowhands handsaws handsels handsets handsome

handy　handyman handymen

hang　bhang hangs whang bhangs change hangar hanged hanger whangs changed changer changes hangars hangdog hangers hanging hangman hangmen hangout hangups

hangs　bhangs whangs

hank　hanks shank thank hanker hankie shanks thanks hankers hankies hanking shanked thanked

hanks　shanks thanks

hant　chant hants chants shanty chanted chanter chantey chantry enchant phantom shantey

hants　chants enchants

hap　chap haps whap chape chaps haply happy shape whaps chapel chapes happed happen mayhap mishap shaped shaper shapes

happy　unhappy

haps　chaps whaps mishaps perhaps

hard　chard hards hardy shard chards harden harder hardly shards diehard hardens hardest hardier hardily hardpan hardtop orchard pochard

hards　chards shards diehards hardship orchards pochards

hare　chare harem hares share chares harems shared sharer shares harelip sharers

harem　harems

hares　chares shares

hark　harks shark charka harked harken sharks charkas harkens harking sharked

harks　sharks

harl　harls harlot harlots

harm　charm harms charms dharma harmed harmer charmed dharmas harmful harming harmony

harms charms

harp harps harpy sharp harped harper sharps harpers harpies harping harpist harpoon sharped sharpen sharper sharpie sharply

harps sharps

harry charry gharry harrying

harsh harsher harshly harshest

hart chart harts charts charted charter

harts charts

has hash hasp hast chase chasm hasps haste hasty phase aghast alohas alphas chased chases chasms chaste hashed hashes haslet hasped hassle hasted hasten pashas phased phases phasic rehash

hash hashed hashes rehash hashing hashish

hasp hasps hasped

hast haste hasty aghast chaste hasted hasten chasten ghastly hastate hastens hastier hastily hasting

haste chaste hasted hasten chasten hastens chastely chastens hastened

hat chat ghat hate hath hats that what chats ghats hatch hated hater hates chatty hatbox haters hating hatpin hatred hatted hatter thatch

hatch thatch hatched hatcher hatches hatchet hatcheck hatchers hatchery hatchets hatching hatchway nuthatch thatched thatches

hate hated hater hates haters hateful

hater haters

hats chats ghats

haul haulm hauls hauled hauler inhaul haulage haulers hauling inhauls

hauls inhauls

haunt haunts haunted haunter haunters haunting

have haven shave behave havens shaved shaven shaver shaves behaved behaves shavers

haven havens shaven

havoc havocked

haw chaw hawk haws shaw thaw chaws hawed hawks hawse pshaw shawl shaws thaws bashaw cashaw chawed cushaw hawing hawked hawker hawser hawses heehaw pshaws shawls thawed

hawed chawed thawed heehawed

hawk hawks hawked hawker goshawk hawkers hawking hawkish

hawks goshawks

haws chaws hawse shaws thaws hawser hawses pshaws bashaws cushaws hawsers heehaws

hawse hawser hawses hawsers

hay hays shay hayed haying haymow sashay

hayed sashayed

hays hayseed sashays

hazan hazans

haze hazed hazel hazes hazels hazelly

hazel hazels hazelly hazelnut

he heh hem hen hep her het hew hex hey she the ache ahem chef chew ghee head heal heap hear heat heck heed heel heft heir held hell helm help heme hemp hems hens hent herb herd here herl herm hern hero hers hest hewn hews khet phew rhea shed shew thee them then thew they when whet whew whey aahed ached aches ahead ashen ashes bathe cache cheap cheat check cheek cheep cheer chefs chela chert chess chest chevy chews chewy ether fiche ghees heads heady heals heaps heard hears heart heath heats heave heavy hecks hedge heeds heels hefts hefty heigh heirs heist helix hello hells helms helps helve hemal hemic hemps hence henna henry hents herbs herby herds herls herma herms herns heron hertz hests hewed hewer hexad hexed hexer hexes hexyl kheth kithe lathe lithe niche ocher oohed other ouphe rheas rheum ruche sadhe sheaf shear sheds sheen sheep sheer sheet sheik shelf shell sherd shewn shews tache theca theft thegn their theme there therm these theta thews thewy tithe usher wheal wheat wheel whelk whelp where whets wheys withe

head ahead heads heady behead headed header airhead beheads bowhead cathead egghead fathead godhead headers headier headily heading headman headmen headpin headset headway hophead hothead jughead pinhead pothead redhead saphead subhead towhead warhead

heads beheads headset airheads bowheads catheads eggheads fatheads headsail headsets headsman headsmen hopheads hotheads pinheads potheads redheads sapheads subheads towheads warheads

heal heals wheal healed healer health wheals healers healing healthy

heals wheals

heap cheap heaps cheapo heaped cheapen cheaper cheapie cheaply cheapos heaping

hear heard hears heart shear hearer hearse hearth hearts hearty shears hearers hearing hearken hearsay

hearses hearten hearths oxheart sheared unheard

heard unheard

hears hearse shears hearsay hearses rehearse

heart hearth hearts hearty hearten hearths oxheart heartens heartier heartily oxhearts

heat cheat heath heats wheat cheats heated heater heaths heathy reheat sheath wheats cheated cheater escheat heaters heathen heather heating preheat reheats sheathe sheaths theater theatre wheaten

heath heaths heathy sheath heathen heather sheathe sheaths heathens heathers heathery sheathed sheathes

heats cheats wheats reheats escheats preheats

heave heaved heaven heaves sheaved sheaves heavenly

heavy heavyset

heck check hecks checks heckle checked checker checkup heckled heckler heckles recheck

hecks checks rechecks

hedge hedged hedger hedges hedgers hedgehog hedgerow

heed heeds heeded heedful heeding wheedle

heel heels wheel heeled heeler wheels heelers heeling heeltap wheelie

heels wheels

heft hefts hefty theft hefted thefts heftier hefting

hefts thefts

heigh height heighten

heir heirs their coheir theirs coheirs heirdom heiress

heirs theirs coheirs heirship

heist heists theist atheist heisted heister atheists heisters heisting theistic

held beheld upheld

helix helixes

hell hello hells shell heller hellos shells shelly hellbox hellcat hellers hellion hellish helloed helluva shellac shelled sheller

hello hellos helloed helloing

hells shells

helm helms helmed helmet helmets helming

helms helmsman helmsmen

help helps whelp helped helper whelps helpers helpful helping whelped

helps whelps

helve helved helves shelve shelved shelves

hem ahem heme hemp hems them hemal hemic hemps theme anthem chemic hemmed hemmer hempen mayhem sachem schema scheme themes

heme theme scheme themes schemed schemer schemes

hemic chemic chemical

hemp hemps hempen

hems anthems mayhems sachems

hen hens hent then when ashen hence henna henry hents hennas hyphen kuchen lichen peahen phenix phenol phenyl thenar thence whence

hence thence whence

henna hennas

hens hyphens lichens peahens

hent hents henting

hep hepcat heptad

her herb herd here herl herm hern hero hers chert ether herbs herby herds herls herma herms herns heron hertz ocher other sherd there therm usher where adhere anther archer bather bother cherry cherts cherub cipher cither cohere cosher cypher dasher dither either ethers father fisher gather gopher gusher herald herbal herbed herded herder herdic hereat hereby herein hereof hereon heresy hereto heriot hermae hermai hermit hernia heroes heroic heroin herons herpes higher hither inhere josher kasher kosher lasher lather lecher lither masher mother nether nigher ochers others pother pusher rasher rather richer rusher sherds sherif sherpa sherry sigher sphere sphery tether ushers washer wether wherry wisher wither zither

herb herbs herby herbal herbed herbage herbier potherb sherbet

herbs potherbs

herd herds sherd herded herder herdic sherds cowherd herdboy herders herding

herds sherds cowherds herdsman herdsmen

here there where adhere cohere hereat hereby herein hereof hereon heresy hereto inhere sphere adhered adheres cohered heretic inhered inheres nowhere sphered spheres thereby therein thereof thereon thereto whereas whereby wherein whereof whereto

herl herls

herm herma herms therm hermae hermai hermit hermits thermae thermal thermic thermos

herma hermae hermai thermae thermal thermals

hern herns hernia cithern herniae hernial hernias

herns citherns

hero heron heroes heroic heroin herons cheroot heroics heroine heroism theroid

heron herons

hers ethers ochers others ushers anthers archers bathers bothers ciphers cithers coshers cyphers dashers dithers fathers fishers gathers gophers gushers herself joshers lashers lathers lechers mashers mithers mothers pushers rushers sighers tethers washers wethers wishers withers zithers

hest chest hests behest chests chesty highest lithest nighest rashest richest

hests chests

het khet whet kheth sheth theta whets cachet chetah ghetto hetman rhetor rochet sachet sheths thetas thetic

hew chew hewn hews phew shew thew whew chews chewy hewed hewer shewn shews thews thewy cashew chewed chewer eschew hewers hewing nephew rechew shewed

hewed chewed shewed eschewed rechewed

hewer chewer hewers chewers

hewn shewn

hews chews shews thews cashews eschews nephews rechews

hex hexad hexed hexer hexes hexyl hexads hexane hexers hexing hexone hexose

hexad hexads

hexer hexers

hey they whey wheys heyday

hi chi hid hie him hin hip his hit chic chid chin chip chit hick hide hied hies high hike hill hilt hind hins hint hips hire hiss hist hits hive shim shin ship shiv thin this whim whip whir whit whiz aphid aphis chick chico chide chief child chili chill chime chimp china chine chink chino chins chips chirk chirp chirr chits ethic hicks hider hides highs hight hiked hikes hills hilly hilts hilum hinds hinge hinny hints hippo hippy hired hirer hires hitch hived hives phial rhino sahib shied shies shift shill shims shine shins shiny ships shire shirk shirr shirt shive shivs spahi sushi thick thief thigh thill thine thing think third thirl which whiff while whims whine whiny whips whipt whirl whirs whish whisk whist white whits whizz

hick chick hicks thick chicks hickey chickee chicken hickeys hickory thicken thicker thicket thickly

hicks chicks

hid chid hide aphid chide chids hider hides aphids chided chides hidden hiders hiding orchid

hide chide hider hides chided chides hiders cowhide hideous rawhide

hider hiders

hides chides cowhides rawhides

hie hied hies chief shied shies thief ashier cahier chiefs chield hieing hiemal mashie shield thieve

hied shied

hies shies ashiest duchies mashies withies

high highs hight thigh higher highly hights thighs highboy highest highway

highs thighs

hight hights hightail

hike hiked hikes

hill chill hills hilly shill thill chilli chills chilly hilled shills thills anthill chilled chiller hillier hilling hillock hilltop

hills chills shills thills anthills hillside

hilly chilly

hilt hilts hilted hilting philter

him shim whim chime chimp shims whims chimed chimes chimps shimmy whimsy

hin chin hind hins hint shin thin china chine chink chino chins hinds hinge hinny hints rhino shine shins shiny thine thing think whine whiny aching behind chinch chines chinks chinos chintz hinder hinged hinger hinges hinted hinter oohing rhinal rhinos shindy shined shiner shines shinny sphinx things thinks thinly urchin whined whiner whines whinny within zechin

hind hinds behind hinder shindy hinders hindgut

hinge hinged hinger hinges

hinny shinny whinny

hins chins shins urchins zechins

hint hints chintz hinted hinter chintzy hinters hinting

hip chip hips ship whip chips hippo hippy ships whips whipt chippy hipped hipper hippie hippos

hippo hippos

hippy chippy

hips chips ships whips hipshot hipster whipsaw

hire hired hirer hires shire hirers rehire shires rehired rehires

hired rehired

hirer hirers

hires shires rehires

his hiss hist this aphis whish whisk whist chisel hispid hissed hisser hisses orchis schism schist spahis whisks whisky whists

hiss   hissed hisser hisses hissers hissing

hist   whist schist whists history schists sophist thistle whistle

hit   chit hits whit chits hitch white whits chitin chiton hither hitter whited whiten whiter whites whitey

hitch   hitched hitches chitchat hitching

hits   chits whits

hive   hived hives shive chives shiver shives archive beehive shivers shivery

hived   archived

hives   chives shives archives beehives

ho   hob hod hoe hog hon hop hot how hoy mho oho rho tho who ahoy chop dhow echo hoar hoax hobo hobs hock hods hoed hoer hoes hogs hoke hold hole holm holp holt holy home homo homy hone hong honk hood hoof hook hoop hoot hope hops hora horn hose host hots hour hove howl hoys mhos phot rhos shod shoe shoo shop shot show thou whoa whom whop abhor ahold chock choir choke choky chomp chops chord chore chose dhole dhoti dhows ephod ephor ethos ghost ghoul hoagy hoard hoary hobby hobos hocks hocus hoers hogan hoist hokes hokey hokku hokum holds holed holes holey hollo holly holms holts homed homer homes homey honed hones honey hongs honks honky honor hooch hoods hooey hoofs hooka hooks hooky hoops hoots hoped hoper hopes horas horde horns horny horse horst horsy hosed hosen hoses hosta hosts hotel hotly hound houri hours house hovel hover howdy howls ichor litho macho nohow phone phony photo phots rhomb shoal shoat shock shoed shoer shoes shoji shone shook shoos shoot shops shore shorn short shote shots shout shove shown shows showy thole thong thorn thoro thorp those wahoo whole whomp whoop whops whore whorl whose

hoar   hoard hoary hoards hoarse hoarded hoarder hoarier hoarsen hoarser

hoard   hoards hoarded hoarder hoarders hoarding

hoax   hoaxed hoaxer hoaxes hoaxers hoaxing

hob   hobo hobs hobby hobos hobble hobnob hoboes phobia

hobby   hobbyist

hobo   hobos hoboes

hock   chock hocks shock chocks hocked hockey shocks chocked hocking shocked shocker

hocks   chocks shocks

hocus   hocused hocusing

hod   hods shod ephod ephods method rhodic shoddy

hods   ephods methods

hoe   hoed hoer hoes shoe hoers shoed shoer shoes echoed echoes hoeing phoebe shoers

hoed   shoed echoed hoedown

hoer   hoers shoer shoers

hoers   shoers

hoes   shoes echoes

hog   hogs hogan hogans hogged hognut hogtie quahog shogun

hogan   hogans mahogany

hogs   hogskin quahogs

hoist   hoists hoisted hoisting

hoke   choke hokes hokey choked choker chokes chokey chokers

hokes   chokes

hokey   chokey

hold   ahold holds aholds behold holden holder holdup uphold beholds holders holding holdout holdups toehold upholds

holds   aholds beholds upholds toeholds

hole   dhole holed holes holey thole whole choler dholes tholed tholes armhole cholera eyehole keyhole manhole pinhole pothole

holed   tholed

holes   dholes tholes armholes eyeholes foxholes keyholes manholes pinholes potholes

hollo   hollos hollow hollowed hollowly

holly   wholly

holm   holms

holp   holpen

holt   holts

holy   unholy

home   homed homer homes homey homely homers

homed   fathomed

homer   homers homeroom

homes   homesick homespun

homo   homonym

hon   hone hong honk honed hones honey hongs honks honky honor phone phony shone thong archon honcho honest honeys honied honies honing honked honker honors honour phoned phones phoney phonic siphon syphon thongs

hone   honed hones honey phone shone honest honeys phoned phones phoney honesty honeyed

honed   phoned siphoned syphoned

hones   honest phones honestly

honey   honeys phoney honeyed honeybee honeydew honeying

hong   hongs thong thongs

hongs   thongs

honk   honks honky honked honker honkers honkies honking

honor   honors honored honoree dishonor honorary honorees honorers honoring

hooch   hooches

hood   hoods hooded hoodoo boyhood hooding hoodlum hoodoos manhood

hooey   phooey

hoof   hoofs hoofed hoofer hoofers hoofing shoofly

hook   hooka hooks hooky shook hookah hookas hooked hooker hookey hookup unhook hookahs hookers hooking hookups pothook unhooks

hooka   hookah hookas hookahs

hooks   pothooks

hoop   hoops whoop hooped hoopla hoopoe whoops hooping hoopoes whooped whoopee

hoops   whoops

hoot   hoots shoot hooted hooter shoots cahoots hooting shooter

hoots   shoots cahoots

hop   chop hope hops shop whop chops hoped hoper hopes shops whops bishop carhop choppy hopers hoping hopped hopper hopple shoppe

hope   hoped hoper hopes hopers hopeful

hoper   hopers

hops   chops shops whops bishops carhops

hora   horas choral horary shoran thorax amphora chorale chorals shorans

horas   amphoras

horde   horded hordes chorded

horn   horns horny shorn thorn horned hornet thorns thorny alphorn bighorn foghorn hornets hornier hornily horning hornito inkhorn leghorn saxhorn tinhorn

horns   thorns alphorns bighorns foghorns inkhorns leghorns saxhorns tinhorns

horny   thorny

horse   horsed horses horsey horsefly horseman horsemen sawhorse

horst   horsts

hose   chose hosed hosen hoses those whose chosen

hosen   chosen

host   ghost hosta hosts ghosts hostas hosted hostel ghosted ghostly hostage hostels hostess hostile hosting hostler

hosta   hostas hostage hostages

hosts   ghosts

hot   hots phot shot dhoti hotel hotly photo phots shote shots dhotis hotbed hotbox hotels hotter photon photos shotes upshot

hotel hotels hotelier

hots phots shots hotshot hotspur upshots

hound hounds hounded foxhound hounding

hour houri hours houris hourly

houri houris

house chouse housed housel houses choused chouses alehouse cathouse doghouse gashouse henhouse hothouse houseboy housefly houseful houseman housemen housesat housesit housetop icehouse madhouse outhouse teahouse

hove hovel hover shove hovels hovers shoved shovel shover shoves hoveled hovered hoverer shovels shovers

hovel hovels shovel hoveled hoveling shoveled

hover hovers shover hovered hoverer hoverers hovering pushover

how dhow howl show dhows howdy howls nohow shown shows showy anyhow howdah howled howler showed shower

howl howls howled howler howlers howling

hoy ahoy hoys hoyden

hub chub hubs chubs hubby chubby hubbly hubbub hubcap hubris

hubby chubby

hubs chubs

hue hued hues

huff chuff huffs huffy chuffs chuffy huffed chuffed huffier huffing huffish shuffle

huffs chuffs

huffy chuffy

hug chug huge hugs thug chugs huger thugs hugely hugest hugged hugger

huge huger hugely hugest

hugs chugs thugs

hula hulas

hulk hulks hulky hulked hulkier hulking

hull hullo hulls hulled huller hullos hullers hulling hulloed

hullo hullos hulloed hulloing

hum chum hump hums chump chums human humic humid humor humph humps humpy humus rhumb thumb thump whump chummy chumps exhume humane humans humble humbly humbug humeri hummed hummer hummus humors humped inhume rhumba rhumbs thumbs thumps whumps

human humane humans humanly inhuman humanely humanism humanist humanity humanize inhumane subhuman

humid humidor humidify humidity humidors

humor humors humoral humored humoring humorist humorous

hump chump humph humps humpy thump whump chumps humped thumps whumps humpier humping thumped thumper whumped

humps chumps thumps whumps

hums chums

hunch hunched hunches hunching

hung hunger hungry hungers

hunk chunk hunks chunks chunky hunker hunkers

hunks chunks

hunt hunts shunt hunted hunter shunts hunters hunting manhunt shunted

hunts shunts huntsman manhunts

hurl churl hurls hurly churls hurled hurler hurlers hurling

hurls churls

hurry hurrying

hurst hursts

hurt hurts hurtle hurtful hurting hurtled hurtles yoghurt

hurts yoghurts

hush shush hushed hushes hushaby hushing shushes

husk husks husky husked husker huskers huskier huskies huskily husking

hut huts shut chute hutch shuts chutes hutted

hutch hutches

huts shuts

hydra hydrae hydras hydrant hydrate hydrants hydrates

hydro hydros hydroid hydrous hydrogen hydroids hydroxyl

hyena hyenas

hying shying

hyla hylas phyla phylae

hymen hymens hymeneal

hymn hymns hymnal hymned hymnals hymning hymnist hymnody

hype hyped hyper hypes hyperon

hyper hyperons

hypha hyphae hyphal

hypo hypos hypoed hypoing hypoxia hypoxic

i

iamb iambs
ibex ibexes
ibis alibis ibises oribis
ice dice iced ices lice mice nice pice rice vice amice diced dices dicey juice nicer price riced ricer rices slice spice trice twice vices voice advice amices apices biceps bodice choice cicely cilice device entice ibices icebox icecap iceman icemen juiced juices malice nicely nicest nicety notice novice office police priced pricer prices pumice ricers sliced slicer slices sluice spiced spices splice thrice triced trices voiced voicer voices
iced diced riced juiced priced sliced spiced triced voiced enticed noticed policed pumiced sluiced spliced
ices dices rices vices amices apices ibices juices nicest prices slices spices trices voices advices bodices calices choices codices cylices devices entices helices indices malices notices novices offices polices pumices radices sluices splices
ichor ichorous
icier dicier juicier spicier
icily juicily
icing dicing icings ricing juicing pricing slicing spicing tricing voicing enticing noticing policing pumicing sluicing splicing
icky dicky kicky micky picky sticky tricky colicky finicky panicky
icon icons iconic helicon lexicon silicon
icons helicons lexicons silicons
ictus ictuses
icy juicy spicy policy
id aid bid did fid gid hid ids kid lid mid rid acid aide aids amid arid avid bide bids chid dido fids gids grid hide idea ides idle idly idol idyl kids laid lids maid nide nidi paid quid raid ride rids said side skid slid tide tidy void wide abide acids acidy acrid aided aides algid amide aphid aside avoid azide biddy bided bides bidet bifid bovid braid bride chide cider druid eider elide felid fetid fluid gelid geoid giddy glide gride grids guide hider hides humid hyoid ideal ideas idiom idiot idled idler idles idols idyll idyls imide kiddy lipid livid lucid lurid maids middy midge midst mucid mysid nides nidus ovoid oxide plaid pride quids rabid raids rapid redid rider rides ridge ridgy

rigid sapid sayid sided sides sidle skids slide snide solid squid staid tepid tidal tided tides timid tumid undid valid vapid video vivid voids widen wider widow width zooid
idea ideal ideas ideals ideate ideally ideated ideates sidearm
ideal ideals ideally idealism idealist idealize
ides aides bides hides nides rides sides tides abides amides asides azides brides chides elides glides grides guides imides irides oxides prides slides widest apsides besides betides bolides borides decides derides divides excides halides pyxides resides strides upsides
idiom idioms
idiot idiots idiotic
idle idled idler idles sidle bridle idlers idlest midleg ridley sidled sidles bridled bridles idlesse lidless
idled sidled bridled
idler idlers
idles idlest sidles bridles idlesse lidless
idly acidly aridly avidly acridly fetidly fluidly lucidly luridly rapidly rigidly solidly tepidly timidly vapidly vividly
idol idols eidola eidolon idolize
ids aids bids fids gids kids lids rids acids chids grids maids midst quids raids skids voids amidst aphids avoids bovids braids druids felids fluids geoids lipids mysids ovoids plaids rapids solids squids zooids
idyl idyll idyls idylls idyllic
idyll idylls idyllic idyllist
if ifs kif rif alif biff coif fife gift iffy jiff kifs life lift miff naif rife riff rifs rift sift tiff waif wife alifs biffs bifid cliff coifs deify drift edify fifed fifer fifes fifth fifty gifts jiffy kalif knife lifer lifts miffs motif naifs nifty quiff reify riffs rifle rifts serif shift sifts skiff sniff spiff stiff swift tiffs unify waifs whiff
iffy jiffy sniffy spiffy
ifs kifs rifs alifs coifs naifs waifs kalifs motifs serifs
igloo igloos
ihram ihrams
ikon eikon ikons eikons
ikons eikons
ileus pileus
ilex ilexes

ilia cilia iliac filial chiliad ciliary ciliate sedilia
ilium cilium milium
ilk bilk milk silk bilks milks milky silks silky bilked milked milker silken
ill bill dill fill gill hill illy kill mill nill pill rill sill till will bills billy chill dilly drill fills filly frill gills grill hills hilly kills krill mills nills pills quill rille rills shill sills silly skill spill still swill thill tills trill twill villa wills axilla billed billet billon billow brills chilli chills chilly drills evilly faille filled filler fillet fillip frills frilly gilled grille grills hilled illume killed killer killie milled miller millet pillar pilled pillow quills rebill refill rilles scilla shills shrill skills spills squill stills stilly swills taille thills thrill tilled tiller trills tuille twills villas willed willow zillah
illy billy dilly filly hilly silly chilly evilly frilly stilly civilly shrilly
image imaged images imagery
imago imagoes
imam imams imamate
imbed imbeds limbed climbed imbedded
imbue imbued imbues
imide imides
imine imines
immix immixed immixing
imp gimp imps limp pimp simp wimp blimp chimp crimp gimps gimpy impel imply limps pimps primp simps skimp wimps wimpy blimps chimps crimps crimpy dimple dimply gimped guimpe impact impair impala impale impart impede impels impend impish import impose impost improv impugn impure impute limped limper limpet limpid limply pimped pimple pimply primps rimple scrimp shrimp simper simple simply skimps skimpy wimple
impel impels impelled impeller
imply dimply limply pimply simply implying
imps gimps limps pimps simps wimps blimps chimps crimps primps skimps glimpse scrimps shrimps
in bin din fin gin hin ink inn kin pin sin tin win yin akin ayin bind bine bins chin coin dine ding dink dins fain find fine fink fins gain gink gins grin hind hins hint inch inks inky inly inns into jink jinn jinx join kina kind kine king kink kino lain line ling link linn lint

liny loin main mina mind mine mink mint minx nine oink pain pine ping pink pins pint piny rain rein rind ring rink ruin sain shin sine sing sink sins skin spin thin tine ting tins tint tiny twin vain vein vina vine viny wain wind wine wing wink wino wins winy zein zinc zing acing again aging aline amain amine aping auxin awing axing ayins azine basin begin being binds bines binge bingo blain blind blink brain brine bring brink briny burin cabin chain china chine chink chino chins cinch cline cling clink coins colin cuing cumin cutin dinar dined diner dines dingo dings dingy dinks dinky doing drain drink dying eking elfin eloin eosin eying faint feint final finch finds fined finer fines finis finks finny fling flint gains gamin ginks glint going grain grind grins groin hinds hinge hinny hints hying icing imine inane inapt incur incus index indri indue inept infer infix ingle ingot inion inked inker inkle inlay inlet inned inner input inset inure inurn jingo jinks jinni jinns joins joint kinds kings kinin kinks kinky kinos koine lapin levin lined linen liner lines linga lingo lings linin links linns lints linty loins lying lysin mains matin mavin minae mince minds mined miner mines minim minks minny minor mints minty minus nines ninja ninny ninon ninth oinks olein opine oping ovine owing pains paint pinch pined pines piney pings pinko pinks pinky pinna pinto pints pinup plain plink point print print quint quoin rains rainy reins renin resin rhino ricin rinds rings rinks rinse robin rosin ruing ruins sabin saint satin savin seine serin shine shins shiny since sines sinew singe sings sinks sinus skein skink skins slain sling slink spine spins spiny stain stein sting stink stint suing suint swain swine swing taint thine thing think tinct tinea tines tinge tings tinny tints toxin train twain twine twins tying unpin urine using veins veiny venin vinas vines vinic vinyl vying wains whine whiny wince winch winds windy wined wines wings winks winos wring zayin zincs zincy zineb zings zinky

inane inanely

inapt inaptly

inch cinch finch pinch winch chinch clinch flinch inched inches cinched cinches finches inching pinched pinches winched winches

incur incurs incurred

incus incuse incuses

index indexed indexer indexes indexers indexing

indri indris

indue indued indues

inert inertia inertial

infer infers inferior infernal infernos inferred inferrer

infix infixed infixing

ingle dingle ingles jingle mingle single tingle atingle cringle dingles jingled mingled singled tingled cringles jinglets kinglets minglers ringlets shingled shingles singlets swingled swingles tinglers wingless

ingot ingots

inion inions minion pinion dominion opinions

ink dink fink gink inks inky jink kink link mink oink pink rink sink tink wink blink brink chink clink dinks dinky drink finks ginks inked inker inkle jinks kinks kinky links minks oinks pinko pinks pinky plink prink rinks sinks skink slink stink think winks zinky blinks brinks chinks clinks dinkey dinkum drinks finked ginkgo inkers inkier inking inkjet kinked linked linker linkup oinked pinked pinkie pinkos plinks prinks shrink sinker skinks slinks slinky stinko stinks stinky thinks tinker tinkle tinkly winked winkle

inked finked kinked linked oinked pinked tinked winked blinked chinked clinked plinked slinked

inker inkers linker sinker tinker blinker clinker drinker blinkers clinkers stinkers thinkers tinkered

inkle tinkle winkle crinkle tinkled winkled crinkled crinkles sprinkle twinkled twinkles wrinkled wrinkles

inks dinks finks ginks jinks kinks links minks oinks pinks rinks sinks winks blinks brinks chinks clinks drinks plinks prinks skinks slinks stinks thinks hijinks shrinks

inky dinky kinky pinky zinky slinky stinky

inlay inlays inlaying

inlet inlets

inly gainly mainly thinly vainly plainly

inn inns jinn linn finny hinny inned inner jinni jinns linns minny ninny pinna tinny binned dinned dinner finned ginned innate inning jinnee linnet minnow pinnas pinned shinny sinned sinner skinny tinned tinner whinny winner winnow zinnia

inned binned dinned finned ginned pinned sinned tinned chinned grinned shinned skinned thinned twinned unpinned

inner dinner sinner tinner winner dinners beginner skinners spinners thinners

inns jinns linns

input inputs

inset insets

inter hinter intern inters sinter tinter winter fainter interne painter anointer disinter interact intercom interest interior intermix internal interned internee internes interred interrex intersex interval painters pointers printers printery quainter sintered splinter sprinter wintered

into pinto intone pintos intoned intoner intones maintop

inure inured inures

inurn inurns inurned inurning

iodic periodic

ion cion ions lion anion cions inion ionic lions onion scion union action amnion anions bionic briony bunion camion cation fusion gabion inions ionium ionize kation legion lesion lotion minion morion motion nation notion onions option pinion potion ration region scions talion unions vision

ionic bionic avionic bionics amnionic avionics

ions cions lions anions inions onions scions unions actions amnions bunions camions cations fusions gabions legions lesions lotions minions morions motions nations notions options pinions potions rations regions talions visions

iota biota iotas

irate pirate emirate irately pirated aspirate emirates levirate

ire dire fire hire lire mire sire tire wire afire aired direr fired fires hired hirer hires mired mires mirex quire shire sired siren sires spire tired tires vireo wired wires zaire admire aspire attire bemire bireme desire direct direly direst empire entire expire faired fairer hirers ireful irenic paired quired quires rehire retire rewire satire shires sirens soiree spired spires squire umpire vireos

iris irises fairish

irk dirk irks kirk chirk dirks irked quirk shirk smirk chirks dirked firkin irking quirks quirky shirks smirks

irked dirked quirked shirked smirked

irks dirks chirks quirks shirks smirks irksome

iron irons irony ironed ironer ironic andiron environ ironers ironies ironing ironist midiron sadiron

irons andirons environs midirons sadirons

is his mis sis wis axis bise cist dais disc dish disk egis fisc fish fist gist hiss hist ibis iris isle iwis kiss kist kris leis lisp list mise miss mist nisi obis pish pois reis rise risk skis this tuis visa vise wise wish wisp aegis aisle amiss anise antis aphis apish apsis arise arris arsis basis bises bison bliss brisk cadis cisco cists crisp cutis daisy deism deist delis disco discs disks etuis exist feist finis fiscs fishy fists foist frisk gismo gists grist guise hajis heist hoist isles islet issue istle joist kakis kepis kissy kists kiwis knish lenis lewis lexis lisle lisps lists loris louis lysis mavis maxis misdo miser missy mists misty moist naris nisus noise noisy oasis orris pavis poise polis prism priss pulis pyxis raise rakis ranis risen riser rises risks risky sakis saris semis sisal sissy swish tapis taxis tipis titis twist visas vised vises visit visor vista wadis waist whish whisk whist wiser wisps wispy wrist yetis yogis yonis zoris

isle aisle isles islet lisle aisled aisles islets lisles misled mislead paisley

isles aisles lisles

islet islets

issue issued issuer issues tissue reissued reissues

istle istles bristle epistle bristled bristles epistles listless thistles whistled whistler whistles wristlet

it bit dit fit hit ita its kit lit nit pit sit tit wit zit adit alit bait bite bits bitt brit chit cite city dits doit edit emit exit fits flit frit gait grit hits itch item kite kith kits knit mite mitt nits obit omit pita pits pity quit rite site sith sits skit slit snit spit suit titi tits twit unit wait whit wite with wits writ ziti zits adits admit afrit aitch ambit amity audit await baits befit bitch biter bites bitts bitty blitz bruit chits cited cites cubit davit debit deity demit digit ditch ditsy ditto ditty ditzy doits droit edits elite emits exits faith fitch fitly flits frith frits fritz fruit gaits glitz grits habit hitch itchy items kited kiter kites kithe kitty knits krait laity legit licit limit liter lithe litho litre merit miter mites mitre mitts nitty obits omits orbit petit pipit pitas pitch pithy piton plait posit quite quits quoit refit remit rites ritzy saith sitar sited sites situp situs skits slits smite smith snits spite spits spitz split sprit suite suits tacit titan titer tithe titis title titre

titty trait trite twits unfit unite units unity visit vital vitta vomit waits white whits witan witch wited wites withe withy witty write writs zizit

ita pita pitas sitar titan vital witan amrita guitar italic litany sitars titans vitals witans

itch aitch bitch ditch fitch hitch itchy pitch witch bitchy glitch itched itches litchi quitch snitch stitch switch twitch bewitch bitched bitches ditched ditches fitches fitchew hitched hitches itchier itching kitchen litchis pitched pitcher pitches witches

itchy bitchy

item items itemed itemize

its bits dits fits hits kits nits pits sits tits wits zits adits baits chits ditsy doits edits emits exits flits frits gaits grits knits obits omits quits skits slits snits spits suits twits units waits whits writs admits ambits audits awaits befits bruits cubits davits debits demits digits droits fruits habits itself kitsch kraits limits merits orbits pipits plaits posits quoits refits remits splits sprits traits visits vomits

ivies civies

ivy privy

iwis kiwis

j

jab jabs jabot jabbed jabber jabiru jabots
jabot jabots
jacal jacals
jack jacks hijack jackal jacked jacket hijacks jackals jackass jackdaw jackets jacking jackleg jackpot skyjack
jacks hijacks jackstay skyjacks
jade jaded jades jadedly jadeite
jaded jadedly
jag jags jaggy jagged jaguar
jail jails jailed jailer jailor jailers jailing jailors
jake jakes
jalap jalaps jalapin
jam jamb jams jambs jammed logjam pajama
jamb jambs jambeau jambone
jams jimjams logjams
japan japans japanned
jape japed japer japes
japer japeries
jar ajar jarl jars jarls jargon jarred
jarl jarls
jato jatos
jaunt jaunts jaunty jaunted jauntier jauntily jaunting
jaw jaws jawed jawing
jay jays deejay
jays deejays
jazz jazzy jazzed jazzier jazzily jazzing jazzman jazzmen
jean jeans
jebel jebels
jeep jeeps jeepers
jeer jeers jeered jeerer jeering
jell jells jelly jelled jellaba jellied jellies jellify jelling
jelly jellying
jerk jerks jerky jerked jerkin jerkier jerkily jerking jerkins
jess jesse jesses
jesse jesses
jest jests jested jester jesters jesting majesty
jet jete jets jetes jetty fanjet inkjet jetsam jetted ramjet

jets jetsam fanjets ramjets
jetty jettying
jewel jewels bejewel jeweled jeweler bejewels jewelers jeweling
jib jibe jibs jibed jiber jibes jibbed jibber jibers jibing
jibe jibed jiber jibes jibers
jiber jibers
jiff jiffy jiffies
jig jigs jigged jigger jiggle jiggly jigsaw
jigs jigsaw jigsaws
jihad jihads
jilt jilts jilted jilting
jimmy jimmying
jingo jingoism jingoist
jink jinks hijinks
jinn jinni jinns
jinx jinxes
jive jived jives
jo job joe jog jot joy dojo jobs jock joes joey jogs john join joke joky jolt josh joss jota jots jowl joys mojo banjo bijou dojos enjoy fjord jocko jocks joeys johns joins joint joist joked joker jokes jokey jolly jolts jolty jones jorum jotas joule joust jowls jowly major mojos
job jobs jobbed jobber
jock jocko jocks jockey jockeys
joe joes joey joeys
joes banjoes
joey joeys
jog jogs jogged jogger joggle
john johns johnny
join joins joint adjoin enjoin joined joiner joints rejoin adjoins conjoin disjoin enjoins joinder joiners joinery joining jointed jointly rejoins subjoin
joins adjoins conjoins disjoins subjoins
joint joints jointed conjoint disjoint jointure
joist joists banjoist
joke joked joker jokes jokey jokers
joker jokers
jokes jokester
jolly jollying
jolt jolts jolty jolted joltier jolting

jorum jorums
josh joshed josher joshes joshers joshing
joss josses
jot jota jots jotas jotted
jota jotas
joule joules
jour adjourn journal journey sojourn
joust jousts jousted jousting
jowl jowls jowly
joy joys enjoy enjoys joyful joyous
joys enjoys
judge judged judger judges adjudge judgers adjudged adjudges forjudge misjudge prejudge
judo judoka judokas
jug juga jugs ajuga jugal jugum ajugas jugate jugful jugged juggle jugums
juga ajuga jugal ajugas jugate
jugal conjugal
jugum jugums
juice juiced juices verjuice
juju jujus jujube jujubes
juke juked jukes jukebox
julep juleps
jumbo jumbos
jump jumps jumpy jumped jumper jumpers jumpier jumpily jumping
junco juncos
junk junks junky junked junker junket junkie junkers junkets junkier junkies junking junkman junkmen
junky junkyard
junto juntos
jupon jupons
jura jural jurat jurats jurally
jural jurally
jurat jurats
jurel jurels
juror jurors conjuror nonjuror
jury injury perjury
jus just jujus justs adjust justle unjust
just justs adjust justle unjust adjusts justice justify justled justles
justs adjusts
jut jute juts jutes jutted
jute jutes

k

ka kab kaf kal kas kat kabs kadi kafs kail kaka kaki kale kame kami kana kaon kaph kart kava kayo okay pika skat weka eskar hooka kabab kabob kafir kakas kakis kalif kames kanas kanji kaons kaphs kapok kappa kaput karat karma karoo karst karts kasha kauri kavas kayak kayos kazoo okapi okays parka pikas polka punka skald skate skats tanka ukase vodka wekas

kab kabs kabab kabob kababs kabala kabobs

kabab kababs

kabob kabobs

kaf kafs kafir kafirs kaftan

kafir kafirs

kaka kakas kakapo kakapos

kaki kakis

kal kale kalif skald alkali jackal kalifs kaliph kalmia kalong kalpak kalpis skalds

kale kalends

kalif kalifs

kame kames

kana kanas

kanji kanjis

kaon kaons

kaph kaphs

kapok kapoks

kappa kappas

karat karate karats

karma karmas

karoo karoos buckaroo

karst karsts

kart karts

kas kakas kasha pikas ukase wekas hookas kasbah kasher parkas polkas punkas tankas ukases vodkas

kat skat skate skats kation skated skater skates

kava kavas

kayak kayaks kayaker kayakers

kayo kayos kayoed kayoing

kazoo kazoos

kebab kebabs

kebob kebobs

keck kecks kecked kecking

kedge kedged kedges kedgeree

keef keefs

keek keeks keeked keeking

keel keels keeled keeling keelson

keels keelsons

keen keens keened keenly keening nankeen

keens nankeens

keep keeps keeper upkeep keepers keeping upkeeps

keeps keepsake

keet keets skeet skeets

keets skeets

kef kefs kefir kefirs

kefir kefirs

keg kegs skeg skegs kegler muskeg

kegs skegs muskegs

kelp kelps kelpy skelp kelpie skelps kelpies skelped

kelps skelps

ken keno kens kenaf kench kendo kenos liken oaken taken token waken woken awaken broken darken harken kenafs kenned kennel kraken likens shaken sicken silken spoken tokens wakens weaken

kenaf kenafs

kench kenches

keno kenos kenosis

kens likens tokens wakens awakens darkens dickens harkens krakens sickens weakens

kepi kepis

kept skeptic

kerb kerbs

kerf kerfs kerfed kerfing

kern kerns kerned kernel kernels kerning

ketch sketch ketches ketchup sketchy ketchups sketched sketcher sketches

kevel kevels

key keys hokey jokey keyed chokey dickey dinkey donkey hickey hockey hookey jockey keying keyway lackey mickey monkey rickey turkey

keyed cockeyed jockeyed monkeyed

keys donkeys hickeys jockeys lackeys monkeys pinkeys rickeys turkeys

khadi khadis

khaki khakis

khan khans khanate

khet kheth

kiang kiangs

kibe kibei kibes kibeis

kibei kibeis

kick kicks kicky kicked kicker kickup kickers kickier kicking kickoff

kicks kickshaw

kid kids skid kiddy skids aikido kidded kidder kiddie kidnap kidney skiddy

kiddy skiddy

kids skids kidskin

kier kiers ickier inkier pokier boskier bulkier cockier corkier dinkier duckier duskier flakier funkier gawkier hulkier huskier jerkier junkier kickier kinkier kookier lankier leakier luckier milkier muckier murkier muskier pawkier perkier peskier pickier porkier punkier quakier riskier rockier shakier silkier smokier snakier sulkier tackier wackier yuckier

kif kifs skiff skiffs

kilim kilims

kill kills skill killed killer killie skills killdee killers killick killies killing killjoy killock skilled skillet

kills skills

kiln kilns

kilo kilos kilobar kiloton

kilt kilts kilted kilter kilters kilting

kin akin kina kind kine king kink kino skin eking kinds kings kinin kinks kinky kinos skink skins asking baking biking bikini bodkin buskin caking catkin coking diking dyking faking firkin gaskin hiking hoking inking irking jerkin joking juking kinder kindle kindly kingly kinked liking making malkin miking nankin napkin nuking piking pipkin poking puking raking siskin skinks skinny taking toking unkind viking waking welkin yoking

kind kinds kinder kindle kindly unkind kindest kindled kindler kindles kindred mankind

kine kinesic kinetic kinetin

king eking kings asking baking biking caking coking diking dyking faking hiking hoking inking irking joking kingly liking making miking nuking piking poking puking raking taking toking viking waking yoking awaking backing balking banking barking basking bilking bonking booking braking bucking bulking bunking burking carking choking cocking cooking corking decking dirking docking ducking erlking evoking finking flaking forking funking gawking hacking hanking harking hawking hocking honking hooking hulking husking jacking jerking junking kecking keeking kicking kingcup kingdom kinglet kingpin kinking lacking larking leaking licking linking locking looking lucking lurking marking masking milking mocking mucking necking nicking nocking oinking packing parking peaking pecking peeking perking picking pinking quaking racking ranking recking reeking risking rocking rooking rucking sacking seeking shaking sicking sinking slaking smoking snaking soaking socking spiking spoking staking stoking sucking sulking tacking talking tanking tasking ticking tucking vikings walking winking working yacking yakking yanking yolking yukking zonking

kings backings bookings erlkings kingship lickings markings packings pickings rankings workings

kink kinks kinky skink kinked skinks kinkier kinking

kinks skinks

kino kinos

kiosk kiosks

kip kips skip skips kipper

kips skips

kir kirk fakir skirl skirr skirt fakirs kirsch kirtle skirls skirrs skirts

kiss kissy kissed kisser kisses kissers kissing

kist kists

kit kite kith kits skit kited kiter kites kithe kitty skits kiters kithed kithes kiting kitsch kitten kittle weskit

kite kited kiter kites kiters

kiter kiters

kith kithe kithed kithes kithing

kithe kithed kithes

kits skits kitsch weskits

kiva kivas

kiwi kiwis

klutz klutzy

knack knacks knacker nicknack

knap knaps knapped

knaps knapsack

knar knars knarred

knave knaves knavery

knead kneads kneaded kneader kneaders kneading

knee kneed kneel knees kneels kneecap kneeing kneeled kneeler kneepad kneepan

kneel kneels kneeled kneeler kneelers kneeling

knell knells knelled knelling

knife knifed penknife

knit knits knitted knitter

knob knobs knobby knobbed

knock knocks knocked knocker knockers knocking knockoff knockout

knoll knolls knolled knolling

knop knops

knot knots knotty bowknot knotted topknot

knots bowknots topknots

knout knouts knouted knouting

know known knows knower knowers knowing unknown

known unknowns

knur knurl knurs knurls knurly knurled

knurl knurls knurly knurled knurlier knurling

koa koan koas koala koans skoal koalas skoals

koala koalas

koan koans

kob kobo kobs kobos kobold

kobo kobold kobolds

koel koels

kohl kohls

koine koines

kola kolas

kolo kolos

kook kooks kooky kookie kookier

kop koph kops kophs koppa kopeck koppas

koph kophs

kor korat korun korats koruna

korun koruna korunas

kos makos arkose bunkos geckos kosher pinkos shakos sickos wackos

kraal kraals

kraft krafts

krait kraits

kraut krauts

kreep kreeps

krone kroner

kudu kudus

kudzu kudzus

kulak kulaks

kurta kurtas

kvas kvass kvasses

kvass kvasses

kyack kyacks

kyak kyaks

kyat kyats

la ala lab lac lad lag lam lap lar law lax lay alar alas blab blah blat clad clam clan clap claw clay cola fila flab flag flak flam flan flap flat flaw flax flay gala glad hula hyla kola labs lace lack lacy lade lads lady lags laic laid lain lair lake lakh laky lama lamb lame lamp lams land lane lank laps lard lark lash lass last late lath laud lava lave lawn laws lays laze lazy mola olla plan plat play slab slag slam slap slat slay tola alack alamo alarm alary alate allay alula atlas balas belay blabs black blade blahs blain blame bland blank blare blast blats blaze bolas bulla bylaw calla cella chela clack claim clamp clams clang clank clans claps clapt claro clary clash clasp class clave claws clays colas delay eclat eland elate fella filar flabs flack flags flail flair flake flaks flaky flame flams flank flans flaps flare flash flask flats flaws flaxy flays galas galax glade glair gland glans glare glary glass glaze hulas hylas inlay jalap koala kolas kulak label labia labor labra laced laces lacks laded laden lades ladle lagan lager laigh laird lairs laity laker lakes lakhs lamas lambs lamed lamer lames lamia lamps lanai lance lands lanes lanky lapel lapin lapse larch lards lardy lares large largo larks larky larva laser lasso lasts latch lated later latex lathe laths lathy latke lauds laugh laved laver laves lawns lawny laxly layer layup lazar lazed lazes lilac llama llano malar molal molar molas moola nyala ollas pepla phyla pilaf pilau place plage plaid plain plait plane plank plans plant plash plate plats platy playa plays plaza polar relax relay salad selah slabs slack slags slain slake slams slang slant slaps slash slate slats slaty slave slays solan solar splat splay tolas uhlan uvula velar villa viola volar xylan

lab blab flab labs slab blabs flabs label labia labor labra slabs flabby labara labels labial labile labium labors labour labret labrum

label labels labeled labeler flabella labelers labeling labelled labeller

labia labial labiate labially labiates

labor labors belabor labored laborer belabors laborers laboring

labs blabs flabs slabs

lac lace lack lacy alack black clack flack glace laced laces lacks lilac place slack blacks clacks glaces glacis laches lacier lacing lacked lackey lactic lacuna lilacs palace placed placer places placet placid slacks solace unlace

lace laced laces place glaces palace placed placer places placet solace unlace emplace palaces placebo placers placets replace solaces unlaced unlaces

laced placed unlaced emplaced replaced

laces glaces places palaces solaces unlaces emplaces replaces

lack alack black clack flack lacks slack blacks clacks lacked lackey slacks blacked blacken blacker blackly clacked lackeys lacking placket slacked slacken slacker slackly

lacks blacks clacks slacks

lacy fallacy prelacy

lad clad glad lade lads lady blade glade laded laden lades ladle salad ballad bladed blades gelada glades ladder laddie ladies lading ladled ladles malady milady salads unclad

lade blade glade laded laden lades bladed blades glades roulade

laded bladed

lades blades glades roulades

ladle ladled ladles ladleful

lads salads ballads

lady malady milady ladybug

lag flag lags slag flags lagan lager plage slags flagon lagans lagged lagger lagoon pelage plagal plages plague silage

lagan lagans

lager villager

lags flags slags

laic laical

laid plaid inlaid plaids relaid mislaid waylaid

lain blain plain slain blains plains plaint delaine explain plainer plainly plaints villain

lair flair glair laird lairs eclair flairs glairs glairy lairds eclairs

laird lairds

lairs flairs glairs eclairs

lake flake laker lakes slake flaked flakes lakers slaked slakes

laker lakers

lakes flakes slakes

lakh lakhs

laky flaky

lam clam flam lama lamb lame lamp lams slam alamo blame clamp clams flame flams lamas lambs lamed lamer lames lamia lamps llama slams aflame alamos bedlam blamed blames calami clammy clamor clamps flamed flamen flames lambda lamely lament lamest lamina laming lammed lampas llamas salami

lama lamas llama llamas clamant

lamas llamas lamasery

lamb lambs lambda clamber lambast lambdas lambent lambert lambkin

lambs lambskin

lame blame flame lamed lamer lames aflame blamed blames flamed flamen flames lamely lament lamest flamens inflame lamella laments

lamed blamed flamed inflamed

lamer inflamer

lames blames flames lamest inflames

lamp clamp lamps clamps lampas clamped lampoon lamprey sunlamp

lamps clamps sunlamps

lams clams flams slams

lanai lanais

lance glance lanced lancer lances lancet balance glanced glances lancers lancets valance balanced balancer balances lancelet parlance valances

land bland eland gland lands elands glands inland island landau landed lander upland blandly calando garland islands landaus landers landing lowland midland outland slander uplands wetland

lands elands glands islands uplands badlands garlands landside landslip landsman landsmen lowlands midlands outlands

lane lanes plane planed planer planes planet biplane deplane planers planets

lanes planes biplanes deplanes

lank blank clank flank lanky plank blanks clanks flanks lankly planks blanked blanket blankly clanked flanked flanker lankier lankily planked

lap clap flap laps slap claps clapt flaps jalap lapel lapin lapse slaps burlap dewlap elapse jalaps lapels lapful lapins lapped lappet lapsed lapses

lapel lapels

lapin lapins jalapin

laps claps flaps lapse slaps elapse jalaps lapsed lapses burlaps dewlaps elapsed elapses lapsing relapse

lapse elapse lapsed lapses elapsed elapses relapse collapse prolapse relapsed relapses

lar alar lard lark alarm alary blare claro clary filar flare glare glary larch lards lardy lares large largo larks larky larva malar molar mylar polar solar velar volar alarms ashlar blared blares cellar claret claros collar dollar flared flares glared glares larded larder lardon larger largos lariat larked larker larrup larvae larval larvas larynx malars medlar molars ocular pillar poplar salary scalar stylar uvular

larch larches

lard lards lardy larded larder lardon bollard collard dullard foulard larders lardier larding lardons lardoon mallard pollard poulard

lards bollards collards dullards foulards mallards pollards poulards

lares blares flares glares declares

large larger enlarge largely largess largest enlarged enlarger enlarges

largo largos

lark larks larky larked larker larking larkish malarky skylark

larks larkspur skylarks

larky malarky

larva larvae larval larvas

laser lasers

lash clash flash plash slash calash flashy lashed lasher lashes splash unlash clashed clashes eyelash flashed flasher flashes goulash lashers lashing plashed plashes slashed slasher slashes splashy

lass class glass lasso classy glassy lasses lassie lassos classed classes classic classis cutlass glassed glasses lassies lassoed lassoer lassoes

lasso lassos lassoed lassoer lassoes lassoers lassoing

last blast lasts blasts lasted laster lastly oblast ballast blasted blastie clastic elastic elastin lastage lasting oblasts outlast plastic plastid

lasts blasts oblasts outlasts

latch latched latches latchet unlatch latchets latching latchkey potlatch

late alate elate lated later latex plate slate alated delate dilate elated elater elates lateen lately latent latest malate oblate palate plated platen plater plates relate slated slater slates velate adulate belated bullate collate deflate delated delates dilated elaters emulate galatea inflate isolate lateens latency

lateral latexes malates oblates ovulate oxalate palates plateau platens prelate prolate related relates slaters sublate ululate violate

lated alated elated plated slated belated delated dilated related adulated collated deflated elatedly emulated inflated isolated ovulated sublated ululated violated

later elater plater slater elaters lateral slaters idolater inflater laterals

latex latexes

lath lathe laths lathy lathed lather lathes blather calathi lathers lathery lathier lathing slather

lathe lathed lather lathes blather lathers lathery slather blathers flathead lathered slathers

latke latkes

laud lauds lauded applaud lauding plaudit

lauds applauds

laugh laughs laughed laugher laughers laughing laughter

lava lavabo lavage baklava

lave clave laved laver laves slave claves lavers slaved slaver slaves enclave enslave klavern palaver slavers slavery

laved slaved enslaved

laver lavers slaver klavern palaver slavers slavery klaverns palavers

laves claves slaves enclaves enslaves

law claw flaw lawn laws bylaw claws flaws lawns lawny bylaws clawed flawed lawful lawman lawmen lawyer outlaw

lawn lawns lawny

laws claws flaws bylaws lawsuit outlaws

lax flax flaxy galax laxly relax flaxen flaxes galaxy laxity smilax

lay clay flay lays play slay allay belay clays delay flays inlay layer layup playa plays relay slays splay allays belays clayey delays flayed inlays layers laying layman laymen layoff layout layups mislay outlay parlay playas played player relays replay slayed slayer splays waylay

layer layers player slayer players slayers waylayer

lays clays flays plays slays allays belays delays inlays relays splays mislays outlays parlays replays waylays

layup layups

lazar lazars

laze blaze glaze lazed lazes ablaze blazed blazer blazes glazed glazes blazers emblaze

lazed blazed glazed emblazed

lazes blazes glazes emblazes

lea flea lead leaf leak leal lean leap leas plea bleak blear bleat clean clear cleat fleam fleas galea gleam glean ileac leach leads leady leafs leafy leaks leaky leans leant leaps learn lease leash least leave leavy palea plead pleas pleat agleam azalea bleach blears bleary bleats cleans clears cleats cleave fleams galeae gleams gleans leachy leaded leaden leader leafed league leaked leaker leally leaned leaner leaped leaper learns learnt leased leaser leases leaved leaven leaves paleae pleach pleads please pleats poleax sleave sleaze sleazo sleazy

leach bleach leachy pleach leached leacher leaches bleached bleacher bleaches leachers leaching pleached pleaches

lead leads leady plead leaded leaden leader pleads implead leaders leadier leading leadoff mislead pleaded

leads pleads leadsman leadsmen misleads

leaf leafs leafy leafed flyleaf leafage leafier leafing leaflet

leak bleak leaks leaky leaked leaker bleaker bleakly leakage leakers leakier leaking

leal leally

lean clean glean leans leant cleans gleans leaned leaner cleaned cleaner cleanly cleanse cleanup gleaned gleaner leaners leanest leaning unclean

leans cleans gleans cleanse cleansed cleanser cleanses

leap leaps leaped leaper leapers leaping

learn learns learnt learned learner unlearn learners learning unlearns

leas fleas lease leash least pleas leased leaser leases please azaleas leasers leashed leashes leasing pleased pleases release unleash

lease leased leaser leases please leasers pleased pleases release released releases sublease unleased

leash leashed leashes unleash leashing

leave cleave leaved leaven leaves sleave cleaved cleaver cleaves leavens sleaves cleavers leavened

lech leched lecher leches lechers lechery leching

led bled fled pled sled ailed baled deled doled filed glede haled holed idled ledge ledgy obled ogled oiled paled piled poled puled riled ruled sleds soled tiled waled wiled addled aisled ambled angled bailed balled bawled belled billed birled boiled bowled bugled bulled burled cabled called ceiled celled coaled coiled cooled cowled culled curled cycled dialed dirled dueled dulled exiled fabled failed felled filled fledge foaled foiled fooled fouled fowled fueled furled gabled galled gelled gilled gledes gulled hailed hauled healed heeled hilled howled hulled hurled jailed jelled keeled killed ladled ledger ledges lolled lulled mailed marled mauled milled misled moiled mulled nailed palled pealed peeled pilled pledge polled pooled pulled purled railed reeled rifled roiled rolled sailed scaled sealed sidled sledge smiled soiled staled styled tabled tailed teledu tholed tilled titled toiled tolled tooled vailed veiled wailed walled whaled whiled willed yawled yelled yowled

ledge   fledge ledger ledges pledge sledge fledged fledges ledgers pledged pledger pledges pledget sledged sledges pledgers pledgets

lee   alee flee glee leek leer lees leet bleed bleep cleek fleer flees fleet gleed glees gleet leech leeks leers leery leets melee sleek sleep sleet asleep baleen bleeds bleeps cleeks coulee fleece fleecy fleers fleets gleets leered leeway mallee melees sleeps sleepy sleets sleety sleeve spleen

leech   leeched leeches leeching

leek   cleek leeks sleek cleeks sleeker

leeks   cleeks

leer   fleer leers leery fleers leered leerier leering

leers   fleers

lees   flees glees melees mallees

leet   fleet gleet leets sleet fleets gleets sleets sleety fleetly sleeted

leets   fleets gleets sleets

left   cleft lefty clefts lefties leftish leftist

leg   legs elegy legal leggy legit allege dogleg elegit legacy legate legato legend legged legion legist legman legmen legume midleg phlegm proleg

legal   illegal legally legalese legalism legalist legality legalize

legit   elegit elegits

legs   doglegs prolegs

lehua   lehuas

lei   leis ileia kleig oleic olein pilei nuclei oleins poleis sleigh

leis   poleis leister leisure

lek   leks lekvar

leman   lemans fugleman nobleman rifleman whaleman

lemma   lemmas dilemma lemmata dilemmas

lemon   lemons lemony lemonade

lemur   lemurs

lend   blend lends blende blends lender blended blender calends kalends lenders lending slender

lends   blends calends kalends

lens   glens flense lenses flensed flenses pollens woolens

lent   blent lento lenten lentic lentil plenty relent silent talent aplenty lentigo lentils opulent polenta relents talents violent

leone   leones

leper   lepers

lept   slept lepton yclept

less   bless lessee lessen lesser lesson lessor unless ageless aimless airless armless artless aweless bedless blessed braless budless earless endless eyeless finless fogless godless gutless hapless hipless hitless hueless iceless idlesse jobless joyless lawless lessees lessens lessons lessors lidless lipless manless napless oarless rayless ribless rimless sapless sexless sinless sunless toeless topless useless wigless witless

lest   blest ablest halest idlest molest palest vilest celesta celeste coolest dullest fullest molests stalest tallest

let   lets aglet culet filet inlet islet letch letup owlet valet aglets amulet anklet armlet auklet ballet billet bullet camlet chalet culets cullet cutlet daleth delete eaglet eyelet filets fillet fletch gallet giblet gimlet goblet goglet gullet hamlet haslet inlets islets lethal letter letups mallet millet muleta mullet nutlet omelet outlet owlets pallet pellet piglet pullet reglet runlet sallet samlet stylet sublet tablet toilet valets varlet violet wallet

letch   fletch letched letches fletcher fletches letching

lets   aglets culets filets inlets islets owlets valets amulets anklets auklets ballets billets bullets camlets chalets cullets cutlets eaglets eyelets fillets gallets giblets gimlets goblets goglets gullets hamlets mallets millets mullets omelets outlets pallets pellets piglets pullets reglets runlets sallets samlets stylets sublets tablets toilets varlets violets wallets

letup   letups

leu   ileum ileus coleus pileus pleura sleuth

lev   leva levy levee level lever levin clever clevis eleven elevon levant leveed levees levels levers levied levies levity

leva   levant elevate levants levator

levee   leveed levees leveeing

level   levels leveled leveler levelers leveling levelled

lever   clever levers levered leveret cleverer cleverly leverage leverets levering

levy   levying

lewd   lewdly

li   lid lie lip lit alif alit blip clip deli flip flit glib glim ilia liar lice lick lids lied lief lien lies lieu life lift like lilt lily limb lime limn limo limp limy line ling link linn lint liny lion lips lira lire lisp list live olio puli slid slim slip slit tali alias alibi alien alifs align alike aline alive belie blimp blind blink blips bliss blitz calix chili cilia click cliff climb clime cline cling clink clips colic colin cylix delis elide elite felid flick flied flier flies fling flint flips flirt flits folia folio gelid glibs glide glint glitz helix iliac ilium kalif kilim kylix liane liars libel libra licht licit licks liege liens lifer lifts ligan light liked liken liker likes lilac lilts limbo limbs limed limen limes limey limit limns limos limps lined linen liner lines linga lingo lings linin links linns lints linty lions lipid liras lisle lisps lists liter lithe litho litre lived liven liver lives livid livre melic oboli olios olive oxlip plica plied plier plink polis pulik pulis relic slice slick slide slime slimy sling slink slips slits solid split styli telic tulip valid

liane   lianes

liar   liars ciliary goliard

libel   libels libeled libeler libelers libeling libelled libelous

libra   library librate librated librates

lice   slice cilice malice police sliced slicer slices splice calices chalice cylices helices license malices policed polices slicers spliced splicer splices

licht   lichts

licit   elicit elicits illicit licitly solicit elicited explicit felicity implicit solicits

lick   click flick licks slick clicks flicks licked slicks clicked clicker colicky cowlick flicked flicker killick licking niblick rollick slicker

licks   clicks flicks slicks cowlicks killicks niblicks rollicks

lid   lids slid elide felid gelid glide slide solid valid bolide elided elides eyelid felids glided glider glides halide lidded pallid slider slides solids stolid

lids   felids solids eyelids

lie   lied lief lien lies lieu alien belie flied flier flies liege liens plied plier aliens allied allies bailie belied belief belies client collie coolie fliers girlie goalie

holier holies inlier killie lieder lieges lierne lilied lilies mealie milieu oilier pliers relied relief relies uglier wilier

lied flied plied allied belied lieder lilied relied applied bellied bullied collied cullied dallied implied jellied jollied rallied replied sallied sullied tallied

lief belief relief beliefs

liege lieges

lien alien liens aliens client alienor clients salient

liens aliens

lies flies allies belies holies lilies relies applies bailies bellies billies bullies chilies collies coolies cullies dailies dallies dillies doilies dollies doolies fellies fillies follies girlies goalies gullies holiest hollies implies jellies jollies killies lollies mollies oiliest rallies replies sallies sillies sullies tallies ugliest wiliest willies

lieu milieu milieus purlieu

life lifer lifers lowlife midlife

lifer lifers

lift lifts lifted lifter uplift airlift lifters lifting liftoff uplifts

lifts airlifts

ligan ligans hooligan mulligan

light alight blight flight lights plight slight alights blights delight lighted alighted blighted daylight delights gaslight lightens lighters lightest lighting lightish penlight plighted skylight slighted slightly sunlight twilight

like alike liked liken liker likes likely likens unlike armlike boxlike catlike dislike godlike henlike hiplike hoelike hoglike kidlike kylikes likened manlike netlike owllike warlike weblike

liked disliked

liken likens likened likeness likening

likes dislikes

lilac lilacs

lilt lilts lilted lilting

lily holily uglily jollily

limb climb limbo limbs climbs limbed limber limbic limbos limbus climbed climber limbate

limbo limbos

limbs climbs

lime clime limed limen limes limey slime blimey climes limeys slimed slimes aliment limeade millime sublime

limed slimed sublimed

limen aliment aliments

limes climes slimes millimes sublimes

limey blimey limeys

limit limits delimit limited delimits limiting

limn limns limner limners

limo limos alimony

limp blimp limps blimps limped limper limpet limpid limply glimpse limpers limpest limpets limping limpkin

limps blimps glimpsed glimpses

limy slimy

line aline cline lined linen liner lines alined alines byline clines feline lineal linear linens liners lineup moline saline spline airline aniline beeline bowline bylines carline choline decline felines hemline hyaline incline lineage lineate lineman linemen lineups malines marline midline milline opaline outline praline ratline recline skyline splined splines unlined

lined alined splined unlined declined inclined outlined reclined

linen linens

liner liners airliner eyeliner incliner jetliner milliner outliner recliner

lines alines clines bylines felines malines airlines anilines beelines bowlines carlines declines hemlines holiness inclines linesman linesmen midlines millines oiliness opalines outlines pralines ratlines reclines skylines ugliness wiliness

ling cling fling linga lingo lings sling ailing baling clings doling filing flings haling holing idling lingam lingas linger lingua ogling oiling paling piling poling puling riling ruling slings soling tiling waling wiling addling ambling angling bailing balling bawling belling billing birling boiling bowling bugling bulling burling cabling calling ceiling clinger coaling codling coiling cooling cowling culling curling cycling darling dealing dialing dirling dueling dulling exiling fabling failing falling fatling feeling felling filings filling foaling foiling fooling fouling fowling fueling furling galling gelling godling gosling gulling hailing hauling healing heeling hilling howling hulling hurling inkling jailing jelling keeling killing ladling lingams lingers lingoes linguae lingual lolling lulling mailing mauling milling moiling mulling nailing palling pealing peeling pilings pilling polling pooling pulling purling railing reeling rifling rilling roiling rolling rulings sailing sapling scaling sealing selling sibling sidling smiling soiling staling styling tabling tailing telling tholing tilling titling toiling tolling tooling vailing veiling wailing walling whaling whiling willing yawling yelling yowling

linga lingam lingas lingams

lings clings flings slings billings callings ceilings darlings dealings failings fatlings feelings fillings goslings inklings killings mailings saplings siblings

linin lining alining

link blink clink links plink slink blinks clinks linked linker linkup plinks slinks slinky blinked blinker clinked clinker linkage linkboy linking linkman linkmen linkups plinked slinked

links blinks clinks plinks slinks

linn linns linnet linnets

lint flint glint lints linty flints flinty glints linted lintel plinth splint blintze glinted lintels lintier linting splints

lints flints glints

linty flinty

lion lions talion billion bullion hellion jillion lioness lionize million mullion pillion talions zillion

lions talions billions bullions hellions jillions millions mullions pillions zillions

lip blip clip flip lips slip blips clips flips lipid oxlip slips tulip aliped caliph fillip kaliph lipids lipoma lipped oxlips slippy tulips

lipid lipids

lips blips clips flips slips oxlips tulips eclipse ellipse fillips

lira liras

lis lisp list bliss delis lisle lisps lists polis pulis cullis enlist holism holist lisles lisped lisper listed listel listen lister mulish owlish oxalis palish polish relish valise

lisle lisles

lisp lisps lisped lisper lispers lisping

list lists enlist holist listed listel listen lister blister cellist cyclist dualist duelist enlists glisten holists listens listers listing oculist realist stylist titlist violist

lists cellists cyclists dualists duelists oculists realists stylists violists

lit alit flit slit blitz elite flits glitz liter lithe litho litre slits split blithe elites eolith glitch glitzy halite iolite litany litchi lither lithia lithic lithos litmus litres litter little oolite polite polity splits

liter literal literacy literary literate literati

lithe blithe lither blithely slithers

litho lithos lithoid

litre litres

live alive lived liven liver lives olive lively livens livers livery olives relive sliver deliver enliven livened livener outlive relived relives slivers

lived relived outlived

liven livens enliven livened livener enlivens livening

liver livers livery sliver deliver delivers delivery liveried liveries slivered

lives olives relives outlives

livid lividity

livre livres

llama llamas

llano llanos

lo lob log loo lop los lot low lox aloe alow blob bloc blot blow bolo clod clog clot cloy floc floe flog flop flow glob glop glow halo kilo kolo load loaf loam loan lobe lobo lobs loch loci lock loco lode loft loge logo logs logy loin loll lone long look loom loon loop loos loot lope lops lord lore lorn lory lose loss lost lota loth lots loud lout love lows milo plod plop plot plow ploy polo silo slob sloe slog slop slot slow solo aglow allot allow alloy aloes aloft aloha alone along aloof aloud below bloat blobs block blocs bloke blond blood bloom blots blown blows blowy bolos cello cloak clock clods clogs clomb clomp clone clops close cloth clots cloud clout clove clown cloys cloze colon color dolor eloin elope felon float flock flocs floes flogs flood floor flops flora floss flour flout flown flows galop gloat globe globs gloom glops glory gloss glove glows gloze hallo hello hollo hullo igloo kilos kolos loach loads loafs loams loamy loans loath lobar lobby lobed lobes lobos local locks locos locus loden lodes lodge loess lofts lofty loges logic logos loins lolls lolly loner longe longs looby looed looie looks looms loons loony loops loopy loose loots loped loper lopes loppy lords lores loris lorry losel loser loses lotah lotas lotto lotus lough louis louse lousy louts loved lover loves lowed lower lowly loyal melon nylon orlop ovolo phlox pilot plods plops plots plows ploys polos pylon salon silos slobs sloes slogs sloop slope slops slosh sloth slots slows solos talon valor xylol zloty

loach loaches

load loads loaded loader reload unload carload loaders loading payload reloads unloads

loads reloads unloads carloads payloads

loaf loafs loafed loafer loafers loafing

loam loams loamy loamed loamier loaming

loan loans loaned loaner loaners loaning

loath loathe loathed loathes loathly loathful loathing

lob blob glob lobe lobo lobs slob blobs globe globs lobar lobby lobed lobes lobos slobs global globed globes globin lobate lobbed lobule

lobar kilobar kilobars

lobby lobbying lobbyist

lobe globe lobed lobes globed globes

lobed globed

lobes globes

lobo lobos globoid

lobs blobs globs slobs lobster

local locale locals locales locally localism locality localize

loch cloche lochia cloches

lock block clock flock locks blocks blocky clocks flocks locked locker locket lockup unlock armlock blocked blocker bullock clocked elflock fetlock flocked hemlock hillock killock lockbox lockers lockets locking lockjaw locknut lockout lockups oarlock padlock pollock rowlock schlock unlocks warlock wedlock

locks blocks clocks flocks unlocks armlocks bullocks elflocks fetlocks gunlocks hemlocks hillocks killocks oarlocks padlocks pollocks rowlocks schlocks warlocks

loco locos

locus locust locusts

lode loden lodes explode implode

lodes explodes implodes lodestar

lodge lodged lodger lodges lodgers dislodge

loft aloft lofts lofty lofted hayloft loftier loftily lofting

lofts haylofts

log clog flog loge logo logs logy slog clogs flogs loges logic logos slogs analog cloggy eulogy logged logger loggia loggie logics logier logjam logman oology putlog slogan unclog

loge loges halogen

logic logics illogic logical dialogic geologic logician zoologic

logo logos

logs clogs flogs slogs analogs putlogs unclogs

logy eulogy oology analogy apology biology ecology geology neology orology trilogy urology zoology

loin eloin loins eloins purloin sirloin soloing

loins eloins purloins sirloins

loll lolls lolly lolled loller lollop lollers lollies lolling lollops

lolly lollygag lollypop

lone alone clone loner cloned clones lonely loners abalone baloney boloney colonel cyclone taloned

loner loners

long along longe longs belong kalong longan longed longer longes longly oblong oolong belongs daylong endlong erelong furlong kalongs longans longbow longest longing longish oblongs oolongs prolong

longe longed longer longes belonged

longs belongs kalongs oblongs furlongs longspur prolongs

loo look loom loon loop loos loot aloof blood bloom flood floor gloom igloo looby looed looie looks looms loons loony loops loopy loose loots sloop abloom bloods bloody blooms bloomy floods flooey floors floozy galoot glooms gloomy halloo igloos loofah looies looing looked looker loomed looped looper loosed loosen looser looses looted looter saloon saloop sloops

looie looies

look looks looked looker lookers looking lookout outlook palooka

looks outlooks

loom bloom gloom looms abloom blooms bloomy glooms gloomy loomed bloomed bloomer gloomed looming

looms blooms glooms

loon loons loony saloon balloon galloon loonier saloons

loons saloons balloons galloons

loop loops loopy sloop looped looper saloop sloops blooper loopers looping saloops

loops sloops saloops

loos loose igloos loosed loosen looser looses halloos loosely loosens loosest loosing

loose loosed loosen looser looses loosened loosener

loot loots galoot looted looter galoots looters looting

loots galoots

lop flop glop lope lops plop slop clops elope flops galop glops loped loper lopes loppy orlop plops slope slops aslope collop dollop eloped eloper elopes floppy gallop galops gloppy jalopy lollop lopers loping lopped lopper orlops sloped slopes sloppy wallop

lope elope loped loper lopes slope aslope eloped eloper elopes lopers sloped slopes elopers

loped eloped sloped galloped walloped

loper eloper lopers galloper

lopes elopes slopes

loppy floppy gloppy sloppy

lops clops flops glops plops slops galops orlops collops dollops gallops lollops wallops

lord lords lorded lordly milord lording warlord

lords lordship warlords

lore lores floret galore colored deplore explore florets implore

lores deplores explores implores

loris colorist florists

lorn forlorn

lory glory calory pillory

los lose loss lost bolos close floss gloss kilos kolos losel loser loses polos silos slosh solos cellos closed closer closes closet filose flossy galosh glossy hallos hellos hollos hullos losers losing losses peplos pilose sloshy volost xylose

lose close losel loser loses closed closer closes closet filose losers pilose xylose amylose closely closers closest closets enclose inclose

losel closely

loser closer losers closers

loses closes closest amyloses encloses incloses peploses

loss floss gloss flossy glossy losses blossom colossi flossed flosses glossae glossal glosses

lost volost volosts

lot blot clot lota loth lots plot slot allot blots cloth clots lotah lotas lotto lotus pilot plots sloth slots zloty allots ballot blotch blotto clothe cloths diglot harlot lotahs lotion lotted ocelot pelota pilots sloths zealot zlotys

lota lotah lotas lotahs pelota pelotas

lotah lotahs

lotas pelotas

loth cloth sloth clothe cloths sloths clothed clothes

lots blots clots plots slots allots pilots ballots diglots flotsam harlots ocelots zealots

lotto blotto

loud aloud cloud clouds cloudy louden louder loudly becloud clouded loudest loudish

lough clough loughs slough cloughs furlough

louse blouse bloused blouses delouse deloused delouses

lousy blousy jealousy

lout clout flout louts clouts flouts bailout clouted fallout flouted flouter loutish pullout sellout

louts clouts flouts bailouts fallouts pullouts sellouts

love clove glove loved lover loves cloven clover cloves gloved glover gloves lovely lovers plover sloven beloved clovers glovers lovebug loverly plovers unloved

loved gloved beloved unloved beloveds

lover clover glover lovers plover clovers pullover

loves cloves gloves lovesick

low alow blow flow glow lows plow slow aglow allow below blown blows blowy clown flown flows glows lowed lower lowly plows slows allows bellow billow blower blowsy blowup blowzy callow clowns fallow fellow flowed flower follow glowed glower hallow hollow inflow lowboy lowers lowery lowest lowing mallow mellow pillow plowed sallow slowed slower slowly tallow wallow willow yellow

lowed flowed glowed plowed slowed allowed bellowed billowed followed hallowed hollowed mellowed pillowed tallowed wallowed yellowed

lower blower flower glower lowers lowery slower blowers lowered deflower flowered floweret follower lowering yellower

lowly slowly hollowly mellowly

lows blows flows glows plows slows allows blowsy bellows billows fallows fellows follows gallows hallows hollows inflows mallows mellows pillows sallows tallows wallows willows yellows

lox phlox

loyal loyally loyalty disloyal loyalist

luau luaus

lube lubes

luce luces lucent lucern lucerns

lucid lucidly lucidity pellucid

luck cluck lucks lucky pluck clucks lucked plucks plucky clucked luckier luckily lucking plucked plucker potluck unlucky

lucks clucks plucks potlucks

lucky plucky unlucky

lues blues clues flues glues slues bluest values reglues unglues

luff bluff fluff luffa luffs sluff bluffs fluffs fluffy luffas luffed sluffs bluffed bluffer fluffed luffing sluffed

luffa luffas

luffs bluffs fluffs sluffs

lug glug luge lugs plug slug glugs kluge luged luges plugs slugs beluga deluge lugged lugger unplug

luge kluge luged luges deluge deluged deluges lugeing

luged deluged

luges deluges

lugs glugs plugs slugs unplugs

lull lulls lulled lullaby lulling

lulu lulus

lum alum glum lump plum slum alums clump filum flume hilum lumen lumps lumpy plumb plume plump plums slump slums velum alumna alumni amylum asylum clumps clumpy clumsy column flumes glumly illume lumbar lumber lumens lumina lummox lumped peplum phylum plumbs plumed plumes plumps slumps vellum volume

lumen lumens

lump clump lumps lumpy plump slump clumps clumpy lumped plumps slumps clumped galumph lumpier lumping lumpish plumped plumper plumply slumped

lumps clumps plumps slumps

lumpy clumpy

lunch lunched lunches luncheon lunching

lune lunes lunette

lung clung flung lunge lungi lungs slung lunged lunges lungis plunge lungers lunging plunged plunger plunges

lunge lunged lunges plunge plunged plungers

lungi lungis plunging

lunt blunt lunts blunts blunted bluntly

lunts blunts

lurch lurched lurches lurching

lure lured lures allure colure velure allured allures colures failure velures

lured allured

lures allures colures failures

lurid luridly

lurk lurks lurked lurking

lush blush flush plush slush lushes lushly slushy blushed blusher blushes flushed flusher flushes slushed slushes

lust lusts lusty lusted luster lustra lustre bluster cluster fluster lustful lustier lustily lusting lustral lustrum

lute elute flute luted lutes dilute eluted elutes fluted flutes gluten plutei salute solute volute diluted dilutes glutens gluteus pluteus pollute saluted saluter salutes solutes voluted volutes

luted eluted fluted diluted saluted voluted polluted

lutes elutes flutes dilutes salutes pollutes

lux flux luxe luxes afflux deluxe efflux fluxed fluxes hallux influx luxate luxury reflux

luxe luxes deluxe fluxed fluxes

luxes fluxes affluxes effluxes refluxes

lye lyes flyer slyer flyers slyest

lyes slyest

lying   flying plying allying belying applying bellying bullying collying cullying
dallying implying jellying jollying outlying rallying replying sallying sullying
tallying
lymph   lymphs lymphoma

lynch   lynched lyncher lynches lynchers
lynching
lynx   lynxes
lyre   lyres
lyric   lyrics lyrical lyricism lyricist
lyse   lysed lyses

lyses   analyses
lysin   lysing lysins
lysis   analysis dialysis
lytic   analytic dialytic
lytta   lyttae

m

ma mac mad mae mag man map mar mat maw may amah bema coma cyma imam lama mace mack macs made mage mags maid mail maim main make mako male mall malm malt mama mana mane many maps marc mare mark marl mart mash mask mass mast mate math mats maud maul maun maws maxi maya mayo maze mazy noma puma soma adman agama amahs amain amass amaze anima aroma atman bemas camas comma derma dogma dolma drama edema enema etyma gamay gamma gemma hamal hemal herma human image imago imams karma lamas leman lemma llama macaw maced maces macho macks macro madam madly mages magic magma maids mails maims mains maize major maker makes makos malar males malls malms malts malty mamas mamba mambo mamma mammy maned manes mange mango mangy mania manic manly manna manor manse manta manus maple maqui march marcs mares marge maria marks marls marly marry marsh marts marvy maser masks mason massy masts match mated mates matey matin matte matzo mauds mauls maund mauve maven mavin mavis maxim maxis mayas maybe mayor mayos mayst mazed mazer mazes myoma nomad nomas pumas sigma simar smack small smalt smart smash smaze somas stoma sumac summa ulema unman woman

mac mace mack macs macaw maced maces macho macks macro smack sumac macing mackle macron macros pomace smacks sumach sumacs

mace maced maces pomace grimace pomaces

maced grimaced

maces pomaces grimaces

mack macks smack mackle smacks mackled mackles smacked

macks smacks

macro macron macros macrons

macs sumacs

mad made madam madly nomad armada madame madams madcap madden madder madman madmen madras maduro nomads pomade remade

madam madame madams

made pomade remade chamade pomaded pomades

mae gemmae hermae mammae summae

mag mage mags image imago mages magic magma damage homage imaged images maggot magnet magpie maguey ohmage

mage image mages damage homage imaged images ohmage damaged damages homager imagery magenta ohmages plumage rummage

mages images damages ohmages plumages rummages

magic magical magician

magma magmatic

maid maids maiden barmaid maidens mermaid

maids barmaids mermaids

mail mails mailed mailer airmail mailbag mailbox mailers mailing maillot mailman mailmen

mails airmails

maim maims maimed maimer maiming

main amain mains domain mainly remain domains maintop remains romaine

mains domains remains mainsail mainstay

maize maizes

major majors majored majoring majority

make maker makes makers remake comaker remakes

maker makers comaker comakers haymaker lawmaker

makes remakes

mako makos

malar malars malaria malarky malarial malarkey

male males female tamale females malefic tamales

males females tamales

mall malls small mallee mallet mallow mallard mallees mallets malleus mallows smaller

malm malms malmsey

malms malmsey malmseys

malt malts malty smalt malted maltha smalts maltase malthas maltier malting maltose smaltos

malts smalts maltster

mama mamas imamate

mamba mambas

mambo mambos

mamma mammae mammal mammas mammals mammary

man mana mane many adman atman human leman maned manes mange mango mangy mania manic manly manna manor manse manta manus unman woman airman ataman atmans badman bagman batman bowman busman cabman caiman carman cayman demand desman dolman firman foeman gagman german gunman hetman humane humans iceman lawman layman legman lemans logman madman manage manege manful manger manges mangle mangos maniac manias manioc manitu mannas manned manner manors manses mantas mantel mantic mantis mantle mantra mantua manual manure merman oilman penman pitman ragman remand seaman shaman socman tinman unmans yeoman

mana manage almanac emanate manacle managed manager manages manakin manatee

mane maned manes humane manege germane maneges

mange manger manges mangers

mango mangos mangoes mangonel

mania maniac manias maniacs egomania maniacal

manic manicure

manly humanly unmanly womanly

manna mannas

manor manors manorial

manse manses

manta mantas

map maps maple maples mapped

maple maples

maqui maquis

mar marc mare mark marl mart march marcs mares marge maria marks marls marly marry marsh marts marvy simar smart fulmar imaret maraca maraud marble marbly marcel margay marges margin marina marine marish marked marker market markka markup marled marlin marmot maroon marque marred marron marrow marshy marten martin martyr marvel palmar remark samara simars smarmy smarts smarty

marc march marcs marcel marcels marched marcher marches

march marched marcher marches marchers marchesa marchese marchesi marching

mare mares imaret maremma

marge marges

maria mariachi

mark marks marked marker market markka markup remark earmark markers markets marking markkaa markups remarks

marks remarks earmarks marksman marksmen

marl marls marly marled marlin marline marlins

marry remarry marrying

marsh marshy marshal marshes marshals marshier

mart marts smart marten martin martyr smarts smarty martens martial martini martins martlet martyrs smarted smarten smarter smartly

marts smarts

maser masers lamasery

mash smash mashed masher mashes mashie mashers mashies mashing quamash smashed smasher smashes smashup

mask masks damask masked masker unmask damasks maskers masking unmasks

masks damasks unmasks

mason masons masonic masonry masonite

mass amass massy massed masses massif amassed amasses massage masseur massifs massing massive

mast masts masted master mastic masters mastery mastics mastiff mastoid topmast

masts topmasts

mat mate math mats match mated mates matey matin matte matzo bemata comate format inmate mateys mating matins matrix matron matted matter mattes mature matzos matzot somata tomato

match matched matches matchup rematch matchbox matching matchups mismatch

mate mated mates matey comate inmate mateys amateur animate bromate climate comates cremate imamate inmates palmate primate

mated animated cremated palmated

mates comates inmates animates bromates climates cremates imamates primates

matey mateys

matin mating matins matinal matinee matings matinees

mats formats

matte matted matter mattes matters smatter mattered smatters

matzo matzos matzot matzoth

maud mauds maudlin

maul mauls mauled mauler maulers mauling

maun maund maunds maunder

maund maunds maunder maunders

mauve mauves

maven mavens

mavin mavins

maw maws

maxi maxim maxis maxims maxixe maxilla maximal maximum maxixes

maxim maxims maximal maximum maximize maximums

may maya mayo gamay mayas maybe mayor mayos mayst dismay mayest mayfly mayhap mayhem maying mayors maypop

maya mayas

mayo mayor mayos mayors mayoral

mayor mayors mayoral mayoress

maze amaze mazed mazer mazes smaze amazed amazes mazers

mazed amazed amazedly

mazer mazers

mazes amazes

me mel mem men met mew acme amen came come cyme dame deme dime dome emeu fame feme fume game hame heme home kame lame lime mead meal mean meat meed meek meet meld mell mels melt memo mems mend menu meow mere merk merl mesa mesh mess mete mewl mews mime mome name nome omen omer pome rime same smew some tame time tome zyme acmes admen aimed ameba ameer amend anime armed blame brume camel cameo cames chime chyme cimex clime comer comes comet crime cymes dames demes dimer dimes domed domes emeer emend emery emeus emmer emmet famed fames femes femme flame flume frame fumed fumes gamed games gimel gimme gnome grime grume hames homed homer homes homey hymen kames lamed lamer lames limed limen limes limey lumen meads meals mealy means meant meany meats meaty medal media medic meeds meets melds melee melic mells melon melts memos menad mends menus meows mercy meres merge merit merle merls merry mesas meshy mesic mesne meson messy metal meted meter metes metre metro

mewed mewls mezzo mimed mimer mimes momes named names neume nomen nomes numen omega omens omers ormer oxime plume pomes prime rhyme rimed rimes rumen semen shame slime smear smell smelt smews spume tamed tamer tames theme timed timer times tomes vimen vomer women yamen zymes

mead meads meadow limeade meadows meadowy

meal meals mealy mealie mealier oatmeal

meals oatmeals

mealy mealybug

mean means meant meany demean meaner meanly demeans meander meanest meanies meaning

means demeans

meant meantime

meat meats meaty meatier nutmeat

meats nutmeats

medal medals medalist

media medial median medians mediant mediate comedian mediated mediates mediator remedial

medic medics medical medicaid medicare medicate medicine

meed meeds

meek meeker meekly meekest

meet meets meeting

mel meld mell mels melt camel gimel melds melee melic mells melon melts smell smelt camels comely enamel gamely gimels homely lamely melded melees mellow melody melons melted namely omelet pomelo pommel smells smelly smelts tamely timely

meld melds melded melding

melee melees cameleer

mell mells smell mellow smells smelly lamella mellows smelled

mells smells

melon melons

mels camels gimels enamels pommels

melt melts smelt melted smelts melting smelted smelter

melts smelts

mem memo mems memos member memoir memory sememe

memo memos memoir memory memoirs

men amen mend menu omen admen amend emend hymen limen lumen menad mends menus nomen numen omens rumen semen vimen women yamen acumen airmen amends badmen bagmen bowmen busmen cabmen carmen cement dement dolmen emends examen flamen foment gagmen gasmen gunmen hymens icemen lament lawmen laymen legmen loment lumens madmen menace menads menage mended mender menhir menial meninx mensal menses mental mentor mermen moment omened penmen pitmen seamen semens stamen tegmen tinmen yamens yeomen

menad menads

mend amend emend mends amends emends mended mender amended amender commend emended menders mending

mends amends emends commends

menu menus

meow meows

mere meres merely merest chimere

meres merest chimeres

merge emerge merged merger merges emerged emerges mergers emergent reemerge submerge

merit merits demerit merited demerits emeritus meriting temerity

merl merle merls merles merlin merlon merlins merlons

merle merles

mesa mesas mesarch

mesh meshy enmesh inmesh meshed meshes meshing

mesic homesick

mesne mesnes demesne demesnes

meson mesons

mess messy messed messes kermess kirmess message messiah messier messily messing

met mete comet emmet metal meted meter metes metro cermet comets emetic emmets gamete helmet kismet metage metals meteor meters method methyl meting metope metres metric metros mettle

metal metals metaled metaling metalize metallic

mete meted meter metes gamete meteor meters ammeter dimeter gametes meteors metered

meted helmeted

meter meters ammeter dimeter metered ammeters cemetery diameter dimeters metering odometer ohmmeter

metes gametes

metre metres

metro metros

mew mewl mews smew mewed mewls smews mewing

mewl mewls

mews smews

mezzo mezzos

mho mhos

mi mid mil mim mir mis mix amid amir emir emit kami mica mice mien miff

mike mild mile milk mill milo mils milt mime mina mind mine mink mint minx mire mirs miry mise miss mist mite mitt mixt omit rami semi admit admix amice amide amigo amine amirs amiss amity comic comix cumin demit elemi emirs emits fermi gamic gamin hemic humic humid imide imine immix lamia limit miaow micas micky micro middy midge midst miens miffs might miked mikes milch miler miles milks milky mills milts mimed mimer mimes mimic minae mince minds mined miner mines minim minks minny minor mints minty minus mired mires mirex mirth mirza misdo miser missy mists misty miter mites mitre mitts mixed mixer mixes mizen ohmic omits osmic remit remix salmi semis smile smirk smite smith swami timid tumid umiak umiaq vomit zamia

miaow miaows miaowed miaowing

mica micas comical domical

mice amice amices pumice dormice micelle pumiced pumices titmice

micky gimmicky

micro micron microbe microns omicron microbar microbes microbic microdot omicrons

mid amid amide humid imide middy midge midst timid tumid amides amidst desmid imides midair midday midden middle midges midget midleg midway

midge midges midget midgets smidgen smidgens

midst amidst

mien miens

miff miffs miffed miffing

might mights mighty almighty mightier mightily

mike miked mikes

mil mild mile milk mill milo mils milt milch miler miles milks milky mills milts smile family homily milady milden milder mildew mildly milers milieu milium milked milker milled miller millet milord simile smilax smiled smiler smiles

mild milden milder mildew mildly mildest mildews mildewy

mile miler miles smile milers simile smiled smiler smiles mileage similes smilers

miler milers smiler

miles smiles

milk milks milky milked milker milkers milkier milking milkman milkmen milksop

milks milksops

mill mills milled miller millet millers millets millime milline milling million sawmill

mills sawmills

milo milord

milt milts

mim mime mimed mimer mimes mimic mimers mimics miming mimosa

mime mimed mimer mimes mimers mimesis

mimer mimers

mimic mimics mimicry mimicked mimicker

mina minae lamina limina lumina numina semina vimina laminae laminar liminal minaret nominal seminal seminar stamina tegmina

minae laminae

mince minced mincer minces mincers

mind minds minded remind mindful minding mindset reminds

minds mindset reminds

mine amine imine mined miner mines amines ermine famine imines miners bromine carmine eminent ermines examine famines jasmine mineral nominee

mined examined

miner miners mineral examiner minerals

mines amines imines ermines famines bromines carmines examines jasmines

minim minims minimal minimize minimums

mink minks

minor minors minority

mint mints minty minted mintage mintier minting varmint

mints varmints

minus terminus

minx minxes

mir amir emir mire mirs miry amirs emirs mired mires mirex mirth mirza smirk admire bemire mirage miring mirror mirzas smirch smirks

mire mired mires mirex admire bemire admired admirer admires bemired bemires demirep

mired admired bemired

mires admires bemires

mirs amirs emirs

mirth mirthful

mirza mirzas

mis mise miss mist amiss misdo miser missy mists misty semis commis demise dermis elemis famish fermis kermis kumiss miscue misdid misers misery misfit mishap mislay misled missal missed misses missus misted mister misuse momism remise remiss

misdo   misdoer misdone misdoers misdoing

mise   miser demise misers misery remise chemise demised demises miserly premise promise remised remises samisen surmise

miser   misers misery miserere miseries promiser

miss   amiss missy kumiss missal missed misses missus remiss dismiss missals missies missile missing mission missive misstep

mist   mists misty misted mister animist atomist chemist mistake misters mistier misting mistook mistral palmist

mists   animists atomists chemists palmists

mite   miter mites smite miters samite smites somite eremite limited limiter mitered samites smiters somites termite vomited

miter   miters mitered mitering

mites   smites samites eremites termites

mitre   mitred mitres

mitt   mitts mitten emitted emitter mittens omitted smitten

mix   mixt admix comix immix mixed mixer mixes remix commix mixers mixing

mixed   admixed immixed remixed unmixed

mixer   mixers

mixes   remixes commixes

mixt   mixture

mo   moa mob mod mog mom mon moo mop mor mos mot mow ammo amok demo homo limo memo moan moas moat mobs mock mode mods mogs moil mojo moke mola mold mole moll molt moly mome moms monk mono mons mood moon moor moos moot mope mops mora more morn mors mort moss most mote moth mots move mown mows moxa smog sumo alamo amole among amour armor demob demon demos emote gismo gizmo humor lemon limos memos moans moats mocha mocks modal model modem modes mogul mohur moils moist mojos mokes molal molar molas molds moldy moles molls molly molto molts momes mommy monad money mongo monks monte month mooch moods moody mooed moola moons moony moors moose moots moped mopes morae moral moray morel mores morns moron morph morro morts mosey mossy motel motes motet moths mothy motif motor motto mould moult mound mount mourn mouse

mousy mouth moved mover moves movie mowed mower moxas moxie promo rumor schmo smock smogs smoke smoky smolt smote sumos tumor

moa   moan moas moat moans moats bemoan moaned

moan   moans bemoan moaned bemoans moaning

moans   bemoans

moat   moats

mob   mobs demob demobs mobbed mobcap mobile

mobs   demobs mobster

mock   mocks smock mocked mocker smocks hammock hummock mammock mockers mockery mocking smocked

mocks   smocks hammocks hummocks mammocks

mod   mode mods modal model modem modes modals models modems modern modest modify modish module

modal   modals modally modality

mode   model modem modes models modems modern modest alamode commode modeled modeler moderns modesty remodel

model   models modeled modeler remodel modelers modeling remodels

modem   modems

modes   modest modesty alamodes commodes immodest modestly

mog   mogs smog mogul smogs moguls

mogs   smogs

mogul   moguls

mohur   mohurs

moil   moils moiled moiling turmoil

moist   moistens moistest moisture

mojo   mojos

moke   mokes smoke smoked smoker smokes smokers

mokes   smokes

mola   molal molar molas molars

molar   molars premolar

molas   molasses

mold   molds moldy molded molder molders moldier molding smolder

mole   amole moles amoles molest molests

moles   amoles molest moleskin molested molester

moll   molls molly mollies mollify mollusk

molt   molto molts smolt molted molten smolts molting

molts   smolts

mom   mome moms momes mommy moment momism momzer

mome   momes moment momenta momento moments

mon   monk mono mons among demon lemon monad money mongo monks monte month almond common daemon daimon demons etymon gammon gnomon kimono lemons lemony mammon monads moneys monger mongst monies monism monist monkey monody montes months salmon sermon simony summon

monad   monads lemonade

money   moneys moneyed moneybag

mongo   mongoose

monk   monks monkey monkeys monkish

mono   kimono monody kimonos monocle monolog

mons   demons lemons commons daemons daimons etymons gammons gnomons mammons monsoon monster salmons sermons summons

monte   montes monteith monteros

month   months

moo   mood moon moor moos moot mooch moods moody mooed moola moons moony moors moose moots mooing moolah moolas mooned moored simoom simoon smooch smooth

mooch   smooch mooched moocher mooches moochers mooching smooched smooches

mood   moods moody moodier moodily

moola   moolah moolas

moon   moons moony mooned simoon moonlet moonlit

moons   moonshot

moor   moors moored moorage mooring

moos   moose schmoos vamoose

moose   vamoose vamoosed vamooses

moot   moots smooth smooths

mop   mope mops moped mopes moping mopish mopped moppet

mope   moped mopes

mor   mora more morn mors mort armor humor morae moral moray morel mores morns moron morph morro morts rumor tumor amoral armors armory clamor enamor humors memory morale morals morass morays morbid moreen morels morgen morgue morion morons morose morphs morros morrow morsel mortal mortar remora rumors termor tremor tumors

mora   morae moral moray amoral morale morals morass morays remora humoral immoral moraine morales morally oxymora remoras

moral   amoral morale morals humoral immoral morales morally moralism moralist morality moralize

moray   morays

more morel mores moreen morels anymore armored armorer humored moreens morello rumored

morel morels morellos

morn morns morning

moron morons moronic oxymoron

morph morphs morphine

morro morros morrow tomorrow

mors armors humors morsel rumors tumors clamors enamors morsels remorse termors tremors

mort morts mortal mortar mortals mortars mortify mortise

mos moss most demos limos memos mosey mossy sumos alamos almost comose cosmos gismos gizmos inmost mimosa mosaic moseys mosque mosses mostly osmose promos samosa upmost utmost vamose

mosey moseys moseyed moseying

moss mossy mosses mossier

most inmost mostly upmost utmost endmost farmost midmost mostest outmost topmost

mot mote moth mots emote motel motes motet moths mothy motif motor motto smote demote emoted emotes marmot motels motets mother motifs motile motion motive motley motmot motors mottle mottos remote

mote emote motel motes motet smote demote emoted emotes motels motets remote demoted demotes promote remoter

motel motels remotely

motes emotes demotes promotes remotest

motet motets

moth moths mothy mother mammoth mothers smother timothy

moths mammoths

motif motifs

motor motors motored motorbus motoring motorist motorize motorman

mots marmots motmots

motto mottos

mould moulds mouldy smoulder

moult moults moulted moulting

mound mounds mounded mounding

mount amount mounts amounts mounted amounted dismount mountain mounting remounts seamount surmount

mourn mourns mourned mourners mournful mourning

mouse moused mouser mousey dormouse titmouse

mouth mouths mouthy mouthed bigmouth mouthful mouthier mouthing vermouth

move moved mover moves movers remove removed remover removes unmoved

moved removed unmoved

mover movers

movie movies

mow mown mows mowed mower haymow mowers mowing unmown

mower mowers

mown unmown

mows haymows

moxa moxas

mu emu mud mug mum mus emus much muck muds muff mugs mule mull mums muon murk muse mush musk muss must mute mutt smug smut amuck amuse camus demur femur gamut humus lemur mucid mucks mucky mucus muddy muffs mufti muggy mulch mulct mules muley mulls mummy mumps munch mungo muons mural murex murks murky murre mused muses mushy music musky mussy musts musty muted mutes mutts muzzy ramus smuts

much muchly

muck amuck mucks mucky mucked mucker muckle shmuck muckers muckier mucking muckles schmuck shmucks

mucks shmucks schmucks

mud muds muddy mudded mudder muddle smudge smudgy

muddy muddying

muff muffs muffed muffin muffle muffing muffins muffled muffler muffles

muffs earmuffs

mufti muftis

mug mugs smug muggy mugged mugger smugly

mulch mulched mulches mulching

mulct mulcts mulcted mulcting

mule mules muley amulet muleta muleys amulets gemmule muletas plumule

mules gemmules plumules

muley muleys

mull mulls mullah mulled mullet mullahs mullets mulling mullion

mum mums mummy mumps mumble mummer

munch munched munches munchies munching munchkin

mungo mungos

muon muons

mural murals

murk murks murky murkier

murre murrey demurred

mus emus muse mush musk muss must amuse camus humus mused muses mushy music musky mussy musts musty ramus amused amuses animus bemuse hummus litmus muscat muscle museum mushed mushes musing musjid muskeg musket muskie muslin mussed mussel musses muster shamus thymus

muse amuse mused muses amused amuses bemuse museum bemused bemuses musette museums

mused amused bemused

muses amuses bemuses shamuses thymuses

mush mushy mushed mushes mushier mushily mushing

music musical musicals musician

musk musky muskeg musket muskie muskegs muskets muskier muskrat

muss mussy mussed mussel musses mussels mussing

must musts musty muster mustang mustard musters

mute muted mutes mutely commute permute

muted commuted permuted

mutes commutes permutes

mutt mutts mutter mutton smutty mutters muttons smutted

my amyl army demy fumy gamy homy limy myna myth rimy amyls atomy balmy barmy beamy dummy enemy filmy foamy gammy gemmy grimy gummy hammy jemmy jimmy loamy mammy mommy mummy mynah mynas myoma myope myrrh mysid myths palmy pygmy roomy rummy seamy slimy spumy stymy swamy tummy wormy yummy

myna mynah mynas mynahs

mynah mynahs

myoma myomas myomata

myope myopes

myrrh myrrhs

mysid mysids

myth myths mythic mythos

na ana nab nae nag nah nap nay anal gnar gnat gnaw kana kina knap knar mana mina myna nabs nags naif nail name naos nape naps narc nard nark nary nave navy snag snap tuna ulna vina arena banal bwana canal china dinar enact fauna final gnarl gnars gnash gnats gnaws gonad henna hyena inane inapt kanas kenaf knack knaps knars knave krona lanai lunar manna menad minae monad mynah mynas nabob nacre nadir naiad naifs nails naive naked named names nanny napes nappy narco narcs nards nares naris narks nasal nasty natal natch nates natty naval navel naves navvy nawab penal penna pinna qanat renal sauna senna snack snafu snags snail snake snaky snaps snare snark snarl snath sonar tonal tunas ulnae ulnas unapt unarm varna venal vinas zonal

nab nabs nabob enable nabbed nabobs unable

nabob nabobs

nacre nacres nacreous

nadir nadirs

nae minae ulnae faunae pennae

nag nags snag snags linage manage menage nagana nagged nagger naggle nonage onager snaggy

nags snags

nah mynah mynahs

naiad naiads naiades

naif naifs

nail nails snail nailed snails tenail hobnail nailing tenails toenail

nails snails tenails hobnails toenails

naive naively naivety

naked snaked nakedly

name named names enamel namely rename enamels renamed renames surname unnamed

named renamed unnamed

names renames namesake surnames

nap knap nape naps snap inapt knaps napes nappy snaps unapt canape catnap kidnap napalm napery napkin napped napper snappy

nape napes canape napery anapest canapes hanaper

napes anapest canapes anapests

nappy snappy

naps knaps snaps catnaps kidnaps synapse

narc narco narcs inarch narcos anarchy monarch

narco narcos narcosis narcotic

nard nards canard canards innards

nards canards innards

nares snares ensnares

nark narks snark snarks

narks snarks

nary binary canary denary senary zonary granary plenary quinary ternary urinary

nasal nasally nasality nasalize

nasty dynasty

natal prenatal

natch snatch snatched snatches

nates agnates donates penates senates cognates khanates magnates phonates quinates ruinates urinates

natty gnatty

nave knave navel naves knaves navels knavery

navel navels

naves knaves

nawab nawabs

ne ane neb nee net new one acne anew bane bine bone cane cone dene dine done dune dyne erne fane fine gene gone hone kine knee knew lane line lone lune mane mine neap near neat nebs neck need neep neon nerd nest nets neuk nevi news newt next nine none ones pane pine pone rune sane sine tine tone tune vane vine wane wine zone acned aline alone amine anear anent annex apnea atone azine benne bines boned boner bones brine caned caner canes chine cline clone coned cones coney crane crone denes dined diner dines drone dunes dynes enema enemy ernes fanes fined finer fines ganef genes genet goner honed hones honey imine inane inept inned inner jones knead kneed kneel knees knell knelt koine krone lanes leone liane lined linen liner lines loner lunes maned manes mesne mined miner mines money neaps nears neath necks needs needy neeps negus neigh neons nerds nerdy nerve nervy nests neuks neume never neves nevus newel newer newly newsy newts nexus nines nonet opine ovine owned owner ozone panel panes panne phone pined pines piney plane pones prone prune renew runes saner scene scone seine shine shone

sines sinew sneak sneer snell spine stone swine tenet thane thine tinea tines toned toner tones tonne tuned tuner tunes twine urine vanes vines waned wanes whine wined wines zineb zoned zones

neap neaps neaped

near anear nears linear neared nearer nearly nearest nearing unearth

neat neath neaten neater neatly beneath cuneate lineate neatens neatest uneaten

neath beneath neatherd

neb nebs zineb nebris nebula

neck necks necked necker neckers necking necktie redneck

necks rednecks

nee knee need neep kneed kneel knees needs needy neeps sneer jinnee kneels needed needer needle sneers sneeze veneer

need kneed needs needy needed needer needle needful needier needing needled needler needles

neep neeps kneepad kneepan

negus neguses

neigh neighs neighed neighbor neighing

neon neons

nerd nerds nerdy

nerve nerved nerves unnerved unnerves

nest nests finest honest nested nester nestle sanest amnesty earnest honesty leanest meanest nesters nesting nestled nestler nestles wannest

net nets genet nonet tenet bonnet brunet burnet cornet cygnet gannet garnet genets hornet jennet linnet magnet nether netted nettle ninety nonets planet rennet sennet signet sonnet spinet tenets

nets genets nonets tenets bonnets brunets burnets cornets cygnets gannets garnets hornets jennets linnets magnets netsuke planets rennets sennets signets sonnets spinets

neuk neuks

neume neumes

never whenever

new anew knew news newt newel newer newly newsy newts renew sinew newels newest newish newton renews sinews sinewy

newel newels

newly newlywed

news newsy renews sinews newsboy newsier newsman newsmen
newt newts newton newtons
nib nibs nibbed nibble
nice nicer nicely nicest nicety cornice
niche niched niches
nick nicks snick nicked nickel nicker snicks dornick finicky nickels nickers nicking panicky snicked snicker
nicks snicks dornicks
nide nides snide cyanide
nides cyanides
nidi nidify
niece nieces
nigh night knight nigher nights nighty knights nighest nightie nightly tonight
night knight nights nighty knighted knightly midnight nightcap nighties sennight twinight
nil anil nill nils anile anils nills nilgai senile tinily zanily
nill nills vanilla
nils anils
nim nims anima anime denim minim nimbi animal animas animes animus denims minims nimble nimbly nimbus paynim
nims denims minims paynims
nine nines canine ninety asinine canines leonine quinine
nines canines boniness puniness quinines zaniness
ninja ninjas
ninon ninons
ninth ninths
nip nipa nips snip nipas nippy snipe snips catnip nipped nipper nipple sniped sniper snipes snippy turnip
nipa nipas
nippy snippy
nips snips turnips
nit knit nits snit unit knits niter nitty snits unite units unity bonito finite ignite lenity manitu nitric nitwit sanity sennit snitch united unites vanity zenith
niter igniters
nits knits snits units sennits
nival carnival
nix nixe nixed nixes nixie fornix nixies nixing phenix
nixe nixed nixes
nixes phenixes
nixie nixies
no nob nod nog nor not now anon enol enow keno kino knob knop knot know leno mono nobs nock node nods noel noes nogg nogs noil noma nome none nook noon nope norm nose nosh nosy nota note noun nous nova nowt snob

snot snow wino annoy anode canoe canon chino donor fanon genoa gnome gonof guano honor kenos kinos knobs knock knoll knops knots knout known knows llano manor minor ninon nobby noble nobly nocks nodal noddy nodes nodus noels nohow noils noise noisy nomad nomas nomen nomes nonce nonet nonyl nooks nooky noons noose nopal noria norms north nosed noses nosey notch noted noter notes notum nouns novae novas novel noway piano porno rhino segno snobs snood snoop snoot snore snort snots snout snows snowy steno synod tenon tenor venom winos xenon
nob knob nobs snob knobs nobby noble nobly snobs hobnob knobby nobble nobles nobody snobby
nobby knobby snobby
noble nobles ennoble ignoble ennobled ennobles nobleman noblemen noblesse
nobly ignobly
nobs knobs snobs hobnobs
nock knock nocks knocks nocked knocked knocker nocking
nocks knocks
nod node nods anode nodal noddy nodes nodus synod anodes monody nodded nodder noddle nodose nodule synods
nodal synodal
node anode nodes anodes
nodes anodes
nods synods
noel noels
noes canoes noesis
nog nogg nogs eggnog noggin
nogg noggin nogging noggins
nogs eggnogs
noil noils
noise noised noises
noma nomad nomas nomads anomaly nomadic
nomad nomads nomadic nomadism
nome gnome nomen nomes gnomes
nomes gnomes
none nonet nonego nonets nonegos
nonet nonets
nonyl nonyls
nook nooks nooky shnook schnook shnooks snooker
nooks schnooks
noon noons noonday nooning
noose noosed nooses burnoose
nopal nopals
nor norm donor honor manor minor noria norms north snore snort tenor anorak donors honors ignore kronor

manors minors norias normal norths signor snored snorer snores snorts tenors
noria norias manorial
norm norms normal
north norths northern northers northing
nose nosed noses nosey lanose nosegay
noses zoonoses
nosh noshed noshes noshing
not knot nota note snot knots notch noted noter notes notum snots cannot cenote denote knotty notary notate noters notice notify noting notion snotty
nota notary notate notable notably notated notates
notch notched notches notching
note noted noter notes cenote denote noters cenotes connote denoted denotes keynote notedly
noted denoted notedly connoted keynoted
noter noters keynoter
notes cenotes denotes connotes keynotes
noun nouns nounal pronoun
nouns pronouns
nous venous vinous acinous burnous heinous ominous ruinous spinous
nova novae novas
novel novels novella novelist novelize novellas
now enow know nowt snow known knows noway snows snowy erenow knower minnow nowise renown snowed winnow
nu gnu nub nun nut anus gnus knur menu nubs nude nuke null numb nuns nuts onus snub snug annul bonus cornu donut ennui genus inure inurn knurl knurs manus menus minus nubby nucha nudes nudge nudie nuked nukes numbs numen nurse nutsy nutty pinup sinus snubs snuff sunup tonus venue
nub nubs snub nubby snubs nubbin nubble nubbly nubile snubby
nubby snubby
nubs snubs
nucha nuchae nuchal
nude nudes denude nudely denuded denudes
nudes denudes
nudge nudged nudges
nudie nudies
nuke nuked nukes
null nullah nullahs nullify nullity
numb numbs benumb numbed number numbly benumbs numbers numbest numbing numbles
numbs benumbs

numen monument
nun nuns nuncio
nurse nursed nurses
nut nuts donut nutsy nutty cobnut donuts hognut minute nutant nutlet

nutmeg nutria nutted peanut pignut tenuti tenuto walnut
nuts nutsy donuts cobnuts hognuts peanuts pignuts walnuts

nyala nyalas
nylon nylons
nymph nympho nymphs nymphal nymphean nymphets

---

o

---

oaf   loaf oafs loafs loafed loafer oafish
oafs   loafs
oak   oaks soak cloak croak oaken oakum soaks cloaks croaks croaky oakums soaked soaker
oaks   soaks cloaks croaks
oakum   oakums
oar   boar hoar oars roar soar board boars hoard hoary oared roars soars aboard bezoar boards coarse hoards hoarse oaring roared roarer soared uproar
oared   roared soared
oars   boars roars soars coarse hoarse bezoars coarsen coarser hoarsen hoarser oarsman oarsmen uproars
oast   boast coast oasts roast toast boasts coasts roasts toasts toasty boasted boaster coastal coasted coaster roasted roaster toasted toaster
oasts   boasts coasts roasts toasts
oat   boat coat goat moat oath oats bloat boats coati coats float gloat goats groat loath moats oaten oaths shoat stoat afloat bloats boated boatel boater coated coatis floats gloats goatee groats loathe shoats stoats throat
oath   loath oaths loathe loathed loathes loathly
oats   boats coats goats moats bloats floats gloats groats shoats stoats throats
obey   obeys obeyed obeyer disobey obeyers obeying
obeys   disobeys
obi   obis obit cobia obits robin cobias globin mobile phobia robing robins
obit   obits probity
oboe   oboes hoboes
oboes   hoboes
oboli   bobolink
occur   occurs reoccur occurred reoccurs
ocean   oceans oceanic oceanaut
ocher   ochers moocher moochers
ochre   ochres
octad   octads
octet   octets
od   cod god hod mod nod odd ode pod rod sod tod yod bode body clod coda code cods dodo food gods good hods hood lode mode mods mood node nods odds odes odic odor plod pods prod quod rode rods rood shod soda sods tody trod wood yodh yods abode anode bipod blood boded bodes brood clods codas coded codes codex diode

dodge dodgy dodos ephod epode erode flood foods geode godly goods goody hoods iodic loden lodes lodge modal model modem modes moods moody nodal noddy nodes nodus oddly odium odors plods prods quods rodeo roods scrod snood sodas stood synod today toddy vodka woods woody yodel yodhs
odd   odds noddy oddly toddy cloddy codded coddle dodder fodder nodded nodder noddle oddity podded rodded shoddy sodded sodden toddle
ode   bode code lode mode node odes rode abode anode boded bodes coded codes codex diode epode erode geode loden lodes model modem modes nodes rodeo yodel abodes anodes bodega decode diodes encode epodes eroded erodes geodes hooded models modems modern modest rodent rodeos strode triode wooded wooden yodels
odes   bodes codes lodes modes nodes abodes anodes diodes epodes erodes geodes modest decodes encodes geodesy modesty triodes
odic   iodic bodice rhodic bodices codices codicil melodic modicum nodical
odium   odiums podium sodium rhodium sodiums rhodiums
odor   odors odored malodor odorant odorous
odors   malodors
of   off oft doff goof hoof loft poof prof roof sofa soft toff toft tofu woof aloft aloof boffo croft doffs feoff gofer gonof goofs goofy hoofs lofts lofty offal offed offer often profs proof roofs scoff sofas softy spoof toffs tofts woofs
off   doff toff boffo doffs feoff offal offed offer scoff toffs coffee coffer coffin coffle cutoff doffed feoffs goffer layoff offals offend offers office offing offish offset payoff runoff scoffs setoff shroff soffit toffee
offal   offals
offed   doffed scoffed
offer   coffer goffer offers coffers offered offerer scoffer goffered offerers offering proffers scoffers
oft   loft soft toft aloft croft lofts lofty often softy tofts crofts lofted soften softer softie softly
often   soften softened softener

ogee   ogees apogee apogees
ogees   apogees
ogham   oghams
ogive   ogives
ogle   ogled ogler ogles dogleg goglet oglers doglegs fogless goglets
ogler   oglers
ogre   ogres ogress ogreish
ogres   ogress ogresses progress
oh   foh ohm oho ohs ooh john kohl ohms oohs pooh aloha johns kohls mohur nohow ohmic oohed poohs
ohm   ohms ohmic ohmage
oho   nohow boohoo
ohs   oohs poohs
oil   boil coil foil moil noil oils oily roil soil toil aboil boils broil coils doily foils moils noils oiled oiler poilu roils roily soils spoil toile toils besoil boiled boiler broils coiled entoil foiled moiled oilcan oilcup oilers oilier oiling oilman poilus recoil roiled soiled spoils spoilt toiled toiler toiles toilet uncoil
oiled   boiled coiled foiled moiled roiled soiled toiled broiled spoiled recoiled uncoiled
oiler   boiler oilers toiler boilers broiler broilers spoilers
oils   boils coils foils moils noils roils soils toils broils spoils besoils entoils oilskin recoils uncoils
oily   doily roily
oink   oinks oinked oinking
okapi   okapis
okay   okays okayed okaying
oke   coke hoke joke moke okes poke soke toke woke yoke awoke bloke broke choke coked cokes evoke hokes hokey joked joker jokes jokey mokes poked poker pokes smoke sokes spoke stoke toked token tokes woken yoked yokel yokes blokes booked broken broker choked choker chokes chokey cooked cooker evoked evokes hooked hooker hookey invoke jokers looked looker pokers revoke rooked smoked smoker smokes spoked spoken spokes stoked stoker stokes stroke tokens yokels
okes   cokes hokes jokes mokes pokes sokes tokes yokes blokes chokes evokes smokes spokes stokes invokes revokes strokes
okra   okras
old   bold cold fold gold hold mold sold told wold ahold colds folds holds

molds moldy olden older oldie scold soldo aholds behold bifold bolder boldly colder coldly enfold folded folder golden holden holder holdup infold kobold molded molder oldest oldies oldish polder resold retold scolds solder unfold untold uphold

olden golden holden beholden embolden

older bolder colder folder holder molder polder solder folders holders molders polders scolder smolder solders beholder folderol scolders smolders soldered

oldie oldies moldier soldier moldiest soldiers soldiery

olein oleins

oleo oleos

olio folio olios folios foliose

olios folios

olive olives

olla ollas cholla collar dollar bollard chollas collage collard collars collate corolla dollars pollard tollage

ollas chollas corollas

om mom oms tom atom bomb boom coma comb come comp dome doom from home homo homy loom mome moms noma nome omen omer omit pome pomp prom romp room soma some tomb tome toms whom womb zoom aroma atoms atomy axiom besom bloom bombs booms bosom broom buxom carom chomp clomb clomp combe combo combs comer comes comet comfy comic comix comma compo comps domed domes dooms gloom gnome groom homed homer homes homey idiom looms momes mommy myoma nomad nomas nomen nomes omber ombre omega omens omers omits oomph pomes promo proms rhomb romps rooms roomy somas stoma stomp tombs tomes venom vomer vomit whomp woman wombs women zombi

omber bomber comber ombers somber bombers combers somberly

ombre hombre ombres hombres sombrero

omega omegas

omen nomen omens women foment loment moment omened yeomen abdomen foments loments momenta momento moments omening

omens abdomens

omer comer homer omers vomer boomer comers homers isomer roomer vomers bloomer boomers isomers roomers

omers comers homers vomers boomers bloomers

omit omits vomit comity somite vomits comitia omitted somites vomited

omits vomits

oms moms toms atoms booms dooms looms proms rooms axioms besoms blooms bosoms brooms caroms glooms grooms idioms venoms

on con don eon hon ion mon one son ton won yon aeon agon anon axon bond bone bong bonk bony boon cion cone conk cons cony coon done dong dons ebon eons exon fond font gone gong goon hone hong honk icon ikon ions iron jeon kaon konk lion lone long loon monk mono mons moon muon neon none noon once ones only onto onus onyx peon pond pone pons pony poon song sons soon tone tong tons tony toon upon wont yond yoni zone zonk zoon aeons agony alone along among ancon anion apron argon arson atone atony axons bacon baron baton bison blond bonds boned boner bones bongo bongs bonks bonny bonus bonze boons boron canon capon cions clone cogon colon conch condo coned cones coney conga congo conic conks conto coons crone crony croon demon donga dongs donor donut drone ebony eikon exons fanon felon fondu fonts frond frons front futon gipon gonad goner gongs gonof goons heron honed hones honey hongs honks honky honor hyson icons ikons inion ionic irons irony jones jupon kaons krona krone lemon leone lions loner longe longs loons loony mason melon meson monad money mongo monks monte month moons moony moron muons neons ninon nonce nonet nonyl noons nylon onion onset ozone paeon peons peony phone phony piton ponds pones poons prone prong pylon radon rayon recon rondo salon scion scone shone sonar sonde songs sonic sonny spoon stone stony swoon talon toned tenon thong tonal toned toner tones tonga tongs tonic tonne tonus toons toyon union wagon wonky wonts wrong xenon yonis zonal zoned zones zonks

once nonce sconce conceal concede conceit concent concept concern concert sconced sconces

one bone cone done gone hone lone none ones pone tone zone alone atone boned boner bones clone coned cones coney crone drone goner honed hones honey jones krone leone loner money nonet ozone phone pones prone scone shone stone toned toner tones zoned

zones agones anyone atoned atoner atones begone boners bygone cloned clones coneys crones debone depone droned drones evzone goners hexone honest honeys intone ironed ironer ketone kroner leones lonely loners moneys mooned nonego nonets ozones phoned phones phoney redone rezone scones sooner stoned stoned stones throne toners undone

ones bones cones hones jones pones tones zones agones atones clones crones drones honest leones ozones phones scones stones ancones boneset bygones debones depones evzones honesty intones ketones lioness oneself rezones thrones umbones

onion onions

onset onsets

onto conto contos pronto contort contour pontoon

onus bonus tonus clonus onuses bonuses nonuser

onyx onyxes

ooh oohs pooh oohed poohs boohoo oohing

oohs poohs

oops coops goops hoops loops poops droops scoops sloops snoops stoops swoops troops whoops saloops

ooze booze oozed oozes boozed boozer boozes snooze boozers snoozed snoozes

oozed boozed snoozed

oozes boozes

oozy boozy woozy floozy

opah opahs

opal copal nopal opals copalm nopals copalms opaline

opals nopals

ope cope dope hope lope mope nope oped open opes pope rope tope coped copes doped doper dopes dopey elope grope hoped hoper hopes loped loper lopes moped mopes myope opens opera popes roped ropes scope slope stope toped topee toper topes trope aslope cooped cooper copeck dopers eloped eloper elopes epopee groped groper gropes hooped hopers kopeck looped looper lopers metope myopes opened opener openly operas pooped propel proper reopen ropery scopes sloped slopes stoped stopes topees topers tropes

oped coped doped hoped loped moped roped toped cooped eloped groped hooped looped pooped sloped stoped drooped popedom scooped snooped stooped swooped trooped whooped

open opens opened opener openly reopen openers opening propend reopens

opera operas operant operate operable operably operants operated operates operatic operator

opes copes dopes hopes lopes mopes popes ropes topes elopes gropes myopes scopes slopes stopes tropes metopes

opine opined opines chopine atropine

oping coping doping hoping loping moping roping toping cooping drooping scooping snooping stooping swooping trooping whooping

opium opiums europium

optic optics optical optician panoptic synoptic

opus opuses octopus

or cor dor for kor mor nor orb orc ore ort tor boor bora bore born bort cord core corf cork corm corn cors door dorm dory fora forb ford fore fork form fort gore gory hora horn lord lore lorn lory moor mora more morn mors mort norm odor orad oral orbs orby orcs ordo ores orgy orle orts oryx orzo poor pore pork port sora sorb sore sori sort tora tore tori torn torr tors tort word wore work worm worn yore zori abhor abort acorn actor adore adorn afore agora aorta aport arbor ardor armor boors boral boras borax bored borer bores boric boron borts ceorl chord chore color coral cords cored corer cores corgi coria corks corky corms corns cornu corny corps corse crore decor dolor donor doors dorky dorms dorsa ephor error favor fetor fiord fjord floor flora fluor foray forbs forby force fordo fords fores forge forgo forks forms forte forth forts forty forum furor glory goral gored gores gorge gorse honor horas horde horns horny horse horst horsy humor ichor ivory ixora jorum juror korat korun labor loran lords lores loris lorry major manor mayor minor moors morae moral moray morel mores morns moron morph morro morts motor noria norms north odors orach orals orate orbed orbit order ordos oread organ oribi oriel orles orlop ormer orris orzos porch pored pores porgy porks porky porno ports prior razor rigor rumor savor score scorn shore shorn short snore snort sopor soras sorbs sorer sores sorgo sorry sorts sorus spoor spore sport store stork storm story sword swore sworn tabor tenor thorn thoro thorp torah toras torch toric torii torsi torsk torso torte torts torus tumor tutor valor vapor vigor visor vizor whore whorl words wordy works world worms wormy worry worse worst worth yores zoris

oral boral coral goral moral orals amoral borals choral corals floral gorals morale morals orally auroral chloral chorale chorals humoral immoral mayoral morales morally

orals borals corals gorals morals chorals

orate borate orated orates borates prorate chlorate decorate priorate prorated prorates

orb forb orbs orby sorb forbs forby orbed orbit sorbs absorb adsorb corbel corbie forbad forbid morbid orbing orbits resorb sorbet

orbed absorbed resorbed

orbit orbits orbital orbited orbiter orbiters orbiting

orbs forbs sorbs absorbs adsorbs resorbs

orby forby

orc orcs force porch torch forced forcer forces orchid orchil orchis scorch

order border orders borders ordered orderer orderly reorder bordered disorder orderers ordering recorder reorders

ordo fordo ordos cordon cordoba cordons fordone

ordos lordosis

ore bore core fore gore lore more ores pore sore tore wore yore adore afore bored borer bores chore cored corer cores crore fores gored gores lores morel mores oread pored pores score shore snore sorer sores spore store swore whore yores adored adorer adores ashore before boreal borers chorea chores corers crores encore floret forego forest furore galore ignore moored moreen morels odored oreads poorer scored scorer scores shored shores snored snorer snores sorely sorest spored spores stored stores torero whored whores

oread oreads toreador

ores bores cores fores gores lores mores pores sores yores adores chores crores forest scores shores snores sorest spores stores whores arbores encores foresaw foresee forests ignores poorest

organ organs organdy organic organon organum organza organism organist organize organons organums organzas

orgy porgy

oribi oribis

oriel oriels

orle orles whorled

orles odorless

orlop orlops

ormer dormer former ormers dormers formerly informer reformer

ort bort fort mort orts port sort tort abort aorta aport borts forte forth forts forty morts north ports short snort sorts sport torte torts worth aborts aortae aortas aortic assort cavort cortex deport effort escort exhort export extort fortes fortis import mortal mortar norths portal ported porter portly report resort retort shorts shorty snorts sorted sorter sortie sports sporty tortes vortex worths worthy

orts borts forts morts ports sorts torts aborts shorts snorts sports cavorts cohorts deports efforts escorts exhorts exports extorts imports reports resorts retorts

oryx oryxes

orzo orzos borzoi borzois

os dos kos los mos ados boos bosh bosk boss coos cosh cost cosy dose doss duos egos epos foss goos gosh hose host josh joss loos lose loss lost mhos moos moss most naos nose nosh nosy ossa pose posh post posy pros rhos rose rosy tosh toss tost twos udos woos zoos adios agios altos ambos arose autos bolos boost bosks bosom bossy bosun bozos capos ceros chaos chose close cocos costa costs cross demos dodos dojos dosed doses dross duros eosin erose ethos faros floss fossa fosse frosh frost ghost gloss goose gross grosz gyros hobos hosed hosen hoses hosta hosts hypos jatos kayos kenos kilos kinos kiosk kolos kudos limos lobos locos logos loose losel loser loses makos mayos memos mojos moose mosey mossy noose nosed noses nosey oleos olios ordos orzos osier osmic ouzos pesos polos posed poser poses posit posse posts prose prosy repos roost rosed roses rosin rotos sagos saros segos shoos silos slosh solos stoss sumos tacos taros those tiros trios tyros umbos whose winos woosh zeros

osier cosier hosier nosier rosier crosier choosier

osmic cosmic osmics

ossa fossa dossal fossae glossae glossal

other bother mother others pother another bothers brother potherb bothered brothers isotherm mothered motherly potherbs smoother smothers smothery

otic biotic erotic exotic miotic notice abiotic aphotic chaotic demotic erotica exotica exotics idiotic noticed notices osmotic parotic zygotic zymotic

otter cotter hotter otters potter rotter totter blotter cotters blotters spotters tottered trotters

ouch couch pouch touch vouch avouch crouch douche grouch ouches pouchy slouch touchy couched couches debouch douched douches grouchy pouched pouches retouch slouchy touched touches vouched voucher vouches

oud loud ouds aloud cloud proud aoudad clouds cloudy louden louder loudly shroud

ouds clouds shrouds

ought bought fought nought sought brought doughty drought besought boughten droughts droughty thoughts unsought

ounce bounce jounce ounces pounce bounced bouncer bounces flounce frounce jounced jounces pounced pounces trounce announce bouncers denounce flounced flounces frounced frounces renounce trounced trounces

ouphe ouphes

our dour four hour jour ours pour sour tour your amour bourg bourn court flour fours gourd houri hours mourn pours scour sours stour tours yours amours bourgs bourse colour course courts detour devour flours floury fourth giaour gourde gourds honour houris hourly labour mourns poured savour scours source soured sourer sourly stours tabour toured velour

ours fours hours pours sours tours yours amours bourse course flours scours stours bourses colours coursed courser courses detours devours giaours honours labours ourself savours tabours velours

oust joust ousts roust jousts ousted ouster rousts jousted ousters rousted

ousts jousts rousts

out bout gout lout outs pout rout tout about bouts clout couth flout gouts gouty grout knout louts mouth outdo outer outgo pouts route routs scout shout snout south spout stout touts trout youth agouti buyout clouts cutout devout dugout flouts grouts knouts layout mahout mouths mouthy mouton outage outbid outcry outdid outfit outfox outing outlaw outlay outlet outran outrun outset outwit payout pigout pouted putout routed router routes scouts shouts snouts spouts

sprout stouts touted trouts tryout youths

outdo outdoes outdone outdoor outdoing outdoors

outer router scouter flouters grouters scouters shouters

outgo outgoing

outs bouts gouts louts pouts routs touts clouts flouts grouts knouts outset scouts shouts snouts spouts stouts trouts buyouts cutouts dugouts layouts mahouts outsell outsets outside outsize outsold payouts pigouts putouts sprouts

ouzel ouzels

ouzo ouzos

ova nova oval novae novas ovals ovary ovate lovage

oval ovals removal

ovals removals

ovate obovate innovate renovate

oven coven ovens woven cloven covens novena proven sloven inwoven novenas

ovens covens

over cover hover lover mover overt rover clover covers covert drover glover govern hovers lovers movers overdo overly plover rovers shover stover trover clovers covered coverup drovers glovers governs hovered hoverer layover loverly overact overage overall overate overawe overbid overbuy overdue overeat overjoy overlap overlay overlie overpay overrun oversaw oversee overtax overtly overtop overuse plovers popover poverty proverb recover remover shovers stovers trovers uncover

overt covert overtax covertly overtake overtime overtone overtook overture overturn

ovine bovine bovines

ovoid ovoids

ovule ovules

ow bow cow how low mow now owe owl own row sow tow vow wow yow alow avow blow bowl bows brow cowl cows crow dhow down enow flow fowl frow glow gowk gown grow howl jowl know lows meow mown mows nowt owed owes owls owns plow prow rows scow show slow snow sown sows stow town tows trow vows wows yowl aglow allow arrow avows below blown blows blowy bowed bowel bower bowie bowls brown brows clown cower cowls cowry crowd crown crows dhows dowdy dowel dower downs downy dowry dowse drown elbow embow endow flown flows fowls frown frows

glows gowan gowks gowns growl grown grows howdy howls jowls jowly known knows lowed lower lowly meows miaow mowed mower nohow noway owing owlet owned owner oxbow plows power prowl prows rowan rowdy rowed rowel rowen rower scowl scows serow shown shows showy slows snows snowy sowed sower stows throw towed towel tower towns trows vowed vowel widow yowls zowie

owe owed owes bowed bowel bower cower dowel dower lowed lower mowed mower power rowed rowel rowen rower sowed sower towed towel tower vowed vowel avowed blower bowels bowers bowery cowers crowed dowels dowers flowed flower glowed glower grower knower lowers lowery lowest mowers plowed powers rowels rowens rowers showed shower slowed slower snowed sowers stowed towels towers trowed trowel vowels

owed bowed lowed mowed rowed sowed towed vowed avowed crowed flowed glowed plowed showed slowed snowed stowed trowed allowed elbowed embowed endowed miaowed widowed

owes lowest prowess slowest

owing bowing lowing mowing rowing sowing towing vowing avowing blowing bowings crowing allowing elbowing embowing endowing miaowing showings throwing widowing

owl bowl cowl fowl howl jowl owls yowl bowls cowls fowls growl howls jowls jowly lowly owlet prowl scowl yowls bowled bowler cowled fowled fowler growls howled howler owlets owlish prowls scowls slowly yowled

owlet owlets

owls bowls cowls fowls howls jowls yowls growls prowls scowls

own down gown mown owns sown town blown brown clown crown downs downy drown flown frown gowns grown known owned owner shown towns browns clowns crowns disown downed downer drowns frowns godown gowned owners owning renown thrown townie unmown uptown

owned downed gowned browned clowned crowned drowned frowned disowned renowned

owner downer owners browner downers clownery frowners

owns downs gowns towns browns clowns crowns drowns frowns disowns godowns renowns

ox box cox fox lox pox sox boxy coxa doxy foxy moxa oxen boxed boxer boxes coxae coxal coxes epoxy foxes moxas moxie oxbow oxeye oxide oxime oxlip phlox poxes proxy redox toxic toxin xerox

oxbow oxbows

oxeye oxeyes

oxide oxides dioxide dioxides monoxide peroxide

oxime oximes

oxlip oxlips

oy boy coy foy goy hoy joy soy toy ahoy boyo boys buoy cloy foys goys hoys joys oyes oyez ploy soys toys troy alloy annoy boyar buoys cloys coyer coyly coypu decoy doyen enjoy envoy foyer goyim loyal ploys royal savoy sepoy toyed toyon

oyes coyest

ozone ozones

p

pa pad pah pal pan pap par pas pat paw pax pay spa nipa opah opal paca pace pack pact pads page paid pail pain pair pale pall palm palp pals paly pane pang pans pant papa paps para pard pare park parr pars part pass past pate path pats pave pawl pawn paws pays pupa span spar spas spat spay spaz tapa upas apace apart copal epact japan kappa koppa nipas nopal opahs opals pacas paced pacer paces packs pacts paddy padre paean paeon pagan paged pager pages pails pains paint pairs palea paled paler pales palls pally palms palmy palpi palps palsy panda pandy panel panes panga pangs panic panne pansy pants panty papal papas papaw paper pappi paras parch pards pared pares pareu parka parks parol parrs parry parse parts party parve pasha pasta paste pasts pasty patch paten pater pates paths patio patly patsy pause pavan paved paver paves pavis pawed pawky pawls pawns paxes payed payee payer pipal pupae pupal repay salpa sepal space spacy spade spahi spake spall spang spank spans spare spark spars spasm spate spats spawn spays stupa tapas topaz typal

paca pacas alpaca alpacas

pacas alpacas

pace apace paced pacer paces space pacers spaced spaces spacey

paced spaced

pacer pacers

paces spaces

pack packs packed packer packet repack unpack mudpack package packers packets packing packman packmen repacks spackle unpacks

packs repacks unpacks mudpacks packsack

pact epact pacts epacts impact compact impacts

pacts epacts impacts compacts

pad pads paddy padre spade padded paddle padres spaded spader spades spadix

padre padres compadre

paean paeans

paeon paeons

pagan pagans paganism

page paged pager pages pagers pipage pageant pageboy pipages rampage seepage unpaged

paged unpaged rampaged

pager pagers

pages pipages rampages seepages

pah opah opahs spahi oompah spahis

paid repaid unpaid prepaid

pail pails pailful

pain pains paint pained painty painful paining painted painter repaint

paint painty painted painter repaint painters painting repaints

pair pairs impair paired repair despair impairs pairing repairs

pairs impairs repairs despairs

pal opal pale pall palm palp pals paly copal nopal opals palea paled paler pales palls pally palms palmy palpi palps palsy papal pipal pupal sepal spall typal appall carpal copalm empale impala impale napalm nopals palace palate paleae palely palest paling palish palled pallet pallid pallor palmar palmed palmer palpus palter paltry pipals sepals spalls

pale palea paled paler pales empale impale paleae palely palest empaled empales impaled impales paletot palette

palea paleae

paled empaled impaled

pales palest empales impales opalesce palestra

pall palls pally spall appall palled pallet pallid pallor spalls appalls pallets palling pallium pallors

palls spalls appalls

palm palms palmy copalm napalm palmar palmed palmer copalms napalms palmary palmate palmers palmier palming palmist palmyra

palms copalms napalms

palmy palmyra palmyras

palp palpi palps palpus palpate

pals opals palsy nopals pipals sepals carpals palsied palsies

palsy palsying

pan pane pang pans pant span japan panda pandy panel panes panga pangs panic panne pansy pants panty spang spank spans bedpan expand frypan japans pandas pander pandit panels pangas panics panned pannes panted pantry panzer sampan spanks trepan tympan

panda pandas

pane panel panes panels empanel impanel paneled propane

panel panels empanel impanel paneled empanels impanels paneling panelist

panes propanes

pang panga pangs spang pangas spangle spangly

panga pangas

panic panics panicky panicked

panne panned pannes spanned spanner japanned spanners

pans pansy spans japans bedpans expanse frypans pansies sampans

pant pants panty panted pantry panther panties pantile panting rampant

pants pantsuit

pap papa paps papal papas papaw paper pappi papacy papaws papaya papers papery papist pappus papule papyri

papa papal papas papaw papacy papaws papaya papayas

papaw papaws

paper papers papery papered endpaper flypaper paperboy papering

par para pard pare park parr pars part spar apart paras parch pards pared pares pareu parka parks parol parrs parry parse parts party parve spare spark spars depart eparch impart parade paramo parang paraph parcel pardon parent pareus pareve parget pariah paries paring parish parity parkas parked parker parlay parley parlor parody parole parols parred parrel parrot parsed parses parson parted partly parure parvis spared sparer spares sparge sparks sparse

para paras parade paramo parang paraph parable paraded parades parados paradox paragon paramos parangs parapet paraphs parasol

paras parasol parasite parasols

parch eparch eparchs eparchy parched parches hipparch parching

pard pards pardon jeopard leopard pardner pardons

pards jeopards leopards

pare pared pares pareu spare parent pareus pareve spared sparer spares aparejo apparel compare pareira paresis prepare sparely sparers sparest

pared spared compared prepared

pares spares paresis sparest compares prepares

pareu pareus

park parka parks spark parkas parked parker sparks parkers parking parkway sparked sparker sparkle

parka parkas

parks sparks

parol parole parols paroled parolee paroles parolees paroling

parr parrs parry parred parrel parrot parrels parried parries parring parrots sparred sparrow

parry parrying

pars parse spars parsed parses parson sparse parsecs parsing parsley parsnip parsons sparser

parse parsed parses sparse parsecs sparser sparsely sparsest

part apart parts party depart impart parted partly departs imparts partake partery partial partied parting partita partite partlet partner partook partway partyer rampart

parts departs imparts ramparts

party partyer partying

parve parvenu parvenus

pas pass past spas upas nipas papas pasha pasta paste pasts pasty spasm tapas bypass kappas koppas lampas pampas pashas passed passel passer passes pastas pasted pastel paster pastes pastor repast salpas spasms stupas

pasha pashas

pass bypass passed passel passer passes compass impasse passade passado passage passant passels passers passing passion passive passkey surpass

past pasta paste pasts pasty pastas pasted pastel paster pastes pastor repast impasto pastels pasters pasties pastime pasting pastors pasture repasts spastic

pasta pastas

paste pasted pastel paster pastes pastels pasters pasterns

pasts repasts

pat pate path pats spat patch paten pater pates paths patio patly patsy patty spate spats apathy patchy patens patent pathos patina patios patois patrol patron patted patten patter pupate spates

patch patchy patched patcher patches despatch dispatch patchers patchier patching

pate paten pater pates spate patens patent paters pupate spates palpate patella patency patents pupated pupates

paten patens patent patency patents patening patented

pater paters paternal

pates spates pupates palpates

path paths apathy pathos empathy pathway towpath warpath

paths towpaths warpaths

patio patios pupation

pats patsy spats patsies

pause paused pauses

pavan pavane pavans pavanes

pave paved paver paves pavers repave repaved repaves unpaved

paved repaved unpaved

paver pavers

paves repaves

pavis pavises

paw pawl pawn paws papaw pawed pawky pawls pawns spawn papaws pawing pawned pawpaw spawns

pawl pawls

pawn pawns spawn pawned spawns pawning spawned

pawns spawns pawnshop

paws papaws pawpaws

pax paxes

pay pays spay payed payee payer repay spays papaya payday payees payers paying paynim payoff payola payout prepay repays spayed

payed spayed

payee payees

payer payers ppayers taxpayer

pays spays repays prepays

pe ape ope pea pee peg pen pep per pet pew aped apes apex cape cope dope epee gape hope hype jape lope mope nape nope oped open opes peag peak peal pean pear peas peat peck peed peek peel peen peep peer pees pegs pelf pelt pend pens pent peon peps peri perk perm pert peso pest pets pews pipe pope rape ripe rope sped spew tape tope type wipe yipe agape apeak apery aspen biped caper capes chape coped copes coupe crape crepe cupel doped doper dopes dopey drape drupe duped duper elope epees expel gaped gaper gapes grape gripe grope hoped hoper hopes hyped hyper hypes impel japed japer japes lapel leper loped loper lopes moped mopes myope napes opens opera paper peace peach peags peaks peals peans pearl pears peart pease peaty peavy pecan pecks pedal peeks peels peens peeps peers peeve pekoe pelfs pelts penal pence pends penna penni penny peons peony pepla peppy perch perdu peril perks perky perms perry perse pesky pesos pests petal peter petit petty pewee piped piper pipes popes raped rapes repel ripen roped ropes rupee scape scope shape slope snipe speak spear speck specs speed spell spelt spend spent sperm spews stipe stope stupe super swipe taped taper tapes taupe tepee toped topee toper topes tripe trope typed types umped upend upper viper wiped wiper wipes

pea peag peak peal pean pear peas peat apeak peace peach peags peaks peals peans pearl pears peart pease peaty peavy speak spear appeal appear peaced peachy peahen peaked pealed peanut pearls pearly peases peavey repeal repeat speaks spears

peace peaced peaceful peacenik

peach peachy impeach peaches peachier

peag peags

peak apeak peaks speak peaked speaks bespeak peaking speaker

peaks speaks bespeaks

peal peals appeal pealed repeal appeals pealing repeals

peals appeals repeals

pean peans peanut peanuts

pear pearl pears peart spear appear pearls pearly spears appears pearled speared

pearl pearls pearly pearled pearlier pearling

pears spears appears

peas pease peases appease peasant

pease peases appease appeased appeases

peat peaty repeat peatier repeats

pecan pecans

peck pecks speck copeck kopeck pecked specks copecks henpeck kopecks pecking specked speckle

pecks specks copecks kopecks henpecks

pedal pedals bipedal pedaled pedaling pedalled

pee epee peed peek peel peen peep peer pees epees peeks peels peens peeps peers peeve rupee speed tepee topee epopee peeing peeked peeled peeler peened peeped peeper peered peeved peeves peewee rupees speech speeds speedy teepee tepees topees toupee

peed speed speeds speedy speeded speeder

peek peeks peeked peeking

peel peels peeled peeler peelers peeling

peen peens peened peening

peep peeps peeped peeper peepers peeping

peer peers peered compeer peerage peeress peering

peers compeers

pees epees rupees tepees topees teepees toupees

peeve peeved peeves

peg pegs pegged
pekoe pekoes
pelf pelfs
pelt pelts spelt pelted pelter peltry pelters pelting
pen open pend pens pent aspen opens penal pence pends penes penna penni penny ripen spend spent upend append arpent aspens dampen deepen depend expend happen hempen holpen impend opened opener openly pences pencil pended penman penmen pennae penned pennia pennis pennon pentad penult penury pigpen reopen repent ripens spends upends
penal penalty penalize
pence pences spencer sixence spencers twopence
pend pends spend upend append depend expend impend pended spends upends appends depends expends impends pendant pendent pending propend stipend suspend upended
pends spends upends appends depends expends impends propends stipends suspends
penna pennae pennant pennants
penni pennia pennis pennies
penny tenpenny
pens opens aspens ripens dampens deepens expense happens pensile pension pensive pigpens reopens
pent spent arpent pentad repent pentads repents serpent
peon peons peony peonage peonies
pep peps pepla peppy peplos peplum pepped pepper pepsin peptic
peps pepsin pepsins
per peri perk perm pert apery caper doper duper gaper hoper hyper japer leper loper opera paper perch perdu peril peris perks perky perms perry perse piper sperm super taper toper upper viper wiper ampere beeper bumper camper capper carper cooper copper cupper damper dapper deeper diaper dipper dopers draper dumper dupers dupery eloper empery expert gapers griper groper hamper harper helper hipper hopers hopper jasper jumper keeper kipper leaper lepers limper lisper looper lopers lopper napery napper nipper operas pamper papers papery pauper peeper pepper perdue perils period perish perked permed permit perron perses person pertly peruke pipers popper proper pumper rapper rasper reaper ripper romper ropery sapper shaper simper sipper sniper sperms superb supers

supper tamper tapers temper tipper topers topper uppers vesper vipers weeper wipers yapper yelper zipper
perch perched perches perching
perdu perdue perdure perdured perdures
peri peril perils period perish imperil perigee periled periods perique periwig
peril perils periled imperils periling perilous
perk perks perky perked perkier perkily perking
perm perms sperm permed permit sperms perming permits permute
perms sperms
perse perses asperse aspersed asperses disperse
pert expert pertly experts pertain perturb
peso pesos
pest pests pester pestle anapest dampest deepest hippest limpest pesters pestled pestles tempest
pests anapests tempests
pet pets petal peter petit petty carpet lappet limpet moppet petals petard peters petite petrel petrol petted puppet sippet tappet tippet
petal petals petaled
peter peters petered petering
petit petite appetite petition
pets lappets limpets moppets puppets sippets tappets tippets
pew pews spew pewee spews pewees pewter spewed
pewee pewees
pews spews
phase phased phases emphases
phew nephew nephews
phial phials
phone phoned phones phoney diaphone earphone phonetic siphoned syphoned
phony symphony
phot photo phots photon photos aphotic photons
photo photon photos
phyla phylae
phyle phyletic
pi pie pig pin pip pit pix epic kepi pica pice pick pied pier pies pigs pika pike pile pill pimp pine ping pink pins pint piny pipe pips pipy pirn pish pita pits pity pixy spin spit spiv tipi apian aping apish aspic epics kepis lapin lipid okapi opine oping opium palpi pappi piano picks picky picot picul piece piers piety piggy pikas piked piker pikes pilaf pilau piled pilei piles pills pilot pimps pinch pined pines piney pings pinko pinks pinky pinna pinto pints pinup pious pipal piped piper

pipes pipit pique pirns pitas pitch pithy piton pivot pixel pixes pixie pizza pupil rapid sapid sepia spica spice spicy spied spiel spies spiff spike spiky spile spill spilt spine spins spiny spire spiry spite spits spitz spivs tapir tapis tempi tepid tipis topic unpin vapid
piano pianos
pica spica apical epical picaro spicae apicals epicarp picador picaros topical typical
pice spice apices spiced spices auspice coppice epicene hospice piceous spicery
pick picks picky pickax picked picker picket pickle pickup nitpick nutpick pickers pickets pickier picking pickled pickles pickups
picks nitpicks
picot picots picotee picotees
picul piculs
pie pied pier pies piece piers piety spied spiel spies apiece copied copier copies cowpie dopier espied espies hippie kelpie magpie pieced piecer pieces pieing pierce pipier potpie rapier spiels weepie yippie yuppie
piece apiece pieced piecer pieces piecers codpiece earpiece eyepiece
pied spied copied espied
pier piers copier dopier pierce pipier rapier bumpier campier copiers dippier dumpier goopier happier humpier jumpier loppier lumpier nappier nippier peppier pierced piercer pierces pulpier rapiers sappier seepier soapier soupier waspier weepier wispier zippier
piers copiers rapiers
pies spies copies espies cowpies dopiest guppies harpies hippies kelpies magpies nappies pipiest poppies potpies puppies yippies yuppies
pig pigs piggy pigeon pigged piggie piglet pignut pigout pigpen pigsty spigot
pigs pigsty pigskin
pika pikas
pike piked piker pikes spike pikers spiked spikes pikeman pikemen
piked spiked
piker pikers
pikes spikes
pilaf pilaff pilafs
pilau pilaus
pile piled pilei piles spile pileus spiles compile pileate pileous
piled compiled
piles spiles compiles

pill pills spill pillar pilled pillow spills lapilli papilla pillage pillars pillbox pilling pillion pillory pillows pillowy spilled

pills spills

pilot pilots copilot piloted copilots piloting

pimp pimps pimped pimple pimply pimping pimples

pin pine ping pink pins pint piny spin aping lapin opine oping pinch pined pines piney pings pinko pinks pinky pinna pinto pints pinup spine spins spiny unpin alpine coping doping duping gaping hatpin hoping hyping japing lapins loping lupine moping opined opines orpine pineal pinery pinged pinier pining pinion pinked pinkie pinkos pinnas pinned pinole pintle pintos pinups piping pippin rapine raping riping roping spinal spined spinel spines spinet supine taping tiepin toping typing umping unpins wiping

pinch pinched pinches pinchers pinchhit pinching

pine opine pined pines piney spine alpine lupine opined opines orpine pineal pinery rapine spined spinel spines spinet supine chopine lupines orpines pinesap pinetum rapines spinets supines vulpine

pined opined spined

pines opines spines pinesap rapines

ping aping oping pings coping doping duping gaping hoping hyping loping moping pinged piping raping riping roping taping toping typing umping wiping bopping bumping burping camping capping carping comping cooping copping craping cupping dapping dipping draping dumping eloping gapping gasping gimping gipping griping groping gulping gypping harping heaping helping hipping hooping hopping humping impinge jumping keeping lapping leaping limping lipping lisping looping lopping lumping mapping mopping napping nipping peeping pepping pimping pinging pinguid pipping pooping popping pulping pumping pupping ramping rapping rasping reaping ripping romping sapping scaping seeping shaping sipping sloping sniping soaping sopping stopping supping swiping tamping tapping tipping topping vamping wapping warping weeping yapping yelping yipping zapping zipping

pings dippings helpings toppings

pink pinko pinks pinky pinked pinkie pinkos pinkeye pinkeys pinkies pinking pinkish

pinko pinkos

pinna pinnas pinnate pinnacle

pins spins lapins unpins hatpins tenpins tiepins

pint pinto pints pintle pintos pintail

pinto pintos

pinup pinups

piny spiny

pious copious

pip pipe pips pipy pipal piped piper pipes pipit pipage pipals pipers pipier piping pipits pipkin pipped pippin

pipal pipals

pipe piped piper pipes pipers bagpipe panpipe pipeful pipette

piper pipers bagpiper piperine

pipes bagpipes panpipes pipestem

pipit pipits

pique piqued piques piquet

pirn pirns

pish apish aspish impish mopish pishes uppish apishly dumpish foppish lumpish waspish wimpish

pit pita pits pity spit pipit pitas pitch pithy piton spite spits spitz armpit pipits pitied pities pitman pitmen pitons pitted spited uppity

pita pitas capital epitaph pitapat

pitas epitasis

pitch pitched pitcher pitches pitchers pitching pitchman pitchmen pitchout

piton pitons

pits spits pipits armpits pulpits

pity uppity pitying

pivot pivots pivotal pivoted pivoting

pix pixy pixel pixes pixie pixels

pixel pixels

pizza pizzas

place placed placer places placet emplace placebo placers placets replace anyplace displace emplaced emplaces misplace placebos placenta replaced replaces

plage plages

plaid plaids

plain plains plaint explain plainer plainly plaints chaplain complain explains plainest

plait plaited plaiting

plan plane plank plans plant planar planed planer planes planet planks plants upland biplane deplane implant planers planets planing planish planked planned planner plantar planted planter replant uplands

plane planed planer planes planet biplane deplane planers planets airplane biplanes deplanes seaplane skiplane warplane

plank planks planked planking plankton

plant plants implant plantar planted planter replant eggplant implants pieplant plantain planters planting replants supplant

plash splash plashed plashes splashy plashing splashed splashes whiplash

plat plate plats platy splat plated platen plater plates splats plateau platens plating platoon platted platter platypi

plate plated platen plater plates plateau platens plateaus plateaux plateful platelet template tinplate

plats splats

platy platypi platypus

play playa plays splay playas played player replay splays airplay display gunplay misplay outplay playact playboy players playful playing playoff playpen replays splayed

playa playas playact playable playacts

plays splays replays airplays displays misplays outplays playsuit

plaza plazas

plea plead pleas pleat pleach pleads please pleats implead pleaded pleased pleases pleated

plead pleads implead pleaded pleading

pleas please pleased pleases pleasant pleasing pleasure

pleat pleats pleated pleating

plebe plebes plebeian

pled pledge coppled coupled dappled dimpled hoppled peopled pledged pledger pledges pledget poppled purpled rimpled rippled rumpled sampled stapled suppled tippled toppled tripled wimpled

plica plicae plicate replica replicas

plied applied implied replied complied supplied

plier pliers pimplier supplier

plink plinks plinked plinking

plod plods explode implode plodded

plop plops plopped

plot plots complot marplot plotted splotch subplot

plots complots marplots subplots

plow plows plowed plowboy plowing plowman

ploy ploys deploy employ deploys employs

ploys deploys

pluck plucks plucky plucked plucker pluckier plucking

plug plugs unplug earplug plugged unplugs

plugs earplugs

plum plumb plume plump plums peplum plumbs plumed plumes plumps peplums plumage plumbed plumber plumery pluming plummet plumped plumper plumply plumule

plumb plumbs plumbed plumber plumbers plumbing

plume plumed plumes

plump plumps plumped plumpers plumping

plunk plunks plunked kerplunk plunking

plus plush pluses nonplus plusses surplus

ply amply apply haply imply reply comply damply deeply dimply limply pimply plying ripply rumply simply supply triply

poach poached poacher poaches poaching

pock pocks pocket yapock pockets yapocks

pocks yapocks

pod pods bipod epode apodal bipods dipody epodes isopod podded podium podsol uropod

pods bipods podsol isopods podsols uropods

poem poems

poet poets poetic poetry poetess poetics poetize

poi pois poilu point poise spoil poilus points pointy poised poises poison spoils spoilt

poilu poilus

point points pointy appoint pointed appoints gunpoint midpoint pinpoint pointers pointier pointing

pois poise poised poises poison poising poisons

poise poised poises porpoise unpoised

poke poked poker pokes spoke pokers spoked spoken spokes bespoke cowpoke

poked spoked

poker pokers

pokes spokes cowpokes

polar bipolar dipolar polarity polarize

pole poled poles dipole poleax poleis dipoles maypole polecat polemic polenta tadpole

poles dipoles maypoles tadpoles

polis polish polished polisher polishes

polka polkas polkaed polkaing

poll polls polled pollen poller pollex pollard pollens pollers polling pollock pollute

polls pollster

polo polos apology

polyp polyps

pome pomes pomelo pomelos

pomp pompom pompon pompano pompoms pompous

pond ponds ponder despond ponders respond

ponds desponds responds

pone pones depone deponed depones propone

pones depones propones

pons capons gipons jupons coupons sponson sponsor tarpons weapons yaupons

pony eponym eponyms

pooch pooches

poof spoof spoofs spoofed

pooh poohs

pool pools spool pooled spools pooling spooled

pools spools

poon poons spoon spoons spoony harpoon lampoon spooned

poons spoons harpoons lampoons

poop poops pooped pooping

poor spoor poorer poorly spoors poorest spoored

pop pope pops popes poppy epopee maypop popgun poplar poplin popped popper popple

pope popes epopee popedom popeyed

pops maypops

porch porches

pore pored pores spore spores

pores spores

pork porks porky porker porkers porkier porkpie

porn porno pornos

porno pornos

port aport ports sport deport export import portal ported porter portly report sports sporty airport carport comport deports exports imports jetport portage portals portend portent porters portico porting portion portray purport rapport reports seaport sported support

ports sports deports airports carports comports jetports purports rapports seaports supports

pose posed poser poses appose depose expose impose oppose posers poseur repose adipose apposed apposes compose deposed deposes dispose exposed exposes imposed imposer imposes opposed opposer opposes poseurs propose purpose reposed reposes suppose

posed apposed deposed exposed imposed opposed reposed composed disposed proposed purposed supposed

poser posers composer imposers opposers proposer

poses apposes deposes adiposes composes disposes proposes purposes supposes

posh poshly

posit posits deposit posited apposite deposits opposite positing position positive positron

posse posses posset

post posts impost posted poster apostil apostle bedpost compost imposts outpost postage postals postbox postern posters postfix posting postman postmen posture postwar

posts bedposts composts outposts

pot pots spot depot potsy potty repot spots capote depots despot potash potato poteen potent potful pother potion potpie potted potter pottle repots sexpot spotty teapot

pots potsy spots depots repots despots potshot sexpots teapots

potty spotty

pouch pouchy pouched pouches pouching

pouf poufs pouffe pouffes

poult poults poultice

pound pounds expound impound pounded pounder compound expounds impounds pounders pounding propound

pour pours poured pouring

pout pouts spout pouted spouts dropout eelpout pouting spouted

pouts spouts dropouts eelpouts

power powers powered empowers manpower powerful powering

pox epoxy poxes cowpox

pram prams

prank pranks prankish

prate prated prates

prawn prawns

pray prays spray prayed prayer sprays praying sprayed

prays sprays

preen preens preened preening

prep preps prepay prepaid prepare prepays prepped preppie

prese preset presence presents preserve

press cypress depress pressed compress espresso expresso pressers pressing pressman pressmen pressors pressure suppress

prey preys osprey preyed lamprey ospreys preying

preys lampreys

price priced pricer prices caprice pricers caprices

prick pricks pricked pricket prickle prickly pinprick prickets pricking prickled prickles

pride prided prides prideful
prier priers
pries priest priestly
prig prigs sprig sprigs prigged spriggy upright
prigs sprigs
prim prime primp primal primed primer primes primly primps primacy primary primate primely primers priming primmed primmer primped
prime primed primer primes primeval
primp primps primped primping
prink prinks sprinkle
print prints sprint printed imprints misprint offprint printers printery printing printout reprints sprinted sprinter surprint
prior priory priorate prioress priories priority
prism prisms prismoid
priss prissy prissier prissily
prize prized prizes
pro proa prod prof prog prom prop pros prow apron proas probe prods proem profs progs promo proms prone prong proof props prose prosy proud prove prowl prows proxy repro aprons improv probed prober probes proems profit prolan proleg prolix promos prompt prongs pronto proofs propel proper propyl prosed proses proton proved proven proves prowls repros sprout uproar uproot uprose
proa proas uproar uproars
probe probed prober probes probers
prod prods prodded prodigy produce product
proem proems
prof profs profit profane profess proffer profile profits profuse
prog progs progeny progged program
prom promo proms promos prompt promise promote prompts
promo promos promoted promoter promotes
prong prongs pronged pronging
proof proofs disproof reproofs
prop props propel proper propyl apropos propane propels propend prophet propjet propman propmen propone propose propped propyls

pros prose prosy proses repros uprose leprose leprosy prosier prosing prosody prosper
prose proses uprose
proud proudly
prove proved proven proves approve proverb approved approves disprove improved improver improves proverbs reproved reproves unproved
prow prowl prows prowls prowess prowled prowler
prowl prowls prowled prowlers prowling
prude prudes prudent prudery prudence
prune pruned prunes prunella
pry spry prying spryer spryly
psalm psalms psalmist psalmody
pshaw pshaws pshawing
psych psycho psyched psyches psychic psychos psychics psyching
pub pubs pubic public
puce puces
puck pucks pucker puckers puckery
puff puffs puffy puffed puffer puffin puffers puffery puffier puffily puffing puffins
pug pugh pugs impugn oppugn pugged
puke puked pukes
pul pule puli pull pulp puls ampul puled pules pulik pulis pulls pulps pulpy pulse ampule ampuls copula cupule papule puling pulled pullet pulley pullup pulped pulque pulsar pulser pulses pulwar
pule puled pules ampule cupule papule ampules cupules opulent papules stipule
pules ampules cupules papules stipules
puli pulik pulis puling
pull pulls pulled pullet pulley pullup ampulla pullets pulleys pulling pullout pullups
pulp pulps pulpy pulped pulpier pulpify pulping pulpits pulpous
puls pulse ampuls pulsar pulser pulses impulse pulsars pulsate repulse
pulse pulser pulses impulses repulsed repulses
puma pumas
pump pumps pumped pumper pumpers pumping pumpkin
pun pung punk puns punt puny spun punch pungs punka punks punky punts punty spunk punchy pundit

punish punkah punkas punkie punned punted punter spunks spunky
punch punchy punched puncher punches keypunch puncheon punchers punchier punching
pung pungs expunge pungent
punk punka punks punky spunk punkah punkas punkie spunks spunky punkahs punkier
punka punkah punkas punkahs
punks spunks
punky spunky
puns punster
punt punts punty punted punter punters punties punting
pup pupa pups pupae pupal pupil puppy pupate pupils pupped puppet
pupa pupae pupal pupate pupated pupates
pupil pupils pupilage
pure puree purer impure pureed purees purely purest guipure
puree pureed purees pureeing
purge purged purger purges
purl purls purled purlin purlieu purling purlins purloin
purr purrs purred spurry purring spurred
purse pursed purser purses cutpurse
pus opus push puss lupus pushy pussy campus carpus corpus coypus opuses palpus pappus pushed pusher pushes pusses quipus rumpus
push pushy pushed pusher pushes pushers pushier pushing pushpin
puss pussy pusses pussier pussies
pussy pussycat
put puts putt input kaput putts putty depute deputy impute inputs putlog putout putrid putter repute sputum
puts inputs
putt putts putty putter putters puttied putties putting sputter
putty puttying
pya pyas
pylon pylons
pyre pyres pyrene pyrenes pyrexia
pyx pyxes pyxie pyxis pyxies
pyxie pyxies

q

qanat qanats
qat qats
qua aqua quad quag quay aquae aquas equal quack quads quaff quags quail quake quaky quale qualm quant quark quart quash quasi quass quays squab squad squat squaw equals equate loquat quacks quaffs quagga quaggy quahog quails quaint quaked quakes qualia qualms quango quanta quants quarks quarry quarte quarto quarts quartz quasar quaver squabs squads squall square squash squats squawk squaws
quack quacks quacked quackery quacking quackish
quad quads squad squads quadded quadrat quadric
quads squads
quaff quaffs quaffed quaffing
quag quags quagga quaggy quaggas
quail quails quailed quailing
quake quaked quakes seaquake
quale equaled
qualm qualms qualmish
quant quanta quants piquant quantal quanted quantic quantum aliquant quantics quantify quantile quanting quantity quantize
quark quarks

quart quarte quarto quarts quartz quartan quarter quartes quartet quartic quartos quartans quartern quarters quartets quartics quartile quartzes
quash squash quashed quasher quashes squashy quashing squashed squashes
quass quasses quassia quassias
quay quays quayage
quean queans cotquean
queen queens queened queendom queening
queer queers queerer queerest queerish
quell quells quelled quelling
quern querns
query querying
quest quests bequest quested bequests conquest inquests questers questing question questors requests
queue queued queues
quick quicken quicker quickie quickly quickens quickest quickies quickset
quid quids squid liquid squids liquids
quids squids liquids
quiet quiets quieted disquiet quietens quieters quieting quietism quietist quietude
quiff quiffs
quill quills squill quillai quilled coquille quilling quillons

quilt quilts quilted quilters quilting
quint quinte quints squint asquint quintal quintan quintain quintals quintans quintets quintile squinted
quip equip quips quipu equips quipus quipped
quips equips quipster
quipu quipus
quire quired quires squire acquire squired acquired acquires enquired enquires esquires inquired inquirer inquires required requires squireen
quirk quirks quirky quirked quirkier quirkily
quirt quirts squirt quirted quirting squirted
quit quite quits acquit equity quitch acquits coquito equites mesquit quitted quitter quittor
quite mesquite
quits acquits
quiz quizzed quizzer quizzes
quod quods
quoin quoins
quoit quoits quoiting
quota quotas quotable quotably
quote quoted quoter quotes misquote
quoth quotha quoths quothed quothing

rabat rabato rabats rabatos

rabbi rabbis rabbit rabbits crabbier crabbing drabbing grabbier grabbing rabbinic rabbitry

race brace grace raced racer races trace braced bracer braces graced graces raceme racers traced tracer traces bracero bracers embrace hyraces racemes raceway retrace terrace tracers tracery

raced braced graced traced embraced retraced terraced

racer bracer racers tracer bracero bracers tracers tracery embracer

races braces graces traces hyraces embraces retraces terraces

rack crack racks track wrack arrack cracks cracky racked racket tracks wracks arracks barrack bracket cracked cracker crackle crackly crackup grackle hatrack hayrack rackets racking tracked tracker

racks cracks tracks wracks arracks barracks hatracks hayracks

racy curacy piracy

rad brad grad orad rads brads farad grade grads radar radii radio radix radon trade abrade cradle farads graded grader grades gradin gradus parade radars raddle radial radian radios radish radium radius radome radons tetrad tirade traded trader trades

radar radars

radio radios radioed radioing

radix radixes

radon radons

rads brads grads farads tetrads

raff draff raffs draffs raffia raffle agraffe giraffe raffias raffish raffled raffles traffic

raffs draffs

raft craft draft graft kraft rafts crafts crafty drafts drafty grafts krafts rafted rafter crafted drafted draftee grafted grafter indraft rafters rafting updraft

rafts crafts drafts grafts krafts updrafts

rag brag crag drag frag raga rage rags brags crags drags frags ragas raged rages scrag sprag borage craggy dragon enrage forage garage mirage ragbag ragged raggle raging raglan ragman ragtag ragtop scrags sprags tragic tragus virago

raga ragas

rage raged rages borage enrage forage garage mirage average barrage borages courage enraged enrages foraged forager forages garages mirages moorage outrage overage peerage rageful storage tragedy umbrage

raged enraged foraged tragedy averaged outraged

rages borages enrages forages garages mirages averages barrages moorages outrages overages peerages storages umbrages

rags brags crags drags frags scrags sprags

rah rahs gerah surah torah gerahs graham hurrah sirrah surahs torahs

rahs gerahs surahs torahs hurrahs sirrahs

raid braid raids afraid braids raided raider braided raiders raiding upbraid

raids braids upbraids

rail brail frail rails trail brails derail railed railer bedrail frailty railers railing railway trailed trailer

rails brails bedrails entrails

rain brain drain grain rains rainy train brains brainy drains grains grainy rained sprain strain trains brained drained drainer grained ingrain moraine murrain rainbow rainier raining rainout refrain retrain sprains strains terrain trained trainee trainer

rains brains drains grains trains sprains strains ingrains murrains refrains retrains

rainy brainy grainy

raise braise fraise praise raised raises braised braises fraises praised praiser praises upraise appraise praisers upraised upraises

raj raja rajs rajah rajas rajahs

raja rajah rajas rajahs

rajah rajahs

rake brake crake drake raked rakee rakes braked brakes crakes drakes kraken rakees strake krakens strakes

raked braked

rakee rakees parakeet

rakes brakes crakes drakes strakes

raki rakis raking rakish braking

rakis rakish rakishly

rale rales morale braless chorale morales

rales braless morales chorales

rally orally jurally morally chorally plurally rallying

ram cram dram gram pram rami ramp rams tram cramp crams drama drams frame grams ihram prams ramps ramus scram tramp trams ziram ashram crambo cramps dramas framed framer frames gramps ihrams paramo ramble ramify ramjet rammed rammer ramous ramped ramrod scrams tramps zirams

rami ramify ceramic framing gourami keramic pyramid

ramp cramp ramps tramp cramps gramps ramped cramped crampon rampage rampant rampart ramping rampion tramped trample

ramps cramps gramps

rams crams drams grams prams trams ihrams scrams zirams ashrams

ran bran rand rang rani rank rant brand brans buran crane crank drank franc frank grand grant loran prank ranch rands randy range rangy ranis ranks rants reran arrant branch brands brandy branks branny burans craned cranes crania cranks cranky cranny errand errant francs franks grands grange granny grants lorans orange orangy outran parang prance pranks rancho rancid rancor random ranged ranger ranges ranked ranker rankle rankly ransom ranted ranter shoran shrank sprang strand trance tyrant uranic

ranch branch rancho ranched rancher ranches ranchos branched branches branchia ranchero ranchers ranching ranchman

rand brand grand rands randy brands brandy errand grands random strand branded errands grandam grandee grander grandly grandma grandpa randies strands veranda

rands brands grands errands strands grandson

randy brandy

rang range rangy grange orange orangy parang ranged ranger ranges sprang arrange derange granger granges oranges orangey parangs rangers ranging strange wrangle

range grange orange ranged ranger ranges arrange derange granger granges oranges orangey rangers strange arranged arranges deranged deranges estrange grangers stranger

rangy orangy

rani ranis crania uranic cranial craning cranium granite uranium

rank crank drank frank prank ranks branks cranks cranky franks pranks ranked ranker rankle rankly shrank cranked franked frankly outrank rankers rankest ranking rankled rankles

ranks branks cranks franks pranks outranks

rant grant rants arrant errant grants ranted ranter tyrant courant currant entrant frantic granted grantee granter grantor hydrant iterant migrant odorant operant ranting spirant tyrants vagrant vibrant warrant

rants grants tyrants currants entrants hydrants migrants odorants operants spirants vagrants warrants

rap crap frap rape raps rapt trap wrap crape craps drape fraps grape graph grapy raped rapes rapid scrap strap traps wraps wrapt craped crapes crappy draped draper drapes enrapt entrap grapes graphs grappa paraph rapids rapier rapine raping rapist rapped rappel rapper sarape satrap scrape scraps serape seraph teraph unwrap

rape crape drape grape raped rapes craped crapes draped draper drapes grapes sarape scrape serape drapers drapery grapery parapet scraped scraper scrapes serapes trapeze

raped craped draped scraped

rapes crapes drapes grapes scrapes serapes

rapid rapids rapidly rapidity

raps craps fraps traps wraps scraps satraps unwraps

rapt wrapt enrapt rapture

rare rarer curare rarefy rarely rarest curares rarebit

rase erase rased rases erased eraser erases phrase erasers phrased phrases

rased erased phrased

rases erases phrases

rash brash crash trash brashy rasher rashes rashly thrash trashy brasher crashed crashes rashest trashed trashes

rasp grasp rasps raspy grasps rasped rasper grasped grasper prasper raspers rasping

rasps grasps

rat brat drat frat rate rath rats brats carat crate frats grate irate jurat karat korat orate prate rated rates ratio ratty sprat wrath aerate berate borate bratty carats cerate cratch crated crater crates curate errata grated grater grates gratis gyrate jurats karate karats krater lyrate orated orates orator pirate prated prates rather ratify rating ration ratios ratite ratoon rattan ratted ratter rattle strata wraths wrathy

rate crate grate irate orate prate rated rates aerate berate borate cerate crated crater crates curate grated grater grates gyrate karate krater lyrate orated orates pirate prated prates aerated aerates berated berates borates cerated cirrate citrate craters curates emirate graters gyrated gyrates hydrate ingrate irately iterate kraters librate lyrated migrate narrate nitrate operate overate pirated prorate serrate titrate vibrate

rated crated grated orated prated aerated berated cerated gyrated lyrated pirated iterated librated migrated narrated nitrated operated prorated serrated vibrated

rates crates grates orates prates aerates berates borates curates gyrates emirates hydrates ingrates iterates librates migrates narrates nitrates operates prorates serrates titrates vibrates

rath wrath rather wraths wrathy

ratio ration oration rations aeration duration gyration orations rational rationed

rats brats frats carats jurats karats

ratty bratty

rave brave crave grave raved ravel raven raves trave braved braver braves craved craven craves graved gravel graven graver graves ravels ravens ravers travel traves bravely bravery bravest caravel deprave engrave gravels gravest raveled ravened travels unravel

raved braved craved graved depraved engraved maravedi

ravel gravel ravels travel bravely caravel gravels raveled travels unravel caravels graveled gravelly raveling traveled traveler travelog unravels

raven craven graven ravens ravened ravening ravenous

raves braves craves graves traves bravest gravest depraves engraves travesty

raw braw craw draw brawl brawn braws crawl craws drawl drawn draws prawn rawer straw trawl traws brawls brawny crawls crawly drawer drawls prawns rawest redraw scrawl sprawl straws strawy thrawn trawls

rawer drawer drawers

ray bray dray fray gray pray rays tray array brays drays foray frays grays moray prays rayed rayer rayon spray stray trays affray arrays astray betray brayed brayer crayon defray drayed estray forays frayed grayed grayer grayly hooray hurray morays prayed prayer rayers raying rayons sprays strays

rayed brayed drayed frayed grayed prayed arrayed forayed sprayed strayed betrayed defrayed hoorayed

rayon crayon rayons crayons crayoned

rays brays drays frays grays prays trays arrays forays morays sprays strays affrays betrays defrays hoorays hurrays

raze braze craze graze razed razee razes brazed brazen brazer brazes crazed crazes grazed grazer grazes razees brazens brazers grazers

razed brazed crazed grazed

razee razees

razes brazes crazes grazes

razor razors

razz razzed razzes frazzle razzing

re are ere ire ore rec red ref reg rem rep res ret rev rex acre area bare bore bred bree brew byre care cere core crew cure dare dire dree drew eyre fare fere fire fore free fret gore gree grew grey gyre hare here hire lire lore lure lyre mare mere mire more ogre ores pare pore prep prey pure pyre rare read real ream reap rear reck redd redo reds reed reef reek reel refs reft regs rein reis rely rend rent repo repp reps resh rest rete rets revs sere sire sore sure tare tire tore tree trek tret urea ware wire wore wren yare yore acred acres adore afire afore agree aired areas areca arena aware azure bared barer bares barre beret blare bored borer bores bread break bream breed brees breve brews byres cadre cared cares caret chare chore cored corer cores creak cream creed creek creel creep crepe crept cress crest crews crore cured cures curet dared dares direr dread dream dreed drees dregs dress eared egret erect erred eyres fared fares feres fired fires flare fores freak freed freer frees fresh frets genre glare gored gores great grebe greed green grees greet greys gyred gyres harem hares hired hirer hires inure jurel kreep lares litre livre lores lucre lured lures lyres mares meres metre mired mires mirex mitre morel mores murex murre nacre nares oared ochre ocrea ogres ombre oread padre pared pares pareu pored pores preen preps press prexy preys puree purer pyres quire rarer reach react reads ready realm reams reaps rearm rears reata rebec rebel rebus rebut recap recks recon recto recur redds redid redox redux reeds reedy reefs reeks reeky reels reeve refer refit refix refry regal rehab reify reign reins relax relay relic remex remit remix renal rends renew renin rents repay repel reply repos repot repps repro reran rerun reset resin rests retch retem retia retie retro retry reuse revel revue sabre scare score scree screw seres share shire shore shred shrew sired siren sires snare snore sorer sores spare spire spore spree stare stere store strep strew surer swore tared tares there three threw tired tires titre tread treat treed trees treks trend tress trets trews ureas uredo vireo wared wares where whore wired wires wreak wreck wrens wrest yores zaire

reach breach preach reached reaches breached breaches outreach preached preacher preaches reaching

react reacts reacted reactor reacting reaction reactive reactors

read bread dread oread reads ready tread breads dreads oreads reader reread thread treads unread already breaded breadth dreaded misread readers readied readies readily reading readmit readout rereads retread spreads threads thready treaded treadle unready

reads breads dreads oreads treads rereads spreads threads misreads retreads

ready already thready unready readying

real realm boreal cereal really realms realty unreal cereals realign realism reality realize realtor

realm realms

ream bream cream dream reams breams creams creamy dreams dreamt dreamy preamp reamed reamer scream stream creamed creamer dreamed dreamer preamps reamers reaming screams streams

reams breams creams dreams screams streams

reap reaps reaped reaper threap reapers reaping reapply

rear rearm rears dreary reared rearms arrears firearm forearm rearing rearmed

rearm rearms firearm forearm rearmed firearms forearms rearming rearmost

rears arrears

reata reatas

rebec rebecs

rebel rebels harebell rebelled trebeled

rebus rebuses

rebut rebuts rebuttal rebutted

rec reck recs areca erect recap recks recon recto recur wreck arecas direct erects recall recant recaps recast recede recent recess rechew recipe recite recked reckon recoil recons recook recopy record recoup rectal rector rectos rectum rectus recurs recuse tenrec wrecks

recap recaps recapped

reck recks wreck recked reckon wrecks freckle freckly recking reckons wrecked wrecker

recks wrecks

recon recons

recto rector rectos erector rectors rectory director erectors

recur recurs recurred

red bred redd redo reds acred aired bared bored cared cored cured dared eared erred fared fired gored gyred hired lured mired oared pared pored redds redid redox redux shred sired tared tired uredo wared wired adored barred blared burred credit dredge faired feared flared furred geared glared hatred inbred inured jarred jeered leered marred mitred moored neared odored paired parred peered poured purred quired reared redact redbud redcap redded redden redder redeem redeye redfin redoes redone redraw redrew redtop reduce roared sabred sacred scared scored seared shared shored shreds sirred snared snored soared soured spared spired spored stared stored teredo toured uredos veered warred whored

redd redds redded redden redder reddens reddest redding reddish

redo redox uredo redoes redone teredo uredos boredom redoing redoubt redound redoxes reredos teredos

redox redoxes

reds shreds

reed breed creed dreed freed greed reeds reedy treed agreed breeds creeds greedy pureed reeded reedit screed breeder decreed freedom inbreed reeding reedits

reeds breeds creeds inbreeds

reedy greedy

reef reefs reefed reefer reefers reefing

reek creek reeks reeky creeks reeked reeking

reeks creeks

reel creel reels creels freely reeled reelect reeling

reels creels

reeve reeves

ref refs reft refer refit refix refry bereft ireful prefab prefer prefix rarefy refers refile refill refine refits reflex reflux reform refuel refuge refund refuse refute

refer prefer refers prefers referee referees referral referred

refit refits refitted

refix prefix refixed refixes prefixed prefixes refixing

refry refrying

reft bereft

reg regs dregs regal barege dreggy forego regain regale regard regent regime regina region regius reglet reglue regnal regret

regal regale regales regalia

regs dregs

reify reifying

reign reigns reigned reigning

rein reins herein reined reining therein wherein

reis ogreish reissue

relax relaxed relaxer relaxes relaxant relaxing

relay relays relayed virelay relaying virelays

relic relics relict relicts derelict

rely barely direly merely purely rarely sorely surely relying sparely

rem harem remex remit remix bireme harems remade remain remake remand remark remedy remind remise remiss remits remora remote remove tremor uremia

remit remits eremite eremites remittal remitted

remix remixed remixes remixing

renal adrenal adrenals

rend rends trend render trends trendy renders rending

rends trends

renew renews renewal renewed renewals

renin renins

rent rents parent rental rented renter current rentals renters renting torrent

rents currents torrents

rep prep repo repp reps crepe crept preps repay repel reply repos repot repps repro strep crepes prepay repack repaid repair repast repave repays repeal repeat repels repent replay report repose repots repros repute streps trepan

repay prepay repays prepays repaying

repel repels repelled

reply replying

repo repos repot report repose repots reports reposed reposes

repos repose reposed reposing

repot repots repotted

repp repps prepped preppie
repro repros reproach reproofs reproved reproves
reps preps streps
rerun reruns
res ores resh rest acres bares bores byres cares cores cress crest cures dares dress eyres fares feres fires fores fresh gores gyres hares hires lares lores lures lyres mares meres mires mores nares ogres pares pores prese press pyres reset resin rests seres sires sores tares tires tress wares wires wrest yores adores afresh arrest azures barest barres blares cadres caress chares chores cresol crests crores direst dressy duress egress flares forest fresco genres glares heresy inures litres livres merest metres mitres nacres ochres ogress ombres padres preset presto purest quires rarest resale rescue reseal resell resent resets reshes reside resign resins resist resold resole resorb resort rested result resume sabres scares scores shares shires shores snares snores sorest spares spires spores stares steres stores stress surest thresh titres unrest whores wrests
reset preset resets
resh fresh afresh reshes thresh freshen fresher freshet freshly refresh reshape
resin resins resinous
rest crest rests wrest arrest barest crests direst forest merest presto purest rarest rested sorest surest unrest wrests armrest arrests crested dearest fairest forests imprest nearest poorest prestos restart restate restful resting restive restock restore sourest sparest trestle wrested wrestle
rests crests wrests arrests armrests
ret fret rete rets tret arete beret caret curet egret frets retch retem retia retie retro retry trets aretes berets carets claret cretin curets egrets ferret floret garret hereto imaret labret pretax pretor pretty regret retail retain retake retard retell retems retied reties retina retire retold retook retort retted return retype secret surety terete terret turret ureter uretic wretch
retch wretch retched retches stretch retching stretchy wretched wretches
rete retem retell retems terete ureter accrete excrete preteen pretend pretest pretext retells secrete ureters
retem retems
retie retied reties sureties
retro retroact
retry retrying

rets frets trets berets carets curets egrets clarets ferrets florets garrets imarets labrets regrets secrets terrets turrets
reuse reused reuses cereuses
rev revs breve revel revue breves brevet pareve prevue revamp reveal revels reverb revere revers revert revery review revile revise revive revoke revolt revues revved
revel revels reveled reveling
revue prevue revues
rex mirex murex prexy
rhea rheas airhead warhead
rheum rheums
rhino rhinos
rho rhos rhomb carhop rhodic rhombs
rhomb rhombs rhombic rhombus rhomboid
rhumb rhumba rhumbs rhumbas
rhyme rhymed rhymes
ria aria rial rias arias atria briar ceria coria curia feria friar maria noria rials riant riata stria triad trial aerial anuria atrial atrias briars briary burial curiae curial feriae ferial ferias friars friary gloria kerria lariat latria myriad narial norias nutria pariah rialto riatas scoria serial striae triads triage yttria
rial rials trial aerial atrial burial curial ferial narial rialto serial aerials burials retrial rialtos serials uxorial
rials aerials burials serials retrials
riant variant variants
rias arias atrias ferias norias anurias glorias nutrias
riata riatas
rib crib drib ribs bribe cribs dribs oribi tribe bribed briber bribes caribe oribis ribald riband ribbed ribbon scribe tribal tribes
ribs cribs dribs
rice price riced ricer rices trice priced pricer prices ricers thrice triced trices avarice caprice pricers
riced priced triced
ricer pricer ricers pricers
rices prices trices avarices caprices matrices
rich enrich richer riches ostrich richest
ricin ricing ricins pricing tricing
rick brick crick prick ricks trick bricks cricks pricks rickey strick tricks tricky bricked brickle cricked cricket derrick pricked pricket prickle prickly rickets rickety rickeys tricked tricker trickle
ricks bricks cricks pricks tricks derricks rickshaw
rid arid grid ride rids acrid bride gride grids lurid pride rider rides ridge ridgy acarid aridly boride bridal brides

bridge bridle deride florid fridge grided grides horrid hybrid irides iridic prided prides putrid ridded ridden riddle riders ridged ridges riding ridley stride torrid
ride bride gride pride rider rides boride brides deride grided grides irides prided prides riders stride astride borides derided derides hayride hydride nitride outride strides trident
rider riders outrider
rides brides grides irides prides borides derides strides hayrides hydrides nitrides outrides
ridge bridge fridge ridged ridges abridge bridged bridges fridges abridged abridges porridge
rids grids acarids hybrids
riel oriel riels oriels
riels oriels
rif rife riff rifs rift drift riffs rifle rifts serif adrift drifts drifty griffe purify riffed riffle rifled rifles rifted serifs sherif shrift strife tariff thrift trifid trifle verify
rife strife strifes
riff riffs griffe riffed riffle tariff griffes griffin midriff riffing riffled riffles sheriff tariffs
riffs tariffs midriffs sheriffs
rifle rifled rifles trifle trifled rifleman riflemen triflers
rifs serifs sherifs
rift drift rifts adrift drifts drifty rifted shrift thrift drifter grifter rifting shrifts thrifty
rifts drifts
rig brig frig grig prig rigs trig brigs frigs grigs prigs right rigid rigor sprig trigs aright bright fright frigid origin rigged rigger righto rights rigors sprigs trigon wright
right aright bright fright righto rights wright righted affright brighten brighter brightly frighten outright rightful righting rightist uprights
rigid frigid rigidly frigidly rigidity
rigor rigors rigorism rigorous
rigs brigs frigs grigs prigs trigs sprigs
rile riled riles virile febrile periled puerile sterile
riled periled
rill drill frill grill krill rille rills trill brills drills frills frilly grille grills rilles shrill thrill trills drilled frilled gorilla grilled grilles rilling shrills shrilly thrills trilled zorille
rille grille rilles drilled frilled grilled trilled shrilled thrilled thriller zorilles
rills brills drills frills grills trills

rim brim grim prim rime rims rimy trim brims crime crimp grime grimy prime primp rimed rimes scrim trims crimes crimps crimpy grimed grimes grimly megrim primal primed primer primes primly primps riming rimmed rimple scrimp scrims shrimp trimly

rime crime grime prime rimed rimes crimes grimed grimes primed primer primes primely primers

rimed grimed primed

rimes crimes grimes primes

rims brims trims scrims crimson megrims

rimy grimy

rind grind rinds grinds brindle grinder

rinds grinds

ring bring rings wring airing baring boring brings caring coring cringe curing daring during earing erring faring firing fringe goring gringo gyring hiring luring miring oaring paring poring ringer siring spring string taring tiring waring wiring wrings adoring barring bearing blaring borings burring cringed cringes cringle earings earring fairing fearing firings flaring fringed fringes furring gearing glaring gringos hearing herring inuring jarring jeering leering marring mitring mooring nearing pairing parings parring peering pouring purring quiring rearing ringers ringing ringlet roaring sabring sacring scaring scoring searing sharing shoring sirring snoring soaring souring sparing spiring sporing springe springs springy staring storing strings stringy syringe tearing touring veering warring wearing whoring wringed wringer

rings brings wrings borings earings parings bearings earrings fairings hearings herrings moorings pairings ringside shorings

rink brink drink prink rinks brinks drinks prinks shrink crinkle crinkly drinker shrinks trinket wrinkle wrinkly

rinks brinks drinks prinks

rinse rinsed rinser rinses

riot riots heriot rioted rioter chariot heriots patriot rioters rioting riotous

riots chariots patriots

rip drip grip ripe rips trip drips dript gripe grips ripen scrip strip tripe trips drippy griped griper gripes grippe ripely ripens riping ripped ripper ripple ripply ripsaw scrips script stripe strips stripy tripes triple triply tripos

ripe gripe ripen tripe griped griper gripes ripely ripens stripe tripes gripers ripened striped striper stripes

ripen ripens ripened ripeness ripening

rips drips grips trips ripsaw scrips strips ripsaws

rise arise risen riser rises arisen arises cerise crises irises risers uprise apprise emprise friseur orrises reprise sunrise uprisen uprises

risen arisen

riser risers

rises arises crises irises apprises emprises nebrises reprises sunrises

risk brisk frisk risks risky frisks frisky risked brisket briskly frisked riskful riskier riskily risking

risks frisks

risky frisky

rite rites trite write barite pyrite sprite triter writer writes azurite barites diorite ferrite merited nitrite pyrites rewrite sorites sprites tritest writers

rites writes barites azurites diorites ferrites nitrites

rival rivals arrival rivaled rivalry arrivals corrival rivaling

rive drive rived riven river rivet arrive derive drivel driven driver drives grivet privet rivers rivets shrive strive thrive trivet arrived arrives deprive derived derives drivels drivers grivets privets riveted riveter shrived shrivel shriven shrives striven strives thrived thriven thrives trivets

rived arrived derived shrived thrived

riven driven

river driver rivers drivers riverbed riverine

rivet grivet privet rivets trivet riveted riveters riveting

riyal riyals

roach broach abroach roaches approach broached broaches encroach reproach

road broad roads abroad broads byroad inroad broadax broaden broader broadly byroads inroads roadbed roadies roadway

roads broads byroads inroads roadshow roadside roadster

roam roams roamed roamer roamers roaming

roan groan roans groans groaned groaner

roans groans

roar roars roared roarer uproar roaring uproars

roars uproars

roast roasts roasted roaster roasting

rob robe robs carob probe robed robes robin roble throb aerobe arroba carobs probed prober probes robbed robber

robing robins robles robots robust strobe throbs

robe probe robed robes aerobe probed prober probes strobe aerobes disrobe microbe probers strobes

robed probed disrobed

robes probes aerobes strobes disrobes microbes

robin robing robins probing

roble robles problem problems

robs carobs throbs

roc rock rocs brock crock frock rocks rocky broche brocks crocks crocus frocks grocer rochet rocked rocker rocket rococo troche

rock brock crock frock rocks rocky brocks crocks frocks rocked rocker rocket bedrock crocked crocket defrock frocked rockers rockets rockier rocking

rocks brocks crocks frocks defrocks

rod prod rode rods trod erode prods rodeo scrod eroded erodes parody ramrod rodded rodent rodeos scrods strode

rode erode rodeo eroded erodes rodent rodeos strode corrode outrode rodents tetrode

rodeo rodeos

rods prods scrods ramrods

roe froe roes froes proem throe heroes proems throes zeroed zeroes

roes froes heroes throes zeroes

rogue brogue drogue rogues brogues drogues

roil broil roils roily broils roiled broiled broiler embroil roiling

roils broils embroils

role roles parole proleg caroled caroler paroled parolee paroles prolegs safrole

roles paroles safroles

roll droll rolls troll drolls drolly enroll rolled roller scroll stroll trolls bedroll corolla drolled enrolls logroll payroll rollers rollick rolling rollway scrolls strolls trolled trolley trollop

rolls drolls trolls scrolls bedrolls logrolls payrolls

romp romps prompt romped romper prompts rompers romping

rondo rondos

rood brood roods broods broody brooded brooder

roods broods

roof proof roofs proofs roofed roofer reproof roofers roofing rooftop sunroof

roofs proofs reproofs sunroofs

rook brook crook rooks rooky brooks crooks rooked rookie brooked crooked rookery rookies rooking rooks brooks crooks

room broom groom rooms roomy brooms grooms roomed roomer roomie barroom bedroom groomed legroom mudroom roomers roomful roomier roomies rooming taproom tearoom

rooms brooms grooms barrooms bedrooms mudrooms taprooms tearooms

roost roosts roosted roosters roosting

root roots rooty rooted rooter uproot cheroot rooters rootier rooting rootlet taproot uproots

roots cheroots taproots

rope grope roped ropes trope groped groper gropes propel proper ropery tropes gropers propels propend towrope

roped groped

ropes gropes tropes towropes

ropy propyl entropy propyls

roque roques roquet baroque croquet croquets piroques

rose arose erose prose rosed roses morose proses rosery uprose cirrose leprose necrose operose roseate rosebud roseola rosette sucrose

rosed necrosed

roses proses necroses neuroses sucroses

rosin rosing rosins rosiny rosined rosiness

rosy prosy leprosy

rot grot rota rote rotl roto rots trot broth froth grots rotas rotes rotos tarot troth trots wrote broths carrot crotch croton erotic froths frothy grotto parrot proton rotary rotate rotche rotgut rotted rotten rotter rotund scrota troths

rota rotas rotary rotate scrota rotated rotates rotator scrotal

rotas protasis

rote rotes wrote garrote protect protein protest rewrote

rotes garrotes protests

rotl

roto rotos croton proton crotons protons

rots grots trots carrots parrots

rouge rouged rouges

rough roughs trough borough brought drought roughed boroughs brougham droughts droughty roughage roughens roughest roughing thorough

round around ground rounds aground grounds rounded roundel rounder roundly roundup grounded grounder roundels rounders roundest rounding roundish roundlet roundups surround

rouse arouse grouse roused rouses aroused arouses carouse groused ca-

roused carousel carouser carouses trousers

roust rousts rousted rousting

rout grout route routs trout grouts routed router routes sprout trouts crouton grouted reroute routers routine routing sprouts

route routed router routes grouted grouters rerouted reroutes sprouted

routs grouts trouts

rove drove grove prove roved rover roves trove droved drover droves grovel groves proved proven proves rovers shrove strove throve trover troves approve drovers grovels improve proverb reprove trovers

roved droved proved approved improved reproved unproved

rover drover rovers trover drovers proverb improver proverbs

roves droves groves proves troves approves improves reproves

row brow crow frow grow prow rows trow arrow brown brows crowd crown crows drown frown frows growl grown grows prowl prows rowan rowdy rowed rowel rowen rower serow throw trows arrows barrow borrow browns browse burrow crowds crowed crowns drowns drowse drowsy escrow farrow frowns frowsy frowzy furrow grower growls growth harrow marrow morrow narrow prowls rowans rowels rowens rowers rowing serows sorrow thrown throws trowed trowel yarrow

rowan rowans

rowdy rowdyism

rowed crowed trowed borrowed burrowed furrowed harrowed narrowed

rowel rowels trowel roweled roweling troweled

rowen rowens

rower grower rowers borrower burrower harrower narrower

rows brows crows frows grows prows trows arrows browse drowse drowsy frowsy serows throws barrows borrows browsed browser browses burrows drowsed drowses escrows farrows furrows harrows marrows morrows narrows sorrows yarrows

royal royals royally royalty royalist

rub drub grub rube rubs ruby drubs grubs rubes ruble scrub shrub cherub grubby rubato rubbed rubber rubble rubbly rubied rubies rubles rubric scrubs shrubs

rube rubes rubella

ruble rubles

rubs drubs grubs scrubs shrubs cherubs

ruche ruches

ruck rucks truck rucked ruckle ruckus struck trucks rucking ruckles trucked trucker truckle

rucks trucks rucksack

rudd rudds ruddy cruddy rudder crudded rudders ruddier ruddock

ruddy cruddy

rude crude prude ruder cruder prudes rudely rudest crudely crudest detrude extrude intrude obtrude prudent prudery ruderal strudel

ruder cruder prudery ruderal extruder intruder obtruder ruderals

rue grue rued rues true cruel cruet gruel grues sprue trued truer trues accrue cruets embrue gruels imbrue rueful sprues truest untrue

rued trued accrued embrued imbrued

rues grues trues sprues truest accrues embrues imbrues

ruff gruff ruffs ruffed ruffle scruff gruffly ruffian ruffled ruffles scruffs scruffy truffle

ruffs scruffs

rug drug ruga rugs drugs rugae rugby shrug frugal rugged rugger rugose shrugs

ruga rugae frugal

rugs drugs shrugs

ruin ruing ruins ruined truing ruinate ruining ruinous

ruing truing accruing embruing imbruing

rule ruled ruler rules curule ferule rulers ferrule feruled ferules misrule

ruled feruled ferruled misruled

ruler rulers

rules ferules misrules

rum drum grum rump rums aurum brume crumb crump drums forum frump grume grump jorum rumba rumen rummy rumor rumps scrum serum strum thrum trump antrum aurums brumal brumes crumbs crumby crummy crumps forums frumps frumpy grumes grumps grumpy jorums labrum quorum rumbas rumble rumbly rummer rumors rumple rumply rumpus sacrum scrums serums struma strums thrums trumps

rumba rumbas

rumen cerumen

rummy crummy

rumor rumors rumored rumoring

rump crump frump grump rumps trump crumps frumps frumpy grumps grumpy rumple rumply rumpus trumps crumped crumpet crumple rumpled rumples trumped trumpet

rumps crumps frumps grumps trumps

rums drums aurums forums jorums scrums serums strums thrums quorums sacrums

run rune rung runs runt brunt drunk grunt korun prune rerun runes rungs runic runny runts runty trunk wrung brunch brunet brunts crunch drunks gerund grungy grunts koruna outrun pruned prunes reruns rundle runlet runnel runner runoff runway shrunk sprung strung trunks

rune prune runes brunet pruned prunes brunets

runes prunes

rung rungs wrung grungy sprung strung grunges

runs reruns outruns

runt brunt grunt runts runty brunts grunts grunted grunter runtier

runts brunts grunts

rupee rupees

rural crural ruralism ruralist ruralize

ruse cruse druse ruses ceruse cruses druses uruses overuse perused peruser peruses viruses

ruses cruses druses uruses choruses citruses overuses walruses

rush brush crush rushy brushy inrush onrush rushed rushee rusher rushes thrush brushed brushes bulrush crushed crusher crushes rushees rushers rushier rushing

rushy brushy

rusk brusk rusks

rust crust rusts rusty trust crusts crusty rusted rustic rustle thrust trusts crusted encrust entrust frustum incrust rustics rustier rustily rusting rustled rustler rustles thrusts trusted trustee

rusts crusts trusts encrusts entrusts incrusts

rusty crusty

rut ruth ruts brute rutty strut truth brutal brutes crutch rutted struts truths

ruth truth truths ruthful

ruts struts

rye ryes dryer fryer dryers fryers spryer

ryot ryots

s

saber sabers sabered sabering
sabin sabins
sable sables usable disable amusable disabled erasable kissable passable reusable
sabot sabots sabotage saboteur
sabra sabras
sabre sabred sabres
sac sack sacs sacks ovisac sachem sachet sacked sacker sacral sacred sacrum
sack sacks sacked sacker ransack sackbut sackers sacking
sacks ransacks
sacs ovisacs
sad sadhe sadhu sadly tsadi pesade sadden sadder saddle sadhes sadhus sadism sadist
sadhe sadhes
sadhu sadhus
safe safer safely safest safety unsafe
sag saga sage sago sags sagas sager sages saggy sagos usage dosage sagely sagest saggar sagged usages visage
saga sagas
sage sager sages usage dosage sagely sagest usages visage corsage dosages massage message passage presage sausage visages
sages sagest usages dosages visages corsages massages messages passages presages sausages
sago sagos isagoge sapsago
sagos sapsagos
sahib sahibs
said unsaid
saiga saigas
sail sails assail sailed sailer sailor assails sailers sailing sailors skysail topsail wassail
sails assails skysails topsails wassails
sain saint fusain saints fusains sainted saintly visaing
saint saints sainted saintly
sake saker sakes forsake
sakes forsakes
saki sakis
sal sale sals salt basal nasal psalm salad salep sales sally salmi salon salpa salsa salts salty salve salvo sisal basalt bursal causal dorsal dossal mensal missal psalms resale salaam salads salami salary saleps salify salina saline saliva sallet sallow salmon salons saloon saloop salpae salpas salsas salted salter salute

salved salver salves salvia salvor salvos sisals tarsal vassal
salad salads
sale salep sales resale saleps resales
salep saleps
sales resales salesman salesmen
sally nasally dorsally sallying
salmi psalmist
salon salons
salpa salpae salpas
sals salsa salsas sisals causals dorsals missals salsify tarsals vassals
salsa salsas
salt salts salty basalt salted salter basalts saltant saltern saltily saltine salting saltish
salts basalts
salve salved salver salves
salvo salvor salvos salvoes
samba sambar sambas sambaed sambars sambaing
same samekh sesame samekhs
samp samps sampan sample sampans sampled sampler samples
sand sands sandy sandal sanded sander sandhi sandals sandbag sandbox sandbur sanders sandhis sandhog sandier sanding sandlot sandman sandmen
sane saner insane sanely sanest
sang linsang sangria
sap saps sapid sappy sapped sapper
sapid sapidity
saps sapsago
sard mansard sardine
sari saris tsarina tsarist
saris tsarist tsarists
sark sarks
sash sashay sashed sashes sashays sashing
sass sassy sassed sasses sassier sassing
sat sated satem sates satin satyr ansate ersatz isatin satang sateen sating satins satiny satire satrap satyrs
sated pulsated
sates pulsates
satin isatin sating satins satiny satinet satinets
satyr satyrs satyric
sauce sauced saucer sauces saucers saucepan
sauna saunas
save saved saver saves savers
saver savers
savin saving savins savings

savor savors savory savored savorer savorers savorier savoring unsavory
savoy savoys
savvy savvying
saw sawn saws sawed jigsaw ripsaw sawfly sawing sawyer seesaw
sawed jigsawed seesawed
saws jigsaws ripsaws seesaws
sax saxes
say says assay essay sayer sayid assays essays sayers saying sayyid
sayer sayers assayer essayer assayers essayers naysayer
says assays essays
scab scabs scabby scabbed scabble scabies
scad scads cascade
scag boscage
scald scalds scalded scaldic scalding
scale scaled scaler scales scalene scalers
scall scalls scallop escallop fiscally scallion scallops
scalp scalps scalped scalpel scalper scalpels scalpers scalping
scam scamp scams scampi scamps scamped scamper
scamp scampi scamps scamped scamper scampers scamping scampish
scan scans scant scants scanty descant discant scandal scanned scanner scanted scantly
scans scansion
scant scants scanty descant discant scanted scantly descants discants scantier scantily scanting
scape escape scaped scapes escaped escapee escaper escapes escapees escapers seascape
scar scare scarf scarp scars scary escarp lascar scarab scarce scared scares scarfs scarps cascara discard escarps lascars mascara piscary scarabs scarcer scarfed scarier scarify scaring scarlet scarped scarper scarred scarves
scare scared scares
scarf scarfs scarfed scarfing
scarp escarp scarps escarps scarped scarper escarped scarping
scars lascars
scary piscary
scat scats muscat scathe muscats scathed scathes scatted
scats muscats
scaup scaups

scend ascend ascends descend scended ascended descends scending

scene scenes obscene scenery

scent ascent scents ascents descent nascent scented crescent descents scenting

schmo schmoes schmoos schmooze

schwa schwas

scion scions

scoff scoffs scoffed scoffer scoffers scoffing scofflaw

scold scolds scolded scolder scolders scolding

scone scones

scoop scoops scooped scoopful scooping

scoot scoots scooted scooter scooters scooting

scop scope scops scopes scopula

scope scopes

score scored scorer scores scorers

scorn scorns scorned scorner scorners scornful scorning

scot ascot ascots mascot scotch scoter scotia mascots scotias

scour scours scoured scourer scourge scourers scourged scourges scouring

scout scouts scouted scouter scouters scouting

scow scowl scows scowls scowled

scowl scowls scowled scowling

scrag scrags scraggy scraggly

scram scrams scramble scrammed

scrap scrape scraps scraped scraper scrapes scrappy scrapers scraping scrapped scrapple

scree screed screen screes screech screens discreet screechy screened screener

screw screws screwy screwed unscrew screwier screwing setscrew unscrews

scrim scrimp scrims scrimps scrimpy scrimped

scrip scrips script scripts adscript scripted

scrod scrods scrodded

scrub scrubs scrubby scrubbed scrubber

scrum scrums

scud scudi scudo scuds escudo escudos scudded

scudo escudo escudos

scuff scuffs scuffed scuffle scuffing scuffled scuffles

scull sculls sculled scullery sculling scullion

sculp sculps sculpt sculpts sculpted sculptor

scum scums scummy scummed

scup scups scupper

scurf scurfs scurfy

scut scuta scute scuts scutch scutes scutum scutage scuttle

scuta scutage scutages

scute scutes

sea seal seam sear seas seat seax seals seams seamy sears seats inseam nausea reseal seabed sealed sealer seaman seamed seamen search seared season seated seaway unseat

seal seals reseal sealed sealer reseals sealant sealers sealery sealing

seals reseals sealskin

seam seams seamy inseam seaman seamed seamen inseams seamier seaming

seams inseams

sear sears search seared searing

seas season disease seasick seaside seasons

seat seats seated unseat caseate roseate seating unseats

seats unseats

sebum sebums

sect sects bisect insect sector bisects dissect insects sectary sectile section sectors

sects bisects insects dissects

sedan sedans

sedge sedges

sedum sedums

see seed seek seel seem seen seep seer sees fusee seeds seedy seeks seels seems seeps seepy seers beseem fusees lessee seeded seeder seeing seeker seemed seemly seeped seesaw seethe unseen

seed seeds seedy seeded seeder allseed aniseed axseeds hayseed linseed seedbed seeders seedier seeding

seeds axseeds allseeds aniseeds hayseeds linseeds

seek seeks seeker seekers seeking

seel seels

seem seems beseem seemed seemly beseems seeming

seems beseems

seen unseen kamseen

seep seeps seepy seeped seepage seepier seeping

seer seers seeress

sees fusees seesaw lessees seesaws

sego segos

segue segued segues segueing

seine seined seines

seize seized seizer seizes

selah selahs

self itself myself herself himself oneself ourself selfish thyself

sell sells resell seller outsell resells sellers selling sellout

sells outsells

semen semens basemen basement casement easement horsemen housemen

semi semis semina seminal seminar semipro

sen send sent hosen risen sends senna sense absent arisen assent chosen lessen loosen resent senary senate sendal sender senega senile senior sennas sennet sennit sensed senses sensor sentry wisent worsen

send sends sendal sender godsend sendals senders sending

sends godsends

senna sennas

sense sensed senses nonsense

sent absent assent resent sentry wisent absents assents consent dissent present resents wisents

sepal sepals

sepoy sepoys

sept septa septet septic septum aseptic septate septets septime septums

septa septate

sera serai serais serape seraph serapes seraphs

serai serais

sere seres serene

serf serfs serfdom

serge serges sergeant

serif serifs

serin serine serins anserine

serow serows

serum serums

serve served server serves deserve observe reserve conserve deserved deserves observed observer observes preserve reserved reserves subserve

servo servos

set seta sets asset beset inset onset reset setae setup upset assets basset closet corset cosset gusset insets offset onsets outset peseta posset preset resets russet setoff setose settee setter settle setups subset sunset upsets

seta setae peseta pesetas

sets assets besets insets onsets resets upsets bassets closets corsets cossets gussets offsets outsets possets presets russets subsets sunsets

setup setups

seven sevens seventh sevenths

sever severe severs several severer severely severest severing severity

sew sewn sews sewed sewer sewage sewers sewing

sewer sewers sewered sewerage sewering

sex sext sexy desex sexed sexes sexts sexier sexing sexism sexist sexpot sextet sexton sexual unisex

sexes desexes

sext sexts sextet sexton sextant sextets sextile sextons

sh ash she shy ashy bash bosh bush cash cosh dash dish fash fish gash gosh gush hash hush josh lash lush mash mesh mush nosh pish posh push rash resh rush sash shad shag shah sham shaw shay shed shew shim shin ship shiv shod shoe shoo shop shot show shun shut tosh tush wash wish abash apish ashen ashes awash blush brash brush bushy clash crash crush cushy fishy flash flesh flush fresh frosh gnash gushy harsh kasha knish leash marsh meshy mushy pasha plash plush pshaw pushy quash rushy shack shade shady shaft shags shake shako shaky shale shall shalt shame shams shank shape shard share shark sharp shave shawl shaws sheaf shear sheds sheen sheep sheer sheet sheik shelf shell sherd shewn shews shied shies shift shill shims shine shins shiny ships shire shirk shirr shirt shive shivs shlep shoal shoat shock shoed shoer shoes shoji shone shook shoos shoot shops shore shorn short shote shots shout shove shown shows showy shred shrew shrub shrug shuck shuns shunt shush shuts shyer shyly slash slosh slush smash stash sushi swash swish trash usher washy welsh whish woosh

shack shacks shackle shackled shackles

shad shade shady shaded shades shadow shadier shadily shading shadoof shadows shadowy

shade shaded shades sunshade

shaft shafts shafted camshaft shafting

shag shags shaggy shagged

shake shaken shaker shakes shakers unshaken

shako shakos

shale shales

shall shallop shallot shallow shalloon shallops shallots shallows

sham shame shams shaman shamas shamed shames shammy shamus ashamed shamans shamble shaming shammed shammer shampoo

shame shamed shames ashamed shameful

shank shanks shanked shanking

shape shaped shaper shapes reshape shapely misshape reshaped reshapes

shard shards

share shared sharer shares sharers

shark sharks sharked sharking

sharp sharps sharped sharpen sharper sharpie sharply sharpens sharpest sharpies sharping

shave shaved shaven shaver shaves shavers

shaw pshaw shawl shaws bashaw cashaw cushaw pshaws shawls bashaws cushaws goshawk

shawl shawls

shaws pshaws bashaws cushaws

shay sashay sashays

she shed shew ashen ashes sheaf shear sheds sheen sheep sheer sheet sheik shelf shell sherd sheth shewn shews usher bashed bashes boshes bushed bushel bushes cashed cashes cashew coshed cosher coshes dashed dasher dashes dished dishes fashed fashes fished fisher fishes gashed gashes gushed gusher gushes hashed hashes hushed hushes joshed josher joshes kasher kosher lashed lasher lashes lushes mashed masher mashes meshed meshes mushed mushes noshed noshes pishes pushed pusher pushes rasher rashes reshes rushed rushee rusher rushes sashed sashes shears sheath sheens sheers sheets sheikh sheiks shekel shells shelly shelty shelve sherds sherif sherpa sherry sheths shewed tushes ushers washed washer washes wished wisher wishes

shear shears sheared shearing

shed sheds bashed bushed cashed coshed dashed dished fashed fished gashed gushed hashed hushed joshed lashed mashed meshed mushed noshed pushed rushed sashed washed wished abashed blushed brushed clashed crashed crushed flashed fleshed flushed gnashed leashed plashed quashed shedder slashed sloshed slushed smashed stashed swashed swished trashed welshed whished wooshed

sheen sheens sheened sheening

sheep sheepdog sheepish sheepman sheepmen

sheer sheers sheered sheerly sheering

sheet sheets sheeted bedsheet sheeting

sheik sheikh sheiks sheikdom

shell shells shelly shellac shelled sheller eggshell nutshell seashell shellacs shellers shellier shelling

sherd sherds

shew shewn shews cashew shewed cashews shewing

shews cashews

shies ashiest mashies bushiest cushiest dashiest fishiest mushiest pushiest rushiest washiest

shift shifts shifty shifted shifters shiftier shiftily shifting

shill shills shilling

shim shims shimmy shimmed shimmer

shin shine shins shiny shindy shined shiner shines shinny bashing bushing cashing coshing dashing dishing fashing fishing gashing gushing hashing hushing joshing lashing mashing meshing mushing noshing pushing rushing sashing shiners shingle shinier shining shinned washing wishing

shine shined shiner shines outshine sunshine

shiny sunshiny

ship ships airship gunship kinship shipman shipped shipper shipway warship worship

ships airships gunships midships shipside warships worships

shire shires

shirk shirks shirked shirkers shirking

shirr shirrs shirred shirring

shirt shirts shirting

shiv shive shivs shiver shives shivers shivery yeshiva

shive shiver shives shivered

shlep shlepp shleps shlepped

shoal shoals shoaly shoaled shoalier shoaling

shoat shoats

shock shocks shocked shocker shockers shocking

shod shoddy shodden

shoe shoed shoer shoes shoers gumshoe shoeing

shoer shoers

shoes gumshoes

shoji shojis

shone outshone

shoo shook shoos shoot shooed shoots shoofly shooing shooter

shoot shoots offshoot shooters shooting

shop shops bishop shoppe bishops shophar shopped shopper shoppes toyshop

shops bishops toyshops

shore ashore shored shores offshore seashore

short shorts shorty shorted shortia shortage shortcut shortens shortias shorting shortish

shot shote shots shotes upshot earshot eyeshot gunshot hipshot hotshot potshot shotgun shotted upshots

shote shotes

shots eyeshots gunshots hotshots potshots

shout shouts shouted washout shouters shouting washouts

shove shoved shovel shover shoves pushover shoveled

show shown shows showy showed shower showers showery showier showing showman showmen showoff

shred shreds shredded shredder

shrew shrews beshrew beshrews shrewder shrewdly shrewish

shrub shrubs shrubby

shrug shrugs shrugged

shuck shucks shucked shucker shuckers shucking

shun shuns shunt shunts shunned shunner shunted

shunt shunts shunted shunting

shut shuts shutout shutter shuttle

shy ashy bushy cushy fishy gushy meshy mushy pushy rushy shyer shyly washy brashy brushy flashy fleshy marshy shyest shying sloshy slushy swishy trashy

si sib sic sin sip sir sis sit six nisi sibs sick side sift sigh sign silk sill silo silt simp sine sing sink sins sips sire sirs site sith sits size apsis arsis aside basic basil basin basis eosin fusil lysin lysis mesic music mysid oasis osier posit quasi resin rosin sibyl sicko sided sides sidle siege sieve sifts sighs sight sigil sigma signs silks silky sills silly silos silts silty silva simar simps since sines sinew singe sings sinks sinus sired siren sires sisal sissy sitar sited sites situp situs sixes sixth sixty sizar sized sizes tarsi torsi using visit

sib sibs sibyl sibyls

sibyl sibyls

sic sick sics basic mesic music sicko basics phasic physic sicked sicken sicker sickie sickle sickly sickos

sick sicko sicked sicken sicker sickie sickle sickly sickos airsick carsick seasick sickbed sickens sickest sicking sickish sickles

sicko sickos

side aside sided sides asides beside inside onside reside upside apsides bedside besides insider offside outside preside resided resides seaside sidearm sidecar sideman sidemen subside topside upsides wayside

sided resided lopsided presided subsided

sides asides apsides besides resides upsides offsides outsides presides sideshow sideslip sidestep subsides topsides waysides

sidle sidled sidles

siege sieged sieges besiege besieged besieges

sieve sieved sieves

sift sifts sifted sifter sifters sifting

sigh sighs sight sighed sigher sights insight sighers sighing sighted sightly

sight sights sighted eyesight insights sighting

sigil sigils

sigma sigmas

sign signs assign design ensign resign signal signed signet signor assigns consign cosigns designs ensigns insigne resigns signals signets signify signing signior signora signors

signs assigns cosigns designs consigns

silk silks silky silken silkier

sill sills silly sillier sillies

silo silos epsilon upsilon

silt silts silty silted siltier silting

silva silvan silvas

simar simars

simp simps simper simple simply simpers simpler

sin sine sing sink sins basin eosin lysin resin rosin since sines sinew singe sings sinks sinus using arsine basing basins busing casing casino cosine cousin dosing easing fusing hosing kamsin losing lysing lysins musing myosin nosing pepsin posing raisin rasing resins rising rosing rosins rosiny sinews sinewy sinful singed singer singes single singly sinker sinned sinner sinter tocsin ursine vising

since sincere sincerer

sine sines sinew arsine cosine sinews sinewy ursine arsines basinet cosines cuisine rosined sinewed

sines arsines cosines business cosiness cuisines easiness nosiness rosiness

sinew sinews sinewy sinewed sinewing

sing singe sings using basing busing casing dosing easing fusing hosing losing lysing musing nosing posing rasing rising rosing singed singer singes single singly vising abasing abusing amusing arising biasing bossing bousing busings bussing casings causing ceasing censing chasing closing cursing cussing dousing dowsing erasing fussing gassing goosing hissing horsing housing kissing lapsing leasing loosing massing messing missing mousing musings mussing noising noosing nursing parsing passing pausing phasing poising prosing pursing raising reusing rinsing rousing sassing sensing singers singing singled singles singlet sousing teasing tensing tossing versing yessing

singe singed singer singes singeing

sings busings casings closings singsong

sink sinks sinker sinkage sinkers sinking

sins basins lysins resins rosins cousins kamsins myosins pepsins raisins tocsins

sip sips gossip siphon sipped sipper sippet

sips gossips

sir sire sirs sired siren sires desire sirdar sirens siring sirrah sirred sirree

sire sired siren sires desire sirens desired desires

sired desired

siren sirens

sires desires

sis apsis arsis basis lysis oasis sisal sissy assist cassis crisis desist diesis ecesis emesis gnosis insist miosis noesis ptosis resist sepsis sisals siskin sister sistra stasis thesis tmesis tussis

sisal sisals

sit site sith sits posit sitar sited sites situp situs visit posits sitars sitcom siting sitten sitter situps visits

sitar sitars

site sited sites felsite hessite posited visited zoisite

sited posited visited

sites felsites

sits posits visits

situp situps

six sixes sixth sixty sixths

sixth sixths

sizar sizars

size sized sizes assize assizes capsize midsize outsize

sized capsized outsized

sizes assizes capsizes outsizes

skald skalds

skat skate skats skated skater skates skaters skating

skate skated skater skates skaters

skean skeans

skee skees skeet skeets

skeet skeets

skeg skegs muskeg muskegs

skein skeins

skelp skelps skelped skelping

skep skepsis skeptic

skew askew skews skewed skewer skewers

ski skid skim skin skip skis skit skids skied skies skiff skill skimp skims skink skins skips skirl skirr skirt skits skive asking buskin gaskin muskie siskin skiddy skiffs skiing skills skimps skimpy skinks skinny skirls skirrs skirts skived skiver skives skivvy weskit

skid skids skiddy nonskid skidded skiddoo

skies boskiest duskiest huskiest peskiest riskiest whiskies

skiff skiffs skiffles

skill skills skilled skillets skillful skilling

skim skimp skims skimps skimpy skimmed skimmer skimped

skimp skimps skimpy skimped skimpier skimping

skin skink skins asking buskin gaskin siskin skinks skinny basking buskins doeskin gaskins hogskin husking kidskin masking oilskin pigskin risking siskins skinful skinned skinner tasking

skink skinks

skins buskins gaskins doeskins hogskins kidskins oilskins pigskins

skip skips skipped skipper

skirl skirls skirled skirling

skirr skirrs skirred skirring

skirt skirts skirted outskirt skirting

skis duskish

skit skits weskit skitter skittle weskits

skive skived skiver skives

skoal skoals

skulk skulks skulked skulking

skull skulls numskull skullcap

skunk skunks skunked skunking

sky dusky husky musky pesky risky skyey frisky skycap skyway whisky

slab slabs slabbed slabber

slack slacks slacked slacken slacker slackly slackens slackers slacking

slag slags slagged

slake slaked slakes

slam slams slammed

slang slangy

slant aslant slants slanted slanting

slap slaps slapped

slash slashed slasher slashes slashers slashing

slat slate slats slaty slated slater slates slaters slather slating slatted

slate slated slater slates slaters

slave slaved slaver slaves enslave slavers slavery enslaved enslaves

slay slays mislay slayed slayer mislays slayers slaying

slays mislays

sled sleds aisled misled sledge bobsled hassled rassled sledded sledder sledged sledges tousled tussled

sleds bobsleds

sleek sleeker sleekest

sleep asleep sleeps sleepy sleeper sleepers sleepier sleepily sleeping

sleet sleets sleety sleeted sleeting

slice sliced slicer slices slicers

slick slicks slicker slickers slickest

slid slide slider slides sliders sliding

slide slider slides sliders mudslide

slim slime slims slimy slimed slimes slimier slimily sliming slimmed slimmer

slime slimed slimes

sling slings brisling goslings hassling nursling quisling rassling slinging tousling tussling

slink slinks slinky slinked slinking

slip slips slippy cowslip slipped slipper slipway

slips cowslips slipshod slipslop

slit slits slither

slob slobs slobber

sloe sloes

slog slogs slogan slogans slogged slogger

sloop sloops

slop slope slops aslope sloped slopes sloppy sloping slopped

slope aslope sloped slopes

slosh sloshy sloshed sloshier sloshing

slot sloth slots sloths slotted

sloth sloths

slow slows slowed slower slowly slowest slowing

slub slubbed

slue slues

sluff sluffs sluffed sluffing

slug slugs slugged slugger

slum slump slums slumps slumber slummed slumped

slump slumps slumped slumping

slur slurb slurp slurs slurbs slurps slurry slurped slurred

slurb slurbs

slurp slurps slurped slurping

slush slushy slushed slushier slushing

slut sluts

sly slyer slyly grisly measly slyest thusly

smack smacks smacked smacking

small smaller dismally smallest smallish smallpox

smalt smalts smaltos

smart smarts smarty smarted smarten smarter smartly outsmart smartass smartens smartest smarties smarting

smash smashed smasher smashes smashup smashers smashing

smear smears smeary besmear smeared besmears smearier smearing

smell smells smelly smelled smellier smelling

smelt smelts smelted smelters smeltery smelting

smew smews

smile smiled smiler smiles

smirk smirks smirked smirking

smite smites

smith smiths smithy gunsmith smithies tinsmith

smock smocks smocked smocking

smog smogs

smoke smoked smoker smokes

smolt smolts

smug smugly smuggle

smut smuts smutch smutty bismuth smutted

snack snacks snacked snacking

snafu snafus snafued snafuing

snag snags snaggy snagged

snail snails

snake snaked snakes

snap snaps snappy snapped snapper

snaps snapshot

snare snared snares ensnare ensnared ensnares

snark snarks

snarl snarls snarled snarling

snath snaths

sneak sneaks sneaky sneaked sneaker sneakers sneakier sneaking

sneer sneers sneered sneering

snell snells

snick snicks snicked snicker snickers snicking

sniff sniffs sniffy sniffed sniffing sniffled sniffles

snip snipe snips sniped sniper snipes snippy parsnip snipers sniping snipped snipper snippet

snipe sniped sniper snipes

snips parsnips

snit snits snitch

snob snobs snobby

snood snoods

snoop snoops snoopy snooped snoopers snooping

snoot snoots snooty

snore snored snorer snores

snort snorts snorted snorting

snot snots snotty

snout snouts

snow snows snowy snowed snowier snowing snowman

snows snowshoe snowsuit

snub snubs snubby snubbed snubber

snuff snuffs snuffy snuffed snuffbox snuffing snuffled snuffles

snug snugly snugged snugger snuggle

so sob sod sol son sop sot sou sow sox soy also peso soak soap soar sobs sock soda sods sofa soft soil soke sold sole solo sols soma some song sons soon soot soph sops sora sorb sore sori sort sots soul soup sour sous sown sows soys arson besom besot bison bosom gesso hyson lasso mason meson pesos soaks soaps soapy soars sober socks socle sodas sofas softy soggy soils sokes solan solar soldo soled soles solid solos solve somas sonar sonde songs sonic sonny sooth soots sooty sopor soppy soras sorbs sorer sores sorgo sorry sorts sorus sotol souls sound soups soupy sours souse south sowed sower torso verso visor

soak soaks soaked soaker soakage soakers soaking

soap soaps soapy soaped soapbox soapier soaping

soaps soapsuds

soar soars soared soaring

sob sobs sober isobar sobbed sobers

sober sobers sobered soberly sobering

sock socks socked socket cassock hassock sockets socking tussock

socks cassocks hassocks tussocks

sod soda sods sodas sodded sodden sodium

soda sodas

sofa sofas insofar

soft softy soften softer softie softly softens softest softies

soil soils besoil soiled besoils soiling subsoil topsoil

soils besoils subsoils topsoils

soke sokes

sol sold sole solo sols solan solar soldo soled soles solid solos solve cresol insole podsol resold resole solace solans solder solely solemn solids soling soloed solute solved solver solves

solan solans solander

solar solaria solarium solarize

sold soldo resold solder outsold solders soldier

sole soled soles insole resole solely solemn console insoles resoled resoles rissole

soled resoled consoled

soles consoles rissoles

solid solids solidly solidify solidity

solo solos soloed soloing soloist

sols consols cresols podsols

solve solved solver solves absolve absolved absolver absolves dissolve resolved resolves solvency solvents unsolved

soma somas somata somatic

some isomer awesome bosomed fulsome irksome isomers lissome noisome someday somehow someone someway twosome winsome woesome

son song sons arson bison hyson mason meson sonar sonde songs sonic sonny arsons damson godson kelson lesson masons mesons orison parson person poison prison reason season sonant sonars sonata sondes sonnet unison

sonar sonars

sonde sondes

song songs

songs songster

sonic masonic subsonic

sons arsons masons mesons damsons godsons kelsons lessons orisons parsons persons poisons prisons reasons seasons

soon sooner bassoon eftsoon gossoon monsoon

soot sooth soots sooty sooted soothe soothed soothes sootier sooting

sooth soothe soothed forsooth soothing soothsay

sop soph sops sopor soppy hyssop isopod sopors sopped

soph sophism sophist

sopor sopors

sops hyssops

sora soras

sorb sorbs absorb adsorb resorb sorbet absorbs adsorbs resorbs sorbets

sorbs absorbs adsorbs resorbs

sore sorer sores sorely sorest bedsore eyesore

sores sorest bedsores eyesores

sorgo sorgos

sori sorites

sort sorts assort resort sorted sorter sortie consort presort resorts sorters sorties sorting

sorts consorts presorts

sot sots besot sotol besots sotols sotted

sotol sotols

sots besots

sou soul soup sour sous souls sound soups soupy sours souse south sought sounds source soured sourer sourly soused souses

soul souls soulful

sound sounds resound sounded sounder soundly unsound resounds sounders sounding

soup soups soupy soupier

sour sours source soured sourer sourly sources sourest souring

sous souse soused souses sousing

souse soused souses

south southern southers southpaw

sow sown sows sowed sower disown sowers sowing

sower sowers

sown disown disowns

soy soys

spa span spar spas spat spay spaz space spacy spade spahi spake spall spang spank spans spare spark spars spasm spate spats spawn spays spaced spaces spacey spaded spader spades spadix spahis spalls spanks spared sparer

spares sparge sparks sparse spasms spates spavin spawns spayed spazes

space spaced spaces spacey spaceman

spade spaded spader spades spaders

spahi spahis

spall spalls

span spang spank spans spanks spancel spandex spangle spangly spaniel spanked spanker spanned spanner

spang spangle spangly spangled spangles

spank spanks spanked spanker spankers spanking

spar spare spark spars spared sparer spares sparge sparks sparse felspar sparely sparers sparest sparged sparges sparing sparked sparker sparkle sparred sparrow sparser

spare spared sparer spares sparely sparers sparest sparerib

spark sparks sparked sparker sparkle sparkers sparking sparkled sparkler sparkles

spars sparse sparser felspars sparsely sparsest sparsity

spas spasm spasms spastic

spasm spasms

spat spate spats spates spatial spatted spatter spatula

spate spates

spawn spawns spawned spawning

spay spays spayed spaying

spaz spazes

speak speaks bespeak speaker bespeaks speakers speaking

spear spears speared spearing

speck specks specked speckle flyspeck specking speckled speckles

sped cusped gasped hasped lisped rasped clasped crisped grasped

speed speeds speedy speeded speeder speeders speedful speedier speedily speeding speedway

spell spells spelled misspell spellers spelling

spend spends suspend spending suspends

sperm sperms

spew spews spewed spewing

spica spicae

spice spiced spices auspice hospice spicery allspice auspices hospices

spied espied

spiel spiels spieler bonspiel spielers

spies espies raspiest waspiest wispiest

spiff spiffs spiffy spiffed spiffier spiffing

spike spiked spikes

spile spiles

spill spills spilled spillage spilling spillway

spilt spilth

spin spine spins spiny spinal spined spinel spines spinet gasping lisping rasping spinach spinals spindle spindly spinets spinier spinner spinney spinoff spinous topspin

spine spined spinel spines spinet

spins spinster topspins

spire aspire spired spires aspired aspires aspirers conspire inspired inspires perspire respired respires suspired suspires

spit spite spits spitz spited despite respite spiting spitter spittle spitzes

spite spited despite despited respited respites spiteful

spiv spivs

splat splats splatter

splay splays display misplay splayed displays misplays splaying

split splits

spoil spoils spoilt despoil spoiled despoils spoilage spoilers spoiling

spoke spoked spoken spokes bespoke misspoke unspoken

spoof spoofs spoofed spoofing

spook spooks spooky spooked spookier spooking

spool spools spooled cesspool spooling

spoon spoons spoony spooned spoonful spooning teaspoon

spoor spoors spoored spooring

spore spores zoospore

sport sports sporty sported passport sportful sportier sporting sportive

spot spots despot spotty despots spotted spotter sunspot

spots despots sunspots

spout spouts spouted spouting

sprag sprags

spray sprays sprayed spraying

spree sprees

sprig sprigs

sprit esprit sprite sprits spritz bowsprit spritzed spritzer spritzes

sprue sprues

spry spryer spryly

spud spuds spudded

spue spues

spume spumed spumes

spun spunk spunks spunky

spunk spunks spunky spunkier

spur spurn spurs spurt spurns spurry spurts hotspur spurned spurred spurted

spurn spurns spurned spurning

spurs hotspurs

spurt spurts spurted spurting

spy espy raspy waspy wispy crispy spying

squab squabs squabby squabble

squad squads squadron

squat squats squatty squatted squatter

squaw squawk squaws squawks squawked

squib squibs squibbed

squid squids

stab stabs stable stabbed stabile stabled stables

stack stacks stacked haystack stacking

staff staffs distaff staffed staffer distaffs staffers staffing tipstaff

stag stage stags stagy staged stager stages stagey hostage lastage onstage postage stagers stagged stagger staging upstage wastage

stage staged stager stages stagey hostage lastage onstage postage stagers upstage wastage hostages offstage upstaged upstages wastages

stain stains abstain distain stained sustain abstains distains stainers staining sustains

stair stairs stairway upstairs

stake staked stakes mistake mistaken mistakes stakeout

stale staled staler stales stalest

stalk stalks stalky stalked stalking

stall stalls install installed distally festally installs stalling stallion

stamp stamps stamped stampede stampers stamping

stand stands standby inkstand standard standbys standing standish standoff standout

stang stangs mustang mustangs

staph staphs

star stare stark stars start costar instar starch stared stares starry starts starve bastard costard costars custard dastard daystar mustard restart starchy stardom staring starkly starlet starlit starred started starter startle starved starves upstart

stare stared stares

stark starkly

stars costars daystars

start starts restart started starter startle upstart restarts starters startled startles upstarts

stash stashed stashes stashing

state estate stated states costate estates hastate restate stately testate apostate aristate gestates misstate prostate restated restates

stave staved staves

stay stays stayed staying

stead steady instead bedstead steadied steadier steadies unsteady

steak steaks

steal osteal steals stealer stealth stealers stealing stealthy

steam steams steamy steamed steamer steamers steamier steaming

steed steeds

steel steels steely steeled steelier steeling

steep steeps steeped steepen steeple steepens steeping steeples

steer steers steered steerage steering

stein steins

stele steles hosteled hosteler

stem stems stemma system stemmas stemmed stemmer systems

steno stenos

step steps instep steppe insteps misstep stepped stepper steppes stepson

steps missteps stepsons

stere stereo steres austere festered fostered mastered mustered oystered pestered pesterer

stern astern sterna sterns cistern eastern sternal asternal cisterns pasterns posterns sternest sternums sternway westerns

stet stets sestet sestets stetson

stets stetsons

stew stews stewed steward stewing stewpan

stich distich pastiche

stick sticks sticky sticked sticker stickle stickup unstick dipstick joystick lipstick stickers stickful stickier sticking stickled stickler stickles stickpin stickups unsticks

stiff stiffs mastiff stiffed mastiffs stiffens stiffest stiffing

stile stiles stiletto

still stills stilly distill stilled bastille distills instills pastille stillest stilling

stilt stilts stilted

sting stings stingy basting besting casting costing dusting easting fasting hasting lasting pasting tasting wasting bastings blasting boasting boosting bursting castings coasting cresting crusting egesting existing feasting foisting frosting ghosting heisting hoisting hustings jousting listings questing roasting roosting rousting stingers stingier stinging stingray toasting trusting trysting twisting wresting yeasting

stink stinko stinks stinky stinkers stinking stinkpot

stint stints stinted stinting

stipe stipel stipes stipend stipends

stir astir stirs bestir stirps bestirs stirred stirrup

stirs bestirs

stoa stoae stoas stoat stoats

stoat   stoats
stob   stobs
stock   stocks stocky restock stocked gunstock restocks stockade stockier stocking stockman stockmen
stoic   stoics stoical
stoke   stoked stoker stokes
stole   stolen stoles diastole pistoled pistoles systoles
stoma   stomas stomach stomata stomachs
stomp   stomps stomped stomping
stone   stones capstone gemstone keystone oilstone
stool   stools stooled barstool stooling
stoop   stoops stooped stooping
stop   estop stope stops stopt estops stoped stopes nonstop stopgap stoping stopped stopper stopple
stope   stoped stopes
stops   estops
store   stored stores restored restores
stork   storks
storm   storms stormy stormed stormier storming
story   storying
stoup   stoups
stour   stours bistoury
stout   stouts
stove   stover stoves
stow   stows bestow stowed bestows stowage stowing
stows   bestows
strap   strapped strapper
straw   straws strawy
stray   astray estray strays strayed straying
strep   streps
strew   strewn strews strewed strewing
stria   striae striate mistrial striated striates
strip   stripe strips stripy striped airstrip outstrip stripers striping stripped stripper
strop   strops strophes stropped
strum   struma strums strumae lustrums nostrums rostrums sistrums strummed strumpet
strut   struts strutted
stub   stubs stubby stubbed stubble
stuck   unstuck
stud   studs study studio studded student studied studies studios testudo
study   studying
stuff   stuffs stuffy stuffed dyestuff stuffier stuffing
stull   stulls
stum   stump stums stumps stumpy costume frustum stumble stummed stumped stumper

stump   stumps stumpy stumped stumpage stumpers stumping
stums   frustums
stun   stung stunk stuns stunt stunts stunned stunner stunted
stunt   stunts stunted stunting stuntman stuntmen
stupa   stupas
sty   busty dusty fusty gusty hasty lusty misty musty nasty pasty rusty style styli stymy tasty testy zesty chesty crusty feisty frosty pigsty stylar styled styles stylet stylus stymie toasty yeasty
style   styled styles stylet epistyle prostyle
styli   stylists stylites stylized stylizes
stymy   stymying
sub   subs subbed subdeb subdue subito sublet submit suborn subset subtle subtly suburb subway
subs   subset subsets subside subsidy subsist subsoil
suck   sucks sucked sucker suckle suckers sucking suckled suckles
sudd   sudden
suds   sudsy
sue   sued sues suet ensue issue suede suets ensued ensues issued issuer issues pursue suedes tissue
sued   suede ensued issued suedes pursued
suede   suedes
sues   ensues issues pursues tissues
suet   suets
sugar   sugars sugary sugared sugaring
suing   pursuing tissuing
suint   suints
suit   suite suits suited suites suitor lawsuit nonsuit pursuit suiting suitors
suite   suited suites unsuited
suits   lawsuits nonsuits pursuits
sulfa   sulfate sulfates
sulk   sulks sulked sulkier sulkies sulking
sully   sullying
sum   sumo sump sums sumac summa sumos sumps assume dorsum gypsum possum resume sumach sumacs summae summed summer summit summon
sumac   sumach sumacs
summa   summae summary
sumo   sumos
sump   sumps sumpter
sums   gypsums possums
sun   sung sunk sunn suns bosun sunny sunup bosuns sunbow sundae sunder sundew sundog sundry sunned sunset suntan sunups unsung
sung   unsung
sunn   sunny sunned sunnier sunning

suns   bosuns sunset sunsets sunspot
sunup   sunups
sup   sups super catsup superb supers supine supped supper supple supply tossup
super   superb supers superego superior superman supernal
sups   tossups
sura   surah suras cesura surahs cesurae
surah   surahs
surd   absurd
sure   surer assure ensure insure surely surest surety usurer assured assures censure closure ensured ensures erasure fissure insured insurer insures leisure measure tonsure usurers
surer   usurer insurers measurer
surf   surfs surfy surfed surfer surface surfeit surfers surfier surfing
surge   surged surges surgeons upsurged upsurges
sutra   sutras
swab   swabs swabbed swabber
swag   swags swagger
swain   swains coxswain
swale   swales
swam   swami swamp swamy swamps swampy swamies swamped
swami   swamies
swamp   swamps swampy swamped swamping
swan   swang swank swans swanky
swank   swanky
swans   swanskin
swap   swaps swapped
sward   swards
swarm   aswarm swarms swarmed swarming
swart   swarth swarthy
swash   swashed swashes swashing
swat   swath swats swatch swathe swaths swathed swathes swatted swatter
swath   swathe swaths swathed swathes swathing unswathe
sway   sways swayed swaying
swear   swears forswear menswear swearing
sweat   sweats sweaty sweated sweater sweatbox sweaters sweatier sweating
sweep   sweeps sweeper sweepers sweeping
sweet   sweets sweeten sweeter sweetie sweetens sweetest sweeties
swell   swells swelled swelling
swift   swiftest
swig   swigs swigged
swill   swills swilled swilling
swim   swims swimmer
swims   swimsuit

swing swinge swings swingy swinged beeswing swingers swinging swingled swingles upswings
swipe swiped swipes
swirl swirls swirly swirled swirling
swish swishy swished swishing
swoon swoons swooned swooning

swoop swoops swooped swooping
swop swops swopped
sword swords password
swore forswore
sworn forsworn
swot swots swotted
syce sycee syces sycees

sycee sycees
sylph sylphs sylphid sylphids
sylva sylvae sylvan sylvas
sync synch syncs syncope
synod synods synodal
syrup syrups syrupy

ta eta ita tab tad tag tam tan tap tar tat tau tav tax anta beta data etas iota jota lota nota pita rota seta stab stag star stay tabs tabu tach tack taco tact tads tael tags tail take talc tale tali talk tall tame tamp tams tang tank tans tapa tape taps tare taro tarp tars tart task tass tats taut tavs taxi zeta adyta altar antae antas aorta attar betas betta biota costa cotta delta dicta dotal fatal fetal gutta hosta iotas jotas junta kurta lotah lotas lytta manta metal natal octad pasta petal pitas quota reata riata rotas scuta septa setae sitar stabs stack staff stage stags stagy staid stain stair stake stale stalk stall stamp stand stang stank staph stare stark stars start stash state stave stays tabby tabes table taboo tabor tacet tache tacit tacks tacky tacos taels taffy taiga tails taint taken taker takes talcs taler tales talks talky tally talon talus tamed tamer tames tamps tango tangs tangy tanka tanks tansy tapas taped taper tapes tapir tapis tardy tared tares targe taros tarot tarps tarry tarsi tarts tasks tasse taste tasty tater tatty taunt taupe tawny taxed taxer taxes taxis tazza testa theta titan total vista vital vitta witan yenta zetas

tab stab tabs tabu stabs tabby tabes table taboo tabor stable tabard tabbed tabled tables tablet taboos tabors tabour

tabby tabbying

table stable tabled tables tablet actable eatable getable mutable notable potable ratable stabled stables tableau tablets votable abatable eatables imitable meltable notables portable potables quotable sortable suitable tableaus tableaux unstable wettable

taboo taboos tabooed tabooing

tabor tabors taboret taborets

tabs stabs

tabu tabular

tach tache attach detach attache

tache attache attached attaches detached detaches mustache

tacit tacitly taciturn

tack stack stack tacks tacky attack stacks tacked tackle attacks stacked tackier tacking tackled tackles

tacks stacks attacks

taco tacos

tact intact stacte tactic contact stactes tactful tactics tactile taction tactual

tad tads octad heptad octads pentad stadia

tads octads heptads pentads

tael taels

tag stag tags stage stags stagy dotage metage outage ragtag staged stager stages stagey tagged tagger

tags stags

taiga taigas

tail tails detail entail oxtail retail tailed taille tailor bobtail cattail curtail entails fantail foxtail oxtails pigtail pintail rattail tailing tailles tailors

tails entails oxtails bobtails cattails curtails fantails foxtails pigtails pintails tailspin

taint taints attaint tainted attaints tainting

take stake taken taker takes betake intake retake staked stakes takers betaken betakes intakes mistake outtake partake retaken retakes takeoff takeout

taken betaken retaken mistaken partaken

taker takers partaker

takes stakes betakes intakes retakes mistakes outtakes partakes

talc talcs talcum talcked

tale stale taler tales staled staler stales talent metaled petaled stalest talents totaled

taler staler

tales stales stalest talesman talesmen

tali italic talion italics staling talions talipes

talk stalk talks talky stalks stalky talked talker stalked talkers talking

talks stalks

talky stalky

tall stall tally stalls taller tallow fatally install stalled tallage tallboy tallest tallied tallies tallish tallith tallows tallowy tallyho totally

tally fatally tallyho totally brutally distally festally mentally mortally tallying tallyman

talon talons taloned

talus taluses

tam tame tamp tams stamp tamed tamer tames tamps ataman bantam stamen stamps tamale tamely tamest taming tamped tamper

tame tamed tamer tames stamen tamely tamest stamens

tames tamest

tamp stamp tamps stamps tamped tamper stamped tamping tampion

tamps stamps

tams bantams

tan tang tank tans stand stang stank tango tangs tangy tanka tanks tansy titan witan botany butane caftan cetane extant kaftan litany mutant natant nutant octane octant rattan satang stance stanch stands stangs stanza sultan suntan tandem tanged tangle tangly tangos tanist tankas tanked tanker tanned tanner tannic tannin tartan titans witans

tang stang tango tangs tangy satang stangs tanged tangle tangly tangos mustang tangelo tangent tangier tanging tangled tangler tangles tangoed

tango tangos tangoed tangoing

tangs stangs mustangs

tank stank tanka tanks tankas tanked tanker tankard tankers tankful tanking

tanka tankas tankard tankards

tans tansy titans witans caftans kaftans rattans sultans suntans tansies tartans

tap tapa tape taps staph tapas taped taper tapes tapir tapis staphs staple tapers taping tapirs tapped tappet

tapa tapas pitapat

tape taped taper tapes tapers tapered

taper tapers tapered tapering

tapes tapestry

tapir tapirs

taps tapster

tar star tare taro tarp tars tart altar attar sitar stare stark stars start tardy tared tares targe taros tarot tarps tarry tarsi tarts altars attars avatar costar datary dotard guitar instar mortar nectar notary petard qintar retard rotary sitars starch stared stares starry starts starve targes target tariff taring tarpon tarsal tarsus tartan tartar tartly votary

tare stare tared tares stared stares hectare

tared stared mortared

tares stares hectares

targe targes target targets targeted

taro taros tarot

tarp tarps tarpon tarpons

tarry starry tarrying

tars stars tarsi altars attars sitars tarsal tarsus avatars costars guitars mortars nectars qintars tarsals tarsier

tarsi tarsier intarsia

tart start tarts starts tartan tartar tartly restart started starter startle tartans tartlet upstart

tarts starts restarts upstarts

task tasks tasked tasking

tass tasse tassel tasses tassels

tasse tassel tasses tassels tasseled

taste tasted taster tastes tasters distaste tasteful

tat tats state tater tatty estate mutate notate potato rotate stated states static stator statue status taters tatted tatter tattle tattoo

tater taters

tau taut taunt taupe taught taunts taupes tauten tautly

taunt taunts taunted taunter taunters taunting

taupe taupes

taut tauten tautly tautens

tav tavs stave atavic octave octavo staved staves tavern

tax taxi taxed taxer taxes taxis ataxia pretax surtax syntax taxers taxied taxing

taxed surtaxed

taxer taxers

taxes surtaxes syntaxes

taxi taxis ataxia taxied taxing ataxias taxicab taxiing taxiway

tazza tazzas

tea teak teal team tear teas teat stead steak steal steam teach teaks teams tears teary tease teats bateau gateau osteal steady steaks steals steams steamy teacup teamed teapot teapoy tearer teased teasel teaser teases teazel teazle

teach teacher teaches teachers teaching

teak steak teaks steaks

teaks steaks

teal steal osteal steals lacteal stealer stealth

team steam teams steams steamy teamed steamed steamer teaming

teams steams teamster

tear tears teary tearer stearic tearful tearing tearoom

teas tease teased teasel teaser teases teasels teasers teasing

tease teased teasel teaser teases teasels teasers

teat teats teatime

tech techs techy catechu technic

ted teds acted bated cited dated doted fated feted gated hated kited lated luted mated meted muted noted rated sated sited teddy toted voted wited abated alated baited basted batted belted bested betted boated bolted booted bunted butted canted carted catted coated crated darted dented dieted dinted dotted dusted edited elated eluted emoted exited farted fasted fatted felted fisted fitted fluted footed gifted grated gusted gutted hafted halted hasted hatted heated hefted hilted hinted hooted hosted hunted hutted jested jetted jilted jolted jotted jutted kilted lasted lifted lilted linted listed lofted looted lotted lusted malted masted matted melted minted misted molted nested netted nutted orated ousted panted parted pasted patted pelted petted pitted plated ported posted potted pouted prated punted quoted rafted ranted ratted rented rested retted rifted rioted rooted rotted routed rusted rutted salted seated sifted silted skated slated sooted sorted sotted spited stated suited tasted tatted tedded tedium tented tested tilted tinted tooted totted touted tufted tutted united vatted vented vested vetted wafted waited wanted wasted welted wetted whited wilted wonted

tee teed teem teen tees steed steel steep steer teems teens teeny teeth anteed bootee esteem goatee lateen poteen sateen settee steeds steels steely steeps steers steeve suttee teeing teemed teensy teepee teeter teethe testee vestee

teed steed anteed steeds

teem teems esteem teemed esteems teeming

teems esteems

teen teens teeny lateen poteen sateen teensy canteen fifteen lateens poteens preteen sateens sixteen teenage teenier umpteen

teens teensy lateens sateens canteens preteens

tees bootees goatees settees suttees testees vestees

teeth teethe teethed eyeteeth sawteeth teething

tell tells telly retell teller patella retells stellar tellers telling

tempo tempos temporal

tempt tempts attempt tempted attempts contempt tempters tempting

ten tend tens tent eaten oaten often paten steno tench tends tenet tenia tenon tenor tense tenth tents attend batten beaten bitten catena detent extend extent fasten fatten gluten gotten hasten intend intent ketene kitten latent latten lenten listen marten mitten molten neaten patens patent patten platen potent rotten sitten soften stench stenos tauten tenace tenail tenant tended tender tendon tenets tennis tenons tenors tenrec tensed tenser tenses tensor tented tenter tenths tenues tenuis tenure tenuti tenuto whiten

tench stench tenches stenches

tend tends attend extend intend tended tender tendon attends bartend contend distend extends intends portend pretend tenders tending tendons tendril

tends attends extends intends bartends contends distends portends pretends

tenet tenets

tenon tenons

tenor tenors

tens tense patens tensed tenser tenses tensor fastens fattens glutens hastens intense kittens lattens listens martens mittens neatens pattens platens softens tautens tensely tensest tensile tensing tension tensors whitens

tense tensed tenser tenses intense pretense

tent tenth tents detent extent intent latent patent potent tented tenter tenths content detente entente extents patents portent stentor tenters tenthly tenting

tenth tenths

tents patents contents portents

tepee tepees

tepid tepidly

terce tercel tercer tercet tercels tercets sesterce

term terms termed termer termor midterm termers terming termite termors

terms midterms

tern stern terns astern eterne extern intern sterna sterns bittern cistern cittern eastern eternal externs gittern interne interns lantern lectern pattern postern saltern sternal sterner sternly sternum ternary ternate ternion western

terns sterns cisterns citterns gitterns lanterns lecterns pasterns patterns posterns salterns westerns

terse terser intersex

test testa tests testy attest cutest detest latest obtest testae tested testee tester teston attests contest daftest detests fastest fattest fittest hottest mostest neatest obtests pretest protest softest testate testees testers testify testily testing testons testudo tritest wettest whitest

testa testae testate testator

tests attests detests obtests contests pretests protests

teth tether tethers

tetra tetrad tetras tetrads tetragon tetrarch

text texts context pretext subtext textile textual texture

texts pretexts subtexts

than thane thank ethane thanes thanks ethanol methane thanked xanthan

thane ethane thanes methane methanes urethane

thank thanks thanked thankful thanking

that thatch

thaw thaws thawed thawing

the thee them then thew they bathe ether kithe lathe lithe other theca theft thegn their theme there therm these theta thews thewy tithe withe anthem anther bathed bather bathes bethel blithe bother cither clothe dither either ethers father gather hither kithed kithes lathed lather lathes lither loathe mother nether others pother rather scathe scythe seethe soothe swathe teethe tether thefts thegns theine theirs theism theist themes thenar thence theory theses thesis thetas thetic tithed tithes wether withed wither withes writhe zither

theft thefts

thegn thegns

their theirs

them theme anthem themes anthems apothem

theme themes

then thenar thence earthen heathen thenars

there thereby therein thereof thereon thereto bothered ethereal fathered gathered gatherer lathered mothered tethered theremin withered

therm thermae thermal thermic isotherm thermals thermion

these theses

theta thetas

thew thews thewy

thick thicken thicker thicket thickly thickens thickest thickets

thigh thighs

thill thills anthill anthills foothill

thin thine thing think things thinks thinly within bathing kithing lathing nothing rethink thinker thinned thinner tithing withing

thine xanthine

thing things bathing lathing anything berthing clothing farthing frothing loathing mouthing northing quothing scathing scything seething soothing swathing teething writhing

think thinks methinks outthink rethinks thinkers thinking

third thirds thirdly

thirl thirls thirled thirling

this thistle

tho thou ethos litho thole thong thorn thoro thorp those author bathos fathom lithos method mythos pathos tholed tholes thongs thorax thorns thorny thorpe thorps though

thole tholed tholes knothole porthole potholes

thong thongs

thorn thorns thorny boxthorn hawthorn lanthorn thornier

thoro thorough

thorp thorpe thorps

thou though thought without

three threes

throb throbs bathrobe throbbed

throe throes

throw thrown throws throwing

thru thrum thrums thrush thrust thrusts thruway

thrum thrums

thud thuds thudded

thug thugs thuggee

thuja thujas

thumb thumbs thumbed thumbing

thump thumps thumped thumpers thumping

thus thusly canthus

thy ethyl lathy mothy pithy withy apathy earthy ethyls filthy frothy heathy methyl mouthy smithy stithy thymol thymus toothy worthy wrathy

ti tic tie til tin tip tit anti otic stir tick tics tide tidy tied tier ties tiff tike tile till tils tilt time tine ting tins tint tiny tipi tips tire tiro titi tits yeti ziti antic antis astir atilt attic batik cacti coati cutie cutin cutis dhoti fetid lytic matin motif mufti optic patio petit ratio retia retie satin stich stick stiff stile still stilt sting stink stint stipe stirs tiara tibia ticks tidal tided tides tiers tiffs tiger tight tikes tilde tiled tiler tiles tills tilth tilts timed timer times timid tinct tinea tines tinge tings tinny tints tipis tipsy tired tires tiros titan titer tithe titis title titre titty tizzy tutti untie until utile vatic yetis

tiara tiaras

tibia tibiae tibial tibias

tic otic tick tics antic attic lytic optic stich stick ticks vatic acetic antics aortic arctic attics biotic bustic critic cystic emetic entice erotic exotic fetich fistic fustic gestic hectic lactic lentic luetic mantic mastic miotic mystic nastic noetic notice optics pectic peptic poetic rustic septic shtick static sticks sticky tactic thetic ticked ticker ticket tickle tictoc uretic

tick stick ticks shtick sticks sticky ticked ticker ticket tickle schtick shticks sticked sticker stickle stickup tickers tickets ticking tickled tickler tickles unstick

ticks sticks shticks schticks unsticks

tics antics attics optics arctics critics emetics exotics mastics mystics poetics rustics tactics

tidal cotidal

tide tided tides betide betided betides peptide riptide

tided betided

tides betides peptides riptides

tidy untidy tidying

tie tied tier ties cutie retie tiers untie auntie citied cities cootie cuties duties footie hogtie pitied pities retied reties softie sortie tieing tiepin tierce untied unties

tied citied pitied retied untied dirtied emptied hogtied jettied partied puttied

tier tiers tierce battier cattier cottier dirtier dottier dustier emptier hastier heftier jettier joltier lintier loftier lustier maltier meatier mintier mistier nattier niftier nuttier pastier peatier pettier rattier rootier runtier rustier siltier sootier tastier tiercel tierces wartier wittier

ties cities cuties duties pities reties unties aunties booties cooties deities dirties ditties empties fifties footies forties hogties jetties kitties laities lefties panties parties pasties patties pieties potties punties putties sixties softies sorties unities

tiff stiff tiffs stiffs tiffed tiffin caitiff mastiff pontiff stiffed stiffen stiffer stiffly tiffany tiffing tiffins

tiffs stiffs caitiffs mastiffs pontiffs

tiger tigers tigerish

tight tights airtight tightens tightest tightwad

tike tikes

tiki tikis

til tile till tils tilt atilt stile still stilt tilde tiled tiler tiles tills tilth tilts until utile dentil futile instil lentil motile pistil pontil stiles stills stilly stilts tildes tilers tiling tilled tiller tilted tilths uptilt

tilde   tildes

tile   stile tiled tiler tiles utile futile motile stiles tilers ductile fertile fictile gentile hostile inutile pantile reptile sectile sextile subtile tactile textile tortile

tiler   tilers

tiles   stiles gentiles pantiles reptiles sextiles textiles

till   still tills stills stilly tilled tiller distill instill stilled tillage tillers tilling

tills   stills distills instills

tils   dentils instils lentils pistils pontils

tilt   atilt stilt tilth tilts stilts tilted tilths uptilt stilted tilting uptilts

tilth   tilths

tilts   stilts

time   timed timer times timely timers airtime bedtime betimes centime daytime pastime ragtime septime teatime timeout wartime

timer   timers

times   betimes airtimes centimes daytimes pastimes ragtimes septimes wartimes

timid   timidly timidity

tin   tine ting tink tins tint tiny cutin matin satin sting stink stint tinct tinea tines tinge tings tinny tints acting bating biting chitin citing cretin dating dentin doting eating feting gating hating isatin kiting lectin luting martin mating matins meting muntin muting mutiny noting outing patina pectin rating retina sating satins satiny siting stings stingy stinko stinks stinky stints tincal tincts tinder tineid tinged tinges tingle tinily tinker tinkle tinkly tinman tinmen tinned tinner tinsel tinted tinter toting voting witing

tinct   tincts extinct distinct instinct tincture

tine   tinea tines tineid cystine destine matinee routine saltine satinet tineids tontine

tines   routines saltines tontines

ting   sting tinge tings acting bating biting citing dating doting eating feting gating hating kiting luting mating meting muting noting outing rating sating siting stings stingy tinged tinges tingle toting voting witing abating atingle baiting basting batting beating belting besting betting boating bolting booting bunting butting canting carting casting catting coating costing crating cutting darting denting dieting dinting dotting dusting easting editing elating eluting emoting exiting farting fasting

fatting felting fitting fluting footing getting grating gusting gutting hafting halting hasting hatting heating hefting henting hilting hinting hitting hooting hosting hunting hurting hutting jesting jetting jilting jolting jotting jutting kilting lasting letting lifting lilting linting listing lofting looting lotting lusting malting matings matting meeting melting minting misting molting nesting netting nutting orating outings panting parting pasting patting pelting petting pitting plating porting posting potting pouting prating punting putting quoting rafting ranting ratings ratting renting resting retting rifting rioting rooting rotting routing rusting rutting salting seating setting sifting silting sitting skating slating smiting sooting sorting spiting stating stinger suiting tasting tatting tenting testing tilting tinging tingled tingler tingles tinting tooting totting touting tufting tutting uniting vatting venting vesting wafting waiting wanting wasting welting westing wetting whiting wilting witting wonting writing

tinge   tinged tinges stingers tingeing untinged

tings   stings matings ratings bastings beatings buntings castings coatings cuttings fittings footings gratings hustings jottings listings meetings partings settings sittings tattings whitings writings

tins   matins satins tinsel cretins dentins lectins martins muntins pectins tinsels

tint   stint tints stints tinted tinter stinted tinting tintype

tints   stints

tiny   mutiny satiny destiny

tip   tipi tips stipe tipis tipsy stipel stipes tipped tipper tippet tipple tiptoe tiptop

tipi   tipis

tips   tipsy tipsier tipster

tire   tired tires attire entire retire satire attired attires retired retiree retires satires

tired   attired retired

tires   attires satires saltires tiresome

tiro   tiros

tit   titi tits petit titan titer tithe titis title titre titty entity otitis petite ratite stitch stithy titans titbit titers tithed tithes titled titles titres titter tittle tittup

titan   titans titanic titanium

titer   titers

tithe   tithed tithes

titi   titis otitis

titis   otitis cystitis mastitis

title   titled titles entitle entitled entitles subtitle untitled

titre   titres

to   tod toe tog tom ton too top tor tot tow toy alto atom atop auto into jato koto onto roto stoa stob stop stow toad tody toed toes toff toft tofu toga togs toil toke tola told toll tolu tomb tome toms tone tong tons tony took tool toon toot tope tops tora tore tori torn torr tors tort tosh toss tost tote tots tour tout town tows toys unto veto actor altos atoll atoms atomy atone atony autos baton canto cento conto ditto estop extol fetor futon gusto jatos junto ketol lento lotto molto motor motto photo pinto piton recto rotos sotol stoae stoas stoat stobs stock stogy stoic stoke stole stoma stomp stone stony stood stook stool stoop stope stops stopt store stork storm story stoss stoup stour stout stove stows toads toady toast today toddy toffs tofts togas toile toils toked token tokes tolas tolls tombs tomes tonal toned toner tones tonga tongs tonic tonne tonus tools toons tooth toots topaz toped topee toper topes topic topis toque torah toras torch toric torii torsi torsk torso torte torts torus total toted totem toter totes touch tough tours touts towed towel tower towns toxic toxin toyed toyon tutor

toad   toads toady toadied toadies

toady   toadying

toast   toasts toasty toasted toaster toasters toasting

tod   tody today toddy stodge stodgy todays toddle todies

today   todays

tody   custody

toe   toed toes tiptoe toeing vetoed vetoes

toed   vetoed dittoed tiptoed

toes   vetoes mottoes tiptoes

toff   toffs cutoff setoff toffee castoff cutoffs liftoff setoffs toffees

toffs   cutoffs castoffs liftoffs

toft   tofts

tog   toga togs stogy togas stogie togged toggle

toga   togas

toil   toile toils entoil toiled toiler toiles toilet entoils toilers toilets toiling

toile   toiled toiler toiles toilet toiletry

toils   toilsome

toke   stoke toked token tokes stoked stoker stokes tokens betoken stokers

toked   stoked

token tokens betoken tokenism

tokes stokes

tola tolas ortolan

told retold untold

toll atoll tolls atolls extoll tolled extolls tollage tolling

tolls atolls

tom atom tomb tome toms atoms atomy stoma stomp tombs tomes atomic bottom custom diatom entomb stomas stomps tomato tomboy tomcat

tomb tombs entomb tomboy entombs tomboys

tombs entombs

tome tomes epitome myotome

tomes epitomes

toms atoms bottoms customs diatoms

ton tone tong tons tony atone atony baton futon piton stone stony tonal toned toner tones tonga tongs tonic tonne tonus atoned atoner atones atonic batons burton button canton carton chiton cotton croton dalton futons intone ketone lepton mouton mutons mutton nekton newton photon piston pitons proton rhyton sexton stoned stones teston toners tongas tonged tongue tonics toning tonnes tonsil triton wanton

tonal tonally atonally tonality

tone atone stone toned toner tones atoned atoner atones intone ketone stones toners acetone atoners intoned intoner intones isotone ketones oxytone peptone

toned atoned intoned buttoned cantoned cottoned

toner atoner toners atoners intoners

tones atones stones acetones isotones peptones

tong tonga tongs tongas tonged tongue tonging tongued tongues

tonga tongas

tonic atonic tonics diatonic

tonne tonnes tonneau cretonne tonneaus

tons batons futons mutons pitons tonsil burtons buttons cantons cartons chitons cottons crotons daltons moutons muttons nektons newtons photons pistons protons rhytons sextons testons tonsils tonsure tritons

tony atony stony antonym cottony metonym

too took tool toon toot stood stook stool stoop tools toons tooth toots betook ratoon retook stooge stools stoops tattoo tooled tooted toothy tootle tootsy

took stook betook retook mistook partook

tool stool tools stools tooled stooled stoolie toolbox tooling

tools stools toolshed

toon toons ratoon cartoon festoon platoon pontoon ratoons

toons ratoons cartoons festoons platoons pontoons

toot tooth toots tooted toothy tootle tootsy toothed tooting tootled tootles tootsie

tooth toothy toothed eyetooth sawtooth

toots tootsy tootsies

top atop stop tope topi tops estop stope stops stopt topaz toped topee toper topes topic topis estops metope octopi ragtop redtop stoped stopes tiptop topees topers topics toping topped topper topple

topaz topazes

tope stope toped topee toper topes metope stoped stopes topees topers isotope metopes

toped stoped

topee topees

toper topers

topes stopes isotopes

topic topics ectopic metopic topical subtopic

tops stops estops autopsy ragtops redtops tiptops topsail topside topsoil topspin

toque toques

tor tora tore tori torn torr tors tort actor fetor motor store stork storm story torah toras torch toric torii torsi torsk torso torte torts torus tutor abator actors attorn bettor cantor captor castor debtor doctor editor extort factor fetors hector lector lictor mentor motors orator pastor pretor rector retort rhetor sector stator storax stored stores storks storms stormy suitor torahs torero torous torpid torpor torque torrid torsks torsos tortes tutors vector victor

tora torah toras storax torahs storage

torah torahs

torch torched torches torchere torching

tore store stored stores torero motored restore toreros tutored

tori toric torii storied stories storing

toric historic rhetoric

torn attorn attorns tornado

torr torrid torrefy torrent

tors torsi torsk torso actors fetors motors torsks torsos tutors abators bettors cantors captors castors debtors doctors editors factors hectors lectors lictors mentors orators pastors pretors rectors rhetors sectors stators suitors torsade torsion vectors victors

torsi torsions

torsk torsks

torso torsos

tort torte torts extort retort tortes contort distort extorts retorts tortile tortoni torture

torte tortes extorted retorted

torts contorts distorts

toss stoss tossed tosses tossup tossing tossups

tost tostada tostado

tot tote tots total toted totem toter totes totals totems toting totted totter

total totals totaled totally subtotal totaling totality

tote toted totem toter totes totems litotes totemic

totem totems totemic totemism

touch touchy retouch touched touches touchier touching

tough toughs toughens

tour stour tours detour stours toured contour detours touring tourism tourist tourney

tours stours detours contours

tout stout touts cutout putout stouts touted cutouts putouts shutout stoutly surtout touting

touts stouts cutouts shutouts

tow stow town tows stows towed towel tower towns bestow kowtow stowed towage toward towels towers towing townie uptown

towed stowed bestowed kowtowed

towel towels toweled toweling

tower towers towered towering

town towns townie uptown midtown townies

towns township townsman townsmen

tows stows bestows kowtows

toxic nontoxic toxicant toxicity

toxin toxins

toy toys toyed toyon toying toyons

toyon toyons

toys toyshop

trace traced tracer traces retrace tracers tracery retraced retraces

track tracks hatrack tracked tracker hatracks trackers tracking

tract tracts attract detract extract retract tractor abstract attracts contract detracts distract extracts protract retracts subtract tractate tractile traction tractors

trade traded trader trades traders

trail trailed trailer contrail entrails trailers trailing

train strain trains retrain strains trained trainee trainer quatrain restrain retrains seatrain strained strainer trainees trainers training

trait   strait traits straits traitor portrait straiten straitly traitors

tram   tramp trams trammel tramped trample tramway

tramp   tramped trample tramping trampled tramples

trap   strap traps entrap satrap flytrap rattrap satraps satrapy trapeze trapped trapper

traps   satraps flytraps rattraps

trash   trashy trashed trashes trashier trashing

trass   strass strasses

trave   travel traves travels traveled traveler travelog traverse travesty

trawl   trawls trawled trawler trawlers trawling

tray   stray trays astray betray estray strays ashtray betrays portray strayed

trays   strays betrays ashtrays portrays

tread   treads retread treaded treadle retreads treading treadled treadles

treat   treats treaty entreat estreat retreat treated entreats entreaty estreats maltreat retreats treaties treating treatise

tree   treed trees entree street entrees streets treeing treetop

trees   entrees

trek   treks trekked trekker

trend   trends trendy trendier trendies

tress   stress actress buttress distress fortress huntress mattress mistress stressed stresses waitress

tret   trets stretch stretti stretto

trews   strews

triad   triads

trial   atrial retrial mistrial retrials

tribe   tribes diatribe

trice   triced trices matrices

trick   strick tricks tricky tricked tricker trickle stricken strickle trickers trickery trickier tricking trickled trickles

tried   retried untried

tries   gantries pantries pastries peltries sentries vestries

trig   trigs trigon trigger trigons

trill   trills trilled trilling trillion

trim   trims trimly trimmed trimmer

trine   citrine latrine citrines doctrine latrines vitrines

trio   trios triode patriot triodes vitriol

trip   strip tripe trips stripe strips stripy tripes triple triply tripos cantrip striped striper stripes tripled triples tripped tripper

tripe   stripe tripes striped stripers

trips   strips cantrips

trite   triter contrite nitrites

trod   strode outrode tetrode trodden

troll   stroll trolls trolled strolled stroller trolleys trolling trollops

troop   troops trooped troopers trooping

trope   tropes

trot   troth trots troths betroth dogtrot trotted trotter

troth   troths betroth betroths

trots   dogtrots

trout   trouts

trove   strove trover troves

trow   trows trowed trowel trowels trowing

troy   destroy

truce   truces

truck   struck trucks trucked trucker truckle truckers trucking truckled truckles

true   trued truer trues truest untrue

trues   truest

trull   trulls

trump   trumps trumped strumpet trumpery trumpets trumping

trunk   trunks

truss   trussed trussing

trust   trusts trusted distrust entrusts mistrust trustees trustful trusties trusting

truth   truths truthful

try   entry retry tryst gantry gentry paltry pantry pastry peltry poetry sentry sultry tetryl trying tryout trysts vestry wintry

tryst   trysts trysted trysting

tsar   tsars tsarina tsarist

tub   stub tuba tube tubs stubs tubal tubas tubby tubed tuber tubes stubby tubers tubing

tuba   tubal tubas saxtuba

tubas   saxtubas

tubby   stubby

tube   tubed tuber tubes tubers

tuber   tubers

tubs   stubs

tuck   stuck tucks tucked tucket tuckets tucking unstuck

tufa   tufas

tuff   stuff tuffs stuffs stuffy stuffed

tuffs   stuffs

tuft   tufts tufty tufted tufting

tug   tugs tugged

tui   etui tuis etuis intuit tuille

tuis   etuis

tule   tules mutule mutules pustule

tules   pustules

tulip   tulips

tulle   tulles

tumor   tumors

tump   stump tumps stumps stumpy stumped stumper

tumps   stumps

tun   stun tuna tune tuns stung stunk stuns stunt tunas tuned tuner tunes tunic attune obtund rotund stunts tundra tuners tuneup tunics tuning tunned tunnel

tuna   tunas tunable

tune   tuned tuner tunes attune tuners tuneup attuned attunes fortune tuneful tuneups

tuned   attuned fortuned

tuner   tuners

tunes   attunes fortunes

tunic   tunics

tuns   stuns

tup   tups cutup letup setup situp stupa stupe cutups letups setups situps stupas stupid stupor tittup tupelo

tups   cutups letups setups situps tittups

tuque   tuques

turd   turds sturdy

turf   turfs turfy

turn   turns return turned turnip upturn nocturn returns turning turnips turnkey turnoff turnout upturns

turns   nocturns

tush   tushes

tusk   tusks

tut   tuts tutu tutor tutti astute tutors tutted tuttis

tutor   tutors tutored tutorial tutoring

tutti   tuttis

tutu   tutus

tux   tuxes tuxedo

twain   twains

twang   twangs twanged twanging

tweak   tweaks tweaked tweaking

tweed   tweeds tweedy tweedle knotweed tweedled tweedles

tweet   tweets tweeted tweeter tweeters tweeting

twerp   twerps

twig   twigs twiggy

twill   twills twilled twilling

twin   twine twins twined twines twinge entwine twinged twinges twining twinkle twinned

twine   twined twines entwine entwined entwines

twirl   twirls twirled twirlers twirling

twist   twists twisted twisters twisting

twit   twits nitwit outwit twitch nitwits outwits twitted twitter

two   twos twofer

twos   twosome

tying   dirtying emptying hogtying jettying partying puttying

tyke   tykes

type   typed types ectype retype ecotype ectypes retyped retypes tintype typeset

typed   retyped

types ectypes ecotypes tintypes		
tyro tyros		
tzar tzarina		

u

udder judder mudder rudder udders judders rudders shudder juddered shudders shuddery

udo judo udos kudos scudo escudo judoka pseudo

udos kudos escudos pseudos

ugh pugh aught bough cough dough faugh laugh lough ought rough tough aughts boughs bought caught chough clough coughs doughs doughy enough faughs fought laughs loughs naught nought roughs slough sought taught though toughs trough

ugly smugly snugly

uhlan uhlans

ukase ukases

ulcer ulcers ulcerate ulcerous

ulna ulnae ulnas

ultra cultrate ultrared

ulu lulu ulus lulus

ulus lulus annulus cumulus famulus hamulus tumulus

um bum cum gum hum lum mum rum sum ump yum alum bump bums chum drum dumb dump fume fumy geum glum grum gums hump hums jump lump mums numb ovum plum puma pump rump rums scum slum stum sumo sump sums swum tump umbo umps album algum alums aurum begum brume bumps bumpy cecum chump chums clump crumb crump cumin datum drums dummy dumps dumpy filum flume forum frump fumed fumes geums grume grump gumbo gummy hilum hokum human humic humid humor humph humps humpy humus ileum ilium jorum jugum jumbo jumps jumpy lumen lumps lumpy mummy mumps neume notum numbs numen oakum odium opium plumb plume plump plums pumas pumps rheum rhumb rumba rumen rummy rumor rumps scrum scums sebum sedum serum slump slums spume spumy strum stump stums sumac summa sumos sumps thrum thumb thump trump tumid tummy tumor tumps umbel umber umbos umbra umiak umiaq umped velum whump yummy

umbel umbels

umber cumber dumber lumber number umbers cumbers lumbers numbers plumber slumber umbered cucumber cumbered encumber lumbered numbered numberer plumbers renumber slumbers umbering

umbo gumbo jumbo umbos gumbos jumbos bumboat gumboot umbones

umbos gumbos jumbos

umbra umbrae umbras umbrage adumbral penumbra umbrages

umiak umiaks

ump bump dump hump jump lump pump rump sump tump umps bumps bumpy chump clump crump dumps dumpy frump grump humph humps humpy jumps jumpy lumps lumpy mumps plump pumps rumps slump stump sumps thump trump tumps umped whump bumped bumper chumps clumps clumpy crumps dumped dumper frumps frumpy grumps grumpy humped jumped jumper lumped plumps pumped pumper rumple rumply rumpus slumps stumps stumpy thumps trumps umping umpire whumps

umped bumped dumped humped jumped lumped pumped clumped crumped plumped slumped stumped thumped trumped whumped

umps bumps dumps humps jumps lumps mumps pumps rumps sumps tumps chumps clumps crumps frumps grumps plumps slumps stumps thumps trumps whumps

unapt unaptly

unarm unarms unarmed unarming

uncle uncles unclean unclear caruncle peduncle unclench

unco bunco junco buncos juncos uncoil uncork buncoed uncoils uncorks uncouth uncover

under sunder asunder blunder bounder founder launder maunder plunder pounder rounder sounder sunders thunder underdo undergo blunders bounders flounder founders grounder launders maunders plunders pounders rounders sounders sundered thunders thundery underarm underbid underbuy undercut underdid underdog underfed underlay underlie underpay underpin undersea undertow

undo sundog undoes undone rundown sundogs sundown undoing

unfix unfixed unfixing

unify unifying

union bunion unions bunions nonunion reunions unionism unionize

unit unite units unity united unites reunite unitary unities uniting unitize

unite united unites disunite reunited reunites

unity disunity immunity impunity

unman gunman unmans unmanly unmanned

unpin unpins unpinned

untie auntie untied unties aunties bounties counties jauntier runtiest untieing

until jauntily

unto junto juntos untold

unzip unzips unzipped

up cup hup pup sup tup yup coup cups pupa pups scup soup sups tups upas upon yaup yups coupe coups croup cupel cutup drupe duped duper duple erupt group guppy jupon layup letup lupus ouphe pinup pupae pupal pupil puppy rupee scaup scups setup situp soups soupy stoup stupa stupe sunup super syrup taupe upend upper upset yaups

upas stupas

upend upends upended upending

upon jupon coupon jupons yaupon coupons yaupons

upper cupper supper uppers crupper cuppers scupper cruppers scuppers uppercut

upset upsets

urban turban urbane exurban turbans suburban urbanely urbanism urbanist urbanite urbanity urbanize

urd curd surd turd urds curds gourd surds turds absurd burden curded curdle gourde gourds hurdle lurdan murder purdah sturdy

urds curds turds gourds

urea ureas bureau bureaus

uredo uredos

urge gurge purge surge urged urges burgee burger gurges purged purger purges surged surges urgent burgees burgeon burgers burgess purgers scourge splurge surgeon surgery upsurge urgency

urged purged surged scourged splurged upsurged

urges gurges purges surges burgess scourges splurges upsurges

uric auric auricle

urine murine taurine figurine taurines

urn   burn turn urns bourn burns burnt churn inurn mourn spurn turns auburn burned burner burnet churns gurney inurns mourns return spurns turned turnip upturn

urns   burns turns churns inurns mourns spurns auburns returns upturns

urus   gurus uruses

us   bus jus mus pus use anus bush buss bust busy crus cusk cusp cuss dusk dust emus feus flus fuse fuss gnus gush gust hush husk just lush lust muse mush musk muss must nous onus opus oust plus push puss ruse rush rusk rust sous thus tush tusk ulus urus used user uses abuse adust amuse ascus babus beaus blush bogus bolus bonus bouse brush brusk busby bused buses bushy busts busty cause cruse crush crust cusec cushy cusks cusps douse druse dusks dusky dusts dusty emeus favus fetus flush focus fucus fused fusee fuses fusil fussy fusty gauss genus gurus gushy gussy gusto gusts gusty gyrus hocus house humus husks husky hussy ictus ileus incus joust jujus justs kudus locus lotus louse lousy luaus lulus lupus lusts lusty manus menus minus mouse mousy mucus mused muses mushy music musky mussy musts musty negus nevus nexus nidus nisus nodus ousts pause pious plush pushy pussy ramus rebus reuse rouse roust ruses rushy rusks rusts rusty shush sinus situs slush sorus souse sushi talus tonus torus truss trust tusks uncus usage users usher using usual usurp usury vagus varus virus zebus

usage   usages sausage sausages

use   fuse muse ruse used user uses abuse amuse bouse bused buses cause cruse cusec douse druse fused fusee fuses house louse mouse mused muses pause reuse rouse ruses souse users abused abuser abuses accuse amused amuses anuses arouse bemuse blouse bouses caused causer causes ceruse chouse clause cruses cusecs defuse disuse doused douses druses effuse excuse fusees grouse housed housel houses incuse infuse misuse moused mouser mousey museum nausea obtuse onuses opuses paused pauses pluses recuse refuse reused reuses roused rouses scouse soused souses spouse unused uruses useful

used   bused fused mused abused amused caused doused housed moused paused reused roused soused unused accused aroused bemused bloused choused defused disused effused excused focused groused hocused infused misused perused recused refused

user   users abuser causer mouser abusers accuser causers infuser mousers nonuser peruser

users   abusers causers accusers infusers nonusers perusers trousers

uses   buses fuses muses ruses abuses amuses anuses bouses causes cruses douses druses houses onuses opuses pauses pluses reuses rouses souses uruses accuses arouses bemuses blouses boluses bonuses chouses clauses defuses disuses effuses excuses fetuses focuses grouses ictuses incuses infuses lotuses minuses misuses neguses nexuses peruses rebuses refuses sinuses spouses taluses viruses

usher   gusher pusher rusher ushers blusher crusher blushers crushers flushers

using   busing fusing musing abusing amusing bousing busings causing dousing pausing accusing arousing bemusing blousing chousing defusing disusing excusing focusing grousing hocusing infusing misusing perusing recusing refusing

usual   unusual usually

usurp   usurps

ut   but cut gut hut jut nut out put rut tut abut auto bout buts butt cute cuts duty futz glut gout guts huts jute juts lout lute mute mutt nuts outs pout puts putt rout ruth ruts scut shut slut smut taut tout tuts about abuts acute autos beaut bouts brute butch butts butyl chute clout couth cutch cuter cutey cutie cutin cutis cutup debut donut elute flout flute futon gamut gluts gouts gouty grout gutsy gutta hutch input jutes kaput klutz knout kraut louts luted lutes mouth muted mutes mutts nutsy nutty outdo outer outgo pouts putts putty rebut route routs rutty scout scuta scute scuts shout shuts sluts smuts snout south spout stout strut sutra touts trout truth tutor tutti uncut uteri utile utter youth

utile   futile futilely

utter   butter cutter gutter mutter putter utters abutter butters buttery clutter cutters uttered abutters aflutter buttered clutters flutters fluttery guttered muttered shutters splutter sputters stutters utterers uttering

uvea   uveas

uvula   uvulae uvular uvulas

v

vac vacs vacua vacant vacate vacuum vivace

vacua evacuate

vague vaguer vaguely vaguest

vail avail vails avails vailed availed prevail travail vailing

vails avails prevails travails

vain vainly

vair vairs

vale vales valet valets rivaled valence

valet valets

valid invalid invalids validate validity

valor valors valorous

value valued values devalue revalue devalued devalues revalued revalues

valve valves bivalve bivalved bivalves

vamp vamps revamp vamped revamps vamping vampire

vamps revamps

van vane vang vans divan pavan vanda vanes vangs divans levant pavane pavans savant silvan sylvan vandas vanish vanity

vanda vandas

vane vanes pavane pavanes

vanes pavanes evanesce

vang vangs evangel

vans divans pavans

vapid vapidly

vapor vapors vapory vaporize vaporous

vara varas

varna varnas

varve varves

vary ovary varying

vase vases

vases canvases

vast avast vastly

vat vats ovate vatic avatar cravat savate vatted

vats cravats

vault vaults vaulted vaulter vaulters vaulting

vaunt avaunt vaunts vaunted vaunting

veal veals reveal reveals

veals reveals

vee veep veer vees levee veeps veers veery leveed levees veered

veep veeps

veer veers veery veered veeries veering

vees levees

veil veils unveil veiled unveils veiling

vein veins veiny devein deveins

veins deveins

velar velarium

veld velds veldt veldts

veldt veldts

venal venally venality

vend vends vended vendee vendor vendue vendees vending vendors vendues

venin venins evening evenings livening ravening

venom venoms envenoms venomous

vent event vents advent events invent vented venter advents convent fervent invents prevent seventh seventy solvent ventage venters venting ventral venture

vents events advents convents prevents solvents

venue avenue venues avenues revenue revenuer revenues

verb verbs adverb reverb verbal verbid adverbs overbid overbuy proverb reverbs verbena verbids verbose

verbs adverbs reverbs proverbs

verge verged verger verges diverge vergers converge diverged diverges

verse averse versed verses adverse diverse obverse oversee reverse aversely converse obverses overseas overseen overseer oversees perverse reversed traverse universe unversed

verso versos oversoul

verst versts overstay overstep

vert avert evert overt verts advert averts covert divert everts invert obvert revert vertex adverts averted convert culvert diverts everted inverts obverts overtax overtly overtop pervert poverty reverts subvert vertigo

verts averts everts adverts diverts obverts converts culverts perverts subverts

verve verves vervet

very every livery revery wavery bravery knavery quavery quivery shivery silvery slavery

vest vests devest divest invest vestal vested vestee vestry bravest devests divests gravest harvest invests vestees vestige vesting vesture

vests devests divests harvests

vet veto vets civet covet duvet rivet vetch brevet civets covets curvet duvets grivet kvetch privet rivets trivet velvet vervet vetoed vetoes vetted

vetch kvetch vetches kvetched kvetches

veto vetoed vetoes vetoing

vets civets covets duvets rivets brevets curvets grivets privets trivets velvets vervets

vex vexed vexes convex vexing

vexed unvexed

vexes convexes

via vial avian vials viand avians aviary caviar gavial jovial salvia trivia viable viands

vial vials gavial jovial eluvial fluvial gavials pluvial trivial

vials gavials

viand viands

vicar vicars vicarage

vice vices advice device novice advices crevice devices novices service viceroy

vices advices devices novices cervices crevices services

video videos

vie vied vies view ivied ivies movie views bevies cavies civies envied envier envies levied levies movies navies review soviet viewed viewer wavier

vied ivied envied levied chevied divvied savvied

vies ivies bevies cavies civies envies levies movies navies chevies civvies gravies navvies peavies privies waviest

view views review viewed viewer preview purview reviews viewers viewing

views previews purviews

vigil vigils vigilant

vigor vigors vigorish vigoroso vigorous

vile viler revile vilely vilest caviler deviled reviled reviles servile

viler caviler cavilers

villa villas village villain villager villages villains villainy villatic

vim vims vimen vimina

vina vinas

vine ovine vines bovine divine ravine vinery bovines cervine corvine divined diviner divines ravines vinegar

vines bovines divines ravines waviness

viny vinyl vinyls

vinyl vinyls

viol viola viols violas violet violin ravioli violate violent violets violins violist

viola violas violate violable violated violates violator

viper vipers viperish viperous

vireo vireos

virga virgas virgate virgates

virtu virtue virtual virtuosi virtuoso virtuous

visa visas ovisac visaed visage devisal ovisacs revisal visages visaing

vise vised vises advise devise revise advised advisee adviser advises devised devises pavises previse revised revises

vised advised devised revised prevised

vises advises devises pavises parvises pelvises previses

visit visits visited revisits visitant visiting visitors

visor visors devisor divisor advisory devisors divisors

vista vistas

vital vitals vitalism vitality vitalize

vitta vittae

vivid vividly

vixen vixens vixenish

vizor vizors

vocal vocals vocally vocalism vocalist vocalize

vodka vodkas

vogue vogues

voice voiced voicer voices invoice invoices

void avoid ovoid voids avoids devoid ovoids voided avoided avoider voiding

voids avoids ovoids

vole voles

volt volts revolt revolts voltage

volva volvas

vomer vomers

vomit vomits vomited vomiting

vote voted voter votes devote voters devoted devotee devotes outvote pivoted

voted devoted pivoted

voter voters nonvoter

votes devotes outvotes

vouch avouch vouched voucher vouches vouchers vouching

vow avow vows avows vowed vowel avowal avowed vowels vowing

vowed avowed avowedly

vowel vowels

vows avows

vug vugs

vying chevying divvying savvying

W

wacko wackos

wad wade wadi wads waddy waded wader wades wadis wadded waddle waders wadies wading

wade waded wader wades waders

wader waders

wadi wadis wadies wading

wafer wafers wafery wafered wafering

waff waffs waffle waffled waffles

waft wafts wafted wafting

wag swag wage wags swags waged wager wages wagon sewage towage wagers wagged waggle waging wagons wigwag

wage waged wager wages sewage towage wagers brewage dowager sewages stowage towages wagered

wager wagers dowager wagered dowagers wagering

wages sewages towages stowages

wagon wagons wagoner wagoners

wags swags wigwags

wahoo wahoos

waif waifs

wail wails bewail wailed bewails wailful wailing

wails bewails

wain swain twain wains swains twains

wains swains twains wainscot

waist waists

wait await waits awaits waited waiter awaited waiters waiting

waits awaits

waive waived waiver waives waivers

wake awake waked waken wakes awaked awaken awakes wakens awakens wakeful wakened

waked awaked

waken awaken wakens awakens wakened awakened reawaken wakening

wakes awakes

wale swale waled wales swales gunwale

wales swales gunwales

walk walks walked walker catwalk jaywalk walkers walking walkout walkway

walks catwalks jaywalks

wall walls walled wallet wallop wallow drywall gadwall swallow wallaby wallets walleye walling wallops wallows

walls drywalls gadwalls

waltz waltzed waltzer waltzes waltzers waltzing

wan swan wand wane want wany bwana dewan gowan rowan swang swank swans twang wands waned wanes

wanly wants bwanas dewans gowans kwanza rowans swanky twangs wander wangle waning wanned wanner wanted wanter wanton

wand wands wander wanders

wane waned wanes

want wants wanted wanter wanton wanters wanting

wap swap waps swaps wapped

waps swaps

war ward ware warm warn warp wars wart wary award aware dwarf sward swarm swart wards wared wares warms warns warps warts warty aswarm awards beware coward dwarfs inward onward prewar pulwar reward swards swarms swarth thwart toward unwary upward warble warded warden warder warier warily waring warmed warmer warmly warmth warned warped warred warren

ward award sward wards awards coward inward onward reward swards toward upward warded warden warder awarded awkward cowards forward hayward inwards leeward onwards outward rewards skyward steward towards upwards wardens warders wayward

wards awards swards cowards inwards onwards rewards towards upwards forwards leewards outwards skywards stewards

ware aware wared wares beware bewared bewares tinware unaware

wared bewared

wares bewares tinwares unawares

warm swarm warms aswarm swarms warmed warmer warmly warmth swarmed warmest warming warmish

warms swarms

warn warns warned warning

warp warps warped warpath warping

wars pulwars warship

wart swart warts warty swarth thwart athwart swarthy thwarts wartier wartime

warts thwarts

wary unwary

was wash wasp wast awash swash washy wasps waspy waste schwas washed washer washes wasted waster wastes

wash awash swash washy washed washer washes carwash eyewash hogwash swashed swashes washday washers

washier washing washout washrag washtub

wasp wasps waspy waspier waspish

wast waste wasted waster wastes wastage wasters wasting wastrel

waste wasted waster wastes wasters wasteful

watch swatch watched watcher watches swatches watchdog watchers watchful watching watchman watchmen

water waters watery watered cutwater waterbed watering waterish waterway

watt watts wattle swatted swatter twattle wattage wattled wattles

wave waved waver waves wavers wavery waverer

waver wavers wavery waverer

waves airwaves

wax waxy waxed waxen waxer waxes earwax waxers waxier waxing

waxer waxers

way away sway ways byway noway sways airway always anyway byways keyway leeway midway runway seaway skyway subway swayed waylay

ways sways always byways airways anyways endways keyways leeways runways seaways skyways subways wayside

we awe ewe owe web wed wee wen wet awed awes ewer ewes owed owes weak weal wean wear webs weds weed week weep weft weir weka weld well welt wend wens wept west wets bowed bowel bower cower dewed dowel dower dwell dwelt fewer hawed hewed hewer jawed jewel lowed lower mewed mowed mower newel newer pawed pewee power rawer rowed rowel rowen rower sawed sewed sewer sowed sower swear sweat sweep sweet swell swept towed towel tower tweak tweed tweet twerp unwed vowed vowel weald weals weans wears weary weave webby wedge wedgy weeds weedy weeks weeny weeps weepy weest wefts weigh weird weirs wekas welds wells welsh welts wench wends wests wetly yawed

weak tweak tweaks weaken weaker weakly tweaked weakens weakest

weal weald weals wealds wealth wealths wealthy

weald wealds

wean weans weaned weaning

wear swear wears weary swears wearer outwear wearers wearied wearier wearily wearing

wears swears outwears

weary wearying

weave weaver weaves inweave weavers inweaves

web webs webby cobweb webbed

webby cobwebby

webs cobwebs

wed awed owed weds bowed dewed hawed hewed jawed lowed mewed mowed pawed rowed sawed sewed sowed towed unwed vowed wedge wedgy yawed avowed brewed chawed chewed clawed clewed crewed crowed flawed flowed glowed gnawed plowed shewed showed skewed slowed snowed spewed stewed stowed thawed trowed viewed wedded wedged wedges

wedge wedged wedges

wee weed week weep weer pewee sweep sweet tweed tweet weeds weedy weeks weeny weeps weepy weest peewee pewees sweeps sweets tweeds tweedy tweets tweeze weeded weeder weekly weenie weeper weepie weever weevil

weed tweed weeds weedy tweeds tweedy weeded weeder hogweed pigweed ragweed seaweed tweedle waxweed weeders weedier weeding

weeds tweeds hogweeds pigweeds ragweeds seaweeds waxweeds

weedy tweedy

week weeks weekly midweek weekday weekend

weep sweep weeps weepy sweeps weeper weepie sweeper weepers weepier weeping

weeps sweeps

weft wefts

weigh aweigh weighs weight weighed weigher outweigh weighers weighing weighted

weir weird weirs weirdo weirdly weirdos

weird weirdo weirdly weirdos

weka wekas

weld welds welded welder welders welding

well dwell swell wells dwells swells unwell dwelled dweller indwell inkwell maxwell swelled

wells dwells swells indwells inkwells maxwells

welsh welshed welsher welshes welshers welshing

welt dwelt welts welted welter indwelt swelter welters welting

wen wend wens rowen wench wends rowens twenty wended

wench wenched wencher wenches wenchers wenching

wend wends wended wending

wens rowens

wept swept upswept

west wests fewest lowest newest rawest wester slowest western westers westing

wet wets wetly wether wetted wetter

whack whacko whacks whacky whacked whackos whackier whacking

whale whaled whaler whales whalers whaleman

wham whams whammo whammy

whang whangs

whap whaps whapped

what whatnot

wheal wheals

wheat wheats wheaten

wheel wheels wheelie cogwheel flywheel pinwheel wheelies

whelk whelks

whelp whelps whelped whelping

when whence

where nowhere whereas whereby wherein whereof whereto anywhere wherever

whet whets whether whetted

whey wheys

whiff whiffs whiffed whiffing whiffled whiffler whiffles

while awhile whiled erewhile

whim whims whimsy whimper

whims whimsy whimsies

whine whined whiner whines

whip whips whipt whipped whippet whipsaw

whips whipsaw whipsaws

whir whirl whirs awhirl whirls whirled whirred

whirl awhirl whirls whirled whirling

whish whished whishing

whisk whisks whisky whisked whiskeys whiskies whisking

whist whists whistled whistler whistles

whit white whits whited whiten whiter whites whitey whitely whitens whitest whither whiting whitish whittle

white whited whiten whiter whites whitey bobwhite nonwhite whitecap whitened whitener

whiz whizz whizzed whizzes

whizz whizzed whizzing

who whoa whom whop whole whomp whoop whops whore whorl whose wholly whomps whoops whoosh whored whores whorls

whom whomp whomps whomped

whomp whomps whomped whomping

whoop whoops whooped whoopee whooping

whop whops whopped whopper

whore whored whores

whorl whorls whorled

whump whumps whumped whumping

wick wicks wicked wicker wicket wickers wickets

wide widen wider widely widens widest widened widener

widen widens widened widener wideness widening

widow widows widowed widower widowers widowing

width widths

wield wields wielded wielder unwieldy wielders wielding

wife wifely alewife henwife midwife oldwife

wig swig twig wigs swigs twigs wigan wight bigwig earwig twiggy wigans wigged wiggle wiggly wights wigwag wigwam

wigan wigans

wight wights

wigs swigs twigs bigwigs earwigs

wild wilds wilder wildly wildcat wildest

wile wiled wiles

will swill twill wills swills twills willed willow swilled twilled willful willies willing willows

wills swills twills

wilt wilts wilted wilting

wimp wimps wimpy wimple wimpish wimpled wimples

win twin wind wine wing wink wino wins winy awing owing swine swing twine twins wince winch winds windy wined wines wings winks winos bowing dewing hawing hewing jawing lowing mewing mowing pawing rewind rowing sawing sewing sowing swinge swings swingy towing twined twines twinge unwind upwind vowing winced winces winded winder window windup winery winged winier wining winked winkle winner winnow winter wintry yawing

wince winced winces

winch winched winches winching

wind winds windy rewind unwind upwind winded winder window windup dwindle inwinds rewinds swindle unwinds windage windbag winders windier winding windows windrow windups

winds inwinds rewinds unwinds windsock

wine swine twine wined wines twined twines winery entwine

wined twined entwined

wines twines entwines wineskin

wing awing owing swing wings bowing dewing hawing hewing jawing lowing mewing mowing pawing rowing sawing sewing sowing swinge swings swingy towing twinge vowing winged yawing avowing blowing bowings brewing chawing chewing clawing clewing crewing crowing drawing flawing flowing glowing gnawing growing knowing lapwing mowings plowing shewing showing slowing snowing spewing stewing stowing swinged swinger swingle thawing trowing twinged twinges upswing viewing winging wingman wingmen wingtip

wings swings bowings drawings gnawings lapwings showings upswings wingspan

wink winks winked winkle chewink twinkle winking winkled winkles

winks chewinks

wino winos

wins twins winsome

wipe swipe wiped wiper wipes swiped swipes wipers wipeout

wiped swiped

wiper wipers

wipes swipes

wire wired wires rewire haywire rewired rewires wiretap

wired rewired

wis iwis wise wish wisp kiwis lewis swish twist wiser wisps wispy brewis newish nowise swishy twists unwise wisdom wisely wisent wisest wished wisher wishes

wise wiser nowise unwise wisely wisent wisest anywise endwise fanwise wisents

wish swish newish swishy wished wisher wishes swished swishes wishers wishful wishing

wisp wisps wispy wispier wispily

wit twit wite with wits twits witan witch wited wites withe withy witty dimwit nitwit outwit switch twitch witans withal withed wither withes within witing

witan witans

witch switch twitch bewitch witches switched switches twitched twitches witchery witching

wite wited wites

with withe withy withal withed wither withes within withers withies withing without

withe withed wither withes withered

wits twits dimwits nitwits outwits

wive wived wives swivel swivels

wives alewives henwives midwives oldwives

wizen wizens wizened wizening

woe woes woeful

woes woesome

wok woke woks awoke woken

woke awoke woken

wolf wolfish

woman womanly laywoman madwoman womanish womanize

womb wombs wombat wombats

women laywomen madwomen

won wont wonky wonts wonder wonned wonted

wont wonts wonted wonting

woo wood woof wool woos swoon swoop woods woody wooed wooer woofs wools woosh woozy swoons swoops swoosh wooded wooden woodsy wooers woofer wooing woolen woolly

wood woods woody wooded wooden woodsy boxwood dogwood inkwood logwood plywood redwood woodcut woodier woodman woodmen

woods woodsy boxwoods dogwoods logwoods plywoods redwoods woodshed woodsier woodsman woodsmen

wooer wooers

woof woofs woofer woofers

wool wools woolen woolly woolens

woos woosh swoosh wooshed wooshes

woosh swoosh wooshed swooshed swooshes wooshing

word sword words wordy byword reword swords worded bywords rewords wordier wordily wording

words swords bywords rewords

wore swore outwore

work works worked worker artwork cutwork legwork network reworks tinwork waxwork workday workers working workman workmen workout

works artworks cutworks gasworks networks tinworks waxworks workshop

world worlds worldly

worm worms wormy wormed cutworm eelworm pinworm wormier worming

worms cutworms eelworms pinworms

worn sworn outworn

worry worrying

worse worsen worser worsened

worst worsted

worth worths worthy unworthy worthier worthies

wound wounds inwound rewound unwound wounded wounding

wove woven inwove inwoven

wow wows bowwow powwow

wows bowwows powwows

wrack wracks

wrap wraps wrapt unwrap unwraps wrapped wrapper

wraps unwraps

wrath wraths wrathy wrathful

wreak wreaks wreaked wreakers wreaking

wreck wrecks wrecked wrecker wreckage wreckers wrecking

wren wrens wrench

wrest wrests wrested wresting wrestled wrestler wrestles

wring wrings wringed wringers wringing

wrist wrists wristlet

writ write writs writer writes writhe rewrite writers writhes writing written

write writer writes rewriter

wrong wrongs wronged wrongful wronging

wry wryly

wurst wursts

wye wyes bowyer lawyer sawyer

wynd wynds

xyz

xebec xebecs
xenia xenias
xenon xenons
xerox xeroxed xeroxing
xi axil axis exit ixia maxi taxi auxin axial axile axils axing axiom exile exist exits lexis maxim maxis moxie nixie oxide oxime pixie pyxie pyxis taxis toxic toxin
xylan xylans
xylem xylems
yacht yachts yachted yachting
yack kyack yacks kyacks yacked yacking
yacks kyacks
yah ayah ayahs aliyah
yak kyak yaks kayak kyaks galyak kayaks yakked
yaks kyaks kayaks
yam yams yamen yamens yammer
yamen yamens
yang yangs
yank yanks yanked yanking
yap yaps yapok yapock yapoks yapped yapper
yapok yapoks
yar yard yare yarn boyar yards yarns boyars yarded yarned yarrow
yard yards yarded halyard lanyard yardage yardarm yarding yardman yardmen
yards halyards lanyards
yarn yarns yarned yarning
yaup yaups yaupon yaupons
yaw yawl yawn yawp yaws yawed yawls yawns yawps yawing yawled yawned yawner
yawl yawls yawled yawling
yawn yawns yawned yawner yawners yawning
yawp yawps
ye aye bye dye eye lye rye wye yea yen yep yes yet yew abye ayes byes dyed dyer dyes eyed eyes lyes oyes oyez ryes wyes yeah yean year yeas yech yegg yell yelp yens yeti bayed buyer coyer doyen dryer dyers flyer foyer fryer gayer guyed hayed hyena keyed layer oxeye payed payee payer rayed rayer sayer shyer skyey slyer toyed yeans yearn years yeast yeggs yells yelps yenta yente yeses yetis
yea yeah yean year yeas yeans yearn years yeast yeaned yearly yearns yeasts yeasty
yean yeans yeaned yeaning

year yearn years yearly yearns midyear yearned yearner
yearn yearns yearned yearner yearners yearning
years midyears
yeas yeast yeasts yeasty yeasted
yeast yeasts yeasty yeasted yeastier yeasting
yegg yeggs
yell yells yelled yeller yellow yellers yelling yellows yellowy
yelp yelps yelped yelper yelpers yelping
yen yens doyen hyena yenta yente doyens hyenas yenned yentas yentes
yens doyens
yenta yentas
yente yentes
yes ayes byes dyes eyes lyes oyes ryes wyes yeses coyest gayest mayest oxeyes shyest slyest yessed yesses yester
yet yeti yetis gayety
yeti yetis
yew yews
yield yields yielded yielder yielders yielding
yin ayin ayins dying eying hying lying tying vying zayin baying buying coying crying drying flying frying guying haying keying laying maying paying plying prying raying saying shying spying toying trying zayins
yip yipe yips yipped yippie
ylem xylem xylems
yob yobs yobbo yobbos
yobbo yobbos
yock yocks
yod yodh yods yodel yodhs yodels
yodel yodels yodeled yodeler yodelers yodeling yodelled
yodh yodhs
yoga yogas
yogi yogic yogis yogini yoginis
yoke yoked yokel yokes yokels
yokel yokels
yolk yolks yolky yolked yolking
yon yond yoni rayon toyon yonis anyone baryon beyond canyon crayon rayons toyons yonder
yond beyond yonder
yoni yonis
yore yores
yores mayoress
you your bayou young yours youth bayous buyout joyous layout payout tryout youths

young youngest youngish
your yours
yours yourself
youth youths youthful
yow yowl yowls yowled
yowl yowls yowled yowling
yuan yuans
yucca yuccas
yuck yucks yucky yuckier
yuk yuks yukked
yule yules guayule
yum yummy
yup yups layup layups yuppie
yups layups
yurt yurts
zag zags zigzag
zags zigzags
zap zaps zapped
zarf zarfs
zax zaxes
zayin zayins
zeal zeals zealot zealots zealous
zebec zebecs
zebra zebras
zebu zebus
zed zeds dazed dozed fazed fuzed gazed hazed lazed mazed oozed razed sized amazed blazed boozed brazed crazed crozed fizzed futzed fuzzed glazed glozed grazed jazzed prized razzed seized
zee zees fuzee razee fuzees razees
zees fuzees razees
zero zeros zeroed zeroes zeroing
zest zests zesty zestful
zeta zetas
zig zigs zigged zigzag
zilch zilches
zinc zincs zincy zinced zincky zincing zincite zincked
zing zings dazing dozing fazing fuzing gazing hazing lazing mazing oozing razing sizing zinged zinger amazing blazing boozing brazing buzzing crazing fizzing futzing fuzzing glazing glozing grazing hazings jazzing prizing razzing seizing sizings zinging
zings hazings glazings
zip zips unzip zippy unzips zipped zipper
zips unzips
ziram zirams
zit ziti zits zizit zither zizith
zizit zizith
zloty zlotys

zoa zoas bezoar
zoea zoeae zoeal zoeas
zombi zombie zombis zombies
zonal azonal zonally
zone ozone zoned zones evzone ozones
    rezone canzone evzones rezoned re-
    zones

zoned rezoned blazoned
zones ozones
zonk zonks zonked zonking
zooid zooidal

zoom zooms zoomed zooming
zoon zoonal
zoos bazoos kazoos
zori zoris zorille

III. THE WORD LISTS

This last part of the Word Finder serves more specialized needs of word game players. Though it pays to check the section during a game, some players will also browse through these pages to familiarize themselves with the lists or even to find choice words for future word games. You never know when a particular ending or combination of high-scoring letters may come in handy.

The Y Problem

The first list below solves a problem of word endings all players face over and over again—for words ending in *y*, when does the *y* change to an *i(e)*? This problem crops up when trying to make the plural of a noun, first person singular of a verb, and comparative form of an adjective when the *y* is involved. Correct spelling counts in all word games, of course, but in board games there is an added problem. If you want to score by tacking an ending onto a word that is already on the board, you must know if the *y* changes or not. If it does, using the ending is against most game rules, because you cannot change letters of a word once they are on the board.

Words With High-Point Letters

The next eight lists are useful for board games that assign point values to letters used in play. Four letters, *j*, *q*, *x*, and *z* are high-scoring letters in such games and can make a big difference in points, even when played as part of short words. You can check these lists during play to find out what word or words to make with the high-scoring letter you have just drawn, or as a resource for identifying and memorizing selected high-point words. At the very least, you should keep in mind words like *jazz* against that lucky day when you have three high-point letters at the same time.

Beginnings and Endings

Sometimes you will find yourself with a group of letters that forms one of the many common beginnings or endings of words, such as *com-* or *-age*. When you want to know what words you can make with any of over 75 different beginnings and endings, this group of lists in this book is just what you need. It present words that will form a valid new word when the particular letters are added. This is especially handy for board games, when you want to score by building on a word that has already been played.

For Scrabble® Players Using the OSPD

The final list in this section will prove invaluable if you use the *Official Scrabble® Players Dictionary* to settle challenges. There are only some 600 words in this book (all valid for play) that are not in the OSPD. But you should check the list before playing a word, when using the OSPD as your final authority.

WHEN, AND WHEN NOT, TO CHANGE THE "Y" TO AN "I"

You can probably spell appropriate forms of the most common words ending in *y* almost without thinking—city, candy, heavy—but how often have you wondered about words you use less often? The plural of *jitney* or *boloney* may well trip you up (yes, boloney can be made into a legitimate plural). So too when it comes to the comparative of the fairly common words *shy* and *wily*.

The handy list presented below is really a mini dictionary of such troublesome endings. It tells you if the word you want to make should end with *ys* or *ies*. And it includes correct spellings for the comparative *er* forms of these words, showing when to use *ier* (most always) and *yer*.

All you have to do is look up the root word in the list. At the nearest correct spelling, you will find the word with the appropriate ending(s), if any. Look up the word *chalky*, for example, and you will quickly find the place where *chaffier*, *chalkier*, and *charier* are listed. The comparative form *chalkier* is obviously the correct choice. When both *ies* and *ys* forms appear, both are acceptable.

Words that end in *-ie*, such as groupie and hippie, do not appear on this list. Neither do words that end in *-er* but that are not comparative forms, as in employer or flyer. Plurals of both these types of nouns take the simple *s* ending.

abbacies	baloneys	bodies	burlier	choppier	cosier
abbeys	bandies	bogeys	busbies	chubbier	cosies
aeries	barflies	bogies	busboys	chummier	costlier
affrays	barmier	boloneys	bushier	chunkier	coteries
agencies	baronies	bonier	busier	chutneys	counties
agonies	battier	bonnier	buys	cicelies	courier
airier	bawdier	boobies	byways	cities	coveys
airways	bays	bookies	cabbies	civies	cowboys
alkalies	beadier	boonies	caddies	civvies	cowries
allays	beamier	booties	cagier	clammier	coyer
alleys	beanies	boskier	calories	claries	cozier
allies	beasties	bossier	campier	classier	crabbier
alloys	beauties	botchier	canaries	clays	craftier
always	beefier	botflies	candies	clergies	craggier
ambries	beerier	bouncier	cannier	cloudier	crankier
angrier	belays	bounties	canopies	cloys	crannies
annoys	belfries	boweries	caraways	clumsier	crappier
anomies	belies	boxier	carboys	cockier	crappies
anyways	bellboys	boys	carnies	cockneys	crazies
apiaries	bellies	brandies	carries	codifier	creakier
applies	beltways	brannier	cashier	codifies	creamier
archways	bennies	brassier	catchier	collies	creepier
argosies	berries	brattier	cattier	colonies	cries
armies	betrays	brawnier	cavities	comedies	crispier
armories	bevies	braxies	cays	comelier	crummier
arrays	beys	brays	chaffier	comfier	crustier
arteries	biddies	breezier	chalkier	comities	cubbies
ashier	biggies	brinier	charier	complies	cuddies
ashtrays	bikeways	brionies	charrier	coneys	cullies
assayer	billies	bubblier	chattier	conies	curacies
assays	binaries	buddies	cheekier	conveys	curries
atomies	biopsies	buggier	cherries	convoys	curtsies
auguries	birdies	buggies	chevies	cookies	curvier
aunties	blarneys	bulkier	chewier	coolies	cushier
aviaries	blasties	bullies	chilies	cooties	cutaways
babies	blockier	bumpier	chillier	copier	cuties
baggier	bloodier	bunchier	chimneys	copies	daddies
bailies	bloomier	bunnies	chippies	corbies	daffier
bakeries	blousier	buoys	chirpier	corkier	dailies
ballys	blowsier	buries	chlamyses	cornier	daintier
balmier	bobbies	burleys	choosier	corries	dainties

620

dairies
daisies
dallier
dallies
dandier
dandies
dashier
dataries
days
deadlier
dearies
decays
decoys
decries
deejays
defies
defrays
deifies
deities
delays
denies
deploys
deputies
derbies
destroys
dexies
deys
diaries
dicier
dillies
dimities
dinghies
dinkier
dinkies
dipodies
dippier
dirtier
dirties
dismays
disobeys
displays
ditties
dizzier
dizzies
doggier
doggies
doilies
dollies
donkeys
doorways
dopier
dories
dossier
dottier
doughier
dowdier
dowdies
downier
dowries
doxies
dozier
draftier
drays
dreamier
drearier
dreggier
dressier

drier
dries
driftier
drippier
droopier
drossier
drowsier
duchies
duckier
dummies
dumpier
duperies
duskier
dustier
duties
earlier
earthier
easier
eateries
ebonies
eddies
edgeways
edgier
edifies
eerier
effigies
eighties
elegies
embays
embodies
emperies
employs
emptier
empties
endways
enemies
energies
enjoys
enmities
entities
entries
envier
envies
envoys
epoxies
equities
espies
essays
eulogies
expiries
facies
faeries
fairies
fairways
falsies
families
fancier
fancies
fannies
faultier
fays
fealties
fellies
felonies
ferities
ferries
fierier

fifties
fillies
filmier
filthier
fineries
fishier
fixities
fizzier
flabbier
flakier
flashier
flays
flies
flimsier
flimsies
floozies
floppier
floppies
fluffier
flurries
foamier
fogeys
fogies
follies
footsies
forays
forties
foxier
foys
frays
freebies
freeways
frenzies
friaries
fries
frostier
fruitier
funkier
funnier
funnies
furies
furrier
fussier
fuzzier
gabbier
gabies
gadflies
gaieties
gainsays
galaxies
galleys
gamier
gangways
gantries
gasifies
gassier
gateways
gaudier
gawkier
gayer
gays
getaways
gharries
giddier
gigglier
girlies
glazier

glories
glossies
goalies
goodies
goofier
gorier
grainier
grannies
grassier
gravies
grayer
grays
grazier
greasier
greedier
greenies
greys
grimier
grislier
grubbier
grungier
guiltier
gullies
gunnies
guys
gypsies
hackies
hackneys
hairier
hallways
hammier
handier
hardier
harpies
harries
hastier
hautboys
hays
hazier
headier
heartier
heavier
heftier
henries
herbier
herdboys
heresies
heydays
hickeys
highboys
highways
hillier
hinnies
hoagies
hoarier
hobbies
holidays
holier
holies
hollies
homelier
homier
homilies
honkies
hornier
horsier
hoys

hubbies
huffier
hulkier
humpier
hungrier
hurrays
hurries
huskier
huskies
hussies
icier
ickier
idiocies
implies
infamies
injuries
inkier
inlays
inlier
ironies
itchier
ivies
ivories
jaggier
jalopies
japeries
jauntier
jays
jazzier
jellies
jemmies
jennies
jerkier
jerseys
jetties
jiffies
jimmies
jitneys
jockeys
joeys
jollier
jollies
joltier
journeys
joys
juicier
jumpier
junkies
juries
kelpies
kerries
kerseys
keys
keyways
kiddies
kidneys
killjoys
kindlier
kinkier
kitties
knobbier
knottier
knurlier
kookier
lacier
laddies
ladies

laities
lampreys
lankier
lardier
lassies
lays
lazier
leadier
leafier
leakier
leerier
leeways
lefties
legacies
leggier
levies
levities
likelier
lilies
limeys
limier
linier
linkboys
linseys
lintier
litanies
livelier
liveries
loamier
lobbies
loftier
logier
lollies
lonelier
longways
loobies
looies
loonier
loppier
lorries
lousier
lovelier
lowboys
lowlier
luckier
lumpier
lustier
luxuries
magueys
maladies
malmseys
maltier
mangier
manlier
margays
marries
marshier
mateys
mayflies
mazier
mealier
meanies
meatier
medleys
melodies
memories
mercies

merrier
messier
mickies
mightier
milkier
mintier
miseries
mislays
misplays
mistier
modifier
modifies
moldier
mollies
mommies
monies
monkeys
moodier
morays
moseys
mossier
mousier
mouthier
movies
muckier
muddier
muleys
mummies
mushier
mutinies
nannies
naperies
nappier
nappies
nastier
nattier
navies
navvies
needier
nervier
newsboys
newsier
niceties
niftier
nineties
ninnies
nippier
nobbier
nobodies
noddies
noisier
noondays
nosegays
nosier
notaries
notifier
notifies
nowadays
nubbier
nubblier
nudities
nuttier
obeys
occupies
oddities
oilier
okays

oozier
orgies
orphreys
orreries
ospreys
ossifies
outcries
outlays
ovaries
overbuys
overlays
pacifier
paddies
pageboys
paisleys
palfreys
palmier
palsies
paltrier
pandies
pannier
pansies
panties
pantries
papacies
paries
parities
parkways
parlays
parleys
parodies
parries
parties
passkeys
pastier
pasties
pastries
patchier
pathways
patsies
patties
pawkier
paydays
pays
peachier
pearlier
peatier
peavies
peltries
pennies
penuries
peonies
peppier
perkier
perries
peskier
pettier
phonier
phonies
pickier
pieties
piggies
pigsties
pimplier
pineries
pinier
pinkies

pipier
piracies
pithier
pities
playboys
plays
plenties
ploys
pluckier
poesies
poetries
pointier
pokier
pokies
policies
polities
ponies
poppies
porkier
portlier
portrays
posies
potpies
potties
prairies
prays
premier
prepays
prettier
pretties
prexies
preys
pries
priories
prissier
privies
prosier
proxies
pudgier
puffier
pulpier
punties
puppies
purifier
purifies
purities
pursier
purveys
pushier
pussier
pussies
putties
pygmies
pyxies
quaggier
quakier
quarrier
quarries
queasier
rabies
raceways
racier
railways
rainier
rallies
ramifies
randies

rapier
rarefies
rarities
raspier
ratifies
rattier
rays
readies
realties
reifies
relays
relies
remedies
repays
replays
replies
reties
retries
rickeys
ridgier
riotries
riskier
ritzier
roadways
rockier
rollways
rookies
roomier
rootier
roperies
rosaries
rosier
rotaries
rowdier
rowdies
rubies
ruddier
rummies
runaways
runnier
runtier
runways
rushier
rustier
safeties
salaries
salifies
sallies
saltier
sandier
sanities
sappier
sashays
sassier
saucier
sauries
savorier
savoys
sawflies
says
scabbier
scalier
scantier
scarier
screwier
scummier
seamier

seaways
seedier
seemlier
seepier
sentries
series
sexier
shabbier
shadier
shaggier
shakier
shammies
shanteys
sharpies
shellier
shelties
sherries
shier
shies
shiftier
shimmies
shindies
shinier
shinnies
shipways
shoalier
shoddier
shoddies
showier
shyer
sicklier
sideways
silkier
sillier
sillies
siltier
simonies
sissies
sixties
skies
skimpier
skinnier
skyways
slays
sleazier
sleepier
slier
slimier
slipways
sloppier
sloshier
slurries
slushier
slyer
smarties
smearier
smellier
smithies
smokier
snakier
snappier
sneakier
snowier
soapier
softies
soggier
someways

sootier
sorrier
soupier
soys
spays
species
speedier
spicier
spies
spiffier
spinier
splays
spongier
spookier
sportier
spottier
sprays
sprier
spryer
spunkier
stays
steadier
steadies
steamier
steelier
stickier
stingier
stockier
stonier
stories
stormier
strays
stubbier
studies
stuffier
sturdier
stymies
subways
sulkier
sulkies
sullies
sundries
sunnier
supplies
sureties
surfier
surreys
surveys
swamies
sways
sweatier
sweeties
tabbies
tackier
taffies
tallboys
tallies
tangier
tardier
tarrier
tarries
tastier
tawnier
taxpayer
teapoys
teddies
teenier

tepefies	tramways	unifies	volleys	weekdays	withies
terrier	trashier	unities	votaries	weeklies	wittier
terries	trays	untidier	wackier	weenies	woodier
theories	treaties	usuries	waddies	weepier	woodsier
thirties	trendier	vagaries	walkways	whackier	woollier
thornier	trickier	valleys	warier	whammies	woollies
thruways	tries	vanities	wartier	wheezier	woozier
tidier	trilbies	varies	washdays	wherries	wordier
tinnier	trolleys	veeries	washier	wheys	workdays
tipsier	trophies	veneries	waspier	whimsies	wormier
tizzies	tubbier	verifier	wavier	whiskies	worrier
toadies	tumefies	verifies	waxier	wigglier	worries
todays	tummies	verities	waylayer	wilier	worthier
toddies	turkeys	vernier	waylays	windier	worthies
todies	turnkeys	vestries	ways	wineries	wrier
tomboys	twenties	viceroys	weaklier	winier	wries
tootsies	typifies	vilifies	wearier	wintrier	wryer
touchier	uglier	vineries	webbier	wirier	yummier
tourneys	uglifies	virelays	wedgier	wispier	zanies
toys	unholier	vivifies	weedier		

WORDS WITH HIGH-POINT LETTERS

There are separate lists below for each of the high-point letters *j*, *q*, *x*, and *z* respectively. In addition, other valuable lists present words that contain two or more of each of the high-point letters. One final list includes words with at least two different high-point letters.

WORDS WITH THE LETTER J

abject
abjectly
acajou
acajous
adjacent
adjoin
adjoined
adjoins
adjourn
adjourns
adjudge
adjudged
adjudges
adjunct
adjuncts
adjure
adjures
adjust
adjusted
adjuster
adjustor
adjusts
adjutant
ajar
aparejo
aparejos
banjo
banjoist
banjos
bejewel
bejewels
benjamin
bijou
bijugate
bijugous
bootjack
cajole
cajoled
cajoler
cajolers
cajolery
cajoles
cajoling
carcajou
conjoin
conjoins
conjoint
conjugal
conjunct
conjure
conjured
conjurer
conjures

conjuror
deejay
deejays
deject
dejected
dejects
demijohn
disjoin
disjoins
disjoint
disjunct
dojo
dojos
donjon
donjons
doorjamb
eject
ejecta
ejected
ejecting
ejection
ejective
ejector
ejectors
ejects
enjoin
enjoins
enjoy
enjoyed
enjoying
enjoys
fanjet
fanjets
fjord
fjords
flapjack
forjudge
frijol
frijole
frijoles
ganjah
ganjahs
hadj
hadji
hadjis
haji
hajis
hajj
hajji
hajjis
hejira
hejiras
hijack
hijacked
hijacker
hijacks

hijinks
inject
injected
injector
injects
injure
injured
injurer
injurers
injures
injuries
injuring
injury
jab
jabs
jabbed
jabber
jabbered
jabberer
jabbers
jabbing
jabiru
jabirus
jabot
jabots
jacamar
jacamars
jacana
jacanas
jacinth
jacinths
jack
jackal
jackals
jackass
jackboot
jackdaw
jackdaws
jacked
jacket
jacketed
jackets
jacking
jackleg
jacklegs
jackpot
jackpots
jacks
jackstay
jaconet
jaconets
jade
jaded
jadedly
jadeite
jadeites

jades
jading
jadish
jag
jagged
jaggedly
jaggier
jaggiest
jagging
jaggy
jags
jaguar
jaguars
jail
jailbait
jailbird
jailed
jailer
jailers
jailing
jails
jake
jakes
jalap
jalaps
jalopies
jalopy
jalousie
jam
jamb
jambone
jamboree
jambs
jammed
jamming
jammings
jams
jangle
jangled
jangler
janglers
jangles
jangling
janitor
janitors
japan
japanned
japans
jape
japed
japer
japeries
japes
jar
jargon
jargons

jarl
jarls
jarred
jarring
jars
jasmine
jasmines
jasper
jaspers
jato
jatos
jaundice
jaunt
jaunted
jauntier
jauntily
jaunting
jaunts
jaunty
java
javelin
javelins
jaw
jawbone
jawboned
jawbones
jawed
jawing
jaws
jay
jaybird
jaybirds
jays
jaywalk
jaywalks
jazz
jazzed
jazzier
jazziest
jazzily
jazzing
jazzman
jazzmen
jazzy
jealous
jealousy
jean
jeans
jeep
jeepers
jeeps
jeer
jeered
jeerer
jeering
jeers

jeez
jejune
jejunum
jell
jelled
jellied
jellies
jelling
jells
jelly
jellying
jemmies
jemmy
jennet
jennets
jennies
jenny
jeopard
jeopards
jeopardy
jerboa
jeremiad
jerk
jerked
jerkier
jerkiest
jerkily
jerkin
jerking
jerkins
jerks
jerky
jerrycan
jersey
jerseys
jess
jesse
jesses
jest
jested
jester
jesters
jesting
jests
jetsam
jet
jetport
jetports
jets
jetted
jettied
jetties
jetting
jettison
jetty
jettying

jewel	jitneys	joked	joyance	jumbo	justs
jeweled	jitter	joker	joyful	jumbos	jut
jeweler	jittered	jokers	joyfully	jump	jute
jewelers	jitters	jokes	joyless	jumped	jutes
jeweling	jittery	joking	joyous	jumper	juts
jewelry	jiujitsu	jokingly	joyously	jumpers	jutted
jewels	jive	jollied	joys	jumpier	jutting
jib	jived	jollier	joystick	jumpiest	juvenile
jibbed	jives	jollies	jubbah	jumpily	kanji
jibber	jiving	jolliest	jubbahs	jumping	kanjis
jibbers	jo	jollify	jubilant	jumps	killjoy
jibbing	job	jollily	jubilate	jumpy	killjoys
jibe	jobbed	jollity	jubilee	junco	lockjaw
jibed	jobber	jolly	jubilees	juncos	logjam
jiber	jobbers	jollying	judge	junction	logjams
jibers	jobbery	jolt	judged	juncture	majority
jibes	jobbing	jolted	judger	jungle	marjoram
jibing	jobless	joltier	judgers	jungles	masjid
jibings	jobs	joltiest	judges	jungly	masjids
jibs	jock	jolting	judging	junior	misjudge
jiffies	jockey	jolts	judgment	juniors	muntjac
jiffy	jockeyed	jolty	judicial	juniper	muntjacs
jig	jockeys	jongleur	judo	junipers	nonjuror
jigged	jocko	jonquil	judoka	junk	object
jigger	jocks	jonquils	judokas	junked	objected
jiggers	jocose	jorum	jug	junker	objector
jigging	jocosely	jorums	jugal	junkers	objects
jiggle	jocosity	josh	jugate	junket	overjoy
jiggled	jocular	joshed	jugful	junketed	pajamas
jiggles	jocund	josher	jugfuls	junkets	perjure
jiggling	jocundly	joshers	jugged	junkie	perjured
jiggly	jodhpur	joshes	jugging	junkies	perjures
jigs	jodhpurs	joshing	juggle	junking	perjury
jigsaw	joe	joss	juggled	junkman	project
jigsawed	joes	josses	juggler	junkmen	projects
jigsaws	joey	jostle	jugglers	junks	propjet
jihad	joeys	jostled	juggles	junkyard	propjets
jihads	jog	jostler	juggling	junta	raj
jillion	jogged	jostlers	jugs	junto	raja
jillions	jogger	jostles	jugular	juntos	rajah
jilt	joggers	jostling	jugulars	jupon	rajahs
jilted	jogging	jot	jugum	jupons	rajas
jilting	joggle	jota	jugums	jura	ramjet
jilts	joggled	jotas	juice	jural	ramjets
jimmied	joggles	jots	juiced	jurally	readjust
jimmies	joggling	jotted	juices	jurat	reject
jimmy	jogs	jotting	juicier	jurats	rejected
jimmying	johannes	jottings	juiciest	jurel	rejects
jingle	john	joule	juicily	jurels	rejoice
jingled	johns	joules	juicing	juridic	rejoiced
jingles	join	jounce	juicy	juries	rejoices
jinglet	joinable	jounces	jujitsu	jurist	rejoin
jinglets	joinder	jouncing	juju	jurists	rejoined
jingling	joined	journal	jujube	juror	rejoins
jingly	joiner	journals	jujubes	jurors	sejant
jingo	joiners	journey	jujus	jury	shoji
jingoes	joinery	journeys	juke	jus	shojis
jingoism	joining	joust	jukebox	jussive	skipjack
jingoist	joins	jousted	juked	just	skyjack
jink	joint	jousting	jukes	justice	skyjacks
jinks	jointed	jousts	julep	justices	slapjack
jinn	jointly	jovial	juleps	justify	sojourn
jinni	joints	jovially	julienne	justle	sojourns
jinns	jointure	jowl	jumble	justled	subject
jinx	joist	jowls	jumbled	justles	subjects
jinxes	joists	jowly	jumbles	justling	subjoin
jitney	joke	joy	jumbling	justness	subjoins

thuja
thujas
turbojet
unjust
unjustly
verjuice

WORDS WITH THE LETTER Q

acequia
acequias
acquaint
acquired
acquit
acquits
adequacy
adequate
aliquant
aliquot
antique
antiqued
antiques
applique
aqua
aquae
aquanaut
aquaria
aquarium
aquatic
aquatint
aqueduct
aqueous
aquifer
aquifers
aquiline
arquebus
asquint
banquet
banquets
baroque
barque
barques
basque
basques
bequeath
bequest
bequests
bezique
beziques
bisque
bisques
bouquet
bouquets
briquet
briquets
brusque
cacique
caciques
caique
caiques
casque
casques
charqui
cheque
cheques
cirque

cirques
claque
claques
clique
cliques
cliquish
coequal
coequals
colloquy
conquer
conquers
conquest
coquet
coquetry
coquets
coquette
coquille
coquina
coquinas
coquito
coquitos
cotquean
critique
croquet
croquets
croquis
cumquat
cumquats
daiquiri
disquiet
eloquent
equable
equably
equal
equaled
equaling
equality
equalize
equally
equals
equate
equated
equates
equating
equation
equator
equerry
equine
equines
equinox
equip
equipage
equipped
equips
equitant
equites
equities
equity
esquire
esquires
frequent
inequity
iniquity
inquest
inquests
inquire
inquired

inquirer
inquires
inquiry
kumquat
kumquats
lacquer
lacquers
liquate
liquated
liquates
liquefy
liqueur
liqueurs
liquid
liquidly
liquids
liquor
liquors
marque
marquee
marquees
marques
marquess
marquis
marquise
masque
masquer
masquers
masques
mesquite
misquote
mosque
mosques
mosquito
mystique
oblique
obloquy
opaque
opaqued
opaquely
opaques
opaquing
pasquil
pasquils
perique
periques
physique
piquancy
piquant
pique
piqued
piques
piquet
piquets
piquing
piroque
piroques
plaque
plaques
pratique
pulque
pulques
qat
qats
qintar
qua
quack

quacked
quackery
quacking
quackish
quacks
quad
quadded
quadding
quadrant
quadrat
quadrate
quadric
quadriga
quadroon
quads
quaestor
quaff
quaffed
quaffing
quaffs
quag
quagga
quaggier
quaggy
quagmire
quagmiry
quags
quahog
quail
quailed
quailing
quails
quaint
quainter
quake
quaked
quakes
quakier
quakiest
quakily
quaking
quaky
qualify
quality
qualm
qualmish
qualms
quamash
quandary
quant
quanta
quantic
quantify
quantity
quantize
quants
quantum
quark
quarks
quarrel
quarried
quarrier
quarries
quarry
quart
quartan
quarter

quartern
quartet
quartic
quartile
quarto
quarts
quartz
quasar
quash
quashed
quashing
quasi
quass
quassia
quatrain
quaver
quavered
quaverer
quavery
quay
quayage
quays
quean
queans
queasier
queasily
queasy
queazy
queen
queendom
queened
queening
queenly
queens
queer
queerer
queerest
queerly
queers
quell
quelled
quelling
quells
quench
quenched
quencher
quenelle
queried
querist
quern
querns
query
querying
quested
quester
questing
question
questor
quetzal
queue
queued
queues
queuing
quibble
quibbled
quibbler
quiche

quick
quicken
quicker
quickest
quickie
quickly
quickset
quid
quiddity
quidnunc
quids
quiet
quieted
quieten
quieter
quieting
quietism
quietist
quietly
quietude
quietus
quill
quillai
quilled
quilling
quillon
quills
quilt
quilted
quilter
quilting
quilts
quinary
quinate
quince
quincunx
quinella
quinine
quinoid
quinsy
quint
quintain
quintal
quintan
quintet
quintile
quints
quip
quipped
quipping
quips
quipster
quipu
quipus
quire
quired
quires
quiring
quirk
quirks
quirky
quirt
quirts
quisling
quitch
quite
quitrent

quitted	squads	squirts	axilla	coaxal	exacters
quitter	squalid	squish	axillae	coaxed	exacting
quitting	squall	squishes	axillar	coaxer	exaction
quittor	squalled	squishy	axillary	coaxers	exactly
quiver	squalls	tequila	axils	coaxes	exacts
quivered	squally	tequilas	axing	coaxial	exalt
quivery	squalor	toque	axiom	coaxing	exalted
quiz	squalors	toques	axioms	coccyx	exalter
quizzed	squander	torque	axis	codex	exalters
quizzer	square	torques	axle	coexist	exalting
quizzes	squared	tranquil	axles	coexists	exalts
quizzing	squarely	tuque	axletree	commix	exam
quod	squarer	tuques	axolotl	commixes	examen
quods	squares	ubiquity	axolotls	complex	examens
quoin	squarest	unequal	axon	conflux	examine
quoins	squaring	unequals	axons	context	examined
quoit	squash	unquote	bandbox	convex	examinee
quoits	squashed	vanquish	bandeaux	convexes	examiner
quorum	squashes	vaquero	bateaux	convexly	examines
quota	squashy	vaqueros	bauxite	cortex	example
quotable	squat		bauxites	cowpox	examples
quotably	squats	**WORDS WITH**	beeswax	cox	exams
quotas	squatted	**THE LETTER**	betwixt	coxa	exarch
quote	squatter	**X**	biaxial	coxae	exarchs
quoted	squatty		bisexual	coxal	excavate
quoter	squaw	addax	bollix	coxalgia	exceed
quotes	squawk	adieux	bollixed	coxalgic	exceeded
quoth	squawked	admix	bollixes	coxcomb	exceeds
quotha	squawks	admixed	borax	coxcombs	excel
quoths	squaws	admixing	boraxes	coxes	excelled
quotient	squeak	affix	box	coxswain	excels
quoting	squeaked	affixed	boxberry	crucifix	except
racquet	squeaker	affixing	boxcar	crux	excepted
racquets	squeaks	afflux	boxcars	cruxes	excepts
request	squeaky	affluxes	boxed	culix	excerpt
requests	squeal	alexia	boxer	cylix	excerpts
requiem	squealed	annex	boxers	deflexed	excess
requiems	squealer	annexed	boxes	deluxe	excesses
require	squeals	annexing	boxier	desex	exchange
required	squeegee	anorexia	boxiest	desexes	excide
requires	squeeze	antefix	boxing	detoxify	excided
requital	squeezed	anxiety	boxwood	dexies	excides
roque	squeezes	anxious	boxwoods	dexter	exciding
roques	squelch	apex	boxy	dextral	excise
roquet	squib	apexes	braxies	dextrose	excised
roquets	squibbed	apoplexy	braxy	dextrous	excising
rorqual	squibs	appendix	broadax	dioxide	excision
rorquals	squid	apraxia	buxom	dioxides	excitant
seaquake	squids	apraxias	buxomly	diplex	excite
sequel	squiggle	apteryx	cachexy	doxies	excited
sequela	squill	asexual	calix	doxology	exciter
sequelae	squills	asphyxia	calx	doxy	exciters
sequels	squint	ataraxia	calxes	duplex	excites
sequence	squinted	ataraxy	calyx	duplexes	exciting
sequent	squints	auxesis	calyxes	dyslexia	exclaim
sequin	squinty	auxetic	carboxyl	earwax	exclaims
sequins	squire	auxin	cathexis	efflux	exclude
sequoia	squired	auxins	caudex	effluxes	excluded
sequoias	squireen	aviatrix	caudexes	elixir	excluder
silique	squires	ax	cervix	elixirs	excludes
siliques	squiring	axe	cervixes	epoxies	excreta
squab	squirm	axed	cicatrix	epoxy	excrete
squabble	squirmed	axel	cimex	ex	excreted
squabby	squirms	axes	climax	exact	excretes
squabs	squirrel	axial	climaxed	exacta	excuse
squad	squirt	axially	climaxes	exacted	excused
squadron	squirted	axil	coax	exacter	excuses
		axile			

excusing
execute
executed
executer
executes
executor
exedra
exegesis
exempla
exemplum
exempt
exempted
exempts
exercise
exergue
exergues
exert
exerted
exerting
exertion
exertive
exerts
exes
exeunt
exhale
exhaled
exhales
exhaling
exhaust
exhausts
exhibit
exhibits
exhort
exhorted
exhorts
exhume
exhumed
exhumes
exhuming
exigency
exigent
exiguous
exile
exiled
exiles
exilic
exiling
exist
existed
existent
existing
exists
exit
exited
exiting
exits
exocarp
exocarps
exodus
exogamy
exogen
exogens
exon
exons
exorable
exorcise
exorcism

exorcist
exordia
exordium
exoteric
exotic
exotics
expand
expanded
expands
expanse
expanses
expect
expected
expects
expedite
expel
expelled
expels
expend
expended
expends
expense
expenses
expert
expertly
experts
expiable
expiate
expiated
expiates
expire
expired
expires
expiries
expiring
expiry
explain
explains
explicit
explode
exploded
explodes
exploit
exploits
explore
explored
explorer
explores
exponent
export
exported
exporter
exports
expose
exposed
exposes
exposing
exposure
expound
expounds
express
expunge
expunged
expunges
exscind
exscinds
extant

extend
extended
extends
extensor
extent
extents
exterior
extern
external
externs
extinct
extol
extolled
extols
extort
extorted
extorts
extra
extract
extracts
extrados
extras
extreme
extremes
extrude
extruded
extrudes
exude
exuded
exudes
exuding
exult
exulted
exulting
exults
exurb
exurbia
exurbs
fabliaux
fax
faxes
fix
fixable
fixate
fixated
fixates
fixating
fixation
fixative
fixed
fixedly
fixer
fixers
fixes
fixing
fixings
fixities
fixity
fixt
fixture
fixtures
flax
flaxen
flaxes
flaxseed
flaxy
flex

flexed
flexes
flexible
flexile
flexing
flexion
flexions
flexor
flexors
flexure
flexures
flummox
flux
fluxed
fluxes
fluxing
fluxion
fluxions
fornix
fox
foxes
foxglove
foxhound
foxier
foxiest
foxiness
foxing
foxtail
foxtails
foxy
galax
galaxies
galaxy
gearbox
hallux
haruspex
hatbox
hatboxes
helix
helixes
hellbox
hex
hexad
hexads
hexagon
hexagons
hexagram
hexane
hexanes
hexapla
hexapod
hexapods
hexed
hexer
hexers
hexes
hexing
hexyl
hoax
hoaxed
hoaxer
hoaxers
hoaxes
hoaxing
hotbox
hotboxes
hydroxyl

hyrax
ibex
ibexes
icebox
iceboxes
ilex
ilexes
immix
immixed
immixes
immixing
index
indexed
indexer
indexers
indexes
indexing
inexact
inexpert
infix
infixed
infixes
infixing
influx
intermix
interrex
intersex
ixia
ixtle
kylix
larynx
larynxes
latexes
lax
laxative
laxity
laxly
laxness
lexical
lexicon
lexicons
lexis
lox
lummox
lummoxes
lux
luxate
luxated
luxates
luxating
luxation
luxe
luxes
luxuries
luxury
lynx
lynxes
mailbox
matchbox
matrix
matrixes
maxi
maxilla
maxillas
maxim
maximal
maximize

maxims
maximum
maximums
maxis
maxwell
maxwells
minx
minxes
mix
mixable
mixed
mixer
mixers
mixes
mixing
mixt
mixture
mixtures
monoxide
moxa
moxas
moxie
murex
murexes
narthex
next
nexus
nexuses
nix
nixed
nixes
nixie
nixing
nontoxic
noxious
onyx
onyxes
orthodox
oryx
oryxes
outfox
outfoxes
overtax
ox
oxblood
oxbloods
oxbow
oxbows
oxen
oxeye
oxeyes
oxford
oxfords
oxheart
oxhearts
oxidant
oxide
oxides
oxidize
oxidized
oxidizer
oxidizes
oxlip
oxlips
oxtail
oxtails

oxygen	relaxed	suffixes	vexed	alcazar	benzoyls
oxygens	relaxes	surtax	vexes	alcazars	benzyl
paradox	relaxing	surtaxed	vexillum	alkalize	benzyls
parallax	remix	surtaxes	vexing	amaze	bezant
paroxysm	remixed	sweatbox	vexingly	amazed	bezants
pax	remixes	syntax	vixen	amazedly	bezel
paxes	remixing	syntaxes	vixenish	amazes	bezels
peroxide	rex	syrinx	vixens	amazing	bezoar
perplex	rondeaux	syrinxes	volvox	amazon	bezoars
phalanx	roux	tableaux	volvoxes	amazons	bizarre
pharynx	salpinx	tax	vortex	amortize	blaze
phenix	sandbox	taxable	vortexes	analyze	blazed
phenixes	sardonyx	taxation	vox	analyzed	blazer
phlox	sax	taxed	wax	analyzes	blazers
phoenix	saxatile	taxer	waxed	aphorize	blazes
pickax	saxes	taxers	waxen	archaize	blazing
pickaxed	saxhorn	taxes	waxer	assize	blazon
pickaxes	saxhorns	taxi	waxers	assizes	blazoned
pillbox	saxtuba	taxicab	waxes	atomize	blazonry
pix	saxtubas	taxicabs	waxier	atomized	blazons
pixes	scolex	taxied	waxiest	atomizer	blintze
pixie	sex	taxiing	waxiness	atomizes	blintzes
pixy	sexed	taxing	waxing	azalea	blizzard
plateaux	sexes	taxis	waxweed	azaleas	blowzy
plexor	sexier	taxonomy	waxweeds	azan	bonanza
plexors	sexiest	taxpayer	waxwork	azans	bonanzas
plexus	sexing	taxying	waxworks	azide	bonze
plexuses	sexism	text	waxy	azides	booze
poleax	sexist	textbook	xebec	azimuth	boozed
poleaxes	sexists	textile	xebecs	azimuths	boozes
pollex	sexless	textiles	xenia	azine	boozing
pontifex	sext	texts	xenias	azines	borzoi
postbox	sextant	textual	xenolith	azoic	borzois
postfix	sextants	texture	xenon	azote	bouzouki
pox	sextet	textured	xenons	azotes	bozo
poxes	sextets	textures	xeric	azoth	bozos
praxis	sextile	thorax	xerox	azoths	braze
praxises	sextiles	thoraxes	xeroxed	azotize	brazed
preaxial	sexton	toolbox	xeroxes	azotized	brazen
preexist	sextons	toxemia	xeroxing	azotizes	brazenly
prefix	sexts	toxemias	xi	azure	brazens
prefixed	sextuple	toxic	xiphoid	azures	brazes
prefixes	sexual	toxicant	xylan	azurite	brazier
pretext	sexy	toxicity	xylans	azurites	braziers
pretexts	six	toxin	xylem	azygous	brazil
prexies	sixes	toxins	xylems	baize	brazils
prexy	sixfold	toxoid	xylene	baizes	brazing
prolix	sixpence	toxoids	xylenes	banzai	breeze
proxies	sixteen	transfix	xylidine	baptize	breezed
proximo	sixth	tux	xyloid	baptized	breezes
proxy	sixths	tuxedo	xylol	baptizer	breezier
pyrexia	sixties	tuxedos	xyster	baptizes	breezily
pyx	sixty	tuxes	xysters	bartizan	breezing
pyxes	smallpox	unfix	zax	bazaar	breezy
pyxides	smilax	unfixed	zaxes	bazaars	bronze
pyxie	smilaxes	unfixes		bazooka	bronzed
pyxies	snuffbox	unfixing	**WORDS WITH**	bazookas	bronzes
pyxis	soapbox	unisex	**THE LETTER**	bedizen	bronzing
radix	sox	unmixed	**Z**	bedizens	bulldoze
radixes	spadix	unvexed		benzene	buzz
reannex	spadixes	uxorial	ablaze	benzenes	buzzard
reflex	sphinx	uxorious	abuzz	benzine	buzzards
reflexed	sphinxes	varix	adz	benzines	buzzer
reflexes	storax	vertex	adzes	benzoic	buzzers
reflux	storaxes	vertexes	agaze	benzol	buzzes
refluxes	suffix	vex	agonize	benzols	cadenza
relax	suffixed	vexation	agonized	benzoyl	
			agonizes		

cadenzas
canalize
canonize
canzone
caponize
capsize
capsized
capsizes
chalaza
chalazas
chintz
chintzes
chutzpa
citizen
citizens
civilize
cloze
cognize
cognized
cognizes
colonize
colza
colzas
coryza
coryzas
coz
cozen
cozenage
cozened
cozening
cozens
cozier
coziest
cozily
cozy
craze
crazed
crazes
crazies
craziest
crazily
crazing
crazy
credenza
croze
crozed
crozes
crozier
cruzado
cruzados
cruzeiro
czar
czardas
czarevna
czarina
czarinas
czarism
czarist
czarists
czaritza
czars
daze
dazed
dazes
dazing
dazzle
dazzled

dazzles
dazzling
demonize
denizen
denizens
deputize
dialyze
dialyzed
dialyzes
dizen
dizened
dizening
dizens
dizzied
dizzier
dizzies
dizziest
dizzily
dizzy
dizzying
doze
dozed
dozen
dozens
dozes
dozier
doziest
dozing
dozy
drizzle
drizzled
drizzles
drizzly
ebonize
ebonizes
eczema
elegize
elegized
elegizes
embezzle
emblaze
emblazed
emblazes
emblazon
energize
entozoon
enzyme
enzymes
epizoic
ersatz
eulogize
evzone
evzones
faradize
faze
fazed
fazes
fazing
feaze
feazes
feeze
feezes
feminize
fez
fezzes
finalize
fizz

fizzed
fizzes
fizzier
fizziest
fizzing
fizzle
fizzled
fizzles
fizzling
fizzy
floozies
floozy
foozle
foozled
foozles
foozling
frazzle
frazzled
frazzles
freeze
freezer
freezers
freezes
freezing
frenzied
frenzies
frenzy
frieze
friezes
friz
frizette
frizzed
frizzing
frizzle
frizzled
frizzles
frizzy
frowzy
froze
frozen
furze
furzes
furzy
fuze
fuzed
fuzee
fuzees
fuzes
fuzing
fuzz
fuzzes
fuzzier
fuzziest
fuzzily
fuzzy
gauze
gauzes
gauzy
gaze
gazebo
gazebos
gazed
gazelle
gazelles
gazer
gazers
gazes

gazette
gazetted
gazettes
gazing
gizmo
gizmos
gizzard
gizzards
glaze
glazed
glazes
glazier
glaziers
glazing
glazings
gloze
glozed
glozes
glozing
graze
grazed
grazer
grazers
grazes
grazier
grazing
grizzle
grizzled
grizzles
grizzly
grosz
guzzle
guzzled
guzzler
guzzlers
guzzles
hafiz
hazan
hazans
hazard
hazarded
hazards
haze
hazed
hazel
hazelly
hazelnut
hazels
hazes
hazier
haziest
haziness
hazing
hazings
hazy
hertz
hoatzin
hoatzins
holozoic
horizon
horizons
howitzer
humanize
huzzah
huzzahs
idealize
idolize

idolized
idolizes
immunize
iodize
iodized
iodizes
iodizing
ionize
ionized
ionizes
ionizing
itemize
itemized
itemizes
izzard
izzards
kazoo
kazoos
kibbutz
kibitz
kibitzed
kibitzer
kibitzes
klutz
klutzes
kolkhoz
kreutzer
lazar
lazars
laze
lazed
lazier
laziest
lazily
laziness
lazing
lazy
legalize
lionize
lionized
lionizes
lizard
lizards
localize
lozenge
lozenges
magazine
mahzor
mahzors
maize
maizes
marzipan
matzo
matzos
mazard
mazards
maze
mazed
mazer
mazers
mazes
mazier
mazing
mazourka
mazuma
mazumas
mazurka

mazurkas
mazy
mazzard
mazzards
melodize
memorize
mestizo
mestizos
metalize
mezuzah
mezuzahs
mezzo
mezzos
minimize
mirza
mirzas
mizzen
mizzens
mizzle
mizzled
mizzles
mizzling
mobilize
moralize
motorize
muezzin
muezzins
muzzle
muzzled
muzzles
muzzling
nasalize
nebulize
notarize
novelize
nuzzle
nuzzled
nuzzles
nuzzling
obelize
obelized
obelizes
ooze
oozed
oozes
oozier
ooziest
oozily
oozing
oozy
optimize
organize
organza
organzas
outsize
outsizes
ouzel
ouzels
oyez
panzer
panzers
paralyze
penalize
piazza
piazzas
pizzle

pizzles	sizars	vizard	zigging	buzzard	jazzier
plaza	size	vizards	zigs	buzzards	jazziest
plazas	sizeable	vizier	zigzag	buzzer	jazzily
poetize	sized	vizor	zigzags	buzzers	jazzing
poetized	sizes	vizors	zinc	buzzes	jazzman
poetizes	sizing	vocalize	zincs	czaritza	jazzmen
polarize	sizings	waltz	zinky	dazzle	jazzy
pretzel	sizzle	waltzed	zip	dazzled	mazzard
pretzels	sizzled	waltzer	zips	dazzles	mazzards
prize	sizzles	waltzers	zircon	dazzling	mezuzah
prized	sizzling	waltzes	zircons	dizzied	mezuzahs
prizes	sleazier	waltzing	zither	dizzier	mezzo
prizing	sleazy	wheeze	zithers	dizzies	mezzos
puzzle	smaze	wheezed	zoa	dizziest	mizzen
puzzled	snazzy	wheezes	zodiac	dizzily	mizzens
puzzler	sneeze	wheezier	zodiacal	dizzy	mizzle
puzzlers	sneezed	wheezing	zodiacs	dizzying	mizzled
puzzles	sneezes	wheezy	zonally	drizzle	mizzles
puzzling	sneezing	whiz	zonary	drizzled	mizzling
raze	snooze	whizz	zone	drizzles	muezzin
razed	snoozed	whizzed	zoned	drizzly	muezzins
razee	snoozes	whizzes	zones	embezzle	muzzle
razees	snoozing	whizzing	zoning	fezzes	muzzled
razes	solarize	wizard	zooid	fizz	muzzles
razing	sozzled	wizardry	zooids	fizzed	muzzling
razor	spitz	wizards	zoology	fizzes	nuzzle
razors	spitzes	wizen	zoophily	fizzier	nuzzled
razz	stanza	wizened	zounds	fizziest	nuzzles
razzed	stanzas	wizening	zygoma	fizzing	nuzzling
razzes	stylize	wizens	zygomas	fizzle	piazza
razzing	stylized	woozier	zygomata	fizzled	piazzas
realize	stylizes	wooziest	zygote	fizzles	pizzle
realized	suzerain	woozy	zygotes	fizzling	pizzles
realizes	swizzle	zanies	zymosis	fizzy	puzzle
rebozo	swizzles	zany	zymotic	frazzle	puzzled
rebozos	tazza	zareba		frazzled	puzzler
rhizoid	tazzas	zarebas	**WORDS WITH**	frazzles	puzzlers
rhizoids	teazel	zarf	**TWO Js**	frizzed	puzzles
rhizome	teazels	zarfs		frizzing	puzzling
rhizomes	teazle	zeal	hajj	frizzle	quizzed
ritzier	terrazzo	zealot	hajji	frizzled	quizzer
ritziest	theorize	zealots	hajjis	frizzles	quizzes
ritzy	tizzies	zealous	jejune	frizzy	quizzing
ruralize	tizzy	zeals	jejunum	fuzz	razz
satirize	topaz	zebec	jiujitsu	fuzzes	razzed
scherzi	topazes	zebecs	jujitsu	fuzzier	razzes
scherzo	trapeze	zebra	juju	fuzziest	razzing
scherzos	trapezes	zebras	jujube	fuzzily	sizzle
schizy	tweeze	zebrine	jujubes	fuzzy	sizzled
schmaltz	tweezed	zebu	jujus	gizzard	sizzles
seize	tweezers	zebus		gizzards	sizzling
seized	tweezes	zed	**WORDS WITH**	grizzle	snazzy
seizer	tweezing	zeds	**TWO Xs**	grizzled	sozzled
seizers	unionize	zemindar		grizzles	swizzle
seizes	unitize	zenith	xerox	grizzly	swizzles
seizin	unitized	zeniths	xeroxed	guzzle	tazza
seizing	unitizes	zero	xeroxes	guzzled	tazzas
seizor	unzip	zeros	xeroxing	guzzler	terrazzo
seizors	unzipped	zest		guzzlers	tizzies
seizure	unzips	zests	**WORDS WITH**	guzzles	tizzy
seizures	urbanize	zeta	**TWO Zs**	huzzah	whizz
seltzer	utilize	zetas		huzzahs	whizzed
seltzers	utilized	zeugma	abuzz	izzard	whizzes
sitzmark	utilizer	zeugmas	azotize	izzards	whizzing
sizable	utilizes	zibeline	azotized	jazz	zigzag
sizably	vaporize	zig	azotizes	jazzed	zigzags
sizar	vitalize	zigged	blizzard		
			buzz		

WORDS WITH TWO DIFFERENT HIGH-SCORING LETTERS				
bezique	equinox	jazzmen	jukebox	quartz	quizzes
beziques	jazz	jazzy	maximize	queazy	quizzing
equalize	jazzed	jeez	oxidize	quetzal	squeeze
	jazzier	jinx	oxidized	quincunx	squeezed
	jazziest	jinxes	oxidizer	quiz	squeezes
	jazzily	jonquil	oxidizes	quizzed	zax
	jazzing	jonquils	quantize	quizzer	zaxes
	jazzman				

BEGINNINGS AND ENDINGS

Here are over 75 lists of words formed by adding a commonly used beginning or ending. Each list includes words up to 8 letters long that contain one of the common prefixes, suffixes, or combining forms covered.

Note that not every possible word formed with the set of first or last letters is included. Only words that, when the beginning or ending letters are removed, stand alone as valid words have been listed. So, in the list for *up-*, the word upshot does appear (up + shot) because shot stands alone as a valid word. Upsilon, on the other hand, does not because the remaining letters *silon* do not form a word. This way, you can look up the list for letters you have available to make a beginning or ending. Then you can either form one of the suggested words by using all of your own letters, or by adding letters to a word already on the game board.

AB-

abash
abashes
abate
abba
abbey
abbeys
abbot
abbots
abduct
abducted
abducts
abed
aberrant
ablaze
ablest
abloom
abnegate
abnormal
abode
abodes
aboil
about
abridge
abridged
abridges
abroach
abroad
absent
absolve
absolved
absolver
absolves
absorb
absorbs
abstain
abstains
abuse
abused
abuser
abusers
abuses
abusing
abutter
abutters
abye

AD-

adage
adages
adapt
adding
address
adduct
adducts
adhere
adit
adits
adjoin
adjoined
adjoins
adjudge
adjudged
adjudges
adjust
adman
admen
admire
admired
admires
admiring
admit
admits
admix
admixed
admixing
adoption
adore
adores
adrenal
adrift
adscript
advent
advents
adverb
adverbs
adverse
advice
advices
adviser
advisers

ANTE-

antedate
antefix

antelope
anteroom
antetype

ANTI-

antibody
antidote
antihero
antimask
antinode
antipode
antipope
antitype
antiwar

AUTO-

autogyro
autoharp
automat
automate
automats
autosome

BE-

bead
beads
beam
bean
bearable
beat
beaver
beavers
bebop
bebops
becalm
becalmed
becalms
became
because
becloud
beclouds
become
becomes
becoming
bedeck
bedecked
bedecks
bedevil

bedevils
bedim
bedimmed
bedims
bedizen
bedizens
befall
befallen
befalls
befell
befit
befits
befog
befogged
befogs
before
befoul
befouled
befouls
befriend
befuddle
beget
begets
begin
begins
begone
begot
begotten
begrudge
begum
begums
begun
behalf
behave
behaves
behaving
behead
beheaded
beheads
beheld
behind
behold
beholder
beholds
behoove
behooved
behooves
bejewel

bejewels
belabor
belabors
belay
belayed
belaying
belays
belie
belied
belies
belittle
belong
belonged
belongs
beloved
beloveds
below
bema
bemas
bemire
bemired
bemires
bemiring
bemoan
bemoaned
bemoans
bemuse
bemuses
beneath
benumb
benumbed
benumbs
bequest
bequests
berate
berated
berates
berating
beseem
beseemed
beseems
beset
besets
beshrew
beshrews
beside
besides
besiege
besieged

besieges
besmear
besmears
besoil
besoiled
besoils
besought
bespeak
bespeaks
bespoke
bestir
bestirs
bestow
bestowed
bestows
betake
betaken
betakes
betaking
betide
betided
betides
betiding
betimes
betoken
betook
betray
betrays
bewail
bewailed
bewails
beware
bewares
bewilder
bewitch

BI-

biannual
bias
biaxial
bicolor
bicuspid
bicycle
bicycled
bicycles
bifocal
bifold
biform
bigot

bijugate
biking
bipedal
biplane
biplanes
bipolar
bisect
bisector
bisects
bisexual
bishop
bishops
bivalent
bivalve
bivalved
bivalves
biweekly

CO-

coact
coacted
coacting
coaction
coactive
coacts
coarse
coat
coauthor
coax
coaxed
coaxer
coaxes
coaxial
coaxing
cobra
cobras
cocoon
cocoons
coed
coeds
coequal
coequals
coexist
coexists
coheir
coheirs
cohere
coif
coifs
coin
coins
coinsure
coma
comaker
comakers
comate
comates
comet
coon
coops
copal
copalm
copalms
copeck
copecks
coped
copier

copiers
copies
copilot
copilots
coping
copious
cored
coring
cosecant
coshed
cosine
cosines
costate
costing
cotenant
cotidal
coupon
covet
covets
coward
cowards

COM-

comate
combat
combats
combe
combed
combust
combusts
comfit
comfits
comfort
comforts
commit
commits
commix
commixes
commode
commodes
commute
commuted
commuter
commutes
compact
compacts
compare
compared
compares
compass
compeer
compeers
compile
compiled
compiler
compiles
comping
complain
complied
complies
complot
complots
comply
comport
comports
compose
composed

composer
composes
compost
composts
compound
compress

CON-

concave
concaved
concaves
concede
conceded
concedes
concent
concents
concord
concords
concur
concurs
condense
condo
condole
condoled
condoles
condone
conduct
conducts
confab
confess
confine
confined
confines
confirm
confirms
conflux
confocal
conform
conforms
confound
confront
confuse
confused
confuses
congee
congees
conjoin
conjoins
conjoint
conjuror
connote
connoted
connotes
consent
conserve
consign
consigns
console
consoled
consoles
consort
consorts
conspire
constat
contact
contacts
contend

contends
content
contents
contest
contests
context
conto
contort
contorts
contour
contours
contract
contrail
contrite
convent
convents
converge
converse
convex
convexes

DE-

dead
dean
debark
debarked
debarks
debarred
debars
debase
debased
debases
debasing
debit
debiting
debits
debone
deboned
debones
deboning
debrief
debriefs
debug
debugged
debugs
debunk
debunks
debut
debuts
decamp
decamped
decamps
decant
decanter
decent
decipher
declaim
declaims
decode
decoded
decodes
decoding
decoy
decrease
decreed
decried
decries

decry
decrying
decurved
deduct
deducted
deducts
deed
deeds
deem
deems
deface
defaced
defaces
defacing
defame
defamed
defames
defaming
default
defaults
defeat
defeats
defend
defended
defender
defends
defile
defiled
defiles
defiling
define
defined
defines
defining
definite
deflexed
deflower
defog
defogged
defogger
defogs
deforce
deforced
deforces
deform
deformed
deforms
defraud
defrauds
defray
defrays
defrock
defrocks
defrost
defrosts
defuse
defused
defuses
defusing
degas
degassed
degrade
degraded
degrades
degrease
delate
delay

delayed
delaying
delays
deled
delight
delights
delimit
delimits
deliver
delivers
delouse
deloused
delouses
deme
demean
demeans
demerit
demerits
demes
demit
demits
demitted
demo
demob
demobbed
demobs
demonism
demos
demote
demy
denary
denature
denote
denoted
denotes
denoting
denude
denudes
depart
departed
departs
depend
depended
depends
deplane
deplanes
deploy
deploys
deport
deported
deports
depose
deposed
deposes
deposing
depot
depots
depress
derail
derailed
derails
deride
derides
deriding
describe
deserve
deserved

deserves
desex
desexes
design
designed
designs
desire
desired
desires
desiring
despite
despoil
despoils
despot
despots
detail
detailed
details
detest
detested
detests
dethrone
detour
detoured
detours
detoxify
detract
detracts
devalue
devalued
devalues
devein
deveins
devest
devested
devests
device
devices
devise
devises
devisor
devisors
devoid
devote
devoted
devotes
devoting
dewan
dewed

DEMI-

demigod
demigods
demijohn
demirep
demireps
demiurge

DI-

dicot
dicots
dido
didoes
diking
dilate
dime

dimeter
dimeters
disable
discant
disinter
divan
divans
diverge
diverges
divest
divested
divests
divine
divined
divines

DIA-

diabase
diabases
diagram
diagrams
dialogic
diameter
diaphone
diastole
diatom
diatoms
diatribe

DIS-

disable
disabuse
disagree
disallow
disarm
disarmed
disarms
disarray
disavow
disavows
disband
disbands
disbar
disbars
disburse
discant
discants
discard
discards
disclaim
disclose
discolor
discord
discords
discount
discover
discuss
disfavor
disgrace
dishonor
disjoin
disjoins
disjoint
dislike
disliked
dislikes

dislodge
disloyal
dismay
dismiss
dismount
disobey
disobeys
disorder
disown
disowned
disowns
dispatch
displace
display
displays
dispose
disposed
disposes
disproof
disprove
disquiet
disrobe
disrobed
disrobes
dissect
dissects
dissent
dissents
dissolve
distally
distaste
distend
distends
distill
distills
distort
distorts
distract
distress
distrust
disunite
disunity
disuse
disused
disuses
disusing

EM-

embalm
embalms
embank
embanked
embanks
embark
embarked
embarks
embattle
embay
embayed
embaying
embays
embed
embedded
embeds
embitter
emblaze
emblazed

emblazes
embodied
embodies
embody
embosom
embosoms
emboss
embossed
embosses
embow
embowed
embowing
embows
embrace
embraced
embracer
embraces
embroil
embroils
emcee
emcees
emend
emended
emending
emends
emit
emits
emmet
emmets
empale
empaled
empales
empaling
emphases
emplace
emplaced
emplaces
employ
employed
employer
employs
empower
empowers
empress
emus

EN-

enable
enabler
enact
enacted
enacting
enactive
enactor
enactors
enacts
encage
encaged
encages
encaging
encamp
encamps
encase
encased
encases
encasing
enchain

enchains
enchant
enchants
enchase
enchased
enchases
encipher
encircle
enclasp
enclasps
enclose
enclosed
encloses
encode
encoded
encoder
encoders
encodes
encoding
encore
encored
encores
encoring
encrust
encrusts
encyst
encysted
encysts
endanger
endear
endeared
endears
ending
endings
endive
endives
endue
endued
endues
enface
enfaced
enfaces
enfacing
enfeeble
enfold
enfolds
enforce
enforced
enforcer
enforces
engage
engaged
engages
engaging
engender
engird
engirded
engirdle
engirds
engorge
engorged
engorges
engrave
engraver
engraves
engross
engulf

engulfed
engulfs
enjoin
enjoins
enjoy
enjoyed
enjoying
enjoys
enlarge
enlarger
enlarges
enlist
enlisted
enlists
enliven
enlivens
enmesh
enmeshes
ennoble
ennobles
enrage
enraged
enrages
enraging
enrapt
enrich
enriches
enroll
enrolled
enrolls
enshrine
enshroud
ensign
ensigns
enslave
enslaved
enslaves
ensue
ensued
ensues
ensuing
ensure
ensured
ensures
ensuring
entail
entailed
entails
entangle
enthrall
enthrone
entire
entitle
entitled
entitles
entoil
entoils
entomb
entombed
entombs
entrails
entrance
entrap
entraps
entreat
entreats
entreaty

entree
entrees
entries
entrust
entrusts
entry
entwine
entwined
entwines
envenom
envenoms
envied
envies
envision

EX-

exact
exacted
exacting
exaction
exacts
exam
examen
examens
example
examples
exarch
exarchs
exchange
excite
excited
excites
exciting
exclaim
exclaims
exhale
exhaled
exhales
exhaling
exit
exits
exon
expend
expended
expends
expert
expertly
explain
explains
export
exported
exporter
exports
expose
exposed
exposes
exposing
expound
expounds
express
extend
extended
extends
extent
extents
extern
externs

extolled
extort
extorts
extract
extracts

FORE-

forearm
forearms
forebear
forebode
forecast
forefoot
forego
foregone
foregoes
forehand
forehead
foreland
foreleg
forelegs
forelock
foreman
foremast
foremen
foremost
forename
forenoon
forepaw
forepaws
forepeak
foreplay
foresaid
foresail
foresaw
foresee
foreseer
foresees
foreskin
forestay
foretell
foretold
foretop
foretops
forewarn
forewent
foreword

IM-

image
imaged
images
imaging
imago
imam
imbed
imbedded
imbeds
immature
immix
immixed
immixes
immixing
immobile
immodest
immoral

immortal
impact
impacted
impacts
impair
impaired
impairs
impale
impaled
impales
impaling
impanel
impanels
impart
imparted
imparter
imparts
impeach
impend
impended
impends
imperil
imperils
impiety
impious
implant
implants
implead
implied
implies
imply
implying
impolicy
impolite
import
imported
importer
imports
impose
imposer
imposers
imposes
imposing
impost
imposter
imposts
impotent
impound
impounds
impress
imprint
imprints
imprison
improper
improve
improves
impulse
impulses
impure
impurity

IN-

inaction
inactive
inapt
inaptly
inarch

inarches
inbeing
inboard
inborn
inbound
inbounds
inbred
inbreed
inbreeds
incase
incased
incases
incasing
incite
incited
inciter
inciters
incites
inciting
inclose
incloses
income
incomes
incoming
increase
incrust
incrusts
incult
indebted
indecent
indeed
indent
indented
indents
indirect
indocile
indoor
indoors
indraft
indrawn
induct
inducted
inducts
indue
indues
indwell
indwells
indwelt
inedible
inexact
inexpert
infamous
infancy
infield
infinite
infirm
infix
infixed
infixes
infixing
inflame
inflamed
inflamer
inflames
inflow
inflows
influx

infold
infolds
inform
informed
informer
informs
infringe
infuse
infused
infuser
infusers
infuses
infusing
infusion
ingoing
ingot
ingrain
ingrains
ingrate
ingrates
ingroup
ingroups
ingrown
ingulf
ingulfed
ingulfs
inhabit
inhabits
inhale
inhaled
inhaler
inhales
inhaling
inhaul
inhauls
inhere
inhuman
inhumane
inion
inions
inlaid
inland
inlander
inlay
inlaying
inlays
inlet
inlets
inmate
inmates
inmesh
inmeshed
inmost
input
inputs
inquest
inquests
inroad
inroads
inrush
inrushes
insane
insanely
insanity
inscribe
insect
insects

insecure
inset
insets
inshore
inside
insider
insiders
insight
insights
insole
inspire
inspired
inspires
install
installs
instance
instar
instead
instep
insteps
instill
instills
insure
insurer
intact
intake
intakes
intend
intended
intends
intense
intent
into
intone
intoned
intoner
intoners
intones
intoning
intrench
invalid
invent
invented
invents
inverse
invest
invested
invests
invoice
invoices
inward
inwards
inweave
inweaves
inwinds
inwound
inwove
inwoven

INTER-

interact
intermix
internee
interred
interrex
intersex

MAL-

maledict
malice
malices
malkin
mallard
mallards
mallee
mallet
mallets
mallow
mallows
malodor
malodors
maltreat

MIS-

miscarry
miscast
mischief
miscount
miscue
miscued
miscues
miscuing
misdeal
misdeals
misdealt
misdeed
misdeeds
misdid
misdo
misdoer
misdoers
misdoing
misdone
misfile
misfiled
misfiles
misfire
misfired
misfires
misfit
misfits
misjudge
mislaid
mislay
mislays
mislead
misleads
misled
mismatch
misplace
misplay
misplays
misprint
misquote
misread
misreads
misrule
misruled
misrules
misshape
missing
misspell
misstate

misstep
missteps
missus
mistake
mistaken
mistakes
mistier
mistook
mistress
mistrial
mistrust
misuse
misused
misuses
misusing

NON-

nonage
noncom
noncoms
nonego
nonegos
nonjuror
nonplus
nonsense
nonskid
nonstop
nonsuit
nonsuits
nontoxic
nonunion
nonuser
nonusers
nonvoter
nonwhite

OVER-

overage
overages
overall
overalls
overate
overbear
overbid
overbids
overbite
overbuy
overbuys
overcame
overcast
overcoat
overcome
overdo
overdone
overdose
overdraw
overdrew
overdue
overeat
overeats
overflow
overgrew
overgrow
overhand
overhang
overhaul

overhead
overhear
overheat
overhung
overjoy
overlaid
overlap
overlaps
overlay
overlays
overleaf
overlie
overload
overlook
overlord
overpass
overplay
overrate
override
overrode
overrun
overruns
oversaw
overseas
oversee
overseen
overseer
oversees
overshoe
overshot
oversoul
overstay
overstep
overtake
overtax
overtime
overtone
overtook
overturn
overview
overwork

POST-

postage
postbox
postdate
postfix
postman
postmark
postmen
postpone

PRE-

preached
preaches
preamble
preaxial
prebend
prebends
precede
preceded
precedes
predate
predated
predates
predial

preen
preens
preexist
preface
prefaced
prefaces
prefix
prefixed
prefixes
preform
preforms
prelate
prelates
premolar
prenatal
prepaid
prepare
prepared
prepares
prepay
prepays
presage
presaged
presages
present
presents
preserve
preset
presets
preside
presided
presides
pretend
pretends
pretense
pretest
pretests
pretext
pretexts
prevail
prevails
prevent
prevents
preview
previews
previse
prevised
previses
prewar

PRO-

proas
probe
probed
proclaim
procure
procured
procurer
procures
product
products
profile
profiled
profiles
profit
profits
profound

profuse
program
programs
prolate
proleg
prolegs
prolong
prolongs
pronoun
pronouns
proof
propane
propanes
propend
propends
propose
proposed
proposes
propound
prostate
prostyle
protest
protests
proton
protons
protract
protrude

RE-

reabsorb
react
reacted
reacting
reaction
reactive
reactor
reactors
reacts
readjust
readmit
readmits
reaffirm
reagent
reagents
realign
realigns
reannex
reappear
reapply
reassert
reassess
reassure
rebirth
rebirths
reborn
rebound
rebounds
rebuff
rebuffed
rebuffs
rebuild
rebuilds
rebuilt
rebus
rebuses
rebut
rebuts

rebutted
recall
recalled
recalls
recant
recanted
recants
recap
recapped
recaps
recast
recasts
recede
receded
recedes
receding
recent
recite
recited
recites
reciting
reclaim
reclaims
recoil
recoiled
recoils
record
recorded
records
recount
recounts
recoup
recouped
recoups
recourse
recover
recovers
recreate
recycle
recycled
recycles
redeem
redeemed
redeems
redesign
redid
redirect
redo
redoes
redoing
redone
redouble
redoubt
redoubts
redress
reelect
reelects
reembark
reenact
reenacts
reenlist
reenter
reenters
reentry
refill
refilled
refills

refine	relocate	reply	restate	revamp	subtitle
refined	remade	replying	restated	revamped	subtopic
refinery	remake	report	restates	revamps	subtotal
refines	remakes	reported	restock	reverse	subtract
refining	remaking	reporter	restocks	reversed	suburban
refinish	remark	reports	restore	revery	suburb
reflex	remarked	repress	restored	review	suburbs
reflexed	remarks	reprint	restores	reviewed	subway
reflexes	remarry	reprints	restrain	reviews	subways
reflux	rematch	repro	restrict	revile	
refluxes	remember	reproof	retail	revises	**SUR-**
reforest	remind	reproofs	retailed	revision	
reform	reminded	repros	retailer	revisit	surah
reformed	reminder	reprove	retails	revisits	surahs
reformer	reminds	reproved	retake	revolt	suras
reforms	remiss	reproves	retaken	revolted	surcoat
refresh	remit	repulse	retakes	revolts	surcoats
refried	remits	repulsed	retaking	reward	surface
refuel	remix	repulses	retell	rewards	surfaced
refueled	remixed	request	retells	rewrote	surfaces
refuels	remixes	requests	retie		surmount
refund	remixing	reran	retied	**SEMI-**	surname
refunded	remodel	reread	reties		surnames
refunds	remodels	rereads	retire	semiarid	surpass
refuse	remount	reroute	retired	semidome	surplus
refused	remounts	rerouted	retires	seminary	surprint
refuses	remove	reroutes	retiring	semipro	surround
refusing	removed	rerun	retold	semipros	surtax
regain	removes	reruns	retook	semitone	surtaxed
regained	removing	resale	retort		surtaxes
regains	rename	resales	retorted	**SUB-**	surtout
rehash	renamed	rescue	retorts		surtouts
rehashed	renames	rescued	retouch	subbed	
rehashes	renaming	rescues	retrace	subdeb	**TRANS-**
rehearse	renew	rescuing	retraced	subdebs	
reheat	renews	research	retraces	subduct	transact
reheated	reopen	resent	retract	subducts	transfix
reheats	reopens	resented	retracts	subdue	transit
reinvest	reorder	resents	retread	subdues	transits
reissue	reorders	reserve	retreads	subgenus	transmit
reissued	repaid	reserved	retreat	subhead	
reissues	repair	reserves	retreats	subheads	**TRI-**
rejoin	repaired	reset	retrench	subhuman	
rejoined	repairs	resets	retrial	subjoin	triad
rejoins	repast	reside	retrials	subjoins	triads
rekindle	repasts	resided	retried	sublate	triage
relaid	repave	resides	retries	sublease	triages
relapse	repaved	residing	retry	sublet	triangle
relapsed	repaves	resign	retrying	sublets	tricolor
relapses	repaving	resigned	return	sublime	tricorn
relate	repay	resigns	returned	sublimed	tricorns
relax	repaying	resole	returns	sublimes	tricot
relaxes	repays	resoled	retying	submerge	tricots
relay	repeal	resoles	retype	submerse	tricycle
relays	repeals	resoling	retyped	submit	trident
release	repeat	resolve	retypes	submits	tridents
released	repeats	resolved	retyping	subplot	tried
releases	repent	resolves	reunify	subplots	trifid
relent	repented	resort	reunion	subserve	trifled
relents	repents	resorted	reunite	subset	trifling
relive	replace	resorts	reunited	subsets	triode
relived	replaced	resound	reunites	subside	triodes
relives	replaces	resounds	reusable	subsided	triply
reliving	replay	resource	reuse	subsides	tritest
reload	replays	respite	reused	subsoil	trivet
reloaded	replied	respited	reuses	subsoils	trivets
reloads	replies	respites	reusing	subsonic	trivia
				subtile	trivial

UN-

unable
unafraid
unaided
unapt
unaptly
unarm
unarmed
unarming
unarms
unaware
unbacked
unbeaten
unbend
unbends
unbent
unbiased
unbidden
unbolted
unborn
unbridle
unbroken
unbuckle
unburden
unbutton
uncanny
uncapped
uncaring
unchain
uncivil
unclad
unclasp
unclean
unclear
unclench
unclog
unclogs
unco
uncoil
uncoils
uncommon
uncooked
uncork
uncorked
uncorks
uncouple
uncouth
uncover
uncovers
uncurl
uncurled
uncurls
uncut
undated
undid
undies
undine
undo
undoes
undoing
undoings
undone
undress
undue
unduly
unearned
unearth

unearths
uneasily
uneasy
uneaten
unending
unequal
unequals
unerring
uneven
unevenly
unfair
unfairly
unfasten
unfed
unfelt
unfilled
unfit
unfix
unfixed
unfixes
unfixing
unfold
unfolded
unfolds
unformed
unfurl
unfurled
unfurls
ungainly
ungodly
unguided
unhand
unhands
unhappy
unharmed
unheard
unheeded
unholier
unholy
unhook
unhooked
unhooks
unionize
unjust
unjustly
unkempt
unkind
unkindly
unknown
unknowns
unlace
unlaced
unlaces
unlacing
unlawful
unleaded
unlearn
unlearns
unleased
unleash
unless
unlike
unlikely
unlined
unlisted
unload
unloaded

unloads
unlock
unlocked
unlocks
unloved
unlucky
unman
unmanly
unmanned
unmans
unmarked
unmask
unmasked
unmasks
unmixed
unmoving
unmown
unnamed
unneeded
unnerved
unnerves
unopened
unpack
unpacked
unpacks
unpaged
unpaid
unpaved
unpin
unpinned
unpins
unplug
unplugs
unpoised
unquote
unravel
unravels
unread
unready
unreal
unreason
unrest
unruly
unsaddle
unsafe
unsalted
unsavory
unscrew
unscrews
unseat
unseated
unseats
unseemly
unseen
unsettle
unshaken
unsocial
unsolved
unsought
unsound
unspoken
unstable
unsteady
unstick
unsticks
unstuck
unsuited

unsung
unswathe
unswayed
untangle
untanned
untested
unthread
untidier
untidy
untie
untied
unties
until
untimely
untinged
untiring
untitled
unto
untold
untoward
untried
untrue
unused
unusual
unveil
unveiled
unveils
unversed
unvexed
unwanted
unwarmed
unwary
unwashed
unwed
unwell
unwieldy
unwind
unwinds
unwise
unwisely
unworthy
unwound
unzip
unzipped
unzips

UNI-

unicorn
unicorns
unicycle
uniform
uniforms
unisex
unison
unities
universe

UNDER-

underarm
underbid
underbuy
undercut
underdid
underdo
underdog
underfed

undergo
underlay
underlie
underpay
underpin
undersea
undertow

UP-

upas
upbeat
upbraid
upbraids
upcast
upcasts
upchuck
upchucks
upcoming
update
updated
updates
updating
updraft
updrafts
upend
upended
upending
upends
upgrade
upgraded
upgrades
upheaval
upheld
uphold
upholds
upkeep
upkeeps
upland
uplands
upmost
upon
upper
uppity
upraise
upraised
upraises
upright
uprights
uprise
uprisen
uprises
uprising
uproar
uproars
uproot
uprooted
uproots
uprose
upset
upsets
upshot
upshots
upside
upsides
upstage
upstages
upstairs

upstart
upstarts
upstream
upsurged
upswept
upswing
upswings
uptight
uptilt
uptilts
uptown
upturn
upturns
upward
upwards

-ABLE

actable
addable
amenable
avowable
bearable
bendable
burnable
capable
eatable
enable
fellable
fixable
fordable
getable
hangable
hateable
joinable
kissable
knowable
laudable
liveable
meltable
mendable
mixable
moldable
moveable
nameable
notable
parable
passable
payable
playable
portable
potable
ratable
readable
ridable
rideable
saleable
saveable
seeable
sizeable
sortable
sparable
suitable
taxable
tenable
usable
useable
washable

wearable
weldable
workable

-ADE

arcade
blockade
brigade
charade
cockade
lemonade
limeade
parade
passade
stockade

-AGE

acreage
adage
average
bandage
baronage
blockage
bondage
breakage
brewage
cartage
clearage
coinage
cordage
corkage
coverage
cubage
damage
dockage
dotage
drainage
drayage
dressage
equipage
footage
forage
frontage
garbage
grillage
haulage
herbage
hostage
lastage
leafage
leakage
leverage
lineage
linkage
manage
massage
menage
message
metage
mileage
mintage
moorage
nonage
ohmage
outage
overage

package
passage
peerage
peonage
pillage
pipage
plumage
portage
postage
pupilage
quayage
rampage
roughage
sackage
seepage
sewage
sewerage
shortage
sinkage
soakage
spillage
spoilage
steerage
stowage
stumpage
tallage
tillage
tollage
tonnage
towage
usage
ventage
vicarage
voltage
wattage
windage
wreckage
yardage

-ANT

buoyant
claimant
clamant
colorant
coolant
couchant
debutant
discant
dormant
errant
gallant
habitant
nutant
odorant
pageant
passant
peasant
pendant
rampant
saltant
sealant
sonant
tenant
toxicant
vacant
vigilant
visitant

-ARY

binary
boundary
canary
denary
dietary
glossary
hoary
honorary
notary
palmary
primary
rotary
sectary

-ATE

alienate
binate
bullate
caseate
cordate
costate
dentate
donate
emirate
fixate
graduate
khanate
legate
limbate
lineate
lobate
luxate
malate
overate
palate
palmate
pileate
primate
priorate
pupate
rebate
rotate
ruinate
ruminate
runagate
tractate
ulcerate
vacate
validate
violate

-DOM

boredom
chiefdom
condom
earldom
freedom
heirdom
kingdom
popedom
queendom
random
serfdom
sheikdom

stardom
wisdom

-EER

cameleer
career
foreseer
overseer

-ENE

epicene
ethylene
sagene

-ENT

anent
assent
cadent
cogent
deferent
docent
existent
fluent
moment
parent
patent
pendent
portent
potent
repent
rodent
student
tangent
violent

-ERY

adultery
archery
artery
beery
bindery
blustery
bowery
brewery
butchery
buttery
clownery
cookery
coopery
creamery
crockery
deanery
drollery
eatery
emery
fishery
foolery
gallery
greenery
hatchery
heathery
joinery
lowery
mastery
mockery

papery
pinery
plumery
printery
puckery
puffery
quackery
rookery
scullery
sealery
showery
smeltery
trickery
trumpery
winery
witchery

-ESS

assess
baroness
burgess
canoness
caress
countess
earless
peeress
poetess
prioress
profess
prowess
seeress

-ETTE

anisette
barbette
brunette
layette
palette
pipette

-FOLD

bifold
billfold
enfold
fivefold
fourfold
gatefold
infold
ninefold
pinfold
sixfold
tenfold
twofold

-FUL

armful
artful
bagful
baleful
baneful
bashful
bellyful
blissful
boastful
brimful

capful
careful
cheerful
colorful
cupful
deathful
deedful
direful
dishful
doleful
doubtful
dreadful
earful
easeful
eventful
eyeful
faithful
fanciful
fateful
fearful
fistful
fitful
forceful
fretful
fruitful
gainful
glassful
gleeful
graceful
grateful
guileful
handful
harmful
hateful
heedful
helpful
hopeful
houseful
hurtful
ireful
joyful
jugful
lapful
lawful
listful
loathful
lustful
manful
mindful
mirthful
mournful
mouthful
needful
pailful
painful
peaceful
pipeful
plateful
playful
potful
powerful
prideful
rageful
rightful
riskful
roomful
rueful

ruthful	partible	lotion	freakish	echoism	hymnist
scoopful	passible	million	ghoulish	egoism	idealist
scornful	vendible	mission	girlish	egotism	idyllist
shameful		mullion	goatish	fatalism	ironist
sinful	**-ICE**	notion	goodish	heroism	jingoist
skillful		onion	greenish	humanism	leftist
skinful	amice	pillion	hashish	idealism	legalist
soulful	bodice	pinion	hawkish	jingoism	legist
speedful	cornice	portion	hellish	legalism	lobbyist
spiteful	dormice	position	huffish	localism	loyalist
spoonful	justice	potion	impish	lyricism	lyricist
sportful	notice	question	longish	momism	medalist
stickful	office	rampion	loutish	moralism	moralist
tactful	poultice	ration	lumpish	nomadism	motorist
tankful		reaction	lungfish	organism	novelist
tasteful	**-IFY**	recision	modish	pacifism	organist
tearful		region	monkish	paganism	palmist
thankful	acidify	scullion	mopish	quietism	panelist
trustful	beatify	section	newish	realism	papist
truthful	beautify	stallion	oafish	rigorism	psalmist
tuneful	classify	station	offish	ruralism	quietist
unlawful	codify	taction	ogreish	sadism	realist
useful	detoxify	tampion	oldish	sexism	rightist
vengeful	edify	traction	owlish	theism	royalist
wailful	fortify	trillion	palish	tokenism	ruralist
wakeful	gasify		parish	totemism	sadist
wasteful	humidify	**-ISH**	perish	tourism	sexist
watchful	justify		pinkish	unionism	soloist
wishful	modify	aspish	planish	urbanism	subsist
wistful	mollify	babyish	polish	virilism	tanist
woeful	notify	banish	punish	vitalism	theist
wrathful	nullify	bearish	quackish	vocalism	tourist
wrongful	pacify	blackish	qualmish		tsarist
youthful	pulpify	blandish	radish	**-IST**	urbanist
	ramify	bleakish	raffish		violist
-HOOD	ratify	blimpish	roundish	alarmist	vocalist
	scarify	blockish	saltish	alienist	
babyhood	signify	blowfish	scampish	annalist	**-ITE**
boyhood	solidify	bluefish	selfish	artist	
girlhood	specify	boarish	sheepish	assist	barite
manhood	testify	bookish	shortish	atomist	bauxite
selfhood		boorish	shrewish	banjoist	campsite
serfhood	**-ION**	boyish	sickish	bassist	cordite
wifehood		brackish	smallish	cabalist	favorite
	abortion	brandish	standish	canoeist	finite
-IAN	action	bullish	tallish	canonist	graphite
	adaption	burnish	tigerish	cellist	jadeite
banian	adoption	catfish	vanish	chartist	martite
civilian	bastion	childish	vigorish	colonist	masonite
comedian	billion	churlish	viperish	colorist	partite
eonian	bullion	clayish	vixenish	copyist	petite
gentian	bunion	clownish	waspish	cultist	ratite
guardian	camion	coltish	waterish	czarist	siderite
logician	cation	devilish	wolfish	dualist	termite
median	champion	dogfish	womanish	duelist	
meridian	ejection	dudish		egoist	**-ITY**
musician	election	dullish	**-ISM**	epeeist	
optician	erection	dumpish		essayist	acidity
plebeian	eruption	duskish	ageism	exist	acridity
radian	eviction	dwarfish	alarmism	fatalist	agility
ruffian	exaction	elfish	alienism	feudist	amenity
	exertion	fairish	atomism	finalist	aridity
-IBLE	faction	famish	bossism	harpist	avidity
	flexion	feverish	cabalism	hedonist	banality
addible	fluxion	fiendish	cynicism	hobbyist	basicity
edible	gabion	finish	czarism	hoist	chastity
fallible	hellion	flourish	demonism	humanist	civility
flexible	inion	foolish	dualism	humorist	crudity
gullible	legion				

cupidity
density
dimity
docility
duality
equality
facility
fatality
finality
fixity
fluidity
futility
humanity
humidity
laxity
legality
lividity
locality
lucidity
majority
minority
mobility
modality
morality
nasality
nullity
obesity
oddity
parity
polarity
polity
priority
rapidity
reality
rigidity
solidity
timidity
tonality
totality
toxicity
urbanity
validity
vanity
venality
virility
vitality

-IUM

barium
conium
gallium
ionium
ischium
labium
medium
podium
radium
sodium
solarium
titanium

-IVE

abortive
active
adaptive
adoptive

archive
costive
ejective
elective
endive
eruptive
exertive
passive
pensive
restive

-IZE

assize
atomize
canalize
canonize
caponize
capsize
civilize
colonize
demonize
deputize
equalize
finalize
humanize
idealize
idolize
ionize
itemize
legalize
lionize
localize
maximize
metalize
mobilize
moralize
motorize
nasalize
notarize
novelize
organize
outsize
penalize
poetize
polarize
realize
ruralize
solarize
unionize
unitize
urbanize
vaporize
vitalize
vocalize

-LESS

ageless
aimless
airless
armless
artless
aweless
baseless
bedless
boneless
bootless

braless
budless
careless
cordless
dateless
deedless
ductless
dustless
earless
endless
eyeless
faceless
fameless
fearless
finless
fireless
flawless
fogless
foldless
foodless
footless
formless
fundless
gateless
godless
hairless
handless
hapless
harmless
headless
heatless
heedless
heirless
helmless
helpless
herbless
hideless
hipless
hitless
holeless
homeless
hoofless
hopeless
hornless
hueless
iceless
jobless
joyless
landless
lawless
leafless
lidless
lifeless
listless
loveless
luckless
maneless
manless
massless
meatless
mindless
moonless
nameless
napless
neckless
needless
noseless

noteless
oarless
odorless
painless
pathless
peerless
rainless
rayless
reckless
reedless
restless
ribless
rimless
rockless
roofless
rootless
ruthless
saltless
sapless
scarless
seedless
selfless
sexless
sighless
sinless
skinless
songless
soulless
spotless
starless
sunless
tactless
tailless
tearless
termless
timeless
tireless
toeless
topless
useless
viewless
waveless
wigless
windless
wingless
wireless
wishless
wordless
workless

-LIKE

godlike
hairlike
hawklike
henlike
hiplike
hoelike
hoglike
homelike
hornlike
hymnlike
ladylike
lamblike
lifelike
nestlike
noselike
songlike

starlike
taillike
tomblike
veillike
warlike
wavelike
weblike

-MENT

abutment
ailment
basement
casement
easement
figment
fragment
hutment
movement
oddment
pavement
payment
pigment
shipment
vestment

-NESS

aptness
archness
aridness
badness
baldness
bareness
baseness
bigness
blueness
boldness
busyness
calmness
canoness
coldness
coolness
coyness
cuteness
daftness
dampness
dankness
darkness
deadness
deafness
dearness
deftness
dryness
dullness
dumbness
evenness
evilness
fairness
fastness
fatness
fellness
fewness
fineness
firmness
fitness
flatness
fondness

foulness
freeness
fullness
gameness
gayness
gladness
glibness
goodness
grayness
hardness
highness
hotness
hugeness
idleness
illness
justness
keenness
kindness
lameness
lateness
laxness
laziness
likeness
limpness
loneness
loudness
lushness
madness
meanness
meekness
mildness
nearness
neatness
newness
niceness
nudeness
numbness
oddness
oldness
oneness
openness
paleness
patness
pertness
poorness
primness
pureness
rankness
rareness
rashness
richness
ripeness
rudeness
sadness
safeness
sageness
saltness
sameness
saneness
setness
shyness
sickness
slyness
smugness
softness
soreness
sourness

sureness
tallness
tameness
tartness
tautness
thinness
trimness
trueness
vainness
vastness
wanness
weakness
wetness
wideness
wildness
witness
wryness

-ORY

armory
auditory
calory
factory
hickory
pillory
theory

-OSE

maltose
mongoose
moose
nodose
noose
propose
rugose
setose
verbose

-OSIS

cyanosis
kenosis
lordosis
miosis
narcosis

-OUS

bayous
bulbous
burnous
callous
caseous
covetous
decorous
dolorous
gorgeous
hideous
humorous
ichorous
joyous
libelous
nacreous
odorous
perilous
piceous
pileous
pious
pompous
pulpous
ramous
ravenous
resinous
rigorous
riotous
ruinous
saporous
serous
spinous
torous

ulcerous
valorous
vaporous
venomous
vigorous
viperous
virtuous
zealous

-SHIP

airship
flagship
hardship
heirship
kingship
kinship
ladyship
lordship
township
warship

-SOME

awesome
dolesome
fearsome
foursome
handsome
irksome
lonesome
tiresome
toilsome
twosome
winsome
woesome

-STER

boaster
booster
dabster
dopester

fluster
forester
gamester
gangster
hipster
huckster
lobster
maltster
master
minister
mobster
molester
monster
muster
oldster
paster
pollster
punster
quester
quipster
roadster
rodster
shyster
songster
spinster
tapster
teamster
tipster

-TH

breadth
daleth
dearth
eleventh
forth
fourth
growth
hath
heighth
seventh
sixth

tenth
tilth
warmth
youth

-WARD

backward
downward
forward
hayward
homeward
inward
landward
leeward
leftward
onward
outward
rearward
selfward
skyward
toward
untoward
upward
wayward
westward
windward

-WAYS

airways
anyways
archways
beltways
bikeways
byways
doorways
edgeways
endways
fairways
freeways
gangways

gateways
getaways
hallways
highways
keyways
longways
parkways
pathways
raceways
railways
roadways
rollways
runways
seaways
shipways
sideways
skyways
slipways
someways
subways
thruways
tramways
walkways

-WISE

anywise
edgewise
fanwise
likewise
nowise
sidewise

FOR SCRABBLE® PLAYERS USING THE OSPD

This list includes all words in the *Word Finder* not found in the current edition of *The Official Scrabble® Players Dictionary*. Only players who are using the OSPD to settle challenges need check the words below. The words are all technically eligible for play in Scrabble®, and in fact many are quite common. But you could be challenged on one of them during play just because the OSPD does not list the word—if you have agreed to the OSPD as your final authority.

aargh
ackee
aerobics
aet
affinal
ageism
ageisms
airplay
airplays
airtime
airtimes
ajuga
ajugas
amaretto
angakok
angakoks
anorexic
antsy
apicals
apteria
apterium
arcanums
arfs
arkose
armlock
armlocks
artsy
auteur
auteurs
autoharp
automat
automats
azlons

backbeat
bagger
baggers
baldies
baldy
ballgame
ballpark
ballsy
ballys
bam
bammed
bamming
bams
bazoo
bazoos
beader
beamer
bearhug
bearhugs
bearwood
bedsheet

beignet
beignets
besoil
besoils
bezazz
bimbo
bleep
bleeps
boathook
bodysuit
bombax
bombings
bondings
bonk
bonked
bonks
boombox
borals
borals
bowie
braless
breadbox
bundt
bundts
burrito
burritos
buyout
buyouts

cabbed
cabbing
calamari
canephor
carbolic
carwash
casbah
casbahs
caseload
cellmate
cep
cepheid
cepheids
ceps
cervid
cheapo
cheapos
chickee
chickees
citator
citators
clammer
clammers
claves
clearage
clearcut

clunky
codded
codding
comix
commis
condo
congrats
contras
coppled
cor
cordelle
cornrow
cornrows
cors
coverup
cowpie
cowpies
crazies
croppies
cursor
cursors
cutbanks

dalton
daltons
dawnings
debitor
departee
desktop
dippings
diskette
ditsy
ditzy
dolma
dolmas
donga
dongas
dorky
drywall
drywalls
duvet
duvets

endgame
exon
exons
expresso

faggy
falafel
farmost
faux
feh
fies
fishworm

flokati
footie
footies
fritz
fundless
futon
futons
futz
futzed
futzes
futzing

gaeing
galleria
gallet
galleted
gallets
gamay
gammy
gasohol
gasohols
gateau
gateaux
gateleg
giddyup
gimme
gimmie
gimmies
giveback
glibs
glitz
glitzy
gloppy
gluepot
gluepots
glug
glugged
glugging
gofer
gofers
goombah
goombahs
goopier
goopiest
goopy
granola
granolas
greenies
grue
grues
grunges
grungier
grungy
gumboot
gumboots

gunky
gunnybag
gussies
gussy

hairnet
hairnets
hambone
hambones
hardnose
havarti
hayfield
heh
henwife
henwives
herbed
herdboy
herdboys
hogskin
hogskins
hon
hosta
hostas
housesat
housesit
hubbly
hummus
hurst
hursts
hyped
hyper
hyping

ickiness
inions
inkjet
ita
ixora

jambone
jasmin
jellaba
jeon
jettier
jettiest
jibings
jicama
jinglet
jinglets
jokey
joky
jones
jumbal
jumbals

kaf
kafs
kal
kasbah
kasbahs
kavakava
kazachok
kazatski
kazatsky
kelep
khet
kheth
khoums
kibbeh
kibei
kibeis
kickball
kickier
kickiest
kicky
killie
killies
kilobyte
kimchi
kina
kinesic
(adj.)
kik
kissy
kleig
klezmer
kluge
kob
kobo
kobs
kolbasi
konk
korat
korats
kreep
kreeps
kreplach
kugel
kukri
kwanza
kwanzas
kyak
kyaks

laetrile
karkish
lastage
latke
latkes
lawbook

lawbooks	modems	paesan	rechew	sozzled	whackos
layup	mojo	paesano	rechewed	spacey	whammo
layups	mojos	paesanos	rechews	spackle	wimp
leaners	momzer	pager	redux	spackled	wimpish
lectin	monoglot	pagers	reedless	spackles	wimps
lectins	moonwalk	panbroil	reg	spacy	wimpy
leftish	mos	parergon	regs	spadixes	wingtip
lekvar	mostest	paygrade	rehab	spandex	wingtips
lekvars	mowings	payout	restroom	spaz	
lendable	muchly	payouts	retro	spazes	xanthan
lept	mudpack	pazazz	ria	spiff	xanthans
letched	mudpacks	peacenik	rias	spiffed	xerox
letching	mudslide	perdure	rif	spiffing	xeroxed
lexeme	muktuk	perdured	rifs	spiffs	xeroxes
lexemes	muktuks	perdures	riskful	spritz	xeroxing
lexemic	munchies	perfumy	roadies	spritzed	xylitol
lexis	munchkin	permed	roadshow	spritzer	
linotype	mutons	perming	ryokan	spritzes	yahrzeit
linted	mysid	philtrum	ryokans	stiffed	yakitori
linting	mysids	pigout		stiffing	yamalka
logman		pigouts		stuntman	yamalkas
lomein		pinkeys	sacring	stuntmen	yatter
lovebug	nachos	pixel	sacrums	sukkot	yattered
lovebugs	naggle	pixels	saggy	sushi	yatters
luged	nah	plumery	salsa	swimwear	yautia
lugeing	natch	plutei	salsas	tech	yautias
luv	naysayer	pluteus	samosa	techs	yech
	neaped	poof	samosas	telepath	yente
marvy	nebris	popsicle	saros	tercer	yentes
masonite	necker	poshly	schizy	toked	yikes
matchup	neckers	poshness	schizzy	toking	ylem
matchups	nerd	presort	schlocky	topspin	yob
maud	nerds	presorts	schtik	topspins	yobbo
mauds	nerdy	promo	scrolled	tostada	yobbos
mayo	neuk	promos	sherpa	tostado	yobs
mayos	neuks	pullup	sherpas	tostados	yock
meatloaf	ninja	pullups	shlep	toyshop	yocks
medevac	ninjas	pulpify	shlepp	toyshops	yuck
medevacs	nixe	pulwar	shlepped	trifecta	yuckier
medflies	nonet	pulwars	shleps	tripwire	yuckiest
medfly	nonets		shmaltzy	tuneup	yucks
megabyte	nonyl		shmuck	tuneups	yucky
megadose	nonyls	qanat	schmucks		yum
meltdown	nuked	qanats	shnook		yuppie
mesnes	nuking	qat	scnooks	ulu	yuppies
messaged	nunatak	qats	sickie	ulus	
mickies	nunataks	quango	sicko	umiaq	
micky	nutsy	quangos	sickos	untieing	
microdot	nuzzler	quantile	sirred	urceolus	zenaida
midlife	nuzzlers	quasher	sirring		zineb
midsize		quillon	sitcom		zinger
mihrab	obconic	quillons	sitcoms	vac	zit
mihrabs	oceanaut	quinte	situp	vacs	zits
miked	ockers	quintes	situps	veggie	zonk
miking	offsides		sleaze	veggies	zonking
mindset	oompah		sleazes		zonks
minicam	orad	rabat	sleazo		zoophily
minicams	orby	rabats	sleazos	wacko	zoris
mo	orzo	rageful	smartass	wackos	zydeco
modals	orzos	ragtop	sotted	weepie	zygoid
modem	outliner	ragtops		whacko	